ACCOUNTING LITERATURE ——INDEX

JEAN LOUIS HECK
Villanova University

ROBERT P. DERSTINE
Villanova University

RONALD J. HUEFNER
State University of New York at Buffalo

McGraw-Hill Publishing Company
New York   St. Louis   San Francisco   Auckland   Bogota   Caracas
Colorado Springs   Hamburg   Lisbon   London   Madrid   Mexico
Milan   Montreal   New Delhi   Oklahoma City   Panama   Paris
San Juan   São Paulo   Singapore   Sydney   Tokyo   Toronto

ACCOUNTING LITERATURE INDEX

ISBN 0-07-042225-7

234567890 WHT WHT 8932109

ACCOUNTING LITERATURE INDEX
Table of Contents

The rapid growth of accounting research over the past 25 years has led to the creation of many new accounting journals. Researchers, teachers, students, and practitioners face a major task in staying abreast of the literature and in locating published works. One may recall that a particular author wrote on a certain subject, but may not recall the journal. Or one may remember seeing an article on a topic in a particular journal, but may have forgotten the author or year of publication. This Index was created to aid in such situations, by creating an extensive source of complete bibliographic references for a large portion of the accounting literature.

Defining the accounting literature is a difficult task. There are about thirty academic or academic/professional journals published in the U.S. and Canada, plus several more published elsewhere in the world. There are numerous professional journals. The boundaries of the accounting literature are unclear. Certainly the field encompasses financial and managerial accounting and auditing; it possibly includes taxation, and often overlaps with related disciplines such as finance. We thus faced a considerable challenge in deciding which journals to include in this Index and which to exclude.

The journals included, and the abbreviation used to reference the journal, are as follows:

Abacus	ABACUS
Accounting and Business Research	ABR
The Accounting Historians Journal	AHJ
Accounting Horizons	ACCHOR
Accounting, Organizations and Society	AOS
The Accounting Review	AR
Advances in Accounting	AIA
Advances in International Accounting	AIIA
Advances in Public Interest Accounting	AIPIA
Advances in Taxation	AIT
Auditing: A Journal of Practice and Theory	AJPT
Contemporary Accounting Research	CAR
Corporate Accounting	CA
The CPA Journal	CPAJ
International Journal of Accounting Education and Research	IJAER
Issues in Accounting Education	IAE
Journal of Accountancy	JOA
Journal of Accounting and Economics	JAEC
Journal of Accounting and Public Policy	JAPP
Journal of Accounting, Auditing and Finance	JAAF
Journal of Accounting Education	JAED
Journal of Accounting Literature	JAL
Journal of Accounting Research	JAR
Journal of Cost Analysis	JCA
Journal of Information Systems	JIS
Journal of the American Taxation Association	JATA
Management Accounting	MA
Research in Accounting Regulation	RIAR
Research in Governmental and Nonprofit Accounting	RIGNA

In selecting these 29 journals for inclusion, we omitted many others. We required that a journal be in existence prior to 1988, thus excluding several which began publication that year. We excluded all but three major professional journals (The Journal of Accountancy, Management Accounting, and the CPA Journal). We excluded any journal already listed in the Finance Literature Index (McGraw-Hill, 1988), most notably the Journal of Business Finance and Accounting. We excluded all but a few foreign journals (Abacus, Accounting and Business Research, Accounting Organizations and Society, and Contemporary Accounting Research). We excluded all but two taxation journals: Advances in Taxation (so as to have all the "Advances" journals) and the Journal of the American Taxation Association (so as to have all the American Accounting Association journals). Finally, some other journals believed to be of limited circulation were omitted.

For twenty-six of the journals, their entire history is included (among these is The Accounting Review, which began in 1926). The three journals for which a complete history is not presented are:

1. The CPA Journal is included from Vol. 42 (1972), when the current journal name was adopted. The contents of the predecessor New York CPA are excluded from the Index.

2. The Journal of Accountancy is included from Vol. 89 (1950) onward. This journal has existed since 1905. Considerations of space and the limited usefulness of the older material led to the exclusion of pre-1950 contents.

3. Management Accounting is included from Vol. 47 (1965-66), when the current journal name was adopted. The contents of the predecessor NAA Bulletin and NACA Bulletin are excluded.

We were also faced with decisions as to what specific items to include. Journals vary among themselves as to the types of items contained, and a given journal may vary over time. We attempted to include all items which constituted articles, including notes, comments, replies, teaching notes, etc. We thus excluded such items as:

- book reviews
- communications from the editor
- committee reports
- discussants of conference papers
- dissertation abstracts
- features, interviews, etc.
- regular columns or departments
- reports on meetings or conferences

Inclusion/exclusion decisions were sometimes difficult to make; we recognize that we may have occasionally been inconsistent.

The data for this Index (authors' names, titles, and page numbers) were taken from the journals' tables of contents. Tables of contents are not error-free; we saw and corrected some errors, but others may remain. Further, we may have inadvertently added new errors of our own. We apologize for any misidentification of your work. If you bring errors to our attention, we will correct them in the next edition.

This Index is organized into two sections. Part One presents a chronological listing of articles, by journal, from the first issue covered through the end of 1988 (in two cases, a journal had not completed its 1988 publication by the time we went to press in April 1989). For consistency and convenience of notation, all journal issues are numbered. Readers desiring exact citations are referred to Appendix A on page 441, where a cross reference for each journal notes any monthly, quarterly, or seasonal names corresponding to particular issues. Part Two of the Index contains all articles listed alphabetically by author. For multiple-authored articles, the citation is repeated in its entirety for each coauthor.

We are grateful to McGraw-Hill for its willingness to undertake the publication of this Index, and to Robert Lynch, Sponsoring Editor for Accounting, for his assistance and support.

We hope this Index proves useful to our colleagues in the academic and practicing professions.

Jean Louis Heck
Villanova University

Robert P. Derstine
Villanova University

Ronald J. Huefner
State University of New York
at Buffalo

PART ONE

JOURNAL
INDEX

ABACUS

Nichols, Donald R. and R. C. Baker. "Testing The Consistency Of Auditors' Prior Distributions And Sampling Results." No. 2, pp. 91-105.

Findlay, M. Chapman, III. "On Market Efficiency And Financial Accounting," No. 2, pp. 106-122.

Peasnell, K. V. "The CCA Depreciation Problem - An Analysis And Proposal," No. 2, pp. 123-140.

Chandra, Gyan and Melvin N. Greenball. "Management Reluctance To Disclosure: An Empirical Study," No. 2, pp. 141-154.

Boatsman, James R. "Why Are There Tigers And Things?," No. 2, pp. 155-167.

Smith, R. G. E. "In Defence Of 'One Type Of Security'," No. 2, pp. 168-179.

Abacus
Volume 14, 1978

Bodenhorn, Diran. "An Economic Approach To Balance Sheets And Income Statements," No. 1, pp. 3-30.

Wolnizer, P. W. "Independence In Auditing: An Imcomplete Notion," No. 1, pp. 31-52.

Parker, R. H. "British Men Of Account," No. 1, pp. 53-65.

Gilling, D. M. and P. J. Stanton. "Changes In The Structure Of The Auditing Profession In Australia," No. 1, pp. 66-80.

Craswell, A. T. "Surrogates In Accounting," No. 1, pp. 81-93.

Walker, R. G. "International Accounting Compromises: The Case Of Consolidation Accounting," No. 2, pp. 97-111.

Garsombke, H. Perrin. "Government-Determined Accounting Rules: An Example," No. 2, pp. 112-121.

Chambers, R. J. "The Use And Abuse Of A Notation: A History Of An Idea," No. 2, pp. 122-144.

Matthews, John. "Accounting, Business And The Economy: Undue Infuence And Dysfunctional Attitudes," No. 2, pp. 145-153.

Whittred, G. P. "Accounting For The Extractive Industries: Use Or Abuse Of The Matching Principle?," No. 2, pp. 154-159.

Skinner, R. C. "Process Costing," No. 2, pp. 160-170.

Clancy, Donald K. "What Is A Convertible Debenture? A Review Of The Literature In The U.S.A.," No. 2, pp. 171-179.

Ma, Ronald, Pramond Pandey and Mark Scott. "Capital Budgeting And Discounted Cash Equivalents," No. 2, pp. 180-187.

Chambers, R. J. "Discounted Cash Equivalents: A Note In Response," No. 2, pp. 188-190.

Abacus
Volume 15, 1979

Tang, Roger Y. W. and K. H. Chan. "Environmental Variables Of International Transfer Pricing: A Japan-United States Comparison," No. 1, pp. 3-12.

Peles, Yoram C. and Meir I. Schneller. "Liquidity Ratios And Industry Averages - New Evidence," No. 1, pp. 13-22.

Ball, Ray, R. G. Walker and G. P. Whittred. "Audit Qualifications And Share Prices," No. 1, pp. 23-34.

Gaertner, James F. "Proposed Alternatives For Accounting For Business Combinations: A Behavioral Study," No. 1, pp. 35-47.

Keane, Simon M. "The Internal Rate Of Return And The Reinvestment Fallacy," No. 1, pp. 48-55.

Schnabel, Jacques A. "One Type Of Security: An Addendum," No. 1, pp. 56-59.

Partington, Graham. "Process Costing: A Comment," No. 1, pp. 60-66.

Chambers, R. J. "Usefulness - The Vanishing Premise In Accounting Standard Setting," No. 2, pp. 71-92.

Davies, J. J. "Accountants' Third Party Liability: A History Of Applied Sociological Jurisprudence," No. 2, pp. 93-112.

Nichols, Donald R. and S. Michael Groomer. "A Study Of The Relative Accuracy Of Executives' Estimates Of Earnings," No. 2, pp. 113-127.

Catt, C. C. and D. W. Rivett. "Fixed Asset Prices And Economic Production Theory," No. 2, pp. 128-135.

Francis, J. R. and B. M. Pollard. "An Investigation Of Nonaudit Fees In Australia," No. 2, pp. 136-144.

Peasnell, K. V. "Capital Budgeting And Discounted Cash Equivalents: Some Clarifying Comments," No. 2, pp. 145-156.

Abacus
Volume 16, 1980

Cramer, Joe J., Jr. and Charles A. Neyhart, Jr. "A Conceptual Framework For Accounting And Reporting By Pension Plans," No. 1, pp. 3-16.

Tippett, Mark. "The 'Agio' Concept Of Interest And The A Priori Foundations Of Current Operating Profit," No. 1, pp. 17-37.

Smith, R. G. E. "One Type Of Security Again," No. 1, pp. 38-47.

Davies, B. and G. P. Whittred. "The Association Between Selected Corporate Attributes And Timeliness In Corporate Reporting: Further Analysis," No. 1, pp. 48-60.

Henderson, Scott and Graham Peirson. "A Note On The Current Cash Equivalent Of Liabilities," No. 1, pp. 61-66.

Skinner, R. C. "Process Costing: Reply To A Comment," No.

1, pp. 67-72.

Ma, Ronald and Mark Scott. "Capital Budgeting And Discounted Cash Equivalents: A Rejoinder," No. 1, pp. 73-75.

Clarke, F. L. "Inflation Accounting And The Accidents Of History," No. 2, pp. 79-99.

Firth, Michael. "Raising Finance And Firms' Corporate Reporting Policies," No. 2, pp. 100-115.

Munter, Paul and Thomas A. Radcliffe. "On The Attributes Of An Asset," No. 2, pp. 116-123.

Helmi, Medhat A. and Murat N. Tanju. "Budget After The Fact: An Auditing Tool For Management Evaluation," No. 2, pp. 124-132.

Williams, Edward E. and M. Chapman Findlay, III. "Beyond Neoclassical Economic Theory As A Foundation For Financial Accounting," No. 2, pp. 133-141.

McNally, Graeme M. and Lee Hock Eng. "Management Accounting Practices And Company Characteristics," No. 2, pp. 142-150.

Mumford, M. J. "An Historical Defence Of Henry Rand Hatfield," No. 2, pp. 151-158.

Abacus
Volume 17, 1981

Yamey, B. S. "The 'Partimenti' Account: A Discarded Practice," No. 1, pp. 3-7.

Trowell, J. R. "Fixed Asset Prices And Economic Production Theory: Comment," No. 1, pp. 8-12.

Stamp, Edward. "Why Can Accounting Not Become A Science Like Physics?," No. 1, pp. 13-27.

Eckel, Norm. "The Income Smoothing Hypothesis Revisited," No. 1, pp. 28-40.

Houghton, K. A. "Law And Accounting: Confusion Surrounding The 'Rule In Garner V. Murray'," No. 1, pp. 41-51.

Peasnell, K. V. "On Capital Budgeting And Income Measurement," No. 1, pp. 52-67.

Chambers, R. J. "The Search For System In Financial Calculation," No. 1, pp. 68-72.

Friedman, Laurence A. and Frank H. Selto. "A Simulation Of The Replacement Cost Lead Indicator Relationship," No. 1, pp. 73-90.

Sterling, Robert R. "Costs (Historical Versus Current) Versus Exit Values," No. 2, pp. 93-129.

Lee, T. A. "A Survey Of Accountants' Opinions On Cash Flow Reporting," No. 2, pp. 130-144.

Zimmer, Ian. "Modelling Lenders' Assessments Of The Ability Of Corporate Borrowers To Repay," No. 2, pp. 145-160.

Mensah, Yaw M. "A Financial Reporting Model For Dependent Market Economies," No. 2, pp. 161-173.

Givoly, D. and J. Ronen. "'Smoothing' Manifestations In Fourth Quarter Results Of Operations: Some Empirical Evidence," No. 2, pp. 174-193.

Abacus
Volume 18, 1982

Chambers, R. J. "Edwards And Bell On Income Measurement In Retrospect," No. 1, pp. 1-39.

Rutherford, B. A. "The Interpretation Of Cash Flow Reports And The Other Allocation Problem," No. 1, pp. 40-49.

Griffin, Paul A. "Foreign Exchange Gains And Losses: Impact On Reported Earnings," No. 1, pp. 50-69.

Stokes, Donald J. "The Nature And Extent Of Contemporary 'Audits' Of Directors' Reports," No. 1, pp. 70-82.

Madan, D. B. "Resurrecting The Discounted Cash Equivalent Flow," No. 1, pp. 83-90.

Houghton, K. A. "Partnership Dissolution: Treatment Of The Overdrawn Capital Of An Insolvent Partner," No. 1, pp. 91-96.

Moonitz, Maurice. "Chambers At The American Institute Of Certified Public Accountants," No. 2, pp. 106-111.

Bedford, Norton M. "The Impact Of Chambers On The Scope Of Accounting: An Analysis And Extension," No. 2, pp. 112-118.

Barton, Allan D. "Chambers' Contribution To Analytical Rigour In Accounting," No. 2, pp. 119-128.

Ma, Ronald. "A Note On The Use Of Selling Prices - Some Examples From The Nineteenth Century," No. 2, pp. 129-138.

Parker, R. H. "Bookkeeping Barter And Current Cash Equivalents In Early New South Wales," No. 2, pp. 139-151.

Lee, Thomas A. "Chambers And Accounting Communication," No. 2, pp. 152-165.

Thomas, Arthur L. "Goals For Joint-Cost Allocation: An Incompatibility In The Literature," No. 2, pp. 166-174.

Mathews, Russell. "Chambers And The Development Of Accounting Theory: A Personal Reminiscence," No. 2, pp. 175-178.

Zeff, Stephen A. "In Appreciation Of Ray Chambers, An Australian Original," No. 2, pp. 179-181.

Stamp, Edward. "R. J. Chambers: Laudatio Viri Veritati Studentis," No. 2, pp. 182-184.

Abacus
Volume 19, 1983

Partington, G. H. and R. H. Chenhall. "Dividends, Distortion And Double Taxation," No. 1, pp. 3-13.

Chambers, R. J. "Accounting For Foreign Business," No. 1, pp. 14-28.

Hirst, Mark. "The Controllability Of Financial Outcomes," No. 1, pp. 29-38.

Williams, Edward E. and M. Chapman Findlay, III. "Is Common Stock Obsolete?," No. 1, pp. 39-55.

Petri, E. and H. Shawky. "Cash Distributions Of Inflationary Gains," No. 1, pp. 56-63.

Wilkins, Trevor and Ian Zimmer. "The Effects Of Alternative Methods Of Accounting For Leases - An Experimental Study," No. 1, pp. 64-75.

Nobes, C. W. "Costs V. Exit Values: A Comment," No. 1, pp. 76-78.

Martinelli, Alvaro. "The Ledger Of Cristianus Lomellinus And Dominicus De Garibaldo, Stewards Of The City Of Genoa (1340-41)," No. 2, pp. 83-118.

Bromwich, M. and M. C. Wells. "The Usefulness Of A Measure Of Wealth," No. 2, pp. 119-129.

Griffin, Paul A. "Management's Preferences For FASB Statement No. 52: Predictive Ability Results," No. 2, pp. 130-138.

Clinch, Greg. "Alternative Hypotheses Concerning Depreciation Of Buildings," No. 2, pp. 139-147.

Bromwich, Michael. "Some Problems With Replacement Cost Asset Measurement For External Accounting Reports With Imperfect Markets," No. 2, pp. 148-161.

Hirst, Mark and Ronald Ma. "Duration And Fisher's Rate Of Return Over Cost," No. 2, pp. 162-170.

Wolnizer, P. W. "Market Prices V. Cost Indexation In Accounting For Steel Inventories," No. 2, pp. 171-188.

Abacus
Volume 20, 1984

Barlev, Benzion. "Theory, Pragmatism And Conservatism In Reflecting The Effects Of Warrants On Diluted EPS," No. 1, pp. 1-15.

McKinnon, Jill L. "Application Of Anglo-American Principles Of Consolidation To Corporate Financial Disclosure In Japan," No. 1, pp. 16-33.

McMickle, Peter L. "'Young Man's Companion' of 1737: America's First Book On Accounting?," No. 1, pp. 34-51.

Morris, Richard D. "Corporate Disclosure In A Substantially Unregulated Environment," No. 1, pp. 52-86.

Bar-Yosef, Sasson and Joshua Livnat. "Investment In Commodities Futures: The Accounting Implications," No. 1, pp. 87-95.

Henderson, Scott and Graham Peirson. "A Note On Accounting And Executory Contracts," No. 1, pp. 96-98.

Chambers, R. J., William S. Hopwood and James C. McKeown. "The Relevance Of Varieties Of Accounting Information: A U.S.A. Survey," No. 2, pp. 99-110.

Archer, G. S. H. and K. V. Peasnell. "Debt Finance And Capital Maintenance In Current Cost Accounting," No. 2, pp. 111-124.

Lee, Tom. "Cash Flows And Net Realizable Values: Further Evidence Of The Intuitive Concepts," No. 2, pp. 125-137.

Smith, R. G. E. "One Type Of Security In Retrospect," No. 2, pp. 138-156.

Boussard, Daniel. "The Impact Of The Definition Of Inflation On The Effectiveness Of Inflation Accounting Adjustments," No. 2, pp. 157-169.

Ashton, R. K. "Garner V. Murray - A Re-Appraisal," No. 2, pp. 170-175.

Abacus
Volume 21, 1985

Lapsley, Irvine. "Risk Capital For A Profitable Public Corporation: Public Dividend Capital Or Equity?," No. 1, pp. 3-18.

Edwards, John Richard. "The Origins And Evolution Of The Double Account System: An Example Of Accounting Innovation," No. 1, pp. 19-43.

Bazley, M., P. Brown and H. Y. Izan. "An Analysis Of Lease Disclosures By Australian Companies," No. 1, pp. 44-62.

Enis, Charles R. and Edward A. Morash. "Accounting For Public Policy Actions: The Case Of Motor Carrier Deregulation," No. 1, pp. 63-83.

Chong, Sebastian and Graeme Dean. "Related Party Transactions: A Preliminary Evaluation Of SFAS 57 And IAS 24," No. 1, pp. 84-100.

Robb, Alan J. "Funds Statements And The Two-Entity Test," No. 1, pp. 101-109.

Vickrey, Don W. "Normative Information Qualities: A Contrast Between Information-Economics And FASB Perspectives," No. 2, pp. 115-129.

Grinyer, John R. "Earned Economic Income - A Theory For Matching," No. 2, pp. 130-148.

Dunlop, Anna. "Bibliographical Notes On Five Examples Of Pacioli's Summa (1494) In Scotland," No. 2, pp. 149-173.

Sullivan, Graham. "Accounting And Legal Implications Of The Interposed Unit Trust Instrument," No. 2, pp. 174-196.

Madan, Dilip B. "Project Evaluation And Accounting Income Forecasts," No. 2, pp. 197-202.

Abacus
Volume 22, 1986

Ashton, R. K. "The Royal Mail Case: A Legal Analysis," No. 1, pp. 3-19.

Stark, A. W. "More On The Discounting Of Residual Income Streams," No. 1, pp. 20-28.

Craswell, A. T. "An Examination Of Alternative Hypotheses Concerning Depreciation Of Buildings," No. 1, pp. 29-38.

Partington, Graham, Jill McKinnon and Carrick Martin. "Funds Statements And The Two-Entity Test: A Response," No. 1, pp. 39-44.

Robb, Alan J. "Funds Statements And The Two-Entity Test: A Reply," No. 1, pp. 45-46.

Houghton, K. A. "Re-Appraisal Of Garner V. Murray: A Comment," No. 1, pp. 47-50.

Ashton, R. K. "Re-Appraisal Of Garner V. Murray: A Reply," No. 1, pp. 51-53.

Baladouni, Vahe. "East India Company's 1783 Balance Of Accounts," No. 2, pp. 59-64.

Clarke, F. L. and G. W. Dean. "Schmidt's 'Betriebswirtschaft' Theory," No. 2, pp. 65-102.

Whittred, Greg. "The Evolution Of Consolidated Financial Reporting In Australia," No. 2, pp. 103-120.

Peasnell, K. V. and D. J. Williams. "Ersatz Academics And Scholar-Saints: The Supply Of Financial Accounting Research," No. 2, pp. 121-135.

Trotman, Ken T. and Ian R. Zimmer. "Revenue Recognition In The Construction Industry: An Experimental Study," No. 2, pp. 136-147.

Nigam, B. M. Lall. "Bahi-Khata: The Pre-Pacioli Indian Double-Entry System Of Bookkeeping," No. 2, pp. 148-161.

Abacus
Volume 23, 1987

Ashton, R. K. "Value To The Owner: A Review And Critique," No. 1, pp. 1-9.

Young, S. David. "Financial Reporting And The Austrian Theory Of Entrepreneurship," No. 1, pp. 10-16.

Gaffikin, M. J. R. "The Methodology of Early Accounting Theorists," No. 1, pp. 17-30.

Mensah, Yaw M. and Gurprit S. Chhatwal. "Accounting For Shrinkage In Continuous Flow Industries: An Expository Note," No. 1, pp. 31-42.

Grinyer, John R. "A New Approach To Depreciation," No. 1, pp. 43-54.

Marsh, J. A. and G. R. Henning. "Some History Of The Debate On Educational Policy Of Accountants In Australia," No. 1, pp. 55-69.

Barlev, Benzion and Yoram C. Peles. "Accounting: The Structure Of A Growing Profession," No. 1, pp. 70-84.

Callen, Jeffrey L. "A Medieval Controversy About Profit And Loss Allocations," No. 1, pp. 85-90.

Bell, Philip W. "Boussard's 'Effectiveness Of Inflation Accounting Adjustments': A Comment," No. 1, pp. 91-92.

Chambers, R. J. "Accounting Education For The Twenty-First Century," No. 2, pp. 97-106.

Findlay, M. C. and E. E. Williams. "Toward A Positive Theory Of Corporate Financial Policy," No. 2. pp. 107-121.

Parker, Lee D. "An Historical Analysis Of Ethical Pronouncements And Debate In The Australian Accounting Profession," No. 2, pp. 122-140.

Craig, Russell and Mark Tippett. "Estimating Current Cost Depreciation Expense Using Numerical Analysis And The STAPOL Technique: A Pedagogic Exposition," No. 2, pp. 141-156.

Taylor, Stephen L. "International Accounting Standards: An Alternative Rationale," No. 2, pp. 157-171.

Gul, Ferdinand A. "The Effects Of Uncertainty Reporting On Lending Officers' Perceptions Of Risk And Additional Information Required," No. 2, pp. 172-181.

Nobes, Christopher W. "The Pre-Pacioli Indian Double-Entry System Of Bookkeeping: A Comment," No. 2, pp. 182-184.

Abacus
Volume 24, 1988

Gray, S. J. "Towards A Theory Of Cultural Influence On The Development Of Accounting Systems Internationally," No. 1, pp. 1-15.

Gaffikin, M. J. R. "Legacy Of The Golden Age: Recent Developments In The Methodology Of Accounting," No. 1, pp. 16-36.

Gwilliam, D. R. "Apportionment In Actions Against Auditors," No. 1, pp. 37-54.

Mepham, M. J. "The Eighteenth-Century Origins Of Cost Accounting," No. 1, pp. 55-74.

Ma, Ronald and Roger Hopkins. "Goodwill - An Example Of Puzzle-Solving In Accounting," No. 1, pp. 75-85.

Fraser, Ian A. M. "Deprival Value Or Value To The Owner? - A Clarification," No. 1, pp. 86-89.

Reeve, Robert C. and Patrick J. Hutchinson. "The Contribution Of Non-U.S. Institutions To Academic Accounting Journals," No. 1, pp. 90-94.

ACCOUNTING AND BUSINESS RESEARCH

Lothian, N. "The Nature Of Redundancy And Its Use In Company Reports And Accounts," No. 23, pp. 216-227.
Keane, Simon M. "The Investment Discount Rate - In Defence Of The Market Rate Of Interest," No. 23, pp. 228-235.
Gee, K. P. and K. V. Peasnell. "A Pragmatic Defence Of Replacement Cost," No. 24, pp. 242-249.
Ma, Ronald and M. C. Miller. "Inflation And The Current Value Illusion," No. 24, pp. 250-263.
Clarke, F. L. "A Closer Look At Sweeney's Stabilised Accounting Proposals," No. 24, pp. 264-275.
Staubus, George J. "The Multiple-Criteria Approach To Making Accounting Decisions," No. 24, pp. 276-288.
Edwards, J. R. "The Accounting Profession And Disclosure In Published Reports, 1925-1935," No. 24, pp. 289-303.
Lee, T. A. and D. Tweedie. "The Private Shareholder: His Sources Of Financial Information And His Understanding Of Reporting Practices," No. 24, pp. 304-314.

Accounting and Business Research
Volume 7, 1976-77

Morgan, John R. and Colin Robinson. "The Comparative Effects Of The UK And Norwegian Oil Taxation Systems On Profitability And Government Revenue," No. 25, pp. 2-16.
Dean, P. N. "Costs, Productivity And Efficiency In The Inland Revenue: An Outsider's View," No. 25, pp. 17-35.
French, E. A. "Physical Capital Maintenance In Income Measurement - An Exemplification," No. 25, pp. 36-44.
Courtis, J. K. "Relationships Between Timeliness In Corporate Reporting And Corporate Attributes," No. 25, pp. 45-56.
Stewart, I. C. "Mergers And The Institutional Environment In The UK 1960-1970," No. 25, pp. 57-63.
Santocki, J. "Meaning And Scope Of Management Audit," No. 25, pp. 64-70.
Shaw, J. C. "Criteria For Consolidation," No. 25, pp. 71-78.
Stamp, Edward. "ED 18 And Current Cost Accounting: A Review Article," No. 26, pp. 83-94.
Nobes, C. W. "Current Cost Accounting: Valuation By Intent?," No. 26, pp. 95-99.
Winsen, Joseph K. "Capital Market Behaviour And Accounting Policy Decisions," No. 26, pp. 100-110.
Chenhall, R. H. and R. Juchau. "Investor Information Needs - An Australian Study," No. 26, pp. 111-119.
Willmer, M. A. P. "A Mathematical Approach To Complex Fraud Problems," No. 26, pp. 120-123.
Bowles, G. N. "Some Thoughts On The Lease Evaluation Solution," No. 26, pp. 124-126.
Middleton, K. A. "Lease Evaluation: Back To Square One," No. 26, p. 127.
Mepham, M. J. and W. E. Stone. "John Mair, M. A. : Author Of The First Classic Book-Keeping Series," No. 26, pp. 128-134.
Parker, Lee. "A Reassessment Of The Role Of Control In Corporate Budgeting," No. 26, pp. 135-143.
McMonnies, P. N. "EEC, UEC, ASC, IASC, IASG, AISG, ICCAP-IFAC, Old Uncle Tom Cobbleigh And All," No. 27, pp. 162-167.
Weetman, Pauline. "Accounting Standards: A Pause For Reflection," No. 27, pp. 168-176.
Buckmaster, Dale A.,Ronald M. Copeland and Paul E. Dascher. "The Relative Predictive Ability Of Three Accounting Models," No. 27, pp. 177-186.
Benjamin, James J. and Keith G. Stanga. "Differences In Disclosure Needs Of Major Users Of Financial Statements," No. 27, pp. 187-192.
Perrin, John R. "CCA And The Appropriation Account," No. 27, pp. 193-202.
Parker, R. H. "Explaining National Differences In Consolidated Accounts," No. 27, pp. 203-207.
Burrows, G. H. "The Lease Evaluation Solution: A Further Comment," No. 27, pp. 208-210.
Grinyer, John R. "The Lease Evaluation Solution: Continued," No. 27, pp. 211-214.
Rutherford, B. A. "Value Added As A Focus Of Attention For Financial Reporting: Some Conceptual Problems," No. 27, pp. 215-220.
Goldberg, L. "The Search For Scouller: An Interim Report," No. 27, pp. 221-235.
Bromwich, Michael. "The General Validity Of Certain 'Current' Value Asset Valuation Bases," No. 28, pp. 242-249.
Estes, Ralph and Marvin Reimer. "A Study Of The Effect Of Qualified Auditors' Opinions On Bankers' Lending Decisions," No. 28, pp. 250-259.
Forker, J. J. "CCA And CPP: A Suggested Basis For Reconciliation," No. 28, pp. 260-269.
Mace, J. R. "A Systems Approach To The Analysis Of Financial Reporting," No. 28, pp. 270-285.
Most, Kenneth S. "The Rise And Fall Of The Matching Principle," No. 28, pp. 286-290.
Muis, Jules W. "Accounting Standard Setting: The Pith And The Pendulum," No. 28, pp. 291-294.
Simon, David S. "The Effect Of A Price Code On Company Profits In A Period Of Inflation," No. 28, pp. 295-299.
Wells, M. C. "Four Cost Accounting Classics: A Review," No. 28, pp. 300-302.
Wolnizer, P. W. "Primary Production Inventories Under Current Value Accounting," No. 28, pp. 303-310.
Popoff, Boris. "Replacement Cost As The Upper Limit Of Value To The Owner," No. 28, p. 311.
Gee, K. P. and K. V. Peasnell. "A Comment On Replacement Cost As The Upper Limit Of Value To The Owner," No. 28, p. 312.

Accounting and Business Research
Volume 8, 1977-78

Tweedie, D. P. "Cash Flows And Realisable Values: The Intuitive Accounting Concepts? An Empirical Test," No. 29, pp. 2-13.
Patz, Dennis H. "A Price Parity Theory Of Translation," No. 29, pp. 14-24.
Perks, R. W. and Leonora Butler. "Accountancy Standards In Practice: The Experience Of SSAP2," No. 29, pp. 25-33.
Gilling, Donald M. "Timeliness In Corporate Reporting: Some Further Comment," No. 29, pp. 34-36.
Emmanuel, C. R. and S. J. Gray. "Segmental Disclosures And The Segment Identification Problem," No. 29, pp. 37-50.
Likierman, J. A. "Analysing Project Cost Escalation: The Case Study Of North Sea Oil," No. 29, pp. 51-57.
Lee, T. A., L. Goldberg and Trevor Johnston. "'The History Of Accounting': Three Reviews," No. 29, pp. 58-67.
Peasnell, K. V. "Interaction Effects In CCA Valuations," No. 30, pp. 82-91.
Earl, Michael and Dean Paxson. "Value Accounting For Currency Transactions," No. 30, pp. 92-100.
Fadel, Hisham and John M. Parkinson. "Liquidity Evaluation By Means Of Ratio Analysis," No. 30, pp. 101-107.
Pound, G. D. "A Review Of EDP Auditing," No. 30, pp. 108-129.
Grinyer, John R. "Holding Gains On Long-Term Liabilities - An Alternative Analysis," No. 30, pp. 130-148.
Barnes, Paul. "The Effect Of A Merger On The Share Price Of The Attacker," No. 31, pp. 162-168.
Emmanuel, C. R. and S. J. Gray. "Segmental Disclosure By Multibusiness Multinational Companies: A Proposal," No. 31, pp. 169-177.
Mepham, M. J. "A Reinstatement Of The Accounting Rate Of Return," No. 31, pp. 178-190.
Parker, Lee D. "Communication In The Corporate Budgetary System," No. 31, pp. 191-207.
Sale, J. Timothy and Robert W. Scapens. "Current Cost Accounting As A Surrogate For Dividend Paying Ability," No. 31, pp. 208-216.
Peasnell, K. V. "Statement Of Accounting Theory And Theory Acceptance," No. 31, pp. 217-225.
Dittman, David A. and Kenneth R. Ferris. "'Profit Centre': A Satisfaction Generating Concept," No. 32, pp. 242-245.
Falk, Haim and James A. Heintz. "Company Risk Relationships Over Consecutive Periods," No. 32, pp. 246-252.
Flink, Solomon J., Assa Birati and Meyer Ungar. "The Impact Of Inflation On The Profits Of Listed Firms In Israel," No. 32, pp. 253-257.
Ma, Ronald and Malcolm C. Miller. "Conceptualising The Liability," No. 32, pp. 258-265.
Tippett, Mark. "The Axioms Of Accounting Measurement," No. 32, pp. 266-278.
Schiff, Allen. "Annual Reports In The United States: A Historical Perspective," No. 32, pp. 279-284.

Accounting and Business Research
Volume 9, 1978-79

Belkaoui, Ahmed. "Accounting Determinants Of Systematic Risk In Canadian Common Stocks: A Multivariate Approach," No. 33, pp. 3-10.
Dev, Susan. "Linear Programming Dual Prices In Management Accounting And Their Interpretation," No. 33, pp. 11-18.
Devon, Philip C. and Richard Kolodny. "Price-Level Reporting And Its Value To Investors," No. 33, pp. 19-24.
Henderson, Scott and Graham Peirson. "Does Accounting Research Matter?," No. 33, pp. 25-34.
James, Simon. "The Report Of The Meade Committee," No. 33, pp. 35-44.
Peasnell, K. V. and L. C. L. Skerratt. "Income-Group Inflation Rates And General Purchasing Power Adjustments: An Empirical Test Of The Heterogeneity Hypothesis," No. 33, pp. 45-60.
Brennan, W. J. "Comment On Value Accounting For Currency Transactions," No. 33, pp. 61-63.
Flower, John. "A Price Parity Theory Of Translation: A Comment," No. 33, pp. 64-65.
Patz, Dennis. "A Price Parity Theory Of Translation: A Reply," No. 33, pp. 66-72.
Clarke, F. L. "Patz On Parities, Exchange Rates And Translation," No. 33, pp. 73-77.
Philips, G. Edward. "Replacement Cost And Owner Wealth," No. 33, pp. 78-80.
Kermode, E. R. "Replacement Cost As Upper Limit Of Value: Further Fallacies," No. 33, p. 81.
Theobald, Michael and John Whitman. "The Variabilities And Correlations Of Stock Market Indices," No. 33, pp. 82-86.
Mumford, Michael. "The End Of A Familiar Inflation Accounting Cycle," No. 34, pp. 98-104.
Silverstone, Rosalie and Allan Williams. "Recruitment, Training, Employment And Careers Of Women Chartered Accountants In England And Wales," No. 34, pp. 105-122.
Parker, Lee D. "Participation In Budget Planning: The Prospects Surveyed," No. 34, pp. 123-138.
Edwards, J. R. and C. Baber. "Dowlais Iron Company: Accounting Policies And Procedures For Profit Measurement And Reporting Purposes," No. 34, pp. 139-151.
Hatherly, David. "Segmentation And The Audit Process," No. 34, pp. 152-156.
Estes, Ralph and Marvin Reimer. "An Experimental Study Of The Differential Effect Of Standard And Qualified Auditors' Opinions On Investors' Price Decisions," No. 34,

Take-Overs In The 1950s," No. 44, pp. 323-330.

Accounting and Business Research
Volume 12, 1981-82

Baxter, William T. "Accounting Standards - Boon Or Curse?," No. 45, pp. 3-10.
Blocher, Edward. "Assessment Of Prior Distributions: The Effect On Required Sample Size In Bayesian Audit Sampling," No. 45, pp. 11-20.
Lapsley, Irvine. "A Case For Depreciation Accounting In UK Health Authorities," No. 45, pp. 21-29.
Hull, J. C. "The Impact Of Stock Relief On The Attractiveness Of Capital Investment Opportunities," No. 45, pp. 30-34.
Lee, John Y. "A New Approach To The Levels Of Assurance Issue In Auditing," No. 45, pp. 35-40.
Macdonald, Graeme. "Taxation And Corporate Finance And Investment," No. 45, pp. 41-54.
Taylor, Martin E. and Robert L. Baker. "An Analysis Of The External Audit Fee," No. 45, pp. 55-60.
Peragallo, E. "Merchandising Of Slaves As Portrayed In The 15th Century Ledger Of Jachomo Badoer, A Venetian Merchant," No. 45, pp. 61-66.
Stone, Richard. "The International Harmonisation Of National Income Accounts," No. 45, pp. 67-79.
Hope, Tony and John Briggs. "Accounting Policy Making - Some Lessons From The Deferred Taxation Debate," No. 46, pp. 83-96.
Manes, R. and R. Verrecchia. "A New Proposal For Setting Intra-Company Transfer Prices," No. 46, pp. 97-104.
Choudhury, N. "Aspects Of Accounting And Internal Control - India 4th Century BC," No. 46, pp. 105-110.
Yamey, B. S. "Two Seventeenth Century Accounting Statements," No. 46, pp. 111-114.
Sutcliffe, Paul. "The Role Of Labour Variances In Harrington Emerson's 'New Gospel Of Efficiency' (1908)," No. 46, pp. 115-123.
Bailey, F. A. "Asset Valuation And Depreciation Under Current Cost Accounting," No. 46, pp. 124-128.
Jones, Rowan and Maurice Pendlebury. "Uniformity V. Flexibility In The Published Accounts Of Local Authorities: The UK Problem And Some European Solutions," No. 46, pp. 129-135.
Hatherly, D. "Accounting And Auditing Standards: Why They Are Inconsistent," No. 46, pp. 136-140.
Liao, Woody M. "Simulating Learning Curve Parameters For Managerial Planning And Control," No. 46, pp. 141-147.
Ogura, E. "The Nakai Family's Bookkeeping System," No. 46, pp. 148-152.
Morris, R. C. "Reporting The Performance Of Investment Intermediaries," No. 47, pp. 163-174.
Bartley, Jon W. and Lewis F. Davidson. "The Entity Concept And Accounting For Interest Costs," No. 47, pp. 175-187.
Burrows, G. H. "Incremental Flows In Project Evaluation," No. 47, pp. 188-192.
Dhingra, H. L. "The Impact Of Accounting Variables On Stock Market Measures Of Risk," No. 47, pp. 193-205.
Simmonds, Kenneth. "Strategic Management Accounting For Pricing: A Case Example," No. 47, pp. 206-214.
Steele, Anthony. "The Accuracy Of Chairmen's Non-Quantified Forecasts: An Exploratory Study," No. 47, pp. 215-230.
Barnes, Paul. "Accounting For Deferred Tax On Depreciable Assets - A Note," No. 47, pp. 231-232.
Skerratt, L. C. L. "Risk Distribution In The Budgetary Process: A Comment," No. 47, pp. 233-235.
Pearcy, Jeff. "Accounting Standards - Boon Or Curse: A Comment," No. 47, pp. 236-237.
Peasnell, K. V. "The Function Of A Conceptual Framework For Corporate Financial Reporting," No. 48, pp. 243-256.
Davison, Alan G. "Auditors' Liability To Third Parties For Negligence," No. 48, pp. 257-264.
French, D. P. and A. H. Russell. "An Approximate Method For The Allocation Of Reciprocal Service Costs," No. 48, pp. 265-272.
Emmanuel, Clive R. and Kenneth P. Gee. "Transfer Pricing: A Fair And Neutral Procedure," No. 48, pp. 273-278.
Parker, L. D. "Corporate Annual Reporting: A Mass Communication Perspective," No. 48, pp. 279-286.
Jones, Rowan H. "Financial Reporting In Nonbusiness Organisations," No. 48, pp. 287-295.
Hines, R. D. "The Usefulness Of Annual Reports: The Anomaly Between The Efficient Markets Hypothesis And Shareholder Surveys," No. 48, pp. 296-309.
Goldberg, Louis. "Murray's Science Of Accountantship," No. 48, pp. 310-312.
Yamey, B. S. "George Peacock, An Early 'Translator' Of Pacioli," No. 48, pp. 313-315.
Macdonald, G. "Capital Maintenance, Borrowing Gains And Income Measurement: A Comment," No. 48, pp. 316-318.
Forker, J. J. "Capital Maintenance, Borrowing Gains And Income Measurement: A Reply," No. 48, pp. 319-320.

Accounting and Business Research
Volume 13, 1982-83

Bhaskar, Krish N. "Use Of Computers In Accountancy Courses," No. 49, pp. 3-10.
McNally, Graeme M., Lee Hock Eng and C. Roy Hasseldine. "Corporate Financial Reporting In New Zealand: An Analysis Of User Preferences, Corporate Characteristics And Disclosure Practices For Discretionary Information," No. 48, pp. 11-20.

Martin, J. W. and Gary John Previts. "The Risk Preference Profiles Of Practising CPAs: Some Tentative Results," No. 49, pp. 21-28.
Davies, J. R. and W. M. McInnes. "The Efficiency And The Accountability Of UK Nationalised Industries," No. 49, pp. 29-41.
Mee, M. J. "The Tasks Of Human Asset Accounting," No. 49, pp. 42-48.
Reeve, James M. "Individual Vs. Group Processing Of Accounting Data - A Field Study," No. 49, pp. 49-55.
Tippett, Mark. "On The Numerical Estimation Of The Loss From Holding Monetary Items," No. 49, pp. 56-62.
Baxter, W. T. "Accounting Standards - Boon Or Curse?: A Reply," No. 49, pp. 63-64.
Bhaskar, Krish N. "Computers And The Choice For Accountancy Syllabuses," No. 50, pp. 83-94.
Gynther, Reg S. "Accounting For Monetary Items Under CCA: A Comment," No. 50, pp. 95-102.
Lee, T. A. "A Note On Users And Uses Of Cash Flow Information," No. 50, pp. 103-106.
Solomons, David. "The Political Implications Of Accounting And Accounting Standard Setting," No. 50, pp. 107-118.
Stamp, Edward. "Does The Chambers' Evidence Support The CoCoA System?," No. 50, pp. 119-127.
Schnabel, Jacques A. "Beta Geared And Ungeared: An Extension," No. 50, pp. 128-130.
Walker, R. G. and G. P. Whittred. "Bank Disclosures Of Secret Reserves: The Impact On The Australian Stock Market," No. 50, pp. 131-142.
Ward, C. W. R. "Property Lease-Or-Buy Decisions," No. 50, pp. 143-150.
Wells, M. C. "Essays In British Accounting Research: A Review," No. 50, pp. 151-158.
Adelberg, Arthur Harris. "The Accounting Syntactic Complexity Formula: A New Instrument For Predicting The Readability Of Selected Accounting Communications," No. 51, pp. 163-176.
Cooke, T. E. and J. J. Glynn. "Taxation Implications Of Companies Purchasing Their Own Shares," No. 51, pp. 177-180.
Harvey, David W. and Soliman Y. Soliman. "Standard Cost Variance Analysis In A Learning Environment," No. 51, pp. 181-190.
Martin, Carrick A. "The Current Cost Of A Quoted Long-Term Liability," No. 51, pp. 191-200.
Pike, R. H. "A Review Of Recent Trends In Capital Budgeting Processes," No. 51, pp. 201-208.
Yamey, B. S. "The First Danish Book On Bookkeeping And Accounts," No. 51, pp. 209-212.
Robb, A. J. "Coincidence Discovered: A Further Example And A Comment," No. 51, pp. 213-214.
Forrester, D. A. R. "German Accounting Principles Applied, A Review Article," No. 51, pp. 215-220.
Arrington, C. Edward, William A. Hillison and Paul F. Williams. "The Psychology Of Expectations Gaps: Why Is There So Much Dispute About Auditor Responsibility?," No. 52, pp. 243-250.
Cowan, T. K. "Accounting In The Real World," No. 52, pp. 251-262.
Edwards, Chris. "The Communication Of Computer Generated Information - A Review Of The Empirical Literature," No. 52, pp. 263-272.
Chen, Joyce T. "A Simplified Integer Programming Approach To Resource Allocation And Profit Budgeting," No. 52, pp. 273-278.
Godwin, Michael and Cedric Sandford. "Simplifying VAT For Small Traders," No. 52, pp. 279-288.
Karathanassis, G. "Empirical Valuation Models: How Useful Have They Been?," No. 52, pp. 289-290.
Schnabel, Jacques A. "On Capital Budgeting With An Unspecified Discount Rate," No. 52, pp. 291-294.
Taffler, R. J. "The Assessment Of Company Solvency And Performance Using A Statistical Model," No. 52, pp. 295-308.
Bird, Peter and F. A. Bailey. "Incremental Plans In Project Evaluation: A Comment," No. 52, pp. 309-310.
Burrows, G. H. "Incremental Plans In Project Evaluation: A Reply," No. 52, pp. 311-312.
Collins, R. "Computers And Accountancy Courses: A Comment," No. 52, pp. 313-315.

Accounting and Business Research
Volume 14, 1983-84

Breakwell, B. "Profit-Sharing And The Finance Acts 1978 To 1983: A Case For A Review Of Incentives," No. 53, pp. 3-14.
Houghton, Keith A. "Audit Reports: Their Impact On The Loan Decision Process And Outcome: An Experiment," No. 53, pp. 15-20.
Lau, Amy Hing-Ling and Hon-Shiang Lau. "Towards A Theory Of Stochastic Exit Value," No. 53, pp. 21-28.
Likierman, Andrew. "Evidence On Accusations Of Manipulating Profitability: Adjustments For Inflation By The Nationalised Industries 1976-81," No. 53, pp. 29-34.
McCaslin, Thomas E. and Keith G. Stanga. "Related Qualities Of Useful Accounting Information," No. 53, pp. 35-42.
Nobes, C. W. "The Evolution Of The Harmonising Provisions Of The 1980 And 1981 Companies Acts," No. 53, pp. 43-54.
Sharp, Robert F. and Eric E. Spires. "Attributability And Distributability Of Profit To Shareholders," No. 53, pp. 55-62.
Stanga, Keith G. and Mikel G. Tiller. "Needs Of Loan Officers For Accounting Information From Large Versus

Accounting and Business Research
Volume 15, 1984-85

Accounting and Business Research
Volume 16, 1985-86

Report," No. 62, pp. 91-98.

Gul, Ferdinand A. "Tolerance For Ambiguity, Auditors' Opinions And Their Effects On Decision Making," No. 62, pp. 99-106.

Smith, L. Douglas and John J. Anderson. "Inflation Accounting And Comparisons Of Corporate Returns On Equity," No. 62, pp. 107-116.

Staubus, George J. "The Market Simulation Theory Of Accounting Measurement," No. 62, pp. 117-132.

Steele, Anthony and Jean Haworth. "Auditors' Views On The Truth And Fairness Of CCA," No. 62, pp. 133-142.

Davidson, I. R. "On 'Contract Value Accounting': A Critique," No. 62, pp. 143-148.

Forker, J. J. "In Defence Of CoVA: A Comment On A Critique," No. 62, pp. 149-150.

McCaslin, Thomas E. and Keith G. Stanga. "Similarities In Measurement Needs Of Equity Investors And Creditors," No. 62, pp. 151-156.

Demirag, Istemi S. "The Treatment Of Exchange Rates In Internal Performance Evaluation," No. 62, pp. 157-164.

Mole, R. H. "Cost Volume Profit Analysis: A Tutorial And Microcomputer Implementation," No. 62, pp. 165-170.

Angus-Leppan, Pam and Vic Fatseas. "The Forecasting Accuracy Of Trainee Accountants Using Judgemental And Statistical Techniques," No. 63, pp. 179-188.

Choudhury, Nandan. "Responsibility Accounting And Controllability," No. 63, pp. 189-198.

Lewis, N. R., L. D. Parker, G. D. Pound and P. Sutcliffe. "Annual Report Readability: The Use Of Readability Techniques," No. 63, pp. 199-214.

Mazhin, Reza. "The Time Series Behaviour Of Reported Current Cost Data," No. 63, pp. 215-220.

Spiceland, J. David and Alan J. Winters. "Market Response Of Stock Distributions: The Effects Of Magnitude, Anticipation, And Cash Returns," No. 63, pp. 221-226.

Walsh, J. Anthony. "Empirical Evidence On Internal Control In Minicomputer-Based Accounting Information Systems," No. 63, pp. 227-234.

Zebda, Awni. "Stochastic Audit Planning And Control Using GERT Simulation," No. 63, pp. 235-244.

Benveniste, Ivor. "Receivers: Double Agents Or Surrogate Liquidators?," No. 63, pp. 245-250.

Edwards, John Richard. "Depreciation And Fixed Asset Valuation In Railway Company Accounts To 1911," No. 63, pp. 251-263.

Barron, Michael. "Year-End Heterogeneity In Calculations Of Industry And Economy Averages Of Accounting Numbers," No. 64, pp. 275-284.

Courtis, J. K. "An Investigation Into Annual Report Readability And Corporate Risk-Return Relationships," No. 64, pp. 285-294.

Day, Judith F. S. "The Use Of Annual Reports By UK Investment Analysts," No. 64, pp. 295-308.

Dorward, Neil. "Overhead Allocations And 'Optimal' Pricing Rules Of Thumb In Oligopolistic Markets," No. 64, pp. 309-318.

Grinyer, John R. "An Alternative To Maximisation Of Shareholders' Wealth," No. 64, pp. 319-326.

Leech, Stewart A. "The Theory And Development Of A Matrix-Based Accounting System," No. 64, pp. 327-342.

Moizer, Peter, Stuart Turley and David Walker. "Reliance On Other Auditors: A UK Study," No. 64, pp. 343-352.

Walton, Peter. "The Export Of British Accounting Legislation To Commonwealth Countries," No. 64, pp. 353-358.

Coulthurst, N. J. "The Application Of The Incremental Principle In Capital Investment Project Evaluation," No. 64, pp. 359-364.

Accounting and Business Research
Volume 17, 1986-87

Ashton, R. K. "The Argyll Foods Case: A Legal Analysis," No. 65, pp. 3-12.

Bhaskar, Krish N. and Bernard C. Williams. "Audit And Control Issues For The Small Computerised Business," No. 65, pp. 13-20.

Choudhury, Nandan. "In Search Of Relevance In Management Accounting Research," No. 65, pp. 21-32.

Coulthurst, N. J. "Accounting For Inflation In Capital Investment. The State Of The Art And Science," No. 65, pp. 33-42.

Diacogiannis, George P. "Some Empirical Evidence On The Intertemporal Stationarity Of Security Return Distributions," No. 65, pp. 43-48.

Keasey, Kevin and Robert Watson. "The Prediction Of Small Company Failure: Some Behavioural Evidence For The UK," No. 65, pp. 49-58.

Lemke, Kenneth W. and Philip P. Powell. "The Gearing Adjustment - An Empirical Study," No. 65, pp. 59-70.

Morris, Richard D. "Lee V. Neuchatel Asphalte Company (1889) And Depreciation Accounting: Two Empirical Studies," No. 65, pp. 71-82.

Harvey-Cook, J. E. and R. J. Taffler. "Graduate Recruitment Procedures In The UK Accountancy Profession: A Preliminary Study," No. 66, pp. 99-108.

Kantor, Jeffrey and Richard Pike. "The Determinants Of The Value Of Unlisted Shares: Opinions Of Professional Valuers In Canada," No. 66, pp. 109-116.

James, Simon. "The Reform Of Personal Taxation: A Review Article," No. 66, pp. 117-124.

Lee, T. A. and A. W. Stark. "Cash Flow Accounting And Capital Budgeting," No. 66, pp. 125-132.

McLeay, Stuart and Susan Fieldsend. "Sector And Size Effects In Ratio Analysis: An Indirect Test Of Ratio Proportionality," No. 66, pp. 133-140.

Tippett, Mark. "Exchange Valuation Rules: Optimal Use Of Specific Price Indices," No. 66, pp. 141-154.

Willett, R. J. "An Axiomatic Theory Of Accounting Measurement," No. 66, pp. 155-172.

Abdolmohammadi, Mohammad J. "Decision Support And Expert Systems In Auditing: A Review And Research Directions," No. 66, pp. 173-185.

Arnold, A. J. and I. Benveniste. "Wealth And Poverty In The English Football League," No. 67, pp. 195-204.

Choudhury, Nandan. "Starting Out In Management Accounting Research," No. 67, pp. 205-220.

Connell, N. A. D. "Expert Systems In Accountancy: A Review Of Some Recent Applications," No. 67, pp. 221-234.

Emmanuel, C. R. and N. Garrod. "On The Segment Identification Issue," No. 67, pp. 235-240.

Gregory, Alan. "Divisional Performance Measurement With Divisions As Lessees Of Head Office Assets," No. 67, pp. 241-246.

Reid, Jean Margo. "Judicial Views On Accounting In Britain Before 1889," No. 67, pp. 247-258.

Wright, Mike and Steve Thompson. "Divestment And The Control Of Divisionalised Firms," No. 67, pp. 259-268.

Walker, R. G. "Australia's ASRB: A Case Study Of Political Activity And Regulatory 'Capture'," No. 67, pp. 269-286.

Abdolmohammadi, Mohammad J. "Bayesian Inference In Auditing: Evidence On The Most Appropriate Assessment Techniques," No. 68, pp. 291-300.

Buckland, R. and E. W. Davis. "Barriers To Entry In The Unlisted Securities Market: The Significance Of Administrative Expenses," No. 68, pp. 301-310.

Mole, R. H. "An Analysis Of The Burden Of Corporation Tax Upon Investment Of Retained Profits In Plant And Machinery," No. 68, pp. 311-318.

Rickwood, Colin, Geoff Coates and Ray Stacey. "Managed Costs And The Capture Of Information," No. 68, pp. 319-326.

Whittington, G. "Positive Accounting Theory: A Review Article," No. 68, pp. 327-336.

Filimon, Radu, Sanford Morton and Soliman Y. Soliman. "Spoilage With A Production Function," No. 68, pp. 337-348.

Messier, William F., Jr. and R. David Plumlee. "The Effects Of Anticipation And Frequency Of Errors On Auditors' Selection Of Substantive Procedures," No. 68, pp. 349-358.

Accounting and Business Research
Volume 18, 1987-88

Peasnell, K. V., L. C. L. Skerratt and C. W. R. Ward. "The Share Price Impact Of UK CCA Disclosures," No. 69, pp. 3-16.

Grinyer, John R. "Revaluation Of Fixed Assets In Accruals Accounting," No. 69, pp. 17-24.

Gwilliam, D. R. "The Auditor, Third Parties And Contributory Negligence," No. 69, pp. 25-36.

Houghton, Keith A. and Peter Robinson. "Experimental Research In Auditing: Field Vs. Laboratory Settings," No. 69, pp. 37-42.

Lee, T. A. "The Search For Correspondence With Economic Reality: A Review Article," No. 69, pp. 43-46.

Morris, Richard D. "Signalling, Agency Theory And Accounting Policy Choice," No. 69, pp. 47-56.

Peel, M. J. and D. A. Peel. "Some Further Empirical Evidence On Predicting Private Company Failure," No. 69, pp. 57-66.

Rogers, Waymond and Thomas J. Housel. "The Effects Of Information And Cognitive Processes On Decision Making," No. 69, pp. 67-74.

Skinner, R. C. "Allocations And The Validity Of The Incremental Principle," No. 69, pp. 75-78.

Ashton, R. K. "The Impact Of Search Costs And Asymmetric Information On Current Value Accounting," No. 70, pp. 99-106.

Bircher, Paul. "Company Law Reform And The Board Of Trade, 1929-1943," No. 70, pp. 107-120.

Duncan, Keith and Ken Moores. "Usefulness Of CCA Information For Investor Decision Making: A Laboratory Experiment," No. 70, pp. 121-132.

Finnie, James. "The Role Of Financial Appraisal In Decisions To Acquire Advanced Manufacturing Technology," No. 70, pp. 133-140.

Keane, Simon M. "Share Tipsters And Fair Advertising," No. 70, pp. 141-148.

Kee, Robert and Bruce Bublitz. "The Role Of Payback In The Investment Process," No. 70, pp. 149-156.

Van Der Tas, L. G. "Measuring Harmonisation Of Financial Reporting Practice," No. 70, pp. 157-169.

Walker, Martin. "The Information Economics Approach To Financial Reporting," No. 70, pp. 170-182.

Haskins, Mark E. and David D. Williams. "The Association Between Client Factors And Audit Fees: A Comparison By Country And By Firm," No. 70, pp. 183-192.

Lyne, Stephen R. "The Role Of The Budget In Medium And Large UK Companies And The Relationship With Budget Pressure And Participation," No. 71, pp. 195-212.

MacArthur, John B. "An Analysis Of The Content Of Corporate Submissions On Proposed Accounting Standards In The UK," No. 71, pp. 213-226.

Moizer, Peter and Jamie Pratt. "The Evaluation Of Performance In Firms Of Chartered Accountants," No. 71, pp. 227-237.

Patz, Dennis H. "Alternative Realities And Price Parity

Translation," No. 71, pp. 239-247.

Pike, Richard, John Sharp and Jeffrey Kantor. "The Role Of Accounting Information In Valuing Unlisted Shares," No. 71, pp. 249-255.

Tishlias, Dennis P. and Peter Chalos. "Product Pricing Behaviour Under Different Costing Systems," No. 71, pp. 257-265.

Estes, Ralph and D. D. Reames. "Effects Of Personal Characteristics On Materiality Decisions: A Multivariate Analysis," No. 72, pp. 291-296.

Jones, M. J. "A Longitudinal Study Of The Readability Of The Chairman's Narratives In The Corporate Reports Of A UK Company," No. 72, pp. 297-305.

Abdel-Karim, Rifaat Ahmed. "The Impact Of The UK Price Codes On Accounting Functions In Organisations: A Power Perspective," No. 72, pp. 307-321.

Keasey, K., R. Watson and P. Wynarczyk. "The Small Company Audit Qualification: A Preliminary Investigation," No. 72, pp. 323-333.

Mear, Ron and Michael Firth. "Risk Perceptions Of Financial Analysts And The Use Of Market And Accounting Data," No. 72, pp. 335-340.

Pike, Richard H. "An Empirical Study Of The Adoption Of Sophisticated Capital Budgeting Practices And Decision-Making Effectiveness," No. 72, pp. 341-351.

Wallace, R. S. O. "Corporate Financial Reporting In Nigeria," No. 72, pp. 352-362.

Ratnatunga, J., R. Pike and G. J. Hooley. "The Application Of Management Accounting Techniques To Marketing," No. 72, pp. 363-370.

Macdonald, Graeme. "An Analysis Of The Reformed Corporation Tax: A Comment And An Extension," No. 72, pp. 371-374.

Mepham, M. J. "Matrix-Based Accounting: A Comment," No. 72, pp. 375-378.

THE ACCOUNTING HISTORIANS JOURNAL

Accounting Historians Journal
Volume 1, 1974

Peragallo, Edward. "Challenges Facing Teachers Of Accounting History," No. 1-4, pp. 5-6.
Previts, Gary John. "Hazy History: Fact And Folklore In Accounting," No. 1-4, pp. 7-9.
Roberts, A. R. "Electronic Methodology: Accounting Oral And Visual History," No. 1-4, pp. 10-12.
Keister, Orville R. "Unexpected Accounting?," No. 1-4, pp. 16-18.
Previts, Gary John. "Old Wine And . . . The New Harvard Bottle," No. 1-4, pp. 19-20.
Flowers, Wm. Baker. "Biography And Accounting History," No. 1-4, pp. 21-22.
Previts, Gary John. "'FASBing': Abracadabra Again?," No. 1-4, pp. 23-24.
Mosich, A. N. "Henry Whitcomb Sweeney," No. 1-4, pp. 25-27.
Morton, James R. "DR Scott," No. 1-4, pp. 27-29.
Smith, William Robert. "John Bennett Canning," No. 1-4, pp. 29-31.
Zeff, Stephen A. "F. R. M. de Paula," No. 1-4, pp. 31-34.

Accounting Historians Journal
Volume 2, 1975

Yamey, Basil S. "Common Costs And Business Decisions: An Historical Note," No. 1-4, pp. 1-2.
Previts, Gary John. "It's About Time . . . Pathways To A New Vista Of Accountancy's Past " No. 1-4, pp. 3-5.
Stone, Williard E. "Who Was Who In Accounting In 1909?," No. 1-4, pp. 6-10.
Kubin, Konrad W. "Accounting For Foreign Currency Translation: Current Problems In Historical Perspective," No. 1-4, pp. 11-16.
Hird, F. M. W. "A Speculation On The Origins Of Accounting," No. 1-4, pp. 17-21.
Shenkir, William G. "Accounting History, The Accounting Historian And The FASB," No. 1-4, pp. 22-24.
Previts, Gary John. "For Example . . . The Value Of Pretending," No. 1-4, pp. 25-26.
Kohler, Eric L. "In All My Years," No. 1-4, pp. 27-30.
Nishikawa, Kojiro. "Historical Studies In Recent Years In Japan," No. 1-4, pp. 31-34.
Spacek, Leonard. "History And Human Nature," No. 1-4, pp. 35-36.
Burns, Thomas J. "The Accounting Hall Of Fame," No. 1-4, pp. 37-39.
Newlove, George Hillis. "In All My Years: Economic And Legal Causes Of Changes In Accounting," No.1-4,pp.40-44.
Baladouni, Vahe. "'It Is Up To Us.' - Arnold J. Toynbee," No. 1-4, pp. 45-48.
Murphy, George J. "Historical Vignette: Benjamin Franklin On Accounting," No. 1-4, pp. 49-50.
Nielsen, Oswald. "In All My Years," No. 1-4, pp. 51-54.
Gurry,Edward James. "Harry Clark Bentley," No.1-4,pp.58-61.
Merino, Barbara Dubis. "Joseph E. Sterrett," No. 1-4, pp. 62-64.
Bryson, Roscoe Eugene, Jr. "Perry Mason," No. 1-4,pp.64-67.
Krzystofik, Anthony T. "Robert Hiester Montgomery," No. 1-4, pp. 67-70.

Accounting Historians Journal
Volume 3, 1976

Chandra, Gyan and Jacob B. Paperman. "Direct Costing Vs. Absorption Costing: A Historical Review," No.1-4,pp.1-9.
Johns, Ralph S. "In All My Years - Classification Of Accounting Service," No. 1-4, pp. 10-12.
Garner, S. Paul. "A Tribute To Federigo Melis: Part I - The Melis Testimonial," No. 1-4, pp. 13-14.
Padroni, Giovanni. "A Tribute To Federigo Melis: Part II - A Profile Of Melis," No. 1-4, pp. 15-17.
Padroni, Giovanni. "A Tribute To Federigo Melis: Part III - A Bibliography Of Melis' Works," No. 1-4, pp. 18-21.
Most, Kenneth S. "How Wrong Was Sombart?," No. 1-4, pp. 22-28.
Paton, W. A. "In All My Years - Notes On Handicapping," No. 1-4, pp. 29-31.
Holmes, William. "Digging In Boston's Accounting Dumps," No. 1-4, pp. 32-39.
Shenkir, William G. "A Perspective On The Measurement Of Earnings And FASB Policymaking," No. 1-4, pp. 40-42.
Spiceland, J. David and Hilary C. Zaunbrecher. "Human Resource Accounting: An Historical Perspective," No. 1-4, pp. 43-49.
Kreiser, Larry. "A Short History Of The Economic Development And Accounting Treatment Of Pension Plans," No. 1-4, pp. 56-62.
Matz, Adolph. "Edward P. Moxey, Jr.," No. 1-4, pp. 63-68.
Mann, Harvey. "John McDonald," No. 1-4, pp. 68-72.
Baladouni, Vahe. "George Soule," No. 1-4, pp. 72-76.
Ziegler, R. E. "Willard J. Graham," No. 1-4, pp. 76-81.

Accounting Historians Journal
Volume 4, 1977

Hatfield, Henry Rand. "A Hatfield Trilogy: 'Zwei Pfadfinder'," No. 1, pp. 2-8.

Homburger, Richard and Gary John Previts. "A Hatfield Trilogy: The Significance Of 'Zwei Pfadfinder'," No. 1, pp. 9-13.
Hatfield, John. "A Hatfield Trilogy: 'Recollections About Father'," No. 1, pp. 14-16.
Antoni, Tito. "The Pisan Document Of Philadelphia," No. 1, pp. 17-24.
Nishikawa, Kojiro. "The Introduction Of Western Bookkeeping Into Japan," No. 1, pp. 25-36.
Costouros, George J. "Development Of An Accounting System In Ancient Athens In Response To Socio-Economic Changes," No. 1, pp. 37-54.
Martinelli, Alvaro. "Business Ventures In Genoa During The Twelfth Century (1156-1158)," No. 1, pp. 55-68.
Kojima, Osamu. "Accounting Textbooks In Seventeenth Century England - Chiefly About Collins' Work," No. 1, pp. 69-78.
Dunlop, Anna B. G. "The Preservation Of Source Materials," No. 1, pp. 79-87.
Potts, James H. "The Evolution Of Budgetary Accounting Theory And Practice In Municipal Accounting From 1870," No. 1, pp. 89-100.
Grandell, Axel. "The Reckoning Board And Tally Stick," No. 1, pp. 101-105.
Stone, Williard E. "Managerial Accounting On The U.S. 1758 Frontier," No. 1, pp. 107-111.
Parker, R. H. "Research Needs In Accounting History," No. 2, pp. 1-28.
Jones, Thomas. "An Analysis Of Bookkeeping As A Branch Of General Education (1842)," No. 2, pp. 29-46.
Wells, M. C. "Some Influences On The Development Of Cost," No. 2, pp. 47-61.
Kiger, Jack E. and Jan R. Williams. "An Emerging Concept Of Income Presentation," No. 2, pp. 63-77.
Lee, G. A. "The Coming Of Age Of Double Entry: The Giovanni Farolfi Ledger Of 1299-1300," No. 2, pp. 79-95.
Brief, Richard P. "The Accountant's Responsibility For Disclosing Bribery: An Historical Note," No. 2, pp. 97-100.
Van Seventer, A. "O. Ten Have (1899-1974)," No. 2, pp. 101-106.
Holmes, William. "A 13th Century Audit Case," No. 2, pp. 107-111.
Haulotte, R. and E. Stevelinck. "A Bit Of Accounting History: Adding The Pages In The Journal," No. 2, pp. 113-116.

Accounting Historians Journal
Volume 5, 1978

Rueschhoff, Norlin. "The Evolution Of Accounting For Corporate Treasury Stock In The United States," No. 1, pp. 1-7.
Boockholdt, J. L. "Influence Of Nineteenth And Early Twentieth Century Railroad Accounting On The Development Of Modern Accounting Theory," No. 1, pp. 9-28.
Williams, John J. "A New Perspective On The Evolution Of Double-Entry Bookkeeping," No. 1, pp. 29-39.
Costouros, George. "Auditing In The Athenian State In The Golden Age (500-300 B.C.)," No. 1, pp. 41-50.
Inoue, Kiyoshi. "The Oldest German Bookkeeping Text," No. 1, pp. 51-65.
Stone, Williard E. "Grammateus Reappears In 1911," No. 1, pp. 67-68.
Heins, John. "The President's Report (1889)," No. 1, pp. 69-71.
Holmes, William. "Benjamin Gilliam's Book - 1700," No. 1, pp. 73-76.
Paton, W. A. "Wandering Into Accounting - Notes On A Writing Career," No. 2, pp. 1-10.
Ansari, Shahid L. and Diana T. Flamholtz. "Management Science And The Development Of Human Resource Accounting," No. 2, pp. 11-35.
Hallbauer, R. C. "Standard Costing And Scientific Management," No. 2, pp. 37-49.
Forrester, D. A. R. "Whether Malcolm's Is Best Or Old Charge & Discharge," No. 2, pp. 51-61.
Holmes, William. "An 18th Century Accounting Projection From Plymouth, Massachusetts," No. 2, pp. 67-70.
Haseman, W. C. "Management Accounting Literature: 1925 And 1975," No. 2, pp. 71-78.
Sprague, Charles E. "Income And Outlay (1889)," No. 2, pp. 79-84.

Accounting Historians Journal
Volume 6, 1979

Dillon, Gadis J. "Corporate Asset Revaluations: 1925-1934," No. 1, pp. 1-15.
Locke, Robert R. "New Insights Of British Entrepreneurial Performance - 1914," No. 1, pp. 17-28.
Carey, John L. "Early Encounters Between CPAs And The SEC," No. 1, pp. 29-37.
Stone, Williard E. "1794 - Middletown, Delaware - From Accounting Records," No. 1, pp. 39-52.
Rhodadoust, T. and Paul Frishkoff. "On Mercantile Accounting In Pre-Industrial Iran," No. 1, pp. 53-62.
Mann, Harvey. "Accounting For Les Forges De Saint-Maurice 1730 - 1936," No. 1, pp. 63-82.
Flesher, Dale L. "Barter Bookkeeping: A Tenacious System,"

No. 1, pp. 83-86.
Cloyd, Helen M. "George Washington As An Accountant," No. 1, pp. 87-91.
Brief, R. P. "Baily's Paradox," No. 1, pp. 93-94.
Locke, Robert R. "Cost Accounting: An Institutional Yardstick For Measuring British Entrepreneurial Performance, Circa 1914," No. 2, pp. 1-22.
Gibson, Robert W. "Development Of Corporate Accounting In Australia," No. 2, pp. 23-38.
Anderson, Paul F. "Distribution Cost Analysis Methodologies, 1901 - 1941," No. 2, pp. 39-51.
Nakanishi, Akira. "On The Life Of Luca Pacioli," No. 2, pp. 53-59.
McKee, Thomas E. "An 1870 Corporate Audit Committee," No. 2, pp. 61-68.

Accounting Historians Journal
Volume 7, 1980

Porter, David M. "The Waltham System And Early American Textile Cost Accounting," No. 1, pp. 1-15.
Chen, Rosita S. and Sheng-Der Pan. "Frederick Winslow Taylor's Contribution To Accounting," No. 1, pp. 17-35.
Givens, Horace R. "Peter Duff: Accountant And Educator," No. 1, pp. 37-42.
Kistler, Linda H. "The Middlesex Canal - An Analysis Of The Accounting and Management," No. 1, pp. 43-57.
Perkins, Edwin J. and Sherry Levinson. "Partnership Accounting In A Nineteenth Century Merchant Banking House," No. 1, pp. 59-68.
Baxter, William T. "The Account Charge And Discharge," No. 1, pp. 69-71.
Ratcliffe, Thomas A. and Paul Munter. "Asset Valuation: An Historical Perspective," No. 1, pp. 73-78.
Chen, Rosita S. and Sheng-Der Pan. "Frederick Winslow Taylor's Contributions To Cost Accounting," No. 2, pp. 1-22.
Mayer-Sommer, Alan P. "Public Accounting In 1929," No. 2, pp. 23-44.
Murphy, George J. "Some Aspects Of Auditing Evolution In Canada," No. 2, pp. 45-61.
Slocum, Elliott L. and Alfred R. Roberts. "The New York School Of Accounts - A Beginning," No. 2, pp. 63-70.
Hagerman, Robert L. "Accounting In The Bible," No. 2, pp. 71-76.

Accounting Historians Journal
Volume 8, 1981

Var, Turgut. "Internal Control For Ottoman Foundations," No. 1, pp. 1-13.
Gaffikin, M. J. R. "The Development Of University And Professional Accountancy Education In New Zealand," No. 1, pp. 15-36.
Andrews, Wesley T., Jr. "The Evolution Of APB Opinion No. 17 'Accounting For Intangible Assets'; A Study Of The U.S. Position On Accounting For Goodwill," No. 1, pp. 37-49.
Gibson, Robert W. and Roger Arnold. "The Development Of Auditing Standards In Australia," No. 1, pp. 51-65.
Baladouni, Vahe. "The Accounting Records Of The East India Company," No. 1, pp. 67-69.
Davis, Harry Zvi. "Note On The First Recorded Audit In The Bible," No. 1, pp. 71-72.
Sugden, Keith F. "A History Of The Abacus," No. 2, pp. 1-22.
Var, Turgut. "Bonsignori Family Estate Accounting 1461 - 1632," No. 2, pp. 23-35.
Edwards, J. R. and Alison Warman. "Discounted Cash Flow And Business Valuation In A Nineteenth Century Merger: A Note," No. 2, pp. 37-50.
Elam, Rick. "The Cultural Significance Of Accounts - The Philosophy Of DR Scott," No. 2, pp. 51-59.
Filios, Vassilios. "Four Schools Of European Accounting Thought," No. 2, pp. 61-78.
Stabler, Henry Francis and Norman X. Dressel. "May And Paton: Two Giants Revisited," No. 2, pp. 79-90.
Paton, William A. "Recalling George Oliver May And Me," No. 2, pp. 91-95.
Stiner, Frederic M., Jr., John C. Williams and Adrian Sclawy. "Vanishing Accounting Journals Due To Paper Deterioration," No. 2, pp. 97-100.

Accounting Historians Journal
Volume 9, 1982

Davis, Harry Zvi. "History Of LIFO," No. 1, pp. 1-23.
Potts, James H. "A Brief History Of Property And Depreciation Accounting In Municipal Accounting," No. 1, pp. 25-37.
Inoue, Kiyoshi. "'Threefold Bookkeeping' By Matthaus Schwarz," No. 1, pp. 39-51.
Freear, John. "The Final Examinations Of The Institute Of Chartered Accountants In England And Wales, 1882 - 1981," No. 1, pp. 53-89.
Brief, Richard P. "Hicks On Accounting," No. 1, pp. 91-101.
Jones, Thomas W. and J. David Smith. "An Historical Perspective Of Net Present Value And Equivalent Annual Cost," No. 1, pp. 103-110.
Van Fleet, David D. and Daniel A. Wren. "History In Today's Business School," No. 1, pp. 111-118.
Sheldahl, Terry K. "Reporting Treasury Stock As An Asset:

Law, Logic, And Economic Substance," No. 2, pp. 1-23.
Crum, Robert P. "Value-Added Taxation: The Roots Run Deep Into Colonial And Early America," No. 2, pp. 25-42.
Hughes, Hugh P. "Some Contributions Of And Some Controversies Surrounding Thomas Jones And Benjamin Franklin Foster," No. 2, pp. 43-51.
Scott, Richard A. and Elizabeth G. Ward. "Carman G. Blough: His Personality And Formative Years," No. 2, pp. 53-60.
Cooper, William D. "Carman G. Blough's Contributions To Accounting: An Overview," No. 2, pp. 61-67.
Wells, M. C. "Taylor's Contribution To Cost Accounting: A Comment," No. 2, pp. 69-77.

Accounting Historians Journal
Volume 10, 1983

Saito, Shizuki. "Asset Revaluation And Cost Basis: Capital Revaluation In Corporate Financial Reports," No. 1, pp. 1-23.
Lee, T. A. "The Early Debate On Financial And Physical Capital," No. 1, pp. 25-50.
Glautier, Michel W. E. "Searching For Accounting Paradigms," No. 1, pp. 51-68.
Boockholdt, James L. "A Historical Perspective On The Auditor's Role: The Early Experience Of The American Railroads," No. 1, pp. 69-86.
Patterson, Jeffrey L. "The Development Of The Concept Of Corporation From Earliest Roman Times To A.D. 476," No. 1, pp. 87-98.
Jones, James W. "A Description Of A Baltimore Merchant's Journal," No. 1, pp. 99-110.
Tucker, James J., III. "The Economic Activity Of A Grain Mill Located In Bald Eagle Valley, Pennsylvania 1868 To 1872," No. 1, pp. 111-117.
Courtis, John K. "Business Goodwill: Conceptual Clarification Via Accounting, Legal And Etymological Perspectives," No. 2, pp. 1-38.
Yeakel, John A. "The Accountant-Historians Of The Incas," No. 2, pp. 39-51.
Jacobsen, Lyle E. "Use Of Knotted String Accounting Records In Old Hawaii And Ancient China," No. 2, pp. 53-61.
Baladouni, Vahe. "Accounting In The Early Years Of The East India Company," No. 2, pp. 63-80.
Broden, Barry C. and Stephen E. Loeb. "Professional Ethics Of CPAs In Tax Practice: An Historical Perspective," No. 2, pp. 81-97.
Kozum, Robert M. "Antecedents Of The Income Tax In Colonial America," No. 2, pp. 99-116.
Slocum, Elliott L. and Alfred R. Roberts. "The Bureau For Placements," No. 2, pp. 117-127.
Choudhury, N. "Vedic Partnership Rules," No. 2, pp. 129-138.

Accounting Historians Journal
Volume 11, 1984

Hopwood, William S. and Karen S. Hreha. "The Interprofessional Tax Altercation," No. 1, pp. 1-18.
Kistler, Linda H., Clairmont P. Carter and Brackston Hinchey. "Planning And Control In The 19th Century Ice Trade," No. 1, pp. 19-30.
Edwards, J. R. and K. M. Webb. "The Development Of Group Accounting In The United Kingdom To 1933," No. 1, pp. 31-61.
Rankin, Larry J. "The Development Of Compilations And Reviews," No. 1, pp. 63-82.
Garbutt, Douglas. "The Significance Of Ancient Mesopotamia In Accounting History," No. 1, pp. 83-101.
Glynn, John J. "The Development Of British Railway Accounting: 1800 - 1911," No. 1, pp. 103-118.
Parker, Lee D. "The Behavioural Impact Of Budgets: Early Accounting Contributions," No. 1, pp. 119-123.
Mann, Harvey. "Thus Spake The Rabbis - The First Income Tax?," No. 1, pp. 125-133.
Vangermeersch, Richard. "A Comment On Some Remarks By Historians Of Cost Accounting On Engineering Contributions To The Subject," No. 1, pp. 135-140.
Taketera, Sadao and Noboru Nishikawa. "Genesis Of Divisional Management And Accounting Systems In The House Of Mitsui, 1710 - 1730," No. 1, pp. 141-149.
Chen, Rosita S. and Sheng-Der Pan. "Taylor's Contribution To Cost Accounting, A Reply," No. 1, pp. 151-161.
Previts, Gary J. "Frameworks Of American Financial Accounting Thought: An Historical Perspective To 1973," No. 2, pp. 1-17.
Stone, Mary S. "The Pension Accounting Myth," No. 2, pp. 19-38.
Murphy, George J. "Early Canadian Financial Statement Disclosure Legislation," No. 2, pp. 39-59.
Dailey, Michael James. "Cyclical Aspects Of Twentieth Century American Accounting," No. 2, pp. 61-75.
Gibson, Robert W. "Episodes In The Australian Tax Accounting Saga," No. 2, pp. 77-99.
Baladouni, Vahe. "Etymological Observations On Some Accounting Terms," No. 2, pp. 101-109.
Swanson, G. A. "The 'Roots' Of Accounting," No. 2, pp. 111-116.
Cooper, William D. "George C. Mathews: An Early Commissioner Of The SEC," No. 2, pp. 117-127.
Ketz, J. Edward. "Tithing And Income Measurement," No. 2, pp. 129-132.
Bloom, Robert and Hans Heymann. "The Ideas Of Stuart Chase On Waste And Inefficiency," No. 2, pp. 133-142.

Accounting Historians Journal
Volume 12, 1985

Stevelinck, Ernest. "Accounting In Ancient Times," No. 1, pp. 1-16.

Razek, Joseph R. "Accounting On The Old Plantation: A Study Of The Financial Records Of An Ante-Bellum Louisiana Sugar Planter," No. 1, pp. 17-36.

Samson, William D. "The Nineteenth Century Income Tax In The South," No. 1, pp. 37-52.

Myers, John H. "Spiraling Upward: Auditing Methods As Described By Montgomery And His Successors," No. 1, pp. 53-72.

Figlewicz, Raymond E., Donald T. Anderson and C. David Strupeck. "The Evolution And Current State Of Financial Accounting Concepts And Standards In The Nonbusiness Sector," No. 1, pp. 73-98.

Samuels, J. M. "The 1904 Congress Of Accountants: National Or International?," No. 1, pp. 99-105.

Copeland, Benny R. "The Story Of The Sixth Rule," No. 1, pp. 107-116.

Givens, Horace R. "A Total Information System For Physicians: C. 1897," No. 1, pp. 117-120.

Goldberg, Louis and Williard E. Stone. "John Caldwell Colt: A Notorious Accountant," No. 1, pp. 121-130.

Sheldahl, Terry K. "America's Earliest Recorded Text In Accounting: Sarjeant's 1789 Book," No. 2, pp. 1-42.

Engstrom, John H. and Randolph A. Shockley. "Financial Reporting For The Georgia Colony," No. 2, pp. 43-58.

Wood, Thomas D. and Anne J. Sylvestre. "The History Of Advertising By Accountants," No. 2, pp. 59-72.

Tucker, James J., III. "The Role Of Stock Dividends In Defining Income, Developing Capital Market Research And Exploring The Economic Consequences Of Accounting Policy Decisions," No. 2, pp. 73-94.

Stone, Williard E. "Barter: Development Of Accounting Practice And Theory," No. 2, pp. 95-108.

Afosa, Kwame. "Financial Administration Of Ancient Ashanti Empire," No. 2, pp. 109-115.

Flesher, Tonya K. and Dale L. Flesher. "James O. McKinsey," No. 2, pp. 117-128.

Accounting Historians Journal
Volume 13, 1986

Doupnik, Timothy S. "The Evolution Of Financial Statement Indexation In Brazil," No. 1, pp. 1-18.

Baladouni, Vahe. "Financial Reporting In The Early Years Of The East India Company," No. 1, pp. 19-30.

Murphy, George J. "A Chronology Of The Development Of Corporate Financial Reporting In Canada," No. 1, pp. 31-62.

Bursal, Nasuhi. "The Use Of Interest As An Element Of Cost In Germany In The 16th And 17th Centuries," No. 1, pp. 63-70.

Parker, Lee D. "The Classical Model Of Control In The Accounting Literature," No. 1, pp. 71-92.

Haskins, Mark E. and David D. Williams. "A Genealogy Of Today's Contributors To Accounting Research," No. 1, pp. 93-101.

Mepham, Michael J. "Accounting Control: An Historical Note," No. 1, pp. 103-107.

Stevelinck, Ernest. "The Many Faces Of Luca Pacioli: Iconographic Research Over Thirty Years," No. 2, pp. 1-18.

Kreiser, Larry and Philip N. Dare. "Shaker Accounting Records At Pleasant Hill: 1830 - 1850," No. 2, pp. 19-36.

Tabb, J. B. and C. B. Frankham. "The Northern Steamship Company: The Depreciation Problem In Nineteenth Century," No. 2, pp. 37-53.

Swanson, G. A. and John C. Gardner. "The Inception And Evolution Of Financial Reporting In The Protestant Episcopal Church In The United States," No. 2, pp. 55-63.

Mills, Patti A. "Financial Reporting And Stewardship Accounting In Sixteenth-Century Spain," No. 2, pp. 65-76.

Vent, Glenn. "Accounting For Gold And Silver Mines: The Development Of Cost Accounting," No. 2, pp. 77-88.

Rayburn, Frank R. "A Chronological Review Of The Authoritative Literature On Interperiod Tax Allocation: 1940 - 1985," No. 2, pp. 89-108.

Birkett, Brenda S. "The Recent History Of Corporate Audit Committees," No. 2, pp. 109-124.

Chatov, Robert. "William O. Douglas On The Transfer Of The Securities Exchange Commission's Authority For The Development Of Rules For Financial Reporting," No. 2, pp. 125-129.

Campbell, Alan D. "The Monetary System, Taxation, And Publicans In The Time Of Christ," No. 2, pp. 131-135.

Sherman, W. Richard. "Where's The 'r' In Debit?," No. 2, pp. 137-143.

Freear, John. "An Accountant In The Bolivian Jungle," No. 2, pp. 145-150.

Davis, Harry Zvi. "Accounting Measurement And Capacity Limits," No. 2, pp. 151-153.

Accounting Historians Journal
Volume 14, 1987

Solomons, David. "The Twilight Of Income Measurement: Twenty-Five Years On," No. 1, pp. 1-6.

Gamble, George O., Brian O'Doherty and Ladelle M. Hyman. "The Development Of Agency Thought: A Citation Analysis Of The Literature," No. 1, pp. 7-26.

Vangermeersch, Richard. "The Diagram Of The Cost System Of Hans Renold Ltd: A Blueprint For Accounting For Robots," No. 1, pp. 27-31.

Graves, O. Finley. "Accounting For Inflation: Henry Sweeney And The German Gold-Mark Model," No. 1, pp. 33-56.

Seville, Mary Alice. "The Evolution Of Voluntary Health And Welfare Organization Accounting: 1910 - 1985," No. 1, pp. 57-82.

Fleischman, Richard K. and R. Penny Marquette. "Municipal Accounting Reform C. 1900: Ohio's Progressive Accountants," No. 1, pp. 83-94.

Mills, Patti A. "The Probative Capacity Of Accounts In Early-Modern Spain," No. 1, pp. 95-108.

Edwards, James Don. "The AICPA's Century Of Progress," No. 1, pp. 111-121.

Coffman, Edward N. "A Synopsis Of Essays On Historical Accounting Topics," No. 1, pp. 123-129.

Staubus, George J. "The Dark Ages Of Cost Accounting: The Role Of Miscues In The Literature," No. 2, pp. 1-18.

Razek, Joseph R. "Ante-Bellum Bank Accounting - A Case Study: The New Orleans Savings Bank In The 1830s," No. 2, pp. 19-39.

Elmore, Robert C. "The Influence Of Tax Legislation On Financial Accounting: A Study Of The Timber Industry, 1905 - 1925," No. 2, pp. 41-57.

Gellein, Oscar S. "Capital Maintenance: A Neglected Notion," No. 2, pp. 59-69.

Mattessich, Richard. "Prehistoric Accounting And The Problem Of Representation: On Recent Archaeological Evidence Of The Middle-East From 8000 B.C. To 3000 B.C.," No. 2, pp. 71-91.

Burns, Thomas J. "Hall Of Fame Induction 1987 - Philip Defliese," No. 2, pp. 93-97.

Roberts, Thomas C. "The American Association Of Public Accountants (1908): Comments," No. 2, pp. 99-103.

Cannon, James G. "The American Association Of Public Accountants (1908): Comments," No. 2, pp. 104-108.

Magill, Harry T. "A Commentary On CPAs 1908 And Today," No. 2, pp. 109-114.

Accounting Historians Journal
Volume 15, 1988

Reid, Jean Margo. "Legal Acceptance Of Accounting Principles In Great Britain And The United States," No. 1, pp. 1-27.

Tyson, Thomas. "The Nature And Function Of Cost Keeping In A Late Nineteenth Century Small Business," No. 1, pp. 29-44.

Vasarhelyi, Miklos, Da Hsein Bao and Joel Berk. "Trends In The Evolution Of Scholarly Accounting Thought: A Quantitative Examination," No. 1, pp. 45-64.

Foran, Nancy and Dahli Gray. "The Evolution Of The Unitary Tax Apportionment Method," No. 1, pp. 65-87.

Melzer, John T. S. "The Rise Of The Price Of Wheat In The 'Bakery In The Street Of The Fishmarket' In The City Of Lima: 1812-1821," No. 1, pp. 89-118.

Parker, R. H. "Select Bibliography Of Works On The History Of Accounting 1981-1987," No. 2, pp. 1-81.

Bricker, Robert J. "Influences From Early Accounting Literature On Contemporary Research," No. 2, pp. 83-98.

Faircloth, Archie. "The Importance Of Accounting To The Shakers," No. 2, pp. 99-108.

Heier, Jan Richard. "A Content Comparison Of Antebellum Plantation Records And Thomas Affleck's Accounting Principles," No. 2, pp. 131-150.

Mepham, Michael J. "The Scottish Enlightenment And The Development Of Accounting," No. 2, pp. 151-176.

16

ACCOUNTING HORIZONS

Accounting Horizons
Volume 1, 1987

Accounting Horizons
Volume 2, 1988

Schrader, William J., Robert E. Malcom and John J. Willingham. "A Partitioned Events View Of Financial Reporting," No. 4, pp. 10-20.

Maloney, David M. and Robert H. Sanborn. "Interactions Between Financial And Tax Accounting Caused By The Tax Reform Act Of 1986," No. 4, pp. 21-28.

Ritchie, P. C., J. E. Rowcroft and B. A. Trenholm. "An Analytical Basis For The Treatment Of Corporate Income Tax," No. 4, pp. 29-40.

Jeter, Debra C. and Paul K. Chaney. "A Financial Statement Analysis Approach To Deferred Taxes." No. 4, pp. 41-49.

Houston, Carol Olson and Gerhard G. Mueller. "Foreign Exchange Rate Hedging And SFAS No. 52 - Relatives Or Strangers?," No. 4, pp. 50-57.

Reider, Barbara and Gary Saunders. "Management Accounting Education: A Defense Of Criticisms," No. 4, pp. 58-62.

Michaelsen, Robert H. "Development Of An Expert Computer System To Assist In The Classification Of Estate Tax Returns," No. 4, pp. 63-70.

Shank, John K. and Vijay Govindarajan. "The Perils Of Cost Allocation Based On Production Volumes," No. 4, pp. 71-79.

Coughlan, John W. "Anomalies In Calculating Earnings Per Share," No. 4, pp. 80-88.

Shaub, Michael K. "Restructuring The Code Of Professional Ethics: A Review Of The Anderson Committee Report And Its Implications," No. 4, pp. 89-97.

ACCOUNTING, ORGANIZATIONS AND SOCIETY

Accounting, Organizations and Society
Volume 1, 1976

Birnberg, J. G. and N. M. Gandhi. "Toward Defining The Accountant's Role In The Evaluation Of Social Programs," No. 1, pp. 5-10.

Bowman, E. H. and M. Haire. "Social Impact Disclosure And Corporate Annual Reports," No. 1, pp. 11-22.

Epstein, M., E. Flamholtz and J. J. McDonough. "Corporate Social Accounting In The U.S.A.: State Of The Art And Future Prospects," No. 1, pp. 23-42.

Hofstedt, T. R. "Behavioral Accounting Research: Pathologies, Paradigms And Prescriptions," No. 1, pp. 43-58.

Gordon, L. A. and D. Miller. "A Contingency Framework For The Design Of Accounting Information Systems," No. 1, pp. 59-70.

Ullmann, A. A. "The Corporate Environmental Accounting System: A Management Tool For Fighting Environmental Degradation," No. 1, pp. 71-80.

Yetton, P. W. "The Interaction Between A Standard Time Incentive Payment Scheme And A Simple Accounting Information System," No. 1, pp. 81-90.

Robertson, J. "When The Name Of The Game Is Changing, How Do We Keep The Score?," No. 1, pp. 91-96.

Sudreau, P. "The Reform Of The Enterprise," No. 1, pp. 97-104.

Renshall, J. M. "Changing Perceptions Behind The Corporate Report," No. 1, pp. 105-110.

Bedford, N. M. "The Corporate Report: A Discussion," No. 1, pp. 111-116.

Acland, D. "The Effects Of Behavioral Indicators On Investor Decisions: An Exploratory Study," No. 2/3, pp. 133-142.

Carper, Wm. B. and J. M. Posey. "The Validity Of Selected Surrogate Measures of Human Resource Value: A Field Study," No. 2/3, pp. 143-152.

Flamholtz, E. "The Impact Of Human Resource Valuation On Management Decisions: A Laboratory Experiment," No. 2/3, pp. 153-166.

Gambling, T. "Systems Dynamics And Human Resource Accounting," No. 2/3, pp. 167-174.

Marques, E. "Human Resource Accounting: Some Questions and Reflections," No. 2/3, pp. 175-178.

Mirvis, P. H. and B. A. Macy. "Accounting For The Costs And Benefits Of Human Resource Development Programs: An Interdisciplinary Approach," No. 2/3, pp. 179-194.

Ogan, P. "Application Of A Human Resource Value Model: A Field Study," No. 2/3, pp. 195-218.

Schwan, E. S. "The Effects Of Human Resource Accounting Data On Financial Decisions: An Empirical Test," No. 2/3, pp. 219-238.

Tomassini, L. A. "Behavioral Research On Human Resource Accounting: A Contingency Framework," No. 2/3, pp. 239-252.

Cannon, J. A. "Applying The Human Resource Account Framework In An International Airline," No. 2/3, pp. 253-264.

Van Den Bergh, R. J. A. and J. Fischer. "Human Resource Accounting - Some Problems In Implementation," No. 2/3, pp. 265-270.

Ashton, R. H. "Deviation-Amplifying Feedback And Unintended Consequences Of Management Accounting Systems," No. 4, pp. 289-300.

Cammann, C. "Effects Of The Use Of Control Systems," No. 4, pp. 301-314.

Charnes, A., C. Colantoni and W.W. Cooper. "A Futurological Justification For Historical Cost And Multi-Dimensional Accounting," No. 4, pp. 315-338.

Rahman, M. and A. M. McCosh. "The Influence Of Organisational And Personal Factors On The Use Of Accounting Information: An Empirical Study," No. 4, pp. 339-356.

San Miguel, J. G. "Human Information Processing And Its Relevance To Accounting: A Laboratory Study," No. 4, pp. 357-374.

Searfoss, D. G. "Some Behavioral Aspects Of Budgeting For Control: An Empirical Study," No. 4, pp. 375-388.

Medawar, C. "The Social Audit: A Political View," No. 4, pp. 389-394.

Accounting, Organizations and Society
Volume 2, 1977

Dierkes, M. and L. E. Preston. "Corporate Social Accounting - Reporting For The Physical Environment: A Critical Review And Implementation Proposal," No. 1, pp. 3-22.

Ferris, K. R. "Perceived Uncertainty And Job Satisfaction In An Accounting Environment," No. 1, pp. 23-28.

Prakash, P. and A. Rappaport. "Information Inductance And Its Significance For Accounting," No. 1, pp. 29-38.

Schroeder, R. G. and L. F. Imdieke. "Local - Cosmopolitan And Bureaucratic Perceptions In Public Accounting Firms," No. 1, pp. 39-46.

Uecker, W. C. "An Inquiry Into The Need For Currently Feasible Extensions Of The Attest Function In Corporate Annual Reports," No. 1, pp. 47-58.

Vogt, R. A. "A Corporate Strategy For Realizing Equal Employment Opportunity," No. 1, pp. 59-80.

Wilcox, K. A. and C. H. Smith. "Role Discrepancies And The Auditor - Client Relationship," No. 1, pp. 81-97.

Ansari, S. L. "An Integrated Approach To Control System Design," No. 2, pp. 101-112.

Argyris, C. "Organziational Learning And Management Information Systems," No. 2, pp. 113-124.

Coppock, R. "Life Among The Environmentalists: An Elaboration On Wildavsky's 'Economics And Environment/ Rationality And Ritual'," No. 2, pp. 125-130.

Crumbley, D. L., M. J. Epstein and L. L. Bravenec. "Tax Impact In Corporate Social Responsibility Decisions And Reporting," No. 2, pp. 131-140.

Gambling, T. "Magic, Accounting And Morale," No. 2, pp. 141-152.

Livingstone, J. L. and K. R. Balachandran. "Cost And Effectiveness Of Physician Peer Review In Reducing Medicare Overutilization," No. 2, pp. 153-164.

Rhode, J. G., J. E. Sorensen and E. E. Lawler, III. "Sources Of Professional Staff Turnover In Public Accounting Firms Revealed By The Exit Interview," No. 2, pp. 165-176.

San Miguel, J. G. "The Behavioral Sciences And Concepts And Standards For Management Planning And Control," No. 2, pp. 177-186.

Birnberg, J. G., I. Hanson Frieze and M. D. Shields. "The Role Of Attribution Theory In Control Systems," No. 3, pp. 189-200.

Cooper, D. and S. Essex. "Accounting Information And Employee Decision Making," No. 3, pp. 201-218.

Grove, H. D., T. J. Mock and K. B. Ehrenreich. "A Review Of Human Resource Accounting Measurement Systems From A Measurement Theory Perspective," No. 3, pp. 219-236.

Lavin, D. "Some Effects Of The Perceived Independence Of The Auditor," No. 3, pp. 237-244.

Libby, R. and B. L. Lewis. "Human Information Processing Research In Accounting: The State Of The Art," No. 3, pp. 245-268.

Uecker, W. C. and W. R. Kinney, Jr. "Judgmental Evaluation Of Sample Results: A Study Of The Type And Severity Of Errors Made By Practising CPAs," No. 3, pp. 269-275.

Lessem, R. "Corporate Social Reporting In Action: An Evaluation Of British, European and American Practice," No. 4, pp. 279-294.

Gordon, F. E., J. G. Rhode and K. A. Merchant. "The Effects Of Salary And Human Resource Accounting Disclosures On Small Group Relations And Performance," No. 4, pp. 295-306.

Welling, P. "A Goal Programming Model For Human Resource Accounting In A CPA Firm," No. 4, pp. 307-316.

Nystrom, P. C. "Managerial Resistance To A Management System," No. 4, pp. 317-322.

Wright, W. F. "Self-Insight Into The Cognitive Processing Of Financial Information," No. 4, pp. 323-332.

San Miguel, J. G., J. K. Shank and V. Govindarajan. "Extending Corporate Accountability: A Survey And Framework For Analysis," No. 4, pp. 333-348.

Grojer, J. E. and A. Stark. "Social Accounting: A Swedish Attempt," No. 4, pp. 349-381.

Accounting, Organizations and Society
Volume 3, 1978

Hopwood, A. G. "Towards An Organizational Perspective For The Study Of Accounting And Information Systems," No. 1, pp. 3-14.

Bariff, M. L. and J. R. Galbraith. "Intraorganizational Power Considerations For Designing Information Systems," No. 1, pp. 15-28.

Den Hertog, J. Friso. "The Role Of Information And Control Systems In The Process Of Organizational Renewal: Roadblock Or Road Bridge?" No. 1, pp. 29-46.

Hedberg, B. and S. Jonsson. "Designing Semi-Confusing Information Systems For Organizations In Changing Environments," No. 1, pp. 47-64.

Waterhouse, J. H. and P. Tiessen. "A Contingency Framework For Management Accounting Systems Research," No. 1, pp. 65-76.

Wildavsky, A. "Policy Analysis Is What Information Systems Are Not," No. 1, pp. 77-88.

Sathe, V. "The Relevance Of Modern Organization Theory For Managerial Accounting," No. 1, pp. 89-92.

Belkaoui, A. "Linguistic Relativity In Accounting," No. 2, pp. 97-104.

Cherns, A. B. "Alienation And Accountancy," No. 2, pp. 105-114.

Flamholtz, E. and E. Cook. "Connotative Meaning And Its Role In Accounting Change: A Field Study," No. 2, pp. 115-140.

Kamin, J. Y. and J. Ronen. "The Smoothing Of Income Numbers: Some Empirical Evidence On Systematic Differences Among Management-Controlled And Owner-Controlled Firms," No. 2, pp. 141-160.

Earl, M. J. "Prototype Systems For Accounting, Information And Control," No. 2, pp. 161-172.

Birnberg, J. C. "Towards A Bibliography Of The French Social Accounting Literature," No. 2, pp. 175-182.

Tokutani, M. and M. Kawano. "A Note On The Japanese Social Accounting Literature," No. 2, pp. 183-188.

Buzby, S. L. and H. Falk. "A Survey Of The Interest In Social Responsibility Accounting By Mutual Funds," No. 3/4, pp. 191-202.

Gordon, L. A., D. F. Larcker and F. D. Tuggle. "Strategic Decision Processes And The Design Of Accounting Information Systems: Conceptual Linkages," No. 3/4, pp. 203-214.

Jablonsky, S. F. and M. W. Dirsmith. "The Pattern Of PPB Rejection: Something About Organizations, Something About PPB," No. 3/4, pp. 215-226.

Maitre, P. "The Measurement Of The Creation And Distribution Of Wealth In A Firm By The Method Of Surplus Accounts," No. 3/4, pp. 227-236.

Swanson, E. B. "The Two Faces Of Organizational Information," No. 3/4, pp. 237-248.

Carlsson, J., P. Ehn, B. Erlander, M. L. Perby and A. Sandberg. "Planning And Control From The Perspective Of Labour: A Short Presentation Of The DEMOS Project," No. 3/4, pp. 249-260.

Jonson, L. C., B. Jonsson and G. Svensson. "The Application Of Social Accounting To Absenteeism And Personnel Turnover," No. 3/4, pp. 261-268.

Accounting, Organizations and Society
Volume 4, 1979

Chandler, A. D., Jr. and H. Daems. "Administrative Coordination, Allocation And Monitoring: A Comparative Analysis Of The Emergence Of Accounting And Organization In The U.S.A. And Europe," No. 1/2, pp. 3-20.

Clancy, D. K. and F. Collins. "Informal Accounting Information Systems: Some Tentative Findings," No. 1/2, pp. 21-30.

Dillard, J. F. "Valance - Instrumentality - Expectancy Model Validation Using Selected Accounting Groups," No. 1/2, pp. 31-38.

Dirsmith, M. W. and S. F. Jablonsky. "MBO, Political Rationality And Information Inductance," No. 1/2, pp. 39-52.

McDonald, D. and A. G. Puxty. "An Inducement - Contribution Approach To Corporate Financial Reporting," No. 1/2, pp. 53-66.

Ricchiute, D. N. "Standard Setting And The Entity - Proprietary Debate," No. 1/2, pp. 67-76.

Brockhoff, K. "A Note On External Social Reporting By German Companies: A Survey Of 1973 Company Reports," No. 1/2, pp. 77-86.

Dierkes, M. "Corporate Social Reporting In Germany: Conceptual Developments And Practical Experience," No. 1/2, pp. 87-108.

Schreuder, H. "Corporate Social Reporting In The Federal Republic Of Germany: An Overview," No. 1/2, pp. 109-122.

Ullmann, A. A. "Corporate Social Reporting: Political Interests And Conflicts In Germany," No. 1/2, pp. 123-134.

Hagg, I. and G. Hedlund. "'Case Studies' In Accounting Research," No. 1/2, pp. 135-143.

Ansari, S. L. "Towards An Open Systems Approach To Budgeting," No. 3, pp. 149-162.

Banbury, J. and J. E. Nahapiet. "Towards A Framework For The Study Of The Antecedents And Consequences Of Information Systems In Organizations," No. 3, pp. 163-178.

Dillard, J. F. and K. R. Ferris. "Sources Of Professional Staff Turnover In Public Accounting Firms: Some Further Evidence," No. 3, pp. 179-186.

Harvey, D. W., J. G. Rhode and K. A. Merchant. "Accounting Aggregation: User Preferences And Decision Making," No. 3, pp. 187-210.

Thornton, D. B. "Information And Institutions In The Capital Market," No. 3, pp. 211-234.

Young, D. W. "Administrative Theory And Administrative Systems: A Synthesis Among Diverging Fields Of Inquiry," No. 3, pp. 235-244.

Amey, L. R. "Towards A New Perspective On Accounting Control," No. 4, pp. 247-258.

Boland, R. J., Jr. "Control, Causality And Information System Requirements," No. 4, pp. 259-272.

Chan, J. L. "Corporate Disclosure In Occupational Safety And Health: Some Empirical Evidence," No. 4, pp. 273-282.

Firth, M. "Consensus Views And Judgment Models In Materiality Decisions," No. 4, pp. 283-296.

Flesher, T. K. and D. L. Flesher. "Managerial Accounting In An Early 19th Century German American Religious Commune," No. 4, pp. 297-304.

Accounting, Organizations and Society
Volume 5, 1980

Burchell, S., C. Clubb, A. Hopwood, J. Hughes and J. Nahapiet. "The Roles Of Accounting In Organizations And Society," No. 1, pp. 5-28.

Flamholtz, E. G. "The Process Of Measurement In Managerial Accounting: A Psycho-Technical Systems Perspective," No. 1, pp. 31-42.

Buckley, J. W. "Policy Models In Accounting: A Critical Commentary," No. 1, pp. 49-64.

Birnberg, J. G. "The Role Of Accounting In Financial Disclosure," No. 1, pp. 71-80.

Charnes, A. and W. W. Cooper. "Auditing And Accounting For Program Efficiency And Management Efficiency In Not-For-Profit Entities," No. 1, pp. 87-108.

Ijiri, Y. and E. C. Kelly. "Multidimensional Accounting And Distributed Databases: Their Implications For Organizations And Society," No. 1, pp. 115-124.

Ansari, S. L. and J. J. McDonough. "Intersubjectivity - The Challenge And Opportunity For Accounting," No. 1, pp.

129-142.

Tinker, A. M. "Towards A Political Economy Of Accounting: An Empirical Illustration Of The Cambridge Controversies," No. 1, pp. 147-160.

Chambers, R. J. "The Myths And Science Of Accounting," No. 1, pp. 167-180.

Benke, R. L., Jr. and J. G. Rhode. "The Job Satisfaction Of Higher Level Employees In Large Certified Public Accounting Firms," No. 2, pp. 187-202.

Bjorn-Andersen, N. and P. H. Pedersen. "Computer Facilitated Changes In The Management Power Structure," No. 2, pp. 203-216.

Newman, D. P. "Prospect Theory: Implications For Information Evaluation," No. 2, pp. 217-230.

Otley, D. T. and A. J. Berry. "Control, Organisation And Accounting," No. 2, pp. 231-246.

Tomkins, C., D. Rosenberg and I. Colville. "The Social Process Of Research: Some Reflections On Developing A Multi-Disciplinary Accounting Project," No. 2, pp. 247-262.

Belkaoui, A. "The Impact Of Socio-Economic Accounting Statements On The Investment Decision: An Empirical Study," No. 3, pp. 263-284.

Holt, R. N. and R. J. Carroll. "Classification Of Commercial Bank Loans Through Policy Capturing," No. 3, pp. 285-296.

McKenna, E. F. "An Analysis Of Leadership Patterns In The Finance Function," No. 3, pp. 297-310.

Kelly-Newton, L. "A Sociological Investigation Of The U.S.A. Mandate For Replacement Cost Disclosures," No. 3, pp. 311-322.

Snowball, D. "Some Effects Of Accounting Expertise And Information Load: An Empirical Study," No. 3, pp. 323-340.

Brooks, L. J., Jr. "An Attitude Survey Approach To The Social Audit: The Southampton Press Experience," No. 3, pp. 341-356.

Cooper, C. L. "Cumulative Trauma And Stress At Work," No. 3, pp. 357-359.

Ferris, K. R., J. F. Dillard and L. Nethercott. "A Comparison Of V-I-E Model Predictions: A Cross-National Study In Professional Accounting Firms," No. 4, pp. 361-368.

Ginzberg, M. J. "An Organizational Contingencies View Of Accounting And Information Systems Implementation," No. 4, pp. 369-382.

Govindarajan, V. "The Objectives Of Financial Statements: An Empirical Study Of The Use Of Cash Flow And Earnings By Security Analysts," No. 4, pp. 383-392.

Harrell, A. M. and H. D. Klick. "Comparing The Impact Of Monetary And Nonmonetary Human Asset Measures On Executive Decision Making," No. 4, pp. 393-400.

Hopper, T. M. "Role Conflicts Of Management Accountants And Their Position Within Organisation Structures," No. 4, pp. 401-412.

Otley, D. T. "The Contingency Theory Of Management Accounting: Achievement And Prognosis," No. 4, pp. 413-428.

Shields, M. D. "Some Effects Of Information Load On Search Patterns Used To Analyze Performance Reports," No. 4, pp. 429-442.

Accounting, Organizations and Society
Volume 6, 1981

Chen, K. H. and E. L. Summers. "A Study Of Reporting Probabilistic Accounting Figures," No. 1, pp. 1-16.

Dillard, J. F. "A Longitudinal Evaluation Of An Occupational Goal-Expectancy Model In Professional Accounting Organizations," No. 1, pp. 17-26.

Hussein, M. Elmutassim. "The Innovative Process In Financial Accounting Standards Setting," No. 1, pp. 27-38.

Macintosh, N. B. "A Contextual Model Of Information Systems," No. 1, pp. 39-52.

Faircloth, A. W. and D. N. Ricchiute. "Ambiguity Intolerance And Financial Reporting Alternatives," No. 1, pp. 53-68.

Shields, M. D., J. G. Birnberg and I. Hanson Frieze. "Attributions, Cognitive Processes And Control Systems," No. 1, pp. 69-96.

Craft, J. A. "Information Disclosure And The Role Of The Accountant In Collective Bargaining," No. 1, pp. 97-107.

Boland, R. J., Jr. "A Study In System Design: C. West Churchman And Chris Argyris," No. 2, pp. 109-118.

Colville, I. "Reconstructing 'Behavioural Accounting'," No. 2, pp. 119-132.

Pratt, J. and J. Jiambalvo. "Relationships Between Leader Behaviors And Audit Team Performance," No. 2, pp. 133-142.

Ramanathan, K. V. and W. L. Weis. "Supplementing Collegiate Financial Statements With Across-Fund Aggregations: An Experimental Inquiry," No. 2, pp. 143-152.

Williams, J. J. "Zero-Base Budgeting: Prospects For Developing A Semi-Confusing Budgeting Information System," No. 2, pp. 153-166.

Polesie, T. "Action And Reaction: Decisive Factors In Developing Accounting Practice," No. 2, pp. 167-174.

Cooper, D. J., D. Hayes and F. Wolf. "Accounting In Organized Anarchies: Understanding And Designing Accounting Systems In Ambiguous Situations," No. 3, pp. 175-192.

Hofstede, G. "Management Control Of Public And Not-For-Profit Activities," No. 3, pp. 193-216.

Glatzer, W. "An Overview Of The International Development

In Macro Social Indicators," No. 3, pp. 219-234.

Parke, R. and J. L. Peterson. "Indicators Of Social Change: Developments In The United States Of America," No. 3, pp. 235-246.

Heard, J. E. and W. J. Bolce. "The Political Significance Of Corporate Social Reporting In The United States Of America," No. 3, pp. 247-254.

Preston, L. E. "Research On Corporate Social Reporting: Directions For Development," No. 3, pp. 255-262.

Bartoshesky, F. "Raymond A. Bauer: A List Of His Works," No. 3, pp. 263-270.

Aranya, N., J. Pollock and J. Amernic. "An Examination Of Professional Commitment In Public Accounting," No. 4, pp. 271-280.

Belkaoui, A. "The Relationship Between Self-Disclosure Style And Attitudes To Responsibility Accounting," No. 4, pp. 281-290.

Dyckman, T. R. "The Intelligence Of Ambiguity," No. 4, pp. 291-300.

Ewusi-Mensah, K. "The External Organizational Environment And Its Impact On Management Information Systems," No. 4, pp. 301-316.

Ferris, K. R. "Organizational Commitment And Performance In A Professional Accounting Firm," No. 4, pp. 317-326.

Purdy, D. "The Provision Of Financial Information To Employees: A Study Of The Reporting Practices Of Some Large Public Companies In The United Kingdom," No. 4, pp. 327-338.

Rosenzweig, K. "An Exploratory Field Study Of The Relationship Between The Controller's Department And Overall Organizational Characteristics," No. 4, pp. 339-354.

Trotman, K. T. and G. W. Bradley. "Associations Between Social Responsibility Disclosure And Characteristics Of Companies," No. 4, pp. 355-362.

Accounting, Organizations and Society
Volume 7, 1982

Dyckman, T. R., R. E. Hoskin and R. J. Swieringa. "An Accounting Change And Information Processing Changes," No. 1, pp. 1-12.

Ferris, K. R. "Perceived Environmental Uncertainty, Organizational Adaptation And Employee Performance: A Longitudinal Study In Professional Accounting Firms," No. 1, pp. 13-26.

Solomon, I., J. L. Krogstad, M. B. Romney, and L. A. Tomassini. "Auditors' Prior Probability Distributions For Account Balances," No. 1, pp. 27-42.

Wilner, N. A. "SFAS 8 And Information Inductance: An Experiment," No. 1, pp. 43-52.

Wiseman, J. "An Evaluation Of Environmental Disclosures Made In Corporate Annual Reports," No. 1, pp. 53-64.

Wright, W. F. "Comparison Of The Lens And Subjective Probability Paradigms For Financial Research Purposes," No. 1, pp. 65-78.

Skousen, C. R. "Public Interest Accounting: A Look At The Issues," No. 1, pp. 79-85.

Benston, G. J. "Accounting And Corporate Accountability," No. 2, pp. 87-106.

Collins, F. "Managerial Accounting Systems And Organizational Control: A Role Perspective," No. 2, pp. 107-122.

Rosenberg, D., C. Tomkins and P. Day. "A Work Role Perspective Of Accountants In Local Government Service Departments," No. 2, pp. 123-138.

Selto, F. H. "Internal Adaptations To Effects Of Changes In Financial Accounting Standards," No. 2, pp. 139-148.

Swieringa, R. J. and J. H. Waterhouse. "Organizational Views Of Transfer Pricing," No. 2, pp. 149-166.

Tinker, A. M., B. D. Merino and M. D. Neimark. "The Normative Origins Of Positive Theories: Ideology And Accounting Thought," No. 2, pp. 167-200.

Aranya, N., R. Lachman and J. Amernic. "Accountants' Job Satisfaction: A Path Analysis," No. 3, pp. 201-216.

Dery, D. "Erring And Learning: An Organizational Analysis," No. 3, pp. 217-224.

Ferris, K. R. "Educational Predictors Of Professional Pay And Performance," No. 3, pp. 225-230.

Libby, R. and B. L. Lewis. "Human Information Processing Research In Accounting: The State Of The Art In 1982," No. 3, pp. 231-286.

Jonsson, S. "Budgetary Behaviour In Local Government - A Case Study Over 3 Years," No. 3, pp. 287-304.

Rorke, C. H. "An Early Pricing Model Regarding The Value Of A Cat: A Historical Note," No. 3, pp. 305-306.

Davis, S. W., K. Menon and G. Morgan. "The Images That Have Shaped Accounting Theory," No. 4, pp. 307-318.

Dirsmith, M. W. and B. L. Lewis. "The Effect Of External Reporting On Managerial Decision Making: Some Antecedent Conditions," No. 4, pp. 319-336.

Dykxhoorn, H. J. and K. E. Sinning. "Perceptions Of Auditor Independence: Its Perceived Effect On The Loan And Investment Decisions Of German Financial Statement Users," No. 4, pp. 337-348.

Johnson, W. B. "The Impact Of Confidence Interval Information On Probability Judgements," No. 4, pp. 349-368.

Pratt, J. and J. Jiambalvo. "Determinants Of Leader Behavior In An Audit Environment," No. 4, pp. 369-380.

Seiler, R. E. and R. W. Bartlett. "Personality Variables As Predictors Of Budget System Characteristics," No. 4, pp. 381-404.

Williams, P. F. "The Predictive Ability Paradox In Behavioral Accounting Research," No. 4, pp. 405-410.

Accounting, Organizations and Society
Volume 8, 1983

Ferris, K. R. and D. F. Larcker. "Explanatory Variables Of Auditor Performance In A Large Public Accounting Firm," No. 1, pp. 1-12.

Jiambalvo, J., D. J. H. Watson and J. V. Baumler. "An Examination Of Performance Evaluation Decisions In CPA Firm Subunits," No. 1, pp. 13-30.

McLeay, S. "Value Added: A Comparative Study," No. 1, pp. 31-56.

Sotto, R. "Scientific Utopia And Accounting," No. 1, pp. 57-72.

Spicer, B. H. and V. Ballew. "Management Accounting Systems And The Economics Of Internal Organization," No. 1, pp. 73-98.

Mushkat, M. "Using Macro-Societal Accounting Data: Some Critical Afterthoughts," No. 1, pp. 99-108.

Birnberg, J. G., L. Turopolec and S. M. Young. "The Organizational Context Of Accounting," No. 2/3, pp. 111-130.

Johnson, H. T. "The Search For Gain In Markets And Firms: A Review Of The Historical Emergence Of Management Accounting Systems," No. 2/3, pp. 139-146.

Flamholtz, E. G. "Accounting, Budgeting And Control Systems In Their Organizational Context: Theoretical And Empirical Perspectives," No. 2/3, pp. 153-170.

Mirvis, P. H. and E. E. Lawler, III. "Systems Are Not Solutions: Issues In Creating Information Systems That Account For The Human Organization," No. 2/3, pp. 175-190.

Mitroff, I. I. and R. O. Mason. "Can We Design Systems For Managing Messes? Or, Why So Many Management Information Systems Are Uninformative," No. 2/3, pp. 195-204.

Markus, M. L. and J. Pfeffer. "Power And The Design And Implementation Of Accounting And Control Systems," No. 2/3, pp. 205-218.

Boland, R. J., Jr. and L. R. Pondy. "Accounting In Organizations: A Union Of Natural And Rational Perspectives," No. 2/3, pp. 223-234.

Hayes, D. C. "Accounting For Accounting: A Story About Managerial Accounting," No. 2/3, pp. 241-250.

Tiessen, P. and J. H. Waterhouse. "Towards A Descriptive Theory Of Management Accounting," No. 2/3, pp. 251-268.

Cooper, D. "Tidiness, Muddle And Things: Commonalities And Divergencies In Two Approaches To Management Accounting Research," No. 2/3, pp. 269-286.

Hopwood, A. G. "On Trying To Study Accounting In The Contexts In Which It Operates," No. 2/3, pp. 287-305.

Brownell, P. "Leadership Style, Budgetary Participation And Managerial Behavior," No. 4, pp. 307-322.

Covaleski, M. A. and M. W. Dirsmith. "Budgeting As A Means For Control And Loose Coupling," No. 4, pp. 323-340.

Kilmann, R. H. "The Costs Of Organization Structure: Dispelling The Myths Of Independent Divisions And Organization-Wide Decision Making," No. 4, pp. 341-360.

Tomkins, C. and R. Groves. "The Everyday Accountant And Researching His Reality," No. 4, pp. 361-374.

Abdel-Khalik, A. R. and B. B. Ajinkya. "An Evaluation Of 'The Everyday Accountant And Researching His Reality'," No. 4, pp. 375-384.

Morgan, G. "Social Science And Accounting Research: A Commentary On Tomkins And Groves," No. 4, pp. 385-388.

Willmott, H. C. "Paradigms For Accounting Research: Critical Reflections On Tomkins And Groves' 'Everyday Accountant And Researching His Reality'," No. 4, pp. 389-406.

Tomkins, C. and R. Groves. "'The Everyday Accountant and Researching His Reality: Further Thoughts'," No. 4, pp. 407-418.

Accounting, Organizations and Society
Volume 9, 1984

Bloom, R., P. T. Elgers and D. Murray. "Functional Fixation In Product Pricing: A Comparison Of Individuals And Groups," No. 1, pp. 1-12.

Daroca, F. P. "Informational Influences On Group Decision Making In A Participative Budgeting Context," No. 1, pp. 13-32.

Gordon, L. A. and V. K. Narayanan. "Management Accounting Systems, Perceived Environmental Uncertainty And Organization Structure: An Empirical Investigation," No. 1, pp. 33-48.

Norris, D. R. and R. E. Niebuhr. "Professionalism, Organizational Commitment And Job Satisfaction In An Accounting Organization," No. 1, pp. 49-60.

Shields, D. "Small CPA Firm Product Differentiation In The Small Business Market," No. 1, pp. 61-80.

Sutton, T. G. "Lobbying Of Accounting Standard-Setting Bodies In The U.K. And The U.S.A.: A Downsian Analysis," No. 1, pp. 81-98.

Maunders, K. T. and B. J. Foley. "Information Disclosure And The Role Of The Accountant In Collective Bargaining - Some Comments," No. 1, pp. 99-106.

Craft, J. A. "A Reply To Maunders And Foley," No. 1, pp. 107-108.

Gordon, L. A., S. Haka and A. G. Schick. "Strategies For Information Systems Implementation: The Case Of Zero Base Budgeting," No. 2, pp. 111-124.

Govindarajan, V. "Appropriateness Of Accounting Data In Performance Evaluation: An Empirical Examination Of Environmental Uncertainty As An Intervening Variable," No. 2, pp. 125-136.

Kida, T. E. "Performance Evaluation And Review Meeting

Governments: An Empirical Study," No. 6, pp. 499-520.
Preston, A. "Interactions And Arrangements In The Process Of Informing," No. 6, pp. 521-540.
Schweikart, J. A. "The Relevance Of Managerial Accounting Information: A Multinational Analysis," No. 6, pp. 541-554.
Willmott, H. "Organising The Profession: A Theoretical And Historical Examination Of The Development Of The Major Accountancy Bodies In The U.K.," No. 6, pp. 555-582.
Chua, Wai Fong. "Theoretical Constructions Of And By The Real," No. 6, pp. 583-597.

Accounting, Organizations and Society
Volume 12, 1987

Bouwman, M. J., P. A. Frishkoff and P. Frishkoff. "How Do Financial Analysts Make Decisions? A Process Model Of The Investment Screening Decision," No. 1, pp. 1-30.
Haka, S. F. "Capital Budgeting Techniques And Firm Specific Contingencies: A Correlational Analysis," No. 1, pp. 31-48.
Macintosh, N. B. and R. L. Daft. "Management Control Systems And Departmental Interdependencies; An Empirical Study," No. 1, pp. 49-64.
Hopwood, A. G. "Accounting And Gender: An Introduction," No. 1, pp. 65-70.
Tinker, T. and M. Neimark. "The Role Of Annual Reports In Gender And Class Contradictions At General Motors: 1917-1976," No. 1, pp. 71-88.
Burrell, G. "No Accounting For Sexuality," No. 1, pp. 89-102.
Crompton, R. "Gender And Accountancy: A Response To Tinker And Neimark," No. 1, pp. 103-110.
Cowen, S. S., L. B. Ferreri and L. D. Parker. "The Impact Of Corporate Characteristics On Social Responsibility Disclosure: A Typology And Frequency-Based Analysis," No. 2, pp. 111-122.
Harte, G. F. and D. L. Owen. "Fighting De-Industrialisation: The Role Of Local Government Social Audits," No. 2, pp. 123-142.
Houghton, K. A. "True And Fair View: An Empirical Study Of Connotative Meaning," No. 2, pp. 143-152.
March, J. G. "Ambiguity And Accounting: The Elusive Link Between Information And Decision Making," No. 2, pp. 153-168.
Williams, P. F. "The Legitimate Concern With Fairness," No. 2, pp. 169-192.
Brown, L. D., J. C. Gardner and M. A. Vasarhelyi. "An Analysis Of The Research Contributions Of 'Accounting, Organizations And Society': 1976-1984," No. 2, pp. 193-204.
Hopwood, A. G. "The Archaeology Of Accounting Systems," No. 3, pp. 207-234.
Miller, P. and T. O'Leary. "Accounting And The Construction Of The Governable Person," No. 3, pp. 235-266.
Boland, R. J., Jr. "Discussion Of 'Accounting And The Construction Of The Governable Person'," No. 3, pp. 267-272.
Puxty, A. G., H. C. Willmott, D. J. Cooper and T. Lowe. "Modes Of Regulation In Advanced Capitalism: Locating Accountancy In Four Countries," No. 3, pp. 273-292.
Swieringa, R. J. and K. E. Weick. "Management Accounting And Action," No. 3, pp. 293-308.
Flamholtz, E. G. "Valuation Of Human Assets In A Securities Brokerage Firm: An Empirical Study," No. 3, pp. 309-318.
Gambling, T. "Accounting For Rituals," No. 3, pp. 319-330.
Mear, R. and M. Firth. "Assessing The Accuracy Of Financial Analyst Security Return Predictions," No. 3, pp. 331-340.
Richardson, A. J. "Accounting As A Legitimating Institution," No. 3, pp. 341-356.
Simons, R. "Accounting Control Systems And Business Strategy: An Empirical Analysis," No. 3, pp. 357-374.
Shields, M. D., I. Solomon and W. S. Waller. "Effects Of Alternative Sample Space Representations On The Accuracy Of Auditors' Uncertainty Judgments," No. 3, pp. 375-388.
Coombs, R. W. "Accounting For The Control Of Doctors: Management Information Systems In Hospitals," No. 3, pp. 389-404.
Cooper, D. J. and T. M. Hopper. "Critical Studies In Accounting," No. 4/5, pp. 407-414.
Armstrong, P. "The Rise Of Accounting Controls In British Capitalist Enterprises," No. 4/5, pp. 415-436.
Hopper, T., J. Storey and H. Willmott. "Accounting For Accounting: Towards The Development Of A Dialectical View," No. 4/5, pp. 437-456.
Knights, D. and D. Collinson. "Disciplining The Shopfloor: A Comparison Of The Disciplinary Effects Of Managerial Psychology And Financial Accounting," No. 4/5, pp. 457-478.
Laughlin, R. C. "Accounting Systems In Organisational Contexts: A Case For Critical Theory," No. 4/5, pp. 479-502.
Lehman, C. and T. Tinker. "The 'Real' Cultural Significance Of Accounts," No. 4/5, pp. 503-522.
Thompson, G. "Inflation Accounting In A Theory Of Calculation," No. 4/5, pp. 523-544.
Ansari, S. and K. J. Euske. "Rational, Rationalizing, And Reifying Uses Of Accounting Data In Organizations," No. 6, pp. 549-570.
Holt, D. L. "Auditors And Base Rates Revisited," No. 6, pp. 571-578.

Lavoie, D. "The Accounting Of Interpretations And The Interpretation Of Accounts: The Communicative Function Of 'The Language Of Business'," No. 6, pp. 579-604.

Accounting, Organizations and Society
Volume 13, 1988

Covaleski, M. A. and M. W. Dirsmith. "The Use Of Budgetary Symbols In The Political Arena: An Historically Informed Field Study," No. 1, pp. 1-24.
Dermer, J. "Control And Organizational Order," No. 1, pp. 25-36.
Hoskin, K. W. and R. H. Macve. "The Genesis Of Accountability: The West Point Connections," No. 1, pp. 37-74.
Soeters, J. and H. Schreuder. "The Interaction Between National And Organizational Cultures In Accounting Firms," No. 1, pp. 75-86.
Waller, W. S. "Slack In Participative Budgeting: The Joint Effect Of A Truth-Inducing Pay Scheme And Risk Preferences," No. 1, pp. 87-100.
Colbert, J. L. "Inherent Risk: An Investigation Of Auditors' Judgments," No. 2, pp. 111-122.
Enis, C. R. "The Impact Of Current-Valued Data On The Predictive Judgments Of Investors," No. 2, pp. 123-146.
Iselin, E. R. "The Effects Of Information Load And Information Diversity On Decision Quality In A Structured Decision Task," No. 2, pp. 147-164.
Tinker, T. "Panglossian Accounting Theories: The Science Of Apologising In Style," No. 2, pp. 165-190.
Williams, J. J. and C. R. Hinings. "A Note On Matching Control System Implications With Organizational Characteristics: ZBB And MBO Revisited," No. 2, pp. 191-200.
Skousen, C. R. and Ji-Liang Yang. "Western Management Accounting And The Economic Reforms Of China," No. 2, pp. 201-206.
Zhou, Zhong Hui. "Chinese Accounting Systems And Practices," No. 2, pp. 207-224.
Chenhall, R. H. and P. Brownell. "The Effect Of Participative Budgeting On Job Satisfaction And Performance: Role Ambiguity As An Intervening Variable," No. 3, pp. 225-234.
Dean, R. A., K. R. Ferris and C. Konstans. "Occupational Reality Shock And Organizational Commitment: Evidence From The Accounting Profession," No. 3, pp. 251-262.
Houghton, K. A. "The Measurement Of Meaning In Accounting: A Critical Analysis Of The Principal Evidence," No. 3, pp. 263-280.
Lukka, K. "Budgetary Biasing In Organizations: Theoretical Framework And Empirical Evidence," No. 3, pp. 281-302.
Spicer, B. H. "Towards An Organizational Theory Of The Transfer Pricing Process," No. 3, pp. 303-324.
Hopwood, A. G. "On Origins And Development: Some Reflections On The 40th Anniversary Of Pergamon Press And The 65th Birthday Of Its Founder, Robert Maxwell," No. 4, pp. 329-332.
Nahapiet, J. "The Rhetoric And Reality Of An Accounting Change: A Study Of Resource Allocation," No. 4, pp. 333-358.
Noreen, E. "The Economics Of Ethics: A New Perspective On Agency Theory," No. 4, pp. 359-370.
Kaplan, S. E., P. M. J. Reckers and S. J. Roark. "An Attribution Theory Analysis Of Tax Evasion Related Judgments," No. 4, pp. 371-380.
Richardson, A. J. "Accounting Knowledge And Professional Privilege," No. 4, pp. 381-396.
Rockness, J. and P. F. Williams. "A Descriptive Study Of Social Responsibility Mutual Funds," No. 4, pp. 397-414.
Czarniawska-Joerges, B. "Dynamics Of Organizational Control: The Case Of Berol Kemi AB," No. 4, pp. 415-430.
Anderson, M. J. "A Comparative Analysis Of Information And Evaluation Behavior Of Professional And Non-Professional Financial Analysts," No. 5, pp. 431-446.
Birnberg, J. G. and C. Snodgrass. "Culture And Control: A Field Study," No. 5, pp. 447-464.
Mia, L. "Managerial Attitude, Motivation And The Effectiveness Of Budget Participation," No. 5, pp. 465-475.
Morgan, G. "Accounting As Reality Construction: Towards A New Epistemology For Accounting Practice," No. 5, pp. 477-485.
Williams, D. D. and M. W. Dirsmith. "The Effects Of Audit Technology On Auditor Efficiency: Auditing And The Timeliness Of Client Earnings Announcements," No. 5, pp. 487-507.
Jonsson, S. and A. Gronlund. "Life With A Sub-Contractor: New Technology And Management Accounting," No. 5, pp. 513-532.
Choudhury, N. "The Seeking Of Accounting Where It Is Not: Towards A Theory Of Non-Accounting In Organizational Settings," No. 6, pp. 549-557.
Colignon, R. and M. Covaleski. "An Examination Of Managerial Accounting Practices As A Process Of Mutual Adjustment," No. 6, pp. 559-579.
Shields, M. D. and W. S. Waller. "A Behavioral Study Of Accounting Variables In Performance-Incentive Contracts," No. 6, pp. 581-594.
Wright, A. "The Impact Of Prior Working Papers On Auditor Evidential Planning Judgments," No. 6, pp. 595-605.
Young, S. M., M. D. Shields and G. Wolf. "Manufacturing Controls And Performance: An Experiment," No. 6, pp. 607-618.

THE ACCOUNTING REVIEW

3, pp. 289-296.

Jackson, J. Hugh. "Teaching Auditing By The Case Method," No. 3, pp. 297-310.

Winter, S. G. "The Next Decade In Accounting," No. 3, pp. 311-322.

Rorem, C. Rufus. "Differential Costs," No. 4, pp. 333-341.

Hatfield, Henry Rand. "An Accounting Paradox," No. 4, pp. 342-344.

Atkins, Paul M. "University Instruction In Industrial Cost Accounting, Part I," No. 4, pp. 345-363.

Drucker, A. P. R. "The Accountant As An Efficiency Expert," No. 4, pp. 364-368.

Porter, Charles H. "Is It Machinery Or Is It Junk?," No. 4, pp. 369-374.

Scott, DR. "Valuation Of Investment Securities," No. 4, pp. 375-382.

Littleton, A. C. "The Evolution Of The Journal Entry," No. 4, pp. 383-396.

Wildman, John R. "Appreciation From The Point Of View Of The Certified Public Accountant," No. 4, pp. 397-406.

Accounting Review
Volume 4, 1929

Canning, J. B. "Some Divergencies of Accounting Theory From Economic Theory," No. 1, pp. 1-8.

Sanders, T. H. "The Uses Of Differential Costs," No. 1, pp. 9-15.

Andersen, Arthur. "Financial And Industrial Investigations," No. 1, pp. 16-22.

Atkins, Paul M. "University Instruction In Industrial Cost Accounting, Part II" No. 1, pp. 23-32.

Frazer, George E. "Accounting In Italy," No. 1, pp. 33-37.

Baily, H. H. "Some Observations On Accounting In France And Germany," No. 1, pp. 38-43.

Robbins, Carl B. "Business Secrets (Part II)," No. 2, pp. 65-79.

Heilman, E. A. "Realized Income," No. 2, pp. 80-87.

Noble, H. S. "Cost Accounting In Great Britain," No. 2, pp. 88-93.

Daines, H. C. "The Changing Objectives Of Accounting," No. 2, pp. 94-110.

Canning, John B. "Hatfield's Paradox," No. 2, pp. 111-115.

Scott, DR. "Depreciation And Repair Costs," No. 2, pp. 116-120.

Lay, Chester F. "Business Policy As Related To Accounting," No. 2, pp. 121-128.

Raper, C. L. "Shall Accounting Instructors Indulge In Outside Practice?," No. 2, pp. 129-130.

Littleton, A. C. "Value And Price In Accounting, (Part II)" No. 3, pp. 147-154.

Robbins, Carl B. "Business Secrets," No. 3, pp. 155-166.

Rorem, C. Rufus. "Replacement Cost In Accounting Valuation," No. 3, pp. 167-174.

Drucker, A. P. R. "Budgeting And The Sales Quota," No. 3, pp. 175-180.

Heckert, J. Brooks. "Methods And Advantages Of Early Closing," No. 3, pp. 181-193.

Burrell, O. K. "An Experiment In Student And Teacher Rating," No. 3, pp. 194-197.

Hornberger, D. J. "Accounting For No-Par Stock Issues," No. 4, pp. 213-217.

Paton, W. A. "The Dividend Code," No. 4, pp. 218-220.

Scott, DR. "Valuation For Depreciation And The Financing Of Replacements," No. 4, pp. 221-226.

Graham, W. J. "Machine Accounting In the Accounting Curriculum," No. 4, pp. 227-233.

Littleton, A. C., Lloyd Morey, David Himmelblau and F. E. Ross. "The International Congress On Accounting," No. 4, pp. 234-246.

Newlove, G. H. "Relative Sales Value Theory Of Allocating Costs," No. 4, pp. 251-254.

Accounting Review
Volume 5, 1930

Graduate Students Of The University Of Illinois. "What Is Appreciation?," No. 1, pp. 1-10.

Carpenter, C. C. "Comments On What Is Appreciation," No. 1, pp. 10-12.

Hatfield, H. R. "Comments On What Is Appreciaiton," No. 1, pp. 12-14.

Wildman, J. R. "Comments On What Is Appreciation," No. 1, pp. 14-15.

Dillavou, E. R. "Comments On Is Appreciation Available For Dividends," No. 1, pp. 22-26.

Hatfield, H. R. "Comments On Is Appreciation Available For Dividends," No. 1, pp. 26-27.

Wildman, J. R. "Comments On Is Appreciation Available For Dividends," No. 1, pp. 27-28.

Hatfield, H. R. "Comments On Should Appreciation Be Brought Into The Accounts?," No. 1, pp. 33-34.

Wildman, J. R. "Comments On Should Appreciation Be Brought Into The Accounts?," No. 1, p. 34.

Barr, Andrew, Jr. "Comments On How Can Appreciation Be Treated In The Accounts?," No. 1, pp. 41-44.

Foster, L. O. "Comments On Is Appreciation A Depreciating Element?," No. 1, pp. 50-53.

Hatfield, H. R. "Comments On Is Appreciation A Depreciating Element?," No. 1, pp. 53-54.

Wildman, J. R. "Comments On Is Appreciation A Depreciating Element?," No. 1, pp. 54-55.

Fisher, Irving. "General Comments On Appreciation," No. 1, pp. 55-57.

Littleton, A. C. "General Comments On Appreciation," No. 1, pp. 57-59.

Krebs, William S. "Asset Appreciation, Its Economic And Accounting Significance," No. 1, pp. 60-69.

Littleton, A. C. "The International Congress On Accounting: Education For The Profession," No. 1, pp. 70-75.

Adams, James P. "Depreciation Accounting And Public Utility Valuation," No. 2, pp. 99-105.

Mason, Perry. "Accounting For Current Depreciation," No. 2. pp. 106-110.

Bauer, John. "Depreciation And Public Utility Valuation," No. 2, pp. 111-116.

Bonbright, James C. "The Concept Of Depreciation As An Accounting Category," No. 2, pp. 117-124.

Nash, L. R. "Depreciation Accounting Methods For Public Utilities," No. 2, pp. 125-141.

Campbell, James A. "Accounting In The Curriculum Of The Small Liberal Arts College," No. 2, pp. 142-145.

Howard, Stanley E. "Accounting Instruction In The Liberal Arts Curriculum," No. 2, pp. 146-149.

Hanslein, John D. "The Position Of Accounting In The Small Liberal Arts College," No. 2, pp. 150-152.

Nerlove, S. H. "Insiders And Corporate Income Streams," No. 2, pp. 153-156.

Fryxell, Carl A. "Should Appreciation Be Brought Into The Accounts," No. 2, pp. 157-158.

Rorem, C. Rufus. "Cost Analysis For Hospitals," No. 2, pp. 159-161.

Schranz, Andrew. "Modern German Accountancy," No. 2, pp. 162-167.

Heckert, J. B. "Comments On The Definition Of Earned Surplus," No. 2, pp. 168-174.

Briggs, L. L. "Accounting In Collegiate Schools Of Business," No. 2, pp. 175-181.

Stevenson, R. A. "Short Tests In Accounting Theory And Practice," No. 2, pp. 182-187.

Stevenson, R. A. "Accounting In The Engineering Curriculum," No. 3, pp. 205-207.

White, James C. "Teaching Of Accounting In Schools Of Engineering," No. 3, pp. 208-212.

Dohr, James L. "Accounting In The Law School," No. 3, pp. 213-214.

Frisbee, Ira N. "Problems In Presenting The Financial Condition Of An Endowed College Or University," No. 3, pp. 215-221.

Shaulis, L. L. "Instruction In Accounting For Liberal Education," No. 3, pp. 222-225.

Guthmann, H. G. "Actuarial Versus Sinking Fund Type Formula For Valuation," No. 3, pp. 226-230.

Schmaltz, Kurt. "The Business Periodicals Of Germany," No. 3, pp. 231-234.

Schmidt, Fritz. "The Importance Of Replacement Value," No. 3, pp. 235-242.

Penndorf, B. "The Relation Of Taxation To The History Of The Balance Sheet," No. 3, pp. 243-251.

Gregory, H. E. "The Current Ratio A Function Of Two Variables," No. 3, pp. 254-256.

Burrell, O. K. and A. B. Stillman. "An Aptitude Test For Accounting," No. 3, pp. 257-262.

Littleton, A. C. "Foreign Accounting Terms," No. 3, p. 262-263.

Sweeney, H. W. "Maintenance Of Capital," No. 4, pp. 277-287.

Cox, C. E. "What Is Cost?," No. 4, pp. 288-297.

Dunham, C. F. "On The Meaning Of 'Capital'," No. 4, pp. 298-300.

Drucker, A. P. R. "Factory Production Under Budgetary Control," No. 4, pp. 301-304.

Voss, Wilhelm. "Corporation Auditing Requirements Under German Commercial Law," No. 4, pp. 305-307.

Taggart, P. "English Public Utility Concerns And Statutory Reserve Funds," No. 4, pp. 308-310.

Kats, P. "A Surmise Regarding The Origin Of Bookkeeping By Double Entry," No. 4, pp. 311-316.

Heilman, E. A. "Coordination Between High-School Bookkeeping And College Accounting Courses," No. 4, pp. 317-320.

Littleton, A. C. "Foreign Accounting Terms," No. 4, pp. 320-322.

Accounting Review
Volume 6, 1931

Wasserman, Max J. "Accounting Practice In France During The Period Of Monetary Inflation (1919-1927)," No. 1, pp. 1-32.

Littleton, A. C. "A Cost Approach to Elementary Bookkeeping," No. 1, pp. 33-37.

Kendrick, Hazen W. "The Need For Accounting In the Law School Curriculum," No. 1, pp. 38-41.

Schlauch, William S. "Contents Of A Mathematics Course For Collegiate Schools Of Business," No. 1, pp. 42-46.

Myer, Joseph C. "Teaching The Accountant The History And Ethics Of His Profession," No. 1, pp. 47-50.

Howard, Stanley E. "Charge And Discharge," No. 1, pp. 51-56.

Baily, H. H. "First-Year Examinations," No. 1, pp. 57-62.

Kunze, H. L. "Liquidation Of Partnership Under Court Administration," No. 1, pp. 62-64.

Littleton, A. C. "Foreign Accounting Terms," No. 1, pp. 64-65.

Paton, W. A. "Economic Theory And Relation to Accounting," No. 2, pp. 89-96.

Walker, C. E. "The History Of The Joint Stock Company," No.

Accounting Review
Volume 7, 1932

Accounting Review
Volume 8, 1933

Goldman, David. "The Accountant In Bankruptcy And Receivership Cases," No. 3, pp. 219-223.

Briggs, L. L. "Dividends On Non-Cumulative Preferred Stock," No. 3, pp. 224-238.

Hasenack, W. "Depression Balance Sheets And Present Day Values," No. 3, pp. 239-242.

Heilman, E. A. "Comments And Questions On The Use Of Ratios," No. 3, pp. 246-247.

Pilcher, D. J. "Three-Fold Presentation Of An Accounting Problem," No. 3, pp. 247-252.

Lund, Reuel I. "Status Of Partner's Loan Accounts In Partnership Dissolution," No. 3, pp. 252-254.

Littleton, A. C. "Socialized Accounts," No. 4 pp. 267-271.

Weidenhammer, Robert. "The Accountant And The Securities Act," No. 4 pp. 272-278.

Schluter, W. C. "Accountancy Under Economic Self-Government," No. 4 pp. 279-284.

Rosenblum, Leo. "The Failure Of The City Of Glasgow Bank," No. 4 pp. 285-291.

Payne, Robert E. "The Importance Of Clarity In Balance Sheet Display," No. 4 pp. 292-301.

Daniels, M. B. "The Valuation Of Fixed Assets," No. 4 pp. 302-316.

Preinreich, Gabriel A. D. "Taxation And The Natural Business Year," No. 4 pp. 317-322.

Sweeney, Henry W. "Income," No. 4 pp. 323-335.

Heckert, J. B. "The Accountant's Part In Determining Standards," No. 4 pp. 342-344.

Burtchett, Floyd F. "Substitute Terminology For 'Stock Dividends'," No. 4 pp. 344-345.

Eaton, R. H. "The Cost Approach," No. 4 pp. 345-348.

Taylor, J. B. "The Field Work Plan," No. 4 pp. 348-350.

Meyer, Harvey G. "The Systems Course," No. 4, p. 350-351.

Accounting Review
Volume 9, 1934

Schmalz, Carl N. "Some Current Problems In Administering The Retail Inventory Method," No. 1, pp. 1-14.

White, Wilford L. "Problems In Determining Total Costs Of Distribution," No. 1, pp. 15-21.

Filbey, Edward J. "Remarks On 'Problems In Determining Total Costs Of Distribution'," No. 1, pp. 21-22.

Atwood, Paul W. "The Manufacturer Looks At His Cost Of Distribution," No. 1, pp. 23-28.

Balch, John. "Some Aspects Of Standard Costs," No. 1, pp. 29-32.

MacLean, H. I. "Unit Costs Of Instruction At The University Of Pennsylvania," No. 1, pp. 33-37.

Hungate, T. L. "Unit Costs In Institutions Of Higher Education," No. 1, pp. 38-43.

Scovill, H. T. "The Accounting Instructor And Local Government Accounting," No. 1, pp. 44-52.

Welcker, William H. "The Public Accountant And Local Government Accounting," No. 1, pp. 53-57.

Elwell, Fayette H. "Governmental Accounting Questions In C.P.A. Examinations," No. 1, pp. 58-60.

Winakor, Arthur H. and Daniel Borth. "Documentation In Accounting Literature," No. 1, pp. 61-68.

Littleton, A. C. "Socialized Accounts (II)," No. 1, pp. 69-74.

Marple, Raymond P. "The Sources Of Capital Surplus," No. 1, pp. 75-81.

Kester, Roy B. "Remarks On 'The Sources Of Capital Surplus'," No. 1, pp. 81-82.

Nelson, Oscar S. "Teaching Accounting Systems," No. 1, pp. 83-89.

Howard, Stanley E. "The Private Business Corporation Under Modern French Law," No. 2, pp. 105-113.

Daniels, Mortimer B. "Principles Of Asset Valuation," No. 2, pp. 114-120.

Paton, William A. "Aspects Of Asset Valuations," No. 2, pp. 122-129.

Wasserman, Max J. "French Enterprise Under Inflation: A Balance Sheet Analysis," No. 2, pp. 130-139.

Littleton, A. C. "The Dividend Base," No. 2, pp. 140-148.

Taggart, Herbert F. "The Relation Of A Cost Accountant To The NRA Codes," No. 2, pp. 149-157.

Hartzell, Elmer. "The Background Of Accounting," No. 2, pp. 158-163.

Peloubet, Maurice E. "Professional Ethics And The Student," No. 2, pp. 164-170.

Neuner, John J. W. "The Status Of Cost Accounting Teaching," No. 2, pp. 171-175.

Lothman, V. O. "The Retail Method Of Inventory," No. 2, pp. 175-178.

Miller, Hermann C. "Standards For A Master's Thesis In Accounting," No. 2, pp. 178-182.

Sanders, T. H. "Reports To Stockholders," No. 3, pp. 201-219.

Briggs, L. L. "Asset Valuation In Dividend Decisions," No. 3, pp. 220-236.

Hatfield, Henry Rand. "Operating Deficit And Paid-In Surplus," No. 3, pp. 237-241.

Nelson, Oscar S. "The Clark Plan Of Retail Accounting," No. 3, pp. 242-246.

Winakor, Arthur H. "Creditors' Protection And Stockholders' Responsibility," No. 3, pp. 247-253.

Boyd, Orton W. "The 'Report And Accounting' Approach," No. 3, pp. 262-267.

Sweeney, Henry W. "How Inflation Affects Balance Sheets," No. 4, pp. 275-299.

Smith, F. P. "Stock-Exchange Margins," No. 4, pp. 300-303.

Littleton, A. C. "Dividends Presuppose Profits," No. 4, pp. 304-311.

Winakor, Arthur H. "Incidence Of Expenses In Accounting," No. 4, pp. 312-318.

Morey, Lloyd. "Principles Of Municipal Accounting," No. 4, pp. 319-325.

Hartzell, Elmer. "Profits In The Steel Industry," No. 4, pp. 326-333.

Fitzpatrick, Paul J. "Transitional Stages Of A Business Failure," No. 4, pp. 337-340.

Benedetto, A. F. "Accounting In Mexico," No. 4, pp. 340-342.

Littleton, A. C. "The Income Approach," No. 4, pp. 342-346.

Accounting Review
Volume 10, 1935

Carmichael, Geoffrey. "Objective Tests In Elementary Accounting," No. 1, pp. 2-4.

Glos, R. E. "The Teaching Of Elementary Accounting," No. 1, pp. 4-6.

Fryxell, C. A. "A Dilemma In Teaching Elementary Accounting," No. 1, pp. 6-7.

Schmidt, Leo A. "Teaching And Testing The Bookkeeping Phase Of Elementary Accounting," No. 1, pp. 8-11.

Wade, Harry H. "Methods Of Teaching A Survey Course In Accounting," No. 1, pp. 11-13.

Gibson, J. C. "Emphasis In Cost Accounting," No. 1, pp. 13-15.

Foster, L. O. "Teaching Cost Accounting," No. 1, pp. 15-17.

Chamberlain, Henry T. "On The Teaching Of Auditing," No. 1, pp. 17-19.

Davies, E. C. "Auditing Teaching Methods," No. 1, pp. 19-21.

Taylor, Jacob B. "The Course In C.P.A. Problems," No. 1, pp. 21-23.

Winter, S. G. "The C.P.A. Review Course," No. 1, pp. 23-26.

Allen, C. E. "The Written Report In Accounting Systems," No. 1, pp. 26-28.

Nerlove, S. H. "Objectives Attainable Through Accounting Research," No. 1, pp. 29-31.

Kohler, E. L. "Some Principles For Terminologists," No. 1, pp. 31-33.

Miller, H. C. "The Master's Thesis," No. 1, pp. 33-49.

McNair, Malcolm P. "Some Proposed Changes In Department Store Accounting Procedure," No. 1, pp. 50-63.

Cassady, Ralph, Jr. "Accounting For Customer Purchases As A Sales Promotional Device," No. 1, pp. 64-68.

Taggart, H. F. "Accounting And Code Regulation," No. 1, pp. 69-74.

Castenholz, W. B. "Accounting And Code Regulation: Comments," No. 1, pp. 75-76.

Morrison, Paul L. "Reports To Stockholders," No. 1, pp. 77-83.

Payne, Robert E. "The Effect Of Recent Laws On Accountancy," No. 1, pp. 84-95.

Sanders, T. H. "The Development Of Accounting Principles," No. 1, pp. 100-102.

Atkinson, Sterling K. "Accounting Treatment Of The Bond Sinking Fund And Reserve," No. 1, pp. 102-106.

Kimball, H. G. "The Importance Of Understanding Income And Profits," No. 2, pp. 131-135.

Frese, Walter F. "Property Rights Of Stockholders Under The 1933 Illinois Business Corporation Act," No. 2, pp. 136-148.

Heilman, E. A. "Accounting And Economics," No. 2, pp. 149-153.

Collins, Clem W. "Accounting And Economics: Comments," No. 2, pp. 154-155.

Theiss, Edwin L. "Accounting And Budgeting," No. 2, pp. 156-161.

Graham, Willard J. "Accounting And Law," No. 2, pp. 162-167.

Taylor, R. Emmett. "Pacioli," No. 2, pp. 168-173.

Borth, Daniel and Arthur H. Winakor. "Some Reflections Of The Scope Of Auditing," No. 2, pp. 174-184.

Sweeney, Henry W. "The Technique Of Stabilized Accounting," No. 2, pp. 185-205.

Hackett, Robert P. "Consistency In Prepaid Expenses," No. 2, pp. 206-209.

Noble, Howard S. "Graduate Study Of Accounting," No. 3, pp. 229-237.

Mason, Perry. "The Financial Aspects Of Depreciation Accounting," No. 3, pp. 238-245.

Ballantine, H. W. and George S. Hills. "Corporate Capital And Restrictions Upon Dividends," No. 3, pp. 246-268.

Littleton, A. C. "Value Or Cost," No. 3, pp. 269-272.

Corstvet, Emma. "Adequacy Of Accounting Records In A Money Economy," No. 3, pp. 273-286.

Young, Walter. "A Method Of Securing A Statement Of Application Of Funds," No. 3, pp. 287-293.

Blayton, Jesse B. "Local Business Concerns As Accounting Laboratories," No. 3, pp. 294-295.

Byrnes, Thomas W. "The Auditing Laboratory At Columbia University," No. 3, pp. 295-298.

Lukas, G. E. "Prepaid Interest," No. 3, pp. 298-301.

Coon, S. J. "Devaluation And Damages," No. 3, pp. 301-302.

Nelson, Edward G. "That Balance-Sheet Approach," No. 4, pp. 313-317.

Mason, Perry. "Depreciation And The Financing Of Replacements," No. 4, pp. 318-324.

Smith, C. Aubrey. "Accounting Practice Under The Securities And Exchange Commission," No. 4, pp. 325-332.

Deinzer, Harvey. "Capital Stock And Surplus: Legal And Accounting Relations," No. 4, pp. 333-344.

Vance, Lawrence L. "Earning-Power Valuation Of Inventory," No. 4, pp. 376-383.
Davis, Albion R. "Some Problems Of Last-In-First-Out Accounting," No. 4, pp. 384-403.

Accounting Review
Volume 18, 1943

Devine, Carl Thomas. "Depreciation Accounting In Utilities," No. 1, pp. 1-8.
Peloubet, Maurice E. "Observations On Cost," No. 1, pp. 9-15.
Linnenberg, Clem C., Jr. "Policies And Procedures In Federal Civilian Procurement," No. 1, pp. 16-25.
Lamden, Charles W. "The Place Of Accounting In Price Control," No. 1, pp. 26-33.
Lundmer, A. Henry. "German Financial Mobilization," No. 1, pp. 34-39.
Clevenger, Earl. "Presenting The Theory Of Debit And Credit," No. 1, pp. 40-44.
Coleman, L. W., Jr. "The Use Of Determinants In The Solution Of Linear Equations," No. 1, pp. 44-48.
Staub, Walter A. "Mode Of Conducting An Audit," No. 2, pp. 91-98.
Scott, DR. "A Simplified Solution Of Circuit Ratio Problems," No. 2, pp. 99-102.
Keith, E. Gordon. "Excess Profits Taxation And Profit Limitation," No. 2, pp. 103-109.
Moyer, C. A. "Social Factors Affecting Obsolescence," No. 2, pp. 110-122.
Tenner, Irving. "Municipal Budgeting In Wartime," No. 2, pp. 123-126.
Boyd, Ralph L. "Examination Objectives," No. 2, pp. 127-135.
Linnenberg, Clem C., Jr. "Policy And Procedures In Federal Civilian Procurement, Part II," No. 2, pp. 136-147.
De Roover, Raymond. "The Lingering Influence Of Medieval Practices," No. 2, pp. 148-151.
Rorem, C. Rufus. "Overhead Costs In Public Welfare," No. 2, pp. 152-155.
Sellie, Clifford N. "Fund Statement Terminology," No. 2, pp. 156-164.
Schlatter, Charles F. "Costs Under Government Contracts," No. 2, pp. 164-167.
May, George O. "The Nature Of The Financial Accounting Process," No. 3, pp. 189-192.
Greer, Howard C. "Structural Fundamentals Of Financial Statements," No. 3, pp. 193-204.
Boursy, Alfred V. "The Name Of Paciolo," No. 3, pp. 205-208.
Scovill, Hiram T. "Wartime Accounting Problems," No. 3, pp. 209-218.
Vance, Lawrence L. "The Authority Of History In Inventory Valuation," No. 3, pp. 219-227.
Fernald, Henry B. "Internal Auditing," No. 3, pp. 228-233.
Lorig, A. N. "Valuing Inventories In Profit And Loss Determination," No. 3, pp. 234-238.
Seldon, Samuel. "Internal Auditing For The State Of New York," No. 3, pp. 239-243.
Brown, Pembroke H. "The Federal Regulatory Commissions," No. 3, pp. 244-248.
Doblin, Ernest M. "Accounting Problems Of Cartels," No. 3, pp. 249-255.
Dixon, Robert L. "The Need For A Statement Of The Principles Underlying Cost Accounting," No. 3, pp. 256-258.
Saliers, Earl A. "Theory Of Repairs, Maintenance, And Betterments," No. 3, pp. 259-261.
Moonitz, Maurice. "Inventories And The Statement Of Funds," No. 3, pp. 262-265.
Blackmore, Charles T. "Economic Obsolescence Of Land," No. 3, pp. 266-268.
Stettler, Howard F. "Classification Of Auditing Questions," No. 4, pp. 293-306.
Littleton, A. C. "Examinations In Auditing," No. 4, pp. 307-316.
Quin, Dick D. "The CPA Examination," No. 4, pp. 317-320.
Bornemann, Alfred. "Accounting Profits: An Institution," No. 4, pp. 321-323.
Blodgett, Ralph H. "The Value Of Economics For The Accountant," No. 4, pp. 324-330.
Brush, Lauren F. "Graphic Analysis Of Expense," No. 4, pp. 331-337.
Saliers, E. A. "Differential Costs," No. 4, pp. 338-339.
Johnson, Arnold W. "Form, Function, And Interpretation Of The Profit And Loss Statement," No. 4, pp. 340-347.
Schmidt, Leo A. "Control Of Detail In Inventory Valuations," No. 4, pp. 348-353.
Oehler, Christian. "Student Achievement And Its Measurement," No. 4, pp. 354-363.
Carr, William. "Professional Accountants Today," No. 4, pp. 364-367.

Accounting Review
Volume 19, 1944

Wilcox, Edward B. "Qualifications For A Professional Career," No. 1, pp. 1-6.
Fernald, Henry B. "Taxes And Employment," No. 1, pp. 7-10.
Paton, William A. "Simplification Of Federal Tax Administration," No. 1, pp. 11-19.
Scovill, Hiram T. "Application Of Funds Made Practical," No. 1, pp. 20-30.
Myer, John N. "Statements Accounting For Balance Sheet Changes," No. 1, pp. 31-38.

Devine, Carl T. "Depreciation And Income Measurement," No. 1, pp. 39-46.
Grady, Paul. "Current Problems In Cost Determinations," No. 1, pp. 47-54.
Anderson, David R. "The Function Of Industrial Controllership," No. 1, pp. 55-65.
Hatfield, Henry Rand. "Replacement And Book Value," No. 1. pp. 66-67.
De Roover, Raymond. "Paciolo Or Pacioli?," No. 1, p. 68.
Taylor, R. Emmett. "The Name Of Pacioli," No. 1, pp. 69-75.
Siddall, K. Y. "Some Postwar Problems Of Industry," No. 1, pp. 76-80.
Gilman, Stephen. "Accounting Principles And The Current Classification," No. 2, pp. 109-116.
Stempf, Victor H. "Termination And Renegotiation," No. 2, pp. 117-130.
Bloom, Ben. "Aptitude Tests For Accounting Students," No. 2, pp. 131-134.
Forbes, John F. "Observations Of A CPA Examiner," No. 2, pp. 135-138.
Mendes, Henry E. "The Development Of Uniform Examinations," No. 2, pp. 139-141.
Webster, Norman E. "Some Early Accountancy Examiners," No. 2, pp. 142-149.
Claire, Richard S. "Training For The Public Accounting Profession," No. 2, pp. 150-158.
Boyd, R. L. "Progress In CPA Legislation," No. 2, pp. 159-163.
Perry, Donald P. "Professional Accounting Practice Today And Tomorrow," No. 2, pp. 164-168.
Prickett, A. L. "General Principles Of Cost Accounting," No. 2, pp. 169-179.
Fiske, Wyman P. "The Teaching Of Cost Accounting," No. 2, pp. 180-186.
Allyn, Robert G. "An Approach To Financial Statement Analysis," No. 2, pp. 187-192.
Vance, Lawrence L. "Current Problems And Accounting Theory," No. 3, pp. 231-237.
Blough, Carman G. "An Approach To Renegotiation," No. 3, pp. 238-247.
Miller, Herbert E. "Reserves For War Contingencies And Postwar Adjustments," No. 3, pp. 248-253.
Deming, W. Edwards. "A View Of The Statistical Method," No. 3, pp. 254-259.
Rice, William B. "Statistical Uses Of Accounting Data," No. 3, pp. 260-265.
Crawford, James R. "Statistical Accounting Procedures," No. 3, pp. 266-269.
Gaa, Lt. Charles J. "Students For Income Determination," No. 3, pp. 270-273.
Bowers, Russell. "Terminology And Form Of The Income Sheet," No. 3, pp. 274-278.
Halterman, J. F. "Accountants In OPA," No. 3, pp. 279-282.
Thurman, Sam D., Jr. "Accountant-Attorney Cooperation," No. 3, pp. 283-289.
Meredith, C. C. "Some Problems Of Labor Union Auditing," No. 3, pp. 290-293.
Hackett, Robert P. "Encumbrance Accounting For Industry," No. 3, pp. 294-297.
Ashley, C. A. "Replacement And Book Value," No. 3, pp. 298-299.
Byrnes, Thomas W. "The Bank Reconcilement," No. 3, pp. 300-301.
Benninger, L. J. "Business And Withholding Taxes," No. 3, pp. 302-305.
Carson, A. B. "Determination Of Merchandise Turnover," No. 3, pp. 306-309.
Sherritt, Lawrence W. "Simplifying The Presentation Of Compound Interest Formulas," No. 3, pp. 310-314.
Finney, H. A. "Principles And Conventions," No. 4, pp. 361-365.
Webster, Norman E. "The Meaning Of 'Public Accountant'," No. 4, pp. 366-376.
Saliers, E. A. "Foreign Exchange Accounting," No. 4, pp. 377-380.
De Roover, Raymond. "Early Accounting Problems Of Foreign Exchange," No. 4, pp. 381-406.
Yamey, Basil S. "Edward Jones's 'English System Of Bookkeeping'," No. 4, pp. 407-415.
Garbade, William H. "Internal Control And The Internal Auditor," No. 4, pp. 416-421.
Nelson, Oscar S. "Cost Principles In Termination Settlements," No. 4, pp. 422-429.
Galitzer, Philip. "The Intra-Family Tax Saving Device," No. 4, pp. 430-434.
Brush, Lauren F. "Accounting Curricula," No. 4, pp. 435-438.
Thomas, L. L. "Methods Of Supervising Local Finances," No. 4, pp. 439-450.

Accounting Review
Volume 20, 1945

Carey, John L. "The Development Of Aptitude Tests For Accountants," No. 1, pp. 1-6.
Boyd, R.L. "Standards For CPA Legislation," No. 1. pp. 7-16.
Smith, C. Aubrey. "Education For The Professional Accountant," No. 1, pp. 17-23.
Bond, Joe. "Accounting Policy Or Economic Philosophy?," No. 1, pp. 24-30.
Kohler, E. L. "Expenditure Controls In The United States Government," No. 1, pp. 31-43.
Gaa, Lt. Charles J. and Lt. Gerald Maxfield. "Accounting Aspects Of Contract Settlement," No. 1, pp. 44-58.

Accounting Review
Volume 21, 1946

Accounting Review
Volume 22, 1947

Accounting Review
Volume 23, 1948

Herbert, Leo. "Comparison Between Governmental And General Accounting," No. 4, pp. 397-400.
Jennings, Alvin R. "Staff Training - Present And Future," No. 4, pp. 401-409.
Flynn, Thomas D. "Public Accountants' Staff Training Program," No. 4, pp. 410-413.
Garner, S. Paul. "The Course In Internal Auditing," No. 4, pp. 414-417.
Broom, H. N. "Method Of Accounting For Inter-Departmental Profits," No. 4, pp. 417-420.
Murphy, Mary E. "Libraries For Students Of Accounting," No. 4, pp. 420-421.

Accounting Review
Volume 24, 1949

Stans, Maurice H. "Modernizing The Income Statement," No. 1, pp. 3-14.
Graham, Willard J. "The Effect Of Changing Price Levels Upon The Determination, Reporting, And Interpretation Of Income," No. 1, pp. 15-26.
Niswonger, C. R. "The Interpretation Of Income In A Period Of Inflated Prices," No. 1, pp. 27-32.
Blocker, John G. "Mismatching Of Costs And Revenues," No. 1, pp. 33-43.
Miller, Herbert E. "The 1948 Revision Of The American Accounting Association's Statement Of Concepts And Standards: A General Appraisal," No. 1, pp. 44-48.
Paton, W. A. "The 1948 Revision Of The American Accounting Association's Statement Of Concepts And Standards: Comments On Item 5 Under 'Expense'," No. 1, pp. 49-53.
Taggart, H. F. "The 1948 Revision Of The American Accounting Association's Statement Of Concepts And Standards: A Critique And Comparison With The 1941 Statement," No. 1, pp. 54-60.
Judd, Frank. "Development Of Cost Accounting Concepts Of Scheduled Airlines," No. 1, pp. 61-67.
Dein, Raymond C. "Original Cost And Public Utility Regulation," No. 1, pp. 68-80.
Scott, DR. "The Influence Of Statistics Upon Accounting Technique And Theory," No. 1, pp. 81-87.
Schmidt, Leo A. "A Secondary Use For The Uniform Achievement Tests," No. 1, pp. 88-89.
Whitney, William H. "Introducing Accounting Majors To Auditing," No. 1, pp. 89-94.
Crum, William F. "Intermediate And Advanced Accounting Advice Sheet," No. 1, pp. 94-96.
Hope, J. William. "The Uniform CPA Examination," No. 2, pp. 123-127.
Newcomer, Hale L. "The CPA Examination," No. 2, pp. 128-135.
Budd, T. A. "The Effects Of A National Testing Program On Accounting Education," No. 2, pp. 140-145.
Miller, Hermann C. "Expense And Accounting Concepts And Standards," No. 2, pp. 146-145.
Child, A. J. E. "Case Studies In Internal Auditing," No. 2, pp. 149-158.
Carson, A. B. "A 'Source And Application Of Funds' Philosophy Of Financial Accounting," No. 2, pp. 159-170.
Grace, John C. "A Controller's Conception Of A Modern Annual Report," No. 2, pp. 171-178.
Coleman, R. W. "The Role Of Accounting In Management," No. 2, pp. 179-183.
Wixon, Rufus. "The Measurement And Administration Of Income," No. 2, pp. 184-190.
Wren, Melvin C. "The Chamber Of The City Of London, 1633-1642," No. 2, pp. 191-198.
Homburger, Richard H. "Forfeited Capital Stock Subscriptions," No. 2, pp. 199-202.
Logan, G. Arnold. "Justification Of And Explanation Of Sinking Fund Reserves," No. 2, pp. 203-206.
Zlatkovich, Charles T. "Teaching The Application Of Funds Statement," No. 2, pp. 206-208.
Heckert, J. Brooks. "A Course In Controllership," No. 2, pp. 208-209.
Cooper, W. W. "Social Accounting: An Invitation To The Accounting Profession," No. 3, pp. 233-238.
Friend, Irwin. "Financial Statements For The Economy," No. 3, pp. 239-247.
Hagen, Everett. "National Accounting Systems And The European Recovery Program," No. 3, pp. 248-253.
Copeland, Morris A. "Social Accounting For Moneyflows," No. 3, pp. 254-264.
Blough, Carman G. "Auditing Standards And Procedures," No. 3, pp. 265-271.
Carey, John L. "Tax Settlement Board Bill," No. 3, p. 272.
Bray, F. Sewell. "The English Universities And The Accounting Profession," No. 3, pp. 273-276.
Borth, Daniel. "Comments On Third Statement Of Accounting Concepts And Standards," No. 3, pp. 277-280.
Littleton, A. C. "Classified Objectives," No. 3, pp. 281-284.
Kelley, Arthur C. "The Presentation Of Corporate Income And Earned Surplus," No. 3, pp. 285-289.
Woomer, Donald B. "LIFO As A Method Of Determining Depreciation," No. 3, pp. 290-295.
Gordon, Dennis. "The Solution Of Process Cost Problems," No. 3, pp. 296-303.
Binkley, M. A. "Components Of The Report Of Financial Changes," No. 3, pp. 304-307.
Goliger, Joseph. "Analysis Of Semi-Variable Expenses," No. 3, pp. 308-310.
Van Sickle, C. L. "Teaching Methods In Accounting Systems," No. 3, pp. 311-314.

Farman, Wilson L. "Teaching Accounting Concepts To The Beginning Student," No. 3, pp. 314-317.
Mautz, R. K. "Using Practical Accounting Experience In Teaching," No. 3, pp. 317-320.
Bordner, H. W. "Financial And Accounting Administration In The Federal Government," No. 4, pp. 341-353.
Nelson, Edward G. "Science And Accounting," No. 4, pp. 354-359.
MacKenzie, D. H. "Contemporary Theories Of Corporate Profits Reporting," No. 4, pp. 360-368.
Spear, Harvey M. "Depreciation Accounting Under Changing Price Levels," No. 4, pp. 369-378.
Weston, J. Fred. "Consistency And Changing Price Levels," No. 4, pp. 379-386.
Benninger, L. J. "The Traditional Vs. The Cost Accounting Concept Of Cost," No. 4, pp. 387-391.
Robbins, George W. "A Pattern For Professional Business Education," No. 4, pp. 392-402.
Emblen, Donald J. "Accounting In The Professional Business Curriculum," No. 4, pp. 403-408.
Revzan, David A. "What Is A Balanced Curriculum In Accounting?," No. 4, pp. 409-413.
Ludmer, Henry. "General Accounting Vs. Tax Accounting," No. 4, pp. 414-422.
Payne, John B. "Financial Administration Of The United Nations," No. 4, pp. 423-431.
Moonitz, Maurice. "Functions Of The Written Examination," No. 4, pp. 432-435.
Mautz, R. K. "Teaching The Significance Of Practical Considerations," No. 4, pp. 435-438.
Bowers, Russell. "On Teaching Depreciation," No. 4, pp. 438-441.

Accounting Review
Volume 25, 1950

Grady, Paul. "Accounting For Fixed Assets And Their Amortization," No. 1, pp. 3-19.
Schmidt, Leo A. "Construction Of Objective Examinations," No. 1, pp. 20-26.
Jacobs, Robert. "Measurement And Guidance In The Field Of Public Accounting," No. 1, pp. 27-34.
King, Earle C. "Current Accounting Problems," No. 1, pp. 35-44.
Davidson, Sidney. "Depreciation And Profit Determination," No. 1, pp. 45-56.
Drake, Milton J. "Reports For Creditors," No. 1, pp. 58-62.
Walter, James E. "Last-In, First-Out," No. 1, pp. 63-75.
Kopta, William. "What Constitutes The Unauthorized Practice Of Law By Accountants In Tax Matters," No. 1, pp. 76-80.
Mautz, R. K. "Accounting For Enterprise Growth," No. 1, pp. 81-88.
Kircher, Paul. "Investments In Corporate Reports," No. 1, pp. 89-93.
Fleig, W. J. "The Use Of Films In Accounting Instruction," No. 1, pp. 94-96.
Bristor, Rolland M. "Some Suggestions On The Teaching Of Principles Of Accounting," No. 1, pp. 96-99.
Broder, Bertram. "An Educational Experiment In Cost Accounting," No. 1, pp. 99-100.
Bailey, George D. "Current Auditing Problems," No. 2, pp. 125-132.
Mason, Perry. "The 1948 Statement Of Concepts And Standards, No. 2, pp. 133-138.
Jones, Ralph Coughenour. "Accounting Concepts And Standards," No. 2, pp. 139-141.
Tiffany, K. C. "Reports For Management," No. 2, pp. 142-148.
Bowers, Russell. "Objections To Index Number Accounting," No. 2, pp. 149-155.
Benninger, L. J. "A Proposed Reconciliation Of Standard And Current Material Costs," No. 2, pp. 156-160.
Gruneberg, Curt. "Is Accountancy A Field Of Science?," No. 2, pp. 161-162.
Noble, Paul L. "A Quantitative Evaluation Of Accounting Curricula," No. 2, pp. 163-169.
Hassler, Russell H. "The Case Method Of Teaching Accounting," No. 2, pp. 170-172.
Dickerson, W. E. "The Courses In Tax Accounting," No. 2, pp. 173-179.
Zraick, Louis E. "The Audit Of Overhead In Companies Handling Both Commercial And Government Contracts," No. 2, pp. 180-183.
Lehnberg, Val B. "Cost Accounting For Motor Freight Lines," No. 2, pp. 184-191.
Littleton, A. C. "A Third Use Value Of Accounting," No. 2, pp. 192-193.
Broom, H. N. "Modified Tabular Presentation Of Gross Profit Variations," No. 2, pp. 193-194.
Gordon, Dennis. "Courses For Students Specializing In Industrial Accounting," No. 2, pp. 194-198.
Broad, Samuel J. "Valuation Of Inventories," No. 3, pp. 227-235.
Vatter, W. J. "Accounting Education For Controllership," No. 3, pp. 236-250.
Brink, Victor Z. "Education For Controllership," No. 3, pp. 251-259.
Heckert, J. Brooks. "Accounting Hall Of Fame," No. 3, pp. 260-261.
Osborn, Richards C. "The Relative Efficiency Of Large, Medium-Sized And Small Business," No. 3, pp. 262-273.
Doyle, Leonard A. "Uses Of Cost Data For Production And Investment Policies," No. 3, pp. 274-282.

Krebs, William S. "Rate Base Problems Presented When Utilities Shift From Retirement To Depreciation Accounting," No. 3, pp. 283-291.

Funk, Roland W. "Recent Developments In Accounting Theory And Practice," No. 3, pp. 292-301.

Landman, J. H. "The Reality Test In Family Partnerships," No. 3, pp. 302-306.

James, Robert M. "Three Major Concepts In Governmental Accounting Theory," No. 3, pp. 307-314.

Pagani, John and William O. Jones. "Price And Mortality Expectations And Valuation Of Inventories," No. 3, pp. 315-319.

Littleton, A. C. "The Social Service Of Accounting," No. 3, pp. 320-321.

Graber, Paul J. "A Plea To Authors," No. 3, pp. 321-322.

Green, David, Jr. "A Reconsideration Of The Course Objectives Of Elementary Accounting," No. 3, pp. 322-326.

Krebs, William S. "Replacement And Retirement Accounting And Rate Base Valuation," No. 4, pp. 351-359.

Herrick, Anson. "A Review Of Recent Developments In Accounting Theory And Practice," No. 4, pp. 360-370.

Rampy, T. R. "Allowable Costs For Air Force Contracts," No. 4, pp. 371-377.

Benninger, L. J. "Standard Costs For Income Determination, Control, And Special Studies," No. 4, pp. 378-383.

Devine, Carl Thomas. "Cost Accounting And Pricing Policies," No. 4, pp. 384-389.

Davidson, Sidney. "The Reserve For Sinking Fund - A Critical Examination," No. 4, pp. 390-394.

Thompson, David W. "Partnership Training Programs," No. 4, pp. 395-401.

Osborn, Richards C. "The Relative Profitability Of Large, Medium-Sized And Small Business," No. 4, pp. 402-411.

Goliger, Josef. "Fixed Charges And Profit," No. 4, pp. 412-416.

Bogart, Fred O. "Accounting For Leaseholds," No. 4, pp. 417-419.

Tenner, Irving. "Balance Sheets For The Federal Government," No. 4, pp. 420-424.

Cannon, Arthur M. "Check List For An Accounting Library," No. 4, pp. 425-440.

Funk, Roland W. "Illustrations To Aid In Explaining The Two Methods Of Pricing Inventory Activity," No. 4, pp. 441-442.

Penz, A.J. "Are Accounting Principles Taught Effectively?," No. 4, pp. 442-444.

Jones, Ralph Coughenour. "A Flexible Test Grading Formula Which Emphasizes Quality," No. 4, pp. 445-448.

Accounting Review
Volume 26, 1951

Moyer, C. A. "Early Developments In American Auditing," No. 1, pp. 3-8.

Carroll, Gay. "Some Challenges To Accounting," No. 1, pp. 9-18.

Miller, Hermann C. "Interim Report Of The Standards Rating Committee," No. 1, pp. 19-21.

Vance, Lawrence L. "How Much Test Checking Is Enough?," No. 1, pp. 22-30.

Nelson, Oscar S. "Capital Gains From Price Level Increases," No. 1, pp. 31-32.

Farman, Wilson L. "Some Basic Assumptions Underlying Social Accounting," No. 1, pp. 33-39.

Campbell, J. D. "Straight-Line Method Of Depreciation," No. 1, pp. 40-42.

Weber, Fred. "Restrictions On Assets," No. 1, pp. 43-44.

Donnell, George R. "What Is A Certified Public Accountant?," No. 1, pp. 45-48.

Greidinger, B. Bernard. "When Are Independent Public Accountants Not In Fact Independent?," No. 1, pp. 49-60.

Amory, Robert, Jr. "Accounting Instruction In Law Schools," No. 1, pp. 61-69.

Boedecker, Karl A. "The Correlation Of Accounting Instruction With Instruction In Other Business Fields," No. 1, pp. 70-76.

Lemke, B. C. "Is Manufacturing Cost An Objective Concept?," No. 1, pp. 77-79.

Beretvas, Andor. "Case Study In Auditing Procedure," No. 1, pp. 80-87.

James, Robert M. "Interrelationships In Governmental Accounting Theory," No. 1, pp. 88-92.

Carrithers, J. M. "Problems And Theories Of Teaching Elementary Accounting," No. 1, pp. 93-101.

Kaulback, Frank S., Jr. "Elementary Accounting And The Non-Accounting Major - A Proposal," No. 1, pp. 102-104.

Lane, Joseph E. "Elementary Accounting And The Non-Accounting Major - A Proposal," No. 1, pp. 105-106.

Kircher, Paul. "The Course In Accounting Theory," No. 1, pp. 106-111.

Taggart, Herbert F. "Cost Accounting Versus Cost Bookkeeping," No. 2, pp. 141-151.

McMullen, Stewart Yarwood. "Clarifying The Balance Sheet," No. 2, pp. 157-166.

Bowers, Russell. "Business Profit And The Price Level," No. 2, pp. 167-178.

Nelson, Oscar S. "Trends And Problems In Governmental And Institutional Accounting," No. 2, pp. 179-184.

Dean, Joel. "Measurement Of Profits For Executive Decisions," No. 2, pp. 185-196.

McGladrey, I. B. "The Audit Report," No. 2, pp. 197-208.

Gordon, Myron J. "Cost Allocations And The Design Of Accounting Systems For Control," No. 2, pp. 209-220.

Walden, Robert E. "A Course In Accounting Theory," No. 2,

pp. 221-225.

Mauriello, Joseph A. "The Relationship Between Accounting And Management," No. 2, pp. 226-231.

Avery, Harold G. "Accounting For Joint Costs," No. 2, pp. 232-238.

Mautz, R. K. "The Intermediate Course In Accounting," No. 2, pp. 239-246.

Scovill, H. T. "Analysis Of A Questionnaire Sent To 1000 Alumni Of The University Of Illinois, College Of Commerce," No. 2, pp. 259-260.

Gellein, Oscar S. "Development Of An Instructional Approach To The Statement Of Funds," No. 2, pp. 260-262.

Matz, Adolph. "The Accounting Senior Seminar In The Wharton School," No. 2, pp. 262-265.

Kelley, Arthur C. "Can Corporate Incomes Be Scientifically Ascertained?," No. 3, pp. 289-298.

Park, Colin. "Working Capital And The Operating Cycle," No. 3, pp. 299-307.

Horn, Frederick E. "Managerial Emphasis In Elementary Accounting," No. 3, pp. 308-312.

Owen, George A. and Richard C. Gerfen. "Can Junior Accountants Be Trained To Write Better?," No. 3, pp. 313-320.

Dinman, Robert. "Orientation And Visual Aids In Teaching Of Auditing," No. 3, pp. 321-326.

Beckett, John A. "A Study Of The Principles Of Allocating Costs," No. 3, pp. 327-333.

Magruder, Bernard F. "Nature Of Reserve For Self-Insurance," No. 3, pp. 334-337.

Raun, Donald L. "The Problem Of Fixed Charges," No. 3, pp. 338-346.

James, Robert M. "Some Aspects Of A Governmental Audit," No. 3, pp. 347-351.

Kerrigan, Harry D. "Accounting Aspects Of Rate-Making In The Public-Utility Field," No. 3, pp. 352-361.

Warriner, Philip. "How Statistical Analysis Can Serve Accountants," No. 3, pp. 362-370.

Eaton, James O. "The Legal Battlefield Of Income Tax Administration," No. 3, pp. 371-383.

Donnell, George R. "Excess Profits Tax Minus Its Technicalities," No. 3, pp. 384-386.

Lordeman, James E., Jr. "Capital And Revenue Expdenditures For Federal Income Tax Purposes," No. 3, pp. 387-394.

Thomas, William E. "One Approach To The Problem Of Communicating Accounting Information," No. 3, pp. 395-399.

Ingraham, Howell A. "Elementary Presentation Of Volume, Cost And Profit Relationships," No. 3, pp. 414-416.

Rushing, Reginald. "ABC's Of Accounting Instruction," No. 3, pp. 417-418.

Littleton, A. C. "Removing The Mysteries From Accounting," No. 3, pp. 418-420.

Carey, John L. "Relationship Of Accountants And Lawyers In Tax Practice," No. 4, pp. 449-455.

Carson, A. B. "An Investment-Recovery-First Concept Of Taxable Profit," No. 4, pp. 456-467.

Litherland, D. A. "Fixed Asset Replacement A Half Century Ago," No. 4, pp. 475-480.

Benninger, L. J. "Needed: A New Concept Of Accounts," No. 4, pp. 481-484.

Goldberg, Louis. "The Funds Statement Reconsidered," No. 4, pp. 485-491.

Shugerman, Abe L. "Historical Costs Vs. Deferred Costs As Basic Concepts For Financial Statement Valuations," No. 4, pp. 492-495.

Kane, John E. "Structural Changes And General Changes In The Price Level In Relation to Financial Reporting," No. 4, pp. 496-502.

Hylton, Delmer P. "Should Financial Statements Show 'Monetary' Or 'Economic' Income?," No. 4, pp. 503-506.

Hendriksen, Eldon S. "The Influence Of Depreciation Accounting On National Income," No. 4, pp. 507-515.

Ives, Kenneth. "The Nature Of The Accounting Unit," No. 4, pp. 516-517.

Meigs, Walter B. "The Expanding Field Of Internal Auditing," No. 4, pp. 518-523.

Goliger, Josef. "The Inventory Challenge," No. 4, pp. 524-525.

Bedford, Norton M. "A Critical Analysis Of Accounting Concepts Of Income," No. 4, pp. 526-537.

Stelson, Hugh E. "Finding The Yield On A Bond," No. 4, pp. 538-539.

Osborn, Richards C. "Plea For Small Business," No. 4, pp. 540-554.

Young, Elmer R. "Controlling Installment Distribution To Partners In A Liquidating Partnership," No. 4, pp. 555-559.

Emery, Kenneth G. "Should Goodwill Be Written Off?," No. 4, pp. 560-567.

Corbin, Donald A. "Accounting And Rising Prices In A Student Co-Operative," No. 4, pp. 568-572.

Carmichael, Vernal H. "Device For Determining And Recording Manufacturing Expense Variances," No. 4, pp. 573-574.

Fordon, John V. "Profit Variations," No. 4, pp. 574-576.

Allyn, Robert G. "The Study Of Philosophy As Part Of The Accounting Students' Training," No. 4, pp. 576-579.

Wright, Howard W. "Federal Accountants Offer Cooperation," No. 4, pp. 579-581.

Accounting Review
Volume 27, 1952

Trumbull, Wendell P. "The All-Inclusive Standard," No. 1, pp. 3-14.

Hill, Thomas M. "An Analysis Of Supplementary Statement No. 2," No. 1, pp. 16-24.

Accounting Review
Volume 28, 1953

Accounting Review
Volume 29, 1954

Beights, D. M. "Opprtunities For A Career In Governmental Accounting," No. 4, pp. 614-619.

Anton, Hector R. "Funds Statement Practices In The United States And Canada," No. 4, pp. 620-627.

Warner, George H. "Depreciation On A Current Basis," No. 4, pp. 628-633.

Odmark, V. E. "Some Aspects Of The Evolution Of Accounting Functions," No. 4, pp. 634-638.

Fergusson, D. A. "Accounting And The Price Level," No. 4, pp. 639-642.

Raby, William L. "Uni-fied Accounting," No. 4, pp. 643-644.

Chenault, Lawrence R. "Business Behavior And The Theory Of The Firm," No. 4, pp. 645-651.

Pinger, R. W. "The Semantics Of Accounting," No. 4, pp. 652-655.

Newton, W. K. "New Developments And Simplified Approaches To Municipal Accounting," No. 4, pp. 656-660.

White, John A. "Accounting Research," No. 4, pp. 661-670.

Sadler, Alton G. "Professional Accountants Library," No. 4, pp. 671-675.

Newlove, G. H. "The Teaching Of Process Costs," No. 4, pp. 676-683.

Braden, Andrew D. "The Blackboard Versus Projected Still Pictures In The Teaching Of Accounting - An Experiment," No. 4, pp. 683-687.

LaSalle, Brother. "An Approach To Ethics," No. 4, pp. 687-689.

Welsch, Glenn A. "Serial Bond Redemption - Bonds Outstanding And Dollar-Period Methods," No. 4, pp. 689-691.

Black, Martin L., Jr. "Student Associate Memberships," No. 4, pp. 691-692.

Accounting Review
Volume 30, 1955

Dein, Raymond C. "Price-Level Adjustments: Fetish In Accounting," No. 1, pp. 3-24.

Morey, Lloyd. "Remarks Before Annual Meeting Of American Accounting Association," No. 1, pp. 25-26.

Gaa, Charles J. "An Experiment In Staff Training: The Advanced Training Center Of The Internal Revenue Service," No. 1, pp. 28-36.

Mason, Perry. "The Price-Level Study Of The American Accounting Association," No. 1, pp. 37-44.

Littleton, A. C. "The Logic Of Accounts," No. 1, pp. 45-47.

Macaulay, Hugh. "Responsibilities Of The Professional Accounting Firms In Continuing The Training Of College Graduates," No. 1, pp. 48-50.

Cunningham, Earle H. "The Need For College Courses In Internal Auditing," No. 1, pp. 51-57.

Smith, C. D. "Comments On Neter's 'Problems In Experimenting With The Application Of Statistical Techniques In Auditing'," No. 1, pp. 70.

Anton, Hector R. "The Funds Statement As An Internal Report To Management," No. 1, pp. 71-79.

Feyerharm, Robert W. "Budgetary Accounting Procedures And Accounting Forms For Small Colleges And Universities," No. 1, pp. 80-85.

Campbell, L. E. "The Responsibility Of The Internal Auditor For Procedures," No. 1. pp. 86-88.

Bower, James B. "Federal Income Tax Practice In The Uniform Certified Public Accountant Examination," No. 1, pp. 89-94.

Walter, James E. "The Treatment Of 'Footnote' Liabilities," No. 1, pp. 95-102.

Coughlan, John W. "Applicability Of The Realization Principle To Money Claims In Common Dollar Accounting," No. 1, pp. 103-113.

Haun, Robert D. "Broad Vs. Narrow Concepts Of Internal Auditing And Internal Control," No. 1. pp. 114-118.

Bastable, Charles W., Jr. "A Revised Concept Of Inventories," No. 1. pp. 130-133.

Mead, Stuart B. "The Machine-Graded Test For Accounting Courses," No. 1, pp. 133-134.

Ashburne, Jim G. "Accounting Training For Non-Accounting Majors," No. 1, pp. 134-139.

Anderson, Wilton T. "A Master Schedule For Partnership Dissolution - Installment Basis," No. 1, pp. 139-144.

Perry, Donald P. "Work Of The Commission On CPA Standards," No. 2, pp. 183-193.

Dohr, James L. "Limitations On The Usefulness Of Price Level Adjustments," No. 2, pp. 198-205.

Fagerberg, Dixon, Jr. "Perspective In The Practice Of Accountancy," No. 2, pp. 211-216.

Trueblood, Robert M. and W. W. Cooper. "Research And Practice In Statistical Applications To Accounting, Auditing, And Management Control," No. 2, pp. 221-229.

Freeman, Roger A. "Reporting And Interpreting The Cost Of State Government," No. 2, pp. 232-239.

Edwards, James Don. "Public Accounting In The United States, 1896-1913," No. 2, pp. 240-251.

Slaton, William H. "Developing Accountants For Atomic Energy," No. 2, pp. 252-256.

Snyder, Ralph W. "Direct Yield Formulas For Serial Bonds," No. 2, pp. 257-267.

Corbin, Donald A. "A Case Study Of Price-Level Adjustments," No. 2, pp. 268-281.

Sih, S. T. "My Experience In Price-Level Adjustments." No. 2, pp. 282-283.

Pye, Malcolm L. "The Undergraduate Accounting Curriculum," No. 2, pp. 284-289.

Addington, Conley R. "Governmental Accounting In The Undergraduate Curriculum," No. 2, pp. 290-292.

Campfield, W.L. "Experiences In Extension Of Staff Training To In-Charge Auditors," No. 2, pp. 293-297.

Larimore, Theodore R. "Renegotiation Accounting," No. 2, pp. 298-306.

Fried, Stephen. "A Short-Cut Method For Simultaneous Tax Computation," No. 2, pp. 316-320.

Hartman, David. "Difficulties With Adjustment Columns - A Solution," No. 2, pp. 336-338.

Edmondson, V. G. "The Statement Of Realization And Liquidation," No. 2, pp. 339-344.

Simons, Harry. "Priority Program Approach To Partnership Liquidation By Installments," No. 2, pp. 344-347.

Latzer, Paul J. "Cost Accountant And Industrial Engineer," No. 2, pp. 348-350.

Husband, George R. "Professor Dein, Mr. Alexander, And Supplementary Statement Number 2," No. 3, pp. 383-399.

De Roover, Raymond. "New Perspectives On The History Of Accounting," No. 3, pp. 405-420.

Beights, David Miers. "Municipal Auditing Standards," No. 3. pp. 421-427.

Marple, Raymond P. "Direct Costing And The Uses Of Cost Data." No. 3, pp. 430-438.

Brummet, R. Lee. "Direct Costing - Should It Be A Controversial Issue?," No. 3, pp. 439-443.

Hay, Robert D. "Management Thinking Concerning Corporate Annual Reports," No. 3, pp. 444-450.

Murphy, Mary E. "Centenary Of The Scottish Institute Of Chartered Accountants," No. 3, pp. 455-462.

Simpson, Clark L. "The Army Audit Agency Goes Professional," No. 3, pp. 463-467.

Goldberg, Louis. "Concepts Of Depreciation," No. 3, pp. 468-484.

Avery, Harold G. "An Analysis Of Missouri's Utility Earnings And Rate Base Formula - A Rejoinder," No. 3, pp. 485-492.

Harvey, John L. "Starting Your Career In Public Accounting," No. 3, pp. 493-499.

Perry, Kenneth W. "Statistical Relationship Of Accounting And Economics," No. 3, pp. 500-506.

Simon, Sidney I. "Legal Decisions On Accounting Reserves," No. 3, pp. 507-514.

Falls, Glenn. "The Financial Value Of Early Tax Deductions For Depreciation," No. 3, pp. 515-518.

Beretvas, Andor. "Management Contracts, Expense Sharing Agreements, And Tax Planning," No. 3, pp. 519-521.

White, John Arch. "Accounting Research," No. 3, pp. 522-532.

Beamer, George C. and Tom Rose. "The Use Of The GATB And The AIA Tests In Predicting Success In Courses In Accounting," No. 3, pp. 533-535.

Van Voorhis, Robert H. "Coordinating Sections Of Courses In Elementary Accounting," No. 3, pp. 535-538.

Lawrence, Charles. "Teaching Responsibilities And Machine-Graded Tests," No. 3, pp. 538-539.

Horngren, Charles T. "Security Analysts And The Price Level." No. 4, pp. 575-581.

Monteverde, Robert J. "Some Notes Of Reservation On The Use Of Sampling Tables In Auditing," No. 4, pp. 582-591.

McMillan, T. E., Jr. "State-Municipal Relations In Financial Control," No. 4, pp. 592-599.

Smith, Stephen Thomas. "Cash Control System In Communistic China," No. 4, pp. 602-604.

Botts, Ralph R. and Fred L. Garlock. "Interest Rates Charged On Installment Purchases," No. 4, pp. 607-616.

Grady, Paul. "Conservation Of Productive Capital Through Recognition Of Current Cost Of Depreciation," No. 4, pp. 617-622.

McDonald, Roderick F. "An Objective Look At Effects Of Income Taxes On Financing Small Business," No. 4, pp. 623-633.

Lorig, Arthur N. "Joint Cost Analysis As An Aid To Management." No. 4, pp. 634-637.

Kent, Arthur H. "The New Internal Auditing And The Need For Specialized Preparatory Training," No. 4, pp. 638-644.

Lawrence, Charles. "A Suggested Program For Cooperation Between Educational Institutions And Small Practitioners," No. 4. pp. 645-650.

Powelson, John P. "Social Accounting." No. 4, pp. 651-659.

Kerrigan, Harry D. "Electronic Data Processor - A Milestone In Machine Method," No. 4, pp. 660-665.

Christenson, Charles. "Construction Of Present Value Tables For Use In Evaluating Capital Investment Opportunities," No. 4. pp. 666-672.

Katzenmeyer, Robert G. "Cost Accounting Context Of Seventeen A.I.A. 'Theory Of Account' Examinations," No. 4, pp. 694-701.

Hay, Leon E. "Statutory Requirements As To Form And Content Of Executors' Reports To Courts," No. 4, pp. 702-705.

Accounting Review
Volume 31, 1956

Greer, Howard C. "Benchmarks And Beacons," No. 1, pp. 3-14.

Carroll, Thomas H. "Attracting And Maintaining A Supply Of Ellective Accounting Teachers," pp. 15-23.

Niswonger, C. Rollin. "The Attraction And Selection Of Accounting Majors," No. 1, pp. 24-32.

Moyer, C. A. "The Attraction And Selection Of Accounting Majors." No. 1, pp. 33-35.

Horne, Gilbert R. "Professional Training For Accountancy In Canada." No. 1, pp. 43-49.

North, Robert D. "Relation Between Scores On The AIA Elementary And Advanced Accounting Achievement Tests," No. 1, pp. 50-55.

Davis, Kenneth L. "The Human Problems Of The Senior

Accounting Review
Volume 32, 1957

Accounting Review
Volume 33, 1958

Accounting Review
Volume 34, 1959

Accounting Review
Volume 35, 1960

Lewis, Ronello B. "The Role Of Accounting In Decision Making," No. 1, pp. 37-44.

Stone, Williard E. "Tax Considerations In Intra-Company Pricing," No. 1, pp. 45-50.

Cyert, Richard M. and John T. Wheeler. "A Proposal For An Integrated Course In Statistics And Accounting," No. 1, pp. 51-59.

McGurr, Francis J. "The Integration Of Statistics And Accounting," No. 1, pp. 60-63.

Jacobsen, Lyle E. "Management Accounting: Content And Approach," No. 1, pp. 64-69.

Berryman, R. G. "Auditing Standards And The Law," No. 1, pp. 70-80.

Simon, Sidney I. "Spin-Offs Vs. Dividends In Kind," No. 1, pp. 81-89.

Singer, Frank A. "Needed: A Glossary To Accompany Audit Reports," No. 1, pp. 90-92.

Cook, John W. "Public Accounting Experience For Private Accountants," No. 1, pp. 93-95.

Watson, Robert H. "Two-Variate Analysis," No. 1, pp. 96-99.

Smith, Helen M. "The Use Of Reserves On The Right-Hand Side Of The Balance Sheet," No. 1, pp. 100-103.

Field, J. E. "Inventory Valuation And The Short-Run Cost Function," No. 1, pp. 104-110.

Murphy, Mary E. "Comparative Professional Accountancy - Netherlands And Belgium," No. 1, pp. 111-116.

Moss, Kermit C. "Admission Of A Partner - Step By Step," No. 1, pp. 123-125.

Cobb, E. Kennedy. "Current Status Of Managerial Accounting As A Course Of Study," No. 1, pp. 125-129.

Lynn, Edward S. "Appropriation-Expenditure Accounting," No. 1, pp. 129-132.

Homburger, Richard H. "Tax Basis Of Partner's Interest Explained By Double Entry," No. 1, pp. 132-134.

Dunn, Clarence L. "Teaching Of Adjusting And Reversing Entries In The Elementary Accounting Courses," No. 1, pp. 135-137.

MacDougall, Colville. "Amortization Of Premiums On Bonds Acquired By Trusts And Estates," No. 1, pp. 137-138.

Walsh, Lawrence M. "Accounting Education In Review," No. 2, pp. 183-189.

Fertig, Paul E. "Organization Of An Accounting Program," No. 2, pp. 190-196.

Matusiak, Louis W. "The Role Of Educators In The American Institute's Professional Development Program," No. 2, pp. 197-202.

Moonitz, Maurice and Carl L. Nelson. "Recent Developments In Accounting Theory," No. 2, pp. 206-217.

Ridilla, Richard A. "A Simplified Statistical Technique For Use In Verifying Accounts Receivable: A Rejoinder," No. 2, pp. 218-222.

McCormick, Edward T. "Reporting To Stockholders," No. 2, pp. 223-227.

Hay, Leon E. "Planning For Profits - How Some Executives Are Doing It," No. 2, pp. 233-237.

Weidenbaum, M. L. "Measures Of The Government Spending Process," No. 2, pp. 238-245.

Sprouse, Robert T. "Accounting Principles And Corporation Statutes," No. 2, pp. 246-257.

Li, David H. "The Nature Of Corporate Residual Equity Under The Entity Concept," No. 2, pp. 258-263.

Kempner, Jack J. "A New Look At The Classification Of Inventories," No. 2, pp. 264-271.

Odmark, V.E. "Current Challenges To Accounting Principles," No. 2, pp. 272-277.

Jaedicke, Robert K. and Carl L. Nelson. "The Allocation Of Income Taxes - A Defense," No. 2, pp. 278-281.

Turner, Clifford L. "Significant Differences Between U.S. and Canadian Requirements For The C.P.A. And C.A. Certificates," No. 2, pp. 282-287.

Dilley, David R. "Accounting Problems Warranting Additional Research," No. 2, pp. 288-298.

Jennings, Robert M. "An Algebraic Model For Working Capital," No. 2, pp. 316-317.

Stone, Vernon W. "A Test For Reversing Entries," No. 2, pp. 318-320.

Newlove, G. H. "The Timing Of Unavoidably Spoiled Units," No. 2, pp. 320-324.

Mastro, Anthony J. and Frank R. Hartman. "An Evaluation Of A Slide-Lecture Method For Teaching A Large Section Of College Auditing," No. 2, pp. 324-329.

Devine, Carl Thomas. "Research Methodology And Accounting Theory Formation," No. 3, pp. 387-399.

Vickers, Douglas. "On The Economics Of Break-Even," No. 3. pp. 405-412.

Flewellen, W. C., Jr. "Concept Of Depreciation Accounting Held By The United States Supreme Court," No. 3, pp. 413-421.

Ross, Myron H. "Depreciation And User Cost," No. 3, pp. 422-428.

Richards, Allen B. "Input-Output Accounting For Business," No. 3, pp. 429-436.

Pye, Malcolm L. "Reasons, Probabilities, And Accounting Principles," No. 3, pp. 437-443.

Campfield, William L. "An Approach To Formulation Of Professional Standards For Internal Auditors," No. 3, pp. 444-448.

Storey, Reed K. "Cash Movements And Periodic Income Determination," No. 3, pp. 449-454.

Lorig, Arthur N. "Training Accountants In Great Britain," No. 3, pp. 455-463.

Smyth, E. Bryan. "Management Accounting In Australia," No. 3, pp. 464-470.

Murphy, Mary E. "Comparative Professional Accountancy - South America," No. 3, pp. 471-475.

Buttimer, Harry. "Statutory Influence On Treasury Stock Accounting," No. 3, pp. 476-481.

Kollaritsch, Felix P. "Can The Balance Sheet Reveal Financial Position?," No. 3, pp. 482-489.

Ferrara, William L. "Idle Capacity As A Loss - Fact Or Fiction," No. 3, pp. 490-496.

Andersson, Henry F. "Allowance For Setup Time Under Standard Costs," No. 3, pp. 497-500.

Koch, Alfred P. "A Fallacy In Accounting For Spoiled Goods," No. 3, pp. 501-502.

Sapienza, S. R. "The Divided House Of Consolidations," No. 3, pp. 503-510.

Koch, Alfred P. "The Unconventional In Accounts Payable," No. 3, pp. 511-514.

Stone, Williard E. "Can Accounting Meet The Challenge Of Liberalized Business Education?," No. 3, pp. 515-520.

LaGrone, Paul G. "The Use Of Visual Aids In Elementary And Intermediate Accounting To Determine Their Practical Value In The Classroom," No. 3, pp. 520-522.

Nielsen, Oswald. "New Challenges In Accounting," No. 4, pp. 583-589.

Dixon, Robert L. "Decreasing Charge Depreciation - A Search For Logic," No. 4, pp. 590-597.

Myers, John H. "Influence Of Salvage Value Upon Choice Of Tax Depreciation Methods," No. 4, pp. 598-602.

Gordon, Myron J. "Scope And Method Of Theory And Research In The Measurement Of Income And Wealth," No. 4, pp. 603-618.

Jones, Gardner M. "Educators, Electrons, And Business Models: A Problem In Synthesis," No. 4, pp. 619-626.

Bierman, Harold, Jr. "Measuring Financial Liquidity," No. 4, pp. 628-632.

Sorter, G. H. and George Benston. "Appraising The Defensive Position Of A Firm: The Interval Measure," No. 4, pp. 633-640.

Weber, G. Fred. "Price Level Accounting," No. 4, pp. 641-649.

Ridilla, Richard A. "A Technique To Adjust Financial Statement Data For Changing Price Levels," No. 4, pp. 650-658.

Mead, George. "Auditing, Management Advisory Services, Social Service, And The Profit Motive," No. 4, pp. 659-666.

Cyert, R. M., G. M. Hinckley and R. J. Monteverde. "Statistical Sampling In The Audit Of The Air Force Motor Vehicle Inventory," No. 4, pp. 667-673.

Li, David H. "The Nature And Treatment Of Dividends Under The Entity Concept," No. 4, pp. 674-679.

Myatt-Price, E. M. "The Twelve At Tattershall," No. 4, pp. 680-685.

Wiener, Julius. "Separation Of Fixed And Variable Costs," No. 4, pp. 686-690.

Woods, Richard S. "Content Of The Accounting Systems Course," No. 4, pp. 720-726.

Boyd, F. Virgil. "A New Look In Accounting Education - The Managerial Approach To Tax Accounting," No. 4, pp. 726-728.

Perry, Kenneth W. "R.T.P.," No. 4, pp. 728-730.

Downing, Glenn D. "Teaching Income Tax Concepts In The Elementary Accounting Course," No. 4, pp. 730-732.

Watson, Robert H. "A Course In Contemporary Literature For Accountants," No. 4, p. 732.

Accounting Review
Volume 36, 1961

Dein, Raymond C. "A Glance Backward At Research In Accounting," No. 1, pp. 1-8.

Bevis, Herman W. "Riding Herd On Accounting Standards," No. 1. pp. 9-16.

Barr, Andrew. "Accounting Research," No. 1, pp. 17-20.

McFarland, Walter B. "Research In Management Accounting By The National Association Of Accountants," No. 1, pp. 21-25.

Powell, Weldon. "Report On The Accounting Research Activities Of The American Institute Of Certified Public Accountants," No. 1, pp. 26-31.

Littlefield, W. Joseph. "Research Program Of Controllers Institute Research Foundation," No. 1, pp. 32-35.

Beckett, John A. "Some Facts Of Federal Fiscal Life And Their Importance To Thinking Americans," No. 1, pp. 36-42.

Kircher, Paul. "Theory And Research In Management Accounting," No. 1, pp. 43-49.

Brown, Victor H. "Rate Of Return: Some Comments On Its Applicability In Capital Budgeting," No. 1, pp. 50-62.

Ferrara, William L. "Overhead Costs And Income Measurement," No. 1. pp. 63-70.

Avery, Harold G. "Depreciation Vs. Inflation," No. 1, pp. 71-74.

Johnson, Arnold W. "'More' On 'Income-Tax-Allocation' Accounting," No. 1, pp. 75-83.

Horngren, Charles T. and George H. Sorter. "'Direct' Costing For External Reporting," No. 1, pp. 84-93.

Homburger, Richard H. "Measurement In Accounting," No. 1, pp. 94-99.

Hay, Leon E. "Executory Reporting - Some Historical Notes," No. 1, pp. 100-104.

Boyd, Virgil and Dale Taylor. "The Magic Words - 'Managerial Accounting'," No. 1, pp. 105-111.

Singer, Frank A. "Management Accounting," No. 1, pp. 112-118.

Dilley, Merrill B. "What Happens To Accounting Majors?," No. 1. pp. 121-123.

Simini, Joseph Peter. "Determining Priorities For Cash Distribution In Partnership Liquidation," No. 1, pp. 123-125.

Rosenfeld, Eugene and Ralph G. Ledley. "An Accounting Course For Majors And Non-Majors," No. 1, pp. 125-128.

Green, David, Jr. "The Direct Method Of Preparing Consolidated Statements," No. 1, pp. 129-137.

Nelson, H. G. "Impact And Validity Of The Ford And Carnegie Reports On Business Education," No. 2, pp. 179-185.

Werntz, William W. "Accounting Education And The Ford And Carnegie Reports," No. 2, pp. 186-190.

Hoover, John Edgar. "FBI Accounting Investigations," No. 2, pp. 197-203.

Tiffany, Kenneth C. "The Future Of Accounting," No. 2, pp. 204-208.

Meyer, Harvey G. "Some Aspects Of Accounting Education," No. 2, pp. 209-212.

Backer, Morton. "The Quantitative Data Course In the Executive Development Program," No. 2, pp. 217-221.

Shillinglaw, Gordon. "Concepts Underlying Interim Financial Statements," No. 2, pp. 222-231.

Lorig, Arthur N. "Training Accountants In Holland And West Germany," No. 2, pp. 232-238.

Reynolds, Issac N. "Selecting The Proper Depreciation Method," No. 2, pp. 239-248.

Windal, Floyd W. "The Accounting Concept Of Realization," No. 2, pp. 249-258.

Niehus, R. J. "Tax-Free Stock Dividends And The New Model Income Statement For German Corporations," No. 2, pp. 259-264.

Li, David H. "Income Taxes And Income Tax Allocation Under The Entity Concept," No. 2, pp. 265-268.

Lawrence, Charles and Byron F. E. Bedwell. "Professional Practice In England And America," No. 2, pp. 269-273.

Hoffman, William H., Jr. "The Theory Of Tax Planning," No. 2, pp. 274-281.

Fox, Harold W. "Statistical Error Concepts Related To Accounting," No. 2, pp. 282-284.

Christiansen, Irving K. "Bringing Reality Into The Accounting Program," No. 2, pp. 293-296.

Moore, Charles N. "Some Experience In Teaching Electronic Data Processing Without A Computer," No. 2, pp. 297-299.

Murph, A. Franklin. "Mathematics In The Accounting Curriculum," No. 2, pp. 299-300.

Bedford, Norton M. and Nicholas Dopuch. "Research Methodology And Accounting Theory - Another Perspective," No. 3, pp. 351-361.

Morse, Ellsworth H., Jr. "The Joint Financial Management Improvement Program In The Federal Government," No. 3, pp. 362-373.

Solomons, David. "Economic And Accounting Concepts Of Income," No. 3, pp. 374-383.

Mattessich, Richard. "Budgeting Models And System Simulation," No. 3, pp. 384-397.

Corbin, Donald A. "Proposals For Improving Funds Statements," No. 3, pp. 398-405.

Staubus, George J. "Nonaccounting For Noninsurance." No. 3, pp. 406-408.

Bierman, Harold, Jr., Lawrence E. Fouraker and Robert K. Jaedicke. "The Use Of Probability And Statistics In Performance Evaluation," No. 3, pp. 409-417.

Weinwurm, Ernest H. "The Importance Of Idle Capacity Costs," No. 3, pp. 418-421.

Ferrara, William L. "The Importance Of Idle Capacity Costs - A Rejoinder," No. 3, pp. 422-424.

Lowe, Howard D. "The Classification Of Corporate Stock Equities," No. 3, pp. 425-433.

Buttimer, Harry. "Dividends And The Law," No. 3, pp. 434-438.

Kollaritsch, Felix. "Austria's Answer To Inflationary Profits And Taxation," No. 3, pp. 439-445.

Fess, Philip E. "The Theory Of Manufacturing Costs," No. 3, pp. 446-453.

Bomeli, Edwin C. "The Accountant's Function In Determination Of Net Income," No. 3, pp. 454-459.

Raun, Donald L. "Accounting For Decisions," No. 3, pp. 460-471.

Richards, Allan B. "A Note On Depreciation And Inventory Valuation Methods Used By Food Companies," No. 3, pp. 472-473.

Stone, Williard E. "Developments In Accounting Instruction," No. 3, pp. 474-477.

Kempner, Jack J. "A Two-Week CPA Coaching Course," No. 3, pp. 477-480.

Zukowska, Wilhelmina H. "Essential Subject Matter For A One-Year Basic Accounting Course Offered To Non-Accounting Majors," No. 3, pp. 481-487.

Milroy, Robert R., Donald F. Istvan and Ray M. Powell. "The Tax Depreciation Muddle," No. 4, pp. 539-547.

Mueller, Gerhard G. "Some Thoughts About The International Congress Of Accountants," No. 4, pp. 548-554.

Murphy, Mary E. "The Seven International Congresses Of Accountants," No. 4, pp. 555-563.

Flanders, Dwight P. "Accountancy, Systematized Learning, And Economics," No. 4, pp. 564-576.

Davidson, H. Justin and Robert M. Trueblood. "Accounting For Decision-Making," No. 4, pp. 577-582.

Bodenhorn, Diran. "An Economist Looks At Industrial Accounting And Depreciation," No. 4, pp. 583-588.

Vatter, William J. "Accounting And Statistics," No. 4, pp. 589-597.

Fess, Philip E. and William L. Ferrara. "The Period Cost Concept For Income Measurement - Can It Be Defended?," No. 4, pp. 598-602.

Briloff, Abraham J. "Price Level Changes And Financial Statements At The Threshold Of The New Frontier," No. 4, pp. 603-607.

Ridilla, Richard A. "Price Level Adjustments To Financial Statements - A Rejoinder," No. 4, pp. 608-612.

Bierman, Harold, Jr. "Depreciable Assets - Timing Of Expense Recognition," No. 4, pp. 613-618.

Harwood, Dale S., Jr. "Yet More On Tax Allocation," No. 4, pp. 619-625.

Swick, Ralph D. "Objectives Of Accounting Education," No. 4, pp. 626-630.

Kohl, Maybelle. "Objectives Of Accounting Education In The Liberal Arts College," No. 4, pp. 631-634.

Williams, Thomas H. and Charles H. Griffin. "Accountancy And Professional Development," No. 4, pp. 637-641.

Zeff, Stephen A. "'Price-Level' Should Be Taught...In The Introductory Course," No. 4, pp. 642-645.

Patrick, A. W. "Burden Rates - Machine Hours Versus Direct Labor Hours," No. 4, pp. 645-647.

Etnier, Don. "Teaching Equivalent Production With A Chart," No. 4, p. 648.

Buttimer, Harry. "The Allocation Of Combined Net Income In Reciprocal Affiliations," No. 4, pp. 649-650.

Accounting Review
Volume 37, 1962

Pilie, Louis H. "Human Relations As A Modern Tonic," No. 1, pp. 1-5.

Rice, Marilyn Young. "Sketch For A Universal Accounting Statement," No. 1, pp. 6-21.

Hylton, Delmer P. "Current Trends In Accounting Theory," No. 1, pp. 22-27.

Raby, William L. "Accounting For Employee Stock Options," No. 1, pp. 28-38.

Mauriello, Joseph A. "The Working Capital Concept - A Restatement," No. 1, pp. 39-43.

Kemp, Patrick S. "Accounting Data For Planning, Motivation, And Control," No. 1, pp. 44-50.

Thacker, Ronald J. "Income Statement Form And Classification," No. 1, pp. 51-55.

Lorig, Arthur N. "On The Logic Of Decreasing Charge Depreciation," No. 1, pp. 56-58.

Sosnick, Stephen H. "Depreciation: the Offsetting-Interest Method," No. 1, pp. 59-66.

Thomas, Arthur L. "Precision And Discounted Services," No. 1, pp. 67-72.

Jennings, Robert M. "Selections From A Pre-Revolutionary Accounting Record," No. 1, pp. 73-75.

Fremgen, James M. "Variable Costing For External Reporting - A Reconsideration," No. 1, pp. 76-81.

Rydell, Ferd. "You Are Being Watched!," No. 1, pp. 82-87.

Murase, Gen. "The Present Status Of The Public Accounting Profession In Japan," No. 1, pp. 88-91.

Lotharius, Richard D. "The Acceptance Of Accounting As A Profession," No. 1, pp. 92-95.

Wales, Stephen H. "Intangible Expenses And Amortizing Intangible Assets," No. 1, pp. 96-98.

Campbell, J. D. "Consolidation Vs. Combination," No. 1, pp. 99-102.

McGowen, George B. "The Flow Of Assets Through A Business Enterprise And The Accounting Flow Equation Based Theron," No. 1, pp. 105-110.

Gibson, Joseph E. "Law And/Or Accounting," No. 1, pp. 110-115.

Dunn, James O. "The Honors Student And Accounting," No. 1, pp. 115-118.

Schonfeld, Hanns-Martin and H. Peter Holzer. "A 'Business' Flow Chart And Its Use As A Teaching Aid," No. 1, pp. 118-120.

Gordon, Dennis. "The Overhead Projector - An Aid In Teaching Accounting," No. 1, pp. 120-121.

Moonitz, Maurice. "Should We Discard The Income Concept?," No. 2, pp. 175-180.

Jaedicke, Robert K. "Accounting Data For Purposes Of Control," No. 2, pp. 181-188.

Vatter, William J. "Fund-Theory View Of Price-Level Adjustments," No. 2, pp. 189-207.

Shillinglaw, Gordon. "Toward A Theory Of Divisional Income Measurement," No. 2, pp. 208-216.

Wade, Harry H. "Comments On Research Bulletins," No. 2, pp. 217-222.

Caplin, Mortimer H. "New Directions In Tax Administration," No. 2, pp. 223-230.

Hofert, Jack. "State Income Taxation - A Suggested Solution To The Present Confusion," No. 2, pp. 231-233.

Pfenning, R. E. "Business Information Systems," No. 2, pp. 234-243.

Jones, Gardner M. "Accounting Innovation And The Psychology Of Change," No. 2, pp. 244-250.

Dopuch, Nicholas. "Metaphysics Of Pragmatism And Accountancy," No. 2, pp. 251-262.

Sapienza, Samuel R. "Pooling Theory And Practice In Business Combinations," No. 2, pp. 263-278.

Drebin, Allan R. "Accounting For Life Insurance As An Investment," No. 2, pp. 279-282.

Burke, John T. "Stock Dividends - Suggestions For Clarification," No. 2, pp. 283-288.

Ladin, Eugene. "The Role Of The Accountant In Operations Analysis," No. 2, pp. 289-294.

Campfield, William L. "A Governmental Agency's Program For Developing Its Professional Accountants," No. 2, pp. 295-299.

Zannetos, Zenon S. "Depreciation And Funds Statements," No. 2, pp. 300-307.

Gregory, John C. "Capital Expenditure Evaluation By Direct Discounting," No. 2, pp. 308-314.

Spiller, Earl A., Jr. "Teaching Consolidated Income Statements - A New Approach," No. 2, pp. 336-342.

Fess, Philip E. "Accounting Instruction Without Rules," No. 2, pp. 342-344.

Weiss, Charles J. "An Adjunct To The Accounting Curriculum: The Business Radio Series," No. 2, pp. 344-345.

Gerber, Quentin N. "Accounting Education Below C.P.A. Standards - An International Approach," No. 2, pp. 346-349.

Sorter, George H. and Charles T. Horngren. "Asset Recognition And Economic Attributes - The Relevant Costing Approach," No. 3, pp. 391-399.

Bierman, Harold, Jr. "Probability, Statistical Decision Theory, And Accounting," No. 3, pp. 400-405.

Boutell, W. S. "The Implementation Of Uniform Standards Of Reporting For National Voluntary Agencies," No. 3, pp. 406-409.

Griffin, Charles H. and Thomas H. Williams. "A Comparative Analysis Of Accounting And Mathematics," No. 3, pp. 410-414.

Kwang, Ching-Wen and Albert Slavin. "The Simple Mathematics Of Variance Analysis," No. 3, pp. 415-432.

Wright, F. Kenneth. "Measuring Project Profitability: Rate Of Return Or Present Value?," No. 3, pp. 433-437.

Wiener, Julius. "The Cost Structure Of The Industrial Enterprise: Pattern Of Analysis," No. 3, pp. 438-451.

Oates, Thomas A. and Milton H. Spencer. "A System Of Retirement Frequencies For Depreciable Assets," No. 3, pp. 452-459.

Stettler, Howard F. "Break-Even Analysis: Its Uses And Misuses," No. 3, pp. 460-463.

Singer, Frank A. "Accounting Is A Matter Of Taste," No. 3, pp. 464-471.

Jacobsen, Lyle E. "Allocation And Attitudes," No. 3, pp. 472-474.

Ashburne, Jim G. "A Forward Looking Statement Of Financial Position," No. 3, pp. 475-478.

Lent, George E. "Accounting Principles And Taxable Income," No. 3, pp. 479-487.

Berg, Kenneth B. "Allowance For Repairs," No. 3, pp. 488-496.

Staubus, George J. "Decreasing Charge Depreciation - Still Searching For Logic," No. 3, pp. 497-501.

Salmonson, R.F. "A Prophetic Analogy?," No. 3, pp. 502-505.

Grimstad, Clayton R. "Thoughts On Continuing Education In Accounting," No. 3, pp. 506-509.

Lawrence, Charles. "Brazil - Education And Accountants," No. 3, pp. 510-514.

Sprouls, R. Clay. "A Role Of Computer Simulation In Accounting Education," No. 3, pp. 515-520.

Gustafson, George A. "The Federal Government Accountants Association," No. 3, pp. 521-522.

Seitelman, Nathan. "An Analysis Of The Auditing Section Of The Certified Public Accountant Examinations, May 1951 to May 1961," No. 3, pp. 547-550.

Frumer, Samuel. "Incorporating Managerial Controls Into Introductory Cost Accounting," No. 3, pp. 551-553.

Singer, Frank A. "Rationale For A Course In Quantitative Methods," No. 3, pp. 554-555.

Woods, Milton. "Law And/Or Accounting - A Footnote," No. 3, p. 556.

Schattke, Rudy and LeRay McAllister. "Large Versus Small Classes In Elementary Accounting," No. 3, pp. 557-561.

Zeff, Stephen A. "Replacement Cost: Member Of The Family, Welcome Guest, Or Intruder?," No. 4, pp. 611-625.

Corbin, Donald A. "The Revolution In Accounting," No. 4, pp. 626-635.

Chang, Emily Chen. "Business Income In Accounting And Economics," No. 4, pp. 636-644.

Schrader, William J. "An Inductive Approach To Accounting Theory," No. 4, pp. 645-649.

Bedford, Norton M. and Vahe Baladouni. "A Communication Theory Approach To Accountancy," No. 4, pp. 650-659.

Vatter, William J. "Another Look At The 1957 Statement," No. 4, pp. 660-669.

Schattke, Rudy. "Expected Income - A Reporting Challenge," No. 4, pp. 670-676.

Drake, David F. "The Service Potential Concept And Inter-Period Tax Allocation," No. 4, pp. 677-684.

Pinkerton, James E. and Stuart Margulies. "Programed Instruction: Its Implication For Accounting Education," No. 4, pp. 685-691.

Gordon, Dennis. "Can Accounting Instruction Be Automated?," No. 4, pp. 692-695.

Brown, R. Gene. "Changing Audit Objectives And Techniques," No. 4, pp. 696-703.

Mogis, Robert C. and Donald Rogoff. "Statistics Offers A Solution To Tommorow's Auditing Complexities," No. 4, pp. 704-707.

Sih, S. T. "Public Accountancy In Hong Kong," No. 4, pp. 708-712.

Zannetos, Zenon S. "Statistical Attributes Of Group Depreciation," No. 4, pp. 713-720.

Moore, Carl L. "The Concept Of The P/V Graph Applied To Capital Investment Planning," No. 4, pp. 721-729.

Moss, Morton F. "Management Services And The CPA Examination," No. 4, pp. 730-740.

Bomeli, Edwin C. "Stock Option Plans - Full Disclosure," No. 4, pp. 741-745.

Buttimer, Harry. "The Evolution Of Stated Capital," No. 4, pp. 746-752.

Ray, J. C. "Accounting For Treasury Stock," No. 4, pp. 753-757.

Jaenicke, Henry R. "Management's Choice To Purchase Or Pool," No. 4, pp. 758-765.

Sterling, Robert R. "Determination Of Goodwill And Bonus On The Admission Of A Partner," No. 4, pp. 766-767.

Andersen, Anker V. "A Defense Of Accounting Education," No. 4, p. 768.

Raun, Donald L. "What Is Accounting?," No. 4, pp. 769-773.

Accounting Review
Volume 38, 1963

Burns, Joseph S., Robert K. Jaedicke and John M. Sangster. "Financial Reporting Of Purchase Contracts Used To Guarantee Large Investments," No. 1, pp. 1-13.

Philips, G. Edward. "The Accretion Concept Of Income," No. 1, pp. 14-25.

Mauriello, Joseph A. "Realization As The Basis For Asset Classification And Measurement," No. 1, pp. 26-28.

Windal, Floyd W. "Legal Background For The Accounting Concept Of Realization," No. 1, pp. 29-36.

DeMaris, E. Joe. "'Success Indicator' Function Of Income Concept Argues Its Further Development," No. 1, pp. 37-45.

Trumbull, Wendell P. "When Is A Liability?," No. 1, pp. 46-51.

Li, David H. "Alternative Accounting Procedures And The Entity Concept," No. 1, pp. 52-55.

Van Horne, James C. "A Look At The Loss Carry-Forward," No. 1, pp. 56-60.

Bierman, Harold, Jr. "A Problem In Expense Recognition," No. 1, pp. 61-63.

Staubus, George J. "Direct, Relevant Or Absorption Costing?," No. 1, pp. 64-74.

Blakely, Edward J. and Peter H. Knutson. "L.I.F.O. Or L.O.F.I. - Which?," No. 1, pp. 75-86.

Wright, F. Kenneth. "Depreciation Theory And The Cost Of Funds," No. 1, pp. 87-90.

Sapienza, Samuel R. "Business Combinations - A Case Study," No. 1, pp. 91-101.

Morey, Lloyd. "Progress Of The Independent Post Audit Program In Illinois," No. 1, pp. 102-108.

Patrick, A. W. and C. L. Quittmeyer. "The CPA And Management Services," No. 1, pp. 109-117.

Mellman, Martin. "Marketing Cost Analysis - Development And Current Practices," No. 1, pp. 118-123.

Alvey, Kenneth L. "Alternative Derivation Of Formulas For The Income Tax Problem," No. 1, pp. 124-125.

Kemp, Patrick S. "Controversies On The Construction Of Financial Statements," No. 1, pp. 126-132.

Farman, Wilson L. and Chi-Ming Hou. "The Balance Of Payments: An Accounting Analysis," No. 1, pp. 133-141.

Mueller, Gerhard G. "The Dimensions Of The International Accounting Problem," No. 1, pp. 142-147.

Wasley, Robert S. "A Revitalized Accounting Curriculum," No. 1, pp. 151-153.

Yager, E. Ben. "An Aid In Explaining 'Funds Provided By Operations'," No. 1, pp. 154-156.

Simini, Joseph Peter. "The Scope Paragraph Of The Audit Report Graphically Illustrated," No. 1, pp. 157-159.

Emblen, Donald J. "When Should Techniques Be Presented?," No. 1, pp. 159-160.

Gustafson, George A. "Working Paper For Preparation Of Cash-Flow Statement," No. 1, pp. 160-167.

Dean, Joel and C. Lowell Harriss. "Railroad Accounting Under The New Depreciation Guidelines And Investment Tax Credit," No. 2, pp. 229-242.

Paton, Wm. A. "The 'Cash-Flow' Illusion," No. 2, pp. 243-251.

Hein, Leonard W. "New British Accounting Recommendations," No. 2, pp. 252-261.

Edey, Harold C. "Company Accounts In Britain: The Jenkins Report," No. 2, pp. 262-265.

Kohler, E. L. "The Jenkins Report," No. 2, pp. 266-269.

Firmin, Peter A. "Dollar Value Lifo: Legitimate Or Not?," No. 2, pp. 270-277.

Davidson, Sidney. "Old Wine Into New Bottles," No. 2, pp. 278-284.

Jacobsen, Lyle E. "The Rise Of The Profit Deferral Notion - The Concept And Practice Of Optimeasurement," No. 2, pp. 285-292.

Lowe, Howard D. "The Essentials Of A General Theory Of Depreciation," No. 2, pp. 293-301.

Seelye, Alfred L. "The Role Of Business Schools In A Changing Evnironment," No. 2, pp. 302-309.

Spencer, Milton H. "Axiomatic Method And Accounting Science," No. 2, pp. 310-316.

Mautz, R. K. "Accounting As A Social Science," No. 2, pp. 317-325.

Zannetos, Zenon S. "Mathematics As A Tool Of Accounting Instruction And Research," No. 2, pp. 326-335.

Gray, Jack, John Willingham and Kenneth Johnston. "A Business Game For The Introductory Course In Accounting," No. 2, pp. 336-346.

Benston, George J. "The Role Of The Firm's Accounting System For Motivation," No. 2, pp. 347-354.

Greene, Edward D. "Changing From Declining Balance To Straight-Line Depreciation," No. 2, pp. 355-362.

McBride, Howard J. "Assigning Tax Loads To Prospective Projects," No. 2, pp. 363-370.

Keister, Orville R. "Commercial Record Keeping In Ancient Mesopotamia," No. 2, pp. 371-376.

Holzer, H. Peter and Hanns-Martin Schonfeld. "The German Solution To The Post-War Price Level Problem," No. 2, pp. 377-381.

Holzer, H. Peter and Hanns-Martin Schonfeld. "The French Approach To The Post-War Price Level Problem," No. 2, pp. 382-388.

Salgado, Ignacio Perez. "Accounting Reports In Chile," No. 2, pp. 389-397.

Kemp, Patrick S. "A 'Current Topics' Course In The Accounting Curriculum?," No. 2, pp. 398-400.

Mandel, B. J. "A Course In Statistical Sampling For Accountants, Auditors And Financial Managers," No. 2, pp. 400-406.

Bedford, Norton M. "The Laws Of Learning And Accounting Instruction," No. 2, pp. 406-408.

Horngren, Charles T. "Teaching Methods And Participation As A Major Law Of Learning," No. 2, pp. 409-411.

Mitchell, Wiley S. "Relationship Of Laws Of Learning To Methods Of Accounting Instruction," No. 2, pp. 411-414.

Goldberg, Louis. "The Present State Of Accounting Theory," No. 3, pp. 457-469.

Vatter, Wm. J. "Sum Of (M3)i," No. 3, pp. 470-477.

Marple, Ray P. "Value-itis," No. 3, pp. 478-482.

Hendriksen, Eldon S. "Purchasing Power And Replacement Cost Concepts - Are They Related?," No. 3, pp. 483-491.

Gibson, James L. "Accounting In The Decision-Making Process," No. 3, pp. 492-500.

Bierman, Harold, Jr. "Measurement And Accounting," No. 3, pp. 501-507.

Hein, Leonard W. "The Auditor And The British Companies Act," No. 3, pp. 508-520.

Campfield, William L. "Critical Paths For Professional Accountants During The New Management Revolution," No. 3, pp. 521-527.

Zannetos, Zenon S. "On The Mathematics Of Variance Analysis," No. 3, pp. 528-533.

Weber, Charles. "The Mathematics Of Variance Analysis," No. 3, pp. 534-539.

McClenon, Paul R. "Cost Finding Through Multiple Correlation Analysis," No. 3, pp. 540-547.

Bennett, J. W. "Measuring Project Profitability: Rate Of Return Or Present Value - A Reply," No. 3, pp. 548-553.

Berg, Kenneth B. and Fred J. Mueller. "Accounting For Investment Credits," No. 3, pp. 554-561.

Taussig, Russell. "Governmental Accounting: Fund Flow Or Service Cost?," No. 3, pp. 562-567.

Raby, Wm. L. and Robert D. Neubig. "Inter-Period Tax Allocation Or Basis Adjustment?," No. 3, pp. 568-576.

Heck, W. R. "Accounting For Warranty Costs," No. 3, pp. 577-578.

Drebin, Allan R. "Recognizing Implicit Interest In Non-Funded Pension Plans," No. 3, pp. 579-583.

Weigand, Robert E. "The Accountant And Marketing Channels," No. 3, pp. 584-590.

Kalinski, B. D. "A Case Of Over-Accounting," No. 3, pp. 591-595.

Brugge, W. G. "The Accountancy Profession In Greece," No. 3, pp. 596-600.

Usry, Milton F. "Developing The Relationship Between Process Cost Accounting Allocations And The Accounting Records," No. 3, pp. 614-619.

Windal, Floyd W. "Analysis Of Changes In Gross Profit," No. 3, pp. 619-622.

Zeff, Stephen A. "Debating Accounting Theory," No. 3, pp. 622-626.

Perry, Kenneth W. "Intercompany Profits And ARB 51," No. 3, pp. 626-628.

Dilley, Merrill B. and David R. Dilley. "College Accounting Courses - 1963," No. 3, pp. 629-632.

Sprouse, Robert T. "Historical Costs And Current Assets - Traditional And Treacherous," No. 4, pp. 687-695.

Philips, G. Edward. "The Revolution In Accounting Theory," No. 4, pp. 696-708.

Woolsey, S. M. "Accounting For Investment Credit," No. 4, pp. 709-713.

Wade, Harry H. "Accounting For The Investment Credit," No. 4, pp. 714-718.

Ferrara, Wm. L. "Relevant Costing - Two Points Of View," No. 4, pp. 719-722.

Fess, Philip E. "The Relevant Costing Concept For Income Measurement - Can It Be Defended?," No. 4, pp. 723-732.

Arnett, Harold E. "Recognition As A Function Of Measurement In The Realization Concept," No. 4, pp. 733-741.

Corbin, Donald A. "Comments On 'The Accretion Concept Of Income'," No. 4, pp. 742-744.

Dopuch, Nicholas. "Mathematical Programming And Accounting Approaches To Incremental Cost Analysis," No. 4, pp. 745-753.

Raun, Donald L. "The Application Of Monte Carlo Analysis To An Inventory Problem," No. 4, pp. 754-758.

Lorig, Arthur N. "Suggested Improvements In Governmental Accounting," No. 4, pp. 759-763.

Bruegman, Donald C. and Gerald D. Brighton. "Institutional Accounting - How It Differs From Commercial Accounting," No. 4, pp. 764-770.

Li, David H. "The Funds Statement Under The Entity Concept," No. 4, pp. 771-775.

Gilles, L. H., Jr. "Statutory Depletion - Subsidy In Disguise?," No. 4, pp. 776-784.

Parker, William M. "Treatment Of Short-Term Credit In The Funds Statement," No. 4, pp. 785-788.

Botts, Ralph R. "Interest And The Truth-In-Lending Bill," No. 4, pp. 789-795.

Hudson, Robert R. "Accounting For Unearned Discount Of Finance Companies," No. 4, pp. 796-801.

Burke, Walter L. "Cost Allocation And Distribution - Merchandise Accounting," No. 4, pp. 802-812.

Anderson, Hershel M. and Fred B. Griffin. "The Accounting Curriculum And Postgraduate Achievement," No. 4, pp. 813-818.

Horwitz, Bertrand. "Depreciation And Cost Stability In Soviet Accounting," No. 4, pp. 819-826.

Andersen, Anker V. "Why Write?," No. 2, pp. 827-830.

Young, Kenneth G. "A Solution Approach To Application Of Funds Problems," No. 2, pp. 830-833.

Green, David, Jr. "A Schema For Interest Formulae," No. 2, pp. 833-834.

Chapin, Ned. "Teaching Business Data Processing With The Aid Of A Computer," No. 2, pp. 835-839.

Pescow, Jerome K. "A Visual Approach To Auditing And Accounting Instruction," No. 2, pp. 839-843.

Accounting Review
Volume 39, 1964

Thomas, Arthur L. "Discounted Services Again: The Homogeneity Problem," No. 1, pp. 1-11.

Briloff, Abraham J. "Needed: A Revolution In The Determination And Application Of Accounting Principles," No. 1, pp. 12-15.

Metcalf, Richard W. "The 'Basic Postulates' In Perspective," No. 1, pp. 16-21.

Greer, Howard C. "The Corporation Stockholder - Accounting's Forgotten Man," No. 1, pp. 22-31.

Tuckerman, Bert. "Objective Consolidation Standards For Foreign Subsidiaries," No. 1, pp. 32-37.

Stone, Williard E. "Legal Implications Of Intracompany Pricing," No. 1, pp. 38-42.

Fremgen, James M. "The Direct Costing Controversy - An Identification Of Issues," No. 1, pp. 43-51.

Baker, Roy E. "The Pension Cost Problem," No. 1, pp. 52-61.

Robinson, Leonard A. and T. P. Hall. "Systems Education And The Accounting Curriculum," No. 1, pp. 62-69.

Holdren, George C. "LIFO And Ratio Analysis," No. 1, pp. 70-85.

Neubig, Robert D. "Sales Growth - Fact Or Fiction?," No. 1, pp. 86-89.

Heebink, David V. "The Optimum Capital Budget," No. 1, pp. 90-93.

Moore, Carl L. "The Present-Value Method And The Replacement Decision," No. 1, pp. 94-102.

Burgher, Peter H. "PERT And The Auditor," No. 1, pp. 103-120.

Allyn, Robert G. "Planning For The C.P.A. Examination In The United States," No. 1, pp. 121-127.

Lamden, Charles W. "The Function Of The State Board Of Accountancy In Improving Reporting Standards In California," No. 1, pp. 128-132.

Wilkinson, Theodore L. "Can Accounting Be An International Language?," No. 1, pp. 133-139.

Ratsch, Herbert. "The New Professional Code For Certified Accountants And Licensed Accountants In The Federal Republic Of Germany," No. 1, pp. 140-144.

Solomon, Kenneth Ira and Howard Gordon Kaplan. "Regulation Of The Accounting Profession In Israel," No. 1, pp. 145-149.

Ziegler, Francis, S. J. and John M. Ivanoff. "A Study Of A Maturity Factor Between Freshman And Sophomore Accounting Students," No. 1, pp. 155-160.

Griffin, Charles H. and Thomas H. Williams. "Simulation In Business Education," No. 1, pp. 160-163.

Landry, Horace J. "Auditing Instruction At The Undergraduate College Level," No. 1, pp. 164-166.

Raby, Wm. L. "A Decision-Making Approach To The First Tax Course," No. 1, pp. 167-172.

Jennings, Robert M. "Prepayals - A Flow Simulation," No. 1, pp. 172-173.

Stettler, Howard F. "Auditing And Accounting Systems: A Marriage Proposal," No. 1, pp. 173-175.

Charnes, A., H. Justin Davidson and K. Kortanck. "On A Mixed Sequential Estimating Procedure With Application To Audit Tests In Accounting," No. 2, pp. 241-250.

Gordon, Myron J. "Postulates, Principles And Research In Accounting," No. 2, pp. 251-263.

Chambers, R. J. "Measurement And Objectivity In Accounting," No. 2, pp. 264-274.

Spacek, Leonard. "A Suggested Solution To The Principles Dilemma," No. 2, pp. 275-284.

Dyckman, Thomas R. "On The Investment Decision," No. 2, pp. 285-295.

Zannetos, Zenon S. "Standard Costs As A First Step To Probabilistic Control: A Theoretical Justification, An Extension And Implications," No. 2, pp. 296-304.

Boutell, W. S. "Business Oriented Computers: A Frame Of Reference," No. 2, pp. 305-311.

Dickens, Robert L. and John O. Blackburn. "Holding Gains On Fixed Assets: An Element Of Business Income?," No. 2, pp. 312-329.

Paine, Neil R. "Uncertainty And Capital Budgeting," No. 2, pp. 330-332.

Golembiewski, Robert T. "Accountancy As A Function Of Organization Theory," No. 2, pp. 333-341.

Reynolds, Isaac N. "A Vanishing Accounting Item - Replacement Accounting?," No. 2, pp. 342-346.

Mauriello, Joseph A. "The All-Inclusive Statement Of Funds," No. 2, pp. 347-357.

Soper, Fred J. and Robert Dolphin, Jr. "Readability And Corporate Annual Reports," No. 2, pp. 358-362.

MacKenzie, Ossian. "Accreditation Of Accounting Curricula," No. 2, pp. 363-370.

Lynn, Edward S. "Education For The Profession," No. 2, pp. 371-376.

Berkow, William F. "Need For Engineering Influence Upon Accounting Procedure," No. 2, pp. 377-386.

Graese, C. E. "Responsibility Reporting To Management," No. 2, pp. 387-391.

Farman, Wilson L. "National Flow-Of-Funds: An Accounting Analysis," No. 2, pp. 392-404.

Holzer, H. Peter and Hanns-Martin Schonfeld. "The 'Funktionale Kontorechnung' Of Walter Thoms," No. 2, pp. 405-413.

Keister, Orville. R. "The Incan Quipu," No. 2, pp. 414-416.

Horngren, Charles T. and George H. Sorter. "An Evaluation Of Some Criticisms Of Relevant Costing," No. 2, pp. 417-420.

Zukowska, Wilhemina H. "Determination Of Goodwill Or Bonus On The Admission Of A Partner - An Alternative Approach," No. 2, pp. 457-460.

Burnet, Mary E. and Arden L. Travis. "A Cooperative Education Program In Public Accounting," No. 2, pp. 460-463.

Brighton, Gerald D. "Image Of The Internal Revenue Service," No. 2, pp. 463-467.

Prince, Thomas R. "Information Systems For Management Control," No. 2, pp. 467-472.

Person, Samuel. "The Integrated Use Of Data Processing Equipment In Teaching Accounting Subjects," No. 2, pp. 473-475.

Pick, John. "A Workshop In Fundamental Accounting," No. 2, pp. 476-481.

Brown, Robert O. "College Entrance Tests And Accounting Grades," No. 2, pp. 481-486.

Willingham, John J. "The Accounting Entity: A Conceptual Model," No. 3, pp. 543-552.

Prince, Thomas R. "The Motivational Assumption For Accounting Theory," No. 3, pp. 553-562.

Lorig, Arthur N. "Some Basic Concepts Of Accounting And Their Implications," No. 3, pp. 563-573.

Thomas, Arthur L. "'Value-Itis' - An Impractical Theorist's Reply," No. 3, pp. 574-581.

Sapienza, Samuel R. "An Examination Of AICPA Research Study No. 5 - Standards For Pooling," No. 3, pp. 582-590.

Luneski, Chris. "Some Aspects Of The Meaning Of Control," No. 3, pp. 591-597.

Woods, Richard S. "Some Dimensions Of Integrated Systems," No. 3, pp. 598-614.

Gomberg, Mandel and Arthur Farber. "The Balance Sheet Of The Future," No. 3, pp. 615-617.

Horwitz, Ronald M. "The Investment Credit, 'Deferred Income Taxes' And Accounting Measurement," No. 3, pp. 618-621.

Winborne, Marilyn G. "The Operating Cycle Concept - Accepted?," No. 3, pp. 622-626.

Goggans, Travis P. "The Accountant's Role In Wage Negotiations," No. 3, pp. 627-630.

Manes, Rene Pierre. "The Grant-In-Aid System For Interstate Highway Construction: An Accounting Or Economic Problem?," No. 3, pp. 631-638.

Stanley, Curtis H. "Cost-Basis Valuations In Transactions Between Entities," No. 3, pp. 639-647.

Jenkins, David O. "Accounting For Funded Industrial Pension Plans," No. 3, pp. 648-653.

Standish, P. E. M. "An Appraisal Of The Teaching And Study Of Auditing," No. 3, pp. 654-666.

Hylton, Delmer P. "Are Consulting And Auditing Compatible? - A Contrary View," No. 3, pp. 667-670.

Williams, Thomas H. and Charles H. Griffin. "Matrix Theory And Cost Allocation," No. 3, pp. 671-678.

Schroderheim, Goran. "Using Mathematical Probability To Estimate The Allowance For Doubtful Accounts," No. 3, pp. 679-684.

Ricks, R. Bruce. "Year To Switch To Straight Line Depreciation," No. 3, pp. 685-688.

Jolivet, Vincent. "The Current French Approach To Inventory Price Level Problems," No. 3, pp. 689-692.

Drebin, Allan R. "A Computer Solution To Cost Or Market Problems," No. 3, pp. 745-749.

DeCoster, Don T. "The Unit Cost Denominator In Process Costing," No. 3, pp. 750-754.

Lentilhon, Robert W. "Determination Of Goodwill And Bonus On Admission Of A Partner," No. 3, pp. 754-756.

Brown, Sandford H. "Teaching The Funds Statement - A Conceptual Approach," No. 3, pp. 756-759.

Noehl, James W. "A Programed Adjustment Procedure," No. 3, pp. 760-764.

Field, J. E. "A Flow Of Funds Approach To Accounting Theory," No. 3, pp. 764-768.

Rozoff, Donald. "Heuristic," No. 3, pp. 768-769.

Burke, Edward J. "Objectivity And Accounting," No. 4, pp. 837-849.

Spiller, Earl A., Jr. "Theory And Practice In The Development Of Accounting," No. 4, pp. 850-859.

Zannetos, Zenon S. "Some Thoughts On Internal Control Systems Of The Firm," No. 4, pp. 860-868.

Cramer, Joe J. "A Note On Pension Trust Accountings," No. 4, pp. 869-875.

Patten, Ronald J. "Intraperiod Income Tax Allocation - A Practical Concept," No. 4, pp. 876-879.

Lentilhon, Robert W. "Direct Costing - Either...Or?," No. 4, pp. 880-883.

Simon, Sidney I. "Cost Accounting And The Law," No. 4, pp. 884-889.

Monson, Norman P. and John A. Tracy. "Stock Rights And Accounting Wrongs," No. 4, pp. 890-893.

Churchill, Neil. "Linear Algebra And Cost Allocations: Some Examples," No. 4, pp. 894-904.

Hobbs, James B. "Volume-Mix-Price/Cost Budget Variance Analysis: A Proper Approach," No. 4, pp. 905-913.

Beranek, William. "A Note On The Equivalence Of Certain Capital Budgeting Criteria," No. 4, pp. 914-916.

Jaedicke, Robert K. and Alexander A. Robichek. "Cost-Volume-Profit Analysis Under Conditions Of Uncertainty," No. 4, pp. 917-926.

Raun, Donald L. "The Limitations Of Profit Graphs, Breakeven Analysis And Budgets," No. 4, pp. 927-945.

Li, David H. "The Objectives Of The Corporation Under The Entity Concept," No. 4, pp. 946-950.

Rappaport, Alfred. "Establishing Objectives For Published Corporate Accounting Reports," No. 4, pp. 951-962.

Birnberg, Jacob. "An Information Oriented Approach To The Presentation Of Common Stockholders' Equity," No. 4, pp. 963-971.

Hirsch, A. Jay. "Accounting For Fixed Assets: A New Perspective," No. 4, pp. 972-978.

Hafner, George F. "Auditing EDP," No. 4, pp. 979-982.

Someya, Kyojiro. "The Use Of Funds Statements In Japan," No. 4, pp. 983-989.

Moreno, Rafael Garcia. "The Unification Of The Professional Teaching Of Accounting In The Americas," No. 4, pp. 990-995.

Mattingly, L. A. "Formation And Development Of The Institute Of Certified Public Accountants Of Greece," No. 4, pp. 996-1003.

Gibbs, George. "Professors' Taxable Income And Deductions," No. 4, pp. 1004-1007.

Welsch, Glenn A. "Some Challenges For Accounting Education," No. 4, pp. 1008-1013.

Brill, Robert J. "A Visual Aid For Explaining Sources And Applications Of Funds," No. 4, pp. 1014-1017.

Gustafson, George A. "Working Paper For Preparation Of Funds Statement," No. 4, pp. 1018-1023.

Smith, C. Aubrey. "The Internship In Accounting Education," No. 4, pp. 1024-1027.

Hay, Leon E. "Graduate Seminars In Accounting Research," No. 4, pp. 1027-1029.

Robinson, William G. "Stepping Stones To The Cost Of Production Report," No. 4, pp. 1029-1033.

Anderson, Wilton T. "Large Classes In Elementary Accounting," No. 4, pp. 1034-1036.

Leer, J. A. "A Logical Approach To The Statement Of Affairs," No. 4, pp. 1036-1039.

Phillips, Lawrence C. "An Application Of Distribution Cost Analysis To A Small Company," No. 4, pp. 1040-1044.

Dyckman, Thomas R. "A Dynamic Case Approach To Management Accounting," No. 4, pp. 1045-1050.

Dilley, Merrill B. and David R. Dilley. "College Accounting Courses - 1964," No. 4, pp. 1050-1053.

Accounting Review
Volume 40, 1965

Cohen, Manuel F. "Current Developments At The SEC," No. 1, pp. 1-8.

Cowan, T. K. "A Resources Theory Of Accounting," No. 1, pp. 9-20.

Grady, Paul. "Inventory Of Generally Accepted Accounting Principles In The USA," No. 1, pp. 21-30.

Manes, R. P. and Vernon L. Smith. "Economic Joint Cost Theory And Accounting Practice," No. 1, pp. 31-35.

Ijiri, Yuji. "Axioms And Structures Of Conventional Accounting Measurement," No. 1, pp. 36-53.

Arnett, Harold E. "Implication Of The Capital Gains And Losses Concept In Practice," No. 1, pp. 54-64.

Zeff, Stephen A. and W. David Maxwell. "Holding Gains On Fixed Assets - A Demurrer," No. 1, pp. 65-75.

Deskins, Jams Wesley. "On The Nature Of The Public Interest," No. 1, pp. 76-81.

Cruse, Rex B., Jr. and Edward L. Summers. "Economics, Accounting Practice And Accounting Research Study No. 3," No. 1, pp. 82-88.

Taylor, R. G. "A Look At Published Interim Reports," No. 1, pp. 89-96.

Linowes, David F. "Nature Of The Accounting Profession," No. 1, pp. 97-104.

Jeynes, Paul H. "A Discipline For Investment Decisions," No. 1, pp. 105-118.

Staubus, George J. "The Association Of Financial Accounting Variables With Common Stock Values," No. 1, pp. 119-134.

O'Donnell, John L. "Relationships Between Reported Earnings And Stock Prices In The Electric Utility Industry," No. 1, pp. 135-143.

Spencer, Charles H. and Thomas S. Barnhisel. "A Decade Of Price-Level Changes - The Effect On The Financial Statements Of Cummins Engine Company," No. 1, pp. 144-153.

Drebin, Allan R. "Price Level Adjustments And Inventory Flow Assumptions," No. 1, pp. 154-162.

Tracy, John A. "A Dissent To The General Price-Level Adjustment Proposal," No. 1, pp. 163-175.

Hirschman, Robert W. "Direct Costing And The Law," No. 1, pp. 176-183.

Keller, Thomas F. "The Investment Tax Credit And The Annual Tax Charge," No. 1, pp. 184-189.

Stone, Williard E. "Accounting Doctoral Programs In AACSB Colleges Of Business Administration," No. 1, pp. 190-195.

Gibson, Robert W. "Comparative Professional Accountancy - Australia," No. 1, pp. 196-203.

Gray, Otha L. "Opinions Of Tax Professors On Tax Courses: A Survey Summary," No. 1, pp. 204-211.

Reininga, Warren. "An Approach To Elementary Accounting," No. 1, pp. 211-214.

Copeland, Ben R. "A Case Study In Gross Profit Analysis," No. 1, pp. 214-219.

Grawoig, Dennis E. "Decision Accounting," No. 1, pp. 220-222.

Thomas, Arthur L. "A Common Dollar Funds Statement," No. 1, pp. 223-230.

Van Horn, Lawrence. "An Experiment With The Case Method In Teaching Federal Income Taxes," No. 1, pp. 230-233.

Mautz, R. K. "Challenges To The Accounting Profession," No. 2, pp. 299-311.

Horngren, Charles T. "How Should We Interpret The Realization Concept?," No. 2, pp. 323-333.

Carson, A. B. "Cash Movement: The Heart Of Income Measurement," No. 2, pp. 334-337.

Bower, James B. and Robert E. Schlosser. "Internal Control - Its True Nature," No. 2, pp. 338-344.

Bruns, William J., Jr. "Inventory Valuation And Management Decisions," No. 2, pp. 345-357.

Rappaport, Alfred. "Lease Capitalization And The Transaction Concept," No. 2, pp. 373-376.

Phillips, Lawrence C. "Accounting For Business Combinations," No. 2, pp. 377-381.

Kollaritsch, Felix P. "International Accounting Practices," No. 2, pp. 382-385.

Mueller, Gerhard G. "Whys And Hows Of International Accounting," No. 2, pp. 386-394.

Kabbes, S. Madonna. "Is Accounting Meeting The Challenge In Europe?," No. 2, pp. 395-400.

Simon, Sidney I. "Fraud In The Balance Sheet," No. 2, pp. 401-406.

Sussman, M. Richard. "Present-Value Short Cuts," No. 2, pp. 407-413.

Corcoran, A. Wayne. "Simultaneous Preparation Of Funds And Cash Flow Statements," No. 2, pp. 440-448.

McLean, James H. "Planning In Corporate Liquidations," No. 2, pp. 448-450.

Pye, Malcolm L. "Footnote On Declining-Balance Depreciation," No. 2, pp. 451-452.

Parker, William M. "Upgrading The Elementary Accounting Course," No. 2, pp. 452-453.

Person, Samuel. "Elementary Accounting With A Systems Approach," No. 2, pp. 454-458.

Rushing, Reginald. "Adjusting Inventories For Consolidated Statements," No. 2, pp. 458-459.

Sommerfeld, Ray. "Teaching Taxes - An Assist," No. 2, p. 460.

Amsbaugh, J. K. "Accrual Calculations With Mutual Holdings," No. 2, pp. 461-462.

Defliese, Philip L. "A Practitioner's View Of The Realization Concept," No. 3, pp. 517-521.

Sprouse, Robert T. "Observations Concerning The Realization Concept," No. 3, pp. 522-526.

Wyatt, Arthur R. "Accounting For Business Combinations: What Next?," No. 3, pp. 527-535.

Eigen, Martin M. "Is Pooling Really Necessary?," No. 3, pp. 536-540.

Bierman, Harold, Jr. "Myths And Accountants," No. 3, pp. 541-546.

Benninger, L. J. "Accounting Theory And Cost Accounting," No. 3, pp. 547-557.

Horrigan, James O. "Some Empirical Bases Of Financial Ratio Analysis," No. 3, pp. 558-568.

Duvall, Richard M. and James Bulloch. "Adjusting Rate Of Return And Present Value For Price-Level Changes," No. 3, pp. 569-573.

Thompson, William W., Jr. and Earl L. Kemper. "Probability Measures For Estimated Data," No. 3, pp. 574-578.

Drinkwater, David and James Don Edwards. "The Nature Of Taxes And The Matching Principle," No. 3, pp. 579-582.

Mateer, William H. "Tax Allocation: A Macro Approach," No. 3, pp. 583-586.

Schulte, Arthur A., Jr. "Compatibility Of Management Consulting And Auditing," No. 3, pp. 587-593.

Campfield, William L. "Professional Status For Internal Auditors," No. 3, pp. 594-598.

Wagner, John W. "Defining Objectivity In Accounting," No. 3, pp. 599-605.

Cramer, Joe J., Jr. "Legal Influences On Pension Trust Accounting," No. 3, pp. 606-616.

Seaman, James L. "Lessons From The Investment Credit," No. 3, pp. 617-621.

Lee, Samuel S. O. "Korean Accounting Revaluation Laws," No. 3, pp. 622-625.

Kublin, Milton. "Acceptability Of A Professional School Of Accountancy," No. 3, pp. 626-635.

Jones, Gardner M. "Linear Algebra For The Neophyte," No. 3, pp. 636-640.

Manes, Rene P. "Comment On Matrix Theory And Cost Allocation," No. 3, pp. 640-643.

Rappaport, Alfred. "Siminar Research On Uniformity," No. 3, pp. 643-648.

Etnier, Don. "A More Interesting Auditing Course," No. 3, pp. 648-649.

Bruns, William J., Jr. "Business Games In Accounting Education," No. 3, pp. 650-653.

Doney, Lloyd D. and Richard C. Neumann. "Teaching Approaches To Elementary Accounting," No. 3, pp. 653-655.

Usry, Milton F. "Recommended Design For Cost Courses," No. 3, pp. 656-659.

Stettler, Howard F. "Accreditation Of Collegiate Accounting Programs," No. 4, pp. 723-730.

Chambers, R. J. "Edwards And Bell On Business Income," No. 4, pp. 731-741.

Kircher, Paul. "Coding Accounting Principles," No. 4, pp. 742-752.

Wilkinson, James R. and Lloyd D. Doney. "Extending Audit And Reporting Boundaries," No. 4, pp. 753-756.

Bradish, Richard D. "Corporate Reporting And The Financial Analyst," No. 4, pp. 757-766.

Churchill, Neil C. and William W. Cooper. "A Field Study Of Internal Auditing," No. 4, pp. 767-781.

Kemp, Patrick S. "The Authority Of The Accounting Principles Board," No. 4, pp. 782-787.

Cowan, Tom K. "Are Truth And Fairness Generally Acceptable?," No. 4, pp. 788-794.

Nielsen, Carl C. "Reporting Joint-Venture Corporations," No. 4, pp. 795-804.

Schattke, R. W. "Financial Reporting Of Antitrust Actions," No. 4, pp. 805-811.

Jerston, Jan E. "Analyst's View Of Deferred Income Taxes," No. 4, pp. 812-813.

Birnberg, Jacob G. "The Reporting Of Executory Contracts," No. 4, pp. 814-820.

Johnson, Glenn L. "The Monetary And Nonmonetary Distinction," No. 4, pp. 821-823.

Hylton, Delmer P. "On Matching Revenue With Expense," No. 4, pp. 824-828.

Wells, M. C. and W. D. J. Cotton. "Holding Gains On Fixed Assets," No. 4, pp. 829-833.

Bogart, Fred O. "Tax Considerations In Partnership Agreements," No. 4, pp. 834-838.

Lowe, Ross E. "Public Accounting Internships," No. 4, pp. 839-846.

Singer, Frank A. "Progress In Programmed Instruction," No. 4, pp. 847-853.

Frank, Werner. "A Computer Application In Process Cost Accounting," No. 4, pp. 854-862.

Jones, H. Milton and Vernon E. Pontius. "Survey Of Accounting Teaching Via Television," No. 4, pp. 863-867.

Goggans, Travis P. "Break-Even Analysis With Curvilinear Functions," No. 4, pp. 867-871.

Nielsen, Gordon L. "The Computer In Accounting Education," No. 4, pp. 871-876.

Sidebotham, Roy. "Comments On The Teacher Development Report," No. 4, pp. 876-879.

Heck, William R. "A Forward Approach To Dollar-Value Lifo," No. 4, pp. 879-880.

Snudden, Leslie W. "A Different Approach To Fund-Flow Problems," No. 4, pp. 880-882.

Accounting Review
Volume 41, 1966

Miller, Herbert E. "Textbooks Or Research," No. 1, pp. 1-7.

Yu, S. C. "Microaccounting And Macroaccounting," No. 1, pp. 8-20.

Deinzer, Harvey T. "Explanation Strains In Financial Accounting," No. 1, pp. 21-31.

Lemke, Kenneth W. "Asset Valuation And Income Theory," No. 1, pp. 32-41.

Nelson, G. Kenneth. "Current And Historical Costs In Financial Statements," No. 1, pp. 42-47.

Vance, L. L. "What The Editor Of An Academic Journal Expects From Authors," No. 1, pp. 48-51.

Green, David, Jr. "Evaluating The Accounting Literature," No. 1, pp. 52-64.

Lauver, R. C. "The Case For Poolings," No. 1, pp. 65-74.

Buckley, John W. "Medicare And Accounting," No. 1, pp. 75-82.

Topiol, Jack. "Accounting For Public Health Nursing Associations," No. 1, pp. 83-91.

Boer, Germain. "Replacement Cost: A Historical Look," No. 1, pp. 92-97.

Baker, Roy E. "Income Of Life Insurance Companies," No. 1, pp. 98-105.

Ferrara, William L. "Should Investment And Financing Decisions Be Separated?," No. 1, pp. 106-114.

Carlisle, Howard M. "Cost Accounting For Advanced Technology Programs," No. 1, pp. 115-120.

Davis, P. Michael. "Marginal Analysis Of Credit Sales," No. 1, pp. 121-126.

Hartman, Maurice A. "A Simplified Solution To Cost Or Market Problems," No. 1, pp. 127-129.

Faux, M. Charles. "A New Matrix Approach To Accounting Training," No. 1, pp. 129-132.

Singer, Frank A. "A Note On 'Teaching Approaches To Elementary Accounting'," No. 1, pp. 133-134.

Ray, J. C. "Graphic Presentation Of Audit Reports," No. 1, pp. 134-138.

Van Ness, Paul H. "To Reverse Or Not To Reverse?," No. 1, pp. 138-141.

Givens, Horace R. "An Application Of Curvilinear Break-Even Analysis," No. 1, pp. 141-143.

Jennings, Robert M. "Graphical Analysis Of Overhead," No. 1, pp. 144-145.

Baladouni, Vahe. "The Accounting Perspective Re-Examined," No. 2, pp. 215-225.

Williams, Doyle Z. "Reporting Loss Carryovers In Financial Statements," No. 2, pp. 226-234.

Comiskey, Eugene E. "Cost Control By Regression Analysis," No. 2, pp. 235-238.

Hanson, Ernest I. "The Budgetary Control Function," No. 2, pp. 239-243.

Furlong, William L. "Minimizing Foreign Exchange Losses," No. 2, pp. 244-252.

Welke, William R. "Accounting Systems In The Curriculum," No. 2, pp. 253-256.

Bower, Richard S., Frank C. Herringer and J. Peter Williamson. "Lease Evaluation," No. 2, pp. 257-265.

Fess, Philip E. "The Working Capital Concept," No. 2, pp.

266-270.

Bierman, Harold, Jr. "A Further Study Of Depreciation," No. 2, pp. 271-274.

Peterson, William A. "Significance Of Prospective Income Data," No. 2, pp. 275-282.

Mautz, R. K. and Donald L. Mini. "Internal Control Evaluation And Audit Program Modification," No. 2, pp. 283-291.

Mobley, Sybil C. "The Realization Concept: A Useful Device," No. 2, pp. 292-296.

DeCoster, Don T. "Measurement Of The Idle-Capacity Variance," No. 2, pp. 297-302.

Allyn, Robert G. "Accreditation Of Accounting Curriculums," No. 2, pp. 303-311.

Stevenson, Richard A. "Corporate Stock Reacquisitons," No. 2, pp. 312-317.

Imke, Frank J. "Relationships In Accounting Theory," No. 2, pp. 318-322.

Heins, Everett B. "A Survey Of Accounting In Junior Colleges," No. 2, pp. 323-326.

Rosenfield, Paul H. and Reed K. Storey. "The Accounting Principles Board - A Correction," No. 2, pp. 327-330.

Anderson, Wilton T. "Recruiting Capable Students To Accounting," No. 2, pp. 331-333.

Jennings, Robert M. "Installment Interest Computations - True And Quoted," No. 2, pp. 333-335.

Lindbeck, Rudolph S. "Conventional Retail - Lower Than Cost Or Market," No. 2, pp. 335-338.

Barker, Raymond F. and Bernard J. Landwehr. "Quantitative Techniques And The Faculty," No. 2, pp. 338-340.

Brown, Robert O. "Predictions Of Accounting Grades," No. 2, pp. 340-343.

Staubus, George J. "Alternative Asset Flow Concepts," No. 3, pp. 397-412.

Drebin, Allan R. "Accounting For Proprietary Research," No. 3, pp. 413-425.

Eaves, B. Curtis. "Operational Axiomatic Accounting Mechanics," No. 3, pp. 426-442.

Chambers, R. J. "A Matter Of Principle," No. 3, pp. 443-457.

Givens, Horace R. "Basic Accounting Postulates," No. 3, pp. 458-463.

Ross, W. R. "Pert/Cost Resource Allocation Procedure," No. 3, pp. 464-473.

Ijiri, Yuji and Robert K. Jaedicke. "Reliability And Objectivity Of Accounting Measurements," No. 3, pp. 474-483.

Briloff, Abraham J. "Old Myths And New Realities In Accountancy," No. 3, pp. 484-495.

Caplan, Edwin H. "Behavioral Assumptions Of Management Accounting," No. 3, pp. 496-509.

Johnson, Glenn L. "Funds-Flow Equations," No. 3, pp. 510-517.

Weiser, Herbert J. "Accounting Education - Present And Future," No. 3, pp. 518-524.

Powell, Ray M. "Career Choices Among Beta Alpha Psi Members," No. 3, pp. 525-534.

Jentz, Gaylord A. "The Case Against The Present CPA Commercial Law Examination," No. 3, pp. 535-541.

Williams, Doyle Z. "A Seminar On The Teaching Of Accounting," No. 3, pp. 541-549.

Penick, Jack G. "ADP Equipment As An Accounting Teaching Tool," No. 3, pp. 549-551.

Malcolm, Robert E. "Decision Tables In Accounting," No. 3, pp. 551-555.

Pattillo, James W. "Rating Student Performance," No. 3, pp. 555-559.

Wright, Howard W. "A Case Of Valuation," No. 3, pp. 559-560.

Prater, George I. "Time-Sharing Computers In Accounting Education," No. 4, pp. 619-625.

Wright, Howard W. "Allocation Of General And Administrative Expenses," No. 4, pp. 626-633.

Larson, Kermit and R. W. Schattke. "Current Cash Equivalent, Additivity, And Financial Action," No. 4, pp. 634-641.

Lim, Ronald S. "The Mathematical Propriety Of Accounting Measurements And Calculations," No. 4, pp. 642-651.

Seiler, Robert E. "Accounting, Information Systems, And Underdeveloped Nations," No. 4, pp. 652-656.

Benston, George J. "Multiple Regression Analysis Of Cost Behavior," No. 4, pp. 657-672.

Chiu, John S. and Don T. DeCoster. "Multiple Product Costing By Multiple Correlation Analysis," No. 4, pp. 673-680.

Vatter, William J. "Income Models, Book Yield, And Rate Of Return," No. 4, pp. 681-698.

Hain, H. P. "Accounting Control In The Zenon Papyri," No. 4, pp. 699-703.

Morrison, Thomas A. "Taxation Of International Investments," No. 4, pp. 704-713.

Raby, William L. "Ethics In Tax Practice," No. 4, pp. 714-720.

Schulte, Arthur A., Jr. "Management Services: A Challenge To Audit Independence?," No. 4, pp. 721-728.

Peirson, Graham. "Three Kinds Of Adjustments For Price Changes," No. 4, pp. 729-736.

Winborne, Marilynn G. and Dee L. Kleespie. "Tax Allocation In Perspective," No. 4, pp. 737-744.

Gross, Harry. "Make Or Buy Decisions In Growing Firms," No. 4, pp. 745-753.

Usry, Milton F. "Cost Accounting On The CPA Examination," No. 4, pp. 754-762.

Hobbs, James B. "Double-Entry And Working Capital Analysis," No. 4, pp. 763-767.

Patten, Ronald J. and Lawrence L. Steinmetz. "What Do Students Think Of Your Elementary Course?," No. 4, pp. 767-772.

Haglund, Byron E. "Inventory: Lower Of Cost Or Market," No. 4, p. 772.

Kistler, Linda H. "Tax Planning In The Elementary Course," No. 4, pp. 773-775.

Accounting Review
Volume 42, 1967

Townsend, Lynn A. "A Career In Business Accounting," No. 1, pp. 1-6.

Paton, W. A. "Some Reflections On Education And Professoring," No. 1, pp. 7-23.

Charnes, A. and W. W. Cooper. "Some Network Characterizations For Mathematical Programming And Accounting Approaches To Planning And Control," No. 1, pp. 24-52.

Goetz, Billy E. "Professorial Obsolescence," No. 1, pp. 53-61.

Sterling, Robert R. "Elements Of Pure Accounting Theory," No. 1, pp. 62-73.

Mills, Robert H. "Investment Loss Reserves For Corporate Bond Investors," No. 1, pp. 74-81.

Bedford, Norton M. "The Nature Of Future Accounting Theory," No. 1, pp. 82-85.

Bernstein, Leopold A. "The Concept Of Materiality," No. 1, pp. 86-95.

Lewis, Charles D. "Tax Deductibility Of Educators' Travel Expenses," No. 1, pp. 96-105.

Rosen, L. S. "Replacement-Value Accounting," No. 1, pp. 106-113.

Mobley, Sybil C. "Revenue Experience As A Guide To Asset Valuation," No. 1, pp. 114-123.

Firmin, Peter A. and James J. Linn. "Accounting Systems Course - A New Concept," No. 1, pp. 124-127.

Welke, William R. "The Accounting Systems Course," No. 1, pp. 127-132.

Gamoneda, R. G. "Time To Double At Compound Interest," No. 1, pp. 132-134.

Ruswinckel, John W. "CCTV Instruction: 1967," No. 1, pp. 134-141.

Hartman, Robert F., Jr. "A New Course: Accounting Services To Management," No. 1, pp. 141-143.

Boer, Germain. "Cash-Flow Statements - Fast," No. 1, pp. 142-146.

Snavely, Howard J. "Accounting Information Criteria," No. 2, pp. 223-232.

Livingstone, John Leslie. "Electric Utility Plant Replacement Costs," No. 2, pp. 233-240.

Chambers, R. J. "Prospective Adventures In Accounting Ideas," No. 2, pp. 241-253.

Horngren, Charles T. "A Contribution Margin Approach to The Analysis Of Capacity Utilization," No. 2, pp. 254-264.

Jensen, Robert E. "A Multiple Regression Model For Cost Control - Assumptions And Limitations," No. 2, pp. 265-273.

Gynther, Reginald S. "Accounting Concepts And Behavioral Hypotheses," No. 2, pp. 274-290.

Arnett, Harold E. "The Concept Of Fairness," No. 2, pp. 291-297.

Zeff, Stephen A. and Robert L. Fossum. "An Analysis Of Large Audit Clients," No. 2, pp. 298-320.

Onsi, Mohamed. "Quantitative Models For Accounting Control," No. 2, pp. 321-330.

Stone, Donald E. "The Objective Of Financial Reporting In The Annual Report," No. 2, pp. 331-337.

Young, T. N. and C. G. Pierson. "Depreciation - Future Service Basis," No. 2, pp. 338-341.

Schneider, Albert J. "Flow-Graph Notation In Accounting," No. 2, pp. 342-348.

Roller, Julius and Thomas H. Williams. "Professional Schools Of Accounting," No. 2, pp. 349-355.

Lowe, Howard D. "Accounting Aid For Developing Countries," No. 2, pp. 356-360.

Bailey, F. A. "A Note On Pert/Cost Resource Allocation," No. 2, p. 361.

Jentz, Gaylord A. "Ten-Year Review Of The CPA Law Examination," No. 2, pp. 362-365.

Neeley, Paden and C. A. Robason. "Governmental Accounting: A Critical Evaluation," No. 2, pp. 366-369.

Mosich, A. N. "Ingenuity In Auditing," No. 2, pp. 369-371.

Mastro, Anthony J. "EDP In One Elementary Course," No. 2, pp. 371-374.

Keister, Orville R. "Consolidations And Intercompany Bond Holdings," No. 2, pp. 375-376.

Sterling, Robert R. "A Case Of Valuation And Learned Cognitive Dissonance," No. 2, pp. 376-378.

Goetz, Billy E. "Transfer Prices: An Exercise In Relevancy And Goal Congruence," No. 3, pp. 435-440.

Rappaport, Alfred. "Sensitivity Analysis In Decision Making," No. 3, pp. 441-456.

Fremgen, James M. "Utility And Accounting Principles," No. 3, pp. 457-467.

Birnberg, Jacob G. and Raghu Nath. "Implications Of Behavioral Science For Managerial Accounting," No. 3, pp. 468-479.

Larson, Kermit D. "Descriptive Validity Of Accounting Calculations," No. 3, pp. 480-488.

Briloff, Abraham J. "Dirty Pooling," No. 3, pp. 489-496.

Hasseldine, C. R. "Mix And Yield Variances," No. 3, pp. 497-515.

Frank, Werner and Rene Manes. "A Standard Cost Application Of Matrix Algebra," No. 3, pp. 516-525.

Dopuch, Nicholas, Jacob G. Birnberg and Joel Demski. "An

Extension Of Standard Cost Variance Analysis," No. 3, pp. 526-536.

Kircher, Paul. "Classification And Coding Of Accounting Information," No. 3, pp. 537-543.

Livingstone, John Leslie. "A Behavioral Study Of Tax Allocation In Electric Utility Regulation," No. 3, pp. 544-552.

Sorensen, James E. "Professional And Bureaucratic Organization In The Public Accounting Firm," No. 3, pp. 553-565.

Zannetos, Zenon S. "Programmed Instruction And Computer Technology," No. 3, pp. 566-571.

Buckley, John W. "Programmed Instruction: With Emphasis On Accounting," No. 3, pp. 572-582.

Anderson, John J. "Integrated Instruction In Computers And Accounting," No. 3, pp. 583-588.

Goetz, Billy E. "Debit, Credit, And Input-Output Tables," No. 3, pp. 589-591.

McCormick, Frank L. "Large Group Instruction In Elementary Accounting," No. 3, p. 592.

Horngren, Charles T. "Process Costing In Perspective: Forget Fifo," No. 3, pp. 593-596.

Carlson, Marvin L. "An Application Of Concepts In The Theory Course," No. 3, pp. 596-598.

Jennings, Robert M. and R. Bruce McCosh. "Construction In Process - A Different Approach," No. 3, pp. 598-600.

Luh, F. S. "Graphical Approach To Process Costing," No. 3, pp. 600-604.

Corbin, Donald A. "On The Feasibility Of Developing Current Cost Information," No. 4, pp. 635-641.

Williams, Thomas H. and Charles H. Griffin. "Income Definition And Measurement: A Structural Approach," No. 4, pp. 642-649.

Staubus, George J. "Current Cash Equivalent For Assets: A Dissent," No. 4, pp. 650-661.

McDonald, Daniel L. "Feasibility Criteria For Accounting Measures," No. 4, pp. 662-679.

Simmons, John K. "A Concept Of Comparability In Financial Reporting," No. 4, pp. 680-692.

McCosh, Andrew M. "Accounting Consistency - Key To Stockholder Information," No. 4, pp. 693-700.

Demski, Joel S. "Accounting System Structured On A Linear Programming Model," No. 4, pp. 701-712.

Kaufman, Felix. "Professional Consulting By CPAs," No. 4, pp. 713-720.

Vatter, William J. "The Use Of Operations Research In American Companies," No. 4, pp. 721-730.

Bierman, Harold, Jr. "Inventory Valuation: The Use Of Market Prices," No. 4, pp. 731-737.

Johnson, Glenn L. and Sherwood W. Newton. "Tax Considerations In Equipment Replacement Decisions," No. 4, pp. 738-746.

Sommerfeld, Ray M. "Tax Implications For The Visiting Professor," No. 4, pp. 747-750.

Chambers, R. J. "Continuously Contemporary Accounting - Additivity And Action," No. 4, pp. 751-757.

Kistler, Linda H. "Stock Option Disclosures Are Inadequate," No. 4, pp. 758-766.

Luneski, Chris. "Continuous Versus Discrete Compounding For Capital Budgeting Decisions," No. 4, pp. 767-771.

Patterson, Robert G. "Materiality And The Economic Environment," No. 4, pp. 772-774.

Seidler, Lee J. "International Accounting - The Ultimate Theory Course," No. 4, pp. 775-781.

Bowen, Earl K. "Mathematics In The Undergraduate Business Curriculum," No. 4, pp. 782-787.

Hawkins, David and Brandt Allen. "Computer Assisted Case Analyses," No. 4, pp. 788-800.

Dilley, Merrill B. "Textbooks Used In Accounting Courses," No. 4, pp. 800-802.

Accounting Review
Volume 43, 1968

Carey, John L. "What Is The Professional Practice Of Accounting?," No. 1, pp. 1-9.

Philips, G. Edward. "Pension Liabilities And Assets," No. 1, pp. 10-17.

Byrne, R. F., A. Charnes, W. W. Cooper and K. Kortanek. "Some New Approaches To Risk," No. 1, pp. 18-37.

Birnberg, Jacob G. and Raghu Nath. "Laboratory Experimentation In Accounting Research," No. 1, pp. 38-45.

Brigham, Eugene F. "The Effects Of Alternative Depreciation Policies On Reported Profits," No. 1, pp. 46-61.

Bierman, Harold, Jr. and Ernest Liu. "The Computation Of Earnings Per Share," No. 1, pp. 62-67.

Taussig, Russell A. and Samuel L. Hayes, III. "Cash Take-Overs And Accounting Valuations," No. 1, pp. 68-74.

Firmin, Peter A. and James J. Linn. "Information Systems And Managerial Accounting," No. 1, pp. 75-82.

Jensen, Robert E. and C. Torben Thomsen. "Statistical Analysis In Cost Measurement And Control," No. 1, pp. 83-93.

Cowan, T. K. "A Pragmatic Approach To Accounting Theory," No. 1, pp. 94-100.

Shwayder, Keith. "A Note On A Contribution Margin Approach To The Analysis Of Capacity Utilization," No. 1, pp. 101-104.

Barrett, William B. "A Functional Approach To Accounting," No. 1, pp. 105-112.

Beaver, William H. "Alternative Accounting Measures As Predictors Of Failure," No. 1, pp. 113-122.

Luh, F. S. "Controlled Cost: An Operational Concept And Statistical Approach To Standard Costing," No. 1, pp. 123-132.

Gossett, Thomas E. and Milton F. Usry. "Process Cost Accounting And Diagrammatical Outlines," No. 1, pp. 133-136.

Burns, Thomas J. "Accounting Courses At Nineteen American Universities," No. 1, pp. 137-147.

Vanasse, Robert W. "Consolidated Position Statements: A Tabular Approach," No. 1, pp. 147-150.

Zeff, Stephen A. "Accounting Journals In Business School Libraries: A Survey," No. 1, pp. 150-153.

Wade, Harry H. "Rationalization Of Schedule G - Income Averaging," No. 1, pp. 154-156.

Brummet, R. Lee, Eric G. Flamholtz and William C. Pyle. "Human Resource Measurement - A Challenge For Accountants," No. 2, pp. 217-224.

LaValle, Irving H. and Alfred Rappaport. "On The Economics Of Acquiring Information Of Imperfect Reliability," No. 2, pp. 225-230.

Iselin, Errol R. "Chambers On Accounting Theory," No. 2, pp. 231-238.

Chambers, Raymond J. "Measures And Values," No. 2, pp. 239-247.

Comiskey, Eugene E. and F. A. Mlynarczyk. "Recognition Of Income By Finance Companies," No. 2, pp. 248-256.

Summers, Edward L. "Observation Of Effects Of Using Alternative Reporting Practices," No. 2, pp. 257-265.

Kell, Walter G. "Public Accounting's Irresistible Force And Immovable Object," No. 2, pp. 266-273.

Buckley, John W., Paul Kircher and Russell L. Mathews. "Methodology In Accounting Theory," No. 2, pp. 274-283.

Horrigan, James O. "A Short History Of Financial Ratio Analysis," No. 2, pp. 284-294.

Hannum, William H. and William Wasserman. "General Adjustments And Price Level Measurement," No. 2, pp. 295-302.

Schachner, Leopold. "Accountability Under Industrial Diversification," No. 2, pp. 303-311.

Farag, Shawki M. "A Planning Model For The Divisionalized Enterprise," No. 2, pp. 312-320.

Hartley, Ronald V. "Operations Research And Its Implications For The Accounting Profession," No. 2, pp. 321-332.

Mobley, Sybil C. "Measures Of Income," No. 2, pp. 333-341.

Caplan, Edwin H. "Behavioral Assumptions Of Management Accounting - Report Of A Field Study," No. 2, pp. 342-362.

Hendrickson, Harvey S. "Some Comments On 'Dirty Pooling'," No. 2, pp. 363-366.

Brief, Richard P. and Joel Owen. "Depreciation And Capital Gains: A 'New' Approach," No. 2, pp. 367-372.

Wells, M. C. "A Note On The Amortization Of Fixed Assets," No. 2, pp. 373-376.

Braunstein, Daniel N. and Richard W. Fortner. "The Design Of Behavioral Research," No. 2, pp. 377-383.

Tambrino, Paul A. "College Placement Accounting In High Schools," No. 2, pp. 383-384.

Copeland, Ronald M. and Michael L. Moore. "Actual Use Of Specialized Accounting Statements," No. 2, pp. 384-386.

Gambling, Trevor E. "LIFO Vs. FIFO Under Conditions Of 'Certainty'," No. 2, pp. 387-389.

Staubus, George J. "Testing Inventory Accounting," No. 3, pp. 413-424.

Jensen, Robert E. "Sensitivity Analysis And Integer Linear Programming," No. 3, pp. 425-446.

Solomons, David. "Breakeven Analysis Under Absorption Costing," No. 3, pp. 447-452.

Bedford, Norton M. and Toshio Iino. "Consistency Reexamined," No. 3, pp. 453-458.

Trumbull, Wendell P. "Differences Between Financial And Tax Depreciation," No. 3, pp. 459-468.

Bruns, William J., Jr. "Accounting Information And Decision-Making: Some Behavioral Hypotheses," No. 3, pp. 469-480.

Sterling, Robert R. "The Going Concern: An Examination," No. 3, pp. 481-502.

Livingstone, John Leslie. "Matrix Algebra And Cost Allocation," No. 3, pp. 503-508.

Mathews, R. L. "Income, Price Changes And The Valuation Controversy In Accounting," No. 3, pp. 509-516.

Morrison, Thomas A. and Stephen L. Buzby. "Effect Of The Investment Tax Credit On The Capitalize-Expense Decision," No. 3, pp. 517-521.

Khemakhem, Abdellatif. "A Simulation Of Management-Decision Behavior: 'Funds' And Income," No. 3, pp. 522-534.

Waugh, James B. "The Interperiod Allocation Of Corporate Income Taxes: A Proposal," No. 3, pp. 535-539.

Copeland, Ronald M. and Ralph D. Licastro. "A Note On Income Smoothing," No. 3, pp. 540-545.

Johnson, Orace. "Some Reservations On The Significance Of Prospective Income Data," No. 3, pp. 546-548.

O'Donnell, John L. "Further Observations On Reported Earnings And Stock Prices," No. 3, pp. 549-553.

Crumbley, D. Larry. "Narrowing The Taxable And Accounting Income Gap For Consolidations," No. 3, pp. 554-564.

Bower, Richard S., Christopher E. Nugent and Donald E. Stone. "Time-Shared Computers In Business Education At Dartmouth," No. 3, pp. 565-582.

Baladouni, Vahe. "Instructional Objectives In Accounting," No. 3, pp. 582-585.

Haseman, Wilber G. "Accountants In Residency Program," No. 3, pp. 585-588.

Thomas, Arthur L. "Estimating The Effective Interest Rate," No. 3, pp. 589-591.

Chatfield, Michael. "A Writing Program In Intermediate Accounting," No. 3, pp. 592-594.

Nichols, Arthur C. and Dennis E. Grawoig. "Accounting Reports With Time As A Variable," No. 4, pp. 631-639.

Cooper, W. W., N. Dopuch and T. F. Keller. "Budgetary Disclosure And Other Suggestions For Improving Accounting," No. 4, pp. 640-648.

Fremgen, James M. "The Going Concern Assumption: A Critical Appraisal," No. 4, pp. 649-656.

Bierman, Harold, Jr. "The Term Structure Of Interest Rates And Accounting For Debt," No. 4, pp. 657-661.

Ijiri, Yuji. "On Budgeting Principles And Budget-Auditing Standards," No. 4, pp. 662-67.

Cushing, Barry E. "Some Observations On Demski's Ex Post Accounting System," No. 4, pp. 668-671.

Demski, Joel S. "Some Observations On Demski's Ex Post Accounting System: A Reply," No. 4, pp. 672-674.

Beaver, William H., John W. Kennelly and William M. Voss. "Predictive Ability As A Criterion For The Evaluation Of Accounting Data," No. 4, pp. 675-683.

Feltham, Gerald A. "The Value Of Information," No. 4, pp. 684-696.

Carmichael, D. R. and R. J. Swieringa. "The Compatibility Of Auditing Independence And Management Services - An Identification Of Issues," No. 4, pp. 697-705.

Gynther, Merle M. "Future Growth Aspects Of The Cash Flow Computation," No. 4, pp. 706-718.

Nurnberg, Hugo. "Present Value Depreciation And Income Tax Allocation," No. 4, pp. 719-729.

Richard, Donald L. "Difficulties In Tax Allocation On General Price-Level Increases," No. 4, pp. 730-737.

Haseman, Wilber C. "An Interpretive Framework For Cost," No. 4, pp. 738-752.

Chumachenko, Nikolai G. "Once Again: The Volume-Mix-Price/Cost Budget Variance Analysis," No. 4, pp. 753-762.

Elliott, Edward L., Jose Larrea and Juan M. Rivera. "Accounting Aid To Developing Countries," No. 4, pp. 763-768.

Clarke, Robert W. "Extension Of The CPA's Attest Function In Corporate Annual Reports," No. 4, pp. 769-776.

Nicol, Robert E. G. "The Accounting Equation Revisited: A Conceptual Accounting Model," No. 4, pp. 777-779.

Windal, Floyd W. "Slaying The Quantitative Goliath," No. 4, pp. 779-781.

Garrison, Ray H. "Methodology Of Lease Capitalization," No. 4, pp. 782-784.

Manes, Rene P. "In A Seminar On Budget Mix Variances," No. 4, pp. 784-787.

Bergolofsky, Henry. "A Proposed Revision Of The Accounting Curriculum," No. 4, pp. 787-788.

Accounting Review
Volume 44, 1969

Raby, William L. "Tax Allocation And Non-Historical Financial Statements," No. 1, pp. 1-11.

Sorter, George H. "An 'Events' Approach To Basic Accounting Theory," No. 1, pp. 12-19.

Brief, Richard P. "An Econometric Analysis Of Goodwill: Some Findings In A Search For Valuation Rules," No. 1, pp. 20-26.

Theil, Henri. "How To Worry About Increased Expenditures," No. 1, pp. 27-31.

Larson, Kermit D. "Implications Of Measurement Theory On Accounting Concept Formulation," No. 1, pp. 38-47.

Livingstone, John Leslie. "Input-Output Analysis For Cost Accounting, Planning And Control," No. 1, pp. 48-64.

Bierman, Harold, Jr. "Accelerated Depreciation And Rate Regulation," No. 1, pp. 65-78.

Carey, John L. "Teachers And Practitioners," No. 1, pp. 79-85.

Horngren, Charles T. "Capacity Utilization And The Efficiency Variance," No. 1, pp. 86-89.

Tracy, John A. "Bayesian Statistical Methods In Auditing," No. 1, pp. 90-98.

Tritschler, Charles A. "Statistical Criteria For Asset Valuation By Specific Price Index," No. 1, pp. 99-123.

Rosen, L. S. and Don T. DeCoster. "'Funds' Statements: A Historical Perspective," No. 1, pp. 124-136.

Brighton, Gerald D. "Accrued Expense Tax Reform - Not Ready In 1954 - Ready In 1969?," No. 1, pp. 137-144.

Most, Kenneth S. "Two Forms Of Experimental Accounts," No. 1, pp. 145-152.

Williams, Doyle Z. "A Profile Of CPA Candidates," No. 1, pp. 153-164.

Copeland, Ronald M. "Textbook Knowledge: Fact Or Fiction," No. 1, pp. 164-167.

Kistler, Linda H. and Robert M. Jennings. "An Accounting Primer Circa 1831," No. 1, pp. 168-173.

Wojdak, Joseph F. and D. Larry Crumbley. "Introducing Important Tax Provisions Into Advanced Accounting," No. 1, pp. 173-175.

Bierman, Harold, Jr. and Sidney Davidson. "The Income Concept - Value Increment Or Earnings Predictor," No. 2, pp. 239-246.

Gynther, Reg S. "Some 'Conceptualizing' On Goodwill," No. 2, pp. 247-255.

Lee, Lucy C. and Norton M. Bedford. "An Information Theory Analysis Of The Accounting Process," No. 2, pp. 256-275.

Paton, W. A. "Postscript On 'Treasury' Shares," No. 2, pp. 276-283.

Stone, Williard E. "Antecedents Of The Accounting Profession," No. 2, pp. 284-291.

Schwab, Bernhard and Robert E. G. Nicol. "From Double-Declining-Balance To Sum-Of-The-Years'-Digits Depreciation: An Optimum Switching Rule," No. 2, pp. 292-296.

Rappaport, Alfred. "Integer Programming And Managerial Analysis," No. 2, pp. 297-299.

Glover, Fred. "Management Decision And Integer Programming," No. 2, pp. 300-303.

Shwayder, Keith. "The Capital Maintenance Rule And The Net Asset Valuation Rule," No. 2, pp. 304-316.

Goldschmidt, Y. and S. Smidt. "Valuing The Firm's Durable Assets For Managerial Information," No. 2, pp. 317-329.

Morrison, Thomas A. and Eugene Kaczka. "A New Application Of Calculus And Risk Analysis To Cost-Volume-Profit Changes," No. 2, pp. 330-343.

Snavely, Howard J. "Current Cost For Long-Lived Assets: A Critical View," No. 2, pp. 344-353.

Revsine, Lawrence. "Some Controversy Concerning 'Controversial Accounting Changes'," No. 2, pp. 354-358.

Corcoran, A. Wayne. "Computers Versus Mathematics," No. 2, pp. 359-374.

Beechy, Thomas H. "Quasi-Debt Analysis Of Financial Leases," No. 2, pp. 375-381.

Beams, Floyd A. "Indications Of Pragmatism And Empiricism In Accounting Thought," No. 2, pp. 382-388.

Buckley, John W. "Programmed And Non-Programmed Instruction: Integration Criteria In Curriculum Design," No. 2, pp. 389-397.

Goetz, Billy E. "The Effect Of A Cost-Plus Contract On Transfer Prices," No. 2, pp. 398-400.

Doney, Lloyd D. "Integrating Accounting And Computerized Data Processing," No. 2, pp. 400-409.

Guerin, Francis J. "An Undergraduate Seminar In Accounting," No. 2, pp. 409-411.

Mautz, R. K. and K. Fred Skousen. "Some Problems In Empirical Research In Accounting," No. 3, pp. 447-456.

Crandall, Robert H. "Information Economics And Its Implications For The Further Development Of Accounting Theory," No. 3, pp. 457-466.

Colantoni, Claude S., Rene P. Manes and Andrew Whinston. "Programming, Profit Rates And Pricing Decisions," No. 3, pp. 467-481.

Arnett, Harold E. "Taxable Income Vs. Financial Income: How Much Uniformity Can We Stand?," No. 3, pp. 482-494.

Hakansson, Nils H. "An Induced Theory Of Accounting Under Risk," No. 3, pp. 495-514.

Benston, George J. "The Value Of The SEC's Accounting Disclosure Requirements," No. 3, pp. 515-532.

Backer, Morton. "Comments On 'The Value Of The SEC's Accounting Disclosure Requirements'," No. 3, pp. 533-538.

Brundage, Marjorie U. and John Leslie Livingstone. "Simulation On A Time-Sharing Computer Utility System," No. 3, pp. 539-545.

Neumann, Frederick L. "The Incidence And Nature Of Consistency Exceptions," No. 3, pp. 546-554.

Sorensen, James E. "Bayesian Analysis In Auditing," No. 3, pp. 555-561.

Wojdak, Joseph F. "A Theoretical Foundation For Leases And Other Executory Contracts," No. 3, pp. 562-570.

Yu, S. C. "A Flow-Of-Resources Statement For Business Enterprises," No. 3, pp. 571-582.

May, Phillip T. "System Control: Computers The Weak Link?," No. 3, pp. 583-592.

Field, John E. "Toward A Multi-Level, Multi-Goal Information System," No. 3, pp. 593-599.

Wagner, John W. "EDP And The Auditor Of The 1970's," No. 3, pp. 600-604.

Helmkamp, John G. "Technical Information Center Management: An Accounting Deficiency," No. 3, pp. 605-610.

Carmichael, D. R. and John J. Willingham. "New Directions In Auditing Education: A Proposal For The Undergraduate Course," No. 3, pp. 611-615.

Higgins, J. Warren. "The Tax Game," No. 3, pp. 615-618.

Currie, Edward M. and John L. Witwer. "Gaining A Foothold In Systems Education," No. 3, pp. 618-623.

Pescow, Jerome K. and Paul A. Tambrino. "Workshop In College Placement Accounting," No. 3, pp. 623-627.

Demski, Joel S. "Decision-Performance Control," No. 4, pp. 669-679.

Fertakis, John P. "On Communication, Understanding, And Relevance In Accounting Reporting," No. 4, pp. 680-691.

Vance, Lawrence L. "The Road To Reform Of Accounting Principles," No. 4, pp. 692-703.

Lev, Baruch. "An Information Theory Analysis Of Budget Variances," No. 4, pp. 704-710.

Call, Dwight V. "Some Salient Factors Often Overlooked In Stock Options," No. 4, pp. 711-719.

Larson, Kermit D. and Nicholas J. Gonedes. "Business Combinations: An Exchange Ratio Determination Model," No. 4, pp. 720-728.

Dockweiler, Raymond C. "The Practicability Of Developing Multiple Financial Statements: A Case Study," No. 4, pp. 729-742.

Ijiri, Yuji and Robert S. Kaplan. "Probabilistic Depreciation And Its Implication For Group Depreciation," No. 4, pp. 743-756.

Simmons, John K. and Jack Gray. "An Investigation Of The Effect Of Differing Accounting Frameworks On The Prediction Of Net Income," No. 4, pp. 757-776.

Langenderfer, Harold Q. and Jack C. Robertson. "A Theoretical Structure For Independent Audits Of Management," No. 4, pp. 777-787.

Rosenfield, Paul. "Reporting Subjunctive Gains And Losses," No. 4, pp. 788-797.

Imdieke, Leroy F. and Jerry J. Weygandt. "Classification Of Convertible Debt," No. 4, pp. 798-805.

Simpson, Richard H. "An Empirical Study Of Possible Income Manipulation," No. 4, pp. 806-817.

Ford, Allen. "Should Cost Be Assigned To Conversion Value?," No. 4, pp. 818-822.

Goetz, Billy E. "A First-Year Accounting Course," No. 4, pp. 823-832.
Beams, Floyd A. "EDP And The Elementary Accounting Course," No. 4, pp. 832-836.
Mecimore, Charles D. "Integrating EDP Into The Elementary Accounting Course - One Approach," No. 4, pp. 837-839.
Hirsch, A. Jay. "Dollar-Value And Retail LIFO: A Diagrammatic Approach," No. 4, pp. 840-842.

Accounting Review
Volume 45, 1970

Wheeler, John T. "Accounting Theory And Research In Perspective," No. 1, pp. 1-10.
Feltham, Gerald A. "Some Quantitative Approaches To Planning For Multiproduct Production Systems," No. 1, pp. 11-26.
Cowie, James B. and James M. Fremgen. "Computers Versus Mathematics: Round 2," No. 1, pp. 27-37.
Hofstedt, Thomas R. and James C. Kinard. "A Strategy For Behavioral Accounting Research," No. 1, pp. 38-54.
Knutson, Peter H. "Income Distribution: The Key to Earnings Per Share," No. 1, pp. 55-68.
Weygandt, Jerry J. "The CPA And His Duty To Silence," No. 1, pp. 69-75.
Demski, Joel S. "The Decision Implementation Interface: Effects Of Alternative Performance Measurement Models," No. 1, pp. 76-87.
Wojdak, Joseph F. "Levels Of Objectivity In The Accounting Process," No. 1, pp. 88-97.
Gambling, Trevor E. and Ahmed Nour. "A Note On Input-Output Analysis: Its Uses In Macro-Economics And Micro-Economics," No. 1, pp. 98-102.
Greer, Willis R., Jr. "Capital Budgeting Analysis With The Timing Of Events Uncertain," No. 1, pp. 103-114.
Jaenicke, Henry R. "Accounting For Restricted Stock Plans And Deferred Stock Plans," No. 1, pp. 115-128.
Wright, F. K. "Dual Variables In Inventory Measurement," No. 1, pp. 129-133.
Dalton, Francis E. and John B. Miner. "The Role Of Accounting Training In Top Mangement Decision-Making," No. 1, pp. 134-139.
Dixon, Robert L. "An Experimental Interview Program To Attract Students To Our Field," No. 1, pp. 140-143.
Crumbley, D. Larry. "Child Care Expense Deduction - A 'Decision Tree' Application," No. 1, pp. 143-145.
Madden, Donald L. "Bridging The Gap Between Business And Academic Environments," No. 1, pp. 145-150.
Thomsen, C. Torben. "Continuous And Consistent Depreciation Formulas," No. 1, pp. 151-158.
Askins, Billy E. "Determining The Effectiveness Of Programmed Instruction - A Training Course Example," No. 1, pp. 159-163.
Hartley, Ronald V. "Some Extensions Of Sensitivity Analysis," No. 2, pp. 223-234.
Carmichael, D. R. "Behavioral Hypotheses Of Internal Control," No. 2, pp. 235-245.
Ijiri, Yuji and Gerald L. Thompson. "Applications Of Mathematical Control Theory To Accounting And Budgeting (The Continuous Wheat Trading Model)," No. 2, pp. 246-258.
Schiff, Michael and Arie Y. Lewin. "The Impact Of People On Budgets," No. 2, pp. 259-268.
Pankoff, Lyn D. and Robert L. Virgil. "On The Usefulness Of Financial Statement Information: A Suggested Research Approach," No. 2, pp. 269-279.
Frank, Werner G. and Jerry J. Weygandt. "Convertible Debt And Earnings Per Share: Pragmatism Vs. Good Theory," No. 2, pp. 280-289.
Jen, Frank C. and Ronald J. Huefner. "Depreciation By Probability-Life," No. 2, pp. 290-298.
Shwayder, Keith. "A Proposed Modification To Residual Income - Interest Adjusted Income," No. 2, pp. 299-307.
Mitchell, G. B. "After-Tax Cost Of Leasing," No. 2, pp. 308-314.
McRae, T. W. "Opportunity And Incremental Cost: An Attempt To Define In Systems Terms," No. 2, pp. 315-321.
Culpepper, Robert C. "A Study Of Some Relationships Between Accounting And Decision-Making Processes," No. 2, pp. 322-332.
Penman, Stephen H. "What Net Asset Value? - An Extension Of A Familiar Debate," No. 2, pp. 333-346.
Shenkir, William G. "Media And Accounting Education," No. 2, pp. 347-350.
Singer, Frank A. "A System Approach To Teaching The Accounting Process," No. 2, pp. 351-364.
Kempner, Jack J. "An Argument For Small Class Size," No. 2, pp. 364-366.
Murphy, G. J. "Algebraic Double Entry," No. 2, pp. 366-369.
Gordon, Myron J. "A Method Of Pricing For A Socialist Economy," No. 3, pp. 427-443.
Sterling, Robert R. "On Theory Construction And Verification," No. 3, pp. 444-457.
Lembke, Valdean C. "Some Considerations In Accounting For Divisive Reorganizations," No. 3, pp. 458-464.
Moonitz, Maurice. "Price-Level Accounting And Scales Of Measurement," No. 3, pp. 465-475.
Littleton, A. C. "Factors Limiting Accounting," No. 3, pp. 476-480.
Groves, Roger, Rene Manes and Robert Sorensen. "The Application Of The Hirsch-Dantzig 'Fixed Charge' Algorithm To Profit Planning: A Formal Statement Of Product Profitability Analysis," No. 3, pp. 481-489.
Barefield, Russell M. "A Model Of Forecast Biasing Behavior," No. 3, pp. 490-501.

Jensen, Robert E. "Empirical Evidence From The Behavioral Sciences: Fish Out Of Water," No. 3, pp. 502-508.
Fertakis, John P. "Empirical Evidence - A Reply," No. 3, pp. 509-512.
Revsine, Lawrence. "On The Correspondence Between Replacement Cost Income And Economic Income," No. 3, pp. 513-523.
Anderson, H. M., J. W. Giese and Jon Booker. "Some Propositions About Auditing," No. 3, pp. 524-531.
Lev, Baruch. "A Comment On 'Business Combinations: An Exchange Ratio Determination Model'," No. 3, pp. 532-534.
Onsi, Mohamed. "A Transfer Pricing System Based On Opportunity Cost," No. 3, pp. 535-543.
Wolk, Harry I. "Current Value Depreciation: A Conceptual Clarification," No. 3, pp. 544-552.
Whitehurst, Frederick D. "The Predictability Of Investor Cash Return From Historical Income Trends Of Common Stocks," No. 3, pp. 553-564.
Manes, Rene P. "Birch Paper Company Revisited: An Exercise In Transfer Pricing," No. 3, pp. 565-572.
Arens, Alvin A., Robert G. May and Geraldine Dominiak. "A Simulated Case For Audit Education," No. 3, pp. 573-578.
Anderson, Wilton T. and Milton F. Usry. "Use Of Theses And Reports In Master's Degree Programs," No. 3, pp. 579-584.
Feltham, Gerald A. and Joel S. Demski. "The Use Of Models In Information Evaluation," No. 4, pp. 623-640.
Johnson, Orace. "Toward An 'Events' Theory Of Accounting," No. 4, pp. 641-653.
Beaver, William H., Paul Kettler and Myron Scholes. "The Association Between Market Determined And Accounting Determined Risk Measures," No. 4, pp. 654-682.
Campfield, William L. "Toward Making Accounting Education Adaptive And Normative," No. 4, pp. 683-689.
Bierman, Harold, Jr. "Investment Decisions And Taxes," No. 4, pp. 690-697.
Cramer, Joe J., Jr. and William J. Schrader. "Depreciation Accounting And The Anomalous Self-Insurance Cost," No. 4, pp. 698-703.
Revsine, Lawrence. "Data Expansion And Conceptual Structure," No. 4, pp. 704-711.
Gynther, Reg S. "Capital Maintenance, Price Changes, And Profit Determination," No. 4, pp. 712-730.
Vickrey, Don W. "Is Accounting A Measurement Discipline?," No. 4, pp. 731-742.
Winjum, James. "Accounting In Its Age Of Stagnation," No. 4, pp. 743-761.
Mobley, Sybil C. "The Challenges Of Socio-Economic Accounting," No. 4, pp. 762-768.
Beechy, Thomas H. "The Cost Of Leasing: Comment And Correction," No. 4, pp. 769-773.
Li, David H. "Audit-Aid: Generalized Computer-Audit Program As An Instructional Device," No. 4, pp. 774-778.
Bird, Francis A. and Phillip A. Jones. "A Decision-Tree Approach To Earnings Per Share," No. 4, pp. 779-783.
Nurnberg, Hugo and Corwin Grube. "Alternative Methods Of Accounting For Business Combinations," No. 4, pp. 783-789.
Deskins, James Wesley, Frederick L. Neumann and Lawrence Revsine. "A Research Methodology Course For Accountants," No. 4, pp. 789-795.
Smith, John H. and John W. Kennelly. "A Seminar In Accounting Research," No. 4, pp. 795-797.

Accounting Review
Volume 46, 1971

Horngren, Charles T. "The Accounting Discipline In 1999," No. 1, pp. 1-11.
McKeown, James C. "An Empirical Test Of A Model Proposed By Chambers," No. 1, pp. 12-29.
Churchman, C. West. "On The Facility, Felicity, And Morality Of Measuring Social Change," No. 1, pp. 30-35.
Jensen, Robert E. "A Cluster Analysis Study Of Financial Performance Of Selected Business Firms," No. 1, pp. 36-56.
Shank, John K. "Income Determination Under Uncertainty: An Application Of Markov Chains," No. 1, pp. 57-74.
Godfrey, James T. and Thomas R. Prince. "The Accounting Model From An Information Systems Perspective," No. 1, pp. 75-89.
Colantoni, Claude S., Rene P. Manes and Andrew Whinston. "A Unified Approach To The Theory Of Accounting And Information Systems," No. 1, pp. 90-102.
Lev, Baruch and Aba Schwartz. "On The Use Of The Economic Concept Of Human Capital In Financial Statements," No. 1, pp. 103-112.
Probst, Frank R. "Probabilistic Cost Controls: A Behavioral Dimension," No. 1, pp. 113-118.
Aly, Hamdi F. and Jack I. Duboff. "Statistical Vs. Judgment Sampling: An Empirical Study Of Auditing The Accounts Receivable Of A Small Retail Store," No. 1, pp. 119-128.
Singhvi, Surendra S. and Harsha B. Desai. "An Empirical Analysis Of The Quality Of Corporate Financial Disclosure," No. 1, pp. 129-138.
Williamson, James E. "The Effects Of Measurement Concepts On The Investment Decisions Of Trustees," No. 1, pp. 139-148.
Winjum, James O. "The Journal Of Thomas Gresham," No. 1, pp. 149-155.
Lampe, James C. "A Time-Sharing Program Library For Accounting Courses," No. 1, pp. 156-159.
Carpenter, Charles G. and Robert H. Strawser. "Initial Experience With Satisfactory-Unsatisfactory Grading In Accounting Courses," No. 1, pp. 160-162.

Goetz, Billy E. "A Problem In Discounted Cash Flow," No. 1, pp. 162-164.

Horwitz, Bertrand and Reza Shabahang. "Published Corporate Accounting Data And General Wage Increases Of The Firm," No. 2, pp. 243-252.

Flamholtz, Eric. "A Model For Human Resource Valuation: A Stochastic Process With Service Rewards," No. 2, pp. 253-267.

Demski, Joel S. "Implementation Effects Of Alternative Performance Measurement Models In A Multivariable Context," No. 2, pp. 268-278.

Comiskey, Eugene E. "Market Response To Changes In Depreciation Accounting," No. 2, pp. 279-285.

Godfrey, James T. "Short-Run Planning In A Decentralized Firm," No. 2, pp. 286-297.

Louderback, Joseph G., III. "Projectability As A Criterion For Income Determination Methods," No. 2, pp. 298-305.

Shwayder, Keith. "Expected And Unexpected Price Level Changes," No. 2, pp. 306-319.

Gonedes, Nicholas J. "Some Evidence On Investor Actions And Accounting Messages - Part I," No. 2, pp. 320-328.

Hofstedt, Thomas R. and Richard R. West. "The APB, Yield Indices, And Predictive Ability," No. 2, pp. 329-337.

Frank, Werner G. and Jerry J. Weygandt. "The APB, Yield Indices, And Predictive Ability: A Reply," No. 2, pp. 338-341.

Laibstain, Samuel. "A New Look At Accounting For Operating Loss Carryforwards," No. 2, pp. 342-351.

Kaplan, Robert S. and Gerald L. Thompson. "Overhead Allocation Via Mathematical Programming Models," No. 2, pp. 352-364.

Dewhirst, John F. "A Conceptual Approach To Pension Accounting," No. 2, pp. 365-373.

Sigloch, Berndt. "Input-Output Analysis And The Cost Model: A Comment," No. 2, pp. 374-375.

Gambling, Trevor E. "Input-Output Analysis And The Cost Model: A Reply," No. 2, pp. 376-379.

Francia, Arthur J. and Robert H. Strawser. "Perceptions Of Financial Reporting Practices By Accounting Educators: An Empirical Study," No. 2, pp. 380-384.

Beechy, Thomas H. and Wayne A. Bernath. "The Measurement Of Economic Activity: An Introductory Accounting Course," No. 2, pp. 385-387.

Casey, Brian J. "Credibility And Cleavage Problems Of The Accounting Profession," No. 2, pp. 387-389.

Herbert, Leo. "A Perspective Of Accounting," No. 3, pp. 433-440.

Sterling, Robert R. and Richard E. Flaherty. "The Role Of Liquidity In Exchange Valuation," No. 3, pp. 441-456.

Abdel-Khalik, A. Rashad. "User Preference Ordering Value: A Model," No. 3, pp. 457-471.

Thomas, Arthur L. "Useful Arbitrary Allocations (With A Comment On the Neutrality Of Financial Accounting Reports)," No. 3, pp. 472-479.

Revsine, Lawrence. "Predictive Ability. Market Prices, And Operating Flows," No. 3, pp. 480-489.

Curry, Dudley W. "Opinion 15 Vs. A Comprehensive Financial Reporting Method For Convertible Debt," No. 3, pp. 490-503.

Chasteen, Lanny G. "An Empirical Study Of Differences In Economic Circumstances As A Justification For Alternative Inventory Pricing Models," No. 3, pp. 504-508.

Carpenter, Charles G. and Robert H. Strawser. "A Study Of The Job Satisfaction Of Academic Accountants," No. 3, pp. 509-518.

Curley, Anthony J. "Conglomerate Earnings Per Share: Real And Transitory Growth," No. 3, pp. 519-528.

Peragallo, Edward. "A Commentary On Vigano's Historical Development Of Ledger Balancing Procedures, Adjustments And Financial Statements During The Fifteenth, Sixteenth, And Seventeenth Centuries," No. 3, pp. 529-534.

Gonedes, Nicholas J. "Some Evidence On Investor Actions And Accounting Messages - Part II," No. 3, pp. 535-551.

Smith, James E. and Nora P. Smith. "Readability: A Measurement Of The Performance Of The Communication Function Of Financial Reporting," No. 3, pp. 552-561.

Robertson, Jack C. and Robert W. Clarke. "Verification Of Management Representations: A First Step Toward Independent Audits Of Management," No. 3, pp. 562-571.

Gonedes, Nicholas J. and Kermit D. Larson. "A Look At 'A Comment On Business Combinations: An Exchange Ratio Determination Model'," No. 3, pp. 572-573.

Sunley, Emil M., Jr. "An Optimum Switch From Double-Declining Balance To Sum-Of-The-Years Digits Depreciation," No. 3, pp. 574-582.

Walgenbach, Paul H. and Werner G. Frank. "A Simulation Model For Applying Audit-Sampling Techniques," No. 3, pp. 583-588.

Perritt, Roscoe D. "Innovations In An Elementary Accounting Program," No. 3, pp. 589-591.

Cloyd, Helen M. "Optimum Course Requirements For Non-accounting Majors," No. 3, pp. 591-594.

Raff, Michael C. "Exposing First-Semester Accounting Students To Accounting Periodicals," No. 3, pp. 594-595.

Lantry, Terry L. "An Experiment," No. 3, pp. 596-597.

DeCoster, Don T. and John Grant Rhode. "The Accountant's Stereotype: Real Or Imagined, Deserved Or Unwarranted," No. 4, pp. 651-664.

Lengermann, Joseph J. "Supposed And Actual Differences In Professional Autonomy Among CPAs As Related to Type Of Work Organization And Size Of Firm," No. 4, pp. 665-675.

McDonough, John H. "The Accountant, Data Collection And Social Exchange," No. 4, pp. 676-685.

Daily, R. Austin. "The Feasibility Of Reporting Forecasted Information," No. 4, pp. 686-692.

Bierman, Harold, Jr. "Discounted Cash Flows, Price Level Adjustments And Expectations," No. 4, pp. 693-699.

Butterworth, John E. and Berndt A. Sigloch. "A Generalized Multi-Stage Input-Output Model And Some Derived Equivalent Systems," No. 4, pp. 700-716.

Huefner, Ronald J. "Analyzing And Reporting Sensitivity Data," No. 4, pp. 717-732.

Ramanathan, K. V. and Alfred Rappaport. "Size, Growth Rates, And Merger Valuation," No. 4, pp. 733-745.

Hartley, Ronald V. "Decision Making When Joint Products Are Involved," No. 4, pp. 746-755.

Lloyd, B. Michl and Jerry J. Weygandt. "Market Value Information For Nonsubsidiary Investments," No. 4, pp. 756-764.

Mock, Theodore J. "Concepts Of Information Value And Accounting," No. 4, pp. 765-778.

Most, Kenneth S. "Gordon's Transfer Price Model For A Socialist Economy: A Comment," No. 4, pp. 779-782.

Abdel-Khalik, A. Rashad. "On Gordon's Model Of Transfer-Pricing System," No. 4, pp. 783-787.

Gordon, M. J. "A Method Of Pricing For A Socialist Economy: A Reply," No. 4, pp. 788-790.

Usry, Milton F. "Cost Accounting In The CPA Examination - Updated," No. 4, pp. 791-796.

Wilkinson, Joseph W. "Designing A Computer-Based Information System: An 'Intermediate' Systems Course," No. 4, pp. 797-799.

Shenkir, William G. "An Exercise For Use In Discussing Audit Evidence," No. 4, pp. 799-801.

Tucker, Marvin W. "A Model For Accounting Flexibility," No. 4, pp. 801-802.

Accounting Review
Volume 47, 1972

Loeb, Stephen E. "Enforcement Of The Code Of Ethics: A Survey," No. 1, pp. 1-10.

Gonedes, Nicholas J. "Efficient Capital Markets And External Accounting," No. 1, pp. 11-21.

Archibald, T. Ross. "Stock Market Reaction To The Depreciation Switch-Back," No. 1, pp. 22-30.

Miller, Henry. "Environmental Complexity And Financial Reports," No. 1, pp. 31-37.

Baskin, Elba F. "The Communicative Effectiveness Of Consistency Exceptions," No. 1, pp. 38-51.

Felix, William L., Jr. "Estimating The Relationship Between Technical Change And Reported Performance," No. 1, pp. 52-63.

Johnson, Orace. "On Taxonomy And Accounting Research," No. 1, pp. 64-74.

Bollom, William J. and Jerry J. Weygandt. "An Examination Of Some Interim Reporting Theories For A Seasonal Business," No. 1, pp. 75-84.

Charnes, A., C. Colantoni, W. W. Cooper and K. O. Kortanek. "Economic Social And Enterprise Accounting And Mathematical Models," No. 1, pp. 85-108.

Sauls, Eugene. "Nonsampling Errors In Accounts Receivable Confirmation," No. 1, pp. 109-115.

Melberg, William F., Jr. "Benishayan Time Series As Models For Debt Processes Over Time," No. 1, pp. 116-133.

Fogler, H. Russell. "Ranking Techniques And Capital Budgeting," No. 1, pp. 134-143.

Currin, David L. and W. Allen Spivey. "A Note On 'Management Decision And Integer Programming'," No. 1, pp. 144-146.

Glover, Fred. "Comment On A Note By Currin And Spivey," No. 1, p. 147.

Flamholtz, Eric G. "On The Use Of The Economic Concept Of Human Capital In Financial Statements: A Comment," No. 1, pp. 148-152.

Lev, Baruch and Aba Schwartz. "On The Use Of The Economic Concept Of Human Capital In Financial Statements: A Reply," No. 1, pp. 153-154.

Frank, Werner G. "Evaluation Of Wage Incentives: Fixed Costs, Revisited," No. 1, pp. 155-160.

McCosh, Andrew M. "The Case Method Of Accounting Instruction And Microwave Television," No. 1, pp. 161-163.

Patten, Ronald J. and Joseph W. Bachman. "Elementary Accounting Profile - 1970," No. 1, pp. 164-167.

Ziegler, John H. "Current Trends In The Teaching Of Auditing," No. 1, pp. 167-170.

Huefner, Ronald J. "An Economic Approach To Price-Index Bias," No. 1, pp. 171-173.

Crumbley, D. Larry. "Introducing Probabilities And Present Value Analysis Into Taxation," No. 1, pp. 173-174.

Anderson, H. M., B. A. Coda and J. W. Giese. "An Experiment With A One-Semester Introductory Accounting Course," No. 1, pp. 175-177.

Schattke, R. W. "An Analysis Of Accounting Principles Board Statement No. 4," No. 2, pp. 233-244.

Frankfurter, G. and B. Horwitz. "The Effects Of Accounting Principles Board Opinion No. 15 On Earnings Per Share: A Simulation Study," No. 2, pp. 245-259.

Smith, Kenneth A. "The Relationship Of Internal Control Evaluation And Audit Sample Size," No. 2, pp. 260-269.

Smith, Charles H., Roy A. Lanier and Martin E. Taylor. "The Need For And Scope Of The Audit Of Management: A Survey Of Attitudes," No. 2, pp. 270-283.

Estes, Ralph W. "Socio-Economic Accounting And External Diseconomies," No. 2, pp. 284-290.

Barefield, Russell M. and Eugene E. Comiskey. "The Smoothing Hypothesis: An Alternative Test," No. 2, pp. 291-298.

Ferrara, William L., Jack C. Hayya and David A. Nachman. "Normalcy Of Profit In The Jaedicke-Robichek Model," No. 2, pp. 299-307.

O'Connor, Melvin C. and James C. Hamre. "Alternative Methods Of Accounting For Long-Term Nonsubsidiary Intercorporate Investments In Common Stock," No. 2, pp. 308-319.

Beaver, William H. and Roland E. Dukes. "Interperiod Tax Allocation, Earnings Expectations, And The Behavior Of Security Prices," No. 2, pp. 320-332.

Bedford, Norton M. and James C. McKeown. "Comparative Analysis Of Net Realizable Value And Replacement Costing," No. 2, pp. 333-338.

Kinney, William R., Jr. "Covariability Of Segment Earnings And Multisegment Company Returns," No. 2, pp. 339-345.

Lea, Richard B. "A Note On The Definition Of Cost Coefficients In A Linear Programming Model," No. 2, pp. 346-350.

Fekrat, M. Ali. "The Conceptual Foundations Of Absorption Costing," No. 2, pp. 351-355.

Gordon, Lawrence A. "Comment On The Value Of R-Square In Regression Analysis," No. 2, pp. 356-357.

Comiskey, Eugene E. "On The Value Of R-Square In Regression Analysis: A Reply," No. 2, pp. 358-359.

Reinhardt, U. E. "Conglomerate Earnings Per Share: Immediate And Post-Merger Effects," No. 2, pp. 360-370.

Curley, Anthony J. "Conglomerate Growth: The Ostrich Effect," No. 2, pp. 371-374.

Harris, John K. and Richard M. Hodgetts. "A Quasi-Consulting Project Involving Accounting And Management Students," No. 2, pp. 375-380.

Markell, William and Wilfred A. Pemberton. "Programmed Instruction In Elementary Accounting - Is It Successful?," No. 2, pp. 381-384.

Patten, Ronald J. and Thomas D. Hubbard. "CPA Review Clinics - An Opportunity For Accounting Educators," No. 2, pp. 385-387.

Schroeder, Joan Gagnon. "Systems And Electronic Data Processing Courses In The Accounting Curriculum," No. 2, pp. 387-389.

Myers, John H. and James R. Kinney. "A Computer Experiment In The Auditing Class," No. 2, pp. 390-392.

Garner, Don E. "New Student Rights And Academic Freedom In The Classroom," No. 2, pp. 393-394.

Copeland, Ronald M. and Michael L. Moore. "Validity Of The 1966 Tax Model As A Research Tool," No. 2, pp. 395-396.

Norgaard, Corine T. "Extending The Boundaries Of The Attest Function," No. 3, pp. 433-442.

Summers, Edward L. "The Audit Staff Assignment Problem: A Linear Programming Analysis," No. 3, pp. 443-453.

Fagerberg, Dixon, Jr. "Concerning Three Mischievous Accounts," No. 3, pp. 454-457.

Heath, Loyd C. "Distinguishing Between Monetary And Nonmonetary Assets And Liabilities In General Price Level Accounting," No. 3, pp. 458-468.

Mattessich, Richard. "Methodological Preconditions And Problems Of A General Theory Of Accounting," No. 3, pp. 469-487.

Chambers, Raymond J. "Measurement In Current Accounting Practices: A Critique," No. 3, pp. 488-509.

Ijiri, Yuji. "Measurement In Current Accounting Practices: A Reply," No. 3, pp. 510-526.

McKeown, James C. "Additivity Of Net Realizable Values," No. 3, pp. 527-532.

Demski, Joel S. and Gerald A. Feltham. "Forecast Evaluation," No. 3, pp. 533-548.

Wolk, Harry I. and A. Douglas Hillman. "Materials Mix And Yield Variances: A Suggested Improvement," No. 3, pp. 549-555.

Corless, John C. "Assessing Prior Distributions For Applying Bayesian Statistics In Auditing," No. 3, pp. 556-566.

Lusk, Edward J. "Discriminant Analysis As Applied To The Resource Allocation Decision," No. 3, pp. 567-575.

Minch, Roland and Enrico Petri. "Matrix Modeling Of Reciprocal Service Cost Allocation," No. 3, pp. 576-580.

Moore, Michael L. and Stephen Buzby. "The Quality Of Corporate Financial Disclosure: A Comment," No. 3, pp. 581-584.

Singhvi, Surendra S. and Harsha B. Desai. "The Quality Of Corporate Financial Disclosure: A Reply," No. 3, pp. 585-586.

Greer, Willis R., Jr. "Discounted Cash Flows, Price Level Adjustments And Expectations: A Comment," No. 3, pp. 587-588.

Bierman, Harold, Jr. "Discounted Cash Flows, Price Level Adjustments And Expectations: A Reply," No. 3, pp. 589-590.

Bruns, William J. "Behavioral Science In The Accounting Curriculum," No. 3, pp. 591-595.

Cramer, Joe J., Jr. "Incompatibility Of Bad Debt 'Expense' With Contemporary Accounting Theory," No. 3, pp. 596-598.

Cushing, Barry E. and Charles H. Smith. "A New Emphasis For Introductory Accounting Instruction," No. 3, pp. 599-601.

Hamre, James C. "A University Accountant Trainee Program," No. 3, pp. 602-603.

McCullers, Levis D. and Relmond P. VanDaniker. "Socio-Economics And Accounting Education," No. 3, pp. 604-606.

Nichols, Gerald E. "Business Consulting For Credit," No. 3, pp. 607-608.

Piaker, Philip M. "The Use Of Medieval Statements For Teaching Accounting," No. 3, pp. 609-610.

Scott, Richard A. "The Study Of Partnership Accounting Through Role Playing," No. 3, pp. 610-612.

Smith, James E. "The Need For A Senior Level Theory Seminar," No. 3, pp. 613-614.

Stettler, Howard F. "An Experiment In Education For The Profession," No. 3, pp. 614-617.

Nurnberg, Hugo. "Discounting Deferred Tax Liabilities," No. 4, pp. 655-665.

Flamholtz, Eric. "Toward A Theory Of Human Resource Value In Formal Organizations," No. 4, pp. 666-678.

Hofstedt, Thomas R. "Some Behavioral Parameters Of Financial Analysis," No. 4, pp. 679-692.

Nakano, Isao. "Noise And Redundancy In Accounting Communications," No. 4, pp. 693-708.

Sterling, Robert R., John O. Tollefson and Richard E. Flaherty. "Exchange Valuation: An Empirical Test," No. 4, pp. 709-721.

Most, Kenneth S. "Sombart's Propositions Revisited," No. 4, pp. 722-734.

Sorensen, James E. and David D. Franks. "The Relative Contribution Of Ability, Self-Esteem And Evaluative Feedback To Performance: Implications For Accounting Systems," No. 4, pp. 735-746.

Shwayder, Keith R. "Accounting For Exchange Rate Fluctuations," No. 4, pp. 747-760.

Morse, Wayne J. "Reporting Production Costs That Follow The Learning Curve Phenomenon," No. 4, pp. 761-773.

Stallman, James C. "A Framework For Evaluating Cost Control Procedures For A Process," No. 4, pp. 774-790.

Abdel-Khalik, A. Rashad. "The Efficient Market Hypothesis And Accounting Data: A Point Of View," No. 4, pp. 791-793.

Dyckman, Thomas R. "Discounted Cash Flows, Price-Level Adjustments And Expectations: A Comment," No. 4, pp. 794-798.

Bierman, Harold, Jr. "Discounted Cash Flows, Price-Level Adjustments And Expectations: A Reply," No. 4, pp. 799-800.

Petersen, Russell J. and Thomas F. Keller. "Asset Valuation, Income Determination And Changing Prices," No. 4, pp. 801-805.

Streuling, G. Fred and Gary L. Holstrum. "Teaching Machines Versus Lectures In Accounting Education: An Experiment," No. 4, pp. 806-810.

Loeb, Stephen E. and James P. Bedingfield. "Teaching Accounting Ethics," No. 4, pp. 811-813.

Block, Max. "Writing For A Public Accounting Practitioners' Magazine," No. 4, pp. 814-818.

Chasteen, Lanny Gordon. "A Graphical Approach To Linear Programming Shadow Prices," No. 4, pp. 819-823.

McCray, John H. "Present Value Of An Annuity - A Formula Approach," No. 4, pp. 824-825.

Mock, Theodore J. "A Decision Tree Approach To The Methodological Decision Process," No. 4, pp. 826-829.

Parker, James E. and Allen Ford. "Dissertation Experiences Of Recent Doctoral Graduates In Accounting," No. 4, pp. 830-833.

Rueschhoff, Norlin G. "The Undergraduate International Accounting Course," No. 4, pp. 833-836.

Sale, J. Timothy. "Using Computerized Budget Simulation Models As A Teaching Device," No. 4, pp. 836-839.

Accounting Review
Volume 48, 1973

Gosman, Martin L. "Characteristics Of Firms Making Accounting Changes," No. 1, pp. 1-11.

Bollom, William John. "Towards A Theory Of Interim Reporting For A Seasonal Business: A Behavioral Approach," No. 1, pp. 12-22.

Arnold, Donald F. and Thomas E. Humann. "Earnings Per Share: An Empirical Test Of The Market Parity And The Investment Value Methods," No. 1, pp. 23-33.

Petersen, Russell J. "Interindustry Estimation Of General Price-Level Impact On Financial Information," No. 1, pp. 34-43.

Meyers, Stephen L. "An Examination Of The Relationship Between Interperiod Tax Allocation And Present-Value Depreciation," No. 1, pp. 44-49.

Friberg, Ronald A. "Probabilistic Depreciation With A Varying Salvage Value," No. 1, pp. 50-60.

Dickhaut, John W. "Alternative Information Structures And Probability Revisions," No. 1, pp. 61-79.

May, Robert G. and Gary L. Sundem. "Cost Of Information And Security Prices: Market Association Tests For Accounting Policy Decisions," No. 1, pp. 80-94.

Jain, Tribhowan N. "Alternative Methods Of Accounting And Decision Making: A Psycho-Linguistical Analysis," No. 1, pp. 95-104.

Corcoran, A. Wayne and Wayne E. Leininger. "Stochastic Process Costing Models," No. 1, pp. 105-114.

Largay, James A., III. "Microeconomic Foundations Of Variable Costing," No. 1, pp. 115-119.

Morse, Ellsworth H., Jr. "Comments On Survey Of Attitudes On Management Auditing," No. 1, pp. 120-122.

Smith, Charles H., Roy A. Lanier and Martin E. Taylor. "Comments On Survey Of Attitudes On Management Auditing: A Reply," No. 1, pp. 123-125.

Moyer, R. Charles and Frank Mastrapasqua. "Socio-Economic Accounting And External Diseconomics: A Comment," No. 1, pp. 126-127.

Gordon, Lawrence A. and Henry Cook, Jr. "Absorption Costing And Fixed Factors Of Production," No. 1, pp. 128-129.

Fekrat, M. Ali. "Absorption Costing And Fixed Factors Of Production: A Reply," No. 1, pp. 130-131.

Littrell, Earl K., III. "A Note On Discounted Cash Flow Examples," No. 1, pp. 132-134.

Goetz, Billy E. "A Note On Discounted Cash Flow Examples: A

Reply," No. 1, pp. 135-136.

DeCoster, Don and George Prater. "An Experimental Study Of The Use Of A Business Game In Elementary Accounting," No. 1, pp. 137-142.

Needles, Belverd E., Jr. "Freedom And Learning: An Approach And First Results," No. 1, pp. 143-148.

Smith, Charles H. "A New Introduction To Accounting: Some Explanations," No. 1, pp. 148-157.

Gosman, Martin L. "An Assessment Of The Recommendations Of The Study Group On Introductory Accounting," No. 1, pp. 158-162.

Edwards, James B. "Should Accounting Students Write Computer Programs?," No. 1, pp. 163-165.

Graham, Curtis C. and Darwin W. Manship. "The Environment Of Reality: An Experiment In Education For Business," No. 1, pp. 166-170.

Modisette, James P. "Audit Practice Set Grading Guide," No. 1, pp. 170-171.

McKeown, James C. "An Effective And Practical Tool For Conveying Test Deck Concepts," No. 1, pp. 172-174.

Francis, M. E. "Accounting And The Evaluation Of Social Programs: A Critical Comment," No. 2, pp. 245-257.

Causey, Denzil Y., Jr. "Foreseeability As A Determinant Of Audit Responsibility," No. 2, pp. 258-267.

Killough, Larry N. and Thomas L. Souders. "A Goal Programming Model For Public Accounting Firms," No. 2, pp. 268-279.

Miller, Malcolm C. "Goodwill - An Aggregation Issue," No. 2, pp. 280-291.

Wolk, Harry I. and Michael G. Tearney. "Income Tax Allocation And Loss Carryforwards: Exploring Uncharted Ground," No. 2, pp. 292-299.

Downes, David and Thomas R. Dyckman. "A Critical Look At The Efficient Market Empirical Research Literature As It Relates To Accounting Information," No. 2, pp. 300-317.

Meyers, Stephen L. "The Stationarity Problem In The Use Of The Market Model Of Security Price Behavior," No. 2, pp. 318-322.

Falk, Haim and Tsvi Ophir. "The Effect Of Risk On The Use Of Financial Statements By Investment Decision-Makers: A Case Study," No. 2, pp. 323-338.

O'Connor, Melvin C. "On The Usefulness Of Financial Ratios To Investors In Common Stock," No. 2, pp. 339-352.

Klammer, Thomas. "The Association Of Capital Budgeting Techniques With Firm Performance," No. 2, pp. 353-364.

Copeland, Ronald M., Arthur J. Francia and Robert H. Strawser. "Students As Subjects In Behavioral Business Research," No. 2, pp. 365-372.

Corcoran, A. Wayne and Wayne E. Leininger. "In-Process Inventories And Multiproduct Production Systems," No. 2, pp. 373-374.

Feltham, Gerald A. "In-Process Inventories And Multiproduct Production Systems: A Comment," No. 2, pp. 375-376.

Bentz, William F. "Input-Output Analysis For Cost Accounting, Planning And Control: A Proof," No. 2, pp. 377-380.

Livingstone, J. Leslie. "Input-Output Analysis For Cost Accounting, Planning And Control: A Reply," No. 2, pp. 381-382.

Nichols, Donald R. "Comparative Analysis Of Net Realizable Value And Replacement Costing - A Comment," No. 2, pp. 383-385.

McKeown, James C. "A Brief Exploration Of The Goal Congruence Of Net Realizable Value," No. 2, pp. 386-388.

Lea, Richard B. "Comments On Mock's Concepts Of Information Value," No. 2, pp. 389-393.

Mock, Theodore J. "Concepts Of Information Value And Accounting: A Reply," No. 2, pp. 394-397.

Stone, Donald E. "Computer Simulation In Financial Accounting," No. 2, pp. 398-409.

Virgil, Robert L., Walter R. Nord and Sterling H. Schoen. "A Classroom Experience In The Behavioral Implications Of Accounting Performance Evaluation Measurements," No. 2, pp. 410-418.

Dascher, Paul E. and Thomas D. Hubbard. "The CPA Review Course - A Second Dimension," No. 2, pp. 418-420.

Bierman, Harold, Jr. "Accounting For Capitalized Leases: Tax Considerations," No. 2, pp. 421-424.

Clary, Duane A. "Blueprint For An Accounting Program In Federal Taxation," No. 2, pp. 425-427.

Olson, Steven K. and Jerry J. Weygandt. "Evolution Of Accounting Changes: Opinion No. 20," No. 2, pp. 428-429.

Streuling, G. Fred and Thomas R. Harper. "Income Tax Questions On The CPA Exam: Recent Changes And Future Outlook," No. 2, pp. 429-432.

Gerboth, Dale L. "Research, Intuition, And Politics In Accounting Inquiry," No. 3, pp. 475-482.

Petri, Enrico. "Holding Gains And Losses As Cost Savings: A Comment On Supplementary Statement No. 2 On Inventory Valuation," No. 3, pp. 483-488.

Wyman, Harold E. "Financial Lease Evaluation Under Conditions Of Uncertainty," No. 3, pp. 489-493.

Shank, John K. and Ronald M. Copeland. "Corporate Personality Theory And Changes In Accounting Methods," No. 3, pp. 494-501.

McDonald, Charles L. "An Empirical Examination Of The Reliability Of Published Predictions Of Future Earnings," No. 3, pp. 502-510.

Dermer, Jerry D. "Cognitive Characteristics And The Perceived Importance Of Information," No. 3, pp. 511-519.

Mock, Theodore J. "The Value Of Budget Information," No. 3, pp. 520-534.

Onsi, Mohamed. "Factor Analysis Of Behavioral Variables Affecting Budgetary Slack," No. 3, pp. 535-548.

Beaver, William H. and Roland E. Dukes. "Interperiod Tax Allocation And Delta-Depreciation Methods: Some

Empirical Results," No. 3, pp. 549-559.

Bailey, Andrew D., Jr. "A Dynamic Programming Approach To The Analysis Of Different Costing Methods In Accounting For Inventories," No. 3, pp. 560-574.

McIntyre, Edward V. "Current-Cost Financial Statements And Common-Stock Investments Decisions," No. 3, pp. 575-585.

Wilson, David A. "A Note On 'Environmental Complexity And Financial Reports'," No. 3, pp. 586-588.

Morse, Wayne J. "A Note On The Relationship Between Human Assets And Human Capital," No. 3, pp. 589-593.

Ophir, Tsvi. "Introducing Probabilities And Present Value Analysis Into Taxation: A Comment," No. 3, p. 594.

Crumbley, D. Larry. "Introducing Probabilities And Present Value Analysis Into Taxation: A Reply," No. 3, pp. 595-597.

Weil, Roman L. "The Algorithm For Lower-Of-Cost-Or-Market Inventory Valuation: Mathematical Notation Makes It Easy," No. 3, p. 598.

Robertson, Jack C. and Charles H. Smith. "Auditing And Professionalism At The Graduate Level," No. 3, pp. 599-602.

Bedingfield, James P. and Stephen E. Loeb. "Attitudes Of Professors Toward Accounting Ethics," No. 3, pp. 603-605.

Brenner, Vincent C. "Some Observations On Student Values And Their Implications For Accounting Education," No. 3, pp. 605-608.

Cattanach, Richard L. and Glyn W. Hanbery. "Audit Planning: An Application Of Network Analysis," No. 3, pp. 609-611.

Granof, Michael H. "Conference Telephone Calls: A Means To Bridge The Academic - 'Real World' Gap," No. 3, pp. 612-614.

Pointer, Larry Gene and Philip W. Ljungdahl. "The Merit Of Using The Case Method In Teaching The Specialized Accounting Courses," No. 3, pp. 614-618.

Beidleman, Carl R. "Income Smoothing: The Role Of Management," No. 4, pp. 653-667.

Clark, John J. and Pieter Elgers. "Forecasted Income Statements: An Investor Perspective," No. 4, pp. 668-678.

Heintz, James A. "Price-Level Restated Financial Statements And Investment Decision Making," No. 4, pp. 679-689.

Brief, Richard P. and Joel Owen. "Present Value Models And The Multi-Asset Problem," No. 4, pp. 690-695.

Ronen, Joshua and Gideon Falk. "Accounting Aggregation And The Entropy Measure: An Experimental Approach," No. 4, pp. 696-717.

Demski, Joel S. "The General Impossibility Of Normative Accounting Standards," No. 4, pp. 718-723.

Ijiri, Yuji and Hiroyuki Itami. "Quadratic Cost-Volume Relationship And Timing Of Demand Information," No. 4, pp. 724-737.

Kaplan, Robert S. "Variable And Self-Service Costs In Reciprocal Allocation Models," No. 4, pp. 738-748.

Weil, Roman L. "Reciprocal Or Mutual Holdings: Allocating Earnings And Selecting The Accounting Method," No. 4, pp. 749-758.

Crumbley, D. Larry. "Behavioral Implications Of Taxation," No. 4, pp. 759-763.

Chasteen, Lanny G. "Implicit Factors In The Evaluation Of Lease Vs. Buy Alternatives," No. 4, pp. 764-767.

Jensen, Daniel L. "Hartley's Demand-Price Analysis In A Case Of Joint Production: A Comment," No. 4, pp. 768-770.

Hartley, Ronald V. "A Note On Quadratic Programming In A Case Of Joint Production: A Reply," No. 4, pp. 771-774.

Scott, Edward R. "Bad Debts: Take Two: A Comment," No. 4, pp. 775-776.

Petersen, Russell J. "Incompatibility Of Bad Debt 'Expense' With Contemporary Accounting Theory: A Comment," No. 4, pp. 777-778.

Cramer, Joe J., Jr. "Bad Debt 'Expense': Not A Member Of The Class Of Data For Measuring Operating Income: A Reply," No. 4, pp. 779-784.

Homburger, Richard H. "The Use Of Medieval Statements For Teaching Accounting: A Comment," No. 4, pp. 785-788.

Piaker, Philip M. "The Use Of Medieval Statements For Teaching Accounting: A Reply," No. 4, p. 789.

Bashan, O., Y. Goldschmidt, G. Levkowitz and L. Shashua. "Laspeyres Indexes For Variance Analysis In Cost Accounting," No. 4, pp. 790-793.

Benjamin, James J. and Donald E. Ricketts. "A Profit Planning Project In The Management Accounting Course," No. 4, pp. 794-797.

Clough, Barbara A. "Towards A Definition Of Experience," No. 4, pp. 798-799.

DeCoster, Don T. and Kavasseri V. Ramanathan. "An Algebraic Aid In Teaching The Differences Between Direct Costing And Full-Absorption Costing Models," No. 4, pp. 800-801.

McCormick, William, Jr. "Trends In Education For Auditors," No. 4, pp. 801-803.

Accounting Review
Volume 49, 1974

Kiger, Jack E. "Volatility In Quarterly Accounting Data," No. 1, pp. 1-7.

Abdel-Khalik, A. Rashad and Edward J. Lusk. "Transfer Pricing - a Synthesis," No. 1, pp. 8-23.

Cushing, Barry E. and Edward B. Deakin. "A Mathematical Approach To The Analysis And Design Of Internal Control Systems," No. 1, pp. 24-41.

Buzby, Stephen L. "Extending The Applicability Of Probabilistic Management Planning And Control Models," No. 1,

Beshara, R. L. "Price-Level Restated Accounting And The Measurement Of Inflation Gains And Losses: A Comment," No. 3, pp. 582-585.

Bradford, William D. "Price-Level Restated Accounting And The Measurement Of Inflation Gains And Losses: A Reply," No. 3, pp. 586-587.

Jensen, D. L. and A. D. Bailey. "Discriminant Analysis As An Aid To Employee Selection: A Comment," No. 3, pp. 588-592.

Welker, Robert B. "Discriminant Analysis As An Aid To Employee Selection: A Reply," No. 3, pp. 593-594.

Paretta, Robert L. and Lester W. Chadwick. "The Sequencing Of Examination Questions And Its Effects On Student Performance," No. 3, pp. 595-601.

Solomon, Lanny. "Improving Student Attitudes In The Beginning Accounting Course," No. 3, pp. 601-605.

Bazley, John D. and Loren A. Nikolai. "A Comparison Of Published Accounting Research And Qualities Of Accounting Faculty And Doctoral Programs," No. 3, pp. 605-610.

Boatsman, J. R. and G. M. Crooch. "An Example Of Controlling The Risk Of A Type II Error For Substantive Tests In Auditing," No. 3, pp. 610-615.

Hawthorne, W. H. and H. C. Herring. "A Quantitative Approach To The Illustration Of The Percentage-Of-Completion Method," No. 3, pp. 615-616.

Lindbeck, R. and R. Rogow. "A Straightforward Decision Rule For Selecting Lower-Of-Cost Or Market Prices: A Contraction," No. 3, p. 617.

Churchill, Neil C. and John K. Shank. "Accounting For Affirmative Action Programs: A Stochastic Flow Approach," No. 4, pp. 643-656.

Abdel-Khalik, A. Rashad. "Advertising Effectiveness And Accounting Policy," No. 4, pp. 657-670.

Ronen, J. and J. L. Livingstone. "An Expectancy Theory Approach To The Motivational Impacts Of Budgets," No. 4, pp. 671-685.

Foster, George. "Accounting Earnings And Stock Prices Of Insurance Companies," No. 4, pp. 686-698.

Hagerman, Robert L. "A Test Of Government Regulation Of Accounting Principles," No. 4, pp. 699-709.

Ashton, Robert H. "User Prediction Models In Accounting: An Alternative Use," No. 4, pp. 710-722.

Prakash, Prem and Alfred Rappaport. "Informational Interdependencies: System Structure Induced By Accounting Information," No. 4, pp. 723-734.

Lucas, Henry C., Jr. "The Use Of An Accounting Information System, Action And Organizational Performance," No. 4, pp. 735-746.

Bodnar, George. "Reliability Modeling Of Internal Control Systems," No. 4, pp. 747-757.

Falk, Haim and James A. Heintz. "Assessing Industry Risk By Ratio Analysis," No. 4, pp. 758-779.

Liao, Mawsen. "Model Sampling: A Stochastic Cost-Volume-Profit Analysis," No. 4, pp. 780-790.

Moriarity, Shane. "Another Approach To Allocating Joint Costs," No. 4, pp. 791-795.

Dyckman, Thomas R. "The Effects Of Restating Financial Statements For Price-Level Changes: A Comment," No. 4, pp. 796-808.

Heintz, James A. "The Effects Of Restating Financial Statements For Price-Level Changes: A Reply," No. 4, pp. 809-814.

McIntyre, Edward V. "The Effects Of Restating Financial Statements For Price-Level Changes: A Reply," No. 4, pp. 815-817.

Barefield, Russell M. and Eugene E. Comiskey. "Segmental Financial Disclosure By Diversified Firms And Security Prices: A Comment," No. 4, pp. 818-821.

Kochanek, Ricahrd F. "Segmental Financial Disclosure By Diversified Firms And Security Prices: A Reply," No. 4, pp. 822-825.

Hayya, Jack, William Ferrara and Erwin Saniga. "Extending The Applicability Of Probabilistic Management Planning And Control Models: A Comment," No. 4, pp. 826-831.

Buzby, Stephen L. "Extending The Applicability Of Probabilistic Management Planning And Control Models: A Reply," No. 4, pp. 832-834.

Hoskins, C. G. "Theory Versus Practice In Risk Analysis: An Empirical Study: A Comment," No. 4, pp. 835-838.

Greer, Willis R., Jr. and Ted D. Skekel. "Theory Versus Practice In Risk Analysis: A Reply," No. 4, pp. 839-843.

Loeb, Stephen E. "The Auditor-Firm Conflict Of Interests: Its Implications For Independence: A Comment," No. 4, pp. 844-847.

Goldman, Arieh and Benzion Barlev. "The Auditor-Firm Conflict Of Interests: Its Implications For Independence: A Reply," No. 4, pp. 848-853.

Aranya, Nissim and Moshe Sarell. "The Auditor-Firm Conflict Of Interests: A Comment," No. 4, pp. 854-856.

Goldman, Arieh and Benzion Barlev. "The Auditor-Firm Conflict Of Interests: Its Implications For Independence: A Reply," No. 4, pp. 857-859.

Liao, Shu S. "The Comparison Of Alternative Income Concepts: A Comment," No. 4, pp. 860-864.

Kratchman, Stanley H., Robert E. Malcom and Richard D. Twark. "The Comparison Of Alternative Income Concepts: A Reply," No. 4, pp. 865-868.

Mepham, M. J. "A Payback Interpretation Of The Annuity Tables," No. 4, pp. 869-870.

Jensen, Robert E. "Truth Versus PHIKTION Versus Something," No. 4, pp. 871-873.

Lossett, Ronald D. and Mohamed Moustafa. "The Nature Of The Demand For Doctorates In Accounting," No. 4, pp. 874-881.

Nikolai, Loren A. and John D. Bazley. "The Organizational

Set Prestige Ranking And Its Impact Upon Accounting Department Faculties," No. 4, pp. 881-888.

McNeill, I. Eugene and Frank Collins. "Personality Tendencies And Learning Modes In Elementary Accounting," No. 4, pp. 888-897.

Belkaoui, Ahmed. "Learning Order And Acceptance Of Accounting Techniques," No. 4, pp. 897-899.

Tennant, Kirk and Charles Lawrence. "Teaching Strategies: Effects On Student Evaluations Of Teachers," No. 4, pp. 899-904.

Stettler, Howard F. "Certificate Programs: Certified Internal Auditor," No. 4, pp. 904-907.

Wyman, Harold E. and Wesley T. Andrews, Jr. "Classifying The Receivable In A Lease Transaction: A Dilemma," No. 4, pp. 908-909.

Accounting Review
Volume 51, 1976

Sunder, Shyam. "Properties Of Accounting Numbers Under Full Costing And Successful-Efforts Costing In The Petroleum Industry," No. 1, pp. 1-18.

Causey, Denzil Y., Jr. "Newly Emerging Standards Of Auditor Responsibility," No. 1, pp. 19-30.

Vickrey, Don W. "General-Price-Level-Adjusted Historical-Cost Statements And The Ratio-Scale View," No. 1, pp. 31-40.

Lavin, David. "Perceptions Of The Independence Of The Auditor," No. 1, pp. 41-50.

Heimann, Stephen R. and Edward J. Lusk. "Decision Flexibility: An Alternative Evaluation Criterion," No. 1, pp. 51-64.

Haseman, William D. and Andrew B. Whinston. "Design Of A Multidimensional Accounting System," No. 1, pp. 65-79.

Meyer, Philip E. "A Framework For Understanding 'Substance Over Form' In Accounting," No. 1, pp. 80-89.

Deakin, Edward B. "Distributions Of Financial Accounting Ratios: Some Empirical Evidence," No. 1, pp. 90-96.

Maxim, L. D., D. E. Cullen and F. X. Cook, Jr. "Optimal Acceptance Sampling Plans For Auditing 'Batched' Stop And Go Vs. Conventional Single-Stage Attributes Plans," No. 1, pp. 97-109.

Barnea, Amir, Joshua Ronen and Simcha Sadan. "Classificatory Smoothing Of Income With Extraordinary Items," No. 1, pp. 110-122.

McKeown, James C. "Computer-Assisted Instruction For Elementary Accounting," No. 1, pp. 123-130.

Carlson, Marvin L. "Toward A New Design For The Intermediate Accounting Course," No. 1, pp. 131-138.

Stolle, Carlton D. "Timing Of The Office Visit: A Factor In Public Accounting Job Selection," No. 1, pp. 139-141.

Capettini, Robert and Thomas E. King. "Exchanges Of Nonmonetary Assets: Some Changes," No. 1, pp. 142-147.

Hamilton, R. E. "Casualty Insurance Recoveries With Coinsurance Clauses: A General Approach," No. 1, pp. 148-150.

McIntyre, Edward V. "A Note On The Joint Variance," No. 1, pp. 151-155.

Revsine, Lawrence. "Surrogates In Income Theory: A Comment," No. 1, pp. 156-159.

Barton, A. D. "Surrogates In Income Theory: A Reply," No. 1, pp. 160-162.

Lau, Amy Hing-Ling and Hon-Shiang Lau. "CVP Analysis Under Uncertainty - A Log Normal Approach: A Comment," No. 1, pp. 163-167.

Hilliard, Jimmy E. and Robert A. Leitch. "CVP Analysis Under Uncertainty - A Log Normal Approach: A Reply," No. 1, pp. 168-171.

Barefield, Russell M., Taylor W. Foster, III and Don Vickrey. "Interpreting The API: A Comment And Extension," No. 1, pp. 172-175.

Marshall, Ronald M. "Interpreting The API: A Reply," No. 1, pp. 176-179.

Hasselback, James R. "Travel Expenses For The Visiting Professor - An Addendum," No. 1, pp. 180-183.

Ijiri, Yuji. "The Price-Level Restatement And Its Dual Interpretation," No. 1, pp. 227-243.

Basi, Bart A., Kenneth J. Carey and Richard D. Twark. "A Comparison Of The Accuracy Of Corporate And Security Analysts' Forecasts Of Earnings," No. 2, pp. 244-254.

Revsine, Lawrence and James B. Thies. "Productivity Changes And Alternative Income Series: A Simulation," No. 2, pp. 255-268.

Hasselback, James R. "An Empirical Examination Of Annual Report Presentation Of The Corporate Income Tax Expense," No. 2, pp. 269-276.

Murphy, George J. "A Numerical Representation Of Some Accounting Conventions," No. 2, pp. 277-286.

Sunder, Shyam. "A Note On Estimating The Economic Impact Of The LIFO Method Of Inventory Valuation," No. 2, pp. 287-291.

Hendricks, James A. "The Impact Of Human Resource Accounting Information On Stock Investment Decisions: An Empirical Study," No. 2, pp. 292-305.

Ogan, Pekin. "A Human Resource Value Model For Professional Service Organizations," No. 2, pp. 306-320.

Lorek, Kenneth S., Charles L. McDonald and Dennis H. Patz. "A Comparative Examination Of Management Forecasts And Box-Jenkins Forecasts Of Earnings," No. 2, pp. 321-330.

Askari, Hossein, Patricia Cain and Richard Shaw. "A Government Tax Subsidy," No. 2, pp. 331-334.

Nichols, Donald R. and Kenneth H. Price. "The Auditor-Firm Conflict: An Analysis Using Concepts Of Exchange Theory," No. 2, pp. 335-346.

**Accounting Review
Volume 52, 1977**

pp. 137-149.

Warren, Carl S. "Characteristics Of Firms Reporting Consistency Exceptions - A Cross-Sectional Analysis," No. 1, pp. 150-161.

McIntyre, Edward V. "Present Value Depreciation And The Disaggregation Problem," No. 1, pp. 162-171.

Weber, Richard P. "Misleading Tax Figures - A Problem For Accountants," No. 1, pp. 172-185.

Peasnell, K. V. "A Note On The Discounted Present Value Concept," No. 1, pp. 186-189.

Magee, Robert P. "Cost Control With Imperfect Parameter Knowledge," No. 1, pp. 190-199.

Frakes, Albert H. "Introductory Accounting Objectives And Intermediate Accounting Performance," No. 1, pp. 200-210.

Castellano, Joseph F. and Harper A. Roehm. "Research In Behavioral Accounting Courses: An Approach," No. 1, pp. 211-215.

Thies, James B. and Lawrence Revsine. "Capital Expenditures Data For Inflation Accounting Studies," No. 1, pp. 216-221.

Call, William L. "General Versus Specific Price-Level Adjustments: A Graphic Analysis," No. 1, pp. 222-228.

Bailey, Andrew D., Jr. and Daniel L. Jensen. "The Two-Dimensional Time Frame Of Common Dollar Statements," No. 1, pp. 229-237.

Matulich, Serge, Loren A. Nikolai and Stevan K. Olson. "Earnings Per Share: A Flow Chart Approach To Teaching Concepts And Procedures," No. 1, pp. 238-247.

Leininger, Wayne E. "Opportunity Costs: Some Definitions And Examples," No. 1, pp. 248-251.

Belkaoui, Ahmed. "The Primacy-Recency Effect, Ego Involvement And The Acceptance Of Accounting Techniques," No. 1, pp. 252-256.

Blum, James D. "Newly Emerging Standards Of Auditor Responsibility: A Comment," No. 1, pp. 257-258.

Causey, Denzil Y., Jr. "Newly Emerging Standards Of Auditor Responsibility: A Reply," No. 1, pp. 259-260.

Flesher, Dale L. "Advertising Effectiveness And Accounting Policy: A Comment," No. 1, pp. 261-263.

Abdel-Khalik, A. Rashad. "Advertising Effectiveness And Accounting Policy: A Reply," No. 1, pp. 264-265.

Mautz, Robert K. and Gary John Previts. "Eric Kohler: An Accounting Original," No. 2, pp. 301-307.

Cushing, Barry E. "On The Possibility Of Optimal Accounting Principles," No. 2, pp. 308-321.

Kissinger, John N. "A General Theory Of Evidence As The Conceptual Foundation In Auditing Theory: Some Comments And Extensions," No. 2, pp. 322-339.

Everest, Gordon C. and Ron Weber. "A Relational Approach To Accounting Models," No. 2, pp. 340-359.

Slavin, Nathan S. "The Elimination Of 'Scienter' In Determining The Auditor's Statutory Liability," No. 2, pp. 360-368.

Kaplan, Robert S. "Purchasing Power Gains On Debt: The Effect Of Expected And Unexpected Inflation," No. 2, pp. 369-378.

Hofstedt, Thomas R. and G. David Hughes. "An Experimental Study Of The Judgmental Element In Disclosure Decisions," No. 2, pp. 379-395.

Hakansson, Nils H. "Interim Disclosure And Public Forecasts: An Economic Analysis And A Framework For Choice," No. 2, pp. 396-416.

Anderson, James A. "The Potential Impact Of Knowledge Of Market Efficiency On Legal Liability Of Auditors," No. 2, pp. 417-426.

Kreiser, Larry. "Maintaining And Improving The Audit Competence Of CPAs: CPA And Selected User Reaction," No. 2, pp. 427-437.

Ronen, Joshua. "The Effect Of Insider Trading Rules On Information Generation And Disclosure By Corporations," No. 2, pp. 438-449.

Barkman, Arnold. "Within-Item Variation: A Stochastic Approach To Audit Uncertainty," No. 2, pp. 450-464.

Bremser, Wayne G., Vincent C. Brenner and Paul E. Dascher. "The Feasibility Of Professional Schools: An Empirical Study," No. 2, pp. 465-473.

Stolle, Carlton D. "Perceived Differences Among Public Accounting Firms Which Affect Job Choices," No. 2, pp. 474-478.

Bottin, Ronald R. "An Investigation Of The Relationship Of The Protestant Ethic Value To Success In Accounting Courses," No. 2, pp. 479-484.

Grinnell, D. Jacque. "Using Linear Programming To Compare Direct And Absorption Costing," No. 2, pp. 485-491.

Martin, Donald D. "Professors' Home Office Expenses: A Recent Development And Economic Extension," No. 2, pp. 492-497.

Willis, Eugene. "The Amount Of A Charitable Contribution Of Property," No. 2, pp. 498-502.

Wyman, Harold E. "Standardized Debt Coverage Ratios," No. 2, pp. 503-507.

Chen, Kung H. and S. J. Lambert. "A Study Of The Consensus On Disclosure Among Public Accountants And Security Analysts: An Alternative Interpretation," No. 2, pp. 508-513.

Chandra, Gyan. "A Study Of The Consensus On Disclosure Among Public Accountants And Security Analysts: An Alternative Interpretation," No. 2, pp. 513-515.

Gibbins, Michael. "Classificatory Smoothing Of Income With Extraordinary Items: Research Implications," No. 2, pp. 516-524.

Barnea, Amir, Joshua Ronen and Simcha Sadan. "Classificatory Smoothing Of Income With Extraordinary Items: A Reply," No. 2, pp. 525-526.

Piper, Roswell M. "The Joint Variance: A Comment," No. 2, pp. 527-533.

Ashton, Robert H. "Objectivity Of Accounting Measures: A Multirule-Multimeasurer Approach," No. 3, pp. 567-575.

Baker, C. Richard. "Management Strategy In A Large Accounting Firm," No. 3, pp. 576-586.

Bromwich, Michael. "The Use Of Present Value Valuation Models In Published Accounting Reports," No. 3, pp. 587-596.

Ferrara, William L. "Probabilistic Approaches To Return On Investment And Residual Income," No. 3, pp. 597-604.

Ferris, Kenneth R. "A Test Of The Expectancy Theory Of Motivation In An Accounting Environment," No. 3, pp. 605-615.

Hamlen, Susan S., William A. Hamlen, Jr. and John T. Tschirhart. "The Use Of Core Theory In Evaluating Joint Cost Allocation Schemes," No. 3, pp. 616-627.

Lessard, Donald R. and Peter Lorange. "Currency Changes And Management Control: Resolving The Centralization/Decentralization Dilemma," No. 3, pp. 628-637.

San Miguel, Joseph G. "The Reliability Of R&D Data In COMPUSTAT And 10-K Reports," No. 3, pp. 638-641.

Savich, Richard S. "The Use Of Accounting Information In Decision Making," No. 3, pp. 642-652.

Schnepper, Jeff A. "The Accountant's Liability Under Rule 10b-5 And Section 10(b) Of The Securities Exchange Act Of 1934: The Hole In Hochfelder," No. 3, pp. 653-657.

Sorensen, James E. and Hugh D. Grove. "Cost-Outcome and Cost-Effectiveness Analysis: Emerging Nonprofit Performance Evaluation Techniques," No. 3, pp. 658-675.

Wright, William F. "Financial Information Processing Models: An Empirical Study," No. 3, pp. 676-689.

Capettini, Robert and Gerald L. Salamon. "Internal Versus External Acquisition Of Services When Reciprocal Services Exist," No. 3, pp. 690-696.

Brandon, Charles H. and Jeffrey E. Jarrett. "Experimenting With Students' Ability To Forecast," No. 3, pp. 697-704.

Burns, David C. and William J. Haga. "Much Ado About Professionalism: A Second Look At Accounting," No. 3, pp. 705-715.

Kiger, Jack E., James B. Wilcox and Jan R. Williams. "Intraperiod Income Tax Allocation With Differential Rates," No. 3, pp. 716-720.

Pawliczek, Ronald. "The Effect Of Different Scoring Plans On Student Performance In An Elementary Accounting Course," No. 3, pp. 721-726.

Willis, Eugene. "Computation Of Gain On Disposition Of Section 1250 Property," No. 3, pp. 727-728.

Zikmund, William G., Ralph F. Catalanello and Steve M. Wegener. "The Accounting Student's Job-Rating Criteria: An Experiment," No. 3, pp. 729-735.

Albrecht, William Steve, Orace Johnson, Larry L. Lookabill and David J. H. Watson. "A Comparison Of The Accuracy Of Corporate And Security Analysts' Forecasts Of Earnings: A Comment," No. 3, pp. 736-740.

Basi, Bart A., Kenneth J. Carey and Richard D. Twark. "A Comparison Of The Accuracy Of Corporate And Security Analysts' Forecasts Of Earnings: A Reply," No. 3, pp. 741-745.

Danos, Paul. "A Revolution In Accounting Thought?: A Comment," No. 3, pp. 746-747.

Wells, M. C. "A Revolution In Accounting Thought?: A Reply," No. 3, pp. 748-750.

Gibbs, Thomas E. "A General Theory Of Evidence As The Conceptual Foundation In Auditing Theory: A Comment," No. 3, pp. 751-755.

Toba, Yoshihide. "A General Theory Of Evidence As The Conceptual Foundation In Auditing Theory: A Reply," No. 3, pp. 756-758.

Riggs, A. James. "An Experimental Study Of The Effects Of Participation, Authoritarianism And Feedback On Cognitive Dissonance In A Standard Setting Situation: A Comment," No. 3, pp. 759-761.

Foran, Michael F. "An Experimental Study Of The Effects Of Participation, Authoritarianism And Feedback On Cognitive Dissonance In A Standard Setting Situation: A Reply," No. 3, pp. 762-764.

Agrawal, Surendra P. "Accounting For The Impact Of Inflation On A Business Enterprise," No. 4, pp. 789-809.

Brief, Richard P. "A Note On 'Rediscovery' And The Rule Of 69," No. 4, pp. 810-812.

Cash, James I, Jr., Andrew D. Bailey, Jr. and Andrew B. Whinston. "A Survey Of Techniques For Auditing EDP-Based Accounting Information Systems," No. 4, pp. 813-832.

Harrell, Adrian M. "The Decision-Making Behavior Of Air Force Officers And The Management Control Process," No. 4, pp. 833-841.

Jensen, Daniel L. "A Class Of Mutually Satisfactory Allocations," No. 4, pp. 842-856.

Bodnar, George and Edward J. Lusk. "Motivational Considerations In Cost Allocation Systems: A Conditioning Theory Approach," No. 4, pp. 857-868.

Magee, Robert P. "The Usefulness Of Commonality Information In Cost Control Decisions," No. 4, pp. 869-880.

Peragallo, Edward. "The Ledger Of Jachomo Badoer," No. 4, pp. 881-892.

Rockness, Howard O. "Expectancy Theory In a Budgetary Setting: An Experimental Examination," No. 4, pp. 893-903.

Tomassini, Lawrence A. "Assessing The Impact Of Human Resource Accounting: An Experimental Study Of Managerial Decision Preferences," No. 4, pp. 904-914.

Dilley, Steven and John J. Wheatley. "Tax Considerations In Research Grants To Faculty," No. 4, pp. 915-924.

Gibbs, Thomas E. and Lynn J. McKell. "Computing The Implicit Interest Rate Under SFAS No. 13," No. 4, pp. 925-929.

Jarnagin, Bill D. and John K. Harris. "Teaching With Multiple Choice Questions," No. 4, pp. 930-934.

Misiewicz, Kevin M. "A Macro-Case Analysis Approach To Tax Research," No. 4, pp. 935-938.

Neyhart, Charles A., Jr. and A. Eugene Abrassart. "Probabilistic Testing And The Evaluation Of Student Performance," No. 4, pp. 939-945.

Schweiger, Bradley J. "A Summary Of Accounting For And Reporting On Accounting Changes," No. 4, pp. 946-949.

Shank, John K. and Neil C. Churchill. "Variance Analysis: A Management Oriented Approach," No. 4, pp. 950-957.

Smith, Ralph E. and Andrew H. Haried. "Exchange Of Nonmonetary Assets: An Interpretation Problem," No. 4, pp. 958-962.

Tidwell, Victor H. and Robert W. Wyndelts. "Graduate Tax Education In AACSB Schools: Where We Stand Today," No. 4, pp. 963-970.

Burton, Eric James. "Toward A Theory Of Corporate Social Accounting: A Comment," No. 4, pp. 971-976.

Tipgos, Manuel A. "Toward A Theory Of Corporate Social Accounting: A Comment," No. 4, pp. 977-983.

Tiessen, Peter and Dennis M. Baker. "Human Information Processing, Decision Style Theory And Accounting Information Systems: A Comment," No. 4, pp. 984-987.

Driver, Michael J. and Theodore J. Mock. "Human Information Processing, Decison Style Theory And Accounting Information Systems: A Reply," No. 4, pp. 988-990.

Accounting Review
Volume 53, 1978

Davis, Darrel W., James R. Boatsman and Elba F. Baskin. "On Generalizing Stock Market Research To A Broader Class Of Markets," No. 1, pp. 1-10.

Dillon, Ray D. and John F. Nash. "The True Relevance Of Relevant Costs," No. 1, pp. 11-17.

Friedman, Laurence A. "An Exit-Price Income Statement," No. 1, pp. 18-30.

Hong, Hai, Robert S. Kaplan and Gershon Mandelker. "Pooling Vs. Purchase: The Effects Of Accounting For Mergers On Stock Prices," No. 1, pp. 31-47.

Kinney, William R., Jr. "ARIMA And Regression In Analytical Review: An Empirical Test," No. 1, pp. 48-60.

Lin, W. Thomas. "Multiple Objective Budgeting Models: A Simulation," No. 1, pp. 61-76.

Neter, John, R. A. Leitch and Stephen E. Fienberg. "Dollar Unit Sampling: Multinomial Bounds For Total Overstatement And Understatement Errors," No. 1, pp. 77-93.

Spicer, Barry H. "Investors, Corporate Social Performance And Information Disclosure: An Empirical Study," No. 1, pp. 94-111.

Watts, Ross L. and Jerold L. Zimmerman. "Towards A Positive Theory Of The Determination Of Accounting Standards," No. 1, pp. 112-134.

Andrews, Wesley T. and Patrick B. McKenzie. "Leading Accounting Departments Revisited," No. 1, pp. 135-138.

Bean, Virginia L. and William G. Mister. "A Partner In Residence Program At The University Of Colorado For National Accountancy Firms," No. 1, pp. 139-142.

Chambers, Andrew D. "Internal Auditing At A University - An Example In Context," No. 1, pp. 143-147.

Frakes, Albert H. and Michael F. Foran. "A Framework For Examining The Evaluative Function Of Accounting Learning Activities," No. 1, pp. 148-154.

Liao, Shu S. "Learner Directed Instruction: Additional Evidence," No. 1, pp. 155-161.

Malcom, Robert E. "A Note On The Effect Of Product Aggregation In Determining Sales Variances," No. 1, pp. 162-169.

Burton, E. James, James C. McKeown and Jeffrey L. Shlosberg. "The Generation And Administration Of Examinations On Interactive Computer Systems," No. 1, pp. 170-178.

Silhan, Peter A. "The Recurring Problem Of Divergent Terminology," No. 1, pp. 179-181.

Stark, Maurice. "A Survey Of Lifo Inventory Application Techniques," No. 1, pp. 182-185.

Throckmorton, Jerry J. and John Talbott. "Computer-Supported Instruction In Financial Statement Analysis," No. 1, pp. 186-191.

Basu, S. and J. R. Hanna. "Interindustry Estimation Of General Price-Level Impact On Financial Information: A Comment," No. 1, pp. 192-197.

Petersen, Russell. "Interindustry Estimation Of General Price-Level Impact On Financial Information: More Data And A Reply," No. 1, pp. 198-203.

Blocher, Edward and Kung H. Chen. "Assessing Industry Risk By Ratio Analysis: A Comment," No. 1, pp. 204-209.

Falk, Haim and James A. Heintz. "Assessing Industry Risk By Ratio Analysis: A Reply," No. 1, pp. 210-215.

Falk, Haim and Lawrence A. Gordon. "Assessing Industry Risk By Ratio Analysis: Validation," No. 1, pp. 216-227.

Collins, Daniel W. and Melvin C. O'Connor. "An Examination Of The Association Between Accounting And Share Price Data In The Extractive Petroleum Industry: A Comment And Extension," No. 1, pp. 228-239.

Eskew, Robert K. "An Examination Of The Association Between Accounting And Share Price Data In The Extractive Petroleum Industry: A Reply," No. 1, pp. 240-246.

Kottas, John F. and Hon-Shiang Lau. "On The Accuracy Of Normalcy Approximation In Stochastic C-V-P Analysis: A Comment," No. 1, pp. 247-251.

Hayya, J. C., W. L. Ferrara and Erwin M. Saniga. "On The Accuracy Of Normalcy Approximation In Stochastic C-V-P Analysis: A Reply," No. 1, pp. 252-259.

Stephens, William L. "Earnings Per Share: A Flow Approach To Teaching Concepts And Procedures: A Comment," No. 1, pp. 260-262.

Thomas, Arthur L. "Arbitrary And Incorrigible Allocations: A Comment," No. 1, pp. 263-269.

Callen, Jeffrey L. "Financial Cost Allocations: A Game Theoretic Approach," No. 2, pp. 303-308.

Chan, James L. "Organizational Consensus Regarding The Relative Importance Of Research Output Indicators," No. 2, pp. 309-323.

Collins, Frank. "The Interaction Of Budget Characteristics And Personality Variables With Budgetary Response Attitudes," No. 2, pp. 324-335.

Demski, Joel S. and Gerald A. Feltham. "Economic Incentives In Budgetary Control Systems," No. 2, pp. 336-359.

Foster, Taylor W., III and Don Vickrey. "The Information Content Of Stock Dividend Announcements," No. 2, pp. 360-370.

Hicks, James O., Jr. "An Examination Of Accounting Interest Groups' Differential Perceptions Of Innovations," No. 2, pp. 371-388.

Kottas, John F., Amy Hing-Ling Lau and Hon-Shiang Lau. "A General Approach to Stochastic Management Planning Models: An Overview," No. 2, pp. 389-401.

Patton, James M. "An Empirical Investigation Of Some Effects Of Consolidating Municipal Financial Reports," No. 2, pp. 402-414.

Petri, Enrico and Roland A. Minch. "A Decision Model For Tax Preference Items," No. 2, pp. 415-428.

Rice, Steven J. "The Information Content Of Fully Diluted Earnings Per Share," No. 2, pp. 429-438.

Ruland, William. "The Accuracy Of Forecasts By Management And By Financial Analysts," No. 2, pp. 439-447.

Scapens, Robert W. "A Neoclassical Measure Of Profit," No. 2, pp. 448-469.

Battista, Marianne S. "The Effect Of Instructional Technology And Learner Characteristics On Cognitive Achievement In College Accounting," No. 2, pp. 477-485.

Crum, William F. "Survey Of Doctoral Programs In The United States," No. 2, pp. 486-494.

Grossman, Steven D. and Robert H. Strawser. "Accounting And Behavioral Concepts: A Classroom Approach," No. 2, pp. 495-500.

Smith, Jay M. "Audit Education For The 1980s," No. 2, pp. 501-509.

Stettler, Howard F. "On Giving Guidance To The CPA Candidate," No. 2, pp. 510-516.

Halperin, Robert. "Misleading Tax Figures - A Problem For Accountants: A Comment," No. 2, pp. 517-519.

Weber, Richard P. "Misleading Tax Figures - A Problem For Accountants: A Reply," No. 2, pp. 520-522.

Tiessen, Peter and J. H. Waterhouse. "The Contingency Theory Of Managerial Accounting: A Comment," No. 2, pp. 523-529.

Hayes, David C. "The Contingency Theory Of Managerial Accounting: A Reply," No. 2, pp. 530-533.

McIntyre, Edward V. "A Note On The Joint Variance: A Reply," No. 2, pp. 534-537.

Basu, S. "The Effects Of Earnings Yield On Assessments Of The Association Between Annual Accounting Income Numbers And Security Prices," No. 3, pp. 599-625.

Schultz, Joseph J., Jr. and Sandra G. Gustavson. "Actuaries' Perceptions Of Variables Affecting The Independent Auditor's Legal Liability," No. 3, pp. 626-641.

Firth, Michael. "Qualified Audit Reports: Their Impact On Investment Decisions," No. 3, pp. 642-650.

Crichfield, Timothy, Thomas Dyckman and Josef Lakonishok. "An Evaluation Of Security Analysts' Forecasts," No. 3, pp. 651-668.

Reneau, J. Hal. "CAV Bounds In Dollar Unit Sampling: Some Simulation Results," No. 3, pp. 669-680.

McGhee, Walter, Michael D. Shields and Jacob G. Birnberg. "The Effects Of Personality On A Subject's Information Processing," No. 3, pp. 681-697.

Kottas, John F. and Hon-Shiang Lau. "Direct Simulation In Stochastic CVP Analysis," No. 3, pp. 698-707.

Hicks, Sam A. "Choosing The Form For Business Tax Incentives," No. 3, pp. 708-716.

Hakansson, Nils H. "Where We Are In Accounting: A Review Of 'Statement On Accounting Theory And Theory Acceptance'," No. 3, pp. 717-725.

Boley, Richard and Paul Danos. "The Use Of LEXIS In Accounting Pedagogy - Preliminary Observations," No. 3, pp. 730-735.

Burns, Jane O. "Professors' Foreign Travel Expenses: Deductible Or Nondeductible?," No. 3, pp. 736-745.

Holder, William W. "Graduate-Level Public Sector Accounting: Status And Forecast," No. 3, pp. 746-751.

Rayburn, Frank R. and E. H. Bonfield. "Schools Of Accountancy: Attitudes And Attitude Structure," No. 3, pp. 752-765.

Blocher, Edward. "Sampling For Integrated Audit Objectives - A Comment," No. 3, pp. 766-772.

Ijiri, Yuji and Robert S. Kaplan. "Sampling For Integrated Audit Objectives - A Replay," No. 3, pp. 773-774.

Palmon, Dan and Lee J. Seidler. "Current Value Reporting Of Real Estate Companies And A Possible Example Of Market Inefficiency," No. 3, pp. 776-790.

Shank, John K. and Richard J. Murdock. "Comparability In The Application Of Reporting Standards: Some Further Evidence," No. 3, pp. 824-835.

Imhoff, Eugene A., Jr. "The Representativeness Of Management Earnings Forecasts," No. 4, pp. 836-850.

Abdel-Khalik, A. Rashad and James C. McKeown. "Understanding Accounting Changes In An Efficient Market: Evidence

Of Differential Reaction," No. 4, pp. 851-868.

Imhoff, Eugene A., Jr. "Employment Effects On Auditor Independence," No. 4, pp. 869-881.

Hughes, John S. "Toward A Contract Basis Of Valuation In Accounting," No. 4, pp. 882-894.

Friedman, Laurence A. "Exit-Price Liabilities: An Analysis Of The Alternatives," No. 4, pp. 895-909.

Ng, David G. "An Information Economics Analysis Of Financial Reporting And External Auditing," No. 4, pp. 910-920.

Foster, Taylor W., III and Don Vickrey. "The Incremental Information Content Of The 10-K," No. 4, pp. 921-934.

Merville, Larry J. and J. William Petty. "Transfer Pricing For The Multinational Firm," No. 4, pp. 935-951.

Ketz, J. Edward. "The Validation Of Some General Price Level Estimating Models," No. 4, pp. 952-960.

Jaggi, Bikki. "A Note On Information Content Of Corporate Annual Earnings Forecasts," No. 4, pp. 961-969.

Lampe, James C. "A Practical EDP Audit-Retrieval System For Education," No. 4, pp. 970-978.

Misiewicz, Kevin M. "The Tax Nucleus Of Gains And Losses," No. 4, pp. 979-984.

Pawliczek, Ronald B. "Modification Of Examinations: A Focus On Individual Weaknesses," No. 4, pp. 985-988.

Burdick, Richard K. and J. Hal Reneau. "Within-Item Variation: A Stochastic Approach To Audit Uncertainty - A Comment," No. 4, pp. 989-992.

Barkman, Arnold I. "Within-Item Variation: A Stochastic Approach To Audit Uncertainty - A Reply," No. 4, pp. 993-996.

Keys, David E. and Curtis Norton. "Estimation Error In Income Determination: A Comment," No. 4, pp. 997-1002.

Albrecht, William Steve. "Estimation Error In Income Determination: A Reply," No. 4, pp. 1003-1004.

Weinstein, Edward A. "Forging Nonprofit Accounting Principles," No. 4, pp. 1005-1016.

Accounting Review
Volume 54, 1979

Prakash, Prem and Shyam Sunder. "The Case Against Separation Of Current Operating Profit And Holding Gain," No. 1, pp. 1-22.

Buzby, Stephen L. and Haim Falk. "Demand For Social Responsibility Information By University Investors," No. 1, pp. 23-37.

Beaver, William H. and Joel S. Demski. "The Nature Of Income Measurement," No. 1, pp. 38-46.

Holmes, William. "Governmental Accounting In Colonial Massachusetts," No. 1, pp. 47-57.

Halperin, Robert. "The Effects Of LIFO Inventory Costing On Resource Allocation: A Public Policy Perspective," No. 1, pp. 58-71.

Norton, Curtis L. and Ralph E. Smith. "A Comparison Of General Price Level And Historical Cost Financial Statements In The Prediction Of Bankruptcy," No. 1, pp. 72-87.

Mayer-Sommer, Alan P. "Understanding And Acceptance Of The Efficient Markets Hypothesis And Its Accounting Implications," No. 1, pp. 88-106.

Eskew, Robert K. "The Forecasting Of Accounting Risk Measures: Some Additional Evidence," No. 1, pp. 107-118.

Nikolai, Loren A. and Rick Elam. "The Pollution Control Tax Incentive: A Non-Incentive," No. 1, pp. 119-131.

Amernic, Joel and Robin Enns. "Levels Of Cognitive Complexity And Design Of An Accounting Curriculum," No. 1, pp. 133-146.

Bailes, Jack C. "Lectures Versus Personalized Instruction: An Experimental Study In Elementary Managerial Accounting," No. 1, pp. 147-154.

Delaney, Patrick R., David E. Keyes, Curtis L. Norton and John R. Simon. "An Admission Test For Intermediate Accounting," No. 1, pp. 155-162.

Pope, Thomas R. "A Flowchart Analysis Of The Federal Tax Concept Of Earnings And Profits," No. 1, pp. 163-169.

Ashton, Robert H. "Some Implications Of Parameter Sensitivity Research For Judgment Modeling In Accounting," No. 1, pp. 170-179.

Blocher, Edward and Clyde Stickney. "Duration And Risk Assessments In Capital Budgeting," No. 1, pp. 180-188.

Jensen, Robert E. "Fantasyland Accounting Research: Let's Make Pretend," No. 1, pp. 189-196.

Ferrara, William L. "Fantasyland Accounting Research: Let's Make Pretend: Comment," No. 1, pp. 197-198.

Snowball, Doug. "Human Resource Accounting Information: A Comment Concerning Demand Characteristics," No. 1, pp. 199-204.

Hendricks, James A. "Human Resource Accounting Information: A Reply Concerning Demand Characteristics," No. 1, pp. 205-208.

Jaggi, Bikki. "A Comment On Motivational Considerations In Cost Allocation Systems: A Conditioning Theory Approach," No. 1, pp. 209-214.

Bodnar, George and Edward Lusk. "Operant Conditioning: A Discussion Of Its Relevance Regarding Institutional Control," No. 1, pp. 215-220.

Brooks, Kenneth and Richard Schroeder. "Management Strategy In A Large Accounting Firm: A Comment," No. 1, pp. 221-223.

Baker, C. Richard. "Management Strategy In A Large Accounting Firm: A Reply," No. 1, p. 224.

Watts, Ross L. and Jerold L. Zimmerman. "The Demand For And Supply Of Accounting Theories: The Market For Excuses," No. 2, pp. 273-305.

Revsine, Lawrence. "Technological Changes And Replacement Costs: A Beginning," No. 2, pp. 306-322.

Yamey, Basil S. "Compound Journal Entries In Early Treatises On Bookkeeping," No. 2, pp. 323-329.

Petri, Enrico and Jack Gelfand. "The Production Function: A New Perspective In Capital Maintenance," No. 2, pp. 330-345.

Abdel-Magid, Moustafa F. "Toward A Better Understanding Of The Role Of Measurement In Accounting," No. 2, pp. 346-357.

Dittman, David and Prem Prakash. "Cost Variance Investigation: Markovian Control Versus Optimal Control," No. 2, pp. 358-373.

Nichols, Donald R., Jeffrey J. Tsay and Paula D. Larkin. "Investor Trading Responses To Differing Characteristics Of Voluntarily Disclosed Earnings Forecasts," No. 2, pp. 376-382.

Hadley, Galen D. and Thomas B. Balke. "A Comparison Of Academic And Practitioner Views Of Current Levels In The Undergraduate Accounting Curriculum," No. 2, pp. 383-389.

Stallman, James C. "A Simplified Graphical Display Of Production And Sales Volume Effects On Absorption Costing Income," No. 2, pp. 390-395.

Wilson, David A. "On The Pedagogy Of Financial Accounting," No. 2, pp. 396-401.

Zeisel, Gerald and Ralph W. Estes. "Accounting And Public Service," No. 2, pp. 402-408.

Johnson, W. Bruce. "A Test Of The Expectancy Theory Of Motivation In An Accounting Environment: A Comment," No. 2, pp. 409-411.

Ferris, Kenneth R. "A Test Of The Expectancy Theory Of Motivation In An Accounting Environment: A Response," No. 2, pp. 412-413.

Liao, Shu S. "The Effect Of The Separation Of Ownership From Control On Accounting Policy Decisions: A Comment," No. 2, pp. 414-416.

Smith, E. Daniel. "The Effect Of The Separation Of Ownership From Control On Accounting Policy Decisions: A Reply," No. 2, pp. 417-420.

Stickney, Clyde P. "Current Issues In The Measurement And Disclosure Of Corporate Income Taxes," No. 2, pp. 421-433.

Lev, Baruch. "The Impact Of Accounting Regulation On The Stock Market: The Case Of Oil And Gas Companies," No. 3, pp. 485-503.

Zimmerman, Jerold L. "The Costs And Benefits Of Cost Allocations," No. 3, pp. 504-521.

Grove, Hugh D. and Richard S. Savich. "Attitude Research In Accounting: A Model For Reliability And Validity Considerations," No. 3, pp. 522-537.

Madeo, Silvia A. "An Empirical Analysis Of Tax Court Decisions In Accumulated Earnings Cases," No. 3, pp. 538-553.

Englebrecht, Ted D. and Robert W. Jamison, Jr. "An Empirical Inquiry Into The Role Of The Tax Court In The Valuation Of Property For Charitable Contribution Purposes," No. 3, pp. 554-562.

Blocher, Edward. "Performance Effects Of Different Audit Staff Assignment Strategies," No. 3, pp. 563-573.

Vatter, William J. "State Of The Art - Non-Business Accounting," No. 3, pp. 574-584.

Brown, Lawrence D. and Michael S. Rozeff. "The Predictive Value Of Interim Reports For Improving Forecasts Of Future Quarterly Earnings," No. 3, pp. 585-591.

Bentz, William F. "Computer Extended Reciprocal Allocation Methods," No. 3, pp. 595-603.

Krogstad, Jack L. and Daniel S. Dexter. "National Automated Accounting Research System - A Challenge For Auditing Education," No. 3, pp. 604-608.

Mehl, Arthur G. and Lucille E. Lammers. "A Report And Analysis Of The Accountancy Faculty Recruiting Surveys Of 1975-1978," No. 3, pp. 609-617.

Morley, Michael F. "The Value Added Statement In Britain," No. 3, pp. 618-629.

Dillard, Jesse F. and James Jiambalvo. "Expectancy Theory In A Budgetary Setting: A Comment," No. 3, pp. 630-634.

Rockness, Howard. "Expectancy Theory In A Budgetary Setting: A Reply," No. 3, pp. 635-636.

Horvitz, Jerome S. and D. R. Finley. "A Macro-Case Analysis Approach To Tax Research - A Comment," No. 3, pp. 637-640.

Misiewicz, Kevin M. "A Macro-Case Analysis Approach To Tax Research - A Reply," No. 3, pp. 641-642.

Chan, K. H., S. F. Lam and Roger Tang. "Probabilistic Approaches To Return On Investment And Residual Income: A Comment," No. 3, pp. 643-649.

Ferrara, William L. "Probabilistic Approaches To Return On Investment And Residual Income: A Reply," No. 3, pp. 650-651.

McCarthy, William E. "An Entity-Relationship View Of Accounting Models," No. 4, pp. 667-686.

Shih, Wei. "A General Decision Model For Cost-Volume-Profit Analysis Under Uncertainty," No. 4, pp. 687-706.

Kenis, Izzettin. "Effects Of Budgetary Goal Characteristics On Managerial Attitudes And Performance," No. 4, pp. 707-721.

Deakin, Edward B., III. "An Analysis Of Differences Between Non-Major Oil Firms Using Successful Efforts And Full Cost Methods," No. 4, pp. 722-734.

Benbasat, Izak and Albert S. Dexter. "Value And Events Approaches To Accounting: An Experimental Evaluation," No. 4, pp. 735-749.

Scott, Richard A. "Owners' Equity, The Anachronistic Element," No. 4, pp. 750-763.

Chambers, R. J. "Canning's 'The Economics Of Accountancy' - After 50 Years," No. 4, pp. 764-775.

Pastena, Victor. "Some Evidence On The SEC's System Of Continuous Disclosure," No. 4, pp. 776-783.

Baker, Kenneth R. and Robert E. Taylor. "A Linear Programming Framework For Cost Allocation And External Acquisition When Reciprocal Services Exist," No. 4, pp. 784-790.

Byars, Richard B. "Income Tax Liability: A Classroom Approach," No. 4, pp. 791-793.

Engstrom, John H. "Public Sector Accounting Education: Status Update And Extension," No. 4, pp. 794-799.

Horvitz, Jerome S. and Herbert L. Jensen. "Systematic Evaluations Of Tax Accounting Textbooks," No. 4, pp. 800-806.

Benis, Martin. "The Non-Consolidated Finance Company Subsidiary," No. 4, pp. 808-814.

Burnett, Tom, Thomas E. King and Valdean C. Lembke. "Equity Method Reporting For Major Finance Company Subsidiaries," No. 4, pp. 815-823.

Abdel-Magid, Moustafa F. "General Price-Level-Adjusted Historical-Cost Statements And The Ratio Scale View: A Comment," No. 4, pp. 825-829.

Vickrey, D. W. "In Defense Of GPLAHCSATRSV," No. 4, pp. 830-839.

Accounting Review
Volume 55, 1980

Dopuch, Nicholas and Shyam Sunder. "FASB's Statements On Objectives And Elements Of Financial Accounting: A Review," No. 1, pp. 1-21.

Baran, Aric, Josef Lakonishok and Aharon R. Ofer. "The Information Content Of General Price Level Adjusted Earnings: Some Empirical Evidence," No. 1, pp. 22-35.

Casey, Cornelius J., Jr. "The Variation In Accounting Information Load: The Effect On Loan Officers' Predictions Of Bankruptcy," No. 1, pp. 36-49.

Pany, Kurt and Philip M. J. Reckers. "The Effects Of Gifts, Discounts, And Client Size On Perceived Auditor Independence," No. 1, pp. 50-61.

Williams, Paul F. "The Evaluative Relevance Of Social Data," No. 1, pp. 62-77.

Dhaliwal, Dan S. "The Effect Of The Firm's Capital Structure On The Choice Of Accounting Methods," No. 1, pp. 78-84.

Hughes, John S. and James H. Scheiner. "Efficiency Properties Of Mutually Satisfactory Cost Allocations," No. 1, pp. 85-95.

Jaggi, Bikki. "Further Evidence On The Accuracy Of Management Forecasts Vis-A-Vis Analysts' Forecasts," No. 1, pp. 96-101.

Boley, Richard and Paul Danos. "Awareness And Usage Of LEXIS By Accounting Educators: A Survey," No. 1, pp. 102-106.

Booker, Jon A. and John K. Harris. "A Project To Enrich The Study Of Financial Reporting," No. 1, pp. 107-110.

Owens, Robert W. "Cash Flow Variance Analysis," No. 1, pp. 111-116.

Pushkin, Ann B. "Presenting Beta Risk To Students," No. 1, pp. 117-122.

Snowball, Doug and William A. Collins. "Televised Accounting Instruction Attitudes And Performance: A Field Experiment," No. 1, pp. 123-133.

Spiceland, J. David, Vincent C. Brenner and Bart P. Hartman. "Standards For Programs And Schools Of Professional Accounting: Accounting Group Perceptions," No. 1, pp. 134-143.

Kaback, Hoffer. "Behind The Balance Sheet: A Case Study In Accounting Analysis," No. 1, pp. 144-167.

Chen, Kung H. and Richard W. Metcalf. "The Relationship Between Pollution Control Record And Financial Indicators Revisited," No. 1, pp. 168-177.

Spicer, Barry H. "The Relationship Between Pollution Control Record And Financial Indicators Revisited: Further Comment," No. 1, pp. 178-185.

Bowman, Robert G. "The Debt Equivalence Of Leases: An Empirical Investigation," No. 2, pp. 237-253.

Samuelson, Richard A. "Should Replacement-Cost Changes Be Included In Income?," No. 2, pp. 254-268.

Hamlen, Susan S., William A. Hamlen, Jr. and John Tschirhart. "The Use Of The Generalized Shapley Allocation In Joint Cost Allocation," No. 2, pp. 269-287.

Bromwich, Michael. "The Possibility Of Partial Accounting Standards," No. 2, pp. 288-300.

Osteryoung, Jerome S., Daniel E. McCarty and Karen Fortin. "A Note On The Optimal Tax Lives For Assets Qualifying For The Investment Tax Credit," No. 2, pp. 301-306.

Schultz, Joseph J., Jr. and Kurt Pany. "The Independent Auditor's Civil Liability - An Overview," No. 2, pp. 319-326.

Klaassen, Jan. "An Accounting Court: The Impact Of The Enterprise Chamber On Financial Reporting In The Netherlands," No. 2, pp. 327-341.

Elgers, Pieter T. "Accounting-Based Risk Predictions: A Re-Examination," No. 3, pp. 389-408.

Whittington, Ray and Gerald Whittenburg. "Judicial Classification Of Debt Versus Equity - An Empirical Study," No. 3, pp. 409-418.

Yamey, Basil S. "The Index To The Ledger: Some Historical Notes," No. 3, pp. 419-425.

Nair, R. D. and Werner G. Frank. "The Impact Of Disclosure And Measurement Practices On International Accounting Classifications," No. 3, pp. 426-450.

Firth, Michael. "Perceptions Of Auditor Independence And Official Ethical Guidelines," No. 3, pp. 451-466.

Anderson, John C. and Alan W. Frankle. "Voluntary Social Reporting: An Iso-Beta Portfolio Analysis," No. 3, pp. 467-479.

Brief, Richard P., Barbara Merino and Ira Weiss. "Cumulative Financial Statements," No. 3, pp. 480-490.

Kida, Thomas E. and Ronald C. Mannino. "Job Selection Criteria Of Accounting Ph.D. Students And Faculty Members," No. 3, pp. 491-500.

Pratt, Jamie. "The Effects Of Personality On A Subject's Information Processing: A Comment," No. 3, pp. 501-506.

Birnberg, Jacob G., Michael D. Shields and Walter McGhee. "The Effects Of Personality On A Subject's Information Processing: A Reply," No. 3, pp. 507-510.

Solomon, Ira and Paul J. Beck. "A Comparison Of General Price Level And Historical Cost Financial Statements In The Prediction Of Bankruptcy: A Comment," No. 3, pp. 511-515.

Norton, Curtis L. and Ralph E. Smith. "A Comparison Of General Price Level And Historical Cost Financial Statements In The Prediction Of Bankruptcy: A Reply," No. 3, pp. 516-521.

Whittred, G. P. "Audit Qualification And The Timeliness Of Corporate Annual Reports," No. 4, pp. 563-577.

Hamlen, Susan S. "A Chance-Constrained Mixed Integer Programming Model For Internal Control Design," No. 4, pp. 578-593.

Senatra, Phillip T. "Role Conflict, Role Ambiguity, And Organizational Climate In A Public Accounting Firm," No. 4, pp. 594-603.

Toba, Yoshihide. "A Semantic Meaning Analysis Of The Ultimate Proposition To Be Verified By Independent Auditors," No. 4, pp. 604-619.

Finnerty, Joseph E., Rick N. Fitzsimmons and Thomas W. Oliver. "Lease Capitalization And Systematic Risk," No. 4, pp. 631-639.

Dittman, David A., Hervey A. Juris and Lawrence Revsine. "Unrecorded Human Assets: A Survey Of Accounting Firms' Training Programs," No. 4, pp. 640-648.

Ashton, Robert H. and Robert E. Hylas. "The Return Of 'Problem' Confirmation Requests By The U.S. Postal Service," No. 4, pp. 649-657.

Baldwin, Bruce A. "On Positioning The Quiz: An Empirical Analysis," No. 4, pp. 664-671.

Horvitz, Jerome S. and Michael J. Tucker. "Clinical Practice Problems In Tax Education," No. 4, pp. 672-679.

Weil, Roman L. "Managing Earnings Using An Insurance Subsidiary: A Case Of Restraint By Sears/Allstate," No. 4, pp. 680-684.

Weinstein, Edward A. "Forging Nonprofit Accounting Principles - An Update," No. 4, pp. 685-691.

Accounting Review
Volume 56, 1981

Bowen, Robert M. "Valuation Of Earnings Components In The Electric Utility Industry," No. 1, pp. 1-22.

Beaver, William H. "Market Efficiency," No. 1, pp. 23-37.

Boatsman, James R. and Elba F. Baskin. "Asset Valuation With Incomplete Markets," No. 1, pp. 38-53.

Nordhauser, Susan L. and John L. Kramer. "Repeal Of The Deferral Privilege For Earnings From Direct Foreign Investments: An Analysis," No. 1, pp. 54-69.

Ro, Byung T. "The Disclosure Of Replacement Cost Accounting Data And Its Effect On Transaction Volumes," No. 1, pp. 70-84.

Balachandran, Bala V. and Ram T. S. Ramakrishnan. "Joint Cost Allocation: A Unified Approach," No. 1, pp. 85-96.

Dykxhoorn, Hans J. and Kathleen E. Sinning. "Wirtschaftsprufer Perception And Auditor Independence," No. 1, pp. 97-107.

Carter, William K. "A Benefits Approach To Certain Accounting Policy Choices," No. 1, pp. 108-114.

Balachandran, K. R., Richard A. Maschmeyer and J. Leslie Livingstone. "Product Warranty Period: A Markovian Approach To Estimation And Analysis Of Repair And Replacement Costs," No. 1, pp. 115-124.

Mayer-Sommer, Alan P. and Stephen E. Loeb. "Fostering More Successful Professional Socialization Among Accounting Students," No. 1, pp. 125-136.

Friedman, Mark E. "The Effect On Achievement Of Using The Computer As A Problem-Solving Tool In The Intermediate Accounting Course," No. 1, pp. 137-143.

Edwards, James B., Robert W. Ingram and Howard P. Sanders. "Developing Teaching Skills In Doctoral Programs: The Current Status And Perceived Needs," No. 1, pp. 144-157.

Spiller, Earl A., Jr. "Capital Expenditure Analysis: An Incident Process Case," No. 1, pp. 158-165.

Swieringa, Robert J. "The Silver-Lined Bonds Of Sunshine Mining," No. 1, pp. 166-176.

Freeman, Robert N. "The Disclosure Of Replacement Cost Accounting Data And Its Effect On Transaction Volumes: A Comment," No. 1, pp. 177-180.

Ro, Byung T. "The Disclosure Of Replacement Cost Accounting Data And Its Effect On Transaction Volumes: A Reply," No. 1, pp. 181-187.

Noreen, Eric and James Sepe. "Market Reactions To Accounting Policy Deliberations: The Inflation Accounting Case," No. 2, pp. 253-269.

Johnson, Johnny R., Robert A. Leitch and John Neter. "Characteristics Of Errors In Accounts Receivable And Inventory Audits," No. 2, pp. 270-293.

Schreuder, Hein. "Employees And The Corporate Social

Report: The Dutch Case," No. 2, pp. 294-308.

Vigeland, Robert L. "The Market Reaction To Statement Of Financial Accounting Standards No. 2," No. 2, pp. 309-325.

Fried, Dov and Allen Schiff. "CPA Switches And Associated Market Reactions," No. 2, pp. 326-341.

Crosby, Michael A. "Bayesian Statistics In Auditing: A Comparison Of Probability Elicitation Techniques," No. 2, pp. 355-365.

Uecker, Wilfred C. "Behavioral Accounting Research As A Source For Experiential Teaching Aids: An Example," No. 2, pp. 366-382.

Revsine, Lawrence. "A Capital Maintenance Approach To Income Measurement," No. 2, pp. 383-389.

Lowenthal, Franklin. "A Decision Model For The Alternative Tax On Capital Gains," No. 2, pp. 390-394.

Dillon, Gadis J. "The Business Combination Process," No. 2, pp. 395-399.

Finley, D. R. and Woody M. Liao. "A General Decision Model For Cost-Volume-Profit Analysis Under Uncertainty: A Comment," No. 2, pp. 400-403.

Shih, Wei. "A General Decision Model For Cost-Volume-Profit Analysis Under Uncertainty: A Reply," No. 2, pp. 404-408.

Uecker, Wilfred C., Arthur P. Brief and William R. Kinney, Jr. "Perception Of The Internal And External Auditor As A Deterrrent To Corporate Irregularities," No. 3, pp. 465-478.

Eichenseher, John W. and Paul Danos. "The Analysis Of Industry-Specific Auditor Concentration: Towards An Explanatory Model," No. 3, pp. 479-492.

Fried, Dov and Joshua Livnat. "Interim Statements: An Analytical Examination Of Alternative Accounting Techniques," No. 3, pp. 493-509.

Johnson, H. Thomas. "Toward A New Understanding Of Nineteenth-Century Cost Accounting," No. 3, pp. 510-518.

Larcker, David F. "The Perceived Importance Of Selected Information Characteristics For Strategic Capital Budgeting Decisions," No. 3, pp. 519-538.

Lee, Geoffrey A. "The Francis Willughby Executorship Accounts, 1672-1682: An Early Double-Entry System In England," No. 3, pp. 539-553.

Carlson, Marvin L. and James W. Lamb. "Constructing A Theory Of Accounting - An Axiomatic Approach," No. 3, pp. 554-573.

Koch, Bruce S. "Income Smoothing: An Experiment," No. 3, pp. 574-586.

Peragallo, Edward. "Choosing Procedures In The 15th Century Ledger Of Jachomo Badoer, A Venetian Merchant," No. 3, pp. 587-595.

Weber, Richard P. and W. C. Stevenson. "Evaluations Of Accounting Journals And Department Quality," No. 3, pp. 596-612.

Howard, Thomas P. "Attitude Measurement: Some Further Considerations," No. 3, pp. 613-621.

Stickney, Clyde P. "A Note On Optimal Tax Depreciation Research," No. 3, pp. 622-625.

Crum, William F. "1980 Survey Of Doctoral Programs In Accounting In The United States," No. 3, pp. 634-641.

Messere, Carl J. and Gilroy J. Zuckerman. "An Alternative Approach To Depreciation Switches," No. 3, pp. 642-652.

Windal, Floyd W. "Publishing For A Varied Public: An Empirical Study," No. 3, pp. 653-658.

Skousen, Clifford R. "A Profile And Index Of The CMA Examination - An Update," No. 3, pp. 659-665.

Wallace, Wanda A. "Internal Control Reporting Practices In The Municipal Sector," No. 3, pp. 666-689.

Lilien, Steven and Victor Pastena. "Intramethod Comparability: The Case Of The Oil And Gas Industry," No. 3, pp. 690-703.

Bejan, Mary. "On The Application Of Rational Choice Theory To Financial Reporting Controversies: A Comment On Cushing," No. 3, pp. 704-712.

Cushing, Barry E. "On The Possibility Of Optimal Accounting Principles: A Restatement," No. 3, pp. 713-718.

Osteryoung, Jerome S., Daniel M. McCarty and Karen Fortin. "A Note On Optimal Depreciation Research - A Comment," No. 3, pp. 719-721.

Maher, Michael W. "The Impact Of Regulation On Controls: Firms' Response To The Foreign Corrupt Practices Act," No. 4, pp. 751-770.

Hirst, Mark K. "Accounting Information And The Evaluation Of Subordinate Performance: A Situational Approach," No. 4, pp. 771-784.

Shockley, Randolph A. "Perceptions Of Auditors' Independence: An Empirical Analysis," No. 4, pp. 785-800.

Balachandran, Bala V. and Andris A. Zoltners. "An Interactive Audit-Staff Scheduling Decision Support System," No. 4, pp. 801-812.

Merchant, Kenneth A. "The Design Of The Corporate Budgeting System: Influences On Managerial Behavioral And Performance," No. 4, pp. 813-829.

Ingram, Robert W. and Ronald M. Copeland. "Municipal Accounting Information And Voting Behavior," No. 4, pp. 830-843.

Brownell, Peter. "Participation In Budgeting, Locus Of Control And Organizational Effectiveness," No. 4, pp. 844-860.

Wolf, Frank M. "The Nature Of Managerial Work: An Investigation Of The Work Of The Audit Manager," No. 4, pp. 861-881.

Bailey, William T. "The Effects Of Audit Reports On Chartered Financial Analysts' Perceptions Of The Sources Of Financial-Statement And Audit-Report Messages," No. 4, pp. 882-896.

Newman, D. Paul. "Coalition Formation In The APB And The FASB: Some Evidence On The Size Principle," No. 4, pp. 897-909.

Raman, K. K. "Financial Reporting And Municipal Bond Rating Changes," No. 4, pp. 910-926.

Hopwood, W. S., J. C. McKeown and P. Newbold. "Power Transformations In Time-Series Models Of Quarterly Earnings Per Share," No. 4, pp. 927-933.

Groomer, S. Michael. "An Experiment In Computer-Assisted Instruction For Introductory Accounting," No. 4, pp. 934-941.

Basu, S. "Market Reactions To Accounting Policy Deliberations: The Inflation Accounting Case Revisited," No. 4, pp. 942-954.

Noreen, Eric and James Sepe. "Market Reactions To Accounting Policy Deliberations: The Inflation Accounting Case Revisited - A Reply," No. 4, pp. 955-958.

Smith, Abbie and Thomas Dyckman. "The Impact Of Accounting Regulation On the Stock Market: The Case Of Oil And Gas Companies: A Comment," No. 4, pp. 959-966.

Ryder, Paul A. "Comments On Wolf's 'The Nature Of Managerial Work' - The Case For Unobtrusive Measures Revisited," No. 4, pp. 967-970.

Wolf, Frank M. "'The Nature Of Managerial Work - The Case For Unobtrusive Measures Revisited' - A Reply," No. 4, pp. 971-974.

Davis, Harry Zvi. "The Effects Of LIFO Inventory Costing On Resource Allocations: A Comment," No. 4, pp. 975-976.

Halperin, Robert. "The Effects Of LIFO Inventory Costing On Resource Allocations: A Reply," No. 4, pp. 977-979.

Lau, Amy Hing-Ling and Hon-Shiang Lau. "A Comment On Shih's General Decision Model For CVP Analysis," No. 4, pp. 980-983.

Shih, Wei. "A Comment On Shih's General Decision Model For CVP Analysis - A Reply," No. 4, pp. 984-985.

Accounting Review
Volume 57, 1982

Collins, Daniel W., Michael S. Rozeff and William K. Salatka. "The SEC's Rejection Of SFAS No. 19: Tests Of Market Price Reversal," No. 1, pp. 1-17.

Dietrich, J. Richard and Robert S. Kaplan. "Empirical Analysis Of The Commercial Loan Classification Decision," No. 1, pp. 18-38.

Danos, Paul and Eugene A. Imhoff. "Auditor Review Of Financial Forecasts: An Analysis Of Factors Affecting Reasonableness Judgments," No. 1, pp. 39-54.

Kinney, William R., Jr. and Wilfred C. Uecker. "Mitigating The Consequences Of Anchoring In Auditor Judgments," No. 1, pp. 55-69.

Kramer, Sandra S. "Blockage: Valuation Of Large Blocks Of Publicly Traded Stocks For Tax Purposes," No. 1, pp. 70-87.

Ballew, Van. "Technological Routineness And Intra-Unit Structure In CPA Firms," No. 1, pp. 88-104.

Gibbins, Michael and Frank M. Wolf. "Auditors' Subjective Decision Environment - The Case Of A Normal External Audit," No. 1, pp. 105-124.

Balachandran, K. R. and Ralph E. Steuer. "An Interactive Model For The CPA Firm Audit Staff Planning Problem With Multiple Objectives," No. 1, pp. 125-140.

Bailey, William T. "An Appraisal Of Research Designs Used To Investigate The Information Content Of Audit Reports," No. 1, pp. 141-146.

Elikai, Fara and Shane Moriarity. "Variance Analysis With PERT/COST," No. 1, pp. 161-170.

Hobbs, James B. and D. R. Bainbridge. "Nonmonetary Exchange Transactions: Clarification Of APB No. 29," No. 1, pp. 171-175.

Lebar, Mary Ann. "A General Semantics Analysis Of Selected Sections Of The 10-K, The Annual Report To Shareholders, And The Financial Press Release," No. 1, pp. 176-189.

Anderson, James A. "A Discussion Of 'Coalition Formation In The APB And The FASB'," No. 1, pp. 190-195.

Newman, D. Paul. "Coalition Formation In The APB And The FASB: A Reply," No. 1, pp. 196-199.

Felix, William L., Jr. and William R. Kinney, Jr. "Research In The Auditor's Opinion Formulation Process: State Of The Art," No. 2, pp. 245-271.

Chow, Chee W. "The Demand For External Auditing: Size, Debt And Ownership Influences," No. 2, pp. 272-291.

Salamon, Gerald L. "Cash Recovery Rates And Measures Of Firm Profitability," No. 2, pp. 292-302.

Nobes, Christopher W. "The Gallerani Account Book Of 1305-1308," No. 2, pp. 303-310.

Weber, Ron. "Audit Trail System Support In Advanced Computer-Based Accounting Systems," No. 2, pp. 311-325.

Chow, Chee W. and Steven J. Rice. "Qualified Audit Opinions And Auditor Switching," No. 2, pp. 326-335.

Cohen, Susan I. and Martin Loeb. "Public Goods, Common Inputs, And The Efficiency Of Full Cost Allocations," No. 2, pp. 336-347.

Vigeland, Robert L. "Dilution Of Earnings Per Share In An Option Pricing Framework," No. 2, pp. 348-357.

Elgers, Pieter T. and Dennis Murray. "The Impact Of The Choice Of Market Index On The Empirical Evaluation Of Accounting Risk Measures," No. 2, pp. 358-375.

Walther, Larry M. "A Comparison Of Estimated And Reported Historical Cost/Constant Dollar Data," No. 2, pp. 376-383.

Leitch, Robert A., John Neter, Robert Plante and Prabhakant Sinha. "Modified Multinomial Bounds For Larger Numbers Of Errors In Audits," No. 2, pp. 384-400.

Howell, William C. and L. Todd Johnson. "An Evaluation Of The Compressed-Course Format For Instruction In Accounting," No. 2, pp. 403-413.

Williamson, Robert W. "Presenting Information Economics To Students," No. 2, pp. 414-419.

Croll, David B. "Cost Accounting In The CPA Examination - Revisited," No. 2, pp. 420-429.

Sepe, James. "The Impact Of The FASB's 1974 GPL Proposal On The Security Price Structure," No. 3, pp. 467-485.

Givoly, Dan and Dan Palmon. "Timeliness Of Annual Earnings Announcements: Some Empirical Evidence," No. 3, pp. 486-508.

Patell, James M. and Mark A. Wolfson. "Good News, Bad News, And The Intraday Timing Of Corporate Disclosures," No. 3, pp. 509-527.

Zeff, Stephen A. "Truth In Accounting: The Ordeal Of Kenneth MacNeal," No. 3, pp. 528-553.

McCarthy, William E. "The REA Accounting Model: A Generalized Framework For Accounting Systems In A Shared Data Environment," No. 3, pp. 554-578.

Verrecchia, Robert E. "An Analysis Of Two Cost Allocation Cases," No. 3, pp. 579-593.

Manes, Rene P., Soong H. Park and Robert Jensen. "Relevant Costs Of Intermediate Goods And Services," No. 3, pp. 594-606.

McIntyre, Edward V. "Interaction Effects Of Inflation Accounting Models And Accounting Techniques," No. 3, pp. 607-618.

Baldwin, Bruce A. and Keith R. Howe. "Secondary-Level Study Of Accounting And Subsequent Performance In The First College Course," No. 3, pp. 619-626.

Patton, James M. "Ratio Analysis And Efficient Markets In Introductory Financial Accounting," No. 3, pp. 627-630.

Warner, Stanley E., Jr. and Frederick D. Whitehurst. "A Graphical Approach To Lower Of Cost Or Market," No. 3, pp. 631-637.

Abdel-Khalik, A. Rashad and Bipin B. Ajinkya. "Returns to Informational Advantages: The Case Of Analysts' Forecast Revisions," No. 4, pp. 661-680.

Mensah, Yaw M. "A Dynamic Approach To The Evaluation Of Input-Variable Cost Center Performance," No. 4, pp. 681-700.

Standish, Peter E. M. and Swee-Im Ung. "Corporate Signaling, Asset Revaluations, And The Stock Prices Of British Companies," No. 4, pp. 701-715.

Outslay, Edmund and James E. Wheeler. "Separating The Annuity And Income Transfer Elements Of Social Security," No. 4, pp. 716-733.

Jiambalvo, James and Jamie Pratt. "Task Complexity And Leadership Effectiveness In CPA Firms," No. 4, pp. 734-750.

Hylas, Robert E. and Robert H. Ashton. "Audit Detection Of Financial Statement Errors," No. 4, pp. 751-765.

Brownell, Peter. "A Field Study Examination Of Budgetary Participation And Locus Of Control," No. 4, pp. 766-777.

Bowen, Robert M. and Gary L. Sundem. "Editorial And Publication Lags In The Accounting And Finance Literature," No. 4, pp. 778-784.

Paolillo, Joseph G. P. and Ralph W. Estes. "An Empirical Analysis Of Career Choice Factors Among Accountants, Attorneys, Engineers, And Physicians," No. 4, pp. 785-793.

Pratt, Jamie and Heidi Hadlich Chrisman. "Teaching The Statement Of Changes In Financial Position: An Empirical Study," No. 4, pp. 794-805.

Schipper, Katherine and Roman L. Weil. "Alternative Accounting Treatments For Pensions," No. 4, pp. 806-824.

Accounting Review
Volume 58, 1983

Christenson, Charles. "The Methodology Of Positive Accounting," No. 1, pp. 1-22.

Leftwich, Richard. "Accounting Information In Private Markets: Evidence From Private Lending Agreements," No. 1, pp. 23-42.

Mepham, Michael J. "Robert Hamilton's Contribution To Accounting," No. 1, pp. 43-57.

Larcker, David F. and V. Parker Lessig. "An Examination Of The Linear And Retrospective Process Tracing Approaches To Judgment Modeling," No. 1, pp. 58-77.

Johnson, W. Bruce. "Representativeness' In Judgmental Predictions Of Corporate Bankruptcy," No. 1, pp. 78-97.

Peragallo, Edward. "Development Of The Compound Entry In The 15th Century Ledger Of Jachomo Badoer. A Venetian Merchant," No. 1, pp. 98-104.

Gombola, Michael J. and J. Edward Ketz. "A Note On Cash Flow And Classification Patterns Of Financial Ratios," No. 1, pp. 105-114.

Frecka, Thomas J. and William S. Hopwood. "The Effects Of Outliers On The Cross-Sectional Distributional Properties Of Financial Ratios," No. 1, pp. 115-128.

Howe, Keith R. and Bruce A. Baldwin. "The Effects Of Evaluative Sequencing On Performance, Behavior, And Attitudes," No. 1, pp. 135-142.

Manes, Rene P. "Demand Elasticities: Supplements To Sales Budget Variance Reports," No. 1, pp. 143-156.

Abdel-Khalik, A. Rashad, Doug A. Snowball and John H. Wragge. "The Effects Of Certain Internal Audit Variables On The Planning Of External Audit Programs," No. 2, pp. 215-227.

Mensah, Yaw M. "The Differential Bankruptcy Predictive Ability Of Specific Price Level Adjustments: Some Empirical Evidence," No. 2, pp. 228-246.

Morse, Dale and Neal Ushman. "The Effect Of Information Announcements On The Market Microstructure," No. 2, pp. 247-258.

Schepanski, Albert and Wilfred Uecker. "Toward A Positive Theory Of Information Evaluation," No. 2, pp. 259-283.

Shields, Michael D. "Effects Of Information Supply And Demand On Judgment Accuracy: Evidence From Corporate Managers," No. 2, pp. 284-303.

Wilson, Robert. "Auditing: Perspectives From Multiperson Decision Theory," No. 2, pp. 305-318.

Jensen, Michael C. "Organization Theory And Methodology," No. 2, pp. 319-339.

Kaplan, Robert S. "Comments On Wilson And Jensen," No. 2, pp. 340-346.

Demski, Joel S. "Comments On Wilson And Jensen," No. 2, pp. 347-349.

Weick, Karl E. "Stress In Accounting Systems," No. 2, pp. 350-369.

Libby, Robert. "Comments On Weick," No. 2, pp. 370-374.

Ross, Stephen A. "Accounting And Economics," No. 2, pp. 375-380.

Hakansson, Nils H. "Comments On Weick And Ross," No. 2, pp. 381-384.

Barlev, Benzion. "Contingent Equity And The Dilutive Effect On EPS," No. 2, pp. 385-393.

Meek, Gary K. "U.S. Securities Market Responses To Alternative Earnings Disclosures Of Non-U.S. Multinational Corporations," No. 2, pp. 394-402.

Dilley, Steven C., Randall B. Hayes and Paul Steinbart. "Development Of A Paradigm For Applied Accounting Research: A Way Of Coping With Subject-Matter Complexity," No. 2, pp. 405-416.

Urbancic, Frank R. "University Library Collections Of Accounting Periodicals," No. 2, pp. 417-427.

Outslay, Edmund, John R. Robinson and Richard Boley. "A Framework For Utilizing Individual Return Problems In Introductory Courses," No. 2, pp. 428-438.

Stickney, Clyde P., Roman L. Weil and Mark A. Wolfson. "Income Taxes And Tax-Transfer Leases: General Electric's Accounting For A Molotov Cocktail," No. 2, pp. 439-459.

Chow, Chee W. "The Impacts Of Accounting Regulation On Bondholder And Shareholder Wealth: The Case Of The Securities Acts," No. 3, pp. 485-520.

Shane, Philip B. and Barry H. Spicer. "Market Response To Environmental Information Produced Outside The Firm," No. 3, pp. 521-538.

White, Richard A. "Employee Preferences For Nontaxable Compensation Offered In A Cafeteria Compensation Plan: An Empirical Study," No. 3, pp. 539-561.

Ingram, Robert W. and Eugene G. Chewning. "The Effect Of Financial Disclosure Regulation On Security Market Behavior," No. 3, pp. 562-580.

Schepanski, Albert A. "Test Of Theories Of Information Processing Behavior In Credit Judgment," No. 3, pp. 581-599.

Chen, Joyce T. "Cost Allocation And External Acquisition Of Services When Self-Services Exist," No. 3, pp. 600-605.

Larcker, David F., Renee E. Reder and Daniel T. Simon. "Trades By Insiders As Evidence Of The Existence Of Economic Consequences Of Accounting Standards," No. 3, pp. 606-620.

Wright, Arnold. "The Impact Of CPA Firm Size On Auditor Disclosure Preferences," No. 3, pp. 621-632.

Jain, Prem. "The Impact Of Accounting Regulation On The Stock Market: The Case Of Oil And Gas Companies: A Further Analysis," No. 3, pp. 633-638.

Reeve, James M. "The Five-Year Accounting Program As A Quality Signal," No. 3, pp. 639-646.

Chow, Chee W. "The Effects Of Job Standard Tightness And Compensation Scheme On Performance: An Exploration Of Linkages," No. 4, pp. 667-685.

Kaplan, Robert S. "Measuring Manufacturing Performance: A New Challenge For Managerial Accounting Research," No. 4, pp. 686-705.

Larcker, David F. and Lawrence Revsine. "The Oil And Gas Accounting Controversy: An Analysis Of Economic Consequences," No. 4, pp. 706-732.

Pesando, James E. and Carol K. Clarke. "Economic Models Of The Labor Market And Pension Accounting: An Exploratory Analysis," No. 4, pp. 733-748.

Wilkins, Trevor and Ian Zimmer. "The Effect Of Leasing And Different Methods Of Accounting For Leases On Credit Evaluations," No. 4, pp. 749-764.

Howard, Thomas P. and Loren A. Nikolai. "Attitude Measurement And Perceptions Of Accounting Faculty Publication Outlets," No. 4, pp. 765-776.

Thomas, Arthur L. "Use Of Microcomputer Spreadsheet Software In Preparing And Grading Complex Accounting Problems," No. 4, pp. 777-786.

Dillard, Jesse F. and Daniel L. Jensen. "The Auditor's Report: An Analysis Of Opinion," No. 4, pp. 787-798.

Nurnberg, Hugo. "Issues In Funds Statement Presentation," No. 4, pp. 799-812.

Chen, Joyce T. "The Effect Of Change Variation On Revenue And Cost Estimations For Break-Even Analysis: A Comment," No. 4, pp. 813-819.

Largay, James A., III and Jack W. Paul. "Market Efficiency And Legal Liability Of Auditors: Comment," No. 4, pp. 820-832.

Anderson, James A. and Kent E. St. Pierre. "Market Efficiency And Legal Liability: A Reply," No. 4, pp. 833-836.

Lowenthal, Franklin. "Product Warranty Period: A Markovian Approach To Estimation And Analysis Of Repair And Replacement Costs - A Comment," No. 4, pp. 837-838.

Accounting Review
Volume 59, 1984

Aranya, Nissim and Kenneth R. Ferris. "A Reexamination Of Accountants' Organizational-Professional Conflict," No. 1, pp. 1-15.

Demski, Joel S., James M. Patell and Mark A. Wolfson. "Decentralized Choice Of Monitoring Systems," No. 1, pp. 16-34.

McCray, John H. "A Quasi-Bayesian Audit Risk Model For Dollar Unit Sampling," No. 1, pp. 35-51.

Ijiri, Yuji and James Noel. "A Reliability Comparison Of The Measurement Of Wealth, Income, And Force," No. 1, pp. 52-63.

Schreuder, Hein and Jan Klaassen. "Confidential Revenue And Profit Forecasts By Management And Financial Analysts: Evidence From The Netherlands," No. 1, pp. 64-77.

Ashton, Robert H. "Integrating Research And Teaching In Auditing: Fifteen Cases On Judgment And Decision Making," No. 1, pp. 78-97.

Arens, Alvin A. and D. Dewey Ward. "The Use Of A Systems Understanding Aid In The Accounting Curriculum," No. 1, pp. 98-108.

Adelberg, Arthur H. and Joseph R. Razek. "The Cloze Procedure: A Methodology For Determining The Understandability Of Accounting Textbooks," No. 1, pp. 109-122.

Swieringa, Robert J. "When Current Is Noncurrent And Vice Versa!," No. 1, pp. 123-130.

Bathke, Allen W., Jr. and Kenneth S. Lorek. "The Relationships Between Time-Series Models And The Security Market's Expectation Of Quarterly Earnings," No. 2, pp. 163-176.

Daley, Lane Alan. "The Valuation Of Reported Pension Measures For Firms Sponsoring Defined Benefit Plans," No. 2, pp. 177-198.

Dharan, Bala G. "Expectation Models And Potential Information Content Of Oil And Gas Reserve Value Disclosures," No. 2, pp. 199-217.

Dworin, Lowell and Richard A. Grimlund. "Dollar Unit Sampling For Accounts Receivable And Inventory," No. 2, pp. 218-241.

St. Pierre, Kent and James A. Anderson. "An Analysis Of Factors Associated With Lawsuits Against Public Accountants," No. 2, pp. 242-263.

Gul, Ferdinand A. "The Joint And Moderating Role Of Personality And Cognitive Style On Decision Making," No. 2, pp. 264-277.

Walker, Martin. "Risk Attitudes, Value-Restricted Preferences And Public Choice Over Lotteries And Information Systems," No. 2, pp. 278-286.

Whittred, Greg and Ian Zimmer. "Timeliness Of Financial Reporting And Financial Distress," No. 2, pp. 287-295.

Williamson, Robert W. "Evidence On Selective Reporting Of Financial Ratios," No. 2, pp. 296-299.

Amernic, Joel H. and Thomas H. Beechy. "Accounting Students' Performance And Cognitive Complexity: Some Empirical Evidence," No. 2, pp. 300-313.

Arnold, Donald F. and Thomas J. Geiselhart. "Practitioners' Views On Five-Year Educational Requirements For CPAs," No. 2, pp. 314-324.

Wallace, Wanda A. "The Effects Of Delays By Accounting Policy-Setters In Reconciling The Accounting Treatment Of Stock Options And Stock Appreciation Rights," No. 2, pp. 325-341.

Zeff, Stephen A. and Sven-Erik Johansson. "The Curious Accounting Treatment Of The Swedish Government Loan To Uddeholm," No. 2, pp. 342-350.

Ashton, Alison Hubbard. "A Field Test Of Implications Of Laboratory Studies Of Decision Making," No.3,pp.361-375.

Baldwin, Bruce A. "Segment Earnings Disclosure And The Ability Of Security Analysts To Forecast Earnings Per Share," No. 3, pp. 376-389.

Kaplan, Robert S. "The Evolution Of Management Accounting," No. 3, pp. 390-418.

King, Raymond D. "The Effect Of Convertible Bond Equity Values On Dilution And Leverage," No. 3, pp. 419-431.

McDonald, Bill and Michael H. Morris. "The Relevance Of SFAS 33 Inflation Accounting Disclosures In The Adjustment Of Stock Prices To Inflation," No. 3, pp. 432-446.

Zeff, Stephen A. "Some Junctures In The Evolution Of The Process Of Establishing Accountng Principles In The U.S.A.: 1917-1972," No. 3, pp. 447-468.

Stone, Mary and Bruce Bublitz. "An Analysis Of The Reliability Of The FASB Data Bank Of Changing Price And Pension Information," No. 3, pp. 469-473.

Brockett, P., A. Charnes, W. W. Cooper and Hong-Chul Shin. "A Chance-Constrained Programming Approach To Cost-Volume-Profit Analysis," No. 3, pp. 474-487.

Marcinko, David and Enrico Petri. "Use Of The Production Function In Calculation Of Standard Cost Variances - An Extension," No. 3, pp. 488-495.

Dockweiler, Raymond C. and Carl G. Willis. "On The Use Of Entry Requirements For Undergraduate Accounting Programs," No. 3, pp. 496-504.

Revsine, Lawrence. "The Rationale Underlying The Functional Currency Choice," No. 3, pp. 505-514.

Chasteen, Lanny. "A Taxonomy Of Price Change Models," No. 3, pp. 515-523.

Smith, Millard E. "A Quasi-Bayesian Audit Risk Model For Dollar Unit Sampling: A Comment," No.3, pp. 524-525.

McCray, John H. "A Quasi-Bayesian Audit Risk Model For Dollar Unit Sampling: A Reply," No. 3, pp. 526-527.

Danos, Paul, Doris L. Holt and Eugene A. Imhoff, Jr. "Bond Raters' Use Of Management Financial Forecasts: An Experiment In Expert Judgment," No. 4, pp. 547-573.

Foster, George, Chris Olsen and Terry Shevlin. "Earnings Releases, Anomalies, And The Behavior Of Security Returns," No. 4, pp. 574-603.

Lamber, Richard A. "Income Smoothing As Rational Equilibrium Behavior," No. 4, pp. 604-618.

Porcano, Thomas M. "Distributive Justice And Tax Policy," No. 4, pp. 619-636.

Waller, William S. and William L. Felix, Jr. "The Effects Of Incomplete Outcome Feedback On Auditors' Self-Perceptions Of Judgment Ability," No. 4, pp. 637-646.

McKee, A. James, Jr., Timothy B. Bell and James R. Boatsman. "Management Preferences Over Accounting Standards: A Replication And Additional Tests," No. 4, pp. 647-659.

Edmonds, Thomas P. "On The Benefits Of Cumulative Exams: An Experimental Study," No. 4, pp. 660-668.

Mann, Harvey. "A Worksheet For Demonstrating The Articulation Of Financial Statements," No. 4, pp. 669-673.

Dunn, W. Marcus and Thomas W. Hall. "An Empirical Analysis Of The Relationships Between CPA Examination Candidate Attributes And Candidate Performance," No. 4, pp. 674-689.

Mohr, Rosanne M. and Steven C. Dilley. "Current Cost And ACRS Depreciation Expense: A Comparison," No. 4, pp. 690-701.

Accounting Review
Volume 60, 1985

Baber, William R. "Budget-Based Compensation And Discretionary Spending," No. 1, pp. 1-9.

Fellingham, John C. and Mark A. Wolfson. "Taxes And Risk Sharing," No. 1, pp. 10-17.

Moore, Michael L., Bert M. Steece and Charles W. Swenson. "Some Empirical Evidence On Taxpayer Rationality," No. 1, pp. 18-32.

Ricks, William E. and John S. Hughes. "Market Reactions To Non-Discretionary Accounting Change, The Case Of Long-Term Investments," No. 1, pp. 33-52.

Staubus, George J. "An Induced Theory Of Accounting Measurement," No. 1, pp. 53-75.

Tsui, Kam-Wah, Ella Mae Matsumura and Kwok-Leung Tsui. "Multinomial-Dirichlet Bounds For Dollar-Unit Sampling In Auditing," No. 1, pp. 76-96.

Umapathy, Srinivasan. "Teaching Behavioral Aspects Of Performance Evaluation: An Experiential Approach," No. 1, pp. 97-108.

Dietrich, J. Richard and James W. Deitrick. "Bond Exchanges In The Airline Industry: Analyzing Public Disclosures," No. 1, pp. 109-126.

Swieringa, Robert J. and Dale Morse. "Accounting For Hybrid Convertible Debentures," No. 1, pp. 127-133.

Ashton, Alison Hubbard. "Does Consensus Imply Accuracy In Accounting Studies Of Decision Making?," No. 2, pp. 173-185.

Bailey, Andrew D., Jr., Gordon Leon Duke, James Gerlach, Chen-En Ko, Rayman D. Meservy and Andrew B. Whinston. "TICOM And The Analysis Of Internal Controls," No. 2, pp. 186-201.

Knapp, Michael C. "Audit Conflict: An Empirical Study Of The Perceived Ability Of Auditors To Resist Management Pressure," No. 2, pp. 202-211.

Libby, Robert, James T. Artman and John J. Willingham. "Process Susceptibility, Control Risk, And Audit Planning," No. 2, pp. 212-230.

Scapens, Robert W. and J. Timothy Sale. "An International Study Of Accounting Practices In Divisionalized Companies And Their Associations With Organizational Variables," No. 2, pp. 231-247.

Schwartz, Kenneth B. and Krishnagopal Menon. "Auditor Switches By Failing Firms," No. 2, pp. 248-261.

Brown, Lawrence D. and John C. Gardner. "Applying Citation Analysis To Evaluate The Research Contributions Of Accounting Faculty And Doctoral Programs," No. 2, pp. 262-277.

Farrelly, Gail E., Kenneth R. Ferris and William R. Reichenstein. "Perceived Risk, Market Risk, And Accounting-Determined Risk Measures," No. 2, pp. 278-288.

Hopwood, William S. and Paul Newbold. "Alternative Interim Reporting Techniques Within A Dynamic Framework: Comments And Extensions," No. 2, pp. 289-294.

Fried, Dov and Joshua Livnat. "Alternative Interim Reporting Techniques Within A Dynamic Framework: A Reply," No. 2, pp. 295-297.

Williams, Paul F. "A Descriptive Analysis Of Authorship In The Accounting Review," No. 2, pp. 300-313.

Drtina, Ralph E. and James A. Largay, III. "Pitfalls In Calculating Cash Flow From Operations," No. 2, pp. 314-326.

Anderson, Kenneth E., Jr. "A Horizontal Equity Analysis Of The Minimum Tax Provisions: An Empirical Study," No. 3, pp. 357-371.

Givoly, Dan. "The Formation Of Earnings Expectations," No. 3, pp. 372-386.

Ham, Jane, Donna Losell and Wally Smieliauskas. "An Empirical Study Of Error Characteristics In Accounting Populations," No. 3, pp. 387-406.

Madeo, Silvia A. and Morton Pincus. "Stock Market Behavior And Tax Rule Changes: The Case Of The Disallowance Of Certain Interest Deductions Claimed By Banks," No. 3, pp. 407-429.

Uecker, Wilfred, Albert Schepanski and Joon Shin. "Toward A Positive Theory Of Information Evaluation: Relevant

Tests Of Competing Models In a Principal-Agency Setting," No. 3, pp. 430-457.

Walker, William S. and Chee W. Chow. "The Self-Selection And Effort Effects Of Standard-Based Employee Contracts: A Framework And Some Empirical Evidence," No. 3, pp. 458-476.

Kaplan, Steven E. and Philip M. J. Reckers. "An Examination Of Auditor Performance Evaluation," No. 3, pp. 477-487.

Neter, John, Johnny R. Johnson and Robert A. Leitch. "Characteristics Of Dollar-Unit Taints And Error Rates In Accounts Receivable And Inventory," No. 3, pp. 488-499.

Short, Daniel G. "A Comparison Of Alternative Methods Of Estimating Constant Dollar Depreciation," No. 3, pp. 500-503.

Srivastava, Rajendra P. "A Note On Internal Control Systems With Control Components In Series," No. 3, pp. 504-507.

Clark, Ronald L. and Robert B. Sweeney. "Admission To Accounting Programs: Using A Discriminant Model As A Classification Procedure," No. 3, pp. 508-518.

Crum, William F. and Don E. Garner. "1983 Survey Of Doctoral Programs In Accounting In The United States And Canada," No. 3, pp. 519-525.

Kilpatrick, Bob, Karl Putnam and Harold Schneider. "Convertible Securities And Earnings Per Share: A Competitive Ranking Algorithm," No. 3, pp. 526-530.

Elliott, John A. and Robert J. Swieringa. "Aetna, The SEC And Tax Benefits Of Loss Carryforwards," No. 3, pp. 531-546.

Rogers, Richard L. and Krishnagopal Menon. "Accounting For Deferred-Payment Notes," No. 3, pp. 547-557.

Biggs, Stanley F. and John J. Wild. "An Investigation Of Auditor Judgment In Analytical Review," No. 4, pp. 607-633.

Fellingham, John C. and D. Paul Newman. "Strategic Considerations In Auditing," No. 4, pp. 634-650.

Haka, Susan F., Lawrence A. Gordon and George E. Pinches. "Sophisticated Capital Budgeting Selection Techniques And Firm Performance," No. 4, pp. 651-669.

Halperin, Robert and Joseph Tzur. "Monetary Compensation And Nontaxable Employee Benefits: An Analytical Perspective," No. 4, pp. 670-680.

Swanson, Edward P., Winston T. Shearon and Lynn R. Thomas. "Predicting Current Cost Operating Profit Using Component Models Incorporating Analysts' Forecasts," No. 4, pp. 681-691.

Cox, Clifford T. "Further Evidence On The Representativeness Of Management Earnings Forecasts," No. 4, pp. 692-701.

Nobes, Christopher W. "International Variations In Perceptions Of Accounting Journals," No. 4, pp. 702-705.

Samuelson, Bruce A. and Brock Murdoch. "The Information Content Of General Price Level Adjusted Earnings: A Comment," No. 4, pp. 706-710.

Lakonsihok, Josef and Aharon R. Ofer. "The Information Content Of General Price Level Adjusted Earnings: A Reply," No. 4, pp. 711-713.

Beck, Paul J. and Ira Solomon. "Sampling Risks And Audit Consequences Under Alternative Testing Approaches," No. 4, pp. 714-723.

Harrell, Adrian, Charles Caldwell and Edwin Doty. "Within-Person Expectancy Theory Predictions Of Accounting Students' Motivation To Achieve Academic Success," No. 4, pp. 724-735.

Johnson, Steven B. "The Economic Function Of Doctoral Programs In Accounting: Alternative Theories And Educational Implications," No. 4, pp. 736-743.

Richardson, A. W. "The Measurement Of The Current Portion Of Long-Term Lease Obligations - Some Evidence From Practice," No. 4, pp. 744-752.

Accounting Review
Volume 61, 1986

Blanchard, Garth A., Chee W. Chow and Eric Noreen. "Information Asymmetry, Incentive Schemes, And Information Biasing: The Case Of Hospital Budgeting Under Rate Regulation," No. 1, pp. 1-15.

Chenhall, Robert H. and Deigan Morris. "The Impact Of Structure, Environment, And Interdependence On The Perceived Usefulness Of Management Accounting Systems," No. 1, pp. 16-35.

Dworin, Lowell and Richard A. Grimlund. "Dollar-Unit Sampling: A Comparison Of The Quasi-Bayesian And Moment Bounds," No. 1, pp. 36-57.

Hassell, John M. and Robert H. Jennings. "Relative Forecast Accuracy And The Timing Of Earnings Forecast Announcements," No. 1, pp. 58-75.

King, Raymond D. and Terrence B. O'Keefe. "Lobbying Activities And Insider Trading," No. 1, pp. 76-90.

Wright, Charlotte J. and James E. Groff. "Uses Of Indexes And Data Bases For Information Release Analysis," No. 1, pp. 91-100.

Butler, Stephen A. "Anchoring In The Judgmental Evaluation Of Audit Samples," No. 1, pp. 101-111.

Licata, Michael P., Robert H. Strawser and Robert B. Welker. "A Note On Participation In Budgeting And Locus Of Control," No. 1, pp. 112-117.

Smieliauskas, Wally. "A Note On Comparison Of Bayesian With Non-Bayesian Dollar-Unit Sampling Bounds For Overstatement Errors In Audits," No. 1, pp. 118-128.

Waymire, Gregory. "Additional Evidence On The Accuracy Of Analyst Forecasts Before And After Voluntary Management Earnings Forecasts," No. 1, pp. 129-142.

Borthick, A. Faye and Ronald L. Clark. "The Role Of Productive Thinking In Affecting Student Learning With Microcomputers In Accounting Education," No. 1, pp. 143-157.

Cargile, Barney R. and Bruce Bublitz. "Factors Contributing To Published Research By Accounting Faculties," No. 1, pp. 158-178.

Jacobs, Fred A., Al L. Hartgraves and Larry H. Beard. "Publication Productivity Of Doctoral Alumni: A Time-Adjusted Model," No. 1, pp. 179-187.

Burgstahler, David and James Jiambalvo. "Sample Error Characteristics And Projection Of Error To Audit Populations," No. 2, pp. 233-248.

Casey, Cornelius, Victor E. McGee and Clyde P. Stickney. "Discriminating Between Reorganized And Liquidated Firms In Bankruptcy," No. 2, pp. 249-262.

Chenhall, Robert H. "Authoritarianism And Participative Budgeting - A Dyadic Analysis," No. 2, pp. 263-272.

Murdoch, Brock. "The Information Content Of FAS 33 Returns On Equity," No. 2, pp. 273-287.

Pastena, Victor and William Ruland. "The Merger/Bankruptcy Alternative," No. 2, pp. 288-301.

Casey, Cornelius and Thomas I. Selling. "The Effect Of Task Predictability And Prior Probability Disclosure On Judgment Quality And Confidence," No. 2, pp. 302-317.

Lere, John C. "Product Pricing Based On Accounting Costs," No. 2, pp. 318-324.

Peles, Yoram C. "A Note On Yield Variance And Mix Variance," No. 2, pp. 325-329.

Thomas, Lynn R. and Edward P. Swanson. "Additional Considerations When Using The FASB Data Bank Of Changing Price Information," No. 2, pp. 330-336.

Kinney, William R., Jr. "Empirical Accounting Research Design For Ph.D. Students," No. 2, pp. 338-350.

Anderson, John C. and James M. Kraushaar. "Measurement Error And Statistical Sampling In Auditing: The Potential Effects," No. 3, pp. 379-399.

DeAngelo, Linda Elizabeth. "Accounting Numbers As Market Valuation Substitutes: A Study Of Management Buyouts Of Public Stockholders," No. 3, pp. 400-420.

Flesher, Dale L. and Tonya K. Flesher. "Ivar Kreuger's Contribution To U.S. Financial Reporting," No. 3, pp. 421-434.

Gaa, James C. "User Primacy In Financial Reporting Rulemaking: A Socal Contract Approach," No. 3, pp. 435-454.

Haka, Susan, Lauren Friedman and Virginia Jones. "Functional Fixation And Interference Theory: A Theoretical And Empirical Investigation," No. 3, pp. 455-474.

Tse, Senyo. "Intra-Year Trends In The Degree Of Association Between Accounting Numbers And Security Prices," No. 3, pp. 475-497.

Weber, Ron. "Data Models Research In Accounting: An Evaluation Of Wholesale Distribution Software," No. 3, pp. 498-518.

Mulford, Charles W. and Eugene Comiskey. "Investment Decisions And The Equity Accounting Standard," No. 3, pp. 519-525.

Sherman, H. David. "Interpreting Hospital Performance With Financial Statement Analysis," No. 3, pp. 526-550.

Brownell, Peter and Morris McInnes. "Budgetary Participation, Motivation, And Managerial Performance," No. 4, pp. 587-600.

Chua, Wai Fong. "Radical Developments In Accounting Thought," No. 4, pp. 601-632.

Danos, Paul and John W. Eichenscher. "Long-Term Trends Toward Seller Concentration In The U.S. Audit Market," No. 4, pp. 633-650.

Dhaliwal, Dan S. "Measurement Of Financial Leverage In The Presence Of Unfunded Pension Obligations," No. 4, pp. 651-661.

Landsman, Wayne. "An Empirical Investigation Of Pension And Property Rights," No. 4, pp. 662-691.

Liberty, Susan E. and Jerold J. Zimmerman. "Labor Union Contract Negotiations And Accounting Choices," No. 4, pp. 692-712.

Bowen, Robert M., David Burgstahler and Lane A. Daley. "Evidence Of The Relationships Between Various Earnings Measures Of Cash Flow," No. 4, pp. 713-725.

Chan, K. Hung and Bajis Dodin. "A Decision Support System For Audit-Staff Scheduling With Precedence Constraints And Due Dates," No. 4, pp. 726-734.

Heck, J. Louis and Wayne G. Bremser. "Six Decades Of The Accounting Review: A Summary Of Author And Institutional Contributors," No. 4, pp. 735-744.

Ijiri, Yuji. "A Framework For Triple-Entry Bookkeeping," No. 4, pp. 745-759.

Wheeler, James E. and Edmund Outslay. "The Phantom Federal Income Taxes Of General Dynamics Corporation," No. 4, pp. 760-774.

Accounting Review
Volume 62, 1987

Abdolmohammadi, Mohammad and Arnold Wright. "An Examination Of The Effects Of Experience And Task Complexity On Audit Judgments," No. 1, pp. 1-13.

Berry, Leonard Eugene, Gordon B. Harwood and Joseph L. Katz. "Performance Of Auditing Procedures By Governmental Auditors: Some Preliminary Evidence," No. 1, pp. 14-28.

Collins, Frank, Paul Munter and Don W. Finn. "The Budgeting Games People Play," No. 1, pp. 29-49.

Conroy, Robert M. and John S. Hughes. "Delegating Information Gathering Decisions," No. 1, pp. 50-66.

Jacobs, Frederic H. and Ronald Marshall. "A Reciprocal Service Cost Approximation," No. 1, pp. 67-78.

Shriver, Keith A. "An Empirical Examination Of The Effects Of Alternative Measurement Techniques On Current Cost Data," No. 1, pp. 79-96.

Steinbart, Paul J. "Materiality: A Case Study Using Expert Systems," No. 1, pp. 97-116.

Swenson, Charles W. "An Analysis Of ACRS During Inflation Periods," No. 1, pp. 117-136.

Beaver, William H. "The Properties Of Sequential Regressions With Multiple Explanatory Variables," No. 1, pp. 137-144.

Francis, Jere R. and Daniel T. Simon. "A Test Of Audit Pricing In The Small-Client Segment Of The U.S. Audit Market," No. 1, pp. 145-157.

Hughes, John S. and William E. Ricks. "Associations Between Forecast Errors And Excess Returns Near To Earnings Announcements," No. 1, pp. 158-175.

Mear, Ross and Michael Firth. "CUE Usage And Self-Insight Of Financial Analysts," No. 1, pp. 176-182.

Nichols, Donald R. "A Model Of Auditors' Preliminary Evaluations Of Internal Control From Audit Data," No. 1, pp. 183-190.

Burgstahler, David. "Inference From Empirical Research," No. 1, pp. 203-214.

Ingram, Robert W. and Russell J. Petersen. "An Evaluation Of AICPA Tests For Predicting The Performance Of Accounting Majors," No. 1, pp. 215-223.

Waller, William S. and William L. Felix, Jr. "Auditors' Covariation Judgments," No. 2, pp. 275-292.

Wilson, G. Peter. "The Incremental Information Content Of The Accrual And Funds Components Of Earnings After Controlling For Earnings," No. 2, pp. 293-322.

Madeo, Silvia A., Albert S. Schepanski and Wilfred C. Uecker. "Modeling Judgments Of Taxpayer Compliance," No. 2, pp. 323-342.

Ziebart, David A. and David H. Kim. "An Examination Of The Market Reactions Associated With SFAS No. 8 And SFAS No. 52," No. 2, pp. 343-357.

Moses, O. Douglas. "Income Smoothing And Incentives: Empirical Tests Using Accounting Changes," No. 2, pp. 358-377.

Halperin, Robert M. and William N. Lanien. "The Effects Of The Thor Power Tool Decision On The LIFO/FIFO Choice," No. 2, pp. 378-384.

Shaw, Wayne H. "Safe Harbor Or Muddy Waters," No. 2, pp. 385-400.

Vruwink, David R. and Janon R. Otto. "Evaluation Of Teaching Techniques For Introductory Accounting Courses," No. 2, pp. 402-408.

Dopuch, Nicholas, Robert W. Holthausen and Richard W. Leftwich. "Predicting Audit Qualifications With Financial And Market Variables," No. 3, pp. 431-454.

Grimlund, Richard A. and William L. Felix, Jr. "Simulation Evidence And Analysis Of Alternative Methods Of Evaluating Dollar-Unit Samples," No. 3, pp. 455-479.

Shevlin, Terry. "Taxes And Off-Balance-Sheet Financing: Research And Development Limited Partnerships," No. 3, pp. 480-509.

Bamber, Linda Smith. "Unexpected Earnings, Firm Size, And Trading Volume Around Quarterly Earnings Announcements," No. 3, pp. 510-532.

Chow, Chee W. and Adrian Wong-Boren. "Voluntary Financial Disclosure By Mexican Corporations," No. 3, pp. 533-541.

Haskins, Mark E. "Client Control Environments: An Examination Of Auditors' Perceptions," No. 3, pp. 542-563.

Brown, Clifton E. and Ira Solomon. "Effects Of Outcome Information On Evaluations Of Management Decisions," No. 3, pp. 564-577.

Knapp, Michael C. "An Empirical Study Of Audit Committee Support For Auditors Involved In Technical Disputes With Client Management," No. 3, pp. 578-588.

Cready, William M. and John K. Shank. "Understanding Accounting Changes In An Efficient Market: A Comment, Replication, And Re-Interpretation," No. 3, pp. 589-596.

McKeown, James C. "Understanding Accounting Changes In An Efficient Market: Analysis Of Variance Issues," No. 3, pp. 597-600.

Gaumnitz, Bruce R. and Joel E. Thompson. "Establishing The Common Stock Equivalence Of Convertible Bonds," No. 3, pp. 601-622.

Harris, Trevor S. and James A. Ohlson. "Accounting Disclosures And The Market's Valuation Of Oil And Gas Properties," No. 4, pp. 651-670.

Moore, Michael L., Bert M. Steece and Charles W. Swenson. "An Analysis Of The Impact Of State Income Tax Rates And Bases On Foreign Investment," No. 4, pp. 671-685.

Halperin, Robert and Bin Srinidhi. "The Effects Of The U.S. Income Tax Regulations' Transfer Pricing Rules On Allocative Efficiency," No. 4, pp. 686-706.

Bernard, Victor L. and Robert G. Ruland. "The Incremental Information Content Of Historical Cost And Current Cost Income Numbers: Time-Series Analyses For 1962-1980," No. 4, pp. 707-722.

Bowen, Robert M., David Burgstahler and Lane A. Daley. "The Incremental Information Content Of Accrual Versus Cash Flows," No. 4, pp. 723-747.

Merino, Barbara D., Bruce S. Koch and Kenneth L. MacRitchie. "Historical Analysis - A Diagnostic Tool For 'Events' Studies: The Impact Of The Securities Act Of 1933," No. 4, pp. 748-762.

Elgers, Pieter, Carolyn Callahan and Elizabeth Strock. "The Effect Of Earnings Yields Upon The Association Between Unexpected Earnings And Security Returns: A Re-Examination," No. 4, pp. 763-773.

Hirst, Mark K. "The Effects Of Setting Budget Goals And Task Uncertainty On Performance: A Theoretical Analysis," No. 4, pp. 774-784.

Maher, John J. "Pension Obligations And The Bond Credit Market: An Empirical Analysis Of Accounting Numbers," No. 4, pp. 785-798.

Knechel, W. Robert and Doug Snowball. "Accounting Internships And Subsequent Academic Performance: An Empirical Study," No. 4, pp. 799-807.

Patell, James M. "Cost Accounting, Process Control, And Product Design: A Case Study Of The Hewlett-Packard Personal Office Computer Division," No. 4, pp. 808-839.

Accounting Review
Volume 63, 1988

Lev, Baruch. "Toward A Theory Of Equitable And Efficient Accounting Policy," No. 1, pp. 1-22.

McGahran, Kathleen T. "SEC Disclosure Regulation And Management Perquisites," No. 1, pp. 23-41.

Magee, Robert P. "Variable Cost Allocation In A Principal/Agent Setting," No. 1, pp. 42-54.

Palmrose, Zoe-Vonna. "An Analysis Of Auditor Litigation And Audit Service Quality," No. 1, pp. 55-73.

Knechel, W. Robert. "The Effectiveness Of Statistical Analytical Review As A Substantive Auditing Procedure: A Simulation Analysis," No. 1, pp. 74-95.

Johnson, W. Bruce and Ramachandran Ramanan. "Discretionary Accounting Changes From 'Successful Efforts' To 'Full Cost' Methods: 1970-76," No. 1, pp. 96-110.

Chow, Chee W., Jean C. Cooper and William S. Waller. "Participative Budgeting: Effects Of A Truth-Inducing Pay Scheme And Information Asymmetry On Slack And Performance," No. 1, pp. 111-122.

Wright, Arnold. "The Comparative Performance Of MBAs Vs. Undergraduate Accounting Majors In Public Accounting," No. 1, pp. 123-136.

Eskew, Robert K. and Robert H. Faley. "Some Determinants Of Student Performance In The First College-Level Financial Accounting Course," No. 1, pp. 137-147.

Biggs, Stanley F., Theodore J. Mock and Paul R. Watkins. "Auditor's Use Of Analytical Review In Audit Program Design," No. 1, pp. 148-161.

Hilton, Ronald W., Robert J. Swieringa and Martha J. Turner. "Product Pricing, Accounting Costs And Use Of Product-Costing Systems," No. 2, pp. 195-218.

Rubin, Marc A. "Municipal Audit Fee Determinants," No. 2, pp. 219-236.

Morris, Michael H. and William D. Nichols. "Consistency Exceptions: Materiality Judgments And Audit Firm Structure," No. 2, pp. 237-254.

Simon, Daniel T. and Jere R. Francis. "The Effects Of Auditor Change On Audit Fees: Tests Of Price Cutting And Price Recovery," No. 2, pp. 255-269.

Lewis, Barry L., James M. Patton and Sharon L. Green. "The Effects Of Information Choice And Information Use On Analysts' Predictions Of Municipal Bond Rating Changes," No. 2, pp. 270-282.

Young, S. David. "The Economic Theory Of Regulation: Evidence From The Uniform CPA Examination," No. 2, pp. 283-291.

Lee, Cheng F. and Chunchi Wu. "Expectation Formation And Financial Ratio Adjustment Processes," No. 2, pp. 292-306.

Harrison, Paul D., Stephen G. West and J. Hal Reneau. "Initial Attributions And Information-Seeking By Superiors And Subordinates In Production Variance Investigations," No. 2, pp. 307-320.

Carslaw, Charles A. P. N. "Anomolies In Income Numbers: Evidence Of Goal Oriented Behavior," No. 2, pp. 321-327.

Bradbury, Michael E. and Shirley C. Calderwood. "Equity Accounting For Reciprocal Stockholdings," No. 2, pp. 330-347.

Davis, Michael L. and James A. Largay, III. "Reporting Consolidated Gains And Losses On Subsidiary Stock Issuances," No. 2, pp. 348-363.

Doran, B. Michal, Daniel W. Collins and Dan S. Dhaliwal. "The Information Of Historical Cost Earnings Relative To Supplemental Reserve-Based Accounting Data In The Extractive Petroleum Industry," No. 3, pp. 389-413.

Horwitz, Bertrand and Daniel Normolle. "Federal Agency R&D Contract Awards And The FASB Rule For Privately-Funded R&D," No. 3, pp. 414-435.

Swanson, G. A. and John C. Gardner. "Not-For-Profit Accounting And Auditing In The Early Eighteenth Century: Some Archival Evidence," No. 3, pp. 436-447.

Thompson, Robert B., II, Chris Olsen and J. Richard Dietrich. "The Influence Of Estimation Period News Events On Standardized Market Model Prediction Errors," No. 3, pp. 448-471.

Kim, K. Kyu. "Organizational Coordination And Performance In Hospital Accounting Information Systems: An Empirical Investigation," No. 3, pp. 472-489.

Bamber, E. Michael and Doug Snowball. "An Experimental Study Of The Effects Of Audit Structure In Uncertain Task Environments," No. 3, pp. 490-504.

Meixner, Wilda F. and Robert B. Welker. "Judgment Consensus And Auditor Experience: An Examination Of Organizational Relations," No. 3, pp. 505-513.

Gordon, Lawrence A. and Michelle M. Hamer. "Rates Of Return And Cash Flow Profiles: An Extension," No. 3, pp. 514-521.

King, Thomas E. and Alan K. Ortegren. "Accounting For Hybrid Securities: The Case Of Adjustable Rate Convertible Notes," No. 3, pp. 522-535.

Daley, Lane A., David W. Senkow and Robert L. Vigeland. "Analysts' Forecasts, Earnings Variability, And Option Pricing: Empirical Evidence," No. 4, pp. 563-585.

Landsman, Wayne R. and Joseph Magliolo. "Cross-Sectional Capital Market Research And Model Specification," No. 4, pp. 586-604.

Balvers, Ronald J., Bill McDonald and Robert E. Miller. "Underpricing Of New Issues And The Choice Of Auditor As A Signal Of Investment Banker Reputation," No. 4, pp. 605-622.

Ashton, Alison Hubbard and Robert H. Ashton. "Sequential Belief Revision In Auditing," No. 4, pp. 623-641.

Lilien, Steven, Martin Mellman and Victor Pastena. "Accounting Changes: Successful Versus Unsuccessful Firms," No. 4, pp. 642-656.

Hines, Ruth D. "Popper's Methodology Of Falsificationism And Accounting Research," No. 4, pp. 657-662.

Francis, Jere R. and Earl R. Wilson. "Auditor Changes: A Joint Test Of Theories Relating To Agency Costs And Auditor Differentiation," No. 4, pp. 663-682.

Maksy, Mostafa M. "Articulation Problems Between The Balance Sheet And The Funds Statement," No. 4, pp. 683-699.

Antle, Rick and Joel S. Demski. "The Controllability Principle In Responsibility Accounting," No. 4, pp. 700-718.

ADVANCES IN ACCOUNTING

The 'Pits' Of Accounting," pp. 113-128.

Dirsmith, Mark and J. Edward Ketz. "A Fifty-Cent Test: An Approach To Teaching Integrity," pp. 129-142.

Stanga, Keith G. "Methods Of Applying LIFO In Practice," pp. 143-152.

Heck, J. Louis and Jiunn C. Huang. "Peer Assessment Versus Citation Analysis Of Contributions To The Accounting Literature," pp. 153-162.

Hull, Rita P., John O. Everett and Steven D. Hall. "Accounting Education: Practitioner's Views On The Value Of A Five-Year Program," pp. 163-178.

Borthick, A. Faye. "Artificial Intelligence In Auditing: Assumptions And Preliminary Development," pp. 179-204.

Schroeder, Richard G. and Kathryn Verreault. "An Empirical Analysis Of Audit Withdrawal Decisions," pp. 205-220.

Kelley, Tim and Loren Margheim. "The Effect Of Audit Billing Arrangement On Underreporting Of Time And Audit Quality Reduction Acts," pp. 221-233.

Advances in Accounting
Volume 5, 1988

Sterling, Robert R. "Confessions Of A Failed Empiricist," pp. 3-36.

Ketz, J. Edward and Walter K. Kunitake. "An Evaluation Of The Conceptual Framework: Can It Resolve The Issues Related To Accounting For Income Taxes?," pp. 37-54.

Bublitz, Bruce O. and Gilroy J. Zuckerman. "Discounting Deferred Taxes: A New Approach," pp. 55-70.

Fries, Clarence E. "A Proposed Procedure For Incorporating Interindustry Relationships In The Design And Analysis Of Empirical Forecasting Studies," pp. 71-84.

Davis, Charles J. and James T. Mackey. "Coalition Costs Through Queueing Theory For Shapley Cost Allocations," pp. 85-110.

Hefzi, Hassan, A. James Ifflander and David B. Smith. "Municipal Bond Market Risk Measures And Bond Ratings," pp. 111-128.

Shriver, Keith A. "A Note On The Estimation Of Current Cost Depreciation," pp. 129-142.

Wilson, Earl R. and R. Penny Marquette. "Evaluating The Effects Of Multicollinearity: A Note On The Use Of Ridge Regression," pp. 143-158.

Abdolmohammadi, M., K. Menon, T. Oliver and S. Umapathy. "Factors Motivating Academic Research In Accounting," pp. 159-174.

Campbell, Terry L., William W. McCartney, Doris M. Taylor and LeRoy A. Franklin. "Job Satisfaction Of Academic Accountants In Southern Business Administration Association Schools," pp. 175-190.

Dunn, W. Marcus and Thomas W. Hall. "Graduate Education And CPA Examination Performance: Some Empirical Evidence," pp. 191-204.

Mulford, Charles W. and Arnold Schneider. "An Empirical Study Of Structural And Controllable Factors Affecting Faculty Evaluations," pp. 205-218.

Mayper, Alan G., Robert B. Walker and Casper E. Wiggins. "Accounting And Review Services: Perceptions Of The Message Within The CPA's Report," pp. 219-232.

Golen, Steven P., Stephen W. Looney and Richard A. White. "An Empirical Examination Of CPA Perceptions Of Communication Barriers Between Auditor And Client," pp. 233-250.

Read, William J. "An Analysis Of Auditor Judgment In Nonstatistical Sampling," pp. 251-266.

Wilson, Arlette C., G. William Glezen and Timothy P. Cronan. "Forecasting Accounting Information For Auditors' Use In Analytical Reviews," pp. 267-276.

ADVANCES IN INTERNATIONAL ACCOUNTING

ADVANCES IN PUBLIC INTEREST ACCOUNTING

ADVANCES IN TAXATION

AUDITING: A JOURNAL OF PRACTICE AND THEORY

Auditing: A Journal of Practice and Theory
Volume 1, 1981-82

Staats, Elmer B. "Auditing As We Enter The 21st Century - What New Challenges Will Have To Be Met," No. 1, pp. 1-11.

Ashton, Robert H. and Robert E. Hylas. "Increasing Confirmation Response Rates," No. 1, pp. 12-22.

Reckers, Philip M. J. and A. J. Stagliano. "Non-Audit Services And Perceived Independence: Some New Evidence," No. 1, pp. 23-37.

Bailey, Andrew D., R. Preston McAfee and Andrew B. Whinston. "An Application Of Complexity Theory To The Analysis Of Internal Control Systems," No. 1, pp. 38-52.

Lea, Richard B. "Recommendations Of The Commission On Auditors' Responsibilities - An Analysis Of The Profession's Responses," No. 1, pp. 53-93.

Burton, John C. and Patricia Fairfield. "Auditing Evolution In A Changing Environment," No. 2, pp. 1-22.

Danos, Paul and Eugene A. Imhoff, Jr. "Forecast Systems, Construction And Attestation," No. 2, pp. 23-34.

Chow, Chee W. and Steven J. Rice. "Qualified Audit Opinions And Share Prices - An Investigation," No. 2, pp. 35-53.

Alderman, C. Wayne and James W. Deitrick. "Auditors' Perceptions Of Time Budget Pressures And Premature Sign-Offs: A Replication And Extension," No. 2, pp. 54-68.

Churchill, N. C., W. W. Cooper and V. Govindarajan. "Effects Of Audits On The Behavior Of Medical Professionals Under The Bennett Amendment," No. 2, pp. 69-90.

Auditing: A Journal of Practice and Theory
Volume 2, 1982-83

Lightner, Sharon M., Steven J. Adams and Kevin M. Lightner. "The Influence Of Situational, Ethical, And Expectancy Theory Variables On Accountants' Underreporting Behavior," No. 1, pp. 1-12.

Davis, Robert R. "An Empirical Evaluation Of Auditors' 'Subject-To' Opinions," No. 1, pp. 13-32.

Mock, Theodore J. and Arnold Wright. "Evaluating The Effectiveness Of Audit Procedures," No. 1, pp. 33-44.

Holstrum, Gary L. and William F. Messier, Jr. "A Review And Integration Of Empirical Research On Materiality," No. 1, pp. 45-63.

Reckers, Philip M. J. and Joseph J. Schultz, Jr. "Individual Versus Group Assisted Evaluations," No. 1, pp. 64-74.

Elliott, Robert K. "Unique Audit Methods: Peat Marwick International," No. 2, pp. 1-12.

Kinney, William R., Jr. "A Note On Compounding Probabilities In Auditing," No. 2, pp. 13-22.

Eichenseher, John W. and David Shields. "The Correlates Of CPA-Firm Change For Publicly-Held Corporations," No. 2, pp. 23-37.

Johnson, Douglas A., Kurt Pany and Richard White. "Audit Reports And The Loan Decision: Actions And Perceptions," No. 2, pp. 38-51.

Kaplan, Robert S. "A Financial Planning Model For An Analytic Review: The Case Of A Savings And Loan Association," No. 2, pp. 52-65.

Wallace, Wanda A. "The Acceptability Of Regression Analysis As Evidence In A Courtroom - Implications For The Auditor," No. 2, pp. 66-90.

Mock, Theodore J. and John J. Willingham. "An Improved Method Of Documenting And Evaluating A System Of Internal Accounting Controls," No. 2, pp. 91-99.

Holder, William W. "Analytical Review Procedures In Planning The Audit: An Application Study," No. 2, pp. 100-107.

Auditing: A Journal of Practice and Theory
Volume 3, 1983-84

Keller, Stuart B. and Lewis F. Davidson. "An Assessment Of Individual Investor Reaction To Certain Qualified Audit Opinions," No. 1, pp. 1-22.

Cushing, Barry E. and James K. Loebbecke. "Analytical Approaches To Audit Risk: A Survey And Analysis," No. 1, pp. 23-41.

Kissinger, John N. "Audit Timing Decisions: A Normative Model, A Practical Heuristic, And Some Empirical Evidence," No. 1, pp. 42-54.

Stephens, Ray G. "An Investigation Of The Descriptiveness Of The General Theory Of Evidence And Auditing," No. 1, pp. 55-74.

Blocher, Edward, Robert S. Esposito and John J. Willingham. "Auditors' Analytical Review Judgments For Payroll Expense," No. 1, pp. 75-91.

Buchman, Thomas A. "The Reliability Of Internal Auditors' Working Papers," No. 1, pp. 92-103.

Finley, D. R. "Normal Form Decision Theory Development Of The Audit Sampling Model," No. 1, pp. 104-115.

Grobstein, Michael and Paul W. Craig. "A Risk Analysis Approach To Auditing," No. 2, pp. 1-16.

Mutchler, Jane F. "Auditors' Perceptions Of The Going-Concern Opinion Decision," No. 2, pp. 17-30.

Ferris, Kenneth R. and Kirk L. Tennant. "An Investigation Of The Impact Of The Qualitative Nature Of Compliance Errors On Internal Control Assessments," No. 2, pp. 31-43.

McConnell, Donald K., Jr. "Auditor Changes And Related Disagreements," No. 2, pp. 44-56.

Robertson, Jack C. "A Defense Of Extant Auditing Theory," No. 2, pp. 57-67.

Biggs, Stanley F. and John J. Wild. "A Note On The Practice Of Analytical Review," No. 2, pp. 68-79.

Jiambalvo, James and William Waller. "Decomposition And Assessments Of Audit Risk," No. 2, pp. 80-88.

Pany, Kurt and Philip M. J. Reckers. "Non-Audit Services And Auditor Independence - A Continuing Problem," No. 2, pp. 89-97.

Auditing: A Journal of Practice and Theory
Volume 4, 1984-85

Kaplan, Steven E. and Philip M. J. Reckers. "An Empirical Examination Of Auditors' Initial Planning Processes," No. 1, pp. 1-19.

DeJong, Douglas V. and John H. Smith. "The Determination Of Audit Responsibilities: An Application Of Agency Theory," No. 1, pp. 20-34.

Sherman, H. David. "Data Envelopment Analysis As A New Managerial Audit Methodology - Test And Evaluation," No. 1, pp. 35-53.

Krogstad, Jack L., Richard T. Ettenson and James Shanteau. "Context And Experience In Auditors' Materiality Judgments," No. 1, pp. 54-74.

Neter, John, Hyo Seuk Kim and Lynford E. Graham. "On Combining Stringer Bounds For Independent Monetary Unit Samples From Several Populations," No. 1, pp. 75-88.

Lin, W. Thomas, Theodore J. Mock and Arnold Wright. "The Use Of The Analytic Hierarchy Process As An Aid In Planning The Nature And Extent Of Audit Procedures," No. 1, pp. 89-99.

Vasarhelyi, Miklos A. "Automation And Changes In The Audit Process," No. 1, pp. 100-106.

Smith, Gerald and Jack L. Krogstad. "Impact Of Sources And Authors On 'Auditing: A Journal Of Practice & Theory' - A Citation Analysis," No. 1, pp. 107-117.

Beck, Paul J. and Ira Solomon. "Ex Post Sampling Risks And Decision Rule Choice In Substantive Testing," No. 2, pp. 1-10.

Dugan, Michael T., James A. Gentry and Keith A. Shriver. "The X-11 Model: A New Analytical Review Technique For The Auditor," No. 2, pp. 11-22.

Firth, Michael. "An Analysis Of Audit Fees And Their Determination In New Zealand," No. 2, pp. 23-37.

Knechel, W. Robert. "A Simulation Model For Evaluating Accounting System Reliability," No. 2, pp. 38-62.

Pillsbury, Ceil Moran. "Limited Assurance Engagements," No. 2, pp. 63-79.

Daroca, Frank P. and William W. Holder. "The Use Of Analytical Procedures In Review And Audit Engagements," No. 2, pp. 80-92.

Tabor, Richard H. and James T. Willis. "Empirical Evidence On The Changing Role Of Analytical Review Procedures," No. 2, pp. 93-109.

Williams, David J. and Anne Lillis. "EDP Audits Of Operating Systems - An Exploratory Study Of The Determinants Of The Prior Probability Of Risk," No. 2, pp. 110-117.

Crosby, Michael A. "The Development Of Bayesian Decision Theoretic Concepts In Attribute Sampling," No. 2, pp. 118-132.

Tamura, H. "Analysis Of The Garstka-Ohlson Bounds," No. 2, pp. 133-142.

Auditing: A Journal of Practice and Theory
Volume 5, 1985-86

Jiambalvo, James and Neil Wilner. "Auditor Evaluation Of Contingent Claims," No. 1, pp. 1-11.

Kaplan, Steven E. "An Examination Of The Effects Of Environment And Explicit Internal Control Evaluation On Planned Audit Hours," No. 1, pp. 12-25.

Levitan, Alan S. and James A. Knoblett. "Indicators Of Exceptions To The Going Concern Assumption," No. 1, pp. 26-39.

Plante, Robert, John Neter and Robert A. Leitch. "Comparative Performance Of Multinomial, Cell, And Stringer Bounds," No. 1, pp. 40-56.

Willingham, John J. and William F. Wright. "Financial Statement Errors And Internal Control Judgments," No. 1, pp. 57-70.

Simon, Daniel T. "The Audit Services Market: Additional Empirical Evidence," No. 1, pp. 71-78.

Blocher, Edward and Joseph Bylinski. "The Influence Of Sample Characteristics In Sample Evaluation," No. 1, pp. 79-90.

Wright, Arnold and Theodore J. Mock. "Towards A Contingency View Of Audit Evidence," No. 1, pp. 91-100.

Abdolmohammadi, Mohammad J. "Efficiency Of The Bayesian Approach In Compliance Testing: Some Empirical Evidence," No. 2, pp. 1-16.

Choo, Freddie. "Job Stress, Job Performance, And Auditor Personality Characteristics," No. 2, pp. 17-34.

Davis, Gordon B. and Ron Weber. "The Impact Of Advanced

Computer Systems On Controls And Audit Procedures: A Theory And An Empirical Test," No. 2, pp. 35-49.

Margheim, Loren and Kurt Pany. "Quality Control, Premature Signoff, And Underreporting Of Time: Some Empirical Findings," No. 2, pp. 50-63.

Srinidhi, B. N. and M. A. Vasarhelyi. "Auditor Judgment Concerning Establishment Of Substantive Tests Based On Internal Control Reliability," No. 2, pp. 64-76.

Bailey, Charles D. and Gene Ballard. "Improving Response Rates To Accounts Receivable Confirmations: An Experiment Using Four Techniques," No. 2, pp. 77-85.

Schroeder, Mary S., Ira Solomon and Don Vickrey. "Audit Quality: The Perceptions Of Audit-Committee Chairpersons And Audit Partners," No. 2, pp. 86-94.

Wright, Arnold. "Performance Evaluation Of Staff Auditors: A Behaviorally Anchored Rating Scale," No. 2, pp. 95-110.

Harrell, Adrian, Eugene Chewning and Martin Taylor. "Organizational-Professional Conflict And The Job Satisfaction And Turnover Intentions Of Internal Auditors," No. 2, pp. 111-121.

Auditing: A Journal of Practice and Theory
Volume 6, 1986-87

Boritz, J. E. and S. Broca. "Scheduling Internal Audit Activities," No. 1, pp. 1-19.

Kreutzfeldt, Richard W. and Wanda A. Wallace. "Error Characteristics In Audit Populations: Their Profile And Relationship To Environmental Factors," No. 1, pp. 20-43.

Meservy, Rayman D., Andrew D. Bailey, Jr. and Paul E. Johnson. "Internal Control Evaluation: A Computational Model Of The Review Process," No. 1, pp. 44-74.

Shpilberg, David and Lynford E. Graham. "Developing ExperTAX: An Expert System For Corporate Tax Accrual And Planning," No. 1, pp. 75-94.

Smith, David B. "Auditor 'Subject To' Opinions, Disclaimers, And Auditor Changes," No. 1, pp. 95-108.

Hansen, James V. and William F. Messier, Jr. "A Preliminary Investigation Of EDP-XPERT," No. 1, pp. 109-123.

Hussein, Mohamed E. A., Vinod B. Bavishi and Jagdish S. Gangolly. "International Similarities And Differences In The Auditor's Report," No. 1, pp. 124-133.

Brown, Paul R. and Vijay Karan. "One Approach For Assessing The Operational Nature Of Auditing Standards: An Analysis Of SAS 9," No. 1, pp. 134-147.

Mutchler, Jane F. "Empirical Evidence Regarding The Auditor's Going-Concern Opinion Decision," No. 1, pp. 148-163.

Biggs, Stanley F., William F. Messier, Jr. and James V. Hansen. "A Descriptive Analysis Of Computer Audit Specialists' Decision-Making Behavior In Advanced Computer Environments," No. 2, pp. 1-21.

Finley, D. R. and J. L. Boockholdt. "A Continuous Constrained Optimization Model For Audit Sampling," No. 2, pp. 22-39.

Kim, Hyo Seuk, John Neter and James T. Godfrey. "Behavior Of Statistical Estimators In Multilocation Audit Sampling," No. 2, pp. 40-58.

Kinney, William R., Jr. "Attention-Directing Analytical Review Using Accounting Ratios: A Case Study," No. 2, pp. 59-73.

Loebbecke, James K. and Paul J. Steinbart. "An Investigation Of The Use Of Preliminary Analytical Review To Provide Substantive Audit Evidence," No. 2, pp. 74-89.

Palmrose, Zoe-Vonna. "Litigation And Independent Auditors: The Role Of Business Failures And Management Fraud," No. 2, pp. 90-103.

Jennings, Marianne, Dan C. Kneer and Philip M. J. Reckers. "A Reexamination Of The Concept Of Materiality: Views Of Auditors, Users And Officers Of The Court," No. 2, pp. 104-115.

Sumners, Glenn E., Richard A. White and Raymond J. Clay, Jr. "The Use Of Engagement Letters In Audit, Review, And Compilation Engagements: An Empirical Study," No. 2, pp. 116-122.

Chow, Chee W., Alan H. McNamee and R. David Plumlee. "Practitioners' Perceptions Of Audit Step Difficulty And Criticalness: Implications For Audit Research," No. 2, pp. 123-133.

Danos, Paul, Doris L. Holt and Andrew D. Bailey, Jr. "The Interaction Of Science And Attestation Standard Formation," No. 2, pp. 134-149.

Auditing: A Journal of Practice and Theory
Volume 7, 1987-88

Farmer, Timothy A., Larry E. Rittenberg and Gregory M. Trompeter. "An Investigation Of The Impact Of Economic And Organizational Factors On Auditor Independence," No. 1, pp. 1-14.

Nair, R. D. and Larry E. Rittenberg. "Messages Perceived From Audit, Review, And Compilation Reports: Extension To More Diverse Groups," No. 1, pp. 15-38.

Pany, Kurt and Philip M. J. Reckers. "Within - Vs. Between - Subjects Experimental Designs: A Study Of Demand Effects," No. 1, pp. 39-53.

Roshwalb, Alan, Roger L. Wright and James Godfrey. "A New Approach For Stratified Sampling In Inventory Cost Estimation," No. 1, pp. 54-70.

Smith, Vernon L., Jeffrey Schatzberg and William S. Waller. "Experimental Economics And Auditing," No. 1, pp. 71-93.

Messier, William F., Jr. and James V. Hansen. "Expert Systems In Auditing: The State Of The Art," No. 1, pp. 94-105.

Marks, Barry R. and K. K. Raman. "Some Additional Evidence On The Determinants Of State Audit Budgets," No. 1, pp. 106-117.

Moizer, Peter and Stuart Turley. "Surrogates For Audit Fees In Concentration Studies," No. 1, pp. 118-123.

Blocher, Edward J. and Jean C. Cooper. "A Study Of Auditors' Analytical Review Performance," No. 2, pp. 1-28.

Ettredge, Michael, Philip B. Shane and David Smith. "Audit Firm Size And The Association Between Reported Earnings And Security Returns," No. 2, pp. 29-42.

Felix, William L., Jr. and Marcia S. Niles. "Research In Internal Control Evaluation," No. 2, pp. 43-60.

Gerlach, James H. "A Model For Testing The Reliability Of Computer Programs And EDP Management: Internal Control Implication," No. 2, pp. 61-76.

Grimlund, Richard A. "Sample Size Planning For The Moment Method Of MUS: Incorporating Audit Judgments," No. 2, pp. 77-104.

Harrell, Adrian A. and Roger Eickhoff. "Auditors' Influence-Orientation And Their Effective Responses To The 'Big Eight' Work Environment," No. 2, pp. 105-118.

Ko, Chen-En, Christopher J. Nachtsheim, Gordon L. Duke and Andrew D. Bailey, Jr. "On The Robustness Of Model-Based Sampling In Auditing," No. 2, pp. 119-136.

Bamber, E. Michael, Linda Smith Bamber and Joseph H. Bylinski. "A Descriptive Study Of Audit Managers' Working Paper Review," No. 2, pp. 137-149.

Coglitore, Frank and R. Glen Berryman. "Analytical Procedures: A Defensive Necessity," No. 2, pp. 150-163.

Wyer, Jean C., Godwin T. White and Ernest C. Janson. "Audits Of Public Companies By Smaller CPA Firms: Clients, Reports, And Quality," No. 2, pp. 164-173.

Daniel, Shirley J. "Some Empirical Evidence About The Assessment Of Audit Risk In Practice," No. 2, pp. 174-181.

Imhoff, Eugene A., Jr. "A Comparison Of Analysts' Accounting Quality Judgments Among CPA Firms' Clients," No. 2, pp. 182-191.

Auditing: A Journal of Practice and Theory
Volume 8, 1988-89

Walker, Norman R. and L. Tim Pierce. "The Price Waterhouse Audit: A State Of The Art Approach," No. 1, pp. 1-22.

Anderson, Urton and Richard A. Young. "Internal Audit Planning In An Interactive Environment," No. 1, pp. 23-42.

Rebele, James E., James A. Heintz and George E. Briden. "Independent Auditor Sensitivity To Evidence Reliability," No. 1, pp. 43-52.

Grimlund, Richard A. and Mary S. Schroeder. "On The Current Use Of The Stringer Method Of MUS: Some New Directions," No. 1, pp. 53-62.

Palmrose, Zoe-Vonna. "Public Accounting Firms And The Acquisition Of Nonaudit Services By Public And Closely-Held Companies," No. 1, pp. 63-71.

Lovata, Linda M. "The Utilization Of Generalized Audit Software," No. 1, pp. 72-86.

Knechel, W. Robert. "The Effectiveness Of Nonstatistical Analytical Review Procedures Used As Substantive Audit Tests," No. 1, pp. 87-107.

Smith, Gerald and Jack L. Krogstad. "A Taxonomy Of Content And Citations In 'Auditing: A Journal Of Practice & Theory'," No. 1, pp. 108-117.

CONTEMPORARY ACCOUNTING RESEARCH

Of Preliminary Audit Strategy By External Auditors," No. 2, pp. 392-411.

Kinney, William R., Jr. "Attestation Research Opportunities: 1987," No. 2, pp. 416-425.

Ro, Byung T. "Firm Size And The Information Content Of Annual Earnings Announcements," No. 2, pp. 438-449.

Dontoh, Alex and Gordon Richardson. "On Interim Information And The Information Content Of Firm Earnings: A State Variable Approach," No. 2, pp. 450-469.

McKeown, James C. and Hossien Shalchi. "A Comparative Examination Of The Time-Series Properties And Predictive Ability Of Annual Historical Cost And General Price Level Adjusted Earnings," No. 2, pp. 485-507.

Amershi, Amin H. and Peter Cheng. "Implementable Equilibria In Accounting Contexts: An Exploratory Study," No. 2, pp. 515-563.

Rockness, Howard O. and Michael D. Shields. "An Empirical Analysis Of The Expenditure Budget In Research And Development," No. 2, pp. 568-581.

Marks, Barry R. and K. K. Raman. "The Effect Of Unfunded Accumulated And Projected Pension Obligations On Governmental Borrowing Costs," No. 2, pp. 595-608.

Chen, Joyce T. and Rene P. Manes. "Distinguishing The Two Forms Of The Constant Percentage Learning Curve Model: A Reply," No. 2, pp. 615-616.

Contemporary Accounting Research
Volume 5, 1988-89

Shields, Michael D., Ira Solomon and William S. Waller. "Auditors' Usage Of Unaudited Book Values When Making Presampling Audit Value Estimates," No. 1, pp. 1-18.

Chung, Dennis Y. and W. Daryl Lindsay. "The Pricing Of Audit Services: The Canadian Perspective," No. 1, pp. 19-46.

Wright, William F. "Empirical Comparison Of Subjective Probability Elicitation Methods," No. 1, pp. 47-57.

Cohen, Susan I. and Martin Loeb. "Improving Performance Through Cost Allocation," No. 1, pp. 70-95.

Banker, Rajiv D., Srikant M. Datar and Ajay Maindiratta. "Unobservable Outcomes And Multiattribute Preferences In The Evaluation Of Managerial Performance," No. 1, pp. 96-124.

Feltham, Gerald A. and Peter O. Christensen. "Firm-Specific Information And Efficient Resource Allocation," No. 1, pp. 133-169.

Amey, Lloyd R. and Jean-Louis Goffin. "Joint Product Decisions: The Variable Proportions Case," No. 1, pp. 174-198.

Darrough, Masako N. "Variance Analysis: A Unifying Cost Function Approach," No. 1, pp. 199-221.

Mensah, Yaw M. "Exercising Budgetary Control In Automated Production Environments," No. 1, pp. 222-249.

Simons, Robert. "Analysis Of The Organizational Characteristics Related To Tight Budget Goals," No. 1.pp.267-283.

Hopwood, William, James McKeown and Jane Mutchler. "The Sensitivity Of Financial Distress Prediction Models To Departures From Normality," No. 1, pp. 284-298.

Richardson, Gordon, Stephan E. Sefcik and Rex Thompson. "Trading Volume Reactions To A Change In Dividend Policy: The Canadian Evidence," No. 1, pp. 299-317.

Hopwood, William S. and Thomas F. Schaefer. "Incremental Information Content Of Earnings And Nonearnings Based Financial Ratios," No. 1, pp. 318-342.

Thornton, Daniel B. "Capital Values In Use Vs. Replacement Costs: Theory And Canadian Evidence," No. 1, pp. 343-370.

Lee, Chi-Wen Jevons. "Inventory Accounting And Earnings/Price Ratio: A Puzzle," No. 1, pp. 371-388.

CORPORATE ACCOUNTING

THE CPA JOURNAL

CPA Journal
Volume 44, 1974

Kramer, Allan. "The Significance Of The Hochfelder Decision," No. 8, pp. 11-14.
Trentin, H. George and Monroe S. Kuttner. "The MAS Body Of Knowledge Study," No. 8. pp. 15-22.
Wolitzer, Philip and Stewart Sandman. "Bridges Between Accounting Educators And Practitioners," No. 8, pp. 23-25.
Newton, Grant W. and James J. Ward, Jr. "Valuation Of A Business In Bankruptcy," No. 8, pp. 26-32.
Chazen, Charles and Ira M. Landis. "Audit Committees - Why And How," No. 8. pp. 33-37.
Tipgos, Manuel A. "Offensive Auditing," No. 9, pp. 19-24.
Wendell, Paul J. "Associations Of CPA Firms," No. 9, pp. 25-28.
Heaney, Terence, Martin Mason and Matthew Minor. "A Closer Look At ESOPs," No. 9, pp. 29-36.
Kreiser, Larry. "Maintaining Professional Competence," No. 9, pp. 37-40.
Blum, James D. and David J. Reiner. "Highlights Of Auditing Standards," No. 9, pp. 41-46.
Bremser, Wayne G. "Peer Review - A Call For Action," No. 10, pp. 15-20.
Grimstad, Clayton R. "New Schools Of Accountancy - Necessary," No. 10, pp. 21-24.
Meckling, William H. and Jerold L. Zimmerman. "Schools Of Accountancy - Accomplish Little," No. 10, pp. 25-30.
Heintz, James A. "Hindsight And Retroactive Restatement," No. 10, pp. 31-34.
Rapp, John. "Discovering And Evaluating Client Problems (Part 1)," No. 10, pp. 35-38.
Holder, William W. "Revenue Recognition In Not-For-Profit Organizations," No. 11, pp. 15-22.
Romney, Marshall. "Fraud And EDP." No. 11. pp. 23-28.
Grinnell, D. Jacque and Richard F. Kochanek. "LIFO Disclosures: Requirements And Restrictions." No. 11, pp. 29-32.
Benjamin, James A. and Robert H. Strawser. "Developments In Lease Accounting," No. 11, pp. 33-36.
Rapp, John. "Discovering And Evaluating Client Problems (Part 2)," No. 11, pp. 37-39.
Hylton, Delmer P. "Are We Communicating?," No. 12, pp. 11-16.
Cumming, John. "Modification In Unaudited Reports," No. 12. pp. 17-22.
Engelbrecht, Ted D. "Corporate Insiders Repayment Dilemma," No. 12, pp. 23-27.
Feinschreiber, Robert. "Minor 1976 Tax Provisions: Major Impact," No. 12, pp. 28-30.
Lurie, Adolph G. "Minimizing Audit Costs (Part 1)," No. 12, pp. 31-34.

CPA Journal
Volume 47, 1977

Feldman, Stewart A. and LeRoy J. Herbert. "The International Accounting Standards Committee," No. 1, pp. 17-22.
Sprouse, Robert. "Understanding Inflation Accounting," No. 1, pp. 23-26.
Sprague, W. Douglas. "The Advertising Dilemma," No. 1, pp. 27-30.
Conway, Charles D. "The Bardahl Formula And Service Companies," No. 1, pp. 31-34.
Lurie, Adolph G. "Minimizing Audit Costs (Part 2)," No. 1, pp. 35-38.
Burns, Thomas J. and Edward N. Coffman. "The Ascending Profession Of Accounting (Part 1)," No. 2, pp. 11-16.
Newman, Barry and Leonard I. Kanarek. "Tax Reform And Net Operating Losses," No. 2, pp. 17-22.
Feinschreiber, Robert. "New Tax Provisions Affect International Operations," No. 2, pp. 23-26.
Godwin, Larry B. "Income Smoothing," No. 2, pp. 27-30.
Paladino, Carl A., Jr. "Financial Forecasts And Our Profession's Future," No. 2, pp. 31-34.
Block, Max. "Trend To Duality In Accounting Standards," No. 3, pp. 11-16.
Lientz, Bennet P. and Ira R. Weiss. "The Vulnerability Of Computer Auditing," No. 3, pp. 17-22.
Rapp, John. "Public Confidence In CPAs," No. 3, pp. 23-26.
Cooper, Kerry and Gerald D. Keim. "Unsettled Issues In Corporate Disclosure," No. 3, pp. 27-30.
Burns, Thomas J. and Edward N. Coffman. "The Ascending Profession Of Accounting (Part 2)," No. 3, pp. 31-36.
Moser, S. Thomas. "Sensitive Corporate Actions: Toward A Resolution," No. 4, pp. 17-22.
Berylson, Kermit J. "ERISA Revolutionizes The Pension Field," No. 4, pp. 23-26.
Weinstein, Edward A. "Disclosure: Too Much Or Too Little?," No. 4, pp. 27-32.
Cunningham, Gary M. "Sub S Corporation Accounting Procedures," No. 4, pp. 37-42.
Newton, Lauren K. "A Process For Assessing Materiality," No. 5, pp. 11-16.
Batzer, R. Kirk. "Accounting For Nonprofit Organizations," No. 5, pp. 17-20.
Mason, John O. and Jonathan J. Davies. "Legal Implications Of EDP Deficiencies," No. 5, pp. 21-24.
Curran, Joseph R. "Disclosure Of Standby Letters Of Credit," No. 5, pp. 31-36.
Dixon, Arthur J. "Commentary On The Metcalf Committee Report," No. 6, pp. 11-20.
Seidler, Lee J. "Major Points In Commission On Auditors' Responsibilities Report," No. 6, pp. 21-24.
Tipgos, Manuel A. "Do We Need New Auditing Standards?," No. 6, pp. 25-30.

Gray, John Y. "Translating Foreign Currency Transactions In Financial Statements," No. 6. pp. 31-36.
Harrison, Robert E. "Some Complexities In Computing 'Earnings And Profits'," No. 6, pp. 37-39.
Kess, Sidney. "Tax Shelters: Are Post Mortems Premature?," No. 7, pp. 11-16.
Flesher, Dale L. "Operations Auditing: For The Independent Auditor," No. 7, pp. 17-21.
Phillips, Lawrence C. and Scott S. Cowen. "Accounting For Debt Restructurings," No. 7, pp. 22-26.
Lambert, Joyce. "Flowcharts Of Recent Statements On Auditing Standards," No. 7, pp. 27-32.
Raabe, Williamm, Jr. and Eugene Willis. "The Conformity Requirement," No. 7, pp. 33-36.
Schachner, Leopold. "Segmental Reporting," No. 8, pp.15-22.
Greenhut, Kenneth. "The Accumulated Earnings Tax - A Call For Repeal," No. 8, pp. 23-26.
Andrews, Wesley T. "Obtaining The Representations Of Legal Counsel," No. 8, pp. 37-40.
Weirich, Thomas R. "Auditing Standards Update," No. 8, pp. 41-45.
Schallman, George C. "Franchisee Accounting - A Specialization Overlooked By CPAs," No. 9, pp. 19-26.
Brown, Marilyn V. "Auditors And Internal Controls: An Analyst's View," No. 9, pp. 27-32.
Leonhardi, Willis A. and Robert W. Newmann. "NAARS And LEXIS: Research Tools," No. 9, pp. 33-40.
Reimer, Steven K. "Tax Considerations In Retirement Plan Distributions," No. 9, pp. 41-46.
Newmiller, John S. and Allen Speiser. "Voluntary Health And Welfare Financial Statements," No. 9, pp. 47-54.
Zuckert, Donald M. "Think About Your Advertising Program," No. 10, pp. 11-14.
Grinnell, D. Jacque and Richard F. Kochanek. "The New Accounting Standards For Leases," No. 10, pp. 15-22.
Stanford, John C. "Compliance Auditing And Loss Contingencies," No. 10, pp. 23-26.
Harmelink, Philip J. and Nancy E. Shurtz. "Tax Effects In Divorce Planning," No. 10, pp. 27-32.
Fee, Francis X., Jr. "Audit Of A Small Manufacturing Company," No. 10, pp. 33-38.
Weinstein, Edward A. "Government As A Client," No. 11, pp. 19-24.
Gordon, Arthur N. "Lessons From A Municipal Fiscal Crisis," No. 11, pp. 25-30.
Loebbecke, James K. "Audit Planning And Company Assistance," No. 11, pp. 31-34.
Lowe, Ronald L. "Auditing The Corporate Information System," No. 11, pp. 35-40.
Rosen, Marvin. "Unclaimed Property - Is It Abandoned?," No. 11, pp. 41-45.
White, Gary E. and Thomas Buchman. "The Continuing Education Requirement: How Effective?," No. 12, pp. 11-16.
Delit, Steven Nelson. "Investigation Of Proposed Acquisitions," No. 12, pp. 17-22.
Crumbley, D. L., P. M. Davis and R. Welker. "A Subchapter S Corporation Is Taxable: Sometimes," No. 12, pp. 23-28.
Goldstein, Michael. "Computer Output Microfilm (COM)," No. 12, pp. 29-32.
Morison, Arthur. "Independence Of The Auditor," No. 12, pp. 33-36.

CPA Journal
Volume 48, 1978

Wood, Thomas D. "Auditors' Concern For Compliance With Laws," No. 1, pp. 17-22.
Neumann, Bruce R., James D. Suver and Ray L. Brown. "Accountants' Role In Zero-Base Budgeting," No. 1, pp. 23-28.
Schachner, Leopold. "Efficiency, Earnings And Equity Capital," No. 1, pp. 29-34.
Reckers, Philip M. J. and Larry H. Beard. "IRS Seeks Auditors' Working Papers," No. 1, pp. 35-40.
Kramer, John L. "Disclosure Of Positions Contrary To The IRC," No. 1, pp. 41-45.
Norton, Curtis. "A.S.R. 190: Liability And Safe Harbor Rules," No. 2, pp. 17-22.
Garsombke, H. Perrin. "A.S.R. 190: Implementation, Costs And Benefits," No. 2, pp. 23-26.
Bailey, Larry. "Secondary Level Assurances," No. 2, pp. 27-32.
Benis, Martin. "Rational Small Business Exceptions To FASB Rules," No. 2, pp. 33-38.
Vargo, Richard J. "Municipal Service Charges - An Opportunity For CPAs," No. 2, pp. 39-43.
Ricchiute, David N. "CPA Responsibility For Detecting Errors Or Irregularities," No. 3, pp. 15-20.
May, Gordon S. and Pieter T. Elgers. "Problems With SEC's Forecast Guidelines," No. 3, pp. 21-26.
Cardona, Ruben and Samuel A. R. Coleridge. "Financing Facilities At Lower Cost," No. 3, pp. 27-30.
Englebrecht, Ted D. and Craig D. Johnson. "Generation-Skipping Transfers Under TRA 1976," No. 3, pp. 31-37.
DeLoach, James W., Jr. "LIFO - Some Important Tax Considerations," No. 3, pp. 38-42.
Werner, Robert H. and Lennard J. Greenberg. "Audits Of CETA Programs," No. 4, pp. 11-20.
Goldwasser, Dan L. "Tax Shelters: CPAs Beware," No. 4, pp. 21-26.
Siegel, Gary and James P. Martin, Jr. "The Need For National Institutional Advertising," No. 4, pp. 27-32.
Bencivenga, Joseph V. "Improving Reviews Of Audit Examinations," No. 4, pp. 33-38.

27-37.

CPA Journal
Volume 52, 1982

CPA Journal
Volume 53, 1983

INTERNATIONAL JOURNAL OF ACCOUNTING
EDUCATION AND RESEARCH

International Journal of Accounting
Education and Research
Volume 1, 1965-66

Wilkinson, Theodore L. "United States Accounting As Viewed By Accountants Of Other Countries," No. 1, pp. 3-14.

Barr, Andrew. "The Influence Of Government Agencies On Accounting Principles With Particular Reference To The Securities And Exchange Commission," No. 1, pp. 15-33.

Kohler, Eric L. "On Developing International Accounting Meanings," No. 1, pp. 35-40.

Queenan, John W. "Challenges In International Auditing," No. 1, pp. 43-51.

Littleton, A. C. "The Continuing Importance Of Basic Concepts," No. 1, pp. 55-65.

Kafer, Karl. "European National Uniform Charts Of Accounts," No. 1, pp. 67-83.

Johansson, Sven-Erik. "An Appraisal Of The Swedish System Of Investment Reserves," No. 1, pp. 85-92.

Bedford, Norton M. "The International Flow Of Accounting Thought," No. 2, pp. 1-7.

Swoboda, Peter. "Comparison Of Consolidated Financial Statements In The United States And West Germany," No. 2, pp. 9-24.

Niehus, Rudolph J. "Stock Corporation Law Reform In Germany And The Public Accountant," No. 2, pp. 35-40.

Lubbert, Jens. "National Accounting - Its Scope And Purpose," No. 2, pp. 43-59.

Kwang, Ching-Wen. "The Economic Accounting System Of State Enterprises In Mainland China," No. 2, pp. 61-99.

Hartmann, Bernhard. "The Effect Of EDP Systems On The Internal Organization Of The Firm," No. 2, pp. 101-117.

International Journal of Accounting
Education and Research
Volume 2, 1966-67

Kosiol, Erich E. "Price Changes, Money Value, And Profit Distribution Within The Framework Of Financial Accounting," No. 1, pp. 1-24.

Littleton, A. C. "The Significance Of Interrelated Concepts In Accounting," No. 1, pp. 25-34.

Weber, Charles. "Income Determination Theory: Some Mathematical And Graphical Approaches," No. 1, pp. 35-47.

Fujita, Yukio. "The Evolution Of Financial Reporting In Japan," No. 1, pp. 49-75.

Ninsuvannakul, Pianchai. "Education For Accountancy In Thailand," No. 1, pp. 77-114.

Zimmerman, V. K. "The Long Shadow Of A Scholar," No. 2, pp. 1-20.

Katano, Ichiro. "Structure Of Accounting For Changing Money Values," No. 2, pp. 21-36.

Mautz, R. K. "The Direction Of Accounting Education," No. 2, pp. 37-46.

Krasensky, Hans. "The Concept Of A Business Asset," No. 2, pp. 47-58.

Kohler, Eric L. "Notes On Activity Accounting," No. 2, pp. 59-64.

Iino, Toshio. "Accounting Principles And Contemporary Legal Thought In Japan," No. 2, pp. 65-87.

Kafer, Karl and V. K. Zimmerman. "Notes On The Evolution Of The Statement Of Sources And Applications Of Funds," No. 2, pp. 89-121.

Farag, Shawki M. "Littleton's Views On Social Accounting - An Elaboration," No. 2, pp. 123-132.

International Journal of Accounting
Education and Research
Volume 3, 1967-68

Kosiol, Erich E. "A Proposal For A General Concept Of Cost," No. 1, pp. 1-19.

Morgan, Robert A. "The Multinational Enterprise And Its Accounting Needs," No. 1, pp. 21-28.

Clapp, Charles L. "National Variations In Accounting Principles And Practices," No. 1, pp. 29-42.

Treffers, Henk C. "The Changing Nature Of The European Accounting Profession," No. 1, pp. 43-54.

Powelson, John P. "National Income Estimates In Latin America," No. 1, pp. 55-65.

Salas, Cesar A. "Accounting Education And Practice In Spanish Latin America," No. 1, pp. 67-85.

Grady, Paul. "Professionalism In Accounting," No. 1, pp. 87-99.

LeMelle, Wilbert E. "The Imperatives Of An Economic Development Program," No. 1, pp. 101-106.

Enthoven, Adolf J. H. "Accounting And Development Programming," No. 1, pp. 107-120.

Beazley, Garnett F., Jr. "An International Implication For Accounting," No. 2, pp. 1-10.

Felt, Howard M. "The Effort And Authority Of The AICPA In The Development of 'Generally-Accepted Accounting Principles'," No. 2, pp. 11-27.

Singhvi, Surendra S. "Characteristics And Implications Of Inadequate Disclosure: A Case Study Of India," No. 2, pp. 29-43.

Yu, S. C. "Is The New U.S. Budget A More Understandable Document?," No. 2, pp. 45-66.

Wasley, R. S. "The Status Of Accountancy And Of Accounting Practices In New Zealand," No. 2, pp. 67-89.

Mueller, G. G. "Accounting Principles Generally Accepted In The United States Versus Those Generally Accepted Elsewhere," No. 2, pp. 91-103.

Duerr, Edwin C. and Mitsuko S. Duerr. "Financing In Northeast Brazil: Problems And Opportunities In A Developing Area," No. 2, pp. 105-116.

Lee, Samuel S. O. "Some Accounting And Philosophical Aspects Of The Third Korean Property Revaluation Law," No. 2, pp. 117-123.

Markell, William. "Accounting Education - Its Importance In Developing Countries: Israel - A Case Study," No. 2, pp. 125-133.

International Journal of Accounting
Education and Research
Volume 4, 1968-69

Ruggles, Richard and Nancy Ruggles. "The Evolution And Present State Of National Economic Accounting," No. 1, pp. 1-16.

Due, John F. "The Institutional Environment And The Tax Structure In Developing Economies," No. 1, pp. 17-27.

Chumachenko, Nikolai and Norton M. Bedford. "Some Distinctive Aspects Of Accounting In The USSR," No. 1, pp. 29-40.

Canning, Robert J. "Selection, Training, And Placement Of Overseas Accounting Personnel," No. 1, pp. 41-50.

Scott, George M. "Private Enterprise Accounting In Developing Nations," No. 1, pp. 51-65.

Hausman, Donald I. "The Foreign Direct Investment Program," No. 1, pp. 67-79.

Linowes, David F. "Commentary On The Foreign Direct Investment Program," No. 1, pp. 81-82.

Bowles, C. C. "International Accounting - A Challenge For Ingenuity," No. 1, pp. 83-97.

Hunziker, A. E. "Commentary To Discussion On International Accounting Challenges," No. 1, pp. 99-100.

Churchill, A. A. "The Balanced Budget In Highway Finance: A Dangerous Concept," No. 1, pp. 101-110.

Shute, John. "Comments On Dr. Churchill's Paper On Highway Finance," No. 1, pp. 111-113.

Farag, Shawki M. "Project Vs. General Development Financing: A Comment," No. 1, pp. 115-119.

Johnson, Eldon L. "International University Responsibilities," No. 1, pp. 121-127.

Elliott, Edward L. "The Managerial Role Of Governmental Accounting In Economic Development," No. 1, pp. 129-136.

Schaller, Howard G. "Thailand: NIDA - An Experiment In Management In The Public And Private Sectors," No. 1, pp. 137-139.

Zeff, Stephen A. "Comments On The NIDA Program," No. 1, pp. 141-143.

Seidler, Lee J. "Teaching Business Administration Overseas: The Case For The Ugly American," No. 1, pp. 145-153.

Fieldcamp, Dale. "International Accounting In An Inflationary Economy," No. 1, pp. 155-164.

Schoenfeld, H. M. "Comments On 'International Accounting In An Inflationary Economy'," No. 1, pp. 165-168.

Van Seventer, A. "The Continuity Postulate In The Dutch Theory Of Business Income," No. 2, pp. 1-19.

Hendriksen, Eldon S. "Disclosure - Insights Into Requirements In The United Kingdom," No. 2, pp. 21-32.

Hakansson, Nils H. "Normative Accounting Theory And The Theory Of Decision," No. 2, pp. 33-47.

Amer, Metwalli B. "Impact Of Public Ownership On The U.A.R. Accounting Profession," No. 2, pp. 49-61.

Gonedes, Nicholas J. "Perception Estimation And Verifiability," No. 2, pp. 63-73.

Chu, Kuo-Chang. "Accountancy Education In The Republic Of China," No. 2, pp. 75-91.

Krieg, Emile. "New Landmarks For Accountancy," No. 2, pp. 93-111.

Niehus, Rudolph J. "Generally Accepted Auditing Principles In Germany," No. 2, pp. 113-124.

International Journal of Accounting
Education and Research
Volume 5, 1969-70

Vatter, William J. "Progress In The Pursuit Of Principles," No. 1, pp. 1-15.

Graebner, Norman A. "Whither Containment?," No. 1, pp. 17-33.

Seidler, Lee J. "Nationalism And The International Transfer Of Accounting Skills," No. 1, pp. 35-45.

Kosiol, Erich E. "Accounting Models As Bases Of Managerial Decisions," No. 1, pp. 47-59.

Mauritz, E. Waldo. "Observations On Accounting In International Finance," No. 1, pp. 61-69.

Aitken, Hugh T. "Accounting Related To Export Credits Insurance And Finance," No. 1, pp. 71-78.

Savoie, Leonard M. "International Dimensions Of Accounting," No. 1, pp. 79-84.

Bomeli, Edward C. "Curricular Recognition Of International Accounting - An Appraisal," No. 1, pp. 85-96.

Baccouche, Mustapha. "The Need For International Accountancy," No. 1, pp. 97-99.

Ogundele, Babatunde. "The Accounting Profession In Nigeria: An International Perspective," No. 1, pp. 101-106.

Rivera, Juan. "Latin American Accounting - A General Perspective," No. 1, pp. 107-108.

Nehrt, Lee C. "Evaluating The Political Climate For Private Investment With Special Application To Tunisia," No. 1, pp. 109-122.

Campfield, William F. "Selected International Trends In Financial Planning And Control In The Public Sector," No. 1, pp. 123-151.

Farag, Shawki M. "The Valuation Of National Capital And The Development Of Accounting Theory," No. 1, pp. 153-169.

Kosiol, Erich E. "An Axiomatic Approach To The Pagatoric Theory Of Financial Income Determination," No. 2, pp. 1-28.

Frishkoff, Paul. "Capitalism And The Development Of Book-keeping: A Reconsideration," No. 2, pp. 29-37.

Tritschler, Charles A. "A Sociological Perspective On Accounting Innovation," No. 2, pp. 39-67.

Schoenfeld, Hanns-Martin. "New German Regulations For The Publication Of Financial Statements," No. 2, pp. 69-88.

Tyra, Anita I. "Financial Disclosure Patterns In Four European Countries," No. 2, pp. 89-101.

Ameiss, Albert P. "Could Swedish Auditing Procedures Result In Greater Corporate Control For U.S. Stockholders?," No. 2, pp. 103-116.

Scott, George M. "A Business Economics Foundation For Accounting: The Dutch Experience," No. 2, pp. 117-131.

International Journal of Accounting Education and Research
Volume 6, 1970-71

Evans, Bergen. "On Authority," No. 1, pp. 1-14.

Jagerhorn, Reginald. "Some Aspects Of Finnish Financial Reporting Practices," No. 1, pp. 15-23.

Dufey, Gunter. "The Outlook For The International Monetary System And Implications For Subsidiary Valuation," No. 1, pp. 25-33.

Jaggi, B. "A Review Of The Accounting Profession In India," No. 1, pp. 35-51.

Carey, John L. "How Can Barriers Against International Accounting Practice Be Eliminated?," No. 1, pp. 53-58.

Thomas, R. Douglas. "The Accountants International Study Group - The First Three Years," No. 1, pp. 59-65.

Mueller, Gerhard G. "Academic Research In International Accounting," No. 1, pp. 67-81.

Bond, Richard R. "Emerging Nations And Emerging Institutions," No. 1, pp. 83-90.

Vandendries, Rene. "Social Accounting And Its Applications In Peru," No. 1, pp. 91-99.

Summers, Edward L. and James Wesley Deskins. "A Classification Schema Of Methods For Reporting Effects Of Resource Price Changes (With Technical Appendix)," No. 1, pp. 101-120.

Gorelik, George. "Enterprise Profit And Profitability Measurements: Soviet-American Convergence," No. 2, pp. 1-14.

Popoff, Boris. "The Price Level Adjustment And Accounting Realism: A Case Study Of A New Zealand Company," No. 2, pp. 15-35.

Yu, S. C. "A Reexamination Of The Going Concern Postulate," No. 2, pp. 37-58.

Smith, Charles H. "The Modern Systems Approach, General System Theory, And Accounting Theory Development In The Age Of Synthesis," No. 2, pp. 59-73.

Cheng, Philip C. "Accounting In Nationalist China," No. 2, pp. 75-88.

Ameiss, Albert P. "Developing Nations And Tax-Ordained Accounting Principles - The Swedish Model," No. 2, pp. 89-102.

Shinawi, Ahmed Abdul Kadir and William F. Crum. "The Emergence Of Professional Accounting In Saudi Arabia," No. 2, pp. 103-110.

International Journal of Accounting Education and Research
Volume 7, 1971-72

Gambling, Trevor E. "Toward A General Theory Of Accounting," No. 1, pp. 1-13.

Most, Kenneth S. "The French Accounting Experiment," No. 1, pp. 15-27.

Abel, Rein. "The Impact Of Environment On Accounting Practices: Germany In The Thirties," No. 1, pp. 29-47.

Willingham, John J. and James E. Sorensen. "The Behavioral Science Milieu Of Accounting," No. 1, pp. 49-63.

Skinner, R. C. "Accounting Information For Decision-Making," No. 1, pp. 65-78.

Weirich, Thomas R., Clarence G. Avery and Henry R. Anderson. "International Accounting: Varying Definitions," No. 1, pp. 79-87.

Jones, Gardner M. and Johannes Kinfu. "The Birth Of An Accounting Profession: The Ethiopian Experience," No. 1, pp. 89-98.

Someya, Kyojiro. "The SLIP Accounting System: Traditional Bookkeeping Procedures In Japan," No. 1, pp. 99-114.

Weber, John A. "Keeping Current On New Developments In Accounting," No. 1, pp. 115-123.

Ameiss, Albert P. "Two Decades Of Change In Foreign Subsidiary Accounting And United States Consolidation Practices," No. 2, pp. 1-22.

Hammer, Richard. "Financial Planning To Avoid Tax Problems," No. 2, pp. 23-34.

Rosenfield, Paul. "Accounting For Foreign Branches And Subsidiaries," No. 2, pp. 35-44.

Wonnacott, Ronald. "U.S. Investment And The Recipient Country," No. 2, pp. 45-54.

Scott, George M. "Financial Control In Multinational Enterprises - The New Challenge To Accountants," No. 2, pp. 55-68.

Moller, George. "The Multinational Executive: Patriot Or Traitor," No. 2, pp. 69-75.

Dufey, Gunter. "Recent Developments In International Money And Capital Markets," No. 2, pp. 77-90.

Neihus, Rudolph. "Harmonized European Economic Community Accounting - A German View Of The Draft Directive For Uniform Accounting Rules," No. 2, pp. 91-125.

International Journal of Accounting Education and Research
Volume 8, 1972-73

Barr, Andrew. "Accounting Yesterday, Today, And Tomorrow," No. 1, pp. 1-15.

Mora, Ricardo E., Jr. "The Accounting Profession In Mexico - And Why," No. 1, pp. 17-24.

Jaruga, Alicja A. "Problems Of Uniform Accounting Principles In Poland," No. 1, pp. 25-41.

Schoenfeld, Hanns-Martin. "Development And Present State Of Cost Theory In Germany," No. 1, pp. 43-65.

Bardsley, R. Geoffrey. "Managing International Financial Transactions," No. 1, pp. 67-76.

McMahon, Terrence J. "Brazil: A Maturing Capital Market Seeks Accelerated Improvements In Accountancy," No. 1, pp. 77-87.

Elliott, Edward L. "Accounting And Economic Development In Latin America," No. 1, pp. 89-97.

Chetkovich, Michael N. "An Appeal For Unity In Establishing Financial Accounting Standards," No. 1, pp. 99-107.

Winjum, James O. "Income Tax Administration In Great Britain," No. 1, pp. 109-116.

Mueller, Gerhard G. "An International View Of Accounting And Disclosure," No. 1, pp. 117-134.

Hanna, John. "An Application And Evaluation Of Selected Alternative Accounting Income Models," No. 1, pp. 135-167.

Chastain, Clark E. "Accounting And Society: A Behavioral View," No. 2, pp. 1-20.

Al Hashim, Dhia D. "Accounting Control Through Purposive Uniformity: An International Perspective," No. 2, pp. 21-32.

Williams, Thomas H. and Charles H. Griffin. "MAS And The Expanded Meaning Of Accounting Education," No. 2, pp. 33-43.

Wright, F. K. "The Valuation Of Tax-Depreciable Assets," No. 2, pp. 45-57.

Glautier, M. W. E. "Roman Accounting: The Influence Of Socioeconomic Factors On The Development Of Accounting Concepts," No. 2, pp. 59-74.

Costouros, George J. "Development Of Banking And Related Bookkeeping Techniques In Ancient Greece (400-300 B.C.)," No. 2, pp. 75-81.

Bait-El-Mal, Mohamed M., Charles H. Smith and Martin E. Taylor. "The Development Of Accounting In Libya," No. 2, pp. 83-101.

Rueschhoff, Norlin G. "U.S. Dollar Based Financial Reporting Of Canadian Multinational Corporations," No. 2, pp. 103-109.

Zappala, Frederick J. "The Current State Of The Accounting Profession In Italy," No. 2, pp. 111-121.

Cheng, Philip C. and Tribhowan N. Jain. "Economic Perspective And Accounting Practices In South Korea," No. 2, pp. 123-139.

International Journal of Accounting Education and Research
Volume 9, 1973-74

Linowes, David F. "Strategies For The Survival Of Our Democratic Institutions," No. 1, pp. 1-12.

Savoie, Leonard M. "Financial And Accounting Aspects In International Business," No. 1, pp. 13-22.

Hauworth, William P. "Problems In The Development Of Worldwide Accounting Standards," No. 1, pp. 23-34.

Nakajima, Seigo. "Economic Growth And Corporate Financial Reporting In Japan," No. 1, pp. 35-41.

Chu, Jose Manuel. "Accounting Principles And Practices In Panama," No. 1, pp. 43-52.

Choi, Frederick D. S. "Financial Disclosure In Relation To The European Capital Market," No. 1, pp. 53-66.

Holzer, H. Peter and Doria Tremblay. "Accounting And Economic Development: The Cases Of Thailand And Tunisia," No. 1, pp. 67-80.

Dascher, Paul E., Charles H. Smith and Robert H. Strawser. "Accounting Curriculum Implications Of The Multinational Corporation," No. 1, pp. 81-97.

Kubin, Konrad W. "The Changing Nature Of International Accounting Courses," No. 1, pp. 99-111.

Enthoven, Adolf J. H. "The Unity Of Accountancy In An International Context," No. 1, pp. 113-133.

Gorelik, George. "Notes On The Development And Problems Of Soviet Uniform Accounting," No. 1, pp. 135-148.

Fredrikson, E. Bruce. "The Valuation Of Noncurrent Foreign Currency Monetary Claims," No. 1, pp. 149-158.

Jaggi, B. L. "Accounting Studies Of Developing Countries: An Assessment," No. 1, pp. 159-170.

Bedford, Norton M. and Jacques P. Gautier. "An International Analytical Comparison Of The Structure And Content Of Annual Reports In The European Economic Community,

Switzerland, And The United States," No. 2, pp. 1-44.

Van Seventer, A. "An Unsettled Problem In The Theory Of Replacing Durable Assets: The Wemelsfelder-Traas Controversy," No. 2, pp. 45-81.

Yu, S. C. "The Several Modes Of Normative Accounting Thought: A Critical Examination," No. 2, pp. 83-104.

Jensen, Daniel L. "The Role Of Interest In Revolving Capital Plans For Cooperative Enterprise," No. 2, pp. 105-109.

Falk, Haim, Samuel Frumer and James A. Heintz. "Accounting For Stock Reacquisitions: Israel And The United States Compared," No. 2, pp. 111-123.

Qureshi, Mahmood A. "Private Enterprise Accounting And Economic Development In Pakistan," No. 2, pp. 125-141.

Burke, Walter L. "Capital Expenditure Analysis," No. 2, pp. 143-154.

Elvik, Kenneth O. "Acquisition Cost Versus Revaluation: A Historical Perspective," No. 2, pp. 155-167.

Neumann, Frederick L. "Career Education In Accounting In The United States: A Current Appraisal," No. 2, pp. 169-179.

International Journal of Accounting
Education and Research
Volume 10, 1974-75

Jaruga, Alicja A. "Recent Developments In Polish Accounting: An International Transaction Emphasis," No. 1, pp. 1-18.

Gorski, Janusz. "The Council For Mutual Economic Assistance: Its Role In The Economic Integration Of Socialist Countries," No. 1, pp. 19-32.

Kupzhasar, Naribaev. "Computer Applications In Soviet Accounting," No. 1, pp. 33-43.

Farag, Shawki M. "The Problem Of Performance Evaluation In International Accounting," No. 1, pp. 45-53.

Radebaugh, Lee H. "The International Dimension Of The Financial Accounting Standards Board: Translation And Disclosure Of Foreign Operations," No. 1, pp. 55-70.

Schoenfeld, Hanns-Martin. "International Influences On The Contemporary Accounting Curriculum: International Accounting Instruction At The University Of Illinois At Urbana-Champaign," No. 1, pp. 71-85.

Scott, George M. "Information Systems And Coordination In Multinational Enterprises," No. 1, pp. 87-105.

Ameiss, Albert P. "International Accounting At The Senior Student Level," No. 1, pp. 107-121.

Deakin, Edward B., Gyles R. Norwood and Charles H. Smith. "The Effect Of Published Earnings Information On Tokyo Stock Exchange Trading," No. 1, pp. 123-136.

Previts, Gary John. "On The Subject Of Methodology And Models For International Accountancy," No. 2, pp. 1-12.

Beekhuizen, Theo and Paul Frishkoff. "A Comparison Of The New Dutch Accounting Act With Generally Accepted American Accounting Principles," No. 2, pp. 13-22.

Kern, Werner. "The Accounting Concept In German Labor-Oriented Business Management," No. 2, pp. 23-35.

Balke, Thomas E. and James E. Sorensen. "Reliability And Validity Of Accounting Data," No. 2, pp. 37-46.

Wolk, Harry I. and Roger W. Briggs. "Accounting Research, Professors, And Practitioners: A Perspective," No. 2, pp. 47-56.

Wasley, Robert S. "The Role Of Management Accounting In New Zealand Business," No. 2, pp. 57-74.

Jaggi, B. L. "The Impact Of The Cultural Environment On Financial Disclosures," No. 2, pp. 75-84.

Brown, Clifford D. "The Emergence Of Income Reporting," No. 2, pp. 85-107.

Gorelik, George. "On The Nature Of Information," No. 2, pp. 109-125.

Skinner, R. C. "Combining LIFO And FIFO," No. 2, pp. 127-134.

International Journal of Accounting
Education and Research
Volume 11, 1975-76

Pomeranz, Felix. "International Auditing Standards," No. 1, pp. 1-13.

Keyserlingk, Alexander N. "International Public Accounting: An Underdeveloped Profession," No. 1, pp. 15-22.

Burnett, R. Andrew. "The Harmonization Of Accounting Principles In The Member Countries Of The European Economic Community," No. 1, pp. 23-30.

Cummings, Joseph P. "The International Accounting Standards Committee: Current And Future Developments," No. 1, pp. 31-37.

Radebaugh, Lee H. "Environmental Factors Influencing The Development Of Accounting Objectives, Standards, And Practices In Peru," No. 1, pp. 39-56.

Fantl, Irving L. "Control And The Internal Audit In The Multinational Firm," No. 1, pp. 57-65.

Van Seventer, A. "Replacement Value Theory In Modern Dutch Accounting," No. 1, pp. 67-94.

Costouros, George J. "Accounting Education And Practice In Greece," No. 1, pp. 95-106.

Ohno, Kimiyoshi, Hideo Ichikawa and Atsuyoshi Kodama. "Recent Changes In Accounting Standards In Japan," No. 1, pp. 107-120.

Choi, Frederick D. S. "Price-Level Adjustments And Foreign Currency Translations: Are They Compatible?," No. 1, pp. 121-143.

Chesebrough, Harry E. "American Management Expertise: Exportable?," No. 1, pp. 145-159.

Brummet, R. Lee. "Internationalism And The Future Of Accounting Education," No. 1, pp. 161-165.

Standish, Peter E. M. "Accounting Responses To Inflation In The European Economic Community," No. 1, pp. 167-184.

Clay, Alvin A. "Undergraduate International Accounting Education," No. 1, pp. 185-192.

Heinen, Edmund. "Goals In Managerial Economics," No. 2, pp. 1-10.

Edwards, James Don and John B. Barrack. "Objectives Of Financial Statements And Inflation Accounting: A Comparison Of Recent British And American Proposals," No. 2, pp. 11-32.

Gandhi, Natwar M. "The Emergence Of The Postindustrial Society And The Future Of The Accounting Function," No. 2, pp. 33-49.

Vickrey, Don W. "Two Views Of Current-Exit Values: Addition And Additivity," No. 2, pp. 51-57.

Gilling, D. M. "Accounting And Social Change," No. 2, pp. 59-71.

Barlev, Benzion. "The Independent Auditor's Report: Study Of A Change," No. 2, pp. 73-90.

Obersteiner, Erich. "The Management Of Liquid Fund Flows Across National Boundaries," No. 2, pp. 91-101.

Said, Kamel E. and Jerry A. Funk. "Planning And Control In Accounting Education: A Model For Subsystem Controls In A Free Market Environment," No. 2, pp. 103-119.

Lev, Baruch. "The Formulation Of Accounting Standards And Rules: A Comparison Of Efforts In Israel And The United States," No. 2, pp. 121-131.

Woelfel, Charles J. "Understanding The Multinationals," No. 2, pp. 133-142.

Pena, Pablo A. "Special Report: A Comparison Of The Accounting Professions Of Colombia And The United States," No. 2, pp. 143-177.

International Journal of Accounting
Education and Research
Volume 12, 1976-77

Richards, William R. "Auditing U.S. Companies With Operations Abroad," No. 1, pp. 1-11.

Garda, J. A. "The Measurement Of Financial Data In Evaluating Overseas Managerial Efficiency," No. 1, pp. 13-17.

Kaocharern, Sukri. "The Development Of The Securities Exchange In Thailand," No. 1, pp. 19-26.

Chang, Lucia S. and Kenneth S. Most. "International Accounting Standards: The Case Of European Oil Companies," No. 1, pp. 27-43.

Needles, Belverd E., Jr. "Implementing A Framework For The International Transfer Of Accounting Technology," No. 1, pp. 45-62.

Piper, Andrew. "Accounting For Overseas Currencies," No. 1, pp. 63-90.

Satubaldin, Sagandyk. "Methods Of Analyzing Profits Of Industrial Enterprises In the USSR," No. 1, pp. 91-99.

Jaruga, Alicja. "Some Developments Of The Auditing Profession In Poland," No. 1, pp. 101-109.

Turk, Ivan. "Recent Professional Statements Of Accounting Principles And Ethics In Yugoslavia," No. 1, pp. 111-120.

Katsuyama, Susumu. "Recent Problems Of The Financial Accounting System In Japan," No. 1, pp. 121-131.

Andrews, Wesley T. and Charles H. Smith. "A Role For Financial Accounting In National Economic Planning In The United States," No. 1, pp. 133-145.

Kortan, Jerzy. "International Economic Organizations And Common Enterprises In Socialist Countries (Principles Of Functioning And Management)," No. 1, pp. 147-165.

Barrett, M. Edgar. "The Extent Of Disclosure In Annual Reports Of Large Companies In Seven Countries," No. 2, pp. 1-25.

Ferris, Kenneth R. and David C. Hayes. "Some Evidence On The Determinants Of Profit Forecast Accuracy In The United Kingdom," No. 2, pp. 27-36.

Barlev, Benzion. "The Initial Selection Of Independent Public Accountants: An Empirical Investigation," No. 2, pp. 37-51.

Baladouni, Vahe. "The Study Of Accounting History," No. 2, pp. 53-67.

Baker, C. Richard. "The Structural Response Of The Large CPA Firm To Its Environment," No. 2, pp. 69-80.

Wu, Frederick H. and Donald W. Hackett. "The Internationalization Of U.S. Public Accounting Firms: An Empirical Study," No. 2, pp. 81-91.

Kim, Seung H. and Paul J. Kuzdrall. "The Simulation Of Financial Strategy Under Fluctuating Exchange Rates Conditions," No. 2, pp. 93-107.

Chen, Kung H. and Edward L. Summers. "Should Accounting Data Be Single-Valued Measurements?," No. 2, pp. 109-125.

Alhashim, Dhia D. "Social Accounting In Egypt," No. 2, pp. 127-141.

Simon, Abraham J. "An Economic And Macroaccounting Framework For Household Nonmarket Production And Its Uses: The Output Side," No. 2, pp. 143-168.

International Journal of Accounting
Education and Research
Volume 13, 1977-78

Baker, H. Kent, Robert H. Chenhall, John A. Haslem and

Roger H. Juchau. "Disclosure Of Material Information: A Cross-National Comparison," No. 1, pp. 1-18.

Belkaoui, Ahmed, Alfred Kahl and Josette Peyrard. "Information Needs Of Financial Analysts: An International Comparison," No. 1, pp. 19-27.

Drury, D. H. "Earnings Per Share: A Canada-United States Comparison," No. 1, pp. 29-51.

Wright, William. "An Empirical Study Of The Professional Socialization Of Accounting Students," No. 1, pp. 53-76.

Ameiss, A. P. "Can British Experience In Profit Forecasting Assist U.S. Firms Interested In Establishing Such Financial Disclosures?," No. 1, pp. 77-91.

Simon, Abraham J. "A Macroaccounting Framework For The Value-Added And Saving Side Of Household Nonmarket Production," No. 1, pp. 93-129.

Luck, Wolfgang. "Recent Changes In The German Professional Certified Public Accountant (Wirtschaftsprufer) Examination," No. 1, pp. 131-140.

Pavlock, Ernest J. "Training Accountants For The Future," No. 1, pp. 141-158.

Polimeni, Ralph S. "Accounting For Forward Exchange Contracts," No. 1, pp. 159-168.

Agrawal, Surendra P. and Rosalie C. Hallbauer. "Advantages Of Replacement Cost Accounting: A Critical Evaluation," No. 2, pp. 1-14.

Copeland, Ronald M. and Robert W. Ingram. "An Evaluation Of Accounting Alternatives For Foreign Currency Transactions," No. 2, pp. 15-26.

Gray, S. J. "Statistical Information And Extensions In European Financial Disclosure," No. 2, pp. 27-40.

Nakano, Isao. "On Monetary-Sacrifice-Based Depreciation," No. 2, pp. 41-55.

Weinstein, Arnold K., Louis Corsini and Ronald Pawliczek. "The Big Eight In Europe," No. 2, pp. 57-71.

Da Costa, Richard C., Jacques C. Bourgeois and William M. Lawson. "A Classification Of International Financial Accounting Practices," No. 2, pp. 73-85.

Peche, Tadeusz. "Instructional Problems In The Modernization Of Accounting Theory," No. 2, pp. 87-104.

Leech, Stewart A. and Denis J. Pratt. "Current Cost Accounting In Australia, New Zealand, And The United Kingdom: A Comparative Study," No. 2, pp. 105-118.

Hoyt, Ronald E. "Profit Measurement In East-West Trade And Industrial Cooperation: Concepts, Criteria, And Special Problems," No. 2, pp. 119-144.

Evans, Thomas G. and William R. Folks, Jr. "SFAS No. 8: Conforming, Coping, Complaining, And Correcting!," No. 1, pp. 33-43.

Piper, Andrew G. "A Note On Translation For Interim Accounts," No. 1, pp. 45-52.

Choi, Frederick D. S. "ASEAN Federation Of Accountants: A New International Accounting Force," No. 1, pp. 53-75.

Morsicato, Helen G. and Lee H. Radebaugh. "Internal Performance Evaluation Of Multinational Enterprise Operations," No. 1, pp. 77-94.

Fekrat, M. A. "Multinational Accounting: A Technical Note," No. 1, pp. 95-103.

Maldonado, Rita M. "Recording And Classifying Transactions In The Balance Of Payments," No. 1, pp. 105-133.

Burns, Jane O. "A Study Of International Accounting Education In The United States," No. 1, pp. 135-145.

Nobes, C. W. "Harmonization Of Accounting Within The European Communites: The Fourth Directive On Company Law," No. 2, pp. 1-16.

Jacobi, Michael H. "The Unit Of Account In Consolidated Financial Statements Of Multinational Enterprises," No. 2, pp. 17-34.

Jaggi, Bikki. "An Analysis Of Corporate Social Reporting In Germany," No. 2, pp. 35-45.

Firth, Michael. "A Cross-Sectional Analysis Of Qualified Audit Reports," No. 2, pp. 47-59.

Kubota, Keiichi. "Information Content Of Accounting Numbers: Evidence On Tokyo Stock Exchange Firms," No. 2, pp. 61-76.

Robb, A. J. "Interim Reports And Their Qualitative Evaluation," No. 2, pp. 77-86.

Murphy, George J. "Financial Statement Disclosure And Corporate Law: The Canadian Experience," No. 2, pp. 87-99.

Markell, William. "A Comparison Of Preparation For The Accounting Profession Among New Zealand, The United Kingdom, And The United States," No. 2, pp. 101-114.

Gniewosz, G. "The Equity Method Of Accounting For Investment In Common Stock: The New Zealand Experience," No. 2, pp. 115-128.

Shuaib, Shuaib A. "Accounting Information And The Development Planning Process In Kuwait," No. 2, pp. 129-141.

Abdeen, Adnan. "The Role Of Accounting In Project Evaluation And Control: The Syrian Experience," No. 2, pp. 143-158.

International Journal of Accounting Education and Research Volume 14, 1978-79

Heinen, Edmund. "Supplemented Multi-Purpose Accounting," No. 1, pp. 1-15.

Boussard, Daniel. "Application Of GST To The Financial Accounting Model," No. 1, pp. 17-37.

Dau, Khalifa. "A Probabilistic Income Determination Theory," No. 1, pp. 39-56.

Firth, Michael. "A Study Of The Consensus Of The Perceived Importance Of Disclosure Of Individual Items In Corporate Annual Reports," No. 1, pp. 57-70.

Arbel, Avner and Bikki Jaggi. "Impact Of Replacement Cost Disclosures Of Investors' Decisions In The United States," No. 1, pp. 71-82.

Shapiro, Alan C. "Evaluation And Control Of Foreign Operations," No. 1, pp. 83-104.

Briston, Richard J. "The Evolution Of Accounting In Developing Countries," No. 1, pp. 105-120.

Ghartey, Ato. "A New Perspective For Accountancy Education In Ghana," No. 1, pp. 121-132.

Ogan, Pekin. "Turkish Accountancy: An Assessment Of Its Effectiveness And Recommendations For Improvements," No. 1, pp. 133-154.

McComb, Desmond. "The International Harmonization Of Accounting: A Cultural Dimension," No. 2, pp. 1-16.

Chen, Kung H. and Thomas E. Balke. "Scale Of Operation, Industry, And Financial Ratios," No. 2, pp. 17-28.

Falk, Haim. "Current Value Accounting Preferences: The Case For Canada," No. 2, pp. 29-46.

Estes, Ralph. "The Profession's Changing Horizons: A Survey Of Practitioners On The Present And Future Importance Of Selected Knowledge And Skills," No. 2, pp. 47-70.

Wu, Frederick H. and Douglas Sharp. "An Empirical Study Of Transfer Pricing Practice," No. 2, pp. 71-99.

Messier, William F., Jr. "SFAS No. 8: Some Implications For MNCS," No. 2, pp. 101-119.

Duangploy, Orapin. "The Sensitivity Of Earnings Per Share To Different Foreign Currency Translation Methods," No. 2, pp. 121-134.

Stanley, Marjorie T. and Stanley B. Block. "Accounting And Economic Aspects Of SFAS No. 8," No. 2, pp. 135-155.

International Journal of Accounting Education and Research Volume 15, 1979-80

Mueller, Gerhard G. "St. Louis To Munich: The Odyssey Of The International Congresses Of Accountants," No. 1, pp. 1-12.

Chetkovich, Michael N. "The International Federation Of Accountants: Its Organization And Goals," No. 1, pp. 13-20.

Sempier, Robert N. "The International Federation Of Accountants: Operating Procedures And Current Progress," No. 1, pp. 21-31.

International Journal of Accounting Education and Research Volume 16, 1980-81

Hayes, Donald J. "The International Accounting Standards Committee - Recent Developments And Current Problems," No. 1, pp. 1-10.

Lawson, G. H. "The Measurement Of Corporate Profitability On A Cash-Flow Basis," No. 1, pp. 11-46.

Alhashim, Dhia D. "Regulation Of Financial Accounting: An International Perspective," No. 1, pp. 47-62.

Hauworth, William P., II. "A Comparison Of Various International Proposals On Inflation Accounting: A Practitioner's View," No. 1, pp. 63-82.

Choi, Frederick D. S. "Primary-Secondary Reporting: A Cross-Cultural Analysis," No. 1, pp. 83-104.

Hoyt, Ronald E. and Lawrence D. Maples. "Accounting For Joint Ventures With The Soviet Bloc And China," No. 1, pp. 105-124.

Arnold, Jerry, William W. Holder and M. Herschel Mann. "International Reporting Aspects Of Segment Disclosure," No. 1, pp. 125-135.

Mintz, Steven M. "Internationalization Of The Accounting Curriculum," No. 1, pp. 137-151.

Bavishi, Vinod B. and Harold E. Wyman. "Foreign Operations Disclosures By U.S.-Based Multinational Corporations: Are They Adequate?," No. 1, pp. 153-168.

Will, Hartmut J. "Computerized Accounting: International Issues," No. 1, pp. 169-207.

Castle, Eric F. "The Problems Of Consolidation Of Accounts Of A Multinational Enterprise: Shell Group Of Companies - Shell Transport And Trading Company, Limited, U.K.," No. 1, pp. 209-219.

Mensah, Yaw M. and Louis F. Biagioni. "The Predictive Ability Of Financial Ratios Using Alternative Translation Methods For Foreign-Currency Financial Statements: A Simulation Study," No. 1, pp. 221-245.

Morsicato, Helen G. and Michael A. Diamond. "An Approach To 'Environmentalizing' MNE Performance Evaluation Systems," No. 1, pp. 247-266.

Comiskey, Eugene E. and Roger E. V. Groves. "United Kingdom Developments In Interperiod Tax Allocation," No. 2, pp. 1-9.

Amernic, Joel H. and Nissim Aranya. "Public Accountants' Independence: Some Evidence In A Canadian Context," No. 2, pp. 11-33.

Parker, L. D. "Corporate Annual Reports: A Failure To Communicate," No. 2, pp. 35-48.

Elam, Rick and Hamid Henaidy. "Transfer Pricing For The Multinational Corporation," No. 2, pp. 49-65.

Skully, Michael T. "Japanese Corporate Structure: Some Factors In Its Development," No. 2, pp. 67-98.

Round, G. D. and B. M. Pollard. "Accounting Theory And History - Lessons To Be Learned," No. 2, pp. 99-123.

Boussard, Daniel. "Accounting As An Artifact: A Methodological Design On Dimensions Of Accounting," No. 2, pp. 125-147.

Machalzina, Klaus and Adolf G. Coenenberg. "Current-Cost Or

Current Purchasing-Power Accounting? An Internationally Based Assessment Of FASB Statement No. 33 On Financial Reporting And Changing Prices," No. 2, pp. 149-162.

Dykxhoorn, Hans J. and Kathleen E. Sinning. "The Independence Issue Concerning German Auditors: A Synthesis," No. 2, pp. 163-181.

International Journal of Accounting
Education and Research
Volume 17, 1981-82

Kullberg, Duane R. "Management Of A Multinational Public Accounting Firm," No. 1, pp. 1-5.

Pomeranz, Felix. "Prospects For International Accounting And Auditing Standards - The Transnationals In Governmental Regulations," No. 1, pp. 7-19.

Fitzgerald, Richard D. "International Harmonization Of Accounting And Reporting," No. 1, pp. 21-32.

Linowes, David F. "The Implications Of Transborder Data-Flow Development For The Accounting Profession," No. 1, pp. 33-41.

Chang, Lucia S. and Kenneth S. Most. "An International Comparison Of Investor Uses Of Financial Statements," No. 1, pp. 43-60.

Nair, R. D. and Werner G. Frank. "The Harmonization Of International Accounting Standards, 1973-1979," No. 1, pp. 61-77.

Abdel-Magid, Moustafa F. "The Theory Of Islamic Banking: Accounting Implications," No. 1, pp. 79-102.

Lefebvre, Chris J. L. "Development Of Belgian Accounting Standards Within The European Economic Community Framework," No. 1, pp. 103-132.

Shields, Janice Christine. "Foreign Language And Accounting Expertise: A Marketable Combination," No. 1,pp. 133-146.

Hussein, Mohamed Elmutassim. "Translation Problems Of International Accounting Standards," No. 1, pp. 147-155.

Hsu, Tsun Tsien. "Recent Business And Accounting Developments In China," No. 1, pp. 157-160.

Burns, Jane O. and Ronald S. Ross. "Establishing International Transfer Pricing Standards For Tax Audits Of Multinational Enterprises," No. 1, pp. 161-179.

Foroughi, Tahirih Khodadoust. "Accounting In Developing Countries Before And After Social Crisis: The Case Of Iran," No. 1, pp. 181-223.

Buckmaster, Dale. "Inflation Gains And Losses From Holding Monetary Assets And Liabilities 1918 To 1936: A Study Of The Development Of Accounting Thought In The United States," No. 2, pp. 1-22.

Leech, Stewart, Denis J. Pratt and W. G. W. Magill. "Asset Revaluations And Inflation In Australia, 1950 To 1975: An Industry Study," No. 2, pp. 23-34.

McComb, Desmond. "International Accounting Standards And The EEC Harmonization Program: A Conflict Of Disparate Objectives," No. 2, pp. 35-48.

Chesley, G. R. and J. H. Scheiner. "The Statement Of Changes In Financial Position: An Empirical Investigation Of Canadian And U.S. Users in Nonpublic Companies," No. 2, pp. 49-58.

Enthoven, Adolph J. H. "International Management Accounting: Its Scope And Standards," No. 2, pp. 59-74.

Barlev, Benzion and Abraham Friedman. "Experience Requirements And The Education Of Certified Public Accountants," No. 2, pp. 75-88.

Turk, Ivan. "Analysis Of Efficiency By Means Of Interrelated Indicators: A Yugoslav Approach," No. 2,pp.89-102.

Riise, Arne. "Norwegian Standards For Annual Reporting Requirements And Chart Of Accounts," No. 2, pp. 103-120.

Givoly, Dan and Josef Lakonishok. "Accounting For Construction Companies, Inflation, And Market Efficiency: Analysis Of An Israeli Case," No. 2, pp. 121-149.

Trotman, K. T. "An Evaluation Of Accounting For Construction Contracts: An International Comparison," No. 2, pp. 151-166.

International Journal of Accounting
Education and Research
Volume 18, 1982-83

Bailey, Derek T. "Accounting In Russia: The European Connection," No. 1, pp. 1-36.

Golub, Steven J. "A Global Perspective To Financial Reporting," No. 1, pp. 37-44.

Luck, Wolfgang. "The Impact Of International Standards And Other Developments On The German Accounting Profession," No. 1, pp. 45-56.

Mirghani, Mohamed A. "A Framework For A Linkage Between Microaccounting And Macroaccounting For Purposes Of Development Planning In Developing Countries," No. 1, pp. 57-68.

Samuels, J. M. and J. C. Oliga. "Accounting Standards In Developing Countries," No. 1, pp. 69-88.

Dahmash, Naim H. "Public Auditing Developments In The Arab States: A Comparative Study," No. 1, pp. 89-114.

Evans, Thomas G. and Martin E. Taylor. "'Bottom Line Compliance' With The IASC: A Comparative Analysis," No. 1, pp. 115-128.

Rivera, Juan M. "The Financial Function Of A U.S. Multinational Company Abroad: A Venezuelan Experience," No. 1, pp. 129-138.

Raymond, Robert H., M. Zafar Iqbal and Eldon L. Schafer. "The Gearing (Leverage) Adjustment: A Historical And Comparative Analysis," No. 1, pp. 139-157.

Choi, Frederick D. S. and Vinod B. Bavishi. "Financial

Accounting Standards: A Multinational Synthesis And Policy Framework," No. 1, pp. 159-183.

Berry, Maureen H. "The Accounting Function In Socialist Economies," No. 1, pp. 185-198.

Doupnik, Timothy S. "Indexation: Brazil's Response To Inflation," No. 1, pp. 199-220.

Violet, William J. "The Development Of International Accounting Standards: An Anthropological Perspective," No. 2, pp. 1-12.

Turley, W. S. "International Harmonization Of Accounting: The Contribution Of The EEC Fourth Directive On Company Law," No. 2, pp. 13-27.

Nance, Jon R. and Roger A. Roemmich. "Foreign Currency Translation: An Evaluation," No. 2, pp. 29-48.

Lister, Roger J. "Accounting As History," No. 2, pp. 49-68.

Jagetia, Lal C. and Evaristus C. Nwadike. "Accounting Systems In Developing Nations: The Nigerian Experience," No. 2, pp. 69-81.

Pendlebury, Maurice and Rowan Jones. "Municipal Disclosure In England: Another Market For Excuses?," No. 2, pp. 83-93.

Agrawal, Surendra P. "Current Cost Accounting In The United Kingdom And The United States: A Comparative Analysis," No. 2, pp. 95-108.

Gebhardt, Guenther. "The Usefulness Of Different Accounting Disclosure Regulations: A German Experience," No. 2, pp. 109-131.

Maingot, Michael. "Published Interim Reports In The United Kingdom," No. 2, pp. 133-149.

Singh, D. R. and Jag Mohan Ahuja. "Corporate Social Reporting In India," No. 2, pp. 151-169.

Rege, Udayan P., W. John Brennan and W. Harold Silvester. "Current Regulatory Practices, Corporate Financial Forecasting, And Takeover Bids," No. 2, pp. 171-175.

Amernic, Joel H., Rabindra Kanungo and Nissim Aranya. "Professional And Work Values Of Accountants: A Cross-Cultural Study," No. 2, pp. 177-192.

International Journal of Accounting
Education and Research
Volume 19, 1983-84

Violet, William J. "A Philosophical Perspective On The Development Of International Accounting Standards," No. 1, pp. 1-13.

Gray, S. J. "International Accounting: A Review Of Academic Research In The United Kingdom," No. 1, pp. 15-42.

Popoff, Boris. "Some Conceptualizing On The True And Fair View," No. 1, pp. 43-54.

Skomp, Stephen E. and C. W. R. Ward. "The Capital Structure Policies Of U.K. Companies: A Comparative Study," No. 1, pp. 55-64.

Hosseini, Ahmad and Raj Aggarwal. "Evaluating Foreign Affiliates: The Impact Of Alternative Foreign Currency Translation Methods," No. 1, pp. 65-87.

Nance, Jon R. and Roger A. Roemmich. "Financial Statement Impact Of Foreign Currency Translation Alternatives," No. 1, pp. 89-113.

Meek, Gary. "The Multiple Earnings Announcements Of Non-U.S. Multinational Enterprises - Implications Of Observed Patterns," No. 1, pp. 115-130.

McClure, Malcolm M. "An Overview Of Rumanian Accounting," No. 1, pp. 131-156.

Agrawal, Surendra P. and Kenneth Rosenzweig. "Some Simpler Methods Of Accounting For The Effects Of Changing Prices," No. 1, pp. 157-171.

Arnold, John., Peter Moizer and Eric Noreen. "Investment Appraisal Methods Of Financial Analysts: A Comparative Study Of U.S. And U.K. Practices," No. 2, pp. 1-18.

McKinnon, S. M. and Paul Janell. "The International Accounting Standards Committee: A Performance Evaluation," No. 2, pp. 19-34.

Aitken, M. J. and M. A. Islam. "Dispelling Arguments Against International Accounting Standards," No. 2, pp. 35-46.

Bloom, Robert. "American And Canadian Accounting Standard Setting: A Comparative Analysis," No. 2, pp. 47-57.

Bailes, Jack C. and Graeme M. McNally. "Cost And Management Accounting Practices In New Zealand," No. 2, pp. 59-71.

Callen, Jeffrey L. and Joshua Livnat. "Is Historical Cost Accounting Possible During Hyperinflation?," No. 2, pp. 73-81.

Fekrat, M. Ali. "Accounting For Forward Exchange Contracts," No. 2, pp. 83-92.

Bursal, Nasuhi I. "The Accounting Environment And Some Recent Developments In Turkey," No. 2, pp. 93-127.

Briston, Richard J. and Ahmed A. El-Ashker. "The Egyptian Accounting System: A Case Study In Western Influence," No. 2, pp. 129-155.

Latanich, Gary A. and John Kaminarides. "Performance Of Accountants In International Business," No.2,pp.157-164.

Amernic, J. H. and B. J. B. Galvin. "Implementing The New Foreign Currency Rules In Canada And The United States: A Challenge To Professional Judgment," No. 2,pp.165-180.

Ndubizu, Gordian A. "Accounting Standards And Economic Development: The Third World In Perspective," No. 2, pp. 181-196.

International Journal of Accounting
Education and Research
Volume 20, 1984-85

Park, Soong. "The Use Of Foreign Financial Statements For

Risk Analysis: An Empirical Test (Korea)," No. 1, pp. 1-15.

McKinnon, Jill. "Cultural Constraints On Audit Independence In Japan," No. 1, pp. 17-43.

Wong-Boren, Adrian and Andrew H. Barnett. "Mexican Market Efficiency: A Study Of The Information Content Of Accounting Numbers," No. 1, pp. 45-70.

Heaston, Patrick H. "Qualification Requirements For Public Accounting In Selected Foreign Countries: A Comparison With The United States," No. 1, pp. 71-94.

Gul, Ferdinand A. and Teoh Hai Yap. "The Effects Of Combined Audit And Management Services On Public Perception Of Auditor Independence In Developing Countries: The Malaysian Case," No. 1, pp. 95-107.

Gray, Dahli. "SFAS No. 52: Progress Or Problem?," No. 1, pp. 109-119.

Abdeen, Adnan. "The Impact Of Accounting Practices On Tax Revenue In Syria," No. 1, pp. 121-139.

Hardman, D. J. "Accounting Development In The Solomon Islands," No. 1, pp. 141-152.

Hall, Thomas W. and H. Jim Snavely. "Translated Financial Statements Can Be Meaningful," No. 1, pp. 153-170.

Aitken, Michael J. and Trevor D. Wise. "The Real Objective Of The International Accounting Standards Committee," No. 1, pp. 171-177.

Houghton, Keith A. and Richard Bell. "Evaluations Of Accounting And Finance Journals: The Australian View," No. 1, pp. 179-187.

Meek, Gary. "Interim Earnings Announcements In The United States By Non-U.S. Multinational Corporations - Responses By The U.S. Securities Market," No. 2, pp. 1-18.

Ooghe, Hubert and Eric Verbaere. "Predicting Business Failure On The Basis Of Accounting Data: The Belgian Experience," No. 2, pp. 19-44.

Berry, Maureen and Alicja Jaruga. "Industrial Accounting In Poland's Reorganized Economy," No. 2, pp. 45-63.

Hooper, Paul, John Page and Karen Smith. "Accountant's Legal Liability: An International Comparison," No. 2, pp. 65-80.

Belkaoui, Ahmed and Mostafa Maksy. "Welfare Of The Common Man And Accounting Disclosure Adequacy: An Empirical Investigation," No. 2, pp. 81-94.

Doost, Roger K. "Alternative Techniques To Measure The Well-Being Of A Region," No. 2, pp. 95-101.

Vangermeersch, Richard. "The Route Of The Seventh Directive Of The EEC On Consolidated Accounts - Slow, Steady, Studied, And Successful," No. 2, pp. 103-118.

Bloom, Robert and Araya Debessay. "A Comparative Analysis Of Recent Pronouncements On Accounting For Changing Prices," No. 2, pp. 119-138.

Pendrill, David. "Contrasting Income Treatment Of Monetary Items In Recent Accounting Standards In New Zealand, The United Kingdom, And The United States," No. 2, pp. 139-154.

Abdeen, Adnan M. and Ugur Yavas. "Current Status Of Accounting Education In Saudi Arabia," No. 2, pp. 155-173.

International Journal of Accounting
Education and Research
Volume 21, 1985-86

Brown, Betty. "The Relationship Between Firm Attributes And Early Adoption Of The Foreign Currency Translation Standard, SFAS No. 52: An Empirical Investigation," No. 1, pp. 1-19.

Heintz, James A. and Jin-Soo Han. "A Study Of Audit Judgments Of Korean CPAs," No. 1, pp. 21-38.

Ziebart, David A. "Exchange Rates And Purchasing Power Parity: Evidence Regarding The Failure Of SFAS No. 52 To Consider Exchange Risk In Hyper-Inflationary Countries," No. 1, pp. 39-51.

Chambers, R. J. "The Functional Utility Of Resale Price Accounting," No. 1, pp. 53-70.

Dheeriya, Prakash L. "A Case For Special Drawing Rights As A Unit Of Account," No. 1, pp. 71-87.

Schweikart, James A. "Contingency Theory As A Framework For Research In International Accounting," No. 1, pp. 89-98.

Markell, William. "Development Of Accounting Education And The Accounting Profession In Third World Countries: Botswana," No. 1, pp. 99-105.

Bloom, Robert and Araya Debessay. "An Appraisal Of The Conceptual Issues On Backlog Depreciation And A Comparative Analysis Of International Accounting Practices," No. 1, pp. 107-121.

Sharkas, Wajdy. "The Effectiveness Of The Supreme Audit Bureau In Kuwait In Monitoring Public Expenditures: An Evaluation," No. 1, pp. 123-142.

Ghartey, J. B. "Accountability, The Threshold Of Political Instability, Underdevelopment, And Misery: The Case Of Africa," No. 1, pp. 143-158.

Burlaud, Alain and Lionel Dahan. "Global Productivity Surplus Accounts," No. 1, pp. 159-169.

Chow, Chee W. and Adrian Wong-Boren. "Audit Firm Size And Audit Quality: Some Evidence From Mexico," No. 2, pp. 1-25.

Simon, Daniel T., Ramachandran Ramanan and Amitabh Dugar. "The Market For Audit Services In India: An Empirical Examination," No. 2, pp. 27-35.

Hopwood, Anthony G. and H. Thomas Johnson. "Accounting

History's Claim To Legitimacy," No. 2, pp. 37-46.

Yagil, Joseph, Ben Amoako-Adu and Jeffrey Kantor. "Capital Cost Allowance (Depreciation) And Capital Budgeting In Canada," No. 2, pp. 47-54.

Talaga, James A. and Gordian Ndubizu. "Accounting And Economic Development: Relationships Among The Paradigms," No. 2, pp. 55-68.

Rushinek, Avi and Sara F. Rushinek. "Additional Fund Allocation Constraints For Common Stock Investments: An Empirical Analysis Of Regional Portfolios In The Common Market And The United States," No. 2, pp. 69-89.

Skinner, R. C. "Cost Allocation In Management And Financial Accounting," No. 2, pp. 91-107.

Purcell, Thomas J., III and James P. Scott. "An Analysis Of The Feasibility Of Harmonizing Financial Reporting Practices Between Member Countries Of The EEC And The OECD," No. 2, pp. 109-131.

Koch, Helmut. "The Concept Of Synchronized Profit And Loss Accounting In Response To Continuous Increases Or Decreases In Prices," No. 2, pp. 133-144.

Juchau, Roger, Mick White and Roger Hopkins. "Tertiary Education Strategies For Accounting In Developing Societies - The Southwest Pacific As A Case Study," No. 2, pp. 145-160.

Ainajjar, Fouad. "Standardization In Accounting Practices: A Comparative International Study," No. 2, pp. 161-176.

International Journal of Accounting
Education and Research
Volume 22, 1986-87

Taylor, Martin E., Thomas G. Evans and Arthur C. Joy. "The Impact Of IASC Accounting Standards On Comparability And Consistency Of International Accounting Reporting Practices," No. 1, pp. 1-9.

Yamaji, Hidetoshi. "Collective Bargaining And Accounting Disclosure: An Inquiry Into The Changes In Accounting Policy," No. 1, pp. 11-23.

Rueschhoff, Norlin G. "International Accounting And Auditing In The U.S. CPA Examination, 1917-86," No. 1, pp. 25-32.

Abdel-Magid, Moustafa F. and Joseph K. Cheung. "Ratio Scales, Foreign Exchange Rates, And The Problem Of Foreign Currency Translation: An Analytical-Empirical Perspective," No. 1, pp. 33-49.

Hoshower, Leon B. and Linda Ann Mandel. "Transfer Pricing Policies Of Diversified U.S.-Based Multinationals," No. 1, pp. 51-59.

Lebow, Marc I. and Rasoul H. Tondkar. "Accounting In The Soviet Union," No. 1, pp. 61-79.

Hove, Mfandaidza R. "Accounting Practices In Developing Countries: Colonialism's Legacy Of Inappropriate Technologies," No. 1, pp. 81-100.

Chan, Anthony Moung-Yin. "The Pattern Of The Theoretical Basis Of IAS: Accounting Theory Models At The International Level," No. 1, pp. 101-117.

Schiff, J. B. "Management Accounting Practices Statement Promulgation: An International Perspective," No. 1, pp. 119-134.

Porcano, Thomas M. "The Perceived Efficacy Of Government Incentives: A Comparative Study Of Seven European Community Countries," No. 1, pp. 135-158.

Bloom, Robert and Araya Debessay. "The Controversial Development Of The Deprival Value Concept," No. 1, pp. 159-172.

Pratt, Jamie and Giorgio Behr. "Environmental Factors, Transaction Costs, And External Reporting: A Cross-Sectional Comparison," No. 2, pp. 1-24.

Duangploy, Orapin, Eugene L. Zieha and Dahli Gray. "SFAS No. 52 And The Statement Of Changes In Financial Position: A Survey And Proposal For Change," No. 2, pp. 25-40.

Carmony, Larry. "Accounting In The Context Of Its Environment: The Uruguayan Case," No. 2, pp. 41-56.

Osiegbu, Patrick I. "The State Of Accounting Education In Nigeria," No. 2, pp. 57-68.

Demirag, Istemi S. "A Review Of The Objectives Of Foreign Currency Translation," No. 2, pp. 69-85.

Rivola-Clay, Anna Maria and Timothy S. Doupnik. "The Progress Of Italian Accounting: Allegro Ma Nontroppo," No. 2, pp. 87-102.

Brooks, LeRoy D. and Dale Buckmaster. "On Monetary Working Capital Maintenance: Theory And Implementation," No. 2, pp. 103-114.

Ndubizu, Gordian A. "Management Preferences For Foreign Currency Standards: An Empirical Analysis," No. 2, pp. 115-130.

Schweikart, James A. "Attitude Measurement And Instrumentation In International Accounting Research," No. 2, pp. 131-141.

Mielke, David E. and Don E. Giacomino. "Cash-Flow Reporting: A Step Toward International Harmonization," No. 2, pp. 143-151.

Ahmed, Sadrudin A. and Daniel Zeghal. "Industry Segment Identification And Social Responsibility Information Disclosure In Selected Canadian Companies," No. 2, pp. 153-167.

Aguirre, Alejandro and Moshe Hagigi. "Accounting, Economic, And Environmental Determinants Of Financial Reporting Practices In Guatemala," No. 2, pp. 169-191.

ISSUES IN ACCOUNTING EDUCATION

Issues in Accounting Education
No Volume No., 1983

Siegel, Gary. "National Study On Professional Accounting Education: Initial Results On Department/Professional School Differences," No. 1, pp. 9-18.

Bergin, J. Lawrence. "The Effect Of Previous Accounting Study On Student Performance In The First College-Level Financial Accounting Course," No. 1, pp. 19-28.

Edmonds, Thomas P. "The Effect Of Environmental Complexity On The Level Of Information Processing By Introductory Accounting Students," No. 1, pp. 29-37.

Lentilhon, Robert W. and Anthony T. Krzystofik. "Professional Examination Preparation In AACSB Accredited And Member Schools," No. 1, pp. 38-49.

Brown, James F., Jr. and Thomas E. Balke. "Accounting Curriculum Comparison By Degree Program Of Schools Intending To Seek AACSB Accreditation," No. 1, pp. 50-59.

Campbell, David R. and Robert W. Williams. "Accreditation Of Accounting Programs: Administrators' Perceptions Of Proposed AACSB Standards," No. 1, pp. 60-70.

Seifrick, John. "The Statement Of Changes In Financial Position: Retain, Repeal, Or Modify?," No. 1, pp. 71-78.

Davis, Charles J. "A Structured Approach To Preparation Of The Statement Of Changes In Financial Position," No. 1, pp. 79-89.

Brill, Robert J. "Analyzing Transactions And The Statement Of Changes In Financial Position: Model," No. 1, pp. 90-94.

Senatra, Phillip T. "The Statement Of Changes In Financial Position: A Flow-Chart Approach To Teaching Concepts And Procedures," No. 1, pp. 95-103.

Frakes, Albert H. "Emphasizing Financial Accounting Theory In Intermediate Accounting," No. 1, pp. 104-114.

Hiltner, Arthur A. "Statistical Sampling In Auditing: A Simulation," No. 1, pp. 115-122.

Scheiner, James H. and Jack E. Kiger. "Generalized Audit Software: A Classroom Approach," No. 1, pp. 123-131.

Wu, Frederick H. "Teaching Accounting Information Systems: A Synthesis," No. 1, pp. 132-145.

Petersen, Russell J. and Richard Grimlund. "CADRAS: Computer Assisted Data Recording And Analysis," No. 1, pp. 146-151.

Andrews, J. Douglas and Betty P. Pytlik. "Revision Techniques For Accountants: Means For More Effective And Efficient Written Communication," No. 1, pp. 152-163.

Lowenthal, Franklin. "The Down Payment Decision," No. 1, pp. 164-167.

Ijiri, Yuji. "New Dimensions In Accounting Education: Computers And Algorithms," No. 1, pp. 168-173.

Issues in Accounting Education
No Volume No., 1984

Williams, Doyle Z. "Schools Of Accounting: Anatomy Of A Movement," No. 1, pp. 13-32.

Beaver, William H. "Incorporating Research Into The Educational Process," No. 1, pp. 33-38.

Bublitz, Bruce and Robert Kee. "Measures Of Research Productivity," No. 1, pp. 39-60.

Hicks, Donald W. and Frederick M. Richardson. "Predicting Early Success In Intermediate Accounting: The Influence Of Entry Examination and GPA," No. 1, pp. 61-67.

O'Doherty, Brian. "Presenting R&D: A Convergence Model And An Algorithm," No. 1, pp. 68-74.

Partington, G. H. "Teaching Process Costing," No. 1, pp. 75-80.

Wu, Frederick H. "Teaching Managerial (Cost) Accounting With Electronic Spreadsheet Software," No. 1, pp. 81-97.

Koch, Bruce S. and Stewart S. Karlinsky. "The Effect Of Federal Income Tax Law Reading Complexity On Students' Task Performance," No. 1, pp. 98-110.

Dillaway, Manson P. "A Tax-Planning Approach For Teaching Corporate Distributions," No. 1, pp. 111-120.

Kneer, Dan C. "The Teaching Of An Effective And Efficient Audit Strategy," No. 1, pp. 121-135.

Umapathy, Srinivasan. "Algorithm-Based Accounting Education: Opportunities And Risks," No. 1, pp. 136-143.

Robinson, Loudell Ellis. "Accounting Theory: Undergraduate Coverage Of The FASB Conceptual Framework," No. 1, pp. 144-148.

Issues in Accounting Education
No Volume No., 1985

Solomons, David. "The AAA's International Lecturer Program: A Passage To India In 1984," No. 1, pp. 1-7.

Madden, Donald L. "Quality Accounting Education As Our Continuing Challenge," No. 1, pp. 8-14.

Alford, R. Mark, Mattie C. Porter and Robert H. Strawser. "Annual Reports Of Departments Of Accounting," No. 1, pp. 15-19.

Moores, Tommy and Gary E. White. "Perceptions Of The Control And Effectiveness Of Schools Of Accountancy," No. 1, pp. 20-27.

Gamble, George O. and Brian O'Doherty. "Citation Indexing And Its Uses In Accounting: An Awareness Survey And Departmental Ranking," No. 1, pp. 28-40.

Rebele, James E. "An Examination Of Accounting Students'

Perceptions Of The Importance Of Communication Skills In Public Accounting," No. 1, pp. 41-50.

Ricchiute, David N. and H. James Williams. "Heuristics, Biases, And Decision Making In Accounting," No. 1, pp. 51-58.

Abdolmohammadi, Mohammad J., Krishnagopal Menon, Thomas W. Oliver and Srinivasan Umapathy. "The Role Of The Doctoral Dissertation In Accounting Research Centers," No. 1, pp. 59-76.

Goosen, Kenneth R. and Jimie Kusel. "Integrating Microcomputer Use Into An Information Systems Course," No. 1, pp. 77-86.

Ketz, J. Edward and James A. Largay, III. "Teaching The 'Funds' Statement Under Alternative Valuation Methods," No. 1, pp. 87-96.

Engle, Terry J. and Rick Elam. "The Status Of Collegiate Auditing Education," No. 1, pp. 97-108.

Haskins, Mark E. and Robert P. Crum. "Cost Allocations: A Classroom Role-Play In Managerial Behavior And Accounting Choices," No. 1, pp. 109-130.

Cherry, Alan A. and Philip M. J. Reckers. "A Study Of The Need For Change In Intermediate Accounting Courses And Textbooks," No. 1, pp. 131-144.

Collins, J. Stephen. "An Effective Method For Teaching The Statement Of Changes In Financial Position," No. 1, pp. 145-156.

Kleckner, Robert A. "The Deregulation Of Public Accounting," No. 1, pp. 157-162.

Issues in Accounting Education
Volume 1, 1986

Baker, Richard E., John R. Simon and Frank P. Bazeli. "An Assessment Of The Learning Style Preferences Of Accounting Majors," No. 1, pp. 1-12.

Canlar, Mehmet. "College-Level Exposure To Accounting Study And Its Effect On Student Performance In The First MBA-Level Financial Accounting Course," No. 1, pp. 13-23.

Wright, Arnold M. "On The Use Of An Available Prior Examination Policy," No. 1, pp. 24-36.

Schroeder, Nicholas W. "Previous Accounting Education And College-Level Accounting Exam Performance," No. 1, pp. 37-47.

Ostrowski, Barbara A. "First-Time Accounting Faculty: The Job Search, Acceptance, And Support Process," No. 1, pp. 48-55.

Hooper, Paul and John Page. "Measuring Teaching Effectiveness By Student Evaluation," No. 1, pp. 56-64.

Seiler, Robert E. and Della A. Pearson. "Work Satisfaction Through Research - An Empirical Test," No. 1, pp. 65-75.

Fetters, Michael, John McKenzie and David Callaghan. "Does The Computer Hinder Accounting Education? An Analysis Of Some Empirical Data," No. 1, pp. 76-85.

Armitage, H. M. and J. E. Boritz. "Integrating Computers Into The Accounting Curriculum," No. 1, pp. 86-101.

Helmi, Medhat A. "Integrating The Microcomputer Into Accounting Education - Approaches And Pitfalls," No. 1, pp. 102-111.

Coombes, Robert J. and Peter H. Eddey. "Accounting Income: The Relationship Between Capital Maintenance And Asset Measurement," No. 1, pp. 112-122.

Monahan, Thomas F. and Bill N. Schwartz. "Stock Dividends Vs. Stock Splits: Normative Vs. Descriptive Approaches To Accounting Education," No. 1, pp. 123-131.

Pearl, Daniel. "Teaching The Statement Of Changes In Financial Position Without Worksheets Or T-Accounts," No. 1, pp. 132-142.

Nurnberg, Hugo. "The Ambiguous High-Low Method," No. 1, pp. 143-147.

Lovata, Linda M. "Experiential Process Costing Project," No. 1, pp. 148-152.

Baldwin, Bruce A. and Dan C. Kneer. "EDP Audit Education And EDP Auditor Characteristics: Empirical Data From Practitioners And Professors," No. 1, pp. 153-167.

Belkaoui, Ahmed. "The Accounting Students' Need For Achievement And Career Aspirations: An Experiment," No. 2, pp. 197-206.

Abdel-Khalik, A. Rashad. "The Computer Held Hostage, Day 1001: A Research Story," No. 2, pp. 207-229.

Bunn, Radie G. "The Professor's Home Office," No. 2, pp. 230-237.

Griffin, Richard B. and Sarah C. Dawkins. "Current Trends In Intermediate Accounting Course Content," No. 2, pp. 238-248.

Robinson, Loudell Ellis and Leonard A. Robinson. "Purchase Discounts Reconsidered," No. 2, pp. 249-260.

Manes, Rene P. and Thomas F. Schaefer. "Relating Financial Leverage To Annual Report Ratios," No. 2, pp. 261-267.

Ajinkya, Bipin, Rowland Atiase and Linda Smith Bamber. "Absorption Versus Direct Costing: Income Reconciliation And Cost-Volume-Profit Analysis," No. 2, pp. 268-281.

Chen, Joyce T. "Full And Direct Costing In Profit Variance Analysis," No. 2, pp. 282-292.

Tomczyk, Stephen and Sangit Chatterjee. "The Impact Of Outliers And Influential Points On The Cost Variance-Investigation Decision," No. 2, pp. 293-301.

Lowenthal, Franklin. "Multiple Splitoff Points," No. 2, pp. 302-308.

Krogstad, Jack L., Gerald Smith and Raymond J. Clay, Jr. "Impact Of A Simulation Of Audit Practice," No. 2, pp. 309-320.

Accounting Principles And Practices," No. 5, pp. 405-413.

Russell, Frank V. "Accounting Firms Can Write Better Long-Form Audit Reports," No. 5, pp. 429-434.

Bordner, H. W. "An Accountant's Guide To Procurement Procedures In The Department Of Defense," No. 6, pp. 464-473.

Inglis, John B. "Recent Statements Show New Techniques In Annual Reporting Are Being Widely Used," No. 6, pp. 474-478.

Harrow, Benjamin. "New Revenue Act Closes Loopholes, Removes Some Perplexities, Adds New Ones," No. 6, pp. 479-485.

Mann, Alan Grant. "How To Train Staff Men To Make An Effective Accounting Organization," No. 6, pp. 486-489.

Wilcox, Ed. B. and Howard C. Greer. "The Case Against Price-Level Adjustments In Income Determination," No. 6, pp. 492-503.

May, George O. "Comment On Wilcox-Greer Paper," No. 6, pp. 504-505.

Journal of Accountancy
Volume 91, 1951

Peloubet, Maurice E. "Choice Of Inventory Methods Depends On Specific Needs Of Each Business," No. 1, pp. 70-77.

Lore, Martin M. "Review Of Significant 1950 Federal Tax Decisions," No. 1, pp. 78-85.

Ankers, Raymond G. "Institute's Vocational Tests Aid In Hiring And Promoting Staff Men," No. 1, pp. 86-91.

Isenberg, William B. "Close Attention To Clients, Sound Staff Training Helps Smaller Practices Grow," No. 1, pp. 92-95.

Nelson, Robert E. "The Dilemma Of The Corporation In Tax Accounting For Dividends In Kind," No. 1, pp. 96-99.

Walker, George T. "Accountant's Present Concept Of Goodwill Depends Upon Unusual Earning Power," No. 1, pp. 100-103.

Stocker, Frederick B., Jr. "Bankers Ask Help Of Accountants In Getting Wider Use Of Standard-Size Bank Checks," No. 1, pp. 104-105.

Bac, Alexander. "Advantages Of 'Break-Even' Income Statement Compared With Conventional Statement," No. 1, pp. 106-111.

Kaplan, Alfred. "How To Establish And Operate Accounts For Small Contractor," No. 1, pp. 112-115.

Spencer, Martin M. "Tax Consequences Arising From Purchase Of Partnership Interest," No. 1, pp. 116-119.

Schilling, B. S., Jr. "Maryland's Uniform Accounting System Expected To Benefit Local Governments," No. 1, pp. 120-123.

Blough, Carman G. "The Accountant's Problems Arising Under SEC's New Revision Of Regulation S-X," No. 2, pp. 238-242.

Casey, William J. and J. K. Lasser. "Decisions To Make Now To Minimize Excess-Profits Tax Liability," No. 2, pp. 243-251.

Flynn, Thomas D. "A Public Accountant's Suggestions To His Client About To Take War Contracts," No. 2, pp. 252-255.

Cloake, T. Reginald. "Accountant's Responsibility In Preparing For Attack," No. 2, pp. 256-259.

Lourie, George B. and Arnold R. Cutler. "Effect Of Henderson Case On Tax Accounting Period Of Deceased Partner," No. 2, pp. 260-265.

Nad, Leon M. "How To Simplify Lifo By Use Of Dollar-Value Method," No. 2, pp. 266-271.

Rawlinson, Charles E. "An Audit Program Designed To Eliminate Year-End Peaks," No. 2, pp. 272-275.

Zitmore, Irving. "How To Decide Whether To Microfilm Business Records, And How To Go About It," No. 2, pp. 276-281.

Bachrach, Michael D. "How To Deal With Inconsistencies In Tax Law On Prepayments, Deferrals, Reserves," No. 2, pp. 282-285.

Deane, William V. "How Westinghouse Organizes Accounting Functions," No. 3, pp. 402-407.

Sanderbeck, Adrian F. "Advice For The New Partner," No. 3, pp. 408-410.

McDonald, Harry A. "Cooperation By SEC, Accountants, Helps Investors," No. 3, pp. 411-415.

Stauffer, Ralph L. "What Bankers Like To Find In Audit Reports," No. 3, pp. 416-421.

Pilie, Louis H. "How To Manage The Accounting Engagement," No. 3, pp. 422-427.

Robertson, Edward H. "Effect Of New Canadian Depreciation Law," No. 3, pp. 428-433.

Goode, Ellis W. "How Motor Carriers Use Punch Card Equipment," No. 3, pp. 434-438.

Weiner, Julian. "Per Diem Costing In Hospitals," No. 3, pp. 439-443.

Mulder, John E. "Continuing Professional Training For Lawyers," No. 3, pp. 444-446.

Willard, Dorothy G. "Accountant's Responsibilities In Income-Tax Work," No. 4, pp. 549-553.

Currier, Donald E. "Accounting Under 1948 Renegotiation Act," No. 4, pp. 554-561.

Morey, Lloyd. "Accounting Principles For Nonprofit Enterprises," No. 4, pp. 562-565.

Stanley, W. F. "Financial Statements Should Show Earnings Per Share," No. 4, pp. 566-569.

Weiss, Arthur. "New Inventory Control System Speeds Orders," No. 4, pp. 570-574.

Feurer, Louis. "Checking Client's Internal Controls," No. 4, pp. 575-579.

Wolfram, Harold W. "Taxpayer Can Lose Benefit Of Statute Of Limitations," No. 4, pp. 580-585.

Scott, F. D. "Inventory Accounting In Grocery Chain," No. 4, pp. 590-594.

Schlesinger, N. E. "Payment For Patent Use - Income Or Capital Gain?," No. 4, pp. 595-599.

Day, Emmett B. "Cash-Balance Approach To Funds Statement," No. 4, pp. 600-603.

McMurry, Robert N. "Choosing The Valuable Accounting Junior," No. 4, pp. 604-609.

Stoy, John M. "Time-Record System For Smaller Accounting Firms," No. 4, pp. 610-612.

Grady, Paul. "Auditing Large-Scale Business Enterprises," No. 5, pp. 678-685.

Robinson, Kenneth W. "Accountant As Expert Witness," No. 5, pp. 686-689.

Mills, Leslie. "Renegotiation Act Of 1951 Analyzed," No. 5, pp. 690-703.

Dolan, Thomas J. "How To Avoid Personal Holding Company Pitfalls," No. 5, pp. 704-709.

Alkire, Durwood L. "How To Handle Net Operating Loss Deductions," No. 5, pp. 710-714.

Reynolds, C. A. "Depreciation Of Assets Contributed By Community," No. 5, pp. 715-717.

Austin, Maurice. "Relations Of Lawyers And CPAs In Tax Practice," No. 6, pp. 805-815.

Fox, John J. "How Emergency Accelerated Amortization Works," No. 6, pp. 816-821.

Beckers, Leonard F. "New Audit Program Relieves Year-End Pressure," No. 6, pp. 822-826.

Jacobs, Perry F. and Seymour Spanier. "How To Make Wage Increases Under Regulation 6," No. 6, pp. 827-832.

Holzman, Robert S. "What Manner Of Tax Do The Courts Say We Have?," No. 6, pp. 833-834.

Journal of Accountancy
Volume 92, 1951

Bock, Russell S. "Relief Provisions Of New Excess-Profits Tax," No. 1, pp. 37-47.

Lipson, Harry A. "Control And Decision-Making Help For Small Retailers," No. 1, pp. 48-51.

Lasser, J. K. "20 Useful Tax Ideas From NYU Tax Institute," No. 1, pp. 52-61.

Griffith, James B. "How Accountants Can Learn About Business Machines," No. 1, pp. 72-81.

Redfern, E. K. "How Weak Accounting Systems Encourage Embezzlement," No. 1, pp. 82-86.

Peloubet, Maurice E. "Costs And Profits Under Government Contracts," No. 1, pp. 87-101.

Andrews, T. Coleman. "AIA Testimony Against Joint Budget Committee," No. 1, pp. 102-106.

Smith, Chas. W. "Current Useful Concepts Of Depreciation For Fixed Assets," No. 2, pp. 166-174.

Zug, Harry C. "Rigid Courses Of Study For CPA Certificates Are Opposed," No. 2, pp. 175-179.

Griswold, Henry J. and Walter W. King. "How To Make Salary Raises Under WSB Regulations," No. 2, pp. 180-183.

Densmore, Seth A. "Special CPA Services For Small Business," No. 2, pp. 184-189.

Paxton, Lloyd. "Accounting During Inflation Behind Iron Curtain," No. 2, pp. 190-197.

Ginder, Willard R. "How To Fix Value Of Close Corporation Stock," No. 2, pp. 198-199.

Jones, Richard F. "Evils Of Hybrid Accounting," No. 2, pp. 206-208.

Carter, K. LeM. "Canadian Legislation For Taxation On Corporate Income," No. 2, pp. 209-213.

Jensen, Wallace M. "Tax Effects Of Splitting A Corporation," No. 3, pp. 294-303.

Hearne, David C. "Using Client's Staff To Cut Costs Of Audit," No. 3, pp. 307-312.

Berger, Robert O., Jr. "Long-Term Debt In Financial Statements," No. 3, pp. 313-315.

Starr, Samuel S. "Renegotiation Appeals In The Tax Court," No. 3, pp. 316-321.

Wehr, P. N., Jr. "Disclosing Fixed-Asset Commitments In Statements," No. 3, pp. 322-325.

Atkinson, S. K. "Non-Manufacturing Costs In Management Decisions," No. 3, pp. 326-330.

Brink, Victor Z. "How Internal Auditing Provides Management Control," No. 4, pp. 421-427.

Stans, Maurice H. "Accounting In A Fire Insurance Program," No. 4, pp. 428-435.

Boughner, Jackson L. "Reviewing The Corporate Federal Income-Tax Return," No. 4, pp. 436-444.

Fagerberg, Dixon, Jr. "Nature Of Business Affects Accounting Services Needed," No. 4, pp. 445-449.

Hodge, William T. "The Unlamented, Self-Represented Taxpayer," No. 4, pp. 450-453.

Foote, Franklin M. "Accountants Need Not Suffer Eyestrain," No. 4, pp. 454-455.

Nelson, W. Porter. "Independent CPA's Part In Cost System Installation," No. 4, pp. 456-459.

Green, Paul M. "Preparing Accounting Data In Price Appeal Cases," No. 5, pp. 549-551.

Morrill, Thomas C. "Uniform Expense Accounting In Fire Insurance Industry," No. 5, pp. 552-561.

Jennings, Alvin R. "Relation Of Internal Control To Independent CPA," No. 5, pp. 562-571.

Cressey, Donald R. "Why Do Trusted Persons Commit Fraud?," No. 5, pp. 576-581.

Mahon, J. J., Jr. "Minimizing Personal Taxes On Executives. Stockholders," No. 5, pp. 582-587.

Stewart, A. Frank. "Individual CPA Should Agree To Statement 23," No. 5, pp. 588-590.

Journal of Accountancy
Volume 96, 1953

Journal of Accountancy
Volume 97, 1954

Journal of Accountancy
Volume 108, 1959

Penney, Louis H. "Inflation And The CPA," No. 1, pp. 23-27.

Stoy, John M. "Accountants And The Small Business Investment Act," No. 1, pp. 28-30.

Hudson, T. W., Jr. "Gifts Through Private Charitable Organizations," No. 1, pp. 31-38.

Horngren, Charles T. "More Useful Financial Statements," No. 1, pp. 39-46.

Purdue, Richard B. and E. Joe DeMaris. "Accounting In The U.S.S.R.," No. 1, pp. 47-57.

Andlauer, Edgar L. "Inventory Management," No. 2, pp. 25-31.

Harris, Reese H., Jr. "The Estate Planning Team," No. 2, pp. 32-36.

Smith, L. Hartley. "A Security Analyst Views Financial Statements," No. 2, pp. 37-41.

Kinnard, William N., Jr. "Advising Clients On Site Selection," No. 2, pp. 42-45.

Barron, J. F. "Tax Equity And Retroactive Tax Adjustments," No. 2, pp. 46-51.

Kohler, Eric L. "Accounting Practices In State Agencies," No. 2, pp. 52-60.

Penney, Louis H. "Continuing Professional Development," No. 3, pp. 31-36.

Defliese, Philip L. "Auditing And Internal Control," No. 3, pp. 37-43.

Tomlinson, Allen, III. "Gift Taxes And Tenancies By The Entirety," No. 3, pp. 44-50.

LaFrance, John W. "Salesmanship In Accounting Practice," No. 3, pp. 51-55.

Pelej, Joseph. "Cost-Cutting Potentials In Small Business," No. 3, pp. 56-61.

Barr, Andrew. "The Independent Accountant And The SEC," No. 4, pp. 32-37.

Paton, William A. "Depreciation - Concept And Measurement," No. 4, pp. 38-43.

Witte, Arthur E. "The Income Statement As A Management Tool," No. 4, pp. 44-48.

Simon, Carl J. "A Survey Of Incentive Compensation Plans," No. 4, pp. 49-57.

Gerver, Eli. "State Taxation Of Interstate Commerce," No. 4, pp. 58-62.

Melvoin, Charles. "Depreciation In Accountants' Reports," No. 5, pp. 34-38.

Craig, John B. "Statistical Sampling In Internal Auditing," No. 5, pp. 39-45.

Belda, Bertrand J. "Income And Expense Planning," No. 5, pp. 46-50.

Schlosser, R. E. "System Mechanization And Small Practitioners," No. 5, pp. 51-54.

Leonard, Robert L. "Accounting Needs Of Local Government," No. 5, pp. 55-59.

Stettler, H. F. "Case Studies For Professional Accounting Training," No. 5, pp. 60-64.

Lewis, Robert W. "An Industry View Of Budgeting," No. 6, pp. 30-36.

Blough, Carman G. "Challenges To The Accounting Profession In The U.S.," No. 6, pp. 37-42.

Griffin, Carleton H. "Changes In Accounting Method," No. 6, pp. 43-50.

Bows, Albert J., Jr. "Creative Accounting Pays Its Way," No. 6, pp. 51-55.

Lewis, Charles A., Jr. "Management Services For Small Clients," No. 6, pp. 56-60.

Nelson, Robert E. "Reproducing Tax Returns," No. 6, pp. 61-64.

Journal of Accountancy
Volume 109, 1960

Richardson, Mark E. "Standards Of Responsibility Of CPAs In Tax Practice," No. 1, pp. 29-33.

Kraayenhof, J. "International Challenges For Accounting," No. 1, pp. 34-38.

Gellhorn, Walter. "Occupational Licensing - A Nationwide Dilemma," No. 1, pp. 39-45.

Wilgus, Ralph E. "Improving Auditor-Client Co-Operation," No. 1, pp. 46-50.

Hamilton, Douglas L. "The Changing Role Of The Controller," No. 1, pp. 51-56.

Sprague, W. D. "Reliance Upon Other Auditors," No. 2, pp. 29-33.

Powell, Weldon. "The Challenge To Research," No. 2, pp. 34-41.

Weitzel, John P. "Practice Before The Treasury," No. 2, pp. 42-46.

Regazzi, John H. "Pitfalls Of Cash Basis For Employee Funds," No. 2, pp. 47-51.

Cook, Edward T. "Revised Contract Cost Principles," No. 2, pp. 52-65.

Catlett, George R. "Relation Of Acceptance To Accounting Principles," No. 3, pp. 33-38.

Thompson, Kenneth L. "Long-Range Planning For A Growing Firm," No. 3, pp. 39-43.

Schaffer, Walter L. "Audits Of Insurance Companies," No. 3, pp. 44-50.

Horvitz, Oscar. "Controlling Truck Costs," No. 3, pp. 51-55.

Bastable, Charles W. "Business Games, Models, And Accounting," No. 3, pp. 56-60.

Miller, Robert E. "Who Should Pay The President's Salary?," No. 3, pp. 61-64.

Olive, George S., Jr. "Management Services - A Local Firm Approach," No. 4, pp. 31-34.

Shirk, Stanley E. "Special Problems Of Bank Audits," No. 4, pp. 35-42.

Griffin, Charles H. and Thomas H. Williams. "Measuring Adequate Disclosure," No. 4, pp. 43-48.

Sharaf, Hussein A. and R. K. Mautz. "An Operational Concept Of Independence," No. 4, pp. 49-54.

White, Robert H. "Municipal Budgets," No. 4, pp. 55-61.

Ruggles, Robert W. "Humanizing Staff Relations," No. 4, pp. 62-65.

Donnelly, Vincent T. "Electromechanical Production Control," No. 4, pp. 66-69.

Hoover, J. Edgar. "The Accountant's Role In The FBI," No. 5, pp. 36-40.

Moonitz, Maurice. "The Changing Concept Of Liabilities," No. 5, pp. 41-46.

Trueblood, Robert M. "Operations Research - A Challenge To Accounting," No. 5, pp. 47-51.

Tomlinson, Allen. "The Gift Tax Credit Against The Estate Tax," No. 5, pp. 52-57.

Blough, Carman G. "Responsibility To Third Parties," No. 5, pp. 58-65.

Schneider, Warren A. "An Auditor Looks At Labor Unions," No. 5, pp. 66-71.

Harrington, Russell C. "Reforming The Federal Tax System," No. 6, pp. 30-35.

Bernstein, Leopold A. "Over-All Checks In Auditing," No. 6, pp. 36-41.

Toan, Arthur B., Jr. "The Auditor And EDP," No. 6, pp. 42-46.

Broucek, Gerald R. "Computer Operation By A CPA Firm," No. 6, pp. 47-50.

Kamp, John N. "Applications Of Subchapter S," No. 6, pp. 51-55.

Malmon, Alvin S. "Pension Plan Contributions," No. 6, pp. 56-59.

Morse, Ellsworth H., Jr. "The Case For Accepting GAO Experience," No. 6, pp. 60-64.

Journal of Accountancy
Volume 110, 1960

Stans, Maurice H. "Current Improvements In Federal Budgeting," No. 1, pp. 27-31.

Coveney, Lloyd I. "Unusual Aspects Of Savings And Loan Audits," No. 1, pp. 32-36.

Goudeket, A. "An Application Of Replacement Value Theory," No. 1, pp. 37-47.

Boyce, L. Fred, Jr. "Installing A Medium-Sized Computer," No. 1, pp. 48-53.

Sebastian, Henry R. "Stock Redemption Problems In Estate Planning," No. 1, pp. 54-60.

Simons, Harry. "What Accountants Think Of Accounting," No. 2, pp. 35-44.

McConnell, Richard J. "The Philadelphia Story," No. 2, pp. 45-52.

Dale, W. Carl. "An Accounting System For A Small CPA Firm," No. 2, pp. 53-59.

Martorano, Lewis A. G. "Sales Forecasting," No. 2, pp. 60-64.

Lewis, Ralph F. "Management Services For Small Clients," No. 3, pp. 39-43.

Love, David. "Differences Between Business And Tax Accounting," No. 3, pp. 44-50.

Herrick, Anson. "Inflation In Accounting," No. 3, pp. 51-56.

Trueblood, Robert M. "Professional And Technical Practitioners In Accounting," No. 3, pp. 57-62.

Rockwood, Charles P. "The Changing Image Of A Profession," No. 4, pp. 35-43.

Catlett, George R. "Factors That Influence Accounting Principles," No. 4, pp. 44-50.

Quinn, James Brian. "Control Of Research And Development Costs," No. 4, pp. 51-58.

Cole, Leroy H. "Accounting For Real Estate Developments," No. 4, pp. 59-63.

Stans, Maurice H. "A Call To Responsibility," No. 5, pp. 39-43.

Coughlan, John W. "Working Capital And Credit Standing," No. 5, pp. 44-52.

Trumbull, Wendell P. "Tax Allocation In Managerial Analysis," No. 5, pp. 53-57.

Lipscomb, Glenard P. "Relations Between CPAs And Non-CPAs," No. 5, pp. 58-62.

Grinaker, Robert L. "The Accountant's Responsibility In Expressing An Opinion," No. 5, pp. 63-69.

Chambers, R. J. "The Conditions Of Research In Accounting," No. 6, pp. 33-39.

Oravec, R. J. "Statistical Inventory Management," No. 6, pp. 40-52.

Puder, A. H. "The Audit Of A Nationwide Company By Local Firms," No. 6, pp. 53-56.

Crovatto, Raymond A. "Data Processing For Small Clients," No. 6, pp. 57-62.

Witschey, Robert E. "CPAs And Noncertified Practitioners," No. 6, pp. 63-71.

Boyce, L. Fred, Jr. "Lamb Among The Ledgers," No. 6, pp. 72-74.

Journal of Accountancy
Volume 111, 1961

Higgins, Thomas G. "The Need For A New Rule On Independence," No. 1, pp. 37-42.

Heath, Leslie A. "An Ounce Of Prevention - Means Dollars To

Your Estate," No. 1, pp. 43-47.

Flowers, W. Baker. "Some Criteria For Post-Statement Disclosure," No. 1, pp. 48-58.

Blank, Virgil F. "Management Concept In Electronic Systems," No. 1, pp. 59-66.

Epps, Max I. "Realistic Accounting Under South American Inflation," No. 1, pp. 67-73.

Zises, Alvin. "Disclosure Of Long-Term Leases," No. 2, pp. 37-47.

Reuben, Milton H. "The Accountant's Part In Estate Planning," No. 2, pp. 48-50.

Arkin, Herbert. "Discovery Sampling In Auditing," No. 2, pp. 51-54.

Learned, Marcel. "How To Set Fees," No. 2, pp. 55-58.

Wheatcroft, G. S. A. "Ethical Restraints On Tax Practice In Great Britain," No. 2, pp. 59-66.

Hennessy, John L. "Recording Lease Obligations," No. 3, pp. 40-46.

Carey, John L. "Higher Accreditation For CPAs," No. 3, pp. 47-53.

Chan, Stephen. "Notes To Financial Statements," No. 3, pp. 54-58.

Mason, Perry. "'Cash Flow' Analysis And Funds Statements," No. 3, pp. 59-72.

Peloubet, Maurice I. "Is Further Uniformity Desirable Or Possible?," No. 4, pp. 35-40.

Spacek, Leonard. "Are Accounting Principles Generally Accepted?," No. 4, pp. 41-46.

Gaa, Charles J. "Uniformity In Accounting Principles," No. 4, pp. 47-50.

Blough, Carman G. "Principles And Procedures," No. 4, pp. 51-53.

Murphy, Mary E. "The British Accounting Tradition In America," No. 4, pp. 54-63.

Baker, Robert L. "Special Farm Tax Problems," No. 4, pp. 64-68.

Perry, Kenneth W. and Warren B. Cutting. "Recruiting For The Small Firm," No. 5, pp. 41-45.

Brown, R. Gene. "Statistical Sampling Tables For Auditors," No. 5, pp. 46-54.

Hoffman, William H., Jr. "Use Of Insurance In Employee Compensation," No. 5, pp. 55-62.

Arnett, Harold E. "What Does 'Objectivity' Mean To Accountants?," No. 5, pp. 63-68.

Sapienza, Samuel R. "Distinguishing Between Purchase And Pooling," No. 6, pp. 35-40.

Hepworth, Samuel R. "Partnership Agreements For CPAs," No. 6, pp. 41-46.

Kaufman, Felix. "Effects Of EDP On Internal Control," No. 6, pp. 47-59.

Johnson, John W. "Creditors' Collection Problems," No. 6, pp. 60-63.

Steiner, Robert A. "An Analysis Of Income Tax Allocation," No. 6, pp. 64-67.

Journal of Accountancy
Volume 112, 1961

May, George O. "Retrospect And Prospect," No. 1, pp. 31-36.

Trueblood, Robert M. "The Management Service Function In Public Accounting," No. 1, pp. 37-44.

Lewis, Ralph F. "Data Processing Centers And The CPA," No. 1, pp. 45-51.

Bordner, H. W. "Fund Concepts As Accounting Postulates," No. 1, pp. 52-60.

Barron, J. F. "Tax Effects Of Inventory Methods," No. 2, pp. 34-40.

Foulk, David G. "Appraising Factoring For A Client," No. 2, pp. 41-46.

Christensen, Oreson H. "Welfare And Pension Plans Disclosure," No. 2, pp. 47-51.

Brausch, John J. "Direct Costing: Progress Or Folly?," No. 2, pp. 52-60.

Ferrara, William L. "Direct Costing: Are Direct Costs Relevant Costs?," No. 2, pp. 61-62.

Re..., Richard C. "On Starting A Practice," No. 2, pp. 63-66.

MacNeill, James H. "Accounting For Inflation Abroad," No. 2, pp. 67-73.

Paton, W. A. "'Deferred Income' - A Misnomer," No. 3, pp. 38-40.

Barker, Richard B. "Dollar-Value Lifo And The Klein Chocolate Case," No. 3, pp. 41-45.

Palamara, Francis J. "Commercial Financing For Accountants' Clients," No. 3, pp. 46-49.

Bach, G. Leland. "Accounting Education For The 1980's," No. 3, pp. 50-54.

Puzey, Russell V. "Accounting Is Communication," No. 3, pp. 55-60.

Hylton, Delmer P. "Some Comments On Materiality," No. 3, pp. 61-64.

Wittus, Erwin Bud. "A CPA Firm's Experience With Punched Tape," No. 3, pp. 65-70.

Welsch, Glenn A. "Budgeting For Management Planning And Control," No. 4, pp. 37-41.

Morse, Ellsworth H., Jr. "GAO Audits Of Management Performance," No. 4, pp. 42-48.

Green, David, Jr. "Financial Statement Working Papers," No. 4, pp. 49-56.

Briloff, Abraham J. "Estate Planning Problems Of Partners," No. 4, pp. 57-64.

Lewis, Charles A., Jr. "Loan Applications To The Small Business Administration," No. 4, pp. 65-70.

Heimbucher, Clifford V. "Fifty-Three Jurisdictions," No. 5, pp. 42-50.

Penney, Louis H. "The Significance Of Mergers Of Accounting Firms," No. 5, pp. 51-58.

Denhardt, J. G., Jr. "Income In Respect Of A Decedent," No. 5, pp. 59-62.

Stringer, Kenneth W. "Some Basic Concepts Of Statistical Sampling In Auditing," No. 5, pp. 63-69.

Bedford, Norton M. "Education For Accounting As A Learned Profession," No. 6, pp. 33-41.

Becker, Benjamin M. and Samuel S. Becker. "Financing A Business Enterprise," No. 6, pp. 42-46.

Rothman, David C. "Pension And Profit-Sharing Plans," No. 6, pp. 47-53.

Haglund, Byron E., Lee J. Adamson and Richard D. Metcalf. "Punched Card Accounting For Small Businesses," No. 6, pp. 54-58.

Journal of Accountancy
Volume 113, 1962

Penney, Louis H. "The American Institute Of CPAs - Past And Future," No. 1, pp. 31-39.

Keogh, Eugene J. "What's Ahead In Federal Tax Legislation," No. 1, pp. 40-44.

Graves, Thomas J. "Problems In Federal Tax Administration," No. 1, pp. 45-52.

Engelmann, Konrad. "Accounting Problems In Developing Countries," No. 1, pp. 53-56.

Meredith, Harlan C. "Fidelity And Surety Bonds," No. 1, pp. 57-63.

Blumenthal, Philip L., Jr. "The Accountant Looks At His Client's Future," No. 1, pp. 64-68.

Bevis, Herman W. "The CPA's Attest Function In Modern Society," No. 2, pp. 28-35.

Richardson, Mark E. "The Accountant And The Tax Law," No. 2, pp. 36-41.

Cannon, Arthur M. "Discussion Notes On 'The Basic Postulates Of Accounting'," No. 2, pp. 42-53.

Kocan, Peter. "Reporting The Operations Of Jointly Owned Companies," No. 2, pp. 54-59.

Higgins, Thomas G. "Professional Ethics: A Time For Reappraisal," No. 3, pp. 29-35.

Kellogg, Irving. "How To Meet The Challenge Of A Successful Client," No. 3, pp. 36-42.

Samuelson, A. T. "Depreciation Of Federal Water Resources Projects," No. 3, pp. 43-48.

Kupfer, T. Milton. "Salvage Value And Useful Life," No. 3, pp. 49-56.

Lorensen, Leonard. "Pension Costs In Selected Financial Statements," No. 3, pp. 57-61.

Lyverse, Sam W. "Inventory Observation," No. 3, pp. 62-64.

Barr, Andrew. "Accountants And The Securities And Exchange Commission," No. 4, pp. 31-37.

Simon, Sidney I. "The Lease-Option Plan - Its Tax And Accounting Implications," No. 4, pp. 38-45.

Williams, Robert W. and Robert I. Leonard. "Financial Reporting By Nonprofit Organizations," No. 4, pp. 46-50.

Hoffman, William H., Jr. "Tax Planning And The Reasonableness Test," No. 4, pp. 51-57.

Lipoff, Carl. "Duplicating And Copying Methods In Practitioners' Offices," No. 4, pp. 58-66.

LaFrance, John W. "Communication With The Client And The Public," No. 5, pp. 39-44.

Grady, Paul. "The Quest For Accounting Principles," No. 5, pp. 45-50.

Beamer, Elmer G. "The Expanding Common Body Of Knowledge Of CPAs," No. 5, pp. 51-54.

Gladstone, William L. "The Co-Operative Housing Corporation," No. 5, pp. 55-58.

Witschey, Robert E. "The Future Of The Local Practitioner," No. 6, pp. 31-36.

Blake, Matthew F. "Professional Association Laws And The CPA," No. 6, pp. 37-46.

Wright, Robert G. "Changing Concepts In EDP Feasibility Studies," No. 6, pp. 47-51.

Mayo, Ralph B. "Administration Of A Tax Practice," No. 6, pp. 52-56.

Nicolson, Miklos Szucs. "Balance Sheets For Partnerships And Proprietors," No. 6, pp. 57-61.

Journal of Accountancy
Volume 114, 1962

Stone, Marvin L. and Arthur E. Witte. "CPA Services For The CPA," No. 1, pp. 31-39.

Wright, Wilmer. "Why Direct Costing Is Rapidly Gaining Acceptance," No. 1, pp. 40-46.

Puder, Richard K. "Local Practitioners Can Use Computers," No. 1, pp. 47-52.

Raby, William L. "Tax Planning And The CPA," No. 1, pp. 53-56.

Corbin, Donald A. and Russell Taussig. "The AICPA Funds Statement Study," No. 1, pp. 57-62.

Hicks, Ernest L. "Materiality: A Useful Audit Tool," No. 1, pp. 63-67.

Brandt, Robert F. "One World In Accounting," No. 1, pp. 68-71.

Queenan, John W. "Postulates: Their Place In Accounting Research," No. 2, pp. 29-33.

McAnly, H. T. "Inventory Pricing," No. 2, pp. 34-39.

Krekstein, I. H. "How Local Firms Can Help Each Other," No. 2, pp. 40-45.

Miller, Herbert E. "How Much Income Tax Allocation?," No. 2, pp. 46-51.

Ready, Robert D. "Auditor's Protection Against Client's Fraud," No. 2, pp. 52-59.
Jennings, Alvin R. "International Standards Of Accounting And Auditing," No. 3, pp. 36-42.
Cannon, Arthur M. "Financial Statements For A Church," No. 3, pp. 43-49.
Steele, Charles G. "An Auditor Samples Statistics," No. 3, pp. 50-56.
Erdahl, C. A. "A Modern Profit Concept In The Retail Selling Field," No. 3, pp. 57-62.
Defliese, Philip L. "Auditor's Responsibility For Fraud Detection," No. 4, pp. 36-44.
Dudick, Thomas S. "Direct Costing - 'Handle With Care'," No. 4, pp. 45-52.
Henning, Fred M. "Health And Welfare Funds - Contributions And Premiums," No. 4, pp. 53-58.
Keller, Thomas F. "The Annual Income Tax Accrual," No. 4, pp. 59-65.
Toan, Arthur B., Jr. "Data Processing, Accounting And Business Administration," No. 5, pp. 43-49.
Brown, R. Gene. "Objective Internal Control Evaluation," No. 5, pp. 50-56.
Marple, Raymond P. "The Balance Sheet - Capital Sources And Composition," No. 5, pp. 57-60.
Sager, William H. "Civil Tax Penalties," No. 5, pp. 61-66.
Graves, Thomas J. "Responsibility Of The Tax Adviser," No. 6, pp. 33-38.
Inglis, John B. "Regulation Of Corporations In Great Britain," No. 6, pp. 39-44.
Schlosser, Robert E. "Accounting System Review Techniques," No. 6, pp. 45-48.
Fremgen, James M. "Involuntary Liquidation Of Lifo Inventories," No. 6, pp. 49-56.
Jaenicke, Henry R. "Ownership Continuity And ARB No. 48," No. 6, pp. 57-63.

Journal of Accountancy
Volume 115, 1963

Cohn, Theodore. "Use Of Punched Tape In Preparing Tax Returns," No. 1, pp. 56-58.
Bromage, Mary C. "A Matter Of Wording," No. 1, pp. 59-62.
Cerf, Alan Robert. "A Survey Of Compliance With Reporting Standards," No. 2, pp. 42-49.
Ashworth, John. "Some Further Data On The Image Of The CPA," No. 2, pp. 50-55.
Birnberg, Jacob G. and Nicholas Dopuch. "A Conceptual Approach To The Framework For Disclosure," No. 2, pp. 56-63.
Becker, Samuel S. "The CPA's Challenge In Estate Planning," No. 2, pp. 64-69.
Kleerekoper, I. "The Economic Approach To Accounting," No. 3, pp. 36-40.
Dickens, Robert L. and Thomas F. Keller. "The Auditor's Responsibility For His Opinion," No. 3, pp. 41-48.
Elliott, Norman J. "Profit Potentials In A Loss Company," No. 3, pp. 49-56.
Manes, Rene Pierre. "Using Computers To Improve Cost Distribution," No. 3, pp. 57-60.
Greer, Howard C. "How To Succeed In Confusing People Without Really Trying," No. 3, pp. 61-65.
Pinter, Alexander, Jr. "My First Year With Punched Tape Accounting," No. 4, pp. 49-53.
Axelson, Kenneth S. "Are Consulting And Auditing Compatible?," No. 4, pp. 54-58.
Anderson, D. S. "Communications Problems Of Financial Reporting," No. 4, pp. 59-64.
Tietjen, A. Carl. "Accounting Principles, Practices And Methods," No. 4, pp. 65-68.
Ingalls, Edmund F. "Accounting Entries For The Investment Tax Credit," No. 5, pp. 37-45.
Wellington, Roger. "Capital Budgeting," No. 5, pp. 46-53.
Sarabia, Antonio R. "The European Common Market," No. 5, pp. 54-58.
Metz, Robert. "How A Reporter Sees The Certified Public Accountant," No. 5, pp. 59-64.
Schiff, Michael. "Reporting For More Profitable Product Management," No. 5, pp. 65-70.
Beyer, Robert. "Integrated Financial Services," No. 6, pp. 30-36.
McLaren, N. Loyall. "Restricted Stock Options," No. 6, pp. 37-42.
Reich, Marion R. "Buy And Sell Agreements Funded By Life Insurance," No. 6, pp. 43-48.
Kocan, Peter. "Geographical Distribution Of Earnings And Assets," No. 6, pp. 49-54.

Journal of Accountancy
Volume 116, 1963

Sargent, Arthur M. "Referrals," No. 1, pp. 40-45.
SyCip, Washington. "Auditors In A Developing Economy," No. 1, pp. 46-48.
Nelson, A. Tom. "Capitalizing Leases - The Effect On Financial Ratios," No. 1, pp. 49-58.
Schley, Norman E. "The CPA And Estate Planning," No. 1, pp. 59-64.
McAnly, H. T. "Administrative Expense And Profit In Product Pricing," No. 2, pp. 33-38.
Donaldson, J. Bruce and Richard D. Hobbet. "The Passing Parade Of 1962 Tax Litigation," No. 2, pp. 39-49.
Hoffman, William H., Jr. and Donald E. Vaughn. "Departmental And Item Profitability For Retailers," No. 2, pp. 50-58.

Dilley, David R. "Professional Writing - Why And How," No. 2, pp. 59-65.
Fluckiger, W. Lynn. "A Philosophy Of Fund Accounting," No. 2, pp. 66-71.
Boni, Gregory M. "Impact Of Electronic Data Processing On Auditing," No. 3, pp. 39-44.
Maddrea, T. Grayson. "Intangibles Should Be Amortizable For Tax Purposes," No. 3, pp. 45-49.
Tracy, John A. "Accounting For Mutual Funds," No. 3, pp. 50-57.
Ives, Martin. "Audit Techniques In Defense Contracting," No. 3, pp. 58-63.
Kohler, Eric L. "Why Not Retain Historical Cost?," No. 4, pp. 35-41.
O'Hara, John B and Richard C. Clelland. "Satisfying Ourselves On Prior Years' Inventories," No. 4, pp. 42-52.
Stettler, Howard F. and Chester B. Vanatta. "Our Changing Profession," No. 4, pp. 53-56.
Backer, Morton. "Accounting Theory, Objectives And Measurements," No. 4, pp. 57-63.
Ford, Gordon. "Planning For Growth Of A CPA Firm," No. 5, pp. 45-51.
Grady, Paul. "Outline For Inventory Of Accounting Principles," No. 5, pp. 52-55.
Tierney, Cecilia. "Price-Level Adjustments - Problem In Perspective," No. 5, pp. 56-60.
Berman, Daniel S. and Bernard S. Cooper. "How The Tax Laws Encourage Corporate Acquisitions," No. 5, pp. 61-64.
Phillippe, Gerald L. "Top Management's Stake In Financial Reporting," No. 6, pp. 37-41.
Moonitz, Maurice. "Why Do We Need 'Postulates' And 'Principles'?," No. 6, pp. 42-46.
Cary, William L. "The SEC And Accounting," No. 6, pp. 47-50.
Bergwerk, Rudolph J. "Data Processing For Small Business," No. 6, pp. 51-54.
Roy, Robert H. and James H. MacNeill. "Study Of The Common Body Of Knowledge For CPAs," No. 6, pp. 55-58.

Journal of Accountancy
Volume 117, 1964

Witschey, Robert E. "The Business Need For Better Accounting Principles," No. 1, pp. 27-31.
Roper, Elmo. "As Others See You," No. 1, pp. 32-36.
Mead, George C. "Professional Responsibility In Reporting," No. 1, pp. 37-43.
Trueger, Paul M. "Profit Guidelines On Defense Contracts," No. 1, pp. 44-48.
Brown, R. Gene. "Automation, Labor Contracts, And CPAs," No. 1, pp. 49-53.
Heath, John, Jr. "Property Valuation Problems And The Accountant," No. 1, pp. 54-58.
Herzog, Asa S. "CPA's Role In Bankruptcy Proceeding," No. 1, pp. 59-69.
Spacek, Leonard. "The Treatment Of Goodwill In The Corporate Balance Sheet," No. 2, pp. 35-40.
Cook, John W. "Additional Rules Of Professional Ethics," No. 2, pp. 41-47.
Denhardt, J. G., Jr. "Estate Accounting," No. 2, pp. 48-56.
Orbach, Sydney C. "Deficiencies In First Filings," No. 2, pp. 57-64.
Squyres, Weldon J. "Tax Planning For Securities Transactions," No. 2, pp. 65-73.
Hill, Henry P. "Your New Bank Client," No. 3, pp. 36-41.
Ray, J. C. "Classification Of Audit Evidence," No. 3, pp. 42-47.
Sullivan, Frank E. "Professional Co-Operation In Estate Planning," No. 3, pp. 48-50.
Salmonson, R. F. "Reporting Earnings After An Acquisition," No. 3, pp. 51-54.
Holmes, William. "The Market Value Of Inventories: A Review," No. 3, pp. 55-59.
Corcoran, A. Wayne. "Matrix Bookkeeping," No. 3, pp. 60-66.
Blake, Matthew F. "Statements On Responsibilities In Tax Practice," No. 4, pp. 37-41.
Rappaport, Donald. "Materiality," No. 4, pp. 42-48.
Kaufman, Stuart F. "Internal Control Principles Applied To Banks," No. 4, pp. 49-55.
Horn, Frederick E. "Managing Cash," No. 4, pp. 56-62.
Richman, Sheldon. "Income Averaging - Tax Relief For The High Income Year," No. 5, pp. 37-41.
Goggans, Travis P. "Liberalized Depreciation And Investment Decisions," No. 5, pp. 42-48.
Sommerfeld, R. M. "The Need For CPA Bank Audits," No. 5, pp. 49-53.
Dill, S. Leland and Donald L. Adams. "Automated Auditing," No. 5, pp. 54-59.
Beyer, Robert. "Profitability Accounting: The Challenge And The Opportunity," No. 6, pp. 33-36.
Philips, G. Edward. "Research In Major Public Accounting Firms," No. 6, pp. 37-40.
Ready, Robert D. "Legal Liability Of The Tax Practitioner," No. 6, pp. 41-46.
Storey, Reed K. "Accounting Principles: AAA And AICPA," No. 6, pp. 47-55.

Journal of Accountancy
Volume 118, 1964

Higgins, W. Rodgers. "Valuation Of Readily Marketable Inventories," No. 1, pp. 25-32.

Bomeli, Edwin C. "Management Reviews By Scandinavian Accountants," No. 1, pp. 33-37.
Alvin, Gerald. "Charitable Contributions: 'Fruit' And 'Tree'," No. 1, pp. 38-42.
Golding, Jordan L. "The Nonauditing Aspects Of EDP Installations," No. 1, pp. 43-46.
Pennington, W. J. "Embezzling: Cases And Cautions," No. 1, pp. 47-51.
Jennings, Alvin R. "Opinions Of The Accounting Principles Board," No. 2, pp. 27-33.
Porter, W. Thomas. "Evaluating Internal Controls In EDP Systems," No. 2, pp. 34-40.
Simonetti, Gilbert, Jr. "Congress Assesses State Taxes On Interstate Business," No. 2, pp. 41-48.
Fess, Philip E. and H. Peter Holzer. "The Diverse Functions Of Accounting," No. 2, pp. 49-52.
Raby, William L. "The Impact Of Income Taxes On Corporate Research," No. 2, pp. 53-56.
Powell, Weldon. "The Development Of Accounting Principles," No. 3, pp. 37-43.
Matusiak, Louis W. and William Salowe. "Mr. CPA, How Good An Executive Are You?," No. 3, pp. 44-50.
Bernstein, Leopold A. "Ratio, Change And Trend Analysis As An Audit Tool," No. 3, pp. 51-55.
Solomon, Kenneth Ira. "Partnership Treatment Of Contributed Property," No. 3, pp. 56-59.
Tarbet, Joseph R. "Benefits Of Income Averaging," No. 3, pp. 60-62.
Weiss, Allen. "Forecasting Collections Of Receivables," No. 3, pp. 63-66.
Miller, Herbert E. "Audited Statements - Are They Really Management's?," No. 4, pp. 43-46.
Tomlinson, Allen, III. "Estate Planning And Administrative Expenses," No. 4, pp. 47-52.
Rosenfield, Paul H. "The Auditor's Standard Report Can Be Improved," No. 4, pp. 53-59.
Gasperow, A. Carl. "Tax Problems Of Country Clubs," No. 4, pp. 60-64.
Macy, Jack. "Change Of Accounting Method Versus Correction Of Error," No. 5, pp. 43-48.
Lennox, John E. "The Accounting Service Bureau: One CPA Firm's Experience," No. 5, pp. 49-54.
Stelzer, Herbert J. "Evaluation Of Internal Control In Small Audits," No. 5, pp. 55-61.
Nichols, Osgood. "The CPA In The Public Eye," No. 6, pp. 33-36.
Catlett, George R. "Controversy Over Uniformity Of Accounting Principles," No. 6, pp. 37-43.
Fox, John L. "'Useful Comparability' In Financial Reporting," No. 6, pp. 44-52.
Graves, Thomas J. "The Future Of Tax Practice," No. 6, pp. 53-57.

Journal of Accountancy
Volume 119, 1965

Solomon, Ezra. "Accounting In The Next Decade," No. 1, pp. 22-26.
Whisler, Thomas L. "The Manager And The Computer," No. 1, pp. 27-32.
Mahon, James J. "Some Observations On World Accounting," No. 1, pp. 33-37.
Murphy, Patrick J. "The Interest Equalization Tax Act," No. 1, pp. 38-45.
Mautz, R. K. "The Place Of Postulates In Accounting," No. 1, pp. 46-49.
Deskins, James Wesley. "Management Services And Management Decisions," No. 1, pp. 50-54.
Berlfein, Harold M. "Personal Holding Companies Under The 1964 Act," No. 1, pp. 55-60.
Blough, Roy. "International Developments Affecting Business," No. 2, pp. 34-39.
Browne, Dudley E. "The New Financial Executive," No. 2, pp. 40-44.
Trueger, Paul M. "Defense Contract Profits - Weighted Guidelines Method," No. 2, pp. 45-50.
Meisky, E. C. "Is Your Corporation 'Controlled'?," No. 2, pp. 51-56.
Kollaritsch, Felix P. "Future Service Potential Value," No. 2, pp. 57-62.
Reeve, John T. "Audits Of Nonprofit Organizations," No. 2, pp. 63-67.
Powell, Weldon. "'Inventory Of Generally Accepted Accounting Principles'," No. 3, pp. 29-35.
Mosher, Roy G. "Employee Benefit Plans: Their Adoption And Operation," No. 3, pp. 36-42.
Beyer, Robert. "Management Services - Time For Decision," No. 3, pp. 43-52.
Taylor, Howard D. "Automatic Data Processing In The Internal Revenue Service," No. 3, pp. 53-56.
Graham, Willard J. and Harold Q. Langenderfer. "Reporting Of Leases: Comment On APB Opinion No. 5," No. 3, pp. 57-62.
Caplin, Mortimer M. and Robert A. Klayman. "Depreciation - 1965 Model," No. 4, pp. 34-42.
Lehmann, Robert S. "A Case History In Co-Operation," No. 4, pp. 43-45.
Ross, Franz E. "Internal Control And Audit Of Real-Time Digital Systems," No. 4, pp. 46-55.
Byron, Earl T. "Stock Options - 1964 Changes," No. 4, pp. 56-63.
Baldwin, Ronald P. "Depreciation Recapture," No. 4, pp. 64-70.
Bedford, Norton M. "The Need For An Extension Of The Accrual Concept," No. 5, pp. 29-33.
Holzman, Robert S. "Thirty Years Of The Gregory Case," No. 5, pp. 34-38.
Rea, Richard C. "Helping A Client Make Up His Mind," No. 5, pp. 39-42.
Hoffman, William H., Jr. "The Buy And Sell Agreement In Estate Planning," No. 5, pp. 43-49.
Elder, Peter and Ernest J. Cholden. "Tax Planning For Foundations," No. 5, pp. 50-54.
Flynn, Thomas D. "Corporate Executives View Accounting Principles," No. 6, pp. 31-36.
Gindlin, Herbert M. "How To Use Short-Term Trusts In Family Tax Planning," No. 6, pp. 37-44.
Alvin, Gerald. "'Prepaid Income' And The Commissioner's Discretion Rule," No. 6, pp. 45-52.
Weinstein, Edward A. "Let The Buyer Beware!," No. 6, pp. 53-60.

Journal of Accountancy
Volume 120, 1965

Linowes, David F. "Professional Organization And Growth," No. 1, pp. 24-29.
Walker, Frank Perry. "A Casualty Insurance Survey For The Smaller Client," No. 1, pp. 30-33.
Hoover, John Edgar. "FBI Investigation Of Fraud," No. 1, pp. 34-39.
Ring, John R. "Professional Ethics Of The Future," No. 1, pp. 40-44.
Pladies, William J. "The Accounting Flow Chart," No. 1, pp. 45-54.
Enthoven, Adolf J. H. "Economic Development And Accountancy," No. 2, pp. 29-35.
Arndt, Robert J. "Auditing The Savings And Loan Associations," No. 2, pp. 36-43.
Metcalf, Richard W. and Joe R. Fritzemeyer. "Taxation Of Interstate Income: A Call To Action," No. 2, pp. 44-46.
Withey, Howard A. and Guy Holman. "Standards Of Accounting For Voluntary Health-Welfare Agencies," No. 2, pp. 47-56.
Davis, LaVaughn. "Corporate Separations," No. 3, pp. 35-42.
Hanson, Robert E. and Don Wharton. "A Local CPA Firm Plans For The Future," No. 3, pp. 43-49.
Ruhe, Karl. "The IRS Position On Allocation Of Intangibles In Business Acquisitions," No. 3, pp. 50-54.
Taylor, Robert G. "The Published Interim Report And The CPA," No. 3, pp. 55-58.
Rea, Richard C. "The Purchase, Sale And Merger Of Small Practices," No. 4, pp. 35-43.
Arkin, Herbert. "Computers And The Audit Test," No. 4, pp. 44-48.
Forer, Henry D. "Tax Planning For Savings And Loan Associations," No. 4, pp. 49-55.
Porter, W. Thomas, Jr. "A Control Framework For Electronic Systems," No. 4, pp. 56-63.
Myers, John H. "Depreciation Disclosure," No. 5, pp. 36-40.
Boutell, Wayne S. "Auditing Through The Computer," No. 5, pp. 41-47.
Sullivan, Brian. "An Introduction To 'Going Public'," No. 5, pp. 48-60.
Carey, John L. "The Integrated Accounting Service," No. 5, pp. 61-64.
Grady, Paul. "The Independent Auditing And Reporting Function Of The CPA," No. 5, pp. 65-71.
Bernstein, Leopold. "Whither Accounting Research?," No. 6, pp. 33-38.
Raymond, Robert H. "Life Insurance Company Vs. Traditional Financial Statements," No. 6, pp. 39-45.
Schley, Norman E. "The Altruistic Brothers Smythe," No. 6, pp. 46-52.
Solomon, Kenneth Ira. "Tax Effects Of Partnership Expansion," No. 6, pp. 53-57.

Journal of Accountancy
Volume 121, 1966

Powell, Weldon. "Extraordinary Items," No. 1, pp. 31-37.
Carey, John L. and William O. Doherty. "The Concept Of Independence - Review And Restatement," No. 1, pp. 38-48.
Gonzalez, J. M. "Highlights Of Proposed Amendment To Consolidated Return Regulations," No. 1, pp. 49-55.
Boyle, Edwin T. "What The Computer Means To The Accounting Profession," No. 1, pp. 56-67.
Perry, Raymond E. "Comprehensive Income Tax Allocation," No. 2, pp. 23-32.
Von Kaschnitz, Egon. "Management Letters For Clients Of Small Accounting Firms," No. 2, pp. 33-38.
Churchill, Neil C. and Richard M. Cyert. "An Experiment In Management Auditing," No. 2, pp. 39-43.
Lundy, Todd S. "The Use Of Data Processing In The Accountant's Office," No. 3, pp. 33-42.
Joplin, H. Bruce. "The Accountant's Role In Management Information Systems," No. 3, pp. 43-46.
McClellan, William A. "Valuation Of Closely Held Securities: Accounting Know-How Is The Key," No. 3, pp. 47-55.
Greer, Howard C. "Anyone For Widgets?," No. 4, pp. 41-49.
Cohen, Martin. "Intercorporate Transactions And Consolidated Returns," No. 4, pp. 50-54.
Stettler, Howard F. "Some Observations On Statistical Sampling In Auditing," No. 4, pp. 55-60.
Hendricks, Arthur G. "Does Your Client Need Long-Term Capital?," No. 5, pp. 36-45.

Miles, Jesse M. "Foreign Tax Liability For U.S. Firms Abroad," No. 5, pp. 46-52.
Linowes, David F. "Government And The Accounting Profession," No. 5, pp. 53-57.
Dodwell, Joseph W. "Operational Auditing: A Part Of The Basic Audit," No. 6, pp. 31-39.
Mills, Robert H. and Abbott L. Brown. "Soviet Economic Development And Accounting," No. 6, pp. 40-46.
Eggan, Hugh M. "Recapture Provisions Of The Internal Revenue Code," No. 6, pp. 47-55.

Journal of Accountancy
Volume 122, 1966

Bevis, Herman W. "Progress And Poverty In Accounting Thought," No. 1, pp. 34-40.
Davis, LaVaughn. "Tax Aspects Of Subsidiary Liquidations," No. 1, pp. 41-48.
Fyffe, Joseph B. "An Accounting System For A Small CPA Practice," No. 1, pp. 49-57.
Zlatkovich, Charles T. "A New Accounting Theory Statement," No. 2, pp. 31-36.
Wasyluka, Ray. "Staff Motivation In The CPA Firm," No. 2, pp. 37-40.
Berger, Bruce. "Installment Sales With Assumed Liabilities," No. 2, pp. 41-47.
Andrews, Victor L. "Should Parent And Captive Finance Companies Be Consolidated?," No. 2, pp. 48-56.
Roy, Robert H. and James H. MacNeill. "Horizons For A Profession: The Common Body Of Knowledge For CPAs," No. 3, pp. 38-50.
Shaw, William R. "Partners' Compensation," No. 3, pp. 51-55.
Hicks, Ernest L. "Comments On 'A Statement Of Basic Accounting Theory'," No. 3, pp. 56-60.
Gladstone, William L. "Tax Aspects Of The Allocation Of Purchase Price Of A Business," No. 4, pp. 36-44.
Sprouse, Robert T. "Accounting For What-You-May-Call-Its," No. 4, pp. 45-53.
Cirtin, Arnold. "Value Analysis - A New Tool For Cost Control," No. 4, pp. 54-58.
Stans, Maurice H. "The Federal Budget Needs Reform," No. 5, pp. 35-41.
Burns, Donald T. "Change In Accounting Method Or Correction Of An Error," No. 5, pp. 42-46.
Jacobson, Daniel. "How To Expand Your Accounting Practice," No. 5, pp. 47-50.
Bows, Albert J., Jr. "Problems In Disclosure Of Segments Of Conglomerate Companies," No. 6, pp. 33-37.
Sommerfeld, Ray M. "Taxation: Education's Orphan," No. 6, pp. 38-44.
Sprague, W. D. and Arthur J. Levy. "Accounting And Law: Is Dual Practice In The Public Interest?," No. 6, pp. 45-52.
Zweig, Jeanne. "Administrative Skills - A Prerequisite For The Smallest Of CPA Firms," No. 6, pp. 53-55.

Journal of Accountancy
Volume 123, 1967

Humphrey, Mitchell O. "Management Letters - Image Builders For The CPA," No. 1, pp. 27-32.
Langenderfer, Harold. "A Problem Of Communication," No. 1, pp. 33-40.
SyCip, Washington Sy. "Professional Practice In Developing Economies," No. 1, pp. 41-45.
Carey, John L. "Accounting Legislation Of The Future," No. 1, pp. 46-51.
Barnes, William T. "The Treasury Department Report On Private Foundations," No. 2, pp. 34-40.
Millar, Victor E. "The Three Levels Of EDP Practice," No. 2, pp. 41-44.
Briloff, Abraham J. "Let The Seller Beware," No. 2, pp. 45-51.
Seidman, J. S. "So You're Going International," No. 2, pp. 52-54.
Blake, Matthew F. "Tax Practice: Responsibilities And Interrelationships," No. 3, pp. 31-37.
Brent, Philip D. "Accounting And Law: Concurrent Practice Is In The Public Interest," No. 3, pp. 38-46.
Call, Donald P. and Paul Kircher. "The Investment Credit Moratorium," No. 3, pp. 47-52.
Stone, Marvin L. "Incorporated CPA Firms - A Modern Vehicle For A Dynamic Profession," No. 3, pp. 53-57.
Burton, John C. and William Roberts. "A Study Of Auditor Changes," No. 4, pp. 31-36.
Fox, John J. "Michigan's Task Force On Expenditure Management," No. 4, pp. 37-42.
Schachner, Leopold. "Corporate Diversification And Financial Reporting," No. 4, pp. 43-50.
Imke, Frank J. "The Future Of The Attest Function," No. 4, pp. 51-58.
Stewart, Dudley. "The Search For A Business Survival Coefficient: The Role Of ROI," No. 4, pp. 59-63.
Jarrow, Sidney F. "Mergers By Accountants And Accounting Firms," No. 5, pp. 37-41.
Larsen, E. John. "The Controversy Over Independent Audits For Banks," No. 5, pp. 42-46.
Trueger, Paul M. "Contractor's Weighted Average Share In Cost Risk (CWAS)," No. 5, pp. 47-55.
Bromage, Mary C. "Sentences That Make Sense," No. 5, pp. 56-60.
Hendrick, Richard Miller. "An Accounting System For An Accounting Office," No. 6, pp. 31-35.
Davis, Gordon B., John Neter and Roger R. Palmer. "An Experimental Study Of Audit Confirmations," No. 6, pp. 36-44.
Studdard, Kenneth. "Planning Effective Gifts - What-When-How-And To Whom?," No. 6, pp. 45-53.
Li, David H. "A Structural Check Of Accounting Input Data In A Computer System," No. 6, pp. 54-57.

Journal of Accountancy
Volume 124, 1967

Freitag, William. "A Status Report On Medicare," No. 1, pp. 27-36.
Petty, William B. "The CPA And Defense Procurement," No. 1, pp. 37-40.
Campfield, William L. "Trends In Auditing Management Plans And Operations," No. 1, pp. 41-46.
Barnett, Bernard. "Estate Administration Expenses," No. 1, pp. 47-51.
Lehmann, Robert S. "One CPA's Experience With Human Relations Training," No. 1, pp. 52-55.
Phoenix, Julius W., Jr. and William D. Bosse. "Accounting For The Cost Of Pension Plans - APB Opinion No. 8," No. 2, pp. 27-37.
Joplin, Bruce. "Local Government Accounting: It's Your Responsibility, Too," No. 2, pp. 38-43.
Briloff, Abraham J. "The Mad, Mad, Mad, Mad World Of 482," No. 2, pp. 44-53.
Witte, Arthur E. "Management Auditing: The Present State Of The Art," No. 2, pp. 54-58.
Berg, Kenneth B., Gerhard G. Mueller and Lauren M. Walker. "Annual Reports Go International," No. 2, pp. 59-64.
Dreher, William A. "Alternatives Available Under APB Opinion No. 8: An Actuary's View," No. 3, pp. 37-51.
Davis, Gordon B. "Standards For Computers And Information Processing," No. 3, pp. 52-57.
Matusiak, Louis W. "Overcoming Obstacles To Merger," No. 3, pp. 58-63.
Phoenix, Julius W., Jr. and William D. Bosse. "Accounting For The Cost Of Pension Plans - More Information On APB No. 8," No. 4, pp. 31-40.
Milston, Martin J. and Theodore Cohn. "Personal And Business Aspects Of Stockholder Agreements," No. 4, pp. 41-45.
Seiler, Robert E. and Harold R. Dilbeck. "Latin America - A Challenge In Developmental Assistance," No. 4, pp. 46-50.
Hall, William D. "Current Problems In Accounting For Leases," No. 5, pp. 35-42.
Usry, Milton F. and John L. Hess. "Planning And Control Of Research And Development Activities," No. 5, pp. 43-48.
Mann, Everett J. "Inflation And Accounting In Brazil," No. 5, pp. 49-53.
Hirschman, Robert W. "A Look At 'Current' Classifications," No. 5, pp. 54-58.
Schulte, Arthur A., Jr. "Compatibility Of Auditing And Management Services: The Viewpoint Of An Outside Observer," No. 6, pp. 29-31.
Hoenemeyer, Frank J. "Compatibility Of Auditing And Management Services: The Viewpoint Of A User Of Financial Statements," No. 6, pp. 32-35.
Devore, Malcolm M. "Compatibility Of Auditing And Management Services: A Viewpoint From Within The Profession," No. 6, pp. 36-39.
Withey, Howard A. "Financial Reporting For Nonprofit Organizations," No. 6, pp. 40-53.

Journal of Accountancy
Volume 125, 1968

David, Irwin T. and Robert M. Trueblood. "The Report Of The President's Commission On Budget Concepts," No. 1, pp. 25-36.
Savoie, Leonard M. "Controversy Over Accounting Principles Board Opinions," No. 1, pp. 37-41.
Inglis, John B. "The British Companies Act Of 1967," No. 1, pp. 42-45.
Stone, Marvin L. "Specialization In The Accounting Profession," No. 2, pp. 25-29.
Reininga, Warren. "The Unknown Materiality Concept," No. 2, pp. 30-35.
Carmichael, D. R. "Tests Of Transactions - Statistical And Otherwise," No. 2, pp. 36-40.
Knutila, Chester. "CPA, Client And Government Agency Co-Operation," No. 2, pp. 41-43.
Barnes, William T. "The CPA's Responsibilities In Tax Practice," No. 3, pp. 27-33.
Lewis, Ralph F. "Managing With And For Distinction," No. 3, pp. 34-38.
Trentin, H. G. "Sampling In Auditing - A Case Study," No. 3, pp. 39-43.
Davis, Gordon B. "The Auditor And The Computer," No. 3, pp. 44-47.
Greer, Howard C. "The Chop Suey Caper," No. 4, pp. 27-34.
Sprouse, Robert T. "Chop Suey, Chain Stores, And Conglomerate Reporting," No. 4, pp. 35-42.
Sandler, Irving J. "Plain Talk About Auditing In An ADPS Environment," No. 4, pp. 43-47.
Burton, John C. "Management Auditing," No. 5, pp. 41-46.
Trueger, Paul M. "Cost Or Pricing Data Under PL 87-653," No. 5, pp. 47-54.
Stettler, Howard F. "CPAs/Auditing/2000," No. 5, pp. 55-60.

Gunther, Samuel P. "Contingent Pay-Outs In Mergers And Acquisitions," No. 6, pp. 33-40.
Hirsch, Rudolph E. "The Value Of Information," No. 6, pp. 41-45.
Greco, Joseph A. "Comments On The Structural Check Of Input Data In A Computer System," No. 6, pp. 46-52.

Journal of Accountancy
Volume 126, 1968

Rappaport, Donald. "New Approaches In Public Education," No. 1, pp. 31-42.
Oehring, Thomas S. "Prepaid Income Developments Since 'Schlude'," No. 1, pp. 43-48.
Mills, Robert H. and Frank Luh. "Financial Reporting Of Commercial Banks," No. 1, pp. 49-54.
Seago, W. E. "Selecting A Medicare Reimbursement Formula," No. 2, pp. 31-41.
Fisch, Jack H. and Martin Mellman. "Poolings Of Interest: The Status Of The Criteria," No. 2, pp. 42-48.
Kraft, William H., Jr. "Statistical Sampling For Auditors: A New Look," No. 2, pp. 49-56.
Galus, Edward R. "Keogh Retirement Plans For CPAs," No. 3, pp. 35-43.
Davidson, H. Justin. "Research In Accounting," No. 3, pp. 44-50.
Richard, Donald L. "An Analysis Of Early Investment Credits," No. 3, pp. 51-55.
Bevis, Herman W. "Contingencies And Probabilities In Financial Statements," No. 4, pp. 37-45.
Ellyson, Robert C. "Planning The Future Growth Of An Accounting Practice - One Approach," No. 4, pp. 46-56.
Herbert, Williard A. "The Burden Of Proof In Tax Fraud Cases," No. 4, pp. 57-60.
Linowes, David F. "Socio-Economic Accounting," No. 5, pp. 37-42.
Ashworth, John. "People Who Become Accountants," No. 5, pp. 43-49.
Holzman, Robert S. "A Critique Of The IRS 'Arm's-Length' Concept," No. 5, pp. 50-53.
Schackne, Stewart. "Incorporating Accounting Practices: Good Idea? Bad Idea?," No. 6, pp. 33-39.
Pacter, Paul A. "Some Recent Examples Of Earnings Reports By Division," No. 6, pp. 40-51.
Smith, C. Aubrey. "The Certified Public Accountant Not In Public Practice," No. 6, pp. 52-56.

Journal of Accountancy
Volume 127, 1969

Burton, John C. "The Seaview Symposium On Financial Reporting," No. 1, pp. 33-38.
Freitag, William. "Medicare And The Hospital Revolution," No. 1, pp. 39-43.
Hoffman, William H., Jr. "Opportunities For Post-Mortem Tax Planning," No. 1, pp. 44-53.
Porter, W. Thomas. "Generalized Computer-Audit Programs," No. 1, pp. 54-62.
Engel, Lee. "The Moment Of Truth In Management Services," No. 2, pp. 33-37.
Schneider, Herman M. and Jack Crestol. "Tax Savings Through Trusts-Custodian Accounts," No. 2, pp. 38-43.
Hull, James C. "A Guide To Better Workpapers," No. 2, pp. 44-52.
Ashworth, John. "The Pursuit Of High Quality Recruits," No. 2, pp. 53-58.
Beyer, Robert. "The Modern Management Approach To A Program Of Social Improvement," No. 3, pp. 37-46.
Bruschi, William C. "Issues Surrounding Qualifying Experience Requirements," No. 3, pp. 47-54.
Johns, Ralph S. and Howard A. Withey. "Authoritative Accounting Guide For Colleges And Universities," No. 3, pp. 55-59.
Schwartz, M. H. "Computer Project Selection In The Business Enterprise," No. 4, pp. 35-43.
Armstrong, Marshall S. "Some Thoughts On Substantial Authoritative Support," No. 4, pp. 44-50.
Kraus, Charles F. "Problems In Identifying Section 38 Property," No. 4, pp. 51-55.
Henderson, William I. "Sale And Liquidation Of A Partnership Interest," No. 5, pp. 39-52.
McCosker, Joseph S. "Backlog Reporting: Challenge To Accountants," No. 5, pp. 53-60.
Pilie, Louis H. "Growth By Merger And Acquisition," No. 5, pp. 61-64.
Jaenicke, Henry R. "Macroeconomics And Accounting Practice," No. 6, pp. 35-39.
Westphal, William H. "The Future Of The CPA In Tax Practice," No. 6, pp. 40-44.
Rosenfield, Paul. "Accounting For Inflation - A Field Test," No. 6, pp. 45-50.
Bird, Francis A. "Interperiod Comparability In Financial Reporting," No. 6, pp. 51-56.

Journal of Accountancy
Volume 128, 1969

Crumbley, D. Larry and Joseph M. Crews. "The Use Of The Installment Tax Method For Revolving Accounts," No. 1, pp. 33-40.
Tracy, John A. "Bayesian Statistical Confidence Intervals For Auditors," No. 1, pp. 41-47.

Weinstein, E. A. "The Achilles Heel Of Retailing: Accounts Payable," No. 1, pp. 48-52.
Olson, Irving J. "Valuation Of A Closely Held Corporation," No. 2, pp. 35-47.
Cobbs, John L. "How The Business Press Views The Accounting Profession," No. 2, pp. 48-51.
Fess, Philip E. and Jerry J. Weygandt. "Cash-Flow Presentations - Trends, Recommendations," No. 2, pp. 52-59.
Carey, John L. "The Origins Of Modern Financial Reporting," No. 3, pp. 35-48.
Brighton, Gerald D. "Bad Debt Deductions Of Officer-Stockholders," No. 3, pp. 49-55.
Hicks, Ernest L. "APB: The First 3600 Days," No. 3, pp. 56-60.
Mitchell, Bert N. "The Black Minority In The CPA Profession," No. 4, pp. 41-48.
Dudick, Thomas S. "Alternative Costing Methods For Reporting And Pricing Purposes," No. 4, pp. 49-54.
Milefsky, Norman R. "Utilization Of Corporate Loss Carryovers," No. 4, pp. 55-61.
Fisch, Jack H. and Martin Mellman. "Accounting For Investments In Affiliated Companies," No. 5, pp. 41-49.
Cunnane, Thomas F. "A Current Survey Of Nonqualified Deferred Compensation Plans," No. 5, pp. 50-55.
Pacter, Paul A. "Reporting Discontinued Operations," No. 5, pp. 56-60.
Davidson, Sidney. "Accounting And Financial Reporting In The Seventies," No. 6, pp. 29-37.
Bassuk, Richard. "The Role Of Accountants In Prototype Employee Benefit Plans," No. 6, pp. 38-44.
Norgaard, Corine T. "The Professional Accountant's View Of Operational Auditing," No. 6, pp. 45-48.

Journal of Accountancy
Volume 129, 1970

Tiedemann, Frank H. "Accounting And Auditing For Regulated Investment Companies," No. 1, pp. 31-39.
Estes, Ralph W. "The Accountant's Social Responsibility," No. 1, pp. 40-43.
Finkenaur, Allen. "Accounting Records For Interperiod Tax Adjustments," No. 1, pp. 44-51.
Fox, Kenneth L. and Philip E. Fess. "Suggested Refinements Of Procedures In Determining Earnings Per Share," No. 1, pp. 52-56.
John, Richard C. and Thomas J. Nissen. "Evaluating Internal Control In EDP Audits," No. 2, pp. 31-38.
Skousen, K. Fred. "Standards For Reporting By Lines Of Business," No. 2, pp. 39-46.
Bergwerk, Rudolph. "Effective Communication Of Financial Data," No. 2, pp. 47-54.
Westphal, William H. "What Is Tax Reform?," No. 2, pp. 55-59.
Ellyson, Robert C. and Barrie S. Shaw. "The Psychological Assessment And Staff Recruiting," No. 3, pp. 35-42.
King, Barry G. "Cost-Effectiveness Analysis: Implications For Accountants," No. 3, pp. 43-49.
Mead, George C. "A Managerial Approach To Governmental Accounting," No. 3, pp. 50-55.
Gustafson, George A. "Status Of Accounting Research Study Nos. 3 And 5," No. 3, pp. 56-60.
Olson, Norman O. "The Auditor In Legal Difficulty - What's The Answer?," No. 4, pp. 39-44.
Throckmorton, Jerry J. "Theoretical Concepts For Interpreting The Investment Credit," No. 4, pp. 45-52.
Messer, Jean F. and Keith H. Burdick. "Profit-Sharing Plans For Closely Held Corporations," No. 4, pp. 53-60.
Lembke, V. C., J. H. Smith and V. H. Tidwell. "Compulsory Continuing Education For CPAs," No. 4, pp. 61-65.
Grenside, J. P. "Accountants' Reports On Profit Forecasts In The U.K.," No. 5, pp. 47-53.
Bakay, Virginia Hicks. "A Review Of Selected Claims Against Public Accountants," No. 5, pp. 54-58.
Posnak, Robert. "The Decline And Fall Of Cratchit...," No. 5, pp. 59-63.
Piersall, Ralph W., Jr. "Pension Costs And The Nonprofit Organization," No. 5, pp. 64-68.
Anderson, Jay H. "Some University Investment And Accounting Concepts," No. 6, pp. 41-48.
Bradish, Richard D. "Accountants In Top Management," No. 6, pp. 49-53.
Imdieke, Leroy F. and Jerry J. Weygandt. "Accounting For That Imputed Discount Factor," No. 6, pp. 54-58.
Trueger, Paul M. "Terminations - Cost Principles And Costing Procedures," No. 6, pp. 59-64.

Journal of Accountancy
Volume 130, 1970

Wharton, Don. "Accounting And Reporting For Companies In The Development Stage," No. 1, pp. 39-52.
Farmer, Jerome. "Auditing And The Computer - A Suggested Program," No. 1, pp. 53-56.
Bernstein, Leopold A. "Reporting The Results Of Operations - A Reassessment Of APB Opinion No. 9," No. 1, pp. 57-61.
Isbell, David B. "The Continental Vending Case: Lessons For The Profession," No. 2, pp. 33-40.
Buckley, John W. "A Perspective On Professional Accounting Education," No. 2, pp. 41-47.
Horwitz, Geoffrey B. "EDP Auditing - The Coming Of Age," No. 2, pp. 48-56.
Kemp, Patrick S. "Criteria For The Selection Of Accounting Methodology," No. 2, pp. 57-61.

Carmichael, D. R. "Auditors' Reports - A Search For Criteria," No. 3, pp. 67-74.
Barker, Phyllis A. "The Value-Added Tax - The Cost To The Businessman," No. 3, pp. 75-79.
Hensley, Clifford F. "The Mathematics Of Life Insurance: An Introduction For The CPA," No. 4, pp. 45-55.
Johnson, Robert T. "What CPAs Should Know About Oil And Gas Tax Shelters," No. 4, pp. 56-62.
Rosenfield, Paul. "The Confusion Between General Price-Level And Current Value Accounting," No. 4, pp. 63-68.
Hartley, Ronald V. and Timothy L. Ross. "MAS And Audit Independence: An Image Problem," No. 5, pp. 42-51.
Lawrence, Charles. "A Study Of A Program Budget For A Small City," No. 5, pp. 52-57.
Pivar, Samuel. "Implementation Of APB Opinions Nos. 16 And 17," No. 5, pp. 58-65.
Douglas, Patricia P. "Accounting For Equity Securities," No. 5, pp. 66-70.
Chazen, Charles and Kenneth I. Solomon. "The 'Unaudited' State Of Affairs," No. 6, pp. 41-45.
Guy, Dan M. and Alan J. Winters. "Unaudited Financial Statements: A Survey," No. 6, pp. 46-53.
Davis, Earl F. and James W. Kelley. "The Engagement Letter And Current Legal Developments," No. 6, pp. 54-59.
Pacter, Paul. "Some Comments On Applying APB Opinion No. 22," No. 6, pp. 60-61.

Journal of Accountancy
Volume 135, 1973

Carmichael, D. R. "Reporting On Forecasts: A U.K. Perspective," No. 1, pp. 36-47.
Morris, William J. and Bernard A. Coda. "Marketable Equity Securities - Valuation Alternatives," No. 1, pp. 48-54.
Hill, Henry P. "Reporting On Uncertainties By Independent Auditors," No. 1, pp. 55-60.
Istvan, Donald F. "Improving Personnel Selection," No. 2, pp. 35-40.
Marlin, John Tepper. "Accounting For Pollution," No. 2, pp. 41-46.
Linowes, David F. "The Accountant's Enlarged Professional Responsibilities," No. 2, pp. 47-51.
Kam, Vernon. "Judgment And The Scientific Trend In Accounting," No. 2, pp. 52-57.
Rea, Richard C. "Some Observations On The Continuation Of A Firm," No. 3, pp. 40-46.
Woolsey, Sam M. "Approach To Solving The Materiality Problem," No. 3, pp. 47-50.
Hagerman, Robert L., Thomas F. Keller and Russell J. Petersen. "Accounting Research And Accounting Principles," No. 3, pp. 51-55.
Isbell, David B. and D. R. Carmichael. "Disclaimers And Liability - The Rhode Island Trust Case," No. 4, pp. 37-42.
Loeb, Stephen E. and Victoria S. Rymer. "The Accounting Paraprofessional," No. 4, pp. 43-49.
Gleim, Irvin N. "Standards Of Disclosure For Supplementary Data," No. 4, pp. 50-57.
McClenon, Paul R. "Operations Of The Cost Accounting Standards Board," No. 4, pp. 58-62.
Moore, Michael R. "Professional Development: The Future Is Now," No. 5, pp. 38-47.
Chambers, Raymond J. "Accounting Principles Or Accounting Policies?," No. 5, pp. 48-53.
Terrell, Junius H. "Minimum Standards For Unaudited Financial Statements," No. 5, pp. 54-60.
Fischer, Paul M. and Martin J. Gregorcich. "Calculating Earnings Per Share," No. 5, pp. 61-71.
Seidler, Lee J. "Accountant: Account For Thyself," No. 6, pp. 38-43.
Loebbecke, James E. and John Neter. "Statistical Sampling In Confirming Receivables," No. 6, pp. 44-50.
Kellogg, Irving. "The CPA As Estate Planner," No. 6, pp. 51-61.

Journal of Accountancy
Volume 136, 1973

Linowes, David F. "The Accounting Profession And Social Progress," No. 1, pp. 32-40.
Tearney, Michael G. "Accounting For Goodwill: A Realistic Approach," No. 1, pp. 41-45.
Langenderfer, Harold Q. "A Conceptual Framework For Financial Reporting," No. 1, pp. 46-55.
Pointer, Larry Gene. "Disclosing Corporate Tax Policy," No. 1, pp. 56-61.
Asebrook, Richard J. and D. R. Carmichael. "Reporting On Forecasts: A Survey Of Attitudes," No. 2, pp. 38-48.
Beaver, William H. "What Should Be The FASB's Objectives?," No. 2, pp. 49-56.
Loeb, Stephen E. and Burt A. Leete. "The Dual Practitioner: CPA, Lawyer Or Both?," No. 2, pp. 57-63.
Sterling, Robert R. "Accounting Research, Education And Practice," No. 3, pp. 44-52.
Shefsky, Lloyd E. and Edward J. Schwartz. "Disclosures And Reporting Under ASR No. 115," No. 3, pp. 53-61.
Dilley, Steven C. and Jerry J. Weygandt. "Measuring Social Responsibility: An Empirical Test," No. 3, pp. 62-70.
Burton, John C. "Some General And Specific Thoughts On The Accounting Environment," No. 4, pp. 40-46.
Aslanian, Paul J. and John T. Duff. "Why Accounting Teachers Are So Academic," No. 4, pp. 47-53.
Bows, Albert J. and Arthur R. Wyatt. "Improving Interim

Financial Reporting," No. 4, pp. 54-59.
Solomon, Kenneth I. and Charles Chazen. "Use Of Legal Opinions In The Audit Process," No. 5, pp. 46-54.
Godick, Neil B. and Richard P. Miller. "Applying APB Opinions Nos. 23 And 24," No. 5, pp. 55-63.
Baker, H. Kent and John A. Haslem. "Information Needs Of Individual Investors," No. 5, pp. 64-69.
Sorensen, James E., John Grant Rhode and Edward E. Lawler, III. "The Generation Gap In Public Accounting," No. 6, pp. 42-50.
Bastable, C. W. "Collegiate Accounting Needs Re-Evaluation," No. 6, pp. 51-57.
Beaver, William H. "Accounting For Marketable Equity Securities," No. 6, pp. 58-64.

Journal of Accountancy
Volume 137, 1974

Mead, Sedgwick, Jr. "Ownership Of Real Estate As A Corporate Investment," No. 1, pp. 42-54.
Buzby, Stephen L. and Haim Falk. "A New Approach To The Funds Statement," No. 1, pp. 55-61.
Schiff, Frederick S. "The Use Of Time-Sharing In The CPA Firm," No. 1, pp. 62-66.
Todd, John T., Paul H. Thompson and Gene Dalton. "Management Control Of Personnel," No. 2, pp. 34-40.
Lambert, Samuel Joseph, III. "Basic Assumptions In Accounting Theory Construction," No. 2, pp. 41-48.
Baris, Marvin L. "Profit Recognition On Real Estate Transactions," No. 2, pp. 49-54.
Gipple, Larry D. and Richard W. Metcalf. "Planning Your Professional Development Program," No. 3, pp. 38-46.
Roberts, Donald M. "A Statistical Interpretation Of SAP No. 54," No. 3, pp. 47-53.
Giese, J. W. and T. P. Klammer. "Achieving The Objectives Of APB Opinion No. 19," No. 3, pp. 54-61.
Buzby, Stephen L. "The Nature Of Adequate Disclosure," No. 4, pp. 38-47.
Regazzi, John H. "Why Aren't Financial Statements Understood?," No. 4, pp. 48-55.
Sharav, Itzhak. "Transfer Pricing - Diversity Of Goals And Practices," No. 4, pp. 56-62.
Jaenicke, Henry R. and Joseph Rascoff. "Segment Disposition: Implementing APB Opinion No. 30," No. 4, pp. 63-69.
Gaede, William G. "Environmental Management Opportunities For The CPA," No. 5, pp. 50-54.
Bedingfield, James P. "The Effect Of Recent Litigation On Audit Practice," No. 5, pp. 55-62.
Greenwald, Bruce M. and Carl D. Harnick. "Corporate Tax Review: The Auditor's Approach," No. 5, pp. 63-70.
DeFilipps, W. J. "Developing A Tax Department In A Growing Organization," No. 6, pp. 63-74.

Journal of Accountancy
Volume 138, 1974

Coleman, Almand R., William G. Shenkir and Williard E. Stone. "Accounting In Colonial Virginia: A Case Study," No. 1, pp. 32-43.
Daily, R. Austin and Robert H. Strawser. "Independent Audits And The Reporting Practices Of Banks," No. 1, pp. 44-49.
Pattillo, James W. "Unity In The Accounting Profession," No. 1, pp. 50-58.
McRae, Thomas W. "Human Resource Accounting As A Management Tool," No. 2, pp. 32-38.
Hicks, Ernest L. "Standards For The Attest Function," No. 2, pp. 39-45.
Corless, John C. and Corine T. Norgaard. "User Reactions To CPA Reports On Forecasts," No. 2, pp. 46-54.
Summers, Edward L. "Accounting Education's New Horizons," No. 3, pp. 56-63.
Carmichael, D. R. "The Assurance Function - Auditing At The Crossroads," No. 3, pp. 64-72.
Rosenfield, Paul and Leonard Lorensen. "Auditors' Responsibilities And The Audit Report," No. 3, pp. 73-83.
Bierman, Harold, Jr., Roland E. Dukes and Thomas R. Dyckman. "Financial Reporting In The Petroleum Industry," No. 4, pp. 58-64.
Coffman, Robert M. "Problems Of Displacement In Public Offerings," No. 4, pp. 65-71.
Revsine, Lawrence and Jerry J. Weygandt. "Accounting For Inflation: The Controversy," No. 4, pp. 72-78.
Cushing, Barry E. "Accounting Changes: The Impact Of APB Opinion No. 20," No. 5, pp. 54-62.
Wittenbach, James L. and Stephen J. Mayer. "A Flowchart Of The Charitable Contribution Rules," No. 5, pp. 63-67.
Smith, Ralph E. and Leroy F. Imdieke. "Accounting For Stock Issued To Employees," No. 5, pp. 68-75.
Altman, Edward I. and Thomas P. McGough. "Evaluation Of A Company As A Going Concern," No. 6, pp. 50-57.
Good, Roy S. "Auditing Single-Employer Pension Funds," No. 6, pp. 58-66.
O'Connor, Melvin C. and Daniel W. Collins. "Toward Establishing User-Oriented Materiality Standards," No. 6, pp. 67-75.

Journal of Accountancy
Volume 139, 1975

Deaton, William C. and Jerry J. Weygandt. "Disclosures

Related To Pension Plans," No. 1, pp. 44-51.

Olson, Wallace E. "A Look At The Responsibility Gap." No. 1, pp. 52-57.

Barden, Horace G. "The Trouble With Accounting Research." No. 1, pp. 58-65.

Sterling, Robert R. "Relevant Financial Reporting In An Age Of Price Changes," No. 2, pp. 42-51.

Lieber, Lawrence and Howard W. Dragutsky. "How Accountants Can Keep Pension Costs Down," No. 2, pp. 52-59.

Calhoun, Charles H., III. "Accounting For Initial Franchise Fees: Is It A Dead Issue?." No. 2, pp. 60-67.

Raby, William and Robert F. Richter. "Conformity Of Tax And Financial Accounting," No. 3, pp. 42-48.

Bastable, C. W. and Jacob D. Merriwether. "Fifo In An Inflationary Environment," No. 3, pp. 49-55.

Summers, Edward L. and Kenneth E. Knight. "The AICPA Studies MAS In CPA Firms." No. 3, pp. 56-64.

Paretta, Robert L. "Designing Management Information Systems: An Overview," No. 4, pp. 42-47.

Bierman, Harold, Jr. and Roland E. Dukes. "Accounting For Research And Development Costs." No. 4, pp. 48-55.

Henry, Evan J. "A New Funds Statement Format For Greater Disclosure," No. 4, pp. 56-62.

Kiesey, Douglas T. and Ernest J. Pavlock. "Trends In Management Education For CPAs." No. 5, pp. 48-53.

Connor, Joseph E. "Discovery Value - The Oil Industry's Untried Method," No. 5, pp. 54-63.

Horn, Frederick E. "Academic Preparation Of The Accountant Of The Future." No. 5, pp. 64-68.

Kratchman, Stanley H., Richard T. Hise and Thomas A. Ulrich. "Management's Decision To Discontinue A Product," No. 6, pp. 50-54.

Gross, Malvern J., Jr. "Report On Nonprofit Accounting." No. 6, pp. 55-59.

Lynn, Bernard B. "Auditing Contractor Compliance With Cost Accounting Standards," No. 6, pp. 60-70.

Journal of Accountancy
Volume 140, 1975

Axelson, Kenneth S. "A Businessman's Views On Disclosure." No. 1, pp. 42-46.

Benson, Benjamin. "The Strategy Of Tax Shelter." No. 1, pp. 47-55.

Wolinsky, Daniel and Arthur L. Breakstone. "Reporting For The Rehabilitation And Sheltered Workshop." No. 1, pp. 56-62.

Cheeseman, Henry R. "How To Create An Inflation Neutral Tax System," No. 2, pp. 44-51.

Rosenfield, Paul. "GPP Accounting - Relevance And Interpretability," No. 2, pp. 52-59.

Burns, David C. and James K. Loebbecke. "Internal Control Evaluation: How The Computer Can Help." No. 2, pp. 60-70.

Chambers, R. J. "NOD, COG And PuPU: See How Inflation Teases!," No. 3, pp. 56-62.

Rosenfield, Paul. "Current Replacement Value Accounting - A Dead End," No. 3, pp. 63-73.

Diamond, Louis H. "Funding Liability Under Union Pension Plans," No. 3, pp. 74-79.

Palmer, Russell E. "It's Time To Stop Talking." No. 4, pp. 60-65.

Chazen, Charles and Kenneth I. Solomon. "The Art Of Defensive Auditing," No. 4, pp. 66-71.

Van Arsdell, Stephen C. "Criteria For Determining Materiality," No. 4, pp. 72-78.

Barcelona, Constance T., Clara C. Lelievre and Thomas W. Lelievre. "The Profession's Underutilized Resource: The Woman CPA," No. 5, pp. 58-64.

Thomas, Arthur L. "The FASB And The Allocation Fallacy." No. 5, pp. 65-68.

Bettauer, Arthur. "Extending Audit Procedures - When And How," No. 5, pp. 69-72.

Bedingfield, James P. "The Current State Of Statistical Sampling And Auditing," No. 6, pp. 48-55.

Lorensen, Leonard. "Gross Profit Method And Interim Financial Information," No. 6, pp. 56-64.

Chandra, Gyan. "Information Needs Of Security Analysts," No. 6, pp. 65-70.

Journal of Accountancy
Volume 141, 1976

Anton, Hector R. "Objectives Of Financial Accounting: Review And Analysis," No. 1. pp. 40-51.

Schaefer, Carl L., Jr. "Lifo - Tax Conformity And Report Disclosure Problems," No. 1, pp. 52-55.

Ramanathan, Kavasseri V., Richard B. Peterson and Michael W. Maher. "Strategic Goals And Performance Criteria." No. 1, pp. 56-64.

Abrego, Gilbert F., Jr. "Applying Word Processing To Accounting Practice," No. 2, pp. 42-45.

Robinson, Daniel D. "Private Philanthropy And Public Needs," No. 2, pp. 46-54.

Climo, Tom. "What's Happening In Britain?." No. 2, pp. 55-59.

Wagman, Barry E. "Political Campaign Accounting - New Opportunities For The CPA." No. 3. pp. 36-41.

McCosh, Andrew M. "Implications Of Sandilands For Non-U.K. Accountants," No. 3, pp. 42-51.

Strait, A. Marvin. "Expanding Your MAS Horizons." No. 3, pp. 52-54.

Fink, Robert S. "The Role Of The Accountant In A Tax Fraud Case," No. 4, pp. 42-48.

Alpern, Anita F. "Staggered Tax Filing Dates: An Idea Whose Time Has Come?," No. 4, pp. 49-51.

Meyers, Stephen L. "A Proposal For Coping With The Allocation Problem," No. 4, pp. 52-56.

Mitchell, Bert N. "The Status Of The Black CPA - An Update," No. 5, pp. 52-58.

Newton, Grant W. "The Practitioner's Role In Debt Settlements," No. 5, pp. 59-63.

Dennis, David M. and William L. Stephens. "Recruitment And Utilization Of Minority Group Members," No. 5, pp. 64-73.

Moseman, Verne R. "Disaster Planning For CPAs," No. 6, pp. 54-56.

Foran, Michael F. and Kavasseri V. Ramanathan. "Selling Options: A New Twist In Securities Trading," No. 6, pp. 57-64.

Thomas, Arthur L. "Evaluating The Effectiveness Of Social Programs." No. 6, pp. 65-71.

Journal of Accountancy
Volume 142, 1976

Previts, Gary John. "The Accountant In Our History: A Bicentennial Overview," No. 1, pp. 45-51.

Winters, Alan J. "Unaudited Statements: Review Procedures And Disclosures," No. 1, pp. 52-59.

Stone, Williard E. "Accounting Records Reveal History: The Virginia Cobbler," No. 1, pp. 60-66.

Mueller, Gerhard G. and Lauren M. Walker. "The Coming Of Age Of Financial Transnational Reporting." No. 1, pp. 67-74.

Blankenship, Ronald C. and Carol A. Schaller. "The CPA, The Small Company And The Computer," No. 2, pp. 46-51.

Herring, Hartwell C., III and Fred A. Jacobs. "The Expected Behavior Of Deferred Tax Credits." No. 2, pp. 52-57.

Bastable, C. W. "Depreciation In An Inflationary Environment." No. 2, pp. 58-66.

Solomon, Kenneth I., Charles Chazen and Barry S. Augenbraun. "Who Judges The Auditor, And How?," No. 2, pp. 67-74.

Smith, Bradford E. "Can CPAs Reach The Public?," No. 3, pp. 56-64.

King, Thomas E. and Valdean C. Lembke. "Reporting Investor Income Under The Equity Method," No. 3, pp. 65-72.

Spearman, Frank H., III. "Financial Reporting For Securities Brokers," No. 3, pp. 73-82.

Harwood, Gordon B. and Roger H. Hermanson. "The Lease-Or-Buy Decision." No. 3, pp. 83-88.

Levine, Arnold I. and E. Stanley Marks. "Accountants' Liability Insurance - Perils And Pitfalls," No. 4, pp. 59-66.

McClure, Melvin T. "Diverse Tax Interpretations Of Accounting Concepts," No. 4, pp. 67-74.

Kay, Robert S. "Disagreements Under Accounting Series Release No. 165." No. 4, pp. 75-84.

Falk, Haim, Bruce G. Gobdel and James H. Naus. "Disclosure For Closely Held Corporations," No. 4, pp. 85-90.

Snavely, H. Jim. "Financial Statement Restatement," No. 4, pp. 91-100.

Johnson, L. Todd and Philip W. Bell. "Current Replacement Costs: A Qualified Opinion." No. 5, pp. 63-71.

Black, Stephen F. and Albert A. Koch. "Replacement Cost - Charting The Uncharted Sea," No. 5, pp. 72-76.

Skousen, K. Fred. "A New Professional Program In Accountancy." No. 5, pp. 77-81.

Nickerson, Charles A. and Robert H. Strawser. "Photography As An Audit Tool," No. 5, pp. 82-86.

Graese, Clifford E. and Joseph R. DeMario. "Revenue Recognition For Long Term Contracts," No. 6, pp. 53-59.

Hepp, Gerald W. "Governmental Financial Statements - A New Look." No. 6, pp. 60-68.

Hampson, J. Jay. "Accountants' Liability - The Significance Of Hochfelder." No. 6, pp. 69-75.

Journal of Accountancy
Volume 143, 1977

Solomon, Kenneth I. and Hyman Muller. "Illegal Payments: Where The Auditor Stands." No. 1, pp. 51-57.

Williams, Wade S. "Illegal Payments: The Legislative Outlook." No. 1, pp. 58-62.

Bastable, C. W. "Why Can't Johnny Account?," No. 1, pp. 63-69.

Derscheid, Vincent K., Raymond Telling and G. W. Tonkin. "Nontax Benefits Of The Incorporation Of A Practice," No. 1, pp. 70-76.

Darling, John R. "Attitudes Toward Advertising By Accountants." No. 2, pp. 48-53.

Haried, Andrew A. and Ralph E. Smith. "Accounting For Marketable Equity Securities," No. 2, pp. 54-61.

Smith, Jack L. "Actuarial Cost Methods - Basics For CPAs." No. 2, pp. 62-66.

Most, Kenneth S. and Arthur Lee Winters. "Focus On Standard Setting - From Trueblood To The FASB," No. 2, pp. 67-75.

Austin, P. Thomas, Joel M. Forster and Robert M. Rosen. "Tax Reform: The New Perspective," No. 3, pp. 48-59.

Lambert, S. J., III and Joyce C. Lambert. "Concepts And Applications In APB Opinion No. 29," No. 3, pp. 60-68.

Jancura, Elise G. and Fred L. Lilly. "SAS No. 3 And The Evaluation Of Internal Control," No. 3, pp. 69-74.

Crumbley, D. Larry, Robert H. Strawser and Herbert L. Jensen. "Accumulated Earnings: A New Court Calculation,"

Alderman, J. Kenneth and C. Wayne Alderman. "Accounting For Leases," No. 6, pp. 74-79.
Crawford, David E. "What The CPA Should Know About Church Tax Changes," No. 6, pp. 80-85.

Journal of Accountancy
Volume 148, 1979

Olson, Wallace E. "The Accounting Profession In The 1980s," No. 1, pp. 54-60.
Chira, Robert. "Deception Of Auditors And False Records," No. 1, pp. 61-72.
Collins, Frank and John A. Yeakel. "Range Estimates In Financial Statements: Help Or Hindrance?," No. 1, pp. 73-78.
Crouse, W. Frank, Maurice C. Paradis and John C. Shaw. "The Client Service Team Approach To Auditing," No. 2, pp. 52-58.
Wise, John A. and Dennis C. Johnson. "Carryover Basis: To Be Given A 'Fresh Start'?," No. 2, pp. 59-64.
Warren, Carl S. "Audit Risk," No. 2, pp. 66-74.
Adkerson, Richard C. "Can Reserve Recognition Accounting Work?," No. 3, pp. 72-81.
Cooper, Kerry, Steven M. Flory, Steven D. Grossman and John C. Groth. "Reserve Recognition Accounting: A Proposed Disclosure Framework," No. 3, pp. 82-91.
Connor, Joseph E. "Reserve Recognition Accounting: Fact Or Fiction?," No. 3, pp. 92-99.
Romney, Marshall B. and W. Steve Albrecht. "The Use Of Investigative Agencies By Auditors," No. 4, pp. 61-67.
Dasburg, John H. and C. Richard Morehead. "Can GAAP Still Support Inventory Valuation After Thor?," No. 4, pp. 68-77.
Loscalzo, Margaret A. "What Is Peer Review All About?," No. 4, pp. 78-82.
Mautz, Robert K. and Robert D. Neary. "Corporate Audit Committee - Quo Vadis?," No. 4, pp. 83-88.
Scott, Richard A. and Rita K. Scott. "Installment Accounting: Is It Inconsistent?," No. 5, pp. 52-59.
Weirich, Thomas R. and George M. Pintar. "Interpretation And Flowchart Of SSARS No. 1," No. 5, pp. 60-66.
Campion, William M. and Richard M. Peters. "Short Interval Scheduling For The Audit Engagement," No. 5, pp. 67-71.
Schwartz, Donald A. "Microcomputers Take Aim On Small Business Clients," No. 6, pp. 57-63.
Grinnell, D. Jacque and Corine T. Norgaard. "Reporting Changes In Accounting Principles - Time For A Change?," No. 6, pp. 64-72.
Press, Israel A. and Herbert Peterson. "Better Planning For Year-End Taxes," No. 6, pp. 73-83.

Journal of Accountancy
Volume 149, 1980

Smith, Bradford E. "Reaching The Public: The CPA's New Image," No. 1, pp. 47-53.
Hanggi, Gerald A., Jr. "Media Advertising As A Practice Development Tool," No. 1, pp. 54-59.
Keane, John G. "The Marketing Perspective: The CPA's New Image," No. 1, pp. 60-66.
Loebbecke, James K. and George R. Zuber. "Evaluating Internal Control," No. 2, pp. 49-57.
Coughlan, John W. "Regulation, Rents And Residuals," No. 2, pp. 58-67.
Krogstad, Jack L. and Marshall B. Romney. "Accounts Receivable Confirmation - An Alternative Auditing Approach," No. 2, pp. 68-73.
Olson, Wallace E. "Self-Regulation - What's Ahead?," No. 3, pp. 46-49.
Sumutka, Alan R. "Questionable Payments And Practices: Why? How? Detection? Prevention?," No. 3, pp. 50-63.
Turner, Jerry L. and Theodore J. Mock. "Economic Considerations In Designing Audit Programs," No. 3, pp. 65-74.
Burton, John C. "A Critical Look At Professionalism And Scope Of Services," No. 4, pp. 48-57.
Bedingfield, James P. "Analyzing The Effect Of CASB Standards On Business," No. 4, pp. 58-67.
Jaenicke, Henry R. "A New Approach To Engagement Management," No. 4, pp. 68-78.
Berliner, Robert W. and Dale L. Gerboth. "FASB Statement No. 33: 'The Great Experiment'," No. 5, pp. 48-54.
Fleming, Mary M. K. "Budgeting Practices In Large CPA Firms," No. 5, pp. 55-62.
Romney, Marshall B., W. Steve Albrecht and David J. Cherrington. "Auditors And The Detection Of Fraud," No. 5, pp. 63-69.
Ellyson, Robert C. and William H. Van Rensselaer. "Sunset - Is The Profession Ready For It?," No. 6, pp. 52-61.
Barnett, Bernard. "The Carryover Basis Election: A Golden Opportunity," No. 6, pp. 62-70.
Rappaport, Alfred. "The Strategic Audit," No. 6, pp. 71-77.

Journal of Accountancy
Volume 150, 1980

Sommer, A. A., Jr. "Corporate Governance: Its Impact On The Profession," No. 1, pp. 52-61.
Goggans, Travis P. "The Use Of Real Estate Tax Shelters In Estate Planning," No. 1, pp. 62-70.
Tussing, Robert T. and Glenn L. Helms. "Training Computer Audit Specialists," No. 1, pp. 71-74.
Anthony, Robert N. "Nonbusiness Financial Reporting: Is There Enough Guidance?," No. 2, pp. 48-54.
Heath, Loyd C. "Is Working Capital Really Working?," No. 2, pp. 55-62.
Czarnecki, Richard E. and Lyle E. Algate. "Using Consultants To Meet CPE Needs," No. 2, pp. 64-68.
Greiner, Larry E. and Alan L. Scharff. "The Challenge Of Cultivating Accounting Firm Executives," No. 3, pp. 57-63.
Ulrich, Thomas A. "The Financial Planning Implications Of Bank Loan Pricing," No. 3, pp. 64-72.
Clay, John R., Dan M. Guy and Dennis R. Meals. "Solving Compilation And Review Practice Problems," No. 3, pp. 74-82.
Ramanathan, Kavasseri V. and William L. Weis. "How To Succeed In Nonbusiness (Without Really Trying): A University Case Study," No. 4, pp. 46-53.
Hickman, James R. "Responding To Clients' Growing Needs: Building An MAS Department," No. 4, pp. 54-61.
Ward, D. Dewey and Jack C. Robertson. "Reliance On Internal Auditors," No. 4, pp. 62-74.
Vanecek, Michael T., Robert F. Zant and Carl Stephen Guynes. "Distributed Data Processing: A New Tool For Accountants," No. 4, pp. 75-83.
Berton, Lee and Barbara Shildneck. "The 75-Year History Of The Journal," No. 5, pp. 48-54.
Kanaga, William S. "International Accounting: The Challenge And The Changes," No. 5, pp. 55-61.
Chenok, Philip B., Douglas R. Carmichael and Thomas P. Kelley. "Accounting And Auditing: The Technical Challenges Ahead," No. 5, pp. 62-70.
Olson, Wallace E. "Our Profession In A Changing World," No. 5, pp. 72-76.
Previts, Gary John and Edward N. Coffman. "Practice And Education: Bridging The Gap," No. 6, pp. 39-46.
Tolstyka, William. "Fee Disputes: How Can We Solve Them?," No. 6, pp. 47-50.
Cowen, Scott S. "Nonaudit Services: How Much Is Too Much?," No. 6, pp. 51-56.

Journal of Accountancy
Volume 151, 1981

Liberty, Robert A. "To Merge Or Not To Merge," No. 1, pp. 52-59.
Chazen, Charles, Richard L. Miller, Jr. and Kenneth I. Solomon. "When The Rules Say: 'See Your Lawyer'," No. 1, pp. 60-70.
Ricchiute, David N. "A Case For Automated Workpapers," No. 1, pp. 71-75.
Akresh, Abraham D. and George Russell Zuber. "Exploring Statistical Sampling," No. 2, pp. 50-56.
Beresford, Dennis R. "Emerging Problems: How The Profession Is Coping," No. 2, pp. 57-60.
Pomeroy, Harlan. "Restrictive Covenants: What The CPA Should Know," No. 2, pp. 61-68.
Dennis, David M. and Robert M. Keith. "Are Litigation Disclosures Inadequate?," No. 3, pp. 54-61.
Arcady, Alex T. and Charles E. Baker. "Interest Cost Accounting: Some Practical Guidance," No. 3, pp. 62-71.
Lynch, B. Michael. "CPE Predictions: 1990s Or Sooner." No. 3, pp. 72-76.
Neuman, David. "Defense Contract Audits: The CPA's Role," No. 4, pp. 42-49.
Taylor, John L. "Lifo: A Different Approach," No. 4, pp. 50-62.
Finney, John E. "Controlling EDP Costs," No. 4, pp. 63-68.
Jarett, Irwin M. "Computer Graphics: A Reporting Revolution?," No. 5, pp. 46-57.
Cohen, Gerald D. and David B. Pearson. "Auditing The Client's Judgments," No. 5, pp. 58-65.
Strauss, Norman N. and Alex T. Arcady. "A New Focus On The 'Bottom Line' And Its Components," No. 5, pp. 66-77.
Steinberg, Harold I., John R. Miller and Terrill E. Menzel. "The Single Audit In Government," No. 6, pp. 56-67.
Gaertner, James F. and John A. Ruhe. "Job-Related Stress In Public Accounting," No. 6, pp. 68-75.
Scott, Robert B., Jr. "A Look At Management Incentive Plans," No. 6, pp. 76-80.

Journal of Accountancy
Volume 152, 1981

Burton, John C. "Emerging Trends In Financial Reporting," No. 1, pp. 54-67.
Hanson, Robert E. and William J. Brown. "CPAs' Workpapers: The IRS Zeros In," No. 1, pp. 68-77.
Austin, Kenneth R. and David C. Langston. "Peer Review: Its Impact On Quality Control," No. 1, pp. 78-82.
Mautz, Robert K. "Financial Reporting: Should Government Emulate Business?," No. 2, pp. 53-60.
Albrecht, W. Steve, Scott W. Brown and David R. Field. "Toward Increased Job Satisfaction Of Practicing CPAs," No. 2, pp. 61-68.
Winters, Alan J. "Avoiding Malpractice Liability Suits," No. 2, pp. 69-74.
Linowes, David F. "Communications Satellites: Their Impact On The CPA," No. 3, pp. 58-67.
Roth, Harold P. "A New Outlet For Energy Audit Data," No. 3, pp. 68-82.
Hall, Thomas W. and A. A. Butler. "Assuring Adequate Attorneys' Replies To Audit Inquiries," No. 3, pp. 83-91.
Lucas, Timothy S. and Betsy Ann Hollowell. "Pension Accounting: The Liability Question," No. 4, pp. 57-67.

Neumann, Frederick L. "The Case For On-The-Job Training," No. 4, pp. 80-91.
Krogstad, Jack L., Maurice Earl Stark, Kenneth L. Fox and Harry O. Lytle, Jr. "The Faculty Residency: A Concept Worth Considering," No. 5, pp. 74-86.
Nair, R. D. and Jerry J. Weygandt. "Let's Fix Deferred Taxes," No. 5, pp. 87-94.
Wynne, Robert C. and Alan Frotman. "Microcomputers: Helping Make Practice Perfect," No. 6, pp. 34-39.
Cohen, Milton H. "Regulation Through Disclosure," No. 6, pp. 52-62.

Journal of Accountancy
Volume 153, 1982

Bastable, C. W. and Stephen L. Fogg. "Indexation: Will Taxpayers Get Its Benefits?," No. 1, pp. 52-61.
Warren, Carl S., Stephen V. N. Yates and George R. Zuber. "Audit Sampling: A Practical Approach," No. 1, pp. 62-72.
Gale, Andrew P. "Computerized Research: An Advanced Tool," No. 1, pp. 73-79.
Daley, Lane A. and Gerhard G. Mueller. "Accounting In The Arena Of World Politics," No. 2, pp. 40-53.
Neuhausen, Benjamin S. "Consolidation And The Equity Method - Time For An Overhaul," No. 2, pp. 54-67.
McAllister, John P. and Mark W. Dirsmith. "How The Client's Business Environment Affects The Audit," No. 2, pp. 68-74.
Hickok, Richard S. "New Guidance For Construction Contractors: 'A Credit Plus'," No. 3, pp. 44-55.
Lorensen, Leonard and Richard J. Haas. "Governmental Accounting: Time For An Accommodation," No. 3, pp. 56-67.
Walther, Larry M. "Commodity Futures: What The Accountant Should Know," No. 3, pp. 68-81.
Burns, Gary W. and D. Scott Peterson. "Accounting For Computer Software," No. 4, pp. 50-59.
Bates, Homer L., Robert W. Ingram and Philip M. J. Reckers. "Auditor-Client Affiliation: The Impact On 'Materiality'," No. 4, pp. 60-63.
Petri, Enrico and Clyde P. Stickney. "Business Combinations: Some Unresolved Issues," No. 4, pp. 64-79.
Hepp, Gerald W. and Thomas W. McRae. "Accounting Standards Overload: Relief Is Needed," No. 5, pp. 52-65.
Clay, John R. and Stephen D. Holton. "Prescribed Form Engagements: Some Practical Guidance," No. 5, pp. 66-79.
Broadus, W. A., Jr. and Joseph F. Moraglio. "Governmental Audit Standards: A New Perspective," No. 5, pp. 80-90.
Biel, Dennis H. and W. C. Stevenson. "Tax Shelters: A Primer For CPAs," No. 6, pp. 54-71.
Van Son, W. Peter, Dan M. Guy and J. Frank Betts. "Engagement Letters: What Practice Shows," No. 6, pp. 72-81.
Ratcliffe, Thomas A. and Paul Munter. "Currency Translation: A New Blueprint," No. 6, pp. 82-90.

Journal of Accountancy
Volume 154, 1982

Klasny, Edward M. and James M. Williams. "Tracking Current Governmental Standards," No. 1, pp. 60-73.
Ross, N. Glenn. "The Canadian Experience," No. 1, pp. 74-81.
Seaman, Jerome F. and Harold H. Hensold, Jr. "Pension Plan Obligations: The 'Real' Impact," No. 1, pp. 82-88.
Alderman, C. Wayne, Dan M. Guy and Dennis R. Meals. "Other Comprehensive Bases Of Accounting: Alternatives To GAAP?," No. 2, pp. 52-63.
Bergherm, Donald E. "The IRS And Business," No. 2, pp. 64-71.
Piteo, Thomas A. "Forward Contracts - Free Market Financial Tools," No. 2, pp. 72-82.
Olson, Wallace E. "Specialization: Search For A Solution," No. 3, pp. 70-79.
Coonrod, Curtis L. and James C. Todderud. "Serving The Federal Election Campaign," No. 3, pp. 80-90.
Brown, Paul R. and Phillip E. Lint. "Co-Teaching: A Key To Auditing Instruction," No. 3, pp. 94-98.
DeNardo, Stephen and John R. Thornton. "Recruiting: The New Horizon," No. 4, pp. 40-49.
Freeman, Robert J. and Craig Douglas Shoulders. "Defining The Governmental Reporting Entity," No. 4, pp. 50-64.
Wittenbach, James L. and Ken Milani. "A Profile Of The CPA In Tax Practice: An Update," No. 4, pp. 65-76.
Raby, William L. "TEFRA: Impact On Taxpayer Compliance," No. 5, pp. 64-73.
Levy, Gregory M. "TEFRA: Its Accounting Implications," No. 5, pp. 74-85.
Van Son, W. Peter and Alan J. Winters. "The Preaudit Conference: A Communication Tool," No. 5, pp. 86-93.
Smith, S. Curtis. "Implementing An FASB Statement," No. 6, pp. 60-65.
Elliott, Merle S. and Monroe S. Kuttner. "MAS: Coming Of Age," No. 6, pp. 66-75.
Anthony, Robert N. "Equity Interest - Its Time Has Come," No. 6, pp. 76-93.

Journal of Accountancy
Volume 155, 1983

Lightner, Sharon M., James J. Leisenring and Alan J. Winters. "Underreporting Chargeable Time," No. 1, pp. 52-57.
Turner, John N. "International Harmonization: A Professional Goal," No. 1, pp. 58-67.
Loebbecke, James K., John F. Mullarkey and George R. Zuber. "Auditing In A Computer Environment," No. 1, pp. 68-78.
Rosenfield, Paul and William C. Dent. "No More Deferred Taxes," No. 2, pp. 44-55.
Wyatt, Arthur R. "Efficient Market Theory: Its Impact On Accounting," No. 2, pp. 56-65.
Bowsher, Charles A. "The GAO And The Accounting Profession," No. 2, pp. 66-72.
Zuber, George R., Robert K. Elliott, William R. Kinney, Jr. and James J. Leisenring. "Using Materiality In Audit Planning," No. 3, pp. 42-55.
Sloan, Donald R. "The Education Of The Professional Accountant," No. 3, pp. 56-61.
Choi, Frederick D. S. and Vinod B. Bavishi. "International Accounting Standards: Issues Needing Attention," No. 3, pp. 62-68.
Raiborn, D. D., Dan M. Guy and Marilyn Zulinski. "Solving Audit Problems In Small Business Engagements," No. 4, pp. 50-59.
Brumfield, Craig A., Robert K. Elliott and Peter D. Jacobson. "Business Risk And The Audit Process," No. 4, pp. 60-69.
Nelson, A. Tom. "Accounting Education's Coming Crisis," No. 4, pp. 70-80.
Phillips, Lawrence C. and Gary John Previts. "Tax Reform: What Are The Issues?," No. 5, pp. 64-75.
Mautz, Robert K. "Self-Regulation - Perils And Problems," No. 5, pp. 76-85.
Larson, Charles B. "Directors For CPA Firms: A Provocative Proposal," No. 5, pp. 86-94.
Williams, Albert S. "Starting A CPA Firm," No. 6, pp. 80-89.
Lucas, Timothy S. and Paul B. W. Miller. "Pension Accounting: Impacting The Financial Statement," No. 6, pp. 90-109.
Enthoven, Adolf J. H. "U.S. Accounting And The Third World," No. 6, pp. 110-118.

Journal of Accountancy
Volume 156, 1983

Solomon, Kenneth Ira, Charles Chazen and Richard L. Miller, Jr. "Compilation And Review: The Safety Factor," No. 1, pp. 50-59.
Miller, Robert D. "Compilation And Review: Standards' Impact On Risk," No. 1, pp. 60-75.
Pacter, Paul A. "The Conceptual Framework: Make No Mystique About It," No. 1, pp. 76-88.
Wiesen, Jeremy and D. R. Carmichael. "High Tech: A Challenge For CPAs," No. 2, pp. 67-73.
Spencer, Lee B., Jr. "The Electronic Library: Impact On Professionals," No. 2, pp. 74-81.
Whittington, Ray, Marilyn Zulinski and James W. Ledwith. "Completeness - The Elusive Assertion," No. 2, pp. 82-92.
Larson, Rholan E. "Self-Regulation: A Professional Step Forward," No. 3, pp. 58-67.
Wheatley, Edward W. "Auditing Your Marketing Performance," No. 3, pp. 68-78.
Holder, William W. "Expenditure And Liability Recognition In Government," No. 3, pp. 79-84.
Rayburn, Frank R. and G. Michael Crooch. "Currency Translation And The Funds Statement: A New Approach," No. 4, pp. 51-63.
Lorensen, Leonard and Paul Rosenfield. "Vested Benefits - A Company's Only Pension Liability," No. 4, pp. 64-77.
Bremser, Wayne G. "Peer Review: Enhancing Quality Control," No. 4, pp. 78-88.
Linowes, David F. "Cutting Government Waste: The Profession's Role," No. 5, pp. 66-77.
Lee, Bernard Z., Rholan E. Larson and Philip B. Chenok. "Issues Confronting The Accounting Profession," No. 5, pp. 78-85.
Raiborn, Mitchell H., Michael R. Lane and D. D. Raiborn. "Purchased Loss Carryforwards: An Unresolved Issue," No. 5, pp. 98-108.
Doll, Barry F. "Staff Turnover: How To Manage It," No. 6, pp. 76-83.
Egger, Roscoe L., Jr. "Maintaining The Viability Of The U.S. Tax System," No. 6, pp. 84-93.

Journal of Accountancy
Volume 157, 1984

Pallais, Don and Robert K. Elliot. "Prospective Financial Statements: Guidelines For A Growing Practice Area," No. 1, pp. 56-71.
Beresford, Dennis R., Lawrence C. Best and Joseph V. Weber. "Accounting For Income Taxes: Change Is Coming," No. 1, pp. 72-79.
Johnson, Ramon E. and Paul T. Peterson. "Current Value Accounting For S&Ls: A Needed Reform?," No. 1, pp. 80-85.
Dillon, Ray D., William R. Feldhaus and Rod P. Farrell. "A Special Area Of Service: Risk Management," No. 2, pp. 50-59.
Gertzman, Stephen F. and Mary-Ellen Hunt. "A Basic Guide To Tax Accounting Opportunities," No. 2, pp. 60-75.
Nielsen, Gordon L. "The Purchase Of An Accounting Practice: Making The Right Choice," No. 2, pp. 76-81.

Barden, Ronald S., James E. Copeland, Jr., Roger H. Hermanson and Leslie Wat. "Going Public - What It Involves," No. 3, pp. 63-76.

Hickok, Richard S. "Looking To The Future: A Key To Success," No. 3, pp. 77-82.

Moe, Thomas O. "Tax Basics Of Buying And Selling A Corporation," No. 3, pp. 83-90.

Mautz, Robert K. "Self-Regulation - Criticisms And A Response," No. 4, pp. 56-67.

Rachlin, Norman S. "Is There (Enough) Life After The Tax Season?," No. 4, pp. 68-77.

Swanson, Edward P. "Accounting For Changing Prices: Some Midcourse Corrections," No. 4, pp. 78-93.

Goldberg, Seymour. "Pension Planning And The CPA," No. 5, pp. 68-76.

Jacobson, Peter D. and Robert K. Elliott. "GAAS: Reconsidering The 'Ten Commandments'," No. 5, pp. 77-89.

Winckler, Susan W. and D. Dewey Ward. "Can City Hall Go Broke? The Going Concern Issue?," No. 5, pp. 90-100.

Cunningham, Michael E. "Push-Down Accounting: Pros And Cons," No. 6, pp. 72-79.

Gavin, Thomas A., Rebecca L. Hicks and Joseph D. Decosimo. "CPAs' Liability To Third Parties," No. 6, pp. 80-91.

Thomas, Paula Bevels and Larry E. Farmer. "Accounting For Stock Options And SARs: The Equality Question," No. 6, pp. 92-98.

Journal of Accountancy
Volume 158, 1984

Fedders, John M. and L. Glenn Perry. "Policing Financial Disclosure Fraud: The SEC's Top Priority," No. 1, pp. 58-67.

Moran, Mark and Gary John Previts. "The SEC And The Profession, 1934-84: The Realities Of Self-Regulation," No. 1, pp. 68-83.

Axline, Larry L. "Are Your Clients Satisfied?," No. 1, pp. 84-90.

Arnold, Jerry L., Alan A. Cherry, Michael A. Diamond and James A. Walker. "Small Business: An Area Ripe For Practice Development," No. 2, pp. 74-83.

Mory, Kenneth J. "Accounting For Regulated Operations: FASB Statement no. 71," No. 2, pp. 84-97.

Bremser, Wayne G. "The AICPA Division For Firms: Problems And A Challenge," No. 2, pp. 98-110.

Minow, Newton N. "Accountants' Liability And The Litigation Explosion," No. 2, pp. 70-90.

Buchholz, David L. and Joseph F. Moraglio. "IRS Access To Auditors' Work Papers: The Supreme Court Decision," No. 3, pp. 91-107.

Robbins, Barry P. and Steven O. Swyers. "Accounting For Income Taxes: Predicting Timing Difference Reversals," No. 3, pp. 108-118.

Vejlupek, Judith R. and Betsy Hollowell Cropsey. "The Hidden Costs Of Postemployment Benefits," No. 4, pp. 84-92.

Bowman, John W. "IRS Procedures," No. 4, pp. 93-108.

Gafford, W. Wade and D. R. Carmichael. "Materiality, Audit Risk And Sampling: A Nuts-And Bolts Approach (Part One)," No. 4, pp. 109-118.

Larson, Rholan E. and Thomas P. Kelley. "Differential Measurement In Accounting Standards: The Concept Makes Sense," No. 5, pp. 78-92.

McCallion, Anne D. and Gregory A. Ray. "Computer Software: An Asset Coming On-Line," No. 5, pp. 93-109.

Lhotka, Joseph D. and Naomi S. Erickson. "Accounting For Software: A Step Forward," No. 5, pp. 110-124.

Gafford, W. Wade and D. R. Carmichael. "Materiality, Audit Risk And Sampling: A Nuts-And-Bolts Approach (Part Two)," No. 5, pp. 125-138.

Jones, Keith L. and Michael L. Hund. "Filing SEC Registration Statements: A View From The Inside," No. 6, pp. 92-107.

Dahl, Shirley J. and Karen L. Hooks. "Women Accountants In A Changing Profession," No. 6, pp. 108-117.

Daroca, Frank P., Gary L. Holstrum and W. Thomas Lin. "Long-Range Planning And Control Of Growth," No. 6, pp. 118-134.

Journal of Accountancy
Volume 159, 1985

Verschoor, Curtis C. "Personal Financial Planning And The CPA," No. 1, pp. 52-59.

Scott, Richard A., Ernest J. Pavlock and Malcolm H. Lathan, Jr. "On-Campus Recruiting: The Students Speak Up," No. 1, pp. 60-75.

Jackson, Betty R. "Stemming Income Tax Evasion," No. 1, pp. 76-80.

Willens, Robert. "Corporate Provisions Of The TRA Of 1984," No. 2, pp. 54-63.

Walker, David M. "Accounting For Reversions From Pension Plans," No. 2, pp. 64-71.

Bohan, Michael P. and Steven Rubin. "Lifo: What Should Be Disclosed?," No. 2, pp. 72-77.

Hermanson, Roger H. and Tad D. Ransopher. "What The Hishon Case Means To CPA Firms," No. 2, pp. 78-80.

Miller, Paul B. W. "The Conceptual Framework: Myths And Realities," No. 3, pp. 62-71.

Ross, Allan John. "Accounting For Hazardous Waste," No. 3, pp. 72-85.

Dillon, Ray D. and J. William Tillett. "Containing The Costs Of Health Care," No. 3, pp. 86-95.

Broadus, W. A., Jr. and Joseph D. Comtois. "The Single Audit Act: A Needed Reform," No. 4, pp. 62-71.

Bleyer, Stephen A. and William R. Stromsem. "Divorce - TRA Style," No. 4, pp. 72-85.

Tanoury, Mark P. and Joel E. Thompson. "Accounting For Junior Stock: Another Look," No. 4, pp. 86-93.

Unger, David L. "The Activity Approach To Personal Financial Planning," No. 4, pp. 94-103.

Stilwell, Martin C. and Robert K. Elliott. "A Model For Expanding The Attest Function," No. 5, pp. 66-81.

Clay, John R. and Dennis R. Meals. "Personal Financial Planning: Two Perspectives," No. 5, pp. 82-97.

Knapp, Michael C. "Avoiding Problem Banks," No. 5, pp. 98-113.

Weinstein, Edward A. and Bradford E. Smith. "Public Service And The Profession," No. 5, pp. 114-120.

Felix, William L., Jr. and Robert S. Roussey. "Statistical Inference And The IRS," No. 6, pp. 38-45.

Johnson, Walter L. "Government Reporting Of Budget Information," No. 6, pp. 46-55.

Barnickol, Karl R., Allan John Ross, Ronald O. Schowalter and Michael J. Walters. "Accounting For Litigation And Claims," No. 6, pp. 56-69.

Dillon, Ray D., Lloyd L. Byars, Craig E. Aronoff and Gale D. Eidson. "The CPA Firm's 'Mission'," No. 6, pp. 70-78.

Journal of Accountancy
Volume 160, 1985

Romney, Marshall B. and Kevin D. Stocks. "How To Buy A Small Computer System," No. 1, pp. 46-63.

Harris, Hubert L., Jr. "Personal Financial Planning: The Competition," No. 1, pp. 64-78.

Fish, Gary L, Larry D. Gipple and Jane E. Katz. "Assessing CPE Needs," No. 1, pp. 79-83.

Levy, Marvin M. "Financial Fraud: Schemes And Indicia," No. 2, pp. 78-88.

Robbins, Barry P. "Perspectives On Tax Basis Financial Statements," No. 2, pp. 89-101.

Dudley, Lola Woodard. "A Critical Look At EPS," No. 2, pp. 102-111.

Corbett, William J. "PR Challenges Facing The Profession," No. 2, pp. 112-122.

Wishon, Keith and Lorin S. Chevalier. "Interest Rate Swaps - Your Rate Or Mine?," No. 3, pp. 63-84.

Flippo, Ronnie G. "The President's Tax Proposals: A View From Capitol Hill," No. 3, pp. 86-88.

Anderson, George D. "A Fresh Look At Standards Of Professional Conduct," No. 3, pp. 91-106.

Block, Stanley B. "Buy-Sell Agreements For Privately Held Corporations," No. 3, pp. 110-124.

Bernard, Clark L. and Douglas Beaven. "Containing The Costs Of Higher Education," No. 4, pp. 78-94.

Ellyson, Robert C., A. Tom Nelson and James H. MacNeill. "Educating Tomorrow's CPAs," No. 4, pp. 95-105.

Mills, Robert H. "Views On Education And Experience Requirements," No. 4, pp. 106-117.

Ciesick, Robert T., Harold L. Monk, Jr. and Ernest J. Pavlock. "The National CPE Curriculum," No. 4, pp. 118-124.

Sack, Robert J. "Commercialism In The Profession: A Threat To Be Managed," No. 4, pp. 125-134.

Erickson, Naomi and David H. Herskovits. "Accounting For Software Costs: Cracking The Code," No. 5, pp. 81-97.

Stepp, James O. "Deferred Taxes: The Discounting Controversy," No. 5, pp. 98-109.

Freeman, Robert J. and Craig D. Shoulders. "Governmental Fund Operating Results: 3 Formats," No. 5, pp. 110-121.

Knight, Lee G. and Ray A. Knight. "Claiming The Home Office Deduction," No. 6, pp. 85-101.

Boucher, Rick. "Why Civil RICO Must Be Reformed," No. 6, pp. 102-110.

Gale, Andrew P. "Data Bases: An Accountant's Choice," No. 6, pp. 111-124.

Goodman, Hortense. "NAARS: The CPA's Electronic Shoe Box," No. 6, pp. 125-132.

Journal of Accountancy
Volume 161, 1986

Barnett, Bernard. "Estate Planning Perils For CPA Partners And Shareholders," No. 1, pp. 68-77.

Barnett, Andrew H. and William J. Read. "Sampling In Small Business Audits," No. 1, pp. 78-90.

Jurinski, James John. "Taxpayer Strategies In A Unitary Tax Audit," No. 1, pp. 91-102.

Willens, Robert. "Consolidated Returns And Affiliated Groups (With A Nod To Wall Street)," No. 2, pp. 60-69.

Mednick, Robert. "The Auditor's Role In Society: A New Approach To Solving The Perception Gap," No. 2, pp. 70-75.

Corbett, William J. "Boosting The Profession With Effective PR," No. 2, pp. 76-82.

Jagolinzer, Philip and John M. Strefeler. "Marital Status And The Taxes We Pay," No. 3, pp. 68-77.

Rosefield, Paul versus Steven Rubin. "Minority Interest: Opposing Views," No. 3, pp. 78-90.

Talwar, Akshay K. "Profit Allocation In CPA Firm Partnership Agreements," No. 3, pp. 91-95.

Grace, J. Peter. "Wielding The Gramm-Rudman Ax," No. 4, pp. 66-72.

Broadus, W. A., Jr. and Joseph D. Comtois. "Tools For The Single Audit," No. 4, pp. 73-81.

Hepp, Gerald W. and William W. Holder. "A New Look In Governmental Audits," No. 4, pp. 82-89.
Pallais, Don and Dan M. Guy. "Prospective Financial Statements," No. 4, pp. 90-99.
Jones, Wm. Jarell and Catherine R. Ward. "Forecasts And Projections For Third-Party Use," No. 4, pp. 100-102.
Weicker, Lowell P., Jr. "The Liability Insurance Crisis: Its Impact On Small Business," No. 5, pp. 66-67.
Stilwell, Martin C. "Prospective Reporting And Small Business Clients," No. 5, pp. 68-87.
Rappaport, Donald. "The Challenge Of The Entrepreneur," No. 5, pp. 88-93.
Upton, Wayne S., Jr. and Carol Lynn Ostergaard. "The FASB Response To Small Business," No. 5, pp. 94-101.
Manegold, James G., Jerry L. Arnold and Michael A. Diamond. "SEC Form S-18: A Boon To Small Business," No. 5, pp. 102-108.
Wishon, Keith. "Plugging The Gaps In GAAP: The FASB's Emerging Issues Task Force," No. 6, pp. 96-107.
Purtill, John S., Jr. and Robert L. Caggiano. "How The CFO Can Lead A Business Turnaround," No. 6, pp. 108-113.
Solomons, David. "The FASB's Conceptual Framework: An Evaluation," No. 6, pp. 114-125.
Sorter, George H. "Accounting For Baseball," No. 6, pp. 126-133.

Journal of Accountancy
Volume 162, 1986

Connor, Joseph E. "Enhancing Public Confidence In The Accounting Profession," No. 1, pp. 76-85.
Willens, Robert. "Taxes And Takeovers," No. 1, pp. 86-96.
Herskowitz, Barry and David A. Kaplowitz. "Asset-Based Revolvers," No. 1, pp. 97-104.
Endsley, Lionel I. and Gary R. Cesnik. "Lifo For Bargain-Purchased Inventories: The Tax Connection," No. 2, pp. 94-101.
Stewart, John E. and Benjamin S. Neuhausen. "Financial Instruments And Transactions: The CPA's Newest Challenge," No. 2, pp. 102-113.
Foley, John C. and Monroe S. Kuttner. "Finding Funds For A Small Business," No. 2, pp. 114-122.
Anderson, George D. and Robert C. Ellyson. "Restructuring Professional Standards: The Anderson Report," No. 3, pp. 92-105.
Bohan, Michael P. and Steven Rubin. "Lifo/Fifo: How Would It Work?," No. 3, pp. 106-114.
Helgeson, James G. and G. Eddy Birrer. "Marketing Plans For Accounting Firms," No. 3, pp. 115-126.
Roussey, Robert S. "The CPA In The Information Age: Today And Tomorrow," No. 4, pp. 94-109.
Wedick, John L., Jr. "Electronic Filing At The IRS: The Goal Is Global," No. 4, pp. 110-119.
Abramson, David H. "The Future Of Accounting: Scenarios For 1996," No. 4, pp. 120-125.
Taylor, Barbara G. and Lane K. Anderson. "Misleading Graphs: Guidelines For The Accountant," No. 4, pp. 126-135.
Willens, Robert. "General Utilities Is Dead: The TRA Of '86 Ends An Era," No. 5, pp. 102-115.
Wiesner, Philip J. "Real Estate Syndications: Is There Life After Tax Reform?," No. 5, pp. 116-127.
Pincus, Karen V. and J. David Pincus. "Public Relations: What CPA Firms Are Doing," No. 5, pp. 128-138.
Diss, William T. "Small Business: Winner Or Loser Under Tax Reform?," No. 6, pp. 164-171.
Johnson, Janice M. and William R. Stromsem. "The TRA And Individuals: A Year-End RX," No. 6, pp. 172-177.
Rothschild, Leonard W., Jr. "Worldwide Unitary Taxation: The End Is In Sight," No. 6, pp. 178-185.

Journal of Accountancy
Volume 163, 1987

Wiese, Donald C. "The Fiscal Year: An Endangered Species Under Tax Reform," No. 1, pp. 78-86.
Hauworth, William P., II and Lailani Moody. "An Accountant's Option Primer: Puts And Calls Demystified," No. 1, pp. 87-97.
Miller, Paul B. W. "The New Pension Accounting (Part 1)," No. 1, pp. 98-108.
Elliott, Robert K. and Peter D. Jacobson. "Two Views On The Auditor's Report: The Last Word Or In Need Of Change?," No. 2, pp. 72-79.
Landsittel, David L. "Two Views On The Auditor's Report: The Last Word Or In Need Of Change?," No. 2, pp. 80-85.
Miller, Paul B. W. "The New Pension Accounting (Part 2)," No. 2, pp. 86-94.
Wishon, Keith and Robert P. Roche. "Making The Switch: Corporation To Partnership," No. 3, pp. 90-95.
Robbins, Barry P. "A Question Of Basis," No. 3, pp. 96-101.
Gaumnitz, Bruce R. and Joel E. Thompson. "In-Substance Defeasance: Costs, Yes; Benefits, No," No. 3, pp. 102-105.
Sack, Robert J. and Robert Tangreti. "ESM: Implications For The Profession," No. 4, pp. 94-101.
Ator, Lloyd G., Jr. and Paul Claytor. "Commerical Banking And The TRA," No. 4, pp. 102-107.
Kaiser, Charles, Jr. "The Challenges Ahead: Now For The Hard Part," No. 4, pp. 108-113.
Droms, William G. "Investment Asset Allocation For PFP Clients," No. 4, pp. 114-118.
Edwards, James Don and Paul J. Miranti, Jr. "The AICPA: A Professional Institution In A Dynamic Society," No. 5, pp. 22-38.
Roberts, Alfred R. "The 'Other' Public Accounting Organizations," No. 5, pp. 41-43.
Zeff, Stephen A. "Leaders Of The Accounting Profession: 14 Who Made A Difference," No. 5, pp. 46-71.
Tucker, James J., III. "Government Oversight In 1917: The Shape Of Things To Come," No. 5, pp. 73-77.
Lowe, Herman J. "Ethics In Our 100-Year History," No. 5, pp. 78-87.
Bishop, Ashton C. and Rasoul H. Tondkar. "Development Of A Professional Code Of Ethics," No. 5, pp. 97-101.
Bialkin, Kenneth J. "Government Antitrust Enforcement And The Rules Of Conduct," No. 5, pp. 105-109.
Davidson, Sidney, and George D. Anderson. "The Development Of Accounting And Auditing Standards," No. 5, pp. 110-126.
Davidson, Sidney. "Addendum - Some Significant Standards," No. 5, pp. 130-135.
Cooper, William D. and Ida B. Robinson. "Who Should Formulate Accounting Principles? The Debate Within The SEC," No. 5, pp. 137-140.
Brief, Richard P. "Corporate Financial Reporting At The Turn Of The Century," No. 5, pp. 142-157.
Barr, Andrew and Irving J. Galpeer. "McKesson & Robbins," No. 5, pp. 159-161.
Sommerfeld, Ray M. and John E. Easton. "The CPA's Tax Practice Today - And How It Got That Way," No. 5, pp. 166-179.
Roth, Harold P. "The Payne-Aldrich Tariff Act Of 1909," No. 5, pp. 181-182.
Gardner, John C. and G. A. Swanson. "From Bercu To Sperry - Significant Legal Landmarks In The Development Of Tax Practice," No. 5, pp. 189-191.
Flesher, Tonya K. "A Turning Point In Tax History," No. 5, pp. 193-194.
Elliott, Robert K. and Peter D. Jacobson. "Audit Technology: A Heritage And A Promise," No. 5, pp. 198-218.
Mednick, Robert and Gary John Previts. "The Scope Of CPA Services: A View Of The Future From The Perspective Of A Century Of Progress," No. 5, pp. 220-238.
Schlosser, Robert E., Bernard Z. Lee and George A. Rabito. "Continuing Professional Education 1887-1987," No. 5, pp. 240-254.
Craig, Quiester. "Toward Integration Of The Accounting Profession," No. 5, pp. 257-258.
Meinert, John R. "The CPA In Business - A Look At Our Past, Present And Future," No. 5, pp. 262-275.
Bowsher, Charles A. "Federal Financial Management: Evolution, Challenges And The Role Of The Accounting Profession," No. 5, pp. 280-294.
Fleischman, Richard K. "Foundation Of The National Municipal League," No. 5, pp. 297-298.
Langenderfer, Harold Q. "Accounting Education's History - A 100-Year Search For Identity," No. 5, pp. 302-331.
Campbell, David R. "The First CPA Review Manual," No. 5, pp. 333-336.
Ried, Glenda, Brenda T. Acken and Elise G. Jancura. "An Historical Perspective On Women In Accounting," No. 5, pp. 338-355.
Amhowitz, Harris J. "The Accounting Profession And The Law: The Misunderstood Victim," No. 5, pp. 356-369.
Cook, J. Michael. "The AICPA At 100: Public Trust And Professional Pride," No. 5, pp. 370-380.
Sperry, John B., Edward C. Spede and Donald W. Hicks. "The Evolution And Current Status Of Peer Review," No. 5, pp. 381-382.
Swain, Frank S. "Reducing Domestic Barriers To A Strong Economy; A Small Business Agenda," No. 6, pp. 110-119.
Harper, Bruce J. and Neil C. Churchill. "Serving Small Business: What CPAs Should Know," No. 6, pp. 120-129.
Reardon, Thomas E. and Judi L. Worthington. "Magnetic Media Reporting: A Solution To Small Business Paperwork?," No. 6, pp. 130-135.
Upton, Wayne S., Jr. "The FASB And Small Business: An Update," No. 6, pp. 136-140.

Journal of Accountancy
Volume 164, 1987

Meinhardt, Joan, Joseph F. Moraglio and Harold I. Steinberg. "Governmental Audits: An Action Plan For Excellence," No. 1, pp. 86-91.
Broadus, W. A., Jr. and Joseph D. Comtois. "The Single Audit: A Progress Report," No. 1, pp. 92-101.
Azorsky, Michael A. "Establishing A Personal Financial Planning Department In Your CPA Firm," No. 1, pp. 102-110.
Bedford, Norton M. and William G. Shenkir. "Reorienting Accounting Education," No. 2, pp. 84-91.
Krebs, Eric H. and Joseph M. Jordan. "The Insurance Industry After The TRA," No. 2, pp. 92-101.
Rosenfield, Paul. "Accounting For Foreign Operations," No. 2, pp. 102-112.
Mednick, Robert. "Accountants' Liability: Coping With The Stampede To The Courtroom," No. 3, pp. 118-125.
Korb, Phillip J., Charles L. Martin, Jr. and Barbara R. Stewart. "Income And Expense Rules After Tax Reform: Helping Clients Cope," No. 3, pp. 126-137.
Kinsman, Michael D. and Bruce Samuelson. "Personal Financial Statements: Valuation Challenges And Solutions," No. 3, pp. 138-150.
Foss, Helga B. and Shaheen Borna. "Employee Leasing After The TRA," No. 3, pp. 151-156.

Journal of Accountancy

Willens, Robert. "Mutual Funds After Tax Reform: Hedging Your Bets," No. 4, pp. 110-115.
Larson, Rholan E. "For The Members, By The Members," No. 4, pp. 116-123.
Banick, Richard S. and Douglas C. Broeker. "Arbitration: An Option For Resolving Claim Against CPAs," No. 4, pp. 124-129.
Ives, Martin. "Accountability And Governmental Financial Reporting," No. 4, pp. 130-134.
Key, Stephen L. and Simon S. Strauss. "Allocating Purchase Price In An Acquisition: A Practical Guide," No. 5, pp. 32-37.
Kautter, David J. "Compensation After Tax Reform (Part 1): The TRA's Two Waves," No. 5, pp. 50-60.
Craco, Louis A. and Deborah E. Cooper. "The Institute As Amicus Curiae: The Key To The Courthouse," No. 5, pp. 70-74.
Creamer, Anthony B., III. "Auditing Beyond U.S. Shores: What The U.S. CPA Should Know," No. 5, pp. 85-96.
Schuetze, Walter. "Disclosure And The Impairment Question," No. 6, pp. 26-32.
Kautter, David J. "Compensation After Tax Reform (Part 2): ESOPs, IRAs And Others," No. 6, pp. 40-48.
Read, William J., John E. Mitchell and Abraham D. Akresh. "Planning Materiality And SAS No. 47," No. 6, pp. 72-79.

Journal of Accountancy
Volume 165, 1988

Wiesner, Philip J. "The TRA's Alternative Minimum Tax (Part 1): How Book Income Can Increase Tax Liability," No. 1, pp. 28-37.
Fowler, Larry. "Tips For Profitable PFP Services," No. 1, pp. 44-52.
Schattke, Rudolph. "Accounting For Computer Software: The Revenue Side Of The Coin." No. 1, pp. 58-70.
Hazard, Albert W. and Raymond E. Perry. "What FASB Statement No. 91 Means For Accountants And Auditors," No. 2, pp. 28-36.
Mears, William H, Jr. and Nadine Gordon Lee. "Traps And Pitfalls For Preparers Of Individual Returns," No. 2, pp. 45-53.
Wiesner, Philip J. and Sherri P. Nadeau. "Alternative Minimum Tax (Part 2): More Headaches Than Aspirin," No. 2, pp. 54-63.
Willens, Robert. "The Revenue Act Of 1987: Why Companies Can Breathe Easier," No. 3, pp. 22-29.
Wiese, Donald C. and Kelly Polich. "The Revenue Act Of 1987: Revenue-Raising Snippets," No. 3, pp. 30-37.
Zuber, George R. "What Auditors Should Know About FASB Statement No. 87," No. 3, pp. 38-48.
Mautz, Robert K. and Louis W. Matusiak. "Concurring Partner Review Revisited," No. 3, pp. 56-63.
Parks, James T. "A Guide To FASB's Overhaul Of Income Tax Accounting," No. 4, pp. 24-35.
Guy, Dan M. and Jerry D. Sullivan. "The Expectation Gap Auditing Standards," No. 4, pp. 36-46.
Podolin, Leonard. "Treasury Raises The Stakes In Circular 230 Proposal," No. 4, pp. 60-69.
Hutto, Gary W. "How To Divest Undervalued Land Without Losing Profits," No. 4, pp. 70-78.
Mahoney, John J., Mark V. Sever and John A. Theis. "Cash Flow: FASB Opens The Floodgates," No. 5, pp. 26-38.
Rezaee, Zabihollah and Grover L. Porter. "Summary Annual Reports: Is Shorter Better?," No. 5, pp. 42-54.
Forrester, Robert. "Tips For Auditing Nonprofit Organizations," No. 5, pp. 56-66.
Baker, Dale E. "Improved Fund Raising: Accounting For Restricted And Unrestricted Funds," No. 5, pp. 68-76.
Turner, Mark A. and Kenneth R. Lambert. "Why The Furor Over UBIT," No. 5, pp. 78-84.
Temkin, Robert H. and Alan J. Winters. "SAS No. 55: The Auditor's New Responsibility For Internal Control," No. 5, pp. 86-98.
Bukofsky, Ward M. and William J. Dunn. "Personal Service Corporations: Down But Not Out," No. 6, pp. 30-37.
Kissin, Warren and Ronald Zulli. "Valuation Of A Closely Held Business," No. 6, pp. 38-48.
Shildneck, Barbara J. "The CPA As Advocate," No. 6, pp. 49-55.

Upton, Wayne S., Jr. and Deborah K. Scott. "What You Should Know About The EITF," No. 6, pp. 56-63.
Johnson, Richard D., Edward M. Klasny and Patrick McNamee. "ASB Proposes New SAS On Compliance Auditing," No. 6, pp. 76-87.
Tierney, Cornelius E. "No Quick Fix For Federal Finances," No. 6, pp. 88-94.

Journal of Accountancy
Volume 166, 1988

Diss, William T. "Estate Planning Tips: Locking In The Advantages," No. 1, pp. 36-45.
Willens, Robert. "The Technical Corrections Act: What Corporations Should Know Now," No. 1, pp. 46-49.
Hall, William D. and Arthur J. Renner. "Lessons That Auditors Ignore At Their Own Risk," No. 1, pp. 50-59.
Roth, Harold P. "Guiding Manufacturers Through The Inventory Capitalization Maze," No. 1, pp. 60-71.
McKee, Thomas E. and W. Edward Stead. "Managing The Professional Accountant," No. 1, pp. 76-86.
Gorman, Jerry. "M&As: The CPA As Acquisition Adviser," No. 2, pp. 36-42.
Willens, Robert. "M&As: The CPA As Tax Adviser," No. 2, pp. 44-52.
Mednick, Robert. "Our Profession In The Year 2000: A Blueprint Of The Future," No. 2, pp. 54-58.
Robbins, Barry P. "FASB's Long Look At Stock Compensation Plans," No. 2, pp. 60-68.
Shenkman, Martin M. "A Real Estate Leasing Checklist: Are Your Clients Making The Most Of Your Services?," No. 2, pp. 78-84.
Carmichael, D. R. "The Auditor's New Guide To Errors, Irregularities And Illegal Acts," No. 3, pp. 40-48.
Miller, Stephen H. "Avoiding Lawsuits," No. 3, pp. 57-65.
Johnson, Gregg D. "Recovering Fees In Bankruptcy," No. 3, pp. 66-70.
Person, Stanley. "1988 Yearend Tax Planning For Small Businesses," No. 4, pp. 29-39.
Powell, Donald F. "Preparing For Tax Season," No. 4, pp. 41-46.
Collins, Stephen H. "1988 Tax Filing Season: Dealing With The Chaos," No. 4, pp. 48-54.
Callahan, Patrick S., Henry R. Jaenicke and Donald L. Neebes. "SASs Nos. 56 And 57: Increasing Audit Effectiveness," No. 4, pp. 56-68.
Gorman, Jerry. "LBO Accounting: Unveiling The Mystery Of Carryover Basis," No. 4, pp. 71-80.
Cholmondeley, Paula H. J. "Seeking The Future: A Game Of Tag," No. 4, pp. 89-94.
Searfoss, D. Gerald and Naomi Erickson. "The Big Unfunded Liability: Postretirement Healthcare Benefits," No. 5, pp. 28-39.
Monk, Harold L., Jr. and Kay W. Tatum. "Applying SAS No. 55 In Audits Of Small Businesses," No. 5, pp. 40-56.
Parks, James T. "How Accounting Standards Are Changing The Home Finance Industry," No. 5, pp. 59-62.
Miller, John R. and Frederick D. Wolf. "A Look At The New Yellow Book: Tomorrow's Government Audits," No. 5, pp. 64-80.
Krzystofik, Anthony T. and Richard Fein. "Does Your Firm Use The Right Approach In Hiring Campus Recruits?," No. 5, pp. 83-88.
Case, Richard. "Interview Techniques For Hiring The Right Candidates," No. 5, pp. 90-96.
Person, Stanley. "Yearend Personal Tax Planning Tips," No. 6, pp. 32-42.
Roussey, Robert S., Ernest L. Ten Eyck and Mimi Blanco-Best. "Three New SASs: Closing The Communications Gap," No. 6, pp. 44-52.
Geiger, Marshall A. "SAS No. 58: Did The ASB Really Listen?," No. 6, pp. 55-57.
Akresh, Abraham D. and Kay W. Tatum. "Audit Sampling - Dealing With The Problems," No. 6, pp. 58-64.
Nichols, John F. "When You're Called To Court As A Witness." No. 6, pp. 66-68.
Humphries, Francis A., Linda M. Plunkett and Rebecca B. Herring. "Let's Make Required CPE Rules Uniform," No. 6, pp. 70-74.

JOURNAL OF ACCOUNTING AND ECONOMICS

**Journal of Accounting and Economics
Volume 1, 1979**

Collins, Daniel W. and Warren T. Dent. "The Proposed Elimination Of Full Cost Accounting In The Extractive Petroleum Industry: An Empirical Assessment Of The Market Consequences," No. 1, pp. 3-44.

Dyckman, Thomas R. and Abbie J. Smith. "Financial Accounting And Reporting By Oil And Gas Producing Companies: A Study Of Information Effects," No. 1, pp. 45-75.

Verrecchia, Robert E. "On The Theory Of Market Information Efficiency," No. 1, pp. 77-90.

Jarrell, Gregg A. "Pro-Producer Regulation And Accounting For Assets: The Case Of Electric Utilities," No. 2, pp. 93-116.

Patell, James M. and Mark A. Wolfson. "Anticipated Information Releases Reflected In Call Option Prices," No. 2, pp. 117-140.

Hagerman, Robert L. and Mark E. Zmijewski. "Some Economic Determinants Of Accounting Policy Choice," No. 2, pp. 141-161.

Givoly, Dan and Josef Lakonishok. "The Information Content Of Financial Analysts' Forecasts Of Earnings: Some Evidence On Semi-Strong Inefficiency," No. 3, pp. 165-185.

Lev, Baruch and Shyam Sunder. "Methodological Issues In The Use Of Financial Ratios," No. 3, pp. 187-210.

Ohlson, James A. "On Financial Disclosure And The Behavior Of Security Prices," No. 3, pp. 211-232.

**Journal of Accounting and Economics
Volume 2, 1980**

Beaver, William, Richard Lambert and Dale Morse. "The Information Content Of Security Prices," No. 1, pp. 3-28.

Foster, George. "Accounting Policy Decisions And Capital Market Research," No. 1, pp. 29-62.

Verrecchia, Robert E. "The Rapidity Of Price Adjustments To Information," No. 1, pp. 63-92.

Watts, Ross L. and Jerold L. Zimmerman. "On The Irrelevance Of Replacement Cost Disclosures For Security Prices," No. 2, pp. 95-106.

Gheyara, Kelly and James Boatsman. "Market Reaction To The 1976 Replacement Cost Disclosures," No. 2, pp. 107-125.

Beaver, William H., Andrew A. Christie and Paul A. Griffin. "The Information Content Of SEC Accounting Series Release No. 190," No. 2, pp. 127-157.

Ro, Byung T. "The Adjustment Of Security Returns to The Disclosure Of Replacement Cost Accounting Information," No. 2, pp. 159-189.

Leftwich, Richard. "Market Failure Fallacies And Accounting Information," No. 3, pp. 193-211.

Wakeman, Lee Macdonald. "Optimal Tax Depreciation," No. 3, pp. 213-237.

**Journal of Accounting and Economics
Volume 3, 1981**

Leftwich, Richard. "Evidence Of The Impact Of Mandatory Changes In Accounting Principles On Corporate Loan Agreements," No. 1, pp. 3-36.

Collins, Daniel W., Michael S. Rozeff and Dan S. Dhaliwal. "The Economic Determinants Of The Market Reaction To Proposed Mandatory Accounting Changes In The Oil And Gas Industry: A Cross-Sectional Analysis," No. 1, pp. 37-71.

Holthausen, Robert W. "Evidence On The Effect Of Bond Covenants And Management Compensation Contracts On The Choice Of Accounting Techniques: The Case Of The Depreciation Switch-Back," No. 1, pp. 73-109.

DeAngelo, Linda Elizabeth. "Auditor Independence, 'Low Balling', And Disclosure Regulation," No. 2, pp. 113-127.

Zmijewski, Mark E. and Robert L. Hagerman. "An Income Strategy Approach To The Positive Theory Of Accounting Standard Setting/Choice," No. 2, pp. 129-149.

Bowen, Robert M., Eric W. Noreen and John M. Lacey. "Determinants Of The Corporate Decision To Capitalize Interest," No. 2, pp. 151-179.

DeAngelo, Linda Elizabeth. "Auditor Size And Audit Quality," No. 3, pp. 183-199.

Foster, George. "Intra-Industry Information Transfers Associated With Earnings Releases," No. 3, pp. 201-232.

Beaver, William H. and Wayne R. Landsman. "Note On The Behavior Of Residual Security Returns For Winner And Loser Portfolios," No. 3, pp. 233-241.

**Journal of Accounting and Economics
Volume 4, 1982**

Hite, Gailen L. and Michael S. Long. "Taxes And Executive Stock Options," No. 1, pp. 3-14.

Beaver, William H., Paul A. Griffin and Wayne R. Landsman. "The Incremental Information Content Of Replacement Cost Earnings," No. 1, pp. 15-39.

Dhaliwal, Dan S., Gerald Salamon and E. Dan Smith. "The Effect Of Owner Versus Management Control On The Choice Of Accounting Methods," No. 1, pp. 41-53.

Whaley, Robert E. and Joseph K. Cheung. "Anticipation Of Quarterly Earnings Announcements: A Test Of Option Market Efficiency," No. 2, pp. 57-83.

Fried, Dov and Dan Givoly. "Financial Analysts' Forecasts Of Earnings: A Better Surrogate For Market Expectations," No. 2, pp. 85-107.

Smith, David B. and Donald R. Nichols. "A Market Test Of Investor Reaction To Disagreements," No. 2, pp. 109-120.

Lustgarten, Steven. "The Impact Of Replacement Cost Disclosure On Security Prices: New Evidence," No. 2, pp. 121-141.

Lilien, Steven and Victor Pastena. "Determinants Of Intra-Method Choice In The Oil And Gas Industry," No. 3, pp. 145-170.

DeAngelo, Linda Elizabeth. "Mandated Successful Efforts And Auditor Choice," No. 3, pp. 171-203.

Jain, Prem C. "Cross-Sectional Association Between Abnormal Returns And Firm Specific Variables," No. 3, pp. 205-228.

**Journal of Accounting and Economics
Volume 5, 1983**

Larcker, David F. "The Association Between Performance Plan Adoption And Corporate Capital Investment," No. 1, pp. 3-30.

Lev, Baruch. "Some Economic Determinants Of Time-Series Properties Of Earnings," No. 1, pp. 31-48.

McNichols, Maureen and James G. Manegold. "The Effect Of The Information Environment On The Relationship Between Financial Disclosure And Security Price Variability," No. 1, pp. 49-74.

Holthausen, Robert W. and Richard W. Leftwich. "The Economic Consequences Of Accounting Choice: Implications Of Costly Contracting And Monitoring," No. 2, pp. 77-117.

Zimmerman, Jerold L. "Taxes And Firm Size," No. 2, pp. 119-149.

Evans, John H., III and James M. Patton. "An Economic Analysis Of Participation In The Municipal Finance Officers Association Certificate Of Conformance Program," No. 2, pp. 151-175.

Verrecchia, Robert E. "Discretionary Disclosure," No. 3, pp. 179-194.

Daley, Lane A. and Robert L. Vigeland. "The Effects Of Debt Covenants And Political Costs On The Choice Of Accounting Methods: The Case Of Accounting For R&D Costs," No. 3, pp. 195-211.

Baber, William R. "Toward Understanding The Role Of Auditing In The Public Sector," No. 3, pp. 213-227.

**Journal of Accounting and Economics
Volume 6, 1984**

Dodd, Peter, Nicholas Dopuch, Robert Holthausen and Richard Leftwich. "Qualified Audit Opinions And Stock Prices: Information Content, Announcement Dates, And Concurrent Disclosures," No. 1, pp. 3-38.

Lys, Thomas. "Mandated Accounting Changes And Debt Covenants: The Case Of Oil And Gas Accounting," No. 1, pp. 39-65.

Dietrich, J. Richard. "Effects Of Early Bond Refundings: An Empirical Investigation Of Security Returns," No. 1, pp. 67-96.

Hughes, John S. and William E. Ricks. "Accounting For Retail Land Sales: Analysis Of A Mandated Change," No. 2, pp. 101-132.

Francis, Jere R. "The Effect Of Audit Firm Size On Audit Prices: A Study Of The Australian Market," No. 2, pp. 133-151.

Smith, David B., Howard Stettler and William Beedles. "An Investigation Of The Information Content Of Foreign Sensitive Payment Disclosures," No. 2, pp. 153-162.

Penman, Stephen H. "Abnormal Returns To Investment Strategies Based On The Timing Of Earnings Reports," No. 3, pp. 165-183.

Kellogg, Robert L. "Accounting Activities, Security Prices, And Class Action Lawsuits," No. 3, pp. 185-204.

Christie, Andrew A., Michael D. Kennelley, J. William King and Thomas F. Schaefer. "Testing For Incremental Information Content In The Presence Of Collinearity," No. 3, pp. 205-217.

Beaver, William H., Paul A. Griffin and Wayne R. Landsman. "Testing For Incremental Information Content In The Presence Of Collinearity: A Comment," No. 3, pp. 219-223.

**Journal of Accounting and Economics
Volume 7, 1985**

Jensen, Michael C. and Jerold L. Zimmerman. "Management Compensation And The Managerial Labor Market," No. 1/3, pp. 3-9.

Murphy, Kevin J. "Corporate Performance And Managerial Remuneration: An Empirical Analysis," No. 1/3, pp. 11-42.

Coughlan, Anne T. and Ronald M. Schmidt. "Executive Compensation, Management Turnover, And Firm Performance: An Empirical Investigation," No. 1/3, pp. 43-66.

Benston, George J. "The Self-Serving Management Hypothesis: Some Evidence," No. 1/3, pp. 67-84.

Healy, Paul. "The Effect Of Bonus Schemes On Accounting Decisions," No. 1/3, pp. 85-107.

Kaplan, Robert S. "Comments On Paul Healy: Evidence On the Effect Of Bonus Schemes On Accounting Procedure And Accrual Decisions," No. 1/3, pp. 109-113.

Brickley, James A., Sanjai Bhagat and Ronald C. Lease. "The Impact Of Long-Range Managerial Compensation Plans On Shareholder Wealth," No. 1/3, pp. 115-129.

Tehranian, Hassan and James F. Waegelein. "Market Reaction To Short-Term Executive Compensation Plan Adoption," No. 1/3, pp. 131-144.

Warner, Jerold B. "Stock Market Reaction To Management Incentive Plan Adoption: An Overview," No. 1/3, pp. 145-149.

Johnson, W. Bruce, Robert P. Magee, Nandu J. Nagarajan and Harry A. Newman. "An Analysis Of The Stock Price Reaction To Sudden Executive Deaths: Implications For The Management Labor Market," No. 1/3, pp. 151-174.

Schwert, G. William. " A Discussion Of CEO Deaths And The Reaction Of Stock Prices," No. 1/3, pp. 175-178.

Lambert, Richard A. and David F. Larcker. "Golden Parachutes, Executive Decision-Making, And Shareholder Wealth," No. 1/3, pp. 179-203.

Rosen, Sherwin. "Commentary On 'Golden Parachutes, Executive Decision-Making, And Shareholder Wealth'," No. 1/3, pp. 205-208.

Lewellen, Wilbur, Claudio Loderer and Ahron Rosenfeld. "Merger Decisions And Executive Stock Ownership In Acquiring Firms," No. 1/3, pp. 209-231.

Mikkelson, Wayne H. and Richard S. Ruback. "Takeovers And Managerial Compensation: A Discussion," No. 1/3, pp. 233-238.

Raviv, Artur. "Management Compensation And The Managerial Labor Market: An Overview," No. 1/3, pp. 239-245.

Meckling, William H. "Three Reflections On Performance Rewards And Higher Education," No. 1/3, pp. 247-251.

Journal of Accounting and Economics
Volume 8, 1986

Palepu, Krishna G. "Predicting Takeover Targets: A Methodological And Empirical Analysis," No. 1, pp. 3-35.

Zimmer, Ian. "Accounting For Interest By Real Estate Developers," No. 1, pp. 37-51.

Trueman, Brett. "Why Do Managers Voluntarily Release Earnings Forecasts?," No. 1, pp. 53-71.

Kinney, William R., Jr. "Audit Technology And Preferences For Auditing Standards," No. 1, pp. 73-89.

Dopuch, Nicholas, Robert W. Holthausen and Richard W. Leftwich. "Abnormal Stock Returns Associated With Media Disclosures Of 'Subject To' Qualified Audit Opinions," No. 2, pp. 93-117.

Hughes, Patricia J. "Signalling By Direct Disclosure Under Asymmetric Information," No. 2, pp. 119-142.

Ayres, Frances L. "Characteristics Of Firms Electing Early Adoption Of SFAS 52," No. 2, pp. 143-158.

Titman, Sheridan and Brett Trueman. "Information Quality And The Valuation Of New Issues," No. 2, pp. 159-172.

Verrecchia, Robert E. "Managerial Discretion In The Choice Among Financial Reporting Alternatives," No. 3, pp. 175-195.

Stickel, Scott E. "The Effect Of Preferred Stock Rating Changes On Preferred And Common Stock Prices," No. 3, pp. 197-215.

El-Gazzar, Samir, Steve Lilien and Victor Pastena. "Accounting For Leases By Lessees," No. 3, pp. 217-237.

Journal of Accounting and Economics
Volume 9, 1987

Healy, Paul M., Sok-Hyon Kang and Krishna G. Palepu. "The Effect Of Accounting Procedure Changes On CEOs' Cash Salary And Bonus Compensation," No. 1, pp. 7-34.

Francis, Jere R. and Sara Ann Reiter. "Determinants Of Corporate Pension Funding Strategy," No. 1, pp. 35-59.

Brown, Lawrence D., Robert L. Hagerman, Paul A. Griffin and Mark E. Zmijewski. "Security Analyst Superiority Relative To Univariate Time-Series Models In Forecasting Quarterly Earnings," No. 1, pp. 61-87.

Clinch, Greg J. and Norman A. Sinclair. "Intra-Industry Information Releases: A Recursive Systems Approach," No. 1, pp. 89-106.

Collins, Daniel W., S. P. Kothari and Judy Dawson Rayburn. "Firm Size And The Information Content Of Prices With Respect To Earnings," No. 2, pp. 111-138.

Beaver, William H., Richard A. Lambert and Stephen G. Ryan. "The Information Content Of Security Prices: A Second Look," No. 2, pp. 139-157.

Brown, Lawrence D., Paul A. Griffin, Robert L. Hagerman and Mark E. Zmijewski. "An Evaluation Of Alternative Proxies For The Market's Assessment Of Unexpected Earnings," No. 2, pp. 159-193.

Freeman, Robert N. "The Association Between Accounting Earnings And Security Returns For Large And Small Firms," No. 2, pp. 195-228.

Christie, Andrew A. "On Cross-Sectional Analysis In Accounting Research," No. 3, pp. 231-258.

Whittred, Greg. "The Derived Demand For Consolidated Financial Reporting," No. 3, pp. 259-285.

Lewellen, Wilbur, Claudio Loderer and Kenneth Martin. "Executive Compensation And Executive Incentive Problems: An Empirical Analysis," No. 3, pp. 287-310.

Journal of Accounting and Economics
Volume 10, 1988

DeAngelo, Linda Elizabeth. "Managerial Competition, Information Costs, And Corporate Governance: The Use Of Accounting Performance Measures In Proxy Contests," No. 1, pp. 3-36.

Wong, Jilnaught. "Political Costs And An Intraperiod Accounting Choice For Export Tax Credits," No. 1, pp. 37-51.

O'Brien, Patricia C. "Analysts' Forecasts As Earnings Expectations," No. 1, pp. 53-83.

Zarowin, Paul. "Non-Linearities And Nominal Contracting Effects: The Case Of The Depreciation Tax Shield," No. 2, pp. 89-110.

Kim, Moshe and Giora Moore. "Economic Vs. Accounting Depreciation," No. 2, pp. 111-125.

Sutton, Timothy G. "The Proposed Introduction Of Current Cost Accounting In The U.K.: Determinants Of Corporate Preference," No. 2, pp. 127-149.

Wong, Jilnaught. "Economic Incentives For The Voluntary Disclosure Of Current Cost Financial Statements," No. 2, pp. 151-167.

Banker, Rajiv D., Srikant M. Datar and Sunder Kekre. "Relevant Costs, Congestion And Stochasticity In Production Environments," No. 3, pp. 171-197.

Thomas, Jacob K. "Corporate Taxes And Defined Benefit Pension Plans," No. 3, pp. 199-237.

McNichols, Maureen. "A Comparison Of The Skewness Of Stock Return Distributions At Earnings And Non-Earnings Announcement Dates," No. 3, pp. 239-273.

Imhoff, Eugene A. and Jacob K. Thomas. "Economic Consequences Of Accounting Standards: The Lease Disclosure Rule Change," No. 4, pp. 277-310.

Lanen, William N. and Rex Thompson. "Stock Price Reactions As Surrogates For Net Cash Flow Effects Of Corporate Policy Decisions," No. 4, pp. 311-334.

Smith, David B. and Susan Pourciau. "A Comparison Of The Financial Characteristics Of December And Non-December Year-End Companies," No. 4, pp. 335-344.

Journal of Accounting and Public Policy
Volume 1, 1982

Benston, George J. "An Analysis Of The Role Of Accounting Standards For Enhancing Corporate Governance And Social Responsibility," No. 1, pp. 5-17.

Amershi, Amin H., Joel S. Demski and Mark A. Wolfson. "Strategic Behavior And Regulation Research In Accounting," No. 1, pp. 19-32.

Merino, Barbara Dubis and Marilyn Dale Neimark. "Disclosure Regulation And Public Policy: A Sociohistorical Reappraisal," No. 1, pp. 33-57.

Aharony, Joseph and Haim Falk. "The Effectiveness Of Electric Utility Price Regulation In The 1970s: A Stochastic Dominance Analysis," No. 1, pp. 59-77.

Horwitz, Bertrand and Richard Kolodny. "Who Is Shortsighted?," No. 2, pp. 79-82.

Schall, Lawrence D. and Gary L. Sundem. "The Investment Tax Credit And The Leasing Industry," No. 2. pp. 83-94.

Arrington, C. Edward, Robert E. Jensen and Masao Tokutani. "Scaling Of Corporate Multivariate Performance Criteria: Subjective Composition Versus The Analytic Hierarchy Process," No. 2, pp. 95-123.

Stickney, Clyde P. and Victor E. McGee. "Effective Corporate Tax Rates: The Effect Of Size, Capital Intensity, Leverage, And Other Factors," No. 2, pp. 125-152.

Kelly, Lauren. "Corporate Lobbying And Changes In Financial Or Operating Activities In Reaction To FAS No. 8," No. 2, pp. 153-173.

Journal of Accounting and Public Policy
Volume 2, 1983

Gordon, Lawrence A. "Federal Capital Investments And Public Policy: The Budgeting Link," No. 1, pp. 1-4.

Ingram, Robert W. "The Importance Of State Accounting Practices For Creditor Decisions," No. 1, pp. 5-17.

Lowe, E. A., A. G. Puxty and R. C. Laughlin. "Simple Theories For Complex Processes: Accounting Policy And The Market For Myopia," No. 1, pp. 19-42.

Pany, Kurt and P. M. J. Reckers. "Auditor Independence And Nonaudit Services: Director Views And Their Policy Implications," No. 1, pp. 43-62.

Goldenberg, David H. and Raymond Chiang. "Systematic Risk And The Theory Of The Firm: A Reexamination," No. 1, pp. 63-72.

Ijiri, Yuji. "On The Accountability-Based Conceptual Framework Of Accounting," No. 2, pp. 75-81.

Dhaliwal, Dan S., Fratern M. Mboya and Russell M. Barefield. "Utilization Of SFAS No. 14 Disclosures In Assessing Operating Risk," No. 2, pp. 83-98.

Euske, K. J. and C. T. Rock, Jr. "Integrating Human Resource Accounting Into The Public Policy Process: An Illustration," No. 2, pp. 99-114.

Zeghal, Daniel. "Industry, Market Structure, And The Informational Content Of Financial Statements," No. 2, pp. 115-131.

Greer, Willis R., Jr. "Where Have All The Deep Discounts Gone?," No. 2, pp. 133-140.

Havens, Harry S. "Accounting And Public Policy," No. 3, pp. 143-146.

Copeland, Ronald M. and Robert W. Ingram. "Municipal Bond Market Recognition Of Pension Reporting Practices," No. 3, pp. 147-165.

Hawkins, C. A. and D. N. Leggett. "The Investment Tax Credit In Capital Replacement: A Simulation," No. 3, pp. 167-187.

Cooper, Kerry and Gerald D. Keim. "The Economic Rationale For The Nature And Extent Of Corporate Financial Disclosure Regulation: A Critical Assessment," No. 3, pp. 189-205.

Belkaoui, Ahmed. "Economic, Political, And Civil Indicators And Reporting And Disclosure Adequacy: Empirical Investigation," No. 3, pp. 207-219.

Aivazian, Varouj A. and Jeffrey L. Callen. "Core Theory And Uniformity In Accounting: Rationalizing The Accounting Rulemaker," No. 4, pp. 225-237.

Halperin, Robert. "The Perceived Instability Of Tax Legislation And Its Effect On Consumption Investment Decisions," No. 4, pp. 239-262.

Volz, William H. "Discovering An Accountant's Tax Accrual Workpapers: Should Auditors Join The Privileged Few?," No. 4, pp. 263-280.

Leete, Burt A. "A Look At The Public Policy Conflict Regarding The Discovery Of Accountants' Tax Accrual Workpapers," No. 4, pp. 281-288.

Hamer, Michelle M. "Failure Prediction: Sensitivity Of Classification Accuracy To Alternative Statistical Methods And Variable Sets," No. 4. pp. 289-307.

Journal of Accounting and Public Policy
Volume 3, 1984

Loeb, Stephen E. "Codes Of Ethics And Self-Regulation For Non-Public Accountants: A Public Policy Perspective," No. 1, pp. 1-8.

Apostolou, Nicholas G., James M. Reeve and Gary A. Giroux. "Accounting Information And Municipal Bond Net Interest Cost: An Empirical Evaluation," No. 1, pp. 9-28.

Robinson, John R. "Tax Reform: Analyzing A Comprehensive Income Tax," No. 1, pp. 29-38.

Edmister, Robert O. and Harry E. Merriken. "Consumer Deposit Demand, Interest Rate Differentials, And Public Welfare," No. 1, pp. 39-54.

Tinker, Anthony. "Theories Of The State And The State Accounting: Economic Reductionism And Political Voluntarism In Accounting Regulation Theory," No. 1, pp. 55-74.

Bernard, Victor L. "A Comment On: 'Effective Corporate Tax Rates'," No. 1, pp. 75-78.

Heuer, Mark A. "Federal Capital Investment Policy: A Role For Accounting," No. 2, pp. 81-89.

Baber, William R. and Pradyot K. Sen. "The Role Of Generally Accepted Reporting Methods In The Public Sector: An Empirical Test," No. 2, pp. 91-106.

Benson, Earl D., Barry R. Marks and K. K. Raman. "State Regulation Of Accounting Practices And Municipal Borrowing Costs," No. 2, pp. 107-122.

Benston, George J. "The Costs Of Complying With A Government Data Collection Program: The FTC's Line Of Business Report," No. 2, pp. 123-137.

Covaleski, Mark A. and Charles J. Davis. "An Empirical Examination Of Capital Expenditure In The Health Sector," No. 2, pp. 139-162.

Johnson, Steven B. and David Solomons. "Institutional Legitimacy And The FASB," No. 3, pp. 165-183.

Silhan, Peter A. "Company Size And The Issue Of Quarterly Segment Reporting," No. 3, pp. 185-197.

Mathews, M. R. "A Suggested Classification For Social Accounting Research," No. 3, pp. 199-221.

Ruland, Robert G. "Duty, Obligation, And Responsibility In Accounting Policy Making," No. 3, pp. 223-237.

Parkinson, J. M. "'Economic, Political, And Civil Indicators And Reporting And Disclosure Adequacy: Empirical Investigation': A Comment," No. 3, pp. 239-248.

Belkaoui, Ahmed. "'Economic, Political, And Civil Indicators And Reporting And Disclosure Adequacy: Empirical Investigation': A Reply," No. 3, pp. 249-250.

Kleiner, Morris M. "Public Policy Implications Of Financial Information Requirements Under The National Labor Relations Act," No. 4, pp. 253-257.

Gordon, Lawrence A. and Fred E. Sellers. "Accounting And Budgeting Systems: The Issue Of Congruency," No. 4, pp. 259-292.

Granof, Michael H. "A Fundamental Flaw Of Debt Limitations For State And Local Governments," No. 4, pp. 293-310.

Beach, John E. "Code Of Ethics: The Professional Catch 22," No. 4, pp. 311-323.

Journal of Accounting and Public Policy
Volume 4, 1985

Revsine, Lawrence. "Comparability: An Analytic Examination," No. 1, pp. 1-12.

Eichenseher, John W. and David Shields. "Corporate Director Liability And Monitoring Preferences," No. 1, pp. 13-31.

Benston, George J. "The Market For Public Accounting Services: Demand, Supply And Regulation," No.1, pp.33-79.

Capettini, Robert, David A. Dittman and Richard C. Morey. "Reimbursement Rate Setting For Medicaid Prescription Drugs Based On Relative Efficiencies," No. 2, pp.83-110.

Reichenstein, William R. and William A. Raabe. "The Effects Of Tax Provisions On Long-Run Investment Prospects," No. 2. pp. 111-121.

Stephens, Ray G., Jesse F. Dillard and David K. Dennis. "Implications Of Formal Grammars For Accounting Policy Development," No. 2, pp. 123-148.

Marks, Barry R. and K. K. Raman. "Pension Ratios As 'Correlates' Of Municipal Pension Underfunding," No. 2, pp. 149-157.

Chatov, Robert. "The Possible New Shape Of Accounting In The United States," No. 3, pp. 161-174.

DeJong, Douglas V. "Class-Action Privileges And Contingent Legal Fees: Investor And Lawyer Incentives To Litigate And The Effect On Audit Quality," No. 3, pp. 175-200.

McKinnon, Jill L. and Graeme L. Harrison. "Cultural Influence On Corporate And Governmental Involvement In Accounting Policy Determination In Japan," No. 3, pp. 201-223.

Stark, A. W. "Inventories, Credit Transactions, And The Marginal Effective Tax Rate," No. 3, pp. 225-231.

Dhaliwal, Dan S. and Eric H. Sorensen. "On Accounting Information And Municipal Bond Interest Cost: A Comment," No. 3, pp. 233-239.

Reeve, James M., Gary A. Giroux and Nicholas G. Apostolou. "Accounting Information And Municipal Bond Interest Cost: Methodological Considerations: Reply To Comment," No. 3, pp. 241-245.

Sharp, Florence C. "The Effects Of Governmental Accounting Methods On Asset-Acquisition Decisions: A Theoretical Model And Three Case Studies," No. 4, pp. 251-276.

Covaleski, Mark A., Mark W. Dirsmith and Stephen F. Jablonsky. "Traditional And Emergent Theories Of Budgeting: An Empirical Analysis," No. 4, pp. 277-300.

Pendlebury, Maurice and Rowan Jones. "Governmental Budgeting As Ex Ante Financial Accounting: The United Kingdom Case," No. 4, pp. 301-316.

Campbell, Terry L. and Douglas W. McNiel. "Stochastic And Nonstochastic Determinants Of Changes In Client-Industry Concentrations For Large Public-Accounting Firms," No. 4, pp. 317-328.

Journal of Accounting and Public Policy
Volume 5, 1986

Journal of Accounting and Public Policy
Volume 6, 1987

Journal of Accounting and Public Policy
Volume 7, 1988

Journal of Accounting, Auditing and Finance
Volume 5, 1981-82

Kinney, William R. Jr. "Predicting Auditor-Initiated Adjustments Using Paired Balance Methods," No. 1, pp. 5-17.

Schnee, Edward J. and Martin E. Taylor. "IRS Access To Accountants' Work Papers - The Rules May Be Changing," No. 1, pp. 18-29.

Dowell, C. Dwayne and James Arthur Hall. "EDP Controls With Audit Cost Implications," No. 1, pp. 30-40.

Hill, Henry P. "Rational Expectations And Accounting Principles," No. 2, pp. 99-109.

Holder, William W. and Kimberly Ham Eudy. "A Framework For Building An Accounting Constitution," No. 2, pp. 110-125.

Shockley, Randolph A. "Perceptions Of Audit Independence: A Conceptual Model," No. 2, pp. 126-143.

Raman, K. K. "Financial Reporting And Municipal Bond Ratings," No. 2, pp. 144-153.

Murray, Dennis. "The Irrelevance Of Lease Capitalization," No. 2, pp. 154-159.

Sorter, George H. "The Emphasis On Cash And Its Impact On The Funds Statement - Sense And Nonsense," No. 3, pp. 188-194.

Johnson, Steven B. and William F. Messier Jr. "The Nature Of Accounting Standards Setting: An Alternative Explanation," No. 3, pp. 195-213.

Dirsmith, Mark W. and John P. McAllister. "The Organic Vs. The Mechanistic Audit," No. 3, pp. 214-228.

St. Pierre, Kent and James Anderson. "An Analysis Of Audit Failures Based On Documented Legal Cases," No. 3, pp. 229-247.

Brown, Paul R. "FASB Responsiveness To Corporate Input," No. 4, pp. 282-290.

Landsittel, David L. and Jerry E. Serlin. "Evaluating The Materiality Of Errors In Financial Statements," No. 4, pp. 291-300.

Wright, Gail B. and Robert D. Taylor. "Reporting Materiality For Investors," No. 4, pp. 301-309.

Whittington, O. Ray and Steven J. Adams. "Temporary Breakdowns Of Internal Control: Implications For External And Internal Auditors," No. 4, pp. 310-319.

Gamble, George O. "An Application Of Current Value Theory To Accounting For Investments In Bonds," No. 4, pp. 320-326.

Kahn, Nathan. "Corporate Motivation For Convertible Bond Debt Exchanges," No. 4, pp. 327-337.

White, Debra and Mike Vanecek. "Intended Use: A Uniform Tax Definition Of Software," No. 4, pp. 338-354.

Journal of Accounting, Auditing and Finance
Volume 6, 1982-83

Altman, Edward I. "Accounting Implications Of Failure Prediction Models," No. 1. pp. 4-19.

Rose, Peter S., Wesley T. Andrews and Gary A. Giroux. "Predicting Business Failure: A Macroeconomic Perspective," No. 1, pp. 20-31.

Schwartz, Kenneth B. "Accounting Changes By Corporations Facing Possible Insolvency," No. 1, pp. 32-43.

Raman, K. K. "Alternative Accounting Measures As Predictors Of Municipal Financial Distress," No. 1, pp. 44-50.

Gormley, R. James. "RICO And The Professional Accountant," No. 1, pp. 51-59.

Dirsmith, Mark W. and John P. McAllister. "The Organic Vs. The Mechanistic Audit: Problems And Pitfalls (Part II)," No. 1, pp. 60-74.

Friedlob, G. Thomas. "How Economic Statisticians View Accounting Profits," No. 2, pp. 100-107.

Munter, Paul and Thomas A. Ratcliffe. "An Assessment Of User Reactions To Lease Accounting Disclosures," No. 2, pp. 108-114.

Ovadia, Arie and Joshua Ronen. "On The Value Of Current-Cost Information," No. 2, pp. 115-129.

Mensah, Yaw M. "The Usefulness Of The Holding Gains And Losses Disclosure," No. 2, pp. 130-141.

Taussig, Russell A. "Impact Of SFAS No. 52 On The Translation Of Foreign Financial Statements Of Companies In Highly Inflationary Economies," No. 2, pp. 142-156.

Karlinsky, Stewart S. "Capital Gains Provisions: Changed By The Tax Act Of 1981, But No Less Complex," No. 2, pp. 157-167.

Campbell, David R. "An Analysis Of The Growth In Public Accounting: Implications For Future Planning Strategies," No. 3, pp. 196-211.

Schieneman, Gary S. "The Accounting Profession Facing The Challenges Of A Changing World," No. 3, pp. 212-226.

Baggett, Walter O. "Internal Control: Insight From A General Systems Theory Perspective," No. 3, pp. 227-233.

Nair, R. D. and Larry E. Rittenberg. "Accounting Costs Of Privately Held Businesses," No. 3, pp. 234-243.

Schwartz, Bill N. "Deferred Taxes: Compliance And Understandability," No. 3, pp. 244-253.

Garsombke, H. Perrin and Gary Allen. "Did SFAS No. 19 Lead To Oil And Gas Company Mergers?," No. 3, pp. 285-298.

Hall, Thomas W. "Inflation And Rates Of Exchange: Support For SFAS No. 52," No. 4, pp. 299-313.

Frankfurter, George M. and Allan E. Young. "Financial Theory: Its Message To The Accountant," No. 4, pp. 314-324.

Monahan, Thomas F. and Lester Barenbaum. "The Use Of Constant Dollar Information To Predict Bond Rating Changes," No. 4, pp. 325-340.

Nix, Harold M. and Henry Wichmann Jr. "The Governmental Audit Report," No. 4, pp. 341-352.

Journal of Accounting, Auditing and Finance
Volume 7, 1983-84

Murray, Dennis and Raymond Johnson. "Differential GAAP And The FASB's Conceptual Framework," No. 1, pp. 4-15.

Gutberlet, Louis G. "An Opportunity - Differential Standards," No. 1, pp. 16-28.

Ketz, J. Edward and Arthur R. Wyatt. "The FASB In A World With Partially Efficient Markets," No. 1, pp. 29-43.

Largay, James A. III. "SFAS No. 52: Expediency Or Principle?," No. 1, pp. 44-53.

Werner, Charles A. and John W. Kostolansky. "Accounting Liabilities Under ERISA," No. 1, pp. 54-64.

Karlinsky, Stewart S. "New Tax Laws Impact On Corporate Financial Reporting," No. 1, pp. 65-76.

Longstreth, Bevis. "The SEC's Role In Financial Disclosure," No. 2, pp. 110-122.

Bublitz, Bruce and Robert Kee. "Do We Need Sunset Requirements For FASB Pronouncements?," No. 2, pp. 123-137.

Holzmann, Oscar J. and Kathryn M. Means. "Accounting For Savings And Loan Mergers: Conflict And Accounting Error," No. 2, pp. 138-150.

Adams, Kerry D. "Hedge Accounting For Anticipatory Hedges Of Short-Term Liabilities," No. 2, pp. 151-163.

Chan, K. Hung and Thomas T. Cheng. "The Recovery Of Nuclear Power Plant Decommissioning Costs," No. 2, pp. 164-177.

McConnell, Donald K., Jr. "Are The Big 8 Increasing Their Share Of The NYSE, AMEX, And OTC Audit Markets?," No. 2, pp. 178-181.

Engstrom, John H. "Pension Reporting By Municipalities," No. 3, pp. 197-211.

Werner, Charles A. and John W. Kostolansky. "Accounting Liabilities Under The Multiemployer Pension Plan Amendments Act," No. 3, pp. 212-224.

Hawkins, Clark A. and Diane Girard. "Replacement Decisions Under The Accelerated Cost Recovery System," No. 3, pp. 225-240.

Everett, John O. and Gary A. Porter. "Safe-Harbor Leasing - Unraveling The Tax Implications," No. 3, pp. 241-256.

St. Pierre, Kent. "Independence And Auditor Sanctions," No. 3, pp. 257-263.

Morris, Michael H. and William D. Nichols. "Pension Accounting And The Balance Sheet: The Potential Effect Of The FASB's Preliminary Views," No. 4, pp. 293-305.

Rue, Joseph C. and Ara G. Volkan. "Financial And Economic Consequences Of The New Pension Accounting Proposals: Is The Gloom Justified?," No. 4, pp. 306-322.

Granof, Michael H. and Daniel G. Short. "Why Do Companies Reject LIFO?," No. 4, pp. 323-333.

Bainbridge, D. R. "Is Dollar-Value LIFO Consistent With Authoritative GAAP?," No. 4, pp. 334-346.

Carmichael, D. R. and Ray Whittington. "The Auditor's Changing Role In Financial Reporting," No. 4, pp. 347-361.

Skerratt, L. C. L. "The Bias In Current Cost Income: An Extension," No. 4, pp. 362-368.

Journal of Accounting, Auditing and Finance
Volume 8, 1984-85

Fulmer, John G., Jr. and James E. Moon. "Tests For Common Stock Equivalency," No. 1, pp. 5-14.

Putnam, Karl and Lynn Thomas. "Does Predictability Change When GAAP Change?," No. 1, pp. 15-23.

Harmon, W. Ken. "Earnings Vs. Funds Flows: An Empirical Investigation Of Market Reaction," No. 1, pp. 24-34.

Boatsman, James R., C. Dwayne Dowell and Janet I. Kimbrell. "Valuing Stock Used For A Business Combination," No. 1, pp. 35-43.

Frishkoff, Paul, Patricia A. Frishkoff and Marinus J. Bouwman. "Use Of Accounting Data In Screening By Financial Analysts," No. 1, pp. 44-53.

Goldschmidt, Yaaqov and Leon Shashua. "Distortion Of Income By SFAS No. 33," No. 1, pp. 54-67.

Horvitz, Jerome S. and Susan Coldwell. "Analysis Of The Arthur Young Decision And Its Potential Impact On Public Accounting," No. 2, pp. 86-99.

Welsh, Mary Jeanne and Jerry E. Trapnell. "Labor Market Models And Employer Accounting For Pensions," No. 2, pp. 100-111.

Beatty, Randolph P. and Steven B. Johnson. "A Market-Based Method Of Classifying Convertible Securities," No. 2, pp. 112-124.

Peavy, John W., III and S. Michael Edgar. "Rating Electric Utility Commercial Paper," No. 2, pp. 125-135.

Puro, Marsha. "Do Large Accounting Firms Collude In The Standards-Setting Process?," No. 3, pp. 165-177.

Young, S. David. "Insider Trading: Why The Concern?," No. 3, pp. 178-183.

Bierman, Harold Jr. "Depreciation And Income Tax Allocation," No. 3, pp. 184-194.

Eichenseher, John W. "The Effects Of Foreign Operations On Domestic Auditor Selection," No. 3, pp. 195-209.

Hall, Thomas W. and Darwin J. Casler. "Using Indexing To Estimate Current Costs - Composite Or Multiple Indexes?," No. 3, pp. 210-224.

Ives, Martin. "The GASB: A Fresh Look At Governmental Accounting And Financial Reporting," No. 4, pp. 253-268.

Goldin, Harrison J. "Changes In Municipal Accounting: The New York City Comptroller's Overview," No. 4, pp. 269-278.

Robbins, Walter A., Nicholas G. Apostolou and Robert H. Strawser. "Municipal Annual Reports And The Information Needs Of Investors," No. 4, pp. 279-292.

Tiller, Mikel G. and R. David Mautz. "The Impact Of State-Mandated Accounting And Auditing Requirements On Municipal Bond Ratings," No. 4, pp. 293-304.

Engstrom, John H. "The Governmental Reporting Entity," No. 4, pp. 305-318.

Journal of Accounting, Auditing and Finance
Volume 9, 1985

Dirsmith, Mark W. and Mark A. Covaleski. "Practice Management Issues In Public Accounting Firms," No. 1, pp. 5-21.

Cooper, W. W., Joanna L. Y. Ho, John E. Hunter and Robert C. Rodgers. "The Impact Of The Foreign Corrupt Practices Act On Internal Control Practices," No. 1, pp. 22-39.

Kahn, Nathan and Allen Schiff. "Tangible Equity Change And The Evolution Of The FASB's Definition Of Income," No. 1, pp. 40-49.

Nurnberg, Hugo and S. Thomas A. Cianciolo. "The Measurement Valuation Allowance: Help For Deferred Taxes," No. 1, pp. 50-59.

Huss, H. Fenwick. "A Contingency Approach To Accounting For Income Taxes," No. 1, pp. 60-66.

Journal of Accounting, Auditing and Finance
Volume 1 (New Series), 1986

Bowsher, Charles A. "Reducing The Federal Deficit: A Critical Challenge," No. 1, pp. 7-16.

Hilke, John C. "Regulatory Compliance Costs And LIFO: No Wonder Small Companies Haven't Switched," No. 1, pp. 17-29.

Cottell, Philip G., Jr. "LIFO Layer Liquidations: Some Empirical Evidence," No. 1, pp. 30-45.

Thode, Stephen F., Ralph E. Drtina and James A. Largay III. "Operating Cash Flows: A Growing Need For Separate Reporting," No. 1, pp. 46-61.

Bierman, Harold Jr. "Common Stock Equivalents, Earnings Per Share And Stock Valuation," No. 1, pp. 62-70.

Kissinger, John N. "In Defense Of Interperiod Income Tax Allocation," No. 2, pp. 90-101.

Gamble, George O. "Property Rights Theory And The Formulation Of Financial Statements," No. 2, pp. 102-117.

Ludman, Earl A. "Insider Trading: The Case For Regulation," No. 2, pp. 118-124.

Rundfelt, Rolf. "Insider Trading: Regulation In Europe," No. 2, pp. 125-130.

Zeff, Stephen A. "Big Eight Firms And The Accounting Literature: The Falloff In Advocacy Writing," No. 2, pp. 131-154.

Benjamin, James J., Steven D. Grossman and Casper E. Wiggins. "The Impact Of Foreign Currency Translation On Reporting During The Phase-In Of SFAS No. 52," No. 3, pp. 177-184.

Brown, Betty C. and Jay T. Brandi. "Security Price Reactions To Changes In Foreign Currency Translation Standards," No. 3, pp. 185-205.

Manegold, James G. "Small-Company Initial Public Offerings: The Impact Of SEC Registration Form S-18," No. 3, pp. 206-221.

Kunitake, Walter K. and Clinton E. White, Jr. "Ethics For Independent Auditors," No. 3, pp. 222-231.

Greenberg, Robert R., Glenn L. Johnson and K. Ramesh. "Earnings Versus Cash Flow As A Predictor Of Future Cash Flow Measures," No. 4, pp. 266-277.

Schaefer, Thomas and Michael Kennelley. "Alternative Cash Flow Measures And Risk-Adjusted Returns," No. 4, pp. 278-287.

Sannella, Alexander J. "An Application Of Income Strategy To Cost Allocation And Segment Reporting," No. 4, pp. 288-304.

Mellman, Martin and Mona E. Seiler. "Structure Needed For Implementing Mandated Accounting Changes," No. 4, pp. 305-318.

Moody, Sharon M. and Dale L. Flesher. "Analysis Of FASB Voting Patterns: Statement Nos. 1-86," No. 4, pp. 319-330.

Journal of Accounting, Auditing and Finance
Volume 2 (New Series), 1987

Fried, Dov and Charles Hosler. "S&Ls, Reporting Changes And The Impact On The GNMA Market," No. 1, pp. 5-23.

Haw, In-Mu, Victor Pastena and Steven Lilien. "The Association Between Market-Based Merger Premiums And Firm's Financial Position Prior To Merger," No. 1, pp. 24-42.

Knauf, Janine B. and Miklos A. Vasarhelyi. "Empirical Characteristics Of Debenture Conversions The Issue Of Equivalency," No. 1, pp. 43-64.

Mielke, David E. and James Seifert. "A Survey On The Effects Of Defeasing Debt," No. 1, pp. 65-78.

Roden, Peyton Foster. "The Financial Implications Of In-Substance Defeasance," No. 1, pp. 79-89.

Kay, Robert S. and Raymond J. Beier. "Leveraged Buyout Accounting," No. 1, pp. 90-97.

Sorter, George H. and Monroe Ingberman. "The Implicit Criteria For The Recognition, Quantification, And Reporting Of Accounting Events," No. 2, pp. 99-116.

Givoly, Dan and Josef Lakonishok. "Aggregate Earnings Expectations And Stock Market Behavior," No. 2, pp. 117-150.

Balachandran, Kashi R. and Bin N. Srinidhi. "A Rationale For Fixed Charge Application," No. 2, pp. 151-183.

Hauworth, William P., II, Valdean C. Lembke and Robert F. Sharp. "The Effects Of Inflation: How They Persist," No. 2, pp. 184-196.

Young, Allan E. "The Securities Industry In Transition: A Normative Perspective," No. 2, pp. 197-201.

Benishay, Haskel. "A Fourth-Degree Polynomial Utility Function And Its Implications For Investors' Responses Toward Four Moments Of The Wealth Distribution," No. 3, pp. 203-238.

Bildersee, John and Nathan Kahn. "A Preliminary Test Of The Presence Of Window Dressing: Evidence From Institutional Stock Trading," No. 3, pp. 239-265.

Katz, Barbara Goody and Joel Owen. "Initial Public Offerings: An Equilibrium Model Of Price Determination," No. 3, pp. 266-298.

Figlewski, Stephen. "The Interaction Between Derivative Securities On Financial Instruments And The Underlying Cash Markets: An Overview," No. 3, pp. 299-318.

Banker, Rajiv D., Srikant M. Datar and Madhav V. Rajan. "Measurement Of Productivity Improvements: An Empirical Analysis," No. 4, pp. 319-354.

Levy, Haim and Young Hoon Byun. "An Empirical Test Of The Black-Scholes Option Pricing Model And The Implied Variance: A Confidence Interval Approach," No. 4, pp. 355-374.

Thies, Clifford F. and Thomas Sturrock. "What Did Inflation Accounting Tell Us?," No. 4, pp. 375-395.

Bierman, Harold Jr. "Accounting For Interest Rate Swaps," No. 4, pp. 396-408.

Foster, George. "Rambo IX: Briloff And The Capital Market," No. 4, pp. 409-430.

Journal of Accounting, Auditing and Finance
Volume 3 (New Series), 1988

Balachandran, Bala V. and Ramachandran Ramanan. "Optimal Internal Control Strategy Under Dynamic Conditions," No. 1, pp. 1-18.

Amit, Raphael and Joshua Livnat. "Diversification, Capital Structure, And Systematic Risk: An Empirical Investigation," No. 1, pp. 19-48.

Wachtel, Paul. "A Look At The World Economy Of The Next Generation: A Comparison Of The United States And Japan," No. 1, pp. 49-61.

Werner, Charles and John Kostolansky. "Legal Aspects Of Accounting For Post-Employment Health Care And Life Insurance Benefits," No. 1, pp. 62-72.

Freund, William C. "Internationalizing Stock Markets," No. 1, pp. 73-77.

Knapp, Michael C. and Fara Elikai. "Auditor Changes: A Note On The Policy Implications Of Recent Analytical And Empirical Research," No. 1, pp. 78-86.

Callen, Jeffrey L. "An Index Number Theory Of Accounting Cost Variances," No. 2, pp. 87-112.

Doran, David T. and Robert Nachtmann. "The Association Of Stock Distribution Announcements And Earnings Performance," No. 2, pp. 113-146.

Marston, Felicia and Robert S. Harris. "Substitutability Of Leases And Debt In Corporate Capital Structures," No. 2, pp. 147-170.

Hilke, John C. "One Step Forward And Two Steps Backward At The SEC?," No. 2, pp. 171-175.

Gormley, R. James. "Developments In Accountants' Liability To Nonclients For Negligence," No. 3, pp. 185-212.

Goldwasser, Dan L. "Policy Considerations In Accountants' Liability To Third Parties For Negligence," No. 3, pp. 217-231.

Sorter, George H., Stanley Siegel and John Slain. "Accountants' Legal Liability: A Determinant Of The Accounting Model," No. 3, pp. 233-243.

Dopuch, Nicholas N. "Implications Of Torts Rules Of The Accountant's Liability For The Accounting Model," No. 3, pp. 245-249.

Nelson, Julianne, Joshua Ronen and Lawrence White. "Legal Liabilities And The Market For Auditing Services," No. 3, pp. 255-295.

Kothari, S. P., Thomas Lys, Clifford W. Smith and Ross L. Watts. "Auditor Liability And Information Disclosure," No. 4, pp. 307-339.

Kripke, Homer. "Some Reactions And Down-to-Earth Reflections On Accountants' Liability," No. 4, pp. 359-367.

Amihud, Yakov and Haim Mendelson. "Liquidity, Volatility, And Exchange Automation," No. 4, pp. 369-395.

134

JOURNAL OF ACCOUNTING EDUCATION

Engstrom, John H. and Floyd W. Windal. "Accounting Education For MBA Students: A Survey," No. 1, pp. 107-121.

Egenolf, Robert V. and Fred Nordhauser. "Public Sector Accounting In The Public Administration Curriculum," No. 1, pp. 123-130.

Anderson, John J. "Using The Statistical Analysis System As An Educational Audit Software System," No. 1,pp.131-144.

Stagliano, A. J. and Frederic M. Stiner, Jr. "Enrollments In Accounting Programs: Trends And Forecasts," No. 1, pp. 145-163.

Bylinski, Joseph H. and Chee W. Chow. "Human Judgment Biases And The Teaching Of Management Accounting," No. 1, pp. 167-172.

Murphy, Roger P. "Local Government's Hidden Resource: University Interns," No. 1, pp. 173-177.

Schwartz, Bill N. and Stephen L. Fogg. "Department Of Accounting Advisory Board: A Method Of Communicating With The Business And Professional Community," No. 1, pp. 179-184.

Campbell, Terry L. "Automating The Systems Understanding AID," No. 1, pp. 185-187.

Chen, Kung H. and S. J. Lambert. "Impurity Of Variable Factory Overhead Variances," No. 1, pp. 189-196.

DeLespinasse, Doris. "Writing Letters To Clients: Connecting Textbook Problems And The Real World," No. 1, pp. 197-200.

Felix, W. L., Jr., Robert G. May, Marcia S. Niles and John R. Thorson. "SCAD: Something New In Auditing Education," No. 2, pp. 5-14.

Baker, Richard E. and John R. Simon. "An Assessment Of The Cognitive Demands Of The Uniform CPA Examination And Implications For CPA Review/Preparation Courses," No. 2, pp. 15-29.

Waller, Thomas C. and Rebecca A. Gallun. "Microcomputer Competency Requirements In The Accounting Industry: A Pilot Study," No. 2, pp. 31-40.

Collier, Henry W. and William A. Mehrens. "Using Multiple Choice Test Items To Improve Classroom Testing Of Professional Accounting Students," No. 2, pp. 41-51.

Fellows, James and James Spence. "Efficiency In Academe: Comparative Advantage Vs. 'Publish Or Perish'," No. 2, pp. 53-60.

Cress, William P. and James B. Pettijohn. "A Survey Of Budget-Related Planning And Control Policies And Procedures," No. 2, pp. 61-78.

Vasarhelyi, Miklos A. and W. Thomas Lin. "EDP Auditing Instruction Using An Interactive Generalized Audit Software," No. 2, pp. 79-89.

Cheung, Joseph K. "Stochastic Dominance As An Approach To Uncertainty In Cost Accounting," No. 2, pp. 91-102.

Hughes, Jesse W. "Revenue And Expenditure Variance Analyses For Local Government," No. 2, pp. 103-114.

Cao, Le Thi and Phillip G. Buchanan. "The Integration Of Behavioral Accounting In Graduate Accounting Curricula," No. 2, pp. 115-121.

Gamble, George O. and Brian O'Doherty. "How Accounting Academicians Can Use Citation Indexing And Analysis For Research," No. 2, pp. 123-144.

Raabe, William A. and William P. Stevens. "Who Is Educating Today's Accountants? Some Observations," No. 2, pp. 147-154.

Beard, Larry H., Fred A. Jacobs and Al L. Hartgraves. "Publications: A Valid Measure Of Faculty Contribution?," No. 2, pp. 155-161.

Brownlee, E. Richard, II. "Actuarial Cost Methods: A Primer," No. 2, pp. 163-169.

Bush, James L., Jr. "A Peer Tutoring Program For Introductory Accounting Courses," No. 2, pp. 171-177.

Howard, Thomas P. "Teaching Ideas For The Commencement Of The Governmental Accounting Course," No. 2, pp. 179-185.

Lere, John C. "Explaining Alternative Standard Cost Entries," No. 2, pp. 187-192.

Journal of Accounting Education
Volume 4, 1986

Bloom, Robert, Araya Debessay and William Markell. "The Development Of Schools Of Accounting And The Underlying Issues," No. 1, pp. 7-29.

Carver, M. Robert, Jr. and Thomas E. King. "Attitudes Of Accounting Practitioners Towards Accounting Faculty And Accounting Education," No. 1, pp. 31-43.

Yost, Gregory C. "The Fifth Year: Reaction In Florida," No. 1, pp. 45-54.

Flesher, Tonya K. and Joyce A. Rescho. "Tax Concepts And Their Importance In The Undergraduate Curriculum," No. 1, pp. 55-68.

Brandon, Charles, Ralph E. Drtina and Donald Plane. "Using Modeling Languages In Mangerial Accounting: An Example For Pricing Decisions," No. 1, pp. 69-80.

Amernic, Joel E. "A Framework For Analyzing Financial Reporting Cases," No. 1, pp. 81-94.

Yunker, Penelope J., Julie A. Sterner and Michael Costigan. "Employment In Accounting: A Comparison Of Recruiter Perceptions With Student Expectations," No. 1,pp.95-112.

Brownlee, E. Richard, II and S. David Young. "Financial Disclosure Regulation And Its Critics," No. 1, pp. 113-126.

Dickens, Thomas L. and Robert M. Harper, Jr. "The Use Of Microcomputers In Intermediate Accounting: Effects On Student Achievement And Attitudes," No. 1, pp. 127-146.

Rouse, Robert, James R. Davis and G. Thomas Friedlob. "The Relevant Experience Criterion For Accounting Accreditation By The AACSB," No. 1, pp. 147-160.

Izard, C. Douglass and James M. Reeve. "Electronic Spreadsheet Technology In The Teaching Of Accounting And Taxation," No. 1, pp. 161-175.

McKell, Lynn J. and Kevin D. Stocks. "An Evaluation Of Computerized Accounting Practice Sets," No. 1, pp. 177-190.

Koshland, Daniel E., Jr. "Anomalous Behavior Patterns," No. 1, pp. 191-192.

O'Keefe, Terrence B. "Financial Statement Analysis In Introductory Financial Accounting For MBAs," No. 1, pp. 195-201.

Gul, Ferdinand A. "Adaption - Innovation As A Factor In Australian Accounting Undergraduates' Subject Interest And Career Preferences," No. 1, pp. 203-209.

Pollard, William B. "Teaching Standard Costs: A Look At Textbook Differences In Overhead Variance Analysis," No. 1, pp. 211-220.

Thompson, Joel E. "Introducing The Capital Budgeting Problem," No. 1, pp. 221-226.

Schmutte, James. "Accounting Internships: The State Of The Art," No. 1, pp. 227-236.

Cronan, Timothy P. and Clarence E. Fries. "MIS And Computer Applications In Accounting Courses - Report Of A Survey," No. 1, pp. 237-244.

Reed, Sarah A. and Thomas P. Klammer. "Perceptions Of National AAA Meetings," No. 2, pp. 5-17.

Alkafaji, Yass and Nicholas Schroeder. "Manual-V-Computerized Practice Sets: A Test For Differences," No. 2, pp. 19-25.

Heck, J. Louis and Jiunn C. Huang. "Contributions To Accounting Literature: A Peer Assessment Of Monographs," No. 2, pp. 27-36.

Friedlob, G. Thomas and Louis P. Ramsay. "Communicating Decision Alternatives Graphically Using The Point Of Indifference," No. 2, pp. 37-49.

Stout, David E. and E. H. Bonfield. "Experimental Evidence On The Relationship Between Class Meeting Time Compression And Accounting Student Performance, Evaluations And Drop-Out Experience," No. 2, pp. 51-62.

Bainbridge, D. Raymond and John W. Paul. "Relating Audit And Internal Control Objectives: A Missing Step In Specifying Compliance Tests," No. 2, pp. 63-74.

Norton, Curtis L. and Thomas S. Wetzel. "The Recognition And Measurement Guidelines Of FASB Concepts No. 5," No. 2, pp. 75-84.

Corman, Eugene J. "A Writing Program For Accounting Courses," No. 2, pp. 85-95.

Haskins, Mark E. and Robert N. Holt. "A Cash Flow Approach To The Statement Of Changes In Financial Position," No. 2, pp. 97-106.

Seville, Mary Alice and Dahli Gray. "Using The Standard-Setting Process To Demystify The Concepts Statements: The Case Of SFAS 76," No. 2, pp. 107-112.

Louderback, Joseph G. and Charles W. McNichols. "A Note On Net Present Value And Internal Rate Of Return Functions In Electronic Spreadsheets," No. 2, pp. 113-116.

Tyson, Thomas N. "Energize Your Accounting Class With A Simulation That's Fun For Students," No. 2, pp. 117-122.

Harper, Robert M., Jr. "Linear Programming In Managerial Accounting: A Misinterpretation Of Shadow Prices," No. 2, pp. 123-130.

Patel, Raman C. "A Note On Inventory Reorder Point Determination," No. 2, pp. 131-140.

Engle, Terry J. and G. W. Joseph. "A Successful Approach To Integrating Computer Assignments Into Accounting Information Systems Courses In A Manner That Complements Theoretical Readings And Classroom Discussions," No. 2, pp. 141-146.

Stern, Myles, Meryle Hirschland and Serge Matulich. "Comment And Reply - 'A Theoretical Deficiency In Accounting For Bonds'," No. 2, pp. 147-151.

Journal of Accounting Education
Volume 5, 1987

Gavin, Thomas A., Rebecca L. Hicks and James H. Scheiner. "Auditors' Common Law Liability: What We Should Be Telling Our Students," No. 1, pp. 1-12.

Stout, David E., Donald E. Wygal and John J. Gorman. "Accounting Student Perceptions Of The Nature And Significance Of Extraordinary Items Data," No. 1, pp. 13-25.

Armstrong, Mary Beth. "Moral Development And Accounting Education," No. 1, pp. 27-43.

Raabe, William A., Robert M. Kozub and Debra L. Sanders. "Attitude Measurement And The Perceptions Of Tax Accounting Faculty Publications Outlets," No. 1, pp. 45-57.

Cox, Clifford T., Ken M. Boze and Lee Schwendig. "Academic Accountants: A Study Of Faculty Characteristics And Career Activities," No. 1, pp. 59-76.

Gruber, Robert A. "Sequencing Exam Questions Relative To Topic Presentation," No. 1, pp. 77-86.

Kreuze, Jerry G. and Gale E. Newell. "Student Ratings Of Accounting Instructors: A Search For Important Determinants," No. 1, pp. 87-98.

Frakes, Albert H. "Survey Of Undergraduate Auditing Education," No. 1, pp. 99-126.

Gingras, Russell T. "Writing And The Certified Public Accountant," No. 1, pp. 127-137.

Courtis, John K. "Putting The Cart Before The Horse," No. 1, pp. 139-144.

Joy, Arthur C. "The Descriptive Case Project For Accounting Information Systems Courses," No. 1, pp. 145-148.

Reimer, Steven C. "On The Interpretation Of The Estimated Intercept In A Regression Of Overhead Cost On Volume," No. 1, pp. 149-153.

Collins, Marilynn. "Incorporating Authoritative Pronouncements With Intermediate And Advanced Accounting Syllabi," No. 1, pp. 155-160.

Briner, Russell F., Diane T. Pearson and James E. Gauntt, Jr. "A Microcomputer Application For Attribute Sampling," No. 1, pp. 161-166.

Bryan, E. Lewis, Alison L. Drews and G. Thomas Friedlob. "Delphic Choice Of Accounting Periodicals For University Libraries," No. 1, pp. 167-174.

Pratt, Jamie. "The Economics Of External Reporting: Three Frameworks For The Classroom," No. 2, pp. 175-185.

Brown, H. Donald and Richard C. Burke. "Accounting Education: A Learning-Styles Study Of Professional-Technical And Future Adaptation Issues," No. 2, pp. 187-206.

Baker, Richard E., John R. Simon and Frank P. Bazeli. "Selecting Instructional Design For Introductory Accounting Based On The Experiential Learning Model," No. 2, pp. 207-226.

DeBerg, Curtis L., H. Fred Mittelstaedt and Philip R. Regier. "Employers' Accounting For Pensions: A Theoretical Approach To Financial Accounting Standards No. 87," No. 2, pp. 227-242.

Bean, Virginia L. and Jeanette N. Medewitz. "Computer Education: A Survey Of Accounting Graduates," No. 2, pp. 243-258.

Sherman, W. Richard. "Internationalizing The Accounting Curriculum," No. 2, pp. 259-275.

Warner, Stanley E., Jr. and Frederick D. Whitehurst. "Inconsistency In Inventory Loss Measurements Under The LCM Rule," No. 2, pp. 277-285.

Marshall, Don C., Kevin M. Misiewicz and W. Ron Singleton. "Applications Of Computer-Assisted Tax Research In Academic Tax Programs," No. 2, pp. 287-296.

Schaefer, Thomas F. "Microcomputer Sensitivity Analyses For Business Combinations," No. 2, pp. 297-306.

Park, Hai G. and Bart P. Hartman. "An Application Of Opportunity Cost For A Short-Run Pricing Decision," No. 2, pp. 307-313.

Taylor, Barbara G., Lane K. Anderson and John T. Sennetti. "SFAC No. 2 Reliability From A Statistical Perspective," No. 2, pp. 315-321.

Zachry, Benny R. "An Investigation Into The Status Of Public Community College Tax Curricula," No. 2, pp. 323-332.

Milne, Ronald A., Glenn A. Vent and Reuben Neumann. "Accounting For Variable Stock Options," No. 2, pp. 333-338.

Stout, David F., E. H. Bonfield and Marianne S. Battista. "Additional Experimental Evidence On The Relationship Between Class Meeting Time Compression And Accounting Student Performance And Evaluations," No. 2, pp. 339-348.

Journal of Accounting Education
Volume 6, 1988

Newton, James D. "Using Student Evaluation Of Teaching In Administrative Control: The Validity Problem," No. 1, pp. 1-14.

Hirsch, Maurice L., Jr. and Janet Duthie Collins. "An Integrated Approach To Communication Skills In An Accounting Curriculum," No. 1, pp. 15-31.

Pratt, Jamie. "A Classification Scheme For Financial Accounting Research." No. 1, pp. 33-54.

Saftner, Donald V. "The Promotion Of Academic Accountants," No. 1, pp. 55-66.

Nance, Jon R. "Capital Budgeting With Continuous Cash Flows: An Application Of Calculus To Managerial Accounting." No. 1, pp. 67-81.

Dinius, Sara H. and Robert B. Rogow. "Application Of The Delphi Method In Identifying Characteristics Big Eight Firms Seek In Entry-Level Accountants," No. 1, pp. 83-101.

Bloom, Robert and Marilynn Collins. "Motivating Students With A Historical Perspective In Financial Accounting Courses." No. 1, pp. 103-115.

Caspari, John A. "Coping With Plagiarism," No. 1, pp. 117-121.

Crockett, James R. and Thomas E. McKee. "A Graphical Approach To Teaching The Relationship Between The Evaluation Of Internal Accounting Controls And Substantive Audit Testing," No. 1, pp. 123-130.

Lehman, Mark W. and Carol M. Lehman. "Interactive Spreadsheet Models Reinforce Accounting Principles." No. 1, pp. 131-137.

Park, Hai G. "A Graphical Analysis Of Profit Variances Under Absorption And Direct Costing," No. 1, pp. 139-147.

Fry, Nicholas E. and Elaine Hobbs Fry. "How Journal Entries Aid The Teaching Of Taxation," No. 1, pp. 149-157.

McClure, Malcolm M. "Internationalization Of The Introductory Financial Accounting Course," No. 1, pp. 159-181.

Chow, Chee W., Michael D. Shields and Adrian Wong-Boren. "A Compilation Of Recent Surveys And Company-Specific Descriptions Of Management Accounting Practices," No. 2, pp. 183-207.

Warner, Stanley E., Jr. and Frederick D. Whitehurst. "The Educational Impact Of Unresolved Conceptual Issues In Interest Capitalization," No. 2, pp. 209-217.

Stout, David E. and Donald E. Wygal. "Making By-Products A Main Product Of Discussion: A Challenge To Accounting Educators," No. 2, pp. 219-233.

Shoenthal, Edward R. "Differences In Competencies Of Newly Licensed Accountants In The United States And Great Britain." No. 2, pp. 235-249.

Smith, Nancy E. "FASB's Conceptual Framework: Is It Being Taught?," No. 2, pp. 251-259.

Alsup, Rodney G., Michael L. Holland and Fred A. Jacobs. "The Perceived Availability Of Resources Which Contribute To Accounting Faculty Productivity," No. 2, pp. 261-277.

Mitchell, Falconer. "High School Accounting And Student Performance In The First Level University Accounting Course: A UK Study," No. 2, pp. 279-291.

Keef, Stephen P. "Preparation For A First Level University Accounting Course: The Experience In New Zealand," No. 2, pp. 293-307.

Skantz, Terrance R. "Budgeting And Profit Variance Analysis Using A Financial Planning Language," No. 2, pp. 309-323.

Welke, William R. "Accounting For 'Negative Salvage'," No. 2, pp. 325-329.

Krause, Paul. "Active Learning For Budgeting Concepts," No. 2, pp. 331-337.

Rosenstein, Stuart and Ronald O. Reed. "An Alternative Approach To Determining Present And Future Value Interest Factors For Annuities Due," No. 2, pp. 339-344.

Chalos, Peter. "A Spreadsheet Analysis Of Different Costing Systems," No. 2, pp. 345-353.

JOURNAL OF ACCOUNTING LITERATURE

JOURNAL OF ACCOUNTING RESEARCH

Journal of Accounting Research
Volume 1, 1963

Chambers, Raymond J. "Why Bother With Postulates?," No. 1, pp. 3-15.

Charnes, A., W. W. Cooper and Y. Ijiri. "Breakeven Budgeting And Programming To Goals," No. 1, pp. 16-41.

Paton, William A. "Accounting And Utilization Of Resources," No. 1, pp. 42-72.

Shillinglaw, Gordon. "The Concept Of Attributable Cost," No. 1, pp. 73-85.

Trueblood, Robert M. "Education For A Changing Profession," No. 1, pp. 86-95.

Davis, Gordon B. "The Application Of Network Techniques To The Planning And Control Of An Audit," No. 1, pp. 96-101.

Li, David H. "The Semantic Aspect Of Communication Theory And Accountancy," No. 1, pp. 102-107.

Davidson, Sidney. "The Day Of Reckoning: Accounting Theory And Management Analysis," No. 2, pp. 117-126.

Devine, Carl T. "The Rule Of Conservatism Reexamined," No. 2, pp. 127-138.

Lindhe, Richard. "Accelerated Depreciation For Income Tax Purposes - A Study Of The Decision And Some Firms Who Made It," No. 2, pp. 139-148.

Smolinski, Edward J. "The Adjunct Method In Consolidations," No. 2, pp. 149-178.

Vatter, William J. "Postulates And Principles," No. 2, pp. 179-197.

Ijiri, Y., F. K. Levy and R. C. Lyon. "A Linear Programming Model For Budgeting And Financial Planning," No. 2, pp. 198-212.

Weingartner, H. M. "The Excess Present Value Index - A Theoretical Basis And Critque," No. 2, pp. 213-224.

Journal of Accounting Research
Volume 2, 1964

Anton, Hector R. "Some Aspects Of Measurement And Accounting," No. 1, pp. 1-9.

Dopuch, Nicholas and David F. Drake. "Accounting Implications Of A Mathematical Programming Approach To The Transfer Price Problem," No. 1, pp. 10-24.

Drebin, Allan R. "'Cash-Flowitis': Malady Or Syndrome?," No. 1, pp. 25-34.

Green, David, Jr. "Towards A Theory Of Interim Reports," No. 1, pp. 35-49.

Sapienza, Samuel R. "Business Combinations And Enterprise Evaluation," No. 1, pp. 50-66.

Taussig, Samuel Russell. "Information Requirements Of Replacement Models," No. 1, pp. 67-79.

Wright, F. K. "Towards A General Theory Of Depreciation," No. 1, pp. 80-90.

Dyckman, Thomas R. "The Effects Of Alternative Accounting Techniques On Certain Management Decisions," No. 1, pp. 91-107.

Yamey, Basil S. "Accounting And The Rise Of Capitalism: Further Notes On A Theme By Sombart," No. 2, pp. 117-136.

Rose, Harold. "Sources And Uses:A British View," No. 2, pp. 137-147.

Mueller, Gerhard G. "Valuing Inventories At Other Than Historical Costs - Some International Differences," No. 2, pp. 148-157.

Hicks, Ernest L. "Materiality," No. 2, pp. 158-171.

Alfred, A. M. "Investment In The Development Districts Of The United Kingdom: Tax And Discounted Cash Flow," No. 2, pp. 172-182.

Sorter, George H., Selwyn W. Becker, T. R. Archibald and W. Beaver. "Corporate Personality As Reflected In Accounting Decisions: Some Preliminary Findings," No. 2, pp. 183-196.

Jacobsen, Lyle E. "The Ancient Inca Empire Of Peru And The Double Entry Accounting Concept," No. 2, pp. 221-228.

Bierman, Harold, Jr. "Recording Obsolescence," No. 2, pp. 229-235.

Anderson, John M. "Dilemmas In Modern Accounting Research," No. 2, pp. 236-238.

Journal of Accounting Research
Volume 3, 1965

Bird, P. A. "Tax Incentives To Capital Investment," No. 1, pp. 1-11.

Brief, Richard P. "Nineteenth Century Accounting Error," No. 1, pp. 12-31.

Chambers, R. J. "Measurement In Accounting," No. 1, pp. 32-62.

Ijiri, Yuji, Robert K. Jaedicke and John L. Livingstone. "The Effect Of Inventory Costing Methods On Full And Direct Costing," No. 1, pp. 63-74.

Johnson, Orace. "Corporate Giving: A Note On Profit Maximization And Accounting Disclosure," No. 1, pp. 75-85.

Livock, D. M. "The Accounts Of The Corporation Of Bristol: 1532 To 1835," No. 1, pp. 86-102.

Thomas, Arthur L. "The Amortization Problem: A Simplified Model And Some Unanswered Questions," No. 1, pp. 103-113.

Benishay, Haskel. "Managerial Controls Of Accounts Receivable: A Deterministic Approach," No. 1, pp. 114-132.

Davidson, Sidney. "LIFO Cost Or Market And Compulsory Tax Reporting Requirements," No. 1, pp. 156-158.

Gambling, Trevor E. "Some Observations On 'Breakeven Budgeting And Programming To Goals'," No. 1, pp. 159-165.

Wright, F. K. "Depreciation And Obsolescence In Current Value Accounting," No. 2, pp. 167-181.

Samuels, J. M. "Opportunity Costing: An Application Of Mathematical Programming," No. 2, pp. 182-191.

Drake, David F. and Nicholas Dopuch. "On The Case For Dichotomizing Income," No. 2, pp. 192-205.

Corcoran, A. Wayne and Ching-wen Kwang. "A Set Theory Approach To Funds-Flow Analysis," No. 2, pp. 206-217.

Langholm, Odd. "Cost Structure And Costing Method: An Empirical Study," No. 2, pp. 218-227.

Purdy, Charles R. "Industry Patterns Of Capacity Or Volume Choice: Their Existence And Rationale," No. 2, pp. 228-241.

McRae, T. W. "Accountancy Training In Scotland," No. 2, pp. 255-260.

Woods, J. H. "Recording Obsolescence: A Note," No. 2, pp. 261-263.

DeCazaux, L. F. G. "On The Budget," No. 2, pp. 264-265.

Journal of Accounting Research
Volume 4, 1966

Carsberg, Bryan V. "The Contribution of P. D. Leake To The Theory Of Goodwill Valuation," No. 1, pp. 1-15.

Flower, J. F. "The Case Of The Profitable Bloodhound," No. 1, pp. 16-36.

Abdel-Khalik, A. Rashad. "Controllership In Egypt," No. 1, pp. 37-46.

Moonitz, Maurice. "Some Reflections On The Investment Credit Experience," No. 1, pp. 47-61.

Schiff, Michael. "Accounting Tactics And The Theory Of The Firm," No. 1, pp. 62-67.

Drebin, Allan R. "The Inventory Calculus," No. 1, pp. 68-86.

Manes, Rene. "A New Dimension To Breakeven Analysis," No. 1, pp. 87-100.

Nielsen, Oswald. "A Predecessor Of Direct Costing," No. 1, pp. 119-120.

Rappaport, Alfred. "Towards A Theory Of Interim Reports: A Modification And An Extension," No. 1, pp. 121-126.

Wright, F. K. "Managerial Controls Of Accounts Receivable: A Comment," No. 1, pp. 127-130.

Benishay, Haskel. "Managerial Controls Of Accounts Receivable: A Reply," No. 1, pp. 131-132.

Vatter, W. J. "Accounting For Leases," No. 2, pp. 133-148.

Parker, William M. "Business Combinations And Accounting Valuation," No. 2, pp. 149-154.

Moonitz, Maurice and Alexander Russ. "Accrual Accounting For Employers' Pension Costs," No. 2, pp. 155-168.

Hatfield, Henry Rand. "Some Variations In Accounting Practice In England, France, Germany And The United States," No. 2, pp. 169-182.

Davidson, Sidney and John M. Kohlmeier. "A Measure Of The Impact Of Some Foreign Accounting Principles," No. 2, pp. 183-212.

Bourn, A. M. "Training For The Accountancy Profession In England And Wales," No. 2, pp. 213-223.

Jensen, Robert E. "An Experimental Design For Study Of Effects Of Accounting Variations In Decision Making," No. 2, pp. 224-238.

Westwick, C. A. "A Graphical Treatment Of Gearing," No. 2, pp. 239-244.

Winborne, M. G. "A Wrinkle On An Intellectual Groove," No. 2, pp. 245-252.

Todd, Kenneth R. "Reporting Equities In Estate Accounting," No. 2, pp. 253-259.

Parker, R. H. "A Note On Savary's 'Le Parfait Negociant'," No. 2, pp. 260-261.

Bruns, William. "The Accounting Period And Its Effect Upon Management Decisions," Supp., pp. 1-14.

Green, David and Joel Segall. "The Predictive Power Of First-Quarter Earnings Reports: A Replication," Supp., pp. 21-36.

Horrigan, James. "The Determination Of Long-Term Credit Standing With Financial Ratios," Supp., pp. 44-62.

Beaver, William. "Financial Ratios As Predictors Of Failure," Supp., pp. 71-111.

Churchill, Neil. "Audit Recommendations And Management Auditing: A Case Study And Some Remarks," Supp., pp. 128-151.

Devine, Carl. "Professional Responsibilities - An Empirical Suggestion," Supp., pp. 160-176.

Trueblood, Robert. "Accounting Principles: The Board And Its Problems," Supp., pp. 183-191.

Dopuch, Nicholas and David Drake. "The Effect Of Alternative Accounting Rules For Nonsubsidiary Investments," Supp., pp. 192-219.

Journal of Accounting Research
Volume 5, 1967

Aharoni, Y. and T. Ophir. "Accounting For Linked Loans," No. 1, pp. 1-26.

Brief, Richard P. "A Late Nineteenth Century Contribution To The Theory Of Depreciation," No. 1, pp. 27-38.

Most, Kenneth S. "The Value Of Inventories," No. 1, pp. 39-50.

Yamey, Basil S. "Fifteenth And Sixteenth Century Manuscripts On The Art Of Bookkeeping," No. 1, pp. 51-76.

Livingstone, John Leslie. "Accelerated Depreciation, Cyclical Asset Expenditures And Deferred Taxes," No. 1, pp. 77-94.

Mathews, Russell. "The Price Level Controversy: A Reply," No. 1, pp. 113-118.

Mattessich, Richard. "Accounting And Analytic Methods: A Comment On Chambers' Review," No. 1, pp. 119-123.

Stamp, Edward. "Some Further Reflections On The Investment Credit," No. 1, pp. 124-128.

Moonitz, Maurice. "Can Laws Coerce Accounting?," No. 1, pp. 129-130.

Baloff, Nicholas and John W. Kennelly. "Accounting Implications Of Product And Process Start-Ups," No. 2, pp. 131-143.

Bierman, Harold, Jr. and Seymour Smidt. "Accounting For Debt And Costs Of Liquidity Under Conditions Of Uncertainty," No. 2, pp. 144-153.

Hain, H. P. "Casting The Account," No. 2, pp. 154-163.

Johnson, Orace. "A Consequential Approach To Accounting For R & D," No. 2, pp. 164-172.

Wright, F. K. "An Evaluation Of Ladelle's Theory Of Depreciation," No. 2, pp. 173-179.

Davidson, H. J., J. Neter and A. S. Petran. "Estimating The Liability For Unredeemed Stamps," No. 2, pp. 186-207.

Chambers, R. J. "Price Variation Accounting - An Improved Representation," No. 2, pp. 215-220.

Dyckman, Thomas R. "Observations On Jensen's Experimental Design For Study Of Effects Of Accounting Variations In Decision Making," No. 2, pp. 221-229.

Jensen, Robert E. "Observations On Jensen's Experimental Design For Study Of Effects Of Accounting Variations In Decision Making: A Rejoinder," No. 2, pp. 230-251.

Benston, George J. "Published Corporate Accounting Data And Stock Prices," Supp., pp. 1-14.

Brown, Philip and Ray Ball. "Some Preliminary Findings On The Association Between The Earnings Of A Firm, Its Industry, And The Economy," Supp., pp. 55-77.

Lawler, John. "The Quest For Accounting Philosophers," Supp., pp. 86-92.

Livingstone, John Leslie. "Accelerated Depreciation And Deferred Taxes: An Empirical Study Of Fluctuating Asset Expenditures," Supp., pp. 93-117.

Manes, Rene P., John Samuels and D. J. Smyth. "Inventories And Sales: A Cross Section Study," Supp., pp. 139-156.

Archibald, T. Ross. "The Return To Straight-Line Depreciation: An Analysis Of A Change In Accounting Method," Supp., pp. 164-180.

Gagnon, Jean-Marie. "Purchase Versus Pooling Of Interests: The Search For A Predictor," Supp., pp. 187-204.

Cook, Doris M. "The Effect Of Frequency Of Feedback On Attitudes And Performance," Supp., pp. 213-224.

Journal of Accounting Research
Volume 6, 1968

Ijiri, Y., J. C. Kinard and F. B. Putney. "An Integrated Evaluation System For Budget Forecasting And Operating Performance With A Classified Budgeting Bibliography," No. 1, pp. 1-28.

Johnson, Orace. "Two General Concepts Of Depreciation," No. 1, pp. 29-37.

McDonald, Daniel L. "A Test Application Of The Feasibility Of Market Based Measures In Accounting," No. 1, pp. 38-49.

Mehta, Dileep R. and Victor L. Andrews. "A Note On Installment Reporting Of Income, Profitability, And Fund Flows," No. 1, pp. 50-57.

Parker, R. H. "Discounted Cash Flow In Historical Perspective," No. 1, pp. 58-71.

Paton, W. A. "Observations On Inflation From An Accounting Stance," No. 1, pp. 72-85.

Shwayder, Keith. "Relevance," No. 1, pp. 86-97.

Bailey, Andrew D., Jr. and Jack Gray. "A Study Of The Importance Of The Planning Horizon On Reports Utilizing Discounted Future Cash Flows," No. 1, pp. 98-105.

Copeland, Ronald M. and William Fredericks. "Extent Of Disclosure," No. 1, pp. 106-113.

Greenball, Melvin N. "The Accuracy Of Different Methods Of Accounting For Earnings - A Simulation Approach," No. 1, pp. 114-129.

Bernhard, Richard N. "Some Problems In Applying Mathematical Programming To Opportunity Costing," No. 1, pp. 143-148.

Brief, Richard P. "Depreciation Theory And Capital Gains," No. 1, pp. 149-152.

Wolk, Harry I. "Accounting For Leases: A Further Examination Of The Issues," No. 1, pp. 153-157.

Ball, Ray and Philip Brown. "An Empirical Evaluation Of Accounting Income Numbers," No. 2, pp. 159-178.

Beaver, William H. "Market Prices, Financial Ratios, And The Prediction Of Failure," No. 2, pp. 179-192.

Brief, Richard P. and Joel Owen. "A Least Squares Allocation Model," No. 2, pp. 193-199.

Estes, Ralph W. "An Assessment Of The Usefulness Of Current Cost And Price-Level Information By Financial Statement Users," No. 2, pp. 200-207.

Fredrikson, E. Bruce. "On The Measurement Of Foreign Income," No. 2, pp. 208-221.

Wright, F. K. "Measuring Asset Services: A Linear Programming Approach," No. 2, pp. 222-236.

DeCoster, Don T. and John P. Fertakis. "Budget-Induced Pressure And Its Relationship To Supervisory Behavior," No. 2, pp. 237-246.

Lev, Baruch. "The Aggregation Problem In Financial Statements: An Informational Approach," No. 2, pp. 247-261.

Voss, William M. "Accelerated Depreciation And Deferred Tax Allocation," No. 2, pp. 262-269.

Forrester, D. A. R. "The Incan Contribution To Double-Entry Accounting," No. 2, p. 283.

Mathews, Russell. "Price Variation Accounting - A Rejoinder," No. 2, pp. 284-285.

Neumann, Fred. "The Auditing Standard Of Consistency," Supp., pp. 1-17.

Greenball, Melvin N. "Evaluation Of The Usefulness To Investors Of Different Accounting Estimators Of Earnings: A Simulation Approach," Supp., pp. 27-49.

Stone, Marvin L. "Problems In Search Of Solutions Through Research," Supp., pp. 59-66.

Beaver, William H. "The Information Content Of Annual Earnings Announcements," Supp., pp. 67-92.

Copeland, Ronald M. "Income Smoothing," Supp., pp. 101-116.

Firmin, Peter A., Seymour S. Goodman, Thomas E. Hendricks and James J. Linn. "University Cost Structure And Behavior: An Empirical Study," Supp., pp. 122-155.

Journal of Accounting Research
Volume 7, 1969

Abel, R. "A Comparative Simulation Of German And U.S. Accounting Principles," No. 1, pp. 1-11.

Brief, Richard P. and Joel Owen. "On The Bias In Accounting Allocations Under Uncertainty," No. 1, pp. 12-16.

Feinschreiber, Robert. "Accelerated Depreciation: A Proposed New Method," No. 1, pp. 17-21.

Hakansson, Nils H. "On The Relevance Of Price-Level Accounting," No. 1, pp. 22-31.

Kaplan, Robert S. "Optimal Investigation Strategies With Imperfect Information," No. 1, pp. 32-43.

Kinney, William R., Jr. "An Environmental Model For Performance Measurement In Multi-Outlet Businesses," No. 1, pp. 44-52.

Rayman, R. A. "An Extension Of The System Of Accounts: The Segregation Of Funds And Value," No. 1, pp. 53-89.

Sterling, Robert R. and Raymond Radosevich. "A Valuation Experiment," No. 1, pp. 90-95.

Demski, Joel S. "Predictive Ability Of Alternative Performance Measurement Models," No. 1, pp. 96-115.

Barton, Richard F. "An Experimental Study Of The Impact Of Competitive Pressures On Overhead Allocation Bids," No. 1, pp. 116-122.

Frank, Werner. "A Study Of The Predictive Significance Of Two Income Measures," No. 1, pp. 123-136.

Strum, Jay E. "Note On 'Two-Sided Shadow Prices'," No. 1, pp. 160-162.

Vatter, William J. "'Time-Adjusted' Depreciation," No. 1, pp. 163-164.

Carsberg, Bryan. "On The Linear Programming Approach To Asset Valuation," No. 2, pp. 165-182.

Wright, F. K. "On The Linear Programming Approach To Asset Valuation," No. 2, pp. 183-187.

Copeland, Ronald M. and Joseph F. Wojdak. "Income Manipulation And The Purchase-Pooling Choice," No. 2, pp. 188-195.

Cushing, Barry E. "An Empirical Study Of Changes In Accounting Policy," No. 2, pp. 196-203.

Drebin, Allan R. "A Fallacy Of Depreciation Translation," No. 2, pp. 204-214.

Dyckman, T. R. "The Investigation Of Cost Variances," No. 2, pp. 215-244.

Livingstone, John Leslie. "Accelerated Depreciation, Tax Allocation, And Cyclical Asset Expenditures Of Large Manufacturing Companies," No. 2, pp. 245-256.

Nurnberg, Hugo. "A Note On The Financial Reporting Of Depreciation And Income Taxes," No. 2, pp. 257-261.

Greenball, M. N. "Appraising Alternative Methods Of Accounting For Accelerated Tax Depreciation: A Relative-Accuracy Approach," No. 2, pp. 262-289.

Lev, Baruch. "Industry Averages As Targets For Financial Ratios," No. 2, pp. 290-299.

Barefield, Russell M. "Comments On A Measure Of Forecasting Performance," No. 2, pp. 324-327.

Bird, Francis A. "A Note On 'The Return To Straight-Line Depreciation'," No. 2, pp. 328-331.

Mitchell, G. B. "Breakeven Analysis And Capital Budgeting," No. 2, pp. 332-338.

Strawser, Robert H., John M. Ivancevich and Herbert L. Lyon. "A Note On The Job Satisfaction Of Accountants In Large And Small CPA Firms," No. 2, pp. 339-345.

Vatter, William J. "More About Leases: A Rejoinder To Professor Wolk," No. 2, pp. 346-349.

Purdy, Charles R., Jay M. Smith and Jack Gray. "The Visibility Of The Auditor's Disclosure Of Deviance From APB Opinion: An Empirical Test," Supp., pp. 1-18.

Stallman, James C. "Toward Experimental Criteria For Judging Disclosure Improvement," Supp., pp. 29-43.

Savoie, Leonard M. "Raising Accounting Standards," Supp., pp. 55-62.

Mlynarczyk, Francis A., Jr. "An Empirical Study Of Accounting Methods And Stock Prices," Supp., pp. 63-81.

Gonedes, Nicholas J. "The Significance Of Selected Accounting Procedures: A Statistical Test," Supp., pp. 90-113.

Mock, Theodore J. "Comparative Values Of Information Structures," Supp., pp. 124-159.

Lev, Baruch. "Testing A Prediction Method For Multivariate Budgets," Supp., pp. 182-197.

Journal of Accounting Research
Volume 8, 1970

Gonedes, Nicholas J. "Accounting For Managerial Control: An Application Of Chance-Constrained Programming." No. 1, pp. 1-20.

Hume, L. J. "The Development Of Industrial Accounting: The Benthams' Contribution," No. 1, pp. 21-33.

Ijiri, Yuji and Robert S Kaplan. "Sequential Models In Probabilistic Depreciation," No. 1, pp. 34-46.

Lemke, Kenneth W. "The Evaluation Of Liquidity: An Analytical Study," No. 1, pp. 47-77.

Lev, Baruch. "The Informational Approach To Aggregation In Financial Statements: Extensions," No. 1, pp. 78-94.

Bernhardt, Irwin and Ronald M. Copeland. "Some Problems In Applying An Information Theory Approach To Accounting Aggregation," No. 1, pp. 95-98.

Ronen, Joshua and George McKinney, III. "Transfer Pricing For Divisional Autonomy," No. 1, pp. 99-112.

Summers, Edward L. and James Wesley Deskins. "A Classification Schema Of Methods For Reporting Effects Of Resource Price Changes," No. 1, pp. 113-117.

West, Richard R. "An Alternative Approach To Predicting Corporate Bond Ratings," No. 1, pp. 118-125.

Horrigan, James O. "An Alternative Approach To Predicting Corporate Bond Ratings: A Comment," No. 1, pp. 126-127.

Peles, Yoram. "Amortization Of Advertising Expenditures In The Financial Statements," No. 1, pp. 128-137.

Cadenhead, Gary M. "Net Realizable Value Redefined," No. 1, pp. 138-140.

Frishkoff, Paul. "Some Recent Trends In Accounting Changes," No. 1, pp. 141-144.

Moonitz, Maurice. "Three Contributions To The Development Of Accounting Principles Prior To 1930," No. 1, pp. 145-155.

Philips, G. Edward. "Error In Accounting Allocations," No. 1, pp. 156-158.

Brenner, Vincent C. "Financial Statement Users' Views Of The Desirability Of Reporting Current Cost Information," No. 2, pp. 159-166.

Brief, Richard P. and Joel Owen. "The Estimation Problem In Financial Accounting," No. 2, pp. 167-177.

Demski, Joel S. "Some Decomposition Results For Information Evaluation," No. 2, pp. 178-198.

Livingstone, John Leslie and Gerald L. Salamon. "Relationship Between The Accounting And The Internal Rate Of Return Measures: A Synthesis And An Analysis." No. 2, pp. 199-216.

Nurnberg, Hugo. "Tax Allocation For Differences In Original Bases," No. 2, pp. 217-231.

Ronen, Joshua. "Capacity And Operating Variances: An Ex Post Approach," No. 2, pp. 232-252.

Dascher, Paul E. and Robert E. Malcolm. "A Note On Income Smoothing In The Chemical Industry," No. 2, pp. 253-259.

White, Gary E. "Discretionary Accounting Decisions And Income Normalization," No. 2, pp. 260-273.

Green, David O. "ERDIAAC," No. 2, pp. 274-281.

Li, Yu-ku. "A Note On 'The Investigation Of Cost Variances'," No. 2, pp. 282-283.

Nelson, G. Kenneth and Robert H. Strawser. "A Note On APB Opinion No. 16," No. 2, pp. 284-289.

Revsine, Lawrence. "Change In Budget Pressure And Its Impact On Supervisor Behavior," No. 2, pp. 290-292.

Skousen, K. Fred. "Chronicle Of Events Surrounding The Segment Reporting Issue," No. 2, pp. 293-299.

Pankoff, Lyn D. and Robert L. Virgil. "Some Preliminary Findings From A Laboratory Experiment On The Usefulness Of Financial Accounting Information To Security Analysts," Supp., pp. 1-48.

Beaver, William H. "The Time Series Behavior Of Earnings," Supp., pp. 62-99.

Ross, Howard. "The Wonderful World Of Accounting," Supp., pp. 108-115.

Frishkoff, Paul. "An Empirical Investigation Of The Concept Of Materiality In Accounting," Supp., pp. 116-129.

Rose, J., W. Beaver, S. Becker and G. Sorter. "Toward An Empirical Measure Of Materiality." Supp., pp. 138-148.

Sauls, Eugene H. "An Experiment On Nonsampling Errors," Supp., pp. 157-171.

Philips, G. Edward and Lucille S. Mayne. "Income Measures And Bank Stock Values," Supp., pp. 178-188.

Journal of Accounting Research
Volume 9, 1971

Ball, Ray. "Index Of Empirical Research In Accounting," No. 1, pp. 1-31.

Dascher, Paul E. and Ronald M. Copeland. "Some Further Evidence On 'Criteria For Judging Disclosure Improvement'," No. 1, pp. 32-39.

Fu, Philip. "Governmental Accounting In China During The Chou Dynasty (1122 B.C. - 256 B.C.)," No. 1, pp. 40-51.

Gagnon, Jean-Marie. "The Purchase-Pooling Choice: Some Empirical Evidence," No. 1, pp. 52-72.

Ijiri, Yuji and Robert S. Kaplan. "A Model For Integrating Sampling Objectives In Auditing," No. 1, pp. 73-87.

Ozan, T. and T. Dyckman. "A Normative Model For Investigation Decisions Involving Multiorigin Cost Variances," No. 1, pp. 88-115.

Frank, Werner G. and Jerry J. Weygandt. "A Prediction Model For Convertible Debentures," No. 1, pp. 116-126.

Kinney, William R., Jr. "Predicting Earnings: Entity Versus Subentity Data," No. 1, pp. 127-136.

Lee, T. A. "The Historical Development Of Internal Control

From The Earliest Times To The End Of The Seventeenth Century," No. 1, pp. 150-157.

Manes, Rene P. "Rejoinder To 'Breakeven Analysis And Capital Budgeting'," No. 1, pp. 158-159.

McCullers, Levis D. "An Alternative To APB Opinion No. 14," No. 1, pp. 160-164.

Shank, John K. "Earnings Per Share, Stock Prices, And APB Opinion No. 15," No. 1, pp. 165-170.

Wells, M. C. "Axioms For Historical Cost Valuation," No. 1, pp. 171-180.

Ijiri, Yuji. "Axioms For Historical Cost Valuation: A Reply," No. 1, pp. 181-187.

Baxter, W. T. and N. H. Carrier. "Depreciation, Replacement Price, And Cost Of Capital," No. 2, pp. 189-214.

Fogelberg, Graeme. "Interim Income Determination: An Examination Of The Effects Of Alternative Measurement Techniques," No. 2, pp. 215-235.

Gonedes, Nicholas J. "Optimal Timing Of Control Messages For A Two-State Markov Process," No. 2, pp. 236-252.

Hinomoto, Hirohide. "Optimum Strategies For Management Information Processing And Control," No. 2, pp. 253-267.

Holstrum, Gary L. "The Effect Of Budget Adaptiveness And Tightness On Managerial Decision Behavior," No. 2, pp. 268-277.

Johnson, Glenn L. and S. Stephen Simik, II. "Multiproduct C-V-P-Analysis Under Uncertainty," No. 2, pp. 278-286.

Loeb, Stephen E. "A Survey Of Ethical Behavior In The Accounting Profession," No. 2, pp. 287-306.

Ronen, Joshua. "Some Effects Of Sequential Aggregation In Accounting On Decision-Making," No. 2, pp. 307-332.

Winjum, James O. "Accounting And The Rise Of Capitalism: An Accountant's View," No. 2, pp. 333-350.

Barefield, Russell M. and Eugene E. Comiskey. "Depreciation Policy And The Behavior Of Corporate Profits," No. 2, pp. 351-358.

Brenner, Vincent C., Claude W. Carmack and Mark G. Weinstein. "An Empirical Test Of The Motivation-Hygiene Theory," No. 2, pp. 359-366.

Chottiner, Sherman and Allan Young. "A Test Of The AICPA Differentiation Between Stock Dividends And Stock Splits," No. 2, pp. 367-374.

Baskin, Elba F. "Comment On 'Some Recent Trends In Accounting Changes'," No. 2, pp. 375-377.

Jarrett, Jeffrey E. "The Principles Of Matching And Realization As Estimation Problems," No. 2, pp. 378-382.

Ross, Timothy L. and Edwin C. Bomeli. "A Comment On Accountants' Job Satisfaction," No. 2, pp. 383-388.

Wilcox, Jarrod W. "A Simple Theory Of Financial Ratios As Predictors Of Failure," No. 2, pp. 389-395.

Martin, Alvin. "An Empirical Test Of The Relevance Of Accounting Information For Investment Decisions," Supp., pp. 1-31.

Barrett, M. Edgar. "Accounting For Intercorporate Investments: A Behavior Field Study ," Supp., pp. 50-65.

Oliphant, Walter J. "The Search For Accounting Principles," Supp., pp. 93-98.

Knutson, Peter H. "An Empirical Study Of The Cost Of Convertible Securities," Supp., pp. 99-112.

May, Robert G. "The Influence Of Quarterly Earnings Announcements On Investor Decisions As Reflected In Common Stock Price Changes," Supp., pp. 119-163.

Greenball, Melvin N. "A Statistical Model Of Earnings Estimation," Supp., pp. 172-190.

Copeland, Ronald M. and John K. Shank. "LIFO And The Diffusion Of Innovation," Supp., pp. 196-224.

Journal of Accounting Research
Volume 10, 1972

Butterworth, John E. "The Accounting System As An Information Function," No. 1, pp. 1-27.

Burt, Oscar R. "A Unified Theory Of Depreciation," No. 1, pp. 28-57.

Demski, Joel. "Information Improvement Bounds," No. 1, pp. 58-76.

Gupta, Manak C. and Ronald J. Huefner. "A Cluster Analysis Study Of Financial Ratios And Industry Characteristics," No. 1, pp. 77-95.

Horwitz, Bertrand and Allan Young. "An Empirical Study Of Accounting Policy And Tender Offers," No. 1, pp. 96-107.

Jarrett, Jeffrey E. "Notes On The Estimation Problem In Financial Accounting," No. 1, pp. 108-112.

Kiger, Jack E. "An Empirical Investigation Of NYSE Volume And Price Reactions To The Announcement Of Quarterly Earnings," No. 1, pp. 113-128.

Mock, Theodore J., Teviah L. Estrin and Miklos A. Vasarhelyi. "Learning Patterns, Decision Approach, And Value Of Information," No. 1, pp. 129-153.

Oliver, Bruce L. "A Study Of Confidence Interval Financial Statements," No. 1, pp. 154-166.

Deakin, Edward B. "A Discriminant Analysis Of Predictors Of Business Failure," No. 1, pp. 167-179.

Dopuch, Nicholas and Ross Watts. "Using Time-Series Models To Assess The Significance Of Accounting Changes," No. 1, pp. 180-194.

Brenner, Vincent C., Ronald M. Copeland, Paul E. Dascher, Arthur J. Francia, Ronald J. Patten and Robert H. Strawser. "Trials And Tribulations Of The Researcher: A Case Study," No. 1, pp. 195-199.

Brenner, Vincent C. and Roland E. Shuey. "An Empirical Study Of Support For APB Opinion No. 16," No. 1, pp. 200-208.

Carpenter, Charles G. and Robert H. Strawser. "Disclosure Of Changes In Accounting Methods," No. 1, pp. 209-216.

Zeff, Stephen A. "Chronology Of Significant Developments In The Establishment Of Accounting Principles In The United States, 1926-1972," No. 1, pp. 217-227.

Barefield, Russell M. "The Effects Of Aggregation On Decision Making Success: A Laboratory Study," No. 2, pp. 229-242.

Demski, Joel. "Optimal Performance Measurement," No. 2, pp. 243-258.

Elliott, J. W. and H. L. Uphoff. "Predicting The Near Term Profit And Loss Statement With An Econometric Model: A Feasibility Study," No. 2, pp. 259-274.

Khandwalla, Pradip N. "The Effect Of Different Types Of Competition On The Use Of Management Controls," No. 2, pp. 275-285.

Marshall, Ronald M. "Determining An Optimal Accounting Information System For An Unidentified User," No. 2, pp. 286-307.

Reilly, Frank K. and Howard F. Stettler. "Factors Influencing Success On The CPA Exam," No. 2, pp. 308-321.

Samuelson, Richard A. "Prediction And Price-Level Adjustment," No. 2, pp. 322-344.

Stone, Williard E. "Abacists Versus Algorists," No. 2, pp. 345-350.

White, Gary E. "Effects Of Discretionary Accounting Policy On Variable And Declining Performance Trends," No. 2, pp. 351-358.

Falk, Haim. "Assessing The Effectiveness Of Accounting Courses Through Facet Analysis," No. 2, pp. 359-375.

Haried, Andrew A. "The Semantic Dimensions Of Financial Statements," No. 2, pp. 376-391.

Patz, Dennis H. and James R. Boatsman. "Accounting Principle Formulation In An Efficient Markets Environment," No. 2, pp. 392-403.

Hubbard, Thomas D. and Robert H. Strawser. "A Test Of 'A Model For Integrating Sampling Objectives In Auditing'," No. 2, pp. 404-406.

Kinney, William R., Jr. "The Auditor's Sampling Objectives: Four Or Two?," No. 2, pp. 407-412.

Ijiri, Yuji and Robert S. Kaplan. "The Auditor's Sampling Objectives: Four Or Two? A Reply," No. 2, pp. 413-416.

Madden, Donald L., Levis D. McCullers and Relmond P. VanDaniker. "The Materiality Of Research And Development Expenditures," No. 2, pp. 417-420.

Ball, Ray. "Changes In Accounting Techniques And Stock Prices," Supp., pp. 1-38.

Ohlson, James. "Analysis Of The Usefulness Of Accounting Data For The Portfolio Decision: A Decision-Theory Approach," Supp., pp. 45-84.

Reilly, Frank K., David L. Morgenson and Marilyn West. "The Predictive Ability Of Alternative Parts Of Interim Financial Statements," Supp., pp. 105-124.

Coates, Robert. "The Predictive Content Of Interim Reports - A Time Series Analysis," Supp., pp. 132-144.

Hopwood, Anthony G. "An Empirical Study Of The Role Of Accounting Data In Performance Evaluation," Supp., pp. 156-182.

Swieringa, Robert J. and Robert H. Moncur. "The Relationship Between Managers' Budget-Oriented Behavior And Selected Attitude, Position, Size, And Performance Measures," Supp., pp. 194-209.

Elias, Nabil. "The Effects Of Human Asset Statements On The Investment Decision: An Experiment," Supp., pp. 215-233.

Flamholtz, Eric G. "Assessing The Validity Of A Theory Of Human Resource Value: A Field Study," Supp., pp. 241-266.

Journal of Accounting Research
Volume 11, 1973

Brief, Richard P. and Joel Owen. "A Reformulation Of The Estimation Problem," No. 1, pp. 1-15.

Firth, Michael A. "An Empirical Examination Of The Applicability Of Adopting The AICPA And NYSE Regulations On Free Share Distributions In The U.K.," No. 1, pp. 16-24.

Foster, George. "Stock Market Reaction To Estimates Of Earnings Per Share By Company Officials," No. 1, pp. 25-37.

Kaplan, Robert S. "A Stochastic Model For Auditing," No. 1, pp. 38-46.

Lee, Geoffrey A. "The Florentine Bank Ledger Fragments Of 1211: Some New Insights," No. 1, pp. 47-61.

McKeown, James C. "Comparative Application Of Market And Cost Based Accounting Models," No. 1, pp. 62-99.

Moore, Michael L. "Management Changes And Discretionary Accounting Decisions," No. 1, pp. 100-107.

Falk, H. and T. Ophir. "The Influence Of Differences In Accounting Policies On Investment Decisions," No. 1, pp. 108-116.

Haried, Andrew A. "Measurement Of Meaning In Financial Reports," No. 1, pp. 117-145.

Harmelink, Philip J. "An Empirical Examination Of The Predictive Ability Of Alternate Sets Of Insurance Company Accounting Data," No. 1, pp. 146-158.

Choi, Frederick D. S. "Financial Disclosure And Entry To The European Capital Market," No. 2, pp. 159-175.

Demski, Joel S. "Rational Choice Of Accounting Method For A Class Of Partnerships," No. 2, pp. 176-190.

Dopuch, N. and J. Ronen. "The Effects Of Alternative Inventory Valuation Methods - An Experimental Study," No. 2, pp. 191-211.

Gonedes, Nicholas J. "Properties Of Accounting Numbers: Models And Tests," No. 2, pp. 212-237.

Kaplan, Robert S. "Statistical Sampling In Auditing With Auxiliary Information Estimators," No. 2, pp. 238-258.

Shwayder, Keith R. "Two 'Wrongs' Making A 'Right'," No. 2, pp. 259-272.

Yu, Seongjae and John Neter. "A Stochastic Model Of The Internal Control System," No. 2, pp. 273-295.

Salamon, Gerald L. "Models Of The Relationship Between The Accounting And Internal Rate Of Return: An Examination Of The Methodology," No. 2, pp. 296-303.

Scott, William R. "A Bayesian Approach To Asset Valuation And Audit Size," No. 2, pp. 304-332.

Nurnberg, Hugo. "A Strange Animal," No. 2, pp. 331-333.

Sunder, Shyam. "Relationship Between Accounting Changes And Stock Prices: Problems Of Measurement And Some Empirical Evidence," Supp., pp. 1-45.

Cumming, John. "An Empirical Evaluation Of Possible Explanations For The Differing Treatment Of Apparently Similar Unusual Events," Supp., pp. 60-95.

Abdel-Khalik, A. Rashad. "The Effect Of Aggregating Accounting Reports On The Quality Of The Lending Decision: An Empirical Investigation," Supp., pp. 104-138.

Wilcox, Jarrod W. "A Prediction Of Business Failure Using Accounting Data," Supp., pp. 163-179.

Lusk, Edward J. "Cognitive Aspects Of Annual Reports: Field Independence/Dependence," Supp., pp. 191-202.

Cherrington, David J. and J. Owen Cherrington. "Appropriate Reinforcement Contingencies In The Budgeting Process," Supp., pp. 225-253.

Journal of Accounting Research
Volume 12, 1974

Blum, Marc. "Failing Company Discriminant Analysis," No. 1, pp. 1-25.

Gonedes, Nicholas J. "Capital Market Equilibrium And Annual Accounting Numbers: Empirical Evidence," No. 1, pp. 26-62.

Jarrett, Jeffrey E. "Bias In Adjusting Asset Values For Changes In The Price Level: An Application Of Estimation Theory," No. 1, pp. 63-66.

Johnson, Glenn L. and S. Stephen Simik, II. "The Use Of Probability Inequalities In Multiproduct C-V-P Analysis Under Uncertainty," No. 1, pp. 67-79.

McRae, Thomas W. "A Citational Analysis Of The Accounting Information Network," No. 1, pp. 80-92.

Ritts, Blaine A. "A Study Of The Impact of APB Opinions Upon Practicing CPAs," No. 1, pp. 93-111.

Spiller, Earl A. and Robert L. Virgil. "Effectiveness Of APB Opinion No. 19 In Improving Funds Reporting," No. 1, pp. 112-142.

Ashton, Robert H. "An Experimental Study Of Internal Control Judgments," No. 1, pp. 143-157.

Warren, Carl S. "Confirmation Informativeness," No. 1, pp. 158-177.

Buckmaster, Dale. "The Incan Quipu And The Jacobsen Hypothesis," No. 1, pp. 178-181.

Dickinson, J. P. "Cost-Volume-Profit Analysis Under Uncertainty," No. 1, pp. 182-187.

Meyer, Philip E. "The APB's Independence And Its Implications For The FASB," No. 1, pp. 188-196.

Barnea, A. and S. Sadan. "On The Decomposition Of The Estimation Problem In Financial Accounting," No. 1, pp. 197-203.

Beaver, W. H. and R. E. Dukes. "Changes In Depreciation Methods: Some Analytical Results," No. 2, pp. 205-215.

Derstine, Robert P. and Ronald J. Huefner. "LIFO-FIFO, Accounting Ratios And Market Risk," No. 2, pp. 216-234.

Friedman, Abraham and Baruch Lev. "A Surrogate Measure For The Firm's Investment In Human Resources," No. 2, pp. 235-250.

Gonedes, Nicholas J. and Yuji Ijiri. "Improving Subjective Probability Assessment For Planning And Control In Team-Like Organizations," No. 2, pp. 251-269.

Magee, Robert P. "Industry-Wide Commonalities In Earnings," No. 2, pp. 270-287.

Morton, James R. "Qualitative Objectives Of Financial Accounting: A Comment On Relevance And Understandability," No. 2, pp. 288-298.

Oliver, Bruce L. "The Semantic Differential: A Device For Measuring The Interprofessional Communication Of Selected Accounting Concepts," No. 2, pp. 299-316.

Becker, Selwyn, Joshua Ronen and George Sorter. "Opportunity Costs - An Experimental Approach," No. 2, pp. 317-329.

Hamilton, Robert E. "The Effect Of Aggregation On Decision-Making Success: A Laboratory Study: A Comment," No. 2, pp. 355-361.

Loeb, Martin. "Comments On Budget Forecasting And Operating Performance," No. 2, pp. 362-366.

Reynolds, Bernard. "Was Shakespeare An Accountant?," No. 2, pp. 367-371.

Zimmerman, Jerold. "Price-Level Restatements: A Technical Note," No. 2, pp. 372-382.

Sorter, George H. and Martin S. Gans. "Opportunities And Implications Of The Report On Objectives Of Financial Statements," Supp., pp. 1-12.

Cyert, Richard M. and Yuji Ijiri. "Problems Of Implementing The Trueblood Objectives Report," Supp., pp. 29-42.

Gonedes, Nicholas J. and Nicholas Dopuch. "Capital Market Equilibrium, Information Production, And Selecting Accounting Techniques: Theoretical Framework And Review Of Empirical Work," Supp., pp. 48-129.

Beaver, William H. and Joel S. Demski. "The Nature Of Financial Accounting Objectives: A Summary And Synthesis," Supp., pp. 170-187.

Journal of Accounting Research
Volume 13, 1975

Baiman, Stanley. "The Evaluation And Choice Of Internal Information Systems Within A Multiperson World," No. 1, pp. 1-15.

Buzby, Stephen L. "Company Size, Listed Versus Unlisted Stocks, And The Extent Of Financial Disclosure," No. 1, pp. 16-37.

Dickhaut, John W. and Ian R. C. Eggleton. "An Examination Of The Processes Underlying Comparative Judgments Of Numerical Stimuli," No. 1, pp. 38-72.

Itami, Hiroyuki. "Evaluation Measures And Goal Congruence Under Uncertainty," No. 1, pp. 73-96.

Kennedy, Henry A. "A Behavioral Study Of The Usefulness Of Four Financial Ratios," No. 1, pp. 97-116.

Kinney, William R., Jr. "A Decision Theory Approach To The Sampling Problem In Auditing," No. 1, pp. 117-132.

Ronen, Joshua and Simcha Sadan. "Classificatory Smoothing: Alternative Income Models," No. 1, pp. 133-149.

Libby, Robert. "Accounting Ratios And The Prediction Of Failure: Some Behavioral Evidence," No. 1, pp. 150-161.

Warren, Carl S. "Uniformity Of Auditing Standards," No. 1, pp. 162-176.

Bruns, William J., Jr. and John H. Waterhouse. "Budgetary Control And Organization Structure," No. 2, pp. 177-203.

Dyer, James C., IV and Arthur J. McHugh. "The Timeliness Of The Australian Annual Report," No. 2, pp. 204-219.

Gonedes, Nicholas J. "Risk, Information, And The Effects Of Special Accounting Items On Capital Market Equilibrium," No. 2, pp. 220-256.

Magee, Robert P. "Cost-Volume-Profit Analysis, Uncertainty And Capital Market Equilibrium," No. 2, pp. 257-266.

Ohlson, James A. "The Complete Ordering Of Information Alternatives For A Class Of Portfolio-Selection Models," No. 2, pp. 267-282.

Foster, George. "Security Price Revaluation Implications Of Sub-Earnings Disclosure," No. 2, pp. 283-292.

Sharpe, I. G. and R. G. Walker. "Asset Revaluations And Stock Market Prices," No. 2, pp. 293-310.

Anderson, John C. and Joseph G. Louderback, III. "Income Manipulation And Purchase-Pooling: Some Additional Results," No. 2, pp. 338-343.

Hughes, John S. "Optimal Timing Of Cost Information," No. 2, pp. 344-349.

Stringer, Kenneth W. "A Statistical Technique For Analytical Review," Supp., pp. 1-9.

Kinney, William R., Jr. "Decision Theory Aspects Of Internal Control System Design/Compliance And Substantive Tests," Supp., pp. 14-29.

Loebbecke, James K. and John Neter. "Considerations In Choosing Statistical Sampling Procedures In Auditing," Supp., pp. 38-52.

Teitlebaum, A. D. and C. F. Robinson. "The Real Risks In Audit Sampling," Supp., pp. 70-91.

Scott, William R. "Auditor's Loss Functions Implicit In Consumption-Investment Models," Supp., pp. 98-117.

Kaplan, Robert S. "Sample Size Computations For Dollar-Unit Sampling," Supp., pp. 126-133.

Journal of Accounting Research
Volume 14, 1976

Ball, Ray, Baruch Lev and Ross Watts. "Income Variation And Balance Sheet Compositions," No. 1, pp. 1-9.

Barrett, M. Edgar. "Financial Reporting Practices: Disclosure And Comprehensiveness In An International Setting," No. 1, pp. 10-26.

Chesley, G. R. "The Elicitation Of, Subjective Probabilities: A Laboratory Study In An Accounting Context," No. 1, pp. 27-48.

Dittman, David A., Hervey A. Juris and Lawrence Revsine. "On The Existence Of Unrecorded Human Assets: An Economic Perspective," No. 1, pp. 49-65.

Eggleton, Ian R. C., Stephen H. Penman and John R. Twombly. "Accounting Changes And Stock Prices: An Examination Of Selected Uncontrolled Variables," No. 1, pp. 66-88.

Gonedes, Nicholas J., Nicholas Dopuch and Stephen H. Penman. "Disclosure Rules, Information-Production, And Capital Market Equilibrium: The Case Of Forecast Disclosure Rules," No. 1, pp. 89-137.

Ward, Bart H. "An Investigation Of The Materiality Construct In Auditing," No. 1, pp. 138-152.

Birnberg, Jacob G. and Dennis P. Slevin. "A Note On The Use Of Confidence Interval Statements In Financial Reporting," No. 1, pp. 153-157.

Boudreaux, Kenneth J. and Stephen A. Zeff. "A Note On The Measure Of Compensation Implicit In Employee Stock Options," No. 1, pp. 158-162.

Collins, Daniel W. "Predicting Earnings With Sub-Entity Data: Some Further Evidence," No. 1, pp. 163-177.

Frishkoff, Paul. "Some Radical Thoughts On Accounting Theory," No. 1, pp. 178-180.

McHugh, A. J. "Relationship Between Accounting And The Internal Rate Of Return Measures," No. 1, pp. 181-186.

Livingstone, J. Leslie and Michael F. Van Breda. "Relationship Between Accounting And The Internal Rate Of Return Measures: A Reply," No. 1, pp. 187-188.

Ansari, Shahid L. "Behavioral Factors In Variance Control: Report On A Laboratory Experiment," No. 2, pp. 189-211.

Cassidy, David B. "Investor Evaluation Of Accounting Information: Some Additional Empirical Evidence," No. 2, pp. 212-229.

Demski, Joel S. "Uncertainty And Evaluation Based On Controllable Performance," No. 2, pp. 230-245.

Patell, James M. "Corporate Forecasts Of Earnings Per Share And Stock Price Behavior: Empirical Tests," No. 2, pp. 246-276.

Sunder, Shyam. "Optimal Choice Between FIFO And LIFO," No. 2, pp. 277-300.

Zimmerman, Jerold L. "Budget Uncertainty And The Allocation Decision In A Nonprofit Organization," No. 2, pp. 301-319.

Moriarity, Shane and F. Hutton Barron. "Modeling The Materiality Judgments Of Audit Partners," No. 2, pp. 320-341.

Burns, Thomas J. and Edward N. Coffman. "The Accounting Hall Of Fame: A Profile Of The Members," No. 2, pp. 342-347.

Shanno, David F. and Roman L. Weil. "The Separate Phases Method Of Accounting For Leveraged Leases: Properties Of The Allocating Rate And An Algorithm For Finding It," No. 2, pp. 348-356.

Smith, Clifford W., Jr. and Jerold L. Zimmerman. "Valuing Employee Stock Option Plans Using Option Pricing Models," No. 2, pp. 357-364.

Ashton, Robert H. "Cognitive Changes Induced By Accounting Changes: Experimental Evidence On The Functional Fixation Hypothesis," Supp., pp. 1-17.

Joyce, Edward J. "Expert Judgment In Audit Program Planning," Supp., pp. 29-60.

Eggleton, Ian R. C. "Patterns, Prototypes, And Predictions: An Exploratory Study," Supp., pp. 68-131.

Swieringa, Robert J., Michael Gibbins, Lars Larsson and Janet Lawson Sweeney. "Experiments In The Heuristics Of Human Information Processing," Supp., pp. 159-187.

Journal of Accounting Research
Volume 15, 1977

Chesley, G. R. "Subjective Probability Elicitation: The Effect Of Congruity Of Datum And Response Mode On Performance," No. 1, pp. 1-11.

Falk, Haim and Joseph C. Miller. "Amortization Of Advertising Expenditures," No. 1, pp. 12-22.

Felix, William L., Jr. and Richard A. Grimlund. "A Sampling Model For Audit Test Of Composite Accounts," No. 1, pp. 23-41.

Feltham, Gerald A. "Cost Aggregation: An Information Economic Analysis," No. 1, pp. 42-70.

Griffin, Paul A. "The Time-Series Behavior Of Quarterly Earnings: Preliminary Evidence," No. 1, pp. 71-83

Harrison, Tom. "Different Market Reactions To Discretionary And Nondiscretionary Accounting Changes," No. 1, pp. 84-107.

Peasnell, K. V. and L. C. L. Skerratt. "How Well Does A Single Index Represent The Nineteen Sandilands Plant And Machinery Indices?," No. 1, pp. 108-119.

Scott, William R. "Group Preference Orderings For Audit And Valuation Alternatives: The Single-Peakedness Condition," No. 1, pp. 120-137.

Vasarhelyi, Miklos Antal. "Man-Machine Planning Systems: A Cognitive Style Examination Of Interactive Decision Making," No. 1, pp. 138-153.

Rockness, Howard O. and Loren A. Nikolai. "An Assessment Of APB Voting Patterns," No. 1, pp. 154-167.

Beja, Avraham and Yair Aharoni. "Some Aspects Of Conventional Accounting Profits In An Inflationary Environment," No. 2, pp. 169-178.

Garstka, Stanley J. "Models For Computing Upper Error Limits In Dollar-Unit Sampling," No. 2, pp. 179-192.

Heimann, Stephen R. and George Richard Chesley. "Audit Sample Sizes For Aggregated Statement Accounts," No. 2, pp. 193-206.

Joy, O. Maurice, Robert H. Litzenberger and Richard W. McEnally. "The Adjustment Of Stock Prices To Announcements Of Unanticipated Changes In Quarterly Earnings," No. 2, pp. 207-225.

Albrecht, W. Steve, Larry L. Lookabill and James C. McKeown. "The Time Series Properties Of Annual Earnings," No. 2, pp. 226-244.

Arnold, Donald F. and Ronald J. Huefner. "Measuring And Evaluating Replacement Costs: An Application," No. 2, pp. 245-252.

Watts, Ross L. and Richard W. Leftwich. "The Time Series Of Annual Accounting Earnings," No. 2, pp. 253-271.

Libby, Robert and Peter C. Fishburn. "Behavioral Models Of Risk Taking In Business Decisions: A Survey And Evaluation," No. 2, pp. 272-292.

Bailey, Andrew D., Jr. and Daniel L. Jensen. "A Note On The Interface Between Compliance And Substantive Tests," No. 2, pp. 293-299.

Chang, Davis L. and Jacob G. Birnberg. "Functional Fixity In Accounting Research: Perspective And New Data," No. 2, pp. 300-312.

Hughes, John S. "Optimal Timing Of Cost Information: Author's Correction," No. 2, pp. 313-316.

Picconi, Mario J. "A Reconsideration Of The Recognition Of Advertising Assets On Financial Statements," No. 2, pp. 317-326.

Schipper, Katherine. "Financial Distress In Private Colleges," Supp., pp. 1-40.

Clark, Terry Nichols. "Fiscal Management Of American Cities: Funds Flow Indicators," Supp., pp. 54-94.

Zimmerman, Jerold L. "The Municipal Accounting Maze: An Analysis Of Political Incentives," Supp., pp. 107-144.

Hansen, Elizabeth S. "Municipal Finances In Perspective: A Look At Interjurisdictional Spending And Revenue Patterns," Supp., pp. 156-201.

Elnicki, Richard A. "Hospital Working Capital: An Empirical Study," Supp., pp. 209-218.

Journal of Accounting Research
Volume 16, 1978

Abdel-khalik, A. Rashad and Jose Espejo. "Expectations Data And The Predictive Value Of Interim Reporting," No. 1, pp. 1-13.

Dittman, David A. and Prem Prakash. "Cost Variance Investigation: Markovian Control Of Markov Processes," No. 1, pp. 14-25.

Gonedes, Nicholas J. "Corporate Signaling, External Accounting, And Capital Market Equilibrium: Evidence On Dividends, Income, And Extraordinary Items," No. 1, pp. 26-79.

Lau, Amy Hing-Ling and Hon-Shiang Lau. "Some Proposed Approaches For Writing Off Capitalized Human Resource Assets," No. 1, pp. 80-102.

Loeb, Martin and Wesley A. Magat. "Soviet Success Indicators And The Evaluation Of Divisional Management," No. 1, pp. 103-121.

Otley, David T. "Budget Use And Managerial Performance," No. 1, pp. 122-149.

Verrecchia, Robert E. "On The Choice Of Accounting Method For Partnerships," No. 1, pp. 150-168.

Uecker, Wilfred C. "A Behavioral Study Of Information System Choice," No. 1, pp. 169-189.

Jacobs, Fredric H. "An Evaluation Of The Effectiveness Of Some Cost Variance Investigation Models," No. 1, pp. 190-203.

Lorek, Kenneth S. and James C. McKeown. "The Effect On Predictive Ability Of Reducing The Number Of Observations On A Time-Series Analysis Of Quarterly Earnings Data," No. 1, pp. 204-214.

Thakkar, Rashmi B. "The Association Between Market-Determined And Accounting-Determined Risk Measures: A Note," No. 1, pp. 215-223.

Chesley, G. R. "Subjective Probability Elicitation Techniques: A Performance Comparison," No. 2, pp. 225-241.

Gray, S. J. "Segment Reporting And The EEC Multinationals," No. 2, pp. 242-253.

Hirsch, Maurice L., Jr. "Disaggregated Probabilistic Accounting Information: The Effect Of Sequential Events On Expected Value Maximization Decisions," No. 2, pp. 254-269.

Ingram, Robert W. "An Investigation Of The Information Content Of (Certain) Social Responsibility Disclosures," No. 2, pp. 270-285.

Lev, Baruch and Henri Theil. "A Maximum Entropy Approach To The Choice Of Asset Depreciation," No. 2, pp. 286-293.

Magee, Robert P. and John W. Dickhaut. "Effects Of Compensation Plans On Heuristics In Cost Variance Investigations," No. 2, pp. 294-314.

Ro, Byung T. "The Disclosure Of Capitalized Lease Information And Stock Prices," No. 2, pp. 315-340.

Sunder, Shyam. "Accuracy Of Exchange Valuation Rules," No. 2, pp. 341-367.

Weber, Ron. "Auditor Decision Making On Overall System Reliability: Accuracy, Consensus, And The Usefulness Of A Simulation Decision Aid," No. 2, pp. 368-388.

Keys, David B. "Confidence Interval Financial Statements: An Empirical Investigation," No. 2, pp. 389-399.

Neumann, Bruce R. and Laurence A. Friedman. "Opportunity Costs: Further Evidence Through An Experimental Replication," No. 2, pp. 400-410.

Brief, Richard P. and Joel Owen. "Accounting For Leveraged Leases: A Comment," No. 2, pp. 411-413.

Mock, Theodore J. and Miklos Antal Vasarhelyi. "A Synthesis Of The Information Economics And Lens Models," No. 2, pp. 414-423.

Peters, Richard M. and Douglas R. Emery. "The Role Of Negative Numbers In The Development Of Double Entry Bookkeeping," No. 2, pp. 424-426.

Benston, George J. and Melvin A. Krasney. "DAAM: The Demand For Alternative Accounting Measurements," Supp., pp.1-30.

Abdel-khalik, A. Rashad and James C. McKeown. "Disclosure Of Estimates Of Holding Gains And The Assessment Of Systematic Risk," Supp., pp. 46-92.

Freeman, Robert N. "On The Association Between Net Monetary Position And Equity Security Prices," Supp., pp.111-145.

Davidson, Sidney and Roman L. Weil. "Income Tax Implications Of Various Methods Of Accounting For Changing Prices," Supp., pp. 154-233.

Short, Daniel G. "The Impact Of Price-Level Adjustment In The Context Of Risk Assessment," Supp., pp. 259-284.

Ketz, J. Edward. "The Effect Of General Price-Level Adjustments On The Predictive Ability Of Financial Ratios," Supp., pp. 273-284.

Journal of Accounting Research
Volume 17, 1979

Atkinson, Anthony A. "Information Incentives In A Standard-Setting Model Of Control," No. 1. pp. 1-22.

Garstka, Stanley J. and Philip A. Ohlson. "Ratio Estimation In Accounting Populations With Probabilities Of Sample Selection Proportional To Size Of Book Values," No. 1, pp. 23-59.

Hillison, William A. "Empirical Investigation Of General Purchasing Power Adjustments On Earnings Per Share And The Movement Of Security Prices," No. 1, pp. 60-73.

Kanodia, Chandra. "Risk Sharing And Transfer Price Systems Under Uncertainty," No. 1, pp. 74-98.

Libby, Robert. "Bankers' And Auditors' Perceptions Of The Message Communicated By The Audit Report," No. 1, pp. 99-122.

Neumann, Bruce R. "An Empirical Investigation Of The Relationship Between An AID Hospital Classification Model And Accounting Measures Of Performance," No. 1, pp. 123-139.

Nichols, Donald R. and Jeffrey J. Tsay. "Security Price Reactions To Long-Range Executive Earnings Forecasts," No. 1, pp. 140-155.

Scott, William R. "Scoring Rules For Probabilistic Reporting," No. 1, pp. 156-178.

Brown, Lawrence D. and Michael S. Rozeff. "Univariate Time-Series Models Of Quarterly Accounting Earnings Per Share: A Proposed Model," No. 1, pp. 179-189.

Lorek, Kenneth S. "Predicting Annual Net Earnings With Quarterly Earnings Time-Series Models," No.1,pp.190-204.

Moriarity, Shane. "Communicating Financial Information Through Multidimensional Graphics," No. 1, pp. 205-224.

Nair, R. D. "Economic Analyses And Accounting Techniques: An Empirical Study," No. 1, pp. 225-242.

Sundem, Gary L. "A Game Theory Model Of The Information Evaluator and The Decision Maker," No. 1, pp. 243-261.

Foster, George. "Briloff And The Capital Market," No. 1, pp. 262-274.

Kinney, William R., Jr. and Carl S. Warren. "The Decision-Theory Approach To Audit Sampling: An Extension And Application To Receivables Confirmation," No. 1, pp. 275-285.

Lusk, Edward J. "A Test Of Differential Performance Peaking For A Disembedding Task," No. 1, pp. 286-294.

Roth, Alvin E. and Robert E. Verrecchia. "The Shapley Value As Applied To Cost Allocations: A Reinterpretation," No. 1, pp. 295-303.

Barlev, Benzion and Haim Levy. "On The Variability Of Accounting Income Numbers," No. 2, pp. 305-315.

Beaver, William H., Roger Clarke and William F. Wright. "The Association Between Unsystematic Security Returns And The Magnitude Of Earnings Forecast Errors," No. 2, pp. 316-340.

Brown, Lawrence D. and Michael S. Rozeff. "Adaptive Expectations, Time-Series Models, And Analyst Forecast Revision," No. 2, pp. 341-351.

Collins, Daniel W. and Richard R. Simonds. "SEC Line-Of-Business Disclosure And Market Risk Adjustments," No. 2, pp. 352-383.

Gonedes, Nicholas J. and Nicholas Dopuch. "Economic Analyses And Accounting Techniques: Perspectives And Proposals," No. 2, pp. 384-410.

Hilton, Ronald W. "The Determinants Of Cost Information Value: An Illustrative Analysis," No. 2, pp. 411-435.

Jiambalvo, James. "Performance Evaluation And Directed Job Effort: Model Development And Analysis In A CPA Firm Setting," No. 2, pp. 436-455.

Kinney, William R., Jr. "Integrating Audit Tests: Regression Analysis And Partitioned Dollar-Unit Sampling," No. 2, pp. 456-475.

Maher, Michael W., Kavasseri V. Ramanathan and Richard B. Peterson. "Preference Congruence, Information Accuracy, And Employee Performance: A Field Study," No. 2, pp. 476-503.

Ohlson, James A. and James M. Patell. "An Introduction To Residual (API) Analysis And The Private Value Of Information And The API And The Design Of Experiments," No. 2, pp. 504-505.

Ohlson, James A. "Residual (API) Analysis And The Private Value Of Information," No. 2, pp. 506-527.

Patell, James M. "The API And The Design Of Experiments," No. 2, pp. 528-549.

Pastena, Victor and Joshua Ronen. "Some Hypotheses On The Pattern Of Management's Informal Disclosures," No. 2, pp. 550-564.

Adelberg, Arthur Harris. "A Methodology For Measuring The Understandability Of Financial Report Messages," No. 2, pp. 565-592.

Frank, Werner G. "An Empirical Analysis Of International Accounting Principles," No. 2, pp. 593-605.

Baker, Robert L. and Ronald M. Copeland. "Evaluation Of The Stratified Regression Estimator For Auditing Accounting Populations," No. 2, pp. 606-617.

Jacobs, Fredric and Kenneth S. Lorek. "A Note On The Time-Series Properties Of Control Data In An Accounting Environment," No. 2, pp. 618-621.

Ng, David S. and Jan Stoeckenius. "Auditing: Incentives And Truthful Reporting," Supp., pp. 1-24.

Libby, Robert. "The Impact Of Uncertainty Reporting On The Loan Decision," Supp., pp. 35-57.

Ramage, John G., Abba M. Krieger and Leslie L. Spero. "An Empirical Study Of Error Characteristics In Audit Populations," Supp., pp. 72-102.

Moriarity, Shane and F. Hutton Barron. "A Judgment-Based Definition Of Materiality," Supp., pp. 114-135.

Kinney, William R., Jr. "The Predictive Power Of Limited Information In Preliminary Analytical Review: An Empirical Study," Supp., pp. 148-165.

Cushing, Barry E., D. Gerald Searfoss and Reed H. Randall. "Materiality Allocation In Audit Planning: A Feasibility Study," Supp., pp. 172-216.

Journal of Accounting Research
Volume 18, 1980

Ashton, Robert H. and Sandra S. Kramer. "Students As

Surrogates In Behavioral Accounting Research: Some Evidence," No. 1, pp. 1-15.

Beck, Paul J. "A Critical Analysis Of The Regression Estimator In Audit Sampling," No. 1, pp. 16-37.

Brown, Robert Moren. "Short-Range Market Reaction To Changes To LIFO Accounting Using Preliminary Earnings Announcement Dates," No. 1, pp. 38-63.

Gray, S. J. "The Impact Of International Accounting Differences From A Security-Analysis Perspective: Some European Evidence," No. 1, pp. 64-76.

Hopwood, William S. "The Transfer Function Relationship Between Earnings And Market-Industry Indices: An Empirical Study," No. 1, pp. 77-90.

Ijiri, Yuji and Robert A. Leitch. "Stein's Paradox And Audit Sampling," No. 1, pp. 91-108.

Ohlson, James A. "Financial Ratios And The Probabilistic Prediction Of Bankruptcy," No. 1, pp. 109-131.

Penman, Stephen H. "An Empirical Investigation Of The Voluntary Disclosure Of Corporate Earnings Forecasts," No. 1, pp. 132-160.

Simunic, Dan A. "The Pricing Of Audit Services: Theory And Evidence," No. 1, pp. 161-190.

Uecker, Wilfred C. "The Effects Of Knowledge Of The User's Decision Model In Simplified Information Evaluation," No. 1, pp. 191-213.

Weber, Ron. "Some Characteristics Of The Free Recall Of Computer Controls By EDP Auditors." No. 1, pp. 214-241.

Bowman, Robert G. "The Importance Of A Market-Value Measurement Of Debt In Assessing Leverage," No. 1, pp. 242-254.

Grant, Edward B. "Market Implications Of Differential Amounts Of Interim Information," No. 1, pp. 255-268.

Ashton, Robert H. and Paul R. Brown. "Descriptive Modeling Of Auditors' Internal Control Judgments: Replication And Extension," No. 1, pp. 269-277.

Brown, Lawrence D., John S. Hughes, Michael S. Rozeff and James H. VanderWeide. "Expectations Data And The Predictive Value Of Interim Reporting: A Comment," No. 1, pp. 278-288.

Hopwood, William S. "On The Automation Of The Box-Jenkins Modeling Procedures: An Algorithm With An Empirical Test," No. 1, pp. 289-296.

Kistner, Klaus-Peter and Timo Salmi. "General Price Level Accounting And Inventory Valuation: A Comment," No. 1, pp. 297-311.

Warren, Carl S. "Uniformity Of Auditing Standards: A Replication," No. 1, pp. 312-324.

Abdel-khalik, A. Rashad and Kamal M. El-Sheshai. "Information Choice And Utilization In An Experiment On Default Prediction," No. 2, pp. 325-342.

Ajinkya, Bipin B. "An Empirical Evaluation Of Line-Of-Business Reporting," No. 2, pp. 343-361.

Belkaoui, Ahmed. "The Interprofessional Linguistic Communication Of Accounting Concepts: An Experiment In Socialinguistics," No. 2, pp. 362-374.

Cohen, Morris A. and Robert Halperin. "Optimal Inventory Order Policy For A Firm Using The LIFO Inventory Costing Method," No. 2, pp. 375-389.

Collins, William A. and William S. Hopwood. "A Multivariate Analysis Of Annual Earnings Forecasts Generated From Quarterly Forecasts Of Financial Analysts And Univariate Time-Series Models," No. 2, pp. 390-406.

Friedman, Laurence A. and Bruce R. Neumann. "The Effects Of Opportunity Costs On Project Investment Decisions: A Replication And Extension," No. 2, pp. 407-419.

Garman, Mark B. and James A. Ohlson. "Information And The Sequential Valuation Of Assets In Arbitrage-Free Economics," No. 2, pp. 420-440.

Gonedes, Nicholas J. "Public Disclosure Rules, Private Information-Production Decisions, And Capital Market Equilibrium," No. 2, pp. 441-476.

Hilton, Ronald W. "Integrating Normative And Descriptive Theories Of Information Processing," No. 2, pp. 477-505.

Kida, Thomas. "An Investigation Into Auditors' Continuity And Related Qualification Judgments," No. 2, pp. 506-523.

Lev, Baruch. "On The Use Of Index Models In Analytical Reviews By Auditors," No. 2, pp. 524-550.

Magee, Robert P. "Equilibria In Budget Participation," No. 2, pp. 551-573.

Oppong, Andrews. "Information Content Of Annual Earnings Announcements Revisited," No. 2, pp. 574-584.

Crosby, Michael A. "Implications Of Prior Probability Elicitation On Auditor Sample Size Decisions," No. 2, pp. 585-593.

Lewis, Barry L. "Expert Judgment In Auditing: An Expected Utility Approach," No. 2, pp. 594-602.

Casey, Cornelius J., Jr. "The Usefulness Of Accounting Ratios For Subjects' Predictions Of Corporate Failure: Replication And Extensions," No. 2, pp. 603-613.

Ingram, Robert W. and Katherine Beal Frazier. "Environmental Performance And Corporate Disclosure," No. 2, pp. 614-622.

Whittred, G. P. "The Timeliness Of The Australian Annual Report: 1972-1977," No. 2, pp. 623-628.

Zimmer, Ian. "A Lens Study Of The Prediction Of Corporate Failure By Bank Loan Officers." No. 2, pp. 629-636.

Dukes, Roland E., Thomas R. Dyckman and John A. Elliott. "Accounting For Research And Development Costs: The Impact On Research And Development Expenditures," Supp., pp. 1-26.

Horwitz, Bertrand N. and Richard Kolodny. "The Economic Effects Of Involuntary Uniformity In The Financial Reporting Of R & D Expenditures," Supp., pp. 38-74.

Evans, John H., III. "Optimal Contracts With Costly Conditional Auditing," Supp., pp. 108-128.

Balachandran, Bala V. and Ram T. S. Ramakrishnan. "Internal Control And External Auditing For Incentive Compensation Schedules," Supp., pp. 140-171.

Baiman, Stanley and Joel S. Demski. "Economically Optimal Performance Evaluation And Control Systems," Supp., pp. 184-220.

Biddle, Gary C. "Accounting Methods And Management Decisions: The Case Of Inventory Costing And Inventory Policy," Supp., pp. 235-280.

Journal of Accounting Research
Volume 19, 1981

Einhorn, Hillel J. and Robin M. Hogarth. "Behavioral Decision Theory: Processes Of Judgment And Choice," No. 1, pp. 1-31.

Ashton, Robert H. "A Descriptive Study Of Information Evaluation," No. 1, pp. 42-61.

Brown, Clifton. "Human Information Processing For Decisions To Investigate Cost Variances," No. 1, pp. 62-85.

Hilton, Ronald W., Robert J. Swieringa and Robert E. Hoskin. "Perception Of Accuracy As A Determinant Of Information Value," No. 1, pp. 86-108.

Hilton, Ronald W. and Robert J. Swieringa. "Perception Of Initial Uncertainty As A Determinant Of Information Value," No. 1, pp. 109-119.

Joyce, Edward J. and Gary C. Biddle. "Anchoring And Adjustment In Probabilistic Inference In Auditing," No. 1, pp. 120-145.

Kessler, Lawrence and Robert H. Ashton. "Feedback And Prediction Achievement In Financial Analysis," No. 1, pp. 146-162.

Beaver, William H. "Econometric Properties Of Alternative Security Return Methods," No. 1, pp. 163-184.

Billera, Louis J., David C. Heath and Robert E. Verrecchia. "A Unique Procedure For Allocating Common Costs From A Production Process," No. 1, pp. 185-196.

Copeland, Ronald M., Ronald L. Taylor and Shari H. Brown. "Observation Error And Bias In Accounting Research," No. 1, pp. 197-207.

Gjesdal, Froystein. "Accounting For Stewardship," No. 1, pp. 208-231.

Brown, Paul R. "A Descriptive Analysis Of Select Input Bases Of The Financial Accounting Standards Board," No. 1, pp. 232-246.

Newman, D. Paul. "An Investigation Of The Distribution Of Power In The APB And FASB," No. 1, pp. 247-262.

Lillestol, Jostein. "A Note On Computing Upper Error Limits In Dollar-Unit Sampling," No. 1, pp. 263-267.

Nobes, C. W. "An Empirical Analysis Of International Accounting Principles: A Comment," No. 1, pp. 268-270.

Verrecchia, Robert E. "On The Relationship Between Volume Reaction And Consensus Of Investors: Implications For Interpreting Tests Of Information Content," No. 1, pp. 271-283.

Cogger, Kenneth O. "A Time-Series Analytic Approach To Aggregation Issues In Accounting Data," No. 2, pp. 285-298.

Gangolly, Jagdish S. "On Joint Cost Allocation: Independent Cost Proportional Scheme (ICPS) And Its Properties," No. 2, pp. 299-312.

Hopwood, William S. and James C. McKeown. "An Evaluation Of Univariate Time-Series Earnings Models And Their Generalization To A Single Input Transfer Function," No. 2, pp. 313-322.

Joyce, Edward J. and Gary C. Biddle. "Are Auditors' Judgments Sufficiently Regressive?," No. 2, pp. 323-349.

Livnat, Joshua. "A Generalization Of The API Methodology As A Way Of Measuring The Association Between Income And Stock Prices," No. 2, pp. 350-359.

Manegold, James G. "Time-Series Properties Of Earnings: A Comparison Of Extrapolative And Component Models," No. 2, pp. 360-373.

Morse, Dale. "Price And Trading Volume Reaction Surrounding Earnings Announcements: A Closer Examination," No. 2, pp. 374-383.

Noreen, Eric and Mark Wolfson. "Equilibrium Warrant Pricing Models And Accounting For Executive Stock Options," No. 2, pp. 384-398.

Ohlson, James A. and A. G. Buckman. "Toward A Theory Of Financial Accounting: Welfare And Public Information," No. 2, pp. 399-433.

Patell, James M. and Mark A. Wolfson. "The Ex Ante And Ex Post Price Effects Of Quarterly Earnings Announcements Reflected In Option And Stock Prices," No. 2, pp. 434-458.

Ronen, J. and J. Livnat. "Incentives For Segment Reporting," No. 2, pp. 459-481.

Schultz, Joseph J., Jr. and Philip M. J. Reckers. "The Impact Of Group Processing On Selected Audit Disclosure Decisions," No. 2, pp. 482-501.

Wallace, Wanda A. "The Association Between Municipal Market Measures And Selected Financial Reporting Practices," No. 2, pp. 502-520.

Firth, Michael. "The Relative Information Content Of The Release Of Financial Results Data By Firms," No. 2, pp. 521-529.

Givoly, Dan and Dan Palmon. "Classification Of Convertible Debt As Common Stock Equivalents: Some Empirical Evidence On The Effects Of APB Opinion 15," No. 2, pp. 530-543.

Joyce, Edward J. and Robert Libby. "Some Accounting Implications Of 'Behavioral Decision Theory: Processes Of Judgment And Choice'," No. 2, pp. 544-550.

Hakansson, Nils H. "On The Policies Of Accounting Disclosure And Measurement: An Analysis Of Economic Incentives," Supp., pp. 1-35.

Leftwich, Richard, Ross L. Watts and Jerold L. Zimmerman. "Voluntary Corporate Disclosure: The Case Of Interim Reporting," Supp., pp. 50-84.

Johnson, Orace. "Some Implications Of The United States Constitution For Accounting Institution Alternatives," Supp., pp. 89-120.

Newman, D. Paul. "The SEC's Influence On Accounting Standards: The Power Of The Veto," Supp., pp. 134-164.

Smith, Abbie J. "The SEC 'Reversal' Of FASB Statement No. 19: An Investigation Of Information Effects," Supp., pp. 174-211.

Journal of Accounting Research
Volume 20, 1982

Benbasat, Izak and Albert S. Dexter. "Individual Differences In The Use Of Decision Support Aids," No. 1, pp. 1-11.

Brownell, Peter. "The Role Of Accounting Data In Performance Evaluation, Budgetary Participation, And Organizational Effectiveness," No. 1, pp. 12-27.

Buckman, A. G. and Bruce L. Miller. "Optimal Investigation Of A Multiple Cost Processes System," No. 1, pp. 28-41.

Duke, Gordon L., John Neter and Robert A. Leitch. "Power Characteristics Of Test Statistics In The Auditing Environment: An Empirical Study," No. 1, pp. 42-67.

Eggleton, Ian R. C. "Intuitive Time-Series Extrapolation," No. 1, pp. 68-102.

Frost, Peter A. and Hirokuni Tamura. "Jackknifed Ratio Estimation In Statistical Auditing," No. 1, pp. 103-120.

Gibbins, Michael. "Regression And Other Statistical Implications For Research On Judgment Using Intercorrelated Data Sources," No. 1, pp. 121-138.

Hall, Thomas W. "An Empirical Test Of The Effect Of Asset Aggregation On Valuation Accuracy," No. 1, pp. 139-151.

Jiambalvo, James. "Measures Of Accuracy And Congruence In The Performance Evaluation Of CPA Personnel: Replication And Extensions," No. 1, pp. 152-161.

Matsumura, Ella Mae and Kam-Wah Tsui. "Stein-Type Poisson Estimators In Audit Sampling," No. 1, pp. 162-170.

Otley, David T. and Francisco J. B. Dias. "Accounting Aggregation And Decision-Making Performance: An Experimental Investigation," No. 1, pp. 171-188.

Pratt, Jamie. "Post-Cognitive Structure: Its Determinants And Relationship To Perceived Information Use And Predictive Accuracy," No. 1, pp. 189-209.

Skinner, R. C. "Fixed Asset Lives And Replacement Cost Accounting," No. 1, pp. 210-226.

Wright, Arnold. "An Investigation Of The Engagement Evaluation Process For Staff Auditors," No. 1, pp. 227-239.

Banks, Doyle W. and William R. Kinney, Jr. "Loss Contingency Reports And Stock Prices: An Empirical Study," No. 1, pp. 240-254.

Silhan, Peter A. "Simulated Mergers Of Existent Autonomous Firms: A New Approach To Segmentation Research," No. 1, pp. 255-262.

Buchman, Thomas A. and John A. Tracy. "Obtaining Responses To Sensitive Questions: Conventional Questionnaire Versus Randomized Response Technique," No. 1,pp.263-271.

DeAngelo, Linda Elizabeth. "Unrecorded Human Assets And The 'Hold-Up' Problem," No. 1, pp. 272-274.

Copeland, Ronald M. and Robert W. Ingram. "The Association Between Municipal Accounting Information And Bond Rating Changes," No. 2, Part I, pp. 275-289.

Emery, Gary W. and Kenneth O. Cogger. "The Measurement Of Liquidity," No. 2, Part I, pp. 290-303.

Godfrey, James T. and Richard W. Andrews. "A Finite Population Bayesian Model For Compliance Testing," No. 2, Part I, pp. 304-315.

Grimlund, Richard A. "An Integration Of Internal Control System And Account Balance Evidence." No. 2, Part I, pp. 316-342.

Hopwood, W. S., J. C. McKeown and P. Newbold. "The Additional Information Content Of Quarterly Earnings Reports: Intertemporal Disaggregation," No. 2, Part I, pp. 343-349.

Kinney, William R., Jr. and Gerald L. Salamon. "Regression Analysis In Auditing: A Comparison Of Alternative Investigation Rules," No. 2, Part I, pp. 350-366.

Ricks, William E. "The Market's Response To The 1974 LIFO Adoptions," No. 2, Part I, pp. 367-387.

Uecker, Wilfred C. "The Quality Of Group Performance In Simplified Information Evaluation," No. 2, Part I, pp. 388-402.

Anderson, Thomas N., Jr. and Thomas E. Kida. "The Cross-Lagged Research Approach: Description And Illustration," No. 2, Part I, pp. 403-414.

Ashton, Alison Hubbard. "The Descriptive Validity Of Normative Decision Theory In Auditing Contexts," No. 2, Part I, pp. 415-428.

Imhoff, Eugene A., Jr. and Paul V. Pare. "Analysis And Comparison Of Earnings Forecast Agents," No. 2, Part I, pp. 429-439.

Ashton, Alison Hubbard. "An Empirical Study Of Budget-Related Predictions Of Corporate Executives," No. 2, Part I, pp. 440-449.

Emery, Douglas A., F. Hutton Barron and William F. Messier, Jr. "Conjoint Measurement And The Analysis Of Noisy Data: A Comment," No. 2, Part I, pp. 450-458.

Kross, William. "Stock Returns And Oil And Gas Pronouncements: Replication And Extension," No. 2, Part I, pp. 459-471.

Pany, Kurt and Charles H. Smith. "Auditor Association With Quarterly Financial Information: An Empirical Test," No. 2, Part I, pp. 472-481.

Scheiner, James H. and Jack E. Kiger. "An Empirical Investigation Of Auditor Involvement In Non-Audit Services," No. 2, Part I, pp. 482-496.

Taylor, William M. and Jerry J. Weygandt. "Accounting For Stock-Based Awards Using The Minimum Value Method," No. 2, Part I, pp. 497-502.

Antle, Rick. "The Auditor As An Economic Agent," No. 2, Part II, pp. 503-527.

Beaver, William H. and Mark A. Wolfson. "Foreign Currency Translation And Changing Prices In Perfect And Complete Markets," No. 2, Part II, pp. 528-550.

Biddle, Gary C. and Frederick W. Lindahl. "Stock Price Reactions To LIFO Adoptions: The Association Beween Excess Returns And LIFO Tax Savings," No. 2, Part II, pp. 551-588.

Christensen, John. "The Determination Of Performance Standards And Participation," No. 2, Part II, pp. 589-603.

Danos, Paul and John W. Eichenseher. "Audit Industry Dynamics: Factors Affecting Changes In Client-Industry Market Shares," No. 2, Part II, pp. 604-616.

Elliott, John A. "'Subject To' Audit Opinions And Abnormal Security Returns: Outcomes And Ambiguities," No. 2, Part II, pp. 617-638.

Freeman, Robert N., James A. Ohlson and Stephen H. Penman. "Book Rate-Of-Return And Prediction Of Earnings Changes: An Empirical Investigation," No. 2, Part II, pp. 639-653.

Joyce, Edward J., Robert Libby and Shyam Sunder. "Using The FASB's Qualitative Characterisitics In Accounting Policy Choices," No. 2, Part II. pp. 654-675.

Selto, Frank H. and Hugh D. Grove. "Voting Power Indices And The Setting Of Financial Accounting Standards: Extensions," No. 2, Part II, pp. 676-688.

Solomon, Ira. "Probability Assessment By Individual Auditors And Audit Teams: An Empirical Investigation," No. 2, Part II, pp. 689-710.

Eger, Carol and John Dickhaut. "An Examination Of The Conservative Information Processing Bias In An Accounting Framework," No. 2, Part II, pp. 711-723.

Hopwood, William S., Paul Newbold and Peter A. Silhan. "The Potential For Gains In Predictive Ability Through Disaggregation: Segmented Annual Earnings," No. 2, pp. 724-732.

Cogger, Kenneth and William Ruland. "A Note On Alternative Tests For Independence Of Financial Time Series," No. 2, pp. 733-737.

Davis, Harry Z. and Nathan Kahn. "Some Additional Evidence On The LIFO-FIFO Choice Using Replacement Cost Data," No. 2, pp. 738-744.

Gaumnitz, Bruce R., Thomas R. Nunamaker, John J. Surdick and Michael F. Thomas. "Auditor Consensus In Internal Control Evaluation And Audit Program Planning," No. 2, Part II, pp. 745-755.

Hamilton, Robert E. and William F. Wright. "Internal Control Judgments And Effects Of Experience Replications And Extensions," No. 2, Part II, pp. 756-765.

Ingram, Robert W. and Ronald M. Copeland. "Municipal Market Measures And Reporting Practices: An Extension," No. 2, Part II. pp. 766-772.

Mayper, Alan G. "Consensus Of Auditors' Materiality Judgments Of Internal Control Weaknesses," No. 2, Part II, pp. 773-783.

Verrecchia, Robert E. "The Use Of Mathematical Models In Financial Accounting," Supp., pp. 1-42.

Swieringa, Robert J. and Karl E. Weick. "An Assessment Of Laboratory Experiments In Accounting," Supp., pp. 56-101.

Demski, Joel S. and David M. Kreps. "Models In Managerial Accounting," Supp., pp. 117-148.

Ball, Ray and George Foster. "Corporate Financial Reporting: A Methodological Review Of Empirical Research," Supp., pp. 161-234.

Lev, Baruch and James A. Ohlson. "Market-Based Empirical Research In Accounting: A Review, Interpretation, And Extension," Supp., pp. 249-322.

Journal of Accounting Research
Volume 21, 1983

Bell, Timothy Barnes. "Market Reaction To Reserve Recognition Accounting," No. 1, pp. 1-17.

Dharan, Bala G. "Identification And Estimation Issues For A Causal Earnings Model," No. 1, pp. 18-41.

Freeman, Robert N. "Alternative Measures Of Profit Margin: An Empirical Study Of The Potential Information Content Of Current Cost Accounting," No. 1, pp. 42-64.

Harrison, Walter T., Jr., Lawrence A. Tomassini and J. Richard Dietrich. "The Use Of Control Groups In Capital Market Research," No. 1, pp. 65-77.

Hoskin, Robert E. "Opportunity Cost And Behavior," No. 1, pp. 78-95.

Menzefricke, Ulrich. "On Sampling Plan Selection With Dollar-Unit Sampling," No. 1, pp. 96-105.

Morse, Dale and Gordon Richardson. "The LIFO/FIFO Decision," No. 1, pp. 106-127.

Murray, Dennis. "The Effect Of Certain Research Design Choices On The Assessment Of The Market's Reaction To LIFO Changes: A Methodological Study," No. 1, pp. 128-140.

Ohlson, James A. "Price-Earnings Ratios And Earnings Capitalization Under Uncertainty." No. 1, pp. 141-154.

Pincus, Morton. "Information Characteristics Of Earnings Announcements And Stock Market Behavior." No. 1, pp. 155-183.

Schipper, Katherine and Rex Thompson. "The Impact Of Merger-Related Regulations On The Shareholders Of Acquiring Firms." No. 1, pp. 184-221.

Sunder, Shyam. "Simpson's Reversal Paradox And Cost Allocation." No. 1, pp. 222-233.

Biggs, Stanley F. and Theodore J. Mock. "An Investigation Of Auditor Decision Processes In The Evaluation Of Internal Controls And Audit Scope Decisions." No. 1, pp. 234-255.

Dharan, Bala G. "Empirical Identification Procedures For Earnings Models." No. 1, pp. 256-270.

Lewis, Barry, Michael D. Shields and S. Mark Young. "Evaluating Human Judgments And Decision Aids." No. 1, pp. 271-285.

Trotman, Ken T., Philip W. Yetton and Ian R. Zimmer. "Individual And Group Judgments Of Internal Control Systems." No. 1, pp. 286-292.

Abdel-khalik, A. Rashad. "Overfitting Bias In The Models Assessing The Predictive Power Of Quarterly Reports." No. 1, pp. 293-296.

Altman, Edward I. "Multidimensional Graphics And Bankruptcy Prediction: A Comment." No. 1, pp. 297-299.

Casey, Cornelius J. "Prior Probability Disclosure And Loan Officers' Judgments: Some Evidence of The Impact." No. 1, pp. 300-307.

Frecka, Thomas J. and Cheng F. Lee. "Generalized Financial Ratio Adjustment Processes And Their Implications." No. 1, pp. 308-316.

Lorek, Kenneth S., Joe D. Icerman and Abdullah A. Abdulkader. "Further Descriptive And Predictive Evidence On Alternative Time-Series Models For Quarterly Earnings." No. 1, pp. 317-328.

Maher, Michael W. and Timothy J. Nantell. "The Tax Effects Of Inflation: Depreciation, Debt, And Miller's Equilibrium Tax Rates." No. 1, pp. 329-340.

Silhan, Peter A. "The Effects Of Segmenting Quarterly Sales And Margins On Extrapolative Forecasts Of Conglomerate Earnings: Extension And Replication." No. 1, pp. 341-347.

Tabor, Richard H. "Internal Control Evaluations And Audit Program Revisions: Some Additional Evidence." No. 1, pp. 348-354.

Bailey, K. E., III, Joseph H. Bylinski and Michael D. Shields. "Effects Of Audit Report Wording Changes On The Perceived Message." No. 2, pp. 355-370.

Baiman, Stanley and John H. Evans, III. "Pre-Decision Information And Participative Management Control Systems." No. 2, pp. 371-395.

Bamber, E. Michael. "Expert Judgment In The Audit Team: A Source Reliability Approach." No. 2, pp. 396-412.

Brown, Clifton. "Effects Of Dynamic Task Environment On The Learning Of Standard Cost Variance Significance." No. 2, pp. 413-431.

Brown, Lawrence D. "Accounting Changes And The Accuracy Of Analysts' Earnings Forecasts." No. 2, pp. 432-443.

Brown, Paul R. "Independent Auditor Judgment In The Evaluation Of Internal Audit Functions." No. 2, pp. 444-455.

Brownell, Peter. "The Motivational Impact Of Management-By-Exception In A Budgetary Context." No. 2, pp. 456-472.

Danos, Paul and Eugene A. Imhoff, Jr. "Factors Affecting Auditor's Evaluations Of Forecasts." No. 2, pp. 473-494.

Dickhaut, John W. and John C. Lere. "Comparison Of Accounting Systems And Heuristics In Selecting Economic Optima." No. 2, pp. 495-513.

Dye, Ronald A. "Communication And Post-Decision Information." No. 2, pp. 514-533.

Nichols, Donald R. and David B. Smith. "Auditor Credibility And Auditor Changes." No. 2, pp. 534-544.

Shockley, Randolph A. and Robert N. Holt. "A Behavioral Investigation Of Supplier Differentiation In The Market For Audit Services." No. 2, pp. 545-564.

Sunder, Shyam and Gregory Waymire. "Marginal Gains In Accuracy Of Valuation From Increasingly Specific Price Indexes: Empirical Evidence For The U.S. Economy." No. 2, pp. 565-580.

Tiller, Mikel G. "The Dissonance Model Of Participative Budgeting: An Empirical Exploration." No. 2, pp. 581-595.

Hirst, Mark K. "Reliance On Accounting Performance Measures, Task Uncertainty, And Dysfunctional Behavior: Some Extensions." No. 2, pp. 596-605.

Lawrence, Edward C. "Reporting Delays For Failed Firms." No. 2, pp. 606-610.

Messier, William F., Jr. "The Effect Of Experience And Firm Type On Materiality/Disclosure Judgments." No. 2, pp. 611-618.

Selto, Frank H. and Hugh D. Grove. "The Predictive Power Of Voting Power Indices: FASB Voting On Statements Of Financial Accounting Standards Nos. 45-69." No. 2, pp. 619-622.

Sterner, Julie A. "An Empirical Evaluation Of SFAS No. 55." No. 2, pp. 623-628.

Waymire, Gregory and Grace Pownall. "Some Evidence On Potential Effects Of Contemporaneous Earnings Disclosures In Tests Of Capital Market Effects Associated With FASB Exposure Draft No. 19." No. 2, pp. 629-643.

Williams, David J. and John O. S. Kennedy. "A Unique Procedure For Allocating Joint Costs From A Production Process?." No. 2, pp. 644-645.

Antle, Rick. "Auditor Indepedence." No. 1, pp. 1-20.

Chambers, Anne E. and Stephen H. Penman. "Timeliness Of Reporting And The Stock Price Reaction To Earnings Announcements." No. 1, pp. 21-47.

Collins, Daniel W. and Warren T. Dent. "A Comparison Of Alternative Testing Methodologies Used In Capital Market Research." No. 1, pp. 48-84.

Elliott, John, Gordon Richardson, Thomas Dyckman and Roland Dukes. "The Impact Of SFAS No.2 On Firm Expenditures On Research And Development: Replications And Extensions." No. 1, pp. 85-102.

Gibbins, Michael. "Propositions About The Psychology Of Professional Judgment In Public Accounting." No. 1, pp. 103-125.

Ingram, Robert W. "Economic Incentives And The Choice Of State Government Accounting Practices." No. 1, pp. 126-144.

Kida, Thomas. "The Effect Of Causality And Specificity On Data Use." No. 1, pp. 145-152.

Kross, William and Douglas A. Schroeder. "An Empirical Investigation Of The Effect Of Quarterly Earnings Announcement Timing On Stock Returns." No. 1, pp.153-176.

Penno, Mark. "Asymmetry Of Pre-Decision Information And Managerial Accounting." No. 1, pp. 177-191.

Stock, Duane and Collin J. Watson. "Human Judgment Accuracy, Multidimensional Graphics, And Humans Versus Models." No. 1, pp. 192-206.

Wilson, Earl R. and Thomas P. Howard. "The Association Between Municipal Market Measures And Selected Financial Reporting Practices: Additional Evidence." No. 1, pp. 207-224.

Dyckman, Thomas R. and Stephen A. Zeff. "Two Decades Of The Journal Of Accounting Research." No. 1, pp. 225-297.

Arrington, C. Edward, William Hillison and Robert E. Jensen. "An Application Of Analytical Hierarchy Process To Model Expert Judgments On Analytical Review Procedures." No. 1, pp. 298-312.

Davison, A. G., Bruce W. Stening and Wan Tai Wai. "Auditor Concentration And The Impact Of Interlocking Directorates." No. 1, pp. 313-317.

Frazier, Katherine Beal, Robert W. Ingram and B. Mack Tennyson. "A Methodology For The Analysis Of Narrative Accounting Disclosures." No. 1, pp. 318-331.

Kida, Thomas. "The Impact Of Hypothesis-Testing Strategies On Auditors' Use Of Judgment Data." No. 1, pp. 332-340.

Ricchiute, David N. "An Empirical Assessment Of The Impact Of Alternative Task Presentation Modes On Decision-Making Research In Auditing." No. 1, pp. 341-350.

Gray, S. J. and Lee H. Radebaugh. "International Segment Disclosures By U.S. and U.K. Multinational Enterprises: A Descriptive Study." No. 1, pp. 351-360.

Houghton, K. A. "Accounting Data And The Prediction Of Business Failure: The Setting Of Priors And The Age Of Data." No. 1, pp. 361-368.

Lorek, Kenneth S. and Allen W. Bathke, Jr. "A Time-Series Analysis Of Nonseasonal Quarterly Earnings Data." No. 1, pp. 369-379.

Mensah, Yaw M. "An Examination Of The Stationarity Of Multivariate Bankruptcy Prediction Models: A Methodological Study." No. 1, pp. 380-395.

Sunder, Shyam and Gregory Waymire. "Accuracy Of Exchange Valuation Rules: Additivity And Unbiased Estimation." No. 1, pp. 396-405.

Watkins, Paul R. "Multidimensional Scaling Measurement And Accounting Research." No. 1, pp. 406-411.

Wescott, Shari H. "Accounting Numbers And Socioeconomic Variables As Predictors Of Municipal General Obligation Bond Ratings." No. 1, pp. 412-423.

Ajinkya, Bipin B. and Michael J. Gift. "Corporate Managers' Earnings Forecasts And Symmetrical Adjustments Of Market Expectations." No. 2, pp. 425-444.

Bernard, Victor L. "The Use Of Market Data And Accounting Data In Hedging Against Consumer Price Inflation." No. 2, pp. 445-466.

Collins, William A., William S. Hopwood and James C. McKeown. "The Predictability Of Interim Earnings Over Alternative Quarters." No. 2, pp. 467-479.

Davis, Harry Z., Nathan Kahn and Etzmun Rozen. "LIFO Inventory Liquidations: An Empirical Study." No. 2, pp. 480-496.

Godfrey, James and John Neter. "Bayesian Bounds For Monetary Unit Sampling In Accounting And Auditing." No. 2, pp. 497-525.

Hagerman, Robert L., Mark E. Zmijewski and Pravin Shah. "The Association Between The Magnitude Of Quarterly Earnings Forecast Errors And Risk-Adjusted Stock Returns." No. 2, pp. 526-540.

Imhoff, Eugene A., Jr. and Gerald J. Lobo. "Information Content Of Analysts' Composite Forecast Revisions." No. 2, pp. 541-554.

Matolcsy, Z. P. "Evidence On The Joint And Marginal Information Content Of Inflation-Adjusted Accounting Income Numbers." No. 2, pp. 555-569.

Menzefricke, Ulrich. "Using Decision Theory For Planning Audit Sample Size With Dollar Unit Sampling." No. 2, pp. 570-587.

Menzefricke, Ulrich and Wally Smieliauskas. "A Simulation Study Of The Performance Of Parametric Dollar Unit Sampling Statistical Procedures." No. 2, pp. 588-604.

Morse, Dale. "An Econometric Analysis Of The Choice Of Daily Versus Monthly Returns In Tests Of Information Content." No. 2, pp. 605-623.

Journal of Accounting Research
Volume 23, 1985

Schachter, Barry. "Open Interest And Consensus Among Investors," No. 2, pp. 907-910.

Schneider, Arnold. "The Reliance Of External Auditors On The Internal Audit Function," No. 2, pp. 911-919.

Ziebart, David A. "Control Of Beta Reliability In Studies Of Abnormal Return Magnitudes: A Methodological Note," No. 2, pp. 920-926.

Bublitz, Bruce, Thomas J. Frecka and James C. McKeown. "Market Association Tests And FASB Statement No. 33 Disclosures: A Reexamination," Supp., pp. 1-23.

Olsen, Chris. "Valuation Implications Of SFAS No. 33 Data For Electric Utility Investors," Supp., pp. 28-47.

Easton, Peter D. "Accounting Earnings And Security Valuation: Empirical Evidence Of The Fundamental Links," Supp., pp. 54-77.

DeJong, Douglas V., Robert Forsythe, Russell J. Lundholm and Wilfred C. Uecker. "A Laboratory Investigation Of The Moral Hazard Problem In An Agency Relationship," Supp., pp. 81-120.

Ransom, Charles R. "The Ex Ante Information Content Of Accounting Information Systems," Supp., pp. 124-139.

Olsen, Chris and J. Richard Dietrich. "Vertical Information Transfers: The Association Between Retailers' Sales Announcements And Suppliers' Security Returns," Supp., pp. 144-166.

Journal of Accounting Research
Volume 24, 1986

Antle, Rick and Abbie Smith. "An Empirical Investigation Of The Relative Performance Evaluation Of Corporate Executives," No. 1, pp. 1-39.

Bamber, Linda Smith. "The Information Content Of Annual Earnings Releases: A Trading Volume Approach," No. 1, pp. 40-56.

Frost, Peter A. and Hirokuni Tamura. "Accuracy Of Auxiliary Information Interval Estimation In Statistical Auditing," No. 1, pp. 57-75.

Jain, Prem C. "Analyses Of The Distribution Of Security Market Model Prediction Errors For Daily Returns Data," No. 1, pp. 76-96.

Palmrose, Zoe-Vonna. "Audit Fees And Auditor Size: Further Evidence," No. 1, pp. 97-110.

Roberts, Donald M. "Stratified Sampling Using A Stochastic Model," No. 1, pp. 111-126.

Rohrbach, Kermit John. "Monetary Unit Acceptance Sampling," No. 1, pp. 127-150.

Shriver, Keith A. "Further Evidence On The Marginal Gains In Accuracy Of Alternative Levels Of Specificity Of The Producer Price Indexes," No. 1, pp. 151-165.

Ayres, Frances L. "A Comment On Corporate Preferences For Foreign Currency Accounting Standards," No. 1, pp. 166-169.

Burgstahler, David and Eric W. Noreen. "Detecting Contemporaneous Security Market Reactions To A Sequence Of Related Events," No. 1, pp. 170-186.

Jain, Prem C. "Relation Beween Market Model Prediction Errors And Omitted Variables: A Methodological Note," No. 1, pp. 187-193.

Margheim, Loren L. "Further Evidence On External Auditors' Reliance On Internal Auditors," No. 1, pp. 194-205.

Ricks, William E. "Firm Size Effects And The Association Between Excess Returns And LIFO Tax Savings," No. 1, pp. 206-216.

Smieliauskas, Wally. "A Simulation Analysis Of The Power Characteristics Of Some Popular Estimators Under Different Risk And Materiality Levels," No. 1, pp. 217-230.

Young, Richard A. "A Note On 'Economically Optimal Performance Evaluation And Control Systems': The Optimality Of Two-Tailed Investigations," No. 1, pp. 231-240.

Brownell, Peter and Mark Hirst. "Reliance On Accounting Information, Budgetary Participation, And Task Uncertainty: Test Of A Three-Way Interaction," No. 2, pp. 241-249.

Demski, Joel S. and David E. M. Sappington. "Line-Item Reporting, Factor Acquisition, And Subcontracting," No. 2, pp. 250-269.

Frederick, David M. and Robert Libby. "Expertise And Auditors' Judgments Of Conjunctive Events," No. 2, pp. 270-290.

Pownall, Grace. "An Empirical Analysis Of The Regulation Of The Defense Contracting Industry: The Cost Accounting Standards Board," No. 2, pp. 291-315.

Sefcik, Stephan E. and Rex Thompson. "An Approach To Statistical Inference In Cross-Sectional Models With Security Abnormal Returns As Dependent Variable," No. 2, pp. 316-334.

Boritz, Jefim Efrim. "The Effect Of Research Method On Audit Planning And Review Judgments," No. 2, pp. 335-348.

Defeo, Victor J. "An Empirical Investigation Of The Speed Of The Market Reaction To Earnings Announcements," No. 2, pp. 349-363.

Tamura, Hirokuni and Peter A. Frost. "Tightening CAV (DUS) Bounds By Using A Parametric Model ," No. 2, pp. 364-371.

Abdel-khalik, A. Rashad, Paul R. Graul and James D. Newton. "Reporting Uncertainty And Assessment Of Risk: Replication And Extension In A Canadian Setting," No. 2, pp. 372-382.

Francis, Jere R. and Donald J. Stokes. "Audit Prices, Product Differentiation, And Scale Economies: Further Evidence From The Australian Market," No. 2, pp. 383-393.

Huss, H. Fenwick and Ramona L. Trader. "A Note On Optimal Sample Sizes In Compliance Tests Using A Formal Bayesian Decision Theoretic Approach For Finite And Infinite Populations," No. 2, pp. 394-399.

Murray, Dennis and Katherine Beal Frazier. "A Within-Subjects Test Of Expectancy Theory In A Public Accounting Environment," No. 2, pp. 400-404.

Palmrose, Zoe-Vonna. "The Effect Of Nonaudit Services On The Pricing Of Audit Services: Further Evidence," No. 2, pp. 405-411.

Robbins, Walter A. and Kenneth R. Austin. "Disclosure Quality In Governmental Financial Reports: An Assessment Of The Appropriateness Of A Compound Measure," No. 2, pp. 412-421.

Srivastava, Rajendra P. "Auditing Functions For Internal Control Systems With Interdependent Documents And Channels," No. 2, pp. 422-426.

Hoskin, Robert E., John S. Hughes and William E. Ricks. "Evidence On The Incremental Information Content Of Additional Firm Disclosures Made Concurrently With Earnings," Supp., pp. 1-32.

Lipe, Robert C. "The Information Contained In The Components Of Earnings," Supp., pp. 37-64.

Magliolo, Joseph. "Capital Market Analysis Of Reserve Recognition Accounting," Supp., pp. 69-108.

Rayburn, Judy. "The Association Of Operating Cash Flow And Accruals With Security Returns," Supp., pp. 112-133.

Stober, Thomas L. "The Incremental Information Content Of Financial Statement Disclosures: The Case Of LIFO Inventory Liquidations," Supp., pp. 138-160.

Wilson, G. Peter. "The Relative Information Content Of Accruals And Cash Flows: Combined Evidence At The Earnings Announcement And Annual Report Release Date," Supp., pp. 165-200.

Journal of Accounting Research
Volume 25, 1987

Bernard, Victor L. "Cross-Sectional Dependence And Problems In Inference In Market-Based Accounting Research," No. 1, pp. 1-48.

Brown, Lawrence D., Gordon D. Richardson and Steven J. Schwager. "An Information Interpretation Of Financial Analyst Superiority In Forecasting Earnings," No. 1, pp. 49-67.

Demski, Joel S. and David E. M. Sappington. "Delegated Expertise," No. 1, pp. 68-89.

Jennings, Robert. "Unsystematic Security Price Movements, Management Earnings Forecasts, And Revisions In Consensus Analyst Earnings Forecasts," No. 1, pp. 90-110.

Balachandran, Bala V. and Ram T. S. Ramakrishnan. "A Theory Of Audit Partnerships: Audit Firm Size And Fees," No. 1, pp. 111-126.

Lau, Amy Hing-Ling. "A Five-State Financial Distress Prediction Model," No. 1, pp. 127-138.

Wild, John J. "The Prediction Performance Of A Structural Model Of Accounting Numbers," No. 1, pp. 139-160.

Wilkerson, Jack E., Jr. "Selecting Experimental And Comparison Samples For Use In Studies Of Auditor Reporting Decisions," No. 1, pp. 161-167.

Atiase, Rowland Kwame. "Market Implications Of Predisclosure Information: Size And Exchange Effects," No. 1, pp. 168-176.

Amershi, Amin H. and Shyam Sunder. "Failure Of Stock Prices To Discipline Managers In A Rational Expectations Economy," No. 2, pp. 177-195.

Baginski, Stephen P. "Intraindustry Information Transfers Associated With Management Forecasts Of Earnings," No. 2, pp. 196-216.

Baiman, Stanley, John H. Evans, III and James Noel. "Optimal Contracts With A Utility-Maximizing Auditor," No. 2, pp. 217-244.

Thompson, Robert B., II, Chris Olsen and J. Richard Dietrich. "Attributes Of News About Firms: An Analysis Of Firm-Specific News Reported In The Wall Street Journal Index," No. 2, pp. 245-274.

Ashton, Robert H., John J. Willingham and Robert K. Elliott. "An Empirical Analysis Of Audit Delay," No. 2, pp. 275-292.

Baber, William R., Eugene H. Brooks and William E. Ricks. "An Empirical Investigation Of The Market For Audit Services In The Public Sector," No. 2, pp. 293-305.

Stevenson, Francis L. "New Evidence On LIFO Adoptions: The Effects Of More Precise Event Dates," No. 2, pp. 306-316.

Stone, Mary. "A Financing Explanation For Overfunded Pension Plan Terminations," No. 2, pp. 317-326.

Harper, Robert M., Jr., William G. Mister and Jerry R. Strawser. "The Impact Of New Pension Disclosure Rules On Perception Of Debt," No. 2, pp. 327-330.

Melumad, Nahum D. and Stefan Reichelstein. "Centralization Versus Delegation And The Value Of Communication," Supp., pp. 1-18.

Suh, Yoon S. "Collusion And Noncontrollable Cost Allocation," Supp., pp. 22-46.

Tehranian, Hassan, Nickolaos G. Travlos and James F. Waegelein. "Management Compensation Contracts And Merger-Induced Abnormal Returns," Supp., pp. 51-76.

Lambert, Richard A. and David F. Larcker. "An Analysis Of The Use Of Accounting And Market Measures Of Performance In Executive Compensation Contracts," Supp., pp. 85-125.

Evans, John H., III and James M. Patton. "Signaling And Monitoring In Public-Sector Accounting," Supp., pp. 130-158.

Lanen, William N. and Robert E. Verrecchia. "Operating Decisions And The Disclosure Of Management Accounting Information," Supp., pp. 165-189.

Journal of Accounting Research
Volume 26, 1988

Cready, William M. "Information Value And Investor Wealth: The Case Of Earnings Announcements." No. 1, pp. 1-27.

Dopuch, Nicholas and Morton Pincus. "Evidence On The Choice Of Inventory Accounting Methods: LIFO Versus FIFO," No. 1, pp. 28-59.

Shaw, Wayne H. "Measuring The Impact Of The Safe Harbor Lease Law On Security Prices," No. 1, pp. 60-81.

Holthausen, Robert W. and Robert E. Verrecchia. "The Effect Of Sequential Information Releases On The Variance Of Price Changes In An Intertemporal Multi-Asset Market," No. 1, pp. 82-106.

Lundholm, Russell J. "Price-Signal Relations In The Presence Of Correlated Public And Private Information," No. 1, pp. 107-118.

Noreen, Eric. "An Empirical Comparison Of Probit And OLS Regression Hypothesis Tests." No. 1, pp. 119-133.

Smith, David B. "An Investigation Of Securities And Exchange Commission Regulation Of Auditor Change Disclosures: The Case Of Accounting Series Release No. 165," No. 1, pp. 134-145.

Jung, Woon-Oh and Young K. Kwon. "Disclosure When The Market Is Unsure Of Information Endowment Of Managers," No. 1, pp. 146-153.

Suh, Yoon. "Noncontrollable Costs And Optimal Performance Measurement," No. 1, pp. 154-168.

Biddle, Gary C. and William E. Ricks. "Analyst Forecast Errors And Stock Price Behavior Near The Earnings Announcement Dates Of LIFO Adopters," No. 2, pp. 169-194.

Dye, Ronald A. "Earnings Management In An Overlapping Generations Model," No. 2, pp. 195-235.

Johnson, W. Bruce and Dan S. Dhaliwal. "LIFO Abandonment," No. 2, pp. 236-272.

Lys, Thomas and Konduru Sivaramakrishnan. "Earnings Expectations And Capital Restructuring: The Case Of Equity-For-Debt Swaps," No. 2, pp. 273-299.

Ronen, Joshua and Kashi R. Balachandran. "An Approach To Transfer Pricing Under Uncertainty," No. 2, pp. 300-314.

Butt, Jane L. "Frequency Judgments Is An Auditing-Related Task," No. 2, pp. 315-330.

Haw, In-Mu and Steven Lustgarten. "Evidence On Income Measurement Properties Of ASR No. 190 And SFAS No. 33 Data," No. 2, pp. 331-352.

Schachter, Barry. "Open Interest In Stock Options Around Quarterly Earnings Announcements," No. 2, pp. 353-372.

McNichols, Maureen and G. Peter Wilson. "Evidence Of Earnings Management From The Provision For Bad Debts," Supp., pp. 1-31.

Hughes, Patricia J. and Eduardo S. Schwartz. "The LIFO/FIFO Choice: An Asymmetric Information Approach," Supp., pp. 41-58.

Mendenhall, Richard R. and William D. Nichols. "Bad News And Differential Market Reactions To Announcements Of Earlier-Quarters Versus Fourth-Quarter Earnings," Supp., pp. 63-86.

Elliott, John A. and Wayne H. Shaw. "Write-Offs As Accounting Procedures To Manage Perceptions," Supp., pp. 91-119.

Trueman, Brett and Sheridan Titman. "An Explanation For Accounting Income Smoothing," Supp., pp. 127-139.

Abdel-Khalik, A. Rashad. "Incentives For Accruing Costs And Efficiency In Regulated Monopolies Subject To ROE Constraint," Supp., pp. 144-174.

JOURNAL OF COST ANALYSIS

Journal of Cost Analysis
Volume 1, 1984

Anthony, Robert N. "Cost Allocation," No. 1, pp. 5-15.

Lucas, William F. "Game Theory And Accounting," No. 1, pp. 17-32.

Green, John E. "Cost Forecasting And Control In The 1980's, From The Perspective Of A Defence Customer," No. 1, pp. 33-58.

Douglas, Evan J. "Pricing For Economic Objectives, Given Search And Price Adjustment Costs," No. 1, pp. 59-74.

Gitman, Lawrence J., Michael D. Joehnk and Peter W. Bacon. "Fundamentals Of Cash Management: Theory And Practice," No. 1, pp. 75-99.

Baseman, LeRoy T. "Cost Growth In The Acquisition Of Weapon Systems: Experience, Causes, Understanding Of And Positive Responses Thereto," No. 1, pp. 101-114.

Tersine, Richard J. and John S. Morris. "Materials Management: Futuristic Orientations," No. 1, pp. 115-130.

Osteryoung, Jerome S. and Gordon G. Abernethy. "Capital Budgeting: A Review," No. 1, pp. 131-142.

Humphries, Kenneth K. "The Cost Engineering Profession," No. 1, pp. 143-147.

McNichols, Gerald R. "The State-Of-The-Art Of Cost Uncertainty Analysis," No. 1, pp. 149-174.

Koenig, Michael E. D. "Cost Containment In Information Systems," No. 1, pp. 175-185.

Maletta, Thomas P. "The Interrelationship Of Taxes And Intercompany Pricing," No. 1, pp. 187-194.

Journal of Cost Analysis
Volume 2, 1985

Augustine, Norman R. "A Viewpoint Of Industry," No. 1, pp. 1-20.

Gilleece, Mary Ann. "DOD Acquisition Management," No. 1, pp. 21-29.

Dalio, Raymond T. "A Macro View Of 1985 And 1986," No. 1, pp. 31-41.

Ortner, Robert. "Outlook 1985," No. 1. pp. 43-46.

Hoaglund, William. "The Federal Budget: After The Election," No. 1. pp. 47-58.

Kirkpatrick, D. L. I. and P. G. Pugh. "Towards The Starship Enterprise - Are The Current Trends In Defence Unit Costs Inexorable?," No. 1, pp. 59-80.

Journal of Cost Analysis
Volume 3, 1986

Harmon, W. Ken, Kay M. Poston and Wayne J. Morse. "Improving Cost Recovery From Federal Grants And Contracts," No. 1, pp. 1-12.

Biery, Frederick P. "The Accuracy Of Military Cost And Schedule Forecasts," No. 1, pp. 13-23.

Truitt, Jack. "The Financial Theory Of The Firm: Capital Budgeting And Divisional Evaluation," No. 1, pp. 25-31.

Schneider, Arnold. "The Effect Of Internal Auditing On External Audit Work," No. 1, pp. 33-40.

Womer, Norman Keith and Ronald C. J. Marcotte. "Airframe Cost Estimation Using An Error Components Model," No. 1, pp. 41-62.

Robinson, Loudell Ellis and Leonard A. Robinson. "Increasing Small Business Profit By Use Of Management Accounting Techniques," No. 1, pp. 63-71.

Beltramo, Michael N. "Findings And Thoughts About Competition In The Procurement Of Weapon Systems," No. 2, pp. 1-11.

Sumners, Glenn E. "Cost Benefit Evaluation Criteria For Public Projects," No. 2, pp. 13-25.

Herbsman, Zohar. "The Bidding Volume Effect On Public Work Cost: A Case Study," No. 2, pp. 27-45.

Schneider, Arnold. "Indirect Cost Allocations And Cost-Plus Pricing Formulas," No. 2, pp. 47-57.

Gordon, Lawrence A., Jack Call and Haim Falk. "Pricing Objectives And Managerial Incentive Plans," No. 2, pp. 59-67.

Benke, Ralph L., Jr. and Ashton Bishop. "Transfer Pricing In An Oligopolistic Market," No. 2, pp. 69-81.

Journal of Cost Analysis
Volume 4, 1987

Gaither, Norman, Donald R. Fraser and William G. Mister. "Accounting For Inventory Carrying Costs," No. 1, pp. 1-6.

Baxendale, Sidney J. and Alan S. Levitan. "The Post Audit Review Of Equipment Replacement Decisions In Capital Intensive Companies," No. 1, pp. 7-15.

Hampton, John J. and Cecilia L. Wagner. "Target Budgeting: The Systematic Allocation Of Resources," No. 1, pp. 17-26.

Camm, Jeffrey D., Thomas R. Gulledge, Jr. and Norman Keith Womer. "Production Rate And Contractor Behavior," No. 1, pp. 27-37.

Kirkpatrick, D. L. I. "The Rising Cost Of Defence Equipment," No. 1, pp. 39-58.

Stump, Evin J. "Composite Learning Curves For Fast Estimating," No. 1. pp. 59-69.

Detweiler, John H., Sean O. Vessey and Arthur J. King. "A Model For Computing Shipyard Overhead," No. 1, pp. 71-93.

Journal of Cost Analysis
Volume 5, 1988

Coffey, Kenneth J. and Jack E. Faires. "Options For Military Retirement System Changes," No. 1, pp. 1-18.

Greenberg, Robert R. "Estimating Cost Functions With Autocorrelated Errors: A Time Series Approach," No. 1, pp. 19-33.

Thibadoux, Greg M., Nicholas Apostolou and Ira S. Greenberg. "The Development Of Not-For-Profit Hospital Cost Models," No. 1, pp. 35-48.

Hinonoto, Hirohide. "Business - Function Productivity And Information Systems," No. 1, pp. 49-61.

Truitt, Jack F. "Capital Rationing: An Annualized Approach," No. 1, pp. 63-75.

JOURNAL OF INFORMATION SYSTEMS

Journal of Information Systems
Volume 1, 1986-87

Grabski, Severin V. "Auditor Participation In Accounting Systems Design: Past Involvement And Future Challenges," No. 1, pp. 3-23.

Fields, Kent T., Heibatollah Sami and Glenn E. Sumners. "Quantification Of The Auditor's Evaluation Of Internal Control In Data Base Systems," No. 1, pp. 24-47.

Garsombke, H. Perrin and Richard H. Tabor. "Factors Explaining The Use Of EDP Audit Techniques," No. 1, pp. 48-66.

Harper, Robert M., Jr. "Internal Control Of Microcomputers In Local Area Networks," No. 1, pp. 67-80.

Fasci, Martha A. "EMAIS - Evaluation By Management Of Automated Information Systems," No. 1, pp. 83-101.

Sena, James A. and Lawrence Murphy Smith. "Designing And Implementing An Integrated Job Cost Accounting System," No. 1, pp. 102-112.

Maris, Terry L. and Robert E. Meier. "A Profile Of Management Consulting Firms," No. 1, pp. 113-117.

Wu, Frederick H. "Spreadsheet Software: A Tool For Teaching Managerial (Cost) And Financial Accounting," No. 1, pp. 121-136.

Kneer, Dan C. "Masters Degree Programs In Accounting Information Systems/EDP Auditing," No. 1, pp. 137-144.

Cherrington, J. Owen and Kevin D. Stocks. "Educating A Management Consultant," No. 1, pp. 145-153.

Weber, Ron. "Toward A Theory Of Artifacts: A Paradigmatic Base For Information Systems Research," No. 2, pp. 3-19.

Bailey, Andrew D. Jr., Karl Hackenbrack, Prabuddha De, and Jesse Dillard. "Artificial Intelligence. Cognitive Science. And Computational Modeling In Auditing Research: A Research Approach," No. 2, pp. 20-40.

Plumlee, R. David and Doug Snowball. "Auditing Your Own System: Some Findings And Implications," No. 2, pp. 41-49.

Golden, Charles W. and Mary R. Golden. "Beyond 'What If': A Risk-Oriented Capital Budgeting Model," No. 2, pp. 53-64.

Greer, Willis R., Jr. and Howard Rockness. "Management Decision Support Systems For A Medical Group Practice," No. 2, pp. 65-79.

Stocks, Kevin D. and Marshall B. Romney. "The Supply And Demand For IS/MAS Graduates," No. 2, pp. 83-100.

Campbell, Terry L. and LeRoy A. Franklin. "Trends And Projections Of IS/MAS Faculty And Courses," No. 2, pp. 101-113.

Burch, John G. "Information Systems: Is It Too Late To Join The Revolution?," No. 2, pp. 114-123.

Journal of Information Systems
Volume 2, 1987-88

Amer, Tarek, Andrew D. Bailey, Jr. and Prabuddha De. "A Review Of The Computer Information Systems Research Related To Accounting And Auditing," No. 1, pp. 3-28.

McCarthy, William E. "Accounting Information Systems: Research Directions And Perspective," No. 1, pp. 29-32.

Reneau, J. Hal and Severin V. Grabski. "A Review Of Research In Computer-Human Interaction And Individual Differences Within A Model For Research In Accounting Information Systems," No. 1, pp. 33-53.

Gal, Graham and Paul Steinbart. "Artificial Intelligence And Research In Accounting Information Systems: Opportunities And Issues," No. 1, pp. 54-62.

Stocks, Kevin D. and Lynn J. McKell. "Accounting Education And Management Advisory Services," No. 1, pp. 65-76.

Borthick, A. Faye. "Course Outline: Systems Issues And Policies," No. 1, pp. 77-80.

Wong-On-Wing, Bernard. "User Involvement In Systems Development: An Attributional Approach," No. 2, pp. 3-14.

Raghunathan, Bhanu and T. S. Raghunathan. "Impact Of Top Management Support On IS Planning," No. 2, pp. 15-23.

O'Leary, Daniel E. "Software Engineering And Research Issues In Accounting Information Systems," No. 2, pp. 24-38.

Liang, Ting-Peng. "Expert Systems As Decision Aids: Issues And Strategies," No. 2, pp. 41-50.

Fields, Kent T. "Assignment Of Audit Responsibility In Computer System Development Projects," No. 2, pp. 51-57.

Togo, Dennis F. "Risk Analysis For Accounting Models Utilizing An Advanced Electronic Spreadsheet Software," No. 2, pp. 61-72.

Levitan, Alan S. "Using A Data Base Management System In An Accounting Information Systems Course," No. 2, pp. 73-78.

Journal of Information Systems
Volume 3, 1988-89

Klersey, George F., Chen-En Ko and Thomas W. Lin. "Use Of A Multi-Attribute Utility Model In Computer System Selection," No. 1, pp. 1-9.

Borthick, A. Faye and James H. Scheiner. "Selection Of Small Business Computer Systems: Structuring A Multi-Criteria Approach," No. 1, pp. 10-29.

Harmon, W. Ken, Kay M. Poston and Paul E. Dascher. "Provision And Inadequacy Of Small Business Computer Controls: A Model And Empirical Test," No. 1, pp. 30-49.

Lederer, Albert L. and Louise Boyer Burky. "Understanding Top Management's Objectives: A Management Information Systems Concern," No. 1, pp. 50-66.

Harper, Robert M., Jr. "AHP Judgment Models Of EDP Auditors' Evaluations Of Internal Control For Local Area Networks," No. 1, pp. 67-86.

Reuber, A. Rebecca. "Opportunities For Accounting Information Systems Research From A Database Perspective," No. 1, pp. 87-103.

Trewin, Janet. "The Need And Opportunity For Field-Based Research In Accounting Information Systems," No. 1, pp. 104-118.

Grossman, Theodore and Shailendra Palvia. "The Design And Implementation Of A Multidimensional Retail Merchandising Information System," No. 1, pp. 119-131.

Raval, Vasant. "A Conceptual Model Of A Curriculum For Accountants," No. 1, pp. 132-152.

Davis, James R. and Robert A. Leitch. "Accounting Information System Courses And Curricula: New Perspectives," No. 1, pp. 153-166.

JOURNAL OF THE AMERICAN TAXATION ASSOCIATION

Journal of the American Taxation Association
Volume 1, 1979-80

Broden, Barry C. and Myron S. Lubell. "The Master's Degree In 'Taxation: An Assessment Of Its Growth And Future," No. 1, pp. 5-14.

Bagley, Ron N. and James W. Jenkins. "Capital Gain Yielding Bonds Produce Higher Than Expected After Tax Bond Yields," No. 1, pp. 15-24.

Jones, Sally Morrow. "The Net Economic Effect Of A 'Widow's Election' In The Community Property States," No. 1, pp. 25-32.

Seago, W. E. and Jerome S. Horvitz. "The Effects Of The Supreme Court's Thor Power Tool Decision On The Balance Of Tax Accounting Power," No. 2, pp. 5-9.

Arnold, Jerry L. and Earl C. Keller. "The Influence Of Accounting Rules On Tax Policy Objectives: An Empirical Investigation," No. 2, pp. 10-16.

Gaffney, Dennis J. and Cynthia D. Dailey. "Property Distributions Of Subchapter S Corporations: Regulation #1.373-1(e)(2) Allocations Not Always Necessary," No. 2, pp. 17-20.

Outslay, Edmund. "The Social Security System: An Evaluation Of Policy Alternatives," No. 2, pp. 21-33.

Burgess, Richard C. and Silvia A. Madeo. "A Simulation Study Of Tax Sheltered Retirement Plans," No. 2, pp. 34-41.

Strefeler, John M. and Jack P. Suyderhoud. "Piggybacking - A Free Ride With No Takers," No. 2, pp. 42-48.

Journal of the American Taxation Association
Volume 2, 1980-81

Lere, John C. "Optimal Depreciation Methods When Marginal Tax Rates Increase," No. 1, pp. 9-15.

Byars, Richard B. and Charles A. Nickerson. "Inter Vivos Gifts: An Anachromism?," No. 1, pp. 16-18.

Broden, Barry C. "Ethical Behavior In IRS Tax Practice," No. 1, pp. 19-28.

Schnee, Edward J. "An Alternative Final Examination - A Tax Debate," No. 1, pp. 29-32.

Boley, Richard and Edmund Outslay. "Conditions Under Which A Dependent Can File A Joint Return: Is The Current Confusion And Complexity Really Necessary?," No. 2, pp. 5-11.

Everett, John O. and David E. Keys. "Quantifying The Poisoning Effect Of Tax Preference Items On The Maximum Tax For A High-Bracket Taxpayer," No. 2, pp. 12-19.

Kramer, John L. and Sandra S. Kramer. "Section 1248(b): The Individual Limitation On Taxing Sales Of CFC Stock Offers Substantial Tax Savings," No. 2, pp. 20-31.

Journal of the American Taxation Association
Volume 3, 1981-82

Ford, Allen and John R. Robinson. "The Proper Charge To Capital: Jarvis And Its Implications," No. 1, pp. 5-10.

Black, Robert L. and Anne G. McMahon. "Graduate Tax Libraries: A Survey Of Their Content And Funding," No. 1, pp. 11-18.

Weiss, Jerold M. and Israel Blumenfrucht. "CPA Examination Tax Problems: An In-Depth Analysis," No. 1, pp. 19-25.

Wyndelts, Robert W. and Anna C. Fowler. "Installment Sales: Temporary Regulations Inconsistent With Judicial Definition Of Payment," No. 1, pp. 26-31.

Jordan, William F. "Capital Recovery Options Under The Economic Recovery Tax Act Of 1981: An Analysis Of Comparative Benefits," No. 2, pp. 5-14.

O'Neil, Cherie Jeanne. "The Targeted Jobs Credit: An Evaluation Of Its Impact On The Employment Decision Process," No. 2, pp. 15-22.

Englebrecht, Ted D. and Robert J. Rolfe. "Noncorporate Lessors Of Equipment Are Still Subject To Administrative And Judicial Scrutiny," No. 2, pp. 23-29.

Bruttomesso, Raymond I. and J. Edward Ketz. "Historical Cost And General Price Level Tax Rates In Seven Industries," No. 2, pp. 30-36.

Journal of the American Taxation Association
Volume 4, 1982-83

Stewart, Dave N. "Use Of LOGIT Analysis To Determine Employment Status For Tax Purposes," No. 1, pp. 5-12.

Byars, Richard B. and Charles A. Nickerson. "Charitable Remainder Trusts - Valuation Methods Yield Inconsistent Results," No. 1, pp. 13-18.

Englebrecht, Ted D. and Robert J. Rolfe. "An Empirical Inquiry Into The Determination Of Dividend Equivalence In Stock Redemptions," No. 1, pp. 19-25.

Schnee, Edward J. and William R. Edwards. "New Preparer Rules: More Or Less Penalty?," No. 1, pp. 26-32.

White, Debra M. and James W. Giese. "Federal Tax Clinic Practice For Accounting Students," No. 1, pp. 33-35.

O'Brien, James P. and William Raabe, Jr. "The Charitable Lead Trust: A Neglected Tax Planning Technique," No. 2, pp. 5-13.

Parker, James E. and Thomas P. Howard. "Leasing As A Means Of Shifting Tax Savings To Non-Taxable Organizations," No. 2, pp. 14-22.

Beranek, William and Edward B. Selby, Jr. "Delayed Depreciation As A Tax Shield," No. 2, pp. 23-34.

O'Neil, Cherie J., Donald V. Saftner and Manson P. Dillaway. "Premature Withdrawals From Individual Retirement Accounts: A Breakeven Analysis," No. 2, pp. 35-43.

Lancaster, Joe and Ted D. Englebrecht. "An Analysis Of The Availability Of Percentage Depletion For Lease Bonuses And Advance Royalties," No. 2, pp. 44-51.

Journal of the American Taxation Association
Volume 5, 1983-84

Robison, Jack. "Tax Court Classification Of Activities Not Engaged In For Profit: Some Empirical Evidence," No. 1, pp. 7-22.

Burns, Jane O. and S. Michael Groomer. "An Analysis Of Tax Court Decisions That Assess The Profit Motive Of Farming-Oriented Operations," No. 1, pp. 23-39.

Izard, C. Douglass and John D. McKinney. "The Certification Of Tax Specialists: Some Empirical Results," No. 1, pp. 40-48.

Boley, Richard and Edmund Outslay. "Doctoral Programs With A Concentration In Taxation: An Examination Of Recent Trends," No. 1, pp. 49-59.

Norton, Curtis L. and John O. Everett. "An Extension Of Jordan's Analysis Of Section 179 Property," No. 1, pp. 60-62.

Jordan, William F. "Capital Recovery Options: A Response And A Note On Changes Resulting From The Tax Equity And Fiscal Responsibility Act Of 1982 (TEFRA)," No. 1, pp. 63-68.

Taylor, Ronald L. and Robert W. Ingram. "WORDS: A New Approach To Determining The Factors Affecting Tax Court Decisions Involving Real Estate Transactions," No. 2, pp. 7-16.

Kramer, Sandra S. "Valuation Of Blocks Of Stock: A Number Of Unresolved Issues Still Remain," No. 2, pp. 17-26.

Johnson, Steven B. "An Economic Perspective On The Certification Of Specialists In Tax Accounting," No. 2, pp. 27-39.

Madeo, Laurence A. and Silvia A. Madeo. "The Equity And Motivating Effects Of The Maximum Tax," No. 2, pp. 40-49.

Gallagher, Michael G. "GCMs, TMs, And AODs - The 'Working Law' Of The Internal Revenue Service," No. 2, pp. 50-59.

Morris, Michael H. and William D. Nichols. "The Election To Capitalize Carrying Charges Following ERTA And TEFRA," No. 2, pp. 60-67.

Gately, Mary Sue. "A Guide To The Tax Treatment Of Corporate Liquidations," No. 2, pp. 68-74.

Jordan, William F. and Rodger G. Holland. "An Empirical Inquiry Into The Determination Of Dividend Equivalence In Stock Redemptions: A Comment," No. 2, pp. 75-80.

Englebrecht, Ted D. and Robert J. Rolfe. "An Empirical Inquiry Into The Determination Of Dividend Equivalence In Stock Redemptions: A Reply," No. 2, pp. 81-84.

Journal of the American Taxation Association
Volume 6, 1984-85

Porcano, Thomas M. "The Perceived Effects Of Tax Policy On Corporate Investment Intentions," No. 1, pp. 7-19.

Enis, Charles R. and Darryl L. Craig. "The Redistribution Of The Income Tax Burden Under A True Flat Tax Structure," No. 1, pp. 20-35.

Jamison, Robert W. and Steven C. Dilley. "Subchapter S In Transition," No. 1, pp. 36-47.

Schnee, Edward J. and Charles W. Caldwell. "Retirement Planning Under Section 403(b)(7): Advantages And Limitations," No. 1, pp. 48-56.

Blumenfrucht, Israel. "Taxation Requirements For The CPA Examination And The Content Of Undergraduate Accounting Curricula," No. 1, pp. 57-65.

Raabe, William A., Kathleen C. Stevens and William P. Stevens. "Tax Textbook Readability: An Application Of The Cloze Method," No. 1, pp. 66-73.

Simonds, Richard R. "Comment On 'Premature Withdrawals From Individual Retirement Accounts: A Breakeven Analysis'," No. 1, pp. 74-76.

O'Neil, Cherie J., Donald V. Saftner and M. Pete Dillaway. "Reply To 'Comment On Premature Withdrawals From Individual Retirement Accounts: A Breakeven Analysis'," No. 1, pp. 77-80.

Jackson, Betty R. and Sally M. Jones. "Salience Of Tax Evasion Penalties Versus Detection Risk," No. 2, pp. 7-17.

Porcano, Judy L. and Thomas M. Porcano. "Incorporating Probability Analysis In Taxpayer Appeal Decisions," No. 2, pp. 18-36.

Bathke, Allen W., Jr., Richard L. Rogers and Jerrold J. Stern. "The Security Market Reaction To Tax Legislation As Reflected In Bond Price Adjustments," No. 2, pp. 37-49.

Ostrowski, Barbara A. "Alternate Indexing Schemes For Nonbusiness Income Taxation: Distributional And Revenue Effects," No. 2, pp. 50-62.

Streer, Paul J. "Obtaining And Preserving Tax-Exempt Status Under Section 501(c)(3): Judicially Developed Factors For Detecting The Presence Of Substantial Nonexempt Activities," No. 2, pp. 63-75.

Brighton, Gerald D. and Robert H. Michaelsen. "Profile Of Tax Dissertations In Accounting: 1967-1984," No. 2, pp. 76-91.

Journal of the American Taxation Association
Volume 7, 1985-86

Pollard, William B. and Ronald M. Copeland. "Evaluating The Robustness Of Multivariate Tax Models To Errors: A Section 162(a)(2) Illustration," No. 1, pp. 7-18.

Milliron, Valerie C. "An Analysis Of The Relationship Between Tax Equity And Tax Complexity," No. 1, pp. 19-33.

Rose, Clarence C. and Cherie J. O'Neil. "The Viewed Importance Of Investment Tax Incentives By Virginia Decision Makers," No. 1, pp. 34-43.

Weber, Richard P. "Allocations Of Consolidated Taxes - Fiction In Financial Statements," No. 1, pp. 44-51.

Crum, Robert P. "Value-Added Tax Collection Alternatives: Their Revenue, Cash Flow, and Micro Tax Policy Effects," No. 1, pp. 52-72.

Reeder, Janis R. and Karen A. Fortin. "Subchapter S In Transition: A Comment," No. 1, pp. 73-75.

Bravenec, Lorence L. "Subchapter S In Transition: A Comment," No. 1, pp. 76-79.

Jamison, Robert W. and Steven C. Dilley. "Subchapter S In Transition: A Reply And Extension," No. 1, pp. 80-88.

McGill, Gary A. and John T. Sennetti. "The Capital Gains Timing Decision: A Quantitative Analysis," No. 2, pp. 7-16.

Porcano, Thomas M. "Corporate Tax Rates: Progressive, Proportional, Or Regressive," No. 2, pp. 17-31.

Parker, James E. "Refunding Non-Callable Bonds: A Tax-Oriented Decision Model," No. 2, pp. 32-47.

Outslay, Edmund and Richard P. Weber. "Minimizing The Tax Cost Of Faculty Research Grants," No. 2, pp. 48-59.

Wiggins, Casper E., D. Larry Crumbley and Nicholas G. Apostolou. "A Critical Analysis Of The Marriage Tax Penalty," No. 2, pp. 60-75.

Hreha, Karen S., Robert F. Sharp and Eugene Willis. "An Analysis Of Two Proposed Cost Recovery Systems," No. 2, pp. 76-84.

Journal of the American Taxation Association
Volume 8, 1986-87

Hreha, Karen S. and Peter A. Silhan. "An Empirical Analysis Of Unitary Apportionment," No. 1, pp. 7-18.

Schmidt, Dennis R. "Apportionment Of Multijurisdictional Corporate Income," No. 1, pp. 19-34.

Collins, Julie H. and John L. Kramer. "An Examination Of The Employer's Pension Plan Choice: Integrated Vs. Non-integrated Plans," No. 1, pp. 35-48.

Carruth, J. Harvey, Harold B. Whitehead and Kenneth E. Anderson. "Maximizing Contributions To Retirement And Deferred Compensation Plans Under Sections 403(b), 401(k), And 457: A Linear Programming Approach," No. 1, pp. 49-72.

Taylor, Martin E. and Caroline D. Stobel. "CPA's Responsibility To Notify Clients Of Tax Law Revisions," No. 1, pp. 73-79.

Boley, Richard and Patrick J. Wilkie. "Practitioners' Views Of The Common Body Of Tax Knowledge For Persons Entering Public Accounting," No. 1, pp. 80-97.

Michaelsen, Robert and William F. Messier, Jr. "Expert Systems In Taxation," No. 2, pp. 7-21.

Long, Susan B. and Judyth A. Swingen. "An Approach To The Measurement Of Tax Law Complexity," No. 2, pp. 22-36.

Streuling, G. Fred, James H. Boyd and Kenneth H. Heller. "Interrelationships Of Sections 731, 736, And 751: A Worksheet Approach," No. 2, pp. 37-49.

Duncan, William A. and Michael A. O'Dell. "Tax Policy And Erroneous Information: An Analysis Of The Interaction Of Inflation, Indexation, And Income Averaging," No. 2, pp. 50-62.

Karlinsky, Stewart S. and Blake Pintar. "Individual Tax Planning Software: A Critical Analysis," No. 2, pp. 63-79.

Journal of the American Taxation Association
Volume 9, 1987-88

Porcano, Thomas M. "Government Tax Incentives And Fixed Asset Acquisitions: A Comparative Study Of Four Industrial Countries," No. 1, pp. 7-23.

Karlinsky, Stewart S. and Bruce S. Koch. "Impact Of Tax Law Complexity On Professionals," No. 1, pp. 24-34.

Michaelsen, Robert H. "An Expert System For Selecting Tax Shelters," No. 1, pp. 35-47.

Larkins, Earnest R. "Professors Who Teach Outside The United States: Tax Planning And Policy Analysis," No. 1, pp. 48-74.

Milani, Ken and Kevin M. Misiewicz. "Enhancing The Tax Learning Experience: Identifying And Using Tax Cases In Introductory Courses," No. 1, pp. 75-85.

Crumbley, D. Larry. "The Evolution Of The ATA: From Orphans, To Outlaws, To Respectability," No. 1, pp. 86-100.

Stiglitz, Joseph E. and Mark A. Wolfson. "Taxation, Information, And Economic Organization," No. 2, pp. 7-18.

Anderson, John C. and Barbara R. McIntosh. "An Analysis Of The Tax And Incentive Considerations Involved In Employee Leasing," No. 2, pp. 19-30.

Helleloid, Richard T. "Hindsight Judgments About Taxpayers' Expectations," No. 2, pp. 31-46.

Hite, Peggy A. "The Effect Of Peer Reporting Behavior On Taxpayer Compliance," No. 2, pp. 47-64.

Manegold, James G. and Stewart S. Karlinsky. "The Security Market Impact Of A Tax Law Change: Possessions Corporation Revisions," No. 2, pp. 65-83.

Milliron, Valerie C. and Daniel R. Toy. "Tax Compliance: An Investigation Of Key Features," No. 2, pp. 84-104.

Gramlich, Jeffrey D., Kenneth F. Abramowicz and James E. Parker. "Refunding Non-Callable Bonds: An Update Of A Tax-Oriented Decision Model In Light Of The Tax Reform Act Of 1986," No. 2, pp. 105-110.

Journal of the American Taxation Association
Volume 10, 1988-89

Anderson, Kenneth E. "A Horizontal Equity Analysis Of The Minimum Tax Provisions: 1976-1986 Tax Acts," No. 1, pp. 7-25.

Chang, Otto H. and Thomas M. McCarty. "Evidence On Judgment Involving The Determination Of Substantial Authority: Tax Practitioners Versus Students," No. 1, pp. 26-39.

Davis, Jon S. and Charles W. Swenson. "The Role Of Experimental Economics In Tax Policy Research," No. 1, pp. 40-59.

Limberg, Stephen T. and Sally Morrow Jones. "An Analysis Of 'Substantiality' Under The Section 704(b) Final Regulations," No. 1, pp. 60-74.

Wilkie, Patrick J. "Corporate Average Effective Tax Rates And Inferences About Relative Tax Preferences," No. 1, pp. 75-88.

Hreha, Karen S. and Peter A. Silhan. "Tax Base Differences Between Worldwide And Water's Edge Methods Of Unitary Taxation," No. 1, pp. 89-98.

DeMoville, Wig. "Understanding Changes In Tax Laws With Variance Analysis," No. 1, pp. 99-103.

MANAGEMENT ACCOUNTING

And Breakeven Analysis - A Different Approach," No. 2, pp. 3-15.
Clason, Donald E. "Clerical Systems And Work Simplification In The Computer Age," No. 2, pp. 19-28.
Bene, Kalman J. "Clerical Work Measurement," No. 2, pp. 29-34.
Evans, William P. and Ronald L. Bosworth. "Computerized Information System (COINS)," No. 2, pp. 36-44.
Current, Kathryn. "Hedging As An Aid In Inventory Cost Control," No. 2, pp. 47-51.
Price, William S., Jr. and Edward J. Neppl. "Automated Inventory Control," No. 2, pp. 52-58.
Howard, David C. "Equivalent Unit Costing (EUCO)," No. 2, pp. 59-63.
Partridge, R. William. "Will The Real Variance, Please, Stand Up," No. 3, pp. 3-9.
Finney, Frederick D. "Pricing Interdivisional Transfers," No. 3, pp. 10-18.
Ott, George W. "Simplified CPM For Contractors," No. 3, pp. 21-25.
Bowen, Richard L., Jr. "Application Of Margin Rates To Credit Analysis," No. 3, pp. 26-31.
Scally, Jerome V. "Successful Management In Transportation Planning And Control," No. 3, pp. 32-45.
Corcoran, A. Wayne. "A Matrix Approach To Process Cost Reporting," No. 3, pp. 48-54.
Hartley, James N. "Problems Of Consistency In Foreign Accounting," No. 3, pp. 55-59.
Elliott, C. Willard. "Quasi-Reorganization Of An International Corporation In The Event Of Currency Devaluation," No. 3, pp. 60-63.
Secrest, Fred G. "From Bookkeeping To Decision Theory," No. 4, pp. 3-9.
Clark, John H. "Financial Control Of Ford Manufacturing Plants," No. 4, pp. 10-15.
Norgaard, Richard L. and Richard H. Pettway. "Evaluating Average Ratios Used In Capital Budgeting," No. 4, pp. 16-20.
Myers, Ronald B. "Performance Review Of Capital Expenditures," No. 4, pp. 21-26.
Peirce, Richard F. "A Resource System For Property Administration," No. 4, pp. 27-33.
Kozik, Eugene. "Computer Augmentation Of Managerial Reasoning," No. 4, pp. 35-43.
Onsi, Mohamed. "Linear Programming: An Accounting Information Model," No. 4, pp. 46-55.
De Francesco, J. Donald. "The Accounting Side Of The Profit-Center Organization," No. 4, pp. 56-60.
Wormley, James T. "Ensuring The Profit Contribution Of A Corporate Data Processing Department," No. 5, pp. 3-12.
Manthey, Philip S. "Profit Planning Using Forecast Schedules," No. 5, pp. 13-30.
Levine, Alan H. "Forecasting Techniques," No. 5, pp. 31-36.
Wright, Wilmer. "Use Of Standard Direct Costing," No. 5, pp. 39-46.
Finnell, Jack C., Leland G. Ayer and Frank B. Harris. "Full Costing In The Oil And Gas Producing Industry," No. 5, pp. 47-52.
Bunch, Robert G. "The Effect Of Payment Terms On Economic Order Quantity Determination," No. 5, pp. 53-63.
Keller, I. Wayne. "The Accountant's Role In The Expanding International Economy," No. 6, pp. 3-7.
Schneider, Herman M. and Peter H. Lengemann. "Optimal Dividend Distribution By German Companies To Their U.S. Parent Corporations," No. 6, pp. 13-20.
Chaump, Donald G. "Reducing Overhead Through The Task-Activity Cycle Ratio Matrix Analysis," No. 6, pp. 23-32.
Erickson, Vernon E. "Mortgage Loan Accounting," No. 6, pp. 36-40.
Barnecut, Leo J., Jr. "Contractor Performance Measurement," No. 6, pp. 43-48.
Morse, Ellsworth H., Jr. "Management Accounting In The Federal Government," No. 6, pp. 55-59.
Lundquist, William H. "Accountants Face New Challenges," No. 7, pp. 3-9.
Aked, H. John. "Control Of Fixed Costs In Relation To Volume," No. 7, pp. 12-20.
Lowell, Samuel B. "Pricing Policies And Methods," No. 7, pp. 23-28.
Kelly, Robert R. "Sales And Use Taxation In Interstate Commerce," No. 7, pp. 29-35.
Christensen, Howard A. "Small Business And Its Accountants: A Case Report," No. 7, pp. 41-45.
Brown, Robert O. "Small Business Controls: The Case A Job Shop," No. 7, pp. 51-54.
Baughman, Gene K. "Economical Processing Of Small Orders," No. 7, pp. 55-58.
Tyran, Michael R. "Management Information Technology In The Space Age," No. 8, pp. 3-13.
Griffin, V. Earl. "Systems Work Below The Corporate Level," No. 8, pp. 14-20.
Furlong, William L. "Risk Income And Alternative Income Concepts," No. 8, pp. 25-29.
Rowlands, John J. "Formula Elements Of Incentive Contracts," No. 8, pp. 30-37.
Gilroy, Walter M. "Investment Control In Fixed Price Defense Contracting," No. 8, pp. 38-42.
Robertson, Leon H. and Tommy P. Hall. "Network Analysis And Financial Planning," No. 8, pp. 43-46.
Ross, Wilbur R. "Accounting Aspects Of PERT/Cost," No. 8, pp. 47-51.
Silvern, David H. and Desmond J. Toal. "EDP - Choosing A Partner," No. 8, pp. 57-60.
Horngren, Charles T. "Motivation And Coordination In Management Control Systems," No. 9, pp. 3-7.

Partridge, R. William. "A Plea For More Standards In Cost Accounting," No. 9, pp. 8-15.
Bonchonsky, Joseph P. "Cost Control For Program Managers," No. 9, pp. 16-24.
Duro, Richard A. "A System Of Research And Development Cost Control," No. 9, pp. 25-30.
Blake, Avery F., Jr. "Unsophisticated Automation Can Break The Paperwork Bottleneck," No. 9, pp. 31-34.
Woolf, Jack J. "A Management Action Reporting System (MARS)," No. 9, pp. 35-40.
Johnson, Hobart S. "Internal Auditing In The Goal Oriented Firm," No. 9, pp. 41-48.
Manthey, Philip S. "An Effective Inventory Control Procedure," No. 9, pp. 53-62.
Beyer, Robert. "Management Information Systems: Who'll Be In Charge?," No. 10, pp. 3-8.
Lee, Richard W. "Top Management's Challenge To The Accountant," No. 10, pp. 9-13.
Mead, George C. "Certification In Management Accounting: Should We Jump On The British Bandwagon?," No. 10, pp. 16-20.
Keller, I. Wayne. "Controlling Contribution," No. 10, pp. 21-32.
Hoverland, H. Arthur and Wilma D. Stricklin. "Management And Accounting Concepts Of Control," No. 10, pp. 33-37.
Ferrara, William L. "Responsibility Reporting Vs. Direct Costing - Is There A Conflict?," No. 10, pp. 43-54.
Sautter, William L. "Product Warranty," No. 10, pp. 55-58.
Grace, William E. "Clerical Work Effectiveness Program - How To Get The Facts," No. 10, pp. 59-62.
Marple, Raymond P. "Management Accounting Is Coming Of Age," No. 11, pp. 3-16.
Shearer, Leonard L. "Direct Costing For Sales Pricing And Profit Planning," No. 11, pp. 17-23.
Cooke, Robert B. "Responsibility Reporting Of Return On Investment," No. 11, pp. 24-29.
Neuhauser, William E. and Dallas H. Bradford. "Should You File A Consolidated Return - Revisited," No. 11, pp. 33-42.
Lowengrub, Jerome. "Internal Reporting For Motion Picture Distributors," No. 11, pp. 45-50.
Eigen, Martin M. "The Share Of Market: A Focal Point For Financial Reporting," No. 11, pp. 51-56.
Eiteman, Dean S. "A Closer Look At Cost Of Capital," No. 11. pp. 57-63.
Nielsen, Oswald. "Canons For Line Of Business Reporting," No. 12, pp. 3-7.
Spiegel, Reed S. "Information Needs For Competing Companies," No. 12, pp. 8-12.
Shultis, Robert L. "Are There Real-Time Financial Statements In Your Future?," No. 12, pp. 13-22.
Hedges, Paul W. "Use Of A Data Processing Service Bureau - A Case Study," No. 12, pp. 23-26.
McIlwain, Arnold P. "Utilizing EDP For Stock Material Inventory Transactions," No. 12, pp. 28-34.
Bill, Robert W., James H. Harrison and Harry R. Maly. "An EDP System For Stores Inventory Control," No. 12, pp. 35-42.
Youell, Harold D. "Inventory Management Through Inventory Ratios," No. 12, pp. 43-46.
Smith, William N. and G. F. Reichenbach. "Maintenance Material Inventory Control," No. 12, pp. 49-53.
Michael, John. "Trading Stamp Accounting," No. 12, pp. 54-61.

Management Accounting
Volume 49, 1967-68

Moles, William A. "Selling The Accounting Services," No. 1, pp. 3-6.
Corcoran, A. Wayne and Ching-Wen Kwang. "Set Theory And Accounting Analysis," No. 1, pp. 7-17.
Hippel, James H. "An Economic Cost Curve Analysis," No. 1, pp. 21-28.
Schubert, Richard F. "Systems Documentation," No. 1, pp. 29-42.
Harrelson, Fred A., Jr. "Document Your Data Processing System," No. 1, pp. 43-49.
Krafft, J. Edward. "A Payback Approach To An Integrated Business System," No. 1, pp. 50-54.
Riley, William J. "Financial Responsibility And Sales Prices," No. 1, pp. 55-62.
Shopoff, Robert W. and William R. Jack. "Organizing, Staffing And Operating The Information Services Function," No. 2, pp. 3-8.
Demski, Joel S. "Analyzing The Effectiveness Of The Traditional Standard Cost Variance Model," No. 2, pp. 9-19.
Juers, Donald A. "Statistical Significance Of Accounting Variances," No. 2, pp. 20-25.
Wilkins, Edwin N. "Forecasting Cash Flow: Some Problems And Some Applications," No. 2, pp. 26-30.
Carson, John R. "Business Games: A Technique For Teaching Decision-Making," No. 2, pp. 31-35.
McLain, Robert K. "Divisional Profit Measurement Using Return On Capital Employed," No. 2, pp. 36-39.
Hromish, Michael. "Maintenance Cost Data For Analysis And Control," No. 2, pp. 40-46.
Register, Levon C. "The Influence Of Taxes On Financial Planning," No. 2, pp. 47-53.
Irish, Robert R. "Management Accounting Developments In The Army Industrial Fund," No. 2, pp. 54-59.
Joplin, Bruce. "Can The Accountant Manage EDP?," No. 3, pp. 3-7.
Gallantier, Alexander J. "Accounting Reports On Research

Management Accounting
Volume 50, 1968-69

Management Accounting
Volume 53, 1971-72

Management Accounting
Volume 54, 1972-73

Management Accounting
Volume 55, 1973-74

Management Accounting
Volume 56, 1974-75

Management Accounting
Volume 57, 1975-76

pp. 41-44.

Pond, Jonathan D. "Capitalizing Leased Assets," No. 7, pp. 45-47.

Gunderson, Russell H. "Capitalization Of Computer Systems Costs," No. 7, pp. 48-50.

Rockness, Howard O., John D. Bazley and Loren A. Nikolai. "Variance Analysis For Pollution Control," No. 7, pp. 51-54.

Weiser, Herbert J. "A Movement Toward Fair And Meaningful Reporting," No. 8, pp. 13-16.

Harris, John K. and Jack L. Krogstad. "Assessing Progress Of The CMA Program," No. 8, pp. 17-23.

Marshall, Juanita. "The Full Disclosure Problem," No. 8, pp. 24-26.

Boone, Alan L. "Wouldn't It Be Nice If - ," No. 8, pp. 27-28.

Spiceland, J. D. and H. C. Zaunbrecher. "The Usefulness Of Human Resource Accounting In Personnel Selection," No. 8, pp. 29-30.

Welling, P. "Introducing The MISA," No. 8, pp. 31-33.

Li, David H. "Homogeneity And Variance Allocation," No. 8, pp. 34-40.

Joehnk, Michael D. and George R. McGrail. "Benefit-Cost Ratios For Family Practice Residency Centers," No. 8, pp. 41-46.

Wycoff, David W. "Profit Determinants," No. 8, pp. 47-48.

Whitt, John D. "Multinationals In Latin America: An Accent On Control," No. 8, pp. 49-50.

Morgan, Lee L. "Business Ethics Start With The Individual," No. 9, pp. 11-14.

Kanaga, William S. "Inflation, Instability And Accounting," No. 9, pp. 15-18.

Lambert, Philip E. "Accrediting Specialties In Public Accounting - A Logical Step," No. 9, pp. 19-22.

Hartman, Bart P., David Laxton and William Walvoord. "A Look At Employee Stock Ownership Plans As Financing Tools," No. 9, pp. 23-28.

Samuelson, Richard A. "Estimating The Replacement Cost Of Inventories And Cost Of Sales," No. 9, pp. 29-32.

Tsay, Jeffrey J. "Human Resource Accounting: A Need For Relevance," No. 9, pp. 33-36.

Lampe, James C. "Electronic Funds Transfer Systems," No. 9, pp. 37-41.

Buchman, Thomas A. and Larry A. Friedman. "Accounting For Certain Marketable Securities," No. 9, pp. 42-44.

Frey, Karen M. "Management Of Foreign Exchange Risk With Forward Contracts," No. 9, pp. 45-48.

Sharp, Norman and Ken Milani. "Hospital Budgeting," No. 9, pp. 49-52.

Hilliard, Jimmy E. and Robert A. Leitch. "Breakeven Analysis Of Alternatives Under Uncertainty," No. 9, pp. 53-57.

Hanson, Walter E. "Big Brother And The Big Eight," No. 10, pp. 15-19.

Donachie, Robert J. "Living With Financial Accounting Standards," No. 10, pp. 20-22.

Howell, Cloyd. "CASB: An Assessment," No. 10, pp. 23-26.

Brandes, James L. "Identifying And Recording Environmental Plant Costs," No. 10, pp. 27-31.

Whittington, Ray. "Social Accounting And The Tragedy Of The Commons," No. 10, pp. 32-34.

Puerta, Ralph. "Discount Rates: Adjusted For Time And Risk," No. 10, pp. 35-40.

Hendricks, James A. "Analysis Of Risk In Capital Budgeting," No. 10, pp. 41-44.

Ryan, Robert J., Jr. "Leveraged Leasing," No. 10, pp. 45-46.

Kim, Suk Hi. "An Integer Programming Model For Direct Foreign Investment Projects," No. 10, pp. 47-50.

Cauthorn, L. Terry. "Whatever Happened To Social Accountants?," No. 10, pp. 55-60.

Boileau, O. C. "Program Management In The Space Age," No. 11, pp. 13-16.

Herzog, Raymond H. "The Numbers Game: What Industry Accountants Can Do For Society," No. 11, pp. 17-19.

Blinn, Mary M. "Detecting Management Fraud: Putting One Past The Auditors?," No. 11, pp. 20-22.

Hansen, David T. "Municipal Accounting And Disclosure," No. 11, pp. 23-24.

Moscove, Stephen A. "Accountants' Legal Liability," No. 11, pp. 25-26.

Davis, James R. "Shared Services: Survival For The Small Business?," No. 11, pp. 27-30.

Cooper, F. Jaimie. "POS Devices: You Don't Have To Be A Giant," No. 11, pp. 31-34.

Alou, Susan and Roger A. Roemmich. "Responsibility Accounting For Banks," No. 11, pp. 35-38.

Morgan, Alan M. "Computer Selection Processes," No. 11, pp. 39-42.

Kasper, Larry J. "Evaluating The Cost Of Financial Leases," No. 11, pp. 43-51.

Grabowski, Roger J. and Lawrence B. Gooch. "Implementing Replacement Cost Disclosure Requirements," No. 12, pp. 13-20.

Choi, Frederick D. S. "Foreign Inflation And Management Decisions," No. 12, pp. 21-27.

Banks, Ina D. "Internal Control Of On-Line And Real-Time Computer Systems," No. 12, pp. 28-30.

Anthony, Paul. "Goodbye Goodwill - Hello Share Of The Market," No. 12, pp. 31-40.

Zolfo, Frank J. and Barry N. Cooper. "Considering The LIFO Election," No. 12, pp. 41-43.

Treacy, John E. "For Direct Costing In The Steel Industry," No. 12, pp. 44-46.

Khtaian, George A. "Strategic Financial Models For A Utility," No. 12, pp. 47-51.

Management Accounting
Volume 59, 1977-78

De Moville, Wig. "Capital Budgeting In Municipalities," No. 1, pp. 17-20.

Kempster, John H. "The Financial Disclosure Problem Of Municipalities," No. 1, pp. 21-23.

Bancroft, D. Stuart. "Financial Management Of A Public School District," No. 1, pp. 24-28.

Giacoletti, Robert R. "The Auditor's Liability For Fraud," No. 1, pp. 29-32.

Bremser, Wayne G. "Reporting On Current Replacement Costs," No. 1, pp. 33-39.

Pillin, Dominic A. "Credit By Exception: A Cash Management Tool," No. 1, pp. 40-42.

McCafferty, Frank. "Basic Elements Of Risk Management," No. 1, pp. 43-45.

Gott, Stanley W. "Can I Save Taxes By Incorporating My Practice?," No. 1, pp. 46-52.

Hampel, Robert E. "Pricing Policies And Profitability," No. 1, pp. 53-56.

McCue, William M. "Hedging Soybeans In The Commodities Market," No. 1, pp. 57-60.

Corbin, Donald A. "SEC Replacement Costs: Suggestions For Full Disclosure," No. 2, pp. 11-18.

Slater, Nathaniel. "Matching Future Cash Payouts To Current Revenue," No. 2, pp. 19-20.

Paul, Terrance D. "Employer-Sponsored Life Insurance: What It Really Costs," No. 2, pp. 21-29.

Worthington, James S. "And Now We Have...," No. 2, pp. 30-32.

Jordan, Raymond B. "Planning, Organizing and Conducting The Annual Physical Inventory," No. 2, pp. 33-36.

Adams, John C. "Two Years On The Road," No. 2, pp. 37-40.

Wyman, Harold E. and J. Edgar McFarland. "Financial Investments And The True Rate Of Return," No. 2, pp. 41-45.

Alexion, John C. "Separate Schools Of Accountancy: Are They Necessary?," No. 3, pp. 11-13.

Bremser, Wayne G., Vincent C. Brenner and Paul E. Dascher. "Schools Of Professional Accountancy: The Management Accountant's View," No. 3, pp. 14-16.

Kimes, J. D. "Handling Stress In The Accounting Profession," No. 3, pp. 17-23.

Malmstrom, Duane. "Accommodating Exchange Rate Fluctuations In Intercompany Pricing And Invoicing," No. 3, pp. 24-28.

Pleak, Ruth E. "An Analysis Of The FASB's Treatment Of Foreign Currency Translation," No. 3, pp. 29-32.

Sibley, A. Michael and Gerald L. Waddle. "The Liquidation Alternative In Business Planning," No. 3, pp. 33-35.

Krupp, James A. G. "Obsolescence: The Neglected Factor," No. 3, pp. 36-40.

Feller, Robert E. "Accounting For Joint Products In The Petroleum Industry," No. 3, pp. 41-44.

Collins, Frank and John J. Willingham. "Contingency Management Approach To Budgeting," No. 3, pp. 45-48.

DeWelt, Robert L. "Replacement Cost - Another Nightmare For Accountants," No. 4, pp. 17-22.

Carlson, Arthur E. "ASR 190 - The Grand Experiment," No. 4, pp. 23-25.

Wells, W. Howard, Jr. "Replacement Cost Accounting: How We Did It," No. 4, pp. 26-28.

Gittes, David L. "GPL Adjusted Income Statements: A Research Study," No. 4, pp. 29-33.

Budge, Bruce P. and Harold L. Jones. "A Management Accounting System For Contract Loggers," No. 4, pp. 34-36.

Anderson, Henry R. "The G & A Overhead Pool: Accounting Tool Or Cop-Out?," No. 4, pp. 37-42.

El Sheshai, Kamal M., Gordon B. Harwood and Roger H. Hermanson. "Cost Volume Profit Analysis With Integer Goal Programming," No. 4, pp. 43-47.

Sollenberger, Harold M. "A Cost Accounting Framework For EDP Management," No. 4, pp. 48-56.

Figler, Homer R. "Retirement: Profit Or Loss?," No. 5, pp. 15-17.

Reckers, Philip M. J. and A. J. Stagliano. "Zero-Base Budgeting," No. 5, pp. 18-20.

Kostolansky, John C. "Budget Control At Corning Glass Works," No. 5, pp. 21-24.

Biagioni, Louis F. and Pekin Ogan. "Human Resource Accounting For Professional Sports Teams," No. 5, pp. 25-29.

Potts, N. Joseph. "Accounting For A Public Television Station," No. 5, pp. 30-33.

Register, Levon C. "How Will Exempt Hospitals Remain Exempt?," No. 5, pp. 34-38.

Allen, John Robert. "The Auditor's Relationship To The Development Of Data Processing Controls," No. 5, pp. 39-42.

Cerullo, Michael J. "The Data Base Concept," No. 5, pp. 43-47.

O'Connor, Norbert C. "Initial Franchise Fee: Revenue Recognition," No. 5, pp. 48-51.

Adkerson, Richard C. "Replacement Cost Accounting: A Time To Move Forward," No. 6, pp. 15-18.

Bailey, Edward J. "The SEC And Replacement Cost: An Urgent Need To Find A Better Answer," No. 6, pp. 19-22.

Berliner, Robert W. "Replacement Cost Accounting: A CPA's View," No. 6, pp. 23-26.

Barbatelli, Ettore. "Implementing ASR 190," No. 6, pp. 27-30.

Johnson, L. Todd. "Current Replacement Costs And Potential Managerial Benefits," No. 6, pp. 31-36.

O'Connor, Melvin C. "NAA-Sponsored Replacement Cost Research," No. 6, pp. 37-42.

Miller, Paul B. W. "What Is Accounting Research Supposed To

Do?," No. 6, pp. 43-47.
Sangeladji, Mohammad A. "Human Resource Accounting: A Refined Measurement Model," No. 6, pp. 48-52.
Alderman, C. Wayne and J. Kenneth Alderman. "The Impact Of Inflation On The Taxation Of Capital Gains And Losses," No. 6, pp. 53-56.
Brueningsen, Arthur F. "SCAT II - A Process For Planning," No. 6, pp. 57-61.
Hagerman, Robert L. "The Metcalf Report: Selling Some Assumptions," No. 7, pp. 13-16.
Randall, Robert F. "Metcalf Subcommittee: Let Accountants Make Reforms," No. 7, pp. 17-18.
Carlson, Timothy B. "Needed: A New Interpretation For Interim Reports," No. 7, pp. 19-22.
Toy, James H. "Responsibility Accounting: A Practical Application," No. 7, pp. 23-26.
Huebner, Robert F., Jr. "Selecting A Retirement Program For A Small Corporation," No. 7, pp. 27-33.
Nagy, Richard J. "Transfer Price Accounting For MNCs," No. 7, pp. 34-38.
Gibson, Charles H. "Budgeting By Objectives: Charlotte's Experience," No. 7, pp. 39-40.
Vanecek, Michael T. "An Overview Of Decision Theory For Management Accountants," No. 7, pp. 41-48.
Henderson, Glenn V., Jr. and Andrew H. Barnett. "Breakeven Present Value: A Pragmatic Approach To Capital Budgeting Under Risk And Uncertainty," No. 7, pp. 49-52.
Singh, Prem S. and Gordon L. Chapman. "Is Linear Approximation Good Enough?," No. 7, pp. 53-55.
Parker, L. D. "Management Accounting And The Corporate Environment," No. 8, pp. 15-20.
Smith, Alan F. "Temporal Method: Temporary Mode?," No. 8, pp. 21-26.
Pansza, Henry G. "Tax Trade-Offs: Investment Credit Versus Depreciation," No. 8, pp. 27-28.
Menees, Elbert L. "Macroaccounting: Why Not?," No. 8, pp. 29-32.
Larson, Steve and C. Mike Merz. "Operations Research At Boise Cascade," No. 8, pp. 33-36.
Woo, John C. H. "Accounting For Inflation: Some International Models," No. 8, pp. 37-43.
Imhoff, Eugene A., Jr. "The Learning Curve And Its Applications," No. 8, pp. 44-46.
Harris, Le Brone C. and William L. Stephens. "The Learning Curve: A Case Study," No. 8, pp. 47-54.
Heaton, Herbert. "Organizing For People," No. 8, pp. 55-58.
Paolasini, Arnold L. "Schools Of Accounting: The Way Of The Future," No. 9, pp. 15-18.
Zoffer, H. J. "Accounting Education And Educated Accountants," No. 9, pp. 19-23.
Springle, Hiram J. "Evaluating Sources Of Capital For Minority Enterprises," No. 9, pp. 24-26.
Vitalone, James W. "Replacement Cost Accounting: A Study Of Its Effect On Growth And Cyclical Stock Characteristics," No. 9, pp. 27-29.
Gillett, J. B. "A Funded Reserve For Major Removals," No. 9, pp. 30-34.
Clancy, Donald K. "The Management Control Problems Of Responsibility Accounting," No. 9, pp. 35-39.
Adrian, James J. "Cost Accounting For A Construction Company," No. 9, pp. 40-44.
Felton, S. K. "Controlling Company-Owned Inventories In Public Warehouses," No. 9, pp. 45-50.
Hancock, Sidney. "An Approach To Hospital Data Processing Development," No. 9, pp. 51-55.
Alonzo, Martin V. "Corporate Strategy For Combating Inflation," No. 9, pp. 57-60.
Taylor, J. Roy. "Liquidation Of LIFO Inventories," No. 10, pp. 13-16.
Ferrara, William L. "The Case For Symmetry In Lease Reporting," No. 10, pp. 17-24.
Blum, James D. "Accounting And Reporting For Leases By Lessees: The Interest Rate Problems," No. 10, pp. 25-28.
Abel, Rein. "The Role Of Costs And Cost Accounting In Price Determination," No. 10, pp. 29-32.
Shaub, H. James. "Transfer Pricing In A Decentralized Organization," No. 10, pp. 33-36.
Mansour, Fathi A. and James H. Sellers. "Comparing Cost Accounting Standards With Existing Accounting Standards," No. 10, pp. 37-42.
Hassan, Nabil, R. Penny Marquette and Joseph M. McKeon, Jr. "Sensitivity Analysis: An Accounting Tool For Decision-Making," No. 10, pp. 43-50.
Klipper, Harold. "Breakeven Analysis With Variable Product Mix," No. 10, pp. 51-54.
Randall, Robert F. "Computer Fraud: A Growing Problem," No. 10, pp. 61-64.
Jaenicke, Henry R. and Patricia A. McConnell. "A Prospectus For Auditor's Responsibilities: The Report Of The Cohen Commission," No. 11, pp. 19-24.
Dudick, Thomas S. "Zero-Base Budgeting In Industry," No. 11, pp. 25-29.
Barbor, John F. "Is LIFO A Valid Accounting Practice?," No. 11, pp. 30-34.
Nusbaum, Edward E., Andrew D. Bailey Jr. and Andrew B. Whinston. "Data-Base Management, Accounting, And Accountants," No. 11, pp. 35-38.
Eichhorn, Frederic G. "A Direct Allocation Financial Data Base For Manufacturing," No. 11, pp. 39-42.
Smith, Jack L. "Needed: Improved Pension Accounting And Reporting," No. 11, pp. 43-46.
Borsuk, Robert M. "Developing A Computer Program For Tax Planning," No. 11, pp. 47-51.
Frishkoff, Paul and Robert Rogowski. "Disclaimers Of Audit Opinion," No. 11, pp. 52-57.

Stanga, Keith G. and James J. Benjamin. "Information Needs Of Bankers," No. 12, pp. 17-21.
Vincenzo, James J. "Replacement Cost Data: What Do You Do With It?," No. 12, pp. 22-26.
Figler, Homer R. "What Should The Management Accountant Know?," No. 12, pp. 27-29.
Billion, Michael M. "To Be Or Not To Be: A Building For Investment Credit?," No. 12, pp. 30-34.
Levine, Jack B. "How A Bank Performs A Customer Profitability Analysis," No. 12, pp. 35-43.
Hennessee, Patrick A. and J. W. Giese. "Accounting For Leveraged ESOPs: Employee Benefit Or Financing Tool?," No. 12, pp. 44-49.
Schnur, Glenn J. "Here Comes Flextime," No. 12, pp. 50-54.
Stoughton, Warner V. "Bringing Up Management Accountants," No. 12, pp. 55-59.
Lambert, Douglas M. "The Distribution Channels Decision: A Problem Of Performance Measurement," No. 12, pp. 60-63.

Management Accounting
Volume 60, 1978-79

Sharav, Itzhak. "Cost Justification Under The Robinson-Patman Act," No. 1, pp. 15-22.
Benedik, John. "Macroeconomics: The Emerging Influence On Accounting Theory," No. 1, pp. 23-26.
Martin, James R. "Computer Time-Sharing Applications In Management Accounting," No. 1, pp. 27-38.
Green, Donald. "To Predict Failure," No. 1, pp. 39-41.
Stoddard, F. Don. "The Accountant's Role In Management," No. 1, pp. 42-45.
Smith, Jack L. "An Alternative Method For Income Tax Allocation," No. 1, pp. 46-50.
Paraszczak, John. "Accounting Soviet Style," No. 1, pp. 51-56.
Barnett, Glen C. "Breeding Cattle For Tax Benefits And Profit," No. 1, pp. 57-59.
Burger, Albert D. and Stuart K. Webster. "The Management Accountant Looks At EPS Vs. ROI: Conflict In Measuring Performance," No. 2, pp. 19-24.
Ericson, Joseph H., Jr. "Standard Cost In Action," No. 2, pp. 25-32.
Tsaklanganos, Angelos A. "Peers, Persuasion, And Horizontal Management," No. 2, pp. 33-37.
Bryant, Keith, Jr. and Carolyn V. Phillips. "Interest On Equity Capital And CASB Standard 414," No. 2, pp. 38-41.
Bartenstein, Edwin. "Different Costs For Different Purposes," No. 2, pp. 42-47.
Hernandez, William H. "Is The Controller An Endangered Species?," No. 2, pp. 48-52.
Simonetti, Gilbert, Jr. "It's Time For Greater Accountability In The Public Sector," No. 3, pp. 13-16.
Kirk, Donald J. "Business And The FASB: The Need For Effective Interaction," No. 3, pp. 17-20.
Thomas, Robert E. "Government Fantasy Or Economic Reality?," No. 3, pp. 21-27.
Hicks, James O., Jr. "The Application Of Exponential Smoothing To Standard Cost Systems," No. 3, pp. 28-32.
Blum, James D. and Herbert L. Jensen. "Accounting For Marketable Securities In Accordance With FASB Statement No. 12," No. 3, pp. 33-42.
Jones, James W. "Rainbows, Catfish, And Other Cash Crops," No. 3, pp. 43-46.
Mullet, Matthew J. "Benefits From Standard Costing In The Restaurant Industry," No. 3, pp. 47-54.
Roemmich, Roger A., Gordon L. Duke and William H. Gates. "Maximizing The Present Value Of Tax Savings From Depreciation," No. 3, pp. 55-57.
O'Connor, Melvin C. and Gyan Chandra. "Replacement Cost Disclosure," No. 3, pp. 58-59.
Perille, P. James and Frederick J. Saathoff. "Why Not Project Financing?," No. 4, pp. 13-16.
Morley, James E., Jr. "Cash Management - Working For The Extra 1% Or 2%," No. 4, pp. 17-22.
Weed, Ralph J. "Financial Sources In The Public Sector," No. 4, pp. 23-28.
Wynant, Larry. "Project Financing For Extractive Ventures," No. 4, pp. 29-35.
Amlung, Martin J., III. "Dollar-Value LIFO," No. 4, pp. 36-40.
Arnett, Harold E. "APB Opinion No. 29: Accounting For Non-monetary Transactions - Some New Perspectives," No. 4, pp. 41-48.
Jackson, Charles B. "Trust Fund Accounting For Multi-Employer Trust Funds," No. 4, pp. 49-54.
Unger, Frank J. "Indexing The Progressive Tax System," No. 4, pp. 55-57.
Coppie, Comer S. "The City: Management By Crisis Or Crisis Management?," No. 5, pp. 13-21.
Connelly, John R., Jr. "Should We License Accountants To Prevent Accounting License?," No. 5, pp. 22-26.
Miller, Paul B. W. "Accounting Research Needs A More Efficient Market," No. 5, pp. 27-34.
Francia, Arthur J., Steven D. Grossman and Robert H. Strawser. "The Attitudes Of Management Accountants," No. 5, pp. 35-40.
Imhoff, Eugene A., Jr. "Management Accounting Techniques: A Survey," No. 5, pp. 41-45.
Largay, James A., III and Ferdinand K. Levy. "Using Segment Reporting And Input-Output Analysis For Managerial Planning," No. 5, pp. 46-50.
Agami, Abdel M. "Accounting For Troubled Debt Restructurings - A Flowchart Approach," No. 5, pp. 51-55.
Mayer-Sommer, Alan P. and Stephen J. Laycock. "Financial

Reporting: Let's Replace Compliance With Competition," No. 6, pp. 14-19.

Dierks, Paul A. "Applying Cost Accounting To Transit System Financing," No. 6, pp. 20-23.

Guthrie, Tommie M. "Measuring Terminal Profitability," No. 6, pp. 24-31.

Blamey, Richard L. "Setting Sewage Treatment User Charge Rates: A Cost/Benefit Approach," No. 6, pp. 32-36.

Melton, Edgar P. and Burton W. Brooks, Jr. "Impact Of GAAP On The Profitability Of Mortgage Bankers," No. 6, pp. 37-43.

Vaughan, R. Allen. "This Hospital Service Forecasts Inflation For Its Fiscal Health," No. 6, pp. 44-47.

Suver, James D. and Bruce R. Neumann. "Capital Budgeting For Hospitals," No. 6, pp. 48-50.

Shirley, Robert E. "Measuring Performance Of A University Accounting Department," No. 6, pp. 51-53.

Teck, Alan. "Beyond FAS No. 8: Defining Other Exposures," No. 6, pp. 54-57.

Tang, Roger Y. W., C. K. Walter and Robert H. Raymond. "Transfer Pricing - Japanese Vs. American Style," No. 7, pp. 12-16.

Cowen, Scott S., Lawrence C. Phillips and Linda Stillabower. "Multinational Transfer Pricing," No. 7, pp. 17-22.

Lucien, Kent. "Transfer Pricing For The Cost Funds In A Commercial Bank," No. 7, pp. 23-24.

Madison, Roland L. "Responsibility Accounting And Transfer Pricing: Approach With Caution," No. 7, pp. 25-29.

Hall, Robert B. "How We Estimate Replacement Costs," No. 7, pp. 30-36.

Severance, Jay and Ronald R. Bottin. "Work-In-Process Inventory Control Through Data Base Concepts," No. 7, pp. 37-41.

Hake, Jack A. and Lanny J. Ryan. "Decision Science And The Management Accountant," No. 7, pp. 42-45.

Burianek, Frank G. "An Actuary's Views On Pension Plan Accounting And Reporting," No. 7, pp. 46-49.

Miller, Paul B. W. "Taxing Capital Gains With Price Indexes," No. 7, pp. 50-52.

Rice, Edward A. "Some Practical Applications Of Target Prices," No. 8, pp. 17-20.

Louderback, Joseph G. and George E. Manners, Jr. "Evaluating Risky Investment Projects," No. 8, pp. 21-23.

Sangeladji, Mohammad A. "True Rate Of Return For Evaluating Capital Investments," No. 8, pp. 24-28.

Lusch, Robert F. and William F. Bentz. "A Variance Approach To Analyzing Changes In Return On Investment," No. 8, pp. 29-34.

Boyles, Jesse V., III. "Energy Accounting," No. 8, pp. 35-41.

White, Denis W. "How A Safety Program Affects The Bottom Line," No. 8, pp. 42-46.

Collier, Boyd and Curtis Carnes. "Convertible Bonds And Financial Reality," No. 8, pp. 47-48.

Grant, Edward B. and Raymond C. Witt. "A Look At Leveraged Leases Under FAS No. 13," No. 8, pp. 49-52.

Ford, Jerry L. "How To Communicate With Management," No. 9, pp. 12-17.

Seiler, Robert E. and Richard W. Sapp. "Just How Satisfied Are Accountants With Their Jobs?," No. 9, pp. 18-21.

Collins, Frank. "Management Accounting And Motivation - The Relationship," No. 9, pp. 22-26.

Meagher, Gary M. "Motivating Accountants," No. 9, pp. 27-30.

Dady, Benjamin L. "How Florida Power & Light Installed Z-B Budgeting," No. 9, pp. 31-34.

Horodowich, Peter. "Evaluating The Write-Off Of Slow-Moving Finished Goods Inventory," No. 9, pp. 35-40.

Kim, Suk H. "Making The Long-Term Investment Decision," No. 9, pp. 41-49.

Imhoff, Eugene A., Jr. and Paul A. Janell. "Opinion No. 29: A New Valuation Method," No. 9, pp. 50-53.

Walker, Michael C. "Determining The Appropriate Discount Rate For Private, Not-For-Profit Organizations," No. 9, pp. 54-56.

Gartenberg, Morris and Robert F. Randall. "From EDP to MIS And Beyond," No. 10, pp. 13-16.

Wood, James H. "How RJR Put Its New MIS On-Line," No. 10, pp. 17-23.

Mayer, James A. "MIS At International Paper: An Integrated Teleprocessing Network," No. 10, pp. 24-27.

Rao, Kailas J. "A Hardware Company Manages Its Inventory The EDP Way," No. 10, pp. 28-32.

Weingard, Marvin. "The Rockford Files: A Case For The Computer," No. 10, pp. 36-38.

Case, Jay C. "Electronic Banking Comes To First-Citizens," No. 10, pp. 39-42.

Cerullo, Michael J. "MIS: What Can Go Wrong?," No. 10, pp. 43-48.

Varrone, James E. and Vincent E. Palmeri, Jr. "EDP Finds A Home At North Haven," No. 10, pp. 49-50.

Ferguson, Linda Wicks. "An Accountant Profiles A Sports Franchise," No. 11, pp. 13-18.

Hazelton, Walter A. "How To Cost Labor Settlements," No. 11, pp. 19-23.

Ginter, Edward M. "Communications And Cost Benefit Aspects Of Employee Safety," No. 11, pp. 24-26.

Dittmer, Gary R. "Inventory Pricing Can Save Costs," No. 11, pp. 27-32.

Lambert, Douglas M. and Howard M. Armitage. "Distribution Costs: The Challenge," No. 11, pp. 33-37.

Davis, Jonathan. "Hood Chooses MIS For Its Frogurt," No. 11, pp. 38-41.

McFarlane, Kentbourne A. W. "Tracking Inflation In Your

Company," No. 11, pp. 42-46.

Harder, David K. "Pricing For Profit In The Printing Industry," No. 11, pp. 47-52.

Most, Kenneth S. "A New Method For Accounting For Oil And Gas Producers," No. 11, pp. 53-58.

Choi, Frederick D. S. "Political Risk - An Accounting Challenge," No. 12, pp. 17-20.

Tse, Paul S. "Evaluating Performance In Multinationals," No. 12, pp. 21-25.

Yamakawa, Thomas T. "How The Strong Yen Influenced Financial Reporting In Japan," No. 12, pp. 26-31.

Malkoff, Alan R. "Foreign Acquisition Analysis: A Suggested Approach," No. 12, pp. 32-36.

Sale, Timothy J. and Karen B. Carroll. "Tax Planning Tools For The Multinational Corporation," No. 12, pp. 37-42.

Benjamin, James J., Paul E. Dascher and Robert G. Morgan. "How Corporate Controllers View The Foreign Corrupt Practices Act," No. 12, pp. 43-45.

Whitt, John D. "Motivating Lower-Level Management Of Mexican Affiliates," No. 12, pp. 46-49.

Chiu, James S. and Davis L. Chang. "Management Accounting In Taiwan," No. 12, pp. 50-55.

Management Accounting
Volume 61, 1979-80

Dennis, Kenneth C. "Hospitals Must Allocate Bad Debts Properly," No. 1, pp. 11-14.

Nestor, Oscar W. and Andrew J. Riddell. "A Home Health Care Agency Cures Itself," No. 1, pp. 15-20.

Millar, James A. "Hospital Equipment Leasing: The Breakeven Discount Rate," No. 1, pp. 21-26.

Ching, Donald F. "How To Isolate Medicare Costs," No. 1, pp. 27-33.

Suver, James D. and F. Theodore Helmer. "Developing Budgetary Models For Greater Hospital Efficiency," No. 1, pp. 34-36.

Jessee, Ken. "Woodland Hospital Computerizes To Reduce Administrative Costs," No. 1, pp. 37-39.

Jablonsky, Stephen F. and Mark W. Dirsmith. "Is Financial Reporting Influencing Internal Decision Making?," No. 1, pp. 40-45.

Bailes, Jack C., James F. Nielsen and Steve Wendell. "Capital Budgeting In The Forest Products Industry," No. 1, pp. 46-51.

Bryant, Keith, Jr. "How A Rental Apartment Was Converted To A Condominium," No. 1, pp. 52-57.

Schulman, Henry N. "Inventory Shrinkage: Is It An Accounting Problem?," No. 2, pp. 15-17.

Hartman, Bart P. and Dan C. Smith. "Improving Credit Collection Responses," No. 2, pp. 18-21.

Ahern, John T., Jr. and Patrick L. Romano. "Managing Inventories And Profits Through GMROI," No. 2, pp. 22-26.

Carper, Wm. Brent, M. Frank Barton, Jr. and Haroldene F. Wunder. "The Future Of Forecasting," No. 2, pp. 27-31.

Simms, Charles A., Jr. "Summarizing The Foreign Earned Income Tax Act Of 1978," No. 2, pp. 32-36.

Rao, Kailas J. "The High Price Of Beef: How One Company Accounts For It," No. 2, pp. 37-40.

Sprinkle, R. David and William E. Hall, Jr. "How To Cope With Reverse Discrimination In Executive Benefit Plans," No. 2, pp. 41-44.

Loretucci, Joseph A. "Financial Leasing: What's The Best Replacement Cycle?," No. 2, pp. 45-48.

Williams, Harold M. "Financial Reporting In A Changing Economic Environment," No. 3, pp. 11-15.

Steakley, Mark E. "Inflation Accounting Techniques: How They Compare," No. 3, pp. 16-18.

Raiborn, D. D. and Thomas A. Ratcliffe. "Are You Accounting For Inflation In Your Capital Budgeting Process?," No. 3, pp. 19-22.

Tsui, Winston W. "Inflation Accounting And Foreign Currency Translation," No. 3, pp. 23-31.

Zieha, Eugene L. and Thomas T. Cheng. "Proposing A More Appropriate Dividend Policy," No. 3, pp. 32-36.

Ferguson, John S. "Decommissioning A Nuclear Plant: The Financial Implications," No. 3, pp. 37-40.

Brewer, Larry W. "Determining Revenue Requirements For Regulated Utilities," No. 3, pp. 41-44.

Campion, William M. and Richard M. Peters. "How To Analyze Manpower Requirements Forecasts," No. 3, pp. 45-51.

Hooper, Paul and John Page. "Better Financial Statements For Corporate Valuation," No. 3, pp. 52-56.

Jones, Gardner M. and David R. L. Gabhart. "Danger: This City Is In Financial Trouble," No. 4, pp. 19-22.

Laible, Steven W. "How Minnesota Improved Its Cities' Financial Reporting," No. 4, pp. 23-29.

Whitmire, Kathryn J. and Philip B. Scheps. "Municipal Pension Plans: The Long Road Back To Financial Soundness," No. 4, pp. 30-33.

Epps, William F. "How Richmond County Learned Fixed-Asset Management," No. 4, pp. 34-39.

Nestor, Joseph. "How Cost Accountants Can Improve Public Housing Programs," No. 4, pp. 40-42.

Henry, James B., Perry Woodside and James B. Edwards. "Public Sector Leasing In South Carolina," No. 4, pp. 43-49.

Brandstedter, Rodney. "Campaign Reporting: A Challenge For Accountants," No. 4, pp. 50-54.

Allen, James L. and Marvin Scher. "Risk Analysis For Non-mathematicians," No. 4, pp. 55-58.

Gartenberg, Morris. "Small Business: A Question Of Survival," No. 5, pp. 14-15.

Wucinich, William. "How To Finance A Small Business," No.

Management Accounting
Volume 68, 1986-87

Management Accounting
Volume 70, 1988-89

RESEARCH IN ACCOUNTING REGULATION

Research in Accounting Regulation
Volume 1, 1987

Parker, Larry M. and Gary John Previts. "Regulation: The Forces Influencing Accounting Practice," Vol. 1, pp. 1-4.

Wallace, Wanda A. "The Economic Role Of The Audit In Free And Regulated Markets: A Review," Vol. 1, pp. 7-34.

Turner, Joanne H. and Daniel L. Jensen. "Recent Episodes In The 'Oversight Cycle' Of Accountancy Self-Regulation," Vol. 1, pp. 35-50.

Johnson, Orace. "Common Law Accounting: The Case Of Goodwill," Vol. 1, pp. 51-77.

Kunitake, Walter K. "SEC Accounting Related Enforcement Actions 1934-1985: A Summary," Vol. 1, pp. 79-87.

St. Pierre, Kent and James M. Reeve. "An Analysis Of Ernst & Ernst v. Hochfelder: Legal And Market Effects A Decade Latter," Vol. 1, pp. 89-101.

O'Leary, Ted and Richard J. Boland, Jr. "Self-Regulation, Public Interest And The Accounting Profession," Vol. 1, pp. 103-121.

O'Leary, Daniel. "Accounting Regulation-Based Expert Systems," Vol. 1, pp. 123-137.

Brown, Richard E. "The Expectations Gap: An Added Dimension - The Case Of Government Auditing," Vol. 1, pp. 139-164.

Sack, Robert J. "The SEC And The Profession: An Exercise In Balance," Vol. 1, pp. 167-175.

Banks, Alexander S. "Informing Stockholders: A Job For Public Accounts In Preference To The Federal Trade Commission," Vol. 1, pp. 177-179.

Burchmore, David W. "SEC Enforcement Of Insider Trading Laws," Vol. 1, pp. 181-189.

Martin, J. W. "A Selected Glossary Of Securities Offering And SEC Accounting Terms," Vol. 1, pp. 191-224.

Research in Accounting Regulation
Volume 2, 1988

Parker, Larry M. and Gary J. Previts. "The 'Yes' Vote For 'Excellence': A Profession More In Consonance With A Changing Society," Vol. 2, pp. 1-4.

Ingram, Robert W. "Costs And Information Effects: Accounting And Auditing Regulation Of Local Governments," Vol. 2, pp. 7-24.

Denning, Karen C. and Kuldeep Shastri. "An Option Pricing Technique For Auditor Review Of Insider Trading," Vol. 2, pp. 25-39.

Knapp, Michael C. "Toward A More Coherent Regulatory Policy For Auditor Changes: An Empirical Study Of Their Impact On Financial Statement Credibility," Vol. 2, pp. 41-59.

Colson, Robert H., Michael W. Maher, Amy J. Broman and Pieter Tiessen. "Audit Pricing Models For Regulation Research: Reliability And Stability," Vol. 2, pp. 61-79.

Chatov, Robert. "The Regulatory Philosophy Of Carmen Blough: A Legacy," Vol. 2, pp. 81-105.

Young, S. David. "Public Accounting Licensure And Service Quality: Issues And Evidence," Vol. 2, pp. 107-121.

Wallace, Wanda A. and Ronald L. Campbell. "State Boards Of Accountancy: Quality Review And Positive Enforcement Program," Vol. 2, pp. 123-154.

Parker, Larry M., John C. Corless and Michael J. Tucker. "Audit Firm Size And Internal Control Assessment: An Experiment," Vol. 2, pp. 155-166.

Pincus, Karen V., William W. Holder and Theodore J. Mock. "The SEC And Fraudulent Financial Reporting," Vol. 2, pp. 167-185.

Flegm, Eugene H. "The Summary Annual Report," Vol. 2, pp. 189-205.

Sampson, Clarence. "Facilitations Of Multinational Securities Offerings," Vol. 2, pp. 207-218.

Martin, J. W. "Selected SEC Financial Statement Requirements - Beyond GAAP," Vol. 2, pp. 219-233.

RESEARCH IN GOVERNMENTAL AND NONPROFIT ACCOUNTING

PART TWO

AUTHOR
INDEX

AAA

Abbey, Dana L. "Production Planning And Cost Reporting For Toys," MA, 1971, Vol. 53, No. 6, pp. 9-11.

Abdallah, Wagdy M. and Donald E. Keller. "Measuring The Multinational's Performance," MA, 1985, Vol. 67, No. 4, pp. 26-30.

Abdallah, Wagdy. "Change The Environment Or Change The System," MA, 1986, Vol. 68, No. 4, pp. 33-37.

Abdeen, Adnan M. and Ugur Yavas. "Current Status Of Accounting Education In Saudi Arabia," IJAER, 1985, Vol. 20, No. 2, pp. 155-173.

Abdeen, Adnan. "The Impact Of Accounting Practices On Tax Revenue In Syria," IJAER, 1984, Vol. 20,No.1,pp.121-139.

Abdeen, Adnan. "The Role Of Accounting In Project Evaluation And Control: The Syrian Experience," IJAER, 1980, Vol. 15, No. 2, pp. 143-158.

Abdelsamad, M. H. and John B. Sperry. "Accounting And Financial Management," AR, 1974, Vol. 49, No. 4, pp. 844-846.

Abdel-Karim, Rifaat Ahmed. "The Impact Of The UK Price Codes On Accounting Functions In Organisations: A Power Perspective," ABR, 1988, Vol. 18, No. 72, pp. 307-321.

Abdel-Khalik, A. Rashad and Bipin B. Ajinkya. "Returns to Informational Advantages: The Case Of Analysts' Forecast Revisions," AR, 1982, Vol. 57, No. 4, pp. 661-680.

Abdel-Khalik, A. Rashad and Edward J. Lusk. "Transfer Pricing - A Synthesis: A Reply," AR, 1975, Vol. 50, No. 2, pp. 356-358.

Abdel-Khalik, A. Rashad and Edward J. Lusk. "Transfer Pricing - a Synthesis," AR, 1974, Vol. 49, No. 1, pp. 8-23.

Abdel-Khalik, A. Rashad and James C. McKeown. "Understanding Accounting Changes In An Efficient Market: Evidence Of Differential Reaction," AR, 1978, Vol. 53, No. 4, pp. 851-868.

Abdel-Khalik, A. Rashad, Charles Chi and Dimitrios Ghicas. "Rationality Of Executive Compensation Schemes And Real Accounting Changes," CAR, 1987-88, Vol. 4, No. 1, pp. 32-60.

Abdel-Khalik, A. Rashad, Doug A. Snowball and John H. Wragge. "The Effects Of Certain Internal Audit Variables On The Planning Of External Audit Programs," AR, 1983, Vol. 58, No. 2, pp. 215-227.

Abdel-Khalik, A. Rashad. "A Critique Of 'Market Reactions To Mandated Interest Capitalization'," CAR, 1985-86, Vol. 2, No. 2, pp. 242-251.

Abdel-Khalik, A. Rashad. "Advertising Effectiveness And Accounting Policy: A Reply," AR, 1977, Vol. 52, No. 1, pp. 264-265.

Abdel-Khalik, A. Rashad. "Advertising Effectiveness And Accounting Policy," AR, 1975, Vol. 50, No. 4,pp.657-670.

Abdel-Khalik, A. Rashad. "An Analysis Of The Attitudes Of A Sample Of The AAA Members Toward The Accounting Review," AR, 1976, Vol. 51, No. 3, pp. 599-611.

Abdel-Khalik, A. Rashad. "Controllership In Egypt," JAR, 1966, Vol. 4, No. 1, pp. 37-46.

Abdel-Khalik, A. Rashad. "Incentives For Accruing Costs And Efficiency In Regulated Monopolies Subject To ROE Constraint," JAR, 1988, Vol. 26, Supp., pp. 144-174.

Abdel-Khalik, A. Rashad. "On Gordon's Model Of Transfer-Pricing System," AR, 1971, Vol. 46, No. 4, pp. 783-787.

Abdel-Khalik, A. Rashad. "On The Efficiency Of Subject Surrogation In Accounting Research," AR, 1974, Vol. 49, No. 4, pp. 743-750.

Abdel-Khalik, A. Rashad. "On The Usefulness Of Financial Ratios To Investors In Common Stock: A Comment," AR, 1974, Vol. 49, No. 3, pp. 547-550.

Abdel-Khalik, A. Rashad. "The Computer Held Hostage, Day 1001: A Research Story," IAE, 1986, Vol. 1, No. 2, pp. 207-229.

Abdel-Khalik, A. Rashad. "The Effect Of Aggregating Accounting Reports On The Quality Of The Lending Decision: An Empirical Investigation," JAR, 1973, Vol. 11, Supp., pp. 104-138.

Abdel-Khalik, A. Rashad. "The Efficient Market Hypothesis And Accounting Data: A Point Of View," AR, 1972, Vol. 47, No. 4, pp. 791-793.

Abdel-Khalik, A. Rashad. "The Entropy Law, Accounting Data, And Relevance To Decision-Making," AR, 1974, Vol. 49, No. 2, pp. 271-283.

Abdel-Khalik, A. Rashad. "User Preference Ordering Value: A Model," AR, 1971, Vol. 46, No. 3, pp. 457-471.

Abdel-khalik, A. R. and B. B. Ajinkya. "An Evaluation Of 'The Everyday Accountant And Researching His Reality'," AOS, 1983, Vol. 8, No. 4, pp. 375-384.

Abdel-khalik, A. Rashad and James C. McKeown. "Disclosure Of Estimates Of Holding Gains And The Assessment Of Systematic Risk," JAR, 1978, Vol. 16, Supp., pp. 46-92.

Abdel-khalik, A. Rashad and Jose Espejo. "Expectations Data And The Predictive Value Of Interim Reporting," JAR, 1978, Vol. 16, No. 1, pp. 1-13.

Abdel-khalik, A. Rashad and Kamal M. El-Sheshai. "Information Choice And Utilization In An Experiment On Default Prediction," JAR, 1980, Vol. 18, No. 2, pp. 325-342.

Abdel-khalik, A. Rashad, Paul R. Graul and James D. Newton. "Reporting Uncertainty And Assessment Of Risk: Replication And Extension In A Canadian Setting," JAR, 1986, Vol. 24, No. 2, pp. 372-382.

Abdel-khalik, A. Rashad. "A Note On The Validity Of The WSJ As A Source Of 'Event' Dates," JAR, 1984, Vol. 22, No. 2, pp. 758-759.

Abdel-khalik, A. Rashad. "Overfitting Bias In The Models Assessing The Predictive Power Of Quarterly Reports," JAR, 1983, Vol. 21, No. 1, pp. 293-296.

Abdel-khalik, A. Rashad. "The Effect Of LIFO-Switching And Firm Ownership On Executives' Pay," JAR, 1985, Vol. 23. No. 2, pp. 427-447.

Abdel-Magid, Moustafa F. and Joseph K. Cheung. "Ratio Scales, Foreign Exchange Rates, And The Problem Of Foreign Currency Translation: An Analytical-Empirical Perspective," IJAER, 1986, Vol. 22, No. 1, pp. 33-49.

Abdel-Magid, Moustafa F. "General Price-Level-Adjusted Historical-Cost Statements And The Ratio Scale View: A Comment," AR, 1979, Vol. 54, No. 4, pp. 825-829.

Abdel-Magid, Moustafa F. "The Theory Of Islamic Banking: Accounting Implications," IJAER, 1981, Vol. 17, No. 1, pp. 79-102.

Abdel-Magid, Moustafa F. "Toward A Better Understanding Of The Role Of Measurement In Accounting," AR, 1979, Vol. 54, No. 2, pp. 346-357.

Abdolmohammadi, Mohammad and Arnold Wright. "An Examination Of The Effects Of Experience And Task Complexity On Audit Judgments," AR, 1987, Vol. 62, No. 1, pp. 1-13.

Abdolmohammadi, Mohammad J. and Paul D. Berger. "A Test Of The Accuracy Of Probability Assessment Techniques In Auditing," CAR, 1986-87, Vol. 3, No. 1, pp. 149-183.

Abdolmohammadi, Mohammad J. "Bayesian Inference In Auditing: Evidence On The Most Appropriate Assessment Techniques," ABR, 1986-87, Vol. 17, No. 68, pp. 291-300.

Abdolmohammadi, Mohammad J. "Bayesian Inference In Substantive Testing: An Ease-Of-Use Criterion," AIA, 1985, Vol. 2, pp. 275-289.

Abdolmohammadi, Mohammad J. "Bayesian Inference Research In Auditing: Some Methodological Suggestions," CAR, 1985-86, Vol. 2, No. 1, pp. 76-94.

Abdolmohammadi, Mohammad J. "Decision Support And Expert Systems In Auditing: A Review And Research Directions," ABR, 1986-87, Vol. 17, No. 66, pp. 173-185.

Abdolmohammadi, Mohammad J. "Efficiency Of The Bayesian Approach In Compliance Testing: Some Empirical Evidence," AJPT, 1985-86, Vol. 5, No. 2, pp. 1-16.

Abdolmohammadi, Mohammad J., Krishnagopal Menon, Thomas W. Oliver and Srinivasan Umapathy. "The Role Of The Doctoral Dissertation In Accounting Research Centers," IAE. 1985, No. 1, pp. 59-76.

Abdolmohammadi, Mohammad. (Wright, Arnold and Mohammad Abdolmohammadi. "Modeling Auditor Weights Of Key Criteria In Evaluating Alternative Sampling Aproaches: A Guide For Researchers," AIA, 1987, Vol. 4, pp. 287-302.)

Abdolmohammadi, M., K. Menon, T. Oliver and S. Umapathy. "Factors Motivating Academic Research In Accounting," AIA, 1988, Vol. 6, pp. 159-174.

Abdulkader, Abdullah A. (Lorek, Kenneth S., Joe D. Icerman and Abdullah A. Abdulkader. "Further Descriptive And Predictive Evidence On Alternative Time-Series Models For Quarterly Earnings," JAR, 1983, Vol. 21, No. 1, pp. 317-328.)

Abel, Rein. "Reflections On APB Opinion No. 26 And Public Utility Practice," CPAJ, 1973, Vol. 43, No. 7, pp. 573-578.

Abel, Rein. "The Impact Of Environment On Accounting Practices: Germany In The Thirties," IJAER, 1971, Vol. 7, No. 1, pp. 29-47.

Abel, Rein. "The Role Of Costs And Cost Accounting In Price Determination," MA, 1978, Vol. 59, No. 10, pp. 29-32.

Abel, R. "A Comparative Simulation Of German And U.S. Accounting Principles," JAR, 1969, Vol. 7, No. 1, pp. 1-11.

Abernethy, Gordon G. (Osteryoung, Jerome S. and Gordon G. Abernethy. "Capital Budgeting: A Review," JCA. 1984, Vol. 1, No. 1, pp. 131-142.)

Abraham, Elizabeth, Carol Loughrey and Hugh Whalen. "Computerized Practice Set In Introductory Financial Accounting," IAE, 1987, Vol. 2, No. 1, pp. 1-12.

Abramowicz, Kenneth F. (Gramlich, Jeffrey D., Kenneth F. Abramowicz and James E. Parker. "Refunding Non-Callable Bonds: An Update Of A Tax-Oriented Decision Model In Light Of The Tax Reform Act Of 1986," JATA, 1988, Vol. 9, No. 2, pp. 105-110.)

Abramson, David H. "The Future Of Accounting: Scenarios For 1996," JOA, 1986, Vol. 162, No. 4, pp. 120-125.

Abranovic, Wynn A. "Probability Plotting For Estimating Time-To-Payment Characteristics For Collections On Accounts Receivable," AR, 1976, Vol. 51, No. 4, pp. 863-874.

Abrassart, A. Eugene. (Neyhart, Charles A., Jr. and A. Eugene Abrassart. "Probabilistic Testing And The Evaluation Of Student Performance," AR, 1977, Vol. 52, No. 4, pp. 939-945.)

Abrassart, A. Eugene. (Neyhart, Charles A., Jr. and A. Eugene Abrassart. "A Scoring Rule For Probabilistic Multiple-Choice Tests," JAED, 1984, Vol. 2, No. 1, pp. 71-81.)

Abrego, Gilbert F., Jr. "Applying Word Processing To Accounting Practice," JOA, 1976, Vol. 141. No. 2. pp. 42-45.

Abs, George, Clayton Grimstad, Robert Hay, W. Asquith Howe, William LaPlace, Francis J. McGurr and William Serraino. "Historical Dates In Accounting," AR, 1954, Vol. 29, No. 3, pp. 486-493.

Acken, Brenda T. (Ried, Glenda, Brenda T. Acken and Elise G. Jancura. "An Historical Perspective On Women In Accounting," JOA, 1987, Vol. 163, No. 5, pp. 338-355.)

Ackoff, Russell L. (Churchman, C. West and Russell L. Ackoff. "Operational Accounting And Operations Research," JOA, 1955, Vol. 99, No. 2, pp. 33-39.)

Acland, D. "The Effects Of Behavioral Indicators On Investor Decisions: An Exploratory Study," AOS, 1976, Vol. 1, No. 2/3, pp. 133-142.

Adamck, Alida M. (Preston, R. Jeffrey and Alida M. Adamek. "Who's Minding The Tax Department?," **MA**, 1983, Vol. 64, No. 11, pp. 24-27.)

Adamson, Lee J. (Haglund, Byron E., Lee J. Adamson and Richard D. Metcalf. "Punched Card Accounting For Small Businesses," **JOA**, 1961, Vol. 112, No. 6, pp. 54-58.)

Adams, Dennis S. "Managing Interest Rate Risk," **CA**, 1986, Vol. 4, No. 3, pp. 49-52.

Adams, Donald L. and John F. Mullarkey. "A Survey Of Audit Software," **JOA**, 1972, Vol. 134, No. 3, pp. 39-66.

Adams, Donald L. (Dill, S. Leland and Donald L. Adams. "Automated Auditing," **JOA**, 1964, Vol. 117, No. 5, pp. 54-59.)

Adams, James P. "Depreciation Accounting And Public Utility Valuation," **AR**, 1930, Vol. 5, No. 2, pp. 99-105.

Adams, Jane B. (Scott, Diana J., Jane B. Adams and Joyce A. Strawser. "Retiree Welfare Benefits Come Out Of Hiding," **CPAJ**, 1988, Vol. 58, No. 11, pp. 26-34.)

Adams, John C. "Two Years On The Road," **MA**, 1977, Vol. 59, No. 2, pp. 37-40.

Adams, Kerry D. "Hedge Accounting For Anticipatory Hedges Of Short-Term Liabilities," **JAAF**, 1984, Vol. 7, No. 2, pp. 151-163.

Adams, Sexton. (Williams, Doyle Z. and Sexton Adams. "Computer Technology And Organizational Change," **MA**, 1968, Vol. 50, No. 1, pp. 44-48.)

Adams, Steven J. and Gerald E. Whittenburg. "How The Energy Tax Act Affects Capital Budgeting," **MA**, 1981, Vol. 63, No. 5, pp. 34-39.

Adams, Steven J. (Lightner, Sharon M., Steven J. Adams and Kevin M. Lightner. "The Influence Of Situational, Ethical, And Expectancy Theory Variables On Accountants' Underreporting Behavior," **AJPT**, 1982-83, Vol. 2, No. 1, pp. 1-12.)

Adams, Steven J. (Whittington, O. Ray and Steven J. Adams. "Temporary Breakdowns Of Internal Control: Implications For External And Internal Auditors," **JAAF**, 1982, Vol. 5, No. 4, pp. 310-319.)

Adam, Paul J. "One Firm's Policies In Training And Compensating Staff Men," **JOA**, 1954, Vol. 98, No. 4, pp. 471-477.

Adar, Zvi, Amir Barnea and Baruch Lev. "A Comprehensive Cost-Volume-Profit Analysis Under Uncertainty," **AR**, 1977, Vol. 52, No. 1, pp. 137-149.

Addams, H. Lon. "Should The Big 8 Teach Communication Skills?," **MA**, 1981, Vol. 62, No. 11, pp. 37-42.

Addington, Conley R. "Governmental Accounting In The Undergraduate Curriculum," **AR**, 1955, Vol. 30, No. 2, pp. 290-292.

Addington, Conley R. "The Undergraduate Course In Income Taxation For Accounting Majors," **AR**, 1957, Vol. 32, No. 1, pp. 93-94.

Adelberg, Arthur Harris. "A Methodology For Measuring The Understandability Of Financial Report Messages," **JAR**, 1979, Vol. 17, No. 2, pp. 565-592.

Adelberg, Arthur Harris. "Narrative Disclosures Contained In Financial Reports: Means Of Communication Or Manipulation?," **ABR**, 1978-79, Vol. 9, No. 35, pp. 179-190.

Adelberg, Arthur Harris. "The Accounting Syntactic Complexity Formula: A New Instrument For Predicting The Readability Of Selected Accounting Communications," **ABR**, 1982-83, Vol. 13, No. 51, pp. 163-176.

Adelberg, Arthur H. and Joseph R. Razek. "The Cloze Procedure: A Methodology For Determining The Understandability Of Accounting Textbooks," **AR**, 1984, Vol. 59, No. 1, pp. 109-122.

Adkerson, Richard C. "Can Reserve Recognition Accounting Work?," **JOA**, 1979, Vol. 148, No. 3, pp. 72-81.

Adkerson, Richard C. "Replacement Cost Accounting: A Time To Move Forward," **MA**, 1977, Vol. 59, No. 6, pp. 15-18.

Adler, Dean A. "Another Look At ERISA," **MA**, 1977, Vol. 58, No. 7, pp. 21-25.

Adler, Herbert S. "Planning For A Successful Acquisition," **CA**, 1984, Vol. 2, No. 4, pp. 42-49.

Adler, Ronald L. "Creative Cost Control In Unemployment Compensation Tax Management," **MA**, 1982, Vol. 63, No. 9, pp. 47-55.

Admon, Kurt. (Goldschmidt, Yaaqov and Kurt Admon. "Measuring Terms Of Trade During Price Level Changes," **ABACUS**, 1977, Vol. 13, No. 1, pp. 28-39.)

Adrian, James J. "Cost Accounting For A Construction Company," **MA**, 1978, Vol. 59, No. 9, pp. 40-44.

Afosa, Kwame. "Financial Administration Of Ancient Ashanti Empire," **AHJ**, 1985, Vol. 12, No. 2, pp. 109-115.

Afterman, Allan B. and Robert D. Bernson. "A Guide To Bank Financing For The Closely Held Company," **CA**, 1983, Vol. 1, No. 3, pp. 33-38.

Agami, Abdel M. "Accounting For Troubled Debt Restructurings - A Flowchart Approach," **MA**, 1978, Vol. 60, No. 5, pp. 51-55.

Agami, Abdel M. "How To Choose Transfer Prices For FSCs," **MA**, 1986, Vol. 67, No. 11, pp. 48-50.

Agami, Abdel M. "The International Accounting Course State Of The Art," **JAED**, 1983, Vol. 1, No. 2, pp. 67-77.

Aggarwal, Raj. "FASB No. 8 And Reported Results Of Multinational Operations: Hazard For Managers And Investors," **JAAF**, 1978, Vol. 1, No. 3, pp. 197-216.

Aggarwal, Raj. (Hosseini, Ahmad and Raj Aggarwal. "Evaluating Foreign Affiliates: The Impact Of Alternative Foreign Currency Translation Methods," **IJAER**, 1983, Vol. 19, No. 1, pp. 65-87.)

Agnich, Joseph F. "How Utilities Account To The Regulators," **MA**, 1981, Vol. 62, No. 8, pp. 17-22.

Agrawal, Surenda P. (Barton, M. Frank, Surenda P. Agrawal and Lynn Rockwell. "Meeting The Challenge Of Japanese Management Concepts," **MA**, 1988, Vol. 70, No. 3, pp. 49-53.)

Agrawal, Surendra P. and Kenneth Rosenzweig. "Some Simpler Methods Of Accounting For The Effects Of Changing Prices," **IJAER**, 1983, Vol. 19, No. 1, pp. 157-171.

Agrawal, Surendra P. and Rosalie C. Hallbauer. "Advantages Of Replacement Cost Accounting: A Critical Evaluation," **IJAER**, 1978, Vol. 13, No. 2, pp. 1-14.

Agrawal, Surendra P. "Accounting For The Impact Of Inflation On A Business Enterprise," **AR**, 1977, Vol. 52, No. 4, pp. 789-809.

Agrawal, Surendra P. "Current Cost Accounting In The United Kingdom And The United States: A Comparative Analysis," **IJAER**, 1983, Vol. 18, No. 2, pp. 95-108.

Agrawal, Surendra P., Rosalie C. Hallbauer and Gerald W. Perritt. "Measurement Of The Current Cost Of Equivalent Productive Capacity," **JAAF**, 1980, Vol. 3, No. 2, pp. 163-173.

Agrawal, Surrendra P. "On The Conceptual Framework Of Accounting," **JAL**, 1987, Vol. 6, pp. 165-178.

Aguirre, Alejandro and Moshe Hagigi. "Accounting, Economic, And Environmental Determinants Of Financial Reporting Practices In Guatemala," **IJAER**, 1987, Vol. 22, No. 2, pp. 169-191.

Aharoni, Yair. (Beja, Avraham and Yair Aharoni. "Some Aspects Of Conventional Accounting Profits In An Inflationary Environment," **JAR**, 1977, Vol. 15, No. 2, pp. 169-178.)

Aharoni, Y. and T. Ophir. "Accounting For Linked Loans," **JAR**, 1967, Vol. 5, No. 1, pp. 1-26.

Aharony, Joseph and Haim Falk. "The Effectiveness Of Electric Utility Price Regulation In The 1970s: A Stochastic Dominance Analysis," **JAPP**, 1982, Vol. 1, No. 1, pp. 59-77.

Aharony, Joseph and Sasson Bar-Yosef. "Tests Of The Impact Of Lifo Adoption On Stockholders: A Stochastic Dominance Approach." **CAR**, 1986-87, Vol. 3, No. 2, pp. 430-444.

Ahern, John T., Jr. and Patrick L. Romano. "Managing Inventories And Profits Through GMROI," **MA**, 1979, Vol. 61, No. 2, pp. 22-26.

Ahituv, Niv, Jonathan Halpern and Hart Will. "Audit Planning: An Algorithmic Approach." **CAR**, 1985-86, Vol. 2, No. 1, pp. 95-110.

Ahmed, Sadrudin A. and Daniel Zeghal. "Industry Segment Identification And Social Responsibility Information Disclosure In Selected Canadian Companies." **IJAER**, 1987, Vol. 22, No. 2, pp. 153-167.

Ahuja, Jag Mohan. (Singh, D. R. and Jag Mohan Ahuja. "Corporate Social Reporting In India," **IJAER**, 1983, Vol. 18, No. 2, pp. 151-169.)

Aiken, M. (Covaleski, M. and M. Aiken. "Accounting And Theories Of Organizations: Some Preliminary Considerations." **AOS**, 1986, Vol. 11, No. 4/5, pp. 297-320.)

Aiken, M., L. Blackett and G. Isaacs. "Modeling Behavioral Interdependencies For Stewardship Reporting," **AR**, 1975, Vol. 50, No. 3, pp. 544-562.

Aiken, William. "The Black Experience In Large Public Accounting Firms," **JOA**, 1972, Vol. 134, No. 2, pp. 60-63.

Ainajjar, Fouad. "Standardization In Accounting Practices: A Comparative International Study," **IJAER**, 1986, Vol. 21, No. 2, pp. 161-176.

Aird, Susan. (Edelstein, Lee and Susan Aird. "Commitment: The Key To Successful Accounting System Implementation," **MA**, 1988, Vol. 70, No. 6, pp. 50-51.)

Airey, C. R. "Depreciation: Left Or Right?," **AR**, 1959, Vol. 34, No. 4, pp. 570-571.

Aislabie, Colin. "The Choice Between Logic, Technique And Pragmatism In The Organizational Use Of Computers," **ABACUS**, 1966, Vol. 2, No. 1, pp. 68-77.

Aitken, Hugh T. "Accounting Related To Export Credits Insurance And Finance," **IJAER**, 1969, Vol. 5, No. 1, pp. 71-78.

Aitken, Michael J. and Trevor D. Wise. "The Real Objective Of The International Accounting Standards Committee," **IJAER**, 1984, Vol. 20, No. 1, pp. 171-177.

Aitken, M. J. and M. A. Islam. "Dispelling Arguments Against International Accounting Standards," **IJAER**, 1984, Vol. 19, No. 2, pp. 35-46.

Aivazian, Varouj A. and Jeffrey L. Callen. "Core Theory And Uniformity In Accounting: Rationalizing The Accounting Rulemaker," **JAPP**, 1983, Vol. 2, No. 4, pp. 225-237.

Ajinkya, Bipin B. and Michael J. Gift. "Corporate Managers' Earnings Forecasts And Symmetrical Adjustments Of Market Expectations," **JAR**, 1984, Vol. 22, No. 2, pp. 425-444.

Ajinkya, Bipin B. "An Empirical Evaluation Of Line-Of-Business Reporting," **JAR**, 1980, Vol. 18, No. 2, pp. 343-361.

Ajinkya, Bipin B. (Abdel-Khalik, A. Rashad and Bipin B. Ajinkya. "Returns to Informational Advantages: The Case Of Analysts' Forecast Revisions," **AR**, 1982, Vol. 57, No. 4, pp. 661-680.)

Ajinkya, Bipin, Rowland Atiase and Linda Smith Bamber. "Absorption Versus Direct Costing: Income Reconciliation And Cost-Volume-Profit Analysis," **IAE**, 1986, Vol. 1, No. 2, pp. 268-281.

Ajinkya, B. B. (Abdel-Khalik, A. R. and B. B. Ajinkya. "An Evaluation Of 'The Everyday Accountant And Researching His Reality'," **AOS**, 1983, Vol. 8, No. 4, pp. 375-384.)

Aked, H. John. "Control Of Fixed Costs In Relation To Volume," **MA**, 1967, Vol. 48, No. 7, pp. 12-20.

Akers, Michael D. and Grover L. Porter. "Expert Systems For Management Accountants," **MA**, 1986, Vol. 67, No. 9, pp. 30-34.

Akers, Michael D. (Porter, Grover L. and Michael D. Akers. "In Defense Of Management Accounting," **MA**, 1987, Vol. 69, No. 5, pp. 58-64.)

Akresh, Abraham D. and D. R. Finley. "Two-Step Attributes Sampling In Auditing," **CPAJ**, 1979, Vol. 49, No. 12, pp. 19-24.

Akresh, Abraham D. and George Russell Zuber. "Exploring Statistical Sampling," **JOA**, 1981, Vol. 151, No. 2, pp. 50-56.

Akresh, Abraham D. and Kay W. Tatum. "Audit Sampling - Dealing With The Problems," **JOA**, 1988, Vol. 166, No. 6, pp. 58-64.

Akresh, Abraham D. and Michael Goldstein. "Point-Of-Sale Accounting Systems: Some Implications For The Auditor," **JOA**, 1978, Vol. 146, No. 6, pp. 68-74.

Akresh, Abraham D. "Observations On Needed Research In Auditing: Materiality And Audit Risk," **AIA**, 1984, Vol. 1, pp. 225-238.

Akresh, Abraham D. "Statistical Sampling In Public Accounting," **CPAJ**, 1980, Vol. 50, No. 7, pp. 20-26.

Akresh, Abraham D. (Read, William J., John E. Mitchell and Abraham D. Akresh. "Planning Materiality And SAS No. 47," **JOA**, 1987, Vol. 164, No. 6, pp. 72-79.)

Akresh, Abraham D., John E. Mitchell and Howard S. Sibelman. "Obtaining Value From An Audit," **CA**, 1987, Vol. 5, No. 1, pp. 15-18.

Akresh, Murray S. (Eisenman, Seymour, Murray S. Akresh and Charles Snow. "Reporting Unusual Events In Income Statements," **CPAJ**, 1979, Vol. 49, No. 6, pp. 23-28.)

Al Hashim, Dhia D. "Accounting Control Through Purposive Uniformity: An International Perspective," **IJAER**, 1973, Vol. 8, No. 2, pp. 21-32.

Albergo, Hal. "Building Better Controls In The Commercial Lending Function," **MA**, 1980, Vol. 61, No. 8, pp. 14-18.

Albert, Anthony B. M. "A Cash Flow Approach To Corporate Credit Analysis," **MA**, 1976, Vol. 57, No. 10, pp. 40-43.

Albery, Michael. "Analysis Versus Interpretation Of Cost," **AR**, 1953, Vol. 28, No. 3, pp. 425-430.

Albrecht, William Steve, Orace Johnson, Larry L. Lookabill and David J. H. Watson. "A Comparison Of The Accuracy Of Corporate And Security Analysts' Forecasts Of Earnings: A Comment," **AR**, 1977, Vol. 52, No. 3, pp. 736-740.

Albrecht, William Steve. "Estimation Error In Income Determination: A Reply," **AR**, 1978, Vol. 53, No. 4, pp. 1003-1004.

Albrecht, William Steve. "Estimation Error In Income Determination," **AR**, 1976, Vol. 51, No. 4, pp. 824-837.

Albrecht, William Steve. "Toward Better And More Efficient Audits," **JOA**, 1977, Vol. 144, No. 6, pp. 48-50.

Albrecht, W. Steve and Marshall B. Romney. "Red-Flagging Management Fraud: A Validation," **AIA**, 1986, Vol. 3, pp. 323-334.

Albrecht, W. Steve, Larry L. Lookabill and James C. McKeown. "The Time Series Properties Of Annual Earnings," **JAR**, 1977, Vol. 15, No. 2, pp. 226-244.

Albrecht, W. Steve, Scott W. Brown and David R. Field. "Toward Increased Job Satisfaction Of Practicing CPAs," **JOA**, 1981, Vol. 152, No. 2, pp. 61-68.

Albrecht, W. Steve. (Romney, Marshall B. and W. Steve Albrecht. "The Use Of Investigative Agencies By Auditors," **JOA**, 1979, Vol. 148, No. 4, pp. 61-67.)

Albrecht, W. Steve. (Romney, Marshall B., W. Steve Albrecht and David J. Cherrington. "Auditors And The Detection Of Fraud," **JOA**, 1980, Vol. 149, No. 5, pp. 63-69.)

Alderman, C. Wayne and James W. Deitrick. "Auditors' Perceptions Of Time Budget Pressures And Premature Sign-Offs: A Replication And Extension," **AJPT**, 1981-82, Vol. 1, No. 2, pp. 54-68.

Alderman, C. Wayne and J. Kenneth Alderman. "The Impact Of Inflation On The Taxation Of Capital Gains And Losses," **MA**, 1977, Vol. 59, No. 6, pp. 53-56.

Alderman, C. Wayne, Dan M. Guy and Dennis R. Meals. "Other Comprehensive Bases Of Accounting: Alternatives To GAAP?," **JOA**, 1982, Vol. 154, No. 2, pp. 52-63.

Alderman, C. Wayne, Glenn E. Sumners and Mary Jeanne Welsh. "The Trend Toward Soft Data In Accounting," **MA**, 1983, Vol. 65, No. 6, pp. 34-39.

Alderman, C. Wayne. "An Empirical Analysis Of The Impact Of Uncertainty Qualifications On The Market Risk Components," **ABR**, 1978-79, Vol. 9, No. 36, pp. 258-266.

Alderman, C. Wayne. (Alderman, J. Kenneth and C. Wayne Alderman. "Accounting For Leases," **JOA**, 1979, Vol. 147, No. 6, pp. 74-79.)

Alderman, C. Wayne. (Deitrick, James W. and C. Wayne Alderman. "Interim Reporting Developments: A Step Toward The Auditor-Of-Record Concept," **JAAF**, 1979, Vol. 2, No. 4, pp. 316-328.)

Alderman, C. Wayne. (Deitrick, James W.. and C. Wayne Alderman and David L. Sayers. "A Profile Of An Accounting Doctoral Program: A Study Of Recent Graduates," **AIA**, 1985, Vol. 2, pp. 69-88.)

Alderman, C. Wayne. (Deitrick, James W. and C. Wayne Alderman. "Pension Plans: What Companies Do - And Do Not - Disclose," **MA**, 1980, Vol. 61, No. 10, pp. 24-29.)

Alderman, C. Wayne. (Robertson, Jack C. and C. Wayne Alderman. "Comparative Auditing Standards," **JAAF**, 1981, Vol. 4, No. 2, pp. 144-161.)

Alderman, J. Kenneth and C. Wayne Alderman. "Accounting For Leases," **JOA**, 1979, Vol. 147, No. 6, pp. 74-79.

Alderman, J. Kenneth. (Alderman, C. Wayne and J. Kenneth Alderman. "The Impact Of Inflation On The Taxation Of Capital Gains And Losses," **MA**, 1977, Vol. 59, No. 6, pp. 53-56.)

Alder, Donald H. "Organizing For International Operations," **MA**, 1969, Vol. 50, No. 9, pp. 28-34.

Alenius, Gunnar. "Improved Municipal Accounting Can Cut Taxes," **JOA**, 1952, Vol. 93, No. 5, pp. 564-567.

Alexander, Charles M. (DiLorenzo, Louis P. and Charles M. Alexander. "Employer's Responsibilities Under 1986 Immigration Act And COBRA," **CPAJ**, 1988, Vol. 58, No. 5, pp. 32-39.)

Alexander, Donald C. "New Internal Revenue Service Rules For Taxpayers' Rulings," **JOA**, 1954, Vol. 97, No. 3, pp. 321-328.

Alexander, Robin A. and John C. Gardner. "Before You Buy HAL," **CA**, 1988, Vol. 6, No. 1, pp. 18-24.

Alexion, John C. "Separate Schools Of Accountancy: Are They Necessary?," **MA**, 1977, Vol. 59, No. 3, pp. 11-13.

Alfano, James B. "Making Auditors' Reports Pure And Simple." **CPAJ**, 1979, Vol. 49, No. 6, pp. 37-41.

Alford, Mark R. and Thomas P. Edmonds. "A Replication: Does Audit Involvement Affect The Quality Of Interim Report Numbers?," **JAAF**, 1981, Vol. 4, No. 3, pp. 255-264.

Alford, R. Mark and Ted D. Skekel. "How The AMT Affects Corporate Decisions," **MA**, 1988, Vol. 70, No. 6, pp. 43-46.

Alford, R. Mark, Mattie C. Porter and Robert H. Strawser. "Forward Accounting - Past, Present And Future," **CPAJ**, 1981, Vol. 51, No. 2, pp. 40-47.

Alford, R. Mark, Mattie C. Porter and Robert H. Strawser. "Annual Reports Of Departments Of Accounting," **IAE**, 1985, No. 1, pp. 15-19.

Alfred, A. M. "Investment In The Development Districts Of The United Kingdom: Tax And Discounted Cash Flow," **JAR**, 1964, Vol. 2, No. 2, pp. 172-182.

Algate, Lyle E. (Czarnecki, Richard E. and Lyle E. Algate. "Using Consultants To Meet CPE Needs," **JOA**, 1980, Vol. 150, No. 2, pp. 64-68.)

Alhashim, Dhia D. and S. Paul Garner. "Postulates For Localized Uniformity In Accounting," **ABACUS**, 1973, Vol. 9, No. 1, pp. 62-72.

Alhashim, Dhia D. "Regulation Of Financial Accounting: An International Perspective," **IJAER**, 1980, Vol. 16, No. 1, pp. 47-62.

Alhashim, Dhia D. "Social Accounting In Egypt," **IJAER**, 1977, Vol. 12, No. 2, pp. 127-141.

Aliber, Robert Z. and Clyde P. Stickney. "Accounting Measures Of Foreign Exchange Exposure: The Long And Short Of It," **AR**, 1975, Vol. 50, No. 1, pp. 44-57.

Alkafaji, Yass and Nicholas Schroeder. "Manual-V-Computerized Practice Sets: A Test For Differences," **JAED**, 1986. Vol. 4, No. 2, pp. 19-25.

Alkier, Michael A. (Hole, Roderick C. and Michael A. Alkier. "German Financial Statements," **MA**, 1974, Vol. 56, No. 1, pp. 28-34.)

Alkire, Durwood L. "How To Handle Net Operating Loss Deductions," **JOA**, 1951, Vol. 91, No. 5, pp. 710-714.

Allan, Robert and Gary Paluba. "Avoiding Type-A Behavior During Tax Season," **CPAJ**, 1985, Vol. 55, No. 3, pp. 75-76.

Allardyce, Fred A. and Kenneth R. Todd, Jr. "Budgeting And Planning Implications Of Tax Credit Carryforwards, **MA**, 1969, Vol. 50, No. 7, pp. 51-56.

Allbright, William R. (Blade, David A. and William R. Allbright. "The Tax Planning Deduction," **CPAJ**, 1980, Vol. 50, No. 3, pp. 35-39.)

Alleman, Raymond H. "Comptrollership At ITT," **MA**, 1985, Vol. 66, No. 11, pp. 24-30.

Alleman, Raymond H. "Why ITT Likes FAS 52," **MA**, 1982, Vol. 64, No. 1, pp. 22-30.

Allen, Brandt R. "Computer Time-Sharing," **MA**, 1969, Vol. 50, No. 9, pp. 36-38.

Allen, Brandt. "The Biggest Computer Frauds: Lessons For CPAs," **JOA**, 1977, Vol. 143, No. 5, pp. 52-63.

Allen, Brandt. (Hawkins, David and Brandt Allen. "Computer Assisted Case Analyses," **AR**, 1967, Vol. 42, No. 4, pp. 788-800.)

Allen, C. B. "The Income Tax - Administrative Aspects," **AR**, 1928, Vol. 3, No. 1, pp. 7-13.

Allen, C. E. "The Growth Of Accounting Instruction Since 1900," **AR**, 1927, Vol. 2, No. 2, pp. 150-166.

Allen, C. E. "The Written Report In Accounting Systems," **AR**, 1935, Vol. 10, No. 1, pp. 26-28.

Allen, Gary. (Garsombke, H. Perrin and Gary Allen. "Did SFAS No. 19 Lead To Oil And Gas Company Mergers?," **JAAF**, 1983, Vol. 6, No. 4, pp. 285-298.)

Allen, James L. and Marvin Scher. "Risk Analysis For Nonmathematicians," **MA**, 1979, Vol. 61, No. 4, pp. 55-58.

Allen, John Robert. "The Auditor's Relationship To The Development Of Data Processing Controls," **MA**, 1977, Vol. 59, No. 5, pp. 39-42.

Allen, Robert F., Colin Park and Saul Pilnick. "The Shadow Organization," **MA**, 1974, Vol. 55, No. 7, pp. 56-60.

Allison, Lisa M. "The Accountant's Role In Acquisition Analysis," **MA**, 1984, Vol. 65, No. 12, pp. 56-60.

Allman, Storm A. "In Search Of Money," **MA**, 1971, Vol. 53, No. 2, pp. 29-32.

Allyn, Robert G. "Accreditation Of Accounting Curriculums," **AR**, 1966, Vol. 41, No. 2, pp. 303-311.

Allyn, Robert G. "An Approach To Financial Statement Analysis," **AR**, 1944, Vol. 19, No. 2, pp. 187-192.

Allyn, Robert G. "Case History Of A Terminated Contract," **AR**, 1945, Vol. 20, No. 4, pp. 410-414.

Allyn, Robert G. "Planning For The C.P.A. Examination In The United States," **AR**, 1964, Vol. 39, No. 1, pp. 121-127.

Allyn, Robert G. "The Study Of Philosophy As Part Of The Accounting Students' Training," **AR**, 1951, Vol. 26, No.

4, pp. 576-579.

Alm, I. W. "Combining Adjusting And Closing Entries," **AR**, 1939, Vol. 14, No. 4, pp. 432-436.

Alonzo, **Martin V.** "Corporate Strategy For Combating Inflation," **MA**, 1978, Vol. 59, No. 9, pp. 57-60.

Alou, **Susan** and Roger A. Roemmich. "Responsibility Accounting For Banks," **MA**, 1977, Vol. 58, No. 11, pp. 35-38.

Alpern, **Anita F.** "Staggered Tax Filing Dates: An Idea Whose Time Has Come?," **JOA**, 1976, Vol. 141, No. 4, pp. 49-51.

Alsup, **Rodney G.** (Dillon, Ray, Rodney G. Alsup and Kel-Ann Eyler. "Telecommunications Costs - How To Identify, Analyze, And Control Them," **MA**, 1988, Vol. 70, No. 2, pp. 50-53.)

Alsup, **Rodney G.,** Michael L. Holland and Fred A. Jacobs. "The Perceived Availability Of Resources Which Contribute To Accounting Faculty Productivity," **JAED**, 1988, Vol. 6, No. 2, pp. 261-277.

Altman, **Edward I.** and Thomas P. McGough. "Evaluation Of A Company As A Going Concern," **JOA**, 1974, Vol. 138, No. 6, pp. 50-57.

Altman, **Edward I.** "Accounting Implications Of Failure Prediction Models," **JAAF**, 1982, Vol. 6, No. 1, pp. 4-19.

Altman, **Edward I.** "Capitalization Of Leases And The Predictability Of Financial Ratios: A Comment," **AR**, 1976, Vol. 51, No. 2, pp. 405-412.

Altman, **Edward I.** "Multidimensional Graphics And Bankruptcy Prediction: A Comment," **JAR**, 1983, Vol. 21, No. 1, pp. 297-299.

Alvarez, **Frank.** "Condominium Accounting," **MA**, 1974, Vol. 56, No. 5, pp. 27-30.

Alvey, **Kenneth L.** "Alternative Derivation Of Formulas For The Income Tax Problem," **AR**, 1963, Vol. 38, No. 1, pp. 124-125.

Alvin, **Gerald.** "Accounting For Investments And Stock Rights: The Market Value Method," **CPAJ**, 1973, Vol. 43, No. 2, pp. 126-131.

Alvin, **Gerald.** "Charitable Contributions: 'Fruit' And 'Tree'," **JOA**, 1964, Vol. 118, No. 1, pp. 38-42.

Alvin, **Gerald.** "'Prepaid Income' And The Commissioner's Discretion Rule," **JOA**, 1965, Vol. 119, No. 6, pp. 45-52.

Aly, **Hamdi F.** and Jack I. Duboff. "Statistical Vs. Judgment Sampling: An Empirical Study Of Auditing The Accounts Receivable Of A Small Retail Store," **AR**, 1971, Vol. 46, No. 1, pp. 119-128.

Amante, **Joseph R.** and Robert L. Graham. "Flexible Budgeting: A Defense Industry Approach," **MA**, 1974, Vol. 55, No. 8, pp. 37-38.

Amato, **Henry N.,** Evan E. Anderson and David W. Harvey. "A General Model Of Future Period Warranty Costs," **AR**, 1976, Vol. 51, No. 4, pp. 854-862.

Ameiss, **Albert P.** "Could Swedish Auditing Procedures Result In Greater Corporate Control For U.S. Stockholders?," **IJAER**, 1970, Vol. 5, No. 2, pp. 103-116.

Ameiss, **Albert P.** "Developing Nations And Tax-Ordained Accounting Principles - The Swedish Model," **IJAER**, 1971, Vol. 6, No. 2, pp. 89-102.

Ameiss, **Albert P.** "International Accounting At The Senior Student Level," **IJAER**, 1974, Vol. 10, No. 1, pp. 107-121.

Ameiss, **Albert P.** "Two Decades Of Change In Foreign Subsidiary Accounting And United States Consolidation Practices," **IJAER**, 1972, Vol. 7, No. 2, pp. 1-22.

Ameiss, **Albert P.** (Terre, Norbert C., Dale W. Warnke and Albert P. Ameiss. "Cost/Benefit Analysis Of Public Projects," **MA**, 1973, Vol. 54, No. 7, pp. 34-37.)

Ameiss, **Albert P.,** Frank J. Ehlen, Charles W. Hutchison, Warren A. Thompson and Harry E. Wood. "Program Management In Missouri's Division Of Mental Health," **MA**, 1973, Vol. 55, No. 9, pp. 31-34.

Ameiss, **A. P.** "Can British Experience In Profit Forecasting Assist U.S. Firms Interested In Establishing Such Financial Disclosures?," **IJAER**, 1977, Vol. 13, No. 1, pp. 77-91.

Amenta, **Michael J.** "Unsettled Issues And Misapplications Of APB Opinion No. 19 As To Treatment Of Extraordinary Items," **CPAJ**, 1972, Vol. 42, No. 8, pp. 640-643.

Amernic, **Joel** and Robin Enns. "Levels Of Cognitive Complexity And Design Of An Accounting Curriculum," **AR**, 1979, Vol. 54, No. 1, pp. 133-146.

Amernic, **Joel E.** "A Framework For Analyzing Financial Reporting Cases," **JAED**, 1986, Vol. 4, No. 1, pp. 81-94.

Amernic, **Joel H.** and Nissim Aranya. "Public Accountants' Independence: Some Evidence In A Canadian Context," **IJAER**, 1981, Vol. 16, No. 2, pp. 11-33.

Amernic, **Joel H.** and Thomas H. Beechy. "Accounting Students' Performance And Cognitive Complexity: Some Empirical Evidence," **AR**, 1984, Vol. 59, No. 2, pp. 300-313.

Amernic, **Joel H.,** Rabindra Kanungo and Nissim Aranya. "Professional And Work Values Of Accountants: A Cross-Cultural Study," **IJAER**, 1983, Vol. 18, No. 2, pp. 177-192.

Amernic, **J. H.** and B. J. B. Galvin. "Implementing The New Foreign Currency Rules In Canada And The United States: A Challenge To Professional Judgment," **IJAER**, 1984, Vol. 19, No. 2, pp. 165-180.

Amernic, **J. H.** "The Roles Of Accounting In Collective Bargaining," **AOS**, 1985, Vol. 10, No. 2, pp. 227-253.

Amernic, **J.** (Aranya, N., J. Pollock and J. Amernic. "An Examination Of Professional Commitment In Public Accounting," **AOS**, 1981, Vol. 6, No. 4, pp. 271-280.)

Amernic, **J.** (Aranya, N., R. Lachman and J. Amernic. "Accountants' Job Satisfaction: A Path Analysis," **AOS**,

1982, Vol. 7, No. 3, pp. 201-216.)

Amershi, **Amin H.** and Peter Cheng. "Implementable Equilibria In Accounting Contexts: An Exploratory Study," **CAR**, 1988, Vol. 4, No. 2, pp. 515-563.

Amershi, **Amin H.** and Shyam Sunder. "Failure Of Stock Prices To Discipline Managers In A Rational Expectations Economy," **JAR**, 1987, Vol. 25, No. 2, pp. 177-195.

Amershi, **Amin H.** "Discussion Of 'A Model Of Standard Setting In Auditing'," **CAR**, 1986-87, Vol. 3, No. 1, pp. 93-101.

Amershi, **Amin H.,** Joel S. Demski and Mark A. Wolfson. "Strategic Behavior And Regulation Research In Accounting," **JAPP**, 1982, Vol. 1, No. 1, pp. 19-32.

Amershi, **Amin H.,** Joel S. Demski and John Fellingham. "Sequential Bayesian Analysis In Accounting," **CAR**, 1984-85, Vol. 1, No. 2, pp. 176-192.

Amer, **Metwalli B.** "Impact Of Public Ownership On The U.A.R. Accounting Profession," **IJAER**, 1969, Vol. 4, No. 2, pp. 49-61.

Amer, **Tarek,** Andrew D. Bailey, Jr. and Prabuddha De. "A Review Of The Computer Information Systems Research Related To Accounting And Auditing," **JIS**, 1987, Vol. 2, No. 1, pp. 3-28.

Amey, **Lloyd R.** and Jean-Louis Goffin. "Joint Product Decisions: The Variable Proportions Case," **CAR**, 1988, Vol. 5, No. 1, pp. 174-198.

Amey, **Lloyd R.** "Budgetary Planning: A Dynamic Reformulation," **ABR**, 1979-80, Vol. 10, No. 37, pp. 17-24.

Amey, **Lloyd R.** "Terborgh's Asset Replacement Formula Reconsidered," **CAR**, 1984-85, Vol. 1, No. 1, pp. 64-76.

Amey, **L. R.** "Towards A New Perspective On Accounting Control," **AOS**, 1979, Vol. 4, No. 4, pp. 247-258.

Amhowitz, **Harris J.** "The Accounting Profession And The Law: The Misunderstood Victim," **JOA**, 1987, Vol. 163, No. 5, pp. 356-369.

Amihud, **Yakov** and Haim Mendelson. "Liquidity, Volatility, And Exchange Automation," **JAAF**, 1988, Vol. 3 (New Series), No. 4, pp. 369-395.

Amit, **Raphael** and Joshua Livnat. "Diversification, Capital Structure, And Systematic Risk: An Empirical Investigation," **JAAF**, 1988, Vol. 3 (New Series), No. 1, pp. 19-48.

Amlung, **Martin J., III.** "Dollar-Value LIFO," **MA**, 1978, Vol. 60, No. 4, pp. 36-40.

Amoako-Adu, **Ben.** (Yagil, Joseph, Ben Amoako-Adu and Jeffrey Kantor. "Capital Cost Allowance (Depreciation) And Capital Budgeting In Canada," **IJAER**, 1986, Vol. 21, No. 2, pp. 47-54.)

Amory, **Robert, Jr.** "Accounting Instruction In Law Schools," **AR**, 1951, Vol. 26, No. 1, pp. 61-69.

Amsbaugh, **J. K.** "Accrual Calculations With Mutual Holdings," **AR**, 1965, Vol. 40, No. 2, pp. 461-462.

Anania, **Joseph V.** (Keegan, Daniel P., Robert G. Eiler and Joseph V. Anania. "An Advanced Cost Management System For The Factory Of The Future," **MA**, 1988, Vol. 70, No. 6, pp. 31-37.)

Andersen, **Anker V.** "A Defense Of Accounting Education," **AR**, 1962, Vol. 37, No. 4, p. 768.

Andersen, **Anker V.** "Current Collection And Credit Practices," **MA**, 1982, Vol. 64, No. 4, pp. 56-60.

Andersen, **Anker V.** "Why Write?," **AR**, 1963, Vol. 38, No. 4, pp. 827-830.

Andersen, **Arthur.** "Financial And Industrial Investigations," **AR**, 1929, Vol. 4, No. 1, pp. 16-22.

Andersen, **John A.** (Brown, James G., Jr. and John A. Andersen. "Sheltering Tax Dollars - Part II," **CPAJ**, 1983, Vol. 53, No. 6, pp. 34-39.)

Andersen, **John A.** (Brown, James G., Jr. and John A. Andersen. "Sheltering Tax Dollars - Part I," **CPAJ**, 1983, Vol. 53, No. 5, pp. 30-43.)

Anderson, **Bruce L.** and Alan M. Hoe. "Company Promotion And The Accountancy Profession In Nineteenth Century Sheffield," **ABR**, 1979-80, Vol. 10, No. 37, pp. 59-64.

Anderson, **Charles M.** "1 + 1 = 3," **MA**, 1987, Vol. 68, No. 10, pp. 28-31.

Anderson, **Charles M., Jr.** "The Capital Budgeting Process," **MA**, 1972, Vol. 54, No. 3, pp. 30-32.

Anderson, **David R.** "The Function Of Industrial Controllership," **AR**, 1944, Vol. 19, No. 1, pp. 55-65.

Anderson, **Donald C.** (Gallia, James J. and Donald C. Anderson. "Finished Goods Movement," **MA**, 1972, Vol. 54, No. 3, pp. 11-14.)

Anderson, **Donald T.** and Barry P. Arlinghaus. "Interest Capitalization For Corporate Taxation," **CPAJ**, 1983, Vol. 53, No. 11, pp. 25-29.

Anderson, **Donald T.** (Figlewicz, Raymond E., Donald T. Anderson and C. David Strupeck. "The Evolution And Current State Of Financial Accounting Concepts And Standards In The Nonbusiness Sector," **AHJ**, 1985. Vol. 12, No. 1, pp. 73-98.)

Anderson, **Donald T.,** Harold I. Dycus and Robert B. Welker. "GAAS And The Small Business Audit," **CPAJ**, 1982, Vol. 52, No. 4, pp. 10-23.

Anderson, **D. S.** "Communications Problems Of Financial Reporting," **JOA**, 1963, Vol. 115, No. 4, pp. 59-64.

Anderson, **Evan E.** (Amato, Henry N., Evan E. Anderson and David W. Harvey. "A General Model Of Future Period Warranty Costs," **AR**, 1976, Vol. 51, No. 4, pp. 854-862.)

Anderson, **Florence.** "How A Foundry Revised Its Standard Cost System," **MA**, 1970, Vol. 51, No. 11, pp. 51-52.

Anderson, **Gary J.,** Gordon B. Harwood and Roger H. Hermanson. "Energy Audits," **CPAJ**, 1979, Vol. 49, No. 1, pp. 31-34.

Anderson, **George D.** and Robert C. Ellyson. "Restructuring Professional Standards: The Anderson Report," **JOA**, 1986,

Vol. 162, No. 3, pp. 92-105.

Anderson, George D. "A Fresh Look At Standards Of Professional Conduct," **JOA**, 1985, Vol. 160, No. 3, pp. 91-106.

Anderson, George D. (Davidson, Sidney, and George D. Anderson. "The Development Of Accounting And Auditing Standards," **JOA**, 1987, Vol. 163, No. 5, pp. 110-126.)

Anderson, Henry R. and D. Dale Bandy. "Understanding The Unitary Tax," **MA**, 1985, Vol. 67, No. 3, pp. 35-43.

Anderson, Henry R. and Rickard P. Schwartz. "The Capital Facility Decision," **MA**, 1971, Vol. 52, No. 8, pp. 28-32.

Anderson, Henry R. "The 150-Hour Requirement: Florida's Experience," **CPAJ**, 1988, Vol. 58, No. 7, pp. 56-63.

Anderson, Henry R. "The G & A Overhead Pool: Accounting Tool Or Cop-Out?," **MA**, 1977, Vol. 59, No. 4, pp. 37-42.

Anderson, Henry R. (Brackney, William O. and Henry R. Anderson. "Regulation Of Cost Accounting: The Answer Or The Abyss," **MA**, 1981, Vol. 63, No. 4, pp. 24-31.)

Anderson, Henry R. (Weirich, Thomas R., Clarence G. Avery and Henry R. Anderson. "International Accounting: Varying Definitions," **IJAER**, 1971, Vol. 7, No. 1, pp. 79-87.)

Anderson, Hershel M. and Fred B. Griffin. "The Accounting Curriculum And Postgraduate Achievement," **AR**, 1963, Vol. 38, No. 4, pp. 813-818.

Anderson, Hershel M. and James W. Giese. "The Auditor's Belief And His Opinion - The Need For Consistency," **CPAJ**, 1973, Vol. 43, No. 1, pp. 49-54.

Anderson, Hershel. (Morris, William and Hershel Anderson. "Audit Scope Adjustments For Internal Control," **CPAJ**, 1976, Vol. 46, No. 7, pp. 15-20.)

Anderson, H. M., B. A. Coda and J. W. Giese. "An Experiment With A One-Semester Introductory Accounting Course," **AR**, 1972, Vol. 47, No. 1, pp. 175-177.

Anderson, H. M., J. W. Giese and Jon Booker. "Some Propositions About Auditing," **AR**, 1970, Vol. 45, No. 3, pp. 524-531.

Anderson, James A. and Kent E. St. Pierre. "Market Efficiency And Legal Liability: A Reply," **AR**, 1983, Vol. 58, No. 4, pp. 833-836.

Anderson, James A. and Morton Pincus. "Market Efficiency And Legal Liability: Some Extensions And An Illustration," **ABR**, 1983-84, Vol. 14, No. 54, pp. 169-181.

Anderson, James A. and Stephen L. Meyers. "Some Limitations Of Efficient Markets Research For The Determination Of Financial Reporting Standards," **ABACUS**, 1975, Vol. 11, No. 1, pp. 18-36.

Anderson, James A. "A Discussion Of 'Coalition Formation In The APB And The FASB'," **AR**, 1982, Vol. 57, No. 1, pp. 190-195.

Anderson, James A. "Information Interactions And Accounting Information User Reactions," **AR**, 1975, Vol. 50, No. 3, pp. 509-511.

Anderson, James A. "The Potential Impact Of Knowledge Of Market Efficiency On Legal Liability Of Auditors," **AR**, 1977, Vol. 52, No. 2, pp. 417-426.

Anderson, James A. (St. Pierre, Kent and James A. Anderson. "An Analysis Of Factors Associated With Lawsuits Against Public Accountants," **AR**, 1984, Vol. 59, No. 2, pp. 242-263.)

Anderson, James. (St. Pierre, Kent and James Anderson. "An Analysis Of Audit Failures Based On Documented Legal Cases," **JAAF**, 1982, Vol. 5, No. 3, pp. 229-247.)

Anderson, Jay H. "Some University Investment And Accounting Concepts," **JOA**, 1970, Vol. 129, No. 6, pp. 41-48.

Anderson, John C. and Alan W. Frankle. "Voluntary Social Reporting: An Iso-Beta Portfolio Analysis," **AR**, 1980, Vol. 55, No. 3, pp. 467-479.

Anderson, John C. and Barbara R. McIntosh. "An Analysis Of The Tax And Incentive Considerations Involved In Employee Leasing," **JATA**, 1988, Vol. 9, No. 2, pp. 19-30.

Anderson, John C. and James M. Kraushaar. "Measurement Error And Statistical Sampling In Auditing: The Potential Effects," **AR**, 1986, Vol. 61, No. 3, pp. 379-399.

Anderson, John C. and Joseph G. Louderback, III. "Income Manipulation And Purchase-Pooling: Some Additional Results," **JAR**, 1975, Vol. 13, No. 2, pp. 338-343.

Anderson, John J. "Computer-Supported Instruction In Managerial Accounting," **AR**, 1976, Vol. 51, No. 3, pp. 612-624.

Anderson, John J. "Integrated Instruction In Computers And Accounting," **AR**, 1967, Vol. 42, No. 3, pp. 583-588.

Anderson, John J. "Using The Statistical Analysis System As An Educational Audit Software System," **JAED**, 1985, Vol. 3, No. 1, pp. 131-144.

Anderson, John J. (Smith, L. Douglas and John J. Anderson. "Inflation Accounting And Comparisons Of Corporate Returns On Equity," **ABR**, 1985-86, Vol. 16, No. 62, pp. 107-116.)

Anderson, John M. "Dilemmas In Modern Accounting Research," **JAR**, 1964, Vol. 2, No. 2, pp. 236-238.

Anderson, Kenneth E. "A Horizontal Equity Analysis Of The Minimum Tax Provisions: 1976-1986 Tax Acts," **JATA**, 1988, Vol. 10, No. 1, pp. 7-25.

Anderson, Kenneth E. (Carruth, J. H., H. B. Whitehead and K. E. Anderson. "Maximizing Contributions To Retirement And Deferred Compensation Plans Under Sections 403(b), 401(k), And 457: A Linear Programming Approach," **JATA**, 1986, Vol.8,No.1,pp.49-72.)

Anderson, Kenneth E., Jr. "A Horizontal Equity Analysis Of The Minimum Tax Provisions: An Empirical Study," **AR**, 1985, Vol. 60, No. 3, pp. 357-371.

Anderson, Lane K. "An Update Of The CASB," **CPAJ**, 1979, Vol. 49, No. 2, pp. 29-35.

Anderson, Lane K. "Expanded Breakeven Analysis For A Multi-

Product Company," **MA**, 1975, Vol. 57, No. 1, pp. 30-32.

Anderson, Lane K. (Koester, Robert J. and Lane K. Anderson. "Accounting For Plant Removal Costs: A Solution," **MA**, 1983, Vol. 65, No. 5, pp. 75-80.)

Anderson, Lane K. (Taylor, Barbara G. and Lane K. Anderson. "Misleading Graphs: Guidelines For The Accountant," **JOA**, 1986, Vol. 162, No. 4, pp. 126-135.)

Anderson, Lane K. (Taylor, Barbara G., Lane K. Anderson and John T. Sennetti. "SFAC No. 2 Reliability From A Statistical Perspective," **JAED**, 1987, Vol. 5, No. 2, pp. 315-321.)

Anderson, Leslie P. and Vergil V. Miller. "Capital Budgeting: A Modified Approach To Capital Allocation," **MA**, 1969, Vol. 50, No. 7, pp. 28-32.

Anderson, Matthew J. "Some Evidence On The Effect Of Verbalizaion On Process: A Methodological Note," **JAR**, 1985, Vol. 23, No. 2, pp. 843-852.

Anderson, M. J. "A Comparative Analysis Of Information And Evaluation Behavior Of Professional And Non-Professional Financial Analysts," **AOS**, 1988, Vol. 13, No. 5, pp. 431-446.

Anderson, Paul F. "Distribution Cost Analysis Methodologies, 1901 - 1941," **AHJ**, 1979, Vol. 6, No. 2, pp. 39-51.

Anderson, Paul F. (Martin, John D., Paul F. Anderson and Arthur J. Keown. "Lease Capitalization And Stock Price Stability: Implications For Accounting," **JAAF**, 1979, Vol. 2, No. 2, pp. 151-164.)

Anderson, Rae D. (Gordon, Dennis and Rae D. Anderson. "Techniques For Handling Increased Enrollments," **AR**, 1958, Vol. 33, No. 3, pp. 486-496.)

Anderson, R. "The Usefulness Of Accounting And Other Information Disclosed In Corporate Annual Reports To Institutional Investors In Australia," **ABR**, 1980-81, Vol. 11, No. 44, pp. 259-266.

Anderson, Thomas E. and Joseph A. Hunt. "Operational Control Through Sampling - An Illustrative Case," **MA**, 1965, Vol. 47, No. 3, pp. 13-17.

Anderson, Thomas L., Jr. "Do Annual Reports Really Communicate?," **MA**, 1982, Vol. 64, No. 3, pp. 15-21.

Anderson, Thomas N., Jr. and Thomas E. Kida. "The Cross-Lagged Research Approach: Description And Illustration," **JAR**, 1982, Vol. 20, No. 2, Part I, pp. 403-414.

Anderson, Urton and Richard A. Young. Internal Audit Planning In An Interactive Environment," **AJPT**, 1988, Vol. 8, No. 1, pp. 23-42.

Anderson, Urton, Robert G. May and Carolyn A. Miles. "Variables Sampling Software: Development And Classroom Testing," **IAE**, 1988, Vol. 3, No. 1, pp. 156-173.

Anderson, Urton. (Marchant, Garry, John R. Robinson, Urton Anderson and Michael S. Schadewald. "A Cognitive Model Of Tax Problem Solving," **AIT**, 1988, Vol. 2, pp. xx-xx.)

Anderson, Wilton T. and Gary John Previts. Accounting Accreditation And Schools Of Accountancy In The United States." **AIA**, 1984, Vol. 1, pp. 89-104.

Anderson, Wilton T. and Milton F. Usry. "Use Of Theses And Reports In Master's Degree Programs," **AR**, 1970, Vol. 45, No. 3, pp. 579-584.

Anderson, Wilton T. "A Master Schedule For Partnership Dissolution - Installment Basis," **AR**, 1955, Vol. 30, No. 1, pp. 139-144.

Anderson, Wilton T. "Large Classes In Elementary Accounting." **AR**, 1964, Vol. 39, No. 4, pp. 1034-1036.

Anderson, Wilton T. "Recruiting Capable Students To Accounting," **AR**, 1966, Vol. 41, No. 2, pp. 331-333.

Anderson, Wilton T. "Suggested Changes In Accounting Education To Meet The Demand Of The Professon," **JAED**, 1983, No. 2, pp. 5-10.

Anderson, Wilton T. "The Admission Of A Partner, Goodwill Method," **AR**, 1957, Vol. 32, No. 1, pp. 646-648.

Andersson, Henry F. "Allowance For Setup Time Under Standard Costs," **AR**, 1960, Vol. 35, No. 3, pp. 497-500.

Anderton, F. Norman. "Centralized Cash Management For A Decentralized Company," **MA**, 1966, Vol. 47, No. 7, pp. 51-58.

Andlauer, Edgar L. "Inventory Management," **JOA**, 1959, Vol. 108, No. 2, pp. 25-31.

Andreae, Roy. "Present-Day Audit Technique," **AR**, 1947, Vol. 22, No. 3, pp. 253-262.

Andrews, Coleman. "Accounting And Management Of Public Affairs." **AR**, 1947, Vol. 22, No. 4, pp. 367-371.

Andrews, C. Roger. "Banking The 'Zero' Way," **MA**, 1971, Vol. 53, No. 3, pp. 31-35.

Andrews, J. Douglas and Betty P. Pytlik. "Revision Techniques For Accountants: Means For More Effective And Efficient Written Communication," **IAE**, 1983, No. 1, pp. 152-163.

Andrews, Richard W. (Godfrey, James T. and Richard W. Andrews. "A Finite Population Bayesian Model For Compliance Testing," **JAR**, 1982, Vol. 20, No. 2, Part I, pp. 304-315.)

Andrews, T. Coleman. "Advances In Governmental Accounting," **AR**, 1947, Vol. 22, No. 1, pp. 23-27.

Andrews, T. Coleman. "AIA Testimony Against Joint Budget Committee," **JOA**, 1951, Vol. 92, No. 1, pp. 102-106.

Andrews, Victor L. "Should Parent And Captive Finance Companies Be Consolidated?," **JOA**, 1966, Vol. 122, No. 2, pp. 48-56.

Andrews, Victor L. (Mehta, Dileep R. and Victor L. Andrews. "A Note On Installment Reporting Of Income, Profitability, And Fund Flows," **JAR**, 1968, Vol. 6, No. 1, pp. 50-57.)

Andrews, Wesley T. and Charles H. Smith. "A Role For Financial Accounting In National Economic Planning In The United States," **IJAER**, 1976, Vol. 12, No. 1, pp. 133-145.

Andrews, Wesley T. and Patrick B. McKenzie. "Leading Accounting Departments Revisited," **AR**, 1978, Vol. 53, No. 1, pp. 135-138.

Andrews, Wesley T. "Obtaining The Representations Of Legal Counsel," **CPAJ**, 1977, Vol. 47, No. 8, pp. 37-40.

Andrews, Wesley T. (Rose, Peter S., Wesley T. Andrews and Gary A. Giroux. "Predicting Business Failure: A Macroeconomic Perspective," **JAAF**, 1982, Vol. 6, No. 1, pp. 20-31.)

Andrews, Wesley T. (Wyman, Harold E. and Wesley T. Andrews, Jr. "Classifying The Receivable In A Lease Transaction: A Dilemma," **AR**, 1975, Vol. 50, No. 4, pp. 908-909.)

Andrews, Wesley T., Jr. "The Evolution Of APB Opinion No. 17 'Accounting For Intangible Assets'; A Study Of The U.S. Position On Accounting For Goodwill," **AHJ**, 1981, Vol. 8, No. 1, pp. 37-49.

Andrews, W. T. "Another Improbable Occurrence," **AR**, 1974, Vol. 49, No. 2, pp. 369-370.

Anell, B. "Exercises In Arbitrariness And Ambiguity - A Study Of Twelve Cost Benefit Analyses Of Industrial Disinvestment Decisions," **AOS**, 1985, Vol. 10, No. 4, pp. 479-492.

Angell, C. Robert. "Preservation And Orderly Destruction Of Records," **MA**, 1970, Vol. 51, No. 9, pp. 47-49.

Angell, Frank J. "Application Of Taxes To Life Insurance," **CPAJ**, 1980, Vol. 50, No. 9, pp. 47-54.

Angell, Frank J. "Taxation Of Life Insurance," **CPAJ**, 1983, Vol. 53, No. 6, pp. 40-48.

Angell, Frank J. "Which Life Insurance Is For You?," **CPAJ**, 1981, Vol. 51, No. 8, pp. 25-31.

Angel, Otto P. and Jay O. Kramer. "Questions On Taxability Of Foreign Income Left Unanswered By Mimeograph 6475," **JOA**, 1950, Vol. 89, No. 6, pp. 496-499.

Angus-Leppan, Pam and Vic Fatseas. "The Forecasting Accuracy Of Trainee Accountants Using Judgemental And Statistical Techniques," **ABR**, 1985-86, Vol. 16, No. 63, pp. 179-188.

Ankers, Raymond G. "College Education As A Requirement For Public Accountants In New York State," **AR**, 1946, Vol. 21, No. 4, pp. 441-444.

Ankers, Raymond G. "Institute's Vocational Tests Aid In Hiring And Promoting Staff Men," **JOA**, 1951, Vol. 91, No. 1, pp. 86-91.

Ankers, Raymond G. "The Question Of Staff Training," **AR**, 1946, Vol. 21, No. 1, pp. 1-7.

Ansari, Shahid L. and Diana T. Flamholtz. "Management Science And The Development Of Human Resource Accounting," **AHJ**, 1978, Vol. 5, No. 2, pp. 11-35.

Ansari, Shahid L. "Behavioral Factors In Variance Control: Report On A Laboratory Experiment," **JAR**, 1976, Vol. 14, No. 2, pp. 189-211.

Ansari, S. and K. J. Euske. "Rational, Rationalizing, And Reifying Uses Of Accounting Data In Organizations," **AOS**, 1987, Vol. 12, No. 6, pp. 549-570.

Ansari, S. L. and J. J. McDonough. "Intersubjectivity - The Challenge And Opportunity For Accounting," **AOS**, 1980, Vol. 5, No. 1, pp. 129-142.

Ansari, S. L. "An Integrated Approach To Control System Design," **AOS**, 1977, Vol. 2, No. 2, pp. 101-112.

Ansari, S. L. "Towards An Open Systems Approach To Budgeting," **AOS**, 1979, Vol. 4, No. 3, pp. 149-162.

Anstine, Patricia A. and Michael E. Scott. "ARCO Establishes Responsibility Accounting At Prudhoe Bay," **MA**, 1980, Vol. 61, No. 9, pp. 13-20.

Antal, A. B. (Dierkes, M. and A. B. Antal. "The Usefulness And Use Of Social Reporting Information," **AOS**, 1985, Vol. 10, No. 1, pp. 29-34.)

Anthony, Joseph H. and Steven C. Dilley. "The Tax Basis Financial Reporting Alternative For Nonpublic Firms," **ACCHOR**, 1988, Vol. 2, No. 3, pp. 41-47.

Anthony, Joseph H. "The Effect Of Information Announcements On Bid/Ask Spreads In The Call Options Market," **CAR**, 1986-87, Vol. 3, No. 2, pp. 460-476.

Anthony, Joseph H. "The New Corporate Alternative Minimum Tax," **CPAJ**, 1987, Vol. 57, No. 12, pp. 68-74.

Anthony, Paul. "Functional Cost Accounting For D. P. Centers," **MA**, 1976, Vol. 58, No. 4, pp. 33-41.

Anthony, Paul. "Goodbye Goodwill - Hello Share Of The Market," **MA**, 1977, Vol. 58, No. 12, pp. 31-40.

Anthony, Robert N. "Cost Allocation," **JCA**, 1984, Vol. 1, No. 1, pp. 5-15.

Anthony, Robert N. "Cost Concepts For Control," **AR**, 1957, Vol. 32, No. 2, pp. 229-234.

Anthony, Robert N. "Equity Interest - Its Time Has Come," **JOA**, 1982, Vol. 154, No. 6, pp. 76-93.

Anthony, Robert N. "Nonbusiness Financial Reporting: Is There Enough Guidance?," **JOA**, 1980, Vol. 150, No. 2, pp. 48-54.

Anthony, Robert N. "The Rebirth Of Cost Accounting," **MA**, 1975, Vol. 57, No. 4, pp. 13-16.

Anthony, Robert N. "We Don't Have The Accounting Concepts We Need," **CPAJ**, 1987, Vol. 57, No. 5, pp. 36-45.

Anthony, Robert N. (Govindarajan, V. and Robert N. Anthony. "How Firms Use Cost Data In Price Decisions," **MA**, 1983, Vol. 65, No. 1, pp. 30-37.)

Anthony, R. N. "Accounting For Subscription Income," **AR**, 1952, Vol. 27, No. 3, pp. 324-328.

Antle, Rick and Abbie Smith. "An Empirical Investigation Of The Relative Performance Evaluation Of Corporate Executives," **JAR**, 1986, Vol. 24, No. 1, pp. 1-39.

Antle, Rick and Abbie Smith. "Measuring Executive Compensation: Methods And Application," **JAR**, 1985, Vol. 23, No. 1, pp. 296-325.

Antle, Rick and Joel S. Demski. "The Controllability Principle In Responsibility Accounting," **AR**, 1988, Vol. 63,

No. 4, pp. 700-718.

Antle, Rick. "Auditor Indepedence," **JAR**, 1984, Vol. 22, No. 1, pp. 1-20.

Antle, Rick. "The Auditor As An Economic Agent," **JAR**, 1982, Vol. 20, No. 2, Part II, pp. 503-527.

Antonio, James F. "Is Government Going Corporate?," **CA**, 1986, Vol. 4, No. 1, pp. 44-50.

Antonio, James F. "Setting Governmental Accounting And Financial Reporting Standards In A Multi-Constituency Environment," **RIGNA**, 1987, Vol. 3, Part B, pp. 137-143.

Antoni, Tito. "The Pisan Document Of Philadelphia," **AHJ**, 1977, Vol. 4, No. 1, pp. 17-24.

Anton, Hector R. "Accounting For Bond Liabilities," **JOA**, 1956, Vol. 102, No. 3, pp. 53-56.

Anton, Hector R. "Funds Statement Practices In The United States And Canada," **AR**, 1954, Vol. 29, No. 4, pp. 620-627.

Anton, Hector R. "Objectives Of Financial Accounting: Review And Analysis," **JOA**, 1976, Vol. 141, No. 1, pp. 40-51.

Anton, Hector R. "Some Aspects Of Measurement And Accounting," **JAR**, 1964, Vol. 2, No. 1, pp. 1-9.

Anton, Hector R. "The Funds Statement As An Internal Report To Management," **AR**, 1955, Vol. 30, No. 1, pp. 71-79.

Anton, Hector R. (Brief, Richard P. and Hector R. Anton. "An Index Of Growth Due To Depreciation," **CAR**, 1986-87, Vol. 3, No. 2, pp. 394-407.)

Aoyagi, Bunji. "Sociological Accounting," **JOA**, 1958, Vol. 106, No. 1, pp. 51-55.

Apostolou, Nicholas G. (Crumbley, D. Larry, Nicholas G. Apostolou and Bob G. Kilpatrick. "Retirement Plan Alternatives," **CPAJ**, 1986, Vol. 56, No. 7, pp. 48-59.)

Apostolou, Nicholas G. (Crumbley, D. Larry, Nicholas G. Apostolou and Casper E. Wiggins. "Tax-Sheltered Plans In Educational And Other Organizations," **CPAJ**, 1984, Vol. 54, No. 4, pp. 22-31.)

Apostolou, Nicholas G. (Cummings, Barbara K., Nicholas G. Apostolou and William G. Mister. "Accounting For Interest Rate Swaps: An Emerging Issue," **ACCHOR**, 1987, Vol. 1, No. 2, pp. 19-24.)

Apostolou, Nicholas G. (Reeve, James M., Gary A. Giroux and Nicholas G. Apostolou. "Accounting Information And Municipal Bond Interest Cost: Methodological Considerations: Reply To Comment," **JAPP**, 1985, Vol. 4, No. 3, pp. 241-245.)

Apostolou, Nicholas G. (Robbins, Walter A. and Nicholas G. Apostolou. "SFAC No. 4: Implications For Nonbusiness Organizations," **CPAJ**, 1981, Vol. 51, No. 8, pp. 32-38.)

Apostolou, Nicholas G. (Robbins, Walter A., Nicholas G. Apostolou and Robert H. Strawser. "Municipal Annual Reports And The Information Needs Of Investors," **JAAF**, 1985, Vol. 8, No. 4, pp. 279-292.)

Apostolou, Nicholas G. (Wiggins, Casper E., D. Larry Crumbley and Nicholas G. Apostolou. "A Critical Analysis Of The Marriage Tax Penalty," **JATA**, 1986, Vol. 7, No. 2, pp. 60-75.)

Apostolou, Nicholas G., Gary A. Giroux and Robert B. Welker. "The Information Content Of Municipal Spending Rate Data," **JAR**, 1985, Vol. 23, No. 2, pp. 853-858.

Apostolou, Nicholas G., Hartwell C. Herring, III and Walter A. Robbins, Jr. "Are Changes Needed In Private Foundation Reporting Practices?," **MA**, 1980, Vol. 62, No. 5, pp. 39-42.

Apostolou, Nicholas G., James M. Reeve and Gary A. Giroux. "Accounting Information And Municipal Bond Net Interest Cost: An Empirical Evaluation," **JAPP**, 1984, Vol. 3, No. 1, pp. 9-28.

Apostolou, Nicholas. (Thibadoux, Greg M., Nicholas Apostolou and Ira S. Greenberg. "The Development Of Not-For-Profit Hospital Cost Models," **JCA**, 1988, Vol. 5, No. 1, pp. 35-48.)

Appleby, B. G. "Correlation Of Costs To Financial Statements," **AR**, 1946, Vol. 21, No. 4, pp. 410-414.

Aranya, Nissim and John T. Wheeler. "Accountants' Personality Types And Their Commitment To Organization And Profession," **CAR**, 1986-87, Vol. 3, No. 1, pp. 184-199.

Aranya, Nissim and Kenneth R. Ferris. "A Reexamination Of Accountants' Organizational-Professional Conflict," **AR**, 1984, Vol. 59, No. 1, pp. 1-15.

Aranya, Nissim and Moshe Sarell. "The Auditor-Firm Conflict Of Interests: A Comment," **AR**, 1975, Vol. 50, No. 4, pp. 854-856.

Aranya, Nissim. "The Influence Of Pressure Groups On Financial Statements In Britain," **ABACUS**, 1974, Vol. 10 No. 1, pp. 3-12.

Aranya, Nissim. (Amernic, Joel H. and Nissim Aranya. "Public Accountants' Independence: Some Evidence In A Canadian Context," **IJAER**, 1981, Vol. 16, No. 2, pp. 11-33.)

Aranya, Nissim. (Amernic, Joel H., Rabindra Kanungo and Nissim Aranya. "Professional And Work Values Of Accountants: A Cross-Cultural Study," **IJAER**, 1983, Vol. 18, No. 2, pp. 177-192.)

Aranya, N., J. Pollock and J. Amernic. "An Examination Of Professional Commitment In Public Accounting," **AOS**, 1981, Vol. 6, No. 4, pp. 271-280.

Aranya, N., R. Lachman and J. Amernic. "Accountants' Job Satisfaction: A Path Analysis," **AOS**, 1982, Vol. 7, No. 3, pp. 201-216.

Arbel, Avner and Bikki Jaggi. "Impact Of Replacement Cost Disclosures Of Investors' Decisions In The United States." **IJAER**, 1978, Vol. 14, No. 1, pp. 71-82.

Arbesfeld, Shirley. (Schiff, Michael and Shirley Arbesfeld. "Goodwill - A Make-Or-Buy Approach," **MA**, 1966, Vol. 47, No. 12, pp. 25-35.)

Arcady, Alex T. and Charles E. Baker. "Interest Cost Accounting: Some Practical Guidance," **JOA**, 1981, Vol. 151, No. 3, pp. 62-71.

Arcady, Alex T. (Strauss, Norman N. and Alex T. Arcady. "A New Focus On The 'Bottom Line' And Its Components," **JOA**, 1981, Vol. 151, No. 5, pp. 66-77.)

Arcady, Alex T. (Weber, Joseph V., Alex T. Arcady and Michael Valine. "Junior Stock For Executive Compensation," **CPAJ**, 1984, Vol. 54, No. 6, pp. 22-29.)

Arceri, Ralph J. "The Mobilehome Park," **MA**, 1975, Vol. 57, No. 3, pp. 49-50.

Archer, G. S. and K. V. Peasnell. "The Current Cost Of A Quoted Long-Term Liability: A Comment," **ABR**, 1984-85, Vol. 15, No. 58, pp. 87-90.

Archer, G. S. H. and K. V. Peasnell. "Debt Finance And Capital Maintenance In Current Cost Accounting," **ABACUS**, 1984, Vol. 20, No. 2, pp. 111-124.

Archibald, T. Ross. "Disclosure Of Accounting Changes: Some Empirical Data," **JOA**, 1971, Vol. 131, No. 4, pp. 34-40.

Archibald, T. Ross. "Stock Market Reaction To The Depreciation Switch-Back," **AR**, 1972, Vol. 47, No. 1, pp. 22-30.

Archibald, T. Ross. "The Return To Straight-Line Depreciation: An Analysis Of A Change In Accounting Method," **JAR**, 1967, Vol. 5, Supp., pp. 164-180.

Archibald, T. R. (Sorter, George H., Selwyn W. Becker, T. R. Archibald and W. Beaver. "Corporate Personality As Reflected In Accounting Decisions: Some Preliminary Findings," **JAR**, 1964, Vol. 2, No. 2, pp. 183-196.)

Arcus, Albert L. and William H. Pietsch. "Planned Performance And The Product Cost Controversy," **MA**, 1970, Vol. 52, No. 3, pp. 9-14.

Arens, Alvin A. and D. Dewey Ward. "The Use Of A Systems Understanding Aid In The Accounting Curriculum," **AR**, 1984, Vol. 59, No. 1, pp. 98-108.

Arens, Alvin A. (Sollenberger, Harold and Alvin A. Arens. "Assessing Information Systems Projects," **MA**, 1973, Vol. 55, No. 3, pp. 37-42.)

Arens, Alvin A., Robert G. May and Geraldine Dominiak. "A Simulated Case For Audit Education," **AR**, 1970, Vol. 45, No. 3, pp. 573-578.

Arens, John Russell. (Milano, Duane R. and John Russell Arens. "Microcomputer Test Banks For Accounting Principles: An Evaluation," **IAE**, 1987, Vol. 2, No. 1, pp. 85-93.)

Aretos, Gust M. "Developing Warehouse Costs," **MA**, 1972, Vol. 54, No. 4, pp. 46-48.

Arevalo, Claire. (May, Gordon S. and Claire Arevalo. "Integrating Effective Writing Skills In The Accounting Curriculum," **JAED**, 1983, Vol. 1, No. 1, pp. 119-126.)

Argyris, C. "Organziational Learning And Management Information Systems," **AOS**, 1977, Vol. 2, No. 2, pp. 113-124.

Ariyo, Ademola. "Economic Considerations In The Choice Of Depreciation Methods: Some Additional Information From Nigeria," **AIIA**, 1988, Vol. 2, pp. 87-97.

Arkin, Herbert. "A Statistician Looks At Accounting," **JOA**, 1958, Vol. 105, No. 4, pp. 66-68.

Arkin, Herbert. "Computers And The Audit Test," **JOA**, 1965, Vol. 120, No. 4, pp. 44-48.

Arkin, Herbert. "Discovery Sampling In Auditing," **JOA**, 1961, Vol. 111, No. 2, pp. 51-54.

Arkin, Herbert. "Statistical Sampling And Internal Control," **CPAJ**, 1976, Vol. 46, No. 1, pp. 15-18.

Arlinghaus, Barry P. (Anderson, Donald T. and Barry P. Arlinghaus. "Interest Capitalization For Corporate Taxation," **CPAJ**, 1983, Vol. 53, No. 11, pp. 25-29.)

Arme, John C. (Huizingh, William and John C. Arme. "The Effect Of Rate Changes On Income Tax Allocation," **MA**, 1965, Vol. 47, No. 4, pp. 17-20.)

Armitage, Howard M. (Lambert, Douglas M. and Howard M. Armitage. "Distribution Costs: The Challenge," **MA**, 1979, Vol. 60, No. 11, pp. 33-37.)

Armitage, H. M. and J. E. Boritz. "Integrating Computers Into The Accounting Curriculum," **IAE**, 1986, Vol. 1, No. 1, pp. 86-101.

Armitage, Jack. "Real Estate Tax Shelter - S Corporation Or Limited Partnership," **CPAJ**, 1986, Vol. 56, No. 5, pp. 34-41.

Armstrong, Charlotte P. "Cash Or Deferred Plans: The 401(k) Advantage," **CA**, 1984, Vol. 2, No. 3, pp. 47-54.

Armstrong, Marshall S. "Some Thoughts On Substantial Authoritative Support," **JOA**, 1969, Vol. 127, No. 4, pp. 44-50.

Armstrong, Mary Beth and Janice I. Vincent. "Public Accounting: A Profession At A Crossroads," **ACCHOR**, 1988, Vol. 2, No. 1, pp. 94-98.

Armstrong, Mary Beth. "Moral Development And Accounting Education," **JAED**, 1987, Vol. 5, No. 1, pp. 27-43.

Armstrong, P. "Changing Management Control Strategies: The Role Of Competition Between Accountancy And Other Organisational Professions," **AOS**, 1985, Vol. 10, No. 2, pp. 129-148.

Armstrong, P. "The Rise Of Accounting Controls In British Capitalist Enterprises," **AOS**, 1987, Vol. 12, No. 4/5, pp. 415-436.

Armstrong, William Y. "Why Only Emergency Facilities?," **AR**, 1946, Vol. 21, No. 4, pp. 390-395.

Arndt, Robert J. "Auditing The Savings And Loan Associations," **JOA**, 1965, Vol. 120, No. 2, pp. 36-43.

Arndt, Terry L. and Richard W. Jones. "Closing The GAAP In Church Accounting," **MA**, 1982, Vol. 64, No. 2, pp. 26-31.

Arnette, Denise A. (Marks, Larry A. and Denise A. Arnette. "Managing Your Banker," **CA**, 1988, Vol. 6, No. 2, pp. 27-30.)

Arnett, Harold E. "APB Opinion No. 29: Accounting For Nonmonetary Transactions - Some New Perspectives," **MA**, 1978, Vol. 60, No. 4, pp. 41-48.

Arnett, Harold E. "Implication Of The Capital Gains And Losses Concept In Practice," **AR**, 1965, Vol. 40, No. 1, pp. 54-64.

Arnett, Harold E. "Recognition As A Function Of Measurement In The Realization Concept," **AR**, 1963, Vol. 38, No. 4, pp. 733-741.

Arnett, Harold E. "Taxable Income Vs. Financial Income: How Much Uniformity Can We Stand?," **AR**, 1969, Vol. 44, No. 3. pp. 482-494.

Arnett, Harold E. "The Concept Of Fairness," **AR**, 1967, Vol. 42, No. 2, pp. 291-297.

Arnett, Harold E. "What Does 'Objectivity' Mean To Accountants?," **JOA**, 1961, Vol. 111, No. 5, pp. 63-68.

Arnett, Robert D. and Edwards R. Fish. "Is Everything Under Control?," **MA**, 1968, Vol. 50, No. 4, pp. 27-29.

Arnoff, E. Leonard. "Operations Research And Decision-Oriented Management Information Systems," **MA**, 1970, Vol. 51. No. 12, pp. 11-16.

Arnold, A. J. and I. Benveniste. "Wealth And Poverty In The English Football League," **ABR**, 1986-87, Vol. 17, No. 67, pp. 195-204.

Arnold, Donald F. and Ronald J. Huefner. "Measuring And Evaluating Replacement Costs: An Application," **JAR**, 1977, Vol. 15, No. 2, pp. 245-252.

Arnold, Donald F. and Thomas E. Humann. "Earnings Per Share: An Empirical Test Of The Market Parity And The Investment Value Methods," **AR**, 1973, Vol. 48, No. 1, pp. 23-33.

Arnold, Donald F. and Thomas J. Geiselhart. "Practitioners' Views On Five-Year Educational Requirements For CPAs," **AR**, 1984, Vol. 59, No. 2, pp. 314-324.

Arnold, Jerry L. and Earl C. Keller. "The Influence Of Accounting Rules On Tax Policy Objectives: An Empirical Investigation," **JATA**, 1980, Vol. 1, No. 2, pp. 10-16.

Arnold, Jerry L. (Manegold, James G., Jerry L. Arnold and Michael A. Diamond. "SEC Form S-18: A Boon To Small Business," **JOA**, 1986, Vol. 161, No. 5, pp. 102-108.)

Arnold, Jerry L., Alan A. Cherry, Michael A. Diamond and James A. Walker. "Small Business: An Area Ripe For Practice Development," **JOA**, 1984, Vol. 158, No. 2, pp. 74-83.

Arnold, Jerry L., William W. Holder and Jan R. Williams. "FASB Should Establish An Accounting Laboratory," **MA**, 1983, Vol. 64, No. 9, pp. 52-55.

Arnold, Jerry, William W. Holder and M. Herschel Mann. "International Reporting Aspects Of Segment Disclosure," **IJAER**, 1980, Vol. 16. No. 1, pp. 125-135.

Arnold, John and Anthony Hope. "Reporting Business Performance," **ABR**, 1974-75. Vol. 5, No. 18, pp. 96-105.

Arnold, John and Peter Moizer. "A Survey Of The Methods Used By UK Investment Analysts To Appraise Investments In Ordinary Shares," **ABR**, 1983-84, Vol. 14, No. 55, pp. 195-208.

Arnold, John. "On The Problem Of Interim Pricing Decisions," **ABR**, 1972-73, Vol. 3, No. 10, pp. 83-91.

Arnold, John. (Moizer, Peter and John Arnold. "Share Appraisal By Investment Analysts - Portfolio Vs. Non-Portfolio Managers," **ABR**, 1983-84, Vol. 14, No. 56, pp. 341-348.)

Arnold, John., Peter Moizer and Eric Noreen. "Investment Appraisal Methods Of Financial Analysts: A Comparative Study Of U.S. And U.K. Practices," **IJAER**, 1984, Vol. 19, No. 2. pp. 1-18.

Arnold, Roger. (Gibson, Robert W. and Roger Arnold. "The Development Of Auditing Standards In Australia," **AHJ**, 1981, Vol. 8, No. 1, pp. 51-65.)

Arnstein, Peter. "Pitfalls In Contract Preparation," **JOA**, 1957, Vol. 103, No. 5, pp. 51-55.

Arnstein, William E. "Price Changes And Profitability," **MA**, 1970, Vol. 51, No. 11, pp. 17-18.

Aronoff, Craig E. (Dillon, Ray D., Lloyd L. Byars, Craig E. Aronoff and Gale D. Eidson. "The CPA Firm's 'Mission'," **JOA**, 1985, Vol. 159, No. 6, pp. 70-78.)

Aronson, Joseph G. "Tax Considerations In Divorce," **CPAJ**, 1981, Vol. 51, No. 1, pp. 11-16.

Aronsson, Joyce and Thomas M. Porcano. "Covenants Not To Compete - Judicial Interpretations," **CPAJ**, 1983, Vol. 53. No. 1, pp. 18-23.

Arrington, Cecil E. and Philip M. J. Reckers. "A Social-Psychological Investigation Into Perceptions Of Tax Evasion," **ABR**, 1984-85, Vol. 15, No. 59, pp. 163-176.

Arrington, C. Edward, Charles D. Bailey and William S. Hopwood. "An Attribution Analysis Of Responsibility Assessment For Audit Performance," **JAR**, 1985, Vol. 23, No. 1. pp. 1-20.

Arrington, C. Edward, Robert E. Jensen and Masao Tokutani. "Scaling Of Corporate Multivariate Performance Criteria: Subjective Composition Versus The Analytic Hierarchy Process," **JAPP**, 1982, Vol. 1, No. 2, pp. 95-123.

Arrington, C. Edward, William A. Hillison and Paul F. Williams. "The Psychology Of Expectations Gaps: Why Is There So Much Dispute About Auditor Responsibility?," **ABR**, 1982-83, Vol. 13, No. 52, pp. 243-250.)

Arrington, C. Edward, William Hillison and Robert E. Jensen. "An Application Of Analytical Hierarchy Process To Model Expert Judgments On Analytical Review Procedures," **JAR**, 1984, Vol. 22, No. 1, pp. 298-312.

Arrington, C. Edward, William Hillison and Rhoda C. Icerman. "Research In Analytical Review: The State Of The Art," **JAL**, 1983, Vol. 2, pp. 151-186.

Arrington, C. Edward. (Holland, Rodger G. and C. Edward Arrington. "Issues Influencing The Decisions Of Accounting Faculty To Relocate," **IAE**, 1987, Vol. 2, No. 1, pp. 57-71.)

Arrington, C. Edward. (Jensen, Robert E. and C. Edward Arrington. "Accounting Education: Turning Wrongs Into Rights In The 1980's," JAED, 1983, Vol. 1, No. 1, pp. 5-18.)

Arthur, Donald, Jr. "Public Relations Fees," JOA, 1956, Vol. 101, No. 4, pp. 41-46.

Artman, James T. (Libby, Robert, James T. Artman and John J. Willingham. "Process Susceptibility, Control Risk, And Audit Planning," AR, 1985, Vol. 60, No. 2, pp. 212-230.)

Asebrook, Richard J. and D. R. Carmichael. "Reporting On Forecasts: A Survey Of Attitudes," JOA, 1973, Vol. 136, No. 2, pp. 38-48.

Ashburne, Jim G. "A Forward Looking Statement Of Financial Position," AR, 1962, Vol. 37, No. 3, pp. 475-478.

Ashburne, Jim G. "Accounting Training For Non-Accounting Majors," AR, 1955, Vol. 30, No. 1, pp. 134-139.

Ashburne, Jim G. "The Five-Year Professional Accounting Program," AR, 1958, Vol. 33, No. 1, pp. 106-110.

Ashby, Rod W. and George D. Funk. "Accounting For Contract Costs And Value In The Forest Products Industry," MA, 1980, Vol. 62, No. 2, pp. 41-44.

Asher, Leslie I. "Accounting For Stock Ownership," MA, 1968, Vol. 50, No. 1, pp. 17-22.

Ashley, C. A. "Replacement And Book Value," AR, 1944, Vol. 19, No. 3, pp. 298-299.

Ashley, C. A. "The Independent Accountant," AR, 1942, Vol. 17, No. 2, pp. 191-193.

Ashton, Alison Hubbard and Robert H. Ashton. "Sequential Belief Revision In Auditing," AR, 1988, Vol. 63, No. 4, pp. 623-641.

Ashton, Alison Hubbard. "A Field Test Of Implications Of Laboratory Studies Of Decision Making," AR, 1984, Vol. 59, No. 3, pp. 361-375.

Ashton, Alison Hubbard. "An Empirical Study Of Budget-Related Predictions Of Corporate Executives," JAR, 1982, Vol. 20, No. 2, Part I, pp. 440-449.

Ashton, Alison Hubbard. "Does Consensus Imply Accuracy In Accounting Studies Of Decision Making?," AR, 1985, Vol. 60, No. 2, pp. 173-185.

Ashton, Alison Hubbard. "The Descriptive Validity Of Normative Decision Theory In Auditing Contexts," JAR, 1982, Vol. 20, No. 2, Part I, pp. 415-428.

Ashton, D. J. "Goal Programming And Intelligent Financial Simulation Models Part I," ABR, 1985-86, Vol. 16, No. 61, pp. 3-10.

Ashton, D. J. "Goal Programming And Intelligent Financial Simulation Models Part II," ABR, 1985-86, Vol. 16, No. 62, pp. 83-90.

Ashton, Robert H. and Paul R. Brown. "Descriptive Modeling Of Auditors' Internal Control Judgments: Replication And Extension," JAR, 1980, Vol. 18, No. 1, pp. 269-277.

Ashton, Robert H. and Robert E. Hylas. "The Return Of 'Problem' Confirmation Requests By The U.S. Postal Service," AR, 1980, Vol. 55, No. 4, pp. 649-657.

Ashton, Robert H. and Robert E. Hylas. "A Study Of The Response To Balance And Invoice Confimation Requests," JAAF, 1981, Vol. 4, No. 4, pp. 325-332.

Ashton, Robert H. and Robert E. Hylas. "Increasing Confirmation Response Rates," AJPT, 1981-82, Vol. 1, No. 1, pp. 12-22.

Ashton, Robert H. and Sandra S. Kramer. "Students As Surrogates In Behavioral Accounting Research: Some Evidence," JAR, 1980, Vol. 18, No. 1, pp. 1-15.

Ashton, Robert H. "A Descriptive Study Of Information Evaluation," JAR, 1981, Vol. 19, No. 1, pp. 42-61.

Ashton, Robert H. "An Experimental Study Of Internal Control Judgments," JAR, 1974, Vol. 12, No. 1, pp. 143-157.

Ashton, Robert H. "Behavioral Implications Of Taxation: A Comment," AR, 1974, Vol. 49, No. 4, pp. 831-833.

Ashton, Robert H. "Cognitive Changes Induced By Accounting Changes: Experimental Evidence On The Functional Fixation Hypothesis," JAR, 1976, Vol. 14, Supp., pp. 1-17.

Ashton, Robert H. "Comment: Some Observations On Auditors' Evaluations Of Internal Accounting Controls," JAAF, 1979, Vol. 3, No. 1, pp. 56-66.

Ashton, Robert H. "Integrating Research And Teaching In Auditing: Fifteen Cases On Judgment And Decision Making," AR, 1984, Vol. 59, No. 1, pp. 78-97.

Ashton, Robert H. "Objectivity Of Accounting Measures: A Multirule-Multimeasurer Approach," AR, 1977, Vol. 52, No. 3, pp. 567-575.

Ashton, Robert H. "Some Implications Of Parameter Sensitivity Research For Judgment Modeling In Accounting," AR, 1979, Vol. 54, No. 1, pp. 170-179.

Ashton, Robert H. "The Predictive-Ability Criterion And User Prediction Models," AR, 1974, Vol. 49, No. 4, pp. 719-732.

Ashton, Robert H. "The Predictive-Ability Criterion And User Prediction Models: A Reply," AR, 1976, Vol. 51, No. 3, pp. 681-682.

Ashton, Robert H. "User Prediction Models In Accounting: An Alternative Use," AR, 1975, Vol. 50, No. 4, pp. 710-722.

Ashton, Robert H. (Ashton, Alison Hubbard and Robert H. Ashton. "Sequential Belief Revision In Auditing," AR, 1988, Vol. 63, No. 4, pp. 623-641.)

Ashton, Robert H. (Hylas, Robert E. and Robert H. Ashton. "Audit Detection Of Financial Statement Errors," AR, 1982, Vol. 57, No. 4, pp. 751-765.)

Ashton, Robert H. (Kessler, Lawrence and Robert H. Ashton. "Feedback And Prediction Achievement In Financial Analysis," JAR, 1981, Vol. 19, No. 1, pp. 146-162.)

Ashton, Robert H. (Lindahl, Frederick W., Craig Emby and Robert H. Ashton. "Empirical Research On LIFO: A Review And Analysis," JAL, 1988, Vol. 7, pp. 310-331.)

Ashton, Robert H., John J. Willingham and Robert K. Elliott. "An Empirical Analysis Of Audit Delay," JAR, 1987, Vol. 25, No. 2, pp. 275-292.

Ashton, R. H. "Deviation-Amplifying Feedback And Unintended Consequences Of Management Accounting Systems," AOS, 1976, Vol. 1, No. 4, pp. 289-300.

Ashton, R. K. "A Statistical Analysis Of Decisions In Revenue Cases By The House Of Lords," ABR, 1984-85, Vol. 15, No. 57, pp. 21-26.

Ashton, R. K. "Accounting For Finance Leases - A Field Test," ABR, 1984-85, Vol. 15, No. 59, pp. 233-238.

Ashton, R. K. "Asset Valuation And Imperfect Markets: An Extension," ABR, 1984-85, Vol. 15, No. 58, pp. 123-128.

Ashton, R. K. "Garner V. Murray - A Re-Appraisal," ABACUS, 1984, Vol. 20, No. 2, pp. 170-175.

Ashton, R. K. "Re-Appraisal Of Garner V. Murray: A Reply," ABACUS, 1986, Vol. 22, No. 1, pp. 51-53.

Ashton, R. K. "The Argyll Foods Case: A Legal Analysis," ABR, 1986-87, Vol. 17, No. 65, pp. 3-12.

Ashton, R. K. "The Effect Of SSAP 16 On Performance Measurement," ABR, 1984-85, Vol. 15, No. 60, pp. 259-264.

Ashton, R. K. "The Impact Of Search Costs And Asymmetric Information On Current Value Accounting," ABR, 1988, Vol. 18, No. 70, pp. 99-106.

Ashton, R. K. "The Royal Mail Case: A Legal Analysis," ABACUS, 1986, Vol. 22, No. 1, pp. 3-19.

Ashton, R. K. "Value To The Owner: A Review And Critique," ABACUS, 1987, Vol. 23, No. 1, pp. 1-9.

Ashworth, John. "People Who Become Accountants," JOA, 1968, Vol. 126, No. 5, pp. 43-49.

Ashworth, John. "Some Further Data On The Image Of The CPA," JOA, 1963, Vol. 115, No. 2, pp. 50-55.

Ashworth, John. "The Pursuit Of High Quality Recruits," JOA, 1969, Vol. 127, No. 2, pp. 53-58.

Ashworth, John. (Lang, Edwin R. and John Ashworth. "Integration In Fact - A Test Of The Professional Accountant As A Citizen," JOA, 1971, Vol. 131, No. 4, pp. 41-46.)

Ash, Ehiel. "Soviet Style Of Teaching Accounting," JAED, 1985, Vol. 3, No. 1, pp. 37-46.

Askari, Hossein, Patricia Cain and Richard Shaw. "A Government Tax Subsidy," AR, 1976, Vol. 51, No. 2, pp. 331-334.

Askew, Robert K. "Leveraged Buyouts: Pros, Cons, And The 'Setup'," CA, 1985, Vol. 3, No. 2, pp. 33-37.

Askins, Billy E. "Determining The Effectiveness Of Programmed Instruction - A Training Course Example," AR, 1970, Vol. 45, No. 1, pp. 159-163.

Aslanian, Paul J. and John T. Duff. "Why Accounting Teachers Are So Academic," JOA, 1973, Vol. 136, No. 4, pp. 47-53.

Asman, Mark F. "CPA-Client Practices In Management Advisory Services," CPAJ, 1975, Vol. 45, No. 5, pp. 22-28.

Atanian, Lynda. (Schaps, Albert L., Warren Kissin, Jay Borow and Lynda Atanian. "Auditing Small Businesses - A New Look," CPAJ, 1984, Vol. 54, No. 10, pp. 12-23.)

Atchison, Michael D. and Robert Sanborn. "Current Classification Criteria Of New Financial Instruments," AIA, 1987, Vol. 5, pp. 99-112.

Atiase, Rowland Kwame. "Market Implications Of Predisclosure Information: Size And Exchange Effects," JAR, 1987, Vol. 25, No. 1, pp. 168-176.

Atiase, Rowland Kwame. "Predisclosure Information, Firm Capitalization, And Security Price Behavior Around Earnings Announcements," JAR, 1985, Vol. 23, No. 1, pp. 21-36.

Atiase, Rowland K. and Senyo Tse. "Stock Valuation Models And Accounting Information: A Review And Synthesis," JAL, 1986, Vol. 5, pp. 1-34.

Atiase, Rowland K., Linda S. Bamber and Robert N. Freeman. "Accounting Disclosures Based On Company Size, Regulations And Capital Markets Evidence," ACCHOR, 1988, Vol. 2. No. 1, pp. 18-26.

Atiase, Rowland. (Ajinkya, Bipin, Rowland Atiase and Linda Smith Bamber. "Absorption Versus Direct Costing: Income Reconciliation And Cost-Volume-Profit Analysis," IAE, 1986, Vol. 1, No. 2, pp. 268-281.)

Atkeson, Thomas C. "Tax Equity And The New Revenue Act," AR, 1956, Vol. 31, No. 2, pp. 194-203.

Atkinson, Anthony A. "Discussion Of 'On The Allocation Of Fixed And Variable Costs From Service Departments'," CAR, 1987-88, Vol. 4, No. 1, pp. 186-193.

Atkinson, Anthony A. "Information Incentives In A Standard-Setting Model Of Control," JAR, 1979, Vol. 17, No. 1, pp. 1-22.

Atkinson, Sterling K. "Accounting Treatment Of The Bond Sinking Fund And Reserve," AR, 1935, Vol. 10, No. 1, pp. 102-106.

Atkinson, S. K. "Non-Manufacturing Costs In Management Decisions," JOA, 1951, Vol. 92, No. 3, pp. 326-330.

Atkins, Paul M. "University Instruction In Industrial Cost Accounting, Part I," AR, 1928, Vol. 3, No. 4, pp. 345-363.

Atkins, Paul M. "University Instruction In Industrial Cost Accounting, Part II," AR, 1929, Vol. 4, No. 1, pp. 23-32.

Atkisson, Curtis T. "Significant Contributions Of Modern Internal Auditing To Management," AR, 1946, Vol. 21, No. 2, pp. 121-127.

Atlas, Martin. "Average Income And Its Use In Taxation," AR, 1938, Vol. 13, No. 2, pp. 124-130.

Atlas, Martin. "Capital-Gains Taxation," AR, 1938, Vol. 13, No. 4, pp. 346-353.

Ator, Lloyd G., Jr. and Paul Claytor. "Commerical Banking And The TRA," JOA, 1987, Vol. 163, No. 4, pp. 102-107.

Atwood, Jesse W. "Motor Freight Reporting," MA, 1969, Vol. 50, No. 5, pp. 53-54.

Atwood, Paul W. "The Manufacturer Looks At His Cost Of Distribution," AR, 1934, Vol. 9, No. 1, pp. 23-28.

Aucoin, Samuel A. "10 Steps To Winning Approval Of A New Reporting System," MA, 1988, Vol. 69, No. 12, pp. 50-54.

Augenbraun, Barry S. "Proposed Audit Report - A Lawyer's View," CPAJ, 1980, Vol. 50, No. 11, pp. 15-20.

Augenbraun, Barry S. (Solomon, Kenneth I., Charles Chazen and Barry S. Augenbraun. "Who Judges The Auditor, And How?," JOA, 1976, Vol. 142, No. 2, pp. 67-74.)

Auger, B. Y. "Presenting...The Budget!," MA, 1981, Vol. 62, No.11, pp. 22-27.

Augustine, Norman R. "A Viewpoint Of Industry," JCA, 1985, Vol. 2, No. 1, pp. 1-20.

Ault, David E. and M. Robert Carver. "The Effect of Pedagogical Format On The Performance Of MBA Students In Graduate-Level Accounting Courses," IAE, 1987, Vol. 2, No. 2, pp. 161-172.

Auster, Rolf. "Option Writing: Strategies And Taxation," JOA, 1977, Vol. 143, No. 5, pp. 64-70.

Austin, L. Allan. (Bostrom, Erik, L. Allan Austin and Robert J. Zenowich. "The ABB Link: Accounting-Based Decisions Improve Planning," CA, 1985, Vol. 3, No. 3, pp. 14-21.

Austin, Kenneth R. and David C. Langston. "Peer Review: Its Impact On Quality Control," JOA, 1981, Vol. 152, No. 1, pp. 78-82.

Austin, Kenneth R. (Robbins, Walter A. and Kenneth R. Austin. "Disclosure Quality In Governmental Financial Reports: An Assessment Of The Appropriateness Of A Compound Measure," JAR, 1986, Vol. 24, No. 2, pp. 412-421.)

Austin, Kenneth R., Robert Strawser and Henry Mixon. "Contingencies And Unasserted Claims: Adequate Answers?," CPAJ, 1985, Vol. 55, No. 9, pp. 48-58.

Austin, Maurice. "Relations Of Lawyers And CPAs In Tax Practice," JOA, 1951, Vol. 91, No. 6, pp. 805-815.

Austin, P. Thomas, Joel M. Forster and Robert M. Rosen. "Tax Reform: The New Perspective," JOA, 1977, Vol. 143, No. 3, pp. 48-59.

Avery, Clarence G. (Weirich, Thomas R., Clarence G. Avery and Henry R. Anderson. "International Accounting: Varying Definitions," IJAER, 1971, Vol. 7, No. 1, pp.79-87.)

Avery, Harold G. and M. Pollack. "Cost And Output Relationships," AR, 1946, Vol. 21, No. 4, pp. 419-424.

Avery, Harold G. "A Study Of Net Worth Comparison," AR, 1954, Vol. 29, No. 1, pp. 114-120.

Avery, Harold G. "Accounting As A Language," AR, 1953, Vol. 28, No. 1, pp. 83-87.

Avery, Harold G. "Accounting For Appraisals," AR, 1940, Vol. 15, No. 3, pp. 394-399.

Avery, Harold G. "Accounting For Intangible Assets," AR, 1942, Vol. 17, No. 4, pp. 354-362.

Avery, Harold G. "Accounting For Joint Costs," AR, 1951, Vol. 26, No. 2, pp. 232-238.

Avery, Harold G. "An Analysis Of Missouri's Utility Earnings And Rate Base Formula - A Rejoinder," AR, 1955, Vol. 30, No. 3, pp. 485-492.

Avery, Harold G. "Capital And Revenue Expenditures," AR, 1941, Vol. 16, No. 3, pp. 274-280.

Avery, Harold G. "Cost Distribution By Regulation," AR, 1959, Vol. 34, No. 2, pp. 250-256.

Avery, Harold G. "Depreciation Vs. Inflation," AR, 1961, Vol. 36, No. 1, pp. 71-74.

Avery, Harold G. "Formal Accounting Laboratory Or Not?," AR, 1958, Vol. 33, No. 2, pp. 309-313.

Avery, Harold G. "Some Aspects Of Public Utility Accounting," AR, 1954, Vol. 29, No. 4, pp. 575-583.

Avery, Harold G. "The Problem Of Idle Equipment," AR, 1940, Vol. 15, No. 4, pp. 469-473.

Avery, Harold G. "The Relative Importance Of Fixed Assets," AR, 1956, Vol. 31, No. 3, pp. 435-438.

Avery, Harold G. "Unbilled Revenues," AR, 1957, Vol. 32, No. 3, pp. 403-405.

Awad, Saber A. (Jones, Gardner M. and Saber A. Awad. "The Use Of Accounting Techniques In Small Firms," MA, 1972, Vol. 53, No. 8, pp. 41-44.)

Axelson, Kenneth S. "A Businessman's Views On Disclosure," JOA, 1975, Vol. 140, No. 1, pp. 42-46.

Axelson, Kenneth S. "Are Consulting And Auditing Compatible?," JOA, 1963, Vol. 115, No. 4, pp. 54-58.

Axelson, Kenneth S. "Facing The Hard Truths About Inflation," MA, 1980, Vol. 61, No. 12, pp. 11-14.

Axline, Larry L. "A Strategy For Personnel Growth," MA, 1976, Vol. 57, No. 11, pp. 38-40.

Axline, Larry L. "Are Your Clients Satisfied?," JOA, 1984, Vol. 158, No. 1, pp. 84-90.

Axline, Larry L. "Planning For Partner Succession," JOA, 1977, Vol. 143, No. 4, pp. 74-78.

Ayer, Leland G. (Belford, William B. and Leland G. Ayer. "Unitization Of Construction Work Orders," MA, 1969, Vol. 51, No. 3, pp. 29-32.)

Ayer, Leland G. (Finnell, Jack C., Leland G. Ayer and Frank B. Harris. "Full Costing In The Oil And Gas Producing Industry," MA, 1967, Vol. 48, No. 5, pp. 47-52.)

Ayres, Frances L. "A Comment On Corporate Preferences For Foreign Currency Accounting Standards," JAR, 1986, Vol. 24, No. 1, pp. 166-169.

Ayres, Frances L. "An Empirical Assessment Of The Effects Of The Investment Tax Credit Legislation On Returns To Equity Securities," JAPP, 1987, Vol. 6, No. 2, pp. 115-137.

Ayres, Frances L. "Characteristics Of Firms Electing Early Adoption Of SFAS 52," JAEC, 1986, Vol. 8, No. 2, pp. 143-158.

Ayres, Frances L. "Models Of Coalition Formation, Reward

Allocation And Accounting Cost Allocations: A Review And Synthesis," JAL, 1985, Vol. 4, pp. 1-32.

Azorsky, Michael A. "Establishing A Personal Financial Planning Department In Your CPA Firm," JOA, 1987, Vol. 164, No. 1, pp. 102-110.

BBB

Baab, John G. (Paroby, Stephen M., John G. Baab and Lewis Kramer. "Controlling Your Computer," CA, 1987, Vol. 5, No. 2, pp. 34-41.)

Babbitt, J. C. (Brady, Edward and J. C. Babbitt. "Inventory Control Systems," MA, 1972, Vol. 54, No. 6, pp. 42-44.)

Baber, C. (Edwards, J. R. and C. Baber. "Dowlais Iron Company: Accounting Policies And Procedures For Profit Measurement And Reporting Purposes," ABR, 1978-79, Vol. 9, No. 34, pp. 139-151.)

Baber, William R. and Pradyot K. Sen. "The Role Of Generally Accepted Reporting Methods In The Public Sector: An Empirical Test," JAPP, 1984, Vol. 3, No. 2, pp. 91-106.

Baber, William R. "A Framework For Making A Class Of Internal Accounting Control Decisions," JAR, 1985, Vol. 23, No. 1, pp. 360-369.

Baber, William R. "Budget-Based Compensation And Discretionary Spending," AR, 1985, Vol. 60, No. 1, pp. 1-9.

Baber, William R. "Toward Understanding The Role Of Auditing In The Public Sector," JAEC, 1983, Vol. 5, No. 3, pp. 213-227.

Baber, William R., Eugene H. Brooks and William E. Ricks. "An Empirical Investigation Of The Market For Audit Services In The Public Sector," JAR, 1987, Vol. 25, No. 2, pp. 293-305.

Babich, George. "The Application Of Information Theory To Accounting Reports: An Appraisal," ABACUS, 1975, Vol. 11, No. 2, pp. 172-181.

Babson, Stanley M., Jr. "Profiling Your Productivity," MA, 1981, Vol. 63, No. 6, pp. 13-17.

Bacas, Paul E. "Content Of The Auditing Course," AR, 1939, Vol. 14, No. 3, pp. 263-266.

Baccouche, Mustapha. "The Need For International Accountancy," IJAER, 1969, Vol. 5, No. 1, pp. 97-99.

Bachman, Joseph W. (Patten, Ronald J. and Joseph W. Bachman. "Elementary Accounting Profile - 1970," AR, 1972, Vol. 47, No. 1, pp. 164-167.)

Bachrach, Michael D. "Accountant's Course When Client Needs Life Insurance," JOA, 1953, Vol. 95, No. 5, pp. 594-596.

Bachrach, Michael D. "Analysis Of King Bill (To Tighten Up Tax Collection)," JOA, 1952, Vol. 94, No. 2, pp.172-177.

Bachrach, Michael D. "How Banks Differ From Ordinary Corporations For Income-Tax Purposes," JOA, 1950, Vol. 89, No. 5, pp. 400-403.

Bachrach, Michael D. "How To Deal With Inconsistencies In Tax Law On Prepayments, Deferrals, Reserves," JOA, 1951, Vol. 91, No. 2, pp. 282-285.

Bachrach, Michael D. "Management Service Referrals," JOA, 1958, Vol. 105, No. 3, pp. 37-39.

Bachrach, Michael D. "Tax Simplification," AR, 1945, Vol. 20, No. 1, pp. 102-103.

Bachtell, George A. "Standard Cost System For A Foundry," MA, 1967, Vol. 49, No. 4, pp. 35-41.

Bach, G. Leland. "Accounting Education For The 1980's," JOA, 1961, Vol. 112, No. 3, pp. 50-54.

Backer, Morton and Paul E. Fertig. "Statistical Sampling And The Accounting Curriculum," AR, 1958, Vol. 33, No. 3. pp. 415-418.

Backer, Morton. "A Model For Current Value Reporting," CPAJ, 1974, Vol. 44, No. 2, pp. 27-34.

Backer, Morton. "Accounting Theory, Objectives And Measurements," JOA, 1963, Vol. 116, No. 4, pp. 57-63.

Backer, Morton. "Comments On 'The Value Of The SEC's Accounting Disclosure Requirements'," AR, 1969, Vol. 44, No. 3, pp. 533-538.

Backer, Morton. "Reporting Profit Expectations," MA, 1972, Vol. 53, No. 8, pp. 33-37.

Backer, Morton. "The Quantitative Data Course In the Executive Development Program," AR, 1961, Vol. 36, No. 2, pp. 217-221.

Backes, Robert W. and Robert J. Glowacki. "Microcomputers: Successful Management And Control," MA, 1983, Vol. 65, No. 3, pp. 48-51.

Backes, Robert W. "Cycle Counting - A Better Method For Achieving Accurate Inventory Records," MA, 1980, Vol. 61, No. 7, pp. 42-46.

Backman, Jules. "Factors Affecting Fee Setting In The Professions," JOA, 1953, Vol. 95, No. 5, pp. 554-566.

Bacon, Peter W. (Gitman, Lawrence J., Michael D. Joehnk and Peter W. Bacon. "Fundamentals Of Cash Management: Theory And Practice," JCA, 1984, Vol. 1, No. 1, pp. 75-99.)

Bacsik, Jeffrey M. and Stephen F. Rizzo. "Review Of Audit Workpapers," CPAJ, 1983, Vol. 53, No. 11, pp. 12-24.

Bae, Alexander. "Advantages Of 'Break-Even' Income Statement Compared With Conventional Statement," JOA, 1951, Vol. 91, No. 1, pp. 106-111.

Bagby, John W. and Philip L. Kintzele. "Management's Responsibilities For Management Reports," CPAJ, 1982, Vol. 52, No. 11, pp 30-39.

Bagby, John W. and Philip L. Kintzele. "Management Discussion And Analysis: Discretionary Disclosures And The Business Segment," ACCHOR, 1987, Vol. 1, No. 1,pp.51-60.

Baggett, Monte R., Richard D. Dole and Jack E. Short. "Accounting And Auditing For Drilling Funds," CPAJ, 1981, Vol. 51, No. 9, pp. 27-37.

Baggett, Samuel M. (Harrison, James F., Jr. and Samuel M. Baggett. "Processing New Ideas," MA, 1974, Vol. 55, No.

10, pp. 25-30.)

Baggett, Walter O. "Internal Control: Insight From A General Systems Theory Perspective," **JAAF**, 1983, Vol. 6, No. 3, pp. 227-233.

Baginski, Stephen P. "Intraindustry Information Transfers Associated With Management Forecasts Of Earnings," **JAR**, 1987, Vol. 25, No. 2, pp. 196-216.

Bagley, Ron N. and James W. Jenkins. "Capital Gain Yielding Bonds Produce Higher Than Expected After Tax Bond Yields," **JATA**, 1979, Vol. 1, No. 1, pp. 15-24.

Bailes, Jack C. and Graeme M. McNally. "Cost And Management Accounting Practices In New Zealand," **IJAER**, 1984, Vol. 19, No. 2, pp. 59-71.

Bailes, Jack C. and Robert L. Edwards. "Productivity Boost: Treating Employees As Independent Contractors," **MA**, 1987, Vol. 69, No. 4, pp. 48-51.

Bailes, Jack C. "Lectures Versus Personalized Instruction: An Experimental Study In Elementary Managerial Accounting," **AR**, 1979, Vol. 54, No. 1, pp. 147-154.

Bailes, Jack C. (Shelton, Fred A. and Jack C. Bailes. "How To Create An Electronic Spreadsheet Budget," **MA**, 1986, Vol. 68, No. 1, pp. 40-47.)

Bailes, Jack C., James F. Nielsen and Steve Wendell. "Capital Budgeting In The Forest Products Industry," **MA**, 1979, Vol. 61, No. 1, pp. 46-51.

Bailes, Jack, Barry Shane and C. Dean Pielstick. "Using Your PC To Project Capital Investment Funds," **MA**, 1988, Vol. 70, No. 1, pp. 59-62.

Bailey, Andrew A., Jr., Warren J. Boe and Thomas Schnack. "The Audit Staff Assignment Problem: A Comment," **AR**, 1974, Vol. 49, No. 3, pp. 572-574.

Bailey, Andrew D. (Ko, Chen-En, Christopher J. Nachtsheim, Gordon L. Duke and Andrew D. Bailey, Jr. "On The Robustness Of Model-Based Sampling In Auditing," **AJPT**, 1988, Vol. 7, No. 2, pp. 119-136.)

Bailey, Andrew D., Jr. and Daniel L. Jensen. "The Two-Dimensional Time Frame Of Common Dollar Statements," **AR**, 1977, Vol. 52, No. 1, pp. 229-237.

Bailey, Andrew D., Jr. and Daniel L. Jensen. "A Note On The Interface Between Compliance And Substantive Tests," **JAR**, 1977, Vol. 15, No. 2, pp. 293-299.

Bailey, Andrew D., Jr. and Jack Gray. "A Study Of The Importance Of The Planning Horizon On Reports Utilizing Discounted Future Cash Flows," **JAR**, 1968, Vol. 6, No. 1, pp. 98-105.

Bailey, Andrew D., Jr. and Warren J. Boe. "Goal And Resource Transfers In The Multigoal Organization," **AR**, 1976, Vol. 51, No. 3, pp. 559-573.

Bailey, Andrew D., Jr. "A Dynamic Programming Approach To The Analysis Of Different Costing Methods In Accounting For Inventories," **AR**, 1973, Vol. 48, No. 3, pp. 560-574.

Bailey, Andrew D., Jr. (Amer, Tarek, Andrew D. Bailey, Jr. and Prabuddha De. "A Review Of The Computer Information Systems Research Related To Accounting And Auditing," **JIS**, 1987, Vol. 2, No. 1, pp. 3-28.)

Bailey, Andrew D., Jr. (Cash, James I. Jr., Andrew D. Bailey, Jr. and Andrew B. Whinston. "A Survey Of Techniques For Auditing EDP-Based Accounting Information Systems," **AR**, 1977, Vol. 52, No. 4, pp. 813-832.)

Bailey, Andrew D., Jr. (Danos, Paul, Doris L. Holt and Andrew D. Bailey, Jr. "The Interaction Of Science And Attestation Standard Formation," **AJPT**, 1986-87, Vol. 6, No. 2, pp. 134-149.)

Bailey, Andrew D., Jr. (Kinney, William R., Jr. and Andrew D. Bailey, Jr. "Regression Analysis As A Means Of Determining Audit Sample Size: A Comment," **AR**, 1976, Vol. 51, No. 2, pp. 395-401.)

Bailey, Andrew D., Jr. (Meservy, Rayman D., Andrew D. Bailey, Jr. and Paul E. Johnson. "Internal Control Evaluation: A Computational Model Of The Review Process," **AJPT**, 1986-87, Vol. 6, No. 1, pp. 44-74.)

Bailey, Andrew D., Jr. (Nusbaum, Edward E., Andrew D. Bailey, Jr. and Andrew B. Whinston. "Data-Base Management, Accounting, And Accountants," **MA**, 1978, Vol. 59, No. 11, pp. 35-38.)

Bailey, Andrew D., Jr., Gordon Leon Duke, James Gerlach, Chen-En Ko, Rayman D. Meservy and Andrew B. Whinston. "TICOM And The Analysis Of Internal Controls," **AR**, 1985, Vol. 60, No. 2, pp. 186-201.

Bailey, Andrew D., Jr., Karl Hackenbrack, Prabuddha De, and Jesse Dillard. "Artificial Intelligence, Cognitive Science, And Computational Modeling In Auditing Research: A Research Approach," **JIS**, 1987, Vol. 1, No. 2, pp. 20-40.

Bailey, Andrew D., R. Preston McAfee and Andrew B. Whinston. "An Application Of Complexity Theory To The Analysis Of Internal Control Systems," **AJPT**, 1981-82, Vol. 1, No. 1, pp. 38-52.

Bailey, A. D. (Jensen, D. L. and A. D. Bailey. "Discriminant Analysis As An Aid To Employee Selection: A Comment," **AR**, 1975, Vol. 50, No. 3, pp. 588-592.)

Bailey, Charles D. and Gene Ballard. "Improving Response Rates To Accounts Receivable Confirmations: An Experiment Using Four Techniques," **AJPT**, 1985-86, Vol. 5, No. 2, pp. 77-85.

Bailey, Charles D. (Arrington, C. Edward, Charles D. Bailey and William S. Hopwood. "An Attribution Analysis Of Responsibility Assessment For Audit Performance," **JAR**, 1985, Vol. 23, No. 1, pp. 1-20.)

Bailey, Charles D., Gordon B. Harwood and William Hopwood. "Removing The Computational Burden From Reciprocal Cost Allocations," **JAED**, 1984, Vol. 2, No. 2, pp. 169-176.

Bailey, Derek T. "Accounting In Russia: The European Connection," **IJAER**, 1982, Vol. 18, No. 1, pp. 1-36.

Bailey, D. T. "Enterprise Accounting In The USSR," **ABR**,

1973-74, Vol. 4, No. 13, pp. 43-59.

Bailey, Edward J. "The SEC And Replacement Cost: An Urgent Need To Find A Better Answer," **MA**, 1977, Vol. 59, No. 6, pp. 19-22.

Bailey, Eldon R. (Swindle, C. Bruce and Eldon R. Bailey. "Determining The Feasibility Of An Internship Program In Public Accounting," **JAED**, 1984, Vol. 2, No. 1, pp. 155-160.)

Bailey, F. A. "A Note On Pert/Cost Resource Allocation," **AR**, 1967, Vol. 42, No. 2, p. 361.

Bailey, F. A. "Asset Valuation And Depreciation Under Current Cost Accounting," **ABR**, 1981-82, Vol. 12, No. 46, pp. 124-128.

Bailey, F. A. (Bird, Peter and F. A. Bailey. "Incremental Plans In Project Evaluation: A Comment," **ABR**, 1982-83, Vol. 13, No. 52, pp. 309-310.)

Bailey, F. A. (Primrose, P. L., F. A. Bailey and R. Leonard. "The Practical Application Of Discounted Cash Flow To Plant Purchase Using An Integrated Suite Of Computer Programs," **ABR**, 1984-85, Vol. 15, No. 57, pp. 27-32.)

Bailey, George D. "Current Auditing Problems," **AR**, 1950, Vol. 25, No. 2, pp. 125-132.

Bailey, George D. "Practical Problems In Governmental Accounting," **AR**, 1939, Vol. 14, No. 1, pp. 52-56.

Bailey, K. E., III, Joseph H. Bylinski and Michael D. Shields. "Effects Of Audit Report Wording Changes On The Perceived Message," **JAR**, 1983, Vol. 21,No. 2,pp.355-370.

Bailey, Larry P. "Impact Of SAS-39 On Nonstatistical Sampling," **CPAJ**, 1982, Vol. 52, No. 6, pp. 38-47.

Bailey, Larry P. "He And His Firm' In The Context Of Independence," **CPAJ**, 1987, Vol. 57, No. 12, pp. 44-57.

Bailey, Larry P. (Stout, David E., Samuel Laibstain and Larry P. Bailey. "Managing Off-Balance-Sheet Financing," **MA**, 1988, Vol. 70, No. 1, pp. 32-39.)

Bailey, Larry. "Secondary Level Assurances," **CPAJ**, 1978, Vol. 48, No. 2, pp. 27-32.

Bailey, William T. "An Appraisal Of Research Designs Used To Investigate The Information Content Of Audit Reports," **AR**, 1982, Vol. 57, No. 1, pp. 141-146.

Bailey, William T. "The Effects Of Audit Reports On Chartered Financial Analysts' Perceptions Of The Sources Of Financial-Statement And Audit-Report Messages," **AR**, 1981. Vol. 56, No. 4, pp. 882-896.

Baily, H. H. "First-Year Examinations," **AR**, 1931, Vol. 6, No. 1, pp. 57-62.

Baily, H. H. "Some Observations On Accounting In France And Germany," **AR**, 1929, Vol. 4, No. 1, pp. 38-43.

Baiman, Stanley and James Noel. "Noncontrollable Costs And Responsibility Accounting," **JAR**, 1985, Vol. 23, No. 2, pp. 486-501.

Baiman, Stanley and Joel S. Demski. "Economically Optimal Performance Evaluation And Control Systems," **JAR**, 1980, Vol. 18, Supp., pp. 184-220.

Baiman, Stanley and John H. Evans, III. "Pre-Decision Information And Participative Management Control Systems," **JAR**, 1983, Vol. 21, No. 2, pp. 371-395.

Baiman, Stanley, John H. Evans, III and James Noel. "Optimal Contracts With A Utility-Maximizing Auditor," **JAR**, 1987, Vol. 25, No. 2, pp. 217-244.

Baiman, Stanley. "Agency Research In Managerial Accounting: A Survey," **JAL**, 1982, Vol. 1, pp. 154-213.

Baiman, Stanley. "The Evaluation And Choice Of Internal Information Systems Within A Multiperson World," **JAR**, 1975, Vol. 13, No. 1, pp. 1-15.

Bainbridge, D. Raymond and John W. Paul. "Relating Audit And Internal Control Objectives: A Missing Step In Specifying Compliance Tests," **JAED**, 1986, Vol. 4, No. 2, pp. 63-74.

Bainbridge, D. Raymond. "Unaudited Statements - Bankers' And CPAs' Perceptions," **CPAJ**, 1979, Vol. 49, No. 12, pp. 11-18.

Bainbridge, D. R. "Is Dollar-Value LIFO Consistent With Authoritative GAAP?," **JAAF**, 1984, Vol. 7, No. 4, pp. 334-346.

Bainbridge, D. R. (Hobbs, James B. and D. R. Bainbridge. "Nonmonetary Exchange Transactions: Clarification Of APB No. 29," **AR**, 1982, Vol. 57, No. 1, pp. 171-175.)

Bain, Craig E. (Smith, L. Murphy and Craig E. Bain. "Computer Graphics For Today's Accountant," **CPAJ**, 1987, Vol. 57, No. 2, pp. 18-35.)

Baird, Jon P. "Computing Product Costs At A Manufacturing Firm," **MA**, 1970, Vol. 51, No. 8, pp. 25-27.

Bait-El-Mal, Mohamed M., Charles H. Smith and Martin E. Taylor. "The Development Of Accounting In Libya," **IJAER**, 1973, Vol. 8, No. 2, pp. 83-101.

Bakay, Virginia and Steven Michel. "Jackpot!," **MA**, 1984, Vol. 65, No. 11, pp. 26-36.

Bakay, Virginia Hicks. "A Review Of Selected Claims Against Public Accountants," **JOA**, 1970, Vol. 129, No. 5, pp. 54-58.

Bakay, Virginia H. (Bullock, James H. and Virginia H. Bakay. "How Las Vegas Casinos Budget," **MA**, 1980, Vol. 62, No. 1, pp. 35-39.)

Baker, Benny L. (Marin, Daniel B. and Benny L. Baker. "How To Avoid The Constructive Dividend Trap," **MA**, 1984, Vol. 66, No. 4, pp. 54-58.)

Baker, Charles E. (Arcady, Alex T. and Charles E. Baker. "Interest Cost Accounting: Some Practical Guidance," **JOA**, 1981, Vol. 151, No. 3, pp. 62-71.)

Baker, C. Richard. "A Day In The Life Of An Audit Partner," **CPAJ**, 1975, Vol. 45, No. 9, pp. 40-44.

Baker, C. Richard. "Accounting Problems In The TV Broadcast Industry," **MA**, 1976, Vol. 57, No. 11, pp. 41-42.

Baker, C. Richard. "An Investigation Of Differences In

Values: Accounting Majors Vs. Nonaccounting Majors," **AR**, 1976, Vol. 51, No. 4, pp. 886-893.

Baker, C. Richard. "Defects In Full-Cost Accounting In The Petroleum Industry," **ABACUS**, 1976, Vol. 12, No. 2, pp. 152-158.

Baker, C. Richard. "Leasing And The Setting Of Accounting Standards: Mapping The Labyrinth," **JAAF**, 1980, Vol. 3, No. 3, pp. 197-206.

Baker, C. Richard. "Management Strategy In A Large Accounting Firm: A Reply," **AR**, 1979, Vol. 54, No. 1, p. 224.

Baker, C. Richard. "Management Strategy In A Large Accounting Firm," **AR**, 1977, Vol. 52, No. 3, pp. 576-586.

Baker, C. Richard. "Some Observations On Student Values And Their Implications For Accounting Education: A Comment," **AR**, 1974, Vol. 49, No. 3, pp. 576-577.

Baker, C. Richard. "The Structural Response Of The Large CPA Firm To Its Environment," **IJAER**, 1977, Vol. 12, No. 2, pp. 69-80.

Baker, Dale E. "Improved Fund Raising: Accounting For Restricted And Unrestricted Funds," **JOA**, 1988, Vol. 165, No. 5, pp. 68-76.

Baker, Dennis M. (Tiessen, Peter and Dennis M. Baker. "Human Information Processing, Decision Style Theory And Accounting Information Systems: A Comment," **AR**, 1977, Vol. 52, No. 4, pp. 984-987.)

Baker, Edward. "Case Study: Corporate Fee For A Non-Profit Organization," **MA**, 1970, Vol. 52, No. 3, pp. 25-26.

Baker, H. Kent and John A. Haslem. "Information Needs Of Individual Investors," **JOA**, 1973, Vol. 136, No. 5, pp. 64-69.

Baker, H. Kent, Robert H. Chenhall, John A. Haslem and Roger H. Juchau. "Disclosure Of Material Information: A Cross-National Comparison," **IJAER**, 1977, Vol. 13, No. 1, pp. 1-18.

Baker, Jack. (Elikai, Fara and Jack Baker. "Empirical Evidence On The Effectiveness Of Quizzes As A Motivational Technique," **IAE**, 1988, Vol. 3, No. 2, pp. 248-254.)

Baker, Joe M. "Examination Of Books And Records For Use In A Criminal Trial," **AR**, 1942, Vol. 17, No. 2, pp. 150-156.

Baker, Kenneth R. and Robert E. Taylor. "A Linear Programming Framework For Cost Allocation And External Acquisition When Reciprocal Services Exist," **AR**, 1979, Vol. 54, No. 4, pp. 784-790.

Baker, Richard E. and John R. Simon. "An Assessment Of The Cognitive Demands Of The Uniform CPA Examination And Implications For CPA Review/Preparation Courses," **JAED**, 1985, Vol. 3, No. 2, pp. 15-29.

Baker, Richard E. (Higley, Wayne M. and Richard E. Baker. "A Comparative Analysis Of Professional Education And Licensure Preparation," **IAE**, 1987, Vol. 2, No. 2, pp. 220-236.)

Baker, Richard E., John R. Simon and Frank P. Bazeli. "Selecting Instructional Design For Introductory Accounting Based On The Experiential Learning Model," **JAED**, 1987, Vol. 5, No. 2, pp. 207-226.

Baker, Richard E., John R. Simon and Frank P. Bazeli. "An Assessment Of The Learning Style Preferences Of Accounting Majors," **IAE**, 1986, Vol. 1, No. 1, pp. 1-12.

Baker, Robert L. and Ronald M. Copeland. "Evaluation Of The Stratified Regression Estimator For Auditing Accounting Populations," **JAR**, 1979, Vol. 17, No. 2, pp. 606-617.

Baker, Robert L. "Special Farm Tax Problems," **JOA**, 1961, Vol. 111, No. 4, pp. 64-68.

Baker, Robert L. "Tax Accounting Problems Of The Farmer," **JOA**, 1957, Vol. 104, No. 3, pp. 51-57.

Baker, Robert L. (Taylor, Martin E. and Robert L. Baker. "An Analysis Of The External Audit Fee," **ABR**, 1981-82, Vol. 12, No. 45, pp. 55-60.)

Baker, Roy E. "Income Of Life Insurance Companies," **AR**, 1966, Vol. 41, No. 1, pp. 98-105.

Baker, Roy E. "The Pension Cost Problem," **AR**, 1964, Vol. 39, No. 1, pp. 52-61.

Baker, R. C. (Nichols, Donald R. and R. C. Baker. "Testing The Consistency Of Auditors' Prior Distributions And Sampling Results," **ABACUS**, 1977, Vol. 13, No. 2, pp. 91-105.)

Balachandran, Bala V. and Andris A. Zoltners. "An Interactive Audit-Staff Scheduling Decision Support System," **AR**, 1981, Vol. 56, No. 4, pp. 801-812.

Balachandran, Bala V. and Nandu J. Nagarajan. "Imperfect Information, Insurance, And Auditors' Legal Liability," **CAR**, 1986-87, Vol. 3, No. 2, pp. 281-301.

Balachandran, Bala V. and Ram T. S. Ramakrishnan. "Joint Cost Allocation: A Unified Approach," **AR**, 1981, Vol. 56, No. 1, pp. 85-96.

Balachandran, Bala V. and Ram T. S. Ramakrishnan. "A Theory Of Audit Partnerships: Audit Firm Size And Fees," **JAR**, 1987, Vol. 25, No. 1, pp. 111-126.

Balachandran, Bala V. and Ram T. S. Ramakrishnan. "Internal Control And External Auditing For Incentive Compensation Schedules," **JAR**, 1980, Vol. 18, Supp., pp. 140-171.

Balachandran, Bala V. and Ramachandran Ramanan. "Optimal Internal Control Strategy Under Dynamic Conditions," **JAAF**, 1988, Vol. 3 (New Series), No. 1, pp. 1-18.

Balachandran, Bala V. "Discussion Of: 'An Analysis Of The Auditor's Uncertainty About Probabilities'," **CAR**, 1985-86, Vol. 2, No. 2, pp. 283-287.

Balachandran, Bala V. (Prince, Thomas R. and Bala V. Balachandran. "An Information System For Administrating Welfare Programs," **RIGNA**, 1987, Vol. 3, Part A, pp. 37-66.)

Balachandran, Bala V., Lode Li and Robert P. Magee. "On The Allocation Of Fixed And Variable Costs From Service Departments," **CAR**, 1987-88, Vol. 4, No. 1, pp. 164-185.

Balachandran, Kashi R. and Bin N. Srinidhi. "A Rationale For Fixed Charge Application," **JAAF**, 1987, Vol. 2 (New Series), No. 2, pp. 151-183.

Balachandran, Kashi R. (Ronen, Joshua and Kashi R. Balachandran. "An Approach To Transfer Pricing Under Uncertainty," **AR**, 1988, Vol. 26, No. 2, pp. 300-314.)

Balachandran, K. R. and Ralph E. Steuer. "An Interactive Model For The CPA Firm Audit Staff Planning Problem With Multiple Objectives," **AR**, 1982, Vol. 57, No. 1, pp. 125-140.

Balachandran, K. R. (Livingstone, J. L. and K. R. Balachandran. "Cost And Effectiveness Of Physician Peer Review In Reducing Medicare Overutilization," **AOS**, 1977, Vol. 2, No. 2, pp. 153-164.)

Balachandran, K. R., Richard A. Maschmeyer and J. Leslie Livingstone. "Product Warranty Period: A Markovian Approach To Estimation And Analysis Of Repair And Replacement Costs," **AR**, 1981, Vol. 56, No. 1, pp. 115-124.

Baladouni, Vahe. "Accounting In The Early Years Of The East India Company," **AHJ**, 1983, Vol. 10, No. 2, pp. 63-80.

Baladouni, Vahe. "East India Company's 1783 Balance Of Accounts," **ABACUS**, 1986, Vol. 22, No. 2, pp. 59-64.

Baladouni, Vahe. "Etymological Observations On Some Accounting Terms," **AHJ**, 1984, Vol. 11, No. 2, pp. 101-109.

Baladouni, Vahe. "Financial Reporting In The Early Years Of The East India Company," **AHJ**, 1986, Vol. 13, No. 1, pp. 19-30.

Baladouni, Vahe. "George Soule," **AHJ**, 1976, Vol. 3, No. 1-4, pp. 72-76.

Baladouni, Vahe. "Instructional Objectives In Accounting," **AR**, 1968, Vol. 43, No. 3, pp. 582-585.

Baladouni, Vahe. "The Accounting Records Of The East India Company," **AHJ**, 1981, Vol. 8, No. 1, pp. 67-69.

Baladouni, Vahe. "The Accounting Perspective Re-Examined," **AR**, 1966, Vol. 41, No. 2, pp. 215-225.

Baladouni, Vahe. "The Study Of Accounting History," **IJAER**, 1977, Vol. 12, No. 2, pp. 53-67.

Baladouni, Vahe. "'It Is Up To Us.' - Arnold J. Toynbee," **AHJ**, 1975, Vol. 2, No. 1-4, pp. 45-48.

Baladouni, Vahe. (Bedford, Norton M. and Vahe Baladouni. "A Communication Theory Approach To Accountancy," **AR**, 1962, Vol. 37, No. 4, pp. 650-659.)

Balch, John. "Some Aspects Of Standard Costs," **AR**, 1934, Vol. 9, No. 1, pp. 29-32.

Baldasaro, P. Michael and Jeffrey R. Hoops. "Tax Act Of 1986 - Corporate Changes," **CPAJ**, 1986, Vol. 56, No. 12, pp. 28-43.

Baldwin, Bruce A. and Dan C. Kneer. "EDP Audit Education And EDP Auditor Characteristics: Empirical Data From Practitioners And Professors," **IAE**, 1986, Vol. 1, No. 1, pp. 153-167.

Baldwin, Bruce A. and Keith R. Howe. "Secondary-Level Study Of Accounting And Subsequent Performance In The First College Course," **AR**, 1982, Vol. 57, No. 3, pp. 619-626.

Baldwin, Bruce A. and Philip M. J. Reckers. "Exploring The Role Of Learning Style Research In Accounting Education Policy," **JAED**, 1984, Vol. 2, No. 2, pp. 63-76.

Baldwin, Bruce A. and Thomas P. Howard. "Intertopical Sequencing Of Examination Questions: An Empirical Evaluation," **JAED**, 1983, Vol. 1, No. 2, pp. 89-95.

Baldwin, Bruce A. "On Positioning The Quiz: An Empirical Analysis," **AR**, 1980, Vol. 55, No. 4, pp. 664-671.

Baldwin, Bruce A. "Segment Earnings Disclosure And The Ability Of Security Analysts To Forecast Earnings Per Share," **AR**, 1984, Vol. 59, No. 3, pp. 376-389.

Baldwin, Bruce A. "The Role Of Difficulty And Discrimination In Constructing Multiple-Choice Examinations: With Guidelines For Practical Application," **JAED**, 1984, Vol. 2, No. 1, pp. 19-28.

Baldwin, Bruce A. "Using The Repeated Measures Model In Accounting Policy Research: The Case Of Segment Reporting," **AIA**, 1987, Vol. 4, pp. 69-82.

Baldwin, Bruce A. (Howe, Keith R. and Bruce A. Baldwin. "The Effects Of Evaluative Sequencing On Performance, Behavior, And Attitudes," **AR**, 1983, Vol. 58, No. 1, pp. 135-142.)

Baldwin, Bruce A. (Watne, Donald A. and Bruce A. Baldwin. "University-Level Education Of Accountants In The People's Republic Of China," **IAE**, 1988, Vol. 3, No. 1, pp. 139-155.)

Baldwin, Ronald P. "Depreciation Recapture," **JOA**, 1965, Vol. 119, No. 4, pp. 64-70.

Baldwin, Rosecrans. "A Practitioner's Plea For More Training In Written English," **AR**, 1956, Vol. 31, No. 3, pp. 358-362.

Baldwin, R. "Problems In Loan Agreements With Unclear Restrictive Clauses," **JOA**, 1953, Vol. 96, No. 2, pp. 190-192.

Balke, Thomas E. and James E. Sorensen. "Reliability And Validity Of Accounting Data," **IJAER**, 1975, Vol. 10, No. 2, pp. 37-46.

Balke, Thomas E. (Brown, James F. Jr and Thomas E. Balke. "Do Accountants Need More Education?," **MA**, 1982, Vol. 64, No. 5, pp. 26-29.)

Balke, Thomas E. (Brown, James F., Jr. and Thomas E. Balke. "Accounting Curriculum Comparison By Degree Program Of Schools Intending To Seek AACSB Accreditation," **IAE**, 1983, No. 1, pp. 50-59.)

Balke, Thomas E. (Chen, Kung H. and Thomas E. Balke. "Scale Of Operation, Industry, And Financial Ratios," **IJAER**, 1979, Vol. 14, No. 2, pp. 17-28.)

Balke, Thomas E. (Hadley, Galen D. and Thomas E. Balke. "A Comparison Of Academic And Practitioner Views Of Current

Levels In The Undergraduate Accounting Curriculum," **AR**, 1979, Vol. 54, No. 2, pp. 383-389.)

Ballantine, H. W. and George S. Hills. "Corporate Capital And Restrictions Upon Dividends," **AR**, 1935, Vol. 10, No. 3, pp. 246-268.

Ballard, Gene. (Bailey, Charles D. and Gene Ballard. "Improving Response Rates To Accounts Receivable Confirmations: An Experiment Using Four Techniques," **AJPT**, 1985-86, Vol. 5, No. 2, pp. 77-85.)

Ballard, William H. "Ten Ways To Better Electronic 'Calc'ulating," **MA**, 1984, Vol. 65, No. 12, pp. 50-54.

Ballew, Van Bennett and O. Ray Whittington. "Litigation Support Engagements - A Growing Practice," **CPAJ**, 1988, Vol. 58, No. 2, pp. 42-47.

Ballew, Van Bennett, Ray Whittington and Marilyn Zulinski. "Shared Audit Engagements," **CPAJ**, 1983, Vol. 53, No. 2, pp. 28-35.

Ballew, Van Bennett. (Whittington, Ray, Van Bennett Ballew and Doyle Z. Williams. "Selecting An Auditor: Times Have Changed," **MA**, 1984, Vol. 65, No. 8, pp. 62-67.)

Ballew, Van. "Technological Routineness And Intra-Unit Structure In CPA Firms," **AR**, 1982, Vol. 57, No. 1, pp. 88-104.

Ballew, V. (Spicer, B. H. and V. Ballew. "Management Accounting Systems And The Economics Of Internal Organization," **AOS**, 1983, Vol. 8, No. 1, pp. 73-98.)

Ballinger, Eddward and Jesse F. Dillard. "The Foreign Corrupt Practices Act," **CPAJ**, 1980, Vol. 50, No. 2, pp. 37-46.

Ball, Donald A. (Wood, Thomas D. and Donald A. Ball. "New Rule 502 And Effective Advertising By CPAs," **JOA**, 1978, Vol. 145, No. 6, pp. 65-71.)

Ball, Jack R. (Cameron, George D., III, Ralph W. Gudmundsen, Jr. and Jack R. Ball. "Accounting Changes: Why CPA's Must Conform," **MA**, 1973, Vol. 54, No. 8, pp. 26-28.)

Ball, Ray and George Foster. "Corporate Financial Reporting: A Methodological Review Of Empirical Research," **JAR**, 1982, Vol. 20, Supp., pp. 161-234.

Ball, Ray and Philip Brown. "An Empirical Evaluation Of Accounting Income Numbers," **JAR**, 1968, Vol. 6, No. 2, pp. 159-178.

Ball, Ray, Baruch Lev and Ross Watts. "Income Variation And Balance Sheet Compositions," **JAR**, 1976, Vol. 14, No. 1, pp. 1-9.

Ball, Ray, R. G. Walker and G. P. Whittred. "Audit Qualifications And Share Prices," **ABACUS**, 1979, Vol. 15, No. 1, pp. 23-34.

Ball, Ray. "Changes In Accounting Techniques And Stock Prices," **JAR**, 1972, Vol. 10, Supp., pp. 1-38.

Ball, Ray. "Index Of Empirical Research In Accounting," **JAR**, 1971, Vol. 9, No. 1, pp. 1-31.

Ball, Ray. (Brown, Philip and Ray Ball. "Some Preliminary Findings On The Association Between The Earnings Of A Firm, Its Industry, And The Economy," **JAR**, 1967, Vol. 5, Supp., pp. 55-77.)

Baloff, Nicholas and John W. Kennelly. "Accounting Implications Of Product And Process Start-ups," **JAR**, 1967, Vol. 5, No. 2, pp. 131-143.

Balvers, Ronald J., Bill McDonald and Robert E. Miller. "Underpricing Of New Issues And The Choice Of Auditor As A Signal Of Investment Banker Reputation," **AR**, 1988, Vol. 63, No. 4, pp. 605-622.

Bamber, E. Michael and Joseph H. Bylinski. "The Effects Of The Planning Memorandum, Time Pressure And Individual Auditor Characteristics On Audit Managers' Review Time Judgments," **CAR**, 1987-88, Vol. 4, No. 1, pp. 127-163.

Bamber, E. Michael and Doug Snowball. "An Experimental Study Of The Effects Of Audit Structure In Uncertain Task Environments," **AR**, 1988, Vol. 63, No. 3, pp. 490-504.

Bamber, E. Michael and Joseph H. Bylinski. "The Audit Team And The Audit Review Process: An Organizational Approach," **JAL**, 1982, Vol. 1, pp. 33-58.

Bamber, E. Michael and Joseph H. Bylinski. "Attribute Sampling: A Review In Light Of SAS No. 39," **JAED**, 1984, Vol. 2, No. 1, pp. 83-97.

Bamber, E. Michael, Linda Smith Bamber and Joseph H. Bylinski. "A Descriptive Study Of Audit Managers' Working Paper Review," **AJPT**, 1988, Vol. 7, No. 2, pp. 137-149.

Bamber, E. Michael, Linda S. Bamber and Gay L. Vincent. "Communication Can Improve Your Audit," **CPAJ**, 1985, Vol. 55, No. 3, pp. 34-38.

Bamber, E. Michael. "Expert Judgment In The Audit Team: A Source Reliability Approach," **JAR**, 1983, Vol. 21, No. 2, pp. 396-412.

Bamber, Linda Smith. "The Information Content Of Annual Earnings Releases: A Trading Volume Approach," **JAR**, 1986, Vol. 24, No. 1, pp. 40-56.

Bamber, Linda Smith. "Unexpected Earnings, Firm Size, And Trading Volume Around Quarterly Earnings Announcements," **AR**, 1987, Vol. 62, No. 3, pp. 510-532.

Bamber, Linda Smith. (Ajinkya, Bipin, Rowland Atiase and Linda Smith Bamber. "Absorption Versus Direct Costing: Income Reconciliation And Cost-Volume-Profit Analysis," **IAE**, 1986, Vol. 1, No. 2, pp. 268-281.)

Bamber, Linda Smith. (Bamber, E. Michael, Linda Smith Bamber and Joseph H. Bylinski. "A Descriptive Study Of Audit Managers' Working Paper Review," **AJPT**, 1988, Vol. 7, No. 2, pp. 137-149.)

Bamber, Linda S. (Atiase, Rowland K., Linda S. Bamber and Robert N. Freeman. "Accounting Disclosures Based On Company Size, Regulations And Capital Markets Evidence," **ACCHOR**, 1988, Vol. 2, No. 1, pp. 18-26.)

Bamber, Linda S. (Bamber, E. Michael, Linda S. Bamber and Gay L. Vincent. "Communication Can Improve Your Audit," **CPAJ**, 1985, Vol. 55, No. 3, pp. 34-38.)

Banbury, J. and J. E. Nahapiet. "Towards A Framework For The Study Of The Antecedents And Consequences Of Information Systems In Organizations," **AOS**, 1979, Vol. 4, No. 3, pp. 163-178.

Bancroft, D. Stuart. "Financial Management Of A Public School District," **MA**, 1977, Vol. 59, No. 1, pp. 24-28.

Bandy, Dale. "Taking Credit Where Credit Is Due," **CPAJ**, 1980, Vol. 50, No. 2, pp. 29-36.

Bandy, D. Dale. (Anderson, Henry R. and D. Dale Bandy. "Understanding The Unitary Tax," **MA**, 1985, Vol. 67, No. 3, pp. 35-43.)

Bangs, Robert B. "The Definition And Measurement Of Income," **AR**, 1940, Vol. 15, No. 3, pp. 353-370.

Banham, Richard L. (Englebrecht, Ted D. and Richard L. Banham. "Earnings And Profits: The Income Tax Dilemma," **JOA**, 1979, Vol. 147, No. 2, pp. 58-65.)

Banick, Richard S. and Douglas C. Broeker. "Arbitration: An Option For Resolving Claim Against CPAs," **JOA**, 1987, Vol. 164, No. 4, pp. 124-129.

Banigan, Russell W. and Jerrold S. Gattegno. "A Breakthrough In Water's-Edge Unitary Legislation," **CPAJ**, 1987, Vol. 57, No. 6, pp. 34-39.

Banister, Harlan. (Loesch, Donald E. and Harlan Banister. "The Accountant's Role In Value Analysis," **MA**, 1967, Vol. 49, No. 3, pp. 52-57.)

Banker, Rajiv D. and James M. Patton. "Analytical Agency Theory And Municipal Accounting: An Introduction And An Application," **RIGNA**, 1987, Vol. 3, Part B, pp. 29-50.

Banker, Rajiv D., Srikant M. Datar and Ajay Maindiratta. "Unobservable Outcomes And Multiattribute Preferences In The Evaluation Of Managerial Performance," **CAR**, 1988, Vol. 5, No. 1, pp. 96-124.

Banker, Rajiv D., Srikant M. Datar and Sunder Kekre. "Relevant Costs, Congestion And Stochasticity In Production Environments," **JAEC**, 1988, Vol. 10, No. 3, pp. 171-197.

Banker, Rajiv D., Srikant M. Datar and Madhav V. Rajan. "Measurement Of Productivity Improvements: An Empirical Analysis," **JAAF**, 1987, Vol. 2 (New Series), No. 4, pp. 319-354.

Banks, Alexander S. "Informing Stockholders: A Job For Public Accounts In Preference To The Federal Trade Commission," **RIAR**, 1987, Vol. 1, pp. 177-179.

Banks, Charles W. "Applying Standard Costs To A Recycled Product: The Automobile Tire," **MA**, 1976, Vol. 58, No. 2, pp. 51-53.

Banks, Doyle W. and William R. Kinney, Jr. "Loss Contingency Reports And Stock Prices: An Empirical Study," **JAR**, 1982, Vol. 20, No. 1, pp. 240-254.

Banks, Doyle W. "The 'Subject To' Qualified Opinion," **CPAJ**, 1985, Vol. 55, No. 3, pp. 26-33.

Banks, Ina D. "Internal Control Of On-Line And Real-Time Computer Systems," **MA**, 1977, Vol. 58, No. 12, pp. 28-30.

Banning, Paul D. "Federal Accountkeeping: Comments," **AR**, 1940, Vol. 15, No. 1, pp. 47-52.

Bao, Ben-Hsien, Da-Hsien Bao and M. A. Vasarhelyi. "A Stochastic Model Of Professional Accountant Turnover," **AOS**, 1986, Vol. 11, No. 3, pp. 289-296.

Bao, Da Hsein. (Vasarhelyi, Miklos, Da Hsein Bao and Joel Berk. "Trends In The Evolution Of Scholarly Accounting Thought: A Quantitative Examination," **AHJ**, 1988, Vol. 15, No. 1, pp. 45-64.)

Bao, Da-Hsien. (Bao, Ben-Hsien, Da-Hsien Bao and M. A. Vasarhelyi. "A Stochastic Model Of Professional Accountant Turnover," **AOS**, 1986, Vol. 11, No. 3, pp. 289-296.)

Bao, D. H. (Bastable, C. W. and D. H. Bao. "The Fiction Of Sales-Mix And Sales-Quantity Variances," **ACCHOR**, 1988, Vol. 2, No. 2, pp. 10-17.)

Baran, Arie, Josef Lakonishok and Aharon R. Ofer. "The Information Content Of General Price Level Adjusted Earnings: Some Empirical Evidence," **AR**, 1980, Vol. 55, No. 1, pp. 22-35.

Barbatelli, Ettore and Carl W. Hagelin. "Replacement Cost Estimating For Financial Reporting," **MA**, 1976, Vol. 57, No. 12, pp. 21-25.

Barbatelli, Ettore Sr. "The Appearance Of Conflict When CPAs Are Consulting," **MA**, 1986, Vol. 68, No. 3, pp. 28-31.

Barbatelli, Ettore. "Implementing ASR 190," **MA**, 1977, Vol. 59, No. 6, pp. 27-30.

Barbor, John F. "Is LIFO A Valid Accounting Practice?," **MA**, 1978, Vol. 59, No. 11, pp. 30-34.

Barcan, Arthur. "Frontiers In Records Management," **JOA**, 1956, Vol. 102, No. 5, pp. 52-59.

Barcelona, Constance T., Clara C. Lelievre and Thomas W. Lelievre. "The Profession's Underutilized Resource: The Woman CPA," **JOA**, 1975, Vol. 140, No. 5, pp. 58-64.

Barcus, Sam W., III. (Boer, Germain B. and Sam W. Barcus, III. "How A Small Company Evaluates Acquisition Of A Minicomputer," **MA**, 1981, Vol. 62, No. 9, pp. 13-23.)

Barden, Horace G. "The Meaning Of Auditing Standards," **JOA**, 1958, Vol. 105, No. 4, pp. 50-56.

Barden, Horace G. "The Trouble With Accounting Research," **JOA**, 1975, Vol. 139, No. 1, pp. 58-65.

Barden, Ronald S., James E. Copeland, Jr., Roger H. Hermanson and Leslie Wat. "Going Public - What It Involves," **JOA**, 1984, Vol. 157, No. 3, pp. 63-76.

Bardsley, R. Geoffrey. "Managing International Financial Transactions," **IJAER**, 1972, Vol. 8, No. 1, pp. 67-76.

Barefield, Russell M. and Eugene E. Comiskey. "The Smoothing Hypothesis: An Alternative Test," **AR**, 1972, Vol. 47, No. 2, pp. 291-298.

Barefield, Russell M. and Eugene E. Comiskey. "Segmental

Financial Disclosure By Diversified Firms And Security Prices: A Comment," **AR**, 1975, Vol. 50, No. 4, pp. 818-821.

Barefield, Russell M. and Eugene E. Comiskey. "Depreciation Policy And The Behavior Of Corporate Profits," **JAR**, 1971, Vol. 9, No. 2, pp. 351-358.

Barefield, Russell M. "A Model Of Forecast Biasing Behavior," **AR**, 1970, Vol. 45, No. 3, pp. 490-501.

Barefield, Russell M. "Comments On A Measure Of Forecasting Performance," **JAR**, 1969, Vol. 7, No. 2, pp. 324-327.

Barefield, Russell M. "The Effects Of Aggregation On Decision Making Success: A Laboratory Study," **JAR**, 1972, Vol. 10, No. 2, pp. 229-242.

Barefield, Russell M. (Beck, Paul J. and Russell M. Barefield. "An Economic Analysis Of Competitive Bidding For Public Sector Audit Engagements," **JAPP**, 1986, Vol. 5, No. 3, pp. 143-165.)

Barefield, Russell M. (Dhaliwal, Dan S., Fratern M. Mboya and Russell M. Barefield. "Utilization Of SFAS No. 14 Disclosures In Assessing Operating Risk," **JAPP**, 1983, Vol. 2, No. 2, pp. 83-98.)

Barefield, Russell M., Taylor W. Foster, III and Don Vickrey. "Interpreting The API: A Comment And Extension," **AR**, 1976, Vol. 51, No. 1, pp. 172-175.

Barenbaum, Lester and Thomas Monahan. "Utilizing Terminal Values In Teaching Time Value Analysis," **JAED**, 1983, Vol. 1, No. 2, pp. 79-88.

Barenbaum, Lester. (Monahan, Thomas F. and Lester Barenbaum. "The Use Of Constant Dollar Information To Predict Bond Rating Changes," **JAAF**, 1983, Vol. 6, No. 4, pp. 325-340.)

Barfield, Jesse T. (Burns, Harold D. and Jesse T. Barfield. "Selecting Accounting Alternatives," **MA**, 1976, Vol. 57, No. 8, pp. 27-28.)

Barfuss, Francois R., Roger D. Musson and David C. Bennett. "Some Significant Differences In U.S. and U.K. Reported Net Income," **CPAJ**, 1982, Vol. 52, No. 2, pp. 44-48.

Barhydt, Dirck, Robert H. Clement, Dan W. Lufkin and A. Jones Yorke. "Planning Concepts In The 'Tentative Statement Of Cost Concepts'," **AR**, 1957, Vol. 32, No. 4, pp. 593-597.

Bariff, M. L. and J. R. Galbraith. "Intraorganizational Power Considerations For Designing Information Systems," **AOS**, 1978, Vol. 3, No. 1, pp. 15-28.

Baris, Marvin L. "Profit Recognition On Real Estate Transactions," **JOA**, 1974, Vol. 137, No. 2, pp. 49-54.

Barker, Fletcher. "Auditing Organizations Handling Escrow Agreements," **JOA**, 1953, Vol. 96, No. 3, pp. 324-330.

Barker, Phyllis A. "The Value-Added Tax - The Cost To The Businessman," **JOA**, 1972, Vol. 134, No. 3, pp. 75-79.

Barker, Raymond F. and Bernard J. Landwehr. "Quantitative Techniques And The Faculty," **AR**, 1966, Vol. 41, No. 2, pp. 338-340.

Barker, Richard B. "Dollar-Value Lifo And The Klein Chocolate Case," **JOA**, 1961, Vol. 112, No. 3, pp. 41-45.

Barker, Robinson F. "The Businessman's Role," **MA**, 1973, Vol. 54, No. 8, pp. 15-16.

Barkman, Arnold I. and John David Jolley, II. "Cost Defenses For Antitrust Cases," **MA**, 1986, Vol. 67, No. 10, pp. 37-40.

Barkman, Arnold I. "Testing The Markov Chain Approach On Accounts Receivable," **MA**, 1981, Vol. 62, No. 7, pp. 48-50.

Barkman, Arnold I. "Within-Item Variation: A Stochastic Approach To Audit Uncertainty - A Reply," **AR**, 1978, Vol. 53, No. 4, pp. 993-996.

Barkman, Arnold. "Within-Item Variation: A Stochastic Approach To Audit Uncertainty," **AR**, 1977, Vol. 52, No. 2, pp. 450-464.

Barlev, Benzion and Abraham Friedman. "Experience Requirements And The Education Of Certified Public Accountants," **IJAER**, 1982, Vol. 17, No. 2, pp. 75-88.

Barlev, Benzion and Arieh Goldman. "Management Advisory Services And Accounting," **ABACUS**, 1974, Vol. 10 No. 1, pp. 74-82.

Barlev, Benzion and Haim Levy. "On The Variability Of Accounting Income Numbers," **JAR**, 1979, Vol. 17, No. 2, pp. 305-315.

Barlev, Benzion and Jeffrey L. Callen. "Total Factor Productivity And Cost Variances: Survey And Analysis," **JAL**, 1986, Vol. 5, pp. 35-56.

Barlev, Benzion and Yoram C. Peles. "Accounting: The Structure Of A Growing Profession," **ABACUS**, 1987, Vol. 23, No. 1, pp. 70-84.

Barlev, Benzion, Dov Fried and Joshua Livnat. "Economic And Financial Reporting Effects Of Inventory Tax Allowances," **CAR**, 1985-86, Vol. 2, No. 2, pp. 288-310.

Barlev, Benzion. "Business Combination And The Creation Of Goodwill," **ABR**, 1972-73, Vol. 3, No. 12, pp. 304-308.

Barlev, Benzion. "Contingent Equity And The Dilutive Effect On EPS," **AR**, 1983, Vol. 58, No. 2, pp. 385-393.

Barlev, Benzion. "On The Measurement Of Materiality," **ABR**, 1971-72, Vol. 2, No. 7, pp. 194-197.

Barlev, Benzion. "The Independent Auditor's Report: Study Of A Change," **IJAER**, 1976, Vol. 11, No. 2, pp. 73-90.

Barlev, Benzion. "The Initial Selection Of Independent Public Accountants: An Empirical Investigation," **IJAER**, 1977, Vol. 12, No. 2, pp. 37-51.

Barlev, Benzion. "Theory, Pragmatism And Conservatism In Reflecting The Effects Of Warrants On Diluted EPS," **ABACUS**, 1984, Vol. 20, No. 1, pp. 1-15.

Barlev, Benzion. (Goldman, Arieh and Benzion Barlev. "The Auditor-Firm Conflict Of Interests: Its Implications For Independence," **AR**, 1974, Vol. 49, No. 4, pp. 707-718.)

Barlev, Benzion. (Goldman, Arieh and Benzion Barlev. "The Auditor-Firm Conflict Of Interests: Its Implications For Independence: A Reply," **AR**, 1975, Vol. 50, No. 4, pp. 848-853.)

Barlev, Benzion. (Goldman, Arieh and Benzion Barlev. "The Auditor-Firm Conflict Of Interests: Its Implications For Independence: A Reply," **AR**, 1975, Vol. 50, No. 4, pp. 857-859.)

Barlev, Benzion. (Sherwood, Kenneth A. and Benzion Barlev. "Materiality - A Note And A Reply," **ABR**, 1972-73, Vol. 3, No. 9, pp. 77-78.)

Barnea, Amir and Harold Bierman, Jr. "Cash Flow Valuation And Depreciation," **AR**, 1973-74, Vol. 4, No. 15, pp. 193-196.

Barnea, Amir, Joshua Ronen and Simcha Sadan. "Classificatory Smoothing Of Income With Extraordinary Items: A Reply," **AR**, 1977, Vol. 52, No. 2, pp. 525-526.

Barnea, Amir, Joshua Ronen and Simcha Sadan. "Classificatory Smoothing Of Income With Extraordinary Items," **AR**, 1976, Vol. 51, No. 1, pp. 110-122.

Barnea, Amir, Simcha Sadan and Michael Schiff. "Conditional Performance Review," **MA**, 1975, Vol. 57, No. 5, pp. 19-22.

Barnea, Amir. (Adar, Zvi, Amir Barnea and Baruch Lev. "A Comprehensive Cost-Volume-Profit Analysis Under Uncertainty," **AR**, 1977, Vol. 52, No. 1, pp. 137-149.)

Barnea, A. and S. Sadan. "On The Decomposition Of The Estimation Problem In Financial Accounting," **JAR**, 1974, Vol. 12, No. 1, pp. 197-203.

Barnea, A., J. Ronen and S. Sadan. "The Implementation Of Accounting Objectives: An Application To Extraordinary Items," **AR**, 1975, Vol. 50, No. 1, pp. 58-68.

Barnecut, Leo J., Jr. "Contractor Performance Measurement," **MA**, 1967, Vol. 48, No. 6, pp. 43-48.

Barnes, Dianne P. "Materiality - An Illusive Concept," **MA**, 1976, Vol. 58, No. 4, pp. 19-20.

Barnes, Donald A. (Le Febvre, Charles N. and Donald A. Barnes. "A Look At Annual Reports Of Employee Benefit Plans," **MA**, 1975, Vol. 57, No. 6, pp. 51-53.)

Barnes, John L. "How To Tell If Standard Costs Are Really Standard," **MA**, 1983, Vol. 64, No. 12, pp. 50-55.

Barnes, Paul. "Accounting For Deferred Tax On Depreciable Assets - A Note," **ABR**, 1981-82, Vol. 12, No. 47, pp. 231-232.

Barnes, Paul. "The Effect Of A Merger On The Share Price Of The Attacker, Revisited," **ABR**, 1984-85, Vol. 15, No. 57, pp. 45-49.

Barnes, Paul. "The Effect Of A Merger On The Share Price Of The Attacker," **ABR**, 1977-78, Vol. 8, No. 31, pp. 162-168.

Barnes, P. and J. Webb. "Management Information Changes And Functional Fixation: Some Experimental Evidence From The Public Sector," **AOS**, 1986, Vol. 11, No. 1, pp. 1-18.

Barnes, William T. "The CPA's Responsibilities In Tax Practice," **JOA**, 1968, Vol. 125, No. 3, pp. 27-33.

Barnes, William T. "The Treasury Department Report On Private Foundations," **JOA**, 1967, Vol. 123, No. 1, pp. 34-40.

Barnett, Andrew H. and F. Fulton Galer. "Scienter Since Hochfelder," **CPAJ**, 1982, Vol. 52, No. 11, pp. 40-45.

Barnett, Andrew H. and James C. Caldwell. "Accounting For Corporate Social Performance: A Survey," **MA**, 1974, Vol. 56, No. 5, pp. 23-26.

Barnett, Andrew H. and William J. Read. "Sampling In Small Business Audits," **JOA**, 1986, Vol. 161, No. 1, pp. 78-90.

Barnett, Andrew H. (Wong-Boren, Adrian and Andrew H. Barnett. "Mexican Market Efficiency: A Study Of The Information Content Of Accounting Numbers," **IJAER**, 1984, Vol. 20, No. 1, pp. 45-70.)

Barnett, Bernard. "Estate Administration Expenses," **JOA**, 1967, Vol. 124, No. 1, pp. 47-51.

Barnett, Bernard. "Estate Planning: A Greater Role For The CPA," **JOA**, 1977, Vol. 143, No. 6, pp. 49-59.

Barnett, Bernard. "Estate Planning Perils For CPA Partners And Shareholders," **JOA**, 1986, Vol. 161, No. 1, pp.68-77.

Barnett, Bernard. "The Carryover Basis Election: A Golden Opportunity," **JOA**, 1980, Vol. 149, No. 6, pp. 62-70.

Barnett, Glen C. "Breeding Cattle For Tax Benefits And Profit," **MA**, 1978, Vol. 60, No. 1, pp. 57-59.

Barnett, William. "Auditing A Limited Partnership Production In The Theater," **JOA**, 1954, Vol. 97, No. 5, pp. 593-598.

Barnhisel, Thomas S. (Spencer, Charles H. and Thomas S. Barnhisel. "A Decade Of Price-Level Changes - The Effect On The Financial Statements Of Cummins Engine Company," **AR**, 1965, Vol. 40, No. 1, pp. 144-153.)

Barnickol, Karl R., Allan John Ross, Ronald O. Schowalter and Michael J. Walters. "Accounting For Litigation And Claims," **JOA**, 1985, Vol. 159, No. 6, pp. 56-69.

Baron, C. David, Douglas A. Johnson, D. Gerald Searfoss and Charles H. Smith. "Uncovering Corporate Irregularities: Are We Closing The Expectation Gap?," **JOA**, 1977, Vol. 144, No. 4, pp. 56-67.

Baron, C. David. (King, Randle R. and C. David Baron. "An Integrated Account Structure For Governmental Accounting And Financial Reporting," **AR**, 1974, Vol. 49, No. 1, pp. 76-87.)

Barr, Andrew and Irving J. Galpeer. "McKesson & Robbins," **JOA**, 1987, Vol. 163, No. 5, pp. 159-161.

Barr, Andrew, Jr. "Comments On How Can Appreciation Be Treated In The Accounts?," **AR**, 1930, Vol. 5, No. 1, pp. 41-44.

Barr, Andrew. "Accountants And The Securities And Exchange Commission," **JOA**, 1962, Vol. 113, No. 4, pp. 31-37.

Barr, Andrew. "Accounting Aspects Of Business Combinations," **AR**, 1959, Vol. 34, No. 2, pp. 175-181.

Bastable, C. W. "Tomorrow's Accounting?," JOA, 1959, Vol. 107, No. 6, pp. 52-58.

Bastable, C. W. "Why Can't Johnny Account?," JOA, 1977, Vol. 143, No. 1, pp. 63-69.

Basu, S. and J. R. Hanna. "Interindustry Estimation Of General Price-Level Impact On Financial Information: A Comment," AR, 1978, Vol. 53, No. 1, pp. 192-197.

Basu, S. "Market Reactions To Accounting Policy Deliberations: The Inflation Accounting Case Revisited," AR, 1981, Vol. 56, No. 4, pp. 942-954.

Basu, S. "The Effects Of Earnings Yield On Assessments Of The Association Between Annual Accounting Income Numbers And Security Prices," AR, 1978, Vol. 53, No. 3, pp. 599-625.

Bates, Homer L., Robert W. Ingram and Philip M. J. Reckers. "Auditor-Client Affiliation: The Impact On 'Materiality'," JOA, 1982, Vol. 153, No. 4, pp. 60-63.

Bates, Robert E. "Auditing The Advanced Computer Systems," MA, 1970, Vol. 51, No. 12, pp. 34-37.

Bathke, Allen W., Jr. and Kenneth S. Lorek. "The Relationships Between Time-Series Models And The Security Market's Expectation Of Quarterly Earnings," AR, 1984, Vol. 59, No. 2, pp. 163-176.

Bathke, Allen W., Jr. (Lorek, Kenneth S. and Allen W. Bathke, Jr. "A Time-Series Analysis Of Nonseasonal Quarterly Earnings Data," JAR, 1984, Vol. 22, No. 1, pp. 369-379.)

Bathke, Allen W., Jr., Richard L. Rogers and Jerrold J. Stern. "The Security Market Reaction To Tax Legislation As Reflected In Bond Price Adjustments," JATA, 1985, Vol. 6, No. 2, pp. 37-49.

Battaglia, Samuel T. (Kucic, A. Ronald and Samuel T. Battaglia. "Matrix Accounting For The Statement Of Changes In Financial Position," MA, 1981, Vol. 62, No. 10, pp. 27-32.)

Battista, George L. "The Selling And Administrative Expenses Dilemma," MA, 1965, Vol. 47, No. 3, pp. 3-8.

Battista, George L. (Crowningshield, Gerald R. and George L. Battista. "Is Conventional Accounting Adequate For A Cost Reduction Program?," MA, 1968, Vol. 49, No. 5, pp. 36-42.)

Battista, G. L. and G. R. Crowningshield. "Cost Behavior And Breakeven Analysis - A Different Approach," MA, 1966, Vol. 48, No. 2, pp. 3-15.

Battista, G. L. (Crowningshield, G. R. and G. L. Battista. "The Accounting Revolution," MA, 1966, Vol. 47, No. 11, pp. 30-38.)

Battista, Marianne S. "The Effect Of Instructional Technology And Learner Characteristics On Cognitive Achievement In College Accounting," AR, 1978, Vol. 53, No. 2, pp. 477-485.

Battista, Marianne S. (Stout, D.F., E.H. Bonfield and M.S. Battista. "Additional Experimental Evidence On The Relationship Between Class Meeting Time Compression And Accounting Student Performance And Evaluations," JAED,1987,Vol. 5,No.2,pp.339-348.)

Batzer, R. Kirk. "Accounting For Nonprofit Organizations," CPAJ, 1977, Vol. 47, No. 5, pp. 17-20.

Batzer, R. Kirk. "Auditing Nonprofit Organizations," CPAJ, 1979, Vol. 49, No. 8, pp. 21-26.

Bauer, Charles A. and Barry P. Robbins. "Accounting Implications Of The 1984 Tax Act," CPAJ, 1984, Vol. 54, No. 9, pp. 46-51.

Bauer, John. "Depreciation And Public Utility Valuation," AR, 1930, Vol. 5, No. 2, pp. 111-116.

Bauer, John. "The Concepts Of Capital And Income In The Regulation Of Public Utilities," AR, 1937, Vol. 12, No. 1, pp. 22-29.

Bauer, Royal D. M. "Keeping The Proper Balance Between Practical And Theoretical Accounting Training," AR, 1942, Vol. 17, No. 3, pp. 233-235.

Baughman, Gene K. "Economical Processing Of Small Orders," MA, 1967, Vol. 48, No. 7, pp. 55-58.

Baughman, Raymond H. "Accounting For Inter-Plant Sales," MA, 1970, Vol. 52, No. 3, pp. 41-43.

Baumler, John V. (Watson, David J. H. and John V. Baumler. "Transfer Pricing: A Behavioral Context," AR, 1975, Vol. 50, No. 3, pp. 466-474.)

Baumler, J. V. (Jiambalvo, J., D. J. H. Watson and J. V. Baumler. "An Examination Of Performance Evaluation Decisions In CPA Firm Subunits," AOS, 1983, Vol. 8, No. 1, pp. 13-30.)

Bavishi, Vinod B. and Harold E. Wyman. "Foreign Operations Disclosures By U.S.-Based Multinational Corporations: Are They Adequate?," IJAER, 1980, Vol. 16, No. 1, pp. 153-168.

Bavishi, Vinod B. "Capital Budgeting Practices At Multinationals," MA, 1981, Vol. 63, No. 2, pp. 32-35.

Bavishi, Vinod B. (Choi, Frederick D. S. and Vinod B. Bavishi. "International Accounting Standards: Issues Needing Attention," JOA, 183, Vol. 155, No. 3,pp.62-68.)

Bavishi, Vinod B. (Choi, Frederick D. S. and Vinod B. Bavishi. "Financial Accounting Standards: A Multinational Synthesis And Policy Framework," IJAER, 1982, Vol. 18, No. 1, pp. 159-183.)

Bavishi, Vinod B. (Hussein, Mohamed E. A., Vinod B. Bavishi and Jagdish S. Gangolly. "International Similarities And Differences In The Auditor's Report," AJPT, 1986-87, Vol. 6, No. 1, pp. 124-133.)

Baxendale, Sidney J. and Alan S. Levitan. "The Post Audit Review Of Equipment Replacement Decisions In Capital Intensive Companies," JCA, 1987, Vol. 4, No. 1, pp.7-15.

Baxter, William T. "Accounting Standards - Boon Or Curse?," ABR, 1981-82, Vol. 12, No. 45, pp. 3-10.

Baxter, William T. "The Account Charge And Discharge," AHJ, 1980, Vol. 7, No. 1, pp. 69-71.

Baxter, W. T. and N. H. Carrier. "Depreciation, Replacement Price, And Cost Of Capital," JAR, 1971, Vol. 9, No. 2, pp. 189-214.

Baxter, W. T. "Accounting Standards - Boon Or Curse?: A Reply," ABR, 1982-83, Vol. 13, No. 49, pp. 63-64.

Baxter, W. T. "Credit, Bills, And Bookkeeping In A Simple Economy," AR, 1946, Vol. 21, No. 2, pp. 154-165.

Baxter, W. T. "Depreciating Assets: The Forward-Looking Approach To Value," ABACUS, 1970, Vol. 6, No. 2, pp. 120-131.

Baxt, R. "Legal Decisions And Accounting Principles," ABACUS, 1967, Vol. 3, No. 1, pp. 83-86.

Bayer, Harmon S. "Planning For Cost Reductions," MA, 1973, Vol. 54, No. 10, pp. 31-36.

Bayliss, R. W. "Input-Output Analysis As An Aid To Financial Control," ABR, 1971-72, Vol. 2, No. 5, pp. 53-59.

Baylis, A. W. "Income Tax Allocation - A Defence," ABACUS, 1971, Vol. 7, No. 2, pp. 161-172.

Bayly, Charles B., Jr. "Lessening Tax Burden On Lump-Sum Income," JOA, 1953, Vol. 96, No. 5, pp. 582-587.

Bay, Max W. "An Experience In Teaching Accountants' Report Writing By Visual Methods," AR, 1953, Vol. 28, No. 1, pp. 113-114.

Bazeli, Frank P. (Baker, Richard E., John R. Simon and Frank P. Bazeli. "An Assessment Of The Learning Style Preferences Of Accounting Majors," IAE, 1986, Vol. 1, No. 1, pp. 1-12.)

Bazeli, Frank P. (Baker, Richard E., John R. Simon and Frank P. Bazeli. "Selecting Instructional Design For Introductory Accounting Based On The Experiential Learning Model," JAED, 1987, Vol. 5, No. 2, pp.207-226.)

Bazley, John D. and Loren A. Nikolai. "A Comparison Of Published Accounting Research And Qualities Of Accounting Faculty And Doctoral Programs," AR, 1975, Vol. 50, No. 3, pp. 605-610.

Bazley, John D. "An Algebraic Aid In Teaching The Differences Between Direct Costing And Full-Absorption Costing Models: A Comment," AR, 1974, Vol. 49, No. 4, p. 838.

Bazley, John D. (Nikolai, Loren A. and John D. Bazley. "The Organizational Set Prestige Ranking And Its Impact Upon Accounting Department Faculties," AR, 1975, Vol. 50, No. 4, pp. 881-888.)

Bazley, John D. (Nikolai, Loren A., John D. Bazley and R. Lee Brummet. "The Measurement Of Corporate Environmental Activity," MA, 1976, Vol. 57, No. 12, pp. 38-40.)

Bazley, John D. (Rockness, Howard O., John D. Bazley and Loren A. Nikolai. "Variance Analysis For Pollution Control," MA, 1977, Vol. 58, No. 7, pp. 51-54.)

Bazley, M., P. Brown and H. Y. Izan. "An Analysis Of Lease Disclosures By Australian Companies," ABACUS, 1985, Vol. 21, No. 1, pp. 44-62.

Beach, John E. "Code Of Ethics: The Professional Catch 22," JAPP, 1984, Vol. 3, No. 4, pp. 311-323.

Beamer, Elmer G. "Continuing Education A Professional Requirement," JOA, 1972, Vol. 133, No. 1, pp. 33-39.

Beamer, Elmer G. "The Expanding Common Body Of Knowledge Of CPAs," JOA, 1962, Vol. 113, No. 5, pp. 51-54.

Beamer, George C. and Tom Rose. "The Use Of The GATB And The AIA Tests In Predicting Success In Courses In Accounting," AR, 1955, Vol. 30, No. 3, pp. 533-535.

Beams, Floyd A. and Paul E. Fertig. "Pollution Control Through Social Cost Conversion," JOA, 1971, Vol. 132, No. 5, pp. 37-42.

Beams, Floyd A. "EDP And The Elementary Accounting Course," AR, 1969, Vol. 44, No. 4, pp. 832-836.

Beams, Floyd A. "Income Reporting: Continuity With Change," MA, 1972, Vol. 54, No. 2, pp. 23-26.

Beams, Floyd A. "Indications Of Pragmatism And Empiricism In Accounting Thought," AR, 1969, Vol. 44, No. 2, pp. 382-388.

Beams, Floyd A. "New Directions In Financial Reporting," MA, 1974, Vol. 55, No. 8, pp. 13-15.

Beams, Floyd A. (Bastable, C. W. and Floyd A. Beams. "Cash Flows And Cash Cows," JAAF, 1981, Vol. 4, No. 3, pp. 248-254.)

Beams, Floyd A. (Cunningham, Gary M. and Floyd A. Beams. "Some Legal Aspects Of The Premature Retirement Of Debt," MA, 1976, Vol. 57, No. 11, pp. 19-21.)

Beam, Thomas J. "Mix Variance In Gross Profit Analysis," MA, 1973, Vol. 55, No. 5, pp. 38-40.

Bean, Virginia L. and Jeanette N. Medewitz. "Computer Education: A Survey Of Accounting Graduates," JAED, 1987, Vol. 5, No. 2, pp. 243-258.

Bean, Virginia L. and William G. Mister. "A Partner In Residence Program At The University Of Colorado For National Accountancy Firms," AR, 1978, Vol. 53, No. 1, pp. 139-142.

Bean, Virginia L. (Watanabe, Judith E., Virginia L. Bean and Justin D. Stolen. "An Empirical Study Of Complexity Experience By Taxpayers," AIT, 1987, Vol. 1, pp. 153-168.)

Beard, Larry H. and Charles W. Caldwell. "Transfer Pricing Can Improve Sales And Credit Cooperation," MA, 1984, Vol. 65, No. 9, pp. 60-65.

Beard, Larry H. and Valarie A. Hoyle. "Cost Accounting Proposal For An Advertising Agency," MA, 1976, Vol. 58, No. 6, pp. 38-40.

Beard, Larry H. (Jacobs, Fred A., Al L. Hartgraves and Larry H. Beard. "Publication Productivity Of Doctoral Alumni: A Time-Adjusted Model," AR, 1986, Vol. 61, No. 1, pp. 179-187.)

Beard, Larry H. (O'Keefe, W. Timothy, Larry H. Beard and Dana S. O'Keefe. "Are U.S. Exporters Benefiting From The FSC?," MA, 1986, Vol. 67, No. 11, pp. 42-47.)

Beard, Larry H. (Reckers, Philip M. J. and Larry H. Beard. "IRS Seeks Auditors' Working Papers," **CPAJ**, 1978, Vol. 48, No. 1, pp. 35-40.)

Beard, Larry H., Fred A. Jacobs and Al L. Hartgraves. "Publications: A Valid Measure Of Faculty Contribution?," **JAED,** 1985, Vol. 3, No. 2, pp. 155-161.

Bearse, Alvah W. "Air Pollution: A Case Study," **MA,** 1971, Vol. 53, No. 3, pp. 16-18.

Bear, James A., Jr. (Shenkir, William G., Glenn A. Welsch and James A. Bear, Jr. "Thomas Jefferson: Management Accountant," **JOA,** 1972, Vol. 133, No. 4, pp. 33-47.)

Beatty, Randolph P. and Steven B. Johnson. "A Market-Based Method Of Classifying Convertible Securities," **JAAF,** 1985, Vol. 8, No. 2, pp. 112-124.

Beatty, Willard C. "Accounting In The Graduate Program Of The Social-Science Student," **AR,** 1941, Vol. 16, No. 2, pp. 155-160.

Beauvais, Edward C. (Kissell, Jeffrey C. and Edward C. Beauvais. "Competition And Local Telephone Company Accounting," **CA,** 1986, Vol. 4, No. 2, pp. 50-58.)

Beaven, Douglas. (Bernard, Clark L. and Douglas Beaven. "Containing The Costs Of Higher Education," **JOA,** 1985, Vol. 160, No. 4, pp. 78-94.)

Beaver, William H. and Joel S. Demski. "The Nature Of Financial Accounting Objectives: A Summary And Synthesis," **JAR,** 1974, Vol. 12, Supp., pp. 170-187.

Beaver, William H. and Joel S. Demski. "The Nature Of Income Measurement," **AR,** 1979, Vol. 54, No. 1, pp. 38-46.

Beaver, William H. and Mark A. Wolfson. "Foreign Currency Translation And Changing Prices In Perfect And Complete Markets," **JAR,** 1982, Vol. 20, No. 2, Part II, pp. 528-550.

Beaver, William H. and Roland E. Dukes. "Interperiod Tax Allocation, Earnings Expectations, And The Behavior Of Security Prices," **AR,** 1972, Vol. 47, No. 2, pp. 320-332.

Beaver, William H. and Roland E. Dukes. "Interperiod Tax Allocation And Delta-Depreciation Methods: Some Empirical Results," **AR,** 1973, Vol. 48, No. 3, pp. 549-559.

Beaver, William H. and Wayne R. Landsman. "Note On The Behavior Of Residual Security Returns For Winner And Loser Portfolios," **JAEC,** 1981, Vol. 3, No. 3, pp. 233-241.

Beaver, William H. "Accounting For Marketable Equity Securities," **JOA,** 1973, Vol. 136, No. 6, pp. 58-64.

Beaver, William H. "Alternative Accounting Measures As Predictors Of Failure," **AR,** 1968, Vol. 43, No. 1, pp. 113-122.

Beaver, William H. "Current Trends In Corporate Disclosure," **JOA,** 1978, Vol. 145, No. 1, pp. 44-52.

Beaver, William H. "Econometric Properties Of Alternative Security Return Methods," **JAR,** 1981, Vol. 19, No. 1, pp. 163-184.

Beaver, William H. "Implications Of Security Price Research For Accounting: A Reply To Bierman," **AR,** 1974, Vol. 49, No. 3, pp. 563-571.

Beaver, William H. "Incorporating Research Into The Educational Process," **IAE,** 1984, No. 1, pp. 33-38.

Beaver, William H. "Market Efficiency," **AR,** 1981, Vol. 56, No. 1, pp. 23-37.

Beaver, William H. "Market Prices, Financial Ratios, And The Prediction Of Failure," **JAR,** 1968, Vol. 6, No. 2, pp. 179-192.

Beaver, William H. "Presidential Address," **ACCHOR,** 1987, Vol. 1, No. 4, pp. 1-6.

Beaver, William H. "Reporting Rules For Marketable Equity Securities," **JOA,** 1971, Vol. 132, No. 4, pp. 57-61.

Beaver, William H. "The Information Content Of Annual Earnings Announcements," **JAR,** 1968, Vol. 6, Supp., pp. 67-92.

Beaver, William H. "The Properties Of Sequential Regressions With Multiple Explanatory Variables," **AR,** 1987, Vol. 62, No. 1, pp. 137-144.

Beaver, William H. "The Time Series Behavior Of Earnings," **JAR,** 1970, Vol. 8, Supp., pp. 62-99.

Beaver, William H. "What Should Be The FASB's Objectives?," **JOA,** 1973, Vol. 136, No. 2, pp. 49-56.

Beaver, William H., Andrew A. Christie and Paul A. Griffin. "The Information Content Of SEC Accounting Series Release No. 190," **JAEC,** 1980, Vol. 2, No. 2, pp. 127-157.

Beaver, William H., John W. Kennelly and William M. Voss. "Predictive Ability As A Criterion For The Evaluation Of Accounting Data," **AR,** 1968, Vol. 43, No. 4, pp. 675-683.

Beaver, William H., Paul A. Griffin and Wayne R. Landsman. "Testing For Incremental Information Content In The Presence Of Collinearity: A Comment," **JAEC,** 1984, Vol. 6, No. 3, pp. 219-223.

Beaver, William H., Paul A. Griffin and Wayne R. Landsman. "The Incremental Information Content Of Replacement Cost Earnings," **JAEC,** 1982, Vol. 4, No. 1, pp. 15-39.

Beaver, William H., Paul Kettler and Myron Scholes. "The Association Between Market Determined And Accounting Determined Risk Measures," **AR,** 1970, Vol. 45, No. 4, pp. 654-682.

Beaver, William H., Richard A. Lambert and Stephen G. Ryan. "The Information Content Of Security Prices: A Second Look," **JAEC,** 1987, Vol. 9, No. 2, pp. 139-157.

Beaver, William H., Roger Clarke and William F. Wright. "The Association Between Unsystematic Security Returns And The Magnitude Of Earnings Forecast Errors," **JAR,** 1979, Vol. 17, No. 2, pp. 316-340.

Beaver, William, Richard Lambert and Dale Morse. "The Information Content Of Security Prices," **JAEC,** 1980, Vol. 2, No. 1, pp. 3-28.

Beaver, William. "Financial Ratios As Predictors Of Failure," **JAR,** 1966, Vol. 4, Supp., pp. 71-111.

Beaver, W. H. and R. E. Dukes. "Changes In Depreciation Methods: Some Analytical Results," **JAR,** 1974, Vol. 12, No. 2, pp. 205-215.

Beaver, W. (Rose, J., W. Beaver, S. Becker and G. Sorter. "Toward An Empirical Measure Of Materiality," **JAR,** 1970, Vol. 8, Supp., pp. 138-148.)

Beaver, W. (Sorter, George H., Selwyn W. Becker, T. R. Archibald and W. Beaver. "Corporate Personality As Reflected In Accounting Decisions: Some Preliminary Findings," **JAR,** 1964, Vol. 2, No. 2, pp. 183-196.)

Beazley, Garnett F., Jr. "An International Implication For Accounting," **IJAER,** 1968, Vol. 3, No. 2, pp. 1-10.

Bebee, Richard F. "A Look At Employee Retirement Benefits," **MA,** 1976, Vol. 57, No. 9, pp. 13-14.

Bebee, Richard F., Lawrence L. Steinmetz and William D. Wilsted. "Managing The Income Number," **MA,** 1975, Vol. 56, No. 8, pp. 40-42.

Beckerley, Edward B. and Richard L. Panich. "RA 87 - Major Provisions For Individual Taxpayers," **CPAJ,** 1988, Vol. 58, No. 7, pp. 64-69.

Beckers, Leonard F. "New Audit Program Relieves Year-End Pressure," **JOA,** 1951, Vol. 91, No. 6, pp. 822-826.

Beckers, Leonard F. "Organizational And Procedural Changes May Help Flatten The Large Firm's Year-End Peak," **JOA,** 1950, Vol. 90, No. 1, pp. 30-35.

Beckers, Leonard F. "The Audit Of Cash," **JOA,** 1955, Vol. 99, No. 3, pp. 35-38.

Becker, Benjamin M. and Samuel S. Becker. "Financing A Business Enterprise," **JOA,** 1961, Vol. 112, No. 6, pp. 42-46.

Becker, Edward A. and K. J. Kim. "Direct Material Variances: Review Of The Mix And Yield Variances," **IAE,** 1988, Vol. 3, No. 1, pp. 1-16.

Becker, James F. "Toward A 'Real' Value Accounting," **AIPIA,** 1988, Vol. 2, pp. 143-155.

Becker, Samuel S. "The CPA's Challenge In Estate Planning," **JOA,** 1963, Vol. 115, No. 2, pp. 64-69.

Becker, Samuel S. (Becker, Benjamin M. and Samuel S. Becker. "Financing A Business Enterprise," **JOA,** 1961, Vol. 112, No. 6, pp. 42-46.)

Becker, Selwyn W. (Sorter, George H., Selwyn W. Becker, T. R. Archibald and W. Beaver. "Corporate Personality As Reflected In Accounting Decisions: Some Preliminary Findings." **JAR,** 1964, Vol. 2, No. 2, pp. 183-196.)

Becker, Selwyn, Joshua Ronen and George Sorter. "Opportunity Costs - An Experimental Approach," **JAR,** 1974, Vol. 12, No. 2, pp. 317-329.

Becker, Stuart. "An Overview Of The Pension Reform Act Of 1974," **CPAJ,** 1975, Vol. 45, No. 2, pp. 27-32.

Becker, S. (Rose, J., W. Beaver, S. Becker and G. Sorter. "Toward An Empirical Measure Of Materiality," **JAR,** 1970, Vol. 8, Supp., pp. 138-148.)

Beckett, John A. "A Study Of The Principles Of Allocating Costs," **AR,** 1951, Vol. 26, No. 3, pp. 327-333.

Beckett, John A. "Some Facts Of Federal Fiscal Life And Their Importance To Thinking Americans," **AR,** 1961, Vol. 36, No. 1, pp. 36-42.

Beck, David. (Gutkin, Sydney A. and David Beck. "Ordinary Loss Denied Post-Liquidation Transferee," **JOA,** 1953, Vol. 95, No. 3, pp. 314-319.)

Beck, G. W. "The Role Of The Auditor In Modern Society," **ABR,** 1972-73, Vol. 3, No. 10, pp. 117-122.

Beck, Paul J. and Ira Solomon. "Ex Post Sampling Risks And Decision Rule Choice In Substantive Testing," **AJPT,** 1984-85, Vol. 4, No. 2, pp. 1-10.

Beck, Paul J. and Ira Solomon. "Sampling Risks And Audit Consequences Under Alternative Testing Approaches," **AR,** 1985, Vol. 60, No. 4, pp. 714-723.

Beck, Paul J. and Russell M. Barefield. "An Economic Analysis Of Competitive Bidding For Public Sector Audit Engagements," **JAPP,** 1986, Vol. 5, No. 3, pp. 143-165.

Beck, Paul J. "A Critical Analysis Of The Regression Estimator In Audit Sampling," **JAR,** 1980, Vol. 18, No. 1, pp. 16-37.

Beck, Paul J. (Solomon, Ira and Paul J. Beck. "A Comparison Of General Price Level And Historical Cost Financial Statements In The Prediction Of Bankruptcy: A Comment," **AR,** 1980, Vol. 55, No. 3, pp. 511-515.)

Beck, Paul J., Ira Solomon and Lawrence A. Tomassini. "Subjective Prior Probability Distributions And Audit Risk," **JAR,** 1985, Vol. 23, No. 1, pp. 37-56.

Beck, Paul J., Thomas J. Frecka and Ira Solomon. "A Model Of The Market For MAS And Audit Services: Knowledge Spillovers And Auditor-Auditee Bonding," **JAL,** 1988, Vol. 7, pp. 50-64.

Beck, Richard P. (Basi, Bart A. and Richard P. Beck. "Accumulated Earnings Vs. Economic Stabilization," **MA,** 1975, Vol. 57, No. 6, pp. 18-20.)

Bedard, Jean, Glen L. Gray and Theodore J. Mock. "Decision Support Systems And Auditing," **AIA,** 1984, Vol. 1, pp. 239-266.

Beddingfield, Ronald. "Human Behavior: The Key To Success In Budgeting," **MA,** 1969, Vol. 51, No. 3, pp. 54-56.

Bedford Norton M. "The Nature Of Business Costs, General Concepts," **AR,** 1957, Vol. 32, No. 1, pp. 8-14.

Bedford, Norton M. and Jacques P. Gautier. "An International Analytical Comparison Of The Structure And Content Of Annual Reports In The European Economic Community, Switzerland, And The United States," **IJAER,** 1974, Vol. 9, No. 2, pp. 1-44.

Bedford, Norton M. and James C. McKeown. "Comparative Analysis Of Net Realizable Value And Replacement Costing," **AR**, 1972, Vol. 47, No. 2, pp. 333-338.

Bedford, Norton M. and Nicholas Dopuch. "Research Methodology And Accounting Theory - Another Perspective," **AR**, 1961, Vol. 36, No. 3, pp. 351-361.

Bedford, Norton M. and Richard E. Ziegler. "The Contributions Of A. C. Littleton To Accounting Thought And Practice," **AR**, 1975, Vol. 50, No. 3, pp. 435-443.

Bedford, Norton M. and Toshio Iino. "Consistency Reexamined," **AR**, 1968, Vol. 43, No. 3, pp. 453-458.

Bedford, Norton M. and Vahe Baladouni. "A Communication Theory Approach To Accountancy," **AR**, 1962, Vol. 37, No. 4, pp. 650-659.

Bedford, Norton M. and William G. Shenkir. "Reorienting Accounting Education," **JOA**, 1987, Vol. 164, No. 2, pp. 84-91.

Bedford, Norton M. "A Critical Analysis Of Accounting Concepts Of Income," **AR**, 1951, Vol. 26, No. 4, pp. 526-537.

Bedford, Norton M. "Accounting And Economic Concepts," **JOA**, 1957, Vol. 103, No. 5, pp. 56-62.

Bedford, Norton M. "Corporate Accountability," **MA**, 1973, Vol. 55, No. 5, pp. 41-44.

Bedford, Norton M. "Education For Accounting As A Learned Profession," **JOA**, 1961, Vol. 112, No. 6, pp. 33-41.

Bedford, Norton M. "Need For Supplementary Data In Interpretation Of Income Reports," **AR**, 1952, Vol. 27, No. 2, pp. 195-201.

Bedford, Norton M. "The Impact Of Chambers On The Scope Of Accounting: An Analysis And Extension," **ABACUS**, 1982, Vol. 18, No. 2, pp. 112-118.

Bedford, Norton M. "The International Flow Of Accounting Thought," **IJAER**, 1966, Vol. 1, No. 2, pp. 1-7.

Bedford, Norton M. "The Laws Of Learning And Accounting Instruction," **AR**, 1963, Vol. 38, No. 2, pp. 406-408.

Bedford, Norton M. "The Nature Of Future Accounting Theory," **AR**, 1967, Vol. 42, No. 1, pp. 82-85.

Bedford, Norton M. "The Need For An Extension Of The Accrual Concept," **JOA**, 1965, Vol. 119, No. 5, pp. 29-33.

Bedford, Norton M. "Using Supplementary Data To Interpret Reported Income," **AR**, 1953, Vol. 28, No. 4, pp. 517-521.

Bedford, Norton M. (Chumachenko, Nikolai and Norton M. Bedford. "Some Distinctive Aspects Of Accounting In The USSR," **IJAER**, 1968, Vol. 4, No. 1, pp. 29-40.)

Bedford, Norton M. (Lee, Lucy C. and Norton M. Bedford. "An Information Theory Analysis Of The Accounting Process," **AR**, 1969, Vol. 44, No. 2, pp. 256-275.)

Bedford, N. M. "The Corporate Report: A Discussion," **AOS**, 1976, Vol. 1, No. 1, pp. 111-116.

Bedingfield, James P. and Myron S. Lubell. "Extension Of The Attest Function To Published Forecasts - An Opinion Survey," **CPAJ**, 1974, Vol. 44, No. 1, pp. 40-45.

Bedingfield, James P. and Stephen E. Loeb. "Attitudes Of Professors Toward Accounting Ethics," **AR**, 1973, Vol. 48, No. 3, pp. 603-605.

Bedingfield, James P. "Analyzing The Effect Of CASB Standards On Business," **JOA**, 1980, Vol. 149, No. 4, pp. 58-67.

Bedingfield, James P. "The Current State Of Statistical Sampling And Auditing," **JOA**, 1975, Vol. 140, No. 6, pp. 48-55.

Bedingfield, James P. "The Effect Of Recent Litigation On Audit Practice," **JOA**, 1974, Vol. 137, No. 5, pp. 55-62.

Bedingfield, James P. (Loeb, Stephen E. and James P. Bedingfield. "Teaching Accounting Ethics," **AR**, 1972, Vol. 47, No. 4, pp. 811-813.)

Bedingfield, James P., Philip M. J. Reckers and A. J. Stagliano. "Assessing The Impact Of Mergers On Bank Performance," **AIA**, 1986, Vol. 3, pp. 149-170.

Bedwell, Byron F. E. (Lawrence, Charles and Byron F. E. Bedwell. "Professional Practice In England And America," **AR**, 1961, Vol. 36, No. 2, pp. 269-273.)

Beechy, Thomas H. and Wayne A. Bernath. "The Measurement Of Economic Activity: An Introductory Accounting Course," **AR**, 1971, Vol. 46, No. 2, pp. 385-387.

Beechy, Thomas H. "Quasi-Debt Analysis Of Financial Leases," **AR**, 1969, Vol. 44, No. 2, pp. 375-381.

Beechy, Thomas H. "The Cost Of Leasing: Comment And Correction," **AR**, 1970, Vol. 45, No. 4, pp. 769-773.

Beechy, Thomas H. (Amernic, Joel H. and Thomas H. Beechy. "Accounting Students' Performance And Cognitive Complexity: Some Empirical Evidence," **AR**, 1984, Vol. 59, No. 2, pp. 300-313.)

Beedles, William. (Smith, David B., Howard Stettler and William Beedles. "An Investigation Of The Information Content Of Foreign Sensitive Payment Disclosures," **JAEC**, 1984, Vol. 6, No. 2, pp. 153-162.)

Beed, Teresa. (Douglas, Patricia, Teresa Beed, Karen Clark and Sylvia Weisenburger. "Surviving Your First Job," **MA**, 1986, Vol. 67, No. 12, pp. 32-35.)

Beekhuizen, Theo and Paul Frishkoff. "A Comparison Of The New Dutch Accounting Act With Generally Accepted American Accounting Principles," **IJAER**, 1975, Vol. 10, No. 2, pp. 13-22.

Beers, J. W. "Training Classes In The Income Tax Unit," **AR**, 1928, Vol. 3, No. 2, pp. 177-183.

Behling, Orlando and Jesse F. Dillard. "Accounting: The Intuitive Challenge," **ACCHOR**, 1987, Vol. 1, No. 2, pp. 35-42.

Behr, Giorgio. (Pratt, Jamie and Giorgio Behr. "Environmental Factors, Transaction Costs, And External Reporting: A Cross-Sectional Comparison," **IJAER**, 1987, Vol. 22, No. 2, pp. 1-24.)

Beidleman, Carl R. "Determinants Of Second-Hand Asset Values," **ABR**, 1973-74, Vol. 4, No. 14, pp. 102-115.

Beidleman, Carl R. "Income Smoothing: The Role Of Manage-

ment," **AR**, 1973, Vol. 48, No. 4, pp. 653-667.

Beidleman, Carl R. "Income Smoothing: The Role Of Management: A Reply," **AR**, 1975, Vol. 50, No. 1, pp. 122-126.

Beier, Raymond J. (Kay, Robert S. and Raymond J. Beier. "Leveraged Buyout Accounting," **JAAF**, 1987, Vol. 2 (New Series), No. 1, pp. 90-97.)

Beights, David Miers. "Municipal Auditing Standards," **AR**, 1955, Vol. 30, No. 3, pp. 421-427.

Beights, David M. "Standards For Admission To The Accounting Profession," **JOA**, 1954, Vol. 97, No. 4, pp. 421-427.

Beights, David M. "The CPA Examination," **AR**, 1952, Vol. 27, No. 3, pp. 346-351.

Beights, D. M. "Opprtunities For A Career In Governmental Accounting," **AR**, 1954, Vol. 29, No. 4, pp. 614-619.

Beights, D. M. "The Accounting Curriculum," **AR**, 1954, Vol. 29, No. 2, pp. 219-223.

Bejan, Mary. "On The Application Of Rational Choice Theory To Financial Reporting Controversies: A Comment On Cushing," **AR**, 1981, Vol. 56, No. 3, pp. 704-712.

Beja, Avraham and Yair Aharoni. "Some Aspects Of Conventional Accounting Profits In An Inflationary Environment," **JAR**, 1977, Vol. 15, No. 2, pp. 169-178.

Bekaert, A. C. "'What's Wrong With Financial Reporting?'," **AR**, 1952, Vol. 27, No. 1, pp. 57-62.

Belda, Bertrand J. "Income And Expense Planning," **JOA**, 1959, Vol. 108, No. 5, pp. 46-50.

Belda, Bertrand J. "Line Of Business Reporting And Product Profitability," **MA**, 1970, Vol. 51, No. 9, pp. 10-12.

Belda, Bertrand J. "Reporting On Forecasts Of Future Developments," **JOA**, 1970, Vol. 130, No. 6, pp. 54-58.

Belford, William B. and Leland G. Ayer. "Unitization Of Construction Work Orders," **MA**, 1969, Vol. 51, No. 3, pp. 29-32.

Belkaoui, Ahmed and James L. Chan. "Professional Value System Of Academic Accountants: An Empirical Inquiry," **AIPIA**, 1988, Vol. 2, pp. 1-28.

Belkaoui, Ahmed and Mostafa Maksy. "Welfare Of The Common Man And Accounting Disclosure Adequacy: An Empirical Investigation," **IJAER**, 1985, Vol. 20, No. 2, pp. 81-94.

Belkaoui, Ahmed, Alfred Kahl and Josette Peyrard. "Information Needs Of Financial Analysts: An International Comparison," **IJAER**, 1977, Vol. 13, No. 1, pp. 19-27.

Belkaoui, Ahmed. "Accounting Determinants Of Systematic Risk In Canadian Common Stocks: A Multivariate Approach," **ABR**, 1978-79, Vol. 9, No. 33, pp. 3-10.

Belkaoui, Ahmed. "Economic, Political, And Civil Indicators And Reporting And Disclosure Adequacy: Empirical Investigation," **JAPP**, 1983, Vol. 2, No. 3, pp. 207-219.

Belkaoui, Ahmed. "Learning Order And Acceptance Of Accounting Techniques," **AR**, 1975, Vol. 50, No. 4, pp. 897-899.

Belkaoui, Ahmed. "Slack Budgeting, Information Distortion And Self-Esteem," **CAR**, 1985-86, Vol. 2, No. 1, pp. 111-123.

Belkaoui, Ahmed. "The Accounting Students' Need For Achievement And Career Aspirations: An Experiment," **IAE**, 1986, Vol. 1, No. 2, pp. 197-206.

Belkaoui, Ahmed. "The Effects Of Diagnostic And Redundant Information On Loan Officer's Restrictions," **ABR**, 1983-84, Vol. 14, No. 55, pp. 249-256.

Belkaoui, Ahmed. "The Interprofessional Linguistic Communication Of Accounting Concepts: An Experiment In Socialinguistics," **JAR**, 1980, Vol. 18, No. 2, pp. 362-374.

Belkaoui, Ahmed. "The Primacy-Recency Effect, Ego Involvement And The Acceptance Of Accounting Techniques," **AR**, 1977, Vol. 52, No. 1, pp. 252-256.

Belkaoui, Ahmed. "'Economic, Political, And Civil Indicators And Reporting And Disclosure Adequacy: Empirical Investigation': A Reply," **JAPP**, 1984, Vol. 3, No. 3, pp. 249-250.

Belkaoui, Ahmed. (Kahl, Alfred and Ahmed Belkaoui. "Bank Annual Report Disclosure Adequacy Internationally," **ABR**, 1980-81, Vol. 11, No. 43, pp. 189-196.)

Belkaoui, A. "Linguistic Relativity In Accounting," **AOS**, 1978, Vol. 3, No. 2, pp. 97-104.

Belkaoui, A. "The Impact Of Socio-Economic Accounting Statements On The Investment Decision: An Empirical Study," No. 3, pp. 263-284.

Belkaoui, A. "The Relationship Between Self-Disclosure Style And Attitudes To Responsibility Accounting," **AOS**, 1981, Vol. 6, No. 4, pp. 281-290.

Bellinghausen, James M. "Preparing For Computers," **MA**, 1968, Vol. 49, No. 7, pp. 9-14.

Belluomini, Frank. "Local Governmental Units: The Going Concern Question," **JOA**, 1977, Vol. 143, No. 6, pp. 60-65.

Bell, Albert L. "Break-Even Charts Versus Marginal Graphs," **MA**, 1969, Vol. 50, No. 6, pp. 32-35.

Bell, Albert L. "College Students' Attitudes Toward Business," **MA**, 1968, Vol. 50, No. 3, pp. 60-64.

Bell, Albert L. "Fixed Assets And Current Costs," **AR**, 1953, Vol. 28. No. 1, pp. 44-53.

Bell, Albert L. "Flexible Budgets And Marginal Cost Pricing," **MA**, 1977, Vol. 58, No. 7, pp. 34-37.

Bell, Jan. (Lewis, Barry L. and Jan Bell. "Decisions Involving Sequential Events: Replications And Extensions," **JAR**, 1985, Vol. 23, No. 1, pp. 228-239.)

Bell, Jay W. "Financial Data In A Management Information System," **MA**, 1968, Vol. 49, No. 10, pp. 23-33.

Bell, Philip W. "Accounting As A Discipline For Study And Practice: 1986," **CAR**, 1986-87, Vol. 3, No. 2, pp. 338-367.

Bell, Philip W. "Boussard's 'Effectiveness Of Inflation Accounting Adjustments': A Comment," **ABACUS**, 1987, Vol. 23, No. 1, pp. 91-92.

Bell, Philip W. (Johnson, L. Todd and Philip W. Bell. "Current Replacement Costs: A Qualified Opinion," JOA, 1976, Vol. 142, No. 5, pp. 63-71.)

Bell, Richard. (Houghton, Keith A. and Richard Bell. "Evaluations Of Accounting And Finance Journals: The Australian View," IJAER, 1984, Vol. 20, No. 1, pp. 179-187.)

Bell, Spurgeon. "Research Work At Ohio State University," AR, 1926, Vol. 1, No. 1, pp. 39-42.

Bell, Timothy Barnes. "Market Reaction To Reserve Recognition Accounting," JAR, 1983, Vol. 21, No. 1, pp. 1-17.

Bell, Timothy B. (McKee, A. James, Jr., Timothy B. Bell and James R. Boatsman. "Management Preferences Over Accounting Standards: A Replication And Additional Tests," AR, 1984, Vol. 59, No. 4, pp. 647-659.)

Bell, William H. "Depreciation And The Price Level," AR, 1948, Vol. 23, No. 2, pp. 126-128.

Belser, F. C. "How The Universities Can Aid The Accounting Profession," AR, 1927, Vol. 2, No. 1, pp. 37-42.

Beltramo, Michael N. "Findings And Thoughts About Competition In The Procurement Of Weapon Systems," JCA, 1986, Vol. 3, No. 2, pp. 1-11.

Benbasat, Izak and Albert S. Dexter. "Individual Differences In The Use Of Decision Support Aids," JAR, 1982, Vol. 20, No. 1, pp. 1-11.

Benbasat, Izak and Albert S. Dexter. "Value And Events Approaches To Accounting: An Experimental Evaluation," AR, 1979, Vol. 54, No. 4, pp. 735-749.

Bence, Alexander A. "Value Analysis For Cost Control And Profit Improvement," MA, 1966, Vol. 47, No. 11, pp. 52-57.

Bencivenga, Joseph V. "Improving Reviews Of Audit Examinations," CPAJ, 1978, Vol. 48, No. 4, pp. 33-38.

Bender, Douglas E. "Foreign Currency Translations - FAS 52 - Part II," CPAJ, 1982, Vol. 52, No. 7, pp. 20-27.

Bender, Douglas E. "Foreign Currency Translation - FAS 52 - Part III," CPAJ, 1982, Vol. 52, No. 8, pp. 40-48.

Bender, Douglas E. "Foreign Currency Translation-FAS 52 - Part I," CPAJ, 1982, Vol. 52, No. 6, pp. 9-15.

Bendock, Charles M. "Measuring Social Costs," MA, 1975, Vol. 56, No. 7, pp. 13-15.

Benedetto, A. F. "Accounting In Mexico," AR, 1934, Vol. 9, No. 4, pp. 340-342.

Benedik, John. "Macroeconomics: The Emerging Influence On Accounting Theory," MA, 1978, Vol. 60, No. 1, pp. 23-26.

Bene, Kalman J. "Clerical Work Measurement," MA, 1966, Vol. 48, No. 2, pp. 29-34.

Benishay, Haskel. "A Fourth-Degree Polynomial Utility Function And Its Implications For Investors' Responses Toward Four Moments Of The Wealth Distribution," JAAF, 1987, Vol. 2 (New Series), No. 3, pp. 203-238.

Benishay, Haskel. "Economic Information In Financial Ratio Analysis: A Note," ABR, 1970-71, Vol. 1, No. 2, pp. 174-179.

Benishay, Haskel. "Managerial Controls Of Accounts Receivable: A Reply," JAR, 1966, Vol. 4, No. 1, pp. 131-132.

Benishay, Haskel. "Managerial Controls Of Accounts Receivable: A Deterministic Approach," JAR, 1965, Vol. 3, No. 1, pp. 114-132.

Benis, Martin and Robert Johnson. "A Case Of Premature Income Recognition," CPAJ, 1973, Vol. 43, No. 10, pp. 863-867.

Benis, Martin and Robert T. Johnson. "Gains And Losses On Early Extinguishment Of Debt," CPAJ, 1975, Vol. 45, No. 11, pp. 39-41.

Benis, Martin, Claire Brody and Robert T. Johnson. "Utilization Of The Small Group Approach To Teaching Intermediate Accounting," AR, 1976, Vol. 51, No. 4, pp. 894-898.

Benis, Martin. "Rational Small Business Exceptions To FASB Rules," CPAJ, 1978, Vol. 48, No. 2, pp. 33-38.

Benis, Martin. "The Non-Consolidated Finance Company Subsidiary," AR, 1979, Vol. 54, No. 4, pp. 808-814.

Benis, Martin. "The Small Client And Representation Letters," JOA, 1978, Vol. 146, No. 3, pp. 78-85.

Benis, Martin. (Johnson, Robert T. and Martin Benis. "The Premature Retirement Of Debt," MA, 1975, Vol. 56, No. 7, pp. 43-44.)

Benis, Martin. (Nakayama, Mie, Steven Lilien and Martin Benis. "Due Process And FAS No. 13," MA, 1981, Vol. 62, No. 10, pp. 49-53.)

Benjamin, Harold. "A Diminishing Depreciation Method Based On A Sine Curve Works With Any Scrap Value," JOA, 1950, Vol. 89, No. 4, pp. 303-309.

Benjamin, James A. and Robert H. Strawser. "Developments In Lease Accounting," CPAJ, 1976, Vol. 46, No. 11, pp. 33-36.

Benjamin, James J. and Donald E. Ricketts. "A Profit Planning Project In The Management Accounting Course," AR, 1973, Vol. 48, No. 4, pp. 794-797.

Benjamin, James J. and Keith G. Stanga. "Differences In Disclosure Needs Of Major Users Of Financial Statements," ABR, 1976-77, Vol. 7, No. 27, pp. 187-192.

Benjamin, James J. and Robert H. Strawser. "The Publication Of Forecasts: An Experiment," ABACUS, 1974, Vol. 10 No. 2, pp. 138-146.

Benjamin, James J. and Steven D. Grossman. "Foreign Currency Translation: An Update," CPAJ, 1981, Vol. 51, No. 2, pp. 48-52.

Benjamin, James J. and Vincent C. Brenner. "Reaction To NYSE White Paper's Call For Disclosure," MA, 1975, Vol. 56, No. 11, pp. 13-18.

Benjamin, James J. and Vincent C. Brenner. "Perceptions Of Journal Quality," AR, 1974, Vol. 49, No. 2, pp. 360-362.

Benjamin, James J. (Brenner, Vincent C. and James J.

Benjamin. "Financial Reporting On Units Of General Purchasing Power," MA, 1976, Vol. 57, No. 12, pp. 15-18.)

Benjamin, James J. (Dalsimer, John Paul, Paul E. Dascher and James J. Benjamin. "An Aspect Of The Profession's Social Commitment," CPAJ, 1979, Vol. 49, No. 11, pp. 13-18.)

Benjamin, James J. (Stanga, Keith G. and James J. Benjamin. "Information Needs Of Bankers," MA, 1978, Vol. 59, No. 12, pp. 17-21.)

Benjamin, James J., Paul E. Dascher and Robert G. Morgan. "How Corporate Controllers View The Foreign Corrupt Practices Act," MA, 1979, Vol. 60, No. 12, pp. 43-45.

Benjamin, James J., Steven D. Grossman and Casper E. Wiggins. "The Impact Of Foreign Currency Translation On Reporting During The Phase-In Of SFAS No. 52," JAAF, 1986, Vol. 1 (New Series), No. 3, pp. 177-184.

Benjamin, James. "The Accuracy Of The Period-End Method For Computing The Current Cost Of Materials Used," ABACUS, 1973, Vol. 9, No. 1, pp. 73-80.

Benjamin, James. "The Effects Of Using Current Costs In The Measurement Of Business Income," ABR, 1972-73, Vol. 3, No. 11, pp. 213-217.

Benjamin, James. (Shearon, Winston, Charles Butler and James Benjamin. "Audit Aspects Of Small Computer Systems," CPAJ, 1980, Vol. 50, No. 8, pp. 17-21.)

Benjamin, Leo J. "Doctors Incorporated?," MA, 1975, Vol. 57, No. 5, pp. 37-39.

Benke, Ralph L., Jr. and Ashton Bishop. "Transfer Pricing In An Oligopolistic Market," JCA, 1986, Vol. 3, No. 2, pp. 69-81.

Benke, Ralph L., Jr. and James Don Edwards. "Should You Use Transfer Pricing To Create Pseudo-Profit Centers?," MA, 1981, Vol. 62, No. 8, pp. 36-39.

Benke, Ralph L., Jr. and John Grant Rhode. "Intent To Turnover Among Higher Level Employees In Large CPA Firms," AIA, 1984, Vol. 1, pp. 157-174.

Benke, Ralph L., Jr., James Don Edwards and Alton R. Wheelock. "Applying An Opportunity Cost General Rule For Transfer Pricing," MA, 1982, Vol. 63, No. 12, pp. 43-51.

Benke, R. L., Jr. and J. G. Rhode. "The Job Satisfaction Of Higher Level Employees In Large Certified Public Accounting Firms," AOS, 1980, Vol. 5, No. 2, pp. 187-202.

Benner-Dale, Carolyn J. "The Hammer Of 'Thor'," MA, 1980, Vol. 62, No. 5, pp. 48-51.

Bennett, A. H. M. "Depreciation And Business Decision-Making," ABR, 1972-73, Vol. 3, No. 9, pp. 3-28.

Bennett, Clinton W. "Management Services By C.P.A.'s," AR, 1958, Vol. 33, No. 4, pp. 602-614.

Bennett, Clinton W. "Rehabilitating A Sick Business," JOA, 1956, Vol. 101, No. 4, pp. 50-53.

Bennett, Clinton W. "Semi-Variable Costs As A Pricing Aid When Prices And Volume Are Declining," JOA, 1950, Vol. 89, No. 3, pp. 228-233.

Bennett, David C. (Barfuss, Francois R., Roger D. Musson and David C. Bennett. "Some Significant Differences In U.S. and U.K. Reported Net Income," CPAJ, 1982, Vol. 52, No. 2, pp. 44-48.)

Bennett, George E. "Assumptions," AR, 1933, Vol. 8, No. 2, pp. 157-159.

Bennett, G. E. "Some Observations On The Application Of Manufacturing Expense To Production," AR, 1926, Vol. 1, No. 1, pp. 1-6.

Bennett, G. E. "The Administration Of College Courses In Accounting'," AR, 1927, Vol. 2, No. 2, pp. 182-188.

Bennett, J. W. "Measuring Project Profitability: Rate Of Return Or Present Value - A Reply," AR, 1963, Vol. 38, No. 3, pp. 548-553.

Bennett, Robert C. "Corporate Divorce And Taxes," MA, 1971, Vol. 52, No. 7, pp. 31-35.

Bennett, Robert E. and James A. Hendricks. "Justifying The Acquisition Of Automated Equipment," MA, 1987, Vol. 69, No. 1, pp. 39-46.

Benninger, Lawrence J. "State Law In Regard To Paid-In Surplus," AR, 1946, Vol. 21, No. 1, pp. 57-60.

Benninger, L. J. "A Proposed Reconciliation Of Standard And Current Material Costs," AR, 1950, Vol. 25, No. 2, pp. 156-160.

Benninger, L. J. "Accounting Theory And Cost Accounting," AR, 1965, Vol. 40, No. 3, pp. 547-557.

Benninger, L. J. "Business And Withholding Taxes," AR, 1944, Vol. 19, No. 3, pp. 302-305.

Benninger, L. J. "Cost Control As Applied To The Smaller Business Organization," AR, 1956, Vol. 31, No. 1, pp. 95-98.

Benninger, L. J. "Development Of Cost Accounting Concepts And Principles," AR, 1954, Vol. 29, No. 1, pp. 27-37.

Benninger, L. J. "Needed: A New Concept Of Accounts," AR, 1951, Vol. 26, No. 4, pp. 481-484.

Benninger, L. J. "Standard Costs For Income Determination, Control, And Special Studies," AR, 1950, Vol. 25, No. 4, pp. 378-383.

Benninger, L. J. "The Traditional Vs. The Cost Accounting Concept Of Cost," AR, 1949, Vol. 24, No. 4, pp. 387-391.

Benson, Benjamin. "Lawyers' Responses To Audit Inquiries - A Continuing Controversy," JOA, 1977, Vol. 144, No. 1, pp. 72-78.

Benson, Benjamin. "The Strategy Of Tax Shelter," JOA, 1975, Vol. 140, No. 1, pp. 47-55.

Benson, Benjamin. (Chazen, Charles and Benjamin Benson. "Fitting GAAP To Smaller Businesses," JOA, 1978, Vol. 145, No. 2, pp. 46-51.)

Benson, Beth A. "Computer Graphics For Financial Management," MA, 1984, Vol. 65, No. 7, pp. 46-49.

Benson, Earl D., Barry R. Marks and K. K. Raman. "Municipal

Borrowing Costs And The Differential Impact Of Accounting Information Across Rating Categories," **RIGNA**, 1986, Vol. 2, pp. 261-273.

Benson, Earl D., Barry R. Marks and K. K. Raman. "State Regulation Of Accounting Practices And Municipal Borrowing Costs," **JAPP**, 1984, Vol. 3, No. 2, pp. 107-122.

Benson, Earl D., Barry R. Marks and K. K. Raman. "The MFOA Certificate Of Conformance And Municipal Borrowing Costs," **AIA**, 1986, Vol. 3, pp. 221-232.

Benson, Frank D. "Effective Operational Budgeting Techniques," **CA**, Vol. 3, No. 3, pp. 3-13.

Benson, Lord. "Discipline In The Accountancy Profession," **CPAJ**, 1983, Vol. 53, No. 7, pp. 10-15.

Benson, Lord. "The Auditor And Fraud - A British View," **CPAJ**, 1986, Vol. 56, No. 7, pp. 14-23.

Benston, George J. and Melvin A. Krasney. "DAAM: The Demand For Alternative Accounting Measurements," **JAR**, 1978, Vol. 16, Supp., pp. 1-30.

Benston, George J. "An Analysis Of The Role Of Accounting Standards For Enhancing Corporate Governance And Social Responsibility," **JAPP**, 1982, Vol. 1, No. 1, pp. 5-17.

Benston, George J. "Multiple Regression Analysis Of Cost Behavior," **AR**, 1966, Vol. 41, No. 4, pp. 657-672.

Benston, George J. "On The Value And Limitations Of Financial Accounting," **CAR**, 1984-85, Vol. 1, No. 1, pp.47-57.

Benston, George J. "Public (U.S.) Compared To Private (U.K.) Regulation Of Corporate Financial Disclosure," **AR**, 1976, Vol. 51, No. 3, pp. 483-498.

Benston, George J. "Published Corporate Accounting Data And Stock Prices," **JAR**, 1967, Vol. 5, Supp., pp. 1-14.

Benston, George J. "The Benefits And Costs To Managers Of Voluntary Accounting Disclosure - A Discussion Of: 'Current Cost: Disclosers And Nondisclosers: Canadian Evidence'," **CAR**, 1986-87, Vol. 3, No. 1, pp. 35-44.

Benston, George J. "The Costs Of Complying With A Government Data Collection Program: The FTC's Line Of Business Report," **JAPP**, 1984, Vol. 3, No. 2, pp. 123-137.

Benston, George J. "The Establishment And Enforcement Of Accounting Standards: Methods, Benefits And Costs," **ABR**, 1980-81, Vol. 11, No. 41, pp. 51-60.

Benston, George J. "The Market For Public Accounting Services: Demand, Supply And Regulation," **JAPP**, 1985, Vol. 4, No. 1, pp. 33-79.

Benston, George J. "The Role Of The Firm's Accounting System For Motivation," **AR**, 1963, Vol. 38, No. 2, pp. 347-354.

Benston, George J. "The Self-Serving Management Hypothesis: Some Evidence," **JAEC**, 1985, Vol. 7, No. 1/3, pp. 67-84.

Benston, George J. "The Value Of The SEC's Accounting Disclosure Requirements," **AR**, 1969, Vol. 44, No. 3, pp. 515-532.

Benston, George. (Sorter, G. H. and George Benston. "Appraising The Defensive Position Of A Firm: The Interval Measure," **AR**, 1960, Vol. 35, No. 4,pp.633-640.)

Benston, G. J. "Accounting And Corporate Accountability," **AOS**, 1982, Vol. 7, No. 2, pp. 87-106.

Benston, G. J. "Rejoinder To 'Accounting And Corporate Accountability: An Extended Comment'," **AOS**, 1984, Vol. 9, No. 3/4, pp. 417-420.

Benton, Bradley W. "Regulatory Implications Of Inflation Accounting," **MA**, 1981, Vol. 63, No. 2, pp. 43-47.

Bentson, Roger. (Gass, Gerald L., Grover McMakin and Roger Bentson. "White Collar Productivity," **MA**, 1987, Vol. 69, No. 3, pp. 33-38.)

Bentz, William F. and Robert F. Lusch. "Now You Can Control Your Product's Market Performance," **MA**, 1980, Vol. 61, No. 7, pp. 17-25.

Bentz, William F. "Computer Extended Reciprocal Allocation Methods," **AR**, 1979, Vol. 54, No. 3, pp. 595-603.

Bentz, William F. "Input-Output Analysis For Cost Accounting, Planning And Control: A Proof," **AR**, 1973, Vol. 48, No. 2, pp. 377-380.

Bentz, William F. "Learning Transfer In Professional Education And Training For Accounting," **AR**, 1975, Vol. 50, No. 2, pp. 370-379.

Bentz, William F. (Lusch, Robert F. and William F. Bentz. "A Variance Approach To Analyzing Changes In Return On Investment," **MA**, 1979, Vol. 60, No. 8, pp. 29-34.)

Benveniste, Ivor. "Receivers: Double Agents Or Surrogate Liquidators?," **ABR**, 1985-86, Vol. 16, No. 63, pp. 245-250.

Benveniste, I. (Arnold, A. J. and I. Benveniste. "Wealth And Poverty In The English Football League," **ABR**, 1986-87, Vol. 17, No. 67, pp. 195-204.)

Benzon, John W. (Kabialis, Edward W. and John W. Benzon. "Accounting For Income Taxes: Proposed Rules," **CPAJ**, 1987, Vol. 57, No. 1, pp. 44-51.)

Beran, David R. "Cost Reduction Through Control Reporting," **MA**, 1982, Vol. 63, No. 10, pp. 29-35.

Beranek, William and Edward B. Selby, Jr. "Delayed Depreciation As A Tax Shield," **JATA**, 1983, Vol. 4, No. 2, pp. 23-34.

Beranek, William. "A Note On The Equivalence Of Certain Capital Budgeting Criteria," **AR**, 1964, Vol. 39, No. 4, pp. 914-916.

Berardino, Joseph F. (O'Halloran, James P. and Joseph F. Berardino. "The Profit Improvement Review: Cutting Out Costs And Increasing Revenues," **CA**, 1983, Vol. 1, No. 1, pp. 54-59.)

Berck, Wayne R. "Evaluation Of Subcontractor Performance," **MA**, 1972, Vol. 53, No. 11, pp. 34-36.

Beresford, Dennis R. and Alexandea H. Mackintosh. "Purchase Business Combinations - Recognition Of Obligations At Acquisition," **CPAJ**, 1985, Vol. 55, No. 8, pp. 36-45.

Beresford, Dennis R. and Bruce J. Rosen. "Accounting For Preacquisition Contingencies," **CPAJ**, 1982, Vol. 52, No. 3, pp. 39-43.

Beresford, Dennis R. and Charles O. Buckner. "Segment Reporting Practices," **CPAJ**, 1978, Vol. 48, No. 12, pp. 37-44.

Beresford, Dennis R. and Mary P. Locatelli. "The Complicated Question Of Accounting For Stock Compensation," **CA**, 1983, Vol. 1, No. 3, pp. 5-13.

Beresford, Dennis R. and Michael H. Sutton. "Short-Term Debt Agreements - Classification Issues," **CPAJ**, 1983, Vol. 53, No. 8, pp. 32-37.

Beresford, Dennis R. and Stewart A. Feldman. "Companies Increase Social Responsibility Disclosure," **MA**, 1976, Vol. 57, No. 9, pp. 51-55.

Beresford, Dennis R. "Deferred Tax Accounting Should Be Changed," **CPAJ**, 1982, Vol. 52, No. 6, pp. 16-23.

Beresford, Dennis R. "Emerging Problems: How The Profession Is Coping," **JOA**, 1981, Vol. 151, No. 2, pp. 57-60.

Beresford, Dennis R. "How Companies Are Reporting Social Performance," **MA**, 1974, Vol. 56, No. 2, pp. 41-44.

Beresford, Dennis R. "The 'Balancing Act' In Setting Accounting Standards," **ACCHOR**, 1988, Vol. 2, No. 1, pp. 1-7.

Beresford, Dennis R. (Neary, Robert D. and Dennis R. Beresford. "Questions And Answers On FASB Inflation Accounting." **CPAJ**, 1979, Vol. 49, No. 6, pp. 11-18.)

Beresford, Dennis R., Lawrence C. Best and Joseph V. Weber. "Accounting For Income Taxes: Change Is Coming," **JOA**, 1984, Vol. 157, No. 1, pp. 72-79.

Beretvas, Andor. "Case Study In Auditing Procedure," **AR**, 1951, Vol. 26, No. 1, pp. 80-87.

Beretvas, Andor. "Case Study In Auditing Procedure," **AR**, 1952, Vol. 27, No. 2, pp. 210-214.

Beretvas, Andor. "Management Contracts, Expense Sharing Agreements, And Tax Planning," **AR**, 1955, Vol. 30, No. 3, pp. 519-521.

Berger, Bruce. "Installment Sales With Assumed Liabilities," **JOA**, 1966, Vol. 122, No. 2, pp. 41-47.

Berger, Paul D. (Abdolmohammadi, Mohammad J. and Paul D. Berger. "A Test Of The Accuracy Of Probability Assessment Techniques In Auditing," **CAR**, 1986-87, Vol. 3, No. 1, pp. 149-183.)

Berger, Robert O., Jr. "Long-Term Debt In Financial Statements," **JOA**, 1951, Vol. 92, No. 3, pp. 313-315.

Bergherm, Donald E. "The IRS And Business," **JOA**, 1982, Vol. 154, No. 2, pp. 64-71.

Bergin, J. Lawrence. "The Effect Of Previous Accounting Study On Student Performance In The First College-Level Financial Accounting Course," **IAE**, 1983, No. 1, pp. 19-28.

Berglind, Bradford L. "Elements Of White-Collar Productivity," **CA**, 1987, Vol. 5, No. 2, pp. 28-33.

Berglund, William J. "Ordering And Controlling Of Supplies - The 'Pattern Accounting' Procedure," **MA**, 1965, Vol. 47, No. 4, pp. 35-40.

Bergolofsky, Henry. "A Proposed Revision Of The Accounting Curriculum," **AR**, 1968, Vol. 43, No. 4, pp. 787-788.

Bergquist, Richard E. "Direct Labor Vs. Machine Hour Costing," **MA**, 1971, Vol. 52, No. 11, pp. 25-28.

Bergstrom, Kenneth H. "For Want Of A Nail," **MA**, 1976, Vol. 58, No. 3, pp. 39-40.

Bergstrom, Kenneth H. "Looking Back," **MA**, 1974, Vol. 55, No. 9, pp. 47-50.

Bergstrom, Kenneth. "Accountant's Role In Building Work Simplification Program," **JOA**, 1953, Vol. 95, No. 4, pp. 449-453.

Bergwerk, Rudolph J. "Data Processing For Small Business," **JOA**, 1963, Vol. 116, No. 6, pp. 51-54.

Bergwerk, Rudolph J. "Personal Financial Counseling By CPAs - A Neglected Service," **JOA**, 1978, Vol. 145, No. 5, pp. 50-58.

Bergwerk, Rudolph. "Effective Communication Of Financial Data," **JOA**, 1970, Vol. 129, No. 2, pp. 47-54.

Berg, Kenneth B. and Fred J. Mueller. "Accounting For Investment Credits," **AR**, 1963, Vol. 38, No. 3, pp. 554-561.

Berg, Kenneth B. "Allowance For Repairs," **AR**, 1962, Vol. 37, No. 3, pp. 488-496.

Berg, Kenneth B., Gerhard G. Mueller and Lauren M. Walker. "Annual Reports Go International," **JOA**, 1967, Vol. 124, No. 2, pp. 59-64.

Berkeley, Edmund C. "The Uses Of Automatic Computers In Financial And Accounting Operations," **JOA**, 1950, Vol. 90, No. 4, pp. 306-311.

Berkey, Marsha A. "Decision Tables For Clerical Procedures," **MA**, 1973, Vol. 55, No. 4, pp. 21-26.

Berkowitz, Bruce. (Branch, Ben and Bruce Berkowitz. "The Predictive Accuracy Of The Business Week Earnings Forecasts." **JAAF**, 1981, Vol. 4, No. 3, pp. 215-219.)

Berkow, William F. "Need For Engineering Influence Upon Accounting Procedure," **AR**, 1964, Vol. 39, No. 2, pp. 377-386.

Berk, Joel. (Vasarhelyi, Miklos, Da Hsein Bao and Joel Berk. "Trends In The Evolution Of Scholarly Accounting Thought: A Quantitative Examination," **AHJ**, 1988, Vol. 15, No. 1, pp. 45-64.)

Berle, A. A., Jr. "Accounting And The Law," **AR**, 1938, Vol. 13, No. 1, pp. 9-15.

Berlfein, Harold M. "Personal Holding Companies Under The 1964 Act," **JOA**, 1965, Vol. 119, No. 1, pp. 55-60.

Berliner, Robert W. and Dale L. Gerboth. "Accounting For Pensions - New FASB Statements," **CPAJ**, 1986, Vol. 56, No. 4, pp. 12-23.

Berliner, Robert W. and Dale L. Gerboth. "FASB Statement No. 33: 'The Great Experiment'," **JOA**, 1980, Vol. 149,

No. 5, pp. 48-54.

Berliner, Robert W. (Basile, Anthony P. and Robert W. Berliner. "Diagnostic Auditing: Identifying Operating Problems Via The Financial Audit," CA, 1985, Vol. 3, No. 2, pp. 44-52.

Berliner, Robert W. "Materiality And Audit Risk - Sharpening The Focus," CPAJ, 1983, Vol. 53, No. 6, pp. 10-19.

Berliner, Robert W. "Replacement Cost Accounting: A CPA's View," MA, 1977, Vol. 59, No. 6, pp. 23-26.

Berman, Daniel S. and Bernard S. Cooper. "How The Tax Laws Encourage Corporate Acquisitions," JOA, 1963, Vol. 116, No. 5, pp. 61-64.

Bernard, Clark L. and Douglas Beaven. "Containing The Costs Of Higher Education," JOA, 1985, Vol. 160, No. 4, pp. 78-94.

Bernard, Victor L. and Robert G. Ruland. "The Incremental Information Content Of Historical Cost And Current Cost Income Numbers: Time-Series Analyses For 1962-1980," AR, 1987, Vol. 62, No. 4, pp. 707-722.

Bernard, Victor L. "A Comment On: 'Effective Corporate Tax Rates'," JAPP, 1984, Vol. 3, No. 1, pp. 75-78.

Bernard, Victor L. "Cross-Sectional Dependence And Problems In Inference In Market-Based Accounting Research," JAR, 1987, Vol. 25, No. 1, pp. 1-48.

Bernard, Victor L. "The Use Of Market Data And Accounting Data In Hedging Against Consumer Price Inflation," JAR, 1984, Vol. 22, No. 2, pp. 445-466.

Bernath, Wayne A. (Beechy, Thomas H. and Wayne A. Bernath. "The Measurement Of Economic Activity: An Introductory Accounting Course," AR, 1971, Vol. 46, No. 2, pp. 385-387.)

Bernhardt, Irwin and Ronald M. Copeland. "Some Problems In Applying An Information Theory Approach To Accounting Aggregation," JAR, 1970, Vol. 8, No. 1, pp. 95-98.

Bernhard, Richard N. "Some Problems In Applying Mathematical Programming To Opportunity Costing," JAR, 1968, Vol. 6, No. 1, pp. 143-148.

Bernheim, Richard C. "The Right Way To Design A Cost Accounting System," MA, 1983, Vol. 65, No. 3, pp. 63-68.

Bernson, Robert D. (Afterman, Allan B. and Robert D. Bernson. "A Guide To Bank Financing For The Closely Held Company," CA, 1983, Vol. 1, No. 3, pp. 33-38.)

Bernstein, Jeffrey. (Schrott, Alfred N., William P. Casciani and Jeffrey Bernstein. "Interest Rate Futures Trading - Part II," CPAJ, 1980, Vol. 50, No. 5, pp. 27-32.)

Bernstein, Jeffrey. (Schrott, Alfred N., William P. Casciani and Jeffrey Bernstein. "Interest Rate Futures Trading - Part I," CPAJ, 1980, Vol. 50, No. 4, pp.16-22.)

Bernstein, Jerome. (Leathers, Park E., James A. Sullivan and Jerome Bernstein. "The CPA Examination - Profile Of The Successful Candidate," AIA, 1984,Vol. 1,pp.105-126.)

Bernstein, Leopold A. "Over-All Checks In Auditing," JOA, 1960, Vol. 109, No. 6, pp. 36-41.

Bernstein, Leopold A. "Ratio, Change And Trend Analysis As An Audit Tool," JOA, 1964, Vol. 118, No. 3, pp. 51-55.

Bernstein, Leopold A. "Reporting The Results Of Operations - A Reassessment Of APB Opinion No. 9," JOA, 1970, Vol. 130, No. 1, pp. 57-61.

Bernstein, Leopold A. "The Concept Of Materiality," AR, 1967, Vol. 42, No. 1, pp. 86-95.

Bernstein, Leopold A. "The CPA's Stake In Financial Statement Analysis," CPAJ, 1975, Vol. 45, No. 2, pp. 23-26.

Bernstein, Leopold. "Whither Accounting Research?," JOA, 1965, Vol. 120, No. 6, pp. 33-38.

Berryman, R. Glen. (Coglitore, Frank and R. Glen Berryman. "Analytical Procedures: A Defensive Necessity," AJPT, 1988, Vol. 7, No. 2, pp. 150-163.)

Berryman, R. G. "Auditing Standards And The Law," AR, 1960, Vol. 35, No. 1, pp. 70-80.

Berry, Anthony. (Otley, David and Anthony Berry. "Risk Distribution In The Budgetary Process," ABR, 1978-79, Vol. 9, No. 36, pp. 325-337.)

Berry, A. J. (Otley, D. T. and A. J. Berry. "Control, Organisation And Accounting," AOS, 1980, Vol. 5, No. 2, pp. 231-246.)

Berry, A. J., T. Capps, D. Cooper, P. Ferguson, T. Hopper and E. A. Lowe. "Management Control In An Area Of The NCB: Rationales Of Accounting Practices In A Public Enterprise," AOS, 1985, Vol. 10, No. 1, pp. 3-28.

Berry, Frank T., Jr. "Some Ramifications Of The Return On Capital Concept," MA, 1968, Vol. 50, No. 3, pp. 36-37.

Berry, Leonard Eugene and Wanda A. Wallace. "Governmental Auditing Research: An Analytic Framework, Assessment Of Past Work, And Future Directions," RIGNA, 1986, Vol. 2, pp. 89-115.

Berry, Leonard Eugene, Gordon B. Harwood and Joseph L. Katz. "Performance Of Auditing Procedures By Governmental Auditors: Some Preliminary Evidence," AR, 1987, Vol. 62, No. 1, pp. 14-28.

Berry, Leonard E. "A New Treatment For Health Care Costs," MA, 1984, Vol. 65, No. 10, pp. 58-61.

Berry, Maureen and Alicja Jaruga. "Industrial Accounting In Poland's Reorganized Economy," IJAER, 1985, Vol. 20, No. 2, pp. 45-63.

Berry, Maureen H. "The Accounting Function In Socialist Economies," IJAER, 1982, Vol. 18, No. 1, pp. 185-198.

Berry, Maureen H. "Why International Cost Accounting Practices Should Be Harmonized," MA, 1981, Vol. 63, No. 2, pp. 36-42.

Berry, Maureen. "Financial Accountability In West German Government," AIIA, 1987, Vol. 1, pp. 39-84.

Berry, R. N. "A Systems Model For Accountants," ABR, 1974-75, Vol. 5, No. 19, pp. 203-212.

Bertholdt, Richard H. "Public Expectations: Meeting The Challenge," CPAJ, 1986, Vol. 56, No. 8, pp. 10-21.

Berton, Lee and Barbara Shildneck. "The 75-Year History Of The Journal," JOA, 1980, Vol. 150, No. 5, pp. 48-54.

Berylson, Kermit J. "ERISA Revolutionizes The Pension Field," CPAJ, 1977, Vol. 47, No. 4, pp. 23-26.

Beshara, R. L. "Price-Level Restated Accounting And The Measurement Of Inflation Gains And Losses: A Comment," AR, 1975, Vol. 50, No. 3, pp. 582-585.

Best, Lawrence C. (Beresford, Dennis R., Lawrence C. Best and Joseph V. Weber. "Accounting For Income Taxes: Change Is Coming," JOA, 1984, Vol. 157 No. 1,pp.72-79.)

Betley, Al J. "Contribution Pricing," MA, 1973, Vol. 54, No. 9, pp. 29-30.

Bettauer, Arthur. "Extending Audit Procedures - When And How," JOA, 1975, Vol. 140, No. 5, pp. 69-72.

Bettauer, Arthur. "External Control - A Necessary Supplement To Internal Control," CPAJ, 1975, Vol. 45, No. 8, pp. 21-24.

Betts, J. Frank. (Van Son, W. Peter, Dan M. Guy and J. Frank Betts. "Engagement Letters: What Practice Shows," JOA, 1982, Vol. 153, No. 6, pp. 72-81.)

Bevis, Donald J. "Audit Programs And Internal Control," JOA, 1955, Vol. 99, No. 6, pp. 46-50.

Bevis, Donald J. "Professional Education For Public Accounting," AR, 1958, Vol. 33, No. 3, pp. 445-449.

Bevis, Herman W. "Contingencies And Probabilities In Financial Statements," JOA, 1968, Vol. 126, No. 4, pp. 37-45.

Bevis, Herman W. "How CPA Exam Is Created, Administered, & Graded," JOA, 1953, Vol. 96, No. 3, pp. 298-308.

Bevis, Herman W. "Progress And Poverty In Accounting Thought," JOA, 1966, Vol. 122, No. 1, pp. 34-40.

Bevis, Herman W. "Riding Herd On Accounting Standards," AR, 1961, Vol. 36. No. 1, pp. 9-16.

Bevis, Herman W. "Streamlining Auditing Techniques," AR, 1957. Vol. 32, No. 1, pp. 26-32.

Bevis, Herman W. "The Accounting Function In Economic Progress," JOA, 1958, Vol. 106, No. 2, pp. 27-34.

Bevis, Herman W. "The CPA's Attest Function In Modern Society," JOA, 1962, Vol. 113, No. 2, pp. 28-35.

Bevis, Herman W. "The CPA's Changing Practice," JOA, 1955, Vol. 100, No. 5, pp. 31-37.

Bexell, J. A. "Accounting At 'Erehwon'," AR, 1927, Vol. 2, No. 2, pp. 172-174.

Beyer, Robert. "Goodwill And Pooling Of Interests: A Re-Assessment," MA, 1969, Vol. 50, No. 6, pp. 9-15.

Beyer, Robert. "Integrated Financial Services," JOA, 1963, Vol. 115, No. 6, pp. 30-36.

Beyer, Robert. "Is Direct Costing The Answer?," JOA, 1955, Vol. 99, No. 4, pp. 45-49.

Beyer, Robert. "Management Information Systems: Who'll Be In Charge?," MA, 1967, Vol. 48, No. 10, pp. 3-8.

Beyer, Robert. "Management Services - Time For Decision," JOA, 1965, Vol. 119, No. 3, pp. 43-52.

Beyer, Robert. "Pilots Of Social Progress," MA, 1972, Vol. 54, No. 1, pp. 11-15.

Beyer, Robert. "Profitability Accounting: The Challenge And The Opportunity," JOA, 1964, Vol. 117, No. 6, pp. 33-36.

Beyer, Robert. "The Modern Management Approach To A Program Of Social Improvement," JOA, 1969, Vol. 127, No. 3, pp. 37-46.

Bhada, Yezdi H. "Dynamic Cost Analysis," MA, 1970, Vol. 52, No. 1, pp. 11-14.

Bhada, Yezdi. "Dynamic Relationships For Accounting Analyses," MA, 1972, Vol. 53, No. 10, pp. 53-57.

Bhagat, Sanjai. (Brickley, James A., Sanjai Bhagat and Ronald C. Lease. "The Impact Of Long-Range Managerial Compensation Plans On Shareholder Wealth," JAEC, 1985, Vol. 7, No. 1/3, pp. 115-129.)

Bhaskar, Krish N. and Bernard C. Williams. "Audit And Control Issues For The Small Computerised Business," ABR, 1986-87, Vol. 17, No. 65, pp. 13-20.

Bhaskar, Krish N. and G. Roland Kaye. "Computers And Accounting Courses: A Reply To Collins," ABR, 1984-85, Vol. 15, No. 59, pp. 239-240.

Bhaskar, Krish N. "Computers And The Choice For Accountancy Syllabuses," ABR, 1982-83, Vol. 13, No. 50, pp. 83-94.

Bhaskar, Krish N. "Use Of Computers In Accountancy Courses," ABR, 1982-83, Vol. 13, No. 49, pp. 3-10.

Bhaskar, Krish. "A Multiple Objective Approach To Capital Budgeting," ABR, 1979-80, Vol. 10, No. 37, pp. 25-46.

Bhaskar, K. N. and R. C. Morris. "The Accuracy Of Brokers' Profits Forecasts In The UK," ABR, 1983-84, Vol. 14, No. 54, pp. 113-124.

Bhaskar, K. N. "Optimal Asset Lives," ABR, 1972-73, Vol. 3, No. 12, pp. 309-316.

Bhaskar, K. N. "Rates Of Return Under Uncertainty," ABR, 1972-73, Vol. 3, No. 9, pp. 40-52.

Bhave, Bhaskar. (Brooks, Donald E. and Bhaskar Bhave. "New And Innovative Financial Instruments Part II," CPAJ, 1987. Vol. 57, No. 8, pp. 38-45.)

Bhave, Bhaskar. (Brooks, Donald E. and Bhaskar Bhave. "New And Innovative Financial Instruments Part I," CPAJ, 1987, Vol. 57, No. 7, pp. 32-37.)

Bhushan, Bhuwan. "Effects Of Inflation And Currency Fluctuation," MA, 1974, Vol. 56, No. 1, pp. 17-19.

Biagioni, Louis F. and Pekin Ogan. "Human Resource Accounting For Professional Sports Teams," MA, 1977, Vol. 59, No. 5, pp. 25-29.

Biagioni, Louis F. (Mensah, Yaw M. and Louis F. Biagioni. "The Predictive Ability Of Financial Ratios Using Alternative Translation Methods For Foreign-Currency Financial Statements: A Simulation Study," IJAER, 1980, Vol. 16, No. 1, pp. 221-245.)

Bialkin, Kenneth J. and Deborah E. Cooper. "Expanding Accountants' Liability: New Trends And Implications,"

CA, 1986, Vol. 4, No. 1, pp. 11-16.

Bialkin, Kenneth J. "Government Antitrust Enforcement And The Rules Of Conduct," **JOA**, 1987, Vol. 163, No. 5, pp. 105-109.

Biddle, Gary C. and Frederick W. Lindahl. "Stock Price Reactions To LIFO Adoptions: The Association Beween Excess Returns And LIFO Tax Savings," **JAR**, 1982, Vol. 20, No. 2, Part II, pp. 551-588.

Biddle, Gary C. and Richard Steinberg. "Allocations Of Joint And Common Costs," **JAL**, 1984, Vol. 3, pp. 1-46.

Biddle, Gary C. and R. Kipp Martin. "Inflation, Taxes, And Optimal Inventory Policies," **JAR**, 1985, Vol. 23, No. 1, pp. 57-83.

Biddle, Gary C. and William E. Ricks. "Analyst Forecast Errors And Stock Price Behavior Near The Earnings Announcement Dates Of LIFO Adopters," **JAR**, 1988, Vol. 26, No. 2, pp. 169-194.

Biddle, Gary C. "Accounting Methods And Management Decisions: The Case Of Inventory Costing And Inventory Policy," **JAR**, 1980, Vol. 18, Supp., pp. 235-280.

Biddle, Gary C. (Joyce, Edward J. and Gary C. Biddle. "Anchoring And Adjustment In Probabilistic Inference In Auditing," **JAR**, 1981, Vol. 19, No. 1, pp. 120-145.)

Biddle, Gary C. (Joyce, Edward J. and Gary C. Biddle. "Are Auditors' Judgments Sufficiently Regressive?," **JAR**, 1981, Vol. 19, No. 2, pp. 323-349.)

Bidwell, Clinton M., III and John R. Riddle, Jr. "Market Inefficiencies - Opportunities For Profits," **JAAF**, 1981, Vol. 4, No. 3, pp. 198-214.

Biel, Dennis H. and W. C. Stevenson. "Tax Shelters: A Primer For CPAs," **JOA**, 1982, Vol. 153, No. 6, pp. 54-71.

Bienz, J. Fred. "The Kelson Happening," **MA**, 1969, Vol. 51, No. 1, pp. 24-26.

Bierman, Harold, Jr. and Ernest Liu. "The Computation Of Earnings Per Share," **AR**, 1968, Vol. 43, No. 1.pp. 62-67.

Bierman, Harold, Jr. and Roland E. Dukes. "Accounting For Research And Development Costs," **JOA**, 1975, Vol. 139, No. 4, pp. 48-55.

Bierman, Harold, Jr. and Seymour Smidt. "Accounting For Debt And Costs Of Liquidity Under Conditions Of Uncertainty," **JAR**, 1967, Vol. 5, No. 2. pp. 144-153.

Bierman, Harold, Jr. and Sidney Davidson. "The Income Concept - Value Increment Or Earnings Predictor," **AR**, 1969, Vol. 44, No. 2, pp. 239-246.

Bierman, Harold, Jr. and Thomas R. Dyckman. "Accounting For Interest During Construction," **ABR**, 1978-79, Vol. 9, No. 36, pp. 267-272.

Bierman, Harold, Jr. "A Case For Immediate Expensing Of Equipment For Tax Purposes," **JOA**, 1977, Vol. 144, No. 4, pp. 87-90.

Bierman, Harold, Jr. "A Further Study Of Depreciation," **AR**, 1966, Vol. 41, No. 2, pp. 271-274.

Bierman, Harold, Jr. "A Problem In Expense Recognition," **AR**, 1963, Vol. 38, No. 1, pp. 61-63.

Bierman, Harold, Jr. "Accelerated Depreciation And Rate Regulation," **AR**, 1969, Vol. 44, No. 1, pp. 65-78.

Bierman, Harold, Jr. "Accounting For Capitalized Leases: Tax Considerations," **AR**, 1973, Vol. 48, No. 2, pp. 421-424.

Bierman, Harold, Jr. "Accounting For Interest Rate Swaps," **JAAF**, 1987, Vol. 2 (New Series), No. 4, pp. 396-408.

Bierman, Harold, Jr. "Capitalization Of A Public Utility And The Measurement Of Income," **AR**, 1957, Vol. 32, No. 1, pp. 21-25.

Bierman, Harold, Jr. "Common Stock Equivalents, Earnings Per Share And Stock Valuation," **JAAF**, 1986, Vol. 1 (New Series), No. 1, pp. 62-70.

Bierman, Harold, Jr. "Creating Shareholder Value," **CA**, 1987, Vol. 5, No. 4, pp. 26-29.

Bierman, Harold, Jr. "Depreciable Assets - Timing Of Expense Recognition," **AR**, 1961, Vol. 36, No. 4, pp. 613-618.

Bierman, Harold, Jr. "Depreciation And Income Tax Allocation," **JAAF**, 1985, Vol. 8, No. 3, pp. 184-194.

Bierman, Harold, Jr. "Discounted Cash Flows, Price Level Adjustments And Expectations," **AR**, 1971, Vol. 46, No. 4, pp. 693-699.

Bierman, Harold, Jr. "Discounted Cash Flows, Price Level Adjustments And Expectations: A Reply," **AR**, 1972, Vol. 47, No. 3, pp. 589-590.

Bierman, Harold, Jr. "Discounted Cash Flows, Price-Level Adjustments And Expectations: A Reply," **AR**, 1972, Vol. 47, No. 4, pp. 799-800.

Bierman, Harold, Jr. "Inventory Valuation: The Use Of Market Prices," **AR**, 1967, Vol. 42, No. 4, pp. 731-737.

Bierman, Harold, Jr. "Investment Decisions And Taxes," **AR**, 1970, Vol. 45, No. 4, pp. 690-697.

Bierman, Harold, Jr. "Measurement And Accounting," **AR**, 1963, Vol. 38, No. 3, pp. 501-507.

Bierman, Harold, Jr. "Measuring Financial Liquidity," **AR**, 1960, Vol. 35, No. 4, pp. 628-632.

Bierman, Harold, Jr. "Myths And Accountants," **AR**, 1965, Vol. 40, No. 3, pp. 541-546.

Bierman, Harold, Jr. "Pricing Intracompany Transfers," **AR**, 1959, Vol. 34, No. 3, pp. 429-432.

Bierman, Harold, Jr. "Probability, Statistical Decision Theory, And Accounting," **AR**, 1962, Vol. 37, No. 3, pp. 400-405.

Bierman, Harold, Jr. "Recording Obsolescence," **JAR**, 1964, Vol. 2, No. 2, pp. 229-235.

Bierman, Harold, Jr. "Regulation, Implied Revenue Requirements, And Methods Of Depreciation," **AR**, 1974, Vol. 49, No. 3, pp. 448-454.

Bierman, Harold, Jr. "The Effect Of Inflation On The Computation Of Income Of Public Utilities," **AR**, 1956, Vol. 31, No. 2, pp. 258-262.

Bierman, Harold, Jr. "The Implications To Accounting Of Efficient Markets And The Capital Asset Pricing Model," **AR**, 1974, Vol. 49, No. 3, pp. 557-562.

Bierman, Harold, Jr. "The Term Structure Of Interest Rates And Accounting For Debt," **AR**, 1968, Vol. 43, No. 4, pp. 657-661.

Bierman, Harold, Jr. (Barnea, Amir and Harold Bierman, Jr. "Cash Flow Valuation And Depreciation," **ABR**, 1973-74, Vol. 4, No. 15, pp. 193-196.)

Bierman, Harold, Jr., Lawrence E. Fouraker and Robert K. Jaedicke. "The Use Of Probability And Statistics In Performance Evaluation," **AR**, 1961, Vol. 36, No. 3, pp. 409-417.

Bierman, Harold, Jr., Roland E. Dukes and Thomas R. Dyckman. "Financial Reporting In The Petroleum Industry," **JOA**, 1974, Vol. 138, No. 4, pp. 58-64.

Bierman, Harold. "Capacity Measures And Financial Accounting," **ABR**, 1974-75, Vol. 5, No. 20, pp. 305-308.

Bierman, Harold. "Extending The Usefulness Of Accrual Accounting," **ACCHOR**, 1988, Vol. 2, No. 3, pp. 10-14.

Biery, Frederick P. "The Accuracy Of Military Cost And Schedule Forecasts," **JCA**, 1986, Vol. 3, No. 1, pp. 13-23.

Biggs, Joseph R. and Ellen J. Long. "Gaining The Competitive Edge With MRP/MRP II," **MA**, 1988, Vol. 69, No. 11, pp. 27-32.

Biggs, Stanley F. and John J. Wild. "An Investigation Of Auditor Judgment In Analytical Review," **AR**, 1985, Vol. 60, No. 4, pp. 607-633.

Biggs, Stanley F. and John J. Wild. "A Note On The Practice Of Analytical Review," **AJPT**, 1983-84, Vol. 3, No. 2, pp. 68-79.

Biggs, Stanley F. and Theodore J. Mock. "An Investigation Of Auditor Decision Processes In The Evaluation Of Internal Controls And Audit Scope Decisions," **JAR**, 1983, Vol. 21, No. 1, pp. 234-255.

Biggs, Stanley F. "Improving Auditor Judgment Through Research: A Problem And Some Potential Solutions," **AIA**, 1985, Vol. 2, pp. 169-184.

Biggs, Stanley F. (Gujarathi, Mahendra R. and Stanley F. Biggs. "Accounting For Purchase Commitments: Some Issues And Recommendations," **ACCHOR**, 1988, Vol. 2, No. 3, pp. 75-82.)

Biggs, Stanley F., Theodore J. Mock and Paul R. Watkins. "Auditor's Use Of Analytical Review In Audit Program Design," **AR**, 1988, Vol. 63, No. 1, pp. 148-161.

Biggs, Stanley F., William F. Messier, Jr. and James V. Hansen. "A Descriptive Analysis Of Computer Audit Specialists' Decision-Making Behavior In Advanced Computer Environments," **AJPT**, 1986-87, Vol. 6, No. 2, pp. 1-21.

Biggs, S. F. "Financial Analysts' Information Search In The Assessment Of Corporte Earning Power," **AOS**, 1984, Vol. 9. No. 3/4, pp. 313-324.

Bildersee, John and Nathan Kahn. "A Preliminary Test Of The Presence Of Window Dressing: Evidence From Institutional Stock Trading," **JAAF**, 1987, Vol. 2 (New Series), No. 3, pp. 239-265.

Bildersee, John S. and Joshua Ronen. "Stock Returns And Real Activity In An Inflationary Environment: The Informational Impact Of FAS No. 33," **CAR**, 1987-88, Vol. 4, No. 1, pp. 89-110.

Bildersee, John S. "The Association Between A Market-Determined Measure Of Risk And Alternative Measures Of Risk," **AR**, 1975, Vol. 50, No. 1, pp. 81-98.

Billera, Louis J., David C. Heath and Robert E. Verrecchia. "A Unique Procedure For Allocating Common Costs From A Production Process," **JAR**, 1981, Vol. 19, No. 1, pp. 185-196.

Billings, Anthony and D. Larry Crumbley. "Bankruptcy Provisions For Limited Partnerships," **CPAJ**, 1987, Vol. 57, No. 2, pp. 58-63.

Billings, Anthony. (Englebrecht, Ted D. and Anthony Billings. "Impact Of TRA 86 On Trusts, Estates And Gifts." **CPAJ**, 1987, Vol. 57, No. 2, pp. 50-57.)

Billings, B. Anthony and D. Larry Crumbley. "Financial Difficulties Of Governmental Units," **CPAJ**, 1988, Vol. 58, No. 10, pp. 52-61.

Billings, B. Anthony. (Roberts, Michael L. and B. Anthony Billings. "Pre-Combination Tax Attributes - TRA 86," **CPAJ**, 1988, Vol. 58, No. 2, pp. 48-55.)

Billion, Michael M. "To Be Or Not To Be: A Building For Investment Credit?," **MA**, 1978, Vol. 59, No. 12, pp. 30-34.

Bill, Robert W., James H. Harrison and Harry R. Maly. "An EDP System For Stores Inventory Control," **MA**, 1967, Vol. 48, No. 12, pp. 35-42.

Binder, John J. "On The Use Of The Multivariate Regression Model In Event Studies," **JAR**, 1985, Vol. 23, No. 1, pp. 370-383.

Bindon, Kathleen Ranney and Edward J. Schnee. "Forward Contracts: Accounting And Tax Implications," **CPAJ**, 1986, Vol. 56, No. 9, pp. 38-51.

Bindon, Kathleen Ranney. (Schnee, Edward J. and Kathleen Ranney Bindon. "Deductions Of Partnership Losses; Strategy And Planning," **CPAJ**, 1986, Vol. 56, No. 10, pp. 74-79.)

Bindon, Kathleen R. and Helen Gernon. "International Accounting Research," **AIA**, 1987, Vol. 4, pp. 43-68.

Bindon, Kathleen. (Burns, Jane O. and Kathleen Bindon. "Evaluating Leases With LP," **MA**, 1980, Vol. 61, No. 8, pp. 48-53.)

Binkley, M. A. "Components Of The Report Of Financial Changes," **AR**, 1949, Vol. 24, No. 3, pp. 304-307.

Binkley, M. A. "The Limitations Of Consistency," **AR**, 1948,

Vol. 23, No. 4, pp. 374-376.

Birati, Assa. (Flink, Solomon J., Assa Birati and Meyer Ungar. "The Impact Of Inflation On The Profits Of Listed Firms In Israel," ABR, 1977-78, Vol. 8, No. 32, pp. 253-257.)

Bircher, Paul. "Company Law Reform And The Board Of Trade, 1929-1943," ABR, 1988, Vol. 18, No. 70, pp. 107-120.

Bird, Francis A. and Phillip A. Jones. "A Decision-Tree Approach To Earnings Per Share," AR, 1970, Vol. 45, No. 4, pp. 779-783.

Bird, Francis A. "A Note On 'The Return To Straight-Line Depreciation'," JAR, 1969, Vol. 7, No. 2, pp. 328-331.

Bird, Francis A. "Interperiod Comparability In Financial Reporting," JOA, 1969, Vol. 127, No. 6, pp. 51-56.

Bird, Francis A., Lewis F. Davidson and Charles H. Smith. "Perceptions Of External Accounting Transfers Under Entity And Proprietary Theory," AR, 1974, Vol. 49, No. 2, pp. 233-244.

Bird, Peter and F. A. Bailey. "Incremental Plans In Project Evaluation: A Comment," ABR, 1982-83, Vol. 13, No. 52, pp. 309-310.

Bird, Peter. "Objectives And Methods Of Financial Reporting: A Generalised Search Procedure," ABR, 1974-75, Vol. 5, No. 19, pp. 162-167.

Bird, Peter. "The Scope Of The Company Audit," ABR, 1970-71, Vol. 1, No. 1, pp. 44-49.

Bird, Peter. "What Is Capital Gearing?," ABR, 1972-73, Vol. 3, No. 10, pp. 92-97.

Bird, P. A. "Tax Incentives To Capital Investment," JAR, 1965, Vol. 3, No. 1, pp. 1-11.

Bird, Ron. "A Reappraisal Of The Share Price Maximisation Criterion," ABR, 1973-74, Vol. 4, No. 14, pp. 127-134.

Birkett, Brenda S. "The Recent History Of Corporate Audit Committees," AHJ, 1986, Vol. 13, No. 2, pp. 109-124.

Birkett, W. P. and R. G. Walker. "Response Of The Australian Accounting Profession To Company Failures In The 1960s," ABACUS, 1971, Vol. 7, No. 2, pp. 97-136.

Birkett, W. P. and R. G. Walker. "Professional Ideas On Research In Accounting: Australia, 1930-49," ABACUS, 1972, Vol. 8, No. 1, pp. 35-60.

Birkett, W. P. "Accounting Inputs," ABACUS, 1968, Vol. 4, No. 2, pp. 164-173.

Birnberg, Jacob G. and Dennis P. Slevin. "A Note On The Use Of Confidence Interval Statements In Financial Reporting," JAR, 1976, Vol. 14, No. 1, pp. 153-157.

Birnberg, Jacob G. and Nicholas Dopuch. "A Conceptual Approach To The Framework For Disclosure," JOA, 1963, Vol. 115, No. 2, pp. 56-63.

Birnberg, Jacob G. and Raghu Nath. "Implications Of Behavioral Science For Managerial Accounting," AR, 1967, Vol. 42, No. 3, pp. 468-479.

Birnberg, Jacob G. and Raghu Nath. "Laboratory Experimentation In Accounting Research," AR, 1968, Vol. 43, No. 1, pp. 38-45.

Birnberg, Jacob G. "The Reporting Of Executory Contracts," AR, 1965, Vol. 40, No. 4, pp. 814-820.

Birnberg, Jacob G. (Chang, Davis L. and Jacob G. Birnberg. "Functional Fixity In Accounting Research: Perspective And New Data," JAR, 1977, Vol. 15, No. 2, pp. 300-312.)

Birnberg, Jacob G. (Dopuch, Nicholas, Jacob G. Birnberg and Joel Demski. "An Extension Of Standard Cost Variance Analysis," AR, 1967, Vol. 42, No. 3, pp. 526-536.)

Birnberg, Jacob G. (Goetz, Billy E. and Jacob G. Birnberg. "A Comment On The Trueblood Report," MA, 1976, Vol. 57, No. 10, pp. 18-20.)

Birnberg, Jacob G. (McGhee, Walter, Michael D. Shields and Jacob G. Birnberg. "The Effects Of Personality On A Subject's Information Processing," AR, 1978, Vol. 53, No. 3, pp. 681-697.)

Birnberg, Jacob G., Michael D. Shields and Walter McGhee. "The Effects Of Personality On A Subject's Information Processing: A Reply," AR, 1980, Vol. 55, No. 3, pp. 507-510.

Birnberg, Jacob. "An Information Oriented Approach To The Presentation Of Common Stockholders' Equity," AR, 1964, Vol. 39, No. 4, pp. 963-971.

Birnberg, J. C. "Towards A Bibliography Of The French Social Accounting Literature," AOS, 1978, Vol. 3, No. 2, pp. 175-182.

Birnberg, J. G. and C. Snodgrass. "Culture And Control: A Field Study," AOS, 1988, Vol. 13, No. 5, pp. 447-464.

Birnberg, J. G. and M. D. Shields. "The Role Of Attention And Memory In Accounting Decisions," AOS, 1984, Vol. 9, No. 3/4, pp. 365-382.

Birnberg, J. G. and N. M. Gandhi. "Toward Defining The Accountant's Role In The Evaluation Of Social Programs," AOS, 1976, Vol. 1, No. 1, pp. 5-10.

Birnberg, J. G. "The Role Of Accounting In Financial Disclosure," AOS, 1980, Vol. 5, No. 1, pp. 71-80.

Birnberg, J. G. (Shields, M. D., J. G. Birnberg and I. Hanson Frieze. "Attributions, Cognitive Processes And Control Systems," AOS, 1981, Vol. 6, No. 1, pp. 69-96.)

Birnberg, J. G., I. Hanson Frieze and M. D. Shields. "The Role Of Attribution Theory In Control Systems," AOS, 1977, Vol. 2, No. 3, pp. 189-200.

Birnberg, J. G., L. Turopolec and S. M. Young. "The Organizational Context Of Accounting," AOS, 1983, Vol. 8, No. 2/3, pp. 111-130.

Birnberg, J. (Wilner, N. and J. Birnberg. "Methodological Problems In Functional Fixation Research: Criticism And Suggestions," AOS, 1986, Vol. 11, No. 1, pp. 71-82.)

Birrer, G. Eddy. (Helgeson, James G. and G. Eddy Birrer. "Marketing Plans For Accounting Firms," JOA, 1986, Vol. 162, No. 3, pp. 115-126.)

Bishop, Ashton C. and Rasoul H. Tondkar. "Development Of A

Professional Code Of Ethics," JOA, 1987, Vol. 163, No. 5, pp. 97-101.

Bishop, Ashton. (Benke, Ralph L., Jr. and Ashton Bishop. "Transfer Pricing In An Oligopolistic Market," JCA, 1986, Vol. 3, No. 2, pp. 69-81.)

Bismack, Thaddeus R. "Management Accounting Implications Of Industrial Steam And Power Plants," MA, 1965, Vol. 47, No. 3, pp. 39-47.

Bitner, Larry N. (Oglesbee, Tom W., Larry N. Bitner and Gail B. Wright. "Measurement Of Incremental Benefits In Computer Enhanced Instruction," IAE, 1988, Vol. 3, No. 2, pp. 365-377.)

Bjorn-Andersen, N. and P. H. Pedersen. "Computer Facilitated Changes In The Management Power Structure," AOS, 1980, Vol. 5, No. 2, pp. 203-216.

Blackburn, John O. (Dickens, Robert L. and John O. Blackburn. "Holding Gains On Fixed Assets: An Element Of Business Income?," AR, 1964, Vol. 39, No. 2, pp. 312-329.)

Blackett, L. (Aiken, M., L. Blackett and G. Isaacs. "Modeling Behavioral Interdependencies For Stewardship Reporting," AR, 1975, Vol. 50, No. 3, pp. 544-562.)

Blackman, Dennis D. (Ortman, Richard F. and Dennis D. Blackman. "Corporate Planning - How Successful Is It?," MA, 1981, Vol. 63, No. 1, pp. 16-24.)

Blackmore, Charles T. "Economic Obsolescene Of Land," AR, 1943, Vol. 18, No. 3, pp. 266-268.

Black, Kenneth, III. (Black, Kenneth, Jr. and Kenneth Black, III. "Insurable Interest And Key-Man Life Insurance," CPAJ, 1987, Vol. 57, No. 8, pp. 46-55.)

Black, Kenneth, Jr. and Kenneth Black, III. "Insurable Interest And Key-Man Life Insurance," CPAJ, 1987, Vol. 57, No. 8, pp. 46-55.

Black, Kenneth, Jr. (Skipper, Harold D., Jr. and Kenneth Black, Jr. "Life Insurance Evaluation For Personal Financial Planning," CPAJ, 1988, Vol. 58, No. 1, pp. 54-63.)

Black, Martin L. "Some Accounting Aspects Of The Tax Exemption For Farmers' Cooperatives," AR, 1948, Vol. 23, No. 3, pp. 254-262.

Black, Martin L., Jr. "Accounting Developments In The Atomic Energy Enterprise," AR, 1952, Vol. 27, No. 1, pp. 25-36.

Black, Martin L., Jr. "Student Associate Memberships," AR, 1954, Vol. 29, No. 4, pp. 691-692.

Black, Robert L. and Anne G. McMahon. "Graduate Tax Libraries: A Survey Of Their Content And Funding," JATA, 1981, Vol. 3, No. 1, pp. 11-18.

Black, Stephen F. and Albert A. Koch. "Replacement Cost - Charting The Uncharted Sea," JOA, 1976, Vol. 142, No. 5, pp. 72-76.

Black, Thomas G. "Government Contracts And Small CPA Firms," CPAJ, 1984, Vol. 54, No. 5, pp. 42-49.

Black, Thomas G. "The Professionalization Of Accounting," MA, 1982, Vol. 64, No. 5, pp. 21-25.

Black, Thomas N., and Donald J. Modenbach. "Profit Planning For Action And Results," MA, 1971, Vol. 52, No. 7, pp. 9-13.

Blade, David A. and Susan A. Durland. "Deductibility Of Vacation Home Expenses," CPAJ, 1979, Vol. 49, No. 4, pp. 29-34.

Blade, David A. and William R. Allbright. "The Tax Planning Deduction," CPAJ, 1980, Vol. 50, No. 3, pp. 35-39.

Blagg, R. Raymond and Kenneth W. Walton. "Functional Time Reporting: Shortcut To Integrating Labor Data," MA, 1984, Vol. 65, No. 12, pp. 34-38.

Blair, A. H. "Installing Bookkeeping System & Equipment For New Client," JOA, 1953, Vol. 96, No. 1, pp. 68-71.

Blair-Smith, Dallas. "How Changes In Corporate Form Affect EPT Liability," JOA, 1952, Vol. 93, No. 2, pp. 181-189.

Blakely, Edward J. and Howard E. Thompson. "Technological Change And Its Effects On Dollar-Value Lifo," MA, 1969, Vol. 51, No. 2, pp. 33-38.

Blakely, Edward J. and Peter H. Knutson. "L.I.F.O. Or L.O.F.I. - Which?," AR, 1963, Vol. 38, No. 1, pp. 75-86.

Blakeney, Roger N., Winford E. Holland and Michael T. Matteson. "The Auditor-Auditee Relationship: Some Behavioral Considerations And Implications For Auditing Education," AR, 1976, Vol. 51, No. 4, pp. 899-906.

Blake, Arthur B. "Interest Is Not A Project Cost," MA, 1976, Vol. 58, No. 1, pp. 41-44.

Blake, Arthur B. "The Asset-Disposal Decision," MA, 1974, Vol. 56, No. 4, pp. 67-70.

Blake, Avery F., Jr. "Unsophisticated Automation Can Break The Paperwork Bottleneck," MA, 1967, Vol. 48, No. 9, pp. 31-34.

Blake, Harold D. and Karen M. Frey. "Information Retrieval," MA, 1976, Vol. 58, No. 3, pp. 47-48.

Blake, Matthew F. "Current Trends In Fringe Benefits," JOA, 1958, Vol. 106, No. 3, pp. 33-40.

Blake, Matthew F. "Deferred Compensation Plans: Employee Stock Options," JOA, 1954, Vol. 98, No. 3, pp. 349-352.

Blake, Matthew F. "Employee Benefit Plans," JOA, 1956, Vol. 102, No. 3, pp. 40-46.

Blake, Matthew F. "Professional Association Laws And The CPA," JOA, 1962, Vol. 113, No. 6, pp. 37-46.

Blake, Matthew F. "Statements On Responsibilities In Tax Practice," JOA, 1964, Vol. 117, No. 4, pp. 37-41.

Blake, Matthew F. "Tax Practice: Responsibilities And Interrelationships," JOA, 1967, Vol. 123, No. 3, pp. 31-37.

Blake, Matthew F. "Taxes And Mergers," JOA, 1956, Vol. 102, No. 1, pp. 27-31.

Blake, Thomas E. and John K. Harris. "An Analysis Of APB Opinion Coverage In The CPA Examination," AR, 1976, Vol.

51, No. 2, pp. 370-375.

Blamey, Richard L. "Setting Sewage Treatment User Charge Rates: A Cost/Benefit Approach," **MA**, 1978, Vol. 60, No. 6, pp. 32-36.

Blanchard, Garth A. and Chee W. Chow. "Allocating Indirect Costs For Improved Management Performance," **MA**, 1983, Vol. 64, No. 9, pp. 38-41.

Blanchard, Garth A., Chee W. Chow and Eric Noreen. "Information Asymmetry, Incentive Schemes, And Information Biasing: The Case Of Hospital Budgeting Under Rate Regulation," **AR**, 1986, Vol. 61, No. 1, pp. 1-15.

Blanco-Best, Mimi. (Roussey, Robert S., Ernest L. Ten Eyck and Mimi Blanco-Best. "Three New SASs: Closing The Communications Gap," **JOA**, 1988, Vol. 166, No. 6, pp. 44-52.)

Blankenship, Ronald C. and Carol A. Schaller. "The CPA, The Small Company And The Computer," **JOA**, 1976, Vol. 142, No. 2, pp. 46-51.

Blank, Virgil F. "Management Concept In Electronic Systems," **JOA**, 1961, Vol. 111, No. 1, pp. 59-66.

Blasi, Ronald W. "Understanding The New Fringe Benefit Law," **MA**, 1985, Vol. 66, No. 12, pp. 43-47.

Blauch, Lloyd E. "The Nature Of A Profession," **JOA**, 1956, Vol. 101, No. 4, pp. 54-57.

Blayton, Jesse B. "Local Business Concerns As Accounting Laboratories," **AR**, 1935, Vol. 10, No. 3, pp. 294-295.

Blazenko, George W. and William R. Scott. "A Model Of Standard Setting In Auditing," **CAR**, 1986-87, Vol. 3, No. 1, pp. 68-92.

Blazer, Barry L. "The Actuary, The CPA, And The Audit Guide," **CPAJ**, 1974, Vol. 44, No. 6, pp. 27-32.

Blecki, Thomas R. (Gourley, Keith C. and Thomas R. Blecki. "Computerized Budgeting At Lord Corporation," **MA**, 1986, Vol. 68, No. 2, pp. 37-40.)

Blewitt, Bert J. "Corporate Accounting And Economics," **MA**, 1974, Vol. 55, No. 9, pp. 11-13.

Bleyer, Stephen A. and William R. Stromsem. "Divorce - TRA Style," **JOA**, 1985, Vol. 159, No. 4, pp. 72-85.

Bline, Dennis M. and Ted D. Skekel. "Effective Classroom Presentation Of FAS 87 Footnote Reconciliation," **IAE**, 1988, Vol. 3, No. 2, pp. 215-227.

Bline, Dennis. (Fairchild, Keith Wm. and Dennis Bline. "Capital Investment Analysis: The Index Method," **IAE**, 1988, Vol. 3, No. 1, pp. 72-78.)

Blinn, Mary M. "Detecting Management Fraud: Putting One Past The Auditors?," **MA**, 1977, Vol. 58, No. 11, pp. 20-22.

Blocher, Edward and Andrew D. Luzi. "Guidance Effects On Analytical Review Decisions," **AIA**, 1987, Vol. 4, pp. 201-214.

Blocher, Edward and Clyde Stickney. "Duration And Risk Assessments In Capital Budgeting," **AR**, 1979, Vol. 54, No. 1, pp. 180-188.

Blocher, Edward and Jack C. Robertson. "Bayesian Sampling Procedures For Auditors: Computer-Assisted Instruction," **AR**, 1976, Vol. 51, No. 2, pp. 359-363.

Blocher, Edward and Joseph Bylinski. "The Influence Of Sample Characteristics In Sample Evaluation," **AJPT**, 1985-86, Vol. 5, No. 1, pp. 79-90.

Blocher, Edward and Kung H. Chen. "Assessing Industry Risk By Ratio Analysis: A Comment," **AR**, 1978, Vol. 53, No. 1, pp. 204-209.

Blocher, Edward J. and Jean C. Cooper. "A Study Of Auditors' Analytical Review Performance," **AJPT**, 1988, Vol. 7, No. 2, pp. 1-28.

Blocher, Edward J., Robert S. Esposito and John J. Willingham. "Auditors' Analytical Review Judgments For Payroll Expense," **AJPT**, 1983-84, Vol. 3, No. 1, pp. 75-91.

Blocher, Edward. "A Computer-Assisted Teaching Aid For Bayesian Variables Audit Sampling," **AIA**, 1985, Vol. 2, pp. 113-148.

Blocher, Edward. "Approaching Analytical Review," **CPAJ**, 1983, Vol. 53, No. 3, pp. 24-33.

Blocher, Edward. "Assessment Of Prior Distributions: The Effect On Required Sample Size In Bayesian Audit Sampling," **ABR**, 1981-82, Vol. 12, No. 45, pp. 11-20.

Blocher, Edward. "CPA Firms' Staff Evaluation Process," **CPAJ**, 1980, Vol. 50, No. 7, pp. 41-47.

Blocher, Edward. "Performance Effects Of Different Audit Staff Assignment Strategies," **AR**, 1979, Vol. 54, No. 3, pp. 563-573.

Blocher, Edward. "Sampling For Integrated Audit Objectives - A Comment," **AR**, 1978, Vol. 53, No. 3, pp. 766-772.

Blocher, E., R. P. Moffie and R. W. Zmud. "Report Format And Task Complexity: Interaction In Risk Judgments," **AOS**, 1986, Vol. 11, No. 6, pp. 457-470.

Blocker, John G. "Mismatching Of Costs And Revenues," **AR**, 1949, Vol. 24, No. 1, pp. 33-43.

Blocker, J. G. "Budgeting In Relation To Standard Costs," **AR**, 1936, Vol. 11, No. 2, pp. 117-124.

Block, J. L. "System Of Accounting For An Iron Works," **AR**, 1926, Vol. 1, No. 3, pp. 1-30.

Block, Linda J. (Farrar, Robert H., William C. Lawler and Linda J. Block. "How CFOs View The CMA Program," **MA**, 1985, Vol. 67, No. 5, pp. 33-37.)

Block, Max. "Any Limits To 'Marketing' CPA Services?," **CPAJ**, 1980, Vol. 50, No. 8, pp. 35-40.

Block, Max. "Duality In The Accounting Profession," **CPAJ**, 1974, Vol. 44, No. 7, pp. 29-34.

Block, Max. "Improving The Credibility Of Financial Statements," **CPAJ**, 1972, Vol. 42, No. 1, pp. 55-61.

Block, Max. "Survival Of The Smaller Practitioner," **CPAJ**, 1981, Vol. 51, No. 6, pp. 32-37.

Block, Max. "Trend To Duality In Accounting Standards," **CPAJ**, 1977, Vol. 47, No. 3, pp. 11-16.

Block, Max. "Write-Up Services And The Auditor's Independence," **CPAJ**, 1975, Vol. 45, No. 3, pp. 25-30.

Block, Max. "Writing For A Public Accounting Practitioners' Magazine," **AR**, 1972, Vol. 47, No. 4, pp. 814-818.

Block, Stanley B. "Buy-Sell Agreements For Privately Held Corporations," **JOA**, 1985, Vol. 160, No. 3, pp. 110-124.

Block, Stanley B. (Stanley, Marjorie T. and Stanley B. Block. "Accounting And Economic Aspects Of SFAS No. 8," **IJAER**, 1979, Vol. 14, No. 2, pp. 135-155.)

Blodgett, Ralph H. "The Value Of Economics For The Accountant," **AR**, 1943, Vol. 18, No. 4, pp. 324-330.

Bloomfield, E. C. and R. Ma. "The Lease Evaluation Solution," **ABR**, 1973-74, Vol. 4, No. 16, pp. 297-302.

Bloom, Robert and Araya Debessay. "The Controversial Development Of The Deprival Value Concept," **IJAER**, 1986, Vol. 22, No. 1, pp. 159-172.

Bloom, Ben. "Aptitude Tests For Accounting Students," **AR**, 1944, Vol. 19, No. 2, pp. 131-134.

Bloom, Robert and Araya Debessay. "A Comparative Analysis Of Recent Pronouncements On Accounting For Changing Prices," **IJAER**, 1985, Vol. 20, No. 2, pp. 119-138.

Bloom, Robert and Araya Debessay. "An Appraisal Of The Conceptual Issues On Backlog Depreciation And A Comparative Analysis Of International Accounting Practices," **IJAER**, 1985, Vol. 21, No. 1, pp. 107-121.

Bloom, Robert and Hans Heymann. "The Concept Of Social Accountability In Accounting Literature," **JAL**, 1986, Vol. 5, pp. 167-182.

Bloom, Robert and Hans Heymann. "The Ideas Of Stuart Chase On Waste And Inefficiency," **AHJ**, 1984, Vol. 11, No. 2, pp. 133-142.

Bloom, Robert and Marilynn Collins. "Motivating Students With A Historical Perspective In Financial Accounting Courses," **JAED**, 1988, Vol. 6, No. 1, pp. 103-115.

Bloom, Robert and M. Ahmed Naciri. "An Analysis Of The Accounting Standard-Setting Framework In Two European Countries: France And The Netherlands," **AIIA**, 1988, Vol. 2, pp. 69-85.

Bloom, Robert, Araya Debessay and William Markell. "The Development Of Schools Of Accounting And The Underlying Issues," **JAED**, 1986, Vol. 4, No. 1, pp. 7-29.

Bloom, Robert. "American And Canadian Accounting Standard Setting: A Comparative Analysis," **IJAER**, 1984, Vol. 19, No. 2, pp. 47-57.

Bloom, Robert. (Debessay, Araya and Robert Bloom. "A Critique Of FAS No. 33," **MA**, 1981, Vol. 62, No. 11, pp. 48-53.)

Bloom, R., P. T. Elgers and D. Murray. "Functional Fixation In Product Pricing: A Comparison Of Individuals And Groups," **AOS**, 1984, Vol. 9, No. 1, pp. 1-12.

Blossom, Christine J. "So You Want To Be A Condominium Treasurer," **MA**, 1984, Vol. 65, No. 12, pp. 61-65.

Blotzer, Joseph R. (Knobloch, John J., Donald C. Schindler and Joseph R. Blotzer. "Maintenance Work Authorization And Control," **MA**, 1970, Vol. 51, No. 11, pp. 19-22.)

Blough, Carman G. "An Approach To Renegotiation," **AR**, 1944, Vol. 19, No. 3, pp. 238-247.

Blough, Carman G. "Auditing Standards And Procedures," **AR**, 1949, Vol. 24, No. 3, pp. 265-271.

Blough, Carman G. "Challenges To The Accounting Profession In The U.S.," **JOA**, 1959, Vol. 108, No. 6, pp. 37-42.

Blough, Carman G. "Principles And Procedures," **JOA**, 1961, Vol. 111, No. 4, pp. 51-53.

Blough, Carman G. "Responsibility To Third Parties," **JOA**, 1960, Vol. 109, No. 5, pp. 58-65.

Blough, Carman G. "Restoration Of Fixed Asset Values To The Balance Sheet," **AR**, 1947, Vol. 22, No. 2, pp. 194-198.

Blough, Carman G. "The Accountant's Problems Arising Under SEC's New Revision Of Regulation S-X," **JOA**, 1951, Vol. 91, No. 2, pp. 238-242.

Blough, Carman G. "The Need For Accounting Principles," **AR**, 1937, Vol. 12, No. 1, pp. 30-36.

Blough, Carman G. "The Role Of Accounting In The Taxing Process," **AR**, 1947, Vol. 22, No. 3, pp. 248-252.

Blough, Roy. "Averaging Income For Tax Purposes," **AR**, 1945, Vol. 20, No. 1, pp. 85-95.

Blough, Roy. "International Developments Affecting Business," **JOA**, 1965, Vol. 119, No. 2, pp. 34-39.

Blumenberg, Sidney. "Tax-Saving Opportunities Available To Estates," **CPAJ**, 1974, Vol. 44, No. 11, pp. 28-32.

Blumenfrucht, Israel. "Taxation Requirements For The CPA Examination And The Content Of Undergraduate Accounting Curricula," **JATA**, 1984, Vol. 6, No. 1, pp. 57-65.

Blumenfrucht, Israel. (Weiss, Jerold M. and Israel Blumenfrucht. "CPA Examination Tax Problems: An In-Depth Analysis," **JATA**, 1981, Vol. 3, No. 1, pp. 19-25.)

Blumenthal, Philip L., Jr. "The Accountant Looks At His Client's Future," **JOA**, 1962, Vol. 113, No. 1, pp. 64-68.

Blumstein, Nathan. "Small Business Liquidation Value Analysis," **MA**, 1976, Vol. 57, No. 12, pp. 41-44.

Blum, James D. and David J. Reiner. "Highlights Of Auditing Standards," **CPAJ**, 1976, Vol. 46, No. 9, pp. 41-46.

Blum, James D. and Herbert L. Jensen. "Accounting For Marketable Securities In Accordance With FASB Statement No. 12," **MA**, 1978, Vol. 60, No. 3, pp. 33-42.

Blum, James D. "Accounting And Reporting For Leases By Lessees: The Interest Rate Problems," **MA**, 1978, Vol. 59, No. 10, pp. 25-28.

Blum, James D. "Decision Tree Analysis For Accounting Decisions," **MA**, 1976, Vol. 58, No. 6, pp. 45-46.

Blum, James D. "Implicit Factors In The Evaluation Of Lease Vs. Buy Alternatives: A Comment," **AR**, 1974, Vol. 49, No. 4, pp. 807-808.

Blum, James D. "Newly Emerging Standards Of Auditor Responsibility: A Comment," **AR**, 1977, Vol. 52, No. 1, pp. 257-258.

Blum, Marc. "Failing Company Discriminant Analysis," **JAR**, 1974, Vol. 12, No. 1, pp. 1-25.

Blyskal, Joanne K. (Siers, Howard L. and Joanne K. Blyskal. "Risk Management Of The Internal Audit Function," **MA**, 1987, Vol. 68, No. 8, pp. 29-35.)

Board, J. L. G. and M. Walker. "Information Content Of SSAP 16 Earnings Changes," **ABR**, 1985-86, Vol. 16, No. 61, pp. 69-72.

Boatsman, J. R. and G. M. Crooch. "An Example Of Controlling The Risk Of A Type II Error For Substantive Tests In Auditing," **AR**, 1975, Vol. 50, No. 3, pp. 610-615.

Boatsman, James R. and Elba F. Baskin. "Asset Valuation With Incomplete Markets," **AR**, 1981, Vol. 56, No. 1, pp. 38-53.

Boatsman, James R. and Jack C. Robertson. "Policy-Capturing On Selected Materiality Judgments," **AR**, 1974, Vol. 49, No. 2, pp. 342-352.

Boatsman, James R. "American Law Schools: Implications For Accounting Education," **JAED**, 1983, Vol. 1, No. 1, pp. 93-117.

Boatsman, James R. "Why Are There Tigers And Things?," **ABACUS**, 1977, Vol. 13, No. 2, pp. 155-167.

Boatsman, James R. (Davis, Darrel W., James R. Boatsman and Elba F. Baskin. "On Generalizing Stock Market Research To A Broader Class Of Markets," **AR**, 1978, Vol. 53, No. 1, pp. 1-10.)

Boatsman, James R. (Durkee, David A., James E. Groff and James R. Boatsman. "The Effect Of Costly Vs. Costless Pension Disclosure On Common Share Prices: The Case Of SFAS 36," **JAL**, 1988, Vol. 7, pp. 180-196.)

Boatsman, James R. (McKee, A. James, Jr., Timothy B. Bell and James R. Boatsman. "Management Preferences Over Accounting Standards: A Replication And Additional Tests," **AR**, 1984, Vol. 59, No. 4, pp. 647-659.)

Boatsman, James R. (Patz, Dennis H. and James R. Boatsman. "Accounting Principle Formulation In An Efficient Markets Environment," **JAR**, 1972, Vol. 10, No. 2, pp. 392-403.)

Boatsman, James R., C. Dwayne Dowell and Janet I. Kimbrell. "Valuing Stock Used For A Business Combination," **JAAF**, 1984, Vol. 8, No. 1, pp. 35-43.

Boatsman, James. (Gheyara, Kelly and James Boatsman. "Market Reaction To The 1976 Replacement Cost Disclosures," **JAEC**, 1980, Vol. 2, No. 2, pp. 107-125.)

Bockanic, William N. (McKeon, Joseph M., Jr. and William N. Bockanic. "Integration Of Law With Accounting: A More Comprehensive Learning Experience," **JAED**, 1984, Vol. 2, No. 2, pp. 127-141.)

Bock, Russell S. "Relief Provisions Of New Excess-Profits Tax," **JOA**, 1951, Vol. 92, No. 1, pp. 37-47.

Bock, Russell S. "Should We Change Our Method Of Taxing The Family?," **JOA**, 1952, Vol. 94, No. 4, pp. 425-433.

Bock, Russell S. "Tax-Saving Opportunities In Deferred Compensation," **JOA**, 1955, Vol. 99, No. 3, pp. 39-44.

Bodenhorn, Diran. "An Economic Approach To Balance Sheets And Income Statements," **ABACUS**, 1978, Vol. 14, No. 1, pp. 3-30.

Bodenhorn, Diran. "An Economist Looks At Industrial Accounting And Depreciation," **AR**, 1961, Vol. 36, No. 4, pp. 583-588.

Bodenhorn, Diran. "An Entity Approach To The Measurement Of Wealth, Income, And Product," **ABACUS**, 1972, Vol. 8, No. 2, pp. 127-144.

Bodnar, George and Edward J. Lusk. "Motivational Considerations In Cost Allocation Systems: A Conditioning Theory Approach," **AR**, 1977, Vol. 52, No. 4, pp. 857-868.

Bodnar, George and Edward Lusk. "Operant Conditioning: A Discussion Of Its Relevance Regarding Institutional Control," **AR**, 1979, Vol. 54, No. 1, pp. 215-220.

Bodnar, George. "Reliability Modeling Of Internal Control Systems," **AR**, 1975, Vol. 50, No. 4, pp. 747-757.

Boedecker, Karl A. "The Correlation Of Accounting Instruction With Instruction In Other Business Fields," **AR**, 1951, Vol. 26, No. 1, pp. 70-76.

Boer, Germain and Harold M. Nix. "Hospital Management And Resource Control," **MA**, 1975, Vol. 57, No. 3, pp. 47-48.

Boer, Germain and John O. Everett. "Information Science And Relevant Accounting Reports," **MA**, 1976, Vol. 57, No. 10, pp. 33-36.

Boer, Germain B. and Sam W. Barcus, III. "How A Small Company Evaluates Acquisition Of A Minicomputer," **MA**, 1981, Vol. 62, No. 9, pp. 13-23.

Boer, Germain. "Cash-Flow Statements - Fast," **AR**, 1967, Vol. 42, No. 1, pp. 142-146.

Boer, Germain. "Replacement Cost: A Historical Look," **AR**, 1966, Vol. 41, No. 1, pp. 92-97.

Boer, Germain. "Solutions In Search Of A Problem: The Case Of Budget Variance Investigation Models," **JAL**, 1984, Vol. 3, pp. 47-70.

Boer, Germain. "Statistical Sampling Concepts: A Review," **CPAJ**, 1973, Vol. 43, No. 6, pp. 487-492.

Boer, Germain. "The Role Of Judgment In Statistical Sampling," **CPAJ**, 1974, Vol. 44, No. 3, pp. 39-44.

Boer, Germain. "What Gross Margins Do Not Tell You," **MA**, 1984, Vol. 66, No. 4, pp. 50-53.

Boe, Warren J. (Bailey, Andrew A., Jr., Warren J. Boe and Thomas Schnack. "The Audit Staff Assignment Problem: A Comment," **AR**, 1974, Vol. 49, No. 3, pp. 572-574.)

Boe, Warren J. (Bailey, Andrew D., Jr. and Warren J. Boe. "Goal And Resource Transfers In The Multigoal Organization," **AR**, 1976, Vol. 51, No. 3, pp. 559-573.)

Bogart, Fred O. "Accounting For Leaseholds," **AR**, 1950, Vol. 25, No. 4, pp. 417-419.

Bogart, Fred O. "Tax Considerations In Partnership Agreements," **AR**, 1965, Vol. 40, No. 4, pp. 834-838.

Bogue, Russell S. "One Firm's Approach To Its Administrative Problems," **JOA**, 1954, Vol. 97, No. 5, pp. 599-602.

Bohan, Michael P. and Steven Rubin. "Lifo: What Should Be Disclosed?," **JOA**, 1985, Vol. 159, No. 2, pp. 72-77.

Bohan, Michael P. and Steven Rubin. "Lifo/Fifo: How Would It Work?," **JOA**, 1986, Vol. 162, No. 3, pp. 106-114.

Bohtling, A. A. A. "Some Notes On Handling Tax And Accounting Problems Of Extraordinary Obsolescence," **JOA**, 1950, Vol. 90, No. 3, pp. 235-237.

Boileau, O. C. "Program Management In The Space Age," **MA**, 1977, Vol. 58, No. 11, pp. 13-16.

Bokemeier, L. Charles. "Revenue Recognition Criteria For State And Local Governments," **RIGNA**, 1988, Vol. 4, pp. 129-157.

Boland, Richard J., Jr. "Fantasies Of Information," **AIPIA**, 1986, Vol. 1, pp. 49-65.

Boland, Richard J., Jr. (O'Leary, Ted and Richard J. Boland, Jr. "Self-Regulation, Public Interest And The Accounting Profession," **RIAR**, 1987, Vol. 1, pp. 103-121.)

Boland, R. J., Jr. and L. R. Pondy. "Accounting In Organizations: A Union Of Natural And Rational Perspectives," **AOS**, 1983, Vol. 8, No. 2/3, pp. 223-234.

Boland, R. J., Jr. and L. R. Pondy. "The Micro Dynamics Of A Budget-Cutting Process: Modes, Models And Structure," **AOS**, 1986, Vol. 11, No. 4/5, pp. 403-422.

Boland, R. J., Jr. "A Study In System Design: C. West Churchman And Chris Argyris," **AOS**, 1981, Vol. 6, No. 2, pp. 109-118.

Boland, R. J., Jr. "Control, Causality And Information System Requirements," **AOS**, 1979, Vol. 4, No. 4, pp. 259-272.

Boland, R. J., Jr. "Discussion Of 'Accounting And The Construction Of The Governable Person'," **AOS**, 1987, Vol. 12, No. 3, pp. 267-272.

Bolce, W. J. (Heard, J. E. and W. J. Bolce. "The Political Significance Of Corporate Social Reporting In The United States Of America," **AOS**, 1981, Vol. 6, No. 3, pp. 247-254.)

Boley, Richard and Edmund Outslay. "Conditions Under Which A Dependent Can File A Joint Return: Is The Current Confusion And Complexity Really Necessary?," **JATA**, 1981, Vol. 2, No. 2, pp. 5-11.

Boley, Richard and Edmund Outslay. "Doctoral Programs With A Concentration In Taxation: An Examination Of Recent Trends," **JATA**, 1983, Vol. 5, No. 1, pp. 49-59.

Boley, Richard and Patrick J. Wilkie. "Practitioners' Views Of The Common Body Of Tax Knowledge For Persons Entering Public Accounting," **JATA**, 1986, Vol. 8, No. 1, pp. 80-97.

Boley, Richard and Paul Danos. "Awareness And Usage Of LEXIS By Accounting Educators: A Survey," **AR**, 1980, Vol. 55, No. 1, pp. 102-106.

Boley, Richard and Paul Danos. "The Use Of LEXIS In Accounting Pedagogy - Preliminary Observations," **AR**, 1978, Vol. 53, No. 3, pp. 730-735.

Boley, Richard. (Danos, Paul and Richard Boley. "Centralized Research In CPA Firms," **CPAJ**, 1980, Vol. 50, No. 3, pp. 10-18.)

Boley, Richard. (Outslay, Edmund, John R. Robinson and Richard Boley. "A Framework For Utilizing Individual Return Problems In Introductory Courses," **AR**, 1983, Vol. 58, No. 2, pp. 428-438.)

Bolling, Rodger A. and Gorman R. Jones. "OID In Nonprofit Property Sales," **CPAJ**, 1986, Vol. 56, No. 8, pp. 32-43.

Bollom, William John. "Towards A Theory Of Interim Reporting For A Seasonal Business: A Behavioral Approach," **AR**, 1973, Vol. 48, No. 1, pp. 12-22.

Bollom, William J. and Jerry J. Weygandt. "An Examination Of Some Interim Reporting Theories For A Seasonal Business," **AR**, 1972, Vol. 47, No. 1, pp. 75-84.

Bollom, William J. "The Employee Report: It's Needed Now," **MA**, 1984, Vol. 66, No. 2, pp. 50-55.

Boll, Dennis M. "How Dutch Pantry Accounts For Standard Costs," **MA**, 1982, Vol. 64, No. 6, pp. 32-35.

Bomblatus, Richard L. "Decision-Making In Middle Management," **MA**, 1974, Vol. 56, No. 2, pp. 22-26.

Bomeli, Edward C. "Curricular Recognition Of International Accounting - An Appraisal," **IJAER**, 1969, Vol. 5, No. 1, pp. 85-96.

Bomeli, Edwin C. "Management Reviews By Scandinavian Accountants," **JOA**, 1964, Vol. 118, No. 1, pp. 33-37.

Bomeli, Edwin C. "Stock Option Plans - Full Disclosure," **AR**, 1962, Vol. 37, No. 4, pp. 741-745.

Bomeli, Edwin C. "The Accountant's Function In Determination Of Net Income," **AR**, 1961, Vol. 36, No. 3, pp. 454-459.

Bomeli, Edwin C. (Ross, Timothy L. and Edwin C. Bomeli. "A Comment On Accountants' Job Satisfaction," **JAR**, 1971, Vol. 9, No. 2, pp. 383-388.)

Bonagura, Robert F. "Delayed Compensation," **JOA**, 1959, Vol. 107, No. 3, pp. 57-62.

Bonbright, James C. "Original Cost As A Rate Base," **AR**, 1945, Vol. 20, No. 4, pp. 441-446.

Bonbright, James C. "The Concept Of Depreciation As An Accounting Category," **AR**, 1930, Vol. 5, No. 2, pp. 117-124.

Bonchonsky, Joseph P. "Cost Control For Program Managers," **MA**, 1967, Vol. 48, No. 9, pp. 16-24.

Bond, Joe. "Accounting Policy Or Economic Philosophy?," **AR**, 1945, Vol. 20, No. 1, pp. 24-30.

Bond, Joe. "Economic Abracadabra," **AR**, 1946, Vol. 21, No. 2, pp. 181-198.

Bond, Richard R. "Emerging Nations And Emerging Institutions," **IJAER**, 1970, Vol. 6, No. 1, pp. 83-90.

Bonfield, E. H. (Rayburn, Frank R. and E. H. Bonfield. "Schools Of Accountancy: Attitudes And Attitude Structure," **AR**, 1978, Vol. 53, No. 3, pp. 752-765.)

Bonfield, E. H. (Stout, David E. and E. H. Bonfield. "Experimental Evidence On The Relationship Between Class Meeting Time Compression And Accounting Student Performance, Evaluations And Drop-Out Experience," **JAED**, 1986, Vol. 4, No. 2, pp. 51-62.)

Bonfield, E. H. (Stout, D. F., E. H. Bonfield and M. S. Battista. "Additional Experimental Evidence On The Relationship Between Class Meeting Time Compression And Accounting Student Performance And Evaluations," **JAED**, 1987, Vol. 5, No. 2, pp. 339-348.)

Bongiorni, Peter J. and Frederic G. Eichhorn. "Keeping A Second Set Of Books - Legally," **MA**, 1979, Vol. 61, No. 6, pp. 30-35.

Bonito, Thomas. "Top-Heavy Rules Affect Pension Plans," **CPAJ**, 1983, Vol. 53, No. 5, pp. 16-23.

Boni, Gregory M. "Impact Of Electronic Data Processing On Auditing," **JOA**, 1963, Vol. 116, No. 3, pp. 39-44.

Boockholdt, James L. "A Historical Perspective On The Auditor's Role: The Early Experience Of The American Railroads," **AHJ**, 1983, Vol. 10, No. 1, pp. 69-86.

Boockholdt, J. L. "Influence Of Nineteenth And Early Twentieth Century Railroad Accounting On The Development Of Modern Accounting Theory," **AHJ**, 1978, Vol. 5, No. 1, pp. 9-28.

Boockholdt, J. L. (Finley, D. R. and J. L. Boockholdt. "A Continuous Constrained Optimization Model For Audit Sampling," **AJPT**, 1986-87, Vol. 6, No. 2, pp. 22-39.)

Boockholdt, J. L. (Hasz, Thomas W. and J. L. Boockholdt. "How Houston Lighting & Power Applied DDP," **MA**, 1983, Vol. 64, No. 9, pp. 56-59.)

Booker, Jon A. and John K. Harris. "A Project To Enrich The Study Of Financial Reporting," **AR**, 1980, Vol. 55, No. 1, pp. 107-110.

Booker, Jon. (Anderson, H. M., J. W. Giese and Jon Booker. "Some Propositons About Auditing," **AR**, 1970, Vol. 45, No. 3, pp. 524-531.)

Book, John W. "Is BOMP Worth The Trouble?," **MA**, 1985, Vol. 66, No. 9, pp. 54-58.

Boone, Alan L. "Wouldn't It Be Nice If - ," **MA**, 1977, Vol. 58, No. 8, pp. 27-28.

Boone, Michael M. "Management Accountants And The Securities Laws," **MA**, 1973, Vol. 54, No. 12, pp. 18-22.

Borden, James P. "An Assessment Of The Impact Of Diagnosis-Related Group (DRG)-Based Reimbursement On The Technical Efficiency Of New Jersey Hospitals Using Data Envelopment Analysis," **JAPP**, 1988, Vol. 7, No. 2, pp. 77-96.

Bordner, Howard W. "Suggestions To The Commission On Organization Of The Executive Branch Of The Government," **AR**, 1948, Vol. 23, No. 4, pp. 360-370.

Bordner, Howard. "Defense Department Policy On Amortization As Cost," **JOA**, 1953, Vol. 95, No. 2, pp. 179-189.

Bordner, H. W. "An Accountant's Guide To Procurement Procedures In The Department Of Defense," **JOA**, 1950, Vol. 90, No. 6, pp. 464-473.

Bordner, H. W. "Consolidated Reports," **AR**, 1938, Vol. 13, No. 3, pp. 289-291.

Bordner, H. W. "Financial And Accounting Administration In The Federal Government," **AR**, 1949, Vol. 24, No. 4, pp. 341-353.

Bordner, H. W. "Fund Concepts As Accounting Postulates," **JOA**, 1961, Vol. 112, No. 1, pp. 52-60.

Borelli, Frank J. and Douglas C. Davis. "Financial Management And Audit Committee," **CA**, 1986, Vol. 4, No. 3, pp. 9-13.

Boritz, Jefim Efrim. "Information Presentation Structures On Audit Planning And Review Judgments," **CAR**, 1984-85, Vol. 1, No. 2, pp. 193-218.

Boritz, Jefim Efrim. "The Effect Of Research Method On Audit Planning And Review Judgments," **JAR**, 1986, Vol. 24, No. 2, pp. 335-348.

Boritz, J. E. and S. Broca. "Scheduling Internal Audit Activities," **AJPT**, 1986-87, Vol. 6, No. 1, pp. 1-19.

Boritz, J. E. (Armitage, H. M. and J. E. Boritz. "Integrating Computers Into The Accounting Curriculum," **IAE**, 1986, Vol. 1, No. 1, pp. 86-101.)

Boritz, J. E., B. G. Gaber and W. M. Lemon. "An Experimental Study Of The Effects Of Elicitation Methods On Review Of Preliminary Audit Strategy By External Auditors," **CAR**, 1988, Vol. 4, No. 2, pp. 392-411.

Borkowski, Joseph. "A System Of Order Entry Profit Analysis," **MA**, 1968, Vol. 49, No. 11, pp. 12-21.

Borna, Shaheen. (Foss, Helga B. and Shaheen Borna. "Employee Leasing After The TRA," **JOA**, 1987, Vol. 164, No. 3, pp. 151-156.)

Bornemann, Alfred. "Accounting Profits: An Institution," **AR**, 1943, Vol. 18, No. 4, pp. 321-323.

Bornemann, Alfred. "Empirical Cost Study And Economic Theory," **AR**, 1945, Vol. 20, No. 3, pp. 327-330.

Bornemann, Alfred. "Improving Depreciable Fixed Asset Accounting," **AR**, 1953, Vol. 28, No. 2, pp. 283-285.

Boros, John L. and Richard E. Thompson. "Distribution Cost Accounting At PPG Industries," **MA**, 1983, Vol. 64, No. 7, pp. 54-59.

Borow, Jay. (Schaps, Albert L., Warren Kissin, Jay Borow and Lynda Atanian. "Auditing Small Businesses - A New Look," **CPAJ**, 1984, Vol. 54, No. 10, pp. 12-23.)

Borsuk, Robert M. "Developing A Computer Program For Tax Planning," **MA**, 1978, Vol. 59, No. 11, pp. 47-51.

Borthick, A. Faye and James H. Scheiner. "Selection Of Small Business Computer Systems: Structuring A Multi-Criteria Approach," **JIS**, 1988, Vol. 3, No. 1, pp. 10-29.

Borthick, A. Faye and Owen D. West. "Expert Systems - A New Tool For The Professional," **ACCHOR**, 1987, Vol. 1, No. 1, pp. 9-16.

Borthick, A. Faye and Ronald L. Clark. "Improving Accounting Majors' Writing Quality: The Role Of Language Analysis In Attention Direction," **IAE**, 1987, Vol. 2, No. 1, pp. 13-27.

Borthick, A. Faye and Ronald L. Clark. "The Role Of Productive Thinking In Affecting Student Learning With Microcomputers In Accounting Education," **AR**, 1986, Vol. 61, No. 1, pp. 143-157.

Borthick, A. Faye and Ronald L. Clark. "Research On Computing In Accounting Education: Opportunities And Impediments," **IAE**, 1987, Vol. 2, No. 2, pp. 173-192

Borthick, A. Faye. "Artificial Intelligence In Auditing: Assumptions And Preliminary Development," **AIA**, 1987, Vol. 5, pp. 179-204.

Borthick, A. Faye. "Audit Implications Of Information Systems," **CPAJ**, 1986, Vol. 56, No. 4, pp. 40-46.

Borthick, A. Faye. "Course Outline: Systems Issues And Policies," **JIS**, 1987, Vol. 2, No. 1, pp. 77-80.

Borth, Daniel and Arthur H. Winakor. "Some Reflections Of The Scope Of Auditing," **AR**, 1935, Vol. 10, No. 2, pp. 174-184.

Borth, Daniel, Jr. "Published Financial Statements Of Banks," **AR**, 1947, Vol. 22, No. 3, pp. 288-294.

Borth, Daniel. "Comments On Third Statement Of Accounting Concepts And Standards," **AR**, 1949, Vol. 24, No. 3, pp. 277-280.

Borth, Daniel. "Donated Fixed Assets," **AR**, 1948, Vol. 23, No. 2, pp. 171-178.

Borth, Daniel. "What Does 'Consistent' Mean In The Short Form Report?," **AR**, 1948, Vol. 23, No. 4, pp. 371-373.

Borth, Daniel. (Winakor, Arthur H. and Daniel Borth. "Documentation In Accounting Literature," **AR**, 1934, Vol. 9, No. 1, pp. 61-68.)

Bort, Richard and Alan G. Seidner. "Investing Surplus Funds: What To Do With Your Everyday Cash," **CA**, 1986, Vol. 4, No. 1, pp. 3-10.

Bosse, William D. (Phoenix, Julius W., Jr. and William D. Bosse. "Accounting For The Cost Of Pension Plans - APB Opinion No. 8," **JOA**, 1967, Vol. 124, No. 2, pp. 27-37.)

Bosse, William D. (Phoenix, Julius W., Jr. and William D. Bosse. "Accounting For The Cost Of Pension Plans - More Information On APB No. 8," **JOA**, 1967, Vol. 124, No. 4, pp. 31-40.)

Bost, Patricia James. "Do Cost Accounting Standards Fill A Gap In Cost Allocation?," **MA**, 1986, Vol. 68, No. 5, pp. 34-36.

Bostrom, Erik, L. Allan Austin and Robert J. Zenowich. "The ABB Link: Accounting-Based Decisions Improve Planning," **CA**, Vol. 3, NO. 3, pp. 14-21.

Bostwick, Charles L. "The Use Of Information Theory In Accounting," **MA**, 1968, Vol. 49, No. 10, pp. 11-17.

Bostwick, William J. (Wagner, Nancy A., Herbert A. O'Keefe and William J. Bostwick. "Audit Committee Functions For Municipalities, Hospitals And Banks," **CPAJ**, 1988, Vol. 58, No. 6, pp. 46-53.)

Bosworth, Ronald L. (Evans, William P. and Ronald L. Bosworth. "Computerized Information System (COINS)," **MA**, 1966, Vol. 48, No. 2, pp. 36-44.)

Bothwell, Chung. "How To Improve Financial Planning With A Budget Manual," **MA**, 1984, Vol. 66, No. 6, pp. 34-38.

Bottin, Ronald R. "An Investigation Of The Relationship Of The Protestant Ethic Value To Success In Accounting Courses," **AR**, 1977, Vol. 52, No. 2, pp. 479-484.

Bottin, Ronald R. (Severance, Jay and Ronald R. Bottin. "Work-In-Process Inventory Control Through Data Base Concepts," **MA**, 1979, Vol. 60, No. 7, pp. 37-41.)

Bottomley, A. (Khanna, R. K. and A. Bottomley. "Costs And Returns On Graduates Of The University Of Bradford," **ABR**, 1970-71, Vol. 1, No. 1, pp. 56-70.)

Botts, Ralph R. and Fred L. Garlock. "Interest Rates Charged On Installment Purchases," **AR**, 1955, Vol. 30, No. 4, pp. 607-616.

Botts, Ralph R. "Interest And The Truth-In-Lending Bill," **AR**, 1963, Vol. 38, No. 4, pp. 789-795.

Boucher, Rick. "Why Civil RICO Must Be Reformed," **JOA**, 1985, Vol. 160, No. 6, pp. 102-110.

Boudreaux, Kenneth J. and Stephen A. Zeff. "A Note On The Measure Of Compensation Implicit In Employee Stock Options," **JAR**, 1976, Vol. 14, No. 1, pp. 158-162.

Bougen, P. (Ogden, S. and P. Bougen. "A Radical Perspective On The Disclosure Of Accounting Information To Trade Unions," **AOS**, 1985, Vol. 10, No. 2, pp. 211-226.)

Boughner, Jackson L. "Reviewing The Corporate Federal Income-Tax Return," **JOA**, 1951, Vol. 92, No. 4, pp. 436-444.

Boulter, Edward M. "The Increasing Importance Of Staff Training Programs," **JOA**, 1954, Vol. 98, No. 2, pp. 173-178.

Bourgeois, Jacques C. (Da Costa, Richard C., Jacques C. Bourgeois and William M. Lawson. "A Classification Of International Financial Accounting Practices," **IJAER**, 1978, Vol. 13, No. 2, pp. 73-85.)

Bourn, A. M. "Training For The Accountancy Profession In England And Wales," **JAR**, 1966, Vol. 4, No. 2, pp. 213-223.

Bourque, Donald D. (Corr, Paul J. and Donald D. Bourque. "Managing In A Reorganization," **MA**, 1988, Vol. 69, No. 7, pp. 33-37.)

Boursy, Alfred V. "The Name Of Paciolo," **AR**, 1943, Vol. 18, No. 3, pp. 205-208.

Boussard, Daniel. "Accounting As An Artifact: A Methodological Design On Dimensions Of Accounting," **IJAER**, 1981, Vol. 16, No. 2, pp. 125-147.

Boussard, Daniel. "Application Of GST To The Financial

Accounting Model," **IJAER**, 1978, Vol. 14, No. 1,pp.17-37.

Boussard, Daniel. "Attributability And Distributability Of Profit To Shareholders: A Note," **ABR**, 1984-85, Vol. 15, No. 60, pp. 271-280.

Boussard, Daniel. "The Impact Of The Definition Of Inflation On The Effectiveness Of Inflation Accounting Adjustments," **ABACUS**, 1984, Vol. 20, No. 2, pp. 157-169.

Boutell, Wayne S. "Auditing Through The Computer," **JOA**, 1965, Vol. 120, No. 5, pp. 41-47.

Boutell, W. S. "Business Oriented Computers: A Frame Of Reference," **AR**, 1964, Vol. 39, No. 2, pp. 305-311.

Boutell, W. S. "The Implementation Of Uniform Standards Of Reporting For National Voluntary Agencies," **AR**, 1962, Vol. 37, No. 3, pp. 406-409.

Bouwman, Marinus J. (Frishkoff, Paul, Patricia A. Frishkoff and Marinus J. Bouwman. "Use Of Accounting Data In Screening By Financial Analysts," **JAAF**, 1984, Vol. 8, No. 1, pp. 44-53.)

Bouwman, M. J. "Expert Vs. Novice Decision Making In Accounting: A Summary," **AOS**, 1984, Vol. 9, No. 3/4,. pp. 325-328.

Bouwman, M. J., P. A. Frishkoff and P. Frishkoff. "How Do Financial Analysts Make Decisions? A Process Model Of The Investment Screening Decision," **AOS**, 1987, Vol. 12, No. 1, pp. 1-30.

Bowen, Earl K. "Mathematics In The Undergraduate Business Curriculum," **AR**, 1967, Vol. 42, No. 4, pp. 782-787.

Bowen, Linda. "Social Responsiveness Of The CPA Profession," **CPAJ**, 1978, Vol. 48, No. 6, pp. 29-35.

Bowen, Richard L., Jr. "Application Of Margin Rates To Credit Analysis," **MA**, 1966, Vol. 48, No. 3, pp. 26-31.

Bowen, Robert M. and Gary L. Sundem. "Editorial And Publication Lags In The Accounting And Finance Literature," **AR**, 1982, Vol. 57, No. 4, pp. 778-784.

Bowen, Robert M. "Valuation Of Earnings Components In The Electric Utility Industry," **AR**, 1981, Vol. 56, No. 1, pp. 1-22.

Bowen, Robert M., David Burgstahler and Lane A. Daley. "Evidence Of The Relationships Between Various Earnings Measures Of Cash Flow," **AR**, 1986, Vol. 61, No. 4, pp. 713-725.

Bowen, Robert M., David Burgstahler and Lane A. Daley. "The Incremental Information Content Of Accrual Versus Cash Flows," **AR**, 1987, Vol. 62, No. 4, pp. 723-747.

Bowen, Robert M., Eric W. Noreen and John M. Lacey. "Determinants Of The Corporate Decision To Capitalize Interest," **JAEC**, 1981, Vol. 3, No. 2, pp. 151-179.

Bowers, Billy B. "Product Costing In The MRP Environment," **MA**, 1982, Vol. 64, No. 6, pp. 24-27.

Bowers, Richard L. "Managing The Company's Cash," **MA**, 1971, Vol. 53, No. 3, pp. 22-26.

Bowers, Russell. "An Efficient Approach To The Teaching Of Accounting," **AR**, 1947, Vol. 22, No. 3, pp. 295-298.

Bowers, Russell. "Business Profit And The Price Level," **AR**, 1951, Vol. 26, No. 2, pp. 167-178.

Bowers, Russell. "Curriculum Building For Prospective Industrial Accountants," **AR**, 1953, Vol. 28,No. 1.pp.58-63.

Bowers, Russell. "Economic And Accounting Concepts," **AR**, 1945, Vol. 20, No. 4, pp. 420-430.

Bowers, Russell. "Objections To Index Number Accounting," **AR**, 1950, Vol. 25, No. 2, pp. 149-155.

Bowers, Russell. "On Teaching Depreciation," **AR**, 1949, Vol. 24, No. 4, pp. 438-441.

Bowers, Russell. "Some Unsettled Problems Of Income," **AR**, 1940, Vol. 15, No. 3, pp. 350-352.

Bowers, Russell. "Terminology And Form Of The Income Sheet," **AR**, 1944, Vol. 19, No. 3, pp. 274-278.

Bowers, Russell. "Tests Of Income Realization," **AR**, 1941, Vol. 16, No. 2, pp. 139-154.

Bowers, Russell. "The Income Tax And The Natural Person," **AR**, 1941, Vol. 16, No. 4, pp. 358-372.

Bower, James B. and Robert E. Schlosser. "Internal Control - Its True Nature," **AR**, 1965, Vol. 40, No. 2, pp. 338-344.

Bower, James B. "A Profession Of Accounting - Or Of Accountancy?," **AR**, 1957, Vol. 32, No. 2, pp. 194-198.

Bower, James B. "Federal Income Tax Practice In The Uniform Certified Public Accountant Examination," **AR**, 1955, Vol. 30, No. 1, pp. 89-94.

Bower, Richard S., Christopher E. Nugent and Donald E. Stone. "Time-Shared Computers In Business Education At Dartmouth," **AR**, 1968, Vol. 43, No. 3, pp. 565-582.

Bower, Richard S., Frank C. Herringer and J. Peter Williamson. "Lease Evaluation," **AR**, 1966, Vol. 41, No. 2, pp. 257-265.

Bower, Ward. "Cutting Outside Legal Fees," **CA**, 1987, Vol. 5, No. 1, pp. 37-40.

Bowles, C. C. "International Accounting - A Challenge For Ingenuity," **IJAER**, 1968, Vol. 4, No. 1, pp. 83-97.

Bowles, G. N. "Some Thoughts On The Lease Evaluation Solution," **ABR**, 1976-77, Vol. 7, No. 26, pp. 124-126.

Bowman, E. H. and M. Haire. "Social Impact Disclosure And Corporate Annual Reports," **AOS**, 1976, Vol. 1, No. 1, pp. 11-22.

Bowman, John W. "IRS Procedures," **JOA**, 1984, Vol. 158, No. 4, pp. 93-108.

Bowman, Robert G. "The Debt Equivalence Of Leases: An Empirical Investigation," **AR**, 1980, Vol. 55, No. 2, pp. 237-253.

Bowman, Robert G. "The Importance Of A Market-Value Measurement Of Debt In Assessing Leverage," **JAR**, 1980, Vol. 18, No. 1, pp. 242-254.

Bowsher, Charles A. "Federal Financial Management: Evolution, Challenges And The Role Of The Accounting Profession," **JOA**, 1987, Vol. 163, No. 5, pp. 280-294.

Bowsher, Charles A. "Reducing The Federal Deficit: A Critical Challenge," **JAAF**, 1986, Vol. 1 (New Series), No. 1, pp. 7-16.

Bowsher, Charles A. "The GAO And The Accounting Profession," **JOA**, 183, Vol. 155, No. 2, pp. 66-72.

Bowsher, Charles A. (Dye, Kenneth M. and Charles A. Bowsher. "Financial Statements For The Sovereign State: The Federal Government Reporting Study," **ACCHOR**, 1987, Vol. 1, No. 1, pp. 17-24.)

Bows, Albert J. and Arthur R. Wyatt. "Improving Interim Financial Reporting," **JOA**, 1973, Vol. 136, No. 4, pp. 54-59.

Bows, Albert J., Jr. "Creative Accounting Pays Its Way," **JOA**, 1959, Vol. 108, No. 6, pp. 51-55.

Bows, Albert J., Jr. "Establishment Of Financial Accounting Standards," **MA**, 1972, Vol. 54, No. 6, pp. 9-12.

Bows, Albert J., Jr. "Problems In Disclosure Of Segments Of Conglomerate Companies," **JOA**, 1966, Vol. 122, No. 6, pp. 33-37.

Boyce, L. Fred, Jr. "Installing A Medium-Sized Computer," **JOA**, 1960, Vol. 110, No. 1, pp. 48-53.

Boyce, L. Fred, Jr. "Lamb Among The Ledgers," **JOA**, 1960, Vol. 110, No. 6, pp. 72-74.

Boydstun, Frank W. "The Pooling Of Outside Income," **JOA**, 1955, Vol. 100, No. 2, pp. 62-65.

Boyd, F. Virgil. "A New Look In Accounting Education - The Managerial Approach To Tax Accounting," **AR**, 1960, Vol. 35, No. 4, pp. 726-728.

Boyd, F. Virgil. (McNichols, Thomas J. and F. Virgil Boyd. "Adjustment Of Fixed Assets To Reflect Price Level Changes," **AR**, 1954, Vol. 29, No. 1, pp. 106-113.)

Boyd, James H. (Heller, Kenneth H. and James H. Boyd. "Professors' Home Office Expenses: A Recent Development," **AR**, 1976, Vol. 51, No. 2, pp. 376-379.)

Boyd, James H. (Streuling, G. Fred, James H. Boyd and Kenneth H. Heller. "Interrelationships Of Sections 731, 736, And 751: A Worksheet Approach," **JATA**, 1987, Vol. 8, No. 2, pp. 37-49.)

Boyd, Orton W. "That Federal Tax Course," **AR**, 1956, Vol. 31, No. 1, pp. 131-135.

Boyd, Orton W. "The 'Report And Accounting' Approach," **AR**, 1934, Vol. 9, No. 3, pp. 262-267.

Boyd, O. W. "Accounting Problems Of The Florida Real Estate Boom," **AR**, 1926, Vol. 1, No. 3, pp. 64-73.

Boyd, Paul and Mary M. K. Fleming. "Productivity: The Controller's Role," **MA**, 1987, Vol. 69, No. 3, pp. 28-32.

Boyd, Ralph L. "A Suggested Program For College Training In Accountancy," **AR**, 1946, Vol. 21, No. 1, pp. 51-56.

Boyd, Ralph L. "Examination Objectives," **AR**, 1943, Vol. 18, No. 2, pp. 127-135.

Boyd, Ralph L. "The Divided Form Of Bank Reconciliation Schedule," **AR**, 1948, Vol. 23, No. 1, pp. 91-93.

Boyd, R. L. "Progress In CPA Legislation," **AR**, 1944, Vol. 19, No. 2, pp. 159-163.

Boyd, R. L. "Standards For CPA Legislation," **AR**, 1945, Vol. 20, No. 1, pp. 7-16.

Boyd, Virgil and Dale Taylor. "The Magic Words - 'Managerial Accounting'," **AR**, 1961, Vol. 36, No. 1, pp. 105-111.

Boyer, Patricia A. and Charles H. Gibson. "How About Earnings Per Share?," **CPAJ**, 1979, Vol. 49, No. 2, pp. 36-42.

Boyer, Robert. "How To Help Your Client Obtain A Bank Loan," **JOA**, 1977, Vol. 144, No. 4, pp. 78-86.

Boyles, Jesse V., III. "Energy Accounting," **MA**, 1979, Vol. 60, No. 8, pp. 35-41.

Boyle, Edwin T. "What The Computer Means To The Accounting Profession," **JOA**, 1966, Vol. 121, No. 1, pp. 56-67.

Boyle, Joseph T. and Thomas L. Holton. "Peer Review In The Accounting Profession - Who Audits The Auditor?," **CPAJ**, 1975, Vol. 45, No. 1, pp. 15-18.

Boyle, Phelim P. "Accounting For Equity Investments Of Life Insurance Companies," **CAR**, 1984-85, Vol. 1, No. 2, pp. 116-175.

Boynton, Charles E., IV and Jack Robison. "Factors Empirically Associated With Federal Tax Trial Case Loads," **AIT**, 1987, Vol. 1, pp. 169-182.

Boze, Ken M. (Cox, Clifford T., Ken M. Boze and Lee Schwendig. "Academic Accountants: A Study Of Faculty Characteristics And Career Activities," **JAED**, 1987, Vol. 5, No. 1, pp. 59-76.)

Brabston, Donald C. "Understanding And Utilizing Standard Costs," **JOA**, 1959, Vol. 107, No. 5, pp. 49-57.

Bracken, Robert M. and Ara G. Volkan. "Cash Flows: A New Reporting Format For Turbulent Times," **MA**, 1988, Vol. 69, No. 7, pp. 38-41.

Brackney, William O. and Henry R. Anderson. "Regulation Of Cost Accounting: The Answer Or The Abyss," **MA**, 1981, Vol. 63, No. 4, pp. 24-31.

Brack, George E. "Allocating Personnel Department Costs," **MA**, 1975, Vol. 56, No. 11, pp. 48-50.

Bradbury, Michael E. and Shirley C. Calderwood. "Equity Accounting For Reciprocal Stockholdings," **AR**, 1988, Vol. 63, No. 2, pp. 330-347.

Braden, Andrew D. "The Blackboard Versus Projected Still Pictures In The Teaching Of Accounting - An Experiment," **AR**, 1954, Vol. 29, No. 4, pp. 683-687.

Braden, Andrew D. "The Need For Simplicity In The Teaching Of Accounting," **AR**, 1954, Vol. 29, No. 3, pp. 499-500.

Bradford, Dalla H. (Neuhauser, William E. and Dallas H. Bradford. "Should You File A Consolidated Return - Revisited," **MA**, 1967, Vol. 48, No. 11, pp. 33-42.)

Bradford, William D. "Price-Level Restated Accounting And The Measurement Of Inflation Gains And Losses: A Reply," **AR**, 1975, Vol. 50, No. 3, pp. 586-587.

Bradford, William D. "Price-Level Restated Accounting And The Measurement Of Inflation Gains And Losses," **AR**.

1974, Vol. 49, No. 2, pp. 296-305.
Bradish, Richard D. "Accountants In Top Management," **JOA,** 1970, Vol. 129, No. 6, pp. 49-53.
Bradish, Richard D. "Corporate Reporting And The Financial Analyst," **AR,** 1965, Vol. 40, No. 4, pp. 757-766.
Bradish, Richard D. (Orton, Bryce B. and Richard D. Bradish. "The Treatment And Disclosure Of Research And Development Expenditures," **MA,** 1969, Vol. 51, No. 1, pp. 31-34.)
Bradley, G. W. (Trotman, K. T. and G. W. Bradley. "Associations Between Social Responsibility Disclosure And Characteristics Of Companies," **AOS,** 1981, Vol. 6, No. 4, pp. 355-362.)
Bradley, Hugh E. "Setting And Controlling Budgets With Regression Analysis," **MA,** 1969, Vol. 51, No. 5, pp. 31-34.
Bradley, Joseph F. "Accounting Aspects Of Protective Provisions In Industrial Preferred Stock," **AR,** 1948, Vol. 23, No. 4, pp. 385-390.
Bradlow, David A. "Positioning The Accounting Firm," **CPAJ,** 1985, Vol. 55, No. 12, pp. 10-19.
Bradow, James R. "Accounting For Deferred Charges - Is More Guidance Needed?," **MA,** 1987, Vol. 68, No. 10, pp. 51-54.
Bradshaw, Thornton F. "Financial Executive's New Place In Management," **JOA,** 1952, Vol. 93, No. 2, pp. 176-180.
Bradshaw, Thornton F. "Planning For Research," **AR,** 1954, Vol. 29, No. 2, pp. 201-207.
Brady, Daniel W. "The Strategic Forces Of Profit," **MA,** 1971, Vol. 52, No. 8, pp. 17-20.
Brady, Edward and J. C. Babbitt. "Inventory Control Systems," **MA,** 1972, Vol. 54, No. 6, pp. 42-44.
Brady, William W. "Accountant's Liability To Third Parties: The Ultramares Case," **AR,** 1938, Vol. 13, No. 4, pp. 395-399.
Braiotta, Louis and Thomas B. Hogan. "Accounting For Compensated Absences," **CPAJ,** 1981, Vol. 51, No. 12, pp. 22-27.
Braiotta, Louis, Jr. "Cash Basis Statement Of Changes," **CPAJ,** 1984, Vol. 54, No. 8, pp. 34-41.
Braitman, Howard L, James J. Klink and Bernard M. Shapiro. "Real Estate Industry Benefits From ERTA 1981," **CPAJ,** 1982, Vol. 52, No. 3, pp. 32-38.
Braly, Scott A. (Perry, Raymond E. and Scott A. Braly. "IRS Access To Audit Workpapers," **CPAJ,** 1981, Vol. 51, No. 9, pp. 13-18.)
Branch, Ben and Bruce Berkowitz. "The Predictive Accuracy Of The Business Week Earnings Forecasts," **JAAF,** 1981, Vol. 4, No. 3, pp. 215-219.
Brandes, James L. "Identifying And Recording Environmental Plant Costs," **MA,** 1977, Vol. 58, No. 10, pp. 27-31.
Brandi, Jay T. (Brown, Betty C. and Jay T. Brandi. "Security Price Reactions To Changes In Foreign Currency Translation Standards," **JAAF,** 1986, Vol. 1 (New Series), No. 3, pp. 185-205.)
Brandon, Charles H. and Jeffrey E. Jarrett. "Experimenting With Students' Ability To Forecast," **AR,** 1977, Vol. 52, No. 3, pp. 697-704.
Brandon, Charles H. and Joseph P. Matoney, Jr. "Social Responsibility Financial Statement," **MA,** 1975, Vol. 57, No. 5, pp. 31-34.
Brandon, Charles, Ralph E. Drtina and Donald Plane. "Using Modeling Languages In Mangerial Accounting: An Example For Pricing Decisions," **JAED,** 1986, Vol. 4, No. 1, pp. 69-80.
Brandstedter, Rodney. "Campaign Reporting: A Challenge For Accountants," **MA,** 1979, Vol. 61, No. 4, pp. 50-54.
Brandt, Robert F. "One World In Accounting," **JOA,** 1962, Vol. 114, No. 1, pp. 68-71.
Brantner, Paul F. "Accounting For Land Development Companies," **MA,** 1973, Vol. 55, No. 2, pp. 15-19.
Brantner, Paul F. "Multi-State Income Taxation," **MA,** 1974, Vol. 56, No. 3, pp. 20-24.
Brantner, Paul F. "Taxation And The Multinational Firm," **MA,** 1973, Vol. 55, No. 4, pp. 11-16.
Braunstein, Daniel N. and Richard W. Fortner. "The Design Of Behavioral Research," **AR,** 1968, Vol. 43, No. 2, pp. 377-383.
Braun, Melvin L. (Leight, Lester A., Melvin L. Braun and William M. Gips. "Review Of Statement On Auditing Procedure No. 47 - 'Subsequent Events'," **CPAJ,** 1972, Vol. 42, No. 2, pp. 123-126.)
Braun, Melvin L. (Wilking, S. Vincent, Melvin L. Braun and William M. Gips. "Pay And Price Control - Phase II," **CPAJ,** 1972, Vol. 42, No. 2, pp. 115-122.)
Brausch, John J. "Direct Costing: Progress Or Folly?," **JOA,** 1961, Vol. 112, No. 2, pp. 52-60.
Brausch, John J. "The Management Accountant's Role In An Office Improvement Program," **MA,** 1970, Vol. 52, No. 2, pp. 42-44.
Bravenec, Lorence L. "Subchapter S In Transition: A Comment," **JATA,** 1985, Vol. 7, No. 1, pp. 76-79.
Bravenec, L. L. (Crumbley, D. L., M. J. Epstein and L. L. Bravenec. "Tax Impact In Corporate Social Responsibility Decisions And Reporting," **AOS,** 1977, Vol. 2, No. 2, pp. 131-140.)
Brayton, Gary N. "Productivity Measure Aids In Profit Analysis," **MA,** 1985, Vol. 66, No. 7, pp. 54-58.
Bray, F. Sewell. "Recent British Accounting Developments," **AR,** 1946, Vol. 21, No. 2, pp. 199-203.
Bray, F. Sewell. "The English Universities And The Accounting Profession," **AR,** 1949, Vol. 24, No. 3, pp. 273-276.
Brazeal, Henry H., Jr. "Large Company Planning Techniques Will Work In Small Multi-Plant Companies," **MA,** 1970, Vol. 52, No. 3, pp. 21-24.
Breakstone, Arthur L. (Wolinsky, Daniel and Arthur L. Breakstone. "Reporting For The Rehabilitation And Sheltered Workshop," **JOA,** 1975, Vol. 140, No. 1, pp. 56-62.)
Breakwell, B. "Profit-Sharing And The Finance Acts 1978 To 1983: A Case For A Review Of Incentives," **ABR,** 1983-84, Vol. 14, No. 53, pp. 3-14.
Breakwell, G. H. (Morris, R. C. and G. H. Breakwell. "Manipulation Of Earnings Figures In The United Kingdom," **ABR,** 1974-75, Vol. 5, No. 19, pp. 177-184.)
Brecht, H. D. "Random Sampling: Benefits And Costs," **CPAJ,** 1983, Vol. 53, No. 9, pp. 30-35.
Breech, Ernest R. "How Did Ford Do It?," **JOA,** 1956, Vol. 101, No. 2, pp. 33-37.
Breen, Robert E. "Consolidating Financial Systems In A Diversified MNC," **CA,** 1986, Vol. 4, No. 3, pp. 25-29.
Bremser, Wayne G. "Acceptance And Continuance Of Clients," **CPAJ,** 1980, Vol. 50, No. 10, pp. 29-36.
Bremser, Wayne G. "Improving The SSARS Engagement Review," **CPAJ,** 1983, Vol. 53, No. 9, pp. 12-19.
Bremser, Wayne G. "Peer Review - A Call For Action," **CPAJ,** 1976, Vol. 46, No. 10, pp. 15-20.
Bremser, Wayne G. "Peer Review: Enhancing Quality Control," **JOA,** 1983, Vol. 156, No. 4, pp. 78-88.
Bremser, Wayne G. "Reporting On Current Replacement Costs," **MA,** 1977, Vol. 59, No. 1, pp. 33-39.
Bremser, Wayne G. "The AICPA Division For Firms: Problems And A Challenge," **JOA,** 1984, Vol. 158, No. 2, pp. 98-110.
Bremser, Wayne G. "The Earnings Characteristics Of Firms Reporting Discretionary Accounting Changes," **AR,** 1975, Vol. 50, No. 3, pp. 563-573.
Bremser, Wayne G. (Heck, J. Louis and Wayne G. Bremser. "Six Decades Of The Accounting Review: A Summary Of Author And Institutional Contributors," **AR,** 1986, Vol. 61, No. 4, pp. 735-744.)
Bremser, Wayne G., Vincent C. Brenner and Paul E. Dascher. "Schools Of Professional Accountancy: The Management Accountant's View," **MA,** 1977, Vol. 59, No. 3, pp. 14-16.
Bremser, Wayne G., Vincent C. Brenner and Paul E. Dascher. "The Feasibility Of Professional Schools: An Empirical Study," **AR,** 1977, Vol. 52, No. 2, pp. 465-473.
Brenizer, Ned W. "A System Of Man-Machine-Material Reporting," **MA,** 1969, Vol. 50, No. 9, pp. 21-22.
Brennan, David B. "Work Measurement For Control Of Clerical Costs," **MA,** 1968, Vol. 49, No. 9, pp. 42-46.
Brennan, W. John. (Rege, Udayan P., W. John Brennan and W. Harold Silvester. "Current Regulatory Practices, Corporate Financial Forecasting, And Takeover Bids," **IJAER,** 1983, Vol. 18, No. 2, pp. 171-175.)
Brennan, W. J. "Comment On Value Accounting For Currency Transactions," **ABR,** 1978-79, Vol. 9, No. 33, pp. 61-63.
Brenner, Elliot M. "Tax Planning For The Disposition Of A Subsidiary," **MA,** 1981, Vol. 63, No. 2, pp. 48-52.
Brenner, George J. "CPAs: Do You Speak Management Accounting?," **MA,** 1975, Vol. 57, No. 3, pp. 29-30.
Brenner, Michael J. "Real Estate Financial Reporting: User's Perspective," **CPAJ,** 1984, Vol. 54, No. 5, pp. 32-35.
Brenner, Vincent C. and James J. Benjamin. "Financial Reporting On Units Of General Purchasing Power," **MA,** 1976, Vol. 57, No. 12, pp. 15-18.
Brenner, Vincent C. and Robert H. Strawser. "Some Observations On Required Continuing Education," **CPAJ,** 1972, Vol. 42, No. 6, pp. 469-474.
Brenner, Vincent C. and Ronald E. Shuey. "An Empirical Study Of Support For APB Opinion No. 16," **JAR,** 1972, Vol. 10, No. 1, pp. 200-208.
Brenner, Vincent C. "Additional Comments On Student Values And Their Implication For Accounting Education," **AR,** 1974, Vol. 49, No. 3, p. 578.
Brenner, Vincent C. "Financial Statement Users' Views Of The Desirability Of Reporting Current Cost Information," **JAR,** 1970, Vol. 8, No. 2, pp. 159-166.
Brenner, Vincent C. "Some Observations On Student Values And Their Implications For Accounting Education," **AR,** 1973, Vol. 48, No. 3, pp. 605-608.
Brenner, Vincent C. (Benjamin, James J. and Vincent C. Brenner. "Reaction To NYSE White Paper's Call For Disclosure," **MA,** 1975, Vol. 56, No. 11, pp. 13-18.)
Brenner, Vincent C. (Benjamin, James J. and Vincent C. Brenner. "Perceptions Of Journal Quality," **AR,** 1974, Vol. 49, No. 2, pp. 360-362.)
Brenner, Vincent C. (Bremser, Wayne G., Vincent C. Brenner and Paul E. Dascher. "Schools Of Professional Accountancy: The Management Accountant's View," **MA,** 1977, Vol. 59, No. 3, pp. 14-16.)
Brenner, Vincent C. (Bremser, Wayne G., Vincent C. Brenner and Paul E. Dascher. "The Feasibility Of Professional Schools: An Empirical Study," **AR,** 1977, Vol. 52, No. 2, pp. 465-473.)
Brenner, Vincent C. (Hartman, Bart P., Vincent C. Brenner. Richard A. Lydecker and Jeffrey M. Wilkinson. "Mission Control Starts In The Controller's Department," **MA,** 1981, Vol. 63, No. 3, pp. 27-32.)
Brenner, Vincent C. (Spiceland, J. David, Vincent C. Brenner and Bart P. Hartman. "Standards For Programs And Schools Of Professional Accounting: Accounting Group Perceptions," **AR,** 1980, Vol. 55, No. 1, pp. 134-143.)
Brenner, Vincent C., Claude W. Carmack and Mark G. Weinstein. "An Empirical Test Of The Motivation-Hygiene Theory," **JAR,** 1971, Vol. 9, No. 2, pp. 359-366.
Brenner, Vincent C., Ronald M. Copeland, Paul E. Dascher, Arthur J. Francia, Ronald J. Patten and Robert H. Strawser. "Trials And Tribulations Of The Researcher: A Case Study," **JAR,** 1972, Vol. 10, No. 1, pp. 195-199.

Brent, Philip D. "Accounting And Law: Concurrent Practice Is In The Public Interest," JOA, 1967, Vol. 123, No. 3, pp. 38-46.

Breslin, Robert W. "Minimizing Your Legal Costs," MA, 1984, Vol. 65, No. 11, pp. 47-51.

Breu, Anthony C. "One Day Closings," MA, 1987, Vol. 68, No. 9, pp. 66-67.

Brewer, Larry W. "Determining Revenue Requirements For Regulated Utilities," MA, 1979, Vol. 61, No. 3.pp.41-44.

Brewster, Robert S. "Controlling Inventory: On-Line Computer Systems," CPAJ, 1975, Vol. 45, No. 9, pp. 35-39.

Bricker, Robert J. "Knowledge Preservation In Accounting: A Citational Study," ABACUS, 1988, Vol. 24, No. 2, pp. 120-131.

Bricker, Robert J. "Influences From Early Accounting Literature On Contemporary Research," AHJ, 1988, Vol. 15, No. 2, pp. 83-98.

Brickley, James A., Sanjai Bhagat and Ronald C. Lease. "The Impact Of Long-Range Managerial Compensation Plans On Shareholder Wealth," JAEC, 1985, Vol. 7, No. 1/3, pp. 115-129.

Briden, George E. (Rebele, James E., James A. Heintz and George E. Briden. "Independent Auditor Sensitivity To Evidence Reliability," AJPT, 1988, Vol. 8, No. 1, pp. 43-52.)

Brief, Arthur P. (Uecker, Wilfred C., Arthur P. Brief and William R. Kinney, Jr. "Perception Of The Internal And External Auditor As A Deterrrent To Corporate Irregularities," AR, 1981, Vol. 56, No. 3, pp. 465-478.)

Brief, Richard P. and Hector R. Anton. "An Index Of Growth Due To Depreciation," CAR, 1986-87, Vol. 3, No. 2, pp. 394-407.

Brief, Richard P. and Joel Owen. "Present Value Models And The Multi-Asset Problem," AR, 1973, Vol. 48, No. 4, pp. 690-695.

Brief, Richard P. and Joel Owen. "On The Bias In Accounting Allocations Under Uncertainty," JAR, 1969, Vol. 7, No. 1, pp. 12-16.

Brief, Richard P. and Joel Owen. "A Reformulation Of The Estimation Problem," JAR, 1973, Vol. 11, No. 1, pp.1-15.

Brief, Richard P. and Joel Owen. "Present Value Models And The Multi-Asset Problem: A Reply," AR, 1974, Vol. 49, No. 4, pp. 819-821.

Brief, Richard P. and Joel Owen. "The Estimation Problem In Financial Accounting," JAR, 1970, Vol. 8, No. 2, pp. 167-177.

Brief, Richard P. and Joel Owen. "Depreciation And Capital Gains: A 'New' Approach," AR, 1968, Vol. 43, No. 2, pp. 367-372.

Brief, Richard P. and Joel Owen. "A Least Squares Allocation Model," JAR, 1968, Vol. 6, No. 2, pp. 193-199.

Brief, Richard P. and Joel Owen. "Accounting For Leveraged Leases: A Comment," JAR, 1978, Vol. 16,No. 2,pp.411-413.

Brief, Richard P. "A Late Nineteenth Century Contribution To The Theory Of Depreciation," JAR, 1967, Vol. 5, No. 1, pp. 27-38.

Brief, Richard P. "A Note On 'Rediscovery' And The Rule Of 69," AR, 1977, Vol. 52. No. 4, pp. 810-812.

Brief, Richard P. "An Econometric Analysis Of Goodwill: Some Findings In A Search For Valuation Rules," AR, 1969, Vol. 44, No. 1, pp. 20-26.

Brief, Richard P. "Corporate Financial Reporting At The Turn Of The Century," JOA. 1987, Vol. 163, No. 5, pp. 142-157.

Brief, Richard P. "Depreciation Theory And Capital Gains," JAR, 1968, Vol. 6, No. 1, pp. 149-152.

Brief, Richard P. "Hicks On Accounting," AHJ, 1982, Vol. 9, No. 1, pp. 91-101.

Brief, Richard P. "Nineteenth Century Accounting Error," JAR, 1965, Vol. 3, No. 1, pp. 12-31.

Brief, Richard P. "The Accountant's Responsibility For Disclosing Bribery: An Historical Note," AHJ, 1977, Vol. 4, No. 2, pp. 97-100.

Brief, Richard P. "The Accountant's Responsibility In Historical Perspective," AR, 1975, Vol. 50, No. 2, pp. 285-297.

Brief, Richard P., Barbara Merino and Ira Weiss. "Cumulative Financial Statements," AR, 1980, Vol. 55, No. 3, pp. 480-490.

Brief, R. P. "Baily's Paradox," AHJ, 1979, Vol. 6, No. 1, pp. 93-94.

Brien, Arthur L. "Effective Reporting For Reimbursement Under Medicare," CPAJ, 1972, Vol. 42, No. 4, pp. 289-296.

Brierton, Nikki. "Managing Your Time Effectively," CA, 1988, Vol. 6, No. 2, pp. 31-39.

Briggs, Douglas H. "Information Requirements Of Users Of Published Corporate Reports - Unit Trusts," ABR, 1975-76, Vol. 6, No. 21, pp. 18-20.

Briggs, John. (Hope, Tony and John Briggs. "Accounting Policy Making - Some Lessons From The Deferred Taxation Debate," ABR, 1981-82, Vol. 12, No. 46, pp. 83-96.)

Briggs, L. L. "Accounting And The Courts," AR, 1931, Vol. 6, No. 3, pp. 184-191.

Briggs, L. L. "Accounting In Collegiate Schools Of Business," AR, 1930, Vol. 5, No. 2, pp. 175-181.

Briggs, L. L. "Asset Valuation In Dividend Decisions," AR, 1934, Vol. 9, No. 3, pp. 220-236.

Briggs, L. L. "Dividends And The General Corporation Statutes," AR, 1933, Vol. 8, No. 2, pp. 130-144.

Briggs, L. L. "Dividends On Non-Cumulative Preferred Stock," AR, 1933, Vol. 8, No. 3, pp. 224-238.

Briggs, L. L. "Property Dividends And Law," AR, 1932, Vol. 7, No. 3, pp. 169-174.

Briggs, L. L. "Rescission Of Dividends," AR, 1932, Vol. 7, No. 4, pp. 233-241.

Briggs, L. L. "Some Legal Aspects Of Stock Rights," AR, 1932, Vol. 7, No. 2, pp. 122-136.

Briggs, Roger W. (Wolk, Harry I. and Roger W. Briggs. "Accounting Research, Professors, And Practitioners: A Perspective," IJAER, 1975, Vol. 10, No. 2, pp. 47-56.)

Brigham, Eugene F. and Timothy J. Nantell. "Normalization Versus Flow Through For Utility Companies Using Liberalized Tax Depreciation," AR, 1974, Vol. 49, No. 3, pp. 436-447.

Brigham, Eugene F. "The Effects Of Alternative Depreciation Policies On Reported Profits," AR, 1968, Vol. 43, No. 1, pp. 46-61.

Brighton, Gerald D. and Robert H. Michaelsen. "Profile Of Tax Dissertations In Accounting: 1967-1984," JATA, 1985, Vol. 6, No. 2, pp. 76-91.

Brighton, Gerald D. "Accrued Expense Tax Reform - Not Ready In 1954 - Ready In 1969?," AR, 1969, Vol. 44, No. 1, pp. 137-144.

Brighton, Gerald D. "An Outline As An Aid In Teaching Tax Accounting For Property," AR, 1957, Vol. 32, No. 1, pp. 123-124.

Brighton, Gerald D. "Bad Debt Deductions Of Officer-Stockholders," JOA, 1969, Vol. 128, No. 3, pp. 49-55.

Brighton, Gerald D. "Book Income - What Is It?," MA, 1965, Vol. 47, No. 1, pp. 58-61.

Brighton, Gerald D. "Image Of The Internal Revenue Service." AR, 1964, Vol. 39, No. 2, pp. 463-467.

Brighton, Gerald D. (Bruegman, Donald C. and Gerald D. Brighton. "Institutional Accounting - How It Differs From Commercial Accounting," AR, 1963, Vol. 38, No. 4, pp. 764-770.)

Brighton, G. D. "Aid To Management Beyond The Audit," AR, 1954, Vol. 29, No. 4, pp. 584-590.

Brill, Alan E. "Reducing Conflict Between Systems Design And Computer Operations," CPAJ, 1975, Vol. 45, No. 4, pp. 39-42.

Brill, Robert J. "A Visual Aid For Explaining Sources And Applications Of Funds," AR, 1964, Vol. 39, No. 4, pp. 1014-1017.

Brill, Robert J. "Analyzing Transactions And The Statement Of Changes In Financial Position: Model," IAE, 1983, No. 1, pp. 90-94.

Briloff, Abraham J. "Accountancy And The Public Interest," AIPIA. 1986, Vol. 1, pp. 1-14.

Briloff, Abraham J. "Dirty Pooling," AR, 1967, Vol. 42, No. 3, pp. 489-496.

Briloff, Abraham J. "Do Management Services Endanger Independence And Objectivity?," CPAJ, 1987, Vol. 57, No. 8, pp. 22-29.

Briloff, Abraham J. "Estate Planning Problems Of Partners," JOA, 1961, Vol. 112, No. 4, pp. 57-64.

Briloff, Abraham J. "Let The Seller Beware," JOA, 1967, Vol. 123, No. 2, pp. 45-51.

Briloff, Abraham J. "Needed: A Revolution In The Determination And Application Of Accounting Principles," AR, 1964, Vol. 39, No. 1, pp. 12-15.

Briloff, Abraham J. "Old Myths And New Realities In Accountancy," AR, 1966, Vol. 41, No. 3, pp. 484-495.

Briloff, Abraham J. "Prescription For Change," MA, 1974, Vol. 56, No. 1, pp. 63-65.

Briloff, Abraham J. "Price Level Changes And Financial Statements At The Threshold Of The New Frontier," AR, 1961. Vol. 36, No. 4, pp. 603-607.

Briloff, Abraham J. "Price Level Changes And Financial Statements: A Critical Reappraisal," AR, 1958, Vol. 33, No. 3. pp. 380-388.

Briloff, Abraham J. "Standards Without Standards / Principles Without Principles / Fairness Without Fairness," AIA. 1986, Vol. 3, pp. 25-50.

Briloff, Abraham J. "The Mad, Mad, Mad, Mad World Of 482," JOA, 1967, Vol. 124, No. 2, pp. 44-53.

Brimson, James A. "How Advanced Manufacturing Technologies Are Reshaping Cost Management," MA, 1986, Vol. 67, No. 9, pp. 25-29.

Briner, Ernst K. "International Tax Management," MA, 1973, Vol. 54, No. 8, pp. 47-50.

Briner, Russell F. "Reporting Obligations For Comparative Financial Statements," CPAJ, 1981, Vol. 51, No. 9, pp. 19-26.

Briner, Russell F., Diane T. Pearson and James E. Gauntt, Jr. "A Microcomputer Application For Attribute Sampling," JAED, 1987, Vol. 5, No. 1, pp. 161-166.

Briner, Russell F., Frank A. Wiebe and Shaker A. Zahra. "Management Accountants: Don't Overlook Quality Circles," MA, 1984, Vol. 66, No. 6, pp. 45-49.

Brinker, Barry J. and Linda York. "Portables: Have Computer, Will Travel," CA, 1987, Vol. 5, No. 4, pp. 5-25.

Brinker, Barry J. "The New Tax Code: How It Affects Corporations." CA. 1987, Vol. 5, No. 1, pp. 3-14.

Brinkman, Donald R. "Minimizing The Loss Of Investment Tax Credits," MA, 1973, Vol. 54, No. 7, pp. 38-40.

Brinkman, Steve. "Productivity Begins With Hiring," MA, 1987. Vol. 69, No. 1, pp. 50-52.

Brink, Victor Z. "Education For Controllership," AR, 1950, Vol. 25, No. 3, pp. 251-259.

Brink, Victor Z. "How Internal Auditing Provides Management Control," JOA, 1951, Vol. 92, No. 4, pp. 421-427.

Brink, Victor Z. "Teaching A Course In Internal Auditing," AR, 1947, Vol. 22, No. 4, pp. 414-416.

Brinton, A. Donald. "Marginal Income And The Pricing Structure," MA, 1972, Vol. 53, No. 12, pp. 40-42.

Brison, Clifford S. "Components Of A Model Permanent File,"

AR, 1946, Vol. 21, No. 3, pp. 310-312.

Briston, Richard J. and Ahmed A. El-Ashker. "The Egyptian Accounting System: A Case Study In Western Influence," IJAER, 1984, Vol. 19, No. 2, pp. 129-155.

Briston, Richard J. "The Evolution Of Accounting In Developing Countries," IJAER, 1978, Vol. 14, No. 1, pp. 105-120.

Briston, R. J. and C. S. Greensted. "Shareholder Behaviour In The New Issues Market: A Final Progress Report," ABR, 1975-76, Vol. 6, No. 22, pp. 125-134.

Briston, R. J., C. R. Tomkins and D. King. "Shareholder Behaviour In The New Issue Market; A Preliminary Report," ABR, 1970-71, Vol. 1, No. 3, pp. 233-241.

Bristor, Rolland M. "Some Suggestions On The Teaching Of Principles Of Accounting," AR, 1950, Vol. 25, No. 1, pp. 96-99.

Bristor, Rolland M. "Training And Recommending Students For Accounting Work In Industry," AR, 1952, Vol. 27, No. 1, pp. 130-133.

Broadston, James A. "Charting Schedule Performance," MA, 1969, Vol. 51, No. 5, pp. 35-40.

Broadston, James A. "Learning Curve Wage Incentives," MA, 1968, Vol. 49, No. 12, pp. 15-23.

Broadston, James A. "Profit By Using Variable Time Allowances," MA, 1968, Vol. 50, No. 2, pp. 26-31.

Broadus, W. A., Jr. and Joseph D. Comtois. "The Single Audit: A Progress Report," JOA, 1987, Vol. 164, No. 1, pp. 92-101.

Broadus, W. A., Jr. and Joseph D. Comtois. "Tools For The Single Audit," JOA, 1986, Vol. 161, No. 4, pp. 73-81.

Broadus, W. A., Jr. and Joseph D. Comtois. "The Single Audit Act: A Needed Reform," JOA, 1985, Vol. 159, No. 4, pp. 62-71.

Broadus, W. A., Jr. and Joseph F. Moraglio. "Governmental Audit Standards: A New Perspective," JOA, 1982, Vol. 153, No. 5, pp. 80-90.

Broad, Samuel J. "Applicability Of Accounting Principles," JOA, 1957, Vol. 104, No. 3, pp. 31-37.

Broad, Samuel J. "Cost: Is It A Binding Principle Or Just A Means To An End?," JOA, 1954, Vol. 97, No. 5, pp. 582-586.

Broad, Samuel J. "Determining Income Under Inflationary Conditions," JOA, 1952, Vol. 93, No. 3, pp. 300-308.

Broad, Samuel J. "Recent Efforts To Increase Significance Of The Figure Of Net Income," JOA, 1950, Vol. 89, No. 5, pp. 376-381.

Broad, Samuel J. "The Capital Principle," AR, 1942, Vol. 17, No. 1, pp. 28-34.

Broad, Samuel J. "The Need For Continuing Changes In Accounting Principles And Practices," JOA, 1950, Vol. 90, No. 5, pp. 405-413.

Broad, Samuel J. "The Progress Of Auditing," JOA, 1955, Vol. 100, No. 3, pp. 38-43.

Broad, Samuel J. "Valuation Of Inventories," AR, 1950, Vol. 25, No. 3, pp. 227-235.

Broad, S. J. "Valuation Of The Business Enterprise: Comments," AR, 1936, Vol. 11, No. 1, pp. 32-34.

Broca, S. (Boritz, J. E. and S. Broca. "Scheduling Internal Audit Activities," AJPT, 1986-87, Vol. 6, No. 1, pp. 1-19.)

Brockett, P., A. Charnes, W. W. Cooper and Hong-Chul Shin. "A Chance-Constrained Programming Approach To Cost-Volume-Profit Analysis," AR, 1984, Vol. 59, No. 3, pp. 474-487.

Brockhoff, K. "A Note On External Social Reporting By German Companies: A Survey Of 1973 Company Reports," AOS, 1979, Vol. 4, No. 1/2, pp. 77-86.

Brock, Horace R. "Petroleum Accounting," JOA, 1956, Vol. 102, No. 6, pp. 53-67.

Brock, Horace. "A Look At Accounting Principles Used By Oil And Gas Producers," AR, 1958, Vol. 33, No. 1, pp. 66-71.

Brock, Horace. "Accounting For Self-Insurance Against Fire Loss - Theory V. Practice," AR, 1959, Vol. 34, No. 2, pp. 257-261.

Brock, Horace. (Klammer, Thomas P. and Horace Brock. "Resolving Accounting Issues Without A Conceptual Framework," CPAJ, 1975, Vol. 45, No. 8, pp. 15-20.)

Broden, Barry C. and Myron S. Lubell. "The Master's Degree In Taxation: An Assessment Of Its Growth And Future," JATA, 1979, Vol. 1, No. 1, pp. 5-14.

Broden, Barry C. and Stephen E. Loeb. "Professional Ethics Of CPAs In Tax Practice: An Historical Perspective," AHJ, 1983, Vol. 10, No. 2, pp. 81-97.

Broden, Barry C. "Ethical Behavior In IRS Tax Practice," JATA, 1980, Vol. 2, No. 1, pp. 19-28.

Broden, Barry C. "Tax Exempt Bond Funds: Beware Tax Traps," CPAJ, 1979, Vol. 49, No. 1, pp. 26-30.

Broden, Barry C. (Lubell, Myron S. and Barry C. Broden. "The Masters Degree In Taxation: An Academic Survey," AR, 1975, Vol. 50, No. 1, pp. 170-176.)

Broder, Bertram. "An Educational Experiment In Cost Accounting," AR, 1950, Vol. 25, No. 1, pp. 99-100.

Broder, Bertram. "The AIA Recruiting Film," AR, 1954, Vol. 29, No. 1, pp. 141-142.

Broder, Paul. (Groves, Roger, Michael Poole and Paul Broder. "Professional Commitments Of The Practising Chartered Accountant In Modern Britain," ABR, 1983-84, Vol. 14, No. 56, pp. 319-332.)

Brody, Claire. (Benis, Martin, Claire Brody and Robert T. Johnson. "Utilization Of The Small Group Approach To Teaching Intermediate Accounting," AR, 1976, Vol. 51, No. 4, pp. 894-898.)

Broecker, Douglas C. (Banick, Richard S. and Douglas C. Broecker. "Arbitration: An Option For Resolving Claim Against CPAs," JOA, 1987, Vol. 164, No. 4, pp. 124-129.)

Brogan, Susan H. and Sherry H. Hogan. "Duty Drawback: 'Found Money' In Refunds," CA, 1985, Vol. 3, pp. 19-25.

Bromage, Mary C. "A Matter Of Wording," JOA, 1963, Vol. 115, No. 1, pp. 59-62.

Bromage, Mary C. "Sentences That Make Sense," JOA, 1967, Vol. 123, No. 5, pp. 56-60.

Bromage, Mary C. "Wording The Management Audit Report," JOA, 1972, Vol. 133, No. 2, pp. 50-57.

Broman, Amy J. (Colson, Robert H., Michael W. Maher, Amy J. Broman and Pieter Tiessen. "Audit Pricing Models For Regulation Research: Reliability And Stability," RIAR, 1988, Vol. 2, pp. 61-79.)

Bromwich, Michael. "Asset Valuation With Imperfect Markets," ABR, 1974-75, Vol. 5, No. 20, pp. 242-253.

Bromwich, Michael. "Individual Purchasing Power Indices And Accounting Reports," ABR, 1974-75, Vol. 5, No. 18, pp. 118-122.

Bromwich, Michael. "Measurement Of Divisional Performance," ABR, 1972-73, Vol. 3, No. 10, pp. 123-132.

Bromwich, Michael. "Some Problems With Replacement Cost Asset Measurement For External Accounting Reports With Imperfect Markets," ABACUS, 1983, Vol. 19, No. 2, pp. 148-161.

Bromwich, Michael. "The General Validity Of Certain 'Current' Value Asset Valuation Bases," ABR, 1976-77, Vol. 7, No. 28, pp. 242-249.

Bromwich, Michael. "The Possibility Of Partial Accounting Standards," AR, 1980, Vol. 55, No. 2, pp. 288-300.

Bromwich, Michael. "The Use Of Present Value Valuation Models In Published Accounting Reports," AR, 1977, Vol. 52, No. 3, pp. 587-596.

Bromwich, M. and M. C. Wells. "The Usefulness Of A Measure Of Wealth," ABACUS, 1983, Vol. 19, No. 2, pp. 119-129.

Brooker, R. P. and J. J. Staunton. "On The Independence Of Auditors," ABACUS, 1966, Vol. 2, No. 2, pp. 172-179.

Brooker, R. P. and T. M. F. Smith. "Business Failures - The English Insolvency Statistics," ABACUS, 1965, Vol. 1, No. 2, pp. 131-149.

Brooker, R. P. "An Aspect Of The Use Of Accounts As Evidence." ABACUS, 1969, Vol. 5, No. 1, pp. 64-77.

Brooker, R. P. "The Background Of Garner V. Murray," ABACUS, 1968, Vol. 4, No. 1, pp. 73-79.

Brooker, R. P. "The Dissolution Of Partnership - Garner V. Murray," ABACUS, 1967, Vol. 3, No. 1, pp. 36-54.

Brooke, Winston. "Training Staff In Use Of Adding Machine," JOA, 1954, Vol. 97, No. 1, pp. 62-63.

Brookner, Lester and Ernest Heilman. "Technical Assistance In Accounting In Turkey," AR, 1960, Vol. 35, No. 1, pp. 33-36.

Brooks, Burton W., Jr. (Melton, Edgar P. and Burton W. Brooks, Jr. "Impact Of GAAP On The Profitability Of Mortgage Bankers," MA, 1978, Vol. 60, No. 6, pp. 37-43.)

Brooks, Donald E. and Bhaskar Bhave. "New And Innovative Financial Instruments Part I," CPAJ, 1987, Vol. 57, No. 7. pp. 32-37.

Brooks, Donald E. and Bhaskar Bhave. "New And Innovative Financial Instruments Part II," CPAJ, 1987, Vol. 57, No. 8. pp. 38-45.

Brooks, Eugene H. (Baber, William R., Eugene H. Brooks and William E. Ricks. "An Empirical Investigation Of The Market For Audit Services In The Public Sector," JAR, 1987, Vol. 25, No. 2, pp. 293-305.)

Brooks, Frederick V. (Courtney, Harley M. and Frederick V. Brooks. "Cumulative Probabilistic Sales Forecasting," MA, 1972, Vol. 53, No. 11, pp. 44-47.)

Brooks, Kenneth and Richard Schroeder. "Management Strategy In A Large Accounting Firm: A Comment," AR, 1979, Vol. 54, No. 1, pp. 221-223.

Brooks, LeRoy D. and Dale Buckmaster. "On Monetary Working Capital Maintenance: Theory And Implementation," IJAER, 1987, Vol. 22, No. 2, pp. 103-114.

Brooks, LeRoy D. (Buckmaster, Dale and LeRoy D. Brooks. "The Effects Of Price-Level Changes On Operating Income," CPAJ, 1974, Vol. 44, No. 5, pp. 49-53.)

Brooks, LeRoy. (Buckmaster, Dale and LeRoy Brooks. "Accounting For Interest And Long-Term Debt In An Inflationary Period," MA, 1982, Vol. 63, No. 11, pp. 26-29.)

Brooks, L. J., Jr. "An Attitude Survey Approach To The Social Audit: The Southampton Press Experience," AOS, 1980, Vol. 5, No. 3, pp. 341-356.

Broom, H. N. "Method Of Accounting For Inter-Departmental Profits," AR, 1948, Vol. 23, No. 4, pp. 417-420.

Broom, H. N. "Modified Tabular Presentation Of Gross Profit Variations," AR, 1950, Vol. 25, No. 2, pp. 193-194.

Brophy, James J. "Audits Of Insurance Companies," JOA, 1956, Vol. 101, No. 6, pp. 29-33.

Brosnan, William T. (Vangermeersch, Richard and William T. Brosnan. "Enhancing Revenues Via Distribution Cost Control." MA, 1985, Vol. 67, No. 2, pp. 56-60.)

Broucek, Gerald R. "Computer Operation By A CPA Firm," JOA, 1960. Vol. 109, No. 6, pp. 47-50.

Brouwer, Curt. "Measuring The Division Manager's Performance," MA, 1984, Vol. 66, No. 6, pp. 30-33.

Brownell, Peter and Mark Hirst. "Reliance On Accounting Information, Budgetary Participation, And Task Uncertainty: Test Of A Three-Way Interaction," JAR, 1986, Vol. 24. No. 2, pp. 241-249.

Brownell, Peter and Morris McInnes. "Budgetary Participation, Motivation, And Managerial Performance," AR, 1986, Vol. 61. No. 4, pp. 587-600.

Brownell, Peter. "A Field Study Examination Of Budgetary Participation And Locus Of Control," AR, 1982, Vol. 57, No. 4. pp. 766-777.

Brownell, Peter. "Budgetary Systems And The Control Of Functionally Differentiated Organizational Activities,"

JAR, 1985, Vol. 23, No. 2, pp. 502-512.

Brownell, Peter. "Participation In The Budgeting Process - When It Works And When It Doesn't," JAL, 1982, Vol. 1, pp. 124-153.

Brownell, Peter. "Participation In Budgeting, Locus Of Control And Organizational Effectiveness," AR, 1981, Vol. 56, No. 4, pp. 844-860.

Brownell, Peter. "The Motivational Impact Of Management-By-Exception In A Budgetary Context," JAR, 1983, Vol. 21, No. 2, pp. 456-472.

Brownell, Peter. "The Role Of Accounting Data In Performance Evaluation, Budgetary Participation, And Organizational Effectiveness," JAR, 1982, Vol. 20, No. 1, pp. 12-27.

Brownell, P. "Leadership Style, Budgetary Participation And Managerial Behavior," AOS, 1983, Vol. 8, No. 4, pp. 307-322.

Brownell, P. (Chenhall, R. H. and P. Brownell. "The Effect Of Participative Budgeting On Job Satisfaction And Performance: Role Ambiguity As An Intervening Variable," AOS, 1988, Vol. 13, No. 3, pp. 225-234.)

Browne, Dudley E. "Preserving The Capability For Accounting Change," MA, 1972, Vol. 53, No. 8, pp. 13-16.

Browne, Dudley E. "Progress In Corporate Financial Reporting," MA, 1969, Vol. 51, No. 1, pp. 7-9.

Browne, Dudley E. "The New Financial Executive," JOA, 1965, Vol. 119, No. 2, pp. 40-44.

Browne, Dudley E. "The Risk/Reward Relationship In Military Procurement," MA, 1971, Vol. 52, No. 9, pp. 9-12.

Browne, Rollin. "Adjustment Of Tax Basis For Depreciation And Depletion: How Present Law Penalizes Taxpayer," JOA, 1950, Vol. 89, No. 3, pp. 192-202.

Brownlee, E. Richard, II and S. David Young. "Financial Disclosure Regulation And Its Critics," JAED, 1986, Vol. 4, No. 1, pp. 113-126.

Brownlee, E. Richard, II and S. David Young. "The SEC And Mandated Disclosure: At The Crossroads," ACCHOR, 1987, Vol. 1, No. 3, pp. 17-24.

Brownlee, E. Richard, II and S. David Young. "Pension Accounting: A New Proposal," CPAJ, 1985, Vol. 55, No. 7, pp. 28-35.

Brownlee, E. Richard, II. "Actuarial Cost Methods: A Primer," JAED, 1985, Vol. 3, No. 2, pp. 163-169.

Brownlee, E. Richard, II. "Capitalizing On Excess Pension Assets," MA, 1986, Vol. 67, No. 7, pp. 43-47.

Brown, Abbott L. (Mills, Robert H. and Abbott L. Brown. "Soviet Economic Development And Accounting," JOA, 1966, Vol. 121, No. 6, pp. 40-46.)

Brown, Arthur A. and Leslie G. Peck. "How Electronic Machines Handle Clerical Work," JOA, 1955, Vol. 99, No. 1, pp. 31-37.

Brown, Betty C. and Jay T. Brandi. "Security Price Reactions To Changes In Foreign Currency Translation Standards," JAAF, 1986, Vol. 1 (New Series), No. 3, pp. 185-205.

Brown, Betty. "The Relationship Between Firm Attributes And Early Adoption Of The Foreign Currency Translation Standard, SFAS No. 52: An Empirical Investigation," IJAER, 1985, Vol. 21, No. 1, pp. 1-19.

Brown, Clifford D. and Priscilla Burnaby. "The Evolution Of The Single Audit: A 20-Year Process," ACCHOR, 1988, Vol. 2, No. 2, pp. 47-52.

Brown, Clifford D. "The Emergence Of Income Reporting," IJAER, 1975, Vol. 10, No. 2, pp. 85-107.

Brown, Clifton E. and Ira Solomon. "Effects Of Outcome Information On Evaluations Of Management Decisions," AR, 1987, Vol. 62, No. 3, pp. 564-577.

Brown, Clifton. "Diagnostic Inference In Performance Evaluation: Effects Of Cause And Event Covariation And Similarity," CAR, 1987-88, Vol. 4, No. 1, pp. 111-126.

Brown, Clifton. "Effects Of Dynamic Task Environment On The Learning Of Standard Cost Variance Significance," JAR, 1983, Vol. 21, No. 2, pp. 413-431.

Brown, Clifton. "Human Information Processing For Decisions To Investigate Cost Variances," JAR, 1981, Vol. 19, No. 1, pp. 62-85.

Brown, C. "Causal Reasoning In Performance Assessment: Effects Of Cause And Effect Temporal Order And Covariation," AOS, 1985, Vol. 10, No. 3, pp. 255-266.

Brown, E. Carey. (Moonitz, Maurice and E. Carey Brown. "The Annuity Method Of Estimating Depreciation," AR, 1939, Vol. 14, No. 4, pp. 424-429.)

Brown, Gene M. "Putting The Corporate Image To Work In The Financial Community," CA, 1986, Vol. 4, No. 3, pp. 4-8.

Brown, George H. "Census Projections: 1970 To 1985," MA, 1973, Vol. 54, No. 7, pp. 11-14.

Brown, Harry G. "Compilation And Review - A Step Forward?," CPAJ, 1979, Vol. 49, No. 5, pp. 18-24.

Brown, Harry G. "Division Of Retained Earnings To Reflect Business Needs," AR, 1957, Vol. 32, No. 2, pp. 258-263.

Brown, Harry G. "Management Counseling For Small Business Firms," JOA, 1955, Vol. 100, No. 1, pp. 36-41.

Brown, Harry L. "Auditing Computer Systems," MA, 1972, Vol. 54, No. 3, pp. 23-26.

Brown, Harry L. "Current Problems Of Real-Time Auditing," MA, 1969, Vol. 50, No. 9, pp. 53-54.

Brown, Harry L. "User Control Of Data Processing," MA, 1976, Vol. 57, No. 9, pp. 22-26.

Brown, H. Donald and Richard C. Burke. "Accounting Education: A Learning-Styles Study Of Professional-Technical And Future Adaptation Issues," JAED, 1987, Vol. 5, No. 2, pp. 187-206.

Brown, James F. Jr and Thomas E. Balke. "Do Accountants Need More Education?," MA, 1982, Vol. 64,No. 5,pp.26-29.

Brown, James F., Jr. and Thomas E. Balke. "Accounting

Intending To Seek AACSB Accreditation," IAE, 1983, No. 1, pp. 50-59.

Brown, James F., Jr. "How U.S. Firms Conduct Strategic Planning," MA, 1986, Vol. 67, No. 8, pp. 38-44.

Brown, James G., Jr. and John A. Andersen. "Sheltering Tax Dollars - Part I," CPAJ, 1983, Vol. 53, No. 5, pp. 30-43.

Brown, James G., Jr. and John A. Andersen. "Sheltering Tax Dollars - Part II," CPAJ, 1983, Vol. 53, No. 6, pp. 34-39.

Brown, James J. "Control In Multi-Division Operations," MA, 1969, Vol. 51, No. 2, pp. 18-20.

Brown, Judy. "Designing An Accounting System For A Small Business," MA, 1975, Vol. 56, No. 12, pp. 27-30.

Brown, Lawrence D. and John C. Gardner. "Applying Citation Analysis To Evaluate The Research Contributions Of Accounting Faculty And Doctoral Programs," AR, 1985, Vol. 60, No. 2, pp. 262-277.

Brown, Lawrence D. and John C. Gardner. "Using Citation Analysis To Assess The Impact Of Journals And Articles On Contemporary Accounting Research (CAR)," JAR, 1985, Vol. 23, No. 1, pp. 84-109.

Brown, Lawrence D. and Mark E. Zmijewski. "The Effect Of Labor Strikes On Security Analysts' Forecast Superiority And On The Association Between Risk-Adjusted Stock Returns And Unexpected Earnings," CAR, 1987-88, Vol. 4, No. 1, pp. 61-75.

Brown, Lawrence D. and Michael S. Rozeff. "Adaptive Expectations, Time-Series Models, And Analyst Forecast Revision," JAR, 1979, Vol. 17, No. 2, pp. 341-351.

Brown, Lawrence D. and Michael S. Rozeff. "Univariate Time-Series Models Of Quarterly Accounting Earnings Per Share: A Proposed Model," JAR, 1979, Vol. 17, No. 1, pp. 179-189.

Brown, Lawrence D. and Michael S. Rozeff. "The Predictive Value Of Interim Reports For Improving Forecasts Of Future Quarterly Earnings," AR, 1979, Vol. 54, No. 3, pp. 585-591.

Brown, Lawrence D. "Accounting Changes And The Accuracy Of Analysts' Earnings Forecasts," JAR, 1983, Vol. 21, No. 2, pp. 432-443.

Brown, Lawrence D. "Discussion Of: 'Market Reactions To Mandated Interest Capitalization'," CAR, 1985-86, Vol. 2, No. 2, pp. 252-258.

Brown, Lawrence D., Gordon D. Richardson and Steven J. Schwager. "An Information Interpretation Of Financial Analyst Superiority In Forecasting Earnings," JAR, 1987, Vol. 25, No. 1, pp. 49-67.

Brown, Lawrence D., John S. Hughes, Michael S. Rozeff and James H. VanderWeide. "Expectations Data And The Predictive Value Of Interim Reporting: A Comment," JAR, 1980, Vol. 18, No. 1, pp. 278-288.

Brown, Lawrence D., Paul A. Griffin, Robert L. Hagerman and Mark E. Zmijewski. "An Evaluation Of Alternative Proxies For The Market's Assessment Of Unexpected Earnings," JAEC, 1987, Vol. 9, No. 2, pp. 159-193.

Brown, Lawrence D., Robert L. Hagerman, Paul A. Griffin and Mark E. Zmijewski. "Security Analyst Superiority Relative To Univariate Time-Series Models In Forecasting Quarterly Earnings," JAEC, 1987, Vol. 9, No. 1, pp. 61-87.

Brown, Lawrence D., Ronald J. Huefner and Joseph Weintrop. "Financial Data Bases In Accounting Doctoral Programs," IAE, 1988, Vol. 3, No. 2, pp. 228-240.

Brown, L. D., J. C. Gardner and M. A. Vasarhelyi. "An Analysis Of The Research Contributions Of 'Accounting, Organizations And Society': 1976-1984," AOS, 1987, Vol. 12, No. 2, pp. 193-204.

Brown, Marilyn V. "Auditors And Internal Controls: An Analyst's View," CPAJ, 1977, Vol. 47, No. 9, pp. 27-32.

Brown, Paul R. and Phillip E. Lint. "Co-Teaching: A Key To Auditing Instruction," JOA, 1982, Vol. 154, No. 3, pp. 94-98.

Brown, Paul R. and Vijay Karan. "One Approach For Assessing The Operational Nature Of Auditing Standards: An Analysis Of SAS 9," AJPT, 1986-87, Vol. 6, No. 1, pp. 134-147.

Brown, Paul R. "A Descriptive Analysis Of Select Input Bases Of The Financial Accounting Standards Board," JAR, 1981, Vol. 19, No. 1, pp. 232-246.

Brown, Paul R. "FASB Responsiveness To Corporate Input," JAAF, 1982, Vol. 5, No. 4, pp. 282-290.

Brown, Paul R. "Independent Auditor Judgment In The Evaluation Of Internal Audit Functions," JAR, 1983, Vol. 21, No. 2, pp. 444-455.

Brown, Paul R. (Ashton, Robert H. and Paul R. Brown. "Descriptive Modeling Of Auditors' Internal Control Judgments: Replication And Extension," JAR, 1980, Vol. 18, No. 1, pp. 269-277.)

Brown, Pembroke H. "The Federal Regulatory Commissions," AR, 1943, Vol. 18, No. 3, pp. 244-248.

Brown, Philip and Ray Ball. "Some Preliminary Findings On The Association Between The Earnings Of A Firm, Its Industry, And The Economy," JAR, 1967, Vol. 5, Supp., pp. 55-77.

Brown, Philip. (Ball, Ray and Philip Brown. "An Empirical Evaluation Of Accounting Income Numbers," JAR, 1968, Vol. 6, No. 2, pp. 159-178.)

Brown, P. (Bazley, M., P. Brown and H. Y. Izan. "An Analysis Of Lease Disclosures By Australian Companies," ABACUS, 1985, Vol. 21, No. 1, pp. 44-62.)

Brown, Ray L. "Management Accountants: Are You Ready For VAT?," MA, 1981, Vol. 63, No. 5, pp. 40-47.

Brown, Ray L. (Neumann, Bruce R., James D. Suver and Ray L. Brown. "Accountants' Role In Zero-Base Budgeting," CPAJ,

1978, Vol. 48, No. 1, pp. 23-28.)

Brown, Richard E. "The Expectations Gap: An Added Dimension - The Case Of Government Auditing," RIAR, 1987, Vol. 1, pp. 139-164.

Brown, Robert D., Ruurd G. Leegstra and Lloyd J. Looram. "Unitary Tax: At The Crossroads? - Part II," CPAJ, 1985, Vol. 55, No. 7, pp. 36-41.

Brown, Robert D., Ruurd G. Leegstra and Lloyd J. Looram. "Unitary Tax: At The Crossroads? - Part I," CPAJ, 1985, Vol. 55, No. 5, pp. 18-25.

Brown, Robert Moren. "Short-Range Market Reaction To Changes To LIFO Accounting Using Preliminary Earnings Announcement Dates," JAR, 1980, Vol. 18, No. 1, pp. 38-63.

Brown, Robert M. and Larry N. Killough. "How PCs Can Solve The Cost Allocation Problem," MA, 1988, Vol. 70, No. 5, pp. 34-38.

Brown, Robert M. (Roth, Harold P. and Robert M. Brown. "Post-Auditing Capital Investments Using IRR And NPV Models," MA, 1982, Vol. 63, No. 8, pp. 29-33.)

Brown, Robert O. "College Entrance Tests And Accounting Grades," AR, 1964, Vol. 39, No. 2, pp. 481-486.

Brown, Robert O. "Predictions Of Accounting Grades," AR, 1966, Vol. 41, No. 2, pp. 340-343.

Brown, Robert O. "Small Business Controls: The Case A Job Shop," MA, 1967, Vol. 48, No. 7, pp. 51-54.

Brown, Robert O. "Using Appraisal Information," MA, 1969, Vol. 51, No. 4, pp. 47-48.

Brown, Russell S. "Measuring Manufacturing Performance: A Targeting Approach," MA, 1980, Vol. 61, No. 12, pp. 25-28.

Brown, R. Gene. "Automation, Labor Contracts, And CPAs," JOA, 1964, Vol. 117, No. 1, pp. 49-53.

Brown, R. Gene. "Changing Audit Objectives And Techniques," AR, 1962, Vol. 37, No. 4, pp. 696-703.

Brown, R. Gene. "Objective Internal Control Evaluation," JOA, 1962, Vol. 114, No. 5, pp. 50-56.

Brown, R. Gene. "Statistical Sampling Tables For Auditors," JOA, 1961, Vol. 111, No. 5, pp. 46-54.

Brown, Sandford H. "Teaching The Funds Statement - A Conceptual Approach," AR, 1964, Vol. 39, No. 3, pp. 756-759.

Brown, Scott W. (Albrecht, W. Steve, Scott W. Brown and David R. Field. "Toward Increased Job Satisfaction Of Practicing CPAs," JOA, 1981, Vol. 152, No. 2, pp. 61-68.)

Brown, Shari H. (Copeland, Ronald M., Ronald L. Taylor and Shari H. Brown. "Observation Error And Bias In Accounting Research," JAR, 1981, Vol. 19, No. 1, pp. 197-207.)

Brown, Victor H. "Rate Of Return: Some Comments On Its Applicability In Capital Budgeting," AR, 1961, Vol. 36, No. 1, pp. 50-62.

Brown, Victor H. "The Tension Between Management Accounting And Financial Reporting," MA, 1987, Vol. 68, No. 11, pp. 39-41.

Brown, William G., Jr. "Exploring Forecast Disclosure," MA, 1974, Vol. 56, No. 6, pp. 19-22.

Brown, William J. (Hanson, Robert E. and William J. Brown. "CPAs' Workpapers: The IRS Zeros In," JOA, 1981, Vol. 152, No. 1, pp. 68-77.)

Browse, R. H. "Tank Content Measurement For Verification Of Liquid Inventory," JOA, 1953, Vol. 95, No. 1, pp. 60-63.

Brozey, Lois A. "Modernizing A Laundry's Accounting System," MA, 1982, Vol. 63, No. 11, pp. 55-59.

Brubaker, John A. "A Data Processing Program For Hospitals," MA, 1973, Vol. 54, No. 9, pp. 21-25.

Bruegelmann, Thomas M., Gaile A. Haessly, Claire P. Wolfangel and Michael Schiff. "How Variable Costing Is Used In Pricing Decisions," MA, 1985, Vol. 66, No. 10, pp. 58-61.

Bruegman, Donald C. and Gerald D. Brighton. "Institutional Accounting - How It Differs From Commercial Accounting," AR, 1963, Vol. 38, No. 4, pp. 764-770.

Brueningsen, Arthur F. "Kodak's Financial Information And Reporting System," MA, 1975, Vol. 57, No. 3, pp. 21-24.

Brueningsen, Arthur F. "SCAT II - A Process For Planning," MA, 1977, Vol. 59, No. 6, pp. 57-61.

Brueningsen, Arthur F. "SCAT - A Process Of Alternatives," MA, 1976, Vol. 58, No. 5, pp. 55-60.

Brugge, W. G. "The Accountancy Profession In Greece," AR, 1963, Vol. 38, No. 3, pp. 596-600.

Brumfield, Craig A., Robert K. Elliott and Peter D. Jacobson. "Business Risk And The Audit Process," JOA, 183, Vol. 155, No. 4, pp. 60-69.

Brumit, Frank. "Toward Effective Computer Utilization," MA, 1968, Vol. 50, No. 4, pp. 19-23.

Brummet, R. Lee, Eric G. Flamholtz and William C. Pyle. "Human Resource Measurement - A Challenge For Accountants," AR, 1968, Vol. 43, No. 2, pp. 217-224.

Brummet, R. Lee, Eric G. Flamholtz and William C. Pyle. "Human Resource Accounting: A Tool To Increase Managerial Effectiveness," MA, 1969, Vol. 51, No. 2, pp. 12-15.

Brummet, R. Lee. "Direct Costing - Should It Be A Controversial Issue?," AR, 1955, Vol. 30, No. 3, pp. 439-443.

Brummet, R. Lee. "Internationalism And The Future Of Accounting Education," IJAER, 1975, Vol. 11, No. 1, pp. 161-165.

Brummet, R. Lee. "Total Performance Measurement," MA, 1973, Vol. 55, No. 5, pp. 11-15.

Brummet, R. Lee. "Try This On Your Class, Professor - A Rejoinder," AR, 1957, Vol. 32, No. 3, pp. 480-484.

Brummet, R. Lee. (Nikolai, Loren A., John D. Bazley and R. Lee Brummet. "The Measurement Of Corporate Environmental Activity," MA, 1976, Vol. 57, No. 12, pp. 38-40.)

Brummet, R. L. and D. A. Thomas. "Accounting System For

Home Builders Aids Control," JOA, 1952, Vol. 94, No. 5, pp. 570-575.

Brundage, Marjorie U. and John Leslie Livingstone. "Simulation On A Time-Sharing Computer Utility System," AR, 1969, Vol. 44, No. 3, pp. 539-545.

Brundage, Percival F. "Influence Of Government Regulation On Development Of Today's Accounting Practices," JOA, 1950, Vol. 90, No. 5, pp. 384-391.

Brundage, Percival F. "Pension Plans From An Accountant's Point Of View," JOA, 1950, Vol. 89, No. 1, pp. 8-15.

Brundage, Percival. "Conclusions OF AIA Study Group On Business Income," JOA, 1952, Vol. 93, No. 2, pp. 190-198.

Bruns, William J. "Behavioral Science In The Accounting Curriculum," AR, 1972, Vol. 47, No. 3, pp. 591-595.

Bruns, William J., Jr. and John H. Waterhouse. "Budgetary Control And Organization Structure," JAR, 1975, Vol. 13, No. 2, pp. 177-203.

Bruns, William J., Jr. "Accounting Information And Decision-Making: Some Behavioral Hypotheses," AR, 1968, Vol. 43. No. 3, pp. 469-480.

Bruns, William J., Jr. "Business Games In Accounting Education." AR, 1965, Vol. 40, No. 3, pp. 650-653.

Bruns, William J., Jr. "Inventory Valuation And Management Decisions," AR, 1965, Vol. 40, No. 2, pp. 345-357.

Bruns, William J., Jr. (McKinnon, Sharon M. and William J. Bruns, Jr. "Evaluating Tasks For Operational Control," MA, 1984, Vol. 66, No. 4, pp. 60-63.)

Bruns, William. "The Accounting Period And Its Effect Upon Management Decisions," JAR, 1966, Vol. 4, Supp., pp. 1-14.

Brunton, Nancy M. "Evaluation Of Overhead Allocations," MA, 1988, Vol. 70, No. 1, pp. 22-26.

Bruschi, William C. "Issues Surrounding Qualifying Experience Requirements," JOA, 1969, Vol. 127, No. 3, pp. 47-54.

Brush, Lauren F. "Accounting Curricula," AR, 1944, Vol. 19, No. 4, pp. 435-438.

Brush, Lauren F. "Graphic Analysis Of Expense," AR, 1943, Vol. 18. No. 4, pp. 331-337.

Bruttomesso, Raymond I. and J. Edward Ketz. "Historical Cost And General Price Level Tax Rates In Seven Industries," JATA, 1982, Vol. 3, No. 2, pp. 30-36.

Bryant, David W. (Krogstad, Jack L., Gary Grudnitski and David W. Bryant. "PERT And PERT/Cost For Audit Planning And Control," JOA, 1977, Vol. 144, No. 5, pp. 82-91.)

Bryant, Julie V. "Proposed: A New Statement Of Changes," MA, 1984, Vol. 65, No. 10, pp. 49-52.

Bryant, Keith, Jr. and Carolyn V. Phillips. "Interest On Equity Capital And CASB Standard 414," MA, 1978, Vol. 60, No. 2, pp. 38-41.

Bryant, Keith, Jr. "How A Rental Apartment Was Converted To A Condominium," MA, 1979, Vol. 61, No. 1, pp. 52-57.

Bryant, Murray J. and Mary Claire Mahaney. "The Politics Of Standard Setting," MA, 1981, Vol. 62, No. 9, pp. 26-34.

Bryan, E. Lewis and L. Stephen Cash. "Forgiveness Of Debt - Income Or Basis Adjustment?," CPAJ, 1985, Vol. 55, No. 8, pp. 30-35.

Bryan, E. Lewis and Robert W. Rouse. "Problems Of The Small Business Audit," CPAJ, 1984, Vol. 54, No. 9, pp. 11-17.

Bryan, E. Lewis, Alison L. Drews and G. Thomas Friedlob. "Delphic Choice Of Accounting Periodicals For University Libraries," JAED, 1987, Vol. 5, No. 1, pp. 167-174.

Bryan, Robert F. "How A Risk Capital Investor Tests Financial Management," JOA, 1952, Vol. 93, No. 5, pp. 568-570.

Bryson, Roscoe Eugene, Jr. "Perry Mason," AHJ, 1975, Vol. 2, No. 1-4, pp. 64-67.

Bublitz, Bruce and Robert Kee. "Do We Need Sunset Requirements For FASB Pronouncements?," JAAF, 1984, Vol. 7, No. 2, pp. 123-137.

Bublitz, Bruce and Robert Kee. "Measures Of Research Productivity," IAE, 1984, No. 1, pp. 39-60.

Bublitz, Bruce O. and Gilroy J. Zuckerman. "Discounting Deferred Taxes: A New Approach," AIA, 1988, Vol. 6, pp. 55-70.

Bublitz, Bruce, Thomas J. Frecka and James C. McKeown. "Market Association Tests And FASB Statement No. 33 Disclosures: A Reexamination," JAR, 1985, Vol. 23, Supp., pp. 1-23.

Bublitz, Bruce. (Cargile, Barney R. and Bruce Bublitz. "Factors Contributing To Published Research By Accounting Faculties," AR, 1986, Vol. 61, No. 1, pp. 158-178.)

Bublitz, Bruce. (Kee, Robert and Bruce Bublitz. "The Role Of Payback In The Investment Process," ABR, 1988, Vol. 18, No. 70, pp. 149-156.)

Bublitz, Bruce. (Stone, Mary and Bruce Bublitz. "An Analysis Of The Reliability Of The FASB Data Bank Of Changing Price And Pension Information," AR, 1984, Vol. 59, No. 3, pp. 469-473.)

Buchanan, Harold, II and Bruce R. Gaumnitz. "Accountants And 'Insider' Trading," ACCHOR, 1987, Vol. 1, No. 4, pp. 7-12.

Buchanan, Philip G. (Cao, Le Thi and Phillip G. Buchanan. "The Integration Of Behavioral Accounting In Graduate Accounting Curricula," JAED, 1985, Vol. 3, No. 2, pp. 115-121.)

Buchele, Robert. (Kircher, Paul and Robert Buchele. "How To Recruit Accounting Personnel," JOA, 1955, Vol. 99, No. 5, pp. 54-59.)

Buchenroth, Kenneth J. "Motivation: Financial And Nonfinancial," MA, 1969, Vol. 51, No. 6, pp. 15-16.

Buchholz, David L. and Joseph F. Moraglio. "IRS Access To Auditors' Work Papers: The Supreme Court Decision," JOA, 1984, Vol. 158, No. 3, pp. 91-107.

Buchmann, **Bettina.** (Schiff, Jonathan B. and Bettina Buchmann. "Shelf Registration Rule 415," **CA**, 1986, Vol. 4, No. 1, pp. 17-23.)

Buchmann, **Thomas A.** and John A. Tracy. "Obtaining Responses To Sensitive Questions: Conventional Questionnaire Versus Randomized Response Technique," **JAR**, 1982, Vol. 20, No. 1, pp. 263-271.

Buchman, **Thomas A.** and Larry A. Friedman. "Accounting For Certain Marketable Securities," **MA**, 1977, Vol. 58, No. 9, pp. 42-44.

Buchman, **Thomas A.** "The Reliability Of Internal Auditors' Working Papers," **AJPT**, 1983-84, Vol. 3, No. 1, pp. 92-103.

Buchman, **Thomas A.** (Geurts, Michael D. and Thomas A. Buchman. "Accounting For 'Shocks' In Forecasts," **MA**, 1981, Vol. 62, No. 10, pp. 21-26.)

Buchman, **Thomas.** (White, Gary E. and Thomas Buchman. "The Continuing Education Requirement: How Effective?," **CPAJ**, 1977, Vol. 47, No. 12, pp. 11-16.)

Buchman, **T. A.** "An Effect Of Hindsight On Predicting Bankruptcy With Accounting Information," **AOS**, 1985, Vol. 10, No. 3, pp. 267-286.

Buckland, **R.** and E. W. Davis. "Barriers To Entry In The Unlisted Securities Market: The Significance Of Administrative Expenses," **ABR**, 1986-87, Vol. 17, No. 68, pp. 301-310.

Buckley, **Adrian** and Eugene McKenna. "Budgetary Control And Business Behaviour," **ABR**, 1971-72, Vol. 2, No. 6, pp. 137-150.

Buckley, **Adrian** and Eugene McKenna. "The Practising Chartered Accountant - Job Attitudes And Professional Values," **ABR**, 1972-73, Vol. 3, No. 11, pp. 197-204.

Buckley, **Adrian.** "A Note On Stock Dividends," **ABR**, 1974-75, Vol. 5, No. 17, pp. 53-60.

Buckley, **Adrian.** "A Profile Of Industrial Acquisitions In 1971," **ABR**, 1971-72, Vol. 2, No. 8, pp. 243-252.

Buckley, **Adrian.** "Beta Geared And Ungeared," **ABR**, 1980-81, Vol. 11, No. 42, pp. 121-126.

Buckley, **Adrian.** "The Distorting Effect Of Surplus Advance Corporation Tax In Project Appraisal," **ABR**, 1974-75, Vol. 5, No. 19, pp. 168-176.

Buckley, **A. A.** "Some Guidelines For Acquisitions," **ABR**, 1970-71, Vol. 1, No. 3, pp. 215-232.

Buckley, **David A.** "Current Problems Of Federal Taxation," **AR**, 1936, Vol. 11, No. 2, pp. 183-184.

Buckley, **John W.** and James R. Goode. "Inventory Valuation And Income Measurement: An Improved System Of Analysis," **ABACUS**, 1976, Vol. 12, No. 1, pp. 34-48.

Buckley, **John W.** and John J. McDonough. "Accounting As A Pluralistic Profession In Practice And Education," **CPAJ**, 1972, Vol. 42, No. 11, pp. 923-929.

Buckley, **John W.** "A Perspective On Professional Accounting Education," **JOA**, 1970, Vol. 130, No. 2, pp. 41-47.

Buckley, **John W.** "Medicare And Accounting," **AR**, 1966, Vol. 41, No. 1, pp. 75-82.

Buckley, **John W.** "Programmed And Non-Programmed Instruction: Integration Criteria In Curriculum Design," **AR**, 1969, Vol. 44, No. 2, pp. 389-397.

Buckley, **John W.** "Programmed Instruction: With Emphasis On Accounting," **AR**, 1967, Vol. 42, No. 3, pp. 572-582.

Buckley, **John W.** "The FASB And Impact Analysis," **MA**, 1976, Vol. 57, No. 10, pp. 13-17.

Buckley, **John W.,** Paul Kircher and Russell L. Mathews. "Methodology In Accounting Theory," **AR**, 1968, Vol. 43, No. 2, pp. 274-283.

Buckley, **J. W.** "Operational Audits By Public Accountants," **ABACUS**, 1966, Vol. 2, No. 2, pp. 159-171.

Buckley, **J. W.** "Policy Models In Accounting: A Critical Commentary," **AOS**, 1980, Vol. 5, No. 1, pp. 49-64.

Buckman, **A. G.** and Bruce L. Miller. "Optimal Investigation Of A Multiple Cost Processes System," **JAR**, 1982, Vol. 20, No. 1, pp. 28-41.

Buckman, **A. G.** (Ohlson, James A. and A. G. Buckman. "Toward A Theory Of Financial Accounting: Welfare And Public Information," **JAR**, 1981, Vol. 19, No. 2, pp. 399-433.)

Buckmaster, **Dale A.,** Ronald M. Copeland and Paul E. Dascher. "The Relative Predictive Ability Of Three Accounting Models," **ABR**, 1976-77, Vol. 7, No. 27, pp. 177-186.

Buckmaster, **Dale** and LeRoy Brooks. "Accounting For Interest And Long-Term Debt In An Inflationary Period," **MA**, 1982, Vol. 63, No. 11, pp. 26-29.

Buckmaster, **Dale** and LeRoy D. Brooks. "The Effects Of Price-Level Changes On Operating Income," **CPAJ**, 1974, Vol. 44, No. 5, pp. 49-53.

Buckmaster, **Dale.** "Inflation Gains And Losses From Holding Monetary Assets And Liabilities 1918 To 1936: A Study Of The Development Of Accounting Thought In The United States," **IJAER**, 1982, Vol. 17, No. 2, pp. 1-22.

Buckmaster, **Dale.** "The Incan Quipu And The Jacobsen Hypothesis," **JAR**, 1974, Vol. 12, No. 1, pp. 178-181.

Buckmaster, **Dale.** (Brooks, LeRoy D. and Dale Buckmaster. "On Monetary Working Capital Maintenance: Theory And Implementation," **IJAER**, 1987, Vol. 22, No. 2, pp. 103-114.)

Buckmaster, **Dale.** (Hassler, Eugene C. and Dale Buckmaster. "Implications Of 'Volatility In Quarterly Accounting Data': A Comment," **AR**, 1975, Vol. 50, No. 1, pp. 127-129.)

Buckner, **Charles O.** (Beresford, Dennis R. and Charles O. Buckner. "Segment Reporting Practices," **CPAJ**, 1978, Vol. 48, No. 12, pp. 37-44.)

Buckwalter, **W. Roy.** "Accrued Depreciation And The Utility Rate Base In Pennsylvania," **AR**, 1942, Vol. 17, No. 3, pp. 265-276.

Budd, **Thomas A.** "The Selection And Educational Training Of Cost Accountants," **AR**, 1948, Vol. 23, No. 2, pp. 183-192.

Budd, **T. A.** "The Effects Of A National Testing Program On Accounting Education," **AR**, 1949, Vol. 24, No. 2, pp. 140-145.

Budge, **Bruce P.** and Harold L. Jones. "A Management Accounting System For Contract Loggers," **MA**, 1977, Vol. 59, No. 4, pp. 34-36.

Buehlmann, **David M.** and Joseph V. Techavichit. "Factors Influencing Final Examination Performance In Large Versus Small Sections Of Accounting Principles," **JAED**, 1984, Vol. 2, No. 1, pp. 127-136.

Buerke, **Edwin A.** "The Small-Business Accountant," **MA**, 1972, Vol. 54, No. 5, pp. 51-52.

Bukofsky, **Ward M.** and William J. Dunn. "Personal Service Corporations: Down But Not Out," **JOA**, 1988, Vol. 165, No. 6, pp. 30-37.

Bulingame, **John F.** "Successful Businesses And Good Managers," **MA**, 1971, Vol. 52, No. 11, pp. 17-18.

Bullard, **John A.** "Price-Level Restatement And Valuation Reporting," **MA**, 1976, Vol. 57, No. 8, pp. 15-18.

Bullen, **Halsey G.** (Hynes, Lynn C. and Halsey G. Bullen. "Financial Instruments: What Should Be Disclosed?," **MA**, 1988, Vol. 69, No. 8, pp. 55-58.)

Bullen, **M. L.** and E. G. Flamholtz. "A Theoretical And Empirical Investigation Of Job Satisfaction And Intended Turnover In The Large CPA Firm," **AOS**, 1985, Vol. 10, No. 3, pp. 287-302.

Bullington, **Jerry B.** (Hubbard, Thomas D. and Jerry B. Bullington. "Positive And Negative Confirmation Requests - A Test," **JOA**, 1972, Vol. 133, No. 3, pp. 48-56.)

Bulloch, **James.** (Duvall, Richard M. and James Bulloch. "Adjusting Rate Of Return And Present Value For Price-Level Changes," **AR**, 1965, Vol. 40, No. 3, pp. 569-573.)

Bullock, **Clayton L.** "Accounting Conventions And Economic Reality," **CPAJ**, 1974, Vol. 44, No. 7, pp. 19-24.

Bullock, **Clayton L.** "Reconciling Economic Depreciation With Tax Allocation," **AR**, 1974, Vol. 49, No. 1, pp. 98-103.

Bullock, **Clinton L.** "Footnotes In Financial Statements," **JOA**, 1956, Vol. 102, No. 1, pp. 39-44.

Bullock, **James H.** and Virginia H. Bakay. "How Las Vegas Casinos Budget," **MA**, 1980, Vol. 62, No. 1, pp. 35-39.

Bull, **Ivan O.** "Personal Financial Statements - Suggestions For Improvement," **CPAJ**, 1984, Vol. 54, No. 12, pp. 38-45.

Bull, **Ivan.** "A Transition From The Profession To Academia," **ACCHOR**, 1987, Vol. 1, No. 3, pp. 85-91.

Bump, **Edwin A.** "Effects Of Learning On Cost Projections," **MA**, 1974, Vol. 55, No. 11, pp. 19-24.

Bunch, **Robert G.** "The Effect Of Payment Terms On Economic Order Quantity Determination," **MA**, 1967, Vol. 48, No. 5, pp. 53-63.

Bund, **Melvin.** "Security In Electronic Data Processing Environment," **CPAJ**, 1975, Vol. 45, No. 2, pp. 33-35.

Bunn, **Radie G.** "The Professor's Home Office," **IAE**, 1986, No. 2, pp. 230-237.

Burchell, **S.,** C. Clubb and A. G. Hopwood. "Accounting In Its Social Context: Towards A History Of Value Added In The United Kingdom," **AOS**, 1985, Vol. 10, No. 4, pp. 381-414.

Burchell, **S.,** C. Clubb, A. Hopwood, J. Hughes and J. Nahapiet. "The Roles Of Accounting In Organizations And Society," **AOS**, 1980, Vol. 5, No. 1, pp. 5-28.

Burchmore, **David W.** "SEC Enforcement Of Insider Trading Laws," **RIAR**, 1987, Vol. 1, pp. 181-189.

Burch, **E. Earl** and William R. Henry. "Opportunity And Incremental Cost: Attempt To Define In Systems Terms: A Comment," **AR**, 1974, Vol. 49, No. 1, pp. 118-123.

Burch, **John G.** "Information Systems: Is It Too Late To Join The Revolution?," **JIS**, 1987, Vol. 1, No. 2, pp. 114-123.

Burch, **John G., Jr.** "Business Games And Simulation Techniques." **MA**, 1969, Vol. 51, No. 6, pp. 49-52.

Burdick, **Keith H.** (Messer, Jean F. and Keith H. Burdick. "Profit-Sharing Plans For Closely Held Corporations," **JOA**, 1970, Vol. 129, No. 4, pp. 53-60.)

Burdick, **Richard K.** and J. Hal Reneau. "Within-Item Variation: A Stochastic Approach To Audit Uncertainty - A Comment," **AR**, 1978, Vol. 53, No. 4, pp. 989-992.

Bures, **Jaroslav P.** "Deflating Long-Term Contract Costs," **MA**, 1975, Vol. 57, No. 2, pp. 43-44.

Bures, **Jaroslav P.** "Time-Framing A PERT Chart," **MA**, 1974, Vol. 56, No. 4, pp. 24-26.

Burgert, **R.** "Reservations About 'Replacement Value' Accounting In The Netherlands," **ABACUS**, 1972, Vol. 8, No. 2, pp. 111-126.

Burger, **Albert D.** and Stuart K. Webster. "The Management Accountant Looks At EPS Vs. ROI: Conflict In Measuring Performance," **MA**, 1978, Vol. 60, No. 2, pp. 19-24.

Burgess, **Richard C.** and Silvia A. Maden. "A Simulation Study Of Tax Sheltered Retirement Plans," **JATA**, 1980, Vol. 1, No. 2, pp. 34-41.

Burgher, **Peter H.** "Features Of An Integrated System Of Financial Controls," **MA**, 1966, Vol. 47, No. 6, pp. 51-54.

Burgher, **Peter H.** "PERT And The Auditor," **AR**, 1964, Vol. 39, No. 1, pp. 103-120.

Burgstahler, **David** and Eric W. Noreen. "Detecting Contemporaneous Security Market Reactions To A Sequence Of Related Events," **JAR**, 1986, Vol. 24, No. 1, pp. 170-186.

Burgstahler, **David** and James Jiambalvo. "Isolation Of Errors In Audit Sampling," **CPAJ**, 1986, Vol. 56, No. 11, pp. 66-71.

Burgstahler, **David** and James Jiambalvo. "Sample Error Characteristics And Projection Of Error To Audit

Populations," **AR**, 1986, Vol. 61, No. 2, pp. 233-248.
Burgstahler, David. "Inference From Empirical Research," **AR**, 1987, Vol. 62, No. 1, pp. 203-214.
Burgstahler, David. (Bowen, Robert M., David Burgstahler and Lane A. Daley. "The Incremental Information Content Of Accrual Versus Cash Flows," **AR**, 1987, Vol. 62, No. 4, pp. 723-747.)
Burgstahler, David. (Bowen, Robert M., David Burgstahler and Lane A. Daley. "Evidence Of The Relationships Between Various Earnings Measures Of Cash Flow," **AR**, 1986, Vol. 61, No. 4, pp. 713-725.)
Burg, Richard L. "An Efficient Foreign Subsidiary Tax Reporting System," **MA**, 1983, Vol. 64, No. 11, pp. 28-30.
Burianek, Frank G. "An Actuary's Views On Pension Plan Accounting And Reporting," **MA**, 1979, Vol. 60, No. 7, pp. 46-49.
Burkert, Ronald L. "Recognizing Inflation In The Capital Budgeting Decision," **MA**, 1971, Vol. 53, No. 5, pp. 40-46.
Burke, Edward J. "Objectivity And Accounting," **AR**, 1964, Vol. 39, No. 4, pp. 837-849.
Burke, John T. "Stock Dividends - Suggestions For Clarification," **AR**, 1962, Vol. 37, No. 2, pp. 283-288.
Burke, Lamar. "Standard Costing In Kaolin Mining," **MA**, 1971, Vol. 52, No. 11, pp. 22-24.
Burke, Mimi. "Reporting On Consistency And Accounting Changes," **CPAJ**, 1973, Vol. 43, No. 6, pp. 475-480.
Burke, Richard C. (Brown, H. Donald and Richard C. Burke. "Accounting Education: A Learning-Styles Study Of Professional-Technical And Future Adaptation Issues," **JAED**, 1987, Vol. 5, No. 2, pp. 187-206.)
Burke, Walter L. "Capital Expenditure Analysis," **IJAER**, 1974, Vol. 9, No. 2, pp. 143-154.
Burke, Walter L. "Cost Allocation And Distribution - Merchandise Accounting," **AR**, 1963, Vol. 38, No. 4, pp. 802-812.
Burkhardt, Dean C. "The Annual Audit," **MA**, 1973, Vol. 55, No. 3, pp. 22-26.
Burky, Louise Boyer. (Lederer, Albert L. and Louise Boyer Burky. "Understanding Top Management's Objectives: A Management Information Systems Concern," **JIS**, 1988, Vol. 3, No. 1, pp. 50-66.)
Burlaud, Alain and Lionel Dahan. "Global Productivity Surplus Accounts," **IJAER**, 1985, Vol. 21, No. 1, pp. 159-169.
Burleson, Harry. "Quasi-Reorganization," **AR**, 1953, Vol. 28, No. 1, pp. 12-16.
Burnaby, Priscilla. (Brown, Clifford D. and Priscilla Burnaby. "The Evolution Of The Single Audit: A 20-Year Process," **ACCHOR**, 1988, Vol. 2, No. 2, pp. 47-52.)
Burnett, R. Andrew. "The Harmonization Of Accounting Principles In The Member Countries Of The European Economic Community," **IJAER**, 1975, Vol. 11, No. 1, pp. 23-30.
Burnett, Tom, Thomas E. King and Valdean C. Lembke. "Equity Method Reporting For Major Finance Company Subsidiaries," **AR**, 1979, Vol. 54, No. 4, pp. 815-823.
Burnet, Mary E. and Arden L. Travis. "A Cooperative Education Program In Public Accounting," **AR**, 1964, Vol. 39, No. 2, pp. 460-463.
Burns, David C. and James K. Loebbecke. "Internal Control Evaluation: How The Computer Can Help," **JOA**, 1975, Vol. 140, No. 2, pp. 60-70.
Burns, David C. and William J. Haga. "Much Ado About Professionalism: A Second Look At Accounting," **AR**, 1977, Vol. 52, No. 3, pp. 705-715.
Burns, David C. "Extending The Study And Evaluation Of Internal Controls," **CPAJ**, 1974, Vol. 44, No. 5, pp. 31-40.
Burns, Donald T. "Change In Accounting Method Or Correction Of An Error," **JOA**, 1966, Vol. 122, No. 5, pp. 42-46.
Burns, Gary W. and D. Scott Peterson. "Accounting For Computer Software," **JOA**, 1982, Vol. 153, No. 4, pp. 50-59.
Burns, Harold D. and Jesse T. Barfield. "Selecting Accounting Alternatives," **MA**, 1976, Vol. 57, No. 8, pp. 27-28.
Burns, Jane O. and Kathleen Bindon. "Evaluating Leases With LP," **MA**, 1980, Vol. 61, No. 8, pp. 48-53.
Burns, Jane O. and Ronald S. Ross. "Establishing International Transfer Pricing Standards For Tax Audits Of Multinational Enterprises," **IJAER**, 1981, Vol. 17, No. 1, pp. 161-179.
Burns, Jane O. and S. Michael Groomer. "An Analysis Of Tax Court Decisions That Assess The Profit Motive Of Farming-Oriented Operations," **JATA**, 1983, Vol. 5, No. 1, pp. 23-39.
Burns, Jane O. "A Study Of International Accounting Education In The United States," **IJAER**, 1979, Vol. 15, No. 1, pp. 135-145.
Burns, Jane O. "Professors' Foreign Travel Expenses: Deductible Or Nondeductible?," **AR**, 1978, Vol. 53, No. 3, pp. 736-745.
Burns, Joseph H. "Managing The Profit Of Conflict," **MA**, 1975, Vol. 57, No. 6, pp. 21-24.
Burns, Joseph S., Robert K. Jaedicke and John M. Sangster. "Financial Reporting Of Purchase Contracts Used To Guarantee Large Investments," **AR**, 1963, Vol. 38, No. 1, pp. 1-13.
Burns, Paul. (Grundy, Graham and Paul Burns. "Taxation-Induced Interdependencies In Project Appraisal," **ABR**, 1979-80, Vol. 10, No. 37, pp. 475-83.)
Burns, Thomas J. and Edward N. Coffman. "The Accounting Hall Of Fame: A Profile Of The Members," **JAR**, 1976, Vol. 14, No. 2, pp. 342-347.
Burns, Thomas J. and Edward N. Coffman. "The Ascending Profession Of Accounting (Part 2)," **CPAJ**, 1977, Vol. 47,

No. 3, pp. 31-36.
Burns, Thomas J. and Edward N. Coffman. "The Ascending Profession Of Accounting (Part 1)," **CPAJ**, 1977, Vol. 47, No. 2, pp. 11-16.
Burns, Thomas J. "Accounting Courses At Nineteen American Universities," **AR**, 1968, Vol. 43, No. 1, pp. 137-147.
Burns, Thomas J. "Hall Of Fame Induction 1987 - Philip Defliese," **AHJ**, 1987, Vol. 14, No. 2, pp. 93-97.
Burns, Thomas J. "The Accounting Hall Of Fame," **AHJ**, 1975, Vol. 2, No. 1-4, pp. 37-39.
Burrell, G. "No Accounting For Sexuality," **AOS**, 1987, Vol. 12, No. 1, pp. 89-102.
Burrell, O. K. and A. B. Stillman. "An Aptitude Test For Accounting," **AR**, 1930, Vol. 5, No. 3, pp. 257-262.
Burrell, O. K. "A Teaching Device In Ratios And Turnovers," **AR**, 1928, Vol. 3, No. 3, pp. 274-277.
Burrell, O. K. "An Experiment In Student And Teacher Rating," **AR**, 1929, Vol. 4, No. 3, pp. 194-197.
Burrill, John C. "Training Accounting Personnel For EDP Systems," **MA**, 1966, Vol. 48, No. 1, pp. 12-16.
Burris, Roland W. "Improving Governmental Financial Reporting And Management: The Illinois Experience And A Proposal For The Federal Government," **RIGNA**, 1987, Vol. 3, Part B, pp. 145-163.
Burrows, G. H. "Incremental Flows In Project Evaluation," **ABR**, 1981-82, Vol. 12, No. 47, pp. 188-192.
Burrows, G. H. "Evolution Of A Lease Solution," **ABACUS**, 1988, Vol. 24, No. 2, pp. 107-119.
Burrows, G. H. "Incremental Plans In Project Evaluation: A Reply," **ABR**, 1982-83, Vol. 13, No. 52, pp. 311-312.
Burrows, G. H. "The Lease Evaluation Solution: A Further Comment," **ABR**, 1976-77, Vol. 7, No. 27, pp. 208-210.
Bursal, Nasuhi I. "The Accounting Environment And Some Recent Developments In Turkey," **IJAER**, 1984, Vol. 19, No. 2, pp. 93-127.
Bursal, Nasuhi. "The Use Of Interest As An Element Of Cost In Germany In The 16th And 17th Centuries," **AHJ**, 1986, Vol. 13, No. 1, pp. 63-70.
Burtchett, Floyd F. "Substitute Terminology For 'Stock Dividends'," **AR**, 1933, Vol. 8, No. 4 pp. 344-345.
Burton, Eric James. "Toward A Theory Of Corporate Social Accounting: A Comment," **AR**, 1977, Vol. 52, No. 4, pp. 971-976.
Burton, E. James, James C. McKeown and Jeffrey L. Shlosberg. "The Generation And Administration Of Examinations On Interactive Computer Systems," **AR**, 1978, Vol. 53, No. 1, pp. 170-178.
Burton, John C. and Patricia Fairfield. "Auditing Evolution In A Changing Environment," **AJPT**, 1981-82, Vol. 1, No. 2, pp. 1-22.
Burton, John C. and William Roberts. "A Study Of Auditor Changes," **JOA**, 1967, Vol. 123, No. 4, pp. 31-36.
Burton, John C. "A Critical Look At Professionalism And Scope Of Services," **JOA**, 1980, Vol. 149, No. 4.pp.48-57.
Burton, John C. "A Symposium On The Conceptual Framework," **JOA**, 1978, Vol. 145, No. 1, pp. 53-58.
Burton, John C. "An Educator Views The Public Accounting Profession," **JOA**, 1971, Vol. 132, No. 3, pp. 47-53.
Burton, John C. "Emerging Trends In Financial Reporting," **JOA**, 1981, Vol. 152, No. 1, pp. 54-67.
Burton, John C. "Fair Presentation: Another View," **CPAJ**, 1975, Vol. 45, No. 6, pp. 13-20.
Burton, John C. "Management Auditing," **JOA**, 1968, Vol. 125, No. 5, pp. 41-46.
Burton, John C. "New Frontiers In Accounting," **CPAJ**, 1980, Vol. 50, No. 9, pp. 14-26.
Burton, John C. "Some General And Specific Thoughts On The Accounting Environment," **JOA**, 1973, Vol. 136, No. 4, pp. 40-46.
Burton, John C. "Symposium On Ethics In Corporate Financial Reporting," **JOA**, 1972, Vol. 133, No. 1, pp. 46-50.
Burton, John C. "The Profession's Institutional Structure In The 1980s," **JOA**, 1978, Vol. 145, No. 4, pp. 63-69.
Burton, John C. "The Seaview Symposium On Financial Reporting," **JOA**, 1969, Vol. 127, No. 1, pp. 33-38.
Burton, John C. (Mautz, Robert K. and John C. Burton. "A Government Accounting Standards Board?," **CPAJ**, 1981, Vol. 51, No. 8, pp. 13-24.)
Burton, John. "Crisis In Accounting: New Controls On The Profession," **CA**, 1986, Vol. 4, No. 4, pp. 15-19.
Burton, Norman L. "Examination Techniques And Methods In Advanced Accounting," **AR**, 1942, Vol. 17, No. 2, pp. 114-118.
Burton, William D. "Controlling Intracompany Freight Costs," **MA**, 1982, Vol. 64, No. 4, pp. 37-41.
Burt, Oscar R. "A Unified Theory Of Depreciation," **JAR**, 1972, Vol. 10, No. 1, pp. 28-57.
Bury, Walter M. "Estate And Gift Taxes Under The New Code," **JOA**, 1954, Vol. 98, No. 3, pp. 371-377.
Bury, W. M. "Elimination Of Double Taxation Of Corporate Income," **JOA**, 1952, Vol. 94, No. 1, pp. 46-52.
Busher, John R. and Gene R. Tyndall. "Logistics Excellence," **MA**, 1987, Vol. 69, No. 2, pp. 32-39.
Bush, James L., Jr. and Reuben F. Stewart. "Vulcan Materials Automates Delivery Ticket Writing," **MA**, 1985, Vol. 67, No. 2, pp. 52-55.
Bush, James L., Jr. "A Peer Tutoring Program For Introductory Accounting Courses," **JAED**, 1985, Vol. 3, No. 2, pp. 171-177.
Bussman, John F. "Condo Taxation - Questions And Answers," **CPAJ**, 1986, Vol. 56, No. 2, pp. 28-31.
Bussman, John F. "Vocabulary: An Integrative Learning Aid For Students In Intermediate Accounting," **AR**, 1976, Vol. 51, No. 2, pp. 380-384.
Butler, A. A. (Hall, Thomas W. and A. A. Butler. "Assuring

Adequate Attorneys' Replies To Audit Inquiries," **JOA**, 1981, Vol. 152, No. 3, pp. 83-91.)

Butler, Charles. (Shearon, Winston, Charles Butler and James Benjamin. "Audit Aspects Of Small Computer Systems," **CPAJ**, 1980, Vol. 50, No. 8, pp. 17-21.)

Butler, Daniel L. (Mickle, Collier E., Jim D. Reed and Daniel L. Butler. "Analyzing The Profitability Of Branch Banks," **MA**, 1985, Vol. 67, No. 6, pp. 61-66.)

Butler, Dean S. "Effectiveness In Negotiations," **MA**, 1966, Vol. 47, No. 10, pp. 19-24.

Butler, John J. "Joint Product Analysis," **MA**, 1971, Vol. 53, No. 6, pp. 12-14.

Butler, Leonora. (Perks, R. W. and Leonora Butler. "Accountancy Standards In Practice: The Experience Of SSAP2," **ABR**, 1977-78, Vol. 8, No. 29, pp. 25-33.)

Butler, Stephen A. "Anchoring In The Judgmental Evaluation Of Audit Samples," **AR**, 1986, Vol. 61, No. 1, pp.101-111.

Butler, Stephen A. "Application Of A Decision Aid In The Judgmental Evaluation Of Substantive Test Of Details Samples," **JAR**, 1985, Vol. 23, No. 2, pp. 513-526.

Butler, Thomas G. (Willens, Robert and Thomas G. Butler. "Tax Ramifications Of Selling A Business - Part II," **CPAJ**, 1986, Vol. 56, No. 4, pp. 24-29.)

Butler, Thomas G. (Willens, Robert and Thomas G. Butler. "Tax Ramifications Of Selling A Business - Part I," **CPAJ**, 1986, Vol. 56, No. 3, pp. 30-35.)

Butterbaugh, Grant J. "Dr. Stands For Debit," **AR**, 1945, Vol. 20, No. 3, pp. 340-343.

Butterworth, John E. and Berndt A. Sigloch. "A Generalized Multi-Stage Input-Output Model And Some Derived Equivalent Systems," **AR**, 1971, Vol. 46, No. 4, pp. 700-716.

Butterworth, John E. "The Accounting System As An Information Function," **JAR**, 1972, Vol. 10, No. 1, pp. 1-27.

Buttimer, Harry. "Dividends And The Law," **AR**, 1961, Vol. 36, No. 3, pp. 434-438.

Buttimer, Harry. "Statutory Influence On Treasury Stock Accounting," **AR**, 1960, Vol. 35, No. 3, pp. 476-481.

Buttimer, Harry. "The Allocation Of Combined Net Income In Reciprocal Affiliations," **AR**, 1961, Vol. 36, No. 4, pp. 649-650.

Buttimer, Harry. "The Evolution Of Stated Capital," **AR**, 1962, Vol. 37, No. 4, pp. 746-752.

Buttross, Thomas E. (Thompson, James H. and Thomas E. Buttross. "Return To Cash Flow," **CPAJ**, 1988, Vol. 58, No. 3, pp. 30-41.)

Butt, Jane L. "Frequency Judgments Is An Auditing-Related Task," **JAR**, 1988, Vol. 26, No. 2, pp. 315-330.

Buxbaum, W. E. "Accounting For Pensions," **MA**, 1983, Vol. 65, No. 4, pp. 28-30.

Buzby, Stephen L. and Haim Falk. "Demand For Social Responsibility Information By University Investors," **AR**, 1979, Vol. 54, No. 1, pp. 23-37.

Buzby, Stephen L. and Haim Falk. "A New Approach To The Funds Statement," **JOA**, 1974. Vol. 137, No. 1, pp. 55-61.

Buzby, Stephen L. and Lester E. Heitger. "Profit Contribution By Market Segment," **MA**, 1976, Vol. 58, No. 5, pp. 42-46.

Buzby, Stephen L. "Company Size, Listed Versus Unlisted Stocks, And The Extent Of Financial Disclosure," **JAR**, 1975, Vol. 13, No. 1, pp. 16-37.

Buzby, Stephen L. "Discussion Of 'Current Cost Disclosers And Nondisclosers: Canadian Evidence'," **CAR**, 1986-87, Vol. 3, No. 1, pp. 45-49.

Buzby, Stephen L. "Extending The Applicability Of Probabilistic Management Planning And Control Models: A Reply," **AR**, 1975, Vol. 50, No. 4, pp. 832-834.

Buzby, Stephen L. "Extending The Applicability Of Probabilistic Management Planning And Control Models," **AR**, 1974, Vol. 49, No. 1, pp. 42-49.

Buzby, Stephen L. "Selected Items Of Information And Their Disclosure In Annual Reports," **AR**, 1974, Vol. 49, No. 3, pp. 423-435.

Buzby, Stephen L. "The Nature Of Adequate Disclosure," **JOA**, 1974, Vol. 137, No. 4, pp. 38-47.

Buzby, Stephen L. (Morrison, Thomas A. and Stephen L. Buzby. "Effect Of The Investment Tax Credit On The Capitalize-Expense Decision," **AR**, 1968, Vol. 43, No. 3, pp. 517-521.)

Buzby, Stephen. (Moore, Michael L. and Stephen Buzby. "The Quality Of Corporate Financial Disclosure: A Comment," **AR**, 1972, Vol. 47, No. 3, pp. 581-584.)

Buzby, S. L. and H. Falk. "A Survey Of The Interest In Social Responsibility Information By Mutual Funds," **AOS**, 1978, Vol. 3, No. 3/4, pp. 191-202.

Byars, Lloyd L. (Dillon, Ray D., Lloyd L. Byars. Craig E. Aronoff and Gale D. Eidson. "The CPA Firm's 'Mission'," **JOA**, 1985, Vol. 159, No. 6, pp. 70-78.)

Byars, Richard B. and Charles A. Nickerson. "Inter Vivos Gifts: An Anachronism?," **JATA**, 1980, Vol. 2, No. 1, pp. 16-18.

Byars, Richard B. and Charles A. Nickerson. "Charitable Remainder Trusts - Valuation Methods Yield Inconsistent Results," **JATA**, 1982, Vol. 4, No. 1, pp. 13-18.

Byars, Richard B. and Thomas P. Klammer. "The Pluses Of The Practical Capacity Concept Of Cost Allocation," **CA**, 1983, Vol. 1, No. 2, pp. 20-25.

Byars, Richard B. "Income Tax Liability: A Classroom Approach," **AR**, 1979, Vol. 54, No. 4, pp. 791-793.

Byerly, Richard A. "Determining The Effective Rate Of Interest On A Series Of Bonds," **AR**, 1941, Vol. 16, No. 3, pp. 281-287.

Byington, Ralph and Paul Munter. "Prospective Financial Statements And Attestation Risk," **CPAJ**, 1988, Vol. 58, No. 2, pp. 34-41.

Bylinski, Joseph H. and Chee W. Chow. "Human Judgment

Biases And The Teaching Of Management Accounting," **JAED**, 1985, Vol. 3, No. 1, pp. 167-172.

Bylinski, Joseph H. (Bailey, K. E., III, Joseph H. Bylinski and Michael D. Shields. "Effects Of Audit Report Wording Changes On The Perceived Message," **JAR**, 1983, Vol. 21, No. 2, pp. 355-370.)

Bylinski, Joseph H. (Bamber E. Michael and Joseph H. Bylinski. "The Effects Of The Planning Memorandum, Time Pressure And Individual Auditor Characteristics On Audit Managers' Review Time Judgments," **CAR**, 1987-88, Vol. 4, No. 1, pp. 127-163.)

Bylinski, Joseph H. (Bamber, E. Michael, Linda Smith Bamber and Joseph H. Bylinski. "A Descriptive Study Of Audit Managers' Working Paper Review," **AJPT**, 1988, Vol. 7, No. 2, pp. 137-149.)

Bylinski, Joseph H. (Bamber, E. Michael and Joseph H. Bylinski. "Attribute Sampling: A Review In Light Of SAS No. 39," **JAED**, 1984, Vol. 2, No. 1, pp. 83-97.)

Bylinski, Joseph H. (Bamber, E. Michael and Joseph H. Bylinski. "The Audit Team And The Audit Review Process: An Organizational Approach," **JAL**, 1982, Vol.1,pp.33-58.)

Bylinski, Joseph. (Blocher, Edward and Joseph Bylinski. "The Influence Of Sample Characteristics In Sample Evaluation," **AJPT**, 1985-86, Vol. 5, No. 1, pp. 79-90.)

Byrd, David B. (Byrd, Sandra D. and David B. Byrd. "Utilizing Task Analysis And Sequencing In Order To More Efficiently Teach Financial Accounting," **IAE**, 1987, Vol. 2, No. 2, pp. 349-360.)

Byrd, Kenneth F. "Differences Between British And American Concept Of 'Market' In Inventory Pricing," **JOA**, 1950, Vol. 89, No. 4, pp. 310-317.

Byrd, Sandra D. and David B. Byrd. "Utilizing Task Analysis And Sequencing In Order To More Efficiently Teach Financial Accounting," **IAE**, 1987, Vol. 2, No. 2, pp. 349-360.

Byrne, Thomas J. "Employee Leasing: A Cost-Saving Solution To An Old Problem?," **CA**, 1985, Vol. 3, No. 3, pp. 60-66.

Byrnes, Thomas W. "Auditing Instruction By The Laboratory Method," **AR**, 1939, Vol. 14, No. 1, pp. 33-37.

Byrnes, Thomas W. "Never Write A Text-Book, Unless," **AR**, 1952, Vol. 27, No. 3, pp. 344-345.

Byrnes, Thomas W. "Private Or Public Accounting," **AR**, 1946, Vol. 21, No. 3, pp. 308-309.

Byrnes, Thomas W. "The Auditing Laboratory At Columbia University," **AR**, 1935, Vol. 10, No. 3, pp. 295-298.

Byrnes, Thomas W. "The Bank Reconcilement," **AR**, 1944, Vol. 19, No. 3, pp. 300-301.

Byrnes, Thomas W. "Vingt Ans Apres," **AR**, 1953, Vol. 28, No. 4, pp. 515-516.

Byrnes, Thomas W. "Where Are You Going, CPA?," **AR**, 1953, Vol. 28. No. 2, p. 177.

Byrne, Gilbert R. "Auditing And Internal Control," **JOA**, 1957. Vol. 103, No. 1, pp. 41-46.

Byrne, R. F., A. Charnes, W. W. Cooper and K. Kortanek. "Some New Approaches To Risk," **AR**, 1968, Vol. 43, No. 1, pp. 18-37.

Byron, Earl T. "Stock Options - 1964 Changes," **JOA**, 1965, Vol. 119, No. 4, pp. 56-63.

Byun, Young Hoon. (Levy, Haim and Young Hoon Byun. "An Empirical Test Of The Black-Scholes Option Pricing Model And The Implied Variance: A Confidence Interval Approach," **JAAF**, 1987, Vol. 2 (New Series), No. 4, pp. 355-374.)

CCC

Caddy, George K. "A Human Value Model," **MA**, 1975, Vol. 56, No. 10, pp. 27-30.

Cadenhead, Gary M. "Net Realizable Value Redefined," **JAR**, 1970, Vol. 8, No. 1, pp. 138-140.

Cadenhead, Gary M. "'Differences In Circumstances': Fact Or Fantasy?," **ABACUS**, 1970, Vol. 6, No. 1, pp. 71-80.

Caggiano, Robert L. (Purtill, John S., Jr. and Robert L. Caggiano. "How The CFO Can Lead A Business Turnaround," **JOA**, 1986, Vol. 161, No. 6, pp. 108-113.)

Cagley, James W. (Lowe, Larry S., C. Richard Roberts and James W. Cagley. "Your Sales Forecast-Marketing Budget Relationship - Is It Consistent?," **MA**, 1980, Vol. 61, No. 7, pp. 29-33.)

Cain, Patricia. (Askari, Hossein, Patricia Cain and Richard Shaw. "A Government Tax Subsidy," **AR**, 1976, Vol. 51, No. 2, pp. 331-334.)

Cairnie, T. R. "Oil And Gas Accounting: A Review Of The Issues And Priorities," **ABR**, 1984-85, Vol. 15, No. 58, pp. 113-122.

Calabro, John P. and Jerry Cohen. "Taking Control of Inventory Shortage," **CA**, 1985, Vol. 3, No. 1. pp. 29-33.

Calas, Robert. "Variance Analysis In Profit Planning," **MA**, 1971, Vol. 53, No. 1, pp. 31-32, 49-51.

Calderwood, Shirley C. (Bradbury, Michael E. and Shirley C. Calderwood. "Equity Accounting For Reciprocal Stockholdings," **AR**, 1988, Vol. 63, No. 2, pp. 330-347.)

Caldwell, Charles W. (Beard, Larry H. and Charles W. Caldwell. "Transfer Pricing Can Improve Sales And Credit Cooperation," **MA**, 1984, Vol. 65, No. 9, pp. 60-65.)

Caldwell, Charles W. (Schnee, Edward J. and Charles W. Caldwell. "Retirement Planning Under Section 403(b)(7): Advantages And Limitations," **JATA**, 1984, Vol. 6, No. 1, pp. 48-56.)

Caldwell, Charles. (Harrell, Adrian, Charles Caldwell and Edwin Doty. "Within-Person Expectancy Theory Predictions Of Accounting Students' Motivation To Achieve Academic Success," **AR**, 1985, Vol. 60, No. 4, pp. 724-735.)

Caldwell, Charles. (Strobel, Caroline and Charles Caldwell. "Rehabilitation Credit Investment Incentives - ERTA

1981," **CPAJ**, 1982, Vol. 52, No. 9, pp. 40-44.)

Caldwell, James C. and Robert W. Ingram. "Management Accountants Respond To Segment Reporting," **MA**, 1976, Vol. 58, No. 5, pp. 37-41.

Caldwell, James C. (Barnett, Andrew H. and James C. Caldwell. "Accounting For Corporate Social Performance: A Survey," **MA**, 1974, Vol. 56, No. 5, pp. 23-26.)

Calhoun, Charles H., III. "Accounting For Initial Franchise Fees: Is It A Dead Issue?," **JOA**, 1975, Vol. 139, No. 2, pp. 60-67.

Calhoun, Donald A. "Computing DISC Profits," **MA**, 1973, Vol. 54, No. 12, pp. 45-46.

Calhoun, Donald A. "Oil And Gas Taxation," **MA**, 1973, Vol. 55, No. 5, pp. 21-24.

Calhoun, Donald A. "Section 931 And The Puerto Rican Program," **MA**, 1974, Vol. 55, No. 9, pp. 18-22.

Calhoun, Donald A. "The Foreign Tax Credit," **MA**, 1975, Vol. 57, No. 3, pp. 41-42.

Call, Donald P. and Paul Kircher. "The Investment Credit Moratorium," **JOA**, 1967, Vol. 123, No. 3, pp. 47-52.

Call, Dwight V. "Some Salient Factors Often Overlooked In Stock Options," **AR**, 1969, Vol. 44, No. 4, pp. 711-719.

Call, Jack. (Gordon, Lawrence A., Jack Call and Haim Falk. "Pricing Objectives And Managerial Incentive Plans," **JCA**, 1986, Vol. 3, No. 2, pp. 59-67.)

Call, William L. "General Versus Specific Price-Level Adjustments: A Graphic Analysis," **AR**, 1977, Vol. 52, No. 1, pp. 222-228.

Call, William L. "Quadratic Cost-Volume Relationship And Timing Of Demand Information: A Comment," **AR**, 1975, Vol. 50, No. 1, pp. 133-137.

Callaghan, David. (Fetters, Michael, John McKenzie and David Callaghan. "Does The Computer Hinder Accounting Education? An Analysis Of Some Empirical Data," **IAE**, 1986, No. 1, pp. 76-85.)

Callahan, Carolyn. (Elgers, Pieter, Carolyn Callahan and Elizabeth Strock. "The Effect Of Earnings Yields Upon The Association Between Unexpected Earnings And Security Returns: A Re-Examination," **AR**, 1987, Vol. 62, No. 4, pp. 763-773.)

Callahan, Patrick S., Henry R. Jaenicke and Donald L. Neebes. "SASs Nos. 56 And 57: Increasing Audit Effectiveness," **JOA**, 1988, Vol. 166, No. 4, pp. 56-68.

Callen, Jeffrey L. and Joshua Livnat. "Is Historical Cost Accounting Possible During Hyperinflation?," **IJAER**, 1984, Vol. 19, No. 2, pp. 73-81.

Callen, Jeffrey L. "A Medieval Controversy About Profit And Loss Allocations," **ABACUS**, 1987, Vol. 23, No.1,pp.85-90.

Callen, Jeffrey L. "An Index Number Theory Of Accounting Cost Variances," **JAAF**, 1988, Vol. 3 (New Series), No. 2, pp. 87-112.

Callen, Jeffrey L. "Financial Cost Allocations: A Game Theoretic Approach," **AR**, 1978, Vol. 53, No.2,pp.303-308.

Callen, Jeffrey L. (Aivazian, Varouj A. and Jeffrey L. Callen. "Core Theory And Uniformity In Accounting: Rationalizing The Accounting Rulemaker," **JAPP**, 1983, Vol. 2, No. 4, pp. 225-237.)

Callen, Jeffrey L. (Barlev, Benzion and Jeffrey L. Callen. "Total Factor Productivity And Cost Variances: Survey And Analysis," **JAL**, 1986, Vol. 5, pp. 35-56.)

Callman, H. William. "U.S. Taxation Of Income Arising From Restitution Of Property Seized By Nazis," **JOA**, 1950, Vol. 89, No. 4, pp. 318-328.

Calvasina, Eugene J. (Calvasina, Richard V. and Eugene J. Calvasina. "Standard Costing Games That Managers Play," **MA**, 1984, Vol. 65, No. 9, pp. 49-51.)

Calvasina, Richard V. and Eugene J. Calvasina. "Standard Costing Games That Managers Play," **MA**, 1984, Vol. 65, No. 9, pp. 49-51.

Cameron, Alex B. "A Review Of Management's Earnings Forecast Research," **JAL**, 1986, Vol. 5, pp. 57-84.

Cameron, Alexander. "Taxes In Organizing A Business Abroad," **JOA**, 1958, Vol. 106, No. 1, pp. 45-50.

Cameron, Donald M. "Computer Use In A Customer Accounting Operation," **MA**, 1971, Vol. 53, No. 4, pp. 17-20.

Cameron, George D., III, Ralph W. Gundmundsen, Jr. and Jack R. Ball. "Accounting Changes: Why CPA's Must Conform," **MA**, 1973, Vol. 54, No. 8, pp. 26-28.

Camilli, Leonard F. "Technical Unification In A Management Information System," **MA**, 1966, Vol. 47, No. 8, pp. 3-8.

Camm, Jeffrey D., Thomas R. Gulledge, Jr. and Norman Keith Womer. "Production Rate And Contractor Behavior," **JCA**, 1987, Vol. 4, No. 1, pp. 27-37.

Cammann, C. "Effects Of The Use Of Control Systems," **AOS**, 1976, Vol. 1, No. 4, pp. 301-314.

Campbell, Alan D. "The Monetary System, Taxation, And Publicans In The Time Of Christ," **AHJ**, 1986, Vol. 13, No. 2, pp. 131-135.

Campbell, David K., James Gaertner and Robert P. Vecchio. "Perceptions Of Promotion And Tenure Criteria: A Survey Of Accounting Educators," **JAED**, 1983, Vol. 1, No. 1, pp. 83-92.

Campbell, David R. and Alfred R. Michenzi. "Revising The Audit Report: A Response To The Expectation Gap," **CPAJ**, 1987, Vol. 57, No. 4, pp. 34-39.

Campbell, David R. and Mary V. Campbell. "Microcomputers For Small Practitioners," **CPAJ**, 1983, Vol. 53, No. 6, pp. 28-33.

Campbell, David R. and Mary V. Campbell. "Prospective Financial Statement Services," **CPAJ**, 1984, Vol. 54, No. 11, pp. 54-64.

Campbell, David R. and Robert G. Morgan. "Publication Activity Of Promoted Accounting Faculty," **IAE**, 1987, Vol. 2, No. 1, pp. 28-43.

Campbell, David R. and Robert W. Williams. "Accreditation Of Accounting Programs: Administrators' Perceptions Of Proposed AACSB Standards," **IAE**, 1983, No. 1, pp. 60-70.

Campbell, David R. "An Analysis Of The Growth In Public Accounting: Implications For Future Planning Strategies," **JAAF**, 1983, Vol. 6, No. 3, pp. 196-211.

Campbell, David R. "How Local Firms Can Document Quality Control," **CPAJ**, 1978, Vol. 48, No. 4, pp. 39-43.

Campbell, David R. "Projection Updating - An Implementation Issue," **CPAJ**, 1980, Vol. 50, No. 4, pp. 23-29.

Campbell, David R. "The First CPA Review Manual," **JOA**, 1987, Vol. 163, No. 5, pp. 333-336.

Campbell, David R. (Ricchiute, David N. and David R. Campbell. "A Need To Bring Educators And Practitioners Together," **CPAJ**, 1979, Vol. 49, No. 3, pp. 35-39.)

Campbell, Donald F., Jr. "Twenty Years Of Social Security," **JOA**, 1956, Vol. 102, No. 2, pp. 27-35.

Campbell, Franklin M. II. "Contractor Cost Risk Determination," **MA**, 1972, Vol. 53, No. 11, pp. 37-40.

Campbell, James A. "Accounting In The Curriculum Of The Small Liberal Arts College," **AR**, 1930, Vol. 5, No. 2, pp. 142-145.

Campbell, Jane E. and Jane F. Mutchler. "The 'Expectations Gap' And Going-Concern Uncertainties," **ACCHOR**, 1988, Vol. 2, No. 1, pp. 42-49.

Campbell, J. D. "Consolidation Vs. Combination," **AR**, 1962, Vol. 37, No. 1, pp. 99-102.

Campbell, J. D. "Straight-Line Method Of Depreciation," **AR**, 1951, Vol. 26, No. 1, pp. 40-42.

Campbell, J. E. "An Application Of Protocol Analysis To The 'Little GAAP' Controversy," **AOS**, 1984, Vol. 9, No. 3/4, pp. 329-342.

Campbell, L. E. "The Responsibility Of The Internal Auditor For Procedures," **AR**, 1955, Vol. 30, No. 1, pp. 86-88.

Campbell, Mary V. (Campbell, David R. and Mary V. Campbell. "Prospective Financial Statement Services," **CPAJ**, 1984, Vol. 54, No. 11, pp. 54-64.)

Campbell, Mary V. (Campbell, David R. and Mary V. Campbell. "Microcomputers For Small Practitioners," **CPAJ**, 1983, Vol. 53, No. 6, pp. 28-33.)

Campbell, Robert J. and Larry J. Rankin. "Regression Analysis In Planning And Testing," **CPAJ**, 1986, Vol. 56, No. 5, pp. 50-59.

Campbell, Roger M. (Schiff, Michael, Roger M. Campbell, Leslie E. Halprin and Judith P. Murphy. "How A Division's Reports Can Reflect Inflation," **MA**, 1982, Vol. 64, No. 4, pp. 32-35.)

Campbell, Ronald L. (Wallace, Wanda A. and Ronald L. Campbell. "State Boards Of Accountancy: Quality Review And Positive Enforcement Program," **RIAR**, 1988, Vol. 2, pp. 123-154.)

Campbell, Terry L. and Douglas W. McNiel. "Stochastic And Nonstochastic Determinants Of Changes In Client-Industry Concentrations For Large Public-Accounting Firms," **JAPP**, 1985, Vol. 4, No. 4, pp. 317-328.

Campbell, Terry L. and LeRoy A. Franklin. "Trends And Projections Of IS/MAS Faculty And Courses," **JIS**, 1987, Vol. 1, No. 2, pp. 101-113.

Campbell, Terry L. "Automating The Systems Understanding AID," **JAED**, 1985, Vol. 3, No. 1, pp. 185-187.

Campbell, Terry L., William W. McCartney, Doris M. Taylor and LeRoy A. Franklin. "Job Satisfaction Of Academic Accountants In Southern Business Administration Association Schools," **AIA**, 1988, Vol. 6, pp. 175-190.

Campfield, William F. "Selected International Trends In Financial Planning And Control In The Public Sector," **IJAER**, 1969, Vol. 5, No. 1, pp. 123-151.

Campfield, William L. "A Blueprint For Appraising And Guiding Audit Staff," **AR**, 1957, Vol. 32, No. 4, pp. 625-629.

Campfield, William L. "A Broad-Gauge Course In Governmental Accounting," **AR**, 1958, Vol. 33, No. 4, pp. 669-675.

Campfield, William L. "A Governmental Agency's Program For Developing Its Professional Accountants," **AR**, 1962, Vol. 37, No. 2, pp. 295-299.

Campfield, William L. "An Approach To Formulation Of Professional Standards For Internal Auditors," **AR**, 1960, Vol. 35, No. 3, pp. 444-448.

Campfield, William L. "Critical Paths For Professional Accountants During The New Management Revolution," **AR**, 1963, Vol. 38, No. 3, pp. 521-527.

Campfield, William L. "Good Judgment And Public Accounting Practice," **AR**, 1952, Vol. 27, No. 1, pp. 73-78.

Campfield, William L. "Professional Status For Internal Auditors," **AR**, 1965, Vol. 40, No. 3, pp. 594-598.

Campfield, William L. "Re-Examination Of Bases And Opportunties For Applying Accounting Judgment," **AR**, 1959, Vol. 34, No. 4, pp. 555-563.

Campfield, William L. "Toward Making Accounting Education Adaptive And Normative," **AR**, 1970, Vol. 45, No. 4, pp. 683-689.

Campfield, William L. "Training For Law And For Public Accounting," **AR**, 1953, Vol. 28, No. 3, pp. 401-411.

Campfield, William L. "Trends In Auditing Management Plans And Operations," **JOA**, 1967, Vol. 124, No. 1, pp. 41-46.

Campfield, W. L. "Experiences In Extension Of Staff Training To In-Charge Auditors," **AR**, 1955, Vol. 30, No. 2, pp. 293-297.

Campion, William M. and Richard M. Peters. "Short Interval Scheduling For The Audit Engagement," **JOA**, 1979, Vol. 148, No. 5, pp. 67-71.

Campion, William M. and Richard M. Peters. "How To Analyze Manpower Requirements Forecasts," **MA**, 1979, Vol. 61, No. 3, pp. 45-51.

Campisi, Sam and Ken T. Trotman. "Auditor Consensus In Going Concern Judgments," **ABR**, 1984-85, Vol. 15, No. 60,

pp. 303-310.

Candee, C. C. "Federal Paperwork And Its Impact On You," **MA**, 1976, Vol. 58, No. 5, pp. 61-62.

Canlar, Mehmet. "College-Level Exposure To Accounting Study And Its Effect On Student Performance In The First MBA-Level Financial Accounting Course," **IAE**, 1986, Vol. 1, No. 1, pp. 13-23.

Canning, John B. "Cost Of Production And Market Price," **AR**, 1931, Vol. 6, No. 3, pp. 161-164.

Canning, John B. "Hatfield's Paradox," **AR**, 1929, Vol. 4, No. 2, pp. 111-115.

Canning, J. B. "Some Divergencies of Accounting Theory From Economic Theory," **AR**, 1929, Vol. 4, No. 1, pp. 1-8.

Canning, Robert J. "Selection, Training, And Placement Of Overseas Accounting Personnel," **IJAER**, 1968, Vol. 4, No. 1, pp. 41-50.

Canning, R. J. "Training For An Accounting Career," **AR**, 1958, Vol. 33, No. 3, pp. 359-367.

Cannon, Arthur M. "Accounting As A Social Force," **JOA**, 1955, Vol. 99, No. 3, pp. 60-66.

Cannon, Arthur M. "Check List For An Accounting Library," **AR**, 1950, Vol. 25, No. 4, pp. 425-440.

Cannon, Arthur M. "Discussion Notes On 'The Basic Postulates Of Accounting'," **JOA**, 1962, Vol. 113, No. 2, pp. 42-53.

Cannon, Arthur M. "Financial Statements For A Church," **JOA**, 1962, Vol. 114, No. 3, pp. 43-49.

Cannon, Arthur M. "Significance Of Auditing Statement 23 In Relation To Accountants' Liability," **JOA**, 1950, Vol. 90, No. 5, pp. 373-378.

Cannon, Arthur M. "Tax Pressures On Accounting Principles And Accountants' Independence," **AR**, 1952, Vol. 27, No. 4, pp. 419-426.

Cannon, Arthur M. "The CPA Standards Report," **JOA**, 1957, Vol. 103, No. 1, pp. 33-40.

Cannon, James G. "The American Association Of Public Accountants (1908): Comments," **AHJ**, 1987, Vol. 14, No. 2, pp. 104-108.

Cannon, J. A. "Applying The Human Resource Account Framework In An International Airline," **AOS**, 1976, Vol. 1, No. 2/3, pp. 253-264.

Cao, Le Thi and Phillip G. Buchanan. "The Integration Of Behavioral Accounting In Graduate Accounting Curricula," **JAED**, 1985, Vol. 3, No. 2, pp. 115-121.

Capelli, Andrew J. and David Winetroub. "Multiemployer Pension Plans: Uncertain Impact On Financial Reporting," **CA**, 1983, Vol. 1, No. 1, pp. 18-23.

Capettini, Robert and Gerald L. Salamon. "Internal Versus External Acquisition Of Services When Reciprocal Services Exist," **AR**, 1977, Vol. 52, No. 3, pp. 690-696.

Capettini, Robert and Thomas E. King. "Exchanges Of Nonmonetary Assets: Some Changes," **AR**, 1976, Vol. 51, No. 1, pp. 142-147.

Capettini, Robert, David A. Dittman and Richard C. Morey. "Reimbursement Rate Setting For Medicaid Prescription Drugs Based On Relative Efficiencies," **JAPP**, 1985, Vol. 4, No. 2, pp. 83-110.

Capettini, Robert. (Harmelink, Philip J. and Robert Capettini. "Income Tax Consequences In Leasing," **CPAJ**, 1979, Vol. 49, No. 3, pp. 29-34.)

Caplan, Edwin H. "Behavioral Assumptions Of Management Accounting - Report Of A Field Study," **AR**, 1968, Vol. 43, No. 2, pp. 342-362.

Caplan, Edwin H. "Behavioral Assumptions Of Management Accounting," **AR**, 1966, Vol. 41, No. 3, pp. 496-509.

Caplan, Edwin H. "Management Accounting And The Behavioral Sciences," **MA**, 1969, Vol. 50, No. 10, pp. 41-45.

Caplan, Edwin H. "Relevance - A 'Will-O'-The-Wisp'," **ABACUS**, 1969, Vol. 5, No. 1, pp. 48-54.

Caplin, Mortimer M. and Robert A. Klayman. "Depreciation - 1965 Model," **JOA**, 1965, Vol. 119, No. 4, pp. 34-42.

Caplin, Mortimer M. "New Directions In Tax Administration," **AR**, 1962, Vol. 37, No. 2, pp. 223-230.

Capps, T. (Berry, A. J., T. Capps, D. Cooper, P. Ferguson, T. Hopper and E. A. Lowe. "Management Control In An Area Of The NCB: Rationales Of Accounting Practices In A Public Enterprise," **AOS**, 1985, Vol. 10, No. 1, pp. 3-28.)

Carbone, Frank J. "Automated Job Costing Helps Mulach Steel Stay Competitive," **MA**, 1980, Vol. 61, No. 12, pp. 29-31.

Carbone, Tobias C. "Are Your Customers Paying On Time?," **MA**, 1975, Vol. 57, No. 5, pp. 46-48.

Cardona, Ruben and Samuel A. R. Coleridge. "Financing Facilities At Lower Cost," **CPAJ**, 1978, Vol. 48, No. 3, pp. 27-30.

Cardullo, J. Patrick and Richard A. Moellenberndt. "The Cost Allocation Problem In A Telecommunications Company," **MA**, 1987, Vol. 69, No. 3, pp. 39-44.

Carey, John L. and William O. Doherty. "The Concept Of Independence - Review And Restatement," **JOA**, 1966, Vol. 121, No. 1, pp. 38-48.

Carey, John L. "Accounting Legislation Of The Future," **JOA**, 1967, Vol. 123, No. 1, pp. 46-51.

Carey, John L. "Early Encounters Between CPAs And The SEC," **AHJ**, 1979, Vol. 6, No. 1, pp. 29-37.

Carey, John L. "Higher Accreditation For CPAs," **JOA**, 1961, Vol. 111, No. 3, pp. 47-53.

Carey, John L. "How Can Barriers Against International Accounting Practice Be Eliminated?," **IJAER**, 1970, Vol. 6, No. 1, pp. 53-58.

Carey, John L. "One Man's View Of The Sixth International Congress On Accounting," **JOA**, 1952, Vol. 94, No. 3, pp. 306-310.

Carey, John L. "Professional Ethics," **JOA**, 1956, Vol. 102, No. 5, pp. 38-41.

Carey, John L. "Relationship Of Accountants And Lawyers In Tax Practice," **AR**, 1951, Vol. 26, No. 4, pp. 449-455.

Carey, John L. "Seventh International Congress," **JOA**, 1957, Vol. 104, No. 6, pp. 34-38.

Carey, John L. "Tax Settlement Board Bill," **AR**, 1949, Vol. 24, No. 3, p. 272.

Carey, John L. "Teachers And Practitioners," **AR**, 1969, Vol. 44, No. 1, pp. 79-85.

Carey, John L. "The Development Of Aptitude Tests For Accountants," **AR**, 1945, Vol. 20, No. 1, pp. 1-6.

Carey, John L. "The Future Of The Profession," **JOA**, 1956, Vol. 101, No. 5, pp. 54-58.

Carey, John L. "The Integrated Accounting Service," **JOA**, 1965, Vol. 120, No. 5, pp. 61-64.

Carey, John L. "The Origins Of Modern Financial Reporting," **JOA**, 1969, Vol. 128, No. 3, pp. 35-48.

Carey, John L. "The Place Of The CPA In Contemporary Society," **JOA**, 1958, Vol. 106, No. 3, pp. 27-32.

Carey, John L. "The Realities Of Professional Ethics," **AR**, 1947, Vol. 22, No. 2, pp. 119-123.

Carey, John L. "What Is The Professional Practice Of Accounting?," **AR**, 1968, Vol. 43, No. 1, pp. 1-9.

Carey, Kenneth J. (Basi, Bart A., Kenneth J. Carey and Richard D. Twark. "A Comparison Of The Accuracy Of Corporate And Security Analysts' Forecasts Of Earnings," **AR**, 1976, Vol. 51, No. 2, pp. 244-254.)

Carey, Kenneth J. (Basi, Bart A., Kenneth J. Carey and Richard D. Twark. "A Comparison Of The Accuracy Of Corporate And Security Analysts' Forecasts Of Earnings: A Reply," **AR**, 1977, Vol. 52, No. 3, pp. 741-745.)

Cargile, Barney R. and Bruce Bublitz. "Factors Contributing To Published Research By Accounting Faculties," **AR**, 1986, Vol. 61, No. 1, pp. 158-178.

Cargile, Barney R. (Fulmer, William E. and Barney R. Cargile. "Ethical Perceptions Of Accounting Students: Does Exposure To A Code Of Professional Ethics Help?," **IAE**, 1987, Vol. 2, No. 2, pp. 207-219.)

Caricofe, Ronald L. "Establishing Standard Costs In The Concrete Pipe Industry," **MA**, 1982, Vol. 63, No. 8, pp. 45-49.

Carlisle, Howard M. "Cost Accounting For Advanced Technology Programs," **AR**, 1966, Vol. 41, No. 1, pp. 115-120.

Carlow, Alan and Bart Johnson. "Overcoming The Mystique Of EDP Auditing," **MA**, 1984, Vol. 66, No. 2, pp. 30-37.

Carlson, Arthur E. "A Case For Current-Cost Reporting," **MA**, 1973, Vol. 54, No. 8, pp. 35-37.

Carlson, Arthur E. "ASR 190 - The Grand Experiment," **MA**, 1977, Vol. 59, No. 4, pp. 23-25.

Carlson, Arthur E. "Automation In Accounting Systems," **AR**, 1957, Vol. 32, No. 2, pp. 224-228.

Carlson, Barbara Mackey and Joanne A. Collins. "Motivating Managers With Positive Reinforcement," **MA**, 1986, Vol. 67, No. 9, pp. 48-51.

Carlson, Harry B. "The Auditor's Dilemmas In Cash-Basis Reporting," **JOA**, 1955, Vol. 100, No. 3, pp. 46-50.

Carlson, Marvin L. and James W. Lamb. "Constructing A Theory Of Accounting - An Axiomatic Approach," **AR**, 1981, Vol. 56, No. 3, pp. 554-573.

Carlson, Marvin L. "An Application Of Concepts In The Theory Course," **AR**, 1967, Vol. 42, No. 3, pp. 596-598.

Carlson, Marvin L. "Toward A New Design For The Intermediate Accounting Course," **AR**, 1976, Vol. 51, No. 1, pp. 131-138.

Carlson, Ronald E. (Schwieger, Bradley J., Wayne R. Wells and Ronald E. Carlson. "Solicitation - Where Do We Stand Today?," **CPAJ**, 1988, Vol. 58, No. 11, pp. 66-70.)

Carlson, Timothy E. "Needed: A New Interpretation For Interim Reports," **MA**, 1978, Vol. 59, No. 7, pp. 19-22.

Carlsson, J., P. Ehn, B. Erlander, M. L. Perby and A. Sandberg. "Planning And Control From The Perspective Of Labour: A Short Presentation Of The DEMOS Project," **AOS**, 1978, Vol. 3, No. 3/4, pp. 249-260.

Carlton, John L. "Security And Computerized Systems," **MA**, 1974, Vol. 55, No. 8, pp. 33-36.

Carmack, Claude W. (Brenner, Vincent C., Claude W. Carmack and Mark G. Weinstein. "An Empirical Test Of The Motivation-Hygiene Theory," **JAR**, 1971, Vol. 9, No. 2, pp. 359-366.)

Carman, Lewis A. "Non-Linear Depreciation," **AR**, 1956, Vol. 31, No. 3, pp. 454-491.

Carman, Lewis A. "Variations In Gross Profits," **AR**, 1953, Vol. 28, No. 3, pp. 422-424.

Carman-Stone, Marie Sandra. "Unabsorbed Overhead: What To Do When Contracts Are Cancelled," **MA**, 1987, Vol. 68, No. 10, pp. 55-57.

Carmichael, Douglas R. "Reconsider The Exposure Draft On Control Risk," **CPAJ**, 1987, Vol. 57, No. 11, pp. 50-57.

Carmichael, Douglas R. "The Cohen Commission In Perspective: Actions And Reactions," **JAAF**, 1979, Vol. 2, No. 4, pp. 294-306.

Carmichael, Douglas R. (Chenok, Philip B., Douglas R. Carmichael and Thomas P. Kelley. "Accounting And Auditing: The Technical Challenges Ahead," **JOA**, 1980, Vol. 150, No. 5, pp. 62-70.)

Carmichael, D. R. and John J. Willingham. "New Directions In Auditing Education: A Proposal For The Undergraduate Course," **AR**, 1969, Vol. 44, No. 3, pp. 611-615.

Carmichael, D. R. and Ray Whittington. "The Auditor's Changing Role In Financial Reporting," **JAAF**, 1984, Vol. 7, No. 4, pp. 347-361.

Carmichael, D. R. and R. J. Swieringa. "The Compatibility Of Auditing Independence And Management Services - An Identification Of Issues," **AR**, 1968, Vol. 43, No. 4, pp. 697-705.

Carmichael, D. R. "Auditors' Reports - A Search For Criteria," **JOA**, 1972, Vol. 134, No. 3, pp. 67-74.

Carmichael, D. R. "Behavioral Hypotheses Of Internal Control," **AR**, 1970, Vol. 45, No. 2, pp. 235-245.

Carmichael, D. R. "Opinions On Internal Control," **JOA**, 1970, Vol. 130, No. 6, pp. 47-53.

Carmichael, D. R. "Reporting On Forecasts: A U.K. Perspective," **JOA**, 1973, Vol. 135, No. 1, pp. 36-47.

Carmichael, D. R. "Standards For Financial Reporting," **JOA**, 1979, Vol. 147, No. 5, pp. 76-84.

Carmichael, D. R. "Tests Of Transactions - Statistical And Otherwise," **JOA**, 1968, Vol. 125, No. 2, pp. 36-40.

Carmichael, D. R. "The Assurance Function - Auditing At The Crossroads," **JOA**, 1974, Vol. 138, No. 3, pp. 64-72.

Carmichael, D. R. "The Auditor's Role And Responsibilities," **JOA**, 1977, Vol. 144, No. 2, pp. 55-60.

Carmichael, D. R. "The Auditor's New Guide To Errors, Irregularities And Illegal Acts," **JOA**, 1988, Vol. 166, No. 3, pp. 40-48.

Carmichael, D. R. (Asebrook, Richard J. and D. R. Carmichael. "Reporting On Forecasts: A Survey Of Attitudes," **JOA**, 1973, Vol. 136, No. 2, pp. 38-48.)

Carmichael, D. R. (Gafford, W. Wade and D. R. Carmichael. "Materiality, Audit Risk And Sampling: A Nuts-And Bolts Approach (Part One)," **JOA**, 1984, Vol. 158, No. 4, pp. 109-118.)

Carmichael, D. R. (Gafford, W. Wade and D. R. Carmichael. "Materiality, Audit Risk And Smapling: A Nuts-And-Bolts Approach (Part Two)," **JOA**, 1984, Vol. 158, No. 5, pp. 125-138.)

Carmichael, D. R. (Isbell, David B. and D. R. Carmichael. "Disclaimers And Liability - The Rhode Island Trust Case," **JOA**, 1973, Vol. 135, No. 4, pp. 37-42.)

Carmichael, D. R. (Swieringa, Robert J. and D. R. Carmichael. "A Positional Analysis Of Internal Control," **JOA**, 1971, Vol. 131, No. 2, pp. 34-43.)

Carmichael, D. R. (Wiesen, Jeremy and D. R. Carmichael. "High Tech: A Challenge For CPAs," **JOA**, 1983, Vol. 156, No. 2, pp. 67-73.)

Carmichael, D. R. (Willingham, John J. and D. R. Carmichael. "The Professional Auditing Subculture," **ABACUS**, 1968, Vol. 4, No. 2, pp. 153-163.)

Carmichael, D. R., Lee J. Seidler and Richard B. Marcus. "Training Young Auditors - A Realistic Approach Through Simulation," **JOA**, 1971, Vol. 131, No. 5, pp. 49-54.

Carmichael, Geoffrey. "Objective Tests In Accounting," **AR**, 1937, Vol. 12, No. 3, pp. 315-317.

Carmichael, Geoffrey. "Objective Tests In Elementary Accounting," **AR**, 1935, Vol. 10, No. 1, pp. 2-4.

Carmichael, Vernal H. "Device For Determining And Recording Manufacturing Expense Variances," **AR**, 1951, Vol. 26, No. 4, pp. 573-574.

Carmony, Larry. "Accounting In The Context Of Its Environment: The Uruguayan Case," **IJAER**, 1987, Vol. 22, No. 2, pp. 41-56.

Carnes, Curtis. (Collier, Boyd and Curtis Carnes. "Convertible Bonds And Financial Reality," **MA**, 1979, Vol. 60, No. 8, pp. 47-48.)

Carpenter, Charles G. and Robert H. Strawser. "Disclosure Of Changes In Accounting Methods," **JAR**, 1972, Vol. 10, No. 1, pp. 209-216.

Carpenter, Charles G. and Robert H. Strawser. "A Study Of The Job Satisfaction Of Academic Accountants," **AR**, 1971, Vol. 46, No. 3, pp. 509-518.

Carpenter, Charles G. and Robert H. Strawser. "Initial Experience With Satisfactory-Unsatisfactory Grading In Accounting Courses," **AR**, 1971, Vol. 46, No. 1, pp. 160-162.

Carpenter, Charles G. and Robert H. Strawser. "Displacement Of Auditors When Clients Go Public," **JOA**, 1971, Vol. 131, No. 6, pp. 55-58.

Carpenter, Charles G. (Curley, Anthony J. and Charles G. Carpenter. "Present Value Models And The Multi-Asset Problem: A Comment," **AR**, 1974, Vol. 49, No. 4, pp. 812-815.)

Carpenter, C. C. "Comments On What Is Appreciation," **AR**, 1930, Vol. 5, No. 1, pp. 10-12.

Carpenter, Frances H. "The Impact Of Financial Reporting Requirements On Municipal Officials' Fixed Asset Acquisition Decisions," **RIGNA**, 1988, Vol. 4, pp. 49-77.

Carpenter, Vivian L. "The Effects Of Interest Group Competition On Funding Government Management Information Systems," **RIGNA**, 1987, Vol. 3, Part A, pp. 67-105.

Carper, Wm. Brent, M. Frank Barton, Jr. and Haroldene F. Wunder. "The Future Of Forecasting," **MA**, 1979, Vol. 61, No. 2, pp. 27-31.

Carper, Wm. B. and J. M. Posey. "The Validity Of Selected Surrogate Measures of Human Resource Value: A Field Study," **AOS**, 1976, Vol. 1, No. 2/3, pp. 143-152.

Carr, William. "Professional Accountants Today," **AR**, 1943, Vol. 18, No. 4, pp. 364-367.

Carreau, David G. "Calendar Variance Reporting," **MA**, 1970, Vol. 51, No. 7, pp. 29-31.

Carrier, N. H. (Baxter, W. T. and N. H. Carrier. "Depreciation, Replacement Price, And Cost Of Capital," **JAR**, 1971, Vol. 9, No. 2, pp. 189-214.)

Carrithers, J. M. and R. K. Mautz. "Arithmetic And Accountancy," **AR**, 1942, Vol. 17, No. 2, pp. 163-170.

Carrithers, J. M. "Problems And Theories Of Teaching Elementary Accounting," **AR**, 1951, Vol. 26, No. 1, pp. 93-101.

Carroll, Gay. "Some Challenges To Accounting," **AR**, 1951, Vol. 26, No. 1, pp. 9-18.

Carroll, Karen B. (Sale, Timothy J. and Karen B. Carroll. "Tax Planning Tools For The Multinational Corporation," **MA**, 1979, Vol. 60, No. 12. pp. 37-42.)

Carroll, Monroe S. "Uniform Hospital Accounting: Comments,"

AR, 1936, Vol. 11, No. 2, pp. 162-163.

Carroll, R. J. (Holt, R. N. and R. J. Carroll. "Classification Of Commercial Bank Loans Through Policy Capturing," **AOS**, 1980, Vol. 5, No. 3, pp. 285-296.)

Carroll, Thomas H. "Attracting And Maintaining A Supply Of Ellective Accounting Teachers," **AR**, 1956, Vol. 31, pp. 15-23.

Carroll, Thomas H. "Education For Business: A Dynamic Concept And Process," **AR**, 1958, Vol. 33, No. 1, pp. 3-10.

Carruth, J. Harvey, Harold B. Whitehead and Kenneth E. Anderson. "Maximizing Contributions To Retirement And Deferred Compensation Plans Under Sections 403(b), 401(k). And 457: A Linear Programming Approach," **JATA**, 1986, Vol. 8, No. 1, pp. 49-72.

Carruth, Paul J. and Thurrell O. McClendon. "How Supervisors React To 'Meeting The Budget' Pressure," **MA**, 1984, Vol. 66, No. 5, pp. 50-54.

Carruth, Paul J., Thurrell O. McClendon and Milton R. Ballard. "What Supervisors Don't Like About Budget Evaluations," **MA**, 1983, Vol. 64, No. 8, pp. 38-45.

Carsberg, Bryan V. "The Contribution of P. D. Leake To The Theory Of Goodwill Valuation," **JAR**, 1966, Vol. 4, No. 1, pp. 1-15.

Carsberg, Bryan, Anthony Hope and R. W. Scapens. "The Objectives Of Published Accounting Reports: Reply To A Comment," **ABR**, 1974-75, Vol. 5, No. 18, pp. 152-155.

Carsberg, Bryan, Anthony Hope and R. W. Scapens. "The Objectives Of Published Accounting Reports," **ABR**, 1973-74, Vol. 4, No. 15, pp. 162-173.

Carsberg, Bryan. "On The Linear Programming Approach To Asset Valuation," **JAR**, 1969, Vol. 7, No. 2, pp. 165-182.

Carscallen, Morley P. "Audit Efficiency," **CPAJ**, 1982, Vol. 52, No. 5, pp. 18-23.

Carslaw, Charles A. P. N. "Anomalies In Income Numbers: Evidence Of Goal Oriented Behavior," **AR**, 1988, Vol. 63, No. 2, pp. 321-327.

Carson, A. B. "A Fund-Change-Statement Approach To The Calculation Of Inflationary Distortion In Conventional Income Measurement," **AR**, 1954, Vol. 29, No. 3, pp. 373-382.

Carson, A. B. "A Method For Speeding The Calculation And Control Of Depreciation Reserves," **AR**, 1953, Vol. 28, No. 2, pp. 239-243.

Carson, A. B. "A System To Reduce Year-End Work By Combining Entries," **JOA**, 1952, Vol. 93, No. 4, pp. 426-433.

Carson, A. B. "A 'Source And Application Of Funds' Philosophy Of Financial Accounting," **AR**, 1949, Vol. 24, No. 2, pp. 159-170.

Carson, A. B. "An Investment-Recovery-First Concept Of Taxable Profit," **AR**, 1951, Vol. 26, No. 4, pp. 456-467.

Carson, A. B. "Cash Movement: The Heart Of Income Measurement," **AR**, 1965, Vol. 40, No. 2, pp. 334-337.

Carson, A. B. "Determination Of Merchandise Turnover," **AR**, 1944, Vol. 19, No. 3, pp. 306-309.

Carson, A. B. "Profile Of A Profession," **JOA**, 1959, Vol. 107, No. 1, pp. 50-56.

Carson, A. B. "The New Internal Revenue Act And The Prosperity Of The Economy," **AR**, 1956, Vol. 31, No. 3, pp. 349-357.

Carson, A. B. "The Terminal-Date-Group Method Of Depreciation Accounting," **JOA**, 1955, Vol. 99, No. 4, pp. 56-62.

Carson, John R. "Business Games: A Technique For Teaching Decision-Making," **MA**, 1967, Vol. 49, No. 2, pp. 31-35.

Carson, William. (Koester, Robert and William Carson. "An Appraisal Of Collegiate Business Students' Understanding Of Price-Level-Adjusted Financial Statements," **AR**, 1976. Vol. 51. No. 3, pp. 625-627.)

Carter, Albert G. "Computing Inventory R.O.I.," **MA**, 1973, Vol. 55. No. 1, pp. 43-45.

Carter, Clairmont P. (Kistler, Linda H., Clairmont P. Carter and Brackston Hinchey. "Planning And Control In The 19th Century Ice Trade," **AHJ**, 1984, Vol. 11, No. 1, pp. 19-30.)

Carter, Jack and Don Tomlinson. "Extending PERT/CPM Into Computerized LOB," **MA**, 1970, Vol. 51, No. 11, pp. 41-44.

Carter, James G. "A Suggested Supplement To Audit Test Programs," **AR**, 1952, Vol. 27, No. 1, pp. 89-93.

Carter, K. LeM. "Canadian Legislation For Taxation On Corporate Income," **JOA**, 1951, Vol. 92, No. 2, pp. 209-213.

Carter, Prickett. "Some Issues Involved In 'Original Cost'." **AR**, 1945, Vol. 20, No. 2, pp. 222-230.

Carter, William E. "Planning Opportunities In A Deflationary Period," **CA**, 1986, Vol. 4, No. 1, pp. 38-43.

Carter, William K. "A Benefits Approach To Certain Accounting Policy Choices," **AR**, 1981, Vol. 56, No. 1, pp. 108-114.

Caruso, Robert L. "Paying Bills The Electronic Way," **MA**, 1984, Vol. 65. No. 10, pp. 24-27.

Carver, M. Robert, Jr. and Thomas E. King. "Attitudes Of Accounting Practitioners Towards Accounting Faculty And Accounting Education," **JAED**, 1986, Vol. 4, No. 1, pp. 31-43.

Carver, M. Robert. (Ault, David E. and M. Robert Carver. "The Effect of Pedagogical Format On The Performance Of MBA Students In Graduate-Level Accounting Courses," **IAE**, 1987, Vol. 2, No. 2, pp. 161-172.)

Cary, William L. "Section 102 May Not Be The Menace Some Tax Men Consider It To Be," **JOA**, 1950, Vol. 89, No. 3, pp. 219-223.

Cary, William L. "The SEC And Accounting," **JOA**, 1963, Vol. 116, No. 6, pp. 47-50.

Casal, Jose. "Barter Accounting In The Puerto Rican Sugar Industry," **MA**, 1969, Vol. 51, No. 2, pp. 48-50.

Casciani, William P. (Schrott, Alfred N., William P. Casciani and Jeffrey Bernstein. "Interest Rate Futures

Trading - Part I," **CPAJ**, 1980, Vol. 50, No. 4, pp. 16-22.)

Casciani, William P. (Schrott, Alfred N., William P. Casciani and Jeffrey Bernstein. "Interest Rate Futures Trading - Part II," **CPAJ**, 1980, Vol. 50, No. 5, pp. 27-32.)

Case, Jay C. "Electronic Banking Comes To First-Citizens," **MA**, 1979, Vol. 60, No. 10, pp. 39-42.

Case, Richard. "Interview Techniques For Hiring The Right Candidates," **JOA**, 1988, Vol. 166, No. 5, pp. 90-96.

Casey, Brian J. "Credibility And Cleavage Problems Of The Accounting Profession," **AR**, 1971, Vol. 46, No. 2, pp. 387-389.

Casey, Cornelius and Norman Bartczak. "Using Operating Cash Flow Data To Predict Financial Distress: Some Extensions," **JAR**, 1985, Vol. 23, No. 1, pp. 384-401.

Casey, Cornelius and Thomas I. Selling. "The Effect Of Task Predictability And Prior Probability Disclosure On Judgment Quality And Confidence," **AR**, 1986, Vol. 61, No. 2, pp. 302-317.

Casey, Cornelius J. "Prior Probability Disclosure And Loan Officers' Judgments: Some Evidence of The Impact," **JAR**, 1983, Vol. 21, No. 1, pp. 300-307.

Casey, Cornelius J., Jr. "The Predictive-Ability Criterion And User Prediction Models: A Comment," **AR**, 1976, Vol. 51, No. 3, pp. 677-680.

Casey, Cornelius J., Jr. "The Usefulness Of Accounting Ratios For Subjects' Predictions Of Corporate Failure: Replication And Extensions," **JAR**, 1980, Vol. 18, No. 2, pp. 603-613.

Casey, Cornelius J., Jr. "The Variation In Accounting Information Load: The Effect On Loan Officers' Predictions Of Bankruptcy," **AR**, 1980, Vol. 55, No. 1, pp. 36-49.

Casey, Cornelius, Victor E. McGee and Clyde P. Stickney. "Discriminating Between Reorganized And Liquidated Firms In Bankruptcy," **AR**, 1986, Vol. 61, No. 2, pp. 249-262.

Casey, Michael P. "International Transfer Pricing," **MA**, 1985, Vol. 67, No. 4, pp. 31-35.

Casey, William J. and J. K. Lasser. "Decisions To Make Now To Minimize Excess-Profits Tax Liability," **JOA**, 1951, Vol. 91, No. 2, pp. 243-251.

Casey, William J. "How To Keep A Close Corporation Alive When The Owner Dies," **JOA**, 1952, Vol. 93, No. 4, pp. 420-425.

Cash, James I, Jr., Andrew D. Bailey, Jr. and Andrew B. Whinston. "A Survey Of Techniques For Auditing EDP-Based Accounting Information Systems," **AR**, 1977, Vol. 52, No. 4, pp. 813-832.

Cash, L. Stephen and Thomas L. Dickens. "Coping With New Auto Record-Keeping Rules," **MA**, 1985, Vol. 67, No. 2, pp. 32-39.

Cash, L. Stephen. (Bryan, E. Lewis and L. Stephen Cash. "Forgiveness Of Debt - Income Or Basis Adjustment?," **CPAJ**, 1985, Vol. 55, No. 8, pp. 30-35.)

Casler, Darwin J. and Thomas W. Hall. "Firm-Specific Asset Valuation Accuracy Using A Composite Price Index," **JAR**, 1985, Vol. 23, No. 1, pp. 110-122.

Casler, Darwin J. (Hall, Thomas W. and Darwin J. Casler. "Using Indexing To Estimate Current Costs - Composite Or Multiple Indexes?," **JAAF**, 1985, Vol. 8, No. 3, pp. 210-224.)

Caspari, John A. "Coping With Plagiarism," **JAED**, 1988, Vol. 6, No. 1, pp. 117-121.

Caspari, John A. "Wherefore Accounting Data - Explanation, Prediction And Decisions," **AR**, 1976, Vol. 51, No. 4, pp. 739-746.

Caspole, John M. "Costing From A Data Bank." **MA**, 1972, Vol. 54, No. 1, pp. 47-50.

Cassady, Ralph, Jr. "Accounting For Customer Purchases As A Sales Promotional Device," **AR**, 1935, Vol. 10, No. 1, pp. 64-68.

Cassidy, David B. "Investor Evaluation Of Accounting Information: Some Additional Empirical Evidence," **JAR**, 1976, Vol. 14, No. 2, pp. 212-229.

Castellano, Joseph F. and Harper A. Roehm. "An Approach To Fairness In Disclosure," **MA**, 1975, Vol. 56, No. 8, pp. 20-22.

Castellano, Joseph F. and Harper A. Roehm. "Research In Behavioral Accounting Courses: An Approach," **AR**, 1977, Vol. 52, No. 1, pp. 211-215.

Castellano, Joseph F. (Roehm, Harper A. and Joseph F. Castellano. "Inflation Accounting: A Compromise," **CPAJ**, 1978, Vol. 48, No. 9, pp. 38-47.)

Castello, Albert P. "The Model Cities Program: An Application Of PPBS," **MA**, 1973, Vol. 54, No. 7, pp. 29-33.

Castenholz, William B. "Selling And Administrative Expense Analysis As A Basis For Sales Control And Cost Reduction," **AR**, 1931, Vol. 6, No. 2, pp. 125-130.

Castenholz, William B. "The Accountant And Changing Monetary Values," **AR**, 1931, Vol. 6, No. 4, pp. 282-288.

Castenholz, W. B. "Accounting And Code Regulation: Comments," **AR**, 1935, Vol. 10, No. 1, pp. 75-76.

Castenholz, W. B. "Bridging The Gap," **AR**, 1927, Vol. 2, No. 3, pp. 237-245.

Castenholz, W. B. "Effects Of The Monthly Profit And Loss Statement," **AR**, 1926, Vol. 1, No. 2, pp. 12-19.

Castenholz, W. B. "Investing In Obsolescence," **AR**, 1928, Vol. 3, No. 3, pp. 269-273.

Castenholz, W. B. "That Application Of Funds Statement," **AR**, 1956, Vol. 31, No. 3, pp. 431-434.

Castenholz, W. B. "The Proper Treatment Of Distribution Costs," **AR**, 1927, Vol. 2, No. 1, pp. 19-27.

Castenholz, W. B. "What Constitutes Material Cost Of Production," **AR**, 1958, Vol. 33, No. 4, pp. 650-653.

Castle, Eric F. "The Problems Of Consolidation Of Accounts Of A Multinational Enterprise: Shell Group Of Companies - Shell Transport And Trading Company, Limited, U.K.," **IJAER**, 1980, Vol. 16, No. 1, pp. 209-219.

Catalanello, Ralph F. (Zikmund, William G., Ralph F. Catalanello and Steve M. Wegener. "The Accounting Student's Job-Rating Criteria: An Experiment," **AR**, 1977, Vol. 52, No. 3, pp. 729-735.)

Catalano, Anthony J. "The Rehabilitation Tax Shelter," **MA**, 1973, Vol. 55, No. 6, pp. 37-40.

Cataldo, Fred. "Make It Happen," **MA**, 1970, Vol. 51, No. 11, pp. 38-40.

Cathey, Jack M. (O'Neil, Cherie J., Jack M. Cathey and Tonya K. Flesher. "An Analysis Of Ph.D. Dissertations In Taxation: 1977-1985," **IAE**, 1988, Vol. 3, No. 1, pp. 120-130.)

Catlett, George R. "Controversy Over Uniformity Of Accounting Principles," **JOA**, 1964, Vol. 118, No. 6, pp. 37-43.

Catlett, George R. "Factors That Influence Accounting Principles," **JOA**, 1960, Vol. 110, No. 4, pp. 44-50.

Catlett, George R. "New Demands On The Profession," **JOA**, 1957, Vol. 104, No. 1, pp. 25-28.

Catlett, George R. "Relation Of Acceptance To Accounting Principles," **JOA**, 1960, Vol. 109, No. 3, pp. 33-38.

Catlett, George R. "Relationship Of Auditing Standards To Detection Of Fraud," **CPAJ**, 1975, Vol. 45, No. 4, pp. 13-22.

Cato, Erle. "Accrued Cost, Not 'Accrued Expenditures' Is The Answer For Government," **AR**, 1959, Vol. 34, No. 3, pp. 392-398.

Cats-Baril, William L., James F. Gatti and D. Jacque Grinnell. "Joint Product Costing In The Semiconductor Industry," **MA**, 1986, Vol. 67, No. 8, pp. 28-38.

Cats-Baril, William, James F. Gatti and D. Jacque Grinnell. "Transfer Pricing Policy In A Dynamic Market," **MA**, 1988, Vol. 69, No. 8, pp. 30-33.

Cattanach, Richard L. and Glyn W. Hanbery. "Audit Planning: An Application Of Network Analysis," **AR**, 1973, Vol. 48, No. 3, pp. 609-611.

Catt, C. C. and D. W. Rivett. "Fixed Asset Prices And Economic Production Theory," **ABACUS**, 1979, Vol. 15, No. 2, pp. 128-135.

Causey, Denzil Y., Jr. "Foreseeability As A Determinant Of Audit Responsibility," **AR**, 1973, Vol. 48, No. 2, pp. 258-267.

Causey, Denzil Y., Jr. "Newly Emerging Standards Of Auditor Responsibility," **AR**, 1976, Vol. 51, No. 1, pp. 19-30.

Causey, Denzil Y., Jr. "Newly Emerging Standards Of Auditor Responsibility: A Reply," **AR**, 1977, Vol. 52, No. 1, pp. 259-260.

Causey, Denzil Y., Jr. "The CPA's Guide To Whistle Blowing," **CPAJ**, 1988, Vol. 58, No. 8, pp. 26-37.

Cauthorn, L. Terry. "Whatever Happened To Social Accountants?," **MA**, 1977, Vol. 58, No. 10, pp. 55-60.

Caygill, Majorie. (Johnson, T. J. and Marjorie Caygill. "The Development Of Accountancy Links In The Commonwealth," **ABR**, 1970-71, Vol. 1, No. 2, pp. 155-173.)

Celi, Louis J. "Critical Issues Facing Senior Financial Executives," **CA**, 1986, Vol. 4, No. 3, pp. 30-38.

Cerf, Alan Robert. "A Survey Of Compliance With Reporting Standards," **JOA**, 1963, Vol. 115, No. 2, pp. 42-49.

Cerf, Alan Robert. "Accounting For Retail Land Sales," **AR**, 1975, Vol. 50, No. 3, pp. 451-465.

Cerf, Alan Robert. "Price Level Changes, Inventory Valuations, And Tax Considerations," **AR**, 1957, Vol. 32, No. 4, pp. 554-565.

Cerf, Alan Robert. "Tax Allocation And Railroad Accounting," **JOA**, 1958, Vol. 106, No. 4, pp. 62-69.

Cerisano, Michael P. "SMS: Social Measurement Systems For The Future - A Practitioner's Preview," **CPAJ**, 1974, Vol. 44, No. 5, pp. 25-30.

Cerullo, Michael J. and John C. Corless. "Auditing Computer Systems," **CPAJ**, 1984, Vol. 54, No. 9, pp. 18-33.

Cerullo, Michael J. "Accountants' Role In Computer Contingency Planning," **CPAJ**, 1981, Vol. 51, No. 1, pp. 22-26.

Cerullo, Michael J. "Controls For Data Base Systems," **CPAJ**, 1982, Vol. 52, No. 1, pp. 30-35.

Cerullo, Michael J. "Data Communications: Opportunity For Accountants," **CPAJ**, 1984, Vol. 54, No. 4, pp. 40-47.

Cerullo, Michael J. "Designing Accounting Information Systems," **MA**, 1985, Vol. 66, No. 12, pp. 37-42.

Cerullo, Michael J. "In-House Computers For CPA Firms," **CPAJ**, 1976, Vol. 46, No. 6, pp. 9-14.

Cerullo, Michael J. "MIS: What Can Go Wrong?," **MA**, 1979, Vol. 60, No. 10, pp. 43-48.

Cerullo, Michael J. "Post-Implementation Evaluation Of Computer Systems," **CPAJ**, 1982, Vol. 52, No. 5, pp. 45-51.

Cerullo, Michael J. "The Data Base Concept," **MA**, 1977, Vol. 59, No. 5, pp. 43-47.

Cerullo, Michael J. "What A Client Should Know About Selecting An EDP Service Bureau," **CPAJ**, 1974, Vol. 44, No. 10, pp. 47-50.

Cerullo, Michael J. (Kolmin, Frank W. and Michael J. Cerullo. "Measuring Productivity And Efficiency," **MA**, 1973, Vol. 55, No. 5, pp. 32-34.)

Cesnik, Gary R. (Endsley, Lionel I. and Gary R. Cesnik. "Lifo For Bargain-Purchased Inventories: The Tax Connection," **JOA**, 1986, Vol. 162, No. 2, pp. 94-101.)

Chadwick, Lester W. (Paretta, Robert L. and Lester W. Chadwick. "The Sequencing Of Examination Questions And Its Effects On Student Performance," **AR**, 1975, Vol. 50, No. 3, pp. 595-601.)

Chalnick, Robert I. (McKeon, Kevin J. and Robert I. Chalnick. "Accounting And Tax Aspects Of GNMA Mortgage-

Backed Securities," **JOA**, 1972, Vol. 134, No. 2, pp. 41-47.)

Chalos, Peter. "A Spreadsheet Analysis Of Different Costing Systems," **JAED**, 1988, Vol. 6, No. 2, pp. 345-353.

Chalos, Peter. "Financial Distress: A Comparative Study Of Individual, Model, And Committee Assessments," **JAR**, 1985, Vol. 23, No. 2, pp. 527-543.

Chalos, Peter. (Tishlias, Dennis P. and Peter Chalos. "Product Pricing Behaviour Under Different Costing Systems," **ABR**, 1988, Vol. 18, No. 71, pp. 257-265.)

Chamberlain, Douglas C. "Capitalization Of Lease Obligations," **MA**, 1975, Vol. 57, No. 6, pp. 37-38.

Chamberlain, Henry T. "On The Teaching Of Auditing," **AR**, 1935, Vol. 10, No. 1, pp. 17-19.

Chambers, Andrew D. "Internal Auditing At A University - An Example In Context," **AR**, 1978, Vol. 53, No. 1, pp. 143-147.

Chambers, Anne E. and Stephen H. Penman. "Timeliness Of Reporting And The Stock Price Reaction To Earnings Announcements," **JAR**, 1984, Vol. 22, No. 1, pp. 21-47.

Chambers, A. D. "Developments In Internal Auditing," **ABR**, 1979-80, Vol. 10, No. 39, pp. 273-284.

Chambers, A. D. "Investment Criteria For EDP Systems," **ABR**, 1974-75, Vol. 5, No. 17, pp. 18-24.

Chambers, D. J., H. S. Singhal, B. D. Taylor and D. L. Wright. "Developing Dividend And Financing Policies With A Computer Terminal," **ABR**, 1970-71, Vol. 1, No. 4, pp. 267-273.

Chambers, Jean. (Doxey, Bobby L. and Jean Chambers. "Making The Most Of Bank Information Systems," **MA**, 1983, Vol. 64, No. 8, pp. 58-61.)

Chambers, John C. and Satinder K. Mullick. "Investment Decision-Making In A Multinational Enterprise," **MA**, 1971, Vol. 53, No. 2, pp. 13-20.

Chambers, John C. and Satinder K. Mullick. "Determining The Acquisition Value Of A Company," **MA**, 1970, Vol. 51, No. 10, pp. 24-31.

Chambers, Raymond J. "Accounting Principles Or Accounting Policies?," **JOA**, 1973, Vol. 135, No. 5, pp. 48-53.

Chambers, Raymond J. "Measurement In Current Accounting Practices: A Critique," **AR**, 1972, Vol. 47, No. 3, pp. 488-509.

Chambers, Raymond J. "Measures And Values," **AR**, 1968, Vol. 43, No. 2, pp. 239-247.

Chambers, Raymond J. "Why Bother With Postulates?," **JAR**, 1963, Vol. 1, No. 1, pp. 3-15.

Chambers, R. J. "A Critical Examination Of Australian Accounting Standards," **ABACUS**, 1975, Vol. 11, No. 2, pp. 136-152.

Chambers, R. J. "A Matter Of Principle," **AR**, 1966, Vol. 41, No. 3, pp. 443-457.

Chambers, R. J. "A Study Of A Price Level Study," **ABACUS**, 1966, Vol. 2, No. 2, pp. 97-118.

Chambers, R. J. "A Study Of A Study Of A Price Level Study," **ABACUS**, 1967, Vol. 3, No. 1, pp. 62-73.

Chambers, R. J. "Accounting Education For The Twenty-First Century," **ABACUS**, 1987, Vol. 23, No. 2, pp. 97-106.

Chambers, R. J. "Accounting For Foreign Business," **ABACUS**, 1983, Vol. 19, No. 1, pp. 14-28.

Chambers, R. J. "Accounting 'One Of The Finest Inventions Of The Human Spirit'," **CAR**, 1984-85, Vol. 1, No. 1, pp. 1-46.

Chambers, R. J. "Asset Revaluations And Stock Dividends," **JOA**, 1958, Vol. 106, No. 2, pp. 55-68.

Chambers, R. J. "Canning's 'The Economics Of Accountancy' - After 50 Years," **AR**, 1979, Vol. 54, No. 4, pp. 764-775.

Chambers, R. J. "Continuously Contemporary Accounting - Additivity And Action," **AR**, 1967, Vol. 42, No. 4, pp. 751-757.

Chambers, R. J. "Continuously Contemporary Accounting: Misunderstandings And Misrepresentations," **ABACUS**, 1976, Vol. 12, No. 2, pp. 137-151.

Chambers, R. J. "Detail For A Blueprint," **AR**, 1957, Vol. 32, No. 2, pp. 206-215.

Chambers, R. J. "Discounted Cash Equivalents: A Note In Response," **ABACUS**, 1978, Vol. 14, No. 2, pp. 188-190.

Chambers, R. J. "Edwards And Bell On Income Measurement In Retrospect," **ABACUS**, 1982, Vol. 18, No. 1, pp. 1-39.

Chambers, R. J. "Edwards And Bell On Business Income," **AR**, 1965, Vol. 40, No. 4, pp. 731-741.

Chambers, R. J. "Financial Information And The Securities Market," **ABACUS**, 1965, Vol. 1, No. 1, pp. 3-30.

Chambers, R. J. "Measurement And Objectivity In Accounting," **AR**, 1964, Vol. 39, No. 2, pp. 264-274.

Chambers, R. J. "Measurement In Accounting," **JAR**, 1965, Vol. 3, No. 1, pp. 32-62.

Chambers, R. J. "NOD, COG And PuPU: See How Inflation Teases!," **JOA**, 1975, Vol. 140, No. 3, pp. 56-62.

Chambers, R. J. "Observation As A Method Of Inquiry," **ABACUS**, 1973, Vol. 9, No. 2, pp. 156-175.

Chambers, R. J. "Price Variation Accounting - An Improved Representation," **JAR**, 1967, Vol. 5, No. 2, pp. 215-220.

Chambers, R. J. "Profit Measurement, Capital Maintenance And Service Potential: A Review Article," **ABACUS**, 1975, Vol. 11, No. 1, pp. 97-104.

Chambers, R. J. "Prospective Adventures In Accounting Ideas," **AR**, 1967, Vol. 42, No. 2, pp. 241-253.

Chambers, R. J. "Pursuit Of An Ideal," **CAR**, 1984-85, Vol. 1, No. 1, pp. 58-63.

Chambers, R. J. "Second Thoughts On Continuously Contemporary Accounting," **ABACUS**, 1970, Vol. 6, No. 1, pp. 39-55.

Chambers, R. J. "Some Observations On 'Structure Of Accounting Theory'," **AR**, 1956, Vol. 31, No. 4, pp. 584-592.

Chambers, R. J. "Stock Market Prices And Accounting Research." **ABACUS**, 1974, Vol. 10 No. 1, pp. 39-54.

Chambers, R. J. "Tax Allocation And Financial Reporting," **ABACUS**, 1968, Vol. 4, No. 2, pp. 99-123.

Chambers, R. J. "The Conditions Of Research In Accounting," **JOA**, 1960, Vol. 110, No. 6, pp. 33-39.

Chambers, R. J. "The Functional Utility Of Resale Price Accounting," **IJAER**, 1985, Vol. 21, No. 1, pp. 53-70.

Chambers, R. J. "The Functions Of Published Financial Statements," **ABR**, 1975-76, Vol. 6, No. 22, pp. 83-94.

Chambers, R. J. "The Mathematics Of Accounting And Estimating," **ABACUS**, 1967, Vol. 3, No. 2, pp. 163-180.

Chambers, R. J. "The Missing Link In Supervision Of The Securities Market," **ABACUS**, 1969, Vol. 5, No. 1, pp. 16-36.

Chambers, R. J. "The Myths And Science Of Accounting," **AOS**, 1980, Vol. 5, No. 1, pp. 167-180.

Chambers, R. J. "The Possibility Of A Normative Accounting Standard," **AR**, 1976, Vol. 51, No. 3, pp. 646-652.

Chambers, R. J. "The Search For System In Financial Calculation," **ABACUS**, 1981, Vol. 17, No. 1, pp. 68-72.

Chambers, R. J. "The Use And Abuse Of A Notation: A History Of An Idea," **ABACUS**, 1978, Vol. 14, No. 2, pp. 122-144.

Chambers, R. J. "Third Thoughts," **ABACUS**, 1974, Vol. 10 No. 2. pp. 129-137.

Chambers, R. J. "Usefulness - The Vanishing Premise In Accounting Standard Setting," **ABACUS**, 1979, Vol. 15, No. 2. pp. 71-92.

Chambers, R. J. "Value To The Owner," **ABACUS**, 1971, Vol. 7, No. 1, pp. 62-72.

Chambers, R. J. "Whatever Happened To CCE?," **AR**, 1976, Vol. 51, No. 2, pp. 385-390.

Chambers, R. J., John W. Kennelly, Thomas W. McRae, Frank K. Reilly and W. Keith Weltmer. "Historical Cost Accounting," **ABACUS**, 1971, Vol. 7, No. 1, p. 39.

Chambers, R. J., William S. Hopwood and James C. McKeown. "The Relevance Of Varieties Of Accounting Information: A U.S.A. Survey," **ABACUS**, 1984, Vol. 20, No. 2, pp. 99-110.

Chan, Anthony Moung-Yin. "The Pattern Of The Theoretical Basis Of IAS: Accounting Theory Models At The International Level," **IJAER**, 1986, Vol. 22, No. 1, pp. 101-117.

Chan, James L. and Marc A. Rubin. "The Role Of Information In A Democracy And In Government Operations: The Public Choice Methodology," **RIGNA**, 1987, Vol. 3, Part B, pp. 3-27.

Chan, James L. and Ronald D. Picur. "Advances In Governmental Accounting: A Review Of Research And Policy," **AIA**, 1986, Vol. 3, pp. 181-220.

Chan, James L. "Fund Reporting And Municipal Credit Risk: A Discussion Of Ingram's Tests," **CAR**, 1986-87, Vol. 3, No. 1. pp. 222-225.

Chan, James L. "Organizational Consensus Regarding The Relative Importance Of Research Output Indicators," **AR**, 1978, Vol. 53, No. 2, pp. 309-323.

Chan, James L. "The Birth Of The Governmental Accounting Standards Board: How? Why? What Next?," **RIGNA**, 1985, Vol. 1, pp. 3-32.

Chan, James L. (Belkaoui, Ahmed and James L. Chan. "Professional Value System Of Academic Accountants: An Empirical Inquiry," **AIPIA**, 1988, Vol. 2, pp. 1-28.)

Chan, J. L. "Corporate Disclosure In Occupational Safety And Health: Some Empirical Evidence," **AOS**, 1979, Vol. 4, No. 4. pp. 273-282.

Chan, K. Hung and Bajis Dodin. "A Decision Support System For Audit-Staff Scheduling With Precedence Constraints And Due Dates," **AR**, 1986, Vol. 61, No. 4, pp. 726-734.

Chan, K. Hung and Peter Tryfos. "Audit Sampling From Skewed Populations And Small Samples," **ABR**, 1983-84, Vol. 14, No. 56, pp. 311-318.

Chan, K. Hung and Thomas T. Cheng. "The Recovery Of Nuclear Power Plant Decommissioning Costs," **JAAF**, 1984, Vol. 7, No. 2, pp. 164-177.

Chan, K. H. (Tang, Roger Y. W. and K. H. Chan. "Environmental Variables Of International Transfer Pricing: A Japan-United States Comparison," **ABACUS**, 1979, Vol. 15, No. 1, pp. 3-12.)

Chan, K. H., S. F. Lam and Roger Tang. "Probabilistic Approaches To Return On Investment And Residual Income: A Comment," **AR**, 1979, Vol. 54, No. 3, pp. 643-649.

Chan, Sau Lan. "Accounting For A Drive-In Diner," **MA**, 1975, Vol. 56. No. 11, pp. 39-42.

Chan, Stephen. "Notes To Financial Statements," **JOA**, 1961, Vol. 111, No. 3, pp. 54-58.

Chan, Stephen. "The Hazards Of Write-Up Work," **CPAJ**, 1972, Vol. 42. No. 8, pp. 635-639.

Chan, Stephen. "The Theory And Practice Of Accountants' Workpapers," **JOA**, 1954, Vol. 97, No. 3, pp. 329-334.

Chandler, A. D., Jr. and H. Daems. "Administrative Coordination, Allocation And Monitoring: A Comparative Analysis Of The Emergence Of Accounting And Organization In The U.S.A. And Europe," **AOS**, 1979, Vol. 4, No. 1/2, pp. 3-20.

Chandler, John S. and Thomas N. Trone. "'Bottom-Up' Budgeting And Control," **MA**, 1982, Vol. 63, No. 8, pp. 37-40.

Chandler, John S. "A Course On The Management Of The Systems Development Processing With Hands-On Computing," **JAED**, 1984, Vol. 2, No. 1, pp. 99-110.

Chandler, John S., Thomas Trone and Michael Weiland. "Decision Support Systems Are For Small Businesses," **MA**, 1983, Vol. 64, No. 10, pp. 34-39.

Chandra, Dyan. (O'Connor, Melvin C. and Gyan Chandra. "Replacement Cost Disclosure," **MA**, 1978, Vol. 60, No. 3, pp. 58-59.)

Chandra, Gyan and Jacob B. Paperman. "Direct Costing Vs. Absorption Costing: A Historical Review," **AHJ**, 1976,

Vol. 3, No. 1-4, pp. 1-9.

Chandra, Gyan and Melvin N. Greenball. "Management Reluctance To Disclosure: An Empirical Study," **ABACUS**, 1977, Vol. 13, No. 2, pp. 141-154.

Chandra, Gyan. "A Study Of The Consensus On Disclosure Among Public Accountants And Security Analysts," **AR**, 1974, Vol. 49, No. 4, pp. 733-742.

Chandra, Gyan. "A Study Of The Consensus On Disclosure Among Public Accountants And Security Analysts: An Alternative Interpretation," **AR**, 1977, Vol. 52, No. 2, pp. 513-515.

Chandra, Gyan. "Information Needs Of Security Analysts," **JOA**, 1975, Vol. 140, No. 6, pp. 65-70.

Chandy, P. R. (Kharabe, Prakash S. and P. R. Chandy. "Private Placements: An Overview For The Financial Executive," **CA**, 1986, Vol. 4, No. 3, pp. 59-65.)

Chaney, Paul K. "Defeasance: Financial Tool Or Window Dressing?," **MA**, 1985, Vol. 67, No. 5, pp. 52-55.

Chaney, Paul K. (Jeter, Debra C. and Paul K. Chaney. "A Financial Statement Analysis Approach To Deferred Taxes," **AH**, 1988, Vol. 2, No. 4, pp. 41-49.)

Chang, Davis L. and Jacob G. Birnberg. "Functional Fixity In Accounting Research: Perspective And New Data," **JAR**, 1977, Vol. 15, No. 2, pp. 300-312.

Chang, Davis L. S. and Shu S. Liao. "Measuring And Disclosing Forecast Reliability," **JOA**, 1977, Vol. 143, No. 5, pp. 76-87.

Chang, Davis L. (Chiu, James S. and Davis L. Chang. "Management Accounting In Taiwan," **MA**, 1979, Vol. 60, No. 12, pp. 50-55.)

Chang, Emily Chen. "Business Income In Accounting And Economics," **AR**, 1962, Vol. 37, No. 4, pp. 636-644.

Chang, Lucia S. and Kenneth S. Most. "International Accounting Standards: The Case Of European Oil Companies," **IJAER**, 1976, Vol. 12, No. 1, pp. 27-43.

Chang, Lucia S. and Kenneth S. Most. "An International Comparison Of Investor Uses Of Financial Statements," **IJAER**, 1981, Vol. 17, No. 1, pp. 43-60.

Chang, Otto H. and Thomas M. McCarty. "Evidence On Judgment Involving The Determination Of Substantial Authority: Tax Practitioners Versus Students," **JATA**, 1988, Vol. 10, No. 1, pp. 26-39.

Chapin, Ned. "Teaching Business Data Processing With The Aid Of A Computer," **AR**, 1963, Vol. 38, No. 4, pp. 835-839.

Chapin, Troy A., Jr. "Selling DCFR," **MA**, 1975, Vol. 57, No. 6, pp. 43-46.

Chapin, Wayne R. (Harris, William T., Jr. and Wayne R. Chapin. "Joint Product Costing," **MA**, 1973, Vol. 54, No. 10, pp. 43-47.)

Chapman, Benson J. "Current LIFO Developments," **CPAJ**, 1975, Vol. 45, No. 10, pp. 27-32.

Chapman, Charles H. "A Small Business Financial Model," **MA**, 1975, Vol. 57, No. 1, pp. 20-22.

Chapman, Gordon L. (Singh, Prem S. and Gordon L. Chapman. "Is Linear Approximation Good Enough?," **MA**, 1978, Vol. 59, No. 7, pp. 53-55.)

Chapman, Gordon. (Kross, William, Gordon Chapman and Kenneth H. Strand. "Fully Diluted Earnings Per Share And Security Returns: Some Additional Evidence," **JAAF**, 1980, Vol. 4, No. 1, pp. 36-46.)

Chapman, H. H. "The Administration Of University Courses In Accounting," **AR**, 1926, Vol. 1, No. 4, pp. 81-84.

Chapman, Robert E. "A Systems Approach To Financial Statements," **MA**, 1965, Vol. 47, No. 4, pp. 29-34.

Charles, Dane W. and R. Scott Miller. "Pension Accounting - Some Unanswered Questions," **CPAJ**, 1980, Vol. 50, No. 2, pp. 19-24.

Charnes, A. and W. W. Cooper. "Auditing And Accounting For Program Efficiency And Management Efficiency In Not-For-Profit Entities," **AOS**, 1980, Vol. 5, No. 1, pp. 87-108.

Charnes, A. and W. W. Cooper. "Some Network Characterizations For Mathematical Programming And Accounting Approaches To Planning And Control," **AR**, 1967, Vol. 42, No. 1, pp. 24-52.

Charnes, A. (Brockett, P., A. Charnes, W. W. Cooper and Hong-Chul Shin. "A Chance-Constrained Programming Approach To Cost-Volume-Profit Analysis," **AR**, 1984, Vol. 59, No. 3, pp. 474-487.)

Charnes, A. (Byrne, R. F., A. Charnes, W. W. Cooper and K. Kortanek. "Some New Approaches To Risk," **AR**, 1968, Vol. 43, No. 1, pp. 18-37.)

Charnes, A., C. Colantoni and W. W. Cooper. "A Futurological Justification For Historical Cost And Multi-Dimensional Accounting," **AOS**, 1976, Vol. 1, No. 4, pp. 315-338.

Charnes, A., C. Colantoni, W. W. Cooper and K. O. Kortanek. "Economic Social And Enterprise Accounting And Mathematical Models," **AR**, 1972, Vol. 47, No. 1, pp. 85-108.

Charnes, A., H. Justin Davidson and K. Kortanek. "On A Mixed Sequential Estimating Procedure With Application To Audit Tests In Accounting," **AR**, 1964, Vol. 39, No. 2, pp. 241-250.

Charnes, A., W. W. Cooper and Y. Ijiri. "Breakeven Budgeting And Programming To Goals," **JAR**, 1963, Vol. 1, No. 1, pp. 16-41.

Chase, Stephen F. "Is Hospital Accounting Different?," **MA**, 1976, Vol. 57, No. 9, pp. 35-40.

Chase, Winsor L. "Use Of Transaction Codes In Operating Report Preparation," **MA**, 1966, Vol. 47, No. 7, pp. 61-63.

Chastain, Clark E. "Accounting And Society: A Behavioral View," **IJAER**, 1973, Vol. 8, No. 2, pp. 1-20.

Chastain, Clark E. "Managing Your Debt For Survival," **MA**, 1983, Vol. 65, No. 6, pp. 20-25.

Chastain, Clark. "How Management Accountants Coped With The Recession," **MA**, 1985, Vol. 66, No. 7, pp. 34-38.

Chasteen, Lanny Gordon. "A Graphical Approach To Linear Programming Shadow Prices," **AR**, 1972, Vol. 47, No. 4, pp. 819-823.

Chasteen, Lanny G. and C. Dwayne Dowell. "Teaching Alternative Income Determination Models Via A Classification Model," **JAED**, 1983, Vol. 1, No. 1, pp. 47-53.

Chasteen, Lanny G. and Marvin S. Keener. "Ranking Convertible Securities For Earnings Per Share: A Graphical Analysis," **IAE**, 1988, Vol. 3, No. 2, pp. 241-247.

Chasteen, Lanny G. "An Empirical Study Of Differences In Economic Circumstances As A Justification For Alternative Inventory Pricing Models," **AR**, 1971, Vol. 46, No. 3. pp. 504-508.

Chasteen, Lanny G. "Economic Circumstances And Inventory Method Selection," **ABACUS**, 1973, Vol. 9, No. 1, pp. 22-27.

Chasteen, Lanny G. "Implicit Factors In The Evaluation Of Lease Vs. Buy Alternatives: A Reply," **AR**, 1974, Vol. 49, No. 4, pp. 809-811.

Chasteen, Lanny G. "Implicit Factors In The Evaluation Of Lease Vs. Buy Alternatives," **AR**, 1973, Vol. 48, No. 4, pp. 764-767.

Chasteen, Lanny G. "Shadow Prices: A Graphical Approach," **MA**, 1972, Vol. 54, No. 3, pp. 27-29.

Chasteen, Lanny. "A Taxonomy Of Price Change Models," **AR**, 1984, Vol. 59, No. 3, pp. 515-523.

Chatfield, Michael. "A Writing Program In Intermediate Accounting," **AR**, 1968, Vol. 43, No. 3, pp. 592-594.

Chatfield, Michael. "The Accounting Review's First Fifty Years," **AR**, 1975, Vol. 50, No. 1, pp. 1-6.

Chatfield, Michael. "The Origins Of Cost Accounting," **MA**, 1971, Vol. 52, No. 12, pp. 11-14.

Chatfield, Michael. "The Role Of Operational Accounting Periods In A Goal-Oriented Control System," **MA**, 1968, Vol. 49, No. 12, pp. 44-48.

Chatov, Robert. "Reexamining The Rules Of The Game: The Dingell Hearings And Beyond," **AIPIA**, 1986, Vol. 1, pp. 15-47.

Chatov, Robert. "The Possible New Shape Of Accounting In The United States," **JAPP**, 1985, Vol. 4, No. 3, pp. 161-174.

Chatov, Robert. "The Regulatory Philosophy Of Carmen Blough: A Legacy," **RIAR**, 1988, Vol. 2, pp. 81-105.

Chatov, Robert. "William O. Douglas On The Transfer Of The Securities Exchange Commission's Authority For The Development Of Rules For Financial Reporting," **AHJ**, 1986, Vol. 13, No. 2, pp. 125-129.

Chatterjee, Sangit. (Tomczyk, Stephen and Sangit Chatterjee. "The Impact Of Outliers And Influential Points On The Cost Variance-Investigation Decision," **IAE**, 1986, No. 2, pp. 293-301.)

Chatters, Carl H. "Present And Future Of Governmental Accounting," **AR**, 1939, Vol. 14, No. 1, pp. 48-51.

Chaump, Donald G. "Reducing Overhead Through The Task-Activity Cycle Ratio Matrix Analysis," **MA**, 1967, Vol. 48, No. 6, pp. 23-32.

Chaykin, Irving J. "More On The Admission Of The New Partner," **AR**, 1953, Vol. 28, No. 3, pp. 431-434.

Chazen, Charles and Benjamin Benson. "Fitting GAAP To Smaller Businesses," **JOA**, 1978, Vol. 145, No. 2, pp. 46-51.

Chazen, Charles and Ira M. Landis. "Audit Committees - Why And How," **CPAJ**, 1976, Vol. 46, No. 8, pp. 33-37.

Chazen, Charles and Kenneth I. Solomon. "The Art Of Defensive Auditing," **JOA**, 1975, Vol. 140, No. 4, pp. 66-71.

Chazen, Charles and Kenneth I. Solomon. "The 'Unaudited' State Of Affairs," **JOA**, 1972, Vol. 134, No. 6, pp. 41-45.

Chazen, Charles, David Kinkade and C. Peter Davis. "A Primer For Novice Restaurant Owners," **CPAJ**, 1985, Vol. 55, No. 11, pp. 10-19.

Chazen, Charles, Richard L. Miller, Jr. and Kenneth I. Solomon. "When The Rules Say: 'See Your Lawyer'," **JOA**, 1981, Vol. 151, No. 1, pp. 60-70.

Chazen, Charles. "An Accountant Looks At The FCPA," **CPAJ**, 1980, Vol. 50, No. 5, pp. 38-45.

Chazen, Charles. "The Profession Today - And Tomorrow," **CPAJ**, 1978, Vol. 48, No. 5, pp. 33-38.

Chazen, Charles. (Solomon, Kenneth I., Charles Chazen and Barry S. Augenbraun. "Who Judges The Auditor, And How?," **JOA**, 1976, Vol. 142, No. 2, pp. 67-74.)

Chazen, Charles. (Solomon, Kenneth I. and Charles Chazen. "Use Of Legal Opinions In The Audit Process," **JOA**, 1973, Vol. 136, No. 5, pp. 46-54.)

Chazen, Charles. (Solomon, Kenneth Ira, Charles Chazen and Richard L. Miller, Jr. "Compilation And Review: The Safety Factor," **JOA**, 183, Vol. 155, No. 6, pp. 50-59.)

Cheatham, Carole A. (Weathers, Henry T. and Carole A. Cheatham. "Earnings Statement For Prediction, Comparison. And Evaluation," **MA**, 1976, Vol. 57, No. 9, pp. 17-18.)

Cheatham, Carole. "Do You Have A Productivity Disease?," **MA**, 1986, Vol. 68, No. 1, pp. 49-51.

Check, C. W. "What The CPA Can Do To Help Small Business," **JOA**, 1959, Vol. 107, No. 6, pp. 29-33.

Cheeseman, Henry R. "How To Create An Inflation Neutral Tax System," **JOA**, 1975, Vol. 140, No. 2, pp. 44-51.

Cheleno, Joseph F. (Hartman, Bart P. and Joseph F. Cheleno. "Estimating Profit And Cash Flow For A New Funeral Home," **MA**, 1979, Vol. 61, No. 5, pp. 35-38.)

Chen, Chao, Philip Fanara, Jr. and Raymond Gorman. "Abandonment Decisions And The Market Value Of The Firm: The Case Of Nuclear Power Project Abandonment," **JAPP**, 1987,

Vol. 6, No. 4, pp. 285-297.

Chen, Joyce T. and Rene P. Manes. "Distinguishing The Two Forms Of The Constant Percentage Learning Curve Model," CAR, 1984-85, Vol. 1, No. 2, pp. 242-252.

Chen, Joyce T. and Rene P. Manes. "Distinguishing The Two Forms Of The Constant Percentage Learning Curve Model: A Reply," CAR, 1988, Vol. 4, No. 2, pp. 615-616.

Chen, Joyce T. "A Simplified Integer Programming Approach To Resource Allocation And Profit Budgeting," ABR, 1982-83, Vol. 13, No. 52, pp. 273-278.

Chen, Joyce T. "Cost Allocation And External Acquisition Of Services When Self-Services Exist," AR, 1983, Vol. 58, No. 3, pp. 600-605.

Chen, Joyce T. "Full And Direct Costing In Profit Variance Analysis," IAE, 1986, No. 2, pp. 282-292.

Chen, Joyce T. "The Effect Of Change Variation On Revenue And Cost Estimations For Break-Even Analysis: A Comment," AR, 1983, Vol. 58, No. 4, pp. 813-819.

Chen, Kung H. and Albert Y. Lew. "A Framework For The Selection Of Representative Financial Ratios: Methodology Note," AIA, 1984, Vol. 1, pp. 63-74.

Chen, Kung H. and Edward L. Summers. "Should Accounting Data Be Single-Valued Measurements?," IJAER, 1977, Vol. 12, No. 2, pp. 109-125.

Chen, Kung H. and Richard W. Metcalf. "The Relationship Between Pollution Control Record And Financial Indicators Revisited," AR, 1980, Vol. 55. No. 1, pp. 168-177.

Chen, Kung H. and S. J. Lambert. "Impurity Of Variable Factory Overhead Variances," JAED, 1985, Vol. 3, No. 1, pp. 189-196.

Chen, Kung H. and S. J. Lambert. "A Study Of The Consensus On Disclosure Among Public Accountants And Security Analysts: An Alternative Interpretation," AR, 1977, Vol. 52, No. 2, pp. 508-513.

Chen, Kung H. and Thomas E. Balke. "Scale Of Operation, Industry, And Financial Ratios," IJAER, 1979, Vol. 14, No. 2, pp. 17-28.

Chen, Kung H. "A Comparison Of Financial Ratios: Historical Cost Versus Price-Level Adjusted Disclosers," AIA, 1986, Vol. 3, pp. 233-254.

Chen, Kung H. (Blocher, Edward and Kung H. Chen. "Assessing Industry Risk By Ratio Analysis: A Comment," AR, 1978, Vol. 53, No. 1, pp. 204-209.)

Chen, Kung H. (Kim, Il-Woon and Kung H. Chen. "Empirical Research On The Information Content Of Financial Leverage: A Review And Critique," JAL, 1987, Vol. 6, pp. 88-110.)

Chen, K. C. W. (Manes, R. P., K. C. W. Chen and R. Greenberg. "Economies Of Scope And Cost-Volume-Profit Analysis For The Multiproduct Firm," JAL, 1985, Vol. 4, pp. 77-112.)

Chen, K. H. and E. L. Summers. "A Study Of Reporting Probabilistic Accounting Figures," AOS, 1981, Vol. 6, No. 1, pp. 1-16.

Chen, Raymond S. "The Treasury Stock Method And Conventional Method In Reciprocal Stockholdings: An Amalgamation: A Comment," AR, 1975, Vol. 50, No. 2, pp. 359-364.

Chen, Rosita S. and Sheng-Der Pan. "Frederick Winslow Taylor's Contributions To Cost Accounting," AHJ, 1980, Vol. 7, No. 2, pp. 1-22.

Chen, Rosita S. and Sheng-Der Pan. "Taylor's Contribution To Cost Accounting, A Reply," AHJ, 1984, Vol. 11, No. 1, pp. 151-161.

Chen, Rosita S. and Sheng-Der Pan. "Frederick Winslow Taylor's Contribution To Accounting," AHJ, 1980, Vol. 7, No. 1, pp. 17-35.

Chen, Rosita S. "Social And Financial Stewardship," AR, 1975, Vol. 50, No. 3, pp. 533-543.

Chenault, Lawrence R. "Business Behavior And The Theory Of The Firm," AR, 1954, Vol. 29, No. 4, pp. 645-651.

Cheney, Paul E. "A Review Of Some Objections To Fair Value Accounting," MA, 1976, Vol. 57, No. 12, pp. 29-30.

Cheng, Peter. (Amershi, Amin H. and Peter Cheng. "Implementable Equilibria In Accounting Contexts: An Exploratory Study," CAR, 1988, Vol. 4, No. 2, pp. 515-563.)

Cheng, Philip C. and Tribhowan N. Jain. "Economic Perspective And Accounting Practices In South Korea," IJAER, 1973, Vol. 8, No. 2, pp. 123-139.

Cheng, Philip C. "Accounting In Nationalist China," IJAER, 1971, Vol. 6, No. 2, pp. 75-88.

Cheng, Thomas T. "Financial Forecasting: Throw Away The Crystal Ball," MA, 1983, Vol. 64, No. 11, pp. 50-52.

Cheng, Thomas T. "Standard Setting And Security Returns: A Time Series Analysis Of FAS No. 8 Events," CAR, 1986-87, Vol. 3, No. 1, pp. 226-241.

Cheng, Thomas T. (Chan, K. Hung and Thomas T. Cheng. "The Recovery Of Nuclear Power Plant Decommissioning Costs," JAAF, 1984, Vol. 7, No. 2, pp. 164-177.)

Cheng, Thomas T. (Zieha, Eugene L. and Thomas T. Cheng. "Proposing A More Appropriate Dividend Policy," MA, 1979, Vol. 61, No. 3, pp. 32-36.)

Chenhall, Robert H. and Deigan Morris. "The Impact Of Structure, Environment, And Interdependence On The Perceived Usefulness Of Management Accounting Systems," AR, 1986, Vol. 61, No. 1, pp. 16-35.

Chenhall, Robert H. "Authoritariansim And Participative Budgeting - A Dyadic Analysis," AR, 1986, Vol. 61, No. 2, pp. 263-272.

Chenhall, Robert H. (Baker, H. Kent, Robert H. Chenhall, John A. Haslem and Roger H. Juchau. "Disclosure Of Material Information: A Cross-National Comparison," IJAER, 1977, Vol. 13, No. 1, pp. 1-18.)

Chenhall, R.H. and P.Brownell. "The Effect Of Participative Budgeting On Job Satisfaction And Performance: Role Ambiguity As An Intervening Variable," AOS, 1988, Vol. 13, No. 3, pp. 225-234.

Chenhall, R. H. and R. Juchau. "Investor Information Needs - An Australian Study," ABR, 1976-77, Vol. 7, No. 26, pp. 111-119.

Chenhall, R. H. (McDougall, F. M. and R. H. Chenhall. "Shareholders And Share Exchange Takeover Offers," ABACUS, 1975, Vol. 11, No. 2, pp. 122-135.)

Chenhall, R. H. (Partington, G. H. and R. H. Chenhall. "Dividends, Distortion And Double Taxation," ABACUS, 1983, Vol. 19, No. 1, pp. 3-13.)

Chenok, Philip B. (Lee, Bernard Z., Rholan E. Larson and Philip B. Chenok. "Issues Confronting The Accounting Profession," JOA, 1983, Vol. 156, No. 5, pp. 78-85.)

Chenok, Philip B., Douglas R. Carmichael and Thomas P. Kelley. "Accounting And Auditing: The Technical Challenges Ahead," JOA, 1980, Vol. 150, No. 5, pp. 62-70.

Cheramy, Shirley J. (Hooks, Karen L. and Shirley J. Cheramy. "Women Accountants - Current Status And Future Prospects," CPAJ, 1988, Vol. 58, No. 5, pp. 18-31.)

Cherns, A. B. "Alienation And Accountancy," AOS, 1978, Vol. 3. No. 2, pp. 105-114.

Cherrington, David J. and J. Owen Cherrington. "Appropriate Reinforcement Contingencies In The Budgeting Process," JAR, 1973. Vol. 11, Supp., pp. 225-253.

Cherrington, David J. (Cherrington, J. Owen and David J. Cherrington. "Budget Games For Fun And Frustration," MA, 1976, Vol. 57, No. 7, pp. 28-32.)

Cherrington, David J. (Romney, Marshall B., W. Steve Albrecht and David J. Cherrington. "Auditors And The Detection Of Fraud," JOA, 1980, Vol. 149, No. 5, pp. 63-69.)

Cherrington, J. Owen and David J. Cherrington. "Budget Games For Fun And Frustration," MA, 1976, Vol. 57, No. 7, pp. 28-32.

Cherrington, J. Owen and Kevin D. Stocks. "Educating A Management Consultant," JIS, 1986, Vol. 1, No. 1, pp. 145-153.

Cherrington, J. Owen. (Cherrington, David J. and J. Owen Cherrington. "Appropriate Reinforcement Contingencies In The Budgeting Process," JAR, 1973, Vol. 11, Supp., pp. 225-253.)

Cherry, Alan A. and Philip M. J. Reckers. "A Study Of The Need For Change In Intermediate Accounting Courses And Textbooks," IAE, 1985, No. 1, pp. 131-144.

Cherry, Alan A. and Phillip M. J. Reckers. "The Introductory Financial Accounting Course: Its Role In The Curriculum For Accounting Majors," JAED, 1983, Vol. 1, No. 1, pp. 71-82.

Cherry, Alan A. (Arnold, Jerry L., Alan A. Cherry, Michael A. Diamond and James A. Walker. "Small Business: An Area Ripe For Practice Development," JOA, 1984, Vol. 158, No. 2. pp. 74-83.)

Cherry, Alan A. (Karlinsky, Stewart S., James G. Manegold and Alan A. Cherry. "Accounting For Deferred Income Taxes: Preparers' Responses To Policy Proposals," AIA, 1987, Vol. 5, pp. 15-38.)

Chesebrough, Harry E. "American Management Expertise: Exportable?," IJAER, 1975, Vol. 11, No. 1, pp. 145-159.

Chesley, George Richard. (Heimann, Stephen R. and George Richard Chesley. "Audit Sample Sizes For Aggregated Statement Accounts," JAR, 1977, Vol. 15, No. 2, pp. 193-206.)

Chesley, G. R. and J. H. Scheiner. "The Statement Of Changes In Financial Position: An Empirical Investigation Of Canadian And U.S. Users in Nonpublic Companies," IJAER, 1982, Vol. 17, No. 2, pp. 49-58.

Chesley, G. R. "Elicitation Of Subjective Probabilities: A Review," AR, 1975, Vol. 50, No. 2, pp. 325-337.

Chesley, G. R. "Interpretation Of Uncertainty Expressions," CAR, 1985-86, Vol. 2, No. 2, pp. 179-221.

Chesley, G. R. "Subjective Probability Elicitation Techniques: A Performance Comparison," JAR, 1978, Vol. 16, No. 2, pp. 225-241.

Chesley, G. R. "Subjective Probability Elicitation: The Effect Of Congruity Of Datum And Response Mode On Performance," JAR, 1977, Vol. 15, No. 1, pp. 1-11.

Chesley, G. R. "The Elicitation Of Subjective Probabilities: A Laboratory Study In An Accounting Context," JAR, 1976. Vol. 14, No. 1, pp. 27-48.

Chesley, G. R. (Larsson, S. and G. R. Chesley. "An Analysis Of The Auditor's Uncertainty About Probabilities," CAR, 1985-86, Vol. 2, No. 2, pp. 259-282.)

Chester, Michael C., Jr. (Holley, Charles L., Edward C. Spede and Michael C. Chester, Jr. "The Push-Down Accounting Controversy," MA, 1987, Vol. 68, No. 7, pp. 39-42.)

Chetkovich, Michael N. "An Appeal For Unity In Establishing Financial Accounting Standards," IJAER, 1972, Vol. 8, No. 1, pp. 99-107.

Chetkovich, Michael N. "Standards Of Disclosure," JOA, 1955. Vol. 100, No. 6, pp. 48-52.

Chetkovich, Michael N. "The International Federation Of Accountants: Its Organization And Goals," IJAER, 1979, Vol. 15, No. 1, pp. 13-20.

Chetkovich, Michael N. (Cummings, Joseph P. and Michael N. Chetkovich. "World Accounting Enters A New Era," JOA, 1978, Vol. 145, No. 4, pp. 52-62.)

Cheung, Joseph K. "Stochastic Dominance As An Approach To Uncertainty In Cost Accounting," JAED, 1985, Vol. 3, No. 2, pp. 91-102.

Cheung, Joseph K. (Abdel-Magid, Moustafa F. and Joseph K. Cheung. "Ratio Scales, Foreign Exchange Rates, And The

Problem Of Foreign Currency Translation: An Analytical-Empirical Perspective," **IJAER**, 1986, Vol. 22, No. 1, pp. 33-49.)

Cheung, Joseph K. (Whaley, Robert E. and Joseph K. Cheung. "Anticipation Of Quarterly Earnings Announcements: A Test Of Option Market Efficiency." **JAEC**, 1982, Vol. 4, No. 2, pp. 57-83.)

Chevalier, Lorin S. (Wishon, Keith and Lorin S. Chevalier. "Interest Rate Swaps - Your Rate Or Mine?," **JOA**, 1985, Vol. 160, No. 3, pp. 63-84.)

Chewning, Eugene G. (Ingram, Robert W. and Eugene G. Chewning. "The Effect Of Financial Disclosure Regulation On Security Market Behavior," **AR**, 1983, Vol. 58, No. 3, pp. 562-580.)

Chewning, Eugene. (Harrell, Adrian, Eugene Chewning and Martin Taylor. "Organizational-Professional Conflict And The Job Satisfaction And Turnover Intentions Of Internal Auditors," **AJPT**, 1985-86, Vol. 5, No. 2, pp. 111-121.)

Chhatwal, Gurprit S. (Mensah, Yaw M. and Gurprit S. Chhatwal. "Accounting For Shrinkage In Continuous Flow Industries: An Expository Note," **ABACUS**, 1987, Vol. 23, No. 1, pp. 31-42.)

Chi, Charles. (Abdel-Khalik, A. Rashad, Charles Chi and Dimitrios Ghicas. "Rationality Of Executive Compensation Schemes And Real Accounting Changes," **CAR**, 1987-88, Vol. 4, No. 1, pp. 32-60.)

Chiang, Raymond. (Goldenberg, David H. and Raymond Chiang. "Systematic Risk And The Theory Of The Firm: A Reexamination," **JAPP**, 1983, Vol. 2, No. 1, pp. 63-72.)

Childs, Wendell M. "Management Of Capital Expenditures," **MA**, 1970, Vol. 51, No. 7, pp. 37-40.

Child, A. J. E. "Case Studies In Internal Auditing," **AR**, 1949, Vol. 24, No. 2, pp. 149-158.

Chilton, Robert C. "Money Talks, Doesn't It?," **MA**, 1976, Vol. 58, No. 2, pp. 29-30.

Ching, Donald F. "How To Isolate Medicare Costs," **MA**, 1979, Vol. 61, No. 1, pp. 27-33.

Chira, Robert. "Deception Of Auditors And False Records," **JOA**, 1979, Vol. 148, No. 1, pp. 61-72.

Chiu, James S. and Davis L. Chang. "Management Accounting In Taiwan," **MA**, 1979, Vol. 60, No. 12, pp. 50-55.

Chiu, John S. and Don T. DeCoster. "Multiple Product Costing By Multiple Correlation Analysis," **AR**, 1966, Vol. 41, No. 4, pp. 673-680.

Chodora, Charles R. "Designing Business Systems For The Third Computer Generation," **MA**, 1968, Vol. 50, No. 1, pp. 29-35.

Choi, Frederick D. S. and Ashwinpaul Sondhi. "SFAS No. 52 And The Funds Statement," **CA**, 1984, Vol. 2, No. 2, pp. 46-56.

Choi, Frederick D. S. and Vinod B. Bavishi. "Financial Accounting Standards: A Multinational Synthesis And Policy Framework," **IJAER**, 1982, Vol. 18, No. 1, pp. 159-183.

Choi, Frederick D. S. and Vinod B. Bavishi. "International Accounting Standards: Issues Needing Attention," **JOA**, 183, Vol. 155, No. 3, pp. 62-68.

Choi, Frederick D. S. "A Cluster Approach To Accounting Harmonization," **MA**, 1981, Vol. 63, No. 2, pp. 26-31.

Choi, Frederick D. S. "ASEAN Federation Of Accountants: A New International Accounting Force," **IJAER**, 1979, Vol. 15, No. 1, pp. 53-75.

Choi, Frederick D. S. "Breaking The Vicious Circle Of Poverty," **MA**, 1974, Vol. 55, No. 12, pp. 25-28.

Choi, Frederick D. S. "Financial Disclosure And Entry To The European Capital Market," **JAR**, 1973, Vol. 11, No. 2, pp. 159-175.

Choi, Frederick D. S. "Financial Disclosure In Relation To A Firm's Capital Costs," **ABR**, 1972-73, Vol. 3, No. 12, pp. 282-292.

Choi, Frederick D. S. "Financial Disclosure In Relation To The European Capital Market," **IJAER**, 1973, Vol. 9, No. 1, pp. 53-66.

Choi, Frederick D. S. "Foreign Inflation And Management Decisions," **MA**, 1977, Vol. 58, No. 12, pp. 21-27.

Choi, Frederick D. S. "Multinational Finance And Management Accounting," **MA**, 1976, Vol. 58, No. 4, pp. 45-48.

Choi, Frederick D. S. "Multinational Financing And Accounting Harmony," **MA**, 1974, Vol. 55, No. 9, pp. 14-17.

Choi, Frederick D. S. "Political Risk - An Accounting Challenge," **MA**, 1979, Vol. 60, No. 12, pp. 17-20.

Choi, Frederick D. S. "Price-Level Adjustments And Foreign Currency Translations: Are They Compatible?," **IJAER**, 1975, Vol. 11, No. 1, pp. 121-143.

Choi, Frederick D. S. "Primary-Secondary Reporting: A Cross-Cultural Analysis," **IJAER**, 1980, Vol. 16, No. 1, pp. 83-104.

Choi, Frederick D. S. "The Development Of Nascent Capital Markets," **MA**, 1975, Vol. 57, No. 3, pp. 18-20.

Chokshi, C. C. "Valuation Of Shares Of Joint Stock Companies," **JOA**, 1954, Vol. 97, No. 1, pp. 38-48.

Cholden, Ernest J. (Elder, Peter and Ernest J. Cholden. "Tax Planning For Foundations," **JOA**, 1965, Vol. 119, No. 5, pp. 50-54.)

Cholmondeley, Paula H. J. "Seeking The Future: A Game Of Tag," **JOA**, 1988, Vol. 166, No. 4, pp. 89-94.

Chong, Sebastian and Graeme Dean. "Related Party Transactions: A Preliminary Evaluation Of SFAS 57 And IAS 24," **ABACUS**, 1985, Vol. 21, No. 1, pp. 84-100.

Choo, Freddie. "Job Stress, Job Performance, And Auditor Personality Characteristics," **AJPT**, 1985-86, Vol. 5, No. 2, pp. 17-34.

Choo, Freddie. "Split-Plot Repeated Measures Designs In Internal Control Judgement Research: A Note," **ABR**, 1983-84, Vol. 14, No. 53, pp. 83-84.

Chottiner, Sherman and Allan Young. "A Test Of The AICPA Differentiation Between Stock Dividends And Stock Splits," **JAR**, 1971, Vol. 9, No. 2, pp. 367-374.

Choudhury, Nandan. "In Search Of Relevance In Management Accounting Research," **ABR**, 1986-87, Vol. 17, No. 65, pp. 21-32.

Choudhury, Nandan. "Incentives For The Divisional Manager," **ABR**, 1985-86, Vol. 16, No. 61, pp. 11-22.

Choudhury, Nandan. "Responsibility Accounting And Controllability," **ABR**, 1985-86, Vol. 16, No. 63, pp. 189-1?8.

Choudhury, Nandan. "Starting Out In Management Accounting Research," **ABR**, 1986-87, Vol. 17, No. 67, pp. 205-220.

Choudhury, N. "Aspects Of Accounting And Internal Control - India 4th Century BC," **ABR**, 1981-82, Vol. 12, No. 46, pp. 105-110.

Choudhury, N. "The Seeking Of Accounting Where It Is Not: Towards A Theory Of Non-Accounting In Organizational Settings," **AOS**, 1988, Vol. 13, No. 6, pp. 549-557.

Choudhury, N. "Vedic Partnership Rules," **AHJ**, 1983, Vol. 10, No. 2, pp. 129-138.

Chown, John. "The Reform Of Corporation Tax," **ABR**, 1970-71, Vol. 1, No. 2, pp. 93-117.

Chow, Chee W. and Adrian Wong-Boren. "Voluntary Financial Disclosure By Mexican Corporations," **AR**, 1987, Vol. 62, No. 3, pp. 533-541.

Chow, Chee W. and Adrian Wong-Boren. "Audit Firm Size And Audit Quality: Some Evidence From Mexico," **IJAER**, 1986, Vol. 21, No. 2, pp. 1-25.

Chow, Chee W. and Rebecca Todd. "Consulting And Internship Opportunities For Accounting Faculty Members: Their Nature And Variables Associated With Their Attainment," **AIA**, 1987, Vol. 4, pp. 111-130.

Chow, Chee W. and Steven J. Rice. "Qualified Audit Opinions And Share Prices - An Investigation," **AJPT**, 1981-82, Vol. 1, No. 2, pp. 35-53.

Chow, Chee W. and Steven J. Rice. "Qualified Audit Opinions And Auditor Switching," **AR**, 1982, Vol. 57, No. 2, pp. 326-335.

Chow, Chee W. and William S. Waller. "Management Accounting And Organizational Control," **MA**, 1982, Vol. 63, No. 10, pp. 36-41.

Chow, Chee W. "Empirical Studies Of The Economic Effects Of Accounting Regulation On Security Prices: Findings, Problems, And Prospects," **JAL**, 1983, Vol. 2, pp. 73-110.

Chow, Chee W. "The Demand For External Auditing: Size, Debt And Ownership Influences," **AR**, 1982, Vol. 57, No. 2, pp. 272-291.

Chow, Chee W. "The Effects Of Job Standard Tightness And Compensation Scheme On Performance: An Exploration Of Linkages," **AR**, 1983, Vol. 58, No. 4, pp. 667-685.

Chow, Chee W. "The Impacts Of Accounting Regulation On Bondholder And Shareholder Wealth: The Case Of The Securities Acts," **AR**, 1983, Vol. 58, No. 3, pp. 485-520.

Chow, Chee W. "Using Cost-Volume-Profit Analysis As An Integrative Framework In Cost/Management Accounting Courses," **JAED**, 1983, Vol. 1, No. 1, pp. 137-139.

Chow, Chee W. (Blanchard, Garth A., Chee W. Chow and Eric Noreen. "Information Asymmetry, Incentive Schemes, And Information Biasing: The Case Of Hospital Budgeting Under Rate Regulation," **AR**, 1986, Vol. 61, No. 1, pp. 1-15.)

Chow, Chee W. (Blanchard, Garth A. and Chee W. Chow. "Allocating Indirect Costs For Improved Management Performance," **MA**, 1983, Vol. 64, No. 9, pp. 38-41.)

Chow, Chee W. (Bylinski, Joseph H. and Chee W. Chow. "Human Judgment Biases And The Teaching Of Management Accounting," **JAED**, 1985, Vol. 3, No. 1, pp. 167-172.)

Chow, Chee W. (Waller, William S. and Chee W. Chow. "The Self-Selection And Effort Effects Of Standard-Based Employee Contracts: A Framework And Some Empirical Evidence," **AR**, 1985, Vol. 60, No. 3, pp. 458-476.)

Chow, Chee W., Alan H. McNamee and R. David Plumlee. "Practitioners' Perceptions Of Audit Step Difficulty And Criticalness: Implications For Audit Research," **AJPT**, 1986-87, Vol. 6, No. 2, pp. 123-133.

Chow, Chee W., Howard R. Toole and Adrian Wong-Boren. "Make Better Decisions: Divide And Conquer," **MA**, 1986, Vol. 68, No. 2, pp. 41-45.

Chow, Chee W., Jean C. Cooper and William S. Waller. "Participative Budgeting: Effects Of A Truth-Inducing Pay Scheme And Information Asymmetry On Slack And Performance," **AR**, 1988, Vol. 63, No. 1, pp. 111-122.

Chow, Chee W., Michael D. Shields and Gerald E. Whittenburg. "The Quality Of Tax Practitioners' Judgments Regarding Substantial Authority: Potential Research Directions And An Exploratory Empirical Investigation," **AIT**, 1988, Vol. 2, pp. xx-xx.

Chow, Chee W., Michael D. Shields and Adrian Wong-Boren. "A Compilation Of Recent Surveys And Company-Specific Descriptions Of Management Accounting Practices," **JAED**, 1988, Vol. 6, No. 2, pp. 183-207.

Chow, Yee-Chuing. "The Concept Of Expense," **AR**, 1939, Vol. 14, No. 4, pp. 340-349.

Chow, Y. C. "The Doctrine Of Proprietorship," **AR**, 1942, Vol. 17, No. 2, pp. 157-162.

Chrisman, Heidi Hadlich. (Pratt, Jamie and Heidi Hadlich Chrisman. "Teaching The Statement Of Changes In Financial Position: An Empirical Study," **AR**, 1982, Vol. 57, No. 4, pp. 794-805.)

Christensen, Howard A. "Small Business And Its Accountants: A Case Report," **MA**, 1967, Vol. 48, No. 7, pp. 41-45.

Christensen, John. "The Determination Of Performance Standards And Participation," **JAR**, 1982, Vol. 20, No. 2, Part II, pp. 589-603.

Christensen, Oreson H. "Welfare And Pension Plans

Disclosure," **JOA**, 1961, Vol. 112, No. 2, pp. 47-51.

Christensen, Peter O. (Feltham, Gerald A. and Peter O. Christensen. "Firm-Specific Information And Efficient Resource Allocation," **CAR**, 1988, Vol. 5, No. 1, pp. 133-169.)

Christenson, Charles. "Construction Of Present Value Tables For Use In Evaluating Capital Investment Opportunities," **AR**, 1955, Vol. 30, No. 4, pp. 666-672.

Christenson, Charles. "The Methodology Of Positive Accounting," **AR**, 1983, Vol. 58, No. 1, pp. 1-22.

Christen, Albert. "Advisory Service To Business: Its Rewards And Hazards," **JOA**, 1954, Vol. 97, No. 4, pp. 460-464.

Christiansen, Irving K. "Bringing Reality Into The Accounting Program," **AR**, 1961, Vol. 36, No. 2, pp. 293-296.

Christie, Andrew A. "On Cross-Sectional Analysis In Accounting Research," **JAEC**, 1987, Vol. 9, No. 3, pp. 231-258.

Christie, Andrew A. (Beaver, William H., Andrew A. Christie and Paul A. Griffin. "The Information Content Of SEC Accounting Series Release No. 190," **JAEC**, 1980, Vol. 2, No. 2, pp. 127-157.)

Christie, Andrew A., Michael D. Kennelley, J. William King and Thomas F. Schaefer. "Testing For Incremental Information Content In The Presence Of Collinearity," **JAEC**, 1984, Vol. 6, No. 3, pp. 205-217.

Christopher, M. G. (Howard, K. and M. G. Christopher. "Price And Discount Rationalisation In A Multiproduct Company," **ABR**, 1972-73, Vol. 3, No. 11, pp. 168-174.)

Christ, Edward C. (Wallace, George R. and Edward C. Christ. "Modern Accounting Can Help Save The Railroads," **MA**, 1970, Vol. 52, No. 6, pp. 15-18.)

Chrysler, Earl and Donald E. Keller. "Preventing Computer Fraud," **MA**, 1988, Vol. 69, No. 10, pp. 28-33.

Chu, Jose Manuel. "Accounting Principles And Practices In Panama," **IJAER**, 1973, Vol. 9, No. 1, pp. 43-52.

Chu, Kuo-Chang. "Accountancy Education In The Republic Of China," **IJAER**, 1969, Vol. 4, No. 2, pp. 75-91.

Chua, Wai Fong. "Of Gods And Demons, Science And Ideology," **AIPIA**, 1988, Vol. 2, pp. 29-46.

Chua, Wai Fong. "Radical Developments In Accounting Thought," **AR**, 1986, Vol. 61, No. 4, pp. 601-632.

Chua, Wai Fong. "Theoretical Constructions Of And By The Real," **AOS**, 1986, Vol. 11, No. 6, pp. 583-597.

Chubb, Timothy D. "Why Computer Conversions Are Tricky," **MA**, 1983, Vol. 65, No. 3, pp. 36-41.

Chumachenko, Nikolai and Norton M. Bedford. "Some Distinctive Aspects Of Accounting In The USSR," **IJAER**, 1968, Vol. 4, No. 1, pp. 29-40.

Chumachenko, Nikolai G. "Once Again: The Volume-Mix-Price/Cost Budget Variance Analysis," **AR**, 1968, Vol. 43, No. 4, pp. 753-762.

Chung, Dennis Y. and W. Daryl Lindsay. "The Pricing Of Audit Services: The Canadian Perspective," **CAR**, 1988, Vol. 5, No. 1, pp. 19-46.

Chung, Tsai Yen. (Jarnagin, Bill D. and Tsai Yen Chung. "Understanding The Accounting For Defined Benefit Pension Plans," **MA**, 1988, Vol. 70, No. 3, pp. 34-42.)

Churchill, A. A. "The Balanced Budget In Highway Finance: A Dangerous Concept," **IJAER**, 1968, Vol. 4, No. 1, pp. 101-110.

Churchill, Neil C. and John K. Shank. "Accounting For Affirmative Action Programs: A Stochastic Flow Approach," **AR**, 1975, Vol. 50, No. 4, pp. 643-656.

Churchill, Neil C. and Myron Uretsky. "Management Accounting Tomorrow," **MA**, 1969, Vol. 50, No. 10, pp. 46-53.

Churchill, Neil C. and Richard M. Cyert. "An Experiment In Management Auditing," **JOA**, 1966, Vol. 121, No. 2, pp. 39-43.

Churchill, Neil C. and William W. Cooper. "A Field Study Of Internal Auditing," **AR**, 1965, Vol. 40, No. 4, pp. 767-781.

Churchill, Neil C. (Harper, Bruce J. and Neil C. Churchill. "Serving Small Business: What CPAs Should Know," **JOA**, 1987, Vol. 163, No. 6, pp. 120-129.)

Churchill, Neil C. (Shank, John K. and Neil C. Churchill. "Variance Analysis: A Management Oriented Approach," **AR**, 1977, Vol. 52, No. 4, pp. 950-957.)

Churchill, Neil. "Audit Recommendations And Management Auditing: A Case Study And Some Remarks," **JAR**, 1966, Vol. 4, Supp., pp. 128-151.

Churchill, Neil. "Linear Algebra And Cost Allocations: Some Examples," **AR**, 1964, Vol. 39, No. 4, pp. 894-904.

Churchill, N. C., W. W. Cooper and V. Govindarajan. "Effects Of Audits On The Behavior Of Medical Professionals Under The Bennett Amendment," **AJPT**, 1981-82, Vol. 1, No. 2, pp. 69-90.

Churchman, C. West and Russell L. Ackoff. "Operational Accounting And Operations Research," **JOA**, 1955, Vol. 99, No. 2, pp. 33-39.

Churchman, C. West. "On The Facility, Felicity, And Morality Of Measuring Social Change," **AR**, 1971, Vol. 46, No. 1, pp. 30-35.

Cianciolo, S. Thomas A. (Nurnberg, Hugo and S. Thomas A. Cianciolo. "The Measurement Valuation Allowance: Help For Deferred Taxes," **JAAF**, 1985, Vol. 9, No. 1, pp. 50-59.)

Ciesick, Robert T., Harold L. Monk, Jr., and Ernest J. Pavlock. "The National CPE Curriculum," **JOA**, 1985, Vol. 160, No. 4, pp. 118-124.

Ciller, Ozer U. "Pricing Employment Contracts," **MA**, 1973, Vol. 55, No. 5, pp. 29-31.

Cirtin, Arnold. "Interest Expense - Is It Really A 'Non-Operating' Expense?," **CPAJ**, 1973, Vol. 43, No. 10, pp. 877-880.

Cirtin, Arnold. "Value Analysis - A New Tool For Cost Control," **JOA**, 1966, Vol. 122, No. 4, pp. 54-58.

Cismoski, David R. and Frederick Toepfer. "How To Allocate The College Budget Objectively," **MA**, 1979, Vol. 61, No. 6, pp. 45-50.

Cisney, Jack E. (Prakash, Som and Jack E. Cisney. "Appraisal And Evaluation Of Internal Financial Reports," **MA**, 1970, Vol. 51, No. 7, pp. 19-24.)

Claiborne, Jerry W. "Review Of APB Opinions No. 23 And 24: Accounting For Income Taxes In Special Areas," **CPAJ**, 1972, Vol. 42, No. 11, pp. 907-914.

Claire, Richard S. "Training For The Public Accounting Profession," **AR**, 1944, Vol. 19, No. 2, pp. 150-158.

Clancy, Donald K. "The Management Control Problems Of Responsibility Accounting," **MA**, 1978, Vol. 59, No. 9, pp. 35-39.

Clancy, Donald K. "What Is A Convertible Debenture? A Review Of The Literature In The U.S.A.," **ABACUS**, 1978, Vol. 14, No. 2, pp. 171-179.

Clancy, Donald K. (Collins, Frank, Robert E. Seiler and Donald K. Clancy. "Budgetary Attitudes: The Effects Of Role Senders, Stress, And Performance Evaluation," **ABR**, 1983-84, Vol. 14, No. 54, pp. 163-168.)

Clancy, Donald K. (Munter, Paul, Donald K. Clancy and Tommy Moores. "Accounting For Futures Contracts," **CPAJ**, 1985, Vol. 55, No. 3, pp. 18-25.)

Clancy, Donald K. (Willits, Stephen D., Donald K. Clancy and Robert J. Freeman. "Public Employee Retirement System Reports: A Study Of Knowledgable User Information Processing Ability," **RIGNA**, 1988, Vol. 4, pp. 3-48.)

Clancy, D. K. and F. Collins. "Informal Accounting Information Systems: Some Tentative Findings," **AOS**, 1979, Vol. 4, No. 1/2, pp. 21-30.

Clancy, Ronald K. (Munter, Paul H., Ronald K. Clancy and C. Tommy Moores. "Accounting For Financial Futures: The Question Of Risk Reduction," **AIA**, 1986, Vol. 3, pp. 51-70.)

Clapp, Charles L. "National Variations In Accounting Principles And Practices," **IJAER**, 1967, Vol. 3, No. 1, pp. 29-42.

Clark, Almer B. "Tax Aspects Of Realty," **MA**, 1972, Vol. 53, No. 7, pp. 39-40.

Clark, John H. "Financial Control Of Ford Manufacturing Plants," **MA**, 1966, Vol. 48, No. 4, pp. 10-15.

Clark, John J. and Pieter Elgers. "Forecasted Income Statements: An Investor Perspective," **AR**, 1973, Vol. 48, No. 4, pp. 668-678.

Clark, John J. (Elgers, Pieter and John J. Clark. "Inclusion Of Budgets In Financial Reports: Investor Needs V. Management Disclosure," **ABR**, 1972-73, Vol. 3, No. 9, pp. 53-61.)

Clark, John. "Costing For Quality At Celanese," **MA**, 1985, Vol. 66, No. 9, pp. 42-46.

Clark, John. "The Labor Mystique," **MA**, 1982, Vol. 64, No. 6, pp. 36-39.

Clark, Karen. (Douglas, Patricia, Teresa Beed, Karen Clark and Sylvia Weisenburger. "Surviving Your First Job," **MA**, 1986, Vol. 67, No. 12, pp. 32-35.)

Clark, Myrtle W., Thomas E. Gibbs and Richard G. Schroeder. "How CPAs Evaluate Internal Auditors," **CPAJ**, 1981, Vol. 51, No. 7, pp. 10-15.

Clark, Myrtle W., Thomas E. Gibbs and Richard G. Schroeder. "CPAs Judge Internal Audit Department Objectivity," **MA**, 1981, Vol. 62, No. 8, pp. 40-43.

Clark, Robert W. "People And Computers," **MA**, 1969, Vol. 51, No. 4, pp. 9-11.

Clark, Ronald L. and James B. McLaughlin. "Controlling The Cost Of Product Defects," **MA**, 1986, Vol. 68, No. 2, pp. 32-35.

Clark, Ronald L. and Robert B. Sweeney. "Admission To Accounting Programs: Using A Discriminant Model As A Classification Procedure," **AR**, 1985, Vol. 60, No. 3, pp. 508-518.

Clark, Ronald L. "Evaluating Continued Existence," **CPAJ**, 1986, Vol. 56, No. 8, pp. 22-31.

Clark, Ronald L. (Borthick, A. Faye and Ronald L. Clark. "The Role Of Productive Thinking In Affecting Student Learning With Microcomputers In Accounting Education," **AR**, 1986, Vol. 61, No. 1, pp. 143-157.)

Clark, Ronald L. (Borthick, A. Faye and Ronald L. Clark. "Research On Computing In Accounting Education: Opportunities And Impediments," **IAE**, 1987, Vol. 2, No. 2, pp. 173-192)

Clark, Ronald L. (Borthick, A. Faye and Ronald L. Clark. "Improving Accounting Majors' Writing Quality: The Role Of Language Analysis In Attention Direction," **IAE**, 1987, Vol. 2, No. 1, pp. 13-27.)

Clark, Ronald L. (Pasewark, William R. and Ronald L. Clark. "Understanding What Went Wrong With The Budget," **CA**, 1988, Vol. 6, No. 1, pp. 48-52.)

Clark, Terry Nichols. "Fiscal Management Of American Cities: Funds Flow Indicators," **JAR**, 1977, Vol. 15, Supp., pp. 54-94.

Clarke, Carol K. (Pesando, James E. and Carol K. Clarke. "Economic Models Of The Labor Market And Pension Accounting: An Exploratory Analysis," **AR**, 1983, Vol. 58, No. 4, pp. 733-748.)

Clarke, F. L. and G. W. Dean. "Schmidt's 'Betriebswirtschaft' Theory," **ABACUS**, 1986, Vol. 22, No. 2, pp. 65-102.

Clarke, F. L. "A Closer Look At Sweeney's Stabilised Accounting Proposals," **ABR**, 1975-76, Vol. 6, No. 24, pp. 264-275.

Clarke, F. L. "A Note On Exchange Rates, Purchasing Power Parities And Translation Procedures," **ABACUS**, 1977, Vol.

Clarke

13, No. 1, pp. 60-66.

Clarke, F. L. "Inflation Accounting And The Accidents Of History," **ABACUS**, 1980, Vol. 16, No. 2, pp. 79-99.

Clarke, F. L. "Patz On Parities, Exchange Rates And Translation," **ABR**, 1978-79, Vol. 9, No. 33, pp. 73-77.

Clarke, F. L. "Some Observations On The Indexation Of Accounts," **ABACUS**, 1975, Vol. 11, No. 2, pp. 107-121.

Clarke, John W. "Statement Of Accounting Policies For War Contract Terminations," **AR**, 1946, Vol. 21, No. 1, pp. 31-36.

Clarke, Robert W. "Extension Of The CPA's Attest Function In Corporate Annual Reports," **AR**, 1968, Vol. 43, No. 4, pp. 769-776.

Clarke, Robert W. (Robertson, Jack C. and Robert W. Clarke. "Verification Of Management Representations: A First Step Toward Independent Audits Of Management," **AR**, 1971, Vol. 46, No. 3, pp. 562-571.)

Clarke, Roger. (Beaver, William H., Roger Clarke and William F. Wright. "The Association Between Unsystematic Security Returns And The Magnitude Of Earnings Forecast Errors," **JAR**, 1979, Vol. 17, No. 2, pp. 316-340.)

Clary, Duane A. "Blueprint For An Accounting Program In Federal Taxation," **AR**, 1973, Vol. 48, No. 2, pp. 425-427.

Clason, Donald E. "Clerical Systems And Work Simplification In The Computer Age," **MA**, 1966, Vol. 48, No. 2, pp. 19-28.

Clay, Alvin A. "Undergraduate International Accounting Education," **IJAER**, 1975, Vol. 11, No. 1, pp. 185-192.

Clay, John R. and Dennis R. Meals. "Personal Financial Planning: Two Perspectives," **JOA**, 1985, Vol. 159, No. 5, pp. 82-97.

Clay, John R. and Stephen D. Holton. "Prescribed Form Engagements: Some Practical Guidance," **JOA**, 1982, Vol. 153, No. 5, pp. 66-79.

Clay, John R., Dan M. Guy and Dennis R. Meals. "Solving Compilation And Review Practice Problems," **JOA**, 1980, Vol. 150, No. 3, pp. 74-82.

Clay, Raymond J., Jr. and Jan R. Williams. "Preparation Guide For Price-Level-Adjusted Financial Statements," **CPAJ**, 1975, Vol. 45, No. 10, pp. 37-44.

Clay, Raymond J., Jr. and M. Herschel Mann. "Modification Of Standards: A Proposed Solution To The Problem Of Increased Accounting Enrollment," **AR**, 1976, Vol. 51, No. 2, pp. 352-358.

Clay, Raymond J., Jr. and William W. Holder. "A Practitioner's Guide To Accounting For Leases," **JOA**, 1977, Vol. 144, No. 2, pp. 61-68.

Clay, Raymond J., Jr. (Krogstad, Jack L., Gerald Smith and Raymond J. Clay, Jr. "Impact Of A Simulation Of Audit Practice," **IAE**, 1986, No. 2, pp. 309-320.)

Clay, Raymond J., Jr. (Sumners, Glenn E., Richard A. White and Raymond J. Clay, Jr. "The Use Of Engagement Letters In Audit, Review, And Compilation Engagements: An Empirical Study," **AJPT**, 1986-87, Vol. 6, No. 2, pp. 116-122.)

Claytor, Paul. (Ator, Lloyd G., Jr. and Paul Claytor. "Commercial Banking And The TRA." **JOA**, 1987, Vol. 163, No. 4, pp. 102-107.)

Cleaver, Goodrich F. "Auditing And Electronic Data Processing," **JOA**, 1958, Vol. 106, No. 5, pp. 48-54.

Clelland, Richard C. (O'Hara, John B and Richard C. Clelland. "Satisfying Ourselves On Prior Years' Inventories," **JOA**, 1963, Vol. 116, No. 4, pp. 42-52.)

Clemens, Peter J., III. "Asset Depreciation Range System...Versus Investment Credit," **MA**, 1972, Vol. 53, No. 7, pp. 25-27.

Clements, Joel and Robert L. Woodall. "Controlled Disbursements: A Cash Management Tool For Growing Concerns," **MA**, 1983, Vol. 64, No. 11, pp. 53-55.

Clement, Robert H. (Barhydt, Dirck, Robert H. Clement, Dan W. Lufkin and A. Jones Yorke. "Planning Concepts In The 'Tentative Statement Of Cost Concepts'," **AR**, 1957, Vol. 32, No. 4, pp. 593-597.)

Clevenger, Earl. "Presenting The Theory Of Debit And Credit," **AR**, 1943, Vol. 18, No. 1, pp. 40-44.

Climo, Tom. "What's Happening In Britain?," **JOA**, 1976, Vol. 141, No. 2, pp. 55-59.

Clinch, Greg J. and Norman A. Sinclair. "Intra-Industry Information Releases: A Recursive Systems Approach," **JAEC**, 1987, Vol. 9, No. 1, pp. 89-106.

Clinch, Greg. "Alternative Hypotheses Concerning Depreciation Of Buildings," **ABACUS**, 1983, Vol. 19, No. 2, pp. 139-147.

Clingman, William F., III. "The Company Car: A Management Decision," **MA**, 1975, Vol. 56, No. 11, pp. 51-55.

Cloake, T. Reginald. "Accountant's Responsibility In Preparing For Attack," **JOA**, 1951, Vol. 91, No. 2, pp. 256-259.

Clohosey, Addison B. "Four Important Trends In Thinking On Federal Taxation," **JOA**, 1950, Vol. 89, No. 2, pp. 132-135.

Clough, Barbara A. "Towards A Definition Of Experience," **AR**, 1973, Vol. 48, No. 4, pp. 798-799.

Clouse, Maclyn L. (Selto, Frank H. and Maclyn L. Clouse. "An Investigation Of Managers' Adaptations To SFAS No. 2: Accounting For Research And Development Costs." **JAR**, 1985, Vol. 23, No. 2, pp. 700-717.)

Cloutier, Clive R. and Barry Mabry. "A Small Bank Adopts A Financial Planning Model," **MA**, 1980, Vol. 61, No. 8, pp. 19-21.

Cloyd, Helen M. "George Washington As An Accountant," **AHJ**, 1979, Vol. 6, No. 1, pp. 87-91.

Cloyd, Helen M. "Optimum Course Requirements For Nonaccounting Majors," **AR**, 1971, Vol. 46, No. 3, pp. 591-594.

Clubb, C. (Burchell, S., C. Clubb, A. Hopwood, J. Hughes and J. Nahapiet. "The Roles Of Accounting In Organizations And Society," **AOS**, 1980, Vol. 5, No. 1, pp. 5-28.)

Clubb, C. (Burchell, S., C. Clubb and A. G. Hopwood. "Accounting In Its Social Context: Towards A History Of Value Added In The United Kingdom," **AOS**, 1985, Vol. 10, No. 4, pp. 381-414.)

Clurman, Herman. "'Perks': Recent Tax Legislation," **JAAF**, 1979, Vol. 2, No. 4, pp. 344-345.

Coad, Fred A. (Faulhaber, Thomas A., Fred A. Coad and Thomas J. Little. "Building A Process Cost Management System From The Bottom Up," **MA**, 1988, Vol. 69, No. 11, pp. 58-62.)

Coakley, James R. and James K. Loebbecke. "The Expectation Of Accounting Errors In Medium-Sized Manufacturing Firms," **AIA**, 1985, Vol. 2, pp. 199-246.

Coates, Geoff. (Rickwood, Colin, Geoff Coates and Ray Stacey. "Managed Costs And The Capture Of Information," **ABR**, 1986-87, Vol. 17, No. 68, pp. 319-326.)

Coates, Robert. "The Predictive Content Of Interim Reports - A Time Series Analysis," **JAR**, 1972, Vol. 10, Supp., pp. 132-144.

Cobbs, John L. "How The Business Press Views The Accounting Profession," **JOA**, 1969, Vol. 128, No. 2, pp. 48-51.

Cobb, E. Kennedy. "Current Status Of Managerial Accounting As A Course Of Study," **AR**, 1960, Vol. 35, No. 1, pp. 125-129.

Coburn, David L., Joseph K. Ellis, III and Duane R. Milano. "Dilemmas In MNC Transfer Pricing," **MA**, 1981, Vol. 63, No. 5, pp. 53-58.

Cochran, Edward B. "What Is A Controller?," **JOA**, 1955, Vol. 100, No. 1, pp. 46-53.

Coda, Bernard A. (Morris, William J. and Bernard A. Coda. "Marketable Equity Securities - Valuation Alternatives," **JOA**, 1973, Vol. 135, No. 1, pp. 48-54.)

Coda, B. A. (Anderson, H. M., B. A. Coda and J. W. Giese. "An Experiment With A One-Semester Introductory Accounting Course," **AR**, 1972, Vol. 47, No. 1, pp. 175-177.)

Coe, Robert K. and Irwin Weinstock. "Evaluating The Accounting Professor's Journal Publications," **JAED**, 1983, Vol. 1, No. 1, pp. 127-129.

Coe, Teddy L. "An Analysis Of The SEC Monitoring Of Prospectuses," **JAAF**, 1979, Vol. 2, No. 3, pp. 244-253.

Coe, Teddy L. "Student Management Consulting Projects In The Accounting Curriculum," **JAED**, 1983, Vol. 1, No. 2, pp. 97-105.

Coe, Teddy L. (Merino, Barbara D. and Teddy L. Coe. "Uniformity In Accounting: A Historical Perspective," **JOA**, 1978, Vol. 146, No. 2, pp. 62-69.)

Coenenberg, Adolf G. (Macharzina, K. and Adolf G. Coenenberg. "Current-Cost Or Current Purchasing-Power Accounting? An Internationally Based Assessment Of FASB Statement No. 33," **IJAER**, 1981, Vol. 16, No. 2, pp. 149-162.)

Coff, Russell. (Flamholtz, Eric G., D. Gerald Searfoss and Russell Coff. "Developing Human Resource Accounting As A Human Resource Decision Support System," **AH**, 1988, Vol. 2, No. 3, pp. 1-9.)

Coffey, Kenneth J. and Jack E. Faires. "Options For Military Retirement System Changes," **JCA**, 1988, Vol. 5, No. 1, pp. 1-18.

Coffman, Edward N. "A Synopsis Of Essays On Historical Accounting Topics," **AHJ**, 1987, Vol. 14, No. 1, pp. 123-129.

Coffman, Edward N. (Burns, Thomas J. and Edward N. Coffman. "The Ascending Profession Of Accounting (Part 2)," **CPAJ**, 1977, Vol. 47, No. 3, pp. 31-36.)

Coffman, Edward N. (Burns, Thomas J. and Edward N. Coffman. "The Ascending Profession Of Accounting (Part 1)," **CPAJ**, 1977, Vol. 47, No. 2, pp. 11-16.)

Coffman, Edward N. (Burns, Thomas J. and Edward N. Coffman. "The Accounting Hall Of Fame: A Profile Of The Members," **JAR**, 1976, Vol. 14, No. 2, pp. 342-347.)

Coffman, Edward N. (Previts, Gary John and Edward N. Coffman. "Practice And Education: Bridging The Gap," **JOA**, 1980, Vol. 150, No. 6, pp. 39-46.)

Coffman, Edward N. (Tondkar, Rasoul H. and Edward N. Coffman. "Teaching Foreign Currency Translation: A Flowchart Approach," **JAED**, 1984, Vol. 2, No. 2, pp. 145-151.)

Coffman, Robert M. "Problems Of Displacement In Public Offerings," **JOA**, 1974, Vol. 138, No. 4, pp. 65-71.

Cogger, Kenneth and William Ruland. "A Note On Alternative Tests For Independence Of Financial Time Series," **JAR**, 1982, Vol. 20, No. 2, pp. 733-737.

Cogger, Kenneth O. "A Time-Series Analytic Approach To Aggregation Issues In Accounting Data," **JAR**, 1981, Vol. 19, No. 2, pp. 285-298.

Cogger, Kenneth O. (Emery, Gary W. and Kenneth O. Cogger. "The Measurement Of Liquidity," **JAR**, 1982, Vol. 20, No. 2, Part I, pp. 290-303.)

Coglitore, Frank and R. Glen Berryman. "Analytical Procedures: A Defensive Necessity," **AJPT**, 1988, Vol. 7, No. 2, pp. 150-163.

Cohen, Albert H. "Guideposts For Revision Of Subchapter C," **JOA**, 1958, Vol. 106, No. 5, pp. 40-47.

Cohen, Albert H. "Professional Conduct In Taxes," **JOA**, 1956, Vol. 101 No. 1, pp. 34-39.

Cohen, Albert H. "Revenue Act Of 1954 - Significant Accounting Changes," **AR**, 1954, Vol. 29, No. 4, pp. 543-551.

Cohen, Albert H. "The Future Of Lease Financing Under New Depreciation Rules," **JOA**, 1954, Vol. 98, No. 2, pp. 189-196.

Cohen, Arthur S. (Siegel, Andrew C., Arthur S. Cohen and

230

Laurence I. Feibel. "ESOPs - The Present And An Imperiled Future? - Part II," **CPAJ**, 1986, Vol. 56, No. 2, pp. 32-35.)

Cohen, Arthur S. (Siegel, Andrew C., Arthur S. Cohen and Laurence I. Feibel. "ESOPs - The Present And An Imperiled Future? - Part I," **CPAJ**, 1986, Vol. 56, No. 1, pp. 14-23.)

Cohen, A. H. "The Impact Of The New Revenue Code Upon Accounting," **AR**, 1956, Vol. 31, No. 2, pp. 206-216.

Cohen, Gerald D. and David B. Pearson. "Auditing The Client's Judgments," **JOA**, 1981, Vol. 151, No. 5, pp. 58-65.

Cohen, Jeffrey M. "Accounting For Modular Housing Manufacturers," **MA**, 1973, Vol. 55, No. 3, pp. 11-14.

Cohen, Jeffrey R. "Ethics & Budgeting," **MA**, 1988, Vol. 70, No. 2, pp. 29-31.

Cohen, Jerry. (Calabro, John P. and Jerry Cohen. "Taking Control of Inventory Shortage," **CA**, 1985, Vol. 3, No. 1, pp. 29-33.)

Cohen, Manuel F. "Current Developments At The SEC," **AR**, 1965, Vol. 40, No. 1, pp. 1-8.

Cohen, Martin. "Intercorporate Transactions And Consolidated Returns," **JOA**, 1966, Vol. 121, No. 4, pp. 50-54.

Cohen, Milton H. "Regulation Through Disclosure," **JOA**, 1981, Vol. 152, No. 6, pp. 52-62.

Cohen, Morris A. and Robert Halperin. "Optimal Inventory Order Policy For A Firm Using The LIFO Inventory Costing Method," **JAR**, 1980, Vol. 18, No. 2, pp. 375-389.

Cohen, Susan I. and Martin Loeb. "Improving Performance Through Cost Allocation," **CAR**, 1988, Vol. 5, No. 1, pp. 70-95.

Cohen, Susan I. and Martin Loeb. "Public Goods, Common Inputs, And The Efficiency Of Full Cost Allocations," **AR**, 1982, Vol. 57, No. 2, pp. 336-347.

Cohn, Theodore. "Use Of Punched Tape In Preparing Tax Returns," **JOA**, 1963, Vol. 115, No. 1, pp. 56-58.

Cohn, Theodore. (Milston, Martin J. and Theodore Cohn. "Personal And Business Aspects Of Stockholder Agreements," **JOA**, 1967, Vol. 124, No. 4, pp. 41-45.)

Coil, Robert F. "Contributions: Monetary Versus Non-Monetary," **MA**, 1975, Vol. 56, No. 10, pp. 35-38.

Colabella, Patrick R. "The Future Tax Practice," **CPAJ**, 1984, Vol. 54, No. 6, pp. 30-35.

Colantoni, Claude S., Rene P. Manes and Andrew Whinston. "A Unified Approach To The Theory Of Accounting And Information Systems," **AR**, 1971, Vol. 46, No. 1, pp. 90-102.

Colantoni, Claude S., Rene P. Manes and Andrew Whinston. "Programming, Profit Rates And Pricing Decisions," **AR**, 1969, Vol. 44, No. 3, pp. 467-481.

Colantoni, C. (Charnes, A., C. Colantoni. W. W. Cooper and K. O. Kortanek. "Economic Social And Enterprise Accounting And Mathematical Models," **AR**, 1972, Vol. 47, No. 1, pp. 85-108.)

Colantoni, C. (Charnes, A., C. Colantoni and W. W. Cooper. "A Futurological Justification For Historical Cost And Multi-Dimensional Accounting," **AOS**, 1976, Vol. 1, No. 4, pp. 315-338.)

Colbert, Janet L. "Audit Risk - Tracing The Evolution," **ACCHOR**, 1987, Vol. 1, No. 3, pp. 49-58.

Colbert, J. L. "Inherent Risk: An Investigation Of Auditors' Judgments," **AOS**, 1988, Vol. 13, No. 2, pp. 111-122.

Colby, Robert W. (Grollman, William K. and Robert W. Colby. "Internal Control For Small Business," **JOA**, 1978, Vol. 146, No. 6, pp. 64-67.)

Coldwell, Susan. (Horvitz, Jerome S. and Susan Coldwell. "Analysis Of The Arthur Young Decision And Its Potential Impact On Public Accounting," **JAAF**, 1985, Vol. 8, No. 2, pp. 86-99.)

Cole, Leroy H. "Accounting For Real Estate Developments," **JOA**, 1960, Vol. 110, No. 4, pp. 59-63.

Cole, Terry D. "How To Obtain Probability Estimates In Capital Expenditure Evaluations: A Practical Approach," **MA**, 1970, Vol. 52, No. 1, pp. 61-64.

Cole, William A. and Stephen H. Wales. Sr. "The Investment Credit," **MA**, 1973, Vol. 54, No. 9, pp. 13-16.

Cole, William Morse. "Theories Of Cost," **AR**, 1936, Vol. 11, No. 1, pp. 4-9.

Coleman, Almand R., William G. Shenkir and Williard E. Stone. "Accounting In Colonial Virginia: A Case Study," **JOA**, 1974, Vol. 138, No. 1, pp 32-43.

Coleman, L. W., Jr. "The Use Of Determinants In The Solution Of Linear Equations," **AR**, 1943, Vol. 18, No. 1, pp. 44-48.

Coleman, Phillip I. "Is Railroad Accounting Off The Track?," **JOA**, 1970, Vol. 130, No. 4, pp. 64-68.

Coleman, Reuben W. (Hopewell, Rita J., Eileen S. Klink and Reuben W. Coleman. "Facing The Ethics Involved In Technical Obsolescence," **MA**, 1984, Vol. 66, No. 6,pp.26-29.)

Coleman, R. W. "The Role Of Accounting In Management," **AR**, 1949, Vol. 24, No. 2, pp. 179-183.

Coleridge, Samuel A. R. (Cardona, Ruben and Samuel A. R. Coleridge. "Financing Facilities At Lower Cost," **CPAJ**, 1978, Vol. 48, No. 3, pp. 27-30.)

Colignon, R. and M. Covaleski. "An Examination Of Managerial Accounting Practices As A Process Of Mutual Adjustment," **AOS**, 1988, Vol. 13, No. 6, pp. 559-579.

Colley, J. Ron and Ara G. Volkan. "Accounting For Goodwill," **ACCHOR**, 1988, Vol. 2, No. 1, pp. 35-41.

Collier, Boyd and Curtis Carnes. "Convertible Bonds And Financial Reality," **MA**, 1979, Vol. 60, No. 8, pp. 47-48.

Collier, Bruce E. (Crooch, G. Michael and Bruce E. Collier. "Reporting Guidelines For Companies In A Stage Of Development," **CPAJ**, 1973, Vol. 43, No. 7, pp. 579-583.)

Collier, Henry W. and William A. Mehrens. "Using Multiple

Choice Test Items To Improve Classroom Testing Of Professional Accounting Students," **JAED**, 1985, Vol. 3, No. 2, pp. 41-51.

Collier, P. and E. W. Davis. "The Management Of Currency Transaction Risk By UK Multinational Companies," **ABR**, 1984-85, Vol. 15, No. 60, pp. 327-334.

Collier, Roger J. "Simulation Of Computer Systems: An Introduction," **MA**, 1973, Vol. 54, No. 11, pp. 45-47.

Collins, Clem W. "Accounting And Economics: Comments," **AR**, 1935, Vol. 10, No. 2, pp. 154-155.

Collins, Daniel W. and Melvin C. O'Connor. "An Examination Of The Association Between Accounting And Share Price Data In The Extractive Petroleum Industry: A Comment And Extension," **AR**, 1978, Vol. 53, No. 1, pp. 228-239.

Collins, Daniel W. and Richard R. Simonds. "SEC Line-Of-Business Disclosure And Market Risk Adjustments," **JAR**, 1979, Vol. 17, No. 2, pp. 352-383.

Collins, Daniel W. and Warren T. Dent. "A Comparison Of Alternative Testing Methodologies Used In Capital Market Research." **JAR**, 1984, Vol. 22, No. 1, pp. 48-84.

Collins, Daniel W. and Warren T. Dent. "The Proposed Elimination Of Full Cost Accounting In The Extractive Petroleum Industry: An Empirical Assessment Of The Market Consequences," **JAEC**, 1979, Vol. 1, No. 1, pp. 3-44.

Collins, Daniel W. "Predicting Earnings With Sub-Entity Data: Some Further Evidence," **JAR**, 1976, Vol. 14, No. 1, pp. 163-177.

Collins, Daniel W. (Doran, B. Michal, D. W. Collins and D. S. Dhaliwal. "The Information Of Historical Cost Earnings Relative To Supplemental Reserve-Based Accounting Data In The Extractive Petroleum Industry," **AR**, 1988, Vol. 63,No. 3,pp. 389-413.)

Collins, Daniel W. (O'Connor, Melvin C. and Daniel W. Collins. "Toward Establishing User-Oriented Materiality Standards," **JOA**, 1974, Vol. 138, No. 6, pp. 67-75.)

Collins, Daniel W., Michael S. Rozeff and Dan S. Dhaliwal. "The Economic Determinants Of The Market Reaction To Proposed Mandatory Accounting Changes In The Oil And Gas Industry: A Cross-Sectional Analysis," **JAEC**, 1981, Vol. 3, No. 1, pp. 37-71.

Collins, Daniel W., Michael S. Rozeff and William K. Salatka. "The SEC's Rejection Of SFAS No. 19: Tests Of Market Price Reversal," **AR**, 1982, Vol. 57, No. 1, pp. 1-17.

Collins, Daniel W., S. P. Kothari and Judy Dawson Rayburn. "Firm Size And The Information Content Of Prices With Respect To Earnings," **JAEC**, 1987, Vol. 9, No. 2, pp. 111-138.

Collins, Francis B. "Business-Type Statements In The Budget Of The United States," **AR**, 1954, Vol. 29, No. 3, pp. 472-479.

Collins, Frank and James L. Porter. "Engagement Withdrawal: The Legal Perils," **JOA**, 1979, Vol. 147, No. 2, pp. 66-71.

Collins, Frank and John A. Yeakel. "Range Estimates In Financial Statements: Help Or Hindrance?," **JOA**, 1979, Vol. 148, No. 1, pp. 73-78.

Collins, Frank and John J. Willingham. "Contingency Management Approach To Budgeting," **MA**, 1977, Vol. 59, No. 3, pp. 45-48.

Collins, Frank, Paul Munter and Don W. Finn. "The Budgeting Games People Play," **AR**, 1987, Vol. 62, No. 1. pp. 29-49.

Collins, Frank, Robert E. Seiler and Donald K. Clancy. "Budgetary Attitudes: The Effects Of Role Senders, Stress, And Performance Evaluation," **ABR**, 1983-84, Vol. 14, No. 54, pp. 163-168.

Collins, Frank. "Management Accounting And Motivation - The Relationship," **MA**, 1979, Vol. 60, No. 9, pp. 22-26.

Collins, Frank. "The Interaction Of Budget Characteristics And Personality Variables With Budgetary Response Attitudes," **AR**, 1978, Vol. 53, No. 2, pp. 324-335.

Collins, Frank. (McNeill, I. Eugene and Frank Collins. "Personality Tendencies And Learning Modes In Elementary Accounting," **AR**, 1975, Vol. 50, No. 4, pp. 888-897.)

Collins, F. "Managerial Accounting Systems And Organizational Control: A Role Perspective," **AOS**, 1982, Vol. 7, No. 2, pp. 107-122.

Collins, F. (Clancy, D. K. and F. Collins. "Informal Accounting Information Systems: Some Tentative Findings," **AOS**, 1979, Vol. 4, No. 1/2, pp. 21-30.)

Collins, George W. "Analysis Of Working Capital," **AR**, 1946, Vol. 21, No. 4, pp. 430-440.

Collins, Janet Duthie. (Hirsch, Maurice L., Jr. and Janet Duthie Collins. "An Integrated Approach To Communication Skills In An Accounting Curriculum," **JAED**, 1988, Vol. 6, No. 1, pp. 15-31.)

Collins, Joanne A. "Case-Mix Accounting Can Help Hospitals Control Costs," **MA**, 1985, Vol. 67, No. 5, pp. 56-59.

Collins, Joanne A. (Carlson, Barbara Mackey and Joanne A. Collins. "Motivating Managers With Positive Reinforcement," **MA**, 1986, Vol. 67, No. 9, pp. 48-51.)

Collins, Joanne A. (Kelley, Patrick J. and Joanne A. Collins. "Good Stuff Bakery: Making More 'Dough' Via Computer Control," **MA**, 1984, Vol. 65, No. 8, pp. 26-30.)

Collins, Julie H. and John L. Kramer. "An Examination Of The Employer's Pension Plan Choice: Integrated Vs. Nonintegrated Plans," **JATA**, 1986, Vol. 8, No. 1, pp. 35-48.

Collins, Julie H. and Valerie C. Milliron. "A Measure Of Professional Accountants' Learning Style," **IAE**, 1987, Vol. 2, No. 2, pp. 193-206

Collins, J. Stephen. "An Effective Method For Teaching The Statement Of Changes In Financial Position," **IAE**, 1985, No. 1, pp. 145-156.

Collins, Marilynn. "Incorporating Authoritative Pronouncements With Intermediate And Advanced Accounting

Syllabi," **JAED**, 1987, Vol. 5, No. 1, pp. 155-160.

Collins, Marilynn. (Bloom, Robert and Marilynn Collins. "Motivating Students With A Historical Perspective In Financial Accounting Courses," **JAED**, 1988, Vol. 6, No. 1, pp. 103-115.)

Collins, R. "Computers And Accountancy Courses: A Comment," **ABR**, 1982-83, Vol. 13, No. 52, pp. 313-315.

Collins, Stephen H. "1988 Tax Filing Seaaon: Dealing With The Chaos," **JOA**, 1988, Vol. 166, No. 4, pp. 48-54.

Collins, Stephen P. "Who Audits The Auditors?," **MA**, 1985, Vol. 66, No. 12, pp. 24-27.

Collins, William A. and William S. Hopwood. "A Multivariate Analysis Of Annual Earnings Forecasts Generated From Quarterly Forecasts Of Financial Analysts And Univariate Time-Series Models," **JAR**, 1980, Vol. 18, No. 2, pp. 390-406.

Collins, William A. (Snowball, Doug and William A. Collins. "Televised Accounting Instruction Attitudes And Performance: A Field Experiment," **AR**, 1980, Vol. 55, No. 1, pp. 123-133.)

Collins, William A., William S. Hopwood and James C. McKeown. "The Predictability Of Interim Earnings Over Alternative Quarters," **JAR**, 1984, Vol. 22, No. 2, pp. 467-479.

Collinson, D. (Knights, D. and D. Collinson. "Disciplining The Shopfloor: A Comparison Of The Disciplinary Effects Of Managerial Psychology And Financial Accounting," **AOS**, 1987, Vol. 12, No. 4/5, pp. 457-478.)

Collison, Jeanne E. (Paretta, Robert L. and Jeanne E. Collison. "Physical Distribution Costs: A Survey," **MA**, 1976, Vol. 58, No. 1, pp. 45-48.)

Collmer, Sheryl. (Holder, William W. and Sheryl Collmer. "Analytical Review Procedures: New Relevance," **CPAJ**, 1980, Vol. 50, No. 11, pp. 29-36.)

Colson, Robert H., Michael W. Maher, Amy J. Broman and Pieter Tiessen. "Audit Pricing Models For Regulation Research: Reliability And Stability," **RIAR**, 1988, Vol. 2, pp. 61-79.

Colville, I. "Reconstructing 'Behavioural Accounting'," **AOS**, 1981, Vol. 6, No. 2, pp. 119-132.

Colville, I. (Tomkins, C., D. Rosenberg and I. Colville. "The Social Process Of Research: Some Reflections On Developing A Multi-Disciplinary Accounting Project," **AOS**, 1980, Vol. 5, No. 2, pp. 247-262.)

Combes, James H. "Communication Gaps: Internal And External," **MA**, 1971, Vol. 53, No. 5, pp. 23-24.

Comer, Robert W. "Brazilian Price-Level Accounting," **MA**, 1975, Vol. 57, No. 4, pp. 41-42.

Comiskey, Eugene E. and Charles W. Mulford. "The Influence Of Accounting Principles On Management Investment Decisions: An Illustration," **ACCHOR**, 1988, Vol. 2, No. 2, pp. 67-72.

Comiskey, Eugene E. and F. A. Mlynarczyk. "Recognition Of Income By Finance Companies," **AR**, 1968, Vol. 43, No. 2, pp. 248-256.

Comiskey, Eugene E. and Roger E. V. Groves. "United Kingdom Developments In Interperiod Tax Allocation," **IJAER**, 1981, Vol. 16, No. 2, pp. 1-9.

Comiskey, Eugene E. "Cost Control By Regression Analysis," **AR**, 1966, Vol. 41, No. 2, pp. 235-238.

Comiskey, Eugene E. "Market Response To Changes In Depreciation Accounting," **AR**, 1971, Vol. 46, No. 2, pp. 279-285.

Comiskey, Eugene E. "On The Value Of R-Square In Regression Analysis: A Reply," **AR**, 1972, Vol. 47, No. 2, pp. 358-359.

Comiskey, Eugene E. (Barefield, Russell M. and Eugene E. Comiskey. "Segmental Financial Disclosure By Diversified Firms And Security Prices: A Comment," **AR**, 1975, Vol. 50, No. 4, pp. 818-821.)

Comiskey, Eugene E. (Barefield, Russell M. and Eugene E. Comiskey. "The Smoothing Hypothesis: An Alternative Test," **AR**, 1972, Vol. 47, No. 2, pp. 291-298.)

Comiskey, Eugene E. (Barefield, Russell M. and Eugene E. Comiskey. "Depreciation Policy And The Behavior Of Corporate Profits," **JAR**, 1971, Vol. 9, No. 2, pp. 351-358.)

Comiskey, Eugene. (Mulford, Charles W. and Eugene Comiskey. "Investment Decisions And The Equity Accounting Standard," **AR**, 1986, Vol. 61, No. 3, pp. 519-525.)

Comiskey, E. E. and R. E. V. Groves. "The Adoption And Diffusion Of An Accounting Innovation," **ABR**, 1971-72, Vol. 2, No. 5, pp. 67-77.

Compton, Ted R. "Auditing And The Paraprofessional," **CPAJ**, 1981, Vol. 51, No. 5, pp. 28-33.

Comtois, Joseph D. (Broadus, W. A., Jr. and Joseph D. Comtois. "The Single Audit Act: A Needed Reform," **JOA**, 1985, Vol. 159, No. 4, pp. 62-71.)

Comtois, Joseph D. (Broadus, W. A., Jr. and Jospeh D. Comtois. "Tools For The Single Audit," **JOA**, 1986, Vol. 161, No. 4, pp. 73-81.)

Comtois, Joseph D. (Broadus, W. A., Jr. and Joseph D. Comtois. "The Single Audit: A Progress Report," **JOA**, 1987, Vol. 164, No. 1, pp. 92-101.)

Conant, Spicer V. "Fifteen Words Or Less," **MA**, 1974, Vol. 55, No. 12, pp. 29-32.

Condie, Frank A. (Skousen, Clifford R. and Frank A. Condie. "Evaluating A Sports Program: Goalposts Vs. Test Tubes," **MA**, 1988, Vol. 70, No. 5, pp. 43-49.)

Condon, Harry I. "How Lightolier's Punched-Card Installation Produces Statements In 6 Instead Of 20 Days," **JOA**, 1950, Vol. 90, No. 2, pp. 136-140.

Conley, Michael J. (Leininger, Wayne E. and Michael J. Conley. "Regression Analysis In Auditing," **CPAJ**, 1980, Vol. 50, No. 10, pp. 43-47.)

Conley, William H. "Accounting In The Junior Colleges," **AR**, 1939, Vol. 14, No. 1, pp. 22-26.

Connally, Catherine E. "An Inside Look At Small Business Reform," **MA**, 1987, Vol. 68, No. 9, pp. 57-60.

Conneen, Andrew M., Jr. "Intermediate-Term Borrowing: An Evolving New Financing Product," **CA**, 1986, Vol. 4, No. 3, pp. 43-48.

Connelly, John R., Jr. "Should We License Accountants To Prevent Accounting License?," **MA**, 1978, Vol. 60, No. 5, pp. 22-26.

Connell, N. A. D. "Expert Systems In Accountancy: A Review Of Some Recent Applications," **ABR**, 1986-87, Vol. 17, No. 67, pp. 221-234.

Connolly, H. Andrew. "Planning A New Cost System: The 'Unfreezing' Stage," **MA**, 1979, Vol. 61, No. 5, pp. 19-24.

Connolly, Robert A. and Mark Hirschey. "Concentration And Profits: A Test Of The Accounting Bias Hypothesis," **JAPP**, 1988, Vol. 7, No. 4, pp. 313-334.

Connors, Suzanne G. "Do Members Read FASB Statements?," **MA**, 1982, Vol. 64, No. 6, pp. 44-45.

Connor, Joseph E. "Accounting For The Upward Float In Foreign Contracts," **JOA**, 1972, Vol. 133, No. 6, pp. 39-44.

Connor, Joseph E. "Control System Priorities For The '80s," **MA**, 1983, Vol. 64, No. 9, pp. 48-51.

Connor, Joseph E. "Discovery Value - The Oil Industry's Untried Method," **JOA**, 1975, Vol. 139, No. 5, pp. 54-63.

Connor, Joseph E. "Enhancing Public Confidence In The Accounting Profession," **JOA**, 1986, Vol. 162, No. 1, pp. 76-85.

Connor, Joseph E. "Measuring Up To Our Maturity," **CPAJ**, 1983, Vol. 53, No. 1, pp. 10-17.

Connor, Joseph E. "Reserve Recognition Accounting: Fact Or Fiction?," **JOA**, 1979, Vol. 148, No. 3, pp. 92-99.

Conroy, Robert M. and John S. Hughes. "Delegating Information Gathering Decisions," **AR**, 1987, Vol. 62, No. 1, pp. 50-66.

Conway, Charles D. "The Bardahl Formula And Service Companies," **CPAJ**, 1977, Vol. 47, No. 1, pp. 31-34.

Conway, Nelson. "Bringing In Partners," **JOA**, 1957, Vol. 103, No. 2, pp. 41-45.

Cook, Charles. (Lankford, Patricia and Charles Cook. "The 'Vital Few' Saves Costs," **MA**, 1986, Vol. 68, No. 2, pp. 54-55.)

Cook, David E. "Inter-Unit Pricing And Your New Pricing Expert: The IRS," **MA**, 1969, Vol. 51, No. 2, pp. 9-11.

Cook, Doris Marie. "The Psychological Impact Of Certain Aspects Of Performance Reports," **MA**, 1968, Vol. 49, No. 11, pp. 26-34.

Cook, Doris M. "The Effect Of Frequency Of Feedback On Attitudes And Performance," **JAR**, 1967, Vol. 5, Supp., pp. 213-224.

Cook, Edward T. "Revised Contract Cost Principles," **JOA**, 1960, Vol. 109, No. 2, pp. 52-65.

Cook, E. (Flamholtz, E. and E. Cook. "Connotative Meaning And Its Role In Accounting Change: A Field Study," **AOS**, 1978, Vol. 3, No. 2, pp. 115-140.)

Cook, Franklin H. "Abandoned Property And The Rate Base," **AR**, 1942, Vol. 17, No. 3, pp. 243-250.

Cook, Franklin H. "The Sale As A Test Of Income Realization," **AR**, 1939, Vol. 14, No. 4, pp. 355-367.

Cook, F. X., Jr. (Maxim, L. D., D. E. Cullen and F. X. Cook, Jr. "Optimal Acceptance Sampling Plans For Auditing 'Batched' Stop And Go Vs. Conventional Single-Stage Attributes Plans," **AR**, 1976, Vol. 51, No. 1, pp. 97-109.)

Cook, Henry, Jr. (Gordon, Lawrence A. and Henry Cook, Jr. "Absorption Costing And Fixed Factors Of Production," **AR**, 1973, Vol. 48, No. 1, pp. 128-129.)

Cook, James S., Jr., Lewis F. Davidson and Charles H. Smith. "Social Costs And Private Accounting," **ABACUS**, 1974, Vol. 10 No. 2, pp. 87-99.

Cook, John S. and Oscar J. Holzmann. "Current Cost And Present Value In Income Theory," **AR**, 1976, Vol. 51, No. 4, pp. 778-787.

Cook, John W. "Additional Rules Of Professional Ethics," **JOA**, 1964, Vol. 117, No. 2, pp. 41-47.

Cook, John W. "Public Accounting Experience For Private Accountants," **AR**, 1960, Vol. 35, No. 1, pp. 93-95.

Cook, J. Darrell. "Profitability Analysis In The Motor Carrier Industry," **MA**, 1973, Vol. 54, No. 11, pp. 48-50.

Cook, J. Michael and Haldon G. Robinson. "Peer Review - The Accounting Profession's Program," **CPAJ**, 1979, Vol. 49, No. 3, pp. 11-16.

Cook, J. Michael and Thomas P. Kelley. "Internal Accounting Control: A Matter Of Law," **JOA**, 1979, Vol. 147, No. 1, pp. 56-64.

Cook, J. Michael. "Special Report: Progress In Financial Accounting And Reporting Since February 1985," **CPAJ**, 1987, Vol. 57, No. 5, pp. 4-25.

Cook, J. Michael. "The AICPA At 100: Public Trust And Professional Pride," **JOA**, 1987, Vol. 163, No. 5, pp. 370-380.

Cooke, Robert B. "Responsibility Reporting Of Return On Investment," **MA**, 1967, Vol. 48, No. 11, pp. 24-29.

Cooke, T. E. and J. J. Glynn. "Taxation Implications Of Companies Purchasing Their Own Shares," **ABR**, 1982-83, Vol. 13, No. 51, pp. 177-180.

Coombes, Robert J. and Peter H. Eddey. "Accounting Income: The Relationship Between Capital Maintenance And Asset Measurement," **IAB**, 1986, Vol. 1, No. 1, pp. 112-122.

Coombes, R. J. and R. B. Tress. "The Financial Implications Of Corporate Share Reacquisitions," **ABACUS**, 1977, Vol. 13, No. 1, pp. 40-51.

Coombe, Lloyd W. and Robert R. Densmore. "How Detroit Edison Improves Its Productivity," **MA**, 1982, Vol. 63, No. 11, pp. 50-54.

Coombs, R. W. "Accounting For The Control Of Doctors: Management Information Systems In Hospitals," **AOS**, 1987, Vol. 12, No. 3, pp. 389-404.

Coon, S. J. "Devaluation And Damages," **AR**, 1935, Vol. 10, No. 3, pp. 301-302.

Coonrod, Curtis L. and James C. Todderud. "Serving The Federal Election Campaign," **JOA**, 1982, Vol. 154, No. 3, pp. 80-90.

Cooper, Barry N. (Zolfo, Frank J. and Barry N. Cooper. "Considering The LIFO Election," **MA**, 1977, Vol. 58, No. 12, pp. 41-43.)

Cooper, Bernard S. (Berman, Daniel S. and Bernard S. Cooper. "How The Tax Laws Encourage Corporate Acquisitions," **JOA**, 1963, Vol. 116, No. 5, pp. 61-64.)

Cooper, C. L. "Cumulative Trauma And Stress At Work," **AOS**, 1980, Vol. 5, No. 3, pp. 357-359.

Cooper, David J. "A Social Analysis Of Corporate Pollution Disclosures: A Comment," **AIPIA**, 1988, Vol. 2, pp. 179-186.

Cooper, David J. "Rationality And Investment Appraisal," **ABR**, 1974-75, Vol. 5, No. 19, pp.198-202.

Cooper, Deborah E. (Bialkin, Kenneth J. and Deborah E. Cooper. "Expanding Accountants' Liability: New Trends And Implications," **CA**, 1986, Vol. 4, No. 1, pp. 11-16.)

Cooper, Deborah E. (Craco, Louis A. and Deborah E. Cooper. "The Institute As Amicus Curiae: The Key To The Courthouse," **JOA**, 1987, Vol. 164, No. 5, pp. 70-74.)

Cooper, D. and S. Essex. "Accounting Information And Employee Decision Making," **AOS**, 1977, Vol. 2, No. 3, pp. 201-218.

Cooper, D. J. and M. J. Sherer. "The Value Of Corporate Accounting Reports: Arguments For A Political Economy Of Accounting," **AOS**, 1984, Vol. 9, No. 3/4, pp. 207-232.

Cooper, D. J. and T. M. Hopper. "Critical Studies In Accounting," **AOS**, 1987, Vol. 12, No. 4/5, pp. 407-414.

Cooper, D. J. (Puxty, A. G., H. C. Willmott, D. J. Cooper and T. Lowe. "Modes Of Regulation In Advanced Capitalism: Locating Accountancy In Four Countries," **AOS**, 1987, Vol. 12, No. 3, pp. 273-292.)

Cooper, D. J., D. Hayes and F. Wolf. "Accounting In Organized Anarchies: Understanding And Designing Accounting Systems In Ambiguous Situations," **AOS**, 1981, Vol. 6, No. 3, pp. 175-192.

Cooper, D. "Tidiness, Muddle And Things: Commonalities And Divergencies In Two Approaches To Management Accounting Research," **AOS**, 1983, Vol. 8, No. 2/3, pp. 269-286.

Cooper, D. (Berry, A. J., T. Capps, D. Cooper, P. Ferguson, T. Hopper and E. A. Lowe. "Management Control In An Area Of The NCB: Rationales Of Accounting Practices In A Public Enterprise," **AOS**, 1985, Vol. 10, No. 1, pp. 3-28.)

Cooper, F. Jaimie. "POS Devices: You Don't Have To Be A Giant," **MA**, 1977, Vol. 58, No. 11, pp. 31-34.

Cooper, Jean C. (Blocher, Edward J. and Jean C. Cooper. "A Study Of Auditors' Analytical Review Performance," **AJPT**, 1988, Vol. 7, No. 2, pp. 1-28.)

Cooper, Jean C. (Chow, Chee W., Jean C. Cooper and William S. Waller. "Participative Budgeting: Effects Of A Truth-Inducing Pay Scheme And Information Asymmetry On Slack And Performance," **AR**, 1988, Vol. 63, No. 1, pp.111-122.)

Cooper, Kerry and Gerald D. Keim. "The Economic Rationale For The Nature And Extent Of Corporate Financial Disclosure Regulation: A Critical Assessment," **JAPP**, 1983, Vol. 2, No. 3, pp. 189-205.

Cooper, Kerry and Gerald D. Keim. "Unsettled Issues In Corporate Disclosure," **CPAJ**, 1977, Vol. 47, No. 3, pp. 27-30.

Cooper, Kerry and Steven Flory. "Lessons From McKesson And Equity Funding," **CPAJ**, 1976, Vol. 46, No. 4, pp. 19-26.

Cooper, Kerry, Steven M. Flory and Steven D. Grossman. "New Ballgame For Oil And Gas Accounting," **CPAJ**, 1979, Vol. 49, No. 1, pp. 11-18.

Cooper, Kerry, Steven M. Flory, Steven D. Grossman and John C. Groth. "Reserve Recognition Accounting: A Proposed Disclosure Framework," **JOA**, 1979, Vol. 148, No. 3, pp. 82-91.

Cooper, Robert S. "Accounting For The Dairy Products Industry," **AR**, 1945, Vol. 20, No. 4, pp. 431-440.

Cooper, Robin and Robert S. Kaplan. "How Cost Accounting Distorts Product Cost," **MA**, 1988, Vol. 69, No. 10, pp. 20-27.

Cooper, Terry. "Replacement Cost And Beta: A Financial Model," **JAAF**, 1980, Vol. 3, No. 2, pp. 138-146.

Cooper, Walter B. "Liability Of Corporate Officers And Employees For Corporate Employment Taxes," **MA**, 1969, Vol. 51, No. 6, pp. 40-41.

Cooper, William D. and Ida B. Robinson. "Who Should Formulate Accounting Principles? The Debate Within The SEC," **JOA**, 1987, Vol. 163, No. 5, pp. 137-140.

Cooper, William D. "Carman G. Blough's Contributions To Accounting: An Overview," **AHJ**, 1982, Vol. 9, No. 2, pp. 61-67.

Cooper, William D. "George C. Mathews: An Early Commissioner Of The SEC," **AHJ**, 1984, Vol. 11, No. 2, pp. 117-127.

Cooper, William D. (Cornick, Michael, William D. Cooper and Susan B. Wilson. "How Do Companies Analyze Overhead?," **MA**, 1988, Vol. 69, No. 12, pp. 41-43.)

Cooper, William D. (Golen, Steven, James Worthington, Greg Thibadoux, William D. Cooper and Ira S. Greenberg. "Flowcharts & Graphics," **CPAJ**, 1986, Vol. 56, No. 3, pp. 12-23.)

Cooper, William D. (Gray, O. Ronald and William D. Cooper. "A Reconsideration Of Accountant-Client Communication Privilege," **CPAJ**, 1986, Vol. 56, No. 8, pp. 54-59.)

Cooper, William D. (Gray, O. Ronald, William D. Cooper and Michael F. Cornick. "A Survey Of Fortune 500 Companies' Interest In Accounting Faculty Residencies," **JAED**, 1984, Vol. 2, No. 2, pp. 177-180.)

Cooper, William W. (Churchill, Neil C. and William W. Cooper. "A Field Study Of Internal Auditing," **AR**, 1965, Vol. 40, No. 4, pp. 767-781.)

Cooper, W. W. and J. M. Crawford. "The Status Of Social Accounting And National Income Statistics In Countries Other Than The United States," **AR**, 1953, Vol. 28, No. 2, pp. 221-238.

Cooper, W. W. "Social Accounting: An Invitation To The Accounting Profession," **AR**, 1949, Vol. 24, No. 3, pp. 233-238.

Cooper, W. W. "Statistical Use Of Accounting Information In Federal Economic Policy Formulation," **AR**, 1948, Vol. 23, No. 3, pp. 244-250.

Cooper, W. W. (Brockett, P., A. Charnes, W. W. Cooper and Hong-Chul Shin. "A Chance-Constrained Programming Approach To Cost-Volume-Profit Analysis," **AR**, 1984, Vol. 59, No. 3, pp. 474-487.)

Cooper, W. W. (Byrne, R. F., A. Charnes, W. W. Cooper and K. Kortanek. "Some New Approaches To Risk," **AR**, 1968, Vol. 43, No. 1, pp. 18-37.)

Cooper, W. W. (Charnes, A. and W. W. Cooper. "Some Network Characterizations For Mathematical Programming And Accounting Approaches To Planning And Control," **AR**, 1967, Vol. 42, No. 1, pp. 24-52.)

Cooper, W. W. (Charnes, A. and W. W. Cooper. "Auditing And Accounting For Program Efficiency And Management Efficiency In Not-For-Profit Entities," **AOS**, 1980, Vol. 5, No. 1, pp. 87-108.)

Cooper, W. W. (Charnes, A., C. Colantoni, W. W. Cooper and K. O. Kortanek. "Economic Social And Enterprise Accounting And Mathematical Models," **AR**, 1972, Vol. 47, No. 1, pp. 85-108.)

Cooper, W. W. (Charnes, A., C. Colantoni and W. W. Cooper. "A Futurological Justification For Historical Cost And Multi-Dimensional Accounting," **AOS**, 1976, Vol. 1, No. 4, pp. 315-338.)

Cooper, W. W. (Charnes, A., W. W. Cooper and Y. Ijiri. "Breakeven Budgeting And Programming To Goals," **JAR**, 1963, Vol. 1, No. 1, pp. 16-41.)

Cooper, W. W. (Churchill, N. C., W. W. Cooper and V. Govindarajan. "Effects Of Audits On The Behavior Of Medical Professionals Under The Bennett Amendment," **AJPT**, 1981-82, Vol. 1, No. 2, pp. 69-90.)

Cooper, W. W. (Kohler, E. L. and W. W. Cooper. "Costs, Prices And Profits: Accounting In The War Program," **AR**, 1945, Vol. 20, No. 3, pp. 267-307.)

Cooper, W. W. (Trueblood, Robert M. and W. W. Cooper. "Research And Practice In Statistical Applications To Accounting, Auditing, And Management Control," **AR**, 1955, Vol. 30, No. 2, pp. 221-229.)

Cooper, W. W., Joanna L. Y. Ho, John E. Hunter and Robert C. Rodgers. "The Impact Of The Foreign Corrupt Practices Act On Internal Control Practices," **JAAF**, 1985, Vol. 9, No. 1, pp. 22-39.

Cooper, W. W., N. Dopuch and T. F. Keller. "Budgetary Disclosure And Other Suggestions For Improving Accounting," **AR**, 1968, Vol. 43, No. 4, pp. 640-648.

Copeland, Ben R. "A Case Study In Gross Profit Analysis," **AR**, 1965, Vol. 40, No. 1, pp. 214-219.

Copeland, Benny R. and Dave Ramzy. "Office Automation: Selecting The Right Communications System," **MA**, 1986, Vol. 68, No. 1, pp. 34-39.

Copeland, Benny R. and Thomas P. Klammer. "Should The IRS Promulgate Generally Accepted Accounting Principles?," **CPAJ**, 1972, Vol. 42, No. 3, pp. 217-220.

Copeland, Benny R. "The Story Of The Sixth Rule," **AHJ**, 1985, Vol. 12, No. 1, pp. 107-116.

Copeland, Benny R. (DeMaris, E. J. and Benny R. Copeland. "Educational Standards For Management Accountants," **JAED**, 1984, Vol. 2, No. 1, pp. 39-53.)

Copeland, Benny R. (DeMaris, E. J. and Benny R. Copeland. "The Critical Need For Educational Standards In Management Accounting," **CA**, 1984, Vol. 2, No. 1, pp. 47-53.)

Copeland, James E., Jr. (Barden, Ronald S., James E. Copeland, Jr., Roger H. Hermanson and Leslie Wat. "Going Public - What It Involves," **JOA**, 1984, Vol. 157, No. 3, pp. 63-76.)

Copeland, Morris A. "Social Accounting For Moneyflows," **AR**, 1949, Vol. 24, No. 3, pp. 254-264.

Copeland, Ronald M. and John K. Shank. "LIFO And The Diffusion Of Innovation," **JAR**, 1971, Vol. 9, Supp., pp. 196-224.

Copeland, Ronald M. and Joseph F. Wojdak. "Income Manipulation And The Purchase-Pooling Choice," **JAR**, 1969, Vol. 7, No. 2, pp. 188-195.

Copeland, Ronald M. and Michael L. Moore. "Validity Of The 1966 Tax Model As A Research Tool," **AR**, 1972, Vol. 47, No. 2, pp. 395-396.

Copeland, Ronald M. and Michael L. Moore. "Actual Use Of Specialized Accounting Statements," **AR**, 1968, Vol. 43, No. 2, pp. 384-386.

Copeland, Ronald M. and Ralph D. Licastro. "A Note On Income Smoothing," **AR**, 1968, Vol. 43, No. 3, pp. 540-545.

Copeland, Ronald M. and Robert W. Ingram. "Municipal Bond Market Recognition Of Pension Reporting Practices," **JAPP**, 1983, Vol. 2, No. 3, pp. 147-165.

Copeland, Ronald M. and Robert W. Ingram. "The Association

Between Municipal Accounting Information And Bond Rating Changes," **JAR**, 1982, Vol. 20, No. 2, Part I, pp. 275-289.

Copeland, Ronald M. and Robert W. Ingram. "An Evaluation Of Accounting Alternatives For Foreign Currency Transactions," **IJAER**, 1978, Vol. 13, No. 2, pp. 15-26.

Copeland, Ronald M. and Ted D. Englebrecht. "Statistical Sampling: An Uncertain Defense Against Legal Liability," **CPAJ**, 1975, Vol. 45, No. 11, pp. 23-28.

Copeland, Ronald M. and William Fredericks. "Extent Of Disclosure," **JAR**, 1968, Vol. 6, No. 1, pp. 106-113.

Copeland, Ronald M. "Income Smoothing," **JAR**, 1968, Vol. 6, Supp., pp. 101-116.

Copeland, Ronald M. "Textbook Knowledge: Fact Or Fiction," **AR**, 1969, Vol. 44, No. 1, pp. 164-167.

Copeland, Ronald M. (Baker, Robert L. and Ronald M. Copeland. "Evaluation Of The Stratified Regression Estimator For Auditing Accounting Populations," **JAR**, 1979, Vol. 17, No. 2, pp. 606-617.)

Copeland, Ronald M. (Bernhardt, Irwin and Ronald M. Copeland. "Some Problems In Applying An Information Theory Approach To Accounting Aggregation," **JAR**, 1970, Vol. 8, No. 1, pp. 95-98.)

Copeland, Ronald M. (Brenner, Vincent C., Ronald M. Copeland, Paul E. Dascher, Arthur J. Francia, Ronald J. Patten and Robert H. Strawser. "Trials And Tribulations Of The Researcher: A Case Study," **JAR**, 1972, Vol. 10, No. 1, pp. 195-199.)

Copeland, Ronald M. (Buckmaster, Dale A., Ronald M. Copeland and Paul E. Dascher. "The Relative Predictive Ability Of Three Accounting Models," **ABR**, 1976-77, Vol. 7, No. 27, pp. 177-186.)

Copeland, Ronald M. (Dascher, Paul E. and Ronald M. Copeland. "Some Further Evidence On 'Criteria For Judging Disclosure Improvement'," **JAR**, 1971, Vol. 9, No. 1, pp. 32-39.)

Copeland, Ronald M. (Ingram, Robert W. and Ronald M. Copeland. "The Association Between Municipal Accounting Numbers And Credit Risk And Return," **AIA**, 1984, Vol. 1, pp. 19-40.)

Copeland, Ronald M. (Ingram, Robert W. and Ronald M. Copeland. "Municipal Accounting Information And Voting Behavior," **AR**, 1981, Vol. 56, No. 4, pp. 830-843.)

Copeland, Ronald M. (Ingram, Robert W. and Ronald M. Copeland. "Municipal Market Measures And Reporting Practices: An Extension," **JAR**, 1982, Vol. 20, No. 2, Part II, pp. 766-772.)

Copeland, Ronald M. (Pollard, William B. and Ronald M. Copeland. "Evaluating The Robustness Of Multivariate Tax Models To Errors: A Section 162(a)(2) Illustration," **JATA**, 1985, Vol. 7, No. 1, pp. 7-18.)

Copeland, Ronald M. (Shank, John K. and Ronald M. Copeland. "Corporate Personality Theory And Changes In Accounting Methods," **AR**, 1973, Vol. 48, No. 3, pp. 494-501.)

Copeland, Ronald M., Arthur J. Francia and Robert H. Strawser. "Students As Subjects In Behavioral Business Research," **AR**, 1973, Vol. 48, No. 2, pp. 365-372.

Copeland, Ronald M., Arthur J. Francia and Robert H. Strawser. "Further Comments On Students As Subjects In Behavioral Business Research," **AR**, 1974, Vol. 49, No. 3, pp. 534-537.

Copeland, Ronald M., Ronald L. Taylor and Shari H. Brown. "Observation Error And Bias In Accounting Research," **JAR**, 1981, Vol. 19, No. 1, pp. 197-207.

Copeland, Thomas E. "Efficient Capital Markets: Evidence And Implications For Financial Reporting," **JAAF**, 1978, Vol. 2, No. 1, pp. 33-48.

Coppie, Comer S. "Fiscal Planning For The Nation's Capital," **MA**, 1975, Vol. 56, No. 8, pp. 15-19.

Coppie, Comer S. "The City: Management By Crisis Or Crisis Management?," **MA**, 1978, Vol. 60, No. 5, pp. 13-21.

Coppock, R. "Life Among The Environmentalists: An Elaboration On Wildavsky's 'Economics And Environment/Rationality And Ritual'," **AOS**, 1977, Vol. 2, No. 2, pp. 125-130.

Corbett, William J. "Boosting The Profession With Effective PR," **JOA**, 1986, Vol. 161, No. 2, pp. 76-82.

Corbett, William J. "PR Challenges Facing The Profession," **JOA**, 1985, Vol. 160, No. 2, pp. 112-122.

Corbin, Donald A. and Russell Taussig. "The AICPA Funds Statement Study," **JOA**, 1962, Vol. 114, No. 1, pp. 57-62.

Corbin, Donald A. "A Case Study Of Price-Level Adjustments," **AR**, 1955, Vol. 30, No. 2, pp. 268-281.

Corbin, Donald A. "A Simple Method For Preparing A Priority Table In Partnership Liquidation By Installments," **AR**, 1956, Vol. 31, No. 2, pp. 313-315.

Corbin, Donald A. "Accounting And Rising Prices In A Student Co-Operative," **AR**, 1951, Vol. 26, No. 4, pp. 568-572.

Corbin, Donald A. "Accounting For Stockholder Growth," **JOA**, 1958, Vol. 105, No. 5, pp. 63-69.

Corbin, Donald A. "Accounting Standards For Research And Development," **MA**, 1975, Vol. 57, No. 4, pp. 47-48.

Corbin, Donald A. "Comments On 'The Accretion Concept Of Income'," **AR**, 1963, Vol. 38, No. 4, pp. 742-744.

Corbin, Donald A. "On The Feasibility Of Developing Current Cost Information," **AR**, 1967, Vol. 42, No. 4, pp. 635-641.

Corbin, Donald A. "Proposals For Improving Funds Statements," **AR**, 1961, Vol. 36, No. 3, pp. 398-405.

Corbin, Donald A. "SEC Replacement Costs: Suggestions For Full Disclosure," **MA**, 1977, Vol. 59, No. 2, pp. 11-18.

Corbin, Donald A. "The Impact Of Changing Prices On A Department Store," **JOA**, 1954, Vol. 97, No. 4, pp. 430-440.

Corbin, Donald A. "The Revolution In Accounting," **AR**, 1962,

Vol. 37, No. 4, pp. 626-635.

Corcoran, A. Wayne and Ching-Wen Kwang. "Set Theory And Accounting Analysis," **MA**, 1967, Vol. 49, No. 1, pp. 7-17.

Corcoran, A. Wayne and Ching-wen Kwang. "A Set Theory Approach To Funds-Flow Analysis," **JAR**, 1965, Vol. 3, No. 2, pp. 206-217.

Corcoran, A. Wayne and Wayne E. Leininger. "Isolating Accounting Variances Via Partitioned Matrices," **AR**, 1975, Vol. 50, No. 1, pp. 184-188.

Corcoran, A. Wayne and Wayne E. Leininger. "Stochastic Process Costing Models," **AR**, 1973, Vol. 48, No. 1, pp. 105-114.

Corcoran, A. Wayne and Wayne E. Leininger. "In-Process Inventories And Multiproduct Production Systems," **AR**, 1973, Vol. 48, No. 2, pp. 373-374.

Corcoran, A. Wayne. "A Matrix Approach To Process Cost Reporting," **MA**, 1966, Vol. 48, No. 3, pp. 48-54.

Corcoran, A. Wayne. "Applied Mathematics And Accounting," **MA**, 1969, Vol. 51, No. 2, pp. 29-32.

Corcoran, A. Wayne. "Computers Versus Mathematics," **AR**, 1969, Vol. 44, No. 2, pp. 359-374.

Corcoran, A. Wayne. "Matrix Bookkeeping," **JOA**, 1964, Vol. 117, No. 3, pp. 60-66.

Corcoran, A. Wayne. "Simultaneous Preparation Of Funds And Cash Flow Statements," **AR**, 1965, Vol. 40, No. 2, pp. 440-448.

Corderman, Douglas G. "ASPR: Some Suggested Changes," **MA**, 1973, Vol. 54, No. 8, pp. 41-44.

Corless, John C. and Corine T. Norgaard. "User Reactions To CPA Reports On Forecasts," **JOA**, 1974, Vol. 138, No. 2, pp. 46-54.

Corless, John C. and Larry M. Parker. "The Impact Of MAS On Auditor Independence: An Experiment," **ACCHOR**, 1987, Vol. 1, No. 3, pp. 25-30.

Corless, John C. "Assessing Prior Distributions For Applying Bayesian Statistics In Auditing," **AR**, 1972, Vol. 47, No. 3, pp. 556-566.

Corless, John C. "Comment On Assessing Prior Distributions For Applying Bayesian Statistics In Auditing: A Reply," **AR**, 1975, Vol. 50, No. 1, pp. 158-159.

Corless, John C. (Cerullo, Michael J. and John C. Corless. "Auditing Computer Systems," **CPAJ**, 1984, Vol. 54, No. 9, pp. 18-33.)

Corless, John C. (Parker, Larry M., John C. Corless and Michael J. Tucker. "Audit Firm Size And Internal Control Assessment: An Experiment," **RIAR**, 1988, Vol. 2, pp. 155-166.)

Corlett, Robert J. (Crankshaw, Carl D. and Robert J. Corlett. "Stock Inventory Control With Data Bases And Analyses," **MA**, 1970, Vol. 51, No. 11, pp. 26-28.)

Corman, Eugene J. "A Writing Program For Accounting Courses," **JAED**, 1986, Vol. 4, No. 2, pp. 85-95.

Corman, James C. "Tax Shelters For Capital Investment - A View On Their Reform," **MA**, 1974, Vol. 55, No. 7, pp. 15-17.

Cornick, Michael F. (Mecimore, Charles D. and Michael F. Cornick. "Banks Should Use Management Accounting Models," **MA**, 1982, Vol. 63, No. 8, pp. 13-18.)

Cornick, Michael F. (Gray, O. Ronald, William D. Cooper and Michael F. Cornick. "A Survey Of Fortune 500 Companies' Interest In Accounting Faculty Residencies," **JAED**, 1984, Vol. 2, No. 2, pp. 177-180.)

Cornick, Michael, William D. Cooper and Susan B. Wilson. "How Do Companies Analyze Overhead?," **MA**, 1988, Vol. 69, No. 12, pp. 41-43.

Cornish, Harold W. "Systems In Small Business," **MA**, 1965, Vol. 47, No. 2, pp. 7-11.

Corr, Arthur V. "A Cost-Effectiveness Approach To Marketing Outlays," **MA**, 1976, Vol. 57, No. 7, pp. 33-36.

Corr, Arthur V. "The Role Of Cost In Pricing," **MA**, 1974, Vol. 56, No. 5, pp. 15-18.

Corr, Paul J. and Donald D. Bourque. "Managing In A Reorganization," **MA**, 1988, Vol. 69, No. 7, pp. 33-37.

Correa, Mathias F. "Recent Developments In Federal Tax Practice," **JOA**, 1954, Vol. 98, No. 5, pp. 599-609.

Corsini, Louis. (Weinstein, Arnold K., Louis Corsini and Ronald Pawliczek. "The Big Eight In Europe," **IJAER**, 1978, Vol. 13, No. 2, pp. 57-71.)

Corstvet, Emma. "Adequacy Of Accounting Records In A Money Economy," **AR**, 1935, Vol. 10, No. 3, pp. 273-286.

Corstvet, Emma. "Adequate Records As An Element In Business Survival," **AR**, 1936, Vol. 11, No. 1, pp. 49-62.

Cortright, Michael F. (Test, Darrell L., John D. Hawley and Michael F. Cortright. "Determining Strategic Value," **MA**, 1987, Vol. 68, No. 12, pp. 39-42.)

Costello, James J. (Steele, Charles G. and James J. Costello. "Summary Annual Reports: An Idea Whose Time Has Come," **CA**, 1984, Vol. 2, No. 4, pp. 4-11.)

Costigan, Michael. (Yunker, Penelope J., Julie A. Sterner and Michael Costigan. "Employment In Accounting: A Comparison Of Recruiter Perceptions With Student Expectations," **JAED**, 1986, Vol. 4, No. 1, pp. 95-112.)

Costouros, George J. "Accounting Education And Practice In Greece," **IJAER**, 1975, Vol. 11, No. 1, pp. 95-106.

Costouros, George J. "Development Of An Accounting System In Ancient Athens In Response To Socio-Economic Changes," **AHJ**, 1977, Vol. 4, No. 1, pp. 37-54.

Costouros, George J. "Development Of Banking And Related Bookkeeping Techniques In Ancient Greece (400-300 B.C.)," **IJAER**, 1973, Vol. 8, No. 2, pp. 75-81.

Costouros, George. "Auditing In The Athenian State In The Golden Age (500-300 B.C.)," **AHJ**, 1978, Vol. 5, No. 1, pp. 41-50.

Cote, Joseph T. "The Concept Of Materiality," **MA**, 1973,

Vol. 55, No. 6, pp. 17-22.

Cotlar, Morton. "Performance Accounting," **MA**, 1975, Vol. 57, No. 2, pp. 33-36.

Cotteleer, Thomas F. "Depreciation: An Accounting Enigma," **MA**, 1971, Vol. 52, No. 8, pp. 23-24.

Cottell, Philip G., Jr. "LIFO Layer Liquidations: Some Empirical Evidence," **JAAF**, 1986, Vol. 1 (New Series), No. 1, pp. 30-45.

Cotter, Arundel. "Why Last-In?," **AR**, 1940, Vol. 15, No. 3, pp. 419-424.

Cotton, W. D. J. (Wells, M. C. and W. D. J. Cotton. "Holding Gains On Fixed Assets," **AR**, 1965, Vol. 40. No. 4, pp. 829-833.)

Cottrell, James L. "Forecasting In Multi-Outlet Business-es," **MA**, 1973, Vol. 54, No. 10, pp. 17-22.

Coughlan, Anne T. and Ronald M. Schmidt. "Executive Compensation, Management Turnover, And Firm Performance: An Empirical Investigation," **JAEC**, 1985, Vol. 7, No. 1/3, pp. 43-66.

Coughlan, John W. "Accounting And Changing Prices," **JOA**, 1957, Vol. 104, No. 2, pp. 42-47.

Coughlan, John W. "Anomalies In Calculating Earnings Per Share," **AH**, 1988, Vol. 2, No. 4, pp. 80-88.

Coughlan, John W. "Applicability Of The Realization Principle To Money Claims In Common Dollar Accounting," **AR**, 1955, Vol. 30, No. 1, pp. 103-113.

Coughlan, John W. "Regulation, Rents And Residuals," **JOA**, 1980, Vol. 149, No. 2, pp. 58-67.

Coughlan, John W. "The Fairfax Embezzlement," **MA**, 1983, Vol. 64, No. 11, pp. 32-39.

Coughlan, John W. "The Guises Of Replacement Cost," **AR**, 1957, Vol. 32, No. 3, pp. 434-447.

Coughlan, John W. "Working Capital And Credit Standing," **JOA**, 1960, Vol. 110, No. 5, pp. 44-52.

Coughlan, John. "Industrial Accounting," **AR**, 1959, Vol. 34, No. 3, pp. 415-428.

Coulthurst, N. J. "Accounting For Inflation In Capital Investment. The State Of The Art And Science," **ABR**, 1986-87, Vol. 17, No. 65, pp. 33-42.

Coulthurst, N. J. "The Application Of The Incremental Principle In Capital Investment Project Evaluation," **ABR**, 1985-86, Vol. 16, No. 64, pp. 359-364.

Courtis, John K. "Business Goodwill: Conceptual Clarification Via Accounting, Legal And Etymological Perspectives," **AHJ**, 1983, Vol. 10, No. 2, pp. 1-38.

Courtis, John K. "Dissolving The Research Mystique," **JAED**, 1984, Vol. 2, No. 1, pp. 29-38.

Courtis, John K. "Putting The Cart Before The Horse," **JAED**, 1987, Vol. 5, No. 1, pp. 139-144.

Courtis, John K. (Pound, G. D. and John K. Courtis. "The Auditor's Liability: A Myth?," **ABR**, 1979-80, Vol. 10, No. 39, pp. 299-306.)

Courtis, J. K. "An Investigation Into Annual Report Readability And Corporate Risk-Return Relationships," **ABR**, 1985-86, Vol. 16, No. 64, pp. 285-294.

Courtis, J. K. "Relationships Between Timeliness In Corporate Reporting And Corporate Attributes," **ABR**, 1976-77, Vol. 7, No. 25, pp. 45-56.

Courtney, Harley M. and Frederick V. Brooks. "Cumulative Probabilistic Sales Forecasting," **MA**, 1972, Vol. 53, No. 11, pp. 44-47.

Covaleski, Mark A. and Charles J. Davis. "An Empirical Examination Of Capital Expenditure In The Health Sector," **JAPP**, 1984, Vol. 3, No. 2, pp. 139-162.

Covaleski, Mark A. and Mark W. Dirsmith. "Social Expectations And Accounting Practices In The Health Sector," **RIGNA**, 1986, Vol. 2, pp. 119-134.

Covaleski, Mark A. (Dirsmith, Mark W., Mark A. Covaleski and John P. McAllister. "Of Paradigms And Metaphors In Auditing Thought," **CAR**, 1985-86, Vol. 2, No. 1, pp. 46-68.)

Covaleski, Mark A. (Dirsmith, Mark W. and Mark A. Covaleski. "Practice Management Issues In Public Accounting Firms," **JAAF**, 1985, Vol. 9, No. 1, pp. 5-21.)

Covaleski, Mark A., Mark W. Dirsmith and Stephen F. Jablonsky. "Traditional And Emergent Theories Of Budgeting: An Empirical Analysis," **JAPP**, 1985, Vol. 4, No. 4, pp. 277-300.

Covaleski, Mark A., Mark W. Dirsmith and Clinton E. White. "Economic Consequences: The Relationship Between Financial Reporting And Strategic Planning. Management And Operating Control Decisions," **CAR**, 1986-87, Vol. 3, No. 2, pp. 408-429.

Covaleski, M. A. and M. W. Dirsmith. "The Budgetary Process Of Power And Politics," **AOS**, 1986, Vol. 11, No. 3, pp. 193-214.

Covaleski, M. A. and M. W. Dirsmith. "Budgeting As A Means For Control And Loose Coupling," **AOS**, 1983, Vol. 8, No. 4, pp. 323-340.

Covaleski, M. A. and M. W. Dirsmith. "The Use Of Budgetary Symbols In The Political Arena: An Historically Informed Field Study," **AOS**, 1988, Vol. 13, No. 1, pp. 1-24.

Covaleski, M. A. (Dirsmith, M. W. and M. A. Covaleski. "Informal Communications, Nonformal Communications And Mentoring In Public Accounting Firms," **AOS**, 1985, Vol. 10, No. 2, pp. 149-170.)

Covaleski, M. and M. Aiken. "Accounting And Theories Of Organizations: Some Preliminary Considerations," **AOS**, 1986, Vol. 11, No. 4/5, pp. 297-320.

Covaleski, M. (Colignon, R. and M. Covaleski. "An Examination Of Managerial Accounting Practices As A Process Of Mutual Adjustment," **AOS**, 1988, Vol. 13, No. 6, pp. 559-579.)

Coveney, Lloyd I. "Unusual Aspects Of Savings And Loan Audits," **JOA**, 1960, Vol. 110, No. 1, pp. 32-36.

Covert, V. F. "Reducing Accounting Costs," **AR**, 1946, Vol. 21, No. 3, pp. 278-282.

Cowan, Tom K. "Are Truth And Fairness Generally Acceptable?," **AR**, 1965, Vol. 40, No. 4, pp. 788-794.

Cowan, Tom K. "Progress Through Dilemma: A Compromise Solution To The Problem Of Accounting For Changing Prices And Values," **ABR**, 1971-72, Vol. 2, No. 5, pp. 38-45.

Cowan, T. K. "A Pragmatic Approach To Accounting Theory," **AR**, 1968, Vol. 43, No. 1, pp. 94-100.

Cowan, T. K. "A Resources Theory Of Accounting," **AR**, 1965, Vol. 40, No. 1, pp. 9-20.

Cowan, T. K. "Accounting In The Real World," **ABR**, 1982-83, Vol. 13, No. 52, pp. 251-262.

Cowen, Scott S. "Nonaudit Services: How Much Is Too Much?," **JOA**, 1980, Vol. 150, No. 6, pp. 51-56.

Cowen, Scott S. (Phillips, Lawrence C. and Scott S. Cowen. "Accounting For Debt Restructurings," **CPAJ**, 1977, Vol. 47, No. 7, pp. 22-26.)

Cowen, Scott S., Lawrence C. Phillips and Linda Stillabower. "Multinational Transfer Pricing," **MA**, 1979, Vol. 60, No. 7, pp. 17-22.

Cowen, S. S., L. B. Ferreri and L. D. Parker. "The Impact Of Corporate Characteristics On Social Responsibility Disclosure: A Typology And Frequency-Based Analysis," **AOS**, 1987, Vol. 12, No. 2, pp. 111-122.

Cowie, James B. and James M. Fremgen. "Computers Versus Mathematics: Round 2," **AR**, 1970, Vol. 45, No. 1, pp. 27-37.

Cowing, John S. "Should Income Be Averaged For Tax Purposes?," **JOA**, 1952, Vol. 93, No. 1, pp. 48-51.

Cowing, John. "Proposals For Averaging Income For Income-Tax Purposes," **JOA**, 1952, Vol. 94, No. 5, pp. 586-593.

Cowin, R. B. "A Problem On The Admission Of A Partner," **AR**, 1932, Vol. 7, No. 2, pp. 137-139.

Cowin, R. B. "Incorporation Of Partnership," **AR**, 1931, Vol. 6, No. 4, pp. 313-315.

Cowin, R. B. "The Cost Formula," **AR**, 1942, Vol. 17, No. 3, pp. 309-311.

Cowton, Christopher J. "The Hero In Accounting History: An Assessment Of The Role Of Biography," **ABR**, 1985-86, Vol. 16, No. 61, pp. 73-77.

Cox, Clifford T. "Earnings Variability, Firm Size, And The Information Content In Management Forecasts Of Annual Earnings," **JAPP**, 1987, Vol. 6, No. 2, pp. 139-153.

Cox, Clifford T. "Further Evidence On The Representativeness Of Management Earnings Forecasts," **AR**, 1985, Vol. 60, No. 4, pp. 692-701.

Cox, Clifford T., Ken M. Boze and Lee Schwendig. "Academic Accountants: A Study Of Faculty Characteristics And Career Activities," **JAED**, 1987, Vol. 5, No. 1, pp. 59-76.

Cox, C. E. "What Is Cost?," **AR**, 1930, Vol. 5, No. 4, pp. 288-297.

Cox, Lanier F. "The CPA Law Examinations," **AR**, 1947, Vol. 22, No. 4, pp. 353-359.

Cox, Robert G. "Conflicting Concepts Of Income For Managerial And Federal Income Tax Purposes," **AR**, 1958, Vol. 33, No. 2, pp. 242-245.

Cox, Robert G. "The Place Of Tax And Fiscal Policy Issues In The Federal Income Tax Course," **AR**, 1957, Vol. 32, No. 1, pp. 95-97.

Coyle, Kathleen A. (Degnan, Theodore E. and Kathleen A. Coyle. "Withholding Provisions Of FIRPTA," **CPAJ**, 1986, Vol. 56, No. 2, pp. 22-27.)

Coyner, Randolph S. and Lawrence J. Stein. "A Classification Scheme For Financial Footnotes," **MA**, 1981, Vol. 62, No. 11, pp. 43-47.

Cozzolino, Joseph M. "Maintenance Cost Controls," **MA**, 1971, Vol. 52, No. 8, pp. 40-43.

Craco, Louis A. and Deborah E. Cooper. "The Institute As Amicus Curiae: The Key To The Courthouse," **JOA**, 1987, Vol. 164, No. 5, pp. 70-74.

Craft, James W. and Kevin P. O'Toole. "Push-Down Accounting - Has Its Time Come?," **CA**, 1984, Vol. 2, No. 2, pp. 57-62.

Craft, J. A. "A Reply To Maunders And Foley," **AOS**, 1984, Vol. 9, No. 1, pp. 107-108.

Craft, J. A. "Information Disclosure And The Role Of The Accountant In Collective Bargaining," **AOS**, 1981, Vol. 6, No. 1, pp. 97-107.

Craig, Darryl L. (Enis, Charles R. and Darryl L. Craig. "The Redistribution Of The Income Tax Burden Under A True Flat Tax Structure," **JATA**, 1984, Vol. 6, No. 1, pp. 20-35.)

Craig, John B. "Statistical Sampling In Internal Auditing," **JOA**, 1959, Vol. 108, No. 5, pp. 39-45.

Craig, Paul W. (Grobstein, Michael and Paul W. Craig. "A Risk Analysis Approach To Auditing," **AJPT**, 1983-84, Vol. 3, No. 2, pp. 1-16.)

Craig, Quiester. "Cost Control: Whose Job?," **MA**, 1975, Vol. 56, No. 9, pp. 22-24.

Craig, Quiester. "Toward Integration Of The Accounting Profession," **JOA**, 1987, Vol. 163, No. 5, pp. 257-258.

Craig, Russell and Mark Tippett. "Estimating Current Cost Depreciation Expense Using Numerical Analysis And The STAPOL Technique: A Pedagogic Exposition," **ABACUS**, 1987, Vol. 23, No. 2, pp. 141-156.

Crain, Gilbert W. "1980 GAAFR: Analysis And Commentary," **CPAJ**, 1982. Vol. 52, No. 2, pp. 17-27.

Crain, Sharon. "What Kind Of Leader Are You?," **MA**, 1985, Vol. 67, No. 3, pp. 24-28.

Cramer, D. H. "What Does The Employer Expect Of The College Graduate?," **AR**, 1957, Vol. 32, No. 1, pp. 15-20.

Cramer, Joe J., Jr. "Income Reporting By Conglomerates," **ABACUS**, 1968, Vol. 4, No. 1, pp. 17-26.

Cramer, Joe J. "A Note On Pension Trust Accountings," **AR**, 1964, Vol. 39, No. 4, pp. 869-875.

Cramer, Joe J., Jr. and Charles A. Neyhart, Jr. "A Comprehensive Accounting Framework For Evaluating Executory Contracts," **JAAF**, 1979, Vol. 2, No. 2, pp. 135-150.

Cramer, Joe J., Jr. and Charles A. Neyhart, Jr. "Accounting For Pensions: A Contemporary Perspective," **CPAJ**, 1976, Vol. 46, No. 6, pp. 19-24.

Cramer, Joe J., Jr. and Charles A. Neyhart, Jr. "A Conceptual Framework For Accounting And Reporting By Pension Plans," **ABACUS**, 1980, Vol. 16, No. 1, pp. 3-16.

Cramer, Joe J., Jr. and Robert H. Strawser. "Perception Of Selected Job Related Factors By Black CPAs," **CPAJ**, 1972, Vol. 42, No. 2, pp. 127-130.

Cramer, Joe J., Jr. and William J. Schrader. "Depreciation Accounting And The Anomalous Self-Insurance Cost," **AR**, 1970, Vol. 45, No. 4, pp. 698-703.

Cramer, Joe J., Jr. "Bad Debt 'Expense': Not A Member Of The Class Of Data For Measuring Operating Income: A Reply," **AR**, 1973, Vol. 48, No. 4, pp. 779-784.

Cramer, Joe J., Jr. "Deferred Income Tax Charges And Credits Are 'Monetary' Items," **ABACUS**, 1975, Vol. 11, No. 2, pp. 153-166.

Cramer, Joe J., Jr. "Incompatibility Of Bad Debt 'Expense' With Contemporary Accounting Theory," **AR**, 1972, Vol. 47, No. 3, pp. 596-598.

Cramer, Joe J., Jr. "Legal Influences On Pension Trust Accounting," **AR**, 1965, Vol. 40, No. 3, pp. 606-616.

Cramer, Joe J., Jr. "Management Accounting Via Computer-Assisted Instruction," **MA**, 1966, Vol. 47, No. 5, pp. 38-45.

Crandall, Arthur L. "Understanding Valuations," **CA**, 1987, Vol. 5, No. 2, pp. 42-46.

Crandall, Robert H. "Information Economics And Its Implications For The Further Development Of Accounting Theory," **AR**, 1969, Vol. 44, No. 3, pp. 457-466.

Crandell, William T. "Financial Statements Of National Wealth And National Income," **AR**, 1936, Vol. 11, No. 3, pp. 271-290.

Crandell, William T. "Income And Its Measurement," **AR**, 1935, Vol. 10, No. 4, pp. 379-400.

Crane, Nicholas E. "A Look At Annual Reports," **JOA**, 1958, Vol. 105, No. 3, pp. 31-36.

Crankshaw, Carl D. and Robert J. Corlett. "Stock Inventory Control With Data Bases And Analyses," **MA**, 1970, Vol. 51, No. 11, pp. 26-28.

Craswell, A. T. "An Examination Of Alternative Hypotheses Concerning Depreciation Of Buildings," **ABACUS**, 1986, Vol. 22, No. 1, pp. 29-38.

Craswell, A. T. "Surrogates In Accounting," **ABACUS**, 1978, Vol. 14, No. 1, pp. 81-93.

Crawford, David E. "What The CPA Should Know About Church Tax Changes," **JOA**, 1979, Vol. 147, No. 6, pp. 80-85.

Crawford, James R. "Statistical Accounting Procedures," **AR**, 1944, Vol. 19, No. 3, pp. 266-269.

Crawford, J. M. (Cooper, W. W. and J. M. Crawford. "The Status Of Social Accounting And National Income Statistics In Countries Other Than The United States," **AR**, 1953, Vol. 28, No. 2, pp. 221-238.)

Cready, William M. and John K. Shank. "Understanding Accounting Changes In An Efficient Market: A Comment, Replication, And Re-Interpretation," **AR**, 1987, Vol. 62, No. 3, pp. 589-596.

Cready, William M. "Information Value And Investor Wealth: The Case Of Earnings Announcements," **JAR**, 1988, Vol. 26, No. 1, pp. 1-27.

Creamer, Anthony B., III. "Auditing Beyond U.S. Shores: What The U.S. CPA Should Know," **JOA**, 1987, Vol. 164, No. 5, pp. 85-96.

Creedon, John J. (Myers, Robert J. and John J. Creedon. "Is Social Security Financially Feasible," **CPAJ**, 1987, Vol. 57, No. 5, pp. 46-55.)

Crescenzi, Adam D. and Jerry Kocher. "Management Support Systems: Opportunity For Controllers," **MA**, 1984, Vol. 65, No. 9, pp. 34-37.

Cressey, Donald R. "Why Do Trusted Persons Commit Fraud?," **JOA**, 1951, Vol. 92, No. 5, pp. 576-581.

Cress, William P. and James B. Pettijohn. "A Survey Of Budget-Related Planning And Control Policies And Procedures," **JAED**, 1985, Vol. 3, No. 2, pp. 61-78.

Crestol, Jack. (Schneider, Herman M. and Jack Crestol. "Tax Savings Through Trusts-Custodian Accounts," **JOA**, 1969, Vol. 127, No. 2, pp. 38-43.)

Crews, Joseph M. (Crumbley, D. Larry and Joseph M. Crews. "The Use Of The Installment Tax Method For Revolving Accounts," **JOA**, 1969, Vol. 128, No. 1, pp. 33-40.)

Crichfield, Timothy, Thomas Dyckman and Josef Lakonishok. "An Evaluation Of Security Analysts' Forecasts," **AR**, 1978, Vol. 53, No. 3, pp. 651-668.

Crick, Trevor. (Kim, Suk H. and Trevor Crick. "How Non-U.S. MNCs Practice Capital Budgeting," **MA**, 1984, Vol. 65, No. 7, pp. 28-31.)

Crick, Trevor. (Kim, Suk H., Trevor Crick and Seung H. Kim. "Do Executives Practice What Academics Preach?," **MA**, 1986, Vol. 68, No. 5, pp. 49-52.)

Crissy, William J. E. (Pashalian, Siroon and William J. E. Crissy. "Are Corporate Annual Reports Difficult, Dull Reading?," **JOA**, 1952, Vol. 94, No. 2, pp. 215-219.)

Crites, Sherman E. "Of Men And Money: The Problem Of The Small Business," **MA**, 1970, Vol. 51, No. 10, pp. 14-16.

Croasdale, Robert. "Markov Chain Models For Motor Insurance," **ABR**, 1971-72, Vol. 2, No. 7, pp. 177-181.

Crockett, James R. and Thomas E. McKee. "A Graphical Approach To Teaching The Relationship Between The Evaluation Of Internal Accounting Controls And

Substantive Audit Testing," **JAED**, 1988, Vol. 6, No. 1, pp. 123-130.

Croll, David B. "Cost Accounting In The CPA Examination - Revisited," **AR**, 1982, Vol. 57, No. 2, pp. 420-429.

Crompton, R. "Gender And Accountancy: A Response To Tinker And Neimark," **AOS**, 1987, Vol. 12, No. 1, pp. 103-110.

Crompton, Walter H. "Transfer Pricing: A Proposal," **MA**, 1972, Vol. 53, No. 10, pp. 46-48.

Cron, William R. (Hayes, Randall B. and William R. Cron. "Changes In Task Unvertainty Induced By Zero-Based Budgeting: Using The Thompson And Hirst Models To Predict Dysfunctional Behaviour," **ABACUS**, 1988, Vol. 24, No. 2, pp. 145-161.)

Cronan, Timothy P. and Clarence E. Fries. "MIS And Computer Applications In Accounting Courses - Report Of A Survey," **JAED**, 1986, Vol. 4, No. 1, pp. 237-244.

Cronan, Timothy P. (Wilson, Arlette C., G. William Glezen and Timothy P. Cronan. "Forecasting Accounting Information For Auditors' Use In Analytical Reviews," **AIA**, 1988, Vol. 6, pp. 267-276.)

Crooch, G. Michael and Bruce E. Collier. "Reporting Guidelines For Companies In A Stage Of Development," **CPAJ**, 1973, Vol. 43, No. 7, pp. 579-583.

Crooch, G. Michael. (Rayburn, Frank R. and G. Michael Crooch. "Currency Translation And The Funds Statement: A New Approach," **JOA**, 1983, Vol. 156, No. 4, pp. 51-63.)

Crooch, G. M. (Boatsman, J. R. and G. M. Crooch. "An Example Of Controlling The Risk Of A Type II Error For Substantive Tests In Auditing," **AR**, 1975, Vol. 50, No. 3. pp. 610-615.)

Cropsey, Betsy Hollowell. (Vejlupek, Judith R. and Betsy Hollowell Cropsey. "The Hidden Costs Of Postemployment Benefits," **JOA**, 1984, Vol. 158, No. 4, pp. 84-92.)

Crosby, Linda Garfield. "Experiences With The Personalized System Of Instruction (PSI) To Teach Elementary Accounting," **JAED**, 1984, Vol. 2, No. 1, pp. 139-143.

Crosby, Michael A. "Bayesian Statistics In Auditing: A Comparison Of Probability Elicitation Techniques," **AR**, 1981, Vol. 56, No. 2, pp. 355-365.

Crosby, Michael A. "Implications Of Prior Probability Elicitation On Auditor Sample Size Decisions," **JAR**, 1980, Vol. 18, No. 2, pp. 585-593.

Crosby, Michael A. "The Development Of Bayesian Decision Theoretic Concepts In Attribute Sampling," **AJPT**, 1984-85, Vol. 4, No. 2, pp. 118-132.

Cross, Joann N. "A Tale Of Woe (Or 10 Mistakes Of A Volunteer Accountant)," **MA**, 1986, Vol. 67, No. 10, pp. 49-51.

Crossman, Paul T. "The Nature Of Management Accounting," **AR**, 1958, Vol. 33, No. 2, pp. 222-227.

Crossman, Paul. "The Function Of The Cost Accountant In Cost Control," **AR**, 1953, Vol. 28, No. 1, pp. 25-31.

Crossman, Paul. "The Genesis Of Cost Control," **AR**, 1953, Vol. 28, No. 4, pp. 522-527.

Crossno, Garlon. "Programmed Requirements Planning," **MA**, 1974, Vol. 55, No. 9, pp. 23-27.

Crouse, W. Frank, Maurice C. Paradis and John C. Shaw. "The Client Service Team Approach To Auditing," **JOA**, 1979, Vol. 148, No. 2, pp. 52-58.

Crovatto, Raymond A. "Data Processing For Small Clients," **JOA**, 1960, Vol. 110, No. 6, pp. 57-62.

Crowningshield, Gerald R. and George L. Battista. "Is Conventional Accounting Adequate For A Cost Reduction Program?," **MA**, 1968, Vol. 49, No. 5, pp. 36-42.

Crowningshield, G. R. and G. L. Battista. "The Accounting Revolution," **MA**, 1966, Vol. 47, No. 11, pp. 30-38.

Crowningshield, G. R. (Battista, G. L. and G. R. Crowningshield. "Cost Behavior And Breakeven Analysis - A Different Approach," **MA**, 1966, Vol. 48, No. 2, pp.3-15.)

Croysdale, Dennis L. "How To Get An Efficient Audit," **MA**, 1985, Vol. 66, No. 12, pp. 28-32.

Crum, Lewis R. "The Role Of Cost Accounting In Cost Control," **AR**, 1953, Vol. 28, No. 3, pp. 363-372.

Crum, Robert P. and Leon B. Hoshower. "The Expanded Nature And Purpose Of Responsibility Accounting," **CA**, 1986, Vol. 4, No. 4, pp. 60-67.

Crum, Robert P. "Using Combined Attributes-Variables Tests," **CPAJ**, 1981, Vol. 51, No. 7, pp. 38-45.

Crum, Robert P. "Value-Added Tax Collection Alternatives: Their Revenue, Cash Flow, and Micro Tax Policy Effects," **JATA**, 1985, Vol. 7, No. 1, pp. 52-72.

Crum, Robert P. "Value-Added Taxation: The Roots Run Deep Into Colonial And Early America," **AHJ**, 1982, Vol. 9, No. 2, pp. 25-42.

Crum, Robert P. (Haskins, Mark E. and Robert P. Crum. "Cost Allocations: A Classroom Role-Play In Managerial Behavior And Accounting Choices," **IAE**, 1985, No. 1, pp. 109-130.)

Crum, Robert P. (Hoshower, Leon B. and Robert P. Crum. "Controlling Service Center Costs," **MA**, 1987, Vol. 69, No. 5, pp. 44-48.)

Crum, Robert P. (Hoshower, Leon B. and Robert P. Crum. "Straightening The Tortuous - And Treacherous - ROI Path," **MA**, 1986, Vol. 68, No. 6, pp. 41-45.)

Crum, Robert P. (Tipgos, Manuel A. and Robert P. Crum. "Applying Management Accounting Concepts To The Health Care Industry," **MA**, 1982, Vol. 64, No. 1, pp. 37-43.)

Crum, William F. and Don E. Garner. "1983 Survey Of Doctoral Programs In Accounting In The United States And Canada," **AR**, 1985, Vol. 60, No. 3, pp. 519-525.

Crum, William F. "1980 Survey Of Doctoral Programs In Accounting In The United States," **AR**, 1981, Vol. 56, No. 3, pp. 634-641.

Crum, William F. "A CPA Examination Topic Frequency Analysis," **AR**, 1956, Vol. 31, No. 1, pp. 122-126.

Crum, William F. "Causes That Underlie Changes In Corporate

Earnings," **MA**, 1972, Vol. 53, No. 8, pp. 38-40.

Crum, William F. "Interim Reports: Do They Meet **MAP** Standards?," **MA**, 1973, Vol. 54, No. 11, pp. 26-28.

Crum, William F. "Intermediate And Advanced Accounting Advice Sheet," **AR**, 1949, Vol. 24, No. 1, pp. 94-96.

Crum, William F. "Survey Of Doctoral Programs In The United States," **AR**, 1978, Vol. 53, No. 2, pp. 486-494.

Crum, William F. "The European Public Accountant," **MA**, 1975, Vol. 56, No. 9, pp. 41-44.

Crum, William F. (Shinawi, Ahmed Abdul Kadir and William F. Crum. "The Emergence Of Professional Accounting In Saudi Arabia," **IJAER**, 1971, Vol. 6, No. 2, pp. 103-110.)

Crumbley, D. Larry, Nicholas G. Apostolou and Casper E. Wiggins. "Tax-Sheltered Plans In Educational And Other Organizations," **CPAJ**, 1984, Vol. 54, No. 4, pp. 22-31.

Crumbley, D. Larry and James R. Hasselback. "The Asset Depreciation Range System," **CPAJ**, 1976, Vol. 46, No. 1, pp. 29-33.

Crumbley, D. Larry and Joseph M. Crews. "The Use Of The Installment Tax Method For Revolving Accounts," **JOA**, 1969, Vol. 128, No. 1, pp. 33-40.

Crumbley, D. Larry and P. Michael Davis. "Accounting And Auditing Problems In Subchapter S Corporations," **JOA**, 1970, Vol. 130, No. 4, pp. 45-51.

Crumbley, D. Larry and Richard S. Savich. "Use Of Human Resource Accounting In Taxation," **AR**, 1975, Vol. 50, No. 1, pp. 112-117.

Crumbley, D. Larry and Robert H. Strawser. "Allocation Of Income Taxes In Segmented Financial Statements," **CPAJ**, 1974, Vol. 44, No. 7, pp. 35-38.

Crumbley, D. Larry and Russell H. Taylor. "Partial Liquidations And Subchapter S," **CPAJ**, 1973, Vol. 43, No. 12, pp. 1067-1072.

Crumbley, D. Larry, Nicholas G. Apostolou and Bob G. Kilpatrick. "Retirement Plan Alternatives," **CPAJ**, 1986, Vol. 56, No. 7, pp. 48-59.

Crumbley, D. Larry, Robert H. Strawser and Herbert L. Jensen. "Accumulated Earnings: A New Court Calculation," **JOA**, 1977, Vol. 143, No. 3, pp. 75-78.

Crumbley, D. Larry. "Behavioral Implications Of Taxation: A Reply," **AR**, 1974, Vol. 49, No. 4, pp. 834-837.

Crumbley, D. Larry. "Behavioral Implications Of Taxation," **AR**, 1973, Vol. 48, No. 4, pp. 759-763.

Crumbley, D. Larry. "Child Care Expense Deduction - A 'Decision Tree' Application," **AR**, 1970, Vol. 45, No. 1, pp. 143-145.

Crumbley, D. Larry. "Introducing Probabilities And Present Value Analysis Into Taxation: A Reply," **AR**, 1973, Vol. 48, No. 3, pp. 595-597.

Crumbley, D. Larry. "Introducing Probabilities And Present Value Analysis Into Taxation," **AR**, 1972, Vol. 47, No. 1, pp. 173-174.

Crumbley, D. Larry. "Multiple Corporations: A Comparison Of Tax Alternatives," **MA**, 1968, Vol. 50, No. 2, pp. 53-61.

Crumbley, D. Larry. "Narrowing The Taxable And Accounting Income Gap For Consolidations," **AR**, 1968, Vol. 43, No. 3, pp. 554-564.

Crumbley, D. Larry. "The Evolution Of The ATA: From Orphans, To Outlaws, To Respectability," **JATA**, 1987, Vol. 9, No. 1, pp. 86-100.

Crumbley, D. Larry. (Bassichis. William H.. D. Larry Crumbley and Carlton D. Stolle. "Caution: Teaching And Research Awards Ahead," **AIT**, 1987, Vol. 1, pp. 199-210.)

Crumbley, D. Larry. (Billings, Anthony and D. Larry Crumbley. "Bankruptcy Provisions For Limited Partnerships," **CPAJ**, 1987, Vol. 57, No. 2, pp. 58-63.)

Crumbley, D. Larry. (Billings, B. Anthony and D. Larry Crumbley. "Financial Difficulties Of Governmental Units," **CPAJ**, 1988, Vol. 58, No. 10, pp. 52-61.)

Crumbley, D. Larry. (Wiggins, Casper E., D. Larry Crumbley and Nicholas G. Apostolou. "A Critical Analysis Of The Marriage Tax Penalty," **JATA**, 1986, Vol. 7, No. 2, pp. 60-75.)

Crumbley, D. Larry. (Wojdak, Joseph F. and D. Larry Crumbley. "Introducing Important Tax Provisions Into Advanced Accounting," **AR**, 1969, Vol. 44, No. 1, pp. 173-175.)

Crumbley, D. L., M. J. Epstein and L. L. Bravenec. "Tax Impact In Corporate Social Responsibility Decisions And Reporting," **AOS**, 1977, Vol. 2, No. 2, pp. 131-140.

Crumbley, D. L., P. M. Davis and R. Welker. "A Subchapter S Corporation Is Taxable: Sometimes," **CPAJ**, 1977, Vol. 47, No. 12, pp. 23-28.

Cruse, Rex B., Jr. and Edward L. Summers. "Economics, Accounting Practice And Accounting Research Study No. 3," **AR**, 1965, Vol. 40, No. 1, pp. 82-88.

Culbertson, William Y. "Expert Systems In Finance," **CA**, 1987, Vol. 5, No. 2, pp. 47-50.

Cullather, James L. "Accounting: Kin To The Humanities?," **AR**, 1959, Vol. 34, No. 4, pp. 525-527.

Cullen, D. E. (Maxim, L. D., D. E. Cullen and F. X. Cook, Jr. "Optimal Acceptance Sampling Plans For Auditing 'Batched' Stop And Go Vs. Conventional Single-Stage Attributes Plans," **AR**, 1976, Vol. 51, No. 1. pp.97-109.)

Culpepper, Robert C. "A Study Of Some Relationships Between Accounting And Decision-Making Processes," **AR**, 1970, Vol. 45, No. 2, pp. 322-332.

Cumming, John. "An Empirical Evaluation Of Possible Explanations For The Differing Treatment Of Apparently Similar Unusual Events," **JAR**, 1973, Vol. 11, Supp., pp. 60-95.

Cumming, John. "Modification In Unaudited Reports," **CPAJ**, 1976, Vol. 46, No. 12, pp. 17-22.

Cummings, Barbara K., Nicholas G. Apostolou and William G. Mister. "Accounting For Interest Rate Swaps: An Emerging Issue," **ACCHOR**, 1987, Vol. 1, No. 2, pp. 19-24.

Cummings, Joseph P. and Michael N. Chetkovich. "World Accounting Enters A New Era," **JOA**, 1978, Vol. 145, No. 4. pp. 52-62.

Cummings, Joseph P. and William L. Rogers. "Developments In International Accounting," **CPAJ**, 1978, Vol. 48, No. 5, pp. 15-20.

Cummings, Joseph P. "The International Accounting Standards Committee: Current And Future Developments," **IJAER**, 1975, Vol. 11, No. 1, pp. 31-37.

Cummings, Joseph P. "The International Accounting Standards Committee - Its Purpose And Status," **CPAJ**, 1974, Vol. 44, No. 9, pp. 50-53.

Cunnane, Thomas F. "A Current Survey Of Nonqualified Deferred Compensation Plans," **JOA**, 1969, Vol. 128, No. 5. pp. 50-55.

Cunningham, Earle H. "The Need For College Courses In Internal Auditing," **AR**, 1955, Vol. 30, No. 1, pp. 51-57.

Cunningham, Gary M. and David E. Reemsnyder. II. "Church Accounting: The Other Side Of Stewardship," **MA**, 1983. Vol. 65, No. 2, pp. 58-62.

Cunningham, Gary M. and Floyd A. Beams. "Some Legal Aspects Of The Premature Retirement Of Debt," **MA**, 1976, Vol. 57, No. 11, pp. 19-21.

Cunningham, Gary M. "Sub S Corporation Accounting Procedures," **CPAJ**, 1977, Vol. 47, No. 4, pp. 37-42.

Cunningham, Gary M. (Hunter, Robert L., Gary M. Cunningham and Thomas G. Evans. "Are Multinational Liquidity Models Worth Their Cost?," **MA**, 1979, Vol. 61, No. 6.pp. 51-56.)

Cunningham, Michael E. "Push-Down Accounting: Pros And Cons," **JOA**, 1984, Vol. 157, No. 6, pp. 72-79.

Curatola, Anthony P., David B. Vicknair and Suzanne R. Pinac Ward. "Earnings Per Share: Alternative Interpretations Of The Three Percent Provision Of APB 15 In Intermediate Accounting Textbooks," **IAE**, 1988, Vol. 3, No. 1. pp. 17-26.

Curley, Anthony J. and Charles G. Carpenter. "Present Value Models And The Multi-Asset Problem: A Comment," **AR**, 1974, Vol. 49, No. 4, pp. 812-815.

Curley, Anthony J. "Conglomerate Earnings Per Share: Real And Transitory Growth," **AR**, 1971, Vol. 46, No. 3, pp. 519-528.

Curley, Anthony J. "Conglomerate Growth: The Ostrich Effect," **AR**, 1972, Vol. 47, No. 2, pp. 371-374.

Curran, Joseph R. "Disclosure Of Standby Letters Of Credit," **CPAJ**, 1977, Vol. 47, No. 5, pp. 31-36.

Current, Kathryn. "Hedging As An Aid In Inventory Cost Control," **MA**, 1966, Vol. 48, No. 2, pp. 47-51.

Currier, Donald E. "Accounting Under 1948 Renegotiation Act," **JOA**, 1951, Vol. 91, No. 4, pp. 554-561.

Currie, Edward M. and John L. Witwer. "Gaining A Foothold In Systems Education," **AR**, 1969, Vol. 44, No. 3, pp. 618-623.

Currie, Edward M. "Acquisition Costing And The Bargaining Area," **MA**, 1974, Vol. 56, No. 3, pp. 29-37.

Currin, David L. and W. Allen Spivey. "A Note On 'Management Decision And Integer Programming'," **AR**, 1972, Vol. 47, No. 1, pp. 144-146.

Curry, Dudley W. "Opinion 15 Vs. A Comprehensive Financial Reporting Method For Convertible Debt," **AR**, 1971, Vol. 46, No. 3, pp. 490-503.

Curtis, John R. "Making Safety Pay," **MA**, 1986, Vol. 68, No. 6, pp. 46-47.

Cushing, Barry E. and Charles H. Smith. "A New Emphasis For Introductory Accounting Instruction," **AR**, 1972, Vol. 47, No. 3, pp. 599-601.

Cushing, Barry E. and Edward B. Deakin. "A Mathematical Approach To The Analysis And Design Of Internal Control Systems," **AR**, 1974, Vol. 49, No. 1, pp. 24-41.

Cushing, Barry E. and Edward B. Deakin. "Firms Making Accounting Changes: A Comment," **AR**, 1974, Vol. 49, No. 1. pp. 104-111.

Cushing, Barry E. and James K. Loebbecke. "Analytical Approaches To Audit Risk: A Survey And Analysis," **AJPT**, 1983-84. Vol. 3, No. 1, pp. 23-41.

Cushing, Barry E. "A Further Note On The Mathematical Approach To Internal Control," **AR**, 1975, Vol. 50, No. 1, pp. 151-154.

Cushing, Barry E. "Accounting Changes: The Impact Of APB Opinion No. 20," **JOA**, 1974, Vol. 138, No. 5, pp. 54-62.

Cushing, Barry E. "An Empirical Study Of Changes In Accounting Policy," **JAR**, 1969, Vol. 7. No. 2,pp.196-203.

Cushing, Barry E. "On The Possibility Of Optimal Accounting Principles," **AR**, 1977, Vol. 52, No. 2, pp. 308-321.

Cushing, Barry E. "On The Possibility Of Optimal Accounting Principles: A Restatement," **AR**, 1981, Vol. 56, No. 3, pp. 713-718.

Cushing, Barry E. "Pricing Internal Computer Services: The Basic Issues," **MA**, 1976, Vol. 57, No. 10, pp. 47-50.

Cushing, Barry E. "Some Observations On Demski's Ex Post Accounting System," **AR**, 1968, Vol. 43, No. 4, pp. 668-671.

Cushing, Barry E. (Parker, James E. and Barry E. Cushing. "Earnings Per Share And Convertible Securities: A Utilitarian Approach," **ABACUS**, 1971, Vol. 7, No. 1, pp. 29-38.)

Cushing, Barry E., D. Gerald Searfoss and Reed H. Randall. "Materiality Allocation In Audit Planning: A Feasibility Study," **JAR**, 1979, Vol. 17, Supp., pp. 172-216.

Cutler, Arnold R. (Lourie, George B. and Arnold R. Cutler. "Effect Of Henderson Case On Tax Accounting Period Of Deceased Partner," **JOA**, 1951, Vol. 91, No. 2, pp. 260-265.)

Cutler, George B. "Developing The Selling Price," **MA**, 1971, Vol. 53. No. 2, pp. 41-42.

Cutting, Warren B. "Profit-Sharing Plans," **JOA**, 1957, Vol.

104, No. 6, pp. 39-42.

Cutting, Warren B. (Perry, Kenneth W. and Warren B. Cutting. "Recruiting For The Small Firm," **JOA**, 1961, Vol. 111, No. 5, pp. 41-45.)

Cyert, Richard M. and John T. Wheeler. "A Proposal For An Integrated Course In Statistics And Accounting," **AR**, 1960, Vol. 35, No. 1, pp. 51-59.

Cyert, Richard M. and Yuji Ijiri. "Problems Of Implementing The Trueblood Objectives Report," **JAR**, 1974, Vol. 12, Supp., pp. 29-42.

Cyert, Richard M. (Churchill, Neil C. and Richard M. Cyert. "An Experiment In Management Auditing," **JOA**, 1966, Vol. 121, No. 2, pp. 39-43.)

Cyert, R. M. "Test-Checking And The Poisson Distribution - A Further Comment," **AR**, 1957, Vol. 32, No. 3, pp. 395-397.

Cyert, R. M. (Trueblood, Robert M. and R. M. Cyert. "Statistical Sampling Applied To Aging Of Accounts Receivable," **JOA**, 1954, Vol. 97, No. 3, pp. 293-298.)

Cyert, R. M., G. M. Hinckley and R. J. Monteverde. "Statistical Sampling In The Audit Of The Air Force Motor Vehicle Inventory," **AR**, 1960, Vol. 35, No. 4, pp. 667-673.

Czajkowski, Peter. (Restall, Lawrence J. and Peter Czajkowski. "Computation Of Lifo Index: A Statistical Sampling Approach," **MA**, 1969, Vol. 51, No. 3, pp. 43-48.)

Czarnecki, Richard E. and Lyle E. Algate. "Using Consultants To Meet CPE Needs," **JOA**, 1980, Vol. 150, No. 2, pp. 64-68.

Czarniawska-Joerges, B. "Dynamics Of Organizational Control: The Case Of Berol Kemi AB," **AOS**, 1988, Vol. 13, No. 4, pp. 415-430.

DDD

Da Costa, Richard C., Jacques C. Bourgeois and William M. Lawson. "A Classification Of International Financial Accounting Practices," **IJAER**, 1978, Vol. 13, No. 2, pp. 73-85.

Dady, Benjamin L. "How Florida Power & Light Installed Z-B Budgeting," **MA**, 1979, Vol. 60, No. 9, pp. 31-34.

Daems, H. (Chandler, A. D., Jr. and H. Daems. "Administrative Coordination, Allocation And Monitoring: A Comparative Analysis Of The Emergence Of Accounting And Organization In The U.S.A. And Europe," **AOS**, 1979, Vol. 4, No. 1/2, pp. 3-20.)

Daft, R. L. (Giroux, G. A., A. G. Mayper and R. L. Daft. "Organization Size, Budget Cycle, And Budget Related Influence In City Governments: An Empirical Study," **AOS**, 1986, Vol. 11, No. 6, pp. 499-520.)

Daft, R. L. (Macintosh, N. B. and R. L. Daft. "Management Control Systems And Departmental Interdependencies: An Empirical Study," **AOS**, 1987. Vol. 12, No. 1, pp. 49-64.)

Dahan, Lionel. (Burlaud, Alain and Lionel Dahan. "Global Productivity Surplus Accounts," **IJAER**, 1985, Vol. 21, No. 1, pp. 159-169.)

Dahl, Shirley J. and Karen L. Hooks. "Women Accountants. Today And Tomorrow," **CPAJ**, 1985, Vol. 55, No. 1, pp. 20-25.

Dahl, Shirley J. and Karen L. Hooks. "Women Accountants In A Changing Profession," **JOA**, 1984, Vol. 158, No. 6, pp. 108-117.

Dahmash, Naim H. "Public Auditing Developments In The Arab States: A Comparative Study," **IJAER**, 1982. Vol. 18. No. 1, pp. 89-114.

Dailey, Cynthia D. (Gaffney, Dennis J. and Cynthia D. Dailey. "Property Distributions Of Subchapter S Corporations: Regulation #1.373-1(e)(2) Allocations Not Always Necessary," **JATA**, 1980, Vol. 1, No. 2, pp. 17-20.)

Dailey, Michael James. "Cyclical Aspects Of Twentieth Century American Accounting," **AHJ**, 1984, Vol. 11, No. 2, pp. 61-75.

Daily, R. Austin and Robert H. Strawser. "Independent Audits And The Reporting Practices Of Banks," **JOA**, 1974, Vol. 138, No. 1, pp. 44-49.

Daily, R. Austin. "The Feasibility Of Reporting Forecasted Information," **AR**, 1971, Vol. 46, No. 4, pp. 686-692.

Daines, H. C. "The Changing Objectives Of Accounting," **AR**, 1929, Vol. 4, No. 2, pp. 94-110.

Dalberth, James. (Piaker, Philip M. and James Dalberth. "Acceptance Of Change Among Accountants: An Examination Of Attitudes Towards Current Controversies," **CPAJ**, 1973, Vol. 43, No. 2, pp. 132-138.)

Dale, Donald M. (Scott, Richard A. and Donald M. Dale. "Interim Testing Of Assets And Liabilities," **CPAJ**, 1984, Vol. 54, No. 11, pp. 22-33.)

Dale, Ernest. "The Accountant's Part In Labor-Management Relations," **JOA**, 1950, Vol. 90, No. 1, pp. 12-25.

Dale, W. Carl. "An Accounting System For A Small CPA Firm," **JOA**, 1960, Vol. 110, No. 2, pp. 53-59.

Daley, Lane Alan. "The Valuation Of Reported Pension Measures For Firms Sponsoring Defined Benefit Plans," **AR**, 1984, Vol. 59, No. 2, pp. 177-198.

Daley, Lane A. and Gerhard G. Mueller. "Accounting In The Arena Of World Politics," **JOA**, 1982, Vol. 153, No. 2, pp. 40-53.

Daley, Lane A. and Robert L. Vigeland. "The Effects Of Debt Covenants And Political Costs On The Choice Of Accounting Methods: The Case Of Accounting For R&D Costs," **JAEC**, 1983, Vol. 5, No. 3, pp. 195-211.

Daley, Lane A. (Bowen, Robert M., David Burgstahler and Lane A. Daley. "The Incremental Information Content Of Accrual Versus Cash Flows," **AR**, 1987, Vol. 62, No. 4, pp. 723-747.)

Daley, Lane A. (Bowen, Robert M., David Burgstahler and Lane A. Daley. "Evidence Of The Relationships Between Various Earnings Measures Of Cash Flow," **AR**, 1986, Vol. 61, No. 4, pp. 713-725.)

Daley, Lane A., David W. Senkow and Robert L. Vigeland. "Analysts' Forecasts, Earnings Variability, And Option Pricing: Empirical Evidence," **AR**, 1988, Vol. 63, No. 4, pp. 563-585.

Dalio, Raymond T. "A Macro View Of 1985 And 1986," **JCA**, 1985, Vol. 2, No. 1, pp. 31-41.

Dalsimer, John Paul, Paul E. Dascher and James J. Benjamin. "An Aspect Of The Profession's Social Commitment," **CPAJ**, 1979, Vol. 49, No. 11, pp. 13-18.

Dalton, Francis E. and John B. Miner. "The Role Of Accounting Training In Top Mangement Decision-Making," **AR**, 1970, Vol. 45, No. 1, pp. 134-139.

Dalton, Gene. (Todd, John T., Paul H. Thompson and Gene Dalton. "Management Control Of Personnel," **JOA**, 1974, Vol. 137, No. 2, pp. 34-40.)

Danford, Fred. "Some Modern Developments In Accounting For Manufacturing Enterprises," **AR**, 1933, Vol. 8, No. 2, pp. 119-121.

Danfy, Richard J. "Analyzing The Return On Investment," **MA**, 1975, Vol. 57, No. 3, pp. 31-32.

Dangerfield, B. C. and E. Stephenson. "Stock Valuation Practices In Consumer Durables Manufacturing Industry," **ABR**, 1973-74, Vol. 4, No. 13, pp. 2-12.

Daniell, E. Roy. "Taxation Of Installment Dealer Finance Reserves," **JOA**, 1954, Vol. 97, No. 2, pp. 201-204.

Daniels, Howard M. "An Evolutionary 5-Year Professional Program," **AR**, 1958, Vol. 33, No. 3, pp. 455-460.

Daniels, Howard M. "Functional Training For The Certified Public Accountant Examination," **AR**, 1947, Vol. 22, No. 2, pp. 166-169.

Daniels, Howard M. "How To Write A Successful Answer To Municipal Accounting Question In CPA Exam," **JOA**, 1950, Vol. 89, No. 4, pp. 329-333.

Daniels, Mortimer B. "Principles Of Asset Valuation," **AR**, 1934, Vol. 9, No. 2, pp. 114-120.

Daniels, M. B. "The Valuation Of Fixed Assets," **AR**, 1933, Vol. 8, No. 4 pp. 302-316.

Daniel, Shirley J. "Some Empirical Evidence About The Assessment Of Audit Risk In Practice," **AJPT**, 1988, Vol. 7, No. 2, pp. 174-181.

Dankowski, Dennis. "Dow Opts For Less - And Gains," **MA**, 1986, Vol. 67, No. 12, pp. 56-57.

Danne, W. H. "Tax Appeal Procedures In The Reorganized Bureau," **JOA**, 1952, Vol. 94, No. 1, pp. 58-61.

Danos, Paul and David Shields. "Referrals From Bankers And Attorneys," **CPAJ**, 1981, Vol. 51, No. 5, pp. 13-19.

Danos, Paul and Eugene A. Imhoff. "Auditor Review Of Financial Forecasts: An Analysis Of Factors Affecting Reasonableness Judgments," **AR**, 1982, Vol. 57, No. 1, pp. 39-54.

Danos, Paul and Eugene A. Imhoff, Jr. "Factors Affecting Auditor's Evaluations Of Forecasts," **JAR**, 1983, Vol. 21, No. 2, pp. 473-494.

Danos, Paul and Eugene A. Imhoff, Jr. "Forecast Systems, Construction And Attestation," **AJPT**, 1981-82, Vol. 1, No. 2, pp. 23-34.

Danos, Paul and John W. Eichenseher. "Long-Term Trends Toward Seller Concentration In The U.S. Audit Market," **AR**, 1986, Vol. 61, No. 4, pp. 633-650.

Danos, Paul and John W. Eichenseher. "Audit Industry Dynamics: Factors Affecting Changes In Client-Industry Market Shares," **JAR**, 1982, Vol. 20, No. 2, Part II, pp. 604-616.

Danos, Paul and Richard Boley. "Centralized Research In CPA Firms," **CPAJ**, 1980, Vol. 50, No. 3, pp. 10-18.

Danos, Paul, Doris L. Holt and Andrew D. Bailey, Jr. "The Interaction Of Science And Attestation Standard Formation," **AJPT**, 1986-87, Vol. 6, No. 2, pp. 134-149.

Danos, Paul, Doris L. Holt and Eugene A. Imhoff, Jr. "Bond Raters' Use Of Management Financial Forecasts: An Experiment In Expert Judgment," **AR**, 1984, Vol. 59, No. 4, pp. 547-573.

Danos, Paul. "A Revolution In Accounting Thought?: A Comment," **AR**, 1977, Vol. 52, No. 3, pp. 746-747.

Danos, Paul. (Boley, Richard and Paul Danos. "The Use Of LEXIS In Accounting Pedagogy - Preliminary Observations," **AR**, 1978, Vol. 53, No. 3, pp. 730-735.)

Danos, Paul. (Boley, Richard and Paul Danos. "Awareness And Usage Of LEXIS By Accounting Educators: A Survey," **AR**, 1980, Vol. 55, No. 1, pp. 102-106.)

Danos, Paul. (Eichenseher, John W. and Paul Danos. "The Analysis Of Industry-Specific Auditor Concentration: Towards An Explanatory Model," **AR**, 1981, Vol. 56, No. 3, pp. 479-492.)

Dare, Philip N. (Kreiser, Larry and Philip N. Dare. "Shaker Accounting Records At Pleasant Hill: 1830 - 1850," **AHJ**, 1986, Vol. 13, No. 1, pp. 19-36.)

Darling, John R. "Attitudes Toward Advertising By Accountants," **JOA**, 1977, Vol. 143, No. 2, pp. 48-53.

Daroca, Frank P. and William W. Holder. "The Use Of Analytical Procedures In Review And Audit Engagements," **AJPT**, 1984-85, Vol. 4, No. 2, pp. 80-92.

Daroca, Frank P., Gary L. Holstrum and W. Thomas Lin. "Long-Range Planning And Control Of Growth," **JOA**, 1984, Vol. 158, No. 6, pp. 118-134.

Daroca, F. P. "Informational Influences On Group Decision Making In A Participative Budgeting Context," **AOS**, 1984, Vol. 9, No. 1, pp. 13-32.

Darrah, Florence J. "Intangible Feminine Assets," **MA**, 1975, Vol. 57, No. 3, pp. 25-28.

Darrell, Norris. "Moral Responsibility In Tax Practice: A

Lawyer's View," **JOA**, 1959, Vol. 107, No. 4, pp. 34-35.

Darrough, Masako N. "Variance Analysis: A Unifying Cost Function Approach," **CAR**, 1988, Vol. 5, No. 1, pp. 199-221.

Das, H. "Organizational And Decision Characteristics And Personality As Determinants Of Control Actions: A Laboratory Experiment," **AOS**, 1986, Vol. 11, No. 3, pp. 215-232.

Das, T. K. (Flamholtz, E. G., T. K. Das and A. S. Tsui. "Toward An Integrative Framework Of Organizational Control," **AOS**, 1985, Vol. 10, No. 1, pp. 35-50.)

Dasburg, John H. and C. Richard Morehead. "Can GAAP Still Support Inventory Valuation After Thor?," **JOA**, 1979, Vol. 148, No. 4, pp. 68-77.

Dascher, Paul E. and Robert E. Malcolm. "A Note On Income Smoothing In The Chemical Industry," **JAR**, 1970, Vol. 8, No. 2, pp. 253-259.

Dascher, Paul E. and Ronald M. Copeland. "Some Further Evidence On 'Criteria For Judging Disclosure Improvement'," **JAR**, 1971, Vol. 9, No. 1, pp. 32-39.

Dascher, Paul E. and Thomas D. Hubbard. "The CPA Review Course - A Second Dimension," **AR**, 1973, Vol. 48, No. 2, pp. 418-420.

Dascher, Paul E. and W. Ken Harmon. "Assessing Microcomputer Risks And Controls For Clients," **CPAJ**, 1984, Vol. 54, No. 5, pp. 36-41.

Dascher, Paul E. and W. Ken Harmon. "The Dark Side Of Small Business Computers," **MA**, 1984, Vol. 65, No. 11, pp. 62-67.

Dascher, Paul E. (Benjamin, James J., Paul E. Dascher and Robert G. Morgan. "How Corporate Controllers View The Foreign Corrupt Practices Act," **MA**, 1979, Vol. 60, No. 12, pp. 43-45.)

Dascher, Paul E. (Bremser, Wayne G., Vincent C. Brenner and Paul E. Dascher. "Schools Of Professional Accountancy: The Management Accountant's View," **MA**, 1977, Vol. 59, No. 3, pp. 14-16.)

Dascher, Paul E. (Bremser, Wayne G., Vincent C. Brenner and Paul E. Dascher. "The Feasibility Of Professional Schools: An Empirical Study," **AR**, 1977, Vol. 52, No. 2, pp. 465-473.)

Dascher, Paul E. (Brenner, Vincent C., Ronald M. Copeland, Paul E. Dascher, Arthur J. Francia, Ronald J. Patten and Robert H. Strawser. "Trials And Tribulations Of The Researcher: A Case Study," **JAR**, 1972, Vol. 10, No. 1, pp. 195-199.)

Dascher, Paul E. (Buckmaster, Dale A., Ronald M. Copeland and Paul E. Dascher. "The Relative Predictive Ability Of Three Accounting Models," **ABR**, 1976-77, Vol. 7, No. 27, pp. 177-186.)

Dascher, Paul E. (Dalsimer, John Paul, Paul E. Dascher and James J. Benjamin. "An Aspect Of The Profession's Social Commitment," **CPAJ**, 1979, Vol. 49, No. 11, pp. 13-18.)

Dascher, Paul E. (Harmon, W. Ken, Kay M. Poston and Paul E. Dascher. "Provision And Inadequacy Of Small Business Computer Controls: A Model And Empirical Test," **JIS**, 1988, Vol. 3, No. 1, pp. 30-49.)

Dascher, Paul E., Charles H. Smith and Robert H. Strawser. "Accounting Curriculum Implications Of The Multinational Corporation," **IJAER**, 1973, Vol. 9, No. 1, pp. 81-97.

Datar, Srikant M. (Banker, Rajiv D., Srikant M. Datar and Ajay Maindiratta. "Unobservable Outcomes And Multiattribute Preferences In The Evaluation Of Managerial Performance," **CAR**, 1988, Vol. 5, No. 1, pp. 96-124.)

Datar, Srikant M. (Banker, Rajiv D., Srikant M. Datar and Madhav V. Rajan. "Measurement Of Productivity Improvements: An Empirical Analysis," **JAAF**, 1987, Vol. 2 (New Series), No. 4, pp. 319-354.)

Datar, Srikant M. (Banker, Rajiv D., Srikant M. Datar and Sunder Kekre. "Relevant Costs, Congestion And Stochasticity In Production Environments," **JAEC**, 1988, Vol. 10, No. 3, pp. 171-197.)

Dau, Khalifa. "A Probabilistic Income Determination Theory," **IJAER**, 1978, Vol. 14, No. 1, pp. 39-56.

Dauber, Nick and Joel G. Siegel. "The Many Facets Of NOLs In Business Arrangements," **CPAJ**, 1982, Vol. 52, No. 2, pp. 37-43.

Daughtrey, Zoel W. (Gulledge, Dexter E. and Zoel W. Daughtrey. "Gambling - A Trade Or Business?," **CPAJ**, 1988, Vol. 58, No. 3, pp. 12-21.)

Davall, Bernard M. and Joseph W. Wilkinson. "Simulating An Accounting Information System Model," **MA**, 1971, Vol. 52, No. 7, pp. 26-30.

Davenport, Frederick. "Financial Management Through MRP," **MA**, 1982, Vol. 63, No. 12, pp. 26-29.

David, Herbert K. "Control Of In-Process Inventory," **MA**, 1969, Vol. 51, No. 6, pp. 27-31.

David, Irwin T. and Robert M. Trueblood. "The Report Of The President's Commission On Budget Concepts," **JOA**, 1968, Vol. 125, No. 1, pp. 25-36.

David, Theodore M. "Appeals In The United States Tax Court," **CPAJ**, 1981, Vol. 51, No. 12, pp. 28-33.

David, Theodore M. "GRITS - Their Role In Estate Planning," **CPAJ**, 1988, Vol. 58, No. 6, pp. 54-58.

David, Theodore M. "Sec. 355 Split-Offs And Brother-Sister Corporations," **CPAJ**, 1983, Vol. 53, No. 9, pp. 36-41.

Davidson, A. N. "Acceptance Of Direct Costing," **MA**, 1970, Vol. 51, No. 9, pp. 35-37.

Davidson, H. Justin and Robert M. Trueblood. "Accounting For Decision-Making," **AR**, 1961, Vol. 36, No. 4, pp. 577-582.

Davidson, H. Justin and Thomas R. Hofstedt. "Published Financial Statements For CPAs," **JOA**, 1972, Vol. 134, No. 1, pp. 31-45.

Davidson, H. Justin. "Accuracy In Statistical Sampling,"

AR, 1959, Vol. 34, No. 3, pp. 356-365.

Davidson, H. Justin. "Research In Accounting," **JOA**, 1968, Vol. 126, No. 3, pp. 44-50.

Davidson, H. Justin. (Charnes, A., H. Justin Davidson and K. Kortanek. "On A Mixed Sequential Estimating Procedure With Application To Audit Tests In Accounting," **AR**, 1964, Vol. 39, No. 2, pp. 241-250.)

Davidson, H. J., J. Neter and A. S. Petran. "Estimating The Liability For Unredeemed Stamps," **JAR**, 1967, Vol. 5, No. 2, pp. 186-207.

Davidson, I. R. "On 'Contract Value Accounting': A Critique," **ABR**, 1985-86, Vol. 16, No. 62, pp. 143-148.

Davidson, Lewis F. (Bartley, Jon W. and Lewis F. Davidson. "The Entity Concept And Accounting For Interest Costs," **ABR**, 1981-82, Vol. 12, No. 47, pp. 175-187.)

Davidson, Lewis F. (Bird, Francis A., Lewis F. Davidson and Charles H. Smith. "Perceptions Of External Accounting Transfers Under Entity And Proprietary Theory," **AR**, 1974, Vol. 49, No. 2, pp. 233-244.)

Davidson, Lewis F. (Cook, James S., Jr., Lewis F. Davidson and Charles H. Smith. "Social Costs And Private Accounting," **ABACUS**, 1974, Vol. 10, No. 2, pp. 87-99.)

Davidson, Lewis F. (Keller, Stuart B. and Lewis F. Davidson. "An Assessment Of Individual Investor Reaction To Certain Qualified Audit Opinions," **AJPT**, 1983-84, Vol. 3, No. 1, pp. 1-22.)

Davidson, Sidney and John M. Kohlmeier. "A Measure Of The Impact Of Some Foreign Accounting Principles," **JAR**, 1966, Vol. 4, No. 2, pp. 183-212.

Davidson, Sidney and Roman L. Weil. "Income Tax Implications Of Various Methods Of Accounting For Changing Prices," **JAR**, 1978, Vol. 16, Supp., pp. 154-233.

Davidson, Sidney and Roman L. Weil. "On Holding Gains And Losses And The Evaluation Of Management: A Comment," **AR**, 1974, Vol. 49, No. 3, pp. 524-527.

Davidson, Sidney, and George D. Anderson. "The Development Of Accounting And Auditing Standards," **JOA**, 1987, Vol. 163, No. 5, pp. 110-126.

Davidson, Sidney. "A Two-Statement Approach To Consolidated Statement Problems," **AR**, 1954, Vol. 29, No. 3, pp. 506-508.

Davidson, Sidney. "A Work Sheet For Statements Of Realization And Liquidation," **AR**, 1952, Vol. 27, No. 1, pp. 133-136.

Davidson, Sidney. "Accelerated Depreciation And The Allocation Of Income Taxes," **AR**, 1958, Vol. 33, No. 2, pp. 173-180.

Davidson, Sidney. "Accounting And Financial Reporting In The Seventies," **JOA**, 1969, Vol. 128, No. 6, pp. 29-37.

Davidson, Sidney. "Accounting Research," **AR**, 1957, Vol. 32, No. 2, pp. 273-280.

Davidson, Sidney. "Addendum - Some Significant Standards," **JOA**, 1987, Vol. 163, No. 5, pp. 130-135.

Davidson, Sidney. "Depreciation And Profit Determination," **AR**, 1950, Vol. 25, No. 1, pp. 45-56.

Davidson, Sidney. "LIFO Cost Or Market And Compulsory Tax Reporting Requirements," **JAR**, 1965, Vol. 3, No. 1, pp. 156-158.

Davidson, Sidney. "Old Wine Into New Bottles," **AR**, 1963, Vol. 38, No. 2, pp. 278-284.

Davidson, Sidney. "Research And Publication By The Accounting Faculty," **AR**, 1957, Vol. 32, No. 1, pp. 114-118.

Davidson, Sidney. "The Day Of Reckoning: Accounting Theory And Management Analysis," **JAR**, 1963, Vol. 1, No. 2, pp. 117-126.

Davidson, Sidney. "The Reserve For Sinking Fund - A Critical Examination," **AR**, 1950, Vol. 25, No. 4, pp. 390-394.

Davidson, Sidney. (Bierman, Harold, Jr. and Sidney Davidson. "The Income Concept - Value Increment Or Earnings Predictor," **AR**, 1969, Vol. 44, No. 2, pp. 239-246.)

Davidson, Sidney. (Miller, Herbert E. and Sidney Davidson. "Accreditation: Two Views," **JOA**, 1978, Vol. 145, No. 3, pp. 56-65.)

Davidson, S. "U.S. Supreme Court Decisions On Public Utility Depreciation," **JOA**, 1953, Vol. 96, No. 3, pp. 331-335.

Davies, B. and G. P. Whittred. "The Association Between Selected Corporate Attributes And Timeliness In Corporate Reporting: Further Analysis," **ABACUS**, 1980, Vol. 16, No. 1, pp. 48-60.

Davies, E. C. "Auditing Teaching Methods," **AR**, 1935, Vol. 10, No. 1, pp. 19-21.

Davies, Jonathan J. (Mason, John O. and Jonathan J. Davies. "Legal Implications Of EDP Deficiencies," **CPAJ**, 1977, Vol. 47, No. 5, pp. 21-24.)

Davies, J. J. "Accountants' Third Party Liability: A History Of Applied Sociological Jurisprudence," **ABACUS**, 1979, Vol. 15, No. 2, pp. 93-112.

Davies, J. R. and W. M. McInnes. "The Efficiency And The Accountability Of UK Nationalised Industries," **ABR**, 1982-83, Vol. 13, No. 49, pp. 29-41.

Davies, M. B. T. "Objectives Of Internal Auditing," **AR**, 1956, Vol. 31, No. 2, pp. 227-233.

Davis, Albion R. "Some Problems Of Last-In-First-Out Accounting," **AR**, 1942, Vol. 17, No. 4, pp. 384-403.

Davis, Charles J. and James T. Mackey. "Coalition Costs Through Queueing Theory For Shapley Cost Allocations," **AIA**, 1988, Vol. 6, pp. 85-110.

Davis, Charles J. "A Structured Approach To Preparation Of The Statement Of Changes In Financial Position," **IAE**, 1983, No. 1, pp. 79-89.

Davis, Charles J. (Covaleski, Mark A. and Charles J. Davis. "An Empirical Examination Of Capital Expenditure In The Health Sector," **JAPP**, 1984, Vol. 3, No. 2, pp. 139-162.)

Davis, C. Peter. (Chazen, Charles, David Kinkade and C.

Davis

Peter Davis. "A Primer For Novice Restaurant Owners," **CPAJ**, 1985, Vol. 55, No. 11, pp. 10-19.)

Davis, Dan D. and Arch Rounsaville. "Modern Sampling Methods," **JOA**, 1959, Vol. 107, No. 6, pp. 45-51.

Davis, Darrel W., James R. Boatsman and Elba F. Baskin. "On Generalizing Stock Market Research To A Broader Class Of Markets," **AR**, 1978, Vol. 53, No. 1, pp. 1-10.

Davis, Douglas C. (Borelli, Frank J. and Douglas C. Davis. "Financial Management And Audit Committee," **CA**, 1986, Vol. 4, No. 3, pp. 9-13.)

Davis, Earl F. and James W. Kelley. "The Engagement Letter And Current Legal Developments," **JOA**, 1972, Vol. 134, No. 6, pp. 54-59.

Davis, Earl F. "Professionalization Of Private Accountants," **MA**, 1970, Vol. 52, No. 5, pp. 49-52.

Davis, E. W. (Buckland, R. and E. W. Davis. "Barriers To Entry In The Unlisted Securities Market: The Significance Of Administrative Expenses," **ABR**, 1986-87, Vol. 17, No. 68, pp. 301-310.)

Davis, E. W. (Collier, P. and E. W. Davis. "The Management Of Currency Transaction Risk By UK Multinational Companies," **ABR**, 1984-85, Vol. 15, No. 60, pp. 327-334.)

Davis, Gordon B. and Ron Weber. "The Impact Of Advanced Computer Systems On Controls And Audit Procedures: A Theory And An Empirical Test," **AJPT**, 1985-86, Vol. 5, No. 2, pp. 35-49.

Davis, Gordon B. "Standards For Computers And Information Processing," **JOA**, 1967, Vol. 124, No. 3, pp. 52-57.

Davis, Gordon B. "The Application Of Network Techniques To The Planning And Control Of An Audit," **JAR**, 1963, Vol. 1, No. 1, pp. 96-101.

Davis, Gordon B. "The Auditor And The Computer," **JOA**, 1968, Vol. 125, No. 3, pp. 44-47.

Davis, Gordon B. (Rittenberg, Larry E. and Gordon B. Davis. "The Roles Of Internal And External Auditors In Auditing EDP Systems," **JOA**, 1977, Vol. 144, No. 6, pp. 51-58.)

Davis, Gordon B., John Neter and Roger R. Palmer. "An Experimental Study Of Audit Confirmations," **JOA**, 1967, Vol. 123, No. 6, pp. 36-44.

Davis, Harry Zvi. "Accounting Measurement And Capacity Limits," **AHJ**, 1986, Vol. 13, No. 2, pp. 151-153.

Davis, Harry Zvi. "History Of LIFO," **AHJ**, 1982, Vol. 9, No. 1, pp. 1-23.

Davis, Harry Zvi. "Note On The First Recorded Audit In The Bible," **AHJ**, 1981, Vol. 8, No. 1, pp. 71-72.

Davis, Harry Zvi. "The Effects Of LIFO Inventory Costing On Resource Allocations: A Comment," **AR**, 1981, Vol. 56, No. 4, pp. 975-976.

Davis, Harry Z. and Nathan Kahn. "Some Additional Evidence On The LIFO-FIFO Choice Using Replacement Cost Data," **JAR**, 1982, Vol. 20, No. 2, pp. 738-744.

Davis, Harry Z., Nathan Kahn and Etzmun Rozen. "LIFO Inventory Liquidations: An Empirical Study," **JAR**, 1984, Vol. 22, No. 2, pp. 480-496.

Davis, James R. and Robert A. Leitch. "Accounting Information System Courses And Curricula: New Perspectives," **JIS**, 1988, Vol. 3, No. 1, pp. 153-166.

Davis, James R. "EDP Control Means Total Control," **MA**, 1977, Vol. 58, No. 7, pp. 41-44.

Davis, James R. "Shared Services: Survival For The Small Business?," **MA**, 1977, Vol. 58, No. 11, pp. 27-30.

Davis, James R. (Rouse, Robert, James R. Davis and G. Thomas Friedlob. "The Relevant Experience Criterion For Accounting Accreditation By The AACSB," **JAED**, 1986, Vol. 4, No. 1, pp. 147-160.)

Davis, Jeffrey J. "Accounting Weaknesses That Could Harm Your Company," **MA**, 1983, Vol. 65, No. 2, pp. 55-57.

Davis, John L. "Accounting For Electrolytic Refining Of Copper," **MA**, 1968, Vol. 50, No. 2, pp. 49-52.

Davis, Jon S. and Charles W. Swenson. "The Role Of Experimental Economics In Tax Policy Research," **JATA**, 1988, Vol. 10, No. 1, pp. 40-59.

Davis, Jonathan. "Hood Chooses MIS For Its Frogurt," **MA**, 1979, Vol. 60, No. 11, pp. 38-41.

Davis, Jordan H. "Inventory Costs And The Property Tax," **MA**, 1971, Vol. 53, No. 1, pp. 18-19.

Davis, Keagle W. "The Information Systems Auditor Of The 1980s," **MA**, 1981, Vol. 62, No. 9, pp. 40-47.

Davis, Keith. (Smith, C. Aubrey and Keith Davis. "Texas Survey Shows Wide Variation In Personnel Practices," **JOA**, 1952, Vol. 93, No. 5, pp. 584-588.)

Davis, Kenneth L. "The Human Problems Of The Senior Accountant," **AR**, 1956, Vol. 31, No. 1, pp. 56-57.

Davis, LaVaughn. "Corporate Separations," **JOA**, 1965, Vol. 120, No. 3, pp. 35-42.

Davis, LaVaughn. "Tax Aspects Of Subsidiary Liquidations," **JOA**, 1966, Vol. 122, No. 1, pp. 41-48.

Davis, Mark W. "Cash Flow Analysis For Feedlot Operations," **MA**, 1973, Vol. 54, No. 12, pp. 38-41.

Davis, Michael L. and James A. Largay, III. "Reporting Consolidated Gains And Losses On Subsidiary Stock Issuances," **AR**, 1988, Vol. 63, No. 2, pp. 348-363.

Davis, P. Michael. "Marginal Analysis Of Credit Sales," **AR**, 1966, Vol. 41, No. 1, pp. 121-126.

Davis, P. Michael. (Crumbley, D. Larry and P. Michael Davis. "Accounting And Auditing Problems In Subchapter S Corporations," **JOA**, 1970, Vol. 130, No. 4. pp. 45-51.)

Davis, P. M. (Crumbley, D. L., P. M. Davis and R. Welker. "A Subchapter S Corporation Is Taxable: Sometimes," **CPAJ**, 1977, Vol. 47, No. 12, pp. 23-28.)

Davis, Robert H. "Production Costing In Open Pit Mining," **MA**, 1971, Vol. 52, No. 7, pp. 39-41.

Davis, Robert R. "An Empirical Evaluation Of Auditors' 'Subject-To' Opinions," **AJPT**, 1982-83, Vol. 2, No. 1, pp. 13-32.

Davis, Robert R. "Ethical Behavior Reexamined," **CPAJ**, 1984, Vol. 54, No. 12, pp. 32-37.

Davis, Stanley W. and Krishnagopal Menon. "The Formation And Termination Of The Cost Accounting Standards Board: Legislative Intervention In Accounting Standard-Setting," **JAPP**, 1987, Vol. 6, No. 3, pp. 185-207.

Davis, S. W., K. Menon and G. Morgan. "The Images That Have Shaped Accounting Theory," **AOS**, 1982, Vol. 7, No. 4, pp. 307-318.

Davison, Alan G. "Auditors' Liability To Third Parties For Negligence," **ABR**, 1981-82, Vol. 12, No. 48, pp. 257-264.

Davison, A. G., Bruce W. Stening and Wan Tai Wai. "Auditor Concentration And The Impact Of Interlocking Directorates," **JAR**, 1984, Vol. 22, No. 1, pp. 313-317.

Davison, Dale L. "The Accumulated Earnings Tax," **MA**, 1973, Vol. 55, No. 5, pp. 25-26.

Dawkins, Sarah C. (Griffin, Richard B. and Sarah C. Dawkins. "Current Trends In Intermediate Accounting Course Content," **IAE**, 1986, No. 2, pp. 238-248.)

Day, Denis W. "How To Reduce Travel And Entertainment Costs," **CA**, 1985, Vol. 3, No. 3, pp. 49-53.

Day, Denis W. "How To Fly The Friendly (Low-Cost) Skies Of T&E," **MA**, 1985, Vol. 66, No. 12, pp. 33-36.

Day, Emmett B. "Cash-Balance Approach To Funds Statement," **JOA**, 1951, Vol. 91, No. 4, pp. 600-603.

Day, James E. "A Screening Model For Investment Proposals," **MA**, 1975, Vol. 56, No. 7, pp. 48-52.

Day, Judith F. S. "The Use Of Annual Reports By UK Investment Analysts," **ABR**, 1985-86, Vol. 16, No.64,pp.295-308.

Day, Kenneth. (Poe, C. Douglas, Gadis J. Dillon and Kenneth Day. "Replacing Fixed Assets In The Construction Industry," **MA**, 1988, Vol. 70, No. 2, pp. 39-43.)

Day, P. (Rosenberg, D., C. Tomkins and P. Day. "A Work Role Perspective Of Accountants In Local Government Service Departments," **AOS**, 1982, Vol. 7, No. 2, pp. 123-138.)

De, Prabuddha. (Amer, Tarek, Andrew D. Bailey, Jr. and Prabuddha De. "A Review Of The Computer Information Systems Research Related To Accounting And Auditing," **JIS**, 1987, Vol. 2, No. 1, pp. 3-28.)

De, Prabuddha. (Bailey, Andrew D., Jr., Karl Hackenbrack, Prabuddha De, and Jesse Dillard. "Artificial Intelligence, Cognitive Science, And Computational Modeling In Auditing Research: A Research Approach," **JIS**, 1987, Vol. 1, No. 2, pp. 20-40.)

DeAngelo, Linda Elizabeth. "Accounting Numbers As Market Valuation Substitutes: A Study Of Management Buyouts Of Public Stockholders," **AR**, 1986, Vol. 61, No. 3, pp. 400-420.

DeAngelo, Linda Elizabeth. "Auditor Independence, 'Low Balling', And Disclosure Regulation," **JAEC**, 1981, Vol. 3, No. 2, pp. 113-127.

DeAngelo, Linda Elizabeth. "Auditor Size And Audit Quality," **JAEC**, 1981, Vol. 3, No. 3, pp. 183-199.

DeAngelo, Linda Elizabeth. "Managerial Competition, Information Costs, And Corporate Governance: The Use Of Accounting Performance Measures In Proxy Contests," **JAEC**, 1988, Vol. 10, No. 1, pp. 3-36.

DeAngelo, Linda Elizabeth. "Mandated Successful Efforts And Auditor Choice," **JAEC**, 1982, Vol. 4, No. 3, pp. 171-203.

DeAngelo, Linda Elizabeth. "Unrecorded Human Assets And The 'Hold-Up' Problem," **JAR**, 1982, Vol. 20, No. 1, pp. 272-274.

Deakin, Edward B. and Michael H. Granof. "Regression Analysis As A Means Of Determining Audit Sample Size," **AR**, 1974, Vol. 49, No. 4, pp. 764-771.

Deakin, Edward B. and Michael H. Granof. "Directing Audit Effort Using Regression Analysis," **CPAJ**, 1976, Vol. 46, No. 2, pp. 29-33.

Deakin, Edward B. and Michael H. Granof. "Accounting For Retail Land Sales Under The New Accounting Guide," **CPAJ**, 1973, Vol. 43, No. 11, pp. 969-976.

Deakin, Edward B. and Michael H. Granof. "Regression Analysis As A Means Of Determining Audit Sample Size: A Reply," **AR**, 1976, Vol. 51, No. 2, pp. 402-404.

Deakin, Edward B. "A Class Project For Risk Analysis In Capital Budgeting," **AR**, 1974, Vol. 49, No. 1,pp.146-149.

Deakin, Edward B. "A Discriminant Analysis Of Predictors Of Business Failure," **JAR**, 1972, Vol. 10, No. 1, pp. 167-179.

Deakin, Edward B. "Accounting Reports, Policy Interventions And The Behavior Of Securities Returns," **AR**, 1976, Vol. 51, No. 3, pp. 590-598.

Deakin, Edward B. "Distributions Of Financial Accounting Ratios: Some Empirical Evidence," **AR**, 1976, Vol. 51, No. 1, pp. 90-96.

Deakin, Edward B. "Impact Of The Retail Land Sales Guide On Reporting Practice," **CPAJ**, 1975, Vol. 45, No. 8, pp. 25-28.

Deakin, Edward B. (Cushing, Barry E. and Edward B. Deakin. "Firms Making Accounting Changes: A Comment," **AR**, 1974, Vol. 49, No. 1, pp. 104-111.)

Deakin, Edward B. (Cushing, Barry E. and Edward B. Deakin. "A Mathematical Approach To The Analysis And Design Of Internal Control Systems," **AR**, 1974, Vol. 49, No. 1, pp. 24-41.)

Deakin, Edward B., Gyles R. Norwood and Charles H. Smith. "The Effect Of Published Earnings Information On Tokyo Stock Exchange Trading," **IJAER**, 1974, Vol. 10, No. 1, pp. 123-136.

Deakin, Edward B., III and Edward L. Summers. "A Survey Of Curriculum Topics Relevant To The Practice Of Management Accounting," **AR**, 1975, Vol. 50, No. 2, pp. 380-383.

Deakin, Edward B., III, Michael H. Granof and Charles H. Smith. "Educational Objectives For An Accounting Program," **AR**, 1974, Vol. 49, No. 3, pp. 584-589.

Deakin, Edward B., III. "An Analysis Of Differences Between Non-Major Oil Firms Using Successful Efforts And Full Cost Methods," **AR**, 1979, Vol. 54, No. 4, pp. 722-734.

Deakin, Michael D. "Pricing For Return On Investment," **MA**, 1975, Vol. 57, No. 6, pp. 43-44.

Dean, Arthur H. "The Relation Of Law And Economics To The Measurement Of Income," **AR**, 1953, Vol. 28, No. 3, pp. 328-342.

Dean, Graeme. (Chong, Sebastian and Graeme Dean. "Related Party Transactions: A Preliminary Evaluation Of SFAS 57 And IAS 24," **ABACUS**, 1985, Vol. 21, No. 1, pp. 84-100.)

Dean, G. W. (Clarke, F. L. and G. W. Dean. "Schmidt's 'Betriebswirtschaft' Theory," **ABACUS**, 1986, Vol. 22, No. 2, pp. 65-102.)

Dean, Joel and C. Lowell Harriss. "Railroad Accounting Under The New Depreciation Guidelines And Investment Tax Credit," **AR**, 1963, Vol. 38, No. 2, pp. 229-242.

Dean, Joel. "Cooperative Research In Cost-Price Relationships," **AR**, 1939, Vol. 14, No. 2, pp. 179-184.

Dean, Joel. "Measurement Of Profits For Executive Decisions," **AR**, 1951, Vol. 26, No. 2, pp. 185-196.

Dean, Joel. "Measurement Of Real Economic Earnings Of A Machinery Manufacturer," **AR**, 1954, Vol. 29, No. 2, pp. 255-266.

Dean, J. "Correlation Analysis Of Cost Variation," **AR**, 1937, Vol. 12, No. 1, pp. 55-60.

Dean, Peter N. "Government Auditing Standards In Twenty-Five Countries," **AIIA**, 1988, Vol. 2, pp. 229-242.

Dean, Peter N. "Nationalised Industry Consumer Councils And The Monitoring Of Financial Performance," **ABR**, 1983-84, Vol. 14, No. 56, pp. 373-382.

Dean, P. N. "Costs, Productivity And Efficiency In The Inland Revenue: An Outsider's View," **ABR**, 1976-77, Vol. 7, No. 25, pp. 17-35.

Dean, P. N. (Sandford, C. T. and P. N. Dean. "Accountants And The Tax System," **ABR**, 1971-72, Vol. 2, No. 5, pp. 3-37.)

Dean, R. A., K. R. Ferris and C. Konstans. "Occupational Reality Shock And Organizational Commitment: Evidence From The Accounting Profession," **AOS**, 1988, Vol. 13, No. 3, pp. 251-262.

Dean, Steven T. and John B. Leake. "Passing Title 'Outside The U.S.' For Tax Purposes," **JOA**, 1952, Vol. 94, No. 4, pp. 457-459.

Deane, William V. "How Westinghouse Organizes Accounting Functions," **JOA**, 1951, Vol. 91, No. 3, pp. 402-407.

Deaton, William C. and Jerry J. Weygandt. "Disclosures Related To Pension Plans," **JOA**, 1975, Vol. 139, No. 1, pp. 44-51.

DeBerg, Curtis L. and Keith A. Shriver. "The Relevance Of Current Cost Accounting Data: A Review And Analysis Of Recent Studies," **JAL**, 1987, Vol. 6, pp. 55-87.

DeBerg, Curtis L., H. Fred Mittelstaedt and Philip R. Regier. "Employers' Accounting For Pensions: A Theoretical Approach To Financial Accounting Standards No. 87," **JAED**, 1987, Vol. 5, No. 2, pp. 227-242.

DeBlasio, Alfred, Jr. "Pension Plans: Exploring The Alternatives," **MA**, 1983, Vol. 65, No. 4, pp. 31-35.

DeBord, Warren A. and Jerry D. Siebel. "Training MIS Users Through Simulation," **MA**, 1982, Vol. 63, No. 7, pp. 36-42.

Debessay, Araya and Robert Bloom. "A Critique Of FAS No. 33," **MA**, 1981, Vol. 62, No. 11, pp. 48-53.

Debessay, Araya. (Bloom, Robert and Araya Debessay. "A Comparative Analysis Of Recent Pronouncements On Accounting For Changing Prices," **IJAER**, 1985, Vol. 20, No. 2, pp. 119-138.)

Debessay, Araya. (Bloom, Robert and Araya Debessay. "An Appraisal Of The Conceptual Issues On Backlog Depreciation And A Comparative Analysis Of International Accounting Practices," **IJAER**, 1985, Vol. 21, No. 1, pp. 107-121.)

Debessay, Araya. (Bloom, Robert and Araya Debessay. "The Controversial Development Of The Deprival Value Concept," **IJAER**, 1986, Vol. 22, No. 1, pp. 159-172.)

Debessay, Araya. (Bloom, Robert, Araya Debessay and William Markell. "The Development Of Schools Of Accounting And The Underlying Issues," **JAED**, 1986, Vol. 4, No. 1, pp. 7-29.)

Debnam, T. F. "Postgraduate Training Of Accounting Teachers For The Small Colleges," **AR**, 1957, Vol. 32, No. 2, pp. 309-312.

DeCazaux, L. F. G. "On The Budget," **JAR**, 1965, Vol. 3, No. 2, pp. 264-265.

DeCoster, Don and George Prater. "An Experimental Study Of The Use Of A Business Game In Elementary Accounting," **AR**, 1973, Vol. 48, No. 1, pp. 137-142.

DeCoster, Don T. and John Grant Rhode. "The Accountant's Stereotype: Real Or Imagined, Deserved Or Unwarranted," **AR**, 1971, Vol. 46, No. 4, pp. 651-664.

DeCoster, Don T. and John P. Fertakis. "Budget-Induced Pressure And Its Relationship To Supervisory Behavior," **JAR**, 1968, Vol. 6, No. 2, pp. 237-246.

DeCoster, Don T. and Kavasseri V. Ramanathan. "An Algebraic Aid In Teaching The Differences Between Direct Costing And Full-Absorption Costing Models," **AR**, 1973, Vol. 48, No. 4, pp. 800-801.

DeCoster, Don T. "Measurement Of The Idle-Capacity Variance," **AR**, 1966, Vol. 41, No. 2, pp. 297-302.

DeCoster, Don T. "The Unit Cost Denominator In Process Costing," **AR**, 1964, Vol. 39, No. 3, pp. 750-754.

DeCoster, Don T. "'Mirror, Mirror On The Wall...' The CPA In The World Of Psychology," **JOA**, 1971, Vol. 132, No. 2, pp. 40-45.

DeCoster, Don T. (Chiu, John S. and Don T. DeCoster.

"Multiple Product Costing By Multiple Correlation Analysis," **AR**, 1966, Vol. 41, No. 4, pp. 673-680.)

DeCoster, Don T. (Foran, Michael F. and Don T. DeCoster. "An Experimental Study Of The Effects Of Participation, Authoritarianism, And Feedback On Cognitive Dissonance In A Standard Setting Situation," **AR**, 1974, Vol. 49, No. 4, pp. 751-763.)

DeCoster, Don T. (Rosen, L. S. and Don T. DeCoster. "'Funds' Statements: A Historical Perspective," **AR**, 1969, Vol. 44, No. 1, pp. 124-136.)

Decker, Thomas J. "MICROMANIA - Or. How To Spend $8,000 And Create A $75,000 Problem," **MA**, 1984, Vol. 66, No. 5, pp. 42-46.

Decker, William E. "Accounting For Shared Appreciation Mortgages," **CPAJ**, 1982, Vol. 52, No. 4, pp. 32-36.

Decker, William E. (Murray, Ronald J., William E. Decker and John W. Joyce. "Pension Accounting: Analysis Of 'Preliminary Views' - Part II," **CPAJ**, 1983, Vol. 53, No. 9, pp. 42-47.)

Decker, William E. (Murray, Ronald J., William E. Decker and John W. Joyce. "Pension Accounting: Analysis Of Preliminary Views - Part I," **CPAJ**, 1983, Vol. 53, No. 8, pp. 10-23.)

Decosimo, Joseph D. (Gavin, Thomas A., Rebecca L. Hicks and Joseph D. Decosimo. "CPAs' Liability To Third Parties," **JOA**, 1984, Vol. 157, No. 6, pp. 80-91.)

Dee, David. "Sales And Cost Deflators," **MA**, 1976, Vol. 58, No. 6, pp. 35-37.

DeFilipps, W. J. "Developing A Tax Department In A Growing Organization," **JOA**, 1974, Vol. 137, No. 6, pp. 63-74.

DeFrancesco, J. Donald. "The Accounting Side Of The Profit-Center Organization," **MA**, 1966, Vol. 48, No. 4, pp. 56-60.

Defee, Robert. "Making The Industrial Engineer A Management Accountant," **MA**, 1983, Vol. 64, No. 8, pp. 52-56.

Defeo, Victor J. "An Empirical Investigation Of The Speed Of The Market Reaction To Earnings Announcements," **JAR**, 1986, Vol. 24, No. 2, pp. 349-363.

Defliese, Philip L. "A Practitioner's View Of The Realization Concept," **AR**, 1965, Vol. 40, No. 3, pp. 517-521.

Defliese, Philip L. "Auditing And Internal Control," **JOA**, 1959, Vol. 108, No. 3, pp. 37-43.

Defliese, Philip L. "Auditor's Responsibility For Fraud Detection," **JOA**, 1962, Vol. 114, No. 4, pp. 36-44.

Defliese, Philip L. "Inflation Accounting: Pursuing The Elusive," **JOA**, 1979, Vol. 147, No. 5, pp. 50-64.

Defliese, Philip L. "The Search For A New Conceptual Framework Of Accounting," **JOA**, 1977, Vol. 144, No. 1, pp. 59-67.

Degnan, James M. (Klink, James J. and James M. Degnan. "New Accounting For Investors In Real Estate Ventures," **CPAJ**, 1980, Vol. 50, No. 1, pp. 11-20.)

Degnan, Theodore E. and Kathleen A. Coyle. "Withholding Provisions Of FIRPTA," **CPAJ**, 1986, Vol. 56, No. 2, pp. 22-27.

Dehne, Carl A. "Needed: A Single Accounting Method For Oil And Gas Producers," **MA**, 1983, Vol. 65, No. 6, pp. 52-58.

Dein, Raymond C. "A Glance Backward At Research In Accounting," **AR**, 1961, Vol. 36, No. 1, pp. 1-8.

Dein, Raymond C. "Original Cost And Public Utility Regulation," **AR**, 1949, Vol. 24, No. 1, pp. 68-80.

Dein, Raymond C. "Price Level Adjustments: Rejoinder To Professor Husband," **AR**, 1956, Vol. 31, No. 1, pp. 58-63.

Dein, Raymond C. "Price-Level Adjustments: Fetish In Accounting," **AR**, 1955, Vol. 30, No. 1, pp. 3-24.

Dein, Raymond C. "The Future Development Of Accounting Theory," **AR**, 1958, Vol. 33, No. 3, pp. 389-400.

Dein, R. C. "Objective Examinations In Elementary Accounting," **AR**, 1942, Vol. 17, No. 2, pp. 101-113.

Deines, Dan S. and David P. Donnelly. "Deferred Income Taxes When Changing To S Corporation," **CPAJ**, 1987, Vol. 57, No. 12, pp. 58-61.

Deines, Dan S. (Ott, Richard L., Dan S. Deines and David P. Donnelly. "The Use Of A Fundamental Practice Set In Intermediate Accounting," **IAE**, 1988, Vol. 3, No. 1, pp. 131-138.)

Deinzer, Harvey T. "Are Leasehold Improvements Taxable Income?," **AR**, 1939, Vol. 14, No. 2, pp. 147-150.

Deinzer, Harvey T. "Explanation Strains In Financial Accounting," **AR**, 1966, Vol. 41, No. 1, pp. 21-31.

Deinzer, Harvey T. "Specialization Or Integration As The Objective Of Graduate Accounting Instruction," **AR**, 1953, Vol. 28, No. 2, pp. 249-257.

Deinzer, Harvey T. "This Treasury-Stock Question," **AR**, 1937, Vol. 12, No. 3, pp. 256-269.

Deinzer, Harvey. "Capital Stock And Surplus: Legal And Accounting Relations," **AR**, 1935, Vol. 10, No. 4, pp. 333-344.

Deitrick, James W. and C. Wayne Alderman. "Interim Reporting Developments: A Step Toward The Auditor-Of-Record Concept," **JAAF**, 1979, Vol. 2, No. 4, pp. 316-328.

Deitrick, James W. and C. Wayne Alderman. "Pension Plans: What Companies Do - And Do Not - Disclose," **MA**, 1980, Vol. 61, No. 10, pp. 24-29.

Deitrick, James W. and Richard H. Tabor. "Improving The Writing Skills Of Accounting Majors: One School's Approach," **AIA**, 1987, Vol. 4, pp. 97-110.

Deitrick, James W. (Alderman, C. Wayne and James W. Deitrick. "Auditors' Perceptions Of Time Budget Pressures And Premature Sign-Offs: A Replication And Extension," **AJPT**, 1981-82, Vol. 1, No. 2, pp. 54-68.)

Deitrick, James W. (Dietrich, J. Richard and James W. Deitrick. "Bond Exchanges In The Airline Industry: Analyzing Public Disclosures," **AR**, 1985, Vol. 60, No. 1, pp. 109-126.)

Deitrick, James W., C. Wayne Alderman and David L. Sayers. "A Profile Of An Accounting Doctoral Program: A Study Of Recent Graduates," **AIA**, 1985, Vol. 2, pp. 69-88.

DeJong, Douglas V. and John H. Smith. "The Determination Of Audit Responsibilities: An Application Of Agency Theory," **AJPT**, 1984-85, Vol. 4, No. 1, pp. 20-34.

DeJong, Douglas V. "Class-Action Privileges And Contingent Legal Fees: Investor And Lawyer Incentives To Litigate And The Effect On Audit Quality," **JAPP**, 1985, Vol. 4, No. 3, pp. 175-200.

DeJong, Douglas V. (Ingram, Robert W. and Douglas V. DeJong. "The Effect Of Regulation On Local Government Disclosure Practices," **JAPP**, 1987, Vol. 6, No. 4, pp. 245-270.)

DeJong, Douglas V., Robert Forsythe and Wilfred C. Uecker. "The Methodology Of Laboratory Markets And Its Implications For Agency Research In Accounting And Auditing," **JAR**, 1985, Vol. 23, No. 2, pp. 753-793.

DeJong, Douglas V., Robert Forsythe, Russell J. Lundholm and Wilfred C. Uecker. "A Laboratory Investigation Of The Moral Hazard Problem In An Agency Relationship." **JAR**, 1985, Vol. 23, Supp., pp. 81-120.

DeLespinasse, Doris. "Writing Letters To Clients: Connecting Textbook Problems And The Real World," **JAED**, 1985, Vol. 3, No. 1, pp. 197-200.

DeLoach, James W., Jr. and David R. Henkel. "New Reasons To Reexamine LIFO," **CA**, 1983, Vol. 1, No. 2, pp. 26-29.

DeLoach, James W., Jr. "LIFO - Some Important Tax Considerations," **CPAJ**, 1978, Vol. 48, No. 3, pp. 38-42.

Delaney, Patrick R., David E. Keyes, Curtis L. Norton and John R. Simon. "An Admission Test For Intermediate Accounting," **AR**, 1979, Vol. 54, No. 1, pp. 155-162.

Delit, Steven Nelson. "Investigation Of Proposed Acquisitions," **CPAJ**, 1977, Vol. 47, No. 12, pp. 17-22.

Delit, Steven N. and Stuart B. Miller. "Watch Your Step-Up: Section 334(b)(2) Liquidations," **CPAJ**, 1981, Vol. 51, No. 11, pp. 44-52.

Dellinger, Roy E. "Bookless Bookkeeping," **MA**, 1971, Vol. 52, No. 11, pp. 31-33.

Deloney, Elise and Clyde L. Posey. "Federal Tax Amnesty: Is It Appropriate?," **CPAJ**, 1987, Vol. 57, No. 7, pp. 38-45.

DeMaagd, Gerald R. and James K. White. "Financing Private Capital With IDBs," **MA**, 1985, Vol. 66, No. 7, pp. 49-52.

DeMario, Joseph R. (Graese, Clifford E. and Joseph R. DeMario. "Revenue Recognition For Long Term Contracts," **JOA**, 1976, Vol. 142, No. 6, pp. 53-59.)

DeMaris, E. Joe. "'Success Indicator' Function Of Income Concept Argues Its Further Development," **AR**, 1963, Vol. 38, No. 1, pp. 37-45.

DeMaris, E. Joe. (Purdue, Richard B. and E. Joe DeMaris. "Accounting In The U.S.S.R.," **JOA**, 1959, Vol. 108, No. 1, pp. 47-57.)

DeMaris, E. J. and Benny R. Copeland. "The Critical Need For Educational Standards In Management Accounting," **CA**, 1984, Vol. 2, No. 1, pp. 47-53.

DeMaris, E. J. and Benny R. Copeland. "Educational Standards For Management Accountants," **JAED**, 1984, Vol. 2, No. 1, pp. 39-53.

DeMoville, Wig. "Understanding Changes In Tax Laws With Variance Analysis," **JATA**, 1988, Vol. 10, No. 1, pp. 99-103.

DeMoville, Wig. "Capital Budgeting In Municipalities," **MA**, 1977, Vol. 59, No. 1, pp. 17-20.

Demarest, Paul W. "Are Labor Unions Accountable?," **MA**, 1968, Vol. 49, No. 12, pp. 37-43.

Dembowski, Sig. "The Management Accountant," **MA**, 1973, Vol. 54, No. 10, pp. 9-12.

Demcak, James A. (Reid, George F. and James A. Demcak. "EDP Audit Implementation With General Purpose Software," **JOA**, 1971, Vol. 132, No. 1, pp. 35-46.)

Deming, John R. "New Guidelines For Extraordinary Items (A Review Of APB Opinion No. 30)," **CPAJ**, 1974, Vol. 44, No. 2, pp. 21-26.

Deming, W. Edwards and T. Nelson Grice. "An Efficient Procedure For Audit Of Accounts Receivable," **MA**, 1970, Vol. 51, No. 9, pp. 17-21.

Deming, W. Edwards. "A View Of The Statistical Method," **AR**, 1944, Vol. 19, No. 3, pp. 254-259.

Deming, W. Edwards. "On A Problem In Standards Of Auditing From The Viewpoint Of Statistical Practice," **JAAF**, 1979, Vol. 2, No. 3, pp. 197-208.

Demirag, Istemi S. "A Review Of The Objectives Of Foreign Currency Translation," **IJAER**, 1987, Vol. 22, No. 2, pp. 69-85.

Demirag, Istemi S. "The Treatment Of Exchange Rates In Internal Performance Evaluation," **ABR**, 1985-86, Vol. 16, No. 62, pp. 157-164.

DeMoville, Wig. "Capital Budgeting In Municipalities," **MA**, 1977, Vol. 59, No. 1, pp. 17-20.

Dempsey, Thomas A. "Lost And Found Department For Advertising Dollars," **MA**, 1967, Vol. 49, No. 4, pp. 51-58.

Dempsey, William A. (Lancioni, Richard A. and William A. Dempsey. "The Critical Role Of Cost Accounting In Distribution Planning And Control," **CA**, 1983, Vol. 1, No. 3, pp. 26-32.)

Demski, Joel S. and David E. M. Sappington. "Delegated Expertise," **JAR**, 1987, Vol. 25, No. 1, pp. 68-89.

Demski, Joel S. and David E. M. Sappington. "Line-Item Reporting, Factor Acquisition, And Subcontracting," **JAR**, 1986, Vol. 24, No. 2, pp. 250-269.

Demski, Joel S. and David M. Kreps. "Models In Managerial Accounting," **JAR**, 1982, Vol. 20, Supp., pp. 117-148.

Demski, Joel S. and Gerald A. Feltham. "Economic Incentives In Budgetary Control Systems," **AR**, 1978, Vol. 53, No. 2, pp. 336-359.

Demski, Joel S. and Gerald A. Feltham. "Forecast Evaluation," **AR**, 1972, Vol. 47, No. 3, pp. 533-548.

Demski, Joel S. and Robert J. Swieringa. "A Cooperative Formulation Of The Audit Choice Problem," **AR**, 1974, Vol. 49, No. 3, pp. 506-513.

Demski, Joel S. "Accounting Research: 1985," **CAR**, 1985-86, Vol. 2, No. 1, pp. 69-75.

Demski, Joel S. "Accounting System Structured On A Linear Programming Model," **AR**, 1967, Vol. 42, No. 4, pp. 701-712.

Demski, Joel S. "An Economic Analysis Of The Chambers' Normative Standard," **AR**, 1976, Vol. 51, No. 3, pp. 653-656.

Demski, Joel S. "Analyzing The Effectiveness Of The Traditional Standard Cost Variance Model," **MA**, 1967, Vol. 49, No. 2, pp. 9-19.

Demski, Joel S. "Choice Among Financial Reporting Alternatives," **AR**, 1974, Vol. 49, No. 2, pp. 221-232.

Demski, Joel S. "Comments On Wilson And Jensen," **AR**, 1983, Vol. 58, No. 2, pp. 347-349.

Demski, Joel S. "Decision-Performance Control," **AR**, 1969, Vol. 44, No. 4, pp. 669-679.

Demski, Joel S. "Implementation Effects Of Alternative Performance Measurement Models In A Multivariable Context," **AR**, 1971, Vol. 46, No. 2, pp. 268-278.

Demski, Joel S. "Predictive Ability Of Alternative Performance Measurement Models," **JAR**, 1969, Vol. 7, No. 1, pp. 96-115.

Demski, Joel S. "Rational Choice Of Accounting Method For A Class Of Partnerships," **JAR**, 1973, Vol. 11, No. 2, pp. 176-190.

Demski, Joel S. "Some Decomposition Results For Information Evaluation," **JAR**, 1970, Vol. 8, No. 2, pp. 178-198.

Demski, Joel S. "Some Observations On Demski's Ex Post Accounting System: A Reply," **AR**, 1968, Vol. 43, No. 4, pp. 672-674.

Demski, Joel S. "The Decision Implementation Interface: Effects Of Alternative Performance Measurement Models," **AR**, 1970, Vol. 45, No. 1, pp. 76-87.

Demski, Joel S. "The General Impossibility Of Normative Accounting Standards," **AR**, 1973, Vol. 48, No. 4, pp. 718-723.

Demski, Joel S. "Uncertainty And Evaluation Based On Controllable Performance," **JAR**, 1976, Vol. 14, No. 2, pp. 230-245.

Demski, Joel S. (Amershi, Amin H., Joel S. Demski and Mark A. Wolfson. "Strategic Behavior And Regulation Research In Accounting," **JAPP**, 1982, Vol. 1, No. 1, pp. 19-32.)

Demski, Joel S. (Amershi, Amin H., Joel S. Demski and John Fellingham. "Sequential Bayesian Analysis In Accounting." **CAR**, 1984-85, Vol. 1, No. 2, pp. 176-192.)

Demski, Joel S. (Antle, Rick and Joel S. Demski. "The Controllability Principle In Responsibility Accounting," **AR**, 1988, Vol. 63, No. 4, pp. 700-718.)

Demski, Joel S. (Baiman, Stanley and Joel S. Demski. "Economically Optimal Performance Evaluation And Control Systems," **JAR**, 1980, Vol. 18, Supp., pp. 184-220.)

Demski, Joel S. (Beaver, William H. and Joel S. Demski. "The Nature Of Income Measurement," **AR**, 1979, Vol. 54, No. 1, pp. 38-46.)

Demski, Joel S. (Beaver, William H. and Joel S. Demski. "The Nature Of Financial Accounting Objectives: A Summary And Synthesis," **JAR**, 1974, Vol. 12, Supp., pp. 170-187.)

Demski, Joel S. (Feltham, Gerald A. and Joel S. Demski. "The Use Of Models In Information Evaluation," **AR**, 1970, Vol. 45, No. 4, pp. 623-640.)

Demski, Joel S., James M. Patell and Mark A. Wolfson. "Decentralized Choice Of Monitoring Systems," **AR**, 1984, Vol. 59, No. 1, pp. 16-34.

Demski, Joel. "Information Improvement Bounds," **JAR**, 1972, vol. 10, No. 1, pp. 58-76.

Demski, Joel. "Optimal Performance Measurement," **JAR**, 1972, Vol. 10, No. 2, pp. 243-258.

Demski, Joel. (Dopuch, Nicholas, Jacob G. Birnberg and Joel Demski. "An Extension Of Standard Cost Variance Analysis." **AR**, 1967, Vol. 42, No. 3, pp. 526-536.)

DeNardo, Stephen and John R. Thornton. "Recruiting: The New Horizon," **JOA**, 1982, Vol. 154, No. 4, pp. 40-49.

Den Hertog, J. Friso. "The Role Of Information And Control Systems In The Process Of Organizational Renewal: Roadblock Or Road Bridge?" No. 1, pp. 29-46.

Denhaan, Alex E. "Dynamic Business Models - A Tool To Meet New Business Challenges," **MA**, 1968, Vol. 49, No. 9, pp. 3-11.

Denhardt, J. G., Jr. "Estate Accounting," **JOA**, 1964, Vol. 117, No. 2, pp. 48-56.

Denhardt, J. G., Jr. "Income In Respect Of A Decedent," **JOA**, 1961, Vol. 112, No. 5, pp. 59-62.

Denholm, Donald H. "Acquisitions - And The Management Accountant," **MA**, 1968, Vol. 50, No. 4, pp. 15-18.

Denker, Dale A. (Diedrich, Andrew J. and Dale A. Denker. "Flexible Budgeting - A Proven Computer Application," **MA**, 1966, Vol. 47, No. 12, pp. 18-24.)

Denning, Karen C. and Kuldeep Shastri. "An Option Pricing Technique For Auditor Review Of Insider Trading," **RIAR**, 1988, Vol. 2, pp. 25-39.

Dennis, David K. (Stephens, Ray G., Jesse F. Dillard and David K. Dennis. "Implications Of Formal Grammars For Accounting Policy Development," **JAPP**, 1985, Vol. 4, No. 2, pp. 123-148.)

Dennis, David M. and Robert M. Keith. "Are Litigation Disclosures Inadequate?," **JOA**, 1981, Vol. 151, No. 3, pp. 54-61.

Dennis, David M. and William L. Stephens. "Recruitment And

Utilization Of Minority Group Members," **JOA**, 1976, Vol. 141, No. 5, pp. 64-73.

Dennis, David M., Jack L. Smith and William J. Ferlita. "The Impact Of ACRS Lives On Deferred Tax Accounting," **MA**, 1986, Vol. 67, No. 9, pp. 39-43.

Dennis, Kenneth C. "Hospitals Must Allocate Bad Debts Properly," **MA**, 1979, Vol. 61, No. 1, pp. 11-14.

Densmore, Robert R. (Coombe, Lloyd W. and Robert R. Densmore. "How Detroit Edison Improves Its Productivity," **MA**, 1982, Vol. 63, No. 11, pp. 50-54.)

Densmore, Seth A. "Special CPA Services For Small Business," **JOA**, 1951, Vol. 92. No. 2, pp. 184-189.

Densmore, Seth. "Statement 23 Makes Auditing More Useful To Small Client," **JOA**, 1952, Vol. 93, No. 5. pp. 557-563.

Dent, Warren T. (Collins, Daniel W. and Warren T. Dent. "A Comparison Of Alternative Testing Methodologies Used In Capital Market Research," **JAR**, 1984, Vol. 22, No. 1, pp. 48-84.)

Dent, Warren T. (Collins, Daniel W. and Warren T. Dent. "The Proposed Elimination Of Full Cost Accounting In The Extractive Petroleum Industry: An Empirical Assessment Of The Market Consequences," **JAEC**, 1979, Vol. 1, No. 1. pp. 3-44.)

Dent, William C. (Homburger, Richard H. and William C. Dent. "Management Accounting Concepts And The Principles Dilemma," **MA**, 1969, Vol. No. 8, pp. 14-15.)

Dent, William C. (Rosenfield, Paul and William C. Dent. "No More Deferred Taxes," **JOA**, 183, Vol. 155, No. 2, pp. 44-55.)

DeOliveira, Fred H. "Management Accounting Techniques For Not-For-Profit Enterprises," **MA**, 1980, Vol. 62, No. 5, pp. 30-34.

DePasquale, Robert J. "Does The Typical Curriculum Prepare You For The CMA Exam?," **MA**, 1985, Vol. 67, No. 5, pp. 44-46.

DePaula, F. R. M. "Financial Organization For 'Management By Exception'," **JOA**, 1952, Vol. 94, No. 3, pp. 318-324.

Depppe, Larry, Don R. Hansen and Stan Jenne. "The 150-Hour Educational Requirement: The History And Message Of The Utah Experience," **ACCHOR**, 1988, Vol. 2, No. 2, pp.53-57.

DeReyna, Ramon Jose, II. "Accounting Achievement In Conventional And Television Classes At The University Of Miami," **AR**, 1959, Vol. 34, No. 4, pp. 651-655.

DeRieux, Jerry S. "The Controversy Over Wage-Price Policies," **MA**, 1972, Vol. 53, No. 8, pp. 17-22.

Derieux, Samuel A. "A GAAP And The Privately Held Company," **Ca**, 1985, No. 3, pp. 29-33.

Dermer, Jerry and Jacob P. Siegel. "The Role Of Behavioral Measures In Accounting For Human Resources," **AR**, 1974, Vol. 49, No. 1, pp. 88-97.

Dermer, Jerry D. "Cognitive Characteristics And The Perceived Importance Of Information," **AR**, 1973, Vol. 48. No. 3, pp. 511-519.,

Dermer, J. D. and J. P. Siegel. "The Role Of Behavioral Measures In Accounting For Human Resources: A Reply." **AR**, 1975, Vol. 50, No. 3, pp. 579-581.

Dermer, J. D. and R. G. Lucas. "The Illusion Of Managerial Control," **AOS**, 1986, Vol. 11, No. 6, pp. 471-482.

Dermer, J. "Control And Organizational Order," **AOS**, 1988, Vol. 13, No. 1, pp. 25-36.

DeRoover, Raymond. "Characteristics Of Bookkeeping Before Paciolo," **AR**, 1938, Vol. 13, No. 2, pp. 144-148.

DeRoover, Raymond. "Early Accounting Problems Of Foreign Exchange," **AR**, 1944, Vol. 19, No. 4, pp. 381-406.

DeRoover, Raymond. "New Perspectives On The History Of Accounting," **AR**, 1955, Vol. 30, No. 3, pp. 405-420.

DeRoover, Raymond. "Paciolo Or Pacioli?," **AR**, 1944, Vol. 19, No. 1, p. 68.

DeRoover, Raymond. "The Lingering Influence Of Medieval Practices," **AR**, 1943, Vol. 18, No. 2, pp. 148-151.

Derscheid, Vincent A., Raymond Telling and G. W. Tonkin. "Nontax Benefits Of The Incorporation Of A Practice," **JOA**, 1977, Vol. 143, No. 1, pp. 70-76.

Derstine, Robert P. and Ronald J. Huefner. "LIFO-FIFO, Accounting Ratios And Market Risk," **JAR**, 1974. Vol. 12, No. 2. pp. 216-234.

Dery, D. "Erring And Learning: An Organizational Analysis," **AOS**, 1982. Vol. 7, No. 3, pp. 217-224.

DeSanctis, Guy. "VAT: Harmful To Our Economic Health," **MA**, 1986, Vol. 68, No. 6, pp. 58-61.

Desai, Harsha B. (Singhvi, Surendra S. and Harsha B. Desai. "An Empirical Analysis Of The Quality Of Corporate Financial Disclosure," **AR**, 1971, Vol. 46, No. 1, pp. 129-138.)

Desai, Harsha B. (Singhvi, Surendra S. and Harsha B. Desai. "The Quality Of Corporate Financial Disclosure: A Reply," **AR**, 1972, Vol. 47, No. 3, pp. 585-586.)

Deskins, James Wesley, Frederick L. Neumann and Lawrence Revsine. "A Research Methodology Course For Accountants," **AR**, 1970, Vol. 45, No. 4, pp. 789-795.

Deskins, James Wesley. "Management Services And Management Decisions," **JOA**, 1965, Vol. 119, No. 1, pp. 50-54.

Deskins, James Wesley. (Summers. Edward L. and James Wesley Deskins. "A Classification Schema Of Methods For Reporting Effects Of Resource Price Changes (With Technical Appendix)," **IJAER**, 1970, Vol. 6, No. 1, pp. 101-120.)

Deskins, James Wesley. (Summers. Edward L. and James Wesley Deskins. "A Classification Schema Of Methods For Reporting Effects Of Resource Price Changes," **JAR**, 1970, Vol. 8, No. 1, pp. 113-117.)

Deskins, Jams Wesley. "On The Nature Of The Public Interest," **AR**, 1965, Vol. 40, No. 1. pp. 76-81.

Deskins, J. W. (Griffin, C. H. and J. W. Deskins. "Development And Application Of Accounting Theory," **ABR**, 1971-72, Vol. 2, No. 8, pp. 308-315.)

DeThomas, Arthur R. and William B. Fredenberger. "Accounting Needs Of Very Small Businesses," **CPAJ**, 1985, Vol. 55. No. 10, pp. 14-25.

Detweiler, John H., Sean O. Vessey and Arthur J. King. "A Model For Computing Shipyard Overhead," **JCA**, 1987, Vol. 4, No. 1, pp. 71-93.

Deur, Jan L. (Leong, Kenneth C. and Jan L. Deur. "Financial Planning And Accounting Control In Telephone Companies," **MA**, 1980, Vol. 62, No. 1, pp. 19-22.)

Deutsch, Richard. "Cases Where Receivables As Tax-Saving Device Failed," **JOA**, 1952, Vol. 94, No. 5, pp. 576-579.

Dev, Susan. "Linear Programming Dual Prices In Management Accounting And Their Interpretation," **ABR**, 1978-79, Vol. 9, No. 33, pp. 11-18.

Dev, Susan. "Problems In Interpreting Prospectus Profit Forecasts," **ABR**, 1972-73, Vol. 3, No. 10, pp. 110-116.

Dev, Susan. "Statements Of Company Prospects," **ABR**, 1973-74, Vol. 4, No. 16, pp. 270-274.

DeValk, Harold G. "The Making Of A CPA Firm," **JOA**, 1972, Vol. 133, No. 2, pp. 31-35.

Devine, Carl Thomas. "Cost Accounting And Pricing Policies," **AR**, 1950. Vol. 25, No. 4, pp. 384-389.

Devine, Carl Thomas. "Depreciation Accounting In Utilities," **AR**, 1943, Vol. 18, No. 1, pp. 1-8.

Devine, Carl Thomas. "Institutional Overhead On Government Projects," **AR**, 1945, Vol. 20, No. 2, pp. 210-215.

Devine, Carl Thomas. "Integration Of Accounting And Economics In The Elementary Accounting Course," **AR**, 1952, Vol. 27. No. 3, pp. 329-333.

Devine, Carl Thomas. "Research Methodology And Accounting Theory Formation," **AR**, 1960, Vol. 35, No. 3, pp.387-399.

Devine, Carl T. "Deferred Maintenance And Improper Depreciation Procedures," **AR**, 1947, Vol. 22, No. 1, pp. 38-44.

Devine, Carl T. "Depreciation And Income Measurement," **AR**, 1944, Vol. 19, No. 1, pp. 39-46.

Devine, Carl T. "The Rule Of Conservatism Reexamined," **JAR**, 1963, Vol. 1, No. 2, pp. 127-138.

Devine, Carl. "Depreciation Policy: Repairs And Replacements," **AR**, 1941, Vol. 16. No. 4, pp. 385-390.

Devine, Carl. "Professional Responsibilities - An Empirical Suggestion," **JAR**, 1966, Vol. 4, Supp., pp. 160-176.

Devlin, Gerald W. "Internal Control Is Not Optional," **MA**, 1975, Vol. 57, No. 2, pp. 49-51.

Devon, Philip C. and Richard Kolodny. "Price-Level Reporting And Its Value To Investors," **ABR**, 1978-79, Vol. 9, No. 33, pp. 19-24.

Devore, Malcolm M. "Compatibility Of Auditing And Management Services: A Viewpoint From Within The Profession," **JOA**, 1967. Vol. 124, No. 6, pp. 36-39.

Devore, Malcolm M. "Reporting On Cash-Basis Statements," **JOA**, 1959. Vol. 107, No. 5, pp. 58-62.

Dew, R. Beresford and Kenneth P. Gee. "Frequency Of Performance Reporting And Managers' Reference For Control - A Note," **ABR**, 1971-72, Vol. 2, No. 7, pp. 234-236.

DeWelt, Robert. "Using Standard Costs With LIFO And FIFO," **MA**, 1976, Vol. 57, No. 11, pp. 25-30.

DeWelt, Robert L. "Labor Measurement And Control," **MA**, 1976, Vol. 58. No. 4, pp. 26-32.

DeWelt, Robert L. "Replacement Cost - Another Nightmare For Accountants," **MA**, 1977, Vol. 59, No. 4, pp. 17-22.

DeWitt, Frank. "Measuring Management Performance," **MA**, 1972, Vol. 54, No. 5, pp. 18-22.

Dewberry, J. Terry. "A New Approach To Business Combinations," **MA**, 1979, Vol. 61, No. 5, pp. 44-51.

Dewhirst, John F. "A Conceptual Approach To Pension Accounting," **AR**, 1971, Vol. 46, No. 2, pp. 365-373.

Dexter, Albert S. (Benbasat, Izak and Albert S. Dexter. "Individual Differences In The Use Of Decision Support Aids," **JAR**, 1982, Vol. 20, No. 1, pp. 1-11.)

Dexter, Albert S. (Benbasat, Izak and Albert S. Dexter. "Value And Events Approaches To Accounting: An Experimental Evaluation," **AR**, 1979, Vol. 54, No. 4, pp. 735-749.)

Dexter, Daniel S. (Krogstad, Jack L. and Daniel S. Dexter. "National Automated Accounting Research System - A Challenge For Auditing Education," **AR**, 1979, Vol. 54, No. 3, pp. 604-608.)

Dhaliwal, Dan S. and Albert A. Schepanski. "On The Use Of Positive Economic Theory To Explain The Choice Of Accounting Methods To Financial Accounting Students," **JAED**, 1984, Vol. 2, No. 2. pp. 89-96.

Dhaliwal, Dan S. and Eric H. Sorensen. "On Accounting Information And Municipal Bond Interest Cost: A Comment," **JAPP**, 1985, Vol. 4, No. 3. pp. 233-239.

Dhaliwal, Dan S. "Cost Allocation And Resource Requirement Planning: An Alternative Approach," **ABR**, 1978-79, Vol. 9, No. 34, pp. 163-168.

Dhaliwal, Dan S. "Improving The Quality Of Corporate Financial Disclosure," **ABR**, 1979-80, Vol. 10, No. 40, pp. 385-392.

Dhaliwal, Dan S. "Measurement Of Financial Leverage In The Presence Of Unfunded Pension Obligations," **AR**, 1986, Vol. 61, No. 4, pp. 651-661.

Dhaliwal, Dan S. "The Effect Of The Firm's Capital Structure On The Choice Of Accounting Methods," **AR**, 1980. Vol. 55, No. 1, pp. 78-84.

Dhaliwal, Dan S. (Collins, D. W., M. S. Rozeff and D. S. Dhaliwal. "The Economic Determinants Of The Market Reaction To Proposed Mandatory Accounting Changes In The Oil And Gas Industry: A Cross-Sectional Analysis," **JAEC**,1981,Vol. 3,No. 1,pp.37-71.)

Dhaliwal, Dan S. (Doran, B. Michal, D. W. Collins and D. S. Dhaliwal. "The Information Of Historical Cost Earnings Relative To Supplemental Reserve-Based Accounting Data In The Extractive Petroleum Industry," **AR**, 1988, Vol.

63, No. 3, pp. 389-413.)

Dhaliwal, Dan S. (Johnson, W. Bruce and Dan S. Dhaliwal. "LIFO Abandonment," **JAR**, 1988, Vol. 26, No. 2, pp. 236-272.)

Dhaliwal, Dan S., Fratern M. Mboya and Russell M. Barefield. "Utilization Of SFAS No. 14 Disclosures In Assessing Operating Risk," **JAPP**, 1983, Vol. 2, No. 2, pp. 83-98.

Dhaliwal, Dan S., Gerald Salamon and E. Dan Smith. "The Effect Of Owner Versus Management Control On The Choice Of Accounting Methods," **JAEC**, 1982, Vol. 4, No. 1, pp. 41-53.

Dharan, Bala G. "Empirical Identification Procedures For Earnings Models," **JAR**, 1983, Vol. 21, No. 1, pp. 256-270.

Dharan, Bala G. "Expectation Models And Potential Information Content Of Oil And Gas Reserve Value Disclosures," **AR**, 1984, Vol. 59, No. 2, pp. 199-217.

Dharan, Bala G. "Identification And Estimation Issues For A Causal Earnings Model," **JAR**, 1983, Vol. 21, No. 1, pp. 18-41.

Dharan, Bala G. "The Effect Of Sales And Collection Disclosures On Cash Flow Forecasting And Income Smoothing," **CAR**, 1986-87, Vol. 3, No. 2, pp. 445-459.

Dheeriya, Prakash L. "A Case For Special Drawing Rights As A Unit Of Account," **IJAER**, 1985, Vol. 21, No. 1, pp. 71-87.

Dhingra, H. L. "The Impact Of Accounting Variables On Stock Market Measures Of Risk," **ABR**, 1981-82, Vol. 12, No. 47, pp. 193-205.

Diacogniannis, George P. "Some Empirical Evidence On The Intertemporal Stationarity Of Security Return Distributions," **ABR**, 1986-87, Vol. 17, No. 65, pp. 43-48.

Diamond, Lee G. and Allan S. Oxman. "Is There Life Insurance After Retirement?," **MA**, 1981, Vol. 62, No. 7, pp. 23-26.

Diamond, Louis H. "Funding Liability Under Union Pension Plans," **JOA**, 1975, Vol. 140, No. 3, pp. 74-79.

Diamond, Michael A. and Bill N. Schwartz. "Dollar-Value Lifo For Manufacturers or Processors," **CPAJ**, 1981, Vol. 51, No. 7, pp. 31-37.

Diamond, Michael A. (Arnold, Jerry L., Alan A. Cherry, Michael A. Diamond and James A. Walker. "Small Business: An Area Ripe For Practice Development," **JOA**, 1984, Vol. 158, No. 2, pp. 74-83.)

Diamond, Michael A. (Manegold, James G., Jerry L. Arnold and Michael A. Diamond. "SEC Form S-18: A Boon To Small Business," **JOA**, 1986, Vol. 161, No. 5, pp. 102-108.)

Diamond, Michael A. (Morsicato, Helen G. and Michael A. Diamond. "An Approach To 'Environmentalizing' MNE Performance Evaluation Systems," **IJAER**, 1980, Vol. 16, No. 1, pp. 247-266.)

Diamond, Michael A. (Schwartz, Bill Neal and Michael A. Diamond. "Is 'Dollar-Value' LIFO For You?," **CPAJ**, 1980, Vol. 50, No. 7, pp. 33-40.)

Diamond, Michael A. (Walendowski, George and Michael A. Diamond. "RRA - Will It Work?," **MA**, 1980, Vol. 61, No. 9, pp. 21-25.)

Dias, Francisco J. B. (Otley, David T. and Francisco J. B. Dias. "Accounting Aggregation And Decision-Making Performance: An Experimental Investigation," **JAR**, 1982, Vol. 20, No. 1, pp. 171-188.)

Dicke, Howard W. "Management Accounting For Research And Development Projects," **MA**, 1969, Vol. 50, No. 9, pp. 40-43.

Dicke, Howard W. "Mini-System Data Processing," **MA**, 1971, Vol. 53, No. 4, pp. 21-25.

Dickens, Robert L. and John O. Blackburn. "Holding Gains On Fixed Assets: An Element Of Business Income?," **AR**, 1964, Vol. 39, No. 2, pp. 312-329.

Dickens, Robert L. and Thomas F. Keller. "The Auditor's Responsibility For His Opinion," **JOA**, 1963, Vol. 115, No. 3, pp. 41-48.

Dickens, Robert L. "A Sabbatical Year In Public Accounting," **AR**, 1956, Vol. 31, No. 4, pp. 617-620.

Dickens, Robert L. "Non-Commercial Curriculum For Accounting Majors," **AR**, 1952, Vol. 27, No. 4, pp. 502-505.

Dickens, Thomas L. and Edward J. Schnee. "Are Sec. 333 Liquidations Still Alive?," **CPAJ**, 1987, Vol. 57, No. 9, pp. 54-63.

Dickens, Thomas L. and Robert M. Harper, Jr. "The Use Of Microcomputers In Intermediate Accounting: Effects On Student Achievement And Attitudes," **JAED**, 1986, Vol. 4, No. 1, pp. 127-146.

Dickens, Thomas L. (Cash, L. Stephen and Thomas L. Dickens. "Coping With New Auto Record-Keeping Rules," **MA**, 1985, Vol. 67, No. 2, pp. 32-39.)

Dickerhoof, Wilford L. "Cutting Costs...Not Worth," **MA**, 1972, Vol. 54, No. 2, pp. 20-22.

Dickerson, W. E. and J. Weldon Jones. "Some Observations On The Statement Of Application Of Funds," **AR**, 1931, Vol. 6, No. 4, pp. 277-281.

Dickerson, W. E. and J. Weldon Jones. "Observations On 'The Equity Method' And Intercorporate Relationships," **AR**, 1933, Vol. 8, No. 3, pp. 200-208.

Dickerson, W. E. "Averaging Income For Tax Purposes," **JOA**, 1958, Vol. 105, No. 5, pp. 27-33.

Dickerson, W. E. "Tax Planning And Tax Research In The Tax Accounting Courses," **AR**, 1957, Vol. 32, No. 1, pp. 98-100.

Dickerson, W. E. "The Courses In Tax Accounting," **AR**, 1950, Vol. 25, No. 2, pp. 173-179.

Dickhaut, John W. and Ian R. C. Eggleton. "An Examination Of The Processes Underlying Comparative Judgments Of Numerical Stimuli," **JAR**, 1975, Vol. 13, No. 1, pp. 38-

72.

Dickhaut, John W. and John C. Lere. "Comparison Of Accounting Systems And Heuristics In Selecting Economic Optima," **JAR**, 1983, Vol. 21, No. 2, pp. 495-513.

Dickhaut, John W. "Alternative Information Structures And Probability Revisions," **AR**, 1973, Vol. 48, No. 1, pp. 61-79.

Dickhaut, John W. (Magee, Robert P. and John W. Dickhaut. "Effects Of Compensation Plans On Heuristics In Cost Variance Investigations," **JAR**, 1978, Vol. 16, No. 2, pp. 294-314.)

Dickhaut, John. (Eger, Carol and John Dickhaut. "An Examination Of The Conservative Information Processing Bias In An Accounting Framework," **JAR**, 1982, Vol. 20, No. 2, Part II, pp. 711-723.)

Dickinson, J. P. "Cost-Volume-Profit Analysis Under Uncertainty," **JAR**, 1974, Vol. 12, No. 1, pp. 182-187.

Diedrich, Andrew J. and Dale A. Denker. "Flexible Budgeting - A Proven Computer Application," **MA**, 1966, Vol. 47, No. 12, pp. 18-24.

Dierkes, M. and A. B. Antal. "The Usefulness And Use Of Social Reporting Information," **AOS**, 1985, Vol. 10, No. 1, pp. 29-34.

Dierkes, M. and L. E. Preston. "Corporate Social Accounting - Reporting For The Physical Environment: A Critical Review And Implementation Proposal," **AOS**, 1977, Vol. 2, No. 1, pp. 3-22.

Dierkes, M. "Corporate Social Reporting In Germany: Conceptual Developments And Practical Experience," **AOS**, 1979, Vol. 4, No. 1/2, pp. 87-108.

Dierks, Paul A. "Applying Cost Accounting To Transit System Financing," **MA**, 1978, Vol. 60, No. 6, pp. 20-23.

Dierks, Paul A. (Johnson, Patricia L. and Paul A. Dierks. "What Are Women Accountants Really Like?," **MA**, 1982, Vol. 63, No. 9, pp. 25-28.)

Dietemann, Gerard J. "Evaluating Multinational Performance Under FAS No. 8," **MA**, 1980, Vol. 61, No. 11, pp. 49-56.

Dietemann, Gerard J. "Measuring Productivity In A Service Company," **MA**, 1988, Vol. 69, No. 8, pp. 48-54.

Dieter, Richard. "Is Lessee Accounting Working?," **CPAJ**, 1979, Vol. 49, No. 8, pp. 13-20.

Dieter, Richard. (Wyatt, Arthur R., Richard Dieter and John E. Stewart. "Tax Allocation Revisited," **CPAJ**, 1984, Vol. 54, No. 3, pp. 10-19.)

Dietrich, J. Richard and James W. Deitrick. "Bond Exchanges In The Airline Industry: Analyzing Public Disclosures," **AR**, 1985, Vol. 60, No. 1, pp. 109-126.

Dietrich, J. Richard and Robert S. Kaplan. "Empirical Analysis Of The Commercial Loan Classification Decision," **AR**, 1982, Vol. 57, No. 1, pp. 18-38.

Dietrich, J. Richard. "Effects Of Early Bond Refundings: An Empirical Investigation Of Security Returns," **JAEC**, 1984, Vol. 6, No. 1, pp. 67-96.

Dietrich, J. Richard. (Harrison, Walter T., Jr., Lawrence A. Tomassini and J. Richard Dietrich. "The Use Of Control Groups In Capital Market Research," **JAR**, 1983, Vol. 21, No. 1, pp. 65-77.)

Dietrich, J. Richard. (Olsen, Chris and J. Richard Dietrich. "Vertical Information Transfers: The Association Between Retailers' Sales Announcements And Suppliers' Security Returns," **JAR**, 1985, Vol. 23, Supp., pp. 144-166.)

Dietrich, J. Richard. (Thompson, Robert B., II, Chris Olsen and J. Richard Dietrich. "Attributes Of News About Firms: An Analysis Of Firm-Specific News Reported In The Wall Street Journal Index," **JAR**, 1987, Vol. 25, No. 2, pp. 245-274.)

Dietrich, J. Richard. (Thompson, Robert B., II, Chris Olsen and J. Richard Dietrich. "The Influence Of Estimation Period News Events On Standardized Market Model Prediction Errors," **AR**, 1988, Vol. 63, No. 3, pp. 448-471.)

Dietrich, Richard and Roman Weil. "Partial Rank Linear Management Information Systems," **AR**, 1974, Vol. 49, No. 4, pp. 846-851.

Dietz, Devon D. and John D. Keane. "Integrating Distributed Processing Within A Central Environment," **MA**, 1980, Vol. 62, No. 5, pp. 43-47.

DiLorenzo, Louis P. and Charles M. Alexander. "Employer's Responsibilities Under 1986 Immigration Act And COBRA," **CPAJ**, 1988, Vol. 58, No. 5, pp. 32-39.

Dilbeck, Harold R. (Seiler, Robert E. and Harold R. Dilbeck. "Latin America - A Challenge In Developmental Assistance," **JOA**, 1967, Vol. 124, No. 4, pp. 46-50.)

Dill, S. Leland and Donald L. Adams. "Automated Auditing," **JOA**, 1964, Vol. 117, No. 5, pp. 54-59.

Dillard, Jesse F. and Daniel L. Jensen. "The Auditor's Report: An Analysis Of Opinion," **AR**, 1983, Vol. 58, No. 4, pp. 787-798.

Dillard, Jesse F. and James Jiambalvo. "Expectancy Theory In A Budgetary Setting: A Comment," **AR**, 1979, Vol. 54, No. 3, pp. 630-634.

Dillard, Jesse F. (Ballinger, Eddward and Jesse F. Dillard. "The Foreign Corrupt Practices Act," **CPAJ**, 1980, Vol. 50, No. 2, pp. 37-46.)

Dillard, Jesse F. (Behling, Orlando and Jesse F. Dillard. "Accounting: The Intuitive Challenge," **ACCHOR**, 1987, Vol. 1, No. 2, pp. 35-42.)

Dillard, Jesse F. (Shank, John K., Jesse F. Dillard and Richard J. Murdock. "CPA's Attitudes Toward 'Subject To' Opinions," **CPAJ**, 1978, Vol. 48, No. 4, pp. 43-47.)

Dillard, Jesse F. (Stephens, Ray G., Jesse F. Dillard and David K. Dennis. "Implications Of Formal Grammars For Accounting Policy Development," **JAPP**, 1985, Vol. 4, No. 2, pp. 123-148.)

Dillard, Jesse. (Bailey, Andrew D., Jr., Karl Hackenbrack,

Prabuddha De, and Jesse Dillard. "Artificial Intelligence, Cognitive Science, And Computational Modeling In Auditing Research: A Research Approach," **JIS**, 1987, Vol. 1, No. 2, pp. 20-40.)

Dillard, J. F. and K. R. Ferris. "Sources Of Professional Staff Turnover In Public Accounting Firms: Some Further Evidence," **AOS**, 1979, Vol. 4, No. 3, pp. 179-186.

Dillard, J. F. "A Longitudinal Evaluation Of An Occupational Goal-Expectancy Model In Professional Accounting Organizations," **AOS**, 1981, Vol. 6, No. 1, pp. 17-26.

Dillard, J. F. "Cognitive Science And Decision Making Research In Accounting," **AOS**, 1984, Vol. 9, No. 3/4, pp. 343-354.

Dillard, J. F. "Valance - Instrumentality - Expectancy Model Validation Using Selected Accounting Groups," **AOS**, 1979, Vol. 4, No. 1/2, pp. 31-38.

Dillard, J. F. (Ferris, K. R., J. F. Dillard and L. Nethercott. "A Comparison Of V-I-E Model Predictions: A Cross-National Study In Professional Accounting Firms," **AOS**, 1980, Vol. 5, No. 4, pp. 361-368.)

Dillavou, E. R. "Comments On Is Appreciation Available For Dividends," **AR**, 1930, Vol. 5, No. 1, pp. 22-26.

Dillavou, E. R. "Desirable Legal Changes In Holding Company Legislation," **AR**, 1933, Vol. 8, No. 1, pp. 43-50.

Dillavou, E. R. "Employee Stock Options," **AR**, 1945, Vol. 20, No. 3, pp. 320-326.

Dillaway, Manson P. "A Tax-Planning Approach For Teaching Corporate Distributions," **IAE**, 1984, No. 1, pp. 111-120.

Dillaway, Manson P. (O'Neil, Cherie J., Donald V. Saftner and Manson P. Dillaway. "Premature Withdrawals From Individual Retirement Accounts: A Breakeven Analysis," **JATA**, 1983, Vol. 4, No. 2, pp. 35-43.)

Dillaway, M. Pete. (O'Neil, Cherie J., Donald V. Saftner and M. Pete Dillaway. "Reply To 'Comment On Premature Withdrawals From Individual Retirement Accounts: A Breakeven Analysis'," **JATA**, 1984, Vol. 6, No. 1, pp. 77-80.)

Dille, Robert J. "Think Metric," **MA**, 1971, Vol. 52, No. 8, pp. 51-52.

Dilley, David R. "Accounting Problems Warranting Additional Research," **AR**, 1960, Vol. 35, No. 2, pp. 288-298.

Dilley, David R. "Professional Writing - Why And How," **JOA**, 1963, Vol. 116, No. 2, pp. 59-65.

Dilley, David R. (Dilley, Merrill B. and David R. Dilley. "College Accounting Courses - 1963," **AR**, 1963, Vol. 38, No. 3, pp. 629-632.)

Dilley, David R. (Dilley, Merrill B. and David R. Dilley. "College Accounting Courses - 1964," **AR**, 1964, Vol. 39, No. 4, pp. 1050-1053.)

Dilley, Merrill B. and David R. Dilley. "College Accounting Courses - 1963," **AR**, 1963, Vol. 38, No. 3, pp. 629-632.

Dilley, Merrill B. and David R. Dilley. "College Accounting Courses - 1964," **AR**, 1964, Vol. 39, No. 4, pp. 1050-1053.

Dilley, Merrill B. "Innovations In Teaching Elementary Accounting," **AR**, 1936, Vol. 11, No. 1, pp. 79-82.

Dilley, Merrill B. "Textbooks Used In Accounting Courses," **AR**, 1967, Vol. 42, No. 4, pp. 800-802.

Dilley, Merrill B. "What Happens To Accounting Majors?," **AR**, 1961, Vol. 36, No. 1, pp. 121-123.

Dilley, Steven and Dennis J. Gaffney. "The Individual Income Tax Computation," **CPAJ**, 1978, Vol. 48, No. 11, pp. 19-23.

Dilley, Steven and John J. Wheatley. "Tax Considerations In Research Grants To Faculty," **AR**, 1977, Vol. 52, No. 4, pp. 915-924.

Dilley, Steven and Joseph M. Kauffman. "The Tax Effects Of Disposing Of A 50 Percent Interest In A Partnership," **CPAJ**, 1978, Vol. 48, No. 7, pp. 23-27.

Dilley, Steven C. and James C. Young. "Brother-Sister Corporations: A Grid Analysis," **CPAJ**, 1984, Vol. 54, No. 1, pp. 10-21.

Dilley, Steven C. and Jerry J. Weygandt. "Measuring Social Responsibility: An Empirical Test," **JOA**, 1973, Vol. 136, No. 3, pp. 62-70.

Dilley, Steven C. "Expanded Scope Audits - Untapped Opportunities?," **CPAJ**, 1975, Vol. 45, No. 12, pp. 30-35.

Dilley, Steven C. "Practical Approaches To Social Accounting," **CPAJ**, 1975, Vol. 45, No. 2, pp. 17-22.

Dilley, Steven C. (Anthony, Joseph H. and Steven C. Dilley. "The Tax Basis Financial Reporting Alternative For Nonpublic Firms," **AH**, 1988, Vol. 2, No. 3, pp. 41-47.)

Dilley, Steven C. (Jamison, Robert W. and Steven C. Dilley. "Subchapter S In Transition," **JATA**, 1984, Vol. 6, No. 1, pp. 36-47.)

Dilley, Steven C. (Jamison, Robert W. and Steven C. Dilley. "Subchapter S In Transition: A Reply And Extension," **JATA**, 1985, Vol. 7, No. 1, pp. 80-88.)

Dilley, Steven C. (Mohr, Rosanne M. and Steven C. Dilley. "Current Cost And ACRS Depreciation Expense: A Comparison," **AR**, 1984, Vol. 59, No. 4, pp. 690-701.)

Dilley, Steven C., Randall B. Hayes and Paul Steinbart. "Development Of A Paradigm For Applied Accounting Research: A Way Of Coping With Subject-Matter Complexity," **AR**, 1983, Vol. 58, No. 2, pp. 405-416.

Dillon, Gadis J. "Allocation And Apportionment Under Reg. 1.861-8," **CPAJ**, 1980, Vol. 50, No. 12, pp. 33-38.

Dillon, Gadis J. "Corporate Asset Revaluations: 1925-1934," **AHJ**, 1979, Vol. 6, No. 1, pp. 1-15.

Dillon, Gadis J. "Getting The Most From Your Forecasting System," **MA**, 1984, Vol. 65, No. 10, pp. 28-32.

Dillon, Gadis J. "The Business Combination Process," **AR**, 1981, Vol. 56, No. 2, pp. 395-399.

Dillon, Gadis J. "The Discount Rate And Lease-Related

Expense," **CPAJ**, 1979, Vol. 49, No. 11, pp. 37-41.

Dillon, Gadis J. (Poe, C. Douglas, Gadis J. Dillon and Kenneth Day. "Replacing Fixed Assets In The Construction Industry," **MA**, 1988, Vol. 70, No. 2, pp. 39-43.)

Dillon, Ray D. and John F. Nash. "The True Relevance Of Relevant Costs," **AR**, 1978, Vol. 53, No. 1, pp. 11-17.

Dillon, Ray D. and J. William Tillett. "Containing The Costs Of Health Care," **JOA**, 1985, Vol. 159, No. 3, pp. 86-95.

Dillon, Ray D., Betty C. Horn and Ernest R. Larkins. "More Value From Fringe Benefit Plans," **CPAJ**, 1986, Vol. 56, No. 11, pp. 40-57.

Dillon, Ray D., Lloyd L. Byars, Craig E. Aronoff and Gale D. Eidson. "The CPA Firm's 'Mission'," **JOA**, 1985, Vol. 159, No. 6, pp. 70-78.

Dillon, Ray D., William R. Feldhaus and Rod P. Farrell. "A Special Area Of Service: Risk Management," **JOA**, 1984, Vol. 157, No. 2, pp. 50-59.

Dillon, Ray, Rodney G. Alsup and Kel-Ann Eyler. "Telecommunications Costs - How To Identify, Analyze, And Control Them," **MA**, 1988, Vol. 70, No. 2, pp. 50-53.

Dilts, David M. and Grant W. Russell. "Accounting For The Factory Of The Future," **MA**, 1985, Vol. 66, No. 10, pp. 34-40.

Dinius, Sara H. and Robert B. Rogow. "Application Of The Delphi Method In Identifying Characteristics Big Eight Firms Seek In Entry-Level Accountants," **JAED**, 1988, Vol. 6. No. 1, pp. 83-101.

Dinius, Sara H. "A Matrix Solution To Process Cost Problems," **IAE**, 1987, Vol. 2, No. 1, pp. 44-56.

Dinman, Robert. "Accounting Machines And The Accounting Curriculum," **AR**, 1953, Vol. 28, No. 4. pp. 577-580.

Dinman, Robert. "Orientation And Visual Aids In Teaching Of Auditing," **AR**, 1951, Vol. 26, No. 3, pp. 321-326.

Dinman, Robert. "Visual Aids Assistance Available," **AR**, 1952, Vol. 27, No. 2, pp. 246-247.

Dino, Lori W. (Dino, Richard N. and Lori W. Dino. "A Sure-Fire Method To Improve Budget Cycling," **MA**, 1980, Vol. 61, No. 7, pp. 34-41.)

Dino, Richard N. and Lori W. Dino. "A Sure-Fire Method To Improve Budget Cycling," **MA**, 1980, Vol. 61, No. 7, pp. 34-41.

Dionise, Robert V. "Differential Cost Concept: Applied To Analysis Of Yield Variances," **MA**, 1971, Vol. 52, No. 7, pp. 36-38.

Dise, Joseph C. "How To Conduct A Training Program For New Staff Assistants," **JOA**, 1950, Vol. 90, No. 2, pp. 132-135.

Dirsmith, Mark and J. Edward Ketz. "A Fifty-Cent Test: An Approach To Teaching Integrity," **AIA**, 1987, Vol. 5, pp. 129-142.

Dirsmith, Mark W. and John P. McAllister. "The Organic Vs. The Mechanistic Audit," **JAAF**, 1982, Vol. 5, No. 3, pp. 214-228.

Dirsmith, Mark W. and John P. McAllister. "The Organic Vs. The Mechanistic Audit: Problems And Pitfalls (Part II)," **JAAF**, 1982, Vol. 6, No. 1, pp. 60-74.

Dirsmith, Mark W. and Mark A. Covaleski. "Practice Management Issues In Public Accounting Firms," **JAAF**, 1985, Vol. 9, No. 1, pp. 5-21.

Dirsmith, Mark W. "Obedience In The Classroom," **JAED**, 1983, Vol. 1, No. 2, pp. 41-50.

Dirsmith, Mark W. (Covaleski, Mark A., Mark W. Dirsmith and Stephen F. Jablonsky. "Traditional And Emergent Theories Of Budgeting: An Empirical Analysis," **JAPP**, 1985, Vol. 4. No. 4. pp. 277-300.)

Dirsmith, Mark W. (Covaleski, Mark A. and Mark W. Dirsmith. "Social Expectations And Accounting Practices In The Health Sector," **RIGNA**, 1986, Vol. 2, pp. 119-134.)

Dirsmith, Mark W. (Covaleski, Mark A., Mark W. Dirsmith and Clinton E. White. "Economic Consequences: The Relationship Between Financial Reporting And Strategic Planning. Mgmt. And Oper. Control Decisions," **CAR**, 1986-87, Vol. 3. No. 2. pp. 408-429.)

Dirsmith, Mark W. (Ferrara, William L., James B. Thies and Mark W. Dirsmith. "The Lease-Purchase Decision," **MA**, 1980, Vol. 61, No. 11, pp. 57-58.)

Dirsmith, Mark W. (Jablonsky, Stephen F. and Mark W. Dirsmith. "Is Financial Reporting Influencing Internal Decision Making?," **MA**, 1979, Vol. 61, No. 1, pp. 40-45.)

Dirsmith, Mark W. (McAllister, John P. and Mark W. Dirsmith. "How The Client's Business Environment Affects The Audit," **JOA**, 1982, Vol. 153, No. 2, pp. 68-74.)

Dirsmith, Mark W., J. Edward Ketz and Ronald J. Teichman. "Vertical And Lateral Considerations Of Undergraduate Accounting Honors Programs," **AIA**, 1986, Vol. 3, pp. 301-322.

Dirsmith, Mark W., Mark A. Covaleski and John P. McAllister. "Of Paradigms And Metaphors In Auditing Thought," **CAR**, 1985-86, Vol. 2, No. 1, pp. 46-68.

Dirsmith, M. W. and B. L. Lewis. "The Effect Of External Reporting On Managerial Decision Making: Some Antecedent Conditions," **AOS**, 1982, Vol. 7, No. 4, pp. 319-336.

Dirsmith, M. W. and M. A. Covaleski. "Informal Communications, Nonformal Communications And Mentoring In Public Accounting Firms," **AOS**, 1985, Vol. 10, No. 2, pp. 149-170.

Dirsmith, M. W. and S. F. Jablonsky. "MBO, Political Rationality And Information Inductance," **AOS**, 1979, Vol. 4. No. 1/2, pp. 39-52.

Dirsmith, M. W. (Covaleski, M. A. and M. W. Dirsmith. "The Budgetary Process Of Power And Politics," **AOS**, 1986, Vol. 11, No. 3, pp. 193-214.)

Dirsmith, M. W. (Covaleski, M. A. and M. W. Dirsmith. "The Use Of Budgetary Symbols In The Political Arena: An

Historically Informed Field Study," **AOS**, 1988, Vol. 13, No. 1, pp. 1-24.)

Dirsmith, M. W. (Covaleski, M. A. and M. W. Dirsmith. "Budgeting As A Means For Control And Loose Coupling," **AOS**, 1983, Vol. 8, No. 4, pp. 323-340.)

Dirsmith, M. W. (Jablonsky, S. F. and M. W. Dirsmith. "The Pattern Of PPB Rejection: Something About Organizations, Something About PPB," **AOS**, 1978, Vol. 3, No. 3/4, pp. 215-226.)

Dirsmith, M. W. (Williams, D. D. and M. W. Dirsmith. "The Effects Of Audit Technology On Auditor Efficiency: Auditing And The Timeliness Of Client Earnings Announcements," **AOS**, 1988, Vol. 13, No. 5, pp. 487-507.)

Diss, William T. "Estate Planning Tips: Locking In The Advantages," **JOA**, 1988, Vol. 166, No. 1, pp. 36-45.

Diss, William T. "Small Business: Winner Or Loser Under Tax Reform?," **JOA**, 1986, Vol. 162, No. 6, pp. 164-171.

Ditkoff, James H. "Financial Tax Accounting At The Cross-roads," **JOA**, 1977, Vol. 144, No. 2, pp. 69-80.

Ditkoff, James H. "State Tax Deductions For Operating Losses," **CPAJ**, 1974, Vol. 44, No. 12, pp. 47-52.

Dittenhofer, Mortimer. "Research In Governmental Accounting And Auditing," **AIIA**, 1988, Vol. 2, pp. 201-203.

Dittman, David A. and Kenneth R. Ferris. "'Profit Centre': A Satisfaction Generating Concept," **ABR**, 1977-78, Vol. 8, No. 32, pp. 242-245.

Dittman, David A. and Prem Prakash. "Cost Variance Investigation: Markovian Control Of Markov Processes," **JAR**, 1978, Vol. 16, No. 1, pp. 14-25.

Dittman, David A. "Transfer Pricing And Decentralization," **MA**, 1972, Vol. 54, No. 5, pp. 47-50.

Dittman, David A. (Capettini, Robert, David A. Dittman and Richard C. Morey. "Reimbursement Rate Setting For Medicaid Prescription Drugs Based On Relative Efficiencies," **JAPP**, 1985, Vol. 4, No. 2, pp. 83-110.)

Dittman, David A., Hervey A. Juris and Lawrence Revsine. "On The Existence Of Unrecorded Human Assets: An Economic Perspective," **JAR**, 1976, Vol. 14, No. 1, pp. 49-65.

Dittman, David A., Hervey A. Juris and Lawrence Revsine. "Unrecorded Human Assets: A Survey Of Accounting Firms' Training Programs," **AR**, 1980, Vol. 55, No. 4, pp. 640-648.

Dittman, David A., Raymond J. Krasniewski and Margaret Smith. "Contracting Strategies For Maximum Benefit In Sales Contracts With Government: The Installment Sale Alternative," **RIGNA**, 1987, Vol. 3, Part A, pp. 107-130.

Dittman, David and Prem Prakash. "Cost Variance Investigation: Markovian Control Versus Optimal Control," **AR**, 1979, Vol. 54, No. 2, pp. 358-373.

Dittmer, Gary R. "Inventory Pricing Can Save Costs," **MA**, 1979, Vol. 60, No. 11, pp. 27-32.

Dittrich, John E. and Donald S. Shannon. "Manpower Development," **MA**, 1975, Vol. 57, No. 4, pp. 29-32.

Dixon, Arthur J. "Commentary On The Metcalf Committee Report," **CPAJ**, 1977, Vol. 47, No. 6, pp. 11-20.

Dixon, Arthur J. "CPAs Face Their Responsibilities," **CPAJ**, 1975, Vol. 45, No. 6, pp. 21-24.

Dixon, Lynwood J. and John M. Thornton, Jr. "The Costs Of Cleaning Up Pollution," **MA**, 1972, Vol. 54, No. 5, pp. 13-17.

Dixon, Robert L. and Harry D. Kerrigan. "Criticisms Of The Tentative Statement Of Accounting Principles," **AR**, 1941, Vol. 16, No. 1, pp. 49-65.

Dixon, Robert L. "An Experimental Interview Program To Attract Students To Our Field," **AR**, 1970, Vol. 45, No. 1, pp. 140-143.

Dixon, Robert L. "Cost Concepts: Special Problems And Definitions," **AR**, 1948, Vol. 23, No. 1, pp. 40-43.

Dixon, Robert L. "Creep," **JOA**, 1953, Vol. 96, No. 1, pp. 48-55.

Dixon, Robert L. "Decreasing Charge Depreciation - A Search For Logic," **AR**, 1960, Vol. 35, No. 4, pp. 590-597.

Dixon, Robert L. "The Need For A Statement Of The Principles Underlying Cost Accounting," **AR**, 1943, Vol. 18, No. 3, pp. 256-258.

Dixon, Robert L., Jr. "Fixed And Variable Costs," **AR**, 1940, Vol. 15, No. 2, pp. 218-221.

Dobbins, Richard. "Institutional Shareholders In The UK Equity Market," **ABR**, 1974-75, Vol. 5, No. 17, pp. 9-17.

Dobbins, Richard. (McRae, Thomas W. and Richard Dobbins. "Behavioural Aspects Of The Inflation Accounting Controversy," **ABR**, 1973-74, Vol. 4, No. 14, pp.135-140.)

Doblin, Ernest M. "Accounting Problems Of Cartels," **AR**, 1943, Vol. 18, No. 3, pp. 249-255.

Dock, V. Thomas, Dan M. Guy and Doyle Z. Williams. "Integrating The Computer In The Classroom: An Approach In Auditing," **AR**, 1974, Vol. 49, No. 1, pp. 149-153.

Dockweiler, Raymond C. and Carl G. Willis. "On The Use Of Entry Requirements For Undergraduate Accounting Programs," **AR**, 1984, Vol. 59, No. 3, pp. 496-504.

Dockweiler, Raymond C. "The Practicability Of Developing Multiple Financial Statements: A Case Study," **AR**, 1969, Vol. 44, No. 4, pp. 729-742.

Dodd, Peter, Nicholas Dopuch, Robert Holthausen and Richard Leftwich. "Qualified Audit Opinions And Stock Prices: Information Content, Announcement Dates, And Concurrent Disclosures," **JAEC**, 1984, Vol. 6, No. 1, pp. 3-38.

Dodge, Robert H. "How Leverage Affects The Cost Of Capital To A Public Utility," **MA**, 1969, Vol. 51, No. 2, pp. 39-44.

Dodin, Bajis. (Chan, K. Hung and Bajis Dodin. "A Decision Support System For Audit-Staff Scheduling With Precedence Constraints And Due Dates," **AR**, 1986, Vol. 61, No. 4, pp. 726-734.)

Dodson, John W. "A Long-Range Forecasting And Planning Technique," **MA**, 1967, Vol. 49, No. 4, pp. 9-18.

Dodwell, Joseph W. "Operational Auditing: A Part Of The Basic Audit," **JOA**, 1966, Vol. 121, No. 6, pp. 31-39.

Doege, Richard L. "Photogrammetrics In Auditing," **JOA**, 1972, Vol. 133, No. 4, pp. 60-63.

Doggett, Ron E. "Managing Working Capital," **MA**, 1980, Vol. 62, No. 6, pp. 19-24.

Doherty, Phillip H. (Muir, Tom P. and Phillip H. Doherty. "How To Turn Canada's FIRA To Your Advantage," **CA**, 1984, Vol. 2, No. 1, pp. 33-37.)

Doherty, William O. (Carey, John L. and William O. Doherty. "The Concept Of Independence - Review And Restatement," **JOA**, 1966, Vol. 121, No. 1, pp. 38-48.)

Dohr, James L. "A Graduate Curriculum In Accounting," **AR**, 1948, Vol. 23, No. 2, pp. 206-208.

Dohr, James L. "Accounting In The Law School," **AR**, 1930, Vol. 5, No. 3, pp. 213-214.

Dohr, James L. "An Introduction To The Art Of Accounting," **AR**, 1947, Vol. 22, No. 2, pp. 151-161.

Dohr, James L. "Budgetary Control And Standard Costs In Industrial Accounting," **AR**, 1932, Vol. 7, No. 1, pp. 31-33.

Dohr, James L. "Business-Law Training For Students Of Accounting," **AR**, 1938, Vol. 13, No. 1, pp. 77-80.

Dohr, James L. "Capital And Surplus In The Corporate Balance Sheet," **AR**, 1939, Vol. 14, No. 1, pp. 38-41.

Dohr, James L. "Current Problems Of Federal Taxation: Comments," **AR**, 1936, Vol. 11, No. 2, pp. 185-186.

Dohr, James L. "Depreciation And The Price Level," **AR**, 1948, Vol. 23, No. 2, pp. 115-118.

Dohr, James L. "Limitations On The Usefulness Of Price Level Adjustments," **AR**, 1955, Vol. 30, No. 2, pp. 198-205.

Dohr, James L. "Materiality - What Does It Mean In Accounting?," **JOA**, 1950, Vol. 90, No. 1, pp. 54-56.

Dohr, James L. "The Next Step In Depreciation Accounting," **JOA**, 1950, Vol. 89, No. 2, pp. 114-119.

Dohr, James L. "The Revenue And Income Principles," **AR**, 1942, Vol. 17, No. 1, pp. 19-27.

Dohr, James L. "What They (Economists) Say About Us (Accountants)," **JOA**, 1953, Vol. 96, No. 2, pp. 167-175.

Dohr, James L. "Work Of The Joint Committee On Income Tax Statistics," **AR**, 1933, Vol. 8, No. 2, pp. 128-129.

Dohr, James L. (May, George O. and James L. Dohr. "Book Value: A Brief Comment On The Stans-Goedert Article," **JOA**, 1955, Vol. 99, No. 4, pp. 42-44.)

Dohr, J. L. "A Legal Analysis Of The Balance Sheet," **AR**, 1928, Vol. 3, No. 2, pp. 117-123.

Dohr, J. L. "Section 220 - Should Corporations Worry?," **AR**, 1928, Vol. 3, No. 1, pp. 23-35.

Dolan, Thomas J. "How To Avoid Personal Holding Company Pitfalls," **JOA**, 1951, Vol. 91, No. 5, pp. 704-709.

Dole, Richard D. (Baggett, Monte R., Richard D. Dole and Jack E. Short. "Accounting And Auditing For Drilling Funds," **CPAJ**, 1981, Vol. 51, No. 9, pp. 27-37.)

Doll, Barry F. "Staff Turnover: How To Manage It," **JOA**, 1983, Vol. 156, No. 6, pp. 76-83.

Dollison, Dwight G. "Accounting For Calf Production," **MA**, 1976, Vol. 58, No. 4, pp. 42-44.

Dolliver, Elson P. (Wood, John P. and Elson P. Dolliver. "Silver Spoons," **MA**, 1975, Vol. 57, No. 1, pp. 18-19.)

Dolphin, Robert, Jr. (Soper, Fred J. and Robert Dolphin, Jr. "Readability And Corporate Annual Reports," **AR**, 1964, Vol. 39, No. 2, pp. 358-362.)

Domínguez, Roberto. "Some Ideas Concerning The Need To Reform Financial Management In The Public Sector Of Developing Countries," **AIIA**, 1988, Vol. 2, pp. 273-284.

Dominiak, Geraldine F. and Joseph G. Louderback, III. "'Present Fairly' And Generally Accepted Accounting Principles," **CPAJ**, 1972, Vol. 42, No. 1, pp. 45-54.

Dominiak, Geraldine. (Arens, Alvin A., Robert G. May and Geraldine Dominiak. "A Simulated Case For Audit Education," **AR**, 1970, Vol. 45, No. 3, pp. 573-578.)

Dominianni, Theresa. (Dropkin, Murray, Vincent Milito, Theresa Dominianni and William La Touche. "Trends In Charities Registration And Reporting," **CPAJ**, 1988, Vol. 58, No. 5, pp. 56-65.)

Domurachi, Mary Ann. (Eichen, Susan P. and Mary Ann Domurachi. "Designing Internal Control Systems For Appropriate Management Control," **CA**, 1986, Vol. 4, No. 4, pp. 20-28.)

Donachie, Robert J. "Living With Financial Accounting Standards," **MA**, 1977, Vol. 58, No. 10, pp. 20-22.

Donadio, Anthony. (Wertz, William F. and Anthony Donadio. "Collateralized Mortgage Obligations," **CPAJ**, 1987, Vol. 57, No. 11, pp. 68-71.)

Donaldson, J. Bruce and Richard D. Hobbet. "The Passing Parade of 1962 Tax Litigation," **JOA**, 1963, Vol. 116, No. 2, pp. 39-49.

Doney, Lloyd D. and Richard C. Neumann. "Teaching Approaches To Elementary Accounting," **AR**, 1965, Vol. 40, No. 3, pp. 653-655.

Doney, Lloyd D. "Coping With Uncertainty In The Make Or Buy Decision," **MA**, 1968, Vol. 50, No. 2, pp. 31-34.

Doney, Lloyd D. "Integrating Accounting And Computerized Data Processing," **AR**, 1969, Vol. 44, No. 2, pp. 400-409.

Doney, Lloyd D. (Wilkinson, James R. and Lloyd D. Doney. "Extending Audit And Reporting Boundaries," **AR**, 1965, Vol. 40, No. 4, pp. 753-756.)

Doney, Lloyd L. (Giacomino, Don E. and Lloyd L. Doney. "The SAI Movement In Manufacturing," **CPAJ**, 1986, Vol. 56, No. 10, pp. 64-73.)

Donham, Philip. "Some Observations On Depreciation Allowances," **AR**, 1946, Vol. 21, No. 4, pp. 415-418.

Donkersloot, Richard, Jr. "Productivity Through Manufacturing Control," **MA**, 1981, Vol. 63, No. 6, pp. 25-32.

Donleavy, G. D. "Aspects Of Hungarian Accounting," **AIIA**, 1987, Vol. 1, pp. 85-109.

Donnell, George R. "Excess Profits Tax Minus Its Technicalities," **AR**, 1951, Vol. 26, No. 3, pp. 384-386.

Donnell, George R. "What Is A Certified Public Accountant?," **AR**, 1951, Vol. 26, No. 1, pp. 45-48.

Donnelly, David P. (Deines, Dan S. and David P. Donnelly. "Deferred Income Taxes When Changing To S Corporation," **CPAJ**, 1987, Vol. 57, No. 12, pp. 58-61.)

Donnelly, David P. (Ott, Richard L., Dan S. Deines and David P. Donnelly. "The Use Of A Fundamental Practice Set In Intermediate Accounting," **IAE**, 1988, Vol. 3, No. 1, pp. 131-138.)

Donnelly, Robert M. "The Controller's Role In Corporate Planning," **MA**, 1981, Vol. 63, No. 3, pp. 13-26.

Donnelly, Vincent T. "Electromechanical Production Control," **JOA**, 1960, Vol. 109, No. 4, pp. 66-69.

Donner, F. G. "General Motors Budgetary Control," **AR**, 1932, Vol. 7, No. 1, pp. 22-30.

D'Onofrio, Joseph. (Porter, Gary and Joseph D'Onofrio. "Deconsolidating Troubled Subsidiaries: A Question Of Control," **CA**, 1987, Vol. 5, No. 3, pp. 32-37.)

Donohue, Roger. "The AICPA 'Guide For Preparation Of Unaudited Financial Statements'," **CPAJ**, 1975, Vol. 45, No. 6, pp. 31-36.

Dontoh, Alex and Gordon Richardson. "On Interim Information And The Information Content Of Firm Earnings: A State Variable Approach," **CAR**, 1988, Vol. 4, No. 2, pp. 450-469.

Doost, Roger K. and Evans Pappas. "Frozen-To-Current Cost Variance," **MA**, 1988, Vol. 69, No. 9, pp. 41-43.

Doost, Roger K. and Karen M. Ligon. "How U.S. And European Accounting Practices Differ," **MA**, 1986, Vol. 68, No. 4, pp. 38-41.

Doost, Roger K. "Alternative Techniques To Measure The Well-Being Of A Region," **IJAER**, 1985, Vol. 20, No. 2, pp. 95-101.

Dopuch, Nicholas and David Drake. "The Effect Of Alternative Accounting Rules For Nonsubsidiary Investments," **JAR**, 1966, Vol. 4, Supp., pp. 192-219.

Dopuch, Nicholas and David F. Drake. "Accounting Implications Of A Mathematical Programming Approach To The Transfer Price Problem," **JAR**, 1964, Vol. 2, No. 1, pp. 10-24.

Dopuch, Nicholas and Morton Pincus. "Evidence On The Choice Of Inventory Accounting Methods: LIFO Versus FIFO," **JAR**, 1988, Vol. 26, No. 1, pp. 28-59.

Dopuch, Nicholas and Ross Watts. "Using Time-Series Models To Assess The Significance Of Accounting Changes," **JAR**, 1972, Vol. 10, No. 1, pp. 180-194.

Dopuch, Nicholas and Shyam Sunder. "FASB's Statements On Objectives And Elements Of Financial Accounting: A Review," **AR**, 1980, Vol. 55, No. 1, pp. 1-21.

Dopuch, Nicholas N. "Implications Of Torts Rules Of The Accountant's Liability For The Accounting Model," **JAAF**, 1988, Vol. 3 (New Series), No. 3, pp. 245-249.

Dopuch, Nicholas, Jacob G. Birnberg and Joel Demski. "An Extension Of Standard Cost Variance Analysis," **AR**, 1967, Vol. 42, No. 3, pp. 526-536.

Dopuch, Nicholas, Robert W. Holthausen and Richard W. Leftwich. "Abnormal Stock Returns Associated With Media Disclosures Of 'Subject To' Qualified Audit Opinions," **JABC**, 1986, Vol. 8, No. 2, pp. 93-117.

Dopuch, Nicholas, Robert W. Holthausen and Richard W. Leftwich. "Predicting Audit Qualifications With Financial And Market Variables," **AR**, 1987, Vol. 62, No. 3, pp. 431-454.

Dopuch, Nicholas. "Mathematical Programming And Accounting Approaches To Incremental Cost Analysis," **AR**, 1963, Vol. 38, No. 4, pp. 745-753.

Dopuch, Nicholas. "Metaphysics Of Pragmatism And Accountancy," **AR**, 1962, Vol. 37, No. 2, pp. 251-262.

Dopuch, Nicholas. (Bedford, Norton M. and Nicholas Dopuch. "Research Methodology And Accounting Theory - Another Perspective," **AR**, 1961, Vol. 36, No. 3, pp. 351-361.)

Dopuch, Nicholas. (Birnberg, Jacob G. and Nicholas Dopuch. "A Conceptual Approach To The Framework For Disclosure," **JOA**, 1963, Vol. 115, No. 2, pp. 56-63.)

Dopuch, Nicholas. (Dodd, Peter, Nicholas Dopuch, Robert Holthausen and Richard Leftwich. "Qualified Audit Opinions And Stock Prices: Information Content, Announcement Dates, And Concurrent Disclosures," **JAEC**, 1984, Vol. 6, No. 1, pp. 3-38.)

Dopuch, Nicholas. (Drake, David F. and Nicholas Dopuch. "On The Case For Dichotomizing Income," **JAR**, 1965, Vol. 3, No. 2, pp. 192-205.)

Dopuch, Nicholas. (Gonedes, Nicholas J. and Nicholas Dopuch. "Capital Market Equilibrium, Information Production, And Selecting Accounting Techniques: Theoretical Framework And Review Of Empirical Work," **JAR**, 1974, Vol. 12, Supp., pp. 48-129.)

Dopuch, Nicholas. (Gonedes, Nicholas J. and Nicholas Dopuch. "Economic Analyses And Accounting Techniques: Perspectives And Proposals," **JAR**, 1979, Vol. 17, No. 2, pp. 384-410.)

Dopuch, Nicholas. (Gonedes, Nicholas J., Nicholas Dopuch and Stephen H. Penman. "Disclosure Rules, Information-Production, And Capital Market Equilibrium: The Case Of Forecast Disclosure Rules," **JAR**, 1976, Vol. 14, No. 1, pp. 89-137.)

Dopuch, N. and J. Ronen. "The Effects Of Alternative Inventory Valuation Methods - An Experimental Study," **JAR**, 1973, Vol. 11, No. 2, pp. 191-211.

Dopuch, N. (Cooper, W. W., N. Dopuch and T. F. Keller. "Budgetary Disclosure And Other Suggestions For Improving Accounting," **AR**, 1968, Vol. 43, No. 4, pp. 640-648.)

Doran, B. Michal, Daniel W. Collins and Dan S. Dhaliwal. "The Information Of Historical Cost Earnings Relative To Supplemental Reserve-Based Accounting Data In The Extractive Petroleum Industry," **AR**, 1988, Vol. 63, No. 3, pp. 389-413.

Doran, David T. and Robert Nachtmann. "The Association Of Stock Distribution Announcements And Earnings Performance," **JAAF**, 1988, Vol. 3 (New Series), No. 2, pp. 113-146.

Dorian, Daniel G. "Management Accounting In A Developing Country," **MA**, 1974, Vol. 55, No. 11, pp. 15-18.

Dorr, Patrick B. "Personal/Business Property: A Bleak Picture," **CPAJ**, 1985, Vol. 55, No. 4, pp. 36-45.

Dorr, Patrick B. "Tax And Economic Aspects Of The Home Office Deduction," **CPAJ**, 1982, Vol. 52, No. 7, pp. 28-36.

Dorr, Patrick, Martha Eining and James E. Groff. "Developing An Accounting Expert System Decision Aid For Classroom Use," **IAE**, 1988, Vol. 3, No. 1, pp. 27-41.

Dorward, Neil. "Overhead Allocations And 'Optimal' Pricing Rules Of Thumb In Oligopolistic Markets," **ABR**, 1985-86, Vol. 16, No. 64, pp. 309-318.

Doty, Edwin. (Harrell, Adrian, Charles Caldwell and Edwin Doty. "Within-Person Expectancy Theory Predictions Of Accounting Students' Motivation To Achieve Academic Success," **AR**, 1985, Vol. 60, No. 4, pp. 724-735.)

Douglas, A. W. "What Should Business Men Know About Accounting?," **AR**, 1927, Vol. 2, No. 1, pp. 43-45.

Douglas, David V. "LIFO: Big Benefits For A Small Company," **MA**, 1981, Vol. 62, No. 10, pp. 40-42.

Douglas, Evan J. "Pricing For Economic Objectives, Given Search And Price Adjustment Costs," **JCA**, 1984, Vol. 1, No. 1, pp. 59-74.

Douglas, Livingston G. "The Hidden Danger In Bond Yields," **MA**, 1987, Vol. 69, No. 3, pp. 51-54.

Douglas, Patricia P. "Accounting For Equity Securities," **JOA**, 1972, Vol. 134, No. 5, pp. 66-70.

Douglas, Patricia P. "Reporting Accounting Information To Top Management," **CA**, 1987, Vol. 5, No. 3, pp. 38-45.

Douglas, Patricia, Teresa Beed, Karen Clark and Sylvia Weisenburger. "Surviving Your First Job," **MA**, 1986, Vol. 67, No. 12, pp. 32-35.

Doupnik, Timothy and Thomas G. Evans. "The Functional Currency Determination: A Strategy To Smooth Income," **AIIA**, 1988, Vol. 2, pp. 169-180.

Doupnik, Timothy S. "Indexation: Brazil's Response To Inflation," **IJAER**, 1982, Vol. 18, No. 1, pp. 199-220.

Doupnik, Timothy S. "The Brazilian System Of Monetary Correction," **AIIA**, 1987, Vol. 1, pp. 111-135.

Doupnik, Timothy S. "The Evolution Of Financial Statement Indexation In Brazil," **AHJ**, 1986, Vol. 13, No. 1, pp. 1-18.

Doupnik, Timothy S. (Rivola-Clay, Anna Maria and Timothy S. Doupnik. "The Progress Of Italian Accounting: Allegro Ma Nontroppo," **IJAER**, 1987, Vol. 22, No. 2, pp. 87-102.)

Dow, Alice S. and Orace Johnson. "The Break-Even Point Concept: Its Development And Expanding Applications," **MA**, 1969, Vol. 50, No. 6, pp. 29-31.

Dowell, C. Dwayne and James Arthur Hall. "EDP Controls With Audit Cost Implications," **JAAF**, 1981, Vol. 5, No. 1, pp. 30-40.

Dowell, C. Dwayne. (Boatsman, James R., C. Dwayne Dowell and Janet I. Kimbrell. "Valuing Stock Used For A Business Combination," **JAAF**, 1984, Vol. 8, No. 1, pp. 35-43.)

Dowell, C. Dwayne. (Chasteen, Lanny G. and C. Dwayne Dowell. "Teaching Alternative Income Determination Models Via A Classification Model," **JAED**, 1983, Vol. 1, No. 1, pp. 47-53.)

Dowis, Robert H., Jr. (Niles, Timothy J. and Robert H. Dowis, Jr. "Accounting For New Plant Construction," **MA**, 1974, Vol. 56, No. 1, pp. 35-38, 43-44.)

Downes, David and Thomas R. Dyckman. "A Critical Look At The Efficient Market Empirical Research Literature As It Relates To Accounting Information," **AR**, 1973, Vol. 48, No. 2, pp. 300-317.

Downing, Glenn D. "Teaching Income Tax Concepts In The Elementary Accounting Course," **AR**, 1960, Vol. 35, No. 4, pp. 730-732.

Doxey, Bobby L. and Jean Chambers. "Making The Most Of Bank Information Systems," **MA**, 1983, Vol. 64, No. 8, pp. 58-61.

Doyle, Arthur H. "Distortion In Ordinary Turnover Rates," **AR**, 1932, Vol. 7, No. 2, pp. 139-142.

Doyle, Leonard A. "Uses Of Cost Data For Production And Investment Policies," **AR**, 1950, Vol. 25, No. 3, pp. 274-282.

Doyle, Robert J. "A New Look At The Scanlon Plan," **MA**, 1970, Vol. 52, No. 3, pp. 48-52.

Dragutsky, Howard W. (Lieber, Lawrence and Howard W. Dragutsky. "How Accountants Can Keep Pension Costs Down," **JOA**, 1975, Vol. 139, No. 2, pp. 52-59.)

Drake, David F. and Nicholas Dopuch. "On The Case For Dichotomizing Income," **JAR**, 1965, Vol. 3, No. 2, pp. 192-205.

Drake, David F. "The Service Potential Concept And Inter-Period Tax Allocation," **AR**, 1962, Vol. 37, No. 4, pp. 677-684.

Drake, David F. (Dopuch, Nicholas and David F. Drake. "Accounting Implications Of A Mathematical Programming Approach To The Transfer Price Problem," **JAR**, 1964, Vol. 2, No. 1, pp. 10-24.)

Drake, David. (Dopuch, Nicholas and David Drake. "The Effect Of Alternative Accounting Rules For Nonsubsidiary Investments," **JAR**, 1966, Vol. 4. Supp., pp. 192-219.)

Drake, Milton J. "Reports For Creditors," **AR**, 1950, Vol. 25, No. 1, pp. 58-62.

Drane, Noel T. "Growth Of Firms And Managerial Capitalism," **ABACUS**, 1966, Vol. 2. No. 1. pp. 49-67.

Drebin, Allan R. "A Computer Solution To Cost Or Market Problems," **AR**, 1964, Vol. 39, No. 3. pp. 745-749.

Drebin, Allan R. "A Fallacy Of Depreciation Translation," **JAR**, 1969, Vol. 7, No. 2, pp. 204-214.

Drebin, Allan R. "Accounting For Life Insurance As An Investment," **AR**, 1962, Vol. 37. No. 2. pp. 279-282.

Drebin, Allan R. "Accounting For Proprietary Research," **AR**, 1966, Vol. 41, No. 3. pp. 413-425.

Drebin, Allan R. "Price Level Adjustments And Inventory Flow Assumptions," **AR**, 1965, Vol. 40, No. 1, pp. 154-162.

Drebin, Allan R. "Recognizing Implicit Interest In Non-Funded Pension Plans," **AR**, 1963, Vol. 38, No. 3. pp. 579-583.

Drebin, Allan R. "The Inventory Calculus," **JAR**, 1966, Vol. 4, No. 1, pp. 68-86.

Drebin, Allan R. "'Cash-Flowitis': Malady Or Syndrome?," **JAR**, 1964, Vol. 2, No. 1, pp. 25-34.

Dreher, William A. "Alternatives Available Under APB Opinion No. 8: An Actuary's View," **JOA**, 1967, Vol. 124, No. 3. pp. 37-51.

Dressel, Norman X. (Stabler, Henry Francis and Norman X. Dressel. "May And Paton: Two Giants Revisited." **AHJ**, 1981, Vol. 8, No. 2. pp. 79-90.)

Drews, Alison L. "Bookkeeping For A Small Business," **MA**, 1975, Vol. 57, No. 4, pp. 33-34.

Drews, Alison L. (Bryan, E. Lewis. Alison L. Drews and G. Thomas Friedlob. "Delphic Choice Of Accounting Periodicals For University Libraries," **JAED**, 1987. Vol. 5, No. 1, pp. 167-174.)

Drexler, Frederick A. "The Client Looks At The CPA Auditor," **CPAJ**, 1975, Vol. 45, No. 1. pp. 29-30.

Drinkwater, David A. "Management Theory And The Budgeting Process," **MA**, 1973, Vol. 54. No. 12. pp. 15-17.

Drinkwater, David and James Don Edwards. "The Nature Of Taxes And The Matching Principle," **AR**, 1965, Vol. 40. No. 3. pp. 579-582.

Driscoll, Donna A., W. Thomas Lin and Paul R. Watkins. "Cost-Volume-Profit Analysis Under Uncertainty: A Synthesis And Framework For Evaluation," **JAL**, 1984, Vol. 3, pp. 85-116.

Driver, Michael and Theodore Mock. "Human Information Processing, Decision Style Theory. And Accounting Information," **AR**, 1975, Vol. 50, No. 3, pp. 490-508.

Driver, Michael J. and Theodore J. Mock. "Human Information Processing. Decison Style Theory And Accounting Information Systems: A Reply," **AR**, 1977, Vol. 52, No. 4. pp. 988-990.

Droege, Mark E. (Phillips, Thomas E. and Mark E. Droege. "Maximizing Cash In Decentralized Organizations," **MA**, 1984, Vol. 66, No. 2. pp. 38-42.)

Droms, William G. "Investment Asset Allocation For PFP Clients," **JOA**, 1987, Vol. 163, No. 4. pp. 114-118.

Dropkin, Murray and Edward Kitrosser. "The Government Audit Maze," **CPAJ**, 1982, Vol. 52. No. 1. pp. 24-29.

Dropkin, Murray, Vincent Milito, Theresa Dominianni and William La Touche. "Trends In Charities Registration And Reporting," **CPAJ**, 1988, Vol. 58. No. 5. pp. 56-65.

Drozdak, Dennis P. and J. Sterling Shuttleworth. "Alternatives To Risk Funding," No. 7, pp. 15-18.

Drtina, Ralph E. and James A. Largay, III. "Pitfalls In Calculating Cash Flow From Operations," **AR**, 1985, Vol. 60, No. 2. pp. 314-326.

Drtina, Ralph E. (Brandon, Charles. Ralph E. Drtina and Donald Plane. "Using Modeling Languages In Mangerial Accounting: An Example For Pricing Decisions." **JAED**, 1986, Vol. 4, No. 1, pp. 69-80.)

Drtina, Ralph E. (Thode, Stephen F., Ralph E. Drtina and James A. Largay, III. "Operating Cash Flows: A Growing Need For Separate Reporting," **JAAF**, 1986. Vol. 1 (New Series), No. 1. pp. 46-61.)

Drucker, A. P. R. "Budgeting And The Sales Quota," **AR**, 1929, Vol. 4, No. 3, pp. 175-180.

Drucker, A. P. R. "Budgeting And Control Of Machinery," **AR**, 1931, Vol. 6, No. 3, pp. 192-196.

Drucker, A. P. R. "Factory Production Under Budgetary Control," **AR**, 1930, Vol. 5, No. 4. pp. 301-304.

Drucker, A. P. R. "The Accountant As An Efficiency Expert." **AR**, 1928, Vol. 3, No. 4, pp. 364-368.

Drucker, Meyer and Mark A. Segal. "Penalties For Federal Tax Crimes: The IRS Arsenal," **MA**, 1984, Vol. 66, No. 1. pp. 32-35.

Drury, D. H. "Earnings Per Share: A Canada-United States Comparison," **IJAER**, 1977, Vol. 13, No. 1, pp. 29-51.

Drury, Edward A. (Stanton, Robert and Edward A. Drury. "Forecasting At Hewlett-Packard: Finding A Better Way," **MA**, 1981, Vol. 62, No. 12. pp. 45-49.)

Duangploy, Orapin. "The Sensitivity Of Earnings Per Share To Different Foreign Currency Translation Methods," **IJAER**, 1979, Vol. 14, No. 2. pp. 121-134.

Duangploy, Orapin, Eugene L. Zieha and Dahli Gray. "SFAS No. 52 And The Statement Of Changes In Financial Position: A Survey And Proposal For Change," **IJAER**, 1987. Vol. 22, No. 2, pp. 25-40.

Dubas, Frank. (Hardiman, Patrick, Arlene Lurie. Frank Dubas and David Schoen. "Internal Control And Financial Integrity In Government Units," **CPAJ**, 1985. Vol. 55. No. 4, pp. 46-51.)

Duboff, Jack I. (Aly, Hamdi F. and Jack I. Duboff. "Statistical Vs. Judgment Sampling: An Empirical Study Of Auditing The Accounts Receivable Of A Small Retail Store," **AR**, 1971, Vol. 46, No. 1, pp. 119-128.)

Duboff, Samuel J. "Recruitment, Selection, And Training," **JOA**, 1959, Vol. 107, No. 3, pp. 50-56.

Dudick, Thomas S. "Alternative Costing Methods For Reporting And Pricing Purposes," **JOA**, 1969, Vol. 128, No. 4, pp. 49-54.

Dudick, Thomas S. "Direct Costing - 'Handle With Care'," **JOA**, 1962, Vol. 114, No. 4, pp. 45-52.

Dudick, Thomas S. "Planning For Profit: Focusing On The Big Picture," **MA**, 1970, Vol. 52, No. 2, pp. 15-19.

Dudick, Thomas S. "Use Of Indicators In Planning For Profits," **MA**, 1969, Vol. 51, No. 5, pp. 16-18.

Dudick, Thomas S. "Zero-Base Budgeting In Industry," **MA**, 1978, Vol. 59, No. 11, pp. 25-29.

Dudley, Lola Woodard. "A Critical Look At EPS," **JOA**, 1985, Vol. 160, No. 2, pp. 102-111.

Due, John F. "The Institutional Environment And The Tax Structure In Developing Economies," **IJAER**, 1968, Vol. 4, No. 1, pp. 17-27.

Duerr, Edwin C. and Mitsuko S. Duerr. "Financing In Northeast Brazil: Problems And Opportunities In A Developing Area." **IJAER**, 1968, Vol. 3, No. 2, pp. 105-116.

Duerr, Mitsuko S. (Duerr, Edwin C. and Mitsuko S. Duerr. "Financing In Northeast Brazil: Problems And Opportunities In A Developing Area," **IJAER**, 1968, Vol. 3, No. 2, pp. 105-116.)

Dufey, Gunter. "Recent Developments In International Money And Capital Markets," **IJAER**, 1972, Vol. 7, No. 2, pp. 77-90.

Dufey, Gunter. "The Outlook For The International Monetary System And Implications For Subsidiary Valuation," **IJAER**, 1970, Vol. 6, No. 1, pp. 15-33.

Duff, John T. (Aslanian, Paul J. and John T. Duff. "Why Accounting Teachers Are So Academic," **JOA**, 1973, Vol. 136, No. 4, pp. 47-53.)

Dugan, Joseph R. "Motivational Psychology And The Management Accountant," **MA**, 1968, Vol. 49, No. 11, pp. 22-25.

Dugan, Michael T. and Christine V. Zavgren. "Bankruptcy Prediction Research: A Valuable Instructional Tool," **IAE**, 1988, Vol. 3, No. 1, pp. 48-64.

Dugan, Michael T. and Keith A. Shriver. "The Importance Of An Environmental Criterion In Applied Business Research." **IAE**, 1988, Vol. 3, No. 1, pp. 42-47.

Dugan, Michael T., James A. Gentry and Keith A. Shriver. "The X-11 Model: A New Analytical Review Technique For The Auditor," **AJPT**, 1984-85, Vol. 4, No. 2, pp. 11-22.

Dugar, Amitabh. (Simon, Daniel T., Ramachandran Ramanan and Amitabh Dugar. "The Market For Audit Services In India: An Empirical Examination," **IJAER**, 1986, Vol. 21, No. 2, pp. 27-35.)

Duke, Gordon Leon. (Bailey, Andrew D., Jr.. Gordon Leon Duke. James Gerlach, Chen-En Ko, Rayman D. Meservy and Andrew B. Whinston. "TICOM And The Analysis Of Internal Controls." **AR**, 1985, Vol. 60, No. 2, pp. 186-201.)

Duke, Gordon L. (Ko, Chen-En, Christopher J. Nachtsheim. Gordon L. Duke and Andrew D. Bailey, Jr. "On The Robustness Of Model-Based Sampling In Auditing," **AJPT**, 1988, Vol. 7, No. 2, pp. 119-136.)

Duke, Gordon L. (Roemmich, Roger A., Gordon L. Duke and William H. Gates. "Maximizing The Present Value Of Tax Savings From Depreciation," **MA**, 1978, Vol. 60, No. 3, pp. 55-57.)

Duke, Gordon L., John Neter and Robert A. Leitch. "Power Characteristics Of Test Statistics In The Auditing Environment: An Empirical Study," **JAR**, 1982, Vol. 20, No. 1. pp. 42-67.

Duke, Jere R. "After The Fire: The Insurance Claim," **MA**, 1974, Vol. 56. No. 3, p. 19.

Dukes, Roland E. (Beaver, William H. and Roland E. Dukes. "Interperiod Tax Allocation, Earnings Expectations, And The Behavior Of Security Prices," **AR**, 1972, Vol. 47, No. 2. pp. 320-332.)

Dukes, Roland E. (Beaver, William H. and Roland E. Dukes. "Interperiod Tax Allocation And Delta-Depreciation Methods: Some Empirical Results," **AR**, 1973, Vol. 48, No. 3. pp. 549-559.)

Dukes, Roland E. (Bierman, Harold, Jr., Roland E. Dukes and Thomas R. Dyckman. "Financial Reporting In The Petroleum Industry," **JOA**, 1974, Vol. 138, No. 4, pp. 58-64.)

Dukes, Roland E. (Bierman, Harold, Jr. and Roland E. Dukes. "Accounting For Research And Development Costs," **JOA**, 1975. Vol. 139, No. 4, pp. 48-55.)

Dukes, Roland E., Thomas R. Dyckman and John A. Elliott. "Accounting For Research And Development Costs: The Impact On Research And Development Expenditures," **JAR**, 1980. Vol. 18, Supp., pp. 1-26.

Dukes, Roland. (Elliott, John, Gordon Richardson. Thomas Dyckman and Roland Dukes. "The Impact Of SFAS No.2 On Firm Expenditures On Research And Development: Replications And Extensions," **JAR**, 1984, Vol. 22, No. 1. pp. 85-102.)

Dukes, R. E. (Beaver, W. H. and R. E. Dukes. "Changes In Depreciation Methods: Some Analytical Results," **JAR**, 1974, Vol. 12. No. 2, pp. 205-215.)

Dukes, William P. (Kagle, Arthur R. and William P. Dukes. "Financial Reporting For Pledges At Educational Institutions," **CPAJ**, 1988. Vol. 58, No. 1, pp. 38-45.)

Dukes, William P. (Kagle, Arthur R. and William P. Dukes. "A Better Method Of Valuing Liabilities In Annuity Agreements," **MA**, 1980, Vol. 61, No. 10, pp. 37-40.)

Duncan, Keith and Ken Moores. "Usefulness Of CCA Information For Investor Decision Making: A Laboratory Experiment," **ABR**, 1988, Vol. 18, No. 70, pp. 121-132.

Duncan, William A. and Michael A. O'Dell. "Tax Policy And Erroneous Information: An Analysis Of The Interaction Of Inflation, Indexation, And Income Averaging," **JATA**, 1987, Vol. 8, No. 2, pp. 50-62.

Duncan, William A., David W. LaRue and P. M. J. Reckers. "An Empirical Examination Of The Influence Of Selected Economic And Non-Economic Variables On Decision Making By Tax Professionals," **AIT**, 1988, Vol. 2, pp. xx-xx.

Duncan, William A., Michael A. O'Dell and Richard L. Panich. "Potential Personal Wealth Redistribution Effects Of Structural Income Tax Reform," **AIT**, 1987, Vol. 1, pp. 1-22.

Duncan, Willis J. "Microfilm: A New Accounting Tool," **MA**, 1971, Vol. 52, No. 7, pp. 16-17.

Dungan, Christopher W., G. Thomas Friedlob and Robert W. Rouse. "The Supreme Court On Tax Accrual Workpapers," **CPAJ**, 1985, Vol. 55, No. 2, pp. 20-27.

Dunham, C. F. "On The Meaning Of 'Capital'," **AR**, 1930, Vol. 5, No. 4, pp. 298-300.

Dunlop, Anna B. G. "The Preservation Of Source Materials," **AHJ**, 1977, Vol. 4, No. 1, pp. 79-87.

Dunlop, Anna. "Bibliographical Notes On Five Examples Of Pacioli's Summa (1494) In Scotland," **ABACUS**, 1985, Vol. 21, No. 2, pp. 149-173.

Dunmore, Paul V. "On The Comparison Of Dollar-Unit And Stratified Mean-Per-Unit Estimators," **CAR**, 1986-87, Vol. 3, No. 1, pp. 125-148.

Dunn, Clarence L. "Helping Accounting Students To Learn How To Analyze A Business Transaction," **AR**, 1956, Vol. 31, No. 3, pp. 501-503.

Dunn, Clarence L. "Instruction Aids In Teaching Basis Of Property Acquired In Certain Tax-Free Exchanges," **AR**, 1956, Vol. 31, No. 1, pp. 129-131.

Dunn, Clarence L. "Teaching Of Adjusting And Reversing Entries In The Elementary Accounting Courses," **AR**, 1960, Vol. 35, No. 1, pp. 135-137.

Dunn, Glen R. "A Proposed Funds Statement For Financial Institutions," **MA**, 1968, Vol. 50, No. 3, pp. 9-12.

Dunn, James O. "The Honors Student And Accounting," **AR**, 1962, Vol. 37, No. 1, pp. 115-118.

Dunn, Keith W. "Clarification Of Auditor's Responsibility," **JOA**, 1958, Vol. 106, No. 2, pp. 49-54.

Dunn, William J. (Bukofsky, Ward M. and William J. Dunn. "Personal Service Corporations: Down But Not Out," **JOA**, 1988, Vol. 165, No. 6, pp. 30-37.)

Dunn, W. Marcus and Thomas W. Hall. "An Empirical Analysis Of The Relatonships Between CPA Examination Candidate Attributes And Candidate Performance," **AR**, 1984, Vol. 59, No. 4, pp. 674-689.

Dunn, W. Marcus and Thomas W. Hall. "Graduate Education And CPA Examination Performance: Some Empirical Evidence," **AIA**, 1988, Vol. 6, pp. 191-204.

DuPree, Jean M. "Users' Preferences For Descriptive Technical Accounting Terms," **ABR**, 1984-85, Vol. 15, No. 60, pp. 281-290.

DuPree, Jean M., Al H. Hartgraves and William H. Thralls. "How Management Accountants Can Communicate Better," **MA**, 1987, Vol. 68, No. 8, pp. 40-43.

Durik, Emil J. "Cost Accounting And Control For Mining Companies," **MA**, 1971, Vol. 53, No. 2, pp. 37-40.

Durkee, David A., James E. Groff and James R. Boatsman. "The Effect Of Costly Vs. Costless Pension Disclosure On Common Share Prices: The Case Of SFAS 36," **JAL**, 1988, Vol. 7, pp. 180-196.

Durland, Susan A. (Blade, David A. and Susan A. Durland. "Deductibility Of Vacation Home Expenses," **CPAJ**, 1979, Vol. 49, No. 4, pp. 29-34.)

Duro, Richard A. "A System Of Research And Development Cost Control," **MA**, 1967, Vol. 48, No. 9, pp. 25-30.

Duro, Richard A. "Don't Forget Your Purchase Order Commitments!," **MA**, 1970, Vol. 51, No. 12, pp. 47-48.

Duty, Glen L. "A Leasing Guide To Taxes," **MA**, 1980, Vol. 62, No. 2, pp. 45-50.

Duvall, Richard M. and James Bulloch. "Adjusting Rate Of Return And Present Value For Price-Level Changes," **AR**, 1965, Vol. 40, No. 3, pp. 569-573.

Dworin, Lowell and Richard A. Grimlund. "Dollar-Unit Sampling: A Comparison Of The Quasi-Bayesian And Moment Bounds," **AR**, 1986, Vol. 61. No. 1. pp. 36-57.

Dworin, Lowell and Richard A. Grimlund. "Dollar Unit Sampling For Accounts Receivable And Inventory," **AR**, 1984, Vol. 59, No. 2, pp. 218-241.

Dyckman, Thomas R. and Abbie J. Smith. "Financial Accounting And Reporting By Oil And Gas Producing Companies: A Study Of Information Effects," **JAEC**, 1979, Vol. 1, No. 1, pp. 45-75.

Dyckman, Thomas R. and Stephen A. Zeff. "Two Decades Of The Journal Of Accounting Research," **JAR**, 1984, Vol. 22, No. 1, pp. 225-297.

Dyckman, Thomas R. "A Dynamic Case Approach To Management Accounting," **AR**, 1964, Vol. 39, No. 4, pp. 1045-1050.

Dyckman, Thomas R. "Credibility And The Formulation Of Accounting Standards Under The Financial Accounting Standards Board," **JAL**, 1988, Vol. 7, pp. 1-30.

Dyckman, Thomas R. "Discounted Cash Flows, Price-Level Adjustments And Expectations: A Comment," **AR**, 1972, Vol. 47, No. 4, pp. 794-798.

Dyckman, Thomas R. "Observations On Jensen's Experimental Design For Study Of Effects Of Accounting Variations In Decision Making," **JAR**, 1967, Vol. 5, No. 2, pp. 221-229.

Dyckman, Thomas R. "On The Investment Decision," **AR**, 1964, Vol. 39, No. 2, pp. 285-295.

Dyckman, Thomas R. "The Effects Of Alternative Accounting Techniques On Certain Management Decisions," **JAR**, 1964, Vol. 2, No. 1, pp. 91-107.

Dyckman, Thomas R. "The Effects Of Restating Financial Statements For Price-Level Changes: A Comment," **AR**, 1975, Vol. 50, No. 4, pp. 796-808.

Dyckman, Thomas R. (Bierman, Harold, Jr. and Thomas R. Dyckman. "Accounting For Interest During Construction," **ABR**, 1978-79, Vol. 9, No. 36, pp. 267-272.)

Dyckman, Thomas R. (Bierman, Harold, Jr., Roland E. Dukes and Thomas R. Dyckman. "Financial Reporting In The Petroleum Industry," **JOA**, 1974, Vol. 138, No. 4, pp. 58-64.)

Dyckman, Thomas R. (Downes, David and Thomas R. Dyckman. "A Critical Look At The Efficient Market Empirical Research Literature As It Relates To Accounting Information," **AR**, 1973, Vol. 48, No. 2, pp. 300-317.)

Dyckman, Thomas R. (Dukes, Roland E., Thomas R. Dyckman and John A. Elliott. "Accounting For Research And Development Costs: The Impact On Research And Development Expenditures," **JAR**, 1980, Vol. 18, Supp., pp. 1-26.)

Dyckman, Thomas, Donna Philbrick and Jens Stephan. "A Comparison Of Event Study Methodologies Using Daily Stock Returns: A Simulation Approach," **JAR**, 1984, Vol. 22. Supp., pp. 1-30.

Dyckman, Thomas. (Crichfield, Timothy, Thomas Dyckman and Josef Lakonishok. "An Evaluation Of Security Analysts' Forecasts," **AR**, 1978, Vol. 53, No. 3, pp. 651-668.)

Dyckman, Thomas. (Elliott, John, Gordon Richardson, Thomas Dyckman and Roland Dukes. "The Impact Of SFAS No.2 On Firm Expenditures On Research And Development: Replications And Extensions," **JAR**, 1984, Vol. 22, No. 1, pp. 85-102.)

Dyckman, Thomas. (Smith, Abbie and Thomas Dyckman. "The Impact Of Accounting Regulation On the Stock Market: The Case Of Oil And Gas Companies: A Comment," **AR**, 1981, Vol. 56. No. 4, pp. 959-966.)

Dyckman, T. R. "The Intelligence Of Ambiguity," **AOS**, 1981, Vol. 6, No. 4, pp. 291-300.

Dyckman, T. R. "The Investigation Of Cost Variances," **JAR**, 1969, Vol. 7, No. 2, pp. 215-244.

Dyckman, T. R., R. E. Hoskin and R. J. Swieringa. "An Accounting Change And Information Processing Changes," **AOS**, 1982, Vol. 7, No. 1, pp. 1-12.

Dyckman, T. (Ozan, T. and T. Dyckman. "A Normative Model For Investigation Decisions Involving Multiorigin Cost Variances," **JAR**, 1971, Vol. 9, No. 1, pp. 88-115.)

Dycus, Harold I. (Anderson, Donald T., Harold I. Dycus and Robert B. Welker. "GAAS And The Small Business Audit," **CPAJ**, 1982. Vol. 52, No. 4, pp. 10-23.)

Dye, G. Kenneth. "Casting Up A Projection," **MA**, 1970, Vol. 51. No. 8, pp. 45-47.

Dye, G. Kenneth. "Graphic Control Of The Capital Plan," **MA**, 1966, Vol. 47. No. 8. pp. 27-35.

Dye, G. Kenneth. "The Slide Rule To Untangle Depreciation," **MA**, 1967, Vol. 49, No. 4, pp. 59-63.

Dye, Kenneth M. and Charles A. Bowsher. "Financial Statements For The Sovereign State: The Federal Government Reporting Study," **ACCHOR**, 1987, Vol. 1, No. 1, pp. 17-24.

Dye, Ronald A. "Communication And Post-Decision Information," **JAR**, 1983, Vol. 21, No. 2, pp. 514-533.

Dye, Ronald A. "Disclosure Of Nonproprietary Information," **JAR**, 1985, Vol. 23, No. 1, pp. 123-145.

Dye, Ronald A. "Earnings Management In An Overlapping Generations Model," **JAR**, 1988, Vol. 26, No. 2, pp. 195-235.

Dye, Ronald A. "Strategic Accounting Choice And The Effects Of Alternative Financial Reporting Requirements," **JAR**, 1985, Vol. 23, No. 2, pp. 544-574.

Dyer, James C. IV and Arthur J. McHugh. "The Timeliness Of The Australian Annual Report," **JAR**, 1975, Vol. 13, No. 2, pp. 204-219.

Dykes, Linda M. (Hermanson, Roger H., Linda M. Dykes and Deborah H. Turner. "Enforced Competition In The Accounting Profession - Does It Make Sense?," **ACCHOR**, 1987, Vol. 1. No. 4, pp. 13-20.)

Dykxhoorn, Hans J. and Kathleen E. Sinning. "The Independence Issue Concerning German Auditors: A Synthesis," **IJAER**, 1981, Vol. 16, No. 2, pp. 163-181.

Dykxhoorn, Hans J. and Kathleen E. Sinning. "Wirtschaftsprufer Perception And Auditor Independence," **AR**, 1981, Vol. 56. No. 1, pp. 97-107.

Dykxhoorn, Hans J. and Kathleen E. Sinning. "The Lack Of Uniformity In Statistical Audit Sampling Terminology," **JAED**, 1984. Vol. 2, No. 2, pp. 153-161.

Dykxhoorn, H. J. and K. E. Sinning. "Perceptions Of Auditor Independence: Its Perceived Effect On The Loan And Investment Decisions Of German Financial Statement Users," **AOS**, 1982, Vol. 7, No. 4, pp. 337-348.

Dyl, E. A. and M. S. Lilly. "A Note On Institutional Contributions To The Accounting Literature," **AOS**, 1985. Vol. 10. No. 2, pp. 171-176.

EEE

Earl, Michael and Dean Paxson. "Value Accounting For Currency Transactions," **ABR**, 1977-78, Vol. 8, No. 30, pp. 92-100.

Earl, M. J. "Prototype Systems For Accounting, Information And Control," **AOS**, 1978, Vol. 3, No. 2, pp. 161-172.

Earnest, Kenneth R. and James C. Lampe. "An Expectancy Theory Investigation Into Causes Of Employee Turnover In

Public Accounting," **AIA**, 1987, Vol. 4, pp. 215-238.

Earnest, Kenneth R. "Applying Motivational Theory In Management Accounting," **MA**, 1979, Vol. 61, No. 6, pp. 41-44.

Earnest, Kenneth R. (Lampe, James C. and Kenneth R. Earnest. "Motivation: A Key To Accountants' Productivity And Turnover," **MA**, 1984, Vol. 65, No. 8, pp. 50-55.)

Easton, John E. (Sommerfeld, Ray M. and John E. Easton. "The CPA's Tax Practice Today - And How It Got That Way," **JOA**, 1987, Vol. 163, No. 5, pp. 166-179.)

Easton, Peter D. "Accounting Earnings And Security Valuation: Empirical Evidence Of The Fundamental Links," **JAR**, 1985, Vol. 23, Supp., pp. 54-77.

Eaton, James O. "The Legal Battlefield Of Income Tax Administration," **AR**, 1951, Vol. 26, No. 3, pp. 371-383.

Eaton, Lawrence N. "Equating Risk With Investment And Performance Evaluation," **MA**, 1970, Vol. 52, No. 6, pp. 19-22.

Eaton, Marquis G. "Advisory Service: New Frontier," **JOA**, 1955, Vol. 100, No. 5, pp. 56-61.

Eaton, Marquis G. "Economics Of Accounting Practice," **JOA**, 1957, Vol. 103, No. 6, pp. 31-35.

Eaton, Marquis G. "What Did Mr. Agran Do?," **JOA**, 1955, Vol. 99, No. 6, pp. 33-39.

Eaton, Marquis. "Financial Reporting In A Changing Society," **JOA**, 1957, Vol. 104, No. 2, pp. 25-31.

Eaton, Marquis. "What Is An Accountant?," **JOA**, 1955, Vol. 99, No. 2, pp. 46-51.

Eaton, R. H. "The Cost Approach," **AR**, 1933, Vol. 8, No. 4 pp. 345-348.

Eaves, B. Curtis. "Operational Axiomatic Accounting Mechanics," **AR**, 1966, Vol. 41, No. 3, pp. 426-442.

Ebey, Carl F. "Why Don't Colleges Depreciate Fixed Assets?," **MA**, 1982, Vol. 64, No. 2, pp. 13-17.

Eckel, Leonard G. "Arbitrary And Incorrigible Allocations," **AR**, 1976, Vol. 51, No. 4, pp. 764-777.

Eckel, Norm and Wayne A. Johnson. "A Model For Screening And Classifying Potential Accounting Majors," **JAED**, 1983, Vol. 1, No. 2, pp. 57-65.

Eckel, Norman and Timothy Ross. "Schools Versus Departments Of Accounting: Is There Really A Difference," **JAED**, 1985, Vol. 3, No. 1, pp. 5-14.

Eckel, Norm. "The Income Smoothing Hypothesis Revisited," **ABACUS**, 1981, Vol. 17, No. 1, pp. 28-40.

Ecton, William W. and James A. Knoblett. "Attitudes Of Management Accountants On The Investment Credit Issue," **MA**, 1970, Vol. 52, No. 3, pp. 36-37.

Eddey, Peter H. (Coombes, Robert J. and Peter H. Eddey. "Accounting Income: The Relationship Between Capital Maintenance And Asset Measurement," **IAE**, 1986, Vol. 1, No. 1, pp. 112-122.)

Edelstein, Lee and Susan Aird. "Commitment: The Key To Successful Accounting System Implementation," **MA**, 1988, Vol. 70, No. 6, pp. 50-51.

Eden, Donald F. "Computerized Inventory Control In A Small Company," **MA**, 1972, Vol. 54, No. 2, pp. 39-42.

Edey, Harold C. "Company Accounts In Britain: The Jenkins Report," **AR**, 1963, Vol. 38, No. 2, pp. 262-265.

Edey, Harold C. "Sandilands And The Logic Of Current Cost," **ABR**, 1978-79, Vol. 9, No. 35, pp. 191-200.

Edey, Harold. "The Nature Of Profit," **ABR**, 1970-71, Vol. 1, No. 1, pp. 50-55.

Edgar, S. Michael. (Peavy, John W., III and S. Michael Edgar. "Rating Electric Utility Commercial Paper," **JAAF**, 1985, Vol. 8, No. 2, pp. 125-135.)

Edler, Florence. "Cost Accounting In The Sixteenth Century," **AR**, 1937, Vol. 12, No. 3, pp. 226-237.

Edmister, Robert O. and Harry E. Merriken. "Consumer Deposit Demand, Interest Rate Differentials, And Public Welfare," **JAPP**, 1984, Vol. 3, No. 1, pp. 39-54.

Edmonds, Dwight M. "A Value Analysis Model," **MA**, 1973, Vol. 54, No. 10, pp. 28-30.

Edmonds, Thomas P. "A Multidimensional Assessment Of Practitioner Perceptions Regarding Microcomputer Course Content," **IAE**, 1988, Vol. 3, No. 1, pp. 65-71.

Edmonds, Thomas P. "On The Benefits Of Cumulative Exams: An Experimental Study," **AR**, 1984, Vol. 59, No. 4, pp. 660-668.

Edmonds, Thomas P. "The Effect Of Environmental Complexity On The Level Of Information Processing By Introductory Accounting Students," **IAE**, 1983, No. 1, pp. 29-37.

Edmonds, Thomas P. (Alford, Mark R. and Thomas P. Edmonds. "A Replication: Does Audit Involvement Affect The Quality Of Interim Report Numbers?," **JAAF**, 1981, Vol. 4, No. 3, pp. 255-264.)

Edmondson, V. G. "Accounting. Legal Difficulties In Determining Trust Income," **JOA**, 1952, Vol. 93, No. 4, pp. 438-445.

Edmondson, V. G. "The Statement Of Realization And Liquidation," **AR**, 1955, Vol. 30, No. 2, pp. 339-344.

Edward, J. R. and K. M. Webb. "The Development Of Group Accounting In The United Kingdom To 1933," **AHJ**, 1984, Vol. 11, No. 1, pp. 31-61.

Edwards, Chris. "The Communication Of Computer Generated Information - A Review Of The Empirical Literature," **ABR**, 1982-83, Vol. 13, No. 52, pp. 263-272.

Edwards, Edgar O. and L. Todd Johnson. "An Indifference Approach To Profit-Volume Analysis," **AR**, 1974, Vol. 49, No. 3, pp. 579-583.

Edwards, Edgar O. "Depreciation Policy Under Changing Price Levels," **AR**, 1954, Vol. 29, No. 2, pp. 267-280.

Edwards, Edgar O. "The Fundamental Character Of Excess Current Income," **ABR**, 1979-80, Vol. 10, No. 40, pp. 375-384.

Edwards, Edgar O. "The State Of Current Value Accounting," **AR**, 1975, Vol. 50, No. 2, pp. 235-245.

Edwards, H. R., Myron S. Kem and Harrison W. Wilder. "The Use Of Accounting In Business Policy Determination," **AR**, 1947, Vol. 22, No. 4, pp. 394-404.

Edwards, James B. and Dean E. Graber. "LIFO: To Switch Or Not To Switch?," **MA**, 1975, Vol. 57, No. 4, pp. 35-40.

Edwards, James B. and Julie A. Heard. "Is Cost Accounting The No. 1 Enemy Of Productivity?," **MA**, 1984, Vol. 65, No. 12, pp. 44-49.

Edwards, James B. "Adjusted DCF Rate Of Return," **MA**, 1973, Vol. 54, No. 7, pp. 45-49.

Edwards, James B. "At The Crossroads," **MA**, 1985, Vol. 67, No. 3, pp. 44-50.

Edwards, James B. "Inflation Accounting For Utilities," **MA**, 1976, Vol. 58, No. 2, pp. 19-23.

Edwards, James B. "People Problems And Human Solutions," **MA**, 1975, Vol. 56, No. 8, pp. 32-34.

Edwards, James B. "Should Accounting Students Write Computer Programs?," **AR**, 1973, Vol. 48, No. 1, pp. 163-165.

Edwards, James B. "The Management Accountant And Creativity," **MA**, 1973, Vol. 55, No. 3, pp. 27-32.

Edwards, James B. (Henry, James B., Perry Woodside and James B. Edwards. "Public Sector Leasing In South Carolina," **MA**, 1979, Vol. 61, No. 4, pp. 43-49.)

Edwards, James B., Robert W. Ingram and Howard P. Sanders. "Developing Teaching Skills In Doctoral Programs: The Current Status And Perceived Needs," **AR**, 1981, Vol. 56, No. 1, pp. 144-157.

Edwards, James Don and Barbara J. Shildneck. "The AICPA's First Century," **MA**, 1987, Vol. 69, No. 3, pp. 57-61.

Edwards, James Don and John B. Barrack. "LIFO Inventory Valuation As An Adjuster For Inflation," **CPAJ**, 1975, Vol. 45, No. 10, pp. 21-26.

Edwards, James Don and John B. Barrack. "Objectives Of Financial Statements And Inflation Accounting: A Comparison Of Recent British And American Proposals," **IJAER**, 1976, Vol. 11, No. 2, pp. 11-32.

Edwards, James Don and John B. Barrack. "A New Method Of Inventory Accounting," **MA**, 1987, Vol. 69, No. 5, pp. 49-57.

Edwards, James Don and Paul J. Miranti, Jr. "The AICPA: A Professional Institution In A Dynamic Society," **JOA**, 1987, Vol. 163, No. 5, pp. 22-38.

Edwards, James Don. "Public Accounting In The United States, 1896-1913," **AR**, 1955, Vol. 30, No. 2, pp. 240-251.

Edwards, James Don. "Reports To Top Management," **AR**, 1957, Vol. 32, No. 1, pp. 56-59.

Edwards, James Don. "The AICPA's Century Of Progress," **AHJ**, 1987, Vol. 14, No. 1, pp. 111-121.

Edwards, James Don. "The Emergence Of Public Accounting In The United States, 1748-1895," **AR**, 1954, Vol. 29, No. 1, pp. 52-63.

Edwards, James Don. "This New Costing Concept - Direct Costing?," **AR**, 1958, Vol. 33, No. 4, pp. 561-567.

Edwards, James Don. (Benke, Ralph L., Jr., James Don Edwards and Alton R. Wheelock. "Applying An Opportunity Cost General Rule For Transfer Pricing," **MA**, 1982, Vol. 63, No. 12, pp. 43-51.)

Edwards, James Don. (Benke, Ralph L., Jr. and James Don Edwards. "Should You Use Transfer Pricing To Create Pseudo-Profit Centers?," **MA**, 1981, Vol. 62, No. 8, pp. 36-39.)

Edwards, James Don. (Drinkwater, David and James Don Edwards. "The Nature Of Taxes And The Matching Principle," **AR**, 1965, Vol. 40, No. 3, pp. 579-582.)

Edwards, James Don. (Heard, Edwin, Constantine Konstans and James Don Edwards. "Demonstrating The Conceptual Significance Of The Matrix Inverse," **AR**, 1974, Vol. 49, No. 2, pp. 377-381.)

Edwards, John Richard. "Depreciation And Fixed Asset Valuation In Railway Company Accounts To 1911," **ABR**, 1985-86, Vol. 16, No. 63, pp. 251-263.

Edwards, John Richard. "The Origins And Evolution Of The Double Account System: An Example Of Accounting Innovation," **ABACUS**, 1985, Vol. 21, No. 1, pp. 19-43.

Edwards, J. R. and Alison Warman. "Discounted Cash Flow And Business Valuation In A Nineteenth Century Merger: A Note," **AHJ**, 1981, Vol. 8, No. 2, pp. 37-50.

Edwards, J. R. and C. Baber. "Dowlais Iron Company: Accounting Policies And Procedures For Profit Measurement And Reporting Purposes," **ABR**, 1978-79, Vol. 9, No. 34, pp. 139-151.

Edwards, J. R. and K. M. Webb. "Use Of Table A By Companies Registering Under The Companies Act 1862," **ABR**, 1984-85, Vol. 15, No. 59, pp. 177-196.

Edwards, J. R. "British Capital Accounting Practices And Business Finance 1852-1919: An Exemplification," **ABR**, 1979-80, Vol. 10, No. 38, pp. 241-258.

Edwards, J. R. "The Accounting Profession And Disclosure In Published Reports, 1925-1935," **ABR**, 1975-76, Vol. 6, No. 24, pp. 289-303.

Edwards, Robert L. (Bailes, Jack C. and Robert L. Edwards. "Productivity Boost: Treating Employees As Independent Contractors," **MA**, 1987, Vol. 69, No. 4, pp. 48-51.)

Edwards, William R. (Schnee, Edward J. and William R. Edwards. "New Preparer Rules: More Or Less Penalty?," **JATA**, 1982, Vol. 4, No. 1, pp. 26-32.)

Egenolf, Robert and G. W. K. Willis. "Status Of Public Sector Accounting Education," **JAED**, 1983, Vol. 1, No. 1, pp. 63-69.

Egenolf, Robert V. and Fred Nordhauser. "Public Sector Accounting In The Public Administration Curriculum,"

JAED, 1985, Vol. 3, No. 1, pp. 123-130.

Eger, Carol and John Dickhaut. "An Examination Of The Conservative Information Processing Bias In An Accounting Framework," **JAR**, 1982, Vol. 20, No. 2, Part II, pp. 711-723.

Eggan, Hugh M. "Recapture Provisions Of The Internal Revenue Code," **JOA**, 1966, Vol. 121, No. 6, pp. 47-55.

Eggers, H. C. "The Evaluation Of Human Assets," **MA**, 1971, Vol. 53, No. 5, pp. 28-30.

Eggert, James R. "Don't Ignore Manufacturers' Duty Drawback," **MA**, 1983, Vol. 64, No. 10, pp. 53-56.

Egger, Roscoe L., Jr. "Maintaining The Viability Of The U.S. Tax System," **JOA**, 1983, Vol. 156, No. 6, pp. 84-93.

Egginton, D. A. "Cash Flow, Profit And Performance Measures For External Reporting: A Rejoinder," **ABR**, 1984-85, Vol. 15, No. 58, pp. 109-112.

Egginton, D. A. "Distributable Profit And The Pursuit Of Prudence," **ABR**, 1980-81, Vol. 11, No. 41, pp. 3-14.

Egginton, D. A. "In Defence Of Profit Measurement: Some Limitations Of Cash Flow And Value Added As Performance Measures For External Reporting," **ABR**, 1983-84, Vol. 14, No. 54, pp. 99-112.

Egginton, D. and R. C. Morris. "Holding Gains On Long-Term Liabilities: A Comment," **ABR**, 1975-76, Vol. 6, No. 23, pp. 177-181.

Eggleton, Ian R. C. "Intuitive Time-Series Extrapolation," **JAR**, 1982, Vol. 20, No. 1, pp. 68-102.

Eggleton, Ian R. C. "Patterns, Prototypes, And Predictions: An Exploratory Study," **JAR**, 1976, Vol. 14, Supp., pp. 68-131.

Eggleton, Ian R. C. (Dickhaut, John W. and Ian R. C. Eggleton. "An Examination Of The Processes Underlying Comparative Judgments Of Numerical Stimuli," **JAR**, 1975, Vol. 13, No. 1, pp. 38-72.)

Eggleton, Ian R. C., Stephen H. Penman and John R. Twombly. "Accounting Changes And Stock Prices: An Examination Of Selected Uncontrolled Variables," **JAR**, 1976, Vol. 14, No. 1, pp. 66-88.

Ehn, P. (Carlsson, J., P. Ehn, B. Erlander, M. L. Perby and A. Sandberg. "Planning And Control From The Perspective Of Labour: A Short Presentation Of The DEMOS Project," **AOS**, 1978, Vol. 3, No. 3/4, pp. 249-260.)

Ehrenreich, K. B. (Grove, H. D., T. J. Mock and K. B. Ehrenreich. "A Review Of Human Resource Accounting Measurement Systems From A Measurement Theory Perspective," **AOS**, 1977, Vol. 2, No. 3, pp. 219-236.)

Ehrsam, Robert. (Lammert, Thomas B. and Robert Ehrsam. "The Human Element: The Real Challenge In Modernizing Cost Systems," **MA**, 1987, Vol. 69, No. 1, pp. 32-37.)

Eichen, Susan P. and Mary Ann Domurachi. "Designing Internal Control Systems For Appropriate Management Control," **CA**, 1986, Vol. 4, No. 4, pp. 20-28.

Eichenseher, John W. and David Shields. "The Correlates Of CPA-Firm Change For Publicly-Held Corporations," **AJPT**, 1982-83, Vol. 2, No. 2, pp. 23-37.

Eichenseher, John W. and David Shields. "Corporate Director Liability And Monitoring Preferences," **JAPP**, 1985, Vol. 4, No. 1, pp. 13-31.

Eichenseher, John W. and Paul Danos. "The Analysis Of Industry-Specific Auditor Concentration: Towards An Explanatory Model," **AR**, 1981, Vol. 56, No. 3, pp. 479-492.

Eichenseher, John W. "The Effects Of Foreign Operations On Domestic Auditor Selection," **JAAF**, 1985, Vol. 8, No. 3, pp. 195-209.

Eichenseher, John W. (Danos, Paul and John W. Eichenseher. "Long-Term Trends Toward Seller Concentration In The U.S. Audit Market," **AR**, 1986, Vol. 61, No. 4, pp. 633-650.)

Eichenseher, John W. (Danos, Paul and John W. Eichenseher. "Audit Industry Dynamics: Factors Affecting Changes In Client-Industry Market Shares," **JAR**, 1982, Vol. 20, No. 2, Part II, pp. 604-616.)

Eichhorn, Frederic G. "A Direct Allocation Financial Data Base For Manufacturing," **MA**, 1978, Vol. 59, No. 11, pp. 39-42.

Eichhorn, Frederic G. (Bongiorni, Peter J. and Frederic G. Eichhorn. "Keeping A Second Set Of Books - Legally," **MA**, 1979, Vol. 61, No. 6, pp. 30-35.)

Eickhoff, Roger. (Harrell, Adrian A. and Roger Eickhoff. "Auditors' Influence-Orientation And Their Effective Responses To The 'Big Eight' Work Environment," **AJPT**, 1988, Vol. 7, No. 2, pp. 105-118.)

Eidson, Gale D. (Dillon, Ray D., Lloyd L. Byars, Craig E. Aronoff and Gale D. Eidson. "The CPA Firm's 'Mission'," **JOA**, 1985, Vol. 159, No. 6, pp. 70-78.)

Eigen, Martin M. "Is Pooling Really Necessary?," **AR**, 1965, Vol. 40, No. 3, pp. 536-540.

Eigen, Martin M. "The Share Of Market: A Focal Point For Financial Reporting," **MA**, 1967, Vol. 48, No. 11, pp. 51-56.

Eiler, Robert G. (Keegan, Daniel P., Robert G. Eiler and Joseph V. Anania. "An Advanced Cost Management System For The Factory Of The Future," **MA**, 1988, Vol. 70, No. 6, pp. 31-37.)

Einhorn, Hillel J. and Robin M. Hogarth. "Behavioral Decision Theory: Processes Of Judgment And Choice," **JAR**, 1981, Vol. 19, No. 1, pp. 1-31.

Eining, Martha. (Dorr, Patrick, Martha Eining and James E. Groff. "Developing An Accounting Expert System Decision Aid For Classroom Use," **IAE**, 1988, Vol. 3, No. 1, pp. 27-41.)

Eisenman, Seymour and Steven B. Lilien. "Accounting Deficiencies In Financial Statements," **CPAJ**, 1978, Vol. 48, No. 7, pp. 28-34.

Eisenman, Seymour, Murray S. Akresh and Charles Snow. "Reporting Unusual Events In Income Statements," **CPAJ**, 1979, Vol. 49, No. 6, pp. 23-28.

Eisenstein, Alex. "Suggestions For The Content Of Corporate Reports," **AR**, 1941, Vol. 16, No. 4, pp. 401-406.

Eiswerth, L. R. (Filer, R. J. and L. R. Eiswerth. "Quality Control And Associated Costs," **MA**, 1966, Vol. 48, No. 1, pp. 37-44.)

Eiteman, Dean S. "A Closer Look At Cost Of Capital," **MA**, 1967, Vol. 48, No. 11, pp. 57-63.

Eiteman, Dean W. "Critical Problems In Accounting For Goodwill," **JOA**, 1971, Vol. 131, No. 3, pp. 46-50.

Elam, Rick and Hamid Henaidy. "Transfer Pricing For The Multinational Corporation," **IJAER**, 1981, Vol. 16, No. 2, pp. 49-65.

Elam, Rick. "Capitalization Of Leases And The Predictability Of Financial Ratios: A Reply," **AR**, 1976, Vol. 51, No. 2, pp. 413-414.

Elam, Rick. "The Cultural Significance Of Accounts - The Philosophy Of DR Scott," **AHJ**, 1981, Vol. 8, No. 2, pp. 51-59.

Elam, Rick. "The Effect Of Lease Data On The Predictive Ability Of Financial Ratios," **AR**, 1975, Vol. 50, No. 1, pp. 25-43.

Elam, Rick. (Engle, Terry J. and Rick Elam. "The Status Of Collegiate Auditing Education," **IAE**, 1985, No. 1, pp. 97-108.)

Elam, Rick. (Nikolai, Loren A. and Rick Elam. "The Pollution Control Tax Incentive: A Non-Incentive," **AR**, 1979, Vol. 54, No. 1, pp. 119-131.)

El Ashker, Ahmed A. (Briston, Richard J. and Ahmed A. El-Ashker. "The Egyptian Accounting System: A Case Study In Western Influence," **IJAER**, 1984, Vol. 19, No. 2, pp. 129-155.)

Elder, Peter and Ernest J. Cholden. "Tax Planning For Foundations," **JOA**, 1965, Vol. 119, No. 5, pp. 50-54.

El Gazzar, Samir, Steve Lilien and Victor Pastena. "Accounting For Leases By Lessees," **JAEC**, 1986, Vol. 8, No. 3, pp. 217-237.

Elgers, Pieter and John J. Clark. "Inclusion Of Budgets In Financial Reports: Investor Needs V. Management Disclosure," **ABR**, 1972-73, Vol. 3, No. 9, pp. 53-61.

Elgers, Pieter T. and Dennis Murray. "The Impact Of The Choice Of Market Index On The Empirical Evaluation Of Accounting Risk Measures," **AR**, 1982, Vol. 57, No. 2, pp. 358-375.

Elgers, Pieter T. "Accounting-Based Risk Predictions: A Re-Examination," **AR**, 1980, Vol. 55, No. 3, pp. 389-408.

Elgers, Pieter T. (May, Gordon S. and Pieter T. Elgers. "Problems With SEC's Forecast Guidelines," **CPAJ**, 1978, Vol. 48, No. 3, pp. 21-26.)

Elgers, Pieter, Carolyn Callahan and Elizabeth Strock. "The Effect Of Earnings Yields Upon The Association Between Unexpected Earnings And Security Returns: A Re-Examination," **AR**, 1987, Vol. 62, No. 4, pp. 763-773.

Elgers, Pieter. (Clark, John J. and Pieter Elgers. "Forecasted Income Statements: An Investor Perspective," **AR**, 1973, Vol. 48, No. 4, pp. 668-678.)

Elgers, P. T. (Bloom, R., P. T. Elgers and D. Murray. "Functional Fixation In Product Pricing: A Comparison Of Individuals And Groups," **AOS**, 1984, Vol. 9, No. 1, pp. 1-12.)

Elias, Nabil and Marc Epstein. "Dimensions Of Corporate Social Reporting," **MA**, 1975, Vol. 56, No. 9, pp. 36-40.

Elias, Nabil. "Behavioral Impact Of Human Resource Accounting," **MA**, 1976, Vol. 57, No. 8, pp. 43-45.

Elias, Nabil. "The Effects Of Human Asset Statements On The Investment Decision: An Experiment," **JAR**, 1972, Vol. 10, Supp., pp. 215-233.

Elikai, Fara and Jack Baker. "Empirical Evidence On The Effectiveness Of Quizzes As A Motivational Technique," **IAE**, 1988, Vol. 3, No. 2, pp. 248-254.

Elikai, Fara and Shane Moriarity. "Variance Analysis With PERT/COST," **AR**, 1982, Vol. 57, No. 1, pp. 161-170.

Elikai, Fara. (Knapp, Michael C. and Fara Elikai. "Auditor Changes: A Note On The Policy Implications Of Recent Analytical And Empirical Research," **JAAF**, 1988, Vol. 3 (New Series), No. 1, pp. 78-86.)

Elkin, Charles. "IRC Section 1244 (A Small Business Aid) - Its Provisions And Necessary Reforms," **CPAJ**, 1973, Vol. 43, No. 11, pp. 955-962.

Ellenberger, Frederick H. "The Accountant And The Time-Share Terminal," **MA**, 1971, Vol. 52, No. 11, pp. 39-40.

Elliott, C. Willard. "Quasi-Reorganization Of An International Corporation In The Event Of Currency Devaluation," **MA**, 1966, Vol. 48, No. 3, pp. 60-63.

Elliott, Edward L. "Accounting And Economic Development In Latin America," **IJAER**, 1972, Vol. 8, No. 1, pp. 89-97.

Elliott, Edward L. "The Managerial Role Of Governmental Accounting In Economic Development," **IJAER**, 1968, Vol. 4, No. 1, pp. 129-136.

Elliott, Edward L., Jose Larrea and Juan M. Rivera. "Accounting Aid To Developing Countries," **AR**, 1968, Vol. 43, No. 4, pp. 763-768.

Elliott, Grover S. "Analyzing The Cost Of Capital," **MA**, 1980, Vol. 62, No. 6, pp. 13-18.

Elliott, Grover S. "Leasing Of Capital Equipment," **MA**, 1975, Vol. 57, No. 6, pp. 39-42.

Elliott, John A. and Duane B. Kennedy. "Estimation And Prediction Of Categorical Models In Accounting Research," **JAL**, 1988, Vol. 7, pp. 202-242.

Elliott, John A. and Robert J. Swieringa. "Aetna, The SEC And Tax Benefits Of Loss Carryforwards," **AR**, 1985, Vol. 60, No. 3, pp. 531-546.

Elliott, John A. and Wayne H. Shaw. "Write-Offs As

Accounting Procedures To Manage Perceptions," **JAR**, 1988, Vol. 26, Supp., pp. 91-119.

Elliott, John A. "'Subject To' Audit Opinions And Abnormal Security Returns: Outcomes And Ambiguities," **JAR**, 1982, Vol. 20, No. 2, Part II, pp. 617-638.

Elliott, John A. (Dukes, Roland E., Thomas R. Dyckman and John A. Elliott. "Accounting For Research And Development Costs: The Impact On Research And Development Expenditures," **JAR**, 1980, Vol. 18, Supp., pp. 1-26.)

Elliott, John, Gordon Richardson, Thomas Dyckman and Roland Dukes. "The Impact Of SFAS No.2 On Firm Expenditures On Research And Development: Replications And Extensions," **JAR**, 1984, Vol. 22, No. 1, pp. 85-102.

Elliott, J. Douglas. "Communications And Automation," **MA**, 1968, Vol. 49, No. 10, pp. 18-22.

Elliott, J. W. and H. L. Uphoff. "Predicting The Near Term Profit And Loss Statement With An Econometric Model: A Feasibility Study," **JAR**, 1972, Vol. 10, No. 2, pp. 259-274.

Elliott, Merle S. and Monroe S. Kuttner. "MAS: Coming Of Age," **JOA**, 1982, Vol. 154, No. 6, pp. 66-75.

Elliott, Norman J. "Another View Of The 1136 Tenants' Corporation Case," **CPAJ**, 1972, Vol. 42, No. 12, pp. 1001-1008.

Elliott, Norman J. "Profit Potentials In A Loss Company," **JOA**, 1963, Vol. 115, No. 3, pp. 49-56.

Elliott, Robert K. and John R. Rogers. "Relating Statistical Sampling To Audit Objectives," **JOA**, 1972, Vol. 134, No. 1, pp. 46-55.

Elliott, Robert K. and Peter D. Jacobson. "Audit Technology: A Heritage And A Promise," **JOA**, 1987, Vol. 163, No. 5, pp. 198-218.

Elliott, Robert K. and Peter D. Jacobson. "Detecting And Deterring Financial Statement Fraud," **CA**, 1986, Vol. 4, No. 4, pp. 34-39.

Elliott, Robert K. and Peter D. Jacobson. "Two Views On The Auditor's Report: The Last Word Or In Need Of Change?," **JOA**, 1987, Vol. 163, No. 2, pp. 72-79.

Elliott, Robert K. and Peter D. Jacobson. "The Treadway Report - Its Potential Impact," **CPAJ**, 1987, Vol. 57, No. 11, pp. 20-35.

Elliott, Robert K. and Peter D. Jacobson. "Assessing The ASB's Ten Exposure Drafts," **CPAJ**, 1987, Vol. 57, No. 12, pp. 16-25.

Elliott, Robert K. "Dinosaurs, Passenger Pigeons, And Financial Accountants," **CPAJ**, 1987, Vol. 57, No. 1, pp. 4-13.

Elliott, Robert K. "Unique Audit Methods: Peat Marwick International," **AJPT**, 1982-83, Vol. 2, No. 2, pp. 1-12.

Elliott, Robert K. (Ashton, Robert H., John J. Willingham and Robert K. Elliott. "An Empirical Analysis Of Audit Delay," **JAR**, 1987, Vol. 25, No. 2, pp. 275-292.)

Elliott, Robert K. (Brumfield, Craig A., Robert K. Elliott and Peter D. Jacobson. "Business Risk And The Audit Process," **JOA**, 183, Vol. 155, No. 4, pp. 60-69.)

Elliott, Robert K. (Jacobson, Peter D. and Robert K. Elliott. "GAAS: Reconsidering The 'Ten Commandments'," **JOA**, 1984, Vol. 157, No. 5, pp. 77-89.)

Elliott, Robert K. (Pallais, Don and Robert K. Elliot. "Prospective Financial Statements: Guidelines For A Growing Practice Area," **JOA**, 1984, Vol. 157, No. 1, pp. 56-71.)

Elliott, Robert K. (Stilwell, Martin C. and Robert K. Elliott. "A Model For Expanding The Attest Function," **JOA**, 1985, Vol. 159, No. 5, pp. 66-81.)

Elliott, Robert K. (Zuber, George R., Robert K. Elliott, William R. Kinney, Jr., and James J. Leisenring. "Using Materiality In Audit Planning," **JOA**, 183, Vol. 155, No. 3, pp. 42-55.)

Elliott, Robert R. (Kelso, Raymond L. and Robert R. Elliott. "Bridging Communications Gap Between Accountants And Managers," **MA**, 1969, Vol. 51, No. 5, pp. 41-43.)

Elliott, V. L. "Functions And Activities Of The Controller's Department," **AR**, 1940, Vol. 15, No. 2, pp. 185-189.

Elliott, W. Larry. "Cost Behavior: A Dynamic Concept," **MA**, 1974, Vol. 55, No. 9, pp. 33-36.

Elliott, W. Larry. "Operational Approach To Cash Management," **MA**, 1976, Vol. 58, No. 6, pp. 20-26.

Ellis, A. C. "Cost Basis In Accounting Must Be Used Unless We Upset Our Whole Business System," **JOA**, 1950, Vol. 90, No. 1, pp. 40-45.

Ellis, Joseph K., III. (Coburn, David L., Joseph K. Ellis, III and Duane R. Milano. "Dilemmas In MNC Transfer Pricing," **MA**, 1981, Vol. 63, No. 5, pp. 53-58.)

Ellis, Loudell O. "Cash Basis Reporting For Churches," **CPAJ**, 1975, Vol. 45, No. 5, pp. 39-44.

Ellis, Loudell O. "Internal Control For Churches And Community Organizations," **CPAJ**, 1974, Vol. 44, No. 5, pp. 45-48.

Ellison, David J. (Raymond, Robert H. and David J. Ellison. "Personal Financial Statements - Benefits Of Experience," **CPAJ**, 1983, Vol. 53, No. 4, pp. 14-23.)

Ellyson, Robert C. and Barrie S. Shaw. "The Psychological Assessment And Staff Recruiting," **JOA**, 1970, Vol. 129, No. 3, pp. 35-42.

Ellyson, Robert C. and William H. Van Rensselaer. "Sunset - Is The Profession Ready For It?," **JOA**, 1980, Vol. 149, No. 6, pp. 52-61.

Ellyson, Robert C. "A 5-Year Education Requirement?," **CPAJ**, 1983, Vol. 53, No. 12, pp. 39-46.

Ellyson, Robert C. "Planning The Future Growth Of An Accounting Practice - One Approach," **JOA**, 1968, Vol. 126, No. 4, pp. 46-56.

Ellyson, Robert C. (Anderson, George D. and Robert C. Ellyson. "Restructuring Professional Standards: The Anderson Report," **JOA**, 1986, Vol. 162, No. 3, pp. 92-105.)

Ellyson, Robert C., A. Tom Nelson and James H. MacNeill. "Educating Tomorrow's CPAs," **JOA**, 1985, Vol. 160, No. 4, pp. 95-105.

Elmore, Robert C. "The Influence Of Tax Legislation On Financial Accounting: A Study Of The Timber Industry, 1905 - 1925," **AHJ**, 1987, Vol. 14, No. 2, pp. 41-57.

Elnicki, Richard A. "Asset Base For Performance Evaluation - A Critique," **MA**, 1968, Vol. 49, No. 12, pp. 55-59.

Elnicki, Richard A. "FOI Simulations For Investment Decisions," **MA**, 1970, Vol. 51, No. 8, pp. 37-41.

Elnicki, Richard A. "Hospital Working Capital: An Empirical Study," **JAR**, 1977, Vol. 15, Supp., pp. 209-218.

Elnicki, Richard A. "The Genesis Of Management Accounting," **MA**, 1971, Vol. 52, No. 10, pp. 15-17.

Elsayed, Mohsen M. and William B. Pollard. "Tax Havens And Other International Techniques," **CPAJ**, 1986, Vol. 56, No. 4, pp. 36-39.

Elvik, Kenneth O. "Acquisition Cost Versus Revaluation: A Historical Perspective," **IJAER**, 1974, Vol. 9, No. 2, pp. 155-167.

Elwell, Fayette H. "Governmental Accounting Questions In C.P.A. Examinations," **AR**, 1934, Vol. 9, No. 1, pp. 58-60.

El Sheshai, Kamal M. (Abdel-khalik, A. Rashad and Kamal M. El-Sheshai. "Information Choice And Utilization In An Experiment On Default Prediction," **JAR**, 1980, Vol. 18, No. 2, pp. 325-342.)

El Sheshai, Kamal M., Gordon B. Harwood and Roger H. Hermanson. "Cost Volume Profit Analysis With Integer Goal Programming," **MA**, 1977, Vol. 59, No. 4, pp. 43-47.

Emanuel, David M. "A Critique Of The Richardson Report," **ABR**, 1978-79, Vol. 9, No. 35, pp. 217-227.

Emblen, Donald J. "Accounting In The Professional Business Curriculum," **AR**, 1949, Vol. 24, No. 4, pp. 403-408.

Emblen, Donald J. "When Should Techniques Be Presented?," **AR**, 1963, Vol. 38, No. 1, pp. 159-160.

Emby, Craig and Michael Gibbins. "Good Judgment In Public Accounting And Justification," **CAR**, 1988, Vol. 4, No. 2, pp. 287-313.

Emby, Craig. (Lindahl, Frederick W., Craig Emby and Robert H. Ashton. "Empirical Research On CPCR: A Review And Analysis," **JAL**, 1988, Vol. 7, pp. 310-331.)

Emery, Douglas R. (Peters, Michael and Douglas R. Emery. "The Role Of Negative Numbers In The Development Of Double Entry Bookkeeping," **JAR**, 1978, Vol. 16, No. 2, pp. 424-426.)

Emery, Douglas R., F. Hutton Barron and William F. Messier, Jr. "Conjoint Measurement And The Analysis Of Noisy Data: A Comment," **JAR**, 1982, Vol. 20, No. 2, Part I, pp. 450-458.)

Emery, Gary W. and Kenneth O. Cogger. "The Measurement Of Liquidity," **JAR**, 1982, Vol. 20, No. 2, Part I, pp. 290-303.

Emery, Kenneth G. "Should Goodwill Be Written Off?," **AR**, 1951, Vol. 26, No. 4, pp. 560-567.

Emin, Hussein D. "The Statement Of Changes In Financial Position: An Alternative Teaching Approach," **JAED**, 1983, Vol. 1, No. 1, pp. 35-45.

Emmanuel, C. R. and S. J. Gray. "Segmental Disclosures And The Segment Identification Problem," **ABR**, 1977-78, Vol. 8, No. 29, pp. 37-50.

Emmanuel, Clive R. and Kenneth P. Gee. "Transfer Pricing: A Fair And Neutral Procedure," **ABR**, 1981-82, Vol. 12, No. 48, pp. 273-278.

Emmanuel, C. R. and N. Garrod. "On The Segment Identification Issue," **ABR**, 1986-87, Vol. 17, No. 67, pp. 235-240.

Emmanuel, C. R. and S. J. Gray. "Segmental Disclosure By Multibusiness Multinational Companies: A Proposal," **ABR**, 1977-78, Vol. 8, No. 31, pp. 169-177.

Emmerich, Herbert. "Federal Administrative Trends And Accountability," **AR**, 1940, Vol. 15, No. 1, pp. 22-30.

Endsley, Lionel I. and Gary R. Cesnik. "Lifo For Bargain-Purchased Inventories: The Tax Connection," **JOA**, 1986, Vol. 162, No. 2, pp. 94-101.

Eng, Lee Hock. (McNally, Graeme M., Lee Hock Eng and C. Roy Hasseldine. "Corporate Financial Reporting In New Zealand," **ABR**, 1982-83, Vol. 13, No. 49, pp. 11-20.)

Eng, Lee Hock. (McNally, Graeme M. and Lee Hock Eng. "Management Accounting Practices And Company Characteristics," **ABACUS**, 1980, Vol. 16, No. 2, pp. 142-150.)

Eng, Richard. (Wiesen, Jeremy and Richard Eng. "Corporate Perks: Disclosure And Tax Considerations," **JAAF**, 1979, Vol. 2, No. 2, pp. 101-121.)

Engber, Michael. "Using Crummey Trusts In Estate Planning," **CPAJ**, 1981, Vol. 51, No. 4, pp. 30-35.

Engel, Lee. "The Moment Of Truth In Management Services," **JOA**, 1969, Vol. 127, No. 2, pp. 33-37.

Engelmann, Konrad. "Accounting Problems In Developing Countries," **JOA**, 1962, Vol. 113, No. 1, pp. 53-56.

Engelmann, Konrad. "In Search Of An Accounting Philosophy," **AR**, 1954, Vol. 29, No. 3, pp. 383-390.

Engelmann, Konrad. "The Impact Of Relativism On Accounting," **AR**, 1952, Vol. 27, No. 3, pp. 361-365.

Engelmann, K. "The Realization Basis Of Determining Income Would Eliminate Distortions Caused By Inflation," **JOA**, 1950, Vol. 90, No. 4, pp. 321-323.

Engelmann, K. "The 'LIFO-OR-MARKET' Plan," **AR**, 1953, Vol. 28, No. 1, pp. 54-57.

Engle, Robert E. "How To Choose The Right Form Of Doing Business," **MA**, 1985, Vol. 66, No. 7, pp. 44-48.

Engle, Robert. (Shipley, Kent and Robert Engle. "We Need

More Ph.D.s In Accounting," **MA**, 1982, Vol. 64, No. 5, pp. 36-41.)

Engle, Terry J. and G. W. Joseph. "A Successful Approach To Integrating Computer Assignments Into Accounting Information Systems Courses," **JAED**, 1986, Vol. 4, No. 2, pp. 141-146.

Engle, Terry J. and Rick Elam. "The Status Of Collegiate Auditing Education," **IAE**, 1985, No. 1, pp. 97-108.

Engle, Terry J. "Training Programs In Large Firms," **CPAJ**, 1984, Vol. 54, No. 4, pp. 15-21.

Englebrecht, Ted D. "Corporate Insiders Repayment Dilemma," **CPAJ**, 1976, Vol. 46, No. 12, pp. 23-27.

Englebrecht, Ted D. and Anthony Billings. "Impact Of TRA 86 On Trusts, Estates And Gifts," **CPAJ**, 1987, Vol. 57, No. 2, pp. 50-57.

Englebrecht, Ted D. and Craig D. Johnson. "Generation-Skipping Transfers Under TRA 1976," **CPAJ**, 1978, Vol. 48, No. 3, pp. 31-37.

Englebrecht, Ted D. and Fred P. Meyer. "Using Qualified Disclaimers In Estate Planning," **CPAJ**, 1986, Vol. 56, No. 9, pp. 66-73.

Englebrecht, Ted D. and Richard L. Banham. "Earnings And Profits: The Income Tax Dilemma," **JOA**, 1979, Vol. 147, No. 2, pp. 58-65.

Englebrecht, Ted D. and Robert J. Rolfe. "An Empirical Inquiry Into The Determination Of Dividend Equivalence In Stock Redemptions: A Reply," **JATA**, 1984, Vol. 5, No. 2, pp. 81-84.

Englebrecht, Ted D. and Robert J. Rolfe. "An Empirical Inquiry Into The Determination Of Dividend Equivalence In Stock Redemptions," **JATA**, 1982, Vol. 4, No. 1, pp. 19-25.

Englebrecht, Ted D. and Robert J. Rolfe. "Noncorporate Lessors Of Equipment Are Still Subject To Administrative And Judicial Scrutiny," **JATA**, 1982, Vol. 3, No. 2, pp. 23-29.

Englebrecht, Ted D. and Robert J. Rolfe. "An Alternative To Education Trusts," **CPAJ**, 1981, Vol. 51, No. 7, pp. 23-30.

Englebrecht, Ted D. and Robert W. Jamison, Jr. "An Empirical Inquiry Into The Role Of The Tax Court In The Valuation Of Property For Charitable Contribution Purposes," **AR**, 1979, Vol. 54, No. 3, pp. 554-562.

Englebrecht, Ted D. (Copeland, Ronald M. and Ted D. Englebrecht. "Statistical Sampling: An Uncertain Defense Against Legal Liability," **CPAJ**, 1975, Vol. 45, No. 11, pp. 23-28.)

Englebrecht, Ted D. (Lancaster, Joe and Ted D. Englebrecht. "An Analysis Of The Availability Of Percentage Depletion For Lease Bonuses And Advance Royalties," **JATA**, 1983, Vol. 4, No. 2, pp. 44-51.)

Englebrecht, Ted D. (Schneider, Kent N. and Ted D. Englebrecht. "Avoiding ITC Recapture In 351 Transfers," **CPAJ**, 1985, Vol. 55, No. 2, pp. 28-35.)

Engstrom, John H. and Floyd W. Windal. "Accounting Education For MBA Students: A Survey," **JAED**, 1985, Vol. 3, No. 1, pp. 107-121.

Engstrom, John H. and Randolph A. Shockley. "Financial Reporting For The Georgia Colony," **AHJ**, 1985, Vol. 12, No. 2, pp. 43-58.

Engstrom, John H. "Pension Reporting By Municipalities," **JAAF**, 1984, Vol. 7, No. 3, pp. 197-211.

Engstrom, John H. "Public Sector Accounting Education: Status Update And Extension," **AR**, 1979, Vol. 54, No. 4, pp. 794-799.

Engstrom, John H. "The Governmental Reporting Entity," **JAAF**, 1985, Vol. 8, No. 4, pp. 305-318.

Enis, Charles R. and Darryl L. Craig. "The Redistribution Of The Income Tax Burden Under A True Flat Tax Structure," **JATA**, 1984, Vol. 6, No. 1, pp. 20-35.

Enis, Charles R. and Edward A. Morash. "Accounting For Public Policy Actions: The Case Of Motor Carrier Deregulation," **ABACUS**, 1985, Vol. 21, No. 1, pp. 63-83.

Enis, Charles R. (Hunt, Herbert G., III and Charles R. Enis. "Economic Analysis Of Broad-Based Income And Consumption Taxes," **AIT**, 1988, Vol. 2, pp. xx-xx.)

Enis, Charles R., William T. Stuart and John J. Hourihan. "Local Revenue Policy In Less Developed Countries: The Case For Energy Consumption Taxation," **AIT**, 1987, Vol. 1, pp. 85-108.

Enis, C. R. "The Impact Of Current-Valued Data On The Predictive Judgments Of Investors," **AOS**, 1988, Vol. 13, No. 2, pp. 123-146.

Enke, Ernest L. "The Accounting Preconditions Of PPB," **MA**, 1972, Vol. 53, No. 7, pp. 33-38.

Enns, Robin. (Amernic, Joel and Robin Enns. "Levels Of Cognitive Complexity And Design Of An Accounting Curriculum," **AR**, 1979, Vol. 54, No. 1, pp. 133-149.

Enrick, Robert L. "Using Sales Equivalency As A Cost Saving Tool," **MA**, 1985, Vol. 66, No. 8, pp. 46-50.

Enright, Richard D. "Standard Costs For Delivery Systems," **MA**, 1974, Vol. 55, No. 7, pp. 34-36.

Enthoven, Adolf J. H. "Accounting And Development Programming," **IJAER**, 1967, Vol. 3, No. 1, pp. 107-120.

Enthoven, Adolf J. H. "Economic Development And Accountancy," **JOA**, 1965, Vol. 120, No. 2, pp. 29-35.

Enthoven, Adolf J. H. "International Management Accounting - A Challenge For Accountants," **MA**, 1980, Vol. 62, No. 3, pp. 25-32.

Enthoven, Adolf J. H. "Standardized Accountancy And Economic Development," **MA**, 1976, Vol. 57, No. 8, pp. 19-23.

Enthoven, Adolf J. H. "The Future Of International Standards In Government Accounting," **AIIA**, 1988, Vol. 2, pp. 205-228.

Enthoven, Adolf J. H. "The Unity Of Accountancy In An International Context," **IJAER**, 1973, Vol. 9, No. 1, pp. 113-133.

Enthoven, Adolf J. H. "U.S. Accounting And The Third World," **JOA**, 183, Vol. 155, No. 6, pp. 110-118.

Enthoven, Adolph J. H. "International Management Accounting: Its Scope And Standards," **IJAER**, 1982, Vol. 17, No. 2, pp. 59-74.

Enthoven, A. J. H. "The Scope For Accountancy Planning In Developing Countries," **ABR**, 1975-76, Vol. 6, No. 22, pp. 135-139.

Epaves, Richard A., Laurence R. Paquette and Michael A. Pearson. "A Flow Chart Conceptualization Of Auditors' Reports On Financial Statements," **AR**, 1976, Vol. 51, No. 4, pp. 913-916.

Epps, Max I. "Realistic Accounting Under South American Inflation," **JOA**, 1961, Vol. 111, No. 1, pp. 67-73.

Epps, William F. "How Richmond County Learned Fixed-Asset Management," **MA**, 1979, Vol. 61, No. 4, pp. 34-39.

Eppston, Harold A. "Accounting Implication Of The Business Cycle," **AR**, 1941, Vol. 16, No. 3, pp. 269-273.

Epstein, Joanne B. (Epstein, Marc J. and Joanne B. Epstein. "An Annotated Bibliography Of Scientific Management And Standard Costing To 1920," **ABACUS**, 1974, Vol. 10 No. 2, pp. 165-174.)

Epstein, Marc J. and Joanne B. Epstein. "An Annotated Bibliography Of Scientific Management And Standard Costing To 1920," **ABACUS**, 1974, Vol. 10 No. 2, pp. 165-174.

Epstein, Marc. (Elias, Nabil and Marc Epstein. "Dimensions Of Corporate Social Reporting," **MA**, 1975, Vol. 56, No. 9, pp. 36-40.)

Epstein, M. J. (Crumbley, D. L., M. J. Epstein and L. L. Bravenec. "Tax Impact In Corporate Social Responsibility Decisions And Reporting," **AOS**, 1977, Vol. 2, No. 2, pp. 131-140.)

Epstein, M., E. Flamholtz and J. J. McDonough. "Corporate Social Accounting In The U.S.A.: State Of The Art And Future Prospects," **AOS**, 1976, Vol. 1, No. 1, pp. 23-42.

Epstein, Ralph C. "Valuation And Other Problems Connected With The Study Of Corporate Profits," **AR**, 1933, Vol. 8, No. 2, pp. 93-98.

Epstein, Stephen and Raymond Showfety. "Section 304: Tax Trap For The Unwary," **CPAJ**, 1975, Vol. 45, No. 12, pp. 27-29.

Erard, Irene C. "Unaudited Financial Statements," **MA**, 1975, Vol. 57, No. 2, pp. 45-48.

Erb, Hester Ellen. "Employee Welfare Funds," **JOA**, 1955, Vol. 100, No. 2, pp. 31-43.

Erdahl, C. A. "A Modern Profit Concept In The Retail Selling Field," **JOA**, 1962, Vol. 114, No. 3, pp. 57-62.

Erickson, Naomi and David H. Herskovits. "Accounting For Software Costs: Cracking The Code," **JOA**, 1985, Vol. 160, No. 5, pp. 81-97.

Erickson, Naomi S. (Lhotka, Joseph D. and Naomi S. Erickson. "Accounting For Software: A Step Forward," **JOA**, 1984, Vol. 158, No. 5, pp. 110-124.)

Erickson, Naomi. (Searfoss, D. Gerald and Naomi Erickson. "The Big Unfunded Liability: Postretirement Healthcare Benefits," **JOA**, 1988, Vol. 166, No. 5, pp. 28-39.)

Erickson, Vernon E. "Mortgage Loan Accounting," **MA**, 1967, Vol. 48, No. 6, pp. 36-40.

Ericson, Joseph H., Jr. "Standard Cost In Action," **MA**, 1978, Vol. 60, No. 2, pp. 25-32.

Eriksen, Edward G. "Budgeting In Retirement," **MA**, 1975, Vol. 56, No. 10, pp. 54-56.

Erlander, B. (Carlsson, J., P. Ehn, B. Erlander, M. L. Perby and A. Sandberg. "Planning And Control From The Perspective Of Labour: A Short Presentation Of The DEMOS Project," **AOS**, 1978, Vol. 3, No. 3/4, pp. 249-260.)

Esenoff, Carl M. "Some Techniques Used Successfully In Running A Medium-Sized Accounting Firm," **JOA**, 1950, Vol. 89, No. 1, pp. 28-33.

Eskew, Robert K. and Robert H. Faley. "Some Determinants Of Student Performance In The First College-Level Financial Accounting Course," **AR**, 1988, Vol. 63, No. 1, pp. 137-147.

Eskew, Robert K. "An Examination Of The Association Between Accounting And Share Price Data In The Extractive Petroleum Industry," **AR**, 1975, Vol. 50, No. 2, pp. 316-324.

Eskew, Robert K. "An Examination Of The Association Between Accounting And Share Price Data In The Extractive Petroleum Industry: A Reply," **AR**, 1978, Vol. 53, No. 1, pp. 240-246.

Eskew, Robert K. "The Forecasting Of Accounting Risk Measures: Some Additional Evidence," **AR**, 1979, Vol. 54, No. 1, pp. 107-119.

Eskridge, Charles V. "Classroom Technique," **AR**, 1946, Vol. 21, No. 3, pp. 306-307.

Espahbodi, Reza and Harvey Hendrikson. "A Discussion Of Cost-Benefit Analysis Methodology: Reply To Comment," **JAPP**, 1987, Vol. 6, No. 3, pp. 219-228.

Espahbodi, Reza and Harvey Hendrikson. "A Cost-Benefit Analysis Of Accounting For Inflation," **JAPP**, 1986, Vol. 5, No. 1, pp. 31-55.

Espejo, Jose. (Abdel-khalik, A. Rashad and Jose Espejo. "Expectations Data And The Predictive Value Of Interim Reporting," **JAR**, 1978, Vol. 16, No. 1, pp. 1-13.)

Esposito, Robert S. (Blocher, Edward, Robert S. Esposito and John J. Willingham. "Auditors' Analytical Review Judgments For Payroll Expense," **AJPT**, 1983-84, Vol. 3, pp. 75-91.)

Essene, John C. "Occupied Japan Revises Accounting For Cooperatives," **JOA**, 1953, Vol. 95, No. 3, pp. 336-344.

Essex, S. (Cooper, D. and S. Essex. "Accounting Information And Employee Decision Making," **AOS**, 1977, Vol. 2, No. 3, pp. 201-218.)

Essner, Warren A. "Review Of Recent Securities And Exchange Commission Regulations Affecting The Securities Industry," **CPAJ**, 1973, Vol. 43, No. 2, pp. 109-114.

Estes, Ralph and D. D. Reames. "Effects Of Personal Characteristics On Materiality Decisions: A Multivariate Analysis," **ABR**, 1988, Vol. 18, No. 72, pp. 291-296.

Estes, Ralph and Marvin Reimer. "An Experimental Study Of The Differential Effect Of Standard And Qualified Auditors' Opinions On Investors' Price Decisions," **ABR**, 1978-79, Vol. 9, No. 34, pp. 157-162.

Estes, Ralph and Marvin Reimer. "A Study Of The Effect Of Qualified Auditors' Opinions On Bankers' Lending Decisions," **ABR**, 1976-77, Vol. 7, No. 28, pp. 250-259.

Estes, Ralph W. "An Assessment Of The Usefulness Of Current Cost And Price-Level Information By Financial Statement Users," **JAR**, 1968, Vol. 6, No. 2, pp. 200-207.

Estes, Ralph W. "Socio-Economic Accounting And External Diseconomies," **AR**, 1972, Vol. 47, No. 2, pp. 284-290.

Estes, Ralph W. "The Accountant's Social Responsibility," **JOA**, 1970, Vol. 129, No. 1, pp. 40-43.

Estes, Ralph W. (Paolillo, Joseph G. P. and Ralph W. Estes. "An Empirical Analysis Of Career Choice Factors Among Accountants, Attorneys, Engineers, And Physicians," **AR**, 1982, Vol. 57, No. 4, pp. 785-793.)

Estes, Ralph W. (Zeisel, Gerald and Ralph W. Estes. "Accounting And Public Service," **AR**, 1979, Vol. 54, No. 2, pp. 402-408.)

Estes, Ralph. "Action Research: Public Utility Regulation - An Opportunity For Research And Service In The Public Interest," **AIPIA**, 1988, Vol. 2, pp. 213-219.

Estes, Ralph. "An Intergenerational Comparison Of Socioeconomic Status Among CPAs, Attorneys, Engineers, And Physicians," **AIA**, 1984, Vol. 1, pp. 1-18.

Estes, Ralph. "Standards For Corporate Social Reporting," **MA**, 1976, Vol. 58, No. 5, pp. 19-22.

Estes, Ralph. "The Profession's Changing Horizons: A Survey Of Practitioners On The Present And Future Importance Of Selected Knowledge And Skills," **IJAER**, 1979, Vol. 14, No. 2, pp. 47-70.

Esteve, Esteban Hernandez. "A Spanish Treatise Of 1706 On Double-Entry Bookkeeping: 'Norte Mercantil Y Cristol De Cuentas' By Gabriel De Souza Brito," **ABR**, 1984-85, Vol. 15, No. 60, pp. 291-296.

Estrin, Teviah L. (Mock, Theodore J., Teviah L. Estrin and Miklos A. Vasarhelyi. "Learning Patterns, Decision Approach, And Value Of Information," **JAR**, 1972, Vol. 10, No. 1, pp. 129-153.)

Etnier, Don. "A More Interesting Auditing Course," **AR**, 1965, Vol. 40, No. 3, pp. 648-649.

Etnier, Don. "Teaching Equivalent Production With A Chart," **AR**, 1961, Vol. 36, No. 4, p. 648.

Etnier, Don. "The Next Best Thing To An Audit Practice Set," **JAED**, 1983, Vol. 1, No. 2, pp. 155-157.

Ettenson, Richard T. (Krogstad, Jack L., Richard T. Ettenson and James Shanteau. "Context And Experience In Auditors' Materiality Judgments," **AJPT**, 1984-85, Vol. 4, No. 1, pp. 54-74.)

Ettredge, Michael, Philip B. Shane and David Smith. "Audit Firm Size And The Association Between Reported Earnings And Security Returns," **AJPT**, 1988, Vol. 7, No. 2, pp. 29-42.

Eudy, Kimberly Ham. (Holder, William W. and Kimberly Ham Eudy. "A Framework For Building An Accounting Constitution," **JAAF**, 1982, Vol. 5, No. 2, pp. 110-125.)

Euske, K. J. and C. T. Rock, Jr. "Integrating Human Resource Accounting Into The Public Policy Process: An Illustration," **JAPP**, 1983, Vol. 2, No. 2, pp. 99-114.

Euske, K. J. (Ansari, S. and K. J. Euske. "Rational, Rationalizing, And Reifying Uses Of Accounting Data In Organizations," **AOS**, 1987, Vol. 12, No. 6, pp. 549-570.)

Evans, Bergen. "On Authority," **IJAER**, 1970, Vol. 6, No. 1, pp. 1-14.

Evans, C. Gilbert. "Crewloading: A Work Control Technique For Modern Management," **MA**, 1970, Vol. 51, No. 8, pp. 31-34.

Evans, Frank E. (Evans, John H., III and Frank E. Evans. "A Small Manufacturer's Success Story," **MA**, 1986, Vol. 68, No. 2, pp. 47-49.)

Evans, John H., III and Frank E. Evans. "A Small Manufacturer's Success Story," **MA**, 1986, Vol. 68, No. 2, pp. 47-49.

Evans, John H., III and James M. Patton. "Signaling And Monitoring In Public-Sector Accounting," **JAR**, 1987, Vol. 25, Supp., pp. 130-158.

Evans, John H., III and James M. Patton. "An Economic Analysis Of Participation In The Municipal Finance Officers Association Certificate Of Conformance Program," **JAEC**, 1983, Vol. 5, No. 2, pp. 151-175.

Evans, John H., III. "Optimal Contracts With Costly Conditional Auditing," **JAR**, 1980, Vol. 18, Supp., pp. 108-128.

Evans, John H., III. (Baiman, Stanley, John H. Evans III and James Noel. "Optimal Contracts With A Utility-Maximizing Auditor," **JAR**, 1987, Vol. 25, No. 2, pp. 217-244.)

Evans, John H., III. (Baiman, Stanley and John H. Evans, III. "Pre-Decision Information And Participative Management Control Systems," **JAR**, 1983, Vol. 21, No. 2, pp. 371-395.)

Evans, J. H., III, B. L. Lewis and J. M. Patton. "An Economic Modeling Approach To Contingency Theory And Management Control," **AOS**, 1986,Vol. 11,No. 6,pp.483-498.

Evans, Thomas G. and Martin E. Taylor. "Bottom Line Compliance' With The IASC: A Comparative Analysis," **IJAER**, 1982, Vol. 18, No. 1, pp. 115-128.

Evans, Thomas G. and William R. Folks, Jr. "SFAS No. 8: Conforming, Coping, Complaining, And Correcting!," **IJAER**, 1979, Vol. 15, No. 1, pp. 33-43.

Evans, Thomas G. "Foreign Currency Translation Practices Abroad," **CPAJ**, 1974, Vol. 44, No. 6, pp. 47-50.

Evans, Thomas G. (Doupnik, Timothy and Thomas G. Evans. "The Functional Currency Determination: A Strategy To Smooth Income," **AIIA**, 1988, Vol. 2, pp. 169-180.)

Evans, Thomas G. (Hunter, Robert L., Gary M. Cunningham and Thomas G. Evans. "Are Multinational Liquidity Models Worth Their Cost?," **MA**, 1979, Vol. 61, No. 6, pp. 51-56.)

Evans, Thomas G. (Taylor, Martin E., Thomas G. Evans and Arthur C. Joy. "The Impact Of IASC Accounting Standards On Comparability And Consistency Of International Accounting Reporting Practices," **IJAER**, 1986, Vol. 22, No. 1, pp. 1-9.)

Evans, Thomas J. "Diversity In Foreign Currency Translation Methods - A Proposal For Uniformity," **CPAJ**, 1974, Vol. 44, No. 2, pp. 41-45.

Evans, William P. and Ronald L. Bosworth. "Computerized Information System (COINS)," **MA**, 1966, Vol. 48, No. 2, pp. 36-44.

Everest, Gordon C. and Ron Weber. "A Relational Approach To Accounting Models," **AR**, 1977, Vol. 52, No. 2, pp. 340-359.

Everett, John O. and David E. Keys. "Quantifying The Poisoning Effect Of Tax Preference Items On The Maximum Tax For A High-Bracket Taxpayer," **JATA**, 1981, Vol. 2, No. 2, pp. 12-19.

Everett, John O. and Gary A. Porter. "Safe-Harbor Leasing - Unraveling The Tax Implications," **JAAF**, 1984, Vol. 7, No. 3, pp. 241-256.

Everett, John O. "ACRS - A Quick And Easy Reference," **CPAJ**, 1982, Vol. 52, No. 7, pp. 12-19.

Everett, John O. (Boer, Germain and John O. Everett. "Information Science And Relevant Accounting Reports," **MA**, 1976, Vol. 57, No. 10, pp. 33-36.)

Everett, John O. (Hull, Rita P., John O. Everett and Steven D. Hall. "Accounting Education: Practitioner's Views On The Value Of A Five-Year Program," **AIA**, 1987, Vol. 5, pp. 163-178.)

Everett, John O. (Norton, Curtis L. and John O. Everett. "An Extension Of Jordan's Analysis Of Section 179 Property," **JATA**, 1983, Vol. 5, No. 1, pp. 60-62.)

Everett, Robert M. "Accounting For Exchange Variation In Local Currency," **MA**, 1968, Vol. 50, No. 2, pp. 15-17.

Ewusi-Mensah, K. "The External Organizational Environment And Its Impact On Management Information Systems," **AOS**, 1981, Vol. 6, No. 4, pp. 301-316.

Eyler, Kel-Ann. (Dillon, Ray, Rodney G. Alsup and Kel-Ann Eyler. "Telecommunications Costs - How To Identify, Analyze, And Control Them," **MA**, 1988, Vol. 70, No. 2, pp. 50-53.)

Ezzamel, Mahmoud A. "On The Assessment Of The Performance Effects Of Multidivisional Structures," **ABR**, 1985-86, Vol. 16, No. 61, pp. 23-34.

Ezzamel, M. A. and K. Hilton. "Divisionalisation In British Industry: A Preliminary Study," **ABR**, 1979-80, Vol. 10, No. 38, pp. 197-214.

Faber, Peter L. "Proposals To Finance Committee On Corporate Acquisitions," **CPAJ**, 1985, Vol. 55, No. 11, pp. 20-27.

Fabricant, Solomon. "Inflation And Current Accounting Practice: An Economist's View," **JOA**, 1971, Vol. 132, No. 6, pp. 39-44.

Fadel, Hisham and John M. Parkinson. "Liquidity Evaluation By Means Of Ratio Analysis," **ABR**, 1977-78, Vol. 8, No. 30, pp. 101-107.

Fader, James A., Jr. "Getting What's Yours When You're The Subcontractor," **MA**, 1984, Vol. 65, No. 8, pp. 32-36.

Fagan, Mark L. "Raising Profits Through Lower Distribution Costs," **CA**, 1987, Vol. 5, No. 1, pp. 26-32.

Fagerberg, Dixon, Jr. "Accounting For Vacation Expense," **MA**, 1969, Vol. 51, No. 6, pp. 47-48.

Fagerberg, Dixon, Jr. "Building And Keeping A Clientele," **JOA**, 1953, Vol. 96, No. 4, pp. 460-463.

Fagerberg, Dixon, Jr. "Concerning Three Mischievous Accounts," **AR**, 1972, Vol. 47, No. 3, pp. 454-457.

Fagerberg, Dixon, Jr. "Nature Of Business Affects Accounting Services Needed," **JOA**, 1951, Vol. 92, No. 4, pp. 445-449.

Fagerberg, Dixon, Jr. "Perspective In The Practice Of Accountancy," **AR**, 1955, Vol. 30, No. 2, pp. 211-216.

Fagerberg, Dixon, Jr. "Spotlight On Personal Accounting," **AR**, 1954, Vol. 29, No. 3, pp. 355-364.

Fagerberg, Dixon, Jr. "The Selling Of Cost Accounting," **MA**, 1974, Vol. 55, No. 12, pp. 23-24.

Fagerberg, Dixon, Jr. "Unmeasured Costs: A Checklist," **MA**, 1974, Vol. 55, No. 8, pp. 29-32.

Fagerberg, Dixon, Jr. "Why Accounting?," **AR**, 1957, Vol. 32, No. 1, pp. 3-7.

Fahey, Bill G. "Production Performance Reporting Under Direct Costing," **MA**, 1970, Vol. 52, No. 5, pp. 9-13.

Fahey, Liam. (Wokutch, Richard E. and Liam Fahey. "A Value Explicit Approach For Evaluating Corporate Social Performance," **JAPP**, 1986, Vol. 5, No. 3, pp. 191-214.)

Fair, Andrew J. and Melvin L. Maisel. "Coping With Taxes On The Second Death," **CPAJ**, 1988, Vol. 58, No. 12, pp. 42-54.

Fair, Larry. "Product Line Accounting: The Proposed Regulation And Its Effects," **MA**, 1968, Vol. 50, No. 3, pp.18-22.

Fairaizl, Alan F. and Satinder K. Mullick. "A Corporate Planning System," **MA**, 1975, Vol. 57, No. 6, pp. 13-17.

Fairchild, Keith Wm. and Dennis Bline. "Capital Investment Analysis: The Index Method," **IAE**, 1988, Vol. 3, No. 1, pp. 72-78.

Faircloth, Archie. "The Importance Of Accounting To The Shakers," **AHJ**, 1988, Vol. 15, No. 2, pp. 99-129.

Faircloth, A. W. and D. N. Ricchiute. "Ambiguity Intolerance And Financial Reporting Alternatives," **AOS**, 1981, Vol. 6, No. 1, pp. 53-68.

Faires, Jack E. (Coffey, Kenneth J. and Jack E. Faires. "Options For Military Retirement System Changes," **JCA**, 1988, Vol. 5, No. 1, pp. 1-18.)

Fairfield, Patricia. (Burton, John C. and Patricia Fairfield. "Auditing Evolution In A Changing Environment," **AJPT**, 1981-82, Vol. 1, No. 2, pp. 1-22.)

Faley, Robert H. (Eskew, Robert K. and Robert H. Faley. "Some Determinants Of Student Performance In The First College-Level Financial Accounting Course," **AR**, 1988, Vol. 63, No. 1, pp. 137-147.)

Falk, Charles Edward and Alan R. Soberman. "Interest-Free Loans After Hardee," **CPAJ**, 1983, Vol. 53, No. 2, pp. 36-41.

Falk, Charles Edward and Alan R. Soberman. "Section 482 After Keller And Foglesong," **CPAJ**, 1982, Vol. 52, No. 9, pp. 30-39.

Falk, Charles Edward and R. Mark Hochberg. "Gift-Leasebacks - When Will They Work?," **CPAJ**, 1984, Vol. 54, No. 10, pp. 24-37.

Falk, Charles Edward and R. Mark Hochberg. "Interest Free Loans - Is Dickman Correct?," **CPAJ**, 1983, Vol. 53, No. 8, pp. 44-51.

Falk, Gideon. (Ronen, Joshua and Gideon Falk. "Accounting Aggregation And The Entropy Measure: An Experimental Approach," **AR**, 1973, Vol. 48, No. 4, pp. 696-717.)

Falk, Haim and James A. Heintz. "Company Risk Relationships Over Consecutive Periods," **ABR**, 1977-78, Vol. 8, No. 32, pp. 246-252.

Falk, Haim and James A. Heintz. "Relative Company Risk Over Time," **ABR**, 1974-75, Vol. 5, No. 17, pp. 25-40.

Falk, Haim and James A. Heintz. "Assessing Industry Risk By Ratio Analysis: A Reply," **AR**, 1978, Vol. 53, No. 1, pp. 210-215.

Falk, Haim and James A. Heintz. "Assessing Industry Risk By Ratio Analysis," **AR**, 1975, Vol. 50, No. 4, pp. 758-779.

Falk, Haim and Joseph C. Miller. "Amortization Of Advertising Expenditures," **JAR**, 1977, Vol. 15, No. 1, pp. 12-22.

Falk, Haim and Lawrence A. Gordon. "Assessing Industry Risk By Ratio Analysis: Validation," **AR**, 1978, Vol. 53, No. 1, pp. 216-227.

Falk, Haim and Tsvi Ophir. "The Effect Of Risk On The Use Of Financial Statements By Investment Decision-Makers: A Case Study," **AR**, 1973, Vol. 48, No. 2, pp. 323-338.

Falk, Haim, Bruce G. Gobdel and James H. Naus. "Disclosure For Closely Held Corporations," **JOA**, 1976, Vol. 142, No. 4, pp. 85-90.

Falk, Haim, Samuel Frumer and James A. Heintz. "Accounting For Stock Reacquisitions: Israel And The United States Compared," **IJAER**, 1974, Vol. 9, No. 2, pp. 111-123.

Falk, Haim. "Assessing The Effectiveness Of Accounting Courses Through Facet Analysis," **JAR**, 1972, Vol. 10, No. 2, pp. 359-375.

Falk, Haim. "Current Value Accounting Preferences: The Case For Canada," **IJAER**, 1979, Vol. 14, No. 2, pp. 29-46.

Falk, Haim. "Financial Statements And Personal Characteristics In Investment Decision Making," **ABR**, 1971-72, Vol. 2, No. 7, pp. 209-222.

Falk, Haim. (Aharony, Joseph and Haim Falk. "The Effectiveness Of Electric Utility Price Regulation In The 1970s: A Stochastic Dominance Analysis," **JAPP**, 1982, Vol. 1, No. 1, pp. 59-77.)

Falk, Haim. (Buzby, Stephen L. and Haim Falk. "Demand For Social Responsibility Information By University Investors," **AR**, 1979, Vol. 54, No. 1, pp. 23-37.)

Falk, Haim. (Buzby, Stephen L. and Haim Falk. "A New Approach To The Funds Statement," **JOA**, 1974, Vol. 137, No. 1, pp. 55-61.)

Falk, Haim. (Gordon, Lawrence A., Jack Call and Haim Falk. "Pricing Objectives And Managerial Incentive Plans," **JCA**, 1986, Vol. 3, No. 2, pp. 59-67.)

Falk, H. and T. Ophir. "The Influence Of Differences In Accounting Policies On Investment Decisions," **JAR**, 1973, Vol. 11, No. 1, pp. 108-116.

Falk, H. (Buzby, S. L. and H. Falk. "A Survey Of The Interest In Social Responsibility Information By Mutual Funds," **AOS**, 1978, Vol. 3, No. 3/4, pp. 191-202.)

Fallon, Daniel F. "Reliability Cycle Sampling For Control Of Inventories," **MA**, 1968, Vol. 50, No. 2, pp. 41-43.

Falls, Glenn. "The Financial Value Of Early Tax Deductions For Depreciation," **AR**, 1955, Vol. 30, No. 3, pp. 515-518.

Fanara, Philip, Jr. (Chen, Chao, Philip Fanara, Jr. and Raymond Gorman. "Abandonment Decisions And The Market Value Of The Firm: The Case Of Nuclear Power Project Abandonment," **JAPP**, 1987, Vol. 6, No. 4, pp. 285-297.)

Fantl, Irving L. "Control And The Internal Audit In The Multinational Firm," **IJAER**, 1975, Vol. 11, No. 1, pp. 57-65.

Fantl, Irving L. "The Case Against International Uniformity," **MA**, 1971, Vol. 52, No. 11, pp. 13-16.

Fantl, Irving L. "Transfer Pricing - Tread Carefully," **CPAJ**, 1974, Vol. 44, No. 12, pp. 42-46.

Farag, Shawki M. "A Planning Model For The Divisionalized Enterprise," **AR**, 1968, Vol. 43, No. 2, pp. 312-320.

Farag, Shawki M. "Littleton's Views On Social Accounting -

An Elaboration," **IJAER**, 1967, Vol. 2, No. 2, pp. 123-132.

Farag, Shawki M. "Project Vs. General Development Financing: A Comment," **IJAER**, 1968, Vol. 4, No. 1, pp. 115-119.

Farag, Shawki M. "The Problem Of Performance Evaluation In International Accounting," **IJAER**, 1974, Vol. 10, No. 1, pp. 45-53.

Farag, Shawki M. "The Valuation Of National Capital And The Development Of Accounting Theory," **IJAER**, 1969, Vol. 5, No. 1, pp. 153-169.

Farber, Arthur. (Gomberg, Mandel and Arthur Farber. "The Balance Sheet Of The Future," **AR**, 1964, Vol. 39, No. 3, pp. 615-617.)

Farley, Anne. (McLaughlin, John K. and Anne Farley. "Resolved: Joint Costs Should Be Allocated (Sometimes)," **CPAJ**, 1988, Vol. 58, No. 1, pp. 46-53.)

Farley, Charles T. "Reporting For United Fund Agencies," **MA**, 1973, Vol. 55, No. 6, pp. 28-30.

Farley, E. Ray. "Picture An Hour," **MA**, 1966, Vol. 47, No. 9, pp. 51-55.

Farman, Wilson L. and Chi-Ming Hou. "The Balance Of Payments: An Accounting Analysis," **AR**, 1963, Vol. 38, No. 1, pp. 133-141.

Farman, Wilson L. "National Flow-Of-Funds: An Accounting Analysis," **AR**, 1964, Vol. 39, No. 2, pp. 392-404.

Farman, Wilson L. "Social Accounting In Subsistence And Family-Production Type Economies," **AR**, 1953, Vol. 28, No. 3, pp. 392-400.

Farman, Wilson L. "Some Basic Assumptions Underlying Social Accounting," **AR**, 1951, Vol. 26, No. 1, pp. 33-39.

Farman, Wilson L. "Teaching Accounting Concepts To The Beginning Student," **AR**, 1949, Vol. 24, No. 3, pp. 314-317.

Farmer, Jerome. "Auditing And The Computer - A Suggested Program," **JOA**, 1970, Vol. 130, No. 1, pp. 53-58.

Farmer, Larry E. (Thomas, Paula Bevels and Larry E. Farmer. "Accounting For Stock Options And SARs: The Equality Question," **JOA**, 1984, Vol. 157, No. 6, pp. 92-98.)

Farmer, Timothy A., Larry E. Rittenberg and Gregory M. Trompeter. "An Investigation Of The Impact Of Economic And Organizational Factors On Auditor Independence," **AJPT**, 1987-88, Vol. 7, No. 1, pp. 1-14.

Farmer, William A. "Multiple Incentive Contracts: An Analytical Technique," **MA**, 1968, Vol. 49, No. 9, pp. 18-24.

Farragher, Edward J. (Kim, Suk H. and Edward J. Farragher. "Current Capital Budgeting Practices," **MA**, 1981, Vol. 62, No. 12, pp. 26-31.)

Farrar, Robert H., William C. Lawler and Linda J. Block. "How CFOs View The CMA Program," **MA**, 1985, Vol. 67, No. 5, pp. 33-37.

Farrell, Rod P. (Dillon, Ray D., William R. Feldhaus and Rod P. Farrell. "A Special Area Of Service: Risk Management," **JOA**, 1984, Vol. 157, No. 2, pp. 50-59.)

Farrelly, Gail E. and Elaine J. Hudson. "How To Teach Introductory Accounting: Student Views," **JAED**, 1985, Vol. 3, No. 1, pp. 47-56.

Farrelly, Gail E., Kenneth R. Ferris and William R. Reichenstein. "Perceived Risk, Market Risk, And Accounting-Determined Risk Measures," **AR**, 1985, Vol. 60, No. 2, pp. 278-288.

Fasci, Martha A. "EMAIS - Evaluation By Management Of Automated Information Systems," **JIS**, 1986, Vol. 1, No. 1, pp. 83-101.

Fasci, Martha A. "The Windfall Profits Tax: Panacea Or Pandora's Box?," **MA**, 1981, Vol. 63, No. 4, pp. 50-53.

Fasci, Martha A., Timothy J. Weiss and Robert L. Worrall. "Everyone Can Use This Cost/Benefit Analysis System," **MA**, 1987, Vol. 68, No. 7, pp. 44-47.

Fatseas, Vic. (Angus-Leppan, Pam and Vic Fatseas. "The Forecasting Accuracy Of Trainee Accountants Using Judgemental And Statistical Techniques," **ABR**, 1985-86, Vol. 16, No. 63, pp. 179-188.)

Faulhaber, Thomas A., Fred A. Coad and Thomas J. Little. "Building A Process Cost Management System From The Bottom Up," **MA**, 1988, Vol. 69, No. 11, pp. 58-62.

Faux, M. Charles. "A New Matrix Approach To Accounting Training," **AR**, 1966, Vol. 41, No. 1, pp. 129-132.

Favaloro, John L. "Retirement Of Partners," **JOA**, 1957, Vol. 103, No. 4, pp. 66-70.

Favaloro, John. "The Special Problems Imposed By The Personal Relationship Existing With Small Clients," **JOA**, 1950, Vol. 89, No. 2, pp. 136-138.

Fawthrop, R. A. "Underlying Problems Of Discounted Cash Flow," **ABR**, 1970-71, Vol. 1, No. 3, pp. 187-198.

Fazzolari, Salvatore D. "How Harsco Integrates Financial & Operational Auditing," **MA**, 1988, Vol. 69, No. 7, pp. 28-32.

Feddeck, Fred C. "Cost Accounting In A Stock Transfer Company," **MA**, 1976, Vol. 58, No. 5, pp. 34-36.

Fedders, John M. and L. Glenn Perry. "Policing Financial Disclosure Fraud: The SEC's Top Priority," **JOA**, 1984, Vol. 158, No. 1, pp. 58-67.

Fee, Francis X., Jr. "Audit Of A Small Manufacturing Company," **CPAJ**, 1977, Vol. 47, No. 10, pp. 33-38.

Fee, Thomas. "Controlling The Audit Fee," **MA**, 1975, Vol. 56, No. 8, pp. 49-51.

Fehrenbach, Arthur. (Talbott, John and Arthur Fehrenbach. "Thoroughbred Breeding - Tax Considerations," **CPAJ**, 1979, Vol. 49, No. 7, pp. 11-16.)

Feibel, Laurence I. (Siegel, Andrew C., Arthur S. Cohen and Laurence I. Feibel. "ESOPs - The Present And An Imperiled Future? - Part I," **CPAJ**, 1986, Vol. 56, No. 1, pp. 14-23.)

Feibel, Laurence I. (Siegel, Andrew C., Arthur S. Cohen and Laurence I. Feibel. "ESOPs - The Present And An Imperiled Future? - Part II," **CPAJ**, 1986, Vol. 56, No. 2, pp. 32-35.)

Fein, Richard. (Krzystofik, Anthony T. and Richard Fein. "Does Your Firm Use The Right Approach In Hiring Campus Recruits?," **JOA**, 1988, Vol. 166, No. 5, pp. 83-88.)

Feinberg, Robert B. "Limitations On NOLs After TRA '86," **CA**, 1987, Vol. 5, No. 3, pp. 10-19.

Feinberg, Stuart A. and Bruce Serlen. "The Crisis In Business Ethics," **CA**, 1988, Vol. 6, No. 1, pp. 36-39.

Feinschreiber, Robert. "Accelerated Depreciation: A Proposed New Method," **JAR**, 1969, Vol. 7, No. 1, pp. 17-21.

Feinschreiber, Robert. "Computing Depreciation Under The New 'Class Life' System," **CPAJ**, 1973, Vol. 43, No. 10, pp. 857-862.

Feinschreiber, Robert. "Cost Accounting Standards Board Issues Rules For Asset Capitalization," **CPAJ**, 1973, Vol. 43, No. 4, pp. 302-305.

Feinschreiber, Robert. "Federal Regulation Of Cost Accounting Begins," **CPAJ**, 1972, Vol. 42, No. 12, pp. 1024-1027.

Feinschreiber, Robert. "Minor 1976 Tax Provisions: Major Impact," **CPAJ**, 1976, Vol. 46, No. 12, pp. 28-30.

Feinschreiber, Robert. "New Tax Provisions Affect International Operations," **CPAJ**, 1977, Vol. 47, No. 2, pp. 23-26.

Feinschreiber, Robert. "Tax Accounting Requirements For Political Candidates And Committees," **CPAJ**, 1972, Vol. 42, No. 8, pp. 654-656.

Feinschreiber, Robert. "Tax Benefits For Domestic International Sales Corporations (DISCs) - Pricing, Profits And Dividends (Part 2 Of 2 Parts)," **CPAJ**, 1972, Vol. 42, No. 3, pp. 221-224.

Feinschreiber, Robert. "Tax Benefits For Domestic International Sales Corporations (DISCs) - How To Qualify (Part 1 Of 2 Parts)," **CPAJ**, 1972, Vol. 42, No. 2, pp. 131-138.

Fekrat, M. Ali. "Absorption Costing And Fixed Factors Of Production: A Reply," **AR**, 1973, Vol. 48, No. 1, pp. 130-131.

Fekrat, M. Ali. "Accounting For Forward Exchange Contracts," **IJAER**, 1984, Vol. 19, No. 2, pp. 83-92.

Fekrat, M. Ali. "Accounting For Forward Exchange Contracts," **AIIA**, 1987, Vol. 1, pp. 249-262.

Fekrat, M. Ali. "The Conceptual Foundations Of Absorption Costing," **AR**, 1972, Vol. 47, No. 2, pp. 351-355.

Fekrat, M. A. "Multinational Accounting: A Technical Note," **IJAER**, 1979, Vol. 15, No. 1, pp. 95-103.

Feldbush, Marvin A. "Participative Budgeting In A Hospital Setting," **MA**, 1981, Vol. 63, No. 3, pp. 43-48.

Feldhaus, William R. (Dillon, Ray D., William R. Feldhaus and Rod P. Farrell. "A Special Area Of Service: Risk Management," **JOA**, 1984, Vol. 157, No. 2, pp. 50-59.)

Feldman, Saul. "A Critical Appraisal Of The Current Asset Concept," **AR**, 1959, Vol. 34, No. 4, pp. 574-578.

Feldman, Stewart A. and LeRoy J. Herbert. "The International Accounting Standards Committee," **CPAJ**, 1977, Vol. 47, No. 1, pp. 17-22.

Feldman, Stewart A. (Beresford, Dennis R. and Stewart A. Feldman. "Companies Increase Social Responsibility Disclosure," **MA**, 1976, Vol. 57, No. 9, pp. 51-55.)

Felix, William L., Jr. and Marcia S. Niles. "Research In Internal Control Evaluation," **AJPT**, 1988, Vol. 7, No. 2, pp. 43-60.

Felix, William L., Jr. and Richard A. Grimlund. "A Sampling Model For Audit Test Of Composite Accounts," **JAR**, 1977, Vol. 15, No. 1, pp. 23-41.

Felix, William L., Jr. and Robert S. Roussey. "Statistical Inference And The IRS," **JOA**, 1985, Vol. 159, No. 6, pp. 38-45.

Felix, William L., Jr. and William R. Kinney, Jr. "Research In The Auditor's Opinion Formulation Process: State Of The Art," **AR**, 1982, Vol. 57, No. 2, pp. 245-271.

Felix, William L., Jr. "Estimating The Relationship Between Technical Change And Reported Performance," **AR**, 1972, Vol. 47, No. 1, pp. 52-63.

Felix, William L., Jr. "Evidence On Alternative Means Of Assessing Prior Probability Distributions; For Audit Decision Making," **AR**, 1976, Vol. 51, No. 4, pp. 800-807.

Felix, William L., Jr. (Grimlund, Richard A. and William L. Felix, Jr. "Simulation Evidence And Analysis Of Alternative Methods Of Evaluating Dollar-Unit Samples," **AR**, 1987, Vol. 62, No. 3, pp. 455-479.)

Felix, William L., Jr. (Waller, William S. and William L. Felix, Jr. "Auditors' Covariation Judgments," **AR**, 1987, Vol. 62, No. 2, pp. 275-292.)

Felix, William L., Jr. (Waller, William S. and William L. Felix, Jr. "The Effects Of Incomplete Outcome Feedback On Auditors' Self-Perceptions Of Judgment Ability," **AR**, 1984, Vol. 59, No. 4, pp. 637-646.)

Felix, W. L., Jr. (Sundem, Gary L. and W. L. Felix, Jr. "Tax Allocation And Security Prices: A Comment," **AR**, 1976, Vol. 51, No. 2, pp. 391-394.)

Felix, W. L., Jr. (Waller, W. S. and W. L. Felix, Jr. "The Auditor And Learning From Experience: Some Conjectures," **AOS**, 1984, Vol. 9, No. 3/4, pp. 383-408.)

Felix, W. L., Jr., Robert G. May, Marcia S. Niles and John R. Thorson. "SCAD: Something New In Auditing Education," **JAED**, 1985, Vol. 3, No. 2, pp. 5-14.

Feller, Robert E. "Accounting For Joint Products In The Petroleum Industry," **MA**, 1977, Vol. 59, No. 3, pp. 41-44.

Feller, Robert E. "Early Contributions To Cost Accounting," **MA**, 1973, Vol. 55, No. 6, pp. 12-16.

Fellingham, John C. and D. Paul Newman. "Strategic

Considerations In Auditing," **AR**, 1985, Vol. 60, No. 4, pp. 634-650.

Fellingham, John C. and Mark A. Wolfson. "Taxes And Risk Sharing," **AR**, 1985, Vol. 60, No. 1, pp. 10-17.

Fellingham, John C., Stephen T. Limberg and Patrick J. Wilkie. "Tax Rates, Tax Shelters And Optimal Portfolios," **AIT**, 1987, Vol. 1, pp. 23-48.

Fellingham, John. (Amershi, Amin H., Joel S. Demski and John Fellingham. "Sequential Bayesian Analysis In Accounting," **CAR**, 1984-85, Vol. 1, No. 2, pp. 176-192.)

Fellows, James A. "Compliance Reporting For U.S. Investment Abroad," **CPAJ**, 1983, Vol. 53, No. 11, pp. 30-38.

Fellows, James A. "Constructive Dividends And The Closely-Held Corporation," **CPAJ**, 1986, Vol. 56, No. 11, pp. 58-65.

Fellows, James A. "Corporate Distributions And Sales After TRA 1986," **CPAJ**, 1987, Vol. 57, No. 2, pp. 44-49.

Fellows, James A. "Foreign Investors In U.S. Real Estate," **CPAJ**, 1983, Vol. 53, No. 7, pp. 30-37.

Fellows, James A. "Investment Tax Credit Recapture For Shareholders Of S Corporations - Part II," **CPAJ**, 1985, Vol. 55, No. 10, pp. 44-51.

Fellows, James A. "Investment Tax Credit Recapture For Shareholders of S Corporations - Part I," **CPAJ**, 1985, Vol. 55, No. 9, pp. 26-33.

Fellows, James A. "Shareholder Loans To S Corporations; Tax Traps?," **CPAJ**, 1985, Vol. 55, No. 5, pp. 44-54.

Fellows, James A. "The Flat-Rate Income Tax," **CPAJ**, 1984, Vol. 54, No. 8, pp. 42-47.

Fellows, James A. "The Myth Of Tax-Free Liquidation," **CPAJ**, 1984, Vol. 54, No. 11, pp. 46-53.

Fellows, James and James Spence. "Efficiency In Academe: Comparative Advantage Vs. 'Publish Or Perish'," **JAED**, 1985, Vol. 3, No. 2, pp. 53-60.

Felsing, Marlyn D. (Wheeler, Robert C., Marlyn D. Felsing and Thomas F. Reilly. "Large Or Small CPA Firms: A Practitioners' Perspective," **CPAJ**, 1987, Vol. 57, No. 4, pp. 29-33.)

Felt, Howard M. and Donald T. Barsky. "Purchase Vs. Lease: Computer Obsolescence," **MA**, 1969, Vol. 51, No. 4, pp. 29-32.

Felt, Howard M. "The Effort And Authority Of The AICPA In The Development of 'Generally-Accepted Accounting Principles'," **IJAER**, 1968, Vol. 3, No. 2, pp. 11-27.

Feltham, Gerald A. and Joel S. Demski. "The Use Of Models In Information Evaluation," **AR**, 1970, Vol. 45, No. 4, pp. 623-640.

Feltham, Gerald A. and Peter O. Christensen. "Firm-Specific Information And Efficient Resource Allocation," **CAR**, 1988, Vol. 5, No. 1, pp. 133-169.

Feltham, Gerald A. "Cost Aggregation: An Information Economic Analysis," **JAR**, 1977, Vol. 15, No. 1, pp. 42-70.

Feltham, Gerald A. "In-Process Inventories And Multiproduct Production Systems: A Comment," **AR**, 1973, Vol. 48, No. 2, pp. 375-376.

Feltham, Gerald A. "John Butterworth's Pioneering Contributions To The Accounting And Information Economics Literature," **CAR**, 1984-85, Vol. 1, No. 1, pp. 87-98.

Feltham, Gerald A. "Some Quantitative Approaches To Planning For Multiproduct Production Systems," **AR**, 1970, Vol. 45, No. 1, pp. 11-26.

Feltham, Gerald A. "The Value Of Information," **AR**, 1968, Vol. 43, No. 4, pp. 684-696.

Feltham, Gerald A. (Demski, Joel S. and Gerald A. Feltham. "Economic Incentives In Budgetary Control Systems," **AR**, 1978, Vol. 53, No. 2, pp. 336-359.)

Feltham, Gerald A. (Demski, Joel S. and Gerald A. Feltham. "Forecast Evaluation," **AR**, 1972, Vol. 47, No. 3, pp. 533-548.)

Felton, S. K. "Controlling Company-Owned Inventories In Public Warehouses," **MA**, 1978, Vol. 59, No. 9, pp. 45-50.

Feltus, Oliver. (Kee, Robert and Oliver Feltus. "The Role Of Abandonment Value In The Investment Decision," **MA**, 1982, Vol. 64, No. 2, pp. 34-42.)

Ferguson, Daniel C. "A CEO's View Of The Controller," **MA**, 1987, Vol. 68, No. 8, pp. 21-23.

Ferguson, Florence J. and Alan Zazoff. "How You Can Control Unemployment Insurance Costs," **MA**, 1985, Vol. 66, No. 9, pp. 48-53.

Ferguson, John S. "Decommissioning A Nuclear Plant: The Financial Implications," **MA**, 1979, Vol. 61, No. 3, pp. 37-40.

Ferguson, Linda Wicks. "An Accountant Profiles A Sports Franchise," **MA**, 1979, Vol. 60, No. 11, pp. 13-18.

Ferguson, P. (Berry, A. J., T. Capps, D. Cooper, P. Ferguson, T. Hopper and E. A. Lowe. "Management Control In An Area Of The NCB: Rationales Of Accounting Practices In A Public Enterprise," **AOS**, 1985, Vol. 10, No. 1, pp. 3-28.)

Fergusson, D. A. "Accounting And The Price Level," **AR**, 1954, Vol. 29, No. 4, pp. 639-642.

Ferlita, William J. (Dennis, David M., Jack L. Smith and William J. Ferlita. "The Impact Of ACRS Lives On Deferred Tax Accounting," **MA**, 1986, Vol. 67, No. 9, pp. 39-43.)

Fern, Richard H. and Manuel A. Tipgos. "Controllers As Business Strategists: A Progress Report," **MA**, 1988, Vol. 69, No. 9, pp. 25-29.

Fern, Richard H. "Vacation Home Rentals Under TRA - Everyone Loses!," **CPAJ**, 1987, Vol. 57, No. 4, pp. 46-51.

Fernald, Henry B. "Internal Auditing," **AR**, 1943, Vol. 18, No. 3, pp. 228-233.

Fernald, Henry B. "Taxes And Employment," **AR**, 1944, Vol. 19, No. 1, pp. 7-10.

Feroz, Ehsan H. "Financial Accounting Standards Setting: A Social Science Perspective," AIA, 1987, Vol. 5, pp. 3-14.

Ferrara, William L, Jack C. Hayya and David A. Nachman. "Normalcy Of Profit In The Jaedicke-Robichek Model," AR, 1972, Vol. 47, No. 2, pp. 299-307.

Ferrara, William L. and Jack C. Hayya. "Toward Probabilistic Profit Budgets," MA, 1970, Vol. 52, No. 4, pp. 23-28.

Ferrara, William L. "A Cash Flow Model For The Future," MA, 1981, Vol. 62, No. 12, pp. 12-21.

Ferrara, William L. "Accounting For Performance Evaluation And Decision-Making," MA, 1976, Vol. 58, No. 6, pp. 13-19.

Ferrara, William L. "Capital Budgeting And Financing Or Leasing Decisions," MA, 1968, Vol. 49, No. 11,pp. 55-63.

Ferrara, William L. "Direct Costing: Are Direct Costs Relevant Costs?," JOA, 1961, Vol. 112, No. 2, pp. 61-62.

Ferrara, William L. "Fantasyland Accounting Research: Let's Make Pretend: Comment," AR, 1979, Vol. 54, No. 1, pp. 197-198.

Ferrara, William L. "Idle Capacity As A Loss - Fact Or Fiction," AR, 1960, Vol. 35, No. 3, pp. 490-496.

Ferrara, William L. "Lease Vs. Purchase: A Quasi-Financing Approach," MA, 1974, Vol. 55, No. 7, pp. 21-26.

Ferrara, William L. "Overhead Costs And Income Measurement," AR, 1961, Vol. 36, No. 1, pp. 63-70.

Ferrara, William L. "Probabilistic Approaches To Return On Investment And Residual Income: A Reply," AR, 1979, Vol. 54, No. 3, pp. 650-651.

Ferrara, William L. "Probabilistic Approaches To Return On Investment And Residual Income," AR, 1977, Vol. 52, No. 3, pp. 597-604.

Ferrara, William L. "Relevant Costing: Footnote To A Controversy," MA, 1970, Vol. 51, No. 7, pp. 45-47.

Ferrara, William L. "Responsibility Reporting Vs. Direct Costing - Is There A Conflict?," MA, 1967, Vol. 48, No. 10, pp. 43-54.

Ferrara, William L. "Should Investment And Financing Decisions Be Separated?," AR, 1966, Vol. 41, No. 1, pp. 106-114.

Ferrara, William L. "The Case For Symmetry In Lease Reporting," MA, 1978, Vol. 59, No. 10, pp. 17-24.

Ferrara, William L. "The Importance Of Idle Capacity Costs - A Rejoinder," AR, 1961, Vol. 36, No. 3, pp. 422-424.

Ferrara, William L. (Fess, Philip E. and William L. Ferrara. "The Period Cost Concept For Income Measurement - Can It Be Defended?," AR, 1961, Vol. 36, No. 4, pp. 598-602.)

Ferrara, William L. (Hoshower, Leon B. and William L. Ferrara. "Deferred Taxes And Consolidations - A Case For Change," MA, 1985, Vol. 67, No. 6, pp. 57-60.)

Ferrara, William L., James B. Thies and Mark W. Dirsmith. "The Lease-Purchase Decision," MA, 1980, Vol. 61, No. 11, pp. 57-58.

Ferrara, William. (Hayya, Jack, William Ferrara and Erwin Saniga. "Extending The Applicability Of Probabilistic Management Planning And Control Models: A Comment," AR, 1975, Vol. 50, No. 4, pp. 826-831.)

Ferrara, Wm. L. "Relevant Costing - Two Points Of View," AR, 1963, Vol. 38, No. 4, pp. 719-722.

Ferrara, W. L. (Hayya, J. C., W. L. Ferrara and Erwin M. Saniga. "On The Accuracy Of Normalcy Approximation In Stochastic C-V-P Analysis: A Reply," AR, 1978, Vol. 53, No. 1, pp. 252-259.)

Ferreri, L. B. (Cowen, S. S., L. B. Ferreri and L. D. Parker. "The Impact Of Corporate Characteristics On Social Responsibility Disclosure: A Typology And Frequency-Based Analysis," AOS, 1987, Vol. 12, No. 2, pp. 111-122.)

Ferris, Kenneth R. and David C. Hayes. "Some Evidence On The Determinants Of Profit Forecast Accuracy In The United Kingdom," IJAER, 1977, Vol. 12, No. 2, pp. 27-36.

Ferris, Kenneth R. and Kirk L. Tennant. "An Investigation Of The Impact Of The Qualitative Nature Of Compliance Errors On Internal Control Assessments," AJPT, 1983-84, Vol. 3, No. 1, pp. 31-43.

Ferris, Kenneth R. "A Test Of The Expectancy Theory Of Motivation In An Accounting Environment," AR, 1977, Vol. 52, No. 3, pp. 605-615.

Ferris, Kenneth R. "A Test Of The Expectancy Theory Of Motivation In An Accounting Environment: A Response," AR, 1979, Vol. 54, No. 2, pp. 412-413.

Ferris, Kenneth R. "Profit Forecast Disclosure: The Effect On Managerial Behaviour," ABR, 1974-75, Vol. 5, No. 18, pp. 133-139.

Ferris, Kenneth R. (Aranya, Nissim and Kenneth R. Ferris. "A Reexamination Of Accountants' Organizational-Professional Conflict," AR, 1984, Vol. 59, No. 1, pp. 1-15.)

Ferris, Kenneth R. (Dittman, David A. and Kenneth R. Ferris. "'Profit Centre': A Satisfaction Generating Concept," ABR, 1977-78, Vol. 8, No. 32, pp. 242-245.)

Ferris, Kenneth R. (Farrelly, Gail E., Kenneth R. Ferris and William R. Reichenstein. "Perceived Risk, Market Risk, And Accounting-Determined Risk Measures," AR, 1985, Vol. 60, No. 2, pp. 278-288.)

Ferris, K. R. and D. F. Larcker. "Explanatory Variables Of Auditor Performance In A Large Public Accounting Firm," AOS, 1983, Vol. 8, No. 1, pp. 1-12.

Ferris, K. R. "Educational Predictors Of Professional Pay And Performance," AOS, 1982, Vol. 7, No. 3, pp. 225-230.

Ferris, K. R. "Organizational Commitment And Performance In A Professional Accounting Firm," AOS, 1981, Vol. 6, No. 4, pp. 317-326.

Ferris, K. R. "Perceived Environmental Uncertainty, Organizational Adaptation And Employee Performance: A Longitudinal Study In Professional Accounting Firms," AOS, 1982, Vol. 7, No. 1, pp. 13-26.

Ferris, K. R. "Perceived Uncertainty And Job Satisfaction In An Accounting Environment," AOS, 1977, Vol. 2, No. 1, pp. 23-28.

Ferris, K. R. (Dean, R. A., K. R. Ferris and C. Konstans. "Occupational Reality Shock And Organizational Commitment: Evidence From The Accounting Profession," AOS, 1988. Vol. 13, No. 3, pp. 251-262.)

Ferris, K. R. (Dillard, J. F. and K. R. Ferris. "Sources Of Professional Staff Turnover In Public Accounting Firms: Some Further Evidence," AOS, 1979, Vol. 4, No. 3, pp. 179-186.)

Ferris, K. R., J. F. Dillard and L. Nethercott. "A Comparison Of V-I-E Model Predictions: A Cross-National Study In Professional Accounting Firms," AOS, 1980, Vol. 5, No. 4, pp. 361-368.

Fertakis, John P. "Empirical Evidence - A Reply," AR, 1970, Vol. 45, No. 3, pp. 509-512.

Fertakis, John P. "On Communication, Understanding, And Relevance In Accounting Reporting," AR, 1969, Vol. 44, No. 4, pp. 680-691.

Fertakis, John P. "Toward A Systems-Oriented Concept Of Controllership," MA, 1968, Vol. 50, No. 4, pp. 5-10.

Fertakis, John P. (DeCoster, Don T. and John P. Fertakis. "Budget-Induced Pressure And Its Relationship To Supervisory Behavior," JAR, 1968, Vol. 6, No. 2, pp. 237-246.)

Fertakis, John. (Truitt, Jack, Albert Frakes and John Fertakis. "A Survey Of The Cost/Managerial Sequence In AACSB Schools," JAED, 1983, Vol. 1, No. 1, pp. 131-135.)

Fertig, Paul E. "Organization Of An Accounting Program," AR, 1960, Vol. 35, No. 2, pp. 190-196.

Fertig, Paul E. (Backer, Morton and Paul E. Fertig. "Statistical Sampling And The Accounting Curriculum," AR, 1958, Vol. 33, No. 3, pp. 415-418.)

Fertig, Paul E. (Beams, Floyd A. and Paul E. Fertig. "Pollution Control Through Social Cost Conversion," JOA, 1971, Vol. 132, No. 5, pp. 37-42.)

Feskoe, Gaffney. "Reducing Currency Risks In A Volatile Foreign Exchange Market," MA, 1980, Vol. 62, No. 3, pp. 19-24.

Fess, Philip E. and H. Peter Holzer. "The Diverse Functions Of Accounting," JOA, 1964, Vol. 118, No. 2, pp. 49-52.

Fess, Philip E. and Jerry J. Weygandt. "Cash-Flow Presentations - Trends, Recommendations," JOA, 1969, Vol. 128, No. 2, pp. 52-59.

Fess, Philip E. and Warren D. Summers. "Comment On The Beamer Report's Recommendation On CPA Examination Qualifying Experience," CPAJ, 1972, Vol. 42, No. 9, pp. 745-748.

Fess, Philip E. and William L. Ferrara. "The Period Cost Concept For Income Measurement - Can It Be Defended?," AR, 1961, Vol. 36, No. 4, pp. 598-602.

Fess, Philip E. "Accounting Instruction Without Rules," AR, 1962, Vol. 37, No. 2, pp. 342-344.

Fess, Philip E. "After A Quarter Century - Revision Of The Standard Short-Form Auditor's Report," CPAJ, 1972, Vol. 42, No. 5, pp. 373-378.

Fess, Philip E. "The Relevant Costing Concept For Income Measurement - Can It Be Defended?," AR, 1963, Vol. 38, No. 4, pp. 723-732.

Fess, Philip E. "The Theory Of Manufacturing Costs," AR, 1961, Vol. 36, No. 3, pp. 446-453.

Fess, Philip E. "The Variable (Direct) Costing Concept In Perspective," MA, 1969, Vol. 50, No. 8, pp. 21-23.

Fess, Philip E. "The Working Capital Concept," AR, 1966, Vol. 41, No. 2, pp. 266-270.

Fess, Philip E. (Fox, Kenneth L. and Philip E. Fess. "Suggested Refinements Of Procedures In Determining Earnings Per Share," JOA, 1970, Vol. 129, No. 1, pp. 52-56.)

Fess, Philip E. and Spencer J. Martin. "Company Forecasts And The Independent Auditor's Inexorable Involvement," CPAJ, 1973, Vol. 43, No. 10, pp. 868-876.

Fetterman, Allen L. "Update On Not-For-Profit Accounting And Reporting," CPAJ, 1988, Vol. 58, No. 3, pp. 22-29.

Fetters, Michael L. and Steven D. Grossman. "Accounting For The Receivable In A Lease Transaction: A Dilemma," AR, 1974, Vol. 49, No. 4, pp. 851-852.

Fetters, Michael, John McKenzie and David Callaghan. "Does The Computer Hinder Accounting Education? An Analysis Of Some Empirical Data," IAE, 1986, Vol. 1, No. 1, pp. 76-85.

Fetter, Frank A. "Reformulation Of The Concepts Of Capital And Income In Economics And Accounting," AR, 1937, Vol. 12, No. 1, pp. 3-12.

Fetyko, David F. and Michael Patterson. "How An Oil Company Analyzes Credit," MA, 1983, Vol. 65, No. 2, pp. 30-34.

Fetyko, David F. "The Company Social Audit," MA, 1975, Vol. 56, No. 10, pp. 31-34.

Fetyko, David F. "Who Shall Train Us?," MA, 1976, Vol. 57, No. 7, pp. 13-14.

Feurer, Louis. "Checking Client's Internal Controls," JOA, 1951, Vol. 91, No. 4, pp. 575-579.

Feyerharm, Robert W. "Budgetary Accounting Procedures And Accounting Forms For Small Colleges And Universities," AR, 1955, Vol. 30, No. 1, pp. 80-85.

Field, David R. (Albrecht, W. Steve, Scott W. Brown and David R. Field. "Toward Increased Job Satisfaction Of Practicing CPAs," JOA, 1981, Vol. 152, No. 2,pp. 61-68.)

Field, Ernest R. "Legal Conflicts And The Study Of Accountancy," AR, 1956, Vol. 31, No. 1, pp. 126-128.

Field, Ernest R. "Representation Before The Treasury," CPAJ, 1974, Vol. 44, No. 10, pp. 32-40.

Field, John E. "Toward A Multi-Level, Multi-Goal Information System," AR, 1969, Vol. 44, No. 3, pp. 593-599.

Field, J. E. "A Flow Of Funds Approach To Accounting Theory," AR, 1964, Vol. 39, No. 3, pp. 764-768.

Field, J. E. "Inventory Valuation And The Short-Run Cost Function," AR, 1960, Vol. 35, No. 1, pp. 104-110.

Fieldcamp, Dale. "International Accounting In An Inflationary Economy," IJAER, 1968, Vol. 4, No. 1, pp. 155-164.

Fieldgrass, V. "Comparative Returns For Institutional Property Investors," ABR, 1974-75, Vol. 5, No. 18, pp. 123-126.

Fields, Kent T. "Assignment Of Audit Responsibility In Computer System Development Projects," JIS, 1988, Vol. 2, No. 2, pp. 51-57.

Fields, Kent T. (Glahn, Gerald L., Kent T. Fields and Jerry E. Trapnell. "How To Evaluate Mixed Risk Capital Projects," MA, 1980, Vol. 62, No. 6, pp. 34-38.)

Fields, Kent T., Gary L. Waters and James H. Thompson. "Accounting For The Costs Of Certain Computer Software," CPAJ, 1986, Vol. 56, No. 1, pp. 32-37.

Fields, Kent T., Heibatollah Sami and Glenn E. Sumners. "Quantification Of The Auditor's Evaluation Of Internal Control In Data Base Systems," JIS, 1986, Vol. 1, No. 1, pp. 24-47.

Fieldsend, Susan. (McLeay, Stuart and Susan Fieldsend. "Sector And Size Effects In Ratio Analysis: An Indirect Test Of Ratio Proportionality," ABR, 1986-87, Vol. 17, No. 66, pp. 133-140.)

Fienberg, Stephen E. (Neter, John, R. A. Leitch and Stephen E. Fienberg. "Dollar Unit Sampling: Multinomial Bounds For Total Overstatement And Understatement Errors," AR, 1978, Vol. 53, No. 1, pp. 77-93.)

Figgie, Harry E. "Improving Your Bottom Line: Cost Reduction Vs. Expansion," CA, 1985, Vol. 3, No. 1, pp. 52-52.

Figler, Homer R. "Accounting For Human Assets," MA, 1975, Vol. 57, No. 5, pp. 23-26.

Figler, Homer R. "Goal-Setting Techniques," MA, 1971, Vol. 53, No. 5, pp. 25-27.

Figler, Homer R. "Managing Stress," MA, 1980, Vol. 62, No. 2, pp. 22-28.

Figler, Homer R. "Retirement: Profit Or Loss?," MA, 1977, Vol. 59, No. 5, pp. 15-17.

Figler, Homer R. "What Should The Management Accountant Know?," MA, 1978, Vol. 59, No. 12, pp. 27-29.

Figlewicz, Raymond E., Donald T. Anderson and C. David Strupeck. "The Evolution And Current State Of Financial Accounting Concepts And Standards In The Nonbusiness Sector," AHJ, 1985, Vol. 12, No. 1, pp. 73-98.

Figlewski, Stephen. "The Interaction Between Derivative Securities On Financial Instruments And The Underlying Cash Markets: An Overview," JAAF, 1987, Vol 2 (New Series), No. 3, pp. 299-318.

Filbey, Edward J. "Remarks On 'Problems In Determining Total Costs Of Distribution'," AR, 1934, Vol. 9, No. 1, pp. 21-22.

Filbey, Edward J. "The Deductibility Of Contributions As Business Expenses," AR, 1931, Vol. 6, No. 3, pp. 197-205.

Filer, R. J. and L. R. Eiswerth. "Quality Control And Associated Costs," MA, 1966, Vol. 48, No. 1, pp. 37-44.

Filimon, Radu, Sanford Morton and Soliman Y. Soliman. "Spoilage With A Production Function," ABR, 1986-87, Vol. 17, No. 68, pp. 337-348.

Filios, Vassilios P. "The French Contribution To The Theory Of Accounting," AIIA, 1987, Vol. 1, pp. 137-151.

Filios, Vassilios P. "The French 'Comptes d'Ordre'," ABR, 1983-84, Vol. 14, No. 53, pp. 89-91.

Filios, Vassilios. "Four Schools Of European Accounting Thought," AHJ, 1981, Vol. 8, No. 2, pp. 61-78.

Filios, V. P. "Some Noteworthy Theories From The French And Swiss Tradition In Accounting," ABR, 1980-81, Vol. 11, No. 44, pp. 267-280.

Filippini, Thomas W. and E. Thomas Thilman. "The Insurance Crisis - An Opportunity," CA, 1987, Vol. 5, No. 2, pp. 10-12.

Filipski, Robert M. "Understanding The New Overhead Capitalization Rules," MA, 1987, Vol. 68, No. 8, pp. 47-49.

Fill, William L. "The Break-Even Chart," AR, 1952, Vol. 27, No. 2, pp. 202-209.

Finch, Gerald L. "Improving The Bottom Line With Budget Incentive Programs," MA, 1987, Vol. 69, No. 4, pp. 42-47.

Findlay, M. Chapman, III. "Financial Lease Evaluation Under Conditions Of Uncertainty: A Comment," AR, 1974, Vol. 49, No. 4, pp. 794-795.

Findlay, M. Chapman, III. "On Market Efficiency And Financial Accounting," ABACUS, 1977, Vol. 13, No. 2, pp. 106-122.

Findlay, M. Chapman, III. (Williams, Edward E. and M. Chapman Findlay, III. "Is Common Stock Obsolete?," ABACUS, 1983, Vol. 19, No. 1, pp. 39-55.)

Findlay, M. Chapman, III. (Williams, Edward E. and M. Chapman Findlay, III. "Beyond Neoclassical Economic Theory As A Foundation For Financial Accounting," ABACUS, 1980, Vol. 16, No. 2, pp. 133-141.)

Findlay, M. C. and E. E. Williams. "Toward A Positive Theory Of Corporate Financial Policy," ABACUS, 1987, Vol. 23, No. 2, pp. 107-121.

Finerty, James J. "Accountants In 1984," MA, 1970, Vol. 51, No. 9, pp. 28-30.

Finerty, James J. "Product Pricing And Investment Analysis," MA, 1971, Vol. 53, No. 6, pp. 15-18.

Fink, Robert S. "The Role Of The Accountant In A Tax Fraud Case," JOA, 1976, Vol. 141, No. 4, pp. 42-48.

Fink, Ronald E. "Using Data Processing In Tax Scheduling," MA, 1970, Vol. 51, No. 8, pp. 48-49.

Finkenaur, Allen. "Accounting Records For Interperiod Tax Adjustments," JOA, 1970, Vol. 129, No. 1, pp. 44-51.

Finley, David R. "Counterexamples To Proposed Dollar-Unit Sampling Algorithm," JAR, 1985, Vol. 23, No. 1, pp. 402-404.

Finley, David R. (Thakkar, Rashmi B., David R. Finley and Woody M. Liao. "A Stochastic Demand CVP Model With Return On Investment Criterion," CAR, 1984-85, Vol. 1, No. 1, pp. 77-86.)

Finley, D. R. and J. L. Boockholdt. "A Continuous Constrained Optimization Model For Audit Sampling," AJPT, 1986-87, Vol. 6, No. 2, pp. 22-39.

Finley, D. R. and Woody M. Liao. "A General Decision Model For Cost-Volume-Profit Analysis Under Uncertainty: A Comment," AR, 1981, Vol. 56, No. 2, pp. 400-403.

Finley, D. R. "Controlling Compliance Testing With Acceptance Sampling," CPAJ, 1978, Vol. 48, No. 12, pp. 30-36.

Finley, D. R. "Normal Form Decision Theory Development Of The Audit Sampling Model," AJPT, 1983-84, Vol. 3, No. 1, pp. 104-115.

Finley, D. R. (Akresh, Abraham D. and D. R. Finley. "Two-Step Attributes Sampling In Auditing," CPAJ, 1979, Vol. 49, No. 12, pp. 19-24.)

Finley, D. R. (Horvitz, Jerome S. and D. R. Finley. "A Macro-Case Analysis Approach To Tax Research - A Comment," AR, 1979, Vol. 54, No. 3, pp. 637-640.)

Finn, Don W. (Collins, Frank, Paul Munter and Don W. Finn. "The Budgeting Games People Play," AR, 1987, Vol. 62, No. 1, pp. 29-49.)

Finn, Frank J. "Integer Programming, Linear Programming And Capital Budgeting," ABACUS, 1973, Vol. 9, No. 2, pp. 180-192.

Finnell, Jack C. "Accounting For Country Clubs: A Different View," MA, 1972, Vol. 54, No. 1, pp. 16-20.

Finnell, Jack C., Leland G. Ayer and Frank B. Harris. "Full Costing In The Oil And Gas Producing Industry," MA, 1967, Vol. 48, No. 5, pp. 47-52.

Finnerty, Joseph E. (Whiteman, Michael J., Anthony T. Krzystofik and Joseph E. Finnerty. "Interest Ruling - Questions For Lenders And Borrowers," CPAJ, 1984, Vol. 54, No. 1, pp. 39-43.)

Finnerty, Joseph E., Rick N. Fitzsimmons and Thomas W. Oliver. "Lease Capitalization And Systematic Risk," AR, 1980, Vol. 55, No. 4, pp. 631-639.

Finney, Frederick D. "Looking At Inflation - Realistically," MA, 1981, Vol. 62, No. 12, pp. 22-25.

Finney, Frederick D. "Pricing Interdivisional Transfers," MA, 1966, Vol. 48, No. 3, pp. 10-18.

Finney, H. A. "Principles And Conventions," AR, 1944, Vol. 19, No. 4, pp. 361-365.

Finney, John E. "Controlling EDP Costs," JOA, 1981, Vol. 151, No. 4, pp. 63-68.

Finney, John E. "Costing In A Data Processing Department," MA, 1974, Vol. 56, No. 4, pp. 29-35.

Finnie, James. "The Role Of Financial Appraisal In Decisions To Acquire Advanced Manufacturing Technology," ABR, 1988, Vol. 18, No. 70, pp. 133-140.

Finston, Howard V. "Managerial Development," JOA, 1956, Vol. 102, No. 1, pp. 32-35.

Fiorenza, Frank A. "Accounting For Unusual Quality-Control Costs," MA, 1969, Vol. 50, No. 6, pp. 53-55.

Firmin, Peter A. and James J. Linn. "Accounting Systems Course - A New Concept," AR, 1967, Vol. 42, No. 1, pp. 124-127.

Firmin, Peter A. and James J. Linn. "Information Systems And Managerial Accounting," AR, 1968, Vol. 43, No. 1, pp. 75-82.

Firmin, Peter A. "Dollar Value Lifo: Legitimate Or Not?," AR, 1963, Vol. 38, No. 2, pp. 270-277.

Firmin, Peter A. "Educating Tomorrow's Accountant - Today," AR, 1957, Vol. 32, No. 4, pp. 569-575.

Firmin, Peter A. "The Five-Year Accounting Program - With Due And Deliberate Speed," AR, 1959, Vol. 34, No. 4, pp. 591-602.

Firmin, Peter A., Seymour S. Goodman, Thomas E. Hendricks and James J. Linn. "University Cost Structure And Behavior: An Empirical Study," JAR, 1968, Vol. 6, Supp., pp. 122-155.

Firth, Michael A. "An Empirical Examination Of The Applicability Of Adopting The AICPA And NYSE Regulations On Free Share Distributions In The U.K.," JAR, 1973, Vol. 11, No. 1, pp. 16-24.

Firth, Michael. "A Cross-Sectional Analysis Of Qualified Audit Reports," IJAER, 1980, Vol. 15, No. 2, pp. 47-59.

Firth, Michael. "A Study Of The Consensus Of The Perceived Importance Of Disclosure Of Individual Items In Corporate Annual Reports," IJAER, 1978, Vol. 14, No. 1, pp. 57-70.

Firth, Michael. "An Analysis Of Audit Fees And Their Determination In New Zealand," AJPT, 1984-85, Vol. 4, No. 2, pp. 23-37.

Firth, Michael. "Auditor-Client Relationships And Their Impact On Bankers' Perceived Lending Decisions," ABR, 1980-81, Vol. 11, No. 43, pp. 179-188.

Firth, Michael. "Perceptions Of Auditor Independence And Official Ethical Guidelines," AR, 1980, Vol. 55, No. 3, pp. 451-466.

Firth, Michael. "Qualified Audit Reports: Their Impact On Investment Decisions," AR, 1978, Vol. 53, No. 3, pp. 642-650.

Firth, **Michael.** "Raising Finance And Firms' Corporate Reporting Policies," **ABACUS,** 1980, Vol. 16, No. 2, pp. 100-115.

Firth, **Michael.** "Shareholder Behaviour Attendant Upon Capitalisation Issues," **ABR,** 1973-74, Vol. 4, No. 13, pp. 23-32.

Firth, **Michael.** "The Impact Of Size. Stock Market Listing, And Auditors On Voluntary Disclosure In Corporate Annual Reports," **ABR,** 1978-79, Vol. 9, No. 36, pp. 273-280.

Firth, **Michael.** "The Relative Information Content Of The Release Of Financial Results Data By Firms," **JAR,** 1981, Vol. 19, No. 2, pp. 521-529.

Firth, **Michael.** (Mear, Ron and Michael Firth. "Risk Perceptions Of Financial Analysts And The Use Of Market And Accounting Data," **ABR,** 1988, Vol. 18, No. 72, pp. 335-340.)

Firth, **Michael.** (Mear, Ross and Michael Firth. "CUE Usage And Self-Insight Of Financial Analysts," **AR,** 1987, Vol. 62, No. 1, pp. 176-182.)

Firth, **M.** "Consensus Views And Judgment Models In Materiality Decisions," **AOS,** 1979. Vol. 4, No. 4, pp. 283-296.

Firth, **M.** (Mear, R. and M. Firth. "Assessing The Accuracy Of Financial Analyst Security Return Predictions," **AOS,** 1987, Vol. 12, No. 3, pp. 331-340.)

Fisch, Jack H. and Martin Mellman. "Accounting For Investments In Affiliated Companies," **JOA,** 1969, Vol. 128, No. 5, pp. 41-49.

Fisch, Jack H. and Martin Mellman. "Poolings Of Interest: The Status Of The Criteria," **JOA,** 1968, Vol. 126, No. 2. pp. 42-48.

Fischer, J. (Van Den Bergh, R. J. A. and J. Fischer. "Human Resource Accounting - Some Problems In Implementation," **AOS,** 1976, Vol. 1, No. 2/3. pp. 265-270.)

Fischer, Paul M. and Martin J. Gregorich. "Calculating Earnings Per Share," **JOA,** 1973, Vol. 135. No. 5, pp. 61-71.

Fischer, **Robert W.** "Clear Responsibility Needed For Internal Control In Banks," **JOA,** 1953, Vol. 95, No. 4, pp. 454-459.

Fish, **Edwards R.** (Arnett, Robert D. and Edwards R. Fish. "Is Everything Under Control?," **MA,** 1968, Vol. 50. No. 4, pp. 27-29.)

Fish, **Gary L,** Larry D. Gipple and Jane E. Katz. "Assessing CPE Needs," **JOA,** 1985, Vol. 160, No. 1. pp. 79-83.

Fishburn, **Peter C.** "Theory Versus Practice In Risk Analysis: An Empirical Study: A Comment," **AR.** 1976. Vol. 51, No. 3, pp. 657-662.

Fishburn, Peter C. (Libby, Robert and Peter C. Fishburn. "Behavioral Models Of Risk Taking In Business Decisions: A Survey And Evaluation," **JAR,** 1977, Vol. 15. No. 2. pp. 272-292.)

Fisher, **Franklin M.** "Accounting Data And The Economic Performance Of Firms," **JAPP,** 1988. Vol. 7. No. 4, pp. 253-260.

Fisher, **Irving.** "General Comments On Appreciation," **AR.** 1930, Vol. 5, No. 1, pp. 55-57.

Fisher, **James.** (Upson, Roger B. and James Fisher. "Sterling-Dollar Forward Exchange Rates," **ABACUS,** 1971, Vol. 7, No. 2, pp. 153-160.)

Fisher, **J.** "Empirical Research Into Information Utility And Acceptability: A Reply," **ABR,** 1974-75, Vol. 5, No. 20, pp. 309-313.

Fisher, **J.** "Financial Information And The Accounting Standards Steering Committee," **ABR,** 1973-74, Vol. 4, No. 16, pp. 275-285.

Fisher, **J.** "Value To The Business - Some Practical Problems," **MA,** 1976. Vol. 58. No. 1, pp. 23-37.

Fisher, **Marguerite.** "Internal Controls: Guidelines For Management Action," **JAAF.** 1978. Vol. 1. No. 4. pp. 349-360.

Fiske, **Wyman P.** "The Teaching Of Cost Accounting," **AR.** 1944, Vol. 19, No. 2, pp. 180-186.

Fiske, **Wyman P.** "Training For The Controllership," **AR.** 1940, Vol. 15, No. 2, pp. 232-237.

Fiske, **W. P.** "The Teaching Of Accounting In An Engineering School," **AR.** 1933. Vol. 8. No. 1, pp. 25-28.

FitzGerald, John Woodward. "Admission Of A New Partner By Investment." **AR.** 1952. Vol. 27, No. 1, pp. 114-118.

Fitzgerald, John Woodward. "Accounting For Variation In Gross Profit," **AR,** 1953, Vol. 28. No. 1. pp. 114-127.

Fitzgerald, **Richard D.** and Eleanor M. Kelley. "International Disclosure Standards - The United Nations Position," **JAAF,** 1979. Vol. 3. No. 1, pp. 5-20.

Fitzgerald, **Richard D.** "International Harmonization Of Accounting And Reporting," **IJAER.** 1981. Vol. 17. No. 1, pp. 21-32.

Fitzpatrick, **Paul J.** "Transitional Stages Of A Business Failure," **AR.** 1934. Vol. 9. No. 4. pp. 337-340.

Fitzsimmons, Rick N. (Finnerty, Joseph E.. Rick N. Fitzsimmons and Thomas W. Oliver. "Lease Capitalization And Systematic Risk," **AR.** 1980. Vol. 55. No. 4, pp. 631-639.)

Fjeld, **E. I.** "An Aid In Grading Papers In Accounting." **AR,** 1927. Vol. 2. No. 3, pp. 280-289.

Fjeld, **E. I.** "Balance-Sheet Form And Classification In Corporate Reports," **AR,** 1936. Vol. 11. No. 3, pp. 211-228.

Fjeld, **E. I.** "Classification And Terminology Of Individual Balance-Sheet Items," **AR.** 1936. Vol. 11. No. 4. pp. 330-344.

Flaherty, **Richard E.** and Bill N. Schwartz. "Earnings Per Share: Compliance And Understandability," **JAAF,** 1980, Vol. 4. No. 1, pp. 47-56.

Flaherty, Richard E. (Sterling, Robert R. and Richard E.

Flaherty. "The Role Of Liquidity In Exchange Valuation," **AR,** 1971. Vol. 46, No. 3, pp. 441-456.)

Flaherty, Richard E. (Sterling, Robert R., John O. Tollefson and Richard E. Flaherty. "Exchange Valuation: An Empirical Test," **AR,** 1972, Vol. 47, No. 4, pp. 709-721.)

Flambholtz, Eric G. (Brummet, R. Lee, Eric G. Flamholtz and William C. Pyle. "Human Resource Accounting: A Tool To Increase Managerial Effectiveness," **MA,** 1969, Vol. 51, No. 2, pp. 12-15.)

Flamholtz, **Diana T.** (Ansari, Shahid L. and Diana T. Flamholtz. "Management Science And The Development Of Human Resource Accounting," **AHJ,** 1978, Vol. 5, No. 2, pp. 11-35.)

Flamholtz, **Eric** and Todd S. Lundy. "Human Resource Accounting For CPA Firms," **CPAJ,** 1975, Vol. 45, No. 10, pp. 45-51.

Flamholtz, **Eric G.** "Assessing The Validity Of A Theory Of Human Resource Value: A Field Study," **JAR,** 1972, Vol. 10. Supp., pp. 241-266.

Flamholtz, **Eric G.** "On The Use Of The Economic Concept Of Human Capital In Financial Statements: A Comment," **AR,** 1972, Vol. 47, No. 1, pp. 148-152.

Flamholtz, **Eric G.** (Brummet, R. Lee, Eric G. Flamholtz and William C. Pyle. "Human Resource Measurement - A Challenge For Accountants," **AR,** 1968, Vol. 43, No. 2, pp. 217-224.)

Flamholtz, **Eric G.,** D. Gerald Searfoss and Russell Coff. "Developing Human Resource Accounting As A Human Resource Decision Support System," **AH,** 1988, Vol. 2, No. 3. pp. 1-9.

Flamholtz, **Eric.** "A Model For Human Resource Valuation: A Stochastic Process With Service Rewards," **AR,** 1971, Vol. 46. No. 2, pp. 253-267.

Flamholtz, **Eric.** "Toward A Theory Of Human Resource Value In Formal Organizations," **AR,** 1972, Vol. 47, No. 4, pp. 666-678.

Flamholtz, **E.** and E. Cook. "Connotative Meaning And Its Role In Accounting Change: A Field Study," **AOS,** 1978, Vol. 3. No. 2, pp. 115-140.

Flamholtz, **E. G.** "Accounting, Budgeting And Control Systems In Their Organizational Context: Theoretical And Empirical Perspectives," **AOS,** 1983, Vol. 8, No. 2/3, pp. 153-170.

Flamholtz, **E. G.** "The Process Of Measurement In Managerial Accounting: A Psycho-Technical Systems Perspective," **AOS,** 1980, Vol. 5, No. 1, pp. 31-42.

Flamholtz, **E. G.** "Valuation Of Human Assets In A Securities Brokerage Firm: An Empirical Study," **AOS,** 1987. Vol. 12. No. 3, pp. 309-318.

Flamholtz, **E. G.** (Bullen, M. L. and E. G. Flamholtz. "A Theoretical And Empirical Investigation Of Job Satisfaction And Intended Turnover In The Large CPA Firm," **AOS,** 1985. Vol. 10, No. 3, pp. 287-302.)

Flamholtz, **E. G.,** T. K. Das and A. S. Tsui. "Toward An Integrative Framework Of Organizational Control," **AOS,** 1985. Vol. 10. No. 1, pp. 35-50.

Flamholtz, **E.** "The Impact Of Human Resource Valuation On Management Decisions: A Laboratory Experiment," **AOS,** 1976. Vol. 1. No. 2/3, pp. 153-166.

Flamholtz, **E.** (Epstein, M., E. Flamholtz and J. J. McDonough. "Corporate Social Accounting In The U.S.A.: State Of The Art And Future Prospects," **AOS,** 1976, Vol. 1. No. 1, pp. 23-42.)

Flanagan, **Raymond M.** "Truth In Negotiations," **MA,** 1969, Vol. 50, No. 8, pp. 55-58.

Flanders, **David P.** "Mechanized Intercompany Transfer System," **MA,** 1969, Vol. 51, No. 4, pp. 49-52.

Flanders, **Dwight P.** "Accountancy. Systematized Learning, And Economics," **AR,** 1961, Vol. 36, No. 4, pp. 564-576.

Flanders, **Dwight P.** "Accounting And Economics: A Note With Special Reference To The Teaching Of Social Accounting," **AR,** 1959, Vol. 34, No. 1, pp. 68-73.

Fleck, **L. H.** "The Incidence Of Abandonment Losses," **AR.** 1926. Vol. 1. No. 2, pp. 48-59.

Flegm, **Eugene H.** "Pension Accounting - The Search For Truth," **CA,** 1984, Vol. 2, No. 3, pp. 30-39.

Flegm, **Eugene H.** "The Summary Annual Report," **RIAR,** 1988, Vol. 2. pp. 189-205.

Fleig, **W. J.** "The Use Of Films In Accounting Instruction," **AR,** 1950. Vol. 25, No. 1, pp. 94-96.

Fleig, **W. J.** "Use Of Slides In Accounting Instruction," **AR,** 1948. Vol. 23, No. 3, pp. 282-288.

Fleischman, **Richard K.** and R. Penny Marquette. "Municipal Accounting Reform C. 1900: Ohio's Progressive Accountants," **AHJ,** 1987. Vol. 14. No. 1, pp. 83-94.

Fleischman, **Richard K.** "Foundation Of The National Municipal League," **JOA,** 1987, Vol. 163, No. 5, pp. 297-298.

Fleming, **Donald A.** (Passage. Howard D. and Donald A. Fleming. "An Integrated Approach To Internal Control Reviews," **MA,** 1980. Vol. 61. No. 8, pp. 29-35.)

Fleming, **Mary M. K.** "Budgeting Practices In Large CPA Firms," **JOA,** 1980, Vol. 149, No. 5, pp. 55-62.

Fleming, **Mary M. K.** (Boyd, Paul and Mary M. K. Fleming. "Productivity: The Controller's Role," **MA,** 1987, Vol. 69, No. 3, pp. 28-32.)

Fleming, **Mary M. K.** (Plaza, Terence J. and Mary M. K. Fleming. "Cost Account Directive - An Effective Management Tool," **MA,** 1987, Vol. 68, No. 11, pp. 49-54.)

Flesher, **Dale L.** and Frances M. McNair. "How Valuable Is The CMA?," **MA,** 1985, Vol. 67, No. 5, pp. 29-32.

Flesher, **Dale L.** and Jalaleddin Soroosh. "Factors Affecting Accountants' Fees," **CPAJ,** 1980, Vol. 50, No. 7, pp. 27-32.

Flesher, Dale L. and Jalaleddin Soroosh. "Controllers Say FAS 33 Is Not Very Useful," MA, 1983, Vol. 64, No. 7, pp. 50-53.

Flesher, Dale L. and Tonya K. Flesher. "Human Resource Accounting In Mississippi Before 1865," ABR, 1979-80, Vol. 10, No. 37A, pp. 124-129.

Flesher, Dale L. and Tonya K. Flesher. "Ivar Kreuger's Contribution To U.S. Financial Reporting," AR, 1986, Vol. 61, No. 3, pp. 421-434.

Flesher, Dale L. "Advertising Effectiveness And Accounting Policy: A Comment," AR, 1977, Vol. 52, No. 1, pp. 261-263.

Flesher, Dale L. "Barter Bookkeeping: A Tenacious System," AHJ, 1979, Vol. 6, No. 1, pp. 83-86.

Flesher, Dale L. "Operations Auditing: For The Independent Auditor," CPAJ, 1977, Vol. 47, No. 7, pp. 17-21.

Flesher, Dale L. (Flesher, Tonya K. and Dale L. Flesher. "James O. McKinsey," AHJ, 1985, Vol. 12, No. 2, pp. 117-128.)

Flesher, Dale L. (Moody, Sharon M. and Dale L. Flesher. "Analysis Of FASB Voting Patterns: Statement Nos. 1-86," JAAF, 1986, Vol. 1 (New Series), No. 4. pp. 319-330.)

Flesher, D. L. (Flesher, T. K. and D. L. Flesher. "Managerial Accounting In An Early 19th Century German American Religious Commune," AOS, 1979, Vol. 4, No. 4, pp. 297-304.)

Flesher, Tonya K. and Dale L. Flesher. "James O. McKinsey," AHJ, 1985, Vol. 12, No. 2, pp. 117-128.

Flesher, Tonya K. and Joyce A. Rescho. "Tax Concepts And Their Importance In The Undergraduate Curriculum," JAED, 1986, Vol. 4, No. 1, pp. 55-68.

Flesher, Tonya K. "A Turning Point In Tax History," JOA, 1987, Vol. 163, No. 5, pp. 193-194.

Flesher, Tonya K. (Flesher, Dale L. and Tonya K. Flesher. "Ivar Kreuger's Contribution To U.S. Financial Reporting," AR, 1986, Vol. 61, No. 3, pp. 421-434.)

Flesher, Tonya K. (Flesher, Dale L. and Tonya K. Flesher. "Human Resource Accounting In Mississippi Before 1865," ABR, 1979-80, Vol. 10, No. 37A, pp. 124-129.)

Flesher, Tonya K. (O'Neil, Cherie J.. Jack M. Cathey and Tonya K. Flesher. "An Analysis Of Ph.D. Dissertations In Taxation: 1977-1985," IAE, 1988, Vol. 3, No. 1, pp. 120-130.)

Flesher, T. K. and D. L. Flesher. "Managerial Accounting In An Early 19th Century German American Religious Commune," AOS, 1979, Vol. 4, No. 4, pp. 297-304.

Flewellen, William C., Jr. "Better Accounting Students - A Critical Problem," MA, 1966, Vol. 47, No. 6, pp. 3-7.

Flewellen, William C., Jr. "Current Trends In Accounting Education," MA, 1968, Vol. 49, No. 5, pp. 3-7.

Flewellen, W. C., Jr. "Concept Of Depreciation Accounting Held By The United States Supreme Court," AR, 1960, Vol. 35, No. 3, pp. 413-421.

Flink, Solomon J., Assa Birati and Meyer Ungar. "The Impact Of Inflation On The Profits Of Listed Firms In Israel," ABR, 1977-78, Vol. 8, No. 32, pp. 253-257.

Flinn, Ronald E. "Income Tax Regulations: A Practitioner's Guide," CPAJ, 1981, Vol. 51, No. 9, pp. 38-45.

Flint, David. "The Role Of The Auditor In Modern Society: An Exploratory Essay," ABR, 1970-71, Vol. 1, No. 4, pp. 287-293.

Flintall, Virginia L. "Should Essay Questions Be Eliminated From The CPA Exam? - An Issue Of Great Importance To The Practice Of Accounting," CPAJ, 1987, Vol. 57, No. 6, pp. 18-25.

Flippo, Ronnie G. "The President's Tax Proposals: A View From Capitol Hill," JOA, 1985, Vol. 160, No. 3, pp. 86-88.

Flock, Henry H. "The Change To Direct Costing In A Multi-Product Company," MA, 1971, Vol. 53, No. 1, pp. 52-55.

Florence, Gary A. "Electric Utility Bond Financing," MA, 1973, Vol. 54, No. 12, pp. 35-37.

Flory, Steven M. and Steven D. Grossman. "New Oil And Gas Accounting Requirements," CPAJ, 1978, Vol. 48, No. 5, pp. 39-43.

Flory, Steven M. (Cooper, Kerry, Steven M. Flory, Steven D. Grossman and John C. Groth. "Reserve Recognition Accounting: A Proposed Disclosure Framework," JOA, 1979, Vol. 148, No. 3, pp. 82-91.)

Flory, Steven M. (Cooper, Kerry, Steven M. Flory and Steven D. Grossman. "New Ballgame For Oil And Gas Accounting," CPAJ, 1979, Vol. 49, No. 1, pp. 11-18.)

Flory, Steven M. (Giroux, Gary A. and Steven M. Flory. "Auditing America's Cities," CPAJ, 1980, Vol. 50, No. 10, pp. 21-28.)

Flory, Steven. (Cooper, Kerry and Steven Flory. "Lessons From McKesson And Equity Funding," CPAJ, 1976, Vol. 46, No. 4, pp. 19-26.)

Flower, John. "A Price Parity Theory Of Translation: A Comment," ABR, 1978-79, Vol. 9, No. 33, pp. 64-65.

Flower, J. F. "A Risk Analysis Approach To Marginal Cost Pricing: A Comment," ABR, 1970-71, Vol. 1, No. 4, pp. 335-339.

Flower, J. F. "Measurement Of Divisional Performance," ABR, 1970-71, Vol. 1, No. 3, pp. 205-214.

Flower, J. F. "The Case Of The Profitable Bloodhound," JAR, 1966, Vol. 4, No. 1, pp. 16-36.

Flowers, Robert E. "Accounting For Certain Off-Balance Sheet Financing," CPAJ, 1986, Vol. 56, No. 2, pp. 36-42.

Flowers, Wm. Baker. "Biography And Accounting History," AHJ, 1974, Vol. 1, No. 1-4, pp. 21-22.

Flowers, W. Baker. "Some Criteria For Post-Statement Disclosure," JOA, 1961, Vol. 111, No. 1, pp. 48-58.

Floyd, Alpha C. "Management Accounting For Churches," MA, 1969, Vol. 50, No. 6, pp. 56-59.

Floyd, Herbert F. (Tucker, Michael J. and Herbert F. Floyd. "Recent Cases Of Reallocation Of Income By IRS," CPAJ, 1987, Vol. 57, No. 12, pp. 62-67.)

Fluckiger, W. Lynn. "A Philosophy Of Fund Accounting," JOA, 1963, Vol. 116, No. 2, pp. 66-71.

Flynn, Thomas D. "A Public Accountant's Suggestions To His Client About To Take War Contracts," JOA, 1951, Vol. 91, No. 2, pp. 252-255.

Flynn, Thomas D. "Corporate Executives View Accounting Principles," JOA, 1965, Vol. 119, No. 6, pp. 31-36.

Flynn, Thomas D. "Public Accountants' Staff Training Program," AR, 1948, Vol. 23, No. 4, pp. 410-413.

Flynn, T. D. "Labor Statistics Bureau Surveys Job Outlook For Accountants," JOA, 1952, Vol. 94, No. 2, pp. 198-201.

Fogelberg, Graeme. "Interim Income Determination: An Examination Of The Effects Of Alternative Measurement Techniques," JAR, 1971, Vol. 9, No. 2, pp. 215-235.

Fogg, Stephen L. (Bastable, C. W. and Stephen L. Fogg. "Indexation: Will Taxpayers Get Its Benefits?," JOA, 1982, Vol. 153, No. 1, pp. 52-61.)

Fogg, Stephen L. (Schwartz, Bill N. and Stephen L. Fogg. "Department Of Accounting Advisory Board: A Method Of Communicating With The Business And Professional Community," JAED, 1985, Vol. 3, No. 1, pp. 179-184.)

Fogler, H. Russell. "Ranking Techniques And Capital Budgeting," AR, 1972, Vol. 47, No. 1, pp. 134-143.

Folbigg, Robert C. (Van Brunt, Roy T. and Robert C. Folbigg. "EDGAR - Informing The Public," CA, 1986, Vol. 4, No. 3, pp. 19-24.)

Foldes, L. P. (Ornhial, A. J. H. and L. P. Foldes. "Tax Uncertainty In Project Evaluation: A Case Study," ABR, 1974-75, Vol. 5, No. 19, pp. 229-230.)

Foley, B. J. (Maunders, K. T. and B. J. Foley. "Information Disclosure And The Role Of The Accountant In Collective Bargaining - Some Comments," AOS, 1984, Vol. 9, No. 1, pp. 99-106.)

Foley, John C. and Monroe S. Kuttner. "Finding Funds For A Small Business," JOA, 1986, Vol. 162, No. 2, pp. 114-122.

Folkenflik, Max and William M. Landau. "The Impact Of The Mann Judd Landau Case," CPAJ, 1988, Vol. 58, No. 10, pp. 32-44.

Folks, William R., Jr. (Evans, Thomas G. and William R. Folks, Jr. "SFAS No. 8: Conforming, Coping, Complaining, And Correcting!," IJAER, 1979, Vol. 15, No. 1, pp. 33-43.)

Folpe, Herbert K. (Robinson, Daniel D. and Herbert K. Folpe. "Joint Costs In Voluntary Health And Welfare Organizations," CPAJ, 1984, Vol. 54, No. 4, pp. 32-39.)

Folsom, Donald J. "A Control Guide For Computer Systems," MA, 1973, Vol. 55, No. 2, pp. 49-53.

Foote, Franklin M. "Accountants Need Not Suffer Eyestrain," JOA, 1951, Vol. 92, No. 4, pp. 454-455.

Foran, Michael F. and Anthony F. McGann. "The Annual Report," MA, 1973, Vol. 55, No. 5, pp. 48-51.

Foran, Michael F. and Don T. DeCoster. "An Experimental Study Of The Effects Of Participation, Authoritarianism, And Feedback On Cognitive Dissonance In A Standard Setting Situation," AR, 1974, Vol. 49, No. 4, pp. 751-763.

Foran, Michael F. and Kavasseri V. Ramanathan. "Selling Options: A New Twist In Securities Trading," JOA, 1976, Vol. 141, No. 6, pp. 57-64.

Foran, Michael F. "An Experimental Study Of The Effects Of Participation, Authoritarianism And Feedback On Cognitive Dissonance In A Standard Setting Situation: A Reply," AR, 1977, Vol. 52, No. 3, pp. 762-764.

Foran, Michael F. (Foran, Nancy J. and Michael F. Foran. "SFAS No. 12 And The Conceptual Framework," ACCHOR, 1987, Vol. 1, No. 4, pp. 43-50.)

Foran, Michael F. (Frakes, Albert H. and Michael F. Foran. "A Framework For Examining The Evaluative Function Of Accounting Learning Activities," AR, 1978, Vol. 53, No. 1, pp. 148-154.)

Foran, Nancy and Dahli Gray. "The Evolution Of The Unitary Tax Apportionment Method," AHJ, 1988, Vol. 15, No. 1, pp. 65-87.

Foran, Nancy J. and Michael F. Foran. "SFAS No. 12 And The Conceptual Framework," ACCHOR, 1987, Vol. 1, No. 4, pp. 43-50.

Forbes, John F. "Observations Of A CPA Examiner," AR, 1944, Vol. 19, No. 2, pp. 135-138.

Ford, Allen and John K. Harris. "The Impact Of Recruiting Practices On Students," CPAJ, 1974, Vol. 44, No. 8, pp. 29-34.

Ford, Allen and John R. Robinson. "The Proper Charge To Capital: Jarvis And Its Implications," JATA, 1981, Vol. 3, No. 1, pp. 5-10.

Ford, Allen. "Selecting A Useful Life For The Investment Credit," MA, 1973, Vol. 54, No. 10, pp. 14-16.

Ford, Allen. "Should Cost Be Assigned To Conversion Value?," AR, 1969, Vol. 44, No. 4, pp. 818-822.

Ford, Allen. "Travel Expenses For A Visiting Professor," AR, 1975, Vol. 50, No. 2, pp. 338-344.

Ford, Allen. (Parker, James E. and Allen Ford. "Dissertation Experiences Of Recent Doctoral Graduates In Accounting," AR, 1972, Vol. 47, No. 4, pp. 830-833.)

Ford, Gordon. "Planning For Growth Of A CPA Firm," JOA, 1963, Vol. 116, No. 5, pp. 45-51.

Ford, Jerry L. "How To Communicate With Management," MA, 1979, Vol. 60, No. 9, pp. 12-17.

Forderhase, F. B. "Notes To Financial Statements," JOA, 1955, Vol. 100, No. 4, pp. 50-55.

Fordon, John V. "Profit Variations," AR, 1951, Vol. 26, No.

4, pp. 574-576.

Forer, Henry D. "Tax Planning For Savings And Loan Associations," **JOA**, 1965, Vol. 120, No. 4, pp. 49-55.

Forker, J. A. "Contract Value Accounting And The Monitoring Of Managerial Performance: An Agency-Based Proposal," **ABR**, 1983-84, Vol. 14, No. 54, pp. 125-138.

Forker, J. J. "Capital Maintenance Concepts, Gains From Borrowing And The Measurement Of Income," **ABR**, 1979-80, Vol. 10, No. 40, pp. 393-402.

Forker, J. J. "Capital Maintenance, Borrowing Gains And Income Measurement: A Reply," **ABR**, 1981-82, Vol. 12, No. 48, pp. 319-320.

Forker, J. J. "CCA And CPP: A Suggested Basis For Reconciliation," **ABR**, 1976-77, Vol. 7, No. 28, pp. 260-269.

Forker, J. J. "In Defence Of CoVA: A Comment On A Critique," **ABR**, 1985-86, Vol. 16, No. 62, pp. 149-150.

Foroughi, Tahirih Khodadoust. "Accounting In Developing Countries Before And After Social Crisis: The Case Of Iran," **IJAER**, 1981, Vol. 17, No. 1, pp. 181-223.

Forrester, D. A. R. "Asset Valuations Before And After Liquidation," **ABR**, 1973-74, Vol. 4, No. 13, pp. 33-42.

Forrester, D. A. R. "Early Canal Company Accounts: Financial And Accounting Aspects Of The Forth And Clyde Navigation, 1768-1816," **ABR**, 1979-80, Vol. 10, No. 37A, pp. 109-123

Forrester, D. A. R. "German Accounting Principles Applied, A Review Article," **ABR**, 1982-83, Vol. 13, No. 51, pp. 215-220.

Forrester, D. A. R. "The Incan Contribution To Double-Entry Accounting," **JAR**, 1968, Vol. 6, No. 2, p. 283.

Forrester, D. A. R. "Whether Malcolm's Is Best Or Old Charge & Discharge," **AHJ**, 1978, Vol. 5, No. 2, pp. 51-61.

Forrester, Robert. "Tips For Auditing Nonprofit Organizations," **JOA**, 1988, Vol. 165, No. 5, pp. 56-66.

Forrester, Robert. (Kropatkin, Philip and Robert Forrester. "The Single Audit - Independence, Materiality And Cost-Effectiveness - Part I," **CPAJ**, 1983, Vol. 53, No. 2, pp. 10-17.)

Forrester, Robert. (Kropatkin, Philip and Robert Forrester. "The Single Audit - Independence, Materiality And Cost-Effectiveness - Part II," **CPAJ**, 1983, Vol. 53, No. 3, pp. 16-23.)

Forster, Joel M. (Austin, P. Thomas, Joel M. Forster and Robert M. Rosen. "Tax Reform: The New Perspective," **JOA**, 1977, Vol. 143, No. 3, pp. 48-59.)

Forster, Joel M., Oliver C. Murray and Edward D. Ryan. "Tax Reform: The New Perspective," **JOA**, 1977, Vol. 143, No. 4, pp. 79-88.

Forsythe, Robert. (DeJong, Douglas V., Robert Forsythe, Russell J. Lundholm and Wilfred C. Uecker. "A Laboratory Investigation Of The Moral Hazard Problem In An Agency Relationship," **JAR**, 1985, Vol. 23, Supp., pp. 81-120.)

Forsythe, Robert. (DeJong, Douglas V., Robert Forsythe and Wilfred C. Uecker. "The Methodology Of Laboratory Markets And Its Implications For Agency Research In Accounting And Auditing," **JAR**, 1985, Vol. 23, No. 2, pp. 753-793.)

Fortin, Karen A. (Osteryoung, Jerome S., Daniel E. McCarty and Karen A. Fortin. "How The New Cost Recovery System Compares With Prior Methods," **MA**, 1981, Vol. 63, No. 5, pp. 13-27.)

Fortin, Karen A. (Reeder, Janis R. and Karen A. Fortin. "Subchapter S In Transition: A Comment," **JATA**, 1985, Vol. 7, No. 1, pp. 73-75.)

Fortin, Karen. (Osteryoung, Jerome S., Daniel E. McCarty and Karen Fortin. "A Note On The Optimal Tax Lives For Assets Qualifying For The Investment Tax Credit," **AR**, 1980, Vol. 55, No. 2, pp. 301-306.)

Fortin, Karen. (Osteryoung, Jerome S., Daniel M. McCarty and Karen Fortin. "A Note On Optimal Depreciation Research - A Comment," **AR**, 1981, Vol. 56, No. 3, pp. 719-721.)

Fortner, Richard W. (Braunstein, Daniel N. and Richard W. Fortner. "The Design Of Behavioral Research," **AR**, 1968, Vol. 43, No. 2, pp. 377-383.)

Fortunato, Frank A. "The Quest For Fairness In Accounting," **MA**, 1972, Vol. 53, No. 7, pp. 15-18.

Foss, E. M. "How To Lose Clients, Or, Watch Your Confirmation Technique," **JOA**, 1952, Vol. 94, No. 1, pp. 67-69.

Foss, Helga B. and Shaheen Borna. "Employee Leasing After The TRA," **JOA**, 1987, Vol. 164, No. 3, pp. 151-156.

Fossum, Robert L. (Zeff, Stephen A. and Robert L. Fossum. "An Analysis Of Large Audit Clients," **AR**, 1967, Vol. 42, No. 2, pp. 298-320.)

Foster, George and Charles T. Horngren. "JIT: Cost Accounting And Cost Management Issues," **MA**, 1987, Vol. 68, No. 12, pp. 19-25.

Foster, George J. "A.R.S. No. 11: Historical Cost Without Perspective," **ABACUS**, 1971, Vol. 7, No. 1, pp. 73-84.

Foster, George J. "Mining Inventories In A Current Price Accounting System," **ABACUS**, 1969, Vol. 5, No. 2, pp. 99-118.

Foster, George, Chris Olsen and Terry Shevlin. "Earnings Releases, Anomalies, And The Behavior Of Security Returns," **AR**, 1984, Vol. 59, No. 4, pp. 574-603.

Foster, George. "Accounting Earnings And Stock Prices Of Insurance Companies," **AR**, 1975, Vol. 50, No. 4, pp. 686-698.

Foster, George. "Accounting Policy Decisions And Capital Market Research," **JAEC**, 1980, Vol. 2, No. 1, pp. 29-62.

Foster, George. "Briloff And The Capital Market," **JAR**, 1979, Vol. 17, No. 1, pp. 262-274.

Foster, George. "Intra-Industry Information Transfers Associated With Earnings Releases," **JAEC**, 1981, Vol. 3,

No. 3, pp. 201-232.

Foster, George. "Quarterly Accounting Data: Time-Series Properties And Predictive-Ability Results," **AR**, 1977, Vol. 52, No. 1, pp. 1-21.

Foster, George. "Rambo IX: Briloff And The Capital Market," **JAAF**, 1987, Vol. 2 (New Series), No. 4, pp. 409-430.

Foster, George. "Security Price Revaluation Implications Of Sub-Earnings Disclosure," **JAR**, 1975, Vol. 13, No. 2, pp. 283-292.

Foster, George. "Stock Market Reaction To Estimates Of Earnings Per Share By Company Officials," **JAR**, 1973, Vol. 11, No. 1, pp. 25-37.

Foster, George. (Ball, Ray and George Foster. "Corporate Financial Reporting: A Methodological Review Of Empirical Research," **JAR**, 1982, Vol. 20, Supp., pp. 161-234.)

Foster, Louis O. "The Asset Approach To Elementary Accounting," **AR**, 1941, Vol. 16, No. 1, pp. 8-14.

Foster, Louis O. (Heckert, J. B., H. F. Taggart, C. L. Van Sickle, R. M. Mikesell, F. W. Woodbridge, Louis O. Foster and T. W. Leland. "Instruction In Methods Of Accounting Control: A Symposium," **AR**, 1937, Vol. 12, No. 2, pp. 114-122.)

Foster, L. O. "Accounting In The Liberal Arts Curriculum," **AR**, 1933, Vol. 8, No. 1, pp. 22-25.

Foster, L. O. "Comments On Is Appreciation A Depreciating Element?," **AR**, 1930, Vol. 5, No. 1, pp. 50-53.

Foster, L. O. "Teaching Cost Accounting," **AR**, 1935, Vol. 10, No. 1, pp. 15-17.

Foster, Taylor W., III and Don Vickrey. "The Incremental Information Content Of The 10-K," **AR**, 1978, Vol. 53, No. 4, pp. 921-934.

Foster, Taylor W., III and Don Vickrey. "The Information Content Of Stock Dividend Announcements," **AR**, 1978, Vol. 53, No. 2, pp. 360-370.

Foster, Taylor W., III, D. Randall Jenkins and Don W. Vickrey. "The Incremental Information Content Of The Annual Report," **ABR**, 1985-86, Vol. 16, No. 62, pp. 91-98.

Foster, Taylor W., III. (Barefield, Russell M., Taylor W. Foster, III and Don Vickrey. "Interpreting The API: A Comment And Extension," **AR**, 1976, Vol. 51, No. 1, pp. 172-175.)

Foster, William C. "Does Pooling Present Fairly?," **CPAJ**, 1974, Vol. 44, No. 12, pp. 36-41.

Foster, William C. "Related-Party Transactions - Some Considerations," **CPAJ**, 1975, Vol. 45, No. 5, pp. 15-21.

Foster, William C. "The Current Financial Reporting Environment," **CPAJ**, 1974, Vol. 44, No. 3, pp. 33-38.

Foulk, David G. "Appraising Factoring For A Client," **JOA**, 1961, Vol. 112, No. 2, pp. 41-46.

Fouraker, Lawrence E. (Bierman, Harold, Jr., Lawrence E. Fouraker and Robert K. Jaedicke. "The Use Of Probability And Statistics In Performance Evaluation," **AR**, 1961, Vol. 36, No. 3, pp. 409-417.)

Fouse, Jacqualyn A. (Ordway, Nicholas and Jacqualyn A. Fouse. "New Rules For Allocating The Purchase Price Of A Business," **MA**, 1988, Vol. 69, No. 11, pp. 50-53.)

Foutz, Paul B. "The Teaching Of International Accounting," **MA**, 1975, Vol. 56, No. 12, pp. 31-33.

Fowler, Anna C. (Wyndelts, Robert W. and Anna C. Fowler. "Installment Sales: Temporary Regulations Inconsistent With Judicial Definition Of Payment," **JATA**, 1981, Vol. 3, No. 1, pp. 26-31.)

Fowler, George C. "Bad Debt Losses," **MA**, 1977, Vol. 58, No. 7, pp. 26-28.

Fowler, Larry. "Tips For Profitable PFP Services," **JOA**, 1988, Vol. 165, No. 1, pp. 44-52.

Fox, Charles N. "Time-Sharing: A Tool For The Modern Accountant," **MA**, 1975, Vol. 57, No. 5, pp. 43-44.

Fox, Harold W. "Statistical Error Concepts Related To Accounting," **AR**, 1961, Vol. 36, No. 2, pp. 282-284.

Fox, Jack V. "How I Started My Own Accounting Business," **MA**, 1983, Vol. 64, No. 10, pp. 48-52.

Fox, John J. "How Emergency Accelerated Amortization Works," **JOA**, 1951, Vol. 91, No. 6, pp. 816-821.

Fox, John J. "Michigan's Task Force On Expenditure Management," **JOA**, 1967, Vol. 123, No. 4, pp. 37-42.

Fox, John L. "Useful Comparability" In Financial Reporting," **JOA**, 1964, Vol. 118, No. 6, pp. 44-52.

Fox, Kenneth L. and Philip E. Fess. "Suggested Refinements Of Procedures In Determining Earnings Per Share," **JOA**, 1970, Vol. 129, No. 1, pp. 52-56.

Fox, Kenneth L. (Krogstad, Jack L., Maurice Earl Stark, Kenneth L. Fox and Harry O. Lytle, Jr. "The Faculty Residency: A Concept Worth Considering," **JOA**, 1981, Vol. 152, No. 5, pp. 74-86.)

Fox, Robert J. and Thomas L. Barton. "Management Control At American Transtech," **MA**, 1986, Vol. 68, No. 3, pp. 37-47.

Fox, Robert J. (Barton, Thomas L. and Robert J. Fox. "Evolution At American Transtech," **MA**, 1988, Vol. 69, No. 10, pp. 49-52.)

Fox, S. "A Structural Approach To Cost Accounting," **ABACUS**, 1967, Vol. 3, No. 2, pp. 153-162.

Foy, Walter A. "Studying Auditing Procedure," **AR**, 1945, Vol. 20, No. 4, pp. 458-464.

Fraedrich, Karl E. "Inflation And Financial Reporting," **MA**, 1974, Vol. 55, No. 10, pp. 18-22.

Frakes, Albert H. and Michael F. Foran. "A Framework For Examining The Evaluative Function Of Accounting Learning Activities," **AR**, 1978, Vol. 53, No. 1, pp. 148-154.

Frakes, Albert H. and William C. Lathen. "A Comparison Of Multiple-Choice And Problem Examinations In Introductory Financial Accounting," **JAED**, 1985, Vol. 3, No. 1, pp. 81-89.

Frakes, Albert H. "Emphasizing Financial Accounting Theory In Intermediate Accounting," **IAE**, 1983, No. 1, pp. 104-114.

Frakes, Albert H. "Introductory Accounting Objectives And Intermediate Accounting Performance," **AR**, 1977, Vol. 52, No. 1, pp. 200-210.

Frakes, Albert H. "Survey Of Undergraduate Auditing Education," **JAED**, 1987, Vol. 5, No. 1, pp. 99-126.

Frakes, Albert. (Truitt, Jack, Albert Frakes and John Fertakis. "A Survey Of The Cost/Managerial Sequence In AACSB Schools," **JAED**, 1983, Vol. 1, No. 1, pp. 131-135.)

Framel, John E. "Managing Information As An Asset," **MA**, 1988, Vol. 70, No. 1, pp. 27-31.

Francia, Arthur J. and Robert H. Strawser. "Perceptions Of Financial Reporting Practices By Accounting Educators: An Empirical Study," **AR**, 1971, Vol. 46, No. 2, pp. 380-384.

Francia, Arthur J. and Robert H. Strawser. "Attitudes Of Management Accountants On The State Of The Art," **MA**, 1972, Vol. 53, No. 11, pp. 21-24.

Francia, Arthur J. (Brenner, Vincent C., Ronald M. Copeland, Paul E. Dascher, Arthur J. Francia, Ronald J. Patten and Robert H. Strawser. "Trials And Tribulations Of The Researcher: A Case Study," **JAR**, 1972, Vol. 10, No. 1, pp. 195-199.)

Francia, Arthur J. (Copeland, Ronald M., Arthur J. Francia and Robert H. Strawser. "Further Comments On Students As Subjects In Behavioral Business Research," **AR**, 1974, Vol. 49, No. 3, pp. 534-537.)

Francia, Arthur J. (Copeland, Ronald M., Arthur J. Francia and Robert H. Strawser. "Students As Subjects In Behavioral Business Research," **AR**, 1973, Vol. 48, No. 2, pp. 365-372.)

Francia, Arthur J. (Ryan, Frank, Arthur J. Francia and Robert H. Strawser. "Professional Football And Information Systems," **MA**, 1973, Vol. 54, No. 9, pp. 43-47.)

Francia, Arthur J., Steven D. Grossman and Robert H. Strawser. "The Attitudes Of Management Accountants," **MA**, 1978, Vol. 60, No. 5, pp. 35-40.

Francis, Jere R. and Daniel T. Simon. "A Test Of Audit Pricing In The Small-Client Segment Of The U.S. Audit Market," **AR**, 1987, Vol. 62, No. 1, pp. 145-157.

Francis, Jere R. and Donald J. Stokes. "Audit Prices, Product Differentiation, And Scale Economies: Further Evidence From The Australian Market," **JAR**, 1986, Vol. 24, No. 2, pp. 383-393.

Francis, Jere R. and Earl R. Wilson. "Auditor Changes: A Joint Test Of Theories Relating To Agency Costs And Auditor Differentiation," **AR**, 1988, Vol. 63, No. 4, pp. 663-682.

Francis, Jere R. and Sara Ann Reiter. "Determinants Of Corporate Pension Funding Strategy," **JAEC**, 1987, Vol. 9, No. 1, pp. 35-59.

Francis, Jere R. "FASB's Preliminary Views On Pension Accounting," **CPAJ**, 1983, Vol. 53, No. 5, pp. 44-52.

Francis, Jere R. "Lobbying Against Proposed Accounting Standards: The Case Of Employers' Pension Accounting," **JAPP**, 1987, Vol. 6, No. 1, pp. 35-57.

Francis, Jere R. "The Effect Of Audit Firm Size On Audit Prices: A Study Of The Australian Market," **JAEC**, 1984, Vol. 6, No. 2, pp. 133-151.

Francis, Jere R. (Gibson, Robert W. and Jere R. Francis. "Accounting For Goodwill - A Study In Permissiveness," **ABACUS**, 1975, Vol. 11, No. 2, pp. 167-171.)

Francis, Jere R. (Simon, Daniel T. and Jere R. Francis. "The Effects Of Auditor Change On Audit Fees: Tests Of Price Cutting And Price Recovery," **AR**, 1988, Vol. 63, No. 2, pp. 255-269.)

Francis, J. R. and B. M. Pollard. "An Investigation Of Nonaudit Fees In Australia," **ABACUS**, 1979, Vol. 15, No. 2, pp. 136-144.

Francis, J. R. "Asset-Size Distribution: Some Research Implications," **ABR**, 1979-80, Vol. 10, No. 37, pp. 54-58.

Francis, M. E. "Accounting And The Evaluation Of Social Programs: A Critical Comment," **AR**, 1973, Vol. 48, No. 2, pp. 245-257.

Francis, M. E. (Sobel, E. L. and M. E. Francis. "Accounting And The Evaluation Of Social Programs: A Reply," **AR**, 1974, Vol. 49, No. 4, pp. 826-830.)

Francis, William B. (Rue, Joseph C., David E. Tosh and William B. Francis. "Accounting For Interest Rate Swaps," **MA**, 1988, Vol. 70, No. 1, pp. 43-49.)

Frank, Neil M. and Akshay K. Talwar. "The Accountant's Role In Labor Negotiations," **CPAJ**, 1988, Vol. 58, No. 12, pp. 56-62.

Frank, Werner and Rene Manes. "A Standard Cost Application Of Matrix Algebra," **AR**, 1967, Vol. 42, No. 3, pp. 516-525.

Frank, Werner G. and Jerry J. Weygandt. "Convertible Debt And Earnings Per Share: Pragmatism Vs. Good Theory," **AR**, 1970, Vol. 45, No. 2, pp. 280-289.

Frank, Werner G. and Jerry J. Weygandt. "The APB, Yield Indices, And Predictive Ability: A Reply," **AR**, 1971, Vol. 46, No. 2, pp. 338-341.

Frank, Werner G. and Jerry J. Weygandt. "A Prediction Model For Convertible Debentures," **JAR**, 1971, Vol. 9, No. 1, pp. 116-126.

Frank, Werner G. "An Empirical Analysis Of International Accounting Principles," **JAR**, 1979, Vol. 17, No. 2, pp. 593-605.

Frank, Werner G. "Evaluation Of Wage Incentives: Fixed Costs, Revisited," **AR**, 1972, Vol. 47, No. 1, pp. 155-160.

Frank, Werner G. "Laspeyres Indexes For Variance Analysis In Cost Accounting: A Comment," **AR**, 1976, Vol. 51, No. 2, pp. 427-431.

Frank, Werner G. "Solving Financial Planning Problems Using Input-Output Models," **AR**, 1974, Vol. 49, No. 2, pp. 371-376.

Frank, Werner G. (Nair, R. D. and Werner G. Frank. "The Impact Of Disclosure And Measurement Practices On International Accounting Classifications," **AR**, 1980, Vol. 55, No. 3, pp. 426-450.)

Frank, Werner G. (Nair, R. D. and Werner G. Frank. "The Harmonization Of International Accounting Standards, 1973-1979," **IJAER**, 1981, Vol. 17, No. 1, pp. 61-77.)

Frank, Werner G. (Walgenbach, Paul H. and Werner G. Frank. "A Simulation Model For Applying Audit-Sampling Techniques," **AR**, 1971, Vol. 46, No. 3, pp. 583-588.)

Frank, Werner. "A Computer Application In Process Cost Accounting," **AR**, 1965, Vol. 40, No. 4, pp. 854-862.

Frank, Werner. "A Study Of The Predictive Significance Of Two Income Measures," **JAR**, 1969, Vol. 7, No. 1, pp. 123-136.

Franke, Reimund. "A Process Model For Costing," **MA**, 1975, Vol. 56, No. 7, pp. 45-47.

Franke, Reimund. "Costing With Matrix Analysis," **MA**, 1976, Vol. 57, No. 10, pp. 44-46.

Frankel, Rachel H. "How To Institute And Automate An Internal Inventory Billing System," **CA**, 1986, Vol. 4, No. 4, pp. 45-51.

Frankfurter, George M. and Allan E. Young. "Financial Theory: Its Message To The Accountant," **JAAF**, 1983, Vol. 6, No. 4, pp. 314-324.

Frankfurter, George M. "Index Funds: Fad Or Foe?," **JAAF**, 1978, Vol. 1, No. 2, pp. 116-123.

Frankfurter, G. and B. Horwitz. "The Effects Of Accounting Principles Board Opinion No. 15 On Earnings Per Share: A Simulation Study," **AR**, 1972, Vol. 47, No. 2, pp. 245-259.

Frankham, C. B. (Tabb, J. B. and C. B. Frankham. "The Northern Steamship Company: The Depreciation Problem In Nineteenth Century," **AHJ**, 1986, Vol. 13, No. 2, pp. 37-53.)

Franke, Alan W. (Anderson, John C. and Alan W. Franke. "Voluntary Social Reporting: An Iso-Beta Portfolio Analysis," **AR**, 1980, Vol. 55, No. 3, pp. 467-479.)

Franklin, Donald R. L. "Profit-Sharing-Trust Retirement Plans," **JOA**, 1953, Vol. 96, No. 5, pp. 600-604.

Franklin, LeRoy A. (Campbell, Terry L., William W. McCartney, Doris M. Taylor and LeRoy A. Franklin. "Job Satisfaction Of Academic Accountants In Southern Business Administration Association Schools," **AIA**, 1988, Vol. 6, pp. 175-190.)

Franklin, LeRoy A. (Campbell, Terry L. and LeRoy A. Franklin. "Trends And Projections Of IS/MAS Faculty And Courses," **JIS**, 1987, Vol. 1, No. 2, pp. 101-113.)

Franks, David D. (Sorensen, James E. and David D. Franks. "The Relative Contribution Of Ability, Self-Esteem And Evaluative Feedback To Performance: Implications For Accounting Systems," **AR**, 1972, Vol. 47, No. 4, pp. 735-746.)

Fraser, Donald R. (Gaither, Norman, Donald R. Fraser and William G. Mister. "Accounting For Inventory Carrying Costs," **JCA**, 1987, Vol. 4, No. 1, pp. 1-6.)

Fraser, Ian A. M. "Deprival Value Or Value To The Owner? - A Clarification," **ABACUS**, 1988, Vol. 24, No. 1, pp. 86-89.

Fraser, I. A. M. and C. W. Nobes. "The Assumed Users In Three Accounting Theories," **ABR**, 1984-85, Vol. 15, No. 58, pp. 144-147.

Fraser, I. A. M. and C. W. Nobes. "Is Sterling Correctly Valued?," **ABR**, 1984-85, Vol. 15, No. 59, pp. 246-247.

Frazer, George E. "Accounting In Italy," **AR**, 1929, Vol. 4, No. 1, pp. 33-37.

Frazier, Harrison L. "Our Experience With Thirteen Period Accounting," **MA**, 1965, Vol. 47, No. 4, pp. 53-58.

Frazier, Katherine Beal, Robert W. Ingram and B. Mack Tennyson. "A Methodology For The Analysis Of Narrative Accounting Disclosures," **JAR**, 1984, Vol. 22, No. 1, pp. 318-331.

Frazier, Katherine Beal. (Ingram, Robert W. and Katherine Beal Frazier. "Environmental Performance And Corporate Disclosure," **JAR**, 1980, Vol. 18, No. 2, pp. 614-622.)

Frazier, Katherine Beal. (Murray, Dennis and Katherine Beal Frazier. "A Within-Subjects Test Of Expectancy Theory In A Public Accounting Environment," **JAR**, 1986, Vol. 24, No. 2, pp. 400-404.)

Frecka, Thomas J. and Cheng F. Lee. "Generalized Financial Ratio Adjustment Processes And Their Implications," **JAR**, 1983, Vol. 21, No. 1, pp. 308-316.

Frecka, Thomas J. and William S. Hopwood. "The Effects Of Outliers On The Cross-Sectional Distributional Properties Of Financial Ratios," **AR**, 1983, Vol. 58, No. 1, pp. 115-128.

Frecka, Thomas J. (Beck, Paul J., Thomas J. Frecka and Ira Solomon. "A Model Of The Market For MAS And Audit Services: Knowledge Spillovers And Auditor-Auditee Bonding," **JAL**, 1988, Vol. 7, pp. 50-64.)

Frecka, Thomas J. (Bublitz, Bruce, Thomas J. Frecka and James C. McKeown. "Market Association Tests And FASB Statement No. 33 Disclosures: A Reexamination," **JAR**, 1985, Vol. 23, Supp., pp. 1-23.)

Frecka, Thomas J. (Stone, Mary S., Thomas J. Frecka and Robert W. Jamison. "Multiemployer Pension Plan Amendments Act," **CPAJ**, 1981, Vol. 51, No. 12, pp. 34-40.)

Fredenberger, William B. (DeThomas, Arthur R. and William B. Fredenberger. "Accounting Needs Of Very Small Businesses," **CPAJ**, 1985, Vol. 55, No. 10, pp. 14-25.)

Fredericks, William. (Copeland, Ronald M. and William Fredericks. "Extent Of Disclosure," **JAR**, 1968, Vol. 6, No. 1, pp. 106-113.)

Frederick, David M. and Robert Libby. "Expertise And Auditors' Judgments Of Conjunctive Events," **JAR**, 1986, Vol. 24, No. 2, pp. 270-290.

Frederick, Marvin L. "Testing The Tests," **JOA**, 1957, Vol. 103, No. 4, pp. 42-47.

Frederick, Marvin L. "The Personality Factor In Accounting Success," **AR**, 1938, Vol. 13, No. 4, pp. 400-403.

Frederick, M. L. "Internship In Accounting - Its Value As A Training For Administrative Positions," **AR**, 1927, Vol. 2, No. 4, pp. 348-353.

Fredrikson, E. Bruce. "On The Measurement Of Foreign Income," **JAR**, 1968, Vol. 6, No. 2, pp. 208-221.

Fredrikson, E. Bruce. "The Valuation Of Noncurrent Foreign Currency Monetary Claims," **IJAER**, 1973, Vol. 9, No. 1, pp. 149-158.

Freean, John. "An Accountant In The Bolivian Jungle," **AHJ**, 1986, Vol. 13, No. 2, pp. 145-150.

Freear, John. "Institute Examinations Behind Barbed Wire 1939-1945," **ABR**, 1979-80, Vol. 10, No. 37A, pp. 143-157.

Freear, John. "Robert Loder, Jacobean Management Accountant," **ABACUS**, 1970, Vol. 6, No. 1, pp. 25-38.

Freear, John. "The Final Examinations Of The Institute Of Chartered Accountants In England And Wales, 1882 - 1981," **AHJ**, 1982, Vol. 9, No. 1, pp. 53-89.

Freedman, Martin and A. J. Stagliano. "A Taxonomic Approach To Defining Industrial Social Costs," **AIA**, 1985, Vol. 2, pp. 3-30.

Freedman, Martin and Bikki Jaggi. "Risk Evaluation Of Firms Disclosing Pollution Information In Financial Statements," **AIA**, 1986, Vol. 3, pp. 113-126.

Freedman, Martin and Bikki Jaggi. "An Analysis Of The Impact Of Corporate Pollution Disclosures Included In Annual Financial Statements On Investors' Decisions," **AIPIA**, 1986, Vol. 1, pp. 193-212.

Freedman, Martin and Bikki Jaggi. "An Analysis Of The Impact Of Corporate Pollution Disclosures: A Reply," **AIPIA**, 1988, Vol. 2, pp. 193-197.

Freedman, Martin S. "A Primer On Fraud And Embezzlement," **MA**, 1973, Vol. 55, No. 4, pp. 36-40.

Freeman, Joe B., Jr. "Flexible Report Generation Programs," **MA**, 1969, Vol. 51, No. 3, pp. 17-22.

Freeman, Joe B., Jr. "PERT/Cost - An Informal Approach To Fundamentals," **MA**, 1966, Vol. 47, No. 8, pp. 19-26.

Freeman, L. Vinson, Jr. "Planning A Retirement Or Pension Program," **MA**, 1972, Vol. 54, No. 2, pp. 35-36.

Freeman, Richard J. "Revenue Recognition And Disclosure On Long-Term Contracts," **MA**, 1976, Vol. 57, No. 7, pp. 43-44.

Freeman, Robert J. and Craig Douglas Shoulders. "Defining The Governmental Reporting Entity," **JOA**, 1982, Vol. 154, No. 4, pp. 50-64.

Freeman, Robert J. and Craig D. Shoulders. "Governmental Fund Operating Results: 3 Formats," **JOA**, 1985, Vol. 160, No. 5, pp. 110-121.

Freeman, Robert J. and Robert B. Scott. "The Essentials Of Hospital Accounting," **CPAJ**, 1985, Vol. 55, No. 1, pp. 40-45.

Freeman, Robert J. (Willits, Stephen D., Donald K. Clancy and Robert J. Freeman. "Public Employee Retirement System Reports: A Study Of Knowledgeable User Information Processing Ability," **RIGNA**, 1988, Vol. 4, pp. 3-48.)

Freeman, Robert N. "Alternative Measures Of Profit Margin: An Empirical Study Of The Potential Information Content Of Current Cost Accounting," **JAR**, 1983, Vol. 21, No. 1, pp. 42-64.

Freeman, Robert N. "On The Association Between Net Monetary Position And Equity Security Prices," **JAR**, 1978, Vol. 16, Supp., pp. 111-145.

Freeman, Robert N. "The Association Between Accounting Earnings And Security Returns For Large And Small Firms," **JAEC**, 1987, Vol. 9, No. 2, pp. 195-228.

Freeman, Robert N. "The Disclosure Of Replacement Cost Accounting Data And Its Effect On Transaction Volumes: A Comment," **AR**, 1981, Vol. 56, No. 1, pp. 177-180.

Freeman, Robert N. (Atiase, Rowland K., Linda S. Bamber and Robert N. Freeman. "Accounting Disclosures Based On Company Size, Regulations And Capital Markets Evidence," **ACCHOR**, 1988, Vol. 2, No. 1, pp. 18-26.)

Freeman, Robert N., James A. Ohlson and Stephen H. Penman. "Book Rate-Of-Return And Prediction Of Earnings Changes: An Empirical Investigation," **JAR**, 1982, Vol. 20, No. 2, Part II, pp. 639-653.

Freeman, Roger A. "Reporting And Interpreting The Cost Of State Government," **AR**, 1955, Vol. 30, No. 2, pp. 232-239.

Freimark, Herbert A. "Governmental Accounting - The Road To Moratorium," **CPAJ**, 1976, Vol. 46, No. 4, pp. 31-34.

Freimuth, Richard C. "Cash Management For Smaller Businesses: A New Technique," **MA**, 1982, Vol. 63, No. 12, pp. 58-60.

Freitag, William. "A Status Report On Medicare," **JOA**, 1967, Vol. 124, No. 1, pp. 27-36.

Freitag, William. "Medicare And The Hospital Revolution," **JOA**, 1969, Vol. 127, No. 1, pp. 39-43.

Freitas, Lewis P. "Monitoring Accounts Receivable," **MA**, 1973, Vol. 55, No. 3, pp. 18-21.

Fremgen, James M. "Capital Budgeting Practices: A Survey," **MA**, 1973, Vol. 54, No. 11, pp. 19-25.

Fremgen, James M. "Involuntary Liquidation Of Lifo Inventories," **JOA**, 1962, Vol. 114, No. 6, pp. 49-56.

Fremgen, James M. "The Direct Costing Controversy - An Identification Of Issues," **AR**, 1964, Vol. 39, No. 1, pp. 43-51.

Fremgen, James M. "The Going Concern Assumption: A Critical Appraisal," **AR**, 1968, Vol. 43, No. 4, pp. 649-656.

Fremgen, James M. "Transfer Pricing And Management Goals," **MA**, 1970, Vol. 52, No. 6, pp. 25-31.

Fremgen, James M. "Utility And Accounting Principles," **AR**, 1967, Vol. 42, No. 3, pp. 457-467.

Fremgen, James M. "Variable Costing For External Reporting - A Reconsideration," **AR**, 1962, Vol. 37, No. 1, pp. 76-81.

Fremgen, James M. (Cowie, James B. and James M. Fremgen. "Computers Versus Mathematics: Round 2," **AR**, 1970, Vol. 45, No. 1, pp. 27-37.)

French, D. P. and A. H. Russell. "An Approximate Method For The Allocation Of Reciprocal Service Costs," **ABR**, 1981-82, Vol. 12, No. 48, pp. 265-272.

French, E. A. "Physical Capital Maintenance In Income Measurement - An Exemplification," **ABR**, 1976-77, Vol. 7, No. 25, pp. 36-44.

Frese, Walter F. "Property Rights Of Stockholders Under The 1933 Illinois Business Corporation Act," **AR**, 1935, Vol. 10, No. 2, pp. 136-148.

Freund, William C. "Internationalizing Stock Markets," **JAAF**, 1988, Vol. 3 (New Series), No. 1, pp. 73-77.

Frey, Karen M. "Management Of Foreign Exchange Risk With Forward Contracts," **MA**, 1977, Vol. 58, No. 9, pp. 45-48.

Frey, Karen M. "Survey Of Price-Level Accounting In Practice," **CPAJ**, 1975, Vol. 45, No. 5, pp. 29-34.

Frey, Karen M. (Blake, Harold D. and Karen M. Frey. "Information Retrieval," **MA**, 1976, Vol. 58, No. 3, pp. 47-48.)

Friberg, Ronald A. "Probabilistic Depreciation With A Varying Salvage Value," **AR**, 1973, Vol. 48, No. 1, pp. 50-60.

Fried, Dov and Allen Schiff. "CPA Switches And Associated Market Reactions," **AR**, 1981, Vol. 56, No. 2, pp. 326-341.

Fried, Dov and Charles Hosler. "S&Ls, Reporting Changes And The Impact On The GNMA Market," **JAAF**, 1987, Vol. 2 (New Series), No. 1, pp. 5-23.

Fried, Dov and Dan Givoly. "Financial Analysts' Forecasts Of Earnings: A Better Surrogate For Market Expectations," **JAEC**, 1982, Vol. 4, No. 2, pp. 85-107.

Fried, Dov and Joshua Livnat. "Alternative Interim Reporting Techniques Within A Dynamic Framework: A Reply," **AR**, 1985, Vol. 60, No. 2, pp. 295-297.

Fried, Dov and Joshua Livnat. "Interim Statements: An Analytical Examination Of Alternative Accounting Techniques," **AR**, 1981, Vol. 56, No. 3, pp. 493-509.

Fried, Dov. "Compensating For Inflation: Shorter Life Vs. Accelerated Depreciation Methods," **JAAF**, 1981, Vol. 4, No. 4, pp. 295-308.

Fried, Dov. (Barlev, Benzion, Dov Fried and Joshua Livnat. "Economic And Financial Reporting Effects Of Inventory Tax Allowances," **CAR**, 1985-86, Vol. 2, No. 2, pp. 288-310.)

Fried, H. Dov. (Schiff, Allen and H. Dov Fried. "Large Companies And The Big Eight: An Overview," **ABACUS**, 1976, Vol. 12, No. 2, pp. 116-124.)

Fried, Stephen. "A Short-Cut Method For Simultaneous Tax Computation," **AR**, 1955, Vol. 30, No. 2, pp. 316-320.

Friedlob, George T. "Federal Tax Management: A Disclosure Problem," **MA**, 1981, Vol. 63, No. 5, pp. 28-33.

Friedlob, G. Thomas and Louis P. Ramsay. "Communicating Decision Alternatives Graphically Using The Point Of Indifference," **JAED**, 1986, Vol. 4, No. 2, pp. 37-49.

Friedlob, G. Thomas, F. Ray Gray, Ralph E. Welton and James D. Sloan. "Combining LIFO And FIFO Inventory Disclosure," **CPAJ**, 1987, Vol. 57, No. 6, pp. 48-53.

Friedlob, G. Thomas. "How Economic Statisticians View Accounting Profits," **JAAF**, 1983, Vol. 6, No. 2, pp. 100-107.

Friedlob, G. Thomas. (Bryan, E. Lewis, Alison L. Drews and G. Thomas Friedlob. "Delphic Choice Of Accounting Periodicals For University Libraries," **JAED**, 1987, Vol. 5, No. 1, pp. 167-174.)

Friedlob, G. Thomas. (Dungan, Christopher W., G. Thomas Friedlob and Robert W. Rouse. "The Supreme Court On Tax Accrual Workpapers," **CPAJ**, 1985, Vol. 55, No. 2, pp. 20-27.)

Friedlob, G. Thomas. (Rouse, Robert, James R. Davis and G. Thomas Friedlob. "The Relevant Experience Criterion For Accounting Accreditation By The AACSB," **JAED**, 1986, Vol. 4, No. 1, pp. 147-160.)

Friedman, Abraham and Baruch Lev. "A Surrogate Measure For The Firm's Investment In Human Resources," **JAR**, 1974, Vol. 12, No. 2, pp. 235-250.

Friedman, Abraham. (Barlev, Benzion and Abraham Friedman. "Experience Requirements And The Education Of Certified Public Accountants," **IJAER**, 1982, Vol. 17, No. 2, pp. 75-88.)

Friedman, Harry and J. Tomilson Hill. "Financial Implications Of Offense And Defense In Corporate Takeovers," **CA**, 1985, Vol. 3, No. 3, pp. 54-59.

Friedman, Larry A. (Buchman, Thomas A. and Larry A. Friedman. "Accounting For Certain Marketable Securities," **MA**, 1977, Vol. 58, No. 9, pp. 42-44.)

Friedman, Laurence A. and Bruce R. Neumann. "The Effects Of Opportunity Costs On Project Investment Decisions: A Replication And Extension," **JAR**, 1980, Vol. 18, No. 2, pp. 407-419.

Friedman, Laurence A. and Frank H. Selto. "A Simulation Of The Replacement Cost Lead Indicator Relationship," **ABACUS**, 1981, Vol. 17, No. 1, pp. 73-90.

Friedman, Laurence A. "An Exit-Price Income Statement," **AR**,

1978, Vol. 53, No. 1, pp. 18-30.

Friedman, Laurence A. "Exit-Price Liabilities: An Analysis Of The Alternatives," AR, 1978, Vol. 53, No. 4, pp. 895-909.

Friedman, Laurence A. "What Is Current Value?," CPAJ, 1978, Vol. 48, No. 11, pp. 24-29.

Friedman, Laurence A. (Neumann, Bruce R. and Laurence A. Friedman. "Opportunity Costs: Further Evidence Through An Experimental Replication," JAR, 1978, Vol. 16, No. 2, pp. 400-410.)

Friedman, Lauren. (Haka, Susan, Lauren Friedman and Virginia Jones. "Functional Fixation And Interference Theory: A Theoretical And Empirical Investigation," AR, 1986, Vol. 61, No. 3, pp. 455-474.)

Friedman, Mark E. "The Effect On Achievement Of Using The Computer As A Problem-Solving Tool In The Intermediate Accounting Course," AR, 1981, Vol. 56, No. 1, pp. 137-143.

Friend, Edward H. "A 1972 Critique On Funding Media For Pension Plans," JOA, 1972, Vol. 134, No. 2, pp. 29-40.

Friend, Irwin. "Financial Statements For The Economy," AR, 1949, Vol. 24, No. 3, pp. 239-247.

Fries, Clarence E. "A Proposed Procedure For Incorporating Interindustry Relationships In The Design And Analysis Of Empirical Forecasting Studies," AIA, 1988, Vol. 6, pp. 71-84.

Fries, Clarence E. (Cronan, Timothy P. and Clarence E. Fries. "MIS And Computer Applications In Accounting Courses - Report Of A Survey," JAED, 1986, Vol. 4, No. 1, pp. 237-244.)

Frieze, Irene. (Olson, Josephine and Irene Frieze. "Women Accountants - Do They Earn As Much As Men?," MA, 1986, Vol. 67, No. 12, pp. 27-31.)

Frieze, I. Hanson. (Birnberg, J. G., I. Hanson Frieze and M. D. Shields. "The Role Of Attribution Theory In Control Systems," AOS, 1977, Vol. 2, No. 3. pp.189-200.)

Frieze, I. Hanson. (Shields, M. D., J. G. Birnberg and I. Hanson Frieze. "Attributions, Cognitive Processes And Control Systems, AOS, 1981, Vol. 6, No. 1, pp. 69-96.)

Frigo, Mark L. (Stone, Peter F. and Mark L. Frigo. "The Neglected Management Letter," CPAJ, 1988, Vol. 58, No. 9, pp. 38-43.)

Frisbee, Ira N. "Accounting For 'Income' Of Municipalities," AR, 1936, Vol. 11, No. 2, pp. 164-169.

Frisbee, Ira N. "Ethics In Management Services," JOA, 1957, Vol. 103, No. 3, pp. 29-34.

Frisbee, Ira N. "Experience As A Necessary Qualification For The CPA Certificate," AR, 1947, Vol. 22, No. 1, pp. 1-5.

Frisbee, Ira N. "How Exercise Of Judgment Affects Application Of Standards In Auditing Field Work," JOA, 1950, Vol. 89, No. 3, pp. 212-218.

Frisbee, Ira N. "How Personal Attributes Of The Auditor Affect The Application Of Auditing Standards," JOA, 1950, Vol. 89, No. 2, pp. 120-124.

Frisbee, Ira N. "Problems In Presenting The Financial Condition Of An Endowed College Or University," AR, 1930, Vol. 5, No. 3, pp. 215-221.

Frisbee, Ira N. "The Application Of Governmental Accounting Principles To Practice," AR, 1939, Vol. 14, No. 1, pp. 27-32.

Frishkoff, Patricia A. and Mary Ellen Phillips. "Materiality In Commercial Bank Inflation Accounting." AIA, 1985, Vol. 2, pp. 31-46.

Frishkoff, Patricia A. "Is Your Controllership Function Out Of Control?," MA, 1986, Vol. 67, No. 9, pp. 45-47.

Frishkoff, Patricia A. (Frishkoff, Paul, Patricia A. Frishkoff and Marinus J. Bouwman. "Use Of Accounting Data In Screening By Financial Analysts." JAAF, 1984, Vol. 8, No. 1, pp. 44-53.)

Frishkoff, Paul and Robert Rogowski. "Disclaimers Of Audit Opinion," MA, 1978, Vol. 59, No. 11, pp. 52-57.

Frishkoff, Paul, Patricia A. Frishkoff and Marinus J. Bouwman. "Use Of Accounting Data In Screening By Financial Analysts," JAAF, 1984, Vol. 8, No. 1.pp.44-53.

Frishkoff, Paul. "An Empirical Investigation Of The Concept Of Materiality In Accounting," JAR, 1970, Vol. 8, Supp., pp. 116-129.

Frishkoff, Paul. "Capitalism And The Development Of Bookkeeping: A Reconsideration," IJAER, 1970, Vol. 5, No. 2, pp. 29-37.

Frishkoff, Paul. "Consistency In Auditing And APB Opinion No. 20," JOA, 1972, Vol. 134, No. 2, pp. 64-70.

Frishkoff, Paul. "Some Radical Thoughts On Accounting Theory," JAR, 1976, Vol. 14, No. 1, pp. 178-180.

Frishkoff, Paul. "Some Recent Trends In Accounting Changes," JAR, 1970, Vol. 8, No. 1, pp. 141-144.

Frishkoff, Paul. (Beekhuizen, Theo and Paul Frishkoff. "A Comparison Of The New Dutch Accounting Act With Generally Accepted American Accounting Principles," IJAER, 1975, Vol. 10, No. 2, pp. 13-22.)

Frishkoff, Paul. (Khodadoust, T. and Paul Frishkoff. "On Mercantile Accounting In Pre-Industrial Iran," AHJ, 1979, Vol. 6, No. 1, pp. 53-62.)

Frishkoff, P. A. (Bouwman, M. J., P. A. Frishkoff and P. Frishkoff. "How Do Financial Analysts Make Decisions? A Process Model Of The Investment Screening Decision," AOS, 1987, Vol. 12, No. 1, pp. 1-30.)

Frishkoff, P. (Bouwman, M. J., P. A. Frishkoff and P. Frishkoff. "How Do Financial Analysts Make Decisions? A Process Model Of The Investment Screening Decision," AOS, 1987, Vol. 12, No. 1, pp. 1-30.)

Fritzemeyer, Joe R. (Metcalf, Richard W. and Joe R. Fritzemeyer. "Taxation Of Interstate Income: A Call To Action," JOA, 1965, Vol. 120, No. 2, pp. 44-46.)

Frizelle, Pamela J. "Accounting And The Other World," MA, 1975, Vol. 57, No. 4, pp. 27-28.

Froebe, John A. "The Use Of Visual Aids In The Teaching Of Accounting," AR, 1959, Vol. 34, No. 4, pp. 655-657.

Frost, Peter A. and Hirokuni Tamura. "Jackknifed Ratio Estimation In Statistical Auditing," JAR, 1982, Vol. 20, No. 1, pp. 103-120.

Frost, Peter A. and Hirokuni Tamura. "Accuracy Of Auxiliary Information Interval Estimation In Statistical Auditing," JAR, 1986, Vol. 24, No. 1, pp. 57-75.

Frost, Peter A. (Tamura, Hirokuni and Peter A. Frost. "Tightening CAV (DUS) Bounds By Using A Parametric Model ," JAR, 1986, Vol. 24, No. 2, pp. 364-371.)

Frotman, Alan. (Wynne, Robert C. and Alan Frotman. "Microcomputers: Helping Make Practice Perfect," JOA, 1981, Vol. 152, No. 6, pp. 34-39.)

Frumer, Samuel. "Incorporating Managerial Controls Into Introductory Cost Accounting," AR, 1962, Vol. 37, No. 3, pp. 551-553.

Frumer, Samuel. (Falk, Haim, Samuel Frumer and James A. Heintz. "Accounting For Stock Reacquisitions: Israel And The United States Compared," IJAER, 1974, Vol. 9, No. 2, pp. 111-123.)

Fry, Elaine Hobbs. (Fry, Nicholas E. and Elaine Hobbs Fry. "How Journal Entries Aid The Teaching Of Taxation," JAED, 1988, Vol. 6, No. 1, pp. 149-157.)

Fry, Nicholas E. and Elaine Hobbs Fry. "How Journal Entries Aid The Teaching Of Taxation," JAED, 1988, Vol. 6, No. 1. pp. 149-157.

Frye, Delbert J. "Combined Costing Method: Absorption And Direct," MA, 1971, Vol. 52, No. 7, pp. 18-20.

Frye, Marion A. "Women's Accounting Societies," AR, 1947, Vol. 22, No. 3, pp. 304-306.

Fryxell, Carl A. "Should Appreciation Be Brought Into The Accounts," AR, 1930, Vol. 5, No. 2, pp. 157-158.

Fryxell, C. A. "A Dilemma In Teaching Elementary Accounting," AR, 1935, Vol. 10, No. 1, pp. 6-7.

Fu, Philip. "Governmental Accounting In China During The Chou Dynasty (1122 B.C. - 256 B.C.)," JAR, 1971, Vol. 9, No. 1, pp. 40-51.

Fuerst, E. "Share Capital In Foreign Exchange Accounting," AR, 1954, Vol. 29, No. 2, pp. 281-285.

Fuglister, Jayne and Richard J. Murdock. "Use Of The Computer In Preparation Of Multiple Choice Examinations: A Multiple Form Generating Program," IAE, 1988, Vol. 3, No. 1, pp. 174-180.

Fujita, Yukio. "The Evolution Of Financial Reporting In Japan," IJAER, 1966, Vol. 2, No. 1, pp. 49-75.

Fullerton, G. G. "Accounting For Variation In Gross Profit." AR, 1952, Vol. 27, No. 2, pp. 244-246.

Fuller, Gerald. (Williams, William J., Gerald Fuller and Roger W. Payne. "Improving Cost Management By Forming An Alliance," CA, 1986, Vol. 4, No. 1, pp. 54-61.)

Fuller, K. John. "Impact Of CASB Standards," CPAJ, 1976, Vol. 46, No. 1, pp. 19-23.

Fulmer, John G., Jr. and James E. Moon. "Tests For Common Stock Equivalency," JAAF, 1984, Vol. 8, No. 1, pp. 5-14.

Fulmer, William E. and Barney R. Cargile. "Ethical Perceptions Of Accounting Students: Does Exposure To A Code Of Professional Ethics Help?," IAE, 1987, Vol. 2, No. 2, pp. 207-219.

Funari, Mario R. "Salesmen's Incentives - For Profit's Sake," MA, 1968, Vol. 49, No. 7, pp. 59-62.

Funk, Jerry A. (Said, Kamel E. and Jerry A. Funk. "Planning And Control In Accounting Education: A Model For Subsystem Controls In A Free Market Environment," IJAER, 1976, Vol. 11, No. 2, pp. 103-119.)

Funk, Roland W. "Illustrations To Aid In Explaining The Two Methods Of Pricing Inventory Activity," AR, 1950, Vol. 25, No. 4, pp. 441-442.

Funk, Roland W. "Recent Developments In Accounting Theory And Practice," AR, 1950, Vol. 25, No. 3, pp. 292-301.

Furlong, Daniel R. (McGrail, George R. and Daniel R. Furlong. "Absorption Break-Even," MA, 1973, Vol. 55, No. 4, pp. 31-35.)

Furlong, William L. and Leon H. Robertson. "Matching Management Decisions And Results," MA, 1968, Vol. 49, No. 12, pp. 3-10.

Furlong, William L. "How To Eliminate The 'Plugging' Of Net Worth For Translated Foreign Currency Financial Statements," MA, 1968, Vol. 49, No. 8, pp. 39-45.

Furlong, William L. "Minimizing Foreign Exchange Losses," AR, 1966, Vol. 41, No. 2, pp. 244-252.

Furlong, William L. "Risk Income And Alternative Income Concepts," MA, 1967, Vol. 48, No. 8, pp. 25-29.

Fusaro, Frank G., Robert A. Gaida and Philip Zimmerman. "Senior Turnover - Seniors Speak Out," CPAJ, 1984, Vol. 54, No. 7, pp. 26-35.

Futhey, Bruce. "Accounting Instructional Staffs In Colleges And Universities," AR, 1941, Vol. 16, No. 1, pp. 109-112.

Futhey, Bruce. "Organizing And Operating A Successful Internship Program," JOA, 1954, Vol. 97, No. 5, pp. 587-592.

Fuyuume, John. "Working With Operating Management," MA, 1965, Vol. 47, No. 1, pp. 51-57.

Fyffe, Joseph B. "An Accounting System For A Small CPA Practice," JOA, 1966, Vol. 122, No. 1, pp. 49-57.

GGG

Gaa, Charles J. "An Experiment In Staff Training: The Advanced Training Center Of The Internal Revenue Service," AR, 1955, Vol. 30, No. 1, pp. 28-36.

Gaa, Charles J. "Income Taxation Of Business In 1952," AR, 1952, Vol. 27, No. 3, pp. 273-283.

Gaa, Charles J. "Uniformity In Accounting Principles," JOA, 1961, Vol. 111, No. 4, pp. 47-50.

Gaa, C. J. (Kirkham, E. J. and C. J. Gaa. "Is There A Theory Basis For Audit Procedure?," AR, 1939, Vol. 14, No. 2, pp. 139-146.)

Gaa, James C. and Charles H. Smith. "Auditors And Deceptive Financial Statements: Assigning Responsibility And Blame," CAR, 1984-85, Vol. 1, No. 2, pp. 219-241.

Gaa, James C. "User Primacy In Financial Reporting Rulemaking: A Socal Contract Approach," AR, 1986, Vol. 61, No. 3, pp. 435-454.

Gaa, Lt. Charles J. and Lt. Gerald Maxfield. "Accounting Aspects Of Contract Settlement," AR, 1945, Vol. 20, No. 1, pp. 44-58.

Gaa, Lt. Charles J. "Students For Income Determination," AR, 1944, Vol. 19, No. 3, pp. 270-273.

Gaber, B. G. (Boritz, J. E., B. G. Gaber and W. M. Lemon. "An Experimental Study Of The Effects Of Elicitation Methods On Review Of Preliminary Audit Strategy By External Auditors," CAR, 1988, Vol. 4, No. 2, pp. 392-411.)

Gabhart, David R. L. (Hardiman, Patrick F., Alan Reinstein and David R. L. Gabhart. "Audit Committees For Governmental Units - How To," CPAJ, 1986, Vol. 56, No. 6, pp. 38-45.)

Gabhart, David R. L. (Jones, Gardner M. and David R. L. Gabhart. "Danger: This City Is In Financial Trouble," MA, 1979, Vol. 61, No. 4, pp. 19-22.)

Gabhart, David R. L. (Roberts, Aubrey C. and David R. L. Gabhart. "Statement Of Funds - A Glimpse Of The Future?," JOA, 1972, Vol. 133, No. 4, pp. 54-59.)

Gabriel, Gerald M. "State Taxation On The Corporate Partner," MA, 1979, Vol. 61, No. 6, pp. 25-29.

Gac, Edward J. (Ruhnka, John C. and Edward J. Gac. "RICO Claims Against CPAs," CPAJ, 1987, Vol. 57, No. 12, pp. 26-43.)

Gac, Edward J. (Scheer, Martha S. and Edward J. Gac. "New Problems For The Unwary In Estate And Gift Tax Valuations: Penalties Under I.R.C. 6660," ACCHOR, 1987, Vol. 1, No. 4, pp. 69-78.)

Gadsby, Edward N. "Listed And Unlisted Securities," JOA, 1958, Vol. 105, No. 4, pp. 30-35.

Gaede, William G. "Environmental Management Opportunities For The CPA," JOA, 1974, Vol. 137, No. 5, pp. 50-54.

Gaertner, James F. and John A. Ruhe. "Job-Related Stress In Public Accounting," JOA, 1981, Vol. 151, No. 6, pp. 68-75.

Gaertner, James F. and Ken Milani. "The TRR Yardstick For Hospital Capital Expenditure Decisions," MA, 1980, Vol. 62, No. 6, pp. 25-33.

Gaertner, James F. "Proposed Alternatives For Accounting For Business Combinations: A Behavioral Study," ABACUS, 1979, Vol. 15, No. 1, pp. 35-47.

Gaertner, James F., Paul E. W. Hemmeter and Marshall K. Pitman. "Employee Turnover In Public Accounting: A New Perspective," CPAJ, 1987, Vol. 57, No. 8, pp. 30-37.

Gaertner, James. (Campbell, David K., James Gaertner and Robert P. Vecchio. "Perceptions Of Promotion And Tenure Criteria: A Survey Of Accounting Educators," JAED, 1983, Vol. 1, No. 1, pp. 83-92.)

Gaffikin, M. J. R. "Legacy Of The Golden Age: Recent Developments In The Methodology Of Accounting," ABACUS, 1988, Vol. 24, No. 1, pp. 16-36.

Gaffikin, M. J. R. "The Development Of University And Professional Accountancy Education In New Zealand," AHJ, 1981, Vol. 8, No. 1, pp. 15-36.

Gaffikin, M. J. R. "The Methodology of Early Accounting Theorists," ABACUS, 1987, Vol. 23, No. 1, pp. 17-30.

Gaffney, Dennis J. and Cynthia D. Dailey. "Property Distributions Of Subchapter S Corporations: Regulation #1.373-1(e)(2) Allocations Not Always Necessary," JATA, 1980, Vol. 1, No. 2, pp. 17-20.

Gaffney, Dennis J. (Dilley, Steven and Dennis J. Gaffney. "The Individual Income Tax Computation," CPAJ, 1978, Vol. 48, No. 11, pp. 19-23.)

Gaffney, Francis M. and Robert F. Wright. "Compensating The Executive In Today's Economic Climate," CPAJ, 1975, Vol. 45, No. 9, pp. 27-30.

Gaffney, Francis M. "Three Proposals To Help Spice Up Executive Compensation Plans," CA, 1983, Vol. 1, No. 4, pp. 13-18.

Gaffney, James J. "A Practical Guide For The CEO In A Troubled Situation," CA, 1985, Vol. 3, No. 2, pp. 53-59.

Gaffney, Mary Anne and Bill N. Schwartz. "Honors Programs In Accounting," IAE, 1988, Vol. 3, No. 1, pp. 79-87.

Gaffney, Mary Anne. "Consolidated Versus Fund-Type Accounting Statements: The Perspectives Of Constituents," JAPP, 1986, Vol. 5, No. 3, pp. 167-189.

Gafford, W. Wade and D. R. Carmichael. "Materiality, Audit Risk And Smapling: A Nuts-And-Bolts Approach (Part Two)," JOA, 1984, Vol. 158, No. 5, pp. 125-138.

Gafford, W. Wade and D. R. Carmichael. "Materiality, Audit Risk And Sampling: A Nuts-And Bolts Approach (Part One)," JOA, 1984, Vol. 158, No. 4, pp. 109-118.

Gagnon, Jean-Marie. "Purchase Versus Pooling Of Interests: The Search For A Predictor," JAR, 1967, Vol. 5, Supp., pp. 187-204.

Gagnon, Jean-Marie. "The Purchase-Pooling Choice: Some Empirical Evidence," JAR, 1971, Vol. 9, No. 1, pp. 52-72.

Gaida, Robert A. (Fusaro, Frank G., Robert A. Gaida and Philip Zimmerman. "Senior Turnover - Seniors Speak Out," CPAJ, 1984, Vol. 54, No. 7, pp. 26-35.)

Gainey, Richard C. "Data Processing You Can Afford," MA, 1974, Vol. 56, No. 4, p. 36, 41-42.

Gaither, John F. "Auditing Military Subcontract Termination Claims," JOA, 1954, Vol. 97, No. 1, pp. 71-76.

Gaither, Norman, Donald R. Fraser and William G. Mister. "Accounting For Inventory Carrying Costs," JCA, 1987, Vol. 4, No. 1, pp. 1-6.

Gal, Graham and Paul Steinbart. "Artificial Intelligence And Research In Accounting Information Systems: Opportunities And Issues," JIS, 1987, Vol. 2, No. 1, pp. 54-62.

Gal, Graham and William E. McCarthy. "Operation Of A Relational Accounting System," AIA, 1986, Vol. 3, pp. 83-112.

Galbraith, J. R. (Bariff, M. L. and J. R. Galbraith. "Intraorganizational Power Considerations For Designing Information Systems," AOS, 1978, Vol. 3, No. 1, pp. 15-28.)

Galbraith, Oliver, III and Jack H. Morse. "Hire Or Overtime? A Best Bet Method," MA, 1972, Vol. 54, No. 1, pp. 42-46.

Gale, Andrew P. "A Breakthrough In Disclosure Retrieval," JOA, 1978, Vol. 146, No. 3, pp. 86-90.

Gale, Andrew P. "Computerized Research: An Advanced Tool," JOA, 1982, Vol. 153, No. 1, pp. 73-79.

Gale, Andrew P. "Data Bases: An Accountant's Choice," JOA, 1985, Vol. 160, No. 6, pp. 111-124.

Galer, F. Fulton. (Barnett, Andrew H. and F. Fulton Galer. "Scienter Since Hochfelder," CPAJ, 1982, Vol. 52, No. 11, pp. 40-45.)

Galitzer, Philip. "Mathematical Formulae And Their Interpretations," AR, 1947, Vol. 22, No. 4, pp. 372-378.

Galitzer, Philip. "The Intra-Family Tax Saving Device," AR, 1944, Vol. 19, No. 4, pp. 430-434.

Gallagher, Michael G. "GCMs, TMs, And AODs - The 'Working Law' Of The Internal Revenue Service," JATA, 1984, Vol. 5, No. 2, pp. 50-59.

Gallantier, Alexander J. "Accounting Reports On Research And Development," MA, 1967, Vol. 49, No. 3, pp. 8-20.

Gallia, James J. and Donald C. Anderson. "Finished Goods Movement," MA, 1972, Vol. 54, No. 3, pp. 11-14.

Galloway, Clair J. "Disclosure Of GAAP Data Of Life Insurance Companies," MA, 1981, Vol. 62, No. 7, pp. 27-31.

Gallun, Rebecca A. (Waller, Thomas C. and Rebecca A. Gallun. "Microcomputer Competency Requirements In The Accounting Industry: A Pilot Study," JAED, 1985, Vol. 3, No. 2, pp. 31-40.)

Galpeer, Irving J. (Barr, Andrew and Irving J. Galpeer. "McKesson & Robbins," JOA, 1987, Vol. 163, No. 5, pp. 159-161.)

Galus, Edward R. "Keogh Retirement Plans For CPAs," JOA, 1968, Vol. 126, No. 3, pp. 35-43.

Galvin, B. J. B. (Amernic, J. H. and B. J. B. Galvin. "Implementing The New Foreign Currency Rules In Canada And The United States: A Challenge To Professional Judgment," IJAER, 1984, Vol. 19, No. 2, pp. 165-180.)

Gambino, Anthony J. and John R. Palmer. "American Accounting Practices - Circa 1776," MA, 1976, Vol. 57, No. 12, pp. 53-56.

Gamble, George O. and Brian O'Doherty. "How Accounting Academicians Can Use Citation Indexing And Analysis For Research," JAED, 1985, Vol. 3, No. 2, pp. 123-144.

Gamble, George O. and Brian O'Doherty. "Citation Indexing And Its Uses In Accounting: An Awareness Survey And Departmental Ranking," IAE, 1985, No. 1, pp. 28-40.

Gamble, George O. "An Application Of Current Value Theory To Accounting For Investments In Bonds," JAAF, 1982, Vol. 5, No. 4, pp. 320-326.

Gamble, George O. "Concepts Of Capital Maintenance," JAAF, 1981, Vol. 4, No. 3, pp. 220-237.

Gamble, George O. "Property Rights Theory And The Formulation Of Financial Statements," JAAF, 1986, Vol. 1 (New Series), pp. 102-117.

Gamble, George O., Brian O'Doherty and Ladelle M. Hyman. "The Development Of Agency Thought: A Citation Analysis Of The Literature," AHJ, 1987, Vol. 14, No. 1, pp. 7-26.

Gambling, Trevor E. and Ahmed Nour. "A Note On Input-Output Analysis: Its Uses In Macro-Economics And Micro-Economics," AR, 1970, Vol. 45, No. 1, pp. 98-102.

Gambling, Trevor E. "A System Dynamics Approach To Human Resource Accounting," AR, 1974, Vol. 49, No. 3, pp. 538-546.

Gambling, Trevor E. "A Technological Model For Use In Input-Output Analysis And Cost Accounting," MA, 1968, Vol. 50, No. 4, pp. 33-38.

Gambling, Trevor E. "Input-Output Analysis And The Cost Model: A Reply," AR, 1971, Vol. 46, No. 2, pp. 376-379.

Gambling, Trevor E. "LIFO Vs. FIFO Under Conditions Of 'Certainty'," AR, 1968, Vol. 43, No. 2, pp. 387-389.

Gambling, Trevor E. "Some Observations On 'Breakeven Budgeting And Programming To Goals'," JAR, 1965, Vol. 3, No. 1, pp. 159-165.

Gambling, Trevor E. "Toward A General Theory Of Accounting," IJAER, 1971, Vol. 7, No. 1, pp. 1-13.

Gambling, Trevor. "Accounting Theory And Inter-Related Processes," ABACUS, 1969, Vol. 5, No. 1, pp. 78-87.

Gambling, T. "Accounting For Rituals," AOS, 1987, Vol. 12, No. 3, pp. 319-330.

Gambling, T. "Magic, Accounting And Morale," AOS, 1977, Vol. 2, No. 2, pp. 141-152.

Gambling, T. "Systems Dynamics And Human Resource Accounting," AOS, 1976, Vol. 1, No. 2/3, pp. 167-174.

Gambling, T. "The Accountant's Guide To The Galaxy,

Including The Profession At The End Of The Universe," **AOS**, 1985, Vol. 10, No. 4, pp. 415-426.

Gammill, Glen M. "Strategic Management Techniques For Insurance Companies," **MA**, 1981, Vol. 62, No. 7, pp. 19-22.

Gamoneda, R. G. "Time To Double At Compound Interest," **AR**, 1967, Vol. 42, No. 1, pp. 132-134.

Gandhi, Natwar M. "The Emergence Of The Postindustrial Society And The Future Of The Accounting Function," **IJAER**, 1976, Vol. 11, No. 2, pp. 33-49.

Gandhi, N. M. (Birnhang, J. G. and N. M. Gandhi. "Toward Defining The Accountant's Role In The Evaluation Of Social Programs," **AOS**, 1976, Vol. 1, No. 1, pp. 5-10.)

Gangolly, Jagdish S. "On Joint Cost Allocation: Independent Cost Proportional Scheme (ICPS) And Its Properties," **JAR**, 1981, Vol. 19, No. 2, pp. 299-312.

Gangolly, Jagdish S. (Hussein, Mohamed E. A., Vinod B. Bavishi, and Jagdish S. Gangolly. "International Similarities And Differences In The Auditor's Report," **AJPT**, 1986-87, Vol. 6, No. 1, pp. 124-133.)

Gannon, John J. and David Parkinson. "Software Development Costs Should Be Expensed," **MA**, 1983, Vol. 65, No. 5, pp. 37-39.

Gans, Martin S. (Sorter, George H. and Martin S. Gans. "Opportunities And Implications Of The Report On Objectives Of Financial Statements," **JAR**, 1974, Vol. 12, Supp., pp. 1-12.)

Ganswindt, Ralph C. "Tax Aspects Of Farms And Ranches," **CPAJ**, 1974, Vol. 44, No. 8, pp. 24-28.

Garbade, William H. "Internal Control And The Internal Auditor," **AR**, 1944, Vol. 19, No. 4, pp. 416-421.

Garbutt, Douglas. "A Systems Approach To The British Industrial Training Act 1964," **ABR**, 1971-72, Vol. 2, No. 5, pp. 60-66.

Garbutt, Douglas. "The Significance Of Ancient Mesopotamia In Accounting History," **AHJ**, 1984, Vol. 11, No. 1, pp. 83-101.

Garcha, Bikramjit S., Gordon B. Harwood and Roger H. Hermanson. "A Study Of The Readership Of The Accounting Review," **JAED**, 1983, Vol. 1, No. 2, pp. 21-39.

Garda, J. A. "The Measurement Of Financial Data In Evaluating Overseas Managerial Efficiency," **IJAER**, 1976, Vol. 12, No. 1, pp. 13-17.

Gardella, Robert R. "Financial Statement Analysis Is Paint-By-The-Numbers Art," **CA**, 1986, Vol. 4, No. 2, pp. 45-49.

Gardner, John C. and G. A. Swanson. "From Bercu To Sperry - Significant Legal Landmarks In The Development Of Tax Practice," **JOA**, 1987, Vol. 163, No. 5, pp. 189-191.

Gardner, John C. (Alexander, Robin A. and John C. Gardner. "Before You Buy HAL," **CA**, 1988, Vol. 6, No. 1, pp. 18-24.)

Gardner, John C. (Brown, Lawrence D. and John C. Gardner. "Using Citation Analysis To Assess The Impact Of Journals And Articles On Contemporary Accounting Research (**CAR**)," **JAR**, 1985, Vol. 23, No. 1, pp. 84-109.)

Gardner, John C. (Brown, Lawrence D. and John C. Gardner. "Applying Citation Analysis To Evaluate The Research Contributions Of Accounting Faculty And Doctoral Programs," **AR**, 1985, Vol. 60, No. 2, pp. 262-277.)

Gardner, John C. (Swanson, G. A. and John C. Gardner. "The Inception And Evolution Of Financial Reporting In The Protestant Episcopal Church In The United States," **AHJ**, 1986, Vol. 13, No. 2, pp. 55-63.)

Gardner, John C. (Swanson, G. A. and John C. Gardner. "Not-For-Profit Accounting And Auditing In The Early Eighteenth Century: Some Archival Evidence," **AR**, 1988, Vol. 63, No. 3, pp. 436-447.)

Gardner, J. C. (Brown, L. D., J. C. Gardner and M. A. Vasarhelyi. "An Analysis Of The Research Contributions Of 'Accounting, Organizations And Society': 1976-1984," **AOS**, 1987, Vol. 12, No. 2, pp. 193-204.)

Gardner, Mona J. and Lucille E. Lammers. "Cost Accounting In Large Banks," **MA**, 1988, Vol. 69, No. 10, pp. 34-40.

Garland, Robert F. "Some Simple Shortcuts From Revenue Earned To Cash-In-The-Till," **MA**, 1970, Vol. 51, No. 9, pp. 22-24.

Garlock, Fred L. (Botts, Ralph R. and Fred L. Garlock. "Interest Rates Charged On Installment Purchases," **AR**, 1955, Vol. 30, No. 4, pp. 607-616.)

Garman, Mark B. and James A. Ohlson. "Information And The Sequential Valuation Of Assets In Arbitrage-Free Economies," **JAR**, 1980, Vol. 18, No. 2, pp. 420-440.

Garner, Don E. "New Student Rights And Academic Freedom In The Classroom," **AR**, 1972, Vol. 47, No. 2, pp. 393-394.

Garner, Don E. (Crum, William F. and Don E. Garner. "1983 Survey Of Doctoral Programs In Accounting In The United States And Canada," **AR**, 1985, Vol. 60, No. 3, pp. 519-525.)

Garner, Paul. "Professional Development Of The Accounting Faculty Member," **AR**, 1957, Vol. 32, No. 2, pp. 297-305.

Garner, Paul. "Some Impressions From The Seventh International Congress Of Accountants," **AR**, 1958, Vol. 33, No. 2, pp. 228-229.

Garner, Paul. "The Challenges Of A Continuing Educational Program For Public Accountants," **AR**, 1959, Vol. 34, No. 2, pp. 226-231.

Garner, S. Paul. "A Tribute To Federigo Melis: Part I - The Melis Testimonial," **AHJ**, 1976, Vol. 3, No. 1-4, pp. 13-14.

Garner, S. Paul. "Elementary Courses In Cost Accounting," **AR**, 1940, Vol. 15, No. 3, pp. 343-349.

Garner, S. Paul. "Historical Development Of Cost Accounting," **AR**, 1947, Vol. 22, No. 4, pp. 385-389.

Garner, S. Paul. "Industrial Accounting Instruction And The National Defense Program," **AR**, 1942, Vol. 17, No. 2, pp.

125-131.

Garner, S. Paul. "The Course In Internal Auditing," **AR**, 1948, Vol. 23, No. 4, pp. 414-417.

Garner, S. Paul. (AlHashim, Dhia D. and S. Paul Garner. "Postulates For Localized Uniformity In Accounting," **ABACUS**, 1973, Vol. 9, No. 1, pp. 62-72.)

Garretson, Donald E. "Business Planning At 3M," **MA**, 1974, Vol. 56, No. 5, pp. 33-36.

Garrett, Linda. (Hunt, Rick, Linda Garrett and C. Mike Merz. "Direct Labor Cost Not Always Relevant At H-P," **MA**, 1985, Vol. 66, No. 8, pp. 58-62.)

Garrett, Richard W. "Implementing The New 'Super' Full-Absorption Rules," **CA**, 1987, Vol. 5, No. 4, pp. 42-47.

Garrison, Frank. "Managing Your Professional Development," **MA**, 1972, Vol. 54, No. 6, pp. 48-51.

Garrison, George C. "Man Vs. Computer: A Personal Success Story," **MA**, 1983, Vol. 65, No. 3, pp. 30-33.

Garrison, Ray H. "Linear Programming In Capital Budgeting," **MA**, 1971, Vol. 52, No. 10, pp. 43-46.

Garrison, Ray H. "Methodology Of Lease Capitalization," **AR**, 1968, Vol. 43, No. 4, pp. 782-784.

Garrod, N. (Emmanuel, C. R. and N. Garrod. "On The Segment Identification Issue," **ABR**, 1986-87, Vol. 17, No. 67, pp. 235-240.)

Garsombke, H. Perrin and Gary Allen. "Did SFAS No. 19 Lead To Oil And Gas Company Mergers?," **JAAF**, 1983, Vol. 6, No. 4, pp. 285-298.

Garsombke, H. Perrin and Richard H. Tabor. "Factors Explaining The Use Of EDP Audit Techniques," **JIS**, 1986, Vol. 1, No. 1, pp. 48-66.

Garsombke, H. Perrin. "A.S.R. 190: Implementation, Costs And Benefits," **CPAJ**, 1978, Vol. 48, No. 2, pp. 23-26.

Garsombke, H. Perrin. "Government-Determined Accounting Rules: An Example," **ABACUS**, 1978, Vol. 14, No. 2, pp. 112-121.

Garstka, Stanley J. and Philip A. Ohlson. "Ratio Estimation In Accounting Populations With Probabilities Of Sample Selection Proportional To Size Of Book Values," **JAR**, 1979, Vol. 17, No. 1, pp. 23-59.

Garstka, Stanley J. "Models For Computing Upper Error Limits In Dollar-Unit Sampling," **JAR**, 1977, Vol. 15, No. 2, pp. 179-192.

Gartenberg, Morris and Robert F. Randall. "From EDP to MIS And Beyond," **MA**, 1979, Vol. 60, No. 10, pp. 13-16.

Gartenberg, Morris. "Current Views On Accounting Issues," **MA**, 1983, Vol. 64, No. 8, p. 64.

Gartenberg, Morris. "How Dow Accounts For Its Energy Use," **MA**, 1980, Vol. 61, No. 9, pp. 10-12.

Gartenberg, Morris. "Small Business: A Question Of Survival," **MA**, 1979, Vol. 61, No. 5, pp. 14-15.

Garton, Steven D. "The Value-Added Tax," **MA**, 1974, Vol. 55, No. 8, pp. 16-18.

Garver, Raymond. "The Evaluation Of A Certain Type Of Property," **AR**, 1932, Vol. 7, No. 1, pp. 70-74.

Gasperow, A. Carl. "Tax Problems Of Country Clubs," **JOA**, 1964, Vol. 118, No. 4, pp. 60-64.

Gass, Gerald L., Grover McMakin and Roger Bentson. "White Collar Productivity," **MA**, 1987, Vol. 69, No. 3, pp. 33-38.

Gately, Mary Sue. "A Guide To The Tax Treatment Of Corporate Liquidations," **JATA**, 1984, Vol. 5, No. 2, pp. 68-74.

Gates, William H. (Roemmich, Roger A., Gordon L. Duke and William H. Gates. "Maximizing The Present Value Of Tax Savings From Depreciation," **MA**, 1978, Vol. 60, No. 3, pp. 55-57.)

Gattegno, Jerrold S. (Banigan, Russell W. and Jerrold S. Gattegno. "A Breakthrough In Water's-Edge Unitary Legislation," **CPAJ**, 1987, Vol. 57, No. 6, pp. 34-39.)

Gatti, James F. (Cats-Baril, William, James F. Gatti and D. Jacque Grinnell. "Transfer Pricing Policy In A Dynamic Market," **MA**, 1988, Vol. 69, No. 8, pp. 30-33.)

Gatti, James F. (Cats-Baril, William L., James F. Gatti and D. Jacque Grinnell. "Joint Product Costing In The Semiconductor Industry," **MA**, 1986, Vol. 67, No. 8, pp. 28-38.)

Gaudin, Donald A. "Building And Controlling A Multi-Divisional Growth Company," **MA**, 1968, Vol. 49, No. 6, pp. 3-8.

Gaumnitz, Bruce R. and Joel E. Thompson. "In-Substance Defeasance: Costs, Yes; Benefits, No," **JOA**, 1987, Vol. 163, No. 3, pp. 102-105.

Gaumnitz, Bruce R. and Joel E. Thompson. "Establishing The Common Stock Equivalence Of Convertible Bonds," **AR**, 1987, Vol. 62, No. 3, pp. 601-622.

Gaumnitz, Bruce R. (Buchanan, Harold, II and Bruce R. Gaumnitz. "Accountants And 'Insider' Trading," **ACCHOR**, 1987, Vol. 1, No. 4, pp. 7-12.)

Gaumnitz, Bruce R., Thomas R. Nunamaker, John J. Surdick and Michael F. Thomas. "Auditor Consensus In Internal Control Evaluation And Audit Program Planning," **JAR**, 1982, Vol. 20, No. 2, Part II, pp. 745-755.

Gauntt, James E., Jr. (Briner, Russell F., Diane T. Pearson and James E. Gauntt, Jr. "A Microcomputer Application For Attribute Sampling," **JAED**, 1987, Vol. 5, No. 1, pp. 161-166.)

Gautier, Jacques P. (Bedford, N. M. and J. P. Gautier. "An International Analytical Comparison Of The Structure And Content Of Annual Reports In The European Economic Community, Switzerland, And The United States," **IJAER**, 1974, Vol. 9, No. 2, pp.1-44.)

Gavin, Thomas A. (Hammer, Edson and Thomas A. Gavin. "How Effective Is Your Supervisor?," **MA**, 1983, Vol. 65, No. 5, pp. 47-52.)

Gavin, Thomas A., Rebecca L. Hicks and Joseph D. Decosimo.

"CPAs' Liability To Third Parties," **JOA**, 1984, Vol. 157, No. 6, pp. 80-91.

Gavin, Thomas A., Rebecca L. Hicks and James H. Scheiner. "Auditors' Common Law Liability: What We Should Be Telling Our Students," **JAED**, 1987, Vol. 5, No. 1, pp. 1-12.

Gavron, Melvin E. "Audits Of Multifamily Housing Enterprises," **CPAJ**, 1978, Vol. 48, No. 10, pp. 13-20.

Gaynor, Edwin W. "Reliability Of Sampling Plans In Auditing," **AR**, 1956, Vol. 31, No. 2, pp. 253-257.

Geary, Raymond R. "The Loner: A Small Firm's Controller Speaks Out," **MA**, 1974, Vol. 56, No. 6, pp. 15-16.

Gebhardt, Guenther. "The Usefulness Of Different Accounting Disclosure Regulations: A German Experience," **IJAER**, 1983, Vol. 18, No. 2, pp. 109-131.

Gee, Edward F. "Banking On Accountants," **JOA**, 1955, Vol. 100, No. 6, pp. 44-47.

Gee, E. A. "The Tale Of The Controlling Account," **AR**, 1926, Vol. 1, No. 4, pp. 76-80.

Gee, Kenneth P. (Dew, R. Beresford and Kenneth P. Gee. "Frequency Of Performance Reporting And Managers' Reference For Control - A Note," **ABR**, 1971-72, Vol. 2, No. 7, pp. 234-236.)

Gee, Kenneth P. (Emmanuel, Clive R. and Kenneth P. Gee. "Transfer Pricing: A Fair And Neutral Procedure," **ABR**, 1981-82, Vol. 12, No. 48, pp. 273-278.)

Gee, K. P. and K. V. Peasnell. "A Comment On Replacement Cost As The Upper Limit Of Value To The Owner," **ABR**, 1976-77, Vol. 7, No. 28, p. 312.

Gee, K. P. and K. V. Peasnell. "A Pragmatic Defence Of Replacement Cost," **ABR**, 1975-76, Vol. 6, No. 24, pp. 242-249.

Geiger, Marshall A. and Herbert G. Hunt, III. "Capital Gain Taxation: A Critical Analysis Of Historical And Current Issues," **AIT**, 1988, Vol. 2, pp. xx-xx.

Geiger, Marshall A. "SAS No. 58: Did The ASB Really Listen?," **JOA**, 1988, Vol. 166, No. 6, pp. 55-57.

Geiler, Louis E. "Analysis Of Uncertainty In Capital Expenditures," **MA**, 1970, Vol. 51, No. 7, pp. 32-36.

Geiselhart, Thomas J. (Arnold, Donald F. and Thomas J. Geiselhart. "Practitioners' Views On Five-Year Educational Requirements For CPAs," **AR**, 1984, Vol. 59, No. 2, pp. 314-324.)

Gelfand, Jack. (Petri, Enrico and Jack Gelfand. "The Production Function: A New Perspective In Capital Maintenance," **AR**, 1979, Vol. 54, No. 2, pp. 330-345.)

Gellein, Oscar S. "Capital Maintenance: A Neglected Notion," **AHJ**, 1987, Vol. 14, No. 2, pp. 59-69.

Gellein, Oscar S. "Cost Allocation: Some Neglected Issues," **CA**, 1987, Vol. 2, No. 3, pp. 40-46.

Gellein, Oscar S. "Development Of An Instructional Approach To The Statement Of Funds," **AR**, 1951, Vol. 26, No. 2, pp. 260-262.

Gellein, Oscar S. "Financial Reporting: The State Of Standard Setting," **AIA**, 1986, Vol. 3, pp. 3-24.

Gellein, Oscar S. "Good Financial Reporting," **CPAJ**, 1983, Vol. 53, No. 11, pp. 39-45.

Gellein, Oscar S. "Periodic Earnings: Income? Or Indicator?," **ACCHOR**, 1987, Vol. 1, No. 2, pp. 59-64.

Gellein, Oscar S. "The Decreasing-Charge Concept Of Cost," **JOA**, 1955, Vol. 100, No. 2, pp. 56-61.

Gellhorn, Walter. "Occupational Licensing - A Nationwide Dilemma," **JOA**, 1960, Vol. 109, No. 1, pp. 39-45.

Gellis, Harold C. "Income Tax Preparation Using The Microcomputer," **CPAJ**, 1987, Vol. 57, No. 10, pp. 30-49.

Gentry, James A. (Dugan, Michael T., James A. Gentry and Keith A. Shriver. "The X-11 Model: A New Analytical Review Technique For The Auditor," **AJPT**, 1984-85, Vol. 4, No. 2, pp. 11-22.)

Gentry, James A., Paul Newbold and David T. Whitford. "Classifying Bankrupt Firms With Funds Flow Components," **JAR**, 1985, Vol. 23, No. 1, pp. 146-160.

Gentry, James A. (Laughlin, Eugene J., James W. Gentry and Carolyn A. May. "Comparison Of Alternative Forms Of Teaching Fundamentals Of Accounting," **AR**, 1976, Vol. 51, No. 2, pp. 347-351.)

Gentzel, Royce L. and Mary Anne Swepston. "The Cardinal Difference In Cash Management," **MA**, 1988, Vol. 69, No. 8, pp. 42-47.

Georgeson, Wayne D. "Valuing A Going-Concern," **MA**, 1976, Vol. 57, No. 12, pp. 26-28.

George, William R. and Kent W. Wheiler. "Practice Development - A Services Marketing Perspective," **CPAJ**, 1986, Vol. 56, No. 10, pp. 30-43.

George, William R. and Richard M. Murray. "Marketing Practices Of CPA Firms," **CPAJ**, 1975, Vol. 45, No. 10, pp. 33-36.

George, William R. (Murray, Richard M. and William R. George. "Managing CPA Personnel - A Marketing Perspective," **CPAJ**, 1979, Vol. 49, No. 7, pp. 17-22.)

Gerber, Donald L. "A Small Information System For Workload Analysis," **MA**, 1971, Vol. 52, No. 9, pp. 13-16.

Gerber, Quentin N. "Accounting Education Below C.P.A. Standards - An International Approach," **AR**, 1962, Vol. 37, No. 2, pp. 346-349.

Gerboth, Dale L. "Accruing The Cost Of Other Postemployment Benefits - The Measurement Problem," **CPAJ**, 1988, Vol. 58, No. 11, pp. 36-44.

Gerboth, Dale L. "Research, Intuition, And Politics In Accounting Inquiry," **AR**, 1973, Vol. 48, No. 3, pp. 475-482.

Gerboth, Dale L. "The Conceptual Framework: Not Definitions, But Professional Values," **ACCHOR**, 1987, Vol. 1, No. 3, pp. 1-8.

Gerboth, Dale L. "'Muddling Through' With The APB," **JOA**, 1972, Vol. 133, No. 5, pp. 42-49.

Gerboth, Dale L. (Berliner, Robert W. and Dale L. Gerboth. "Accounting For Pensions - New FASB Statements," **CPAJ**, 1986, Vol. 56, No. 4, pp. 12-23.)

Gerboth, Dale L. (Berliner, Robert W. and Dale L. Gerboth. "FASB Statement No. 33: 'The Great Experiment'," **JOA**, 1980, Vol. 149, No. 5, pp. 48-54.)

Gerfen, Richard C. (Owen, George A. and Richard C. Gerfen. "Can Junior Accountants Be Trained To Write Better?," **AR**, 1951, Vol. 26, No. 3, pp. 313-320.)

Gerlach, James H. "A Model For Testing The Reliability Of Computer Programs And EDP Management: Internal Control Implication," **AJPT**, 1988, Vol. 7, No. 2, pp. 61-76.

Gerlach, James. (Bailey, Andrew D., Jr., Gordon Leon Duke, James Gerlach, Chen-En Ko, Rayman D. Meservy and Andrew B. Whinston. "TICOM And The Analysis Of Internal Controls," **AR**, 1985, Vol. 60, No. 2, pp. 186-201.)

Gernon, Helen. (Bindon, Kathleen R. and Helen Gernon. "International Accounting Research," **AIA**, 1987, Vol. 4, pp. 43-68.)

Gertzman, Stephen F. and Mary-Ellen Hunt. "A Basic Guide To Tax Accounting Opportunities," **JOA**, 1984, Vol. 157, No. 2, pp. 60-75.

Gerver, Eli. "Partnership Distributions," **JOA**, 1958, Vol. 105, No. 2, pp. 42-49.

Gerver, Eli. "State Taxation Of Interstate Commerce," **JOA**, 1959, Vol. 108, No. 4, pp. 58-62.

Gessford, Glen N. "Utilizing CPM/Cost In Nondefense Industries," **MA**, 1968, Vol. 49, No. 5, pp. 52-57.

Getzelman, John C. "Financial Analysis In An Inflationary Environment," **MA**, 1975, Vol. 56, No. 9, pp. 31-35.

Geurts, Michael D. and Thomas A. Buchman. "Accounting For 'Shocks' In Forecasts," **MA**, 1981, Vol. 62, No. 10, pp. 21-26.

Geurts, William T. "A Simple Way To Account For Loss Reserves For Loan Receivables," **MA**, 1985, Vol. 66, No. 10, pp. 66-69.

Ghartey, Ato. "A New Perspective For Accountancy Education In Ghana," **IJAER**, 1978, Vol. 14, No. 1, pp. 121-132.

Ghartey, J. B. "Accountability, The Threshold Of Political Instability, Underdevelopment, And Misery: The Case Of Africa," **IJAER**, 1985, Vol. 21, No. 1, pp. 143-158.

Gheyara, Kelly and James Boatsman. "Market Reaction To The 1976 Replacement Cost Disclosures," **JAEC**, 1980, Vol. 2, No. 2, pp. 107-125.

Ghicas, Dimitrios. (Abdel-Khalik, A. Rashad, Charles Chi and Dimitrios Ghicas. "Rationality Of Executive Compensation Schemes And Real Accounting Changes," **CAR**, 1987-88, Vol. 4, No. 1, pp. 32-60.)

Giacoletti, Robert R. "The Auditor's Liability For Fraud," **MA**, 1977, Vol. 59, No. 1, pp. 29-32.

Giacomino, Don E. and David E. Mielke. "Preparation And Use Of Cash Flow Statements," **CPAJ**, 1987, Vol. 57, No. 3, pp. 30-35.

Giacomino, Don E. and David E. Mielke. "Using The Statement Of Cash Flows To Analyze Corporate Performance," **MA**, 1988, Vol. 69, No. 11, pp. 54-57.

Giacomino, Don E. and Lloyd L. Doney. "The SAI Movement In Manufacturing," **CPAJ**, 1986, Vol. 56, No. 10, pp. 64-73.

Giacomino, Don E. "University Controllers: Are They Management Accountants?," **MA**, 1980, Vol. 61, No. 12, pp. 32-35.

Giacomino, Don E. (Mielke, David E. and Don E. Giacomino. "Cash-Flow Reporting: A Step Toward International Harmonization," **IJAER**, 1987, Vol. 22, No. 2, pp. 143-151.)

Giacomino, Don E. (Mielke, David E. and Don E. Giacomino. "Ratio Analysis Using The New Statement Of Cash Flows," **CA**, 1988, Vol. 6, No. 1, pp. 10-17.)

Giardina, Edward. "Call Option Reporting," **JOA**, 1978, Vol. 146, No. 1, pp. 72-77.

Gibbins, Michael and Frank M. Wolf. "Auditors' Subjective Decision Environment - The Case Of A Normal External Audit," **AR**, 1982, Vol. 57, No. 1, pp. 105-124.

Gibbins, Michael. "Classificatory Smoothing Of Income With Extraordinary Items: Research Implications," **AR**, 1977, Vol. 52, No. 2, pp. 516-524.

Gibbins, Michael. "Propositions About The Psychology Of Professional Judgment In Public Accounting," **JAR**, 1984, Vol. 22, No. 1, pp. 103-125.

Gibbins, Michael. "Regression And Other Statistical Implications For Research On Judgment Using Intercorrelated Data Sources," **JAR**, 1982, Vol. 20, No. 1, pp. 121-138.

Gibbins, Michael. (Emby, Craig and Michael Gibbins. "Good Judgment In Public Accounting And Justification," **CAR**, 1988, Vol. 4, No. 2, pp. 287-313.)

Gibbins, Michael. (Swieringa, Robert J., Michael Gibbins, Lars Larsson and Janet Lawson Sweeney. "Experiments In The Heuristics Of Human Information Processing," **JAR**, 1976, Vol. 14, Supp., pp. 159-187.)

Gibbons, Charles C. "Meeting The Challenge Of Technical Work," **MA**, 1969, Vol. 51, No. 2, pp. 16-17.

Gibbs, George. "Accounting Fundamentals: Guides To Human Judgment," **ABR**, 1972-73, Vol. 3, No. 11, pp. 205-212.

Gibbs, George. "Accounting Principles 'Generally Accepted': By Whom?," **ABR**, 1970-71, Vol. 1, No. 1, pp. 39-43.

Gibbs, George. "New Cost Accounting Concepts," **AR**, 1958, Vol. 33, No. 1, pp. 96-101.

Gibbs, George. "Professors' Taxable Income And Deductions," **AR**, 1964, Vol. 39, No. 4, pp. 1004-1007.

Gibbs, Thomas E. and Lynn J. McKell. "Computing The Implicit Interest Rate Under SFAS No. 13," **AR**, 1977, Vol. 52, No. 4, pp. 925-929.

Gibbs, Thomas E. "A General Theory Of Evidence As The Conceptual Foundation In Auditing Theory: A Comment," **AR**, 1977, Vol. 52, No. 3, pp. 751-755.

Gibbs, Thomas E. (Clark, Myrtle W., Thomas E. Gibbs and Richard G. Schroeder. "How CPAs Evaluate Internal Auditors," **CPAJ**, 1981, Vol. 51, No. 7, pp. 10-15.)

Gibbs, Thomas E. (Clark, Myrtle W., Thomas E. Gibbs and Richard G. Schroeder. "CPAs Judge Internal Audit Department Objectivity," **MA**, 1981, Vol. 62, No. 8, pp. 40-43.)

Gibson, Charles H. and John Daniel Williams. "Should Common Stock Equivalents Be Considered In Earnings Per Share?," **CPAJ**, 1973, Vol. 43, No. 3, pp. 209-213.

Gibson, Charles H. "Budgeting By Objectives: Charlotte's Experience," **MA**, 1978, Vol. 59, No. 7, pp. 39-40.

Gibson, Charles H. "How Industry Perceives Financial Ratios," **MA**, 1982, Vol. 63, No. 10, pp. 13-19.

Gibson, Charles H. "IRS Audit Techniques - Accumulated Earnings Tax," **CPAJ**, 1975, Vol. 45, No. 4, pp. 23-26.

Gibson, Charles H. (Boyer, Patricia A. and Charles H. Gibson. "How About Earnings Per Share?," **CPAJ**, 1979, Vol. 49, No. 2, pp. 36-42.)

Gibson, Charles H. (Schroeder, Nicholas W. and Charles H. Gibson. "Using Microcomputers To Improve Written Communication," **CPAJ**, 1987, Vol. 57, No. 10, pp. 50-57.)

Gibson, Charles H., Thomas P. Klammer and Sarah A. Reed. "The Cash Flow Statement," **CPAJ**, 1986, Vol. 56, No. 11, pp. 18-39.

Gibson, Charles. "Financial Ratios In Annual Reports," **CPAJ**, 1982, Vol. 52, No. 9, pp. 18-29.

Gibson, Charles. "Quasi-Reorganizations In Practice," AH, 1988, Vol. 2, No. 3, pp. 83-89.

Gibson, James L. "Accounting In The Decision-Making Process," **AR**, 1963, Vol. 38, No. 3, pp. 492-500.

Gibson, Joseph E. "Law And/Or Accounting," **AR**, 1962, Vol. 37, No. 1, pp. 110-115.

Gibson, J. C. "A Standard Cost Problem," **AR**, 1927, Vol. 2, No. 4, pp. 362-387.

Gibson, J. C. "Emphasis In Cost Accounting," **AR**, 1935, Vol. 10, No. 1, pp. 13-15.

Gibson, Robert W. and Jere R. Francis. "Accounting For Goodwill - A Study In Permissiveness," ABACUS, 1975, Vol. 11, No. 2, pp. 167-171.

Gibson, Robert W. and Roger Arnold. "The Development Of Auditing Standards In Australia," AHJ, 1981, Vol. 8, No. 1, pp. 51-65.

Gibson, Robert W. "Comparative Professional Accountancy - Australia," **AR**, 1965, Vol. 40, No. 1, pp. 196-203.

Gibson, Robert W. "Development Of Corporate Accounting In Australia," AHJ, 1979, Vol. 6, No. 2, pp. 23-38.

Gibson, Robert W. "Episodes In The Australian Tax Accounting Saga," AHJ, 1984, Vol. 11, No. 2, pp. 77-99.

Gibson, R. W. "Accounting For Monetary Items Under CCA," ABR, 1980-81, Vol. 11, No. 44, pp. 281-290.

Giese, James W. (Anderson, Hershel M. and James W. Giese. "The Auditor's Belief And His Opinion - The Need For Consistency," **CPAJ**, 1973, Vol. 43, No. 1, pp. 49-54.)

Giese, James W. (White, Debra M. and James W. Giese. "Federal Tax Clinic Practice For Accounting Students," **JATA**, 1982, Vol. 4, No. 1, pp. 33-35.)

Giese, J. W. and T. P. Klammer. "Achieving The Objectives Of APB Opinion No. 19," JOA, 1974, Vol. 137, No. 3, pp. 54-61.

Giese, J. W. (Anderson, H. M., B. A. Coda and J. W. Giese. "An Experiment With A One-Semester Introductory Accounting Course," **AR**, 1972, Vol. 47, No. 1, pp. 175-177.)

Giese, J. W. (Anderson, H. M., J. W. Giese and Jon Booker. "Some Propositons About Auditing," **AR**, 1970, Vol. 45, No. 3, pp. 524-531.)

Giese, J. W. (Hennessee, Patrick A. and J. W. Giese. "Accounting For Leveraged ESOPs: Employee Benefit Or Financing Tool?," **MA**, 1978, Vol. 59, No. 12, pp. 44-49.)

Giesler, Conrad. "Budgeting For Multiple Operations," **MA**, 1971, Vol. 53, No. 4, pp. 15-16.

Giesler, Conrad. "Compensating Sales Reps," **MA**, 1980, Vol. 61, No. 10, pp. 34-36.

Gift, Michael J. (Ajinkya, Bipin B. and Michael J. Gift. "Corporate Managers' Earnings Forecasts And Symmetrical Adjustments Of Market Expectations," **JAR**, 1984, Vol. 22, No. 2, pp. 425-444.)

Gilbert, Julie Y. and David E. Keys. "Enforcing The NAA Standards Of Ethical Conduct," **MA**, 1986, Vol. 67, No. 7, pp. 30-33.

Gilbert, Michael H. "The Asset Value Of The Human Organization," **MA**, 1970, Vol. 52, No. 1, pp. 25-28.

Gilchrist, Michael, Diane D. Pattison and Ronald J. Kudla. "Controlling Indirect Costs With Headcount Forecast Algorithms," **MA**, 1985, Vol. 67, No. 2, pp. 46-51.

Gill, Charles W. "Foreign Exchange Exposures Under FASB 8 And 52," **CPAJ**, 1982, Vol. 52, No. 10, pp. 24-31.

Gillece, Mary Ann. "DOD Acquisition Management," **JCA**, 1985, Vol. 2, No. 1, pp. 21-29.

Gilles, L. H., Jr. "Statutory Depletion - Subsidy In Disguise?," **AR**, 1963, Vol. 38, No. 4, pp. 776-784.

Gillespie, Jackson F. "An Application Of Learning Curves To Standard Costing," **MA**, 1981, Vol. 63, No. 3, pp. 63-65.

Gillespie, Jackson F., Janis R. Reeder and John H. Wragge. "Safeguarding Your Spreadsheet," **MA**, 1985, Vol. 66, No. 11, pp. 38-42.

Gillett, J. B. "A Funded Reserve For Major Removals," **MA**, 1978, Vol. 59, No. 9, pp. 30-34.

Gillick, James V. "A Hard Look At Forecasts," **CPAJ**, 1976, Vol. 46, No. 4, pp. 39-42.

Gilling, Donald M. "Timeliness In Corporate Reporting: Some Further Comment," ABR, 1977-78, Vol. 8, No. 29, pp. 34-36.

Gilling, D. M. and P. J. Stanton. "Changes In The Structure Of The Auditing Profession In Australia," ABACUS, 1978, Vol. 14, No. 1, pp. 66-80.

Gilling, D. M. "Accounting And Social Change," IJAER, 1976, Vol. 11, No. 2, pp. 59-71.

Gilman, Stephen. "Accounting Principles And The Current Classification," **AR**, 1944, Vol. 19, No. 2, pp. 109-116.

Gilman, Stephen. "Correspondence Courses In The Accounting Education Program," **AR**, 1946, Vol. 21, No. 4, pp. 396-403.

Gilman, Stephen. "Is College The Only Way?," **AR**, 1937, Vol. 12. No. 2, pp. 105-110.

Gilmore, Michael J. (Schwartz, Richard and Michael J. Gilmore. "Auditing Pension Costs And Disclosures," **CPAJ**, 1988, Vol. 58, No. 6, pp. 16-25.)

Gilroy, Walter M. "Investment Control In Fixed Price Defense Contracting," **MA**, 1967, Vol. 48, No. 8, pp. 38-42.

Giltinan, John W. "Customs Drawback," **MA**, 1973, Vol. 54, No. 10, pp. 23-27.

Ginder, Willard R. "How To Fix Value Of Close Corporation Stock," JOA, 1951, Vol. 92, No. 2, pp. 198-199.

Gindlin, Herbert M. "How To Use Short-Term Trusts In Family Tax Planning," JOA, 1965, Vol. 119, No. 6, pp. 37-44.

Gingras, Russell T. "Writing And The Certified Public Accountant," JAED, 1987, Vol. 5, No. 1, pp. 127-137.

Ginter, Edward M. "Communications And Cost Benefit Aspects Of Employee Safety," **MA**, 1979, Vol. 60, No. 11, pp. 24-26.

Ginzberg, M. J. "An Organizational Contingencies View Of Accounting And Information Systems Implementation," AOS, 1980, Vol. 5, No. 4, pp. 369-382.

Giordano, Robert J. "Controlling Accounts Payable," **MA**, 1973, Vol. 54, No. 11, pp. 34-36.

Giovinazzo, Vincent J. and John F. Nash. "Selecting Accounting Software Packages," **CPAJ**, 1982, Vol. 52, No. 10, pp. 40-45.

Giovinazzo, Vincent J. "Accounting Problems That Nobody Talks About," **MA**, 1982, Vol. 64, No. 4, pp. 14-19.

Giovinazzo, Vincent J. "Designing Focused Information Systems," **MA**, 1984, Vol. 66, No. 5, pp. 34-41.

Giovinazzo, Vincent J. "Speeding Up Interim Closings," **MA**, 1981, Vol. 63, No. 6, pp. 51-59.

Giovinazzo, Vincent J. (Nash, John F. and Vincent J. Giovinazzo. "Selecting Computer Hardware," **CPAJ**, 1982, Vol. 52, No. 9, pp. 57-63.)

Gipple, Larry D. and Richard W. Metcalf. "Planning Your Professional Development Program," JOA, 1974, Vol. 137, No. 3, pp. 38-46.

Gipple, Larry D. (Fish, Gary L., Larry D. Gipple and Jane E. Katz. "Assessing CPE Needs," JOA, 1985, Vol. 160, No. 1, pp. 79-83.)

Gips, William M. (Leight, Lester A., Melvin L. Braun and William M. Gips. "Review Of Statement On Auditing Procedure No. 47 - 'Subsequent Events'," **CPAJ**, 1972, Vol. 42, No. 2, pp. 123-126.)

Gips, William M. (Wilking, S. Vincent, Melvin L. Braun and William M. Gips. "Pay And Price Control - Phase II," **CPAJ**, 1972, Vol. 42, No. 2, pp. 115-122.)

Girard, Diane. (Hawkins, Clark A. and Diane Girard. "Replacement Decisions Under The Accelerated Cost Recovery System," **JAAF**, 1984, Vol. 7, No. 3, pp. 225-240.)

Girard, Ross M. "Accounting Data Needed In Renegotiation Cases," JOA, 1952, Vol. 94, No. 6, pp. 692-696.

Girard, Ross M. "Some Specific Points For Accountants To Consider In Dealing With Renegotiation," JOA, 1950, Vol. 89, No. 3, pp. 238-239.

Giroux, Gary A. and Stanley H. Kratchman. "How Banks Forecast," **MA**, 1980, Vol. 61, No. 11, pp. 39-44.

Giroux, Gary A. and Steven M. Flory. "Auditing America's Cities," **CPAJ**, 1980, Vol. 50, No. 10, pp. 21-28.

Giroux, Gary A. (Apostolou, Nicholas G., James M. Reeve and Gary A. Giroux. "Accounting Information And Municipal Bond Net Interest Cost: An Empirical Evaluation," **JAPP**, 1984, Vol. 3, No. 1, pp. 9-28.)

Giroux, Gary A. (Apostolou, Nicholas G., Gary A. Giroux and Robert B. Welker. "The Information Content Of Municipal Spending Rate Data," **JAR**, 1985, Vol. 23, No. 2, pp. 853-858.)

Giroux, Gary A. (Reeve, James M., Gary A. Giroux and Nicholas G. Apostolou. "Accounting Information And Municipal Bond Interest Cost: Methodological Considerations: Reply To Comment," **JAPP**, 1985, Vol. 4, No. 3, pp. 241-245.)

Giroux, Gary A. (Rose, Peter S., Wesley T. Andrews and Gary A. Giroux. "Predicting Business Failure: A Macroeconomic Perspective," **JAAF**, 1982, Vol. 6, No. 1, pp. 20-31.)

Giroux, Gary A. (Rowe, Thomas M. and Gary A. Giroux. "Diocesan Financial Disclosure: A Quality Assessment," **JAPP**, 1986, Vol. 5, No. 1, pp. 57-74.)

Giroux, Gary and Casper Wiggins. "Intergovernmental Grants And Local Needs," **JAPP**, 1987, Vol. 6, No. 3, pp. 169-183.

Giroux, Gary, Steven Grossman and Stanley Kratchman. "What FAS No. 33 Does To Bank Financial Statements," **MA**, 1981, Vol. 62, No. 7, pp. 42-47.

Giroux, G. A., A. G. Mayper and R. L. Daft. "Organization Size, Budget Cycle, And Budget Related Influence In City Governments: An Empirical Study," AOS, 1986, Vol. 11, No. 6, pp. 499-520.

Gitman, Lawrence J., Michael D. Joehnk and Peter W. Bacon. "Fundamentals Of Cash Management: Theory And Practice," **JCA**, 1984, Vol. 1, No. 1, pp. 75-99.

Gittes, David L. "GPL Adjusted Income Statements: A Research Study," **MA**, 1977, Vol. 59, No. 4, pp. 29-33.

Gittes, David L. "Negative Goodwill Paradox," **CPAJ**, 1978, Vol. 48. No. 12, pp. 45-48.

Giuliani, William J. "Needed: Tax Reform To Save The U.S. Economy," **MA**, 1981, Vol. 63, No. 5, pp. 48-52.

Givens, Horace R. "A Total Information System For Physicians: C. 1897," **AHJ**, 1985, Vol. 12, No. 1, pp. 117-120.

Givens, Horace R. "An Application Of Curvilinear Break-Even Analysis," **AR**, 1966, Vol. 41, No. 1, pp. 141-143.

Givens, Horace R. "Basic Accounting Postulates," **AR**, 1966, Vol. 41, No. 3, pp. 458-463.

Givens, Horace R. "Peter Duff: Accountant And Educator," **AHJ**, 1980, Vol. 7, No. 1, pp. 37-42.

Givoly, Dan and Dan Palmon. "Classification Of Convertible Debt As Common Stock Equivalents: Some Empirical Evidence On The Effects Of APB Opinion 15," **JAR**, 1981, Vol. 19, No. 2, pp. 530-543.

Givoly, Dan and Dan Palmon. "Timeliness Of Annual Earnings Announcements: Some Empirical Evidence," **AR**, 1982, Vol. 57, No. 3, pp. 486-508.

Givoly, Dan and Josef Lakonishok. "The Information Content Of Financial Analysts' Forecasts Of Earnings: Some Evidence On Semi-Strong Inefficiency," **JAEC**, 1979, Vol. 1, No. 3, pp. 165-185.

Givoly, Dan and Josef Lakonishok. "Aggregate Earnings Expectations And Stock Market Behavior," **JAAF**, 1987, Vol. 2 (New Series), No. 2, pp. 117-150.

Givoly, Dan and Josef Lakonishok. "Properties Of Analysts' Forecasts Of Earnings: A Review And Analysis Of The Research," **JAL**, 1984, Vol. 3, pp. 117-152.

Givoly, Dan and Josef Lakonishok. "Accounting For Construction Companies, Inflation, And Market Efficiency: Analysis Of An Israeli Case," **IJAER**, 1982, Vol. 17, No. 2, pp. 121-149.

Givoly, Dan, Joshua Ronen and Allen Schiff. "Does Audit Involvement Affect The Quality Of Interim Report Numbers?," **JAAF**, 1978, Vol. 1, No. 4, pp. 361-372.

Givoly, Dan. "The Formation Of Earnings Expectations," **AR**, 1985, Vol. 60, No. 3, pp. 372-386.

Givoly, Dan. (Fried, Dov and Dan Givoly. "Financial Analysts' Forecasts Of Earnings: A Better Surrogate For Market Expectations," **JAEC**, 1982, Vol. 4, No. 2, pp. 85-107.)

Givoly, D. and J. Ronen. "'Smoothing' Manifestations In Fourth Quarter Results Of Operations: Some Expirical Evidence," **ABACUS**, 1981, Vol. 17, No. 2, pp. 174-193.

Gjesdal, Froystein. "Accounting For Stewardship," **JAR**, 1981, Vol. 19, No. 1, pp. 208-231.

Gladstone, William L. "Tax Aspects Of The Allocation Of Purchase Price Of A Business," **JOA**, 1966, Vol. 122, No. 4, pp. 36-44.

Gladstone, William L. "The Co-Operative Housing Corporation," **JOA**, 1962, Vol. 113, No. 5, pp. 55-58.

Glahn, Gerald L., Kent T. Fields and Jerry E. Trapnell. "How To Evaluate Mixed Risk Capital Projects," **MA**, 1980, Vol. 62, No. 6, pp. 34-38.

Glatzer, W. "An Overview Of The International Development In Macro Social Indicators," **AOS**, 1981, Vol. 6, No. 3, pp. 219-234.

Glausser, Gary G. (Kilzer, James R. and Gary G. Glausser. "Closing The Small Business Management Gap," **MA**, 1984, Vol. 65, No. 11, pp. 57-61.)

Glautier, Michel W. E. "Searching For Accounting Paradigms," **AHJ**, 1983, Vol. 10, No. 1, pp. 51-68.

Glautier, M. W. E. "Roman Accounting: The Influence Of Socioeconomic Factors On The Development Of Accounting Concepts," **IJAER**, 1973, Vol. 8, No. 2, pp. 59-74.

Gleason, Alan. (Kaufman, Felix and Alan Gleason. "The Effect Of Growth On The Adequacy Of Depreciation Allowances," **AR**, 1953, Vol. 28, No. 4, pp. 539-544.)

Gleim, Irvin N. and John B. Wallace, Jr. "Probabilistically Answered Examinations: A Field Test," **AR**, 1974, Vol. 49, No. 2, pp. 363-366.

Gleim, Irvin N. "Standards Of Disclosure For Supplementary Data," **JOA**, 1973, Vol. 135, No. 4, pp. 50-57.

Glen, Roy H. (Littrell, Earl K. and Roy H. Glen. "Playing The Consulting Game," **MA**, 1982, Vol. 63, No. 7, pp. 56-60.)

Glenn, Neil B. and William J. Scheurer. "Examining The Debate Over Tax Credits," **JOA**, 1970, Vol. 130, No. 3, pp. 63-66.

Glezen, G. William and James A. Millar. "An Empirical Investigation Of Stockholder Reaction To Disclosures Required By ASR No. 250," **JAR**, 1985, Vol. 23, No. 2, pp. 859-870.

Glezen, G. William and James A. Millar. "An Analysis Of Trends And Sources Of Published Funded Accounting Research," **AIA**, 1987, Vol. 4, pp. 83-96.

Glezen, G. William. (Kunitake, Walter K., Andrew D. Luzi and G. William Glezen. "Analytical Review For Audit And Review Engagements," **CPAJ**, 1985, Vol. 55, No. 4, pp. 18-27.)

Glezen, G. William. (Russell, Keith A. and G. William Glezen. "An Investigation Of Certain Interactions Between Large CPA Firms And Accounting Educators," **JAED**, 1984, Vol. 2, No. 1, pp. 55-69.)

Glezen, G. William. (Wilson, Arlette C., G. William Glezen and Timothy P. Cronan. "Forecasting Accounting Information For Auditors' Use In Analytical Reviews," **AIA**, 1988, Vol. 6, pp. 267-276.)

Glos, R. E. "The Teaching Of Elementary Accounting," **AR**, 1935, Vol. 10, No. 1, pp. 4-6.

Glover, Fred. "Comment On A Note By Currin And Spivey," **AR**, 1972, Vol. 47, No. 1, p. 147.

Glover, Fred. "Management Decision And Integer Programming," **AR**, 1969, Vol. 44, No. 2, pp. 300-303.

Glowacki, Robert J. (Backes, Robert W. and Robert J. Glowacki. "Microcomputers: Successful Management And Control," **MA**, 1983, Vol. 65, No. 3, pp. 48-51.)

Gluick, L. "What's Wrong With Our Textbooks?," **AR**, 1947, Vol. 22, No. 1, pp. 36-37.

Glynn, John J. "The Development Of British Railway Accounting: 1800 - 1911," **AHJ**, 1984, Vol. 11, No. 1, pp. 103-118.

Glynn, John R. "Computer Program: A Profitable By-Product," **MA**, 1971, Vol. 52, No. 11, pp. 41-42.

Glynn, J. J. (Cooke, T. E. and J. J. Glynn. "Taxation Implications Of Companies Purchasing Their Own Shares," **ABR**, 1982-83, Vol. 13, No. 51, pp. 177-180.)

Gniewosz, G. "The Equity Method Of Accounting For Investment In Common Stock: The New Zealand Experience," **IJAER**, 1980, Vol. 15, No. 2, pp. 115-128.

Gniewosz, G. "Significant Influence' Through Board Representation: Some Conflicts And Controversies," **ABR**, 1979-80, Vol. 10, No. 39, pp. 285-290.

Gobdel, Bruce G. (Falk, Haim, Bruce G. Gobdel and James H. Naus. "Disclosure For Closely Held Corporations," **JOA**, 1976, Vol. 142, No. 4, pp. 85-90.)

Goddu, George A. "Wage Controls - A Synopsis," **CPAJ**, 1972, Vol. 42, No. 10, pp. 812-818.

Godfrey, James and John Neter. "Bayesian Bounds For Monetary Unit Sampling In Accounting And Auditing," **JAR**, 1984, Vol. 22, No. 2, pp. 497-525.

Godfrey, James T. and Richard W. Andrews. "A Finite Population Bayesian Model For Compliance Testing," **JAR**, 1982, Vol. 20, No. 2, Part I, pp. 304-315.

Godfrey, James T. and Thomas R. Prince. "The Accounting Model From An Information Systems Perspective," **AR**, 1971, Vol. 46, No. 1, pp. 75-89.

Godfrey, James T. and William R. Pasewark. "Controlling Quality Costs," **MA**, 1988, Vol. 69, No. 9, pp. 48-51.

Godfrey, James T. "Short-Run Planning In A Decentralized Firm," **AR**, 1971, Vol. 46, No. 2, pp. 286-297.

Godfrey, James T. (Kim, Hyo Seuk, John Neter and James T. Godfrey. "Behavior Of Statistical Estimators In Multilocation Audit Sampling," **AJPT**, 1986-87, Vol. 6, No. 2, pp. 40-58.)

Godfrey, James. (Roshwalb, Alan, Roger L. Wright, and James Godfrey. "A New Approach For Stratified Sampling In Inventory Cost Estimation," **AJPT**, 1987-88, Vol. 7, No. 1. pp. 54-70.)

Godick, Neil B. and Richard P. Miller. "Applying APB Opinions Nos. 23 And 24," **JOA**, 1973, Vol. 136, No. 5, pp. 55-63.

Godwin, Larry B. "CPA And User Opinions On Increased Corporate Disclosure," **CPAJ**, 1975, Vol. 45, No. 7, pp. 31-35.

Godwin, Larry B. "Income Smoothing," **CPAJ**, 1977, Vol. 47, No. 2, pp. 27-30.

Godwin, Larry B. "Outlook For Public Internal Control Reports," **CPAJ**, 1978, Vol. 48, No. 11, pp. 13-18.

Godwin, Michael and Cedric Sandford. "Simplifying VAT For Small Traders," **ABR**, 1982-83, Vol. 13, No. 52, pp. 279-288.

Goedert, John Philip. "How Progressive Are Our Tax Laws?," **JOA**, 1958, Vol. 105, No. 3, pp. 40-45.

Goedert, John P. "Income And Transfer Taxes," **JOA**, 1956, Vol. 102, No. 1, pp. 45-50.

Goedert, John P. (Stans, Maurice H. and John P. Goedert. "What Is Book Value?," **JOA**, 1955, Vol. 99, No. 1, pp. 38-46.)

Goelzer, Daniel L. "The Opinion-Shopping Controversy," **CA**, 1986, Vol. 4, No. 4, pp. 9-14.

Goetz, Billy E. and Jacob G. Birnberg. "A Comment On The Trueblood Report," **MA**, 1976, Vol. 57, No. 10, pp. 18-20.

Goetz, Billy E. "A First-Year Accounting Course," **AR**, 1969, Vol. 44, No. 4, pp. 823-832.

Goetz, Billy E. "A Note On Discounted Cash Flow Examples: A Reply," **AR**, 1973, Vol. 48, No. 1, pp. 135-136.

Goetz, Billy E. "A Problem In Discounted Cash Flow," **AR**, 1971, Vol. 46, No. 1, pp. 162-164.

Goetz, Billy E. "Compensate For Spoilage By Planning Overruns," **MA**, 1971, Vol. 52, No. 10, pp. 49-52.

Goetz, Billy E. "Debit, Credit, And Input-Output Tables," **AR**, 1967, Vol. 42, No. 3, pp. 589-591.

Goetz, Billy E. "Professional Obsolescence," **AR**, 1967, Vol. 42, No. 1, pp. 53-61.

Goetz, Billy E. "The Corporate Utility Transform," **MA**, 1975, Vol. 56, No. 12, pp. 43-44.

Goetz, Billy E. "The Effect Of A Cost-Plus Contract On Transfer Prices," **AR**, 1969, Vol. 44, No. 2, pp. 398-400.

Goetz, Billy E. "The Management Of Objectives," **MA**, 1973, Vol. 55, No. 2, pp. 35-38.

Goetz, Billy E. "Transfer Prices: An Exercise In Relevancy And Goal Congruence," **AR**, 1967, Vol. 42, No. 3, pp. 435-440.

Goffin, Jean-Louis. (Amey, Lloyd R. and Jean-Louis Goffin. "Joint Product Decisions: The Variable Proportions Case," **CAR**, 1988, Vol. 5, No. 1, pp. 174-198.)

Goffinet, Oliver L. "Limitations In Developing Top-Level Executives," **MA**, 1971, Vol. 53, No. 1, pp. 20-22.

Goggans, Travis P. and John Del Walker. "Selection Of Property For Gifting," **CPAJ**, 1987, Vol. 57, No. 8, pp. 56-63.

Goggans, Travis P. and Ruby Kuhmichel. "Estate Planning For Subchapter S Stockholders," **CPAJ**, 1980, Vol. 50, No. 9, pp. 33-40.

Goggans, Travis P. "Break-Even Analysis With Curvilinear Functions," **AR**, 1965, Vol. 40, No. 4, pp. 867-871.

Goggans, Travis P. "Impact Of Gift And Estate Tax Changes," **CPAJ**, 1982, Vol. 52, No. 1, pp. 12-23.

Goggans, Travis P. "Liberalized Depreciation And Investment

Decisions," **JOA**, 1964, Vol. 117, No. 5, pp. 42-48.

Goggans, Travis P. "The Accountant's Role In Wage Negotiations," **AR**, 1964, Vol. 39, No. 3, pp. 627-630.

Goggans, Travis P. "The Use Of Real Estate Tax Shelters In Estate Planning," **JOA**, 1980, Vol. 150, No. 1, pp. 62-70.

Goggans, Travis P. "The Use Of Trusts As Estate Planning Tools," **CPAJ**, 1979, Vol. 49, No. 9, pp. 19-24.

Goggin, W. J. "A Method Of Solving Accounting Problems," **AR**, 1926, Vol. 1, No. 4, pp. 63-75.

Goggin, Zane. "Two Sides Of Gain Sharing," **MA**, 1986, Vol. 68, No. 4, pp. 47-51.

Goggi, Stephen C. "New Business Plan: Goggi Fountain Service," **MA**, 1976, Vol. 58, No. 2, pp. 48-50.

Golbert, Albert S. "Pitfalls Of DISC," **MA**, 1973, Vol. 55, No. 1, pp. 52-55.

Gold, Bela. "Practical Productivity Analysis For Management Accountants," **MA**, 1980, Vol. 61, No. 11, pp. 31-38.

Goldberg, Louis and Williard E. Stone. "John Caldwell Colt: A Notorious Accountant," **AHJ**, 1985, Vol. 12, No. 1, pp. 121-130.

Goldberg, Louis S. "Lawyers And CPAs: A Study Of Methods Of Practice," **JOA**, 1971, Vol. 131, No. 4, pp. 53-57.

Goldberg, Louis. "Concepts Of Depreciation," **AR**, 1955, Vol. 30, No. 3, pp. 468-484.

Goldberg, Louis. "Murray's Science Of Accountantship," **ABR**, 1981-82, Vol. 12, No. 48, pp. 310-312.

Goldberg, Louis. "The Exposition Of Fundamental Accounting Procedure," **AR**, 1953, Vol. 28, No. 2, pp. 280-281.

Goldberg, Louis. "The Funds Statement Reconsidered," **AR**, 1951, Vol. 26, No. 4, pp. 485-491.

Goldberg, Louis. "The Present State Of Accounting Theory," **AR**, 1963, Vol. 38, No. 3, pp. 457-469.

Goldberg, L. "A Note On Current Assets," **ABACUS**, 1965, Vol. 1, No. 1, pp. 31-45.

Goldberg, L. "The Search For Scouller: An Interim Report," **ABR**, 1976-77, Vol. 7, No. 27, pp. 221-235.

Goldberg, L. (Lee, T. A., L. Goldberg and Trevor Johnston. "The History Of Accounting': Three Reviews," **ABR**, 1977-78, Vol. 8, No. 29, pp. 58-67.)

Goldberg, Seymour. "Pension Planning And The CPA," **JOA**, 1984, Vol. 157, No. 5, pp. 68-76.

Goldenberg, David H. and Raymond Chiang. "Systematic Risk And The Theory Of The Firm: A Reexamination," **JAPP**, 1983, Vol. 2, No. 1, pp. 63-72.

Golden, Charles W. and Mary R. Golden. "Beyond 'What If': A Risk-Oriented Capital Budgeting Model," **JIS**, 1987, Vol. 1, No. 2, pp. 53-64.

Golden, Mary R. (Golden, Charles W. and Mary R. Golden. "Beyond 'What If': A Risk-Oriented Capital Budgeting Model," **JIS**, 1987, Vol. 1, No. 2, pp. 53-64.)

Goldin, Harrison J. "Changes In Municipal Accounting: The New York City Comptroller's Overview," **JAAF**, 1985, Vol. 8, No. 4, pp. 269-278.

Goldin, Harrison J. "Improving New York City's Financial Reporting: A Ten Year Retrospective," **RIGNA**, 1987, Vol. 3, Part B, pp. 165-174.

Golding, Jordan L. "The Nonauditing Aspects Of EDP Installations," **JOA**, 1964, Vol. 118, No. 1, pp. 43-46.

Goldman, Arieh and Benzion Barlev. "The Auditor-Firm Conflict Of Interests: Its Implications For Independence: A Reply," **AR**, 1975, Vol. 50, No. 4, pp. 857-859.

Goldman, Arieh and Benzion Barlev. "The Auditor-Firm Conflict Of Interests: Its Implications For Independence," **AR**, 1974, Vol. 49, No. 4, pp. 707-718.

Goldman, Arieh and Benzion Barlev. "The Auditor-Firm Conflict Of Interests: Its Implications For Independence: A Reply," **AR**, 1975, Vol. 50, No. 4, pp. 848-853.

Goldman, Arieh. (Barlev, Benzion and Arieh Goldman. "Management Advisory Services And Accounting." **ABACUS**, 1974, Vol. 10 No. 1, pp. 74-82.)

Goldman, David. "The Accountant In Bankruptcy And Receivership Cases," **AR**, 1933, Vol. 8, No. 3, pp. 219-223.

Goldschmidt, Yaaqov and Kurt Admon. "Measuring Terms Of Trade During Price Level Changes," **ABACUS**, 1977, Vol. 13, No. 1, pp. 28-39.

Goldschmidt, Yaaqov and Leon Shashua. "Distortion Of Income By SFAS No. 33," **JAAF**, 1984, Vol. 8. No. 1, pp. 54-67.

Goldschmidt, Yaaqov. (Shashua, Leon, Yaaqov Goldschmidt and Dorikam Shadmon. "Control Charts For Citrus Packing Plants," **MA**, 1975, Vol. 56, No. 9, pp. 19-21.)

Goldschmidt, Yaaqov. (Shashua, Leon and Yaaqov Goldschmidt. "Laspeyres Indexes For Variance Analysis In Cost Accounting: A Reply," **AR**, 1976, Vol. 51, No. 2, pp. 432-433.)

Goldschmidt, Y. and S. Smidt. "Valuing The Firm's Durable Assets For Managerial Information," **AR**, 1969, Vol. 44, No. 2, pp. 317-329.

Goldschmidt, Y. (Bashan, O., Y. Goldschmidt, G. Levkowitz and L. Shashua. "Laspeyres Indexes For Variance Analysis In Cost Accounting," **AR**, 1973, Vol. 48, No. 4, pp. 790-793.)

Goldschmidt, Y. (Shashua, L., Y. Goldschmidt and A. Melnik. "The Predictive Value Of Interim Reports And Budgets," **ABACUS**, 1973, Vol. 9, No. 2, pp. 176-179.)

Goldstein, Kenneth Lee. "Dividends Paid Or Received - Recent Developments," **CPAJ**, 1986, Vol. 56, No. 1, pp. 46-49.

Goldstein, Leo. "Unfunded Pension Liabilities May Be Dangerous To Corporate Health," **MA**, 1980, Vol. 61, No. 10, pp. 20-23.

Goldstein, Michael. "Computer Output Microfilm (COM)," **CPAJ**, 1977, Vol. 47, No. 12, pp. 29-32.

Goldstein, Michael. "Management Of Staff Retention," **CPAJ**, 1982, Vol. 52, No. 12, pp. 12-17.

Goldstein, Michael. (Akresh, Abraham D. and Michael Goldstein. "Point-Of-Sale Accounting Systems: Some Implications For The Auditor," **JOA**, 1978, Vol. 146, No. 6, pp. 68-74.)

Goldstein, Murray. (Livingstone, John Leslie and Murray Goldstein. "FASB Experiment In Inflation Disclosures," **CPAJ**, 1980, Vol. 50, No. 6, pp. 34-41.)

Goldstein, Richard L. and Dewey Golkin. "Tax Considerations For S Corporations After 1982," **CPAJ**, 1986, Vol. 56, No. 8, pp. 44-53.

Goldstein, Robert H. and Stephen B. Zimmerman. "Help For Small-To-Medium-Size Distributors," **CPAJ**, 1978, Vol. 48, No. 10, pp. 21-25.

Goldwasser, Dan L. "Another Look At Accountants' Liability - Part I," **CPAJ**, 1985, Vol. 55, No. 8, pp. 22-29.

Goldwasser, Dan L. "Damage Control For CPAs," **CPAJ**, 1986, Vol. 56, No. 12, pp. 50-57.

Goldwasser, Dan L. "Liability Exposure In Compilation And Review," **CPAJ**, 1980, Vol. 50, No. 9, pp. 27-32.

Goldwasser, Dan L. "Policy Considerations In Accountants' Liability To Third Parties For Negligence," **JAAF**, 1988, Vol. 3 (New Series), No. 3, pp. 217-231.

Goldwasser, Dan L. "Recent Developments In Accountants' Negligence Suits," **CPAJ**, 1985, Vol. 55, No. 12, pp. 20-25.

Goldwasser, Dan L. "Shopping For Professional Liability Insurance," **CPAJ**, 1980, Vol. 50, No. 4, pp. 41-47.

Goldwasser, Dan L. "Suing For Fees?," **CPAJ**, 1982, Vol. 52, No. 6, pp. 34-37.

Goldwasser, Dan L. "Tax Shelters: CPAs Beware," **CPAJ**, 1978, Vol. 48, No. 4, pp. 21-26.

Goldwasser, Dan L. "The Accountant As Middleman," **CPAJ**, 1985, Vol. 55, No. 9, pp. 42-47.

Golembiewski, Robert T. "Accountancy As A Function Of Organization Theory," **AR**, 1964, Vol. 39, No. 2, pp. 333-341.

Golen, Stephen P. and Richard A. White. "Communicating Effectively With Clients," **CPAJ**, 1983, Vol. 53, No. 12, pp. 12-17.

Golen, Steven P., Stephen W. Looney and Richard A. White. "An Empirical Examination Of CPA Perceptions Of Communication Barriers Between Auditor And Client," **AIA**, 1988, Vol. 6, pp. 233-250.

Golen, Steven, James Worthington, Greg Thibadoux, William D. Cooper and Ira S. Greenberg. "Flowcharts & Graphics," **CPAJ**, 1986, Vol. 56, No. 3, pp. 12-23.

Golick, Edward A. "Robotics: A Way To Higher Productivity," **CA**, 1985, Vol. 3, No. 2, pp. 22-25.

Goliger, Josef. "Fixed Charges And Profit," **AR**, 1950, Vol. 25, No. 4, pp. 412-416.

Goliger, Josef. "The Inventory Challenge," **AR**, 1951, Vol. 26, No. 4, pp. 524-525.

Goliger, Joseph. "Analysis Of Semi-Variable Expenses," **AR**, 1949, Vol. 24, No. 3, pp. 308-310.

Golkin, Dewey. (Goldstein, Richard L. and Dewey Golkin. "Tax Considerations For S Corporations After 1982," **CPAJ**, 1986, Vol. 56, No. 8, pp. 44-53.)

Golub, Steven J. "A Global Perspective To Financial Reporting," **IJAER**, 1982, Vol. 18, No. 1, pp. 37-44.

Gomberg, Mandel and Arthur Farber. "The Balance Sheet Of The Future," **AR**, 1964, Vol. 39, No. 3, pp. 615-617.

Gombola, Michael J. and J. Edward Ketz. "A Note On Cash Flow And Classification Patterns Of Financial Ratios," **AR**, 1983, Vol. 58, No. 1, pp. 105-114.

Gonedes, Nicholas J. and Kermit D. Larson. "A Look At 'A Comment On 'Business Combinations: An Exchange Ratio Determination Model'," **AR**, 1971, Vol. 46, No. 3, pp. 572-573.

Gonedes, Nicholas J. and Nicholas Dopuch. "Economic Analyses And Accounting Techniques: Perspectives And Proposals," **JAR**, 1979, Vol. 17, No. 2, pp. 384-410.

Gonedes, Nicholas J. and Nicholas Dopuch. "Capital Market Equilibrium, Information Production, And Selecting Accounting Techniques: Theoretical Framework And Review Of Empirical Work," **JAR**, 1974, Vol. 12, Supp., pp. 48-129.

Gonedes, Nicholas J. and Yuji Ijiri. "Improving Subjective Probability Assessment For Planning And Control In Team-Like Organizations," **JAR**, 1974, Vol. 12, No. 2, pp. 251-269.

Gonedes, Nicholas J. "Accounting For Managerial Control: An Application Of Chance-Constrained Programming," **JAR**, 1970, Vol. 8, No. 1, pp. 1-20.

Gonedes, Nicholas J. "Capital Market Equilibrium And Annual Accounting Numbers: Empirical Evidence," **JAR**, 1974, Vol. 12. No. 1, pp. 26-62.

Gonedes, Nicholas J. "Corporate Signaling, External Accounting, And Capital Market Equilibrium: Evidence On Dividends, Income, And Extraordinary Items," **JAR**, 1978. Vol. 16. No. 1, pp. 26-79.

Gonedes, Nicholas J. "Efficient Capital Markets And External Accounting," **AR**, 1972, Vol. 47. No. 1, pp. 11-21.

Gonedes, Nicholas J. "On Livestock Cost Accounting: A General Proposal," **MA**, 1968, Vol. 50, No. 3, pp. 47-50.

Gonedes, Nicholas J. "Optimal Timing Of Control Messages For A Two-State Markov Process," **JAR**, 1971, Vol. 9, No. 2, pp. 236-252.

Gonedes, Nicholas J. "Perception Estimation And Verifiability," **IJAER**, 1969, Vol. 4, No. 2, pp. 63-73.

Gonedes, Nicholas J. "Properties Of Accounting Numbers: Models And Tests," **JAR**, 1973, Vol. 11, No. 2, pp. 212-237.

Gonedes, Nicholas J. "Public Disclosure Rules, Private Information-Production Decisions, And Capital Market Equilibrium," **JAR**, 1980, Vol. 18, No. 2, pp. 441-476.

Gonedes, Nicholas J. "Risk, Information, And The Effects Of Special Accounting Items On Capital Market Equilibrium," **JAR**, 1975, Vol. 13, No. 2, pp. 220-256.

Gonedes, Nicholas J. "Some Evidence On Investor Actions And Accounting Messages - Part II," **AR**, 1971, Vol. 46, No. 3, pp. 535-551.

Gonedes, Nicholas J. "Some Evidence On Investor Actions And Accounting Messages - Part I," **AR**, 1971, Vol. 46, No. 2, pp. 320-328.

Gonedes, Nicholas J. "The Significance Of Selected Accounting Procedures: A Statistical Test," **JAR**, 1969, Vol. 7, Supp., pp. 90-113.

Gonedes, Nicholas J. (Larson, Kermit D. and Nicholas J. Gonedes. "Business Combinations: An Exchange Ratio Determination Model," **AR**, 1969, Vol. 44, No. 4, pp. 720-728.)

Gonedes, Nicholas J., Nicholas Dopuch and Stephen H. Penman. "Disclosure Rules, Information-Production, And Capital Market Equilibrium: The Case Of Forecast Disclosure Rules," **JAR**, 1976, Vol. 14, No. 1, pp. 89-137.

Gonzalez, Jose L. "Time Management...Or Learning How To Say No," **MA**, 1987, Vol. 68, No. 10, pp. 38-40.

Gonzalez, J. M. "Highlights Of Proposed Amendment To Consolidated Return Regulations," **JOA**, 1966, Vol. 121, No. 1, pp. 49-55.

Gooch, Lawrence B. (Grabowski, Roger J. and Lawrence B. Gooch. "Implementing Replacement Cost Disclosure Requirements," **MA**, 1977, Vol. 58, No. 12, pp. 13-20.)

Good, Roy S. "Auditing Single-Employer Pension Funds," **JOA**, 1974, Vol. 138, No. 6, pp. 58-66.

Goode, Ellis W. "How Motor Carriers Use Punch Card Equipment," **JOA**, 1951, Vol. 91, No. 3, pp. 434-438.

Goode, James R. (Buckley, John W. and James R. Goode. "Inventory Valuation And Income Measurement: An Improved System Of Analysis," **ABACUS**, 1976, Vol. 12, No. 1, pp. 34-48.)

Goodman, Hortense. "NAARS: The CPA's Electronic Shoe Box," **JOA**, 1985, Vol. 160, No. 6, pp. 125-132.

Goodman, Leonard and Roland Lipka. "Property Transfers Under Section 351," **CPAJ**, 1981, Vol. 51, No. 3, pp. 42-48.

Goodman, Leonard and Stanley Rier. "The Impact Of TRA-86 On The Taxation Of Business," **CPAJ**, 1987, Vol. 57, No. 5, pp. 66-71.

Goodman, Leonard. "An Analysis Of The Effectiveness Of Public Accounting Internship Programs At Major New York City CPA Firms," **JAED**, 1983, Vol. 1, No. 2, pp. 159-162.

Goodman, Leonard. "Corporate Liquidations, Distributions, And Reorganizations After TEFRA," **CA**, 1983, Vol. 1, No. 4, pp. 46-50.

Goodman, Leonard. (Lipka, Roland and Leonard Goodman. "Planning For Retirement: Section 402 Election," **CPAJ**, 1983, Vol. 53, No. 4, pp. 44-53.)

Goodman, Leonard. (Rier, Stanley and Leonard Goodman. "The Tax Reform Act Of 1984 - Part III," **CPAJ**, 1985, Vol. 55, No. 2, pp. 44-47.)

Goodman, Leonard. (Rier, Stanley and Leonard Goodman. "Changes To Tax On Individuals - TRA 1986," **CPAJ**, 1986, Vol. 56, No. 12, pp. 16-27.)

Goodman, Leonard. (Rier, Stanley and Leonard Goodman. "The Tax Reform Act Of 1984 - Part II," **CPAJ**, 1985, Vol. 55, No. 3, pp. 39-43.)

Goodman, Leonard. (Rier, Stanley and Leonard Goodman. "The Tax Reform Act Of 1984 - Part I," **CPAJ**, 1985, Vol. 55, No. 1, pp. 26-33.)

Goodman, Seymour S. (Firmin, Peter A., Seymour S. Goodman, Thomas J. Hendricks and James J. Linn. "University Cost Structure And Behavior: An Empirical Study," **JAR**, 1968, Vol. 6, Supp., pp. 122-155.)

Goodwin, Ken. "Inflation Accounting: A Bit Of Philosophy And A Lot Of Simplification," **ABR**, 1979-80, Vol. 10, No. 38, pp. 187-196.

Goolsby, John L. "Integrated Accounting Systems: A Practical Approach," **MA**, 1969, Vol. 51, No. 3, pp. 11-13.

Goosen, Kenneth R. and Jimie Kusel. "Integrating Microcomputer Use Into An Information Systems Course," **IAE**, 1985, No. 1, pp. 77-86.

Gopez, Eduardo C. "Auditing With Accent On The Income Statement," **AR**, 1954, Vol. 29, No. 4, pp. 571-574.

Gordon, Arthur N. "Lessons From A Municipal Fiscal Crisis," **CPAJ**, 1977, Vol. 47, No. 11, pp. 25-30.

Gordon, Dennis and Rae D. Anderson. "Techniques For Handling Increased Enrollments," **AR**, 1958, Vol. 33, No. 3, pp. 486-496.

Gordon, Dennis. "Can Accounting Instruction Be Automated?," **AR**, 1962, Vol. 37, No. 4, pp. 692-695.

Gordon, Dennis. "Courses For Students Specializing In Industrial Accounting," **AR**, 1950, Vol. 25, No. 2, pp. 194-198.

Gordon, Dennis. "The Overhead Projector - An Aid In Teaching Accounting," **AR**, 1962, Vol. 37, No. 1, pp. 120-121.

Gordon, Dennis. "The Solution Of Process Cost Problems," **AR**, 1949, Vol. 24, No. 3, pp. 296-303.

Gordon, F. E., J. G. Rhode and K. A. Merchant. "The Effects Of Salary And Human Resource Accounting Disclosures On Small Group Relations And Performance," **AOS**, 1977, Vol. 2, No. 4, pp. 295-306.

Gordon, I. M. and M. R. Mathews. "The Attitudes Of The Members Of Three Canadian Accounting Organizations Toward Continuing Education," **AIIA**, 1987, Vol. 1, pp. 357-382.

Gordon, James W. "Protecting Your Retirement Nest Egg," **MA**, 1987, Vol. 68, No. 12, pp. 30-33.

Gordon, Lawrence A. and Fred E. Sellers. "Accounting And Budgeting Systems: The Issue Of Congruency," **JAPP**, 1984, Vol. 3, No. 4, pp. 259-292.

Gordon, Lawrence A. and Henry Cook, Jr. "Absorption Costing And Fixed Factors Of Production," **AR**, 1973, Vol. 48, No. 1, pp. 128-129.

Gordon, Lawrence A. and Michelle M. Hamer. "Rates Of Return And Cash Flow Profiles: An Extension," **AR**, 1988, Vol. 63, No. 3, pp. 514-521.

Gordon, Lawrence A. "Allocating Service Departments' Costs: Methodology And Case Study," **ABR**, 1974-75, Vol. 5, No. 17, pp. 3-8.

Gordon, Lawrence A. "Comment On The Value Of R-Square In Regression Analysis," **AR**, 1972, Vol. 47, No. 2, pp. 356-357.

Gordon, Lawrence A. "Differential Rate Of Return Method For Reporting Holding Gains Earned By Fixed Assets," **ABR**, 1972-73, Vol. 3, No. 11, pp. 228-234.

Gordon, Lawrence A. "Federal Capital Investments And Public Policy: The Budgeting Link," **JAPP**, 1983, Vol. 2, No. 1, pp. 1-4.

Gordon, Lawrence A. "The Return On Investment And The Cost Of Capital," **MA**, 1976, Vol. 57, No. 8, pp. 37-40.

Gordon, Lawrence A. (Falk, Haim and Lawrence A. Gordon. "Assessing Industry Risk By Ratio Analysis: Validation," **AR**, 1978, Vol. 53, No. 1, pp. 216-227.)

Gordon, Lawrence A. (Haka, Susan F., Lawrence A. Gordon and George E. Pinches. "Sophisticated Capital Budgeting Selection Techniques And Firm Performance," **AR**, 1985, Vol. 60, No. 4, pp. 651-669.)

Gordon, Lawrence A., Jack Call and Haim Falk. "Pricing Objectives And Managerial Incentive Plans," **JCA**, 1986, Vol. 3, No. 2, pp. 59-67.

Gordon, Lawrence A., Morris M. Kleiner and R. Natarajan. "Federal Capital Expenditures And Budget Deficits: Gross National Product And Labor Implications," **JAPP**, 1986, Vol. 5, No. 4, pp. 217-232.

Gordon, L. A. and D. Miller. "A Contingency Framework For The Design Of Accounting Information Systems," **AOS**, 1976, Vol. 1, No. 1, pp. 59-70.

Gordon, L. A. and V. K. Narayanan. "Management Accounting Systems, Perceived Environmental Uncertainty And Organization Structure: An Empirical Investigation," **AOS**, 1984, Vol. 9, No. 1, pp. 33-48.

Gordon, L. A., D. F. Larcker and F. D. Tuggle. "Strategic Decision Processes And The Design Of Accounting Information Systems: Conceptual Linkages," **AOS**, 1978, Vol. 3, No. 3/4, pp. 203-214.

Gordon, L. A., S. Haka and A. G. Schick. "Strategies For Information Systems Implementation: The Case Of Zero Base Budgeting," **AOS**, 1984, Vol. 9, No. 2, pp. 111-124.

Gordon, Myron J. "A Method Of Pricing For A Socialist Economy," **AR**, 1970, Vol. 45, No. 3, pp. 427-443.

Gordon, Myron J. "Cost Allocations And The Design Of Accounting Systems For Control," **AR**, 1951, Vol. 26, No. 2, pp. 209-220.

Gordon, Myron J. "Postulates, Principles And Research In Accounting," **AR**, 1964, Vol. 39, No. 2, pp. 251-263.

Gordon, Myron J. "Scope And Method Of Theory And Research In The Measurement Of Income And Wealth," **AR**, 1960, Vol. 35, No. 4, pp. 603-618.

Gordon, Myron J. "The Managerial Use Of Data Obtainable In Conjunction With LIFO," **AR**, 1956, Vol. 31, No. 2, pp. 234-243.

Gordon, Myron J. "The Valuation Of Accounts At Current Cost," **AR**, 1953, Vol. 28, No. 3, pp. 373-384.

Gordon, M. J. "A Method Of Pricing For A Socialist Economy: A Reply," **AR**, 1971, Vol. 46, No. 4, pp. 788-790.

Gorelik, George. "Enterprise Profit And Profitability Measurements: Soviet-American Convergence," **IJAER**, 1971, Vol. 6, No. 2, pp. 1-14.

Gorelik, George. "Notes On The Development And Problems Of Soviet Uniform Accounting," **IJAER**, 1973, Vol. 9, No. 1, pp. 135-148.

Gorelik, George. "On The Nature Of Information," **IJAER**, 1975, Vol. 10, No. 2, pp. 109-125.

Gorelik, George. "Soviet Accounting, Planning And Control," **ABACUS**, 1974, Vol. 10, No. 1, pp. 13-25.

Gorman, Jerry. "LBO Accounting: Unveiling The Mystery Of Carryover Basis," **JOA**, 1988, Vol. 166, No. 4, pp. 71-80.

Gorman, Jerry. "M&As: The CPA As Acquisition Adviser," **JOA**, 1988, Vol. 166, No. 2, pp. 36-42.

Gorman, John J. (Stout, David E., Donald E. Wygal and John J. Gorman. "Accounting Student Perceptions Of The Nature And Significance Of Extraordinary Items Data," **JAED**, 1987, Vol. 5, No. 1, pp. 13-25.)

Gorman, Raymond. (Chen, Chao, Philip Fanara, Jr. and Raymond Gorman. "Abandonment Decisions And The Market Value Of The Firm: The Case Of Nuclear Power Project Abandonment," **JAPP**, 1987, Vol. 6, No. 4, pp. 285-297.)

Gormley, R. James. "Developments In Accountants' Liability To Nonclients For Negligence," **JAAF**, 1988, Vol. 3 (New Series), No. 3, pp. 185-212.

Gormley, R. James. "Professional Risks In Purchase Audits And Reviews," **JAAF**, 1980, Vol. 3, No. 4, pp. 293-312.

Gormley, R. James. "RICO And The Professional Accountant," **JAAF**, 1982, Vol. 6, No. 1, pp. 51-59.

Gorski, Janusz. "The Council For Mutual Economic Assistance: Its Role In The Economic Integration Of Socialist Countries," **IJAER**, 1974, Vol. 10, No. 1, pp. 19-32.

Gosman, Martin L. "An Assessment Of The Recommendations Of The Study Group On Introductory Accounting," **AR**, 1973, Vol. 48, No. 1, pp. 158-162.

Gosman, Martin L. "Characteristics Of Firms Making Accounting Changes," **AR**, 1973, Vol. 48, No. 1, pp. 1-11.

Gosman, Martin L. "Firms Making Accounting Changes: A

Reply," **AR**, 1974, Vol. 49, No. 1, pp. 112-117.

Gossett, Thomas E. and Milton F. Usry. "Process Cost Accounting And Diagrammatical Outlines," **AR**, 1968, Vol. 43, No. 1, pp. 133-136.

Gott, Stanley W. "Can I Save Taxes By Incorporating My Practice," **MA**, 1977, Vol. 59, No. 1, pp. 46-52.

Gotthilf, Daniel L. "Prescription Pre-Billing," **MA**, 1966, Vol. 48, No. 1, pp. 27-33.

Goudeket, A. "An Application Of Replacement Value Theory," **JOA**, 1960, Vol. 110, No. 1, pp. 37-47.

Goudeket, A. "How Dutch Financial Statements Reflect Inflation," **JOA**, 1952, Vol. 94, No. 4, pp. 448-456.

Goudie, A. W. and G. Meeks. "Medium Term Projections Of Companies' Financial Flows: A Disaggregated Approach," **ABR**, 1980-81, Vol. 11, No. 44, pp. 291-302.

Gough, Daniel J. "The CPA's Role In An Acquisition," **CPAJ**, 1985, Vol. 55, No. 6, pp. 44-53.

Gould, Douglas P. "Opportunity Accounting For Product Line Decisions," **MA**, 1969, Vol. 50, No. 8, pp. 33-38.

Gourley, B. M. "Projects To Enrich The Study Of Financial Reporting," **JAED**, 1983, Vol. 1, No. 2, pp. 143-148.

Gourley, Keith C. and Thomas R. Blecki. "Computerized Budgeting At Lord Corporation," **MA**, 1986, Vol. 68, No. 2, pp. 37-40.

Govindarajan, Vijayaraghavan. "Objectives Of Financial Reporting By Business Enterprises: Some Evidence Of User Preference," **JAAF**, 1979, Vol. 2, No. 4, pp. 339-343.

Govindarajan, Vijay. (Shank, John K. and Vijay Govindarajan. "The Perils Of Cost Allocation Based On Production Volumes," **AH**, 1988, Vol. 2, No. 4, pp. 71-79.)

Govindarajan, V. and A. K. Gupta. "Linking Control Systems To Business Unit Strategy: Impact On Performance," **AOS**, 1985, Vol. 10, No. 1, pp. 51-66.

Govindarajan, V. and John K. Shank. "Cash Sufficiency: The Missing Link In Strategic Planning," **CA**, 1984, Vol. 2, No. 1, pp. 23-32.

Govindarajan, V. and Robert N. Anthony. "How Firms Use Cost Data In Price Decisions," **MA**, 1983, Vol. 65, No. 1, pp. 30-37.

Govindarajan, V. "Appropriateness Of Accounting Data In Performance Evaluation: An Empirical Examination Of Environmental Uncertainty As An Intervening Variable," **AOS**, 1984, Vol. 9, No. 2, pp. 125-136.

Govindarajan, V. "The Objectives Of Financial Statements: An Empirical Study Of The Use Of Cash Flow And Earnings By Security Analysts," **AOS**, 1980, Vol. 5, No. 4, pp. 383-392.

Govindarajan, V. "Use Of Accounting Data In Product Pricing," **CA**, 1984, Vol. 2, No. 2, pp. 38-45.

Govindarajan, V. (Churchill, N. C., W. W. Cooper and V. Govindarajan. "Effects Of Audits On The Behavior Of Medical Professionals Under The Bennett Amendment," **AJPT**, 1981-82, Vol. 1, No. 2, pp. 69-90.)

Govindarajan, V. (San Miguel, J. G., J. K. Shank and V. Govindarajan. "Extending Corporate Accountability: A Survey And Framework For Analysis," **AOS**, 1977, Vol. 2, No. 4, pp. 333-348.)

Govindarajan, V. (San Miguel, J. G. and V. Govindarajan. "The Contingent Relationship Between The Controller And Internal Audit Functions In Large Organizations," **AOS**, 1984, Vol. 9, No. 2, pp. 179-188.)

Graber, Dean E. "Professional Specialization In Perspective," **JOA**, 1972, Vol. 133, No. 5, pp. 58-62.

Graber, Dean E. "Ethics Enforcement - How Effective?," **CPAJ**, 1979, Vol. 49, No. 9, pp. 11-18.

Graber, Dean E. (Edwards, James B. and Dean E. Graber. "LIFO: To Switch Or Not To Switch?," **MA**, 1975, Vol. 57, No. 4, pp. 35-40.)

Graber, Paul J. "A Plea To Authors," **AR**, 1950, Vol. 25, No. 3, pp. 321-322.

Graber, Paul J. "Report Of Committee On Revision Of The Statement Of Principles: Assets," **AR**, 1948, Vol. 23, No. 1, pp. 12-16.

Grabowski, Roger J. and Lawrence B. Gooch. "Implementing Replacement Cost Disclosure Requirements," **MA**, 1977, Vol. 58, No. 12, pp. 13-20.

Grabski, Severin V. "Auditor Participation In Accounting Systems Design: Past Involvement And Future Challenges," **JIS**, 1986, Vol. 1, No. 1, pp. 3-23.

Grabski, Severin V. "Transfer Pricing In Complex Organizations: A Review And Integration Of Recent Empirical And Analytical Research," **JAL**, 1985, Vol. 4, pp. 33-76.

Grabski, Severin V. (Reneau, J. Hal and Severin V. Grabski. "A Review Of Research In Computer-Human Interaction And Individual Differences Within A Model For Research In Accounting Information Systems," **JIS**, 1987, Vol. 2, No. 1, pp. 33-53.)

Grace, John C. "A Controller's Conception Of A Modern Annual Report," **AR**, 1949, Vol. 24, No. 2, pp. 171-178.

Grace, J. Peter. "Wielding The Gramm-Rudman Ax," **JOA**, 1986, Vol. 161, No. 4, pp. 66-72.

Grace, William E. "Clerical Work Effectiveness Program - How To Get The Facts," **MA**, 1967, Vol. 48, No. 10, pp. 59-62.

Grace, William E. "Planning And Organizing A Work Measurement Program," **MA**, 1970, Vol. 52, No. 1, pp. 29-56.

Graduate Students Of The University Of Illinois. "Is Appreciation Available For Dividends?," **AR**, 1930, Vol. 5, No. 1, pp. 15-22.

Grady, Paul. "A Broader View Of Internal Control," **JOA**, 1957, Vol. 103, No. 5, pp. 36-41.

Grady, Paul. "Accounting For Fixed Assets And Their Amortization," **AR**, 1950, Vol. 25, No. 1, pp. 3-19.

Grady, Paul. "Auditing Large-Scale Business Enterprises," **JOA**, 1951, Vol. 91, No. 5, pp. 678-685.

Grady, Paul. "Conservation Of Productive Capital Through Recognition Of Current Cost Of Depreciation," **AR**, 1955, Vol. 30, No. 4, pp. 617-622.

Grady, Paul. "Current Problems In Cost Determinations," **AR**, 1944, Vol. 19, No. 1, pp. 47-54.

Grady, Paul. "Economic Depreciation," **JOA**, 1959, Vol. 107, No. 4, pp. 54-60.

Grady, Paul. "Inventory Of Generally Accepted Accounting Principles In The USA," **AR**, 1965, Vol. 40, No. 1, pp. 21-30.

Grady, Paul. "Outline For Inventory Of Accounting Principles," **JOA**, 1963, Vol. 116, No. 5, pp. 52-55.

Grady, Paul. "Professionalism In Accounting," **IJAER**, 1967, Vol. 3, No. 1, pp. 87-99.

Grady, Paul. "Standards Of Disclosure For Changing Price Levels," **JOA**, 1952, Vol. 94, No. 5, pp. 565-569.

Grady, Paul. "The CPA's Role At Stockholder Meetings," **JOA**, 1956, Vol. 101, No. 5, pp. 31-35.

Grady, Paul. "The Increasing Emphasis On Accounting As a Social Force," **AR**, 1948, Vol. 23, No. 3, pp. 266-275.

Grady, Paul. "The Independent Auditing And Reporting Function Of The CPA," **JOA**, 1965, Vol. 120, No. 5, pp. 65-71.

Grady, Paul. "The Quest For Accounting Principles," **JOA**, 1962, Vol. 113, No. 5, pp. 45-50.

Graebner, Norman A. "Whither Containment?," **IJAER**, 1969, Vol. 5, No. 1, pp. 53-59.

Graese, Clifford E. and Joseph R. DeMario. "Revenue Recognition For Long Term Contracts," **JOA**, 1976, Vol. 142, No. 6, pp. 53-59.

Graese, C. E. "Responsibility Reporting To Management," **AR**, 1964, Vol. 39, No. 2, pp. 387-391.

Graff, F. W. "Objective Tests In Accounting," **AR**, 1933, Vol. 8, No. 1, pp. 73-77.

Graham, Curtis C. and Darwin W. Manship. "The Environment Of Reality: An Experiment In Education For Business," **AR**, 1973, Vol. 48, No. 1, pp. 166-170.

Graham, Gerald. (Lewis, Tom D., Thomas A. Shimerda and Gerald Graham. "What The Academic Advisor Needs To Know About Job Placement," **JAED**, 1983, Vol. 1, No. 2, pp. 135-142.)

Graham, H. L. and D. C. Johnson. "An EDP System For Integrated Payroll," **MA**, 1966, Vol. 47, No. 12, pp. 36-43.

Graham, Lynford E. "Analytical Review Techniques: Some Neglected Tools," **CPAJ**, 1981, Vol. 51, No. 10, pp. 18-24.

Graham, Lynford E. "Audit Risk - Part V," **CPAJ**, 1985, Vol. 55, No. 12, pp. 26-35.

Graham, Lynford E. "Audit Risk - Part I," **CPAJ**, 1985, Vol. 55, No. 8, pp. 12-21.

Graham, Lynford E. "Audit Risk - Part II," **CPAJ**, 1985, Vol. 55, No. 9, pp. 34-41.

Graham, Lynford E. "Audit Risk - Part III," **CPAJ**, 1985, Vol. 55, No. 10, pp. 36-43.

Graham, Lynford E. "Audit Risk - Part IV," **CPAJ**, 1985, Vol. 55, No. 11, pp. 38-47.

Graham, Lynford E. (Neter, John, Hyo Seuk Kim and Lynford E. Graham. "On Combining Stringer Bounds For Independent Monetary Unit Samples From Several Populations," **AJPT**, 1984-85, Vol. 4, No. 1, pp. 75-88.)

Graham, Lynford E. (Shpilberg, David and Lynford E. Graham. "Developing ExperTAX: An Expert System For Corporate Tax Accrual And Planning," **AJPT**, 1986-87, Vol. 6, No. 1, pp. 75-94.)

Graham, Robert F. "Valuation For Profit Determination," **AR**, 1940, Vol. 15, No. 2, pp. 145-165.

Graham, Robert L. (Amante, Joseph R. and Robert L. Graham. "Flexible Budgeting: A Defense Industry Approach," **MA**, 1974, Vol. 55, No. 8, pp. 37-38.)

Graham, Willard J. and Harold Q. Langenderfer. "Reporting Of Leases: Comment On APB Opinion No. 5," **JOA**, 1965, Vol. 119, No. 3, pp. 57-62.

Graham, Willard J. "Accounting And Law," **AR**, 1935, Vol. 10, No. 2, pp. 162-167.

Graham, Willard J. "Accounting Education, Ethics And Training," **AR**, 1939, Vol. 14, No. 3, pp. 258-262.

Graham, Willard J. "Accounting In The Law-School Curriculum," **AR**, 1939, Vol. 14, No. 1, pp. 14-21.

Graham, Willard J. "Allocation Of Income Taxes," **JOA**, 1959, Vol. 107, No. 1, pp. 57-67.

Graham, Willard J. "Colleges And The Profession," **JOA**, 1956, Vol. 101, No. 2, pp. 45-50.

Graham, Willard J. "Comprehensive Examinations Vs. Course Credits," **AR**, 1933, Vol. 8, No. 1, pp. 39-42.

Graham, Willard J. "Depreciation And Capital Replacement In An Inflationary Economy," **AR**, 1959, Vol. 34, No. 3, pp. 367-375.

Graham, Willard J. "Income Tax Allocation," **AR**, 1959, Vol. 34, No. 1, pp. 14-27.

Graham, Willard J. "The Effect Of Changing Price Levels Upon The Determination, Reporting, And Interpretation Of Income," **AR**, 1949, Vol. 24, No. 1, pp. 15-26.

Graham, Willard J. "The Price Level Research Project," **AR**, 1954, Vol. 29, No. 2, ppp. 208-214.

Graham, W. J. "Machine Accounting In the Accounting Curriculum," **AR**, 1929, Vol. 4, No. 4, pp. 227-233.

Graichen, Raymond E. "Buying And Selling A Corporate Business," **JOA**, 1959, Vol. 107, No. 4, pp. 45-53.

Graichen, Raymond E. "Pension, Profit-Sharing And Bonus Plans," **JOA**, 1958, Vol. 106, No. 2, pp. 42-48.

Graichen, Raymond E. "Today's Depreciation Deduction," **JOA**, 1957, Vol. 104, No. 6, pp. 27-33.

Gram, Harold A. "The Social Responsibility Of Business," **MA**, 1969, Vol. 50, No. 9, pp. 26-27.

Gramlich, Jeffrey D., Kenneth F. Abramowicz and James E.

Parker. "Refunding Non-Callable Bonds: An Update Of A Tax-Oriented Decision Model In Light Of The Tax Reform Act Of 1986," **JATA**, 1988, Vol. 9, No. 2, pp. 105-110.

Grandell, Axel. "The Reckoning Board And Tally Stick," **AHJ**, 1977, Vol. 4, No. 1, pp. 101-105.

Grande, Vincent B. "Installment Method Of Accounting," **MA**, 1976, Vol. 57, No. 7, pp. 37-38.

Granof, Michael H. and Charles H. Smith. "Accounting And The Evaluation Of Social Programs: A Comment," **AR**, 1974, Vol. 49, No. 4, pp. 822-825.

Granof, Michael H. and Daniel G. Short. "Why Do Companies Reject LIFO?," **JAAF**, 1984, Vol. 7, No. 4, pp. 323-333.

Granof, Michael H. "A Fundamental Flaw Of Debt Limitations For State And Local Governments," **JAPP**, 1984, Vol. 3, No. 4, pp. 293-310.

Granof, Michael H. "Conference Telephone Calls: A Means To Bridge The Academic - 'Real World' Gap," **AR**, 1973, Vol. 48, No. 3, pp. 612-614.

Granof, Michael H. "Financial Evaluation Of Labor Contracts," **MA**, 1973, Vol. 55, No. 1, pp. 38-42.

Granof, Michael H. "Governmental Standard Setting In Perspective," **JOA**, 1979, Vol. 147, No. 3, pp. 56-64.

Granof, Michael H. "Operational Auditing Standards For Audits Of Government Services," **CPAJ**, 1973, Vol. 43, No. 12, pp. 1079-1085.

Granof, Michael H. (Deakin, Edward B. and Michael H. Granof. "Accounting For Retail Land Sales Under The New Accounting Guide," **CPAJ**, 1973, Vol. 43, No. 11, pp. 969-976.)

Granof, Michael H. (Deakin, Edward B. and Michael H. Granof. "Regression Analysis As A Means Of Determining Audit Sample Size," **AR**, 1974, Vol. 49, No. 4, pp. 764-771.)

Granof, Michael H. (Deakin, Edward B. and Michael H. Granof. "Directing Audit Effort Using Regression Analysis," **CPAJ**, 1976, Vol. 46, No. 2, pp. 29-33.)

Granof, Michael H. (Deakin, Edward B., III, Michael H. Granof and Charles H. Smith. "Educational Objectives For An Accounting Program," **AR**, 1974, Vol. 49, No. 3, pp. 584-589.)

Granof, Michael H. (Deakin, Edward B. and Michael H. Granof. "Regression Analysis As A Means Of Determining Audit Sample Size: A Reply," **AR**, 1976, Vol. 51, No. 2, pp. 402-404.)

Grant, Edward B. and Raymond C. Witt. "A Look At Leveraged Leases Under FAS No. 13," **MA**, 1979, Vol. 60, No. 8, pp. 49-52.

Grant, Edward B. "Market Implications Of Differential Amounts Of Interim Information," **JAR**, 1980, Vol. 18, No. 1, pp. 255-268.

Grant, Keith E. "Accounting For Deferred Income Tax Debits," **MA**, 1972, Vol. 53, No. 8, pp. 45-47.

Grau, Francis C. "Accounting For Real Estate Joint Ventures," **MA**, 1975, Vol. 57, No. 6, pp. 47-50.

Graul, Paul R. and Kenneth W. Lemke. "On The Economic Substance Of Deferred Taxes," **ABACUS**, 1976, Vol. 12, No. 1, pp. 14-33.

Graul, Paul R. (Abdel-khalik, A. Rashad, Paul R. Graul and James D. Newton. "Reporting Uncertainty And Assessment Of Risk: Replication And Extension In A Canadian Setting," **JAR**, 1986, Vol. 24, No. 2, pp. 372-382.)

Graul, Paul R. (Lemke, Kenneth W. and Paul R. Graul. "Deferred Taxes - An 'Explicit Cost' Solution To The Discounting Problem," **ABR**, 1980-81, Vol. 11, No. 44, pp. 309-315.)

Graves, O. Finley. "Accounting For Inflation: Henry Sweeney And The German Gold-Mark Model," **AHJ**, 1987, Vol. 14, No. 1, pp. 33-56.

Graves, Thomas J. "Depreciation Problems," **JOA**, 1956, Vol. 102, No. 4, pp. 43-46.

Graves, Thomas J. "Problems In Federal Tax Administration," **JOA**, 1962, Vol. 113, No. 1, pp. 45-52.

Graves, Thomas J. "Reimbursed Expenses," **JOA**, 1958, Vol. 105, No. 6, pp. 27-34.

Graves, Thomas J. "Responsibility Of The Tax Adviser," **JOA**, 1962, Vol. 114, No. 6, pp. 33-38.

Graves, Thomas J. "The Future Of Tax Practice," **JOA**, 1964, Vol. 118, No. 6, pp. 53-57.

Grawoig, Dennis E. "Decision Accounting," **AR**, 1965, Vol. 40, No. 1, pp. 220-222.

Grawoig, Dennis E. (Nichols, Arthur C. and Dennis E. Grawoig. "Accounting Reports With Time As A Variable," **AR**, 1968, Vol. 43, No. 4, pp. 631-639.)

Gray, Charles H. "How To Plan Audit Engagement To Cut Down Man Hours," **JOA**, 1953, Vol. 95, No. 5, pp. 588-593.

Gray, Dahli. "Corporate Preferences For Foreign Currency Accounting Standards," **JAR**, 1984, Vol. 22, No. 2, pp. 760-764.

Gray, Dahli. "Improving Hospital Accounting And Reporting," **MA**, 1982, Vol. 64, No. 1, pp. 49-53.

Gray, Dahli. "Opportunities In Advanced Computer Systems," **CPAJ**, 1982, Vol. 52, No. 12, pp. 37-45.

Gray, Dahli. "SFAS No. 52: Progress Or Problem?," **IJAER**, 1984, Vol. 20, No. 1, pp. 109-119.

Gray, Dahli. (Duangploy, Orapin, Eugene L. Zieha and Dahli Gray. "SFAS No. 52 And The Statement Of Changes In Financial Position: A Survey And Proposal For Change," **IJAER**, 1987, Vol. 22, No. 2, pp. 25-40.)

Gray, Dahli. (Foran, Nancy and Dahli Gray. "The Evolution Of The Unitary Tax Apportionment Method," **AHJ**, 1988, Vol. 15, No. 1, pp. 65-87.)

Gray, Dahli. (Seville, Mary Alice and Dahli Gray. "Using The Standard-Setting Process To Demystify The Concepts Statements: The Case Of SFAS 76," **JAED**, 1986, Vol. 4, No. 2, pp. 107-112.)

Gray, F. Ray. (Friedlob, G. Thomas, F. Ray Gray, Ralph E. Welton and James D. Sloan. "Combining LIFO And FIFO Inventory Disclosure," **CPAJ**, 1987, Vol. 57, No. 6, pp. 48-53.)

Gray, Glen L. (Bedard, Jean, Glen L. Gray and Theodore J. Mock. "Decision Support Systems And Auditing," **AIA**, 1984, Vol. 1, pp. 239-266.)

Gray, Jack and Diane Matson. "Early Warning Systems," **MA**, 1987, Vol. 69, No. 2, pp. 50-55.

Gray, Jack, John Willingham and Kenneth Johnston. "A Business Game For The Introductory Course In Accounting," **AR**, 1963, Vol. 38, No. 2, pp. 336-346.

Gray, Jack. (Bailey, Andrew D., Jr. and Jack Gray. "A Study Of The Importance Of The Planning Horizon On Reports Utilizing Discounted Future Cash Flows," **JAR**, 1968, Vol. 6, No. 1, pp. 98-105.)

Gray, Jack. (Mautz, R. K. and Jack Gray. "Some Thoughts On Research Needs In Accounting," **JOA**, 1970, Vol. 130, No. 3, pp. 54-62.)

Gray, Jack. (Purdy, Charles R., Jay M. Smith and Jack Gray. "The Visibility Of The Auditor's Disclosure Of Deviance From APB Opinion: An Empirical Test," **JAR**, 1969, Vol. 7, Supp., pp. 1-18.)

Gray, Jack. (Simmons, John K. and Jack Gray. "An Investigation Of The Effect Of Differing Accounting Frameworks On The Prediction Of Net Income," **AR**, 1969, Vol. 44, No. 4, pp. 757-776.)

Gray, John Y. "Translating Foreign Currency Transactions In Financial Statements," **CPAJ**, 1977, Vol. 47, No. 6, pp. 31-36.

Gray, Otha L. "Opinions Of Tax Professors On Tax Courses: A Survey Summary," **AR**, 1965, Vol. 40, No. 1, pp. 204-211.

Gray, O. Ronald and William D. Cooper. "A Reconsideration Of Accountant-Client Communication Privilege," **CPAJ**, 1986, Vol. 56, No. 8, pp. 54-59.

Gray, O. Ronald, William D. Cooper and Michael F. Cornick. "A Survey Of Fortune 500 Companies' Interest In Accounting Faculty Residencies," **JAED**, 1984, Vol. 2, No. 2, pp. 177-180.

Gray, Sidney J. (Meek, Gary K. and Sidney J. Gray. "The Value Added Statement: An Innovation For U.S. Companies?," **ACCHOR**, 1988, Vol. 2, No. 2, pp. 73-81.)

Gray, S. J. and C. B. Roberts. "International Accounting Education: A Survey Of University Courses In The UK," **ABR**, 1983-84, Vol. 14, No. 55, pp. 267-270.

Gray, S. J. and Lee H. Radebaugh. "International Segment Disclosures By U.S. and U.K. Multinational Enterprises: A Descriptive Study," **JAR**, 1984, Vol. 22, No. 1, pp. 351-360.

Gray, S. J. and M. C. Wells. "A Further Comment On Asset Values And Income Measurement," **ABR**, 1974-75, Vol. 5, No. 18, pp. 91-95.

Gray, S. J. and M. C. Wells. "Asset Values And Ex Post Income," **ABR**, 1972-73, Vol. 3, No. 11, pp. 163-167.

Gray, S. J. "Accounting Values And Inflation: A Review," **ABACUS**, 1977, Vol. 13, No. 1, pp. 67-77.

Gray, S. J. "International Accounting: A Review Of Academic Research In The United Kingdom," **IJAER**, 1983, Vol. 19, No. 1, pp. 15-42.

Gray, S. J. "Price Changes And Company Profits In The Securities Market," **ABACUS**, 1975, Vol. 11, No. 1, pp. 71-85.

Gray, S. J. "Segment Reporting And The EEC Multinationals," **JAR**, 1978, Vol. 16, No. 2, pp. 242-253.

Gray, S. J. "Statistical Information And Extensions In European Financial Disclosure," **IJAER**, 1978, Vol. 13, No. 2, pp. 27-40.

Gray, S. J. "The Impact Of International Accounting Differences From A Security-Analysis Perspective: Some European Evidence," **JAR**, 1980, Vol. 18, No. 1, pp. 64-76.

Gray, S. J. "Towards A Theory Of Cultural Influence On The Development Of Accounting Systems Internationally," **ABACUS**, 1988, Vol. 24, No. 1, pp. 1-15.

Gray, S. J. (Emmanuel, C. R. and S. J. Gray. "Segmental Disclosures And The Segment Identification Problem," **ABR**, 1977-78, Vol. 8, No. 29, pp. 37-50.)

Gray, S. J. (Emmanuel, C. R. and S. J. Gray. "Segmental Disclosure By Multibusiness Multinational Companies: A Proposal," **ABR**, 1977-78, Vol. 8, No. 31, pp. 169-177.)

Gray, W. R. (Madden, J. T., R. A. Stevenson and W. R. Gray. "The Place Of Accounting In The Commerce Curriculum," **AR**, 1928, Vol. 3, No. 2, pp. 189-207.)

Grayson, John D. "The Controller's Function In Predetermining Profit Through Forecasting," **JOA**, 1950, Vol. 90, No. 3, pp. 216-219.

Greco, Joseph A. "Comments On The Structural Check Of Input Data In A Computer System," **JOA**, 1968, Vol. 125, No. 6, pp. 46-52.

Green, Cynthia B. "The Use And Usefulness Of Governmental Financial Reports: The Perspective Of Citizen-Taxpayer Organizations," **RIGNA**, 1987, Vol. 3, Part B, pp. 189-213.

Green, David and Joel Segall. "The Predictive Power Of First-Quarter Earnings Reports: A Replication," **JAR**, 1966, Vol. 4, Supp., pp. 21-36.

Green, David O. and Clyde P. Stickney. "No Price Level Adjusted Statements, Please (Pleas)," **CPAJ**, 1974, Vol. 44, No. 1, pp. 25-33.

Green, David O. "ERDIAAC," **JAR**, 1970, Vol. 8, No. 2, pp. 274-281.

Green, David, Jr. and George H. Sorter. "Accounting For Obsolescence - A Proposal," **AR**, 1959, Vol. 34, No. 3, pp. 433-441.

Green, David, Jr. "A Reconsideration Of The Course

Objectives Of Elementary Accounting," **AR**, 1950, Vol. 25, No. 3, pp. 322-326.

Green, David, Jr. "A Schema For Interest Formulae," **AR**, 1963, Vol. 38, No. 4, pp. 833-834.

Green, David, Jr. "Evaluating Student Competence," **AR**, 1952, Vol. 27, No. 4, pp. 544-551.

Green, David, Jr. "Evaluating The Accounting Literature," **AR**, 1966, Vol. 41, No. 1, pp. 52-64.

Green, David, Jr. "Financial Statement Working Papers," **JOA**, 1961, Vol. 112, No. 4, pp. 49-56.

Green, David, Jr. "The Direct Method Of Preparing Consolidated Statements," **AR**, 1961, Vol. 36, No. 1, pp. 129-137.

Green, David, Jr. "Towards A Theory Of Interim Reports," **JAR**, 1964, Vol. 2, No. 1, pp. 35-49.

Green, Donald. "To Predict Failure," **MA**, 1978, Vol. 60, No. 1, pp. 39-41.

Green, Gary I. and Earl A. Wilcox. "Find The Right Software Through Specifications," **MA**, 1982, Vol. 63, No. 7, pp. 43-50.

Green, Jeffrey D. "Systems Documentation, Internal Control, And The Auditor's Responsibilities," **CPAJ**, 1974, Vol. 44, No. 7, pp. 25-28.

Green, John E. "Cost Forecasting And Control In The 1980's, From The Perspective Of A Defence Customer," **JCA**, 1984, Vol. 1, No. 1, pp. 33-58.

Green, John E. "Developing Capitalization Rates," **MA**, 1972, Vol. 54, No. 3, pp. 33-36.

Green, Paul M. "Accounting In the Stabilization Program," **AR**, 1945, Vol. 20, No. 2, pp. 148-155.

Green, Paul M. "Preparing Accounting Data In Price Appeal Cases," **JOA**, 1951, Vol. 92, No. 5, pp. 549-551.

Green, Paul M. "Preserving The Benefits Of the Holding Company," **AR**, 1933, Vol. 8, No. 1, pp. 51-57.

Green, Paul M. "Some Problems In Government Accounting," **AR**, 1936, Vol. 11, No. 2, pp. 141-148.

Green, Richard C. (Owen, George A. and Richard C. Green. "Training Staff Accountants To Write More Effective Reports," **JOA**, 1952, Vol. 93, No. 5, pp. 589-595.)

Green, Robert. (Kadin, Morris B. and Robert Green. "Computerization In The Medium-Sized CPA Firm," **JOA**, 1971, Vol. 131, No. 2, pp. 44-49.)

Green, Sharon L. (Lewis, Barry L., James M. Patton and Sharon L. Green. "The Effects Of Information Choice And Information Use On Analysts' Predictions Of Municipal Bond Rating Changes," **AR**, 1988, Vol. 63, No. 2, pp. 270-282.)

Green, William H. "Developing Key Personnel," **MA**, 1972, Vol. 53, No. 12, pp. 23-24.

Greenball, Melvin N. "A Statistical Model Of Earnings Estimation," **JAR**, 1971, Vol. 9, Supp., pp. 172-190.

Greenball, Melvin N. "Evaluation Of The Usefulness To Investors Of Different Accounting Estimators Of Earnings: A Simulation Approach," **JAR**, 1968, Vol. 6, Supp., pp. 27-49.

Greenball, Melvin N. "The Accuracy Of Different Methods Of Accounting For Earnings - A Simulation Approach," **JAR**, 1968, Vol. 6, No. 1, pp. 114-129.

Greenball, Melvin N. (Chandra, Gyan and Melvin N. Greenball. "Management Reluctance To Disclosure: An Empirical Study," **ABACUS**, 1977, Vol. 13, No. 2, pp. 141-154.)

Greenball, M. N. "Appraising Alternative Methods Of Accounting For Accelerated Tax Depreciation: A Relative-Accuracy Approach," **JAR**, 1969, Vol. 7.No. 2.pp. 262-289.

Greenball, M. N. "Estimating An Entity's Capital Investment, Earnings And Rate-Of-Return: An Econometric Approach," **ABACUS**, 1973, Vol. 9, No. 1, pp. 44-61.

Greenball, M. N. "The Predictive-Ability Criterion: Its Relevance In Evaluating Accounting Data," **ABACUS**, 1971, Vol. 7, No. 1, pp. 1-7.

Greenberger, Robert M. (Nadel, Eugene and Robert M. Greenberger. "Condos Or Co-Ops For Good 'Shelter'," **CPAJ**, 1981, Vol. 51, No. 11, pp. 9-19.)

Greenberg, Ira S. (Golen, Steven, James Worthington, Greg Thibadoux, William D. Cooper and Ira S. Greenberg. "Flowcharts & Graphics," **CPAJ**, 1986, Vol. 56, No. 3, pp. 12-23.)

Greenberg, Ira S. (Thibadoux, Greg M., Nicholas Apostolou and Ira S. Greenberg. "The Development Of Not-For-Profit Hospital Cost Models," **JCA**, 1988, Vol. 5, No. 1, pp. 35-48.)

Greenberg, Lennard J. (Werner, Robert H. and Lennard J. Greenberg. "Auditing And Reporting For CETA Programs," **CPAJ**, 1978, Vol. 48, No. 6, pp. 27-28.)

Greenberg, Lennard J. (Werner, Robert H. and Lennard J. Greenberg. "Audits Of CETA Programs," **CPAJ**, 1978, Vol. 48, No. 4, pp. 13-20.)

Greenberg, Ralph. "Adaptive Estimation: An Alternative To The Traditional Stationarity Assumption," **JAR**, 1984, Vol. 22, No. 2, pp. 719-730.

Greenberg, Robert R. "Estimating Cost Functions With Autocorrelated Errors: A Time Series Approach," **JCA**, 1988, Vol. 5, No. 1, pp. 19-33.

Greenberg, Robert R., Glenn L. Johnson and K. Ramesh. "Earnings Versus Cash Flow As A Predictor Of Future Cash Flow Measures," **JAAF**, 1986, Vol. 1 (New Series). No. 4, pp. 266-277.

Greenberg, R. (Manes, R. P., K. C. W. Chen and R. Greenberg. "Economies Of Scope And Cost-Volume-Profit Analysis For The Multiproduct Firm," **JAL**, 1985, Vol. 4, pp. 77-112.)

Greene, Alan K. (Mandel, George. Alan K. Greene and Stuart A. Simel. "Brookhaven Internal Revenue Service Center," **CPAJ**, 1976, Vol. 46, No. 3, pp. 21-24.)

Greene, Edward D. "Changing From Declining Balance To Straight-Line Depreciation," **AR**, 1963, Vol. 38, No. 2, pp. 355-362.

Greene, Howard F. "Cost Problems Encountered In CPA Examinations," **AR**, 1946, Vol. 21, No. 2, pp. 148-153.

Greene, Howard F. "Technical Preparation For The C.P.A. Examination," **AR**, 1935, Vol. 10, No. 4, pp. 401-405.

Greene, Robert E. "Obtaining Bank Credit," **MA**, 1976, Vol. 57, No. 10, pp. 37-39.

Greenhut, Kenneth. "The Accumulated Earnings Tax - A Call For Repeal," **CPAJ**, 1977, Vol. 47, No. 8, pp. 23-26.

Greensted, C. S. (Briston, R. J. and C. S. Greensted. "Shareholder Behaviour In The New Issues Market: A Final Progress Report," **ABR**, 1975-76, Vol. 6, No. 22, pp. 125-134.)

Greenstein, Mary and Richard L. Pannell. "A Vital Indexing Tool," **CPAJ**, 1978, Vol. 48, No. 9, pp. 26-31.

Greenstein, Mary. (Pannell, Richard L. and Mary Greenstein. "How To Find Answers To Technical Questions," **CPAJ**, 1982, Vol. 52, No. 3, pp. 13-25.)

Greenwald, Bruce and Gary Oberlander. "IRS Audits Of EDP Systems," **MA**, 1975, Vol. 56, No. 10, pp. 13-15.

Greenwald, Bruce M. and Carl D. Harnick. "Corporate Tax Review: The Auditor's Approach," **JOA**, 1974, Vol. 137, No. 5, pp. 63-70.

Greenwald, William I. "Amortization Schedules For Motion Pictures," **AR**, 1952, Vol. 27, No. 3, pp. 339-343.

Greer, Howard C. "A Council On Accounting Research," **AR**, 1932, Vol. 7, No. 3, pp. 176-181.

Greer, Howard C. "Anyone For Widgets?," **JOA**, 1966, Vol. 121, No. 4, pp. 41-49.

Greer, Howard C. "Application Of Accounting Rules And Standards To Financial Statements," **AR**, 1938, Vol. 13, No. 4, pp. 333-345.

Greer, Howard C. "Benchmarks And Beacons," **AR**, 1956, Vol. 31, No. 1, pp. 3-14.

Greer, Howard C. "Comments On The Statement Of Accounting Principles: A Reply," **AR**, 1937, Vol. 12, No. 1, pp. 79-82.

Greer, Howard C. "Depreciation And The Price Level," **AR**, 1948, Vol. 23, No. 2, pp. 129-131.

Greer, Howard C. "How To Succeed In Confusing People Without Really Trying," **JOA**, 1963, Vol. 115, No. 3, pp. 61-65.

Greer, Howard C. "Managerial Accounting - Twenty Years From Now," **AR**, 1954, Vol. 29, No. 2, pp. 175-185.

Greer, Howard C. "One Eight-Day Week Would Improve The Calendar," **JOA**, 1971, Vol. 132, No. 6, pp. 45-51.

Greer, Howard C. "Restoration Of Fixed Asset Values To The Balance Sheet," **AR**, 1947, Vol. 22, No. 2, pp. 203-206.

Greer, Howard C. "Structural Fundamentals Of Financial Statements," **AR**, 1943, Vol. 18, No. 3, pp. 193-204.

Greer, Howard C. "The Chop Suey Caper," **JOA**, 1968, Vol. 125, No. 4, pp. 27-34.

Greer, Howard C. "The Corporation Stockholder - Accounting's Forgotten Man," **AR**, 1964, Vol. 39, No. 1, pp. 22-31.

Greer, Howard C. "The Present Status Of Accounting Teaching," **AR**, 1933, Vol. 8, No. 1, pp. 62-68.

Greer, Howard C. "The Technique Of Distribution Cost Accounting," **AR**, 1931, Vol. 6, No. 2, pp. 136-139.

Greer, Howard C. "Treatment Of Income Taxes In Corporation Income Statements," **AR**, 1945, Vol. 20, No. 1, pp. 96-101.

Greer, Howard C. "What Are Accepted Principles Of Accounting?," **AR**, 1938, Vol. 13, No. 1, pp. 25-30.

Greer, Howard C. "Where Teaching Lags Behind Practice," **AR**, 1928, Vol. 3, No. 3, pp. 289-296.

Greer, Howard C. (Wilcox, Ed. B. and Howard C. Greer. "The Case Against Price-Level Adjustments In Income Determination," **JOA**, 1950, Vol. 90, No. 6, pp. 492-503.)

Greer, Willis R., Jr. and Howard Rockness. "Management Decision Support Systems For A Medical Group Practice," **JIS**, 1987, Vol. 1, No. 2, pp. 65-79.

Greer, Willis R., Jr. and Leonard E. Morrissey, Jr. "Accounting Rule-Making In A World Of Efficient Markets," **JAAF**, 1978, Vol. 2, No. 1, pp. 49-57.

Greer, Willis R., Jr. and Shu S. Liao. "Weapon Pricing Models For Defense Acquisition Policy," **JAPP**, 1987, Vol. 6, No. 4, pp. 271-284.

Greer, Willis R., Jr. and Ted D. Skekel. "Theory Versus Practice In Risk Analysis: A Reply," **AR**, 1975, Vol. 50, No. 4, pp. 839-843.

Greer, Willis R., Jr. "Better Motivation For Time-Constrained Sequential Production Processes," **MA**, 1972, Vol. 54, No. 2, pp. 15-19.

Greer, Willis R., Jr. "Capital Budgeting Analysis With The Timing Of Events Uncertain," **AR**, 1970, Vol. 45, No. 1, pp. 103-114.

Greer, Willis R., Jr. "Discounted Cash Flows, Price Level Adjustments And Expectations: A Comment," **AR**, 1972, Vol. 47, No. 3, pp. 587-588.

Greer, Willis R., Jr. "Inflation And Asset Performance Measurement," **MA**, 1976, Vol. 57, No. 7, pp. 49-52.

Greer, Willis R., Jr. "Sales Compensation: Conflict And Harmony," **MA**, 1974, Vol. 55, No. 9, pp. 37-41.

Greer, Willis R., Jr. "Theory Versus Practice In Risk Analysis: An Empirical Study," **AR**, 1974, Vol. 49, No. 3, pp. 496-505.

Greer, Willis R., Jr. "Theory Versus Practice In Risk Analysis: An Empirical Study: A Reply," **AR**, 1976, Vol. 51, No. 3, p. 663.

Greer, Willis R., Jr. "Where Have All The Deep Discounts Gone?," **JAPP**, 1983, Vol. 2, No. 2, pp. 133-140.

Gregorcich, Martin J. (Fischer, Paul M. and Martin J.

Gregorich. "Calculating Earnings Per Share," **JOA**, 1973, Vol. 135, No. 5, pp. 61-71.)

Gregory, Alan. "Divisional Performance Measurement With Divisions As Lessees Of Head Office Assets," **ABR**, 1986-87, Vol. 17, No. 67, pp. 241-246.

Gregory, Arthur J. "Operational Audit Of The Engineering Function," **MA**, 1973, Vol. 55, No. 3, pp. 43-47.

Gregory, H. E. "The Current Ratio A Function Of Two Variables," **AR**, 1930, Vol. 5, No. 3, pp. 254-256.

Gregory, John C. "Capital Expenditure Evaluation By Direct Discounting," **AR**, 1962, Vol. 37, No. 2, pp. 308-314.

Gregory, Robert H. and Edward L. Wallace. "Work Sheet For Funds Statement Problems," **AR**, 1953, Vol. 28, No. 1, pp. 88-97.

Gregory, Robert H. "A Critique Of Accounting Trends And Techniques - 1951 Edition," **AR**, 1952, Vol. 27, No. 3, pp. 300-312.

Gregory, Robert H. "Computers And Accounting Systems: A Bibliography," **AR**, 1956, Vol. 31, No. 2, pp. 278-285.

Gregory, Wm. R. "Unaudited, But OK?," **JOA**, 1978, Vol. 145, No. 2, pp. 61-65.

Greidinger, B. Bernard. "When Are Independent Public Accountants Not In Fact Independent?," **AR**, 1951, Vol. 26, No. 1, pp. 49-60.

Greiner, Larry E. and Alan L. Scharff. "The Challenge Of Cultivating Accounting Firm Executives," **JOA**, 1980, Vol. 150, No. 3, pp. 57-63.

Greipel, Rudolph C. "Accounting For Nonmonetary Transactions - A Review Of APB Statement No. 29," **CPAJ**, 1974, Vol. 44, No. 1, pp. 34-39.

Greipel, Rudolph C. "Review Of APB Opinion No. 20 - 'Accounting Changes'," **CPAJ**, 1972, Vol. 42, No. 1, pp. 17-25.

Grenside, J. P. "Accountants' Reports On Profit Forecasts In The U.K.," **JOA**, 1970, Vol. 129, No. 5, pp. 47-53.

Gressis, Nicolas. (Holzmann, Oscar J. and Nicolas Gressis. "Covariability Of Segment Earnings And Multisegment Company Returns: A Comment," **AR**, 1974, Vol. 49, No. 1, pp. 132-139.)

Gress, Edward J. "Application Of Replacement Cost Accounting: A Case Study," **ABACUS**, 1972, Vol. 8, No. 1, pp. 3-12.

Grey, Alfred. "A 'One Economy' Concept Of Financial Accounting And Reporting," **AR**, 1952, Vol. 27, No. 1, pp. 119-123.

Griffin, Carleton H. "Changes In Accounting Method," **JOA**, 1959, Vol. 108, No. 6, pp. 43-50.

Griffin, Charles H. and Thomas H. Williams. "A Comparative Analysis Of Accounting And Mathematics," **AR**, 1962, Vol. 37, No. 3, pp. 410-414.

Griffin, Charles H. and Thomas H. Williams. "Simulation In Business Education," **AR**, 1964, Vol. 39, No. 1, pp. 160-163.

Griffin, Charles H. and Thomas H. Williams. "Measuring Adequate Disclosure," **JOA**, 1960, Vol. 109, No. 4, pp. 43-48.

Griffin, Charles H. "Co-Operative Education For Business," **AR**, 1958, Vol. 33, No. 4, pp. 664-669.

Griffin, Charles H. "Pedagogical Implications Of The Materiality Concept," **AR**, 1959, Vol. 34, No. 2, pp. 298-300.

Griffin, Charles H. "Petroleum Products Costing," **JOA**, 1958, Vol. 105, No. 3, pp. 46-52.

Griffin, Charles H. "Use Of Yield Data To Cut Purchase Costs," **JOA**, 1958, Vol. 106, No. 3, pp. 51-55.

Griffin, Charles H. (Williams, Thomas H. and Charles H. Griffin. "MAS And The Expanded Meaning Of Accounting Education," **IJAER**, 1973, Vol. 8, No. 2, pp. 33-43.)

Griffin, Charles H. (Williams, Thomas H. and Charles H. Griffin. "Accountancy And Professional Development," **AR**, 1961, Vol. 36, No. 4, pp. 637-641.)

Griffin, Charles H. (Williams, Thomas H. and Charles H. Griffin. "On The Nature Of Empirical Verification In Accounting," **ABACUS**, 1969, Vol. 5, No. 2, pp. 143-180.)

Griffin, Charles H. (Williams, Thomas H. and Charles H. Griffin. "Matrix Theory And Cost Allocation," **AR**, 1964, Vol. 39, No. 3, pp. 671-678.)

Griffin, Charles H. (Williams, Thomas H. and Charles H. Griffin. "Income Definition And Measurement: A Structural Approach," **AR**, 1967, Vol. 42, No. 4, pp. 642-649.)

Griffin, C. E. "The Economic Significance Of Recent Price Legislation," **AR**, 1939, Vol. 14, No. 1, pp. 42-47.

Griffin, C. H. and J. W. Deskins. "Development And Application Of Accounting Theory," **ABR**, 1971-72, Vol. 2, No. 8, pp. 308-315.

Griffin, Fred B. (Anderson, Hershel M. and Fred B. Griffin. "The Accounting Curriculum And Postgraduate Achievement," **AR**, 1963, Vol. 38, No. 4, pp. 813-818.)

Griffin, Paul A. "Foreign Exchange Gains And Losses: Impact On Reported Earnings," **ABACUS**, 1982, Vol. 18, No. 1, pp. 50-69.

Griffin, Paul A. "Management's Preferences For FASB Statement No. 52: Predictive Ability Results," **ABACUS**, 1983, Vol. 19, No. 2, pp. 130-138.

Griffin, Paul A. "The Association Between Relative Risk And Risk Estimates Derived From Quarterly Earnings And Dividends," **AR**, 1976, Vol. 51, No. 3, pp. 499-515.

Griffin, Paul A. "The Time-Series Behavior Of Quarterly Earnings: Preliminary Evidence," **JAR**, 1977, Vol. 15, No. 1, pp. 71-83

Griffin, Paul A. (Beaver, William H., Andrew A. Christie and Paul A. Griffin. "The Information Content Of SEC Accounting Series Release No. 190," **JAEC**, 1980, Vol. 2, No. 2, pp. 127-157.)

Griffin, Paul A. (Beaver, William H., Paul A. Griffin and Wayne R. Landsman. "Testing For Incremental Information Content In The Presence Of Collinearity: A Comment," **JAEC**, 1984, Vol. 6, No. 3, pp. 219-223.)

Griffin, Paul A. (Beaver, William H., Paul A. Griffin and Wayne R. Landsman. "The Incremental Information Content Of Replacement Cost Earnings," **JAEC**, 1982, Vol. 4, No. 1, pp. 15-39.)

Griffin, Paul A. (Brown, Lawrence D., Paul A. Griffin, Robert L. Hagerman and Mark E. Zmijewski. "An Evaluation Of Alternative Proxies For The Market's Assessment Of Unexpected Earnings," **JAEC**, 1987, Vol. 9, No. 2, pp. 159-193.)

Griffin, Paul A. (Brown, Lawrence D., Paul A. Griffin, Robert L. Hagerman, Paul A. Griffin and Mark E. Zmijewski. "Security Analyst Superiority Relative To Univariate Time-Series Models In Forecasting Quarterly Earnings," **JAEC**, 1987, Vol. 9, No. 1, pp. 61-87.)

Griffin, Richard B. and Sarah C. Dawkins. "Current Trends In Intermediate Accounting Course Content," **IAE**, 1986, Vol. 1, No. 2, pp. 238-248.

Griffin, V. Earl. "Systems Work Below The Corporate Level," **MA**, 1967, Vol. 48, No. 8, pp. 14-20.

Griffith, Donald K. "Weaknesses Of Index-Number Accounting," **AR**, 1937, Vol. 12, No. 2, pp. 123-132.

Griffith, James B. "How Accountants Can Learn About Business Machines," **JOA**, 1951, Vol. 92, No. 1, pp. 72-81.

Grimes, J. A. "The Income Tax - Depletion And Depreciation," **AR**, 1928, Vol. 3, No. 2, pp. 161-176.

Grimlund, Richard A. and Mary S. Schroeder. "On The Current Use Of The Stringer Method Of MUS: Some New Directions," **AJPT**, 1988, Vol. 8, No. 1, pp. 53-62.

Grimlund, Richard A. and William L. Felix, Jr. "Simulation Evidence And Analysis Of Alternative Methods Of Evaluating Dollar-Unit Samples," **AR**, 1987, Vol. 62, No. 3, pp. 455-479.

Grimlund, Richard A. "A Proposal For Implementing The FASB's 'Reasonably Possible' Disclosure Provision For Product Warranty Liabilities," **JAR**, 1985, Vol. 23, No. 2, pp. 575-594.

Grimlund, Richard A. "An Integration Of Internal Control System And Account Balance Evidence," **JAR**, 1982, Vol. 20, No. 2, Part I, pp. 316-342.

Grimlund, Richard A. "Sample Size Planning For The Moment Method Of MUS: Incorporating Audit Judgments," **AJPT**, 1988, Vol. 7, No. 2, pp. 77-104.

Grimlund, Richard A. (Dworin, Lowell and Richard A. Grimlund. "Dollar-Unit Sampling: A Comparison Of The Quasi-Bayesian And Moment Bounds," **AR**, 1986, Vol. 61, No. 1, pp. 36-57.)

Grimlund, Richard A. (Dworin, Lowell and Richard A. Grimlund. "Dollar Unit Sampling For Accounts Receivable And Inventory," **AR**, 1984, Vol. 59, No. 2, pp. 218-241.)

Grimlund, Richard A. (Felix, William L., Jr. and Richard A. Grimlund. "A Sampling Model For Audit Test Of Composite Accounts," **JAR**, 1977, Vol. 15, No. 1, pp. 23-41.)

Grimlund, Richard. (Petersen, Russell J. and Richard Grimlund. "CADRAS: Computer Assisted Data Recording And Analysis," **IAE**, 1983, No. 1, pp. 146-151.)

Grimstad, Clayton R. "New Schools Of Accountancy - Necessary," **CPAJ**, 1976, Vol. 46, No. 10, pp. 21-24.

Grimstad, Clayton R. "Thoughts On Continuing Education In Accounting," **AR**, 1962, Vol. 37, No. 3, pp. 506-509.

Grimstad, Clayton. (Abs, George, Clayton Grimstad, Robert Hay, W. Asquith Howe, William LaPlace, Francis J. McGurr and William Serrano. "Historical Dates In Accounting," **AR**, 1954, Vol. 29, No. 3, pp. 486-493.)

Grinaker, Robert L. "The Accountant's Responsibility In Expressing An Opinion," **JOA**, 1960, Vol. 110, No. 5, pp. 63-69.

Grindle, Howard, Charles W. Caldwell and Caroline D. Strobel. "RDLP: A Tax Shelter That Provides Benefits For Everyone," **MA**, 1985, Vol. 67, No. 1, pp. 44-47.

Griner, E. H. and A. W. Stark. "Cash Recovery Rates, Accounting Rates Of Return, And The Estimation Of Economic Performance," **JAPP**, 1988, Vol. 7, No. 4, pp. 293-311.

Grinnell, D. Jacque and Corine T. Norgaard. "Reporting Changes In Accounting Principles - Time For A Change?," **JOA**, 1979, Vol. 148, No. 6, pp. 64-72.

Grinnell, D. Jacque and Corine T. Norgaard. "Reporting Changes In Financial Position," **MA**, 1972, Vol. 54, No. 3, pp. 15-22.

Grinnell, D. Jacque and Richard F. Kochanek. "The New Accounting Standards For Leases," **CPAJ**, 1977, Vol. 47, No. 10, pp. 15-22.

Grinnell, D. Jacque and Richard F. Kochanek. "LIFO Disclosures: Requirements And Restrictions," **CPAJ**, 1976, Vol. 46, No. 11, pp. 29-32.

Grinnell, D. Jacque. "Activity Levels And The Disposition Of Volume Variances," **MA**, 1975, Vol. 57, No. 2, pp. 29-32.

Grinnell, D. Jacque. "Product Mix Decisions: Direct Costing Vs. Absorption Costing," **MA**, 1976, Vol. 58, No. 2, pp. 36-42.

Grinnell, D. Jacque. "Using Linear Programming To Compare Direct And Absorption Costing," **AR**, 1977, Vol. 52, No. 2, pp. 485-491.

Grinnell, D. Jacque. (Cats-Baril, William L., James F. Gatti and D. Jacque Grinnell. "Joint Product Costing In The Semiconductor Industry," **MA**, 1986, Vol. 67, No. 8, pp. 28-38.)

Grinnell, D. Jacque. (Cats-Baril, William, James F. Gatti and D. Jacque Grinnell. "Transfer Pricing Policy In A Dynamic Market," **MA**, 1988, Vol. 69, No. 8, pp. 30-33.)

Grinyer, John R. and Iain W. Symon. "Maintenance Of Capital Intact: An Unnecessary Abstraction?," **ABR**, 1979-80, Vol.

10, No. 40, pp. 403-414.

Grinyer, John R. and Richard W. Lewis. "Valuation And Meaningful Accounts," **ABR**, 1971-72, Vol. 2, No. 8, pp. 275-283.

Grinyer, John R. "A New Approach To Depreciation," **ABACUS**, 1987, Vol. 23, No. 1, pp. 43-54.

Grinyer, John R. "An Alternative To Maximisation Of Shareholders' Wealth," **ABR**, 1985-86, Vol. 16, No. 64, pp. 319-326.

Grinyer, John R. "Earned Economic Income - A Theory For Matching," **ABACUS**, 1985, Vol. 21, No. 2, pp. 130-148.

Grinyer, John R. "Financial Planning Models Incorporating Dividend Growth Elements," **ABR**, 1972-73, Vol. 3, No. 10, pp. 145-155.

Grinyer, John R. "Holding Gains On Long-Term Liabilities - An Alternative Analysis," **ABR**, 1977-78, Vol. 8, No. 30, pp. 130-148.

Grinyer, John R. "Holding Gains And Long-Term Liabilities: A Rigorous Analysis," **ABR**, 1974-75, Vol. 5, No. 20, pp. 292-297.

Grinyer, John R. "Revaluation Of Fixed Assets In Accruals Accounting," **ABR**, 1987-88, Vol. 18, No. 69, pp. 17-24.

Grinyer, John R. "The Lease Evaluation Solution: A Comment And Alternative," **ABR**, 1974-75, Vol. 5, No. 19, pp. 231-234.

Grinyer, John R. "The Lease Evaluation Solution: Continued," **ABR**, 1976-77, Vol. 7, No. 27, pp. 211-214.

Grinyer, Peter H. and Jeff Wooller. "An Overview Of A Decade Of Corporate Modelling In The UK," **ABR**, 1980-81, Vol. 11, No. 41, pp. 41-50.

Griswold, Erwin N. "Lawyers, Accountants, And Taxes," **JOA**, 1955, Vol. 99, No. 4, pp. 33-41.

Griswold, Erwin N. "The Tax Practice Problem I," **JOA**, 1955, Vol. 100, No. 6, pp. 29-35.

Griswold, Henry J. and Walter W. King. "How To Make Salary Raises Under WSB Regulations," **JOA**, 1951, Vol. 92, No. 2, pp. 180-183.

Gritta, Richard D. "Capitalizing Net Lease Rentals: A Comment," **MA**, 1974, Vol. 56, No. 5, pp. 37-39.

Grobstein, Michael and Paul W. Craig. "A Risk Analysis Approach To Auditing," **AJPT**, 1983-84, Vol. 3, No. 2, pp. 1-16.

Groebner, David F. (Merz, Mike and David F. Groebner. "Ethics And The CPA Industry," **MA**, 1982, Vol. 64, No. 3, pp. 44-48.)

Groff, James E. (Dorr, Patrick, Martha Eining and James E. Groff. "Developing An Accounting Expert System Decision Aid For Classroom Use," **IAE**, 1988, Vol. 3, No. 1, pp. 27-41.)

Groff, James E. (Durkee, David A., James E. Groff and James R. Boatsman. "The Effect Of Costly Vs. Costless Pension Disclosure On Common Share Prices: The Case Of SFAS 36," **JAL**, 1988, Vol. 7, pp. 180-196.)

Groff, James E. (Wright, Charlotte J. and James E. Groff. "Uses Of Indexes And Data Bases For Information Release Analysis," **AR**, 1986, Vol. 61, No. 1, pp. 91-100.)

Grohe, Ronald E. (Weiss, Steven P. and Ronald E. Grohe. "Complying With The Inventory Capitalization Rules," **MA**, 1988, Vol. 70, No. 2, pp. 44-49.)

Grojer, J. E. and A. Stark. "Social Accounting: A Swedish Attempt," **AOS**, 1977, Vol. 2, No. 4, pp. 349-381.

Grollman, William K. and Robert W. Colby. "Internal Control For Small Business," **JOA**, 1978, Vol. 146, No. 6, pp. 64-67.

Grollman, William K. "Independence Of Auditors And Applicability To International Engagements," **CPAJ**, 1973, Vol. 43, No. 4, pp. 286-291.

Grollman, William K. "Professional Development For Smaller Firms," **CPAJ**, 1976, Vol. 46, No. 5, pp. 29-33.

Gronlund, A. (Jonsson, S. and A. Gronlund. "Life With A Sub-Contractor: New Technology And Management Accounting," **AOS**, 1988, Vol. 13, No. 5, pp. 513-532.)

Groomer, S. Michael. "An Experiment In Computer-Assisted Instruction For Introductory Accounting," **AR**, 1981, Vol. 56, No. 4, pp. 934-941.

Groomer, S. Michael. (Burns, Jane O. and S. Michael Groomer. "An Analysis Of Tax Court Decisions That Assess The Profit Motive Of Farming-Oriented Operations," **JATA**, 1983, Vol. 5, No. 1, pp. 23-39.)

Groomer, S. Michael. (Nichols, Donald R. and S. Michael Groomer. "A Study Of The Relative Accuracy Of Executives' Estimates Of Earnings," **ABACUS**, 1979, Vol. 15, No. 2, pp. 113-127.)

Gross, Harry. "Make Or Buy Decisions In Growing Firms," **AR**, 1966, Vol. 41, No. 4, pp. 745-753.

Gross, Malvern J., Jr. "State Compliance Reporting For Non-profit Organizations," **CPAJ**, 1975, Vol. 45, No. 4, pp. 33-38.

Gross, Malvern J. "An Accountant Looks At The 'Total Return' Approach For Endowment Funds," **CPAJ**, 1973, Vol. 43, No. 11, pp. 977-984.

Gross, Malvern J. "Uniform Financial Reporting By Philanthropic Organizations," **CPAJ**, 1975, Vol. 45, No. 6, pp. 25-30.

Gross, Malvern J., Jr. "Nonprofit Accounting: The Continuing Revolution," **JOA**, 1977, Vol. 143, No. 6, pp. 66-76.

Gross, Malvern J., Jr. "Report On Nonprofit Accounting," **JOA**, 1975, Vol. 139, No. 6, pp. 55-59.

Grossfield, Abraham. "Brokerage Firm Solves Management Problems With Advanced Computer," **MA**, 1970, Vol. 52, No. 6, pp. 34-36.

Grossman, Steven D. and Robert H. Strawser. "Accounting And Behavioral Concepts: A Classroom Approach," **AR**, 1978, Vol. 53, No. 2, pp. 495-500.

Grossman, Steven D. (Benjamin, James J. and Steven D.

Grossman. "Foreign Currency Translation: An Update," **CPAJ**, 1981, Vol. 51, No. 2, pp. 48-52.)

Grossman, Steven D. (Benjamin, James J., Steven D. Grossman and Casper E. Wiggins. "The Impact Of Foreign Currency Translation On Reporting During The Phase-In Of SFAS No. 52," **JAAF**, 1986, Vol. 1 (New Series), No. 3, pp. 177-184.)

Grossman, Steven D. (Cooper, Kerry, Steven M. Flory, Steven D. Grossman and John C. Groth. "Reserve Recognition Accounting: A Proposed Disclosure Framework," **JOA**, 1979, Vol. 148, No. 3, pp. 82-91.)

Grossman, Steven D. (Cooper, Kerry, Steven M. Flory and Steven D. Grossman. "New Ballgame For Oil And Gas Accounting," **CPAJ**, 1979, Vol. 49, No. 1, pp. 11-18.)

Grossman, Steven D. (Fetters, Michael L. and Steven D. Grossman. "Accounting For The Receivable In A Lease Transaction: A Dilemma," **AR**, 1974, Vol. 49, No. 4, pp. 851-852.)

Grossman, Steven D. (Flory, Steven M. and Steven D. Grossman. "New Oil And Gas Accounting Requirements," **CPAJ**, 1978, Vol. 48, No. 5, pp. 39-43.)

Grossman, Steven D. (Francia, Arthur J., Steven D. Grossman and Robert H. Strawser. "The Attitudes Of Management Accountants," **MA**, 1978, Vol. 60, No. 5, pp. 35-40.)

Grossman, Steven D. (Jensen, Herbert L. and Steven D. Grossman. "Accounting Applications Of Covariance Analysis," **ABR**, 1978-79, Vol. 9, No. 36, pp. 300-308.)

Grossman, Steven D., Alan G. Mayper and Robert B. Welker. "Oil And Gas Disclosures - The FASB Reacts," **CPAJ**, 1983, Vol. 53, No. 5, pp. 24-29.

Grossman, Steven D., Stanley H. Kratchman and Robert B. Welker. "Comment: The Effect Of Replacement Cost Disclosures On Security Prices," **JAAF**, 1981, Vol. 4, No. 2, pp. 136-143.

Grossman, Steven. (Giroux, Gary, Steven Grossman and Stanley Kratchman. "What FAS No. 33 Does To Bank Financial Statements," **MA**, 1981, Vol. 62, No. 7, pp. 42-47.)

Grossman, Theodore and Shailendra Palvia. "The Design And Implementation Of A Multidimensional Retail Merchandising Information System," **JIS**, 1988, Vol. 3, No. 1, pp. 119-131.

Groth, John C. (Cooper, Kerry, Steven M. Flory, Steven D. Grossman and John C. Groth. "Reserve Recognition Accounting: A Proposed Disclosure Framework," **JOA**, 1979, Vol. 148, No. 3, pp. 82-91.)

Grove, Hugh D. and Richard S. Savich. "Attitude Research In Accounting: A Model For Reliability And Validity Considerations," **AR**, 1979, Vol. 54, No. 3, pp. 522-537.

Grove, Hugh D. (Selto, Frank H. and Hugh D. Grove. "Voting Power Indices And The Setting Of Financial Accounting Standards: Extensions," **JAR**, 1982, Vol. 20, No. 2, Part II, pp. 676-688.)

Grove, Hugh D. (Selto, Frank H. and Hugh D. Grove. "The Predictive Power Of Voting Power Indices: FASB Voting On Statements Of Financial Accounting Standards Nos. 45-69," **JAR**, 1983, Vol. 21, No. 2, pp. 619-622.)

Grove, Hugh D. (Sorensen, James E. and Hugh D. Grove. "Cost-Outcome and Cost-Effectiveness Analysis: Emerging Nonprofit Performance Evaluation Techniques," **AR**, 1977, Vol. 52, No. 3, pp. 658-675.)

Grove, H. D., T. J. Mock and K. B. Ehrenreich. "A Review Of Human Resource Accounting Measurement Systems From A Measurement Theory Perspective," **AOS**, 1977, Vol. 2, No. 3, pp. 219-236.

Groves, Roger E. V. (Comiskey, Eugene E. and Roger E. V. Groves. "United Kingdom Developments In Interperiod Tax Allocation," **IJAER**, 1981, Vol. 16, No. 2, pp. 1-9.)

Groves, Roger, Michael Poole and Paul Broder. "Professional Commitments Of The Practising Chartered Accountant In Modern Britain," **ABR**, 1983-84, Vol. 14, No. 56, pp. 319-332.

Groves, Roger, Rene Manes and Robert Sorensen. "The Application Of The Hirsch-Dantzig 'Fixed Charge' Algorithm To Profit Planning: A Formal Statement Of Product Profitability Analysis," **AR**, 1970, Vol. 45, No. 3, pp. 481-489.

Groves, R. E. V. and R. Harrison. "Bank Loans And Small Business Financing In Britain," **ABR**, 1973-74, Vol. 4, No. 15, pp. 227-233.

Groves, R. E. V. (Comiskey, E. E. and R. E. V. Groves. "The Adoption And Diffusion Of An Accounting Innovation," **ABR**, 1971-72, Vol. 2, No. 5, pp. 67-77.)

Groves, R. (Tomkins, C. and R. Groves. "The Everyday Accountant and Researching His Reality: Further Thoughts'," **AOS**, 1983, Vol. 8, No. 4, pp. 407-418.)

Groves, R. (Tomkins, C. and R. Groves. "The Everyday Accountant And Researching His Reality," **AOS**, 1983, Vol. 8, No. 4, pp. 361-374.)

Growe, Gary A. and Philip G. Kaplan. "Surviving The IRS Tax Accrual Decision," **MA**, 1985, Vol. 66, No. 8, pp. 42-45.

Grube, Corwin. (Nurnberg, Hugo and Corwin Grube. "Alternative Methods Of Accounting For Business Combinations," **AR**, 1970, Vol. 45, No. 4, pp. 783-789.)

Gruber, Robert A. "Sequencing Exam Questions Relative To Topic Presentation," **JAED**, 1987, Vol. 5, No. 1, pp. 77-86.

Grudnitski, Gary. (Harrison, Walter T., Jr. and Gary Grudnitski. "Bondholder And Stockholder Reactions To Discretionary Accounting Changes," **JAPP**, 1987, Vol. 6, No. 2, pp. 87-113.)

Grudnitski, Gary. (Krogstad, Jack L., Gary Grudnitski and David W. Bryant. "PERT And PERT/Cost For Audit Planning And Control," **JOA**, 1977, Vol. 144, No. 5, pp. 82-91.)

Grundy, Graham and Paul Burns. "Taxation-Induced Interdependencies In Project Appraisal," **ABR**, 1979-80, Vol. 10, No. 37, pp. 47-53.

Grundy, Richard A. "Hospital Accounting," MA, 1971, Vol. 52, No. 9, pp. 45-47.

Gruneberg, Curt. "Is Accountancy A Field Of Science?," AR, 1950, Vol. 25, No. 2, pp. 161-162.

Guberman, Harvey C. (Kaplan, Gene P. and Harvey C. Guberman. "Financing In Chapter 11 - Back From The Depths," CA, 1986, Vol. 4, No. 2, pp. 26-38.)

Guck, Henry H. "The Psychology Of Management Audits," MA, 1974, Vol. 56, No. 3, pp. 41-44.

Gudmundsen, Ralph W., Jr. (Cameron, George D., III, Ralph W. Gudmundsen, Jr. and Jack R. Ball. "Accounting Changes: Why CPA's Must Conform," MA, 1973, Vol. 54, No. 8, pp. 26-28.)

Guequierre, John P. "A Need For A Non-Redundant System," MA, 1972, Vol. 53, No. 12, pp. 25-28.

Guerin, Francis J. "An Undergraduate Seminar In Accounting," AR, 1969, Vol. 44, No. 2, pp. 409-411.

Guinn, Robert E. "The Use Of Microcomputers In The First Auditing Course," IAE, 1988, Vol. 3, No. 1, pp. 88-95.

Gujarathi, Mahendra R. and Stanley F. Biggs. "Accounting For Purchase Commitments: Some Issues And Recommendations," AH, 1988, Vol. 2, No. 3, pp. 75-82.

Gul, Ferdinand A. and Teoh Hai Yap. "The Effects Of Combined Audit And Management Services On Public Perception Of Auditor Independence In Developing Countries: The Malaysian Case," IJAER, 1984, Vol. 20, No. 1, pp. 95-107.

Gul, Ferdinand A. "Adaption - Innovation As A Factor In Australian Accounting Undergraduates' Subject Interest And Career Preferences," JAED, 1986, Vol. 4, No. 1, pp. 203-209.

Gul, Ferdinand A. "The Effects Of Uncertainty Reporting On Lending Officers' Perceptions Of Risk And Additional Information Required," ABACUS, 1987, Vol. 23, No. 2, pp. 172-181.

Gul, Ferdinand A. "The Joint And Moderating Role Of Personality And Cognitive Style On Decision Making," AR, 1984, Vol. 59, No. 2, pp. 264-277.

Gul, Ferdinand A. "Tolerance For Ambiguity, Auditors' Opinions And Their Effects On Decision Making," ABR, 1985-86, Vol. 16, No. 62, pp. 99-106.

Gul, F. A. "A Note On The Relationship Between Age, Experience, Cognitive Styles And Accountants' Decision Confidence," ABR, 1983-84, Vol. 14, No. 53, pp. 85-88.

Gul, F. A. "An Empirical Study Of The Usefulness Of Human Resources Turnover Costs In Australian Accounting Firms," AOS, 1984, Vol. 9, No. 3/4, pp. 233-240.

Gulden, Douglas J. and Charles J. Stokes. "Simultaneous Calculation Of Federal And State Income Taxes, A Suggested Method," AR, 1954, Vol. 29, No. 3, pp. 501-502.

Guldig, John F. "Redesigning Accounts Payable," MA, 1983, Vol. 65, No. 3, pp. 42-47.

Gullapalli, Sambo Murty. "Simulating A Cash Budget For A Small Manufacturer," MA, 1979, Vol. 61, No. 5,pp. 25-29.

Gulledge, Dexter E. and Zoel W. Daughtrey. "Gambling - A Trade Or Business?," CPAJ, 1988, Vol. 58, No. 3, pp. 12-21.

Gulledge, Thomas R., Jr. (Camm, Jeffrey D., Thomas R. Gulledge, Jr. and Norman Keith Womer. "Production Rate And Contractor Behavior," JCA, 1987, Vol. 4, No. 1, pp. 27-37.)

Gunderson, Russell H. "Capitalization Of Computer Systems Costs," MA, 1977, Vol. 58, No. 7, pp. 48-50.

Gunders, Henry. "Clerical Work Measurement," JOA, 1956, Vol. 101, No. 2, pp. 38-44.

Gunn, Sanford. (Johnson, Orace and Sanford Gunn. "Conflict Resolution: The Market And/Or Accounting?," AR, 1974, Vol. 49, No. 4, pp. 649-663.)

Gunnarson, Arthur B. "There Yesterday-Here Today-Where Tomorrow?," MA, 1969, Vol. 50, No. 10, pp. 32-35.

Gunther, Samuel P. "Accounting And Tax Aspects Of Securities Reacquisitions," CPAJ, 1975, Vol. 45, No. 12, pp. 18-22.

Gunther, Samuel P. "Contingent Pay-Outs In Mergers And Acquisitions," JOA, 1968, Vol. 125, No. 6, pp. 33-40.

Gunther, Samuel P. "Lingering Pooling Problems," CPAJ, 1973, Vol. 43, No. 6, pp. 459-464.

Gunther, Samuel P. "The CPA's Role In Mergers And Acquisitions," JOA, 1979, Vol. 147, No. 2, pp. 47-57.

Gupta, A. K. (Govindarajan, V. and A. K. Gupta. "Linking Control Systems To Business Unit Strategy: Impact On Performance," AOS, 1985, Vol. 10, No. 1, pp. 51-66.)

Gupta, Manak C. and Ronald J. Huefner. "A Cluster Analysis Study Of Financial Ratios And Industry Characteristics," JAR, 1972, Vol. 10, No. 1, pp. 77-95.

Gurry, Edward James. "Harry Clark Bentley," AHJ, 1975, Vol. 2, No. 1-4, pp. 58-61.

Gusbee, Charles H. "Bond Discount Or Premium At Refunding," AR, 1946, Vol. 21, No. 1, pp. 61-66.

Gustafson, George A. "Is Accounting Theory Defunct?," AR, 1952, Vol. 27, No. 2, pp. 236-244.

Gustafson, George A. "Status Of Accounting Research Study Nos. 1 And 3," JOA, 1970, Vol. 129, No. 3, pp. 56-60.

Gustafson, George A. "The Federal Government Accountants Association," AR, 1962, Vol. 37, No. 3, pp. 521-522.

Gustafson, George A. "Working Paper For Preparation Of Cash-Flow Statement," AR, 1963, Vol. 38, No. 1, pp. 160-167.

Gustafson, George A. "Working Paper For Preparation Of Funds Statement," AR, 1964, Vol. 39,No. 4, pp.1018-1023.

Gustavson, Sandra G. (Schultz, Joseph J., Jr. and Sandra G. Gustavson. "Actuaries' Perceptions Of Variables Affecting The Independent Auditor's Legal Liability," AR, 1978, Vol. 53, No. 3, pp. 626-641.)

Gutberlet, Louis G. "An Opportunity - Differential Standards," JAAF, 1983, Vol. 7, No. 1, pp. 16-28.

Gutberlet, Louis G. "Compilation And Review Of Financial Statements By An Accountant," JAAF, 1980, Vol. 3, No. 4, pp. 313-338.

Guthmann, H. G. "Actuarial Versus Sinking Fund Type Formula For Valuation," AR, 1930, Vol. 5, No. 3, pp. 226-230.

Guthrie, Art. "Modern Semantics Can Help Accounting," JOA, 1972, Vol. 133, No. 6, pp. 56-63.

Guthrie, Tommie M. "Measuring Terminal Profitability," MA, 1978, Vol. 60, No. 6, pp. 24-31.

Gutkin, Sydney A. and David Beck. "Ordinary Loss Denied Post-Liquidation Transferee," JOA, 1953, Vol. 95, No. 3, pp. 314-319.

Guy, Dan M. and Alan J. Winters. "Unaudited Financial Statements: A Survey," JOA, 1972, Vol. 134, No. 6, pp. 46-53.

Guy, Dan M. and Herschel Mann. "A Practical Guide For Reporting On Limited Examinations Of Financial Statements," CPAJ, 1973, Vol. 43, No. 7, pp. 555-562.

Guy, Dan M. and Jerry D. Sullivan. "The Expectation Gap Auditing Standards," JOA, 1988, Vol. 165, No. 4, pp. 36-46.

Guy, Dan M. "A Proposed Statement Of Audit Responsibility For Projected Financial Statements," CPAJ, 1972, Vol. 42, No. 12, pp. 1009-1018.

Guy, Dan M. "Auditing Projected Financial Statements," MA, 1972, Vol. 54, No. 5, pp. 33-37.

Guy, Dan M. (Alderman, C. Wayne, Dan M. Guy and Dennis R. Meals. "Other Comprehensive Bases Of Accounting: Alternatives To GAAP?," JOA, 1982, Vol. 154, No. 2, pp. 52-63.)

Guy, Dan M. (Clay, John R., Dan M. Guy and Dennis R. Meals. "Solving Compilation And Review Practice Problems," JOA, 1980, Vol. 150, No. 3, pp. 74-82.)

Guy, Dan M. (Dock, V. Thomas, Dan M. Guy and Doyle Z. Williams. "Integrating The Computer In The Classroom: An Approach In Auditing," AR, 1974, Vol. 49, No. 1, pp. 149-153.)

Guy, Dan M. (Ingram, Robert W., Dan M. Guy, Issam J. Merei and Robert T. Justis. "Disclosure Practices In Unaudited Financial Statements Of Small Businesses," JOA, 1977, Vol. 144, No. 2, pp. 81-86.)

Guy, Dan M. (Pallais, Don and Dan M. Guy. "Prospective Financial Statements," JOA, 1986, Vol. 161, No. 4, pp. 90-99.)

Guy, Dan M. (Raiborn, D. D., Dan M. Guy and Marilyn Zulinski. "Solving Audit Problems In Small Business Engagements," JOA, 183, Vol. 155, No. 4, pp. 50-59.)

Guy, Dan M. (Van Son, W. Peter, Dan M. Guy and J. Frank Betts. "Engagement Letters: What Practice Shows," JOA, 1982, Vol. 153, No. 6, pp. 72-81.)

Guy, Dan M., Patricia E. Harris and Doyle Z. Williams. "Client Perceptions Of A Local CPA Firm," CPAJ, 1979, Vol. 49, No. 3, pp. 17-22.

Guynes, Carl Stephen, Michael T. Vanecek and Robert F. Zant. "Security Of Telecommunication Systems," CPAJ, 1979, Vol. 49, No. 10, pp. 31-34.

Guynes, Carl Stephen. (Vanecek, Michael T., Robert F. Zant and Carl Stephen Guynes. "Distributed Data Processing: A New Tool For Accountants," JOA, 1980, Vol. 150, No. 4, pp. 75-83.)

Gwilliam, D. R. "Apportionment In Actions Against Auditors," ABACUS, 1988, Vol. 24, No. 1, pp. 37-54.

Gwilliam, D. R. "The Auditor, Third Parties And Contributory Negligence," ABR, 1987-88, Vol. 18, No. 69, pp. 25-36.

Gynther, Merle M. "Future Growth Aspects Of The Cash Flow Computation," AR, 1968, Vol. 43, No. 4, pp. 706-718.

Gynther, Reg S. "Accounting For Monetary Items Under CCA: A Comment," ABR, 1982-83, Vol. 13, No. 50, pp. 95-102.

Gynther, Reg S. "Capital Maintenance, Price Changes, And Profit Determination," AR, 1970, Vol. 45, No. 4, pp. 712-730.

Gynther, Reg S. "Some 'Conceptualizing' On Goodwill," AR, 1969, Vol. 44, No. 2, pp. 247-255.

Gynther, Reg S. "Why Use General Purchasing Power?," ABR, 1973-74, Vol. 4, No. 14, pp. 141-156.

Gynther, Reginald S. "Accounting Concepts And Behavioral Hypotheses," AR, 1967, Vol. 42, No. 2, pp. 274-290.

HHH

Haase, William B. "How Outside And Internal Auditors Work Together," CPAJ, 1974, Vol. 44, No. 1, pp. 46-50.

Haas, Raymond. "U.S. Tax Policies Hurt U.S. Multinationals," CPAJ, 1988, Vol. 58, No. 10, pp. 62-73.

Haas, Richard J. (Harrell, Rhett D. and Richard J. Haas. "Selecting An External Auditor For Government Organizations - Part I," CPAJ, 1984, Vol. 54, No. 9, pp. 34-45.)

Haas, Richard J. (Lorensen, Leonard and Richard J. Haas. "Governmental Accounting: Time For An Accommodation," JOA, 1982, Vol. 153, No. 3, pp. 56-67.)

Haas, Robert J. (Harrell, Rhett D. and Robert J. Haas. "Selecting An External Auditor For Government Organizations - Part II," CPAJ, 1984, Vol. 54, No. 10, pp. 62-72.)

Hackenbrack, Karl. (Bailey, Andrew D., Jr., Karl Hackenbrack, Prabuddha De, and Jesse Dillard. "Artificial Intelligence, Cognitive Science, And Computational Modeling In Auditing Research: A Research Approach," JIS, 1987, Vol. 1, No. 2, pp. 20-40.)

Hackenburg, P. Richard. "Proposed Solutions To The Insurance Availability/Affordability Crisis," CA, 1987,

Vol. 5, No. 2, pp. 3-6.

Hackett, Donald W. (Wu, Frederick H. and Donald W. Hackett. "The Internationalization Of U.S. Public Accounting Firms: An Empirical Study," IJAER, 1977, Vol. 12, No. 2, pp. 81-91.)

Hackett, Robert P. "A Second Course In Accountancy," AR, 1933, Vol. 8, No. 2, p. 160.

Hackett, Robert P. "Consistency In Prepaid Expenses," AR, 1935, Vol. 10, No. 2, pp. 206-209.

Hackett, Robert P. "Encumbrance Accounting For Industry," AR, 1944, Vol. 19, No. 3, pp. 294-297.

Hackett, Robert P. "Government Accounting In The Education Of The Public Accountant," AR, 1938, Vol. 13, No. 4, pp. 390-391.

Hackett, Robert P. "Property Accounts For Municipalities," AR, 1937, Vol. 12, No. 1, pp. 64-67.

Hackett, R. P. "Recent Developments In Governmental And Institutional Accounting," AR, 1933, Vol. 8, No. 2, pp. 122-127.

Hackett, Steven W. (Weber, Joseph V., John J. Mahoney, Jr. and Steven W. Hackett. "Inventory Costing Under TRA 86 - Part I," CPAJ, 1988, Vol. 58, No. 5, pp. 66-71.)

Hackett, Steven W. (Weber, Joseph V., John J. Mahoney, Jr. and Steven W. Hackett. "Inventory Costing Under TRA 86 - Part III," CPAJ, 1988, Vol. 58, No. 8, pp. 64-69.)

Hackett, Steven W. (Weber, Joseph V., John J. Mahoney, Jr. and Steven W. Hackett. "Inventory Costing Under TRA 86 - Part II," CPAJ, 1988, Vol. 58, No. 6, pp. 26-33.)

Hadley, Galen D. and Thomas E. Balke. "A Comparison Of Academic And Practitioner Views Of Current Levels In The Undergraduate Accounting Curriculum," AR, 1979, Vol. 54, No. 2, pp. 383-389.

Hadnott, Bennie L. "Audit Evidence - What Kind And How Much," CPAJ, 1979, Vol. 49, No. 10, pp. 23-30.

Haessly, Gaile A. (Bruegelmann, Thomas M., Gaile A. Haessly, Claire P. Wolfangel and Michael Schiff. "How Variable Costing Is Used In Pricing Decisions," MA, 1985, Vol. 66, No. 10, pp. 58-61.)

Hafner, George F. "Auditing EDP," AR, 1964, Vol. 39, No. 4, pp. 979-982.

Hafter, Richard A. and Robert C. Sparks. "Can You Evaluate Your R&D Spending?," MA, 1986, Vol. 67, No. 7, pp. 53-55.

Haga, William J. (Burns, David C. and William J. Haga. "Much Ado About Professionalism: A Second Look At Accounting," AR, 1977, Vol. 52, No. 3, pp. 705-715.)

Hagen, Everett. "National Accounting Systems And The European Recovery Program," AR, 1949, Vol. 24, No. 3, pp. 248-253.

Hagerman, Robert L. and Mark E. Zmijewski. "Some Economic Determinants Of Accounting Policy Choice," JAEC, 1979, Vol. 1, No. 2, pp. 141-161.

Hagerman, Robert L. "A Test Of Government Regulation Of Accounting Principles," AR, 1975, Vol. 50, No. 4, pp. 699-709.

Hagerman, Robert L. "Accounting In The Bible," AHJ, 1980, Vol. 7, pp. 71-76.

Hagerman, Robert L. "The Metcalf Report: Selling Some Assumptions," MA, 1978, Vol. 59, No. 7, pp. 13-16.

Hagerman, Robert L. (Brown, Lawrence D., Paul A. Griffin, Robert L. Hagerman and Mark E. Zmijewski. "An Evaluation Of Alternative Proxies For The Market's Assessment Of Unexpected Earnings," JAEC, 1987, Vol. 9, No. 2, pp. 159-193.)

Hagerman, Robert L. (Brown, Lawrence D., Robert L. Hagerman, Paul A. Griffin and Mark E. Zmijewski. "Security Analyst Superiority Relative To Univariate Time-Series Models In Forecasting Quarterly Earnings," JAEC, 1987, Vol. 9, No. 1, pp. 61-87.)

Hagerman, Robert L. (Zmijewski, Mark E. and Robert L. Hagerman. "An Income Strategy Approach To The Positive Theory Of Accounting Standard Setting/Choice," JAEC, 1981, Vol. 3, No. 2, pp. 129-149.)

Hagerman, Robert L., Mark E. Zmijewski and Pravin Shah. "The Association Between The Magnitude Of Quarterly Earnings Forecast Errors And Risk-Adjusted Stock Returns," JAR, 1984, Vol. 22, No. 2, pp. 526-540.

Hagerman, Robert L., Thomas F. Keller and Russell J. Petersen. "Accounting Research And Accounting Principles," JOA, 1973, Vol. 135, No. 3, pp. 51-55.

Hager, Hampton C. "Cash Management And The Cash Cycle," MA, 1976, Vol. 57, No. 9, pp. 19-21.

Hagg, I. and G. Hedlund. "'Case Studies' In Accounting Research," AOS, 1979, Vol. 4, No. 1/2, pp. 135-143.

Hagigi, Moshe. (Aguirre, Alejandro and Moshe Hagigi. "Accounting, Economic, And Environmental Determinants Of Financial Reporting Practices In Guatemala," IJAER, 1987, Vol. 22, No. 2, pp. 169-191.)

Hagler, J. Larry. "The Franchise Fee," MA, 1974, Vol. 56, No. 1, pp. 49-51.

Hagler, J. Larry. (Thomas, Paula B. and J. Larry Hagler. "Induced Conversions Of Convertible Debt: Beware Of The Pitfalls," MA, 1987, Vol. 68, No. 12, pp. 52-55.)

Hagler, J. Larry. (Thomas, Paula B. and J. Larry Hagler. "Push Down Accounting: A Descriptive Assessment," AH, 1988, Vol. 2, No. 3, pp. 26-31.)

Haglund, Byron E. "Inventory: Lower Of Cost Or Market," AR, 1966, Vol. 41, No. 4, p. 772.

Haglund, Byron E., Lee J. Adamson and Richard D. Metcalf. "Punched Card Accounting For Small Businesses," JOA, 1961, Vol. 112, No. 6, pp. 54-58.

Haidinger, Timothy P. "Negotiate For Profits," MA, 1970, Vol. 52, No. 6, pp. 23-24.

Haidinger, Timothy P. "The Case For Continuous Discounting," MA, 1968, Vol. 49, No. 6, pp. 57-61.

Hain, H. P. "Accounting Control In The Zenon Papyri," AR, 1966, Vol. 41, No. 4, pp. 699-703.

Hain, H. P. "Casting The Account," JAR, 1967, Vol. 5, No. 2, pp. 154-163.

Hainkel, Michael. (Horvitz, Jerome S. and Michael Hainkel. "The IRS Summons Power And Its Effect On The Independent Auditor," JAAF, 1981, Vol. 4, No. 2, pp. 114-127.)

Haire, M. (Bowman, E. H. and M. Haire. "Social Impact Disclosure And Corporate Annual Reports," AOS, 1976, Vol. 1, No. 1, pp. 11-22.)

Haka, Susan F., Lawrence A. Gordon and George E. Pinches. "Sophisticated Capital Budgeting Selection Techniques And Firm Performance," AR, 1985, Vol. 60, No. 4, pp. 651-669.

Haka, Susan, Lauren Friedman and Virginia Jones. "Functional Fixation And Interference Theory: A Theoretical And Empirical Investigation," AR, 1986, Vol. 61, No. 3, pp. 455-474.

Haka, S. F. "Capital Budgeting Techniques And Firm Specific Contingencies: A Correlational Analysis," AOS, 1987, Vol. 12, No. 1, pp. 31-48.

Haka, S. (Gordon, L. A., S. Haka and A. G. Schick. "Strategies For Information Systems Implementation: The Case Of Zero Base Budgeting," AOS, 1984, Vol. 9, No. 2, pp. 111-124.)

Hakala, Gregory. "Measuring Costs With Machine Hours," MA, 1985, Vol. 67, No. 4, pp. 57-61.

Hakansson, Nils H. "An Induced Theory Of Accounting Under Risk," AR, 1969, Vol. 44, No. 3, pp. 495-514.

Hakansson, Nils H. "Comments On Weick And Ross," AR, 1983, Vol. 58, No. 2, pp. 381-384.

Hakansson, Nils H. "Interim Disclosure And Public Forecasts: An Economic Analysis And A Framework For Choice," AR, 1977, Vol. 52, No. 2, pp. 396-416.

Hakansson, Nils H. "Normative Accounting Theory And The Theory Of Decision," IJAER, 1969, Vol. 4, No. 2, pp. 33-47.

Hakansson, Nils H. "On The Policies Of Accounting Disclosure And Measurement: An Analysis Of Economic Incentives," JAR, 1981, Vol. 19, Supp., pp. 1-35.

Hakansson, Nils H. "On The Relevance Of Price-Level Accounting," JAR, 1969, Vol. 7, No. 1, pp. 22-31.

Hakansson, Nils H. "Where We Are In Accounting: A Review Of 'Statement On Accounting Theory And Theory Acceptance'," AR, 1978, Vol. 53, No. 3, pp. 717-725.

Hakansson, Nils H., J. Gregory Kunkel and James A. Ohlson. "A Comment On Verrecchia's No Trading 'Theorem'," JAR, 1984, Vol. 22, No. 2, pp. 765-767.

Hale, Jack A. and Lanny J. Ryan. "Decision Science And The Management Accountant," MA, 1979, Vol. 60, No. 7, pp. 42-45.

Haley, Brian W. and Thomas A. Ratcliffe. "Accounting For Incentive Stock Options," CPAJ, 1982, Vol. 52, No. 10, pp. 32-39.

Haley, Brian W. and Thomas A. Ratcliffe. "ERTA And Incentive Stock Options," CPAJ, 1982, Vol. 52, No. 9, pp. 45-56.

Half, Robert. "A Better Job...Yours For The Asking," MA, 1976, Vol. 58, No. 6, pp. 54-57.

Half, Robert. "Burnout Or Cop-Out?," MA, 1985, Vol. 66, No. 7, pp. 29-33.

Half, Robert. "Do Management Accountants Have An Image Problem?," MA, 1980, Vol. 62, No. 2, pp. 10-13.

Half, Robert. "Keeping The Best - Employee Retention In Public Accounting," CPAJ, 1982, Vol. 52, No. 8, pp. 34-39.

Hall, Edmund J. and Richard J. Kolkmann. "A Vote For The Probabilistic Pro Forma Income Statement," MA, 1976, Vol. 57, No. 7, pp. 45-48.

Hall, Ed. "Inventory Accounting For Atomic Energy Process Materials," JOA, 1953, Vol. 96, No. 1, pp. 62-67.

Hall, Foster E. "Current Defense Contract Termination Rules," JOA, 1953, Vol. 95, No. 4, pp. 440-448.

Hall, James Arthur. (Dowell, C. Dwayne and James Arthur Hall. "EDP Controls With Audit Cost Implications," JAAF, 1981, Vol. 5, No. 1, pp. 30-40.)

Hall, Joe. "Representation Without Taxation," MA, 1972, Vol. 53, No. 9, pp. 36-38.

Hall, Otto L. "Mark-Up Based On Assets Employed," MA, 1971, Vol. 52, No. 8, pp. 48-49.

Hall, Robert B. "How We Estimate Replacement Costs," MA, 1979, Vol. 60, No. 7, pp. 30-36.

Hall, Steven D. (Hull, Rita P., John O. Everett and Steven D. Hall. "Accounting Education: Practitioner's Views On The Value Of A Five-Year Program," AIA, 1987, Vol. 5, pp. 163-178.)

Hall, Thomas W. and A. A. Butler. "Assuring Adequate Attorneys' Replies To Audit Inquiries," JOA, 1981, Vol. 152, No. 3, pp. 83-91.

Hall, Thomas W. and Darwin J. Casler. "Using Indexing To Estimate Current Costs - Composite Or Multiple Indexes?," JAAF, 1985, Vol. 8, No. 3, pp. 210-224.

Hall, Thomas W. and H. Jim Snavely. "Translated Financial Statements Can Be Meaningful," IJAER, 1984, Vol. 20, No. 1, pp. 153-170.

Hall, Thomas W. "An Empirical Test Of The Effect Of Asset Aggregation On Valuation Accuracy," JAR, 1982, Vol. 20, No. 1, pp. 139-151.

Hall, Thomas W. "Inflation And Rates Of Exchange: Support For SFAS No. 52," JAAF, 1983, Vol. 6, No. 4, pp. 299-313.

Hall, Thomas W. "Inventory Carrying Costs: A Case Study," MA, 1974, Vol. 55, No. 7, pp. 37-39.

Hall, Thomas W. "Post-Completion Audit Procedure," MA, 1975, Vol. 57, No. 3, pp. 33-37.

Hall, Thomas W. (Casler, Darwin J. and Thomas W. Hall. "Firm-Specific Asset Valuation Accuracy Using A Composite Price Index," **JAR**, 1985, Vol. 23,No. 1, pp.110-122.)

Hall, Thomas W. (Dunn, W. Marcus and Thomas W. Hall. "Graduate Education And CPA Examination Performance: Some Empirical Evidence," **AIA**, 1988, Vol. 6, pp. 191-204.)

Hall, Thomas W. (Dunn, W. Marcus and Thomas W. Hall. "An Empirical Analysis Of The Relationships Between CPA Examination Candidate Attributes And Candidate Performance," **AR**, 1984, Vol. 59, No. 4, pp. 674-689.)

Hall, Tommy P. (Robertson, Leon H. and Tommy P. Hall. "Network Analysis And Financial Planning," **MA**, 1967, Vol. 48, No. 8, pp. 43-46.)

Hall, T. P. (Robinson, Leonard A. and T. P. Hall. "Systems Education And The Accounting Curriculum," **AR**, 1964, Vol. 39, No. 1, pp. 62-69.)

Hall, William D. and Arthur J. Renner. "Lessons That Auditors Ignore At Their Own Risk," **JOA**, 1988, Vol. 166, No. 1, pp. 50-59.

Hall, William D. "An Acceptable Scope Of Practice," **CPAJ**, 1988, Vol. 58, No. 2, pp. 24-33.

Hall, William D. "Current Problems In Accounting For Leases," **JOA**, 1967, Vol. 124, No. 5, pp. 35-42.

Hall, William E., Jr. (Sprinkle, R. David and William E. Hall, Jr. "How To Cope With Reverse Discrimination In Executive Benefit Plans," **MA**, 1979, Vol. 61, No. 2, pp. 41-44.)

Hallbauer, Rosalie C. "How Orchestras Measure Internal Performance," **MA**, 1980, Vol. 61, No. 8, pp. 54-57.

Hallbauer, Rosalie C. (Agrawal, Surendra P., Rosalie C. Hallbauer and Gerald W. Perritt. "Measurement Of The Current Cost Of Equivalent Productive Capacity," **JAAF**, 1980, Vol. 3, No. 2, pp. 163-173.)

Hallbauer, Rosalie C. (Agrawal, Surendra P. and Rosalie C. Hallbauer. "Advantages Of Replacement Cost Accounting: A Critical Evaluation," **IJAER**, 1978, Vol. 13, No. 2, pp. 1-14.)

Hallbauer, R. C. "Standard Costing And Scientific Management," **AHJ**, 1978, Vol. 5, No. 2, pp. 37-49.

Halliwell, Paul D. "Basic Principles Of Pension Funding And APB Opinion No. 8." **MA**, 1969, Vol. 51, No. 1, pp. 15-19.

Halperin, Robert and Bin Srinidhi. "The Effects Of The U.S. Income Tax Regulations' Transfer Pricing Rules On Allocative Efficiency," **AR**, 1987, Vol. 62, No. 4, pp. 686-706.

Halperin, Robert and Joseph Tzur. "Monetary Compensation And Nontaxable Employee Benefits: An Analytical Perspective," **AR**, 1985, Vol. 60, No. 4, pp. 670-680.

Halperin, Robert M. and William N. Lanien. "The Effects Of The Thor Power Tool Decision On The LIFO/FIFO Choice," **AR**, 1987, Vol. 62, No. 2, pp. 378-384.

Halperin, Robert. "Misleading Tax Figures - A Problem For Accountants: A Comment," **AR**, 1978, Vol. 53, No. 2, pp. 517-519.

Halperin, Robert. "The Effects Of LIFO Inventory Costing On Resource Allocations: A Reply," **AR**, 1981, Vol. 56, No. 4, pp. 977-979.

Halperin, Robert. "The Effects Of LIFO Inventory Costing On Resource Allocation: A Public Policy Perspective," **AR**, 1979, Vol. 54, No. 1, pp. 58-71.

Halperin, Robert. "The Perceived Instability Of Tax Legislation And Its Effect On Consumption Investment Decisions," **JAPP**, 1983, Vol. 2, No. 4, pp. 239-262.

Halperin, Robert. (Cohen. Morris A. and Robert Halperin. "Optimal Inventory Order Policy For A Firm Using The LIFO Inventory Costing Method," **JAR**, 1980, Vol. 18, No. 2, pp. 375-389.)

Halpern, Jonathan. (Ahituv, Niv. Jonathan Halpern and Hart Will. "Audit Planning: An Algorithmic Approach." **CAR**, 1985-86, Vol. 2, No. 1, pp. 95-110.)

Halprin, Leslie E. (Schiff, Michael, Roger M. Campbell, Leslie E. Halprin and Judith P. Murphy. "How A Division's Reports Can Reflect Inflation." **MA**, 1982, Vol. 64, No. 4, pp. 32-35.)

Halterman, J. F. "Accountants In OPA." **AR**, 1944, Vol. 19, No. 3, pp. 279-282.

Halt, Donald R. "Aesop Revisited: A Management Fable Of The '80s," **MA**, 1986, Vol. 68, No. 3, pp. 48-50.

Ham, Jane, Donna Losell and Wally Smieliauskas. "An Empirical Study Of Error Characteristics In Accounting Populations," **AR**, 1985, Vol. 60, No. 3, pp. 387-406.

Ham, Jane, Donna Losell and Wally Smieliauskas. "Some Empirical Evidence On The Stability Of Accounting Error Characteristics Over Time," **CAR**, 1987-88, Vol. 4, No. 1, pp. 210-226.

Ham, Jane, Donna Losell and Wally Smieliauskas. "A Note On The Neutrality Of Internal Control Systems In Audit Practice," **CAR**, 1985-86, Vol. 2, No. 2. pp. 311-317.

Hamdallah, Ahmed El-Sayed and William Ruland. "The Decision To Terminate Overfunded Pension Plans." **JAPP**, 1986, Vol. 5, No. 2, pp. 77-91.

Hamer, John G. (Kistler, Linda H. and John G. Hamer. "Understanding The New Statement Of Cash Flows," **CA**, 1988, Vol. 6, No. 1, pp. 3-9.)

Hamer, Michelle M. "Failure Prediction: Sensitivity Of Classification Accuracy To Alternative Statistical Methods And Variable Sets," **JAPP**, 1983, Vol. 2, No. 4, pp. 289-307.

Hamer, Michelle M. (Gordon. Lawrence A. and Michelle M. Hamer. "Rates Of Return And Cash Flow Profiles: An Extension," **AR**, 1988, Vol. 63, No. 3, pp. 514-521.)

Hamill, Edwin N. "Utilizing PEM In A Capital Program," **MA**, 1967, Vol. 49, No. 3, pp. 21-24.

Hamilton, Benjamin P., Jr. "Which Information For Stockholders?," **MA**, 1968, Vol. 50, No. 4, pp. 13-14.

Hamilton, Douglas L. "The Changing Role Of The Controller," **JOA**, 1960, Vol. 109, No. 1, pp. 51-56.

Hamilton, Robert E. and William F. Wright. "Internal Control Judgments And Effects Of Experience Replications And Extensions," **JAR**, 1982, Vol. 20, No. 2, Part II, pp. 756-765.

Hamilton, Robert E. "The Effect Of Aggregation On Decision-Making Success: A Laboratory Study: A Comment," **JAR**, 1974, Vol. 12, No. 2, pp. 355-361.

Hamilton, R. E. "Casualty Insurance Recoveries With Coinsurance Clauses: A General Approach," **AR**, 1976, Vol. 51, No. 1, pp. 148-150.

Hamlen, Susan S. "A Chance-Constrained Mixed Integer Programming Model For Internal Control Design," **AR**, 1980, Vol. 55, No. 4, pp. 578-593.

Hamlen, Susan S., William A. Hamlen, Jr. and John T. Tschirhart. "The Use Of Core Theory In Evaluating Joint Cost Allocation Schemes," **AR**, 1977, Vol. 52, No. 3, pp. 616-627.

Hamlen, Susan S., William A. Hamlen, Jr. and John Tschirhart. "The Use Of The Generalized Shapley Allocation In Joint Cost Allocation," **AR**, 1980, Vol. 55, No. 2, pp. 269-287.

Hamlen, William A., Jr. (Hamlen, Susan S., William A. Hamlen, Jr. and John T. Tschirhart. "The Use Of Core Theory In Evaluating Joint Cost Allocation Schemes," **AR**, 1977, Vol. 52, No. 3, pp. 616-627.)

Hamlen, William A., Jr. (Hamlen, Susan S., William A. Hamlen, Jr. and John Tschirhart. "The Use Of The Generalized Shapley Allocation In Joint Cost Allocation," **AR**, 1980, Vol. 55, No. 2, pp. 269-287.)

Hamman, Paul E. "The Audit Of Machine Records," **JOA**, 1956, Vol. 101, No. 3, pp. 56-61.

Hammer, Edson and Thomas A. Gavin. "How Effective Is Your Supervisor?," **MA**, 1983, Vol. 65, No. 5, pp. 47-52.

Hammer, Richard. "Financial Planning To Avoid Tax Problems," **IJAER**, 1972, Vol. 7, No. 2, pp. 23-34.

Hammond, James E. "Statistics On The Profession." **JOA**, 1957, Vol. 104, No. 5, pp. 42-49.

Hammond, W. Rogers. "Electronic Data Processing And The Accounting Faculty," **AR**, 1957, Vol. 32, No. 4, pp. 576-579.

Hampel, Robert E. "Pricing Policies And Profitability," **MA**, 1977, Vol. 59, No. 1, pp. 53-56.

Hampson, J. Jay. "Accountants' Liability - The Significance Of Hochfelder," **JOA**, 1976, Vol. 142, No. 6, pp. 69-75.

Hampton, John J. and Cecilia L. Wagner. "Target Budgeting: The Systematic Allocation Of Resources," **JCA**, 1987, Vol. 4, No. 1, pp. 17-26.

Hampton, Robert, III. "A World Of Differences In Accounting And Reporting," **MA**, 1980, Vol. 62, No. 3, pp. 14-18.

Hamre, James C. "A University Accountant Trainee Program," **AR**, 1972, Vol. 47, No. 3, pp. 602-603.

Hamre, James C. (O'Connor, Melvin C. and James C. Hamre. "Alternative Methods Of Accounting For Long-Term Nonsubsidiary Intercorporate Investments In Common Stock." **AR**, 1972, Vol. 47, No. 2, pp. 308-319.)

Han, Jin-Soo. (Heintz, James A. and Jin-Soo Han. "A Study Of Audit Judgments Of Korean CPAs," **IJAER**, 1985, Vol. 21, No. 1, pp. 21-38.)

Hanbery, Glyn W. (Cattanach, Richard L. and Glyn W. Hanbery. "Audit Planning: An Application Of Network Analysis." **AR**, 1973, Vol. 48, No. 3, pp. 609-611.)

Hancock, Sidney. "An Approach To Hospital Data Processing Development." **MA**, 1978, Vol. 59, No. 9, pp. 51-55.

Handler, Kenneth I. "Tying The Key Executive To The Firm," **CA**, 1986, Vol. 4, No. 3, pp. 53-58.

Handy, Charles B. "The Conversion Option: A Proposed Method Of Valuation." **MA**, 1974, Vol. 55, No. 12, pp. 38-42.

Handy, Gene R. and Roscoe Perritt. "Account Monitoring And Cash Management," **MA**, 1976, Vol. 58, No. 3, pp. 29-31.

Hanggi, Gerald A., Jr. "Media Advertising As A Practice Development Tool," **JOA**, 1980, Vol. 149, No. 1, pp. 54-59.

Hanigsberg, Oscar and Laurence Keiser. "Preparer Penalties: A New Look - Part I," **CPAJ**, 1980, Vol. 50, No. 3, pp. 19-22.

Hanigsberg, Oscar and Laurence Keiser. "Preparer Penalties: A New Look - Part II." **CPAJ**, 1980, Vol. 50, No. 4, pp. 48-54.

Hanks, George F. and Pamela L. Murphy. "A Look At Accounting For Small Manufacturers," **MA**, 1984, Vol. 65, No. 10, pp. 40-44.

Hanks, George F. "Formal Certification Of Specialties: A Necessary Step?," **CPAJ**, 1979, Vol. 49, No. 3, pp. 23-28.

Hanks, George F. "Rx For Better Management: Critical Success Factors." **MA**, 1988, Vol. 70, No. 4, pp. 45-49.

Hanna, John. "An Application And Evaluation Of Selected Alternative Accounting Income Models," **IJAER**, 1972, Vol. 8, No. 1, pp. 135-167.

Hanna, J. R. (Basu, S. and J. R. Hanna. "Interindustry Estimation Of General Price-Level Impact On Financial Information: A Comment," **AR**, 1978, Vol. 53, No. 1, pp. 192-197.)

Hannon, James P. "Continuing Professional Education For A CPA Firm," **CPAJ**, 1980, Vol. 50, No. 1, pp. 21-25.

Hannon, James P. "Quality Control Standards: Peer Review," **CPAJ**, 1979, Vol. 49, No. 9, pp. 33-38.

Hannon, John M. "Lease Accounting: A Current Controversy," **MA**, 1976, Vol. 58, No. 4, pp. 25-28.

Hannum, William H. and William Wasserman. "General Adjustments And Price Level Measurement," **AR**, 1968, Vol. 43, No. 2, pp. 295-302.

Hanold, Terrance. "Accounting Vs. Management Information Systems," **CPAJ**, 1972, Vol. 42, No. 7, pp. 557-560.

Hanouille, Leon. (Harding, Susan, Leon Hanouille, Joseph C. Rue and Ara G. Volkan. "Why LBOs Are Popular," **MA**, 1985, Vol. 67, No. 6, pp. 51-56.)

Hansen, David T. "Municipal Accounting And Disclosure," **MA**, 1977, Vol. 58, No. 11, pp. 23-24.

Hansen, Don R. and Timothy L. Shaftel. "Sampling For Integrated Auditing Objectives," **AR**, 1977, Vol. 52, No. 1, pp. 109-123.

Hansen, Don R. (Depppe, Larry, Don R. Hansen and Stan Jenne. "The 150-Hour Educational Requirement: The History And Message Of The Utah Experience," **ACCHOR**, 1988, Vol. 2, No. 2, pp. 53-57.)

Hansen, Elizabeth S. "Municipal Finances In Perspective: A Look At Interjurisdictional Spending And Revenue Patterns," **JAR**, 1977, Vol. 15, Supp., pp. 156-201.

Hansen, James V. and William F. Messier, Jr. "A Preliminary Investigation Of EDP-XPERT," **AJPT**, 1986-87, Vol. 6, No. 1, pp. 109-123.

Hansen, James V. (Biggs, Stanley F., William F. Messier, Jr. and James V. Hansen. "A Descriptive Analysis Of Computer Audit Specialists' Decision-Making Behavior In Advanced Computer Environments," **AJPT**, 1986-87, Vol. 6, No. 2, pp. 1-21.)

Hansen, James V. (Messier, William F., Jr. and James V. Hansen. "Expert Systems In Auditing: The State Of The Art," **AJPT**, 1987-88, Vol. 7, No. 1, pp. 94-105.)

Hansen, Palle. "An Operational Cost Information Model," **ABACUS**, 1970, Vol. 6, No. 2, pp. 154-168.

Hanshaw, Nancy F., Thomas A. Ulrich and Charles J. Hollon. "Save Time, Money, And Taxes - Lease Your Employees," **MA**, 1986, Vol. 67, No. 10, pp. 30-36.

Hanslein, John D. "The Position Of Accounting In The Small Liberal Arts College," **AR**, 1930, Vol. 5, No. 2, pp. 150-152.

Hanson, Alan. (Sprigg, William T., Alan Hanson and Larry Steffens. "Controlling And Tracking Unit Costs," **MA**, 1976, Vol. 58, No. 5, pp. 47-54.)

Hanson, Arthur W. "The Relation Of Cost Accounting To The Budgetary Control Problem," **AR**, 1932, Vol. 7, No. 1, pp. 34-37.

Hanson, Charles A. "Life Insurance Accounting," **MA**, 1975, Vol. 57, No. 2, pp. 37-38.

Hanson, Ernest I. "The Budgetary Control Function," **AR**, 1966, Vol. 41, No. 2, pp. 239-243.

Hanson, Kermit O. "Graphic Presentation In CPA's Reports," **JOA**, 1957, Vol. 104, No. 3, pp. 58-63.

Hanson, Robert E. and Charles R. Lees. "IRS Examination Of Accountants' Workpapers," **JOA**, 1977, Vol. 143, No. 4, pp. 60-65.

Hanson, Robert E. and Don Wharton. "A Local CPA Firm Plans For The Future," **JOA**, 1965, Vol. 120, No. 3, pp. 43-49.

Hanson, Robert E. and William J. Brown. "CPAs' Workpapers: The IRS Zeros In," **JOA**, 1981, Vol. 152, No. 1, pp. 68-77.

Hanson, Walter E. "Big Brother And The Big Eight," **MA**, 1977, Vol. 58, No. 10, pp. 15-19.

Hanson, Walter E. "Peer Review, Illegal Payments, And Lawyers' Letters," **MA**, 1976, Vol. 58, No. 4, pp. 15-18.

Haqiqi, Abdul Wassay and Felix Pomeranz. "Accounting Needs Of Islamic Banking," **AIIA**, 1987, Vol. 1, pp. 153-168.

Harbour, James E. "Just In Time, Not Just In Case," **CA**, 1985, Vol. 3, No. 2, pp. 5-9.

Harder, David K. "Pricing For Profit In The Printing Industry," **MA**, 1979, Vol. 60, No. 11, pp. 47-52.

Hardiman, Patrick F., Alan Reinstein and David R. L. Gabhart. "Audit Committees For Governmental Units - How To," **CPAJ**, 1986, Vol. 56, No. 6, pp. 38-45.

Hardiman, Patrick F., Quentin Squires and Robert Smith. "Audit Quality For Governmental Units - Part I," **CPAJ**, 1987, Vol. 57, No. 9, pp. 22-33.

Hardiman, Patrick F., Quentin Squires and Robert Smith. "Audit Quality For Governmental Units - Part II," **CPAJ**, 1987, Vol. 57, No. 11, pp. 58-67.

Hardiman, Patrick, Arlene Lurie, Frank Dubas and David Schoen. "Internal Control And Financial Integrity In Government Units," **CPAJ**, 1985, Vol. 55, No. 4, pp. 46-51.

Harding, George G. "Mechanized Maintenance Scheduling," **MA**, 1973, Vol. 54, No. 9, pp. 36-38.

Harding, Susan, Leon Hanouille, Joseph C. Rue and Ara G. Volkan. "Why LBOs Are Popular," **MA**, 1985, Vol. 67, No. 6, pp. 51-56.

Hardman, D. J. "Accounting Development In The Solomon Islands," **IJAER**, 1984, Vol. 20, No. 1, pp. 141-152.

Hardy, John W. and E. Dee Hubbard. "Internal Reporting Guidelines: Their Coverage In Cost Accounting Texts," **AR**, 1976, Vol. 51, No. 4, pp. 917-921.

Hardy, John W. "Financing With R&D Partnerships Reduces Risk," **MA**, 1984, Vol. 65, No. 7, pp. 56-59.

Hardy, John W. "How ERTA And TEFRA Affect Capital Budgeting Decisions," **MA**, 1983, Vol. 64, No. 10, pp. 20-23.

Hardy, John W. (Hubbard, E. Dee, Kevin D. Stocks and John W. Hardy. "A Comprehensive Project For Managerial Accounting," **JAED**, 1984, Vol. 2, No. 1, pp. 111-125.)

Hardy, John W., Bryce B. Orton and J. Weldon Moffit. "Bonus Systems DO Motivate," **MA**, 1986, Vol. 68, No. 5, pp. 58-61.

Haried, Andrew A. and LeRoy R. Imdieke. "Reporting On Brother-Sister Affiliations," **CPAJ**, 1978, Vol. 48, No. 12, pp. 13-20.

Haried, Andrew A. and Ralph E. Smith. "Accounting For Marketable Equity Securities," **JOA**, 1977, Vol. 143, No. 2, pp. 54-61.

Haried, Andrew A. "Measurement Of Meaning In Financial Reports," **JAR**, 1973, Vol. 11, No. 1, pp. 117-145.

Haried, Andrew A. "The Semantic Dimensions Of Financial Statements," **JAR**, 1972, Vol. 10, No. 2, pp. 376-391.

Haried, Andrew H. (Smith, Ralph E. and Andrew H. Haried. "Exchange Of Nonmonetary Assets: An Interpretation Problem," **AR**, 1977, Vol. 52, No. 4, pp. 958-962.)

Harkins, Jeffrey L. and John Mills. "Annual Reports: A Pedagogical Tool For Intermediate Accounting," **AIA**, 1985, Vol. 2, pp. 149-168.

Harlan, Stephen D. "Practical Interpretations Of SAP No. 54 ('The Auditor's Study And Evaluation Of Internal Control')," **CPAJ**, 1974, Vol. 44, No. 3, pp. 21-26.

Harmelink, Philip J. and Nancy E. Shurtz. "Tax Effects In Divorce Planning," **CPAJ**, 1977, Vol. 47, No. 10, pp. 27-32.

Harmelink, Philip J. and Robert Capettini. "Income Tax Consequences In Leasing," **CPAJ**, 1979, Vol. 49, No. 3, pp. 29-34.

Harmelink, Philip J. "An Empirical Examination Of The Predictive Ability Of Alternate Sets Of Insurance Company Accounting Data," **JAR**, 1973, Vol. 11, No. 1, pp. 146-158.

Harmon, W. Ken, Kay M. Poston and Paul E. Dascher. "Provision And Inadequacy Of Small Business Computer Controls: A Model And Empirical Test," **JIS**, 1988, Vol. 3, No. 1, pp. 30-49.

Harmon, W. Ken, Kay M. Poston and Wayne J. Morse. "Improving Cost Recovery From Federal Grants And Contracts," **JCA**, 1986, Vol. 3, No. 1, pp. 1-12.

Harmon, W. Ken. (Dascher, Paul E. and W. Ken Harmon. "The Dark Side Of Small Business Computers," **MA**, 1984, Vol. 65, No. 11, pp. 62-67.)

Harmon, W. Ken. "Earnings Vs. Funds Flows: An Empirical Investigation Of Market Reaction," **JAAF**, 1984, Vol. 8, No. 1, pp. 24-34.

Harmon, W. Ken. (Dascher, Paul E. and W. Ken Harmon. "Assessing Microcomputer Risks And Controls For Clients," **CPAJ**, 1984, Vol. 54, No. 5, pp. 36-41.)

Harnick, Carl D. (Greenwald, Bruce M. and Carl D. Harnick. "Corporate Tax Review: The Auditor's Approach," **JOA**, 1974, Vol. 137, No. 5, pp. 63-70.)

Harold, Gilbert. "Profits In A Theory," **AR**, 1939, Vol. 14, No. 3, pp. 309-312.

Harper, Betty S. and Phil Harper. "Religious Reporting: Is It The Gospel Truth?," **MA**, 1988, Vol. 69, No. 8, pp. 34-39.

Harper, Bruce J. and Neil C. Churchill. "Serving Small Business: What CPAs Should Know," **JOA**, 1987, Vol. 163, No. 6, pp. 120-129.

Harper, Donald O. "Project Management As A Control And Planning Tool In The Decentralized Company," **MA**, 1968, Vol. 50, No. 3, pp. 29-33.

Harper, Phil. (Harper, Betty S. and Phil Harper. "Religious Reporting: Is It The Gospel Truth?," **MA**, 1988, Vol. 69, No. 8, pp. 34-39.)

Harper, Robert M. and Michael J. R. Hoffman. "EDP Record Retention," **CPAJ**, 1985, Vol. 55, No. 6, pp. 54-62.

Harper, Robert M., Jr. "AHP Judgment Models Of EDP Auditors' Evaluations Of Internal Control For Local Area Networks," **JIS**, 1988, Vol. 3, No. 1, pp. 67-86.

Harper, Robert M., Jr. "Internal Control Of Microcomputers In Local Area Networks," **JIS**, 1986, Vol. 1, No. 1, pp. 67-80.

Harper, Robert M., Jr. "Linear Programming In Managerial Accounting: A Misinterpretation Of Shadow Prices," **JAED**, 1986, Vol. 4, No. 2, pp. 123-130.

Harper, Robert M., Jr. (Dickens, Thomas L. and Robert M. Harper, Jr. "The Use Of Microcomputers In Intermediate Accounting: Effects On Student Achievement And Attitudes," **JAED**, 1986, Vol. 4, No. 1, pp. 127-146.)

Harper, Robert M., Jr., William G. Mister and Jerry R. Strawser. "The Impact Of New Pension Disclosure Rules On Perception Of Debt," **JAR**, 1987, Vol. 25, No. 2, pp. 327-330.

Harper, Thomas R. (Streuling, G. Fred and Thomas R. Harper. "Income Tax Questions On The CPA Exam: Recent Changes And Future Outlook," **AR**, 1973, Vol. 48, No. 2, pp. 429-432.)

Harrell, Adrian A. and Roger Eickhoff. "Auditors' Influence-Orientation And Their Effective Responses To The 'Big Eight' Work Environment," **AJPT**, 1988, Vol. 7, No. 2, pp. 105-118.

Harrell, Adrian M. and Michael J. Stahl. "Need For Achievement, Need For Affiliation And The Academic Performance And Career Intentions Of Accounting Students," **JAED**, 1983, Vol. 1, No. 2, pp. 149-153.

Harrell, Adrian M. "The Air Force Switches To Management Accounting," **MA**, 1971, Vol. 52, No. 10, pp. 11-14.

Harrell, Adrian M. "The Decision-Making Behavior Of Air Force Officers And The Management Control Process," **AR**, 1977, Vol. 52, No. 4, pp. 833-841.

Harrell, Adrian, Charles Caldwell and Edwin Doty. "Within-Person Expectancy Theory Predictions Of Accounting Students' Motivation To Achieve Academic Success," **AR**, 1985, Vol. 60, No. 4, pp. 724-735.

Harrell, Adrian, Eugene Chewning, and Martin Taylor. "Organizational-Professional Conflict And The Job Satisfaction And Turnover Intentions Of Internal Auditors," **AJPT**, 1985-86, Vol. 5, No. 2, pp. 111-121.

Harrell, A. M. and H. D. Klick. "Comparing The Impact Of Monetary And Nonmonetary Human Asset Measures On Executive Decision Making," **AOS**, 1980, Vol. 5, No. 4, pp. 393-400.

Harrell, A. M. and J. J. Stahl. "McClelland's Trichotomy Of Needs Theory And The Job Satisfaction And Work Performance Of CPA Firm Professionals," **AOS**, 1984, Vol. 9, No.

3/4, pp. 241-252.

Harrell, Rhett D. and Richard J. Haas. "Selecting An External Auditor For Government Organizations - Part I," **CPAJ**, 1984, Vol. 54, No. 9, pp. 34-45.

Harrell, Rhett D. and Robert J. Haas. "Selecting An External Auditor For Government Organizations - Part II," **CPAJ**, 1984, Vol. 54, No. 10, pp. 62-72.

Harrelson, Fred A., Jr. "Document Your Data Processing System," **MA**, 1967, Vol. 49, No. 1, pp. 43-49.

Harrill, E. Reece and Thomas E. Richards. "A Total Systems Approach To Governmental Accounting," **MA**, 1972, Vol. 53, No. 11, pp. 14-20.

Harrington, Emmett S. "Important Issues Being Discussed By The Accounting Principles Board," **MA**, 1970, Vol. 52, No. 6, pp. 9-14.

Harrington, Russell C. "Reforming The Federal Tax System," **JOA**, 1960, Vol. 109, No. 6, pp. 30-35.

Harris, Frank B. (Finnell, Jack C., Leland G. Ayer and Frank B. Harris. "Full Costing In The Oil And Gas Producing Industry," **MA**, 1967, Vol. 48, No. 5, pp. 47-52.)

Harris, Gould L. "An Application Of Standard Costs In The Field Of Distribution," **AR**, 1931, Vol. 6, No. 2, pp. 118-124.

Harris, Hubert L., Jr. "Personal Financial Planning: The Competition," **JOA**, 1985, Vol. 160, No. 1, pp. 64-78.

Harris, John K. and Jack L. Krogstad. "Assessing Progress Of The CMA Program," **MA**, 1977, Vol. 58, No. 8, pp. 17-23.

Harris, John K. and Jack L. Krogstad. "A Profile And Index Of The CMA Examination," **AR**, 1976, Vol. 51, No. 3, pp. 637-641.

Harris, John K. and Richard M. Hodgetts. "A Quasi-Consulting Project Involving Accounting And Management Students," **AR**, 1972, Vol. 47, No. 2, pp. 375-380.

Harris, John K. (Blake, Thomas E. and John K. Harris. "An Analysis Of APB Opinion Coverage In The CPA Examination," **AR**, 1976, Vol. 51, No. 2, pp. 370-375.)

Harris, John K. (Booker, Jon A. and John K. Harris. "A Project To Enrich The Study Of Financial Reporting," **AR**, 1980, Vol. 55, No. 1, pp. 107-110.)

Harris, John K. (Ford, Allen and John K. Harris. "The Impact Of Recruiting Practices On Students," **CPAJ**, 1974, Vol. 44, No. 8, pp. 29-34.)

Harris, John K. (Jarnagin, Bill D. and John K. Harris. "Teaching With Multiple Choice Questions," **AR**, 1977, Vol. 52, No. 4, pp. 930-934.)

Harris, John K. (Krogstad, Jack L. and John K. Harris. "The CMA Examination: A Content Analysis," **MA**, 1974, Vol. 56, No. 4, pp. 21-23.)

Harris, Joseph P. "Does Federal Accounting And Auditing Need Overhauling?," **AR**, 1940, Vol. 15, No. 1, pp. 1-21.

Harris, Le Brone C. and William L. Stephens. "The Learning Curve: A Case Study," **MA**, 1978, Vol. 59, No. 8, pp. 47-54.

Harris, Patricia E. (Guy, Dan M., Patricia E. Harris and Doyle Z. Williams. "Client Perceptions Of A Local CPA Firm," **CPAJ**, 1979, Vol. 49, No. 3, pp. 17-22.)

Harris, Paul V. "A Review Of Investment Credit And Recapture," **MA**, 1969, Vol. 50, No. 6, pp. 49-52.

Harris, Paul V. "Tax Deductibility Of Contested Taxes And Legal Expenses," **MA**, 1966, Vol. 47, No. 8, pp. 36-40.

Harris, Reese H., Jr. "The Estate Planning Team," **JOA**, 1959, Vol. 108, No. 2, pp. 32-36.

Harris, Robert S. (Marston, Felicia and Robert S. Harris. "Substitutability Of Leases And Debt In Corporate Capital Structures," **JAAF**, 1988, Vol. 3 (New Series), No. 2, pp. 147-170.)

Harris, Trevor S. and James A. Ohlson. "Accounting Disclosures And The Market's Valuation Of Oil And Gas Properties," **AR**, 1987, Vol. 62, No. 4, pp. 651-670.

Harris, William T., Jr. and Wayne R. Chapin. "Joint Product Costing," **MA**, 1973, Vol. 54, No. 10, pp. 43-47.

Harrison, Graeme L. (McKinnon, Jill L. and Graeme L. Harrison. "Cultural Influence On Corporate And Governmental Involvement In Accounting Policy Determination In Japan," **JAPP**, 1985, Vol. 4, No. 3, pp. 201-223.)

Harrison, G. L. and J. L. McKinnon. "Culture And Accounting Change: A New Perspective On Corporate Reporting Regulation And Accounting Policy Formulation," **AOS**, 1986, Vol. 11, No. 3, pp. 233-252.)

Harrison, James F., Jr. and Samuel M. Baggett. "Processing New Ideas," **MA**, 1974, Vol. 55, No. 10, pp. 25-30.

Harrison, James H. (Bill, Robert W., James H. Harrison and Harry R. Maly. "An EDP System For Stores Inventory Control," **MA**, 1967, Vol. 48, No. 12, pp. 35-42.)

Harrison, John P. "In EDP, Organization Breeds Success," **MA**, 1968, Vol. 49, No. 7, pp. 33-36.

Harrison, Paul D., Stephen G. West and J. Hal Reneau. "Initial Attributions And Information-Seeking By Superiors And Subordinates In Production Variance Investigations," **AR**, 1988, Vol. 63, No. 2, pp. 307-320.

Harrison, Robert E. "Some Complexities In Computing 'Earnings And Profits'," **CPAJ**, 1977, Vol. 47, No. 6, pp. 37-39.

Harrison, R. (Groves, R. E. V. and R. Harrison. "Bank Loans And Small Business Financing In Britain," **ABR**, 1973-74, Vol. 4, No. 15, pp. 227-233.)

Harrison, Steven R. "South Central Bell And The Treadway Commission Report," **MA**, 1988, Vol. 70, No. 2, pp. 21-27.

Harrison, Tom. "Different Market Reactions To Discretionary And Nondiscretionary Accounting Changes," **JAR**, 1977, Vol. 15, No. 1, pp. 84-107.

Harrison, Walter T., Jr. and Gary Grudnitski. "Bondholder And Stockholder Reactions To Discretionary Accounting

Changes," **JAPP**, 1987, Vol. 6, No. 2, pp. 87-113.

Harrison, Walter T., Jr., Lawrence A. Tomassini and J. Richard Dietrich. "The Use Of Control Groups In Capital Market Research," **JAR**, 1983, Vol. 21, No. 1, pp. 65-77.

Harrison, W. L. "Message From The American Society," **AR**, 1926, Vol. 1, No. 1, pp. 70-73.

Harriss, C. Lowell. (Dean, Joel and C. Lowell Harriss. "Railroad Accounting Under The New Depreciation Guidelines And Investment Tax Credit," **AR**, 1963, Vol. 38, No. 2, pp. 229-242.)

Harrow, Benjamin. "A Review Of The Proposed New Internal Revenue Code," **JOA**, 1954, Vol. 97, No. 5, pp. 572-581.

Harrow, Benjamin. "A Review Of The Proposed New Internal Revenue Code," **JOA**, 1954, Vol. 97, No. 6, pp. 688-697.

Harrow, Benjamin. "A Review Of The Proposed New Internal Revenue Code," **JOA**, 1954, Vol. 98, No. 2, pp. 179-184.

Harrow, Benjamin. "A Review Of The Proposed New Internal Revenue Code," **JOA**, 1954, Vol. 98, No. 1, pp. 72-81.

Harrow, Benjamin. "An Analysis Of The Revenue Act Of 1950 With Its Provisions And How They Will Operate," **JOA**, 1950, Vol. 90, No. 5, pp. 398-404.

Harrow, Benjamin. "Changes In EPT Under 1951 Revenue Act," **JOA**, 1952, Vol. 93, No. 1, pp. 37-43.

Harrow, Benjamin. "New Changes In Federal Income-Tax Law," **JOA**, 1953, Vol. 96, No. 4, pp. 438-443.

Harrow, Benjamin. "New Revenue Act Closes Loopholes, Removes Some Perplexities, Adds New Ones," **JOA**, 1950, Vol. 90, No. 6, pp. 479-485.

Harrow, Benjamin. "New Tax Situations Under Revenue Act Of 1951," **JOA**, 1951, Vol. 92, No. 6, pp. 676-682.

Hart, Allen M. "Review Of 'Reports On Internal Control' - SAP No. 49," **CPAJ**, 1972, Vol. 42, No. 9, pp. 717-722.

Hart, H. "A Review Of Some Major Recent Developments In The Management Accounting Field," **ABR**, 1980-81, Vol. 11, No. 42, pp. 99-116.

Hart, James R. and Randall W. Luecke. "Corporate Health Care Costs: A Strategy For Containment," **CA**, 1984, Vol. 2, No. 4, pp. 12-21.

Harte, G. F. and D. L. Owen. "Fighting De-Industrialisation: The Role Of Local Government Social Audits," **AOS**, 1987, Vol. 12, No. 2, pp. 123-142.

Hartgraves Al H. (DuPree, Jean M., Al H. Hartgraves and William H. Thralls. "How Management Accountants Can Communicate Better," **MA**, 1987, Vol. 68, No. 8, pp. 40-43.)

Hartgraves, Al and W. Elbert Jones. "Use Of Generic Titles By Unlicensed Accountants," **CPAJ**, 1979, Vol. 49, No. 12, pp. 33-38.

Hartgraves, Al L. and William C. Tuthill. "How Cash Flow Reporting Should Be Changed," **MA**, 1986, Vol. 67, No. 10, pp. 41-45.

Hartgraves, Al L. (Beard, Larry H., Fred A. Jacobs and Al L. Hartgraves. "Publications: A Valid Measure Of Faculty Contribution?," **JAED**, 1985, Vol. 3, No. 2, pp. 155-161.)

Hartgraves, Al L. (Jacobs, Fred A., Al L. Hartgraves and Larry H. Beard. "Publication Productivity Of Doctoral Alumni: A Time-Adjusted Model," **AR**, 1986, Vol. 61, No. 1, pp. 179-187.)

Hartgraves, Robert F., Jr. "Controlling Expenses In A Large Changing Company," **CA**, 1985, Vol. 3, No. 4, pp. 59-65.

Hartley, James N. "Problems Of Consistency In Foreign Accounting," **MA**, 1966, Vol. 48, No. 3, pp. 55-59.

Hartley, Ronald V. and Timothy L. Ross. "MAS And Audit Independence: An Image Problem," **JOA**, 1972, Vol. 134, No. 5, pp. 42-51.

Hartley, Ronald V. "A Note On Quadratic Programming In A Case Of Joint Production: A Reply," **AR**, 1973, Vol. 48, No. 4, pp. 771-774.

Hartley, Ronald V. "Cost Prediction And Allocation: An Incident Process Case," **IAE**, 1987, Vol. 2, No. 1, pp. 141-151.

Hartley, Ronald V. "Decision Making When Joint Products Are Involved," **AR**, 1971, Vol. 46, No. 4, pp. 746-755.

Hartley, Ronald V. "Linear Programming: Some Implications For Management Accounting," **MA**, 1969, Vol. 51, No. 5, pp. 48-49.

Hartley, Ronald V. "Operations Research And Its Implications For The Accounting Profession," **AR**, 1968, Vol. 43, No. 2, pp. 321-332.

Hartley, Ronald V. "Some Extensions Of Sensitivity Analysis," **AR**, 1970, Vol. 45, No. 2, pp. 223-234.

Hartl, Robert J. "The Linear Total Revenue Curve In Cost-Volume-Profit Analysis," **MA**, 1975, Vol. 56, No. 9, pp. 49-52.

Hartman, A. A. "Notes On Dairy-Animal Valuation," **AR**, 1942, Vol. 17, No. 3, pp. 311-313.

Hartman, Bart P. and Dan C. Smith. "Improving Credit Collection Responses," **MA**, 1979, Vol. 61, No. 2, pp. 18-21.

Hartman, Bart P. and H. C. Zaunbrecher. "Comparability And Objectivity Of Exit Value Accounting: A Comment," **AR**, 1976, Vol. 51, No. 4, pp. 927-929.

Hartman, Bart P. and Joseph F. Cheleno. "Estimating Profit And Cash Flow For A New Funeral Home," **MA**, 1979, Vol. 61, No. 5, pp. 35-38.

Hartman, Bart P. and Richard A. White. "Why Not Try A Cafeteria Compensation Plan?," **MA**, 1984, Vol. 66, No. 4, pp. 44-47.

Hartman, Bart P. "The Management Accountant's Role In Deleting A Product Line," **MA**, 1983, Vol. 65, No. 2, pp. 63-66.

Hartman, Bart P. (Park, Hai G. and Bart P. Hartman. "An Application Of Opportunity Cost For A Short-Run Pricing Decision," **JAED**, 1987, Vol. 5, No. 2, pp. 307-313.)

Hartman, Bart P. (Spiceland, J. David, Vincent C. Brenner and Bart P. Hartman. "Standards For Programs And Schools Of Professional Accounting: Accounting Group Perceptions," **AR**, 1980, Vol. 55, No. 1, pp. 134-143.)

Hartman, Bart P. (Swad, Randy G. and Bart P. Hartman. "Financial Accounting And Reporting Of ESOPs," **CPAJ**, 1980, Vol. 50, No. 1, pp. 37-42.)

Hartman, Bart P., David Laxton and William Walvoord. "A Look At Employee Stock Ownership Plans As Financing Tools," **MA**, 1977, Vol. 58, No. 9, pp. 23-28.

Hartman, Bart P., Vincent C. Brenner, Richard A. Lydecker and Jeffrey M. Wilkinson. "Mission Control Starts In The Controller's Department," **MA**, 1981, Vol. 63, No. 3, pp. 27-32.

Hartman, David. "Accounting For Repossessions And Trade-Ups," **AR**, 1939, Vol. 14, No. 3, pp. 267-271.

Hartman, David. "Difficulties With Adjustment Columns - A Solution," **AR**, 1955, Vol. 30, No. 2, pp. 336-338.

Hartman, Frank R. (Mastro, Anthony J. and Frank R. Hartman. "An Evaluation Of A Slide-Lecture Method For Teaching A Large Section Of College Auditing," **AR**, 1960, Vol. 35, No. 2, pp. 324-329.)

Hartman, Marlene. (Lightner, Sharon and Marlene Hartman. "Inventory Of Computer Software Designed For Use In Accounting Curriculum: Student Materials And Test Banks," **JAED**, 1985, Vol. 3, No. 1, pp. 15-35.)

Hartman, Maurice A. "A Simplified Solution To Cost Or Market Problems," **AR**, 1966, Vol. 41, No. 1, pp. 127-129.

Hartman, Robert F., Jr. "A New Course: Accounting Services To Management," **AR**, 1967, Vol. 42, No. 1, pp. 141-143.

Hartmann, Bernhard. "The Effect Of EDP Systems On The Internal Organization Of The Firm," **IJAER**, 1966, Vol. 1, No. 2, pp. 101-117.

Harton, William R., Jr. "Program Planning And Control Through The Budgetary Process," **AR**, 1954, Vol. 29, No. 3, pp. 423-428.

Hartzell, Elmer. "Profits In The Steel Industry," **AR**, 1934, Vol. 9, No. 4, pp. 326-333.

Hartzell, Elmer. "The Background Of Accounting," **AR**, 1934, Vol. 9, No. 2, pp. 158-163.

Harvey, David W. and Soliman Y. Soliman. "Standard Cost Variance Analysis In A Learning Environment," **ABR**, 1982-83, Vol. 13, No. 51, pp. 181-190.

Harvey, David W. "Financial Planning Information For Production Start-Ups," **AR**, 1976, Vol. 51, No. 4, pp. 838-845.

Harvey, David W. (Amato, Henry N., Evan E. Anderson and David W. Harvey. "A General Model Of Future Period Warranty Costs," **AR**, 1976, Vol. 51, No. 4, pp. 854-862.)

Harvey, D. W., J. G. Rhode and K. A. Merchant. "Accounting Aggregation: User Preferences And Decision Making," **AOS**, 1979, Vol. 4, No. 3, pp. 187-210.

Harvey, Gilman C., Jr. "Mathematics Is Bypassing The Accountant," **MA**, 1969, Vol. 50, No. 6, pp. 47-48.

Harvey, John L. "Starting Your Career In Public Accounting," **AR**, 1955, Vol. 30, No. 3, pp. 493-499.

Harvey, J. H. and P. M. McCollum. "Automated Internal Auditing Tools," **MA**, 1966, Vol. 47, No. 2, pp. 44-50.

Harvey-Cook, J. E. and R. J. Taffler. "Graduate Recruitment Procedures In The UK Accountancy Profession: A Preliminary Study," **ABR**, 1986-87, Vol. 17, No. 66, pp. 99-108.

Harwell, Jeff L, William S. Nichols, III and Scott D. Steffler. "Recent Developments In The Presentation Of Earnings Per Share," **AR**, 1974, Vol. 49, No. 4, pp. 852-853.

Harwood, Dale S., Jr. "Yet More On Tax Allocation," **AR**, 1961, Vol. 36, No. 4, pp. 619-625.

Harwood, Gordon B. and Roger H. Hermanson. "The Lease-Or-Buy Decision," **JOA**, 1972, Vol. 142, No. 3, pp. 83-88.

Harwood, Gordon B. (Anderson, Gary J., Gordon B. Harwood and Roger H. Hermanson. "Energy Audits," **CPAJ**, 1979, Vol. 49, No. 1, pp. 31-34.)

Harwood, Gordon B. (Bailey, Charles D., Gordon B. Harwood and William Hopwood. "Removing The Computational Burden From Reciprocal Cost Allocations," **JAED**, 1984, Vol. 2, No. 2, pp. 169-176.)

Harwood, Gordon B. (Berry, Leonard Eugene, Gordon B. Harwood and Joseph L. Katz. "Performance Of Auditing Procedures By Governmental Auditors: Some Preliminary Evidence," **AR**, 1987, Vol. 62, No. 1, pp. 14-28.)

Harwood, Gordon B. (El Sheshai, Kamal M., Gordon B. Harwood and Roger H. Hermanson. "Cost Volume Profit Analysis With Integer Goal Programming," **MA**, 1977, Vol. 59, No. 4, pp. 43-47.)

Harwood, Gordon B. (Garcha, Bikramjit S., Gordon B. Harwood and Roger H. Hermanson. "A Study Of The Readership Of The Accounting Review," **JAED**, 1983, Vol. 1, No. 2, pp. 21-39.)

Hasbrouck, H. C. "Public Utilities View Net-Plant Balance-Sheet Concept," **JOA**, 1952, Vol. 94, No. 4, pp. 460-467.

Haseman, Wilber C. "An Interpretive Framework For Cost," **AR**, 1968, Vol. 43, No. 4, pp. 738-752.

Haseman, Wilber C. (Moss, Morton F. and Wilber C. Haseman. "Some Comments On The Applicability Of Direct Costing To Decision Making," **AR**, 1957, Vol. 32, No. 2, pp. 184-193.)

Haseman, Wilber G. "Accountants In Residency Program," **AR**, 1968, Vol. 43, No. 3, pp. 585-588.

Haseman, William D. and Andrew B. Whinston. "Design Of A Multidimensional Accounting System," **AR**, 1976, Vol. 51, No. 1, pp. 65-79.

Haseman, W. C. "Management Accounting Literature: 1925 And 1975," **AHJ**, 1978, Vol. 5, No. 2, pp. 71-78.

Hasenack, W. "Depression Balance Sheets And Present Day Values," **AR**, 1933, Vol. 8, No. 3, pp. 239-242.

Haskins, Mark E. and Alfred J. Nanni, Jr. "Toward Attribute

Models Of Accounting Control Systems: Qualitative Versus Quantitative Approaches," **JAL**, 1987, Vol. 6, pp. 111-130.

Haskins, Mark E. and David D. Williams. "A Genealogy Of Today's Contributors To Accounting Research," **AHJ**, 1986, Vol. 13, No. 1, pp. 93-101.

Haskins, Mark E. and David D. Williams. "The Association Between Client Factors And Audit Fees: A Comparison By Country And By Firm," **ABR**, 1988, Vol. 18, No. 70, pp. 183-192.

Haskins, Mark E. and David D. Williams. "Corporate Mergers And Auditors' Client Portfolios," **ACCHOR**, 1988, Vol. 2, No. 1, pp. 77-87.

Haskins, Mark E. and Robert L. Henarie. "Attributes And Audit Impact Of Client's Control Environment," **CPAJ**, 1985, Vol. 55, No. 7, pp. 18-27.

Haskins, Mark E. and Robert N. Holt. "A Cash Flow Approach To The Statement Of Changes In Financial Position," **JAED**, 1986, Vol. 4, No. 2, pp. 97-106.

Haskins, Mark E. and Robert P. Crum. "Cost Allocations: A Classroom Role-Play In Managerial Behavior And Accounting Choices," **IAE**, 1985, No. 1, pp. 109-130.

Haskins, Mark E. "Client Control Environments: An Examination Of Auditors' Perceptions," **AR**, 1987, Vol. 62, No. 3, pp. 542-563.

Haslem, John A. (Baker, H. Kent and John A. Haslem. "Information Needs Of Individual Investors," **JOA**, 1973, Vol. 136, No. 5, pp. 64-69.)

Haslem, John A. (Baker, H. Kent, Robert H. Chenhall, John A. Haslem and Roger H. Juchau. "Disclosure Of Material Information: A Cross-National Comparison," **IJAER**, 1977, Vol. 13, No. 1, pp. 1-18.)

Hassan, Nabil, R. Penny Marquette and Joseph M. McKeon, Jr. "Sensitivity Analysis: An Accounting Tool For Decision-Making," **MA**, 1978, Vol. 59, No. 10, pp. 43-50.

Hasselback, James R. "An Empirical Examination Of Annual Report Presentation Of The Corporate Income Tax Expense," **AR**, 1976, Vol. 51, No. 2, pp. 269-276.

Hasselback, James R. "Travel Expenses For The Visiting Professor - An Addendum," **AR**, 1976, Vol. 51, No. 1, pp. 180-183.

Hasselback, James R. (Crumbley, D. Larry and James R. Hasselback. "The Asset Depreciation Range System," **CPAJ**, 1976, Vol. 46, No. 1, pp. 29-33.)

Hasseldine, C. Roy. (McNally, Graeme M., Lee Hock Eng and C. Roy Hasseldine. "Corporate Financial Reporting In New Zealand," **ABR**, 1982-83, Vol. 13, No. 49, pp. 11-20.)

Hasseldine, C. R. "Mix And Yield Variances," **AR**, 1967, Vol. 42, No. 3, pp. 497-515.

Hassell, John M. and Robert H. Jennings. "Relative Forecast Accuracy And The Timing Of Earnings Forecast Announcements," **AR**, 1986, Vol. 61, No. 1, pp. 58-75.

Hassler, Eugene C. and Dale Buckmaster. "Implications Of 'Volatility In Quarterly Accounting Data': A Comment," **AR**, 1975, Vol. 50, No. 1, pp. 127-129.

Hassler, Russell H. "The Case Method Of Teaching Accounting," **AR**, 1950, Vol. 25, No. 2, pp. 170-172.

Hassler, Russell H. (Ward, Lewis B. and Russell H. Hassler. "A Critical Evaluation Of The Institute Personnel Selection & Testing Program," **JOA**, 1950, Vol. 90, No. 2, pp. 113-121.)

Hastings, John E. Jr, Albert P. Ameiss and Charles R. Kuehl. "CMA Review - The Monsanto Experience," **MA**, 1976, Vol. 57, No. 8, pp. 57-60.

Hasz, Thomas W. and J. L. Boockholdt. "How Houston Lighting & Power Applied DDP," **MA**, 1983, Vol. 64, No. 9, pp. 56-59.

Hatfield, Henry Rand. "A Hatfield Trilogy: 'Zwei Pfadfinder'," **AHJ**, 1977, Vol. 4, No. 1, pp. 2-8.

Hatfield, Henry Rand. "Accounting Trivia," **AR**, 1940, Vol. 15, No. 3, pp. 417-419.

Hatfield, Henry Rand. "An Accounting Paradox," **AR**, 1928, Vol. 3, No. 4, pp. 342-344.

Hatfield, Henry Rand. "Operating Deficit And Paid-In Surplus," **AR**, 1934, Vol. 9, No. 3, pp. 237-241.

Hatfield, Henry Rand. "Replacement And Book Value," **AR**, 1944, Vol. 19, No. 1, pp. 66-67.

Hatfield, Henry Rand. "Some Variations In Accounting Practice In England, France, Germany And The United States," **JAR**, 1966, Vol. 4, No. 2, pp. 169-182.

Hatfield, Henry R. "A Fable," **AR**, 1932, Vol. 7, No. 3, p. 175.

Hatfield, Henry R. "What They Say About Depreciation," **AR**, 1936, Vol. 11, No. 1, pp. 18-25.

Hatfield, H. R. and A. C. Littleton. "A Check-List Of Early Bookkeeping Texts," **AR**, 1932, Vol. 7, No. 3, pp. 194-206.

Hatfield, H. R. "Comments On Is Appreciation Available For Dividends," **AR**, 1930, Vol. 5, No. 1, pp. 26-27.

Hatfield, H. R. "Comments On Is Appreciation A Depreciating Element?," **AR**, 1930, Vol. 5, No. 1, pp. 53-54.

Hatfield, H. R. "Comments On Should Appreciation Be Brought Into The Accounts?," **AR**, 1930, Vol. 5, No. 1, pp. 33-34.

Hatfield, H. R. "Comments On What Is Appreciaiton," **AR**, 1930, Vol. 5, No. 1, pp. 12-14.

Hatfield, Jack D. "How To Establish An Effective Records Retention Program," **MA**, 1980, Vol. 61, No. 9, pp. 55-57.

Hatfield, John. "A Hatfield Trilogy: 'Recollections About Father'," **AHJ**, 1977, Vol. 4, No. 1, pp. 14-16.

Hathaway, Bruce R. "Controlling New Facilities Costs," **MA**, 1975, Vol. 56, No. 10, pp. 47-49.

Hathaway, Wade W., Jr. "How We Documented Our Internal Accounting Control Systems," **MA**, 1981, Vol. 63, No. 4, pp. 65-71.

Hatherly, David J. "Evaluating The Effects Of Interrelated

Evidence Sources," **ABR**, 1985-86, Vol. 16, No. 61, pp. 35-46.

Hatherly, David. "Linking Internal Control And Substantive Tests: A Note," **ABR**, 1975-76, Vol. 6, No. 21, pp. 63-66.

Hatherly, David. "Segmentation And The Audit Process," **ABR**, 1978-79, Vol. 9, No. 34, pp. 152-156.

Hatherly, D. "Accounting And Auditing Standards: Why They Are Inconsistent," **ABR**, 1981-82, Vol. 12, No. 46, pp. 136-140.

Haulotte, R. and E. Stevelinck. "A Bit Of Accounting History: Adding The Pages In The Journal," **AHJ**, 1977, Vol. 4, No. 2, pp. 113-116.

Haun, Richard R. "Accounting For The Horse Racing Business," **MA**, 1976, Vol. 58, No. 2, pp. 43-47.

Haun, Robert D. and Leo Herbert. "Grading Of The American Institute of Accountants' Examination Papers," **AR**, 1952, Vol. 27, No. 4, pp. 523-529.

Haun, Robert D. "Broad Vs. Narrow Concepts Of Internal Auditing And Internal Control," **AR**, 1955, Vol. 30, No. 1, pp. 114-118.

Haun, R. D. "Two Present-Day Problems Of General Financial Accounting," **AR**, 1933, Vol. 8, No. 2, pp. 117-118.

Hausman, Donald I. "The Foreign Direct Investment Program," **IJAER**, 1968, Vol. 4, No. 1, pp. 67-79.

Haussener, Donald P. (Mullick, Satinder K. and Donald P. Haussner. "Production Decisions For New Products," **MA**, 1974, Vol. 56, No. 2, pp. 27-32.)

Hauworth, William P. and L. Joe Moravy. "Accounting For Expanded Use Of Option Transactions," **CPAJ**, 1987, Vol. 57, No. 5, pp. 56-65.

Hauworth, William P. "Problems In The Development Of Worldwide Accounting Standards," **IJAER**, 1973, Vol. 9, No. 1, pp. 23-34.

Hauworth, William P., II and Lailani Moody. "An Accountant's Option Primer: Puts And Calls Demystified," **JOA**, 1987, Vol. 163, No. 1, pp. 87-97.

Hauworth, William P., II, Valdean C. Lembke and Robert F. Sharp. "The Effects Of Inflation: How They Persist," **JAAF**, 1987, Vol. 2 (New Series). No. 2, pp. 184-196.

Hauworth, William P., II. "A Comparison Of Various International Proposals On Inflation Accounting: A Practitioner's View," **IJAER**, 1980, Vol. 16, No. 1, pp. 63-82.

Havens, Harry S. "Accounting And Public Policy," **JAPP**, 1983, Vol. 2, No. 3, pp. 143-146.

Havis, Kenneth R. (Needles, Belverd E., Jr. and Kenneth R. Havis. "Financial Reporting Of Regulated Investment Companies: A Survey," **JOA**, 1971, Vol. 131, No. 1, pp. 52-59.)

Haw, In-Mu and Byung T. Ro. "An Analysis Of The Impact Of Corporate Pollution Disclosures: A Comment," **AIPIA**, 1988, Vol. 2, pp. 187-191.

Haw, In-Mu and Steven Lustgarten. "Evidence On Income Measurement Properties Of ASR No. 190 And SFAS No. 33 Data," **JAR**, 1988, Vol. 26, No. 2, pp. 331-352.

Haw, In-Mu, Victor Pastena and Steven Lilien. "The Association Between Market-Based Merger Premiums And Firm's Financial Position Prior To Merger," **JAAF**, 1987, Vol. 2 (New Series), No. 1, pp. 24-42.

Hawes, Richard K. "Financial Futures: Today's Cash Management Alternatives," **MA**, 1983, Vol. 65, No. 6, pp. 26-29.

Hawkins, Clark A. and Diane Girard. "Replacement Decisions Under The Accelerated Cost Recovery System," **JAAF**, 1984, Vol. 7, No. 3, pp. 225-240.

Hawkins, C. A. and D. N. Leggett. "The Investment Tax Credit In Capital Replacement: A Simulation," **JAPP**, 1983, Vol. 2, No. 3, pp. 167-187.

Hawkins, David and Brandt Allen. "Computer Assisted Case Analyses," **AR**, 1967, Vol. 42, No. 4, pp. 788-800.

Hawkins, William M. "An EDP General Accounting System In Concept And In Force," **MA**, 1970, Vol. 52, No. 4, pp. 11-14.

Hawley, John D. (Test, Darrell L., John D. Hawley and Michael F. Cortright. "Determining Strategic Value," **MA**, 1987, Vol. 68, No. 12, pp. 39-42.)

Haworth, Jean. (Steele, Anthony and Jean Haworth. "Auditors' Views On The Truth And Fairness Of CCA," **ABR**, 1985-86, Vol. 16, No. 62, pp. 133-142.)

Hawthorne, W. H. and H. C. Herring. "A Quantitative Approach To The Illustration Of The Percentage-Of-Completion Method," **AR**, 1975, Vol. 50,No. 3,pp. 615-616.

Hay, Leon E. "A Form For Trustees' Reports," **JOA**, 1956, Vol. 101, No. 1, pp. 50-54.

Hay, Leon E. "Executorship Reporting - Some Historical Notes," **AR**, 1961, Vol. 36, No. 1, pp. 100-104.

Hay, Leon E. "Graduate Seminars In Accounting Research," **AR**, 1964, Vol. 39, No. 4, pp. 1027-1029.

Hay, Leon E. "Planning For Profits - How Some Executives Are Doing It," **AR**, 1960, Vol. 35, No. 2, pp. 233-237.

Hay, Leon E. "Statutory Requirements As To Form And Content Of Executors' Reports To Courts," **AR**, 1955, Vol. 30, No. 4, pp. 702-705.

Hay, Leon E. "The Myth Of The Charge And Discharge Statement," **AR**, 1956, Vol. 31, No. 4, pp. 632-635.

Hay, Robert D. "Management Thinking Concerning Corporate Annual Reports," **AR**, 1955, Vol. 30, No. 3, pp. 444-450.

Hay, Robert. (Abs, George, Clayton Grimstad, Robert Hay, W. Asquith Howe, William LaPlace, Francis J. McGurr and William Serrano. "Historical Dates In Accounting," **AR**, 1954, Vol. 29, No. 3, pp. 486-493.)

Hayes, David C. "The Contingency Theory Of Managerial Accounting," **AR**, 1977, Vol. 52, No. 1, pp. 22-39.

Hayes, David C. "The Contingency Theory Of Managerial Accounting: A Reply," **AR**, 1978, Vol. 53, No. 2, pp. 530-533.

Hayes, David C. (Ferris, Kenneth R. and David C. Hayes. "Some Evidence On The Determinants Of Profit Forecast Accuracy In The United Kingdom," **IJAER**, 1977, Vol. 12, No. 2, pp. 27-36.)

Hayes, Donald J. "The International Accounting Standards Committee - Recent Developments And Current Problems," **IJAER**. 1980, Vol. 16, No. 1, pp. 1-10.

Hayes, D. C. "Accounting For Accounting: A Story About Managerial Accounting," **AOS**, 1983, Vol. 8, No. 2/3, pp. 241-250.

Hayes, D. (Cooper, D. J., D. Hayes and F. Wolf. "Accounting In Organized Anarchies: Understanding And Designing Accounting Systems In Ambiguous Situations," **AOS**, 1981, Vol. 6, No. 3, pp. 175-192.)

Hayes, Randall B. and William R. Cron. "Changes In Task Unvertainty Induced By Zero-Based Budgeting: Using The Thompson And Hirst Models To Predict Dysfunctional Behaviour," **ABACUS**, 1988, Vol. 24, No. 2, pp. 145-161.

Hayes, Randall B. (Dilley, Steven C., Randall B. Hayes and Paul Steinbart. "Development Of A Paradigm For Applied Accounting Research: A Way Of Coping With Subject-Matter Complexity," **AR**, 1983, Vol. 58, No. 2, pp. 405-416.)

Hayes, Samuel L., III. (Taussig, Russell A. and Samuel L. Hayes, III. "Cash Take-Overs And Accounting Valuations." **AR**, 1968, Vol. 43, No. 1, pp. 68-74.)

Hayes, William D. "How A Practitioner In Smaller Community Sets Fees, Pays Staff, Maintains Records," **JOA**, 1950, Vol. 89, No. 3, pp. 224-227.

Hays, James R. "Manpower Control For Manufacturing," **MA**, 1972, Vol. 53, No. 10, pp. 31-37.

Hayya, Jack C. (Ferrara, William L. and Jack C. Hayya. "Toward Probabilistic Profit Budgets," **MA**, 1970, Vol. 52. No. 4, pp. 23-28.)

Hayya, Jack C. (Ferrara, William L, Jack C. Hayya and David A. Nachman,. "Normalcy Of Profit In The Jaedicke-Robichek Model," **AR**, 1972, Vol. 47, No. 2, pp. 299-307.)

Hayya, Jack, William Ferrara and Erwin Saniga. "Extending The Applicability Of Probabilistic Management Planning And Control Models: A Comment," **AR**, 1975, Vol. 50, No. 4. pp. 826-831.

Hayya, J. C., W. L. Ferrara and Erwin M. Saniga. "On The Accuracy Of Normalcy Approximation In Stochastic C-V-P Analysis: A Reply," **AR**, 1978, Vol. 53, No. 1, pp. 252-259.

Hazard, Albert W. and Raymond E. Perry. "What FASB Statement No. 91 Means For Accountants And Auditors," **JOA**, 1988. Vol. 165, No. 2, pp. 28-36.

Hazard, Jeffrey. "Are You Wasting Time With Your Micro?." **MA**. 1986, Vol. 67, No. 11, pp. 58-61.

Hazelton, Walter A. "How To Cost Labor Settlements," **MA**, 1979, Vol. 60, No. 11, pp. 19-23.

Hazelton, Walter A. "The Ins And Outs Of Foreign Trade." **MA**, 1987, Vol. 69, No. 6, pp. 53-58.

Hazlehurst, Blackburn H. "Auditor/Actuary Relations Under ERISA: As An Actuary Sees It," **JOA**, 1978, Vol. 146, No. 1, pp. 58-65.

Heagy, Cynthia D. and Peter L. McMickle. "An Empirical Investigation Of The Accounting Systems Course: Academic Practice Versus Practitioner Needs," **IAE**, 1988, Vol. 3, No. 1. pp. 96-107.

Healy, Paul and Thomas Lys. "Auditor Changes Following Big Eight Mergers With Non-Big Eight Audit Firms," **JAPP**, 1986, Vol. 5, No. 4, pp. 251-265.

Healy, Paul M., Sok-Hyon Kang and Krishna G. Palepu. "The Effect Of Accounting Procedure Changes On CEOs' Cash Salary And Bonus Compensation," **JAEC**, 1987, Vol. 9, No. 1, pp. 7-34.

Healy, Paul. "The Effect Of Bonus Schemes On Accounting Decisions," **JAEC**, 1985, Vol. 7, No. 1/3, pp. 85-107.

Healy, Robert E. "Acquistions And Mergers - Management Problems," **MA**, 1969, Vol. 50, No. 9, pp. 9-11.

Healy, Robert E. "The Next Step In Accounting." **AR**, 1938. Vol. 13, No. 1, pp. 1-8.

Heamon, John W. "Deferring Mortgage Origination Expenses," **MA**. 1973, Vol. 54, No. 11, pp. 43-44.

Heamon, John W. "Inventory And Financing Procedures For A Mortgage Banker," **MA**, 1969, Vol. 51, No. 6, pp. 32-34.

Heaney, Terence, Martin Mason and Matthew Minor. "A Closer Look At ESOPs," **CPAJ**, 1976, Vol. 46, No. 9. pp. 29-36.

Heard, Edwin, Constantine Konstans and James Don Edwards. "Demonstrating The Conceptual Significance Of The Matrix Inverse," **AR**, 1974, Vol. 49, No. 2, pp. 377-381.

Heard, Julie A. (Edwards, James B. and Julie A. Heard. "Is Cost Accounting The No. 1 Enemy Of Productivity?," **MA**, 1984, Vol. 65, No. 12, pp. 44-49.)

Heard, J. E. and W. J. Bolce. "The Political Significance Of Corporate Social Reporting In The United States Of America," **AOS**, 1981, Vol. 6, No. 3, pp. 247-254.

Hearne, David C. "Using Client's Staff To Cut Costs Of Audit," **JOA**, 1951, Vol. 92, No. 3, pp. 307-312.

Heaston, Patrick H. "Qualification Requirements For Public Accounting In Selected Foreign Countries: A Comparison With The United States," **IJAER**, 1984, Vol. 20, No. 1, pp. 71-94.

Heath, David C. (Billera. Louis J., David C. Heath and Robert E. Verrecchia. "A Unique Procedure For Allocating Common Costs From A Production Process," **JAR**, 1981, Vol. 19. No. 1, pp. 185-196.)

Heath, John, Jr. "Optimizing Cash Flow And Tax Benefits In New Plant Construction," **MA**, 1971, Vol. 52, No. 9, pp. 35-38.

Heath, John, Jr. "Property Valuation Problems And The Accountant," **JOA**, 1964, Vol. 117, No. 1, pp. 54-58.

Heath, Leslie A. "An Ounce Of Prevention - Means Dollars To Your Estate," **JOA**, 1961, Vol. 111, No. 1, pp. 43-47.

Heath, Leslie A. "What An Accounting Student Should Know," **AR**, 1942, Vol. 17, No. 3, pp. 313-315.

Heath, Loyd C. and Paul Rosenfield. "Solvency: The Forgotten Half Of Financial Reporting," **JOA**, 1979, Vol. 147, No. 1, pp. 48-55.

Heath, Loyd C. "Accounting, Communication, And The Pygmalion Syndrome," **ACCHOR**, 1987, Vol. 1, No. 1, pp. 1-8.

Heath, Loyd C. "Distinguishing Between Monetary And Nonmonetary Assets And Liabilities In General Price Level Accounting," **AR**, 1972, Vol. 47, No. 3, pp. 458-468.

Heath, Loyd C. "Is Working Capital Really Working?," **JOA**, 1980, Vol. 150, No. 2, pp. 55-62.

Heath, Loyd C. "Let's Scrap The 'Funds' Statement," **JOA**, 1978, Vol. 146, No. 4, pp. 94-103.

Heaton, Herbert. "Organizing For People," **MA**, 1978, Vol. 59, No. 8, pp. 55-58.

Hecht, Gerhard. "The New Management Information Systems: Should Auld Accounting Be Forgot?," **MA**, 1969, Vol. 50, No. 9, pp. 15-16.

Heck, J. Louis and Jiunn C. Huang. "Contributions To Accounting Literature: A Peer Assessment Of Monographs," **JAED**, 1986, Vol. 4, No. 2, pp. 27-36.

Heck, J. Louis and Jiunn C. Huang. "Peer Assessment Versus Citation Analysis Of Contributions To The Accounting Literature," **AIA**, 1987, Vol. 5, pp. 153-162.

Heck, J. Louis and Wayne G. Bremser. "Six Decades Of The Accounting Review: A Summary Of Author And Institutional Contributors," **AR**, 1986, Vol. 61, No. 4, pp. 735-744.

Heck, William R. "A Forward Approach To Dollar-Value Lifo," **AR**, 1965, Vol. 40, No. 4, pp. 879-880.

Heck, W. R. "Accounting For Warranty Costs," **AR**, 1963, Vol. 38, No. 3, pp. 577-578.

Heckert, J. Brooks. "A Course In Controllership," **AR**, 1949, Vol. 24, No. 2, pp. 208-209.

Heckert, J. Brooks. "Accounting Hall Of Fame," **AR**, 1950, Vol. 25, No. 3, pp. 260-261.

Heckert, J. Brooks. "Methods And Advantages Of Early Closing," **AR**, 1929, Vol. 4, No. 3, pp. 181-193.

Heckert, J. B. "Comments On The Definition Of Earned Surplus," **AR**, 1930, Vol. 5, No. 2, pp. 168-174.

Heckert, J. B. "The Accountant's Part In Determining Standards," **AR**, 1933, Vol. 8, No. 4 pp. 342-344.

Heckert, J. B., H. F. Taggart, C. L. Van Sickle, R. M. Mikesell, F. W. Woodbridge, Louis O. Foster and T. W. Leland. "Instruction In Methods Of Accounting Control: A Symposium," **AR**, 1937, Vol. 12. No. 2. pp. 114-122.

Heckman, H. M. "Standards Of Accounting Training," **AR**, 1933, Vol. 8, No. 2, pp. 110-112.

Hedberg, B. and S. Jonsson. "Designing Semi-Confusing Information Systems For Organizations In Changing Environments," **AOS**, 1978, Vol. 3. No. 1. pp. 47-64.

Hedges, Paul W. "Use Of A Data Processing Service Bureau - A Case Study," **MA**, 1967, Vol. 48. No. 12. pp. 23-26.

Hedish, Norman D. "Account Classification And Principle Codification," **AR**, 1959, Vol. 34, No. 4, pp. 660-662.

Hedlund, G. (Hagg, I. and G. Hedlund. "Case Studies' In Accounting Research," **AOS**, 1979, Vol. 4, No. 1/2, pp. 135-143.)

Heebink, David V. "The Optimum Capital Budget," **AR**, 1964, Vol. 39, No. 1, pp. 90-93.

Hefzi, Hassan, A. James Ifflander and David B. Smith. "Municipal Bond Market Risk Measures And Bond Ratings," **AIA**, 1988, Vol. 6, pp. 111-128.

Heier, Jan Richard. "A Content Comparison Of Antebellum Plantation Records And Thomas Affleck's Accounting Principles," **AHJ**, 1988, Vol. 15, No. 2, pp. 131-150.

Heightchew, Robert E., Jr. "Strategies For Marketing Your Accounting Practice," **CPAJ**, 1987, Vol. 57, No. 9, pp. 64-74.

Heilman, Ernest. (Brookner. Lester and Ernest Heilman. "Technical Assistance In Accounting In Turkey," **AR**, 1960, Vol. 35, No. 1, pp. 33-36.)

Heilman, E. A. "Accounting And Economics," **AR**, 1935, Vol. 10, No. 2, pp. 149-153.

Heilman, E. A. "Comments And Questions On The Use Of Ratios," **AR**, 1933, Vol. 8, No. 3, pp. 246-247.

Heilman, E. A. "Coordination Between High-School Bookkeeping And College Accounting Courses," **AR**, 1930, Vol. 5, No. 4, pp. 317-320.

Heilman, E. A. "Realized Income," **AR**, 1929, Vol. 4, No. 2, pp. 80-87.

Heilman, E. A. "Roundtable On Examinations In Accounting - Opening Remarks," **AR**, 1942, Vol. 17, No. 2, p. 100.

Heimann, Stephen R. and Edward J. Lusk. "Decision Flexibility: An Alternative Evaluation Criterion," **AR**, 1976, Vol. 51, No. 1, pp. 51-64.

Heimann, Stephen R. and George Richard Chesley. "Audit Sample Sizes For Aggregated Statement Accounts," **JAR**, 1977, Vol. 15, No. 2, pp. 193-206.

Heimbucher, Clifford V. "Fifty-Three Jurisdictions," **JOA**, 1961, Vol. 112, No. 5, pp. 42-50.

Hein, Clarence D. and Keith R. Shwayder. "Some Accounting Problems In Divesting Former Acquisitions," **CPAJ**, 1974, Vol. 44, No. 11, pp. 33-38.

Hein, Leonard W. "J. Lee Nicholson: Pioneer Cost Accountant," **AR**, 1959, Vol. 34, No. 1, pp. 106-111.

Hein, Leonard W. "New British Accounting Recommendations," **AR**, 1963, Vol. 38, No. 2, pp. 252-261.

Hein, Leonard W. "The Auditor And The British Companies Act," **AR**, 1963, Vol. 38, No. 3, pp. 508-520.

Hein, Leonard W. "The Course In Computers - Is It Accounting? Mathematics? Engineering?," **AR**, 1959, Vol. 34, No. 1, pp. 132-134.

Hein, Leonard W. "The Management Accountant And The Integrated Information System," **MA**, 1968, Vol. 49, No. 10, pp. 34-38.

Heinen, Edmund. "Goals In Managerial Economics," **IJAER**, 1976, Vol. 11, No. 2, pp. 1-10.

Heinen, Edmund. "Supplemented Multi-Purpose Accounting," **IJAER**, 1978, Vol. 14, No. 1, pp. 1-15.

Heins, Everett B. "A Survey Of Accounting In Junior Colleges," **AR**, 1966, Vol. 41, No. 2, pp. 323-326.

Heins, John. "The President's Report (1889)," **AHJ**, 1978, Vol. 5, No. 1, pp. 69-71.

Heins, Robert H. "Steam Power As A Production Cost," **MA**, 1972, Vol. 53, No. 10, pp. 25-26.

Heintz, James A. and Jin-Soo Han. "A Study Of Audit Judgments Of Korean CPAs," **IJAER**, 1985, Vol. 21, No. 1, pp. 21-38.

Heintz, James A. "Hindsight And Retroactive Restatement," **CPAJ**, 1976, Vol. 46, No. 10, pp. 31-34.

Heintz, James A. "Price-Level Restated Financial Statements And Investment Decision Making," **AR**, 1973, Vol. 48, No. 4, pp. 679-689.

Heintz, James A. "The Effects Of Restating Financial Statements For Price-Level Changes: A Reply," **AR**, 1975, Vol. 50, No. 4, pp. 809-814.

Heintz, James A. (Falk, Haim and James A. Heintz. "Assessing Industry Risk By Ratio Analysis: A Reply," **AR**, 1978, Vol. 53, No. 1, pp. 210-215.)

Heintz, James A. (Falk, Haim and James A. Heintz. "Company Risk Relationships Over Consecutive Periods," **ABR**, 1977-78, Vol. 8, No. 32, pp. 246-252.)

Heintz, James A. (Falk, Haim and James A. Heintz. "Assessing Industry Risk By Ratio Analysis," **AR**, 1975, Vol. 50, No. 4, pp. 758-779.)

Heintz, James A. (Falk, Haim and James A. Heintz. "Relative Company Risk Over Time," **ABR**, 1974-75, Vol. 5, No. 17, pp. 25-40.)

Heintz, James A. (Falk, Haim, Samuel Frumer and James A. Heintz. "Accounting For Stock Reacquisitions: Israel And The United States Compared," **IJAER**, 1974, Vol. 9, No. 2, pp. 111-123.)

Heintz, James A. (Rebele, James E., James A. Heintz and George E. Briden. "Independent Auditor Sensitivity To Evidence Reliability," **AJPT**, 1988, Vol. 8, No. 1, pp. 43-52.)

Heitger, Lester E. "Data Base Considerations For Electric Utilities," **MA**, 1976, Vol. 57, No. 9, pp. 31-33.

Heitger, Lester E. (Buzby, Stephen L. and Lester E. Heitger. "Profit Contribution By Market Segment," **MA**, 1976, Vol. 58, No. 5, pp. 42-46.)

Helgeson, James G. and G. Eddy Birrer. "Marketing Plans For Accounting Firms," **JOA**, 1986, Vol. 162, No. 3, pp. 115-126.

Helleloid, Richard T. "Hindsight Judgments About Taxpayers' Expectations," **JATA**, 1988, Vol. 9, No. 2, pp. 31-46.

Heller, Kenneth H. and James H. Boyd. "Professors' Home Office Expenses: A Recent Development," **AR**, 1976, Vol. 51, No. 2, pp. 376-379.

Heller, Kenneth H. (Streuling, G. Fred, James H. Boyd and Kenneth H. Heller. "Interrelationships Of Sections 731, 736, And 751: A Worksheet Approach," **JATA**, 1987, Vol. 8, No. 2, pp. 37-49.)

Helmer, F. Theodore. (Suver, James D. and F. Theodore Helmer. "Developing Budgetary Models For Greater Hospital Efficiency," **MA**, 1979, Vol. 61, No. 1, pp. 34-36.)

Helmi, Medhat A. and Murat N. Tanju. "Budget After The Fact: An Auditing Tool For Management Evaluation," **ABACUS**, 1980, Vol. 16, No. 2, pp. 124-132.

Helmi, Medhat A. "Integrating The Microcomputer Into Accounting Education - Approaches And Pitfalls." **IAE**, 1986. Vol. 1, No. 1, pp. 102-111.

Helmkamp, John G. "Technical Information Center Management: An Accounting Deficiency," **AR**, 1969, Vol. 44, No. 3, pp. 605-610.

Helms, Glenn L. (Tussing. Robert T. and Glenn L. Helms. "Training Computer Audit Specialists," **JOA**, 1980, Vol. 150, No. 1, pp. 71-74.)

Helpern, Stephen R. (Wright, Robert F. and Stephen R. Helpern. "Corporate Business Combinations - A New Look At The Basic Tax And Accounting Considerations," **CPAJ**, 1973, Vol. 43, No. 5, pp. 361-368.)

Helstein, Richard S. "Guidelines For Professional Liability Insurance Coverage," **CPAJ**, 1973, Vol. 43, No. 10, pp. 849-856.

Helstein, Richard S. "Privileged Communications For CPAs," **JOA**, 1970, Vol. 130, No. 6, pp. 39-46.

Helstein, Richard S. "Why Attorneys Should Welcome An Accountant-Client Privilege Bill," **CPAJ**, 1975, Vol. 45, No. 9, pp. 31-34.

Hemmeter, Paul E. W. (Gaertner, James F., Paul E. W. Hemmeter and Marshall K. Pitman. "Employee Turnover In Public Accounting: A New Perspective," **CPAJ**, 1987, Vol. 57, No. 8, pp. 30-37.)

Henaidy, Hamid. (Elam, Rick and Hamid Henaidy. "Transfer Pricing For The Multinational Corporation," **IJAER**, 1981, Vol. 16, No. 2, pp. 49-65.)

Henarie, Robert L. (Haskins, Mark E. and Robert L. Henarie. "Attributes And Audit Impact Of Client's Control Environment," **CPAJ**, 1985, Vol. 55, No. 7, pp. 18-27.)

Henderson, A. D. "Accounting As Taught At Antioch," **AR**, 1927, Vol. 2, No. 1, pp. 55-58.

Henderson, Frederick A. "EBDI: A Radical Approach To Paper Work," **CA**, 1988, Vol. 6, No. 1, pp. 40-45.

Henderson, Glenn V., Jr. and Andrew H. Barnett. "Breakeven Present Value: A Pragmatic Approach To Capital Budgeting

Under Risk And Uncertainty," **MA**, 1978, Vol. 59, No. 7, pp. 49-52.

Henderson, Robert H. "Day Care: A Business Operated For Profit," **MA**, 1975, Vol. 56, No. 10, pp. 39-42.

Henderson, Scott and Graham Peirson. "Does Accounting Research Matter?," **ABR**, 1978-79, Vol. 9, No. 33, pp. 25-34.

Henderson, Scott and Graham Peirson. "A Note On The Current Cash Equivalent Of Liabilities," **ABACUS**, 1980, Vol. 16, No. 1, pp. 61-66.

Henderson, Scott and Graham Peirson. "A Note On Accounting And Executory Contracts," **ABACUS**, 1984, Vol. 20, No. 1, pp. 96-98.

Henderson, William I. "Sale And Liquidation Of A Partnership Interest," **JOA**, 1969, Vol. 127, No. 5, pp. 39-52.

Hendrick, Richard Miller. "An Accounting System For An Accounting Office," **JOA**, 1967, Vol. 123, No. 6, pp. 31-35.

Hendricks, Arthur G. "Audits Of Federal Credit Unions," **JOA**, 1958, Vol. 105, No. 2, pp. 56-59.

Hendricks, Arthur G. "Does Your Client Need Long-Term Capital?," **JOA**, 1966, Vol. 121, No. 5, pp. 36-45.

Hendricks, Arthur G. "The Initial Audit Engagement," **CPAJ**, 1979, Vol. 49, No. 5, pp. 9-17.

Hendricks, James A. "Analysis Of Risk In Capital Budgeting," **MA**, 1977, Vol. 58, No. 10, pp. 41-44.

Hendricks, James A. "Cost Accounting For Factory Automation," **MA**, 1988, Vol. 70, No. 6, pp. 24-30.

Hendricks, James A. "Human Resource Accounting Information: A Reply Concerning Demand Characteristics," **AR**, 1979, Vol. 54, No. 1, pp. 205-208.

Hendricks, James A. The Impact Of Human Resource Accounting Information On Stock Investment Decisions: An Empirical Study," **AR**, 1976, Vol. 51, No. 2, pp. 292-305.

Hendricks, James A. (Bennett, Robert E. and James A. Hendricks. "Justifying The Acquisition Of Automated Equipment," **MA**, 1987, Vol. 69, No. 1, pp. 39-46.)

Hendricks, James A. (Keys, David E. and James A. Hendricks. "The Ethics Of Accounting Research," **JAED**, 1984, Vol. 2, No. 2, pp. 77-88.)

Hendricks, Thomas E. (Firmin, Peter A., Seymour S. Goodman, Thomas E. Hendricks and James J. Linn. "University Cost Structure And Behavior: An Empirical Study," **JAR**, 1968, Vol. 6, Supp., pp. 122-155.)

Hendrickson, Harvey S. "Some Comments On 'Dirty Pooling'," **AR**, 1968, Vol. 43, No. 2, pp. 363-366.

Hendrickson, Harvey. (Espahbodi, Reza and Harvey Hendrickson. "A Cost-Benefit Analysis Of Accounting For Inflation," **JAPP**, 1986, Vol. 5, No. 1, pp. 31-55.)

Hendrickson, H. S. "The Changing Content Of The CPA Examination," **JOA**, 1971, Vol. 132, No. 1, pp. 60-67.

Hendriksen, Eldon S. "Disclosure - Insights Into Requirements In The United Kingdom," **IJAER**, 1969, Vol. 4, No. 2, pp. 21-32.

Hendriksen, Eldon S. "Purchasing Power And Replacement Cost Concepts - Are They Related?," **AR**, 1963, Vol. 38, No. 3, pp. 483-491.

Hendriksen, Eldon S. "The Influence Of Depreciation Accounting On National Income," **AR**, 1951, Vol. 26, No. 4, pp. 507-515.

Hendriksen, Eldon S. "The Treatment Of Income Taxes By The 1957 AAA Statement," **AR**, 1958, Vol. 33, No. 2, pp. 216-221.

Hendrikson, Harvey. (Espahbodi, Reza and Harvey Hendrikson. "A Discussion Of Cost-Benefit Analysis Methodology: Reply To Comment," **JAPP**, 1987, Vol. 6, No. 3, pp. 219-228.)

Henke, Emerson O. "Performance Evaluation For Not-For-Profit Organizations," **JOA**, 1972, Vol. 133, No. 6, pp. 51-55.

Henke, Emerson. "Teaching Accounting By Principle And Convention," **AR**, 1958, Vol. 33, No. 2, pp. 302-305.

Henkel, David R. (DeLoach, James W., Jr. and David R. Henkel. "New Reasons To Reexamine LIFO," **CA**, 1983, Vol. 1, No. 2, pp. 26-29.)

Hennessee, Patrick A. and J. W. Giese. "Accounting For Leveraged ESOPs: Employee Benefit Or Financing Tool?," **MA**, 1978, Vol. 59, No. 12, pp. 44-49.

Hennessy, John H., Jr. "Ad Hoc Research In Small Companies," **MA**, 1969, Vol. 51, No. 1, pp. 27-30.

Hennessy, John L. "Recording Lease Obligations," **JOA**, 1961, Vol. 111, No. 3, pp. 40-46.

Hennessy, J. H., Jr. "Is A Standard Cost System The Answer?," **JOA**, 1958, Vol. 105, No. 6, pp. 57-63.

Hennessy, Vincent C. "Accounting For Pension Liabilities Created By ERISA," **JAAF**, 1978, Vol. 1, No. 4, pp. 317-330.

Hennig, James F. "Win-Win Negotiations," **CA**, 1987, Vol. 5, No. 1, pp. 51-55.

Henning, Fred M. "Health And Welfare Funds - Contributions And Premiums," **JOA**, 1962, Vol. 114, No. 4, pp. 53-58.

Henning, G. R. (Marsh, J. A. and G. R. Henning. "Some History Of The Debate On Educational Policy Of Accountants In Australia," **ABACUS**, 1987, Vol. 23, No. 1, pp. 55-69.)

Henriques, Donald A. "Accounting For The Acquisition Of Farm Produce," **MA**, 1971, Vol. 52, No. 10, pp. 27-30.

Henry, Evan J. "A New Funds Statement Format For Greater Disclosure," **JOA**, 1975, Vol. 139, No. 4, pp. 56-62.

Henry, James B. "Leasing: Cost Measurement And Disclosure," **MA**, 1974, Vol. 55, No. 11, pp. 42-47.

Henry, James B. (Roenfeldt, Rodney L. and James B. Henry. "Lease Vs. Debt Purchase Of Automobiles," **MA**, 1976, Vol. 58, No. 4, pp. 49-56.)

Henry, James B., Perry Woodside and James B. Edwards.

"Public Sector Leasing In South Carolina," **MA**, 1979, Vol. 61, No. 4, pp. 43-49.

Henry, William R. (Burch, E. Earl and William R. Henry. "Opportunity And Incremental Cost: Attempt To Define In Systems Terms: A Comment," **AR**, 1974, Vol. 49, No. 1, pp. 118-123.)

Hensler, Emil J., Jr. "Accounting For Small Nonprofit Organizations," **MA**, 1973, Vol. 54, No. 7, pp. 41-44.

Hensley, Clifford F. "The Mathematics Of Life Insurance: An Introduction For The CPA," **JOA**, 1972, Vol. 134, No. 4, pp. 45-55.

Hensley, R. Dale. "Border Zone Limits For Materiality," **MA**, 1974, Vol. 55, No. 12, pp. 15-17.

Hensold, Harold H., Jr. (Seaman, Jerome F. and Harold H. Hensold, Jr. "Pension Plan Obligations: The 'Real' Impact," **JOA**, 1982, Vol. 154, No. 1, pp. 82-88.)

Hepp, Gerald W. and Thomas W. McRae. "Accounting Standards Overload: Relief Is Needed," **JOA**, 1982, Vol. 153, No. 5, pp. 52-65.

Hepp, Gerald W. and William W. Holder. "A New Look In Governmental Audits," **JOA**, 1986, Vol. 161, No. 4, pp. 82-89.

Hepp, Gerald W. "Governmental Financial Statements - A New Look," **JOA**, 1976, Vol. 142, No. 6, pp. 60-68.

Hepworth, Samuel R. "Direct Costing - The Case 'Against'," **AR**, 1954, Vol. 29, No. 1, pp. 94-99.

Hepworth, Samuel R. "Partnership Agreements For CPAs," **JOA**, 1961, Vol. 111, No. 6, pp. 41-46.

Hepworth, Samuel R. "Smoothing Periodic Income," **AR**, 1953, Vol. 28, No. 1, pp. 32-39.

Herbert, Leo. "A Perspective Of Accounting," **AR**, 1971, Vol. 46, No. 3, pp. 433-440.

Herbert, Leo. "Comparison Between Governmental And General Accounting," **AR**, 1948, Vol. 23, No. 4, pp. 397-400.

Herbert, Leo. "How To Prepare Working Papers, Reports, For Small Audits," **JOA**, 1952, Vol. 93, No. 6, pp. 698-704.

Herbert, Leo. "Modern Accounting Methods For Governmental Units," **AR**, 1956, Vol. 31, No. 4, pp. 628-631.

Herbert, Leo. "Practical Sampling For Auditors," **AR**, 1946, Vol. 21, No. 4, pp. 386-389.

Herbert, Leo. (Haun, Robert D. and Leo Herbert. "Grading Of The American Institute Of Accountants' Examination Papers," **AR**, 1952, Vol. 27, No. 4, pp. 523-529.)

Herbert, LeRoy J. (Feldman, Stewart A. and LeRoy J. Herbert. "The International Accounting Standards Committee," **CPAJ**, 1977, Vol. 47, No. 1, pp. 17-22.)

Herbert, Williard A. "The Burden Of Proof In Tax Fraud Cases," **JOA**, 1968, Vol. 126, No. 4, pp. 57-60.

Herbsman, Zohar. "The Bidding Volume Effect On Public Work Cost: A Case Study," **JCA**, 1986, Vol. 3, No. 2, pp. 27-45.

Herhold, Susan, Robert W. Parry and James M. Patton. "Behavioral Research In Municipal Accounting," **RIGNA**, 1987, Vol. 3, Part B, pp. 71-109.

Hereth, Russell and John Talbott. "TRA 86 - Its Impact On Thoroughbred Investments," **CPAJ**, 1988, Vol. 58, No. 4, pp. 30-37.

Hermanson, Roger H. and Catherine E. Miles. "Fine-Tuning The Predictive Model Of The American Accounting Association 1971-72 And 1972-73 Committees On Future Professorial Supply And Demand," **AR**, 1976, Vol. 51, No. 4, pp. 875-885.

Hermanson, Roger H. and Tad D. Ransopher. "What The Hishon Case Means To CPA Firms," **JOA**, 1985, Vol. 159, No. 2, pp. 78-80.

Hermanson, Roger H. "A Senior Level Accounting Seminar For Honors Students," **AR**, 1974, Vol. 49, No. 3, pp. 595-597.

Hermanson, Roger H. (Anderson, Gary J., Gordon B. Harwood and Roger H. Hermanson. "Energy Audits," **CPAJ**, 1979, Vol. 49, No. 1, pp. 31-34.)

Hermanson, Roger H. (Barden, Ronald S., James E. Copeland, Jr., Roger H. Hermanson and Leslie Wat. "Going Public - What It Involves," **JOA**, 1984, Vol. 157,No. 3,pp. 63-76.)

Hermanson, Roger H. (El Sheshai, Kamal M., Gordon B. Harwood and Roger H. Hermanson. "Cost Volume Profit Analysis With Integer Goal Programming," **MA**, 1977, Vol. 59, No. 4, pp. 43-47.)

Hermanson, Roger H. (Garcha, Bikramjit S., Gordon B. Harwood and Roger H. Hermanson. "A Study Of The Readership Of The Accounting Review," **JAED**, 1983, Vol. 1, No. 2, pp. 21-39.)

Hermanson, Roger H. (Harwood, Gordon B. and Roger H. Hermanson. "The Lease-Or-Buy Decision," **JOA**, 1976, Vol. 142, No. 3, pp. 83-88.)

Hermanson, Roger H., Linda M. Dykes and Deborah H. Turner. "Enforced Competition In The Accounting Profession - Does It Make Sense?," **ACCHOR**, 1987, Vol. 1, No. 4, pp. 13-20.

Herman, Michael P. "Uniform Cost Accounting Standards: Are They Necessary?," **MA**, 1972, Vol. 53, No. 10, pp. 15-19.

Hernandez, William H. "Is The Controller An Endangered Species?," **MA**, 1978, Vol. 60, No. 2, pp. 48-52.

Hernandez, William H. "Pricing Policies Under Inflation," **MA**, 1982, Vol. 63, No. 7, pp. 51-55.

Herrick, Anson. "A Review Of Recent Developments In Accounting Theory And Practice," **AR**, 1950, Vol. 25, No. 4, pp. 360-370.

Herrick, Anson. "A Review Of The Work Of The Accounting Procedure Committee," **JOA**, 1954, Vol. 98, No. 5, pp. 627-638.

Herrick, Anson. "Inflation In Accounting," **JOA**, 1960, Vol. 110, No. 3, pp. 51-56.

Herringer, Frank C. (Bower, Richard S., Frank C. Herringer and J. Peter Williamson. "Lease Evaluation," **AR**, 1966, Vol. 41, No. 2, pp. 257-265.)

Herring, Dora R. "Statistical Estimations Of Historical

Distribution Cost," **MA**, 1969, Vol. 51, No. 4, pp. 42-46.

Herring, Hartwell C., III and Fred A. Jacobs. "The Expected Behavior Of Deferred Tax Credits," **JOA**, 1976, Vol. 142, No. 2, pp. 52-57.

Herring, Hartwell C., III. (Apostolou, Nicholas G., Hartwell C. Herring, III and Walter A. Robbins, Jr. "Are Changes Needed In Private Foundation Reporting Practices," **MA**, 1980, Vol. 62, No. 5, pp. 39-42.)

Herring, Hartwell C., III. (Jacobs, Fred A. and Hartwell C. Herring, III. "The Impact Of Proposed **CASB** Standards," **MA**, 1976, Vol. 58, No. 3, pp. 13-14.)

Herring, Hartwell C., III. (Jacobs, Fred A. and Hartwell C. Herring, III. "Salary Compression In The Academic Marketplace: Some Empirical Evidence," **IAE**, 1987, Vol. 2, No. 2, pp. 237-250.)

Herring, H. C. (Hawthorne, W. H. and H. C. Herring. "A Quantitative Approach To The Illustration Of The Percentage-Of-Completion Method," **AR**, 1975, Vol. 50, No. 3, pp. 615-616.)

Herring, Rebecca B. (Humphries, Francis A., Linda M. Plunkett and Rebecca B. Herring. "Let's Make Required CPE Rules Uniform," **JOA**, 1988, Vol. 166, No. 6, pp. 70-74.)

Herskovits, David H. (Erickson, Naomi and David H. Herskovits. "Accounting For Software Costs: Cracking The Code," **JOA**, 1985, Vol. 160, No. 5, pp. 81-97.)

Herskowitz, Barry and David A. Kaplowitz. "Asset-Based Revolvers," **JOA**, 1986, Vol. 162, No. 1, pp. 97-104.

Herst, James T. "Safeguards Against Credit Abuse," **CA**, 1988, Vol. 6, No. 2, pp. 40-43.

Hertz, Ronald S. "Standards Overload - A Euphemism," **CPAJ**, 1983, Vol. 53, No. 10, pp. 24-33.

Herz, Theodore. "Government Auditing Needs," **JOA**, 1956, Vol. 101, No. 5, pp. 40-53.

Herzberg, Arno. "How To Handle Tax And Accounting Problems Of Dealers' Reserves In Installment Financing," **JOA**, 1950, Vol. 90, No. 4, pp. 330-334.

Herzlinger, Regina E. and William S. Krasker. "Measuring The Economic Performance Of For-Profit And Nonprofit Organizations," **RIGNA**, 1986, Vol. 2, pp. 151-172.

Herzog, Asa S. "CPA's Role In Bankruptcy Proceeding," **JOA**, 1964, Vol. 117, No. 1, pp. 59-69.

Herzog, Donald R. "Pricing Engineering Work For Defense Contracts," **MA**, 1970, Vol. 52, No. 3, pp. 32-35.

Herzog, Raymond H. "The Numbers Game: What Industry Accountants Can Do For Society," **MA**, 1977, Vol. 58, No. 11, pp. 17-19.

Hess, John L. (Usry, Milton F. and John L. Hess. "Planning And Control Of Research And Development Activities," **JOA**, 1967, Vol. 124, No. 5, pp. 43-48.)

Heuer, Mark A. "Federal Capital Investment Policy: A Role For Accounting," **JAPP**, 1984, Vol. 3, No. 2, pp. 81-89.

Heuser, Forrest L. "Control Vs. Cost Of Control," **MA**, 1970, Vol. 51, No. 8, pp. 17-19.

Heuser, Forrest L. "Financial Statement Analysis For Management," **MA**, 1969, Vol. 50, No. 6, pp. 23-28.

Heuser, Forrest L. "The Question Of Uniform Accounting Standards," **MA**, 1969, Vol. 51, No. 1, pp. 20-23.

Hewitt, LeRoy A. "Appraising The Firm's Collection Policy," **MA**, 1966, Vol. 47, No. 7, pp. 34-39.

Heymann, Hans. (Bloom, Robert and Hans Heymann. "The Concept Of Social Accountability In Accounting Literature," **JAL**, 1986, Vol. 5, pp. 167-182.)

Heymann, Hans. (Bloom, Robert and Hans Heymann. "The Ideas Of Stuart Chase On Waste And Inefficiency," **AHJ**, 1984, Vol. 11, No. 2, pp. 133-142.)

Hickerson, William C. (Skertich, John M. and William C. Hickerson. "Record Retention Program," **MA**, 1972, Vol. 53, No. 8, pp. 23-28.)

Hickman, James R. "A Marketing Plan For CPA Firms," **CPAJ**, 1978, Vol. 48, No. 7, pp. 35-37.

Hickman, James R. "Responding To Clients' Growing Needs: Building An MAS Department," **JOA**, 1980, Vol. 150, No. 4, pp. 54-61.

Hickok, Richard S. "Looking To The Future: A Key To Success," **JOA**, 1984, Vol. 157, No. 3, pp. 77-82.

Hickok, Richard S. "Management Comment Letters," **CPAJ**, 1972, Vol. 42, No. 12, pp. 993-1000.

Hickok, Richard S. "New Guidance For Construction Contractors: 'A Credit Plus'," **JOA**, 1982, Vol. 153, No. 3, pp. 44-55.

Hickok, Richard S. "The Impact On Corporate Accountants Of Future Issues Affecting The Accounting Profession," **CA**, 1984, Vol. 2, No. 4, pp. 28-33.

Hicks, Carl F., Jr. and L. Lee Schmidt, Jr. "Post-Auditing The Capital Investment Decision," **MA**, 1971, Vol. 53, No. 2, pp. 24-28.

Hicks, Donald W. and Frederick M. Richardson. "Predicting Early Success In Intermediate Accounting: The Influence Of Entry Examination and GPA," **IAE**, 1984, No. 1, pp. 61-67.

Hicks, Donald W. (Sperry, John B., Edward C. Spede and Donald W. Hicks. "The Evolution And Current Status Of Peer Review," **JOA**, 1987, Vol. 163, No. 5, pp. 381-382.)

Hicks, Ernest L. "APB: The First 3600 Days," **JOA**, 1969, Vol. 128, No. 3, pp. 56-60.

Hicks, Ernest L. "Comments On 'A Statement Of Basic Accounting Theory'," **JOA**, 1966, Vol. 122, No. 3, pp. 56-60.

Hicks, Ernest L. "Materiality," **JAR**, 1964, Vol. 2, No. 2, pp. 158-171.

Hicks, Ernest L. "Materiality: A Useful Audit Tool," **JOA**, 1962, Vol. 114, No. 1, pp. 63-67.

Hicks, Ernest L. "Standards For The Attest Function," **JOA**, 1974, Vol. 138, No. 2, pp. 39-45.

Hicks, James O., Jr. "An Examination Of Accounting Interest Groups' Differential Perceptions Of Innovations," **AR**, 1978, Vol. 53, No. 2, pp. 371-388.

Hicks, James O., Jr. "The Application Of Exponential Smoothing To Standard Cost Systems," **MA**, 1978, Vol. 60, No. 3, pp. 28-32.

Hicks, Rebecca L. (Gavin, Thomas A., Rebecca L. Hicks and James H. Scheiner. "Auditors' Common Law Liability: What We Should Be Telling Our Students," **JAED**, 1987, Vol. 5, No. 1, pp. 1-12.)

Hicks, Rebecca L. (Gavin, Thomas A., Rebecca L. Hicks and Joseph D. Decosimo. "CPAs' Liability To Third Parties," **JOA**, 1984, Vol. 157, No. 6, pp. 80-91.)

Hicks, Sam A. "Choosing The Form For Business Tax Incentives," **AR**, 1978, Vol. 53, No. 3, pp. 708-716.

Higgins, J. C. and E. J. Opdebeeck. "The Microcomputer As A Tool In Financial Planning And Control: Some Survey Results," **ABR**, 1983-84, Vol. 14, No. 56, pp. 333-340.

Higgins, J. Warren. "The Tax Game," **AR**, 1969, Vol. 44, No. 3, pp. 615-618.

Higgins, Thomas G. and Wallace E. Olson. "Restating The Ethics Code: A Decision For The Times," **JOA**, 1972, Vol. 133, No. 3, pp. 33-39.

Higgins, Thomas G. "Division Of Fees," **JOA**, 1957, Vol. 103, No. 1, pp. 47-52.

Higgins, Thomas G. "Homer St. Clair Pace (1879-1942) - Co-Founder Of Pace College," **CPAJ**, 1972, Vol. 42, No. 6, pp. 475-478.

Higgins, Thomas G. "Professional Ethics And Public Opinion," **JOA**, 1958, Vol. 106, No. 5, pp. 34-39.

Higgins, Thomas G. "Professional Ethics: A Time For Reappraisal," **JOA**, 1962, Vol. 113, No. 3, pp. 29-35.

Higgins, Thomas G. "The Need For A New Rule On Independence," **JOA**, 1961, Vol. 111, No. 1, pp. 37-42.

Higgins, W. Rodgers. "Valuation Of Readily Marketable Inventories," **JOA**, 1964, Vol. 118, No. 1, pp. 25-32.

Highleyman, Wilbur H. "The Economics Of Business Mini's," **MA**, 1971, Vol. 53, No. 4, pp. 12-14.

Higley, Wayne M. and Richard E. Baker. "A Comparative Analysis Of Professional Education And Licensure Preparation," **IAE**, 1987, Vol. 2, No. 2, pp. 220-236.

Hildebrand, Glendon R. "Let's Look At Financial Reporting By Smaller Businesses," **MA**, 1982, Vol. 63, No. 10, pp. 42-47.

Hilgert, J. R. "Methods Of Controlling Distribution Costs," **AR**, 1927, Vol. 2, No. 3, pp. 254-262.

Hilke, John C. "One Step Forward And Two Steps Backward At The SEC?," **JAAF**, 1988, Vol. 3 (New Series), No. 2, pp. 171-175.

Hilke, John C. "Regulatory Compliance Costs And LIFO: No Wonder Small Companies Haven't Switched," **JAAF**, 1986, Vol. 1 (New Series), No. 1, pp. 17-29.

Hill, Dan J. and Garold L. Rutherford. "Computerized Financial Data Reporting System," **MA**, 1976, Vol. 58, No. 1, pp. 57-60.

Hill, Gordon M. "Three Major Technical Problems," **JOA**, 1955, Vol. 100, No. 2, pp. 44-48.

Hill, Gordon. "CPA's Difficulty In Expressing Opinion On Cash-Basis Statement," **JOA**, 1953, Vol. 96, No. 3, pp. 309-315.

Hill, Harrell B. "At Western Electric The Accent Is On Professional," **MA**, 1975, Vol. 57, No. 3, pp. 15-17.

Hill, Henry P. "An Accountant Looks At Statistics," **JOA**, 1958, Vol. 105, No. 4, pp. 57-65.

Hill, Henry P. "Rational Expectations And Accounting Principles," **JAAF**, 1982, Vol. 5, No. 2, pp. 99-109.

Hill, Henry P. "Reporting On Uncertainties By Independent Auditors," **JOA**, 1973, Vol. 135, No. 1, pp. 55-60.

Hill, Henry P. "Your New Bank Client," **JOA**, 1964, Vol. 117, No. 3, pp. 36-41.

Hill, J. Tomilson. (Freidman, Harry and J. Tomilson Hill. "Financial Implications Of Offense And Defense In Corporate Takeovers," **CA**, 1985, Vol. 3, No. 3, pp. 54-59.

Hill, Jack. "Livestock Accounting," **MA**, 1975, Vol. 57, No. 4, pp. 43-46.

Hill, Thomas M. and William T. Jerome, III. "Accounting In The Executive Program," **AR**, 1956, Vol. 31, No. 3, pp. 411-417.

Hill, Thomas M. "An Analysis Of Supplementary Statement No. 2," **AR**, 1952, Vol. 27, No. 1, pp. 16-24.

Hill, Thomas M. "Some Arguments Against The Inter-Period Allocation Of Income Taxes," **AR**, 1957, Vol. 32, No. 3, pp. 357-361.

Hill, T. M. "A Criticism Of 'Joint Cost Analysis As An Aid To Management'," **AR**, 1956, Vol. 31, No. 2, pp. 204-205.

Hillhouse, A. M. and K. Bodo Lang. "German Federal Audit Court," **AR**, 1952, Vol. 27, No. 4, pp. 530-543.

Hilliard, Jimmy E. and Robert A. Leitch. "Breakeven Analysis Of Alternatives Under Uncertainty," **MA**, 1977, Vol. 58, No. 9, pp. 53-57.

Hilliard, Jimmy E. and Robert A. Leitch. "CVP Analysis Under Uncertainty - A Log Normal Approach: A Reply," **AR**, 1976, Vol. 51, No. 1, pp. 168-171.

Hilliard, Jimmy E. and Robert A. Leitch. "Cost-Volume-Profit Analysis Under Uncertainty: A Log Normal Approach," **AR**, 1975, Vol. 50, No. 1, pp. 69-80.

Hillison, William A. and Paul F. Williams. "Confidentiality Of Student Records: The Professor's Obligation," **JAED**, 1983, Vol. 1, No. 1, pp. 55-62.

Hillison, William A. "Empirical Investigation Of General Purchasing Power Adjustments On Earnings Per Share And The Movement Of Security Prices," **JAR**, 1979, Vol. 17, No. 1, pp. 60-73.

Hillison, William A. (Arrington, C. Edward, William A. Hillison and Paul F. Williams. "The Psychology Of

Expectations Gaps: Why Is There So Much Dispute About Auditor Responsibility?," **ABR**, 1982-83, Vol. 13, No. 52, pp. 243-250.)

Hillison, William and Michael Kennelley. "The Economics Of Nonaudit Services," **AH**, 1988, Vol. 2, No. 3, pp. 32-40.

Hillison, William. (Arrington, C. Edward, William Hillison and Rhoda C. Icerman. "Research In Analytical Review: The State Of The Art," **JAL**, 1983, Vol. 2, pp. 151-186.)

Hillison, William. (Arrington, C. Edward, William Hillison and Robert E. Jensen. "An Application Of Analytical Hierarchy Process To Model Expert Judgments On Analytical Review Procedures," **JAR**, 1984, Vol. 22, No. 1, pp. 298-312.)

Hillman, A. Douglas. (Wolk, Harry I. and A. Douglas Hillman. "Materials Mix And Yield Variances: A Suggested Improvement," **AR**, 1972, Vol. 47, No. 3, pp. 549-555.)

Hills, George S. (Ballantine, H. W. and George S. Hills. "Corporate Capital And Restrictions Upon Dividends," **AR**, 1935, Vol. 10, No. 3, pp. 246-268.)

Hiltner, Arthur A. "Statistical Sampling In Auditing: A Simulation," **IAE**, 1983, Vol. 1, No. 1, pp. 115-122.

Hilton, K. (Ezzamel, M. A. and K. Hilton. "Divisionalisation In British Industry: A Preliminary Study," **ABR**, 1979-80, Vol. 10, No. 38, pp. 197-214.)

Hilton, Ronald W. and Robert J. Swieringa. "Perception Of Initial Uncertainty As A Determinant Of Information Value," **JAR**, 1981, Vol. 19, No. 1, pp. 109-119.

Hilton, Ronald W. "Integrating Normative And Descriptive Theories Of Information Processing," **JAR**, 1980, Vol. 18, No. 2, pp. 477-505.

Hilton, Ronald W. "Interdependence Between The Information Evaluator And The Decision Maker," **CAR**, 1986-87, Vol. 3, No. 1, pp. 50-67.

Hilton, Ronald W. "The Determinants Of Cost Information Value: An Illustrative Analysis," **JAR**, 1979, Vol. 17, No. 2, pp. 411-435.

Hilton, Ronald W., Robert J. Swieringa and Robert E. Hoskin. "Perception Of Accuracy As A Determinant Of Information Value," **JAR**, 1981, Vol. 19,No. 1,pp. 86-108.

Hilton, Ronald W., Robert J. Swieringa and Martha J. Turner. "Product Pricing, Accounting Costs And Use Of Product-Costing Systems," **AR**, 1988, Vol. 63, No. 2, pp. 195-218.

Himmelblau, David. "Auditor's Responsibilities To Third Parties," **AR**, 1933, Vol. 8, No. 2, pp. 99-104.

Himmelblau, David. "Effect Of The Adoption Of The Classification Of Accounting Service On Accounting Instruction," **AR**, 1931, Vol. 6, No. 4, pp. 298-304.

Himmelblau, David. "Some Corporate Problems Created By Income Tax Laws," **AR**, 1927, Vol. 2, No. 3, pp. 263-277.

Himmelblau, David. "Some Problems In Property Accounting," **AR**, 1928, Vol. 3, No. 2, pp. 149-160.

Himmelblau, David. "The Refinancing Balance Sheet," **AR**, 1927, Vol. 2, No. 4, pp. 339-347.

Himmelblau, David. (Littleton. A. C., Lloyd Morey, David Himmelblau and F. E. Ross. "The International Congress On Accounting," **AR**, 1929, Vol. 4, No. 4, pp. 234-246.)

Hinchey, Brackston. (Kistler, Linda H., Clairmont P. Carter and Brackston Hinchey. "Planning And Control In The 19th Century Ice Trade," **AHJ**, 1984, Vol. 11, No. 1, pp. 19-30.)

Hinckley, G. M. (Cyert, R. M., G. M. Hinckley and R. J. Monteverde. "Statistical Sampling In The Audit Of The Air Force Motor Vehicle Inventory," **AR**, 1960, Vol. 35, No. 4, pp. 667-673.)

Hinderer, Harry. "Management Practices For Growing Medium-Sized Firm," **JOA**, 1953, Vol. 95, No. 2, pp. 198-205.

Hindman, William R. and Floyd F. Kettering, Jr. "Integrated MIS: A Case Study," **MA**, 1973, Vol. 55, No. 2, pp. 20-27.

Hines, Dorothy L., Douglas A. Johnson and William V. Lennox. "The Semiconductor Industry Controller: A Profile," **MA**, 1982, Vol. 63, No. 12, pp. 30-35.

Hines, Ruth D. "Popper's Methodology Of Falsificationism And Accounting Research," **AR**, 1988, Vol. 63, No. 4, pp. 657-662.

Hines, R. D. "The Implications Of Stock Market Reaction (Non-Reaction) For Financial Accounting Standard Setting," **ABR**, 1984-85, Vol. 15, No. 57, pp. 3-14.

Hines, R. D. "The Usefulness Of Annual Reports: The Anomaly Between The Efficient Markets Hypothesis And Shareholder Surveys," **ABR**, 1981-82, Vol. 12, No. 48, pp. 296-309.

Hinings, C. R. (Williams, J. J. and C. R. Hinings. "A Note On Matching Control System Implications With Organizational Characteristics: ZBB And MBO Revisited," **AOS**, 1988, Vol. 13, No. 2, pp. 191-200.)

Hinomoto, Hirohide. "Optimum Strategies For Management Information Processing And Control," **JAR**, 1971, Vol. 9, No. 2, pp. 253-267.

Hinonoto, Hirohide. "Business - Function Productivity And Information Systems," **JCA**, 1988, Vol. 5, No. 1, pp. 49-61.

Hinson, Dolan R. "Time-Adjusted Capital Budgeting Models," **MA**, 1975, Vol. 57, No. 1, pp. 55-58.

Hinton, Thomas L. "Capital Investment: International Paper Fights Back," **MA**, 1983, Vol. 65, No. 1, pp. 41-44.

Hippel, James H. "An Economic Cost Curve Analysis," **MA**, 1967, Vol. 49, No. 1, pp. 21-28.

Hird, F. M. W. "A Speculation On The Origins Of Accounting," **AHJ**, 1975, Vol. 2, No. 1-4, pp. 17-21.

Hirsch, A. Jay. "Accounting For Fixed Assets: A New Perspective," **AR**, 1964, Vol. 39, No. 4, pp. 972-978.

Hirsch, A. Jay. "Dollar-Value And Retail LIFO: A Diagrammatic Approach," **AR**, 1969, Vol. 44, No. 4, pp. 840-842.

Hirsch, Julius. "Choosing Between Capehart Amendment And CPR 22," **JOA**, 1952, Vol. 93, No. 1, pp. 76-81.

Hirsch, Maurice L., Jr. and Janet Duthie Collins. "An Integrated Approach To Communication Skills In An Accounting Curriculum," **JAED**, 1988, Vol. 6, No. 1, pp. 15-31.

Hirsch, Maurice L., Jr. "Disaggregated Probabilistic Accounting Information: The Effect Of Sequential Events On Expected Value Maximization Decisions," **JAR**, 1978, Vol. 16, No. 2, pp. 254-269.

Hirsch, Rudolph E. "The Value Of Information," **JOA**, 1968, Vol. 125, No. 6, pp. 41-45.

Hirschey, Mark and Jerry J. Weygandt. "Amortization Policy For Advertising And Research And Development Expenditures," **JAR**, 1985, Vol. 23, No. 1, pp. 326-335.

Hirschey, Mark. (Connolly, Robert A. and Mark Hirschey. "Concentration And Profits: A Test Of The Accounting Bias Hypothesis," **JAPP**, 1988, Vol. 7, No. 4, pp. 313-334.)

Hirschland, Meryle. (Stern, Myles, Meryle Hirschland and Serge Matulich. "Comment And Reply - 'A Theoretical Deficiency In Accounting For Bonds'," **JAED**, 1986, Vol. 4, No. 2, pp. 147-151.)

Hirschman, Robert W. "A Look At 'Current' Classifications." **JOA**, 1967, Vol. 124, No. 5, pp. 54-58.

Hirschman, Robert W. "Direct Costing And The Law," **AR**, 1965, Vol. 40, No. 1, pp. 176-183.

Hirshfield, Arthur S. (O'Riordan, Maureen and Arthur S. Hirshfield. "Aspects Of The Profession's Code Of Ethics," **CPAJ**, 1982, Vol. 52, No. 8, pp. 30-33.)

Hirst, Mark and Ronald Ma. "Duration And Fisher's Rate Of Return Over Cost," **ABACUS**, 1983, Vol. 19, No. 2. pp. 162-170.

Hirst, Mark K. "Accounting Information And The Evaluation Of Subordinate Performance: A Situational Approach," **AR**, 1981, Vol. 56, No. 4, pp. 771-784.

Hirst, Mark K. "Reliance On Accounting Performance Measures, Task Uncertainty, And Dysfunctional Behavior: Some Extensions," **JAR**, 1983, Vol. 21, No. 2,pp. 596-605.

Hirst, Mark K. "The Effects Of Setting Budget Goals And Task Uncertainty On Performance: A Theoretical Analysis," **AR**, 1987, Vol. 62, No. 4, pp. 774-784.

Hirst, Mark. "The Controllability Of Financial Outcomes," **ABACUS**, 1983, Vol. 19, No. 1, pp. 29-38.

Hirst, Mark. (Brownell, Peter and Mark Hirst. "Reliance On Accounting Information, Budgetary Participation, And Task Uncertainty: Test Of A Three-Way Interaction," **JAR**, 1986, Vol. 24, No. 2, pp. 241-249.)

Hirzel, Patrick S. and Jeffrey D. Mamorsky. "Fiduciary Audits: Defusing The Pension Time Bomb," **CA**, 1983, Vol. 1, No. 1, pp. 60-63.

Hise, Richard T. (Kratchman, Stanley H., Richard T. Hise and Thomas A. Ulrich. "Management's Decision To Discontinue A Product," **JOA**, 1975, Vol. 139, No. 6,pp. 50-54.)

Hise, Richard T. (Strawser, Robert H., J. Patrick Kelly and Richard T. Hise. "What Causes Stress For Management Accountants?," **MA**, 1987, Vol. 63, No. 9, pp. 32-37.)

Hise, Richard T., Stanley H. Kratchman and Theodore H. Mattheiss. "Involvement Of The Undergraduate Accounting Curriculum With Distribution Cost Analysis," **AR**, 1974, Vol. 49, No. 1, pp. 153-157.

Hite, Gailen L. and Michael S. Long. "Taxes And Executive Stock Options," **JAEC**, 1982, Vol. 4, No. 1, pp. 3-14.

Hite, Peggy A. and Timothy O'Grady. "The Substantial Understatement Penalty: An Update," **CPAJ**, 1988, Vol. 58, No. 4, pp. 64-68.

Hite, Peggy A. and David A. Jerman. "Partial Liquidation - Then And Now," **CPAJ**, 1987, Vol. 57, No. 3, pp. 36-40.

Hite, Peggy A. and Denis J. Rice. "The Continuity Of Interest Doctrine," **CPAJ**, 1986, Vol. 56, No. 11, pp. 72-79.

Hite, Peggy A. "Qualifications For A Tax Specialist: Some Tax Partners' Views," **AIT**, 1987, Vol. 1, pp. 183-198.

Hite, Peggy A. "The Effect Of Peer Reporting Behavior On Taxpayer Compliance," **JATA**, 1988, Vol. 9, No. 2, pp. 47-64.

Ho, Joanna L. Y. (Cooper, W. W., Joanna L. Y. Ho, John E. Hunter and Robert C. Rodgers. "The Impact Of The Foreign Corrupt Practices Act On Internal Control Practices," **JAAF**, 1985, Vol. 9, No. 1, pp. 22-39.)

Hoaglund, William. "The Federal Budget: After The Election," **JCA**, 1985, Vol. 2, No. 1, pp. 47-58.

Hobbett, Richard D. (Donaldson, J. Bruce and Richard D. Hobbet. "The Passing Parade Of 1962 Tax Litigation," **JOA**, 1963, Vol. 116, No. 2, pp. 39-49.)

Hobbs, H. Kendall and Mohamed E. Hussein. "Internal Control Methods For Small Business," **CPAJ**, 1985, Vol. 55, No. 5, pp. 26-35.

Hobbs, James B. and D. R. Bainbridge. "Nonmonetary Exchange Transactions: Clarification Of APB No. 29," **AR**, 1982, Vol. 57, No. 1, pp. 171-175.

Hobbs, James B. "Double-Entry And Working Capital Analysis," **AR**, 1966, Vol. 41, No. 4, pp. 763-767.

Hobbs, James B. "Volume-Mix-Price/Cost Budget Variance Analysis: A Proper Approach," **AR**, 1964, Vol. 39, No. 4, pp. 905-913.

Hobbs, William, III. "Contribution Reporting For Consumer Products," **MA**, 1970, Vol. 52, No. 5, pp. 22-24.

Hobson, Charles J. (Pelfrey, Sandra and Charles J. Hobson. "Keeping Employees Physically Fit Can Be Cost Efficient," **MA**, 1984, Vol. 65, No. 12, pp. 39-43.)

Hochberg, R. Mark. (Falk, Charles Edward and R. Mark Hochberg. "Gift-Leasebacks - When Will They Work?," **CPAJ**, 1984, Vol. 54, No. 10, pp. 24-37.)

Hochberg, R. Mark. (Falk, Charles Edward and R. Mark Hochberg. "Interest Free Loans - Is Dickman Correct?," **CPAJ**, 1983, Vol. 53, No. 8, pp. 44-51.)

287

Hochman, Joel. (Krausz, Joshua, Joel Hochman and Allen Schiff. "The Impact Of Taxation On Project Valuation For Alternative Depreciation Methods," **ACCHOR**, 1987, Vol. 1, No. 3, pp. 31-40.)

Hocke, Clayton A. (Kern, Charles L., Charles A. Neyhart, Jr. and Clayton A. Hocke. "Statistical Risk And Sample Reliability," **CPAJ**, 1973, Vol. 43, No. 1, pp. 55-60.)

Hodgetts, Richard M. (Harris, John K. and Richard M. Hodgetts. "A Quasi-Consulting Project Involving Accounting And Management Students," **AR**, 1972, Vol. 47, No. 2, pp. 375-380.)

Hodge, William T. "The Unlamented, Self-Represented Taxpayer," **JOA**, 1951, Vol. 92, No. 4, pp. 450-453.

Hoecker, Olivia J. and Dorothy M. Watson. "Risk Management: More Than Insurance," **MA**, 1984, Vol. 66, No. 2, pp. 22-29.

Hoeflick, Charles J. "Auditing Of Construction Contracts," **MA**, 1966, Vol. 48, No. 1, pp. 51-56.

Hoenemeyer, Frank J. "Compatibility Of Auditing And Management Services: The Viewpoint Of A User Of Financial Statements," **JOA**, 1967, Vol. 124, No. 6, pp. 32-35.

Hoe, Alan M. (Anderson, Bruce L. and Alan M. Hoe. "Company Promotion And The Accountancy Profession In Nineteenth Century Sheffield," **ABR**, 1979-80, Vol. 10, No. 37, pp. 59-64.)

Hofert, Jack. "State Income Taxation - A Suggested Solution To The Present Confusion," **AR**, 1962, Vol. 37, No. 2, pp. 231-233.

Hofer, Charles R. "Analysis Of Fixed Costs In Inventory," **MA**, 1970, Vol. 52, No. 3, pp. 15-17.

Hoffman, Harold L. "Preparation & Presentation Of Accounting Data In Litigation," **JOA**, 1952, Vol. 94, No. 4, pp. 434-441.

Hoffman, Michael J. R. and Brian Langemeier. "Tax Planning For Divorced Couples Under TRA 86," **CPAJ**, 1988, Vol. 58, No. 5, pp. 40-47.

Hoffman, Michael J. R. and Richard A. White. "Tax Planning For Employee Home Offices - Part II," **CPAJ**, 1985, Vol. 55, No. 12, pp. 50-55.

Hoffman, Michael J. R. and Richard A. White. "Tax Planning For Employee Home Offices - Part I," **CPAJ**, 1985, Vol. 55, No. 11, pp. 48-56.

Hoffman, Michael J. R. (Harper, Robert M. and Michael J. R. Hoffman. "EDP Record Retention," **CPAJ**, 1985, Vol. 55, No. 6, pp. 54-62.)

Hoffman, William H., Jr. and Donald E. Vaughn. "Departmental And Item Profitability For Retailers," **JOA**, 1963, Vol. 116, No. 2, pp. 50-58.

Hoffman, William H., Jr. "Opportunities For Post-Mortem Tax Planning," **JOA**, 1969, Vol. 127, No. 1, pp. 44-53.

Hoffman, William H., Jr. "Tax Planning And The Reasonableness Test," **JOA**, 1962, Vol. 113, No. 4, pp. 51-57.

Hoffman, William H., Jr. "The Buy And Sell Agreement In Estate Planning," **JOA**, 1965, Vol. 119, No. 5, pp. 43-49.

Hoffman, William H., Jr. "The Theory Of Tax Planning," **AR**, 1961, Vol. 36, No. 2, pp. 274-281.

Hoffman, William H., Jr. "Use Of Insurance In Employee Compensation," **JOA**, 1961, Vol. 111, No. 5, pp. 55-62.

Hofstede, G. "Management Control Of Public And Not-For-Profit Activities," **AOS**, 1981, Vol. 6,No. 3,pp. 193-216.

Hofstedt, Thomas R. and G. David Hughes."An Experimental Study Of The Judgmental Element In Disclosure Decisions," **AR**, 1977, Vol. 52, No. 2, pp. 379-395.

Hofstedt, Thomas R. and James C. Kinard. "A Strategy For Behavioral Accounting Research," **AR**, 1970, Vol. 45, No. 1, pp. 38-54.

Hofstedt, Thomas R. and Richard R. West. "The APB, Yield Indices, And Predictive Ability," **AR**, 1971, Vol. 46, No. 2, pp. 329-337.

Hofstedt, Thomas R. "Some Behavioral Parameters Of Financial Analysis," **AR**, 1972, Vol. 47, No. 4, pp. 679-692.

Hofstedt, Thomas R. (Davidson, H. Justin and Thomas R. Hofstedt. "Published Financial Statements For CPAs," **JOA**, 1972, Vol. 134, No. 1, pp. 31-45.)

Hofstedt, T. R. "Behavioral Accounting Research: Pathologies, Paradigms And Prescriptions," **AOS**, 1976, Vol. 1, No. 1, pp. 43-58.

Hogan, Thomas B. (Braiotta, Louis and Thomas B. Hogan. "Accounting For Compensated Absences," **CPAJ**, 1981, Vol. 51, No. 12, pp. 22-27.)

Hogan, Sherry H. (Brogan, Susan H. and Sherry H. Hogan. "Duty Drawback: 'Found Money' In Refunds," **CA**, 1985, Vol. 3, No. 4, pp. 19-25.

Hogarth, Robin M. (Einhorn, Hillel J. and Robin M. Hogarth. "Behavioral Decision Theory: Processes Of Judgment And Choice," **JAR**, 1981, Vol. 19, No. 1, pp. 1-31.)

Holder, Carolyn S. (Holder, William W. and Carolyn S. Holder. "Problems Of Income Determination For Service Industries," **CPAJ**, 1986, Vol. 56, No. 10, pp. 54-63.)

Holder, William W. and Carolyn S. Holder. "Problems Of Income Determination For Service Industries," **CPAJ**, 1986, Vol. 56, No. 10, pp. 54-63.

Holder, William W. and Kimberly Ham Eudy. "A Framework For Building An Accounting Constitution," **JAAF**, 1982, Vol. 5, No. 2, pp. 110-125.

Holder, William W. and Sheryl Collmer. "Analytical Review Procedures: New Relevance," **CPAJ**, 1980, Vol. 50, No. 11, pp. 29-36.

Holder, William W. "Analytical Review Procedures In Planning The Audit: An Application Study," **AJPT**, 1982-83, Vol. 2, No. 2, pp. 100-107.

Holder, William W. "Expenditure And Liability Recognition In Government," **JOA**, 1983, Vol. 156, No. 3, pp. 79-84.

Holder, William W. "Graduate-Level Public Sector Accounting: Status And Forecast," **AR**, 1978, Vol. 53, No. 3, pp. 746-751.

Holder, William W. "Revenue Recognition In Not-For-Profit Organizations," **CPAJ**, 1976, Vol. 46, No. 11, pp. 15-22.

Holder, William W. (Arnold, Jerry, William W. Holder and M. Herschel Mann. "International Reporting Aspects Of Segment Disclosure," **IJAER**, 1980, Vol. 16, No. 1, pp. 125-135.)

Holder, William W. (Arnold, Jerry L., William W. Holder and Jan R. Williams. "FASB Should Establish An Accounting Laboratory," **MA**, 1983, Vol. 64, No. 9, pp. 52-55.)

Holder, William W. (Clay, Raymond J., Jr. and William W. Holder. "A Practitioner's Guide To Accounting For Leases," **JOA**, 1977, Vol. 144, No. 2, pp. 61-68.)

Holder, William W. (Daroca, Frank P. and William W. Holder. "The Use Of Analytical Procedures In Review And Audit Engagements," **AJPT**, 1984-85, Vol. 4, No. 2, pp. 80-92.)

Holder, William W. (Hepp, Gerald W. and William W. Holder. "A New Look In Governmental Audits," **JOA**, 1986, Vol. 161, No. 4, pp. 82-89.)

Holder, William W. (Pincus, Karen V., William W. Holder and Theodore J. Mock. "The SEC And Fraudulent Financial Reporting," **RIAR**, 1988, Vol. 2, pp. 167-185.)

Holder, William W., E. John Larsen and Doyle Z. Williams. "Educational Requirements For Public Accounting," **CPAJ**, 1985, Vol. 55, No. 12, pp. 36-49.

Holdren, George C. "LIFO And Ratio Analysis," **AR**, 1964, Vol. 39, No. 1, pp. 70-85.

Hole, Roderick C. and Michael A. Alkier. "German Financial Statements," **MA**, 1974, Vol. 56, No. 1, pp. 28-34.

Holgate, H. C. F. "Auditing The Contingent Liabilities Of British Banks," **AR**, 1941, Vol. 16, No. 2, pp. 207-208.

Holland, Michael L. (Alsup, Rodney G., Michael L. Holland and Fred A. Jacobs. "The Perceived Availability Of Resources Which Contribute To Accounting Faculty Productivity," **JAED**, 1988, Vol. 6, No. 2, pp. 261-277.)

Holland, Rodger G. and C. Edward Arrington. "Issues Influencing The Decisions Of Accounting Faculty To Relocate," **IAE**, 1987, Vol. 2, No. 1, pp. 57-71.

Holland, Rodger G. (Jordan, William F. and Rodger G. Holland. "An Empirical Inquiry Into The Determination Of Dividend Equivalence In Stock Redemptions: A Comment," **JATA**, 1984, Vol. 5, No. 2, pp. 75-80.)

Holland, Winford E. (Blakeney, Roger N., Winford E. Holland and Michael T. Matteson. "The Auditor-Auditee Relationship: Some Behavioral Considerations And Implications For Auditing Education," **AR**, 1976, Vol. 51, No. 4, pp. 899-906.)

Hollander, Stanley C. "Malachy Postlethwayt's British Mercantile College, 1755," **AR**, 1953, Vol. 28, No. 3, pp. 434-438.

Hollen, Thomas W. "Investment Credit: Are You Getting Your Share?," **MA**, 1984, Vol. 66, No. 4, pp. 64-68.

Holley, Charles L., Edward C. Spede and Michael C. Chester, Jr. "The Push-Down Accounting Controversy," **MA**, 1987, Vol. 68, No. 7, pp. 39-42.

Hollon, Charles J. (Hanshaw, Nancy F., Thomas A. Ulrich and Charles J. Hollon. "Save Time, Money, And Taxes - Lease Your Employees," **MA**, 1986, Vol. 67, No. 10, pp. 30-36.)

Holloway, Frank B. "The Non-Profits Can Benefit From Cost Accounting," **MA**, 1968, Vol. 50, No. 3, pp. 13-14.

Hollowell, Betsy Ann. (Lucas, Timothy S. and Betsy Ann Hollowell. "Pension Accounting: The Liability Question," **JOA**, 1981, Vol. 152, No. 4, pp. 57-67.)

Holman, Guy. (Withey, Howard A. and Guy Holman. "Standards Of Accounting For Voluntary Health-Welfare Agencies," **JOA**, 1965, Vol. 120, No. 2, pp. 47-56.)

Holmes, Geoffrey. "Earnings Per Share: A Measure Of Sustainable Growth," **ABR**, 1970-71, Vol. 1, No. 2, pp. 118-144.

Holmes, James D. J. "An Introductory Course In The Field Of Electronic Data Processing," **AR**, 1959, Vol. 34, No. 3, pp. 463-464.

Holmes, James R. (Tipgos, Manuel A., James R. Holmes and Gerald H. Lander. "The Management Accountant Today: A Status Report," **MA**, 1983, Vol. 65, No. 5, pp. 53-57.)

Holmes, Robert W. "Update Your Cost Accounting System," **MA**, 1970, Vol. 51, No. 8, pp. 14-16.

Holmes, William. "A 13th Century Audit Case," **AHJ**, 1977, Vol. 4, No. 2, pp. 107-111.

Holmes, William. "An 18th Century Accounting Projection From Plymouth, Massachusetts," **AHJ**, 1978, Vol. 5, No. 2, pp. 67-70.

Holmes, William. "Benjamin Gilliam's Book - 1700," **AHJ**, 1978, Vol. 5, No. 1, pp. 73-76.

Holmes, William. "Digging In Boston's Accounting Dumps," **AHJ**, 1976, Vol. 3, No. 1-4, pp. 32-39.

Holmes, William. "Governmental Accounting In Colonial Massachusetts," **AR**, 1979, Vol. 54, No. 1, pp. 47-57.

Holmes, William. "Materiality - Through The Looking Glass," **JOA**, 1972, Vol. 133, No. 2, pp. 44-49.

Holmes, William. "The Market Value Of Inventories: A Review," **JOA**, 1964, Vol. 117, No. 3, pp. 55-59.

Holstrum, Gary L. and Eugene H. Sauls. "The Opportunity Cost Transfer Price," **MA**, 1973, Vol. 54, No. 11, pp. 29-33.

Holstrum, Gary L. and William F. Messier, Jr. "A Review And Integration Of Empirical Research On Materiality," **AJPT**, 1982-83, Vol. 2, No. 1, pp. 45-63.

Holstrum, Gary L. "Sources Of Error And Inconsistency In Audit Judgment," **AIA**, 1987, Vol. 4, pp. 179-200.

Holstrum, Gary L. "The Effect Of Budget Adaptiveness And Tightness On Managerial Decision Behavior," **JAR**, 1971, Vol. 9, No. 2, pp. 268-277.

Holstrum, Gary L. (Daroca, Frank P., Gary L. Holstrum and W. Thomas Lin. "Long-Range Planning And Control Of

Growth," **JOA**, 1984, Vol. 158, No. 6, pp. 118-134.)

Holstrum, Gary L. (Larson, Kermit D. and Gary L. Holstrum. "Financial Accounting Standards In The United States: 1973 - ?," **ABACUS**, 1973, Vol. 9, No. 1, pp. 3-15.)

Holstrum, Gary L. (Streuling, G. Fred and Gary L. Holstrum. "Teaching Machines Versus Lectures In Accounting Education: An Experiment," **AR**, 1972, Vol. 47, No. 4, pp. 806-810.)

Holt, Doris L. (Danos, Paul, Doris L. Holt and Andrew D. Bailey, Jr. "The Interaction Of Science And Attestation Standard Formation," **AJPT**, 1986-87, Vol. 6, No. 2, pp. 134-149.)

Holt, Doris L. (Danos, Paul, Doris L. Holt and Eugene A. Imhoff, Jr. "Bond Raters' Use Of Management Financial Forecasts: An Experiment In Expert Judgment," **AR**, 1984, Vol. 59, No. 4, pp. 547-573.)

Holt, D. L. "Auditors And Base Rates Revisited," **AOS**, 1987, Vol. 12, No. 6, pp. 571-578.

Holt, Robert N. (Haskins, Mark E. and Robert N. Holt. "A Cash Flow Approach To The Statement Of Changes In Financial Position," **JAED**, 1986, Vol. 4, No. 2, pp. 97-106.)

Holt, Robert N. (Shockley, Randolph A. and Robert N. Holt. "A Behavioral Investigation Of Supplier Differentiation In The Market For Audit Services," **JAR**, 1983, Vol. 21, No. 2, pp. 545-564.)

Holt, R. N. and R. J. Carroll. "Classification Of Commercial Bank Loans Through Policy Capturing," **AOS**, 1980, Vol. 5, No. 3, pp. 285-296.

Holt, William L. "A Short Analysis Of Depreciation," **MA**, 1971, Vol. 52, No. 8, pp. 21-22.

Holthausen, Robert W. and Richard W. Leftwich. "The Economic Consequences Of Accounting Choice: Implications Of Costly Contracting And Monitoring," **JAEC**, 1983, Vol. 5, No. 2, pp. 77-117.

Holthausen, Robert W. and Robert E. Verrecchia. "The Effect Of Sequential Information Releases On The Variance Of Price Changes In An Intertemporal Multi-Asset Market," **JAR**, 1988, Vol. 26, No. 1, pp. 82-106.

Holthausen, Robert W. "Evidence On The Effect Of Bond Covenants And Management Compensation Contracts On The Choice Of Accounting Techniques: The Case Of The Depreciation Switch-Back," **JAEC**, 1981, Vol. 3, No. 1, pp. 73-109.

Holthausen, Robert W. (Dopuch, Nicholas, Robert W. Holthausen and Richard W. Leftwich. "Abnormal Stock Returns Associated With Media Disclosures Of 'Subject To' Qualified Audit Opinions," **JAEC**, 1986, Vol. 8, No. 2, pp. 93-117.)

Holthausen, Robert W. (Dopuch, Nicholas, Robert W. Holthausen and Richard W. Leftwich. "Predicting Audit Qualifications With Financial And Market Variables," **AR**, 1987, Vol. 62, No. 3, pp. 431-454.)

Holthausen, Robert. (Dodd, Peter, Nicholas Dopuch, Robert Holthausen and Richard Leftwich. "Qualified Audit Opinions And Stock Returns: Information Content, Announcement Dates, And Concurrent Disclosures," **JAEC**, 1984, Vol. 6, No. 1, pp. 3-38.)

Holton, Stephen D. (Clay, John R. and Stephen D. Holton. "Prescribed Form Engagements: Some Practical Guidance," **JOA**, 1982, Vol. 153, No. 5, pp. 66-79.)

Holton, Thomas L. "Reports On Nonprofit Organizations," **JOA**, 1959, Vol. 107, No. 4, pp. 61-67.

Holton, Thomas L. (Boyle, Joseph T. and Thomas L. Holton. "Peer Review In The Accounting Profession - Who Audits The Auditor?," **CPAJ**, 1975, Vol. 45, No. 1, pp. 15-18.)

Holzer, H. Peter and Doria Tremblay. "Accounting And Economic Development: The Cases Of Thailand And Tunisia," **IJAER**, 1973, Vol. 9, No. 1, pp. 67-80.

Holzer, H. Peter and Hanns-Martin Schonfeld. "The German Solution To The Post-War Price Level Problem," **AR**, 1963, Vol. 38, No. 2, pp. 377-381.

Holzer, H. Peter and Hanns-Martin Schonfeld. "The 'Funktionale Kontorechnung' Of Walter Thoms," **AR**, 1964, Vol. 39, No. 2, pp. 405-413.

Holzer, H. Peter and Hanns-Martin Schonfeld. "The French Approach To The Post-War Price Level Problem," **AR**, 1963, Vol. 38, No. 2, pp. 382-388.

Holzer, H. Peter. (Fess, Philip E. and H. Peter Holzer. "The Diverse Functions Of Accounting," **JOA**, 1964, Vol. 118, No. 2, pp. 49-52.)

Holzer, H. Peter. (Schonfeld, Hanns-Martin and H. Peter Holzer. "A 'Business' Flow Chart And Its Use As A Teaching Aid," **AR**, 1962, Vol. 37. No. 1, pp. 118-120.)

Holzer, H. P. "Corporate Financial Reporting In West-Germany," **AR**, 1959, Vol. 34, No. 3, pp. 399-402.

Holzmann, Oscar J. and Kathryn M. Means. "Accounting For Savings And Loan Mergers: Conflict And Accounting Error," **JAAF**, 1984, Vol. 7, No. 2, pp. 138-150.

Holzmann, Oscar J. and Nicolas Gressis. "Covariability Of Segment Earnings And Multisegment Company Returns: A Comment," **AR**, 1974, Vol. 49, No. 1, pp. 132-139.

Holzmann, Oscar J. (Cook, John S. and Oscar J. Holzmann. "Current Cost And Present Value In Income Theory," **AR**, 1976, Vol. 51, No. 4, pp. 778-787.)

Holzman, Robert S. "A Critique Of The IRS 'Arm's-Length' Concept," **JOA**, 1968, Vol. 126, No. 5, pp. 50-53.

Holzman, Robert S. "The Gregory Case," **JOA**, 1955, Vol. 100, No. 1, pp. 54-58.

Holzman, Robert S. "Thirty Years Of The Gregory Case," **JOA**, 1965, Vol. 119, No. 5, pp. 34-38.

Holzman, Robert S. "What Manner Of Tax Do The Courts Say We Have?," **JOA**, 1951, Vol. 91, No. 6, pp. 833-834.

Homburger, Richard and Gary John Previts. "A Hatfield Trilogy: The Significance Of 'Zwei Pfadfinder'," **AHJ**, 1977, Vol. 4, No. 1, pp. 9-13.

Homburger, Richard H. and William C. Dent. "Management Accounting Concepts And The Principles Dilemma," **MA**, 1969, Vol. 50, No. 8, pp. 14-15.

Homburger, Richard H. "A Study Of History - Gateway To Perspective," **AR**, 1958, Vol. 33, No. 3, pp. 501-503.

Homburger, Richard H. "Forfeited Capital Stock Subscriptions," **AR**, 1949, Vol. 24, No. 2, pp. 199-202.

Homburger, Richard H. "Measurement In Accounting," **AR**, 1961, Vol. 36, No. 1, pp. 94-99.

Homburger, Richard H. "Tax Basis Of Partner's Interest Explained By Double Entry," **AR**, 1960, Vol. 35, No. 1, pp. 132-134.

Homburger, Richard H. "The Graduate Course In Accounting Theory - Seminar Style," **AR**, 1957, Vol. 32, No. 3, pp. 485-487.

Homburger, Richard H. "The Use Of Medieval Statements For Teaching Accounting: A Comment," **AR**, 1973, Vol. 48, No. 4, pp. 785-788.

Hong, Hai, Robert S. Kaplan and Gershon Mandelker. "Pooling Vs. Purchase: The Effects Of Accounting For Mergers On Stock Prices," **AR**, 1978, Vol. 53, No. 1, pp. 31-47.

Hong, Han Kang. "Control Theory Approach To Process Costing," **ABR**, 1984-85, Vol. 15, No. 58, pp. 129-133.

Hong, Han Kang. "Reciprocal Service Costs Allocation And Sensitivity Analysis," **ABR**, 1980-81, Vol. 11, No. 42, pp. 117-120.

Honig, Lawrence E. "Theory Vs. Practice: Parsimony As Referee," **JAAF**, 1978, Vol. 1, No. 3, pp. 231-236.

Hook, Bill B. (Johnson, Douglas A., Steve Kaplan and Bill B. Hook. "Looking For Mr. Overhead: An Expanded Role For Management Accountants," **MA**, 1983, Vol. 65, No. 5, pp. 65-70.)

Hook, Bill. (Shoemaker, Charles and Bill Hook. "Developing Bidding Factors For A Quality Assurance Department," **MA**, 1970, Vol. 51, No. 7, pp. 41-44.)

Hooks, Karen L. and Shirley J. Cheramy. "Women Accountants - Current Status And Future Prospects," **CPAJ**, 1988, Vol. 58, No. 5, pp. 18-31.

Hooks, Karen L. (Dahl, Shirley J. and Karen L. Hooks. "Women Accountants In A Changing Profession," **JOA**, 1984, Vol. 158, No. 6, pp. 108-117.)

Hooks, Karen L. (Dahl, Shirley J. and Karen L. Hooks. "Women Accountants, Today And Tomorrow," **CPAJ**, 1985, Vol. 55, No. 1, pp. 20-25.)

Hooley, G. J. (Ratnatunga, J., R. Pike and G. J. Hooley. "The Application Of Management Accounting Techniques To Marketing," **ABR**, 1988, Vol. 18, No. 72, pp. 363-370.)

Hooper, H. Paul. (Page, John R. and H. Paul Hooper. "How To Buy A Computer," **CPAJ**, 1979, Vol. 49, No. 9, pp. 39-45.)

Hooper, Paul and John Page. "Better Financial Statements For Corporate Valuation," **MA**, 1979, Vol. 61, No. 3, pp. 52-56.

Hooper, Paul and John Page. "Measuring Teaching Effectiveness By Student Evaluation," **IAE**, 1986, Vol. 1, No. 1, pp. 56-64.

Hooper, Paul and John Page. "Organizing Business Data Processing Systems," **CPAJ**, 1983, Vol. 53, No. 8, pp. 24-31.

Hooper, Paul and John Page. "The Legal Environment Of Public Accounting," **CPAJ**, 1984, Vol. 54, No. 6, pp. 36-39.

Hooper, Paul, John Page and Karen Smith. "Accountant's Legal Liability: An International Comparison," **IJAER**, 1985, Vol. 20, No. 2, pp. 65-80.

Hoops, Jeffrey R. "The Investment Tax Credit - What Qualifies?," **CPAJ**, 1979, Vol. 49, No. 10, pp. 17-22.

Hoops, Jeffrey R. (Baldasaro, P. Michael and Jeffrey R. Hoops. "Tax Act Of 1986 - Corporate Changes," **CPAJ**, 1986, Vol. 56, No. 12, pp. 28-43.)

Hoover, John Edgar. "Accounting Investigations Of The FBI," **MA**, 1968, Vol. 49, No. 12, pp. 11-14.

Hoover, John Edgar. "FBI Accounting Investigations," **AR**, 1961, Vol. 36, No. 2, pp. 197-203.

Hoover, John Edgar. "FBI Investigation Of Fraud," **JOA**, 1965, Vol. 120, No. 1, pp. 34-39.

Hoover, J. Edgar. "The Accountant's Role In The FBI," **JOA**, 1960, Vol. 109, No. 5, pp. 36-40.

Hope, Anthony. (Arnold, John and Anthony Hope. "Reporting Business Performance," **ABR**, 1974-75, Vol. 5, No. 18, pp. 96-105.)

Hope, Anthony. (Carsberg, Bryan, Anthony Hope and R. W. Scapens. "The Objectives Of Published Accounting Reports: Reply To A Comment," **ABR**, 1974-75, Vol. 5, No. 18, pp. 152-155.)

Hope, Anthony. (Carsberg, Bryan, Anthony Hope and R. W. Scapens. "The Objectives Of Published Accounting Reports," **ABR**, 1973-74, Vol. 4, No. 15, pp. 162-173.)

Hope, J. William. "New Markets For Ideas," **AR**, 1953, Vol. 28, No. 1, pp. 3-7.

Hope, J. William. "Restriction Would Strengthen The Profession," **AR**, 1945, Vol. 20, No. 2, pp. 194-197.

Hope, J. William. "The Uniform CPA Examination," **AR**, 1949, Vol. 24, No. 2, pp. 123-127.

Hope, Tony and John Briggs. "Accounting Policy Making - Some Lessons From The Deferred Taxation Debate," **ABR**, 1981-82, Vol. 12, No. 46, pp. 83-96.

Hopewell, Rita J. and Harold N. Myklebust. "Stimulating Faculty To Use Computers," **JAED**, 1984, Vol. 2, No. 1, pp. 161-162.

Hopewell, Rita J., Eileen S. Klink and Reuben W. Coleman. "Facing The Ethics Involved In Technical Obsolescence," **MA**, 1984, Vol. 66, No. 6, pp. 26-29.

Hopkins, Roger. (Juchau, Roger, Mick White and Roger Hopkins. "Tertiary Education Strategies For Accounting In Developing Societies - The Southwest Pacific As A

Case Study," **IJAER**, 1986, Vol. 21, No. 2, pp. 145-160.)

Hopkins, Roger. (Ma, Ronald and Roger Hopkins. "Goodwill - An Example Of Puzzle-Solving In Accounting," **ABACUS**, 1988, Vol. 24, No. 1, pp. 75-85.)

Hopkins, Ruth P. "Japanese Business Practices," **MA**, 1974, Vol. 56, No. 1, pp. 52-53.

Hopper, T. M. "Role Conflicts Of Management Accountants And Their Position Within Organisation Structures," **AOS**, 1980, Vol. 5, No. 4, pp. 401-412.

Hopper, T. M. (Cooper, D. J. and T. M. Hopper. "Critical Studies In Accounting," **AOS**, 1987, Vol. 12, No. 4/5, pp. 407-414.)

Hopper, T. (Berry, A. J., T. Capps, D. Cooper, P. Ferguson, T. Hopper and E. A. Lowe. "Management Control In An Area Of The NCB: Rationales Of Accounting Practices In A Public Enterprise," **AOS**, 1985, Vol. 10, No. 1, pp. 3-28.)

Hopper, T., J. Storey and H. Willmott. "Accounting For Accounting: Towards The Development Of A Dialectical View," **AOS**, 1987, Vol. 12, No. 4/5, pp. 437-456.

Hopwood, Anthony G. and H. Thomas Johnson. "Accounting History's Claim To Legitimacy," **IJAER**, 1986, Vol. 21, No. 2, pp. 37-46.

Hopwood, Anthony G. "An Empirical Study Of The Role Of Accounting Data In Performance Evaluation," **JAR**, 1972, Vol. 10, Supp., pp. 156-182.

Hopwood, Anthony G. "Leadership Climate And The Use Of Accounting Data In Performance Evaluation," **AR**, 1974, Vol. 49, No. 3, pp. 485-495.

Hopwood, A. G. "Accounting And Gender: An Introduction," **AOS**, 1987, Vol. 12, No. 1, pp. 65-70.

Hopwood, A. G. "On Origins And Development: Some Reflections On The 40th Anniversary Of Pergamon Press And The 65th Birthday Of Its Founder, Robert Maxwell," **AOS**, 1988, Vol. 13, No. 4, pp. 329-332.

Hopwood, A. G. "On Trying To Study Accounting In The Contexts In Which It Operates," **AOS**, 1983, Vol. 8, No. 2/3, pp. 287-305.

Hopwood, A. G. "The Archaeology Of Accounting Systems," **AOS**, 1987, Vol. 12, No. 3, pp. 207-234.

Hopwood, A. G. "The Tale Of A Committee That Never Reported: Disagreements On Intertwining Accounting With The Social," **AOS**, 1985, Vol. 10, No. 3, pp. 361-377.

Hopwood, A. G. "Towards An Organizational Perspective For The Study Of Accounting And Information Systems," **AOS**, 1978, Vol. 3, No. 1, pp. 3-14.

Hopwood, A. G. (Burchell, S., C. Clubb and A. G. Hopwood. "Accounting In Its Social Context: Towards A History Of Value Added In The United Kingdom," **AOS**, 1985, Vol. 10, No. 4, pp. 381-414.)

Hopwood, A. (Burchell, S., C. Clubb, A. Hopwood, J. Hughes and J. Nahapiet. "The Roles Of Accounting In Organizations And Society," **AOS**, 1980, Vol. 5, No. 1, pp. 5-28.)

Hopwood, William S. and James C. McKeown. "The Incremental Informational Content Of Interim Expenses Over Interim Sales," **JAR**, 1985, Vol. 23, No. 1, pp. 161-174.

Hopwood, William S. and James C. McKeown. "An Evaluation Of Univariate Time-Series Earnings Models And Their Generalization To A Single Input Transfer Function," **JAR**, 1981, Vol. 19, No. 2, pp. 313-322.

Hopwood, William S. and Karen S. Hreha. "The Interprofessional Tax Altercation," **AHJ**, 1984, Vol. 11, No. 1, pp. 1-18.

Hopwood, William S. and Paul Newbold. "Alternative Interim Reporting Techniques Within A Dynamic Framework: Comments And Extensions," **AR**, 1985, Vol. 60, No. 2, pp. 289-294.

Hopwood, William S. and Thomas F. Schaefer. "Incremental Information Content Of Earnings And Nonearnings Based Financial Ratios," **CAR**, 1988, Vol. 5, No. 1, pp. 318-342.

Hopwood, William S. "On The Automation Of The Box-Jenkins Modeling Procedures: An Algorithm With An Empirical Test," **JAR**, 1980, Vol. 18, No. 1, pp. 289-296.

Hopwood, William S. "The Transfer Function Relationship Between Earnings And Market-Industry Indices: An Empirical Study," **JAR**, 1980, Vol. 18, No. 1, pp. 77-90.

Hopwood, William S. (Arrington, C. Edward, Charles D. Bailey and William S. Hopwood. "An Attribution Analysis Of Responsibility Assessment For Audit Performance," **JAR**, 1985, Vol. 23, No. 1, pp. 1-20.)

Hopwood, William S. (Chambers, R. J., William S. Hopwood and James C. McKeown. "The Relevance Of Varieties Of Accounting Information: A U.S.A. Survey," **ABACUS**, 1984, Vol. 20, No. 2, pp. 99-110.)

Hopwood, William S. (Collins, William A., William S. Hopwood and James C. McKeown. "The Predictability Of Interim Earnings Over Alternative Quarters," **JAR**, 1984, Vol. 22, No. 2, pp. 467-479.)

Hopwood, William S. (Collins, William A. and William S. Hopwood. "A Multivariate Analysis Of Annual Earnings Forecasts Generated From Quarterly Forecasts Of Financial Analysts And Univariate Time-Series Models," **JAR**, 1980, Vol. 18, No. 2, pp.390-406.)

Hopwood, William S. (Frecka. Thomas J. and William S. Hopwood. "The Effects Of Outliers On The Cross-Sectional Distributional Properties Of Financial Ratios," **AR**, 1983, Vol. 58, No. 1, pp. 115-128.)

Hopwood, William S., Paul Newbold and Peter A. Silhan. "The Potential For Gains In Predictive Ability Through Disaggregation: Segmented Annual Earnings," **JAR**, 1982, Vol. 20, No. 2, pp. 724-732.

Hopwood, William, James McKeown and Jane Mutchler. "The Sensitivity Of Financial Distress Prediction Models To Departures From Normality," **CAR**, 1988, Vol. 5, No. 1,

pp. 284-298.

Hopwood, William. (Bailey, Charles D., Gordon B. Harwood and William Hopwood. "Removing The Computational Burden From Reciprocal Cost Allocations," **JAED**, 1984, Vol. 2, No. 2, pp. 169-176.)

Hopwood, W. S., J. C. McKeown and P. Newbold. "Power Transformations In Time-Series Models Of Quarterly Earnings Per Share," **AR**, 1981, Vol. 56, No. 4, pp. 927-933.

Hopwood, W. S., J. C. McKeown and P. Newbold. "The Additional Information Content Of Quarterly Earnings Reports: Intertemporal Disaggregation," **JAR**, 1982, Vol. 20, No. 2, Part I, pp. 343-349.

Hord, Warner H. "A Neglected Area Of Accounting Valuation," **AR**, 1942, Vol. 17, No. 4, pp. 335-347.

Hord, Warner H. "Bond Discount And Debt Expense In Terms Of Consistent Accounting," **AR**, 1940, Vol. 15, No. 2, pp. 211-217.

Hord, Warner H. "The Flow Of Property As A Basis Of Internal Control," **AR**, 1939, Vol. 14, No. 3, pp. 272-284.

Horn, Betty C. (Dillon, Ray D., Betty C. Horn and Ernest R. Larkins. "More Value From Fringe Benefit Plans," **CPAJ**, 1986, Vol. 56, No. 11, pp. 40-57.)

Horn, Frederick E. "Academic Preparation Of The Accountant Of The Future," **JOA**, 1975, Vol. 139, No. 5, pp. 64-68.

Horn, Frederick E. "Managerial Emphasis In Elementary Accounting," **AR**, 1951, Vol. 26, No. 3, pp. 308-312.

Horn, Frederick E. "Managing Cash," **JOA**, 1964, Vol. 117, No. 4, pp. 56-62.

Hornberger, D. J. "Accounting Control In College Fraternal Organizations," **AR**, 1926, Vol. 1, No. 3, pp. 89-92.

Hornberger, D. J. "Accounting For No-Par Stocks During The Depression," **AR**, 1933, Vol. 8, No. 1, pp. 58-62.

Hornberger, D. J. "Accounting For No-Par Stock Issues," **AR**, 1929, Vol. 4, No. 4, pp. 213-217.

Horne, Gilbert R. "Professional Training For Accountancy In Canada," **AR**, 1956, Vol. 31, No. 1, pp. 43-49.

Horne, John M. "EDP Controls To Check Fraud," **MA**, 1974, Vol. 56, No. 4, pp. 43-46.

Horngren, Charles T. and George H. Sorter. "An Evaluation Of Some Criticisms Of Relevant Costing," **AR**, 1964, Vol. 39, No. 2, pp. 417-420.

Horngren, Charles T. and George H. Sorter. "Direct' Costing For External Reporting," **AR**, 1961, Vol. 36, No. 1, pp. 84-93.

Horngren, Charles T. "A Contribution Margin Approach to The Analysis Of Capacity Utilization," **AR**, 1967, Vol. 42, No. 2, pp. 254-264.

Horngren, Charles T. "Accounting Principles: Private Or Public Sector?," **JOA**, 1972, Vol. 133, No. 5, pp. 37-41.

Horngren, Charles T. "Capacity Utilization And The Efficiency Variance," **AR**, 1969, Vol. 44, No. 1, pp. 86-89.

Horngren, Charles T. "Disclosure: What Next?," **AR**, 1958, Vol. 33, No. 1, pp. 84-92.

Horngren, Charles T. "Disclosure: 1957," **AR**, 1957, Vol. 32, No. 4, pp. 598-604.

Horngren, Charles T. "How Should We Interpret The Realization Concept?," **AR**, 1965, Vol. 40, No. 2, pp. 323-333.

Horngren, Charles T. "More Useful Financial Statements," **JOA**, 1959, Vol. 108, No. 1, pp. 39-46.

Horngren, Charles T. "Motivation And Coordination In Management Control Systems," **MA**, 1967, Vol. 48, No. 9, pp. 3-7.

Horngren, Charles T. "Process Costing In Perspective: Forget Fifo," **AR**, 1967, Vol. 42, No. 3, pp. 593-596.

Horngren, Charles T. "Security Analysts And The Price Level," **AR**, 1955, Vol. 30, No. 4, pp. 575-581.

Horngren, Charles T. "Stock Dividends And The Entity Theory," **AR**, 1957, Vol. 32, No. 3, pp. 379-385.

Horngren, Charles T. "Teaching Methods And Participation As A Major Law Of Learning," **AR**, 1963, Vol. 38, No. 2, pp. 409-411.

Horngren, Charles T. "The Accounting Discipline In 1999," **AR**, 1971, Vol. 46, No. 1, pp. 1-11.

Horngren, Charles T. "The Funds Statement," **JOA**, 1956, Vol. 101, No. 1, pp. 55-59.

Horngren, Charles T. (Foster, George and Charles T. Horngren. "JIT: Cost Accounting And Cost Management Issues," **MA**, 1987, Vol. 68, No. 12, pp. 19-25.)

Horngren, Charles T. (Sorter, George H. and Charles T. Horngren. "Asset Recognition And Economic Attributes - The Relevant Costing Approach," **AR**, 1962, Vol. 37, No. 3. pp. 391-399.)

Horodowich, Peter. "Evaluating The Write-Off Of Slow-Moving Finished Goods Inventory," **MA**, 1979, Vol. 60, No. 9, pp. 35-40.

Horrigan, James O. "A Short History Of Financial Ratio Analysis," **AR**, 1968, Vol. 43, No. 2, pp. 284-294.

Horrigan, James O. "An Alternative Approach To Predicting Corporate Bond Ratings: A Comment," **JAR**, 1970, Vol. 8, No. 1, pp. 126-127.

Horrigan, James O. "Some Empirical Bases Of Financial Ratio Analysis," **AR**, 1965, Vol. 40, No. 3, pp. 558-568.

Horrigan, James. "The Determination Of Long-Term Credit Standing With Financial Ratios," **JAR**, 1966, Vol. 4, Supp., pp. 44-62.

Horvitz, Jerome S. and D. R. Finley. "A Macro-Case Analysis Approach To Tax Research - A Comment," **AR**, 1979, Vol. 54, No. 3, pp. 637-640.

Horvitz, Jerome S. and Herbert L. Jensen. "Systematic Evaluations Of Tax Accounting Textbooks," **AR**, 1979, Vol. 54, No. 4, pp. 800-806.

Horvitz, Jerome S. and Michael Hainkel. "The IRS Summons Power And Its Effect On The Independent Auditor," **JAAF**, 1981, Vol. 4, No. 2, pp. 114-127.

Horvitz, **Jerome S.** and Michael J. Tucker. "Clinical Practice Problems In Tax Education," **AR**, 1980, Vol. 55, No. 4, pp. 672-679.

Horvitz, **Jerome S.** and Oliver Ray Whittington, III. "Responsibilities In Tax Practice," **CPAJ**, 1978, Vol. 48, No. 10, pp. 26-31.

Horvitz, **Jerome S.** and Susan Coldwell. "Analysis Of The Arthur Young Decision And Its Potential Impact On Public Accounting," **JAAF**, 1985, Vol. 8, No. 2, pp. 86-99.

Horvitz, **Jerome S.** (Seago, W. E. and Jerome S. Horvitz. "The Effects Of The Supreme Court's Thor Power Tool Decision On The Balance Of Tax Accounting Power," **JATA**, 1980, Vol. 1, No. 2, pp. 5-9.)

Horvitz, **Jerome S.** (Seiler, Robert E. and Jerome S. Horvitz. "The Partnership Decision - The Hishon Case," **CPAJ**, 1985, Vol. 55, No. 1, pp. 12-19.)

Horvitz, **Oscar.** "Controlling Truck Costs," **JOA**, 1960, Vol. 109, No. 3, pp. 51-55.

Horwitz, **Bertrand** and Allan Young. "An Empirical Study Of Accounting Policy And Tender Offers," **JAR**, 1972, Vol. 10, No. 1, pp. 96-107.

Horwitz, **Bertrand** and Allan Young. "The Case For Asset Disclosure Of Treasury Stock," **CPAJ**, 1975, Vol. 45, No. 3, pp. 31-33.

Horwitz, **Bertrand** and Daniel Normolle. "Federal Agency R&D Contract Awards And The FASB Rule For Privately-Funded R&D," **AR**, 1988, Vol. 63, No. 3, pp. 414-435.

Horwitz, **Bertrand** and Reza Shabahang. "Published Corporate Accounting Data And General Wage Increases Of The Firm," **AR**, 1971, Vol. 46, No. 2, pp. 243-252.

Horwitz, **Bertrand** and Richard Kolodny. "The Impact Of Rule Making On R&D Investments Of Small High-Technology Firms," **JAAF**, 1981, Vol. 4, No. 2, pp. 102-113.

Horwitz, **Bertrand** and Richard Kolodny. "Who Is Short-sighted?," **JAPP**, 1982, Vol. 1, No. 2, pp. 79-82.

Horwitz, **Bertrand N.** and Richard Kolodny. "The Economic Effects Of Involuntary Uniformity In The Financial Reporting Of R & D Expenditures," **JAR**, 1980, Vol. 18, Supp., pp. 38-74.

Horwitz, **Bertrand.** "Depreciation And Cost Stability In Soviet Accounting," **AR**, 1963, Vol. 38, No. 4, pp. 819-826.

Horwitz, **B.** and R. Kolodny. "Segment Reporting: Hindsight After Ten Years," **JAAF**, 1980, Vol. 4, No. 1, pp. 20-35.

Horwitz, **B.** (Frankfurter, G. and B. Horwitz. "The Effects Of Accounting Principles Board Opinion No. 15 On Earnings Per Share: A Simulation Study," **AR**, 1972, Vol. 47, No. 2, pp. 245-259.)

Horwitz, **Geoffrey B.** "EDP Auditing - The Coming Of Age," **JOA**, 1970, Vol. 130, No. 2, pp. 48-56.

Horwitz, **Ronald M.** "The Investment Credit, 'Deferred Income Taxes' And Accounting Measurement," **AR**, 1964, Vol. 39, No. 3, pp. 618-621.

Hoshower, **Leon B.** and Linda Ann Mandel. "Transfer Pricing Policies Of Diversified U.S.-Based Multinationals," **IJAER**, 1986, Vol. 22, No. 1, pp. 51-59.

Hoshower, **Leon B.** and Robert P. Crum. "Controlling Service Center Costs," **MA**, 1987, Vol. 69, No. 5, pp. 44-48.

Hoshower, **Leon B.** and Robert P. Crum. "Straightening The Tortuous - And Treacherous - ROI Path," **MA**, 1986, Vol. 68, No. 6, pp. 41-45.

Hoshower, **Leon B.** and William L. Ferrara. "Deferred Taxes And Consolidations - A Case For Change," **MA**, 1985, Vol. 67, No. 6, pp. 57-60.

Hoshower, **Leon B.** (Crum, Robert P. and Leon B. Hoshower. "The Expanded Nature And Purpose Of Responsibility Accounting," **CA**, 1986, Vol. 4, No. 4, pp. 60-67.)

Hosick, **Ted R.** "Effect Of Direct Costing On Company's Accounting," **JOA**, 1953, Vol. 96, No. 4, pp. 444-448.

Hoskin, **K. W.** and R. H. Macve. "Accounting And The Examination: A Genealogy Of Disciplinary Power," **AOS**, 1986, Vol. 11, No. 2, pp. 105-136.

Hoskin, **K. W.** and R. H. Macve. "The Genesis Of Accountability: The West Point Connections," **AOS**, 1988, Vol. 13, No. 1, pp. 37-74.

Hoskin, **Robert E.** "Opportunity Cost And Behavior," **JAR**, 1983, Vol. 21, No. 1, pp. 78-95.

Hoskin, **Robert E.** (Hilton, Ronald W., Robert J. Swieringa and Robert E. Hoskin. "Perception Of Accuracy As A Determinant Of Information Value," **JAR**, 1981, Vol. 19, No. 1, pp. 86-108.)

Hoskin, **Robert E.**, John S. Hughes and William E. Ricks. "Evidence On The Incremental Information Content Of Additional Firm Disclosures Made Concurrently With Earnings," **JAR**, 1986, Vol. 24, Supp., pp. 1-32.

Hoskin, **R. E.** (Dyckman, T. R., R. E. Hoskin and R. J. Swieringa. "An Accounting Change And Information Processing Changes," **AOS**, 1982, Vol. 7, No. 1, pp. 1-12.)

Hoskins, **C. G.** "Theory Versus Practice In Risk Analysis: An Empirical Study: A Comment," **AR**, 1975, Vol. 50, No. 4, pp. 835-838.

Hosler, **Charles.** (Fried, Dov and Charles Hosler. "S&Ls, Reporting Changes And The Impact On The GNMA Market," **JAAF**, 1987, Vol. 2 (New Series), No. 1, pp. 5-23.)

Hosmer, **W. A.** "The Effect Of Direct Charges To Surplus On The Measurement Of Income," **AR**, 1938, Vol. 13, No. 1, pp. 31-54.

Hosseini, **Ahmad** and Raj Aggarwal. "Evaluating Foreign Affiliates: The Impact Of Alternative Foreign Currency Translation Methods," **IJAER**, 1983, Vol. 19, No. 1, pp. 65-87.

Houghton, **John W., Jr.** "Foreign Long-Term Debt Translation," **MA**, 1974, Vol. 56, No. 3, pp. 17-18.

Houghton, **Keith A.** and Peter Robinson. "Experimental Research In Auditing: Field Vs. Laboratory Settings," **ABR**, 1987-88, Vol. 18, No. 69, pp. 37-42.

Houghton, **Keith A.** and Ratna Sengupta. "The Effect Of Prior Probability Disclosure And Information Set Construction On Bankers' Ability To Predict Failure," **JAR**, 1984, Vol. 22, No. 2, pp. 768-775.

Houghton, **Keith A.** and Richard Bell. "Evaluations Of Accounting And Finance Journals: The Australian View," **IJAER**, 1984, Vol. 20, No. 1, pp. 179-187.

Houghton, **Keith A.** "Audit Reports: Their Impact On The Loan Decision Process And Outcome: An Experiment," **ABR**, 1983-84, Vol. 14, No. 53, pp. 15-20.

Houghton, **K. A.** "A Note On 'Harsh Effects' And Accounting For Partnership Liquidations: Myth And Reality," **ABR**, 1984-85, Vol. 15, No. 57, pp. 15-20.

Houghton, **K. A.** "Accounting Data And The Prediction Of Business Failure: The Setting Of Priors And The Age Of Data," **JAR**, 1984, Vol. 22, No. 1, pp. 361-368.

Houghton, **K. A.** "Law And Accounting: Confusion Surrounding The 'Rule In Garner V. Murray'," **ABACUS**, 1981, Vol. 17, No. 1, pp. 41-51.

Houghton, **K. A.** "Partnership Dissolution: Treatment Of The Overdrawn Capital Of An Insolvent Partner," **ABACUS**, 1982, Vol. 18, No. 1, pp. 91-96.

Houghton, **K. A.** "Re-Appraisal Of Garner V. Murray: A Comment," **ABACUS**, 1986, Vol. 22, No. 1, pp. 47-50.

Houghton, **K. A.** "The Measurement Of Meaning In Accounting: A Critical Analysis Of The Principal Evidence," **AOS**, 1988, Vol. 13, No. 3, pp. 263-280.

Houghton, **K. A.** "True And Fair View: An Empirical Study Of Connotative Meaning," **AOS**, 1987, Vol. 12, No. 2, pp. 143-152.

Houk, **Lawrence E.** "Credit Card/EDP Control Of Engineering Drawings," **MA**, 1969, Vol. 51, No. 2, pp. 45-47.

Houlihan, **William A.** and Ashwinpaul C. Sondhi. "De Facto Capitalization Of Operating Leases: The Effect On Debt Capacity," **CA**, 1984, Vol. 2, No. 3, pp. 3-13.

Hourihan, **John J.** (Enis, Charles R., William T. Stuart and John J. Hourihan. "Local Revenue Policy In Less Developed Countries: The Case For Energy Consumption Taxation." **AIT**, 1987, Vol. 1, pp. 85-108.)

House, **William C., Jr.** "The Usefulness Of Sensitivity Analysis In Capital Investment Decisions," **MA**, 1966, Vol. 47, No. 6, pp. 22-29.

Housel, **Thomas J.** (Rogers, Waymond and Thomas J. Housel. "The Effects Of Information And Cognitive Processes On Decision Making," **ABR**, 1987-88, Vol. 18, No. 69, pp. 67-74.)

Houston, **Carol Olson** and Gerhard G. Mueller. "Foreign Exchange Rate Hedging And SFAS No. 52 - Relatives Or Strangers?," **AH**, 1988, Vol. 2, No. 4, pp. 50-57.

Houston, **William S., Jr.** "Vocational Rehabilitation Workshop Costs," **MA**, 1974, Vol. 56, No. 2, pp. 15-21.

Hou, **Chi-Ming.** (Farman, Wilson L. and Chi-Ming Hou. "The Balance Of Payments: An Accounting Analysis," **AR**, 1963, Vol. 38, No. 1, pp. 133-141.)

Hove, **Mfandaidza R.** "Accounting Practices In Developing Countries: Colonialism's Legacy Of Inappropriate Technologies," **IJAER**, 1986, Vol. 22, No. 1, pp. 81-100.

Hover, **Ellis T.** "Practical Details Of Acquisitions," **MA**, 1971, Vol. 52, No. 12, pp. 33-36.

Hoverland, **H. Arthur** and Wilma D. Stricklin. "Management And Accounting Concepts Of Control," **MA**, 1967, Vol. 48, No. 10, pp. 33-37.

Hovey, **Dann F.** "Memo To FASB: A Cash Flow Statement Suggestion," **MA**, 1986, Vol. 68, No. 5, pp. 63-67.

Howard, **David C.** "Cost/Schedule Control Systems," **MA**, 1976, Vol. 58, No. 4, pp. 21-25.

Howard, **David C.** "Equivalent Unit Costing (EUCO)," **MA**, 1966, Vol. 48, No. 2, pp. 59-63.

Howard, **K.** and M. G. Christopher. "Price And Discount Rationalisation In A Multiproduct Company," **ABR**, 1972-73, Vol. 3, No. 11, pp. 168-174.

Howard, **Stanley E.** "Accounting Instruction In The Liberal Arts Curriculum," **AR**, 1930, Vol. 5, No. 2, pp. 146-149.

Howard, **Stanley E.** "Accounting In A Liberal Arts Curriculum," **AR**, 1936, Vol. 11, No. 2, pp. 149-154.

Howard, **Stanley E.** "Business Partnerships In France Before 1807," **AR**, 1932, Vol. 7, No. 4, pp. 242-257.

Howard, **Stanley E.** "Charge And Discharge," **AR**, 1931, Vol. 6, No. 1, pp. 51-56.

Howard, **Stanley E.** "Concepts Of Capital And Income," **AR**, 1937, Vol. 12, No. 1, pp. 1-2.

Howard, **Stanley E.** "Public Rules For Private Accounting In France, 1673 And 1807," **AR**, 1932, Vol. 7, No. 2, pp. 91-102.

Howard, **Stanley E.** "The Private Business Corporation Under Modern French Law," **AR**, 1934, Vol. 9, No. 2, pp. 105-113.

Howard, **Stanley E.** "The Societe Anonyme," **AR**, 1933, Vol. 8, No. 1, pp. 11-21.

Howard, **S. E.** "Some Cost Problems In University Accounting," **AR**, 1926, Vol. 1, No. 4, pp. 55-62.

Howard, **Thomas P.** and Loren A. Nikolai. "Attitude Measurement And Perceptions Of Accounting Faculty Publication Outlets," **AR**, 1983, Vol. 58, No. 4, pp. 765-776.

Howard, **Thomas P.** "Attitude Measurement: Some Further Considerations," **AR**, 1981, Vol. 56, No. 3, pp. 613-621.

Howard, **Thomas P.** "Teaching Ideas For The Commencement Of The Governmental Accounting Course," **JAED**, 1985, Vol. 3, No. 2, pp. 179-185.

Howard, **Thomas P.** (Baldwin, Bruce A. and Thomas P. Howard. "Intertopical Sequencing Of Examination Questions: An Empirical Evaluation," **JAED**, 1983, Vol. 1, No. 2, pp. 89-95.)

Howard, **Thomas P.** (Parker, James E. and Thomas P. Howard. "Leasing As A Means Of Shifting Tax Savings To Non-

291

Taxable Organizations," **JATA**, 1983, Vol. 4, No. 2, pp. 14-22.)

Howard, Thomas P. (Wilson, Earl R. and Thomas P. Howard. "The Association Between Municipal Market Measures And Selected Financial Reporting Practices: Additional Evidence," **JAR**, 1984, Vol. 22, No. 1, pp. 207-224.)

Howard, Thomas P. (Wilson, Earl R. and Thomas P. Howard. "Information For Municipal Bond Investment Decisions: Synthesis Of Prior Research, An Extension And Policy Implications," **RIGNA**, 1985, Vol. 1, pp. 213-263.)

Howe, Jerry T. "Managing Accounts Receivable Effectively," **MA**, 1983, Vol. 65, No. 2, pp. 35-39.

Howe, Keith R. and Bruce A. Baldwin. "The Effects Of Evaluative Sequencing On Performance, Behavior, And Attitudes," **AR**, 1983, Vol. 58, No. 1, pp. 135-142.

Howe, Keith R. (Baldwin, Bruce A. and Keith R. Howe. "Secondary-Level Study Of Accounting And Subsequent Performance In The First College Course," **AR**, 1982, Vol. 57, No. 3, pp. 619-626.)

Howe, W. Asquith. (Abs, George, Clayton Grimstad, Robert Hay, W. Asquith Howe, William LaPlace, Francis J. McGurr and William Serraino. "Historical Dates In Accounting," **AR**, 1954, Vol. 29, No. 3, pp. 486-493.)

Howell, Cloyd. "CASB: An Assessment," **MA**, 1977, Vol. 58, No. 10, pp. 23-26.

Howell, F. S. "How To Obtain Progress Payments On Government Contracts," **JOA**, 1952, Vol. 94, No. 1, pp. 53-57.

Howell, Harry. "Pricing Exports Under The Foreign Assistance Act Of 1948," **AR**, 1948, Vol. 23, No. 3, pp. 235-243.

Howell, Robert A. and Stephen R. Soucy. "The New Manufacturing Environment: Major Trends For Management Accountants," **MA**, 1987, Vol. 69, No. 1, pp. 21-27.

Howell, Robert A. and Stephen R. Soucy. "Operating Controls In The New Manufacturing Environment," **MA**, 1987, Vol. 69, No. 4, pp. 25-31.

Howell, Robert A. and Stephen R. Soucy. "Management Reporting In The New Manufacturing Environment," **MA**, 1988, Vol. 69, No. 8, pp. 22-29.

Howell, Robert A. and Stephen R. Soucy. "Cost Accounting In The New Manufacturing Environment," **MA**, 1987, Vol. 69, No. 2, pp. 42-48.

Howell, Robert A. and Stephen R. Soucy. "Capital Investment Analysis In The New Manufacturing Environment," **MA**, 1987, Vol. 69, No. 5, pp. 26-32.

Howell, William C. and L. Todd Johnson. "An Evaluation Of The Compressed-Course Format For Instruction In Accounting," **AR**, 1982, Vol. 57, No. 2, pp. 403-413.

Hoyle, Joe. "Mandatory Auditor Rotation: The Arguments And An Alternative," **JOA**, 1978, Vol. 145, No. 5, pp. 69-78.

Hoyle, Valarie A. (Beard, Larry H. and Valarie A. Hoyle. "Cost Accounting Proposal For An Advertising Agency," **MA**, 1976, Vol. 58, No. 6, pp. 38-40.)

Hoyt, Ronald E. and Lawrence D. Maples. "Accounting For Joint Ventures With The Soviet Bloc And China," **IJAER**, 1980, Vol. 16, No. 1, pp. 105-124.

Hoyt, Ronald E. and Michel Legault. "A Discriminant Analysis Of Soviet Decision-Making Behavior In Selecting United States Suppliers Of Goods And Services," **AIIA**, 1987, Vol. 1, pp. 263-285.

Hoyt, Ronald E. "Profit Measurement In East-West Trade And Industrial Cooperation: Concepts, Criteria, And Special Problems," **IJAER**, 1978, Vol. 13, No. 2, pp. 119-144.

Hreha, Karen S. and Peter A. Silhan. "An Empirical Analysis Of Unitary Apportionment," **JATA**, 1986, Vol. 8, No. 1, pp. 7-18.

Hreha, Karen S. and Peter A. Silhan. "Tax Base Differences Between Worldwide And Water's Edge Methods Of Unitary Taxation," **JATA**, 1988, Vol. 10, No. 1, pp. 89-98.

Hreha, Karen S. (Hopwood, William S. and Karen S. Hreha. "The Interprofessional Tax Altercation," **AHJ**, 1984, Vol. 11, No. 1, pp. 1-18.)

Hreha, Karen S., Robert F. Sharp and Eugene Willis. "An Analysis Of Two Proposed Cost Recovery Systems," **JATA**, 1986, Vol. 7, No. 2, pp. 76-84.

Hreha, Karen. (Schnee, Edward J. and Karen Hreha. "Capital Gains And Boot In Reorganizations," **CPAJ**, 1987, Vol. 57, No. 4, pp. 40-45.)

Hromish, Michael. "Maintenance Cost Data For Analysis And Control," **MA**, 1967, Vol. 49, No. 2, pp. 40-46.

Hsieh, David A. (Lee, Chi-wen Jevons and David A. Hsieh. "Choice Of Inventory Accounting Methods: Comparative Analyses Of Alternative Hypotheses," **JAR**, 1985, Vol. 23, No. 2, pp. 468-485.)

Hsu, Tsun Tsien. "Recent Business And Accounting Developments In China," **IJAER**, 1981, Vol. 17, No. 1, pp. 157-160.

Huang, Jiunn C. (Heck, J. Louis and Jiunn C. Huang. "Peer Assessment Versus Citation Analysis Of Contributions To The Accounting Literature," **AIA**, 1987, Vol. 5, pp. 153-162.)

Huang, Jiunn C. (Heck, J. Louis and Jiunn C. Huang. "Contributions To Accounting Literature: A Peer Assessment Of Monographs," **JAED**, 1986, Vol. 4, No. 2, pp. 27-36.)

Hubbard, Charles L. "On-Going Control Of Cash And Income," **MA**, 1975, Vol. 57, No. 2, pp. 20-24.

Hubbard, E. Dee, Kevin D. Stocks and John W. Hardy. "A Comprehensive Project For Managerial Accounting," **JAED**, 1984, Vol. 2, No. 1, pp. 111-125.

Hubbard, E. Dee. (Hardy, John W. and E. Dee Hubbard. "Internal Reporting Guidelines: Their Coverage In Cost Accounting Texts," **AR**, 1976, Vol. 51, No. 4, pp. 917-921.)

Hubbard, Paull F. "Asset Redeployment: An Old Practice Come To Life," **CA**, 1985, Vol. 3, No. 1, pp. 24-28.

Hubbard, Thomas D. and Jerry B. Bullington. "Positive And Negative Confirmation Requests - A Test," **JOA**, 1972, Vol. 133, No. 3, pp. 48-56.

Hubbard, Thomas D. and Joyce C. Lambert. "Current And Proposed Unaudited Statement Standards," **CPAJ**, 1978, Vol. 48, No. 8, pp. 35-42.

Hubbard, Thomas D. and Robert H. Strawser. "The Auditor And Statistical Sampling," **CPAJ**, 1973, Vol. 43, No. 8, pp. 670-673.

Hubbard, Thomas D. and Robert H. Strawser. "A Test Of 'A Model For Integrating Sampling Objectives In Auditing'." **JAR**, 1972, Vol. 10, No. 2, pp. 404-406.

Hubbard, Thomas D. (Dascher, Paul E. and Thomas D. Hubbard. "The CPA Review Course - A Second Dimension," **AR**, 1973, Vol. 48, No. 2, pp. 418-420.)

Hubbard, Thomas D. (Patten, Ronald J. and Thomas D. Hubbard. "CPA Review Clinics - An Opportunity For Accounting Educators," **AR**, 1972, Vol. 47, No. 2, pp. 385-387.)

Hubler, Myron J., Jr. "New Areas Of Creativity In The Accounting-Finance Function," **MA**, 1969, Vol. 50, No. 8, pp. 16-17.

Hudson, Elaine J. (Farrelly, Gail E. and Elaine J. Hudson. "How To Teach Introductory Accounting: Student Views," **JAED**, 1985, Vol. 3, No. 1, pp. 47-56.)

Hudson, J. (McRoberts, H. A. and J. Hudson. "Auditing Program Evaluations: The Canadian Case," **AOS**, 1985, Vol. 10, No. 4, pp. 493-502.)

Hudson, Robert R. "Accounting For Unearned Discount Of Finance Companies," **AR**, 1963, Vol. 38, No. 4, pp. 796-801.

Hudson, Robert R. "Small Loan Company Audits," **JOA**, 1957, Vol. 103, No. 5, pp. 42-45.

Hudson, T. W., Jr. "Gifts Through Private Charitable Organizations," **JOA**, 1959, Vol. 108, No. 1, pp. 31-38.

Huebner, Robert F., Jr. "Selecting A Retirement Program For A Small Corporation," **MA**, 1978, Vol. 59, No. 7, pp. 27-33.

Huefner, Ronald J. "Accounting System For Earnings Per Share," **MA**, 1972, Vol. 53, No. 9, pp. 29-35.

Huefner, Ronald J. "An Economic Approach To Price-Index Bias," **AR**, 1972, Vol. 47, No. 1, pp. 171-173.

Huefner, Ronald J. "Analysis Of CASB Disclosure Statements," **MA**, 1976, Vol. 57, No. 12, pp. 45-48.

Huefner, Ronald J. "Analyzing And Reporting Sensitivity Data," **AR**, 1971, Vol. 46, No. 4, pp. 717-732.

Huefner, Ronald J. "The Minimum Income Tax," **MA**, 1976, Vol. 57, No. 7, pp. 18-22.

Huefner, Ronald J. (Arnold, Donald F. and Ronald J. Huefner. "Measuring And Evaluating Replacement Costs: An Application," **JAR**, 1977, Vol. 15, No. 2, pp. 245-252.)

Huefner, Ronald J. (Brown, Lawrence D., Ronald J. Huefner and Joseph Weintrop. "Financial Data Bases In Accounting Doctoral Programs," **IAE**, 1988, Vol. 3, No. 2, pp. 228-240.)

Huefner, Ronald J. (Derstine, Robert P. and Ronald J. Huefner. "LIFO-FIFO, Accounting Ratios And Market Risk," **JAR**, 1974, Vol. 12, No. 2, pp. 216-234.)

Huefner, Ronald J. (Gupta, Manak C. and Ronald J. Huefner. "A Cluster Analysis Study Of Financial Ratios And Industry Characteristics," **JAR**, 1972, Vol. 10, No. 1, pp. 77-95.)

Huefner, Ronald J. (Jen, Frank C. and Ronald J. Huefner. "Depreciation By Probability-Life," **AR**, 1970, Vol. 45, No. 2, pp. 290-298.)

Hufford, Kenneth W. "Accounting Laboratories In Collegiate Schools Of Business," **AR**, 1939, Vol. 14, No. 2, pp. 178-179.

Hughes, Abner E. "Other Income," **JOA**, 1956, Vol. 102, No. 6. pp. 42-47.

Hughes, G. David. (Hofstedt, Thomas R. and G. David Hughes. "An Experimental Study Of The Judgmental Element In Disclosure Decisions," **AR**, 1977, Vol. 52, No. 2, pp. 379-395.)

Hughes, Hugh P. "Some Contributions Of And Some Controversies Surrounding Thomas Jones And Benjamin Franklin Foster," **AHJ**, 1982, Vol. 9, No. 2, pp. 43-51.

Hughes, Jesse W. "Revenue And Expenditure Variance Analyses For Local Government," **JAED**, 1985, Vol. 3, No. 2, pp. 103-114.

Hughes, John S. and James H. Scheiner. "Efficiency Properties Of Mutually Satisfactory Cost Allocations," **AR**. 1980, Vol. 55, No. 1, pp. 85-95.

Hughes, John S. and William E. Ricks. "Associations Between Forecast Errors And Excess Returns Near To Earnings Announcements," **AR**, 1987, Vol. 62, No. 1, pp. 158-175.

Hughes, John S. and William E. Ricks. "Accounting For Retail Land Sales: Analysis Of A Mandated Change," **JAEC**, 1984, Vol. 6, No. 2, pp. 101-132.

Hughes, John S. and William E. Ricks. "Market Reactions To Mandated Interest Capitalization," **CAR**, 1985-86, Vol. 2, No. 2, pp. 222-241.

Hughes, John S. "Optimal Internal Audit Timing," **AR**, 1977, Vol. 52, No. 1, pp. 56-68.

Hughes, John S. "Optimal Timing Of Cost Information: Author's Correction," **JAR**, 1977, Vol. 15, No. 2, pp. 313-316.

Hughes, John S. "Optimal Timing Of Cost Information," **JAR**, 1975, Vol. 13, No. 2, pp. 344-349.

Hughes, John S. "Toward A Contract Basis Of Valuation In Accounting," **AR**, 1978, Vol. 53, No. 4, pp. 882-894.

Hughes, John S. (Brown, Lawrence D., John S. Hughes, Michael S. Rozeff and James H. VanderWeide. "Expectations Data And The Predictive Value Of Interim

Reporting: A Comment," **JAR**, 1980, Vol. 18, No. 1, pp. 278-288.)

Hughes, **John S.** (Conroy, Robert M. and John S. Hughes. "Delegating Information Gathering Decisions," **AR**, 1987, Vol. 62, No. 1, pp. 50-66.)

Hughes, **John S.** (Hoskin, Robert E., John S. Hughes and William E. Ricks. "Evidence On The Incremental Information Content Of Additional Firm Disclosures Made Concurrently With Earnings," **JAR**, 1986, Vol. 24, Supp., pp. 1-32.)

Hughes, **John S.** (Ricks, William E. and John S. Hughes. "Market Reactions To Non-Discretionary Accounting Change, The Case Of Long-Term Investments," **AR**, 1985, Vol. 60, No. 1, pp. 33-52.)

Hughes, **J.** (Burchell, S., C. Clubb, A. Hopwood, J. Hughes and J. Nahapiet. "The Roles Of Accounting In Organizations And Society," **AOS**, 1980, Vol. 5, No. 1, pp. 5-28.)

Hughes, **Lyle F.** and Charles A. Olson. "Computer-Assisted Financial Planning," **MA**, 1969, Vol. 50, No. 8, pp. 24-27.

Hughes, **Patricia J.** and Eduardo S. Schwartz. "The LIFO/FIFO Choice: An Asymmetric Information Approach," **JAR**, 1988, Vol. 26, Supp., pp. 41-58.

Hughes, **Patricia J.** "Signalling By Direct Disclosure Under Asymmetric Information," **JAEC**, 1986, Vol. 8, No. 2, pp. 119-142.

Hughes, **Raymond E.** "Controlling Healthcare Costs Through Integrated' PPOs," **CA**, 1986, Vol. 4, No. 2, pp. 22-25.

Hughey, **David A.** "Integrated Processing Gets Marketing Edge," **MA**, 1970, Vol. 52, No. 6, pp. 37-38.

Huizingh, **William** and John C. Arme. "The Effect Of Rate Changes On Income Tax Allocation," **MA**, 1965, Vol. 47, No. 4, pp. 17-20.

Hulen, **Myron** and William Kenny. "Taxation Of A Visiting Professorship After Tax Reform," **IAE**, 1988, Vol. 3, No. 2, pp. 255-269.

Hull, **G. L.** "Plant Appraisals - Their Treatment In The Accounts," **AR**, 1927, Vol. 2, No. 4, pp. 303-326.

Hull, **James C.** "A Guide To Better Workpapers," **JOA**, 1969, Vol. 127, No. 2, pp. 44-52.

Hull, **J. C.** "The Impact Of Stock Relief On The Attractiveness Of Capital Investment Opportunities," **ABR**, 1981-82, Vol. 12, No. 45, pp. 30-34.

Hull, **Rita P.** and Cheryl Mitchem. "Practitioners' Views On Communications Between Predecessor And Successor Auditors And Accountants," **ACCHOR**, 1987, Vol. 1, No. 1, pp. 61-70.

Hull, **Rita P.**, John O. Everett and Steven D. Hall. "Accounting Education: Practitioner's Views On The Value Of A Five-Year Program," **AIA**, 1987, Vol. 5, pp. 163-178.

Humann, **Thomas E.** (Arnold, Donald F. and Thomas E. Humann. "Earnings Per Share: An Empirical Test Of The Market Parity And The Investment Value Methods," **AR**, 1973, Vol. 48, No. 1, pp. 23-33.)

Hume, **L. J.** "The Development Of Industrial Accounting: The Benthams' Contribution," **JAR**, 1970, Vol. 8, No. 1, pp. 21-33.

Humer, **Kenneth G.** "Full-Absorption Cost: A Managerial Dilemma?," **MA**, 1974, Vol. 56, No. 6, pp. 53-57.

Humphrey, **Mitchell O.** "Management Letters - Image Builders For The CPA," **JOA**, 1967, Vol. 123, No. 1, pp. 27-32.

Humphries, **Francis A.**, Linda M. Plunkett and Rebecca B. Herring. "Let's Make Required CPE Rules Uniform," **JOA**, 1988, Vol. 166, No. 6, pp. 70-74.

Humphries, **Kenneth K.** "The Cost Engineering Profession," **JCA**, 1984, Vol. 1, No. 1, pp. 143-147.

Hund, **Michael L.** (Jones, Keith L. and Michael L. Hund. "Filing SEC Registration Statements: A View From The Inside," **JOA**, 1984, Vol. 158, No. 6, pp. 92-107.)

Hungate, **T. L.** "Unit Costs In Institutions Of Higher Education," **AR**, 1934, Vol. 9, No. 1, pp. 38-43.

Hunt, **Herbert G., III** and Charles R. Enis. "Economic Analysis Of Broad-Based Income And Consumption Taxes," **AIT**, 1988, Vol. 2, pp. xx-xx.

Hunt, **Herbert G., III.** "Federal Tax Reform: Analysis Of Two Consumption Taxes," **AIT**, 1987, Vol. 1, pp. 109-130.

Hunt, **Herbert G., III.** "Potential Determinants Of Corporate Inventory Accounting Decisions," **JAR**, 1985, Vol. 23, No. 2, pp. 448-467.

Hunt, **Herbert G., III.** "The Separation Of Corporate Ownership And Control: Theory, Evidence And Implications," **JAL**, 1986, Vol. 5, pp. 85-124.

Hunt, **Herbert G., III.** (Geiger, Marshall A. and Herbert G. Hunt, III. "Capital Gain Taxation: A Critical Analysis Of Historical And Current Issues," **AIT**, 1988, Vol. 2, pp. xx-xx.)

Hunt, **Joseph A.** (Anderson, Thomas E. and Joseph A. Hunt. "Operational Control Through Sampling - An Illustrative Case," **MA**, 1965, Vol. 47, No. 3, pp. 13-17.)

Hunt, **Mary-Ellen.** (Gertzman, Stephen F. and Mary-Ellen Hunt. "A Basic Guide To Tax Accounting Opportunities," **JOA**, 1984, Vol. 157, No. 2, pp. 60-75.)

Hunt, **Rick**, Linda Garrett and C. Mike Merz. "Direct Labor Cost Not Always Relevant At H-P," **MA**, 1985, Vol. 66, No. 8, pp. 58-62.

Hunt, **Stanley M.** "Conducting A Social Inventory," **MA**, 1974, Vol. 56, No. 4, pp. 15-16.

Hunter, **Joel.** "Accounting In Management," **JOA**, 1955, Vol. 100, No. 5, pp. 62-65.

Hunter, **Joel.** "The Auditing Function In The Federal Government," **AR**, 1942, Vol. 17, No. 3, pp. 221-232.

Hunter, **John E.** (Cooper, W. W., Joanna L. Y. Ho, John E. Hunter and Robert C. Rodgers. "The Impact Of The Foreign Corrupt Practices Act On Internal Control Practices," **JAAF**, 1985, Vol. 9, No. 1, pp. 22-39.)

Hunter, **Robert L.**, Gary M. Cunningham and Thomas G. Evans. "Are Multinational Liquidity Models Worth Their Cost?," **MA**, 1979, Vol. 61, No. 6, pp. 51-56.

Hunziker, **A. E.** "Commentary To Discussion On International Accounting Challenges," **IJAER**, 1968, Vol. 4, No. 1, pp. 99-100.

Hurley, **Richard E.** "Interest Penalty And Estimated Taxes Revisited," **CPAJ**, 1982, Vol. 52, No. 11, pp. 24-29.

Hurni, **M. L.** "Some Implications Of The Use Of Computers In Industry," **AR**, 1954, Vol. 29, No. 3, pp. 447-455.

Hurst, **Kenneth.** "Other Deductions," **JOA**, 1956, Vol. 102, No. 6, pp. 48-52.

Husband, **George R.** "A Critique Of The Revised Statement Of Accounting Principles," **AR**, 1942, Vol. 17, No. 3, pp. 283-293.

Husband, **George R.** "A Reply To Mr. Cotter," **AR**, 1940, Vol. 15, No. 4, pp. 510-513.

Husband, **George R.** "A Training Program For The Certified Public Accountant's Staff," **AR**, 1947, Vol. 22, No. 2, pp. 124-130.

Husband, **George R.** "Accounting Postulates: An Analysis Of The Tentative Statement Of Accounting Principles," **AR**, 1937, Vol. 12, No. 4, pp. 386-400.

Husband, **George R.** "Another Look At Cost Or Market Which-ever Is Lower," **AR**, 1946, Vol. 21, No. 2, pp. 115-120.

Husband, **George R.** "Effective Teaching," **AR**, 1947, Vol. 22, No. 4, pp. 411-414.

Husband, **George R.** "Professor Dein, Mr. Alexander, And Supplementary Statement Number 2," **AR**, 1955, Vol. 30, No. 3, pp. 383-399.

Husband, **George R.** "Rationalization In The Accounting Measurement Of Income," **AR**, 1954, Vol. 29, No. 1, pp. 3-14.

Husband, **George R.** "That Thing Which The Accountant Calls Income," **AR**, 1946, Vol. 21, No. 3, pp. 247-253.

Husband, **George R.** "The Bad-Debt Estimate: A Deduction From Gross Sales," **AR**, 1942, Vol. 17, No. 2, pp. 178-190.

Husband, **George R.** "The Corporate-Entity Fiction And Accounting Theory," **AR**, 1938, Vol. 13, No. 3, pp. 241-252.

Husband, **George R.** "The Entity Concept In Accounting," **AR**, 1954, Vol. 29, No. 4, pp. 552-563.

Husband, **George R.** "The First-In, Last-Out Method Of Inventory Valuation," **AR**, 1940, Vol. 15, No. 2, pp. 190-195.

Husband, **W. H.** "The Accrual Principle Applied To Bank Accounting," **AR**, 1926, Vol. 1, No. 2, pp. 85-89.

Huskey, **H. D.** and V. R. Huskey. "Electronic Computers Aiding Management Control," **JOA**, 1952, Vol. 93, No. 1, pp. 69-75.

Huskey, **V. R.** (Huskey, H. D. and V. R. Huskey. "Electronic Computers Aiding Management Control," **JOA**, 1952, Vol. 93, No. 1, pp. 69-75.)

Huss, **H. Fenwick** and Ramona L. Trader. "A Note On Optimal Sample Sizes In Compliance Tests Using A Formal Bayesian Decision Theoretic Approach For Finite And Infinite Populations," **JAR**, 1986, Vol. 24, No. 2, pp. 394-399.

Huss, **H. Fenwick.** "A Contingency Approach To Accounting For Income Taxes," **JAAF**, 1985, Vol. 9, No. 1, pp. 60-66.

Huss, **H. Fenwick.** (Trader, Ramona L. and H. Fenwick Huss. "An Investigation Of The Possible Effects Of Nonsampling Error On Inference In Auditing: A Bayesian Analysis," **CAR**, 1987-88, Vol. 4, No. 1, pp. 227-239.)

Huss, **Jerry S.** "Better Budgeting For CPA Firms," **JOA**, 1977, Vol. 144, No. 5, pp. 64-73.

Hussein, **Mohamed Elmutassim.** "Consulting As An Instruction Tool In Accounting," **AIA**, 1985, Vol. 2, pp. 101-112.

Hussein, **Mohamed Elmutassim.** "Translation Problems Of International Accounting Standards," **IJAER**, 1981, Vol. 17, No. 1, pp. 147-155.

Hussein, **Mohamed Elmuttasim** and J. Edward Ketz. "Ruling Elites Of The FASB: A Study Of The Big Eight," **JAAF**, 1980, Vol. 3, No. 4, pp. 354-367.

Hussein, **Mohamed E. A.**, Vinod B. Bavishi, and Jagdish S. Gangolly. "International Similarities And Differences In The Auditor's Report," **AJPT**, 1986-87, Vol. 6, No. 1, pp. 124-133.

Hussein, **Mohamed E.** (Hobbs, H. Kendall and Mohamed E. Hussein. "Internal Control Methods For Small Business," **CPAJ**, 1985, Vol. 55, No. 5, pp. 26-35.)

Hussein, **M. Elmutassim.** "The Innovative Process In Financial Accounting Standards Setting," **AOS**, 1981, Vol. 6, No. 1, pp. 27-38.

Hutchinson, **Patrick J.** (Reeve, Robert C. and Patrick J. Hutchinson. "The Contribution Of Non-U.S. Institutions To Academic Accounting Journals," **ABACUS**, 1988, Vol. 24, No. 1, pp. 90-94.)

Hutchinson, **P. J.**, J. A. Piper and G. A. Ray. "The Financing Of Rapid Growth Firms Up To Flotation," **ABR**, 1974-75, Vol. 5, No. 18, pp. 145-151.

Hutchinson, **P. J.**, J. A. Piper and G. H. Ray. "The Financial Control Of Rapid-Growth Firms Up To Flotation," **ABR**, 1974-75, Vol. 5, No. 19, pp. 222-228.

Hutchison, **William P.** "Professional Development," **JOA**, 1957, Vol. 104, No. 5, pp. 31-36.

Hutton, **Clifford E.**, Barbara Stoops and Michael J. Tucker. "Losses Caused By Drought," **CPAJ**, 1984, Vol. 54, No. 3, pp. 40-49.

Hutton, **Edwin W.** "A CPA's Evaluation Of The Business Computer Utility," **JOA**, 1971, Vol. 131, No. 3, pp.51-56.

Hutton, **Marguerite R.** and Woody M. Liao. "A CPA's Responsibility: Ethics And Tax Penalties," **CPAJ**, 1985, Vol. 55, No. 10, pp. 26-35.

Hutto, **Gary W.** "How To Divest Undervalued Land Without Losing Profits," **JOA**, 1988, Vol. 165, No. 4, pp. 70-78.

Hylas

Hylas, Robert E. and Robert H. Ashton. "Audit Detection Of Financial Statement Errors," **AR**, 1982, Vol. 57, No. 4, pp. 751-765.

Hylas, Robert E. (Ashton, Robert H. and Robert E. Hylas. "The Return Of 'Problem' Confirmation Requests By The U.S. Postal Service," **AR**, 1980, Vol. 55, No. 4, pp. 649-657.)

Hylas, Robert E. (Ashton, Robert H. and Robert E. Hylas. "A Study Of The Response To Balance And Invoice Confimation Requests," **JAAF**, 1981, Vol. 4, No. 4, pp. 325-332.)

Hylas, Robert E. (Ashton, Robert H. and Robert E. Hylas. "Increasing Confirmation Response Rates," **AJPT**, 1981-82, Vol. 1, No. 1, pp. 12-22.)

Hylton, Delmer P. "Accounting Principles: Their General Acceptance And Application," **AR**, 1954, Vol. 29, No. 1, pp. 127-129.

Hylton, Delmer P. "Are Consulting And Auditing Compatible? - A Contrary View," **AR**, 1964, Vol. 39, No. 3, pp. 667-670.

Hylton, Delmer P. "Are We Communicating?," **CPAJ**, 1976, Vol. 46, No. 12, pp. 11-16.

Hylton, Delmer P. "Current Trends In Accounting Theory," **AR**, 1962, Vol. 37, No. 1, pp. 22-27.

Hylton, Delmer P. "Needed: More Informative And Understandable Financial Statements From Governmental Units," **AR**, 1957, Vol. 32, No. 1, pp. 51-54.

Hylton, Delmer P. "On Matching Revenue With Expense," **AR**, 1965, Vol. 40, No. 4, pp. 824-828.

Hylton, Delmer P. "Should Financial Statements Show 'Monetary' Or 'Economic' Income?," **AR**, 1951, Vol. 26, No. 4, pp. 503-506.

Hylton, Delmer P. "Some Comments On Materiality," **JOA**, 1961, Vol. 112, No. 3, pp. 61-64.

Hyman, Ladelle M. (Gamble, George O., Brian O'Doherty and Ladelle M. Hyman. "The Development Of Agency Thought: A Citation Analysis Of The Literature," **AHJ**, 1987, Vol. 14, No. 1, pp. 7-26.)

Hynes, Lynn C. and Halsey G. Bullen. "Financial Instruments: What Should Be Disclosed?," **MA**, 1988, Vol. 69, No. 8, pp. 55-58.

III

Ibarrche, Santiago. (Seglund, Ragnor and Santiago Ibarreche. "Just-In-Time: The Accounting Implications," **MA**, 1984, Vol. 66, No. 2, pp. 43-45.)

Icerman, Joe D. (Lorek, Kenneth S., Joe D. Icerman and Abdullah A. Abdulkader. "Further Descriptive And Predictive Evidence On Alternative Time-Series Models For Quarterly Earnings," **JAR**, 1983, Vol. 21, No. 1, pp. 317-328.)

Icerman, Rhoda C. (Arrington, C. Edward, William Hillison and Rhoda C. Icerman. "Research In Analytical Review: The State Of The Art," **JAL**, 1983, Vol. 2, pp. 151-186.)

Ichikawa, Hideo. (Ohno, Kimiyoshi, Hideo Ichikawa and Atsuyoshi Kodama. "Recent Changes In Accounting Standards In Japan," **IJAER**, 1975, Vol. 11, No. 1, pp. 107-120.)

Ifflander, A. James. (Hefzi, Hassan, A. James Ifflander and David B. Smith. "Municipal Bond Market Risk Measures And Bond Ratings," **AIA**, 1988, Vol. 6, pp. 111-128.)

Iino, Toshio. "Accounting Principles And Contemporary Legal Thought In Japan," **IJAER**, 1967, Vol. 2, No. 2, pp. 65-87.

Iino, Toshio. (Bedford, Norton M. and Toshio Iino. "Consistency Reexamined," **AR**, 1968, Vol. 43, No. 3, pp. 453-458.)

Ijiri, Yuji and Gerald L. Thompson. "Applications Of Mathematical Control Theory To Accounting And Budgeting (The Continuous Wheat Trading Model)," **AR**, 1970, Vol. 45, No. 2, pp. 246-258.

Ijiri, Yuji and Hiroyuki Itami. "Quadratic Cost-Volume Relationship And Timing Of Demand Information: A Reply," **AR**, 1975, Vol. 50, No. 1, pp. 138-139.

Ijiri, Yuji and Hiroyuki Itami. "Quadratic Cost-Volume Relationship And Timing Of Demand Information," **AR**, 1973, Vol. 48, No. 4, pp. 724-737.

Ijiri, Yuji and James Noel. "A Reliability Comparison Of The Measurement Of Wealth, Income, And Force," **AR**, 1984, Vol. 59, No. 1, pp. 52-63.

Ijiri, Yuji and Robert A. Leitch. "Stein's Paradox And Audit Sampling," **JAR**, 1980, Vol. 18, No. 1, pp. 91-108.

Ijiri, Yuji and Robert K. Jaedicke. "Reliability And Objectivity Of Accounting Measurements," **AR**, 1966, Vol. 41, No. 3, pp. 474-483.

Ijiri, Yuji and Robert S. Kaplan. "Probabilistic Depreciation And Its Implication For Group Depreciation," **AR**, 1969, Vol. 44, No. 4, pp. 743-756.

Ijiri, Yuji and Robert S. Kaplan. "The Four Objectives Of Sampling In Auditing: Representative, Corrective, Protective And Preventive," **MA**, 1970, Vol. 52, No. 6, pp. 42-44.

Ijiri, Yuji and Robert S. Kaplan. "Sequential Models In Probabilistic Depreciation," **JAR**, 1970, Vol. 8, No. 1, pp. 34-46.

Ijiri, Yuji and Robert S. Kaplan. "Sampling For Integrated Audit Objectives - A Replay," **AR**, 1978, Vol. 53, No. 3, pp. 773-774.

Ijiri, Yuji and Robert S. Kaplan. "The Auditor's Sampling Objectives: Four Or Two? A Reply," **JAR**, 1972, Vol. 10, No. 2, pp. 413-416.

Ijiri, Yuji and Robert S. Kaplan. "A Model For Integrating Sampling Objectives In Auditing," **JAR**, 1971, Vol. 9, No. 1, pp. 73-87.

Ijiri, Yuji, Robert K. Jaedicke and John L. Livingstone. "The Effect Of Inventory Costing Methods On Full And Direct Costing," **JAR**, 1965, Vol. 3, No. 1, pp. 63-74.

Ijiri, Yuji. "A Framework For Triple-Entry Bookkeeping," **AR**, 1986, Vol. 61, No. 4, pp. 745-759.

Ijiri, Yuji. "Accounting Matrices And Three-Dimensional Arrays," **IAE**, 1988, Vol. 3, No. 2, pp. 270-285.

Ijiri, Yuji. "An Application Of Input-Output Analysis To Some Problems In Cost Accounting," **MA**, 1968, Vol. 49, No. 8, pp. 49-61.

Ijiri, Yuji. "Axioms And Structures Of Conventional Accounting Measurement," **AR**, 1965, Vol. 40, No. 1, pp. 36-53.

Ijiri, Yuji. "Axioms For Historical Cost Valuation: A Reply," **JAR**, 1971, Vol. 9, No. 1, pp. 181-187.

Ijiri, Yuji. "Cash-Flow Accounting And Its Structure," **JAAF**, 1978, Vol. 1, No. 4, pp. 331-348.

Ijiri, Yuji. "Critique Of The APB Fundamentals Statement," **JOA**, 1971, Vol. 132, No. 5, pp. 43-50.

Ijiri, Yuji. "Measurement In Current Accounting Practices: A Reply," **AR**, 1972, Vol. 47, No. 3, pp. 510-526.

Ijiri, Yuji. "New Dimensions In Accounting Education: Computers And Algorithms," **IAE**, 1983, No. 1, pp. 168-173.

Ijiri, Yuji. "On Budgeting Principles And Budget-Auditing Standards," **AR**, 1968, Vol. 43, No. 4, pp. 662-67.

Ijiri, Yuji. "On The Accountability-Based Conceptual Framework Of Accounting," **JAPP**, 1983, Vol. 2, No. 2, pp. 75-81.

Ijiri, Yuji. "The Price-Level Restatement And Its Dual Interpretation," **AR**, 1976, Vol. 51, No. 2, pp. 227-243.

Ijiri, Yuji. "Three Postulates Of Momentum Accounting," **ACCHOR**, 1987, Vol. 1, No. 1, pp. 25-34.

Ijiri, Yuji. (Cyert, Richard M. and Yuji Ijiri. "Problems Of Implementing The Trueblood Objectives Report," **JAR**, 1974, Vol. 12, Supp., pp. 29-42.)

Ijiri, Yuji. (Gonedes, Nicholas J. and Yuji Ijiri. "Improving Subjective Probability Assessment For Planning And Control In Team-Like Organizations," **JAR**, 1974, Vol. 12, No. 2, pp. 251-269.)

Ijiri, Y. and E. C. Kelly. "Multidimensional Accounting And Distributed Databases: Their Implications For Organizations And Society," **AOS**, 1980, Vol. 5, No. 1, pp. 115-124.

Ijiri, Y. (Charnes, A., W. W. Cooper and Y. Ijiri. "Breakeven Budgeting And Programming To Goals," **JAR**, 1963, Vol. 1, No. 1, pp. 16-41.)

Ijiri, Y., F. K. Levy and R. C. Lyon. "A Linear Programming Model For Budgeting And Financial Planning," **JAR**, 1963, Vol. 1, No. 2, pp. 198-212.

Ijiri, Y., J. C. Kinard and F. B. Putney. "An Integrated Evaluation System For Budget Forecasting And Operating Performance With A Classified Budgeting Bibliography," **JAR**, 1968, Vol. 6, No. 1, pp. 1-28.

Ilett, Frank, Jr. "Cost Of Capital In Hospital Financing," **MA**, 1976, Vol. 57, No. 8, pp. 46-48.

Imbro, Andrew. "New Products And Their Related Costs," **MA**, 1971, Vol. 53, No. 2, pp. 43-44.

Imdieke, LeRoy R. (Haried, Andrew A. and LeRoy R. Imdieke. "Reporting On Brother-Sister Affiliations," **CPAJ**, 1978, Vol. 48, No. 12, pp. 13-20.)

Imdieke, Leroy F. and Jerry J. Weygandt. "Classification Of Convertible Debt," **AR**, 1969, Vol. 44, No. 4, pp. 798-805.

Imdieke, Leroy F. and Jerry J. Weygandt. "Accounting For That Imputed Discount Factor," **JOA**, 1970, Vol. 129, No. 6, pp. 54-58.

Imdieke, Leroy F. (Smith, Ralph E. and Leroy F. Imdieke. "Accounting For Stock Issued To Employees," **JOA**, 1974, Vol. 138, No. 5, pp. 68-75.)

Imdieke, Leroy F. (Smith, Ralph E. and Leroy F. Imdieke. "Accounting For Interest Cost," **CPAJ**, 1980, Vol. 50, No. 4, pp. 30-40.)

Imdieke, L. F. (Schroeder, R. G. and L. F. Imdieke. "Local - Cosmopolitan And Bureaucratic Perceptions In Public Accounting Firms," **AOS**, 1977, Vol. 2, No. 1, pp. 39-46.)

Imhoff, Eugene A. and Jacob K. Thomas. "Economic Consequences Of Accounting Standards: The Lease Disclosure Rule Change," **JAEC**, 1988, Vol. 10, No. 4, pp. 277-310.

Imhoff, Eugene A. (Danos, Paul and Eugene A. Imhoff. "Auditor Review Of Financial Forecasts: An Analysis Of Factors Affecting Reasonableness Judgments," **AR**, 1982, Vol. 57, No. 1, pp. 39-54.)

Imhoff, Eugene A., Jr. and Gerald J. Lobo. "Information Content Of Analysts' Composite Forecast Revisions," **JAR**, 1984, Vol. 22, No. 2, pp. 541-554.

Imhoff, Eugene A., Jr. and Paul V. Pare. "Analysis And Comparison Of Earnings Forecast Agents," **JAR**, 1982, Vol. 20, No. 2, Part I, pp. 429-439.

Imhoff, Eugene A., Jr. and Paul A. Janell. "Opinion No. 29: A New Valuation Method," **MA**, 1979, Vol. 60, No. 9, pp. 50-53.

Imhoff, Eugene A., Jr. "A Closer Look At Management Forecasts," **MA**, 1980, Vol. 61, No. 11, pp. 18-23.

Imhoff, Eugene A., Jr. "A Comparison Of Analysts' Accounting Quality Judgments Among CPA Firms' Clients," **AJPT**, 1988, Vol. 7, No. 2, pp. 182-191.

Imhoff, Eugene A., Jr. "Analytical Review Of Income Elements," **JAAF**, 1981, Vol. 4, No. 4, pp. 333-351.

Imhoff, Eugene A., Jr. "Employment Effects On Auditor Independence," **AR**, 1978, Vol. 53, No. 4, pp. 869-881.

Imhoff, Eugene A., Jr. "Evaluating Accounting Alternatives," **MA**, 1981, Vol. 63, No. 4, pp. 56-64.

Imhoff, Eugene A., Jr. "Income Smoothing: The Role Of Management: A Comment," **AR**, 1975, Vol. 50, No. 1, pp.

Of Governmental Financial Reporting: A Summary And Analysis," **RIGNA**, 1987, Vol. 3, Part B, pp. 227-235.

Ives, Martin. "Accountability And Governmental Financial Reporting," **JOA**, 1987, Vol. 164, No. 4, pp. 130-134.

Ives, Martin. "Audit Techniques In Defense Contracting," **JOA**, 1963, Vol. 116, No. 3, pp. 58-63.

Ives, Martin. "The GASB: A Fresh Look At Governmental Accounting And Financial Reporting," **JAAF**, 1985, Vol. 8, No. 4, pp. 253-268.

Ivy, Madie and Robert Willens. "Final Sec. 385 Regs.: Debt V. Equity," **CPAJ**, 1981, Vol. 51, No. 7, pp. 16-22.

Ivy, Madie and Robert Willens. "Proposed Section 385 Regs. Bring Order From Chaos," **CPAJ**, 1980, Vol. 50, No. 10, pp. 13-20.

Izan, H. Y. (Bazley, M., P. Brown and H. Y. Izan. "An Analysis Of Lease Disclosures By Australian Companies," **ABACUS**, 1985, Vol. 21, No. 1, pp. 44-62.)

Izard, C. Douglass and James M. Reeve. "Electronic Spreadsheet Technology In The Teaching Of Accounting And Taxation," **JAED**, 1986, Vol. 4, No. 1, pp. 161-175.

Izard, C. Douglass and John D. McKinney. "The Certification Of Tax Specialists: Some Empirical Results," **JATA**, 1983, Vol. 5, No. 1, pp. 40-48.

JJJ

Jablonsky, Stephen F. and Mark W. Dirsmith. "Is Financial Reporting Influencing Internal Decision Making?," **MA**, 1979, Vol. 61, No. 1, pp. 40-45.

Jablonsky, Stephen F. (Covaleski, Mark A., Mark W. Dirsmith and Stephen F. Jablonsky. "Traditional And Emergent Theories Of Budgeting: An Empirical Analysis," **JAPP**, 1985, Vol. 4, No. 4, pp. 277-300.)

Jablonsky, S. F. and M. W. Dirsmith. "The Pattern Of PPB Rejection: Something About Organizations, Something About PPB," **AOS**, 1978, Vol. 3, No. 3/4, pp. 215-226.

Jablonsky, S. F. (Dirsmith, M. W. and S. F. Jablonsky. "MBO, Political Rationality And Information Inductance," **AOS**, 1979, Vol. 4, No. 1/2, pp. 39-52.)

Jack, Sybil M. "An Historical Defence Of Single Entry Book-Keeping," **ABACUS**, 1966, Vol. 2, No. 2, pp. 137-158.

Jack, Sybil M. "On F. P. Barnard, The Casting Counter And The Counting Board," **ABACUS**, 1967, Vol. 3, No. 1, pp. 80-82.

Jack, William R. (Shopoff, Robert W. and William R. Jack. "Organizing, Staffing And Operating The Information Services Function," **MA**, 1967, Vol. 49, No. 2, pp. 3-8.)

Jackson, Betty R. and Pauline R. Jaouen. "Influencing Taxpayer Compliance Through Sanction Threat Or Appeals To Conscience," **AIT**, 1988, Vol. 2, pp. xx-xx.

Jackson, Betty R. and Sally M. Jones. "Salience Of Tax Evasion Penalties Versus Detection Risk," **JATA**, 1985, Vol. 6, No. 2, pp. 7-17.

Jackson, Betty R. and Valerie C. Milliron. "Tax Compliance Research, Findings, Problems And Prospects," **JAL**, 1986, Vol. 5, pp. 125-166.

Jackson, Betty R. "Stemming Income Tax Evasion," **JOA**, 1985, Vol. 159, No. 1, pp. 76-80.

Jackson, Charles B. "Trust Fund Accounting For Multi-Employer Trust Funds," **MA**, 1978, Vol. 60, No. 4, pp. 49-54.

Jackson, David H. "New Product Management," **MA**, 1974, Vol. 56, No. 1, pp. 54-56.

Jackson, Jerry R. "Do Tax Shelters Really Reduce Taxes?," **MA**, 1976, Vol. 57, No. 11, pp. 43-45.

Jackson, J. Hugh. "Teaching Auditing By The Case Method," **AR**, 1928, Vol. 3, No. 3, pp. 297-310.

Jackson, J. H. "Audit Certificates And Reports," **AR**, 1926, Vol. 1, No. 3, pp. 45-63.

Jackson, J. H. "Present Tendencies In Commercial Education," **AR**, 1926, Vol. 1, No. 2, pp. 1-11.

Jackson-Cox, J., J. E. M. Thirkell and J. McQueeney. "The Disclosure Of Company Information To Trade Unions: The Relevance Of The ACAS Code Of Practice On Disclosure," **AOS**, 1984, Vol. 9, No. 3/4, pp. 253-274.

Jacobi, Bardo G. (Mowry, Glenn P. and Bardo G. Jacobi. "Planning Communications In A Computer Network," **MA**, 1970, Vol. 51, No. 12, pp. 38-40.)

Jacobi, Michael H. "The Unit Of Account In Consolidated Financial Statements Of Multinational Enterprises," **IJAER**, 1980, Vol. 15, No. 2, pp. 17-34.

Jacobs, Fred A. and Hartwell C. Herring, III. "Salary Compression In The Academic Marketplace: Some Empirical Evidence," **IAE**, 1987, Vol. 2, No. 2, pp. 237-250.

Jacobs, Fred A. and Hartwell C. Herring, III. "The Impact Of Proposed CASB Standards," **MA**, 1976, Vol. 58, No. 3, pp. 13-14.

Jacobs, Fred A. (Alsup, Rodney G., Michael L. Holland and Fred A. Jacobs. "The Perceived Availability Of Resources Which Contribute To Accounting Faculty Productivity," **JAED**, 1988, Vol. 6, No. 2, pp. 261-277.)

Jacobs, Fred A. (Beard, Larry H., Fred A. Jacobs and Al L. Hartgraves. "Publications: A Valid Measure Of Faculty Contribution?," **JAED**, 1985, Vol. 3, No. 2, pp. 155-161.)

Jacobs, Fred A. (Herring, Hartwell C., III and Fred A. Jacobs. "The Expected Behavior Of Deferred Tax Credits," **JOA**, 1976, Vol. 142, No. 2, pp. 52-57.)

Jacobs, Fred A. (Tyson, Thomas N. and Fred A. Jacobs. "Segment Reporting In The Banking Industry: Does It Meet The Criteria Of The Conceptual Framework?," **ACCHOR**, 1987, Vol. 1, No. 4, pp. 35-42.)

Jacobs, Fred A., Al L. Hartgraves and Larry H. Beard. "Publication Productivity Of Doctoral Alumni: A Time-Adjusted Model," **AR**, 1986, Vol. 61, No. 1, pp. 179-187.

Jacobs, Frederic H. and Ronald Marshall. "A Reciprocal Service Cost Approximation," **AR**, 1987, Vol. 62, No. 1,

pp. 67-78.

Jacobs, Fredric and Kenneth S. Lorek. "A Note On The Time-Series Properties Of Control Data In An Accounting Environment," **JAR**, 1979, Vol. 17, No. 2, pp. 618-621.

Jacobs, Fredric and Ronald Marshall. "A Note On The Choice Structure Of Cost Variance Investigation Models," **JAL**, 1984, Vol. 3, pp. 71-84.

Jacobs, Fredric H. "An Evaluation Of The Effectiveness Of Some Cost Variance Investigation Models," **JAR**, 1978, Vol. 16, No. 1, pp. 190-203.

Jacobs, Perry F. and Seymour Spanier. "How To Make Wage Increases Under Regulation 6," **JOA**, 1951, Vol. 91, No. 6, pp. 827-832.

Jacobs, Robert and Arthur E. Traxler. "What Manner Of Man Is The Average Accountant?," **JOA**, 1954, Vol. 97, No. 4, pp. 465-469.

Jacobs, Robert. "Measurement And Guidance In The Field Of Public Accounting," **AR**, 1950, Vol. 25, No. 1, pp. 27-34.

Jacobsen, Lyle E. "Allocation And Attitudes," **AR**, 1962, Vol. 37, No. 3, pp. 472-474.

Jacobsen, Lyle E. "Management Accounting: Content And Approach," **AR**, 1960, Vol. 35, No. 1, pp. 64-69.

Jacobsen, Lyle E. "The Ancient Inca Empire Of Peru And The Double Entry Accounting Concept," **JAR**, 1964, Vol. 2, No. 2, pp. 221-228.

Jacobsen, Lyle E. "The Rise Of The Profit Deferral Notion - The Concept And Practice Of Optimeasurement," **AR**, 1963, Vol. 38, No. 2, pp. 285-292.

Jacobsen, Lyle E. "Use Of Knotted String Accounting Records In Old Hawaii And Ancient China," **AHJ**, 1983, Vol. 10, No. 2, pp. 53-61.

Jacobson, Daniel. "How To Expand Your Accounting Practice," **JOA**, 1966, Vol. 122, No. 5, pp. 47-50.

Jacobson, Peter D. and Robert K. Elliott. "GAAS: Reconsidering The 'Ten Commandments'," **JOA**, 1984, Vol. 157, No. 5, pp. 77-89.

Jacobson, Peter D. (Brumfield, Craig A., Robert K. Elliott and Peter D. Jacobson. "Business Risk And The Audit Process," **JOA**, 183, Vol. 155, No. 4, pp. 60-69.)

Jacobson, Peter D. (Elliott, Robert K. and Peter D. Jacobson. "Audit Technology: A Heritage And A Promise," **JOA**, 1987, Vol. 163, No. 5, pp. 198-218.)

Jacobson, Peter D. (Elliott, Robert K. and Peter D. Jacobson. "Two Views On The Auditor's Report: The Last Word Or In Need Of Change?," **JOA**, 1987, Vol. 163, No. 2, pp. 72-79.)

Jacobson, Peter D. (Elliott, Robert K. and Peter D. Jacobson. "The Treadway Report - Its Potential Impact," **CPAJ**, 1987, Vol. 57, No. 11, pp. 20-35.)

Jacobson, Peter D. (Elliott, Robert K. and Peter D. Jacobson. "Assessing The ASB's Ten Exposure Drafts," **CPAJ**, 1987, Vol. 57, No. 12, pp. 16-25.)

Jacobson, Peter D. (Elliott, Robert K. and Peter D. Jacobson. "Detecting And Deterring Financial Statement Fraud," **CA**, 1986, Vol. 4, No. 4, pp. 34-39.)

Jaedicke, Robert K. and Alexander A. Robichek. "Cost-Volume-Profit Analysis Under Conditions Of Uncertainty," **AR**, 1964, Vol. 39, No. 4, pp. 917-926.

Jaedicke, Robert K. and Carl L. Nelson. "The Allocation Of Income Taxes - A Defense," **AR**, 1960, Vol. 35, No. 2, pp. 278-281.

Jaedicke, Robert K. "Accounting Data For Purposes Of Control," **AR**, 1962, Vol. 37, No. 2, pp. 181-188.

Jaedicke, Robert K. "Production Method Changes And The Hormel Wage Plan," **AR**, 1959, Vol. 34, No. 2, pp. 266-280.

Jaedicke, Robert K. "Some Notes On Product-Combination Decisions," **AR**, 1958, Vol. 33, No. 4, pp. 596-601.

Jaedicke, Robert K. (Bierman, Harold, Jr., Lawrence E. Fouraker and Robert K. Jaedicke. "The Use Of Probability And Statistics In Performance Evaluation," **AR**, 1961, Vol. 36, No. 3, pp. 409-417.)

Jaedicke, Robert K. (Burns, Joseph S., Robert K. Jaedicke and John M. Sangster. "Financial Reporting Of Purchase Contracts Used To Guarantee Large Investments," **AR**, 1963, Vol. 38, No. 1, pp. 1-13.)

Jaedicke, Robert K. (Ijiri, Yuji, Robert K. Jaedicke and John L. Livingstone. "The Effect Of Inventory Costing Methods On Full And Direct Costing," **JAR**, 1965, Vol. 3, No. 1, pp. 63-74.)

Jaedicke, Robert K. (Ijiri, Yuji and Robert K. Jaedicke. "Reliability And Objectivity Of Accounting Measurements," **AR**, 1966, Vol. 41, No. 3, pp. 474-483.)

Jaenicke, Henry R. and Joseph Rascoff. "Segment Disposition: Implementing APB Opinion No. 30," **JOA**, 1974, Vol. 137, No. 4, pp. 63-69.

Jaenicke, Henry R. and Patricia A. McConnell. "A Prospectus For Auditor's Responsibilities: The Report Of The Cohen Commission," **MA**, 1978, Vol. 59, No. 11, pp. 19-24.

Jaenicke, Henry R. "A New Approach To Engagement Management," **JOA**, 1980, Vol. 149, No. 4, pp. 68-78.

Jaenicke, Henry R. "Accounting For Restricted Stock Plans And Deferred Stock Plans," **AR**, 1970, Vol. 45, No. 1, pp. 115-128.

Jaenicke, Henry R. "Macroeconomics And Accounting Practice," **JOA**, 1969, Vol. 127, No. 6, pp. 35-39.

Jaenicke, Henry R. "Management's Choice To Purchase Or Pool," **AR**, 1962, Vol. 37, No. 4, pp. 758-765.

Jaenicke, Henry R. "Ownership Continuity And ARB No. 48," **JOA**, 1962, Vol. 114, No. 6, pp. 57-63.

Jaenicke, Henry R. (Callahan, Patrick S., Henry R. Jaenicke and Thomas L. Neebes. "SASs Nos. 56 And 57: Increasing Audit Effectiveness," **JOA**, 1988, Vol. 166, No. 4, pp. 56-61.)

Jagerhorn, Reginald. "Some Aspects Of Finnish Financial Reporting Practices," **IJAER**, 1970, Vol. 6, No. 1, pp.

15-23.

Jagetia, Lal C. and Evaristus C. Nwadike. "Accounting Systems In Developing Nations: The Nigerian Experience," **IJAER**, 1983, Vol. 18, No. 2, pp. 69-81.

Jaggi, Bikki and Hon-Shiang Lau. "Toward A Model For Human Resource Valuation," **AR**, 1974, Vol. 49, No. 2, pp. 321-329.

Jaggi, Bikki and Hon-Shiang Lau. "Toward A Model For Human Resource Valuation: A Reply," **AR**, 1975, Vol. 50, No. 2, pp. 348-350.

Jaggi, Bikki. "A Comment On Motivational Considerations In Cost Allocation Systems: A Conditioning Theory Approach," **AR**, 1979, Vol. 54, No. 1, pp. 209-214.

Jaggi, Bikki. "A Note On Information Content Of Corporate Annual Earnings Forecasts," **AR**, 1978, Vol. 53, No. 4, pp. 961-969.

Jaggi, Bikki. "An Analysis Of Corporate Social Reporting In Germany," **IJAER**, 1980, Vol. 15, No. 2, pp. 35-45.

Jaggi, Bikki. "Further Evidence On The Accuracy Of Management Forecasts Vis-A-Vis Analysts' Forecasts," **AR**, 1980, Vol. 55, No. 1, pp. 96-101.

Jaggi, Bikki. "Human Resources Are Assets," **MA**, 1976, Vol. 57, No. 8, pp. 41-42.

Jaggi, Bikki. (Arbel, Avner and Bikki Jaggi. "Impact Of Replacement Cost Disclosures Of Investors' Decisions In The United States," **IJAER**, 1978, Vol. 14, No. 1, pp. 71-82.)

Jaggi, Bikki. (Freedman, Martin and Bikki Jaggi. "An Analysis Of The Impact Of Corporate Pollution Disclosures: A Reply," **AIPIA**, 1988, Vol. 2, pp. 193-197.)

Jaggi, Bikki. (Freedman, Martin and Bikki Jaggi. "An Analysis Of The Impact Of Corporate Pollution Disclosures Included In Annual Financial Statements On Investors' Decisions," **AIPIA**, 1986, Vol. 1, pp. 193-212.)

Jaggi, Bikki. (Freedman, Martin and Bikki Jaggi. "Risk Evaluation Of Firms Disclosing Pollution Information In Financial Statements," **AIA**, 1986, Vol. 3, pp. 113-126.)

Jaggi, B. L. "Accounting Studies Of Developing Countries: An Assessment," **IJAER**, 1973, Vol. 9, No. 1, pp. 159-170.

Jaggi, B. L. "The Impact Of The Cultural Environment On Financial Disclosures," **IJAER**, 1975, Vol. 10, No. 2, pp. 75-84.

Jaggi, B. "A Review Of The Accounting Profession In India," **IJAER**, 1970, Vol. 6, No. 1, pp. 35-51.

Jagolinzer, Philip and John M. Strefeler. "Marital Status And The Taxes We Pay," **JOA**, 1986, Vol. 161, No. 3, pp. 68-77.

Jahn, Jerome J. and Douglas E. Norberg. "The Barchris Decision - Liability For All," **MA**, 1968, Vol. 50, No. 3, pp. 54-56.

Jain, Prem C. "Analyses Of The Distribution Of Security Market Model Prediction Errors For Daily Returns Data," **JAR**, 1986, Vol. 24, No. 1, pp. 76-96.

Jain, Prem C. "Cross-Sectional Association Between Abnormal Returns And Firm Specific Variables," **JAEC**, 1982, Vol. 4, No. 3, pp. 205-228.

Jain, Prem C. "Relation Beween Market Model Prediction Errors And Omitted Variables: A Methodological Note," **JAR**, 1986, Vol. 24, No. 1, pp. 187-193.

Jain, Prem. "The Impact Of Accounting Regulation On The Stock Market: The Case Of Oil And Gas Companies: A Further Analysis," **AR**, 1983, Vol. 58, No. 3, pp. 633-638.

Jain, Tribhowan N. "Alternative Methods Of Accounting And Decision Making: A Psycho-Linguistical Analysis," **AR**, 1973, Vol. 48, No. 1, pp. 95-104.

Jain, Tribhowan N. (Cheng, Philip C. and Tribhowan N. Jain. "Economic Perspective And Accounting Practices In South Korea," **IJAER**, 1973, Vol. 8, No. 2, pp. 123-139.)

James, Donald. "Proposed Budget-Auditing Standards," **MA**, 1974, Vol. 55, No. 11, pp. 30-32.

James, Edwin P. "Certification Of Cost Or Pricing Data Under Defense Contracts," **MA**, 1969, Vol. 50, No. 8, pp. 47-51.

James, Edwin P. "Defense Contract Change Orders: Pricing," **MA**, 1970, Vol. 52, No. 1, pp. 71-73.

James, Edwin P. "Defense Contractors Weighted Average Share In Cost Risk (CWAS)," **MA**, 1968, Vol. 49, No. 5, pp. 45-51.

James, Edwin P. "Weighted Guidelines Profit On Defense Contracts," **MA**, 1965, Vol. 47, No. 4, pp. 3-13.

James, Robert M. "Interrelationships In Governmental Accounting Theory," **AR**, 1951, Vol. 26, No. 1, pp. 88-92.

James, Robert M. "Some Aspects Of A Governmental Audit," **AR**, 1951, Vol. 26, No. 3, pp. 347-351.

James, Robert M. "Three Major Concepts In Governmental Accounting Theory," **AR**, 1950, Vol. 25, No. 3, pp. 307-314.

James, Simon. "The Reform Of Personal Taxation: A Review Article," **ABR**, 1986-87, Vol. 17, No. 66, pp. 117-124.

James, Simon. "The Report Of The Meade Committee," **ABR**, 1978-79, Vol. 9, No. 33, pp. 35-44.

Jameson, William J. "Co-Operation Between Professions," **JOA**, 1956, Vol. 102, No. 5, pp. 42-45.

Jamison, Robert W. and Steven C. Dilley. "Subchapter S In Transition," **JATA**, 1984, Vol. 6, No. 1, pp. 36-47.

Jamison, Robert W. and Steven C. Dilley. "Subchapter S In Transition: A Reply And Extension," **JATA**, 1985, Vol. 7, No. 1, pp. 80-88.

Jamison, Robert W. (Stone, Mary S., Thomas J. Frecka and Robert W. Jamison. "Multiemployer Pension Plan Amendments Act," **CPAJ**, 1981, Vol. 51, No. 12, pp. 34-40.)

Jamison, Robert W., Jr. (Englebrecht, Ted D. and Robert W. Jamison, Jr. "An Empirical Inquiry Into The Role Of The Tax Court In The Valuation Of Property For Charitable Contribution Purposes," **AR**, 1979, Vol. 54, No. 3, pp. 554-562.)

Jancura, Elise G. and Fred L. Lilly. "SAS No. 3 And The Evaluation Of Internal Control," **JOA**, 1977, Vol. 143, No. 3, pp. 69-74.

Jancura, Elise G. (Ried, Glenda, Brenda T. Acken and Elise G. Jancura. "An Historical Perspective On Women In Accounting," **JOA**, 1987, Vol. 163, No. 5, pp. 338-355.)

Janell, Paul A. and Raymond M. Kinnunen. "Portrait Of The Divisional Controller," **MA**, 1980, Vol. 61, No. 12, pp. 15-19.

Janell, Paul A. (Imhoff, Eugene A., Jr. and Paul A. Janell. "Opinion No. 29: A New Valuation Method," **MA**, 1979, Vol. 60, No. 9, pp. 50-53.)

Janell, Paul. (McKinnon, S. M. and Paul Janell. "The International Accounting Standards Committee: A Performance Evaluation," **IJAER**, 1984, Vol. 19, No. 2, pp. 19-34.)

Janin, Harry. "Partners And Partnerships," **JOA**, 1956, Vol. 102, No. 3, pp. 47-52.

Janson, Ernest C. (White, Godwin T., Jean C. Wyer and Ernest C. Janson. "Peer Review: Proposed Regulations And Current Compliance," **ACCHOR**, 1988, Vol. 2, No. 2, pp. 27-30.)

Janson, Ernest C. (White, Godwin T., Jean C. Wyer and Ernest C. Janson. "Uncertainty Reporting - Impact Of Proposed Changes," **CPAJ**, 1987, Vol. 57, No. 9, pp. 46-53.)

Janson, Ernest C. (Wyer, Jean C., Godwin T. White and Ernest C. Janson. "Audits Of Public Companies By Smaller CPA Firms: Clients, Reports, And Quality," **AJPT**, 1988, Vol. 7, No. 2, pp. 164-173.)

Janusky, Dominic R. "Plant Forecasting At Burroughs," **MA**, 1985, Vol. 66, No. 9, pp. 59-62.

Jaouen, Pauline R. (Jackson, Betty R. and Pauline R. Jaouen. "Influencing Taxpayer Compliance Through Sanction Threat Or Appeals To Conscience," **AIT**, 1988, Vol. 2, pp. xx-xx.)

Jardine, Linda A. and Randall W. Luecke. "FAS 81: Disclosing Postretirement Benefits," **MA**, 1985, Vol. 67, No. 4, pp. 51-54.

Jarett, Irwin M. "Computer Graphics: A Reporting Revolution?," **JOA**, 1981, Vol. 151, No. 5, pp. 46-57.

Jarnagin, Bill D. and John K. Harris. "Teaching With Multiple Choice Questions," **AR**, 1977, Vol. 52, No. 4, pp. 930-934.

Jarnagin, Bill D. and Tsai Yen Chung. "Understanding The Accounting For Defined Benefit Pension Plans," **MA**, 1988, Vol. 70, No. 3, pp. 34-42.

Jarrell, Gregg A. "Pro-Producer Regulation And Accounting For Assets: The Case Of Electric Utilities," **JAEC**, 1979, Vol. 1, No. 2, pp. 93-116.

Jarrett, Art P. "Manufacturing Power Substations: An Accounting Practice Report," **MA**, 1971, Vol. 52, No. 9, pp. 39-42.

Jarrett, Art P. "We Control Costs At Their Source," **MA**, 1966, Vol. 47, No. 6, pp. 30-35.

Jarrett, Jeffrey E. "Bias In Adjusting Asset Values For Changes In The Price Level: An Application Of Estimation Theory," **JAR**, 1974, Vol. 12, No. 1, pp. 63-66.

Jarrett, Jeffrey E. "Notes On The Estimation Problem In Financial Accounting," **JAR**, 1972, Vol. 10, No. 1, pp. 108-112.

Jarrett, Jeffrey E. "The Principles Of Matching And Realization As Estimation Problems," **JAR**, 1971, Vol. 9, No. 2, pp. 378-382.

Jarrett, Jeffrey E. (Brandon, Charles H. and Jeffrey E. Jarrett. "Experimenting With Students' Ability To Forecast," **AR**, 1977, Vol. 52, No. 3, pp. 697-704.)

Jarrow, Sidney F. "Mergers By Accountants And Accounting Firms," **JOA**, 1967, Vol. 123, No. 5, pp. 37-41.

Jaruga, Alicja A. "Problems Of Uniform Accounting Principles In Poland," **IJAER**, 1972, Vol. 8, No. 1, pp. 25-41.

Jaruga, Alicja A. "Recent Developments In Polish Accounting: An International Transaction Emphasis," **IJAER**, 1974, Vol. 10, No. 1, pp. 1-18.

Jaruga, Alicja. A. "Some Developments Of The Auditing Profession In Poland," **IJAER**, 1976, Vol. 12, No. 1, pp. 101-109.

Jaruga, Alicja. (Berry, Maureen and Alicja Jaruga. "Industrial Accounting In Poland's Reorganized Economy," **IJAER**, 1985, Vol. 20, No. 2, pp. 45-63.)

Jasinowski, Jerry J. "After The Crash," **MA**, 1988, Vol. 69, No. 7, pp. 12-15.

Jaskie, Walter E. "Pension Fund Accounting," **MA**, 1974, Vol. 55, No. 12, pp. 43-46.

Jasper, Geraldine F. (Smith, Clarence O. and Geraldine F. Jasper. "Using The Computer In Audit Work," **MA**, 1972, Vol. 54, No. 4, pp. 34-38.)

Jauch, Roger and Michael Skigen. "Human Resource Accounting: A Critical Evaluation," **MA**, 1974, Vol. 55, No. 11, pp. 33-36.

Jaycock, Stephen J. (Mayer-Sommer, Alan P. and Stephen J. Laycock. "Financial Reporting: Let's Replace Compliance With Competition," **MA**, 1978, Vol. 60, No. 6, pp. 14-19.)

Jayson, Susan. "Filing Into The Future With EDGAR," **MA**, 1985, Vol. 66, No. 12, pp. 20-23.

Jayson, Susan. "Pension Update: An Interview With Consultant Larry B. Wiltse," **MA**, 1988, Vol. 70, No. 3, pp. 20-23.

Jayson, Susan. "Tax Reform And Its Impact," **MA**, 1985, Vol. 66, No. 9, pp. 20-28.

Jean, William H. "Operations Research For The Accountant," **MA**, 1968, Vol. 49, No. 6, pp. 27-31.

Jeffries, Kenneth R. "Materiality As Defined By The Courts," **CPAJ**, 1981, Vol. 51, No. 10, pp. 13-17.

Jen, Frank C. and Ronald J. Huefner. "Depreciation By Probability-Life," **AR**, 1970, Vol. 45, No. 2, pp. 290-298.

Jenkins, David O. "Accounting For Funded Industrial Pension Plans," **AR**, 1964, Vol. 39, No. 3, pp. 648-653.

Jenkins, David O. "Pitfalls In Using Discounted Cash Flows For Mutually Exclusive Proposals," **MA**, 1970, Vol. 52, No. 4, pp. 33-37.

Jenkins, D. Randall. (Foster, Taylor W., III, D. Randall Jenkins and Don W. Vickrey. "The Incremental Information Content Of The Annual Report," **ABR**, 1985-86, Vol. 16, No. 62, pp. 91-98.)

Jenkins, James W. (Bagley, Ron N. and James W. Jenkins. "Capital Gain Yielding Bonds Produce Higher Than Expected After Tax Bond Yields," **JATA**, 1979, Vol. 1, No. 1, pp. 15-24.)

Jenkins, Martha E. and Loudell Ellis Robinson. "The Corporate Audit Committee," **MA**, 1985, Vol. 67, No. 6, pp. 31-35.

Jenkins, William L. "Nonprofit Hospital Accounting System," **MA**, 1973, Vol. 54, No. 12, pp. 23-27.

Jenne, Stanley Earl. "The Development Of Monetary Unit Sampling In Auditing Literature," **JAL**, 1986, Vol. 5, pp. 205-220.

Jenne, Stan. (Depppe, Larry, Don R. Hansen and Stan Jenne. "The 150-Hour Educational Requirement: The History And Message Of The Utah Experience," **ACCHOR**, 1988, Vol. 2, No. 2, pp. 53-57.)

Jennings, Alvin R. "Accounting Research," **AR**, 1958, Vol. 33, No. 4, pp. 547-554.

Jennings, Alvin R. "An Analysis Of New Developments In Auditing Procedures And Standards," **JOA**, 1950, Vol. 90, No. 3, pp. 190-200.

Jennings, Alvin R. "Challenges In Financial Reporting," **JOA**, 1958, Vol. 105, No. 1, pp. 28-34.

Jennings, Alvin R. "CPAs, Bankers Help Each Other To Help Clients," **JOA**, 1953, Vol. 95, No. 6, pp. 706-708.

Jennings, Alvin R. "International Standards Of Accounting And Auditing," **JOA**, 1962, Vol. 114, No. 3, pp. 36-42.

Jennings, Alvin R. "New Developments In Auditing By Independent CPAs," **JOA**, 1953, Vol. 96, No. 1, pp. 37-47.

Jennings, Alvin R. "Opinions Of The Accounting Principles Board," **JOA**, 1964, Vol. 118, No. 2, pp. 27-33.

Jennings, Alvin R. "Relation Of Internal Control To Independent CPA," **JOA**, 1951, Vol. 92, No. 5, pp. 562-571.

Jennings, Alvin R. "Staff Training - Present And Future," **AR**, 1948, Vol. 23, No. 4, pp. 401-409.

Jennings, Marianne M. (Reckers, Philip M. J., Dan C. Kneer and Marianne M. Jennings. "Concepts Of Materiality And Disclosure," **CPAJ**, 1984, Vol. 54, No. 12, pp. 20-31.)

Jennings, Marianne, Dan C. Kneer and Philip M. J. Reckers. "A Reexamination Of The Concept Of Materiality: Views Of Auditors, Users And Officers Of The Court," **AJPT**, 1986-87, Vol. 6, No. 2, pp. 104-115.

Jennings, Robert and Laura Starks. "Information Content And The Speed Of Stock Price Adjustment," **JAR**, 1985, Vol. 23, No. 1, pp. 336-350.

Jennings, Robert H. (Hassell, John M. and Robert H. Jennings. "Relative Forecast Accuracy And The Timing Of Earnings Forecast Announcements," **AR**, 1986, Vol. 61, No. 1, pp. 58-75.)

Jennings, Robert M. and R. Bruce McCosh. "Construction In Process - A Different Approach," **AR**, 1967, Vol. 42, No. 3, pp. 598-600.

Jennings, Robert M. "An Algebraic Model For Working Capital," **AR**, 1960, Vol. 35, No. 2, pp. 316-317.

Jennings, Robert M. "Graphical Analysis Of Overhead," **AR**, 1966, Vol. 41, No. 1, pp. 144-145.

Jennings, Robert M. "Installment Interest Computations - True And Quoted," **AR**, 1966, Vol. 41, No. 2, pp. 333-335.

Jennings, Robert M. "Prepayals - A Flow Simulation," **AR**, 1964, Vol. 39, No. 1, pp. 172-173.

Jennings, Robert M. "Selections From A Pre-Revolutionary Accounting Record," **AR**, 1962, Vol. 37, No. 1, pp. 73-75.

Jennings, Robert M. (Kistler, Linda H. and Robert M. Jennings. "An Accounting Primer Circa 1831," **AR**, 1969, Vol. 44, No. 1, pp. 168-173.)

Jennings, Robert. "Unsystematic Security Price Movements, Management Earnings Forecasts, And Revisions In Consensus Analyst Earnings Forecasts," **JAR**, 1987, Vol. 25, No. 1, pp. 90-110.

Jensen, Daniel L. "A Class Of Mutually Satisfactory Allocations," **AR**, 1977, Vol. 52, No. 4, pp. 842-856.

Jensen, Daniel L. "Hartley's Demand-Price Analysis In A Case Of Joint Production: A Comment," **AR**, 1973, Vol. 48, No. 4, pp. 768-770.

Jensen, Daniel L. "The Role Of Cost In Pricing Joint Products: A Case Of Production In Fixed Proportions," **AR**, 1974, Vol. 49, No. 3, pp. 465-476.

Jensen, Daniel L. "The Role Of Interest In Revolving Capital Plans For Cooperative Enterprise," **IJAER**, 1974, Vol. 9, No. 2, pp. 105-109.

Jensen, Daniel L. (Bailey, Andrew D., Jr. and Daniel L. Jensen. "The Two-Dimensional Time Frame Of Common Dollar Statements," **AR**, 1977, Vol. 52, No. 1, pp. 229-237.)

Jensen, Daniel L. (Bailey, Andrew D., Jr. and Daniel L. Jensen. "A Note On The Interface Between Compliance And Substantive Tests," **JAR**, 1977, Vol. 15, No. 2, pp. 293-299.)

Jensen, Daniel L. (Dillard, Jesse F. and Daniel L. Jensen.

"The Auditor's Report: An Analysis Of Opinion," **AR**, 1983, Vol. 58, No. 4, pp. 787-798.)

Jensen, Daniel L. (Turner, Joanne H. and Daniel L. Jensen. "Recent Episodes In The 'Oversight Cycle' Of Accountancy Self-Regulation," **RIAR**, 1987, Vol. 1, pp. 35-50.)

Jensen, D. L. and A. D. Bailey. "Discriminant Analysis As An Aid To Employee Selection: A Comment," **AR**, 1975, Vol. 50, No. 3, pp. 588-592.

Jensen, Herbert L. and Robert W. Wyndelts. "Through The Looking Glass: An Empirical Look At Discrimination In The Federal Income Tax Rate Structure," **AR**, 1976, Vol. 51, No. 4, pp. 846-853.

Jensen, Herbert L. and Steven D. Grossman. "Accounting Applications Of Covariance Analysis," **ABR**, 1978-79, Vol. 9, No. 36, pp. 300-308.

Jensen, Herbert L. "Allocating Tax Liabilities In Consolidated Returns," **MA**, 1983, Vol. 64, No. 12, pp. 56-62.

Jensen, Herbert L. "Cost Analyses Of Commercial Bank Portfolios," **MA**, 1982, Vol. 64, No. 4, pp. 47-51.

Jensen, Herbert L. (Blum, James D. and Herbert L. Jensen. "Accounting For Marketable Securities In Accordance With FASB Statement No. 12," **MA**, 1978, Vol. 60, No. 3, pp. 33-42.)

Jensen, Herbert L. (Crumbley, D. Larry, Robert H. Strawser and Herbert L. Jensen. "Accumulated Earnings: A New Court Calculation," **JOA**, 1977, Vol. 143, No. 3, pp. 75-78.)

Jensen, Herbert L. (Horvitz, Jerome S. and Herbert L. Jensen. "Systematic Evaluations Of Tax Accounting Textbooks," **AR**, 1979, Vol. 54, No. 4, pp. 800-806.)

Jensen, James A. and H. Gary Larson. "Records Management For Pollution Abatement Programs: Meeting EPA Requirements," **MA**, 1980, Vol. 61, No. 9, pp. 37-41.

Jensen, Michael C. and Jerold L. Zimmerman. "Management Compensation And The Managerial Labor Market," **JAEC**, 1985, Vol. 7, No. 1/3, pp. 3-9.

Jensen, Michael C. "Organization Theory And Methodology," **AR**, 1983, Vol. 58, No. 2, pp. 319-339.

Jensen, Robert E. and C. Edward Arrington. "Accounting Education: Turning Wrongs Into Rights In The 1980's," **JAED**, 1983, Vol. 1, No. 1, pp. 5-18.

Jensen, Robert E. and C. Torben Thomsen. "Statistical Analysis In Cost Measurement And Control," **AR**, 1968, Vol. 43, No. 1, pp. 83-93.

Jensen, Robert E. "A Cluster Analysis Study Of Financial Performance Of Selected Business Firms," **AR**, 1971, Vol. 46, No. 1, pp. 36-56.

Jensen, Robert E. "A Multiple Regression Model For Cost Control - Assumptions And Limitations," **AR**, 1967, Vol. 42, No. 2, pp. 265-273.

Jensen, Robert E. "An Experimental Design For Study Of Effects Of Accounting Variations In Decision Making," **JAR**, 1966, Vol. 4, No. 2, pp. 224-238.

Jensen, Robert E. "Capital Budgeting Under Risk And Inflation: A Pedagogical Guide," **AIA**, 1986, Vol. 3, pp. 255-280.

Jensen, Robert E. "Empirical Evidence From The Behavioral Sciences: Fish Out Of Water," **AR**, 1970, Vol. 45, No. 3, pp. 502-508.

Jensen, Robert E. "Fantasyland Accounting Research: Let's Make Pretend," **AR**, 1979, Vol. 54, No. 1, pp. 189-196.

Jensen, Robert E. "Observations On Jensen's Experimental Design For Study Of Effects Of Accounting Variations In Decision Making: A Rejoinder," **JAR**, 1967, Vol. 5, No. 2, pp. 230-251.

Jensen, Robert E. "Sensitivity Analysis And Integer Linear Programming," **AR**, 1968, Vol. 43, No. 3, pp. 425-446.

Jensen, Robert E. "The Befuddled Merchant Of Venice: More On The 'Misuse' Of Accounting Rates Of Return Vis-A-Vis Economic Rates Of Return," **AIPIA**, 1986, Vol. 1, pp. 113-166.

Jensen, Robert E. "Truth Versus PHIKTION Versus Something," **AR**, 1975, Vol. 50, No. 4, pp. 871-873.

Jensen, Robert E. (Arrington, C. Edward, Robert E. Jensen and Masao Tokutani. "Scaling Of Corporate Multivariate Performance Criteria: Subjective Composition Versus The Analytic Hierarchy Process," **JAPP**, 1982, Vol. 1, No. 2, pp. 95-123.)

Jensen, Robert E. (Arrington, C. Edward, William Hillison and Robert E. Jensen. "An Application Of Analytical Hierarchy Process To Model Expert Judgments On Analytical Review Procedures," **JAR**, 1984, Vol. 22, No. 1, pp. 298-312.)

Jensen, Robert. (Manes, Rene P., Soong H. Park and Robert Jensen. "Relevant Costs Of Intermediate Goods And Services," **AR**, 1982, Vol. 57, No. 3, pp. 594-606.)

Jensen, Wallace M. "Tax Effects Of Splitting A Corporation," **JOA**, 1951, Vol. 92, No. 3, pp. 294-303.

Jensen, William S. "Problem Identification In Accounting Research," **MA**, 1973, Vol. 55, No. 6, pp. 49-52.

Jentz, Gaylord A. "Ten-Year Review Of The CPA Law Examination," **AR**, 1967, Vol. 42, No. 2, pp. 362-365.

Jentz, Gaylord A. "The Case Against The Present CPA Commercial Law Examination," **AR**, 1966, Vol. 41, No. 3, pp. 535-541.

Jepsen, Victor. "The Objective Versus Problem Type Accounting Test," **AR**, 1948, Vol. 23, No. 3, p. 308-309.

Jerman, David A. (Hite, Peggy A. and David A. Jerman. "Partial Liquidation - Then And Now," **CPAJ**, 1987, Vol. 57, No. 3, pp. 36-40.)

Jerome, William T. (Hill, Thomas M. and William T. Jerome, III. "Accounting In The Executive Program," **AR**, 1956, Vol. 31, No. 3, pp. 411-417.)

Jerston, Jan E. "Analyst's View Of Deferred Income Taxes,"

AR, 1965, Vol. 40, No. 4, pp. 812-813.

Jessee, Ken. "Woodland Hospital Computerizes To Reduce Administrative Costs," **MA**, 1979, Vol. 61, No. 1, pp. 37-39.

Jeter, Debra C. and Paul K. Chaney. "A Financial Statement Analysis Approach To Deferred Taxes," **AH**, 1988, Vol. 2, No. 4, pp. 41-49.

Jewett, Grandjean G. "Survey Of Presently Available Electronic Computers," **JOA**, 1953, Vol. 96, No. 2, pp. 182-189.

Jewett, Grandjean G. "The Distribution Of Overhead With Electronic Calculators," **JOA**, 1954, Vol. 97, No. 6, pp. 698-701.

Jeynes, Paul H. "A Discipline For Investment Decisions," **AR**, 1965, Vol. 40, No. 1, pp. 105-118.

Jeynes, Paul H. (Slesinger, Reuben E. and Paul H. Jeynes. "Profit Incentive: Earnings Less Cost of Capital," **ABR**, 1971-72, Vol. 2, No. 7, pp. 163-176.)

Jiambalvo, James and Jamie Pratt. "Task Complexity And Leadership Effectiveness In CPA Firms," **AR**, 1982, Vol. 57, No. 4, pp. 734-750.

Jiambalvo, James and Neil Wilner. "Auditor Evaluation Of Contingent Claims," **AJPT**, 1985-86, Vol. 5, No. 1, pp. 1-11.

Jiambalvo, James and William Waller. "Decomposition And Assessments Of Audit Risk," **AJPT**, 1983-84, Vol. 3, No. 2, pp. 80-88.

Jiambalvo, James. "Measures Of Accuracy And Congruence In The Performance Evaluation Of CPA Personnel: Replication And Extensions," **AR**, 1982, Vol. 20, No. 1, pp. 152-161.

Jiambalvo, James. "Performance Evaluation And Directed Job Effort: Model Development And Analysis In A CPA Firm Setting," **JAR**, 1979, Vol. 17, No. 2, pp. 436-455.

Jiambalvo, James. "Prediction Achievement And Simulated Decision Makers As An Extension Of The Predictive Ability Criterion: Some Comments," **AR**, 1976, Vol. 51, No. 3, pp. 666-671.

Jiambalvo, James. (Burgstahler, David and James Jiambalvo. "Isolation Of Errors In Audit Sampling," **CPAJ**, 1986, Vol. 56, No. 11, pp. 66-71.)

Jiambalvo, James. (Burgstahler, David and James Jiambalvo. "Sample Error Characteristics And Projection Of Error To Audit Populations," **AR**, 1986, Vol. 61, No. 2, pp. 233-248.)

Jiambalvo, James. (Dillard, Jesse F. and James Jiambalvo. "Expectancy Theory In A Budgetary Setting: A Comment," **AR**, 1979, Vol. 54, No. 3, pp. 630-634.)

Jiambalvo, James. (Waller, William and James Jiambalvo. "The Use Of Normative Models In Human Information Processing Research In Accounting," **JAL**, 1984, Vol. 3, pp. 201-226.)

Jiambalvo, J. (Pratt, J. and J. Jiambalvo. "Relationships Between Leader Behaviors And Audit Team Performance," **AOS**, 1981, Vol. 6, No. 2, pp. 133-142.)

Jiambalvo, J. (Pratt, J. and J. Jiambalvo. "Determinants Of Leader Behavior In An Audit Environment," **AOS**, 1982, Vol. 7, No. 4, pp. 369-380.)

Jiambalvo, J., D. J. H. Watson and J. V. Baumler. "An Examination Of Performance Evaluation Decisions In CPA Firm Subunits," **AOS**, 1983, Vol. 8, No. 1, pp. 13-30.

Joehnk, Michael D. and George R. McGrail. "Benefit-Cost Ratios For Family Practice Residency Centers," **MA**, 1977, Vol. 58, No. 8, pp. 41-46.

Joehnk, Michael D. (Gitman, Lawrence J., Michael D. Joehnk and Peter W. Bacon. "Fundamentals Of Cash Management: Theory And Practice," **JCA**, 1984, Vol. 1, No. 1, pp. 75-99.)

Johansson, Sven-Erik. "An Appraisal Of The Swedish System Of Investment Reserves," **IJAER**, 1965, Vol. 1, No. 1, pp. 85-92.

Johansson, Sven-Erik. (Zeff, Stephen A. and Sven-Erik Johansson. "The Curious Accounting Treatment Of The Swedish Government Loan To Uddeholm," **AR**, 1984, Vol. 59, No. 2, pp. 342-350.)

John, Richard C. and Thomas J. Nissen. "Evaluating Internal Control In EDP Audits," **JOA**, 1970, Vol. 129, No. 2, pp. 31-38.

John, Richard C. "Improve Your Technical Writing," **MA**, 1976, Vol. 58, No. 3, pp. 49-52.

John, Richard C. "Parolee Counseling Service," **MA**, 1975, Vol. 57, No. 5, pp. 27-30.

Johns, Cort M. "Credit Information: A Management Tool," **MA**, 1971, Vol. 53, No. 3, pp. 27-30.

Johns, Gordon M. "Reflections On The Wheat Committee Recommendations," **CPAJ**, 1972, Vol. 42, No. 7, pp. 533-541.

Johns, Ralph S. and Howard A. Withey. "Authoritative Accounting Guide For Colleges And Universities," **JOA**, 1969, Vol. 127, No. 3, pp. 55-59.

Johns, Ralph S. "A Brief Guide For Preparing Good Audit Work Papers," **JOA**, 1954, Vol. 98, No. 1, pp. 45-53.

Johns, Ralph S. "Allocation Of Income Taxes," **JOA**, 1958, Vol. 106, No. 3, pp. 41-50.

Johns, Ralph S. "Authoritative Accounting Guide For Nonprofit Institutions," **JOA**, 1954, Vol. 97, No. 3, pp. 299-306.

Johns, Ralph S. "In All My Years - Classification Of Accounting Service," **AHJ**, 1976, Vol. 3, No. 1-4, pp. 10-12.

Johnson, Arnold W. "Form, Function, And Interpretation Of The Profit And Loss Statement," **AR**, 1943, Vol. 18, No. 4, pp. 340-347.

Johnson, Arnold W. "'More' On 'Income-Tax-Allocation' Accounting," **AR**, 1961, Vol. 36, No. 1, pp. 75-83.

Johnson, Bart. "Should You Convert To In-House EDP?," **MA**, 1983, Vol. 65, No. 3, pp. 52-57.

Johnson, Bart. "Why Your Company Needs Three Accounting Systems," **MA**, 1984, Vol. 66, No. 3, pp. 39-46.

Johnson, Bart. (Carlow, Alan and Bart Johnson. "Overcoming The Mystique Of EDP Auditing," **MA**, 1984, Vol. 66, No. 2, pp. 30-37.)

Johnson, Charles E. "A Case Against The Idea Of An All-Purpose Concept Of Business Income," **AR**, 1954, Vol. 29, No. 2, pp. 224-243.

Johnson, Charles E. "A Course In Income Taxation For Non-Accounting Majors?," **AR**, 1957, Vol. 32, No. 1, pp. 90-92.

Johnson, Charles E. "Elements In Solving Shortage Of Accounting Personnel," **JOA**, 1953, Vol. 96, No. 6, pp. 695-702.

Johnson, Charles E. "Inventory Valuation - The Accountant's Achilles Heel," **AR**, 1954, Vol. 29, No. 1, pp. 15-26.

Johnson, Craig D. (Englebrecht, Ted D. and Craig D. Johnson. "Generation-Skipping Transfers Under TRA 1976," **CPAJ**, 1978, Vol. 48, No. 3, pp. 31-37.)

Johnson, Dennis C. (Wise, John A. and Dennis C. Johnson. "Carryover Basis: To Be Given A 'Fresh Start'?," **JOA**, 1979, Vol. 148, No. 2, pp. 59-64.)

Johnson, Douglas A. and Kurt Pany. "Expose Or Cover-Up: Will An Employee Blow The Whistle?," **MA**, 1981, Vol. 63, No. 1, pp. 32-36.

Johnson, Douglas A. and Kurt Pany. "Forecasts, Auditor Review, And Bank Loan Decisions," **JAR**, 1984, Vol. 22, No. 2, pp. 731-743.

Johnson, Douglas A. (Baron, C. David, Douglas A. Johnson, D. Gerald Searfoss and Charles H. Smith. "Uncovering Corporate Irregularities: Are We Closing The Expectation Gap?," **JOA**, 1977, Vol. 144, No. 4, pp. 56-67.)

Johnson, Douglas A. (Hines, Dorothy L., Douglas A. Johnson and William V. Lennox. "The Semiconductor Industry Controller: A Profile," **MA**, 1982, Vol. 63, No. 12, pp. 30-35.)

Johnson, Douglas A. (Pany, Kurt and Douglas A. Johnson. "The Death (Perhaps Timely) Of An Audit Report: Some Empirical Results," **AIA**, 1985, Vol. 2, pp. 247-260.)

Johnson, Douglas A., Kurt Pany and Richard White. "Audit Reports And The Loan Decision: Actions And Perceptions," **AJPT**, 1982-83, Vol. 2, No. 2, pp. 38-51.

Johnson, Douglas A., Steve Kaplan and Bill B. Hook. "Looking For Mr. Overhead: An Expanded Role For Management Accountants," **MA**, 1983, Vol. 65, No. 5, pp. 65-70.

Johnson, D. C. (Graham. H. L. and D. C. Johnson. "An EDP System For Integrated Payroll," **MA**, 1966, Vol. 47, No. 12, pp. 36-43.)

Johnson, Eldon L. "International University Responsibilities," **IJAER**, 1968, Vol. 4, No. 1, pp. 121-127.

Johnson, Eugene A. "The Controllership Function," **MA**, 1972, Vol. 53, No. 9, pp. 45-48.

Johnson, Everett C. "The Income-Tax Treatment Of Partners And Partnerships," **JOA**, 1954, Vol. 98, No. 3, pp. 360-365.

Johnson, Frank P. and Charles F. Muenzberg. "Can Cost Analysis Improve Your Mortgage Loan Function?," **MA**, 1980, Vol. 61, No. 8, pp. 22-25.

Johnson, Glenn L. and Sherwood W. Newton. "Tax Considerations In Equipment Replacement Decisions," **AR**, 1967, Vol. 42, No. 4, pp. 738-746.

Johnson, Glenn L. and S. Stephen Simik, II. "The Use Of Probability Inequalities In Multiproduct C-V-P Analysis Under Uncertainty," **JAR**, 1974, Vol. 12, No. 1, pp. 67-79.

Johnson, Glenn L. and S. Stephen Simik, II. "Multiproduct C-V-P-Analysis Under Uncertainty," **JAR**, 1971, Vol. 9, No. 2, pp. 278-286.

Johnson, Glenn L. "Funds-Flow Equations," **AR**, 1966, Vol. 41, No. 3, pp. 510-517.

Johnson, Glenn L. "The Monetary And Nonmonetary Distinction," **AR**, 1965, Vol. 40, No. 4, pp. 821-823.

Johnson, Glenn L. (Greenberg, Robert R., Glenn L. Johnson and K. Ramesh. "Earnings Versus Cash Flow As A Predictor Of Future Cash Flow Measures," **JAAF**, 1986, Vol. 1 (New Series), No. 4, pp. 266-277.)

Johnson, Gregg D. "Recovering Fees In Bankruptcy," **JOA**, 1988. Vol. 166, No. 3, pp. 66-70.

Johnson, Hans V. "Merchant-Accountants," **MA**, 1976, Vol. 58, No. 4, pp. 57-61.

Johnson, Hobart S. "Internal Auditing In The Goal Oriented Firm," **MA**, 1967, Vol. 48, No. 9, pp. 41-48.

Johnson, H. Thomas and Dennis A. Loewe. "How Weyerhaeuser Manages Corporate Overhead Costs," **MA**, 1987, Vol. 69, No. 2, pp. 20-26.

Johnson, H. Thomas and Robert S. Kaplan. "The Rise And Fall Of Management Accounting," **MA**, 1987, Vol. 68, No. 7, pp. 22-30.

Johnson, H. Thomas. "Activity-Based Information: A Blueprint For World-Class Management," **MA**, 1988, Vol. 69, No. 12, pp. 23-30.

Johnson, H. Thomas. "The Role Of Accounting History In The Study Of Modern Business Enterprise," **AR**, 1975, Vol. 50, No. 3, pp. 444-450.

Johnson, H. Thomas. "Toward A New Understanding Of Nineteenth-Century Cost Accounting," **AR**, 1981, Vol. 56, No. 3, pp. 510-518.

Johnson, H. Thomas. (Hopwood, Anthony G. and H. Thomas Johnson. "Accounting History's Claim To Legitimacy," **IJAER**, 1986, Vol. 21, No. 2, pp. 37-46.)

Johnson, H. T. "The Search For Gain In Markets And Firms: A Review Of The Historical Emergence Of Management

Accounting Systems," **AOS**, 1983, Vol. 8, No. 2/3, pp. 139-146.

Johnson, James T. "Is The Trust Fund Theory Of Capital Stock Dead?," **AR**, 1959, Vol. 34, No. 4, pp. 609-611.

Johnson, Janice M. and William R. Stromsem. "The TRA And Individuals: A Year-End RX," **JOA**, 1986, Vol. 162, No. 6, pp. 172-177.

Johnson, John W. "Creditors' Collection Problems," **JOA**, 1961, Vol. 111, No. 6, pp. 60-63.

Johnson, Johnny R. (Neter, John, Johnny R. Johnson and Robert A. Leitch. "Characteristics Of Dollar-Unit Taints And Error Rates In Accounts Receivable And Inventory," **AR**, 1985, Vol. 60, No. 3, pp. 488-499.)

Johnson, Johnny R. (Roemmich, Roger A., Johnny R. Johnson and Robert R. Rice. "Pictures That Lie: The Abuse Of Graphs In Annual Reports," **MA**, 1980, Vol. 62, No. 4, pp. 50-57.)

Johnson, Johnny R., Robert A. Leitch and John Neter. "Characteristics Of Errors In Accounts Receivable And Inventory Audits," **AR**, 1981, Vol. 56, No. 2, pp. 270-293.

Johnson, Keith. "One Company's Forecasting," **CPAJ**, 1974, Vol. 44, No. 9, pp. 47-49.

Johnson, Kenneth P. "The Auditor's Responsibility To Detect Fraud - II," **CPAJ**, 1981, Vol. 51, No. 1, pp. 17-21.

Johnson, Kenneth P. "The Auditor's Responsibility To Detect Fraud - III," **CPAJ**, 1981, Vol. 51, No. 2, pp. 23-34.

Johnson, Kenneth P. "The Auditor's Responsibility To Detect Fraud - I," **CPAJ**, 1980, Vol. 50, No. 12, pp. 10-20.

Johnson, Kenneth P. "The Auditor's Responsibility To Detect Fraud - IV," **CPAJ**, 1981, Vol. 51, No. 3, pp. 22-28.

Johnson, Lester E. "Using LIFO To Measure Performance," **MA**, 1982, Vol. 64, No. 6, pp. 28-31.

Johnson, L. Todd and Philip W. Bell. "Current Replacement Costs: A Qualified Opinion," **JOA**, 1976, Vol. 142, No. 5, pp. 63-71.

Johnson, L. Todd. "Current Replacement Costs And Potential Managerial Benefits," **MA**, 1977, Vol. 59, No. 6, pp. 31-36.

Johnson, L. Todd. "Extending The Attest Function To Interim Reports," **CPAJ**, 1974, Vol. 44, No. 6, pp. 43-46.

Johnson, L. Todd. "Non-Arm's-Length Transactions: The Auditor's Responsibility," **CPAJ**, 1974, Vol. 44, No. 11, pp. 39-42.

Johnson, L. Todd. (Edwards, Edgar O. and L. Todd Johnson. "An Indifference Approach To Profit-Volume Analysis," **AR**, 1974, Vol. 49, No. 3, pp. 579-583.)

Johnson, L. Todd. (Howell, William C. and L. Todd Johnson. "An Evaluation Of The Compressed-Course Format For Instruction In Accounting," **AR**, 1982, Vol. 57, No. 2, pp. 403-413.)

Johnson, Merlyn K. "A System Of Modified Direct Costing For Planning And Control," **MA**, 1968, Vol. 49, No. 10, pp. 51-56.

Johnson, Orace and Sanford Gunn. "Conflict Resolution: The Market And/Or Accounting?," **AR**, 1974, Vol. 49, No. 4, pp. 649-663.

Johnson, Orace. "A Consequential Approach To Accounting For R & D," **JAR**, 1967, Vol. 5, No. 2, pp. 164-172.

Johnson, Orace. "Common Law Accounting: The Case Of Goodwill," **RIAR**, 1987, Vol. 1, pp. 51-77.

Johnson, Orace. "Contraequity Accounting For R&D," **AR**, 1976, Vol. 51, No. 4, pp. 808-823.

Johnson, Orace. "Corporate Giving: A Note On Profit Maximization And Accounting Disclosure," **JAR**, 1965, Vol. 3, No. 1, pp. 75-85.

Johnson, Orace. "On Taxonomy And Accounting Research," **AR**, 1972, Vol. 47, No. 1, pp. 64-74.

Johnson, Orace. "Some Implications Of The United States Constitution For Accounting Institution Alternatives," **JAR**, 1981, Vol. 19, Supp., pp. 89-120.

Johnson, Orace. "Some Reservations On The Significance Of Prospective Income Data," **AR**, 1968, Vol. 43, No. 3, pp. 546-548.

Johnson, Orace. "The Art of Enquiry: A Seminar In Accounting Research," **AR**, 1974, Vol. 49, No. 1, pp. 159-165.

Johnson, Orace. "Toward An 'Events' Theory Of Accounting," **AR**, 1970, Vol. 45, No. 4, pp. 641-653.

Johnson, Orace. "Two General Concepts Of Depreciation," **JAR**, 1968, Vol. 6, No. 1, pp. 29-37.

Johnson, Orace. (Albrecht, William Steve, Orace Johnson, Larry L. Lookabill and David J. H. Watson. "A Comparison Of The Accuracy Of Corporate And Security Analysts' Forecasts Of Earnings: A Comment," **AR**, 1977, Vol. 52, No. 3, pp. 736-740.)

Johnson, Orace. (Dow, Alice S. and Orace Johnson. "The Break-Even Point Concept: Its Development And Expanding Applications," **MA**, 1969, Vol. 50, No. 6, pp. 29-31.)

Johnson, Patricia L. and Paul A. Dierks. "What Are Women Accountants Really Like?," **MA**, 1982, Vol. 63, No. 9, pp. 25-28.

Johnson, Paul E. (Meservy, Rayman D., Andrew D. Bailey, Jr. and Paul E. Johnson. "Internal Control Evaluation: A Computational Model Of The Review Process," **AJPT**, 1986-87, Vol. 6, No. 1, pp. 44-74.)

Johnson, Ramon E. and Paul T. Peterson. "Current Value Accounting For S&Ls: A Needed Reform?," **JOA**, 1984, Vol. 157, No. 1, pp. 80-85.

Johnson, Raymond. (Murray, Dennis and Raymond Johnson. "Differential GAAP And The FASB's Conceptual Framework," **JAAF**, 1983, Vol. 7, No. 1, pp. 4-15.)

Johnson, Richard D., Edward M. Klasny and Patrick McNamee. "ASB Proposes New SAS On Compliance Auditing," **JOA**, 1988, Vol. 165, No. 6, pp. 76-87.

Johnson, Robert L. "Michigan's New Tax," **JOA**, 1955, Vol. 99, No. 2, pp. 56-60.

Johnson, Robert T. and Martin Benis. "The Premature Retirement Of Debt," **MA**, 1975, Vol. 56, No. 7, pp. 43-44.

Johnson, Robert T. "Full-Cost Vs. Conventional Accounting In The Petroleum Industry," **CPAJ**, 1972, Vol. 42, No. 6, pp. 479-484.

Johnson, Robert T. "What CPAs Should Know About Oil And Gas Tax Shelters," **JOA**, 1972, Vol. 134, No. 4, pp. 56-62.

Johnson, Robert T. (Benis, Martin and Robert T. Johnson. "Gains And Losses On Early Extinguishment Of Debt," **CPAJ**, 1975, Vol. 45, No. 11, pp. 39-41.)

Johnson, Robert T. (Benis, Martin, Claire Brody and Robert T. Johnson. "Utilization Of The Small Group Approach To Teaching Intermediate Accounting," **AR**, 1976, Vol. 51, No. 4, pp. 894-898.)

Johnson, Robert W. "Random Samples In Audit Tests," **JOA**, 1957, Vol. 104, No. 6, pp. 43-48.

Johnson, Robert W. "Statistical Techniques For Auditing Need Deeper Study," **JOA**, 1953, Vol. 96, No. 3, pp. 336-340.

Johnson, Robert. (Benis, Martin and Robert Johnson. "A Case Of Premature Income Recognition," **CPAJ**, 1973, Vol. 43, No. 10, pp. 863-867.)

Johnson, Roger D. and Jack J. Beren. "Commodity Straddle: A Viable Tax-Shelter," **MA**, 1973, Vol. 55, No. 5, pp. 35-37.

Johnson, R. Bruce. "Managing The Microcomputer Explosion," **CA**, 1984, Vol. 2, No. 2, pp. 30-37.

Johnson, Sandra J. and Thomas M. Porcano. "The Safe Harbor Lease - Tax Implications," **CPAJ**, 1983, Vol. 53, No. -9, pp. 20-29.

Johnson, Steven B. and David Solomons. "Institutional Legitimacy And The FASB," **JAPP**, 1984, Vol. 3, No. 3, pp. 165-183.

Johnson, Steven B. and William F. Messier, Jr. "The Nature Of Accounting Standards Setting: An Alternative Explanation," **JAAF**, 1982, Vol. 5, No. 3, pp. 195-213.

Johnson, Steven B. "An Economic Perspective On The Certification Of Specialists In Tax Accounting," **JATA**, 1984, Vol. 5, No. 2, pp. 27-39.

Johnson, Steven B. "The Economic Function Of Doctoral Programs In Accounting: Alternative Theories And Educational Implications," **AR**, 1985, Vol. 60, No. 4, pp. 736-743.

Johnson, Steven B. (Beatty, Randolph P. and Steven B. Johnson. "A Market-Based Method Of Classifying Convertible Securities," **JAAF**, 1985, Vol. 8, No. 2, pp. 112-124.)

Johnson, Steven C. "An Accounting System For Joint Ventures," **MA**, 1973, Vol. 54, No. 10, pp. 37-38.

Johnson, T. J. and Marjorie Caygill. "The Development Of Accountancy Links In The Commonwealth," **ABR**, 1970-71, Vol. 1, No. 2, pp. 155-173.

Johnson, W. Bruce and Dan S. Dhaliwal. "LIFO Abandonment," **JAR**, 1988, Vol. 26, No. 2, pp. 236-272.

Johnson, W. Bruce and Lawrence Revsine. "Financial Reporting Standards, Agency Costs, And Shareholder Intervention," **JAL**, 1988, Vol. 7, pp. 94-124.

Johnson, W. Bruce and Ramachandran Ramanan. "Discretionary Accounting Changes From 'Successful Efforts' To 'Full Cost' Methods: 1970-76," **AR**, 1988, Vol. 63, No. 1, pp. 96-110.

Johnson, W. Bruce, Robert P. Magee, Nandu J. Nagarajan and Harry A. Newman. "An Analysis Of The Stock Price Reaction To Sudden Executive Deaths: Implications For The Management Labor Market," **JAEC**, 1985, Vol. 7, No. 1/3, pp. 151-174.

Johnson, W. Bruce. "A Test Of The Expectancy Theory Of Motivation In An Accounting Environment: A Comment," **AR**, 1979, Vol. 54, No. 2, pp. 409-411.

Johnson, W. Bruce. "Representativeness' In Judgmental Predictions Of Corporate Bankruptcy," **AR**, 1983, Vol. 58, No. 1, pp. 78-97.

Johnson, W. B. "The Impact Of Confidence Interval Information On Probability Judgements," **AOS**, 1982, Vol. 7, No. 4, pp. 349-368.

Johnson, Walter J. "Government Reporting Of Budget Information," **JOA**, 1985, Vol. 159, No. 6, pp. 46-55.

Johnson, Wayne A. (Eckel, Norm and Wayne A. Johnson. "A Model For Screening And Classifying Potential Accounting Majors," **JAED**, 1983, Vol. 1, No. 2, pp. 57-65.)

Johnston, Donald J., W. Morley Lemon and Frederick L. Neumann. "The Canadian Study Of The Role Of The Auditor," **JAAF**, 1980, Vol. 3, No. 3, pp. 251-263.

Johnston, Kenneth. (Gray, Jack, John Willingham and Kenneth Johnston. "A Business Game For The Introductory Course In Accounting," **AR**, 1963, Vol. 38, No. 2, pp. 336-346.)

Johnston, Trevor. (Lee, T. A., L. Goldberg and Trevor Johnston. "The History Of Accounting': Three Reviews," **ABR**, 1977-78, Vol. 8, No. 29, pp. 58-67.)

Jolivet, Vincent. "The Current French Approach To Inventory Price Level Problems," **AR**, 1964, Vol. 39, No. 3, pp. 689-692.

Jolley, John David, II. (Barkman, Arnold I. and John David Jolley, II. "Cost Defenses For Antitrust Cases," **MA**, 1986, Vol. 67, No. 10, pp. 37-40.)

Jones, Colin J. "Accounting Standards: A Blind Alley?," **ABR**, 1974-75, Vol. 5, No. 20, pp. 273-279.

Jones, C. S. "An Empirical Study Of The Role Of Management Accounting Systems Following Takeover Or Merger," **AOS**, 1985, Vol. 10, No. 2, pp. 177-200.

Jones, C. S. "An Empirical Study Of The Evidence For Contingency Theories Of Management Accounting Systems In

Conditions Of Rapid Change," **AOS**, 1985, Vol. 10, No. 3, pp. 303-328.

Jones, David C. "The Use Of Accounting For Municipal Management Purposes," **AIIA**, 1988, Vol. 2, pp. 295-306.

Jones, Frederick L. "Current Techniques In Bankruptcy Prediction," **JAL**, 1987, Vol. 6, pp. 131-164.

Jones, Gardner M. and David R. L. Gabhart. "Danger: This City Is In Financial Trouble," **MA**, 1979, Vol. 61, No. 4, pp. 19-22.

Jones, Gardner M. and Johannes Kinfu. "The Birth Of An Accounting Profession: The Ethiopian Experience," **IJAER**, 1971, Vol. 7, No. 1, pp. 89-98.

Jones, Gardner M. and Saber A. Awad. "The Use Of Accounting Techniques In Small Firms," **MA**, 1972, Vol. 53, No. 8, pp. 41-44.

Jones, Gardner M. "Accounting Innovation And The Psychology Of Change," **AR**, 1962, Vol. 37, No. 2, pp. 244-250.

Jones, Gardner M. "Educators, Electrons, And Business Models: A Problem In Synthesis," **AR**, 1960, Vol. 35, No. 4, pp. 619-626.

Jones, Gardner M. "Linear Algebra For The Neophyte," **AR**, 1965, Vol. 40, No. 3, pp. 636-640.

Jones, Gardner M. "Some Problems In Accounting For Land Development," **MA**, 1968, Vol. 49, No. 12, pp. 27-33.

Jones, Gardner M. "University Responses To EDP," **AR**, 1958, Vol. 33, No. 4, pp. 645-649.

Jones, Gardner M. (Sadhwani, Arjan T. and Gardner M. Jones. "Accounting For The Carrying Charges On Land," **MA**, 1973, Vol. 54, No. 11, pp. 40-42.)

Jones, Gene K. "Capital Budgeting: A Modified Approach To Simplify Sound Investment Decisions," **MA**, 1969, Vol. 50, No. 7, pp. 33-34.

Jones, Gorman R. (Bolling, Rodger A. and Gorman R. Jones. "OID In Nonpublic Property Sales," **CPAJ**, 1986, Vol. 56, No. 8, pp. 32-43.)

Jones, Harold L. (Budge, Bruce P. and Harold L. Jones. "A Management Accounting System For Contract Loggers," **MA**, 1977, Vol. 59, No. 4, pp. 34-36.)

Jones, H. Milton and Vernon E. Pontius. "Survey Of Accounting Teaching Via Television," **AR**, 1965, Vol. 40, No. 4, pp. 863-867.

Jones, James W. "A Description Of A Baltimore Merchant's Journal," 1983, Vol. 10, No. 1, pp. 99-110.

Jones, James W. "Accounting For Amusement Parks," **MA**, 1971, Vol. 52, No. 10, pp. 20-21.

Jones, James W. "Accounting Practices In Ship Chandlery," **MA**, 1973, Vol. 55, No. 2, pp. 28-30.

Jones, James W. "Pitfalls Of Misinformation: A Case Study," **MA**, 1970, Vol. 51, No. 12, pp. 17-19.

Jones, James W. "Rainbows, Catfish, And Other Cash Crops," **MA**, 1978, Vol. 60, No. 3, pp. 43-46.

Jones, James W. "Tobacco Auction Warehouse Accounting," **MA**, 1974, Vol. 55, No. 10, pp. 35-38.

Jones, Jeffrey C. "Financial Instruments: Historical Cost V. Fair Value," **CPAJ**, 1988, Vol. 58, No. 8, pp. 56-63.

Jones, J. Weldon. "The Execution Of The Federal Budget," **AR**, 1942, Vol. 17, No. 2, pp. 88-93.

Jones, J. Weldon. (Dickerson, W. E. and J. Weldon Jones. "Observations On 'The Equity Method' And Intercorporate Relationships," **AR**, 1933, Vol. 8, No. 3, pp. 200-208.)

Jones, J. Weldon. (Dickerson, W. E. and J. Weldon Jones. "Some Observations On The Statement Of Application Of Funds," **AR**, 1931, Vol. 6, No. 4, pp. 277-281.)

Jones, Keith L. and Michael L. Hund. "Filing SEC Registration Statements: A View From The Inside," **JOA**, 1984, Vol. 158, No. 6, pp. 92-107.

Jones, Lou. "Competitor Cost Analysis At Caterpillar," **MA**, 1988, Vol. 70, No. 4, pp. 32-39.

Jones, M. J. "A Longitudinal Study Of The Readability Of The Chairman's Narratives In The Corporate Reports Of A UK Company," **ABR**, 1988, Vol. 18, No. 72, pp. 297-305.

Jones, Philip A. Sr. "The Computer: A Cost-Benefit Analysis," **MA**, 1971, Vol. 53, No. 1, pp. 23-25.

Jones, Phillip A. (Bird, Francis A. and Phillip A. Jones. "A Decision-Tree Approach To Earnings Per Share," **AR**, 1970, Vol. 45, No. 4, pp. 779-783.)

Jones, Ralph Coughenour. "A Flexible Test Grading Formula Which Emphasizes Quality," **AR**, 1950, Vol. 25, No. 4, pp. 445-448.

Jones, Ralph Coughenour. "Accounting Concepts And Standards," **AR**, 1950, Vol. 25, No. 2, pp. 139-141.

Jones, Ralph Coughenour. "Current Practice In Teaching Elementary Accounting," **AR**, 1937, Vol. 12, No. 2, pp. 174-180.

Jones, Ray G. "Analyzing Initial And Growth Financing For Small Businesses," **MA**, 1979, Vol. 61, No. 5, pp. 30-34.

Jones, Ray G., Jr. "You Can Call It Earnings, You Can Call It Income, Or....," **MA**, 1982, Vol. 63, No. 11, pp. 16-25.

Jones, Richard F. "Evils Of Hybrid Accounting," **JOA**, 1951, Vol. 92, No. 2, pp. 206-208.

Jones, Richard W. (Arndt, Terry L. and Richard W. Jones. "Closing The GAAP In Church Accounting," **MA**, 1982, Vol. 64, No. 2, pp. 26-31.)

Jones, Robert L. "Cost Control For Engineering Programs," **MA**, 1966, Vol. 47, No. 10, pp. 25-32.

Jones, Rowan and Maurice Pendlebury. "Uniformity V. Flexibility In The Published Accounts Of Local Authorities: The UK Problem And Some European Solutions," **ABR**, 1981-82, Vol. 12, No. 46, pp. 129-135.

Jones, Rowan H. "Accounting In English Local Government From The Middle Ages To C. 1835," **ABR**, 1984-85, Vol. 15, No. 59, pp. 197-210.

Jones, Rowan H. "Converting The Recognized Needs Of Municipal Financial Report Users Into Responsive Accounting Systems," **AIIA**, 1988, Vol. 2, pp. 285-293.

Jones, Rowan H. "Financial Reporting In Nonbusiness Organisations," **ABR**, 1981-82, Vol. 12, No. 48, pp. 287-295.

Jones, Rowan. (Pendlebury, Maurice and Rowan Jones. "Governmental Budgeting As Ex Ante Financial Accounting: The United Kingdom Case," **JAPP**, 1985, Vol. 4, No. 4, pp. 301-316.)

Jones, Rowan. (Pendlebury, Maurice and Rowan Jones. "Municipal Disclosure In England: Another Market For Excuses?," **IJAER**, 1983, Vol. 18, No. 2, pp. 83-93.)

Jones, Sally Morrow. "The Net Economic Effect Of A 'Widow's Election' In The Community Property States," **JATA**, 1979, Vol. 1, No. 1, pp. 25-32.

Jones, Sally Morrow. (Limberg, Stephen T. and Sally Morrow Jones. "An Analysis Of 'Substantiality' Under The Section 704(b) Final Regulations," **JATA**, 1988, Vol. 10, No. 1, pp. 60-74.)

Jones, Sally M. (Jackson, Betty R. and Sally M. Jones. "Salience Of Tax Evasion Penalties Versus Detection Risk," **JATA**, 1985, Vol. 6, No. 2, pp. 7-17.)

Jones, Thomas W. and J. David Smith. "An Historical Perspective Of Net Present Value And Equivalent Annual Cost," **AHJ**, 1982, Vol. 9, No. 1, pp. 103-110.

Jones, Thomas. "An Analysis Of Bookkeeping As A Branch Of General Education (1842)," **AHJ**, 1977, Vol. 4, No. 2, pp. 29-46.

Jones, Virginia. (Haka, Susan, Lauren Friedman and Virginia Jones. "Functional Fixation And Interference Theory: A Theoretical And Empirical Investigation," **AR**, 1986, Vol. 61, No. 3, pp. 455-474.)

Jones, Walter. "A Procedure To Find Optimal Overrun Quantity," **MA**, 1970, Vol. 51, No. 8, pp. 35-36.

Jones, William O. (Pagani, John and William O. Jones. "Price And Mortality Expectations And Valuation Of Inventories," **AR**, 1950, Vol. 25, No. 3, pp. 315-319.)

Jones, William V. "Setting Up Production Standards," **MA**, 1972, Vol. 54, No. 2, pp. 37-38.

Jones, Wm. Jarell and Catherine R. Ward. "Forecasts And Projections For Third-Party Use," **JOA**, 1986, Vol. 161, No. 4, pp. 100-102.

Jones, W. Elbert. (Hartgraves, Al and W. Elbert Jones. "Use Of Generic Titles By Unlicensed Accountants," **CPAJ**, 1979, Vol. 49, No. 12, pp. 33-38.)

Jonez, John W. (Wright, Michael A. and John W. Jonez. "Material Burdening: Management Accounting CAN Support Competitive Strategy," **MA**, 1987, Vol. 69, No. 2, pp. 27-31.)

Jonson, L. C., B. Jonsson and G. Svensson. "The Application Of Social Accounting To Absenteeism And Personnel Turnover," **AOS**, 1978, Vol. 3, No. 3/4, pp. 261-268.

Jonsson, B. (Jonson, L. C., B. Jonsson and G. Svensson. "The Application Of Social Accounting To Absenteeism And Personnel Turnover," **AOS**, 1978, Vol. 3, No. 3/4, pp. 261-268.)

Jonsson, S. and A. Gronlund. "Life With A Sub-Contractor: New Technology And Management Accounting," **AOS**, 1988, Vol. 13, No. 5, pp. 513-552.

Jonsson, S. "Budgetary Behaviour In Local Government - A Case Study Over 3 Years," **AOS**, 1982, Vol. 7, No. 3, pp. 287-304.

Jonsson, S. (Hedberg, B. and S. Jonsson. "Designing Semi-Confusing Information Systems For Organizations In Changing Environments," **AOS**, 1978, Vol. 3, No. 1, pp. 47-64.)

Joplin, Bruce. "Can The Accountant Manage EDP?," **MA**, 1967, Vol. 49, No. 3, pp. 3-7.

Joplin, Bruce. "Local Government Accounting: It's Your Responsibility, Too," **JOA**, 1967, Vol. 124, No. 2, pp. 38-43.

Joplin, Bruce. "What Business Are We In? Information!," **MA**, 1970, Vol. 51, No. 10, pp. 36-39.

Joplin, H. Bruce. "The Accountant's Role In Management Information Systems," **JOA**, 1966, Vol. 121, No. 3, pp. 43-46.

Jordan, Joseph M. (Krebs, Eric H. and Joseph M. Jordan. "The Insurance Industry After The TRA," **JOA**, 1987, Vol. 164, No. 2, pp. 92-101.)

Jordan, Raymond B. "Cost Reduction: A 'Get Tough' Action Plan," **MA**, 1984, Vol. 65, No. 11, pp. 37-46.

Jordan, Raymond B. "Negotiating Overhead Expense With Confidence," **MA**, 1969, Vol. 51, No. 6, pp. 35-39.

Jordan, Raymond B. "Planning, Organizing and Conducting The Annual Physical Inventory," **MA**, 1977, Vol. 59, No. 2, pp. 33-36.

Jordan, William F. and Rodger G. Holland. "An Empirical Inquiry Into The Determination Of Dividend Equivalence In Stock Redemptions: A Comment," **JATA**, 1984, Vol. 5, No. 2, pp. 75-80.

Jordan, William F. "Capital Recovery Options Under The Economic Recovery Tax Act Of 1981: An Analysis Of Comparative Benefits," **JATA**, 1982, Vol. 3, No. 2, pp. 5-14.

Jordan, William F. "Capital Recovery Options: A Response And A Note On Changes Resulting From The Tax Equity And Fiscal Responsibility Act Of 1982 (TEFRA)," **JATA**, 1983, Vol. 5, No. 1, pp. 63-68.

Jorgensen, Jerry L. (Mano, Ronald M. and Jerry L. Jorgensen. "Assisting Clients In Insurance Evaluation," **CPAJ**, 1981, Vol. 51, No. 1, pp. 27-32.)

Joseph, G. W. (Engle, Terry J. and G. W. Joseph. "A Successful Approach To Integrating Computer Assignments Into Accounting Information Systems Courses," **JAED**, 1986, Vol. 4, No. 2, pp. 141-146.)

Joy, Arthur C. "The Descriptive Case Project For Accounting Information Systems Courses," **JAED**, 1987, Vol. 5, No. 1,

pp. 145-148.

Joy, Arthur C. (Taylor, Martin E., Thomas G. Evans and Arthur C. Joy. "The Impact Of IASC Accounting Standards On Comparability And Consistency Of International Accounting Reporting Practices," **IJAER**, 1986, Vol. 22, No. 1, pp. 1-9.)

Joy, O. Maurice, Robert H. Litzenberger and Richard W. McEnally. "The Adjustment Of Stock Prices To Announcements Of Unanticipated Changes In Quarterly Earnings," **JAR**, 1977, Vol. 15, No. 2, pp. 207-225.

Joyce, Edward J. and Gary C. Biddle. "Anchoring And Adjustment In Probabilistic Inference In Auditing, **JAR**, 1981, Vol. 19, No. 1, pp. 120-145.

Joyce, Edward J. and Gary C. Biddle. "Are Auditors' Judgments Sufficiently Regressive?," **JAR**, 1981, Vol. 19, No. 2, pp. 323-349.

Joyce, Edward J. and Robert Libby. "Behavioral Studies Of Audit Decision Making," **JAL**, 1982, Vol. 1, pp. 103-123.

Joyce, Edward J. and Robert Libby. "Some Accounting Implications Of 'Behavioral Decision Theory': Processes Of Judgment And Choice'," **JAR**, 1981, Vol. 19, No. 2, pp. 544-550.

Joyce, Edward J. "Expert Judgment In Audit Program Planning," **JAR**, 1976, Vol. 14, Supp., pp. 29-60.

Joyce, Edward J., Robert Libby and Shyam Sunder. "Using The FASB's Qualitative Characterisitics In Accounting Policy Choices," **JAR**, 1982, Vol. 20, No. 2, Part II,pp.654-675.

Joyce, James E. "The Overhead Mystique," **MA**, 1968, Vol. 50, No. 3, pp. 43-46.

Joyce, John W. (Murray, Ronald J., William E. Decker and John W. Joyce. "Pension Accounting: Analysis Of 'Preliminary Views' - Part II," **CPAJ**, 1983, Vol. 53, No. 9, pp. 42-47.)

Joyce, John W. (Murray, Ronald J., William E. Decker and John W. Joyce. "Pension Accounting: Analysis Of Preliminary Views - Part I," **CPAJ**, 1983, Vol. 53, No. 8, pp. 10-23.)

Juchau, Roger H. (Baker, H. Kent, Robert H. Chenhall, John A. Haslem and Roger H. Juchau. "Disclosure Of Material Information: A Cross-National Comparison," **IJAER**, 1977, Vol. 13, No. 1, pp. 1-18.)

Juchau, Roger, Mick White and Roger Hopkins. "Tertiary Education Strategies For Accounting In Developing Societies - The Southwest Pacific As A Case Study, **IJAER**, 1986, Vol. 21, No. 2, pp. 145-160.

Juchau, R. (Chenhall, R. H. and R. Juchau. "Investor Information Needs - An Australian Study," **ABR**, 1976-77, Vol. 7, No. 26, pp. 111-119.)

Judd, Frank. "An Approach To Interim Reporting," **MA**, 1970, Vol. 52, No. 4, pp. 21-22.

Judd, Frank. "Development Of Cost Accounting Concepts Of Scheduled Airlines," **AR**, 1949, Vol. 24, No. 1, pp.61-67.

Judd, Frank. "Organizing For Forward Motion," **MA**, 1974, Vol. 55, No. 10, pp. 23-24.

Juers, Donald A. "Statistical Significance Of Accounting Variances," **MA**, 1967, Vol. 49, No. 2, pp. 20-25.

Jung, Woon-Oh and Young K. Kwon. "Disclosure When The Market Is Unsure Of Information Endowment Of Managers," **JAR**, 1988, Vol. 26, No. 1, pp. 146-153.

Jurinski, James John. "A Primer On The Unitary Business Concept," **CPAJ**, 1986, Vol. 56, No. 9, pp. 52-65.

Jurinski, James John. "Taxpayer Strategies In A Unitary Tax Audit," **JOA**, 1986, Vol. 161, No. 1, pp. 91-102.

Juris, Hervey A. (Dittman, David A., Hervey A. Juris and Lawrence Revsine. "Unrecorded Human Assets: A Survey Of Accounting Firms' Training Programs," **AR**, 1980, Vol. 55, No. 4, pp. 640-648.)

Juris, Hervey A. (Dittman, David A., Hervey A. Juris and Lawrence Revsine. "On The Existence Of Unrecorded Human Assets: An Economic Perspective," **JAR**, 1976, Vol. 14, No. 1, pp. 49-65.)

Juskow, David J. "Is Your Credit Policy Effective?," **MA**, 1983, Vol. 64, No. 8, pp. 34-37.

Justis, Robert T. (Ingram, Robert W., Dan M. Guy, Issam J. Merei and Robert T. Justis. "Disclosure Practices In Unaudited Financial Statements Of Small Businesses," **JOA**, 1977, Vol. 144, No. 2, pp. 81-86.)

KKK

Kaback, Hoffer. "Behind The Balance Sheet: A Case Study In Accounting Analysis," **AR**, 1980, Vol. 55, No. 1, pp. 144-167.

Kabbes, S. Madonna. "Is Accounting Meeting The Challenge In Europe?," **AR**, 1965, Vol. 40, No. 2, pp. 395-400.

Kabialis, Edward W. and John W. Benzon. "Accounting For Income Taxes: Proposed Rules," **CPAJ**, 1987, Vol. 57, No. 1, pp. 44-51.

Kaczka, Eugene. (Morrison, Thomas A. and Eugene Kaczka. "A New Application Of Calculus And Risk Analysis To Cost-Volume-Profit Changes," **AR**, 1969, Vol. 44, No. 2, pp. 330-343.)

Kadel, J. Henry. "Contribution Reporting," **MA**, 1972, Vol. 54, No. 5, pp. 40-46.

Kadin, Morris B. and Robert Green. "Computerization In The Medium-Sized CPA Firm," **JOA**, 1971, Vol. 131, No. 2, pp. 44-49.

Kaercher, Jacque E. "A General Retrieval System," **MA**, 1972, Vol. 54, No. 6, pp. 27-30.

Kafer, Karl and V. K. Zimmerman. "Notes On The Evolution Of The Statement Of Sources And Applications Of Funds," **IJAER**, 1967, Vol. 2, No. 2, pp. 89-121.

Kafer, Karl. "European National Uniform Charts Of Accounts," **IJAER**, 1965, Vol. 1, No. 1, pp. 67-83.

Kagle, Arthur R. and William P. Dukes. "Financial Reporting For Pledges At Educational Institutions," **CPAJ**, 1988, Vol. 58, No. 1, pp. 38-45.

Kagle, Arthur R. and William P. Dukes. "A Better Method Of Valuing Liabilities In Annuity Agreements," **MA**, 1980, Vol. 61, No. 10, pp. 37-40.

Kahl, Alfred and Ahmed Belkaoui. "Bank Annual Report Disclosure Adequacy Internationally," **ABR**, 1980-81, Vol. 11, No. 43, pp. 189-196.

Kahl, Alfred. (Belkaoui, Ahmed, Alfred Kahl and Josette Peyrard. "Information Needs Of Financial Analysts: An International Comparison," **IJAER**, 1977, Vol. 13, No. 1, pp. 19-27.)

Kahn, Nathan and Allen Schiff. "Tangible Equity Change And The Evolution Of The FASB's Definition Of Income." **JAAF**, 1985, Vol. 9, No. 1, pp. 40-49.

Kahn, Nathan. "Corporate Motivation For Convertible Bond Debt Exchanges," **JAAF**, 1982, Vol. 5, No. 4, pp. 327-337.

Kahn, Nathan. (Bildersee, John and Nathan Kahn. "A Preliminary Test Of The Presence Of Window Dressing: Evidence From Institutional Stock Trading," **JAAF**, 1987, Vol. 2 (New Series), No. 3, pp. 239-265.)

Kahn, Nathan. (Davis, Harry Z. and Nathan Kahn. "Some Additional Evidence On The LIFO-FIFO Choice Using Replacement Cost Data," **JAR**, 1982, Vol. 20, No. 2, pp. 738-744.)

Kahn, Nathan. (Davis, Harry Z., Nathan Kahn and Etzmun Rozen. "LIFO Inventory Liquidations: An Empirical Study," **JAR**, 1984, Vol. 22, No. 2, pp. 480-496.)

Kaiser, Charles, Jr. "The Challenges Ahead: Now For The Hard Part," **JOA**, 1987, Vol. 163, No. 4, pp. 108-113.

Kalbers, Lawrence P. "Electronic Spreadsheets: Powerful And Flexible Educational Tools," **JAED**, 1984, Vol. 2, No. 2, pp. 163-168.

Kalinski, B. D. "A Case Of Over-Accounting," **AR**, 1963, Vol. 38, No. 3, pp. 591-595.

Kallimanis, William S. "Product Contribution Analysis For Multi-Product Pricing," **MA**, 1968, Vol. 49, No. 11, pp. 3-11.

Kam, Vernon. "Judgment And The Scientific Trend In Accounting," **JOA**, 1973, Vol. 135, No. 2, pp. 52-57.

Kam, Vernon. "The Determination Of 'Substantial Authoritative Support," **CPAJ**, 1972, Vol. 42, No. 9, pp. 723-728.

Kaminarides, John. (Latanich, Gary A. and John Kaminarides. "Performance Of Accountants In International Business," **IJAER**, 1984, Vol. 19, No. 2, pp. 157-164.)

Kamin, J. Y. and J. Ronen. "The Smoothing Of Income Numbers: Some Empirical Evidence On Systematic Differences Among Management-Controlled And Owner-Controlled Firms," **AOS**, 1978, Vol. 3, No. 2, pp. 141-160.

Kamp, John N. "Applications Of Subchapter S," **JOA**, 1960, Vol. 109, No. 6, pp. 51-55.

Kanaga, William S. "Inflation, Instability And Accounting," **MA**, 1977, Vol. 58, No. 9, pp. 15-18.

Kanaga, William S. "International Accounting: The Challenge And The Changes," **JOA**, 1980, Vol. 150, No. 5, pp. 55-61.

Kanarek, Leonard I. (Newman, Barry and Leonard I. Kanarek. "Tax Reform And Net Operating Losses," **CPAJ**, 1977, Vol. 47, No. 2, pp. 17-22.)

Kane, John E. "Depreciation And Maintenance Of Capital During Inflation," **JOA**, 1952, Vol. 94, No. 6, pp. 697-701.

Kane, John E. "Keeping Up With Economic Trends," **JOA**, 1955, Vol. 99, No. 3, pp. 45-48.

Kane, John E. "Structural Changes And General Changes In The Price Level In Relation to Financial Reporting," **AR**, 1951, Vol. 26, No. 4, pp. 496-502.

Kane, Robert L., Jr. and Arthur E. Traxler. "Predicting CPA Examination Results," **AR**, 1954, Vol. 29, No. 4, pp. 564-570.

Kane, Robert L., Jr. "Suggestions To Examination Candidates," **JOA**, 1955, Vol. 99, No. 1, pp. 47-49.

Kang, Sok-Hyon. (Healy, Paul M., Sok-Hyon Kang and Krishna G. Palepu. "The Effect Of Accounting Procedure Changes On CEOs' Cash Salary And Bonus Compensation," **JAEC**, 1987, Vol. 9, No. 1, pp. 7-34.)

Kanodia, Chandra S. "Stochastic Monitoring And Moral Hazard," **JAR**, 1985, Vol. 23, No. 1, pp. 175-193.

Kanodia, Chandra. "Risk Sharing And Transfer Price Systems Under Uncertainty," **JAR**, 1979, Vol. 17, No. 1, pp. 74-98.

Kanter, Howard A. and Marshall K. Pitman. "An Auditing Curriculum For The Future," **IAE**, 1987, Vol. 2, No. 2, pp. 251-263.

Kantor, Jeffrey and Richard Pike. "The Determinants Of The Value Of Unlisted Shares: Opinions Of Professional Valuers In Canada," **ABR**, 1986-87, Vol. 17, No. 66, pp. 109-116.

Kantor, Jeffrey. (Pike, Richard, John Sharp and Jeffrey Kantor. "The Role Of Accounting Information In Valuing Unlisted Shares," **ABR**, 1988, Vol. 18, No. 71, pp. 249-255.)

Kantor, Jeffrey. (Yagil, Joseph, Ben Amoako-Adu and Jeffrey Kantor. "Capital Cost Allowance (Depreciation) And Capital Budgeting In Canada," **IJAER**, 1986, Vol. 21, No. 2, pp. 47-54.)

Kanungo, Rabindra. (Amernic, Joel H., Rabindra Kanungo and Nissim Aranya. "Professional And Work Values Of Accountants: A Cross-Cultural Study," **IJAER**, 1983, Vol. 18, No. 2, pp. 177-192.)

Kaocharern, Sukri. "The Development Of The Securities Exchange In Thailand," **IJAER**, 1976, Vol. 12, No. 1, pp. 19-26.

Kaplan, Alfred. "How To Establish And Operate Accounts For Small Contractor," **JOA**, 1951, Vol. 91,No. 1,pp. 112-115.

Kaplan, Ben. "Accounting Concerns For Nonprofit Institutions," **CA**, 1986, Vol. 4, No. 2, pp. 59-63.

Kaplan, Gene P. "Refinancing Your Company - Trauma Or Opportunity?," **CA**, 1985, Vol. 3, No. 1, pp. 5-11.

Kaplan, Gene P. and Harvey C. Guberman. "Financing In Chapter 11 - Back From The Depths," **CA**, 1986, Vol. 4, No. 2, pp. 26-38.

Kaplan, Howard Gordon. (Solomon, Kenneth Ira and Howard Gordon Kaplan. "Regulation Of The Accounting Profession In Israel," **AR**, 1964, Vol. 39, No. 1, pp. 145-149.)

Kaplan, Maurice C. and Daniel M. Reaugh. "Accounting, Reports To Stockholders, And The SEC," **AR**, 1939, Vol. 14, No. 3, pp. 203-235.

Kaplan, Mitchell and Leonard Jay Schultz. "Deductibility Of Education Expense," **CPAJ**, 1978, Vol. 48, No. 11, pp. 37-40.

Kaplan, Mitchell. (Schultz, Leonard Jay and Mitchell Kaplan. "Let's 'Co-Op' Erate," **CPAJ**, 1981, Vol. 51, No. 2, pp. 35-39.)

Kaplan, Mitchell. (Schultz, Leonard Jay and Mitchell Kaplan. "Tax Aspects Of Damage Settlements," **CPAJ**, 1981, Vol. 51, No. 11, pp. 28-31.)

Kaplan, Mitchell. (Schultz, Leonard Jay and Mitchell Kaplan. "Tax Aspects Of Marital Settlements," **CPAJ**, 1980, Vol. 50, No. 5, pp. 33-37.)

Kaplan, Philip G. (Growe, Gary A. and Philip G. Kaplan. "Surviving The IRS Tax Accrual Decision," **MA**, 1985, Vol. 66, No. 8, pp. 42-45.)

Kaplan, Richard L. "Accountants' Liability And Audit Failures: When The Umpire Strikes Out," **JAPP**, 1987, Vol. 6, No. 1, pp. 1-8.

Kaplan, Robert S. "A Financial Planning Model For An Analytic Review: The Case Of A Savings And Loan Association," **AJPT**, 1982-83, Vol. 2, No. 2, pp. 52-65.

Kaplan, Robert S. and Gerald L. Thompson. "Overhead Allocation Via Mathematical Programming Models," **AR**, 1971, Vol. 46, No. 2, pp. 352-364.

Kaplan, Robert S. and Ulf Peter Welam. "Overhead Allocation With Imperfect Markets And Nonlinear Technology," **AR**, 1974, Vol. 49, No. 3, pp. 477-484.

Kaplan, Robert S. "A Stochastic Model For Auditing," **JAR**, 1973, Vol. 11, No. 1, pp. 38-46.

Kaplan, Robert S. "Comments On Paul Healy: Evidence On the Effect Of Bonus Schemes On Accounting Procedure And Accrual Decisions," **JAEC**, 1985, Vol. 7, No. 1/3, pp. 109-113.

Kaplan, Robert S. "Comments On Wilson And Jensen," **AR**, 1983, Vol. 58, No. 2, pp. 340-346.

Kaplan, Robert S. "Measuring Manufacturing Performance: A New Challenge For Managerial Accounting Research," **AR**, 1983, Vol. 58, No. 4, pp. 686-705.

Kaplan, Robert S. "Optimal Investigation Strategies With Imperfect Information," **JAR**, 1969, Vol. 7, No. 1, pp. 32-43.

Kaplan, Robert S. "Purchasing Power Gains On Debt: The Effect Of Expected And Unexpected Inflation," **AR**, 1977, Vol. 52, No. 2, pp. 369-378.

Kaplan, Robert S. "Sample Size Computations For Dollar-Unit Sampling," **JAR**, 1975, Vol. 13, Supp., pp. 126-133.

Kaplan, Robert S. "Statistical Sampling In Auditing With Auxiliary Information Estimators," **JAR**, 1973, Vol. 11, No. 2, pp. 238-258.

Kaplan, Robert S. "The Evolution Of Management Accounting," **AR**, 1984, Vol. 59, No. 3, pp. 390-418.

Kaplan, Robert S. "Variable And Self-Service Costs In Reciprocal Allocation Models," **AR**, 1973, Vol. 48, No. 4, pp. 738-748.

Kaplan, Robert S. (Cooper, Robin and Robert S. Kaplan. "How Cost Accounting Distorts Product Cost," **MA**, 1988, Vol. 69, No. 10, pp. 20-27.)

Kaplan, Robert S. (Dietrich, J. Richard and Robert S. Kaplan. "Empirical Analysis Of The Commercial Loan Classification Decision," **AR**, 1982, Vol. 57, No. 1, pp. 18-38.)

Kaplan, Robert S. (Hong, Hai, Robert S. Kaplan and Gershon Mandelker. "Pooling Vs. Purchase: The Effects Of Accounting For Mergers On Stock Prices," **AR**, 1978, Vol. 53, No. 1, pp. 31-47.)

Kaplan, Robert S. (Ijiri, Yuji and Robert S. Kaplan. "The Four Objectives Of Sampling In Auditing: Representative, Corrective, Protective And Preventive," **MA**, 1970, Vol. 52, No. 6, pp. 42-44.)

Kaplan, Robert S. (Ijiri, Yuji and Robert S. Kaplan. "A Model For Integrating Sampling Objectives In Auditing," **JAR**, 1971, Vol. 9, No. 1, pp. 73-87.)

Kaplan, Robert S. (Ijiri, Yuji and Robert S. Kaplan. "Probabilistic Depreciation And Its Implication For Group Depreciation," **AR**, 1969, Vol. 44, No. 4, pp. 743-756.)

Kaplan, Robert S. (Ijiri, Yuji and Robert S. Kaplan. "Sequential Models In Probabilistic Depreciation," **JAR**, 1970, Vol. 8, No. 1, pp. 34-46.)

Kaplan, Robert S. (Ijiri, Yuji and Robert S. Kaplan. "The Auditor's Sampling Objectives: Four Or Two? A Reply," **JAR**, 1972, Vol. 10, No. 2, pp. 413-416.)

Kaplan, Robert S. (Ijiri, Yuji and Robert S. Kaplan. "Sampling For Integrated Audit Objectives - A Replay," **AR**, 1978, Vol. 53, No. 3, pp. 773-774.)

Kaplan, Robert S. (Johnson, H. Thomas and Robert S. Kaplan. "The Rise And Fall Of Management Accounting," **MA**, 1987, Vol. 68, No. 7, pp. 22-30.)

Kaplan, R. S. "The Role For Empirical Research In Management Accounting," **AOS**, 1986, Vol. 11, No. 4/5, pp. 429-452.

Kaplan, Steven E. and Philip M. J. Reckers. "Noneconomic

Contributors To Tax Evasion: A Replication," **AIA**, 1987, Vol. 4, pp. 13-32.

Kaplan, Steven E. and Philip M. J. Reckers. "An Empirical Examination Of Auditors' Initial Planning Processes," **AJPT**, 1984-85, Vol. 4, No. 1, pp. 1-19.

Kaplan, Steven E. and Philip M. J. Reckers. "An Examination Of Auditor Performance Evaluation," **AR**, 1985, Vol. 60, No. 3, pp. 477-487.

Kaplan, Steven E. and Philip M. J. Reckers. "An Empirical Examination Of The Effect Of Orientation Information On Audit Judgments," **AIA**, 1986, Vol. 3, pp. 335-357.

Kaplan, Steven E. "An Examination Of The Effects Of Environment And Explicit Internal Control Evaluation On Planned Audit Hours," **AJPT**, 1985-86, Vol. 5, No. 1, pp. 12-25.

Kaplan, Steven E. "An Examination Of The Effect Of Presentation Format On Auditor's Expected Value Judgments," **AH**, 1988, Vol. 2, No. 3, pp. 90-95.

Kaplan, Steven E. "The Effect Of Combining Compliance And Substantive Tasks On Auditor Consensus," **JAR**, 1985, Vol. 23, No. 2, pp. 871-877.

Kaplan, Steven. "Evaluation Of Research On Expectancy Theory Predictions Of Auditor Effort Judgments," **AIA**, 1984, Vol. 1, pp. 175-196.

Kaplan, Steve. (Johnson, Douglas A., Steve Kaplan and Bill B. Hook. "Looking For Mr. Overhead: An Expanded Role For Management Accountants," **MA**, 1983, Vol. 65, No. 5, pp. 65-70.)

Kaplan, S. E., P. M. J. Reckers and S. J. Roark. "An Attribution Theory Analysis Of Tax Evasion Related Judgments," **AOS**, 1988, Vol. 13, No. 4, pp. 371-380.

Kaplowitz, David A. (Herskowitz, Barry and David A. Kaplowitz. "Asset-Based Revolvers," **JOA**, 1986, Vol. 162, No. 1, pp. 97-104.)

Kapnick, Harvey. "Public Accountability - A Challenge For The Accounting Profession," **CPAJ**, 1974, Vol. 44, No. 10, pp. 29-31.

Kapnick, Harvey. "Responsibilities Of The Accounting Profession," **MA**, 1972, Vol. 53, No. 9, pp. 21-24.

Kapnick, Harvey. "Responsibility And Detection In Management Fraud," **CPAJ**, 1976, Vol. 46, No. 5, pp. 19-24.

Kapoor, M. Rai. "Accounting Students' Attributes And Performance: Some Empirical Evidence On General Education," **IAE**, 1988, Vol. 3, No. 1, pp. 108-119.

Karan, Vijay. (Brown, Paul R. and Vijay Karan. "One Approach For Assessing The Operational Nature Of Auditing Standards: An Analysis Of SAS 9," **AJPT**, 1986-87, Vol. 6, No. 1, pp. 134-147.)

Karasyk, Joseph. "The Net Worth Method In Tax Evasion Cases," **CPAJ**, 1979, Vol. 49, No. 4, pp. 35-40.

Karathanassis, G. "Empirical Valuation Models: How Useful Have They Been?," **ABR**, 1982-83, Vol. 13, No. 52, pp. 289-290.

Karchner, Quentin L., Jr. "How One Plant Automated Its Collection Of Data," **MA**, 1980, Vol. 62, No. 3, pp. 45-48.

Kare, Dilip D. and C. Don Wiggins. "How To Estimate The Effect Of A Stock Repurchase," **MA**, 1987, Vol. 68, No. 11, pp. 55-57.

Karlinsky, Stewart S. and Blake Pintar. "Individual Tax Planning Software: A Critical Analysis," **JATA**, 1987, Vol. 8, No. 2, pp. 63-79.

Karlinsky, Stewart S. and Bruce S. Koch. "Impact Of Tax Law Complexity On Professionals," **JATA**, 1987, Vol. 9, No. 1, pp. 24-34.

Karlinsky, Stewart S. "Capital Gains Provisions: Changed By The Tax Act Of 1981, But No Less Complex," **JAAF**, 1983, Vol. 6, No. 2, pp. 157-167.

Karlinsky, Stewart S. "New Tax Laws Impact On Corporate Financial Reporting," **JAAF**, 1983, Vol. 7, No. 1, pp. 65-76.

Karlinsky, Stewart S. (Koch, Bruce S. and Stewart S. Karlinsky. "The Effect Of Federal Income Tax Law Reading Complexity On Students' Task Performance," **IAE**, 1984, No. 1, pp. 98-110.)

Karlinsky, Stewart S. (Manegold, James G. and Stewart S. Karlinsky. "The Security Market Impact Of A Tax Law Change: Possessions Corporation Revisions," **JATA**, 1988, Vol. 9, No. 2, pp. 65-83.)

Karlinsky, Stewart S. (Milliron, Valerie C., Paul R. Watkins and Stewart S. Karlinsky. "Policy Judgments Of Taxpayers: An Analysis Of Criteria Employed," **AIT**, 1988, Vol. 2, pp. xx-xx.)

Karlinsky, Stewart S., James G. Manegold and Alan A. Cherry. "Accounting For Deferred Income Taxes: Preparers' Responses To Policy Proposals," **AIA**, 1987, Vol. 5, pp. 15-38.

Karrenbrock, W. E. "Proof Of Surplus Accruing To A Holding Company When The Investment In A Subsidiary Is Carried At Cost," **AR**, 1958, Vol. 33, No. 3, pp. 461-468.

Karvelis, Leon J., Jr. "The Use And Usefulness Of Governmental Financial Reports: The Perspective Of Municipal Investors," **RIGNA**, 1987, Vol. 3, Part B, pp. 175-188.

Kask, Alex W. "Regression And Correlation Analysis," **CPAJ**, 1979, Vol. 49, No. 10, pp. 35-41.

Kasper, Larry J. "Evaluating The Cost Of Financial Leases," **MA**, 1977, Vol. 58, No. 11, pp. 43-51.

Kastantin, Joseph T. "Revolving Credit: Not Just For The 'Fortune 500'," **MA**, 1986, Vol. 68, No. 2, pp. 50-53.

Katano, Ichiro. "Structure Of Accounting For Changing Money Values," **IJAER**, 1967, Vol. 2, No. 2, pp. 21-36.

Katon, William E. "Property Utilization & Accounting In Federal Government," **JOA**, 1953, Vol. 96, No. 3, pp. 316-323.

Kats, P. "A Surmise Regarding The Origin Of Bookkeeping By Double Entry," **AR**, 1930, Vol. 5, No. 4, pp. 311-316.

Katsoris, Constantine N. "In Defense Of Capital Gains," **CPAJ**, 1974, Vol. 44, No. 4, pp. 39-54.

Katsuyama, Susumu. "Recent Problems Of The Financial Accounting System In Japan," **IJAER**, 1976, Vol. 12, No. 1, pp. 121-131.

Katzenmeyer, Robert G. "Cost Accounting Context Of Seventeen A.I.A. 'Theory Of Account' Examinations," **AR**, 1955, Vol. 30, No. 4, pp. 694-701.

Katz, Adam M., Kevin O'Toole and Linda Trotta. "TRA-1986 And The Hotel/Restaurant Industry," **CPAJ**, 1987, Vol. 57, No. 7, pp. 46-51.

Katz, Barbara Goody and Joel Owen. "Initial Public Offerings: An Equilibrium Model Of Price Determination," **JAAF**, 1987, Vol. 2 (New Series), No. 3, pp. 266-298.

Katz, Jane E. (Fish, Gary L, Larry D. Gipple and Jane E. Katz. "Assessing CPE Needs," **JOA**, 1985, Vol. 160, No. 1, pp. 79-83.)

Katz, Joseph L. (Berry, Leonard Eugene, Gordon B. Harwood and Joseph L. Katz. "Performance Of Auditing Procedures By Governmental Auditors: Some Preliminary Evidence," **AR**, 1987, Vol. 62, No. 1, pp. 14-28.)

Katz, Wilber G. "Accounting Problems In Corporate Distributions," **AR**, 1941, Vol. 16, No. 3, pp. 244-261.

Kauffman, Joseph M. (Dilley, Steven and Joseph M. Kauffman. "The Tax Effects Of Disposing Of A 50 Percent Interest In A Partnership," **CPAJ**, 1978, Vol. 48, No. 7, pp. 23-27.)

Kaufman, Felix and Alan Gleason. "The Effect Of Growth On The Adequacy Of Depreciation Allowances," **AR**, 1953, Vol. 28, No. 4, pp. 539-544.

Kaufman, Felix and Leo A. Schmidt. "Auditing Electronic Records," **AR**, 1957, Vol. 32, No. 1, pp. 33-41.

Kaufman, Felix. "Admission Of The New Partner," **AR**, 1952, Vol. 27, No. 2, pp. 247-248.

Kaufman, Felix. "Effects Of EDP On Internal Control," **JOA**, 1961, Vol. 111, No. 6, pp. 47-59.

Kaufman, Felix. "Professional Consulting By CPAs," **AR**, 1967, Vol. 42, No. 4, pp. 713-720.

Kaufman, Felix. "The Computer, The Accountant And The Next Decade," **JOA**, 1971, Vol. 132, No. 2, pp. 33-39.

Kaufman, Stuart F. "Internal Control Principles Applied To Banks," **JOA**, 1964, Vol. 117, No. 4, pp. 49-55.

Kaulback, Frank S., Jr. "Accounting Problems Of Price Control," **AR**, 1952, Vol. 27, No. 1, pp. 37-43.

Kaulback, Frank S., Jr. "Elementary Accounting And The Non-Accounting Major - A Proposal," **AR**, 1951, Vol. 26, No. 1, pp. 102-104.

Kaulback, Frank S., Jr. "The Faculty Residency Program," **AR**, 1954, Vol. 29, No. 2, pp. 194-195.

Kautter, David J. "Compensation After Tax Reform (Part 2): ESOPs, IRAs And Others," **JOA**, 1987, Vol. 164, No. 6, pp. 40-48.

Kautter, David J. "Compensation After Tax Reform (Part 1): The TRA's Two Waves," **JOA**, 1987, Vol. 164, No. 5, pp. 50-60.

Kawano, M. (Tokutani, M. and M. Kawano. "A Note On The Japanese Social Accounting Literature," **AOS**, 1978, Vol. 3, No. 2, pp. 183-188.)

Kay, Philip W. and Robert O. Wagner. "Is There An Optimum Verification Cycle Of Property Records?," **MA**, 1967, Vol. 49, No. 4, pp. 25-32.

Kay, Robert S. and Raymond J. Beier. "Leveraged Buyout Accounting," **JAAF**, 1987, Vol. 2 (New Series), No. 1, pp. 90-97.

Kay, Robert S. "Disagreements Under Accounting Series Release No. 165," **JOA**, 1976, Vol. 142, No. 4, pp. 75-84.

Kay, Robert S. "The Cohen Commission Report: Some Compliments, Some Criticisms," **JAAF**, 1979, Vol. 2, No. 4, pp. 307-315.

Kaye, G. Roland. (Bhaskar, Krish N. and G. Roland Kaye. "Computers And Accounting Courses: A Reply To Collins," **ABR**, 1984-85, Vol. 15, No. 59, pp. 239-240.)

Kazenski, Paul M. (Means, Kathryn M. and Paul M. Kazenski. "Improving Internal Control Can Cut Audit Costs," **MA**, 1987, Vol. 68, No. 7, pp. 48-51.)

Kazenski, Paul M. (Means, Kathryn M. and Paul M. Kazenski. "SFAS 91: New Dilemmas," **ACCHOR**, 1987, Vol. 1, No. 4, pp. 63-68.)

Kazenski, Paul M. (Means, Kathryn M. and Paul M. Kazenski. "SFAS 34: A Recipe For Diversity," **AH**, 1988, Vol. 2, No. 3, pp. 62-67.)

Keane, John D. (Dietz, Devon D. and John D. Keane. "Integrating Distributed Processing Within A Central Environment," **MA**, 1980, Vol. 62, No. 5, pp. 43-47.)

Keane, John G. "The Marketing Perspective: The CPA's New Image," **JOA**, 1980, Vol. 149, No. 1, pp. 60-66.

Keane, Simon M. "Portfolio Theory, Corporate Objectives And The Disclosure Of Accounting Data," **ABR**, 1973-74, Vol. 4, No. 15, pp. 210-219.

Keane, Simon M. "Share Tipsters And Fair Advertising," **ABR**, 1988, Vol. 18, No. 70, pp. 141-148.

Keane, Simon M. "Some Aspects Of The Cost Of Debt," **ABR**, 1974-75, Vol. 5, No. 20, pp. 298-304.

Keane, Simon M. "The Internal Rate Of Return And The Reinvestment Fallacy," **ABACUS**, 1979, Vol. 15, No. 1, pp. 48-55.

Keane, Simon M. "The Investment Discount Rate - In Defence Of The Market Rate Of Interest," **ABR**, 1975-76, Vol. 6, No. 23, pp. 228-235.

Kearns, Francis and William S. Myott. "Expediting The Scheduling Of Staff Work," **CPAJ**, 1984, Vol. 54, No. 6, pp. 12-21.

Keasey, Kevin and Robert Watson. "The Prediction Of Small

Company Failure: Some Behavioural Evidence For The UK," **ABR**, 1986-87, Vol. 17, No. 65, pp. 49-58.

Keasey, K., R. Watson and P. Wynarczyk. "The Small Company Audit Qualification: A Preliminary Investigation," **ABR**, 1988, Vol. 18, No. 72, pp. 323-333.

Kee, Robert and Bruce Bublitz. "The Role Of Payback In The Investment Process," **ABR**, 1988, Vol. 18, No. 70, pp. 149-156.

Kee, Robert and Oliver Feltus. "The Role Of Abandonment Value In The Investment Decision," **MA**, 1982, Vol. 64, No. 2, pp. 34-42.

Kee, Robert. (Bublitz, Bruce and Robert Kee. "Do We Need Sunset Requirements For FASB Pronouncements?," **JAAF**, 1984, Vol. 7, No. 2, pp. 123-137.)

Kee, Robert. (Bublitz, Bruce and Robert Kee. "Measures Of Research Productivity," **IAE**, 1984, No. 1, pp. 39-60.)

Keef, Stephen P. "Preparation For A First Level University Accounting Course: The Experience In New Zealand," **JAED**, 1988, Vol. 6, No. 2, pp. 293-307.

Keegan, Daniel P., Robert G. Eiler and Joseph V. Anania. "An Advanced Cost Management System For The Factory Of The Future," **MA**, 1988, Vol. 70, No. 6, pp. 31-37.

Keener, Marvin S. (Chasteen, Lanny G. and Marvin S. Keener. "Ranking Convertible Securities For Earnings Per Share: A Graphical Analysis," **IAE**, 1988, Vol. 3, No. 2, pp. 241-247.)

Keenoy, C. L. "The Impact Of Automation On The Field Of Accounting," **AR**, 1958, Vol. 33, No. 2, pp. 230-236.

Keesee, Donald G. "An Alternative To Hedging In Foreign Investments," **MA**, 1970, Vol. 52, No. 1, pp. 74-76.

Keim, Gerald D. (Cooper, Kerry and Gerald D. Keim. "Unsettled Issues In Corporate Disclosure," **CPAJ**, 1977, Vol. 47, No. 3, pp. 27-30.)

Keim, Gerald D. (Cooper, Kerry and Gerald D. Keim. "The Economic Rationale For The Nature And Extent Of Corporate Financial Disclosure Regulation: A Critical Assessment," **JAPP**, 1983, Vol. 2, No. 3, pp. 189-205.)

Keiser, Laurence. "Preparer Penalties," **CPAJ**, 1981, Vol. 51. No. 6, pp. 21-23.

Keiser, Laurence. (Hanigsberg, Oscar and Laurence Keiser. "Preparer Penalties: A New Look - Part I," **CPAJ**, 1980, Vol. 50, No. 3, pp. 19-22.)

Keiser, Laurence. (Hanigsberg, Oscar and Laurence Keiser. "Preparer Penalties: A New Look - Part II," **CPAJ**, 1980, Vol. 50, No. 4, pp. 48-54.)

Keiser, Lawrence. (Schell, Wayne M. and Lawrence Keiser. "Digesting The Passive Activity Rules," **CPAJ**, 1988, Vol. 58. No. 8, pp. 46-55.)

Keister, Orville R. "Cable TV: Clearing Up The Financial Picture," **MA**, 1983, Vol. 64, No. 10, pp. 43-47.

Keister, Orville R. "Commercial Record Keeping In Ancient Mesopotamia," **AR**, 1963, Vol. 38, No. 2, pp. 371-376.

Keister, Orville R. "Consolidations And Intercompany Bond Holdings," **AR**, 1967, Vol. 42, No. 2, pp. 375-376.

Keister, Orville R. "Internal Control For Churches," **MA**, 1974, Vol. 55, No. 7, pp. 40-42.

Keister, Orville R. "LIFO And Inflation," **MA**, 1975, Vol. 56, No. 11, pp. 27-31.

Keister, Orville R. "Test Your Acronym Skills," **MA**, 1985, Vol. 67, No. 2, pp. 68-71.

Keister, Orville R. "The Influence Of Mesopotamian Record-Keeping," **ABACUS**, 1970, Vol. 6, No. 2, pp. 169-181.

Keister, Orville R. "Unexpected Accounting?," **AHJ**, 1974, Vol. 1. No. 1-4, pp. 16-18.

Keister, Orville, R. "The Incan Quipu," **AR**, 1964, Vol. 39, No. 2, pp. 414-416.

Keith, E. Gordon. "Excess Profits Taxation And Profit Limitation," **AR**, 1943, Vol. 18, No. 2, pp. 103-109.

Keith, Robert M. (Dennis, David M. and Robert M. Keith. "Are Litigation Disclosures Inadequate?," **JOA**, 1981, Vol. 151. No. 3, pp. 54-61.)

Kekre, Sunder. (Banker, Rajiv D., Srikant M. Datar and Sunder Kekre. "Relevant Costs, Congestion And Stochasticity In Production Environments," **JAEC**, 1988, Vol. 10. No. 3, pp. 171-197.)

Kell, Walter G. "Public Accounting's Irresistible Force And Immovable Object," **AR**, 1968, Vol. 43, No. 2, pp. 266-273.

Kell, Walter G. "Should The Accounting Entity Be Personified?," **AR**, 1953, Vol. 28, No. 1, pp. 40-43.

Kell, Walter G. "The Commission's Long Run Goals," **AR**, 1958. Vol. 33. No. 2, pp. 198-205.

Keller, Donald E. (Abdallah, Wagdy M. and Donald E. Keller. "Measuring The Multinational's Performance," **MA**, 1985, Vol. 67. No. 4, pp. 26-30.)

Keller, Donald E. (Chrysler, Earl and Donald E. Keller. "Preventing Computer Fraud," **MA**, 1988, Vol. 69, No. 10, pp. 28-33.)

Keller, Donald E. (Krause, Paul and Donald E. Keller. "Bringing World-Class Manufacturing And Accounting To A Small Company," **MA**, 1988, Vol. 70, No. 5, pp. 28-33.)

Keller, Earl C. (Arnold, Jerry L. and Earl C. Keller. "The Influence Of Accounting Rules On Tax Policy Objectives: An Empirical Investigation," **JATA**, 1980, Vol. 1, No. 2, pp. 10-16.)

Keller, I. Wayne. "All Accounting Is Management Accounting," **MA**, 1976, Vol. 58, No. 5, pp. 13-15.

Keller, I. Wayne. "Budgeting For Small Business," **JOA**, 1959. Vol. 107, No. 1, pp. 44-49.

Keller, I. Wayne. "Concepts, Standards, And Rules," **MA**, 1973, Vol. 54, No. 11, pp. 13-15.

Keller, I. Wayne. "Controlling Contribution," **MA**, 1967, Vol. 48. No. 10, pp. 21-32.

Keller, I. Wayne. "Planning Corporate Social Performance,"

MA, 1975, Vol. 56, No. 12, pp. 19-24.

Keller, I. Wayne. "The Accountant's Role In The Expanding International Economy," MA, 1967, Vol. 48, No. 6, pp. 3-7.

Keller, I. Wayne. "The Link Between Accounting And Management," MA, 1969, Vol. 50, No. 10, pp. 36-40.

Keller, Stuart B. and Lewis F. Davidson. "An Assessment Of Individual Investor Reaction To Certain Qualified Audit Opinions," AJPT, 1983-84, Vol. 3, No. 1, pp. 1-22.

Keller, Thomas F. "Another Look At Financial Disclosure," MA, 1969, Vol. 50, No. 6, pp. 19-22.

Keller, Thomas F. "The Annual Income Tax Accrual," JOA, 1962, Vol. 114, No. 4, pp. 59-65.

Keller, Thomas F. "The Investment Tax Credit And The Annual Tax Charge," AR, 1965, Vol. 40, No. 1, pp. 184-189.

Keller, Thomas F. (Dickens, Robert L. and Thomas F. Keller. "The Auditor's Responsibility For His Opinion," JOA, 1963, Vol. 115, No. 3, pp. 41-48.)

Keller, Thomas F. (Hagerman, Robert L., Thomas F. Keller and Russell J. Petersen. "Accounting Research And Accounting Principles," JOA, 1973, Vol. 135, No. 3, pp. 51-55.)

Keller, Thomas F. (Petersen, Russell J. and Thomas F. Keller. "Asset Valuation, Income Determination And Changing Prices," AR, 1972, Vol. 47, No. 4, pp. 801-805.)

Keller, T. F. (Cooper, W. W., N. Dopuch and T. F. Keller. "Budgetary Disclosure And Other Suggestions For Improving Accounting," AR, 1968, Vol. 43, No. 4, pp. 640-648.)

Kelley, Arthur C. "Can Corporate Incomes Be Scientifically Ascertained?," AR, 1951, Vol. 26, No. 3, pp. 289-298.

Kelley, Arthur C. "Comments On The 1957 Revision Of Corporate Accounting And Reporting Standards," AR, 1958, Vol. 33, No. 2, pp. 214-215.

Kelley, Arthur C. "Cost Analysis Of A Cost-Plus Contract," AR, 1942, Vol. 17, No. 4, pp. 370-375.

Kelley, Arthur C. "Definitive Income Determinations: The Measurement Of Corporate Incomes On An Objective Scientific Basis," AR, 1948, Vol. 23, No. 2, pp. 148-153.

Kelley, Arthur C. "In Defense Of The Accountant," AR, 1936, Vol. 11, No. 1, pp. 63-65.

Kelley, Arthur C. "Is Accountancy A Science?," AR, 1941, Vol. 16, No. 3, pp. 231-233.

Kelley, Arthur C. "The Presentation Of Corporate Income And Earned Surplus," AR, 1949, Vol. 24, No. 3, pp. 285-289.

Kelley, Edward H. "Strategies For A Successful Job Search," MA, 1987, Vol. 69, No. 4, pp. 32-36.

Kelley, Edward H. "Toward Better Collections," MA, 1985, Vol. 67, No. 3, pp. 30-34.

Kelley, Eleanor M. (Fitzgerald, Richard D. and Eleanor M. Kelley. "International Disclosure Standards - The United Nations Position," JAAF, 1979, Vol. 3, No. 1, pp. 5-20.)

Kelley, James W. (Davis, Earl F. and James W. Kelley. "The Engagement Letter And Current Legal Developments," JOA, 1972, Vol. 134, No. 6, pp. 54-59.)

Kelley, Patrick J. and Joanne A. Collins. "Good Stuff Bakery: Making More 'Dough' Via Computer Control," MA, 1984, Vol. 65, No. 8, pp. 26-30.

Kelley, Thomas P. and David V. Roscetti. "Auditor/Actuary Relations Under ERISA: From The Auditor's Standpoint," JOA, 1978, Vol. 146, No. 1, pp. 66-71.

Kelley, Thomas P. "Accounting Standards Overload - Time For Action?," CPAJ, 1982, Vol. 52, No. 5, pp. 10-17.

Kelley, Thomas P. "Compilation And Review - A Revolution In Practice," CPAJ, 1979, Vol. 49, No. 4, pp. 19-28.

Kelley, Thomas P. "The Dingell Hearings And Related AICPA Initiatives," AIPIA, 1988, Vol. 2, pp. 157-165.

Kelley, Thomas P. (Chenok, Philip B., Douglas R. Carmichael and Thomas P. Kelley. "Accounting And Auditing: The Technical Challenges Ahead," JOA, 1980, Vol. 150, No. 5, pp. 62-70.)

Kelley, Thomas P. (Cook, J. Michael and Thomas P. Kelley. "Internal Accounting Control: A Matter Of Law," JOA, 1979, Vol. 147, No. 1, pp. 56-64.)

Kelley, Thomas P. (Larson, Rholan E. and Thomas P. Kelley. "Differential Measurement In Accounting Standards: The Concept Makes Sense," JOA, 1984, Vol. 158, No. 5, pp. 78-92.)

Kelley, Tim and Loren Margheim. "The Effect Of Audit Billing Arrangement On Underreporting Of Time And Audit Quality Reduction Acts," AIA, 1987, Vol. 5, pp. 221-233.

Kelley, Tim and Robert E. Seiler. "Auditor Stress And Time Budgets," CPAJ, 1982, Vol. 52, No. 12, pp. 24-36.

Kellogg, Irving. "How To Meet The Challenge Of A Successful Client," JOA, 1962, Vol. 113, No. 3, pp. 36-42.

Kellogg, Irving. "The CPA As Estate Planner," JOA, 1973, Vol. 135, No. 6, pp. 51-61.

Kellogg, Robert L. "Accounting Activities, Security Prices, And Class Action Lawsuits," JAEC, 1984, Vol. 6, No. 3, pp. 185-204.

Kelly, E. C. (Ijiri, Y. and E. C. Kelly. "Multidimensional Accounting And Distributed Databases: Their Implications For Organizations And Society," AOS, 1980, Vol. 5, No. 1, pp. 115-124.)

Kelly, J. Patrick. (Strawser, Robert H., J. Patrick Kelly and Richard T. Hise. "What Causes Stress For Management Accountants?," MA, 1982, Vol. 63, No. 9, pp. 32-37.)

Kelly, Lauren. "Corporate Lobbying And Changes In Financial Or Operating Activities In Reaction To FAS No. 8," JAPP, 1982, Vol. 1, No. 2, pp. 153-173.

Kelly, Lauren. "Corporate Management Lobbying On FAS No. 8: Some Further Evidence," JAR, 1985, Vol. 23, No. 2, pp. 619-632.

Kelly, Lauren. "Positive Theory Research: A Review," JAL, 1983, Vol. 2, pp. 111-150.

Kelly, Lincoln G. "Value To Individual Of Adherence To Code Of Ethics," JOA, 1953, Vol. 96, No. 5, pp. 577-581.

Kelly, Robert R. "Growing Role Of Corporate Tax Administration," MA, 1969, Vol. 50, No. 7, pp. 47-50.

Kelly, Robert R. "Sales And Use Taxation In Interstate Commerce," MA, 1967, Vol. 48, No. 7, pp. 29-35.

Kelly, Thomas H. (Bartlett, Ralph T. and Thomas H. Kelly. "Will FAS No. 33 Solve Inflation Accounting Problems?," MA, 1980, Vol. 61, No. 10, pp. 11-14.)

Kelly, Warren H. "Cost Accounting And Control Of Routine Operations," MA, 1975, Vol. 57, No. 5, pp. 15-18.

Kelly, William E. "Computer Systems: Slaves Or Masters?," MA, 1971, Vol. 53, No. 4, pp. 9-11.

Kelly-Newton, L. "A Sociological Investigation Of The U.S.A. Mandate For Replacement Cost Disclosures," AOS, 1980, Vol. 5, No. 3, pp. 311-322.

Kelsey, Richard L. (Rhode, John Grant, Gary M. Whitsell and Richard L. Kelsey. "An Analysis Of Client-Industry Concentrations For Large Public Accounting Firms," AR, 1974, Vol. 49, No. 4, pp. 772-788.)

Kelso, Raymond L. and Robert R. Elliott. "Bridging Communications Gap Between Accountants And Managers," MA, 1969, Vol. 51, No. 5, pp. 41-43.

Kem, Myron S. (Edwards, H. R., Myron S. Kem and Harrison W. Wilder. "The Use Of Accounting In Business Policy Determination," AR, 1947, Vol. 22, No. 4, pp. 394-404.)

Kemp, Patrick S. "A Further Look At Fairness In Accounting," MA, 1973, Vol. 54, No. 7, pp. 15-16.

Kemp, Patrick S. "A 'Current Topics' Course In The Accounting Curriculum?," AR, 1963, Vol. 38, No. 2, pp. 398-400.

Kemp, Patrick S. "Accounting Data For Planning, Motivation, And Control," AR, 1962, Vol. 37, No. 1, pp. 44-50.

Kemp, Patrick S. "Contribution Margin Reporting For Diversified Companies," MA, 1968, Vol. 49, No. 9, pp. 14-17.

Kemp, Patrick S. "Controversies On The Construction Of Financial Statements," AR, 1963, Vol. 38, No. 1, pp. 126-132.

Kemp, Patrick S. "Criteria For The Selection Of Accounting Methodology," JOA, 1970, Vol. 130, No. 2, pp. 57-61.

Kemp, Patrick S. "Financial Forecasts And Projections," CPAJ, 1986, Vol. 56, No. 7, pp. 34-41.

Kemp, Patrick S. "Post-Completion Audits Of Capital Investment Projects," MA, 1966, Vol. 47, No. 12, pp. 49-54.

Kemp, Patrick S. "The Authority Of The Accounting Principles Board," AR, 1965, Vol. 40, No. 4, pp. 782-787.

Kemp, Robert S., Jr. "An Examination Of The Relationship Of Unfunded Vested Pension Liabilities And Selected Elements Of Firm Value," AIA, 1987, Vol. 5, pp. 59-72.

Kemper, Earl L. (Thompson, William W., Jr. and Earl L. Kemper. "Probability Measures For Estimated Data," AR, 1965, Vol. 40, No. 3, pp. 574-578.)

Kempner, Jack J. "A New Look At The Classification Of Inventories," AR, 1960, Vol. 35, No. 2, pp. 264-271.

Kempner, Jack J. "A Two-Week CPA Coaching Course," AR, 1961, Vol. 36, No. 3, pp. 477-480.

Kempner, Jack J. "An Argument For Small Class Size," AR, 1970, Vol. 45, No. 2, pp. 364-366.

Kempner, Jack J. "Funds Statement Practices Of Certified Public Accounting Firms," AR, 1957, Vol. 32, No. 1, pp. 71-82.

Kempner, Jack J. "Revaluation And Depreciation Of Plant Assets," AR, 1952, Vol. 27, No. 4, pp. 506-513.

Kempster, John H. "The Financial Disclosure Problem Of Municipalities," MA, 1977, Vol. 59, No. 1, pp. 21-23.

Kendall, Donald R., Jr. "How To Evaluate A Lease," CA, 1983, Vol. 1, No. 4, pp. 32-45.

Kendrick, Hazen W. "The Need For Accounting In the Law School Curriculum," AR, 1931, Vol. 6, No. 1, pp. 38-41.

Kendrick, H. W. "The Relationship Of Cost Accounting To Income Determination," AR, 1948, Vol. 23, No. 1, pp. 35-39.

Kenis, Izzettin. "Effects Of Budgetary Goal Characteristics On Managerial Attitudes And Performance," AR, 1979, Vol. 54, No. 4, pp. 707-721.

Kennedy, Duane B. (Elliott, John A. and Duane B. Kennedy. "Estimation And Prediction Of Categorical Models In Accounting Research," JAL, 1988, Vol. 7, pp. 202-242.)

Kennedy, Henry A. "A Behavioral Study Of The Usefulness Of Four Financial Ratios," JAR, 1975, Vol. 13, No. 1, pp. 97-116.

Kennedy, John O. S. (Williams, David J. and John O. S. Kennedy. "A Unique Procedure For Allocating Joint Costs From A Production Process?," JAR, 1983, Vol. 21, No. 2, pp. 644-645.)

Kennelley, Michael D. (Christie, Andrew A., Michael D. Kennelley, J. William King and Thomas F. Schaefer. "Testing For Incremental Information Content In The Presence Of Collinearity," JAEC, 1984, Vol. 6, No. 3, pp. 205-217.)

Kennelley, Michael. (Hillison, William and Michael Kennelley. "The Economics Of Nonaudit Services," AH, 1988. Vol. 2, No. 3, pp. 32-40.)

Kennelley, Michael. (Schaefer, Thomas and Michael Kennelley. "Alternative Cash Flow Measures And Risk-Adjusted Returns," JAAF, 1986, Vol. 1 (New Series), No. 4, pp. 278-287.)

Kennelly, John W. (Baloff, Nicholas and John W. Kennelly. "Accounting Implications Of Product And Process Start-ups," JAR, 1967, Vol. 5, No. 2, pp. 131-143.)

Kennelly, John W. (Beaver, William H., John W. Kennelly and William M. Voss. "Predictive Ability As A Criterion For The Evaluation Of Accounting Data," **AR**, 1968, Vol. 43, No. 4, pp. 675-683.)

Kennelly, John W. (Chambers, R. J., John W. Kennelly, Thomas W. McRae, Frank K. Reilly and W. Keith Weltmer. "Historical Cost Accounting," **ABACUS**, 1971, Vol. 7, No. 1, p. 39.)

Kennelly, John W. (Smith, John H. and John W. Kennelly. "A Seminar In Accounting Research," **AR**, 1970, Vol. 45, No. 4, pp. 795-797.)

Kenny, William. (Hulen, Myron and William Kenny. "Taxation Of A Visiting Professorship After Tax Reform," **IAE**, 1988, Vol. 3, No. 2, pp. 255-269.)

Kent, Arthur H. "The New Internal Auditing And The Need For Specialized Preparatory Training," **AR**, 1955, Vol. 30, No. 4, pp. 638-644.

Kent, D. and M. Theobald. "The Imputation System, Cost Of Capital And Dividend Policy," **ABR**, 1980-81, Vol. 11, No. 41, pp. 61-65.

Kent, Ralph E. "Certified Public Accountancy - Toward A Learned Profession," **CPAJ**, 1974, Vol. 44, No. 11, pp. 25-27.

Kent, Ralph E. "Liability Of Auditors," **JOA**, 1958, Vol. 106, No. 3, pp. 61-66.

Keogh, Eugene J. "What's Ahead In Federal Tax Legislation," **JOA**, 1962, Vol. 113, No. 1, pp. 40-44.

Keoppen, David R. "Using The FASB's Conceptual Framework: Fitting The Pieces Together," **ACCHOR**, 1988, Vol. 2, No. 2, pp. 18-26.

Keown, Arthur J. (Martin, John D., Paul F. Anderson and Arthur J. Keown. "Lease Capitalization And Stock Price Stability: Implications For Accounting," **JAAF**, 1979, Vol. 2, No. 2, pp. 151-164.)

Kermis, George F. and S. Mahapatra. "An Empirical Study Of The Effects Of Time Pressure On Audit Time Allocations," **AIA**, 1985, Vol. 2, pp. 261-274.

Kermode, E. R. "Replacement Cost As Upper Limit Of Value: Further Fallacies," **ABR**, 1978-79, Vol. 9, No. 33, p. 81.

Kern, Charles L., Charles A. Neyhart, Jr. and Clayton A. Hocke. "Statistical Risk And Sample Reliability," **CPAJ**, 1973, Vol. 43, No. 1, pp. 55-60.

Kern, Donald F. (Levy, Louis E. and Donald F. Kern. "SAP No. 49, 'Reports On Internal Control,' - Small Step Or Giant Leap?," **CPAJ**, 1972, Vol. 42, No. 12, pp. 1019-1023.)

Kern, Werner. "The Accounting Concept In German Labor-Oriented Business Management," **IJAER**, 1975, Vol. 10, No. 2, pp. 23-35.

Kerr, H. W. T. "Handling Working Capital In Discounted Cash Flow Calculations," **ABR**, 1970-71, Vol. 1, No. 4, pp. 294-299.

Kerrigan, Harry D. "Accounting Aspects Of Rate-Making In The Public-Utility Field," **AR**, 1951, Vol. 26, No. 3, pp. 352-361.

Kerrigan, Harry D. "Accounting For Stock Dividends Received," **AR**, 1938, Vol. 13, No. 2, pp. 166-173.

Kerrigan, Harry D. "Accounting For Stock Dividends Paid," **AR**, 1937, Vol. 12, No. 4, pp. 369-385.

Kerrigan, Harry D. "Analysis Of Variation In Net Profit," **AR**, 1937, Vol. 12, No. 4, pp. 430-432.

Kerrigan, Harry D. "Corporate Distributions As Income To Stockholders," **AR**, 1938, Vol. 13, No. 4, pp. 366-378.

Kerrigan, Harry D. "Electronic Data Processor - A Milestone In Machine Method," **AR**, 1955, Vol. 30, No. 4, pp. 660-665.

Kerrigan, Harry D. "Intermediate Accounting Instruction - Circa, 1955," **AR**, 1956, Vol. 31, No. 3, pp. 418-422.

Kerrigan, Harry D. "Limitations On Stock Dividends," **AR**, 1937, Vol. 12, No. 2, pp. 238-255.

Kerrigan, Harry D. "Major Influences On Accounting Education," **AR**, 1959, Vol. 34, No. 3, pp. 403-414.

Kerrigan, Harry D. "Recent Data On Accounting Majors And Programs," **AR**, 1959, Vol. 34, No. 2, pp. 262-265.

Kerrigan, Harry D. "Some Current Problems In The Teaching Of Accounting," **AR**, 1952, Vol. 27, No. 1, pp. 79-88.

Kerrigan, Harry D. "Stock Dividends In Trust Distributions," **AR**, 1937, Vol. 12, No. 2, pp. 93-104.

Kerrigan, Harry D. "Taxability Of Stock Dividends Under Federal And State Laws," **AR**, 1936, Vol. 11, No. 4, pp. 373-387.

Kerrigan, Harry D. "Whither Accounting?," **AR**, 1937, Vol. 12, No. 1, pp. 61-63.

Kerrigan, Harry D. (Dixon, Robert L. and Harry D. Kerrigan. "Criticisms Of The Tentative Statement Of Accounting Principles," **AR**, 1941, Vol. 16, No. 1, pp. 49-65.)

Kess, Sidney. "Tax Shelters: Are Post Mortems Premature?," **CPAJ**, 1977, Vol. 47, No. 7, pp. 11-16.

Kesselman, Jerome J. "Federal Income Taxation In The Graduate Accounting Program," **AR**, 1957, Vol. 32, No. 1, pp. 101-103.

Kesselman, Jerome J. "The CPA Curriculum," **JOA**, 1957, Vol. 103, No. 4, pp. 61-65.

Kessler, Lawrence and Robert H. Ashton. "Feedback And Prediction Achievement In Financial Analysis," **JAR**, 1981, Vol. 19, No. 1, pp. 146-162.

Kessler, Louis M. "Professional Education," **JOA**, 1956, Vol. 102, No. 6, pp. 32-37.

Kessler, Stuart. "IRA Discontent," **CPAJ**, 1980, Vol. 50, No. 1, pp. 43-49.

Kessler, Stuart. "The Will Of George Washington," **CPAJ**, 1984, Vol. 54, No. 1, pp. 22-31.

Kester, Roy B. "Education For Professional Accountancy," **AR**, 1936, Vol. 11, No. 2, pp. 99-105.

Kester, Roy B. "Remarks On The Sources Of Capital Surplus'," **AR**, 1934, Vol. 9, No. 1, pp. 81-82.

Kester, Roy B. "The Practitioner's Responsibilities For Accountancy Education," **AR**, 1938, Vol. 13, No. 3, pp. 259-264.

Kester, R. B. "The Importance Of The Controller," **AR**, 1928, Vol. 3, No. 3, pp. 237-251.

Kettering, Floyd F., Jr. (Hindman, William R. and Floyd F. Kettering, Jr. "Integrated MIS: A Case Study," **MA**, 1973, Vol. 55, No. 2, pp. 20-27.)

Kettler, Paul. (Beaver, William H., Paul Kettler and Myron Scholes. "The Association Between Market Determined And Accounting Determined Risk Measures," **AR**, 1970, Vol. 45, No. 4, pp. 654-682.)

Ketz, J. Edward and Arthur R. Wyatt. "The FASB In A World With Partially Efficient Markets," **JAAF**, 1983, Vol. 7, No. 1, pp. 29-43.

Ketz, J. Edward and James A. Largay, III. "Teaching The 'Funds' Statement Under Alternative Valuation Methods," **IAE**, 1985, No. 1, pp. 87-96.

Ketz, J. Edward and James A. Largay, III. "Reporting Income And Cash Flows From Operations," **ACCHOR**, 1987, Vol. 1, No. 2, pp. 9-18.

Ketz, J. Edward and Walter K. Kunitake. "An Evaluation Of The Conceptual Framework: Can It Resolve The Issues Related To Accounting For Income Taxes?," **AIA**, 1988, Vol. 6, pp. 37-54.

Ketz, J. Edward and Walter K. Kunitake. "Demand For And Supply Of SEC Courses," **JAED**, 1985, Vol. 3, No. 1, pp. 91-106.

Ketz, J. Edward. "Accounting For Business Combinations In An Age Of Changing Prices," **ABR**, 1983-84, Vol. 14, No. 55, pp. 209-216.

Ketz, J. Edward. "The Effect Of General Price-Level Adjustments On The Predictive Ability Of Financial Ratios," **JAR**, 1978, Vol. 16, Supp., pp. 273-284.

Ketz, J. Edward. "The Validation Of Some General Price Level Estimating Models," **AR**, 1978, Vol. 53, No. 4, pp. 952-960.

Ketz, J. Edward. "Tithing And Income Measurement," **AHJ**, 1984, Vol. 11, No. 2, pp. 129-132.

Ketz, J. Edward. (Bruttomesso, Raymond I. and J. Edward Ketz. "Historical Cost And General Price Level Tax Rates In Seven Industries," **JATA**, 1982, Vol. 3, No. 2, pp. 30-36.)

Ketz, J. Edward. (Dirsmith, Mark and J. Edward Ketz. "A Fifty-Cent Test: An Approach To Teaching Integrity," **AIA**, 1987, Vol. 5, pp. 129-142.)

Ketz, J. Edward. (Dirsmith, Mark W. J., Edward Ketz and Ronald J. Teichman. "Vertical And Lateral Considerations Of Undergraduate Accounting Honors Programs," **AIA**, 1986, Vol. 3, pp. 301-322.)

Ketz, J. Edward. (Gombola, Michael J. and J. Edward Ketz. "A Note On Cash Flow And Classification Patterns Of Financial Ratios," **AR**, 1983, Vol. 58, No. 1, pp. 105-114.)

Ketz, J. Edward. (Hussein, Mohamed Elmuttasim and J. Edward Ketz. "Ruling Elites Of The FASB: A Study Of The Big Eight," **JAAF**, 1980, Vol. 3, No. 4, pp. 354-367.)

Key, Stephen L. and Simon S. Strauss. "Allocating Purchase Price In An Acquisition: A Practical Guide," **JOA**, 1987, Vol. 164, No. 5, pp. 32-37.

Keyes, David E. (Delaney, Patrick R., David E. Keyes, Curtis L. Norton and John R. Simon. "An Admission Test For Intermediate Accounting," **AR**, 1979, Vol. 54, No. 1, pp. 155-162.)

Keyserlingk, Alexander N. "International Public Accounting: An Underdeveloped Profession," **IJAER**, 1975, Vol. 11, No. 1, pp. 15-22.

Keys, David E. and Curtis Norton. "Estimation Error In Income Determination: A Comment," **AR**, 1978, Vol. 53, No. 4, pp. 997-1002.

Keys, David E. and James A. Hendricks. "The Ethics Of Accounting Research," **JAED**, 1984, Vol. 2, No. 2, pp. 77-88.

Keys, David E. "Confidence Interval Financial Statements: An Empirical Investigation," **JAR**, 1978, Vol. 16, No. 2, pp. 389-399.

Keys, David E. "Six Problems In Accounting For N/C Machines," **MA**, 1986, Vol. 68, No. 5, pp. 38-47.

Keys, David E. (Everett, John O. and David E. Keys. "Quantifying The Poisoning Effect Of Tax Preference Items On The Maximum Tax For A High-Bracket Taxpayer," **JATA**, 1981, Vol. 2, No. 2, pp. 12-19.)

Khandwalla, Pradip N. "The Effect Of Different Types Of Competition On The Use Of Management Controls," **JAR**, 1972, Vol. 10, No. 2, pp. 275-285.

Khanna, R. K. and A. Bottomley. "Costs And Returns On Graduates Of The University Of Bradford," **ABR**, 1970-71, Vol. 1, No. 1, pp. 56-70.

Khanna-Bardouille, R. "Comparative Costs Of Undergraduate Education At The University Of Bradford 1966-67 And 1969-70," **ABR**, 1972-73, Vol. 3, No. 9, pp. 70-76.

Kharabe, Prakash S. and P. R. Chandy. "Private Placements: An Overview For The Financial Executive," **CA**, 1986, Vol. 4, No. 3, pp. 59-65.

Khemakhem, Abdellatif. "A Simulation Of Management-Decision Behavior: 'Funds' And Income," **AR**, 1968, Vol. 43, No. 3, pp. 522-534.

Khodadoust, T. and Paul Frishkoff. "On Mercantile Accounting In Pre-Industrial Iran," **AHJ**, 1979, Vol. 6, No. 1, pp. 53-62.

Khtaian, George A. "Strategic Financial Models For A Utility," **MA**, 1977, Vol. 58, No. 12, pp. 47-51.

Kida, Thomas E. and Ronald C. Mannino. "Job Selection Criteria Of Accounting Ph.D. Students And Faculty

Members," **AR**, 1980, Vol. 55, No. 3, pp. 491-500.

Kida, Thomas E. (Anderson, Thomas N., Jr. and Thomas E. Kida. "The Cross-Lagged Research Approach: Description And Illustration," **JAR**, 1982, Vol. 20, No. 2, Part I, pp. 403-414.)

Kida, Thomas. "An Investigation Into Auditors' Continuity And Related Qualification Judgments," **JAR**, 1980, Vol. 18, No. 2, pp. 506-523.

Kida, Thomas. "The Effect Of Causality And Specificity On Data Use," **JAR**, 1984, Vol. 22, No. 1, pp. 145-152.

Kida, Thomas. "The Impact Of Hypothesis-Testing Strategies On Auditors' Use Of Judgment Data," **JAR**, 1984, Vol. 22, No. 1, pp. 332-340.

Kida, T. E. "Performance Evaluation And Review Meeting Characteristics In Public Accounting Firms," **AOS**, 1984, Vol. 9, No. 2, pp. 137-148.

Kiefer, Gene H. "Systems Auditing With Test Decks," **MA**, 1972, Vol. 53, No. 12, pp. 14-18.

Kiesey, Douglas T. and Ernest J. Pavlock. "Trends In Management Education For CPAs," **JOA**, 1975, Vol. 139, No. 5, pp. 48-53.

Kiger, Jack E. and Carl S. Warren. "Visiting Professorships," **AR**, 1975, Vol. 50, No. 2, pp. 387-391.

Kiger, Jack E. and Jan R. Williams. "An Emerging Concept Of Income Presentation," **AHJ**, 1977, Vol. 4, No. 2, pp. 63-77.

Kiger, Jack E. "An Empirical Investigation of NYSE Volume And Price Reactions To The Announcement Of Quarterly Earnings," **JAR**, 1972, Vol. 10, No. 1, pp. 113-128.

Kiger, Jack E. "Implications Of Volatility In Quarterly Accounting Data: A Reply," **AR**, 1975, Vol. 50, No. 1, pp. 130-132.

Kiger, Jack E. "Volatility In Quarterly Accounting Data," **AR**, 1974, Vol. 49, No. 1, pp. 1-7.

Kiger, Jack E. (Scheiner, James H. and Jack E. Kiger. "An Empirical Investigation Of Auditor Involvement In Non-Audit Services," **JAR**, 1982, Vol. 20, No. 2, Part I, pp. 482-496.)

Kiger, Jack E. (Scheiner, James H. and Jack E. Kiger. "Generalized Audit Software: A Classroom Approach," **IAE**, 1983, No. 1, pp. 123-131.)

Kiger, Jack E., James B. Wilcox and Jan R. Williams. "Intraperiod Income Tax Allocation With Differential Rates," **AR**, 1977, Vol. 52, No. 3, pp. 716-720.

Killian, G. E. "Auditing For Payables And Contingent Liabilities," **JOA**, 1952, Vol. 93, No. 1, pp. 60-65.

Killough, Larry N. and Hian C. Koh. "The Going-Concern Concept," **CPAJ**, 1986, Vol. 56, No. 7, pp. 24-33.

Killough, Larry N. and Thomas L. Souders. "A Goal Programming Model For Public Accounting Firms," **AR**, 1973, Vol. 48, No. 2, pp. 268-279.

Killough, Larry N. "Does Management Accounting Have A Theoretical Structure?," **MA**, 1972, Vol. 53, No. 10, pp. 20-22.

Killough, Larry N. "Systems Framework For Capital Expenditure Program Development," **MA**, 1970, Vol. 52, No. 4, pp. 29-32.

Killough, Larry N. (Brown, Robert M. and Larry N. Killough. "How PCs Can Solve The Cost Allocation Problem," **MA**, 1988, Vol. 70, No. 5, pp. 34-38.)

Kilmann, R. H. "The Costs Of Organization Structure: Dispelling The Myths Of Independent Divisions And Organization-Wide Decision Making," **AOS**, 1983, Vol. 8, No. 4, pp. 341-360.

Kilpatrick, Bob G. (Crumbley, D. Larry, Nicholas G. Apostolou and Bob G. Kilpatrick. "Retirement Plan Alternatives," **CPAJ**, 1986, Vol. 56, No. 7, pp. 48-59.)

Kilpatrick, Bob, Karl Putnam and Harold Schneider. "Convertible Securities And Earnings Per Share: A Competitive Ranking Algorithm," **AR**, 1985, Vol. 60, No. 3, pp. 526-530.

Kilvington, Kenneth W. "The Management Accountant: A British Study," **MA**, 1975, Vol. 56, No. 11, pp. 32-38.

Kilzer, James R. and Gary G. Glausser. "Closing The Small Business Management Gap," **MA**, 1984, Vol. 65, No. 11, pp. 57-61.

Kim, David H. (Ziebart, David A. and David H. Kim. "An Examination Of The Market Reactions Associated With SFAS No. 8 And SFAS No. 52," **AR**, 1987, Vol. 62, No. 2, pp. 343-357.)

Kim, Hyo Seuk, John Neter and James T. Godfrey. "Behavior Of Statistical Estimators In Multilocation Audit Sampling," **AJPT**, 1986-87, Vol. 6, No. 2, pp. 40-58.

Kim, Hyo Seuk. (Neter, John, Hyo Seuk Kim and Lynford E. Graham. "On Combining Stringer Bounds For Independent Monetary Unit Samples From Several Populations," **AJPT**, 1984-85, Vol. 4, No. 1, pp. 75-88.)

Kim, Il-Woon and Kung H. Chen. "Empirical Research On The Information Content Of Financial Leverage: A Review And Critique," **JAL**, 1987, Vol. 6, pp. 88-110.

Kim, K. J. (Becker, Edward A. and K. J. Kim. "Direct Material Variances: Review Of The Mix And Yield Variances," **IAE**, 1988, Vol. 3, No. 1, pp. 1-16.)

Kim, K. Kyu. "Organizational Coordination And Performance In Hospital Accounting Information Systems: An Empirical Investigation," **AR**, 1988, Vol. 63, No. 3, pp. 472-489.

Kim, Moshe and Giora Moore. "Economic Vs. Accounting Depreciation," **JAEC**, 1988, Vol. 10, No. 2, pp. 111-125.

Kim, Seung H. and Paul J. Kuzdrall. "The Simulation Of Financial Strategy Under Fluctuating Exchange Rates Conditions," **IJAER**, 1977, Vol. 12, No. 2, pp. 93-107.

Kim, Seung H. (Kim, Suk H., Trevor Crick and Seung H. Kim. "Do Executives Practice What Academics Preach?," **MA**, 1986, Vol. 68, No. 5, pp. 49-52.)

Kim, Suk Hi. "An Integer Programming Model For Direct

Foreign Investment Projects," **MA**, 1977, Vol. 58, No. 10, pp. 47-50.

Kim, Suk H. and Edward J. Farragher. "Current Capital Budgeting Practices," **MA**, 1981, Vol. 62, No. 12, pp. 26-31.

Kim, Suk H. and Trevor Crick. "How Non-U.S. MNCs Practice Capital Budgeting," **MA**, 1984, Vol. 65, No. 7, pp. 28-31.

Kim, Suk H. "Making The Long-Term Investment Decision," **MA**, 1979, Vol. 60, No. 9, pp. 41-49.

Kim, Suk H., Trevor Crick and Seung H. Kim. "Do Executives Practice What Academics Preach?," **MA**, 1986, Vol. 68, No. 5, pp. 49-52.

Kimball, H. G. "Depreciation And Savings," **AR**, 1935, Vol. 10, No. 4, pp. 365-369.

Kimball, H. G. "The Importance Of Understanding Income And Profits," **AR**, 1935, Vol. 10, No. 2, pp. 131-135.

Kimbrell, Janet I. (Boatsman, James R., C. Dwayne Dowell and Janet I. Kimbrell. "Valuing Stock Used For A Business Combination," **JAAF**, 1984, Vol. 8, No. 1, pp. 35-43.)

Kimelman, Johannes. "Material Mix And Yield Variances," **MA**, 1969, Vol. 50, No. 6, pp. 42-43.

Kimes, James D. "20 Attributes Of An Effective Manager," **MA**, 1988, Vol. 70, No. 1, pp. 50-53.

Kimes, James D. "Are Your Really Managing Your Inventory?," **MA**, 1984, Vol. 65, No. 8, pp. 70-73.

Kimes, James D. "Donating Inventory Can Improve Profitability," **MA**, 1985, Vol. 66, No. 8, pp. 38-41.

Kimes, James D. "Making Your Meetings Count," **MA**, 1987, Vol. 68, No. 7, pp. 56-59.

Kimes, J. D. "Handling Stress In The Accounting Profession," **MA**, 1977, Vol. 59, No. 3, pp. 17-23.

Kimmill, Dennis Lee. "Consolidation Models At Acquisition: Purchase And Pooling Of Interest Methods," **MA**, 1976, Vol. 51, No. 3, pp. 628-632.

Kinard, James C. (Hofstedt, Thomas R. and James C. Kinard. "A Strategy For Behavioral Accounting Research," **AR**, 1970, Vol. 45, No. 1, pp. 38-54.)

Kinard, J. C. (Ijiri, Y., J. C. Kinard and F. B. Putney. "An Integrated Evaluation System For Budget Forecasting And Operating Performance With A Classified Budgeting Bibliography," **JAR**, 1968, Vol. 6, No. 1, pp. 1-28.)

Kindelan, James W. "Techniques Of Auditing Fire Loss Insurance Claims," **JOA**, 1954, Vol. 98, No. 5, pp. 639-642.

Kinfu, Johannes. (Jones, Gardner M. and Johannes Kinfu. "The Birth Of An Accounting Profession: The Ethiopian Experience," **IJAER**, 1971, Vol. 7, No. 1, pp. 89-98.)

King Walter W. (Griswold, Henry J. and Walter W. King. "How To Make Salary Raises Under WSB Regulations," **JOA**, 1951, Vol. 92, No. 2, pp. 180-183.)

King, Alfred M. "Accounting Problems Raised By A Foreign Subsidy," **MA**, 1966, Vol. 47, No. 11, pp. 23-29.

King, Alfred M. "Budgeting Foreign Exchange Losses," **MA**, 1969, Vol. 51, No. 4, pp. 39-41.

King, Alfred M. "Check-Account Payroll System," **MA**, 1970, Vol. 51, No. 12, pp. 49-50.

King, Alfred M. "Fair Value Reporting," **MA**, 1975, Vol. 56, No. 9, pp. 25-30.

King, Alfred M. "Price-Level Restatement: Solution Or Problem?," **MA**, 1976, Vol. 58, No. 5, pp. 16-18.

King, Anthony W. "Fair-Value Accounting," **MA**, 1975, Vol. 57, No. 4, pp. 24-26.

King, Arthur J. (Detweiler, John H., Sean O. Vessey and Arthur J. King. "A Model For Computing Shipyard Overhead," **JCA**, 1987, Vol. 4, No. 1, pp. 71-93.)

King, Barry G. "Cost-Effectiveness Analysis: Implications For Accountants," **JOA**, 1970, Vol. 129, No. 3, pp. 43-49.

King, D. (Briston, R. J., C. R. Tomkins and D. King. "Shareholder Behaviour In The New Issue Market: A Preliminary Report," **ABR**, 1970-71, Vol. 1, No. 3, pp. 233-241.)

King, Earle C. "Current Accounting Problems," **AR**, 1950, Vol. 25, No. 1, pp. 35-44.

King, Earle C. "Presentation Of Pertinent Data In Financial Statements," **AR**, 1948, Vol. 23, No. 4, pp. 345-354.

King, Edmund B. "A Control System Of Profitability Of New Products," **MA**, 1968, Vol. 49, No. 11, pp. 35-42.

King, J. William. (Christie, Andrew A., Michael D. Kennelley, J. William King and Thomas F. Schaefer. "Testing For Incremental Information Content In The Presence Of Collinearity," **JAEC**, 1984, Vol. 6, No. 3, pp. 205-217.)

King, Karl G. (Welke, William R. and Karl G. King. "Using The Computer As An Audit Tool," **CPAJ**, 1972, Vol. 42, No. 11, pp. 930-935.)

King, Randle R. and C. David Baron. "An Integrated Account Structure For Governmental Accounting And Financial Reporting," **AR**, 1974, Vol. 49, No. 1, pp. 76-87.

King, Raymond D. and Terrence B. O'Keefe. "Lobbying Activities And Insider Trading," **AR**, 1986, Vol. 61, No. 1, pp. 76-90.

King, Raymond D. "The Effect Of Convertible Bond Equity Values On Dilution And Leverage," **AR**, 1984, Vol. 59, No. 3, pp. 419-431.

King, Robert W. "Effect Of Inventory Valuation Methods On Profits," **AR**, 1947, Vol. 22, No. 1, pp. 45-53.

King, Thomas E. and Alan K. Ortegren. "Accounting For Hybrid Securities: The Case Of Adjustable Rate Convertible Notes," **AR**, 1988, Vol. 63, No. 3, pp. 522-535.

King, Thomas E. and Valdean C. Lembke. "Reporting Investor Income Under The Equity Method," **JOA**, 1976, Vol. 142, No. 3, pp. 65-72.

King, Thomas E. "Accounting Standards For Reporting

Unincorporated Partnerships In Corporate Financial Statements," **JAAF**, 1979, Vol. 2, No. 3, pp. 209-223.

King, Thomas E. (Burnett, Tom, Thomas E. King and Valdean C. Lembke. "Equity Method Reporting For Major Finance Company Subsidiaries," **AR**, 1979, Vol. 54, No. 4, pp. 815-823.)

King, Thomas E. (Capettini, Robert and Thomas E. King. "Exchanges Of Nonmonetary Assets: Some Changes," **AR**, 1976, Vol. 51, No. 1, pp. 142-147.)

King, Thomas E. (Carver, M. Robert, Jr. and Thomas E. King. "Attitudes Of Accounting Practitioners Towards Accounting Faculty And Accounting Education," **JAED**, 1986, Vol. 4, No. 1, pp. 31-43.)

Kinkade, David. (Chazen, Charles, David Kinkade and C. Peter Davis. "A Primer For Novice Restaurant Owners," **CPAJ**, 1985, Vol. 55, No. 11, pp. 10-19.)

Kinnard, William N., Jr. "Advising Clients On Site Selection," **JOA**, 1959, Vol. 108, No. 2, pp. 42-45.

Kinney, James R. (Myers, John H. and James R. Kinney. "A Computer Experiment In The Auditing Class," **AR**, 1972, Vol. 47, No. 2, pp. 390-392.)

Kinney, Robert L. "Why Pension Funds Are Looking At Real Estate," **MA**, 1980, Vol. 61, No. 10, pp. 15-19.

Kinney, William R., Jr. and Andrew D. Bailey, Jr. "Regression Analysis As A Means Of Determining Audit Sample Size: A Comment," **AR**, 1976, Vol. 51, No. 2, pp. 395-401.

Kinney, William R., Jr. and Carl S. Warren. "The Decision-Theory Approach To Audit Sampling: An Extension And Application To Receivables Confirmation," **JAR**, 1979, Vol. 17, No. 1, pp. 275-285.

Kinney, William R., Jr. and Gerald L. Salamon. "Regression Analysis In Auditing: A Comparison Of Alternative Investigation Rules," **JAR**, 1982, Vol. 20, No. 2, Part I, pp. 350-366.

Kinney, William R., Jr. and Wilfred C. Uecker. "Mitigating The Consequences Of Anchoring In Auditor Judgments," **AR**, 1982, Vol. 57, No. 1, pp. 55-69.

Kinney, William R., Jr. "A Decision Theory Approach To The Sampling Problem In Auditing," **JAR**, 1975, Vol. 13, No. 1, pp. 117-132.

Kinney, William R., Jr. "A Note On Compounding Probabilities In Auditing," **AJPT**, 1982-83, Vol. 2, No. 2, pp. 13-22.

Kinney, William R., Jr. "An Environmental Model For Performance Measurement In Multi-Outlet Businesses," **JAR**, 1969, Vol. 7, No. 1, pp. 44-52.

Kinney, William R., Jr. "ARIMA And Regression In Analytical Review: An Empirical Test," **AR**, 1978, Vol. 53, No. 1, pp. 48-60.

Kinney, William R., Jr. "Attention-Directing Analytical Review Using Accounting Ratios: A Case Study," **AJPT**, 1986-87, Vol. 6, No. 2, pp. 59-73.

Kinney, William R., Jr. "Attestation Research Opportunities: 1987," **CAR**, 1988, Vol. 4, No. 2, pp. 416-425.

Kinney, William R., Jr. "Audit Technology And Preferences For Auditing Standards," **JAEC**, 1986, Vol. 8, No. 1, pp. 73-89.

Kinney, William R., Jr. "Covariability Of Segment Earnings And Multisegment Company Returns: A Reply," **AR**, 1974, Vol. 49, No. 1, pp. 140-145.

Kinney, William R., Jr. "Covariability Of Segment Earnings And Multisegment Company Returns," **AR**, 1972, Vol. 47, No. 2, pp. 339-345.

Kinney, William R., Jr. "Decision Theory Aspects Of Internal Control System Design/Compliance And Substantive Tests," **JAR**, 1975, Vol. 13, Supp., pp. 14-29.

Kinney, William R., Jr. "Empirical Accounting Research Design For Ph.D. Students," **AR**, 1986, Vol. 61, No. 2, pp. 338-350.

Kinney, William R., Jr. "Integrating Audit Tests: Regression Analysis And Partitioned Dollar-Unit Sampling," **JAR**, 1979, Vol. 17, No. 2, pp. 456-475.

Kinney, William R., Jr. "Predicting Earnings: Entity Versus Subentity Data," **JAR**, 1971, Vol. 9, No. 1, pp. 127-136.

Kinney, William R., Jr. "Predicting Auditor-Initiated Adjustments Using Paired Balance Methods," **JAAF**, 1981, Vol. 5, No. 1, pp. 5-17.

Kinney, William R., Jr. "Quantitative Applications In Auditing," **JAL**, 1983, Vol. 2, pp. 187-204.

Kinney, William R., Jr. "The Auditor's Sampling Objectives: Four Or Two?," **JAR**, 1972, Vol. 10, No. 2, pp. 407-412.

Kinney, William R., Jr. "The Predictive Power Of Limited Information In Preliminary Analytical Review: An Empirical Study," **JAR**, 1979, Vol. 17, Supp., pp. 148-165.

Kinney, William R., Jr. "The Use Of Time-Shared Interactive Computer In Audit Education," **AR**, 1974, Vol. 49, No. 3, pp. 590-594.

Kinney, William R., Jr. (Banks, Doyle W. and William R. Kinney, Jr. "Loss Contingency Reports And Stock Prices: An Empirical Study," **JAR**, 1982, Vol. 20, No. 1, pp. 240-254.)

Kinney, William R., Jr. (Felix, William L., Jr. and William R. Kinney, Jr. "Research In The Auditor's Opinion Formulation Process: State Of The Art," **AR**, 1982, Vol. 57, No. 2, pp. 245-271.)

Kinney, William R., Jr. (Uecker, Wilfred C., Arthur P. Brief and William R. Kinney, Jr. "Perception Of The Internal And External Auditor As A Deterrent To Corporate Irregularities," **AR**, 1981, Vol. 56, No. 3, pp. 465-478.)

Kinney, William R., Jr. (Zuber, George R., Robert K.

Elliott, William R. Kinney, Jr., and James J. Leisenring. "Using Materiality In Audit Planning," **JOA**, 183, Vol. 155, No. 3, pp. 42-55.)

Kinney, W. R., Jr. (Uecker, W. C. and W. R. Kinney, Jr. "Judgmental Evaluation Of Sample Results: A Study Of The Type And Severity Of Errors Made By Practising CPAs," **AOS**, 1977, Vol. 2, No. 3, pp. 269-275.)

Kinnunen, Raymond M. (Janell, Paul A. and Raymond M. Kinnunen. "Portrait Of The Divisional Controller," **MA**, 1980, Vol. 61, No. 12, pp. 15-19.)

Kinsman, Michael D. and Bruce Samuelson. "Personal Financial Statements: Valuation Challenges And Solutions," **JOA**, 1987, Vol. 164, No. 3, pp. 138-150.

Kintzele, Philip L. (Bagby, John W. and Philip L. Kintzele. "Management's Responsibilities For Management Reports," **CPAJ**, 1982, Vol. 52, No. 11, pp. 30-39.)

Kintzele, Philip L. (Bagby, John W. and Philip L. Kintzele. "Management Discussion And Analysis: Discretionary Disclosures And The Business Segment," **ACCHOR**, 1987, Vol. 1, No. 1, pp. 51-60.)

Kirby, Barbara J. "Establishing Control Through Computer Systems Development," **CA**, 1983, Vol. 1, No. 3, pp. 39-43.

Kircher, Paul and Robert Buchele. "How To Recruit Accounting Personnel," **JOA**, 1955, Vol. 99, No. 5, pp. 54-59.

Kircher, Paul. "Accounting Entries And National Accounts," **AR**, 1953, Vol. 28, No. 2, pp. 191-198.

Kircher, Paul. "Classification And Coding Of Accounting Information," **AR**, 1967, Vol. 42, No. 3, pp. 537-543.

Kircher, Paul. "Coding Accounting Principles," **AR**, 1965, Vol. 40, No. 4, pp. 742-752.

Kircher, Paul. "Investments In Corporate Reports," **AR**, 1950, Vol. 25, No. 1, pp. 89-93.

Kircher, Paul. "Seven Major Problems In Handling The New Industrial Pension Plans," **JOA**, 1950, Vol. 90, No. 4, pp. 290-300.

Kircher, Paul. "Study Of A Successful Computer System," **JOA**, 1957, Vol. 104, No. 4, pp. 59-65.

Kircher, Paul. "The Course In Accounting Theory," **AR**, 1951, Vol. 26, No. 1, pp. 106-111.

Kircher, Paul. "Theory And Research In Management Accounting," **AR**, 1961, Vol. 36, No. 1, pp. 43-49.

Kircher, Paul. (Buckley, John W., Paul Kircher and Russell L. Mathews. "Methodology In Accounting Theory," **AR**, 1968, Vol. 43, No. 2, pp. 274-283.)

Kircher, Paul. (Call, Donald P. and Paul Kircher. "The Investment Credit Moratorium," **JOA**, 1967, Vol. 123, No. 3, pp. 47-52.)

Kircher, Paul. (Rothchild, Richard M. and Paul Kircher. "Projecting Capital Needs," **JOA**, 1955, Vol. 100, No. 3, pp. 51-56.)

Kiringoda, Dayal. (Sadhwani, Arjan T., M. H. Sarhan and Dayal Kiringoda. "Just-In-Time: An Inventory System Whose Time Has Come," **MA**, 1985, Vol. 67, No. 6, pp. 36-44.)

Kirk, Donald J. "Business And The FASB: The Need For Effective Interaction," **MA**, 1978, Vol. 60, No. 3, pp. 17-20.

Kirk, Donald J. "Looking Back On Fourteen Years At The FASB:The Education Of A Standard Setter," **ACCHOR**, 1988, Vol. 2, No. 1, pp. 8-17.

Kirk, Donald J. "The FASB: Serving Its Constituency," **MA**, 1976, Vol. 57, No. 12, pp. 11-14.

Kirk, Donald J. "The Impact Of Management Accounting On GAAP," **MA**, 1985, Vol. 67, No. 1, pp. 26-30.

Kirkham, Edward J. "Depreciation Under The Income Tax," **AR**, 1936, Vol. 11, No. 4, pp. 345-372.

Kirkham, E. J. and C. J. Gaa. "Is There A Theory Basis For Audit Procedure?," **AR**, 1939, Vol. 14, No. 2,pp. 139-146.

Kirkman, P. R. A. "What Can We Learn From Published Accounts In The USA?," **ABR**, 1970-71, Vol. 1, No. 4, pp. 329-334.

Kirkpatrick, D. L. I. and P. G. Pugh. "Towards The Starship Enterprise - Are The Current Trends In Defence Unit Costs Inexorable?," **JCA**, 1985, Vol. 2, No. 1, pp. 59-80.

Kirkpatrick, D. L. I. "The Rising Cost Of Defence Equipment," **JCA**, 1987, Vol. 4, No. 1, pp. 39-58.

Kirkpatrick, John L. "The Gaps In International GAAP," **CA**, 1985, Vol. 3, No. 4, pp. 3-10.

Kirschbaum, Robert T. "Measuring Profitability In The Equipment Rental Business," **MA**, 1972, Vol. 53, No. 7, pp. 41-45.

Kirschner, Daniel. "Construction Audit Services For Owners," **CPAJ**, 1979, Vol. 49, No. 1, pp. 19-25.

Kissell, Jeffrey C. and Edward C. Beauvais. "Competition And Local Telephone Company Accounting," **CA**, 1986, Vol. 4, No. 2, pp. 50-58.

Kissin, Warren and Ronald Zulli. "Valuation Of A Closely Held Business," **JOA**, 1988, Vol. 165, No. 6, pp. 38-48.

Kissin, Warren. (Schaps, Albert L., Warren Kissin, Jay Borow and Lynda Atanian. "Auditing Small Businesses - A New Look," **CPAJ**, 1984, Vol. 54, No. 10, pp. 12-23.)

Kissinger, John N. "A General Theory Of Evidence As The Conceptual Foundation In Auditing Theory: Some Comments And Extensions," **AR**, 1977, Vol. 52, No. 2, pp. 322-339.

Kissinger, John N. "Audit Timing Decisions: A Normative Model. A Practical Heuristic, And Some Empirical Evidence," **AJPT**, 1983-84, Vol. 3, No. 1, pp. 42-54.

Kissinger, John N. "In Defense Of Interperiod Income Tax Allocation," **JAAF**, 1986, Vol. 1 (New Series), No. 2, pp. 90-101.

Kistler, Linda H. and John G. Hamer. "Understanding The New Statement Of Cash Flows," **CA**, 1988, Vol. 6, No. 1, pp. 3-9.

Kistler, Linda H. and Robert M. Jennings. "An Accounting Primer Circa 1831," **AR**, 1969, Vol. 44, No. 1, pp. 168-173.

Kistler, Linda H. "Stock Option Disclosures Are Inadequate," **AR**, 1967, Vol. 42, No. 4, pp. 758-766.

Kistler, Linda H. "Tax Planning In The Elementary Course," **AR**, 1966, Vol. 41, No. 4, pp. 773-775.

Kistler, Linda H. "The Middlesex Canal - An Analysis Of The Accounting and Management," **AHJ**, 1980, Vol. 7, No. 1, pp. 43-57.

Kistler, Linda H., Clairmont P. Carter and Brackston Hinchey. "Planning And Control In The 19th Century Ice Trade," **AHJ**, 1984, Vol. 11, No. 1, pp. 19-30.

Kistner, Klaus-Peter and Timo Salmi. "General Price Level Accounting And Inventory Valuation: A Comment," **JAR**, 1980, Vol. 18, No. 1, pp. 297-311.

Kitchen, J. "Fixed Asset Values: Ideas On Depreciation 1892-1914," **ABR**, 1978-79, Vol. 9, No. 36, pp. 281-291.

Kitchen, J. "The Accounts Of British Holding Company Groups: Some Thoughts On Development In The Early Years," **ABR**, 1971-72, Vol. 2, No. 6, pp. 114-136.

Kitrosser, Edward. (Dropkin, Murray and Edward Kitrosser. "The Government Audit Maze," **CPAJ**, 1982, Vol. 52, No. 1, pp. 24-29.)

Klaassen, Jan. "An Accounting Court: The Impact Of The Enterprise Chamber On Financial Reporting In The Netherlands," **AR**, 1980, Vol. 55, No. 2, pp. 327-341.

Klaassen, Jan. (Schreuder, Hein and Jan Klaassen. "Confidential Revenue And Profit Forecasts By Management And Financial Analysts: Evidence From The Netherlands," **AR**, 1984, Vol. 59, No. 1, pp. 64-77.)

Klammer, Thomas P. and Horace Brock. "Resolving Accounting Issues Without A Conceptual Framework," **CPAJ**, 1975, Vol. 45, No. 8, pp. 15-20.

Klammer, Thomas P. (Byars, Richard B. and Thomas P. Klammer. "The Pluses Of The Practical Capacity Concept Of Cost Allocation," **CA**, 1983, Vol. 1, No. 2, pp. 20-25.)

Klammer, Thomas P. (Copeland, Benny R. and Thomas P. Klammer. "Should The IRS Promulgate Generally Accepted Accounting Principles?," **CPAJ**, 1972, Vol. 42, No. 3, pp. 217-220.)

Klammer, Thomas P. (Gibson, Charles H., Thomas P. Klammer and Sarah A. Reed. "The Cash Flow Statement," **CPAJ**, 1986, Vol. 56, No. 11, pp. 18-39.)

Klammer, Thomas P. (Reed, Sarah A. and Thomas P. Klammer. "Perceptions Of National AAA Meetings," **JAED**, 1986, Vol. 4, No. 2, pp. 5-17.)

Klammer, Thomas. "The Association Of Capital Budgeting Techniques With Firm Performance," **AR**, 1973, Vol. 48, No. 2, pp. 353-364.

Klammer, T. P. (Giese, J. W. and T. P. Klammer. "Achieving The Objectives Of APB Opinion No. 19," **JOA**, 1974, Vol. 137, No. 3, pp. 54-61.)

Klarman, Herbert E. "Do Hospitals Need Cost Accounting To Solve Efficiency And Rate-Making Problems?," **JOA**, 1950, Vol. 89, No. 5, pp. 396-399.

Klasny, Edward M. and James M. Williams. "Tracking Current Governmental Standards," **JOA**, 1982, Vol. 154, No. 1, pp. 60-73.

Klasny, Edward M. (Johnson, Richard D., Edward M. Klasny and Patrick McNamee. "ASB Proposes New SAS On Compliance Auditing," **JOA**, 1988, Vol. 165, No. 6, pp. 76-87.)

Klayman, Robert A. (Caplin, Mortimer M. and Robert A. Klayman. "Depreciation - 1965 Model," **JOA**, 1965, Vol. 119, No. 4, pp. 34-42.)

Kleckner, Robert A. "The Deregulation Of Public Accounting," **IAE**, 1985, No. 1, pp. 157-162.

Kleerekoper, I. "The Economic Approach To Accounting," **JOA**, 1963, Vol. 115, No. 3, pp. 36-40.

Kleespie, Dee L. (Winborne, Marilynn G. and Dee L. Kleespie. "Tax Allocation In Perspective," **AR**, 1966, Vol. 41, No. 4, pp. 737-744.)

Klein, Michael F., Jr. "Tax Upheaval In The Private Pension System," **CA**, 1983, Vol. 1, No. 2, pp. 35-41.

Klein, Richard B. "Inter-Country Purchasing Power Index Numbers," **MA**, 1972, Vol. 54, No. 2. pp. 28-32.

Kleiner, Morris M. "Public Policy Implications Of Financial Information Requirements Under The National Labor Relations Act," **JAPP**, 1984, Vol. 3, No. 4, pp. 253-257.

Kleiner, Morris M. (Gordon, Lawrence A., Morris M. Kleiner and R. Natarajan. "Federal Capital Expenditures And Budget Deficits: Gross National Product And Labor Implications," **JAPP**, 1986, Vol. 5, No. 4, pp. 217-232.)

Klersey, George F., Chen-En Ko and Thomas W. Lin. "Use Of A Multi-Attribute Utility Model In Computer System Selection," **JIS**, 1988, Vol. 3, No. 1, pp. 1-9.

Klick, H. D. (Harrell, A. M. and H. D. Klick. "Comparing The Impact Of Monetary And Nonmonetary Human Asset Measures On Executive Decision Making," **AOS**, 1980, Vol. 5, No. 4, pp. 393-400.)

Klingler, John P. and James B. Savage. "Deciphering The New Accounting For Income Tax Rules," **MA**, 1988, Vol. 70, No. 2, pp. 32-38.

Klink, Eileen S. (Hopewell, Rita J., Eileen S. Klink and Reuben W. Coleman. "Facing The Ethics Involved In Technical Obsolescence," **MA**, 1984, Vol. 66, No. 6, pp. 26-29.)

Klink, James J. and James M. Degnan. "New Accounting For Investors In Real Estate Ventures," **CPAJ**, 1980, Vol. 50, No. 1, pp. 11-20.

Klink, James J. "Accounting For Real Estate Sales - It's A New Ball Game," **CPAJ**, 1974, Vol. 44, No. 2, pp. 35-40.

Klink, James J. (Braitman, Howard L. James J. Klink and Bernard M. Shapiro. "Real Estate Industry Benefits From ERTA 1981," **CPAJ**, 1982, Vol. 52, No. 3, pp. 32-38.)

Klion, Stanley R. "MAS Practice: Are The Critics Justified?," **JOA**, 1978, Vol. 145, No. 6, pp. 72-78.

Klipper, Harold. "Breakeven Analysis With Variable Product Mix," **MA**, 1978, Vol. 59, No. 10, pp. 51-54.

Knapp, Michael C. and Bart H. Ward. "An Integrative Analysis Of Audit Conflict: Sources, Consequences And Resolution," **AIA**, 1987, Vol. 4, pp. 267-286.

Knapp, Michael C. and Fara Elikai. "Auditor Changes: A Note On The Policy Implications Of Recent Analytical And Empirical Research," **JAAF**, 1988, Vol. 3 (New Series), No. 1, pp. 78-86.

Knapp, Michael C. "An Empirical Study Of Audit Committee Support For Auditors Involved In Technical Disputes With Client Management," **AR**, 1987, Vol. 62, No. 3, pp. 578-588.

Knapp, Michael C. "Audit Conflict: An Empirical Study Of The Perceived Ability Of Auditors To Resist Management Pressure," **AR**, 1985, Vol. 60, No. 2, pp. 202-211.

Knapp, Michael C. "Avoiding Problem Banks," **JOA**, 1985, Vol. 159, No. 5, pp. 98-113.

Knapp, Michael C. "The Bank Audit: More Challenge And Risk," **CPAJ**, 1984, Vol. 54, No. 2, pp. 16-22.

Knapp, Michael C. "Toward A More Coherent Regulatory Policy For Auditor Changes: An Empirical Study Of Their Impact On Financial Statement Credibility," **RIAR**, 1988, Vol. 2, pp. 41-59.

Knauf, Janine B. and Miklos A. Vasarhelyi. "Empirical Characteristics Of Debenture Conversions The Issue Of Equivalency," **JAAF**, 1987, Vol. 2 (New Series), No. 1, pp. 43-64.

Knauf, Lawrence B. "Increasing Cash Flow In Corporate Acquisitions After TEFRA," **CA**, 1983, Vol. 1, No. 2, pp. 3-12.

Knauth, Oswald W. "An Executive Looks At Accountancy," **JOA**, 1957, Vol. 103, No. 1, pp. 29-32.

Knechel, W. Robert and Doug Snowball. "Accounting Internships And Subsequent Academic Performance: An Empirical Study," **AR**, 1987, Vol. 62, No. 4, pp. 799-807.

Knechel, W. Robert. "A Simulation Model For Evaluating Accounting System Reliability," **AJPT**, 1984-85, Vol. 4, No. 2, pp. 38-62.

Knechel, W. Robert. "A Stochastic Model Of Error Generation In Accounting Systems," **ABR**, 1984-85, Vol. 15, No. 59, pp. 211-222.

Knechel, W. Robert. "An Analysis Of Alternative Error Assumptions In Modeling The Reliability Of Accounting Systems." **JAR**, 1985, Vol. 23, No. 1, pp. 194-212.

Knechel, W. Robert. "The Effectiveness Of Nonstatistical Analytical Review Procedures Used As Substantive Audit Tests," **AJPT**, 1988, Vol. 8, No. 1, pp. 87-107.

Knechel, W. Robert. "The Effectiveness Of Statistical Analytical Review As A Substantive Auditing Procedure: A Simulation Analysis," **AR**, 1988, Vol. 63, No. 1, pp. 74-95.

Knechel, W. Robert. "The Use Of Quantitative Models In The Review And Evaluation Of Internal Control: A Survey And Review," **JAL**, 1983, Vol. 2, pp. 205-219.

Kneer, Dan C. and Joseph W. Wilkinson. "Data-Base Management Systems: Do You Know Enough To Choose?," **MA**, 1984, Vol. 66, No. 3, pp. 30-38.

Kneer, Dan C. and Kurt Pany. "SAS 43 - Explanation And Analysis," **CPAJ**, 1983, Vol. 53, No. 8, pp. 38-43.

Kneer, Dan C. "Masters Degree Programs In Accounting Information Systems/EDP Auditing," **JIS**, 1986, Vol. 1, No. 1, pp. 137-144.

Kneer, Dan C. "The Teaching Of An Effective And Efficient Audit Strategy," **IAE**, 1984, No. 1, pp. 121-135.

Kneer, Dan C. (Baldwin, Bruce A. and Dan C. Kneer. "EDP Audit Education And EDP Auditor Characteristics: Empirical Data From Practitioners And Professors," **IAE**, 1986, Vol. 1, No. 1, pp. 153-167.)

Kneer, Dan C. (Jennings, Marianne, Dan C. Kneer and Philip M. J. Reckers. "A Reexamination Of The Concept Of Materiality: Views Of Auditors, Users And Officers Of The Court," **AJPT**, 1986-87, Vol. 6, No. 2, pp. 104-115.)

Kneer, Dan C. (Reckers, Philip M. J., Dan C. Kneer and Marianne M. Jennings. "Concepts Of Materiality And Disclosure," **CPAJ**, 1984, Vol. 54, No. 12, pp. 20-31.)

Knight, Kenneth E. (Summers, Edward L. and Kenneth E. Knight. "The AICPA Studies MAS In CPA Firms," **JOA**, 1975, Vol. 139, No. 3, pp. 56-64.)

Knight, Lee G. and Ray A. Knight. "Claiming The Home Office Deduction," **JOA**, 1985, Vol. 160, No. 6, pp. 85-101.

Knight, Lee G. and Ray A. Knight. "An Update On Tax-Free Reorganizations," **CPAJ**, 1988, Vol. 58, No. 11, pp. 58-64.

Knight, Lee G. and Ray A. Knight. "Possibility For A Captive Insurance Subsidiary," **CPAJ**, 1988, Vol. 58, No. 5, pp. 48-55.

Knight, Lee G., Ray A. Knight and Jep Robertson. "Tax Status Of Hybrid Securities," **CPAJ**, 1988, Vol. 58, No. 9, pp. 44-50.

Knight, Ray A. (Knight, Lee G. and Ray A. Knight. "Possibility For A Captive Insurance Subsidiary," **CPAJ**, 1988, Vol. 58, No. 5, pp. 48-55.)

Knight, Ray A. (Knight, Lee G. and Ray A. Knight. "Claiming The Home Office Deduction," **JOA**, 1985, Vol. 160, No. 6, pp. 85-101.)

Knight, Ray A. (Knight, Lee G. and Ray A. Knight. "An Update On Tax-Free Reorganizations," **CPAJ**, 1988, Vol. 58, No. 11, pp. 58-64.)

Knight, Ray A. (Knight, Lee G., Ray A. Knight and Jep Robertson. "Tax Status Of Hybrid Securities," **CPAJ**, 1988, Vol. 58, No. 9, pp. 44-50.)

Knight, Robert G. "Accounting Education - From The Point Of View Of The Business Employer," **AR**, 1953, Vol. 28, No. 3, pp. 343-349.

Knight, Roger N. and Gregory B. Tomlinson. "The Internal Auditor And The Annual Audit," **MA**, 1976, Vol. 58, No. 6, pp. 27-28.

Knight, Royal E. and Donald R. Zook. "Controllers And CPAs Evaluate Relevance Of Education Topics," **MA**, 1982, Vol. 64, No. 5, pp. 30-35.

Knights, David. "Risk, Financial Self-Discipline, And Commodity Relations: An Analysis Of The Growth And Development Of Life Insurance In Contemporary Capitalism," **AIPIA**, 1988, Vol. 2, pp. 47-69.

Knights, D. and D. Collinson. "Disciplining The Shopfloor: A Comparison Of The Disciplinary Effects Of Managerial Psychology And Financial Accounting," **AOS**, 1987, Vol. 12, No. 4/5, pp. 457-478.

Knittel, Roger F. "Help Wanted - Accountants," **AR**, 1939, Vol. 14, No. 2, pp. 158-162.

Knoblett, James A. (Ecton, William W. and James A. Knoblett. "Attitudes Of Management Accountants On The Investment Credit Issue," **MA**, 1970, Vol. 52, No. 3, pp. 36-37.)

Knoblett, James A. (Levitan, Alan S. and James A. Knoblett. "Indicators Of Exceptions To The Going Concern Assumption," **AJPT**, 1985-86, Vol. 5, No. 1, pp. 26-39.)

Knobloch, John J., Donald C. Schindler and Joseph R. Blotzer. "Maintenance Work Authorization And Control," **MA**, 1970, Vol. 51, No. 11, pp. 19-22.

Knoll, Christopher H. "Confirming Brokers' Accounts With Customers On A Test Basis," **JOA**, 1954, Vol. 97, No. 6, pp. 685-687.

Knoll, M. "Auditor's Report - Society's Expectations V. Realities," **ABR**, 1975-76, No. 23, pp. 182-200.

Knopp, Russell. "Jobs And Juniors," **AR**, 1939, Vol. 14, No. 4, pp. 391-395.

Knortz, Herbert C. "The New Financial Environment," **MA**, 1975, Vol. 56, No. 9, pp. 13-18.

Knowles, Asa S. and William C. White. "Teaching Load Of Accounting Instructors," **AR**, 1940, Vol. 15, No. 2, pp. 166-169.

Knowlton, Don. "The Semantics Of Annual Reports," **AR**, 1947, Vol. 22, No. 4, pp. 360-366.

Knutila, Chester. "CPA, Client And Government Agency Co-Operation," **JOA**, 1968, Vol. 125, No. 2, pp. 41-43.

Knutson, Peter H. "An Empirical Study Of The Cost Of Convertible Securities," **JAR**, 1971, Vol. 9, Supp., pp. 99-112.

Knutson, Peter H. "Income Distribution: The Key to Earnings Per Share," **AR**, 1970, Vol. 45, No. 1, pp. 55-68.

Knutson, Peter H. (Blakely, Edward J. and Peter H. Knutson. "L.I.F.O. Or L.O.F.I. - Which?," **AR**, 1963, Vol. 38, No. 1, pp. 75-86.)

Ko, Chen-En, Christopher J. Nachtsheim, Gordon L. Duke and Andrew D. Bailey, Jr. "On The Robustness Of Model-Based Sampling In Auditing," **AJPT**, 1988, Vol. 7, No. 2, pp. 119-136.

Ko, Chen-En. (Bailey, Andrew D., Jr., Gordon Leon Duke, James Gerlach, Chen-En Ko, Rayman D. Meservy and Andrew B. Whinston. "TICOM And The Analysis Of Internal Controls," **AR**, 1985, Vol. 60, No. 2, pp. 186-201.)

Ko, Chen-En. (Klersey, George F., Chen-En Ko and Thomas W. Lin. "Use Of A Multi-Attribute Utility Model In Computer System Selection," **JIS**, 1988, Vol. 3, No. 1, pp. 1-9.)

Kocan, Peter. "Geographical Distribution Of Earnings And Assets," **JOA**, 1963, Vol. 115, No. 6, pp. 49-54.

Kocan, Peter. "Reporting The Operations Of Jointly Owned Companies," **JOA**, 1962, Vol. 113, No. 2, pp. 54-59.

Koch, Albert A. (Black, Stephen F. and Albert A. Koch. "Replacement Cost - Charting The Uncharted Sea," **JOA**, 1976, Vol. 142, No. 5, pp. 72-76.)

Koch, Alfred P. "A Fallacy In Accounting For Spoiled Goods," **AR**, 1960, Vol. 35, No. 3, pp. 501-502.

Koch, Alfred P. "The Unconventional In Accounts Payable," **AR**, 1960, Vol. 35, No. 3, pp. 511-514.

Koch, Bruce S. and Stewart S. Karlinsky. "The Effect Of Federal Income Tax Law Reading Complexity On Students' Task Performance," **IAE**, 1984, No. 1, pp. 98-110.

Koch, Bruce S. "Income Smoothing: An Experiment," **AR**, 1981, Vol. 56, No. 3, pp. 574-586.

Koch, Bruce S. (Karlinsky, Stewart S. and Bruce S. Koch. "Impact Of Tax Law Complexity On Professionals," **JATA**, 1987, Vol. 9, No. 1, pp. 24-34.)

Koch, Bruce S. (Merino, Barbara D., Bruce S. Koch and Kenneth L. MacRitchie. "Historical Analysis - A Diagnostic Tool For 'Events' Studies: The Impact Of The Securities Act Of 1933," **AR**, 1987, Vol. 62, No. 4, pp. 748-762.)

Koch, Bruce S. (Reed, Sarah A. and Bruce S. Koch. "The Race: A View From The 'Pits' Of Accounting," **AIA**, 1987, Vol. 5, pp. 113-128.)

Koch, Donald G. "A Plan For Distributing Deferred Compensation To High-Bracket Executives," **MA**, 1980, Vol. 61, No. 10, pp. 30-33.

Koch, Helmut. "The Concept Of Synchronized Profit And Loss Accounting In Response To Continuous Increases Or Decreases In Prices," **IJAER**, 1986, Vol. 21, No. 2, pp. 133-144.

Kochanek, Ricahrd F. "Segmental Financial Disclosure By Diversified Firms And Security Prices: A Reply," **AR**, 1975, Vol. 50, No. 4, pp. 822-825.

Kochanek, Richard Frank. "Segmental Financial Disclosure By Diversified Firms And Security Prices," **AR**, 1974, Vol. 49, No. 2, pp. 245-258.

Kochanek, Richard F. and Corine T. Norgaard. "Student Perceptions Of Alternative Accounting Careers - Part II," **CPAJ**, 1985, Vol. 55, No. 6, pp. 26-33.

Kochanek, Richard F. and Corine T. Norgaard. "Analyzing The Components Of Operating Cash Flow: The Charter Company," **ACCHOR**, 1988, Vol. 2, No. 1, pp. 58-66.

Kochanek, Richard F. and Corine T. Norgaard. "Student Perceptions Of Alternative Accounting Careers - Part I," **CPAJ**, 1985, Vol. 55, No. 5, pp. 36-43.

Kochanek, Richard F. (Grinnell, D. Jacque and Richard F. Kochanek. "LIFO Disclosures: Requirements And Restrictions," **CPAJ**, 1976, Vol. 46, No. 11, pp. 29-32.)

Kochanek, Richard F. (Grinnell, D. Jacque and Richard F. Kochanek. "The New Accounting Standards For Leases," **CPAJ**, 1977, Vol. 47, No. 10, pp. 15-22.)

Kochanek, Richard, Bimal Prodhan and Harold Wyman. "CMAs Can Learn From The U.K. Experience," **MA**, 1985, Vol. 67, No. 5, pp. 38-42.

Kocher, Jerry. (Crescenzi, Adam D. and Jerry Kocher. "Management Support Systems: Opportunity For Controllers," **MA**, 1984, Vol. 65, No. 9, pp. 34-37.)

Kodama, Atsuyoshi. (Ohno, Kimiyoshi, Hideo Ichikawa and Atsuyoshi Kodama. "Recent Changes In Accounting Standards In Japan," **IJAER**, 1975, Vol. 11, No. 1, pp. 107-120.)

Koeblitz, William M. (Novak, Frank S. and William M. Koeblitz. "Pensions: The Surprise Package In Corporate Marriage," **MA**, 1984, Vol. 65, No. 7, pp. 50-55.)

Koehler, John T. "Renegotiation Board Will Favor Efficient Contractors," **JOA**, 1952, Vol. 93, No. 6, pp. 689-693.

Koehler, Robert W. "Statistical Variance Control: Through Performance Reports And On-The-Spot Observation," **MA**, 1969, Vol. 51, No. 6, pp. 42-46.

Koehler, Robert W. "The Effect Of Internship Programs On Subsequent College Performance," **AR**, 1974, Vol. 49, No. 2. pp. 382-384.

Koehler, Robert W. "The Relevance Of Probability Statistics To Accounting Variance Control," **MA**, 1968, Vol. 50, No. 2. pp. 35-41.

Koenig, Michael E. D. "Cost Containment In Information Systems," **JCA**, 1984, Vol. 1, No. 1, pp. 175-185.

Koester, Robert and William Carson. "An Appraisal Of Collegiate Business Students' Understanding Of Price-Level-Adjusted Financial Statements," **AR**, 1976, Vol. 51, No. 3, pp. 625-627.

Koester, Robert J. and Lane K. Anderson. "Accounting For Plant Removal Costs: A Solution," **MA**, 1983, Vol. 65, No. 5, pp. 75-80.

Koh, Hian C. (Killough, Larry N. and Hian C. Koh. "The Going-Concern Concept," **CPAJ**, 1986, Vol. 56, No. 7, pp. 24-33.)

Kohl, Maybelle. "Objectives Of Accounting Education In The Liberal Arts College," **AR**, 1961, Vol. 36, No. 4, pp. 631-634.

Kohler, Eric L. "Accounting Practices In State Agencies," **JOA**, 1959, Vol. 108, No. 2, pp. 52-60.

Kohler, Eric L. "Depreciation And The Price Level," **AR**, 1948, Vol. 23, No. 2, pp. 131-136.

Kohler, Eric L. "Examinations Of The American Institute Of Accountants," **AR**, 1927, Vol. 2, No. 4, pp. 354-361.

Kohler, Eric L. "In All My Years," **AHJ**, 1975, Vol. 2, No. 1-4, pp. 27-30.

Kohler, Eric L. "Notes On Activity Accounting," **IJAER**, 1967, Vol. 2, No. 2, pp. 59-64.

Kohler, Eric L. "On Developing International Accounting Meanings," **IJAER**, 1965, Vol. 1, No. 1, pp. 35-40.

Kohler, Eric L. "Restoration Of Fixed Asset Values To The Balance Sheet," **AR**, 1947, Vol. 22, No. 2, pp. 200-203.

Kohler, Eric L. "Why Not Retain Historical Cost?," **JOA**, 1963, Vol. 116, No. 4, pp. 35-41.

Kohler, E. L. and W. W. Cooper. "Costs, Prices And Profits: Accounting In The War Program," **AR**, 1945, Vol. 20, No. 3, pp. 267-307.

Kohler, E. L. "A C.P.A. Problem," **AR**, 1931, Vol. 6, No. 4, pp. 308-310.

Kohler, E. L. "A Federal Income-Tax Chart For 1936," **AR**, 1935, Vol. 10, No. 4, pp. 406-407.

Kohler, E. L. "Accounting Concepts And National Income," **AR**, 1952, Vol. 27, No. 1, pp. 50-56.

Kohler, E. L. "Aspects Of National Income," **AR**, 1953, Vol. 28, No. 2, p. 178.

Kohler, E. L. "Essential Elements In A Program Of Internal Audit," **AR**, 1953, Vol. 28, No. 1, pp. 17-24.

Kohler, E. L. "Expenditure Controls In The United States Government," **AR**, 1945, Vol. 20, No. 1, pp. 31-43.

Kohler, E. L. "Grading C.P.A. Papers," **AR**, 1932, Vol. 7, No. 1, pp. 67-68.

Kohler, E. L. "Needed: A Research Plan For Accountancy," **AR**, 1932, Vol. 7, No. 1, pp. 1-10.

Kohler, E. L. "Solution To Problem In December Issue," **AR**, 1932, Vol. 7, No. 2, pp. 142-144.

Kohler, E. L. "Some Principles For Terminologists," **AR**, 1935, Vol. 10, No. 1, pp. 31-33.

Kohler, E. L. "Some Tentative Propositions Underlying Consolidated Reports," **AR**, 1938, Vol. 13, No. 1, pp. 63-72.

Kohler, E. L. "Standards: A Dialogue," **AR**, 1935, Vol. 10, No. 4, pp. 370-378.

Kohler, E. L. "Tendencies In Balance Sheet Construction," **AR**, 1926, Vol. 1, No. 4, pp. 1-11.

Kohler, E. L. "The Concept Of Earned Surplus," **AR**, 1931, Vol. 6, No. 3, pp. 206-217.

Kohler, E. L. "The Development Of Accounting For Regulatory Purposes By The Federal Power Commission," **AR**, 1946, Vol. 21, No. 1, pp. 19-30.

Kohler, E. L. "The Jenkins Report," **AR**, 1963, Vol. 38, No.

2, pp. 266-269.

Kohler, E. L. "The TVA And Its Power-Accounting Problems," **AR**, 1948, Vol. 23, No. 1, pp. 44-62.

Kohler, E. L. "Two C.P.A. Problems," **AR**, 1932, Vol. 7, No. 4, pp. 296-300.

Kohler, Marcel F. and Adolph Matz. "Swiss Financial Reporting And Auditing Practices," **ABACUS**, 1968, Vol. 4, No. 1, pp. 3-16.

Kohlmeier, John M. (Davidson, Sidney and John M. Kohlmeier. "A Measure Of The Impact Of Some Foreign Accounting Principles," **JAR**, 1966, Vol. 4, No. 2, pp. 183-212.)

Kohlmeier, John M. (Krueger, Donald A. and John M. Kohlmeier. "Financial Modeling And 'What If' Budgeting," **MA**, 1972, Vol. 53, No. 11, pp. 25-30.)

Koisiol, Erich. "Annual Financial Statements Of German Corporations," **AR**, 1938, Vol. 13, No. 2, pp. 183-190.

Kojima, Osamu. "Accounting Textbooks In Seventeenth Century England - Chiefly About Collins' Work," **AHJ**, 1977, Vol. 4, No. 1, pp. 69-78.

Kojima, Osamu. "Macghie's 'The Principles Of Book-Keeping' - The Second Scottish Book On Accounting," **ABR**, 1979-80, Vol. 10, No. 37A, pp. 102-108.

Kokkila, Leonard M. and Louis A. Werbaneth, Jr. "The Public Practice Of Accounting: An Experimental Program," **AR**, 1974, Vol. 49, No. 1, pp. 157-159.

Kokula, John F. "The Many Roles Of The Plant Controller," **MA**, 1986, Vol. 67, No. 11, pp. 38-41.

Kole, Michael A. "Controlling Costs With A Database System," **MA**, 1988, Vol. 69, No. 12, pp. 31-35.

Kolkmann, Richard J. (Hall, Edmund J. and Richard J. Kolkmann. "A Vote For The Probabilistic Pro Forma Income Statement," **MA**, 1976, Vol. 57, No. 7, pp. 45-48.)

Kollaritsch, Felix P. "Can The Balance Sheet Reveal Financial Position?," **AR**, 1960, Vol. 35, No. 3, pp. 482-489.

Kollaritsch, Felix P. "Future Service Potential Value," **JOA**, 1965, Vol. 119, No. 2, pp. 57-62.

Kollaritsch, Felix P. "International Accounting Practices," **AR**, 1965, Vol. 40, No. 2, pp. 382-385.

Kollaritsch, Felix P. "Job Migration Patterns Of Accountants," **MA**, 1968, Vol. 50, No. 1, pp. 52-54.

Kollaritsch, Felix P. "Unbalanced Bidding Vs. Income And Performance Measurement," **MA**, 1970, Vol. 51, No. 11, pp. 34-37.

Kollaritsch, Felix. "Austria's Answer To Inflationary Profits And Taxation," **AR**, 1961, Vol. 36, No. 3, pp. 439-445.

Kolmin, Frank W. and Michael J. Cerullo. "Measuring Productivity And Efficiency," **MA**, 1973, Vol. 55, No. 5, pp. 32-34.

Kolodny, Richard. (Devon, Philip C. and Richard Kolodny. "Price-Level Reporting And Its Value To Investors," **ABR**, 1978-79, Vol. 9, No. 33, pp. 19-24.)

Kolodny, Richard. (Horwitz, Bertrand and Richard Kolodny. "The Impact Of Rule Making On R&D Investments Of Small High-Technology Firms," **JAAF**, 1981, Vol. 4, No. 2, pp. 102-113.)

Kolodny, Richard. (Horwitz, Bertrand and Richard Kolodny. "Who Is Shortsighted?," **JAPP**, 1982, Vol. 1, No. 2, pp. 79-82.)

Kolodny, Richard. (Horwitz, Bertrand N. and Richard Kolodny. "The Economic Effects Of Involuntary Uniformity In The Financial Reporting Of R & D Expenditures," **JAR**, 1980, Vol. 18, Supp., pp. 38-74.)

Kolodny, R. (Horwitz, B. and R. Kolodny. "Segment Reporting: Hindsight After Ten Years," **JAAF**, 1980, Vol. 4, No. 1, pp. 20-35.)

Konrath, Larry F. "Foreign Exchange Versus Purchasing Power Gains And Losses," **MA**, 1972, Vol. 53, No. 11, pp. 41-43.

Konrath, Larry F. "Public Accountability Of Colleges And Universities," **CPAJ**, 1976, Vol. 46, No. 2, pp. 25-28.

Konrath, Larry F. "The CPA's Risk In Evaluating Internal Control," **JOA**, 1971, Vol. 132, No. 4, pp. 53-56.

Konstans, Constantine. "The Potential Of Multiple-Access-Computer Service Bureaus," **MA**, 1968, Vol. 49, No. 7, pp. 37-42.

Konstans, Constantine. (Heard, Edwin, Constantine Konstans and James Don Edwards. "Demonstrating The Conceptual Significance Of The Matrix Inverse," **AR**, 1974, Vol. 49, No. 2, pp. 377-381.)

Konstans, C. (Dean, R. A., K. R. Ferris and C. Konstans. "Occupational Reality Shock And Organizational Commitment: Evidence From The Accounting Profession," **AOS**, 1988, Vol. 13, No. 3, pp. 251-262.)

Kopta, William A. "Managerial Utility Of Accounting In A Period Of Adjustment," **AR**, 1954, Vol. 29, No. 3, pp. 369-372.

Kopta, William. "What Constitutes The Unauthorized Practice Of Law By Accountants In Tax Matters," **AR**, 1950, Vol. 25, No. 1, pp. 76-80.

Korb, Phillip J., Charles L. Martin, Jr., and Barbara R. Stewart. "Income And Expense Rules After Tax Reform: Helping Clients Cope," **JOA**, 1987, Vol. 164, No. 3, pp. 126-137.

Kordes, Frans G. "Court Of Audit, A European Phenomenon: The Situation In The Netherlands," **AIIA**, 1988, Vol. 2, pp. 243-253.

Korf, Jack H. "Management Accounting Control By Remote Output," **MA**, 1969, Vol. 51, No. 5, pp. 44-47.

Korn, S. Winton. "Tax Aspects Of A Complete Liquidation Of A Corporation," **CPAJ**, 1973, Vol. 43, No. 6, pp. 465-474.

Kornbluth, J. S. H. "Accounting In Multiple Objective Linear Programming," **AR**, 1974, Vol. 49, No. 2, pp. 284-295.

Kortanek, K. O. (Charnes, A., C. Colantoni, W. W. Cooper and K. O. Kortanek. "Economic Social And Enterprise Accounting And Mathematical Models," **AR**, 1972, Vol. 47. No. 1, pp. 85-108.)

Kortanek, K. (Byrne, R. F., A. Charnes, W. W. Cooper and K. Kortanek. "Some New Approaches To Risk," **AR**, 1968, Vol. 43, No. 1, pp. 18-37.)

Kortanek, K. (Charnes, A., H. Justin Davidson and K. Kortanek. "On A Mixed Sequential Estimating Procedure With Application To Audit Tests In Accounting," **AR**, 1964, Vol. 39, No. 2, pp. 241-250.)

Kortan, Jerzy. "International Economic Organizations And Common Enterprises In Socialist Countries (Principles Of Functioning And Management)," **IJAER**, 1976, Vol. 12, No. 1, pp. 147-165.

Koshland, Daniel E., Jr. "Anomalous Behavior Patterns," **JAED**, 1986, Vol. 4, No. 1, pp. 191-192.

Kosiol, Erich E. "A Proposal For A General Concept Of Cost," **IJAER**, 1967, Vol. 3, No. 1, pp. 1-19.

Kosiol, Erich E. "Accounting Models As Bases Of Managerial Decisions," **IJAER**, 1969, Vol. 5, No. 1, pp. 47-59.

Kosiol, Erich E. "An Axiomatic Approach To The Pagatoric Theory Of Financial Income Determination," **IJAER**, 1970, Vol. 5, No. 2, pp. 1-28.

Kosiol, Erich E. "Price Changes, Money Value, And Profit Distribution Within The Framework Of Financial Accounting," **IJAER**, 1966, Vol. 2, No. 1, pp. 1-24.

Kosiol, E. "Bases Of Valuation In German Corporate Balance Sheets," **AR**, 1937, Vol. 12, No. 4, pp. 355-360.

Kostolansky, John C. "Budget Control At Corning Glass Works," **MA**, 1977, Vol. 59, No. 5, pp. 21-24.

Kostolansky, John W. (Werner, Charles A. and John W. Kostolansky. "Accounting Liabilities Under ERISA," **JAAF**, 1983, Vol. 7, No. 1, pp. 54-64.)

Kostolansky, John W. (Werner, Charles A. and John W. Kostolansky. "Accounting Liabilities Under The Multiemployer Pension Plan Amendments Act," **JAAF**, 1984, Vol. 7, No. 3, pp. 212-224.)

Kostolansky, John. (Werner, Charles and John Kostolansky. "Legal Aspects Of Accounting For Post-Employment Health Care And Life Insurance Benefits," **JAAF**, 1988, Vol. 3 (New Series), No. 1, pp. 62-72.)

Kothari, S. P. (Collins, Daniel W., S. P. Kothari and Judy Dawson Rayburn. "Firm Size And The Information Content Of Prices With Respect To Earnings," **JAEC**, 1987, Vol. 9, No. 2, pp. 111-138.)

Kothari, S. P., Thomas Lys, Clifford W. Smith and Ross L. Watts. "Auditor Liability And Information Disclosure," **JAAF**, 1988, Vol. 3 (New Series), No. 4, pp. 307-339.

Kottas, John F. and Hon-Shiang Lau. "Direct Simulation In Stochastic CVP Analysis," **AR**, 1978, Vol. 53, No. 3, pp. 698-707.

Kottas, John F. and Hon-Shiang Lau. "On The Accuracy Of Normalcy Approximation In Stochastic C-V-P Analysis: A Comment," **AR**, 1978, Vol. 53, No. 1, pp. 247-251.

Kottas, John F., Amy Hing-Ling Lau and Hon-Shiang Lau. "A General Approach to Stochastic Management Planning Models: An Overview," **AR**, 1978, Vol. 53, No. 2, pp. 389-401.

Kovlak, Daniel L. "Understanding Your Town's Financial Report," **MA**, 1984, Vol. 66, No. 6, pp. 53-58.

Kovlak, Daniel L. "What You Should Know About Repos," **MA**, 1986, Vol. 67, No. 11, pp. 52-56.

Kovlak, Daniel L. (Wood, Venita M. and Daniel L. Kovlak. "What Is The GASB?," **CPAJ**, 1987, Vol. 57, No. 3, pp. 18-23.)

Kozik, Eugene. "Computer Augmentation Of Managerial Reasoning," **MA**, 1966, Vol. 48, No. 4, pp. 35-43.

Koziol, David S. "How The Constraint Theory Improved A Job-Shop Operation," **MA**, 1988, Vol. 69, No. 11, pp. 44-49.

Kozub, Robert M. (Raabe, William A., Robert M. Kozub and Debra L. Sanders. "Attitude Measurement And The Perceptions Of Tax Accounting Faculty Publications Outlets," **JAED**, 1987, Vol. 5, No. 1, pp. 45-57.)

Kozum, Robert M. "Antecedents Of The Income Tax In Colonial America," **AHJ**, 1983, Vol. 10, No. 2, pp. 99-116.

Kraayenhof, J. "International Challenges For Accounting," **JOA**, 1960, Vol. 109, No. 1, pp. 34-38.

Kracke, Edward A. "Inventories: From Fetish To Creed," **AR**, 1941, Vol. 16, No. 2, pp. 175-182.

Kracke, E. A. "Restoration Of Fixed Asset Values To The Balance Sheet," **AR**, 1947, Vol. 22, No. 2, pp. 208-210.

Krafft, J. Edward. "A Payback Approach To An Integrated Business System," **MA**, 1967, Vol. 49, No. 1, pp. 50-54.

Kraft, Kyle K. "Measuring Production Efficiency," **MA**, 1983, Vol. 64, No. 12, pp. 40-43.

Kraft, William H., Jr. "Multiple Regression Analysis Of Labor Rates," **MA**, 1971, Vol. 52, No. 7, pp. 50-53.

Kraft, William H., Jr. "Statistical Sampling For Auditors: A New Look," **JOA**, 1968, Vol. 126, No. 2, pp. 49-56.

Kramer, Allan. "The Significance Of The Hochfelder Decision," **CPAJ**, 1976, Vol. 46, No. 8, pp. 11-14.

Kramer, Dan G. "Personal Financial Statements," **CPAJ**, 1974, Vol. 44, No. 9, pp. 31-34.

Kramer, Jay O. "Developments In Taxability Of Corporate Stock Redemptions," **JOA**, 1952, Vol. 94, No. 2, pp. 189-194.

Kramer, Jay O. "The Thin Corporation Problem," **JOA**, 1953. Vol. 96, No. 4, pp. 449-451.

Kramer, Jay O. "The Thin Incorporation Problem Today," **JOA**, 1958, Vol. 106, No. 6, pp. 48-51.

Kramer, Jay O. (Angel, Otto P. and Jay O. Kramer. "Questions On Taxability Of Foreign Income Left Unanswered By Mimeograph 6475," **JOA**, 1950, Vol. 89, No. 6, pp. 496-499.)

Kramer, John F. "Staff Training In Smaller Firms," **JOA**,

311

Kramer, John L. and Sandra S. Kramer. "Section 1248(b): The Individual Limitation On Taxing Sales Of CFC Stock Offers Substantial Tax Savings," JATA, 1981, Vol. 2, No. 2, pp. 20-31.

Kramer, John L. "Accounting Theory: Revolution Or Evolution?," MA, 1974, Vol. 55, No. 10, pp. 31-34.

Kramer, John L. "Disclosure Of Positions Contrary To The IRC," CPAJ, 1978, Vol. 48, No. 1, pp. 41-45.

Kramer, John L. (Collins, Julie H. and John L. Kramer. "An Examination Of The Employer's Pension Plan Choice: Integrated Vs. Nonintegrated Plans," JATA, 1986, Vol. 8, No. 1, pp. 35-48.)

Kramer, John L. (Nordhauser, Susan L. and John L. Kramer. "Repeal Of The Deferral Privilege For Earnings From Direct Foreign Investments: An Analysis," AR, 1981, Vol. 56, No. 1, pp. 54-69.)

Kramer, Lewis. (Paroby, Stephen M., John G. Baab and Lewis Kramer. "Controlling Your Computer," CA, 1987, Vol. 5, No. 2, pp. 34-41.)

Kramer, Robert. "A Control Program For Construction Projects," MA, 1970, Vol. 52, No. 4, pp. 38-41.

Kramer, Sandra S. "Blockage: Valuation Of Large Blocks Of Publicly Traded Stocks For Tax Purposes," AR, 1982, Vol. 57, No. 1, pp. 70-87.

Kramer, Sandra S. "Valuation Of Blocks Of Stock: A Number Of Unresolved Issues Still Remain," JATA, 1984, Vol. 5, No. 2, pp. 17-26.

Kramer, Sandra S. (Ashton, Robert H. and Sandra S. Kramer. "Students As Surrogates In Behavioral Accounting Research: Some Evidence," JAR, 1980, Vol. 18, No. 1, pp. 1-15.)

Kramer, Sandra S. (Kramer, John L. and Sandra S. Kramer. "Section 1248(b): The Individual Limitation On Taxing Sales Of CFC Stock Offers Substantial Tax Savings," JATA, 1981, Vol. 2, No. 2, pp. 20-31.)

Krasensky, Hans. "The Concept Of A Business Asset," IJAER, 1967, Vol. 2, No. 2, pp. 47-58.

Krasker, William S. (Herzlinger, Regina E. and William S. Krasker. "Measuring The Economic Performance Of For-Profit And Nonprofit Organizations," RIGNA, 1986, Vol. 2, pp. 151-172.)

Krasney, Melvin A. (Benston, George J. and Melvin A. Krasney. "DAAM: The Demand For Alternative Accounting Measurements," JAR, 1978, Vol. 16, Supp., pp. 1-30.)

Krasney, Melvin. "Accounting Controls For Corporate EDP Costs," MA, 1971, Vol. 52, No. 9, pp. 17-18.

Krasniewski, Raymond J. (Dittman, David A., Raymond J. Krasniewski and Margaret Smith. "Contracting Strategies For Maximum Benefit In Sales Contracts With Government: The Installment Sale Alternative," RIGNA, 1987, Vol. 3, Part A, pp. 107-130.)

Krasts, Aivars. "The Impact Of Inflation Rates On Investment Appraisal, Performance, And Financial Measures," CA, 1983, Vol. 1, No. 4, pp. 19-25.

Kratchan, Stanley H. (Giroux, Gary A. and Stanley H. Kratchman. "How Banks Forecast," MA, 1980, Vol. 61, No. 11, pp. 39-44.)

Kratchman, Stanley H. (Grossman, Steven D., Stanley H. Kratchman and Robert B. Welker. "Comment: The Effect Of Replacement Cost Disclosures On Security Prices," JAAF, 1981, Vol. 4, No. 2, pp. 136-143.)

Kratchman, Stanley H. (Hise, Richard T., Stanley H. Kratchman and Theodore H. Mattheiss. "Involvement Of The Undergraduate Accounting Curriculum With Distribution Cost Analysis," AR, 1974, Vol. 49, No. 1, pp. 153-157.)

Kratchman, Stanley H., Richard T. Hise and Thomas A. Ulrich. "Management's Decision To Discontinue A Product," JOA, 1975, Vol. 139, No. 6, pp. 50-54.

Kratchman, Stanley H., Robert E. Malcom and Richard D. Twark. "The Comparison Of Alternative Income Concepts: A Reply," AR, 1975, Vol. 50, No. 4, pp. 865-868.

Kratchman, Stanley H., Robert E. Malcom and Richard D. Twark. "Alternative Income Concepts And Relative Performance Evaluations: A Reply," AR, 1976, Vol. 51, No. 2, pp. 421-426.

Kratchman, Stanley H., Robert E. Malcom and Richard D. Twark. "An Intra-Industry Comparison Of Alternative Income Concepts And Relative Performance Evaluations," AR, 1974, Vol. 49, No. 4, pp. 682-689.

Kratchman, Stanley. (Giroux, Gary, Steven Grossman and Stanley Kratchman. "What FAS No. 33 Does To Bank Financial Statements," MA, 1981, Vol. 62, No. 7, pp. 42-47.)

Krause, Paul and Donald E. Keller. "Bringing World-Class Manufacturing And Accounting To A Small Company," MA, 1988, Vol. 70, No. 5, pp. 28-33.

Krause, Paul. "Active Learning For Budgeting Concepts," JAED, 1988, Vol. 6, No. 2, pp. 331-337.

Kraushaar, James M. (Anderson, John C. and James M. Kraushaar. "Measurement Error And Statistical Sampling In Auditing: The Potential Effects," AR, 1986, Vol. 61, No. 3, pp. 379-399.)

Kraus, Charles F. "Problems In Identifying Section 38 Property," JOA, 1969, Vol. 127, No. 4, pp. 51-55.

Krausz, Joshua, Joel Hochman and Allen Schiff. "The Impact Of Taxation On Project Valuation For Alternative Depreciation Methods," ACCHOR, 1987, Vol. 1, No. 3, pp. 31-40.

Krebs, Eric H. and Joseph M. Jordan. "The Insurance Industry After The TRA," JOA, 1987, Vol. 164, No. 2, pp. 92-101.

Krebs, William S. "An Analysis Of Missouri's Utility Earnings And Rate Base Formula," AR, 1954, Vol. 29, No. 3, pp. 429-446.

Krebs, William S. "Asset Appreciation, Its Economic And Accounting Significance," AR, 1930, Vol. 5, No. 1, pp. 60-69.

Krebs, William S. "Depreciation And Valuation For A Utility With Only One Plant," AR, 1958, Vol. 33, No. 2, pp. 256-264.

Krebs, William S. "Rate Base Problems Presented When Utilities Shift From Retirement To Depreciation Accounting," AR, 1950, Vol. 25, No. 3, pp. 283-291.

Krebs, William S. "Replacement And Retirement Accounting And Rate Base Valuation," AR, 1950, Vol. 25, No. 4, pp. 351-359.

Krebs, W. S. "Public-Utility Depreciation In Its Relation to The Rate Base," AR, 1939, Vol. 14, No. 2, pp. 93-107.

Krebs, W. S. "Purchases Discounts," AR, 1926, Vol. 1, No. 1, pp. 9-15.

Kreiser, Larry and Philip N. Dare. "Shaker Accounting Records At Pleasant Hill: 1830 - 1850," AHJ, 1986, Vol. 13, No. 2, pp. 19-36.

Kreiser, Larry. "A New Model For Accounting For Pension Costs," CPAJ, 1975, Vol. 45, No. 6, pp. 37-41.

Kreiser, Larry. "A Short History Of The Economic Development And Accounting Treatment Of Pension Plans," AHJ, 1976, Vol. 3, No. 1-4, pp. 56-62.

Kreiser, Larry. "Maintaining And Improving The Audit Competence Of CPAs: CPA And Selected User Reaction," AR, 1977, Vol. 52, No. 2, pp. 427-437.

Kreiser, Larry. "Maintaining Professional Competence," CPAJ, 1976, Vol. 46, No. 9, pp. 37-40.

Krekstein, I. H. "How Local Firms Can Help Each Other," JOA, 1962, Vol. 114, No. 2, pp. 40-45.

Kren, Leslie and Woody M. Liao. "The Role Of Accounting Information In The Control Of Organizations: A Review Of The Evidence," JAL, 1988, Vol. 7, pp. 280-309.

Kreps, David M. (Demski, Joel S. and David M. Kreps. "Models In Managerial Accounting," JAR, 1982, Vol. 20, Supp., pp. 117-148.)

Kress, Thomas C. "Management Principles Revisited - Or How Dad Ran His Grocery Store," MA, 1984, Vol. 65, No. 8, pp. 46-49.

Kreutzfeldt, Richard W. and Wanda A. Wallace. "Error Characteristics In Audit Populations: Their Profile And Relationship To Environmental Factors," AJPT, 1986-87, Vol. 6, No. 1, pp. 20-43.

Kreuze, Jerry G. and Gale E. Newell. "Student Ratings Of Accounting Instructors: A Search For Important Determinants," JAED, 1987, Vol. 5, No. 1, pp. 87-98.

Kreuze, Jerry G. (Newell, Gale E. and Jerry G. Kreuze. "Improving The Audit Process," MA, 1987, Vol. 69, No. 2, pp. 56-59.)

Krieger, Abba M. (Ramage, John G., Abba M. Krieger and Leslie L. Spero. "An Empirical Study Of Error Characteristics In Audit Populations," JAR, 1979, Vol. 17, Supp., pp. 72-102.)

Krieg, Emile. "New Landmarks For Accountancy," IJAER, 1969, Vol. 4, No. 2, pp. 93-111.

Krilich, James H. "A Look At The Copper Industry," MA, 1976, Vol. 57, No. 9, pp. 37-38.

Krinsky, I., W. D. Rotenberg and D. B. Thornton. "Takeovers: A Synthesis," JAL, 1988, Vol. 7, pp. 243-279.

Kripke, Homer. "Some Reactions And Down-to-Earth Reflections On Accountants' Liability," JAAF, 1988, Vol. 3 (New Series), No. 4, pp. 359-367.

Kripke, Homer. "The Objective Of Financial Accounting Should Be To Provide Information For The Serious Investor," CPAJ, 1972, Vol. 42, No. 5, pp. 389-398.

Kripke, Homer. "Where Are We On Securities Disclosure After The Advisory Committee Report?," JAAF, 1978, Vol. 2, No. 1, pp. 4-32.

Krise, Shirley A. "Certain Tax Implications Of Professional Sports," CPAJ, 1975, Vol. 45, No. 4, pp. 27-32.

Krogstad, Jack L. and Daniel S. Dexter. "National Automated Accounting Research System - A Challenge For Auditing Education," AR, 1979, Vol. 54, No. 3, pp. 604-608.

Krogstad, Jack L. and John K. Harris. "The CMA Examination: A Content Analysis," MA, 1974, Vol. 56, No. 4, pp. 21-23.

Krogstad, Jack L. and Marshall B. Romney. "Accounts Receivable Confirmation - An Alternative Auditing Approach," JOA, 1980, Vol. 149, No. 2, pp. 68-73.

Krogstad, Jack L. (Harris, John K. and Jack L. Krogstad. "Assessing Progress Of The CMA Program," MA, 1977, Vol. 58, No. 8, pp. 17-23.)

Krogstad, Jack L. (Harris, John K. and Jack L. Krogstad. "A Profile And Index Of The CMA Examination," AR, 1976, Vol. 51, No. 3, pp. 637-641.)

Krogstad, Jack L. (Smith, Gerald and Jack L. Krogstad. "Impact Of Sources And Authors On 'Auditing: A Journal Of Practice & Theory' - A Citation Analysis," AJPT, 1984-85, Vol. 4, No. 1, pp. 107-117.)

Krogstad, Jack L. (Smith, Gerald and Jack L. Krogstad. "A Taxonomy Of Content And Citations In 'Auditing: A Journal Of Practice & Theory'," AJPT, 1988, Vol. 8, No. 1, pp. 108-117.)

Krogstad, Jack L. (Solomon, Ira, Lawrence A. Tomassini, Marshall B. Romney and Jack L. Krogstad. "Probability Elicitation In Auditing: Additional Evidence On The Equivalent Prior Sample Method," AIA, 1984, Vol. 1, pp. 267-290.)

Krogstad, Jack L. (Treadway, James C., Jr., Jack L. Krogstad and Shirley A. Sunderland. "Financial Reporting And Public Confidence," CA, 1986, Vol. 4, No. 4, pp. 4-8.)

Krogstad, Jack L., Gary Grudnitski and David W. Bryant.

"PERT And PERT/Cost For Audit Planning And Control," **JOA**, 1977, Vol. 144, No. 5, pp. 82-91.

Krogstad, Jack L., Gerald Smith and Raymond J. Clay, Jr. "Impact Of A Simulation Of Audit Practice," **IAE**, 1986, Vol. 1, No. 2, pp. 309-320.

Krogstad, Jack L., Maurice Earl Stark, Kenneth L. Fox and Harry O. Lytle, Jr. "The Faculty Residency: A Concept Worth Considering," **JOA**, 1981, Vol. 152, No. 5, pp. 74-86.

Krogstad, Jack L., Richard T. Ettenson and James Shanteau. "Context And Experience In Auditors' Materiality Judgments," **AJPT**, 1984-85, Vol. 4, No. 1, pp. 54-74.

Krogstad, J. L. (Solomon, I., J. L. Krogstad, M. B. Romney, and L. A. Tomassini. "Auditors' Prior Probability Distributions For Account Balances," **AOS**, 1982, Vol. 7, No. 1, pp. 27-42.)

Kroll, Stanley. "Commodity Hedging - For Insurance And Profit," **CPAJ**, 1972, Vol. 42, No. 4, pp. 303-307.

Kropatkin, Philip and Robert Forrester. "The Single Audit - Independence, Materiality And Cost-Effectiveness - Part II," **CPAJ**, 1983, Vol. 53, No. 3, pp. 16-23.

Kropatkin, Philip and Robert Forrester. "The Single Audit - Independence, Materiality And Cost-Effectiveness - Part I," **CPAJ**, 1983, Vol. 53, No. 2, pp. 10-17.

Kross, William and Douglas A. Schroeder. "An Empirical Investigation Of The Effect Of Quarterly Earnings Announcement Timing On Stock Returns," **JAR**, 1984, Vol. 22, No. 1, pp. 153-176.

Kross, William, Gordon Chapman and Kenneth H. Strand. "Fully Diluted Earnings Per Share And Security Returns: Some Additional Evidence," **JAAF**, 1980, Vol. 4, No. 1, pp. 36-46.

Kross, William. "Stock Returns And Oil And Gas Pronouncements: Replication And Extension," **JAR**, 1982, Vol. 20, No. 2, Part I, pp. 459-471.

Krueger, Charles A. and Richard L. Townsend. "The Controller's Role In Controlling Construction Costs," **MA**, 1988, Vol. 70, No. 6, pp. 38-42.

Krueger, Charles A. "Ratio Analysis: Using Spreadsheets For Better Management Reports," **CA**, 1987, Vol. 5, No. 2, pp. 17-27.

Krueger, Donald A. and John M. Kohlmeier. "Financial Modeling And 'What If' Budgeting," **MA**, 1972, Vol. 53, No. 11, pp. 25-30.

Krupp, James A. G. "Obsolescence: The Neglected Factor," **MA**, 1977, Vol. 59. No. 3, pp. 36-40.

Krzystofik, Anthony T. and Richard Fein. "Does Your Firm Use The Right Approach In Hiring Campus Recruits?," **JOA**, 1988, Vol. 166, No. 5, pp. 83-88.

Krzystofik, Anthony T. "Robert Hiester Montgomery," **AHJ**, 1975, Vol. 2, No. 1-4, pp. 67-70.

Krzystofik, Anthony T. (Lentilhon, Robert W. and Anthony T. Krzystofik. "Professional Examination Preparation In AACSB Accredited And Member Schools," **IAE**, 1983, No. 1, pp. 38-49.)

Krzystofik, Anthony T. (Whiteman, Michael J., Anthony T. Krzystofik and Joseph E. Finnerty. "Interest Ruling - Questions For Lenders And Borrowers," **CPAJ**, 1984, Vol. 54, No. 1, pp. 39-43.)

Krzystofik, Anthony T. (Whiteman, Michael J. and Anthony T. Krzystofik. "401(k) Plans: A Time To Act," **MA**, 1986, Vol. 68, No. 3, pp. 33-35.)

Krzystofik, Anthony T., Stephen E. Loeb and Doyle Z. Williams. "How To Review Audit Training," **CPAJ**, 1978, Vol. 48, No. 7, pp. 11-16.

Krzystofik, Anthony T. "Integrating Testing And Evaluation In Education For Public Accounting," **CPAJ**, 1986, Vol. 56, No. 1, pp. 24-31.

Kubin, Konrad W. "Accounting For Foreign Currency Translation: Current Problems In Historical Perspective," **AHJ**, 1975, Vol. 2, No. 1-4, pp. 11-16.

Kubin, Konrad W. "The Changing Nature Of International Accounting Courses," **IJAER**, 1973, Vol. 9, No. 1, pp. 99-111.

Kublin, Milton. "Acceptability Of A Professional School Of Accountancy," **AR**, 1965, Vol. 40, No. 3, pp. 626-635.

Kubota, Keiichi. "Information Content Of Accounting Numbers: Evidence On Tokyo Stock Exchange Firms," **IJAER**, 1980, Vol. 15, No. 2, pp. 61-76.

Kucic, A. Ronald and Samuel T. Battaglia. "Matrix Accounting For The Statement Of Changes In Financial Position," **MA**, 1981, Vol. 62, No. 10, pp. 27-32.

Kuhmichel, Ruby. (Goggans, Travis P. and Ruby Kuhmichel. "Estate Planning For Subchapter S Stockholders," **CPAJ**, 1980, Vol. 50, No. 9, pp. 33-40.)

Kujawa, Daniel. "A Banker's Approach To Business Loans," **MA**, 1971, Vol. 52, No. 12, pp. 24-27.

Kukla, Ronald J. (Gilchrist, Michael, Diane D. Pattison and Ronald J. Kudla. "Controlling Indirect Costs With Headcount Forecast Algorithms," **MA**, 1985, Vol. 67, No. 2, pp. 46-51.)

Kulkarni, Deepak. "The Valuation Of Liabilities," **ABR**, 1979-80, Vol. 10, No. 39, pp. 291-298.

Kullberg, Duane R. "Management Of A Multinational Public Accounting Firm," **IJAER**, 1981, Vol. 17, No. 1, pp. 1-5.

Kunitake, Walter K. and Clinton E. White, Jr. "Ethics For Independent Auditors," **JAAF**, 1986, Vol. 1 (New Series), No. 3, pp. 222-231.

Kunitake, Walter K. "SEC Accounting Related Enforcement Actions 1934-1985: A Summary," **RIAR**, 1987, Vol. 1, pp. 79-87.

Kunitake, Walter K. (Ketz, J. Edward and Walter K. Kunitake. "Demand For And Supply Of SEC Courses," **JAED**, 1985, Vol. 3, No. 1, pp. 91-106.)

Kunitake, Walter K. (Ketz, J. Edward and Walter K. Kunitake. "An Evaluation Of The Conceptual Framework: Can It Resolve The Issues Related To Accounting For Income Taxes?," **AIA**, 1988, Vol. 6, pp. 37-54.)

Kunitake, Walter K., Andrew D. Luzi and G. William Glezen. "Analytical Review For Audit And Review Engagements," **CPAJ**, 1985, Vol. 55, No. 4, pp. 18-27.

Kunitzky, Sergius. (Lev, Baruch and Sergius Kunitzky. "On The Association Between Smoothing Measures And The Risk Of Common Stocks," **AR**, 1974, Vol. 49, No. 2, pp. 259-270.)

Kunkel, J. Gregory. "Continuous Auditing By Exception," **MA**, 1974, Vol. 56, No. 1, pp. 45-48.

Kunkel, J. Gregory. (Hakansson, Nils H., J. Gregory Kunkel and James A. Ohlson. "A Comment On Verrecchia's No Trading 'Theorem'," **JAR**, 1984, Vol. 22, No. 2, pp. 765-767.)

Kunreuther, Oscar R. "Enhancing Your Practice With EDP," **CPAJ**, 1976, Vol. 46, No. 1, pp. 11-14.

Kunze, Harry L. "A New Form Of Funds Statement," **AR**, 1940, Vol. 15, No. 2, pp. 222-224.

Kunze, Harry L. "How To Study Accounting," **AR**, 1931, Vol. 6, No. 4, pp. 316-317.

Kunze, Harry L. "Priority Of Taxes Under The Bankruptcy Act," **AR**, 1936, Vol. 11, No. 2, pp. 125-129.

Kunze, Harry L. "State Taxation Of Corporate Income," **AR**, 1935, Vol. 10, No. 4, pp. 345-364.

Kunze, H. L. "Liquidation Of Partnership Under Court Administration," **AR**, 1931, Vol. 6, No. 1, pp. 62-64.

Kupfer, T. Milton. "Salvage Value And Useful Life," **JOA**, 1962, Vol. 113, No. 3, pp. 49-56.

Kupzhasar, Naribaev. "Computer Applications In Soviet Accounting," **IJAER**, 1974, Vol. 10, No. 1, pp. 33-43.

Kurtz, Cornelius. "The Cost Of Human Depreciation - Ostrich Liability?," **AR**, 1957, Vol. 32, No. 3, pp. 413-418.

Kusel, Jimie. (Goosen, Kenneth R. and Jimie Kusel. "Integrating Microcomputer Use Into An Information Systems Course," **IAE**, 1985, No. 1, pp. 77-86.)

Kusel, Jimie. (Moore, P. Michael, Thomas H. Oxner and Jimie Kusel. "Determining Common Stock Equivalency Of Convertible Securities: A Teaching Approach," **IAE**, 1987, Vol. 2, No. 1, pp. 152-156.)

Kushell, C. J., Jr. "Organization Of Financial Department Aids Management," **JOA**, 1952, Vol. 93, No. 3, pp. 330-332.

Kuttner, Monroe S. (Elliott, Merle S. and Monroe S. Kuttner. "MAS: Coming Of Age," **JOA**, 1982, Vol. 154, No. 6, pp. 66-75.)

Kuttner, Monroe S. (Foley, John C. and Monroe S. Kuttner. "Finding Funds For A Small Business," **JOA**, 1986, Vol. 162, No. 2, pp. 114-122.)

Kuttner, Monroe S. (Trentin, H. George and Monroe S. Kuttner. "The MAS Body Of Knowledge Study," **CPAJ**, 1976, Vol. 46, No. 8, pp. 15-22.)

Kuzdrall, Paul J. (Kim, Seung H. and Paul J. Kuzdrall. "The Simulation Of Financial Strategy Under Fluctuating Exchange Rates Conditions," **IJAER**, 1977, Vol. 12, No. 2, pp. 93-107.)

Kwang, Ching-Wen and Albert Slavin. "The Simple Mathematics Of Variance Analysis," **AR**, 1962, Vol. 37, No. 3, pp. 415-432.

Kwang, Ching-Wen. "The Economic Accounting System Of State Enterprises In Mainland China," **IJAER**, 1966, Vol. 1, No. 2, pp. 61-99.

Kwang, Ching-Wen. (Corcoran, A. Wayne and Ching-Wen Kwang. "Set Theory And Accounting Analysis," **MA**, 1967, Vol. 49, No. 1, pp. 7-17.)

Kwang, Ching-wen. (Corcoran, A. Wayne and Ching-wen Kwang. "A Set Theory Approach To Funds-Flow Analysis," **JAR**, 1965, Vol. 3, No. 2, pp. 206-217.)

Kwatinetz, Michael. (Palmon, Dan and Michael Kwatinetz. "The Significant Role Interpretation Plays In The Implementation Of SFAS No. 13," **JAAF**, 1980, Vol. 3, No. 3, pp. 207-226.)

Kwon, Young K. (Jung, Woon-Oh and Young K. Kwon. "Disclosure When The Market Is Unsure Of Information Endowment Of Managers," **JAR**, 1988, Vol. 26, No. 1, pp. 146-153.)

Ky, Liem. "Making The Right Cost Distribution Decision," **MA**, 1983, Vol. 65, No. 1, pp. 38-40.

Kyd, Charles W. "Managing The Financial Demands Of Growth," **MA**, 1981, Vol. 63, No. 6, pp. 33-43.

LLL

Label, Wayne A. (Maupin, Rebekah J. and Wayne A. Label. "Profiting From A Management Buyout," **MA**, 1987, Vol. 68, No. 10, pp. 32-34.)

Label, Wayne A. (Seiler, Robert E. and Wayne A. Label. "Impact Of Curricular Changes Upon Professional Staff Training Efforts," **AR**, 1974, Vol. 49, No. 4, pp. 854-859.)

Labus, Henry L. "The Fusion Of Cost Accounting And Industrial Engineering," **MA**, 1968, Vol. 50, No. 1, pp. 57-59.

Lacey, John M. "Replacement Cost Accounting: Another Answer," **CPAJ**, 1976, Vol. 46, No. 3, pp. 13-20.

Lacey, John M. (Bowen, Robert M., Eric W. Noreen and John M. Lacey. "Determinants Of The Corporate Decision To Capitalize Interest," **JAEC**, 1981, Vol. 3, No. 2, pp. 151-179.)

Lachan, R. (Aranya, N., R. Lachman and J. Amernic. "Accountants' Job Satisfaction: A Path Analysis," **AOS**, 1982, Vol. 7, No. 3, pp. 201-216.)

Ladd, Eldon. "How To Evaluate Financial Software," **MA**, 1985, Vol. 66, No. 7, pp. 39-42.

Ladin, Eugene. "The Role Of The Accountant In Operations Analysis," **AR**, 1962, Vol. 37, No. 2, pp. 289-294.

LaFrance, John W. "Communication With The Client And The Public," **JOA**, 1962, Vol. 113, No. 5, pp. 39-44.

LaFrance, John W. "Interpreting Reports For Management," **JOA**, 1958, Vol. 105, No. 2, pp. 60-65.

LaFrance, John W. "Salesmanship In Accounting Practice," **JOA**, 1959, Vol. 108, No. 3, pp. 51-55.

Lafferty, George W. "Influences Of Law On The Independent Auditor In The Examination Of Local Government Accounts," **JOA**, 1950, Vol. 90, No. 2, pp. 122-126.

Lafrentz, Arthur F. "CPAs And Surety Executives," **JOA**, 1956, Vol. 101, No. 2, pp. 51-55.

LaGrone, Paul G. "The Use Of Visual Aids In Elementary And Intermediate Accounting To Determine Their Practical Value In The Classroom," **AR**, 1960, Vol. 35, No. 3, pp. 520-522.

Lahey, James. "Toward A More Understandable Auditor's Report," **JOA**, 1972, Vol. 133, No. 4, pp. 48-53.

Laible, Steven W. "How Minnesota Improved Its Cities' Financial Reporting," **MA**, 1979, Vol. 61, No. 4, pp. 23-29.

Laibstain, Samuel. "A New Look At Accounting For Operating Loss Carryforwards," **AR**, 1971, Vol. 46, No. 2, pp. 342-351.

Laibstain, Samuel. "Accounting For Income Taxes - Recent Developments," **CPAJ**, 1983, Vol. 53, No. 7, pp. 16-23.

Laibstain, Samuel. "Income Tax Accounting For Business Combinations," **CPAJ**, 1988, Vol. 58, No. 12, pp. 32-40.

Laibstain, Samuel. "Reduction In Tax Basis From The ITC," **CPAJ**, 1984, Vol. 54, No. 7, pp. 44-51.

Laibstain, Samuel. (Stout, David E.. Samuel Laibstain and Larry P. Bailey. "Managing Off-Balance-Sheet Financing," **MA**, 1988, Vol. 70, No. 1, pp. 32-39.)

Lake, Robert C. "The Maximum Tax On Earned Income - A Graphical Illustration," **AR**, 1976, Vol. 51, No. 3, pp. 644-645.

Lakin, Leonard. "What The Accountant Must Know About Secured Transactions," **JOA**, 1971, Vol. 131, No. 1, pp. 60-65.

Lakonishok, Josef. (Baran, Arie. Josef Lakonishok and Aharon R. Ofer. "The Information Content Of General Price Level Adjusted Earnings: Some Empirical Evidence," **AR**, 1980, Vol. 55, No. 1, pp. 22-35.)

Lakonishok, Josef. (Crichfield. Timothy. Thomas Dyckman and Josef Lakonishok. "An Evaluation Of Security Analysts' Forecasts," **AR**, 1978, Vol. 53, No. 3, pp. 651-668.)

Lakonishok, Josef. (Givoly. Dan and Josef Lakonishok. "Aggregate Earnings Expectations And Stock Market Behavior," **JAAF**, 1987, Vol. 2 (New Series). No. 2, pp. 117-150.)

Lakonishok, Josef. (Givoly. Dan and Josef Lakonishok. "Properties Of Analysts' Forecasts Of Earnings: A Review And Analysis Of The Research," **JAL**. 1984, Vol. 3, pp. 117-152.)

Lakonishok, Josef. (Givoly. Dan and Josef Lakonishok. "The Information Content Of Financial Analysts' Forecasts Of Earnings: Some Evidence On Semi-Strong Inefficiency," **JAEC**, 1979, Vol. 1, No. 3, pp. 165-185.)

Lakonishok, Josef. (Givoly. Dan and Josef Lakonishok. "Accounting For Construction Companies. Inflation. And Market Efficiency: Analysis Of An Israeli Case," **IJAER**, 1982, Vol. 17, No. 2, pp. 121-149.)

Lakonsihok, Josef and Aharon R. Ofer. "The Information Content Of General Price Level Adjusted Earnings: A Reply," **AR**, 1987, Vol. 60, No. 4, pp. 711-713.

LaLonde, Bernard J. (Lambert. Douglas M. and Bernard J. La Londe. "Inventory Carrying Costs," **MA**, 1976, Vol. 58, No. 2, pp. 31-35.)

Lam, S. F. (Chan. K. H., S. F. Lam and Roger Tang. "Probabilistic Approaches To Return On Investment And Residual Income: A Comment," **AR**, 1979, Vol. 54, No. 3, pp. 643-649.)

Lam, Wai P. "Management Representation On Audit Committees," **CPAJ**, 1975, Vol. 45, No. 11, pp. 33-38.

Lamb, James W. (Carlson. Marvin L. and James W. Lamb. "Constructing A Theory Of Accounting - An Axiomatic Approach," **AR**, 1981, Vol. 56, No. 3, pp. 554-573.)

Lamber, Richard A. "Income Smoothing As Rational Equilibrium Behavior," **AR**, 1984, Vol. 59, No. 4, pp. 604-618.

Lambers, Guy W. "Computers Used As Accounting Tools," **MA**, 1966, Vol. 47, No. 5, pp. 29-37.

Lambert, Douglas M. and Bernard J. La Londe. "Inventory Carrying Costs," **MA**, 1976, Vol. 58, No. 2, pp. 31-35.

Lambert, Douglas M. and Howard M. Armitage. "Distribution Costs: The Challenge," **MA**, 1979, Vol. 60, No. 11, pp. 33-37.

Lambert, Douglas M. "The Distribution Channels Decision: A Problem Of Performance Measurement," **MA**, 1978, Vol. 59, No. 12, pp. 60-63.

Lambert, Joyce C. and S. J. Lambert. III. "Review Of Interim Financial Information," **CPAJ**, 1979. Vol. 49, No. 9, pp. 25-32.

Lambert, Joyce C. and S. J. Lambert. III. "Tentative Report On Internal Accounting Control," **CPAJ**, 1979. Vol. 49, No. 5, pp. 25-29.

Lambert, Joyce C. "Proposed Code Of Professional Conduct," **MA**, 1974, Vol. 55, No. 8, pp. 19-22.

Lambert, Joyce C. "Reports. Reports. And More Reports," **CPAJ**, 1983, Vol. 53, No. 4, pp. 24-31.

Lambert, Joyce C. (Hubbard. Thomas D. and Joyce C. Lambert. "Current And Proposed Unaudited Statement Standards," **CPAJ**, 1978, Vol. 48, No. 3, pp. 35-42.)

Lambert, Joyce C. (Lambert. S. J., III and Joyce C. Lambert. "Concepts And Applications In APB Opinion No.

29," **JOA**, 1977, Vol. 143, No. 3, pp. 60-68.)

Lambert, Joyce. "Flowcharts Of Recent Statements On Auditing Standards," **CPAJ**, 1977, Vol. 47, No. 7, pp. 27-32.

Lambert, Kenneth R. (Turner, Mark A. and Kenneth R. Lambert. "Why The Furor Over UBIT," **JOA**, 1988, Vol. 165, No. 5, pp. 78-84.)

Lambert, Philip E. "Accrediting Specialties In Public Accounting - A Logical Step," **MA**, 1977, Vol. 58, No. 9, pp. 19-22.

Lambert, Richard A. and David F. Larcker. "Executive Compensation Effects Of Large Corporate Acquisitions," **JAPP**, 1987, Vol. 6, No. 4, pp. 231-243.

Lambert, Richard A. and David F. Larcker. "An Analysis Of The Use Of Accounting And Market Measures Of Performance In Executive Compensation Contracts," **JAR**, 1987, Vol. 25, Supp., pp. 85-125.

Lambert, Richard A. and David F. Larcker. "Golden Parachutes. Executive Decision-Making, And Shareholder Wealth," **JAEC**, 1985, Vol. 7, No. 1/3, pp. 179-203.

Lambert, Richard A. "Variance Investigation In Agency Settings," **JAR**, 1985, Vol. 23, No. 2, pp. 633-647.

Lambert, Richard A. (Beaver, William H., Richard A. Lambert and Stephen G. Ryan. "The Information Content Of Security Prices: A Second Look," **JAEC**, 1987, Vol. 9, No. 2, pp. 139-157.)

Lambert, Richard. (Beaver, William, Richard Lambert and Dale Morse. "The Information Content Of Security Prices," **JAEC**, 1980, Vol. 2, No. 1, pp. 3-28.)

Lambert, Samuel Joseph, III. "Basic Assumptions In Accounting Theory Construction," **JOA**, 1974, Vol. 137, No. 2, pp. 41-48.

Lambert, S. J. (Chen, Kung H. and S. J. Lambert. "A Study Of The Consensus On Disclosure Among Public Accountants And Security Analysts: An Alternative Interpretation," **AR**, 1977, Vol. 52, No. 2, pp. 508-513.)

Lambert, S. J. (Chen, Kung H. and S. J. Lambert. "Impurity Of Variable Factory Overhead Variances," **JAED**, 1985, Vol. 3. No. 1, pp. 189-196.)

Lambert, S. J., III and Joyce C. Lambert. "Concepts And Applications In APB Opinion No. 29," **JOA**, 1977, Vol. 143. No. 3, pp. 60-68.

Lambert, S. J., III. (Lambert, Joyce C. and S. J. Lambert III. "Review Of Interim Financial Information," **CPAJ**, 1979. Vol. 49, No. 9, pp. 25-32.)

Lambert, S. J., III. (Lambert, Joyce C. and S. J. Lambert, III. "Tentative Report On Internal Accounting Control," **CPAJ**, 1979. Vol. 49, No. 5, pp. 25-29.)

Lambrix, Robert J. (Singhvi, Surendra S. and Robert J. Lambrix. "Investment Versus Financing Decisions," **MA**, 1984, Vol. 65, No. 9, pp. 54-56.)

Lamden, Charles W. "The Function Of The State Board Of Accountancy In Improving Reporting Standards In California," **AR**, 1964, Vol. 39, No. 1, pp. 128-132.

Lamden, Charles W. "The Place Of Accounting In Price Control," **AR**, 1943, Vol. 18, No. 1, pp. 26-33.

Lammers, Lucille E. "1985-86 Contract Terms For Incoming Accounting Faculty," **AIA**, 1987, Vol. 4, pp. 153-178.

Lammers, Lucille E. (Gardner, Mona J. and Lucille E. Lammers. "Cost Accounting In Large Banks," **MA**, 1988, Vol. 69, No. 10, pp. 34-40.)

Lammers, Lucille E. (Mehl, Arthur G. and Lucille E. Lammers. "A Report And Analysis Of The Accountancy Faculty Recruiting Surveys Of 1975-1978," **AR**, 1979, Vol. 54, No. 3, pp. 609-617.)

Lammert, Thomas B. and Gregory J. Stratis. "Uniform Capitalization Rules Are Here To Stay," **MA**, 1987, Vol. 69, No. 6, pp. 31-33.

Lammert, Thomas B. and Robert Ehrsam. "The Human Element: The Real Challenge In Modernizing Cost Systems," **MA**, 1987, Vol. 69, No. 1, pp. 32-37.

Lammie, H. R. "Return On Capital Employed," **JOA**, 1958, Vol. 106, No. 2, pp. 35-41.

Lampe, James C. and Kenneth R. Earnest. "Motivation: A Key To Accountants' Productivity And Turnover," **MA**, 1984, Vol. 65. No. 8, pp. 50-55.

Lampe, James C. "A Practical EDP Audit-Retrieval System For Education," **AR**, 1978, Vol. 53, No. 4, pp. 970-978.

Lampe, James C. "A Time-Sharing Program Library For Accounting Courses," **AR**, 1971, Vol. 46, No. 1, pp. 156-159.

Lampe, James C. "Electronic Funds Transfer Systems," **MA**, 1977. Vol. 59, pp. 37-41.

Lampe, James C. "The Trend Toward Automated Capital Investment Decisions," **MA**, 1971, Vol. 52, No. 10, pp. 37-42.

Lampe, James C. (Earnest. Kenneth R. and James C. Lampe. "An Expectancy Theory Investigation Into Causes Of Employee Turnover In Public Accounting," **AIA**, 1987, Vol. 4, pp. 215-238.)

Lancaster, Joe and Ted D. Englebrecht. "An Analysis Of The Availability Of Percentage Depletion For Lease Bonuses And Advance Royalties," **JATA**, 1983, vol. 4, No. 2, pp. 44-51.

Lancioni, Richard A. and William A. Dempsey. "The Critical Role Of Cost Accounting In Distribution Planning And Control," **CA**, 1983, Vol. 1, No. 3, pp. 26-32.

Landagora, Dustin C. (Neumann, Bruce R. and Dustin C. Landagora. "Measuring Divisional Performance For An Oil Company," **MA**, 1982, Vol. 63, No. 9, pp. 41-46.)

Landau, William M. (Folkenflik, Max and William M. Landau. "The Impact Of The Mann Judd Landau Case," **CPAJ**, 1988, Vol. 58, No. 10, pp. 32-44.)

Lander, Gerald H. and Alan Reinstein. "Identifying A Common Body Of Knowledge For Management Accounting," **IAE**, 1987, Vol. 2, No. 2, pp. 264-280.

Lander, Gerald H. (Tipgos, Manuel A., James R. Holmes and

Gerald H. Lander. "The Management Accountant Today: A Status Report," **MA**, 1983, Vol. 65, No. 5, pp. 53-57.)

Landis, Ira M. (Chazen, Charles and Ira M. Landis. "Audit Committees - Why And How," **CPAJ**, 1976, Vol. 46, No. 8, pp. 33-37.)

Landman, J. H. "The Reality Test In Family Partnerships," **AR**, 1950, Vol. 25, No. 3, pp. 302-306.

Landry, Horace J. "Auditing Instruction At The Undergraduate College Level," **AR**, 1964, Vol. 39, No. 1, pp. 164-166.

Landsittel, David L. and Jerry E. Serlin. "Evaluating The Materiality Of Errors In Financial Statements," **JAAF**, 1982, Vol. 5, No. 4, pp. 291-300.

Landsittel, David L. "Two Views On The Auditor's Report: The Last Word Or In Need Of Change?," **JOA**, 1987, Vol. 163, No. 2, pp. 80-85.

Landsman, Wayne R. and Joseph Magliolo. "Cross-Sectional Capital Market Research And Model Specification," **AR**, 1988, Vol. 63, No. 4, pp. 586-604.

Landsman, Wayne R. (Beaver, William H., Paul A. Griffin and Wayne R. Landsman. "The Incremental Information Content Of Replacement Cost Earnings," **JAEC**, 1982, Vol. 4, No. 1, pp. 15-39.)

Landsman, Wayne R. (Beaver, William H., Paul A. Griffin and Wayne R. Landsman. "Testing For Incremental Information Content In The Presence Of Collinearity: A Comment," **JAEC**, 1984, Vol. 6, No. 3, pp. 219-223.)

Landsman, Wayne R. (Beaver, William H. and Wayne R. Landsman. "Note On The Behavior Of Residual Security Returns For Winner And Loser Portfolios," **JAEC**, 1981, Vol. 3, No. 3, pp. 233-241.)

Landsman, Wayne. "An Empirical Investigation Of Pension And Property Rights," **AR**, 1986, Vol. 61, No. 4, pp. 662-691.

Landwehr, Bernard J. (Barker, Raymond F. and Bernard J. Landwehr. "Quantitative Techniques And The Faculty," **AR**, 1966, Vol. 41, No. 2, pp. 338-340.)

Lane, Joe. "Methods And Techniques Of Presenting Accounting Career Opportunities To High School And Preparatory School Students," **AR**, 1954, Vol. 29, No. 3, pp. 502-505.

Lane, Joseph E. "Elementary Accounting And The Non-Accounting Major - A Proposal," **AR**, 1951, Vol. 26, No. 1, pp. 105-106.

Lane, Michael R. (Raiborn, Mitchell H., Michael R. Lane and D. D. Raiborn. "Purchased Loss Carryforwards: An Unresolved Issue," **JOA**, 1983, Vol. 156, No. 5, pp. 98-108.)

Lane, Michael R. (Raiborn, Mitchell H., Michael R. Lane and D. D. Raiborn. "Accounting For 'That Other' Prior Period Adjustment," **MA**, 1985, Vol. 67, No. 1, pp. 39-43.)

Lanen, William N. and Rex Thompson. "Stock Price Reactions As Surrogates For Net Cash Flow Effects Of Corporate Policy Decisions," **JAEC**, 1988, Vol. 10, No. 4, pp. 311-334.

Lanen, William N. and Robert E. Verrecchia. "Operating Decisions And The Disclosure Of Management Accounting Information," **JAR**, 1987, Vol. 25, Supp., pp. 165-189.

Lang, Edwin R. and John Ashworth. "Integration In Fact - A Test Of The Professional Accountant As A Citizen," **JOA**, 1971, Vol. 131, No. 4, pp. 41-46.

Lang, Fred R. "Cost Accounting Standards And Financial Auditing," **MA**, 1975, Vol. 56, No. 10, pp. 21-23.

Lang, K. Bodo. (Hillhouse, A. M. and K. Bodo Lang. "German Federal Audit Court," **AR**, 1952, Vol. 27, No. 4, pp. 530-543.)

Lang, Richard C. and Charles F. Lursen. "The Captive Finance Company: Profitability And Control Reporting," **MA**, 1970, Vol. 51, No. 11, pp. 45-50.

Lange, Otto K. "Counting Chickens Before And After They Hatch," **MA**, 1975, Vol. 57, No. 5, pp. 35-36.

Langemeier, Brian. (Hoffman, Michael J. R. and Brian Langemeier. "Tax Planning For Divorced Couples Under TRA 86," **CPAJ**, 1988, Vol. 58, No. 5, pp. 40-47.)

Langenderfer, Harold Q. and Ernest H. Weinwurm. "Bringing Accounting Curricula Up-To-Date," **AR**, 1956, Vol. 31, No. 3, pp. 423-430.

Langenderfer, Harold Q. and Jack C. Robertson. "A Theoretical Structure For Independent Audits Of Management," **AR**, 1969, Vol. 44, No. 4, pp. 777-787.

Langenderfer, Harold Q. "A Conceptual Framework For Financial Reporting," **JOA**, 1973, Vol. 136, No. 1, pp. 46-55.

Langenderfer, Harold Q. "Accounting Education's History - A 100-Year Search For Identity," **JOA**, 1987, Vol. 163, No. 5, pp. 302-331.

Langenderfer, Harold Q. (Graham, Willard J. and Harold Q. Langenderfer. "Reporting Of Leases: Comment On APB Opinion No. 5," **JOA**, 1965, Vol. 119, No. 3, pp. 57-62.)

Langenderfer, Harold. "A Problem Of Communication," **JOA**, 1967, Vol. 123, No. 1, pp. 33-40.

Langer, Clarence. "Derivations Of Accounting Terminology," **MA**, 1971, Vol. 52, No. 9, pp. 43-44.

Langer, Clarence. "Paciolo - Patriarch Of Accounting," **AR**, 1958, Vol. 33, No. 3, pp. 482-484.

Langholm, Odd. "Cost Structure And Costing Method: An Empirical Study," **JAR**, 1965, Vol. 3, No. 2, pp. 218-227.

Langston, David C. (Austin, Kenneth R. and David C. Langston. "Peer Review: Its Impact On Quality Control," **JOA**, 1981, Vol. 152, No. 1, pp. 78-82.)

Lanham, James S. "Group Method Of Depreciation," **AR**, 1947, Vol. 22, No. 2, pp. 170-174.

Lanien, William N. (Halperin, Robert M. and William N. Lanien. "The Effects Of The Thor Power Tool Decision On The LIFO/FIFO Choice," **AR**, 1987, Vol. 62, No. 2, pp. 378-384.)

Lanier, Roy A. (Smith, Charles H., Roy A. Lanier and Martin E. Taylor. "Comments On Survey Of Attitudes On

Management Auditing: A Reply," **AR**, 1973, Vol. 48, No. 1, pp. 123-125.)

Lanier, Roy A. (Smith, Charles H. and Roy A. Lanier. "The Audit Of Management: Report On A Field Study," **MA**, 1970, Vol. 51, No. 12, pp. 24-26.)

Lanier, Roy A. (Smith, Charles H., Roy A. Lanier and Martin E. Taylor. "The Need For And Scope Of The Audit Of Management: A Survey Of Attitudes," **AR**, 1972, Vol. 47, No. 2, pp. 270-283.)

Lanigar, Mary E. "Doing Business As Partnership Or Corporation," **JOA**, 1955, Vol. 99, No. 5, pp. 48-53.

Lanigar, Mary E. "Estate And Trust Income," **JOA**, 1956, Vol. 102, No. 4, pp. 37-42.

Lankford, Patricia and Charles Cook. "The 'Vital Few' Saves Costs," **MA**, 1986, Vol. 68, No. 2, pp. 54-55.

Lantry, Terry L. "An Experiment," **AR**, 1971, Vol. 46, No. 3, pp. 596-597.

LaPlace, William. (Abs, George, Clayton Grimstad, Robert Hay, W. Asquith Howe, William LaPlace, Francis J. McGurr and William Serraino. "Historical Dates In Accounting," **AR**, 1954, Vol. 29, No. 3, pp. 486-493.)

Lapsley, Irvine. "A Case For Depreciation Accounting In UK Health Authorities," **ABR**, 1981-82, Vol. 12, No. 45, pp. 21-29.

Lapsley, Irvine. "Capital Budgeting, Public Service Organizations And UK Government Policy," **JAPP**, 1988, Vol. 7, No. 1, pp. 65-74.

Lapsley, Irvine. "Financial Objectives, Productive Efficiency And The Regulation Of A Subsidised State Monopoly," **ABR**, 1983-84, Vol. 14, No. 55, pp. 217-228.

Lapsley, Irvine. "Risk Capital For A Profitable Public Corporation: Public Dividend Capital Or Equity?," **ABACUS**, 1985, Vol. 21, No. 1, pp. 3-18.

LaRue, David W. (Duncan, William A., David W. LaRue and P. M. J. Reckers. "An Empirical Examination Of The Influence Of Selected Economic And Non-Economic Variables On Decision Making By Tax Professionals," **AIT**, 1988, Vol. 2, pp. xx-xx.)

Larcker, David F. and Lawrence Revsine. "The Oil And Gas Accounting Controversy: An Analysis Of Economic Consequences," **AR**, 1983, Vol. 58, No. 4, pp. 706-732.

Larcker, David F. and V. Parker Lessig. "An Examination Of The Linear And Retrospective Process Tracing Approaches To Judgment Modeling," **AR**, 1983, Vol. 58, No. 1, pp. 58-77.

Larcker, David F. "The Association Between Performance Plan Adoption And Corporate Capital Investment," **JAEC**, 1983, Vol. 5, No. 1, pp. 3-30.

Larcker, David F. "The Perceived Importance Of Selected Information Characteristics For Strategic Capital Budgeting Decisions," **AR**, 1981, Vol. 56, No. 3, pp. 519-538.

Larcker, David F. (Lambert, Richard A. and David F. Larcker. "Golden Parachutes, Executive Decision-Making, And Shareholder Wealth," **JAEC**, 1985, Vol. 7, No. 1/3, pp. 179-203.)

Larcker, David F. (Lambert, Richard A. and David F. Larcker. "An Analysis Of The Use Of Accounting And Market Measures Of Performance In Executive Compensation Contracts," **JAR**, 1987, Vol. 25, Supp., pp. 85-125.)

Larcker, David F. (Lambert, Richard A. and David F. Larcker. "Executive Compensation Effects Of Large Corporate Acquisitions," **JAPP**, 1987, Vol. 6, No. 4, pp. 231-243.)

Larcker, David F., Renee E. Reder and Daniel T. Simon. "Trades By Insiders As Evidence Of The Existence Of Economic Consequences Of Accounting Standards," **AR**, 1983, Vol. 58, No. 3, pp. 606-620.

Larcker, D. F. (Ferris, K. R. and D. F. Larcker. "Explanatory Variables Of Auditor Performance In A Large Public Accounting Firm," **AOS**, 1983, Vol. 8, No. 1, pp. 1-12.)

Larcker, D. F. (Gordon, L. A., D. F. Larcker and F. D. Tuggle. "Strategic Decision Processes And The Design Of Accounting Information Systems: Conceptual Linkages," **AOS**, 1978, Vol. 3, No. 3/4, pp. 203-214.)

Largay, James A., III and Ferdinand K. Levy. "Using Segment Reporting And Input-Output Analysis For Managerial Planning," **MA**, 1978, Vol. 60, No. 5, pp. 46-50.

Largay, James A., III and Jack W. Paul. "Market Efficiency And Legal Liability Of Auditors: Comment," **AR**, 1983, Vol. 58, No. 4, pp. 820-832.

Largay, James A., III. "Microeconomic Foundations Of Variable Costing," **AR**, 1973, Vol. 48, No. 1, pp. 115-119.

Largay, James A., III. "SFAS No. 52: Expediency Or Principle?," **JAAF**, 1983, Vol. 7, No. 1, pp. 44-53.

Largay, James A., III. (Davis, Michael L. and James A. Largay, III. "Reporting Consolidated Gains And Losses On Subsidiary Stock Issuances," **AR**, 1988, Vol. 63, No. 2, pp. 348-363.)

Largay, James A., III. (Drtina, Ralph E. and James A. Largay, III. "Pitfalls In Calculating Cash Flow From Operations," **AR**, 1985, Vol. 60, No. 2, pp. 314-326.)

Largay, James A., III. (Ketz, J. Edward and James A. Largay, III. "Reporting Income And Cash Flows From Operations," **ACCHOR**, 1987, Vol. 1, No. 2, pp. 9-18.)

Largay, James A., III. (Ketz, J. Edward and James A. Largay, III. "Teaching The 'Funds' Statement Under Alternative Valuation Methods," **IAE**, 1985, No. 1, pp. 87-96.)

Largay, James A., III. (Thode, Stephen F., Ralph E. Drtina and James A. Largay, III. "Operating Cash Flows: A Growing Need For Separate Reporting," **JAAF**, 1986, Vol. 1 (New Series), No. 1, pp. 46-61.)

Larimore, L. Keith. "Break-Even Analysis For Higher Education," **MA**, 1974, Vol. 56, No. 3, pp. 25-28.

Larimore, Theodore R. "Renegotiation Accounting," **AR**, 1955, Vol. 30, No. 2, pp. 298-306.

Larimore, T. R. "Accounting Administration Of Unemployment Insurance," **AR**, 1945, Vol. 20, No. 3, pp. 331-339.

Larimore, T. R. "Accounting In The Small Liberal-Arts College," **AR**, 1937, Vol. 12, No. 2, pp. 180-183.

Larkin, Joseph J. "Strategic Marketing Of Public Accounting Services," **CPAJ**, 1981, Vol. 51, No. 9, pp. 46-51.

Larkin, Paula D. (Nichols, Donald R., Jeffrey J. Tsay and Paula D. Larkin. "Investor Trading Responses To Differing Characteristics Of Voluntarily Disclosed Earnings Forecasts," **AR**, 1979, Vol. 54, No. 2, pp. 376-382.)

Larkin, Richard F. "Certain Nonprofit Organizations - Proposed Audit Guide," **CPAJ**, 1980, Vol. 50, No. 11, pp. 45-49.

Larkins, Earnest R. "Professors Who Teach Outside The United States: Tax Planning And Policy Analysis," **JATA**, 1987, Vol. 9, No. 1, pp. 48-74.

Larkins, Ernest R. (Dillon, Ray D., Betty C. Horn and Ernest R. Larkins. "More Value From Fringe Benefit Plans," **CPAJ**, 1986, Vol. 56, No. 11, pp. 40-57.)

Larracey, Susan A. "Hospital Planning For Cost-Effectiveness," **MA**, 1982, Vol. 64, No. 1, pp. 44-48.

Larrea, Jose. (Elliott, Edward L., Jose Larrea and Juan M. Rivera. "Accounting Aid To Developing Countries," **AR**, 1968, Vol. 43, No. 4, pp. 763-768.)

Larsen, E. John. "The Controversy Over Independent Audits For Banks," **JOA**, 1967, Vol. 123, No. 5, pp. 42-46.

Larsen, E. John. (Holder, William W., E. John Larsen and Doyle Z. Williams. "Educational Requirements For Public Accounting," **CPAJ**, 1985, Vol. 55, No. 12, pp. 36-49.)

Larsen, John B. (Lasusa, Peter R. and John B. Larsen. "Accounting For Hedged Transactions," **CPAJ**, 1978, Vol. 48, No. 6, pp. 17-24.)

Larsen, Roy E. "The Crisis In Education," **JOA**, 1956, Vol. 101, No. 1, pp. 29-33.

Larson, Bruce. "LIFO Reports Current Position," **MA**, 1976, Vol. 57, No. 8, pp. 34-36.

Larson, Charles B. "Directors For CPA Firms: A Provocative Proposal," **JOA**, 183, Vol. 155, No. 5, pp. 86-94.

Larson, H. Gary. (Jensen, James A. and H. Gary Larson. "Records Management For Pollution Abatement Programs: Meeting EPA Requirements," **MA**, 1980, Vol. 61, No. 9, pp. 37-41.)

Larson, Kermit and R. W. Schattke. "Current Cash Equivalent, Additivity, And Financial Action," **AR**, 1966, Vol. 41, No. 4, pp. 634-641.

Larson, Kermit D. and Gary L. Holstrum. "Financial Accounting Standards In The United States: 1973 - ?," **ABACUS**, 1973, Vol. 9, No. 1, pp. 3-15.

Larson, Kermit D. and Nicholas J. Gonedes. "Business Combinations: An Exchange Ratio Determination Model," **AR**, 1969, Vol. 44, No. 4, pp. 720-728.

Larson, Kermit D. and R. W. Schattke. "A Note On Vickrey's Comment," **AR**, 1975, Vol. 50, No. 1, p. 147.

Larson, Kermit D. "Descriptive Validity Of Accounting Calculations," **AR**, 1967, Vol. 42, No. 3, pp. 480-488.

Larson, Kermit D. "Implications Of Measurement Theory On Accounting Concept Formulation," **AR**, 1969, Vol. 44, No. 1, pp. 38-47.

Larson, Kermit D. (Gonedes, Nicholas J. and Kermit D. Larson. "A Look At 'A Comment On 'Business Combinations: An Exchange Ratio Determination Model'," **AR**, 1971, Vol. 46, No. 3, pp. 572-573.)

Larson, Lowell E. "Church Accounting," **JOA**, 1957, Vol. 103, No. 5, pp. 28-35.

Larson, Raymond L. "Decentralization In Real Life," **MA**, 1974, Vol. 55, No. 9, pp. 28-32.

Larson, Raymond L. "Transfer Pricing In A Commercial Bank - A Differing Viewpoint," **MA**, 1971, Vol. 53, No. 6, pp. 19-22.

Larson, Rholan E. and Thomas P. Kelley. "Differential Measurement In Accounting Standards: The Concept Makes Sense," **MA**, 1984, Vol. 158, No. 5, pp. 78-92.

Larson, Rholan E. "For The Members, By The Members," **JOA**, 1987, Vol. 164, No. 4, pp. 116-123.

Larson, Rholan E. "Self-Regulation: A Professional Step Forward," **JOA**, 1983, Vol. 156, No. 3, pp. 58-67.

Larson, Rholan E. (Lee, Bernard Z., Rholan E. Larson and Philip B. Chenok. "Issues Confronting The Accounting Profession," **JOA**, 1983, Vol. 156, No. 5, pp. 78-85.)

Larson, Steve and C. Mike Merz. "Operations Research At Boise Cascade," **MA**, 1978, Vol. 59, No. 8, pp. 33-36.

Larsson, Lars. (Swieringa, Robert J., Michael Gibbins, Lars Larsson and Janet Lawson Sweeney. "Experiments In The Heuristics Of Human Information Processing," **JAR**, 1976, Vol. 14, Supp., pp. 159-187.)

Larsson, S. and G. R. Chesley. "An Analysis Of The Auditor's Uncertainty About Probabilities," **CAR**, 1985-86, Vol. 2, No. 2, pp. 259-282.

LaSalle, Brother. "An Approach To Ethics," **AR**, 1954, Vol. 29, No. 4, pp. 687-689.

LaSalle, Brother. "Factors Contributing To Success In Public Accounting," **AR**, 1956, Vol. 31, No. 2, pp. 315-316.

LaSalle, Brother. "Basic Research In Accounting," **AR**, 1959, Vol. 34, No. 4, pp. 603-608.

LaSalle, Brother. "The Philosophy Of Accounting (Continued)," **AR**, 1958, Vol. 33, No. 2, pp. 254-255.

Lasser, J. K. "20 Useful Tax Ideas From NYU Tax Institute," **JOA**, 1951, Vol. 92, No. 1, pp. 52-61.

Lasser, J. K. "Auditing Program Of Audit Bureau Of Circulations," **JOA**, 1953, Vol. 96, No. 4, pp. 464-469.

Lasser, J. K. "How CPA Serves His Client In The Art Of Tax Planning," **JOA**, 1952, Vol. 93, No. 6, pp. 678-688.

Lasser, J. K. "How To Analyze Business Taxpayer To Get Minimum Taxes Under Higher 1950 - 1951 Tax Rates," **JOA**, 1950, Vol. 90, No. 5, pp. 379-383.

Lasser, J. K. "How To Defer Compensation To Obtain Minimum Tax To Both Employee And Employer," **JOA**, 1950, Vol. 89, No. 1, pp. 42-47.

Lasser, J. K. "How To Raise Executives' Take-Home Pay Under Wage Control And Tax Laws," **JOA**, 1952, Vol. 93, No. 2, pp. 166-175.

Lasser, J. K. "Increasing Charitable Deduction By Non-Cash Gifts," **JOA**, 1953, Vol. 95, No. 6, pp. 701-705.

Lasser, J. K. "Treasurers Define The Nature Of Advertising Items," **JOA**, 1954, Vol. 97, No. 4, pp. 428-429.

Lasser, J. K. (Casey, William J. and J. K. Lasser. "Decisions To Make Now To Minimize Excess-Profits Tax Liability," **JOA**, 1951, Vol. 91, No. 2, pp. 243-251.)

Lasser, S. Jay. "Organizing Preparation Of Tax Returns In CPA's Office," **JOA**, 1953, Vol. 95, No. 2, pp. 190-197.

Lassila, Dennis R. "Divorce Taxation After The 1984 Act," **CPAJ**, 1985, Vol. 55, No. 2, pp. 36-43.

Lasusa, Peter R. and John B. Larsen. "Accounting For Hedged Transactions," **CPAJ**, 1978, Vol. 48, No. 6, pp. 17-24.

Latanich, Gary A. and John Kaminarides. "Performance Of Accountants In International Business," **IJAER**, 1984, Vol. 19, No. 2, pp. 157-164.

Lathan, Malcolm H., Jr. (Rouse, Robert W. and Malcolm H. Lathan, Jr. "Improving The Confirmation Process," **CPAJ**, 1986, Vol. 56, No. 12, pp. 58-61.)

Lathan, Malcolm H., Jr. (Scott, Richard A., Ernest J. Pavlock and Malcolm H. Lathan, Jr. "On-Campus Recruiting: The Students Speak Up," **JOA**, 1985, Vol. 159, No. 1, pp. 60-75.)

Lathan, Malcolm H., Jr., Barbara A. Ostrowski, Ernest J. Pavlock and Richard A. Scott. "Recruiting Entry Level Staff: Gender Differences," **CPAJ**, 1987, Vol. 57, No. 1, pp. 30-43.

Lathen, William C. (Frakes, Albert H. and William C. Lathen. "A Comparison Of Multiple-Choice And Problem Examinations In Introductory Financial Accounting," **JAED**, 1985, Vol. 3, No. 1, pp. 81-89.)

LaTouche, William. (Dropkin, Murray, Vincent Milito, Theresa Dominianni and William La Touche. "Trends In Charities Registration And Reporting," **CPAJ**, 1988, Vol. 58, No. 5, pp. 56-65.)

Latzer, Paul J. "Cost Accountant And Industrial Engineer," **AR**, 1955, Vol. 30, No. 2, pp. 348-350.

Lau, Amy Hing-Ling and Hon-Shiang Lau. "Improving Present Value Analysis With A Programmable Calculator," **MA**, 1979, Vol. 61, No. 5, pp. 52-58.

Lau, Amy Hing-Ling and Hon-Shiang Lau. "CVP Analysis Under Uncertainty - A Log Normal Approach: A Comment," **AR**, 1976, Vol. 51, No. 1, pp. 163-167.

Lau, Amy Hing-Ling and Hon-Shiang Lau. "A Comment On Shih's General Decision Model For CVP Analysis," **AR**, 1981, Vol. 56, No. 4, pp. 980-983.

Lau, Amy Hing-Ling and Hon-Shiang Lau. "Some Proposed Approaches For Writing Off Capitalized Human Resource Assets," **JAR**, 1978, Vol. 16, No. 1, pp. 80-102.

Lau, Amy Hing-Ling and Hon-Shiang Lau. "CVP Analysis With Stochastic Price-Demand Functions And Shortage-Surplus Costs," **CAR**, 1987-88, Vol. 4, No. 1, pp. 194-209.

Lau, Amy Hing-Ling and Hon-Shiang Lau. "Towards A Theory Of Stochastic Exit Value," **ABR**, 1983-84, Vol. 14, No. 53, pp. 21-28.

Lau, Amy Hing-Ling. "A Five-State Financial Distress Prediction Model," **JAR**, 1987, Vol. 25, No. 1, pp. 127-138.

Lau, Amy Hing-Ling. (Kottas, John F., Amy Hing-Ling Lau and Hon-Shiang Lau. "A General Approach to Stochastic Management Planning Models: An Overview," **AR**, 1978, Vol. 53, No. 2, pp. 389-401.)

Lau, Hon-Shiang. (Jaggi, Bikki and Hon-Shiang Lau. "Toward A Model For Human Resource Valuation," **AR**, 1974, Vol. 49, No. 2, pp. 321-329.)

Lau, Hon-Shiang. (Jaggi, Bikki and Hon-Shiang Lau. "Toward A Model For Human Resource Valuation: A Reply," **AR**, 1975, Vol. 50, No. 2, pp. 348-350.)

Lau, Hon-Shiang. (Kottas, John F., Amy Hing-Ling Lau and Hon-Shiang Lau. "A General Approach to Stochastic Management Planning Models: An Overview," **AR**, 1978, Vol. 53, No. 2, pp. 389-401.)

Lau, Hon-Shiang. (Kottas, John F. and Hon-Shiang Lau. "On The Accuracy Of Normalcy Approximation In Stochastic C-V-P Analysis: A Comment," **AR**, 1978, Vol. 53, No. 1, pp. 247-251.)

Lau, Hon-Shiang. (Kottas, John F. and Hon-Shiang Lau. "Direct Simulation In Stochastic CVP Analysis," **AR**, 1978, Vol. 53, No. 3, pp. 698-707.)

Lau, Hon-Shiang. (Lau, Amy Hing-Ling and Hon-Shiang Lau. "Towards A Theory Of Stochastic Exit Value," **ABR**, 1983-84, Vol. 14, No. 53, pp. 21-28.)

Lau, Hon-Shiang. (Lau, Amy Hing-Ling and Hon-Shiang Lau. "Some Proposed Approaches For Writing Off Capitalized Human Resource Assets," **JAR**, 1978, Vol. 16, No. 1, pp. 80-102.)

Lau, Hon-Shiang. (Lau, Amy Hing-Ling and Hon-Shiang Lau. "A Comment On Shih's General Decision Model For CVP Analysis," **AR**, 1981, Vol. 56, No. 4, pp. 980-983.)

Lau, Hon-Shiang. (Lau, Amy Hing-Ling and Hon-Shiang Lau. "CVP Analysis With Stochastic Price-Demand Functions And Shortage-Surplus Costs," **CAR**, 1987-88, Vol. 4, No. 1, pp. 194-209.)

Lau, Hon-Shiang. (Lau, Amy Hing-Ling and Hon-Shiang Lau. "Improving Present Value Analysis With A Programmable Calculator," **MA**, 1979, Vol. 61, No. 5, pp. 52-58.)

Lau, Hon-Shiang. (Lau, Amy Hing-Ling and Hon-Shiang Lau. "CVP Analysis Under Uncertainty - A Log Normal Approach: A Comment," AR, 1976, Vol. 51, No. 1, pp. 163-167.)

Laughlin, Eugene J. (Martin, James R. and Eugene J. Laughlin. "A Graphic Approach To Variance Analysis Emphasizes Concepts Rather Than Mechanics," IAE, 1988, Vol. 3, No. 2, pp. 351-364.)

Laughlin, Eugene J., James W. Gentry and Carolyn A. May. "Comparison Of Alternative Forms Of Teaching Fundamentals Of Accounting," AR, 1976, Vol. 51, No. 2, pp. 347-351.

Laughlin, R. C. "Accounting Systems In Organisational Contexts: A Case For Critical Theory," AOS, 1987, Vol. 12, No. 4/5, pp. 479-502.

Laughlin, R. C. (Lowe, E. A., A. G. Puxty and R. C. Laughlin. "Simple Theories For Complex Processes: Accounting Policy And The Market For Myopia," JAPP, 1983, Vol. 2, No. 1, pp. 19-42.)

Laurent, Mark. "Protect Your Pension Surplus From Interest Rate Risk," MA, 1988, Vol. 70, No. 3, pp. 24-28.

Lauver, R. C. "The Case For Poolings," AR, 1966, Vol. 41, No. 1, pp. 65-74.

Lauzen, Leo G. "Small Business Failures Are Controllable," CA, 1985, Vol. 3, No. 3, pp. 34-39.

Lauzen, Leo. "Franchising: Another Strategy To Start Your Own Business," MA, 1984, Vol. 66, No. 1, pp. 50-53.

LaValle, Irving H. and Alfred Rappaport. "On The Economics Of Acquiring Information Of Imperfect Reliability," AR, 1968, Vol. 43, No. 2, pp. 225-230.

Lavely, Joseph A. "Inflation: Does The Firm Benefit?," MA, 1975, Vol. 56, No. 12, pp. 16-18.

Laverdiere, Raymond G. (McKee, Tim C. and Raymond G. Laverdiere. "Maximizing Depreciation Benefits," MA, 1987, Vol. 68, No. 12, pp. 35-38.)

Lavin, David. "Perceptions Of The Independence Of The Auditor," AR, 1976, Vol. 51, No. 1, pp. 41-50.

Lavin, D. "Some Effects Of The Perceived Independence Of The Auditor," AOS, 1977, Vol. 2, No. 3, pp. 237-244.

Lavoie, D. "The Accounting Of Interpretations And The Interpretation Of Accounts: The Communicative Function Of 'The Language Of Business'," AOS, 1987, Vol. 12, No. 6, pp. 579-604.

Lawler, Edward E., III. (Sorensen, James E., John Grant Rhode and Edward E. Lawler. III. "The Generation Gap In Public Accounting," JOA, 1973, Vol. 136. No. 6, pp. 42-50.)

Lawler, E. E., III. (Mirvis, P. H. and E. E. Lawler, III. "Systems Are Not Solutions: Issues In Creating Information Systems That Account For The Human Organization," AOS, 1983, Vol. 8, No. 2/3, pp. 175-190.)

Lawler, E. E., III. (Rhode, J. G., J. E. Sorensen and E. E. Lawler, III. "Sources Of Professional Staff Turnover In Public Accounting Firms Revealed By The Exit Interview," AOS, 1977, Vol. 2, No. 2, pp. 165-176.)

Lawler, John. "Accounting: A Bridge Across The Generation Gap," JOA, 1971, Vol. 131, No. 5, pp. 44-48.

Lawler, John. "The Quest For Accounting Philosophers," JAR, 1967, Vol. 5, Supp., pp. 86-92.

Lawler, William C. (Farrar, Robert H., William C. Lawler and Linda J. Block. "How CFOs View The CMA Program," MA, 1985, Vol. 67, No. 5, pp. 33-37.)

Lawrence, Charles and Byron F. E. Bedwell. "Professional Practice In England And America," AR, 1961, Vol. 36, No. 2, pp. 269-273.

Lawrence, Charles. "A Study Of A Program Budget For A Small City," JOA, 1972, Vol. 134, No. 5, pp. 52-57.

Lawrence, Charles. "A Suggested Program For Cooperation Between Educational Institutions And Small Practitioners," AR, 1955, Vol. 30, No. 4, pp. 645-650.

Lawrence, Charles. "Brazil - Education And Accountants," AR, 1962, Vol. 37, No. 3, pp. 510-514.

Lawrence, Charles. "Professional Responsibilities In Referral Fees," JOA, 1958, Vol. 106, No. 3, pp. 61-60.

Lawrence, Charles. "Teaching Responsibilities And Machine-Graded Tests," AR, 1955, Vol. 30, No. 3, pp. 538-539.

Lawrence, Charles. "Why Not Improve Your Presention Of The 'Statement Of Changes'?," CPAJ, 1974, Vol. 44, No. 5, pp. 41-44.

Lawrence, Charles. (Tennant, Kirk and Charles Lawrence. "Teaching Strategies: Effects On Student Evaluations Of Teachers," AR, 1975, Vol. 50, No. 4, pp. 899-904.)

Lawrence, Edward C. "Reporting Delays For Failed Firms," JAR, 1983, Vol. 21, No. 2, pp. 606-610.

Lawrence, Edward C. "What Should Banks Disclose?," MA, 1982, Vol. 63, No. 11, pp. 39-46.

Lawrence, W. B. "Cost Accounting Versus The Pricing System," AR, 1945, Vol. 20, No. 2, pp. 177-181.

Lawrence, W. B. "Teaching Cost Accounting," AR, 1933, Vol. 8, No. 2, pp. 155-157.

Lawson, Gerald H. "Joint Cost Analysis As An Aid To Management - A Rejoinder," AR, 1956, Vol. 31, No. 3, pp. 439-443.

Lawson, Gerald H. "Joint Cost Analysis As An Aid To Management - A Further Note," AR, 1957. Vol. 32, No. 3, pp. 431-433.

Lawson, G. H. and A. W. Stark. "The Concept Of Profit For Fund Raising," ABR, 1975-76, Vol. 6, No. 21, pp. 21-41.

Lawson, G. H. "The Measurement Of Corporate Profitability On A Cash-Flow Basis," IJAER, 1980. Vol. 16, No. 1, pp. 11-46.

Lawson, G. H. "The Measurement Of Corporate Performance On A Cash Flow Basis: A Reply To Mr. Egginton," ABR, 1984-85, Vol. 15, No. 58, pp. 99-108.

Lawson, William M. (Da Costa, Richard C., Jacques C. Bourgeois and William M. Lawson. "A Classification Of International Financial Accounting Practices," IJAER, 1978, Vol. 13, No. 2, pp. 73-85.)

Laxton, David. (Hartman, Bart P., David Laxton and William Walvoord. "A Look At Employee Stock Ownership Plans As Financing Tools," MA, 1977, Vol. 58, No. 9, pp. 23-28.)

Lay, Chester F. "A Study Of Public Accounting Personnel From the Viewpoint Of Professional Advancement," AR, 1931, Vol. 6, No. 3, pp. 218-229.

Lay, Chester F. "Business Policy As Related To Accounting." AR, 1929, Vol. 4, No. 2, pp. 121-128.

Lay, C. F. "The Growth Of The Controller And The Business Administration Curriculum," AR, 1928, Vol. 3, No. 1, pp. 43-52.

Lazenby, C. D. "The Economic Accounting Approach," AR, 1927, Vol. 2. No. 4, pp. 397-408.

Lazere, Monroe R. "The Roles Of The Secured Lender And The Borrower's CPA," CPAJ, 1972, Vol. 42, No. 4, pp. 308-313.

Lea, Richard B. "A Note On The Definition Of Cost Coefficients In A Linear Programming Model," AR, 1972, Vol. 47, No. 2, pp. 346-350.

Lea, Richard B. "Comments On Mock's Concepts Of Information Value," AR, 1973, Vol. 48, No. 2, pp. 389-393.

Lea, Richard B. "Recommendations Of The Commission On Auditors' Responsibilities - An Analysis Of The Profession's Responses," AJPT, 1981-82, Vol. 1, No. 1, pp. 53-93.

Leach, Jack R. "Cost Control At A New Plant," MA, 1970, Vol. 51, No. 8, pp. 23-24.

Leake, John B. (Dean, Steven T. and John B. Leake. "Passing Title 'Outside The U.S.' For Tax Purposes," JOA, 1952, Vol. 94, No. 4, pp. 457-459.)

Learned, Marcel. "How To Set Fees," JOA, 1961, Vol. 111, No. 1, pp. 55-58.

Leary, Neil. "Minimizing Export Cash Flow Delays," MA, 1984, Vol. 65, No. 10, pp. 33-39.

Lease, Ronald C. (Brickley, James A., Sanjai Bhagat and Ronald C. Lease. "The Impact Of Long-Range Managerial Compensation Plans On Shareholder Wealth," JAEC, 1985. Vol. 7, No. 1/3, pp. 115-129.)

Leathers, Park E., James A. Sullivan and Jerome Bernstein. "The CPA Examination - Profile Of The Successful Candidate," AIA, 1984, Vol. 1, pp. 105-126.

Leaton, Edward K. "Comments On TEFRA's Pension Provisions," CPAJ, 1983, Vol. 53, No. 3, pp. 40-48.

Leavitt, Gary S. and Richard W. Sapp. "Who's Minding The Store?: Inventory Control For Bars And Clubs," MA, 1980, Vol. 62. No. 5, pp. 13-24.

Lebar, Mary Ann. "A General Semantics Analysis Of Selected Sections Of The 10-K, The Annual Report To Shareholders, And The Financial Press Release," AR, 1982, Vol. 57, No. 1, pp. 176-189.

Lebow, Marc I. and Rasoul H. Tondkar. "Accounting In The Soviet Union," IJAER, 1986, Vol. 22, No. 1, pp. 61-79.

Lederer, Albert L. and Louise Boyer Burky. "Understanding Top Management's Objectives: A Management Information Systems Concern," JIS, 1988, Vol. 3, No. 1, pp. 50-66.

Ledley, Ralph G. (Rosenfeld, Eugene and Ralph G. Ledley. "An Accounting Course For Majors And Non-Majors," AR, 1961, Vol. 36, No. 1, pp. 125-128.)

Ledwith, James W. (Whittington, Ray, Marilyn Zulinski and James W. Ledwith. "Completeness - The Elusive Assertion," JOA, 1983, Vol. 156, No. 2, pp. 82-92.)

Lee, Bernard Z. (Schlosser, Robert E., Bernard Z. Lee and George A. Rabito. "Continuing Professional Education 1887-1987," JOA, 1987, Vol. 163, No. 5, pp. 240-254.)

Lee, Bernard Z., Rholan E. Larson and Philip B. Chenok. "Issues Confronting The Accounting Profession," JOA, 1983, Vol. 156, No. 5, pp. 78-85.

Lee, Cheng F. and Chunchi Wu. "Expectation Formation And Financial Ratio Adjustment Processes," AR, 1988. Vol. 63. No. 2, pp. 292-306.

Lee, Cheng F. (Frecka, Thomas J. and Cheng F. Lee. "Generalized Financial Ratio Adjustment Processes And Their Implications," JAR, 1983, Vol. 21, No. 1, pp. 308-316.)

Lee, Chi-Wen Jevons. "Accounting Infrastructure And Economic Development," JAPP, 1987, Vol. 6, No. 2, pp. 75-85.

Lee, Chi-Wen Jevons. "Inventory Accounting And Earnings/Price Ratios: A Puzzle," CAR, 1988, Vol. 5, No. 1, pp. 371-388.

Lee, Chi-Wen Jevons. "The Speed Of Adjustment Of Financial Ratios: An Error-In-Variable Problem," JAR, 1984, Vol. 22, No. 2, pp. 776-781.

Lee, Chi-wen Jevons and David A. Hsieh. "Choice Of Inventory Accounting Methods: Comparative Analyses Of Alternative Hypotheses," JAR, 1985, Vol. 23, No. 2, pp. 468-485.

Lee, Chi-wen Jevons. "Stochastic Properties Of Cross-Sectional Financial Data," JAR, 1985, Vol. 23, No. 1, pp. 213-227.

Lee, Frederick C. "Healthcare Coalitions And Corporations: A Partnership For Lower Costs," CA, 1986, Vol. 4, No. 2, pp. 11-16.

Lee, Geoffrey Alan. "The Development Of Italian Bookkeeping 1211-1300," ABACUS, 1973, Vol. 9, No. 2, pp. 137-155.

Lee, Geoffrey A. "The Florentine Bank Ledger Fragments Of 1211: Some New Insights," JAR, 1973, Vol. 11, No. 1, pp. 47-61.

Lee, Geoffrey A. "The Francis Willughby Executorship Accounts, 1672-1682; An Early Double-Entry System In England," AR, 1981, Vol. 56, No. 3, pp. 539-553.

Lee, George A. "Internal Auditor's Function In Annual Audit," JOA, 1953, Vol. 96, No. 6, pp. 711-713.

Lee, G. A. "The Coming Of Age Of Double Entry: The Giovanni

Farolfi Ledger Of 1299-1300," **AHJ**, 1977, Vol. 4, No. 2, pp. 79-95.

Lee, **John Y.** "A New Approach To The Levels Of Assurance Issue In Auditing," **ABR**, 1981-82, Vol. 12, No. 45, pp. 35-40.

Lee, **John Y.** "Developing A Pricing System For A Small Business," **MA**, 1987, Vol. 68, No. 9, pp. 50-53.

Lee, **Lucy C.** and Norton M. Bedford. "An Information Theory Analysis Of The Accounting Process," **AR**, 1969, Vol. 44, No. 2, pp. 256-275.

Lee, **Lyman S.** "Feedback - A Key To Engineering Cost Control," **MA**, 1966, Vol. 48, No. 1, pp. 45-50.

Lee, **Mary M.** "The Challenge Of EDP Auditing," **MA**, 1988, Vol. 69, No. 9, pp. 52-53.

Lee, **Nadine Gordon.** (Mears, William H. Jr. and Nadine Gordon Lee. "Traps And Pitfalls For Preparers Of Individual Returns," **JOA**, 1988, Vol. 165, No. 2, pp. 45-53.)

Lee, **Richard W.** "Top Management's Challenge To The Accountant," **MA**, 1967, Vol. 48, No. 10, pp. 9-13.

Lee, **Samuel S. O.** "Korean Accounting Revaluation Laws," **AR**, 1965, Vol. 40, No. 3, pp. 622-625.

Lee, **Samuel S. O.** "Some Accounting And Philosophical Aspects Of The Third Korean Property Revaluation Law," **IJAER**, 1968, Vol. 3, No. 2, pp. 117-123.

Lee, **Stanley B., Jr.** "The 1969 Tax Reform Act And Employee Moving Expenses," **MA**, 1972, Vol. 53, No. 7, pp. 31-32.

Lee, **S. L.** and C. W. R. Ward. "The Investment Performance Of Property Unit Trusts Evaluated By Stochastic Dominance," **ABR**, 1980-81, Vol. 11, No. 44, pp. 303-308.

Lee, **Thomas A.** "Chambers And Accounting Communication," **ABACUS**, 1982, Vol. 18, No. 2, pp. 152-165.

Lee, **Tom.** "Cash Flows And Net Realizable Values: Further Evidence Of The Intuitive Concepts," **ABACUS**, 1984, Vol. 20, No. 2, pp. 125-137.

Lee, **T. A.** and A. W. Stark. "Cash Flow Accounting And Capital Budgeting," **ABR**, 1986-87, Vol. 17, No. 66, pp. 125-132.

Lee, **T. A.** and D. P. Tweedie. "Accounting Information: An Investigation Of Private Shareholders' Understanding," **ABR**, 1975-76, Vol. 6, No. 21, pp. 3-17.

Lee, **T. A.** and D. P. Tweedie. "Accounting Information: An Investigation Of Private Shareholder Usage," **ABR**, 1974-75, Vol. 5, No. 20, pp. 280-291.

Lee, **T. A.** and D. Tweedie. "The Private Shareholder: His Sources Of Financial Information And His Understanding Of Reporting Practices," **ABR**, 1975-76, Vol. 6, No. 24, pp. 304-314.

Lee, **T. A.** "A Note On Users And Uses Of Cash Flow Information," **ABR**, 1982-83, Vol. 13, No. 50, pp. 103-106.

Lee, **T. A.** "A Survey Of Accountants' Opinions On Cash Flow Reporting," **ABACUS**, 1981, Vol. 17, No. 2, pp. 130-144.

Lee, **T. A.** "Accounting For Goodwill," **ABR**, 1972-73, Vol. 3, No. 11, pp. 175-196.

Lee, **T. A.** "Cash Flow Accounting, Profit And Performance Measurement: A Response To A Challenge," **ABR**, 1984-85, Vol. 15, No. 58, pp. 93-98.

Lee, **T. A.** "Empirical Research Into Information Utility And Acceptability," **ABR**, 1974-75, Vol. 5, No. 18, pp. 140-144.

Lee, **T. A.** "Enterprise Income: Survival Or Decline And Fall?," **ABR**, 1973-74, Vol. 4, No. 15, pp. 178-192.

Lee, **T. A.** "Goodwill: An Example Of Will-O'-The-Wisp Accounting," **ABR**, 1970-71, Vol. 1, No. 4, pp. 318-328.

Lee, **T. A.** "Psychological Aspects Of Accounting," **ABR**, 1971-72, Vol. 2, No. 7, pp. 223-233.

Lee, **T. A.** "Reporting Cash Flows And Net Realisable Values," **ABR**, 1980-81, Vol. 11, No. 42, pp. 163-170.

Lee, **T. A.** "The Accounting Entity Concept, Accounting Standards And Inflation Accounting," **ABR**, 1979-80, Vol. 10, No. 38, pp. 176-186.

Lee, **T. A.** "The Early Debate On Financial And Physical Capital," **AHJ**, 1983, Vol. 10, No. 1, pp. 25-50.

Lee, **T. A.** "The Evolution And Revolution Of Financial Accounting: A Review Article," **ABR**, 1978-79, Vol. 9, No. 36, pp. 292-299.

Lee, **T. A.** "The Historical Development Of Internal Control From The Earliest Times To The End Of The Seventeenth Century," **JAR**, 1971, Vol. 9, No. 1, pp. 150-157.

Lee, **T. A.** "The Search For Correspondence With Economic Reality: A Review Article," **ABR**, 1987-88, Vol. 18, No. 69, pp. 43-46.

Lee, **T. A.** "Utility And Relevance - The Search For Reliable Accounting Information," **ABR**, 1970-71, Vol. 1, No. 3, pp. 242-249.

Lee, **T. A.**, L. Goldberg and Trevor Johnston. "The History Of Accounting's Three Reviews," **ABR**, 1977-78, Vol. 8, No. 29, pp. 58-67.

Leech, **Stewart A.** and Denis J. Pratt. "Current Cost Accounting In Australia, New Zealand, And The United Kingdom: A Comparative Study," **IJAER**, 1978, Vol. 13, No. 2, pp. 105-118.

Leech, **Stewart A.** "Profitability, Rates Of Return And Prices Justification," **ABACUS**, 1974, Vol. 10, No. 2, pp. 147-159.

Leech, **Stewart A.** "The Theory And Development Of A Matrix-Based Accounting System," **ABR**, 1985-86, Vol. 16, No. 64, pp. 327-342.

Leech, **Stewart**, Denis J. Pratt and W. G. W. Magill. "Asset Revaluations And Inflation In Australia, 1950 To 1975: An Industry Study," **IJAER**, 1982, Vol. 17, No. 2, pp. 23-34.

Leegstra, **Ruurd G.** (Brown, Robert D., Ruurd G. Leegstra and Lloyd J. Looram. "Unitary Tax: At The Crossroads? - Part I," **CPAJ**, 1985, Vol. 55, No. 5, pp. 18-25.)

Leegstra, **Ruurd G.** (Brown, Robert D., Ruurd G. Leegstra and Lloyd J. Looram. "Unitary Tax: At The Crossroads? - Part II," **CPAJ**, 1985, Vol. 55, No. 7, pp. 36-41.)

Leer, **J. A.** "A Logical Approach To The Statement Of Affairs," **AR**, 1964, Vol. 39, No. 4, pp. 1036-1039.

Lees, **Charles R.** "Moral Responsibility In Tax Practice: A CPA's View," **JOA**, 1959, Vol. 107, No. 4, pp. 30-33.

Lees, **Charles R.** (Hanson, Robert E. and Charles R. Lees. "IRS Examination Of Accountants' Workpapers," **JOA**, 1977, Vol. 143, No. 4, pp. 60-65.)

Leete, **Burt A.** "A Look At The Public Policy Conflict Regarding The Discovery Of Accountants' Tax Accrual Workpapers," **JAPP**, 1983, Vol. 2, No. 4, pp. 281-288.

Leete, **Burt A.** (Loeb, Stephen E. and Burt A. Leete. "The Dual Practitioner: CPA, Lawyer Or Both?," **JOA**, 1973, Vol. 136, No. 2, pp. 57-63.)

Lefebvre, **Charles N.** and Donald A. Barnes. "A Look At Annual Reports Of Employee Benefit Plans," **MA**, 1975, Vol. 57, No. 6, pp. 51-53.

Lefebvre, **Chris J. L.** "Development Of Belgian Accounting Standards Within The European Economic Community Framework," **IJAER**, 1981, Vol. 17, No. 1, pp. 103-132.

Lefkowitz, **Burton T.** "Preliminary Review For Acquisitions And Mergers," **CPAJ**, 1978, Vol. 48, No. 9, pp. 13-18.

Leftwich, **Richard W.** (Dopuch, Nicholas, Robert W. Holthausen and Richard W. Leftwich. "Abnormal Stock Returns Associated With Media Disclosures Of 'Subject To' Qualified Audit Opinions," **JAEC**, 1986, Vol. 8, No. 2, pp. 93-117.)

Leftwich, **Richard W.** (Dopuch, Nicholas, Robert W. Holthausen and Richard W. Leftwich. "Predicting Audit Qualifications With Financial And Market Variables," **AR**, 1987, Vol. 62, No. 3, pp. 431-454.)

Leftwich, **Richard W.** (Holthausen, Robert W. and Richard W. Leftwich. "The Economic Consequences Of Accounting Choice: Implications Of Costly Contracting And Monitoring," **JAEC**, 1983, Vol. 5, No. 2, pp. 77-117.)

Leftwich, **Richard W.** (Watts, Ross L. and Richard W. Leftwich. "The Time Series Of Annual Accounting Earnings," **JAR**, 1977, Vol. 15, No. 2, pp. 253-271.)

Leftwich, **Richard**, Ross L. Watts and Jerold L. Zimmerman. "Voluntary Corporate Disclosure: The Case Of Interim Reporting," **JAR**, 1981, Vol. 19, Supp., pp. 50-84.

Leftwich, **Richard.** "Accounting Information In Private Markets: Evidence From Private Lending Agreements," **AR**, 1983, Vol. 58, No. 1, pp. 23-42.

Leftwich, **Richard.** "Evidence Of The Impact Of Mandatory Changes In Accounting Principles On Corporate Loan Agreements," **JAEC**, 1981, Vol. 3, No. 1, pp. 3-36.

Leftwich, **Richard.** "Market Failure Fallacies And Accounting Information," **JAEC**, 1980, Vol. 2, No. 3, pp. 193-211.

Leftwich, **Richard.** (Dodd, Peter, Nicholas Dopuch, Robert Holthausen and Richard Leftwich. "Qualified Audit Opinions And Stock Prices: Information Content, Announcement Dates, And Concurrent Disclosures," **JAEC**, 1984, Vol. 6, No. 1, pp. 3-38.)

Legault, **Michel.** (Hoyt, Ronald E. and Michel Legault. "A Discrimminant Analysis Of Soviet Decision-Making Behavior In Selecting United States Suppliers Of Goods And Services," **AIIA**, 1987, Vol. 1, pp. 263-285.)

Legge, **H. Allan, Jr.** "Surviving The End Of Bad Debt Reserves," **CPAJ**, 1987, Vol. 57, No. 7, pp. 52-55.

Leggett, **D. N.** (Hawkins, C. A. and D. N. Leggett. "The Investment Tax Credit In Capital Replacement: A Simulation," **JAPP**, 1983, Vol. 2, No. 3, pp. 167-187.)

Lehmann, **Robert S.** "A Case History In Co-Operation," **JOA**, 1965, Vol. 119, No. 4, pp. 43-45.

Lehmann, **Robert S.** "One CPA's Experience With Human Relations Training," **JOA**, 1967, Vol. 124, No. 1, pp. 52-55.

Lehman, **Carol M.** (Lehman, Mark W. and Carol M. Lehman. "Interactive Spreadsheet Models Reinforce Accounting Principles," **JAED**, 1988, Vol. 6, No. 1, pp. 131-137.)

Lehman, **Cheryl R.** "Accounting Ethics: Surviving Survival Of The Fittest," **AIPIA**, 1988, Vol. 2, pp. 71-82.

Lehman, **C.** and T. Tinker. "The 'Real' Cultural Significance Of Accounts," **AOS**, 1987, Vol. 12, No. 4/5, pp. 503-522.

Lehman, **Mark W.** and Carol M. Lehman. "Interactive Spreadsheet Models Reinforce Accounting Principles," **JAED**, 1988, Vol. 6, No. 1, pp. 131-137.

Lehnberg, **Val B.** "Cost Accounting For Motor Freight Lines," **AR**, 1950, Vol. 25, No. 2, pp. 184-191.

Lehnberg, **Val B.** "Cost Accounting For Motor Freight Terminals," **AR**, 1952, Vol. 27, No. 2, pp. 215-220.

Leight, **Lester A.**, Melvin L. Braun and William M. Gips. "Review Of Statement On Auditing Procedure No. 47 - 'Subsequent Events'," **CPAJ**, 1972, Vol. 42, No. 2, pp. 123-126.

Leininger, **Wayne E.** and Michael J. Conley. "Regression Analysis In Auditing," **CPAJ**, 1980, Vol. 50, No. 10, pp. 43-47.

Leininger, **Wayne E.** "Opportunity Costs: Some Definitions And Examples," **AR**, 1977, Vol. 52, No. 1, pp. 248-251.

Leininger, **Wayne E.** (Corcoran, A. Wayne and Wayne E. Leininger. "Isolating Accounting Variances Via Partitioned Matrices," **AR**, 1975, Vol. 50, No. 1, pp. 184-188.)

Leininger, **Wayne E.** (Corcoran, A. Wayne and Wayne E. Leininger. "Stochastic Process Costing Models," **AR**, 1973, Vol. 48, No. 1, pp. 105-114.)

Leininger, **Wayne E.** (Corcoran, A. Wayne and Wayne E. Leininger. "In-Process Inventories And Multiproduct Production Systems," **AR**, 1973, Vol. 48, No. 2, pp. 373-374.)

Leisenring, **James J.** (Lightner, Sharon M., James J.

Leisenring and Alan J. Winters. "Underreporting Charge-able Time," **JOA**, 183, Vol. 155, No. 1, pp. 52-57.)

Leisenring, James J. (Zuber, George R., Robert K. Elliott, William R. Kinney, Jr., and James J. Leisenring. "Using Materiality In Audit Planning," **JOA**, 183, Vol. 155, No. 3, pp. 42-55.)

Leitch, Robert A. (Davis, James R. and Robert A. Leitch. "Accounting Information System Courses And Curricula: New Perspectives," **JIS**, 1988, Vol. 3, No. 1, pp. 153-166.)

Leitch, Robert A. (Duke, Gordon L., John Neter and Robert A. Leitch. "Power Characteristics Of Test Statistics In The Auditing Environment: An Empirical Study," **JAR**, 1982, Vol. 20, No. 1, pp. 42-67.)

Leitch, Robert A. (Hilliard, Jimmy E. and Robert A. Leitch. "Cost-Volume-Profit Analysis Under Uncertainty: A Log Normal Approach," **AR**, 1975, Vol. 50, No. 1, pp. 69-80.)

Leitch, Robert A. (Hilliard, Jimmy E. and Robert A. Leitch. "CVP Analysis Under Uncertainty - A Log Normal Approach: A Reply," **AR**, 1976, Vol. 51, No. 1, pp. 168-171.)

Leitch, Robert A. (Hilliard, Jimmy E. and Robert A. Leitch. "Breakeven Analysis Of Alternatives Under Uncertainty," **MA**, 1977, Vol. 58, No. 9, pp. 53-57.)

Leitch, Robert A. (Ijiri, Yuji and Robert A. Leitch. "Stein's Paradox And Audit Sampling," **JAR**, 1980, Vol. 18, No. 1, pp. 91-108.)

Leitch, Robert A. (Johnson, Johnny R., Robert A. Leitch and John Neter. "Characteristics Of Errors In Accounts Receivable And Inventory Audits," **AR**, 1981, Vol. 56, No. 2, pp. 270-293.)

Leitch, Robert A. (Neter, John, Johnny R. Johnson and Robert A. Leitch. "Characteristics Of Dollar-Unit Taints And Error Rates In Accounts Receivable And Inventory," **AR**, 1985, Vol. 60, No. 3, pp. 488-499.)

Leitch, Robert A. (Plante, Robert, John Neter and Robert A. Leitch. "Comparative Performance Of Multinomial, Cell, And Stringer Bounds," **AJPT**, 1985-86, Vol. 5, No. 1, pp. 40-56.)

Leitch, Robert A., John B. Barrack and Sue H. McKinley. "Controlling Your Cash Resources," **MA**, 1980, Vol. 62, No. 4, pp. 58-63.

Leitch, Robert A., John Neter, Robert Plante and Prabhakant Sinha. "Modified Multinomial Bounds For Larger Numbers Of Errors In Audits," **AR**, 1982, Vol. 57, No. 2, pp. 384-400.

Leitch, R. A. (Neter, John, R. A. Leitch and Stephen E. Fienberg. "Dollar Unit Sampling: Multinomial Bounds For Total Overstatement And Understatement Errors," **AR**, 1978, Vol. 53, No. 1, pp. 77-93.)

Leivian, Gregory M. "How To Communicate Financial Data More Effectively," **MA**, 1980, Vol. 62, No. 1, pp. 31-34.

Leland, Thomas W. "Educational Prerequisites For The Certificate," **AR**, 1945, Vol. 20, No. 2, pp. 191-193.

Leland, Thomas W. "Helping The Small Client With Budget Problems," **JOA**, 1955, Vol. 100, No. 4, pp. 56-61.

Leland, Thomas W. "Report Of Committee On Revision Of The Statement Of Principles: Revenue. Expense," **AR**, 1948, Vol. 23, No. 1, pp. 16-23.

Leland, T. W. (Heckert, J. B., H. F. Taggart, C. L. Van Sickle, R. M. Mikesell, F. W. Woodbridge, Louis O. Foster and T. W. Leland. "Instruction In Methods Of Accounting Instruction: A Symposium," **AR**, 1937, Vol. 12, No. 2, pp. 114-122.)

Lelievre, Clara C. (Barcelona, Constance T., Clara C. Lelievre and Thomas W. Lelievre. "The Profession's Underutilized Resource: The Woman CPA," **JOA**, 1975, Vol. 140, No. 5, pp. 58-64.)

Lelievre, Thomas W. (Barcelona, Constance T., Clara C. Lelievre and Thomas W. Lelievre. "The Profession's Underutilized Resource: The Woman CPA," **JOA**, 1975, Vol. 140, No. 5, pp. 58-64.)

LeMaster, Eustace. "Accounting For Nonferrous Mines," **JOA**, 1957, Vol. 104, No. 5, pp. 57-63.

LeMelle, Wilbert J. "The Imperatives Of An Economic Development Program," **IJAER**, 1967, Vol. 3, No. 1, pp. 101-106.

Lembke, Valdean C. and Howard R. Toole. "Differences In Depreciation Methods And The Analysis Of Supplemental Current-Cost And Replacement Cost Data," **JAAF**, 1981, Vol. 4, No. 2, pp. 128-135.

Lembke, Valdean C. and John H. Smith. "Replacement Costs: An Analysis Of Financial Statement And Tax Policy Effects," **JAAF**, 1980, Vol. 3, No. 2, pp. 147-162.

Lembke, Valdean C. "Some Considerations In Accounting For Divisive Reorganizations," **AR**, 1970, Vol. 45, No. 3, pp. 458-464.

Lembke, Valdean C. (Burnett, Tom, Thomas E. King and Valdean C. Lembke. "Equity Method Reporting For Major Finance Company Subsidiaries," **AR**, 1979, Vol. 54, No. 4, pp. 815-823.)

Lembke, Valdean C. (Hauworth, William P., II, Valdean C. Lembke and Robert F. Sharp. "The Effects Of Inflation: How They Persist," **JAAF**, 1987, Vol. 2 (New Series), No. 2, pp. 184-196.)

Lembke, Valdean C. (King, Thomas E. and Valdean C. Lembke. "Reporting Investor Income Under The Equity Method," **JOA**, 1976, Vol. 142, No. 3, pp. 65-72.)

Lembke, V. C. (Smith, J. H., V. H. Tidwell and V. C. Lembke. "An Analysis Of Participation In Continuing Education," **JOA**, 1972, Vol. 133, No. 1, pp. 40-45.)

Lembke, V. C., J. H. Smith and V. H. Tidwell. "Compulsory Continuing Education For CPAs," **JOA**, 1970, Vol. 129, No. 4, pp. 61-65.

Lemke, B. C. "Is Manufacturing Cost An Objective Concept?," **AR**, 1951, Vol. 26, No. 1, pp. 77-79.

Lemke, B. C. "The Treatment Of Unamortized Discount And Expense Applicable To Bonds Refunded Before Maturity," **AR**, 1947, Vol. 22, No. 4, pp. 379-384.

Lemke, Kenneth W. and Paul R. Graul. "Deferred Taxes - An 'Explicit Cost' Solution To The Discounting Problem," **ABR**, 1980-81, Vol. 11, No. 44, pp. 309-316.

Lemke, Kenneth W. and Philip P. Powell. "The Gearing Adjustment - An Empirical Study," **ABR**, 1986-87, Vol. 17, No. 65, pp. 59-70.

Lemke, Kenneth W. "Asset Valuation And Income Theory," **AR**, 1966, Vol. 41, No. 1, pp. 32-41.

Lemke, Kenneth W. "Capital Maintenance And Confusion," **ABACUS**, 1974, Vol. 10 No. 1, pp. 26-38.

Lemke, Kenneth W. "In Defence Of The 'Profit Centre' Concept," **ABACUS**, 1970, Vol. 6, No. 2, pp. 182-189.

Lemke, Kenneth W. "The Evaluation Of Liquidity: An Analytical Study," **JAR**, 1970, Vol. 8, No. 1, pp. 47-77.

Lemke, Kenneth W. (Graul, Paul R. and Kenneth W. Lemke. "On The Economic Substance Of Deferred Taxes," **ABACUS**, 1976, Vol. 12, No. 1, pp. 14-33.)

Lemke, Lester C., Jr. "Status Index Reporting," **MA**, 1968, Vol. 49, No. 9, pp. 25-34.

Lemon, James D. "Problems In Mine Evaluation," **MA**, 1971, Vol. 53, No. 3, pp. 46-48.

Lemon, W. Morley. (Johnston, Donald J., W. Morley Lemon and Frederick L. Neumann. "The Canadian Study Of The Role Of The Auditor," **JAAF**, 1980, Vol. 3, No. 3, pp. 251-263.)

Lemon, W. M. (Boritz, J. E., B. G. Gaber and W. M. Lemon. "An Experimental Study Of The Effects Of Elicitation Methods On Review Of Preliminary Audit Strategy By External Auditors," **CAR**, 1988, Vol. 4, No. 2, pp. 392-411.)

Lengermann, Joseph J. "Supposed And Actual Differences In Professional Autonomy Among CPAs As Related to Type Of Work Organization And Size Of Firm," **AR**, 1971, Vol. 46, No. 4, pp. 665-675.

Lenihan, John F. "Applied Programming Packages Are Growing In Importance," **MA**, 1970, Vol. 51, No. 7, pp. 12-14.

Lenihan, Stephen J. "Chartier Revisited - Alternative Tax And The Net Operating Loss," **CPAJ**, 1975, Vol. 45, No. 11, pp. 29-32.

Lennos, William V. (Hines, Dorothy L., Douglas A. Johnson and William V. Lennox. "The Semiconductor Industry Controller: A Profile," **MA**, 1982, Vol. 63, No. 12, pp. 30-35.)

Lennox, John E. "The Accounting Service Bureau: One CPA Firm's Experience," **JOA**, 1964, Vol. 118, No. 5, pp. 49-54.

Lent, Charles W. "The Socio-Economic Assistance Program," **MA**, 1975, Vol. 57, No. 2, pp. 11-13.

Lent, George E. "Accounting Principles And Taxable Income," **AR**, 1962, Vol. 37, No. 3, pp. 479-487.

Lentilhon, Robert W. and Anthony T. Krzystofik. "Professional Examination Preparation In AACSB Accredited And Member Schools," **IAE**, 1983, No. 1, pp. 38-49.

Lentilhon, Robert W. "Determination Of Goodwill And Bonus On Admission Of A Partner," **AR**, 1964, Vol. 39, No. 3, pp. 754-756.

Lentilhon, Robert W. "Direct Costing - Either...Or?," **AR**, 1964, Vol. 39, No. 4, pp. 880-883.

Lentini, Lawrence. "Using Ratio Estimation In Observing Inventories," **CPAJ**, 1981, Vol. 51, No. 6, pp. 24-31.

Leonard, Herman B. "Measuring And Reporting The Financial Condition Of Public Organizations," **RIGNA**, 1985, Vol. 1, pp. 117-148.

Leonard, Robert I. (Williams, Robert W. and Robert I. Leonard. "Financial Reporting By Nonprofit Organizations," **JOA**, 1962, Vol. 113, No. 4, pp. 46-50.)

Leonard, Robert L. "Accounting Needs Of Local Government," **JOA**, 1959, Vol. 108, No. 5, pp. 55-59.

Leonard, R. (Primrose, P. L., F. A. Bailey and R. Leonard. "The Practical Application Of Discounted Cash Flow To Plant Purchase Using An Integrated Suite Of Computer Programs," **ABR**, 1984-85, Vol. 15, No. 57, pp. 27-32.)

Leonard, W. G. "Accumulated Depreciation - Balance Sheet Presentation," **AR**, 1959, Vol. 34, No. 4, pp. 572-573.

Leonard, W. G. "Comments On 'Accounting And Reporting Standards For Corporate Financial Statements - 1957 Revision'," **AR**, 1958, Vol. 33, No. 3, pp. 401-402.

Leone, Barry P. and Thomas S. Rose. "Installing A Microcomputer Based Accounting System: One Company's Experience," **MA**, 1987, Vol. 68, No. 11, pp. 34-38.

Leong, Kenneth C. and Jan L. Deur. "Financial Planning And Accounting Control In Telephone Companies," **MA**, 1980, Vol. 62, No. 1, pp. 19-22.

Leonhardi, Willis A. and Robert W. Newmann. "NAARS And LEXIS: Research Tools," **CPAJ**, 1977, Vol. 47, No. 9, pp. 33-40.

Leonhardi, Willis. "Bad Debts In The Profit-And-Loss Statement," **AR**, 1941, Vol. 16, No. 3, pp. 234-243.

Lere, John C. "Explaining Alternative Standard Cost Entries," **JAED**, 1985, Vol. 3, No. 2, pp. 187-192.

Lere, John C. "Optimal Depreciation Methods When Marginal Tax Rates Increase," **JATA**, 1980, Vol. 2, No. 1, pp. 9-15.

Lere, John C. "Product Pricing Based On Accounting Costs," **AR**, 1986, Vol. 61, No. 2, pp. 318-324.

Lere, John C. (Dickhaut, John W. and John C. Lere. "Comparison Of Accounting Systems And Heuristics In Selecting Economic Optima," **JAR**, 1983, Vol. 21, No. 2, pp. 495-513.)

Leslie, John E. "How To Build, Maintain, And Use A Professional Library For An Accounting Firm," **JOA**, 1950, Vol. 89, No. 5, pp. 392-395.

Leslie, John E. "Impact Of 1951 Tax Law On Year-End

Securities Transactions," **JOA**, 1951, Vol. 92, No. 6, pp. 683-687.

Lessard, Donald R. and Peter Lorange. "Currency Changes And Management Control: Resolving The Centralization/Decentralization Dilemma," **AR**, 1977, Vol. 52, No. 3, pp. 628-637.

Lessem, R. "Corporate Social Reporting In Action: An Evaluation Of British, European and American Practice," **AOS**, 1977, Vol. 2, No. 4, pp. 279-294.

Lesser, Frederic E. "Does Your Transfer Pricing Make Cents?," **MA**, 1987, Vol. 69, No. 6, pp. 43-47.

Lesser, Frederic E. "Will The Real Cost Please Stand Up?," **MA**, 1986, Vol. 68, No. 5, pp. 29-31.

Lessig, V. Parker. (Larcker, David F. and V. Parker Lessig. "An Examination Of The Linear And Retrospective Process Tracing Approaches To Judgment Modeling," **AR**, 1983, Vol. 58, No. 1, pp. 58-77.)

Leverett, E. J., Jr. (Trieschmann, James S. and E. J. Leverett, Jr. "What A CPA Needs To Know About General Liability Insurance," **CPAJ**, 1975, Vol. 45, No. 8, pp. 34-37.)

Lev, Baruch and Aba Schwartz. "On The Use Of The Economic Concept Of Human Capital In Financial Statements: A Reply," **AR**, 1972, Vol. 47, No. 1, pp. 153-154.

Lev, Baruch and Aba Schwartz. "On The Use Of The Economic Concept Of Human Capital In Financial Statements," **AR**, 1971, Vol. 46, No. 1, pp. 103-112.

Lev, Baruch and Henri Theil. "A Maximum Entropy Approach To The Choice Of Asset Depreciation," **JAR**, 1978, Vol. 16, No. 2, pp. 286-293.

Lev, Baruch and James A. Ohlson. "Market-Based Empirical Research In Accounting: A Review, Interpretation, And Extension," **JAR**, 1982, Vol. 20, Supp., pp. 249-322.

Lev, Baruch and Kenneth W. Taylor. "Accounting Recognition Of Imputed Interest On Equity: An Empirical Investigation," **JAAF**, 1979, Vol. 2, No. 3, pp. 232-243.

Lev, Baruch and Sergius Kunitzky. "On The Association Between Smoothing Measures And The Risk Of Common Stocks," **AR**, 1974, Vol. 49, No. 2, pp. 259-270.

Lev, Baruch and Shyam Sunder. "Methodological Issues In The Use Of Financial Ratios," **JAEC**, 1979, Vol. 1, No. 3, pp. 187-210.

Lev, Baruch. "A Comment On 'Business Combinations: An Exchange Ratio Determination Model'," **AR**, 1970, Vol. 45, No. 3, pp. 532-534.

Lev, Baruch. "An Information Theory Analysis Of Budget Variances," **AR**, 1969, Vol. 44, No. 4, pp. 704-710.

Lev, Baruch. "Industry Averages As Targets For Financial Ratios," **JAR**, 1969, Vol. 7, No. 2, pp. 290-299.

Lev, Baruch. "On The Use Of Index Models In Analytical Reviews By Auditors," **JAR**, 1980, Vol. 18, No. 2, pp. 524-550.

Lev, Baruch. "Some Economic Determinants Of Time-Series Properties Of Earnings," **JAEC**, 1983, Vol. 5, No. 1, pp. 31-48.

Lev, Baruch. "Testing A Prediction Method For Multivariate Budgets," **JAR**, 1969, Vol. 7, Supp., pp. 182-197.

Lev, Baruch. "The Aggregation Problem In Financial Statements: An Informational Approach," **JAR**, 1968, Vol. 6, No. 2, pp. 247-261.

Lev, Baruch. "The Formulation Of Accounting Standards And Rules: A Comparison Of Efforts In Israel And The United States," **IJAER**, 1976, Vol. 11, No. 2, pp. 121-131.

Lev, Baruch. "The Impact Of Accounting Regulation On The Stock Market: The Case Of Oil And Gas Companies," **AR**, 1979, Vol. 54, No. 3, pp. 485-503.

Lev, Baruch. "The Informational Approach To Aggregation In Financial Statements: Extensions," **JAR**, 1970, Vol. 8, No. 1, pp. 78-94.

Lev, Baruch. "Toward A Theory Of Equitable And Efficient Accounting Policy," **AR**, 1988, Vol. 63, No. 1, pp. 1-22.

Lev, Baruch. (Adar, Zvi, Amir Barnea and Baruch Lev. "A Comprehensive Cost-Volume-Profit Analysis Under Uncertainty," **AR**, 1977, Vol. 52, No. 1, pp. 137-149.)

Lev, Baruch. (Ball, Ray, Baruch Lev and Ross Watts. "Income Variation And Balance Sheet Compositions," **JAR**, 1976, Vol. 14, No. 1, pp. 1-9.)

Lev, Baruch. (Friedman, Abraham and Baruch Lev. "A Surrogate Measure For The Firm's Investment In Human Resources," **JAR**, 1974, Vol. 12, No. 2, pp. 235-250.)

Levcy, Gary D. "The Second Aim," **MA**, 1974, Vol. 55, No. 12, pp. 47-50.

Levine, Alan H. "Forecasting Techniques," **MA**, 1967, Vol. 48, No. 5, pp. 31-36.

Levine, Arnold I. and E. Stanley Marks. "Accountants' Liability Insurance - Perils And Pitfalls," **JOA**, 1976, Vol. 142, No. 4, pp. 59-66.

Levine, Jack B. "How A Bank Performs A Customer Profitability Analysis," **MA**, 1978, Vol. 59, No. 12, pp. 35-43.

Levinson, Sherry. (Perkins, Edwin J. and Sherry Levinson. "Partnership Accounting In A Nineteenth Century Merchant Banking House," **AHJ**, 1980, Vol. 7, No. 1, pp. 59-68.)

Levitan, Alan S. and James A. Knoblett. "Indicators Of Exceptions To The Going Concern Assumption," **AJPT**, 1985-86, Vol. 5, No. 1, pp. 26-39.

Levitan, Alan S. "Getting Out Of A Partnership - II," **CPAJ**, 1981, Vol. 51, No. 4, pp. 36-41.

Levitan, Alan S. "Getting Out Of A Partnership - I," **CPAJ**, 1981, Vol. 51, No. 3, pp. 15-21.

Levitan, Alan S. "Using A Data Base Management System In An Accounting Information Systems Course," **JIS**, 1988, Vol. 2, No. 2, pp. 73-78.

Levitan, Alan S. (Baxendale, Sidney J. and Alan S. Levitan. "The Post Audit Review Of Equipment Replacement Decisions In Capital Intensive Companies," **JCA**, 1987, Vol.

4, No. 1, pp. 7-15.)

Levitt, Arthur. "The Modern Approach To Public Audits," **MA**, 1974, Vol. 55, No. 8, pp. 44-46.

Levkowitz, G. (Bashan, O., Y. Goldschmidt, G. Levkowitz and L. Shashua. "Laspeyres Indexes For Variance Analysis In Cost Accounting," **AR**, 1973, Vol. 48, No. 4, pp. 790-793.)

Levy, Arthur J. (Sprague, W. D. and Arthur J. Levy. "Accounting And Law: Is Dual Practice In The Public Interest?," **JOA**, 1966, Vol. 122, No. 6, pp. 45-52.)

Levy, Ferdinand K. "On The Definition Of A Good Decision Or Solution To A Problem," **ABACUS**, 1972, Vol. 8, No. 1, pp. 61-67.

Levy, Ferdinand K. (Largay, James A., III and Ferdinand K. Levy. "Using Segment Reporting And Input-Output Analysis For Managerial Planning," **MA**, 1978, Vol. 60, No. 5, pp. 46-50.)

Levy, F. K. (Ijiri, Y., F. K. Levy and R. C. Lyon. "A Linear Programming Model For Budgeting And Financial Planning," **JAR**, 1963, Vol. 1, No. 2, pp. 198-212.)

Levy, Gregory M. "TEFRA: Its Accounting Implications," **JOA**, 1982, Vol. 154, No. 5, pp. 74-85.

Levy, Gregory M. (Neier, Dennis S. and Gregory M. Levy. "Centralized Review Of Financial Statements And Accountants' Reports," **CPAJ**, 1982, Vol. 52. No. 8, pp. 12-21.)

Levy, Haim and Young Hoon Byun. "An Empirical Test Of The Black-Scholes Option Pricing Model And The Implied Variance: A Confidence Interval Approach," **JAAF**, 1987, Vol. 2 (New Series), No. 4, pp. 355-374.

Levy, Haim. (Barlev, Benzion and Haim Levy. "On The Variability Of Accounting Income Numbers," **JAR**, 1979, Vol. 17, No. 2, pp. 305-315.)

Levy, Louis E. and Donald F. Kern. "SAP No. 49, 'Reports On Internal Control,' - Small Step Or Giant Leap?," **CPAJ**, 1972, Vol. 42, No. 12, pp. 1019-1023.

Levy, Louis E. "Off Balance Sheet Financing," **MA**, 1969, Vol. 50, No. 9, pp. 12-14.

Levy, Marvin M. "Financial Fraud: Schemes And Indicia," **JOA**, 1985, Vol. 160, No. 2, pp. 78-88.

Levy, Saul. "Audit Working Papers And Liability," **JOA**, 1956, Vol. 101, No. 5, pp. 36-39.

Levy, Saul. "Internal Control And Responsibility," **JOA**, 1957, Vol. 103, No. 2, pp. 29-33.

Levy, Saul. "Legal Hazards In Public Accounting," **JOA**, 1955, Vol. 99, No. 5, pp. 37-39.

Levy, Saul. "Special Reports And Nonstandard Opinions," **JOA**, 1957, Vol. 103, No. 6, pp. 48-52.

Levy, Saul. "The C. I. T. Case," **JOA**, 1955, Vol. 100, No. 4, pp. 31-42.

Levy, Saul. "The Long-Form Report," **JOA**, 1956, Vol. 101, No. 3, pp. 44-48.

Levy, Saul. "The Scope And Limitations Of Accounting Practice In Federal Income Taxation," **JOA**, 1950, Vol. 89, No. 6, pp. 470-479.

Lew, Albert Y. (Chen, Kung H. and Albert Y. Lew. "A Framework For The Selection Of Representative Financial Ratios: Methodology Note," **AIA**, 1984, Vol. 1, pp. 63-74.)

Lewellen, Wilbur, Claudio Loderer and Kenneth Martin. "Executive Compensation And Executive Incentive Problems: An Empirical Analysis," **JAEC**, 1987, Vol. 9, No. 3, pp. 287-310.

Lewellen, Wilbur, Claudio Loderer and Ahron Rosenfeld. "Merger Decisions And Executive Stock Ownership In Acquiring Firms," **JAEC**, 1985, Vol. 7, No. 1/3, pp. 209-231.

Lewin, Arie Y. (Schiff, Michael and Arie Y. Lewin. "The Impact Of People On Budgets," **AR**, 1970, Vol. 45, No. 2, pp. 259-268.)

Lewis, Barry L. and Jan Bell. "Decisions Involving Sequential Events: Replications And Extensions," **JAR**, 1985, Vol. 23, No. 1, pp. 228-239.

Lewis, Barry L. "Expert Judgment In Auditing: An Expected Utility Approach," **JAR**, 1980, Vol. 18, No. 2, pp. 594-602.

Lewis, Barry L., James M. Patton and Sharon L. Green. "The Effects Of Information Choice And Information Use On Analysts' Predictions Of Municipal Bond Rating Changes," **AR**, 1988, Vol. 63, No. 2, pp. 270-282.

Lewis, Barry, Michael D. Shields and S. Mark Young. "Evaluating Human Judgments And Decision Aids," **JAR**, 1983, Vol. 21, No. 1, pp. 271-285.

Lewis, B. L. (Dirsmith, M. W. and B. L. Lewis. "The Effect Of External Reporting On Managerial Decision Making: Some Antecedent Conditions," **AOS**, 1982, Vol. 7, No. 4, pp. 319-336.)

Lewis, B. L. (Evans, J. H., III, B. L. Lewis and J. M. Patton. "An Economic Modeling Approach To Contingency Theory And Management Control," **AOS**, 1986, Vol. 11, No. 6, pp. 483-498.)

Lewis, B. L. (Libby, R. and B. L. Lewis. "Human Information Processing Research In Accounting: The State Of The Art In 1982," **AOS**, 1982, Vol. 7, No. 3, pp. 231-286.)

Lewis, B. L. (Libby, R. and B. L. Lewis. "Human Information Processing Research In Accounting: The State Of The Art," **AOS**, 1977, Vol. 2, No. 3, pp. 245-268.)

Lewis, Charles A., Jr. "Are There 'Principles' Of Accounting?," **AR**, 1959, Vol. 34, No. 2, pp. 239-241.

Lewis, Charles A., Jr. "Loan Applications To The Small Business Administration," **JOA**, 1961, Vol. 112, No. 4, pp. 65-70.

Lewis, Charles A., Jr. "Management Services For Small Clients," **JOA**, 1959, Vol. 108, No. 6, pp. 56-60.

Lewis, Charles D. "Tax Deductibility Of Educators' Travel Expenses," **AR**, 1967, Vol. 42, No. 1, pp. 96-105.

Lewis, Eldon C. "Successful Interface Between Accounting And Management," **MA**, 1969, Vol. 50, No. 7, pp. 19-21.
Lewis, Fletcher. "Some Legal And Accounting Questions Presented By The Michigan General Corporation Act," **AR**, 1933, Vol. 8, No. 2, pp. 145-154.
Lewis, Merrill T., W. Thomas Lin and Doyle Z. Williams. "The Economic Status Of Accounting Educators: An Empirical Study," **AIA**, 1984, Vol. 1, pp. 127-144.
Lewis, N. R., L. D. Parker and P. Sutcliffe. "Financial Reporting To Employees: The Pattern Of Development 1919 To 1979," **AOS**, 1984, Vol. 9, No. 3/4, pp. 275-290.
Lewis, N. R., L. D. Parker, G. D. Pound and P. Sutcliffe. "Annual Report Readability: The Use Of Readability Techniques," **ABR**, 1985-86, Vol. 16, No. 63, pp. 199-214.
Lewis, N., L. D. Parker and P. Sutcliffe. "Financial Reporting To Employees: Towards A Research Framework," **ABR**, 1983-84, Vol. 14, No. 55, pp. 229-240.
Lewis, Ralph F. "Data Processing Centers And The CPA," **JOA**, 1961, Vol. 110, No. 1, pp. 45-51.
Lewis, Ralph F. "Management Services For Small Clients," **JOA**, 1960, Vol. 110, No. 3, pp. 39-43.
Lewis, Ralph F. "Managing With And For Distinction," **JOA**, 1968, Vol. 125, No. 3, pp. 34-38.
Lewis, Richard W. (Grinyer, John R. and Richard W. Lewis. "Valuation And Meaningful Accounts," **ABR**, 1971-72, Vol. 2, No. 8, pp. 275-283.)
Lewis, Robert W. "An Industry View Of Budgeting," **JOA**, 1959, Vol. 108, No. 6, pp. 30-36.
Lewis, Ronello B. "The Role Of Accounting In Decision Making," **AR**, 1960, Vol. 35, No. 1, pp. 37-44.
Lewis, Tom D. "Did You Say What You Said Or Did You Say What I Think You Said?," **MA**, 1985, Vol. 67, No. 2, pp. 40-45.
Lewis, Tom D., Thomas A. Shimerda and Gerald Graham. "What The Academic Advisor Needs To Know About Job Placement," **JAED**, 1983, Vol. 1, No. 2, pp. 135-142.
Lewis, William F. "Auditing On-Line Computer Systems," **JOA**, 1971, Vol. 132, No. 4, pp. 47-52.
Lhotka, Joseph D. and Naomi S. Erickson. "Accounting For Software: A Step Forward," **JOA**, 1984, Vol. 158, No. 5, pp. 110-124.
Li, David H. "A Structural Check Of Accounting Input Data In A Computer System," **JOA**, 1967, Vol. 123, No. 6, pp. 54-57.
Li, David H. "Alternative Accounting Procedures And The Entity Concept," **AR**, 1963, Vol. 38, No. 1, pp. 52-55.
Li, David H. "Audit-Aid: Generalized Computer-Audit Program As An Instructional Device," **AR**, 1970, Vol. 45, No. 4, pp. 774-778.
Li, David H. "Cost Accounting Standards Board: A Progress Report," **MA**, 1973, Vol. 54, No. 12, pp. 11-14.
Li, David H. "Homogeneity And Variance Allocation," **MA**, 1977, Vol. 58, No. 8, pp. 34-40.
Li, David H. "Income Taxes And Income Tax Allocation Under The Entity Concept," **AR**, 1961, Vol. 36, No. 2, pp. 265-268.
Li, David H. "The Funds Statement Under The Entity Concept," **AR**, 1963, Vol. 38, No. 4, pp. 771-775.
Li, David H. "The Nature And Treatment Of Dividends Under The Entity Concept," **AR**, 1960, Vol. 35, No. 4, pp. 674-679.
Li, David H. "The Nature Of Corporate Residual Equity Under The Entity Concept," **AR**, 1960, Vol. 35, No. 2, pp. 258-263.
Li, David H. "The Objectives Of The Corporation Under The Entity Concept," **AR**, 1964, Vol. 39, No. 4, pp. 946-950.
Li, David H. "The Semantic Aspect Of Communication Theory And Accountancy," **JAR**, 1963, Vol. 1, No. 1, pp. 102-107.
Li, Lode. (Balachandran, Bala V., Lode Li and Robert P. Magee. "On The Allocation Of Fixed And Variable Costs From Service Departments," **CAR**, 1987-88, Vol. 4, No. 1, pp. 164-185.)
Li, Yu-ku. "A Note On 'The Investigation Of Cost Variances'," **JAR**, 1970, Vol. 8, No. 2, pp. 282-283.
Liang, Ting-Peng. "Expert Systems As Decision Aids: Issues And Strategies," **JIS**, 1988, Vol. 2, No. 2, pp. 41-50.
Liao, Mawsen. "A Matrix Approach To The Depreciation Lapse Schedule Preparation," **AR**, 1976, Vol. 51, No. 2, pp. 364-369.
Liao, Mawsen. "Equal-Cost Analysis," **MA**, 1976, Vol. 57, No. 10, pp. 51-53.
Liao, Mawsen. "Model Sampling: A Stochastic Cost-Volume-Profit Analysis," **AR**, 1975, Vol. 50, No. 4, pp. 780-790.
Liao, Mawsen. "Modified Payback Analysis," **MA**, 1976, Vol. 58, No. 3, pp. 19-21.
Liao, Mawsen. "The Effect Of Change Variation On Revenue And Cost Estimations For Breakeven Analysis," **AR**, 1976, Vol. 51, No. 4, pp. 922-926.
Liao, Shu S. "Human Assets, Human Resources and Managerial Decisions," **MA**, 1974, Vol. 56, No. 5, pp. 19-22.
Liao, Shu S. "Learner Directed Instruction: Additional Evidence," **AR**, 1978, Vol. 53, No. 1, pp. 155-161.
Liao, Shu S. "Responsibility Centers," **MA**, 1973, Vol. 55, No. 1, pp. 46-48.
Liao, Shu S. "The Comparison Of Alternative Income Concepts: A Comment," **AR**, 1975, Vol. 50, No. 4, pp. 860-864.
Liao, Shu S. "The Effect Of The Separation Of Ownership From Control On Accounting Policy Decisions: A Comment," **AR**, 1979, Vol. 54, No. 2, pp. 414-416.
Liao, Shu S. "The Learning Curve: Wright's Model Vs. Crawford's Model," **IAE**, 1988, Vol. 3, No. 2, pp. 302-315.
Liao, Shu S. "The Matching Concept And Cost Allocation," **ABR**, 1978-79, Vol. 9, No. 35, pp. 228-236.

Liao, Shu S. "Three-Step Analysis Measures Productivity," **MA**, 1975, Vol. 57, No. 2, pp. 25-28.
Liao, Shu S. (Chang, Davis L. S. and Shu S. Liao. "Measuring And Disclosing Forecast Reliability," **JOA**, 1977, Vol. 143, No. 5, pp. 76-87.)
Liao, Shu S. (Greer, Willis R., Jr. and Shu S. Liao. "Weapon Pricing Models For Defense Acquisition Policy," **JAPP**, 1987, Vol. 6, No. 4, pp. 271-284.)
Liao, Woody M. "Simulating Learning Curve Parameters For Managerial Planning And Control," **ABR**, 1981-82, Vol. 12, No. 46, pp. 141-147.
Liao, Woody M. "Streamlining Small Business Performance Reporting," **MA**, 1983, Vol. 64, No. 10, pp. 25-29.
Liao, Woody M. (Finley, D. R. and Woody M. Liao. "A General Decision Model For Cost-Volume-Profit Analysis Under Uncertainty: A Comment," **AR**, 1981, Vol. 56, No. 2, pp. 400-403.)
Liao, Woody M. (Hutton, Marguerite R. and Woody M. Liao. "A CPA's Responsibility: Ethics And Tax Penalties," **CPAJ**, 1985, Vol. 55, No. 10, pp. 26-35.)
Liao, Woody M. (Kren, Leslie and Woody M. Liao. "The Role Of Accounting Information In The Control Of Organizations: A Review Of The Evidence," **JAL**, 1988, Vol. 7, pp. 280-309.)
Liao, Woody M. (Thakkar, Rashmi B., David R. Finley and Woody M. Liao. "A Stochastic Demand CVP Model With Return On Investment Criterion," **CAR**, 1984-85, Vol. 1, No. 1, pp. 77-86.)
Libby, Robert and Peter C. Fishburn. "Behavioral Models Of Risk Taking In Business Decisions: A Survey And Evaluation," **JAR**, 1977, Vol. 15, No. 2, pp. 272-292.
Libby, Robert, James T. Artman and John J. Willingham. "Process Susceptibility, Control Risk, And Audit Planning," **AR**, 1985, Vol. 60, No. 2, pp. 212-230.
Libby, Robert. "Accounting Ratios And The Prediction Of Failure: Some Behavioral Evidence," **JAR**, 1975, Vol. 13, No. 1, pp. 150-161.
Libby, Robert. "Availability And The Generation Of Hypotheses In Analytical Review," **JAR**, 1985, Vol. 23, No. 2, pp. 648-667.
Libby, Robert. "Bankers' And Auditors' Perceptions Of The Message Communicated By The Audit Report," **JAR**, 1979, Vol. 17, No. 1, pp. 99-122.
Libby, Robert. "Comments On Weick," **AR**, 1983, Vol. 58, No. 2, pp. 370-374.
Libby, Robert. "Prediction Achievement And Simulated Decision Makers As An Extension Of The Predictive Ability Criterion: A Reply," **AR**, 1976, Vol. 51, No. 3, pp. 672-676.
Libby, Robert. "The Early Impact Of APB Opinions No. 16 And 17 - An Empirical Study," **CPAJ**, 1972, Vol. 42, No. 10, pp. 837-842.
Libby, Robert. "The Impact Of Uncertainty Reporting On The Loan Decision," **JAR**, 1979, Vol. 17, Supp., pp. 35-57.
Libby, Robert. "The Use Of Simulated Decision Makers In Information Evaluation," **AR**, 1975, Vol. 50, No. 3, pp. 475-489.
Libby, Robert. (Frederick, David M. and Robert Libby. "Expertise And Auditors' Judgments Of Conjunctive Events," **JAR**, 1986, Vol. 24, No. 2, pp. 270-290.)
Libby, Robert. (Joyce, Edward J. and Robert Libby. "Some Accounting Implications Of 'Behavioral Decision Theory: Processes Of Judgment And Choice'," **JAR**, 1981, Vol. 19, No. 2, pp. 544-550.)
Libby, Robert. (Joyce, Edward J., Robert Libby and Shyam Sunder. "Using The FASB's Qualitative Characterisitics In Accounting Policy Choices," **JAR**, 1982, Vol. 20, No. 2. Part II, pp. 103-123.)
Libby, Robert. (Joyce, Edward J. and Robert Libby. "Behavioral Studies Of Audit Decision Making," **JAL**, 1982, Vol. 1, pp. 103-123.)
Libby, R. and B. L. Lewis. "Human Information Processing Research In Accounting: The State Of The Art In 1982," **AOS**, 1982, Vol. 7, No. 3, pp. 231-286.
Libby, R. and B. L. Lewis. "Human Information Processing Research In Accounting: The State Of The Art," **AOS**, 1977, Vol. 2, No. 3, pp. 245-268.
Liberatore, Joseph. "Stock Option Plans Make Sense," **MA**, 1987, Vol. 68, No. 9, pp. 46-48.
Liberty, Robert A. "To Merge Or Not To Merge," **JOA**, 1981, Vol. 151, No. 1, pp. 52-59.
Liberty, Susan E. and Jerold J. Zimmerman. "Labor Union Contract Negotiations And Accounting Choices," **AR**, 1986, Vol. 61, No. 4, pp. 692-712.
Licastro, Ralph D. (Copeland, Ronald M. and Ralph D. Licastro. "A Note On Income Smoothing," **AR**, 1968, Vol. 43, No. 3, pp. 540-545.)
Licata, Michael P., Robert H. Strawser and Robert B. Welker. "A Note On Participation In Budgeting And Locus Of Control," **AR**, 1986, Vol. 61, No. 1, pp. 112-117.
Lieberman, Arthur Z. and Andrew B. Whinston. "A Structuring Of An Events-Accounting Information System," **AR**, 1975, Vol. 50, No. 2, pp. 246-258.
Lieber, Lawrence and Howard W. Dragutsky. "How Accountants Can Keep Pension Costs Down," **JOA**, 1975, Vol. 139, No. 2, pp. 52-59.
Lientz, Bennet P. and Ira R. Weiss. "The Vulnerability Of Computer Auditing," **CPAJ**, 1977, Vol. 47,No. 3,pp. 17-22.
Liggio, Carl D. "The Expectation Gap: The Accountant's Legal Waterloo?," **CPAJ**, 1975, Vol. 45, No. 7, pp. 23-30.
Lightner, Kevin M. (Lightner, Sharon M., Steven J. Adams and Kevin M. Lightner. "The Influence Of Situational, Ethical, And Expectancy Theory Variables On Accountants' Underreporting Behavior," **AJPT**, 1982-83, Vol. 2, No. 1, pp. 1-12.)

Lightner, Sharon and Marlene Hartman. "Inventory Of Computer Software Designed For Use In Accounting Curriculum: Student Materials And Test Banks," **JAED**, 1985, Vol. 3, No. 1, pp. 15-35.

Lightner, Sharon M., James J. Leisenring and Alan J. Winters. "Underreporting Chargeable Time," **JOA**, 183, Vol. 155, No. 1, pp. 52-57.

Lightner, Sharon M., Steven J. Adams and Kevin M. Lightner. "The Influence Of Situational, Ethical, And Expectancy Theory Variables On Accountants' Underreporting Behavior," **AJPT**, 1982-83, Vol. 2, No. 1, pp. 1-12.

Ligon, Karen M. (Doost, Roger K. and Karen M. Ligon. "How U.S. And European Accounting Practices Differ," **MA**, 1986, Vol. 68, No. 4, pp. 38-41.)

Likierman, Andrew. "Evidence On Accusations Of Manipulating Profitability: Adjustments For Inflation By The Nationalised Industries 1976-81," **ABR**, 1983-84, Vol. 14, No. 53, pp. 29-34.

Likierman, J. A. "Analysing Project Cost Escalation: The Case Study Of North Sea Oil," **ABR**, 1977-78, Vol. 8, No. 29, pp. 51-57.

Lilien, Steven and Victor Pastena. "Intramethod Comparability: The Case Of The Oil And Gas Industry," **AR**, 1981, Vol. 56, No. 3, pp. 690-703.

Lilien, Steven and Victor Pastena. "Determinants Of Intra-Method Choice In The Oil And Gas Industry," **JAEC**, 1982, Vol. 4, No. 3, pp. 145-170.

Lilien, Steven B. (Eisenman, Seymour and Steven B. Lilien. "Accounting Deficiencies In Financial Statements," **CPAJ**, 1978, Vol. 48, No. 7, pp. 28-34.)

Lilien, Steven, Martin Mellman and Victor Pastena. "Accounting Changes: Successful Versus Unsuccessful Firms," **AR**, 1988, Vol. 63, No. 4, pp. 642-656.

Lilien, Steven. (Haw, In-Mu, Victor Pastena and Steven Lilien. "The Association Between Market-Based Merger Premiums And Firm's Financial Position Prior To Merger," **JAAF**, 1987, Vol. 2 (New Series), No. 1, pp. 24-42.)

Lilien, Steven. (Nakayama, Mie, Steven Lilien and Martin Benis. "Due Process And FAS No. 13," **MA**, 1981, Vol. 62, No. 10, pp. 49-53.)

Lilien, Steve. (El-Gazzar, Samir, Steve Lilien and Victor Pastena. "Accounting For Leases By Lessees," **JAEC**, 1986, Vol. 8, No. 3, pp. 217-237.)

Liljeblad, Ragnar. "Depreciation Of Industrial Plant," **AR**, 1937, Vol. 12, No. 4, pp. 361-368.

Lillestol, Jostein. "A Note On Computing Upper Error Limits In Dollar-Unit Sampling," **JAR**, 1981, Vol. 19, No. 1, pp. 263-267.

Lillie, John. "A Practical Method For Evaluation Of Investments," **MA**, 1966, Vol. 47, No. 10, pp. 3-7.

Lillis, Anne. (Williams, David J. and Anne Lillis. "EDP Audits Of Operating Systems - An Exploratory Study Of The Determinants Of The Prior Probability Of Risk," **AJPT**, 1984-85, Vol. 4, No. 2, pp. 110-117.)

Lilly, Fred L. (Jancura, Elise G. and Fred L. Lilly. "SAS No. 3 And The Evaluation Of Internal Control," **JOA**, 1977, Vol. 143, No. 3, pp. 69-74.)

Lilly, Lewis. "Restrictive Legislation And Its Concomitants," **AR**, 1945, Vol. 20, No. 2, pp. 198-200.

Lilly, M. S. (Dyl, E. A. and M. S. Lilly. "A Note On Institutional Contributions To The Accounting Literature," **AOS**, 1985, Vol. 10, No. 2, pp. 171-176.)

Lim, Ronald S. "The Mathematical Propriety Of Accounting Measurements And Calculations," **AR**, 1966, Vol. 41, No. 4, pp. 642-651.

Limberg, Stephen T. and Bill N. Schwartz. "Should You Use Multiple Asset Accounts?," **CPAJ**, 1981, Vol. 51, No. 10, pp. 25-31.

Limberg, Stephen T. and Sally Morrow Jones. "An Analysis Of 'Substantiality' Under The Section 704(b) Final Regulations," **JATA**, 1988, Vol. 10, No. 1, pp. 60-74.

Limberg, Stephen T. "Incorporating Economic Uncertainty Into The Tax Planning Curricula," **AIA**, 1987, Vol. 4, pp. 131-152.

Limberg, Stephen T. (Fellingham, John C., Stephen T. Limberg and Patrick J. Wilkie. "Tax Rates, Tax Shelters And Optimal Portfolios," **AIT**, 1987, Vol. 1, pp. 23-48.)

Lin, W. Thomas. (Klersey, George F., Chen-En Ko and Thomas W. Lin. "Use Of A Multi-Attribute Utility Model In Computer System Selection," **JIS**, 1988, Vol. 3, No. 1, pp. 1-9.)

Lin, W. Thomas, Theodore J. Mock and Arnold Wright. "The Use Of The Analytic Hierarchy Process As An Aid In Planning The Nature And Extent Of Audit Procedures," **AJPT**, 1984-85, Vol. 4, No. 1, pp. 89-99.

Lin, W. Thomas. "Multiple Objective Budgeting Models: A Simulation," **AR**, 1978, Vol. 53, No. 1, pp. 61-76.

Lin, W. Thomas. (Daroca, Frank P., Gary L. Holstrum and W. Thomas Lin. "Long-Range Planning And Control Of Growth," **JOA**, 1984, Vol. 158, No. 6, pp. 118-134.)

Lin, W. Thomas. (Driscoll, Donna A., W. Thomas Lin and Paul R. Watkins. "Cost-Volume-Profit Analysis Under Uncertainty: A Synthesis And Framework For Evaluation," **JAL**, 1984, Vol. 3, pp. 85-116.)

Lin, W. Thomas. (Lewis, Merrill T., W. Thomas Lin and Doyle Z. Williams. "The Economic Status Of Accounting Educators: An Empirical Study," **AIA**, 1984, Vol. 1, pp. 127-144.)

Lin, W. Thomas. (Vasarhelyi, Miklos A. and W. Thomas Lin. "EDP Auditing Instruction Using An Interactive Generalized Audit Software," **JAED**, 1985, Vol. 3, No. 2, pp. 79-89.)

Lincoln, John. "Innovative Financing For Growing Companies," **CA**, 1985, Vol. 3, No. 1, pp. 12-18.

Lindahl, Frederick W. "Accounting Standards And Olson's Theory Of Collection Action," **JAPP**, 1987, Vol. 6, No. 1, pp. 59-72.

Lindahl, Frederick W. (Biddle, Gary C. and Frederick W. Lindahl. "Stock Price Reactions To LIFO Adoptions: The Association Beween Excess Returns And LIFO Tax Savings," **JAR**, 1982, Vol. 20, No. 2, Part II, pp. 551-588.)

Lindahl, Frederick W., Craig Emby and Robert H. Ashton. "Empirical Research On LIFO: A Review And Analysis," **JAL**, 1988, Vol. 7, pp. 310-331.

Lindbeck, Rudolph S. "Conventional Retail - Lower Than Cost Or Market," **AR**, 1966, Vol. 41, No. 2, pp. 335-338.

Lindbeck, R. and R. Rogow. "A Straightforward Decision Rule For Selecting Lower-Of-Cost Or Market Prices: A Contraction," **AR**, 1975, Vol. 50, No. 3, p. 617.

Linder, Robert E. "HUD Guide For Public Housing Agency Audits," **CPAJ**, 1979, Vol. 49, No. 11, pp. 19-24.

Lindgren, John H., Jr. (Pearson, Michael A., John H. Lindgren, Jr. and Buddy L. Myers. "A Preliminary Analysis Of AudSEC Voting Patterns," **JAAF**, 1979, Vol. 2, No. 2, pp. 122-134.)

Lindhe, Richard. "Accelerated Depreciation For Income Tax Purposes - A Study Of The Decision And Some Firms Who Made It," **JAR**, 1963, Vol. 1, No. 2, pp. 139-148.

Lindsay, Daryl, Morina Rennie, George Murphy and Harold Silvester. "Independence Of External Auditors: A Canadian Perspective," **AIIA**, 1987, Vol. 1, pp. 169-189.

Lindsay, W. Daryl. (Chung, Dennis Y. and W. Daryl Lindsay. "The Pricing Of Audit Services: The Canadian Perspective," **CAR**, 1988, Vol. 5, No. 1, pp. 19-46.)

Lindsey, Bradford A. "Forecasting For Control," **MA**, 1976, Vol. 58, No. 3, pp. 41-43.

Link, Robert F. "Sales Up, Profits Down: Sales Price Lag," **MA**, 1970, Vol. 52, No. 4, pp. 19-20.

Linn, James J. (Firmin, Peter A. and James J. Linn. "Information Systems And Managerial Accounting," **AR**, 1968, Vol. 43, No. 1, pp. 75-82.)

Linn, James J. (Firmin, Peter A. and James J. Linn. "Accounting Systems Course - A New Concept," **AR**, 1967, Vol. 42, No. 1, pp. 124-127.)

Linn, James J. (Firmin, Peter A., Seymour S. Goodman, Thomas E. Hendricks and James J. Linn. "University Cost Structure And Behavior: An Empirical Study," **JAR**, 1968, Vol. 6, Supp., pp. 122-155.)

Linnenberg, Clem C., Jr. "Policies And Procedures In Federal Civilian Procurement," **AR**, 1943, Vol. 18, No. 1, pp. 16-25.

Linnenberg, Clem C., Jr. "Policy And Procedures In Federal Civilian Procurement, Part II," **AR**, 1943, Vol. 18, No. 2, pp. 136-147.

Linowes, David F. "Commentary On The Foreign Direct Investment Program," **IJAER**, 1968, Vol. 4, No. 1, pp. 81-82.

Linowes, David F. "Communications Satellites: Their Impact On The CPA," **JOA**, 1981, Vol. 152, No. 3, pp. 58-67.

Linowes, David F. "Cutting Government Waste: The Profession's Role," **JOA**, 1983, Vol. 156, No. 5, pp. 66-77.

Linowes, David F. "Government And The Accounting Profession," **JOA**, 1966, Vol. 121, No. 5, pp. 53-57.

Linowes, David F. "Nature Of The Accounting Profession." **AR**, 1965, Vol. 40, No. 1, pp. 97-104.

Linowes, David F. "Professional Organization And Growth," **JOA**, 1965, Vol. 120, No. 1, pp. 24-29.

Linowes, David F. "Socio-Economic Accounting," **JOA**, 1968, Vol. 126, No. 5, pp. 37-42.

Linowes, David F. "Strategies For The Survival Of Our Democratic Institutions," **IJAER**, 1973, Vol. 9, No. 1, pp. 1-12.

Linowes, David F. "The Accountant's Enlarged Professional Responsibilities," **JOA**, 1973, Vol. 135, No. 2, pp. 47-51.

Linowes, David F. "The Accounting Profession And Social Progress," **JOA**, 1973, Vol. 136, No. 1, pp. 32-40.

Linowes, David F. "The Implications Of Transborder Data-Flow Development For The Accounting Profession," **IJAER**, 1981, Vol. 17, No. 1, pp. 33-41.

Lint, Phillip E. (Brown, Paul R. and Phillip E. Lint. "Co-Teaching: A Key To Auditing Instruction," **JOA**, 1982, Vol. 154, No. 3, pp. 94-98.)

Lipe, Robert C. "The Information Contained In The Components Of Earnings," **JAR**, 1986, Vol. 24, Supp., pp. 37-64.

Lipka, Roland and Leonard Goodman. "Planning For Retirement: Section 402 Election," **CPAJ**, 1983, Vol. 53, No. 4, pp. 44-53.

Lipka, Roland. (Goodman, Leonard and Roland Lipka. "Property Transfers Under Section 351," **CPAJ**, 1981, Vol. 51, No. 3, pp. 42-48.)

Lipkin, Lawrence. "The Dynamic Equation Of Accounting," **AR**, 1959, Vol. 34, No. 1, pp. 134-135.

Lipoff, Carl. "Duplicating And Copying Methods In Practitioners' Offices," **JOA**, 1962, Vol. 113, No. 4, pp. 58-66.

Lippitt, Vernon G. "Accountants And Sales Forecasters - Partners For Profits," **MA**, 1968, Vol. 49, No. 7, pp. 51-58.

Lipscomb, Glenard P. "Relations Between CPAs And Non-CPAs," **JOA**, 1960, Vol. 110, No. 5, pp. 58-62.

Lipsher, Laurence E. "Selecting A Minicomputer," **JOA**, 1979, Vol. 147, No. 6, pp. 61-65.

Lipsky, Daniel. "A New Role For The Accounting Instructor," **AR**, 1945, Vol. 20, No. 3, pp. 344-347.

Lipson, Harry A. "Control And Decision-Making Help For Small Retailers," **JOA**, 1951, Vol. 92, No. 1, pp. 48-51.

Lister, Roger J. "Accounting As History," **IJAER**, 1983, Vol. 18, No. 2, pp. 49-68.

Lister, Roger J. "Werner Sombart's 'Der Moderne Kapitalismus': An Apotheosis Of Double-Entry Accounting?," **ABR**,

1984-85, Vol. 15, No. 59, pp. 229-232.

Lister, R. J. "Financing An Acquisition," **ABR**, 1972-73, Vol. 3, No. 9, pp. 62-69.

Listro, John P. "The AICPA Discussion Draft For Non-Profit Organizations," **CPAJ**, 1978. Vol. 48, No. 6, pp. 25-26.

Litherland, D. A. "Fixed Asset Replacement A Half Century Ago," **AR**, 1951, Vol. 26, No. 4. pp. 475-480.

Little, Arthur S. "The Frequency Of 'Often'," **AR**, 1947, Vol. 22, No. 2. pp. 162-165.

Little, Thomas J. (Faulhaber, Thomas A., Fred A. Coad and Thomas J. Little. "Building A Process Cost Management System From The Bottom Up," **MA**, 1988, Vol. 69, No. 11, pp. 58-62.)

Littlefield, W. Joseph. "Research Program Of Controllers Institute Research Foundation," **AR**, 1961, Vol. 36, No. 1, pp. 32-35.

Littleton, A. C. "A Cost Approach to Elementary Bookkeeping," **AR**, 1931, Vol. 6, No. 1, pp. 33-37.

Littleton, A. C. "A Genealogy For 'Cost Or Market'," **AR**, 1941, Vol. 16, No. 2, pp. 161-166.

Littleton, A. C. "A Reply," **AR**, 1953. Vol. 28, No. 1, pp. 8-11.

Littleton, A. C. "A Third Use Value Of Accounting," **AR**, 1950, Vol. 25, No. 2, pp. 192-193.

Littleton, A. C. "Accounting Rediscovered," **AR**, 1958, Vol. 33, No. 2, pp. 246-253.

Littleton, A. C. "Capital And Surplus," **AR**, 1932, Vol. 7, No. 4, pp. 290-293.

Littleton, A. C. "Choice Among Alternatives," **AR**, 1956, Vol. 31, No. 3, pp. 363-370.

Littleton, A. C. "Classified Objectives," **AR**, 1949, Vol. 24, No. 3, pp. 281-284.

Littleton, A. C. "Concepts Of Income Underlying Accounting," **AR**, 1937, Vol. 12, No. 1, pp. 13-21.

Littleton, A. C. "Contrasting Theories Of Profit," **AR**, 1936, Vol. 11, No. 1, pp. 10-14.

Littleton, A. C. "Dividends Presuppose Profits," **AR**, 1934, Vol. 9, No. 4, pp. 304-311.

Littleton, A. C. "Early Transaction Analysis," **AR**, 1931, Vol. 6, No. 3, pp. 179-183.

Littleton, A. C. "Evolution Of The Ledger Account," **AR**, 1926, Vol. 1, No. 4, pp. 12-23.

Littleton, A. C. "Examinations In Auditing," **AR**, 1943, Vol. 18, No. 4, pp. 307-316.

Littleton, A. C. "Factors Limiting Accounting," **AR**, 1970, Vol. 45, No. 3, pp. 476-480.

Littleton, A. C. "Foreign Accounting Terms," **AR**, 1930, Vol. 5, No. 4, pp. 320-322.

Littleton, A. C. "Foreign Accounting Terms," **AR**, 1930, Vol. 5, No. 3, pp. 262-263.

Littleton, A. C. "Foreign Accounting Terms," **AR**, 1931, Vol. 6, No. 2, pp. 147-149.

Littleton, A. C. "Foreign Accounting Terms," **AR**, 1931, Vol. 6, No. 1, pp. 64-65.

Littleton, A. C. "General Comments On Appreciation," **AR**, 1930, Vol. 5, No. 1, pp. 57-59.

Littleton, A. C. "Guidance Tests For Accounting Students," **AR**, 1946, Vol. 21, No. 4, pp. 404-409.

Littleton, A. C. "Independent Study," **AR**, 1933, Vol. 8, No. 2, pp. 160-161.

Littleton, A. C. "Italian Double Entry In Early England," **AR**, 1926, Vol. 1, No. 2, pp. 60-71.

Littleton, A. C. "Old And New In Management And Accounting," **AR**, 1954, Vol. 29, No. 2, pp. 196-200.

Littleton, A. C. "Paciolo And Modern Accounting," **AR**, 1928, Vol. 3, No. 2, pp. 131-140.

Littleton, A. C. "Questions On Accounting Standards," **AR**, 1941, Vol. 16, No. 4, pp. 330-340.

Littleton, A. C. "Removing The Mysteries From Accounting," **AR**, 1951, Vol. 26, No. 3, pp. 418-420.

Littleton, A. C. "Research Work At The University Of Illinois," **AR**, 1926, Vol. 1, No. 1, pp. 31-38.

Littleton, A. C. "Significance Of Invested Cost," **AR**, 1952, Vol. 27, No. 2, pp. 167-173.

Littleton, A. C. "Socialized Accounts (II)," **AR**, 1934, Vol. 9, No. 1, pp. 69-74.

Littleton, A. C. "Socialized Accounts," **AR**, 1933, Vol. 8, No. 4 pp. 267-271.

Littleton, A. C. "Suggestions For The Revision Of The Tentative Statement Of Accounting Principles," **AR**, 1939, Vol. 14, No. 1, pp. 57-64.

Littleton, A. C. "Tests For Principles," **AR**, 1938, Vol. 13, No. 1, pp. 16-24.

Littleton, A. C. "The Antecedents Of Double-Entry," **AR**, 1927, Vol. 2, No. 2, pp. 140-149.

Littleton, A. C. "The Continuing Importance Of Basic Concepts," **IJAER**, 1965, Vol. 1, No. 1, pp. 55-65.

Littleton, A. C. "The Dividend Base," **AR**, 1934, Vol. 9, No. 2. pp. 140-148.

Littleton, A. C. "The Evolution Of The Journal Entry," **AR**, 1928, Vol. 3, No. 4, pp. 383-396.

Littleton, A. C. "The Income Approach," **AR**, 1934, Vol. 9, No. 4, pp. 342-346.

Littleton, A. C. "The International Congress On Accounting: Education For The Profession," **AR**, 1930, Vol. 5, No. 1, pp. 70-75.

Littleton, A. C. "The Logic Of Accounts," **AR**, 1955, Vol. 30, No. 1, pp. 45-47.

Littleton, A. C. "The Meaning Of Accounting Education," **AR**, 1942, Vol. 17, No. 3, pp. 215-220.

Littleton, A. C. "The Professional College," **AR**, 1936, Vol. 11, No. 2, pp. 109-116.

Littleton, A. C. "The Relation Of Function To Principles," **AR**, 1938, Vol. 13, No. 3, pp. 233-240.

Littleton, A. C. "The Significance Of Interrelated Concepts In Accounting," **IJAER**, 1966, Vol. 2, No. 1, pp. 25-34.

Littleton, A. C. "The Social Service Of Accounting," **AR**, 1950, Vol. 25, No. 3, pp. 320-321.

Littleton, A. C. "Two Fables Of Bookkeeping," **AR**, 1927, Vol. 2, No. 4, pp. 388-396.

Littleton, A. C. "Value And Price In Accounting, (Part II)" No. 3, pp. 147-154.

Littleton, A. C. "Value Or Cost," **AR**, 1935, Vol. 10, No. 3, pp. 269-272.

Littleton, A. C. "What Is Profit?," **AR**, 1928, Vol. 3, No. 3, pp. 278-288.

Littleton, A. C. (Hatfield, H. R. and A. C. Littleton. "A Check-List Of Early Bookkeeping Texts," **AR**, 1932, Vol. 7, No. 3, pp. 194-206.)

Littleton, A. C., Lloyd Morey, David Himmelblau and F. E. Ross. "The International Congress On Accounting," **AR**, 1929, Vol. 4, No. 4, pp. 234-246.

Littrell, Earl K. and Roy H. Glen. "Playing The Consulting Game," **MA**, 1982, Vol. 63, No. 7, pp. 56-60.

Littrell, Earl K. "Designing A Profit-Sharing Plan For A Service Company," **MA**, 1980, Vol. 62, No. 4, pp. 47-49.

Littrell, Earl K. "High Tech: The Challenge To Management Accounting," **MA**, 1984, Vol. 66, No. 4, pp. 33-36.

Littrell, Earl K. "Optimizing Control Costs," **MA**, 1971, Vol. 52, No. 10, pp. 22-24.

Littrell, Earl K., III. "A Note On Discounted Cash Flow Examples," **AR**, 1973, Vol. 48, No. 1, pp. 132-134.

Litzenberger, Robert H. (Joy, O. Maurice, Robert H. Litzenberger and Richard W. McEnally. "The Adjustment Of Stock Prices To Announcements Of Unanticipated Changes In Quarterly Earnings," **JAR**, 1977, Vol. 15, No. 2, pp. 207-225.)

Liu, Ernest. (Bierman, Harold, Jr. and Ernest Liu. "The Computation Of Earnings Per Share," **AR**, 1968, Vol. 43, No. 1, pp. 62-67.)

Lively, Charles L. "Improving Profit Potential Of Contractors." **CPAJ**, 1978, Vol. 48, No. 10, pp. 32-39.

Livingstone, John Leslie and Gerald L. Salamon. "Relationship Between The Accounting And The Internal Rate Of Return Measures: A Synthesis And An Analysis," **JAR**, 1970. Vol. 8, No. 2, pp. 199-216.

Livingstone, John Leslie and Murray Goldstein. "FASB Experiment In Inflation Disclosures," **CPAJ**, 1980, Vol. 50, No. 6, pp. 34-41.

Livingstone, John Leslie and Richard M. Steinberg. "SEC's Proposed Internal Control Reporting Rules," **CPAJ**, 1979, Vol. 49, No. 12. pp. 39-43.

Livingstone, John Leslie. "A Behavioral Study Of Tax Allocation In Electric Utility Regulation," **AR**, 1967, Vol. 42, No. 3, pp. 544-552.

Livingstone, John Leslie. "Accelerated Depreciation And Deferred Taxes: An Empirical Study Of Fluctuating Asset Expenditures," **JAR**, 1967, Vol. 5, Supp., pp. 93-117.

Livingstone, John Leslie. "Accelerated Depreciation, Tax Allocation. And Cyclical Asset Expenditures Of Large Manufacturing Companies," **JAR**, 1969, Vol. 7, No. 2, pp. 245-256.

Livingstone, John Leslie. "Accelerated Depreciation, Cyclical Asset Expenditures And Deferred Taxes," **JAR**, 1967, Vol. 5, No. 2, pp. 77-94.

Livingstone, John Leslie. "Electric Utility Plant Replacement Costs," **AR**, 1967, Vol. 42, No. 2, pp. 233-240.

Livingstone, John Leslie. "Input-Output Analysis For Cost Accounting, Planning And Control," **AR**, 1969, Vol. 44, No. 1, pp. 48-64.

Livingstone, John Leslie. "Matrix Algebra And Cost Allocation." **AR**, 1968, Vol. 43, No. 3, pp. 503-508.

Livingstone, John Leslie. (Brundage, Marjorie U. and John Leslie Livingstone. "Simulation On A Time-Sharing Computer Utility System," **AR**, 1969, Vol. 44, No. 3, pp. 539-545.)

Livingstone, John L. (Ijiri, Yuji, Robert K. Jaedicke and John L. Livingstone. "The Effect Of Inventory Costing Methods On Full And Direct Costing," **JAR**, 1965, Vol. 3, No. 1, pp. 63-74.)

Livingstone, J. Leslie and Michael F. Van Breda. "Relationship Between Accounting And The Internal Rate Of Return Measures: A Reply," **JAR**, 1976, Vol. 14. No. 1, pp. 187-188.

Livingstone, J. Leslie. "Input-Output Analysis For Cost Accounting, Planning And Control: A Reply," **AR**, 1973, Vol. 48, No. 2, pp. 381-382.

Livingstone, J. Leslie. "Organization Goals And The Budget Process," **ABACUS**, 1975, Vol. 11, No. 1, pp. 37-48.

Livingstone, J. Leslie. (Balachandran, K. R., Richard A. Maschmeyer and J. Leslie Livingstone. "Product Warranty Period: A Markovian Approach To Estimation And Analysis Of Repair And Replacement Costs," **AR**, 1981, Vol. 56, No. 1. pp. 115-124.)

Livingstone, J. L. and K. R. Balachandran. "Cost And Effectiveness Of Physician Peer Review In Reducing Medicare Overutilization," **AOS**, 1977, Vol. 2, No. 2. pp. 153-164.

Livingstone, J. L. (Ronen, J. and J. L. Livingstone. "An Expectancy Theory Approach To The Motivational Impacts Of Budgets," **AR**, 1975, Vol. 50, No. 4, pp. 671-685.)

Livnat, Joshua. "A Generalization Of The APL Methodology As A Way Of Measuring The Association Between Income And Stock Prices," **JAR**, 1981, Vol. 19. No. 2. pp. 350-359.

Livnat, Joshua. (Amit, Raphael and Joshua Livnat. "Diversification, Capital Structure, And Systematic Risk: An Empirical Investigation," **JAAF**, 1988, Vol. 3 (New Series), No. 1, pp. 19-48.)

Livnat, Joshua. (Barlev, Benzion, Dov Fried and Joshua Livnat. "Economic And Financial Reporting Effects Of

Inventory Tax Allowances," **CAR**, 1985-86, Vol. 2, No. 2, pp. 288-310.)

Livnat, Joshua. (Bar-Yosef, Sasson and Joshua Livnat. "Auditor Selection: An Incentive-Signalling Approach," **ABR**, 1983-84, Vol. 14, No. 56, pp. 301-310.)

Livnat, Joshua. (Bar-Yosef, Sasson and Joshua Livnat. "Investment In Commodities Futures: The Accounting Implications," **ABACUS**, 1984, Vol. 20, No. 1, pp. 87-95.)

Livnat, Joshua. (Callen, Jeffrey L. and Joshua Livnat. "Is Historical Cost Accounting Possible During Hyperinflation?," **IJAER**, 1984, Vol. 19, No. 2, pp. 73-81.)

Livnat, Joshua. (Fried, Dov and Joshua Livnat. "Alternative Interim Reporting Techniques Within A Dynamic Framework: A Reply," **AR**, 1985, Vol. 60, No. 2, pp. 295-297.)

Livnat, Joshua. (Fried, Dov and Joshua Livnat. "Interim Statements: An Analytical Examination Of Alternative Accounting Techniques," **AR**, 1981, Vol. 56, No. 3, pp. 493-509.)

Livnat, J. (Ronen, J. and J. Livnat. "Incentives For Segment Reporting," **JAR**, 1981, Vol. 19, No. 2, pp. 459-481.)

Livock, D. M. "The Accounts Of The Corporation Of Bristol: 1532 To 1835," **JAR**, 1965, Vol. 3, No. 1, pp. 86-102.

Ljungdahl, Philip W. "Enterprise Account System For Agricultural Businesses," **MA**, 1971, Vol. 52, No. 10, pp. 31-36.

Ljungdahl, Philip W. (Pointer, Larry Gene and Philip W. Ljungdahl. "The Merit Of Using The Case Method In Teaching The Specialized Accounting Courses," **AR**, 1973, Vol. 48, No. 3, pp. 614-618.)

Ljungdahl, Philip W. (Stolle, Carlton D. and Philip W. Ljungdahl. "Lower Of Cost Or Market Decision Matrix," **AR**, 1974, Vol. 49, No. 4, pp. 841-843.)

Lloyd, A. J. (Owen, D. L. and A. J. Lloyd. "The Use Of Financial Information In Plant Level Collective Bargaining," **AOS**, 1985, Vol. 10, No. 3, pp. 329-352.)

Lloyd, B. Michl and Jerry J. Weygandt. "Market Value Information For Nonsubsidiary Investments," **AR**, 1971, Vol. 46, No. 4, pp. 756-764.

Lobel, Jerome. "Auditing In The New Systems Environment," **JOA**, 1971, Vol. 132, No. 3, pp. 63-67.

Lobo, Gerald J. (Imhoff, Eugene A., Jr. and Gerald J. Lobo. "Information Content Of Analysts' Composite Forecast Revisions," **JAR**, 1984, Vol. 22, No. 2, pp. 541-554.)

Locatelli, Mary P. (Beresford, Dennis R. and Mary P. Locatelli. "The Complicated Question Of Accounting For Stock Compensation," **CA**, 1983, Vol. 1, No. 3, pp. 5-13.)

Lockett, Peter P. "Capitalization Of Interest In The Light Of Recent SEC Developments," **CPAJ**, 1975, Vol. 45, No. 1, pp. 31-35.

Locke, Robert R. "Cost Accounting: An Institutional Yardstick For Measuring British Entrepreneurial Performance, Circa 1914," **AHJ**, 1979, Vol. 6, No. 2, pp. 1-22.

Locke, Robert R. "New Insights Of British Entrepreneurial Performance - 1914," **AHJ**, 1979, Vol. 6, No. 1, pp. 17-28.

Lockitch, Percy A. "Health And Welfare Fund Audits," **JOA**, 1958, Vol. 105, No. 1, pp. 43-48.

Lockwood, Jeremiah. "Early University Education In Accountancy," **AR**, 1938, Vol. 13, No. 2, pp. 131-143.

Lococo, Lawrence J. "Selecting The Right Transfer Pricing Model," **MA**, 1983, Vol. 64, No. 9, pp. 42-45.

Loderer, Claudio. (Lewellen, Wilbur, Claudio Loderer and Kenneth Martin. "Executive Compensation And Executive Incentive Problems: An Empirical Analysis," **JAEC**, 1987, Vol. 9, No. 3, pp. 287-310.)

Loderer, Claudio. (Lewellen, Wilbur, Claudio Loderer and Ahron Rosenfeld. "Merger Decisions And Executive Stock Ownership In Acquiring Firms," **JAEC**, 1985, Vol. 7, No. 1/3, pp. 209-231.)

Loeb, Isidor. "The Place Of Accounting Instruction," **AR**, 1927, Vol. 2, No. 1, pp. 46-47.

Loeb, Martin and Wesley A. Magat. "Soviet Success Indicators And The Evaluation Of Divisional Management," **JAR**, 1978, Vol. 16, No. 1, pp. 103-121.

Loeb, Martin. "Comments On Budget Forecasting And Operating Performance," **JAR**, 1974, Vol. 12, No. 2, pp. 362-366.

Loeb, Martin. (Cohen, Susan I. and Martin Loeb. "Public Goods, Common Inputs, And The Efficiency Of Full Cost Allocations," **AR**, 1982, Vol. 57, No. 2, pp. 336-347.)

Loeb, Martin. (Cohen, Susan I. and Martin Loeb. "Improving Performance Through Cost Allocation," **CAR**, 1988, Vol. 5, No. 1, pp. 70-95.)

Loeb, Stephen E. and Burt A. Leete. "The Dual Practitioner: CPA, Lawyer Or Both?," **JOA**, 1973, Vol. 136, No. 2, pp. 57-63.

Loeb, Stephen E. and James P. Bedingfield. "Teaching Accounting Ethics," **AR**, 1972, Vol. 47, No. 4, pp. 811-813.

Loeb, Stephen E. and Victoria S. Rymer. "The Accounting Paraprofessional," **JOA**, 1973, Vol. 135, No. 4, pp. 43-49.

Loeb, Stephen E. "A Code Of Ethics For CPAs In Industry: A Survey," **JOA**, 1971, Vol. 132, No. 6, pp. 52-60.

Loeb, Stephen E. "A Survey Of Ethical Behavior In The Accounting Profession," **JAR**, 1971, Vol. 9, No. 2, pp. 287-306.

Loeb, Stephen E. "Accounting Regulation: Some Further Research Questions," **JAPP**, 1986, Vol. 5, No. 1, pp. 1-4.

Loeb, Stephen E. "Codes Of Ethics And Self-Regulation For Non-Public Accountants: A Public Policy Perspective," **JAPP**, 1984, Vol. 3, No. 1, pp. 1-8.

Loeb, Stephen E. "Enforcement Of The Code Of Ethics: A Survey," **AR**, 1972, Vol. 47, No. 1, pp. 1-10.

Loeb, Stephen E. "Population Aging: Some Accounting Considerations," **JAPP**, 1987, Vol. 6, No. 3, pp. 157-167.

Loeb, Stephen E. "Teaching Students Accounting Ethics: Some Crucial Issues," **IAE**, 1988, Vol. 3, No. 2, pp. 316-329.

Loeb, Stephen E. "The Auditor-Firm Conflict Of Interests: Its Implications For Independence: A Comment," **AR**, 1975, Vol. 50, No. 4, pp. 844-847.

Loeb, Stephen E. (Bedingfield, James P. and Stephen E. Loeb. "Attitudes Of Professors Toward Accounting Ethics," **AR**, 1973, Vol. 48, No. 3, pp. 603-605.)

Loeb, Stephen E. (Broden, Barry C. and Stephen E. Loeb. "Professional Ethics Of CPAs In Tax Practice: An Historical Perspective," **AHJ**, 1983, Vol. 10, No. 2, pp. 81-97.)

Loeb, Stephen E. (Krzystofik, Anthony T., Stephen E. Loeb and Doyle Z. Williams. "How To Review Audit Training," **CPAJ**, 1978, Vol. 48, No. 7, pp. 11-16.)

Loeb, Stephen E. (Mayer-Sommer, Alan P. and Stephen E. Loeb. "Fostering More Successful Professional Socialization Among Accounting Students," **AR**, 1981, Vol. 56, No. 1, pp. 125-136.)

Loebbecke, James K. and George R. Zuber. "Evaluating Internal Control," **JOA**, 1980, Vol. 149, No. 2, pp. 49-57.

Loebbecke, James K. and John Neter. "Considerations In Choosing Statistical Sampling Procedures In Auditing," **JAR**, 1975, Vol. 13, Supp., pp. 38-52.

Loebbecke, James K. and John Neter. "Statistical Sampling In Confirming Receivables," **JOA**, 1973, Vol. 135, No. 6, pp. 44-50.

Loebbecke, James K. and Paul J. Steinbart. "An Investigation Of The Use Of Preliminary Analytical Review To Provide Substantive Audit Evidence," **AJPT**, 1986-87, Vol. 6, No. 2, pp. 74-89.

Loebbecke, James K. "Audit Planning And Company Assistance," **CPAJ**, 1977, Vol. 47, No. 11, pp. 31-34.

Loebbecke, James K. (Burns, David C. and James K. Loebbecke. "Internal Control Evaluation: How The Computer Can Help," **JOA**, 1975, Vol. 140, No. 2, pp. 60-70.)

Loebbecke, James K. (Coakley, James R. and James K. Loebbecke. "The Expectation Of Accounting Errors In Medium-Sized Manufacturing Firms," **AIA**, 1985, Vol. 2, pp. 199-246.)

Loebbecke, James K. (Cushing, Barry E. and James K. Loebbecke. "Analytical Approaches To Audit Risk: A Survey And Analysis," **AJPT**, 1983-84, Vol. 3, No. 1, pp. 23-41.)

Loebbecke, James K., John F. Mullarkey and George R. Zuber. "Auditing In A Computer Environment," **JOA**, 183, Vol. 155, No. 1, pp. 68-78.

Loesch, Donald E. and Harlan Banister. "The Accountant's Role In Value Analysis," **MA**, 1967, Vol. 49, No. 3, pp. 52-57.

Loewe, Dennis A. (Johnson, H. Thomas and Dennis A. Loewe. "How Weyerhaeuser Manages Corporate Overhead Costs," **MA**, 1987, Vol. 69, No. 2, pp. 20-26.)

Loewe, Dennis. "How Weyerhaeuser Made Its MIS Work," **MA**, 1982, Vol. 63, No. 7, pp. 16-22.

Loft, A. "Towards A Critical Understanding Of Accounting: The Case Of Cost Accounting In The U.K., 1914-1925," **AOS**, 1986, Vol. 11, No. 2, pp. 137-170.

Logan, George T., Jr. "The Direct Costing Controversy," **MA**, 1968, Vol. 50, No. 1, pp. 9-12.

Logan, G. Arnold. "Justification Of And Explanation Of Sinking Fund Reserves," **AR**, 1949, Vol. 24, No. 2, pp. 203-206.

Logan, Robert J. "Auditing Compliance With Phase IV Regulations," **CPAJ**, 1974, Vol. 44, No. 3, pp. 27-32.

Logue, Dennis E. "Shareholder Wealth And Management Compensation," **CA**, 1984, Vol. 2, No. 1, pp. 38-46.

Logue, Robert P. "Matching Costs With Revenues In The Flour-Milling Industry," **AR**, 1941, Vol. 16, No. 2, pp. 196-206.

Lomax, Victor W., Jr. and Earl R. Wilson. "Predicting Failure Of Private Colleges: Financial And Nonfinancial Determinants," **RIGNA**, 1986, Vol. 2, pp. 213-232.

Long, Ellen J. (Biggs, Joseph R. and Ellen J. Long. "Gaining The Competitive Edge With MRP/MRP II," **MA**, 1988, Vol. 69, No. 11, pp. 27-32.)

Long, Michael S. (Hite, Gailen L. and Michael S. Long. "Taxes And Executive Stock Options," **JAEC**, 1982, Vol. 4, No. 1, pp. 3-14.)

Long, Susan B. and Judyth A. Swingen. "An Approach To The Measurement Of Tax Law Complexity," **JATA**, 1987, Vol. 8, No. 2, pp. 22-36.

Longstreth, Bevis. "The SEC's Role In Financial Disclosure," **JAAF**, 1984, Vol. 7, No. 2, pp. 110-122.

Lookabill, Larry L. "Some Additional Evidence On The Time Series Properties Of Accounting Earnings," **AR**, 1976, Vol. 51, No. 4, pp. 724-738.

Lookabill, Larry L. (Albrecht, W. Steve, Larry L. Lookabill and James C. McKeown. "The Time Series Properties Of Annual Earnings," **JAR**, 1977, Vol. 15, No. 2, pp. 226-244.)

Lookabill, Larry L. (Albrecht, William Steve, Orace Johnson, Larry L. Lookabill and David J. H. Watson. "A Comparison Of The Accuracy Of Corporate And Security Analysts' Forecasts Of Earnings: A Comment," **AR**, 1977, Vol. 52, No. 3, pp. 736-740.)

Looney, Stephen W. (Golen, Steven P., Stephen W. Looney and Richard A. White. "An Empirical Examination Of CPA Perceptions Of Communication Barriers Between Auditor And Client," **AIA**, 1988, Vol. 6, pp. 233-250.)

Looram, Lloyd J. (Brown, Robert D., Ruurd G. Leegstra and Lloyd J. Looram. "Unitary Tax: At The Crossroads? - Part II," CPAJ, 1985, Vol. 55, No. 7, pp. 36-41.)

Looram, Lloyd J. (Brown, Robert D., Ruurd G. Leegstra and Lloyd J. Looram. "Unitary Tax: At The Crossroads? - Part I," CPAJ, 1985, Vol. 55, No. 5, pp. 18-25.)

Lorange, Peter. (Lessard, Donald R. and Peter Lorange. "Currency Changes And Management Control: Resolving The Centralization/Decentralization Dilemma," AR, 1977, Vol. 52, No. 3, pp. 628-637.)

Lordeman, James E., Jr. "Capital And Revenue Expdenditures For Federal Income Tax Purposes," AR, 1951, Vol. 26, No. 3, pp. 387-394.

Lorek, Kenneth S. and Allen W. Bathke, Jr. "A Time-Series Analysis Of Nonseasonal Quarterly Earnings Data," JAR, 1984, Vol. 22, No. 1, pp. 369-379.

Lorek, Kenneth S. and James C. McKeown. "The Effect On Predictive Ability Of Reducing The Number Of Observations On A Time-Series Analysis Of Quarterly Earnings Data," JAR, 1978, Vol. 16, No. 1, pp. 204-214.

Lorek, Kenneth S. "Predicting Annual Net Earnings With Quarterly Earnings Time-Series Models," JAR, 1979, Vol. 17, No. 1, pp. 190-204.

Lorek, Kenneth S. (Bathke, Allen W., Jr. and Kenneth S. Lorek. "The Relationships Between Time-Series Models And The Security Market's Expectation Of Quarterly Earnings," AR, 1984, Vol. 59, No. 2, pp. 163-176.)

Lorek, Kenneth S. (Jacobs, Fredric and Kenneth S. Lorek. "A Note On The Time-Series Properties Of Control Data In An Accounting Environment," JAR, 1979, Vol. 17, No. 2, pp. 618-621.)

Lorek, Kenneth S., Charles L. McDonald and Dennis H. Patz. "A Comparative Examination Of Management Forecasts And Box-Jenkins Forecasts Of Earnings," AR, 1976, Vol. 51, No. 2, pp. 321-330.

Lorek, Kenneth S., Joe D. Icerman and Abdullah A. Abdulkader. "Further Descriptive And Predictive Evidence On Alternative Time-Series Models For Quarterly Earnings," JAR, 1983, Vol. 21, No. 1, pp. 317-328.

Lorensen, Leonard and Paul Rosenfield. "Vested Benefits - A Company's Only Pension Liability," JOA, 1983, Vol. 156, No. 4, pp. 64-77.

Lorensen, Leonard and Richard J. Haas. "Governmental Accounting: Time For An Accommodation," JOA, 1982, Vol. 153, No. 3, pp. 56-67.

Lorensen, Leonard. "Gross Profit Method And Interim Financial Information," JOA, 1975, Vol. 140, No. 6, pp. 56-64.

Lorensen, Leonard. "Pension Costs In Selected Financial Statements," JOA, 1962, Vol. 113, No. 3, pp. 57-61.

Lorensen, Leonard. "The Temporal Principle Of Translation," JOA, 1972, Vol. 134, No. 2, pp. 48-54.

Lorensen, Leonard. (Rosenfield, Paul and Leonard Lorensen. "Auditors' Responsibilities And The Audit Report," JOA, 1974, Vol. 138, No. 3, pp. 73-83.)

Lorentz, John M. (Schwartz, Richard and John M. Lorentz. "Postemployment Benefits Other Than Pensions," CPAJ, 1986, Vol. 56, No. 5, pp. 16-23.)

Lorenzi, Peter. (Schick, Allen G. and Peter Lorenzi. "Bureaucratic And Political Models Of The University Budgetary Process: Consensus On Departmental Merit," RIGNA, 1986, Vol. 2, pp. 191-211.)

Loretucci, Joseph A. "Financial Leasing: What's The Best Replacement Cycle?," MA, 1979, Vol. 61, No. 2, pp. 45-48.

Lore, Martin M. "Review Of Important 1951 Federal Tax Decisions," JOA, 1952, Vol. 93, No. 3, pp. 309-314.

Lore, Martin M. "Review Of Significant 1950 Federal Tax Decisions," JOA, 1951, Vol. 91, No. 1, pp. 78-85.

Lorig, Arthur N. "A Non-Thesis Program For Masters' Candidates," AR, 1958, Vol. 33, No. 1, pp. 126-128.

Lorig, Arthur N. "A Reply On 'Structure Of Accounting Theory," AR, 1956, Vol. 31, No. 4, pp. 593-595.

Lorig, Arthur N. "Accounting Postulates: An Analysis Of The Tentative Statement Of Accounting Principles: Comments," AR, 1937, Vol. 12, No. 4, pp. 401-403.

Lorig, Arthur N. "Classification Of Municipal Income And Expenditures," AR, 1937, Vol. 12, No. 2, pp. 163-173.

Lorig, Arthur N. "Cost Accounting And Classification Of Municipal Expenditures," AR, 1936, Vol. 11, No. 3, pp. 291-295.

Lorig, Arthur N. "Determining The Current Financial Position Of A City," AR, 1941, Vol. 16, No. 1, pp. 41-48.

Lorig, Arthur N. "Joint Cost Analysis As An Aid To Management," AR, 1955, Vol. 30, No. 4, pp. 634-637.

Lorig, Arthur N. "On The Logic Of Decreasing Charge Depreciation," AR, 1962, Vol. 37, No. 1, pp. 56-58.

Lorig, Arthur N. "Replying To 'A Further Note' On Joint Cost Analysis," AR, 1958, Vol. 33, No. 1, pp. 35-36.

Lorig, Arthur N. "Some Basic Concepts Of Accounting And Their Implications," AR, 1964, Vol. 39, No. 3, pp. 563-573.

Lorig, Arthur N. "Suggested Improvements In Governmental Accounting," AR, 1963, Vol. 38, No. 4, pp. 759-763.

Lorig, Arthur N. "Training Accountants In Holland And West Germany," AR, 1961, Vol. 36, No. 2, pp. 232-238.

Lorig, Arthur N. "Training Accountants In Great Britain," AR, 1960, Vol. 35, No. 3, pp. 455-463.

Lorig, A. N. "Valuing Inventories In Profit And Loss Determination," AR, 1943, Vol. 18, No. 3, pp. 234-238.

Loscalzo, Margaret A. "What Is Peer Review All About?," JOA, 1979, Vol. 148, No. 4, pp. 78-82.

Loscalzo, Margaret. "Preparing For Quality Review," CPAJ, 1988, Vol. 58, No. 12, pp. 24-30.

Loschen, Leslie R. "Accounting Aspects Of Self Insurance Programs," JOA, 1955, Vol. 99, No. 1, pp. 50-55.

Losell, Donna. (Ham, Jane, Donna Losell and Wally Smieliauskas. "An Empirical Study Of Error Characteristics In Accounting Populations," AR, 1985, Vol. 60, No. 3, pp. 387-406.)

Losell, Donna. (Ham, Jane, Donna Losell and Wally Smieliauskas. "A Note On The Neutrality Of Internal Control Systems In Audit Practice," CAR, 1985-86, Vol. 2. No. 2, pp. 311-317.)

Losell, Donna. (Ham, Jane, Donna Losell and Wally Smieliauskas. "Some Empirical Evidence On The Stability Of Accounting Error Characteristics Over Time," CAR, 1987-88, Vol. 4, No. 1, pp. 210-226.)

Lossett, Ronald D. and Mohamed Moustafa. "The Nature Of The Demand For Doctorates In Accounting," AR, 1975, Vol. 50, No. 4, pp. 874-881.

Lotharius, Richard D. "The Acceptance Of Accounting As A Profession," AR, 1962, Vol. 37, No. 1, pp. 92-95.

Lothian, N. "The Nature Of Redundancy And Its Use In Company Reports And Accounts," ABR, 1975-76, Vol. 6, No. 23. pp. 216-227.

Lothman, V. O. "The Retail Method Of Inventory," AR, 1934, Vol. 9. No. 2, pp. 175-178.

Louderback, Joseph G. and Charles W. McNichols. "A Note On Net Present Value And Internal Rate Of Return Functions In Electronic Spreadsheets," JAED, 1986, Vol. 4, No. 2, pp. 113-116.

Louderback, Joseph G. and George E. Manners, Jr. "Integrating ROI And CVP," MA, 1981, Vol. 62, No. 10, pp. 33-39.

Louderback, Joseph G. and George E. Manners, Jr. "Evaluating Risky Investment Projects," MA, 1979, Vol. 60, No. 8. pp. 21-23.

Louderback, Joseph G. "Another Approach To Allocating Joint Costs: A Comment," AR, 1976, Vol. 51, No. 3, pp. 683-685.

Louderback, Joseph G., III. "Projectability As A Criterion For Income Determination Methods," AR, 1971, Vol. 46, No. 2, pp. 298-305.

Louderback, Joseph G., III. (Anderson, John C. and Joseph G. Louderback. III. "Income Manipulation And Purchase-Pooling: Some Additional Results," JAR, 1975, Vol. 13, No. 2, pp. 338-343.)

Louderback, Joseph G., III. (Dominiak, Geraldine F. and Joseph G. Louderback, III. "'Present Fairly' And Generally Accepted Accounting Principles," CPAJ, 1972, Vol. 42, No. 1, pp. 45-54.)

Loughlin, John F. "Cattle Accounting," MA, 1974, Vol. 56. No. 6, pp. 29-35.

Loughrey, Carol. (Abraham, Elizabeth, Carol Loughrey and Hugh Whalen. "Computerized Practice Set In Introductory Financial Accounting," IAE, 1987, Vol. 2, No. 1, pp. 1-12.)

Lourie, George B. and Arnold R. Cutler. "Effect Of Henderson Case On Tax Accounting Period Of Deceased Partner," JOA, 1951, Vol. 91, No. 2, pp. 260-265.

Louwers, Pieter C. "The European Public Accountant: A Different View," MA, 1975, Vol. 57, No. 3, pp. 43-46.

Lovata, Linda M. "Experiential Process Costing Project," IAE, 1986, Vol. 1, No. 1, pp. 148-152.

Lovata, Linda M. "The Utilization Of Generalized Audit Software," AJPT, 1988, Vol. 8, No. 1, pp. 72-86.

Love, David. "Differences Between Business And Tax Accounting." JOA, 1960, Vol. 110, No. 3, pp. 44-50.

Lowe, E. A. (Berry, A. J., T. Capps, D. Cooper, P. Ferguson. T. Hopper and E. A. Lowe. "Management Control In An Area Of The NCB: Rationales Of Accounting Practices In A Public Enterprise," AOS, 1985, Vol. 10, No. 1, pp. 3-28.)

Lowe, E. A., A. G. Puxty and R. C. Laughlin. "Simple Theories For Complex Processes: Accounting Policy And The Market For Myopia," JAPP, 1983, Vol. 2, No. 1, pp. 19-42.

Lowe, Herman J. "Ethics In Our 100-Year History," JOA, 1987. Vol. 163, No. 5, pp. 78-87.

Lowe, Howard D. "Accounting Aid For Developing Countries," AR, 1967, Vol. 42, No. 2, pp. 356-360.

Lowe, Howard D. "Standards Overload: What Must Be Done," MA, 1987, Vol. 68, No. 12, pp. 57-61.

Lowe, Howard D. "The Classification Of Corporate Stock Equities," AR, 1961, Vol. 36, No. 3, pp. 425-433.

Lowe, Howard D. "The Essentials Of A General Theory Of Depreciation," AR, 1963, Vol. 38, No. 2, pp. 293-301.

Lowe, Larry S., C. Richard Roberts and James W. Cagley. "Your Sales Forecast-Marketing Budget Relationship - Is It Consistent?," MA, 1980, Vol. 61, No. 7, pp. 29-33.

Lowe, Ronald L. "Auditing The Corporate Information System," CPAJ, 1977, Vol. 47, No. 11, pp. 35-40.

Lowe, Ronald L. "Management Involvement In EDP Planning," CPAJ, 1980, Vol. 50, No. 6, pp. 28-33.

Lowe, Ross E. "Public Accounting Internships," AR, 1965. Vol. 40, No. 4, pp. 839-846.

Lowe, T. (Puxty, A. G., H. C. Willmott, D. J. Cooper and T. Lowe. "Modes Of Regulation In Advanced Capitalism: Locating Accountancy In Four Countries," AOS, 1987, Vol. 12, No. 3, pp. 273-292.)

Lowell, Robert P. "Usury: What The Accountant Should Know," MA, 1972, Vol. 53, No. 8, pp. 29-32.

Lowell, Samuel B. "Pricing Policies And Methods," MA, 1967, Vol. 48. No. 7, pp. 23-28.

Lowengrub, Jerome. "Internal Reporting For Motion Picture Distributors," MA, 1967, Vol. 48, No. 11, pp. 45-50.

Lowenthal, Franklin. "A Decision Model For The Alternative Tax On Capital Gains," AR, 1981, Vol. 56, No. 2, pp. 390-394.

Lowenthal, Franklin. "Multiple Splitoff Points," IAE, 1986,

Vol. 1, No. 2, pp. 302-308.

Lowenthal, Franklin. "Product Warranty Period: A Markovian Approach To Estimation And Analysis Of Repair And Replacement Costs - A Comment," **AR**, 1983, Vol. 58, No. 4, pp. 837-838.

Lowenthal, Franklin. "The Down Payment Decision," **IAE**, 1983, No. 1, pp. 164-167.

Lowles, D. C. "Some Results Of Cost Analysis In Industrial Distribution," **AR**, 1931, Vol. 6, No. 2, pp. 131-135.

Loxton, John M. "Use Of Computer To Facilitate Audit Of Transportation Charges," **MA**, 1970, Vol. 51, No. 7, pp. 16-18.

Loy, David. (Mathur, Ike and David Loy. "Foreign Currency Translation: Survey Of Corporate Treasurers," **MA**, 1981, Vol. 63, No. 3, pp. 33-42.)

Loy, L. David and Howard R. Toole. "Accounting For Discounted Convertible Bond Exchanges: A Survey Of Results," **JAAF**, 1980, Vol. 3, No. 3, pp. 227-243.

Lubar, Melvin M. "A Computer Interviews A Sole Practitioner," **CPAJ**, 1974, Vol. 44, No. 11, pp. 43-45.

Lubas, Daniel P. "Developing A Computerized General Ledger System," **MA**, 1976, Vol. 57, No. 11, pp. 53-56.

Lubbert, Jens. "National Accounting - Its Scope And Purpose," **IJAER**, 1966, Vol. 1, No. 2, pp. 43-59.

Lubell, Myron S. and Barry C. Broden. "The Masters Degree In Taxation: An Academic Survey," **AR**, 1975, Vol. 50, No. 1, pp. 170-176.

Lubell, Myron S. (Bedingfield, James P. and Myron S. Lubell. "Extension Of The Attest Function To Published Forecasts - An Opinion Survey," **CPAJ**, 1974, Vol. 44, No. 1, pp. 40-45.)

Lubell, Myron S. (Broden, Barry C. and Myron S. Lubell. "The Master's Degree In Taxation: An Assessment Of Its Growth And Future," **JATA**, 1979, Vol. 1, No. 1, pp. 5-14.)

Lubin, Millicent E. and Jeffrey D. Summa. "New Section 338 - History And Purpose," **CPAJ**, 1984, Vol. 54, No. 8, pp. 18-23.

Lucas, Henry C., Jr. "The Implementation Of Computer-Based Models," **MA**, 1976, Vol. 57, No. 8, pp. 49-50.

Lucas, Henry C., Jr. "The Use Of An Accounting Information System, Action And Organizational Performance," **AR**, 1975, Vol. 50, No. 4, pp. 735-746.

Lucas, R. G. (Dermer, J. D. and R. G. Lucas. "The Illusion Of Managerial Control," **AOS**, 1986, Vol. 11, No. 6, pp. 471-482.)

Lucas, Timothy S. and Betsy Ann Hollowell. "Pension Accounting: The Liability Question," **JOA**, 1981, Vol. 152, No. 4, pp. 57-67.

Lucas, Timothy S. and Paul B. W. Miller. "Pension Accounting: Impacting The Financial Statement," **JOA**, 183, Vol. 155, No. 6, pp. 90-109.

Lucas, William F. "Game Theory And Accounting," **JCA**, 1984, Vol. 1, No. 1, pp. 17-32.

Lucas, William H. and Thomas L. Morrison. "Management Accounting For Construction Contracts," **MA**, 1981, Vol. 63, No. 5, pp. 59-65.

Lucien, Kent. "Transfer Pricing For The Cost Funds In A Commercial Bank," **MA**, 1979, Vol. 60, No. 7, pp. 23-24.

Luck, Wolfgang. "Recent Changes In The German Professional Certified Public Accountant (Wirtschaftsprufer) Examination," **IJAER**, 1977, Vol. 13, No. 1, pp. 131-140.

Luck, Wolfgang. "The Impact Of International Standards And Other Developments On The German Accounting Profession," **IJAER**, 1982, Vol. 18, No. 1, pp. 45-56.

Ludman, Earl A. "Insider Trading: The Case For Regulation," **JAAF**, 1986, Vol. 1 (New Series), No. 2, pp. 118-124.

Ludmer, Henry. "General Accounting Vs. Tax Accounting," **AR**, 1949, Vol. 24, No. 4, pp. 414-422.

Luecke, Randall W. "Diversifying Revenue Sources: A Key To Hospital Survival," **CA**, 1986, Vol. 4, No. 2, pp. 3-10.

Luecke, Randall W. (Hart, James R. and Randall W. Luecke. "Corporate Health Care Costs: A Strategy For Containment," **CA**, 1984, Vol. 2, No. 4, pp. 12-21.)

Luecke, Randall W. (Jardine, Linda L. and Randall W. Luecke. "FAS 81: Disclosing Postretirement Benefits," **MA**, 1985, Vol. 67, No. 4, pp. 51-54.)

Luepker, LaVern W. "Budgeting - Boon Or Bust?," **MA**, 1969, Vol. 50, No. 8, pp. 31-32.

Lufkin, Dan W. (Barhydt, Dirck, Robert H. Clement, Dan W. Lufkin and A. Jones Yorke. "Planning Concepts In The 'Tentative Statement Of Cost Concepts'," **AR**, 1957, Vol. 32, No. 4, pp. 593-597.)

Luh, Frank. (Mills, Robert H. and Frank Luh. "Financial Reporting Of Commercial Banks," **JOA**, 1968, Vol. 126, No. 1, pp. 49-54.)

Luh, F. S. "Controlled Cost: An Operational Concept And Statistical Approach To Standard Costing," **AR**, 1968, Vol. 43, No. 1, pp. 123-132.

Luh, F. S. "Graphical Approach To Process Costing," **AR**, 1967, Vol. 42, No. 3, pp. 600-604.

Luh, Martin J., Jr. "Forecasting And Budgeting In A Research Firm," **MA**, 1972, Vol. 53, No. 12, pp. 35-39.

Lukas, G. E. "Prepaid Interest," **AR**, 1935, Vol. 10, No. 3, pp. 298-301.

Luke, Hugh D. "Dynamic Accounting For Effective Management," **MA**, 1970, Vol. 51, No. 11, pp. 11-13.

Lukka, K. "Budgetary Biasing In Organizations: Theoretical Framework And Empirical Evidence," **AOS**, 1988, Vol. 13, No. 3, pp. 281-302.

Lumer, Marc. (Weiner, David P. and Marc Lumer. "Accountants For The Public Interest: A Brief History," **CPAJ**, 1975, Vol. 45, No. 3, pp. 18-20.)

Lundahl, Melvin O. "Appreciation And The Statutes," **AR**, 1932, Vol. 7, No. 3, pp. 189-193.

Lundholm, Russell J. "Price-Signal Relations In The Presence Of Correlated Public And Private Information," **JAR**, 1988, Vol. 26, No. 1, pp. 107-118.

Lundholm, Russell J. (DeJong, Douglas V., Robert Forsythe, Russell J. Lundholm and Wilfred C. Uecker. "A Laboratory Investigation Of The Moral Hazard Problem In An Agency Relationship," **JAR**, 1985, Vol. 23, Supp., pp. 81-120.)

Lundmer, A. Henry. "German Financial Mobilization," **AR**, 1943, Vol. 18, No. 1, pp. 34-39.

Lundquist, William H. "Accountants Face New Challenges," **MA**, 1967, Vol. 48, No. 7, pp. 3-9.

Lundy, Todd S. "The Use Of Data Processing In The Accountant's Office," **JOA**, 1966, Vol. 121, No. 3, pp. 33-42.

Lundy, Todd S. (Flamholtz, Eric and Todd S. Lundy. "Human Resource Accounting For CPA Firms," **CPAJ**, 1975, Vol. 45, No. 10, pp. 45-51.)

Lund, Reuel I. "Realizable Value As A Measurement Of Gross Income," **AR**, 1941, Vol. 16, No. 4, pp. 373-384.

Lund, Reuel I. "Status Of Partner's Loan Accounts In Partnership Dissolution," **AR**, 1933, Vol. 8, No. 3, pp. 252-254.

Luneski, Chris. "Continuous Versus Discrete Compounding For Capital Budgeting Decisions," **AR**, 1967, Vol. 42, No. 4, pp. 767-771.

Luneski, Chris. "Some Aspects Of The Meaning Of Control," **AR**, 1964, Vol. 39, No. 3, pp. 591-597.

Luper, Oral L. and Paul Rosenfield. "The APB Statement On Basic Concepts And Principles," **JOA**, 1971, Vol. 131, No. 1, pp. 46-51.

Lurie, Adolph G. "Minimizing Audit Costs (Part 2)," **CPAJ**, 1977, Vol. 47, No. 1, pp. 35-38.

Lurie, Adolph G. "Minimizing Audit Costs (Part 1)," **CPAJ**, 1976, Vol. 46, No. 12, pp. 31-34.

Lurie, Adolph. "Segment Reporting - Past, Present And Future," **CPAJ**, 1979, Vol. 49, No. 8, pp. 27-30.

Lurie, Arlene. (Hardiman, Patrick, Arlene Lurie. Frank Dubas and David Schoen. "Internal Control And Financial Integrity In Government Units," **CPAJ**, 1985, Vol. 55, No. 4, pp. 46-51.)

Lursen, Charles F. (Lang, Richard C. and Charles F. Lursen. "The Captive Finance Company: Profitability And Control Reporting," **MA**, 1970, Vol. 51, No. 11, pp. 45-50.)

Lusch, Robert F. and William F. Bentz. "A Variance Approach To Analyzing Changes In Return On Investment," **MA**, 1979, Vol. 60, No. 8, pp. 29-34.

Lusch, Robert F. (Bentz, William F. and Robert F. Lusch. "Now You Can Control Your Product's Market Performance," **MA**, 1980, Vol. 61, No. 7, pp. 17-25.)

Lusk, Edward J. "A Test Of Differential Performance Peaking For A Disembedding Task," **JAR**, 1979, Vol. 17, No. 1, pp. 286-294.

Lusk, Edward J. "Cognitive Aspects Of Annual Reports: Field Independence/Dependence," **JAR**, 1973, Vol. 11, Supp., pp. 191-202.

Lusk, Edward J. "Discriminant Analysis As Applied To The Resource Allocation Decision," **AR**, 1972, Vol. 47. No. 3, pp. 567-575.

Lusk, Edward J. "Hospital Investment Evaluation," **ABR**, 1973-74, Vol. 4, No. 16, pp. 303-314.

Lusk, Edward J. "Normal Assumptions In Decision Making." **ABR**, 1972-73, Vol. 3, No. 10, pp. 133-144.

Lusk, Edward J. "Post-Auditing The Capital Investment Decision - A Strategic Extension," **ABR**, 1971-72, Vol. 2, No. 8, pp. 284-286.

Lusk, Edward J. (Abdel-Khalik, A. Rashad and Edward J. Lusk. "Transfer Pricing - A Synthesis: A Reply," **AR**, 1975, Vol. 50, No. 2, pp. 356-358.)

Lusk, Edward J. (Abdel-Khalik, A. Rashad and Edward J. Lusk. "Transfer Pricing - a Synthesis," **AR**, 1974, Vol. 49, No. 1, pp. 8-23.)

Lusk, Edward J. (Bodnar, George and Edward J. Lusk. "Motivational Considerations In Cost Allocation Systems: A Conditioning Theory Approach," **AR**, 1977, Vol. 52, No. 4, pp. 857-868.)

Lusk, Edward J. (Heimann, Stephen R. and Edward J. Lusk. "Decision Flexibility: An Alternative Evaluation Criterion," **AR**, 1976, Vol. 51, No. 1, pp. 51-64.)

Lusk, Edward. (Bodnar, George and Edward Lusk. "Operant Conditioning: A Discussion Of Its Relevance Regarding Institutional Control," **AR**, 1979, Vol. 54, No. 1, pp. 215-220.)

Lustgarten, Steven. "The Impact Of Replacement Cost Disclosure On Security Prices: New Evidence," **JAEC**, 1982, Vol. 4, No. 2, pp. 121-141.

Lustgarten, Steven. (Haw, In-Mu and Steven Lustgarten. "Evidence On Income Measurement Properties Of ASR No. 190 And SFAS No. 33 Data," **JAR**, 1988, Vol. 26, No. 2, pp. 331-352.)

Lutchen, Mark D. and Gerald M. Ward. "Microcomputer Implementation: A Practical, Realistic, And Surefire Strategy," **CA**, 1983, Vol. 1, No. 3, pp. 21-25.

Lutz, Edward O. "A Practice Of Your Own," **JOA**, 1956, Vol. 102, No. 4, pp. 51-55.

Lutz, Sara A. "Pension Plan Disclosures: What They Mean," **MA**, 1982, Vol. 63, No. 10, pp. 48-54.

Luzi, Andrew D. (Blocher, Edward and Andrew D. Luzi. "Guidance Effects On Analytical Review Decisions," **AIA**, 1987, Vol. 4, pp. 201-214.)

Luzi, Andrew D. (Kunitake, Walter K., Andrew D. Luzi and G. William Glezen. "Analytical Review For Audit And Review Engagements," **CPAJ**, 1985, Vol. 55, No. 4, pp. 18-27.)

Lydecker, Ricahrd A. (Hartman, Bart P., Vincent C. Brenner, Richard A. Lydecker and Jeffrey M. Wilkinson. "Mission Control Starts In The Controller's Department," **MA**, 1981, Vol. 63, No. 3, pp. 27-32.)

Lynam, Nicholas E. "A Brief Explanation Of EBDI," **CA**, 1988, Vol. 6, No. 1, pp. 46-47.

Lynch, B. Michael. "CPE Predictions: 1990s Or Sooner," **JOA**, 1981, Vol. 151, No. 3, pp. 72-76.

Lynch, Elliott. "Telecommunications: AT&T Has A Few Suggestions," **MA**, 1984, Vol. 65. No. 10, pp. 45-48.

Lynch, Robert W. "Fraud And Negligence Penalties Under The 1986 Code," **CPAJ**, 1988, Vol. 58, No. 1, pp. 64-68.

Lynch, Thomas Edward. "Responsibility For Corporate Financial Reports," **MA**, 1970, Vol. 51, No. 11, pp. 14-16.

Lynch, Thomas E. "Reporting Requirements For Equity Securities," **MA**, 1972, Vol. 54, No. 6, pp. 23-26.

Lyne, Stephen R. "The Role Of The Budget In Medium And Large UK Companies And The Relationship With Budget Pressure And Participation," **ABR**, 1988, Vol. 18, No. 71, pp. 195-212.

Lynn, Bernard B. "Auditing Contractor Compliance With Cost Accounting Standards," **JOA**, 1975, Vol. 139, No. 6, pp. 60-70.

Lynn, Edward S. "Appropriation-Expenditure Accounting," **AR**, 1960, Vol. 35, No. 1, pp. 129-132.

Lynn, Edward S. "Education For The Profession," **AR**, 1964, Vol. 39, No. 2, pp. 371-376.

Lynn, Susan A. "Segmenting The CPA Services Market," **AIA**, 1987, Vol. 4. pp. 239-266.

Lyons, Norman R. "Segregation Of Functions In EFTS," **JOA**, 1978, Vol. 146, No. 4, pp. 89-93.

Lyon, George C. "Fixed Characteristics Of Variable Costs," **MA**, 1973, Vol. 55, No. 4, pp. 27-30.

Lyon, Herbert L. (Strawser, Robert H., John M. Ivancevich and Herbert L. Lyon. "A Note On The Job Satisfaction Of Accountants In Large And Small CPA Firms," **JAR**, 1969, Vol. 7, No. 2, pp. 339-345.)

Lyon, R. C. (Ijiri, Y., F. K. Levy and R. C. Lyon. "A Linear Programming Model For Budgeting And Financial Planning," **JAR**, 1963, Vol. 1, No. 2, pp. 198-212.)

Lys, Thomas and Konduru Sivaramakrishnan. "Earnings Expectations And Capital Restructuring: The Case Of Equity-For-Debt Swaps," **JAR**, 1988, Vol. 26, No. 2, pp. 273-299.

Lys, Thomas. "Mandated Accounting Changes And Debt Covenants: The Case Of Oil And Gas Accounting," **JAEC**, 1984, Vol. 6, No. 1, pp. 39-65.

Lys, Thomas. (Healy, Paul and Thomas Lys. "Auditor Changes Following Big Eight Mergers With Non-Big Eight Audit Firms," **JAPP**, 1986, Vol. 5. No. 4, pp. 251-265.)

Lys, Thomas. (Kothari, S. P., Thomas Lys. Clifford W. Smith and Ross L. Watts. "Auditor Liability And Information Disclosure," **JAAF**, 1988, Vol. 3 (New Series), No. 4, pp. 307-339.)

Lytle, Harry O., Jr. (Krogstad, Jack L., Maurice Earl Stark, Kenneth L. Fox and Harry O. Lytle, Jr. "The Faculty Residency: A Concept Worth Considering," **JOA**, 1981, Vol. 152, No. 5, pp. 74-86.)

Lyverse, Sam W. "Inventory Observation," **JOA**, 1962, Vol. 113, No. 3, pp. 62-64.

Lyzenga, Frank A. "Mechanized Financial Exhibits," **MA**, 1970, Vol. 52, No. 3, pp. 44-47.

MMM

Ma, Ronald and Eric Sowey. "The Linear Aggregation Coefficient And The Multiple User Case," **ABR**, 1979-80, Vol. 10, No. 38, pp. 215-220.

Ma, Ronald and Malcolm C. Miller. "Conceptualising The Liability," **ABR**, 1977-78, Vol. 8, No. 32, pp. 258-265.

Ma, Ronald and Mark Scott. "Capital Budgeting And Discounted Cash Equivalents: A Rejoinder," **ABACUS**, 1980, Vol. 16, No. 1, pp. 73-75.

Ma, Ronald and M. C. Miller. "Inflation And The Current Value Illusion," **ABR**, 1975-76, Vol. 6, No. 24, pp. 250-263.

Ma, Ronald and Roger Hopkins. "Goodwill - An Example Of Puzzle-Solving In Accounting," **ABACUS**, 1988, Vol. 24, No. 1, pp. 75-85.

Ma, Ronald, Pramond Pandey and Mark Scott. "Capital Budgeting And Discounted Cash Equivalents," **ABACUS**, 1978, Vol. 14, No. 2, pp. 180-187.

Ma, Ronald. "A Comparative Review Of Some Price Level Accounting Systems," **ABACUS**, 1965, Vol. 1, No. 2, pp. 107-130.

Ma, Ronald. "A Note On The Boundary Values Of The Certainty Equivalent Coefficient," **ABR**, 1979-80, Vol. 10, No. 40, pp. 415-420.

Ma, Ronald. "A Note On The Use Of Selling Prices - Some Examples From The Nineteenth Century," **ABACUS**, 1982, Vol. 18, No. 2, pp. 129-138.

Ma, Ronald. "Accounting For Long Term Leases," **ABACUS**, 1972, Vol. 8, No. 1, pp. 21-34.

Ma, Ronald. "Comparative Analysis Of Lease Evaluation Models: A Review Article," **ABR**, 1980-81, Vol. 11, No. 42. pp. 153-162.

Ma, Ronald. "Equity Accounting And Investment Value," **ABR**, 1971-72, Vol. 2, No. 6, pp. 151-155.

Ma, Ronald. "On Chambers' Second Thoughts," **ABACUS**, 1974, Vol. 10 No. 2, pp. 124-128.

Ma, Ronald. "Project Appraisal In A Divisionalized Company," **ABACUS**, 1969, Vol. 5, No. 2, pp. 132-142.

Ma, Ronald. "Value To The Owner Revisited," **ABACUS**, 1976, Vol. 12, No. 2, pp. 159-165.

Ma, Ronald. (Hirst, Mark and Ronald Ma. "Duration And Fisher's Rate Of Return Over Cost," **ABACUS**, 1983, Vol. 19, No. 2, pp. 162-170.)

Ma, R. (Bloomfield, E. C. and R. Ma. "The Lease Evaluation Solution," **ABR**, 1973-74, Vol. 4, No. 16, pp. 297-302.)

Maas, R. W. "In Defence Of Estate Duty," **ABR**, 1972-73, Vol. 3. No. 9, pp. 29-35.

Mabert, V. A. and R. C. Radcliffe. "A Forecasting Methodology As Applied To Financial Time Series," **AR**, 1974, Vol. 49. No. 1, pp. 61-75.

Mabry, Barry. (Cloutier, Clive R. and Barry Mabry. "A Small Bank Adopts A Financial Planning Model," **MA**, 1980, Vol. 61. No. 8, pp. 19-21.)

MacArthur, John B. "An Analysis Of The Content Of Corporate Submissions On Proposed Accounting Standards In The UK," **ABR**, 1988, Vol. 18, No. 71, pp. 213-226.

Macaulay, Hugh. "Responsibilities Of The Professional Accounting Firms In Continuing The Training Of College Graduates," **AR**, 1955, Vol. 30, No. 1, pp. 48-50.

MacDonald, George A. (Parsons, Vinson A. and George A. MacDonald. "Standard Cost And Control System," **MA**, 1970, Vol. 52. No. 5, pp. 19-21.)

MacDonald, J. A. "The Concept Of A National Comptroller (Accountant)," **AIIA**, 1988, Vol. 2, pp. 263-272.

MacDougall, Colville. "Amortization Of Premiums On Bonds Acquired By Trusts And Estates," **AR**, 1960, Vol. 35, No. 1. pp. 137-138.

MacDougall, Colville. "Statutory Requirements As To Form And Content Of Executors' Reports To Courts - A Rejoinder," **AR**, 1956, Vol. 31, No. 2, pp. 317-318.

Macdonald, Graeme. "An Analysis Of The Reformed Corporation Tax: A Comment And An Extension," **ABR**, 1988, Vol. 18, No. 72. pp. 371-374.

Macdonald, Graeme. "Can A Corporation Tax Under An Expenditure Tax Regime Be Non-Distortionary?," **ABR**, 1980-81, Vol. 11, No. 41, pp. 66-70.

Macdonald, Graeme. "Deprival Value: Its Use And Abuse," **ABR**. 1973-74, Vol. No. 16, pp. 263-269.

Macdonald, Graeme. "Taxation And Corporate Finance And Investment," **ABR**, 1981-82, Vol. 12, No. 45, pp. 41-54.

Macdonald, G. "Capital Maintenance, Borrowing Gains And Income Measurement: A Comment," **ABR**, 1981-82, Vol. 12, No. 48. pp. 316-318.

Macdonald, Ray W. "A Few Pointers On Accounting For Management," **MA**, 1966, Vol. 47, No. 7, pp. 3-8.

Mace, J. R. "A Systems Approach To The Analysis Of Financial Reporting," **ABR**, 1976-77, Vol. 7, No. 28, pp. 270-285.

Mace, Sherburne F. "Accounting - Italian Concept," **MA**, 1969, Vol. 50, No. 4, pp. 52-53.

MacFarland, G. A. "Accounting In The Wharton School," **AR**, 1927, Vol. 2. No. 2, pp. 175-177.

MacGillivray, C. K. "Auditors' Consulting Services," **JOA**, 1956, Vol. 101, No. 4, pp. 58-62.

Macharzina, Klaus and Adolf G. Coenenberg. "Current-Cost Or Current Purchasing-Power Accounting? An Internationally Based Assessment Of FASB Statement No. 33 On Financial Reporting And Changing Prices," **IJAER**, 1981, Vol. 16, No. 2, pp. 149-162.

Macharzina, Klaus. "Recent Advances In European Accounting: An Assessment By Use Of The Accounting Culture Concept," **AIIA**. 1988, Vol. 2, pp. 131-146.

Macintosh, N. B. and R. L. Daft. "Management Control Systems And Departmental Interdependencies: An Empirical Study," **AOS**, 1987, Vol. 12, No. 1, pp. 49-64.

Macintosh, N. B. "A Contextual Model Of Information Systems," **AOS**, 1981, Vol. 6, No. 1, pp. 39-52.

Macintyre, Donald K. "Marketing Costs: A New Look," **MA**, 1983, Vol. 64, No. 9, pp. 21-28.

MacKenzie, D. H. "Contemporary Theories Of Corporate Profits Reporting," **AR**, 1949, Vol. 24, No. 4, pp. 360-368.

MacKenzie, Ossian. "Accreditation Of Accounting Curricula," **AR**, 1964, Vol. 39, No. 2, pp. 363-370.

Mackay, Archibald E. (Rehmet, Ralph and Archibald E. Mackay. "The Division For Firms," **CPAJ**, 1981, Vol. 51, No. 2, pp. 15-22.)

Mackenzie, D. H. "The Logic Of The Cost And Revenue Approach," **AR**, 1947, Vol. 22, No. 1, pp. 12-17.

Mackey, James T. (Davis, Charles J. and James T. Mackey. "Coalition Costs Through Queueing Theory For Shapley Cost Allocations," **AIA**, 1988, Vol. 6, pp. 85-110.)

Mackey, Jim. "11 Key Issues In Manufacturing Accounting," **MA**, 1987, Vol. 68, No. 7, pp. 32-37.

Mackey, J. T. "Allocating Opportunity Costs," **MA**, 1983, Vol. 64, No. 9, pp. 33-37.

Mackintosh, Alexandea H. (Beresford, Dennis R. and Alexandea H. Mackintosh. "Purchase Business Combinations - Recognition Of Obligations At Acquisition," **CPAJ**, 1985, Vol. 55, No. 8, pp. 36-45.)

Mackler, I. M. "A Suggestion For The Measurement Of Solvency," **AR**, 1942, Vol. 17, No. 4, pp. 348-353.

Mack. Kenneth. "Computer Fraud And Fidelity Bonding," **CPAJ**, 1982, Vol. 52, No. 10, pp. 18-23.

MacLean, H. I. "Unit Costs Of Instruction At The University Of Pennsylvania," **AR**, 1934, Vol. 9, No. 1, pp. 33-37.

MacLeod, R. K. "The Percentage Depletion Controversy," **JOA**, 1955, Vol. 99, No. 2, pp. 40-45.

MacNeill, James H. "A Time To Reprogram Our Accounting Minds," **CPAJ**, 1978, Vol. 48, No. 8, pp. 19-26.

MacNeill, James H. "Accounting For Inflation Abroad," **JOA**, 1961, Vol. 112, No. 2, pp. 67-73.

MacNeill, James H. (Ellyson, Robert C., A. Tom Nelson and James H. MacNeill. "Educating Tomorrow's CPAs," **JOA**, 1985, Vol. 160, No. 4, pp. 95-105.)

MacNeill, James H. (Roy, Robert H. and James H. MacNeill. "Study Of The Common Body Of Knowledge For CPAs," **JOA**, 1963, Vol. 116, No. 6, pp. 55-58.)

MacNeill, James H. (Roy, Robert H. and James H. MacNeill. "Horizons For A Profession: The Common Body Of Knowledge

For CPAs," JOA, 1966, Vol. 122, No. 3, pp. 38-50.)

MacRitchie, Kenneth L. (Merino, Barbara D., Bruce S. Koch and Kenneth L. MacRitchie. "Historical Analysis - A Diagnostic Tool For 'Events' Studies: The Impact Of The Securities Act Of 1933," AR, 1987, Vol. 62, No. 4. pp. 748-762.)

Macve, R. H. (Hoskin, K. W. and R. H. Macve. "The Genesis Of Accountability: The West Point Connections," AOS, 1988, Vol. 13, No. 1, pp. 37-74.)

Macve, R. H. (Hoskin, K. W. and R. H. Macve. "Accounting And The Examination: A Genealogy Of Disciplinary Power," AOS, 1986, Vol. 11, No. 2. No. 2, pp. 105-136.)

Macy, B. A. (Mirvis. P. H. and Macy, B. A. "Accounting For The Costs And Benefits Of Human Resource Development Programs: An Interdisciplinary Approach," AOS, 1976, Vol. 1, No. 2/3, pp. 179-194.)

Macy, Jack. "Change Of Accounting Method Versus Correction Of Error," JOA, 1964. Vol. 118. No. 5, pp. 43-48.

Madan, Dilip B. "Project Evaluation And Accounting Income Forecasts," ABACUS, 1985. Vol. 21. No. 2. pp. 197-202.

Madan, D. B. "Resurrecting The Discounted Cash Equivalent Flow," ABACUS, 1982. Vol. 18. No. 1. pp. 83-90.

Madden, Donald L. "Bridging The Gap Between Business And Academic Environments," AR, 1970. Vol. 45, No. 1. pp. 145-150.

Madden, Donald L. "Quality Accounting Education As Our Continuing Challenge," IAE, 1985. No. 1, pp. 8-14.

Madden, Donald L. "The CMA Examination: A Step Toward Professionalism," MA, 1974. Vol. 56. No. 4. pp. 17-20.

Madden, Donald L., Levis D. McCullers and Relmond P. VanDaniker. "The Materiality Of Research And Development Expenditures," JAR, 1972. Vol. 10. No. 2. pp. 417-420.

Madden, Donald L., Levis D. McCullers and Relmond P. VanDaniker. "Classification Of Research And Development Expenditures: A Guide To Better Accounting," CPAJ, 1972, Vol. 42. No. 2, pp. 139-142.

Madden, J. T., R. A. Stevenson and W. R. Gray. "The Place Of Accounting In The Commerce Curriculum," AR, 1928, Vol. 3, No. 2. pp. 189-207.

Maddison, L. B. "Joys And Sorrows Of Practice V. Employment," JOA, 1952. Vol. 93. No. 2. pp. 199-203.

Maddrea, T. Grayson. "Intangibles Should Be Amortizable For Tax Purposes," JOA, 1963. Vol. 116. No. 3. pp. 45-49.

Maddrea, T. G. "Doing Constructive Work Does Not Destroy Independence. Should Not Interfere With Opinion," JOA, 1950, Vol. 90. No. 4. pp. 324-329.

Maddrea, T. G. "Tax Problems Of Real-Estate Developers," JOA, 1957. Vol. 104, No. 2. pp. 48-53.

Madeo, Laurence A. and Silvia A. Madeo. "The Equity And Motivating Effects Of The Maximum Tax," JATA. 1984, Vol. 5, No. 2. pp. 40-49.

Madeo, Silvia A. and Morton Pincus. "Stock Market Behavior And Tax Rule Changes: The Case Of The Disallowance Of Certain Interest Deductions Claimed By Banks," AR, 1985, Vol. 60. No. 3. pp. 407-429.

Madeo, Silvia A. "An Empirical Analysis Of Tax Court Decisions In Accumulated Earnings Cases," AR, 1979. Vol. 54. No. 3, pp. 538-553.

Madeo, Silvia A. (Burgess, Richard C. and Silvia A. Madeo. "A Simulation Study Of Tax Sheltered Retirement Plans," JATA, 1980. Vol. 1. No. 2. pp. 34-41.)

Madeo, Silvia A. (Madeo. Laurence A. and Silvia A. Madeo. "The Equity And Motivating Effects Of The Maximum Tax," JATA. 1984. Vol. 5. No. 2. pp. 40-49.)

Madeo, Silvia A., Albert S. Schepanski and Wilfred C. Uecker. "Modeling Judgments Of Taxpayer Compliance," AR, 1987. Vol. 62. No. 2. pp. 323-342.

Madison, Jim. "The 'Make Or Buy' Decision," MA, 1973. Vol. 54. No. 8. pp. 32-34.

Madison, Roland L. "Responsibility Accounting And Transfer Pricing: Approach With Caution," MA, 1979. Vol. 60. No. 7. pp. 25-29.

Magat, Wesley A. (Loeb, Martin and Wesley A. Magat. "Soviet Success Indicators And The Evaluation Of Divisional Management," JAR, 1978. Vol. 16. No. 1. pp. 103-121.)

Magee, Robert P. and John W. Dickhaut. "Effects Of Compensation Plans On Heuristics In Cost Variance Investigations," JAR, 1978. Vol. 16. No. 2. pp. 294-314.

Magee, Robert P. "A Simulation Analysis Of Alternative Cost Variance Investigation Models," AR, 1976. Vol. 51. No. 3. pp. 529-544.

Magee, Robert P. "Cost Control With Imperfect Parameter Knowledge," AR, 1977. Vol. 52. No. 1. pp. 190-199.

Magee, Robert P. "Cost Of Information And Security Prices: A Comment," AR, 1974. Vol. 49. No. 4. pp. 788-790.

Magee, Robert P. "Cost-Volume-Profit Analysis, Uncertainty And Capital Market Equilibrium," JAR, 1975. Vol. 13. No. 2. pp. 257-266.

Magee, Robert P. "Equilibria In Budget Participation," JAR, 1980. Vol. 18. No. 2. pp. 551-573.

Magee, Robert P. "Industry-Wide Commonalities In Earnings," JAR, 1974. Vol. 12. No. 2. pp. 270-287.

Magee, Robert P. "The Usefulness Of Commonality Information In Cost Control Decisions," AR, 1977. Vol. 52. No. 4. pp. 869-880.

Magee, Robert P. "Variable Cost Allocation In A Principal/ Agent Setting," AR, 1988. Vol. 63. No. 1. pp. 42-54.

Magee, Robert P. (Balachandran. Bala V.. Lode Li and Robert P. Magee. "On The Allocation Of Fixed And Variable Costs From Service Departments," CAR, 1987-88. Vol. 4. No. 1. pp. 164-185.)

Magee, Robert P. (Johnson, W. Bruce, Robert P. Magee. Nandu J. Nagarajan and Harry A. Newman. "An Analysis Of The Stock Price Reaction To Sudden Executive Deaths: Implications For The Management Labor Market," JAEC, 1985.

Vol. 7. No. 1/3, pp. 151-174.)

Magill, Harry T. "A Commentary On CPAs 1908 And Today," AHJ, 1987, Vol. 14, No. 2, pp. 109-114.

Magill, W. G. W. (Leech, Stewart, Denis J. Pratt and W. G. W. Magill. "Asset Revaluations And Inflation In Australia, 1950 To 1975: An Industry Study," IJAER, 1982, Vol. 17, No. 2, pp. 23-34.)

Magliolo, Joseph. "Capital Market Analysis Of Reserve Recognition Accounting," JAR, 1986, Vol. 24, Supp., pp. 69-108.

Magliolo, Joseph. (Landsman. Wayne R. and Joseph Magliolo. "Cross-Sectional Capital Market Research And Model Specification," AR, 1988, Vol. 63, No. 4, pp. 586-604.)

Maglione, Lawrence G. (McGinnis, Edward C. and Lawrence G. Maglione. "Taking VisiCalc To The Limit," MA, 1984, Vol. 65, No. 7, pp. 41-45.)

Magruder, Bernard F. "Nature Of Reserve For Self-Insurance," AR, 1951, Vol. 26, No. 3, pp. 334-337.

Mahaney, Mary Claire. (Bryant, Murray J. and Mary Claire Mahaney. "The Politics Of Standard Setting," MA, 1981, Vol. 62. No. 9, pp. 26-34.)

Mahapatra, S. (Kermis, George F. and S. Mahapatra. "An Empirical Study Of The Effects Of Time Pressure On Audit Time Allocations," AIA, 1985, Vol. 2, pp. 261-274.)

Maher, John J. "Pension Obligations And The Bond Credit Market: An Empirical Analysis Of Accounting Numbers," AR, 1987, Vol. 62, No. 4, pp. 785-798.

Maher, Michael W. and Ramachandran Ramanan. "Does Internal Auditing Improve Managerial Performance?," MA, 1988, Vol. 69, No. 9, pp. 54-56.

Maher, Michael W. and Timothy J. Nantell. "The Tax Effects Of Inflation: Depreciation, Debt, And Miller's Equilibrium Tax Rates," JAR, 1983, Vol. 21, No. 1, pp. 329-340.

Maher, Michael W. "The Impact Of Regulation On Controls: Firms' Response To The Foreign Corrupt Practices Act," AR, 1981, Vol. 56, No. 4, pp. 751-770.

Maher, Michael W. (Colson, Robert H., Michael W. Maher, Amy J. Broman and Pieter Tiessen. "Audit Pricing Models For Regulation Research: Reliability And Stability," RIAR, 1988, Vol. 2, pp. 61-79.)

Maher, Michael W. (Ramanathan. Kavasseri V.. Richard B. Peterson and Michael W. Maher. "Strategic Goals And Performance Criteria," JOA, 1976, Vol. 141. No. 1. pp. 56-64.)

Maher, Michael W., Kavasseri V. Ramanathan and Richard B. Peterson. "Preference Congruence. Information Accuracy. And Employee Performance: A Field Study," JAR, 1979, Vol. 17. No. 2, pp. 476-503.

Mahon, James J. "Some Observations On World Accounting." JOA, 1965, Vol. 119, No. 1, pp. 33-37.

Mahon, James J. "Whither International Accounting Standards?," CPAJ, 1983. Vol. 53. No. 12, pp. 30-38.

Mahon, J. J., Jr. "Minimizing Personal Taxes On Executives, Stockholders," JOA, 1951. Vol. 92. No. 5, pp. 582-587.

Mahoney, John J. "Earnings Per Share And The Insensitive Denominator," MA, 1970, Vol. 52, No. 1, pp. 15-20.

Mahoney, John J., Jr. (Weber, Joseph V., John J. Mahoney, Jr. and Steven W. Hackett. "Inventory Costing Under TRA 86 - Part II," CPAJ, 1988. Vol. 58. No. 6. pp. 26-33.)

Mahoney, John J., Jr. (Weber, Joseph V., John J. Mahoney, Jr. and Steven W. Hackett. "Inventory Costing Under TRA 86 - Part I," CPAJ, 1988. Vol. 58. No. 5. pp. 66-71.)

Mahoney, John J., Jr. (Weber, Joseph V., John J. Mahoney, Jr. and Steven W. Hackett. "Inventory Costing Under TRA 86 - Part III," CPAJ, 1988. Vol. 58. No. 8. pp. 64-69.)

Mahoney, John J., Mark V. Sever and John A. Theis. "Cash Flow: FASB Opens The Floodgates," JOA, 1988, Vol. 165. No. 5. pp. 26-38.

Mahoney, Thomas A. and Ralph Rehmet. "A Small CPA Firm Looks At The Regulation Question," CA. 1986. Vol. 4. No. 4. pp. 29-33.

Mahrle, Benjamin C. "Social Clubs: Accounting For Unrelated Business Income," MA, 1972, Vol. 54. No. 1. pp. 21-24.

Maindiratta, Ajay. (Banker, Rajiv D.. Srikant M. Datar and Ajay Maindiratta. "Unobservable Outcomes And Multiattribute Preferences In The Evaluation Of Managerial Performance," CAR, 1988. Vol. 5, No. 1. pp. 96-124.)

Maingot, Michael. "Published Interim Reports In The United Kingdom," IJAER, 1983. Vol. 18. No. 2. pp. 133-149.

Maisel, Melvin L. (Fair, Andrew J. and Melvin L. Maisel. "Coping With Taxes On The Second Death," CPAJ, 1988. Vol. 58. No. 12. pp. 42-54.)

Maitre, P. "The Measurement Of The Creation And Distribution Of Wealth In A Firm By The Method Of Surplus Accounts," AOS. 1978. Vol. 3, No. 3/4. pp. 227-236.

Maksy, Mostafa M. "Articulation Problems Between The Balance Sheet And The Funds Statement," AR, 1988. Vol. 63. No. 4. pp. 683-699.

Maksy, Mostafa M. "The Use Of Inflation-Adjusted Accounting Data By US Banks," ABR, 1984-85, Vol. 15. No. 57. pp. 37-44.

Maksy, Mostafa. (Belkaoui. Ahmed and Mostafa Maksy. "Welfare Of The Common Man And Accounting Disclosure Adequacy: An Empirical Investigation," IJAER, 1985. Vol. 20. No. 2. pp. 81-94.)

Malcolm, Robert E. "Decision Tables In Accounting," AR, 1966. Vol. 41. No. 3. pp. 551-555.

Malcolm, Robert E. (Dascher, Paul E. and Robert E. Malcolm. "A Note On Income Smoothing In The Chemical Industry," JAR, 1970. Vol. 8. No. 2. pp. 253-259.)

Malcom, Robert E. "A Note On The Effect Of Product Aggregation In Determining Sales Variances," AR, 1978. Vol. 53. No. 1. pp. 162-169.

Malcom, Robert E. (Kratchman, Stanley H., Robert E. Malcom

and Richard D. Twark. "The Comparison Of Alternative Income Concepts: A Reply," **AR**, 1975, Vol. 50, No. 4, pp. 865-868.)

Malcom, Robert E. (Kratchman, Stanley H., Robert E. Malcom and Richard D. Twark. "Alternative Income Concepts And Relative Performance Evaluations: A Reply," **AR**, 1976, Vol. 51, No. 2, pp. 421-426.)

Malcom, Robert E. (Kratchman, Stanley H., Robert E. Malcom and Richard D. Twark. "An Intra-Industry Comparison Of Alternative Income Concepts And Relative Performance Evaluations," **AR**, 1974, Vol. 49, No. 4, pp. 682-689.)

Malcom, Robert E. (Schrader, William J. and Robert E. Malcom. "A Note On Accounting Theory Construction And Verification," **ABACUS**, 1973, Vol. 9, No. 1, pp. 93-98.)

Malcom, Robert E. (Schrader, William J., Robert E. Malcom and John J. Willingham. "A Partitioned Events View Of Financial Reporting," **AH**, 1988, Vol. 2, No. 4, pp. 10-20.)

Malcom, Robert E. (Winarchick, James S. and Robert E. Malcom. "General Purchasing Power Accounting," **MA**, 1976, Vol. 58, No. 1, pp. 38-40.)

Maldonado, Rita M. "Recording And Classifying Transactions In The Balance Of Payments," **IJAER**, 1979, Vol. 15, No. 1, pp. 105-133.

Maletta, Thomas P. "The Interrelationship Of Taxes And Intercompany Pricing," **JCA**, 1984, Vol. 1, No. 1, pp. 187-194.

Malkoff, Alan R. "Foreign Acquisition Analysis: A Suggested Approach," **MA**, 1979, Vol. 60, No. 12, pp. 32-36.

Mallery, Gary. "Statistical Sampling And Auditing," **MA**, 1969, Vol. 51, No. 2, pp. 51-53.

Mallinson, A. H. "A Risk Analysis Approach To Profits Forecasts," **ABR**, 1973-74, Vol. 4, No. 14, pp. 83-95.

Malloy, John. "Making Price Decisions In A Small Business," **MA**, 1984, Vol. 66, No. 6, pp. 50-52.

Malmon, Alvin S. "Pension Plan Contributions," **JOA**, 1960, Vol. 109, No. 6, pp. 56-59.

Malmstrom, Duane. "Accommodating Exchange Rate Fluctuations In Intercompany Pricing And Invoicing," **MA**, 1977, Vol. 59, No. 3, pp. 24-28.

Maloney, David M. and Robert H. Sanborn. "Interactions Between Financial And Tax Accounting Caused By The Tax Reform Act Of 1986," **AH**, 1988, Vol. 2, No. 4, pp. 21-28.

Maly, Harry R. (Bill, Robert W., James H. Harrison and Harry R. Maly. "An EDP System For Stores Inventory Control," **MA**, 1967, Vol. 48, No. 12, pp. 35-42.)

Mammone, James L. "A Practical Approach To Productivity Measurement," **MA**, 1980, Vol. 62, No. 1, pp. 40-45.

Mammone, James L. "Productivity Measurement: A Conceptual Overview," **MA**, 1980, Vol. 61, No. 12, pp. 36-42.

Mamorsky, Jeffrey D. (Hirzel, Patrick S. and Jeffrey D. Mamorsky. "Fiduciary Audits: Defusing The Pension Time Bomb," **CA**, 1983, Vol. 1, No. 1, pp. 60-63.)

Manchester, Harlan R. "Sales-Use Tax Administration," **MA**, 1972, Vol. 54, No. 6, pp. 31-34.

Mandel, B. J. "A Course In Statistical Sampling For Accountants, Auditors And Financial Managers," **AR**, 1963, Vol. 38, No. 2, pp. 400-406.

Mandel, George, Alan K. Greene and Stuart A. Simel. "Brookhaven Internal Revenue Service Center," **CPAJ**, 1976, Vol. 46, No. 3, pp. 21-24.

Mandel, Linda Ann. (Hoshower, Leon B. and Linda Ann Mandel. "Transfer Pricing Policies Of Diversified U.S.-Based Multinationals," **IJAER**, 1986, Vol. 22, No. 1, pp. 51-59.)

Mandelker, Gershon. (Hong, Hai, Robert S. Kaplan and Gershon Mandelker. "Pooling Vs. Purchase: The Effects Of Accounting For Mergers On Stock Prices," **AR**, 1978, Vol. 53, No. 1, pp. 31-47.)

Mandich, Donald R. "Devaluation, Revaluation - Re-Evaluation?," **MA**, 1970, Vol. 52, No. 2, pp. 27-29.

Manegold, James G. and Stewart S. Karlinsky. "The Security Market Impact Of A Tax Law Change: Possessions Corporation Revisions," **JATA**, 1988, Vol. 9, No. 2, pp. 65-83.

Manegold, James G. "Small-Company Initial Public Offerings: The Impact Of SEC Registration Form S-18," **JAAF**, 1986, Vol. 1 (New Series), No. 3, pp. 206-221.

Manegold, James G. "Time-Series Properties Of Earnings: A Comparison Of Extrapolative And Component Models," **JAR**, 1981, Vol. 19, No. 2, pp. 360-373.

Manegold, James G. (Karlinsky, Stewart S., James G. Manegold and Alan A. Cherry. "Accounting For Deferred Income Taxes: Preparers' Responses To Policy Proposals," **AIA**, 1987, Vol. 5, pp. 15-38.)

Manegold, James G. (McNichols, Maureen and James G. Manegold. "The Effect Of The Information Environment On The Relationship Between Financial Disclosure And Security Price Variability," **JAEC**, 1983, Vol. 5, No. 1, pp. 49-74.)

Manegold, James G., Jerry L. Arnold and Michael A. Diamond. "SEC Form S-18: A Boon To Small Business," **JOA**, 1986, Vol. 161, No. 5, pp. 102-108.

Manes, Rene Pierre. The Grant-In-Aid System For Interstate Highway Construction: An Accounting Or Economic Problem?," **AR**, 1964, Vol. 39, No. 3, pp. 631-638.

Manes, Rene Pierre. "Using Computers To Improve Cost Distribution," **JOA**, 1963, Vol. 115, No. 3, pp. 57-60.

Manes, Rene P. and Thomas F. Schaefer. "Relating Financial Leverage To Annual Report Ratios," **IAE**, 1986, Vol. 1, No. 2, pp. 261-267.

Manes, Rene P. "Birch Paper Company Revisited: An Exercise In Transfer Pricing," **AR**, 1970, Vol. 45, No. 3, pp. 565-572.

Manes, Rene P. "Demand Elasticities: Supplements To Sales

Budget Variance Reports," **AR**, 1983, Vol. 58, No. 1, pp. 143-156.

Manes, Rene P. "In A Seminar On Budget Mix Variances," **AR**, 1968, Vol. 43, No. 4, pp. 784-787.

Manes, Rene P. "Rejoinder To 'Breakeven Analysis And Capital Budgeting'," **JAR**, 1971, Vol. 9, No. 1, pp. 158-159.

Manes, Rene P. "The Expense Of Expected Idle Capacity," **MA**, 1969, Vol. 50, No. 7, pp. 37-41.

Manes, Rene P. (Chen, Joyce T. and Rene P. Manes. "Distinguishing The Two Forms Of The Constant Percentage Learning Curve Model," **CAR**, 1984-85, Vol. 1, No. 2, pp. 242-252.)

Manes, Rene P. (Chen, Joyce T. and Rene P. Manes. "Distinguishing The Two Forms Of The Constant Percentage Learning Curve Model: A Reply," **CAR**, 1988, Vol. 4, No. 2, pp. 615-616.)

Manes, Rene P. (Colantoni, Claude S., Rene P. Manes and Andrew Whinston. "Programming, Profit Rates And Pricing Decisions," **AR**, 1969, Vol. 44, No. 3, pp. 467-481.)

Manes, Rene P. (Colantoni, Claude S., Rene P. Manes and Andrew Whinston. "A Unified Approach To The Theory Of Accounting And Information Systems," **AR**, 1971, Vol. 46, No. 1, pp. 90-102.)

Manes, Rene P., John Samuels and D. J. Smyth. "Inventories And Sales: A Cross Section Study," **JAR**, 1967, Vol. 5, Supp., pp. 139-156.

Manes, Rene P., Soong H. Park and Robert Jensen. "Relevant Costs Of Intermediate Goods And Services," **AR**, 1982, Vol. 57, No. 3, pp. 594-606.

Manes, Rene. "A New Dimension To Breakeven Analysis," **JAR**, 1966, Vol. 4, No. 1, pp. 87-100.

Manes, Rene. (Frank, Werner and Rene Manes. "A Standard Cost Application Of Matrix Algebra," **AR**, 1967, Vol. 42, No. 3, pp. 516-525.)

Manes, Rene. (Groves, Roger, Rene Manes and Robert Sorensen. "The Application Of The Hirsch-Dantzig 'Fixed Charge' Algorithm To Profit Planning: A Formal Statement Of Product Profitability Analysis," **AR**, 1970, Vol. 45, No. 3, pp. 481-489.)

Manes, R. and R. Verrecchia. "A New Proposal For Setting Intra-Company Transfer Prices," **ABR**, 1981-82, Vol. 12, No. 46, pp. 97-104.

Manes, R. P. and Vernon L. Smith. "Economic Joint Cost Theory And Accounting Practice," **AR**, 1965, Vol. 40, No. 1, pp. 31-35.

Manes, R. P., K. C. W. Chen and R. Greenberg. "Economies Of Scope And Cost-Volume-Profit Analysis For The Multiproduct Firm," **JAL**, 1985, Vol. 4, pp. 77-112.

Manes, Rene P. "Comment On Matrix Theory And Cost Allocation," **AR**, 1965, Vol. 40, No. 3, pp. 640-643.

Manley, P. S. "Clarence Hatry," **ABACUS**, 1976, Vol. 12, No. 1, pp. 49-60.

Manley, P. S. "Gerard Lee Bevan And The City Equitable Companies," **ABACUS**, 1973, Vol. 9, No. 2, pp. 107-115.

Mann, Alan Grant. "How To Train Staff Men To Make An Effective Accounting Organization," **JOA**, 1950, Vol. 90, No. 6, pp. 486-489.

Mann, Clifton D. "Evaluating The Cost In A Lease Proposal," **MA**, 1971, Vol. 53, No. 1, pp. 56-58.

Mann, Everett J. "Accounting In West Germany," **JOA**, 1956, Vol. 102, No. 3, pp. 57-62.

Mann, Everett J. "Cash Flow Earnings - New Concept In Security Analysis," **AR**, 1958, Vol. 33, No. 3, pp. 423-426.

Mann, Everett J. "Inflation And Accounting In Brazil," **JOA**, 1967, Vol. 124, No. 5, pp. 49-53.

Mann, Everett J. "Management And Industrial Accounting In Western Europe," **AR**, 1956, Vol. 31, No. 2, pp. 244-252.

Mann, Everett J. "Putting Idle Cash To Work To Earn Its Own Keep," **JOA**, 1954, Vol. 97, No. 5, pp. 565-571.

Mann, Everett J. "Toward A Better Federal Income Tax," **AR**, 1953, Vol. 28, No. 3, pp. 356-362.

Mann, E. J. "Executive Compensation Plans: Legal, But Are They Ethical?," **JOA**, 1952, Vol. 93, No. 3, pp. 324-329.

Mann, Harvey. "A Worksheet For Demonstrating The Articulation Of Financial Statements," **AR**, 1984, Vol. 59, No. 4, pp. 669-673.

Mann, Harvey. "Accounting For Les Forges De Saint-Maurice 1730 - 1936," **AHJ**, 1979, Vol. 6, No. 1, pp. 63-82.

Mann, Harvey. "John McDonald," **AHJ**, 1976, Vol. 3, No. 1-4, pp. 68-72.

Mann, Harvey. "Thus Spake The Rabbis - The First Income Tax?," **AHJ**, 1984, Vol. 11, No. 1, pp. 125-133.

Mann, Herschel. (Guy, Dan M. and Herschel Mann. "A Practical Guide For Reporting On Limited Examinations Of Financial Statements," **CPAJ**, 1973, Vol. 43, No. 7, pp. 555-562.)

Mann, M. Herschel. (Arnold, Jerry, William W. Holder and M. Herschel Mann. "International Reporting Aspects Of Segment Disclosure," **IJAER**, 1980, Vol. 16, No. 1, pp. 125-135.)

Mann, M. Herschel. (Clay, Raymond J., Jr. and M. Herschel Mann. "Modification Of Standards: A Proposed Solution To The Problem Of Increased Accounting Enrollment," **AR**, 1976, Vol. 51, No. 2, pp. 352-358.)

Manner, George E. (Louderback, Joseph G. and George E. Manners, Jr. "Evaluating Risky Investment Projects," **MA**, 1979, Vol. 60, No. 8, pp. 21-23.)

Manners, George E., Jr. "Use Of Predetermined Costs In The Life Insurance Industry," **MA**, 1968, Vol. 50, No. 2, pp. 44-48.

Manners, George E., Jr. (Louderback, Joseph G. and George E. Manners, Jr. "Integrating ROI And CVP," **MA**, 1981, Vol. 62, No. 10, pp. 33-39.)

Mannino, Ronald C. (Kida, Thomas E. and Ronald C. Mannino. "Job Selection Criteria Of Accounting Ph.D. Students And Faculty Members," **AR**, 1980, Vol. 55, No. 3, pp. 491-500.)

Mannis, Norm. "How Small Business Can Meet The New Challenges Of Retirement Planning," **CA**, 1985, Vol. 3, No. 3, pp. 44-48.

Mano, Ronald M. and Jerry L. Jorgensen. "Assisting Clients In Insurance Evaluation," **CPAJ**, 1981, Vol. 51, No. 1, pp. 27-32.

Mansfield, Harvey C. "The Reorganization Of Federal Accounting," **AR**, 1940, Vol. 15, No. 1, pp. 53-61.

Mansfield, Mark D. "Covering The Bases - Documenting Your Micro Programs," **MA**, 1985, Vol. 66, No. 11, pp. 44-47.

Mansfield, Mark D. "Plugging The DP Gap: Small Computers For Big Business," **MA**, 1983, Vol. 65, No. 3, pp. 58-62.

Manship, Darwin W. (Graham, Curtis C. and Darwin W. Manship. "The Environment Of Reality: An Experiment In Education For Business," **AR**, 1973, Vol. 48, No. 1, pp. 166-170.)

Mansour, Fathi A. and James H. Sellers. "Comparing Cost Accounting Standards With Existing Accounting Standards," **MA**, 1978, Vol. 59, No. 10, pp. 37-42.

Manthey, Philip S. "An Effective Inventory Control Procedure," **MA**, 1967, Vol. 48, No. 9, pp. 53-62.

Manthey, Philip S. "Profit Planning Using Forecast Schedules," **MA**, 1967, Vol. 48, No. 5, pp. 15-30.

Manthey, Philip S. "Scheduling And Profit Planning By Utilizing The Ratio-Analysis Method Of Linear Programming," **MA**, 1966, Vol. 47, No. 10, pp. 33-43.

Manthey, Philip S. "Time Task Range And Maintenance Account Technique," **MA**, 1970, Vol. 52, No. 2, pp. 35-38.

Maples, Lawrence D. (Hoyt, Ronald E. and Lawrence D. Maples. "Accounting For Joint Ventures With The Soviet Bloc And China," **IJAER**, 1980, Vol. 16, No. 1, pp. 105-124.)

Marais, M. Laurentius, James M. Patell and Mark A. Wolfson. "The Experimental Design Of Classification Models: An Application Of Recursive Partitioning And Bootstrapping To Commercial Bank Loan Classifications," **JAR**, 1984, Vol. 22, Supp., pp. 87-114.

Marais, M. Laurentius. "An Application Of The Bootstrap Method To The Analysis Of Squared, Standardized Market Model Prediction Errors," **JAR**, 1984, Vol. 22, Supp. pp. 34-54.

Marcella, Alfred J., Jr. "Disaster Recovery Planning - Business As Usual?," **CA**, 1985, Vol. 3, No. 1, pp. 53-61.

Marcella, Alfred J., Jr. "Disaster Recovery Planning - The Next Step," **CA**, 1985, Vol. 3, No. 2, pp. 60-66.

March, J. G. "Ambiguity And Accounting: The Elusive Link Between Information And Decision Making," **AOS**, 1987, Vol. 12, No. 2, pp. 153-168.

Marchant, Garry, John R. Robinson, Urton Anderson and Michael S. Schadewald. "A Cognitive Model Of Tax Problem Solving," **AIT**, 1988, Vol. 2, pp. xx-xx.

Marchione, Murray J. "International Financing Of Construction Projects," **MA**, 1970, Vol. 52, No. 4, pp. 42-45.

Marcinko, David and Enrico Petri. "Use Of The Production Function In Calculation Of Standard Cost Variances - An Extension," **AR**, 1984, Vol. 59, No. 3, pp. 488-495.

Marcotte, Ronald C. J. (Womer, Norman Keith and Ronald C. J. Marcotte. "Airframe Cost Estimation Using An Error Components Model," **JCA**, 1986, Vol. 3, No. 1, pp. 41-62.)

Marcus, Richard B. (Carmichael, D. R., Lee J. Seidler and Richard B. Marcus. "Training Young Auditors - A Realistic Approach Through Simulation," **JOA**, 1971, Vol. 131, No. 5, pp. 49-54.)

Marcus, Sumner. "Determining Renegotiable Business, Allowable Costs," **JOA**, 1952, Vol. 94, No. 1, pp. 38-45.

Marcus, S. Wesley. "Staff Training," **JOA**, 1958, Vol. 105, No. 3, pp. 60-64.

Marder, Louis. "Suggestions For The Final C.P.A. Review," **AR**, 1939, Vol. 14, No. 2, pp. 177-178.

Margheim, Loren and Kurt Pany. "Quality Control, Premature Signoff, And Underreporting Of Time: Some Empirical Findings," **AJPT**, 1985-86, Vol. 5, No. 2, pp. 50-63.

Margheim, Loren L. "Further Evidence On External Auditors' Reliance On Internal Auditors," **JAR**, 1986, Vol. 24, No. 1, pp. 194-205.

Margheim, Loren. (Kelley, Tim and Loren Margheim. "The Effect Of Audit Billing Arrangement On Underreporting Of Time And Audit Quality Reduction Acts," **AIA**, 1987, Vol. 5, pp. 221-233.)

Margolis, Julius. "The Classification Of Sectors In Social Accounts," **AR**, 1953, Vol. 28, No. 2, pp. 178-185.

Marin, Daniel B. and Benny L. Baker. "How To Avoid The Constructive Dividend Trap," **MA**, 1984, Vol. 66, No. 4, pp. 54-58.

Marino, Francis A. "Corn Products: Evolution Of Tax Doctrine," **CPAJ**, 1980, Vol. 50, No. 11, pp. 21-28.

Marino, Frank. "Creation Of Income In Federal Taxation," **CPAJ**, 1982, Vol. 52, No. 12, pp. 46-50.

Maris, Terry L. and Robert E. Meier. "A Profile Of Management Consulting Firms," **JIS**, 1986, Vol. 1, No. 1, pp. 113-117.

Markell, William and Wilfred A. Pemberton. "Programmed Instruction In Elementary Accounting - Is It Successful?," **AR**, 1972, Vol. 47, No. 2, pp. 381-384.

Markell, William. "A Comparison Of Preparation For The Accounting Profession Among New Zealand, The United Kingdom, And The United States," **IJAER**, 1980, Vol. 15, No. 2, pp. 101-114.

Markell, William. "Accounting Education - Its Importance In Developing Countries: Israel - A Case Study," **IJAER**, 1968, Vol. 3, No. 2, pp. 125-133.

Markell, William. "Development Of Accounting Education And The Accounting Profession In Third World Countries: Botswana," **IJAER**, 1985, Vol. 21, No. 1, pp. 99-105.

Markell, William. (Bloom, Robert, Araya Debessay and William Markell. "The Development Of Schools Of Accounting And The Underlying Issues," **JAED**, 1986, Vol. 4, No. 1, pp. 7-29.)

Marks, Barry R. and Krishnamurthy K. Raman. "The Importance Of Pension Data For Municipal And State Creditor Decisions: Replications And Extensions," **JAR**, 1985, Vol. 23, No. 2, pp. 878-886.

Marks, Barry R. and K. K. Raman. "Some Additional Evidence On The Determinants Of State Audit Budgets," **AJPT**, 1987-88, Vol. 7, No. 1, pp. 106-117.

Marks, Barry R. and K. K. Raman. "Pension Ratios As 'Correlates' Of Municipal Pension Underfunding," **JAPP**, 1985, Vol. 4, No. 2, pp. 149-157.

Marks, Barry R. and K. K. Raman. "The Effect Of Unfunded Accumulated And Projected Pension Obligations On Governmental Borrowing Costs," **CAR**, 1988, Vol. 4, No. 2, pp. 595-608.

Marks, Barry R. and K. K. Raman. "The Information Content Of Unfunded Pension Obligations For Municipal Bond Ratings: An Empirical Evaluation," **AIA**, 1987, Vol. 4, pp. 33-42.

Marks, Barry R. and K. K. Raman. "State Audit Budgets And Market Assessments Of Credit Risk," **JAPP**, 1986, Vol. 5, No. 4, pp. 233-250.

Marks, Barry R. (Benson, Earl D., Barry R. Marks and K. K. Raman. "The MFOA Certificate Of Conformance And Municipal Borrowing Costs," **AIA**, 1986, Vol. 3, pp. 221-232.)

Marks, Barry R. (Benson, Earl D., Barry R. Marks and K. K. Raman. "State Regulation Of Accounting Practices And Municipal Borrowing Costs," **JAPP**, 1984, Vol. 3, No. 2, pp. 107-122.)

Marks, Barry R. (Benson, Earl D., Barry R. Marks and K. K. Raman. "Municipal Borrowing Costs And The Differential Impact Of Accounting Information Across Rating Categories," **RIGNA**, 1986, Vol. 2, pp. 261-273.)

Marks, Barry R., K. K. Raman and Earl R. Wilson. "Toward Understanding The Determinants Of Pension Underfunding In The Public Sector," **JAPP**, 1988, Vol. 7, No. 3, pp. 157-183.

Marks, E. Stanley. (Levine, Arnold I. and E. Stanley Marks. "Accountants' Liability Insurance - Perils And Pitfalls," **JOA**, 1976, Vol. 142, No. 4, pp. 59-66.)

Marks, Larry A. and Denise A. Arnette. "Managing Your Banker," **CA**, 1988, Vol. 6, No. 2, pp. 27-30.

Markus, M. L. and J. Pfeffer. "Power And The Design And Implementation Of Accounting And Control Systems," **AOS**, 1983, Vol. 8, No. 2/3, pp. 205-218.

Markwalder, Alice S. "A Vote For Profit Forecasting," **MA**, 1974, Vol. 56, No. 6, pp. 23-25.

Marlin, John Tepper. "Accounting For Pollution," **JOA**, 1973, Vol. 135, No. 2, pp. 41-46.

Maroli, Alfred J. (VanAlstine, Robert W. and Alfred J. Maroli. "Proposed Accounting Model For State And Local Governments," **CPAJ**, 1983, Vol. 53, No. 2, pp. 42-51.)

Marple, Charles T. "Operations Control Plan," **MA**, 1968, Vol. 50, No. 3, pp. 23-26.

Marple, Ray P. "Value-itis," **AR**, 1963, Vol. 38, No. 3, pp. 478-482.

Marple, Raymond P. "Direct Costing And The Uses Of Cost Data," **AR**, 1955, Vol. 30, No. 3, pp. 430-438.

Marple, Raymond P. "Management Accounting Is Coming Of Age," **MA**, 1967, Vol. 48, No. 11, pp. 3-16.

Marple, Raymond P. "The Balance Sheet - Capital Sources And Composition," **JOA**, 1962, Vol. 114, No. 5, pp. 57-60.

Marple, Raymond P. "The Sources Of Capital Surplus," **AR**, 1934, Vol. 9, No. 1, pp. 75-81.

Marple, Raymond P. "Try This On Your Class, Professor," **AR**, 1956, Vol. 31, No. 3, pp. 492-497.

Marple, R. P. "Combining The Forecast And Flexible Budgets," **AR**, 1946, Vol. 21, No. 2, pp. 140-147.

Marques, E. "Human Resource Accounting: Some Questions and Reflections," **AOS**, 1976, Vol. 1, No. 2/3, pp. 175-178.

Marquette, Jesse F. (Marquette, R. Penny and Jesse F. Marquette. "Improving Models Of Municipal Bond Rating Changes: Surrogation Of Subjective Bias," **RIGNA**, 1986, Vol. 2, pp. 235-259.)

Marquette, R. Penny and Jesse F. Marquette. "Improving Models Of Municipal Bond Rating Changes: Surrogation Of Subjective Bias," **RIGNA**, 1986, Vol. 2, pp. 235-259.

Marquette, R. Penny. (Fleischman, Richard K. and R. Penny Marquette. "Municipal Accounting Reform C. 1900: Ohio's Progressive Accountants," **AHJ**, 1987, Vol. 14, No. 1, pp. 83-94.)

Marquette, R. Penny. (Hassan, Nabil, R. Penny Marquette and Joseph M. McKeon, Jr. "Sensitivity Analysis: An Accounting Tool For Decision-Making," **MA**, 1978, Vol. 59, No. 10, pp. 43-50.)

Marquette, R. Penny. (Wilson, Earl R. and R. Penny Marquette. "Evaluating The Effects Of Multicollinearity: A Note On The Use Of Ridge Regression," **AIA**, 1988, Vol. 6, pp. 143-158.)

Marquette, R. Penny. (Wrege, William T. and R. Penny Marquette. "Measurement Focus And Basis Of Accounting (GASB)," **CPAJ**, 1988, Vol. 58, No. 12, pp. 64-70.)

Marquis, Linda M. and Virginia M. Moore. "Proposed Federal Computer Systems Protection Act," **CPAJ**, 1980, Vol. 50, No. 12, pp. 29-32.

Marriner, Sheila. "The Ministry Of Munitions 1915-19 And Government Accounting Procedures," **ABR**, 1979-80, Vol. 10, No. 37A, pp. 130-142.

Marsh, J. A. and G. R. Henning. "Some History Of The

Debate On Educational Policy Of Accountants In Australia," **ABACUS**, 1987, Vol. 23, No. 1, pp. 55-69.

Marshall, Don C., Kevin M. Misiewicz and W. Ron Singleton. "Applications Of Computer-Assisted Tax Research In Academic Tax Programs," **JAED**, 1987, Vol. 5, No. 2, pp. 287-296.

Marshall, Juanita. "The Full Disclosure Problem," **MA**, 1977, Vol. 58, No. 8, pp. 24-26.

Marshall, Ronald M. "Determining An Optimal Accounting Information System For An Unidentified User," **JAR**, 1972, Vol. 10, No. 2, pp. 286-307.

Marshall, Ronald M. "Interpreting The API," **AR**, 1975, Vol. 50, No. 1, pp. 99-111.

Marshall, Ronald M. "Interpreting The API: A Reply," **AR**, 1976, Vol. 51, No. 1, pp. 176-179.

Marshall, Ronald. (Jacobs, Frederic H. and Ronald Marshall. "A Reciprocal Service Cost Approximation," **AR**, 1987, Vol. 62, No. 1, pp. 67-78.)

Marshall, Ronald. (Jacobs, Fredric and Ronald Marshall. "A Note On The Choice Structure Of Cost Variance Investigation Models," **JAL**, 1984, Vol. 3, pp. 71-84.)

Marshall, William H. "George's Business Problems," **MA**, 1975, Vol. 57, No. 2, pp. 17-19.

Marston, Felicia and Robert S. Harris. "Substitutability Of Leases And Debt In Corporate Capital Structures," **JAAF**, 1988, Vol. 3 (New Series), No. 2, pp. 147-170.

Martin, Alvin. "An Empirical Test Of The Relevance Of Accounting Information For Investment Decisions," **JAR**, 1971, Vol. 9, Supp., pp. 1-31.

Martin, Carrick A. "The Current Cost Of A Quoted Long-Term Liability: A Reply," **ABR**, 1984-85, Vol. 15, No. 58, pp. 91-92.

Martin, Carrick A. "The Current Cost Of A Quoted Long-Term Liability," **ABR**, 1982-83, Vol. 13, No. 51, pp. 191-200.

Martin, Carrick. (Partington, Graham, Jill McKinnon and Carrick Martin. "Funds Statements And The Two-Entity Test: A Response," **ABACUS**, 1986, Vol. 22, No. 1, pp. 39-44.)

Martin, Charles L., Jr. (Korb, Phillip J., Charles L. Martin, Jr., and Barbara R. Stewart. "Income And Expense Rules After Tax Reform: Helping Clients Cope," **JOA**, 1987, Vol. 164, No. 3, pp. 126-137.)

Martin, Charles L., Jr. (Sedaghat, Ali M. and Charles L. Martin, Jr. "Perceptions Of Accounting Faculty Regarding Proposed Changes In The CPA Examination," **IAE**, 1988, Vol. 3, No. 2, pp. 409-422.)

Martin, C. A. "Programmed Learning And The Teaching Of Accounting," **ABACUS**, 1965, Vol. 1, No. 1, pp. 92-96.

Martin, Donald D. "Professors' Home Office Expenses: A Recent Development And Economic Extension," **AR**, 1977, Vol. 52, No. 2, pp. 492-497.

Martin, Howard. "Breaking Through The Breakeven Barriers," **MA**, 1985, Vol. 66, No. 11, pp. 31-34.

Martin, James P., Jr. (Siegel, Gary and James P. Martin, Jr. "The Need For National Institutional Advertising," **CPAJ**, 1978, Vol. 48, No. 4, pp. 27-32.)

Martin, James R. and Eugene J. Laughlin. "A Graphic Approach To Variance Analysis Emphasizes Concepts Rather Than Mechanics," **IAE**, 1988, Vol. 3, No. 2, pp. 351-364.

Martin, James R. "Computer Time-Sharing Applications In Management Accounting," **MA**, 1978, Vol. 60, No. 1, pp. 27-38.

Martin, James R. "Dedicated Microcomputer Software For The Enrichment Of Cost And Managerial Accounting Education," **IAE**, 1987, Vol. 2, pp. 361-372.

Martin, James R. "Integrating The Major Concepts And Techniques Of Cost And Managerial Accounting: A Recommendation," **IAE**, 1987, Vol. 2, No. 1, pp. 72-84.

Martin, John D., Paul F. Anderson and Arthur J. Keown. "Lease Capitalization And Stock Price Stability: Implications For Accounting," **JAAF**, 1979, Vol. 2, No. 2, pp. 151-164.

Martin, John E. "Justifying Price Differentials," **MA**, 1965, Vol. 47, No. 3, pp. 56-62.

Martin, J. W. and Gary John Previts. "The Risk Preference Profiles Of Practising CPAs: Some Tentative Results," **ABR**, 1982-83, Vol. 13, No. 49, pp. 21-28.

Martin, J. W. and Susan R. Whisnant. "Why Johnny Can't Audit," **CPAJ**, 1982, Vol. 52, No. 11, pp. 10-17.

Martin, J. W. "A Selected Glossary Of Securities Offering And SEC Accounting Terms," **RIAR**, 1987, Vol. 1, pp. 191-224.

Martin, J. W. "Identifying Critical Internal Controls," **CPAJ**, 1980, Vol. 50, No. 9, pp. 41-46.

Martin, J. W. "Risk Interpretation Of Reporting Standards," **CPAJ**, 1979, Vol. 49, No. 11, pp. 31-36.

Martin, J. W. "Selected SEC Financial Statement Requirements - Beyond GAAP," **RIAR**, 1988, Vol. 2, pp. 219-233.

Martin, J. W. (Whisnant, Susan R. and J. W. Martin. "What Is Cycle Auditing?," **MA**, 1982, Vol. 64, No. 4, pp. 52-55.)

Martin, Kenneth. (Lewellen, Wilbur, Claudio Loderer and Kenneth Martin. "Executive Compensation And Executive Incentive Problems: An Empirical Analysis," **JAEC**, 1987, Vol. 9, No. 3, pp. 287-310.)

Martin, Larry R. "How We Lowered Our Audit Fees," **MA**, 1983, Vol. 64, No. 10, pp. 30-32.

Martin, O. R. "Surplus Arising Through Revaluation," **AR**, 1927, Vol. 2, No. 2, pp. 111-123.

Martin, R. Kipp. (Biddle, Gary C. and R. Kipp Martin. "Inflation, Taxes, And Optimal Inventory Policies," **JAR**, 1985, Vol. 23, No. 1, pp. 57-83.)

Martin, Spencer J. and Gerald P. Votta. "Accounting And Nonaccounting Factors In Valuing Stock Of Closed Corporations," **CPAJ**, 1972, Vol. 42, No. 11, pp. 901-906.

Martin, Spencer J. (Fess, Philip E. and Spencer J. Martin. "Company Forecasts And The Independent Auditor's Inexorable Involvement," **CPAJ**, 1973, Vol. 43, No. 10, pp. 868-876.)

Martin, T. Leroy. "Overcapitalization Has Little Meaning," **AR**, 1941, Vol. 16, No. 4, pp. 407-427.

Martinelli, Alvaro. "Business Ventures In Genoa During The Twelfth Century (1156-1158)," **AHJ**, 1977, Vol. 4, No. 1, pp. 55-68.

Martinelli, Alvaro. "Notes On The Origin Of Double Entry Bookkeeping," **ABACUS**, 1977, Vol. 13, No. 1, pp. 3-27.

Martinelli, Alvaro. "The Ledger Of Cristianus Lomellinus And Dominicus De Garibaldo, Stewards Of The City Of Genoa (1340-41)," **ABACUS**, 1983, Vol. 19, No. 2, pp. 83-118.

Martinez, Alonso. (Schwallie, Edward H. and Alonso Martinez. "Managing In A High Inflationary Environment," **MA**, 1987, Vol. 69, No. 4, pp. 21-24.)

Martorano, Lewis A. G. "Sales Forecasting," **JOA**, 1960, Vol. 110, No. 2, pp. 60-64.

Maschmeyer, Richard A. (Balachandran, K. R., Richard A. Maschmeyer and J. Leslie Livingstone. "Product Warranty Period: A Markovian Approach To Estimation And Analysis Of Repair And Replacement Costs," **AR**, 1981, Vol. 56, No. 1, pp. 115-124.)

Mason, Alister K. (Stamp, Edward and Alister K. Mason. "Current Cost Accounting: British Panacea Or Quagmire?," **JOA**, 1977, Vol. 143, No. 4, pp. 66-73.)

Mason, Eli. "A Proposal For Restructuring The Profession," **CPAJ**, 1975, Vol. 45, No. 7, pp. 19-22.

Mason, John O. and Jonathan J. Davies. "Legal Implications Of EDP Deficiencies," **CPAJ**, 1977, Vol. 47, No. 5, pp. 21-24.

Mason, John O., Jr. "Stock Valuation Theories And Rate Of Return Analysis," **MA**, 1971, Vol. 53, No. 6, pp. 46-50.

Mason, Martin. (Heaney, Terence, Martin Mason and Matthew Minor. "A Closer Look At ESOPs," **CPAJ**, 1976, Vol. 46, No. 9, pp. 29-36.)

Mason, Perry. "Accounting For Current Depreciation," **AR**, 1930, Vol. 5, No. 2, pp. 106-110.

Mason, Perry. "Depreciation And The Financing Of Replacements," **AR**, 1935, Vol. 10, No. 4, pp. 318-324.

Mason, Perry. "Illustrations Of The Early Treatment Of Depreciation," **AR**, 1933, Vol. 8, No. 3, pp. 209-218.

Mason, Perry. "Problems In Handling Of Large Sections In Accounting By The Lecture Method," **AR**, 1948, Vol. 23, No. 2, pp. 179-182.

Mason, Perry. "Profits And Surplus Available For Dividends," **AR**, 1932, Vol. 7, No. 1, pp. 61-66.

Mason, Perry. "Recent Trends In Depreciation Decisions," **AR**, 1939, Vol. 14, No. 1, pp. 1-13.

Mason, Perry. "The 1948 Statement Of Concepts And Standards, No. 2, pp. 133-138.

Mason, Perry. "The Financial Aspects Of Depreciation Accounting," **AR**, 1935, Vol. 10, No. 3, pp. 238-245.

Mason, Perry. "The Price-Level Study Of The American Accounting Association," **AR**, 1955, Vol. 30, No. 1, pp. 37-44.

Mason, Perry. "The Supreme Court On Public-Utility Depreciation," **AR**, 1936, Vol. 11, No. 3, pp. 234-270.

Mason, Perry. "The Use Of Costs In Setting Selling Prices," **AR**, 1926, Vol. 1, No. 2, pp. 72-76.

Mason, Perry. "Treatment Of Depreciation In The Interstate Commerce Commission Valuation Cases," **AR**, 1928, Vol. 3, No. 2, pp. 141-148.

Mason, Perry. "'Cash Flow' Analysis And Funds Statements," **JOA**, 1961, Vol. 111, No. 3, pp. 59-72.

Mason, R. O. (Mitroff, I. I. and R. O. Mason. "Can We Design Systems For Managing Messes? Or, Why So Many Management Information Systems Are Uninformative," **AOS**, 1983, Vol. 8, No. 2/3, pp. 195-204.)

Masonson, Leslie N. "Collection Acceleration: A Cash Management Primer," **CA**, 1983, Vol. 1, No. 1, pp. 34-44.

Massel, Mark S. "Accounting Training For The Government Service," **AR**, 1945, Vol. 20, No. 1, pp. 206-209.

Mastrapasqua, Frank. (Moyer, R. Charles and Frank Mastrapasqua. "Socio-Economic Accounting And External Diseconomics: A Comment," **AR**, 1973, Vol. 48, No. 1, pp. 126-127.)

Mastro, Anthony J. and Frank R. Hartman. "An Evaluation Of A Slide-Lecture Method For Teaching A Large Section Of College Auditing," **AR**, 1960, Vol. 35, No. 2, pp. 324-329.

Mastro, Anthony J. "EDP In One Elementary Course," **AR**, 1967, Vol. 42, No. 2, pp. 371-374.

Mastromano, Frank M. "A Data Base Concept," **MA**, 1970, Vol. 52, No. 4, pp. 15-18.

Mastromano, Frank M. "Information Technology Applied To Profit Planning," **MA**, 1968, Vol. 50, No. 2, pp. 22-25.

Mastromano, Frank M. "The Changing Nature Of The EDP Audit," **MA**, 1980, Vol. 62, No. 1, pp. 27-30.

Mateer, William H. "Tax Allocation: A Macro Approach," **AR**, 1965, Vol. 40, No. 3, pp. 583-586.

Materne, Douglas W. and Richard Vangermeersch. "Capitalizing Personnel-Retention Costs," **MA**, 1973, Vol. 55, No. 5, pp. 27-28.

Mathews, George C. "Accounting In The Regulation Of Security Sales," **AR**, 1938, Vol. 13, No. 3, pp. 225-232.

Mathews, M. R. "A Suggested Classification For Social Accounting Research," **JAPP**, 1984, Vol. 3, No. 3, pp. 199-221.

Mathews, M. R. (Gordon, I. M. and M. R. Mathews. "The Attitudes Of The Members Of Three Canadian Accounting Organizations Toward Continuing Education," **AIIA**, 1987, Vol. 1, pp. 357-382.)

Mathews, Russell L. (Buckley, John W., Paul Kircher and Russell L. Mathews. "Methodology In Accounting Theory," AR, 1968, Vol. 43, No. 2, pp. 274-283.)

Mathews, Russell. "Chambers And The Development Of Accounting Theory: A Personal Reminiscence," ABACUS, 1982, Vol. 18, No. 2, pp. 175-178.

Mathews, Russell. "Inflation And Company Finance," AR, 1960, Vol. 35, No. 1, pp. 8-18.

Mathews, Russell. "Price Variation Accounting - A Rejoinder," JAR, 1968, Vol. 6, No. 2, pp. 284-285.

Mathews, Russell. "The Price Level Controversy: A Reply," JAR, 1967, Vol. 5, No. 1, pp. 113-118.

Mathews, R. L. "A Computer Programming Approach To The Design Of Accounting Systems," ABACUS, 1967, Vol. 3, No. 2, pp. 133-152.

Mathews, R. L. "Income, Price Changes And The Valuation Controversy In Accounting," AR, 1968, Vol. 43, No. 3, pp. 509-516.

Mathur, Ike and David Loy. "Foreign Currency Translation: Survey Of Corporate Treasurers," MA, 1981, Vol. 63, No. 3, pp. 33-42.

Matolcsy, Z. P. "Evidence On The Joint And Marginal Information Content Of Inflation-Adjusted Accounting Income Numbers," JAR, 1984, Vol. 22, No. 2, pp. 555-569.

Matoney, Joseph P., Jr. (Brandon, Charles H. and Joseph P. Matoney, Jr. "Social Responsibility Financial Statement," MA, 1975, Vol. 57, No. 5, pp. 31-34.)

Matson, Diane. (Gray, Jack and Diane Matson. "Early Warning Systems," MA, 1987, Vol. 69, No. 2, pp. 50-55.)

Matsuda, Hiromu. "Introduction Of Standard Cost Accounting In Japan," MA, 1976, Vol. 57, No. 7, pp. 25-27.

Matsumura, Ella Mae and Kam-Wah Tsui. "Stein-Type Poisson Estimators In Audit Sampling," JAR, 1982, Vol. 20, No. 1, pp. 162-170.

Matsumura, Ella Mae. (Tsui, Kam-Wah, Ella Mae Matsumura and Kwok-Leung Tsui. "Multinomial-Dirichlet Bounds For Dollar-Unit Sampling In Auditing," AR, 1985, Vol. 60, No. 1, pp. 76-96.)

Matteson, Michael T. (Blakeney, Roger N., Winford E. Holland and Michael T. Matteson. "The Auditor-Auditee Relationship: Some Behavioral Considerations And Implications For Auditing Education," AR, 1976, Vol. 51, No. 4, pp. 899-906.)

Mattessich, Richard V. "Fritz Schmidt (1882-1950) And His Pioneering Work Of Current Value Accounting In Comparison To Edwards And Bell's Theory," CAR, 1985-86, Vol. 2, No. 2, pp. 157-178.

Mattessich, Richard. "Accounting And Analytic Methods: A Comment On Chambers' Review," JAR, 1967, Vol. 5, No. 1, pp. 119-123.

Mattessich, Richard. "Budgeting Models And System Simulation," AR, 1961, Vol. 36, No. 3, pp. 384-397.

Mattessich, Richard. "Mathematical Models In Business Accounting," AR, 1958, Vol. 33, No. 3, pp. 472-481.

Mattessich, Richard. "Methodological Preconditions And Problems Of A General Theory Of Accounting," AR, 1972, Vol. 47, No. 3, pp. 469-487.

Mattessich, Richard. "On The Evolution Of Theory Construction In Accounting: A Personal Account," ABR, 1979-80, Vol. 10, No. 37A, pp. 158-173.

Mattessich, Richard. "Prehistoric Accounting And The Problem Of Representation: On Recent Archaeological Evidence Of The Middle-East From 8000 B.C. To 3000 B.C.," AHJ, 1987, Vol. 14, No. 2, pp. 71-91.

Mattessich, Richard. "The Constellation Of Accountancy And Economics," AR, 1956, Vol. 31, No. 4, pp. 551-564.

Mattessich, Richard. "The Market Value Method According To Sterling: A Review Article," ABACUS, 1971, Vol. 7, No. 2, pp. 176-193.

Mattheiss, Theodore H. (Hise, Richard T., Stanley H. Kratchman and Theodore H. Mattheiss. "Involvement Of The Undergraduate Accounting Curriculum With Distribution Cost Analysis," AR, 1974, Vol. 49, No. 1, pp. 153-157.)

Matthews, John. "Accounting, Business And The Economy: Undue Infuence And Dysfunctional Attitudes," ABACUS, 1978, Vol. 14, No. 2, pp. 145-153.

Mattingly, L. A. "Formation And Development Of The Institute Of Certified Public Accountants Of Greece," AR, 1964, Vol. 39, No. 4, pp. 996-1003.

Mattingly, Peter W. (Wassner, Neil A. and Peter W. Mattingly. "Spreading Ownership In Corporate America - An ESOP Fable," CA, 1985, Vol. 3, No. 2, pp. 38-43.)

Matulich, Serge, Loren A. Nikolai and Stevan K. Olson. "Earnings Per Share: A Flow Chart Approach To Teaching Concepts And Procedures," AR, 1977, Vol. 52, No. 1, pp. 238-247.

Matulich, Serge. "A Theoretical Deficiency In Accounting For Bonds," JAED, 1984, Vol. 2, No. 2, pp. 52-62.

Matulich, Serge. (Stern, Myles, Meryle Hirschland and Serge Matulich. "Comment And Reply - 'A Theoretical Deficiency In Accounting For Bonds'," JAED, 1986, Vol. 4, No. 2, pp. 147-151.)

Matusiak, Louis W. and William Salowe. "Mr. CPA. How Good An Executive Are You?," JOA, 1964, Vol. 118, No. 3, pp. 44-50.

Matusiak, Louis W. "Overcoming Obstacles To Merger," JOA, 1967, Vol. 124, No. 3, pp. 58-63.

Matusiak, Louis W. "The Role Of Educators In The American Institute's Professional Development Program," AR, 1960, Vol. 35, No. 2, pp. 197-202.

Matusiak, Louis W. (Mautz, Robert K. and Louis W. Matusiak. "Concurring Partner Review Revisited," JOA, 1988, Vol. 165, No. 3, pp. 56-63.)

Matz, Adolph. "Accounting As A Tool For Economy In German Business," AR, 1940, Vol. 15, No. 2, pp. 177-184.

Matz, Adolph. "Edward P. Moxey, Jr.," AHJ, 1976, Vol. 3. No. 1-4, pp. 63-68.

Matz, Adolph. "Electronics In Accounting." AR, 1946, Vol. 21, No. 4, pp. 371-379.

Matz, Adolph. "Teaching Standard Costs And Flexible Budget With Three- And Two-Variance Methods," AR, 1948, Vol. 23, No. 3, pp. 309-313.

Matz, Adolph. "The Accounting Senior Seminar In The Wharton School," AR, 1951, Vol. 26, No. 2, pp. 262-265.

Matz, Adolph. (Kohler, Marcel F. and Adolph Matz. "Swiss Financial Reporting And Auditing Practices," ABACUS, 1968, Vol. 4, No. 1, pp. 3-16.)

Matz, A. "Cost Accounting In Germany," AR, 1940, Vol. 15, No. 3, pp. 371-379.

Matz, A. "Problems In Designing An Accounting System," AR, 1945, Vol. 20, No. 2, pp. 216-221.

Matz, A. "The Position Of The German Accountant," AR, 1938, Vol. 13, No. 4, pp. 392-394.

Mauldin, Elaine G. "How Not-For-Profit Organizations Should Value Investments," MA, 1980, Vol. 62, No. 5, pp. 35-38.

Mauldon, R. G., Henry P. Schapper and D. W. G. Treloar. "A Managerial Accounting System For Australian Agriculture," ABACUS, 1968, Vol. 4, No. 1, pp. 39-50.

Maund, D. and G. R. Young. "Equity Accounting And Investment Value: Another View," ABR, 1973-74, Vol. 4, No. 15, pp. 207-209.

Maunders, K. T. and B. J. Foley. "Information Disclosure And The Role Of The Accountant In Collective Bargaining - Some Comments," AOS, 1984, Vol. 9, No. 1, pp. 99-106.

Maunders, K. T. "Financial Management In The Soviet Industrial Enterprise," ABR, 1971-72, Vol. 2, No. 8, pp. 298-307.

Maupin, Rebekah J. and Wayne A. Label. "Profiting From A Management Buyout," MA, 1987, Vol. 68, No. 10, pp. 32-34.

Maurer, Lawrence J. "MNCs Gain New Freedom Under FAS 52 Flexibility," MA, 1983, Vol. 65, No. 6, pp. 30-33.

Mauriello, Joseph A. "Realization As The Basis For Asset Classification And Measurement," AR, 1963, Vol. 38, No. 1, pp. 26-28.

Mauriello, Joseph A. "The All-Inclusive Statement Of Funds." AR, 1964, Vol. 39, No. 2, pp. 347-357.

Mauriello, Joseph A. "The Relationship Between Accounting And Management," AR, 1951, Vol. 26, No. 2, pp. 226-231.

Mauriello, Joseph A. "The Working Capital Concept - A Restatement," AR, 1962, Vol. 37, No. 1, pp. 39-43.

Mauriello, Joseph A. (Mautner, Oscar and Joseph A. Mauriello. "Complementary Accounting Through The General Ledger." AR, 1953, Vol. 28, No. 4, pp. 565-569.)

Mauriel, John J. "Evaluation And Control Of Overseas Operations." MA, 1969, Vol. 50, No. 9, pp. 35-39.

Mauritz, E. Waldo. "Observations On Accounting In International Finance," IJAER, 1969, Vol. 5, No. 1, pp. 61-69.

Maus, William J. "How To Calculate The Cost Of Capital In A Privately-Owned Company," MA, 1980, Vol. 61, No. 12, pp. 20-24.

Maus, William J. "The Monetary Side Of International Trade," MA, 1974, Vol. 55, No. 10, pp. 13-17.

Mautner, Oscar and Joseph A. Mauriello. "Complementary Accounting Through The General Ledger," AR, 1953, Vol. 28, No. 4, pp. 565-569.

Mautz, Robert K. and Gary John Previts. "Eric Kohler: An Accounting Original," AR, 1977, Vol. 52, No. 2, pp. 301-307.

Mautz, Robert K. and John C. Burton. "A Government Accounting Standards Board?," CPAJ, 1981, Vol. 51, No. 8, pp. 13-24.

Mautz, Robert K. and Louis W. Matusiak. "Concurring Partner Review Revisited," JOA, 1988, Vol. 165, No. 3. pp. 56-63.

Mautz, Robert K. "Internal And External Auditors: How Do They Relate?," CA, 1985, Vol. 3, No. 4, pp. 56-58.

Mautz, Robert K. and Robert D. Neary. "Corporate Audit Committee - Quo Vadis?," JOA, 1979, Vol. 148, No. 4, pp. 83-88.

Mautz, Robert K. "Accounting And Statistics," AR, 1945. Vol. 20, No. 4, pp. 399-409.

Mautz, Robert K. "Accounting Objectives - The Conservative View," CPAJ, 1973, Vol. 43, No. 9, pp. 771-778.

Mautz, Robert K. "Accounting Principles - How Can They Be Made More Authoritative?," CPAJ, 1973, Vol. 43, No. 3, pp. 185-192.

Mautz, Robert K. "Financial Reporting: Should Government Emulate Business?," JOA, 1981, Vol. 152, No. 2, pp. 53-60.

Mautz, Robert K. "Self-Regulation - Criticisms And A Response," JOA, 1984, Vol. 157, No. 4, pp. 56-67.

Mautz, Robert K. "Self-Regulation - Perils And Problems," JOA, 183, Vol. 155, No. 5, pp. 76-85.

Mautz, R. David. (Tiller, Mikel G. and R. David Mautz. "The Impact Of State-Mandated Accounting And Auditing Requirements On Municipal Bond Ratings," JAAF, 1985, Vol. 8, No. 4, pp. 293-304.)

Mautz, R. K. and Donald L. Mini. "Internal Control Evaluation And Audit Program Modification," AR, 1966, Vol. 41, No. 2, pp. 283-291.

Mautz, R. K. and Jack Gray. "Some Thoughts On Research Needs In Accounting," JOA, 1970, Vol. 130, No. 3. pp. 54-62.

Mautz, R. K. and K. Fred Skousen. "Some Problems In Empirical Research In Accounting," AR, 1969, Vol. 44, No. 3. pp. 447-456.

Mautz, R. K. and R. Schlosser. "Internal Control Techniques," JOA, 1957, Vol. 104, No. 4, pp. 43-48.

Mautz, R. K. "A New Technique For Reporting Financial

Transactions," **JOA**, 1952, Vol. 94. No. 1, pp. 82-87.

Mautz, R. K. "Accounting As A Social Science," **AR**, 1963, Vol. 38, No. 2, pp. 317-325.

Mautz, R. K. "Accounting For Enterprise Growth," **AR**, 1950, Vol. 25, No. 1, pp. 81-88.

Mautz, R. K. "Challenges To The Accounting Profession." **AR**, 1965. Vol. 40. No. 2. pp. 299-311.

Mautz, R. K. "Emphasis On Reporting Could Settle Income Statement Dispute," **JOA**, 1953, Vol. 96, No. 2. pp. 212-216.

Mautz, R. K. "Evidence. Judgment. And The Auditor's Opinion," **JOA**, 1959, Vol. 107, No. 4, pp. 40-44.

Mautz, R. K. "Profit-Sharing Bonus Payments In The Income Statement." **AR**, 1947, Vol. 22, No. 1. pp. 54-57.

Mautz, R. K. "Reliability Of Audit Evidence." **JOA**, 1958, Vol. 105. No. 5, pp. 40-47.

Mautz, R. K. "Revising The 'Tentative Statement'," **AR**, 1941, Vol. 16, No. 1. pp. 66-74.

Mautz, R. K. "Standards For The Review Of Internal Control," **AR**, 1958, Vol. 106, No. 1. pp. 27-31.

Mautz, R. K. "Teaching The Significance Of Practical Considerations," **AR**, 1949, Vol. 24, No. 4. pp. 435-438.

Mautz, R. K. "The 1957 Statement Of Accounting And Reporting Standards," **AR**, 1957, Vol. 32. No. 4, pp. 547-553.

Mautz, R. K. "The Direction Of Accounting Education," **IJAER**, 1967, Vol. 2. No. 2. pp. 37-46.

Mautz, R. K. "The Intermediate Course In Accounting," **AR**, 1951, Vol. 26. No. 2, pp. 239-246.

Mautz, R. K. "The Place Of Postulates In Accounting." **JOA**, 1965, Vol. 119. No. 1. pp. 46-49.

Mautz, R. K. "Using Practical Accounting Experience In Teaching." **AR**, 1949, Vol. 24. No. 3. pp. 317-320.

Mautz, R. K. "Where Do We Go From Here?." **AR**, 1974, Vol. 49, No. 2. pp. 353-360.

Mautz, R. K. "Will Accounting Education Improve?." **JOA**, 1955. Vol. 100. No. 2. pp. 53-55.

Mautz, R. K. (Carrithers, J. M. and R. K. Mautz. "Arithmetic And Accountancy," **AR**, 1942. Vol. 17, No. 2. pp. 163-170.)

Mautz, R. K. (Perry, K. W. and R. K. Mautz. "Theory Cases For Undergraduate Courses." **AR**, 1956, Vol. 31. No. 3. pp. 497-500.)

Mautz, R. K. (Sharaf, Hussein A. and R. K. Mautz. "An Operational Concept Of Independence." **JOA**, 1960. Vol. 109. No. 4. pp. 49-54.)

Maxfield, Lt. Gerald. (Gaa, Lt. Charles J. and Lt. Gerald Maxfield. "Accounting Aspects Of Contract Settlement," **AR**, 1945, Vol. 20. No. 1, pp. 44-58.)

Maxim, L. D., D. E. Cullen and F. X. Cook, Jr. "Optimal Acceptance Sampling Plans For Auditing 'Batched' Stop And Go Vs. Conventional Single-Stage Attributes Plans." **AR**, 1976. Vol. 51. No. 1, pp. 97-109.

Maxwell, Arthur D. and W. Howard Taylor. "A Study Of Accounting Curricula," **AR**, 1942, Vol. 17. No. 2. pp. 141-149.

Maxwell, Arthur D. "Answering Examination Questions." **AR**, 1956, Vol. 31. No. 4. pp. 636-645.

Maxwell. W. David. (Zeff, Stephen A. and W. David Maxwell. "Holding Gains On Fixed Assets - A Demurrer," **AR**, 1965. Vol. 40, No. 1, pp. 65-75.)

May, Carolyn A. (Laughlin, Eugene J., James W. Gentry and Carolyn A. May. "Comparison Of Alternative Forms Of Teaching Fundamentals Of Accounting." **AR**, 1976, Vol. 51. No. 2. pp. 347-351.)

May, George O. and James L. Dohr. "Book Value: A Brief Comment On The Stans-Goedert Article." **JOA**, 1955. Vol. 99, No. 4. pp. 42-44.

May, George O. "A Comment On Mr. Greer's Benchmarks And Beacons," **AR**, 1956, Vol. 31. No. 4. pp. 581-583.

May, George O. "Business Combinations." **JOA**, 1957. Vol. 103. No. 4. pp. 33-36.

May, George O. "Comment On Wilcox-Greer Paper," **JOA**, 1950. Vol. 90, No. 6, pp. 504-505.

May, George O. "Generally Accepted Accounting Principles." **JOA**, 1958. Vol. 105, No. 1. pp. 23-27.

May, George O. "Income Accounting And Social Revolution," **JOA**, 1957. Vol. 103. No. 6. pp. 36-41.

May, George O. "Limitations On The Significance Of Invested Cost." **AR**, 1952, Vol. 27. No. 4. pp. 436-440.

May, George O. "Retrospect And Prospect," **JOA**, 1961. Vol. 112. No. 1. pp. 31-36.

May, George O. "Stock Dividends And Concepts Of Income." **JOA**, 1953. Vol. 96, No. 4. pp. 427-431.

May, George O. "Teaching Accounting To Nontechnical Students," **AR**, 1945, Vol. 20. No. 2. pp. 131-138.

May, George O. "The Choice Before Us." **JOA**. 1950. Vol. 89. No. 3. pp. 206-211.

May, George O. "The Nature Of The Financial Accounting Process, **AR**, 1943, Vol. 18. No. 3. pp. 189-192.

May, George O. "Three Discussions Of Financial Accounting And Inflation," **JOA**, 1952. Vol. 93. No. 3. pp. 294-299.

May, George O. "Truth And Usefulness In Accounting." **JOA**, 1950, Vol. 89, No. 5. p. 387.

May, Gordon S. and Claire Arevalo. "Integrating Effective Writing Skills In The Accounting Curriculum." **JAED**, 1983, Vol. 1, No. 1. pp. 119-126.

May, Gordon S. and Douglas K. Schneider. "Reporting Accounting Changes: Are Stricter Guidelines Needed?," **AH**, 1988, Vol. 2, No. 3, pp. 68-74.

May, Gordon S. and Pieter T. Elgers. "Problems With SEC's Forecast Guidelines," **CPAJ**, 1978. Vol. 48. No. 3. pp. 21-26.

May, Gordon S. "Professional Development In Medium-Size Firms," **CPAJ**, 1976, Vol. 46. No. 3. pp. 35-39.

May, Paul A. "The Budgeting Process." **MA**, 1973. Vol. 54,

No. 7, pp. 19-25.

May, Phillip T. "System Control: Computers The Weak Link?," **AR**, 1969, Vol. 44, No. 3, pp. 583-592.

May, Robert G. and Gary L. Sundem. "Cost Of Information And Security Prices: Market Association Tests For Accounting Policy Decisions," **AR**, 1973, Vol. 48, No. 1, pp. 80-94.

May, Robert G. and Gary L. Sundem. "Cost Of Information And Security Prices: A Reply," **AR**, 1974, Vol. 49, No. 4, pp. 791-793.

May, Robert G. and Gary L. Sundem. "Research For Accounting Policy: An Overview," **AR**, 1976, Vol. 51, No. 4, pp. 747-763.

May, Robert G. "The Influence Of Quarterly Earnings Announcements On Investor Decisions As Reflected In Common Stock Price Changes," **JAR**, 1971, Vol. 9, Supp., pp. 119-163.

May, Robert G. (Anderson, Urton, Robert G. May and Carolyn A. Miles. "Variables Sampling Software: Development And Classroom Testing," **IAE**, 1988, Vol. 3, No. 1, pp. 156-173.)

May, Robert G. (Arens, Alvin A., Robert G. May and Geraldine Dominiak. "A Simulated Case For Audit Education," **AR**, 1970, Vol. 45, No. 3, pp. 573-578.)

May, Robert G. (Felix, W. L., Jr., Robert G. May, Marcia S. Niles and John R. Thorson. "SCAD: Something New In Auditing Education," **JAED**, 1985, Vol. 3, No. 2, pp. 5-14.)

Mayer, Emilio. "Taxation Of Foreign Businessman Visiting The U.S.," **JOA**, 1953, Vol. 95, No. 1, pp. 56-59.

Mayer, Gerhard. "Determining Basis, Gain Or Loss; Capital Gains And Losses," **JOA**, 1954, Vol. 98. No. 3, pp. 309-319.

Mayer, Harry O. "Cost Accounting Standards," **MA**, 1975. Vol. 57. No. 4, pp. 17-20.

Mayer, James A. "MIS At International Paper: An Integrated Teleprocessing Network," **MA**, 1979, Vol. 60, No. 10, pp. 24-27.

Mayer, Raymond R. "The Role Of The Accountant In Equipment Replacement Analyses," **AR**, 1958. Vol. 33. No. 4. pp. 637-644.

Mayer, Stephen J. (Wittenbach, James L. and Stephen J. Mayer. "A Flowchart Of The Charitable Contribution Rules," **JOA**, 1974, Vol. 138, No. 5, pp. 63-67.)

Mayer-Sommer, Alan P. and Stephen E. Loeb. "Fostering More Successful Professional Socialization Among Accounting Students," **AR**, 1981, Vol. 56, No. 1, pp. 125-136.

Mayer-Sommer, Alan P. and Stephen J. Laycock. "Financial Reporting: Let's Replace Compliance With Competition," **MA**, 1978, Vol. 60, No. 6, pp. 14-19.

Mayer-Sommer, Alan P. "A Historical Case Study Of Planning And Control Under Uncertainty: The Weapons Acquisition Process For The U.S. Ironclad Monitor." **JAPP**, 1988. Vol. 7. No. 3. pp. 201-249.

Mayer-Sommer, Alan P. "Bargaining Skills: Because Being Right Is Not Enough," **MA**, 1981, Vol. 62, No. 11. pp. 28-36.

Mayer-Sommer, Alan P. "Public Accounting In 1929," **AHJ**. 1980. Vol. 7. No. 2. pp. 23-44.

Mayer-Sommer, Alan P. "Understanding And Acceptance Of The Efficient Markets Hypothesis And Its Accounting Implications." **AR**, 1979, Vol. 54. No. 1. pp. 88-106.

Maynard, Gilbert P. "Business Income And National Income: A Contrast Of Concepts," **AR**, 1952, Vol. 27, No. 2, pp. 189-194.

Maynard, Gilbert P. "Modifications Of Accounting Data In National-Income Estimation," **AR**, 1953, Vol. 28, No. 2. pp. 199-210.

Mayne, Lucille S. (Philips, G. Edward and Lucille S. Mayne. "Income Measures And Bank Stock Values," **JAR**, 1970. Vol. 8. Supp., pp. 178-188.)

Mayo, Ralph B. "Administration Of A Tax Practice," **JOA**. 1962. Vol. 113, No. 6, pp. 52-56.

Mayo, Robert P. "Economic Expansion In 1972." **MA**. 1972. Vol. 53. No. 11. pp. 11-13.

Mayotte, Russell J. "How One Utility Allocates Steam Service Costs," **MA**, 1980, Vol. 61, No. 9, pp. 26-36.

Mayper, Alan G. "Consensus Of Auditors' Materiality Judgments Of Internal Control Weaknesses," **JAR**, 1982, Vol. 20. No. 2, Part II, pp. 773-783.

Mayper, Alan G. (Grossman, Steven D., Alan G. Mayper and Robert B. Welker. "Oil And Gas Disclosures - The FASB Reacts." **CPAJ**, 1983. Vol. 53. No. 5. pp. 24-29.)

Mayper, Alan G., Robert B. Walker and Casper E. Wiggins. "Accounting And Review Services: Perceptions Of The Message Within The CPA's Report," **AIA**, 1988, Vol. 6. pp. 219-232.

Mayper, A. G. (Giroux, G. A., A. G. Mayper and R. L. Daft. "Organization Size, Budget Cycle. And Budget Related Influence In City Governments: An Empirical Study," **AOS**, 1986. Vol. 11. No. 6. pp. 499-520.)

Mays, Robert L., Jr. "Divisional Performance Measurement And Transfer Prices," **MA**, 1982, Vol. 63, No. 10, pp. 20-28.

Mazhin, Reza. "The Time Series Behaviour Of Reported Current Cost Data," **ABR**, 1985-86, Vol. 16, No. 63, pp. 215-220.

Mazurkiewicz, Gerard T. (Wright, James M. and Gerard T. Mazurkiewicz. "Accounting For Contract Revenue: Builders' Burden?," **MA**, 1988, Vol. 69, No. 7, pp. 49-54.)

Mboya, Fratern M. (Dhaliwal, Dan S., Fratern M. Mboya and Russell M. Barefield. "Utilization Of SFAS No. 14 Disclosures In Assessing Operating Risk," **JAPP**, 1983, Vol. 2. No. 2. pp. 83-98.)

McAfee, R. Preston. (Bailey, Andrew D., R. Preston McAfee and Andrew B. Whinston. "An Application Of Complexity Theory To The Analysis Of Internal Control Systems," **AJPT**, 1981-82, Vol. 1, No. 1, pp. 38-52.)

McAllister, Don. "Unprincipled Administration." **ABACUS**, 1970, Vol. 6, No. 1, pp. 81-87.

McAllister, John P. and Mark W. Dirsmith. "How The Client's Business Environment Affects The Audit," **JOA**, 1982, Vol. 153, No. 2, pp. 68-74.

McAllister, John P. (Dirsmith, Mark W. and John P. McAllister. "The Organic Vs. The Mechanistic Audit: Problems And Pitfalls (Part II)," **JAAF**, 1982, Vol. 6, No. 1, pp. 60-74.)

McAllister, John P. (Dirsmith, Mark W. and John P. McAllister. "The Organic Vs. The Mechanistic Audit," **JAAF**, 1982, Vol. 5, No. 3, pp. 214-228.)

McAllister, John P. (Dirsmith, Mark W., Mark A. Covaleski and John P. McAllister. "Of Paradigms And Metaphors In Auditing Thought," **CAR**, 1985-86, Vol. 2, No. 1, pp. 46-68.)

McAllister, LeRay. (Schattke, Rudy and LeRay McAllister. "Large Versus Small Classes In Elementary Accounting," **AR**, 1962, Vol. 37, No. 3, pp. 557-561.)

McAnly, Herbert T. "How LIFO Began." **MA**, 1975, Vol. 56, No. 11, pp. 24-26.

McAnly, Herbert T. "The Current Status Of Lifo." **JOA**, 1958, Vol. 105, No. 5, pp. 55-62.

McAnly, H. T. "Administrative Expense And Profit In Product Pricing." **JOA**, 1963, Vol. 116, No. 2, pp. 33-38.

McAnly, H. T. "Inventory Pricing," **JOA**, 1962, Vol. 114, No. 2, pp. 34-39.

McAnly, H. T. "The Case For Lifo," **JOA**, 1953, Vol. 95, No. 6, pp. 691-700.

McArthur, Donald S. "Operations Research." **MA**, 1975, Vol. 57, No. 1, pp. 45-48.

McBride, Howard J. "Assigning Tax Loads To Prospective Projects," **AR**, 1963, Vol. 38, No. 2, pp. 363-370.

McCabe, George M. and George N. Sanderson. "Abandonment Value In Capital Budgeting: Another View," **MA**, 1984, Vol. 65, No. 7, pp. 32-36.

McCabe, Kelly S. (Pasewark, William R. and Kelly S. McCabe. "Preparing And Maintaining A Budget Manual." **MA**, 1988, Vol. 69, No. 11, pp. 33-36.)

McCabe, Kevin P. "Accounting For Motion Picture Films." **CPAJ**, 1974, Vol. 44, No. 12, pp. 53-55.

McCafferty, Frank. "Basic Elements Of Risk Management." **MA**, 1977, Vol. 59, No. 1, pp. 43-45.

McCallion, Anne D. (Ray, Gregory A. and Anne D. McCallion. "FASB's Due Process Tackles Accounting For Computer Software Costs." **CA**, 1985, Vol. 3, No. 4, ppp. 31-40.

McCallion, Anne D. and Gregory A. Ray. "Computer Software: An Asset Coming On-Line. **JOA**, 1984, Vol. 158, No. 5, pp. 93-109.

McCallion, Anne D. (Ray, Gregory A. and Anne D. McCallion. "Accounting For Computer Software: The FASB Approach." **MA**, 1985, Vol. 66, No. 8, pp. 51-57.)

McCallum, John S. "A Note On Professor Robbins' Paper On Capital Budgeting Under Risky Conditions." **JAAF**, 1978, Vol. 1, No. 4, pp. 373-376.

McCarthy, William E. "Accounting Information Systems: Research Directions And Perspective." **JIS**, 1987, Vol. 2, No. 1, pp. 29-32.

McCarthy, William E. "An Entity-Relationship View Of Accounting Models," **AR**, 1979, Vol. 54, No. 4, pp. 667-686.

McCarthy, William E. "The REA Accounting Model: A Generalized Framework For Accounting Systems In A Shared Data Environment," **AR**, 1982, Vol. 57, No. 3, pp. 554-578.

McCarthy, William E. (Gal, Graham and William E. McCarthy. "Operation Of A Relational Accounting System." **AIA**, 1986, Vol. 3, pp. 83-112.)

McCartney, Willliam W. (Campbell, Terry L., William W. McCartney, Doris M. Taylor and LeRoy A. Franklin. "Job Satisfaction Of Academic Accountants In Southern Business Administration Association Schools." **AIA**, 1988, Vol. 6, pp. 175-190.)

McCarty, Daniel E. (Osteryoung, Jerome S., Daniel E. McCarty and Karen A. Fortin. "How The New Cost Recovery System Compares With Prior Methods." **MA**, 1981, Vol. 63, No. 5, pp. 13-27.)

McCarty, Daniel E. (Osteryoung, Jerome S., Daniel E. McCarty and Karen Fortin. "A Note On The Optimal Tax Lives For Assets Qualifying For The Investment Tax Credit." **AR**, 1980, Vol. 55, No. 2, pp. 301-306.)

McCarty, Daniel M. (Osteryoung, Jerome S., Daniel M. McCarty and Karen Fortin. "A Note On Optimal Depreciation Research - A Comment." **AR**, 1981, Vol. 56, No. 3, pp. 719-721.)

McCarty, Thomas M. (Chang, Otto H. and Thomas M. McCarty. "Evidence On Judgment Involving The Determination Of Substantial Authority: Tax Practitioners Versus Students." **JATA**, 1988, Vol. 10, No. 1, pp. 26-39.)

McCaslin, Thomas E. and Keith G. Stanga. "Similarities In Measurement Needs Of Equity Investors And Creditors." **ABR**, 1985-86, Vol. 16, No. 62, pp. 151-156.

McCaslin, Thomas E. and Keith G. Stanga. "Related Qualities Of Useful Accounting Information," **ABR**, 1983-84, Vol. 14, No. 53, pp. 35-42.

McCaslin, Thomas E. (Munter, Paul and Thomas E. McCaslin. "Risk And Materiality In An Audit." **CPAJ**, 1984, Vol. 54, No. 11, pp. 34-45.)

McClellan, William A. "Valuation Of Closely Held Securities: Accounting Know-How Is The Key." **JOA**, 1966, Vol. 121, No. 3, pp. 47-55.

McClendon, Thurrell O. (Carruth, Paul J. and Thurrell O. McClendon. "How Supervisors React To 'Meeting The Budget' Pressure," **MA**, 1984, Vol. 66, No. 5, pp. 50-54.)

McClenon, Paul R. "Capitalization Criteria: A CASB Study," **MA**, 1980, Vol. 62, No. 6, pp. 39-43.

McClenon, Paul R. "Cost Finding Through Multiple Correlation Analysis," **AR**, 1963, Vol. 38, No. 3, pp. 540-547.

McClenon, Paul R. "Operations Of The Cost Accounting Standards Board," **JOA**, 1973, Vol. 135, No. 4, pp. 58-62.

McClure, Malcolm M. "An Overview Of Rumanian Accounting," **IJAER**, 1983, Vol. 19, No. 1, pp. 131-156.

McClure, Malcolm M. "Internationalization Of The Introductory Financial Accounting Course," **JAED**, 1988, Vol. 6, No. 1, pp. 159-181.

McClure, Melvin T. "Diverse Tax Interpretations Of Accounting Concepts," **JOA**, 1976, Vol. 142, No. 4, pp. 67-74.

McCollum, Paul. "Computer System Audit," **MA**, 1969, Vol. 50, No. 9, pp. 51-52.

McCollum, P. M. (Harvey, J. H. and P. M. McCollum. "Automated Internal Auditing Tools," **MA**, 1965, Vol. 47, No. 2, pp. 44-50.)

McComb, Desmond. "International Accounting Standards And The EEC Harmonization Program: A Conflict Of Disparate Objectives." **IJAER**, 1982, Vol. 17, No. 2, pp. 35-48.

McComb, Desmond. "The International Harmonization Of Accounting: A Cultural Dimension," **IJAER**, 1979, Vol. 14, No. 2, pp. 1-16.

McConnell, Donald K., Jr. "Are The Big 8 Increasing Their Share Of The NYSE, AMEX, And OTC Audit Markets?," **JAAF**, 1984, Vol. 7, No. 2, pp. 178-181.

McConnell, Donald K., Jr. "Auditor Changes And Related Disagreements," **AJPT**, 1983-84, Vol. 3, No. 2, pp. 44-56.

McConnell, Patricia A. (Jaenicke, Henry R. and Patricia A. McConnell. "A Prospectus For Auditor's Responsibilities: The Report Of The Cohen Commission," **MA**, 1978, Vol. 59, No. 11, pp. 19-24.)

McConnell, Richard J. "The Philadelphia Story," **JOA**, 1960, Vol. 110, No. 2, pp. 45-52.

McConnell, Thomas P. "Hidden Resources In The Dues Dollar," **MA**, 1969, Vol. 51, No. 6, pp. 24-26.

McCormick, Edward T. "Reporting To Stockholders," **AR**, 1960, Vol. 35, No. 2, pp. 223-227.

McCormick, Frank L. "Large Group Instruction In Elementary Accounting," **AR**, 1967, Vol. 42, No. 3, p. 592.

McCormick, William, Jr. "Trends In Education For Auditors," **AR**, 1973, Vol. 48, No. 4, pp. 801-803.

McCosh, Andrew M. and Richard R. Vancil. "Reconciling Sandilands With Current Purchasing Power Adjustments," **ABR**, 1975-76, Vol. 6, No. 23, pp. 162-170.

McCosh, Andrew M. "Accounting Consistency - Key To Stockholder Information," **AR**, 1967, Vol. 42, No. 4, pp. 693-700.

McCosh, Andrew M. "Computerized Cost Classification System." **MA**, 1972, Vol. 53, No. 10, pp. 42-45.

McCosh, Andrew M. "Implications Of Sandilands For Non-U.K. Accountants," **JOA**, 1976, Vol. 141, No. 3, pp. 42-51.

McCosh, Andrew M. "The Case Method Of Accounting Instruction And Microwave Television," **AR**, 1972, Vol. 47, No. 1, pp. 161-164.

McCosh, A. M. (Rahman, M. and A. M. McCosh. "The Influence Of Organisational And Personal Factors On The Use Of Accounting Information: An Empirical Study," **AOS**, 1976, Vol. 1, No. 4, pp. 339-356.)

McCosh, R. Bruce. "Internship Programs In Accounting." **AR**, 1957, Vol. 32, No. 2, pp. 306-308.

McCosh, R. Bruce. (Jennings, Robert M. and R. Bruce McCosh. "Construction In Process - A Different Approach," **AR**, 1967, Vol. 42, No. 3, pp. 598-600.)

McCosker, Joseph S. "Backlog Reporting: Challenge To Accountants." **JOA**, 1969, Vol. 127, No. 5, pp. 53-60.

McCowen, George B. "Replacement Cost Of Goods Sold." **AR**, 1937, Vol. 12, No. 3, pp. 270-277.

McCowen, George B. "The Accountant As An Artist." **AR**, 1946, Vol. 21, No. 2, pp. 204-211.

McCoy, James R. "Report Of Committee On Revision Of The Statement Of Principles: Equities," **AR**, 1948, Vol. 23, No. 1, pp. 23-27.

McCoy, Robert E. and Robert C. Robinson. "Positioning For The Upturn After Surviving The Downturn." **MA**, 1984, Vol. 65, No. 9, pp. 24-28.

McCray, John H. "A Quasi-Bayesian Audit Risk Model For Dollar Unit Sampling: A Reply," **AR**, 1984, Vol. 59, No. 3, pp. 526-527.

McCray, John H. "A Quasi-Bayesian Audit Risk Model For Dollar Unit Sampling." **AR**, 1984, Vol. 59, No. 1, pp. 35-51.

McCray, John H. "Present Value Of An Annuity - A Formula Approach." **AR**, 1972, Vol. 47, No. 4, pp. 824-825.

McCray, John H. "Ratio And Difference Estimation In Auditing." **MA**, 1973, Vol. 55, No. 6, pp. 45-48.

McCredie, H. "The Theory And Practice Of Accounting." **AR**, 1957, Vol. 32, No. 2, pp. 216-223.

McCue, James J. "Credit Union Election Results By Computer." **MA**, 1970, Vol. 51, No. 10, p. 17.

McCue, William M. "Hedging Soybeans In The Commodities Market." **MA**, 1977, Vol. 59, No. 1, pp. 57-60.

McCullers, Levis D. and Relmond P. Van Daniker. "Professionalism In Accounting." **CPAJ**, 1974, Vol. 44, No. 8, pp. 39-42.

McCullers, Levis D. and Relmond P. VanDaniker. "Socio-Economics And Accounting Education," **AR**, 1972, Vol. 47, No. 3, pp. 604-606.

McCullers, Levis D. "An Alternative To APB Opinion No. 14," **JAR**, 1971, Vol. 9, No. 1, pp. 160-164.

McCullers, Levis D. (Madden, Donald L., Levis D. McCullers and Relmond P. VanDaniker. "Classification Of Research And Development Expenditures: A Guide To Better Accounting," CPAJ, 1972, Vol. 42, No. 2, pp. 139-142.)

McCullers, Levis D. (Madden, Donald L., Levis D. McCullers and Relmond P. VanDaniker. "The Materiality Of Research And Development Expenditures," JAR, 1972, Vol. 10, No. 2, pp. 417-420.)

McDaniel, Lloyd W. (Messer, Jean F. and Lloyd W. McDaniel. "Accounting For Country Clubs," MA, 1971, Vol. 52, No. 12, pp. 21-23.)

McDermott, John P. "Making A Manual Cost System Work For You," MA, 1982, Vol. 64, No. 6, pp. 40-43.

McDevitt, Edward J. "Ethics And A Change Of Auditors," JOA, 1955, Vol. 99, No. 5, pp. 46-47.

McDevitt, Edward. "Paper: How To Specify, Plan, And Buy Economically," JOA, 1953, Vol. 95, No. 4, pp. 460-466.

McDonald, Bill and Michael H. Morris. "The Functional Specifications Of Financial Ratios: An Empirical Examination," ABR, 1984-85, Vol. 15. No. 59, pp. 223-228.

McDonald, Bill and Michael H. Morris. "The Relevance Of SFAS 33 Inflation Accounting Disclosures In The Adjustment Of Stock Prices To Inflation," AR, 1984, Vol. 59, No. 3, pp. 432-446.

McDonald, Bill. (Balvers, Ronald J., Bill McDonald and Robert E. Miller. "Underpricing Of New Issues And The Choice Of Auditor As A Signal Of Investment Banker Reputation," AR, 1988, Vol. 63. No. 4, pp. 605-622.)

McDonald, Charles L. and Michael H. Sutton. "In-Substance Defeasance: Implementation Issues," CA, 1984, Vol. 2, No. 4, pp. 22-27.

McDonald, Charles L. "An Empirical Examination Of The Reliability Of Published Predictions Of Future Earnings," AR, 1973, Vol. 48, No. 3, pp. 502-510.

McDonald, Charles L. (Lorek, Kenneth S., Charles L. McDonald and Dennis H. Patz. "A Comparative Examination Of Management Forecasts And Box-Jenkins Forecasts Of Earnings," AR, 1976, Vol. 51, No. 2, pp. 321-330.)

McDonald, Daniel L. "A Test Application Of The Feasibility Of Market Based Measures In Accounting," JAR, 1968, Vol. 6, No. 1, pp. 38-49.

McDonald, Daniel L. "Feasibility Criteria For Accounting Measures," AR, 1967, Vol. 42, No. 4, pp. 662-679.

McDonald, D. and A. G. Puxty. "An Inducement - Contribution Approach To Corporate Financial Reporting," AOS, 1979, Vol. 4, No. 1/2, pp. 53-66.

McDonald, Harry A. "Cooperation By SEC Accountants, Helps Investors," JOA, 1951, Vol. 91, No. 3, pp. 411-415.

McDonald, Martin J., Jr. "Profit-Volume And Net Profit Percentages Computed On Cost," MA, 1968, Vol. 49, No. 10, pp. 46-50.

McDonald, Roderick F. "An Objective Look At Effects Of Income Taxes On Financing Small Business," AR, 1955, Vol. 30, No. 4, pp. 623-633.

McDonough, John H. "The Accountant, Data Collection And Social Exchange," AR, 1971, Vol. 46, No. 4, pp. 676-685.

McDonough, John J. "The MBA And The Accounting Profession," CPAJ, 1973, Vol. 43, No. 4, pp. 292-301.

McDonough, John J. (Buckley, John W. and John J. McDonough. "Accounting As A Pluralistic Profession In Practice And Education," CPAJ, 1972, Vol. 42, No. 11, pp. 923-929.)

McDonough, J. J. (Ansari, S. L. and J. J. McDonough. "Intersubjectivity - The Challenge And Opportunity For Accounting," AOS, 1980, Vol. 5, No. 1, pp. 129-142.)

McDonough, J. J. (Epstein, M., E. Flamholtz and J. J. McDonough. "Corporate Social Accounting In The U.S.A.: State Of The Art And Future Prospects, AOS, 1976, Vol. 1, No. 1, pp. 23-42.)

McDonough, Wallace. "Controlling Relocation Costs," CA, 1987, Vol. 5, No. 1, pp. 33-36.

McDougall, F. M. and R. H. Chenhall. "Shareholders And Share Exchange Takeover Offers," ABACUS, 1975, Vol. 11, No. 2, pp. 122-135.

McDougall, F. M. "Factors Influencing The Outcome Of Take-Over Offers," ABACUS, 1974, Vol. 10 No. 2, pp. 111-123.

McEachren, John W. "Accounting Reform In Washington," JOA, 1955, Vol. 100, No. 3, pp. 29-33.

McElvain, David P. "Keying The Short-Run Capital Flow To Return-On-Investment Objectives," MA, 1967, Vol. 49, No. 4, pp. 3-8.

McElvain, David P. "Profit Plan Pricing," MA, 1970, Vol. 52, No. 3, pp. 27-31.

McElwee, Leonard F. "A Set Of Programs For Total Cost Improvement," MA, 1968, Vol. 49, No. 10, pp. 57-64.

McElwee, Leonard F. "Planning And Launching An EFP Program," MA, 1966, Vol. 48, No. 1. pp. 3-11.

McElwee, Leonard F. "Sustaining Error-Free Performance," MA, 1967, Vol. 49, No. 4, pp. 42-50.

McEnally, Richard W. (Joy, O. Maurice, Robert H. Litzenberger and Richard W. McEnally. "The Adjustment Of Stock Prices To Announcements Of Unanticipated Changes In Quarterly Earnings," JAR, 1977, Vol. 15, No. 2, pp. 207-225.)

McFarland, J. Edgar. (Wyman, Harold E. and J. Edgar McFarland. "Financial Investments And The True Rate Of Return," MA, 1977, Vol. 59, No. 2, pp. 41-45.)

McFarland, Walter B. "Cost Analysis For Equipment Replacement," AR, 1947, Vol. 22, No. 1, pp. 58-64.

McFarland, Walter B. "How Standard Costs Are Being Used Today For Control, Budgeting, Pricing: A Survey," JOA, 1950, Vol. 89, No. 2, pp. 125-131.

McFarland, Walter B. "Research In Management Accounting By The National Association Of Accountants," AR, 1961, Vol. 36, No. 1, pp. 21-25.

McFarland, Walter B. "Research In Management Accounting By NAA," MA, 1970, Vol. 51, No. 9, pp. 31-34.

McFarland, Walter B. "The Basic Theory Of Standard Costs," AR, 1939, Vol. 14, No. 2, pp. 151-157.

McFarland, Walter B. "The Economics Of Business Costs," AR, 1940, Vol. 15, No. 2, pp. 196-204.

McFarlane, Kentbourne A. W. "Tracking Inflation In Your Company," MA, 1979, Vol. 60, No. 11, pp. 42-46.

McGahran, Kathleen T. "SEC Disclosure Regulation And Management Perquisites," AR, 1988, Vol. 63, No. 1, pp. 23-41.

McGann, Anthony F. (Foran, Michael F. and Anthony F. McGann. "The Annual Report," MA, 1973, Vol. 55, No. 5, pp. 48-51.)

McGee, Robert W. "Accounting After Tax Reform," CPAJ, 1987, Vol. 57, No. 1, pp. 52-55.

McGee, Robert W. "How The New Tax Law Affects Individuals," MA, 1986, Vol. 68, No. 6, pp. 22-26.

McGee, Robert W. "How The New Tax Law Affects Business," MA, 1986, Vol. 68, No. 4, pp. 54-57.

McGee, Victor E. (Casey, Cornelius, Victor E. McGee and Clyde P. Stickney. "Discriminating Between Reorganized And Liquidated Firms In Bankruptcy," AR, 1986, Vol. 61, No. 2. pp. 249-262.)

McGee, Victor E. (Stickney, Clyde P. and Victor E. McGee. "Effective Corporate Tax Rates: The Effect Of Size, Capital Intensity, Leverage, And Other Factors," JAPP, 1982. Vol. 1, No. 2. pp. 125-152.)

McGee, Wesley O. and David T. Norman. "Profit And Growth Through Sales Compensation," MA, 1976, Vol. 58, No. 6, pp. 32-34.

McGhee, Walter, Michael D. Shields and Jacob G. Birnberg. "The Effects Of Personality On A Subject's Information Processing," AR, 1978, Vol. 53, No. 3, pp. 681-697.

McGhee, Walter. (Birnberg, Jacob G., Michael D. Shields and Walter McGhee. "The Effects Of Personality On A Subject's Information Processing: A Reply," AR, 1980. Vol. 55, No. 3, pp. 507-510.)

McGill, Gary A. and John T. Sennetti. "The Capital Gains Timing Decision: A Quantitative Analysis," JATA, 1986, Vol. 7. No. 2, pp. 7-16.

McGinnis, Edward C. and Lawrence G. Maglione. "Taking VisiCalc To The Limit," MA, 1984, Vol. 65, No. 7, pp. 41-45.

McGladrey, I. B. "Problems In Assuming Proper Responsibility," AR. 1947, Vol. 22, No. 3, pp. 273-280.

McGladrey, I. B. "The Audit Report," AR, 1951, Vol. 26, No. 2. pp. 197-208.

McGough, Philip. "The Legal Significance Of The Par Value Of Common Stock: What Accounting Educators Should Know," IAE. 1988, Vol. 3, No. 2, pp. 330-350.

McGough, Thomas P. (Altman, Edward I. and Thomas P. McGough. "Evaluation Of A Company As A Going Concern." JOA. 1974, Vol. 138, No. 6, pp. 50-57.)

McGowen, George B. "The Flow Of Assets Through A Business Enterprise And The Accounting Flow Equation Based Thereon," AR, 1962, Vol. 37, No. 1, pp. 105-110.

McGowen, Joseph and Bruce Rosborough. "Priming Your Lender's Pump," CA, 1985, Vol. 3. No. 1. pp. 19-23.

McGrail, George R. and Daniel R. Furlong. "Absorption Break-Even," MA, 1973, Vol. 55, No. 4, pp. 31-35.

McGrail, George R. (Joehnk, Michael D. and George R. McGrail. Benefit-Cost Ratios For Family Practice Residency Centers," MA, 1977, Vol. 58, No. 8, pp. 41-46.)

McGrath, Earl J. "Education, Profession & Public Affairs." JOA. 1958, Vol. 105, No. 4, pp. 44-49.

McGuigan, Harold C. "Internal Control Over Inventories In Manufacturing Concerns," JOA, 1954, Vol. 97, No. 3, pp. 335-338.

McGurr, Francis J. "The Integration Of Statistics And Accounting," AR, 1960, Vol. 35, No. 1, pp. 60-63.

McGurr, Francis, J. (Abs, George, Clayton Grimstad, Robert Hay, W. Asquith Howe, William LaPlace, Francis J. McGurr and William Serraino. "Historical Dates In Accounting." AR, 1954, Vol. 29, No. 3, pp. 486-493.)

McHugh, Arthur J. (Dyer, James C. IV and Arthur J. McHugh. "The Timeliness Of The Australian Annual Report," JAR, 1975, Vol. 13, No. 2, pp. 204-219.)

McHugh, A. J. "Relationship Between Accounting And The Internal Rate Of Return Measures," JAR, 1976, Vol. 14, No. 1, pp. 181-186.

McHugh, William J. "ERISA - A New Audit Headache For Management," MA, 1976, Vol. 57, No. 10, pp. 21-28.

McIlhattan, Robert D. "How Cost Management Systems Can Support The JIT Philosophy," MA, 1987, Vol. 69, No. 3, pp. 20-27.

McIlwain, Arnold P. "Utilizing EDP For Stock Material Inventory Transactions," MA, 1967, Vol. 48, No. 12, pp. 28-34.

McInnes, Morris. (Brownell, Peter and Morris McInnes. "Budgetary Participation, Motivation, And Managerial Performance," AR, 1986, Vol. 61, No. 4, pp. 587-600.)

McInnes, W. M. (Davies, J. R. and W. M. McInnes. "The Efficiency And The Accountability Of UK Nationalised Industries." ABR, 1982-83, Vol. 13, No. 49, pp. 29-41.)

McIntire, L. B. "Income Taxes And Capital Investment," AR, 1945. Vol. 20, No. 4, pp. 415-419.

McIntosh, Barbara R. (Anderson, John C. and Barbara R. McIntosh. "An Analysis Of The Tax And Incentive Considerations Involved In Employee Leasing," JATA. 1988. Vol. 9, No. 2, pp. 19-30.)

McIntyre, Edward V. "A Note On The Joint Variance: A Reply," AR, 1978, Vol. 53, No. 2, pp. 534-537.

McIntyre, Edward V. "A Note On The Joint Variance," AR. 1976, Vol. 51. No. 1, pp. 151-155.

McIntyre, Edward V. "An Algebraic Aid In Teaching The

Differences Between Direct Costing And Full-Absorption Costing Models: An Extension," **AR**, 1974, Vol. 49, No. 4, pp. 839-840.

McIntyre, Edward V. "Current-Cost Financial Statements And Common-Stock Investments Decisions," **AR**, 1973, Vol. 48, No. 3, pp. 575-585.

McIntyre, Edward V. "Interaction Effects Of Inflation Accounting Models And Accounting Techniques," **AR**, 1982, Vol. 57, No. 3, pp. 607-618.

McIntyre, Edward V. "Present Value Depreciation And The Disaggregation Problem," **AR**, 1977, Vol. 52, No. 1, pp. 162-171.

McIntyre, Edward V. "The Effects Of Restating Financial Statements For Price-Level Changes: A Reply," **AR**, 1975, Vol. 50, No. 4, pp. 815-817.

McKague, W. A. "Canadian Examinations," **AR**, 1945, Vol. 20, No. 2, pp. 204-205.

McKee, A. James, Jr., Timothy B. Bell and James R. Boatsman. "Management Preferences Over Accounting Standards: A Replication And Additional Tests," **AR**, 1984, Vol. 59, No. 4, pp. 647-659.

McKee, Thomas E. and W. Edward Stead. "Managing The Professional Accountant," **JOA**, 1988, Vol. 166, No. 1, pp. 76-86.

McKee, Thomas E. "An 1870 Corporate Audit Committee," **AHJ**, 1979, Vol. 6, No. 2, pp. 61-68.

McKee, Thomas E. "Auditing Under The Foreign Corrupt Practices Act," **CPAJ**, 1979, Vol. 49, No. 8, pp. 31-36.

McKee, Thomas E. "Developments In Analytical Review," **CPAJ**, 1982, Vol. 52, No. 1, pp. 36-42.

McKee, Thomas E. "Expert Systems: The Final Frontier?," **CPAJ**, 1986, Vol. 56, No. 7, pp. 42-47.

McKee, Thomas E. "What Happened To Judgmental Sampling?," **CPAJ**, 1984, Vol. 54, No. 5, pp. 24-31.

McKee, Thomas E. "Why Can't Accountants Deal With Uncertainty About Enterprise Continuity?," **MA**, 1986, Vol. 68, No. 1, pp. 24-29.

McKee, Thomas E. (Crockett, James R. and Thomas E. McKee. "A Graphical Approach To Teaching The Relationship Between The Evaluation Of Internal Accounting Controls And Substantive Audit Testing," **JAED**, 1988, Vol. 6, No. 1, pp. 123-130.)

McKee, Tim C. and Raymond G. Laverdiere. "Maximizing Depreciation Benefits," **MA**, 1987, Vol. 68, No. 12, pp. 35-38.

McKee, Wayne W. "Small Businesses Can Be Computerized," **MA**, 1972, Vol. 53, No. 10, pp. 49-52.

McKell, Lynn J. and Kevin D. Stocks. "An Evaluation Of Computerized Accounting Practice Sets," **JAED**, 1986, Vol. 4, No. 1, pp. 177-190.

McKell, Lynn J. (Gibbs, Thomas E. and Lynn J. McKell. "Computing The Implicit Interest Rate Under SFAS No. 13," **AR**, 1977, Vol. 52, No. 4, pp. 925-929.)

McKell, Lynn J. (Stocks, Kevin D. and Lynn J. McKell. "Accounting Education And Management Advisory Services," **JIS**, 1987, Vol. 2, No. 1, pp. 65-76.)

McKenna, Eugene. (Buckley, Adrian and Eugene McKenna. "Budgetary Control And Business Behaviour," **ABR**, 1971-72, Vol. 2, No. 6, pp. 137-150.)

McKenna, Eugene. (Buckley, Adrian and Eugene McKenna. "The Practising Chartered Accountant - Job Attitudes And Professional Values," **ABR**, 1972-73, Vol. 3, No. 11, pp. 197-204.)

McKenna, E. F. "An Analysis Of Leadership Patterns In The Finance Function," **AOS**, 1980, Vol. 5, No. 3, pp. 297-310.

McKenzie, John. (Fetters, Michael, John McKenzie and David Callaghan. "Does The Computer Hinder Accounting Education? An Analysis Of Some Empirical Data," **IAE**, 1986, Vol. 1, No. 1, pp. 76-85.)

McKenzie, Patrick B. "An Alternative Learning Curve Formula," **IAE**, 1987, Vol. 2, No. 2, pp. 383-387.

McKenzie, Patrick B. "Multiple Optima And Sensitivity Analysis In The Product Mix Problem," **ABR**, 1974-75, Vol. 5, No. 19, pp. 213-221.

McKenzie, Patrick B. (Andrews, Wesley T. and Patrick B. McKenzie. "Leading Accounting Departments Revisited," **AR**, 1978, Vol. 53, No. 1, pp. 135-138.)

McKeon, Joseph M., Jr. and William N. Bockanic. "Integration Of Law With Accounting: A More Comprehensive Learning Experience," **JAED**, 1984, Vol. 2, No. 2, pp. 127-141.

McKeon, Joseph M., Jr. (Hassan, Nabil, R. Penny Marquette and Joseph M. McKeon, Jr. "Sensitivity Analysis: An Accounting Tool For Decision-Making," **MA**, 1978, Vol. 59, No. 10, pp. 43-50.)

McKeon, Kevin J. and Robert I. Chalnick. "Accounting And Tax Aspects Of GNMA Mortgage-Backed Securities," **JOA**, 1972, Vol. 134, No. 2, pp. 41-47.

McKeown, James C. and Hossien Shalchi. "A Comparative Examination Of The Time-Series Properties And Predictive Ability Of Annual Historical Cost And General Price Level Adjusted Earnings," **CAR**, 1988, Vol. 4, No. 2, pp. 485-507.

McKeown, James C. "A Brief Exploration Of The Goal Congruence Of Net Realizable Value," **AR**, 1973, Vol. 48, No. 2, pp. 386-388.

McKeown, James C. "Additivity Of Net Realizable Values," **AR**, 1972, Vol. 47, No. 3, pp. 527-532.

McKeown, James C. "An Effective And Practical Tool For Conveying Test Deck Concepts," **AR**, 1973, Vol. 48, No. 1, pp. 172-174.

McKeown, James C. "An Empirical Test Of A Model Proposed By Chambers," **AR**, 1971, Vol. 46, No. 1, pp. 12-29.

McKeown, James C. "Comparative Application Of Market And Cost Based Accounting Models," **JAR**, 1973, Vol. 11, No. 1, pp. 62-99.

McKeown, James C. "Computer-Assisted Instruction For Elementary Accounting," **AR**, 1976, Vol. 51, No. 1, pp. 123-130.

McKeown, James C. "Understanding Accounting Changes In An Efficient Market: Analysis Of Variance Issues," **AR**, 1987, Vol. 62, No. 3, pp. 597-600.

McKeown, James C. (Abdel-Khalik, A. Rashad and James C. McKeown. "Understanding Accounting Changes In An Efficient Market: Evidence Of Differential Reaction," **AR**, 1978, Vol. 53, No. 4, pp. 851-868.)

McKeown, James C. (Abdel-khalik, A. Rashad and James C. McKeown. "Disclosure Of Estimates Of Holding Gains And The Assessment Of Systematic Risk," **JAR**, 1978, Vol. 16, Supp., pp. 46-92.)

McKeown, James C. (Albrecht, W. Steve, Larry L. Lookabill and James C. McKeown. "The Time Series Properties Of Annual Earnings," **JAR**, 1977, Vol. 15, No. 2, pp. 226-244.)

McKeown, James C. (Bedford, Norton M. and James C. McKeown. "Comparative Analysis Of Net Realizable Value And Replacement Costing," **AR**, 1972, Vol. 47, No. 2, pp. 333-338.)

McKeown, James C. (Bublitz, Bruce, Thomas J. Frecka and James C. McKeown. "Market Association Tests And FASB Statement No. 33 Disclosures: A Reexamination," **JAR**, 1985, Vol. 23, Supp., pp. 1-23.)

McKeown, James C. (Burton, E. James, James C. McKeown and Jeffrey L. Shlosberg. "The Generation And Administration Of Examinations On Interactive Computer Systems," **AR**, 1978, Vol. 53, No. 1, pp. 170-178.)

McKeown, James C. (Chambers, R. J., William S. Hopwood and James C. McKeown. "The Relevance Of Varieties Of Accounting Information: A U.S.A. Survey," **ABACUS**, 1984, Vol. 20, No. 2, pp. 99-110.)

McKeown, James C. (Collins, William A., William S. Hopwood and James C. McKeown. "The Predictability Of Interim Earnings Over Alternative Quarters," **JAR**, 1984, Vol. 22, No. 2, pp. 467-479.)

McKeown, James C. (Hopwood, William S. and James C. McKeown. "An Evaluation Of Univariate Time-Series Earnings Models And Their Generalization To A Single Input Transfer Function," **JAR**, 1981, Vol. 19, No. 2, pp. 313-322.)

McKeown, James C. (Hopwood, William S. and James C. McKeown. "The Incremental Informational Content Of Interim Expenses Over Interim Sales," **JAR**, 1985, Vol. 23, No. 1, pp. 161-174.)

McKeown, James C. (Lorek, Kenneth S. and James C. McKeown. "The Effect On Predictive Ability Of Reducing The Number Of Observations On A Time-Series Analysis Of Quarterly Earnings Data," **JAR**, 1978, Vol. 16, No. 1, pp. 204-214.)

McKeown, James C. (Picur, Ronald D. and James C. McKeown. "Alternative Income Concepts And Relative Performance Evaluations: A Comment And Extension," **AR**, 1976, Vol. 51, No. 2, pp. 415-420.)

McKeown, James C. (Silhan, Peter A. and James C. McKeown. "Further Evidence On The Usefulness Of Simulated Mergers," **JAR**, 1985, Vol. 23, No. 1, pp. 416-426.)

McKeown, James. (Hopwood, William, James McKeown and Jane Mutchler. "The Sensitivity Of Financial Distress Prediction Models To Departures From Normality," **CAR**, 1988, Vol. 5, No. 1, pp. 284-298.)

McKeown, J. C. (Hopwood, W. S., J. C. McKeown and P. Newbold. "Power Transformations In Time-Series Models Of Quarterly Earnings Per Share," **AR**, 1981, Vol. 56, No. 4, pp. 927-933.)

McKeown, J. C. (Hopwood, W. S., J. C. McKeown and P. Newbold. "The Additional Information Content Of Quarterly Earnings Reports: Intertemporal Disaggregation," **JAR**, 1982, Vol. 20, No. 2, Part I, pp. 343-349.)

McKinley, Sue H. (Leitch, Robert A., John B. Barrack and Sue H. McKinley. "Controlling Your Cash Resources," **MA**, 1980, Vol. 62, No. 4, pp. 58-63.)

McKinley, Sue, Kurt Pany and Philip M. J. Reckers. "An Examination Of The Influence Of CPA Firm Type, Size, And MAS Provision On Loan Officer Decisions And Perceptions," **JAR**, 1985, Vol. 23, No. 2, pp. 887-896.

McKinney, George, III. (Ronen, Joshua and George McKinney, III. "Transfer Pricing For Divisional Autonomy," **JAR**, 1970, Vol. 8, No. 1, pp. 99-112.)

McKinney, John D. (Izard, C. Douglass and John D. McKinney. "The Certification Of Tax Specialists: Some Empirical Results," **JATA**, 1983, Vol. 5, No. 1, pp. 40-48.)

McKinnon, Jill L. and Graeme L. Harrison. "Cultural Influence On Corporate And Governmental Involvement In Accounting Policy Determination In Japan," **JAPP**, 1985, Vol. 4, No. 3, pp. 201-223.

McKinnon, Jill L. "Application Of Anglo-American Principles Of Consolidation To Corporate Financial Disclosure In Japan," **ABACUS**, 1984, Vol. 20, No. 1, pp. 16-33.

McKinnon, Jill. "Cultural Constraints On Audit Independence In Japan," **IJAER**, 1984, Vol. 20, No. 1, pp. 17-43.

McKinnon, Jill. (Partington, Graham, Jill McKinnon and Carrick Martin. "Funds Statements And The Two-Entity Test: A Response," **ABACUS**, 1986, Vol. 22, No. 1, pp. 39-44.)

McKinnon, J. L. (Harrison, G. L. and J. L. McKinnon. "Culture And Accounting Change: A New Perspective On Corporate Reporting Regulation And Accounting Policy Formulation," **AOS**, 1986, Vol. 11, No. 3, pp. 233-252.)

McKinnon, Sharon M. and William J. Bruns, Jr. "Evaluating Tasks For Operational Control," **MA**, 1984, Vol. 66, No. 4, pp. 60-63.

McKinnon, S. M. and Paul Janell. "The International Accounting Standards Committee: A Performance Evaluation," **IJAER**, 1984, Vol. 19, No. 2, pp. 19-34.

McLain, Robert K. "Divisional Profit Measurement Using Return On Capital Employed," **MA**, 1967, Vol. 49, No. 2, pp. 36-39.

McLaney, James P. "Actionable-Asset Reporting," **MA**, 1973, Vol. 54, No. 11, pp. 37-39.

McLaney, James P. "Asset Forecasting: A Defense Industry Technique," **MA**, 1969, Vol. 51, No. 3, pp. 33-35.

McLaren, N. Loyall. "Restricted Stock Options," **JOA**, 1963, Vol. 115, No. 6, pp. 37-42.

McLaren, N. Loyall. "Rotation Of Auditors," **JOA**, 1958, Vol. 106, No. 1, pp. 41-44.

McLaughlin, James B. (Clark, Ronald L. and James B. McLaughlin. "Controlling The Cost Of Product Defects," **MA**, 1986, Vol. 68, No. 2, pp. 32-35.)

McLaughlin, John K. and Anne Farley. "Resolved: Joint Costs Should Be Allocated (Sometimes)," **CPAJ**, 1988, Vol. 58, No. 1. pp. 46-53.

McLaughlin, William J. "Data Processing In A Manufacturing Industry - A Case Study," **MA**, 1966, Vol. 47, No. 11, pp. 41-51.

McLaughlin, W. T. "What Have You Done For Yourself Lately?," **MA**, 1970, Vol. 51, No. 7, p. 15.

McLean, James H. "Planning In Corporate Liquidations," **AR**, 1965, Vol. 40, No. 2, pp. 448-450.

McLeay, Stuart and Susan Fieldsend. "Sector And Size Effects In Ratio Analysis: An Indirect Test Of Ratio Proportionality," **ABR**, 1986-87, Vol. 17, No. 66, pp. 133-140.

McLeay, S. "Value Added: A Comparative Study," **AOS**, 1983, Vol. 8, No. 1, pp. 31-56.

McMahan, John L. "Controlling Corporate Insurance Costs," **MA**, 1973, Vol. 54, No. 9, pp. 39-42.

McMahan, John W. "Basic Education For Accounting In Business," **AR**, 1946, Vol. 21, No. 2, pp. 135-139.

McMahon, Anne G. (Black, Robert L. and Anne G. McMahon. "Graduate Tax Libraries: A Survey Of Their Content And Funding," **JATA**, 1981, Vol. 3, No. 1, pp. 11-18.)

McMahon, Terrence J. "Brazil: A Maturing Capital Market Seeks Accelerated Improvements In Accountancy," **IJAER**, 1972, Vol. 8, No. 1, pp. 77-87.

McMakinm, Grover. (Gass, Gerald L., Grover McMakin and Roger Bentson. "White Collar Productivity," **MA**, 1987, Vol. 69, No. 3, pp. 33-38.)

McMickle, Peter L. "'Young Man's Companion' of 1737: America's First Book On Accounting?," **ABACUS**, 1984, Vol. 20, No. 1, pp. 34-51.

McMickle, Peter L. (Heagy, Cynthia D. and Peter L. McMickle. "An Empirical Investigation Of The Accounting Systems Course: Academic Practice Versus Practitioner Needs," **IAE**, 1988, Vol. 3, No. 1, pp. 96-107.)

McMillan, T. E., Jr. "State-Municipal Relations In Financial Control," **AR**, 1955, Vol. 30, No. 4, pp. 592-599.

McMonnies, P. N. "Corporate Reporting In The Future," **ABR**, 1975-76, Vol. 6, No. 22, pp. 95-106.

McMonnies, P. N. "EEC, UEC, ASC, IASC, IASG, AISG, ICCAP-IFAC, Old Uncle Tom Cobbleigh And All," **ABR**, 1976-77, Vol. 7, No. 27, pp. 162-167.

McMullen, Kenneth E. "The Management Accountant And Program Control," **MA**, 1968, Vol. 49, No. 6, pp. 35-42.

McMullen, Stewart Yarwood. "Clarifying The Balance Sheet," **AR**, 1951, Vol. 26, No. 2, pp. 157-166.

McMullen, Stewart Yarwood. "Replacement Value Of Lifo Inventories Should Be Disclosed In Balance-Sheet," **JOA**, 1950, Vol. 89, No. 6, pp. 480-486.

McMurry, Robert N. "Choosing The Valuable Accounting Junior," **JOA**, 1951, Vol. 91, No. 4, pp. 604-609.

McNaboe, Eugene J. "Flexible Budgeting Through Electronic Data Processing," **MA**, 1966, Vol. 47, No. 7, pp. 9-16.

McNair, C. J. and William Mosconi. "Measuring Performance In An Advanced Manufacturing Environment," **MA**, 1987, Vol. 69, No. 1, pp. 28-31.

McNair, Frances M. (Flesher, Dale L. and Frances M. McNair. "How Valuable Is The CMA?," **MA**, 1985, Vol. 67, No. 5, pp. 29-32.)

McNair, Malcolm P. "Some Proposed Changes In Department Store Accounting Procedure," **AR**, 1935, Vol. 10, No. 1, pp. 50-63.

McNally, Graeme M. and Lee Hock Eng. "Management Accounting Practices And Company Characteristics," **ABACUS**, 1980, Vol. 16, No. 2, pp. 142-150.

McNally, Graeme M. (Bailes, Jack C. and Graeme M. McNally. "Cost And Management Accounting Practices In New Zealand," **IJAER**, 1984, Vol. 19, No. 2, pp. 59-71.)

McNally, Graeme M., Lee Hock Eng and C. Roy Hasseldine. "Corporate Financial Reporting In New Zealand," **ABR**, 1982-83, Vol. 13, No. 49, pp. 11-20.

McNally, G. M. "Profit Centres And Transfer Prices - Are They Necessary?," **ABR**, 1973-74, Vol. 4, No. 13, pp. 13-22.

McNamee, Alan H. (Chow, Chee W., Alan H. McNamee and R. David Plumlee. "Practitioners' Perceptions Of Audit Step Difficulty And Criticalness: Implications For Audit Research," **AJPT**, 1986-87, Vol. 6, No. 2, pp. 123-133.)

McNamee, Patrick. (Johnson, Richard D., Edward M. Klasny and Patrick McNamee. "ASB Proposes New SAS On Compliance Auditing," **JOA**, 1988, Vol. 165, No. 6, pp. 76-87.)

McNeill, I. Eugene and Frank Collins. "Personality Tendencies And Learning Modes In Elementary Accounting," **AR**, 1975, Vol. 50, No. 4, pp. 888-897.

McNichols, Charles W. (Louderback, Joseph G. and Charles W. McNichols. "A Note On Net Present Value And Internal Rate Of Return Functions In Electronic Spreadsheets," **JAED**, 1986, Vol. 4, No. 2, pp. 113-116.)

McNichols, Gerald R. "The State-Of-The-Art Of Cost Uncertainty Analysis," **JCA**, 1984, Vol. 1, No. 1, pp. 149-174.

McNichols, Maureen and G. Peter Wilson. "Evidence Of Earnings Management From The Provision For Bad Debts," **JAR**, 1988, Vol. 26, Supp., pp. 1-31.

McNichols, Maureen and James G. Manegold. "The Effect Of The Information Environment On The Relationship Between Financial Disclosure And Security Price Variability," **JAEC**, 1983, Vol. 5, No. 1, pp. 49-74.

McNichols, Maureen. "A Comparison Of The Skewness Of Stock Return Distributions At Earnings And Non-Earnings Announcement Dates," **JAEC**, 1988, Vol. 10, No. 3, pp. 239-273.

McNichols, Thomas J. and F. Virgil Boyd. "Adjustment Of Fixed Assets To Reflect Price Level Changes," **AR**, 1954, Vol. 29, No. 1, pp. 106-113.

McNiel, Douglas W. (Campbell, Terry L. and Douglas W. McNiel. "Stochastic And Nonstochastic Determinants Of Changes In Client-Industry Concentrations For Large Public-Accounting Firms," **JAPP**, 1985, Vol. 4, No. 4, pp. 317-328.)

McQueary, Glenn M., II and Michael P. Risdon. "How We Comply With The Foreign Corrupt Practices Act," **MA**, 1979, Vol. 61, No. 5, pp. 39-43.

McQueeney, J. (Jackson-Cox, J., J. E. M. Thirkell and J. McQueeney. "The Disclosure Of Company Information To Trade Unions: The Relevance Of The ACAS Code Of Practice On Disclosure," **AOS**, 1984, Vol. 9, No. 3/4, pp. 253-274.)

McRae, Angus. "Credit Review Analysis," **MA**, 1971, Vol. 52, No. 12, pp. 28-32.

McRae, Thomas W. and Richard Dobbins. "Behavioural Aspects Of The Inflation Accounting Controversy," **ABR**, 1973-74, Vol. 4, No. 14, pp. 135-140.

McRae, Thomas W. "A Citational Analysis Of The Accounting Information Network," **JAR**, 1974, Vol. 12, No. 1, pp. 80-92.

McRae, Thomas W. "Human Resource Accounting As A Management Tool," **JOA**, 1974, Vol. 138, No. 2, pp. 32-38.

McRae, Thomas W. (Chambers, R. J., John W. Kennelly, Thomas W. McRae, Frank K. Reilly and W. Keith Weltmer. "Historical Cost Accounting," **ABACUS**, 1971, Vol. 7, No. 1, p. 39.)

McRae, Thomas W. (Hepp, Gerald W. and Thomas W. McRae. "Accounting Standards Overload: Relief Is Needed," **JOA**, 1982, Vol. 153, No. 5, pp. 52-65.)

McRae, T. W. "A Further Note On The Definition Of Incremental And Opportunity Cost," **AR**, 1974, Vol. 49, No. 1, pp. 124-125.

McRae, T. W. "Accountancy Training In Scotland," **JAR**, 1965, Vol. 3, No. 2, pp. 255-260.

McRae, T. W. "Financial Control Of R. & D. Activity - A Study In Applied Accounting," **ABACUS**, 1968, Vol. 4, No. 2, pp. 124-141.

McRae, T. W. "Opportunity And Incremental Cost: An Attempt To Define In Systems Terms," **AR**, 1970, Vol. 45, No. 2, pp. 315-321.

McRae, T. W. "The Behavioural Critique Of Accounting," **ABR**, 1970-71, Vol. 1, No. 2, pp. 83-92.

McRae, T. W. "The Evaluation Of Investment In Computers," **ABACUS**, 1970, Vol. 6, No. 1, pp. 56-70.

McRoberts, H. A. and J. Hudson. "Auditing Program Evaluations: The Canadian Case," **AOS**, 1985, Vol. 10, No. 4, pp. 493-502.

Mead, George C. "A Managerial Approach To Governmental Accounting," **JOA**, 1970, Vol. 129, No. 3, pp. 50-55.

Mead, George C. "Certification In Management Accounting: Should We Jump On The British Bandwagon?," **MA**, 1967, Vol. 48, No. 10, pp. 16-20.

Mead, George C. "Professional Responsibility In Reporting," **JOA**, 1964, Vol. 117, No. 1, pp. 37-43.

Mead, George. "Auditing, Management Advisory Services, Social Service, And The Profit Motive," **AR**, 1960, Vol. 35, No. 4, pp. 659-666.

Mead, Sedgwick, Jr. "Ownership Of Real Estate As A Corporate Investment," **JOA**, 1974, Vol. 137, No. 1, pp. 42-54.

Mead, Stuart B. and John W. Ruswinckel. "The Lecture System In Elementary Accounting," **AR**, 1959, Vol. 34, No. 1, pp. 130-131.

Mead, Stuart B. "A Federal Tax Course For Non-Accounting Students," **AR**, 1957, Vol. 32, No. 4, pp. 652-653.

Mead, Stuart B. "Disposition Of Special Post-War Reserves At Close Of World War II," **AR**, 1952, Vol. 27, No. 4, pp. 496-501.

Mead, Stuart B. "The Machine-Graded Test For Accounting Courses," **AR**, 1955, Vol. 30, No. 1, pp. 133-134.

Meagher, Gary M. "Motivating Accountants," **MA**, 1979, Vol. 60, No. 9, pp. 27-30.

Meals, Dennis R. (Alderman, C. Wayne, Dan M. Guy and Dennis R. Meals. "Other Comprehensive Bases Of Accounting: Alternatives To GAAP," **JOA**, 1982, Vol. 154, No. 2, pp. 52-63.)

Meals, Dennis R. (Clay, John R. and Dennis R. Meals. "Personal Financial Planning: Two Perspectives," **JOA**, 1985, Vol. 159, No. 5, pp. 82-97.)

Meals, Dennis R. (Clay, John R., Dan M. Guy and Dennis R. Meals. "Solving Compilation And Review Practice Problems," **JOA**, 1980, Vol. 150, No. 3, pp. 74-82.)

Means, Kathryn M. and Paul M. Kazenski. "SFAS 91: New Dilemmas," **ACCHOR**, 1987, Vol. 1, No. 4, pp. 63-68.

Means, Kathryn M. and Paul M. Kazenski. "Improving Internal Control Can Cut Audit Costs," **MA**, 1987, Vol. 68, No. 7, pp. 48-51.

Means, Kathryn M. and Paul M. Kazenski. "SFAS 34: A Recipe For Diversity," **AH**, 1988, Vol. 2, No. 3, pp. 62-67.

Means, Kathryn M. (Holzmann, Oscar J. and Kathryn M. Means. "Accounting For Savings And Loan Mergers: Conflict And Accounting Error," **JAAF**, 1984, Vol. 7, No. 2, pp. 138-150.)

Mear, Ron and Michael Firth. "Risk Perceptions Of Financial Analysts And The Use Of Market And Accounting Data," **ABR**, 1988, Vol. 18, No. 72, pp. 335-340.

Mear, Ross and Michael Firth. "CUE Usage And Self-Insight Of Financial Analysts," **AR**, 1987, Vol. 62, No. 1, pp. 176-182.

Mear, R. and M. Firth. "Assessing The Accuracy Of Financial Analyst Security Return Predictions," **AOS**, 1987, Vol. 12, No. 3, pp. 331-340.

Mears, William H, Jr. and Nadine Gordon Lee. "Traps And Pitfalls For Preparers Of Individual Returns," **JOA**, 1988, Vol. 165, No. 2, pp. 45-53.

Mechem, Leon E. (Poe, Gary D. and Leon E. Mechem. "How Total Factor Productivity Works," **MA**, 1983, Vol. 64, No. 12, pp. 44-46.)

Mecimore, Charles D. and Michael F. Cornick. "Banks Should Use Management Accounting Models," **MA**, 1982, Vol. 63, No. 8, pp. 13-18.

Mecimore, Charles D. and Robert G. Morgan. "Flowcharting: An Effective Teaching Tool," **JAED**, 1983, Vol. 1, No. 2, pp. 163-167.

Mecimore, Charles D. "Classifying And Selecting Financial Ratios," **MA**, 1968, Vol. 49, No. 6, pp. 11-17.

Mecimore, Charles D. "Integrating EDP Into The Elementary Accounting Course - One Approach," **AR**, 1969, Vol. 44, No. 4, pp. 837-839.

Mecimore, Charles D. "Locating And Evaluating Unprofitable Products Or Segments Of A Business Firm," **MA**, 1970, Vol. 52, No. 1, pp. 57-60.

Mecimore, Charles D. "Some Empirical Distributions Of Financial Ratios," **MA**, 1968, Vol. 50, No. 1, pp. 13-16.

Meckler, Jack M. (Rossitch, Eugene and Jack M. Meckler. "Foreign Currency Exposure Control," **MA**, 1973, Vol. 55, No. 1, pp. 29-32, 37.)

Meckling, William H. and Jerold L. Zimmerman. "Schools Of Accountancy - Accomplish Little," **CPAJ**, 1976, Vol. 46, No. 10, pp. 25-30.

Meckling, William H. "Relevant Thinking For Investment Decisions," **MA**, 1966, Vol. 47, No. 6, pp. 8-11.

Meckling, William H. "Three Reflections On Performance Rewards And Higher Education," **JAEC**, 1985, Vol. 7, No. 1/3, pp. 247-251.

Medawar, C. "The Social Audit: A Political View," **AOS**, 1976, Vol. 1, No. 4, pp. 389-394.

Meddaugh, E. James. "Toward The Limited Review For Unaudited Statements," **JOA**, 1977, Vol. 143, No. 6, pp. 77-80.

Medewitz, Jeanette N. (Bean, Virginia L. and Jeanette N. Medewitz. "Computer Education: A Survey Of Accounting Graduates," **JAED**, 1987, Vol. 5, No. 2, pp. 243-258.)

Medford, William L. "Key Item Reporting," **MA**, 1969, Vol. 51, No. 2, pp. 21-26.

Medlin, Jo Anne. (Schneider, Kent N. and Jo Anne Medlin. "Depreciation Rules After TRA 86," **CPAJ**, 1988, Vol. 58. No. 1, pp. 18-25.)

Mednick, Robert and Gary John Previts. "The Scope Of CPA Services: A View Of The Future From The Perspective Of A Century Of Progress," **JOA**, 1987, Vol. 163, No. 5, pp. 220-238.

Mednick, Robert. "Accountants' Liability: Coping With The Stampede To The Courtroom," **JOA**, 1987, Vol. 164, No. 3, pp. 118-125.

Mednick, Robert. "Call For New Standards Of Attestation," **CPAJ**, 1984, Vol. 54, No. 8, pp. 12-17.

Mednick, Robert. "Our Profession In The Year 2000: A Blueprint Of The Future," **JOA**, 1988, Vol. 166, No. 2, pp. 54-58.

Mednick, Robert. "Proposed Attestation Standards - A Major Step Forward," **CPAJ**, 1985, Vol. 55, No. 5, pp. 10-17.

Mednick, Robert. "The Auditor's Role In Society: A New Approach To Solving The Perception Gap," **JOA**, 1986, Vol. 161, No. 2, pp. 70-75.

Medsker, Leland L. "Qualifications Required By Law Of C.P.A. Candidates," **AR**, 1940, Vol. 15, No. 1, pp. 100-102.

Mee, M. J. "The Tasks Of Human Asset Accounting," **ABR**, 1982-83, Vol. 13, No. 49, pp. 42-48.

Meek, Gary K. and Sidney J. Gray. "The Value Added Statement: An Innovation For U.S. Companies?," **ACCHOR**, 1988, Vol. 2, No. 2, pp. 73-81.

Meek, Gary K. "Adding An International Dimension To The Introductory Course," **JAED**, 1985, Vol. 3, No. 1, pp. 57-68.

Meek, Gary K. "U.S. Securities Market Responses To Alternative Earnings Disclosures Of Non-U.S. Multinational Corporations," **AR**, 1983, Vol. 58, No. 2, pp. 394-402.

Meek, Gary. "Competition Spurs Worldwide Harmonization," **MA**, 1984, Vol. 66, No. 2, pp. 47-49.

Meek, Gary. "Interim Earnings Announcements In The United States By Non-U.S. Multinational Corporations - Responses By The U.S. Securities Market," **IJAER**, 1985, Vol. 20, No. 2, pp. 1-18.

Meek, Gary. "The Multiple Earnings Announcements Of Non-U.S. Multinational Enterprises - Implications Of Observed Patterns," **IJAER**, 1983, Vol. 19, No. 1, pp. 115-130.

Meeks, G. (Goudie, A. W. and G. Meeks. "Medium Term Projections Of Companies' Financial Flows: A Disaggregated Approach," **ABR**, 1980-81, Vol. 11, No. 44, pp. 291-302.)

Mehl, Arthur G. and Lucille E. Lammers. "A Report And Analysis Of The Accountancy Faculty Recruiting Surveys Of 1975-1978," **AR**, 1979, Vol. 54, No. 3, pp. 609-617.

Mehler, Edmund W. "Capital Budgeting: Theory And Practice," **MA**, 1976, Vol. 58, No. 3, pp. 32-38.

Mehrens, William A. (Collier, Henry W. and William A. Mehrens. "Using Multiple Choice Test Items To Improve Classroom Testing Of Professional Accounting Students," **JAED**, 1985, Vol. 3, No. 2, pp. 41-51.)

Mehta, Dileep R. and Victor L. Andrews. "A Note On Installment Reporting Of Income, Profitability, And Fund Flows," **JAR**, 1968, Vol. 6, No. 1, pp. 50-57.

Meier, Donald M. "Developing A Reserve For Loan Losses," **MA**, 1980, Vol. 61, No. 8, pp. 36-38.

Meier, Robert E. (Maris, Terry L. and Robert E. Meier. "A Profile Of Management Consulting Firms," **JIS**, 1986, Vol. 1. No. 1, pp. 113-117.)

Meigs, Walter B. "The Expanding Field Of Internal Auditing," **AR**, 1951, Vol. 26, No. 4, pp. 518-523.

Meinert, John R. "The CPA In Business - A Look At Our Past, Present And Future," **JOA**, 1987, Vol. 163, No. 5, pp. 262-275.

Meinhardt, Joan, Joseph F. Moraglio and Harold I. Steinberg. "Governmental Audits: An Action Plan For Excellence," **JOA**, 1987, Vol. 164, No. 1, pp. 86-91.

Meisky, E. C. "Is Your Corporation 'Controlled'?," **JOA**, 1965, Vol. 119, No. 2, pp. 51-56.

Meixner, Wilda F. and Robert B. Welker. "Judgment Consensus And Auditor Experience: An Examination Of Organizational Relations," **AR**, 1988, Vol. 63, No. 3, pp. 505-513.

Melang, Thomas E. "Accounting Controls For Professional Service Firms," **MA**, 1971, Vol. 53, No. 1, pp. 26-30.

Melberg, William F., Jr. "Benishayan Time Series As Models For Debt Processes Over Time," **AR**, 1972, Vol. 47, No. 1, pp. 116-133.

Melicher, Ronald W. (Vaughn, Donald E. and Ronald W. Melicher. "Capitalizing Net Lease Rentals," **MA**, 1974, Vol. 55, No. 7, pp. 27-33.)

Mellman, Martin and Mona E. Seiler. "Structure Needed For Implementing Mandated Accounting Changes," **JAAF**, 1986, Vol. 1 (New Series), No. 4, pp. 305-318.

Mellman, Martin. "Classifying Segments For Line-Of-Business Reporting," **CPAJ**, 1974, Vol. 44, No. 8, pp. 17-23.

Mellman, Martin. "Marketing Cost Analysis - Development And Current Practices," **AR**, 1963, Vol. 38, No. 1, pp. 118-123.

Mellman, Martin. (Fisch, Jack H. and Martin Mellman. "Accounting For Investments In Affiliated Companies," **JOA**, 1969, Vol. 128, No. 5, pp. 41-49.)

Mellman, Martin. (Fisch, Jack H. and Martin Mellman. "Poolings Of Interest: The Status Of The Criteria," **JOA**, 1968, Vol. 126, No. 2, pp. 42-48.)

Mellman, Martin. (Lilien, Steven, Martin Mellman and Victor Pastena. "Accounting Changes: Successful Versus Unsuccessful Firms," **AR**, 1988, Vol. 63, No. 4, pp. 642-656.)

Mellors, J. "Capital Allowances And The Incentive To Invest," **ABR**, 1970-71, Vol. 1, No. 3, pp. 199-204.

Melnik, A. (Shashua, L., Y. Goldschmidt and A. Melnik. "The Predictive Value Of Interim Reports And Budgets," **ABACUS**, 1973, Vol. 9, No. 2, pp. 176-179.)

Melton, Edgar P. and Burton W. Brooks, Jr. "Impact Of GAAP On The Profitability Of Mortgage Bankers," **MA**, 1978, Vol. 60, No. 6, pp. 37-43.

Melumad, Nahum D. and Stefan Reichelstein. "Centralization Versus Delegation And The Value Of Communication," **JAR**, 1987, Vol. 25, Supp., pp. 1-18.

Melvoin, Charles. "Depreciation In Accountants' Reports," **JOA**, 1959, Vol. 108, No. 5, pp. 34-38.

Melzer, John T. S. "The Rise Of The Price Of Wheat In The 'Bakery In The Street Of The Fishmarket' In The City Of Lima: 1812-1821," **AHJ**, 1988, Vol. 15, No. 1, pp. 89-118.

Mendelson, Haim. (Amihud, Yakov and Haim Mendelson. "Liquidity, Volatility, And Exchange Automation," **JAAF**, 1988, Vol. 3 (New Series), No. 4, pp. 369-395.)

Mendenhall, Richard R. and William D. Nichols. "Bad News And Differential Market Reactions To Announcements Of Earlier-Quarters Versus Fourth-Quarter Earnings," **JAR**, 1988, Vol. 26, Supp., pp. 63-86.

Mendes, Henry E. "The Development Of Uniform Examinations," **AR**, 1944, Vol. 19, No. 2, pp. 139-141.

Mendus, Sharon L. (Van Sickle, Robert W. and Sharon L. Mendus. "Producing Financial Statements Faster," **MA**, 1984, Vol. 66, No. 2, pp. 58-61.)

Menees, Elbert L. "Macroaccounting: Why Not?," **MA**, 1978, Vol. 59, No. 8, pp. 29-32.

Menke, Warren W. (Ray, Delmas D. and Warren W. Menke. "Benefit-Cost Analysis: A Challenge For Accountants," **MA**, 1970, Vol. 52, No. 2, pp. 7-14.)

Menon, Krishnagopal and Kenneth B. Schwartz. "An Empirical Investigation Of Audit Qualification Decisions In The Presence Of Going Concern Uncertainties," **CAR**, 1986-87, Vol. 3, No. 2, pp. 302-315.

Menon, Krishnagopal. (Abdolmohammadi, Mohammad J., Krishnagopal Menon, Thomas W. Oliver and Srinivasan Umapathy. "The Role Of The Doctoral Dissertation In Accounting Research Centers," **IAE**, 1985, No. 1, pp. 59-76.)

Menon, Krishnagopal. (Davis, Stanley W. and Krishnagopal Menon. "The Formation And Termination Of The Cost Accounting Standards Board: Legislative Intervention In Accounting Standard-Setting," **JAPP**, 1987, Vol. 6, No. 3, pp. 185-207.)

Menon, Krishnagopal. (Rogers, Richard L. and Krishnagopal Menon. "Accounting For Deferred-Payment Notes," **AR**, 1985, Vol. 60, No. 3, pp. 547-557.)

Menon, Krishnagopal. (Schwartz, Kenneth B. and Krishnagopal

Menon. "Auditor Switches By Failing Firms," **AR**, 1985, Vol. 60, No. 2, pp. 248-261.)

Menon, K. (Abdolmohammadi, M., K. Menon, T. Oliver and S. Umapathy. "Factors Motivating Academic Research In Accounting," **AIA**, 1988, Vol. 6, pp. 159-174.)

Menon, K. (Davis, S. W., K. Menon and G. Morgan. "The Images That Have Shaped Accounting Theory," **AOS**, 1982, Vol. 7, No. 4, pp. 307-318.)

Mensah, Yaw M. and Gurprit S. Chhatwal. "Accounting For Shrinkage In Continuous Flow Industries: An Expository Note," **ABACUS**, 1987, Vol. 23, No. 1, pp. 31-42.

Mensah, Yaw M. and Louis F. Biagioni. "The Predictive Ability Of Financial Ratios Using Alternative Translation Methods For Foreign-Currency Financial Statements: A Simulation Study," **IJAER**, 1980, Vol. 16, No. 1, pp. 221-245.

Mensah, Yaw M. "A Dynamic Approach To The Evaluation Of Input-Variable Cost Center Performance," **AR**, 1982, Vol. 57, No. 4, pp. 681-700.

Mensah, Yaw M. "A Financial Reporting Model For Dependent Market Economies," **ABACUS**, 1981, Vol. 17, No. 2, pp. 161-173.

Mensah, Yaw M. "An Examination Of The Stationarity Of Multivariate Bankruptcy Prediction Models: A Methodological Study," **JAR**, 1984, Vol. 22, No. 1, pp. 380-395.

Mensah, Yaw M. "Exercising Budgetary Control In Automated Production Environments," **CAR**, 1988, Vol. 5, No. 1, pp. 222-249.

Mensah, Yaw M. "The Differential Bankruptcy Predictive Ability Of Specific Price Level Adjustments: Some Empirical Evidence," **AR**, 1983, Vol. 58, No. 2, pp. 228-246.

Mensah, Yaw M. "The Usefulness Of The Holding Gains And Losses Disclosure," **JAAF**, 1983, Vol. 6, No. 2, pp. 130-141.

Menssen, Merle D. "A Contract Price Policy For Multinationals," **MA**, 1988, Vol. 70, No. 4, pp. 27-32.

Menssen, M. D. "Eliminating Low Profit Product Lines," **MA**, 1981, Vol. 62, No. 9, pp. 24-25.

Mentzel, Alvin J. and Leonard J. Proscia. "Financial Forecasts - State Of The Art," **CPAJ**, 1980, Vol. 50, No. 7, pp. 12-19.

Menzefricke, Ulrich and Wally Smieliauskas. "A Comparison Of The Stratified Difference Estimator With Some Monetary-Unit Sampling Estimators," **CAR**, 1987-88, Vol. 4, No. 1, pp. 240-251.

Menzefricke, Ulrich and Wally Smieliauskas. "A Survey Of Simulation Studies In Statistical Auditing," **JAL**, 1987, Vol. 6, pp. 26-54.

Menzefricke, Ulrich and Wally Smieliauskas. "A Simulation Study Of The Performance Of Parametric Dollar Unit Sampling Statistical Procedures," **JAR**, 1984, Vol. 22, No. 2, pp. 588-604.

Menzefricke, Ulrich and Wally Smieliauskas. "On Sample Size Allocation In Auditing," **CAR**, 1988, Vol. 4, No. 2, pp. 314-336.

Menzefricke, Ulrich. "On Sampling Plan Selection With Dollar-Unit Sampling," **JAR**, 1983, Vol. 21, No. 1, pp. 96-105.

Menzefricke, Ulrich. "Using Decision Theory For Planning Audit Sample Size With Dollar Unit Sampling," **JAR**, 1984, Vol. 22, No. 2, pp. 570-587.

Menzel, Terrill E. (Steinberg, Harold I., John R. Miller and Terrill E. Menzel. "The Single Audit In Government," **JOA**, 1981, Vol. 151, No. 6, pp. 56-67.)

Mconske, Norman R. "Accounting Interns To The Rescue." **MA**, 1982, Vol. 64, No. 5, pp. 42-47.

Mepham, Michael J. "Accounting Control: An Historical Note," **AHJ**, 1986, Vol. 13, No. 1, pp. 103-107.

Mepham, Michael J. "Robert Hamilton's Contribution To Accounting," **AR**, 1983, Vol. 58, No. 1, pp. 43-57.

Mepham, Michael J. "The Scottish Enlightenment And The Development Of Accounting," **AHJ**, 1988, Vol. 15, No. 2, pp. 151-176.

Mepham, M. J. and W. E. Stone. "John Mair, M. A.: Author Of The First Classic Book-Keeping Series," **ABR**, 1976-77, Vol. 7, No. 26, pp. 128-134.

Mepham, M. J. "A Note To 'A Reinstatement Of The Accounting Rate Of Return'," **ABR**, 1979-80, Vol. 10, No. 37, pp. 74-75.

Mepham, M. J. "A Reinstatement Of The Accounting Rate Of Return." **ABR**, 1977-78, Vol. 8, No. 31, pp. 178-190.

Mepham, M. J. "Matrix-Based Accounting: A Comment," **ABR**, 1988, Vol. 18, No. 72, pp. 375-378.

Mepham, M. J. "The Eighteenth-Century Origins Of Cost Accounting," **ABACUS**, 1988, Vol. 24, No. 1, pp. 55-74.

Mepham, M. J. "A Payback Interpretation Of The Annuity Tables," **AR**, 1975, Vol. 50, No. 4, pp. 869-870.

Merchant, Kenneth A. and Robert Simons. "Research And Control In Complex Organizations: An Overview," **JAL**, 1986, Vol. 5, pp. 183-204.

Merchant, Kenneth A. "The Design Of The Corporate Budgeting System: Influences On Managerial Behavioral And Performance," **AR**, 1981, Vol. 56, No. 4, pp. 813-829.

Merchant, K. A. "Budgeting And The Propensity To Create Budgetary Slack," **AOS**, 1985, Vol. 10, No. 2, pp. 201-210.

Merchant, K. A. "Influences On Departmental Budgeting: An Empirical Examination Of A Contingency Model," **AOS**, 1984, Vol. 9, No. 3/4, pp. 291-310.

Merchant, K. A. "Organizational Controls And Discretionary Program Decision Making: A Field Study," **AOS**, 1985, Vol. 10, No. 1, pp. 67-86.

Merchant, K. A. (Gordon, F. E., J. G. Rhode and K. A. Merchant. "The Effects Of Salary And Human Resource Accounting Disclosures On Small Group Relations And Performance," **AOS**, 1977, Vol. 2, No. 4, pp. 295-306.)

Merchant, K. A. (Harvey, D. W., J. G. Rhode and K. A. Merchant. "Accounting Aggregation: User Preferences And Decision Making," **AOS**, 1979, Vol. 4, No. 3, pp. 187-210.)

Meredith, C. C. "Some Problems Of Labor Union Auditing," **AR**, 1944, Vol. 19, No. 3, pp. 290-293.

Meredith, Harlan C. "Fidelity And Surety Bonds," **JOA**, 1962, Vol. 113, No. 1, pp. 57-63.

Meredith, James E., Jr. "Accounting's Contribution To The Selection Of Business Investments," **MA**, 1968, Vol. 49, No. 8, pp. 3-11.

Merei, Issam J. (Ingram, Robert W., Dan M. Guy, Issam J. Merei and Robert T. Justis. "Disclosure Practices In Unaudited Financial Statements Of Small Businesses," **JOA**, 1977, Vol. 144, No. 2, pp. 81-86.)

Merino, Barbara Dubis and Marilyn Dale Neimark. "Disclosure Regulation And Public Policy: A Sociohistorical Reappraisal," **JAPP**, 1982, Vol. 1, No. 1, pp. 33-57.

Merino, Barbara Dubis. "Joseph E. Sterrett," **AHJ**, 1975, Vol. 2, No. 1-4, pp. 62-64.

Merino, Barbara D. and Teddy L. Coe. "Uniformity In Accounting: A Historical Perspective," **JOA**, 1978, Vol. 146, No. 2, pp. 62-69.

Merino, Barbara D. "Development Of American Accounting From 1876 To 1976," **CPAJ**, 1976, Vol. 46, No. 6, pp. 31-36.

Merino, Barbara D., Bruce S. Koch and Kenneth L. MacRitchie. "Historical Analysis - A Diagnostic Tool For 'Events' Studies: The Impact Of The Securities Act Of 1933," **AR**, 1987, Vol. 62, No. 4, pp. 748-762.

Merino, Barbara. (Brief, Richard P., Barbara Merino and Ira Weiss. "Cumulative Financial Statements," **AR**, 1980, Vol. 55, No. 3, pp. 480-490.)

Merino, B. D. (Tinker, A. M., B. D. Merino and M. D. Neimark. "The Normative Origins Of Positive Theories: Ideology And Accounting Thought," **AOS**, 1982, Vol. 7, No. 2, pp. 167-200.)

Merklein, Ernest A., Jr. "Environmental Risk Management: A New Approach To Pollution Insurance," **CA**, 1987, Vol. 5, No. 2, pp. 7-9.

Merlo, Jacques. "Management Accounting In The Airlines With Optical Reading Computers," **MA**, 1969, Vol. 51, No. 1, pp. 35-37.

Merrett, A. J. and G. D. Newbould. "A Theoretical And Empirical Procedure For The Measurement Of The Economic Income Of Corporations," **AIA**, 1985, Vol. 2, pp. 47-68.

Merriken, Harry E. (Edmister, Robert O. and Harry E. Merriken. "Consumer Deposit Demand, Interest Rate Differentials, And Public Welfare," **JAPP**, 1984, Vol. 3, No. 1, pp. 39-54.)

Merrill, Susan. (Sardinas, Joseph L., Jr. and Susan Merrill. "Regulation Of International Data Communications And The Effect Upon Multinational Corporations," **AIIA**, 1987, Vol. 1, pp. 305-315.)

Merriwether, Jacob D. (Bastable, C. W. and Jacob D. Merriwether. "Fifo In An Inflationary Environment," **JOA**, 1975, Vol. 139, No. 3, pp. 49-55.)

Merville, Larry J. and J. William Petty. "Transfer Pricing For The Multinational Firm," **AR**, 1978, Vol. 53, No. 4, pp. 935-951.

Mervin, Michael N. "Robinson-Patman Act Cost Justification And CPAs," **JOA**, 1971, Vol. 131, No. 6, pp. 59-62.

Merz, C. Mike. "Measuring Sales Forecast Accuracy," **MA**, 1975, Vol. 57, No. 1, pp. 53-54.

Merz, C. Mike. (Hunt, Rick, Linda Garrett and C. Mike Merz. "Direct Labor Cost Not Always Relevant At H-P," **MA**, 1985, Vol. 66, No. 8, pp. 58-62.)

Merz, C. Mike. (Larson, Steve and C. Mike Merz. "Operations Research At Boise Cascade," **MA**, 1978, Vol. 59, No. 8, pp. 33-36.)

Merz, Gary L. "How To Plan For A Small Business Tax Audit," **MA**, 1983, Vol. 65, No. 4, pp. 68-71.

Merz, Mike and David F. Groebner. "Ethics And The CPA Industry," **MA**, 1982, Vol. 64, No. 3, pp. 44-48.

Meschke, Marvin F. "Keeping Track Of Office Assets Via Computer," **MA**, 1984, Vol. 66, No. 1, pp. 38-41.

Meservy, Rayman D., Andrew D. Bailey, Jr. and Paul E. Johnson. "Internal Control Evaluation: A Computational Model Of The Review Process," **AJPT**, 1986-87, Vol. 6, No. 1, pp. 44-74.

Meservy, Raymon D. (Bailey, Andrew D., Jr., Gordon Leon Duke, James Gerlach, Chen-En Ko, Rayman D. Meservy and Andrew B. Whinston. "TICOM And The Analysis Of Internal Controls," **AR**, 1985, Vol. 60, No. 2, pp. 186-201.)

Mesko, John J. "How We Valued Our Closely Held Corporation," **MA**, 1982, Vol. 63, No. 9, pp. 41-42.

Messer, Jean F. and Keith H. Burdick. "Profit-Sharing Plans For Closely Held Corporations," **JOA**, 1970, Vol. 129, No. 4, pp. 53-60.

Messer, Jean F. and Lloyd W. McDaniel. "Accounting For Country Clubs," **MA**, 1971, Vol. 52, No. 12, pp. 21-23.

Messere, Carl J. and Gilroy J. Zuckerman. "An Alternative Approach To Depreciation Switches," **AR**, 1981, Vol. 56, No. 3, pp. 642-652.

Messier, William F., Jr. and Arnold Schneider. "A Hierarchical Approach To The External Auditor's Evaluation Of The Internal Auditing Function," **CAR**, 1988, Vol. 4, No. 2, pp. 337-353.

Messier, William F., Jr. and James V. Hansen. "Expert Systems In Auditing: The State Of The Art," **AJPT**, 1987-88, Vol. 7, No. 1, pp. 94-105.

Messier, William F., Jr. and R. David Plumlee. "The Effects Of Anticipation And Frequency Of Errors On Auditors' Selection Of Substantive Procedures," **ABR**, 1986-87, Vol. 17, No. 68, pp. 349-358.

Messier, William F., Jr. "SFAS No. 8: Some Implications For MNCS," IJAER, 1979, Vol. 14, No. 2, pp. 101-119.

Messier, William F., Jr. "The Effect Of Experience And Firm Type On Materiality/Disclosure Judgments," **JAR**, 1983, Vol. 21, No. 2, pp. 611-618.

Messier, William F., Jr. (Biggs, Stanley F., William F. Messier, Jr. and James V. Hansen. "A Descriptive Analysis Of Computer Audit Specialists' Decision-Making Behavior In Advanced Computer Environments," **AJPT**, 1986-87, Vol. 6, No. 2, pp. 1-21.)

Messier, William F., Jr. (Emery, Douglas R., F. Hutton Barron and William F. Messier, Jr. "Conjoint Measurement And The Analysis Of Noisy Data: A Comment," **JAR**, 1982, Vol. 20, No. 2, Part I, pp. 450-458.)

Messier, William F., Jr. (Hansen, James V. and William F. Messier, Jr. "A Preliminary Investigation Of EDP-XPERT," **AJPT**, 1986-87, Vol. 6, No. 1, pp. 109-123.)

Messier, William F., Jr. (Holstrum, Gary L. and William F. Messier, Jr. "A Review And Integration Of Empirical Research On Materiality," **AJPT**, 1982-83, Vol. 2, No. 1, pp. 45-63.)

Messier, William F., Jr. (Johnson, Steven B. and William F. Messier, Jr. "The Nature Of Accounting Standards Setting: An Alternative Explanation," **JAAF**, 1982, Vol. 5, No. 3, pp. 195-213.)

Messier, William F., Jr. (Michaelsen, Robert and William F. Messier, Jr. "Expert Systems In Taxation," **JATA**, 1987, Vol. 8, No. 2, pp. 7-21.)

Metcalf, Richard D. (Haglund, Byron E., Lee J. Adamson and Richard D. Metcalf. "Punched Card Accounting For Small Businesses," **JOA**, 1961, Vol. 112, No. 6, pp. 54-58.)

Metcalf, Richard W. and Harry I. Wolk. "Applied Fixed Overhead Accounting: A Proposal," **MA**, 1971, Vol. 52, No. 8, pp. 25-27.

Metcalf, Richard W. and Joe R. Fritzemeyer. "Taxation Of Interstate Income: A Call To Action," **JOA**, 1965, Vol. 120, No. 2, pp. 44-46.

Metcalf, Richard W. "The 'Basic Postulates' In Perspective," **AR**, 1964, Vol. 39, No. 1, pp. 16-21.

Metcalf, Richard W. (Chen, Kung H. and Richard W. Metcalf. "The Relationship Between Pollution Control Record And Financial Indicators Revisited," **AR**, 1980, Vol. 55, No. 1, pp. 168-177.)

Metcalf, Richard W. (Gipple, Larry D. and Richard W. Metcalf. "Planning Your Professional Development Program," **JOA**, 1974, Vol. 137, No. 3, pp. 38-46.)

Metcalf, R. W. and G. D. Welch. "Basic Accounting Theory: A Set Of Three Postulates," **MA**, 1968, Vol. 49, No. 10, pp. 3-10.

Metz, Robert. "How A Reporter Sees The Certified Public Accountant," **JOA**, 1963, Vol. 115, No. 5, pp. 59-64.

Mey, Abram. "Replacement Value Accounting Theory: The 'Circular Flow' And The Circulation Of Value," **AIIA**, 1988, Vol. 2, pp. 3-21.

Mey, Abram. "Theodore Limperg And His Theory Of Values And Costs," **ABACUS**, 1966, Vol. 2, No. 1, pp. 3-23.

Meyer, Fred P. (Englebrecht, Ted D. and Fred P. Meyer. "Using Qualified Disclaimers In Estate Planning," **CPAJ**, 1986, Vol. 56, No. 9, pp. 66-73.)

Meyer, Harvey G. "Some Aspects Of Accounting Education," **AR**, 1961, Vol. 36, No. 2, pp. 209-212.

Meyer, Harvey G. "The Systems Course," **AR**, 1933, Vol. 8, No. 4, p. 350-351.

Meyer, Harvey G. "The Use Of Problems, Cases And Practice Sets In The Elementary Course," **AR**, 1933, Vol. 8, No. 1, pp. 33-36.

Meyer, J. W. "Social Environments And Organizational Accounting," **AOS**, 1986, Vol. 11, No. 4, pp. 345-356.

Meyer, Philip E. "A Framework For Understanding 'Substance Over Form' In Accounting," **AR**, 1976, Vol. 51, No. 1, pp. 80-89.

Meyer, Philip E. "The Accounting Entity," **ABACUS**, 1973, Vol. 9, No. 2, pp. 116-126.

Meyer, Philip E. "The APB's Independence And Its Implications For The FASB," **JAR**, 1974, Vol. 12, No. 1, pp. 188-196.

Meyers, Stephen L. "A Proposal For Coping With The Allocation Problem," **JOA**, 1976, Vol. 141, No. 4, pp. 52-56.

Meyers, Stephen L. "Accounting For Long-Term Notes," **MA**, 1973, Vol. 55, No. 1, pp. 49-51.

Meyers, Stephen L. "An Examination Of The Relationship Between Interperiod Tax Allocation And Present-Value Depreciation," **AR**, 1973, Vol. 48, No. 1, pp. 44-49.

Meyers, Stephen L. "Present Value Models And The Multi-Asset Problem: A Comment," **AR**, 1974, Vol. 49, No. 4, pp. 816-818.

Meyers, Stephen L. "The Stationarity Problem In The Use Of The Market Model Of Security Price Behavior," **AR**, 1973, Vol. 48, No. 2, pp. 318-322.

Meyers, Stephen L. (Anderson, James A. and Stephen L. Meyers. "Some Limitations Of Efficient Markets Research For The Determination Of Financial Reporting Standards," **ABACUS**, 1975, Vol. 11, No. 1, pp. 18-36.)

Mezner, Edward. "Advantages To A Business Which Result From Abandoning December 31 Closing Date," **JOA**, 1950, Vol. 90, No. 5, pp. 392-397.

Mia, L. "Managerial Attitude, Motivation And The Effectiveness Of Budget Participation," **AOS**, 1988, Vol. 13, No. 5, pp. 465-475.

Michaelsen, Robert and William F. Messier, Jr. "Expert Systems In Taxation," **JATA**, 1987, Vol. 8, No. 2, pp. 7-21.

Michaelsen, Robert H. "An Expert System For Selecting Tax Shelters," **JATA**, 1987, Vol. 9, No. 1, pp. 35-47.

Michaelsen, Robert H. "Development Of An Expert Computer System To Assist In The Classification Of Estate Tax Returns," AH, 1988, Vol. 2, No. 4, pp. 63-70.

Michaelsen, Robert H. (Brighton, Gerald D. and Robert H. Michaelsen. "Profile Of Tax Dissertations In Accounting: 1967-1984," **JATA**, 1985, Vol. 6, No. 2, pp. 76-91.)

Michaels, Andrew J. "Establishing A PERT System," **MA**, 1971, Vol. 53, No. 4, pp. 26-32.

Michaels, Lawrence T. "A Control Framework For Factory Automation," **MA**, 1988, Vol. 69, No. 11, pp. 37-43.

Michael, John. "Trading Stamp Accounting," **MA**, 1967, Vol. 48, No. 12, pp. 54-61.

Michel, Steven. (Bakay, Virginia and Steven Michel. "Jackpot!," **MA**, 1984, Vol. 65, No. 11, pp. 26-36.)

Michelsen, Neil R. "Auditing And Other Services For Banks," **CPAJ**, 1978, Vol. 48, No. 11, pp. 30-36.

Michenzi, Alfred R. (Campbell, David R. and Alfred R. Michenzi. "Revising The Audit Report: A Response To The Expectation Gap," **CPAJ**, 1987, Vol. 57, No. 4, pp. 34-39.)

Michi, Richard A. (Rollin, Arthur S. and Richard A. Michi. "The Outlook For Tax Shelters," **CPAJ**, 1973, Vol. 43, No. 12, pp. 1063-1066.)

Mickel, Frederick B. "Stress: Race To The Bottom Line," **MA**, 1981, Vol. 62, No. 10, pp. 15-20.

Mickle, Collier E., Jim D. Reed and Daniel L. Butler. "Analyzing The Profitability Of Branch Banks," **MA**, 1985, Vol. 67, No. 6, pp. 61-66.

Middleton, K. A. "Lease Evaluation: Back To Square One," **ABR**, 1976-77, Vol. 7, No. 26, p. 127.

Mielke, David E. and Don E. Giacomino. "Cash-Flow Reporting: A Step Toward International Harmonization," **IJAER**, 1987, Vol. 22, No. 2, pp. 143-151.

Mielke, David E. and Don E. Giacomino. "Ratio Analysis Using The New Statement Of Cash Flows," **CA**, 1988, Vol. 6, No. 1, pp. 10-17.

Mielke, David E. and James Seifert. "A Survey On The Effects Of Defeasing Debt," **JAAF**, 1987, Vol. 2 (New Series), No. 1, pp. 65-78.

Mielke, David E. and Robert B. Yahr. "Business Combinations And FASB Statement No. 87," **CA**, 1987, Vol. 5, No. 4, pp. 30-37.

Mielke, David E. (Giacomino, Don E. and David E. Mielke. "Using The Statement Of Cash Flows To Analyze Corporate Performance," **MA**, 1988, Vol. 69, No. 11, pp. 54-57.)

Mielke, David E. (Giacomino, Don E. and David E. Mielke. "Preparation And Use Of Cash Flow Statements," **CPAJ**, 1987, Vol. 57, No. 3, pp. 30-35.)

Mihalek, Paul H., Anne J. Rich and Carl S. Smith. "Ethics And Management Accountants," **MA**, 1987, Vol. 69, No. 6, pp. 34-36.

Mikesell, R. M. "Statement Of Source And Application Of Funds Without Formal Working Papers," AR, 1959, Vol. 34, No. 2, pp. 300-301.

Mikesell, R. M. "Wanted: More Cost Accounting For Government," AR, 1947, Vol. 22, No. 3, pp. 241-247.

Mikesell, R. M. (Heckert, J. B., H. F. Taggart, C. L. Van Sickle, R. M. Mikesell, F. W. Woodbridge, Louis O. Foster and T. W. Leland. "Instruction In Methods Of Accounting Control: A Symposium," **AR**, 1937, Vol. 12, No. 2, pp. 114-122.)

Mikkelson, Wayne H. and Richard S. Ruback. "Takeovers And Managerial Compensation: A Discussion," **JAEC**, 1985, Vol. 7, No. 1/3, pp. 233-238.

Milani, Ken and Kevin M. Misiewicz. "Enhancing The Tax Learning Experience: Identifying And Using Tax Cases In Introductory Courses," **JATA**, 1987, Vol. 9, No. 1, pp. 75-85.

Milani, Ken. "LIFO And Its Limitations," **MA**, 1975, Vol. 57, No. 6, pp. 31-32.

Milani, Ken. "The Relationship Of Participation In Budget-Setting To Industrial Supervisor Performance And Attitudes: A Field Study," **AR**, 1975, Vol. 50, No. 2, pp. 274-284.

Milani, Ken. (Gaertner, James F. and Ken Milani. "The TRR Yardstick For Hospital Capital Expenditure Decisions," **MA**, 1980, Vol. 62, No. 6, pp. 25-33.)

Milani, Ken. (Sharp, Norman and Ken Milani. "Hospital Budgeting," **MA**, 1977, Vol. 58, No. 9, pp. 49-52.)

Milani, Ken. (Wittenbach, James L. and Ken Milani. "A Profile Of The CPA In Tax Practice: An Update," **JOA**, 1982, Vol. 154, No. 4, pp. 65-76.)

Milano, Duane R. and John Russell Arens. "Microcomputer Test Banks For Accounting Principles: An Evaluation," **IAE**, 1987, Vol. 2, No. 1, pp. 85-93.

Milano, Duane R. (Coburn, David L., Joseph K. Ellis, III and Duane R. Milano. "Dilemmas In MNC Transfer Pricing," **MA**, 1981, Vol. 63, No. 5, pp. 53-58.)

Milefsky, Norman R. "Utilization Of Corporate Loss Carryovers," **JOA**, 1969, Vol. 128, No. 4, pp. 55-61.

Miles, Carolyn A. (Anderson, Urton, Robert G. May and Carolyn A. Miles. "Variables Sampling Software: Development And Classroom Testing," **IAE**, 1988, Vol. 3, No. 1, pp. 156-173.)

Miles, Catherine E. "The Objectives And Material Contents Of Elementary Accounting Courses For Accounting Majors And Of Courses For Majors In Fields Other Than Accounting," **AR**, 1954, Vol. 29, No. 4, pp. 601-604.

Miles, Catherine E. (Hermanson, Roger H. and Catherine E. Miles. "Fine-Tuning The Predictive Model Of The American Accounting Association 1971-72 And 1972-73 Committees On Future Professorial Supply And Demand," **AR**, 1976, Vol. 51, No. 4, pp. 875-885.)

Miles, Jesse M. "Foreign Tax Liability For U.S. Firms Abroad," **JOA**, 1966, Vol. 121, No. 5, pp. 46-52.

Milito, Vincent. (Dropkin, Murray, Vincent Milito, Theresa

Dominianni and William La Touche. "Trends In Charities Registration And Reporting," **CPAJ**, 1988, Vol. 58, No. 5, pp. 56-65.)

Milko, Edward M. "Auditing: Through The Computer Or Around?," **MA**, 1970, Vol. 52, No. 2, pp. 45-48.

Millar, James A. "Hospital Equipment Leasing: The Breakeven Discount Rate," **MA**, 1979, Vol. 61, No. 1, pp. 21-26.

Millar, James A. "Split Or Dividend: Do The Words Really Matter?," **AR**, 1977, Vol. 52, No. 1, pp. 52-55.

Millar, James A. (Glezen, G. William and James A. Millar. "An Empirical Investigation Of Stockholder Reaction To Disclosures Required By ASR No. 250," **JAR**, 1985, Vol. 23, No. 2, pp. 859-870.)

Millar, James A. (Glezen, G. William and James A. Millar. "An Analysis Of Trends And Sources Of Published Funded Accounting Research," **AIA**, 1987, Vol. 4, pp. 83-96.)

Millar, Victor E. "The Three Levels Of EDP Practice," **JOA**, 1967, Vol. 123, No. 2, pp. 41-44.

Miller, Bruce L. (Buckman, A. G. and Bruce L. Miller. "Optimal Investigation Of A Multiple Cost Processes System," **JAR**, 1982, Vol. 20, No. 1, pp. 28-41.)

Miller, Carrol R. "Are Accountants The Public's Protectors?," **MA**, 1973, Vol. 54, No. 11, pp. 16-18.

Miller, D. (Gordon, L. A. and D. Miller. "A Contingency Framework For The Design Of Accounting Information Systems," **AOS**, 1976, Vol. 1, No. 1, pp. 59-70.)

Miller, Edward M. "Why Overstated Earnings Affect Stock Prices But Not The Reverse - An Important Asymmetry," **JAAF**, 1980, Vol. 4, No. 1, pp. 6-19.

Miller, Henry. "Environmental Complexity And Financial Reports," **AR**, 1972, Vol. 47, No. 1, pp. 31-37.

Miller, Herbert E. and Sidney Davidson. "Accreditation: Two Views," **JOA**, 1978, Vol. 145, No. 3, pp. 56-65.

Miller, Herbert E. "Accounting Statements For Publication," **AR**, 1942, Vol. 17, No. 3, pp. 251-256.

Miller, Herbert E. "Audited Statements - Are They Really Management's?," **JOA**, 1964, Vol. 118, No. 4, pp. 43-46.

Miller, Herbert E. "How Much Income Tax Allocation?," **JOA**, 1962, Vol. 114, No. 2, pp. 46-51.

Miller, Herbert E. "Internship Training In Accounting," **AR**, 1945, Vol. 20, No. 2, pp. 187-190.

Miller, Herbert E. "Quasi-Reorganizations In Reverse," **AR**, 1948, Vol. 23, No. 2, pp. 154-157.

Miller, Herbert E. "Reserves For War Contingencies And Postwar Adjustments," **AR**, 1944, Vol. 19, No. 3, pp. 248-253.

Miller, Herbert E. "Surplus Reserves," **AR**, 1947, Vol. 22, No. 2, pp. 147-150.

Miller, Herbert E. "Textbooks Or Research," **AR**, 1966, Vol. 41, No. 1, pp. 1-7.

Miller, Herbert E. "The 1948 Revision Of The American Accounting Association's Statement Of Concepts And Standards: A General Appraisal," **AR**, 1949, Vol. 24, No. 1, pp. 44-48.

Miller, Herman C. "A Suggested Program Of Education For The Accountant," **AR**, 1938, Vol. 13, No. 2, pp. 191-198.

Miller, Herman C. "The Place Of Governmental Accounting In The Syllabus," **AR**, 1939, Vol. 14, No. 2, pp. 176-177.

Miller, Herman C. (Weimer, Arthur M. and Herman C. Miller. "The Attraction And Selection Of Accounting Teachers," **AR**, 1956, Vol. 31, No. 3, pp. 407-410.)

Miller, Herman C. "A Five-Year Plan For Training Specialists," **AR**, 1933, Vol. 8, No. 1, pp. 36-38.

Miller, Hermann C. "Cost Inspection In The United States Navy," **AR**, 1942, Vol. 17, No. 2, pp. 94-99.

Miller, Hermann C. "Expense And Accounting Concepts And Standards," **AR**, 1949, Vol. 24, No. 2, pp. 146-145.

Miller, Hermann C. "Interim Report Of The Standards Rating Committee," **AR**, 1951, Vol. 26, No. 1, pp. 19-21.

Miller, Hermann C. "Standards For A Master's Thesis In Accounting," **AR**, 1934, Vol. 9, No. 2, pp. 178-182.

Miller, H. C. "The Master's Thesis," **AR**, 1935, Vol. 10, No. 1, pp. 33-49.

Miller, Jeffrey G. (Nanni, Alfred J., Jeffrey G. Miller and Thomas E. Vollmann. "What Shall We Account For?," **MA**, 1988, Vol. 69, No. 7, pp. 42-48.)

Miller, Jerry D. "Accounting For Warrants And Convertible Bonds," **MA**, 1973, Vol. 54, No. 7, pp. 26-28.

Miller, John R. and Frederick D. Wolf. "A Look At The New Yellow Book: Tomorrow's Government Audits," **JOA**, 1988, Vol. 166, No. 6, pp. 64-80.

Miller, John R. (Steinberg, Harold I., John R. Miller and Terrill E. Menzel. "The Single Audit In Government," **JOA**, 1981, Vol. 151, No. 6, pp. 56-67.)

Miller, Joseph C. (Falk, Haim and Joseph C. Miller. "Amortization Of Advertising Expenditures," **JAR**, 1977, Vol. 15, No. 1, pp. 12-22.)

Miller, Kenneth C. "The Intangible Drilling Deduction," **JOA**, 1955, Vol. 100, No. 3, pp. 40-45.

Miller, Malcolm C. "Goodwill - An Aggregation Issue," **AR**, 1973, Vol. 48, No. 2, pp. 280-291.

Miller, Malcolm C. (Ma, Ronald and Malcolm C. Miller. "Conceptualising The Liability," **ABR**, 1977-78, Vol. 8, No. 32, pp. 258-265.)

Miller, Max J. "Supplying Economic Data To Unions," **JOA**, 1956, Vol. 101, No. 1, pp. 40-49.

Miller, M. C. (Ma, Ronald and M. C. Miller. "Inflation And The Current Value Illusion," **ABR**, 1975-76, Vol. 6, No. 24, pp. 250-263.)

Miller, Paul B. W. "A New View Of Comparability," **JOA**, 1978, Vol. 146, No. 2, pp. 70-77.

Miller, Paul B. W. "Accounting Research Needs A More Efficient Market," **MA**, 1978, Vol. 60, No. 5, pp. 27-34.

Miller, Paul B. W. "Taxing Capital Gains With Price Indexes," **MA**, 1979, Vol. 60, No. 7, pp. 50-52.

Miller, Paul B. W. "The Conceptual Framework: Myths And Realities," **JOA**, 1985, Vol. 159, No. 3, pp. 62-71.

Miller, Paul B. W. "The Contributions Of The Financial Accounting Standards Board To Accounting Education," **AIA**, 1984, Vol. 1, pp. 145-156.

Miller, Paul B. W. "The New Pension Accounting (Part 1)," **JOA**, 1987, Vol. 163, No. 1, pp. 98-108.

Miller, Paul B. W. "The New Pension Accounting (Part 2)," **JOA**, 1987, Vol. 163, No. 2, pp. 86-94.

Miller, Paul B. W. "The Use Of Effective Tax Rates," **MA**, 1969, Vol. 50, No. 7, pp. 57-59.

Miller, Paul B. W. "What Is Accounting Research Supposed To Do?," **MA**, 1977, Vol. 59, No. 6, pp. 43-47.

Miller, Paul B. W. (Lucas, Timothy S. and Paul B. W. Miller. "Pension Accounting: Impacting The Financial Statement," **JOA**, 183, Vol. 155, No. 6, pp. 90-109.)

Miller, P. and T. O'Leary. "Accounting And The Construction Of The Governable Person," **AOS**, 1987, Vol. 12, No. 3, pp. 235-266.

Miller, Rene A. "Interim Financial Accounting And Reporting - Review Of APB Opinion No. 28," **CPAJ**, 1973, Vol. 43, No. 9, pp. 755-762.

Miller, Richard D. "Accounting And Labor Relations - Inter-related Responsibilities," **MA**, 1971, Vol. 53, No. 5, pp. 15-19.

Miller, Richard L., Jr. (Chazen, Charles, Richard L. Miller, Jr. and Kenneth I. Solomon. "When The Rules Say: 'See Your Lawyer," **JOA**, 1981, Vol. 151, No. 1, pp. 60-70.)

Miller, Richard L., Jr. (Solomon, Kenneth Ira, Charles Chazen and Richard L. Miller, Jr. "Compilation And Review: The Safety Factor," **JOA**, 183, Vol. 155, No. 6, pp. 50-59.)

Miller, Richard P. and Norman N. Strauss. "SFAS No. 52: The FASB Tackles Foreign Currency Translation...Again," **CA**, 1983, Vol. 1, No. 1, pp. 3-17.

Miller, Richard P. (Godick, Neil B. and Richard P. Miller. "Applying APB Opinions Nos. 23 And 24," **JOA**, 1973, Vol. 136, No. 5, pp. 55-63.)

Miller, Robert A. "MAS Consultant's Role In Asset-Based Financing," **CPAJ**, 1982, Vol. 52, No. 4, pp. 24-31.

Miller, Robert D. and Terry L. Robinson. "Performance Reports Based On Direct Costing: A Case Study," **MA**, 1970, Vol. 51, No. 10, pp. 43-47.

Miller, Robert D. "A Short-Cut Method To Calculate Declining Balance Depreciation," **MA**, 1970, Vol. 52, No. 1, pp. 68-70.

Miller, Robert D. "Compilation And Review: Standards' Impact On Risk," **JOA**, 1983, Vol. 156, No. 1, pp. 60-75.

Miller, Robert D. "Governmental Oversight Of The Role Of Auditors," **CPAJ**, 1986, Vol. 56, No. 9, pp. 20-37.

Miller, Robert D. "Proposed Standards Of Attestation - Solution Or First Step?," **CPAJ**, 1985, Vol. 55, No. 6, pp. 10-25.

Miller, Robert E. "Who Should Pay The President's Salary?," **JOA**, 1960, Vol. 109, No. 3, pp. 61-64.

Miller, Robert E. (Balvers, Ronald J., Bill McDonald and Robert E. Miller. "Underpricing Of New Issues And The Choice Of Auditor As A Signal Of Investment Banker Reputation," **AR**, 1988, Vol. 63, No. 4, pp. 605-622.)

Miller, R. Scott. (Charles, Dane W. and R. Scott Miller. "Pension Accounting - Some Unanswered Questions," **CPAJ**, 1980, Vol. 50, No. 2, pp. 19-24.)

Miller, Stephanie. "International Accounting - Users Beware!," **MA**, 1984, Vol. 66, No. 2, p. 46.

Miller, Stephen H. "Avoiding Lawsuits," **JOA**, 1988, Vol. 166, No. 3, pp. 57-65.

Miller, Stuart B. (Delit, Steven N. and Stuart B. Miller. "Watch Your Step-Up: Section 334(b)(2) Liquidations," **CPAJ**, 1981, Vol. 51, No. 11, pp. 44-52.)

Miller, Vergil V. (Anderson, Leslie P. and Vergil V. Miller. "Capital Budgeting: A Modified Approach To Capital Allocation," **MA**, 1969, Vol. 50, No. 7, pp. 28-32.)

Miller, Walter I. "Air Force Accounting," **JOA**, 1956, Vol. 102, No. 4, pp. 47-50.

Millians, Paul M. "Profit Planning And Budgetary Control," **AR**, 1947, Vol. 22, No. 1, pp. 65-67.

Milligan, Bruce L. "Contribution Margin In Decision Making," **MA**, 1969, Vol. 51, No. 4, pp. 33-38.

Milliron, Valerie C. and Daniel R. Toy. "Tax Compliance: An Investigation Of Key Features," **JATA**, 1988, Vol. 9, No. 2, pp. 84-104.

Milliron, Valerie C. "A Behavioral Study Of The Meaning And Influence Of Tax Complexity," **JAR**, 1985, Vol. 23, No. 2, pp. 794-816.

Milliron, Valerie C. "An Analysis Of The Relationship Between Tax Equity And Tax Complexity," **JATA**, 1985, Vol. 7, No. 1, pp. 19-33.

Milliron, Valerie C. (Collins, Julie H. and Valerie C. Milliron. "A Measure Of Professional Accountants' Learning Style," **IAE**, 1987, Vol. 2, No. 2, pp. 193-206)

Milliron, Valerie C. (Jackson, Betty R. and Valerie C. Milliron. "Tax Compliance Research, Findings, Problems And Prospects," **JAL**, 1986, Vol. 5, pp. 125-166.)

Milliron, Valerie C., Paul R. Watkins and Stewart S. Karlinsky. "Policy Judgments Of Taxpayers: An Analysis Of Criteria Employed," **AIT**, 1988, Vol. 2, pp. xx-xx.

Mills, John. (Harkins, Jeffrey L. and John Mills. "Annual Reports: A Pedagogical Tool For Intermediate Accounting," **AIA**, 1985, Vol. 2, pp. 149-168.)

Mills, Leslie. "Renegotiation Act Of 1951 Analyzed," **JOA**, 1951, Vol. 91, No. 5, pp. 690-703.

Mills, Patti A. "Financial Reporting And Stewardship Accounting In Sixteenth-Century Spain," **AHJ**, 1986, Vol.

13, No. 2, pp. 65-76.

Mills, Patti A. "The Probative Capacity Of Accounts In Early-Modern Spain," **AHJ**, 1987, Vol. 14, No. 1, pp. 95-108.

Mills, Robert H. "Proposed Changes In The Uniform Examination," **CPAJ**, 1988, Vol. 58, No. 4, pp. 38-43.

Mills, Robert H. and Abbott L. Brown. "Soviet Economic Development And Accounting," **JOA**, 1966, Vol. 121, No. 6, pp. 40-46.

Mills, Robert H. and Frank Luh. "Financial Reporting Of Commercial Banks," **JOA**, 1968, Vol. 126, No. 1, pp. 49-54.

Mills, Robert H. "Investment Loss Reserves For Corporate Bond Investors," **AR**, 1967, Vol. 42, No. 1, pp. 74-81.

Mills, Robert H. "Post-Baccalaureate Education For CPAs: Educational Capacity And Perceived Academic Quality Of Accounting Students," **ACCHOR**, 1987, Vol. 1, No. 2, pp. 49-58.

Mills, Robert H. "Views On Education And Experience Requirements," **JOA**, 1985, Vol. 160, No. 4, pp. 106-117.

Mills, William B. "Drawing Up A Budgeting System For An Ad Agency," **MA**, 1983, Vol. 65, No. 6, pp. 46-51.

Milne, Frank and Ron Weber. "Regulation And The Auditing Profession In The USA: The Metcalf Subcommittee's Recommendations Re-Examined," **ABR**, 1980-81, Vol. 11, No. 43, pp. 197-206.

Milne, Ronald A. and Glenn A. Vent. "Publication Productivity: A Comparison Of Accounting Faculty Members Promoted In 1981 and 1984," **IAE**, 1987, Vol. 2, No. 1, pp. 94-102.

Milne, Ronald A., Glenn A. Vent and Reuben Neumann. "Accounting For Variable Stock Options," **JAED**, 1987, Vol. 5, No. 2, pp. 333-338.

Milroy, Robert R., Donald F. Istvan and Ray M. Powell. "The Tax Depreciation Muddle," **AR**, 1961, Vol. 36, No. 4, pp. 539-547.

Milston, Martin J. and Theodore Cohn. "Personal And Business Aspects Of Stockholder Agreements," **JOA**, 1967, Vol. 124, No. 4, pp. 41-45.

Minch, Roland A. and Enrico Petri. "Reporting Income For Reciprocal Parent-Subsidiary Stockholdings," **CPAJ**, 1975, Vol. 45, No. 7, pp. 36-40.

Minch, Roland A. (Petri, Enrico and Roland A. Minch. "A Decision Model For Tax Preference Items," **AR**, 1978, Vol. 53, No. 2, pp. 415-428.)

Minch, Roland and Enrico Petri. "Matrix Modeling Of Reciprocal Service Cost Allocation," **AR**, 1972, Vol. 47, No. 3, pp. 576-580.

Minch, Roland. (Petri, Enrico and Roland Minch. "Evaluation Of Resource Acquisiton Decisions By The Partitioning Of Holding Activity," **AR**, 1974, Vol. 49, No. 3, pp. 455-464.)

Minch, Roland. (Petri, Enrico and Roland Minch. "The Treasury Stock Method And Conventional Method In Reciprocal Stockholdings - An Amalgamation," **AR**, 1974, Vol. 49, No. 2, pp. 330-341.)

Minch, Roland. (Petri, Enrico and Roland Minch. "The Treasury Stock Method And Conventional Method In Reciprocal Stockholdings: An Amalgamation: A Reply," **AR**, 1975, Vol. 50, No. 2, pp. 365-369.)

Minch, Roland. (Petri, Enrico and Roland Minch. "Contemporary Inflation Accounting Proposals: An Analysis And An Alternative," **ABACUS**, 1975, Vol. 11, No. 2, pp. 182-192.)

Minch, Roland. (Petri, Enrico and Roland Minch. "Capacity Variance: Responsibility And Control," **MA**, 1972, Vol. 53, No. 10, pp. 38-41.)

Miner, John B. (Dalton, Francis E. and John B. Miner. "The Role Of Accounting Training In Top Mangement Decision-Making," **AR**, 1970, Vol. 45, No. 1, pp. 134-139.)

Mini, Donald L. (Mautz, R. K. and Donald L. Mini. "Internal Control Evaluation And Audit Program Modification," **AR**, 1966, Vol. 41, No. 2, pp. 283-291.)

Minor, Matthew. (Heaney, Terence, Martin Mason and Matthew Minor. "A Closer Look At ESOPs," **CPAJ**, 1976, Vol. 46, No. 9, pp. 29-36.)

Minow, Newton N. "Accountants' Liability And The Litigation Explosion," **JOA**, 1984, Vol. 158, No. 3, pp. 70-90.

Mintz, Seymour D. "Tax Effects In Liquidating A Corporate Structure," **CPAJ**, 1980, Vol. 50, No. 3, pp. 29-34.

Mintz, Steven M. "Internationalization Of The Accounting Curriculum," **IJAER**, 1980, Vol. 16, No. 1, pp. 137-151.

Miotto, Neil J. "Evaluating Internal Accounting Controls," **MA**, 1980, Vol. 62, No. 1, pp. 15-18.

Miranti, Paul J., Jr. (Edwards, James Don and Paul J. Miranti, Jr. "The AICPA: A Professional Institution In A Dynamic Society," **JOA**, 1987, Vol. 163, No. 5, pp. 22-38.)

Mires, H. F. "The Income Tax - Collection Aspects," **AR**, 1928, Vol. 3, No. 1, pp. 1-6.

Mirghani, Mohamed A. "A Framework For A Linkage Between Microaccounting And Macroaccounting For Purposes Of Development Planning In Developing Countries," **IJAER**, 1982, Vol. 18, No. 1, pp. 57-68.

Mirvis, P. H. and B. A. Macy. "Accounting For The Costs And Benefits Of Human Resource Development Programs: An Interdisciplinary Approach," **AOS**, 1976, Vol. 1, No. 2/3, pp. 179-194.

Mirvis, P. H. and E. E. Lawler, III. "Systems Are Not Solutions: Issues In Creating Information Systems That Account For The Human Organization," **AOS**, 1983, Vol. 8, No. 2/3, pp. 175-190.

Mischler, James J. "Taxation Of War Loss Recoveries," **AR**, 1946, Vol. 21, No. 3, pp. 283-287.

Misiewicz, Kevin M. "A Macro-Case Analysis Approach To Tax Research," **AR**, 1977, Vol. 52, No. 4, pp. 935-938.

Misiewicz, Kevin M. "A Macro-Case Analysis Approach To Tax Research - A Reply," **AR**, 1979, Vol. 54, No. 3, pp. 641-642.

Misiewicz, Kevin M. "Ethical Guidelines For Tax Practitioners," **CPAJ**, 1981, Vol. 51, No. 10, pp. 42-50.

Misiewicz, Kevin M. "The Role Of LEXIS In Tax Research," **CPAJ**, 1979, Vol. 49, No. 2, pp. 23-28.

Misiewicz, Kevin M. "The Tax Nucleus Of Gains And Losses," **AR**, 1978, Vol. 53, No. 4, pp. 979-984.

Misiewicz, Kevin M. (Marshall, Don C., Kevin M. Misiewicz and W. Ron Singleton. "Applications Of Computer-Assisted Tax Research In Academic Tax Programs," **JAED**, 1987, Vol. 5, No. 2, pp. 287-296.)

Misiewicz, Kevin M. (Milani, Ken and Kevin M. Misiewicz. "Enhancing The Tax Learning Experience: Identifying And Using Tax Cases In Introductory Courses," **JATA**, 1987, Vol. 9, No. 1, pp. 75-85.)

Mister, William G. "Note On The Interpretation Of Standard Cost Variances," **JAED**, 1983, Vol. 1, No. 2, pp. 51-56.

Mister, William G. (Bean, Virginia L. and William G. Mister. "A Partner In Residence Program At The University Of Colorado For National Accountancy Firms," **AR**, 1978, Vol. 53, No. 1, pp. 139-142.)

Mister, William G. (Cummings, Barbara K., Nicholas G. Apostolou and William G. Mister. "Accounting For Interest Rate Swaps: An Emerging Issue," **ACCHOR**, 1987, Vol. 1, No. 2, pp. 19-24.)

Mister, William G. (Gaither, Norman, Donald R. Fraser and William G. Mister. "Accounting For Inventory Carrying Costs," **JCA**, 1987, Vol. 4, No. 1, pp. 1-6.)

Mister, William G. (Harper, Robert M., Jr., William G. Mister and Jerry R. Strawser. "The Impact Of New Pension Disclosure Rules On Perception Of Debt," **JAR**, 1987, Vol. 25, No. 2, pp. 327-330.)

Mitchell, Bert N. "Materiality In Financial Statement Preparation - The Auditors' Dilemma," **CPAJ**, 1972, Vol. 42, No. 8, pp. 644-650.

Mitchell, Bert N. "The Black Minority In The CPA Profession," **JOA**, 1969, Vol. 128, No. 4, pp. 41-48.

Mitchell, Bert N. "The Status Of The Black CPA - An Update," **JOA**, 1976, Vol. 141, No. 5, pp. 52-58.

Mitchell, Falconer. "High School Accounting And Student Performance In The First Level University Accounting Course: A UK Study," **JAED**, 1988, Vol. 6, No. 2, pp. 279-291.

Mitchell, F. "School Accounting Qualifications And Student Performance In First Level University Accounting Examinations," **ABR**, 1984-85, Vol. 15, No. 58, pp. 81-86.

Mitchell, Gibson E. "The Make-Or-Buy Decision - A Case Study," **MA**, 1967, Vol. 49, No. 3, pp. 41-51.

Mitchell, G. B. "After-Tax Cost Of Leasing," **AR**, 1970, Vol. 45, No. 2, pp. 308-314.

Mitchell, G. B. "Breakeven Analysis And Capital Budgeting," **JAR**, 1969, Vol. 7, No. 2, pp. 332-338.

Mitchell, James A. "A Practical Cost System For The Small Manufacturer," **JOA**, 1954, Vol. 98, No. 4, pp. 478-482.

Mitchell, John E. (Akresh, Abraham D., John E. Mitchell and Howard S. Sibelman. "Obtaining Value From An Audit," **CA**, 1987, Vol. 5, No. 1, pp. 15-18.)

Mitchell, John E. (Read, William J., John E. Mitchell and Abraham D. Akresh. "Planning Materiality And SAS No. 47," **JOA**, 1987, Vol. 164, No. 6, pp. 72-79.)

Mitchell, John R. "The Do's And Don'ts Of Management Advisory Services," **CPAJ**, 1972, Vol. 42, No. 10, pp. 831-836.

Mitchell, Wiley S. "Relationship Of Laws Of Learning To Methods Of Accounting Instruction," **AR**, 1963, Vol. 38, No. 2, pp. 411-414.

Mitchem Cheryl. (Hull, Rita P. and Cheryl Mitchem. "Practitioners' Views On Communications Between Predecessor And Successor Auditors And Accountants," **ACCHOR**, 1987, Vol. 1, No. 1, pp. 61-70.)

Mitroff, I. I. and R. O. Mason. "Can We Design Systems For Managing Messes? Or, Why So Many Management Information Systems Are Uninformative," **AOS**, 1983, Vol. 8, No. 2/3, pp. 195-204.

Mittelstaedt, H. Fred. (DeBerg, Curtis L., H. Fred Mittelstaedt and Philip R. Regier. "Employers' Accounting For Pensions: A Theoretical Approach To Financial Accounting Standards No. 87," **JAED**, 1987, Vol. 5, No. 2, pp. 227-242.)

Mixon, Henry. (Austin, Kenneth R., Robert Strawser and Henry Mixon. "Contingencies And Unasserted Claims: Adequate Answers?," **CPAJ**, 1985, Vol. 55, No. 9, pp. 48-58.)

Mlynarczyk, Francis A., Jr. "An Empirical Study Of Accounting Methods And Stock Prices," **JAR**, 1969, Vol. 7, Supp., pp. 63-81.

Mlynarczyk, F. A. (Comiskey, Eugene E. and F. A. Mlynarczyk. "Recognition Of Income By Finance Companies," **AR**, 1968, Vol. 43, No. 2, pp. 248-256.)

Mobley, Sybil C. "Measures Of Income," **AR**, 1968, Vol. 43, No. 2, pp. 333-341.

Mobley, Sybil C. "Revenue Experience As A Guide To Asset Valuation," **AR**, 1967, Vol. 42, No. 1, pp. 114-123.

Mobley, Sybil C. "The Challenges Of Socio-Economic Accounting," **AR**, 1970, Vol. 45, No. 4, pp. 762-768.

Mobley, Sybil C. "The Realization Concept: A Useful Device," **AR**, 1966, Vol. 41, No. 2, pp. 292-296.

Mock, Edward J. "Post-Completion Audits Of Capital Projects," **MA**, 1967, Vol. 49, No. 3, pp. 25-32.

Mock, Theodore J. and Arnold Wright. "Evaluating The Effectiveness Of Audit Procedures," **AJPT**, 1982-83, Vol. 2, No. 1, pp. 33-44.

Mock, Theodore J. and John J. Willingham. "An Improved

Method Of Documenting And Evaluating A System Of Internal Accounting Controls," **AJPT**, 1982-83, Vol. 2, No. 2, pp. 91-99.

Mock, Theodore J. and Miklos Antal Vasarhelyi. "A Synthesis Of The Information Economics And Lens Models," **JAR**, 1978, Vol. 16, No. 2, pp. 414-423.

Mock, Theodore J. "A Decision Tree Approach To The Methodological Decision Process," **AR**, 1972, Vol. 47, No. 4, pp. 826-829.

Mock, Theodore J. "Comparative Values Of Information Structures," **JAR**, 1969, Vol. 7, Supp., pp. 124-159.

Mock, Theodore J. "Concepts Of Information Value And Accounting: A Reply," **AR**, 1973, Vol. 48, No. 2, pp. 394-397.

Mock, Theodore J. "Concepts Of Information Value And Accounting," **AR**, 1971, Vol. 46, No. 4, pp. 765-778.

Mock, Theodore J. "The Value Of Budget Information," **AR**, 1973, Vol. 48, No. 3, pp. 520-534.

Mock, Theodore J. (Bedard, Jean, Glen L. Gray and Theodore J. Mock. "Decision Support Systems And Auditing," **AIA**, 1984, Vol. 1, pp. 239-266.)

Mock, Theodore J. (Biggs, Stanley F., Theodore J. Mock and Paul R. Watkins. "Auditor's Use Of Analytical Review In Audit Program Design," **AR**, 1988, Vol. 63, No. 1, pp. 148-161.)

Mock, Theodore J. (Biggs, Stanley F. and Theodore J. Mock. "An Investigation Of Auditor Decision Processes In The Evaluation Of Internal Controls And Audit Scope Decisions," **JAR**, 1983, Vol. 21, No. 1, pp. 234-255.)

Mock, Theodore J. (Driver, Michael J. and Theodore J. Mock. "Human Information Processing, Decison Style Theory And Accounting Information Systems: A Reply," **AR**, 1977, Vol. 52, No. 4, pp. 988-990.)

Mock, Theodore J. (Lin, W. Thomas, Theodore J. Mock and Arnold Wright. "The Use Of The Analytic Hierarchy Process As An Aid In Planning The Nature And Extent Of Audit Procedures," **AJPT**, 1984-85, Vol. 4, No. 1, pp. 89-99.)

Mock, Theodore J. (Pincus, Karen V., William W. Holder and Theodore J. Mock. "The SEC And Fraudulent Financial Reporting," **RIAR**, 1988, Vol. 2, pp. 167-185.)

Mock, Theodore J. (Turner, Jerry L. and Theodore J. Mock. "Economic Considerations In Designing Audit Programs," **JOA**, 1980, Vol. 149, No. 3, pp. 65-74.)

Mock, Theodore J. (Wright, Arnold and Theodore J. Mock. "Towards A Contingency View Of Audit Evidence," **AJPT**, 1985-86, Vol. 5, No. 1, pp. 91-100.)

Mock, Theodore J., Teviah L. Estrin and Miklos A. Vasarhelyi. "Learning Patterns, Decision Approach, And Value Of Information," **JAR**, 1972, Vol. 10, No. 1, pp. 129-153.

Mock, Theodore. (Driver, Michael and Theodore Mock. "Human Information Processing, Decision Style Theory, And Accounting Information," **AR**, 1975, Vol. 50, No. 3, pp. 490-508.)

Mock, T. J. (Grove, H. D., T. J. Mock and K. B. Ehrenreich. "A Review Of Human Resource Accounting Measurement Systems From A Measurement Theory Perspective," **AOS**, 1977, Vol. 2, No. 3, pp. 219-236.)

Modenbach, Donald J. (Black, Thomas N., and Donald J. Modenbach. "Profit Planning For Action And Results," **MA**, 1971, Vol. 52, No. 7, pp. 9-13.)

Modisette, James P. "Audit Practice Set Grading Guide," **AR**, 1973, Vol. 48, No. 1, pp. 170-171.

Moe, Thomas O. "Tax Basics Of Buying And Selling A Corporation," **JOA**, 1984, Vol. 157, No. 3, pp. 83-90.

Moellenberndt, Richard A. (Cardullo, J. Patrick and Richard A. Moellenberndt. "The Cost Allocation Problem In A Telecommunications Company," **MA**, 1987, Vol. 69, No. 3, pp. 39-44.)

Moffie, R. P. (Blocher, E., R. P. Moffie and R. W. Zmud. "Report Format And Task Complexity: Interaction In Risk Judgments," **AOS**, 1986, Vol. 11, No. 6, pp. 457-470.)

Moffit, J. Weldon. (Hardy, John W., Bryce B. Orton and J. Weldon Moffit. "Bonus Systems DO Motivate," **MA**, 1986, Vol. 68, No. 5, pp. 58-61.)

Mogis, Robert C. and Donald Rogoff. "Statistics Offers A Solution To Tomorrow's Auditing Complexities," **AR**, 1962, Vol. 37, No. 4, pp. 704-707.

Mohr, Rosanne M. and Steven C. Dilley. "Current Cost And ACRS Depreciation Expense: A Comparison," **AR**, 1984, Vol. 59, No. 4, pp. 690-701.

Mohr, Rosanne M. "The Segmental Reporting Issue: A Review Of The Empirical Research," **JAL**, 1983, Vol. 2, pp. 39-72.

Mohr, Rosanne M. "Unconsolidated Finance Subsidiaries: Characteristics And Debt/Equity Effects," **ACCHOR**, 1988, Vol. 2, No. 1, pp. 27-34.

Moizer, Peter and Jamie Pratt. "The Evaluation Of Performance In Firms Of Chartered Accountants," **ABR**, 1988, Vol. 18, No. 71, pp. 227-237.

Moizer, Peter and John Arnold. "Share Appraisal By Investment Analysts - Portfolio Vs. Non-Portfolio Managers," **ABR**, 1983-84, Vol. 14, No. 56, pp. 341-348.

Moizer, Peter and Stuart Turley. "Surrogates For Audit Fees In Concentration Studies," **AJPT**, 1987-88, Vol. 7, No. 1, pp. 118-123.

Moizer, Peter, Stuart Turley and David Walker. "Reliance On Other Auditors: A UK Study," **ABR**, 1985-86, Vol. 16, No. 64, pp. 343-352.

Moizer, Peter. (Arnold, John and Peter Moizer. "A Survey Of The Methods Used By UK Investment Analysts To Appraise Investments In Ordinary Shares," **ABR**, 1983-84, Vol. 14, No. 55, pp. 195-208.)

Moizer, Peter. (Arnold, John., Peter Moizer and Eric Noreen. "Investment Appraisal Methods Of Financial

Analysts: A Comparative Study Of U.S. And U.K. Practices," **IJAER**, 1984, Vol. 19, No. 2, pp. 1-18.)

Mole, R. H. "An Analysis Of The Burden Of Corporation Tax Upon Investment Of Retained Profits In Plant And Machinery," **ABR**, 1986-87, Vol. 17, No. 68, pp. 311-318.

Mole, R. H. "Cost Volume Profit Analysis: A Tutorial And Microcomputer Implementation," **ABR**, 1985-86, Vol. 16, No. 62, pp. 165-170.

Moles, William A. "Selling The Accounting Services," **MA**, 1967, Vol. 49, No. 1, pp. 3-6.

Molinelli, James J. "A Computer Dilemma," **MA**, 1968, Vol. 50, No. 2, p. 21.

Moller, George. "The Multinational Executive: Patriot Or Traitor," **IJAER**, 1972, Vol. 7, No. 2, pp. 69-75.

Monahan, Thomas F. and Bill N. Schwartz. "Stock Dividends Vs. Stock Splits: Normative Vs. Descriptive Approaches To Accounting Education," **IAE**, 1986, Vol. 1, No. 1, pp. 123-131.

Monahan, Thomas F. and Lester Barenbaum. "The Use Of Constant Dollar Information To Predict Bond Rating Changes," **JAAF**, 1983, Vol. 6, No. 4, pp. 325-340.

Monahan, Thomas. (Barenbaum, Lester and Thomas Monahan. "Utilizing Terminal Values In Teaching Time Value Analysis," **JAED**, 1983, Vol. 1, No. 2, pp. 79-88.)

Moncur, Robert H. (Swieringa, Robert J. and Robert H. Moncur. "The Relationship Between Managers' Budget-Oriented Behavior And Selected Attitude, Position, Size, And Performance Measures," **JAR**, 1972, Vol. 10, Supp., pp. 194-209.)

Moncal, Chris. "Caution: RICO Can Hurt You," **MA**, 1985, Vol. 66, No. 10, pp. 62-65.

Monk, Harold L., Jr. and Kay W. Tatum. "Applying SAS No. 55 In Audits Of Small Businesses," **JOA**, 1988, Vol. 166, No. 5, pp. 40-56.

Monk, Harold L., Jr. (Ciesick, Robert T., Harold L. Monk, Jr., and Ernest J. Pavlock. "The National CPE Curriculum," **JOA**, 1985, Vol. 160, No. 4, pp. 118-124.)

Monson, Norman P. and John A. Tracy. "Stock Rights And Accounting Wrongs," **AR**, 1964, Vol. 39, No. 4, pp. 890-893.

Monteverde, Robert J. "Some Notes Of Reservation On The Use Of Sampling Tables In Auditing," **AR**, 1955, Vol. 30, No. 4, pp. 582-591.

Monteverde, Robert J. (Trueblood, Robert M. and Robert J. Monteverde. "A Bibliography On The Application Of Statistical Methods To Accounting And Auditing," **AR**, 1954, Vol. 29, No. 2, pp. 251-254.)

Monteverde, R. J. (Cyert, R. M., G. M. Hinckley and R. J. Monteverde. "Statistical Sampling In The Audit Of The Air Force Motor Vehicle Inventory," **AR**, 1960, Vol. 35, No. 4, pp. 667-673.)

Montgomery, John L. "Appraising Capital Expenditures," **MA**, 1965, Vol. 47, No. 1, pp. 3-10.

Montgomery, Robert H. "The Curse Of Balancing," **JOA**, 1950, Vol. 90, No. 2, p. 127.

Moody, Lailani. (Hauworth, William P., II and Lailani Moody. "An Accountant's Option Primer: Puts And Calls Demystified," **JOA**, 1987, Vol. 163, No. 1, pp. 87-97.)

Moody, Robert G. "Management Accounting Customer Service," **MA**, 1971, Vol. 52, No. 9, pp. 48-50.

Moody, Sharon M. and Dale L. Flesher. "Analysis Of FASB Voting Patterns: Statement Nos. 1-86," **JAAF**, 1986, Vol. 1 (New Series), No. 4, pp. 319-330.

Moon, James E. (Fulmer, John G., Jr. and James E. Moon. "Tests For Common Stock Equivalency," **JAAF**, 1984, Vol. 8, No. 1, pp. 5-14.)

Moon, Philip. "Competitive Tendering And Under-Capacity: An Incident Process Case," **IAE**, 1988, Vol. 3, No. 2, pp. 445-452.

Moonitz, Maurice and Alexander Russ. "Accrual Accounting For Employers' Pension Costs," **JAR**, 1966, Vol. 4, No. 2, pp. 155-168.

Moonitz, Maurice and Carl L. Nelson. "Recent Developments In Accounting Theory," **AR**, 1960, Vol. 35, No. 2, pp. 206-217.

Moonitz, Maurice and E. Carey Brown. "The Annuity Method Of Estimating Depreciation," **AR**, 1939, Vol. 14, No. 4, pp. 424-429.

Moonitz, Maurice. "Adaptations To Price-Level Changes," **AR**, 1948, Vol. 23, No. 2, pp. 137-147.

Moonitz, Maurice. "Can Laws Coerce Accounting?," **JAR**, 1967, Vol. 5, No. 1, pp. 129-130.

Moonitz, Maurice. "Chambers At The American Institute Of Certified Public Accountants," **ABACUS**, 1982, Vol. 18, No. 2, pp. 106-111.

Moonitz, Maurice. "Chambers On The Price Level Study," **ABACUS**, 1967, Vol. 3, No. 1, pp. 55-61.

Moonitz, Maurice. "Functions Of The Written Examination," **AR**, 1949, Vol. 24, No. 4, pp. 432-435.

Moonitz, Maurice. "Income Taxes In Financial Statements," **AR**, 1957, Vol. 32, No. 2, pp. 175-183.

Moonitz, Maurice. "Inventories And The Statement Of Funds," **AR**, 1943, Vol. 18, No. 3, pp. 262-265.

Moonitz, Maurice. "Price-Level Accounting And Scales Of Measurement," **AR**, 1970, Vol. 45, No. 3, pp. 465-475.

Moonitz, Maurice. "Reporting On The Flow Of Funds," **AR**, 1956, Vol. 31, No. 3, pp. 375-385.

Moonitz, Maurice. "Should We Discard The Income Concept?," **AR**, 1962, Vol. 37, No. 2, pp. 175-180.

Moonitz, Maurice. "Some Reflections On The Investment Credit Experience," **JAR**, 1966, Vol. 4, No. 1, pp. 47-61.

Moonitz, Maurice. "The Case Against Lifo," **JOA**, 1953, Vol. 95, No. 6, pp. 682-690.

Moonitz, Maurice. "The Changing Concept Of Liabilities," **JOA**, 1960, Vol. 109, No. 5, pp. 41-46.

Moonitz, Maurice. "The Entity Approach To Consolidated Statements," **AR**, 1942, Vol. 17, No. 3, pp. 236-242.

Moonitz, Maurice. "Three Contributions To The Development Of Accounting Principles Prior To 1930," **JAR**, 1970, Vol. 8, No. 1, pp. 145-155.

Moonitz, Maurice. "Why Do We Need 'Postulates' And 'Principles'?," **JOA**, 1963, Vol. 116, No. 6, pp. 42-46.

Moonitz, Maurice. (Stamp, Edward and Maurice Moonitz. "International Auditing Standards - Part I," **CPAJ**, 1982, Vol. 52, No. 6, pp. 24-33.)

Moonitz, Maurice. (Stamp, Edward and Maurice Moonitz. "International Auditing Standards - Part II," **CPAJ**, 1982, Vol. 52, No. 7, pp. 48-53.)

Moore, Carl L. "An Extension Of Break-Even Analysis," **MA**, 1969, Vol. 50, No. 9, pp. 55-58.

Moore, Carl L. "The Concept Of The P/V Graph Applied To Capital Investment Planning," **AR**, 1962, Vol. 37, No. 4, pp. 721-729.

Moore, Carl L. "The Present-Value Method And The Replacement Decision," **AR**, 1964, Vol. 39, No. 1, pp. 94-102.

Moore, Charles N. "Some Experience In Teaching Electronic Data Processing Without A Computer," **AR**, 1961, Vol. 36, No. 2, pp. 297-299.

Moore, Francis E. "An Auditing Teacher Looks At The CPA Examination In Auditing," **AR**, 1947, Vol. 22, No. 1, pp. 6-11.

Moore, Giora. "Depreciation, Inflation And Capital Replacement," **CAR**, 1986-87, Vol. 3, No. 2, pp. 375-393.

Moore, Giora. (Kim, Moshe and Giora Moore. "Economic Vs. Accounting Depreciation," **JAEC**, 1988, Vol. 10, No. 2, pp. 111-125.)

Moore, James. "Push-Down Accounting: FAS 200?," **MA**, 1988, Vol. 70, No. 5, pp. 53-58.

Moore, Laurence J. and David F. Scott, Jr. "Long-Range Planning And The Decentralized Firm," **MA**, 1971, Vol. 53, No. 5, pp. 35-39.

Moore, Michael L. and Stephen Buzby. "The Quality Of Corporate Financial Disclosure: A Comment," **AR**, 1972, Vol. 47, No. 3, pp. 581-584.

Moore, Michael L. "Management Changes And Discretionary Accounting Decisions," **JAR**, 1973, Vol. 11, No. 1, pp. 100-107.

Moore, Michael L. (Copeland, Ronald M. and Michael L. Moore. "Actual Use Of Specialized Accounting Statements," **AR**, 1968, Vol. 43, No. 2, pp. 384-386.)

Moore, Michael L. (Copeland, Ronald M. and Michael L. Moore. "Validity Of The 1966 Tax Model As A Research Tool," **AR**, 1972, Vol. 47, No. 2, pp. 395-396.)

Moore, Michael L. (Swenson, Charles W. and Michael L. Moore. "Use Of Input-Output Analysis In Tax Research," **AIT**, 1987, Vol. 1, pp. 49-84.)

Moore, Michael L., Bert M. Steece and Charles W. Swenson. "An Analysis Of The Impact Of State Income Tax Rates And Bases On Foreign Investment," **AR**, 1987, Vol. 62, No. 4, pp. 671-685.

Moore, Michael L., Bert M. Steece and Charles W. Swenson. "Some Empirical Evidence On Taxpayer Rationality," **AR**, 1985, Vol. 60, No. 1, pp. 18-32.

Moore, Michael R. "A Management Audit Of The EDP Center," **MA**, 1968, Vol. 49, No. 7, pp. 23-32.

Moore, Michael R. "Advancing Computer Auditing In The Seventies," **CPAJ**, 1972, Vol. 42, No. 9, pp. 729-734.

Moore, Michael R. "Professional Development: The Future Is Now," **JOA**, 1973, Vol. 135, No. 5, pp. 38-47.

Moore, P. Michael, Thomas H. Oxner and Jimie Kusel. "Determining Common Stock Equivalency Of Convertible Securities: A Teaching Approach," **IAE**, 1987, Vol. 2, No. 1, pp. 152-156.

Moore, Virginia M. (Marquis, Linda M. and Virginia M. Moore. "Proposed Federal Computer Systems Protection Act," **CPAJ**, 1980, Vol. 50, No. 12, pp. 29-32.)

Moore, Winsor C. "Taxation Of Treasury Stock Dividends," **JOA**, 1954, Vol. 97, No. 2, pp. 179-187.

Moores, C. Tommy. (Munter, Paul H., Ronald K. Clancy and C. Tommy Moores. "Accounting For Financial Futures: The Question Of Risk Reduction," **AIA**, 1986, Vol. 3, pp. 51-70.)

Moores, Ken. (Duncan, Keith and Ken Moores. "Usefulness Of CCA Information For Investor Decision Making: A Laboratory Experiment," **ABR**, 1988, Vol. 18, No. 70, pp. 121-132.)

Moores, K. and G. T. Steadman. "The Comparative Viewpoints Of Groups Of Accountants: More On The Entity-Proprietary Debate," **AOS**, 1986, Vol. 11, No. 1, pp. 19-34.

Moores, Tommy and Gary E. White. "Perceptions Of The Control And Effectiveness Of Schools Of Accountancy," **IAE**, 1985, No. 1, pp. 20-27.

Moores, Tommy. (Munter, Paul and Tommy Moores. "Transfers Of Receivables With Recourse," **CPAJ**, 1984, Vol. 54, No. 7, pp. 52-60.)

Moores, Tommy. (Munter, Paul, Donald K. Clancy and Tommy Moores. "Accounting For Futures Contracts," **CPAJ**, 1985, Vol. 55, No. 3, pp. 18-25.)

Mora, Ricardo E., Jr. "The Accounting Profession In Mexico - And Why," **IJAER**, 1972, Vol. 8, No. 1, pp. 17-24.

Moraglio, Joseph F. "Improve The Federal Governments Financial Management," **CPAJ**, 1988, Vol. 58, No. 11, pp. 46-57.

Moraglio, Joseph F. (Broadus, W. A., Jr. and Joseph F. Moraglio. "Governmental Audit Standards: A New Perspective," **JOA**, 1982, Vol. 153, No. 5, pp. 80-90.)

Moraglio, Joseph F. (Buchholz, David L. and Joseph F. Moraglio. "IRS Access To Auditors' Work Papers: The Supreme Court Decision," **JOA**, 1984, Vol. 158, No. 3, pp. 91-107.)

Moraglio, Joseph F. (Meinhardt, Joan, Joseph F. Moraglio and Harold I. Steinberg. "Governmental Audits: An Action Plan For Excellence," **JOA**, 1987, Vol. 164, No. 1, pp. 86-91.)

Moran, Mark and Gary John Previts. "The SEC And The Profession, 1934-84: The Realities Of Self-Regulation," **JOA**, 1984, Vol. 158, No. 1, pp. 68-83.

Morash, Edward A. (Enis, Charles R. and Edward A. Morash. "Accounting For Public Policy Actions: The Case Of Motor Carrier Deregulation," **ABACUS**, 1985, Vol. 21, No. 1, pp. 63-83.)

Moravy, L. Joe. (Hauworth, William P. and L. Joe Moravy. "Accounting For Expanded Use Of Option Transactions," **CPAJ**, 1987, Vol. 57, No. 5, pp. 56-65.)

Morehead, C. Richard. (Dasburg, John H. and C. Richard Morehead. "Can GAAP Still Support Inventory Valuation After Thor?," **JOA**, 1979, Vol. 148, No. 4, pp. 68-77.)

Moreno, Rafael Garcia. "The Unification Of The Professional Teaching Of Accounting In The Americas," **AR**, 1964, Vol. 39, No. 4, pp. 990-995.

Morey, Lloyd. "Accounting Principles For Nonprofit Enterprises," **JOA**, 1951, Vol. 91, No. 4, pp. 562-565.

Morey, Lloyd. "Accounting Procedures For Universities And Colleges," **AR**, 1932, Vol. 7, No. 1, pp. 54-60.

Morey, Lloyd. "Better Applications Of Recognized Principles Would Improve University Accounting," **JOA**, 1950, Vol. 90, No. 3, pp. 201-210.

Morey, Lloyd. "Financial Reporting In The Federal Government," **AR**, 1942, Vol. 17, No. 2, pp. 73-81.

Morey, Lloyd. "Finding Correct Principles Of Public Accounts," **AR**, 1927, Vol. 2, No. 3, pp. 213-222.

Morey, Lloyd. "Fund And Property Accounts In Governmental Accounting," **AR**, 1926, Vol. 1, No. 2, pp. 77-84.

Morey, Lloyd. "Greater Recognition Is Needed Of Applicable Principles In Governmental And Institutional Accounting," **AR**, 1958, Vol. 33, No. 3, pp. 469-471.

Morey, Lloyd. "Illinois Finances," **JOA**, 1957, Vol. 103, No. 4, pp. 37-41.

Morey, Lloyd. "Illinois Municipal Audit Law Contains Best Current Practices," **JOA**, 1952, Vol. 94, No. 2, pp. 195-197.

Morey, Lloyd. "National Committee Issues Guide For Municipal Accounting," **JOA**, 1952, Vol. 94, No. 5, pp. 594-601.

Morey, Lloyd. "Principles Of Municipal Accounting," **AR**, 1934, Vol. 9, No. 4, pp. 319-325.

Morey, Lloyd. "Progress Of The Independent Post Audit Program In Illinois," **AR**, 1963, Vol. 38, No. 1, pp. 102-108.

Morey, Lloyd. "Remarks Before Annual Meeting Of American Accounting Association," **AR**, 1955, Vol. 30, No. 1, pp. 25-26.

Morey, Lloyd. "Trends In Governmental Accounting," **AR**, 1948, Vol. 23, No. 3, pp. 227-234.

Morey, Lloyd. (Littleton, A. C., Lloyd Morey, David Himmelblau and F. E. Ross. "The International Congress On Accounting," **AR**, 1929, Vol. 4, No. 4, pp. 234-246.)

Morey, Richard C. (Capettini, Robert, David A. Dittman and Richard C. Morey. "Reimbursement Rate Setting For Medicaid Prescription Drugs Based On Relative Efficiencies," **JAPP**, 1985, Vol. 4, No. 2, pp. 83-110.)

Morgan, E. A. (Williams, J. J., J. D. Newton and E. A. Morgan. "The Integration Of Zero-Based Budgeting With Management-By-Objectives: An Empirical Inquiry," **AOS**, 1985, Vol. 10, No. 4, pp. 457-478.)

Morgan, Alan M. "Computer Selection Processes," **MA**, 1977, Vol. 58, No. 11, pp. 39-42.

Morgan, Dana Smith and Fred W. Morgan. "How Confimation Reporting Can Be Applied To Market Control Systems," **MA**, 1980, Vol. 61, No. 7, pp. 26-28.

Morgan, Fred W. (Morgan, Dana Smith and Fred W. Morgan. "How Confimation Reporting Can Be Applied To Market Control Systems," **MA**, 1980, Vol. 61, No. 7, pp. 26-28.)

Morgan, G. "Accounting As Reality Construction: Towards A New Epistemology For Accounting Practice," **AOS**, 1988, Vol. 13, No. 5, pp. 477-485.

Morgan, G. "Social Science And Accounting Research: A Commentary On Tomkins And Groves," **AOS**, 1983, Vol. 8, No. 4, pp. 385-388.

Morgan, G. (Davis, S. W., K. Menon and G. Morgan. "The Images That Have Shaped Accounting Theory," **AOS**, 1982, Vol. 7, No. 4, pp. 307-318.)

Morgan, John R. and Colin Robinson. "The Comparative Effects Of The UK And Norwegian Oil Taxation Systems On Profitability And Government Revenue," **ABR**, 1976-77, Vol. 7, No. 25, pp. 2-16.

Morgan, Lee L. "Business Ethics Start With The Individual," **MA**, 1977, Vol. 58, No. 9, pp. 11-14.

Morgan, Robert A. "Regulation, Deregulation Or Self-Regulation?," **MA**, 1981, Vol. 63, No. 4, pp. 54-55.

Morgan, Robert A. "The Bottom Line: Part II," **MA**, 1985, Vol. 67, No. 2, pp. 62-67.

Morgan, Robert A. "The Bottom Line: Part IV," **MA**, 1985, Vol. 67, No. 6, pp. 67-69.

Morgan, Robert A. "The Bottom Line: Part I," **MA**, 1985, Vol. 67, No. 1, pp. 32-38.

Morgan, Robert A. "The Bottom Line: Part III," **MA**, 1985, Vol. 67, No. 3, pp. 51-53.

Morgan, Robert A. "The Multinational Enterprise And Its Accounting Needs," **IJAER**, 1967, Vol. 3, No. 1, pp. 21-28.

Morgan, Robert G. (Benjamin, James J., Paul E. Dascher and Robert G. Morgan. "How Corporate Controllers View The Foreign Corrupt Practices Act," **MA**, 1979, Vol. 60, No. 12, pp. 43-45.)

Morgan, Robert G. (Campbell, David R. and Robert G. Morgan.

"Publication Activity Of Promoted Accounting Faculty," **IAE**, 1987, Vol. 2, No. 1, pp. 28-43.)

Morgan, Robert G. (Mecimore, Charles D. and Robert G. Morgan. "Flowcharting: An Effective Teaching Tool," **JAED**, 1983, Vol. 1, No. 2. pp. 163-167.)

Morgan, Robert G., Jalaleddin Soroosh and Charles J. Woelfel. "Are Ethics Dangerous To Your Job?," **MA**, 1985, Vol. 66, No. 8, pp. 24-32.

Morgan, W. F. "The Auditor's Report On Municipal Revenue Bonds," **JOA**, 1954, Vol. 97, No. 3, pp. 316-320.

Morgenson, David L. (Reilly, Frank K., David L. Morgenson and Marilyn West. "The Predictive Ability Of Alternative Parts Of Interim Financial Statements," **JAR**, 1972, Vol. 10, Supp., pp. 105-124.)

Moriarity, Shane and F. Hutton Barron. "A Judgment-Based Definition Of Materiality," **JAR**, 1979, Vol. 17, Supp., pp. 114-135.

Moriarity, Shane and F. Hutton Barron. "Modeling The Materiality Judgments Of Audit Partners," **JAR**, 1976, Vol. 14, No. 2, pp. 320-341.

Moriarity, Shane. "Another Approach To Allocating Joint Costs: A Reply," **AR**, 1976, Vol. 51, No. 3. pp. 686-687.

Moriarity, Shane. "Another Approach To Allocating Joint Costs," **AR**, 1975, Vol. 50, No. 4. pp. 791-795.

Moriarity, Shane. "Communicating Financial Information Through Multidimensional Graphics," **JAR**, 1979, Vol. 17, No. 1, pp. 205-224.

Moriarity, Shane. (Elikai, Fara and Shane Moriarity. "Variance Analysis With PERT/COST," **AR**, 1982, Vol. 57, No. 1, pp. 161-170.)

Morison, Arthur. "Independence Of The Auditor," **CPAJ**, 1977, Vol. 47, No. 12, pp. 33-36.

Morison, A. M. C. "A Model For Accounting For Inflation," **ABR**, 1974-75, Vol. 5, No. 17. pp. 41-52.

Morley, James E., Jr. "Cash Management - Working For The Extra 1% Or 2%," **MA**, 1978, Vol. 60, No. 4. pp. 17-22.

Morley, Michael F. "The Value Added Statement In Britain," **AR**, 1979, Vol. 54, No. 3, pp. 618-629.

Morrill, Thomas C. "Uniform Expense Accounting In Fire Insurance Industry," **JOA**, 1951, Vol. 92, No. 5, pp. 552-561.

Morris, Augustus. "Discount Bonds Are Useful As Tax-Planning Instruments," **JOA**, 1953, Vol. 95, No. 3, pp. 305-309.

Morris, Augustus. "Getting Maximum Tax Savings For Farmers," **JOA**, 1950, Vol. 89, No. 6, pp. 490-495.

Morris, Deigan. (Chenhall, Robert H. and Deigan Morris. "The Impact Of Structure, Environment, And Interdependence On The Perceived Usefulness Of Management Accounting Systems," **AR**, 1986, Vol. 61, No. 1, pp. 16-35.)

Morris, Edwin R. "The Role Of The Accountant In Direct-Placement Financing," **JOA**, 1954, Vol. 98, No. 1, pp. 82-88.

Morris, John S. (Tersine, Richard J. and John S. Morris. "Materials Management: Futuristic Orientations," **JCA**, 1984, Vol. 1, No. 1, pp. 115-130.)

Morris, Michael H. and James L. Wittenbach. "The First Year Of Safe Harbor Leasing Activity: A Look At Objectives And Results," **AIT**, 1987, Vol. 1, pp. 131-152.

Morris, Michael H. and William D. Nichols. "Pension Accounting And The Balance Sheet: The Potential Effect Of The FASB's Preliminary Views," **JAAF**, 1984, Vol. 7, No. 4, pp. 293-305.

Morris, Michael H. and William D. Nichols. "The Election To Capitalize Carrying Charges Following ERTA And TEFRA," **JATA**, 1984, Vol. 5, No. 2, pp. 60-67.

Morris, Michael H. and William D. Nichols. "Consistency Exceptions: Materiality Judgments And Audit Firm Structure," **AR**, 1988, Vol. 63, No. 2, pp. 237-254.

Morris, Michael H. (McDonald, Bill and Michael H. Morris. "The Functional Specifications Of Financial Ratios: An Empirical Examination," **ABR**, 1984-85, Vol. 15, No. 59, pp. 223-228.)

Morris, Michael H. (McDonald, Bill and Michael H. Morris. "The Relevance Of SFAS 33 Inflation Accounting Disclosures In The Adjustment Of Stock Prices To Inflation," **AR**, 1984, Vol. 59, No. 3, pp. 432-446.)

Morris, Michael H. (Pattillo, James W., Michael H. Morris and William D. Nichols. "The Materiality Principle: Problems And Possible Solutions," **CA**, 1983, Vol. 1, No. 3, pp. 44-51.)

Morris, Peter F. "Widget Pricing," **MA**, 1969, Vol. 51, No. 6, pp. 12-14.

Morris, Richard D. "Corporate Disclosure In A Substantially Unregulated Environment," **ABACUS**, 1984, Vol. 20, No. 1, pp. 52-86.

Morris, Richard D. "Lee V. Neuchatel Asphalte Company (1889) And Depreciation Accounting: Two Empirical Studies," **ABR**, 1986-87, Vol. 17, No. 65, pp. 71-82.

Morris, Richard D. "Signalling, Agency Theory And Accounting Policy Choice," **ABR**, 1987-88, Vol. 18, No. 69, pp. 47-56.

Morris, R. C. and G. H. Breakwell. "Manipulation Of Earnings Figures In The United Kingdom," **ABR**, 1974-75, Vol. 5, No. 19, pp. 177-184.

Morris, R. C. "Evidence Of The Impact Of Inflation Accounting On Share Prices," **ABR**, 1974-75, Vol. 5, No. 18, pp. 82-90.

Morris, R. C. "Reporting The Performance Of Investment Intermediaries," **ABR**, 1981-82, Vol. 12, No. 47, pp. 163-174.

Morris, R. C. "The Comparability Of Oil Company Accounts: A Comment," **ABR**, 1975-76, Vol. 6, No. 21, pp. 70-78.

Morris, R. C. (Bhaskar, K. N. and R. C. Morris. "The Accuracy Of Brokers' Profits Forecasts In The UK," **ABR**, 1983-84, Vol. 14, No. 54, pp. 113-124.)

Morris, R. C. (Egginton, D. and R. C. Morris. "Holding Gains On Long-Term Liabilities: A Comment," **ABR**, 1975-76, Vol. 6, No. 23, pp. 177-181.)

Morris, Timothy. "A Different Approach To A Customer's Bankruptcy Reorganization," **CA**, 1986, Vol. 4, No. 2, pp. 39-44.

Morris, William and Hershel Anderson. "Audit Scope Adjustments For Internal Control," **CPAJ**, 1976, Vol. 46, No. 7, pp. 15-20.

Morris, William J. and Bernard A. Coda. "Marketable Equity Securities - Valuation Alternatives," **JOA**, 1973, Vol. 135, No. 1, pp. 48-54.

Morrison, Lloyd F. "Some Accounting Limitations Of Statement Interpretation," **AR**, 1952, Vol. 27, No. 4, pp. 490-495.

Morrison, Paul L. "Reports To Stockholders," **AR**, 1935, Vol. 10, No. 1, pp. 77-83.

Morrison, Paul L. "The Interest Of The Investor In Accounting Principles," **AR**, 1937, Vol. 12, No. 1, pp. 37-42.

Morrison, Thomas A. and Eugene Kaczka. "A New Application Of Calculus And Risk Analysis To Cost-Volume-Profit Changes," **AR**, 1969, Vol. 44, No. 2, pp. 330-343.

Morrison, Thomas A. and Stephen L. Buzby. "Effect Of The Investment Tax Credit On The Capitalize-Expense Decision," **AR**, 1968, Vol. 43, No. 3, pp. 517-521.

Morrison, Thomas A. "Taxation Of International Investments," **AR**, 1966, Vol. 41, No. 4, pp. 704-713.

Morrison, Thomas L. (Lucas, William H. and Thomas L. Morrison. "Management Accounting For Construction Contracts," **MA**, 1981, Vol. 63, No. 5. pp. 59-65.)

Morrissey, Leonard E., Jr. (Greer, Willis R., Jr. and Leonard E. Morrissey, Jr. "Accounting Rule-Making In A World Of Efficient Markets," **JAAF**, 1978, Vol. 2, No. 1. pp. 49-57.)

Morse, Dale and Gordon Richardson. "The LIFO/FIFO Decision," **JAR**, 1983, Vol. 21, No. 1, pp. 106-127.

Morse, Dale and Neal Ushman. "The Effect Of Information Announcements On The Market Microstructure," **AR**, 1983, Vol. 58. No. 2, pp. 247-258.

Morse, Dale. "An Econometric Analysis Of The Choice Of Daily Versus Monthly Returns In Tests Of Information Content," **JAR**, 1984, Vol. 22, No. 2, pp. 605-623.

Morse, Dale. "Price And Trading Volume Reaction Surrounding Earnings Announcements: A Closer Examination," **JAR**, 1981, Vol. 19, No. 2, pp. 374-383.

Morse, Dale. (Beaver, William, Richard Lambert and Dale Morse. "The Information Content Of Security Prices," **JAEC**, 1980, Vol. 2, No. 1, pp. 3-28.)

Morse, Dale. (Swieringa, Robert J. and Dale Morse. "Accounting For Hybrid Convertible Debentures," **AR**, 1985, Vol. 60, No. 1, pp. 127-133.)

Morse, Ellsworth H., Jr. "Comments On Survey Of Attitudes On Management Auditing," **AR**, 1973, Vol. 48, No. 1, pp. 120-122.

Morse, Ellsworth H., Jr. "GAO Audits Of Management Performance," **JOA**, 1961, Vol. 112, No. 4, pp. 42-48.

Morse, Ellsworth H., Jr. "Management Accounting In The Federal Government," **MA**, 1967, Vol. 48, No. 6, pp. 55-59.

Morse, Ellsworth H., Jr. "Performance And Operational Auditing," **JOA**, 1971, Vol. 131, No. 6, pp. 41-46.

Morse, Ellsworth H., Jr. "The Case For Accepting GAO Experience," **JOA**, 1960, Vol. 109, No. 6, pp. 60-64.

Morse, Ellsworth H., Jr. "The Joint Financial Management Improvement Program In The Federal Government," **AR**, 1961, Vol. 36, No. 3, pp. 362-373.

Morse, Wayne J. and Harold P. Roth. "Why Quality Costs Are Important," **MA**, 1987, Vol. 69, No. 5, pp. 42-43.

Morse, Wayne J. and Imogene A. Posey. "Income Taxes Do Make A Difference In C-V-P Analysis," **MA**, 1979, Vol. 61, No. 6, pp. 20-24.

Morse, Wayne J. (Roth, Harold P. and Wayne J. Morse. "What Are Your Client's Quality Costs?," **CPAJ**, 1988, Vol. 58, No. 4, pp. 54-63.)

Morse, Wayne J. and James H. Scheiner. "Cost Minimisation, Return On Investment, Residual Income: Alternative Criteria For Inventory Models," **ABR**, 1978-79, Vol. 9, No. 36, pp. 320-324.

Morse, Wayne J. "A Note On The Relationship Between Human Assets And Human Capital," **AR**, 1973, Vol. 48, No. 3, pp. 589-593.

Morse, Wayne J. "Estimating The Human Capital Associated With An Organization," **ABR**, 1975-76, Vol. 6, No. 21, pp. 48-56.

Morse, Wayne J. "Reporting Production Costs That Follow The Learning Curve Phenomenon," **AR**, 1972, Vol. 47, No. 4, pp. 761-773.

Morse, Wayne J. "The Use Of Learning Curves In Financial Accounting," **CPAJ**, 1974, Vol. 44, No. 1, pp. 51-57.

Morse, Wayne J. "Toward A Model For Human Resource Valuation: A Comment," **AR**, 1975, Vol. 50, No. 2. pp. 345-347.

Morse, Wayne J. (Harmon, W. Ken, Kay M. Poston and Wayne J. Morse. "Improving Cost Recovery From Federal Grants And Contracts," **JCA**, 1986, Vol. 3, No. 1, pp. 1-12.)

Morse, Wayne J. (Roth, Harold P. and Wayne J. Morse. "Let's Help Measure And Report Quality Costs," **MA**, 1983, Vol. 65, No. 2, pp. 50-54.)

Morsicato, Helen G. and Lee H. Radebaugh. "Internal Performance Evaluation Of Multinational Enterprise Operations," **IJAER**, 1979, Vol. 15, No. 1, pp. 77-94.

Morsicato, Helen G. and Michael A. Diamond. "An Approach To

'Environmentalizing' MNE Performance Evaluation Systems," **IJAER**, 1980, Vol. 16. No. 1, pp. 247-266.

Mortensen, Clair M. "Estate & Trust Taxation From CPA's Point Of View," **JOA**, 1953, Vol. 96, No. 2. pp. 206-211.

Morton, James R. "DR Scott," **AHJ**, 1974, Vol. 1, No. 1-4, pp. 27-29.

Morton, James R. "Qualitative Objectives Of Financial Accounting: A Comment On Relevance And Understandability," **JAR**, 1974, Vol. 12, No. 2, pp. 288-298.

Morton, Sanford. (Filimon, Radu, Sanford Morton and Soliman Y. Soliman. "Spoilage With A Production Function," **ABR**, 1986-87, Vol. 17, No. 68, pp. 337-348.)

Mory, Kenneth J. "Accounting For Regulated Operations: FASB Statement no. 71," **JOA**, 1984, Vol. 158, No. 2, pp. 84-97.

Mory, Kenneth J. "How South Central Bell Confirms Accounts Receivable," **MA**, 1983, Vol. 65, No. 2, pp. 40-43.

Mory, Kenneth J. (Tanju, Murat N. and Kenneth J. Mory. "How South Central Bell Handles Inflation Accounting," **MA**, 1982, Vol. 64, No. 1, pp. 54-58.)

Mosconi, William. (McNair, C. J. and William Mosconi. "Measuring Performance In An Advanced Manufacturing Environment," **MA**, 1987, Vol. 69, No. 1, pp. 28-31.)

Moscove, Stephen A. "Accountants' Legal Liability," **MA**, 1977, Vol. 58, No. 11, pp. 25-26.

Moseley, Roger. "The Controller: A Mythical Executive?," **MA**, 1972, Vol. 53, No. 9, pp. 42-44.

Moseman, Verne R. "Disaster Planning For CPAs," **JOA**, 1976, Vol. 141, No. 6, pp. 54-56.

Moser, S. Thomas. "Sensitive Corporate Actions: Toward A Resolution," **CPAJ**, 1977, Vol. 47, No. 4, pp. 17-22.

Moses, O. Douglas. "Factors Explaining Performance In Graduate Level Accounting," **IAE**, 1987, Vol. 2, No. 2, pp. 281-291.

Moses, O. Douglas. "Income Smoothing And Incentives: Empirical Tests Using Accounting Changes," **AR**, 1987, Vol. 62, No. 2, pp. 358-377.

Mosher, Roy G. "Employee Benefit Plans: Their Adoption And Operation," **JOA**, 1965, Vol. 119, No. 3, pp. 36-42.

Mosich, A. N. "Henry Whitcomb Sweeney," **AHJ**, 1974, Vol. 1, No. 1-4, pp. 25-27.

Mosich, A. N. "Impact Of Merger Accounting On Post-Merger Financial Reports," **MA**, 1965, Vol. 47, No. 4, pp. 21-28.

Mosich, A. N. "Ingenuity In Auditing," **AR**, 1967, Vol. 42, No. 2, pp. 369-371.

Moskowitz, Jerald I. "What's Your Business Worth?," **MA**, 1988, Vol. 69, No. 9, pp. 30-36.

Mosler, Stanley D. "A Value Added Base For G&A On Government Contracts," **MA**, 1970, Vol. 52. No. 6, pp. 45-48.

Moss, Kermit C. "Admission Of A Partner - Step By Step," **AR**, 1960, Vol. 35, No. 1, pp. 123-125.

Moss, Kermit C. "Paper Grading - An Accounting Instructor's Dilemma," **AR**, 1957, Vol. 32, No. 1, pp. 125-127.

Moss, Kermit C. "Practice Set Procedures In American Colleges And Universities," **AR**, 1957, Vol. 32, No. 4, pp. 650-652.

Moss, Morton F. and Wilber C. Haseman. "Some Comments On The Applicability Of Direct Costing To Decision Making," **AR**, 1957, Vol. 32, No. 2, pp. 184-193.

Moss, Morton F. "Management Services And The CPA Examination," **AR**, 1962, Vol. 37, No. 4, pp. 730-740.

Moss, Morton F. "The Presentation Of Errors In Valuation," **AR**, 1954, Vol. 29, No. 2, pp. 308-310.

Mosso, David. "Standards Overload - No Simple Solution," **CPAJ**, 1983, Vol. 53, No. 10, pp. 12-23.

Most, Kenneth S. and Arthur Lee Winters. "Focus On Standard Setting - From Trueblood To The FASB," **JOA**, 1977, Vol. 143, No. 2, pp. 67-75.

Most, Kenneth S. "A Comparative Study Of The Accounts Of Seven Major Oil Companies," **ABR**. 1973-74. Vol. 4, No. 16, pp. 242-250.

Most, Kenneth S. "A New Method For Accounting For Oil And Gas Producers," **MA**, 1979, Vol. 60, No. 11, pp. 53-58.

Most, Kenneth S. "An Accountant Looks At Social Accounting," **ABR**, 1971-72, Vol. 2, No. 8, pp. 264-274.

Most, Kenneth S. "Depreciation Expense And The Effect Of Inflation," **JAR**, 1984, Vol. 22, No. 2, pp. 782-788.

Most, Kenneth S. "Gordon's Transfer Price Model For A Socialist Economy: A Comment," **AR**, 1971, Vol. 46, No. 4, pp. 779-782.

Most, Kenneth S. "How Wrong Was Sombart?," **AHJ**, 1976, Vol. 3, No. 1-4, pp. 22-28.

Most, Kenneth S. "Oil Company Accounting: Not So Comparable? A Reply," **ABR**, 1975-76, Vol. 6, No. 21, pp. 67-69.

Most, Kenneth S. "Sombart's Propositions Revisited," **AR**, 1972, Vol. 47, No. 4, pp. 722-734.

Most, Kenneth S. "Some Notes On The Obsolescence Of Accounting Textbooks," **AR**, 1974, Vol. 49, No. 3, pp. 598-600.

Most, Kenneth S. "The Cost Center Problem In The Oil Industry," **MA**, 1972, Vol. 54, No. 6, pp. 39-41.

Most, Kenneth S. "The French Accounting Experiment," **IJAER**, 1971, Vol. 7, No. 1, pp. 15-27.

Most, Kenneth S. "The Planning Hypothesis As A Basis For Accounting Theory," **ABACUS**, 1973, Vol. 9, No. 2, pp. 127-136.

Most, Kenneth S. "The Rise And Fall Of The Matching Principle," **ABR**, 1976-77, Vol. 7, No. 28, pp. 286-290.

Most, Kenneth S. "The Value Of Inventories," **JAR**, 1967, Vol. 5, No. 1, pp. 39-50.

Most, Kenneth S. "Two Forms Of Experimental Accounts," **AR**, 1969, Vol. 44, No. 1, pp. 145-152.

Most, Kenneth S. (Chang, Lucia S. and Kenneth S. Most. "An International Comparison Of Investor Uses Of Financial Statements," **IJAER**, 1981, Vol. 17, No. 1, pp. 43-60.)

Most, Kenneth S. (Chang, Lucia S. and Kenneth S. Most. "International Accounting Standards: The Case Of European Oil Companies," **IJAER**, 1976, Vol. 12, No. 1. pp. 27-43.)

Mott, Charles H. "Forecast Disclosure," **MA**, 1973, Vol. 55, No. 1, pp. 17-18.

Mottola, Anthony J. and Matthew E. Silverman. "Managing Telecommunications Costs," **CA**, 1987, Vol. 5, No. 1, pp. 19-25.

Mourelatos, Anthony. "Bankruptcy," **MA**, 1975, Vol. 57, No. 1, pp. 33-34.

Moustafa, Mohamed. (Lossett, Ronald D. and Mohamed Moustafa. "The Nature Of The Demand For Doctorates In Accounting," **AR**, 1975, Vol. 50, No. 4, pp. 874-881.)

Mowry, Glenn P. and Bardo G. Jacobi. "Planning Communications In A Computer Network," **MA**, 1970, Vol. 51, No. 12. pp. 38-40.

Moyer, C. A. "Audit Programs And Standards, Principles, And Procedures," **JOA**, 1952, Vol. 94, No. 6, pp. 687-691.

Moyer, C. A. "Early Developments In American Auditing," **AR**, 1951, Vol. 26, No. 1, pp. 3-8.

Moyer, C. A. "Economic Aspects Of Fixed-Capital Obsolescence," **AR**, 1939, Vol. 14, No. 3, pp. 285-296.

Moyer, C. A. "Professional Accounting Education," **AR**, 1945, Vol. 20, No. 2, pp. 182-186.

Moyer, C. A. "Should Obsolescence Be Separately Accrued?," **AR**. 1940, Vol. 15, No. 2, pp. 225-231.

Moyer, C. A. "Social Factors Affecting Obsolescence," **AR**. 1943, Vol. 18, No. 2, pp. 110-122.

Moyer, C. A. "Some Common Misconceptions Relating To Accounting Education," **AR**, 1957, Vol. 32, No. 4, pp. 531-535.

Moyer, C. A. "The Attraction And Selection Of Accounting Majors," **AR**, 1956, Vol. 31, No. 1, pp. 33-35.

Moyer, C. A. "The Problem Of Selecting Standards," **AR**, 1948, Vol. 23, No. 2, pp. 193-199.

Moyer, J. K. "The Income Tax - Accounting Aspects," **AR**, 1928, Vol. 3, No. 1, pp. 18-22.

Moyer, R. Charles and Frank Mastrapasqua. "Socio-Economic Accounting And External Diseconomies: A Comment," **AR**, 1973, Vol. 48, No. 1, pp. 126-127.

Moyle, James H. "Justifying Retrofit Projects," **MA**, 1987, Vol. 68, No. 10, pp. 59-61.

Mueller, A. Theodore. "The Ratio And Proportion Method Of Preparing A Program Of Priorities For Cash Distribution In Partnership Liquidation," **AR**, 1959, Vol. 34, No. 3, pp. 469-472.

Mueller, Fred J. (Berg, Kenneth B. and Fred J. Mueller. "Accounting For Investment Credits," **AR**, 1963, Vol. 38, No. 3, pp. 554-561.)

Mueller, Gerhard G. and Lauren M. Walker. "The Coming Of Age Of Financial Transnational Reporting," **JOA**, 1976, Vol. 142, No. 1, pp. 67-74.

Mueller, Gerhard G. "Academic Research In International Accounting," **IJAER**, 1970, Vol. 6, No. 1, pp. 67-81.

Mueller, Gerhard G. "An International View Of Accounting And Disclosure," **IJAER**, 1972, Vol. 8, No. 1. pp. 117-134.

Mueller, Gerhard G. "Some Thoughts About The International Congress Of Accountants," **AR**, 1961, Vol. 36, No. 4. pp. 548-554.

Mueller, Gerhard G. "St. Louis To Munich: The Odyssey Of The International Congresses Of Accountants," **IJAER**, 1979, Vol. 15, No. 1, pp. 1-12.

Mueller, Gerhard G. "The Dimensions Of The International Accounting Problem," **AR**, 1963, Vol. 38, No. 1, pp. 142-147.

Mueller, Gerhard G. "Valuing Inventories At Other Than Historical Costs - Some International Differences," **JAR**, 1964, Vol. 2, No. 2, pp. 148-157.

Mueller, Gerhard G. "Whys And Hows Of International Accounting," **AR**, 1965, Vol. 40, No. 2, pp. 386-394.

Mueller, Gerhard G. (Berg, Kenneth B., Gerhard G. Mueller and Lauren M. Walker. "Annual Reports Go International," **JOA**, 1967, Vol. 124, No. 2, pp. 59-64.)

Mueller, Gerhard G. (Daley, Lane A. and Gerhard G. Mueller. "Accounting In The Arena Of World Politics," **JOA**, 1982, Vol. 153, No. 2, pp. 40-53.)

Mueller, Gerhard G. (Houston, Carol Olson and Gerhard G. Mueller. "Foreign Exchange Rate Hedging And SFAS No. 52 - Relatives Or Strangers?," **AH**, 1988, Vol. 2. No. 4, pp. 50-57.)

Mueller, G. G. "Accounting Principles Generally Accepted In The United States Versus Those Generally Accepted Elsewhere," **IJAER**, 1968, Vol. 3, No. 2, pp. 91-103.

Mueller, Robert K. "How The Changing Role Of The Board Will Affect Controllers," **MA**, 1985, Vol. 67, No. 6, pp. 22-30.

Muench, F. William, Jr. "Computer Time-Sharing For CPAs," **JOA**, 1979, Vol. 147, No. 1, pp. 65-69.

Muenzberg, Charles F. (Johnson, Frank P. and Charles F. Muenzberg. "Can Cost Analysis Improve Your Mortgage Loan Function?," **MA**, 1980, Vol. 61, No. 8, pp. 22-25.)

Mufti, Amer. (Smith, James F. and Amer Mufti. "Using The Relational Database," **MA**, 1985, Vol. 67, No. 4, pp. 43-50.)

Muir, Tom P. and Phillip H. Doherty. "How To Turn Canada's FIRA To Your Advantage," **CA**, 1984, Vol. 2, No. 1, pp. 33-37.

Muis, Jules W. "Accounting Standard Setting: The Pith And The Pendulum," **ABR**, 1976-77, Vol. 7, No. 28, pp. 291-294.

Mulder, John E. "Continuing Professional Training For

Lawyers," **JOA**, 1951, Vol. 91, No. 3, pp. 444-446.

Mulford, Charles W. and Arnold Schneider. "An Empirical Study Of Structural And Controllable Factors Affecting Faculty Evaluations," **AIA**, 1988, Vol. 6, pp. 205-218.

Mulford, Charles W. and Eugene Comiskey. "Investment Decisions And The Equity Accounting Standard," **AR**, 1986, Vol. 61, No. 3, pp. 519-525.

Mulford, Charles W. "The Importance Of A Market Value Measurement Of Debt In Leverage Ratios: Replication And Extensions," **JAR**, 1985, Vol. 23. No. 2, pp. 897-906.

Mulford, Charles W. "The Usefulness Of Current-Cost Measures Of Debt In Assessing Systematic Risk: Extending The Provisions Of SFAS No. 33," **JAPP**, 1986, Vol. 5, No. 1, pp. 21-29.

Mulford, Charles W. (Comiskey, Eugene E. and Charles W. Mulford. "The Influence Of Accounting Principles On Management Investment Decisions: An Illustration," **ACCHOR**, 1988, Vol. 2, No. 2, pp. 67-72.)

Mullarkey, John F. (Adams, Donald L. and John F. Mullarkey. "A Survey Of Audit Software," **JOA**, 1972, Vol. 134, No. 3, pp. 39-66.)

Mullarkey, John F. (Loebbecke, James K., John F. Mullarkey and George R. Zuber. "Auditing In A Computer Environment," **JOA**, 183, Vol. 155. No. 1, pp. 68-78.)

Mullen, Louis E. "Spotlight On Estimated Economic Life Of Depreciable Assets," **CPAJ**, 1973, Vol. 43, No. 8, pp. 662-666.

Muller, Hyman. (Solomon, Kenneth I. and Hyman Muller. "Illegal Payments: Where The Auditor Stands," **JOA**, 1977, Vol. 143, No. 1, pp. 51-57.)

Mullet, Matthew J. "Benefits From Standard Costing In The Restaurant Industry," **MA**, 1978, Vol. 60, No. 3, pp. 47-54.

Mullick, Satinder K. and Donald P. Haussener. "Production Decisions For New Products," **MA**, 1974, Vol. 56, No. 2, pp. 27-32.

Mullick, Satinder K. (Chambers, John C. and Satinder K. Mullick. "Determining The Acquisition Value Of A Company," **MA**, 1970, Vol. 51, No. 10, pp. 24-31.)

Mullick, Satinder K. (Chambers, John C. and Satinder K. Mullick. "Investment Decision-Making In A Multinational Enterprise," **MA**, 1971, Vol. 53. No. 2, pp. 13-20.)

Mullick, Satinder K. (Fairaizl, Alan F. and Satinder K. Mullick. "A Corporate Planning System," **MA**, 1975, Vol. 57, No. 6, pp. 13-17.)

Mulligan, Richard G. "An Alternative To Uniform Cost Accounting Standards," **MA**, 1970, Vol. 51, No. 10, pp. 18-20.

Mulligan, Richard G. "Forecasting And Recording Profits For Incentive Type Contracts (PERT/Fee)," **MA**, 1966, Vol. 47, No. 10, pp. 48-56.

Mullis, Elbert N., Jr. "Variable Budgeting For Financial Planning And Control," **MA**, 1975, Vol. 56, No. 8, pp. 43-45.

Mumford, Michael J. "Memorial: Professor Edward Stamp," **ACCHOR**, 1987, Vol. 1, No. 1, pp. 71-74.

Mumford, Michael. "Objectivity And The Accounting Profession," **ABR**, 1970-71, Vol. 1. No. 4, pp. 284-286.

Mumford, Michael. "The End Of A Familiar Inflation Accounting Cycle," **ABR**, 1978-79, Vol. 9. No. 34, pp. 98-104.

Mumford, M. J. "An Historical Defence Of Henry Rand Hatfield," **ABACUS**, 1980, Vol. 16, No. 2, pp. 151-158.

Mumford, M. J. "Fiftieth Anniversary Of The Accounting Review," **ABR**, 1975-76, Vol. 6. No. 22. p. 149.

Mumford, M. J. "The 1952 Study, Accounting For Inflation: A Review Article," **ABR**, 1983-84, Vol. 14, No. 53. pp. 71-82.

Mundee, C. Roy, Jr. "Primer On The Professional Corporation," **MA**, 1975, Vol. 56, No. 7. pp. 25-28.

Munter, Paul and Stephen D. Willits. "Understanding The New Pension Math," **MA**, 1986, Vol. 68. No. 6, pp. 34-39.

Munter, Paul and Thomas A. Radcliffe. "On The Attributes Of An Asset," **ABACUS**, 1980, Vol. 16, No. 2, pp. 116-123.

Munter, Paul and Thomas A. Ratcliffe. "Going Concern Questions," **CPAJ**, 1981, Vol. 51, No. 8, pp. 39-45.

Munter, Paul and Thomas A. Ratcliffe. "Disclosure Of Long-Term Obligations," **CPAJ**, 1981, Vol. 51, No. 10, pp. 32-41.

Munter, Paul and Thomas A. Ratcliffe. "A Synthesis Of Compilation And Review Standards - Part II." **CPAJ**, 1982, Vol. 52, No. 8, pp. 22-29.

Munter, Paul and Thomas A. Ratcliffe. "Accounting For Real Estate Projects - Part I," **CPAJ**, 1983, Vol. 53, No. 6, pp. 20-27.

Munter, Paul and Thomas A. Ratcliffe. "Accounting For Research And Development Activities," **CPAJ**, 1983, Vol. 53, No. 4, pp. 54-65.

Munter, Paul and Thomas A. Ratcliffe. "Special Reports," **CPAJ**, 1982, Vol. 52, No. 2. pp. 28-36.

Munter, Paul and Thomas A. Ratcliffe. "Accounting For Real Estate Projects - Part II," **CPAJ**, 1983. Vol. 53, No. 7, pp. 38-44.

Munter, Paul and Thomas A. Ratcliffe. "Impact Of Computer Processing On Financial Audits," **CPAJ**, 1985, Vol. 55, No. 1, pp. 34-39.

Munter, Paul and Thomas A. Ratcliffe. "An Assessment Of User Reactions To Lease Accounting Disclosures," **JAAF**, 1983, Vol. 6, No. 2, pp. 108-114.

Munter, Paul and Thomas E. McCaslin. "Risk And Materiality In An Audit," **CPAJ**, 1984, Vol. 54. No. 11, pp. 34-45.

Munter, Paul and Tommy Moores. "Transfers Of Receivables With Recourse," **CPAJ**, 1984, Vol. 54. No. 7. pp. 52-60.

Munter, Paul H., Ronald K. Clancy and C. Tommy Moores. "Accounting For Financial Futures: The Question Of Risk Reduction," **AIA**, 1986, Vol. 3, pp. 51-70.

Munter, Paul, Donald K. Clancy and Tommy Moores. "Accounting For Futures Contracts," **CPAJ**, 1985, Vol. 55, No. 3, pp. 18-25.

Munter, Paul. "Personal Financial Statements - Accountants' Reporting Responsibilities," **CPAJ**, 1984, Vol. 54, No. 8, pp. 24-33.

Munter, Paul. (Byington, Ralph and Paul Munter. "Prospective Financial Statements And Attestation Risk," **CPAJ**, 1988, Vol. 58, No. 2, pp. 34-41.)

Munter, Paul. (Collins, Frank, Paul Munter and Don W. Finn. "The Budgeting Games People Play," **AR**, 1987, Vol. 62, No. 1, pp. 29-49.)

Munter, Paul. (Ratcliffe, Thomas A. and Paul Munter. "Auditors' Responsibility Regarding Supplementary Information," **CPAJ**, 1981, Vol. 51, No. 3, pp. 36-41.)

Munter, Paul. (Ratcliffe, Thomas A. and Paul Munter. "Reporting By Defined Benefit Pension Plans," **CPAJ**, 1980, Vol. 50, No. 12, pp. 39-43.)

Munter, Paul. (Ratcliffe, Thomas A. and Paul Munter. "Asset Valuation: An Historical Perspective," **AHJ**, 1980, Vol. 7. No. 1. pp. 73-78.)

Munter, Paul. (Ratcliffe, Thomas A. and Paul Munter. "Currency Translation: A New Blueprint," **JOA**, 1982, Vol. 153. No. 6, pp. 82-90.)

Munter, Paul. (Ratcliffe, Thomas A. and Paul Munter. "A Synthesis Of Compilation And Review Standards - Part I," **CPAJ**, 1982, Vol. 52, No. 7, pp. 37-47.)

Munter, Paul. (Ratcliffe, Thomas A. and Paul Munter. "Implementing FAS No. 33: A Case Example," **MA**, 1981, Vol. 62. No. 8, pp. 44-52.)

Murase, Gen. "Accounting In Japan And The New Japanese Certified Public Accountant Law," **JOA**, 1950, Vol. 89, No. 4, pp. 334-339.

Murase, Gen. "The Present Status Of The Public Accounting Profession In Japan," **AR**, 1962, Vol. 37, No. 1, pp. 88-91.

Murdick, Robert G. (Wood, Edwin A. and Robert G. Murdick. "A Practical Solution To Forecasting Problems," **MA**, 1980, Vol. 61, No. 11, pp. 45-48.)

Murdoch, Brock. "The Information Content Of FAS 33 Returns On Equity," **AR**, 1986, Vol. 61, No. 2, pp. 273-287.

Murdoch, Brock. (Samuelson, Bruce A. and Brock Murdoch. "The Information Content Of General Price Level Adjusted Earnings: A Comment," **AR**, 1985, Vol. 60, No. 4. pp. 706-710.)

Murdock, Richard J. (Fuglister, Jayne and Richard J. Murdock. "Use Of The Computer In Preparation Of Multiple Choice Examinations: A Multiple Form Generating Program," **IAE**, 1988, Vol. 3, No. 1, pp. 174-180.)

Murdock, Richard J. (Shank, John K., Jesse F. Dillard and Richard J. Murdock. "CPA's Attitudes Toward 'Subject To' Opinions," **CPAJ**, 1978, Vol. 48, No. 8. pp. 43-47.)

Murdock, Richard J. (Shank, John K. and Richard J. Murdock. "Comparability In The Application Of Reporting Standards: Some Further Evidence," **AR**, 1978, Vol. 53, No. 4, pp. 824-835.)

Murph, A. Franklin. "Mathematics In The Accounting Curriculum," **AR**, 1961, Vol. 36, No. 2, pp. 299-300.

Murphy, George J. "A Chronology Of The Development Of Corporate Financial Reporting In Canada," **AHJ**, 1986, Vol. 13, No. 1, pp. 31-62.

Murphy, George J. "A Numerical Representation Of Some Accounting Conventions," **AR**, 1976, Vol. 51, No. 2, pp. 277-286.

Murphy, George J. "Early Canadian Financial Statement Disclosure Legislation," **AHJ**, 1984, Vol. 11, No. 2, pp. 39-59.

Murphy, George J. "Financial Statement Disclosure And Corporate Law: The Canadian Experience," **IJAER**, 1980, Vol. 15, No. 2, pp. 87-99.

Murphy, George J. "Historical Vignette: Benjamin Franklin On Accounting," **AHJ**, 1975, Vol. 2, No. 1-4. pp. 49-50.

Murphy, George J. "Price Changes," **ABR**, 1971-72, Vol. 2. No. 6, pp. 110-113.

Murphy, George J. "Some Aspects Of Auditing Evolution In Canada," **AHJ**, 1980, Vol. 7, No. 2, pp. 45-61.

Murphy, George J. "The Choice And Consequences Of Generally Accepted Accounting Alternatives," **IAE**, 1987, Vol. 2, No. 2, pp. 373-382.

Murphy, George. (Lindsay, Daryl, Morina Rennie, George Murphy and Harold Silvester. "Independence Of External Auditors: A Canadian Perspective," **AIIA**, 1987, Vol. 1, pp. 169-189.)

Murphy, G. J. "Algebraic Double Entry," **AR**, 1970, Vol. 45. No. 2, pp. 366-369.

Murphy, Judith P. (Schiff, Michael, Roger M. Campbell, Leslie E. Halprin and Judith P. Murphy. "How A Division's Reports Can Reflect Inflation," **MA**, 1982, Vol. 64. No. 4, pp. 32-35.)

Murphy, Kevin J. "Corporate Performance And Managerial Remuneration: An Empirical Analysis," **JAEC**, 1985, Vol. 7, No. 1/3, pp. 11-42.

Murphy, Mary E. "Accounting In The Liberal Arts College," **AR**, 1952, Vol. 27, No. 4, pp. 517-522.

Murphy, Mary E. "Centenary Of The Scottish Institute Of Chartered Accountants," **AR**, 1955, Vol. 30, No. 3, pp. 455-462.

Murphy, Mary E. "Comparative Professional Accountancy," **AR**, 1958, Vol. 33. No. 4, pp. 615-621.

Murphy, Mary E. "Comparative Professional Accountancy - Australia," **AR**, 1959, Vol. 34, No. 1, pp. 46-51.

Murphy, Mary E. "Comparative Professional Accountancy - South America," **AR**, 1960, Vol. 35, No. 3, pp. 471-475.

Murphy, Mary E. "Comparative Professional Accountancy - Netherlands And Belgium," **AR**, 1960, Vol. 35, No. 1, pp.

111-116.

Murphy, Mary E. "Education And Training Of English Accountants," AR, 1938, Vol. 13, No. 4, pp. 404-423.

Murphy, Mary E. "Effect Of British And American Institutes On Accounting," JOA, 1952, Vol. 94, No. 2, pp. 202-207.

Murphy, Mary E. "Effect On Financial Reporting Of Law, Research," JOA, 1952, Vol. 94, No. 3, pp. 328-335.

Murphy, Mary E. "Fulbrighter In The Antipodes," AR, 1954, Vol. 29, No. 3, pp. 413-422.

Murphy, Mary E. "Libraries For Students Of Accounting," AR, 1948, Vol. 23, No. 4, pp. 420-421.

Murphy, Mary E. "Proposed Amendment Of British Company Law," AR, 1946, Vol. 21, No. 1, pp. 37-46.

Murphy, Mary E. "Role Of Accountants In The British Nationalization Program," AR, 1952, Vol. 27, No. 1, pp. 63-72.

Murphy, Mary E. "The British Accounting Tradition In America," JOA, 1961, Vol. 111, No. 4, pp. 54-63.

Murphy, Mary E. "The Profession Of Accountancy In England: The Public, The Government. And The Profession," AR, 1940, Vol. 15, No. 3, pp. 328-342.

Murphy, Mary E. "The Profession Of Accountancy In England: The Client And The Investor," AR, 1940, Vol. 15, No. 2, pp. 241-260.

Murphy, Mary E. "The Rise Of The Profession Of Accountancy In England," AR, 1940, Vol. 15, No. 1, pp. 62-70.

Murphy, Mary E. "The Seven International Congresses Of Accountants," AR, 1961, Vol. 36, No. 4, pp. 555-563.

Murphy, Mary E. "The Teaching Of Social Accounting: A Research Planning Paper," AR, 1957, Vol. 32, No. 4, pp. 630-645.

Murphy, Pamela L. (Hanks, George F. and Pamela L. Murphy. "A Look At Accounting For Small Manufacturers," MA, 1984, Vol. 65, No. 10, pp. 40-44.)

Murphy, Patrick J. "The Interest Equalization Tax Act," JOA, 1965, Vol. 119, No. 1, pp. 38-45.

Murphy, Richard C. "A Computer Model Approach To Budgeting," MA, 1975, Vol. 56, No. 12, pp. 34-36.

Murphy, Robert J. "Service Bureaus And The Bookkeeping Function," MA, 1971, Vol. 50, No. 3, pp. 36-38.

Murphy, Roger P. "Local Government's Hidden Resource: University Interns," JAED, 1985, Vol. 3, No. 1, pp. 173-177.

Murray, Daniel R. "How Management Accountants Can Make A Manufacturing Control System More Effective," MA, 1981, Vol. 63, No. 1, pp. 25-31.

Murray, Dennis and Katherine Beal Frazier. "A Within-Subjects Test Of Expectancy Theory In A Public Accounting Environment," JAR, 1986, Vol. 24, No. 2, pp. 400-404.

Murray, Dennis and Raymond Johnson. "Differential GAAP And The FASB's Conceptual Framework," JAAF, 1983, Vol. 7, No. 1, pp. 4-15.

Murray, Dennis. "The Effect Of Certain Research Design Choices On The Assessment Of The Market's Reaction To LIFO Changes: A Methodological Study," JAR, 1983, Vol. 21, No. 1, pp. 128-140.

Murray, Dennis. "The Irrelevance Of Lease Capitalization." JAAF, 1982, Vol. 5, No. 2, pp. 154-159.

Murray, Dennis. (Elgers, Pieter T. and Dennis Murray. "The Impact Of The Choice Of Market Index On The Empirical Evaluation Of Accounting Risk Measures," AR, 1982, Vol. 57, No. 2, pp. 358-375.)

Murray, D. (Bloom, R., P. T. Elgers and D. Murray. "Functional Fixation In Product Pricing: A Comparison Of Individuals And Groups," AOS, 1984, Vol. 9, No. 1, pp. 1-12.)

Murray, John P. "How An Information Center Improved Productivity," MA, 1984, Vol. 65, No. 9, pp. 38-44.

Murray, John R. "Sensitivity Analysis In The Return On Investment Computation," MA, 1969, Vol. 50, No. 9, pp. 23-25.

Murray, Lawrence M. "Management Audit Of Divisional Performance," MA, 1973, Vol. 54, No. 9, pp. 26-28.

Murray, Oliver C. (Forster, Joel M., Oliver C. Murray and Edward D. Ryan. "Tax Reform: The New Perspective," JOA, 1977, Vol. 143, No. 4, pp. 79-88.)

Murray, Richard M. and William R. George. "Managing CPA Personnel - A Marketing Perspective," CPAJ, 1979, Vol. 49, No. 7, pp. 17-22.

Murray, Richard M. (George, William R. and Richard M. Murray. "Marketing Practices Of CPA Firms," CPAJ, 1975, Vol. 45, No. 10, pp. 33-36.)

Murray, Ronald J., William E. Decker and John W. Joyce. "Pension Accounting: Analysis Of Preliminary Views - Part II," CPAJ, 1983, Vol. 53, No. 9, pp. 42-47.

Murray, Ronald J., William E. Decker and John W. Joyce. "Pension Accounting: Analysis Of Preliminary Views - Part I," CPAJ, 1983, Vol. 53, No. 8, pp. 10-23.

Mushkat, M. "Using Macro-Societal Accounting Data: Some Critical Afterthoughts," AOS, 1983, Vol. 1, pp. 99-108.

Musson, Roger D. (Barfuss, Francois R., Roger D. Musson and David C. Bennett. "Some Significant Differences In U.S. and U.K. Reported Net Income," CPAJ, 1982, Vol. 52, No. 2, pp. 44-48.)

Mutchler, Jane F. "A Multivariate Analysis Of The Auditor's Going-Concern Opinion Decision," JAR, 1985, Vol. 23, No. 2, pp. 668-682.

Mutchler, Jane F. "Auditors' Perceptions Of The Going-Concern Opinion Decision," AJPT, 1983-84, Vol. 3, No. 2, pp. 17-30.

Mutchler, Jane F. "Empirical Evidence Regarding The Auditor's Going-Concern Opinion Decision," AJPT, 1986-87, Vol. 6, No. 1, pp. 148-163.

Mutchler, Jane F. (Campbell, Jane E. and Jane F. Mutchler. "The 'Expectations Gap' And Going-Concern Uncertainties," ACCHOR, 1988, Vol. 2, No. 1, pp. 42-49.)

Mutchler, Jane F., Joanne H. Turner and David D. Williams. "The Performance Of Female Versus Male Accounting Students," IAE, 1987, Vol. 2, No. 1, pp. 103-111.

Mutchler, Jane. (Hopwood, William, James McKeown and Jane Mutchler. "The Sensitivity Of Financial Distress Prediction Models To Departures From Normality," CAR, 1988, Vol. 5, No. 1, pp. 284-298.)

Myatt-Price, E. M. "Examples Of Techniques In Medieval Building Accounts," ABACUS, 1966, Vol. 2, No. 1, pp. 41-48.

Myatt-Price, E. M. "The Twelve At Tattershall," AR, 1960, Vol. 35, No. 4, pp. 680-685.

Myddelton, D. R. "Consolidated Nationalised Industries Accounts 1948-1970: Published Figures Adjusted For Currency Debasement," ABR, 1971-72, Vol. 2, No. 6, pp. 83-109.

Myer, John N. "Fallacies In The Balance Sheet Approach," AR, 1946, Vol. 21, No. 1, pp. 8-12.

Myer, John N. "Statements Accounting For Balance Sheet Changes," AR, 1944, Vol. 19, No. 1, pp. 31-38.

Myer, John N. "The Backward Art Of Teaching Accounting," AR, 1946, Vol. 21, No. 2, pp. 128-134.

Myer, Joseph C. "Teaching The Accountant The History And Ethics Of His Profession," AR, 1931, Vol. 6, No. 1, pp. 47-50.

Myers, Buddy L. (Pearson, Michael A., John H. Lindgren, Jr. and Buddy L. Myers. "A Preliminary Analysis Of AudSEC Voting Patterns," JAAF, 1979, Vol. 2, No. 2, pp. 122-134.)

Myers, Fredric T. "Filing Pro Forma Financial Statements," MA, 1975, Vol. 57, No. 6, pp. 25-26.

Myers, John H. and James R. Kinney. "A Computer Experiment In The Auditing Class," AR, 1972, Vol. 47, No. 2, pp. 390-392.

Myers, John H. "A Set Of New Financial Statements," JOA, 1971, Vol. 131, No. 2, pp. 50-57.

Myers, John H. "Accelerated Amortization Of Emergency Facilities In Financial Statements," JOA, 1955, Vol. 99, No. 2, pp. 52-55.

Myers, John H. "Depreciation Disclosure," JOA, 1965, Vol. 120, No. 5, pp. 36-40.

Myers, John H. "Footnotes," AR, 1959, Vol. 34, No. 3, pp. 381-388.

Myers, John H. "Influence Of Salvage Value Upon Choice Of Tax Depreciation Methods," AR, 1960, Vol. 35, No. 4, pp. 598-602.

Myers, John H. "Inventory Disclosure In Annual Reports," JOA, 1955, Vol. 100, No. 1, pp. 42-45.

Myers, John H. "More Efficient Utilization Of Teaching Staff," AR, 1959, Vol. 34, No. 2, pp. 221-225.

Myers, John H. "Presentation Of Long-Term Lease Liabilities In The Balance Sheet," AR, 1948, Vol. 23, No. 3, pp. 289-295.

Myers, John H. "Special Inventory Problems Of The Dealer In Collectors' Items," AR, 1953, Vol. 28, No. 4, pp. 562-564.

Myers, John H. "Spiraling Upward: Auditing Methods As Described By Montgomery And His Successors," AHJ, 1985, Vol. 12, No. 1, pp. 53-72.

Myers, John H. "The Critical Event And Recognition Of Net Profit," AR, 1959, Vol. 34, No. 4, pp. 528-532.

Myers, John H. "Useful Formulae For DDB And SYD Depreciation," AR, 1958, Vol. 33, No. 1, pp. 93-95.

Myers, John H. "Useful Variations In Short-Form Audit Report," JOA, 1953, Vol. 96, No. 5, pp. 588-599.

Myers, Robert J. and John J. Creedon. "Is Social Security Financially Feasible," CPAJ, 1987, Vol. 57, No. 5, pp. 46-55.

Myers, Ronald E. "Performance Review Of Capital Expenditures," MA, 1966, Vol. 48, No. 4, pp. 21-26.

Myklebust, Harold N. (Hopewell, Rita J. and Harold N. Myklebust. "Stimulating Faculty To Use Computers," JAED, 1984, Vol. 2, No. 1, pp. 161-162.)

Myott, William S. (Kearns, Francis and William S. Myott. "Expediting The Scheduling Of Staff Work," CPAJ, 1984, Vol. 54, No. 6, pp. 12-21.)

NNN

Nachman, David A. (Ferrara, William L., Jack C. Hayya and David A. Nachman.. "Normalcy Of Profit In The Jaedicke-Robichek Model," AR, 1972, Vol. 47, No. 2, pp. 299-307.)

Nachtmann, Robert. (Doran, David T. and Robert Nachtmann. "The Association Of Stock Distribution Announcements And Earnings Performance," JAAF, 1988, Vol. 3 (New Series), No. 2, pp. 113-146.)

Nachtsheim, Christopher J. (Ko, Chen-En, Christopher J. Nachtsheim, Gordon L. Duke and Andrew D. Bailey, Jr. "On The Robustness Of Model-Based Sampling In Auditing," AJPT, 1988, Vol. 7, No. 2, pp. 119-136.)

Naciri, M. Ahmed. (Bloom, Robert and M. Ahmed Naciri. "An Analysis Of The Accounting Standard-Setting Framework In Two European Countries: France And The Netherlands," AIIA, 1988, Vol. 2, pp. 69-85.)

Nad, Leon M. "How To Simplify Lifo By Use Of Dollar-Value Method," JOA, 1951, Vol. 91, No. 2, pp. 266-271.

Nadeau, Sherri P. (Wiesner, Philip J. and Sherri P. Nadeau. "Alternative Minimum Tax (Part 2): More Headaches Than Aspirin," JOA, 1988, Vol. 165, No. 2, pp. 54-63.)

Nadel, Eugene and Robert M. Greenberger. "Condos Or Co-Ops For Good 'Shelter'," CPAJ, 1981, Vol. 51, No. 11, pp. 9-19.

Nadel, Eugene. "Theft Losses, Insurance And Taxability," **CPAJ**, 1980, Vol. 50, No. 8, pp. 11-16.

Nadel, Robert B. "Computer Consulting For The Smaller Firm: Opportunity Or Trap?," **CPAJ**, 1988, Vol. 58, No. 4, pp. 18-29.

Nadel, Robert B. "Computer Auditing - Has Its Time Come?," **CPAJ**, 1987, Vol. 57, No. 3, pp. 24-29.

Nagarajan, Nandu J. (Balachandran, Bala V. and Nandu J. Nagarajan. "Imperfect Information, Insurance, And Auditors' Legal Liability," **CAR**, 1986-87, Vol. 3, No. 2, pp. 281-301.)

Nagarajan, Nandu J. (Johnson, W. Bruce, Robert P. Magee, Nandu J. Nagarajan and Harry A. Newman. "An Analysis Of The Stock Price Reaction To Sudden Executive Deaths: Implications For The Management Labor Market," **JAEC**, 1985, Vol. 7, No. 1/3, pp. 151-174.)

Naggar, Ali. "Oil And Gas Accounting: Where Wall Street Stands," **JOA**, 1978, Vol. 146, No. 3, pp. 72-77.

Nagy, Richard J. "Transfer Price Accounting For MNCs," **MA**, 1978, Vol. 59, No. 7, pp. 34-38.

Nahapiet, J. E. (Banbury, J. and J. E. Nahapiet. "Towards A Framework For The Study Of The Antecedents And Consequences Of Information Systems In Organizations," **AOS**, 1979, Vol. 4, No. 3, pp. 163-178.)

Nahapiet, J. "The Rhetoric And Reality Of An Accounting Change: A Study Of Resource Allocation," **AOS**, 1988, Vol. 13, No. 4, pp. 333-358.

Nahapiet, J. (Burchell, S., C. Clubb, A. Hopwood, J. Hughes and J. Nahapiet. "The Roles Of Accounting In Organizations And Society," **AOS**, 1980, Vol. 5, No. 1, pp. 5-28.)

Nair, R. D. and Jerry J. Weygandt. "Let's Fix Deferred Taxes," **JOA**, 1981, Vol. 152, No. 5, pp. 87-94.

Nair, R. D. and Larry E. Rittenberg. "Messages Perceived From Audit, Review, And Compilation Reports: Extension To More Diverse Groups," **AJPT**, 1987-88, Vol. 7, No. 1, pp. 15-38.

Nair, R. D. and Larry E. Rittenberg. "Accounting Costs Of Privately Held Businesses," **JAAF**, 1983, Vol. 6, No. 3, pp. 234-243.

Nair, R. D. and Werner G. Frank. "The Impact Of Disclosure And Measurement Practices On International Accounting Classifications," **AR**, 1980, Vol. 55, No. 3, pp. 426-450.

Nair, R. D. and Werner G. Frank. "The Harmonization Of International Accounting Standards, 1973-1979," **IJAER**, 1981, Vol. 17, No. 1, pp. 61-77.

Nair, R. D. "Economic Analyses And Accounting Techniques: An Empirical Study," **JAR**, 1979, Vol. 17, No. 1, pp. 225-242.

Nakajima, Seigo. "Economic Growth And Corporate Financial Reporting In Japan," **IJAER**, 1973, Vol. 9, No. 1, pp. 35-41.

Nakanishi, Akira. "On The Life Of Luca Pacioli," **AHJ**, 1979, Vol. 6, No. 2, pp. 53-59.

Nakano, Isao. "Noise And Redundancy In Accounting Communications," **AR**, 1972, Vol. 47, No. 4, pp. 693-708.

Nakano, Isao. "On Monetary-Sacrifice-Based Depreciation," **IJAER**, 1978, Vol. 13, No. 2, pp. 41-55.

Nakano, Isao. "The Usefulness Of Probabilistic Accounting Data," **ABACUS**, 1976, Vol. 12, No. 2, pp. 125-136.

Nakayama, Mic, Steven Lilien and Martin Benis. "Due Process And FAS No. 13," **MA**, 1981, Vol. 62, No. 10, pp. 49-53.

Namazi, Mohammad. "Theoretical Developments Of Principal-Agent Employment Contract In Accounting: The State Of The Art," **JAL**, 1985, Vol. 4, pp. 113-163.

Nance, Jon R. and Roger A. Roemmich. "Financial Statement Impact Of Foreign Currency Translation Alternatives," **IJAER**, 1983, Vol. 19, No. 1, pp. 89-113.

Nance, Jon R. and Roger A. Roemmich. "Foreign Currency Translation: An Evaluation," **IJAER**, 1983, Vol. 18, No. 2, pp. 29-48.

Nance, Jon R. "Capital Budgeting With Continuous Cash Flows: An Application Of Calculus To Managerial Accounting," **JAED**, 1988, Vol. 6, No. 1, pp. 67-81.

Nanni, Alfred J., Jeffrey G. Miller and Thomas E. Vollmann. "What Shall We Account For?," **MA**, 1988, Vol. 69, No. 7, pp. 42-48.

Nanni, Alfred J., Jr. (Haskins, Mark E. and Alfred J. Nanni, Jr. "Toward Attribute Models Of Accounting Control Systems: Qualitative Versus Quantitative Approaches," **JAL**, 1987, Vol. 6, pp. 111-130.)

Nanni, A. J., Jr. "An Exploration Of The Mediating Effects Of Auditor Experience And Position In Internal Accounting Control Evaluation," **AOS**, 1984, Vol. 9, No. 2, pp. 149-164.

Nantell, Timothy J. (Brigham, Eugene F. and Timothy J. Nantell. "Normalization Versus Flow Through For Utility Companies Using Liberalized Tax Depreciation," **AR**, 1974, Vol. 49, No. 3, pp. 436-447.)

Nantell, Timothy J. (Maher, Michael W. and Timothy J. Nantell. "The Tax Effects Of Inflation: Depreciation, Debt, And Miller's Equilibrium Tax Rates," **JAR**, 1983, Vol. 21, No. 1, pp. 329-340.)

Narayanan, V. K. (Gordon, L. A. and V. K. Narayanan. "Management Accounting Systems, Perceived Environmental Uncertainty And Organization Structure: An Empirical Investigation," **AOS**, 1984, Vol. 9, No. 1, pp. 33-48.)

Nash, Arthur L. "Audits For Credit Purposes," **JOA**, 1956, Vol. 101, No. 6, pp. 44-48.

Nash, Arthur L. "Banker Says Some Audit Reports Are Still Not Good Enough," **JOA**, 1952, Vol. 94, No. 5, pp. 560-564.

Nash, John F. and Vincent J. Giovinazzo. "Selecting Computer Hardware," **CPAJ**, 1982, Vol. 52, No. 9, pp. 57-63.

Nash, John F. "A Note On Cost-Volume-Profit Analysis And Price Elasticity," **AR**, 1975, Vol. 50, No. 2, pp. 384-386.

Nash, John F. (Dillon, Ray D. and John F. Nash. "The True Relevance Of Relevant Costs," **AR**, 1978, Vol. 53, No. 1, pp. 11-17.)

Nash, John F. (Giovinazzo, Vincent J. and John F. Nash. "Selecting Accounting Software Packages," **CPAJ**, 1982, Vol. 52, No. 10, pp. 40-45.)

Nash, L. R. "Depreciation Accounting Methods For Public Utilities," **AR**, 1930, Vol. 5, No. 2, pp. 125-141.

Nassimbene, Raymond. "The National Income And Product Account," **AR**, 1953, Vol. 28, No. 2, pp. 211-220.

Nassimbene, Raymond. "The Use Of Double-Entry Accounting In National Income Accounts," **AR**, 1954, Vol. 29, No. 1, pp. 74-83.

Natarajan, R. (Gordon, Lawrence A., Morris M. Kleiner and R. Natarajan. "Federal Capital Expenditures And Budget Deficits: Gross National Product And Labor Implications," **JAPP**, 1986, Vol. 5, No. 4, pp. 217-232.)

Nath, Raghu. (Birnberg, Jacob G. and Raghu Nath. "Laboratory Experimentation In Accounting Research," **AR**, 1968, Vol. 43, No. 1, pp. 38-45.)

Nath, Raghu. (Birnberg, Jacob G. and Raghu Nath. "Implications Of Behavioral Science For Managerial Accounting," **AR**, 1967, Vol. 42, No. 3, pp. 468-479.)

Nathan, Kevin. "Do Firms Pay To Pool?: Some Empirical Evidence," **JAPP**, 1988, Vol. 7, No. 3, pp. 185-200.

Naus, James H. (Falk, Haim, Bruce G. Gobdel and James H. Naus. "Disclosure For Closely Held Corporations," **JOA**, 1976, Vol. 142, No. 4, pp. 85-90.)

Navarro, Murray. "The Selection And Audit Of Tax Returns," **CPAJ**, 1976, Vol. 46, No. 4, pp. 27-30.

Nave, David R. "The Davis Problem In Divorce And Separation," **CPAJ**, 1984, Vol. 54, No. 11, pp. 16-21.

Naylor, E. E. "Budgetary And Proprietary Accounts Of The Federal Government," **AR**, 1940, Vol. 15, No. 4, pp. 485-494.

Ndubizu, Gordian A. "Accounting Standards And Economic Development: The Third World In Perspective," **IJAER**, 1984, Vol. 19, No. 2, pp. 181-196.

Ndubizu, Gordian A. "Analysis Of The Economic Consequences Of Foreign Currency Standards: A Classification Issue," **AIIA**, 1988, Vol. 2, pp. 181-198.

Ndubizu, Gordian A. "Management Preferences For Foreign Currency Standards: An Empirical Analysis," **IJAER**, 1987, Vol. 22, No. 2, pp. 115-130.

Ndubizu, Gordian. (Talaka, James A. and Gordian Ndubizu. "Accounting And Economic Development: Relationships Among The Paradigms," **IJAER**, 1986, Vol. 21, No. 2, pp. 55-68.)

Neary, Robert D. and Dennis R. Beresford. "Questions And Answers On FASB Inflation Accounting," **CPAJ**, 1979, Vol. 49, No. 6, pp. 11-18.

Neary, Robert D. (Mautz, Robert K. and Robert D. Neary. "Corporate Audit Committee - Quo Vadis?," **JOA**, 1979, Vol. 148, No. 4, pp. 83-88.)

Neebes, Doanld L. (Callahan, Patrick S., Henry R. Jaenicke and Donald L. Neebes. "SASs Nos. 56 And 57: Increasing Audit Effectiveness," **JOA**, 1988, Vol. 166, No. 4, pp. 56-68.)

Neebes, Donald L. and William G. Roost. "The ASB's Ten 'Expectation Gap' Proposals - Will They Do The Job?," **CPAJ**, 1987, Vol. 57, No. 10, pp. 22-29.

Needham, James J. "Current Financial Reporting Issues," **CPAJ**, 1973, Vol. 43, No. 8, pp. 657-661.

Needle, Sheldon. "Microcomputer Accounting In Large Corporations," **CA**, 1986, Vol. 4, No. 2, pp. 64-68.

Needles, Belverd E., Jr. and Kenneth R. Havis. "Financial Reporting Of Regulated Investment Companies: A Survey," **JOA**, 1971, Vol. 131, No. 1, pp. 52-59.

Needles, Belverd E., Jr. "Budgeting Techniques: Subjective To Probabilistic," **MA**, 1971, Vol. 53, No. 6, pp. 39-45.

Needles, Belverd E., Jr. "Freedom And Learning: An Approach And First Results," **AR**, 1973, Vol. 48, No. 1, pp. 143-148.

Needles, Belverd E., Jr. "Implementing A Framework For The International Transfer Of Accounting Technology," **IJAER**, 1976, Vol. 12, No. 1, pp. 45-62.

Needles, Belverd E., Jr. (Skousen, K. Fred and Belverd E. Needles, Jr. "A Conceptual Framework For Analyzing And Evaluating Managerial Decisions," **MA**, 1969, Vol. 50, No. 5, pp. 9-11.)

Neely, Paden and C. A. Robason. "Governmental Accounting: A Critical Evaluation," **AR**, 1967, Vol. 42, No. 2, pp. 366-369.

Neely, Fred T. "Finding Transposition Errors With Rule Of Nine," **JOA**, 1953, Vol. 96, No. 4, pp. 470-473.

Neely, Fred T. "The Easy Addition Of Numbers In Sequence," **JOA**, 1955, Vol. 100, No. 2, pp. 49-52.

Neely, L. Paden. (Robason, Goyne A. and L. Paden Neely. "Financial Reporting In Municipalities," **MA**, 1970, Vol. 51, No. 9, pp. 45-46.)

Nehrt, Lee C. "Evaluating The Political Climate For Private Investment With Special Application To Tunisia," **IJAER**, 1969, Vol. 5, No. 1, pp. 109-122.

Neier, Dennis S. and Gregory M. Levy. "Centralized Review Of Financial Statements And Accountants' Reports," **CPAJ**, 1982, Vol. 52, No. 8, pp. 12-21.

Neihus, Rudolph. "Harmonized European Economic Community Accounting - A German View Of The Draft Directive For Uniform Accounting Rules," **IJAER**, 1972, Vol. 7, No. 2, pp. 91-125.

Neilsen, Oswald. "Direct Costing - The Case 'For'," **AR**, 1954, Vol. 29, No. 1, pp. 89-93.

Neimark, Marilyn Dale. (Merino, Barbara Dubis and Marilyn

Dale Neimark. "Disclosure Regulation And Public Policy: A Sociohistorical Reappraisal," **JAPP**, 1982, Vol. 1, No. 1, pp. 33-57.)

Neimark, M. and T. Tinker. "The Social Construction Of Management Systems," **AOS**, 1986, Vol. 11, No. 4/5, pp. 369-396.

Neimark, M. D. (Tinker, A. M., B. D. Merino and M. D. Neimark. "The Normative Origins Of Positive Theories: Ideology And Accounting Thought," **AOS**, 1982, Vol. 7, No. 2, pp. 167-200.)

Neimark, M. (Tinker, T. and M. Neimark. "The Role Of Annual Reports In Gender And Class Contradictions At General Motors: 1917-1976," **AOS**, 1987, Vol. 12, No. 1, pp. 71-88.)

Nelson, A. Tom. "Accounting Education's Coming Crisis," **JOA**, 183, Vol. 155, No. 4, pp. 70-80.

Nelson, A. Tom. "Accounting In A Decade - Trade Or Profession?," **CPAJ**, 1978, Vol. 48, No. 6, pp. 11-16.

Nelson, A. Tom. "Capitalizing Leases - The Effect On Financial Ratios," **JOA**, 1963, Vol. 116, No. 1, pp. 49-58.

Nelson, A. Tom. (Ellyson, Robert C., A. Tom Nelson and James H. MacNeill. "Educating Tomorrow's CPAs," **JOA**, 1985, Vol. 160, No. 2, pp. 95-105.)

Nelson, Carl L. "Use Of Accounting Data In National-Income Estimation," **AR**, 1953, Vol. 28, No. 2, pp. 186-190.

Nelson, Carl L. (Jaedicke, Robert K. and Carl L. Nelson. "The Allocation Of Income Taxes - A Defense," **AR**, 1960, Vol. 35, No. 2, pp. 278-281.)

Nelson, Carl L. (Moonitz, Maurice and Carl L. Nelson. "Recent Developments In Accounting Theory," **AR**, 1960, Vol. 35, No. 2, pp. 206-217.)

Nelson, Don A. "More Effective Strategic Planning For Organizations," **CPAJ**, 1984, Vol. 54, No. 5, pp. 18-23.

Nelson, Edward G. "A Brief Study Of Balance Sheets," **AR**, 1947, Vol. 22, No. 4, pp. 341-352.

Nelson, Edward G. "A Note On Principles Of Accounting," **AR**, 1939, Vol. 14, No. 4, pp. 350-354.

Nelson, Edward G. "Science And Accounting," **AR**, 1949, Vol. 24, No. 4, pp. 354-359.

Nelson, Edward G. "That Balance-Sheet Approach," **AR**, 1935, Vol. 10, No. 4, pp. 313-317.

Nelson, Edward G. "The Relation Between The Balance Sheet And The Profit-And-Loss Statement," **AR**, 1942, Vol. 17, No. 2, pp. 132-140.

Nelson, G. Kenneth and Robert H. Strawser. "A Note On APB Opinion No. 16," **JAR**, 1970, Vol. 8, No. 2, pp. 284-289.

Nelson, G. Kenneth. "An Internship Program For Accounting Majors," **AR**, 1952, Vol. 27, No. 3, pp. 382-385.

Nelson, G. Kenneth. "Current And Historical Costs In Financial Statements," **AR**, 1966, Vol. 41, No. 1, pp. 42-47.

Nelson, H. G. "Impact And Validity Of The Ford And Carnegie Reports On Business Education," **AR**, 1961, Vol. 36, No. 2, pp. 179-185.

Nelson, Jeanne H. "Behavioral Implications Of Internal Auditing," **MA**, 1973, Vol. 55, No. 4, pp. 52-56.

Nelson, Julianne, Joshua Ronen and Lawrence White. "Legal Liabilities And The Market For Auditing Services," **JAAF**, 1988, Vol. 3 (New Series), No. 3, pp. 255-295.

Nelson, Oscar S. "Capital Gains From Price Level Increases," **AR**, 1951, Vol. 26, No. 1, pp. 31-32.

Nelson, Oscar S. "Cost Principles In Termination Settlements," **AR**, 1944, Vol. 19, No. 4, pp. 422-429.

Nelson, Oscar S. "Teaching Accounting Systems," **AR**, 1934, Vol. 9, No. 1, pp. 83-89.

Nelson, Oscar S. "Testing Obsolescence In Fixed Assets," **AR**, 1945, Vol. 20, No. 4, pp. 447-457.

Nelson, Oscar S. "The Clark Plan Of Retail Accounting," **AR**, 1934, Vol. 9, No. 3, pp. 242-246.

Nelson, Oscar S. "Trends And Problems In Governmental And Institutional Accounting," **AR**, 1951, Vol. 26, No. 2, pp. 179-184.

Nelson, Robert E. "Increasing The Speed And Accuracy Of Filling Out Tax Returns," **JOA**, 1954, Vol. 98, No. 4, pp. 491-497.

Nelson, Robert E. "Reproducing Tax Returns," **JOA**, 1959, Vol. 108, No. 6, pp. 61-64.

Nelson, Robert E. "The Dilemma Of The Corporation In Tax Accounting For Dividends In Kind," **JOA**, 1951, Vol. 91, No. 1, pp. 96-99.

Nelson, Robert H. "The Momentum Theory Of Goodwill," No. 4, pp. 491-499.

Nelson, Thomas G. "Post-Retirement Benefits: The Tip Of A Financial Iceberg," **MA**, 1987, Vol. 68, No. 7, pp. 52-55.

Nelson, William G. IV. "Two Cost-Of-Capital Standards?," **MA**, 1966, Vol. 47, No. 9, pp. 29-32.

Nelson, W. Dale. "A Guide To Accounting For Costs Of Discontinued Operations," **MA**, 1981, Vol. 62, No. 10, pp. 43-48.

Nelson, W. Porter. "Independent CPA's Part In Cost System Installation," **JOA**, 1951, Vol. 92, No. 4, pp. 456-459.

Nemec, Marilyn J. "Reporting In Consolidated Statements The Sale Of A Subsidiary's Stock," **CPAJ**, 1973, Vol. 43, No. 3, pp. 214-217.

Neppl, Edward J. (Price, William S., Jr. and Edward J. Neppl. "Automated Inventory Control," **MA**, 1966, Vol. 48, No. 2, pp. 52-58.)

Nerlove, S. H. "Insiders And Corporate Income Streams," **AR**, 1930, Vol. 5, No. 2, pp. 153-156.

Nerlove, S. H. "Objectives Attainable Through Accounting Research," **AR**, 1935, Vol. 10, No. 1, pp. 29-31.

Nestor, Joseph. "How Cost Accountants Can Improve Public Housing Programs," **MA**, 1979, Vol. 61, No. 4, pp. 40-42.

Nestor, Oscar W. and Andrew J. Riddell. "A Home Health Care Agency Cures Itself," **MA**, 1979, Vol. 61, No. 1, pp. 15-20.

Neter, John, Hyo Seuk Kim and Lynford E. Graham. "On Combining Stringer Bounds For Independent Monetary Unit Samples From Several Populations," **AJPT**, 1984-85, Vol. 4, No. 1, pp. 75-88.

Neter, John, Johnny R. Johnson and Robert A. Leitch. "Characteristics Of Dollar-Unit Taints And Error Rates In Accounts Receivable And Inventory," **AR**, 1985, Vol. 60, No. 3, pp. 488-499.

Neter, John, R. A. Leitch and Stephen E. Fienberg. "Dollar Unit Sampling: Multinomial Bounds For Total Overstatement And Understatement Errors," **AR**, 1978, Vol. 53, No. 1, pp. 77-93.

Neter, John. "Applicability Of Statistical Sampling Techniques To The Confirmation Of Accounts Receivable," **AR**, 1956, Vol. 31, No. 1, pp. 82-94.

Neter, John. "Problems In Experimenting With The Application Of Statistical Techniques In Auditing," **AR**, 1954, Vol. 29, No. 4, pp. 591-600.

Neter, John. "Sampling Tables: An Important Statistical Tool For Auditors," **AR**, 1952, Vol. 27, No. 4, pp. 475-483.

Neter, John. (Davis, Gordon B., John Neter and Roger R. Palmer. "An Experimental Study Of Audit Confirmations," **JOA**, 1967, Vol. 123, No. 6, pp. 36-44.)

Neter, John. (Duke, Gordon L., John Neter and Robert A. Leitch. "Power Characteristics Of Test Statistics In The Auditing Environment: An Empirical Study," **JAR**, 1982, Vol. 20, No. 1, pp. 42-67.)

Neter, John. (Godfrey, James and John Neter. "Bayesian Bounds For Monetary Unit Sampling In Accounting And Auditing," **JAR**, 1984, Vol. 22, No. 2, pp. 497-525.)

Neter, John. (Johnson, Johnny R., Robert A. Leitch and John Neter. "Characteristics Of Errors In Accounts Receivable And Inventory Audits," **AR**, 1981, Vol. 56, No. 2, pp. 270-293.)

Neter, John. (Kim, Hyo Seuk, John Neter and James T. Godfrey. "Behavior Of Statistical Estimators In Multilocation Audit Sampling," **AJPT**, 1986-87, Vol. 6, No. 2, pp. 40-58.)

Neter, John. (Leitch, Robert A., John Neter, Robert Plante and Prabhakant Sinha. "Modified Multinomial Bounds For Larger Numbers Of Errors In Audits," **AR**, 1982, Vol. 57, No. 2, pp. 384-400.)

Neter, John. (Loebbecke, James K. and John Neter. "Statistical Sampling In Confirming Receivables," **JOA**, 1973, Vol. 135, No. 6, pp. 44-50.)

Neter, John. (Loebbecke, James K. and John Neter. "Considerations In Choosing Statistical Sampling Procedures In Auditing," **JAR**, 1975, Vol. 13, Supp., pp. 38-52.)

Neter, John. (Plante, Robert, John Neter and Robert A. Leitch. "Comparative Performance Of Multinomial, Cell, And Stringer Bounds," **AJPT**, 1985-86, Vol. 5, No. 1, pp. 40-56.)

Neter, John. (Yu, Seongjae and John Neter. "A Stochastic Model Of The Internal Control System," **JAR**, 1973, Vol. 11, No. 2, pp. 273-295.)

Neter, J. (Davidson, H. J., J. Neter and A. S. Petran. "Estimating The Liability For Unredeemed Stamps," **JAR**, 1967, Vol. 5, No. 2, pp. 186-207.)

Neth, John T. "Program Budgets For A Marketing Group," **MA**, 1966, Vol. 47, No. 10, pp. 8-17.

Nethercott, L. (Ferris, K. R., J. F. Dillard and L. Nethercott. "A Comparison Of V-I-E Model Predictions: A Cross-National Study In Professional Accounting Firms," **AOS**, 1980, Vol. 5, No. 4, pp. 361-368.)

Neubauer, John C. "The Accounting Aid Society," **JOA**, 1971, Vol. 131, No. 5, pp. 55-59.

Neubert, Helmut. "Money Flow And The Firm," **AR**, 1959, Vol. 34, No. 1, pp. 84-90.

Neubig, Robert D. "Sales Growth - Fact Or Fiction?," **AR**, 1964, Vol. 39, No. 1, pp. 86-89.

Neubig, Robert D. (Raby, Wm. L. and Robert D. Neubig. "Inter-Period Tax Allocation Or Basis Adjustment?," **AR**, 1963, Vol. 38, No. 3, pp. 568-576.)

Neuhausen, Benjamin S. "Consolidation And The Equity Method - Time For An Overhaul," **JOA**, 1982, Vol. 153, No. 2, pp. 54-67.

Neuhausen, Benjamin S. "The Seventh Directive Requires Consolidated Reporting For European Operations," **CA**, 1984, Vol. 2, No. 3, pp. 20-29.

Neuhausen, Benjamin S. (Stewart, John E. and Benjamin S. Neuhausen. "Financial Instruments And Transactions: The CPA's Newest Challenge," **JOA**, 1986, Vol. 162, No. 2, pp. 102-113.)

Neuhausen, Benjamin S. (Stewart, John E. and Benjamin S. Neuhausen. "Understanding And Implementing The New Pension Rules," **CA**, 1987, Vol. 5, No. 1, pp. 41-50.)

Neuhauser, William E. and Dallas H. Bradford. "Should You File A Consolidated Return - Revisited," **MA**, 1967, Vol. 48, No. 11, pp. 33-42.

Neumann, Bruce R. and Dustin C. Landagora. "Measuring Divisional Performance For An Oil Company," **MA**, 1982, Vol. 63, No. 9, pp. 41-46.

Neumann, Bruce R. and Laurence A. Friedman. "Opportunity Costs: Further Evidence Through An Experimental Replication," **JAR**, 1978, Vol. 16, No. 2, pp. 400-410.

Neumann, Bruce R. "An Empirical Investigation Of The Relationship Between An AID Hospital Classification Model And Accounting Measures Of Performance," **JAR**, 1979, Vol. 17, No. 1, pp. 123-139.

Neumann, Bruce R. "Future Directions Of Health Care Accounting Research," **RIGNA**, 1986, Vol. 2, pp. 173-187.

Neumann, Bruce R. (Friedman, Laurence A. and Bruce R. Neumann. "The Effects Of Opportunity Costs On Project Investment Decisions: A Replication And Extension," **JAR**,

1980, Vol. 18, No. 2, pp. 407-419.)

Neumann, Bruce R. (Selto, Frank H. and Bruce R. Neumann. "A Further Guide To Research On The Economic Consequences Of Accounting Information," **ABR**, 1980-81. Vol. 11, No. 44, pp. 317-322.)

Neumann, Bruce R. (Suver, James D. and Bruce R. Neumann. "Patient Mix And Breakeven Analysis," **MA**, 1977, Vol. 58, No. 7, pp. 38-40.)

Neumann, Bruce R. (Suver, James D. and Bruce R. Neumann. "Capital Budgeting For Hospitals," **MA**, 1978, Vol. 60, No. 6, pp. 48-50.(Suver, James D. and Bruce R. Neumann. "Capital Budgeting For Hospitals," **MA**, 1978, Vol. 60, No. 6, pp. 48-50.)

Neumann, Bruce R., James D. Suver and Ray L. Brown. "Accountants' Role In Zero-Base Budgeting," **CPAJ**, 1978, Vol. 48, No. 1, pp. 23-28.

Neumann, Frederick L. "Career Education In Accounting In The United States: A Current Appraisal," **IJAER**, 1974, Vol. 9, No. 2, pp. 169-179.

Neumann, Frederick L. "Narrowing The Breach," **CPAJ**, 1978, Vol. 48, No. 10, pp. 40-44.

Neumann, Frederick L. "The Case For On-The-Job Training," **JOA**, 1981, Vol. 152, No. 4, pp. 80-91.

Neumann, Frederick L. "The Incidence And Nature Of Consistency Exceptions," **AR**, 1969, Vol. 44, No. 3, pp. 546-554.

Neumann, Frederick L. "Effect Of Circumstances On..." Accounting Education," **AR**, 1974, Vol. 49, No. 2, pp. 366-368.

Neumann, Frederick L. (Deskins, James Wesley, Frederick L. Neumann and Lawrence Revsine. "A Research Methodology Course For Accountants," **AR**, 1970, Vol. 45, No. 4, pp. 789-795.)

Neumann, Fred. "The Auditing Standard Of Consistency," **JAR**, 1968, Vol. 6, Supp., pp. 1-17.

Neumann, Reuben. (Milne, Ronald A., Glenn A. Vent and Reuben Neumann. "Accounting For Variable Stock Options," **JAED**, 1987, Vol. 5, No. 2, pp. 333-338.)

Neumann, Richard C. (Doney, Lloyd D. and Richard C. Neumann. "Teaching Approaches To Elementary Accounting," **AR**, 1965, Vol. 40, No. 3, pp. 653-655.)

Neuman, David. "Defense Contract Audits: The CPA's Role," **JOA**, 1981, Vol. 151, No. 4, pp. 42-49.

Neuman, Frederick L. (Johnston, Donald J., W. Morley Lemon and Frederick L. Neumann. "The Canadian Study Of The Role Of The Auditor," **JAAF**, 1980, Vol. 3, No. 3, pp. 251-263.)

Neuner, John J. W. "The Status Of Cost Accounting Teaching," **AR**, 1934, Vol. 9, No. 2, pp. 171-175.

Nevling, Robert E. "Records And Procedures For Joint Pole Use," **MA**, 1970, Vol. 51, No. 12, pp. 44-46.

Newbold, Paul. (Gentry, James A., Paul Newbold and David T. Whitford. "Classifying Bankrupt Firms With Funds Flow Components," **JAR**, 1985, Vol. 23, No. 1, pp. 146-160.)

Newbold, Paul. (Hopwood, William S., Paul Newbold and Peter A. Silhan. "The Potential For Gains In Predictive Ability Through Disaggregation: Segmented Annual Earnings," **JAR**, 1982, Vol. 20, No. 2, pp. 724-732.)

Newbold, Paul. (Hopwood, William S. and Paul Newbold. "Alternative Interim Reporting Techniques Within A Dynamic Framework: Comments And Extensions," **AR**, 1985, Vol. 60, No. 2, pp. 289-294.)

Newbold, P. (Hopwood, W. S., J. C. McKeown and P. Newbold. "Power Transformations In Time-Series Models Of Quarterly Earnings Per Share," **AR**, 1981, Vol. 56, No. 4, pp. 927-933.)

Newbold, P. (Hopwood, W. S., J. C. McKeown and P. Newbold. "The Additional Information Content Of Quarterly Earnings Reports: Intertemporal Disaggregation," **JAR**, 1982, Vol. 20, No. 2, Part I, pp. 343-349.)

Newbould, G. D. (Merrett, A. J. and G. D. Newbould. "A Theoretical And Empirical Procedure For The Measurement Of The Economic Income Of Corporations," **AIA**, 1985, Vol. 2, pp. 47-68.)

Newbould, G. D., S. J. Stray and K. W. Wilson. "Shareholders' Interests And Acquisition Activity," **ABR**, 1975-76, Vol. 6, No. 23, pp. 201-215.

Newcomer, Hale L. "Report Of Committee On Revision Of The Statement Of Principles: Introductory Statement," **AR**, 1948, Vol. 23, No. 1, pp. 7-12.

Newcomer, Hale L. "The CPA Examination," **AR**, 1949, Vol. 24, No. 2, pp. 128-135.

Newell, Gale E. and Jerry G. Kreuze. "Improving The Audit Process," **MA**, 1987, Vol. 69, No. 2, pp. 56-59.

Newell, Gale E. "Should Humans Be Reported As Assets?," **MA**, 1972, Vol. 54, No. 6, pp. 13-16.

Newell, Gale E. (Kreuze, Jerry G. and Gale E. Newell. "Student Ratings Of Accounting Instructors: A Search For Important Determinants," **JAED**, 1987, Vol. 5, No. 1, pp. 87-98.)

Newkirk, Thomas. "Improving Financial Information Systems In Local Government," **MA**, 1982, Vol. 63, No. 7, pp. 23-28.

Newlove, George Hillis. "In All My Years: Economic And Legal Causes Of Changes In Accounting," **AHJ**, 1975, Vol. 2, No. 1-4, pp. 40-44.

Newlove, G. H. "Columnar Realization And Liquidation Statement," **AR**, 1946, Vol. 21, No. 1, pp. 78-81.

Newlove, G. H. "Graduate Courses In Accounting," **AR**, 1927, Vol. 2, No. 2, pp. 167-171.

Newlove, G. H. "Graduate Schools Of Business," **AR**, 1926, Vol. 1, No. 3, pp. 74-79.

Newlove, G. H. "New Techniques In Consolidations," **AR**, 1953, Vol. 28, No. 4, pp. 500-504.

Newlove, G. H. "Relative Sales Value Theory Of Allocating

Costs," **AR**, 1929, Vol. 4, No. 4, pp. 251-254.

Newlove, G. H. "The Teaching Of Process Costs," **AR**, 1954, Vol. 29, No. 4, pp. 676-683.

Newlove, G. H. "The Teaching Of Cost Accounting," **AR**, 1931, Vol. 6, No. 2, pp. 113-117.

Newlove, G. H. "The Timing Of Unavoidably Spoiled Units," **AR**, 1960, Vol. 35, No. 2, pp. 320-324.

Newmann, Robert W. (Leonhardi, Willis A. and Robert W. Newmann. "NAARS And LEXIS: Research Tools," **CPAJ**, 1977, Vol. 47, No. 9, pp. 33-40.)

Newman, Barry and David L. Treiger. "Michelin And State Taxation Of Imports," **CPAJ**, 1976, Vol. 46, No. 7, pp. 33-36.

Newman, Barry and Leonard I. Kanarek. "Tax Reform And Net Operating Losses," **CPAJ**, 1977, Vol. 47, No. 2, pp. 17-22.

Newman, Benjamin. "Auditing Standards Should Require More Competent Evidence For Fixed Assets," **JOA**, 1950, Vol. 89, No. 6, pp. 510-512.

Newman, D. Paul. "An Investigation Of The Distribution Of Power In The APB And FASB," **JAR**, 1981, Vol. 19, No. 1, pp. 247-262.

Newman, D. Paul. "Coalition Formation In The APB And The FASB: Some Evidence On The Size Principle," **AR**, 1981, Vol. 56, No. 4, pp. 897-909.

Newman, D. Paul. "Coalition Formation In The APB And The FASB:A Reply," **AR**, 1982, Vol. 57, No. 1, pp. 196-199.

Newman, D. Paul. "The SEC's Influence On Accounting Standards: The Power Of The Veto," **JAR**, 1981, Vol. 19, Supp., pp. 134-164.

Newman, D. Paul. (Fellingham, John C. and D. Paul Newman. "Strategic Considerations In Auditing," **AR**, 1985, Vol. 60, No. 4, pp. 634-650.)

Newman, D. P. "Prospect Theory: Implications For Information Evaluation," **AOS**, 1980, Vol. 5, No. 2, pp. 217-230.

Newman, Harry A. (Johnson, W. Bruce, Robert P. Magee, Nandu J. Nagarajan and Harry A. Newman. "An Analysis Of The Stock Price Reaction To Sudden Executive Deaths: Implications For The Management Labor Market," **JAEC**, 1985, Vol. 7, No. 1/3, pp. 151-174.)

Newman, Maurice S. "Accounting For Research And Development Expenditures," **CPAJ**, 1974, Vol. 44, No. 4, pp. 55-58.

Newman, Maurice S. "Computer-Assisted Professional Competence," **ACCHOR**, 1988, Vol. 2, No. 1, pp. 50-57.

Newmark, Richard H. "Gross-Up" Of Foreign Dividends," **MA**, 1966, Vol. 47, No. 5, pp. 47-54.

Newmiller, John S. and Allen Speiser. "Voluntary Health And Welfare Financial Statements," **CPAJ**, 1977, Vol. 47, No. 9, pp. 47-54.

Newton, Don P. "Computer Impact On Standard Costs," **MA**, 1968, Vol. 50, No. 4, pp. 24-26.

Newton, Fred J. "Restoring Public Confidence In Government Contractors," **MA**, 1986, Vol. 67, No. 12, pp. 51-55.

Newton, Grant W. and James J. Ward, Jr. "Valuation Of A Business In Bankruptcy," **CPAJ**, 1976, Vol. 46, No. 8, pp. 26-32.

Newton, Grant W. "Management Accountant: Catalyst For Change," **MA**, 1976, Vol. 58, No. 1, pp. 52-56.

Newton, Grant W. "The Practitioner's Role In Debt Settlements," **JOA**, 1976, Vol. 141, No. 5, pp. 59-63.

Newton, James D. "Using Student Evaluation Of Teaching In Administrative Control: The Validity Problem," **JAED**, 1988, Vol. 6, No. 1, pp. 1-14.

Newton, James D. (Abdel-khalik, A. Rashad, Paul R. Graul and James D. Newton. "Reporting Uncertainty And Assessment Of Risk: Replication And Extension In A Canadian Setting," **JAR**, 1986, Vol. 24, No. 2, pp. 372-382.)

Newton, J. D. (Williams, J. J., J. D. Newton and E. A. Morgan. "The Integration Of Zero-Based Budgeting With Management-By-Objectives: An Empirical Inquiry," **AOS**, 1985, Vol. 10, No. 4, pp. 457-478.)

Newton, Lauren K. "A Process For Assessing Materiality," **CPAJ**, 1977, Vol. 47, No. 5, pp. 11-16.

Newton, Lauren K. "The Risk Factor In Materiality Decisions," **AR**, 1977, Vol. 52, No. 1, pp. 97-108.

Newton, Sherwood W. (Johnson, Glenn L. and Sherwood W. Newton. "Tax Considerations In Equipment Replacement Decisions," **AR**, 1967, Vol. 42, No. 4, pp. 738-746.)

Newton, W. K. "New Developments And Simplified Approaches To Municipal Accounting," **AR**, 1954, Vol. 29, No. 4, pp. 656-660.

Neyhart, Charles A. (Cramer, Joe J., Jr. and Charles A. Neyhart, Jr. "A Conceptual Framework For Accounting And Reporting By Pension Plans," **ABACUS**, 1980, Vol. 16, No. 1, pp. 3-16.)

Neyhart, Charles A., Jr. and A. Eugene Abrassart. "A Scoring Rule For Probabilistic Multiple-Choice Tests," **JAED**, 1984, Vol. 2, No. 1, pp. 71-81.

Neyhart, Charles A., Jr. and A. Eugene Abrassart. "Probabilistic Testing And The Evaluation Of Student Performance," **AR**, 1977, Vol. 52, No. 4, pp. 939-945.

Neyhart, Charles A., Jr. (Cramer, Joe J., Jr. and Charles A. Neyhart, Jr. "A Comprehensive Accounting Framework For Evaluating Executory Contracts," **JAAF**, 1979, Vol. 2, No. 2, pp. 135-150.)

Neyhart, Charles A., Jr. (Cramer, Joe J., Jr. and Charles A. Neyhart, Jr. "Accounting For Pensions: A Contemporary Perspective," **CPAJ**, 1976, Vol. 46, No. 6, pp. 19-24.)

Neyhart, Charles A., Jr. (Kern, Charles L., Charles A. Neyhart, Jr. and Clayton A. Hocke. "Statistical Risk And Sample Reliability," **CPAJ**, 1973, Vol. 43, No. 1, pp. 55-60.)

Ng, David G. "An Information Economics Analysis Of Financial Reporting And External Auditing," **AR**, 1978, Vol. 53, No. 4, pp. 910-920.

Ng, **David S.** and Jan Stoeckenius. "Auditing: Incentives And Truthful Reporting," **JAR**, 1979, Vol. 17, Supp., pp. 1-24.

Nichols, **Arthur C.** and Dennis E. Grawoig. "Accounting Reports With Time As A Variable." **AR**, 1968, Vol. 43, No. 4, pp. 631-639.

Nichols, **Donald R.** and David B. Smith. "Auditor Credibility And Auditor Changes," **JAR**, 1983, Vol. 21, No. 2, pp. 534-544.

Nichols, **Donald R.** and James E. Parker. "An Alternative To Liquidity As A Basis For Exchange Valuation," **ABACUS**, 1972, Vol. 8, No. 1, pp. 68-74.

Nichols, **Donald R.** and Jeffrey J. Tsay. "Security Price Reactions To Long-Range Executive Earnings Forecasts," **JAR**, 1979, Vol. 17, No. 1. pp. 140-155.

Nichols, **Donald R.** and Kenneth H. Price. "The Auditor-Firm Conflict: An Analysis Using Concepts Of Exchange Theory," **AR**, 1976, Vol. 51. No. 2. pp. 335-346.

Nichols, **Donald R.** and R. C. Baker. "Testing The Consistency Of Auditors' Prior Distributions And Sampling Results," **ABACUS**, 1977, Vol. 13. No. 2, pp. 91-105.

Nichols, **Donald R.** and S. Michael Groomer. "A Study Of The Relative Accuracy Of Executives' Estimates Of Earnings," **ABACUS**, 1979, Vol. 15, No. 2, pp. 113-127.

Nichols, **Donald R.** "A Model Of Auditors' Preliminary Evaluations Of Internal Control From Audit Data," **AR**, 1987, Vol. 62, No. 1, pp. 183-190.

Nichols, **Donald R.** "Comparative Analysis Of Net Realizable Value And Replacement Costing - A Comment," **AR**, 1973, Vol. 48, No. 2, pp. 383-385.

Nichols, **Donald R.** "PPBS: A Challenge To Non-Profit Accounting," **MA**, 1969, Vol. 51, No. 5. pp. 12-13.

Nichols, **Donald R.** "The Effect Of Extraordinary Items On Predictions Of Earnings," **ABACUS**, 1973, Vol. 9, No. 1, pp. 81-92.

Nichols, **Donald R.** "The 'Never-To-Recur Unusual Item' - A Critique Of APB Opinion No. 30," **CPAJ**, 1974, Vol. 44, No. 3, pp. 45-48.

Nichols, **Donald R.** (Smith, David B. and Donald R. Nichols. "A Market Test Of Investor Reaction To Disagreements." **JAEC**, 1982, Vol. 4, No. 2, pp. 109-120.)

Nichols, **Donald R.**, Jeffrey J. Tsay and Paula D. Larkin. "Investor Trading Responses To Differing Characteristics Of Voluntarily Disclosed Earnings Forecasts." **AR**, 1979, Vol. 54, No. 2, pp. 376-382.

Nichols, **Gerald E.** "Accounting And The Total Information System," **MA**, 1971, Vol. 52, No. 9, pp. 27-30.

Nichols, **Gerald E.** "Business Consulting For Credit," **AR**, 1972, Vol. 47, No. 3, pp. 607-608.

Nichols, **Gerald E.** "On The Nature Of Management Information," **MA**, 1969, Vol. 50, No. 8, pp. 9-13.

Nichols, **John F.** "When You're Called To Court As A Witness," **JOA**, 1988, Vol. 166. No. 6, pp. 66-68.

Nichols, **John R.** "An Accounts Payable Application Of EDP." **MA**, 1966, Vol. 47, No. 7. pp. 17-33.

Nichols, **Osgood.** "The CPA In The Public Eye," **JOA**, 1964, Vol. 118, No. 6, pp. 33-36.

Nichols, **William D.** (Mendenhall, Richard R. and William D. Nichols. "Bad News And Differential Market Reactions To Announcements Of Earlier-Quarters Versus Fourth-Quarter Earnings," **JAR**, 1988, Vol. 26, Supp., pp. 63-86.)

Nichols, **William D.** (Morris, Michael H. and William D. Nichols. "Pension Accounting And The Balance Sheet: The Potential Effect Of The FASB's Preliminary Views," **JAAF**, 1984, Vol. 7, No. 4, pp. 293-305.)

Nichols, **William D.** (Morris, Michael H. and William D. Nichols. "Consistency Exceptions: Materiality Judgments And Audit Firm Structure," **AR**, 1988, Vol. 63, No. 2, pp. 237-254.)

Nichols, **William D.** (Morris, Michael H. and William D. Nichols. "The Election To Capitalize Carrying Charges Following ERTA And TEFRA," **JATA**, 1984. Vol. 5. No. 2, pp. 60-67.)

Nichols, **William D.** (Pattillo, James W., Michael H. Morris and William D. Nichols. "The Materiality Principle: Problems And Possible Solutions," **CA**, 1983. Vol. 1, No. 3, pp. 44-51.)

Nichols, **William S.** (Harwell, Jeff L, William S. Nichols, III and Scott D. Steffler. "Recent Experiments In The Presentation Of Earnings Per Share," **AR**, 1974, Vol. 49, No. 4, pp. 852-853.)

Nickerson, **Charles A.** and Robert H. Strawser. "Photography As An Audit Tool," **JOA**, 1976, Vol. 142. No. 5, pp. 82-86.

Nickerson, **Charles A.** (Byars, Richard B. and Charles A. Nickerson. "Inter Vivos Gifts: An Anachronism?," **JATA**, 1980, Vol. 2. No. 1, pp. 16-18.)

Nickerson, **Charles A.** (Byars, Richard B. and Charles A. Nickerson. "Charitable Remainder Trusts - Valuation Methods Yield Inconsistent Results," **JATA**, 1982, Vol. 4, No. 1, pp. 13-18.)

Nickerson, **Charles A.,** Larry Gene Pointer and Robert H. Strawser. "Attitudes Of Financial Executives Toward Interim Financial Statements," **CPAJ**, 1975, Vol. 45, No. 3, pp. 21-24.

Nickerson, **Clarence B.** "Inventory Reserves As An Element Of Inventory Policy," **AR**, 1937, Vol. 12, No. 4, pp. 345-354.

Nicol, **Robert E. G.** "The Accounting Equation Revisited: A Conceptual Accounting Model," **AR**, 1968, Vol. 43, No. 4, pp. 777-779.

Nicol, **Robert E. G.** (Schwab. Bernhard and Robert E. G. Nicol. "From Double-Declining-Balance To Sum-Of-The-Years'-Digits Depreciation: An Optimum Switching Rule," **AR**, 1969, Vol. 44, No. 2, pp. 292-296.)

Nicolson, **Miklos Szucs.** "Balance Sheets For Partnerships And Proprietors," **JOA**, 1962, Vol. 113. No. 6, pp. 57-61.

Niebuhr, **R. E.** (Norris, D. R. and R. E. Niebuhr. "Professionalism, Organizational Commitment And Job Satisfaction In An Accounting Organization," **AOS**, 1984, Vol. 9, No. 1, pp. 49-60.)

Niehus, **Rudolph J.** "Generally Accepted Auditing Principles In Germany." **IJAER**, 1969, Vol. 4, No. 2, pp. 113-124.

Niehus, **Rudolph J.** "Stock Corporation Law Reform In Germany And The Public Accountant," **IJAER**, 1966, Vol. 1, No. 2, pp. 25-41.

Niehus, **R. J.** "Tax-Free Stock Dividends And The New Model Income Statement For German Corporations," **AR**, 1961. Vol. 36. No. 2, pp. 259-264.

Nielsen, **Carl C.** "Reporting Joint-Venture Corporations." **AR**, 1965. Vol. 40. No. 4, pp. 795-804.

Nielsen, **Gordon L.** "The Computer In Accounting Education," **AR**, 1965, Vol. 40, No. 4, pp. 871-876.

Nielsen, **Gordon L.** "The Purchase Of An Accounting Practice: Making The Right Choice," **JOA**, 1984, Vol. 157, No. 2, pp. 76-81.

Nielsen, **James F.** (Bailes, Jack C., James F. Nielsen and Steve Wendell. "Capital Budgeting In The Forest Products Industry," **MA**, 1979, Vol. 61, No. 1, pp. 46-51.)

Nielsen, **Oswald.** "A Predecessor Of Direct Costing," **JAR**, 1966, Vol. 4, No. 1, pp. 119-120.

Nielsen, **Oswald.** "Canons For Line Of Business Reporting," **MA**, 1967, Vol. 48, No. 12, pp. 3-7.

Nielsen, **Oswald.** "Depreciation As A Function Of Revenue," **AR**, 1938, Vol. 13, No. 3, pp. 265-274.

Nielsen, **Oswald.** "How Direct Costing Works For Small Manufacturer," **JOA**, 1953, Vol. 96, No. 2, pp. 197-205.

Nielsen, **Oswald.** "In All My Years," **AHJ**, 1975, Vol. 2, No. 1-4. pp. 51-54.

Nielsen, **Oswald.** "New Challenges In Accounting," **AR**, 1960. Vol. 35. No. 4, pp. 583-589.

Nielsen, **Oswald.** "The Nature And Importance Of Variances From Standard Cost Of Production," **MA**, 1969, Vol. 50, No. 5, pp. 16-20.

Nielsen, **Oswald.** "The Role Of Variance In Managerial Control," **MA**, 1969, Vol. 51, No. 4, pp. 26-28.

Nielson, **Richard P.** "Market Piggybacking For Nonprofits: A Shared-Costs-Based Self-Subsidization Strategy," **CA**. 1984, Vol. 2, No. 2, pp. 13-23.

Nigam, **B. M. Lall.** "Bahi-Khata: The Pre-Pacioli Indian Double-Entry System Of Bookkeeping." **ABACUS**, 1986. Vol. 22, No. 2, pp. 148-161.

Nikolai, **Loren A.** and John D. Bazley. "The Organizational Set Prestige Ranking And Its Impact Upon Accounting Department Faculties," **AR**, 1975, Vol. 50, No. 4. pp. 881-888.

Nikolai, **Loren A.** and Rick Elam. "The Pollution Control Tax Incentive: A Non-Incentive," **AR**, 1979, Vol. 54. No. 1. pp. 119-131.

Nikolai, **Loren A.** (Bazley, John D. and Loren A. Nikolai. "A Comparison Of Published Accounting Research And Qualities Of Accounting Faculty And Doctoral Programs," **AR**. 1975, Vol. 50. No. 3, pp. 605-610.)

Nikolai, **Loren A.** (Howard, Thomas P. and Loren A. Nikolai. "Attitude Measurement And Perceptions Of Accounting Faculty Publication Outlets," **AR**, 1983, Vol. 58, No. 4, pp. 765-776.)

Nikolai, **Loren A.** (Matulich. Serge, Loren A. Nikolai and Stevan K. Olson. "Earnings Per Share: A Flow Chart Approach To Teaching Concepts And Procedures," **AR**, 1977, Vol. 52. No. 1, pp. 238-247.)

Nikolai, **Loren A.** (Rockness, Howard O., John D. Bazley and Loren A. Nikolai. "Variance Analysis For Pollution Control," **MA**, 1977, Vol. 58, No. 7, pp. 51-54.)

Nikolai, **Loren A.** (Rockness, Howard O. and Loren A. Nikolai. "An Assessment Of APB Voting Patterns," **JAR**, 1977, Vol. 15, No. 1, pp. 154-167.)

Nikolai, **Loren A.,** John D. Bazley and R. Lee Brummet. "The Measurement Of Corporate Environmental Activity," **MA**, 1976, Vol. 57, No. 12, pp. 38-40.

Niles, **Marcia S.** (Felix, William L., Jr. and Marcia S. Niles. "Research In Internal Control Evaluation," **AJPT**, 1988, Vol. 7, No. 2, pp. 43-60.)

Niles, **Marcia S.** (Felix, W. L., Jr., Robert G. May, Marcia S. Niles and John R. Thorson. "SCAD: Something New In Auditing Education," **JAED**, 1985, Vol. 3, No. 2. pp. 5-14.)

Niles, **Timothy J.** and Robert H. Dowis, Jr. "Accounting For New Plant Construction," **MA**, 1974, Vol. 56, No. 1, pp. 35-38, 43-44.

Nilsson, **Henry G.** "Three Methods Of Fixing Fees For Public Accounting Work, And Advantages Of Each," **JOA**, 1950, Vol. 90, No. 1, pp. 36-39.

Ninsuvannakul, **Pianchai.** "Education For Accountancy In Thailand," **IJAER**, 1966, Vol. 2, No. 1, pp. 77-114.

Nishikawa, **Kojiro.** "Historical Studies In Recent Years In Japan," **AHJ**, 1975, Vol. 2. No. 1-4. pp. 31-34.

Nishikawa, **Kojiro.** "The Introduction Of Western Bookkeeping Into Japan," **AHJ**, 1977, Vol. 4, No. 1, pp. 25-36.

Nishikawa, **Noboru.** (Taketera, Sadao and Noboru Nishikawa. "Genesis Of Divisional Management And Accounting Systems In The House Of Mitsui, 1710 - 1730," **AHJ**, 1984, Vol. 11, No. 1, pp. 141-149.)

Nissen, **Thomas J.** (John, Richard C. and Thomas J. Nissen. "Evaluating Internal Control In EDP Audits," **JOA**, 1970. Vol. 129. No. 2. pp. 31-38.)

Nissley, **Warren W.** "Education For Professional Accountancy: Comments," **AR**, 1936, Vol. 11, No. 2, pp. 105-108.

Nissley, **Warren W.** "Recruitment For The Profession," **AR**, 1947. Vol. 22, No. 1, pp. 18-22.

Nissley, Warren W. "Use Of Short-Term 'Capital' Loans Growing, Bankers Need Income Statement More Than Balance-Sheet," **JOA**, 1950, Vol. 89, No. 3, pp. 203-205.

Nissley, Warren W. (Wood, Ben D., Arthur E. Traxler and Warren W. Nissley. "College Accounting Testing Program," **AR**, 1948, Vol. 23, No. 1, pp. 63-83.)

Nissley, W. W. "Bureau For Placing Junior Accountants," **AR**, 1926, Vol. 1, No. 1, pp. 64-68.

Nissley, W. W. "Progress Of The Bureau For Placements," **AR**, 1928, Vol. 3, No. 1, pp. 36-42.

Niswonger, C. Rollin. "The Attraction And Selection Of Accounting Majors," **AR**, 1956, Vol. 31, No. 1, pp. 24-32.

Niswonger, C. R. "The Interpretation Of Income In A Period Of Inflated Prices," **AR**, 1949, Vol. 24, No. 1, pp. 27-32.

Nix, Harold M. and Henry Wichmann, Jr. "The Governmental Audit Report," **JAAF**, 1983, Vol. 6, No. 4, pp. 341-352.

Nix, Harold M. (Boer, Germain and Harold M. Nix. "Hospital Management And Resource Control," **MA**, 1975, Vol. 57, No. 3, pp. 47-48.)

Nobes, Christopher W. "Classification Of Financial Accounting Practices," **AIIA**, 1987, Vol. 1, pp. 1-22.

Nobes, Christopher W. "International Variations In Perceptions Of Accounting Journals," **AR**, 1985, Vol. 60, No. 4, pp. 702-705.

Nobes, Christopher W. "The Gallerani Account Book Of 1305-1308," **AR**, 1982, Vol. 57, No. 2, pp. 303-310.

Nobes, Christopher W. "The Pre-Pacioli Indian Double-Entry System Of Bookkeeping: A Comment," **ABACUS**, 1987, Vol. 23, No. 2, pp. 182-184.

Nobes, C. W. "A Review Of The Translation Debate," **ABR**, 1979-80, Vol. 10, No. 40, pp. 421-431.

Nobes, C. W. "An Empirical Analysis Of International Accounting Principles: A Comment," **JAR**, 1981, Vol. 19, No. 1, pp. 268-270.

Nobes, C. W. "Costs V. Exit Values: A Comment," **ABACUS**, 1983, Vol. 19, No. 1, pp. 76-78.

Nobes, C. W. "Current Cost Accounting: Valuation By Intent?," **ABR**, 1976-77, Vol. 7, No. 26, pp. 95-99.

Nobes, C. W. "Harmonization Of Accounting Within The European Communites: The Fourth Directive On Company Law," **IJAER**, 1980, Vol. 15, No. 2, pp. 1-16.

Nobes, C. W. "Imputation Systems Of Corporation Tax Within The EEC," **ABR**, 1979-80, Vol. 10, No. 38, pp. 221-231.

Nobes, C. W. "The Evolution Of The Harmonising Provisions Of The 1980 And 1981 Companies Acts," **ABR**, 1983-84, Vol. 14, No. 53, pp. 43-54.

Nobes, C. W. (Fraser, I. A. M. and C. W. Nobes. "The Assumed Users In Three Accounting Theories," **ABR**, 1984-85, Vol. 15, No. 58, pp. 144-147.)

Nobes, C. W. (Fraser, I. A. M. and C. W. Nobes. "Is Sterling Correctly Valued?," **ABR**, 1984-85, Vol. 15, No. 59, pp. 246-247.)

Noble, Howard S. "A Cost Approach To Elementary Accounting," **AR**, 1933, Vol. 8, No. 1, pp. 29-33.

Noble, Howard S. "Graduate Study Of Accounting," **AR**, 1935, Vol. 10, No. 3, pp. 229-237.

Noble, H. S. "Cost Accounting In Great Britain," **AR**, 1929, Vol. 4, No. 2, pp. 88-93.

Noble, H. S. "Some Cost Accounting Concepts Of Wider Application," **AR**, 1926, Vol. 1, No. 4, pp. 48-54.

Noble, H. S. "The Relation Of Business Organization To Accounting," **AR**, 1927, Vol. 2, No. 3, pp. 232-236.

Noble, Paul L. "A Quantitative Evaluation Of Accounting Curricula," **AR**, 1950, Vol. 25, No. 2, pp. 163-169.

Noble, T. B. "How Client And Auditor Can Help Each Other Get Most Effective Audits At Least Cost," **JOA**, 1950, Vol. 89, No. 6, pp. 506-509.

Nodar, Andrew L. "Coca-Cola Writes An Accounting Procedures Manual," **MA**, 1986, Vol. 68, No. 4, pp. 52-53.

Noel, James. (Baiman, Stanley and James Noel. "Noncontrollable Costs And Responsibility Accounting," **JAR**, 1985, Vol. 23, No. 2, pp. 486-501.)

Noel, James. (Baiman, Stanley, John H. Evans, III and James Noel. "Optimal Contracts With A Utility-Maximizing Auditor," **JAR**, 1987, Vol. 25, No. 2, pp. 217-244.)

Noel, James. (Ijiri, Yuji and James Noel. "A Reliability Comparison Of The Measurement Of Wealth, Income, And Force," **AR**, 1984, Vol. 59, No. 1, pp. 52-63.)

Noehl, James W. "A Programed Adjustment Procedure," **AR**, 1964, Vol. 39, No. 3, pp. 760-764.

Noke, Christopher. "Accounting For Bailiffship In Thirteenth Century England," **ABR**, 1980-81, Vol. 11, No. 42, pp. 137-152.

Noltemeyer, Vincent E. "Cost Accounting Practices In The Wood Conversion Industry," **MA**, 1970, Vol. 52, No. 5, pp. 45-48.

Norberg, Douglas E. (Jahn, Jerome J. and Douglas E. Norberg. "The Barchris Decision - Liability For All," **MA**, 1968, Vol. 50, No. 3, pp. 54-56.)

Nord, Walter R. (Virgil, Robert L., Walter R. Nord and Sterling H. Schoen. "A Classroom Experience In The Behavioral Implications Of Accounting Performance Evaluation Measurements," **AR**, 1973, Vol. 48, No. 2, pp. 410-418.)

Nordby, David B. "Controlling And Estimating Labor Costs In The Construction Industry," **MA**, 1970, Vol. 51, No. 11, pp. 23-25.

Nordhauser, Fred. (Egenolf, Robert V. and Fred Nordhauser. "Public Sector Accounting In The Public Administration Curriculum," **JAED**, 1985, Vol. 3, No. 1, pp. 123-130.)

Nordhauser, Susan L. and John L. Kramer. "Repeal Of The Deferral Privilege For Earnings From Direct Foreign Investments: An Analysis," **AR**, 1981, Vol. 56, No. 1, pp. 54-69.

Noreen, Eric and James Sepe. "Market Reactions To Accounting Policy Deliberations: The Inflation Accounting Case," **AR**, 1981, Vol. 56, No. 2, pp. 253-269.

Noreen, Eric and James Sepe. "Market Reactions To Accounting Policy Deliberations: The Inflation Accounting Case Revisited - A Reply," **AR**, 1981, Vol. 56, No. 4, pp. 955-958.

Noreen, Eric and Mark Wolfson. "Equilibrium Warrant Pricing Models And Accounting For Executive Stock Options," **JAR**, 1981, Vol. 19, No. 2, pp. 384-398.

Noreen, Eric W. "Comment: Measuring The Compensation Element In Employee Stock Option Plans," **JAAF**, 1979, Vol. 3, No. 1, pp. 67-69.

Noreen, Eric W. (Bowen, Robert M., Eric W. Noreen and John M. Lacey. "Determinants Of The Corporate Decision To Capitalize Interest," **JAEC**, 1981, Vol. 3, No. 2, pp. 151-179.)

Noreen, Eric W. (Burgstahler, David and Eric W. Noreen. "Detecting Contemporaneous Security Market Reactions To A Sequence Of Related Events," **JAR**, 1986, Vol. 24, No. 1, pp. 170-186.)

Noreen, Eric. "An Empirical Comparison Of Probit And OLS Regression Hypothesis Tests," **JAR**, 1988, Vol. 26, No. 1, pp. 119-133.

Noreen, Eric. (Arnold, John., Peter Moizer and Eric Noreen. "Investment Appraisal Methods Of Financial Analysts: A Comparative Study Of U.S. And U.K. Practices," **IJAER**, 1984, Vol. 19, No. 2, pp. 1-18.)

Noreen, Eric. (Blanchard, Garth A., Chee W. Chow and Eric Noreen. "Information Asymmetry, Incentive Schemes, And Information Biasing: The Case Of Hospital Budgeting Under Rate Regulation," **AR**, 1986, Vol. 61, No. 1, pp. 1-15.)

Noreen, E. "The Economics Of Ethics: A New Perspective On Agency Theory," **AOS**, 1988, Vol. 13, No. 4, pp. 359-370.

Norgaard, Corine T. "Extending The Boundaries Of The Attest Function," **AR**, 1972, Vol. 47, No. 3, pp. 433-442.

Norgaard, Corine T. "Operational Auditing: A Part Of The Control Process," **MA**, 1972, Vol. 53, No. 9, pp. 25-28.

Norgaard, Corine T. "The Professional Accountant's View Of Operational Auditing," **JOA**, 1969, Vol. 128, No. 6, pp. 45-48.

Norgaard, Corine T. (Corless, John C. and Corine T. Norgaard. "User Reactions To CPA Reports On Forecasts," **JOA**, 1974, Vol. 138, No. 2, pp. 46-54.)

Norgaard, Corine T. (Grinnell, D. Jacque and Corine T. Norgaard. "Reporting Changes In Accounting Principles - Time For A Change?," **JOA**, 1979, Vol. 148, No. 6, pp. 64-72.)

Norgaard, Corine T. (Grinnell, D. Jacque and Corine T. Norgaard. "Reporting Changes In Financial Position," **MA**, 1972, Vol. 54, No. 3, pp. 15-22.)

Norgaard, Corine T. (Kochanek, Richard F. and Corine T. Norgaard. "Analyzing The Components Of Operating Cash Flow: The Charter Company," **ACCHOR**, 1988, Vol. 2, No. 1, pp. 58-66.)

Norgaard, Corine T. (Kochanek, Richard F. and Corine T. Norgaard. "Student Perceptions Of Alternative Accounting Careers - Part I," **CPAJ**, 1985, Vol. 55, No. 5, pp. 36-43.)

Norgaard, Corine T. (Kochanek, Richard F. and Corine T. Norgaard. "Student Perceptions Of Alternative Accounting Careers - Part II," **CPAJ**, 1985, Vol. 55, No. 6, pp. 26-33.)

Norgaard, Richard L. and Richard H. Pettway. "Evaluating Average Ratios Used In Capital Budgeting," **MA**, 1966, Vol. 48, No. 4, pp. 16-20.

Norman, David T. (McGee, Wesley O. and David T. Norman. "Profit And Growth Through Sales Compensation," **MA**, 1976, Vol. 58, No. 6, pp. 32-34.)

Normolle, Daniel. (Horwitz, Bertrand and Daniel Normolle. "Federal Agency R&D Contract Awards And The FASB Rule For Privately-Funded R&D," **AR**, 1988, Vol. 63, No. 3, pp. 414-435.)

Norris, D. R. and R. E. Niebuhr. "Professionalism, Organizational Commitment And Job Satisfaction In An Accounting Organization," **AOS**, 1984, Vol. 9, No. 1, pp. 49-60.

Norris, James C., Jr. "Accountants And Engineers: Closing The Communications Gap," **MA**, 1972, Vol. 54, No. 6, pp. 17-19.

Norstrom, Carl J. "The Deprival Value Of Durable Assets," **ABR**, 1984-85, Vol. 15, No. 60, pp. 265-270.

North, Paul. "An Application Of Direct Costing," **MA**, 1970, Vol. 51, No. 7, pp. 48-50.

North, Robert D. "Relation Between Scores On The AIA Elementary And Advanced Accounting Achievement Tests," **AR**, 1956, Vol. 31, No. 1, pp. 50-55.

Norton, Curtis L. and John O. Everett. "An Extension Of Jordan's Analysis Of Section 179 Property," **JATA**, 1983, Vol. 5, No. 1, pp. 60-62.

Norton, Curtis L. and Ralph E. Smith. "A Comparison Of General Price Level And Historical Cost Financial Statements In The Prediction Of Bankruptcy: A Reply," **AR**, 1980, Vol. 55, No. 3, pp. 516-521.

Norton, Curtis L. and Ralph E. Smith. "A Comparison Of General Price Level And Historical Cost Financial Statements In The Prediction Of Bankruptcy," **AR**, 1979, Vol. 54, No. 1, pp. 72-87.

Norton, Curtis L. and Thomas S. Wetzel. "The Recognition And Measurement Guidelines Of FASB Concepts No. 5," **JAED**, 1986, Vol. 4, No. 2, pp. 75-84.

Norton, Curtis L. "Pension Accounting: Effects Of Early Adoption," **CPAJ**, 1988, Vol. 58, No. 3, pp. 46-51.

Norton, Curtis L. (Delaney, Patrick R., David E. Keyes,

Curtis L. Norton and John R. Simon. "An Admission Test For Intermediate Accounting." **AR**, 1979, Vol. 54, No. 1, pp. 155-162.)

Norton, Curtis. "A.S.R. 190: Liability And Safe Harbor Rules." **CPAJ**, 1978, Vol. 48, No. 2, pp. 17-22.

Norton, Curtis. (Keys, David E. and Curtis Norton. "Estimation Error In Income Determination: A Comment," **AR**, 1978, Vol. 53, No. 4, pp. 997-1002.)

Norton, Paul T., Jr. "Depreciation Accounting." **JOA**, 1958, Vol. 105, No. 6, pp. 35-40.

Norton, Roger L. "The Controller And Pension Plans," **AR**, 1953, Vol. 28, No. 2, pp. 170-176.

Norwood, Gyles R. (Deakin, Edward B., Gyles R. Norwood and Charles H. Smith. "The Effect Of Published Earnings Information On Tokyo Stock Exchange Trading," **IJAER**, 1974, Vol. 10, No. 1, pp. 123-136.)

Nottingham, C. "Conceptual Framework For Improved Computer Audits," **ABR**, 1975-76, Vol. 6, No. 22, pp. 140-148.

Nour, Ahmed. (Gambling, Trevor E. and Ahmed Nour. "A Note On Input-Output Analysis: Its Uses In Macro-Economics And Micro-Economics," **AR**, 1970, Vol. 45, No. 1, pp. 98-102.)

Novak, Frank S. and William M. Koeblitz. "Pensions: The Surprise Package In Corporate Marriage," **MA**, 1984, Vol. 65, No. 7, pp. 50-55.

Nugent, Christopher E. (Bower, Richard S., Christopher E. Nugent and Donald E. Stone. "Time-Shared Computers In Business Education At Dartmouth," **AR**, 1968, Vol. 43, No. 3, pp. 565-582.)

Nunamaker, Thomas R. (Gaumnitz, Bruce R., Thomas R. Nunamaker, John J. Surdick and Michael F. Thomas. "Auditor Consensus In Internal Control Evaluation And Audit Program Planning," **JAR**, 1982, Vol. 20, No. 2, Part II, pp. 745-755.)

Nunamaker, Thomas R. (Truitt, Jack F. and Thomas R. Nunamaker. "Self-Insurance Should Be Accrued," **MA**, 1987, Vol. 68, No. 9, pp. 62-65.)

Nurnberg, Hugo and Corwin Grube. "Alternative Methods Of Accounting For Business Combinations," **AR**, 1970, Vol. 45, No. 4, pp. 783-789.

Nurnberg, Hugo and S. Thomas A. Cianciolo. "The Measurement Valuation Allowance: Help For Deferred Taxes," **JAAF**, 1985, Vol. 9, No. 1, pp. 50-59.

Nurnberg, Hugo, Clyde P. Stickney and Roman L. Weil. "Combining Stockholders' Equity Accounts Under Pooling Of Interests Method," **AR**, 1975, Vol. 50, No. 1, pp. 179-183.

Nurnberg, Hugo. "A Note On The Financial Reporting Of Depreciation And Income Taxes," **JAR**, 1969, Vol. 7, No. 2, pp. 257-261.

Nurnberg, Hugo. "A Strange Animal," **JAR**, 1973, Vol. 11, No. 2, pp. 331-333.

Nurnberg, Hugo. "Annual And Interim Financial Reporting Of Changes In Accounting Estimates," **ACCHOR**, 1988, Vol. 2, No. 3, pp. 15-25.

Nurnberg, Hugo. "Changes In Tax Rates Under The Deferred And Liability Methods Of Interperiod Tax Allocation," **ACCHOR**, 1987, Vol. 1, No. 3, pp. 59-68.

Nurnberg, Hugo. "Discounting Deferred Tax Liabilities," **AR**, 1972, Vol. 47, No. 4, pp. 655-665.

Nurnberg, Hugo. "Income Tax Allocation Under SFAS 96," **CPAJ**, 1988, Vol. 58, No. 7, pp. 34-47.

Nurnberg, Hugo. "Issues In Funds Statement Presentation." **AR**, 1983, Vol. 58, No. 4, pp. 799-812.

Nurnberg, Hugo. "Leases, Purchase Commitments, And Pensions Revisited," **CPAJ**, 1973, Vol. 43, No. 5, pp. 375-389.

Nurnberg, Hugo. "Present Value Depreciation And Income Tax Allocation," **AR**, 1968, Vol. 43, No. 4, pp. 719-729.

Nurnberg, Hugo. "Some Of The Essential Provisons Of Opinion No. 8," **AR**, 1974, Vol. 49, No. 1, pp. 165-176.

Nurnberg, Hugo. "Tax Allocation For Differences In Original Bases," **JAR**, 1970, Vol. 8, No. 2, pp. 217-231.

Nurnberg, Hugo. "The Ambiguous High-Low Method." **IAE**, 1986, Vol. 1, No. 1, pp. 143-147.

Nusbaum, Edward E., Andrew D. Bailey, Jr. and Andrew B. Whinston. "Data-Base Management, Accounting, And Accountants." **MA**, 1978, Vol. 59, No. 11, pp. 35-38.

Nwadike, Evaristus C. (Jagetia, Lal C. and Evaristus C. Nwadike. "Accounting Systems In Developing Nations: The Nigerian Experience," **IJAER**, 1983, Vol. 18, No. 2, pp. 69-81.)

Nye, Paul E. "Training For An Accounting Career: A Public Accountant's View." **AR**, 1958, Vol. 33, No. 2, pp. 187-192.

Nystrom, P. C. "Managerial Resistance To A Management System," **AOS**, 1977, Vol. 2, No. 4, pp. 317-322.

OOO

Oakleaf, Robert B. "Retail Trade ROI." **MA**, 1972, Vol. 54, No. 4, pp. 25-26.

Oakleaf, Robert B. "The Mall: Treasure Trove Or Trap." **MA**, 1970, Vol. 51, No. 12, pp. 41-43.

Oates, Thomas A. and Milton H. Spencer. "A System Of Retirement Frequencies For Depreciable Assets." **AR**, 1962, Vol. 37, No. 3, pp. 452-459.

Obersteiner, Erich. "The Management Of Liquid Fund Flows Across National Boundaries." **IJAER**, 1976, Vol. 11, No. 2, pp. 91-101.

O'Brien, James P. and William Raabe, Jr. "The Charitable Lead Trust: A Neglected Tax Planning Technique," **JATA**, 1983, Vol. 4, No. 2, pp. 5-13.

O'Brien, John L. "A Look At Accounting Legislation," **JOA**, 1958, Vol. 105, No. 1, pp. 39-42.

O'Brien, Patricia C. "Analysts' Forecasts As Earnings Expectations," **JAEC**, 1988, Vol. 10, No. 1, pp. 53-83.

Obrock, Raymond F. "Statistical Inventory Sampling," **JOA**, 1958, Vol. 105, No. 3, pp. 53-59.

O'Connell, J. Fred. "How We Simplified Administrative Tasks," **MA**, 1984, Vol. 66, No. 6, pp. 40-44.

O'Connor, Melvin C. and Daniel W. Collins. "Toward Establishing User-Oriented Materiality Standards," **JOA**, 1974, Vol. 138, No. 6, pp. 67-75.

O'Connor, Melvin C. and Gyan Chandra. "Replacement Cost Disclosure," **MA**, 1978, Vol. 60, No. 3, pp. 58-59.

O'Connor, Melvin C. and James C. Hamre. "Alternative Methods Of Accounting For Long-Term Nonsubsidiary Intercorporate Investments In Common Stock," **AR**, 1972, Vol. 47, No. 2, pp. 308-319.

O'Connor, Melvin C. "NAA-Sponsored Replacement Cost Research," **MA**, 1977, Vol. 59, No. 6, pp. 37-42.

O'Connor, Melvin C. "On The Usefulness Of Financial Ratios To Investors In Common Stock: A Reply," **AR**, 1974, Vol. 49, No. 3, pp. 551-556.

O'Connor, Melvin C. "On The Usefulness Of Financial Ratios To Investors In Common Stock," **AR**, 1973, Vol. 48, No. 2, pp. 339-352.

O'Connor, Melvin C. (Collins, Daniel W. and Melvin C. O'Connor. "An Examination Of The Association Between Accounting And Share Price Data In The Extractive Petroleum Industry: A Comment And Extension," **AR**, 1978, Vol. 53, No. 1, pp. 228-239.)

O'Connor, Norbert C. "Initial Franchise Fee: Revenue Recognition." **MA**, 1977, Vol. 59, No. 5, pp. 48-51.

O'Dell, Michael A. (Duncan, William A. and Michael A. O'Dell. "Tax Policy And Erroneous Information: An Analysis Of The Interaction Of Inflation, Indexation, And Income Averaging," **JATA**, 1987, Vol. 8, No. 2, pp. 50-62.)

O'Dell, Michael A. (Duncan, William A., Michael A. O'Dell and Richard L. Panich. "Potential Personal Wealth Redistribution Effects Of Structural Income Tax Reform," **AIT**, 1987, Vol. 1, pp. 1-22.)

Odiorne, George S. "The New Generation And The Accounting Profession," **JOA**, 1971, Vol. 131, No. 5, pp. 39-43.

Odmark, V. E. "Current Challenges To Accounting Principles," **AR**, 1960, Vol. 35, No. 2, pp. 272-277.

Odmark, V. E. "Some Aspects Of The Evolution Of Accounting Functions," **AR**, 1954, Vol. 29, No. 4, pp. 634-638.

O'Doherty, Brian. "Presenting R&D: A Convergence Model And An Algorithm." **IAE**, 1984, No. 1, pp. 68-74.

O'Doherty, Brian. (Gamble, George O. and Brian O'Doherty. "Citation Indexing And Its Uses In Accounting: An Awareness Survey And Departmental Ranking," **IAE**, 1985, No. 1, pp. 28-40.)

O'Doherty, Brian. (Gamble, George O., Brian O'Doherty and Ladelle M. Hyman. "The Development Of Agency Thought: A Citation Analysis Of The Literature," **AHJ**, 1987, Vol. 14, No. 1, pp. 7-26.)

O'Doherty, Brian. (Gamble, George O. and Brian O'Doherty. "How Accounting Academicians Can Use Citation Indexing And Analysis For Research," **JAED**, 1985, Vol. 3, No. 2, pp. 123-144.)

Odom, George T. "Employee Information System," **MA**, 1971, Vol. 53, No. 5, pp. 20-22.

Odom, Lofton B. "The 80 Percent Limitation And The 2.4-Martini Lunch," **CA**, 1987, Vol. 5, No. 3, pp. 26-31.

O'Donnell, John L. "Further Observations On Reported Earnings And Stock Prices," **AR**, 1968, Vol. 43, No. 3, pp. 549-553.

O'Donnell, John L. "Relationships Between Reported Earnings And Stock Prices In The Electric Utility Industry," **AR**, 1965, Vol. 40, No. 1, pp. 135-143.

O'Donnell, Robert G. "How Users Analyze Financial Statements," **CA**, 1986, Vol. 4, No. 3, pp. 14-18.

Oehler, Christian. "Student Achievement And Its Measurement," **AR**, 1943, Vol. 18, No. 4, pp. 354-363.

Oehler, Christian. "Theory And Practice," **AR**, 1942, Vol. 17, No. 3, pp. 277-282.

Oehm, J. Kent. "Controlling Professional Manpower Costs," **MA**, 1973, Vol. 54, No. 9, pp. 31-35.

Oehring, Thomas S. "Prepaid Income Developments Since 'Schlude'," **JOA**, 1968, Vol. 126, No. 1, pp. 43-48.

Ofer, Aharon R. (Baran, Arie, Josef Lakonishok and Aharon R. Ofer. "The Information Content Of General Price Level Adjusted Earnings: Some Empirical Evidence," **AR**, 1980, Vol. 55, No. 1, pp. 22-35.)

Ofer, Aharon R. (Lakonishok, Josef and Aharon R. Ofer. "The Information Content Of General Price Level Adjusted Earnings: A Reply," **AR**, 1985, Vol. 60, No. 4, pp. 711-713.)

Ogan, Pekin. "A Human Resource Value Model For Professional Service Organizations," **AR**, 1976, Vol. 51, No. 2, pp. 306-320.

Ogan, Pekin. "Turkish Accountancy: An Assessment Of Its Effectiveness And Recommendations For Improvements," **IJAER**, 1978, Vol. 14, No. 1, pp. 133-154.

Ogan, Pekin. (Biagioni, Louis F. and Pekin Ogan. "Human Resource Accounting For Professional Sports Teams," **MA**, 1977, Vol. 59, No. 5, pp. 25-29.)

Ogan, P. "Application Of A Human Resource Value Model: A Field Study," **AOS**, 1976, Vol. 1, No. 2/3, pp. 195-218.

Ogden, S. and P. Bougen. "A Radical Perspective On The Disclosure Of Accounting Information To Trade Unions," **AOS**, 1985, Vol. 10, No. 2, pp. 211-226.

Ogden, Warde B. "Survey Investigates Accounting For Pension Costs," **JOA**, 1952, Vol. 93, No. 1, pp. 44-47.

Oglesbee, Tom W., Larry N. Bitner and Gail B. Wright. "Measurement Of Incremental Benefits In Computer Enhanced

Instruction," **IAE**, 1988, Vol. 3. No. 2, pp. 365-377.

O'Grady, Timothy. (Hite, Peggy A. and Timothy O'Grady. "The Substantial Understatement Penalty: An Update," **CPAJ**, 1988, Vol. 58, No. 4, pp. 64-68.)

Ogundele, Babatunde. "The Accounting Profession In Nigeria: An International Perspective," **IJAER**, 1969, Vol. 5, No. 1, pp. 101-106.

Ogura, E. "The Nakai Family's Bookkeeping System," **ABR**, 1981-82, Vol. 12, No. 46, pp. 148-152.

O'Halloran, James P. and Joseph F. Berardino. "The Profit Improvement Review: Cutting Out Costs And Increasing Revenues," **CA**, 1983, Vol. 1, No. 1, pp. 54-59.

O'Hara, John B and Richard C. Clelland. "Satisfying Ourselves On Prior Years' Inventories," **JOA**, 1963, Vol. 116, No. 4, pp. 42-52.

Ohlson, James A. and A. G. Buckman. "Toward A Theory Of Financial Accounting: Welfare And Public Information," **JAR**, 1981, Vol. 19, No. 2, pp. 399-433.

Ohlson, James A. and James M. Patell. "An Introduction To Residual (API) Analysis And The Private Value Of Information And The API And The Design Of Experiments," **JAR**, 1979, Vol. 17, No. 2, pp. 504-505.

Ohlson, James A. "Financial Ratios And The Probabilistic Prediction Of Bankruptcy," **JAR**, 1980, Vol. 18, No. 1, pp. 109-131.

Ohlson, James A. "On Financial Disclosure And The Behavior Of Security Prices," **JAEC**, 1979, Vol. 1, No. 3, pp. 211-232.

Ohlson, James A. "On The Nature Of Income Measurement: The Basic Results," **CAR**, 1987-88, Vol. 4, No. 1, pp. 1-15.

Ohlson, James A. "Price-Earnings Ratios And Earnings Capitalization Under Uncertainty," **JAR**, 1983, Vol. 21, No. 1, pp. 141-154.

Ohlson, James A. "Residual (API) Analysis And The Private Value Of Information," **JAR**, 1979, Vol. 17, No. 2, pp. 506-527.

Ohlson, James A. "The Complete Ordering Of Information Alternatives For A Class Of Portfolio-Selection Models," **JAR**, 1975, Vol. 13, No. 2, pp. 267-282.

Ohlson, James A. (Freeman, Robert N., James A. Ohlson and Stephen H. Penman. "Book Rate-Of-Return And Prediction Of Earnings Changes: An Empirical Investigation," **JAR**, 1982, Vol. 20, No. 2, Part II, pp. 639-653.)

Ohlson, James A. (Garman, Mark B. and James A. Ohlson. "Information And The Sequential Valuation Of Assets In Arbitrage-Free Economies," **JAR**, 1980, Vol. 18, No. 2, pp. 420-440.)

Ohlson, James A. (Hakansson, Nils H., J. Gregory Kunkel and James A. Ohlson. "A Comment On Verrecchia's No Trading 'Theorem'," **JAR**, 1984, Vol. 22, No. 2, pp. 765-767.)

Ohlson, James A. (Harris, Trevor S. and James A. Ohlson. "Accounting Disclosures And The Market's Valuation Of Oil And Gas Properties," **AR**, 1987, Vol. 62, No. 4, pp. 651-670.)

Ohlson, James A. (Lev, Baruch and James A. Ohlson. "Market-Based Empirical Research In Accounting: A Review, Interpretation, And Extension," **JAR**, 1982, Vol. 20, Supp., pp. 249-322.)

Ohlson, James. "Analysis Of The Usefulness Of Accounting Data For The Portfolio Decision: A Decision-Theory Approach," **JAR**, 1972, Vol. 10, Supp., pp. 45-84.

Ohlson, Phlip A. (Garstka, Stanley J. and Philip A. Ohlson. "Ratio Estimation In Accounting Populations With Probabilities Of Sample Selection Proportional To Size Of Book Values," **JAR**, 1979, Vol. 17, No. 1, pp. 23-59.)

Ohno, Kimiyoshi, Hideo Ichikawa and Atsuyoshi Kodama. "Recent Changes In Accounting Standards In Japan," **IJAER**, 1975, Vol. 11, No. 1, pp. 107-120.

O'Keefe, Dana S. (O'Keefe, W. Timothy, Larry H. Beard and Dana S. O'Keefe. "Are U.S. Exporters Benefiting From The FSC?," **MA**, 1986, Vol. 67, No. 11, pp. 42-47.)

O'Keefe, Herbert A. (Wagner, Nancy A., Herbert A. O'Keefe and William J. Bostwick. "Audit Committee Functions For Municipalities, Hospitals And Banks," **CPAJ**, 1988, Vol. 58, No. 6, pp. 46-53.)

O'Keefe, Herbert A., Jr. "Increasing The Productivity Of Local Governments," **MA**, 1976, Vol. 57, No. 9, pp. 43-44.

O'Keefe, Terrence B. and Soliman Y. Soliman. "Do Managers Believe The Efficient Market Hypothesis? Additional Evidence," **ABR**, 1984-85, Vol. 15, No. 58, pp. 67-80.

O'Keefe, Terrence B. "Financial Statement Analysis In Introductory Financial Accounting For MBAs," **JAED**, 1986, Vol. 4, No. 1, pp. 195-201.

O'Keefe, Terrence B. (King, Raymond D. and Terrence B. O'Keefe. "Lobbying Activities And Insider Trading," **AR**, 1986, Vol. 61, No. 1, pp. 76-90.)

O'Keefe, W. Timothy, Larry H. Beard and Dana S. O'Keefe. "Are U.S. Exporters Benefiting From The FSC?," **MA**, 1986, Vol. 67, No. 11, pp. 42-47.

Okopny, D. Robert and Jerry R. Strawser. "A Management Guide To Prospective Financial Statements," **CA**, 1988, Vol. 6, No. 2, pp. 52-57.

Okubara, Linda L. (Pearson, Mark W. and Linda L. Okubara. "Restructurings And Impairment Of Value: A Growing Controversy," **ACCHOR**, 1987, Vol. 1, No. 1, pp. 35-42.)

O'Larnic, Thomas J. (Smith, Gene L. and Thomas J. O'Larnic. "Estimating Accounting Reserves With Quantitative Methods," **MA**, 1984, Vol. 66, No. 5, pp. 59-62.)

O'Leary, Daniel E. "Software Engineering And Research Issues In Accounting Information Systems," **JIS**, 1988, Vol. 2, No. 2, pp. 24-38.

O'Leary, Daniel. "Accounting Regulation-Based Expert Systems," **RIAR**, 1987, Vol. 1, pp. 123-137.

O'Leary, Ted and Richard J. Boland. Jr. "Self-Regulation, Public Interest And The Accounting Profession," **RIAR**,

1987, Vol. 1, pp. 103-121.

O'Leary, T. "Observations On Corporate Financial Reporting In The Name Of Politics," **AOS**, 1985, Vol. 10, No. 1, pp. 87-104.

O'Leary, T. (Miller, P. and T. O'Leary. "Accounting And The Construction Of The Governable Person," **AOS**, 1987, Vol. 12, No. 3, pp. 235-266.)

Olenick, Arnold J. "Dangers Ahead For Professional Corporations," **CPAJ**, 1972, Vol. 42, No. 11, pp. 915-922.

Oliga, J. C. (Samuels, J. M. and J. C. Oliga. "Accounting Standards In Developing Countries," **IJAER**, 1982, Vol. 18, No. 1, pp. 69-88.)

Oliphant, Walter J. "The Search For Accounting Principles," **JAR**, 1971, Vol. 9, Supp., pp. 93-98.

Olive, George S. "Practical Prerequisites For The Certificate," **AR**, 1945, Vol. 20, No. 2, pp. 201-203.

Olive, George S., Jr. "Management Services - A Local Firm Approach," **JOA**, 1960, Vol. 109, No. 4, pp. 31-34.

Oliver, Bruce L. "A Study Of Confidence Interval Financial Statements," **JAR**, 1972, Vol. 10, No. 1, pp. 154-166.

Oliver, Bruce L. "The Semantic Differential: A Device For Measuring The Interprofessional Communication Of Selected Accounting Concepts," **JAR**, 1974, Vol. 12, No. 2. pp. 299-316.

Oliver, Fred M. "Municipal Governments' Accounting And Reporting For Federal Grants," **CPAJ**, 1973, Vol. 43, No. 12, pp. 1073-1078.

Oliver, Thomas W. (Abdolmohammadi, Mohammad J., Krishnagopal Menon, Thomas W. Oliver and Srinivasan Umapathy. "The Role Of The Doctoral Dissertation In Accounting Research Centers," **IAE**, 1985, No. 1, pp. 59-76.)

Oliver, Thomas W. (Finnerty, Joseph E., Rick N. Fitzsimmons and Thomas W. Oliver. "Lease Capitalization And Systematic Risk," **AR**, 1980, Vol. 55, No. 4, pp. 631-639.)

Oliver, T. (Abdolmohammadi, M., K. Menon, T. Oliver and S. Umapathy. "Factors Motivating Academic Research In Accounting," **AIA**, 1988, Vol. 6, pp. 159-174.)

Oliverio, Mary Ellen. "The Audit As A Scientific Investigation," **CPAJ**, 1984, Vol. 54, No. 10, pp. 52-61.

Olsen Chris. (Foster, George, Chris Olsen and Terry Shevlin. "Earnings Releases, Anomalies, And The Behavior Of Security Returns," **AR**, 1984, Vol. 59, No. 4, pp. 574-603.)

Olsen, Chris and J. Richard Dietrich. "Vertical Information Transfers: The Association Between Retailers' Sales Announcements And Suppliers' Security Returns," **JAR**, 1985, Vol. 23, Supp., pp. 144-166.

Olsen, Chris. "Valuation Implications Of SFAS No. 33 Data For Electric Utility Investors," **JAR**, 1985, Vol. 23, Supp., pp. 28-47.

Olsen, Chris. (Thompson, Robert B., II, Chris Olsen and J. Richard Dietrich. "Attributes Of News About Firms: An Analysis Of Firm-Specific News Reported In The Wall Street Journal Index," **JAR**, 1987, Vol. 25, No. 2, pp. 245-274.)

Olsen, Chris. (Thompson, Robert B., II, Chris Olsen and J. Richard Dietrich. "The Influence Of Estimation Period News Events On Standardized Market Model Prediction Errors," **AR**, 1988, Vol. 63, No. 3, pp. 448-471.)

Olson, Charles A. (Hughes, Lyle F. and Charles A. Olson. "Computer-Assisted Financial Planning," **MA**, 1969, Vol. 50, No. 8, pp. 24-27.)

Olson, Irving J. "Valuation Of A Closely Held Corporation," **JOA**, 1969, Vol. 128, No. 2, pp. 35-47.

Olson, John F. "A Manager's Guide To Avoiding Insider Trading Liability," **MA**, 1987, Vol. 68, No. 11, pp. 26-29.

Olson, Josephine and Irene Frieze. "Women Accountants - Do They Earn As Much As Men?," **MA**, 1986, Vol. 67, No. 12, pp. 27-31.

Olson, Lyle H. "What Of The Appraiser?," **AR**, 1932, Vol. 7, No. 3. pp. 207-213.

Olson, Norman O. "The Auditor In Legal Difficulty - What's The Answer?," **JOA**, 1970, Vol. 129, No. 4, pp. 39-44.

Olson, Robert S. "Cost And Tax Considerations In The Small Business Parent-Subsidiary Relationship," **MA**, 1966, Vol. 47, No. 10, pp. 44-47.

Olson, Robert S. "The Franchise Agreement," **MA**, 1971, Vol. 52, No. 12, pp. 37-44.

Olson, Stevan K. (Matulich, Serge, Loren A. Nikolai and Stevan K. Olson. "Earnings Per Share: A Flow Chart Approach To Teaching Concepts And Procedures," **AR**, 1977, Vol. 52, No. 1, pp. 238-247.)

Olson, Steven K. and Jerry J. Weygandt. "Evolution Of Accounting Changes: Opinion No. 20," **AR**, 1973, Vol. 48, No. 2. pp. 428-429.

Olson, Wallace E. "A Look At The Responsibility Gap," **JOA**, 1975, Vol. 139, No. 1, pp. 52-57.

Olson, Wallace E. "Financial Reporting - Fact Or Fiction?," **JOA**, 1977, Vol. 144, No. 1, pp. 68-71.

Olson, Wallace E. "How Should A Profession Be Disciplined?," **JOA**, 1978, Vol. 145, No. 5, pp. 59-68.

Olson, Wallace E. "Our Profession In A Changing World," **JOA**, 1980, Vol. 150, No. 5, pp. 72-76.

Olson, Wallace E. "Self-Regulation - What's Ahead?," **JOA**, 1980, Vol. 149, No. 2, pp. 46-49.

Olson, Wallace E. "Specialization: Search For A Solution," **JOA**, 1982, Vol. 154, No. 3, pp. 70-79.

Olson, Wallace E. "The Accounting Profession In The 1980s," **JOA**, 1979, Vol. 148, No. 1, pp. 54-60.

Olson, Wallace E. (Higgins, Thomas G. and Wallace E. Olson. "Restating The Ethics Code: A Decision For The Times," **JOA**, 1972, Vol. 133, No. 3, pp. 33-39.)

Omlor, John J. "Management Information System For Direct Planning, Forecasting And Budgeting," **MA**, 1970, Vol. 51, No. 9, pp. 13-16.

O'Neal, Curtis H. "Professional Service Associations: Assets And Liabilities," **MA**, 1970, Vol. 52, No. 5, pp. 41-44.

O'Neil, Cherie Jeanne. "The Targeted Jobs Credit: An Evaluation Of Its Impact On The Employment Decision Process," **JATA**, 1982, Vol. 3, No. 2, pp. 15-22.

O'Neil, Cherie J. (Rose, Clarence C. and Cherie J. O'Neil. "The Viewed Importance Of Investment Tax Incentives By Virginia Decision Makers," **JATA**, 1985, Vol. 7, No. 1, pp. 34-43.)

O'Neil, Cherie J. (Saftner, Donald V. and Cherie J. O'Neil. "Early Withdrawals From Individual Retirement Accounts (IRAs) After The 1986 Tax Reform Act," **JAPP**, 1988, Vol. 7, No. 2, pp. 113-136.)

O'Neil, Cherie J., Donald V. Saftner and M. Pete Dillaway. "Reply To 'Comment On Premature Withdrawals From Individual Retirement Accounts: A Breakeven Analysis'," **JATA**, 1984, Vol. 6, No. 1, pp. 77-80.

O'Neil, Cherie J., Donald V. Saftner and Manson P. Dillaway. "Premature Withdrawals From Individual Retirement Accounts: A Breakeven Analysis," **JATA**, 1983, Vol. 4, No. 2, pp. 35-43.

O'Neil, Cherie J., Jack M. Cathey and Tonya K. Flesher. "An Analysis Of Ph.D. Dissertations In Taxation: 1977-1985," **IAE**, 1988, Vol. 3, No. 1, pp. 120-130.

Onis, Linda M. "Why Go Private?," **MA**, 1984, Vol. 66, No. 3, pp. 51-54.

Onsi, Mohamed. "A Transfer Pricing System Based On Opportunity Cost," **AR**, 1970, Vol. 45, No. 3, pp. 535-543.

Onsi, Mohamed. "Factor Analysis Of Behavioral Variables Affecting Budgetary Slack," **AR**, 1973, Vol. 48, No. 3, pp. 535-548.

Onsi, Mohamed. "Linear Programming: An Accounting Information Model," **MA**, 1966, Vol. 48, No. 4, pp. 46-55.

Onsi, Mohamed. "Quantitative Models For Accounting Control," **AR**, 1967, Vol. 42, No. 2, pp. 321-330.

Onsi, Mohamed. "'Transfer Pricing System Based On Opportunity Costs': A Reply," **AR**, 1974, Vol. 49, No. 1, pp. 129-131.

Ooghe, Hubert and Eric Verbaere. "Predicting Business Failure On The Basis Of Accounting Data: The Belgian Experience," **IJAER**, 1985, Vol. 20, No. 2, pp. 19-44.

Opdebeeck, E. J. (Higgins, J. C. and E. J. Opdebeeck. "The Microcomputer As A Tool In Financial Planning And Control: Some Survey Results," **ABR**, 1983-84, Vol. 14, No. 56, pp. 333-340.)

Ophir, Tsvi. "Introducing Probabilities And Present Value Analysis Into Taxation: A Comment," **AR**, 1973, Vol. 48, No. 3, pp. 589-594.

Ophir, Tsvi. (Falk, Haim and Tsvi Ophir. "The Effect Of Risk On The Use Of Financial Statements By Investment Decision-Makers: A Case Study," **AR**, 1973, Vol. 48, No. 2, pp. 323-338.)

Ophir, T. (Aharoni, Y. and T. Ophir. "Accounting For Linked Loans," **JAR**, 1967, Vol. 5, No. 1, pp. 1-26.)

Ophir, T. (Falk, H. and T. Ophir. "The Influence Of Differences In Accounting Policies On Investment Decisions," **JAR**, 1973, Vol. 11, No. 1, pp. 108-116.)

Oppenheim, Richard K. "Word Processing For First Time Users," **CPAJ**, 1981, Vol. 51, No. 4, pp. 11-18.

Oppong, Andrews. "Information Content Of Annual Earnings Announcements Revisited," **JAR**, 1980, Vol. 18, No. 2, pp. 574-584.

Oravec, R. J. "Statistical Inventory Management," **JOA**, 1960, Vol. 110, No. 6, pp. 40-52.

Orbach, Kenneth N. and Robert H. Strawser. "Public Disclosure Requirements For CPA Firms?," **CPAJ**, 1979, Vol. 49, No. 2, pp. 15-22.

Orbach, Kenneth N. and William D. Samson. "An Open Letter To Congress: Leasing Little Lisa," **MA**, 1983, Vol. 64, No. 9, pp. 46-47.

Orbach, Sydney C. "Deficiencies In First Filings," **JOA**, 1964, Vol. 117, No. 2, pp. 57-64.

Ordway, Nicholas and Jacqualyn A. Fouse. "New Rules For Allocating The Purchase Price Of A Business," **MA**, 1988, Vol. 69, No. 11, pp. 50-53.

Orhnial, A. J. H. and L. P. Foldes. "Tax Uncertainty In Project Evaluation: A Case Study," **ABR**, 1974-75, Vol. 5, No. 19, pp. 229-230.

O'Riordan, Maureen and Arthur S. Hirshfield. "Aspects Of The Profession's Code Of Ethics," **CPAJ**, 1982, Vol. 52, No. 8, pp. 30-33.

Orr, George W., Jr. "The President's Job Is Easier," **MA**, 1975, Vol. 56, No. 12, pp. 25-26.

Ortegren, Alan K. (King, Thomas E. and Alan K. Ortegren. "Accounting For Hybrid Securities: The Case Of Adjustable Rate Convertible Notes," **AR**, 1988, Vol. 63, No. 3, pp. 522-535.)

Ortman, Richard F. and Dennis D. Blackman. "Corporate Planning - How Successful Is It?," **MA**, 1981, Vol. 63, No. 1, pp. 16-24.

Ortman, Richard F. "The Effects On Investment Analysis Of Alternative Reporting Procedures For Diversified Firms," **AR**, 1975, Vol. 50, No. 2, pp. 298-304.

Ortner, James L. "Management: A Productive Or Standby Asset," **MA**, 1970, Vol. 51, No. 9, pp. 7-9.

Ortner, Robert. "Outlook 1985," **JCA**, 1985, Vol. 2, No. 1, pp. 43-46.

Orton, Bryce B. and Richard D. Bradish. "The Treatment And Disclosure Of Research And Development Expenditures," **MA**, 1969, Vol. 51, No. 1, pp. 31-34.

Orton, Bryce B. (Hardy, John W., Bryce B. Orton and J. Weldon Moffit. "Bonus Systems DO Motivate," **MA**, 1986, Vol. 68, No. 5, pp. 58-61.)

Osborne, Kent L. "Performing A Cost Segregation Analysis,"

CA, 1988, Vol. 6, No. 2, pp. 11-26.

Osborn, Richards C. "Plea For Small Business," **AR**, 1951, Vol. 26, No. 4, pp. 540-554.

Osborn, Richards C. "Statutory Renegotiation: A Critique," **AR**, 1947, Vol. 22, No. 2, pp. 175-186.

Osborn, Richards C. "The Relative Efficiency Of Large, Medium-Sized And Small Business," **AR**, 1950, Vol. 25, No. 3, pp. 262-273.

Osborn, Richards C. "The Relative Profitability Of Large, Medium-Sized And Small Business," **AR**, 1950, Vol. 25, No. 4, pp. 402-411.

Osiegbu, Patrick I. "The State Of Accounting Education In Nigeria," **IJAER**, 1987, Vol. 22, No. 2, pp. 57-68.

Osler, Paul W. "Long-Range Forecasts: Where Do We Go From Here," **MA**, 1971, Vol. 52, No. 7, pp. 21-23.

Ostalkiewicz, Clarence J. "Market Mix: The Key To Profitability," **MA**, 1969, Vol. 50, No. 5, pp. 28-30.

Ostergaard, Carol Lynn. (Upton, Wayne S., Jr. and Carol Lynn Ostergaard. "The FASB Response To Small Business," **JOA**, 1986, Vol. 161, No. 5, pp. 94-101.)

Osteryoung, Jerome S. and Gordon G. Abernethy. "Capital Budgeting: A Review," **JCA**, 1984, Vol. 1, No. 1, pp. 131-142.

Osteryoung, Jerome S., Daniel E. McCarty and Karen A. Fortin. "How The New Cost Recovery System Compares With Prior Methods," **MA**, 1981, Vol. 63, No. 5, pp. 13-27.

Osteryoung, Jerome S., Daniel E. McCarty and Karen Fortin. "A Note On The Optimal Tax Lives For Assets Qualifying For The Investment Tax Credit," **AR**, 1980, Vol. 55, No. 2, pp. 301-306.

Osteryoung, Jerome S., Daniel M. McCarty and Karen Fortin. "A Note On Optimal Depreciation Research - A Comment," **AR**, 1981, Vol. 56, No. 3, pp. 719-721.

Ostlund, A. Clayton. "Advertising - In The Public Interest?," **JOA**, 1978, Vol. 145, No. 1, pp. 59-63.

Ostlund, H. J. "Cost Research In The Field Of Distribution," **AR**, 1932, Vol. 7, No. 1, pp. 48-53.

Ostlund, H. J. "The Robinson-Patman Act And Quantity Discounts," **AR**, 1939, Vol. 14, No. 4, pp. 402-408.

Ostrowski, Barbara A. "Alternate Indexing Schemes For Nonbusiness Income Taxation: Distributional And Revenue Effects," **JATA**, 1985, Vol. 6, No. 2, pp. 50-62.

Ostrowski, Barbara A. "First-Time Accounting Faculty: The Job Search, Acceptance, And Support Process," **IAE**, 1986, Vol. 1, No. 1, pp. 48-55.

Ostrowski, Barbara A. (Lathan, Malcolm H., Jr., Barbara A. Ostrowski, Ernest J. Pavlock and Richard A. Scott. "Recruiting Entry Level Staff: Gender Differences," **CPAJ**, 1987, Vol. 57, No. 1, pp. 30-43.)

Ostwald, Phillip F. (White, Gary E. and Phillip F. Ostwald. "Life Cycle Costing," **MA**, 1976, Vol. 57, No. 7, pp. 39-40.)

Otley, David and Anthony Berry. "Risk Distribution In The Budgetary Process," **ABR**, 1978-79, Vol. 9, No. 36, pp. 325-337.

Otley, David T. and Francisco J. B. Dias. "Accounting Aggregation And Decision-Making Performance: An Experimental Investigation," **JAR**, 1982, Vol. 20, No. 1, pp. 171-188.

Otley, David T. "Budget Use And Managerial Performance," **JAR**, 1978, Vol. 16, No. 1, pp. 122-149.

Otley, D. T. and A. J. Berry. "Control, Organisation And Accounting," **AOS**, 1980, Vol. 5, No. 2, pp. 231-246.

Otley, D. T. "The Contingency Theory Of Management Accounting: Achievement And Prognosis," **AOS**, 1980, Vol. 5, No. 4, pp. 413-428.

O'Toole, Kevin P. (Craft, James W. and Kevin P. O'Toole. "Push-Down Accounting - Has Its Time Come?," **CA**, 1984, Vol. 2, No. 2, pp. 57-62.)

O'Toole, Kevin. (Katz, Adam M., Kevin O'Toole and Linda Trotta. "TRA-1986 And The Hotel/Restaurant Industry," **CPAJ**, 1987, Vol. 57, No. 7, pp. 46-51.)

Ott, George W. "Simplified CPM For Contractors," **MA**, 1966, Vol. 48, No. 3, pp. 21-25.

Ott, Richard L. "Pretest Reviews In Intermediate Accounting: An Empirical Analysis," **IAE**, 1988, Vol. 3, No. 2, pp. 378-387.

Ott, Richard L., Dan S. Deines and David P. Donnelly. "The Use Of A Fundamental Practice Set In Intermediate Accounting," **IAE**, 1988, Vol. 3, No. 1, pp. 131-138.

Otto, Janon R. (Vruwink, David R. and Janon R. Otto. "Evaluation Of Teaching Techniques For Introductory Accounting Courses," **AR**, 1987, Vol. 62, No. 2, pp. 402-408.)

Outslay, Edmund and James E. Wheeler. "Separating The Annuity And Income Transfer Elements Of Social Security," **AR**, 1982, Vol. 57, No. 4, pp. 716-733.

Outslay, Edmund and Richard P. Weber. "Minimizing The Tax Cost Of Faculty Research Grants," **JATA**, 1986, Vol. 7, No. 2, pp. 48-59.

Outslay, Edmund, John R. Robinson and Richard Boley. "A Framework For Utilizing Individual Return Problems In Introductory Courses," **AR**, 1983, Vol. 58, No. 2, pp. 428-438.

Outslay, Edmund. "The Social Security System: An Evaluation Of Policy Alternatives," **JATA**, 1980, Vol. 1, No. 2, pp. 21-33.

Outslay, Edmund. (Boley, Richard and Edmund Outslay. "Doctoral Programs With A Concentration In Taxation: An Examination Of Recent Trends," **JATA**, 1983, Vol. 5, No. 1, pp. 49-59.)

Outslay, Edmund. (Boley, Richard and Edmund Outslay. "Conditions Under Which A Dependent Can File A Joint Return: Is The Current Confusion And Complexity Really Necessary?," **JATA**, 1981, Vol. 2, No. 2, pp. 5-11.)

Outslay, Edmund. (Wheeler, James E. and Edmund Outslay. "The Phantom Federal Income Taxes Of General Dynamics Corporation," **AR**, 1986, Vol. 61, No. 4, pp. 760-774.)

Ovadia, Arie and Joshua Ronen. "On The Value Of Current-Cost Information," **JAAF**, 1983, Vol. 6, No. 2, pp. 115-129.

Ovadia, Arie and Joshua Ronen. "General Price-Level Adjustment And Replacement Cost Accounting As Special Cases Of The Index Number Problem," **JAAF**, 1980, Vol. 3, No. 2, pp. 113-137.

Owen, D. L. and A. J. Lloyd. "The Use Of Financial Information By Trade Union Negotiators In Plant Level Collective Bargaining," **AOS**, 1985, Vol. 10, No. 3, pp. 329-352.

Owen, D. L. (Harte, G. F. and D. L. Owen. "Fighting De-Industrialisation: The Role Of Local Government Social Audits," **AOS**, 1987, Vol. 12, No. 2, pp. 123-142.)

Owen, George A. and Richard C. Gerfen. "Can Junior Accountants Be Trained To Write Better?," **AR**, 1951, Vol. 26, No. 3, pp. 313-320.

Owen, George A. and Richard C. Green. "Training Staff Accountants To Write More Effective Reports," **JOA**, 1952, Vol. 93, No. 5, pp. 589-595.

Owen, Henry H. "How To Evaluate Your Cost Accounting Department," **MA**, 1982, Vol. 63, No. 9, pp. 29-31.

Owen, Joel. (Brief, Richard P. and Joel Owen. "Present Value Models And The Multi-Asset Problem," **AR**, 1973, Vol. 48, No. 4, pp. 690-695.)

Owen, Joel. (Brief, Richard P. and Joel Owen. "Depreciation And Capital Gains: A 'New' Approach," **AR**, 1968. Vol. 43. No. 2, pp. 367-372.)

Owen, Joel. (Brief, Richard P. and Joel Owen. "On The Bias In Accounting Allocations Under Uncertainty," **JAR**, 1969, Vol. 7, No. 1, pp. 12-16.)

Owen, Joel. (Brief, Richard P. and Joel Owen. "Present Value Models And The Multi-Asset Problem: A Reply," **AR**, 1974, Vol. 49, No. 4, pp. 819-821.)

Owen, Joel. (Brief, Richard P. and Joel Owen. "The Estimation Problem In Financial Accounting," **JAR**, 1974, Vol. 8, No. 2, pp. 167-177.)

Owen, Joel. (Brief, Richard P. and Joel Owen. "A Reformulation Of The Estimation Problem," **JAR**, 1973, Vol. 11, No. 1, pp. 1-15.)

Owen, Joel. (Brief, Richard P. and Joel Owen. "Accounting For Leveraged Leases: A Comment," **JAR**, 1978, Vol. 16, No. 2, pp. 411-413.)

Owen, Joel. (Brief, Richard P. and Joel Owen. "A Least Squares Allocation Model," **JAR**, 1968, Vol. 6, No. 2, pp. 193-199.)

Owen, Joel. (Katz, Barbara Goody and Joel Owen. "Initial Public Offerings: An Equilibrium Model Of Price Determination," **JAAF**, 1987, Vol. 2 (New Series). No. 3, pp. 266-298.)

Owen, Linda S. "Partners In The Workplace," **MA**, 1986, Vol. 68, No. 6, pp. 53-57.

Owens, Richard N. "Surplus Accounts Of Iron And Steel Corporations," **AR**, 1936, Vol. 11, No. 2, pp. 171-178.

Owens, Richard N. "The Place Of The Business Management Course In The Curriculum," **AR**, 1937, Vol. 12, No. 2, pp. 183-187.

Owens, Richard N. "What Is A Security?," **AR**, 1942, Vol. 17, No. 3, pp. 303-308.

Owens, Richard N. "What Is An Independent Accountant?," **AR**, 1941, Vol. 16, No. 4, pp. 391-400.

Owens, Robert W. "Cash Flow Variance Analysis," **AR**, 1980, Vol. 55, No. 1, pp. 111-116.

Oxman, Allan S. (Diamond, Lee G. and Allan S. Oxman. "Is There Life Insurance After Retirement?," **MA**, 1981, Vol. 62, No. 7, pp. 23-26.)

Oxner, Thomas H. (Moore, P. Michael. Thomas H. Oxner and Jimie Kusel. "Determining Common Stock Equivalency Of Convertible Securities: A Teaching Approach," **IAE**, 1987, Vol. 2, No. 1, pp. 152-156.)

Ozan, T. and T. Dyckman. "A Normative Model For Investigation Decisions Involving Multiorigin Cost Variances," **JAR**, 1971, Vol. 9, No. 1, pp. 88-115.

Ozer, Jan Lee. "Tax Planning For Software Acquisitions," **CPAJ**, 1983, Vol. 53, No. 3, pp. 34-39.

PPP

Pacter, Paul A. "A Synopsis Of APB Opinion No. 21," **JOA**, 1972, Vol. 133, No. 3, pp. 57-67.

Pacter, Paul A. "Line-Of-Business Earnings Disclosures In Recent SEC Filings," **JOA**, 1970, Vol. 130, No. 4, pp. 52-63.

Pacter, Paul A. "Reporting Discontinued Operations," **JOA**, 1969, Vol. 128, No. 5, pp. 56-60.

Pacter, Paul A. "Some Recent Examples Of Earnings Reports By Division," **JOA**, 1968, Vol. 126, No. 6, pp. 40-51.

Pacter, Paul A. "The Conceptual Framework: Make No Mystique About It," **JOA**, 1983, Vol. 156, No. 1, pp. 76-88.

Pacter, Paul A. "The FASB At Ten: A View From Within," **CA**, 1983, Vol. 1, No. 1, pp. 24-33.

Pacter, Paul. "Applying APB Opinion No. 18 - Equity Method," **JOA**, 1971, Vol. 132, No. 3, pp. 54-62.

Pacter, Paul. "Some Comments On Applying APB Opinion No. 22," **JOA**, 1972, Vol. 134, No. 6, pp. 60-61.

Paddock, Harold E. "Production Waste - Its Nature And Its Accounting," **AR**, 1958, Vol. 33, No. 1, pp. 50-55.

Paden-Bost, Patricia J. "Making Money Control A Management Issue," **MA**, 1982, Vol. 64, No. 5, pp. 48-51.

Padroni, Giovanni. "A Tribute To Federgio Melis: Part II - A Profile Of Melis," **AHJ**, 1976, Vol. 3, No.1-4.pp.15-17.

Padroni, Giovanni. "A Tribute To Federgio Melis: Part III - A Bibliography Of Melis' Works," **AHJ**, 1976, Vol. 3, No. 1-4. pp. 18-21.

Pagani, John and William O. Jones. "Price And Mortality Expectations And Valuation Of Inventories," **AR**, 1950, Vol. 25. No. 3. pp. 315-319.

Pagano, Dominic F. "New Cookie Development," **MA**, 1974, Vol. 56, No. 2, pp. 37-40.

Pagano, Dominic F. "The Line Manager's Role In Bakery Operations," **MA**, 1972, Vol. 54, No. 3, pp. 43-47.

Pagano, Thomas G. "Measuring Customer Profitability In A Commercial Bank," **MA**, 1975, Vol. 56, No. 11, pp. 43-47.

Page, John R. and H. Paul Hooper. "How To Buy A Computer," **CPAJ**, 1979, Vol. 49, No. 9, pp. 39-45.

Page, John. (Hooper, Paul and John Page. "Measuring Teaching Effectiveness By Student Evaluation," **IAE**, 1986. Vol. 1, No. 1, pp. 56-64.)

Page, John. (Hooper, Paul and John Page. "Organizing Business Data Processing Systems," **CPAJ**, 1983, Vol. 53, No. 8, pp. 24-31.)

Page, John. (Hooper, Paul and John Page. "The Legal Environment Of Public Accounting," **CPAJ**, 1984, Vol. 54, No. 6, pp. 36-39.)

Page, John. (Hooper, Paul and John Page. "Better Financial Statements For Corporate Valuation," **MA**, 1979, Vol. 61, No. 3, pp. 52-56.)

Page, John. (Hooper, Paul, John Page and Karen Smith. "Accountant's Legal Liability: An International Comparison," **IJAER**, 1985, Vol. 20, No. 2, pp. 65-80.)

Page, Michael J. "Corporate Financial Reporting And The Small Independent Company," **ABR**, 1983-84, Vol. 14, No. 55, pp. 271-282.

Page, Pamela. "Reimbursing Travel Expenses," **MA**, 1972, Vol. 54, No. 5, pp. 38-39.

Pain, George R. "A Case Study In Auditing A Medium Scale Computer Installation," **MA**, 1966, Vol. 47, No. 12, pp. 55-63.

Paine, Neil R. "Uncertainty And Capital Budgeting," **AR**, 1964, Vol. 39, No. 2, pp. 330-332.

Paladino, Carl A., Jr. "Financial Forecasts And Our Profession's Future," **CPAJ**, 1977, Vol. 47, No. 2, pp. 31-34.

Palamara, Francis J. "Commercial Financing For Accountants' Clients," **JOA**, 1961, Vol. 112, No. 3, pp. 46-49.

Palepu, Krishna G. "Predicting Takeover Targets: A Methodological And Empirical Analysis," **JAEC**, 1986, Vol. 8, No. 1. pp. 3-35.

Palepu, Krishna G. (Healy, Paul M., Sok-Hyon Kang and Krishna G. Palepu. "The Effect Of Accounting Procedure Changes On CEOs' Cash Salary And Bonus Compensation," **JAEC**, 1987, Vol. 9, No. 1, pp. 7-34.)

Pallais, Don and Dan M. Guy. Prospective Financial Statements." **JOA**, 1986, Vol. 161, No. 4, pp. 90-99.

Pallais, Don and Robert K. Elliot. "Prospective Financial Statements: Guidelines For A Growing Practice Area," **JOA**, 1984, Vol. 157, No. 1, pp. 56-71.

Palm, Arthur O. "Net Operating Losses," **JOA**, 1956, Vol. 102, No. 5, pp. 59-67.

Palmeri, Vincent E., Jr. (Varrone, James E. and Vincent E. Palmeri. Jr. "EDP Finds A Home At North Haven," **MA**, 1979, Vol. 60, No. 10, pp. 49-50.)

Palmer, B. Thomas. "Management Reports For Multiproduct Plants," **MA**, 1970, Vol. 52, No. 2, pp. 30-34.

Palmer, John R. (Gambino, Anthony J. and John R. Palmer. "American Accounting Practices - Circa 1776," **MA**, 1976, Vol. 57, No. 12, pp. 53-56.)

Palmer, Roger R. (Davis, Gordon B., John Neter and Roger R. Palmer. "An Experimental Study Of Audit Confirmations," **JOA**, 1967, Vol. 123, No. 6, pp. 36-44.)

Palmer, Russell E. "Audit Committees - Are They Effective? An Auditor's View," **JOA**, 1977, Vol. 144, No. 3, pp. 76-79.

Palmer, Russell E. "It's Time To Stop Talking," **JOA**, 1975, Vol. 140, No. 4, pp. 60-65.

Palmon, Dan and Lee J. Seidler. "Current Value Reporting Of Real Estate Companies And A Possible Example Of Market Inefficiency," **AR**, 1978, Vol. 53, No. 3, pp. 776-790.

Palmon, Dan and Michael Kwatinetz. "The Significant Role Interpretation Plays In The Implementation Of SFAS No. 13," **JAAF**, 1980, Vol. 3, No. 3, pp. 207-226.

Palmon, Dan. (Givoly, Dan and Dan Palmon. "Timeliness Of Annual Earnings Announcements: Some Empirical Evidence," **AR**, 1982, Vol. 57, No. 3, pp. 486-508.)

Palmon, Dan. (Givoly, Dan and Dan Palmon. "Classification Of Convertible Debt As Common Stock Equivalents: Some Empirical Evidence On The Effects Of APB Opinion 15," **JAR**, 1981, Vol. 19, No. 2, pp. 530-543.)

Palmrose, Zoe-Vonna. "An Analysis Of Auditor Litigation And Audit Service Quality," **AR**, 1988, Vol. 63, No. 1, pp. 55-73.

Palmrose, Zoe-Vonna. "Audit Fees And Auditor Size: Further Evidence," **JAR**, 1986, Vol. 24, No. 1, pp. 97-110.

Palmrose, Zoe-Vonna. "Litigation And Independent Auditors: The Role Of Business Failures And Management Fraud," **AJPT**, 1986-87, Vol. 6, No. 2, pp. 90-103.

Palmrose, Zoe-Vonna. "Public Accounting Firms And The Acquisition Of Nonaudit Services By Public And Closely-Held Companies," **AJPT**, 1988, Vol. 8, No. 1, pp. 63-71.

Palmrose, Zoe-Vonna. "The Effect Of Nonaudit Services On The Pricing Of Audit Services: Further Evidence," **JAR**, 1986, Vol. 24, No. 2, pp. 405-411.

Paluba, Gary. (Allan, Robert and Gary Paluba. "Avoiding Type-A Behavior During Tax Season," **CPAJ**, 1985, Vol. 55, No. 3, pp. 75-76.)

Palvia, Shailendra. (Grossman, Theodore and Shailendra

Palvia. "The Design And Implementation Of A Multidimensional Retail Merchandising Information System." **JIS**. 1988. Vol. 3. No. 1, pp. 119-131.)

Pan, Sheng-Der. (Chen, Rosita S. and Sheng-Der Pan. "Taylor's Contribution To Cost Accounting. A Reply." **AHJ.** 1984. Vol. 11. No. 1. pp. 151-161.)

Pan, Sheng-Der. (Chen, Rosita S. and Sheng-Der Pan. "Frederick Winslow Taylor's Contribution To Accounting." **AHJ.** 1980. Vol. 7. No. 1. pp. 17-35.)

Pan, Sheng-Der. (Chen, Rosita S. and Sheng-Der Pan. "Frederick Winslow Taylor's Contributions To Cost Accounting," **AHJ.** 1980. Vol. 7. No. 2. pp. 1-22.)

Pandey, Pramond. (Ma. Ronald. Pramond Pandey and Mark Scott. "Capital Budgeting And Discounted Cash Equivalents." **ABACUS.** 1978. Vol. 14. No. 2. pp. 180-187.)

Panich, Richard L. (Beckerley. Edward B. and Richard L. Panich. "RA 87 - Major Provisions For Individual Taxpayers." **CPAJ.** 1988. Vol. 58. No. 7. pp. 64-69.)

Panich, Richard L. (Duncan. William A.. Michael A. O'Dell and Richard L. Panich. "Potential Personal Wealth Redistribution Effects Of Structural Income Tax Reform." **AIT.** 1987. Vol. 1. pp. 1-22.)

Pankoff, Lyn D. and Robert L. Virgil. "Some Preliminary Findings From A Laboratory Experiment On The Usefulness Of Financial Accounting Information To Security Analysts." **JAR.** 1970. Vol. 8. Supp.. pp. 1-48.

Pankoff, Lyn D. and Robert L. Virgil. "On The Usefulness Of Financial Statement Information: A Suggested Research Approach." **AR.** 1970. Vol. 45. No. 2. pp. 269-279.

Pannell, Richard L. and Mary Greenstein. "How To Find Answers To Technical Questions." **CPAJ.** 1982. Vol. 52. No. 3. pp. 13-25.

Pannell, Richard L. (Greenstein. Mary and Richard L. Pannell. "A Vital Indexing Tool." **CPAJ.** 1978. Vol. 48. No. 9. pp. 26-31.)

Pansza, Henry G. "Task-Cost Analysis Of Construction In Progress." **MA.** 1976. Vol. 58. No. 6. pp. 41-44.

Pansza, Henry G. "Tax Trade-Offs: Investment Credit Versus Depreciation." **MA.** 1978. Vol. 59. No. 8. pp. 27-28.

Pany, Kurt and Charles H. Smith. "Auditor Association With Quarterly Financial Information: An Empirical Test." **JAR.** 1982. Vol. 20. No. 2. Part I. pp. 472-481.

Pany, Kurt and Douglas A. Johnson. "The Death (Perhaps Timely) Of An Audit Report: Some Empirical Results." **AIA.** 1985. Vol. 2. pp. 247-260.

Pany, Kurt and Philip M. J. Reckers. "Within - Vs. Between - Subjects Experimental Designs: A Study Of Demand Effects." **AJPT.** 1987-88. Vol. 7. No. 1. pp. 39-53.

Pany, Kurt and Philip M. J. Reckers. "Auditor Performance Of MAS: A Study Of Its Effects On Decisions And Perceptions." **ACCHOR.** 1988. Vol. 2. No. 1. pp. 31-38.

Pany, Kurt and Philip M. J. Reckers. "Non-Audit Services And Auditor Independence - A Continuing Problem." **AJPT.** 1983-84. Vol. 3. No. 2. pp. 89-97.

Pany, Kurt and Philip M. J. Reckers. "The Effects Of Gifts. Discounts. And Client Size On Perceived Auditor Independence." **AR.** 1980. Vol. 55. No. 1. pp. 50-61.

Pany, Kurt and P. M. J. Reckers. "Auditor Independence And Nonaudit Services: Director Views And Their Policy Implications." **JAPP.** 1983. Vol. 2. No. 1. pp. 43-62.

Pany, Kurt. (Johnson. Douglas A.. Kurt Pany and Richard White. "Audit Reports And The Loan Decision: Actions And Perceptions." **AJPT.** 1982-83. Vol. 2. No. 2. pp. 38-51.)

Pany, Kurt. (Johnson. Douglas A. and Kurt Pany. "Expose Or Cover-Up: Will An Employee Blow The Whistle?." **MA.** 1981. Vol. 63. No. 1. pp. 32-36.)

Pany, Kurt. (Johnson. Douglas A. and Kurt Pany. "Forecasts. Auditor Review. And Bank Loan Decisions." **JAR.** 1984. Vol. 22. No. 2. pp. 731-743.)

Pany, Kurt. (Kneer. Dan C. and Kurt Pany. "SAS 43 - Explanation And Analysis." **CPAJ.** 1983. Vol. 53. No. 8. pp. 38-43.)

Pany, Kurt. (Margheim. Loren and Kurt Pany. "Quality Control. Premature Signoff. And Underreporting Of Time: Some Empirical Findings." **AJPT.** 1985-86. Vol. 5. No. 2. pp. 50-63.)

Pany, Kurt. (McKinley. Sue. Kurt Pany and Philip M. J. Reckers. "An Examination Of The Influence Of CPA Firm Type. Size. And MAS Provision On Loan Officer Decisions And Perceptions." **JAR.** 1985. Vol. 20. No. 2. pp. 887-896.)

Pany, Kurt. (Schultz. Joseph J.. Jr. and Kurt Pany. "The Independent Auditor's Civil Liability - An Overview." **AR.** 1980. Vol. 55. No. 2. pp. 319-326.)

Paolasini, Arnold L. "Schools Of Accounting: The Way Of The Future." **MA.** 1978. Vol. 59. No. 9. pp. 15-18.

Paolillo, Joseph G. P. and Ralph W. Estes. "An Empirical Analysis Of Career Choice Factors Among Accountants. Attorneys. Engineers. And Physicians." **AR.** 1982. Vol. 57. No. 4. pp. 785-793.

Paperman, Jacob B. (Chandra. Gyan and Jacob B. Paperman. "Direct Costing Vs. Absorption Costing: A Historical Review." **MA.** 1976. Vol. 3. No. 1-4. pp. 1-9.)

Pape, Moritz E. "Costs And Inventory Values In The Glue Industry." **AR.** 1959. Vol. 34. No. 1. pp. 52-58.

Pappas, Evans. (Doost. Roger K. and Evans Pappas. "Frozen-To-Current Cost Variance." **MA.** 1988. Vol. 69. No. 9. pp. 41-43.)

Paquette, Laurence R. (Epaves. Richard A.. Laurence R. Paquette and Michael A. Pearson. "A Flow Chart Conceptualization Of Auditors' Reports On Financial Statements." **AR.** 1976. Vol. 51. No. 4. pp. 913-916.)

Paradis, Maurice C. (Crouse. W. Frank. Maurice C. Paradis and John C. Shaw. "The Client Service Team Approach To Auditing." **JOA.** 1979. Vol. 148. No. 2. pp. 52-58.)

Paraszczak, John. "Accounting Soviet Style," **MA**, 1978, Vol. 60. No. 1, pp. 51-56.

Pare, Paul V. (Imhoff, Eugene A., Jr. and Paul V. Pare. "Analysis And Comparison Of Earnings Forecast Agents," **JAR.** 1982. Vol. 20, No. 2, Part I. pp. 429-439.)

Paretta, Robert L. and Jeanne E. Collison. "Physical Distribution Costs: A Survey," **MA**, 1976, Vol. 58, No. 1, pp. 45-48.

Paretta, Robert L. and Lester W. Chadwick. "The Sequencing Of Examination Questions And Its Effects On Student Performance." **AR.** 1975, Vol. 50, No. 3, pp. 595-601.

Paretta, Robert L. "Designing Management Information Systems: An Overview," **JOA**, 1975, Vol. 139, No. 4, pp. 42-47.

Park. Colin. "Community Service And The CPA," **JOA**, 1958. Vol. 106, No. 4, pp. 43-47.

Park. Colin. "Comparing The Gross And Net Price Methods," **AR.** 1952. Vol. 27, No. 4, pp. 552-554.

Park. Colin. "Thought Processes In Creative Accounting." **AR.** 1958. Vol. 33, No. 3, pp. 441-444.

Park. Colin. "Working Capital And The Operating Cycle," **AR**, 1951. Vol. 26, No. 3, pp. 299-307.

Park. Colin. (Allen, Robert F., Colin Park and Saul Pilnick. "The Shadow Organization," **MA**, 1974, Vol. 55. No. 7. pp. 11-14.)

Park. Hai G. and Bart P. Hartman. "An Application Of Opportunity Cost For A Short-Run Pricing Decision," **JAED**, 1987. Vol. 5, No. 2, pp. 307-313.

Park. Hai G. "A Graphical Analysis Of Profit Variances Under Absorption And Direct Costing," **JAED**, 1988, Vol. 6. No. 1, pp. 139-147.

Park. Soong H. (Manes, Rene P.. Soong H. Park and Robert Jensen. "Relevant Costs Of Intermediate Goods And Services." **AR.** 1982, Vol. 57, No. 3. pp. 594-606.)

Park. Soong. "The Use Of Foreign Financial Statements For Risk Analysis: An Empirical Test (Korea)," **IJAER**, 1984. Vol. 20. No. 1, pp. 1-15.

Parke, R. and J. L. Peterson. "Indicators Of Social Change: Developments In The United States Of America," **AOS**, 1981. Vol. 6. No. 3. pp. 235-246.

Parker. James E. and Allen Ford. "Dissertation Experiences Of Recent Doctoral Graduates In Accounting." **AR**, 1972. Vol. 47. No. 4. pp. 830-833.

Parker. James E. and Barry E. Cushing. "Earnings Per Share And Convertible Securities: A Utilitarian Approach." **ABACUS.** 1971. Vol. 7. No. 1. pp. 29-38.

Parker. James E. and Thomas P. Howard. "Leasing As A Means Of Shifting Tax Savings To Non-Taxable Organizations." **JATA.** 1983. Vol. 4. No. 2. pp. 14-22.

Parker. James E. "Accounting And Ecology: A Perspective," **JOA.** 1971. Vol. 132. No. 4. pp. 41-46.

Parker. James E. "Comparability And Objectivity Of Exit Value Accounting: A Reply," **AR.** 1976, Vol. 51, No. 4. pp. 930-933.

Parker. James E. "Impact Of Price-Level Accounting." **AR**. 1977. Vol. 52. No. 1, pp. 69-96.

Parker. James E. "Refunding Non-Callable Bonds: A Tax-Oriented Decision Model," **JATA**, 1986. Vol. 7. No. 2, pp. 32-47.

Parker. James E. "Testing Comparability And Objectivity Of Exit Value Accounting." **AR.** 1975. Vol. 50. No. 3. pp. 512-524.

Parker. James E. (Gramlich. Jeffrey D.. Kenneth F. Abramowicz and James E. Parker. "Refunding Non-Callable Bonds: An Update Of A Tax-Oriented Decision Model In Light Of The Tax Reform Act Of 1986." **JATA**. 1988. Vol. 9. No. 2. pp. 105-110.)

Parker. James E. (Nichols. Donald R. and James E. Parker. "An Alternative To Liquidity As A Basis For Exchange Valuation." **ABACUS.** 1972. Vol. 8. No. 1. pp. 68-74.)

Parker. Larry M. and Gary John Previts. "Regulation: The Forces Influencing Accounting Practice," **RIAR.** 1987. Vol. 1. pp. 1-4.

Parker. Larry M. and Gary J. Previts. "The 'Yes' Vote For 'Excellence': A Profession More In Consonance With A Changing Society." **RIAR.** 1988. Vol. 2. pp. 1-4.

Parker. Larry M. (Corless. John C. and Larry M. Parker. "The Impact Of MAS On Auditor Independence: An Experiment." **ACCHOR.** 1987. Vol. 1. No. 3. pp. 25-30.)

Parker. Larry M. (Tucker. Michael J. and Larry M. Parker. "Losses On Nonrecourse Loans - Tax Shelters," **CPAJ**. 1984. Vol. 54. No. 1. pp. 32-38.)

Parker. Larry M., John C. Corless and Michael J. Tucker. "Audit Firm Size And Internal Control Assessment: An Experiment." **RIAR.** 1988. Vol. 2. pp. 155-166.

Parker. Lee D. "An Historical Analysis Of Ethical Pronouncements And Debate In The Australian Accounting Profession." **ABACUS.** 1987. Vol. 23. No. 2. pp. 122-140.

Parker. Lee D. "Communication In The Corporate Budgetary System." **ABR.** 1977-78. Vol. 8. No. 31. pp. 191-207.

Parker. Lee D. "Divisional Performance Measurement: Beyond An Exclusive Profit Test." **ABR.** 1978-79. Vol. 9. No. 36. pp. 309-319.

Parker. Lee D. "Goal Congruence: A Misguided Accounting Concept." **ABACUS.** 1976. Vol. 12. No. 1. pp. 3-13.

Parker. Lee D. "Participation In Budget Planning: The Prospects Surveyed." **ABR.** 1978-79. Vol. 9. No. 34. pp. 123-138.

Parker. Lee D. "Polemical Themes In Social Accounting: A Scenario For Standard Setting." **AIPIA.** 1986. Vol. 1. pp. 67-93.

Parker. Lee D. "The Behavioural Impact Of Budgets: Early Accounting Contributions," **AHJ**, 1984, Vol. 11. No. 1. pp. 119-123.

Parker. Lee D. "The Classical Model Of Control In The

Accounting Literature," **AHJ**, 1986, Vol. 13, No. 1, pp. 71-92.

Parker, Lee. "A Reassessment Of The Role Of Control In Corporate Budgeting," **ABR**, 1976-77, Vol. 7, No. 26, pp. 135-143.

Parker, L. D. "Coincidence Discovered: Fifty Years On," **ABR**, 1980-81, Vol. 11, No. 42, pp. 171-172.

Parker, L. D. "Corporate Annual Reports: A Failure To Communicate," **IJAER**, 1981, Vol. 16, No. 2, pp. 35-48.

Parker, L. D. "Corporate Annual Reporting: A Mass Communication Perspective," **ABR**, 1981-82, Vol. 12, No. 48, pp. 279-286.

Parker, L. D. "Management Accounting And The Corporate Environment," **MA**, 1978, Vol. 59, No. 8, pp. 15-20.

Parker, L. D. (Cowen, S. S., L. B. Ferreri and L. D. Parker. "The Impact Of Corporate Characteristics On Social Responsibility Disclosure: A Typology And Frequency-Based Analysis," **AOS**, 1987, Vol. 12, No. 2, pp. 111-122.)

Parker, L. D. (Lewis, N. R., L. D. Parker, G. D. Pound and P. Sutcliffe. "Annual Report Readability: The Use Of Readability Techniques," **ABR**, 1985-86, Vol. 16, No. 63, pp. 199-214.)

Parker, L. D. (Lewis, N. R., L. D. Parker and P. Sutcliffe. "Financial Reporting To Employees: The Pattern Of Development 1919 To 1979," **AOS**, 1984, Vol. 9, No. 3/4, pp. 275-290.)

Parker, L. D. (Lewis, N., L. D. Parker and P. Sutcliffe. "Financial Reporting To Employees: Towards A Research Framework," **ABR**, 1983-84, Vol. 14, No. 55, pp. 229-240.)

Parker, R. H. "A Note On Savary's 'Le Parfait Negociant'," **JAR**, 1966, Vol. 4, No. 2, pp. 260-261.

Parker, R. H. "Accounting History: A Select Bibliography," **ABACUS**, 1965, Vol. 1, No. 1, pp. 62-84.

Parker, R. H. "Bookkeeping Barter And Current Cash Equivalents In Early New South Wales," **ABACUS**, 1982, Vol. 18, No. 2, pp. 139-151.

Parker, R. H. "British Men Of Account," **ABACUS**, 1978, Vol. 14, No. 1, pp. 53-65.

Parker, R. H. "Discounted Cash Flow In Historical Perspective," **JAR**, 1968, Vol. 6, No. 1, pp. 58-71.

Parker, R. H. "Explaining National Differences In Consolidated Accounts," **ABR**, 1976-77, Vol. 7, No. 27, pp. 203-207.

Parker, R. H. "Lower Of Cost And Market In Britain And The United States: An Historical Survey," **ABACUS**, 1965, Vol. 1, No. 2, pp. 156-172.

Parker, R. H. "Principles And Practice In Translating Foreign Currencies: An Essay In Comparative Accounting," **ABACUS**, 1970, Vol. 6, No. 2, pp. 144-153.

Parker, R. H. "Research Needs In Accounting History," **AHJ**, 1977, Vol. 4, No. 2, pp. 1-28.

Parker, R. H. "Select Bibliography Of Works On The History Of Accounting 1981-1987," **AHJ**, 1988, Vol. 15, No. 2, pp. 1-81.

Parker, William M. "Business Combinations And Accounting Valuation," **JAR**, 1966, Vol. 4, No. 2, pp. 149-154.

Parker, William M. "Treatment Of Short-Term Credit In The Funds Statement," **AR**, 1963, Vol. 38, No. 4, pp. 785-788.

Parker, William M. "Upgrading The Elementary Accounting Course," **AR**, 1965, Vol. 40, No. 2, pp. 452-453.

Parkinson, C. Northcote. "Our Overheads Are Overhigh," **MA**, 1969, Vol. 51, No. 5, pp. 9-11.

Parkinson, David. (Gannon, John J. and David Parkinson. "Software Development Costs Should Be Expensed," **MA**, 1983, Vol. 65, No. 5, pp. 37-39.)

Parkinson, John M. (Fadel, Hisham and John M. Parkinson. "Liquidity Evaluation By Means Of Ratio Analysis," **ABR**, 1977-78, Vol. 8, No. 30, pp. 101-107.)

Parkinson, J. M. "Economic, Political, And Civil Indicators And Reporting And Disclosure Adequacy: Empirical Investigation': A Comment," **JAPP**, 1984, Vol. 3, No. 3, pp. 239-248.

Parkison, Paul W. "Investment Decision-Making: Conventional Methods Vs. Game Theory," **MA**, 1971, Vol. 53, No. 3, pp. 13-15.

Parks, James T. "A Guide To FASB's Overhaul Of Income Tax Accounting," **JOA**, 1988, Vol. 165, No. 4, pp. 24-35.

Parks, James T. "How Accounting Standards Are Changing The Home Finance Industry," **JOA**, 1988, Vol. 166, No. 5, pp. 59-62.

Parks, James. (Willingham, John and James Parks. "Internal Control Analysis - A Solution," **CPAJ**, 1982, Vol. 52, No. 5, pp. 24-35.)

Paroby, Stephen M. and William J. Barrett. "Reducing The Risk Of Computer Fraud," **CA**, 1987, Vol. 5, No. 4, pp. 59-62.

Paroby, Stephen M. and William J. Barrett. "Preventing Computer Fraud - A Message For Management," **CPAJ**, 1987, Vol. 57, No. 11, pp. 36-49.

Paroby, Stephen M., John G. Baab and Lewis Kramer. "Controlling Your Computer," **CA**, 1987, Vol. 5, No. 2, pp. 34-41.

Parr, Charles D. "Networks: The Vital Link," **CA**, 1986, Vol. 4, No. 1, pp. 51-53.

Parrott, William H. "The Allocation Of Pension Costs To Periods Of Time," **MA**, 1969, Vol. 50, No. 8, pp. 39-42.

Parry, Robert W. (Herhold, Susan, Robert W. Parry and James M. Patton. "Behavioral Research In Municipal Accounting," **RIGNA**, 1987, Vol. 3, Part B, pp. 71-109.)

Parry, Robert W., Jr. "A Digest Of Authoritative Pronouncements On Governmental Accounting And Reporting," **RIGNA**, 1985, Vol. 1, pp. 77-84.

Parry, Robert W., Jr. "Defining The Municipal Entity," **MA**, 1982, Vol. 64, No. 3, pp. 50-55.

Parsons, David W. "Financial Planning Services - Part I," **CPAJ**, 1986, Vol. 56, No. 2, pp. 14-21.

Parsons, David W. "Financial Planning Services - Part II," **CPAJ**, 1986, Vol. 56, No. 3, pp. 42-47.

Parsons, R. David. "Converting Taxes To Employee Benefits," **MA**, 1983, Vol. 65, No. 4, pp. 54-58.

Parsons, Vinson A. and George A. MacDonald. "Standard Cost And Control System," **MA**, 1970, Vol. 52, No. 5, pp. 19-21.

Partington, Graham, Jill McKinnon and Carrick Martin. "Funds Statements And The Two-Entity Test: A Response," **ABACUS**, 1986, Vol. 22, No. 1, pp. 39-44.

Partington, Graham. "Process Costing: A Comment," **ABACUS**, 1979, Vol. 15, No. 1, pp. 60-66.

Partington, G. H. and R. H. Chenhall. "Dividends, Distortion And Double Taxation," **ABACUS**, 1983, Vol. 19, No. 1, pp. 3-13.

Partington, G. H. "Teaching Process Costing," **IAE**, 1984, No. 1, pp. 75-80.

Partridge, R. William. "A Plea For More Standards In Cost Accounting," **MA**, 1967, Vol. 48, No. 9, pp. 8-15.

Partridge, R. William. "Will The Real Variance, Please, Stand Up," **MA**, 1966, Vol. 48, No. 3, pp. 3-9.

Pasewark, William R. and Kelly S. McCabe. "Preparing And Maintaining A Budget Manual," **MA**, 1988, Vol. 69, No. 11, pp. 33-36.

Pasewark, William R. and Ronald L. Clark. "Understanding What Went Wrong With The Budget," **CA**, 1988, Vol. 6, No. 1, pp. 48-52.

Pasewark, William R., Jerry R. Strawser and Jack E. Wilkerson, Jr. "Empirical Evidence On The Association Between Characteristics Of Graduating Accounting Students And Recruiting Decisions," **IAE**, 1988, Vol. 3, No. 2, pp. 388-401.

Pashalian, Siroon and William J. E. Crissy. "Are Corporate Annual Reports Difficult, Dull Reading?," **JOA**, 1952, Vol. 94, No. 2, pp. 215-219.

Passage, Howard D. and Donald A. Fleming. "An Integrated Approach To Internal Control Reviews," **MA**, 1980, Vol. 61, No. 8, pp. 29-35.

Pastena, Victor and Joshua Ronen. "Some Hypotheses On The Pattern Of Management's Informal Disclosures," **JAR**, 1979, Vol. 17, No. 2, pp. 550-564.

Pastena, Victor and William Ruland. "The Merger/Bankruptcy Alternative," **AR**, 1986, Vol. 61, No. 2, pp. 288-301.

Pastena, Victor. "Some Evidence On The SEC's System Of Continuous Disclosure," **AR**, 1979, Vol. 54, No. 4, pp. 776-783.

Pastena, Victor. (El-Gazzar, Samir, Steve Lilien and Victor Pastena. "Accounting For Leases By Lessees," **JAEC**, 1986, Vol. 8, No. 3, pp. 217-237.)

Pastena, Victor. (Haw, In-Mu, Victor Pastena and Steven Lilien. "The Association Between Market-Based Merger Premiums And Firm's Financial Position Prior To Merger," **JAAF**, 1987, Vol. 2 (New Series), No. 1, pp. 24-42.)

Pastena, Victor. (Lilien, Steven and Victor Pastena. "Intramethod Comparability: The Case Of The Oil And Gas Industry," **AR**, 1981, Vol. 56, No. 3, pp. 690-703.)

Pastena, Victor. (Lilien, Steven, Martin Mellman and Victor Pastena. "Accounting Changes: Successful Versus Unsuccessful Firms," **AR**, 1988, Vol. 63, No. 4, pp. 642-656.)

Pastena, Victor. (Lilien, Steven and Victor Pastena. "Determinants Of Intra-Method Choice In The Oil And Gas Industry," **JAEC**, 1982, Vol. 4, No. 3, pp. 145-170.)

Patchin, Peter J. "Estimating Property Taxes," **MA**, 1972, Vol. 54, No. 4, pp. 39-42.

Patel, Raman C. "A Note On Inventory Reorder Point Determination," **JAED**, 1986, Vol. 4, No. 2, pp. 131-140.

Patell, James M. and Mark A. Wolfson. "Good News, Bad News, And The Intraday Timing Of Corporate Disclosures," **AR**, 1982, Vol. 57, No. 3, pp. 509-527.

Patell, James M. and Mark A. Wolfson. "The Ex Ante And Ex Post Price Effects Of Quarterly Earnings Announcements Reflected In Option And Stock Prices," **JAR**, 1981, Vol. 19, No. 2, pp. 434-458.

Patell, James M. and Mark A. Wolfson. "Anticipated Information Releases Reflected In Call Option Prices," **JAEC**, 1979, Vol. 1, No. 2, pp. 117-140.

Patell, James M. "Corporate Forecasts Of Earnings Per Share And Stock Price Behavior: Empirical Tests," **JAR**, 1976, Vol. 14, No. 2, pp. 246-276.

Patell, James M. "Cost Accounting, Process Control, And Product Design: A Case Study Of The Hewlett-Packard Personal Office Computer Division," **AR**, 1987, Vol. 62, No. 4, pp. 808-839.

Patell, James M. "The API And The Design Of Experiments," **JAR**, 1979, Vol. 17, No. 2, pp. 528-549.

Patell, James M. (Demski, Joel S., James M. Patell and Mark A. Wolfson. "Decentralized Choice Of Monitoring Systems," **AR**, 1984, Vol. 59, No. 1, pp. 16-34.)

Patell, James M. (M.M. Laurentius, J.M. Patell and M.A. Wolfson. "The Experimental Design Of Classification Models: An Application Of Recursive Partitioning And Bootstrapping To Commercial Bank Loan Classifications," **JAR**, 1984, Vol. 22, Supp., pp. 87-114.)

Patell, James M. (Ohlson, James A. and James M. Patell. "An Introduction To Residual (API) Analysis And The Private Value Of Information And The API And The Design Of Experiments," **JAR**, 1979, Vol. 17, No. 2, pp. 504-505.)

Paton, Scott N. "Negotiating Strategy And Tactics," **CA**, 1988, Vol. 6, No. 1, pp. 53-58.

Paton, William A. "Accounting And Utilization Of Resources," **JAR**, 1963, Vol. 1, No. 1, pp. 42-72.

Paton, William A. "Aspects Of Asset Valuations," **AR**, 1934,

Vol. 9, No. 2, pp. 122-129.

Paton, William A. "Depreciation - Concept And Measurement," **JOA**, 1959, Vol. 108, No. 4. pp. 38-43.

Paton, William A. "Measuring Profits Under Inflation Conditions: A Serious Problem For Accountants," **JOA**, 1950, Vol. 89, No. 1, pp. 16-27.

Paton, William A. "Presentation Of Bond Discount." **AR**, 1937, Vol. 12, No. 3, pp. 285-289.

Paton, William A. "Recalling George Oliver May And Me," **AHJ**, 1981, Vol. 8, No. 2, pp. 91-95.

Paton, William A. "Simplification Of Federal Tax Administration," **AR**, 1944, Vol. 19, No. 1. pp. 11-19.

Paton, Wm. A. "The 'Cash-Flow' Illusion." **AR**. 1963. Vol. 38, No. 2, pp. 243-251.

Paton, W. A. "Accounting Problems Of The Depression." **AR**, 1932. Vol. 7, No. 4, pp. 258-267.

Paton, W. A. "Comments On The Cost Principle." **AR**. 1942. Vol. 17, No. 1, pp. 10-18.

Paton, W. A. "Depreciation And The Price Level." **AR**. 1948. Vol. 23, No. 2, pp. 118-123.

Paton, W. A. "Distribution Costs And Inventory Values." **AR**. 1927. Vol. 2, No. 3, pp. 246-253.

Paton, W. A. "Earmarks Of A Profession - And The APB." **JOA**. 1971. Vol. 131, No. 1, pp. 37-45.

Paton, W. A. "Economic Theory And Relation to Accounting," **AR**, 1931. Vol. 6, No. 2, pp. 89-96.

Paton, W. A. "In All My Years - Notes On Handicapping," **AHJ**, 1976, Vol. 3, No. 1-4, pp. 29-31.

Paton, W. A. "Limitations Of Financial And Operating Ratios," **AR**, 1928, Vol. 3, No. 3. pp. 252-260.

Paton, W. A. "Observations On Inflation From An Accounting Stance," **JAR**, 1968. Vol. 6. No. 1. pp. 72-85.

Paton, W. A. "Postscript On 'Treasury' Shares." **AR**. 1969. Vol. 44, No. 2, pp. 276-283.

Paton, W. A. "Premature Revenue Recognition." **JOA**. 1953. Vol. 96, No. 4. pp. 432-437.

Paton, W. A. "Restoration Of Fixed Asset Values To The Balance Sheet," **AR**, 1947. Vol. 22. No. 2. pp. 198-200.

Paton, W. A. "Some Reflections On Education And Professoring." **AR**, 1967. Vol. 42. No. 1. pp. 7-23.

Paton, W. A. "The 1948 Revision Of The American Accounting Association's Statement Of Concepts And Standards: Comments On Item 5 Under 'Expense'," **AR**, 1949, Vol. 24. No. 1, pp. 49-53.

Paton, W. A. "The Dividend Code." **AR**, 1929, Vol. 4. No. 4. pp. 218-220.

Paton, W. A. "Transactions Between Affiliates." **AR**. 1945. Vol. 20, No. 3, pp. 255-266.

Paton, W. A. "Valuation Of The Business Enterprise." **AR**. 1936. Vol. 11. No. 1. pp. 26-31.

Paton, W. A. "Wandering Into Accounting - Notes On A Writing Career." **AHJ**, 1978. Vol. 5. No. 2. pp. 1-10.

Paton, W. A. "Deferred Income' - A Misnomer." **JOA**. 1961. Vol. 112, No. 3. pp. 38-40.

Patrick, A. W. and C. L. Quittmeyer. "The CPA And Management Services," **AR**, 1963. Vol. 38. No. 1. pp. 109-117.

Patrick, A. W. "A Proposal For Determining The Significance Of Variations From Standard." **AR**. 1957. Vol. 32. No. 4. pp. 587-592.

Patrick, A. W. "Burden Rates - Machine Hours Versus Direct Labor Hours." **AR**. 1961. Vol. 36. No. 4. pp. 645-647.

Patrick, A. W. "Some Observations On The Break-Even Chart." **AR**. 1958. Vol. 33. No. 4, pp. 573-580.

Patrick, William F. "Cash Flow And Return On Investment - A Supplement To FAS 33." **CPAJ**. 1981. Vol. 51. No. 3. pp. 29-35.

Patten, Ronald J. and Joseph W. Bachman. "Elementary Accounting Profile - 1970." **AR**. 1972. Vol. 47. No. 1. pp. 164-167.

Patten, Ronald J. and Lawrence L. Steinmetz. "What Do Students Think Of Your Elementary Course?." **AR**. 1966. Vol. 41. No. 4, pp. 767-772.

Patten, Ronald J. and Thomas D. Hubbard. "CPA Review Clinics - An Opportunity For Accounting Educators." **AR**. 1972. Vol. 47. No. 2, pp. 385-387.

Patten, Ronald J. "Intraperiod Income Tax Allocation - A Practical Concept." **AR**. 1964. Vol. 39. No. 4. pp. 876-879.

Patten, Woolvin. "Handling Tax Fraud Cases." **JOA**. 1957. Vol. 103. No. 3. pp. 58-63.

Patterson, Jeffrey L. "The Development Of The Concept Of Corporation From Earliest Roman Times To A.D. 476." **AHJ**. 1983. Vol. 10. No. 1. pp. 87-98.

Patterson, John R. "Decision Making Applications Of Direct Cost Information." **MA**. 1968. Vol. 49. No. 5. pp. 11-22.

Patterson, Michael. (Fetkyo, David F. and Michael Patterson. "How An Oil Company Analyzes Credit." **MA**. 1983. Vol. 65. No. 2. pp. 30-34.)

Patterson, Mike C. "Inventory File Accuracy: A Key Ingredient To Planning." **CA**. 1986. Vol. 4. No. 4. pp. 52-55.

Patterson, Robert G. "Materiality And The Economic Environment," **AR**, 1967. Vol. 42. No. 4. pp. 772-774.

Pattillo, James W. and Jerry D. Siebel. "Factors Affecting The Materiality Judgment," **CPAJ**. 1974. Vol. 44. No. 7. pp. 39-44.

Pattillo, James W. "A Study In Instant Information." **MA**. 1969. Vol. 50, No. 9, pp. 17-20.

Pattillo, James W. "Communication Through Reports." **MA**. 1969. Vol. 51. No. 4. pp. 19-22.

Pattillo, James W. "Rating Student Performance." **AR**. 1966. Vol. 41, No. 3. pp. 555-559.

Pattillo, James W. "Unity In The Accounting Profession." **JOA**. 1974. Vol. 138. No. 1. pp. 50-58.

Pattillo, James W., Michael H. Morris and William D. Nichols. "The Materiality Principle: Problems And Possible Solutions," **CA**, 1983, Vol. 1, No. 3, pp. 44-51.

Pattinson, W. Richard. "Excess And Obsolete Inventory Control." **MA**, 1974. Vol. 55, No. 12, pp. 35-37.

Pattison, Diane D. (Gilchrist, Michael, Diane D. Pattison and Ronald J. Kudla. "Controlling Indirect Costs With Headcount Forecast Algorithms," **MA**, 1985, Vol. 67, No. 2. pp. 46-51.)

Pattison, Fred S. "Accounting For Behavior," **MA**, 1973, Vol. 54. No. 10, p. 13.

Patton, James M. "An Empirical Investigation Of Some Effects Of Consolidating Municipal Financial Reports." **AR**. 1978. Vol. 53. No. 2, pp. 402-414.

Patton, James M. "Ratio Analysis And Efficient Markets In Introductory Financial Accounting," **AR**, 1982, Vol. 57. No. 3. pp. 627-630.

Patton, James M. "The Governmental Financial Reporting Entity: A Review And Analysis," **RIGNA**, 1985, Vol. 1. pp. 85-116.

Patton, James M. (Banker, Rajiv D. and James M. Patton. "Analytical Agency Theory And Municipal Accounting: An Introduction And An Application," **RIGNA**, 1987, Vol. 3. Part B, pp. 29-50.)

Patton, James M. (Evans, John H., III and James M. Patton. "An Economic Analysis Of Participation In The Municipal Finance Officers Association Certificate Of Conformance Program." **JAEC**. 1983, Vol. 5, No. 2, pp. 151-175.)

Patton, James M. (Evans, John H., III and James M. Patton. "Signaling And Monitoring In Public-Sector Accounting," **JAR**. 1987, Vol. 25, Supp., pp. 130-158.)

Patton, James M. (Herhold, Susan, Robert W. Parry and James M. Patton. "Behavioral Research In Municipal Accounting," **RIGNA**, 1987, Vol. 3, Part B, pp. 71-109.)

Patton, James M. (Lewis, Barry L., James M. Patton and Sharon L. Green. "The Effects Of Information Choice And Information Use On Analysts' Predictions Of Municipal Bond Rating Changes," **AR**, 1988, Vol. 63, No. 2, pp. 270-282.)

Patton, J. M. (Evans, J. H., III, B. L. Lewis and J. M. Patton. "An Economic Modeling Approach To Contingency Theory And Management Control", **AOS**, 1986, Vol. 11, No. 6. pp. 483-498.)

Patton, Ronald J. (Brenner, Vincent C., Ronald M. Copeland, Paul E. Dascher, Arthur J. Francia, Ronald J. Patten and Robert H. Strawser. "Trials And Tribulations Of The Researcher: A Case Study." **JAR**, 1972, Vol. 10, No. 1. pp. 195-199.)

Patz, Dennis H. and James R. Boatsman. "Accounting Principle Formulation In An Efficient Markets Environment." **JAR**, 1972, Vol. 10, No. 2, pp. 392-403.

Patz, Dennis H. "A Price Parity Theory Of Translation." **ABR**. 1977-78, Vol. 8, No. 29. pp. 14-24.

Patz, Dennis H. "Alternative Realities And Price Parity Translation." **ABR**. 1988, Vol. 18, No. 71. pp. 239-247.

Patz, Dennis H. (Lorek, Kenneth S., Charles L. McDonald and Dennis H. Patz. "A Comparative Examination Of Management Forecasts and Box-Jenkins Forecasts Of Earnings." **AR**. 1976. Vol. 51. No. 2, pp. 321-330.)

Patz, Dennis. "A Price Parity Theory Of Translation: A Reply." **ABR**. 1978-79, Vol. 9, No. 33, pp. 66-72.

Patz, D. H. "Price Parity Translation: Methodology And Implementation," **ABR**, 1980-81, Vol. 11, No. 43, pp. 207-216.

Paul, Herbert M. "Financial Counseling By CPAs." **CPAJ**. 1974. Vol. 44, No. 9, pp. 39-46.

Paul, Jack W. "Presenting Hypothesis Testing By Analogy." **JAED**. 1983. Vol. 1. No. 2, pp. 107-121.

Paul, Jack W. (Largay, James A., III and Jack W. Paul. "Market Efficiency And Legal Liability Of Auditors: Comment." **AR**, 1983, Vol. 58, No. 4. pp. 820-832.)

Paul, John W. (Bainbridge, D. Raymond and John W. Paul. "Relating Audit And Internal Control Objectives: A Missing Step In Specifying Compliance Tests." **JAED**. 1986. Vol. 4. No. 2. pp. 63-74.)

Paul, Terrance D. "Employer-Sponsored Life Insurance: What It Really Costs." **MA**, 1977. Vol. 59. No. 2. pp. 21-29.

Paul, William B. "Excess Profits Tax." **AR**, 1952, Vol. 27. No. 1. pp. 44-49.

Paulsen, Neil E. "Software Development Costs Should Be Capitalized." **MA**, 1983, Vol. 65, No. 5, pp. 40-42.

Pavlock, Ernest J. "Training Accountants For The Future." **IJAER**. 1977. Vol. 13. No. 1. pp. 141-158.

Pavlock, Ernest J. (Ciesick, Robert T., Harold L. Monk. Jr., and Ernest J. Pavlock. "The National CPE Curriculum." **JOA**, 1985, Vol. 160, No. 4. pp. 118-124.)

Pavlock, Ernest J. (Kiesey, Douglas T. and Ernest J. Pavlock. "Trends In Management Education For CPAs." **JOA**. 1975. Vol. 139, No. 5, pp. 48-53.)

Pavlock, Ernest J. (Lathan, Malcolm H., Jr., Barbara A. Ostrowski, Ernest J. Pavlock and Richard A. Scott. "Recruiting Entry Level Staff: Gender Differences." **CPAJ**. 1987, Vol. 57. No. 1. pp. 30-43.)

Pavlock, Ernest J. (Scott, Richard A., Ernest J. Pavlock and Malcolm H. Lathan, Jr. "On-Campus Recruiting: The Students Speak Up," **JOA**, 1985, Vol. 159, No. 1, pp. 60-75.)

Pavony, William H. "Budgeting New Plant Ventures." **MA**. 1969. Vol. 50, No. 7, pp. 35-36.

Pawliczek, Ronald B. "Modification Of Examinations: A Focus On Individual Weaknesses," **AR**, 1978, Vol. 53, No. 4, pp. 985-988.

Pawliczek, Ronald. "The Effect Of Different Scoring Plans On Student Performance In An Elementary Accounting Course." **AR**. 1977. Vol. 52. No. 3, pp. 721-726.

Pawliczek, Ronald. (Weinstein, Arnold K., Louis Corsini and Ronald Pawliczek. "The Big Eight In Europe." **IJAER**.

1978, Vol. 13, No. 2, pp. 57-71.)

Paxson, Dean. (Earl, Michael and Dean Paxson. "Value Accounting For Currency Transactions," **ABR**, 1977-78, Vol. 8, No. 30, pp. 92-100.)

Paxton, Lloyd. "Accounting During Inflation Behind Iron Curtain," **JOA**, 1951, Vol. 92, No. 2, pp. 190-197.

Payne, John B. "Federal Accountkeeping," **AR**, 1940, Vol. 15, No. 1, pp. 31-46.

Payne, John B. "Financial Administration Of The United Nations," **AR**, 1949, Vol. 24, No. 4, pp. 423-431.

Payne, Robert E. "Net Worth Under The Delaware And Michigan Corporation Laws," **AR**, 1933, Vol. 8, No. 1, pp. 1-10.

Payne, Robert E. "The Effect Of Recent Laws On Accountancy," **AR**, 1935, Vol. 10, No. 1, pp. 84-95.

Payne, Robert E. "The Importance Of Clarity In Balance Sheet Display," **AR**, 1933, Vol. 8, No. 4, pp. 292-301.

Payne, Roger W. (Williams, William J., Gerald Fuller and Roger W. Payne. "Improving Cost Management By Forming An Alliance," **CA**, 1986, Vol. 4, No. 1, pp. 54-61.)

Paynter, John W. "The Department Store Controller's Part In Business Policy," **AR**, 1947, Vol. 22, No. 4, pp. 390-393.

Peacock, Eileen. "Why Errors Occur In Accounting Systems," **MA**, 1988, Vol. 70, No. 2, pp. 54-56.

Peak, George W. "Auditing Assessment Accuracy," **AR**, 1940, Vol. 15, No. 2, pp. 238-240.

Pearce, Douglas K. and Sara A. Reiter. "Regression Strategies When Multicollinearity Is A Problem: A Methodological Note," **JAR**, 1985, Vol. 23, No. 1, pp. 405-407.

Pearcy, Jeff. "Accounting Standards - Boon Or Curse: A Comment," **ABR**, 1981-82, Vol. 12, No. 47, pp. 236-237.

Pearl, Daniel. "Teaching The Statement Of Changes In Financial Position Without Worksheets Or T-Accounts," **IAE**, 1986, Vol. 1, No. 1, pp. 132-142.

Pearson, David B. "Will Accreditation Improve The Quality Of Education?," **JOA**, 1979, Vol. 147, No. 4, pp. 53-58.

Pearson, David B. (Cohen, Gerald D. and David B. Pearson. "Auditing The Client's Judgments," **JOA**, 1981, Vol. 151, No. 5, pp. 58-65.)

Pearson, Della A. (Seiler, Robert E. and Della A. Pearson. "Work Satisfaction Through Research - An Empirical Test," **IAE**, 1986, Vol. 1, No. 1, pp. 65-75.)

Pearson, Della A., Robert E. Seiler and Ira R. Weiss. "Why Do Management Accountants Feel Disliked?," **MA**, 1982, Vol. 63, No. 9, pp. 14-19.

Pearson, Diane T. (Briner, Russell F., Diane T. Pearson and James E. Gauntt, Jr. "A Microcomputer Application For Attribute Sampling," **JAED**, 1987, Vol. 5, No. 1, pp. 161-166.)

Pearson, George, Jr. "Ten Warnings For The Accountant On The Witness Stand," **JOA**, 1952, Vol. 94, No. 1, pp. 78-81.

Pearson, John A. "Paragon Pricing," **MA**, 1986, Vol. 67, No. 12, pp. 41-43.

Pearson, Mark W. and Linda L. Okubara. "Restructurings And Impairment Of Value: A Growing Controversy," **ACCHOR**, 1987, Vol. 1, No. 1, pp. 35-42.

Pearson, Michael A. (Epaves, Richard A., Laurence R. Paquette and Michael A. Pearson. "A Flow Chart Conceptualization Of Auditors' Reports On Financial Statements," **AR**, 1976, Vol. 51, No. 4, pp. 913-916.)

Pearson, Michael A., John H. Lindgren, Jr. and Buddy L. Myers. "A Preliminary Analysis Of AudSEC Voting Patterns," **JAAF**, 1979, Vol. 2, No. 2, pp. 122-134.

Peasnell, K. V. and D. J. Williams. "Ersatz Academics And Scholar-Saints: The Supply Of Financial Accounting Research," **ABACUS**, 1986, Vol. 22, No. 2, pp. 121-135.

Peasnell, K. V. and L. C. L. Skerratt. "Income-Group Inflation Rates And General Purchasing Power Adjustments: An Empirical Test Of The Heterogeneity Hypothesis," **ABR**, 1978-79, Vol. 9, No. 33, pp. 45-60.

Peasnell, K. V. and L. C. L. Skerratt. "How Well Does A Single Index Represent The Nineteen Sandilands Plant And Machinery Indices?," **JAR**, 1977, Vol. 15, No. 1, pp. 108-119.

Peasnell, K. V. "A Note On The Discounted Present Value Concept," **AR**, 1977, Vol. 52, No. 1, pp. 186-189.

Peasnell, K. V. "Capital Budgeting And Discounted Cash Equivalents: Some Clarifying Comments," **ABACUS**, 1979, Vol. 15, No. 2, pp. 145-156.

Peasnell, K. V. "Interaction Effects In CCA Valuations," **ABR**, 1977-78, Vol. 8, No. 30, pp. 82-91.

Peasnell, K. V. "On Capital Budgeting And Income Measurement," **ABACUS**, 1981, Vol. 17, No. 1, pp. 52-67.

Peasnell, K. V. "Statement Of Accounting Theory And Theory Acceptance," **ABR**, 1977-78, Vol. 8, No. 31, pp. 217-225.

Peasnell, K. V. "The CCA Depreciation Problem - An Analysis And Proposal," **ABACUS**, 1977, Vol. 13, No. 2, pp.123-140.

Peasnell, K. V. "The Function Of A Conceptual Framework For Corporate Financial Reporting," **ABR**, 1981-82, Vol. 12, No. 48, pp. 243-256.

Peasnell, K. V. "The Objectives Of Published Accounting Reports: A Comment," **ABR**, 1974-75, Vol. 5, No. 17, pp. 71-76.

Peasnell, K. V. (Archer, G. S. and K. V. Peasnell. "The Current Cost Of A Quoted Long-Term Liability: A Comment," **ABR**, 1984-85, Vol. 15, No. 58, pp. 87-90.)

Peasnell, K. V. (Archer, G. S. H. and K. V. Peasnell. "Debt Finance And Capital Maintenance In Current Cost Accounting," **ABACUS**, 1984, Vol. 20, No. 2, pp. 111-124.)

Peasnell, K. V. (Gee, K. P. and K. V. Peasnell. "A Comment On Replacement Cost As The Upper Limit Of Value To The Owner," **ABR**, 1976-77, Vol. 7, No. 28, p. 312.)

Peasnell, K. V. (Gee, K. P. and K. V. Peasnell. "A Pragmatic Defence Of Replacement Cost," **ABR**, 1975-76, Vol.

6, No. 24, pp. 242-249.)

Peasnell, K. V. (Skerratt, L. C. L. and K. V. Peasnell. "Anti-Dilution Of Earnings Per Share," **ABR**, 1975-76, Vol. 6, No. 21, pp. 57-62.)

Peasnell, K. V., L. C. L. Skerratt and C. W. R. Ward. "The Share Price Impact Of UK CCA Disclosures," **ABR**, 1987-88, Vol. 18, No. 69, pp. 3-16.

Peavy, John W., III and S. Michael Edgar. "Rating Electric Utility Commercial Paper," **JAAF**, 1985, Vol. 8, No. 2, pp. 125-135.

Peavy, Waymon G. "Corporations Used To Avoid Income Tax On Shareholders," **JOA**, 1954, Vol. 98, No. 3, pp. 353-359.

Peavy, Waymon G. "Organizations And Reorganizations," **JOA**, 1956, Vol. 102, No. 2, pp. 36-40.

Peche, Tadeusz. "Instructional Problems In The Modernization Of Accounting Theory," **IJAER**, 1978, Vol. 13, No. 2, pp. 87-104.

Peck, Leslie G. (Brown, Arthur A. and Leslie G. Peck. "How Electronic Machines Handle Clerical Work," **JOA**, 1955, Vol. 99, No. 1, pp. 31-37.)

Pedelahore, J. Earl. "Case For The Dissent," **JOA**, 1956, Vol. 102, No. 6, pp. 38-41.

Pedersen, P. H. (Bjorn-Andersen, N. and P. H. Pedersen. "Computer Facilitated Changes In The Management Power Structure," **AOS**, 1980, Vol. 5, No. 2, pp. 203-216.)

Peel, D. A. (Peel, M. J. and D. A. Peel. "Some Further Empirical Evidence On Predicting Private Company Failure," **ABR**, 1987-88, Vol. 18, No. 69, pp. 57-66.)

Peel, M. J. and D. A. Peel. "Some Further Empirical Evidence On Predicting Private Company Failure," **ABR**, 1987-88, Vol. 18, No. 69, pp. 57-66.

Peirce, Richard F. "A Course In Electronic Data Processing In The Accounting Curriculum," **AR**, 1956, Vol. 31, No. 2, pp. 309-313.

Peirce, Richard F. "A Resource System For Property Administration," **MA**, 1966, Vol. 48, No. 4, pp. 27-33.

Peirce, Richard F. "Changes In Management Methods Resulting From Advanced EDP Systems," **MA**, 1966, Vol. 47, No. 8, pp. 9-15.

Peirce, Richard F. "Managing An Information Systems Activity," **MA**, 1968, Vol. 50, No. 1, pp. 23-28.

Peirson, Graham. "Three Kinds Of Adjustments For Price Changes," **AR**, 1966, Vol. 41, No. 4, pp. 729-736.

Peirson, Graham. (Henderson, Scott and Graham Peirson. "A Note On The Current Cash Equivalent Of Liabilities," **ABACUS**, 1980, Vol. 16, No. 1, pp. 61-66.)

Peirson, Graham. (Henderson, Scott and Graham Peirson. "A Note On Accounting And Executory Contracts," **ABACUS**, 1984, Vol. 20, No. 1, pp. 96-98.)

Peirson, Graham. (Henderson, Scott and Graham Peirson. "Does Accounting Research Matter?," **ABR**, 1978-79, Vol. 9, No. 33, pp. 25-34.)

Pelej, Joseph. "Budgeting And Accounting," **JOA**, 1958, Vol. 105, No. 6, pp. 64-68.

Pelej, Joseph. "Cost-Cutting Potentials In Small Business," **JOA**, 1959, Vol. 108, No. 3, pp. 56-61.

Pelej, Joseph. "How Will Business Electronics Affect The Auditor's Work?," **JOA**, 1954, Vol. 98, No. 1, pp. 36-44.

Pelej, Joseph. "The Place Of The Methods Group Within The Organization," **JOA**, 1954, Vol. 98, No. 6, pp. 723-735.

Peles, Yoram C. and Meir I. Schneller. "Liquidity Ratios And Industry Averages - New Evidence," **ABACUS**, 1979, Vol. 15, No. 1, pp. 13-22.

Peles, Yoram C. "A Note On Yield Variance And Mix Variance," **AR**, 1986, Vol. 61, No. 2, pp. 325-329.

Peles, Yoram C. (Barlev, Benzion and Yoram C. Peles. "Accounting: The Structure Of A Growing Profession," **ABACUS**, 1987, Vol. 23, No. 1, pp. 70-84.)

Peles, Yoram. "Amortization Of Advertising Expenditures In The Financial Statements," **JAR**, 1970, Vol. 8, No. 1, pp. 128-137.

Pelfrey, Sandra and Charles J. Hobson. "Keeping Employees Physically Fit Can Be Cost Efficient," **MA**, 1984, Vol. 65, No. 12, pp. 39-43.

Pellicelli, Giorgio. "The Axiomatic Method In Business Economics: A First Approach," **ABACUS**, 1969, Vol. 5, No. 2, pp. 119-131.

Peloubet, Maurice E. "Accountants' Failure To Deal With Effects Of Inflation," **JOA**, 1953, Vol. 96, No. 6, pp. 714-722.

Peloubet, Maurice E. "An Analysis Of The Effects Of Taxation On Inventory Accounting And Policies," **JOA**, 1950, Vol. 89, No. 2, pp. 139-143.

Peloubet, Maurice E. "Are Profits Necessary?," **AR**, 1947, Vol. 22, No. 2, pp. 141-146.

Peloubet, Maurice E. "Art Or Science," **AR**, 1945, Vol. 20, No. 4, pp. 391-398.

Peloubet, Maurice E. "Choice Of Inventory Methods Depends On Specific Needs Of Each Business," **JOA**, 1951, Vol. 91, No. 1, pp. 70-77.

Peloubet, Maurice E. "Costs And Profits Under Government Contracts," **JOA**, 1951, Vol. 92, No. 1, pp. 87-101.

Peloubet, Maurice E. "Depreciation And The Price Level," **AR**, 1948, Vol. 23, No. 2, pp. 123-126.

Peloubet, Maurice E. "Disclosure Of Current Value Of Lifo Inventories Is Not Normally Useful," **JOA**, 1950, Vol. 89, No. 6, pp. 487-489.

Peloubet, Maurice E. "Is Further Uniformity Desirable Or Possible?," **JOA**, 1961, Vol. 111, No. 4, pp. 35-40.

Peloubet, Maurice E. "Observations On Cost," **AR**, 1943, Vol. 18, No. 1, pp. 9-15.

Peloubet, Maurice E. "Professional Ethics And The Student," **AR**, 1934, Vol. 9, No. 2, pp. 164-170.

Peloubet, Maurice E. "The Cost Accountant In The Modern World," **JOA**, 1955, Vol. 99, No. 3, pp. 55-59.

Peloubet, Maurice E. "The Problem Of Communication." **JOA**, 1956, Vol. 102, No. 1, pp. 36-38.

Peltz, Julius. "Taxation Of Income Resulting From Lease Cancellation," **JOA**, 1954, Vol. 97, No. 2, pp. 205-213.

Peltz, Julius. "When Do Rental Arrangements Create Personal Holding Company Income?," **JOA**, 1950, Vol. 90, No. 3, pp. 238-241.

Pemberton, K. G. (Rands, C. A., R. Vause and K. G. Pemberton. "Using Computers In Small Company Cash Management," **ABR**, 1973-74, Vol. 4, No. 16, pp. 251-262.)

Pemberton, Wilfred A. (Markell, William and Wilfred A. Pemberton. "Programmed Instruction In Elementary Accounting - Is It Successful?," **AR**, 1972, Vol. 47, No. 2, pp. 381-384.)

Pena, Pablo A. "Special Report: A Comparison Of The Accounting Professions Of Colombia And The United States," **IJAER**, 1976, Vol. 11, No. 2, pp. 143-177.

Pendlebury, Maurice and Rowan Jones. "Governmental Budgeting As Ex Ante Financial Accounting: The United Kingdom Case," **JAPP**, 1985, Vol. 4, No. 4, pp. 301-316.

Pendlebury, Maurice and Rowan Jones. "Municipal Disclosure In England: Another Market For Excuses?," **IJAER**, 1983, Vol. 18, No. 2, pp. 83-93.

Pendlebury, Maurice. (Jones, Rowan and Maurice Pendlebury. "Uniformity V. Flexibility In The Published Accounts Of Local Authorities: The UK Problem And Some European Solutions," **ABR**, 1981-82, Vol. 12, No. 46, pp. 129-135.)

Pendrill, David. "Contrasting Income Treatment Of Monetary Items In Recent Accounting Standards In New Zealand, The United Kingdom, And The United States," **IJAER**, 1985, Vol. 20, No. 2, pp. 139-154.

Penick, Jack G. "ADP Equipment As An Accounting Teaching Tool," **AR**, 1966, Vol. 41, No. 3, pp. 549-551.

Penman, Stephen H. "Abnormal Returns To Investment Strategies Based On The Timing Of Earnings Reports," **JAEC**, 1984, Vol. 6, No. 3, pp. 165-183.

Penman, Stephen H. "An Empirical Investigation Of The Voluntary Disclosure Of Corporate Earnings Forecasts," **JAR**, 1980, Vol. 18, No. 1, pp. 132-160.

Penman, Stephen H. "What Net Asset Value? - An Extension Of A Familiar Debate," **AR**, 1970, Vol. 45, No. 2, pp. 333-346.

Penman, Stephen H. (Chambers, Anne E. and Stephen H. Penman. "Timeliness Of Reporting And The Stock Price Reaction To Earnings Announcements," **JAR**, 1984, Vol. 22, No. 1, pp. 21-47.)

Penman, Stephen H. (Eggleton, Ian R. C., Stephen H. Penman and John R. Twombly. "Accounting Changes And Stock Prices: An Examination Of Selected Uncontrolled Variables," **JAR**, 1976, Vol. 14, No. 1, pp. 66-88.)

Penman, Stephen H. (Freeman, Robert N., James A. Ohlson and Stephen H. Penman. "Book Rate-Of-Return And Prediction Of Earnings Changes: An Empirical Investigation," **JAR**, 1982, Vol. 20, No. 2, Part II, pp. 639-653.)

Penman, Stephen H. (Gonedes, Nicholas J., Nicholas Dopuch and Stephen H. Penman. "Disclosure Rules. Information-Production, And Capital Market Equilibrium: The Case Of Forecast Disclosure Rules," **JAR**, 1976, Vol. 14, No. 1, pp. 89-137.)

Penndorf, B. "The Relation Of Taxation To The History Of The Balance Sheet," **AR**, 1930, Vol. 5, No. 3, pp. 243-251.

Penney, Louis H. "Continuing Professional Development," **JOA**, 1959, Vol. 108, No. 3, pp. 31-36.

Penney, Louis H. "Inflation And The CPA." **JOA**, 1959, Vol. 108, No. 1, pp. 23-27.

Penney, Louis H. "The American Institute Of CPAs - Past And Future," **JOA**, 1962, Vol. 113, No. 1, pp. 31-39.

Penney, Louis H. "The Significance Of Mergers Of Accounting Firms," **JOA**, 1961, Vol. 112, No. 5, pp. 51-58.

Penney, Louis H. "Why Research," **AR**, 1960, Vol. 35, No. 1, pp. 1-7.

Penney, L. H. "Financial Statements For Credit Purposes," **JOA**, 1957, Vol. 104, No. 3, pp. 46-50.

Pennington, Lee R. "How FBI Accountant-Investigators Catch Criminals," **JOA**, 1952, Vol. 93, No. 4, pp. 456-463.

Pennington, W. J. "Cost Analysis Procedures For Newspaper Publishers," **JOA**, 1955, Vol. 99, No. 3, pp. 49-54.

Pennington, W. J. "Embezzling: Cases And Cautions," **JOA**, 1964, Vol. 118, No. 1, pp. 47-51.

Penno, Mark. "A Note On The Value Of Information Given Asymmetric Information And Self-Reporting," **CAR**, 1986-87, Vol. 3, No. 2, pp. 368-374.

Penno, Mark. "Asymmetry Of Pre-Decision Information And Managerial Accounting," **JAR**, 1984, Vol. 22, No. 1, pp. 177-191.

Penno, Mark. "Informational Issues In The Financial Reporting Process," **JAR**, 1985, Vol. 23, No. 1, pp. 240-255.

Penny, Hugh R. "Guide To Computer-Assisted Auditing Techniques," **CA**, 1983, Vol. 1, No. 1, pp. 45-53.

Pentrack, Wayne G. "Last-In First-Out Accounting For Inventories," **CPAJ**, 1985, Vol. 55, No. 7, pp. 42-48.

Penz, A. J. "Are Accounting Principles Taught Effectively?," **AR**, 1950, Vol. 25, No. 4, pp. 442-444.

Peoples, John. "Preparation Of Consolidated Statements," **JOA**, 1957, Vol. 104, No. 2, pp. 32-36.

Peragallo, Edward. "A Commentary On Vigano's Historical Development Of Ledger Balancing Procedures, Adjustments And Financial Statements During The Fifteenth, Sixteenth, And Seventeenth Centuries," **AR**, 1971, Vol. 46, No. 3, pp. 529-534.

Peragallo, Edward. "Challenges Facing Teachers Of Accounting History," **AHJ**, 1974, Vol. 1, No. 1-4, pp. 5-6.

Peragallo, Edward. "Choosing Procedures In The 15th Century Ledger Of Jachomo Badoer, A Venetian Merchant," **AR**, 1981, Vol. 56, No. 3, pp. 587-595.

Peragallo, Edward. "Development Of The Compound Entry In The 15th Century Ledger Of Jachomo Badoer, A Venetian Merchant," **AR**, 1983, Vol. 58, No. 1, pp. 98-104.

Peragallo, Edward. "Jachomo Badoer. Renaissance Man Of Commerce, And His Ledger," **ABR**, 1979-80, Vol. 10, No. 37A, pp. 93-101.

Peragallo, Edward. "Origin Of The Trial Balance," **AR**, 1956, Vol. 31, No. 3, pp. 389-394.

Peragallo, Edward. "The Ledger Of Jachomo Badoer," **AR**, 1977, Vol. 52, No. 4, pp. 881-892.

Peragallo, E. "Merchandising Of Slaves As Portrayed In The 15th Century Ledger Of Jachomo Badoer, A Venetian Merchant," **ABR**, 1981-82, Vol. 12, No. 45, pp. 61-66.

Perby, M. L. (Carlsson, J., P. Ehn, B. Erlander, M. L. Perby and A. Sandberg. "Planning And Control From The Perspective Of Labour: A Short Presentation Of The DEMOS Project," **AOS**, 1978, Vol. 3, No. 3/4, pp. 249-260.)

Perera, M. H. B. "Accounting And Its Environment In Sri Lanka," **ABACUS**, 1975, Vol. 11, No. 1, pp. 86-96.

Perille, P. James and Frederick J. Saathoff. "Why Not Project Financing?," **MA**, 1978, Vol. 60, No. 4, pp. 13-16.

Perkins, Barbara D. "Internal Control For The Small Business," **MA**, 1982, Vol. 63, No. 8, pp. 43-44.

Perkins, Deborah. "Unemployment Insurance: A Cost Worth Controlling," **CA**, 1987, Vol. 5, No. 4, pp. 63-69.

Perkins, Edwin J. and Sherry Levinson. "Partnership Accounting In A Nineteenth Century Merchant Banking House," **AHJ**, 1980, Vol. 7, No. 1, pp. 59-68.

Perks, R. W. and Leonora Butler. "Accountancy Standards In Practice: The Experience Of SSAP2," **ABR**, 1977-78, Vol. 8, No. 29, pp. 25-33.

Perler, Julius. "Profit Sharing And Smaller Clients," **JOA**, 1956, Vol. 101, No. 2, pp. 56-61.

Perna, George D. Sr. "Contractor Performance Measurement," **MA**, 1972, Vol. 54, No. 5, pp. 23-24.

Perna, George D. "Inventory Systems Simulation - A Case Study," **MA**, 1968, Vol. 49, No. 11, pp. 50-54.

Perrin, John R. "CCA And The Appropriation Account," **ABR**, 1976-77, Vol. 7, No. 27, pp. 193-202.

Perrin, John R. "Illusory Holding Gains On Long Term Debt," **ABR**, 1973-74, Vol. 4, No. 15, pp. 234-236.

Perritt, Gerald W. (Agrawal, Surendra P., Rosalie C. Hallbauer and Gerald W. Perritt. "Measurement Of The Current Cost Of Equivalent Productive Capacity," **JAAF**, 1980, Vol. 3, No. 2, pp. 163-173.)

Perritt, Roscoe D. "Innovations In An Elementary Accounting Program." **AR**, 1971, Vol. 46, No. 3, pp. 589-591.

Perritt, Roscoe. (Handy, Gene R. and Roscoe Perritt. "Account Monitoring And Cash Management," **MA**, 1976, Vol. 58, No. 3, pp. 29-31.)

Perry, Clyde. "Computerized Estimating," **MA**, 1975, Vol. 56, No. 7, pp. 37-42.

Perry, Donald M. "So You Want A Small Computer!," **MA**, 1970, Vol. 52, No. 5, pp. 29-31.

Perry, Donald P. "How The Uniform CPA Examination Is Made Up, Graded, And Administered," **JOA**, 1950, Vol. 89, No. 2, pp. 108-113.

Perry, Donald P. "Professional Accounting Practice Today And Tomorrow," **AR**, 1944, Vol. 19, No. 2, pp. 164-168.

Perry, Donald P. "Training For The Profession," **JOA**, 1955, Vol. 100, No. 5, pp. 66-71.

Perry, Donald P. "Work Of The Commission On CPA Standards," **AR**, 1955, Vol. 30, No. 2, pp. 183-193.

Perry, Kenneth W. and Lauren M. Walker. "Use Of Visual Aids In the Teaching Of Accounting," **AR**, 1957, Vol. 32, No. 3, pp. 477-480.

Perry, Kenneth W. and Warren B. Cutting. "Recruiting For The Small Firm," **JOA**, 1961, Vol. 111, No. 5, pp. 41-45.

Perry, Kenneth W. "Accounting And Economics Reciprocally Indebted," **AR**, 1958, Vol. 33, No. 3, pp. 450-454.

Perry, Kenneth W. "Intercompany Profits And ARB 51," **AR**, 1963, Vol. 38, No. 3, pp. 626-628.

Perry, Kenneth W. "R.T.P.," **AR**, 1960, Vol. 35, No. 4, pp. 728-730.

Perry, Kenneth W. "Statistical Relationship Of Accounting And Economics," **AR**, 1955, Vol. 30, No. 3, pp. 500-506.

Perry, Kenneth W. "The Faculty Fellowship And Accounting Education," **AR**, 1958, Vol. 33, No. 1, pp. 123-126.

Perry, Kenneth W. "The Profession's Responsibility In Attracting Students," **AR**, 1959, Vol. 34, No. 3, pp. 465-469.

Perry, Kenneth W. "The Role Of The Accountancy Club In Accounting Education," **AR**, 1957, Vol. 32, No. 4, pp. 648-650.

Perry, Kenneth W. "Young Eyes On Accounting," **AR**, 1958, Vol. 33, No. 4, pp. 556-558.

Perry, K. W. and R. K. Mautz. "Theory Cases For Undergraduate Courses," **AR**, 1956, Vol. 31, No. 3, pp. 497-500.

Perry, L. Glenn. "The SEC's Enforcement Activities," **CPAJ**, 1984, Vol. 54, No. 4, pp. 9-14.

Perry, L. Glenn. (Fedders, John M. and L. Glenn Perry. "Policing Financial Disclosure Fraud: The SEC's Top Priority," **JOA**, 1984, Vol. 158, No. 1, pp. 58-67.)

Perry, Raymond E. and John Van Camp. "The FASB Takes A Long-Awaited Look At Accounting For Corporate Income Taxes," **CA**, 1983, Vol. 1, No. 4, pp. 3-12.

Perry, Raymond E. and Scott A. Braly. "IRS Access To Audit Workpapers," **CPAJ**, 1981, Vol. 51, No. 9, pp. 13-18.

Perry, Raymond E. "Comprehensive Income Tax Allocation," **JOA**, 1966, Vol. 121, No. 2, pp. 23-32.

Perry, Raymond E. (Hazard, Albert W. and Raymond E. Perry.

"What FASB Statement No. 91 Means For Accountants And Auditors," **JOA**, 1988, Vol. 165, No. 2, pp. 28-36.)

Perry, Richard S. "An Approach To Elementary Accounting For Non-Business Students," **AR**, 1959, Vol. 34, No. 3, pp. 472-476.

Perry, William E. and Henry C. Warner. "Systems Auditability: Friend Or Foe?," **JOA**, 1978, Vol. 145, No. 2, pp. 52-60.

Person, Samuel. "Elementary Accounting With A Systems Approach." **AR**, 1965, Vol. 40, No. 2, pp. 454-458.

Person, Samuel. "The Integrated Use Of Data Processing Equipment In Teaching Accounting Subjects." **AR**, 1964, Vol. 39, No. 2, pp. 473-475.

Person, Stanley. "1988 Yearend Tax Planning For Small Businesses," **JOA**, 1988, Vol. 166, No. 4, pp. 29-39.

Person, Stanley. "A Microcomputer In A Small CPA Firm." **CPAJ**, 1984, Vol. 54, No. 3, pp. 20-26.

Person, Stanley. "Yearend Personal Tax Planning Tips." **JOA**, 1988, Vol. 166, No. 6, pp. 32-42.

Pesando, James E. and Carol K. Clarke. "Economic Models Of The Labor Market And Pension Accounting: An Exploratory Analysis," **AR**, 1983, Vol. 58, No. 4, pp. 733-748.

Pescow, Jerome K. and Paul A. Tambrino. "Workshop In College Placement Accounting." **AR**, 1969, Vol. 44, No. 3, pp. 623-627.

Pescow, Jerome K. "A Visual Approach To Auditing And Accounting Instruction," **AR**, 1963, Vol. 38, No. 4, pp. 839-843.

Peters, James F. "State Taxation Of Personal Service Income," **CPAJ**, 1980, Vol. 50, No. 10, pp. 37-42.

Peters, Richard D. "Distributor Profit Measurement." **MA**, 1972, Vol. 54, No. 2, pp. 47-48.

Peters, Richard M. and Douglas R. Emery. "The Role Of Negative Numbers In The Development Of Double Entry Bookkeeping," **JAR**, 1978, Vol. 16, No. 2, pp. 424-426.

Peters, Richard M. (Campion, William M. and Richard M. Peters. "How To Analyze Manpower Requirements Forecasts," **MA**, 1979, Vol. 61, No. 3, pp. 45-51.)

Peters, Richard M. (Campion, William M. and Richard M. Peters. "Short Interval Scheduling For The Audit Engagement," **JOA**, 1979, Vol. 148, No. 5, pp. 67-71.)

Petersen, Russell J. and Richard Grimlund. "CADRAS: Computer Assisted Data Recording And Analysis," **IAE**, 1983, No. 1, pp. 146-151.

Petersen, Russell J. and Thomas F. Keller. "Asset Valuation, Income Determination And Changing Prices," **AR**, 1972, Vol. 47, No. 4, pp. 801-805.

Petersen, Russell J. "A Portfolio Analysis Of General Price Level Restatement," **AR**, 1975, Vol. 50, No. 3, pp. 525-532.

Petersen, Russell J. "Incompatibility Of Bad Debt 'Expense' With Contemporary Accounting Theory: A Comment," **AR**, 1973, Vol. 48, No. 4, pp. 777-778.

Petersen, Russell J. "Interindustry Estimation Of General Price-Level Impact On Financial Information," **AR**, 1973, Vol. 48, No. 1, pp. 34-43.

Petersen, Russell J. "Price-Level Changes And Company Wealth," **MA**, 1973, Vol. 54, No. 8, pp. 17-20.

Petersen, Russell J. (Hagerman, Robert L., Thomas F. Keller and Russell J. Petersen. "Accounting Research And Accounting Principles," **JOA**, 1973, Vol. 135, No. 3, pp. 51-55.)

Petersen, Russell J. (Ingram, Robert W. and Russell J. Petersen. "An Evaluation Of AICPA Tests For Predicting The Performance Of Accounting Majors," **AR**, 1987, Vol. 62, No. 1, pp. 215-223.)

Petersen, Russell. "Interindustry Estimation Of General Price-Level Impact On Financial Information: More Data And A Reply," **AR**, 1978, Vol. 53, No. 1, pp. 198-203.

Peterson, Carroll. "More Perils Of Automation Fever." **MA**, 1984, Vol. 65, No. 5, pp. 47-48.

Peterson, D. Scott. (Burns, Gary W. and D. Scott Peterson. "Accounting For Computer Software," **JOA**, 1982, Vol. 153, No. 4, pp. 50-59.)

Peterson, George A. "A Budget And Cost Estimating System For A Medium-Sized Public Accounting Firm," **JOA**, 1950, Vol. 90, No. 3, pp. 220-225.

Peterson, Herbert. (Press, Israel A. and Herbert Peterson. "Better Planning For Year-End Taxes," **JOA**, 1979, Vol. 148, No. 6, pp. 73-83.)

Peterson, J. L. (Parke, R. and J. L. Peterson. "Indicators Of Social Change: Developments In The United States Of America," **AOS**, 1981, Vol. 6, No. 3, pp. 235-246.)

Peterson, Norman D. "Error Control In EDP Systems." **MA**, 1970, Vol. 52, No. 5, pp. 34-36.

Peterson, Paul T. (Johnson, Ramon E. and Paul T. Peterson. "Current Value Accounting For S&Ls: A Needed Reform?," **JOA**, 1984, Vol. 157, No. 1, pp. 80-85.)

Peterson, Peter G. "Productivity Is Not A Dirty Word." **MA**, 1972, Vol. 54, No. 3, pp. 57-59.

Peterson, Raymond H. and Alyce Zahorsky. "Telephone Company Develops New Cost Standards." **MA**, 1988, Vol. 70, No. 6, pp. 47-49.

Peterson, Richard B. (Maher, Michael W., Kavasseri V. Ramanathan and Richard B. Peterson. "Preference Congruence, Information Accuracy, And Employee Performance: A Field Study," **JAR**, 1979, Vol. 17, No. 2, pp. 476-503.)

Peterson, Richard B. (Ramanathan, Kavasseri V., Richard B. Peterson and Michael W. Maher. "Strategic Goals And Performance Criteria," **JOA**, 1976, Vol. 141, No. 1, pp. 56-64.)

Peterson, Sandra E. "Accounting For Human Resources." **MA**, 1972, Vol. 53, No. 12, pp. 19-22.

Peterson, William A. "Significance Of Prospective Income Data." **AR**, 1966, Vol. 41, No. 2, pp. 275-282.

Petran, A. S. (Davidson, H. J., J. Neter and A. S. Petran. "Estimating The Liability For Unredeemed Stamps," **JAR**, 1967, Vol. 5, No. 2, pp. 186-207.)

Petrello, George J. (Sedki, S. Sam and George J. Petrello. "The Accounting Practitioners Accounting Educators Dialogue - A Short Survey," **JAED**, 1984, Vol. 2, No. 1, pp. 163-166.)

Petri, Enrico and Clyde P. Stickney. "Business Combinations: Some Unresolved Issues," **JOA**, 1982, Vol. 153, No. 4, pp. 64-79.

Petri, Enrico and Jack Gelfand. "The Production Function: A New Perspective In Capital Maintenance," **AR**, 1979, Vol. 54, No. 2, pp. 330-345.

Petri, Enrico and Roland A. Minch. "A Decision Model For Tax Preference Items," **AR**, 1978, Vol. 53, No. 2, pp. 415-428.

Petri, Enrico and Roland Minch. "Contemporary Inflation Accounting Proposals: An Analysis And An Alternative." **ABACUS**, 1975, Vol. 11, No. 2, pp. 182-192.

Petri, Enrico and Roland Minch. "The Treasury Stock Method And Conventional Method In Reciprocal Stockholdings - An Amalgamation," **AR**, 1974, Vol. 49, No. 2, pp. 330-341.

Petri, Enrico and Roland Minch. "The Treasury Stock Method And Conventional Method In Reciprocal Stockholdings: An Amalgamation: A Reply," **AR**, 1975, Vol. 50, No. 2, pp. 365-369.

Petri, Enrico and Roland Minch. "Capacity Variance: Responsibility And Control," **MA**, 1972, Vol. 53, No. 10, pp. 38-41.

Petri, Enrico and Roland Minch. "Evaluation Of Resource Acquisiton Decisions By The Partitioning Of Holding Activity," **AR**, 1974, Vol. 49, No. 3, pp. 455-464.

Petri, Enrico. "Holding Gains And Losses As Cost Savings: A Comment On Supplementary Statement No. 2 On Inventory Valuation," **AR**, 1973, Vol. 48, No. 3, pp. 483-488.

Petri, Enrico. "Income Reporting And APB Opinion No. 18." **MA**, 1974, Vol. 56, No. 6, pp. 49-52.

Petri, Enrico. "On Holding Gains And Losses And The Evaluation Of Management: A Reply," **AR**, 1974, Vol. 49, No. 3, pp. 528-529.

Petri, Enrico. "Sales To Controlled Corporations," **MA**, 1973, Vol. 55, No. 2, pp. 42-44.

Petri, Enrico. "Use Of Capitalized Cost In Repeated Replacement Problems," **MA**, 1969, Vol. 51, No. 3, pp. 49-53.

Petri, Enrico. (Marcinko, David and Enrico Petri. "Use Of The Production Function In Calculation Of Standard Cost Variances - An Extension," **AR**, 1984, Vol. 59, No. 3, pp. 488-495.)

Petri, Enrico. (Minch, Roland A. and Enrico Petri. "Reporting Income For Reciprocal Parent-Subsidiary Stockholdings," **CPAJ**, 1975, Vol. 45, No. 7, pp. 36-40.)

Petri, Enrico. (Minch, Roland and Enrico Petri. "Matrix Modeling Of Reciprocal Service Cost Allocation," **AR**, 1972, Vol. 47, No. 3, pp. 576-580.)

Petri, Enrico. (Seagle, John P. and Enrico Petri. "Gift Vs. Estate Transfer: The Method Of Equated Rates," **AR**, 1977, Vol. 52, No. 1, pp. 124-136.)

Petri, E. and H. Shawky. "Cash Distributions Of Inflationary Gains," **ABACUS**, 1983, Vol. 19, No. 1, pp. 56-63.

Petruzzi, Christopher R. "Mergers And The Double Taxation Of Corporate Income," **JAPP**, 1988, Vol. 7, No. 2, pp. 97-111.

Pettijohn, James B. (Cress, William P. and James B. Pettijohn. "A Survey Of Budget-Related Planning And Control Policies And Procedures," **JAED**, 1985, Vol. 3, No. 2, pp. 61-78.)

Pettway, Richard H. (Norgaard, Richard L. and Richard H. Pettway. "Evaluating Average Ratios Used In Capital Budgeting," **MA**, 1966, Vol. 48, No. 4, pp. 16-20.)

Petty, J. William and John M. Pinkerton. "The Stock-Repurchase Decision: A Market Perspective," **JAAF**, 1978, Vol. 1, No. 2, pp. 99-115.

Petty, J. William. (Merville, Larry J. and J. William Petty. "Transfer Pricing For The Multinational Firm," **AR**, 1978, Vol. 53, No. 4, pp. 935-951.)

Petty, William B. "The CPA And Defense Procurement." **JOA**, 1967, Vol. 124, No. 1, pp. 37-40.

Peyrard, Josette. (Belkaoui, Ahmed, Alfred Kahl and Josette Peyrard. "Information Needs Of Financial Analysts: An International Comparison," **IJAER**, 1977, Vol. 13, No. 1, pp. 19-27.)

Pfau, Pamela R. "Computer Abuse," **CA**, 1985, Vol. 3, No. 4, pp. 46-51.

Pfeffer, J. (Markus, M. L. and J. Pfeffer. "Power And The Design And Implementation Of Accounting And Control Systems," **AOS**, 1983, Vol. 8, No. 2/3, pp. 205-218.)

Pfenning, R. E. "Business Information Systems," **AR**, 1962, Vol. 37, No. 2, pp. 234-243.

Philbrick, Donna. (Dyckman, Thomas, Donna Philbrick and Jens Stephan. "A Comparison Of Event Study Methodologies Using Daily Stock Returns: A Simulation Approach," **JAR**, 1984, Vol. 22, Supp., pp. 1-30.)

Philips, D. C. "Systems Theory - A Discredited Philosophy." **ABACUS**, 1969, Vol. 5, No. 1, pp. 3-15.

Philips, G. Edward and Lucille S. Mayne. "Income Measures And Bank Stock Values," **JAR**, 1970, Vol. 8, Supp., pp. 178-188.

Philips, G. Edward. "An Entity-Value For Assets And Equities," **ABACUS**, 1968, Vol. 4, No. 2, pp. 142-152.

Philips, G. Edward. "Error In Accounting Allocations," **JAR**, 1970, Vol. 8, No. 1, pp. 156-158.

Philips, G. Edward. "Pension Liabilities And Assets," **AR**, 1968, Vol. 43, No. 1, pp. 10-17.

Philips, G. Edward. "Replacement Cost And Owner Wealth," **ABR**, 1978-79, Vol. 9, No. 33, pp. 78-80.

Philips, G. Edward. "Research In Major Public Accounting Firms," **JOA**, 1964, Vol. 117, No. 6, pp. 37-40.

Philips, G. Edward. "The Accretion Concept Of Income," **AR**, 1963, Vol. 38, No. 1, pp. 14-25.

Philips, G. Edward. "The Revolution In Accounting Theory," **AR**, 1963, Vol. 38, No. 4, pp. 696-708.

Phillippe, Gerald L. "Top Management's Stake In Financial Reporting," **JOA**, 1963, Vol. 116, No. 6, pp. 37-41.

Phillips, Carolyn V. (Bryant, Keith, Jr. and Carolyn V. Phillips. "Interest On Equity Capital And CASB Standard 414," **MA**, 1978, Vol. 60, No. 2, pp. 38-41.)

Phillips, Jay A. "Tax Factors Affecting Operation Of Closely-Held Corporation," **JOA**, 1953, Vol. 95, No. 2, pp. 166-175.

Phillips, Lawrence C. and Gary John Previts. "Tax Reform: What Are The Issues?," **JOA**, 183, Vol. 155, No. 5, pp. 64-75.

Phillips, Lawrence C. and Scott S. Cowen. "Accounting For Debt Restructurings," **CPAJ**, 1977, Vol. 47, No. 7, pp. 22-26.

Phillips, Lawrence C. "Accounting For Business Combinations," **AR**, 1965, Vol. 40, No. 2, pp. 377-381.

Phillips, Lawrence C. "An Application Of Distribution Cost Analysis To A Small Company," **AR**, 1964, Vol. 39, No. 4, pp. 1040-1044.

Phillips, Lawrence C. (Cowen, Scott S., Lawrence C. Phillips and Linda Stillabower. "Multinational Transfer Pricing," **MA**, 1979, Vol. 60, No. 7, pp. 17-22.)

Phillips, Mary Ellen. (Frishkoff, Patricia A. and Mary Ellen Phillips. "Materiality In Commercial Bank Inflation Accounting," **AIA**, 1985, Vol. 2, pp. 31-46.)

Phillips, Thomas E. and Mark E. Droege. "Maximizing Cash In Decentralized Organizations," **MA**, 1984, Vol. 66, No. 2, pp. 38-42.

Philo, Philip. "The Savings Game," **MA**, 1970, Vol. 51, No. 8, pp. 28-30.

Phipps, David W. (Stone, Mary S., Walter A. Robbins and David W. Phipps. "Disclosure Practices Of Public Employee Retirement Systems: An Analysis Of Incentives To Adopt Alternative Standards," **RIGNA**, 1987, Vol. 3, Part A, pp. 149-180.)

Phoenix, Julius W., Jr. and William D. Bosse. "Accounting For The Cost Of Pension Plans - More Information On APB No. 8," **JOA**, 1967, Vol. 124, No. 4, pp. 31-40.

Phoenix, Julius W., Jr. and William D. Bosse. "Accounting For The Cost Of Pension Plans - APB Opinion No. 8," **JOA**, 1967, Vol. 124, No. 2, pp. 27-37.

Piaker, Philip M. and James Dalberth. "Acceptance Of Change Among Accountants: An Examination Of Attitudes Towards Current Controversies," **CPAJ**, 1973, Vol. 43, No. 2, pp. 132-138.

Piaker, Philip M. "The Distinctive Characteristics Of Small Company Audits," **CPAJ**, 1972, Vol. 42, No. 1, pp. 37-44.

Piaker, Philip M. "The Use Of Medieval Statements For Teaching Accounting: A Reply," **AR**, 1973, Vol. 48, No. 4, p. 789.

Piaker, Philip M. "The Use Of Medieval Statements For Teaching Accounting," **AR**, 1972, Vol. 47, No. 3, pp. 609-610.

Picard, Harry L. "Continuity Of An Accounting Practice," **CPAJ**, 1976, Vol. 46, No. 4, pp. 35-38.

Picconi, Mario J. "A Reconsideration Of The Recognition Of Advertising Assets On Financial Statements," **JAR**, 1977, Vol. 15, No. 2, pp. 317-326.

Pickford, Michael. "The Incremental Costing Of University Expansion," **ABR**, 1972-73, Vol. 3, No. 11, pp. 218-227.

Picking, Bruce G. "Auditing Standards," **ABR**, 1973-74, Vol. 4, No. 13, pp. 60-70.

Pick, John. "A Workshop In Fundamental Accounting," **AR**, 1964, Vol. 39, No. 2, pp. 476-481.

Picur, Ronald D. and James C. McKeown. "Alternative Income Concepts And Relative Performance Evaluations: A Comment And Extension," **AR**, 1976, Vol. 51, No. 2, pp. 415-420.

Picur, Ronald D. (Chan, James L. and Ronald D. Picur. "Advances In Governmental Accounting: A Review Of Research And Policy," **AIA**, 1986, Vol. 3, pp. 181-220.)

Pidock, Wayne L. "Accounting For Net Salvage," **MA**, 1970, Vol. 52, No. 6, pp. 49-52.

Pielstick, C. Dean. (Bailes, Jack, Barry Shane and C. Dean Pielstick. "Using Your PC To Project Capital Investment Funds," **MA**, 1988, Vol. 70, No. 1, pp. 59-62.)

Pierce, Happy. "Leasing And The Lessee," **MA**, 1975, Vol. 57, No. 6, pp. 33-36.

Pierce, L. Tim. (Walker, Norman R. and L. Tim Pierce. "The Price Waterhouse Audit: A State Of The Art Approach," **AJPT**, 1988, Vol. 8, No. 1, pp. 1-22.)

Pierce, Melville. "Taxability Of Prepayments In U.S., Canada & Britain," **JOA**, 1953, Vol. 96, No. 1, pp. 72-78.

Pierpont, W. K. "Statistical Data On Depreciation Bases," **AR**, 1948, Vol. 23, No. 3, pp. 251-253.

Pierpont, W. K. "The Classification And Control Of Navy Expenditures," **AR**, 1946, Vol. 21, No. 2, pp. 172-180.

Pierpont, W. K. "The Classification And Control Of Navy Expenditures," **AR**, 1946, Vol. 21, No. 1, pp. 70-77.

Piersall, Ralph W., Jr. "Pension Costs And The Nonprofit Organization," **JOA**, 1970, Vol. 129, No. 5, pp. 64-68.

Pierson, C. G. (Young, T. N. and C. G. Pierson. "Depreciation - Future Service Basis," **AR**, 1967, Vol. 42, No. 2, pp. 338-341.)

Pietsch, William H. (Arcus, Albert L. and William H. Pietsch. "Planned Performance And The Product Cost Controversy," **MA**, 1970, Vol. 52, No. 3, pp. 9-14.)

Pike, Richard H. "An Empirical Study Of The Adoption Of Sophisticated Capital Budgeting Practices And Decision-Making Effectiveness," **ABR**, 1988, Vol. 18, No. 72, pp. 341-351.

Pike, Richard H. "Owner-Manager Conflict And The Role Of The Payback Method," **ABR**, 1985-86, Vol. 16, No. 61, pp. 47-52.

Pike, Richard, John Sharp and Jeffrey Kantor. "The Role Of Accounting Information In Valuing Unlisted Shares," **ABR**, 1988, Vol. 18, No. 71, pp. 249-255.

Pike, Richard. (Kantor, Jeffrey and Richard Pike. "The Determinants Of The Value Of Unlisted Shares: Opinions Of Professional Valuers In Canada," **ABR**, 1986-87, Vol. 17, No. 66, pp. 109-116.)

Pike, R. H. "A Review Of Recent Trends In Capital Budgeting Processes," **ABR**, 1982-83, Vol. 13, No. 51, pp. 201-208.

Pike, R. (Ratnatunga, J., R. Pike and G. J. Hooley. "The Application Of Management Accounting Techniques To Marketing," **ABR**, 1988, Vol. 18, No. 72, pp. 363-370.)

Pilcher, D. J. "Five Basic Accounting Concepts," **AR**, 1933, Vol. 8, No. 1, pp. 70-73.

Pilcher, D. J. "The Accounting Equation," **AR**, 1932, Vol. 7, No. 4, pp. 294-296.

Pilcher, D. J. "Three-Fold Presentation Of An Accounting Problem," **AR**, 1933, Vol. 8, No. 3, pp. 247-252.

Pilie, Louis H. "Client Help Program Study: A Comparative Survey," **JOA**, 1954, Vol. 98, No. 4, pp. 465-470.

Pilie, Louis H. "Growth By Merger And Acquisition," **JOA**, 1969, Vol. 127, No. 5, pp. 61-64.

Pilie, Louis H. "How To Manage The Accounting Engagement," **JOA**, 1951, Vol. 91, No. 3, pp. 422-427.

Pilie, Louis H. "Human Relations As A Modern Tonic," **AR**, 1962, Vol. 37, No. 1, pp. 1-5.

Pillin, Dominic A. "Credit By Exception: A Cash Management Tool," **MA**, 1977, Vol. 59, No. 1, pp. 40-42.

Pillsbury, Ceil Moran. "Limited Assurance Engagements," **AJPT**, 1984-85, Vol. 4, No. 2, pp. 63-79.

Pillsbury, Wilbur F. "Labor's View Of Financial Reports," **JOA**, 1958, Vol. 105, No. 6, pp. 46-56.

Pilnick, Saul. (Allen, Robert F., Colin Park and Saul Pilnick. "The Shadow Organization," **MA**, 1974, Vol. 55, No. 7, pp. 11-14.)

Pinches, George E. (Haka, Susan F., Lawrence A. Gordon and George E. Pinches. "Sophisticated Capital Budgeting Selection Techniques And Firm Performance," **AR**, 1985, Vol. 60, No. 4, pp. 651-669.)

Pincus, J. David. (Pincus, Karen V. and J. David Pincus. "Public Relations: What CPA Firms Are Doing," **JOA**, 1986, Vol. 162, No. 5, pp. 128-138.)

Pincus, Karen V. and J. David Pincus. "Public Relations: What CPA Firms Are Doing," **JOA**, 1986, Vol. 162, No. 5, pp. 128-138.

Pincus, Karen V., William W. Holder and Theodore J. Mock. "The SEC And Fraudulent Financial Reporting," **RIAR**, 1988, Vol. 2, pp. 167-185.

Pincus, Morton. "Information Characteristics Of Earnings Announcements And Stock Market Behavior," **JAR**, 1983, Vol. 21, No. 1, pp. 155-183.

Pincus, Morton. (Anderson, James A. and Morton Pincus. "Market Efficiency And Legal Liability: Some Extensions And An Illustration," **ABR**, 1983-84, Vol. 14, No. 54, pp. 169-181.)

Pincus, Morton. (Dopuch, Nicholas and Morton Pincus. "Evidence On The Choice Of Inventory Accounting Methods: LIFO Versus FIFO," **JAR**, 1988, Vol. 26, No. 1, pp. 28-59.)

Pincus, Morton. (Madeo, Silvia A. and Morton Pincus. "Stock Market Behavior And Tax Rule Changes: The Case Of The Disallowance Of Certain Interest Deductions Claimed By Banks," **AR**, 1985, Vol. 60, No. 3, pp. 407-429.)

Pinger, R. W. "The Semantics Of Accounting," **AR**, 1954, Vol. 29, No. 4, pp. 652-655.

Pinkerton, James E. and Stuart Margulies. "Programed Instruction: Its Implication For Accounting Education," **AR**, 1962, Vol. 37, No. 4, pp. 685-691.

Pinkerton, John M. (Petty, J. William and John M. Pinkerton. "The Stock-Repurchase Decision: A Market Perspective," **JAAF**, 1978, Vol. 1, No. 2, pp. 99-115.)

Pintar, Blake. (Karlinsky, Stewart S. and Blake Pintar. "Individual Tax Planning Software: A Critical Analysis," **JATA**, 1978, Vol. 8, No. 2, pp. 63-79.)

Pintar, George M. (Weirich, Thomas R. and George M. Pintar. "Interpretation And Flowchart Of SSARS No. 1," **JOA**, 1979, Vol. 148, No. 5, pp. 60-66.)

Pinter, Alexander, Jr. "My First Year With Punched Tape Accounting," **JOA**, 1963, Vol. 115, No. 4, pp. 49-53.

Piper, Andrew G. "A Note On Translation For Interim Accounts," **IJAER**, 1979, Vol. 15, No. 1, pp. 45-52.

Piper, Andrew. "Accounting For Overseas Currencies," **IJAER**, 1976, Vol. 12, No. 1, pp. 63-90.

Piper, J. A. (Hutchinson, P. J., J. A. Piper and G. A. Ray. "The Financing Of Rapid Growth Firms Up To Flotation," **ABR**, 1974-75, Vol. 5, No. 18, pp. 145-151.)

Piper, J. A. (Hutchinson, P. J., J. A. Piper and G. H. Ray. "The Financial Control Of Rapid-Growth Firms Up To Flotation," **ABR**, 1974-75, Vol. 5, No. 19, pp. 222-228.)

Piper, Roswell M. "Engineering Standards And Standard Costs," **MA**, 1976, Vol. 58, No. 3, pp. 44-46.

Piper, Roswell M. "The Joint Variance: A Comment," **AR**, 1977, Vol. 52, No. 2, pp. 527-533.

Pipkin, John B., II. "Put Your Banker To Work," **MA**, 1970, Vol. 51, No. 8, pp. 42-44.

Piron, Stephen F. "Restoring Business Information Controls," **MA**, 1980, Vol. 62, No. 6, pp. 53-54.

Pirrong, Gordon D. "New Rules For Long-Term Construction Projects," **MA**, 1987, Vol. 69, No. 6, pp. 48-52.

No. 1, pp. 7-19.

Porcano, Thomas M. (Aronsson, Joyce and Thomas M. Porcano. "Covenants Not To Compete - Judicial Interpretations," **CPAJ**, 1983, Vol. 53, No. 1, pp. 18-23.)

Porcano, Thomas M. (Johnson, Sandra J. and Thomas M. Porcano. "The Safe Harbor Lease - Tax Implications," **CPAJ**, 1983, Vol. 53, No. 9, pp. 20-29.)

Porcano, Thomas M. (Porcano, Judy L. and Thomas M. Porcano. "Incorporating Probability Analysis In Taxpayer Appeal Decisions," **JATA**, 1985, Vol. 6, No. 2, pp. 18-36.)

Poreba, Edward. "Alternative Minimum Tax - Application To Individuals," **CPAJ**, 1988, Vol. 58, No. 3, pp. 52-59.

Porter, Charles H. "Is It Machinery Or Is It Junk?," **AR**, 1928, Vol. 3, No. 4, pp. 369-374.

Porter, David M. "The Waltham System And Early American Textile Cost Accounting," **AHJ**, 1980, Vol. 7, No. 1, pp. 1-15.

Porter, Gary A. (Everett, John O. and Gary A. Porter. "Safe-Harbor Leasing - Unraveling The Tax Implications," **JAAF**, 1984, Vol. 7, No. 3, pp. 241-256.)

Porter, Gary and Joseph D'Onofrio. "Deconsolidating Troubled Subsidiaries: A Question Of Control," **CA**, 1987, Vol. 5, No. 3, pp. 32-37.

Porter, Grover H. (Akers, Michael D. and Grover L. Porter. "Expert Systems For Management Accountants," **MA**, 1986, Vol. 67, No. 9, pp. 30-34.)

Porter, Grover L. and Michael D. Akers. "In Defense Of Management Accounting," **MA**, 1987, Vol. 69, No. 5, pp. 58-64.

Porter, Grover L. (Rezaee, Zabihollah and Grover L. Porter. "Summary Annual Reports: Is Shorter Better?," **JOA**, 1988, Vol. 165, No. 5, pp. 42-54.)

Porter, James L. (Collins, Frank and James L. Porter. "Engagement Withdrawal: The Legal Perils," **JOA**, 1979, Vol. 147, No. 2, pp. 66-71.)

Porter, James W. "Using Client's Personnel To Save Audit Time," **JOA**, 1953, Vol. 96, No. 2, pp. 193-196.

Porter, Mattie C. (Alford, R. Mark, Mattie C. Porter and Robert H. Strawser. "Annual Reports Of Departments Of Accounting," **IAE**, 1985, No. 1, pp. 15-19.)

Porter, Mattie C. (Alford, R. Mark, Mattie C. Porter and Robert H. Strawser. "Forward Accounting - Past, Present And Future," **CPAJ**, 1981, Vol. 51, No. 2, pp. 40-47.)

Porter, W. Thomas, Jr. "A Control Framework For Electronic Systems," **JOA**, 1965, Vol. 120, No. 4, pp. 56-63.

Porter, W. Thomas, Jr. "Time And Self-Management," **JOA**, 1978, Vol. 145, No. 6, pp. 58-64.

Porter, W. Thomas. "Evaluating Internal Controls In EDP Systems," **JOA**, 1964, Vol. 118, No. 2, pp. 34-40.

Porter, W. Thomas. "Generalized Computer-Audit Programs," **JOA**, 1969, Vol. 127, No. 1, pp. 54-62.

Posey, Clyde L. (Deloney, Elise and Clyde L. Posey. "Federal Tax Amnesty: Is It Appropriate?," **CPAJ**, 1987, Vol. 57, No. 7, pp. 38-45.)

Posey, Imogene A. (Morse, Wayne J. and Imogene A. Posey. "Income Taxes Do Make A Difference In C-V-P Analysis," **MA**, 1979, Vol. 61, No. 6, pp. 20-24.)

Posey, J. Marion. "Professional Schools Of Accountancy: A Promising Alternative," **MA**, 1976, Vol. 57, No. 7, pp. 15-17.

Posey, J. M. (Carper, Wm. B. and J. M. Posey. "The Validity Of Selected Surrogate Measures of Human Resource Value: A Field Study," **AOS**, 1976, Vol. 1, No. 2/3, pp. 143-152.)

Posnak, Robert. "The Decline And Fall Of Cratchit....," **JOA**, 1970, Vol. 129, No. 5, pp. 59-63.

Possett, Richard W. "Measuring Productive Costs In The Service Sector," **MA**, 1980, Vol. 62, No. 4, pp. 16-24.

Poston, Kay M. (Harmon, W. Ken, Kay M. Poston and Paul E. Dascher. "Provision And Inadequacy Of Small Business Computer Controls: A Model And Empirical Test," **JIS**, 1988, Vol. 3, No. 1, pp. 30-49.)

Poston, Kay M. (Harmon, W. Ken, Kay M. Poston and Wayne J. Morse. "Improving Cost Recovery From Federal Grants And Contracts," **JCA**, 1986, Vol. 3, No. 1, pp. 1-12.)

Poswolsky, Melvyn and Akshay K. Talwar. "Employee Business Expense Deductions Under TRA 1986," **CPAJ**, 1987, Vol. 57, No. 10, pp. 70-77.

Potter, John C. "Confirmation Of Receivables," **JOA**, 1957, Vol. 104, No. 1, pp. 45-49.

Potts, James H. "A Brief History Of Property And Depreciation Accounting In Municipal Accounting," **AHJ**, 1982, Vol. 9, No. 1, pp. 25-37.

Potts, James H. The Evolution Of Budgetary Accounting Theory And Practice In Municipal Accounting From 1870," **AHJ**, 1977, Vol. 4, No. 1, pp. 89-100.

Potts, N. Joseph. "Accounting For A Public Television Station," **MA**, 1977, Vol. 59, No. 5, pp. 30-33.

Pound, G. D. and John K. Courtis. "The Auditor's Liability: A Myth?," **ABR**, 1979-80, Vol. 10, No. 39, pp. 299-306.

Pound, G. D. and B. M. Pollard. "Accounting Theory And History - Lessons To Be Learned," **IJAER**, 1981, Vol. 16, No. 2, pp. 99-123.

Pound, G. D. "A Review Of EDP Auditing," **ABR**, 1977-78, Vol. 8, No. 30, pp. 108-129.

Pound, G. D. (Lewis, N. R., L. D. Parker, G. D. Pound and P. Sutcliffe. "Annual Report Readability: The Use Of Readability Techniques," **ABR**, 1985-86, Vol. 16, No. 63, pp. 199-214.)

Pourciau, Susan. (Smith, David B. and Susan Pourciau. "A Comparison Of The Financial Characteristics Of December And Non-December Year-End Companies," **JAEC**, 1988, Vol. 10, No. 4, pp. 335-344.)

Powell, Donald F. "Preparing For Tax Season," **JOA**, 1988, Vol. 166, No. 4, pp. 41-46.

Powell, Philip P. (Lemke, Kenneth W. and Philip P. Powell. "The Gearing Adjustment - An Empirical Study," **ABR**, 1986-87, Vol. 17, No. 65, pp. 59-70.)

Powell, Ray M. "Career Choices Among Beta Alpha Psi Members," **AR**, 1966, Vol. 41, No. 3, pp. 525-534.

Powell, Ray M. (Milroy, Robert R., Donald F. Istvan and Ray M. Powell. "The Tax Depreciation Muddle," **AR**, 1961, Vol. 36, No. 4, pp. 539-547.)

Powell, Weldon. "Business Separations," **JOA**, 1957, Vol. 103, No. 3, pp. 54-57.

Powell, Weldon. "CPA's Responsibility For Events After Statement Date," **JOA**, 1953, Vol. 95, No. 6, pp. 709-713.

Powell, Weldon. "Extraordinary Items," **JOA**, 1966, Vol. 121, No. 1, pp. 31-37.

Powell, Weldon. "Report On The Accounting Research Activities Of The American Institute Of Certified Public Accountants," **AR**, 1961, Vol. 36, No. 1, pp. 26-31.

Powell, Weldon. "The Challenge To Research," **JOA**, 1960, Vol. 109, No. 2, pp. 34-41.

Powell, Weldon. "The Development Of Accounting Principles," **JOA**, 1964, Vol. 118, No. 3, pp. 37-43.

Powell, Weldon. "Inventory Of Generally Accepted Accounting Principles'," **JOA**, 1965, Vol. 119, No. 3, pp. 29-35.

Powelson, John P. "Economic Accounting In The U.S.," **JOA**, 1958, Vol. 105, No. 6, pp. 41-45.

Powelson, John P. "National Income Estimates In Latin America," **IJAER**, 1967, Vol. 3, No. 1, pp. 55-65.

Powelson, John P. "Social Accounting," **AR**, 1955, Vol. 30, No. 4, pp. 651-659.

Powers, Ollie S. (Strobel, Caroline D. and Ollie S. Powers. "Accounting For Inventories: Where We Stand," **CPAJ**, 1981, Vol. 51, No. 5, pp. 41-46.)

Pownall, Grace. "An Empirical Analysis Of The Regulation Of The Defense Contracting Industry: The Cost Accounting Standards Board," **JAR**, 1986, Vol. 24, No. 2, pp. 291-315.

Pownall, Grace. (Waymire, Gregory and Grace Pownall. "Some Evidence On Potential Effects Of Contemporaneous Earnings Disclosures In Tests Of Capital Market Effects Associated With FASB Exposure Draft No. 19," **JAR**, 1983, Vol. 21, No. 2, pp. 629-643.)

Prakash, Prem and Alfred Rappaport. "Informational Interdependencies: System Structure Induced By Accounting Information," **AR**, 1975, Vol. 50, No. 4, pp. 723-734.

Prakash, Prem and Shyam Sunder. "The Case Against Separation Of Current Operating Profit And Holding Gain," **AR**, 1979, Vol. 54, No. 1, pp. 1-22.

Prakash, Prem. (Dittman, David A. and Prem Prakash. "Cost Variance Investigation: Markovian Control Of Markov Processes," **JAR**, 1978, Vol. 16, No. 1, pp. 14-25.)

Prakash, Prem. (Dittman, David and Prem Prakash. "Cost Variance Investigation: Markovian Control Versus Optimal Control," **AR**, 1979, Vol. 54, No. 2, pp. 358-373.)

Prakash, P. and A. Rappaport. "Information Inductance And Its Significance For Accounting," **AOS**, 1977, Vol. 2, No. 1, pp. 29-38.

Prakash, Som and Jack E. Cisney. "Appraisal And Evaluation Of Internal Financial Reports," **MA**, 1970, Vol. 51, No. 7, pp. 19-24.

Prater, George I. "Time-Sharing Computers In Accounting Education," **AR**, 1966, Vol. 41, No. 4, pp. 619-625.

Prater, George. (DeCoster, Don and George Prater. "An Experimental Study Of The Use Of A Business Game In Elementary Accounting," **AR**, 1973, Vol. 48, No. 1, pp. 137-142.)

Pratt, Denis J. "Capital Maintenance Adjustment Under The Financial (Real) Capital Concept," No. 2, pp. 170-178.

Pratt, Denis J. (Leech, Stewart A. and Denis J. Pratt. "Current Cost Accounting In Australia, New Zealand, And The United Kingdom: A Comparative Study," **IJAER**, 1978, Vol. 13, No. 2, pp. 105-118.)

Pratt, Denis J. (Leech, Stewart, Denis J. Pratt and W. G. W. Magill. "Asset Revaluations And Inflation In Australia, 1950 To 1975: An Industry Study," **IJAER**, 1982, Vol. 17, No. 2, pp. 23-34.)

Pratt, James W. "The Need For Attested Interim Statements Of Public Companies, And Attendant Implications," **CPAJ**, 1973, Vol. 43, No. 5, pp. 390-395.

Pratt, Jamie and Giorgio Behr. "Environmental Factors, Transaction Costs, And External Reporting: A Cross-Sectional Comparison," **IJAER**, 1987, Vol. 22, No. 2, pp. 1-24.

Pratt, Jamie and Heidi Hadlich Chrisman. "Teaching The Statement Of Changes In Financial Position: An Empirical Study," **AR**, 1982, Vol. 57, No. 4, pp. 794-805.

Pratt, Jamie. "A Classification Scheme For Financial Accounting Research," **JAED**, 1988, Vol. 6, No. 1, pp. 33-54.

Pratt, Jamie. "Post-Cognitive Structure: Its Determinants And Relationship To Perceived Information Use And Predictive Accuracy," **JAR**, 1982, Vol. 20, No. 1, pp. 189-209.

Pratt, Jamie. "The Economics Of External Reporting: Three Frameworks For The Classroom," **JAED**, 1987, Vol. 5, No. 2, pp. 175-185.

Pratt, Jamie. "The Effects Of Personality On A Subject's Information Processing: A Comment," **AR**, 1980, Vol. 55, No. 3, pp. 501-506.

Pratt, Jamie. (Jiambalvo, James and Jamie Pratt. "Task Complexity And Leadership Effectiveness In CPA Firms," **AR**, 1982, Vol. 57, No. 4, pp. 734-750.)

Pratt, Jamie. (Moizer, Peter and Jamie Pratt. "The Evaluation Of Performance In Firms Of Chartered Accountants," **ABR**, 1988, Vol. 18, No. 71, pp. 227-237.)

Pratt, J. and J. Jiambalvo. "Determinants Of Leader Behavior In An Audit Environment," AOS, 1982, Vol. 7, No. 4, pp. 369-380.

Pratt, J. and J. Jiambalvo. "Relationships Between Leader Behaviors And Audit Team Performance," AOS, 1981, Vol. 6, No. 2, pp. 133-142.

Pratt, J. "SFAS No. 2: Auditor Evaluations And Input To The Home Office," AOS, 1985, Vol. 10, No. 4. pp. 427-442.

Pratt, Robert R. "Wanted: Management Accountants For U.S. Orchestras," MA, 1971, Vol. 52, No. 7, pp. 24-25.

Precious, J. R. and D. R. Wood. "Corporate Modelling: When Success Can Be A Long-Term Forecast." ABR, 1974-75, Vol. 5, No. 20, pp. 254-272.

Preinreich, Gabriel A. D. "Accounting Terminology," AR, 1933, Vol. 8, No. 2, pp. 113-116.

Preinreich, Gabriel A. D. "Stock Yields, Stock Dividends And Inflation," AR, 1932, Vol. 7, No. 4, pp. 273-289.

Preinreich, Gabriel A. D. "Taxation And The Natural Business Year," AR, 1933, Vol. 8, No. 4 pp. 317-322.

Preinreich, Gabriel A. D. "The Fair Value And Yield Of Common Stock," AR, 1936, Vol. 11. No. 2. pp. 130-140.

Preinreich, Gabriel A. D. "The Law Of Goodwill," AR, 1936, Vol. 11, No. 4, pp. 317-329.

Preinreich, Gabriel A. D. "The Principles Of Public-Utility Depreciation," AR, 1938, Vol. 13, No. 2, pp. 149-165.

Preinreich, Gabriel A. D. "Valuation And Amortization," AR, 1937, Vol. 12, No. 3, pp. 209-225.

Prenger, Al J. "Divisional Controllership," MA, 1972, Vol. 54, No. 5, pp. 29-32.

Press, Israel A. and Herbert Peterson. "Better Planning For Year-End Taxes," JOA, 1979, Vol. 148, No. 6, pp. 73-83.

Preston, A. "Interactions And Arrangements In The Process Of Informing," AOS, 1986, Vol. 11, No. 6, pp. 521-540.

Preston, L. E. "Research On Corporate Social Reporting: Directions For Development," AOS, 1981, Vol. 6, No. 3, pp. 255-262.

Preston, L. E. (Dierkes, M. and L. E. Preston. "Corporate Social Accounting - Reporting For The Physical Environment: A Critical Review And Implementation Proposal," AOS, 1977, Vol. 2, No. 1, pp. 3-22.)

Preston, R. Jeffrey and Alida M. Adamek. "Who's Minding The Tax Department?," MA, 1983. Vol. 64, No. 11. pp. 24-27.

Prest, A. P. L. "Review Of Unaudited Interim Statements," JOA, 1957, Vol. 104, No. 4, pp. 49-53.

Preu, F. L. and J. F. Schoen. "Accounting For Emergency Relief Funds," AR, 1940, Vol. 15, No. 2, pp. 170-176.

Previts, Gary John and Edward N. Coffman. "Practice And Education: Bridging The Gap," AR, 1980, Vol. 150, No. 6, pp. 39-46.

Previts, Gary John and Terry K. Sheldahl. "Accounting And 'Countinghouses': An Analysis And Commentary." ABACUS, 1977, Vol. 13, No. 1, pp. 52-59.

Previts, Gary John. "For Example . . . The Value Of Pretending," AHJ, 1975, Vol. 2, No. 1-4, pp. 25-26.

Previts, Gary John. "Hazy History: Fact And Folklore In Accounting," AHJ, 1974, Vol. 1, No. 1-4, pp. 7-9.

Previts, Gary John. "It's About Time . . . Pathways To A New Vista Of Accountancy's Past," AHJ, 1975, Vol. 2, No. 1-4, pp. 3-5.

Previts, Gary John. "Old Wine And . . . The New Harvard Bottle," AHJ, 1974, Vol. 1, No. 1-4. pp. 19-20.

Previts, Gary John. "On The Subject Of Methodology And Models For International Accountancy," IJAER. 1975, Vol. 10, No. 2, pp. 1-12.

Previts, Gary John. "Origins Of American Accounting," CPAJ, 1976, Vol. 46, No. 5, pp. 13-18.

Previts, Gary John. "The Accountant In Our History: A Bicentennial Overview," JOA, 1976, Vol. 142, No. 1, pp. 45-51.

Previts, Gary John. "'FASBing': Abracadabra Again?," AHJ, 1974, Vol. 1, No. 1-4, pp. 23-24.

Previts, Gary John. (Anderson, Wilton T. and Gary John Previts. "Accounting Accreditation And Schools Of Accountancy In The United States." AIA, 1984, Vol. 1, pp. 89-104.)

Previts, Gary John. (Homburger, Richard and Gary John Previts. "A Hatfield Trilogy: The Significance Of 'Zwei Pfadfinder'," AHJ, 1977, Vol. 4. No. 1. pp. 9-13.)

Previts, Gary John. (Martin, J. W. and Gary John Previts. "The Risk Preference Profiles Of Practising CPAs: Some Tentative Results," ABR, 1982-83, Vol. 13, No. 49, pp. 21-28.)

Previts, Gary John. (Mautz, Robert K. and Gary John Previts. "Eric Kohler: An Accounting Original," AR, 1977, Vol. 52, No. 2, pp. 301-307.)

Previts, Gary John. (Mednick, Robert and Gary John Previts. "The Scope Of CPA Services: A View Of The Future From The Perspective Of A Century Of Progress," JOA, 1987. Vol. 163, No. 5, pp. 220-238.)

Previts, Gary John. (Moran, Mark and Gary John Previts. "The SEC And The Profession, 1934-84: The Realities Of Self-Regulation," JOA, 1984, Vol. 158, No. 1, pp. 68-83.)

Previts, Gary John. (Parker, Larry M. and Gary John Previts. "Regulation: The Forces Influencing Accounting Practice," RIAR, 1987, Vol. 1, pp. 1-4.)

Previts, Gary John. (Phillips, Lawrence C. and Gary John Previts. "Tax Reform: What Are The Issues?," JOA, 183, Vol. 155, No. 5, pp. 64-75.)

Previts, Gary J. "Frameworks Of American Financial Accounting Thought: An Historical Perspective To 1973," AHJ, 1984, Vol. 11, No. 2, pp. 1-17.

Previts, Gary J. (Parker, Larry M. and Gary J. Previts. "The 'Yes' Vote For 'Excellence': A Profession More In Consonance With A Changing Society," RIAR, 1988, Vol. 2,

pp. 1-4.)

Price, Harry R. "Qualifications For College Accounting Teachers," AR, 1957, Vol. 32, No. 1, pp. 83-89.

Price, Kenneth H. (Nichols, Donald R. and Kenneth H. Price. "The Auditor-Firm Conflict: An Analysis Using Concepts Of Exchange Theory," AR, 1976, Vol. 51, No. 2. pp. 335-346.)

Price, William G. F. "Common Aims Of Bankers, Accountants, Borrowers," JOA, 1953, Vol. 96, No. 4, pp. 474-477.

Price, William S., Jr. and Edward J. Neppl. "Automated Inventory Control," MA, 1966, Vol. 48, No. 2, pp. 52-58.

Prickett, A. L. "Development Of High School Commercial Curriculum And University Courses," AR, 1928, Vol. 3, No. 1, pp. 53-68.

Prickett, A. L. "General Principles Of Cost Accounting." AR, 1944, Vol. 19, No. 2, pp. 169-179.

Prickett, A. L. "Labor Turnover Rate And Cost," AR, 1931, Vol. 6, No. 4, pp. 261-276.

Prickett, A. L. "Suggestions For Beginning Teachers In Accounting," AR, 1947, Vol. 22, No. 4, pp. 405-411.

Prickett, A. L. "The Master's Degree With Courses In Business, Yesterday, Today, And Tomorrow," AR, 1958, Vol. 33, No. 1, pp. 76-83.

Pridemore, Charles. "Software: Expense Or Capitalize?," MA, 1983. Vol. 65, No. 5, pp. 33-36.

Primrose, P. L., F. A. Bailey and R. Leonard. "The Practical Application Of Discounted Cash Flow To Plant Purchase Using An Integrated Suite Of Computer Programs," ABR, 1984-85, Vol. 15, No. 57, pp. 27-32.

Prince, Thomas R. and Bala V. Balachandran. "An Information System For Administrating Welfare Programs," RIGNA, 1987, Vol. 3, Part A, pp. 37-66.

Prince, Thomas R. "Information Systems For Management Control," AR, 1964, Vol. 39, No. 2, pp. 467-472.

Prince, Thomas R. "The Motivational Assumption For Accounting Theory," AR, 1964, Vol. 39, No. 3, pp. 553-562.

Prince, Thomas R. (Godfrey, James T. and Thomas R. Prince. "The Accounting Model From An Information Systems Perspective," AR, 1971, Vol. 46, No. 1, pp. 75-89.)

Pritchard, Robert T. "Shakespeare And Accounting," AR, 1946. Vol. 21, No. 1, pp. 67-69.

Pritchett, James C. "Cost Control In A Logging Operation," MA, 1975, Vol. 57, No. 3, pp. 51-53.

Probst, Frank R. "Probabilistic Cost Controls: A Behavioral Dimension," AR, 1971, Vol. 46, No. 1, pp. 113-118.

Prodhan, Bimal. (Kochanek, Richard, Bimal Prodhan and Harold Wyman. "CMAs Can Learn From The U.K. Experience," MA, 1985, Vol. 67, No. 5, pp. 38-42.)

Proscia, Leonard J. (Mentzel, Alvin J. and Leonard J. Proscia. "Financial Forecasts - State Of The Art," CPAJ, 1980. Vol. 50. No. 7, pp. 12-19.)

Prouty, Morton D., Jr. "The Business Environment: How Shall We Account For It?," MA, 1971, Vol. 52, No. 10, pp. 18-19.

Prudden, David W. "A More-Informative Payroll Deduction Register," MA, 1965, Vol. 47, No. 2, pp. 37-41.

Pryor, John. "What The Small Business Owner Should Know About Accounting," MA, 1983, Vol. 64, No. 11, pp. 42-45.

Pryor, LeRoy. "Profit Planning With Probabilities," MA, 1970, Vol. 51, No. 10, pp. 32-35.

Pryor, Leroy J. "Simulation: Budgeting For A 'What If...'," JOA, 1970, Vol. 130, No. 5, pp. 59-63.

Puder, A. H. "The Audit Of A Nationwide Company By Local Firms." JOA, 1960, Vol. 110, No. 6, pp. 53-56.

Puder, Richard K. "Local Practitioners Can Use Computers," JOA, 1962, Vol. 114, No. 1, pp. 47-52.

Puerta, Ralph. "Discount Rates: Adjusted For Time And Risk," MA, 1977, Vol. 58, No. 10, pp. 35-40.

Pugh, P. G. (Kirkpatrick, D. L. I. and P. G. Pugh. "Towards The Starship Enterprise - Are The Current Trends In Defence Unit Costs Inexorable?," JCA, 1985, Vol. 2, No. 1. pp. 59-80.)

Purcell, Thomas J., III and James P. Scott. "An Analysis Of The Feasibility Of Harmonizing Financial Reporting Practices Between Member Countries Of The EEC And The OECD." IJAER, 1986, Vol. 21, No. 2, pp. 109-131.

Purdue, Richard B. and E. Joe DeMaris. "Accounting In The U.S.S.R.," JOA, 1959, Vol. 108, No. 1, pp. 47-57.

Purdy, Charles R. and Donald E. Ricketts. "Analysis Of Rate. Efficiency, And Utilization Variances," MA, 1974. Vol. 56, No. 5, pp. 49-52.

Purdy, Charles R. "Industry Patterns Of Capacity Or Volume Choice: Their Existence And Rationale," JAR, 1965, Vol. 3. No. 2. pp. 228-241.

Purdy, Charles R. (Ricketts, Donald E. and Charles R. Purdy. "The Effect Of Cost-Volume-Profit Structure On Full And Direct Costing Net Income: A Generalizable Approach," AR, 1974, Vol. 49, No. 3, pp. 603-607.)

Purdy, Charles R., Jay M. Smith and Jack Gray. "The Visibility Of The Auditor's Disclosure Of Deviance From APB Opinion: An Empirical Test," JAR, 1969, Vol. 7, Supp., pp. 1-18.

Purdy, D. "The Provision Of Financial Information To Employees: A Study Of The Reporting Practices Of Some Large Public Companies In The United Kingdom," AOS, 1981. Vol. 6, No. 4, pp. 327-338.

Puro, Marsha. "Audit Firm Lobbying Before The Financial Accounting Standards Board: An Empirical Study," JAR, 1984. Vol. 22, No. 2, pp. 624-646.

Puro, Marsha. "Do Large Accounting Firms Collude In The Standards-Setting Process?," JAAF, 1985, Vol. 8, No. 3, pp. 165-177.

Purtill, John S., Jr. and Robert L. Caggiano. "How The CFO Can Lead A Business Turnaround," JOA, 1986, Vol. 161, No. 6. pp. 108-113.

Pushkin, Ann B. "Presenting Beta Risk To Students." **AR**, 1980, Vol. 55, No. 1, pp. 117-122.

Pusker, Henri C. "The Effect Of The 'Maximum Tax' On Tax Planning And Avoidance," **CPAJ**, 1973, Vol. 43, No. 7, pp. 567-572.

Putnam, Karl and Lynn Thomas. "Does Predictability Change When GAAP Change?," **JAAF**, 1984, Vol. 8, No. 1, pp. 15-23.

Putnam, Karl. (Kilpatrick, Bob, Karl Putnam and Harold Schneider. "Convertible Securities And Earnings Per Share: A Competitive Ranking Algorithm," **AR**, 1985, Vol. 60, No. 3, pp. 526-530.)

Putney, F. B. (Ijiri, Y., J. C. Kinard and F. B. Putney. "An Integrated Evaluation System For Budget Forecasting And Operating Performance With A Classified Budgeting Bibliography," **JAR**, 1968, Vol. 6, No. 1, pp. 1-28.)

Putterill, Martin S. "Information Systems For Road Maintenance Management: A Value For Money Approach," **RIGNA**, 1987, Vol. 3, Part A, pp. 131-145.

Puxty, Anthony G. "Social Accounting As Immanent Legitimation: A Critique Of A Technicist Ideology." **AIPIA**, 1986, Vol. 1, pp. 95-111.

Puxty, A. G. (Lowe, E. A., A. G. Puxty and R. C. Laughlin. "Simple Theories For Complex Processes: Accounting Policy And The Market For Myopia," **JAPP**, 1983, Vol. 2, No. 1, pp. 19-42.)

Puxty, A. G. (McDonald, D. and A. G. Puxty. "An Inducement - Contribution Approach To Corporate Financial Reporting," **AOS**, 1979, Vol. 4, No. 1/2, pp. 53-66.)

Puxty, A. G., H. C. Willmott, D. J. Cooper and T. Lowe. "Modes Of Regulation In Advanced Capitalism: Locating Accountancy In Four Countries," **AOS**, 1987, Vol. 12, No. 3, pp. 273-292.

Puzey, Russell V. "Accounting Is Communication." **JOA**, 1961, Vol. 112, No. 3, pp. 55-60.

Pye, Malcolm L. "Footnote On Declining-Balance Depreciation," **AR**, 1965, Vol. 40, No. 2, pp. 451-452.

Pye, Malcolm L. "Income Determination And The Non-Profit Institution," **AR**, 1957, Vol. 32, No. 4, pp. 612-621.

Pye, Malcolm L. "Reasons, Probabilities, And Accounting Principles," **AR**, 1960, Vol. 35, No. 3, pp. 437-443.

Pye, Malcolm L. "The Presentation Of Installment Transactions," **AR**, 1953, Vol. 28, No. 2, pp. 282-283.

Pye, Malcolm L. "The Undergraduate Accounting Curriculum." **AR**, 1955, Vol. 30, No. 2, pp. 284-289.

Pyle, William C. (Brummet, R. Lee, Eric G. Flamholtz and William C. Pyle. "Human Resource Accounting: A Tool To Increase Managerial Effectiveness," **MA**, 1969, Vol. 51, No. 2, pp. 12-15.)

Pyle, William C. (Brummet, R. Lee, Eric G. Flamholtz and William C. Pyle. "Human Resource Measurement - A Challenge For Accountants," **AR**, 1968, Vol. 43, No. 2, pp. 217-224.)

Pytlik, Betty P. (Andrews, J. Douglas and Betty P. Pytlik. "Revision Techniques For Accountants: Means For More Effective And Efficient Written Communication." **IAE**, 1983, No. 1, pp. 152-163.)

QQQ

Quackenbush, James E. "A Comment On The Undergraduate Accounting Curriculum," **MA**, 1969, Vol. 50, No. 8, p. 20.

Queenan, John W. "Challenges In International Auditing." **IJAER**, 1965, Vol. 1, No. 1, pp. 43-51.

Queenan, John W. "Facing Legal Liability Risks In A Public Accounting Practice," **JOA**, 1954, Vol. 98, No. 5, pp. 618-626.

Queenan, John W. "Lawyers And CPAs," **JOA**, 1956, Vol. 102, No. 5, pp. 46-49.

Queenan, John W. "Postulates: Their Place In Accounting Research." **JOA**, 1962, Vol. 114, No. 2, pp. 29-33.

Queenan, John W. "Presentation Of Special Reports," **JOA**, 1957, Vol. 103, No. 2, pp. 34-40.

Queenan, John W. "The Process Of Developing Accepted Accounting Standards," **JOA**, 1954, Vol. 98, No. 1, pp. 58-65.

Queenan, John W. "The Public Accountant Of Today And Tomorrow," **AR**, 1946, Vol. 21, No. 3, pp. 254-260.

Queenan, J. W. "The Role Of The Public Accountant In Contract Termination," **AR**, 1945, Vol. 20, No. 1, pp. 59-63.

Quin, Dick D. "The CPA Examination," **AR**, 1943, Vol. 18, No. 4, pp. 317-320.

Quinn, James Brian. "Control Of Research And Development Costs," **JOA**, 1960, Vol. 110, No. 4, pp. 51-58.

Quire, Catherine DeMotte. "Pioneers In Accounting," **AR**, 1947, Vol. 22, No. 1, pp. 74-79.

Quittmeyer, C. L. (Patrick, A. W. and C. L. Quittmeyer. "The CPA And Management Services," **AR**, 1963, Vol. 38, No. 1, pp. 109-117.)

Qureshi, Mahmood A. "Private Enterprise Accounting And Economic Development In Pakistan," **IJAER**, 1974, Vol. 9, No. 2, pp. 125-141.

RRR

Raabe, William A. and William P. Stevens. "Who Is Educating Today's Accountants? Some Observations," **JAED**, 1985, Vol. 3, No. 2, pp. 147-154.

Raabe, William A. (Reichenstein, William R. and William A. Raabe. "Investment Returns And Inflation Neutrality Under Alternate Tax Structures: Investment And Public Policy Implications," **AIT**, 1988, Vol. 2, pp. xx-xx.)

Raabe, William A. (Reichenstein, William R. and William A. Raabe. "The Effects Of Tax Provisions On Long-Run Investment Prospects," **JAPP**, 1985, Vol. 4, No. 2, pp. 111-121.)

Raabe, William A. (Stevens, William P., Kathleen C. Stevens and William A. Raabe. "FASB Statements In The Classroom: A Study Of Readability," **AIA**, 1985, Vol. 2, pp. 89-100.)

Raabe, William A., Kathleen C. Stevens and William P. Stevens. "Tax Textbook Readability: An Application Of The Cloze Method," **JATA**, 1984, Vol. 6, No. 1, pp. 66-73.

Raabe, William A., Robert M. Kozub and Debra L. Sanders. "Attitude Measurement And The Perceptions Of Tax Accounting Faculty Publications Outlets," **JAED**, 1987, Vol. 5, No. 1, pp. 45-57.

Raabe, William, Jr. and Eugene Willis. "The Conformity Requirement," **CPAJ**, 1977, Vol. 47, No. 7, pp. 33-36.

Raabe, William, Jr. (O'Brien, James P. and William Raabe, Jr. "The Charitable Lead Trust: A Neglected Tax Planning Technique," **JATA**, 1983, Vol. 4, No. 2, pp. 5-13.)

Rabas, Clarence R. "An Accounting Guide For Retail Land Sales," **MA**, 1976, Vol. 57, No. 9, pp. 41-42.

Rabel, Frederick K. "Show Surplus Restrictions From Treasury Stock Purchases," **JOA**, 1953, Vol. 95, No. 5, pp. 572-579.

Rabinowitz, Sidney I. "Treatment Of Prepaid Expenses On The Cash Basis Of Accounting," **AR**, 1940, Vol. 15, No. 4, pp. 474-484.

Rabito, George A. (Schlosser, Robert E., Bernard Z. Lee and George A. Rabito. "Continuing Professional Education 1887-1987," **JOA**, 1987, Vol. 163, No. 5, pp. 240-254.)

Rabun, Ted M. "Accounting And Labor Relations," **MA**, 1966, Vol. 47, No. 5, pp. 14-17.

Raby, William and Robert F. Richter. "Conformity Of Tax And Financial Accounting," **JOA**, 1975, Vol. 139, No. 3, pp. 42-48.

Raby, William L. "Accounting For Employee Stock Options," **AR**, 1962, Vol. 37, No. 1, pp. 28-38.

Raby, William L. "Advocacy Vs. Independence In Tax Liability Accrual," **JOA**, 1972, Vol. 133, No. 3, pp. 40-47.

Raby, William L. "Ethics In Tax Practice," **AR**, 1966, Vol. 41, No. 4, pp. 714-720.

Raby, William L. "Tax Allocation And Non-Historical Financial Statements," **AR**, 1969, Vol. 44, No. 1, pp. 1-11.

Raby, William L. "Tax Planning And The CPA," **JOA**, 1962, Vol. 114, No. 1, pp. 53-56.

Raby, William L. "TEFRA: Impact On Taxpayer Compliance," **JOA**, 1982, Vol. 154, No. 5, pp. 64-73.

Raby, William L. "The Impact Of Income Taxes On Corporate Research," **JOA**, 1964, Vol. 118, No. 2, pp. 53-56.

Raby, William L. "The Raby Corporations," **AR**, 1952, Vol. 27, No. 3, pp. 359-360.

Raby, William L. "The Two Faces Of Accounting," **AR**, 1959, Vol. 34, No. 3, pp. 452-461.

Raby, William L. "Uni-fied Accounting," **AR**, 1954, Vol. 29, No. 4, pp. 643-644.

Raby, Wm. L. and Robert D. Neubig. "Inter-Period Tax Allocation Or Basis Adjustment?," **AR**, 1963, Vol. 38, No. 3, pp. 568-576.

Raby, Wm. L. "A Decision-Making Approach To The First Tax Course." **AR**, 1964, Vol. 39, No. 1, pp. 167-172.

Rachleff, Mark L. "Hedging In The Futures Market," **CA**, 1984, Vol. 2, No. 4, pp. 34-41.

Rachlin, Norman S. "Is There (Enough) Life After The Tax Season?," **JOA**, 1984, Vol. 157, No. 4, pp. 68-77.

Rachlin, Norman S. "New Thoughts On Partner Compensation." **JOA**, 1979, Vol. 147, No. 6, pp. 66-73.

Rachui, Charles. "Percentage Of Completion Accounting," **MA**, 1974, Vol. 56, No. 6, pp. 41-44.

Radcliffe, R. C. (Mabert, V. A. and R. C. Radcliffe. "A Forecasting Methodology As Applied To Financial Time Series," **AR**, 1974, Vol. 49, No. 1, pp. 61-75.)

Radcliffe, Thomas A. (Munter, Paul and Thomas A. Radcliffe. "On The Attributes Of An Asset," **ABACUS**, 1980, Vol. 16, No. 2, pp. 116-123.)

Radebaugh, Lee H. "Environmental Factors Influencing The Development Of Accounting Objectives, Standards, And Practices In Peru," **IJAER**, 1975, Vol. 11, No. 1, pp. 39-56.

Radebaugh, Lee H. "The International Dimension Of The Financial Accounting Standards Board: Translation And Disclosure Of Foreign Operations," **IJAER**, 1974, Vol. 10, No. 1, pp. 55-70.

Radebaugh, Lee H. (Gray, S. J. and Lee H. Radebaugh. "International Segment Disclosures By U.S. and U.K. Multinational Enterprises: A Descriptive Study," **JAR**, 1984, Vol. 22, No. 1, pp. 351-360.)

Radebaugh, Lee H. (Morsicato, Helen G. and Lee H. Radebaugh. "Internal Performance Evaluation Of Multinational Enterprise Operations," **IJAER**, 1979, Vol. 15, No. 1, pp. 77-94.)

Radosevich, Raymond. (Sterling, Robert R. and Raymond Radosevich. "A Valuation Experiment," **JAR**, 1969, Vol. 7, No. 1, pp. 90-95.)

Raff, Michael C. "Exposing First-Semester Accounting Students To Accounting Periodicals," **AR**, 1971, Vol. 46, No. 3, pp. 594-595.

Raghunathan, Bhanu and T. S. Raghunathan. "Impact Of Top Management Support On IS Planning," **JIS**, 1988, Vol. 2, No. 2, pp. 15-23.

Raghunathan, T. S. (Raghunathan, Bhanu and T. S. Raghunathan. "Impact Of Top Management Support On IS Planning," **JIS**, 1988, Vol. 2, No. 2, pp. 15-23.)

Rahman, M. and A. A. M. McCosh. "The Influence Of Organisational And Personal Factors On The Use Of Accounting Information: An Empirical Study," **AOS**, 1976, Vol. 1, No.

4, pp. 339-356.

Rahman, M. Zubaidur and Robert W. Scapens. "Financial Reporting By Multinational Enterprises: Accounting Policy Choice In A Developing Country," **JAPP**, 1988, Vol. 7, No. 1, pp. 29-42.

Raiborn, D. D. and Thomas A. Ratcliffe. "Are You Accounting For Inflation In Your Capital Budgeting Process?," **MA**, 1979, Vol. 61, No. 3, pp. 19-22.

Raiborn, D. D. (Raiborn, Mitchell H., Michael R. Lane and D. D. Raiborn. "Purchased Loss Carryforwards: An Unresolved Issue," **JOA**, 1983, Vol. 156, No. 5, pp. 98-108.)

Raiborn, D. D. (Raiborn, Mitchell H., Michael R. Lane and D. D. Raiborn. "Accounting For 'That Other' Prior Period Adjustment," **MA**, 1985, Vol. 67, No. 1, pp. 39-43.)

Raiborn, D. D. (Raiborn, Mitchell H. and D. D. Raiborn. "Defining The Boundaries Of GAAP," **CPAJ**, 1984, Vol. 54, No. 7, pp. 10-25.)

Raiborn, D. D. (Rouse, Robert W. and D. D. Raiborn. "Completeness - The Perplexing Assertion." **CPAJ**, 1986, Vol. 56, No. 9, pp. 74-77.)

Raiborn, D. D., Dan M. Guy and Marilyn Zulinski. "Solving Audit Problems In Small Business Engagements," **JOA**, 183, Vol. 155, No. 4, pp. 50-59.

Raiborn, Mitchell H. and D. D. Raiborn. "Defining The Boundaries Of GAAP," **CPAJ**, 1984, Vol. 54, No. 7, pp. 10-25.

Raiborn, Mitchell H. "Systems Planning For Performance Evaluation," **MA**, 1971, Vol. 53, No. 2, pp. 21-23.

Raiborn, Mitchell H., Michael R. Lane and D. D. Raiborn. "Purchased Loss Carryforwards: An Unresolved Issue," **JOA**, 1983, Vol. 156, No. 5, pp. 98-108.

Raiborn, Mitchell H., Michael R. Lane and D. D. Raiborn. "Accounting For 'That Other' Prior Period Adjustment," **MA**, 1985, Vol. 67, No. 1, pp. 39-43.

Rajan, Madhav V. (Banker, Rajiv D., Srikant M. Datar and Madhav V. Rajan. "Measurement Of Productivity Improvements: An Empirical Analysis," **JAAF**, 1987, Vol. 2 (New Issues), No. 4, pp. 319-354.)

Rakes, Harold W. "Grass Roots Forecasting." **MA**, 1974, Vol. 56, No. 3, pp. 38-40.

Ramage, John G., Abba M. Krieger and Leslie L. Spero. "An Empirical Study Of Error Characteristics In Audit Populations," **JAR**, 1979, Vol. 17, Supp., pp. 72-102.

Ramakrishnan, Ram T. S. (Balachandran, Bala V. and Ram T. S. Ramakrishnan. "Joint Cost Allocation: A Unified Approach," **AR**, 1981, Vol. 56, No. 1, pp. 85-96.)

Ramakrishnan, Ram T. S. (Balachandran, Bala V. and Ram T. S. Ramakrishnan. "Internal Control And External Auditing For Incentive Compensation Schedules," **JAR**, 1980, Vol. 18, Supp., pp. 140-171.)

Ramakrishnan, Ram T. S. (Balachandran, Bala V. and Ram T. S. Ramakrishnan. "A Theory Of Audit Partnerships: Audit Firm Size And Fees," **JAR**, 1987, Vol. 25, No. 1, pp. 111-126.)

Raman, Krishnamurthy K. "Assessing Credit Risk On Municipal Short-Term Debt," **AIA**, 1986, Vol. 3, pp. 171-180.

Raman, Krishnamurthy K. (Marks, Barry R. and Krishnamurthy K. Raman. "The Importance Of Pension Data For Municipal And State Creditor Decisions: Replications And Extensions," **JAR**, 1985, Vol. 23, No. 2, pp. 878-886.)

Raman, K. K. "Alternative Accounting Measures As Predictors Of Municipal Financial Distress," **JAAF**, 1982, Vol. 6, No. 1, pp. 44-50.

Raman, K. K. "Financial Reporting And Municipal Bond Ratings," **JAAF**, 1982, Vol. 5, No. 2, pp. 144-153.

Raman, K. K. "Financial Reporting And Municipal Bond Rating Changes," **AR**, 1981, Vol. 56, No. 4, pp. 910-926.

Raman, K. K. "Municipal Financial Reporting: Monitoring 'Full' Accountability," **JAAF**, 1981, Vol. 4, No. 4, pp. 352-359.

Raman, K. K. "The Tiebout Hypothesis: Implications For Municipal Financial Reporting," **JAAF**, 1979, Vol. 3, No. 1, pp. 31-41.

Raman, K. K. (Benson, Earl D., Barry R. Marks and K. K. Raman. "State Regulation Of Accounting Practices And Municipal Borrowing Costs," **JAPP**, 1984, Vol. 3, No. 2, pp. 107-122.)

Raman, K. K. (Benson, Earl D., Barry R. Marks and K. K. Raman. "Municipal Borrowing Costs And The Differential Impact Of Accounting Information Across Rating Categories," **RIGNA**, 1986, Vol. 2, pp. 261-273.)

Raman, K. K. (Marks, Barry R. and K. K. Raman. "The Information Content Of Unfunded Pension Obligations For Municipal Bond Ratings: An Empirical Evaluation," **AIA**, 1987, Vol. 4, pp. 33-42.)

Raman, K. K. (Marks, Barry R. and K. K. Raman. "Pension Ratios As 'Correlates' Of Municipal Pension Underfunding," **JAPP**, 1985, Vol. 4, No. 2, pp. 149-157.)

Raman, K. K. (Marks, Barry R. and K. K. Raman. "Some Additional Evidence On The Determinants Of State Audit Budgets," **AJPT**, 1987-88, Vol. 7, No. 1, pp. 106-117.)

Raman, K. K. (Marks, Barry R. and K. K. Raman. "State Audit Budgets And Market Assessments Of Credit Risk," **JAPP**, 1986, Vol. 5, No. 4, pp. 233-250.)

Raman, K. K. (Marks, Barry R. and K. K. Raman. "The Effect Of Unfunded Accumulated And Projected Pension Obligations On Governmental Borrowing Costs," **CAR**, 1988, Vol. 4, No. 2, pp. 595-608.)

Raman, K. K. (Marks, Barry R., K. K. Raman and Earl R. Wilson. "Toward Understanding The Determinants Of Pension Underfunding In The Public Sector," **JAPP**, 1988, Vol. 7, No. 3, pp. 157-183.)

Ramanan, Ramachandran. (Balachandran, Bala V. and Ramachandran Ramanan. "Optimal Internal Control Strategy Under Dynamic Conditions," **JAAF**, 1988, Vol. 3 (New Series), No. 1, pp. 1-18.)

Ramanan, Ramachandran. (Johnson, W. Bruce and Ramachandran Ramanan. "Discretionary Accounting Changes From 'Successful Efforts' To 'Full Cost' Methods: 1970-76," **AR**, 1988, Vol. 63, No. 1, pp. 96-110.)

Ramanan, Ramachandran. (Maher, Michael W. and Ramachandran Ramanan. "Does Internal Auditing Improve Managerial Performance?," **MA**, 1988, Vol. 69, No. 9, pp. 54-56.)

Ramanan, Ramachandran. (Simon, Daniel T., Ramachandran Ramanan and Amitabh Dugar. "The Market For Audit Services In India: An Empirical Examination," **IJAER**, 1986, Vol. 21, No. 2, pp. 27-35.)

Ramanathan, Kavasseri V. and William L. Weis. "How To Succeed In Nonbusiness (Without Really Trying): A University Case Study," **JOA**, 1980, Vol. 150, No. 4, pp. 46-53.

Ramanathan, Kavasseri V. "Toward A Theory Of Corporate Social Accounting," **AR**, 1976, Vol. 51, No. 3, pp. 516-528.

Ramanathan, Kavasseri V. (DeCoster, Don T. and Kavasseri V. Ramanathan. "An Algebraic Aid In Teaching The Differences Between Direct Costing And Full-Absorption Costing Models," **AR**, 1973, Vol. 48, No. 4, pp. 800-801.)

Ramanathan, Kavasseri V. (Foran, Michael F. and Kavasseri V. Ramanathan. "Selling Options: A New Twist In Securities Trading," **JOA**, 1976, Vol. 141, No. 6, pp. 57-64.)

Ramanathan, Kavasseri V. (Maher, Michael W., Kavasseri V. Ramanathan and Richard B. Peterson. "Preference Congruence, Information Accuracy, And Employee Performance: A Field Study," **JAR**, 1979, Vol. 17, No. 2, pp. 476-503.)

Ramanathan, Kavasseri V., Richard B. Peterson and Michael W. Maher. "Strategic Goals And Performance Criteria," **JOA**, 1976, Vol. 141, No. 1, pp. 56-64.

Ramanathan, K. V. and Alfred Rappaport. "Size, Growth Rates, And Merger Valuation," **AR**, 1971, Vol. 46, No. 4, pp. 733-745.

Ramanathan, K. V. and W. L. Weis. "Supplementing Collegiate Financial Statements With Across-Fund Aggregations: An Experimental Inquiry," **AOS**, 1981, Vol. 6, No. 2, pp. 143-152.

Ramanathan, K. V. (Schreuder, H. and K. V. Ramanathan. "Accounting And Corporate Accountability: An Extended Comment," **AOS**, 1984, Vol. 9, No. 3/4, pp. 409-416.)

Ramanathan, K. V. (Schreuder, H. and K. V. Ramanathan. "Accounting And Corporate Accountability: A Postscript," **AOS**, 1984, Vol. 9, No. 3/4, pp. 421-423.)

Rambow, Earl A. "Direct Costing The Company's Aircraft," **MA**, 1971, Vol. 52, No. 10, pp. 25-26.

Ramen, K. K. (Benson, Earl D., Barry R. Marks and K. K. Raman. "The MFOA Certificate Of Conformance And Municipal Borrowing Costs," **AIA**, 1986, Vol. 3, pp. 221-232.)

Ramesh, K. (Greenberg, Robert R., Glenn L. Johnson and K. Ramesh. "Earnings Versus Cash Flow As A Predictor Of Future Cash Flow Measures," **JAAF**, 1986, Vol. 1 (New Series), No. 4, pp. 266-277.)

Rampy, Brig. Gen. T. R. "How The U.S. Air Force Audits Supplier's Accounts On Procurement Contracts," **JOA**, 1950, Vol. 90, No. 4, pp. 301-305.

Rampy, Brig. Gen. T. R. "The Accountant's Role In Our Present Economy," **AR**, 1952, Vol. 27, No. 4, pp. 467-471.

Rampy, T. R. "Allowable Costs For Air Force Contracts," **AR**, 1950, Vol. 25, No. 4, pp. 371-377.

Ramsay, Louis P. (Friedlob, G. Thomas and Louis P. Ramsay. "Communicating Decision Alternatives Graphically Using The Point Of Indifference," **JAED**, 1986, Vol. 4, No. 2, pp. 37-49.)

Ramzy, Dave. (Copeland, Benny R. and Dave Ramzy. "Office Automation: Selecting The Right Communications System," **MA**, 1986, Vol. 68, No. 1, pp. 34-39.)

Ranck, J. Harold, Jr. "Avoiding The Pitfalls In Sales Forecasting," **MA**, 1986, Vol. 68, No. 3, pp. 51-55.

Randall, L. J. "Deduction Of Mine Development And Exploration Costs," **JOA**, 1952, Vol. 94, No. 3, pp. 325-327.

Randall, Maury R. (Sumutka, Alan R. and Maury R. Randall. "Some Tax Advantaged Investments - Part I," **CPAJ**, 1984, Vol. 54, No. 2, pp. 10-15.)

Randall, Maury R. (Sumutka, Alan R. and Maury R. Randall. "Some Tax Advantaged Investments - Part II," **CPAJ**, 1984, Vol. 54, No. 3, pp. 27-33.)

Randall, Reed H. (Cushing, Barry E., D. Gerald Searfoss and Reed H. Randall. "Materiality Allocation In Audit Planning: A Feasibility Study," **JAR**, 1979, Vol. 17, Supp., pp. 172-216.)

Randall, Robert F. "Computer Fraud: A Growing Problem," **MA**, 1978, Vol. 59, No. 10, pp. 61-64.

Randall, Robert F. "Metcalf Subcommittee: Let Accountants Make Reforms," **MA**, 1978, Vol. 59, No. 7, pp. 17-18.

Randall, Robert F. (Gartenberg, Morris and Robert F. Randall. "From EDP to MIS And Beyond," **MA**, 1979, Vol. 60, No. 10, pp. 13-16.)

Rands, C. A., R. Vause and K. G. Pemberton. "Using Computers In Small Company Cash Management," **ABR**, 1973-74, Vol. 4, No. 16, pp. 251-262.

Rankin, Calvin H. "Treasury Stock: A Source Of Profit Or Loss?," **AR**, 1940, Vol. 15, No. 1, pp. 71-76.

Rankin, Larry J. "The Development Of Compilations And Reviews," **AHJ**, 1984, Vol. 11, No. 1, pp. 63-82.

Rankin, Larry J. (Campbell, Robert J. and Larry J. Rankin. "Regression Analysis In Planning And Testing," **CPAJ**, 1986, Vol. 56, No. 5, pp. 50-59.)

Ransom, Charles R. "The Ex Ante Information Content Of Accounting Information Systems," **JAR**, 1985, Vol. 23, Supp., pp. 124-139.

Ransopher, Tad D. (Hermanson, Roger H. and Tad D. Ransopher. "What The Hishon Case Means To CPA Firms," **JOA**, 1985, Vol. 159, No. 2, pp. 78-80.)

Ranzal, Gerald H. "Foreign Investment In U.S. Real Property," **CPAJ**, 1981, Vol. 51, No. 6, pp. 9-14.

Rao, Kailas J. "A Hardware Company Manages Its Inventory The EDP Way," **MA**, 1979, Vol. 60, No. 10, pp. 28-32.

Rao, Kailas J. "The High Price Of Beef: How One Company Accounts For It," **MA**, 1979, Vol. 61, No. 2, pp. 37-40.

Raper, C. L. "Shall Accounting Instructors Indulge In Outside Practice?," **AR**, 1929, Vol. 4, No. 2, pp. 129-130.

Rapp, John. "Discovering And Evaluating Client Problems (Part 2)," **CPAJ**, 1976, Vol. 46, No. 11, pp. 37-39.

Rapp, John. "Discovering And Evaluating Client Problems (Part 1)," **CPAJ**, 1976, Vol. 46, No. 10, pp. 35-38.

Rapp, John. "Evaluating The Marketing Operations Of An Acquisition Candidate," **CPAJ**, 1974, Vol. 44, No. 8, pp. 35-38.

Rapp, John. "Public Confidence In CPAs," **CPAJ**, 1977, Vol. 47, No. 3, pp. 23-26.

Rappaport, Alfred. "Establishing Objectives For Published Corporate Accounting Reports," **AR**, 1964, Vol. 39, No. 4, pp. 951-962.

Rappaport, Alfred. "Integer Programming And Managerial Analysis," **AR**, 1969, Vol. 44, No. 2, pp. 297-299.

Rappaport, Alfred. "Lease Capitalization And The Transaction Concept," **AR**, 1965, Vol. 40, No. 2, pp. 373-376.

Rappaport, Alfred. "Sensitivity Analysis In Decision Making," **AR**, 1967, Vol. 42, No. 3, pp. 441-456.

Rappaport, Alfred. "Siminar Research On Uniformity," **AR**, 1965, Vol. 40, No. 3, pp. 643-648.

Rappaport, Alfred. "The Strategic Audit," **JOA**, 1980, Vol. 149, No. 6, pp. 71-77.

Rappaport, Alfred. "Towards A Theory Of Interim Reports: A Modification And An Extension," **JAR**, 1966, Vol. 4, No. 1, pp. 121-126.

Rappaport, Alfred. (LaValle, Irving H. and Alfred Rappaport. "On The Economics Of Acquiring Information Of Imperfect Reliability," **AR**, 1968, Vol. 43, No. 2, pp. 225-230.)

Rappaport, Alfred. (Prakash, Prem and Alfred Rappaport. "Informational Interdependencies: System Structure Induced By Accounting Information," **AR**, 1975, Vol. 50, No. 4, pp. 723-734.)

Rappaport, Alfred. (Ramanathan, K. V. and Alfred Rappaport. "Size, Growth Rates, And Merger Valuation," **AR**, 1971, Vol. 46, No. 4, pp. 733-745.)

Rappaport, A. (Prakash, P. and A. Rappaport. "Information Inductance And Its Significance For Accounting," **AOS**, 1977, Vol. 2, No. 1, pp. 29-38.)

Rappaport, Donald. "Materiality," **JOA**, 1964, Vol. 117, No. 4, pp. 42-48.

Rappaport, Donald. "New Approaches In Public Education," **JOA**, 1968, Vol. 126, No. 1, pp. 31-42.

Rappaport, Donald. "The Challenge Of The Entrepreneur," **JOA**, 1986, Vol. 161, No. 5, pp. 88-93.

Rappaport, Louis H. "Accountant's Responsiblity For Events After Balance-Sheet Date," **JOA**, 1953, Vol. 95, No. 3, pp. 332-335.

Rappaport, Louis H. "Lawyers And Accountants In SEC Engagements," **JOA**, 1959, Vol. 107, No. 6, pp. 34-40.

Rappaport, Percy. "Inside The Budget Bureau," **JOA**, 1956, Vol. 101, No. 3, pp. 31-37.

Raptis, James. "College Instruction - A Student's Viewpoint," **AR**, 1952, Vol. 27, No. 4, pp. 431-435.

Rascoff, Joseph. (Jaenicke, Henry R. and Joseph Rascoff. "Segment Disposition: Implementing APB Opinion No. 30," **JOA**, 1974, Vol. 137, No. 4, pp. 63-69.)

Rasmussen, William G. "Alabama Gas Corp. Estimates Unbilled Energy," **MA**, 1981, Vol. 62, No. 8, pp. 23-27.

Ratcliffe, Thomas A. and Paul Munter. "Auditors' Responsibility Regarding Supplementary Information," **CPAJ**, 1981, Vol. 51, No. 3, pp. 36-41.

Ratcliffe, Thomas A. and Paul Munter. "Reporting By Defined Benefit Pension Plans," **CPAJ**, 1980, Vol. 50, No. 12, pp. 39-43.

Ratcliffe, Thomas A. and Paul Munter. "A Synthesis Of Compilation And Review Standards - Part I," **CPAJ**, 1982, Vol. 52, No. 7, pp. 37-47.

Ratcliffe, Thomas A. and Paul Munter. "Implementing FAS No. 33: A Case Example," **MA**, 1981, Vol. 62, No. 8, pp. 44-52.

Ratcliffe, Thomas A. and Paul Munter. "Asset Valuation: An Historical Perspective," **AHJ**, 1980, Vol. 7, No. 1, pp. 73-78.

Ratcliffe, Thomas A. and Paul Munter. "Currency Translation: A New Blueprint," **JOA**, 1982, Vol. 153, No. 6, pp. 82-90.

Ratcliffe, Thomas A. (Haley, Brian W. and Thomas A. Ratcliffe. "Accounting For Incentive Stock Options," **CPAJ**, 1982, Vol. 52, No. 10, pp. 32-39.)

Ratcliffe, Thomas A. (Haley, Brian W. and Thomas A. Ratcliffe. "ERTA And Incentive Stock Options," **CPAJ**, 1982, Vol. 52, No. 9, pp. 45-56.)

Ratcliffe, Thomas A. (Munter, Paul and Thomas A. Ratcliffe. "Accounting For Real Estate Projects - Part I," **CPAJ**, 1983, Vol. 53, No. 6, pp. 20-27.)

Ratcliffe, Thomas A. (Munter, Paul and Thomas A. Ratcliffe. "A Synthesis Of Compilation And Review Standards - Part II," **CPAJ**, 1982, Vol. 52, No. 8, pp. 22-29.)

Ratcliffe, Thomas A. (Munter, Paul and Thomas A. Ratcliffe. "Accounting For Real Estate Projects - Part II," **CPAJ**, 1983, Vol. 53, No. 7, pp. 38-44.)

Ratcliffe, Thomas A. (Munter, Paul and Thomas A. Ratcliffe. "Disclosure Of Long-Term Obligations," **CPAJ**, 1981, Vol. 51, No. 10, pp. 32-41.)

Ratcliffe, Thomas A. (Munter, Paul and Thomas A. Ratcliffe. "Impact Of Computer Processing On Financial Audits," **CPAJ**, 1985, Vol. 55, No. 1, pp. 34-39.)

Ratcliffe, Thomas A. (Munter, Paul and Thomas A. Ratcliffe. "An Assessment Of User Reactions To Lease Accounting Disclosures," **JAAF**, 1983, Vol. 6, No. 2, pp. 108-114.)

Ratcliffe, Thomas A. (Munter, Paul and Thomas A. Ratcliffe. "Special Reports," **CPAJ**, 1982, Vol. 52, No. 2, pp. 28-36.)

Ratcliffe, Thomas A. (Munter, Paul and Thomas A. Ratcliffe. "Accounting For Research And Development Activities," **CPAJ**, 1983, Vol. 53, No. 4, pp. 54-65.)

Ratcliffe, Thomas A. (Munter, Paul and Thomas A. Ratcliffe. "Going Concern Questions," **CPAJ**, 1981, Vol. 51, No. 8, pp. 39-45.)

Ratcliffe, Thomas A. (Raiborn, D. D. and Thomas A. Ratcliffe. "Are You Accounting For Inflation In Your Capital Budgeting Process?," **MA**, 1979, Vol. 61, No. 3, pp. 19-22.)

Ratnatunga, J., R. Pike and G. J. Hooley. "The Application Of Management Accounting Techniques To Marketing," **ABR**, 1988, Vol. 18, No. 72, pp. 363-370.

Ratoff, Steven B. "Auditing Phase II Price Control Compliance," **CPAJ**, 1973, Vol. 43, No. 2, pp. 115-120.

Ratsch, Herbert. "The New Professional Code For Certified Accountants And Licensed Accountants In The Federal Republic Of Germany," **AR**, 1964, Vol. 39, No. 1, pp. 140-144.

Raun, Donald L. "Accounting For Decisions," **AR**, 1961, Vol. 36, No. 3, pp. 460-471.

Raun, Donald L. "Income: A Measurement Of Currently Added Purchasing Power Through Operations," **AR**, 1952, Vol. 27, No. 3, pp. 352-358.

Raun, Donald L. "Product-Mix Analysis By Linear Programming," **MA**, 1966, Vol. 47, No. 5, pp. 3-13.

Raun, Donald L. "Profit Planning And Game Theory," **MA**, 1966, Vol. 47, No. 11, pp. 3-10.

Raun, Donald L. "The Application Of Monte Carlo Analysis To An Inventory Problem," **AR**, 1963, Vol. 38, No. 4, pp. 754-758.

Raun, Donald L. "The Limitations Of Profit Graphs, Break-even Analysis And Budgets," **AR**, 1964, Vol. 39, No. 4, pp. 927-945.

Raun, Donald L. "The Problem Of Fixed Charges," **AR**, 1951, Vol. 26, No. 3, pp. 338-346.

Raun, Donald L. "What Is Accounting?," **AR**, 1962, Vol. 37, No. 4, pp. 769-773.

Raval, Vasant. "A Conceptual Model Of A Curriculum For Accountants," **JIS**, 1988, Vol. 3, No. 1, pp. 132-152.

Raviv, Artur. "Management Compensation And The Managerial Labor Market: An Overview," **JAEC**, 1985, Vol. 7, No. 1/3, pp. 239-245.

Rawcliffe, George A. "Accounting Concepts For Managerial Decison-Making," **MA**, 1972, Vol. 53, No. 10, pp. 23-24.

Rawlinson, Charles E. "An Audit Program Designed To Eliminate Year-End Peaks," **JOA**, 1951, Vol. 91, No. 2, pp. 272-275.

Ray, Delmas D. and Warren W. Menke. "Benefit-Cost Analysis: A Challenge For Accountants," **MA**, 1970, Vol. 52, No. 2, pp. 7-14.

Ray, Delmas D. "Faculty Responsibility With Respect To Correcting Certain Defects In The Accountant's Education," **AR**, 1957, Vol. 32, No. 4, pp. 580-586.

Ray, Gregory A. and Anne D. McCallion. "Accounting For Computer Software: The FASB Approach," **MA**, 1985, Vol. 66, No. 8, pp. 51-57.

Ray, Gregory A. (McCallion, Anne D. and Gregory A. Ray. "Computer Software: An Asset Coming On-Line," **JOA**, 1984, Vol. 158, No. 5, pp. 93-109.)

Ray, G. A. (Hutchinson, P. J., J. A. Piper and G. A. Ray. "The Financing Of Rapid Growth Firms Up To Flotation," **ABR**, 1974-75, Vol. 5, No. 18, pp. 145-151.)

Ray, G. H. (Hutchinson, P. J., J. A. Piper and G. H. Ray. "The Financial Control Of Rapid-Growth Firms Up To Flotation," **ABR**, 1974-75, Vol. 5, No. 19, pp. 222-228.)

Ray, J. C. "Accounting For Treasury Stock," **AR**, 1962, Vol. 37, No. 4, pp. 753-757.

Ray, J. C. "Classification Of Audit Evidence," **JOA**, 1964, Vol. 117, No. 3, pp. 42-47.

Ray, J. C. "Graphic Presentation Of Audit Reports," **AR**, 1966, Vol. 41, No. 1, pp. 134-138.

Rayburn, Frank R. and E. H. Bonfield. "Schools Of Accountancy: Attitudes And Attitude Structure," **AR**, 1978, Vol. 53, No. 3, pp. 752-765.

Rayburn, Frank R. and G. Michael Crooch. "Currency Translation And The Funds Statement: A New Approach," **JOA**, 1983, Vol. 156, No. 4, pp. 51-63.

Rayburn, Frank R. "A Chronological Review Of The Authoritative Literature On Interperiod Tax Allocation: 1940 - 1985," **AHJ**, 1986, Vol. 13, No. 2, pp. 89-108.

Rayburn, Frank R. "Discounting Of Deferred Income Taxes: An Argument For Reconsideration," **ACCHOR**, 1987, Vol. 1, No. 1, pp. 43-50.

Rayburn, Judy Dawson. (Collins, Daniel W., S. P. Kothari and Judy Dawson Rayburn. "Firm Size And The Information Content Of Prices With Respect To Earnings," **JAEC**, 1987, Vol. 9, No. 2, pp. 111-138.)

Rayburn, Judy. "The Association Of Operating Cash Flow And Accruals With Security Returns," **JAR**, 1986, Vol. 24, Supp., pp. 112-133.

Rayburn, L. Gayle. "Analysis Of Current Marketing Cost Methods," **CPAJ**, 1973, Vol. 43, No. 11, pp. 985-991.

Rayburn, L. Gayle. "Marketing Costs - Accountants To The Rescue." **MA**, 1981, Vol. 62. No. 7. pp. 32-41.

Rayburn, L. Gayle. "Recruitment Of Women Accountants," **JOA**, 1971, Vol. 132, No. 5, pp. 51-57.

Rayman, R. A. "Accounting Reform: Standardisation, Stabilisation Or Segregation?," **ABR**, 1970-71, Vol. 1, No. 4, pp. 300-308.

Rayman, R. A. "An Extension Of The System Of Accounts: The Segregation Of Funds And Value." **JAR**, 1969, Vol. 7, No. 1, pp. 53-89.

Raymond, Robert H. and David J. Ellison. "Personal Financial Statements - Benefits Of Experience," **CPAJ**, 1983, Vol. 53, No. 4, pp. 14-23.

Raymond, Robert H. "History Of The Flexible Budget," **MA**, 1966, Vol. 47, No. 12, pp. 9-15.

Raymond, Robert H. "Life Insurance Company Vs. Traditional Financial Statements," **JOA**, 1965, Vol. 120, No. 6, pp. 39-45.

Raymond, Robert H., M. Zafar Iqbal and Eldon L. Schafer. "The Gearing (Leverage) Adjustment: A Historical And Comparative Analysis," **IJAER**, 1982, Vol. 18. No. 1, pp. 139-157.

Razek, Joseph R. "Accounting On The Old Plantation: A Study Of The Financial Records Of An Ante-Bellum Louisiana Sugar Planter," **AHJ**, 1985, Vol. 12, No. 1, pp. 17-36.

Razek, Joseph R. "Ante-Bellum Bank Accounting - A Case Study: The New Orleans Savings Bank In The 1830s," **AHJ**, 1987, Vol. 14, No. 2, pp. 19-39.

Razek, Joseph R. (Adelberg. Arthur H. and Joseph R. Razek. "The Cloze Procedure: A Methodology For Determining The Understandability Of Accounting Textbooks." **AR**, 1984, Vol. 59, No. 1, pp. 109-122.)

Rea, Richard C. "Helping A Client Make Up His Mind." **JOA**, 1965, Vol. 119, No. 5, pp. 39-4?.

Rea, Richard C. "On Starting A Practice." **JOA**, 1961, Vol. 112, No. 2, pp. 63-66.

Rea, Richard C. "Some Observations On The Continuation Of A Firm," **JOA**, 1973, Vol. 135, No. 3, pp. 40-46.

Rea, Richard C. "The Purchase. Sale And Merger Of Small Practices," **JOA**, 1965, Vol. 120, No. 4, pp. 35-43.

Rea, Richard C. "What Makes A Good Managing Partner?," **JOA**, 1979, Vol. 147, No. 6, pp. 55-60.

Read, William J., John E. Mitchell and Abraham D. Akresh. "Planning Materiality And SAS No. 47." **JOA**, 1987, Vol. 164, No. 6, pp. 72-79.

Read, William J. and Stephen Tomczyk. "An Argument For Complete Financial Disclosure By Public Accounting Firms," **ACCHOR**, 1988, Vol. 2. No. 2. pp. 39-46.

Read, William J. "An Analysis Of Auditor Judgment In Non-statistical Sampling," **AIA**, 1988, Vol. 6. pp. 251-266.

Read, William J. (Barnett, Andrew H. and William J. Read. "Sampling In Small Business Audits," **JOA**, 1986, Vol. 161, No. 1, pp. 78-90.)

Read, W. H. "Cost Accounting Concepts: Introductory Statement," **AR**, 1948, Vol. 23, No. 1, pp. 28-31.

Read, W. H. "The War Department Classification Of Accounts," **AR**, 1947, Vol. 22, No. 3, pp. 281-287.

Ready, Robert D. "Auditor's Protection Against Client's Fraud," **JOA**, 1962, Vol. 114, No. 2, pp. 52-59.

Ready, Robert D. "Legal Liability Of The Tax Practitioner," **JOA**, 1964, Vol. 117, No. 6, pp. 41-46.

Reames, D. D. (Estes, Ralph and D. D. Reames. "Effects Of Personal Characteristics On Materiality Decisions: A Multivariate Analysis," **ABR**, 1988, Vol. 18, No. 72, pp. 291-296.)

Reardon, Thomas E. and Judi L. Worthington. "Magnetic Media Reporting: A Solution To Small Business Paperwork?," **JOA**, 1987, Vol. 163, No. 6, pp. 130-135.

Reaugh, Daniel M. (Kaplan, Maurice C. and Daniel M. Reaugh. "Accounting, Reports To Stockholders, And The SEC," **AR**, 1939, Vol. 14, No. 3, pp. 203-235.)

Rebele, James E. "An Examination Of Accounting Students' Perceptions Of The Importance Of Communication Skills In Public Accounting," **IAB**, 1985, No. 1, pp. 41-50.

Rebele, James E., James A. Heintz and George E. Briden. "Independent Auditor Sensitivity To Evidence Reliability," **AJPT**, 1988, Vol. 8. No. 1. pp. 43-52.

Reckers, Philip M. J. and A. J. Stagliano. "The CPA's Nonaudit Services," **CPAJ**, 1980, Vol. 50, No. 2, pp. 25-28.

Reckers, Philip M. J. and A. J. Stagliano. "Non-Audit Services And Perceived Independence: Some New Evidence," **AJPT**, 1981-82, Vol. 1, No. 1, pp. 23-37.

Reckers, Philip M. J. and A. J. Stagliano. "Zero-Base Budgeting," **MA**, 1977, Vol. 59, No. 5, pp. 18-20.

Reckers, Philip M. J. and Joseph J. Schultz, Jr. "Individual Versus Group Assisted Evaluations," **AJPT**, 1982-83, Vol. 2, No. 1, pp. 64-74.

Reckers, Philip M. J. and Larry H. Beard. "IRS Seeks Auditors' Working Papers," **CPAJ**, 1978, Vol. 48, No. 1, pp. 35-40.

Reckers, Philip M. J. and Martin E. Taylor. "Peer Review - At The State Level," **CPAJ**, 1979, Vol. 49, No. 1, pp. 35-41.

Reckers, Philip M. J. and Martin E. Taylor. "Consistency In Auditors' Evaluations Of Internal Accounting Controls," **JAAF**, 1979, Vol. 3, No. 1, pp. 42-55.

Reckers, Philip M. J. and Martin E. Taylor. "FAS No. 8 - Does It Distort Financial Statements?," **CPAJ**, 1978, Vol. 48, No. 8, pp. 31-34.

Reckers, Philip M. J. "The Impact Of Selected Behavioral Variables On Disclosure Decisions," **AIA**, 1984, Vol. 1, pp. 197-224.

Reckers, Philip M. J. (Arrington. Cecil E. and Philip M. J. Reckers. "A Social-Psychological Investigation Into Perceptions Of Tax Evasion," **ABR**, 1984-85, Vol. 15, No. 59, pp. 163-176.)

Reckers, Philip M. J. (Baldwin, Bruce A. and Philip M. J. Reckers. "Exploring The Role Of Learning Style Research In Accounting Education Policy," **JAED**, 1984, Vol. 2, No. 2, pp. 63-76.)

Reckers, Philip M. J. (Bates, Homer L., Robert W. Ingram and Philip M. J. Reckers. "Auditor-Client Affiliation: The Impact On 'Materiality'," **JOA**, 1982, Vol. 153, No. 4. pp. 60-63.)

Reckers, Philip M. J. (Bedingfield, James P., Philip M. J. Reckers and A. J. Stagliano. "Assessing The Impact Of Mergers On Bank Performance," **AIA**, 1986, Vol. 3, pp. 149-170.)

Reckers, Philip M. J. (Cherry, Alan A. and Phillip M. J. Reckers. "The Introductory Financial Accounting Course: Its Role In The Curriculum For Accounting Majors," **JAED**, 1983, Vol. 1, No. 1, pp. 71-82.)

Reckers, Philip M. J. (Cherry, Alan A. and Philip M. J. Reckers. "A Study Of The Need For Change In Intermediate Accounting Courses And Textbooks," **IAB**, 1985, No. 1, pp. 131-144.)

Reckers, Philip M. J. (Jennings, Marianne, Dan C. Kneer and Philip M. J. Reckers. "A Reexamination Of The Concept Of Materiality: Views Of Auditors, Users And Officers Of The Court," **AJPT**, 1986-87, Vol. 6, No. 2, pp. 104-115.)

Reckers, Philip M. J. (Kaplan, Steven E. and Philip M. J. Reckers. "An Empirical Examination Of The Effect Of Orientation Information On Audit Judgments," **AIA**, 1986, Vol. 3, pp. 335-357.)

Reckers, Philip M. J. (Kaplan, Steven E. and Philip M. J. Reckers. "An Examination Of Auditor Performance Evaluation," **AR**, 1985, Vol. 60, No. 3, pp. 477-487.)

Reckers, Philip M. J. (Kaplan, Steven E. and Philip M. J. Reckers. "An Empirical Examination Of Auditors' Initial Planning Processes," **AJPT**, 1984-85, Vol. 4, No. 1, pp. 1-19.)

Reckers, Philip M. J. (Kaplan, Steven E. and Philip M. J. Reckers. "Noneconomic Contributors To Tax Evasion: A Replication," **AIA**, 1987, Vol. 4, pp. 13-32.)

Reckers, Philip M. J. (McKinley. Sue, Kurt Pany and Philip M. J. Reckers. "An Examination Of The Influence Of CPA Firm Type, Size, And MAS Provision On Loan Officer Decisions And Perceptions," **JAR**, 1985, Vol. 23, No. 2, pp. 887-896.)

Reckers, Philip M. J. (Pany, Kurt and Philip M. J. Reckers. "Auditor Performance Of MAS: A Study Of Its Effects On Decisions And Perceptions," **ACCHOR**, 1988, Vol. 2, No. 2, pp. 31-38.)

Reckers, Philip M. J. (Pany, Kurt and Philip M. J. Reckers. "Within - Vs. Between - Subjects Experimental Designs: A Study Of Demand Effects," **AJPT**, 1987-88, Vol. 7, No. 1, pp. 39-53.)

Reckers, Philip M. J. (Pany, Kurt and Philip M. J. Reckers. "Non-Audit Services And Auditor Independence - A Continuing Problem," **AJPT**, 1983-84, Vol. 3, No. 2. pp. 89-97.)

Reckers, Philip M. J. (Pany, Kurt and Philip M. J. Reckers. "The Effects Of Gifts, Discounts, And Client Size On Perceived Auditor Independence," **AR**, 1980, Vol. 55, No. 1. pp. 50-61.)

Reckers, Philip M. J. (Schultz, Joseph J., Jr. and Philip M. J. Reckers. "The Impact Of Group Processing On Selected Audit Disclosure Decisions," **JAR**, 1981, Vol. 19. No. 2, pp. 482-501.)

Reckers, Philip M. J. (Schwartz, Bill N. and Philip M. J. Reckers. "User Attitudes Toward Selected Professional Developments," **ACCHOR**, 1987, Vol. 1. No. 2, pp. 43-48.)

Reckers, Philip M. J., Dan C. Kneer and Marianne M. Jennings. "Concepts Of Materiality And Disclosure," **CPAJ**, 1984. Vol. 54, No. 12. pp. 20-31.

Reckers, P. M. J. (Duncan, William A., David W. LaRue and P. M. J. Reckers. "An Empirical Examination Of The Influence Of Selected Economic And Non-Economic Variables On Decision Making By Tax Professionals," **AIT**, 1988, Vol. 2. pp. xx-xx.)

Reckers, P. M. J. (Kaplan, S. E., P. M. J. Reckers and S. J. Roark. "An Attribution Theory Analysis Of Tax Evasion Related Judgments," **AOS**, 1988, Vol. 13, No. 4, pp. 371-380.)

Reckers, P. M. J. (Pany, Kurt and P. M. J. Reckers. "Auditor Independence And Nonaudit Services: Director Views And Their Policy Implications," **JAPP**, 1983, Vol. 2, No. 1, pp. 43-62.)

Redd, Robert O. "The Controller And Energy Management," **MA**, 1981, Vol. 62, No. 9, pp. 48-51.

Reddington, Donald A. "Control Methods For Small Business," **MA**, 1973, Vol. 55, No. 3, pp. 15-17.

Reder, Renee E. (Larcker, David F., Renee E. Reder and Daniel T. Simon. "Trades By Insiders As Evidence Of The Existence Of Economic Consequences Of Accounting Standards," **AR**, 1983, Vol. 58, No. 3, pp. 606-620.)

Redfern, E. K. "How Weak Accounting Systems Encourage Embezzlement," **JOA**, 1951, Vol. 92, No. 1, pp. 82-86.

Redman, Lipman. "How The Reorganized Bureau Of Internal Revenue Will Work," **JOA**, 1952, Vol. 93, No. 5, pp. 571-577.

Reed, Jim D. (Mickle, Collier E., Jim D. Reed and Daniel L. Butler. "Analyzing The Profitability Of Branch Banks," **MA**, 1985, Vol. 67, No. 6, pp. 61-66.)

Reed, Joel. "Are Auditors Sentinels For Society?," **CPAJ**, 1976. Vol. 46, No. 6, pp. 15-18.

Reed, Richard A. "Consolidation Accounting," **MA**, 1972, Vol. 54. No. 2, pp. 33-34.

Reed, Ronald O. (Rosenstein, Stuart and Ronald O. Reed. "An

Alternative Approach To Determining Present And Future Value Interest Factors For Annuities Due," **JAED**, 1988, Vol. 6, No. 2, pp. 339-344.)

Reed, **Sarah A.** and Bruce S. Koch. "The Race: A View From The 'Pits' Of Accounting," **AIA**, 1987, Vol. 5, pp. 113-128.

Reed, **Sarah A.** and Thomas P. Klammer. "Perceptions Of National AAA Meetings," **JAED**, 1986, Vol. 4. No. 2, pp. 5-17.

Reed, **Sarah A.** "The Impact Of Nonmonetary Performance Measures Upon Budgetary Decision Making In The Public Sector," **JAPP**, 1986, Vol. 5, No. 2, pp. 111-140.

Reed, **Sarah A.** (Gibson, Charles H., Thomas P. Klammer and Sarah A. Reed. "The Cash Flow Statement," **CPAJ**, 1986, Vol. 56, No. 11, pp. 18-39.)

Reeder, **Janis R.** and Karen A. Fortin. "Subchapter S In Transition: A Comment," **JATA**, 1985, Vol. 7, No. 1, pp. 73-75.

Reeder, **Janis R.** (Gillespie, Jackson F., Janis R. Reeder and John H. Wragge. "Safeguarding Your Spreadsheet," **MA**, 1985, Vol. 66, No. 11, pp. 38-42.)

Reemsnyder, **David E., II.** (Cunningham, Gary M. and David E. Reemsnyder, II. "Church Accounting: The Other Side Of Stewardship," **MA**, 1983, Vol. 65, No. 2, pp. 58-62.)

Reetz, **Wilfred.** "Reports Should Be Written Chiefly For Use By Management," **JOA**, 1952, Vol. 93, No. 4, pp. 451-455.

Reetz, **W.** "The Contractor's Organization For Terminations," **AR**, 1945, Vol. 20, No. 1, pp. 68-75.

Reeve, **James M.** and Keith G. Stanga. "The LIFO Pooling Decision: Some Empirical Results From Accounting Practice," **ACCHOR**, 1987, Vol. 1, No. 2. pp. 25-34.

Reeve, **James M.** and Keith G. Stanga. "Balance Sheet Impact Of Using LIFO: An Empirical Study." **ACCHOR**, 1987, Vol. 1, No. 3, pp. 9-16.

Reeve, **James M.** "Individual Vs. Group Processing Of Accounting Data - A Field Study," **ABR**, 1982-83, Vol. 13, No. 49, pp. 49-55.

Reeve, **James M.** "The Five-Year Accounting Program As A Quality Signal," **AR**, 1983. Vol. 58, No. 3, pp. 639-646.

Reeve, **James M.** (Apostolou, Nicholas G., James M. Reeve and Gary A. Giroux. "Accounting Information And Municipal Bond Net Interest Cost: An Empirical Evaluation," **JAPP**, 1984, Vol. 3, No. 1, pp. 9-28.)

Reeve, **James M.** (Izard, C. Douglass and James M. Reeve. "Electronic Spreadsheet Technology In The Teaching Of Accounting And Taxation," **JAED**, 1986, Vol. 4. No. 1, pp. 161-175.)

Reeve, **James M.** (St. Pierre, Kent and James M. Reeve. "An Analysis Of Ernst & Ernst v. Hochfelder: Legal And Market Effects A Decade Latter," **RIAR**, 1987, Vol. 1, pp. 89-101.)

Reeve, **James M.** (Sullivan, William G. and James M. Reeve. "Xventure: Expert Systems To The Rescue," **MA**, 1988, Vol. 70, No. 4, pp. 51-58.)

Reeve, **James M.,** Gary A. Giroux and Nicholas G. Apostolou. "Accounting Information And Municipal Bond Interest Cost: Methodological Considerations: Reply To Comment," **JAPP**, 1985, Vol. 4, No. 3, pp. 241-245.

Reeve, **John T.** "Audits Of Nonprofit Organizations," **JOA**, 1965, Vol. 119, No. 2, pp. 63-67.

Reeve, **John T.** "Could Your Company Pass A Government Contract Inspection?," **MA**, 1981, Vol. 62, No. 9, pp. 52-58.

Reeve, **Robert C.** and Patrick J. Hutchinson. "The Contribution Of Non-U.S. Institutions To Academic Accounting Journals," **ABACUS**, 1988, Vol. 24, No. 1, pp. 90-94.

Regazzi, **John H.** "Pitfalls Of Cash Basis For Employee Funds," **JOA**, 1960, Vol. 109, No. 2, pp. 47-51.

Regazzi, **John H.** "The Accounting Picture In The Television Industry," **JOA**, 1955, Vol. 99, No. 5, pp. 60-66.

Regazzi, **John H.** "Why Aren't Financial Statements Understood?," **JOA**, 1974, Vol. 137, No. 4, pp. 48-55.

Rege, **Udayan P.,** W. John Brennan and W. Harold Silvester. "Current Regulatory Practices, Corporate Financial Forecasting, And Takeover Bids," **IJAER**, 1983, Vol. 18, No. 2, pp. 171-175.

Regier, **Philip R.** (DeBerg, Curtis L.. H. Fred Mittelstaedt and Philip R. Regier. "Employers' Accounting For Pensions: A Theoretical Approach To Financial Accounting Standards No. 87," **JAPP**, 1987, Vol. 5, No. 2, pp. 227-242.)

Register, **Levon C.** "How Will Exempt Hospitals Remain Exempt?," **MA**, 1977, Vol. 59, No. 5, pp. 34-38.

Register, **Levon C.** "The Influence Of Taxes On Financial Planning," **MA**, 1967, Vol. 49, No. 2, pp. 47-53.

Rehmet, **Ralph** and Archibald E. Mackay. "The Division For Firms," **CPAJ**, 1981, Vol. 51. No. 2, pp. 15-22.

Rehmet, **Ralph.** (Mahoney, Thomas A. and Ralph Rehmet. "A Small CPA Firm Looks At The Regulation Question," **CA**, 1986, Vol. 4, No. 4, pp. 29-33.)

Reichardt, **Karl E.** "Capitalizing Costs Of Information Systems," **MA**, 1974, Vol. 55, No. 10, pp. 39-43.

Reichelstein, **Stefan.** (Melumad, Nahum D. and Stefan Reichelstein. "Centralization Versus Delegation And The Value Of Communication," **JAR**, 1987, Vol. 25, Supp., pp. 1-18.)

Reichel, **Kenneth.** (Taub, Lewis J. and Kenneth Reichel. "Year-End Tax Planning - TRA 86." **CPAJ**, 1986, Vol. 56, No. 12, pp. 44-49.)

Reichenbach, **G. F.** (Smith, William N. and G. F. Reichenbach. "Maintenance Material Inventory Control." **MA**, 1967, Vol. 48, No. 12, pp. 49-53.)

Reichenstein, **William R.** and William A. Raabe. "Investment Returns And Inflation Neutrality Under Alternate Tax Structures: Investment And Public Policy Implications,"

AIT, 1988, Vol. 2, pp. xx-xx.

Reichenstein, **William R.** and William A. Raabe. "The Effects Of Tax Provisions On Long-Run Investment Prospects," **JAPP**, 1985, Vol. 4, No. 2, pp. 111-121.

Reichenstein, **William R.** (Farrelly, Gail E., Kenneth R. Ferris and William R. Reichenstein. "Perceived Risk, Market Risk. And Accounting-Determined Risk Measures," **AR**, 1985, Vol. 60, No. 2, pp. 278-288.)

Reich, **Marion R.** "Accounting For Time Charges In A Public Accounting Practice," **JOA**, 1954, Vol. 97, No. 3, pp. 307-311.

Reich, **Marion R.** "Buy And Sell Agreements Funded By Life Insurance," **JOA**, 1963, Vol. 115, No. 6, pp. 43-48.

Reich, **Marion R.** "Do Accountants Die Young?," **JOA**, 1956, Vol. 101, No. 6, pp. 49-51.

Reid, **George F.** and James A. Demcak. "EDP Audit Implementation With General Purpose Software," **JOA**, 1971, Vol. 132, No. 1, pp. 35-46.

Reid, **Jean Margo.** "Judicial Intervention In Accounting Behavior: A Reevaluation Of The Nineteenth Century Experience," **JAPP**, 1987, Vol. 6, No. 1, pp. 9-34.

Reid, **Jean Margo.** "Judicial Views On Accounting In Britain Before 1889," **ABR**, 1986-87, Vol. 17, No. 67, pp. 247-258.

Reid, **Jean Margo.** "Legal Acceptance Of Accounting Principles In Great Britain And The United States," **AHJ**, 1988. Vol. 15, No. 1, pp. 1-27.

Reider, **Barbara** and Gary Saunders. "Management Accounting Education: A Defense Of Criticisms," **AH**, 1988, Vol. 2, No. 4. pp. 58-62.

Reifer, **David.** "Sale Of Rental Housing Units: Ordinary Income Or Capital Gain?," **JOA**, 1954, Vol. 97, No. 4, pp. 449-459.

Reighard, **John J.** "A Problem In Income Taxes," **AR**, 1933. Vol. 8, No. 1, pp. 68-70.

Reighard, **John J.** "Earnings Statements In Periods Of Prosperity And Depression," **AR**, 1932, Vol. 7, No. 2, pp. 107-114.

Reiling, **Henry B.** and Russell A. Taussig. "Recent Liability Cases - Implications For Accountants," **JOA**, 1970, Vol. 130, No. 3, pp. 39-53.

Reiling, **Herman T.** "Procedure For Tax Refunds Over $200,000 Explained," **JOA**, 1953, Vol. 95, No. 5, pp. 567-571.

Reilly, **Frank K.** and Howard F. Stettler. "Factors Influencing Success On The CPA Exam," **JAR**, 1972, Vol. 10, No. 2, pp. 308-321.

Reilly, **Frank K.** (Chambers, R. J., John W. Kennelly, Thomas W. McRae, Frank K. Reilly and W. Keith Weltmer. "Historical Cost Accounting," **ABACUS**, 1971, Vol. 7, No. 1, p. 39.)

Reilly, **Frank K.,** David L. Morgenson and Marilyn West. "The Predictive Ability Of Alternative Parts Of Interim Financial Statements," **JAR**, 1972, Vol. 10, Supp., pp. 105-124.

Reilly, **Robert F.** "Evaluating An Acquisition Candidate Is Easier Than You Think," **MA**, 1980, Vol. 61, No. 7, pp. 47-51.

Reilly, **Thomas F.** (Wheeler, Robert C., Marlyn D. Felsing and Thomas F. Reilly. "Large Or Small CPA Firms: A Practitioners' Perspective," **CPAJ**, 1987, Vol. 57, No. 4, pp. 29-33.)

Reimers, **J. Morgan.** "Cost/Production Evaluation Through 'Level Of Buoyancy' Correlations," **MA**, 1965, Vol. 47, No. 1, pp. 30-34.

Reimers, **J. Morgan.** "The Functions Of Return On Investment," **MA**, 1968, Vol. 49, No. 9, pp. 55-59.

Reimer, **Clarence F.** "Major Differences Between Net Income For Accounting Purposes And For Federal Income Taxes," **AR**, 1948, Vol. 23, No. 3, pp. 305-307.

Reimer, **Marvin.** (Estes, Ralph and Marvin Reimer. "An Experimental Study Of The Differential Effect Of Standard And Qualified Auditors' Opinions On Investors' Price Decisions," **ABR**, 1978-79, Vol. 9, No. 34, pp. 157-162.)

Reimer, **Marvin.** (Estes, Ralph and Marvin Reimer. "A Study Of The Effect Of Qualified Auditors' Opinions On Bankers' Lending Decisions," **ABR**, 1976-77, Vol. 7, No. 28, pp. 250-259.)

Reimer, **Steven C.** "On The Interpretation Of The Estimated Intercept In A Regression Of Overhead Cost On Volume," **JAED**, 1987, Vol. 5, No. 1, pp. 149-153.

Reimer, **Steven K.** "Tax Considerations In Retirement Plan Distributions," **CPAJ**, 1977, Vol. 47, No. 9, pp. 41-46.

Reiner, **David J.** (Blum, James D. and David J. Reiner. "Highlights Of Auditing Standards," **CPAJ**, 1976, Vol. 46, No. 9, pp. 41-46.)

Reinhardt, **U. E.** "Conglomerate Earnings Per Share: Immediate And Post-Merger Effects," **AR**, 1972, Vol. 47, No. 2, pp. 360-370.

Reininga, **Warren.** "An Approach To Elementary Accounting." **AR**, 1965, Vol. 40, No. 1, pp. 211-214.

Reininga, **Warren.** "The Unknown Materiality Concept," **JOA**, 1968, Vol. 125, No. 2, pp. 30-35.

Reinstein, **Alan** and Jack E. Smith. "CPA Firms' Performance Appraisal Procedures," **CPAJ**, 1983, Vol. 53, No. 10, pp. 48-55.

Reinstein, **Alan.** "Improving Cost Allocations For Auto Dealers." **MA**, 1982, Vol. 63, No. 12, pp. 52-57.

Reinstein, **Alan.** (Hardiman, Patrick F., Alan Reinstein and David R. L. Gabhart. "Audit Committees For Governmental Units - How To," **CPAJ**, 1988, Vol. 56, No. 6, pp. 38-45.)

Reinstein, **Alan.** (Lander, Gerald H. and Alan Reinstein. "Indentifying A Common Body Of Knowledge For Management Accounting." **IAE**, 1987, Vol. 2, No. 2, pp. 264-280.)

Reiter, **Sara Ann.** (Francis, Jere R. and Sara Ann Reiter. "Determinants Of Corporate Pension Funding Strategy,"

JAEC, 1987, Vol. 9, No. 1, pp. 35-59.)

Reiter, Sara A. (Pearce, Douglas K. and Sara A. Reiter. "Regression Strategies When Multicollinearity Is A Problem: A Methodological Note," JAR, 1985, Vol. 23, No. 1, pp. 405-407.)

Reklau, David L. "Accounting For Investments In Joint Ventures - A Reexamination," JOA, 1977, Vol. 144, No. 3, pp. 96-103.

Rembar, Charles. "The Practice Of Taxes: One Attorney's Point Of View," JOA, 1954, Vol. 97, No. 5, pp. 549-564.

Reneau, J. Hal and Severin V. Grabski. "A Review Of Research In Computer-Human Interaction And Individual Differences Within A Model For Research In Accounting Information Systems," JIS, 1987, Vol. 2, No. 1, pp. 33-53.

Reneau, J. Hal. "Auditing In A Data Base Environment," JOA, 1977, Vol. 144, No. 6, pp. 59-65.

Reneau, J. Hal. "CAV Bounds In Dollar Unit Sampling: Some Simulation Results," AR, 1978, Vol. 53, No. 3, pp. 669-680.

Reneau, J. Hal. (Burdick, Richard K. and J. Hal Reneau. "Within-Item Variation: A Stochastic Approach To Audit Uncertainty - A Comment," AR, 1978, Vol. 53, No. 4, pp. 989-992.)

Reneau, J. Hal. (Harrison, Paul D., Stephen G. West and J. Hal Reneau. "Initial Attributions And Information-Seeking By Superiors And Subordinates In Production Variance Investigations," AR, 1988, Vol. 63, No. 2, pp. 307-320.)

Renk, Richard C. "Casualty Insurance: Loss Control Is Cost Control," MA, 1971, Vol. 52, No. 7, pp. 42-44.

Renner, Arthur J. (Hall, William D. and Arthur J. Renner. "Lessons That Auditors Ignore At Their Own Risk," JOA, 1988, Vol. 166, No. 1, pp. 50-59.)

Rennie, Morina. (Lindsay, Daryl, Morina Rennie, George Murphy and Harold Silvester. "Independence Of External Auditors: A Canadian Perspective," AIIA, 1987, Vol. 1, pp. 169-189.)

Reno, Edwin S. "The Rules Of Depreciation," JOA, 1956, Vol. 101, No. 5, pp. 59-64.

Renshall, J. M. "Changing Perceptions Behind The Corporate Report," AOS, 1976, Vol. 1, No. 1, pp. 105-110.

Rescho, Joyce A. (Flesher, Tonya K. and Joyce A. Rescho. "Tax Concepts And Their Importance In The Undergraduate Curriculum," JAED, 1986, Vol. 4, No. 1, pp. 55-68.)

Resenberg, D. (Tomkins, C., D. Rosenberg and I. Colville. "The Social Process Of Research: Some Reflections On Developing A Multi-Disciplinary Accounting Project," AOS, 1980, Vol. 5, No. 2, pp. 247-262.)

Restall, Lawrence J. and Peter Czajkowski. "Computation Of Lifo Index: A Statistical Sampling Approach," MA, 1969, Vol. 51, No. 3, pp. 43-48.

Retz, David J. "Business Combinations: Pooling Or Purchase?," MA, 1973, Vol. 54, No. 8, pp. 45-46.

Reuben, Milton H. "The Accountant's Part In Estate Planning," JOA, 1961, Vol. 111, No. 2, pp. 48-50.

Reuber, A. Rebecca. "Opportunities For Accounting Information Systems Research From A Database Perspective," JIS, 1988, Vol. 3, No. 1, pp. 87-103.

Reves, William F. "The Human Side Of Auditing," AR, 1946, Vol. 21, No. 1, pp. 82-84.

Revsine, Lawrence and James B. Thies. "Price Level Adjusted Replacement Cost Data," JOA, 1977, Vol. 143, No. 5, pp. 71-75.

Revsine, Lawrence and James B. Thies. "Productivity Changes And Alternative Income Series: A Simulation," AR, 1976, Vol. 51, No. 2, pp. 255-268.

Revsine, Lawrence and Jerry J. Weygandt. "Accounting For Inflation: The Controversy," JOA, 1974, Vol. 138, No. 4, pp. 72-78.

Revsine, Lawrence. "A Capital Maintenance Approach To Income Measurement," AR, 1981, Vol. 56, No. 2, pp. 383-389.

Revsine, Lawrence. "Change In Budget Pressure And Its Impact On Supervisor Behavior," JAR, 1970, Vol. 8, No. 2, pp. 290-292.

Revsine, Lawrence. "Comparability: An Analytic Examination," JAPP, 1985, Vol. 4, No. 1, pp. 1-12.

Revsine, Lawrence. "Data Expansion And Conceptual Structure," AR, 1970, Vol. 45, No. 4, pp. 704-711.

Revsine, Lawrence. "On The Correspondence Between Replacement Cost Income And Economic Income," AR, 1970, Vol. 45, No. 3, pp. 513-523.

Revsine, Lawrence. "Predictive Ability, Market Prices, And Operating Flows," AR, 1971, Vol. 46, No. 3, pp. 480-489.

Revsine, Lawrence. "Some Controversy Concerning 'Controversial Accounting Changes'," AR, 1969, Vol. 44, No. 3, pp. 354-358.

Revsine, Lawrence. "Surrogates In Income Theory: A Comment," AR, 1976, Vol. 51, No. 1, pp. 156-159.

Revsine, Lawrence. "Technological Changes And Replacement Costs: A Beginning," AR, 1979, Vol. 54, No. 2, pp. 306-322.

Revsine, Lawrence. "The Preferability Dilemma," JOA, 1977, Vol. 144, No. 3, pp. 80-89.

Revsine, Lawrence. "The Rationale Underlying The Functional Currency Choice," AR, 1984, Vol. 59, No. 3, pp. 505-514.

Revsine, Lawrence. (Deskins, James Wesley, Frederick L. Neumann and Lawrence Revsine. "A Research Methodology Course For Accountants," AR, 1970, Vol. 45, No. 4, pp. 789-795.)

Revsine, Lawrence. (Dittman, David A., Hervey A. Juris and Lawrence Revsine. "Unrecorded Human Assets: A Survey Of Accounting Firms' Training Programs," AR, 1980, Vol. 55, No. 4, pp. 640-648.)

Revsine, Lawrence. (Dittman, David A., Hervey A. Juris and Lawrence Revsine. "On The Existence Of Unrecorded Human Assets: An Economic Perspective," JAR, 1976, Vol. 14, No. 1, pp. 49-65.)

Revsine, Lawrence. (Johnson, W. Bruce and Lawrence Revsine. "Financial Reporting Standards, Agency Costs, And Shareholder Intervention," JAL, 1988, Vol. 7, pp. 94-124.)

Revsine, Lawrence. (Larcker, David F. and Lawrence Revsine. "The Oil And Gas Accounting Controversy: An Analysis Of Economic Consequences," AR, 1983, Vol. 58, No. 4, pp. 706-732.)

Revsine, Lawrence. (Thies, James B. and Lawrence Revsine. "Capital Expenditures Data For Inflation Accounting Studies," AR, 1977, Vol. 52, No. 1, pp. 216-221.)

Revzan, David A. "What Is A Balanced Curriculum In Accounting?," AR, 1949, Vol. 24, No. 4, pp. 409-413.

Revzan, Henry A. "A Guide To Auditing Insurance Programs," MA, 1984, Vol. 65, No. 10, pp. 53-57.

Reynolds, Bernard. "Was Shakespeare An Accountant?," JAR, 1974, Vol. 12, No. 2, pp. 367-371.

Reynolds, C. A. "Depreciation Of Assets Contributed By Community," JOA, 1951, Vol. 91, No. 5, pp. 715-717.

Reynolds, Donald. "Accrual Accounting: For Banks," MA, 1971, Vol. 53, No. 3, pp. 39-41.

Reynolds, Isaac N. "A Vanishing Accounting Item - Replacement Accounting?," AR, 1964, Vol. 39, No. 2, pp. 342-346.

Reynolds, Issac N. "Selecting The Proper Depreciation Method," AR, 1961, Vol. 36, No. 2, pp. 239-248.

Rezaee, Zabihollah and Grover L. Porter. "Summary Annual Reports: Is Shorter Better?," JOA, 1988, Vol. 165, No. 5, pp. 42-54.

Rhoads, John L. "Tax Considerations For A Small Business," MA, 1975, Vol. 56, No. 7, pp. 20-24.

Rhode, John Grant, Gary M. Whitsell and Richard L. Kelsey. "An Analysis Of Client-Industry Concentrations For Large Public Accounting Firms," AR, 1974, Vol. 49, No. 4, pp. 772-788.

Rhode, John Grant. (Benke, Ralph L., Jr. and John Grant Rhode. "Intent To Turnover Among Higher Level Employees In Large CPA Firms," AIA, 1984, Vol. 1, pp. 157-174.)

Rhode, John Grant. (DeCoster, Don T. and John Grant Rhode. "The Accountant's Stereotype: Real Or Imagined, Deserved Or Unwarranted," AR, 1971, Vol. 46, No. 4, pp. 651-664.)

Rhode, John Grant. (Sorensen, James E., John Grant Rhode and Edward E. Lawler, III. "The Generation Gap In Public Accounting," JOA, 1973, Vol. 136, No. 6, pp. 42-50.)

Rhode, J. G. (Benke, R. L., Jr. and J. G. Rhode. "The Job Satisfaction Of Higher Level Employees In Large Certified Public Accounting Firms," AOS, 1980, Vol. 5, No. 2, pp. 187-202.)

Rhode, J. G. (Gordon, F. E., J. G. Rhode and K. A. Merchant. "The Effects Of Salary And Human Resource Accounting Disclosures On Small Group Relations And Performance," AOS, 1977, Vol. 2, No. 4, pp. 295-306.)

Rhode, J. G. (Harvey, D. W., J. G. Rhode and K. A. Merchant. "Accounting Aggregation: User Preferences And Decision Making," AOS, 1979, Vol. 4, No. 3, pp. 187-210.)

Rhode, J. G., J. E. Sorensen and E. E. Lawler, III. "Sources Of Professional Staff Turnover In Public Accounting Firms Revealed By The Exit Interview," AOS, 1977, Vol. 2, No. 2, pp. 165-176.

Rhys, D. G. "Anatomy Of A Merger," ABR, 1971-72, Vol. 2, No. 5, pp. 46-52.

Rhys, D. G. "Sub-Optimal Production Runs: A Case Study," ABR, 1973-74, Vol. 4, No. 15, pp. 174-177.

Ricchiute, David N. and David R. Campbell. "A Need To Bring Educators And Practitioners Together," CPAJ, 1979, Vol. 49, No. 3, pp. 35-39.

Ricchiute, David N. and H. James Williams. "Heuristics, Biases, And Decision Making In Accounting," IAE, 1985, No. 1, pp. 51-58.

Ricchiute, David N. "A Case For Automated Workpapers," JOA, 1981, Vol. 151, No. 1, pp. 71-75.

Ricchiute, David N. "An Empirical Assessment Of The Impact Of Alternative Task Presentation Modes On Decision-Making Research In Auditing," JAR, 1984, Vol. 22, No. 1, pp. 341-350.

Ricchiute, David N. "CPA Responsibility For Detecting Errors Or Irregularities," CPAJ, 1978, Vol. 48, No. 3, pp. 15-20.

Ricchiute, David N. "Overauditing - The State Of The Art?," CPAJ, 1983, Vol. 53, No. 3, pp. 9-15.

Ricchiute, D. N. "Standard Setting And The Entity - Proprietary Debate," AOS, 1979, Vol. 4, No. 1/2, pp. 67-76.

Ricchiute, D. N. (Faircloth, A. W. and D. N. Ricchiute. "Ambiguity Intolerance And Financial Reporting Alternatives," AOS, 1981, Vol. 6, No. 1, pp. 53-68.)

Rice, Denis J. (Hite, Peggy A. and Denis J. Rice. "The Continuity Of Interest Doctrine," CPAJ, 1986, Vol. 56, No. 11, pp. 72-79.)

Rice, Edward A. "Some Practical Applications Of Target Prices," MA, 1979, Vol. 60, No. 8, pp. 17-20.

Rice, Marilyn Young. "Sketch For A Universal Accounting Statement," AR, 1962, Vol. 37, No. 1, pp. 6-21.

Rice, Robert R. (Roemmich, Roger A., Johnny R. Johnson and Robert R. Rice. "Pictures That Lie: The Abuse Of Graphs In Annual Reports," MA, 1980, Vol. 62, No. 4, pp. 50-57.)

Rice, Steven J. "The Information Content Of Fully Diluted Earnings Per Share," AR, 1978, Vol. 53, No. 2, pp. 429-438.

Rice, Steven J. (Chow, Chee W. and Steven J. Rice.

"Qualified Audit Opinions And Auditor Switching," **AR**, 1982, Vol. 57, No. 2, pp. 326-335.)

Rice, Steven J. (Chow, Chee W. and Steven J. Rice. "Qualified Audit Opinions And Share Prices - An Investigation," **AJPT**, 1981-82, Vol. 1, No. 2, pp. 35-53.)

Rice, William B. "Statistical Controls Applied To Financial Statements," **AR**, 1946, Vol. 21, No. 3, pp. 267-271.

Rice, William B. "Statistical Uses Of Accounting Data," **AR**, 1944, Vol. 19, No. 3, pp. 260-265.

Rich, Anne J. "The Certificate In Management Accounting - Its Development And Acceptance," **CA**, 1984, Vol. 2, No. 3, pp. 55-60.

Rich, Anne J. "The Controller Who Said 'No'," **MA**, 1985, Vol. 66, No. 8, pp. 34-37.

Rich, Anne J. (Mihalek, Paul H., Anne J. Rich and Carl S. Smith. "Ethics And Management Accountants," **MA**, 1987, Vol. 69, No. 6, pp. 34-36.)

Richard, Donald L. "An Analysis Of Early Investment Credits," **JOA**, 1968, Vol. 126, No. 3, pp. 51-55.

Richard, Donald L. "Difficulties In Tax Allocation On General Price-Level Increases," **AR**, 1968, Vol. 43, No. 4, pp. 730-737.

Richards, Allan B. "A Note On Depreciation And Inventory Valuation Methods Used By Food Companies," **AR**, 1961, Vol. 36, No. 3, pp. 472-473.

Richards, Allen B. "Input-Output Accounting For Business," **AR**, 1960, Vol. 35, No. 3, pp. 429-436.

Richards, Ferry E. "The Multinational Corporation's Borrowing Decision," **MA**, 1976, No. 8, pp. 51-52.

Richards, Jon C. "A Need For Communicating Uncertainties," **MA**, 1976, Vol. 57, No. 8, pp. 24-26.

Richards, Stephen D. "Relocating The Corporate Executive," **CA**, 1988, Vol. 6, No. 2, pp. 44-51.

Richards, Thomas E. (Harrill, E. Reece and Thomas E. Richards. "A Total Systems Approach To Management Accounting," **MA**, 1972, Vol. 53, No. 11, pp. 14-20.)

Richards, William R. "Auditing U.S. Companies With Operations Abroad," **IJAER**, 1976, Vol. 12, No. 1, pp. 1-11.

Richardson, A. J. "Accounting As A Legitimating Institution," **AOS**, 1987, Vol. 12, No. 3, pp. 341-356.

Richardson, A. J. "Accounting Knowledge And Professional Privilege," **AOS**, 1988, Vol. 13, No. 4, pp. 381-396.

Richardson, A. W. "The Measurement Of The Current Portion Of Long-Term Lease Obligations - Some Evidence From Practice," **AR**, 1985, Vol. 60, No. 4, pp. 744-752.

Richardson, Charles P. "Managing Staff: A Concern For Corporate Finance," **CA**, 1986, Vol. 4, No. 4, pp. 40-44.

Richardson, Dana R. "Auditing EFTS," **JOA**, 1978, Vol. 146, No. 4, pp. 81-88.

Richardson, Frederick M. and C. T. Wright. "Standards Overload: A Case For Accountant Judgment," **CPAJ**, 1986, Vol. 56, No. 10, pp. 44-53.

Richardson, Frederick M. (Hicks, Donald W. and Frederick M. Richardson. "Predicting Early Success In Intermediate Accounting: The Influence Of Entry Examination and GPA," **IAE**, 1984, No. 1, pp. 61-67.)

Richardson, Gordon D. (Brown, Lawrence D., Gordon D. Richardson and Steven J. Schwager. "An Information Interpretation Of Financial Analyst Superiority In Forecasting Earnings," **JAR**, 1987, Vol. 25, No. 1, pp. 49-67.)

Richardson, Gordon, Stephan E. Sefcik and Rex Thompson. "Trading Volume Reactions To A Change In Dividend Policy: The Canadian Evidence," **CAR**, 1988, Vol. 5, No. 1, pp. 299-317.

Richardson, Gordon. (Dontoh, Alex and Gordon Richardson. "On Interim Information And The Information Content Of Firm Earnings: A State Variable Approach," **CAR**, 1988, Vol. 4, No. 2, pp. 450-469.)

Richardson, Gordon. (Elliott, John, Gordon Richardson, Thomas Dyckman and Roland Dukes. "The Impact Of SFAS No.2 On Firm Expenditures On Research And Development: Replications And Extensions," **JAR**, 1984, Vol. 22, No. 1, pp. 85-102.)

Richardson, Gordon. (Morse, Dale and Gordon Richardson. "The LIFO/FIFO Decision," **JAR**, 1983, Vol. 21, No. 1, pp. 106-127.)

Richardson, Mark E. "Dividends And Stock Redemptions," **JOA**, 1956, Vol. 102, No. 2, pp. 49-57.

Richardson, Mark E. "Standards Of Responsibility Of CPAs In Tax Practice," **JOA**, 1960, Vol. 109, No. 1, pp. 29-33.

Richardson, Mark E. "The Accountant's Position In The Field Of Taxation," **JOA**, 1954, Vol. 98, No. 2, pp. 166-172.

Richardson, Mark E. "The Accountant And The Tax Law," **JOA**, 1962, Vol. 113, No. 2, pp. 36-41.

Richardson, Mark E. "The Tax Practice 'Quarrel'," **JOA**, 1955, Vol. 100, No. 1, pp. 27-29.

Richardson, Steve D. "Uniform Accounting Standards For Government Contractors," **MA**, 1969, Vol. 50, No. 5, pp. 26-27.

Richman, Sheldon. "Income Averaging - Tax Relief For The High Income Year," **JOA**, 1964, Vol. 117, No. 5, pp. 37-41.

Richter, Robert F. "A Review Of APB Opinion No. 22: 'Disclosure Of Accounting Policies'," **CPAJ**, 1973, Vol. 43, No. 1, pp. 27-36.

Richter, Robert F. (Raby, William and Robert F. Richter. "Conformity Of Tax And Financial Accounting," **JOA**, 1975, Vol. 139, No. 3, pp. 42-48.)

Ricketts, Donald E. and Charles R. Purdy. "The Effect Of Cost-Volume-Profit Structure On Full And Direct Costing Net Income: A Generalizable Approach," **AR**, 1974, Vol. 49, No. 3, pp. 603-607.

Ricketts, Donald E. (Benjamin, James J. and Donald E. Ricketts. "A Profit Planning Project In The Management Accounting Course," **AR**, 1973, Vol. 48, No. 4, pp. 794-797.)

Ricketts, Donald E. (Purdy, Charles R. and Donald E. Ricketts. "Analysis Of Rate, Efficiency, And Utilization Variances," **MA**, 1974, Vol. 56, No. 5, pp. 49-52.)

Rickey, Kenneth R. "Control Cost Accounting," **MA**, 1970, Vol. 51, No. 10, pp. 9-13.

Rickey, Kenneth R. "Cost Of Capital - Determination And Use," **MA**, 1964, Vol. 47, No. 6, pp. 14-19.

Rickey, Kenneth R. "Earnings Per Share: Management And The Investor," **MA**, 1969, Vol. 51, No. 6, pp. 9-11.

Ricks, Charles V. "Preplanning For A One-Month Liquidation," **MA**, 1966, Vol. 47, No. 9, pp. 43-49.

Ricks, R. Bruce. "Year To Switch To Straight Line Depreciation," **AR**, 1964, Vol. 39, No. 3, pp. 685-688.

Ricks, William E. and John S. Hughes. "Market Reactions To Non-Discretionary Accounting Change, The Case Of Long-Term Investments," **AR**, 1985, Vol. 60, No. 1, pp. 33-52.

Ricks, William E. "Firm Size Effects And The Association Between Excess Returns And LIFO Tax Savings," **JAR**, 1986, Vol. 24, No. 1, pp. 206-216.

Ricks, William E. "The Market's Response To The 1974 LIFO Adoptions," **JAR**, 1982, Vol. 20, No. 2, Part I, pp. 367-387.

Ricks, William E. (Baber, William R., Eugene H. Brooks and William E. Ricks. "An Empirical Investigation Of The Market For Audit Services In The Public Sector," **JAR**, 1987, Vol. 25, No. 2, pp. 293-305.)

Ricks, William E. (Biddle, Gary C. and William E. Ricks. "Analyst Forecast Errors And Stock Price Behavior Near The Earnings Announcement Dates Of LIFO Adopters," **JAR**, 1988, Vol. 26, No. 2, pp. 169-194.)

Ricks, William E. (Hoskin, Robert E., John S. Hughes and William E. Ricks. "Evidence On The Incremental Information Content Of Additional Firm Disclosures Made Concurrently With Earnings," **JAR**, 1986, Vol. 24, Supp., pp. 1-32.)

Ricks, William E. (Hughes, John S. and William E. Ricks. "Accounting For Retail Land Sales: Analysis Of A Mandated Change," **JAEC**, 1984, Vol. 6, No. 2, pp. 101-132.)

Ricks, William E. (Hughes, John S. and William E. Ricks. "Associations Between Forecast Errors And Excess Returns Near To Earnings Announcements," **AR**, 1987, Vol. 62, No. 1. pp. 158-175.)

Ricks, William E. (Hughes, John S. and William E. Ricks. "Market Reactions To Mandated Interest Capitalization," **CAR**, 1985-86, Vol. 2, No. 2, pp. 222-241.)

Ricks, William. "Market Assessment Of Alternative Accounting Methods: A Review Of The Empirical Evidence," **JAL**, 1982, Vol. 1, pp. 59-102.

Rickwood, Colin, Geoff Coates and Ray Stacey. "Managed Costs And The Capture Of Information," **ABR**, 1986-87, Vol. 17, No. 68, pp. 319-326.

Riddell, Andrew J. (Nestor, Oscar W. and Andrew J. Riddell. "A Home Health Care Agency Cures Itself," **MA**, 1979, Vol. 61, No. 1, pp. 15-20.)

Riddle, John R., Jr. (Bidwell, Clinton M., III and John R. Riddle, Jr. "Market Inefficiencies - Opportunities For Profits," **JAAF**, 1981, Vol. 4, No. 3, pp. 198-214.)

Ridilla, Richard A. "A Simplified Statistical Technique For Use In Verifying Accounts Receivable: A Rejoinder," **AR**, 1960, Vol. 35, No. 2, pp. 218-222.

Ridilla, Richard A. "A Simplified Statistical Technique For Use In Verifying Accounts Receivable," **AR**, 1959, Vol. 34, No. 4, pp. 547-554.

Ridilla, Richard A. "A Technique To Adjust Financial Statement Data For Changing Price Levels," **AR**, 1960, Vol. 35, No. 4, pp. 650-658.

Ridilla, Richard A. "Price Level Adjustments To Financial Statements - A Rejoinder," **AR**, 1961, Vol. 36, No. 4, pp. 608-612.

Ried, Glenda E. "Legal Compliance Audits For Municipalities," **CPAJ**, 1986, Vol. 56, No. 6, pp. 46-55.

Ried, Glenda, Brenda T. Acken and Elise G. Jancura. "An Historical Perspective On Women In Accounting," **JOA**, 1987, Vol. 163, No. 5, pp. 338-355.

Riener, John. "Are You Really Managing Your T&E System?," **MA**, 1981, Vol. 63, No. 6, pp. 44-50.

Rier, Stanley and Leonard Goodman. "The Tax Reform Act Of 1984 - Part III," **CPAJ**, 1985, Vol. 55, No. 2, pp. 44-47.

Rier, Stanley and Leonard Goodman. "The Tax Reform Act Of 1984 - Part I," **CPAJ**, 1985, Vol. 55, No. 1, pp. 26-33.

Rier, Stanley and Leonard Goodman. "Changes To Tax On Individuals - TRA 1986," **CPAJ**, 1986, Vol. 56, No. 12, pp. 16-27.

Rier, Stanley and Leonard Goodman. "The Tax Reform Act Of 1984 - Part III," **CPAJ**, 1985, Vol. 55, No. 3, pp. 39-43.

Rier, Stanley. (Goodman, Leonard and Stanley Rier. "The Impact Of TRA-86 On The Taxation Of Business," **CPAJ**, 1987, Vol. 57, No. 5, pp. 66-71.)

Riggs, A. James. "An Experimental Study Of The Effects Of Participation, Authoritarianism And Feedback On Cognitive Dissonance In A Standard Setting Situation: A Comment," **AR**, 1977, Vol. 52, No. 3, pp. 759-761.

Rigsby, John T. (Siegel, Philip H. and John T. Rigsby. "The Relationship Of Accounting Internships And Subsequent Professional Performance," **IAE**, 1988, Vol. 3, No. 2, pp. 423-432.)

Riise, Arne. "Norwegian Standards For Annual Reporting Requirements And Chart Of Accounts," **IJAER**, 1982, Vol. 17, No. 2, pp. 103-120.

Riley, Kevin. "Productive Hours Analysis For A Small Shop," **MA**, 1973, Vol. 54, No. 7, pp. 17-18.

Riley, Robert C. "Comparison Of Results Of AIA Achievement

Test With ACE Psychological Examination," **AR**, 1958, Vol. 33, No. 1, pp. 128-130.

Riley, William B. and G. Stevenson Smith. "Interest Rate Swaps: Disclosure And Recognition," **CPAJ**, 1987, Vol. 57, No. 1, pp. 64-70.

Riley, William J. "Financial Responsibility And Sales Prices," **MA**, 1967, Vol. 49, No. 1, pp. 55-62.

Rinehard, Jack R. "Economic Purchase Quantity Calculations," **MA**, 1970, Vol. 52, No. 3, pp. 18-20.

Ring, John R. "Professional Ethics Of The Future," **JOA**, 1965, Vol. 120, No. 1, pp. 40-44.

Ring, R. Warner. "Current Developments In The Public Accounting Profession," **AR**, 1958, Vol. 33, No. 2, pp. 181-186.

Ringelberg, Elizabeth J. (Weirich, Thomas R. and Elizabeth J. Ringelberg. "Omitted Audit Procedures," **CPAJ**, 1984, Vol. 54, No. 3, pp. 34-39.)

Rini, Charles T. (Sibley, A. M. and Charles T. Rini. "How Often Should You Pay Dividends?," **MA**, 1974, Vol. 56, No. 5, pp. 40-42.)

Risdon, Michael P. (McQueary, Glenn M., II and Michael P. Risdon. "How We Comply With The Foreign Corrupt Practices Act," **MA**, 1979, Vol. 61, No. 5, pp. 39-43.)

Rismiller, Gary H. "A Product Line Case Study," **MA**, 1970, Vol. 52, No. 6, pp. 39-41.

Ritchey, James S. "Acquisition Valuation: DCF Can Be Misleading," **MA**, 1983, Vol. 64, No. 7, pp. 24-31.

Ritchie, P. C., J. E. Rowcroft and B. A. Trenholm. "An Analytical Basis For The Treatment Of Corporate Income Tax," **AH**, 1988, Vol. 2, No. 4, pp. 29-40.

Rittenberg, Larry E. and Gordon B. Davis. "The Roles Of Internal And External Auditors In Auditing EDP Systems," **JOA**, 1977, Vol. 144, No. 6, pp. 51-58.

Rittenberg, Larry E. (Farmer, Timothy A., Larry E. Rittenberg and Gregory M. Trompeter. "An Investigation Of The Impact Of Economic And Organizational Factors On Auditor Independence," **AJPT**, 1987-88, Vol. 7, No. 1, pp. 1-14.)

Rittenberg, Larry E. (Nair, R. D. and Larry E. Rittenberg. "Messages Perceived From Audit, Review, And Compilation Reports: Extension To More Diverse Groups," **AJPT**, 1987-88, Vol. 7, No. 1, pp. 15-38.)

Rittenberg, Larry E. (Nair, R. D. and Larry E. Rittenberg. "Accounting Costs Of Privately Held Businesses," **JAAF**, 1983, Vol. 6, No. 3, pp. 234-243.)

Ritts, Blaine A. "A Study Of The Impact of APB Opinions Upon Practicing CPAs," **JAR**, 1974, Vol. 12, No. 1, pp. 93-111.

Rivera, Juan M. "Price-Adjusted Financial Information And Investment Returns In A Highly Inflationary Economy: An Evaluation," **AIIA**, 1987, Vol. 1, pp. 287-304.

Rivera, Juan M. "The Financial Function Of A U.S. Multinational Company Abroad: A Venezuelan Experience," **IJAER**, 1982, Vol. 18, No. 1, pp. 129-138.

Rivera, Juan M. (Elliott, Edward L., Jose Larrea and Juan M. Rivera. "Accounting Aid To Developing Countries," **AR**, 1968, Vol. 43, No. 4, pp. 763-768.)

Rivera, Juan. "Latin American Accounting - A General Perspective," **IJAER**, 1969, Vol. 5, No. 1, pp. 107-108.

Rivett, D. W. (Catt, C. C. and D. W. Rivett. "Fixed Asset Prices And Economic Production Theory," **ABACUS**, 1979, Vol. 15, No. 2, pp. 128-135.)

Rivola-Clay, Anna Maria and Timothy S. Doupnik. "The Progress Of Italian Accounting: Allegro Ma Nontroppo," **IJAER**, 1987, Vol. 22, No. 2, pp. 87-102.

Rizzo, Stephen F. (Bacsik, Jeffrey M. and Stephen F. Rizzo. "Review Of Audit Workpapers," **CPAJ**, 1983, Vol. 53, No. 11, pp. 12-24.)

Ro, Byung T. "Firm Size And The Information Content Of Annual Earnings Announcements," **CAR**, 1988, Vol. 4, No. 2, pp. 438-449.

Ro, Byung T. "The Adjustment Of Security Returns to The Disclosure Of Replacement Cost Accounting Information," **JAEC**, 1980, Vol. 2, No. 2, pp. 159-189.

Ro, Byung T. "The Disclosure Of Replacement Cost Accounting Data And Its Effect On Transaction Volumes," **AR**, 1981, Vol. 56, No. 1, pp. 70-84.

Ro, Byung T. "The Disclosure Of Capitalized Lease Information And Stock Prices," **JAR**, 1978, Vol. 16, No. 2, pp. 315-340.

Ro, Byung T. "The Disclosure Of Replacement Cost Accounting Data And Its Effect On Transaction Volumes: A Reply," **AR**, 1981, Vol. 56, No. 1, pp. 181-187.

Ro, Byung T. (Haw, In-Mu and Byung T. Ro. "An Analysis Of The Impact Of Corporate Pollution Disclosures: A Comment," **AIPIA**, 1988, Vol. 2, pp. 187-191.)

Roark, S. J. (Kaplan, S. E., P. M. J. Reckers and S. J. Roark. "An Attribution Theory Analysis Of Tax Evasion Related Judgments," **AOS**, 1988, Vol. 13, No. 4, pp. 371-380.)

Robason, C. A. (Neeley, Paden and C. A. Robason. "Governmental Accounting: A Critical Evaluation," **AR**, 1967, Vol. 42, No. 2, pp. 366-369.)

Robason, Goyne A. and L. Paden Neely. "Financial Reporting In Municipalities," **MA**, 1970, Vol. 51, No. 9, pp. 45-46.

Robb, Alan J. "Funds Statements And The Two-Entity Test," **ABACUS**, 1985, Vol. 21, No. 1, pp. 101-109.

Robb, Alan J. "Funds Statements And The Two-Entity Test: A Reply," **ABACUS**, 1986, Vol. 22, No. 1, pp. 45-46.

Robb, A. J. "Coincidence Discovered: A Further Example And A Comment," **ABR**, 1982-83, Vol. 13, No. 51, pp. 213-214.

Robb, A. J. "Interim Reports And Their Qualitative Evaluation," **IJAER**, 1980, Vol. 15, No. 2, pp. 77-86.

Robbins, Barry P. and Steven O. Swyers. "Accounting For Income Taxes: Predicting Timing Difference Reversals," **JOA**, 1984, Vol. 158, No. 3, pp. 108-118.

Robbins, Barry P. "A Question Of Basis," **JOA**, 1987, Vol. 163, No. 3, pp. 96-101.

Robbins, Barry P. "Accounting For Income Taxes: Deferred And Liability Methods," **CPAJ**, 1986, Vol. 56, No. 3, pp. 36-41.

Robbins, Barry P. "FASB's Long Look At Stock Compensation Plans," **JOA**, 1988, Vol. 166, No. 2, pp. 60-68.

Robbins, Barry P. "Perspectives On Tax Basis Financial Statements," **JOA**, 1985, Vol. 160, No. 2, pp. 89-101.

Robbins, Barry P. "The Modified-Units-Of-Production Method Of Depreciation," **CA**, 1984, Vol. 2, No. 2, pp. 24-29.

Robbins, Barry P. (Bauer, Charles A. and Barry P. Robbins. "Accounting Implications Of The 1984 Tax Act," **CPAJ**, 1984, Vol. 54, No. 9, pp. 46-51.)

Robbins, Carl B. "Business Secrets," **AR**, 1929, Vol. 4, No. 3, pp. 155-166.

Robbins, Carl B. "Business Secrets (Part II)," **AR**, 1929, Vol. 4, No. 2, pp. 65-79.

Robbins, George W. "A Pattern For Professional Business Education," **AR**, 1949, Vol. 24, No. 4, pp. 392-402.

Robbins, Sidney M. "Risk Analysis In Capital Budgeting," **JAAF**, 1977, Vol. 1, No. 1, pp. 5-18.

Robbins, Walter A. and Kenneth R. Austin. "Disclosure Quality In Governmental Financial Reports: An Assessment Of The Appropriateness Of A Compound Measure," **JAR**, 1986, Vol. 24, No. 2, pp. 412-421.

Robbins, Walter A. and Nicholas G. Apostolou. "SFAC No. 4: Implications For Nonbusiness Organizations," **CPAJ**, 1981, Vol. 51, No. 8, pp. 32-38.

Robbins, Walter A. and Robert W. Ingram. "Financial Reporting Of Health Maintenance Organizations," **CPAJ**, 1987, Vol. 57, No. 2, pp. 36-43.

Robbins, Walter A. and William D. Sampson. "Auditing Federally Assisted Programs," **CPAJ**, 1985, Vol. 55, No. 9, pp. 12-25.

Robbins, Walter A. "Consensus Between Preparers And Users Of Municipal Annual Reports: An Empirical Analysis," **ABR**, 1983-84, Vol. 14, No. 54, pp. 157-162.

Robbins, Walter A. "The Importance Of Selected Information Items To Municipal Bond Analysts And Their Disclosure In Municipal Annual Reports: An Empirical Assessment," **RIGNA**, 1988, Vol. 4, pp. 103-127.

Robbins, Walter A. (Stone, Mary S., Walter A. Robbins and David W. Phipps. "Disclosure Practices Of Public Employee Retirement Systems: An Analysis Of Incentives To Adopt Alternative Standards," **RIGNA**, 1987, Vol. 3, Part A, pp. 149-180.)

Robbins, Walter A., Jr. (Apostolou, Nicholas G., Hartwell C. Herring, III and Walter A. Robbins, Jr. "Are Changes Needed In Private Foundation Reporting Practices?," **MA**, 1980, Vol. 62, No. 5, pp. 39-42.)

Robbins, Walter A., Nicholas G. Apostolou and Robert H. Strawser. "Municipal Annual Reports And The Information Needs Of Investors," **JAAF**, 1985, Vol. 8, No. 4, pp. 279-292.

Roberge, Michael D. "Pricing For Government Contractors," **MA**, 1973, Vol. 54, No. 12, pp. 28-34.

Robert, R. "The Accountant In Literature," **JOA**, 1957, Vol. 103, No. 3, pp. 64-66.

Roberts, Alfred R. "The 'Other' Public Accounting Organizations," **JOA**, 1987, Vol. 163, No. 5, pp. 41-43.

Roberts, Alfred R. (Slocum, Elliott L. and Alfred R. Roberts. "The New York School Of Accounts - A Beginning," **AHJ**, 1980, Vol. 7, No. 2, pp. 63-70.)

Roberts, Alfred R. (Slocum, Elliott L. and Alfred R. Roberts. "The Bureau For Placements," **AHJ**, 1983, Vol. 10, No. 2, pp. 117-127.)

Roberts, Aubrey C. and David R. L. Gabhart. "Statement Of Funds - A Glimpse Of The Future?," **JOA**, 1972, Vol. 133, No. 4, pp. 54-59.

Roberts, A. R. "Electronic Methodology: Accounting Oral And Visual History," **AHJ**, 1974, Vol. 1, No. 1-4, pp. 10-12.

Roberts, C. B. (Gray, S. J. and C. B. Roberts. "International Accounting Education: A Survey Of University Courses In The UK," **ABR**, 1983-84, Vol. 14, No. 55, pp. 267-270.)

Roberts, C. Richard. (Lowe, Larry S., C. Richard Roberts and James W. Cagley. "Your Sales Forecast-Marketing Budget Relationship - Is It Consistent?," **MA**, 1980, Vol. 61, No. 7, pp. 29-33.)

Roberts, Donald M. and Phil D. Wedemeyer. "Assessing The Likelihood Of Financial Statement Errors Using A Discriminant Model," **JAL**, 1988, Vol. 7, pp. 133-146.

Roberts, Donald M. "A Statistical Interpretation Of SAP No. 54," **JOA**, 1974, Vol. 137, No. 3, pp. 47-53.

Roberts, Donald M. "Stratified Sampling Using A Stochastic Model," **JAR**, 1986, Vol. 24, No. 1, pp. 111-126.

Roberts, Donald. "Controlling Audit Risk - A Method For Optimal Sample Design," **JAAF**, 1980, Vol. 4, No. 1, pp. 57-69.

Roberts, Frank C. "Accounting For Multinational Operations," **MA**, 1970, Vol. 52, No. 2, pp. 20-26.

Roberts, Frank L. "How Statutory Renegotiation Of Military Procurement Contracts Works Today," **JOA**, 1950, Vol. 89, No. 3, pp. 234-237.

Roberts, Harry K. "To Keep Or Not To Keep - A Record Retention Program," **MA**, 1966, Vol. 47, No. 8, pp. 58-62.

Roberts, J. and R. Scapens. "Accounting Systems And Systems Of Accountability - Understanding Accounting Practices In Their Organisational Contexts," **AOS**, 1985, Vol. 10, No. 4, pp. 443-456.

Roberts, Michael L. and B. Anthony Billings. "Pre-Combination Tax Attributes - TRA 86," **CPAJ**, 1988, Vol. 58, No. 2, pp. 48-55.

Roberts, Thomas C. "The American Association Of Public

Accountants (1908): Comments," **AHJ**, 1987, Vol. 14, No. 2, pp. 99-103.

Roberts, William. (Burton, John C. and William Roberts. "A Study Of Auditor Changes," **JOA**, 1967, Vol. 123, No. 4, pp. 31-36.)

Robertson, A. Haeworth. "Is Social Security Financially Feasible? Part I," **CPAJ**, 1987, Vol. 57, No. 4, pp. 18-28.

Robertson, Edward H. "Effect Of New Canadian Depreciation Law," **JOA**, 1951, Vol. 91, No. 3. pp. 428-433.

Robertson, Jack C. and Charles H. Smith. "Auditing And Professionalism At The Graduate Level," **AR**, 1973, Vol. 48, No. 3, pp. 599-602.

Robertson, Jack C. and C. Wayne Alderman. "Comparative Auditing Standards," **JAAF**, 1981, Vol. 4, No. 2, pp. 144-161.

Robertson, Jack C. and Robert W. Clarke. "Verification Of Management Representations: A First Step Toward Independent Audits Of Management," **AR**, 1971, Vol. 46, No. 3, pp. 562-571.

Robertson, Jack C. "A Defense Of Extant Auditing Theory," **AJPT**, 1983-84, Vol. 3, No. 2, pp. 57-67.

Robertson, Jack C. "Analysts' Reactions To Auditors' Messages In Qualified Reports," **ACCHOR**, 1988, Vol. 2, No. 2, pp. 82-89.

Robertson, Jack C. "Eye On The SEC: Complying With Reporting Requirements," **CA**, 1984, Vol. 2, No. 1, pp. 3-15.

Robertson, Jack C. (Blocher, Edward and Jack C. Robertson. "Bayesian Sampling Procedures For Auditors: Computer-Assisted Instruction," **AR**, 1976, Vol. 51, No. 2, pp. 359-363.)

Robertson, Jack C. (Boatsman, James R. and Jack C. Robertson. "Policy-Capturing On Selected Materiality Judgments," **AR**, 1974, Vol. 49, No. 2, pp. 342-352.)

Robertson, Jack C. (Langenderfer, Harold Q. and Jack C. Robertson. "A Theoretical Structure For Independent Audits Of Management," **AR**, 1969, Vol. 44, No. 4, pp. 777-787.)

Robertson, Jack C. (Ward, D. Dewey and Jack C. Robertson. "Reliance On Internal Auditors," **JOA**, 1980, Vol. 150, No. 4, pp. 62-74.)

Robertson, Jep. (Knight, Lee G., Ray A. Knight and Jep Robertson. "Tax Status Of Hybrid Securities," **CPAJ**, 1988, Vol. 58, No. 9, pp. 44-50.)

Robertson, J. "When The Name Of The Game Is Changing, How Do We Keep The Score?," **AOS**, 1976, Vol. 1, No. 1, pp. 91-96.

Robertson, Leon H. and Tommy P. Hall. "Network Analysis And Financial Planning," **MA**, 1967, Vol. 48, No. 8, pp. 43-46.

Robertson, Leon H. "Profitability Commission Plans Relating Sales Compensation To Profitability," **MA**, 1968, Vol. 49, No. 10, pp. 39-45.

Robertson, Leon H. (Furlong, William L. and Leon H. Robertson. "Matching Management Decisions And Results," **MA**, 1968, Vol. 49, No. 12, pp. 3-10.)

Robertson, Wilson A. "Make Friends With Your Computer," **MA**, 1965, Vol. 47, No. 3, pp. 30-34.

Robichek, Alexander A. (Jaedicke, Robert K. and Alexander A. Robichek. "Cost-Volume-Profit Analysis Under Conditions Of Uncertainty," **AR**, 1964, Vol. 39, No. 4, pp. 917-926.)

Robinson, Colin. (Morgan, John R. and Colin Robinson. "The Comparative Effects Of The UK And Norwegian Oil Taxation Systems On Profitability And Government Revenue," **ABR**, 1976-77, Vol. 7, No. 25, pp. 2-16.)

Robinson, C. F. (Teitlebaum, A. D. and C. F. Robinson. "The Real Risks In Audit Sampling," **JAR**, 1975, Vol. 13, Supp., pp. 70-91.)

Robinson, Daniel D. and Herbert K. Folpe. "Joint Costs In Voluntary Health And Welfare Organizations," **CPAJ**, 1984, Vol. 54, No. 4, pp. 32-39.

Robinson, Daniel D. "Private Philanthropy And Public Needs," **JOA**, 1976, Vol. 141, No. 2, pp. 46-54.

Robinson, Haldon G. (Cook, J. Michael and Haldon G. Robinson. "Peer Review - The Accounting Profession's Program," **CPAJ**, 1979, Vol. 49, No. 3, pp. 11-16.)

Robinson, Ida B. (Cooper, William D. and Ida B. Robinson. "Who Should Formulate Accounting Principles? The Debate Within The SEC," **JOA**, 1987, Vol. 163, No. 5, pp. 137-140.)

Robinson, Jay E. "Work Simplification Methods To Save Time And Money," **JOA**, 1951, Vol. 92, No. 6, pp. 697-699.

Robinson, John R. "Tax Reform: Analyzing A Comprehensive Income Tax," **JAPP**, 1984, Vol. 3, No. 1, pp. 29-38.

Robinson, John R. (Ford, Allen and John R. Robinson. "The Proper Charge To Capital: Jarvis And Its Implications," **JATA**, 1981, Vol. 3, No. 1, pp. 5-10.)

Robinson, John R. (Marchant, Garry, John R. Robinson, Urton Anderson and Michael S. Schadewald. "A Cognitive Model Of Tax Problem Solving," **AIT**, 1988, Vol. 2, pp. xx-xx.)

Robinson, John R. (Outslay, Edmund, John R. Robinson and Richard Boley. "A Framework For Utilizing Individual Return Problems In Introductory Courses," **AR**, 1983, Vol. 58, No. 2, pp. 428-438.)

Robinson, J. S. "Some Doubtful Elements Of Cost," **AR**, 1926, Vol. 1, No. 3, pp. 80-88.

Robinson, Kenneth W. "Accountant As Expert Witness," **JOA**, 1951, Vol. 91, No. 5, pp. 686-689.

Robinson, Leonard A. and Loudell Ellis Robinson. "Treatment Of The Material Price Variance," **AIA**, 1986, Vol. 3, pp. 255-280.

Robinson, Leonard A. and Loudell Ellis Robinson. "Steering A Boat Maker Through Cost Shoals," **MA**, 1983, Vol. 64, No. 7, pp. 60-66.

Robinson, Leonard A. and Milton J. Alexander. "Are Accountants Adjusting To Change?," **MA**, 1971, Vol. 53, No. 5, pp. 11-14.

Robinson, Leonard A. and T. P. Hall. "Systems Education And The Accounting Curriculum," **AR**, 1964, Vol. 39, No. 1, pp. 62-69.

Robinson, Leonard A. (Robinson, Loudell Ellis and Leonard A. Robinson. "Purchase Discounts Reconsidered," **IAE**, 1986, Vol. 1, No. 2, pp. 249-260.)

Robinson, Leonard A. (Robinson, Loudell Ellis and Leonard A. Robinson. "Increasing Small Business Profit By Use Of Management Accounting Techniques," **JCA**, 1986, Vol. 3, No. 1, pp. 63-71.)

Robinson, Leonard A. (Tripp, Thomas W. and Leonard A. Robinson. "The How And Why Of The Acquisition Decision," **MA**, 1983, Vol. 65, No. 1, pp. 48-53.)

Robinson, Loudell Ellis and Leonard A. Robinson. "Increasing Small Business Profit By Use Of Management Accounting Techniques," **JCA**, 1986, Vol. 3, No. 1, pp. 63-71.

Robinson, Loudell Ellis and Leonard A. Robinson. "Purchase Discounts Reconsidered," **IAE**, 1986, Vol. 1, No. 2, pp. 249-260.

Robinson, Loudell Ellis. "Accounting Theory: Undergraduate Coverage Of The FASB Conceptual Framework," **IAE**, 1984, No. 1, pp. 144-148.

Robinson, Loudell Ellis. (Jenkins, Martha E. and Loudell Ellis Robinson. "The Corporate Audit Committee," **MA**, 1985, Vol. 67, No. 6, pp. 31-35.)

Robinson, Loudell Ellis. (Robinson, Leonard A. and Loudell Ellis Robinson. "Steering A Boat Maker Through Cost Shoals," **MA**, 1983, Vol. 64, No. 7, pp. 60-66.)

Robinson, Loudell Ellis. (Robinson, Leonard A. and Loudell Ellis Robinson. "Treatment Of The Material Price Variance," **AIA**, 1986, Vol. 3, pp. 255-280.)

Robinson, Michael A. and John E. Timmerman. "Vendor Analysis Supports JIT Manufacturing," **MA**, 1987, Vol. 69, No. 6, pp. 20-24.

Robinson, Peter. (Houghton, Keith A. and Peter Robinson. "Experimental Research In Auditing: Field Vs. Laboratory Settings," **ABR**, 1987-88, Vol. 18, No. 69, pp. 37-42.)

Robinson, Robert C. (McCoy, Robert E. and Robert C. Robinson. "Positioning For The Upturn After Surviving The Downturn," **MA**, 1984, Vol. 65, No. 9, pp. 24-28.)

Robinson, Terry L. (Miller, Robert D. and Terry L. Robinson. "Performance Reports Based On Direct Costing: A Case Study," **MA**, 1970, Vol. 51, No. 10, pp. 43-47.)

Robinson, William G. "Stepping Stones To The Cost Of Production Report," **AR**, 1964, Vol. 39, No. 4, pp. 1029-1033.

Robison, Jack. "Tax Court Attendance: A Learning Tool In Advanced Tax Classes," **IAE**, 1988, Vol. 3, No. 2, pp. 402-408.

Robison, Jack. "Tax Court Classification Of Activities Not Engaged In For Profit: Some Empirical Evidence," **JATA**, 1983, Vol. 5, No. 1, pp. 7-22.

Robison, Jack. (Boynton, Charles E., IV and Jack Robison. "Factors Empirically Associated With Federal Tax Trial Case Loads," **AIT**, 1987, Vol. 1, pp. 169-182.)

Roche, Robert P. (Wishon, Keith and Robert P. Roche. "Making The Switch: Corporation To Partnership," **JOA**, 1987, Vol. 163, No. 3, pp. 90-95.)

Rock, C. T., Jr. (Euske, K. J. and C. T. Rock, Jr. "Integrating Human Resource Accounting Into The Public Policy Process: An Illustration," **JAPP**, 1983, Vol. 2, No. 2, pp. 99-114.)

Rock, Milton L. and Martin Sikora. "Accounting For Merger Mania," **MA**, 1987, Vol. 68, No. 10, pp. 20-26.

Rockness, Howard O. and Loren A. Nikolai. "An Assessment Of APB Voting Patterns," **JAR**, 1977, Vol. 15, No. 1, pp. 154-167.

Rockness, Howard O. and Michael D. Shields. "An Empirical Analysis Of The Expenditure Budget In Research And Development," **CAR**, 1988, Vol. 4, No. 2, pp. 568-581.

Rockness, Howard O. "Expectancy Theory In a Budgetary Setting: An Experimental Examination," **AR**, 1977, Vol. 52, No. 4, pp. 893-903.

Rockness, Howard O. (Rockness, Joanne, Paul Schlachter and Howard O. Rockness. "Hazardous Waste Disposal, Corporate Disclosure, And Financial Performance In The Chemical Industry," **AIPIA**, 1986, Vol. 1, pp. 167-191.)

Rockness, Howard O., John D. Bazley and Loren A. Nikolai. "Variance Analysis For Pollution Control," **MA**, 1977, Vol. 58, No. 7, pp. 51-54.

Rockness, Howard. "Expectancy Theory In A Budgetary Setting: A Reply," **AR**, 1979, Vol. 54, No. 3, pp. 635-636.

Rockness, Howard. (Greer, Willis R., Jr. and Howard Rockness. "Management Decision Support Systems For A Medical Group Practice," **JIS**, 1987, Vol. 1, No. 2, pp. 65-79.)

Rockness, H. O. and M. D. Shields. "Organizational Control Systems In Research And Development," **AOS**, 1984, Vol. 9. No. 2, pp. 165-178.

Rockness, Joanne W. and Paul Schlachter. "Directions For Social Accounting Research: A Survey Of Potential Data Sources," **AIPIA**, 1988, Vol. 2, pp. 83-94.

Rockness, Joanne, Paul Schlachter and Howard O. Rockness. "Hazardous Waste Disposal, Corporate Disclosure, And Financial Performance In The Chemical Industry," **AIPIA**, 1986, Vol. 1, pp. 167-191.

Rockness, J. and P. F. Williams. "A Descriptive Study Of Social Responsibility Mutual Funds," **AOS**, 1988, Vol. 13, No. 4, pp. 397-414.

Rockwell, Lynn. (Barton, M. Frank, Surenda P. Agrawal and

Lynn Rockwell. "Meeting The Challenge Of Japanese Management Concepts," **MA**, 1988, Vol. 70, No. 3, pp. 49-53.)

Rockwood, Charles P. "The Changing Image Of A Profession," **JOA**, 1960, Vol. 110, No. 4, pp. 35-43.

Roden, Peyton Foster. "The Financial Implications Of In-Substance Defeasance," **JAAF**, 1987, Vol. 2 (New Issues), No. 1, pp. 79-89.

Roderick, Richard M. "Can You Still Say, 'You're Fired!'?," **MA**, 1986, Vol. 67, No. 10, pp. 24-29.

Roderick, Richard M. "Redesigning An Accounting Department For Corporate And Personal Goals," **MA**, 1984, Vol. 65, No. 8, pp. 56-61.

Rodgers, Edward W. "Systems Education In The Business School," **MA**, 1971, Vol. 53, No. 6, pp. 35-38.

Rodgers, Robert C. (Cooper, W. W., Joanna L. Y. Ho, John E. Hunter and Robert C. Rodgers. "The Impact Of The Foreign Corrupt Practices Act On Internal Control Practices," **JAAF**, 1985, Vol. 9, No. 1, pp. 22-39.)

Roebuck, Derek. "Law And Business Studies," **ABACUS**, 1965, Vol. 1, No. 2, pp. 173-187.

Roebuck, Derek. "Law And Business Studies," **ABACUS**, 1965, Vol. 1, No. 1, pp. 46-61.

Roehm, Harger A. (Castellano, Joseph F. and Harper A. Roehm. "An Approach To Fairness In Disclosure," **MA**, 1975, Vol. 56, No. 8, pp. 20-22.)

Roehm, Harper A. and Joseph F. Castellano. "Inflation Accounting: A Compromise," **CPAJ**, 1978, Vol. 48, No. 9, pp. 38-47.

Roehm, Harper A. (Castellano, Joseph F. and Harper A. Roehm. "Research In Behavioral Accounting Courses: An Approach," **AR**, 1977, Vol. 52, No. 1, pp. 211-215.)

Roemmich, Roger A. (Alou, Susan and Roger A. Roemmich. "Responsibility Accounting For Banks," **MA**, 1977, Vol. 58, No. 11, pp. 35-38.)

Roemmich, Roger A. (Nance, Jon R. and Roger A. Roemmich. "Foreign Currency Translation: An Evaluation," **IJAER**, 1983, Vol. 18, No. 2, pp. 29-48.)

Roemmich, Roger A. (Nance, Jon R. and Roger A. Roemmich. "Financial Statement Impact Of Foreign Currency Translation Alternatives," **IJAER**, 1983, Vol. 19, No. 1, pp. 89-113.)

Roemmich, Roger A., Gordon L. Duke and William H. Gates. "Maximizing The Present Value Of Tax Savings From Depreciation," **MA**, 1978, Vol. 60, No. 3, pp. 55-57.

Roemmich, Roger A., Johnny R. Johnson and Robert R. Rice. "Pictures That Lie: The Abuse Of Graphs In Annual Reports," **MA**, 1980, Vol. 62, No. 4, pp. 50-57.

Roenfeldt, Rodney L. and James B. Henry. "Lease Vs. Debt Purchase Of Automobiles," **MA**, 1976, Vol. 58, No. 4, pp. 49-56.

Roesner, Paul I. "The Lease Or Buy Decision In 'Truck Fleet' Expansion," **MA**, 1972, Vol. 53, No. 7, pp. 46-48.

Rogers, Donald R. and R. W. Schattke. "Buy-Outs Of Stock Options: Compensation Or Capital?," **JOA**, 1972, Vol. 134, No. 2, pp. 55-59.

Rogers, John R. (Elliott, Robert K. and John R. Rogers. "Relating Statistical Sampling To Audit Objectives," **JOA**, 1972, Vol. 134, No. 1, pp. 46-55.)

Rogers, Richard L. and Jerrold J. Stern. "When Should LIFO Liquidated Inventories Be Replaced?," **MA**, 1986, Vol. 68, No. 5, pp. 53-57.

Rogers, Richard L. and Krishnagopal Menon. "Accounting For Deferred-Payment Notes," **AR**, 1985, Vol. 60, No. 3, pp. 547-557.

Rogers, Richard L. (Bathke, Allen W., Jr., Richard L. Rogers and Jerrold J. Stern. "The Security Market Reaction To Tax Legislation As Reflected In Bond Price Adjustments," **JATA**, 1985, Vol. 6, No. 2, pp. 37-49.)

Rogers, Waymond and Thomas J. Housel. "The Effects Of Information And Cognitive Processes On Decision Making," **ABR**, 1987-88, Vol. 18, No. 69, pp. 67-74.

Rogers, William L. (Cummings, Joseph P. and William L. Rogers. "Developments In International Accounting," **CPAJ**, 1978, Vol. 48, No. 5, pp. 15-20.)

Rogness, Earl C. "For Export: Accounting Expertise," **MA**, 1977, Vol. 58, No. 7, pp. 19-20.

Rogoff, Donald. (Mogis, Robert C. and Donald Rogoff. "Statistics Offers A Solution To Tomorrow's Auditing Complexities," **AR**, 1962, Vol. 37, No. 4, pp. 704-707.)

Rogoff, Joel J. "Accounting And Tax Aspects Of Private Hedge Funds," **JOA**, 1971, Vol. 131, No. 3, pp. 35-45.

Rogowski, Robert. (Frishkoff, Paul and Robert Rogowski. "Disclaimers Of Audit Opinion," **MA**, 1978, Vol. 59, No. 11, pp. 52-57.)

Rogow, Robert B. (Dinius, Sara H. and Robert B. Rogow. "Application Of The Delphi Method In Identifying Characteristics Big Eight Firms Seek In Entry-Level Accountants," **JAED**, 1988, Vol. 6, No. 1, pp. 83-101.)

Rogow, R. (Lindbeck, R. and R. Rogow. "A Straightforward Decision Rule For Selecting Lower-Of-Cost Or Market Prices: A Contraction," **AR**, 1975, Vol. 50, No. 3, p. 617.)

Rohrbach, Kermit John. "Monetary Unit Acceptance Sampling," **JAR**, 1986, Vol. 24, No. 1, pp. 127-150.

Rolfe, Robert J. (Englebrecht, Ted D. and Robert J. Rolfe. "Noncorporate Lessors Of Equipment Are Still Subject To Administrative And Judicial Scrutiny," **JATA**, 1982, Vol. 3, No. 2, pp. 23-29.)

Rolfe, Robert J. (Englebrecht, Ted D. and Robert J. Rolfe. "An Alternative To Education Trusts," **CPAJ**, 1981, Vol. 51, No. 7, pp. 23-30.)

Rolfe, Robert J. (Englebrecht, Ted D. and Robert J. Rolfe. "An Empirical Inquiry Into The Determination Of Dividend Equivalence In Stock Redemptions: A Reply," **JATA**, 1984,

Vol. 5, No. 2, pp. 81-84.)

Rolfe, Robert J. (Englebrecht, Ted D. and Robert J. Rolfe. "An Empirical Inquiry Into The Determination Of Dividend Equivalence In Stock Redemptions," **JATA**, 1982, Vol. 4, No. 1, pp. 19-25.)

Roller, Julius and Thomas H. Williams. "Professional Schools Of Accounting," **AR**, 1967, Vol. 42, No. 2, pp. 349-355.

Rollin, Arthur S. and Richard A. Michi. "The Outlook For Tax Shelters," **CPAJ**, 1973, Vol. 43, No. 12, pp. 1063-1066.

Romano, Michael B. "Goodwill...A Dilemma," **MA**, 1975, Vol. 57, No. 1, pp. 39-44.

Romano, Patrick L. (Ahern, John T., Jr. and Patrick L. Romano. "Managing Inventories And Profits Through GMROI," **MA**, 1979, Vol. 61, No. 2, pp. 22-26.)

Romney, Marshall B. and Kevin D. Stocks. "How To Buy A Small Computer System," **JOA**, 1985, Vol. 160, No. 1, pp. 46-63.

Romney, Marshall B. and W. Steve Albrecht. "The Use Of Investigative Agencies By Auditors," **JOA**, 1979, Vol. 148, No. 4, pp. 61-67.

Romney, Marshall B. "Teaching Accounting Information Systems Using A Case Study Approach," **JAED**, 1984, Vol. 2, No. 1, pp. 145-154.

Romney, Marshall B. (Albrecht, W. Steve and Marshall B. Romney. "Red-Flagging Management Fraud: A Validation," **AIA**, 1986, Vol. 3, pp. 323-334.)

Romney, Marshall B. (Krogstad, Jack L. and Marshall B. Romney. "Accounts Receivable Confirmation - An Alternative Auditing Approach," **JOA**, 1980, Vol. 149, No. 2, pp. 68-73.)

Romney, Marshall B. (Solomon, Ira, Lawrence A. Tomassini, Marshall B. Romney and Jack L. Krogstad. "Probability Elicitation In Auditing: Additional Evidence On The Equivalent Prior Sample Method," **AIA**, 1984, Vol. 1, pp. 267-290.)

Romney, Marshall B. (Stocks, Kevin D. and Marshall B. Romney. "The Supply And Demand For IS/MAS Graduates," **JIS**, 1987, Vol. 1, No. 2, pp. 83-100.)

Romney, Marshall B., W. Steve Albrecht and David J. Cherrington. "Auditors And The Detection Of Fraud," **JOA**, 1980, Vol. 149, No. 5, pp. 63-69.

Romney, Marshall B., W. Steve Albrecht and David J. Cherrington. "Red-Flagging The White Collar Criminal," **MA**, 1980, Vol. 61, No. 9, pp. 51-54.

Romney, Marshall. "Fraud And EDP," **CPAJ**, 1976, Vol. 46, No. 11, pp. 23-28.

Romney, Marshall. "The Use Of Microcomputers In Accounting Education," **JAED**, 1983, Vol. 1, No. 2, pp. 11-19.

Romney, M. B. (Solomon, I., J. L. Krogstad, M. B. Romney, and L. A. Tomassini. "Auditors' Prior Probability Distributions For Account Balances," **AOS**, 1982, Vol. 7, No. 1, pp. 27-42.)

Ronen, Joshua and George McKinney, III. "Transfer Pricing For Divisional Autonomy," **JAR**, 1970, Vol. 8, No. 1, pp. 99-112.

Ronen, Joshua and Gideon Falk. "Accounting Aggregation And The Entropy Measure: An Experimental Approach," **AR**, 1973, Vol. 48, No. 4, pp. 696-717.

Ronen, Joshua and Kashi R. Balachandran. "An Approach To Transfer Pricing Under Uncertainty," **JAR**, 1988, Vol. 26, No. 2, pp. 300-314.

Ronen, Joshua and Michael Schiff. "The Setting Of Financial Accounting Standards - Private Or Public?," **JOA**, 1978, Vol. 145, No. 3, pp. 66-73.

Ronen, Joshua and Simcha Sadan. "Accounting Classification As A Tool For Income Prediction," **JAAF**, 1980, Vol. 3, No. 4, pp. 339-353.

Ronen, Joshua and Simcha Sadan. "Classificatory Smoothing: Alternative Income Models," **JAR**, 1975, Vol. 13, No. 1, pp. 133-149.

Ronen, Joshua. "Capacity And Operating Variances: An Ex Post Approach," **JAR**, 1970, Vol. 8, No. 2, pp. 232-252.

Ronen, Joshua. "Nonaggregation Versus Disaggregation Of Variances," **AR**, 1974, Vol. 49, No. 1, pp. 50-60.

Ronen, Joshua. "Some Effects Of Sequential Aggregation In Accounting On Decision-Making," **JAR**, 1971, Vol. 9, No. 2, pp. 307-332.

Ronen, Joshua. "The Effect Of Insider Trading Rules On Information Generation And Disclosure By Corporations," **AR**, 1977, Vol. 52, No. 2, pp. 438-449.

Ronen, Joshua. "Transfer Pricing - A Synthesis: A Comment," **AR**, 1975, Vol. 50, No. 2, pp. 351-355.

Ronen, Joshua. (Barnea, Amir, Joshua Ronen and Simcha Sadan. "Classificatory Smoothing Of Income With Extraordinary Items: A Reply," **AR**, 1977, Vol. 52, No. 2, pp. 525-526.)

Ronen, Joshua. (Barnea, Amir, Joshua Ronen and Simcha Sadan. "Classificatory Smoothing Of Income With Extraordinary Items," **AR**, 1976, Vol. 51, No. 1, pp. 110-122.)

Ronen, Joshua. (Becker, Selwyn, Joshua Ronen and George Sorter. "Opportunity Costs - An Experimental Approach," **JAR**, 1974, Vol. 12, No. 2, pp. 317-329.)

Ronen, Joshua. (Bildersee, John S. and Joshua Ronen. "Stock Returns And Real Activity In An Inflationary Environment: The Informational Impact Of FAS No. 33," **CAR**, 1987-88, Vol. 4, No. 1, pp. 89-110.)

Ronen, Joshua. (Givoly, Dan, Joshua Ronen and Allen Schiff. "Does Audit Involvement Affect The Quality Of Interim Report Numbers?," **JAAF**, 1978, Vol. 1, No. 4, pp. 361-372.)

Ronen, Joshua. (Nelson, Julianne, Joshua Ronen and Lawrence White. "Legal Liabilities And The Market For Auditing

Services," **JAAF**, 1988, Vol. 3 (New Series), No. 3, pp. 255-295.)

Ronen, Joshua. (Ovadia, Arie and Joshua Ronen. "General Price-Level Adjustment And Replacement Cost Accounting As Special Cases Of The Index Number Problem," **JAAF**, 1980, Vol. 3, No. 2, pp. 113-137.)

Ronen, Joshua. (Ovadia, Arie and Joshua Ronen. "On The Value Of Current-Cost Information," **JAAF**, 1983, Vol. 6, No. 2. pp. 115-129.)

Ronen, Joshua. (Pastena, Victor and Joshua Ronen. "Some Hypotheses On The Pattern Of Management's Informal Disclosures," **JAR**, 1979, Vol. 17, No. 2, pp. 550-564.)

Ronen, J. and J. Livnat. "Incentives For Segment Reporting," **JAR**, 1981, Vol. 19, No. 2, pp. 459-481.)

Ronen, J. and J. L. Livingstone. "An Expectancy Theory Approach To The Motivational Impacts Of Budgets," **AR**, 1975, Vol. 50, No. 4, pp. 671-685.

Ronen, J. (Barnea, A., J. Ronen and S. Sadan. "The Implementation Of Accounting Objectives: An Application To Extraordinary Items," **AR**, 1975, Vol. 50, No. 1, pp. 58-68.)

Ronen, J. (Dopuch, N. and J. Ronen. "The Effects Of Alternative Inventory Valuation Methods - An Experimental Study," **JAR**, 1973, Vol. 11, No. 2, pp. 191-211.)

Ronen, J. (Givoly, D. and J. Ronen. "'Smoothing' Manifestations In Fourth Quarter Results Of Operations: Some Expirical Evidence," **ABACUS**, 1981, Vol. 17, No. 2, pp. 174-193.)

Ronen, J. (Kamin, J. Y. and J. Ronen. "The Smoothing Of Income Numbers: Some Empirical Evidence On Systematic Differences Among Management-Controlled And Owner-Controlled Firms," **AOS**, 1978, Vol. 3, No. 2, pp. 141-160.)

Roof, Bradley M. "A Personal Information System Checkup," **MA**, 1982, Vol. 63, No. 7, pp. 29-35.

Roost, William G. (Neebes, Donald L. and William G. Roost. "The ASB's Ten 'Expectation Gap' Proposals - Will They Do The Job?," **CPAJ**, 1987, Vol. 57, No. 10, pp. 22-29.)

Root, Steven J. (Willson, James D. and Steven J. Root. "A Practical Guide To Operational Auditing," **CA**, 1983, Vol. 1, No. 2, pp. 13-19.)

Roper, Elmo. "As Others See You," **JOA**, 1964, Vol. 117, No. 1, pp. 32-36.

Rorem, C. Rufus. "Accounting Theory: A Critique Of The Tentative Statement Of Accounting Principles," **AR**, 1937, Vol. 12, No. 2, pp. 133-136.

Rorem, C. Rufus. "Cost Analysis For Hospitals," **AR**, 1930, Vol. 5, No. 2, pp. 159-161.

Rorem, C. Rufus. "Differential Costs," **AR**, 1928, Vol. 3, No. 4, pp. 333-341.

Rorem, C. Rufus. "Overhead Costs In Public Welfare," **AR**, 1943, Vol. 18, No. 2, pp. 152-155.

Rorem, C. Rufus. "Replacement Cost In Accounting Valuation," **AR**, 1929, Vol. 4, No. 3, pp. 167-174.

Rorem, C. Rufus. "Social Control Through Accounts," **AR**, 1928, Vol. 3, No. 3, pp. 261-268.

Rorem, C. Rufus. "The Costs Of Medical Care," **AR**, 1932, Vol. 7, No. 1, pp. 38-41.

Rorem, C. Rufus. "Uniform Hospital Accounting," **AR**, 1936, Vol. 11, No. 2, pp. 157-162.

Rorem, C. R. "Similarities Of Accounting And Statistical Method," **AR**, 1927, Vol. 2, No. 1, pp. 10-18.

Rorke, C. H. "An Early Pricing Model Regarding The Value Of A Cat: A Historical Note," **AOS**, 1982, Vol. 7, No. 3, pp. 305-306.

Rosbe, Robert L. "Corpus And Income In Trust Accounting," **AR**, 1939, Vol. 14, No. 4, pp. 374-380.

Roscetti, David V. (Kelley, Thomas P. and David V. Roscetti. "Auditor/Actuary Relations Under ERISA: From The Auditor's Standpoint," **JOA**, 1978, Vol. 146, No. 1, pp. 66-71.)

Rose, Clarence C. and Cherie J. O'Neil. "The Viewed Importance Of Investment Tax Incentives By Virginia Decision Makers," **JATA**, 1985, Vol. 7, No. 1, pp. 34-43.

Rose, Edward M. and John M. Tucker. "The CPA And The Media," **CPAJ**, 1985, Vol. 55, No. 3, pp. 11-17.

Rose, Harold. "Sources And Uses:A British View," **JAR**, 1964, Vol. 2, No. 2, pp. 137-147.

Rose, J., W. Beaver, S. Becker and G. Sorter. "Toward An Empirical Measure Of Materiality," **JAR**, 1970, Vol. 8, Supp., pp. 138-148.

Rose, Peter S., Wesley T. Andrews and Gary A. Giroux. "Predicting Business Failure: A Macroeconomic Perspective," **JAAF**, 1982, Vol. 6, No. 1. pp. 20-31.

Rose, Tawn A. "Microcomputers For Financial Consulting," **MA**, 1984, Vol. 65, No. 8, pp. 42-45.

Rose, Thomas S. (Leone, Barry P. and Thomas S. Rose. "Installing A Microcomputer Based Accounting System: One Company's Experience," **MA**, 1987, Vol. 68, No. 11, pp. 34-38.)

Rose, Tom. (Beamer, George C. and Tom Rose. "The Use Of The GATB And The AIA Tests In Predicting Success In Courses In Accounting," **AR**, 1955, Vol. 30, No. 3, pp. 533-535.)

Rosefield, Paul and Steven Rubin. "Minority Interest: Opposing Views," **JOA**, 1986, Vol. 161, No. 3, pp. 78-90.

Rosen, Bruce J. (Beresford, Dennis R. and Bruce J. Rosen. "Accounting For Preacquisition Contingencies," **CPAJ**, 1982, Vol. 52, No. 3, pp. 39-43.)

Rosen, Corey. "ESOPs: More Attractive Then Ever," **CA**, 1988, Vol. 6, No. 1, pp. 25-30.

Rosen, L. S. and Don T. DeCoster. "'Funds' Statements: A Historical Perspective," **AR**, 1969, Vol. 44, No. 1, pp. 124-136.

Rosen, L. S. "Replacement-Value Accounting," **AR**, 1967, Vol. 42, No. 1, pp. 106-113.

Rosen, Marvin. "Unclaimed Property - Is It Abandoned?," **CPAJ**, 1977, Vol. 47, No. 11, pp. 41-45.

Rosen, Robert M. (Austin, P. Thomas, Joel M. Forster and Robert M. Rosen. "Tax Reform: The New Perspective," **JOA**, 1977, Vol. 143, No. 3, pp. 48-59.)

Rosen, Robert W. "Misuse Of Standards In Decision Making," **MA**, 1969, Vol. 50, No. 5, pp. 14-15.

Rosen, Sherwin. "Commentary On 'Golden Parachutes, Executive Decision-Making, And Shareholder Wealth'," **JAEC**, 1985, Vol. 7, No. 1/3, pp. 205-208.

Rosenbaum, D. Hugh. "How To Set Up And Use Captive Insurers," **CA**, 1987, Vol. 5, No. 2, pp. 13-16.

Rosenberg, D., C. Tomkins and P. Day. "A Work Role Perspective Of Accountants In Local Government Service Departments," **AOS**, 1982, Vol. 7, No. 2, pp. 123-138.

Rosenberg, Rita F. J. "SSARS In Action," **CPAJ**, 1985, Vol. 55, No. 2, pp. 10-19.

Rosenblum, Leo. "The Failure Of The City Of Glasgow Bank," **AR**, 1933, Vol. 8, No. 4 pp. 285-291.

Rosenfeld, Ahron. (Lewellen, Wilbur, Claudio Loderer and Ahron Rosenfeld. "Merger Decisions And Executive Stock Ownership In Acquiring Firms," **JAEC**, 1985, Vol. 7, No. 1/3. pp. 209-231.)

Rosenfeld, Eugene and Ralph G. Ledley. "An Accounting Course For Majors And Non-Majors," **AR**, 1961, Vol. 36, No. 1. pp. 125-128.

Rosenfeld, Eugene. "Uniformity In Accounting For Treasury Stock And Its Disposition," **CPAJ**, 1973, Vol. 43, No. 9, pp. 763-770.

Rosenfeld, Paul and Leonard Lorensen. "Auditors' Responsibilities And The Audit Report," **JOA**, 1974, Vol. 138, No. 3, pp. 73-83.

Rosenfeld, Paul and William C. Dent. "No More Deferred Taxes," **JOA**, 183, Vol. 155, No. 2, pp. 44-55.

Rosenfeld, Paul H. and Reed K. Storey. "The Accounting Principles Board - A Correction," **AR**, 1966, Vol. 41, No. 2. pp. 327-330.

Rosenfeld, Paul H. "The Auditor's Standard Report Can Be Improved," **JOA**, 1964, Vol. 118, No. 4, pp. 53-59.

Rosenfeld, Paul. "Accounting For Foreign Branches And Subsidiaries," **IJAER**, 1972, Vol. 7, No. 2, pp. 35-44.

Rosenfeld, Paul. "Accounting For Foreign Operations," **JOA**, 1987, Vol. 164, No. 2, pp. 102-112.

Rosenfeld, Paul. "Accounting For Inflation - A Field Test," **JOA**, 1969, Vol. 127, No. 6, pp. 45-50.

Rosenfeld, Paul. "Current Replacement Value Accounting - A Dead End," **JOA**, 1975, Vol. 140, No. 3, pp. 63-73.

Rosenfeld, Paul. "General Price-level Accounting And Foreign Operations," **JOA**, 1971, Vol. 131, No. 2, pp. 58-65.

Rosenfeld, Paul. "GPP Accounting - Relevance And Interpretability," **JOA**, 1975, Vol. 140, No. 2, pp. 52-59.

Rosenfeld, Paul. "Reporting Subjunctive Gains And Losses," **AR**, 1969. Vol. 44, No. 4, pp. 788-797.

Rosenfeld, Paul. "The Confusion Between General Price-Level And Current Value Accounting," **JOA**, 1972, Vol. 134, No. 4, pp. 63-68.

Rosenfeld, Paul. (Heath, Loyd C. and Paul Rosenfeld. "Solvency: The Forgotten Half Of Financial Reporting," **JOA**, 1979, Vol. 147, No. 1, pp. 48-55.)

Rosenfeld, Paul. (Lorensen, Leonard and Paul Rosenfeld. "Vested Benefits - A Company's Only Pension Liability," **JOA**, 1983, Vol. 156, No. 4, pp. 64-77.)

Rosenfeld, Paul. (Luper, Oral L. and Paul Rosenfeld. "The APB Statement On Basic Concepts And Principles," **JOA**, 1971. Vol. 131, No. 1, pp. 46-51.)

Rosenkampff, A. H. "The Preparation Of Students For The C.P.A. Examination," **AR**, 1927, Vol. 2, No. 3, pp. 278-279.

Rosenstein, Stuart and Ronald O. Reed. "An Alternative Approach To Determining Present And Future Value Interest Factors For Annuities Due," **JAED**, 1988, Vol. 6, No. 2, pp. 339-344.

Rosenzweig, Kenneth. "Companies Are Not Using FAS 33 Data," **MA**, 1985, Vol. 66, No. 10, pp. 51-57.

Rosenzweig, Kenneth. (Agrawal, Surendra P. and Kenneth Rosenzweig. "Some Simpler Methods Of Accounting For The Effects Of Changing Prices," **IJAER**, 1983, Vol. 19, No. 1. pp. 157-171.)

Rosenzweig, K. "An Exploratory Field Study Of The Relationship Between The Controller's Department And Overall Organizational Characteristics," **AOS**, 1981, Vol. 6, No. 4, pp. 339-354.

Rosenzweig, Paul. "Outside Computer Service For On-Line Data Processing," **CPAJ**, 1976, Vol. 46, No. 3, pp. 25-29.

Roshwalb, Alan, Roger L. Wright, and James Godfrey. "A New Approach For Stratified Sampling In Inventory Cost Estimation," **AJPT**, 1987-88, Vol. 7, No. 1, pp. 54-70.

Ross, Allan John. "Accounting For Hazardous Waste," **JOA**, 1985, Vol. 159, No. 3, pp. 72-85.

Ross, Allan John. (Barnickol, Karl R., Allan John Ross, Ronald O. Schowalter and Michael J. Walters. "Accounting For Litigation And Claims," **JOA**, 1985, Vol. 159, No. 6, pp. 56-69.)

Ross, Barbara. "The Accounts Of The Stewards Of The Talbot Household At Blakemere: An Example Of Medieval Accounting Practice," **ABACUS**, 1968, Vol. 4, No. 1, pp. 51-72.

Ross, E. Chadwick. "FAS 87 - What It Means For Business," **MA**, 1986, Vol. 67, No. 9, pp. 20-24.

Ross, Franz E. "Internal Control And Audit Of Real-Time Digital Systems," **JOA**, 1965, Vol. 119, No. 4, pp. 46-55.

Ross, F. E. "Installment Sales Of Real Estate," **AR**, 1926, Vol. 1, No. 4, pp. 24-36.

Ross, F. E. (Littleton, A. C., Lloyd Morey, David Himmelblau and F. E. Ross. "The International Congress

On Accounting," **AR**, 1929, Vol. 4, No. 4, pp. 234-246.)

Ross, Howard. "The Wonderful World Of Accounting," **JAR**, 1970, Vol. 8, Supp., pp. 108-115.

Ross, Joel E. "The Impact Of Information Systems," **MA**, 1974, Vol. 56, No. 2, pp. 33-36.

Ross, Mary E. H. "Income-Tax Position Of Family Partnership Since 1951 Act," **JOA**, 1953, Vol. 95, No. 4. pp. 425-435.

Ross, Myron H. "Depreciation And User Cost," **AR**, 1960, Vol. 35, No. 3, pp. 422-428.

Ross, N. Glenn. "The Canadian Experience," **JOA**, 1982, Vol. 154, No. 1, pp. 74-81.

Ross, Richard L. "Surviving A Pink Slip," **MA**, 1983, Vol. 65, No. 2, pp. 44-49.

Ross, Ronald S. (Burns, Jane O. and Ronald S. Ross. "Establishing International Transfer Pricing Standards For Tax Audits Of Multinational Enterprises," **IJAER**, 1981, Vol. 1, No. 1, pp. 161-179.)

Ross, Stephen A. "Accounting And Economics," **AR**, 1983, Vol. 58, No. 2, pp. 375-380.

Ross, Timothy L. and Edwin C. Bomeli. "A Comment On Accountants' Job Satisfaction," **JAR**, 1971, Vol. 9, No. 2, pp. 383-388.

Ross, Timothy L. (Hartley, Ronald V. and Timothy L. Ross. "MAS And Audit Independence: An Image Problem," **JOA**, 1972, Vol. 134, No. 5, pp. 42-51.)

Ross, Timothy. (Eckel, Norman and Timothy Ross. "Schools Versus Departments Of Accounting: Is There Really A Difference," **JAED**, 1985, Vol. 3, No. 1, pp. 5-14.)

Ross, Wilbur R. "Accounting Aspects Of PERT/Cost," **MA**, 1967, Vol. 48, No. 8, pp. 47-51.

Ross, W. R. "Pert/Cost Resource Allocation Procedure," **AR**, 1966, Vol. 41, No. 3, pp. 464-473.

Rossell, James H. "Calculation Vs. An Understanding Of Net Operating Loss," **AR**, 1958, Vol. 33, No. 1. pp. 120-123.

Rossitch, Eugene and Jack M. Meckler. "Foreign Currency Exposure Control," **MA**, 1973, Vol. 55, No. 1, pp. 29-32, 37.

Rossman, William H. "Allocation Of Equipment Cost In The Heavy Construction Industry," **MA**, 1969, Vol. 51, No. 5, pp. 14-15.

Rotenberg, W. D. (Krinsky, I., W. D. Rotenberg and D. B. Thornton. "Takeovers: A Synthesis," **JAL**, 1988, Vol. 7, pp. 243-279.)

Roth, Alvin E. and Robert E. Verrecchia. "The Shapley Value As Applied To Cost Allocations: A Reinterpretation," **JAR**, 1979, Vol. 17, No. 1, pp. 295-303.

Roth, Harold P. and Wayne J. Morse. "What Are Your Client's Quality Costs?," **CPAJ**, 1988, Vol. 58, No. 4, pp. 54-63.

Roth, Harold P. and Robert M. Brown. "Post-Auditing Capital Investments Using IRR And NPV Models," **MA**, 1982, Vol. 63, No. 8, pp. 29-33.

Roth, Harold P. and Wayne J. Morse. "Let's Help Measure And Report Quality Costs," **MA**, 1983, Vol. 65, No. 2, pp. 50-54.

Roth, Harold P. "A New Outlet For Energy Audit Data," **JOA**, 1981, Vol. 152, No. 3, pp. 68-82.

Roth, Harold P. "Guiding Manufacturers Through The Inventory Capitalization Maze," **JOA**, 1988, Vol. 166, No. 1, pp. 60-71.

Roth, Harold P. "New Rules For Inventory Costing," **MA**, 1987, Vol. 68, No. 9, pp. 32-36.

Roth, Harold P. "The Payne-Aldrich Tariff Act Of 1909," **JOA**, 1987, Vol. 163, No. 5, pp. 181-182.

Roth, Harold P. (Morse, Wayne J. and Harold P. Roth. "Why Quality Costs Are Important," **MA**, 1987, Vol. 69, No. 5, pp. 42-43.)

Rothchild, Richard M. and Paul Kircher. "Projecting Capital Needs," **JOA**, 1955, Vol. 100, No. 3, pp. 51-56.

Rothkopf, Mitchell. "No More Essay Questions On The Uniform CPA Examination," **ACCHOR**, 1987, Vol. 1, No. 4, pp. 79-86.

Rothman, David C. "Pension And Profit-Sharing Plans," **JOA**, 1961, Vol. 112, No. 6, pp. 47-53.

Rothman, Frederick H. "Tax-Exempt Organizations Face New Hurdles - Part II," **CPAJ**, 1988, Vol. 58, No. 8, pp. 38-44.

Rothman, Frederick H. "Tax-Exempt Organizations Face New Hurdles - Part I," **CPAJ**, 1988, Vol. 58, No. 7, pp. 48-55.

Rothschild, Leonard W., Jr. "Worldwide Unitary Taxation: The End Is In Sight," **JOA**, 1986, Vol. 162, No. 6, pp. 178-185.

Rothstein, Eugene L. "Problems In The Treatment Of Research And Development Costs," **MA**, 1965, Vol. 47, No. 3, pp. 9-12.

Roufaiel, Nazik S. "Electronic Tutor: A Tool For Financial Accounting Education," **IAE**, 1988, Vol. 3, No. 1. pp. 181-198.

Rounsaville, Arch. (Davis, Dan D. and Arch Rounsaville. "Modern Sampling Methods," **JOA**, 1959, Vol. 107, No. 6, pp. 45-51.)

Rouse, Robert W. and D. D. Raiborn. "Completeness - The Perplexing Assertion," **CPAJ**, 1986. Vol. 56, No. 9, pp. 74-77.

Rouse, Robert W. and Malcolm H. Lathan, Jr. "Improving The Confirmation Process," **CPAJ**, 1986, Vol. 56, No. 12, pp. 58-61.

Rouse, Robert W. and Randolph A. Shockley. "Setting Realistic Expectations For Publishing In Leading Accounting Research Journals," **JAED**, 1984, Vol. 2, No. 2, pp. 43-52.

Rouse, Robert W. "Reporting On Internal Controls Of Service Organizations," **CPAJ**, 1985, Vol. 55, No. 11, pp. 28-37.

Rouse, Robert W. (Bryan, E. Lewis and Robert W. Rouse. "Problems Of The Small Business Audit," **CPAJ**, 1984, Vol.

54, No. 9, pp. 11-17.)

Rouse, Robert W. (Dungan, Christopher W., G. Thomas Friedlob and Robert W. Rouse. "The Supreme Court On Tax Accrual Workpapers," **CPAJ**, 1985, Vol. 55, No. 2, pp. 20-27.)

Rouse, Robert, James R. Davis and G. Thomas Friedlob. "The Relevant Experience Criterion For Accounting Accreditation By The AACSB," **JAED**, 1986, Vol. 4, No. 1, pp. 147-160.

Rouselle, Arthur L., Jr. "The ERTA Bonus: R&D Can Reduce Your Taxes," **MA**, 1983, Vol. 65, No. 4, pp. 72-78.

Roussey, Robert S. "The CPA In The Information Age: Today And Tomorrow," **JOA**, 1986, Vol. 162, No. 4, pp. 94-109.

Roussey, Robert S. "Third-Party Review Of The Computer Service Center," **JOA**, 1978, Vol. 146, No. 2, pp. 78-82.

Roussey, Robert S. (Felix, William L., Jr. and Robert S. Roussey. "Statistical Inference And The IRS," **JOA**, 1985, Vol. 159, No. 6, pp. 38-45.)

Roussey, Robert S., Ernest L. Ten Eyck and Mimi Blanco-Best. "Three New SASs: Closing The Communications Gap," **JOA**, 1988, Vol. 166, No. 6, pp. 44-52.

Rowbury, James G., Jr. "Timber 'Depletion'," **AR**, 1947, Vol. 22, No. 2, pp. 187-193.

Rowcroft, J. E. (Ritchie, P. C., J. E. Rowcroft and B. A. Trenholm. "An Analytical Basis For The Treatment Of Corporate Income Tax," **AH**, 1988, Vol. 2, No. 4, pp. 29-40.)

Rowe, Edward R. "The Federal Government Reporting Study (Canada And The United States)," **AIIA**, 1988, Vol. 2, pp. 255-261.

Rowe, Thomas M. and Gary A. Giroux. "Diocesan Financial Disclosure: A Quality Assessment," **JAPP**, 1986, Vol. 5, No. 1, pp. 57-74.

Rowlands, John J. "Formula Elements Of Incentive Contracts," **MA**, 1967, Vol. 48, No. 8, pp. 30-37.

Rowles, Barry M. "Application Of Statistical Sampling Techniques To LIFO Inventory Valuation," **AR**, 1954, Vol. 29, No. 2, pp. 244-250.

Rowley, C. Stevenson. "Implications Of SFAS 80 To Grain Merchandising," **CPAJ**, 1985, Vol. 55, No. 10, pp. 52-62.

Roy, Robert H. and James H. MacNeill. "Horizons For A Profession: The Common Body Of Knowledge For CPAs," **JOA**, 1966, Vol. 122, No. 3, pp. 38-50.

Roy, Robert H. and James H. MacNeill. "Study Of The Common Body Of Knowledge For CPAs," **JOA**, 1963, Vol. 116, No. 6, pp. 55-58.

Roy, S. Paul. "A Strategy For More Efficient Audit Sample Determination," **ABR**, 1983-84, Vol. 14, No. 55, pp. 241-248.

Rozeff, Michael S. (Brown, Lawrence D. and Michael S. Rozeff. "Adaptive Expectations, Time-Series Models, And Analyst Forecast Revision," **JAR**, 1979, Vol. 17, No. 2, pp. 341-351.)

Rozeff, Michael S. (Brown, Lawrence D. and Michael S. Rozeff. "Univariate Time-Series Models Of Quarterly Accounting Earnings Per Share: A Proposed Model," **JAR**, 1979, Vol. 17, No. 1, pp. 179-189.)

Rozeff, Michael S. (Brown, Lawrence D., John S. Hughes, Michael S. Rozeff and James H. VanderWeide. "Expectations Data And The Predictive Value Of Interim Reporting: A Comment," **JAR**, 1980, Vol. 18, No. 1, pp. 278-288.)

Rozeff, Michael S. (Brown, Lawrence D. and Michael S. Rozeff. "The Predictive Value Of Interim Reports For Improving Forecasts Of Future Quarterly Earnings," **AR**, 1979, Vol. 54, No. 3, pp. 585-591.)

Rozeff, Michael S. (Collins, Daniel W., Michael S. Rozeff and William K. Salatka. "The SEC's Rejection Of SFAS No. 19: Tests Of Market Price Reversal," **AR**, 1982, Vol. 57. No. 1, pp. 1-17.)

Rozeff, Michael S. (Collins, D W., M. S. Rozeff and D. S. Dhaliwal. "The Economic Determinants Of The Market Reaction To Proposed Mandatory Accounting Changes In The Oil And Gas Industry: A Cross-Sectional Analysis," **JAEC**,1981,Vol.3,No.1,pp.37-71.)

Rozen, Etzmun. (Davis, Harry Z., Nathan Kahn and Etzmun Rozen. "LIFO Inventory Liquidations: An Empirical Study," **JAR**, 1984, Vol. 22, No. 2, pp. 480-496.)

Rozoff, Donald. "Heuristic," **AR**, 1964, Vol. 39, No. 3, pp. 768-769.

Ruback, Richard S. (Mikkelson, Wayne H. and Richard S. Ruback. "Takeovers And Managerial Compensation: A Discussion," **JAEC**, 1985, Vol. 7, No. 1/3, pp. 233-238.)

Rubenstein, Daniel Blake. "Crisis Of Identity - A Canadian Observation," **CPAJ**, 1986, Vol. 56, No. 6, pp. 24-37.

Rubin, Marc A. "A Theory Of Demand For Municipal Audits And Audit Contracts," **RIGNA**, 1987, Vol. 3, Part A, pp. 3-33.

Rubin, Marc A. "Municipal Audit Fee Determinants," **AR**, 1988, Vol. 63, No. 2, pp. 219-236.

Rubin, Marc A. (Chan, James L. and Marc A. Rubin. "The Role Of Information In A Democracy And In Government Operations: The Public Choice Methodology," **RIGNA**, 1987, Vol. 3. Part B, pp. 3-27.)

Rubin, Steven. (Bohan, Michael P. and Steven Rubin. "Lifo/Fifo: How Would It Work?," **JOA**, 1986, Vol. 162, No. 3. pp. 106-114.)

Rubin, Steven. (Bohan, Michael P. and Steven Rubin. "Lifo: What Should Be Disclosed?," **JOA**, 1985, Vol. 159, No. 2, pp. 72-77.)

Rubin, Steven. (Rosefield, Paul versus Steven Rubin. "Minority Interest: Opposing Views," **JOA**, 1986, Vol. 161, No. 3. pp. 78-90.)

Rubinfien, David. "Bank Check Automation," **JOA**, 1957, Vol. 103, No. 3, pp. 41-47.

Rucker, Ranald G. "Cost Analysis By Standards In The

Accounts," **AR**, 1939, Vol. 14, No. 4, pp. 368-373.

Rue, Joseph C. and Ara G. Volkan. "Financial And Economic Consequences Of The New Pension Accounting Proposals: Is The Gloom Justified?," **JAAF**, 1984, Vol. 7, No. 4, pp. 306-322.

Rue, Joseph C. and David E. Tosh. "Continuing Unresolved Issues Of Pension Accounting," **ACCHOR**, 1987, Vol. 1, No. 4, pp. 21-28.

Rue, Joseph C. and David E. Tosh. "Should We Consolidate Finance Subsidiaries?," **MA**, 1987, Vol. 68, No. 10, pp. 45-50.

Rue, Joseph C. (Harding, Susan, Leon Hanouille, Joseph C. Rue and Ara G. Volkan. "Why LBOs Are Popular," **MA**, 1985, Vol. 67, No. 6, pp. 51-56.)

Rue, Joseph C. (Tosh, David E. and Joseph C. Rue. "The Effects Of Unconsolidated Finance Subsidiary Debt On Market Estimates Of Systematic Risk," **JAL**, 1988, Vol. 7, pp. 157-173.)

Rue, Joseph C., David E. Tosh and William B. Francis. "Accounting For Interest Rate Swaps," **MA**, 1988, Vol. 70, No. 1, pp. 43-49.

Rue, Joseph. (Volkan, Ara and Joseph Rue. "The Case Against Deferred Taxes," **MA**, 1985, Vol. 66, No. 9, pp. 30-35.)

Rueschhoff, Donald S. "Inventory Profits," **MA**, 1975, Vol. 57, No. 1, pp. 15-17.

Rueschhoff, Norlin G. "International Accounting And Auditing In The U.S. CPA Examination, 1917-86," **IJAER**, 1986, Vol. 22, No. 1, pp. 25-32.

Rueschhoff, Norlin G. "The Intrinsic Uniformity Of International Accounting," **AIIA**, 1987, Vol. 1, pp. 23-38.

Rueschhoff, Norlin G. "The Undergraduate International Accounting Course," **AR**, 1972. Vol. 47, No. 4, pp. 833-836.

Rueschhoff, Norlin G. "U.S. Dollar Based Financial Reporting Of Canadian Multinational Corporations," **IJAER**, 1973, Vol. 8, No. 2, pp. 103-109.

Rueschhoff, Norlin. "The Evolution Of Accounting For Corporate Treasury Stock In The United States," **AHJ**, 1978, Vol. 5, No. 1, pp. 1-7.

Ruggles, Nancy. (Ruggles, Richard and Nancy Ruggles. "The Evolution And Present State Of National Economic Accounting," **IJAER**, 1968, Vol. 4, No. 1, pp. 1-16.)

Ruggles, Richard and Nancy Ruggles. "The Evolution And Present State Of National Economic Accounting," **IJAER**, 1968, Vol. 4, No. 1, pp. 1-16.

Ruggles, Robert W. "Humanizing Staff Relations," **JOA**, 1960, Vol. 109, No. 4, pp. 62-65.

Ruggles, Robert W. "Need To Clarify Accountant's Opinion On Interim Reports," **JOA**, 1953, Vol. 95, No. 1, pp. 51-55.

Ruhe, John A. (Gaertner, James F. and John A. Ruhe. "Job-Related Stress In Public Accounting," **JOA**, 1981, Vol. 151, No. 6, pp. 68-75.)

Ruhe, Karl. "The IRS Position On Allocation Of Intangibles In Business Acquisitions," **JOA**, 1965, Vol. 120, No. 3, pp. 50-54.

Ruhnka, John C. and Edward J. Gac. "RICO Claims Against CPAs," **CPAJ**, 1987, Vol. 57, No. 12, pp. 26-43.

Ruhnka, John C. "Regulation Of The Investment Advisor," **CPAJ**, 1986, Vol. 56, No. 4, pp. 30-35.

Ruland, Robert G. "Duty, Obligation, And Responsibility In Accounting Policy Making," **JAPP**, 1984, Vol. 3, No. 3, pp. 223-237.

Ruland, Robert G. (Bernard, Victor L. and Robert G. Ruland. "The Incremental Information Content Of Historical Cost And Current Cost Income Numbers: Time-Series Analyses For 1962-1980," **AR**, 1987, Vol. 62, No. 4, pp. 707-722.)

Ruland, William. "The Accuracy Of Forecasts By Management And By Financial Analysts," **AR**, 1978, Vol. 53, No. 2, pp. 439-447.

Ruland, William. (Cogger, Kenneth and William Ruland. "A Note On Alternative Tests For Independence Of Financial Time Series," **JAR**, 1982, Vol. 20, No. 2, pp. 733-737.)

Ruland, William. (Hamdallah, Ahmed El-Sayed and William Ruland. "The Decision To Terminate Overfunded Pension Plans," **JAPP**, 1986, Vol. 5, No. 2, pp. 77-91.)

Ruland, William. (Pastena, Victor and William Ruland. "The Merger/Bankruptcy Alternative," **AR**, 1986, Vol. 61, No. 2, pp. 288-301.)

Rumble, Clayton T. "So You Still Have Not Adopted LIFO," **MA**, 1983, Vol. 65, No. 4, pp. 59-67.

Rundfelt, Rolf. "Insider Trading: Regulation In Europe," **JAAF**, 1986, Vol. 1 (New Series), No. 2, pp. 125-130.

Runk, George D. (Ashby, Rod W. and George D. Funk. "Accounting For Contract Costs And Value In The Forest Products Industry," **MA**, 1980, Vol. 62, No. 2, pp. 41-44.)

Rupli, R. G. "How To Improve Profits Through Simulation," **MA**, 1973, Vol. 55, No. 5, pp. 16-20.

Rushinek, Avi and Sara F. Rushinek. "Additional Fund Allocation Constraints For Common Stock Investments: An Empirical Analysis Of Regional Portfolios In The Common Market And The United States," **IJAER**, 1986, Vol. 21, No. 2, pp. 69-89.

Rushinek, Sara F. (Rushinek, A. and S. F. Rushinek. "Additional Fund Allocation Constraints For Common Stock Investments: An Empirical Analysis Of Regional Portfolios In The Common Market And The United States," **IJAER**, 1986, Vol. 21, No. 2, pp. 68-89.)

Rushing, Reginald. "ABC's Of Accounting Instruction," **AR**, 1951, Vol. 26, No. 3, pp. 417-418.

Rushing, Reginald. "Adjusting Inventories For Consolidated Statements," **AR**, 1965, Vol. 40, No. 2, pp. 458-459.

Rushkoff, Marvin. "The New Role Of The Physician-Businessman," **CPAJ**, 1988, Vol. 58, No. 9, pp. 30-37.

Russ, Alexander. (Moonitz, Maurice and Alexander Russ.

"Accrual Accounting For Employers' Pension Costs," **JAR**, 1966, Vol. 4, No. 2, pp. 155-168.)

Russell, A. H. (French, D. P. and A. H. Russell. "An Approximate Method For The Allocation Of Reciprocal Service Costs," **ABR**, 1981-82, Vol. 12, No. 48, pp. 265-272.)

Russell, Frank V. "Accounting Firms Can Write Better Long-Form Audit Reports," **JOA**, 1950, Vol. 90, No. 5, pp. 429-434.

Russell, Grant W. (Dilts, David M. and Grant W. Russell. "Accounting For The Factory Of The Future," **MA**, 1985, Vol. 66, No. 10, pp. 34-40.)

Russell, Keith A. and G. William Glezen. "An Investigation Of Certain Interactions Between Large CPA Firms And Accounting Educators," **JAED**, 1984, Vol. 2, No. 1, pp. 55-69.

Russell, Keith A. "So You Want To Be An Expert Witness," **MA**, 1985, Vol. 66, No. 9, pp. 36-39.

Russell, Ralph C. "Formulae For Calculating Standard Cost Variances," **AR**, 1947, Vol. 22, No. 3, pp. 307-312.

Russo, Joseph A., Jr. "Escalations In Commercial Leases," **CPAJ**, 1985, Vol. 55, No. 4, pp. 28-35.

Russo, Joseph A., Jr. "Input-Output Analysis For Financial Decision-Making," **MA**, 1976, Vol. 58, No. 3, pp. 22-24.

Ruswinckel, John W. "CCTV Instruction: 1967," **AR**, 1967, Vol. 42, No. 1, pp. 134-141.

Ruswinckel, John W. (Mead, Stuart B. and John W. Ruswinckel. "The Lecture System In Elementary Accounting," **AR**, 1959, Vol. 34, No. 1, pp. 130-131.)

Ruswinckel, J. W. "A Report On The Use Of Visual Aids In The Teaching Of Accounting," **AR**, 1952, Vol. 27, No. 3, pp. 370-375.

Rutherford, B. A. "Published Statements Of Value Added: A Survey Of Three Years' Experience," **ABR**, 1980-81, Vol. 11, No. 41, pp. 15-28.

Rutherford, B. A. "The Interpretation Of Cash Flow Reports And The Other Allocation Problem," **ABACUS**, 1982, Vol. 18, No. 1, pp. 40-49.

Rutherford, B. A. "Value Added As A Focus Of Attention For Financial Reporting: Some Conceptual Problems," **ABR**, 1976-77, Vol. 7, No. 27, pp. 215-220.

Rutherford, Garold L. (Hill, Dan J. and Garold L. Rutherford. "Computerized Financial Data Reporting System," **MA**, 1976, Vol. 58, No. 1, pp. 57-60.)

Ryan, Edward D. "International Tax Problems And The Financial Officer," **MA**, 1975, Vol. 57, No. 4, pp. 49-51.

Ryan, Edward D. (Forster, Joel M., Oliver C. Murray and Edward D. Ryan. "Tax Reform: The New Perspective," **JOA**, 1977. Vol. 143, No. 4, pp. 79-88.)

Ryan, Frank, Arthur J. Francia and Robert H. Strawser. "Professional Football And Information Systems," **MA**, 1973. Vol. 54, No. 9, pp. 43-47.

Ryan, F. J. O. "A True And Fair View'," **ABACUS**, 1967, Vol. 3, No. 2, pp. 95-108.

Ryan, Lanny J. (Hale, Jack A. and Lanny J. Ryan. "Decision Science And The Management Accountant," **MA**, 1979, Vol. 60, No. 7, pp. 42-45.)

Ryan, Louis A. "Organizing For Management Services," **JOA**, 1957. Vol. 103, No. 2, pp. 46-50.

Ryan, Robert J., Jr. "Leveraged Leasing," **MA**, 1977, Vol. 58, No. 10, pp. 45-46.

Ryan, Stephen G. (Beaver, William H., Richard A. Lambert and Stephen G. Ryan. "The Information Content Of Security Prices: A Second Look," **JAEC**, 1987, Vol. 9, No. 2, pp. 139-157.)

Rydell, Ferd. "You Are Being Watched!," **AR**, 1962, Vol. 37, No. 1, pp. 82-87.

Ryder, Paul A. "Comments On Wolf's 'The Nature Of Managerial Work' - The Case For Unobtrusive Measures Revisited," **AR**, 1981, Vol. 56, No. 4, pp. 967-970.

Ryder, Paul A. "The Role Of Behavioral Measures In Accounting For Human Resources: A Comment," **AR**, 1975, Vol. 50, No. 3, pp. 574-578.

Rymer, Victoria S. (Loeb, Stephen E. and Victoria S. Rymer. "The Accounting Paraprofessional," **JOA**, 1973, Vol. 135, No. 4, pp. 43-49.)

SSS

Saathoff, Fredrick J. (Perille, P. James and Frederick J. Saathoff. "Why Not Project Financing?," **MA**, 1978, Vol. 60, No. 4, pp. 13-16.)

Sabol, Thomas A. "Purchasing A Computer," **MA**, 1972, Vol. 54, No. 4, pp. 43-45.

Saccone, John P. "LIFO Fundamentals," **MA**, 1976, Vol. 57, No. 8, pp. 29-33.

Sack, Robert J. and Robert Tangreti. "ESM: Implications For The Profession," **JOA**, 1987, Vol. 163, No. 4, pp. 94-101.

Sack, Robert J. "Commercialism In The Profession: A Threat To Be Managed," **JOA**, 1985, Vol. 160, No. 4, pp. 125-134.

Sack, Robert J. "The SEC And The Profession: An Exercise In Balance," **RIAR**, 1987, Vol. 1, pp. 167-175.

Sackmary, Stephen M. "Spoilage Control: An Accounting Approach," **MA**, 1976, Vol. 47, No. 8, pp. 51-57.

Sadan, Simcha. (Barnea, Amir, Joshua Ronen and Simcha Sadan. "Classificatory Smoothing Of Income With Extraordinary Items: A Reply," **AR**, 1977, Vol. 52, No. 2, pp. 525-526.)

Sadan, Simcha. (Barnea, Amir, Joshua Ronen and Simcha Sadan. "Classificatory Smoothing Of Income With Extraordinary Items," **AR**, 1976, Vol. 51, No. 1, pp. 110-122.)

Sadan, Simcha. (Barnea, Amir, Simcha Sadan and Michael Schiff. "Conditional Performance Review," **MA**, 1975, Vol. 57, No. 5, pp. 19-22.)

Sadan, Simcha. (Ronen, Joshua and Simcha Sadan. "Classificatory Smoothing: Alternative Income Models," JAR, 1975, Vol. 13, No. 1, pp. 133-149.)
Sadan, Simcha. (Ronen, Joshua and Simcha Sadan. "Accounting Classification As A Tool For Income Prediction," JAAF, 1980, Vol. 3, No. 4, pp. 339-353.)
Sadan, S. (Barnea, A. and S. Sadan. "On The Decomposition Of The Estimation Problem In Financial Accounting," JAR, 1974, Vol. 12, No. 1, pp. 197-203.)
Sadan, S. (Barnea, A., J. Ronen and S. Sadan. "The Implementation Of Accounting Objectives: An Application To Extraordinary Items," AR, 1975, Vol. 50, No. 1, pp. 58-68.)
Sadhwani, Arjan T. and Gardner M. Jones. "Accounting For The Carrying Charges On Land," MA, 1973, Vol. 54, No. 11, pp. 40-42.
Sadhwani, Arjan T. and M. H. Sarhan. "Electronic Systems Enhance JIT Operations," MA, 1987, Vol. 69, No. 6, pp. 25-30.
Sadhwani, Arjan T. (Tyson, Thomas and Arjan T. Sadhwani. "Bar Codes Speed Factory Floor Reporting," MA, 1988, Vol. 69, No. 10, pp. 41-46.)
Sadhwani, Arjan T., M. H. Sarhan and Dayal Kiringoda. "Just-In-Time: An Inventory System Whose Time Has Come," MA, 1985, Vol. 67, No. 6, pp. 36-44.
Sadler, Alton G. "Professional Accountants Library," AR, 1954, Vol. 29, No. 4, pp. 671-675.
Sadler, Alton S. "The Accounting Teacher Turns To Electronic Data Processing," AR, 1958, Vol. 33, No. 3, pp. 496-501.
Safran, Ronald A. (Wu, Frederick H. and Ronald A. Safran. "A Practical Approach For Evaluating EDP Controls," CPAJ, 1987, Vol. 57, No. 10, pp. 58-69.)
Saftner, Donald V. and Cherie J. O'Neil. "Early Withdrawals From Individual Retirement Accounts (IRAs) After The 1986 Tax Reform Act," JAPP, 1988, Vol. 7, No. 2, pp. 113-136.
Saftner, Donald V. "The Promotion Of Academic Accountants," JAED, 1988, Vol. 6, No. 1, pp. 55-66.
Saftner, Donald V. (O'Neil, Cherie J., Donald V. Saftner and Manson P. Dillaway. "Premature Withdrawals From Individual Retirement Accounts: A Breakeven Analysis," JATA, 1983, Vol. 4, No. 2, pp. 35-43.)
Saftner, Donald V. (O'Neil, Cherie J., Donald V. Saftner and M. Pete Dillaway. "Reply To Comment On Premature Withdrawals From Individual Retirement Accounts: A Breakeven Analysis'," JATA, 1984, Vol. 6, No. 1, pp. 77-80.)
Sager, William H. "Civil Tax Penalties," JOA, 1962, Vol. 114, No. 5, pp. 61-66.
Said, Kamal E. "A Goal-Oriented Budgetary Process," MA, 1975, Vol. 56, No. 7, pp. 31-36.
Said, Kamel E. and Jerry A. Funk. "Planning And Control In Accounting Education: A Model For Subsystem Controls In A Free Market Environment," IJAER, 1976, Vol. 11, No. 2, pp. 103-119.
St. Pierre, Kent and James Anderson. "An Analysis Of Audit Failures Based On Documented Legal Cases," JAAF, 1982, Vol. 5, No. 3, pp. 229-247.
St. Pierre, Kent and James A. Anderson. "An Analysis Of Factors Associated With Lawsuits Against Public Accountants," AR, 1984, Vol. 59, No. 2, pp. 242-263.
St. Pierre, Kent and James M. Reeve. "An Analysis Of Ernst & Ernst v. Hochfelder: Legal And Market Effects A Decade Latter," RIAR, 1987, Vol. 1, pp. 89-101.
St. Pierre, Kent E. (Anderson, James A. and Kent E. St. Pierre. "Market Efficiency And Legal Liability: A Reply," AR, 1983, Vol. 58, No. 4, pp. 833-836.)
St. Pierre, Kent. "Independence And Auditor Sanctions," JAAF, 1984, Vol. 7, No. 3, pp. 257-263.
Saito, Shizuki. "Asset Revaluation And Cost Basis: Capital Revaluation In Corporate Financial Reports," AHJ, 1983, Vol. 10, No. 1, pp. 1-23.
Salamon, Gerald L. "Cash Recovery Rates And Measures Of Firm Profitability," AR, 1982, Vol. 57, No. 2, pp. 292-302.
Salamon, Gerald L. "Models Of The Relationship Between The Accounting And Internal Rate Of Return: An Examination Of The Methodology," JAR, 1973, Vol. 11, No. 2, pp. 296-303.
Salamon, Gerald L. "On The Validity Of Accounting Rate Of Return In Cross-Sectional Analysis: Theory, Evidence, And Implications," JAPP, 1988, Vol. 7, No. 4, pp. 267-292.
Salamon, Gerald L. (Capettini, Robert and Gerald L. Salamon. "Internal Versus External Acquisition Of Services When Reciprocal Services Exist," AR, 1977, Vol. 52, No. 3, pp. 690-696.)
Salamon, Gerald L. (Kinney, William R., Jr. and Gerald L. Salamon. "Regression Analysis In Auditing: A Comparison Of Alternative Investigation Rules," JAR, 1982, Vol. 20, No. 2, Part I, pp. 350-366.)
Salamon, Gerald L. (Livingstone, John Leslie and Gerald L. Salamon. "Relationship Between The Accounting And The Internal Rate Of Return Measures: A Synthesis And An Analysis," JAR, 1970, Vol. 8, No. 2, pp. 199-216.)
Salamon, Gerald L, Wilfred C. Uecker and Richard Simmons. "Prediction Achievement And Simulated Decision Makers As An Extension Of The Predictive Ability Criterion: Some Comments," AR, 1976, Vol. 51, No. 3, pp. 664-665.
Salamon, Gerald. (Dhaliwal, Dan S., Gerald Salamon and E. Dan Smith. "The Effect Of Owner Versus Management Control On The Choice Of Accounting Methods," JAEC, 1982, Vol. 4, No. 1, pp. 41-53.)
Salas, Cesar A. "Accounting Education And Practice In

Spanish Latin America," IJAER, 1967, Vol. 3, No. 1, pp. 67-85.
Salatka, William K. (Collins, Daniel W., Michael S. Rozeff and William K. Salatka. "The SEC's Rejection Of SFAS No. 19: Tests Of Market Price Reversal," AR, 1982, Vol. 57, No. 1, pp. 1-17.)
Sale, J. Timothy and Robert W. Scapens. "The Control Of Capital Investment In Divisionalized Companies," MA, 1982. Vol. 64, No. 4, pp. 24-29.
Sale, J. Timothy and Robert W. Scapens. "Current Cost Accounting As A Surrogate For Dividend Paying Ability," ABR, 1977-78, Vol. 8, No. 31, pp. 208-216.
Sale, J. Timothy. "Using Computerized Budget Simulation Models As A Teaching Device," AR, 1972, Vol. 47, No. 4, pp. 836-839.
Sale, J. Timothy. (Scapens, Robert W. and J. Timothy Sale. "An International Study Of Accounting Practices In Divisionalized Companies And Their Associations With Organizational Variables," AR, 1985, Vol. 60, No. 2, pp. 231-247.)
Sale, J. Timothy. (Walter, Herbert E., II and J. Timothy Sale. "Financial Reporting: A Two-Perspective Issue," MA, 1981, Vol. 62, No. 12, pp. 32-37.)
Sale, Timothy J. and Karen B. Carroll. "Tax Planning Tools For The Multinational Corporation," MA, 1979, Vol. 60, No. 12, pp. 37-42.
Salgado, Ignacio Perez. "Accounting Reports In Chile," AR, 1963, Vol. 38, No. 2, pp. 389-397.
Saliers, Earl A. "An Accounting Curriculum," AR, 1933, Vol. 8, No. 2, pp. 159-160.
Saliers, Earl A. "Notes On The Contrasting Concepts Of Accounting And Economics," AR, 1941, Vol. 16, No. 3, pp. 296-301.
Saliers, Earl A. "The Louisiana Civil Code," AR, 1931, Vol. 6, No. 4, pp. 294-297.
Saliers, Earl A. "Theory Of Repairs, Maintenance, And Betterments," AR, 1943, Vol. 18, No. 3, pp. 259-261.
Saliers, E. A. "Differential Costs," AR, 1943, Vol. 18, No. 4, pp. 338-339.
Saliers, E. A. "Foreign Exchange Accounting," AR, 1944, Vol. 19, No. 4, pp. 377-380.
Saliers, E. A. "Inadequate Depreciation Methods," AR, 1937, Vol. 12, No. 3, pp. 303-306.
Salmi, Timo. (Kistner, Klaus-Peter and Timo Salmi. "General Price Level Accounting And Inventory Valuation: A Comment," JAR, 1980, Vol. 18, No. 1, pp. 297-311.)
Salmonson, R. F. "A Prophetic Analogy?," AR, 1962, Vol. 37, No. 3, pp. 502-505.
Salmonson, R. F. "CPA's Negligence, Third Parties And The Future," AR, 1959, Vol. 34, No. 1, pp. 91-96.
Salmonson, R. F. "Qualifications For College Accounting Teachers: A Rebuttal," AR, 1957, Vol. 32, No. 4, pp. 622-624.
Salmonson, R. F. "Reporting Earnings After An Acquisition," JOA, 1964, Vol. 117, No. 3, pp. 51-54.
Salmonson, R. F. "Third Party Actions Against Accountants," AR, 1957, Vol. 32, No. 3, pp. 389-394.
Salowe, William. (Matusiak, Louis W. and William Salowe. "Mr. CPA, How Good An Executive Are You?," JOA, 1964, Vol. 118, No. 3, pp. 44-50.)
Salter, John H. and Marilyn P. Salter. "A Volunteer Treasurer's Survival Guide," MA, 1983, Vol. 64, No. 8, pp. 46-51.
Salter, Marilyn P. (Salter, John H. and Marilyn P. Salter. "A Volunteer Treasurer's Survival Guide," MA, 1983, Vol. 64, No. 8, pp. 46-51.)
Sami, Heibatollah and Jerry E. Trapnell. "Inflation-Adjusted Data And Security Prices: Some Empirical Evidence," AIA, 1987, Vol. 5, pp. 39-58.
Sami, Heibatollah. (Fields, Kent T., Heibatollah Sami and Glenn E. Sumners. "Quantification Of The Auditor's Evaluation Of Internal Control In Data Base Systems," JIS, 1986, Vol. 1, No. 1, pp. 24-47.)
Sampson, Clarence. "Facilitations Of Multinational Securities Offerings," RIAR, 1988, Vol. 2, pp. 207-218.
Sampson, William D. (Robbins, Walter A. and William D. Sampson. "Auditing Federally Assisted Programs," CPAJ, 1985, Vol. 55, No. 9, pp. 12-25.)
Samson, Thomas F. "Computer Auditing," CPAJ, 1974, Vol. 44, No. 4, pp. 67-74.
Samson, William D. and Edward J. Schnee. "Tax Planning: Damage And Injury Payments," CPAJ, 1986, Vol. 56, No. 5, pp. 24-33.
Samson, William D. "The Accountant As Hero," MA, 1988, Vol. 70, No. 1, pp. 40-42.
Samson, William D. "The Nineteenth Century Income Tax In The South," AHJ, 1985, Vol. 12, No. 1, pp. 37-52.
Samson, William D. (Orbach, Kenneth N. and William D. Samson. "An Open Letter To Congress: Leasing Little Lisa," MA, 1983, Vol. 64, No. 9, pp. 46-47.)
Samuels, John. (Manes, Rene P., John Samuels and D. J. Smyth. "Inventories And Sales: A Cross Section Study," JAR, 1967, Vol. 5, Supp., pp. 139-156.)
Samuels, J. M. and J. C. Oliga. "Accounting Standards In Developing Countries," IJAER, 1982, Vol. 18, No. 1, pp. 69-88.
Samuels, J. M. "Opportunity Costing: An Application Of Mathematical Programming," JAR, 1965, Vol. 3, No. 2, pp. 182-191.
Samuels, J. M. "The 1904 Congress Of Accountants: National Or International?," AHJ, 1985, Vol. 12, No. 1, pp. 99-105.
Samuelson, A. T. "Accounting Vs. Federal Regulation - Is There An Emerging Discipline?," MA, 1965, Vol. 47, No. 2, pp. 14-21.

Samuelson, A. T. "Depreciation Of Federal Water Resources Projects," **JOA**, 1962, Vol. 113, No. 3, pp. 43-48.

Samuelson, A. T. "The New Postal Service: A Managerial Challenge," **MA**, 1972, Vol. 53, No. 12, pp. 11-13.

Samuelson, Bruce A. and Brock Murdoch. "The Information Content Of General Price Level Adjusted Earnings: A Comment," **AR**, 1985, Vol. 60, No. 4, pp. 706-710.

Samuelson, Bruce. (Kinsman, Michael D. and Bruce Samuelson. "Personal Financial Statements: Valuation Challenges And Solutions," **JOA**, 1987, Vol. 164, No. 3, pp. 138-150.)

Samuelson, L. A. "Discrepancies Between The Roles Of Budgeting," **AOS**, 1986, Vol. 11. No. 1, pp. 35-46.

Samuelson, Richard A. "Estimating The Replacement Cost Of Inventories And Cost Of Sales," **MA**, 1977, Vol. 58, No. 9, pp. 29-32.

Samuelson, Richard A. "Prediction And Price-Level Adjustment," **JAR**, 1972, Vol. 10, No. 2, pp. 322-344.

Samuelson, Richard A. "Should Replacement-Cost Changes Be Included In Income?," **AR**, 1980, Vol. 55, No. 2, pp. 254-268.

Samuelson, John L. "Simplified Employee Pensions," **MA**, 1988, Vol. 70, No. 3, pp. 29-31.

San Miguel, Joseph G. "The Reliability Of R&D Data In COMPUSTAT And 10-K Reports," **AR**, 1977, Vol. 52, No. 3, pp. 638-641.

San Miguel, J. G. and V. Govindarajan. "The Contingent Relationship Between The Controller And Internal Audit Functions In Large Organizations," **AOS**, 1984, Vol. 9, No. 2, pp. 179-188.

San Miguel, J. G. "Human Information Processing And Its Relevance To Accounting: A Laboratory Study," **AOS**, 1976, Vol. 1, No. 4, pp. 357-374.

San Miguel, J. G. "The Behavioral Sciences And Concepts And Standards For Management Planning And Control," **AOS**, 1977, Vol. 2, No. 2, pp. 177-186.

San Miguel, J. G., J. K. Shank and V. Govindarajan. "Extending Corporate Accountability: A Survey And Framework For Analysis," **AOS**, 1977, Vol. 2, No. 4, pp. 333-348.

Sanborn, Robert H. "An Evaluation And Critique Of The Changes Provided By Statement Of Financial Accounting Concepts No. 6," **ACCHOR**, 1987, Vol. 1, No. 3, pp. 41-48.

Sanborn, Robert H. (Maloney, David M. and Robert H. Sanborn. "Interactions Between Financial And Tax Accounting Caused By The Tax Reform Act Of 1986," **AH**, 1988, Vol. 2, No. 4, pp. 21-28.)

Sanborn, Robert. (Atchison, Michael D. and Robert Sanborn. "Current Classification Criteria Of New Financial Instruments," **AIA**, 1987, Vol. 5, pp. 99-112.)

Sandberg, A. (Carlsson, J., P. Ehn, B. Erlander, M. L. Perby and A. Sandberg. "Planning And Control From The Perspective Of Labour: A Short Presentation Of The DEMOS Project," **AOS**, 1978, Vol. 3, No. 3/4, pp. 249-260.)

Sandberg, E. L. "Premature Retirement Of Bonds Outstanding - Adjustment Of Unamortized Bond Expense," **AR**, 1932, Vol. 7, No. 1, pp. 68-70.

Sandbulte, Arend J. "Sales And Revenue Forecasting," **MA**, 1969, Vol. 51, No. 6, pp. 17-23.

Sanderbeck, Adrian F. "Advice For The New Partner," **JOA**, 1951, Vol. 91, No. 3, pp. 408-410.

Sanders, Debra L. and Robert W. Wyndelts. "An Examination Of Tax Practitioners' Decisions Under Uncertainty," **AIT**, 1988, Vol. 2, pp. xx-xx.

Sanders, Debra L. (Raabe, William A., Robert M. Kozub and Debra L. Sanders. "Attitude Measurement And The Perceptions Of Tax Accounting Faculty Publications Outlets," **JAED**, 1987, Vol. 5, No. 1, pp. 45-57.)

Sanders, Howard P. (Edwards, James B., Robert W. Ingram and Howard P. Sanders. "Developing Teaching Skills In Doctoral Programs: The Current Status And Perceived Needs," **AR**, 1981, Vol. 56, No. 1, pp. 144-157.)

Sanders, Thomas Henry. "An Analysis Of The Forces Which Are Shaping The Future Of Accountancy," **JOA**, 1950, Vol. 90, No. 4, pp. 282-289.

Sanders, T. H. "Accounting Research: Objectives And Methods," **AR**, 1940, Vol. 15, No. 1, pp. 77-88.

Sanders, T. H. "Comments On The Statement Of Accounting Principles," **AR**, 1937, Vol. 12. No. 1, pp. 76-79.

Sanders, T. H. "Influence Of The Securities And Exchange Commission Upon Accounting Principles," **AR**, 1936, Vol. 11, No. 1, pp. 66-73.

Sanders, T. H. "Reports To Stockholders," **AR**, 1934, Vol. 9, No. 3, pp. 201-219.

Sanders, T. H. "The Development Of Accounting Principles," **AR**, 1935, Vol. 10, No. 1, pp. 100-102.

Sanders, T. H. "The Uses Of Differential Costs," **AR**, 1929, Vol. 4, No. 1, pp. 9-15.

Sanders, W. L., Jr. (Schuchart, J. A. and W. L. Sanders, Jr. "Pension Fund Consideration," **MA**, 1972, Vol. 53, No. 9, pp. 49-54.)

Sanderson, George N. (McCabe, George M. and George N. Sanderson. "Abandonment Value In Capital Budgeting: Another View," **MA**, 1984, Vol. 65, No. 7, pp. 32-36.)

Sanderson, Glen R. and Iris I. Varner. "What's Wrong With Corporate Codes Of Conduct?," **MA**, 1984, Vol. 66, No. 1, pp. 28-31.

Sandford, Cedric. (Godwin, Michael and Cedric Sandford. "Simplifying VAT For Small Traders," **ABR**, 1982-83, Vol. 13, No. 52, pp. 279-288.)

Sandford, C. T. and P. N. Dean. "Accountants And The Tax System," **ABR**, 1971-72, Vol. 2, No. 5, pp. 3-37.

Sandford, C. T., J. R. M. Willis and D. J. Ironside. "An Accessions Tax The Problem Of Trusts," **ABR**, 1972-73, Vol. 3, No. 12, pp. 263-281.

Sandler, Irving J. "Plain Talk About Auditing In An ADPS Environment," **JOA**, 1968, Vol. 125, No. 4, pp. 43-47.

Sandman, Stewart. (Wolitzer, Philip and Stewart Sandman. "Bridges Between Accounting Educators And Practitioners," **CPAJ**, 1976, Vol. 46, No. 8, pp. 23-25.)

Sands, J. E. "Deferred Tax Credits Are Liabilities," **AR**, 1959, Vol. 34, No. 4, pp. 584-590.

Sandstrom, Scott. "Tax Strategies In Planning For College Costs," **CPAJ**, 1986, Vol. 56, No. 3, pp. 24-29.

Sangeladji, Mohammad A. "Effect Of Different Cost Behaviors On 'EOQ' (Economic Order Quantity): Practice Note," **AIA**, 1984, Vol. 1, pp. 75-88.

Sangeladji, Mohammad A. "Human Resource Accounting: A Refined Measurement Model," **MA**, 1977, Vol. 59, No. 6, pp. 48-52.

Sangeladji, Mohammad A. "True Rate Of Return For Evaluating Capital Investments," **MA**, 1979, Vol. 60, No. 8, pp. 24-28.

Sangster, John M. (Burns, Joseph S., Robert K. Jaedicke and John M. Sangster. "Financial Reporting Of Purchase Contracts Used To Guarantee Large Investments," **AR**, 1963. Vol. 38, No. 1, pp. 1-13.)

Saniga, Erwin M. (Hayya, J. C., W. L. Ferrara and Erwin M. Saniga. "On The Accuracy Of Normalcy Approximation In Stochastic C-V-P Analysis: A Reply," **AR**, 1978, Vol. 53, No. 1, pp. 252-259.)

Saniga, Erwin. (Hayya, Jack, William Ferrara and Erwin Saniga. "Extending The Applicability Of Probabilistic Management Planning And Control Models: A Comment," **AR**, 1975, Vol. 50, No. 4, pp. 826-831.)

Sannella, Alexander J. "An Application Of Income Strategy To Cost Allocation And Segment Reporting," **JAAF**, 1986, Vol. 1 (New Series), No. 4, pp. 288-304.

Santocki, J. "Meaning And Scope Of Management Audit," **ABR**, 1976-77, Vol. 7, No. 25, pp. 64-70.

Sapienza, Samuel R. "Admission To Graduate Business School," **AR**, 1959, Vol. 34, No. 1, pp. 30-35.

Sapienza, Samuel R. "An Examination Of AICPA Research Study No. 5 - Standards For Pooling," **AR**, 1964, Vol. 39, No. 3. pp. 582-590.

Sapienza, Samuel R. "Business Combinations And Enterprise Evaluation," **JAR**, 1964, Vol. 2, No. 1, pp. 50-66.

Sapienza, Samuel R. "Business Combinations - A Case Study," **AR**, 1963, Vol. 38, No. 1, pp. 91-101.

Sapienza, Samuel R. "Distinguishing Between Purchase And Pooling," **JOA**, 1961, Vol. 111, No. 6, pp. 35-40.

Sapienza, Samuel R. "Pooling Theory And Practice In Business Combinations," **AR**, 1962, Vol. 37, No. 2, pp. 263-278.

Sapienza, S. R. "The Divided House Of Consolidations," **AR**, 1960, Vol. 35, No. 3, pp. 503-510.

Sapp, Richard W. and Robert E. Seiler. "Accounting For Performance: Stressful - But Satisfying," **MA**, 1980, Vol. 62, No. 2, pp. 29-35.

Sapp, Richard W. (Leavitt, Gary S. and Richard W. Sapp. "Who's Minding The Store?: Inventory Control For Bars And Clubs," **MA**, 1980, Vol. 62, No. 5, pp. 13-24.)

Sapp, Richard W. (Seiler, Robert E. and Richard W. Sapp. "Just How Satisfied Are Accountants With Their Jobs?," **MA**, 1979, Vol. 60, No. 9, pp. 18-21.)

Sappington, David E. M. (Demski, Joel S. and David E. M. Sappington. "Line-Item Reporting, Factor Acquisition, And Subcontracting," **JAR**, 1986, Vol. 24, No. 2, pp. 250-269.)

Sappington, David E. M. (Demski, Joel S. and David E. M. Sappington. "Delegated Expertise," **JAR**, 1987, Vol. 25, No. 1, pp. 68-89.)

Sarabia, Antonio R. "The European Common Market," **JOA**, 1963, Vol. 115, No. 5, pp. 54-58.

Sardinas, Joseph L., Jr. and Susan Merrill. "Regulation Of International Data Communications And The Effect Upon Multinational Corporations," **AIIA**, 1987, Vol. 1, pp. 305-315.

Sarell, Moshe. (Aranya, Nissim and Moshe Sarell. "The Auditor-Firm Conflict Of Interests: A Comment," **AR**, 1975, Vol. 50, No. 4, pp. 854-856.)

Sargent, Arthur M. "Referrals," **JOA**, 1963, Vol. 116, No. 1, pp. 40-45.

Sargent, Arthur M. "Successful Meetings And Conferences," **JOA**, 1959, Vol. 107, No. 6, pp. 41-44.

Sargent, Arthur M. "There Is No Mystery," **AR**, 1952, Vol. 27. No. 3, pp. 292-297.

Sarhan, M. H. (Sadhwani, Arjan T. and M. H. Sarhan. "Electronic Systems Enhance JIT Operations," **MA**, 1987, Vol. 69, No. 6, pp. 25-30.)

Sarhan, M. H. (Sadhwani, Arjan T., M. H. Sarhan and Dayal Kiringoda. "Just-In-Time: An Inventory System Whose Time Has Come," **MA**, 1985, Vol. 67, No. 6, pp. 36-44.)

Sartain, Kenneth C. "The Competence Of Microfilmed Audit Evidence," **CPAJ**, 1981, Vol. 51, No. 6, pp. 15-20.

Sartoris, William. "Transfer Pricing In A Commercial Bank," **MA**, 1971, Vol. 52, No. 8, pp. 33-34.

Sasaki, Harold D. "Planning And Controlling Research Development Costs," **MA**, 1969, Vol. 50, No. 9, pp. 44-50.

Sathe, V. "The Relevance Of Modern Organization Theory For Managerial Accounting," **AOS**, 1978, Vol. 3, No. 1, pp. 89-92.

Satubaldin, Sagandyk. "Methods Of Analyzing Profits Of Industrial Enterprises In the USSR," **IJAER**, 1976, Vol. 12. No. 1, pp. 91-99.

Sauers, Dale G. "Analyzing Inventory Systems," **MA**, 1986, Vol. 67, No. 11, pp. 30-36.

Sauer, John R. "Psychology And Accounting: The Odd Couple?," **MA**, 1980, Vol. 62, No. 2, pp. 14-17.

Sauls, Eugene H. "An Experiment On Nonsampling Errors," **JAR**, 1970, Vol. 8, Supp., pp. 157-171.

Sauls, Eugene H. (Holstrum, Gary L. and Eugene H. Sauls. "The Opportunity Cost Transfer Price," **MA**, 1973, Vol. 54, No. 11, pp. 29-33.)

Sauls, Eugene. "Nonsampling Errors In Accounts Receivable Confirmation," **AR**, 1972, Vol. 47, No. 1, pp. 109-115.

Saunders, Gary. (Reider, Barbara and Gary Saunders. "Management Accounting Education: A Defense Of Criticisms," **AH**, 1988, Vol. 2, No. 4, pp. 58-62.)

Sautter, William L. "Product Warranty," **MA**, 1967, Vol. 48, No. 10, pp. 55-58.

Sautter, William L. "Projected Cash Needs," **MA**, 1971, Vol. 52, No. 8, pp. 11-16.

Savage, Allan H. "Management Accounting In Mexico," **MA**, 1969, Vol. 50, No. 4, pp. 45-51.

Savage, Charles L. "Review Of APB Opinion No. 28 - 'Early Extinguishment Of Debt'," **CPAJ**, 1973, Vol. 43, No. 4, pp. 283-285.

Savage, James B. (Klingler, John P. and James B. Savage. "Deciphering The New Accounting For Income Tax Rules," **MA**, 1988, Vol. 70, No. 2, pp. 32-38.)

Savage, Linda and Joel Siegel. "Disposal Of A Segment Of A Business," **CPAJ**, 1978, Vol. 48, No. 9, pp. 32-37.

Savich, Richard S. "Organizing Audits In EDP Environments," **CPAJ**, 1980, Vol. 50, No. 8, pp. 22-28.

Savich, Richard S. "The Use Of Accounting Information In Decision Making," **AR**, 1977, Vol. 52, No. 3, pp. 642-652.

Savich, Richard S. (Crumbley, D. Larry and Richard S. Savich. "Use Of Human Resource Accounting In Taxation," **AR**, 1975, Vol. 50, No. 1, pp. 112-117.)

Savich, Richard S. (Grove, Hugh D. and Richard S. Savich. "Attitude Research In Accounting: A Model For Reliability And Validity Considerations," **AR**, 1979, Vol. 54, No. 3, pp. 522-537.)

Savidge, David F. "Analysis And Measurement Of Administrative Work - A Case Study," **MA**, 1966, Vol. 47, No. 7, pp. 41-50.

Savoie, Leonard M. "Controversy Over Accounting Principles Board Opinions," **JOA**, 1968, Vol. 125, No. 1, pp. 37-41.

Savoie, Leonard M. "Financial And Accounting Aspects In International Business," **IJAER**, 1973, Vol. 9, No. 1, pp. 13-22.

Savoie, Leonard M. "International Dimensions Of Accounting," **IJAER**, 1969, Vol. 5, No. 1, pp. 79-84.

Savoie, Leonard M. "Price-Level Accounting, Practical Politics, And Tax Relief," **MA**, 1977, Vol. 58, No. 7, pp. 15-18.

Savoie, Leonard M. "Raising Accounting Standards," **JAR**, 1969, Vol. 7, Supp., pp. 55-62.

Sawyer, Albert E. "Accounting And Distribution Techniques As Voluntary Devices To Eliminate Abuses In Marketing," **AR**, 1939, Vol. 14, No. 2, pp. 108-116.

Sawyer, John D. "Proposed Treasury Regs. On Tax Shelter Opinions," **CPAJ**, 1981, Vol. 51, No. 4, pp. 25-29.

Sawyer, Lawrence B. "Modern Internal Auditing - The New Profession," **AR**, 1975, Vol. 50, No. 1, pp. 176-178.

Sax, Franklin S. "The Lease-Or-Purchase Decision - Present Value Method," **MA**, 1965, Vol. 47, No. 2, pp. 55-61.

Saxe, Emanuel. "An Interesting Problem In Estate Tax Apportionment," **CPAJ**, 1974, Vol. 44, No. 10, pp. 51-53.

Saxe, Emanuel. "Education For Public Accountancy," **AR**, 1947, Vol. 22, No. 1, pp. 28-35.

Saxe, Emanuel. "Retain The Present Auditor's Standard Report," **CPAJ**, 1981, Vol. 51, No. 4, pp. 19-24.

Saxe, Emanuel. "Some Notes On The Teaching Of A Course In Estate And Trust Accounting," **AR**, 1948, Vol. 23, No. 1, pp. 93-96.

Saxe, Emanuel. "Unaudited Financial Statements: Rules, Risks And Recommendations," **CPAJ**, 1972, Vol. 42, No. 6, pp. 457-464.

Sayers, David L. (Deitrick, James W., C. Wayne Alderman and David L. Sayers. "A Profile Of An Accounting Doctoral Program: A Study Of Recent Graduates," **AIA**, 1985, Vol. 2, pp. 69-88.)

Scally, Jerome V. "Successful Management In Transportation Planning And Control," **MA**, 1966, Vol. 48, No. 3, pp. 32-45.

Scapens, Robert W. and J. Timothy Sale. "An International Study Of Accounting Practices In Divisionalized Companies And Their Associations With Organizational Variables," **AR**, 1985, Vol. 60, No. 2, pp. 231-247.

Scapens, Robert W. "A Neoclassical Measure Of Profit," **AR**, 1978, Vol. 53, No. 2, pp. 448-469.

Scapens, Robert W. (Rahman, M. Zubaidur and Robert W. Scapens. "Financial Reporting By Multinational Enterprises: Accounting Policy Choice In A Developing Country," **JAPP**, 1988, Vol. 7, No. 1, pp. 29-42.)

Scapens, Robert W. (Sale, J. Timothy and Robert W. Scapens. "Current Cost Accounting As A Surrogate For Dividend Paying Ability," **ABR**, 1977-78, Vol. 8, No. 31, pp. 208-216.)

Scapens, Robert W. (Sale, J. Timothy and Robert W. Scapens. "The Control Of Capital Investment In Divisionalized Companies," **MA**, 1982, Vol. 64, No. 4, pp. 24-29.)

Scapens, R. W. (Carsberg, Bryan, Anthony Hope and R. W. Scapens. "The Objectives Of Published Accounting Reports: Reply To A Comment," **ABR**, 1974-75, Vol. 5, No. 18, pp. 152-155.)

Scapens, R. (Roberts, J. and R. Scapens. "Accounting Systems And Systems Of Accountability - Understanding Accounting Practices In Their Organisational Contexts," **AOS**, 1985, Vol. 10, No. 4, pp. 443-456.)

Scapens, R. W. (Carsberg, Bryan, Anthony Hope and R. W. Scapens. "The Objectives Of Published Accounting Reports," **ABR**, 1973-74, Vol. 4, No. 15, pp. 162-173.)

Scarpo, Joseph A., Jr. "Auto Dealers Lag In Transfer Pricing," **MA**, 1984, Vol. 66, No. 1, pp. 54-56.

Schachner, Leopold. "Accountability Under Industrial Diversification," **AR**, 1968, Vol. 43, No. 2, pp. 303-311.

Schachner, Leopold. "An Accounting For Cost Of Equity Capital," **CPAJ**, 1975, Vol. 45, No. 12, pp. 13-17.

Schachner, Leopold. "Corporate Diversification And Financial Reporting," **JOA**, 1967, Vol. 123, No. 4, pp. 43-50.

Schachner, Leopold. "Efficiency, Earnings And Equity Capital," **CPAJ**, 1978, Vol. 48, No. 1, pp. 29-34.

Schachner, Leopold. "Published Forecasts And Internal Budgets," **CPAJ**, 1975, Vol. 45, No. 1, pp. 19-24.

Schachner, Leopold. "Return On Investment - Its Values, Determination And Uses," **CPAJ**, 1973, Vol. 43, No. 4, pp. 277-282.

Schachner, Leopold. "Segmental Reporting," **CPAJ**, 1977, Vol. 47, No. 8, pp. 15-22.

Schachter, Barry. "Open Interest And Consensus Among Investors," **JAR**, 1985, Vol. 23, No. 2, pp. 907-910.

Schachter, Barry. "Open Interest In Stock Options Around Quarterly Earnings Announcements," **JAR**, 1988, Vol. 26, No. 2, pp. 353-372.

Schackne, Stewart. "Incorporating Accounting Practices: Good Idea? Bad Idea?," **JOA**, 1968, Vol. 126, No. 6, pp. 33-39.

Schadewald, Michael S. (Marchant, Garry, John R. Robinson, Urton Anderson and Michael S. Schadewald. "A Cognitive Model Of Tax Problem Solving," **AIT**, 1988, Vol. 2, pp. xx-xx.)

Schaefer, Carl L., Jr. "Lifo - Tax Conformity And Report Disclosure Problems," **JOA**, 1976, Vol. 141, No. 1, pp. 52-55.

Schaefer, Hadley P. "Comments On The Audits Of School Districts," **AR**, 1957, Vol. 32, No. 3, pp. 428-430.

Schaefer, Hadley P. "The Distribution Cost Problem," **AR**, 1958, Vol. 33, No. 4, pp. 625-631.

Schaefer, Thomas and Michael Kennelley. "Alternative Cash Flow Measures And Risk-Adjusted Returns," **JAAF**, 1986, Vol. 1 (New Series), No. 4, pp. 278-287.

Schaefer, Thomas F. "Microcomputer Sensitivity Analyses For Business Combinations," **JAED**, 1987, Vol. 5, No. 2, pp. 297-306.

Schaefer, Thomas F. (Christie, Andrew A., Michael D. Kennelley, J. William King and Thomas F. Schaefer. "Testing For Incremental Information Content In The Presence Of Collinearity," **JAEC**, 1984, Vol. 6, No. 3, pp. 205-217.)

Schaefer, Thomas F. (Hopwood, William S. and Thomas F. Schaefer. "Incremental Information Content Of Earnings And Nonearnings Based Financial Ratios," **CAR**, 1988, Vol. 5, No. 1, pp. 318-342.)

Schaefer, Thomas F. (Manes, Rene P. and Thomas F. Schaefer. "Relating Financial Leverage To Annual Report Ratios," **IAE**, 1986, Vol. 1, No. 2, pp. 261-267.)

Schaefer, T. F. "The Information Content Of Current Cost Income Relative To Dividends And Historical Cost Income," **JAR**, 1984, Vol. 22, No. 2, pp. 647-656.

Schafer, Eldon L. (Raymond, Robert H., M. Zafar Iqbal and Eldon L. Schafer. "The Gearing (Leverage) Adjustment: A Historical And Comparative Analysis," **IJAER**, 1982, Vol. 18, No. 1, pp. 139-157.)

Schaffer, Walter L. "Accounting Procedures & Methods Under The New Revenue Code," **JOA**, 1954, Vol. 98, No. 3, pp. 320-327.

Schaffer, Walter L. "Audits Of Insurance Companies," **JOA**, 1960, Vol. 109, No. 3, pp. 44-50.

Schall, Lawrence D. and Gary L. Sundem. "The Investment Tax Credit And The Leasing Industry," **JAPP**, 1982, Vol. 1, No. 2, pp. 83-94.

Schaller, Caral A. (Blankenship, Ronald C. and Carol A. Schaller. "The CPA, The Small Company And The Computer," **JOA**, 1976, Vol. 142, No. 2, pp. 46-51.)

Schaller, Carol A. "The Revolution Of EFTS," **JOA**, 1978, Vol. 146, No. 4, pp. 74-80.

Schaller, Howard G. "Thailand: NIDA - An Experiment In Management In The Public And Private Sectors," **IJAER**, 1968, Vol. 4, No. 1, pp. 137-139.

Schallman, George C. "Franchisee Accounting - A Specialization Overlooked By CPAs," **CPAJ**, 1977, Vol. 47, No. 9, pp. 19-26.

Schanz, William. "Financial Pitfalls In International Operations," **MA**, 1969, Vol. 50, No. 8, pp. 43-46.

Schapper, Henry P. (Mauldon, R. G., Henry P. Schapper and D. W. G. Treloar. "A Managerial Accounting System For Australian Agriculture," **ABACUS**, 1968, Vol. 4, No. 1, pp. 39-50.)

Schaps, Albert L., Warren Kissin, Jay Borow and Lynda Atanian. "Auditing Small Businesses - A New Look," **CPAJ**, 1984, Vol. 54, No. 10, pp. 12-23.

Scharff, Alan L. (Greiner, Larry E. and Alan L. Scharff. "The Challenge Of Cultivating Accounting Firm Executives," **JOA**, 1980, Vol. 150, No. 3, pp. 57-63.)

Schattke, Rudolph. "Accounting For Computer Software: The Revenue Side Of The Coin," **JOA**, 1988, Vol. 165, No. 1, pp. 58-70.

Schattke, Rudy and LeRay McAllister. "Large Versus Small Classes In Elementary Accounting," **AR**, 1962, Vol. 37, No. 3, pp. 557-561.

Schattke, Rudy. "Expected Income - A Reporting Challenge," **AR**, 1962, Vol. 37, No. 4, pp. 670-676.

Schattke, R. W. "Accounting Principles Board Statement 4 - Promise For The Future," **CPAJ**, 1972, Vol. 42, No. 7, pp. 552-556.

Schattke, R. W. "An Analysis Of Accounting Principles Board Statement No. 4," **AR**, 1972, Vol. 47, No. 2, pp. 233-244.

Schattke, R. W. "Financial Reporting Of Antitrust Actions,"

AR, 1965, Vol. 40, No. 4, pp. 805-811.

Schattke, R. W. (Larson, Kermit and R. W. Schattke. "Current Cash Equivalent, Additivity, And Financial Action," **AR**, 1966, Vol. 41, No. 4, pp. 634-641.)

Schattke, R. W. (Larson, Kermit D. and R. W. Schattke. "A Note On Vickrey's Comment," **AR**, 1975, Vol. 50, No. 1, p. 147.)

Schattke, R. W. (Rogers, Donald R. and R. W. Schattke. "Buy-Outs Of Stock Options: Compensation Or Capital?," **JOA**, 1972, Vol. 134, No. 2, pp. 55-59.)

Schatzberg, Jeffrey. (Smith, Vernon L., Jeffrey Schatzberg and William S. Waller. "Experimental Economics And Auditing," **AJPT**, 1987-88, Vol. 7, No. 1, pp. 71-93.)

Schatz, William H. (Seifried, Jerome F. and William H. Schatz. "Accounting Control Of Government Contract And Commercial Program Activity," **MA**, 1970, Vol. 51, No. 9, pp. 38-44.)

Scheer, Martha S. and Edward J. Gac. "New Problems For The Unwary In Estate And Gift Tax Valuations: Penalties Under I.R.C. 6660," **ACCHOR**, 1987, Vol. 1, No. 4, pp. 69-78.

Scheiner, James H. and Jack E. Kiger. "An Empirical Investigation Of Auditor Involvement In Non-Audit Services." **JAR**, 1982, Vol. 20, No. 2, Part I, pp. 482-496.

Scheiner, James H. and Jack E. Kiger. "Generalized Audit Software: A Classroom Approach," **IAE**, 1983, No. 1, pp. 123-131.

Scheiner, James H. "An Empirical Assessment Of The Impact Of SEC Nonaudit Service Disclosure Requirements On Independent Auditors And Their Clients," **JAR**, 1984, Vol. 22, No. 2, pp. 789-797.

Scheiner, James H. (Borthick, A. Faye and James H. Scheiner. "Selection Of Small Business Computer Systems: Structuring A Multi-Criteria Approach," **JIS**, 1988, Vol. 3, No. 1, pp. 10-29.)

Scheiner, James H. (Gavin, Thomas A., Rebecca L. Hicks and James H. Scheiner. "Auditors' Common Law Liability: What We Should Be Telling Our Students," **JAED**, 1987, Vol. 5, No. 1, pp. 1-12.)

Scheiner, James H. (Hughes, John S. and James H. Scheiner. "Efficiency Properties Of Mutually Satisfactory Cost Allocations," **AR**, 1980, Vol. 55, No. 1, pp. 85-95.)

Scheiner, James H. (Morse, Wayne J. and James H. Scheiner. "Cost Minimisation, Return On Investment, Residual Income: Alternative Criteria For Inventory Models," **ABR**, 1978-79, Vol. 9, No. 36, pp. 320-324.)

Scheiner, J. H. (Chesley, G. R. and J. H. Scheiner. "The Statement Of Changes In Financial Position: An Empirical Investigation Of Canadian And U.S. Users In Nonpublic Companies," **IJAER**, 1982, Vol. 17, No. 2, pp. 49-58.)

Schell, Wayne M. and Lawrence Keiser. "Digesting The Passive Activity Rules," **CPAJ**, 1988, Vol. 58, No. 8, pp. 46-55.

Schenk, Ronald J. "Interim Financial Statements For Contractors: A Case Study," **MA**, 1976, Vol. 58, No. 3, pp. 15-18.

Schepanski, Albert A. "Test Of Theories Of Information Processing Behavior In Credit Judgment," **AR**, 1983, Vol. 58, No. 3, pp. 581-599.

Schepanski, Albert A. (Dhaliwal, Dan S. and Albert A. Schepanski. "On The Use Of Positive Economic Theory To Explain The Choice Of Accounting Methods To Financial Accounting Students," **JAED**, 1984, Vol. 2, No. 2, pp. 89-96.)

Schepanski, Albert and Wilfred Uecker. "Toward A Positive Theory Of Information Evaluation," **AR**, 1983, Vol. 58, No. 2, pp. 259-283.

Schepanski, Albert S. (Madeo, Silvia A., Albert S. Schepanski and Wilfred C. Uecker. "Modeling Judgments Of Taxpayer Compliance," **AR**, 1987, Vol. 62, No. 2, pp. 323-342.)

Schepanski, Albert. (Uecker, Wilfred, Albert Schepanski and Joon Shin. "Toward A Positive Theory Of Information Evaluation: Relevant Tests Of Competing Models In a Principal-Agency Setting," **AR**, 1985, Vol. 60, No. 3, pp. 430-457.)

Scheps, Philip B. (Whitmire, Kathryn J. and Philip B. Scheps. "Municipal Pension Plans: The Long Road Back To Financial Soundness," **MA**, 1979, Vol. 61, No. 4, pp. 30-33.)

Scher, Marvin. (Allen, James L. and Marvin Scher. "Risk Analysis For Nonmathematicians," **MA**, 1979, Vol. 61, No. 4, pp. 55-58.)

Scheurer, William J. (Glenn, Neil B. and William J. Scheurer. "Examining The Debate Over Tax Credits," **JOA**, 1970, Vol. 130, No. 3, pp. 63-66.)

Schick, Allen G. and Peter Lorenzi. "Bureaucratic And Political Models Of The University Budgetary Process: Consensus On Departmental Merit," **RIGNA**, 1986, Vol. 2, pp. 191-211.

Schick, A. G. (Gordon, L. A., S. Haka and A. G. Schick. "Strategies For Information Systems Implementation: The Case Of Zero Base Budgeting," **AOS**, 1984, Vol. 9, No. 2, pp. 111-124.)

Schiedler, Patricia L. "Using Accounting Information To Assess Risk," **MA**, 1981, Vol. 62, No. 12, pp. 38-44.

Schieneman, Gary S. "International Accounting: Issues And Perspective," **JAAF**, 1979, Vol. 3, No. 1, pp. 21-30.

Schieneman, Gary S. "The Accounting Profession Facing The Challenges Of A Changing World," **JAAF**, 1983, Vol. 6, No. 3, pp. 212-226.

Schiff, Allen and H. Dov Fried. "Large Comapnies And The Big Eight: An Overview," **ABACUS**, 1976, Vol. 12, No. 2, pp. 116-124.

Schiff, Allen I. (Schiff, Jonathan B. and Allen I. Schiff.

"High-Tech Cost Accounting For The F-16," **MA**, 1988, Vol. 70, No. 3, pp. 43-48.)

Schiff, Allen. "Annual Reports In The United States: A Historical Perspective," **ABR**, 1977-78, Vol. 8, No. 32, pp. 279-284.

Schiff, Allen. (Fried, Dov and Allen Schiff. "CPA Switches And Associated Market Reactions," **AR**, 1981, Vol. 56, No. 2, pp. 326-341.)

Schiff, Allen. (Givoly, Dan, Joshua Ronen and Allen Schiff. "Does Audit Involvement Affect The Quality Of Interim Report Numbers?," **JAAF**, 1978, Vol. 1, No. 4, pp. 361-372.)

Schiff, Allen. (Kahn, Nathan and Allen Schiff. "Tangible Equity Change And The Evolution Of The FASB's Definition Of Income," **JAAF**, 1985, Vol. 9, No. 1, pp. 40-49.)

Schiff, Allen. (Krausz, Joshua, Joel Hochman and Allen Schiff. "The Impact Of Taxation On Project Valuation For Alternative Depreciation Methods," **ACCHOR**, 1987, Vol. 1, No. 3, pp. 31-40.)

Schiff, Frederick S. "The Use Of Time-Sharing In The CPA Firm," **JOA**, 1974, Vol. 137, No. 1, pp. 62-66.

Schiff, Jonathan B. and Allen I. Schiff. "High-Tech Cost Accounting For The F-16," **MA**, 1988, Vol. 70, No. 3, pp. 43-48.

Schiff, Jonathan B. and Bettina Buchmann. "Shelf Registration Rule 415," **CA**, 1986, Vol. 4, No. 1, pp. 17-23.

Schiff, Jonathan B. and Elizabeth M. Tolan. "Technical Inquiry Systems For The Accounting Profession," **CA**, 1987, Vol. 5, No. 2, pp. 51-53.

Schiff, Jonathan B. "A Management Accounting Reading Guide For Students," **MA**, 1980, Vol. 61, No. 7, p. 58.

Schiff, Jonathan B. "An Unusual Financing Source: Will It Spur New Disclosure Rules?," **MA**, 1986, Vol. 68, No. 4, pp. 42-45.

Schiff, Jonathan B. "Surprise Losses In Quarterly Earnings Reports," **MA**, 1985, Vol. 67, No. 1, pp. 52-53.

Schiff, J. B. "Management Accounting Practices Statement Promulgation: An International Perspective," **IJAER**, 1986, Vol. 22, No. 1, pp. 119-134.

Schiff, Michael and Arie Y. Lewin. "The Impact Of People On Budgets," **AR**, 1970, Vol. 45, No. 2, pp. 259-268.

Schiff, Michael and Shirley Arbesfeld. "Goodwill - A Make-Or-Buy Approach," **MA**, 1966, Vol. 47, No. 12, pp. 25-35.

Schiff, Michael, George H. Sorter and Jeremy L. Wiesen. "The Evolving Role Of Corporate Audit Committees," **JAAF**, 1977, Vol. 1, No. 1, pp. 19-44.

Schiff, Michael, Roger M. Campbell, Leslie E. Halprin and Judith P. Murphy. "How A Division's Reports Can Reflect Inflation," **MA**, 1982, Vol. 64, No. 4, pp. 32-35.

Schiff, Michael. "A Closer Look At Variable Costing," **MA**, 1987, Vol. 68, No. 8, pp. 36-39.

Schiff, Michael. "A Note On Transfer Pricing And Industry Segment Reporting," **JAAF**, 1979, Vol. 2, No. 3, pp. 224-231.

Schiff, Michael. "Accounting Tactics And The Theory Of The Firm," **JAR**, 1966, Vol. 4, No. 1, pp. 62-67.

Schiff, Michael. "Benefits Of Immediate Writeoffs," **MA**, 1976, Vol. 58, No. 6, pp. 11-12.

Schiff, Michael. "Cheers For Thirteen," **CPAJ**, 1978, Vol. 48, No. 12, pp. 21-29.

Schiff, Michael. "Distribution Cost Analysis," **JOA**, 1958, Vol. 105, No. 2, pp. 37-41.

Schiff, Michael. "Physical Distribution: A Cost Analysis," **MA**, 1972, Vol. 53, No. 8, pp. 48-50.

Schiff, Michael. "Reporting For More Profitable Product Management," **JOA**, 1963, Vol. 115, No. 5, pp. 65-70.

Schiff, Michael. "The Accounting Accreditation Planning Committee," **CPAJ**, 1980, Vol. 50, No. 8, pp. 29-34.

Schiff, Michael. "Transfer Pricing For Public Reporting: A Case Study," **ABR**, 1979-80, Vol. 10, No. 40, pp. 440-443.

Schiff, Michael. "What Happens To Depreciation," **JOA**, 1959, Vol. 107, No. 3, pp. 37-41.

Schiff, Michael. (Barnea, Amir, Simcha Sadan and Michael Schiff. "Conditional Performance Review," **MA**, 1975, Vol. 57, No. 5, pp. 19-22.)

Schiff, Michael. (Bruegelmann, Thomas M., Gaile A. Haessly, Claire P. Wolfangel and Michael Schiff. "How Variable Costing Is Used In Pricing Decisions," **MA**, 1985, Vol. 66, No. 10, pp. 58-61.)

Schiff, Michael. (Ronen, Joshua and Michael Schiff. "The Setting Of Financial Accounting Standards - Private Or Public?," **JOA**, 1978, Vol. 145, No. 3, pp. 66-73.)

Schilit, W. Keith. "Financing Your Business," **MA**, 1987, Vol. 68, No. 8, pp. 50-54.

Schilit, W. Keith. "Venture Capital: A Guide For CPAs," **CPAJ**, 1988, Vol. 58, No. 2, pp. 56-61.

Schilling, B. S., Jr. "Maryland's Uniform Accounting System Expected To Benefit Local Governments," **JOA**, 1951, Vol. 91, No. 1, pp. 120-123.

Schindler, Donald C. (Knobloch, John J., Donald C. Schindler and Joseph R. Blotzer. "Maintenance Work Authorization And Control," **MA**, 1970, Vol. 51, No. 11, pp. 19-22.)

Schipper, Katherine and Rex Thompson. "The Impact Of Merger-Related Regulations Using Exact Distributions Of Test Statistics," **JAR**, 1985, Vol. 23, No. 1, pp. 408-415.

Schipper, Katherine and Rex Thompson. "The Impact Of Merger-Related Regulations On The Shareholders Of Acquiring Firms," **JAR**, 1983, Vol. 21, No. 1, pp. 184-221.

Schipper, Katherine and Roman L. Weil. "Alternative Accounting Treatments For Pensions," **AR**, 1982, Vol. 57, No. 4, pp. 806-824.

Schipper, Katherine, John R. Twombly and Roman L. Weil.

"Financial Lease Evaluation Under Conditions Of Uncertainty: A Comment," **AR**, 1974, Vol. 49, No. 4, pp. 796-801.

Schipper, Katherine. "Financial Distress In Private Colleges," **JAR**, 1977, Vol. 15, Supp., pp. 1-40.

Schireson, Bert. "Towards A New Accounting," **AR**, 1957, Vol. 32, No. 2, pp. 253-257.

Schisler, Herbert N. "Fraud Possible With Best System If Rules Are Not Followed," **JOA**, 1953, Vol. 95, No. 2, pp. 176-178.

Schlachter, Paul. (Rockness, Joanne W. and Paul Schlachter. "Directions For Social Accounting Research: A Survey Of Potential Data Sources," **AIPIA**, 1988, Vol. 2, pp. 83-94.)

Schlachter, Paul. (Rockness, Joanne, Paul Schlachter and Howard O. Rockness. "Hazardous Waste Disposal, Corporate Disclosure, And Financial Performance In The Chemical Industry," **AIPIA**, 1986, Vol. 1, pp. 167-191.)

Schlag, Rene C. "Accounting For Taxes Of Foreign Subsidiaries - A Simplified Approach," **MA**, 1979, Vol. 61, No. 6, pp. 15-19.

Schlatter, Charles F. "Costs Under Government Contracts," **AR**, 1943, Vol. 18, No. 2, pp. 164-167.

Schlatter, Charles F. "Fixed Expense," **AR**, 1945, Vol. 20, No. 2, pp. 156-162.

Schlatter, Chas. F. "Market Profits On The Operating Statement," **AR**, 1942, Vol. 17, No. 2, pp. 171-177.

Schlauch, William S. "Contents Of A Mathematics Course For Collegiate Schools Of Business," **AR**, 1931, Vol. 6, No. 1, pp. 42-46.

Schlesinger, N. E. "Payment For Patent Use - Income Or Capital Gain?," **JOA**, 1951, Vol. 91, No. 4, pp. 595-599.

Schley, Norman E. "Cost Cutting In A Declining Economy," **JOA**, 1971, Vol. 131, No. 6, pp. 47-54.

Schley, Norman E. "The Altruistic Brothers Smythe," **JOA**, 1965, Vol. 120, No. 6, pp. 46-52.

Schley, Norman E. "The CPA And Estate Planning," **JOA**, 1963, Vol. 116, No. 1, pp. 59-64.

Schlick, James D. "Implementing Project Management Methods," **CA**, 1987, Vol. 5, No. 3, pp. 46-63.

Schlosser, Robert E. "Accounting System Review Techniques," **JOA**, 1962, Vol. 114, No. 6, pp. 45-48.

Schlosser, Robert E. (Bower, James B. and Robert E. Schlosser. "Internal Control - Its True Nature," **AR**, 1965, Vol. 40, No. 2, pp. 338-344.)

Schlosser, Robert E., Bernard Z. Lee and George A. Rabito. "Continuing Professional Education 1887-1987," **JOA**, 1987, Vol. 163, No. 5, pp. 240-254.

Schlosser, R. E. "System Mechanization And Small Practitioners," **JOA**, 1959, Vol. 108, No. 5, pp. 51-54.

Schlosser, R. (Mautz, R. K. and R. Schlosser. "Internal Control Techniques," **JOA**, 1957, Vol. 104, No. 4, pp. 43-48.)

Schluter, W. C. "Accountancy Under Economic Self-Government," **AR**, 1933, Vol. 8, No. 4 pp. 279-284.

Schmaltz, Kurt. "The Business Periodicals Of Germany," **AR**, 1930, Vol. 5, No. 3, pp. 231-234.

Schmalz, Carl N. "Some Current Problems In Administering The Retail Inventory Method," **AR**, 1934, Vol. 9, No. 1, pp. 1-14.

Schmidt, Dennis R. "Apportionment Of Multijurisdictional Corporate Income," **JATA**, 1986, Vol. 8, No. 1, pp. 19-34.

Schmidt, Fritz. "Is Appreciation Profit?," **AR**, 1931, Vol. 6, No. 4, pp. 289-293.

Schmidt, Fritz. "The Importance Of Replacement Value," **AR**, 1930, Vol. 5, No. 3, pp. 235-242.

Schmidt, Leo A. "A Secondary Use For The Uniform Achievement Tests," **AR**, 1949, Vol. 24, No. 1, pp. 88-89.

Schmidt, Leo A. "Construction Of Objective Examinations," **AR**, 1950, Vol. 25, No. 1, pp. 20-26.

Schmidt, Leo A. "Control Of Detail In Inventory Valuations," **AR**, 1943, Vol. 18, No. 4, pp. 348-353.

Schmidt, Leo A. "Teaching And Testing The Bookkeeping Phase Of Elementary Accounting," **AR**, 1935, Vol. 10, No. 1, pp. 8-11.

Schmidt, Leo A. "Testing The Tests," **AR**, 1937, Vol. 12, No. 3, pp. 317-320.

Schmidt, Leo A. (Kaufman, Felix and Leo A. Schmidt. "Auditing Electronic Records," **AR**, 1957, Vol. 32, No. 1, pp. 33-41.)

Schmidt, L. A. "The Problem Method In The Beginning Course," **AR**, 1928, Vol. 3, No. 2, pp. 184-188.

Schmidt, L. Lee, Jr. (Hicks, Carl F., Jr. and L. Lee Schmidt, Jr. "Post-Auditing The Capital Investment Decision," **MA**, 1971, Vol. 53, No. 2, pp. 24-28.)

Schmidt, Ronald M. (Coughlan, Anne T. and Ronald M. Schmidt. "Executive Compensation, Management Turnover, And Firm Performance: An Empirical Investigation," **JAEC**, 1985, Vol. 7, No. 1/3, pp. 43-66.)

Schmidt, Ronald R. "Erosion Of Profits Through Asset Losses," **MA**, 1970, Vol. 52, No. 6, pp. 53-54.

Schmitz, Marvin N. "Taxation Of Foreign Exchange Gains And Losses," **MA**, 1976, Vol. 58, No. 1, pp. 49-51.

Schmutte, James. "Accounting Internships: The State Of The Art," **JAED**, 1986, Vol. 4, No. 1, pp. 227-236.

Schmutte, James. "The Socializational Effect Of The On-Campus Recruiting Phase Of The Placement Process," **IAE**, 1987, Vol. 2, No. 2, pp. 292-312.

Schnabel, Jacques A. "Beta Geared And Ungeared: An Extension," **ABR**, 1982-83, Vol. 13, No. 50, pp. 128-130.

Schnabel, Jacques A. "On Capital Budgeting With An Unspecified Discount Rate," **ABR**, 1982-83, Vol. 13, No. 52, pp. 291-294.

Schnabel, Jacques A. "One Type Of Security: An Addendum," **ABACUS**, 1979, Vol. 15, No. 1, pp. 56-59.

Schnack, Thomas. (Bailey, Andrew A., Jr., Warren J. Boe and Thomas Schnack. "The Audit Staff Assignment Problem: A Comment," **AR**, 1974, Vol. 49, No. 3, pp. 572-574.)

Schnee, Edward J. and Charles W. Caldwell. "Retirement Planning Under Section 403(b)(7): Advantages And Limitations," **JATA**, 1984, Vol. 6, No. 1, pp. 48-56.

Schnee, Edward J. and Karen Hreha. "Capital Gains And Boot In Reorganizations," **CPAJ**, 1987, Vol. 57, No. 4, pp. 40-45.

Schnee, Edward J. and Kathleen Ranney Bindon. "Deductions Of Partnership Losses; Strategy And Planning," **CPAJ**, 1986, Vol. 56, No. 10, pp. 74-79.

Schnee, Edward J. and Martin E. Taylor. "Accountants' Workpapers - Recent IRS Developments," **CPAJ**, 1980, Vol. 50, No. 2, pp. 13-18.

Schnee, Edward J. and Martin E. Taylor. "IRS Access To Accountants' Work Papers - The Rules May Be Changing," **JAAF**, 1981, Vol. 5, No. 1, pp. 18-29.

Schnee, Edward J. and William R. Edwards. "New Preparer Rules: More Or Less Penalty?," **JATA**, 1982, Vol. 4, No. 1, pp. 26-32.

Schnee, Edward J. "An Alternative Final Examination - A Tax Debate," **JATA**, 1980, Vol. 2, No. 1, pp. 29-32.

Schnee, Edward J. (Bindon, Kathleen Ranney and Edward J. Schnee. "Forward Contracts: Accounting And Tax Implications," **CPAJ**, 1986, Vol. 56, No. 9, pp. 38-51.)

Schnee, Edward J. (Dickens, Thomas L. and Edward J. Schnee. "Are Sec. 333 Liquidations Still Alive?," **CPAJ**, 1987, Vol. 57, No. 9, pp. 54-63.)

Schnee, Edward J. (Samson, William D. and Edward J. Schnee. "Tax Planning: Damage And Injury Payments," **CPAJ**, 1986, Vol. 56, No. 5, pp. 24-33.)

Schneiderman, Irwin. "1136 Tenants' Corporation Vs. Max Rothenberg & Co. - Some Legal Considerations," **CPAJ**, 1972, Vol. 42, No. 6, pp. 465-468.

Schneider, Albert J. "Flow-Graph Notation In Accounting," **AR**, 1967, Vol. 42, No. 2, pp. 342-348.

Schneider, Arnold. "Consensus Among Auditors In Evaluating The Internal Audit Function," **ABR**, 1984-85, Vol. 15, No. 60, pp. 297-302.

Schneider, Arnold. "Indirect Cost Allocations And Cost-Plus Pricing Formulas," **JCA**, 1986, Vol. 3, No. 2, pp. 47-57.

Schneider, Arnold. "Modeling External Auditors' Evaluations Of Internal Auditing," **JAR**, 1984, Vol. 22, No. 2, pp. 657-678.

Schneider, Arnold. "The Effect Of Internal Auditing On External Audit Work," **JCA**, 1986, Vol. 3, No. 1, pp. 33-40.

Schneider, Arnold. "The Reliance Of External Auditors On The Internal Audit Function," **JAR**, 1985, Vol. 23, No. 2, pp. 911-919.

Schneider, Arnold. (Messier, William F., Jr. and Arnold Schneider. "A Hierarchical Approach To The External Auditor's Evaluation Of The Internal Auditing Function," **CAR**, 1988, Vol. 4, No. 2, pp. 337-353.)

Schneider, Arnold. (Mulford, Charles W. and Arnold Schneider. "An Empirical Study Of Structural And Controllable Factors Affecting Faculty Evaluations," **AIA**, 1988, Vol. 6, pp. 205-218.)

Schneider, Douglas K. (May, Gordon S. and Douglas K. Schneider. "Reporting Accounting Changes: Are Stricter Guidelines Needed?," **AH**, 1988, Vol. 2, No. 3, pp. 68-74.)

Schneider, Harold. (Kilpatrick, Bob, Karl Putnam and Harold Schneider. "Convertible Securities And Earnings Per Share: A Competitive Ranking Algorithm," **AR**, 1985, Vol. 60, No. 3, pp. 526-530.)

Schneider, Herman M. and Jack Crestol. "Tax Savings Through Trusts-Custodian Accounts," **JOA**, 1969, Vol. 127, No. 2, pp. 38-43.

Schneider, Herman M. and Peter H. Lengemann. "Optimal Dividend Distribution By German Companies To Their U.S. Parent Corporations," **MA**, 1967, Vol. 48, No. 6, pp. 13-20.

Schneider, Kent N. and Jo Anne Medlin. "Depreciation Rules After TRA 86," **CPAJ**, 1988, Vol. 58, No. 1, pp. 18-25.

Schneider, Kent N. and Ted D. Englebrecht. "Avoiding ITC Recapture In 351 Transfers," **CPAJ**, 1985, Vol. 55, No. 2, pp. 28-35.

Schneider, Lester J. "Should Your Company Consider Defense Contracts?," **MA**, 1968, Vol. 49, No. 6, pp. 46-51.

Schneider, Warren A. "An Auditor Looks At Labor Unions," **JOA**, 1960, Vol. 109, No. 5, pp. 66-71.

Schneidman, Arnold. "Need For Auditors' Computer Education," **CPAJ**, 1979, Vol. 49, No. 6, pp. 29-36.

Schneller, Meir I. (Peles, Yoram C. and Meir I. Schneller. "Liquidity Ratios And Industry Averages - New Evidence," **ABACUS**, 1979, Vol. 15, No. 1, pp. 13-22.)

Schnepper, Jeff A. "The Accountant's Liability Under Rule 10b-5 And Section 10(b) Of The Securities Exchange Act Of 1934: The Hole In Hochfelder," **AR**, 1977, Vol. 52, No. 3, pp. 653-657.

Schnur, Glenn J. "Here Comes Flextime," **MA**, 1978, Vol. 59, No. 12, pp. 50-54.

Schoen, David. (Hardiman, Patrick, Arlene Lurie, Frank Dubas and David Schoen. "Internal Control And Financial Integrity In Government Units," **CPAJ**, 1985, Vol. 55, No. 4, pp. 46-51.)

Schoen, J. F. (Preu, F. L. and J. F. Schoen. "Accounting For Emergency Relief Funds," **AR**, 1940, Vol. 15, No. 2, pp. 170-176.)

Schoen, Sterling H. (Virgil, Robert L., Walter R. Nord and Sterling H. Schoen. "A Classroom Experience In The Behavioral Implications Of Accounting Performance Evaluation Measurements," **AR**, 1973, Vol. 48, No. 2, pp.

410-418.)

Schoenfeld, Hanns-Martin. "Development And Present State Of Cost Theory In Germany," IJAER, 1972, Vol. 8, No. 1. pp. 43-65.

Schoenfeld, Hanns-Martin. "International Influences On The Contemporary Accounting Curriculum: International Accounting Instruction At The University Of Illinois At Urbana-Champaign," IJAER, 1974, Vol. 10, No. 1. pp. 71-85.

Schoenfeld, Hanns-Martin. "New German Regulations For The Publication Of Financial Statements," IJAER, 1970, Vol. 5, No. 2, pp. 69-88.

Schoenfeld, H. M. "Comments On 'International Accounting In An Inflationary Economy'," IJAER, 1968, Vol. 4, No. 1. pp. 165-168.

Schoenthal, Edward R. "Contingent Legal Liabilities," CPAJ, 1976, Vol. 46, No. 3, pp. 30-34.

Schoff, Charles J. (VanAlstine, Robert W. and Charles J. Schoff. "Auditing State And Local Governments," CPAJ, 1984, Vol. 54, No. 1, pp. 44-49.)

Schofield, William M. "An Effective Internal Management Reporting System," MA, 1966, Vol. 48, No. 1, pp. 17-26.

Scholefield, H. H. "Replacement Of Equipment," ABR, 1971-72, Vol. 2, No. 8, pp. 316-324.

Scholes, Myron. (Beaver, William H., Paul Kettler and Myron Scholes. "The Association Between Market Determined And Accounting Determined Risk Measures," AR, 1970, Vol. 45, No. 4, pp. 654-682.)

Scholl, Robert. "Managing The Scientific Mind," MA, 1973, Vol. 55, No. 3, pp. 48-50.

Schomo, Robert G. "Testing Internal Control In An EDP System," MA, 1973, Vol. 54, No. 10. pp. 39-42.

Schonfeld, Hanns-Martin and H. Peter Holzer. "A 'Business' Flow Chart And Its Use As A Teaching Aid," AR, 1962, Vol. 37, No. 1, pp. 118-120.

Schonfeld, Hanns-Martin. (Holzer, H. Peter and Hanns-Martin Schonfeld. "The German Solution To The Post-War Price Level Problem," AR, 1963, Vol. 38, No. 2. pp. 377-381.)

Schonfeld, Hanns-Martin. (Holzer, H. Peter and Hanns-Martin Schonfeld. "The 'Funktionale Kontorechnung' Of Walter Thoms," AR, 1964, Vol. 39, No. 2, pp. 405-413.)

Schonfeld, Hanns-Martin. (Holzer, H. Peter and Hanns-Martin Schonfeld. "The French Approach To The Post-War Price Level Problem," AR, 1963, Vol. 38, No. 2. pp. 382-388.)

Schotanus, Eugene L. "A Strategy For Coping With Exchange Risks," MA, 1971, Vol. 52, No. 7, pp. 45-49.

Schowalter, Ronald O. (Barnickol, Karl R., Allan John Ross, Ronald O. Schowalter and Michael J. Walters. "Accounting For Litigation And Claims," JOA, 1985, Vol. 159, No. 6, pp. 56-69.)

Schrader, William J. and Robert E. Malcom. "A Note On Accounting Theory Construction And Verification," ABACUS, 1973, Vol. 9, No. 1, pp. 93-98.

Schrader, William J. "An Inductive Approach To Accounting Theory," AR, 1962, Vol. 37, No. 4, pp. 645-649.

Schrader, William J. "Business Combinations," AR. 1958, Vol. 33, No. 1, pp. 72-75.

Schrader, William J. (Cramer, Joe J., Jr. and William J. Schrader. "Depreciation Accounting And The Anomalous Self-Insurance Cost," AR, 1970, Vol. 45, No. 4, pp. 698-703.)

Schrader, William J., Robert E. Malcom and John J. Willingham. "A Partitioned Events View Of Financial Reporting," AH, 1988, Vol. 2, No. 4, pp. 10-20.

Schramm, John E., Jr. "Financial Accounting And Reporting For Municipalities," CPAJ, 1972, Vol. 42, No. 4, pp. 297-302.

Schramm, John E., Jr. "Municipal Accounting And Reporting (Part 2)," CPAJ, 1976, Vol. 46, No. 6, pp. 25-30.

Schramm, John E., Jr. "Municipal Accounting And Reporting (Part 1)," CPAJ, 1976, Vol. 46, No. 5, pp. 25-28.

Schranz, Andrew. "Modern German Accountancy," AR, 1930, Vol. 5, No. 2, pp. 162-167.

Schranz, A. "Recent Tendencies In German Business Economics," AR, 1937, Vol. 12, No. 3, pp. 278-284.

Schreiner, Ernst H. "Contracted EDP In A Small Business," MA, 1972, Vol. 54, No. 1, pp. 25-28.

Schreuder, Hein and Jan Klaassen. "Confidential Revenue And Profit Forecasts By Management And Financial Analysts: Evidence From The Netherlands," AR, 1984, Vol. 59, No. 1, pp. 64-77.

Schreuder, Hein. "Employees And The Corporate Social Report: The Dutch Case," AR, 1981, Vol. 56, No. 2, pp. 294-308.

Schreuder, H. and K. V. Ramanathan. "Accounting And Corporate Accountability: An Extended Comment," AOS, 1984, Vol. 9, No. 3/4, pp. 409-416.

Schreuder, H. and K. V. Ramanathan. "Accounting And Corporate Accountability: A Postscript." AOS, 1984, Vol. 9, No. 3/4, pp. 421-423.

Schreuder, H. "Corporate Social Reporting In The Federal Republic Of Germany: An Overview," AOS, 1979, Vol. 4, No. 1/2, pp. 109-122.

Schreuder, H. (Soeters, J. and H. Schreuder. "The Interaction Between National And Organizational Cultures In Accounting Firms," AOS, 1988, Vol. 13, No. 1, pp. 75-86.)

Schroderheim, Goran. "Using Mathematical Probability To Estimate The Allowance For Doubtful Accounts," AR, 1964, Vol. 39, No. 3, pp. 679-684.

Schroeder, Douglas A. (Kross, William and Douglas A. Schroeder. "An Empirical Investigation Of The Effect Of Quarterly Earnings Announcement Timing On Stock Returns," JAR, 1984, Vol. 22, No. 1, pp. 153-176.)

Schroeder, Joan Gagnon. "Systems And Electronic Data Processing Courses In The Accounting Curriculum," AR, 1972, Vol. 47, No. 2, pp. 387-389.

Schroeder, Mary S. (Grimlund, Richard A. and Mary S. Schroeder. "On The Current Use Of The Stringer Method Of MUS: Some New Directions," AJPT, 1988, Vol. 8, No. 1, pp. 53-62.)

Schroeder, Mary S., Ira Solomon, and Don Vickrey. "Audit Quality: The Perceptions Of Audit-Committee Chairpersons And Audit Partners," AJPT, 1985-86, Vol. 5, No. 2, pp. 86-94.

Schroeder, Nicholas W. and Charles H. Gibson. "Using Microcomputers To Improve Written Communication," CPAJ, 1987, Vol. 57, No. 10, pp. 50-57.

Schroeder, Nicholas W. "Previous Accounting Education And College-Level Accounting Exam Performance," IAE, 1986, Vol. 1, No. 1, pp. 37-47.

Schroeder, Nicholas. (Alkafaji, Yass and Nicholas Schroeder. "Manual-V-Computerized Practice Sets: A Test For Differences," JAED, 1986, Vol. 4, No. 2, pp. 19-25.)

Schroeder, Richard G. and Kathryn Verreault. "An Empirical Analysis Of Audit Withdrawal Decisions," AIA, 1987, Vol. 5, pp. 205-220.

Schroeder, Richard G. (Clark, Myrtle W., Thomas E. Gibbs and Richard G. Schroeder. "How CPAs Evaluate Internal Auditors," CPAJ, 1981, Vol. 51, No. 7, pp. 10-15.)

Schroeder, Richard G. (Clark, Myrtle W., Thomas E. Gibbs and Richard G. Schroeder. "CPAs Judge Internal Audit Department Objectivity," MA, 1981, Vol. 62, No. 8, pp. 40-43.)

Schroeder, Richard. (Brooks, Kenneth and Richard Schroeder. "Management Strategy In A Large Accounting Firm: A Comment," AR, 1979, Vol. 54, No. 1, pp. 221-223.)

Schroeder, R. G. and L. F. Imdieke. "Local - Cosmopolitan And Bureaucratic Perceptions In Public Accounting Firms," AOS, 1977, Vol. 2, No. 1, pp. 39-46.

Schroeder, William J., Jr. "EDP: Who Will Assess Its Value?," MA, 1975, Vol. 56, No. 9, pp. 45-48.

Schroeder, William J., Jr. "Toward A Documentless System Of Inventory Control And Material Accounting," MA, 1965, Vol. 47, No. 4, pp. 41-49.

Schrott, Alfred N., William P. Casciani and Jeffrey Bernstein. "Interest Rate Futures Trading - Part II," CPAJ, 1980, Vol. 50, No. 5, pp. 27-32.

Schrott, Alfred N., William P. Casciani and Jeffrey Bernstein. "Interest Rate Futures Trading - Part I," CPAJ, 1980, Vol. 50, No. 4, pp. 16-22.

Schubert, Richard F. "Systems Documentation," MA, 1967, Vol. 49, No. 1. pp. 29-42.

Schuchart, J. A. and W. L. Sanders, Jr. "Pension Fund Consideration," MA, 1972, Vol. 53, No. 9, pp. 49-54.

Schuckman, Dean P. "A 'How-To' Look At Dollar-Value LIFO," MA, 1975, Vol. 57, No. 6, pp. 27-30.

Schueler, Robert H. "The Systems Concept," MA, 1974, Vol. 55, No. 12, pp. 33-34.

Schuetze, Walter. "Disclosure And The Impairment Question," JOA, 1987, Vol. 164, No. 6, pp. 26-32.

Schulman, Henry N. "Inventory Shrinkage: Is It An Accounting Problem?," MA, 1979, Vol. 61, No. 2, pp. 15-17.

Schulte, Arthur A., Jr. "Compatibility Of Auditing And Management Services: The Viewpoint Of An Outside Observer," JOA, 1967, Vol. 124, No. 6, pp. 29-31.

Schulte, Arthur A., Jr. "Compatibility Of Management Consulting And Auditing," AR, 1965, Vol. 40, No. 3, pp. 587-593.

Schulte, Arthur A., Jr. "Management Services: A Challenge To Audit Independence?," AR, 1966, Vol. 41, No. 4, pp. 721-728.

Schulte, R. Gregg. "One More Time: Direct Costing Versus Absorption Costing," MA, 1975, Vol. 57, No. 5, pp. 11-14.

Schultz, Glenn V. "Financial Systems Development," MA, 1974, Vol. 55, No. 8, pp. 23-26.

Schultz, Joseph J., Jr. and Kurt Pany. "The Independent Auditor's Civil Liability - An Overview," AR, 1980, Vol. 55, No. 2, pp. 319-326.

Schultz, Joseph J., Jr. and Philip M. J. Reckers. "The Impact Of Group Processing On Selected Audit Disclosure Decisions," JAR, 1981, Vol. 19, No. 2, pp. 482-501.

Schultz, Joseph J., Jr. and Sandra G. Gustavson. "Actuaries' Perceptions Of Variables Affecting The Independent Auditor's Legal Liability," AR, 1978, Vol. 53, No. 3. pp. 626-641.

Schultz, Joseph J., Jr. (Reckers, Philip M. J. and Joseph J. Schultz, Jr. "Individual Versus Group Assisted Evaluations," AJPT, 1982-83, Vol. 2, No. 1. pp. 64-74.)

Schultz, Leonard Jay and Mitchell Kaplan. "Tax Aspects Of Marital Settlements," CPAJ, 1980, Vol. 50, No. 5, pp. 33-37.

Schultz, Leonard Jay and Mitchell Kaplan. "Let's 'Co-Op' Erate," CPAJ, 1981, Vol. 51, No. 2. pp. 35-39.

Schultz, Leonard Jay and Mitchell Kaplan. "Tax Aspects Of Damage Settlements," CPAJ, 1981, Vol. 51, No. 11, pp. 28-31.

Schultz, Leonard Jay. (Kaplan, Mitchell and Leonard Jay Schultz. "Deductibility Of Education Expense," CPAJ, 1978, Vol. 48, No. 11, pp. 37-40.)

Schulze, Michael E. "An Interim Billing System," MA, 1973, Vol. 55, No. 5, pp. 45-47.

Schwab, Bernhard and Robert E. G. Nicol. "From Double-Declining-Balance To Sum-Of-The-Years'-Digits Depreciation: An Optimum Switching Rule," AR, 1969, Vol. 44, No. 2. pp. 292-296.

Schwab, Richard J. "A Contribution Approach To Transfer Pricing," MA, 1975, Vol. 56, No. 8, pp. 46-48.

Schwager, Steven J. (Brown, Lawrence D., Gordon D.

Richardson and Steven J. Schwager. "An Information Interpretation Of Financial Analyst Superiority In Forecasting Earnings," **JAR**, 1987, Vol. 25, No. 1, pp. 49-67.)

Schwallie, Edward H. and Alonso Martinez. "Managing In A High Inflationary Environment," **MA**, 1987, Vol. 69, No. 4, pp. 21-24.

Schwan, Edward S. "Process Costing Via Reaction Accounting," **MA**, 1974, Vol. 56, No. 3, pp. 45-50.

Schwan, E. S. "The Effects Of Human Resource Accounting Data On Financial Decisions: An Empirical Test," **AOS**, 1976, Vol. 1, No. 2/3, pp. 219-238.

Schwartz, Aba. (Lev, Baruch and Aba Schwartz. "On The Use Of The Economic Concept Of Human Capital In Financial Statements," **AR**, 1971, Vol. 46, No. 1, pp. 103-112.)

Schwartz, Aba. (Lev, Baruch and Aba Schwartz. "On The Use Of The Economic Concept Of Human Capital In Financial Statements: A Reply," **AR**, 1972, Vol. 47, No. 1, pp. 153-154.)

Schwartz, Bill Neal and Michael A. Diamond. "Is 'Dollar-Value' LIFO For You?," **CPAJ**, 1980, Vol. 50, No. 7, pp. 33-40.

Schwartz, Bill N. and David E. Stout. "A Comparison Of Practitioner And Educator Opinions On Tax Education Requirements For Undergraduate Accounting Majors," **IAE**, 1987, Vol. 2, No. 1, pp. 112-126.

Schwartz, Bill N. and Philip M. J. Reckers. "User Attitudes Toward Selected Professional Developments," **ACCHOR**, 1987, Vol. 1, No. 2, pp. 43-48.

Schwartz, Bill N. and Stephen L. Fogg. "Department Of Accounting Advisory Board: A Method Of Communicating With The Business And Professional Community," **JAED**, 1985, Vol. 3, No. 1, pp. 179-184.

Schwartz, Bill N. "Deferred Taxes: Compliance And Understandability," **JAAF**, 1983, Vol. 6, No. 3, pp. 244-253.

Schwartz, Bill N. "Dollar Value LIFO - Evaluating One Experience," **CPAJ**, 1982, Vol. 52, No. 4, pp. 42-46.

Schwartz, Bill N. "Income Tax Allocation: It Is Time For A Change," **JAAF**, 1981, Vol. 4, No. 3, pp. 238-247.

Schwartz, Bill N. (Diamond, Michael A. and Bill N. Schwartz. "Dollar-Value Lifo For Manufacturers or Processors," **CPAJ**, 1981, Vol. 51, No. 7, pp. 31-37.)

Schwartz, Bill N. (Flaherty, Richard E. and Bill N. Schwartz. "Earnings Per Share: Compliance And Understandability," **JAAF**, 1980, Vol. 4, No. 1, pp. 47-56.)

Schwartz, Bill N. (Gaffney, Mary Anne and Bill N. Schwartz. "Honors Programs In Accounting," **IAE**, 1988, Vol. 3, No. 1, pp. 79-87.)

Schwartz, Bill N. (Limberg, Stephen T. and Bill N. Schwartz. "Should You Use Multiple Asset Accounts?," **CPAJ**, 1981, Vol. 51, No. 10, pp. 25-31.)

Schwartz, Bill N. (Monahan, Thomas F. and Bill N. Schwartz. "Stock Dividends Vs. Stock Splits: Normative Vs. Descriptive Approaches To Accounting Education," **IAE**, 1986, Vol. 1, No. 1, pp. 123-131.)

Schwartz, Bill. "An Investigation Of Publications In Accounting Journals 1970-1982," **JAED**, 1984, Vol. 2, No. 2, pp. 97-110.

Schwartz, Charles M. "Inflation And Accounting Principles," **CPAJ**, 1972, Vol. 42, No. 10, pp. 823-830.

Schwartz, Donald A. "Microcomputers Take Aim On Small Business Clients," **JOA**, 1979, Vol. 148, No. 6, pp. 57-63.

Schwartz, Donald A. "Punched Tape Accounting For Smaller Business," **JOA**, 1959, Vol. 107, No. 5, pp. 37-42.

Schwartz, Eduardo S. (Hughes, Patricia J. and Eduardo S. Schwartz. "The LIFO/FIFO Choice: An Asymmetric Information Approach," **JAR**, 1988, Vol. 26, Supp., pp. 41-58.)

Schwartz, Edward J. (Shefsky, Lloyd E. and Edward J. Schwartz. "Disclosures And Reporting Under ASR No. 115," **JOA**, 1973, Vol. 136, No. 3, pp. 53-61.)

Schwartz, Kenneth B. and Krishnagopal Menon. "Auditor Switches By Failing Firms," **AR**, 1985, Vol. 60, No. 2, pp. 248-261.

Schwartz, Kenneth B. "Accounting Changes By Corporations Facing Possible Insolvency," **JAAF**, 1982, Vol. 6, No. 1, pp. 32-43.

Schwartz, Kenneth B. (Menon, Krishnagopal and Kenneth B. Schwartz. "An Empirical Investigation Of Audit Qualification Decisions In The Presence Of Going Concern Uncertainties," **CAR**, 1986-87, Vol. 3, No. 2.pp.302-315.)

Schwartz, M. H. "Computer Project Selection In The Business Enterprise," **JOA**, 1969, Vol. 127, No. 4, pp. 35-43.

Schwartz, Richard and John M. Lorentz. "Postemployment Benefits Other Than Pensions," **CPAJ**, 1986, Vol. 56, No. 5, pp. 16-23.

Schwartz, Richard and Michael J. Gilmore. "Auditing Pension Costs And Disclosures," **CPAJ**, 1988, Vol. 58, No. 6, pp. 16-25.

Schwartz, Rickard P. (Anderson, Henry R. and Rickard P. Schwartz. "The Capital Facility Decision," **MA**, 1971, Vol. 52, No. 8, pp. 28-32.)

Schwarzbach, Henry R. and Richard G. Vangermeersch. "Why We Should Account For The 4th Cost Of Manufacturing," **MA**, 1983, Vol. 65, No. 1, pp. 24-29.

Schwarzbach, Henry R. "A Current Overview Of The MIS Audit," **MA**, 1980, Vol. 62, No. 1, pp. 23-26.

Schwarzbach, Henry R. "The Impact Of Automation On Accounting For Indirect Costs," **MA**, 1985, Vol. 67, No. 6, pp. 45-50.

Schweiger, Bradley J. "A Summary Of Accounting For And Reporting On Accounting Changes," **AR**, 1977, Vol. 52, No. 4, pp. 946-949.

Schweikart, James A. "Attitude Measurement And Instrumentation In International Accounting Research," **IJAER**, 1987,

Vol. 22, No. 2, pp. 131-141.

Schweikart, James A. "Contingency Theory As A Framework For Research In International Accounting," **IJAER**, 1985, Vol. 21. No. 1, pp. 89-98.

Schweikart, James A. "We Must End Consolidation Of Foreign Subsidiaries," **MA**, 1981, Vol. 63, No. 2, pp. 15-25.

Schweikart, J. A. "The Relevance Of Managerial Accounting Information: A Multinational Analysis," **AOS**, 1986, Vol. 11. No. 6, pp. 541-554.

Schwendig, Lee. (Cox, Clifford T., Ken M. Boze and Lee Schwendig. "Academic Accountants: A Study Of Faculty Characteristics And Career Activities," **JAED**, 1987, Vol. 5, No. 1, pp. 59-76.)

Schwersenz, Jack. "Marketing Your Services," **CPAJ**, 1979, Vol. 49, No. 10, pp. 11-16.

Schwert, G. William. "A Discussion Of CEO Deaths And The Reaction Of Stock Prices," **JAEC**, 1985, Vol. 7, No. 1/3, pp. 175-178.

Schwieger, Bradley J., Wayne R. Wells and Ronald E. Carlson. "Solicitation - Where Do We Stand Today?," **CPAJ**, 1988, Vol. 58, No. 11, pp. 66-70.

Sclawy, Adrian. (Stiner, Frederic M., Jr., John C. Williams and Adrian Sclawy. "Vanishing Accounting Journals Due To Paper Deterioration," **AHJ**, 1981, Vol. 8, No. 2, pp. 97-100.)

Scorgie, M. B. "Rate Of Return," **ABACUS**, 1965, Vol. 1, No. 1, pp. 85-91.

Scotto, Anthony P. "Effectively Achieving Due Diligence Objectives," **CA**, 1986, Vol. 4, No. 1, pp. 24-29.

Scott, David F., Jr. (Moore, Laurence J. and David F. Scott, Jr. "Long-Range Planning And The Decentralized Firm," **MA**, 1971, Vol. 53, No. 5, pp. 35-39.)

Scott, Deborah K. (Upton, Wayne S., Jr. and Deborah K. Scott. "What You Should Know About The EITF," **JOA**, 1988, Vol. 165, No. 6, pp. 56-63.)

Scott, Diana J., Jane B. Adams and Joyce A. Strawser. "Retiree Welfare Benefits Come Out Of Hiding," **CPAJ**, 1988, Vol. 58, No. 11, pp. 26-34.

Scott, DR. "A Simplified Solution Of Circuit Ratio Problems," **AR**, 1943, Vol. 18, No. 2, pp. 99-102.

Scott, DR. "Conservatism In Inventory Valuations," **AR**, 1926, Vol. 1, No. 1, pp. 18-21.

Scott, DR. "Defining And Accounting For Depreciation," **AR**, 1945, Vol. 20, No. 3, pp. 308-315.

Scott, DR. "Depreciation And Repair Costs," **AR**, 1929, Vol. 4. No. 2, pp. 116-120.

Scott, DR. "Responsibilities Of Accountants In A Changing Economy," **AR**, 1939, Vol. 14, No. 4, pp. 396-401.

Scott, DR. "Role Of Accounting In Public Utility Regulation," **AR**, 1947, Vol. 22, No. 3, pp. 227-240.

Scott, DR. "Selling Accounting Short," **AR**, 1940, Vol. 15, No. 4, pp. 507-510.

Scott, DR. "The Basis For Accounting Principles," **AR**, 1941, Vol. 16, No. 4, pp. 341-348.

Scott, DR. "The Influence Of Statistics Upon Accounting Technique And Theory," **AR**, 1949, Vol. 24, No. 1, pp. 81-87.

Scott, DR. "The Tentative Statement Of Principles," **AR**, 1937, Vol. 12, No. 3, pp. 296-302.

Scott, DR. "Trends In The Technique And Tools Of Management," **AR**, 1937, Vol. 12, No. 2, pp. 138-144.

Scott, DR. "Unity In Accounting Theory," **AR**, 1931, Vol. 6, No. 2, pp. 106-112.

Scott, DR. "Valuation For Depreciation And The Financing Of Replacements," **AR**, 1929, Vol. 4, No. 4, pp. 221-226.

Scott, DR. "Valuation Of Investment Securities," **AR**, 1928, Vol. 3. No. 4, pp. 375-382.

Scott, Edward R. "Bad Debts: Take Two: A Comment," **AR**, 1973, Vol. 48, No. 4, pp. 775-776.

Scott, F. D. "Inventory Accounting In Grocery Chain," **JOA**, 1951, Vol. 91, No. 4, pp. 590-594.

Scott, George M. "A Business Economics Foundation For Accounting: The Dutch Experience," **IJAER**, 1970, Vol. 5, No. 2, pp. 117-131.

Scott, George M. "A Business Economics Foundation For Accounting: The Dutch Experience," **ABR**, 1970-71, Vol. 1, No. 4, pp. 309-317.

Scott, George M. "Accounting And Economic Reform In The Soviet Union," **ABACUS**, 1969, Vol. 5, No. 1, pp. 55-63.

Scott, George M. "Currency Exchange Rates And Accounting Translation: A Mis-Marriage?," **ABACUS**, 1975, Vol. 11, No. 1, pp. 58-70.

Scott, George M. "Financial Control In Multinational Enterprises - The New Challenge To Accountants," **IJAER**, 1972, Vol. 7, No. 2, pp. 55-68.

Scott, George M. "Information Systems And Coordination In Multinational Enterprises," **IJAER**, 1974, Vol. 10, No. 1, pp. 87-105.

Scott, George M. "Private Enterprise Accounting In Developing Nations," **IJAER**, 1968, Vol. 4, No. 1, pp. 51-65.

Scott, George. (Vanecek, Michael T. and George Scott. "Data Bases - The Auditor's Dilemma," **CPAJ**, 1980, Vol. 50, No. 1, pp. 26-36.)

Scott, James P. (Purcell, Thomas J., III and James P. Scott. "An Analysis Of The Feasibility Of Harmonizing Financial Reporting Practices Between Member Countries Of The EEC And The OECD," **IJAER**, 1986, Vol. 21, No. 2, pp. 109-131.)

Scott, Mark. (Ma, Ronald and Mark Scott. "Capital Budgeting And Discounted Cash Equivalents: A Rejoinder," **ABACUS**, 1980, Vol. 16, No. 1, pp. 73-75.)

Scott, Mark. (Ma, Ronald, Pramond Pandey and Mark Scott. "Capital Budgeting And Discounted Cash Equivalents," **ABACUS**, 1978, Vol. 14, No. 2, pp. 180-187.)

Scott, Michael E. (Anstine, Patricia A. and Michael E.

Scott. "ARCO Establishes Responsibility Accounting At Prudhoe Bay," **MA**. 1980. Vol. 61, No. 9. pp. 13-20.)

Scott, Richard A. and Donald M. Dale. "Interim Testing Of Assets And Liabilities," **CPAJ**, 1984, Vol. 54, No. 11, pp. 22-33.

Scott, Richard A. and Elizabeth G. Ward. "Carman G. Blough: His Personality And Formative Years," **AHJ**, 1982, Vol. 9, No. 2. pp. 53-60.

Scott, Richard A. and Rita K. Scott. "Installment Accounting: Is It Inconsistent?," **JOA**, 1979, Vol. 148, No. 5. pp. 52-59.

Scott, Richard A. "Owners' Equity. The Anachronistic Element," **AR**, 1979. Vol. 54. No. 4, pp. 750-763.

Scott, Richard A. "The Study Of Partnership Accounting Through Role Playing," **AR**, 1972. Vol. 47. No. 3. pp. 610-612.

Scott, Richard A. (Lathan. Malcolm H., Jr., Barbara A. Ostrowski, Ernest J. Pavlock and Richard A. Scott. "Recruiting Entry Level Staff: Gender Differences," **CPAJ**, 1987, Vol. 57, No. 1. pp. 30-43.)

Scott, Richard A., Ernest J. Pavlock and Malcolm H. Lathan, Jr. "On-Campus Recruiting: The Students Speak Up," **JOA**. 1985. Vol. 159, No. 1, pp. 60-75.

Scott, Rita K. (Scott. Richard A. and Rita K. Scott. "Installment Accounting: Is It Inconsistent?," **JOA**, 1979, Vol. 148, No. 5, pp. 52-59.)

Scott, Robert B. (Freeman, Robert J. and Robert B. Scott. "The Essentials Of Hospital Accounting," **CPAJ**, 1985. Vol. 55, No. 1, pp. 40-45.)

Scott, Robert B., Jr. "A Look At Management Incentive Plans," **JOA**, 1981, Vol. 151. No. 6. pp. 76-80.

Scott, William R. "A Bayesian Approach To Asset Valuation And Audit Size," **JAR**, 1973. Vol. 11. No. 2, pp. 304-332.

Scott, William R. "Auditor's Loss Functions Implicit In Consumption-Investment Models," **JAR**. 1975. Vol. 13. Supp.. pp. 98-117.

Scott, William R. "Economic Effects Of A Mandated Audit In A Contingent-Claims Production Economy," **CAR**. 1988. Vol. 4. No. 2. pp. 354-388.

Scott, William R. "Group Preference Orderings For Audit And Valuation Alternatives: The Single-Peakedness Condition," **JAR**, 1977. Vol. 15. No. 1. pp. 120-137.

Scott, William R. "Scoring Rules For Probabilistic Reporting." **JAR**, 1979. Vol. 17. No. 1. pp. 156-178.

Scott, William R. "The State Of The Art Of Academic Research In Auditing," **JAL**. 1984. Vol. 3. pp. 153-200.

Scott, William R. (Blazenko, George W. and William R. Scott. "A Model Of Standard Setting In Auditing," **CAR**. 1986-87, Vol. 3. No. 1. pp. 68-92.)

Scovil, E. G. "Systems For Small Business With Suddenly Expanded Volume," **JOA**. 1952. Vol. 94. No. 6. pp. 702-707.

Scovill, Hiram T. "Application Of Funds Made Practical," **AR**. 1944. Vol. 19, No. 1. pp. 20-30.

Scovill, Hiram T. "Wartime Accounting Problems," **AR**. 1943. Vol. 18, No. 3. pp. 209-218.

Scovill, H. T. "An Effort To Define Business Income," **AR**. 1952. Vol. 27. No. 4, pp. 458-466.

Scovill, H. T. "Analysis Of A Questionnaire Sent To 1000 Alumni Of The University Of Illinois. College Of Commerce," **AR**. 1951. Vol. 26. No. 2. pp. 259-260.

Scovill, H. T. "Education For Public Accounting On The Collegiate Level," **AR**. 1946. Vol. 21, No. 3. pp. 261-266.

Scovill, H. T. "Premium On Redemption Of Preferred-Stock Issues," **AR**. 1940. Vol. 15, No. 2. pp. 205-210.

Scovill, H. T. "Reflections Of Twenty-Five Years In The American Accounting Association," **AR**. 1941. Vol. 16. No. 2. pp. 167-174.

Scovill, H. T. "Some Tentative Propositions Underlying Consolidated Reports: Comments," **AR**. 1938. Vol. 13. No. 1. pp. 73-76.

Scovill, H. T. "The Accounting Instructor And Local Government Accounting," **AR**. 1934. Vol. 9. No. 1. pp. 44-52.

Scovill, H. T. "The Junior Accountant: His Problems. Responsibilities, And Training," **AR**. 1938. Vol. 13. No. 4. pp. 354-365.

Scudiere, Paul M. "Justifying Proposals To Save Energy," **MA**. 1980. Vol. 61. No. 9. pp. 42-50.

Seagle, John P. and Enrico Petri. "Gift Vs. Estate Transfer: The Method Of Equated Rates," **AR**. 1977. Vol. 52, No. 1, pp. 124-136.

Seago, W. E. and Jerome S. Horvitz. "The Effects Of The Supreme Court's Thor Power Tool Decision On The Balance Of Tax Accounting Power," **JATA**. 1980. Vol. 1. No. 2. pp. 5-9.

Seago, W. E. "Medicare: Accounting Methods And Social Goals," **JOA**. 1971. Vol. 132. No. 2. pp. 46-53.

Seago, W. E. "Selecting A Medicare Reimbursement Formula," **JOA**. 1968. Vol. 126. No. 2. pp. 31-41.

Seaman, James L. "Lessons From The Investment Credit," **AR**. 1965, Vol. 40. No. 3. pp. 617-621.

Seaman, Jerome F. and Harold H. Hensold. Jr. "Pension Plan Obligations: The 'Real' Impact," **JOA**. 1982. Vol. 154. No. 1, pp. 82-88.

Searfoss, D. Gerald and Naomi Erickson. "The Big Unfunded Liability: Postretirement Healthcare Benefits," **JOA**. 1988. Vol. 166. No. 5, pp. 28-39.

Searfoss, D. Gerald. (Cushing, Barry E.. D. Gerald Searfoss and Reed H. Randall. "Materiality Allocation In Audit Planning: A Feasibility Study," **JAR**. 1979. Vol. 17. Supp.. pp. 172-216.)

Searfoss, D. Gerald. (Flamholtz. Eric G.. D. Gerald Searfoss and Russell Coff. "Developing Human Resource Accounting As A Human Resource Decision Support System,"

AHJ, 1988. Vol. 2, No. 3, pp. 1-9.)

Searfoss, D. G. "Some Behavioral Aspects Of Budgeting For Control: An Empirical Study," **AOS**, 1976, Vol. 1, No. 4, pp. 375-388.

Searfoss, Gerald. (Baron, C. David, Douglas A. Johnson, D. Gerald Searfoss and Charles H. Smith. "Uncovering Corporate Irregularities: Are We Closing The Expectation Gap?," **JOA**, 1977, Vol. 144, No. 4, pp. 56-67.)

Seaton, Lloyd, Jr. "Standard Costing Developments And Applications," **MA**, 1970, Vol. 52, No. 1, pp. 65-67.

Sebastian, Henry J. "Stock Redemption Problems In Estate Planning," **JOA**. 1960, Vol. 110, No. 1, pp. 54-60.

Secoy, Thomas G. "A CPA's Opinion On Management Performance," **JOA**, 1971, Vol. 132, No. 1, pp. 53-59.

Secrest, Fred G. "From Bookkeeping To Decision Theory," **MA**, 1966, Vol. 48, No. 4, pp. 3-9.

Sedaghat, Ali M. and Charles L. Martin, Jr. "Perceptions Of Accounting Faculty Regarding Proposed Changes In The CPA Examination," **IAE**, 1988, Vol. 3, No. 2, pp. 409-422.

Sedki. S. Sam and George J. Petrello. "The Accounting Practitioners Accounting Educators Dialogue - A Short Survey," **JAED**, 1984, Vol. 2. No. 1, pp. 163-166.

Seed, Allen H., III. "Cost Accounting In The Age Of Robotics," **MA**. 1984. Vol. 66, No. 4, pp. 39-43.

Seed, Allen H., III. "Management Accounting For Software Development," **CA**, 1984, Vol. 2, No. 3, pp. 14-19.

Seed, Allen H., III. "Strategic Planning: The Cutting Edge Of Management Accounting," **MA**, 1980, Vol. 61, No. 11. pp. 10-15.

Seed, Allen H., III. "The Rational Abuse Of Accounting Information," **MA**, 1970, Vol. 51, No. 7, pp. 9-11.

Seed, Allen H., III. "Using Cash Flows To Measure Business Unit Performance," **CA**, 1983, Vol. 1, No. 3. pp. 14-20.

Seed, Allen H., III. "Utilizing The Funds Statement," **MA**, 1976. Vol. 57, No. 11, pp. 15-18.

Seelye, Alfred L. "The Role Of Business Schools In A Changing Evnironment," **AR**, 1963. Vol. 38. No. 2. pp. 302-309.

Sefcik, Stephan E. and Rex Thompson. "An Approach To Statistical Inference In Cross-Sectional Models With Security Abnormal Returns As Dependent Variable," **JAR**. 1986, Vol. 24. No. 2, pp. 316-334.

Sefcik, Stephan E. (Richardson, Gordon, Stephan E. Sefcik and Rex Thompson. "Trading Volume Reactions To A Change In Dividend Policy: The Canadian Evidence," **CAR**, 1988, Vol. 5. No. 1, pp. 299-317.)

Segal, Mark A. (Drucker, Meyer and Mark A. Segal. "Penalties For Federal Tax Crimes: The IRS Arsenal," **MA**. 1984. Vol. 66, No. 1, pp. 32-35.)

Segall, Joel. (Green, David and Joel Segall. "The Predictive Power Of First-Quarter Earnings Reports: A Replication," **JAR**, 1966, Vol. 4, Supp., pp. 21-36.)

Seglund, Ragnor and Santiago Ibarreche. "Just-In-Time: The Accounting Implications," **MA**, 1984, Vol. 66, No. 2, pp. 43-45.

Seider, Robert J. "Concern Over Opinions Of The Accounting Principles Board," **MA**, 1969, Vol. 50, No. 7. pp. 15-16.

Seidler, Lee J. "Accountant: Account For Thyself," **JOA**. 1973, Vol. 135, No. 6, pp. 38-43.

Seidler, Lee J. "Adding Up The Change In Accounting," **CPAJ**, 1985, Vol. 55, No. 7, pp. 12-17.

Seidler, Lee J. "An Income Approach To The Translation Of Foreign Currency Financial Statements," **CPAJ**, 1972, Vol. 42. No. 1. pp. 26-36.

Seidler, Lee J. "International Accounting - The Ultimate Theory Course," **AR**, 1967, Vol. 42, No. 4, pp. 775-781.

Seidler, Lee J. "Major Points In Commission On Auditors' Responsibilities Report," **CPAJ**, 1977, Vol. 47, No. 6. pp. 21-24.

Seidler, Lee J. "Nationalism And The International Transfer Of Accounting Skills," **IJAER**, 1969, Vol. 5, No. 1, pp. 35-45.

Seidler, Lee J. "Teaching Business Administration Overseas: The Case For The Ugly American," **IJAER**, 1968, Vol. 4, No. 1. pp. 145-153.

Seidler, Lee J. "The Cohen Commission After One Year: A Personal View," **JAAF**, 1979, Vol. 2, No. 4, pp. 285-293.

Seidler, Lee J. (Carmichael, D. R., Lee J. Seidler and Richard B. Marcus. "Training Young Auditors - A Realistic Approach Through Simulation," **JOA**, 1971, Vol. 131, No. 5, pp. 49-54.)

Seidler, Lee J. (Palmon, Dan and Lee J. Seidler. "Current Value Reporting Of Real Estate Companies And A Possible Example Of Market Inefficiency," **AR**, 1978, Vol. 53, No. 3. pp. 776-790.)

Seidman, Albert G. "Conglomerates And The Federal Trade Commission," **MA**. 1970, Vol. 51, No. 10, pp. 21-23.

Seidman, J. S. "A Brief Introduction To The New Internal Revenue Code," **JOA**, 1954, Vol. 98, No. 3, pp. 291-293.

Seidman, J. S. "A Comparison Of Tax Advantages Of A Corporation V. Partnership Or Sole Proprietorship," **JOA**, 1950. Vol. 90. No. 2. pp. 104-112.

Seidman, J. S. "Catching Up With Employee Frauds," **AR**. 1939, Vol. 14. No. 4, pp. 415-423.

Seidman, J. S. "Should A Federal Tax Bar Be Organized?," **AR**. 1936, Vol. 11, No. 2, pp. 179-182.

Seidman, J. S. "So You're Going International," **JOA**, 1967. Vol. 123. No. 2, pp. 52-54.

Seidman, J. S. "Taxes: Friend Or Foe?," **JOA**, 1955, Vol. 100, No. 5, pp. 51-55.

Seidman, J. S. "The Future Of The Accounting Profession," **JOA**, 1959, Vol. 107, No. 3, pp. 29-36.

Seidman, L. William. "The End Of The Great Green Eyeshade," **JOA**, 1972. Vol. 133, No. 1, pp. 51-55.

Seidman, Nelson B. "The Determination Of Stockholder Income," **AR**, 1956, Vol. 31, No. 1, pp. 64-70.

Seidner, Alan G. (Bort, Richard and Alan G. Seidner. "Investing Surplus Funds: What To Do With Your Everyday Cash," CA, 1986, Vol. 4, No. 1. pp. 3-10.)

Seifert, James. (Mielke, David E. and James Seifert. "A Survey On The Effects Of Defeasing Debt," JAAF, 1987, Vol. 2 (New Issues), No. 1. pp. 65-78.)

Seifrick, John. "The Statement Of Changes In Financial Position: Retain, Repeal, Or Modify?," IAE, 1983, No. 1, pp. 71-78.

Seifried, Jerome F. and William H. Schatz. "Accounting Control Of Government Contract And Commercial Program Activity," MA, 1970, Vol. 51, No. 9, pp. 38-44.

Seiler, Mona E. (Mellman, Martin and Mona E. Seiler. "Structure Needed For Implementing Mandated Accounting Changes," JAAF, 1986, Vol. 1 (New Series), No. 4, pp. 305-318.)

Seiler, Robert E. and Della A. Pearson. "Work Satisfaction Through Research - An Empirical Test," IAE, 1986, Vol. 1, No. 1, pp. 65-75.

Seiler, Robert E. and Harold R. Dilbeck. "Latin America - A Challenge In Developmental Assistance," JOA, 1967, Vol. 124, No. 4, pp. 46-50.

Seiler, Robert E. and Jerome S. Horvitz. "The Partnership Decision - The Hishon Case," CPAJ, 1985, Vol. 55, No. 1, pp. 12-19.

Seiler, Robert E. and Richard W. Sapp. "Just How Satisfied Are Accountants With Their Jobs?," MA, 1979, Vol. 60, No. 9, pp. 18-21.

Seiler, Robert E. and Wayne A. Label. "Impact Of Curricular Changes Upon Professional Staff Training Efforts," AR, 1974, Vol. 49, No. 4, pp. 854-859.

Seiler, Robert E. "A Simplified Three-Variance Technique," AR, 1956, Vol. 31, No. 3. pp. 500-501.

Seiler, Robert E. "Accounting For Guaranteed Wage Plans," AR, 1956, Vol. 31, No. 3. pp. 401-406.

Seiler, Robert E. "Accounting. Information Systems. And Underdeveloped Nations," AR, 1966, Vol. 41, No. 4. pp. 652-656.

Seiler, Robert E. "Improvements In External Reporting By Use Of Direct Costing," AR, 1959, Vol. 34, No. 1. pp. 59-66.

Seiler, Robert E. (Collins, Frank, Robert E. Seiler and Donald K. Clancy. "Budgetary Attitudes: The Effects Of Role Senders, Stress, And Performance Evaluation," ABR, 1983-84, Vol. 14, No. 54, pp. 163-168.)

Seiler, Robert E. (Kelley, Tim and Robert E. Seiler. "Auditor Stress And Time Budgets," CPAJ, 1982, Vol. 52, No. 12, pp. 24-36.)

Seiler, Robert E. (Pearson, Della A., Robert E. Seiler and Ira R. Weiss. "Why Do Management Accountants Feel Disliked?," MA, 1982, Vol. 63, No. 9, pp. 14-19.)

Seiler, Robert E. (Sapp, Richard W. and Robert E. Seiler. "Accounting For Performance: Stressful - But Satisfying," MA, 1980, Vol. 62, No. 2. pp. 29-35.)

Seiler, R. E. and R. W. Bartlett. "Personality Variables As Predictors Of Budget System Characteristics," AOS, 1982, Vol. 7, No. 4, pp. 381-404.

Seitelman, Nathan. "An Analysis Of The Auditing Section Of The Certified Public Accountant Examinations. May 1951 to May 1961," AR, 1962, Vol. 37, No. 3, pp. 547-550.

Seitelman, Nathan. "Has A.R.B. 29 Settled The Problem Of Inventory Valuation?," AR, 1953, Vol. 28, No. 4. pp. 550-553.

Seitelman, Nathan. "The Depletion Problem," AR, 1953, Vol. 28, No. 1, pp. 102-109.

Selby, Edward B., Jr. (Beranek, William and Edward B. Selby, Jr. "Delayed Depreciation As A Tax Shield," JATA, 1983, Vol. 4, No. 2, pp. 23-34.)

Seldon, Samuel. "Internal Auditing For The State Of New York," AR, 1943, Vol. 18, No. 3, pp. 239-243.

Sellers, Fred E. (Gordon, Lawrence A. and Fred E. Sellers. "Accounting And Budgeting Systems: The Issue Of Congruency," JAPP, 1984, Vol. 3, No. 4. pp 259-292.)

Sellers, James H. (Mansour, Fathi A. and James H. Sellers. "Comparing Cost Accounting Standards With Existing Accounting Standards," MA, 1978, Vol. 59, No. 10. pp. 37-42.)

Sellie, Clifford N. "Fund Statement Terminology," AR, 1943, Vol. 18, No. 2, pp. 156-164.

Selling, Thomas I. and Clyde P. Stickney. "Accounting Measures Of Unfunded Pension Liabilities And Expected Present Value Of Future Pension Cash Flows," JAPP, 1986, Vol. 5, No. 4, pp. 267-285.

Selling, Thomas I. (Casey, Cornelius and Thomas I. Selling. "The Effect Of Task Predictability And Prior Probability Disclosure On Judgment Quality And Confidence," AR, 1986, Vol. 61, No. 2, pp. 302-317.)

Selto, Frank H. and Bruce R. Neumann. "A Further Guide To Research On The Economic Consequences Of Accounting Information," ABR, 1980-81, Vol. 11, No. 44. pp. 317-322.

Selto, Frank H. and Hugh D. Grove. "Voting Power Indices And The Setting Of Financial Accounting Standards: Extensions," JAR, 1982, Vol. 20, No. 2, Part II, pp. 676-688.

Selto, Frank H. and Hugh D. Grove. "The Predictive Power Of Voting Power Indices: FASB Voting On Statements Of Financial Accounting Standards Nos. 45-69," JAR, 1983, Vol. 21, No. 2, pp. 619-622.

Selto, Frank H. and Maclyn L. Clouse. "An Investigation Of Managers' Adaptations To SFAS No. 2: Accounting For Research And Development Costs," JAR, 1985, Vol. 23, No. 2, pp. 700-717.

Selto, Frank H. (Friedman, Laurence A. and Frank H. Selto. "A Simulation Of The Replacement Cost Lead Indicator Relationship," ABACUS, 1981, Vol. 17, No. 1, pp. 73-90.)

Selto, F. H. "Internal Adaptations To Effects Of Changes In Financial Accounting Standards," AOS, 1982, Vol. 7, No. 2. pp. 139-148.

Sempier, Robert N. "The International Federation Of Accountants: Operating Procedures And Current Progress," IJAER, 1979, Vol. 15, No. 1, pp. 21-31.

Sena, James A. and Lawrence Murphy Smith. "Designing And Implementing An Integrated Job Cost Accounting System," JIS, 1986, Vol. 1, No. 1, pp. 102-112.

Senatra, Phillip T. "Role Conflict, Role Ambiguity. And Organizational Climate In A Public Accounting Firm," AR, 1980, Vol. 55, No. 4, pp. 594-603.

Senatra, Phillip T. "The Statement Of Changes In Financial Position: A Flow-Chart Approach To Teaching Concepts And Procedures," IAE, 1983, No. 1, pp. 95-103.

Sengupta, Ratna. (Houghton, Keith A. and Ratna Sengupta. "The Effect Of Prior Probability Disclosure And Information Set Construction On Bankers' Ability To Predict Failure," JAR, 1984, Vol. 22, No. 2, pp. 768-775.)

Senkow, David W. (Daley, Lane A., David W. Senkow and Robert L. Vigeland. "Analysts' Forecasts, Earnings Variability, And Option Pricing: Empirical Evidence," AR, 1988, Vol. 63, No. 4, pp. 563-585.)

Senna, Donald J. "Understanding Troubled Debt Restructuring," MA, 1982, Vol. 63, No. 8. pp. 26-28.

Sennetti, John T. (McGill, Gary A. and John T. Sennetti. "The Capital Gains Timing Decision: A Quantitative Analysis," JATA, 1986, Vol. 7, No. 2, pp. 7-16.)

Sennetti, John T. (Taylor, Barbara G., Lane K. Anderson and John T. Sennetti. "SFAC No. 2 Reliability From A Statistical Perspective," JAED, 1987, Vol. 5, No. 2, pp. 315-321.)

Senn, Stanley A. "British And American Auditing Differences," JOA, 1955, Vol. 100, No. 3, pp. 57-63.

Sen, Pradyot K. (Baber, William R. and Pradyot K. Sen. "The Role Of Generally Accepted Reporting Methods In The Public Sector: An Empirical Test," JAPP, 1984, Vol. 3, No. 2. pp. 91-106.)

Sepe, James. "The Impact Of The FASB's 1974 GPL Proposal On The Security Price Structure," AR, 1982, Vol. 57, No. 3, pp. 467-485.

Sepe, James. (Noreen, Eric and James Sepe. "Market Reactions To Accounting Policy Deliberations: The Inflation Accounting Case Revisited - A Reply," AR, 1981, Vol. 56, No. 4. pp. 955-958.)

Sepe, James. (Noreen, Eric and James Sepe. "Market Reactions To Accounting Policy Deliberations: The Inflation Accounting Case," AR, 1981, Vol. 56, No. 2. pp. 253-269.)

Serlen, Bruce. (Feinberg, Stuart A. and Bruce Serlen. "The Crisis In Business Ethics," CA, 1988, Vol. 6, No. 1, pp. 36-39.)

Serlin, Henry. "Accounting Through Income And Surplus," AR, 1942, Vol. 17, No. 3, pp. 294-302.

Serlin, Jerry E. (Landsittel, David L. and Jerry E. Serlin. "Evaluating The Materiality Of Errors In Financial Statements," JAAF, 1982, Vol. 5, No. 4. pp. 291-300.)

Serraino, William. (Abs, George, Clayton Grimstad, Robert Hay, W. Asquith Howe, William LaPlace, Francis J. McGurr and William Serraino. "Historical Dates In Accounting," AR, 1954, Vol. 29, No. 3. pp. 486-493.)

Severance, Jay and Ronald R. Bottin. "Work-In-Process Inventory Control Through Data Base Concepts," MA, 1979, Vol. 60, No. 7, pp. 37-41.

Sever, Mark V. (Mahoney, John J., Mark V. Sever and John A. Theis. "Cash Flow: FASB Opens The Floodgates," JOA, 1988, Vol. 165, No. 5, pp. 26-38.)

Seville, Mary Alice and Dahli Gray. "Using The Standard-Setting Process To Demystify The Concepts Statements: The Case Of SFAS 76," JAED, 1986, Vol. 4, No. 2, pp. 107-112.

Seville, Mary Alice. "Accounting And Auditing Of Human Service Organizations," CPAJ, 1987, Vol. 57, No. 9, pp. 34-45.

Seville, Mary Alice. "The Evolution Of Voluntary Health And Welfare Organization Accounting: 1910 - 1985," AHJ, 1987, Vol. 14, No. 1, pp. 57-82.

Sexton, Robert E. "The Accountant's Role In Management - A Company's Experience," MA, 1968, Vol. 50, No. 4, pp. 11-12.

Shabahang, Reza. (Horwitz, Bertrand and Reza Shabahang. "Published Corporate Accounting Data And General Wage Increases Of The Firm," AR, 1971, Vol. 46, No. 2, pp. 243-252.)

Shadmon, Dorikam. (Shashua, Leon, Yaaqov Goldschmidt and Dorikam Shadmon. "Control Charts For Citrus Packing Plants," MA, 1975, Vol. 56, No. 9, pp. 19-21.)

Shaftel, Timothy L. (Hansen, Don R. and Timothy L. Shaftel. "Sampling For Integrated Auditing Objectives," AR, 1977, Vol. 52, No. 1, pp. 109-123.)

Shafton, Robert M. "Why Corporations Need An Annual Legal Review," MA, 1981, Vol. 63, No. 5, pp. 66-69.

Shah, Pravin. (Hagerman, Robert L., Mark E. Zmijewski and Pravin Shah. "The Association Between The Magnitude Of Quarterly Earnings Forecast Errors And Risk-Adjusted Stock Returns," JAR, 1984, Vol. 22, No. 2, pp. 526-540.)

Shalchi, Hossien. (McKeown, James C. and Hossien Shalchi. "A Comparative Examination Of The Time-Series Properties And Predictive Ability Of Annual Historical Cost And General Price Level Adjusted Earnings," CAR, 1988, Vol. 4, No. 2, pp. 485-507.)

Shamberg, Stephen C. "Can Controllers Avoid Legal Problems?," MA, 1987, Vol. 68, No. 9, pp. 18-24.

Shamis, Gary S. (Shank, John K. and Gary S. Shamis.

"Reporting Foreign Currency Adjustments: A Disclosure Perspective," **JOA**, 1979, Vol. 147, No. 4, pp. 59-67.)

Shane, Barry. (Bailes, Jack, Barry Shane and C. Dean Pielstick. "Using Your PC To Project Capital Investment Funds," **MA**, 1988, Vol. 70, No. 1, pp. 59-62.)

Shane, Philip B. and Barry H. Spicer. "Market Response To Environmental Information Produced Outside The Firm." **AR**, 1983, Vol. 58, No. 3, pp. 521-538.

Shane, Philip B. (Ettredge, Michael, Philip B. Shane and David Smith. "Audit Firm Size And The Association Between Reported Earnings And Security Returns," **AJPT**, 1988, Vol. 7, No. 2, pp. 29-42.)

Shank, John K. and Gary S. Shamis. "Reporting Foreign Currency Adjustments: A Disclosure Perspective," **JOA**, 1979, Vol. 147, No. 4, pp. 59-67.

Shank, John K. and Neil C. Churchill. "Variance Analysis: A Management Oriented Approach." **AR**, 1977, Vol. 52, No. 4, pp. 950-957.

Shank, John K. and Richard J. Murdock. "Comparability In The Application Of Reporting Standards: Some Further Evidence," **AR**, 1978, Vol. 53, No. 4, pp. 824-835.

Shank, John K. and Ronald M. Copeland. "Corporate Personality Theory And Changes In Accounting Methods." **AR**, 1973, Vol. 48, No. 3, pp. 494-501.

Shank, John K. and Vijay Govindarajan. "The Perils Of Cost Allocation Based On Production Volumes," **AH**, 1988, Vol. 2, No. 4, pp. 71-79.

Shank, John K. "Earnings Per Share, Stock Prices, And APB Opinion No. 15," **JAR**, 1971, Vol. 9, No. 1, pp. 165-170.

Shank, John K. "Income Determination Under Uncertainty: An Application Of Markov Chains." **AR**, 1971, Vol. 46, No. 1, pp. 57-74.

Shank, John K. "The Pursuit Of Accounting Standards - Whither And Whence," **CPAJ**, 1974, Vol. 44, No. 4, pp. 59-62.

Shank, John K. (Churchill, Neil C. and John K. Shank. "Accounting For Affirmative Action Programs: A Stochastic Flow Approach." **AR**, 1975, Vol. 50, No. 4, pp. 643-656.)

Shank, John K. (Copeland, Ronald M. and John K. Shank. "LIFO And The Diffusion Of Innovation," **JAR**, 1971, Vol. 9, Supp., pp. 196-224.)

Shank, John K. (Cready, William M. and John K. Shank. "Understanding Accounting Changes In An Efficient Market: A Comment, Replication, And Re-Interpretation." **AR**, 1987, Vol. 62, No. 3, pp. 589-596.)

Shank, John K. (Govindarajan, V. and John K. Shank. "Cash Sufficiency: The Missing Link In Strategic Planning." **CA**, 1984, Vol. 2, No. 1, pp. 23-32.)

Shank, John K., Jesse F. Dillard and Richard J. Murdock. "CPA's Attitudes Toward 'Subject To' Opinions," **CPAJ**, 1978, Vol. 48, No. 8, pp. 43-47.

Shank, J. K. (San Miguel, J. G., J. K. Shank and V. Govindarajan. "Extending Corporate Accountability: A Survey And Framework For Analysis." **AOS**, 1977, Vol. 2, No. 4, pp. 333-348.)

Shannon, Donald S. and William T. Stevens. "How Debt Refunding Can Cause Decision Conflicts," **MA**, 1983, Vol. 65, No. 6, pp. 40-44.

Shannon, Donald S. (Dittrich, John E. and Donald S. Shannon. "Manpower Development," **MA**, 1975, Vol. 57, No. 4, pp. 29-32.)

Shanno, David F. and Roman L. Weil. "The Separate Phases Method Of Accounting For Leveraged Leases: Properties Of The Allocating Rate And An Algorithm For Finding It," **JAR**, 1976, Vol. 14, No. 2, pp. 348-356.

Shanteau, James. (Krogstad, Jack L., Richard T. Ettenson and James Shanteau. "Context And Experience In Auditors' Materiality Judgments," **AJPT**, 1984-85, Vol. 4, No. 1, pp. 54-74.)

Shapiro, Alan C. "Evaluation And Control Of Foreign Operations," **IJAER**, 1978, Vol. 14, No. 1, pp. 83-104.

Shapiro, Bernard M. (Braitman, Howard L., James J. Klink and Bernard M. Shapiro. "Real Estate Industry Benefits From ERTA 1981," **CPAJ**, 1982, Vol. 52, No. 3, pp. 32-38.)

Shapiro, Theodore. "Going Private: Accounting And Tax Considerations," **CPAJ**, 1975, Vol. 45, No. 11, pp. 17-22.

Sharaf, Hussein A. and R. K. Mautz. "An Operational Concept Of Independence," **AR**, 1960, Vol. 109, No. 4, pp. 49-54.

Sharav, Itzhak. "Cost Justification Under The Robinson-Patman Act," **MA**, 1978, Vol. 60, No. 1, pp. 15-22.

Sharav, Itzhak. "The CPA And The Public Policy Makers: Rent Controls As A Case," **CPAJ**, 1972, Vol. 42, No. 7, pp. 561-565.

Sharav, Itzhak. "Transfer Pricing - Diversity Of Goals And Practices," **JOA**, 1974, Vol. 137, No. 4, pp. 56-62.

Sharits, Earl C. "Business Income And The Cash Basis," **AR**, 1954, Vol. 29, No. 3, pp. 494-499.

Sharkas, Wajdy. "The Effectiveness Of The Supreme Audit Bureau In Kuwait In Monitoring Public Expenditures: An Evaluation," **IJAER**, 1985, Vol. 21, No. 1, pp. 123-142.

Sharp, Douglas. "The Effect Of Direct Costing On The Relative Size Of Financial Ratios," **MA**, 1970, Vol. 52, No. 5, pp. 14-18.

Sharp, Douglas. (Wu, Frederick H. and Douglas Sharp. "An Empirical Study Of Transfer Pricing Practice," **IJAER**, 1979, Vol. 14, No. 2, pp. 71-99.)

Sharp, Florence C. and Robert W. Ingram. "Measuring The Periodic Performance Of Government: Policy And Research Issues," **RIGNA**, 1985, Vol. 1, pp. 149-179.

Sharp, Florence C. "The Effects Of Governmental Accounting Methods On Asset-Acquisition Decisions: A Theoretical Model And Three Case Studies," **JAPP**, 1985, Vol. 4, No. 4, pp. 251-276.

Sharp, Harold E. "Control And Management Of Indirect Expenses," **MA**, 1973, Vol. 54, No. 8, pp. 21-25.

Sharp, John. (Pike, Richard, John Sharp and Jeffrey Kantor. "The Role Of Accounting Information In Valuing Unlisted Shares," **ABR**, 1988, Vol. 18, No. 71, pp. 249-255.)

Sharp, Norman and Ken Milani. "Hospital Budgeting," **MA**, 1977, Vol. 58, No. 9, pp. 49-52.

Sharp, Robert A. (Skousen, K. Fred, Robert A. Sharp and Russell K. Tolman. "Corporate Disclosure Of Budgetary Data." **JOA**, 1972, Vol. 133, No. 5, pp. 50-57.)

Sharp, Robert F. and Eric E. Spires. "Attributability And Distributability Of Profit To Shareholders," **ABR**, 1983-84, Vol. 14, No. 53, pp. 55-62.

Sharp, Robert F. "Comparison Of Conventional And Adjusted Performance Measures Under Simulated Price Stabilization." **JAPP**, 1986, Vol. 5, No. 2, pp. 93-110.

Sharp, Robert F. (Hauworth, William P., II, Valdean C. Lembke and Robert F. Sharp. "The Effects Of Inflation: How They Persist," **JAAF**, 1987, Vol. 2 (New Issues), No. 2, pp. 184-196.)

Sharp, Robert F. (Hreha, Karen S., Robert F. Sharp and Eugene Willis. "An Analysis Of Two Proposed Cost Recovery Systems," **JATA**, 1986, Vol. 7, No. 2, pp. 76-84.)

Sharpe, Ian G. "Econometric Model Building In Financial Management," **ABACUS**, 1974, Vol. 10 No. 1, pp. 55-73.

Sharpe, I. G. and R. G. Walker. "Asset Revaluations And Stock Market Prices," **JAR**, 1975, Vol. 13, No. 2, pp. 293-310.

Shartle, R. B. "How Scientific Sampling Controls Accuracy In Invoicing," **JOA**, 1952, Vol. 94, No. 2, pp. 167-171.

Shashua, Leon and Yaaqov Goldschmidt. "Laspeyres Indexes For Variance Analysis In Cost Accounting: A Reply," **AR**, 1976, Vol. 51, No. 2, pp. 432-433.

Shashua, Leon, Yaaqov Goldschmidt and Dorikam Shadmon. "Control Charts For Citrus Packing Plants," **MA**, 1975, Vol. 56, No. 9, pp. 19-21.

Shashua, Leon. (Goldschmidt, Yaaqov and Leon Shashua. "Distortion Of Income By SFAS No. 33," **JAAF**, 1984, Vol. 8, No. 1, pp. 54-67.)

Shashua, L. (Bashan, O., Y. Goldschmidt, G. Levkowitz and L. Shashua. "Laspeyres Indexes For Variance Analysis In Cost Accounting," **AR**, 1973, Vol. 48, No. 4, pp. 790-793.)

Shashua, L., Y. Goldschmidt and A. Melnik. "The Predictive Value Of Interim Reports And Budgets," **ABACUS**, 1973, Vol. 9, No. 2, pp. 176-179.

Shastri, Kuldeep. (Denning, Karen C. and Kuldeep Shastri. "An Option Pricing Technique For Auditor Review Of Insider Trading," **RIAR**, 1988, Vol. 2, pp. 25-39.)

Shaub, H. James. "Transfer Pricing In A Decentralized Organization," **MA**, 1978, Vol. 59, No. 10, pp. 33-36.

Shaub, Larry N. "Minimum Required Payment Of Estimated Federal Income Tax," **MA**, 1975, Vol. 57, No. 2, pp. 39-42.

Shaub, Michael K. "Restructuring The Code Of Professional Ethics: A Review Of The Anderson Committee Report And Its Implications," **AH**, 1988, Vol. 2, No. 4, pp. 89-97.

Shaulis, L. L. "Instruction In Accounting For Liberal Education," **AR**, 1930, Vol. 5, No. 3, pp. 222-225.

Shawky, H. (Petri, E. and H. Shawky. "Cash Distributions Of Inflationary Gains," **ABACUS**, 1983, Vol. 19, No. 1, pp. 56-63.)

Shaw, Barrie S. (Ellyson, Robert C. and Barrie S. Shaw. "The Psychological Assessment And Staff Recruiting," **JOA**, 1970, Vol. 129, No. 3, pp. 35-42.)

Shaw, Delphine R. (Tietze, Armin R. and Delphine R. Shaw. "OPUS: A New Concept For Mastering Cost," **MA**, 1986, Vol. 68, No. 2, pp. 27-31.)

Shaw, John C. (Crouse, W. Frank, Maurice C. Paradis and John C. Shaw. "The Client Service Team Approach To Auditing," **JOA**, 1979, Vol. 148, No. 2, pp. 52-58.)

Shaw, J. C. "Criteria For Consolidation," **ABR**, 1976-77, Vol. 7, No. 25, pp. 71-78.

Shaw, Richard. (Askari, Hossein, Patricia Cain and Richard Shaw. "A Government Tax Subsidy," **AR**, 1976, Vol. 51, No. 2, pp. 331-334.)

Shaw, T. T. "Changes In Methods Of Accounting," **JOA**, 1957, Vol. 104, No. 5, pp. 50-56.

Shaw, T. T. "Corporate Liquidations," **JOA**, 1956, Vol. 102, No. 2, pp. 41-48.

Shaw, T. T. "Scope And Limitation Of Tax Practice," **JOA**, 1957, Vol. 104, No. 2, pp. 37-41.

Shaw, T. T. "Tax Effects Of Corporate Distributions And Adjustments," **JOA**, 1954, Vol. 98, No. 3, pp. 328-348.

Shaw, Wayne H. "Measuring The Impact Of The Safe Harbor Lease Law On Security Prices," **JAR**, 1988, Vol. 26, No. 1, pp. 60-81.

Shaw, Wayne H. "Safe Harbor Or Muddy Waters," **AR**, 1987, Vol. 62, No. 2, pp. 385-400.

Shaw, Wayne H. (Elliott, John A. and Wayne H. Shaw. "Write-Offs As Accounting Procedures To Manage Perceptions," **JAR**, 1988, Vol. 26, Supp., pp. 91-119.)

Shaw, William L. (Taussig, Russell A. and William L. Shaw. "Accounting For Productivity: A Practical Approach," **MA**, 1985, Vol. 66, No. 11, pp. 48-52.)

Shaw, William R. "Partners' Compensation," **JOA**, 1966, Vol. 122, No. 3, pp. 51-55.

Shayeb, David. "Inventory Valuation Problems: Ten Causes And Solutions," **CA**, 1986, Vol. 4, No. 1, pp. 30-37.

Shea, Edward T. "Unmeasured Direct-Labor Payment Plan," **MA**, 1972, Vol. 54, No. 4, pp. 27-28.

Shearer, Leonard L. "Direct Costing For Sales Pricing And Profit Planning," **MA**, 1967, Vol. 48, No. 11, pp. 17-23.

Shearon, Winston T. (Swanson, Edward P., Winston T. Shearon and Lynn R. Thomas. "Predicting Current Cost Operating

Profit Using Component Models Incorporating Analysts' Forecasts," **AR**, 1985, Vol. 60, No. 4, pp. 681-691.)

Shearon, Winston, Charles Butler and James Benjamin. "Audit Aspects Of Small Computer Systems," **CPAJ**, 1980, Vol. 50, No. 8, pp. 17-21.

Sheffey, Michael B. "The Amount Of A Charitable Contribution Of Property: A Decision-Tree Approach," **AR**, 1976, Vol. 51, No. 3, pp. 642-643.

Sheffield, Susie and William B. Pollard. "Tax Preparer Penalties," **CPAJ**, 1985, Vol. 55, No. 6, pp. 34-43.

Shefsky, Lloyd E. and Edward J. Schwartz. "Disclosures And Reporting Under ASR No. 115," **JOA**, 1973, Vol. 136, No. 3, pp. 53-61.

Sheldahl, Terry K. "America's Earliest Recorded Text In Accounting: Sarjeant's 1789 Book," **AHJ**, 1985, Vol. 12, No. 2, pp. 1-42.

Sheldahl, Terry K. "Reporting Treasury Stock As An Asset: Law, Logic, And Economic Substance," **AHJ**, 1982, Vol. 9, No. 2, pp. 1-23.

Sheldahl, Terry K. "Toward A Code Of Professional Ethics For Management Accountants," **MA**, 1980, Vol. 62, No. 2, pp. 36-40.

Sheldahl, Terry K. (Previts, Gary John and Terry K. Sheldahl. "Accounting And 'Countinghouses': An Analysis And Commentary," **ABACUS**, 1977, Vol. 13, No. 1, pp. 52-59.)

Sheldah, Terry K. "Ethical Dilemmas In Management Accounting," **MA**, 1986, Vol. 67, No. 7, pp. 34-41.

Shellenberger, John S. (Smith, E. Wakefield and John S. Shellenberger. "Some Unpublished Audit Reports," **JOA**, 1970, Vol. 130, No. 5, pp. 45-52.)

Shelton, Fred A. and Jack C. Bailes. "How To Create An Electronic Spreadsheet Budget," **MA**, 1986, Vol. 68, No. 1, pp. 40-47.

Shen, Paul. "Cash Flow Budgeting For The Importer," **MA**, 1980, Vol. 62, No. 3, pp. 33-35.

Shenkir, William G. and Robert H. Strawser. "Auditing And Management Advisory Services: A Conflict Of Roles," **ABACUS**, 1972, Vol. 8, No. 1, pp. 13-20.

Shenkir, William G. "A Perspective On The Measurement Of Earnings And FASB Policymaking," **AHJ**, 1976, Vol. 3, No. 1-4, pp. 40-42.

Shenkir, William G. "Accounting History, The Accounting Historian And The FASB," **AHJ**, 1975, Vol. 2, No. 1-4. pp. 22-24.

Shenkir, William G. "An Exercise For Use In Discussing Audit Evidence," **AR**, 1971, Vol. 46, No. 4, pp. 799-801.

Shenkir, William G. "Media And Accounting Education," **AR**, 1970, Vol. 45, No. 2, pp. 347-350.

Shenkir, William G. (Bedford, Norton M. and William G. Shenkir. "Reorienting Accounting Education," **JOA**, 1987, Vol. 164, No. 2, pp. 84-91.)

Shenkir, William G. (Coleman, Almand R., William G. Shenkir and Williard E. Stone. "Accounting In Colonial Virginia: A Case Study," **JOA**, 1974, Vol. 138, No. 1, pp. 32-43.)

Shenkir, William G., Glenn A. Welsch and James A. Bear, Jr. "Thomas Jefferson: Management Accountant," **JOA**, 1972, Vol. 133, No. 4, pp. 33-47.

Shenkir, William G., Thomas L. Wheelen and Robert H. Strawser. "The Making Of An Accountant," **CPAJ**, 1973, Vol. 43, No. 3, pp. 218-221.

Shenkman, Martin M. "A Real Estate Leasing Checklist: Are Your Clients Making The Most Of Your Services?," **JOA**, 1988, Vol. 166, No. 2, pp. 78-84.

Sherer, Harvey. "Modern Trends In Financial Reporting For Colleges And Universities Over Past 20 Years," **JOA**, 1950, Vol. 90, No. 3, pp. 211-212.

Sherer, M. J. (Cooper, D. J. and M. J. Sherer. "The Value Of Corporate Accounting Reports: Arguments For A Political Economy Of Accounting," **AOS**, 1984, Vol. 9, No. 3/4, pp. 207-232.)

Sherman, H. David. "Data Envelopment Analysis As A New Managerial Audit Methodology - Test And Evaluation," **AJPT**, 1984-85, Vol. 4, No. 1, pp. 35-53.

Sherman, H. David. "Interpreting Hospital Performance With Financial Statement Analysis," **AR**, 1986, Vol. 61, No. 3, pp. 526-550.

Sherman, H. David. "Measurement Of Hospital Performance And Implications For Accounting," **RIGNA**, 1986, Vol. 2, pp. 135-150.

Sherman, Samuel J. "Anatomy Of Medical Expense Deductions," **CPAJ**, 1972, Vol. 42, No. 3, pp. 205-216.

Sherman, Samuel J. "Medical Expense Deductions Updated," **CPAJ**, 1974, Vol. 44, No. 6, pp. 33-42.

Sherman, W. Richard. "Internationalizing The Accounting Curriculum," **JAED**, 1987, Vol. 5, No. 2, pp. 259-275.

Sherman, W. Richard. "Where's The 'r' In Debit?," **AHJ**, 1986, Vol. 13, No. 2, pp. 137-143.

Sherritt, Lawrence W. "Simplifying The Presentation Of Compound Interest Formulas," **AR**, 1944, Vol. 19, No. 3, pp. 310-314.

Sherwood, Kenneth A. and Benzion Barlev. "Materiality - A Note And A Reply," **ABR**, 1972-73, Vol. 3, No. 9, pp. 77-78.

Shevlin, Terry. "Taxes And Off-Balance-Sheet Financing: Research And Development Limited Partnerships," **AR**, 1987, Vol. 62, No. 3, pp. 480-509.

Shevlin, Terry. (Foster, George, Chris Olsen and Terry Shevlin. "Earnings Releases, Anomalies, And The Behavior Of Security Returns," **AR**, 1984, Vol. 59, No. 4, pp. 574-603.)

Shields, David. (Danos, Paul and David Shields. "Referrals From Bankers And Attorneys," **CPAJ**, 1981, Vol. 51, No. 5, pp. 13-19.)

Shields, David. (Eichenseher, John W. and David Shields.

"The Correlates Of CPA-Firm Change For Publicly-Held Corporations," **AJPT**, 1982-83, Vol. 2, No. 2, pp. 23-37.)

Shields, David. (Eichenseher, John W. and David Shields. "Corporate Director Liability And Monitoring Preferences," **JAPP**, 1985, Vol. 4, No. 1, pp. 13-31.)

Shields, D. "Small CPA Firm Product Differentiation In The Small Business Market," **AOS**, 1984, Vol. 9, No. 1, pp. 61-80.

Shields, Janice Christine. "Foreign Language And Accounting Expertise: A Marketable Combination," **IJAER**, 1981, Vol. 17, No. 1, pp. 133-146.

Shields, Michael D. "Effects Of Information Supply And Demand On Judgment Accuracy: Evidence From Corporate Managers," **AR**, 1983, Vol. 58, No. 2, pp. 284-303.

Shields, Michael D. (Bailey, K. E., III, Joseph H. Bylinski and Michael D. Shields. "Effects Of Audit Report Wording Changes On The Perceived Message," **JAR**, 1983, Vol. 21, No. 2, pp. 355-370.)

Shields, Michael D. (Birnberg, Jacob G., Michael D. Shields and Walter McGhee. "The Effects Of Personality On A Subject's Information Processing: A Reply," **AR**, 1980, Vol. 55, No. 3, pp. 507-510.)

Shields, Michael D. (Chow, Chee W., Michael D. Shields and Adrian Wong-Boren. "A Compilation Of Recent Surveys And Company-Specific Descriptions Of Management Accounting Practices," **JAED**, 1988, Vol. 6, No. 2, pp. 183-207.)

Shields, Michael D. (Chow, C. W., M. D. Shields and G. E. Whittenburg. "The Quality Of Tax Practitioners' Judgments Regarding Substantial Authority: Potential Research Directions And An Exploratory Empirical Investigation," **AIT**, 1988, Vol. 2, pp.)

Shields, Michael D. (Lewis, Barry, Michael D. Shields and S. Mark Young. "Evaluating Human Judgments And Decision Aids," **JAR**, 1983, Vol. 21, No. 1, pp. 271-285.)

Shields, Michael D. (McGhee, Walter, Michael D. Shields and Jacob G. Birnberg. "The Effects Of Personality On A Subject's Information Processing," **AR**, 1978, Vol. 53. No. 3, pp. 681-697.)

Shields, Michael D. (Rockness, Howard O. and Michael D. Shields. "An Empirical Analysis Of The Expenditure Budget In Research And Development," **CAR**, 1988, Vol. 4, No. 2, pp. 568-581.)

Shields, Michael D., Ira Solomon and William S. Waller. "Auditors' Usage Of Unaudited Book Values When Making Presampling Audit Value Estimates," **CAR**, 1988, Vol. 5, No. 1, pp. 1-18.

Shields, M. D. and W. S. Waller. "A Behavioral Study Of Accounting Variables In Performance-Incentive Contracts," **AOS**, 1988, Vol. 13, No. 6, pp. 581-594.

Shields, M. D. "A Predecisional Approach To The Measurement Of The Demand For Information In A Performance Report," **AOS**, 1984, Vol. 9, No. 3/4, pp. 355-364.

Shields, M. D. "Some Effects Of Information Load On Search Patterns Used To Analyze Performance Reports," **AOS**, 1980, Vol. 5, No. 4, pp. 429-442.

Shields, M. D. (Birnberg, J. G. and M. D. Shields. "The Role Of Attention And Memory In Accounting Decisions," **AOS**, 1984, Vol. 9, No. 3/4, pp. 365-382.)

Shields, M. D. (Birnberg, J. G., I. Hanson Frieze and M. D. Shields. "The Role Of Attribution Theory In Control Systems," **AOS**, 1977, Vol. 2, No. 3, pp. 189-200.)

Shields, M. D. (Rockness, H. O. and M. D. Shields. "Organizational Control Systems In Research And Development," **AOS**, 1984, Vol. 9, No. 2, pp. 165-178.)

Shields, M. D. (Young, S. M., M. D. Shields and G. Wolf. "Manufacturing Controls And Performance: An Experiment," **AOS**, 1988, Vol. 13, No. 6, pp. 607-618.)

Shields, M. D., I. Solomon and W. S. Waller. "Effects Of Alternative Sample Space Representations On The Accuracy Of Auditors' Uncertainty Judgments," **AOS**, 1987, Vol. 12, No. 3, pp. 375-388.

Shields, M. D., J. G. Birnberg and I. Hanson Frieze. "Attributions, Cognitive Processes And Control Systems," **AOS**, 1981, Vol. 6, No. 1, pp. 69-96.

Shield, Hans J. "Allocation Of Income Taxes," **JOA**, 1957, Vol. 103, No. 4, pp. 53-60.

Shiflett, Arnold D. "How We Automated Our Accounting Department," **MA**, 1983, Vol. 64, No. 12, pp. 34-39.

Shih, Michael S. H. and Shyam Sunder. "Design And Tests Of An Efficient Search Algorithm For Accurate Linear Valuation Systems," **CAR**, 1987-88, Vol. 4, No. 1, pp. 16-31.

Shih, Wei. "A Comment On Shih's General Decision Model For CVP Analysis - A Reply," **AR**, 1981, Vol. 56, No. 4, pp. 984-985.

Shih, Wei. "A General Decision Model For Cost-Volume-Profit Analysis Under Uncertainty," **AR**, 1979, Vol. 54, No. 4. pp. 687-706.

Shih, Wei. "A General Decision Model For Cost-Volume-Profit Analysis Under Uncertainty: A Reply," **AR**, 1981, Vol. 56, No. 2, pp. 404-408.

Shildneck, Barbara J. "The CPA As Advocate," **JOA**, 1988, Vol. 165, No. 6, pp. 49-55.

Shildneck, Barbara J. (Edwards, James Don and Barbara J. Shildneck. "The AICPA's First Century," **MA**, 1987, Vol. 69, No. 3, pp. 57-61.)

Shildneck, Barbara. (Berton, Lee and Barbara Shildneck. "The 75-Year History Of The Journal," **JOA**, 1980, Vol. 150, No. 5, pp. 48-54.)

Shillinglaw, Gordon. "Concepts Underlying Interim Financial Statements," **AR**, 1961, Vol. 36, No. 2, pp. 222-231.

Shillinglaw, Gordon. "Leasing And Financial Statements," **AR**, 1958, Vol. 33, No. 4, pp. 581-592.

Shillinglaw, Gordon. "The Concept Of Attributable Cost," **JAR**, 1963, Vol. 1, No. 1, pp. 73-85.

Shillinglaw, Gordon. "Toward A Theory Of Divisional Income

Measurement," **AR**, 1962, Vol. 37, No. 2, pp. 208-216.

Shimerda, Thomas A. (Lewis, Tom D., Thomas A. Shimerda and Gerald Graham. "What The Academic Advisor Needs To Know About Job Placement," **JAED**, 1983, Vol. 1, No. 2, pp. 135-142.)

Shimme, Shinshichiro. "Introduction Of Double-Entry Book-keeping Into Japan," **AR**, 1937, Vol. 12, No. 3, pp. 290-295.

Shim, Jae K. "An Econometric Investigation On Forecasting Cash Inflows For Budgeting," **AIA**, 1986, Vol. 3, pp. 71-82.

Shin, Hong-Chul. (Brockett, P., A. Charnes, W. W. Cooper and Hong-Chul Shin. "A Chance-Constrained Programming Approach To Cost-Volume-Profit Analysis," **AR**, 1984, Vol. 59, No. 3, pp. 474-487.)

Shin, Joon. (Uecker, Wilfred, Albert Schepanski and Joon Shin. "Toward A Positive Theory Of Information Evaluation: Relevant Tests Of Competing Models In a Principal-Agency Setting," **AR**, 1985, Vol. 60, No. 3, pp. 430-457.)

Shinawi, Ahmed Abdul Kadir and William F. Crum. "The Emergence Of Professional Accounting In Saudi Arabia," **IJAER**, 1971, Vol. 6, No. 2, pp. 103-110.

Shinneman, William J. "Product Evaluation Using The Assigned-Value Approach," **MA**, 1968, Vol. 49, No. 9, pp. 35-40.

Shipley, Kent and Robert Engle. "We Need More Ph.D.s In Accounting," **MA**, 1982, Vol. 64, No. 5, pp. 36-41.

Shirk, Stanley E. "Is There More Than One Set Of Generally Accepted Accounting Principles?," **JOA**, 1950, Vol. 90, No. 3, pp. 226-234.

Shirk, Stanley E. "Special Problems Of Bank Audits," **JOA**, 1960, Vol. 109, No. 4, pp. 35-42.

Shirley, Robert E. "Measuring Performance Of A University Accounting Department," **MA**, 1978, Vol. 60, No. 6, pp. 51-53.

Shirley, Robert E. (Wheeler, Dennie L. and Robert E. Shirley. "Minimizing The LIFO Pool Sample," **MA**, 1976, Vol. 58, No. 6, pp. 47-53.)

Shirley, Tim. "The Leveraged ESOT As A Financing Tool," **MA**, 1981, Vol. 63, No. 1, pp. 49-52.

Shlosberg, Jeffrey L. (Burton, E. James, James C. McKeown and Jeffrey L. Shlosberg. "The Generation And Administration Of Examinations On Interactive Computer Systems," **AR**, 1978, Vol. 53, No. 1, pp. 170-178.)

Shockley, Randolph A. and Robert N. Holt. "A Behavioral Investigation Of Supplier Differentiation In The Market For Audit Services," **JAR**, 1983, Vol. 21, No. 2, pp. 545-564.

Shockley, Randolph A. "Perceptions Of Audit Independence: A Conceptual Model," **JAAF**, 1982, Vol. 5, No. 2, pp. 126-143.

Shockley, Randolph A. "Perceptions Of Auditors' Independence: An Empirical Analysis," **AR**, 1981, Vol. 56, No. 4, pp. 785-800.

Shockley, Randolph A. (Engstrom, John H. and Randolph A. Shockley. "Financial Reporting For The Georgia Colony," **AHJ**, 1985, Vol. 12, No. 2, pp. 43-58.)

Shockley, Randolph A. (Rouse, Robert W. and Randolph A. Shockley. "Setting Realistic Expectations For Publishing In Leading Accounting Research Journals," **JAED**, 1984, Vol. 2, No. 2, pp. 43-52.)

Shoemaker, Charles and Bill Hook. "Developing Bidding Factors For A Quality Assurance Department," **MA**, 1970, Vol. 51, No. 7, pp. 41-44.

Shoenthal, Edward R. "Differences In Competencies Of Newly Licensed Accountants In The United States And Great Britain,". **JAED**, 1988, Vol. 6, No. 2, pp. 235-249.

Shomler, Russell P. "Guideposts From Collegiate To Practicing Senior," **AR**, 1953, Vol. 28. No. 4, pp. 534-538.

Shonting, D. M. and L. D. Stone. "Auditing Electronic Systems," **JOA**, 1958, Vol. 106, No. 4. pp. 54-61.

Shonting, D. M. "Accounting For 'Income' Of Municipalities: Comments," **AR**, 1936, Vol. 11, No. 2, pp. 169-170.

Shopoff, Robert W. and William R. Jack. "Organizing, Staffing And Operating The Information Services Function," **MA**, 1967, Vol. 49, No. 2, pp. 3-8.

Short, Daniel G. "A Comparison Of Alternative Methods Of Estimating Constant Dollar Depreciation," **AR**, 1985, Vol. 60, No. 3, pp. 500-503.

Short, Daniel G. "The Impact Of Price-Level Adjustment In The Context Of Risk Assessment," **JAR**, 1978, Vol. 16, Supp., pp. 259-284.

Short, Daniel G. (Granof, Michael H. and Daniel G. Short. "Why Do Companies Reject LIFO?," **JAAF**, 1984, Vol. 7, No. 4, pp. 323-333.)

Short, Jack E. (Baggett, Monte R., Richard D. Dole and Jack E. Short. "Accounting And Auditing For Drilling Funds," **CPAJ**, 1981, Vol. 51, No. 9, pp. 27-37.)

Shoulders, Craig Douglas. (Freeman, Robert J. and Craig Douglas Shoulders. "Defining The Governmental Reporting Entity," **JOA**, 1982, Vol. 154, No. 4, pp. 50-64.)

Shoulders, Craig D. "Criteria For Identifying The Municipal Organizational Reporting Entity," **RIGNA**, 1987, Vol. 3, Part A, pp. 181-206.

Shoulders, Craig D. (Freeman, Robert J. and Craig D. Shoulders. "Governmental Fund Operating Results: 3 Formats," **JOA**, 1982, Vol. 154, No. 5, pp. 110-121.)

Showfety, Raymond. (Epstein, Stephen and Raymond Showfety. "Section 304: Tax Trap For The Unwary," **CPAJ**, 1975, Vol. 45, No. 12, pp. 27-29.)

Shpilberg, David and Lynford E. Graham. "Developing ExperTAX: An Expert System For Corporate Tax Accrual And Planning," **AJPT**, 1986-87, Vol. 6, No. 1, pp. 75-94.

Shriver, Keith A. "A Note On The Estimation Of Current Cost Depreciation," **AIA**, 1988, Vol. 6, pp. 129-142.

Shriver, Keith A. "An Empirical Examination Of The Effects Of Alternative Measurement Techniques On Current Cost Data," **AR**, 1987, Vol. 62, No. 1, pp. 79-96.

Shriver, Keith A. "Further Evidence On The Marginal Gains In Accuracy Of Alternative Levels Of Specificity Of The Producer Price Indexes," **JAR**, 1986, Vol. 24, No. 1, pp. 151-165.

Shriver, Keith A. (DeBerg, Curtis L. and Keith A. Shriver. "The Relevance Of Current Cost Accounting Data: A Review And Analysis Of Recent Studies," **JAL**, 1987, Vol. 6, pp. 55-87.)

Shriver, Keith A. (Dugan, Michael T. and Keith A. Shriver. "The Importance Of An Environmental Criterion In Applied Business Research," **IAE**, 1988, Vol. 3, No. 1, pp. 42-47.)

Shriver, Keith A. (Dugan, Michael T., James A. Gentry and Keith A. Shriver. "The X-11 Model: A New Analytical Review Technique For The Auditor," **AJPT**, 1984-85, Vol. 4, No. 2, pp. 11-22.)

Shriver, Keith A. (Swanson, Edward P. and Keith A. Shriver. "The Accounting-For-Changing-Prices Experiment: A Valid Test Of Usefulness?," **ACCHOR**, 1987, Vol. 1, No. 3, pp. 69-78.)

Shuaib, Shuaib A. "Accounting Information And The Development Planning Process In Kuwait," **IJAER**, 1980, Vol. 15. No. 2, pp. 129-141.

Shuey, Ronald E. (Brenner, Vincent C. and Ronald E. Shuey. "An Empirical Study Of Support For APB Opinion No. 16," **JAR**, 1972, Vol. 10, No. 1, pp. 200-208.)

Shugerman, Abe L. "Historical Costs Vs. Deferred Costs As Basic Concepts For Financial Statement Valuations," **AR**, 1951, Vol. 26, No. 4, pp. 492-495.

Shultis, Robert L. "Are There Real-Time Financial Statements In Your Future?," **MA**, 1967, Vol. 48, No. 12. pp. 13-22.

Shultis, Robert L. "Must Accountants' Writing Be So Dull?," **MA**, 1969, Vol. 51, No. 4, pp. 23-25.

Shurtz, Nancy E. (Harmelink, Philip J. and Nancy E. Shurtz. "Tax Effects In Divorce Planning," **CPAJ**, 1977, Vol. 47, No. 10, pp. 27-32.)

Shuster, Harvey L. and Paul D. Warner. "Micros For Small Business: The Time Is Now," **MA**, 1984, Vol. 65, No. 9, pp. 45-48.

Shute, John. "Comments On Dr. Churchill's Paper On Highway Finance," **IJAER**. 1968, Vol. 4, No. 1, pp. 111-113.

Shuttleworth, J. Sterling. (Drozdak, Dennis P. and J. Sterling Shuttleworth. "Alternatives To Risk Funding," No. 7, pp. 15-18.)

Shwayder, Keith R. "Accounting For Exchange Rate Fluctuations," **AR**, 1972, Vol. 47, No. 4, pp. 747-760.

Shwayder, Keith R. "Two 'Wrongs' Making A 'Right'," **JAR**, 1973. Vol. 11, No. 2, pp. 259-272.

Shwayder, Keith R. (Hein, Clarence D. and Keith R. Shwayder. "Some Accounting Problems In Divesting Former Acquisitions," **CPAJ**, 1974, Vol. 44, No. 11, pp. 33-38.)

Shwayder, Keith. "A Critique Of Economic Income As An Accounting Concept," **ABACUS**, 1967, Vol. 3, No. 1, pp. 23-35.

Shwayder, Keith. "A Note On A Contribution Margin Approach To The Analysis Of Capacity Utilization," **AR**, 1968, Vol. 43. No. 1, pp. 101-104.

Shwayder, Keith. "A Proposed Modification To Residual Income - Interest Adjusted Income," **AR**, 1970, Vol. 45, No. 2, pp. 299-307.

Shwayder, Keith. "Expected And Unexpected Price Level Changes," **AR**, 1971, Vol. 46, No. 2, pp. 306-319.

Shwayder, Keith. "Relevance," **JAR**, 1968, Vol. 6, No. 1, pp. 86-97.

Shwayder, Keith. "The Capital Maintenance Rule And The Net Asset Valuation Rule," **AR**, 1969, Vol. 44, No. 2, pp. 304-316.

Sias, Carleton P. "Financial Communication With Graphics," **MA**, 1970, Vol. 51, No. 10, pp. 40-42.

Sias, Randall G. "Pricing Bank Services," **MA**, 1985, Vol. 67, No. 1, pp. 48-50.

Sibelman, Howard S. (Akresh, Abraham D., John E. Mitchell and Howard S. Sibelman. "Obtaining Value From An Audit," **CA**, 1987, Vol. 5, No. 1, pp. 15-18.)

Sibley, A. Michael and Gerald L. Waddle. "The Liquidation Alternative In Business Planning," **MA**, 1977, Vol. 59, No. 3, pp. 33-35.

Sibley, A. M. and Charles T. Rini. "How Often Should You Pay Dividends?," **MA**, 1974, Vol. 56, No. 5, pp. 40-42.

Siddall, K. Y. "Some Postwar Problems Of Industry," **AR**, 1944, Vol. 19, No. 1, pp. 76-80.

Sidebotham, Roy. "An Accounting Framework For Local Authorities." **ABACUS**, 1966, Vol. 2, No. 1, pp. 24-40.

Sidebotham, Roy. "Comments On The Teacher Development Report," **AR**, 1965, Vol. 40, No. 4, pp. 876-879.

Siebel, Jerry D. (DeBord, Warren A. and Jerry D. Siebel. "Training MIS Users Through Simulation," **MA**, 1982. Vol. 63, No. 9, pp. 36-42.)

Siebel, Jerry D. (Pattillo, James W. and Jerry D. Siebel. "Factors Affecting The Materiality Judgment," **CPAJ**, 1974, Vol. 44, No. 7, pp. 39-44.)

Siebers, Ted. "Accounting For Commodity Futures," **MA**, 1985, Vol. 66, No. 10, pp. 42-47.

Siegel, Andrew C., Arthur S. Cohen and Laurence I. Feibel. "ESOPs - The Present And An Imperiled Future? - Part II," **CPAJ**, 1986, Vol. 56, No. 2, pp. 32-35.

Siegel, Andrew C., Arthur S. Cohen and Laurence I. Feibel. "ESOPs - The Present And An Imperiled Future? - Part I," **CPAJ**, 1986, Vol. 56, No. 1, pp. 14-23.

Siegel, Gary and James P. Martin, Jr. "The Need For National Institutional Advertising," **CPAJ**, 1978, Vol.

48, No. 4, pp. 27-32.

Siegel, Gary. "National Study On Professional Accounting Education: Initial Results On Department/Professional School Differences," **IAE**, 1983. No. 1. pp. 9-18.

Siegel, Gary. "Specialization And Segmentation In The Accounting Profession," **JOA**, 1977. Vol. 144. No. 5. pp. 74-81.

Siegel, Jacob P. (Dermer, Jerry and Jacob P. Siegel. "The Role Of Behavioral Measures In Accounting For Human Resources," **AR**, 1974, Vol. 49. No. 1, pp. 88-97.)

Siegel, Joel G. and Roberta M. Siegel. "About Small Business Computers," **CPAJ**, 1984, Vol. 54. No. 6, pp. 40-45.

Siegel, Joel G. (Dauber, Nick and Joel G. Siegel. "The Many Facets Of NOLs In Business Arrangements." **CPAJ**, 1982. Vol. 52. No. 2, pp. 37-43.)

Siegel, Joel. (Savage, Linda and Joel Siegel. "Disposal Of A Segment Of A Business." **CPAJ**, 1978. Vol. 48, No. 9. pp. 32-37.)

Siegel, J. P. (Dermer, J. D. and J. P. Siegel. "The Role Of Behavioral Measures In Accounting For Human Resources: A Reply," **AR**, 1975. Vol. 50, No. 3, pp. 579-581.)

Siegel, Philip H. and John T. Rigsby. "The Relationship Of Accounting Internships And Subsequent Professional Performance," **IAE**, 1988. Vol. 3, No. 2, pp. 423-432.

Siegel, Philip H. "Auditor Performance And Educational Preparation: An Analysis," **IAE**, 1987. Vol. 2. No. 1, pp. 127-140.

Siegel, Roberta M. (Siegel, Joel G. and Roberta M. Siegel. "About Small Business Computers," **CPAJ**, 1984. Vol. 54. No. 6, pp. 40-45.)

Siegel, Stanley. (Sorter, George H.. Stanley Siegel and John Slain. "Accountants' Legal Liability: A Determinant Of The Accounting Model," **JAAF**, 1988. Vol. 3 (New Series), No. 3, pp. 233-243.)

Sienkiewicz, Casimir A. "Bank Accounting Problems." **JOA**. 1957. Vol. 104, No. 4, pp. 38-42.

Siers, Howard L. and Joanne K. Blyskal. "Risk Management Of The Internal Audit Function." **MA**. 1987. Vol. 68, No. 8. pp. 29-35.

Sigloch, Berndt A. (Butterworth. John E. and Berndt A. Sigloch. "A Generalized Multi-Stage Input-Output Model And Some Derived Equivalent Systems," **AR**, 1971. Vol. 46. No. 4, pp. 700-716.)

Sigloch, Berndt. "Input-Output Analysis And The Cost Model: A Comment," **AR**, 1971. Vol. 46. No. 2, pp. 374-375.

Sih, S. T. "My Experience In Price-Level Adjustments." **AR**. 1955, Vol. 30, No. 2, pp. 282-283.

Sih, S. T. "Public Accountancy In Hong Kong." **AR**. 1962. Vol. 37, No. 4, pp. 708-712.

Sikora, Martin. (Rock, Milton L. and Martin Sikora. "Accounting For Merger Mania." **MA**. 1987. Vol. 68. No. 10, pp. 20-26.)

Silex, Karl H. (Towles, Martin F. and Karl H. Silex. "Dollar-Value LIFO And Its Effect On Profits." **MA**. 1975. Vol. 57, No. 1, pp. 27-29.)

Silhan, Peter A. and James C. McKeown. "Further Evidence On The Usefulness Of Simulated Mergers." **JAR**. 1985. Vol. 23, No. 1, pp. 416-426.

Silhan, Peter A. "Company Size And The Issue Of Quarterly Segment Reporting," **JAPP**, 1984, Vol. 3. No. 3, pp. 185-197.

Silhan, Peter A. "Management Accounting Is Research." **MA**. 1982. Vol. 64, No. 3, pp. 38-42.

Silhan, Peter A. "Simulated Mergers Of Existent Autonomous Firms: A New Approach To Segmentation Research." **JAR**. 1982. Vol. 20, No. 1. pp. 255-262.

Silhan, Peter A. "The Effects Of Segmenting Quarterly Sales And Margins On Extrapolative Forecasts Of Conglomerate Earnings: Extension And Replication," **JAR**. 1983. Vol. 21. No. 1, pp. 341-347.

Silhan, Peter A. "The Recurring Problem Of Divergent Terminology," **AR**, 1978. Vol. 53. No. 1. pp. 179-181.

Silhan, Peter A. (Hopwood, William S.. Paul Newbold and Peter A. Silhan. "The Potential For Gains In Predictive Ability Through Disaggregation: Segmented Annual Earnings," **JAR**, 1982. Vol. 20. No. 2. pp. 724-732.)

Silhan, Peter A. (Hreha, Karen S. and Peter A. Silhan. "Tax Base Differences Between Worldwide And Water's Edge Methods Of Unitary Taxation," **JATA**, 1988. Vol. 10. No. 1, pp. 89-98.)

Silhan, Peter A. (Hreha, Karen S. and Peter A. Silhan. "An Empirical Analysis Of Unitary Apportionment," **JATA**. 1986, Vol. 8. No. 1, pp. 7-18.)

Silverman, Herbert R. "When Should Clients Use Commercial Financing?," **JOA**. 1955, Vol. 99. No. 6. pp. 51-55.

Silverman, Matthew E. (Mottola. Anthony J. and Matthew E. Silverman. "Managing Telecommunications Costs." **CA**. 1987, Vol. 5, No. 1. pp. 19-25.)

Silverman, O. Jay. "Extermination Planning." **AR**. 1945. Vol. 20. No. 3. pp. 316-319.

Silvern, David H. and Desmond J. Toal. "EDP - Choosing A Partner," **MA**. 1967, Vol. 48. No. 8. pp. 57-60.

Silvern, David H. "Product Opportunity Analysis." **MA**. 1969. Vol. 50, No. 6. pp. 44-46.

Silvern, David H. "The Venture: A Basis For Accounting Theory," **MA**. 1975. Vol. 56, No. 8. pp. 27-31.

Silverstone, Rosalie and Allan Williams. "Recruitment. Training, Employment And Careers Of Women Chartered Accountants In England And Wales." **ABR**. 1978-79, Vol. 9, No. 34, pp. 105-122.

Silvester, Harold. (Lindsay. Daryl. Morina Rennie. George Murphy and Harold Silvester. "Independence Of External Auditors: A Canadian Perspective," **AIIA**. 1987. Vol. 1. pp. 169-189.)

Silvester, W. Harold. (Rege, Udayan P.. W. John Brennan and W. Harold Silvester. "Current Regulatory Practices, Corporate Financial Forecasting, And Takeover Bids," **IJAER**. 1983. Vol. 18, No. 2. pp. 171-175.)

Simel, Stuart A. (Mandel, George, Alan K. Greene and Stuart A. Simel. "Brookhaven Internal Revenue Service Center," **CPAJ**. 1976. Vol. 46. No. 3, pp. 21-24.)

Simich, Stevan and Robert Strauss. "The Energy Audit," **JOA**, 1978. Vol. 146, No. 5, pp. 52-59.

Simik, S. Stephen, II. (Johnson, Glenn L. and S. Stephen Simik. II. "Multiproduct C-V-P-Analysis Under Uncertainty." **JAR**, 1971, Vol. 9, No. 2, pp. 278-286.)

Simik, S. Stephen, II. (Johnson, Glenn L. and S. Stephen Simik. II. "The Use Of Probability Inequalities In Multiproduct C-V-P Analysis Under Uncertainty," **JAR**, 1974, Vol. 12, No. 1, pp. 67-79.)

Simini, Joseph Peter. "Determining Priorities For Cash Distribution In Partnership Liquidation," **AR**, 1961, Vol. 36. No. 1, pp. 123-125.

Simini, Joseph Peter. "The Scope Paragraph Of The Audit Report Graphically Illustrated," **AR**, 1963, Vol. 38, No. 1. pp. 157-159.

Simkin, Mark G. "Computer Crime: Lessons And Direction." **CPAJ**. 1981. Vol. 51, No. 12, pp. 10-16.

Simmonds, Kenneth. "Strategic Management Accounting For Pricing: A Case Example," **ABR**, 1981-82, Vol. 12, No. 47, pp. 206-214.

Simmonds, K. and R. Vause. "Cost Estimating Under Uncertainty." **ABR**. 1970-71, Vol. 1, No. 1, pp. 3-10.

Simmons, John K. and Jack Gray. "An Investigation Of The Effect Of Differing Accounting Frameworks On The Prediction Of Net Income," **AR**, 1969, Vol. 44. No. 4, pp. 757-776.

Simmons, John K. "A Concept Of Comparability In Financial Reporting." **AR**, 1967, Vol. 42, No. 4, pp. 680-692.

Simmons, Peter G. "Performance Reporting As A Means Of Labor Cost Control," **MA**, 1965, Vol. 47, No. 2, pp. 32-36.

Simmons, Richard. (Salamon, Gerald L.. Wilfred C. Uecker and Richard Simmons. "Prediction Achievement And Simulated Decision Makers As An Extension Of The Predictive Ability Criterion: Some Comments," **AR**, 1976, Vol. 51. No. 3. pp. 664-665.)

Simms, Charles A., Jr. "Summarizing The Foreign Earned Income Tax Act Of 1978," **MA**, 1979, Vol. 61, No. 2, pp. 32-36.

Simon, Abraham J. "A Macroaccounting Framework For The Value-Added And Saving Side Of Household Nonmarket Production." **IJAER**, 1977. Vol. 13, No. 1, pp. 93-129.

Simon, Abraham J. "An Economic And Macroaccounting Framework For Household Nonmarket Production And Its Uses: The Output Side," **IJAER**, 1977. Vol. 12, No. 2, pp. 143-168.

Simon, Carl J. "A Survey Of Incentive Compensation Plans." **JOA**. 1959. Vol. 108, No. 4, pp. 49-57.

Simon, Daniel T. and Jere R. Francis. "The Effects Of Auditor Change On Audit Fees: Tests Of Price Cutting And Price Recovery," **AR**, 1988, Vol. 63. No. 2, pp. 255-269.

Simon, Daniel T. "The Audit Services Market: Additional Empirical Evidence," **AJPT**, 1985-86, Vol. 5, No. 1, pp. 71-78.

Simon, Daniel T. (Francis, Jere R. and Daniel T. Simon. "A Test Of Audit Pricing In The Small-Client Segment Of The U.S. Audit Market," **AR**, 1987, Vol. 62, No. 1, pp. 145-157.)

Simon, Daniel T. (Larcker, David F.. Renee E. Reder and Daniel T. Simon. "Trades By Insiders As Evidence Of The Existence Of Economic Consequences Of Accounting Standards," **AR**, 1983, Vol. 58. No. 3, pp. 606-620.)

Simon, Daniel T., Ramachandran Ramanan and Amitabh Dugar. "The Market For Audit Services In India: An Empirical Examination," **IJAER**, 1986, Vol. 21. No. 2, pp. 27-35.

Simon, David S. "The Effect Of A Price Code On Company Profits In A Period Of Inflation," **ABR**, 1976-77, Vol. 7. No. 28. pp. 295-299.

Simon, John R. (Baker. Richard E.. John R. Simon and Frank P. Bazeli. "An Assessment Of The Learning Style Preferences Of Accounting Majors," **IAE**. 1986. Vol. 1. No. 1. pp. 1-12.)

Simon, John R. (Baker. Richard E. and John R. Simon. "An Assessment Of The Cognitive Demands Of The Uniform CPA Examination And Implications For CPA Review/Preparation Courses," **JAED**, 1985, Vol. 3, No. 2, pp. 15-29.)

Simon, John R. (Baker, Richard E.. John R. Simon and Frank P. Bazeli. "Selecting Instructional Design For Introductory Accounting Based On The Experiential Learning Model," **JAED**. 1987. Vol. 5. No. 2. pp. 207-226.)

Simon, John R. (Delaney, Patrick R.. David E. Keyes. Curtis L. Norton and John R. Simon. "An Admission Test For Intermediate Accounting," **AR**, 1979, Vol. 54. No. 1, pp. 155-162.)

Simon, Sidney I. "Consolidated Statements And The Law," **AR**, 1953. Vol. 28. No. 4, pp. 505-514.

Simon, Sidney I. "Cost Accounting And The Law," **AR**, 1964, Vol. 39. No. 4, pp. 884-889.

Simon, Sidney I. "Cost Or Market Before The Bar." **AR**. 1956. Vol. 31. No. 4, pp. 621-624.

Simon, Sidney I. "Court Decisions And Income Determination." **JOA**. 1953, Vol. 96, No. 6, pp. 683-694.

Simon, Sidney I. "Court Decisions Concerning Goodwill," **AR**. 1956. Vol. 31. No. 2, pp. 272-277.

Simon, Sidney I. "Fraud In The Balance Sheet," **AR**, 1965, Vol. 40. No. 2, pp. 401-406.

Simon, Sidney I. "Legal Decisions On The Accounting For Corporate Surplus," **AR**, 1956, Vol. 31. No. 1,pp.104-108.

Simon, Sidney I. "Legal Decisions On Accounting Reserves." AR, 1955, Vol. 30, No. 3, pp. 507-514.

Simon, Sidney I. "Spin-Offs Vs. Dividends In Kind," AR, 1960, Vol. 35, No. 1, pp. 81-89.

Simon, Sidney I. "The Accounting For Trading Stamps," AR, 1957, Vol. 32, No. 3, pp. 398-402.

Simon, Sidney I. "The Lease-Option Plan - Its Tax And Accounting Implications," JOA, 1962, Vol. 113, No. 4. pp. 38-45.

Simon, Sidney I. "The Right Side Of Accumulated Depreciation," AR, 1959, Vol. 34, No. 1, pp. 97-105.

Simonds, Richard R. "Comment On 'Premature Withdrawals From Individual Retirement Accounts: A Breakeven Analysis'." JATA, 1984, Vol. 6, No. 1, pp. 74-76.

Simonds, Richard R. (Collins, Daniel W. and Richard R. Simonds. "SEC Line-Of-Business Disclosure And Market Risk Adjustments," JAR, 1979, Vol. 17, No. 2, pp. 352-383.)

Simonetti, Gilbert, Jr. "Congress Assesses State Taxes On Interstate Business," JOA, 1964, Vol. 118, No. 2, pp. 41-48.

Simonetti, Gilbert, Jr. "It's Time For Greater Accountability In The Public Sector," MA, 1978, Vol. 60, No. 3, pp. 13-16.

Simons, Donald R. and Jerry J. Weygandt. "Stock Options Revised: Accounting For Option Buy-Outs," CPAJ, 1973, Vol. 43, No. 9, pp. 779-783.

Simons, Harry. "Continuity In Consolidated Statements," AR, 1956, Vol. 31, No. 4, pp. 652-662.

Simons, Harry. "Priority Program Approach To Partnership Liquidation By Installments," AR, 1955, Vol. 30, No. 2, pp. 344-347.

Simons, Harry. "Success On The CPA Examination - Product Of Classroom Or Practice?," AR, 1957, Vol. 32, No. 4, pp. 605-611.

Simons, Harry. "What Accountants Think Of Accounting." JOA, 1960, Vol. 110, No. 2, pp. 35-44.

Simons, Robert. "Analysis Of The Organizational Characteristics Related To Tight Budget Goals." CAR, 1988, Vol. 5, No. 1, pp. 267-283.

Simons, Robert. (Merchant, Kenneth A. and Robert Simons. "Research And Control In Complex Organizations: An Overview," JAL, 1986, Vol. 5, pp. 183-204.)

Simons, R. "Accounting Control Systems And Business Strategy: An Empirical Analysis," AOS, 1987, Vol. 12. No. 3, pp. 357-374.

Simpson, Clark L. "Controls In Mutual Security Agency Abroad." AR, 1953, Vol. 28, No. 1, pp. 79-82.

Simpson, Clark L. "Public Accounting De Luxe." AR, 1948, Vol. 23, No. 3, pp. 263-265.

Simpson, Clark L. "The Army Audit Agency Goes Professional." AR, 1955, Vol. 30, No. 3, pp. 463-467.

Simpson, Richard H. "An Empirical Study Of Possible Income Manipulation," AR, 1969, Vol. 44, No. 4, pp. 806-817.

Simpson, Robert M. "Forest-Products Industry Accounting." JOA, 1957, Vol. 104, No. 3, pp. 38-45.

Simunic, Dan A. "Auditing, Consulting, And Auditor Independence," JAR, 1984, Vol. 22, No. 2, pp. 679-702.

Simunic, Dan A. "The Pricing Of Audit Services: Theory And Evidence," JAR, 1980, Vol. 18, No. 1, pp. 161-190.

Sinclair, Kenneth P. and James A. Talbott, Jr. "Using Breakeven Analysis When Cost Behavior Is Unknown," MA, 1986, Vol. 68, No. 1, pp. 52-55.

Sinclair, Norman A. (Clinch, Greg J. and Norman A. Sinclair. "Intra-Industry Information Releases: A Recursive Systems Approach," JAEC, 1987, Vol. 9, No. 1, pp. 89-106.)

Sine, Edward P. "Accounting For Dividends," AR, 1953, Vol. 28, No. 3, pp. 320-324.

Singer, Frank A. "A Goofy Glossary For Accountants," AR, 1958, Vol. 33, No. 3, p. 485.

Singer, Frank A. "A Note On 'Teaching Approaches To Elementary Accounting'," AR, 1966, Vol. 41, No. 1, pp. 133-134.

Singer, Frank A. "A System Approach To Teaching The Accounting Process," AR, 1970, Vol. 45, No. 2, pp. 351-364.

Singer, Frank A. "Accounting Is A Matter Of Taste," AR, 1962, Vol. 37, No. 3, pp. 464-471.

Singer, Frank A. "Fixing 'Fixed Assets'," AR, 1957, Vol. 32, No. 1, pp. 104-106.

Singer, Frank A. "Management Accounting," AR, 1961, Vol. 36, No. 1, pp. 112-118.

Singer, Frank A. "Mixed Meanings: An Added Responsibility For Accounting Teachers," AR, 1956, Vol. 31, No. 4, pp. 663-666.

Singer, Frank A. "Needed: A Glossary To Accompany Audit Reports," AR, 1960, Vol. 35, No. 1, pp. 90-92.

Singer, Frank A. "Progress In Programmed Instruction," AR, 1965, Vol. 40, No. 4, pp. 847-853.

Singer, Frank A. "Rationale For A Course In Quantitative Methods," AR, 1962, Vol. 37, No. 3, pp. 554-555.

Singer, Frank A. "'Depreciation' - Better Left Unsaid," AR, 1957, Vol. 32, No. 3, pp. 406-412.

Singer, I. Michael. "Universal Life: Insurance Of The Future?," CPAJ, 1984, Vol. 54, No. 7, pp. 36-43.

Singh, D. R. and Jag Mohan Ahuja. "Corporate Social Reporting In India," IJAER, 1983, Vol. 18, No. 2, pp. 151-169.

Singh, Prem S. and Gordon L. Chapman. "Is Linear Approximation Good Enough?," MA, 1978, Vol. 59, No. 7, pp. 53-55.

Singhal, H. S. (Chambers, D. J., H. S. Singhal, B. D. Taylor and D. L. Wright. "Developing Dividend And Financing Policies With A Computer Terminal," ABR, 1970-71, Vol. 1, No. 4, pp. 267-273.)

Singhvi, Surendra S. and Harsha B. Desai. "An Empirical Analysis Of The Quality Of Corporate Financial Disclosure," AR, 1971, Vol. 46, No. 1, pp. 129-138.

Singhvi, Surendra S. and Harsha B. Desai. "The Quality Of Corporate Financial Disclosure: A Reply," AR, 1972, Vol. 47, No. 3, pp. 585-586.

Singhvi, Surendra S. and Robert J. Lambrix. "Investment Versus Financing Decisions," MA, 1984, Vol. 65, No. 9, pp. 54-56.

Singhvi, Surendra S. "Characteristics And Implications Of Inadequate Disclosure: A Case Study Of India," IJAER, 1968, Vol. 3, No. 2, pp. 29-43.

Singhvi, Surendra S. "Corporate Financial Disclosure: Nature And Media," MA, 1968, Vol. 50, No. 3, pp. 15-17.

Singhvi, Surendra. "What Is The Real Bottom Line?," MA, 1983, Vol. 64, No. 8, pp. 25-27.

Singleton, W. Ron. "A Comparative Analysis Of Tax Expenditure Budget Trends," AIT, 1988, Vol. 2, pp. xx-xx.

Singleton, W. Ron. (Marshall, Don C., Kevin M. Misiewicz and W. Ron Singleton. "Applications Of Computer-Assisted Tax Research In Academic Tax Programs," JAED, 1987, Vol. 5, No. 2, pp. 287-296.)

Sinha, Prabhakant. (Leitch, Robert A., John Neter, Robert Plante and Prabhakant Sinha. "Modified Multinomial Bounds For Larger Numbers Of Errors In Audits," AR, 1982, Vol. 57, No. 2, pp. 384-400.)

Sinning, Kathleen E. (Dykxhoorn, Hans J. and Kathleen E. Sinning. "The Lack Of Uniformity In Statistical Audit Sampling Terminology," JAED, 1984, Vol. 2, No. 2, pp. 153-161.)

Sinning, Kathleen E. (Dykxhoorn, Hans J. and Kathleen E. Sinning. "Wirtschaftsprufer Perception And Auditor Independence," AR, 1981, Vol. 56, No. 1, pp. 97-107.)

Sinning, Kathleen E. (Dykxhoorn, Hans J. and Kathleen E. Sinning. "The Independence Issue Concerning German Auditors: A Synthesis," IJAER, 1981, Vol. 16, No. 2, pp. 163-181.)

Sinning, K. E. (Dykxhoorn, H. J. and K. E. Sinning. "Perceptions Of Auditor Independence: Its Perceived Effect On The Loan And Investment Decisions Of German Financial Statement Users," AOS, 1982, Vol. 7, No. 4, pp. 337-348.)

Sinnott, John T. "The Insurance Problem: Affordability Vs. Availability," CA, 1987, Vol. 5, No. 1, pp. 56-63.

Sisco, Anthony F., Jr. "Overhead Variance Analysis And Corrective Action," MA, 1973, Vol. 55, No. 4, pp. 45-47.

Sivaramakrishnan, Konduru. (Lys, Thomas and Konduru Sivaramakrishnan. "Earnings Expectations And Capital Restructuring: The Case Of Equity-For-Debt Swaps," JAR, 1988, Vol. 26, No. 2, pp. 273-299.)

Sizer, John. "A Risk Analysis Approach To Marginal Cost Pricing," ABR, 1970-71, Vol. 1, No. 1, pp. 30-38.

Sizer, John. "Hardwood, Softwood And Plywood Company: A Case Study," ABR, 1970-71, Vol. 1, No. 3, pp. 250-257.

Sizer, John. "Performance Assessment In Institutions Of Higher Education Under Conditions Of Financial Stringency. Contraction And Changing Needs: A Management Accounting Perspective," ABR, 1980-81, Vol. 11, No. 43, pp. 227-242.

Sizer, John. "Pricing Policy In Inflation: A Management Accountant's Perspective," ABR, 1975-76, Vol. 6, No. 22, pp. 107-124.

Sizer, John. "Some Difficulties Facing Organisers Of Interfirm Comparison Schemes," ABR, 1973-74, Vol. 4, No. 14, pp. 116-126.

Skaar, Christopher, Jr. (Worthley, Stephen G. and Christopher Skaar, Jr. "Managing Information Through Banks," MA, 1982, Vol. 64, No. 2, pp. 52-58.)

Skantz, Terrance R. "Budgeting And Profit Variance Analysis Using A Financial Planning Language," JAED, 1988, Vol. 6, No. 2, pp. 309-323.

Skekel, Ted D. and O. Ray Whittington. "Management Reports' On Financial Statements," CPAJ, 1979, Vol. 49, No. 7, pp. 32-37.

Skekel, Ted D. (Alford, R. Mark and Ted D. Skekel. "How The AMT Affects Corporate Decisions," MA, 1988, Vol. 70, No. 6, pp. 43-46.)

Skekel, Ted D. (Bline, Dennis M. and Ted D. Skekel. "Effective Classroom Presentation Of FAS 87 Footnote Reconciliation," IAE, 1988, Vol. 3, No. 2, pp. 215-227.)

Skekel, Ted D. (Greer, Willis R., Jr. and Ted D. Skekel. "Theory Versus Practice In Risk Analysis: A Reply," AR, 1975, Vol. 50, No. 4, pp. 839-843.)

Skerratt, L. C. L. and K. V. Peasnell. "Anti-Dilution Of Earnings Per Share," ABR, 1975-76, Vol. 6, No. 21, pp. 57-62.

Skerratt, L. C. L. "Risk Distribution In The Budgetary Process: A Comment," ABR, 1981-82, Vol. 12, No. 47, pp. 233-235.

Skerratt, L. C. L. "The Bias In Current Cost Income: An Extension," JAAF, 1984, Vol. 7, No. 4, pp. 362-368.

Skerratt, L. C. L. (Peasnell, K. V. and L. C. L. Skerratt. "Income-Group Inflation Rates And General Purchasing Power Adjustments: An Empirical Test Of The Heterogeneity Hypothesis," ABR, 1978-79, Vol. 9, No. 33, pp. 45-60.)

Skerratt, L. C. L. (Peasnell, K. V., L. C. L. Skerratt and C. W. R. Ward. "The Share Price Impact Of UK CCA Disclosures," ABR, 1987-88, Vol. 18, No. 69, pp. 3-16.)

Skerratt, L. C. L. (Peasnell, K. V. and L. C. L. Skerratt. "How Well Does A Single Index Represent The Nineteen Sandilands Plant And Machinery Indices?," JAR, 1977, Vol. 15, No. 1, pp. 108-119.)

Skertich, John M. and William C. Hickerson. "Record Retention Program," MA, 1972, Vol. 53, No. 8, pp. 23-28.

Skigen, Michael. (Jauch, Roger and Michael Skigen. "Human Resource Accounting: A Critical Evaluation," **MA**, 1974, Vol. 55, No. 11, pp. 33-36.)

Skinner, Allen. "Accounting For R&D Costs," **MA**, 1971, Vol. 52, No. 11, pp. 29-30.

Skinner, R. C. "Accounting Information For Decision-Making," **IJAER**, 1971, Vol. 7, No. 1, pp. 65-78.

Skinner, R. C. "Allocations And The Validity Of The Incremental Principle," **ABR**, 1987-88, Vol. 18, No. 69, pp. 75-78.

Skinner, R. C. "Combining LIFO And FIFO," **IJAER**, 1975, Vol. 10, No. 2, pp. 127-134.

Skinner, R. C. "Cost Allocation In Management And Financial Accounting," **IJAER**, 1986, Vol. 21, No. 2, pp. 91-107.

Skinner, R. C. "Fixed Asset Lives And Replacement Cost Accounting," **JAR**, 1982, Vol. 20, No. 1, pp. 210-226.

Skinner, R. C. "Process Costing," **ABACUS**, 1978, Vol. 14, No. 2, pp. 160-170.

Skinner, R. C. "Process Costing: Reply To A Comment," **ABACUS**, 1980, Vol. 16, No. 1, pp. 67-72.

Skipper, Harold D., Jr. and Kenneth Black, Jr. "Life Insurance Evaluation For Personal Financial Planning," **CPAJ**, 1988, Vol. 58, No. 1, pp. 54-63.

Skomp, Stephen E. and C. W. R. Ward. "The Capital Structure Policies Of U.K. Companies: A Comparative Study," **IJAER**, 1983, Vol. 19, No. 1, pp. 55-64.

Skousen, Clifford R. and Frank A. Condie. "Evaluating A Sports Program: Goalposts Vs. Test Tubes," **MA**, 1988, Vol. 70, No. 5, pp. 43-49.

Skousen, Clifford R. "A Profile And Index Of The CMA Examination - An Update," **AR**, 1981, Vol. 56, No. 3, pp. 659-665.

Skousen, C. R. and Ji-Liang Yang. "Western Management Accounting And The Economic Reforms Of China," **AOS**, 1988, Vol. 13, No. 2, pp. 201-206.

Skousen, C. R. "Public Interest Accounting: A Look At The Issues," **AOS**, 1982, Vol. 7, No. 1, pp. 79-85.

Skousen, K. Fred and Belverd E. Needles, Jr. "A Conceptual Framework For Analyzing And Evaluating Managerial Decisions," **MA**, 1969, Vol. 50, No. 5, pp. 9-11.

Skousen, K. Fred and Robert K. Zimmer. "Controllership Obsolescence: Fact Or Fiction," **MA**, 1970, Vol. 51, No. 12, pp. 20-23.

Skousen, K. Fred, Robert A. Sharp and Russell H. Tolman. "Corporate Disclosure Of Budgetary Data," **JOA**, 1972, Vol. 133, No. 5, pp. 50-57.

Skousen, K. Fred. "A Format For Reporting Segment Profits," **MA**, 1971, Vol. 52, No. 12, pp. 15-20.

Skousen, K. Fred. "A New Professional Program In Accountancy," **JOA**, 1976, Vol. 142, No. 5, pp. 77-81.

Skousen, K. Fred. "Accounting Education: The New Professionalism," **JOA**, 1977, Vol. 144, No. 1, pp. 54-58.

Skousen, K. Fred. "Chronicle Of Events Surrounding The Segment Reporting Issue," **JAR**, 1970, Vol. 8, No. 2, pp. 293-299.

Skousen, K. Fred. "Standards For Reporting By Lines Of Business," **JOA**, 1970, Vol. 129, No. 2, pp. 39-46.

Skousen, K. Fred. (Mautz, R. K. and K. Fred Skousen. "Some Problems In Empirical Research In Accounting," **AR**, 1969, Vol. 44, No. 3, pp. 447-456.)

Skudrna, Vincent J. "The Status Of EDP Auditing," **CPAJ**, 1982, Vol. 52, No. 3, pp. 26-31.

Skully, Michael T. "Japanese Corporate Structure: Some Factors In Its Development," **IJAER**, 1981, Vol. 16, No. 2, pp. 67-98.

Slain, John. (Sorter, George H., Stanley Siegel and John Slain. "Accountnats' Legal Liability: A Determinant Of The Accounting Model," **JAAF**, 1988, Vol. 3 (New Series), No. 3, pp. 233-243.)

Slater, Nathaniel. "Matching Future Cash Payouts To Current Revenue," **MA**, 1977, Vol. 59, No. 2, pp. 19-20.

Slaton, William H. "Developing Accountants For Atomic Energy," **AR**, 1955, Vol. 30, No. 2, pp. 252-256.

Slavin, Albert. (Kwang, Ching-Wen and Albert Slavin. "The Simple Mathematics Of Variance Analysis," **AR**, 1962, Vol. 37, No. 3, pp. 415-432.)

Slavin, Nathan S. "The Elimination Of 'Scienter' In Determining The Auditor's Statutory Liability," **AR**, 1977, Vol. 52, No. 2, pp. 360-368.

Slaybaugh, Charles J. "Inventory Management Program," **MA**, 1971, Vol. 53, No. 1, pp. 13-17.

Slayter, W. Edwin. "Accounting For Freight Costs On Company Trucks," **MA**, 1965, Vol. 47, No. 1, pp. 35-38.

Slepian, Steven L. "How A Proposed Accounting Change Threatened An Industry," **MA**, 1985, Vol. 67, No. 5, pp. 47-51.

Slesinger, Reuben E. and Paul H. Jeynes. "Profit Incentive: Earnings Less Cost of Capital," **ABR**, 1971-72, Vol. 2, No. 7, pp. 163-176.

Slesinger, Reuben E. "Conglomeration: Growth And Techniques," **ABR**, 1970-71, Vol. 1, No. 2, pp. 145-154.

Slevin, Dennis P. (Birnberg, Jacob G. and Dennis P. Slevin. "A Note On The Use Of Confidence Interval Statements In Financial Reporting," **JAR**, 1976, Vol. 14, No. 1, pp. 153-157.)

Slipkowsky, John N. "The Volvo Way Of Financial Reporting," **MA**, 1988, Vol. 70, No. 4, pp. 22-26.

Sloan, Donald R. "The Education Of The Professional Accountant," **JOA**, 1983, Vol. 155, No. 3, pp. 56-61.

Sloan, James D. (Friedlob, G. Thomas, F. Ray Gray, Ralph E. Welton and James D. Sloan. "Combining LIFO And FIFO Inventory Disclosure," **CPAJ**, 1987, Vol. 57, No. 6, pp. 48-53.)

Sloan, Stephen B. "How Milliken Measures Training Program Effectiveness," **MA**, 1981, Vol. 63, No. 1, pp. 37-41.

Slocum, Elliott L. and Alfred R. Roberts. "The New York School Of Accounts - A Beginning," **AHJ**, 1980, Vol. 7, No. 2, pp. 63-70.

Slocum, Elliott L. and Alfred R. Roberts. "The Bureau For Placements," **AHJ**, 1983, Vol. 10, No. 2, pp. 117-127.

Slutzker, David R. "A Proposal To Computerize The Accounting System," **MA**, 1969, Vol. 51, No. 3, pp. 23-28.

Smails, R. G. H. "Some Aspects Of Depreciation," **AR**, 1927, Vol. 2. No. 2, pp. 101-110.

Smalls, Isaac S. "Hospital Cost Controls," **MA**, 1973, Vol. 54, No. 9, pp. 17-20.

Smidt, Seymour. (Bierman, Harold, Jr. and Seymour Smidt. "Accounting For Debt And Costs Of Liquidity Under Conditions Of Uncertainty," **JAR**, 1967, Vol. 5, No. 2, pp. 144-153.)

Smidt, S. (Goldschmidt, Y. and S. Smidt. "Valuing The Firm's Durable Assets For Managerial Information," **AR**, 1969, Vol. 44, No. 2, pp. 317-329.)

Smieliauskas, Wally. "A Note On Comparison Of Bayesian With Non-Bayesian Dollar-Unit Sampling Bounds For Overstatement Errors In Audits," **AR**, 1986, Vol. 61, No. 1, pp. 118-128.

Smieliauskas, Wally. "A Simulation Analysis Of The Power Characteristics Of Some Popular Estimators Under Different Risk And Materiality Levels," **JAR**, 1986, Vol. 24, No. 1, pp. 217-230.

Smieliauskas, Wally. "Control Of Sampling Risks In Auditing," **CAR**, 1986-87, Vol. 3, No. 1, pp. 102-124.

Smieliauskas, Wally. "Sensitivity Analysis Of The Realized Risks Of Auditing With Uncertainty Concerning Internal Control Evaluations," **JAR**, 1985, Vol. 23, No. 2, pp. 718-739.

Smieliauskas, Wally. (Ham, Jane, Donna Losell and Wally Smieliauskas. "An Empirical Study Of Error Characteristics In Accounting Populations," **AR**, 1985, Vol. 60, No. 3, pp. 387-406.)

Smieliauskas, Wally. (Ham, Jane, Donna Losell and Wally Smieliauskas. "Some Empirical Evidence On The Stability Of Accounting Error Characteristics Over Time," **CAR**, 1987-88, Vol. 4, No. 1, pp. 210-226.)

Smieliauskas, Wally. (Ham, Jane, Donna Losell and Wally Smieliauskas. "A Note On The Neutrality Of Internal Control Systems In Audit Practice," **CAR**, 1985-86, Vol. 2. No. 2, pp. 311-317.)

Smieliauskas, Wally. (Menzefricke, Ulrich and Wally Smieliauskas. "A Simulation Study Of The Performance Of Parametric Dollar Unit Sampling Statistical Procedures," **JAR**, 1984, Vol. 22, No. 2, pp. 588-604.)

Smieliauskas, Wally. (Menzefricke, Ulrich and Wally Smieliauskas. "On Sample Size Allocation In Auditing," **CAR**, 1988, Vol. 4, No. 2, pp. 314-336.)

Smieliauskas, Wally. (Menzefricke, Ulrich and Wally Smieliauskas. "A Survey Of Simulation Studies In Statistical Auditing," **JAL**, 1987, Vol. 6, pp. 26-54.)

Smieliauskas, Wally. (Menzefricke, Ulrich and Wally Smieliauskas. "A Comparison Of The Stratified Difference Estimator With Some Monetary-Unit Sampling Estimators," **CAR**, 1987-88, Vol. 4, No. 1, pp. 240-251.)

Smith, Abbie and Thomas Dyckman. "The Impact Of Accounting Regulation On the Stock Market: The Case Of Oil And Gas Companies: A Comment," **AR**, 1981, Vol. 56, No. 4, pp. 959-966.

Smith, Abbie J. "The SEC 'Reversal' Of FASB Statement No. 19: An Investigation Of Information Effects," **JAR**, 1981, Vol. 19, Supp., pp. 174-211.

Smith, Abbie J. (Dyckman, Thomas R. and Abbie J. Smith. "Financial Accounting And Reporting By Oil And Gas Producing Companies: A Study Of Information Effects," **JAEC**, 1979, Vol. 1, No. 1, pp. 45-75.)

Smith, Abbie. (Antle, Rick and Abbie Smith. "An Empirical Investigation Of The Relative Performance Evaluation Of Corporate Executives," **JAR**, 1986, Vol. 24, No. 1, pp. 1-39.)

Smith, Abbie. (Antle, Rick and Abbie Smith. "Measuring Executive Compensation: Methods And Application," **JAR**, 1985, Vol. 23, No. 1, pp. 296-325.)

Smith, Alan F. "Oil Production And Accounting In The Extractive Industry," **ABACUS**, 1974, Vol. 10 No. 2, pp. 100-110.

Smith, Alan F. "Purchased Goodwill Is An Investment: Treat It As Such," **MA**, 1969, Vol. 51, No. 5, pp. 19-22.

Smith, Alan F. "Temporal Method: Temporary Mode?," **MA**, 1978, Vol. 59, No. 8, pp. 21-26.

Smith, Alden C. "Audit Engagement Doesn't Need Detailed Description," **JOA**, 1952, Vol. 93, No. 2, pp. 210-213.

Smith, Bradford E. "Can CPAs Reach The Public?," **JOA**, 1976, Vol. 142. No. 3, pp. 56-64.

Smith, Bradford E. "Reaching The Public: The CPA's New Image," **JOA**, 1980, Vol. 149, No. 1, pp. 47-53.

Smith, Bradford E. (Weinstein, Edward A. and Bradford E. Smith. "Public Service And The Profession," **JOA**, 1985, Vol. 159, No. 5, pp. 114-120.)

Smith, C. Aubrey and Keith Davis. "Texas Survey Shows Wide Variation In Personnel Practices," **JOA**, 1952, Vol. 93, No. 5, pp. 584-588.

Smith, C. Aubrey. "Accountancy: Circa 2000 A.D.," **AR**, 1954, Vol. 29, No. 1, pp. 64-71.

Smith, C. Aubrey. "Accounting Practice Under The Securities And Exchange Commission," **AR**, 1935, Vol. 10, No. 4, pp. 325-332.

Smith, C. Aubrey. "Education For The Professional Accountant," **AR**, 1945, Vol. 20, No. 1, pp. 17-23.

Smith, C. Aubrey. "Postgraduate Curricula In Accounting," **AR**, 1948, Vol. 23, No. 2, pp. 200-205.

Smith, C. Aubrey. "The Certified Public Accountant Not In

Public Practice," **JOA**, 1968. Vol. 126. No. 6, pp. 52-56.

Smith, C. Aubrey. "The Internship In Accounting Education," **AR**, 1964, Vol. 39, No. 4, pp. 1024-1027.

Smith, C. Aubrey. "The Next Step - A Professional School Of Accounting," **AR**, 1956, Vol. 31. No. 4. pp. 565-572.

Smith, C. D. "Comments On Neter's 'Problems In Experimenting With The Application Of Statistical Techniques In Auditing'," **AR**, 1955, Vol. 30, No. 1. p. 70.

Smith, C. D. "Three Cases Where Scientific Sampling Halved Clerical Time," **JOA**, 1952, Vol. 94, No. 1, pp. 62-66.

Smith, C. H. (Wilcox, K. A. and C. H. Smith. "Role Discrepancies And The Auditor - Client Relationship," **AOS**, 1977, Vol. 2, No. 1, pp. 81-97.)

Smith, Caleb A. "How Can Accounting Be Integrated With Economics?," **AR**, 1952, Vol. 27. No. 1, pp. 100-103.

Smith, Carl S. (Mihalek, Paul H., Anne J. Rich and Carl S. Smith. "Ethics And Management Accountants," **MA**, 1987, Vol. 69, No. 6, pp. 34-36.)

Smith, Charles H. and Roy A. Lanier, "The Audit Of Management: Report On A Field Study," **MA**, 1970, Vol. 51, No. 12, pp. 24-26.

Smith, Charles H. "A New Introduction To Accounting: Some Explanations," **AR**, 1973, Vol. 48, No. 1, pp. 148-157.

Smith, Charles H. "The Modern Systems Approach, General System Theory, And Accounting Theory Development In The Age Of Synthesis," **IJAER**, 1971, Vol. 6, No. 2, pp. 59-73.

Smith, Charles H. (Andrews, Wesley T. and Charles H. Smith. "A Role For Financial Accounting In National Economic Planning In The United States," **IJAER**, 1976, Vol. 12, No. 1, pp. 133-145.)

Smith, Charles H. (Bait-El-Mal, Mohamed M., Charles H. Smith and Martin E. Taylor. "The Development Of Accounting In Libya," **IJAER**, 1973, Vol. 8, No. 2. pp. 83-101.)

Smith, Charles H. (Baron, C. David, Douglas A. Johnson, D. Gerald Searfoss and Charles H. Smith. "Uncovering Corporate Irregularities: Are We Closing The Expectation Gap?," **JOA**, 1977, Vol. 144, No. 4, pp. 56-67.)

Smith, Charles H. (Bird, Francis A., Lewis F. Davidson and Charles H. Smith. "Perceptions Of External Accounting Transfers Under Entity And Proprietary Theory," **AR**, 1974, Vol. 49, No. 2, pp. 233-244.)

Smith, Charles H. (Cook, James S., Jr., Lewis F. Davidson and Charles H. Smith. "Social Costs And Private Accounting," **ABACUS**, 1974, Vol. 10 No. 2, pp. 87-99.)

Smith, Charles H. (Cushing, Barry E. and Charles H. Smith. "A New Emphasis For Introductory Accounting Instruction," **AR**, 1972, Vol. 47, No. 3, pp. 599-601.)

Smith, Charles H. (Dascher, Paul E., Charles H. Smith and Robert H. Strawser. "Accounting Curriculum Implications Of The Multinational Corporation," **IJAER**, 1973, Vol. 9, No. 1, pp. 81-97.)

Smith, Charles H. (Deakin, Edward B., III. Michael H. Granof and Charles H. Smith. "Educational Objectives For An Accounting Program," **AR**, 1974, Vol. 49. No. 3, pp. 584-589.)

Smith, Charles H. (Deakin, Edward B., Gyles R. Norwood and Charles H. Smith. "The Effect Of Published Earnings Information On Tokyo Stock Exchange Trading," **IJAER**, 1974, Vol. 10, No. 1, pp. 123-136.)

Smith, Charles H. (Gaa, James C. and Charles H. Smith. "Auditors And Deceptive Financial Statements: Assigning Responsibility And Blame," **CAR**, 1984-85, Vol. 1, No. 2, pp. 219-241.)

Smith, Charles H. (Granof, Michael H. and Charles H. Smith. "Accounting And The Evaluation Of Social Programs: A Comment," **AR**, 1974, Vol. 49. No. 4, pp. 822-825.)

Smith, Charles H. (Ishikawa, Akira and Charles H. Smith. "A Feedforward Control System For Organizational Planning And Control," **ABACUS**, 1972, Vol. 8, No. 2, pp. 163-180.)

Smith, Charles H. (Pany, Kurt and Charles H. Smith. "Auditor Association With Quarterly Financial Information: An Empirical Test," **JAR**, 1982, Vol. 20, No. 2, Part I, pp. 472-481.)

Smith, Charles H. (Robertson, Jack C. and Charles H. Smith. "Auditing And Professionalism At The Graduate Level," **AR**, 1973, Vol. 48, No. 1, pp. 599-602.)

Smith, Charles H., Roy A. Lanier and Martin E. Taylor. "The Need For And Scope Of The Audit Of Management: A Survey Of Attitudes," **AR**, 1972, Vol. 47, No. 2, pp. 270-283.

Smith, Charles H., Roy A. Lanier and Martin E. Taylor. "Comments On Survey Of Attitudes On Management Auditing: A Reply," **AR**, 1973, Vol. 48, No. 1, pp. 123-125.

Smith, Charles J., Jr. "The Class Life System," **MA**, 1973, Vol. 55, No. 2, pp. 45-48.

Smith, Charles T., Jr. "Accounting For Poultry Projects," **MA**, 1969, Vol. 50, No. 5, pp. 48-52.

Smith, Charles W. "Prudent Investment Theory In Public Utility Rate Making," **AR**, 1946, Vol. 21, No. 3, pp. 288-305.

Smith, Charles W. "Uniform System Of Accounts Of The Federal Power Commission," **AR**, 1937. Vol. 12, No. 2, pp. 153-162.

Smith, Chas. W. "Current Useful Concepts Of Depreciation For Fixed Assets," **JOA**, 1951, Vol. 92, No. 2, pp. 166-174.

Smith, Chris, Richard Whipp and Hugh Willmott. "Case-Study Research In Accounting: Methodological Breakthrough Or Ideological Weapon?," **AIPIA**, 1988, Vol. 2, pp. 95-120.

Smith, Clarence O. and Geraldine F. Jasper. "Using The Computer In Audit Work," **MA**, 1972, Vol. 54, No. 4, pp. 34-38.

Smith, Clifford W. (Kothari, S. P., Thomas Lys, Clifford W. Smith and Ross L. Watts. "Auditor Liability And Information Disclosure," **JAAF**, 1988, Vol. 3 (New Series), No.

4. pp. 307-339.)

Smith, Clifford W., Jr. and Jerold L. Zimmerman. "Valuing Employee Stock Option Plans Using Option Pricing Models," **JAR**, 1976, Vol. 14, No. 2, pp. 357-364.

Smith, Dan C. (Hartman. Bart P. and Dan C. Smith. "Improving Credit Collection Responses," **MA**, 1979, Vol. 61. No. 2, pp. 18-21.)

Smith, Dan Throop. "U.S. Tax Policy Objectives," **JOA**, 1958, Vol. 105, No. 1, pp. 35-38.

Smith, David B. and Donald R. Nichols. "A Market Test Of Investor Reaction To Disagreements," **JAEC**, 1982, Vol. 4, No. 2. pp. 109-120.

Smith, David B. and Susan Pourciau. "A Comparison Of The Financial Characteristics Of December And Non-December Year-End Companies," **JAEC**, 1988, Vol. 10, No. 4, pp. 335-344.

Smith, David B. "An Investigation Of Securities And Exchange Commission Regulation Of Auditor Change Disclosures: The Case Of Accounting Series Release No. 165." **JAR**, 1988, Vol. 26, No. 1, pp. 134-145.

Smith, David B. "Auditor 'Subject To' Opinions, Disclaimers, And Auditor Changes," **AJPT**, 1986-87, Vol. 6, No. 1. pp. 95-108.

Smith, David B. (Hefzi, Hassan, A. James Ifflander and David B. Smith. "Municipal Bond Market Risk Measures And Bond Ratings," **AIA**, 1988, Vol. 6, pp. 111-128.)

Smith, David B. (Nichols, Donald R. and David B. Smith. "Auditor Credibility And Auditor Changes," **JAR**, 1983, Vol. 21. No. 2, pp. 534-544.)

Smith, David B., Howard Stettler and William Beedles. "An Investigation Of The Information Content Of Foreign Sensitive Payment Disclosures," **JAEC**, 1984, Vol. 6, No. 2. pp. 153-162.

Smith, David R. "Recognition, Validation And Processing Of Accounts Payable," **MA**, 1970, Vol. 52, No. 2, pp. 39-41.

Smith, David. (Ettredge, Michael, Philip B. Shane and David Smith. "Audit Firm Size And The Association Between Reported Earnings And Security Returns," **AJPT**, 1988, Vol. 7, No. 2, pp. 29-42.)

Smith, E. Daniel. "The Effect Of The Separation Of Ownership From Control On Accounting Policy Decisions," **AR**, 1976, Vol. 51, No. 4, pp. 707-723.

Smith, E. Daniel. "The Effect Of The Separation Of Ownership From Control On Accounting Policy Decisions: A Reply," **AR**, 1979, Vol. 54, No. 2, pp. 417-420.

Smith, E. Dan. (Dhaliwal, Dan S., Gerald Salamon and E. Dan Smith. "The Effect Of Owner Versus Management Control On The Choice Of Accounting Methods," **JAEC**, 1982, Vol. 4, No. 1. pp. 41-53.)

Smith, E. Wakefield and John S. Shellenberger. "Some Unpublished Audit Reports," **JOA**, 1970, Vol. 130, No. 5, pp. 45-52.

Smith, Edward Paul. "Training Contractor Personnel In Termination Principles And Procedures," **AR**, 1945, Vol. 20, No. 1, pp. 76-84.

Smith, F. P. "Stock-Exchange Margins," **AR**, 1934, Vol. 9, No. 4. pp. 300-303.

Smith, Frank P. "Accounting Provisions Of The Investment Company Act," **AR**, 1941, Vol. 16, No. 1, pp. 1-7.

Smith, Frank P. "Accounting Reports For Management Investment Companies," **AR**, 1940, Vol. 15, No. 3, pp. 301-320.

Smith, Frank P. "Accounting Requirements Of Stock Exchanges, 1933," **AR**, 1937, Vol. 12, No. 2, pp. 145-152.

Smith, Frank P. "Financing The Steel Industry," **AR**, 1939, Vol. 14, No. 4, pp. 331-339.

Smith, Frank P. "Lot Release Cost Accounting In The Aviation Industry," **AR**, 1947, Vol. 22, No. 1, pp. 68-73.

Smith, Frank P. "Research And Faculty Development," **AR**, 1959, Vol. 34, No. 3, pp. 349-355.

Smith, Frank P. "Stock Exchange Listing Requirements, And Publicity," **AR**, 1936, Vol. 11, No. 1, pp. 35-39.

Smith, Frank P. "Surplus Adjustments In The Iron And Steel Industry," **AR**, 1938, Vol. 13, No. 4. pp. 379-389.

Smith, Frank P. "University Costs Of Government Contracts," **AR**, 1948, Vol. 23, No. 2, pp. 158-170.

Smith, G. Stevenson and M. S. Tseng. "Benefit-Cost Analysis As A Performance Indicator," **MA**, 1986, Vol. 67, No. 12, pp. 44-49.

Smith, G. Stevenson. (Riley, William B. and G. Stevenson Smith. "Interest Rate Swaps: Disclosure And Recognition," **CPAJ**, 1987, Vol. 57, No. 1. pp. 64-70.)

Smith, Gene L. and Thomas J. O'Larnic. "Estimating Accounting Reserves With Quantitative Methods," **MA**, 1984. Vol. 66, No. 5, pp. 59-62.

Smith, Gene L. "Accounting For PACs," **MA**, 1984, Vol. 66. No. 1. pp. 58-62.

Smith, Gene L. "Improving Productivity In The Controller's Organization," **MA**, 1986, Vol. 67, No. 7. pp. 49-51.

Smith, Gerald and Jack L. Krogstad. "Impact Of Sources And Authors On 'Auditing: A Jorunal Of Practice & Theory' - A Citation Analysis," **AJPT**, 1984-85, Vol. 4, No. 1, pp. 107-117.

Smith, Gerald and Jack L. Krogstad. "A Taxonomy Of Content And Citations In 'Auditing: A Journal Of Practice & Theory'," **AJPT**, 1988, Vol. 8, No. 1, pp. 108-117.

Smith, Gerald. (Krogstad, Jack L., Gerald Smith and Raymond J. Clay, Jr. "Impact Of A Simulation Of Audit Practice." **IAE**, 1986, Vol. 1, No. 2, pp. 309-320.)

Smith, Gerald. (Wolfe, Donald N. and Gerald Smith. "Planning The Audit In A Distressed Industry," **CPAJ**, 1988. Vol. 58. No. 10, pp. 46-50.)

Smith, Harvey. (Stephenson, James C. and Harvey Smith. "A New Marketing Information System," **MA**, 1974, Vol. 56, No. 2, pp. 11-14.)

Smith, Helen M. "The Use Of Reserves On The Right-Hand Side

Of The Balance Sheet," **AR**, 1960, Vol. 35, No. 1, pp. 100-103.

Smith, Henry C. "New, Realistic Tax Treatment Of Involuntary Conversion," **JOA**, 1952, Vol. 94, No. 3, pp. 311-317.

Smith, Herbert L. "The Natural Christmas Tree Industry," **MA**, 1973, Vol. 55, No. 6, pp. 9-11.

Smith, J. David. (Jones, Thomas W. and J. David Smith. "An Historical Perspective Of Net Present Value And Equivalent Annual Cost," **AHJ**, 1982, Vol. 9, No. 1, pp. 103-110.)

Smith, J. H. (Lembke, V. C., J. H. Smith and V. H. Tidwell. "Compulsory Continuing Education For CPAs," **JOA**, 1970, Vol. 129, No. 4, pp. 61-65.)

Smith, J. H., V. H. Tidwell and V. C. Lembke. "An Analysis Of Participation In Continuing Education," **JOA**, 1972, Vol. 133, No. 1, pp. 40-45.

Smith, Jack E. (Reinstein, Alan and Jack E. Smith. "CPA Firms' Performance Appraisal Procedures," **CPAJ**, 1983, Vol. 53, No. 10, pp. 48-55.)

Smith, Jack L. "Actuarial Cost Methods - Basics For CPAs," **JOA**, 1977, Vol. 143, No. 2, pp. 62-66.

Smith, Jack L. "An Alternative Method For Income Tax Allocation," **MA**, 1978, Vol. 60, No. 1, pp. 46-50.

Smith, Jack L. "Needed: Improved Pension Accounting And Reporting," **MA**, 1978, Vol. 59, No. 11, pp. 43-46.

Smith, Jack L. (Dennis, David M., Jack L. Smith and William J. Ferlita. "The Impact Of ACRS Lives On Deferred Tax Accounting," **MA**, 1986, Vol. 67, No. 9, pp. 39-43.)

Smith, James E. and Nora P. Smith. "Readability: A Measurement Of The Performance Of The Communication Function Of Financial Reporting," **AR**, 1971, Vol. 46, No. 3, pp. 552-561.

Smith, James E. "The Need For A Senior Level Theory Seminar," **AR**, 1972, Vol. 47, No. 3, pp. 613-614.

Smith, James F. and Amer Mufti. "Using The Relational Database," **MA**, 1985, Vol. 67, No. 4, pp. 43-50.

Smith, Jay M. "Audit Education For The 1980s," **AR**, 1978, Vol. 53, No. 2, pp. 501-509.

Smith, Jay M. (Purdy, Charles R., Jay M. Smith and Jack Gray. "The Visibility Of The Auditor's Disclosure Of Deviance From APB Opinion: An Empirical Test," **JAR**, 1969, Vol. 7, Supp., pp. 1-18.)

Smith, Jay M., Dale Taylor and Harold Western. "Experiment In Modularized Learning For Intermediate Accounting," **AR**, 1974, Vol. 49, No. 2, pp. 385-390.

Smith, John H. and John W. Kennelly. "A Seminar In Accounting Research," **AR**, 1970, Vol. 45, No. 4, pp. 795-797.

Smith, John H. (DeJong, Douglas V. and John H. Smith. "The Determination Of Audit Responsibilities: An Application Of Agency Theory," **AJPT**, 1984-85, Vol. 4, No. 1, pp. 20-34.)

Smith, John H. (Lembke, Valdean C. and John H. Smith. "Replacement Costs: An Analysis Of Financial Statement And Tax Policy Effects," **JAAF**, 1980, Vol. 3, No. 2, pp. 147-162.)

Smith, John J. "Machine Hours In An Absorption Cost System," **MA**, 1966, Vol. 47, No. 6, pp. 55-61.

Smith, John L. "Improving Reported Earnings," **MA**, 1981, Vol. 63, No. 3, pp. 49-52.

Smith, Karen. (Hooper, Paul, John Page and Karen Smith. "Accountant's Legal Liability: An International Comparison," **IJAER**, 1985, Vol. 20, No. 2, pp. 65-80.)

Smith, Kenneth A. "The Relationship Of Internal Control Evaluation And Audit Sample Size," **AR**, 1972, Vol. 47, No. 2, pp. 260-269.

Smith, Kenneth J. "Differential Cost Analysis Techniques In Occupational Health Promotion Evaluation," **ACCHOR**, 1988, Vol. 2, No. 2, pp. 58-66.

Smith, Kenneth L. "A Regulatory View Of The Tax Allocation Controversy," **MA**, 1966, Vol. 48, No. 1, pp. 57-62.

Smith, Kenneth L. "Capital Gains And Losses In Accounting," **AR**, 1939, Vol. 14, No. 2, pp. 126-138.

Smith, L. Douglas and John J. Anderson. "Inflation Accounting And Comparisons Of Corporate Returns On Equity," **ABR**, 1985-86, Vol. 16, No. 62, pp. 107-116.

Smith, L. Hartley. "A Security Analyst Views Financial Statements," **JOA**, 1959, Vol. 108, No. 2, pp. 37-41.

Smith, L. Murphy and Craig E. Bain. "Computer Graphics For Today's Accountant," **CPAJ**, 1987, Vol. 57, No. 2, pp. 18-35.

Smith, L. Murphy. (Thompson, James H., James S. Worthington and L. Murphy Smith. "An Inconsistency In The Method Of Accounting For Changes In Estimate: Variable Stock Plans," **ACCHOR**, 1987, Vol. 1, No. 4, pp. 29-34.)

Smith, L. Murphy. (Wiggins, Casper E., Jr. and L. Murphy Smith. "A Generalized Audit Simulation Tool For Evaluating The Reliability Of Internal Controls," **CAR**, 1986-87, Vol. 3, No. 2, pp. 316-337.)

Smith, Lawrence Murphy. (Sena, James A. and Lawrence Murphy Smith. "Designing And Implementing An Integrated Job Cost Accounting System," **JIS**, 1986, Vol. 1, No. 1, pp. 102-112.)

Smith, Larry L. "Using Labor Information To Measure Productivity," **MA**, 1983, Vol. 64, No. 12, pp. 47-49.

Smith, Malcolm and Richard Taffler. "Improving The Communication Function Of Published Accounting Statements," **ABR**, 1983-84, Vol. 14, No. 54, pp. 139-146.

Smith, Margaret. (Dittman, David A., Raymond J. Krasniewski and Margaret Smith. "Contracting Strategies For Maximum Benefit In Sales Contracts With Government: The Installment Sale Alternative," **RIGNA**, 1987, Vol. 3. Part A, pp. 107-130.)

Smith, Millard E. "A Quasi-Bayesian Audit Risk Model For Dollar Unit Sampling: A Comment," **AR**, 1984, Vol. 59, No.

3, pp. 524-525.

Smith, Nancy E. "FASB's Conceptual Framework: Is It Being Taught?," **JAED**, 1988, Vol. 6, No. 2, pp. 251-259.

Smith, Nora P. (Smith, James E. and Nora P. Smith. "Readability: A Measurement Of The Performance Of The Communication Function Of Financial Reporting," **AR**, 1971, Vol. 46, No. 3, pp. 552-561.)

Smith, Paul F. "Deferred Compensation Plans After The 1969 Tax Reform Act," **MA**, 1970, Vol. 52, No. 1, pp. 21-24.

Smith, R. G. E. "A Proposal: One Type Of Security?," **ABACUS**, 1975, Vol. 11, No. 1, pp. 3-17.

Smith, R. G. E. "In Defence Of 'One Type Of Security'," **ABACUS**, 1977, Vol. 13, No. 2, pp. 168-179.

Smith, R. G. E. "One Type Of Security Again," **ABACUS**, 1980, Vol. 16, No. 1, pp. 38-47.

Smith, R. G. E. "One Type Of Security In Retrospect," **ABACUS**, 1984, Vol. 20, No. 2, pp. 138-156.

Smith, R. Bob. "The Professional Obligations Imposed By Auditing Standards," **JOA**, 1954, Vol. 98, No. 4, pp. 498-501.

Smith, Ralph E. and Andrew H. Haried. "Exchange Of Nonmonetary Assets: An Interpretation Problem," **AR**, 1977, Vol. 52, No. 4, pp. 958-962.

Smith, Ralph E. and Leroy F. Imdieke. "Accounting For Interest Cost," **CPAJ**, 1980, Vol. 50, No. 4, pp. 30-40.

Smith, Ralph E. and Leroy F. Imdieke. "Accounting For Stock Issued To Employees," **JOA**, 1974, Vol. 138, No. 5, pp. 68-75.

Smith, Ralph E. (Haried, Andrew A. and Ralph E. Smith. "Accounting For Marketable Equity Securities," **JOA**, 1977, Vol. 143, No. 2, pp. 54-61.)

Smith, Ralph E. (Norton, Curtis L. and Ralph E. Smith. "A Comparison Of General Price Level And Historical Cost Financial Statements In The Prediction Of Bankruptcy," **AR**, 1979, Vol. 54, No. 1, pp. 72-87.)

Smith, Ralph E. (Norton, Curtis L. and Ralph E. Smith. "A Comparison Of General Price Level And Historical Cost Financial Statements In The Prediction Of Bankruptcy: A Reply," **AR**, 1980, Vol. 55, No. 3, pp. 516-521.)

Smith, Robert. (Hardiman, Patrick F., Quentin Squires and Robert Smith. "Audit Quality For Governmental Units - Part I," **CPAJ**, 1987, Vol. 57, No. 9, pp. 22-33.)

Smith, Robert. (Hardiman, Patrick F., Quentin Squires and Robert Smith. "Audit Quality For Governmental Units - Part II," **CPAJ**, 1987, Vol. 57, No. 11, pp. 58-67.)

Smith, S. Curtis. "Implementing An FASB Statement," **JOA**, 1982, Vol. 154, No. 6, pp. 60-65.

Smith, Stephen Thomas. "Cash Control System In Communistic China," **AR**, 1955, Vol. 30, No. 4, pp. 602-604.

Smith, T. M. F. (Brooker, R. P. and T. M. F. Smith. "Business Failures - The English Insolvency Statistics," **ABACUS**, 1965, Vol. 1, No. 2, pp. 131-149.)

Smith, Vernon L. (Manes, R. P. and Vernon L. Smith. "Economic Joint Cost Theory And Accounting Practice," **AR**, 1965, Vol. 40, No. 1, pp. 31-35.)

Smith, Vernon L., Jeffrey Schatzberg and William S. Waller. "Experimental Economics And Auditing," **AJPT**, 1987-88, Vol. 7, No. 1, pp. 71-93.

Smith, William N. and G. F. Reichenbach. "Maintenance Material Inventory Control," **MA**, 1967, Vol. 48, No. 12, pp. 49-53.

Smith, William Robert. "John Bennett Canning," **AHJ**, 1974, Vol. 1, No. 1-4, pp. 29-31.

Smith, William R. "A Surrogate Model For Income Reporting," **MA**, 1974, Vol. 56, No. 6, pp. 45-48.

Smith, Willis A. "International Accounting Standards - An Update," **CPAJ**, 1980, Vol. 50, No. 6, pp. 22-27.

Smith, Willis A. "Tax Allocation Revisited - Another Viewpoint," **CPAJ**, 1984, Vol. 54, No. 9, pp. 52-56.

Smith, Willis A. "The Revised AICPA Rules Of Conduct - 'To Serve The Public Interest'," **CPAJ**, 1973, Vol. 43, No. 11, pp. 963-968.

Smolinski, Edward J. "The Adjunct Method In Consolidations," **JAR**, 1963, Vol. 1, No. 2, pp. 149-178.

Smyth, D. J. (Manes, Rene P., John Samuels and D. J. Smyth. "Inventories And Sales: A Cross Section Study," **JAR**, 1967, Vol. 5, Supp., pp. 139-156.)

Smyth, E. Bryan. "Management Accounting In Australia," **AR**, 1960, Vol. 35, No. 3, pp. 464-470.

Smyth, J. E. "A Case For National Income Accounting In The Accounting Curriculum," **AR**, 1959, Vol. 34, No. 3, pp. 376-380.

Smyth, J. E. "An Attempt To Formulate Elementary Classwork Problems In Social Accounting," **AR**, 1954, Vol. 29, No. 2, pp. 313-323.

Snavely, Howard J. "Accounting Information Criteria," **AR**, 1967, Vol. 42, No. 2, pp. 223-232.

Snavely, Howard J. "Current Cost For Long-Lived Assets: A Critical View," **AR**, 1969, Vol. 44, No. 2, pp. 344-353.

Snavely, Howard J. "Needed: An Accounting Constitution," **MA**, 1987, Vol. 68, No. 11, pp. 43-47.

Snavely, H. Jim and Larry M. Walther. "Earnings And The FASB - For Better Or Worse?," **MA**, 1983, Vol. 64, No. 8, pp. 28-33.

Snavely, H. Jim. "Financial Statement Restatement," **JOA**, 1976, Vol. 142, No. 4, pp. 91-100.

Snavely, H. Jim. "Pooling Should Be Mandatory," **CPAJ**, 1975, Vol. 45, No. 12, pp. 23-26.

Snavely, H. Jim. (Hall, Thomas W. and H. Jim Snavely. "Translated Financial Statements Can Be Meaningful," **IJAER**, 1984, Vol. 20, No. 1, pp. 153-170.)

Sneed, Florence R., Clair J. Nixon and Steven D. Grossman. "Auditing Agricultural Producers And Cooperatives," **CPAJ**, 1983, Vol. 53, No. 12, pp. 47-53.

Snellgrove, William F. "A Cost Accounting System For

Service Companies," **MA**, 1971, Vol. 52, No. 8, pp. 35-39.

Snelling, Donald E. "Short-Term Investment Of Excess Cash," **MA**, 1969, Vol. 50, No. 5, pp. 31-35.

Snodgrass, C. (Birnberg, J. G. and C. Snodgrass. "Culture And Control: A Field Study," **AOS**, 1988, Vol. 13, No. 5, pp. 447-464.)

Snow, Charles. (Eisenman, Seymour, Murray S. Akresh and Charles Snow. "Reporting Unusual Events In Income Statements," **CPAJ**, 1979, Vol. 49, No. 6, pp. 23-28.)

Snowball, Doug A. (Abdel-Khalik, A. Rashad, Doug A. Snowball and John H. Wragge. "The Effects Of Certain Internal Audit Variables On The Planning Of External Audit Programs," **AR**, 1983, Vol. 58, No. 2, pp. 215-227.)

Snowball, Doug and William A. Collins. "Televised Accounting Instruction Attitudes And Performance: A Field Experiment," **AR**, 1980, Vol. 55, No. 1, pp. 123-133.

Snowball, Doug. "Human Resource Accounting Information: A Comment Concerning Demand Characteristics," **AR**, 1979, Vol. 54, No. 1, pp. 199-204.

Snowball, Doug. "On The Integration Of Accounting Research On Human Information Processing," **ABR**, 1979-80, Vol. 10, No. 39, pp. 307-318.

Snowball, Doug. (Bamber, E. Michael and Doug Snowball. "An Experimental Study Of The Effects Of Audit Structure In Uncertain Task Environments," **AR**, 1988, Vol. 63, No. 3, pp. 490-504.)

Snowball, Doug. (Knechel, W. Robert and Doug Snowball. "Accounting Internships And Subsequent Academic Performance: An Empirical Study," **AR**, 1987, Vol. 62, No. 4, pp. 799-807.)

Snowball, Doug. (Plumlee, R. David and Doug Snowball. "Auditing Your Own System: Some Findings And Implications," **JIS**, 1987, Vol. 1, No. 2, pp. 41-49.)

Snowball, D. "Accounting Laboratory Experiments On Human Judgment: Some Characteristics And Influences," **AOS**, 1986, Vol. 11, No. 1, pp. 47-70.

Snowball, D. "Some Effects Of Accounting Expertise And Information Load: An Empirical Study," **AOS**, 1980, Vol. 5, No. 3, pp. 323-340.

Snudden, Leslie W. "A Different Approach To Fund-Flow Problems," **AR**, 1965, Vol. 40, No. 4, pp. 880-882.

Snyder, Daniel R. "Cost Analysis And Control Of RDT&E Projects," **MA**, 1971, Vol. 53, No. 3, pp. 42-45.

Snyder, Jerome. "The Future Of Financial Reporting," **AR**, 1954, Vol. 29, No. 3, pp. 480-485.

Snyder, Ralph W. "A Yield Formula For Irregular Installment Payments," **AR**, 1954, Vol. 29, No. 3, pp. 457-464.

Snyder, Ralph W. "Approximate Amortization Of Bond Premiums By 'Payments Outstanding' (Or 'Sum Of Digits') Method," **AR**, 1959, Vol. 34, No. 2, pp. 182-194.

Snyder, Ralph W. "Direct Yield Formulas For Serial Bonds." **AR**, 1955, Vol. 30, No. 2, pp. 257-267.

Snyder, Ralph W. "Some More Notes On The Bond Yield Problem: Serial Bonds," **AR**, 1953, Vol. 28, No. 3, pp. 412-421.

Snyder, Ralph W. "Some Notes On The Bond Yield Problem." **AR**, 1952, Vol. 27, No. 3, pp. 334-338.

Snyder, Ralph W. (Stelson, Hugh E. and Ralph W. Snyder. "Note On Installment Loan Rebates," **AR**, 1954, Vol. 29, No. 1, pp. 72-73.)

Snyder, Ralph W. (Stelson, Hugh E. and Ralph W. Snyder. "Finding The Rate Of Interest," **AR**, 1953, Vol. 28, No. 4, pp. 554-561.)

Sobel, E. L. and M. E. Francis. "Accounting And The Evaluation Of Social Programs: A Reply," **AR**, 1974, Vol. 49, No. 4, pp. 826-830.

Soberman, Alan R. (Falk, Charles Edward and Alan R. Soberman. "Interest-Free Loans After Hardee," **CPAJ**, 1983, Vol. 53, No. 2, pp. 36-41.)

Soberman, Alan R. (Falk, Charles Edward and Alan R. Soberman. "Section 482 After Keller And Foglesong," **CPAJ**, 1982, Vol. 52, No. 9, pp. 30-39.)

Soeters, J. and H. Schreuder. "The Interaction Between National And Organizational Cultures In Accounting Firms," **AOS**, 1988, Vol. 13, No. 1, pp. 75-86.

Solari, Jerome P. and Don J. Summa. "Profile Of The CPA In Tax Practice," **JOA**, 1972, Vol. 133, No. 6, pp. 45-50.

Soliman, Soliman Y. (Filimon, Radu, Sanford Morton and Soliman Y. Soliman. "Spoilage With A Production Function," **ABR**, 1986-87, Vol. 17, No. 68, pp. 337-348.)

Soliman, Soliman Y. (Harvey, David W. and Soliman Y. Soliman. "Standard Cost Variance Analysis In A Learning Environment," **ABR**, 1982-83, Vol. 13, No. 51, pp. 181-190.)

Soliman, Soliman Y. (O'Keefe, Terrence B. and Soliman Y. Soliman. "Do Managers Believe The Efficient Market Hypothesis? Additional Evidence," **ABR**, 1984-85, Vol. 15, No. 58, pp. 67-80.)

Sollenberger, Harold and Alvin A. Arens. "Assessing Information Systems Projects," **MA**, 1973, Vol. 55, No. 3, pp. 37-42.

Sollenberger, Harold M. "A Cost Accounting Framework For EDP Management," **MA**, 1977, Vol. 59, No. 4, pp. 48-56.

Sollenberger, Harold M. "Financial Planning And Control For Political Campaigns," **MA**, 1976, Vol. 57, No. 12, pp. 31-37.

Sollenberger, Harold M. "Management Information Systems: A Charge To Users And Cost Control," **MA**, 1970, Vol. 52, No. 5, pp. 25-28.

Solodar, Donald J. "What The New York Stock Exchange Is Doing About Insider Trading," **MA**, 1987, Vol. 69, No. 5, pp. 22-25.

Solomon, Ezra. "Accounting In The Next Decade," **JOA**, 1965, Vol. 119, No. 1, pp. 22-26.

Solomon, Ira and Paul J. Beck. "A Comparison Of General

Price Level And Historical Cost Financial Statements In The Prediction Of Bankruptcy: A Comment," **AR**, 1980, Vol. 55, No. 3, pp. 511-515.

Solomon, Ira, Lawrence A. Tomassini, Marshall B. Romney and Jack L. Krogstad. "Probability Elicitation In Auditing: Additional Evidence On The Equivalent Prior Sample Method," **AIA**, 1984, Vol. 1, pp. 267-290.

Solomon, Ira. "Multi-Auditor Judgment/Decision Making Research," **JAL**, 1987, Vol. 6, pp. 1-25.

Solomon, Ira. "Probability Assessment By Individual Auditors And Audit Teams: An Empirical Investigation," **JAR**, 1982, Vol. 20, No. 2, Part II, pp. 689-710.

Solomon, Ira. (Beck, Paul J. and Ira Solomon. "Ex Post Sampling Risks And Decision Rule Choice In Substantive Testing," **AJPT**, 1984-85, Vol. 4, No. 2, pp. 1-10.)

Solomon, Ira. (Beck, Paul J. and Ira Solomon. "Sampling Risks And Audit Consequences Under Alternative Testing Approaches," **AR**, 1985, Vol. 60, No. 4, pp. 714-723.)

Solomon, Ira. (Beck, Paul J., Ira Solomon and Lawrence A. Tomassini. "Subjective Prior Probability Distributions And Audit Risk," **JAR**, 1985, Vol. 23, No. 1, pp. 37-56.)

Solomon, Ira. (Beck, Paul J., Thomas J. Frecka and Ira Solomon. "A Model Of The Market For MAS And Audit Services: Knowledge Spillovers And Auditor-Auditee Bonding," **JAL**, 1988, Vol. 7, pp. 50-64.)

Solomon, Ira. (Brown, Clifton E. and Ira Solomon. "Effects Of Outcome Information On Evaluations Of Management Decisions," **AR**, 1987, Vol. 62, No. 3, pp. 564-577.)

Solomon, Ira. (Schroeder, Mary S., Ira Solomon, and Don Vickrey. "Audit Quality: The Perceptions Of Audit-Committee Chairpersons And Audit Partners," **AJPT**, 1985-86, Vol. 5, No. 2, pp. 86-94.)

Solomon, Ira. (Shields, Michael D., Ira Solomon and William S. Waller. "Auditors' Usage Of Unaudited Book Values When Making Presampling Audit Value Estimates," **CAR**, 1988, Vol. 5, No. 1, pp. 1-18.)

Solomon, I. (Shields, M. D., I. Solomon and W. S. Waller. "Effects Of Alternative Sample Space Representations On The Accuracy Of Auditors' Uncertainty Judgments," **AOS**, 1987, Vol. 12, No. 3, pp. 375-388.)

Solomon, I., J. L. Krogstad, M. B. Romney, and L. A. Tomassini. "Auditors' Prior Probability Distributions For Account Balances," **AOS**, 1982, Vol. 7, No. 1, pp. 27-42.

Solomon, Kenneth Ira and Howard Gordon Kaplan. "Regulation Of The Accounting Profession In Israel," **AR**, 1964, Vol. 39, No. 1, pp. 145-149.

Solomon, Kenneth Ira, Charles Chazen and Richard L. Miller, Jr. "Compilation And Review: The Safety Factor," **JOA**, 183, Vol. 155, No. 6, pp. 50-59.

Solomon, Kenneth Ira. "Partnership Treatment Of Contributed Property," **JOA**, 1964, Vol. 118, No. 3, pp. 56-59.

Solomon, Kenneth Ira. "Tax Effects Of Partnership Expansion," **JOA**, 1965, Vol. 120, No. 6, pp. 53-57.

Solomon, Kenneth I. and Charles Chazen. "Use Of Legal Opinions In The Audit Process," **JOA**, 1973, Vol. 136, No. 5, pp. 46-54.

Solomon, Kenneth I. and Hyman Muller. "Illegal Payments: Where The Auditor Stands," **JOA**, 1977, Vol. 143, No. 1, pp. 51-57.

Solomon, Kenneth I. (Chazen, Charles and Kenneth I. Solomon. "The Art Of Defensive Auditing," **JOA**, 1975, Vol. 140, No. 4, pp. 66-71.)

Solomon, Kenneth I. (Chazen, Charles, Richard L. Miller, Jr. and Kenneth I. Solomon. "When The Rules Say: 'See Your Lawyer,'" **JOA**, 1981, Vol. 151, No. 1, pp. 60-70.)

Solomon, Kenneth I. (Chazen, Charles and Kenneth I. Solomon. "The 'Unaudited' State Of Affairs," **JOA**, 1972, Vol. 134, No. 6, pp. 41-45.)

Solomon, Kenneth I., Charles Chazen and Barry S. Augenbraun. "Who Judges The Auditor, And How?," **JOA**, 1976, Vol. 142, No. 2, pp. 67-74.

Solomon, Lanny. "Improving Student Attitudes In The Beginning Accounting Course," **AR**, 1975, Vol. 50, No. 3, pp. 601-605.

Solomon, Morton B. "The Contingent Bailout In Pooling Of Interests," **CPAJ**, 1973, Vol. 43, No. 8, pp. 667-669.

Solomons, David. "Accounting For Changing Price Levels: Recent British Views," **JOA**, 1954, Vol. 97, No. 6, pp. 702-707.

Solomons, David. "Accounting Research In The United States: A Survey Of Current Organisational Activity," **ABR**, 1970-71, Vol. 1, No. 1, pp. 11-17.

Solomons, David. "Breakeven Analysis Under Absorption Costing," **AR**, 1968, Vol. 43, No. 3, pp. 447-452.

Solomons, David. "Economic And Accounting Concepts Of Income," **AR**, 1961, Vol. 36, No. 3, pp. 374-383.

Solomons, David. "The AAA's International Lecturer Program: A Passage To India In 1984," **IAE**, 1985, Vol. 1, No. 1, pp. 1-7.

Solomons, David. "The FASB's Conceptual Framework: An Evaluation," **JOA**, 1986, Vol. 161, No. 6, pp. 114-125.

Solomons, David. "The Political Implications Of Accounting And Accounting Standard Setting," **ABR**, 1982-83, Vol. 13, No. 50, pp. 107-118.

Solomons, David. "The Politicization Of Accounting," **JOA**, 1978, Vol. 146, No. 5, pp. 65-72.

Solomons, David. "The Twilight Of Income Measurement: Twenty-Five Years On," **AHJ**, 1987, Vol. 14, No. 1, pp. 1-6.

Solomons, David. (Johnson, Steven B. and David Solomons. "Institutional Legitimacy And The FASB," **JAPP**, 1984, Vol. 3, No. 3, pp. 165-183.)

Someya, Kyojiro. "The SLIP Accounting System: Traditional Bookkeeping Procedures In Japan," **IJAER**, 1971, Vol. 7, No. 1, pp. 99-114.

Someya, Kyojiro. "The Use Of Funds Statements In Japan," AR, 1964, Vol. 39, No. 4, pp. 983-989.

Sommer, A. A., Jr. "Corporate Governance: Its Impact On The Profession," JOA, 1980, Vol. 150, No. 1, pp. 52-61.

Sommer, A. A., Jr. "The Lion And The Lamb: Can The Profession Live With 'Cooperative Regulation'?," JOA, 1978, Vol. 145, No. 4, pp. 70-75.

Sommerfeld, Ray M. and John E. Easton. "The CPA's Tax Practice Today - And How It Got That Way," JOA, 1987, Vol. 163, No. 5, pp. 166-179.

Sommerfeld, Ray M. "Statement Of President Ray M. Sommerfeld On Proposed Changes In The Uniform CPA Examination," ACCHOR, 1987, Vol. 1, No. 4, pp. 87-91.

Sommerfeld, Ray M. "Tax Implications For The Visiting Professor," AR, 1967, Vol. 42, No. 4, pp. 747-750.

Sommerfeld, Ray M. "Taxation: Education's Orphan," JOA, 1966, Vol. 122, No. 6, pp. 38-44.

Sommerfeld, Ray. "Teaching Taxes - An Assist," AR, 1965, Vol. 40, No. 2, p. 460.

Sommerfeld, R. M. "The Need For CPA Bank Audits," JOA, 1964, Vol. 117, No. 5, pp. 49-53.

Sonderegger, Emory O. "Qualifications For Accounting Students To Meet The Needs Of Business Firms," AR, 1959, Vol. 34, No. 1, pp. 112-123.

Sondhi, Ashwinpaul C. (Houlihan, William A. and Ashwinpaul C. Sondhi. "De Facto Capitalization Of Operating Leases: The Effect On Debt Capacity," CA, 1984, Vol. 2, No. 3, pp. 3-13.)

Sondhi, Ashwinpaul. (Choi, Frederick D. S. and Ashwinpaul Sondhi. "SFAS No. 52 And The Funds Statement," CA, 1984, Vol. 2, No. 2, pp. 46-56.)

Soper, Fred J. and Robert Dolphin, Jr. "Readability And Corporate Annual Reports," AR, 1964, Vol. 39, No. 2, pp. 358-362.

Soper, Herbert D. "Inventory Reserves: Why And When," AR, 1948, Vol. 23, No. 4, pp. 391-396.

Sorensen, Eric H. (Dhaliwal, Dan S. and Eric H. Sorensen. "On Accounting Information And Municipal Bond Interest Cost: A Comment," JAPP, 1985, Vol. 4, No. 3, pp. 233-239.)

Sorensen, James E. and David D. Franks. "The Relative Contribution Of Ability, Self-Esteem And Evaluative Feedback To Performance: Implications For Accounting Systems," AR, 1972, Vol. 47, No. 4, pp. 735-746.

Sorensen, James E. and Hugh D. Grove. "Cost-Outcome and Cost-Effectiveness Analysis: Emerging Nonprofit Performance Evaluation Techniques," AR, 1977, Vol. 52, No. 3, pp. 658-675.

Sorensen, James E. "Bayesian Analysis In Auditing," AR, 1969, Vol. 44, No. 3, pp. 555-561.

Sorensen, James E. "Professional And Bureaucratic Organization In The Public Accounting Firm," AR, 1967, Vol. 42, No. 3, pp. 553-565.

Sorensen, James E. (Balke, Thomas E. and James E. Sorensen. "Reliability And Validity Of Accounting Data," IJAER, 1975, Vol. 10, No. 2, pp. 37-46.)

Sorensen, James E. (Willingham, John J. and James E. Sorensen. "The Behavioral Science Milieu Of Accounting," IJAER, 1971, Vol. 7, No. 1, pp. 49-63.)

Sorensen, James E., John Grant Rhode and Edward E. Lawler, III. "The Generation Gap In Public Accounting," JOA, 1973, Vol. 136, No. 6, pp. 42-50.

Sorensen, Jim L. "Common Sense In Computer Security," CPAJ, 1972, Vol. 42, No. 5, pp. 379-382.

Sorensen, J. E. (Rhode, J. G., J. E. Sorensen and E. E. Lawler III. "Sources Of Professional Staff Turnover In Public Accounting Firms Revealed By The Exit Interview," AOS, 1977, Vol. 2, No. 2, pp. 165-176.)

Sorensen, Robert. (Groves, Roger, Rene Manes and Robert Sorensen. "The Application Of The Hirsch-Dantzig 'Fixed Charge' Algorithm To Profit Planning: A Formal Statement Of Product Profitability Analysis," AR, 1970, Vol. 45, No. 3, pp. 481-489.)

Sorkin, Ira Lee. "Inside Insider Trading," CA, 1988, Vol. 6, No. 1, pp. 31-35.

Soroosh, Jalaleddin. (Flesher, Dale L. and Jalaleddin Soroosh. "Controllers Say FAS 33 Is Not Very Useful," MA, 1983, Vol. 64, No. 7, pp. 50-53.)

Soroosh, Jalaleddin. (Flesher, Dale L. and Jalaleddin Soroosh. "Factors Affecting Accountants' Fees," CPAJ, 1980, Vol. 50, No. 7, pp. 27-32.)

Soroosh, Jalaleddin. (Morgan, Robert G., Jalaleddin Soroosh and Charles J. Woelfel. "Are Ethics Dangerous To Your Job?," MA, 1985, Vol. 66, No. 8, pp. 24-32.)

Soroosh, Jalal. "Why Accountants Oppose IRS Access To Work Papers," MA, 1988, Vol. 69, No. 12, pp. 44-49.

Sorter, George H. and Charles T. Horngren. "Asset Recognition And Economic Attributes - The Relevant Costing Approach," AR, 1962, Vol. 37, No. 3, pp. 391-399.

Sorter, George H. and Martin S. Gans. "Opportunities And Implications Of The Report On Objectives Of Financial Statements," JAR, 1974, Vol. 12, Supp., pp. 1-12.

Sorter, George H. and Monroe Ingberman. "The Implicit Criteria For The Recognition, Quantification, And Reporting Of Accounting Events," JAAF, 1987, Vol. 2 (New Issues), No. 2, pp. 99-116.

Sorter, George H. "Accounting For Baseball," JOA, 1986, Vol. 161, No. 6, pp. 126-133.

Sorter, George H. "An 'Events' Approach To Basic Accounting Theory," AR, 1969, Vol. 44, No. 1, pp. 12-19.

Sorter, George H. "Notes On Funds Provided By Operations," AR, 1959, Vol. 34, No. 2, p. 302.

Sorter, George H. "The Emphasis On Cash And Its Impact On The Funds Statement - Sense And Nonsense," JAAF, 1982, Vol. 5, No. 3, pp. 188-194.

Sorter, George H. (Green, David, Jr. and George H. Sorter. "Accounting For Obsolescence - A Proposal," AR, 1959, Vol. 34, No. 3, pp. 433-441.)

Sorter, George H. (Horngren, Charles T. and George H. Sorter. "An Evaluation Of Some Criticisms Of Relevant Costing," AR, 1964, Vol. 39, No. 2, pp. 417-420.)

Sorter, George H. (Horngren, Charles T. and George H. Sorter. "'Direct' Costing For External Reporting," AR, 1961, Vol. 36, No. 1, pp. 84-93.)

Sorter, George H. (Ingberman, Monroe and George H. Sorter. "The Role Of Financial Statements In An Efficient Market," JAAF, 1978, Vol. 2, No. 1, pp. 58-62.)

Sorter, George H. (Schiff, Michael, George H. Sorter and Jeremy L. Wiesen. "The Evolving Role Of Corporate Audit Committees," JAAF, 1977, Vol. 1, No. 1, pp. 19-44.)

Sorter, George H., Selwyn W. Becker, T. R. Archibald and W. Beaver. "Corporate Personality As Reflected In Accounting Decisions: Some Preliminary Findings," JAR, 1964, Vol. 2, No. 2, pp. 183-196.

Sorter, George H., Stanley Siegel and John Slain. "Accountants' Legal Liability: A Determinant Of The Accounting Model," JAAF, 1988, Vol. 3 (New Series), No. 3, pp. 233-243.

Sorter, George. (Becker, Selwyn, Joshua Ronen and George Sorter. "Opportunity Costs - An Experimental Approach," JAR, 1974, Vol. 12, No. 2, pp. 317-329.)

Sorter, G. H. and George Benston. "Appraising The Defensive Position Of A Firm: The Interval Measure," AR, 1960, Vol. 35, No. 4, pp. 633-640.

Sorter, G. (Rose, J., W. Beaver, S. Becker and G. Sorter. "Toward An Empirical Measure Of Materiality," JAR, 1970, Vol. 8, Supp., pp. 138-148.)

Sosnick, Stephen H. "Depreciation: the Offsetting-Interest Method," AR, 1962, Vol. 37, No. 1, pp. 59-66.

Sotto, R. "Scientific Utopia And Accounting," AOS, 1983, Vol. 8, No. 1, pp. 57-72.

Soucy, Stehen R. (Howell, Robert A. and Stephen R. Soucy. "Cost Accounting In The New Manufacturing Environment," MA, 1987, Vol. 69, No. 2, pp. 42-48.)

Soucy, Stehen R. (Howell, Robert A. and Stephen R. Soucy. "Management Reporting In The New Manufacturing Environment," MA, 1988, Vol. 69, No. 8, pp. 22-29.)

Soucy, Stephen R. (Howell, Robert A. and Stephen R. Soucy. "The New Manufacturing Environment: Major Trends For Management Accountants," MA, 1987, Vol. 69, No. 1, pp. 21-27.)

Soucy, Stephen R. (Howell, Robert A. and Stephen R. Soucy. "Capital Investment Analysis In The New Manufacturing Environment," MA, 1987, Vol. 69, No. 5, pp. 26-32.)

Soucy, Stephen R. (Howell, Robert A. and Stephen R. Soucy. "Operating Controls In The New Manufacturing Environment," MA, 1987, Vol. 69, No. 4, pp. 25-31.)

Souders, Thomas L. (Killough, Larry N. and Thomas L. Souders. "A Goal Programming Model For Public Accounting Firms," AR, 1973, Vol. 48, No. 2, pp. 268-279.)

Southerland, Edwin W. "Financial Personnel Recruitment," MA, 1974, Vol. 56, No. 6, pp. 17-18.

Sowey, Eric. (Ma, Ronald and Eric Sowey. "The Linear Aggregation Coefficient And The Multiple User Case," ABR, 1979-80, Vol. 10, No. 38, pp. 215-220.)

Spacek, Leonard. "A Suggested Solution To The Principles Dilemma," AR, 1964, Vol. 39, No. 2, pp. 275-284.

Spacek, Leonard. "Are Accounting Principles Generally Accepted?," JOA, 1961, Vol. 111, No. 4, pp. 41-46.

Spacek, Leonard. "Can Accounting Principles Be Defined?," JOA, 1958, Vol. 106, No. 6, pp. 40-47.

Spacek, Leonard. "History And Human Nature," AHJ, 1975, Vol. 2, No. 1-4, pp. 35-36.

Spacek, Leonard. "The Need For An Accounting Court," AR, 1958, Vol. 33, No. 3, pp. 368-379.

Spacek, Leonard. "The Treatment Of Goodwill In The Corporate Balance Sheet," JOA, 1964, Vol. 117, No. 2, pp. 35-40.

Spacek, Leonard. "Umpiring The Earnings Per Share Results," MA, 1969, Vol. 50, No. 7, pp. 9-14.

Spanier, Seymour. (Jacobs, Perry F. and Seymour Spanier. "How To Make Wage Increases Under Regulation 6," JOA, 1951, Vol. 91, No. 6, pp. 827-832.)

Sparks, Robert C. "How To Survive A Business Divorce," MA, 1987, Vol. 68, No. 10, pp. 42-44.

Sparks, Robert C. (Hafter, Richard A. and Robert C. Sparks. "Can You Evaluate Your R&D Spending?," MA, 1986, Vol. 67, No. 7, pp. 53-55.)

Spearman, Frank H., III. "Financial Reporting For Securities Brokers," JOA, 1976, Vol. 142, No. 3, pp. 73-82.

Spear, Harvey M. "Depreciation Accounting Under Changing Price Levels," AR, 1949, Vol. 24, No. 4, pp. 369-378.

Spears, J. Steven. "Applying The Unitary Business Concept To Diverse Businesses," CPAJ, 1988, Vol. 58, No. 6, pp. 34-45.

Spede, Edward C. (Holley, Charles L., Edward C. Spede and Michael C. Chester, Jr. "The Push-Down Accounting Controversy," MA, 1987, Vol. 68, No. 7, pp. 39-42.)

Spede, Edward C. (Sperry, John B., Edward C. Spede and Donald W. Hicks. "The Evolution And Current Status Of Peer Review," JOA, 1987, Vol. 163, No. 5, pp. 381-382.)

Speiser, Allen. (Newmiller, John S. and Allen Speiser. "Voluntary Health And Welfare Financial Statements," CPAJ, 1977, Vol. 47, No. 9, pp. 47-54.)

Spencer, Charles H. and Thomas S. Barnhisel. "A Decade Of Price-Level Changes - The Effect On The Financial Statements Of Cummins Engine Company," AR, 1965, Vol. 40, No. 1, pp. 144-153.

Spencer, Charles H. "The Bad Debt Deduction Of Savings And Loan Associations," AR, 1956, Vol. 31, No. 2, pp. 263-271.

Spencer, Lee B., Jr. "The Electronic Library: Impact On Professionals," JOA, 1983, Vol. 156, No. 2, pp. 74-81.

Spencer, Martin M. "Tax Consequences Arising From Purchase Of Partnership Interest," JOA, 1951, Vol. 91, No. 1, pp. 116-119.

Spencer, Martin M. "Taxation Of Couples, Married And Unmarried," CPAJ, 1975, Vol. 45, No. 2, pp. 11-16.

Spencer, Martin M. (Tilt, James T. and Martin M. Spencer. "Marriage Penalties Persist In Tax Laws," CPAJ, 1983, Vol. 53, No. 1, pp. 38-44.)

Spencer, Milton H. "Axiomatic Method And Accounting Science," AR, 1963, Vol. 38, No. 2, pp. 310-316.

Spencer, Milton H. (Oates, Thomas A. and Milton H. Spencer. "A System Of Retirement Frequencies For Depreciable Assets," AR, 1962, Vol. 37, No. 3, pp. 452-459.)

Spence, James. (Fellows, James and James Spence. "Efficiency In Academe: Comparative Advantage Vs. 'Publish Or Perish'," JAED, 1985, Vol. 3, No. 2, pp. 53-60.)

Spero, Leslie L. (Ramage, John G., Abba M. Krieger and Leslie L. Spero. "An Empirical Study Of Error Characteristics In Audit Populations," JAR, 1979, Vol. 17, Supp., pp. 72-102.)

Sperry, John B. (Abdelsamad, M. H. and John B. Sperry. "Accounting And Financial Management," AR, 1974, Vol. 49, No. 4, pp. 844-846.)

Sperry, John B., Edward C. Spede and Donald W. Hicks. "The Evolution And Current Status Of Peer Review," JOA, 1987, Vol. 163, No. 5, pp. 381-382.

Spiceland, J. David and Alan J. Winters. "Market Response Of Stock Distributions: The Effects Of Magnitude, Anticipation, And Cash Returns," ABR, 1985-86, Vol. 16, No. 63, pp. 221-226.

Spiceland, J. David and Hilary C. Zaunbrecher. "Human Resource Accounting: An Historical Perspective," AHJ, 1976, Vol. 3, No. 1-4, pp. 43-49.

Spiceland, J. David, Vincent C. Brenner and Bart P. Hartman. "Standards For Programs And Schools Of Professional Accounting: Accounting Group Perceptions," AR, 1980, Vol. 55, No. 1, pp. 134-143.

Spiceland, J. David. "A CPA Preparation Program For Non-Accounting Majors," JAED, 1983, Vol. 1, No. 2, pp. 169-171.

Spiceland, J. D. and H. C. Zaunbrecher. "The Usefulness Of Human Resource Accounting In Personnel Selection," MA, 1977, Vol. 58, No. 8, pp. 29-30.

Spicer, Barry H. "Investors, Corporate Social Performance And Information Disclosure: An Empirical Study," AR, 1978, Vol. 53, No. 1, pp. 94-111.

Spicer, Barry H. "The Relationship Between Pollution Control Record And Financial Indicators Revisited: Further Comment," AR, 1980, Vol. 55, No. 1, pp. 178-185.

Spicer, Barry H. (Shane, Philip B. and Barry H. Spicer. "Market Response To Environmental Information Produced Outside The Firm," AR, 1983, Vol. 58, No. 3, pp. 521-538.)

Spicer, B. H. and V. Ballew. "Management Accounting Systems And The Economics Of Internal Organization," AOS, 1983, Vol. 8, No. 1, pp. 73-98.

Spicer, B. H. "Towards An Organizational Theory Of The Transfer Pricing Process," AOS, 1988, Vol. 13, No. 3, pp. 303-324.

Spiegel, Reed S. "Information Needs For Competing Companies," MA, 1967, Vol. 48, No. 12, pp. 8-12.

Spiegel, Reed S. "The Accountant, The Marketing Manager And Profit," MA, 1974, Vol. 55, No. 7, pp. 18-20.

Spiller, Earl A. and Robert L. Virgil. "Effectiveness Of APB Opinion No. 19 In Improving Funds Reporting," JAR, 1974, Vol. 12, No. 1, pp. 112-142.

Spiller, Earl A., Jr. "Capital Expenditure Analysis: An Incident Process Case," AR, 1981, Vol. 56, No. 1, pp. 158-165.

Spiller, Earl A., Jr. "Return On Investment: A Need For Special Purpose Information," ACCHOR, 1988, Vol. 2, No. 2, pp. 1-9.

Spiller, Earl A., Jr. "Teaching Consolidated Income Statements - A New Approach," AR, 1962, Vol. 37, No. 2, pp. 336-342.

Spiller, Earl A., Jr. "Theory And Practice In The Development Of Accounting," AR, 1964, Vol. 39, No. 4, pp. 850-859.

Spindell, Robert F. "Emeloid Reversal Upholds Business Insurance Agreements," JOA, 1952, Vol. 93, No. 5, pp. 578-583.

Spires, Eric E. (Sharp, Robert F. and Eric E. Spires. "Attributability And Distributability Of Profit To Shareholders," ABR, 1983-84, Vol. 14, No. 53, pp. 55-62.)

Spivey, W. Allen. (Currin, David L. and W. Allen Spivey. "A Note On 'Management Decision And Integer Programming'," AR, 1972, Vol. 47, No. 1, pp. 144-146.)

Sprague, Charles E. "Income And Outlay (1889)," AHJ, 1978, Vol. 5, No. 2, pp. 79-84.

Sprague, Ralph H., Jr. "System Support For A Financial Planning Model," MA, 1972, Vol. 53, No. 12, pp. 29-34.

Sprague, William. "Fraud, The Accountant, And Internal Control," JOA, 1955, Vol. 100, No. 3, pp. 34-39.

Sprague, William D. "Interim Financial Reporting And Continuous Auditing," CPAJ, 1975, Vol. 45, No. 7, pp. 15-18.

Sprague, William D. "The Testing Of Internal Control," JOA, 1956, Vol. 101, No. 3, pp. 49-55.

Sprague, W. Douglas. "The Advertising Dilemma," CPAJ, 1977, Vol. 47, No. 1, pp. 27-30.

Sprague, W. D. and Arthur J. Levy. "Accounting And Law: Is Dual Practice In The Public Interest?," JOA, 1966, Vol. 122, No. 6, pp. 45-52.

Sprague, W. D. "Reliance Upon Other Auditors," JOA, 1960, Vol. 109, No. 2, pp. 29-33.

Sprague, W. D. "The Case For Universal Professional Development," CPAJ, 1973, Vol. 43, No. 9, pp. 747-754.

Sprigg, William T., Alan Hanson and Larry Steffens. "Controlling And Tracking Unit Costs," MA, 1976, Vol. 58, No. 5, pp. 47-54.

Springle, Hiram J. "Evaluating Sources Of Capital For Minority Enterprises," MA, 1978, Vol. 59, No. 9, pp. 24-26.

Sprinkle, R. David and William E. Hall, Jr. "How To Cope With Reverse Discrimination In Executive Benefit Plans," MA, 1979, Vol. 61, No. 2, pp. 41-44.

Sprouls, R. Clay. "A Role Of Computer Simulation In Accounting Education," AR, 1962, Vol. 37, No. 3, pp. 515-520.

Sprouse, Robert T. "Accounting For What-You-May-Call-Its," JOA, 1966, Vol. 122, No. 4, pp. 45-53.

Sprouse, Robert T. "Accounting Principles And Corporation Statutes," AR, 1960, Vol. 35, No. 2, pp. 246-257.

Sprouse, Robert T. "Chop Suey, Chain Stores, And Conglomerate Reporting," JOA, 1968, Vol. 125, No. 4, pp. 35-42.

Sprouse, Robert T. "Historical Costs And Current Assets - Traditional And Treacherous," AR, 1963, Vol. 38, No. 4, pp. 687-695.

Sprouse, Robert T. "Legal Concepts Of The Corporation," AR, 1958, Vol. 33, No. 1, pp. 37-49.

Sprouse, Robert T. "Observations Concerning The Realization Concept," AR, 1965, Vol. 40, No. 3, pp. 522-526.

Sprouse, Robert T. "The Importance Of Earnings In The Conceptual Framework," JOA, 1978, Vol. 145, No. 1, pp. 64-71.

Sprouse, Robert T. "The Significance Of The Concept Of The Corporation In Accounting Analyses," AR, 1957, Vol. 32, No. 3, pp. 369-378.

Sprouse, Robert. "Understanding Inflation Accounting," CPAJ, 1977, Vol. 47, No. 1, pp. 23-26.

Sprtel, Frank J. "Employee Retirement Income Security Act," MA, 1976, Vol. 57, No. 9, pp. 15-16.

Spurr, William A. "How To Construct A Price Index For Lifo Inventories," JOA, 1952, Vol. 93, No. 2, pp. 204-209.

Squires, James W. IV. "The Perfect Fit: Minicomputers And Medium-Sized Companies," MA, 1984, Vol. 66, No. 1, pp. 42-48.

Squires, Quentin. (Hardiman, Patrick F., Quentin Squires and Robert Smith. "Audit Quality For Governmental Units - Part I," CPAJ, 1987, Vol. 57, No. 9, pp. 22-33.)

Squires, Quentin. (Hardiman, Patrick F., Quentin Squires and Robert Smith. "Audit Quality For Governmental Units - Part II," CPAJ, 1987, Vol. 57, No. 11, pp. 58-67.)

Squyres, Weldon J. "Tax Planning For Securities Transactions," JOA, 1964, Vol. 117, No. 2, pp. 65-73.

Srinidhi, Bin N. (Balachandran, Kashi R. and Bin N. Srinidhi. "A Rationale For Fixed Charge Application," JAAF, 1987, Vol. 2 (New Issues), No. 2, pp. 151-183.)

Srinidhi, Bin. (Halperin, Robert and Bin Srinidhi. "The Effects Of The U.S. Income Tax Regulations' Transfer Pricing Rules On Allocative Efficiency," AR, 1987, Vol. 62, No. 4, pp. 686-706.)

Srinidhi, B. N. and M. A. Vasarhelyi. "Auditor Judgment Concerning Establishment Of Substantive Tests Based On Internal Control Reliability," AJPT, 1985-86, Vol. 5, No. 2, pp. 64-76.

Srivastava, Rajendra P. "A Note On Internal Control Systems With Control Components In Series," AR, 1985, Vol. 60, No. 3, pp. 504-507.

Srivastava, Rajendra P. "Auditing Functions For Internal Control Systems With Interdependent Documents And Channels," JAR, 1986, Vol. 24, No. 2, pp. 422-426.

Staats, Elmer B. "Auditing As We Enter The 21st Century - What New Challenges Will Have To Be Met," AJPT, 1981-82, Vol. 1, No. 1, pp. 1-11.

Staats, Elmer B. "Grant Audits: A New Vista For CPAs." JOA, 1979, Vol. 147, No. 4, pp. 68-72.

Staats, Elmer B. "Information Needs In An Era Of Change," MA, 1968, Vol. 50, No. 2, pp. 11-15.

Staats, Elmer B. "The History Of Standard No. 409," MA, 1975, Vol. 57, No. 4, pp. 21-23.

Staats, Elmer B. "The Role Of The Accountant In The 70's," MA, 1972, Vol. 53, No. 10, pp. 13-14.

Staats, Elmer B. "Uniform Cost Accounting Standards In Negotiated Defense Contracts," MA, 1969, Vol. 50, No. 5, pp. 21-25.

Staats, Elmer B. (Wyatt, Arthur R. and Elmer B. Staats. "Who Should Set Governmental Accounting Standards?," JOA, 1979, Vol. 147, No. 3, pp. 65-70.)

Stabler, Henry Francis and Norman X. Dressel. "May And Paton: Two Giants Revisited," AHJ, 1981, Vol. 8, No. 2, pp. 79-90.

Stacey, Nicholas A. H. "The Accountant In Literature," AR, 1958, Vol. 33, No. 1, pp. 102-105.

Stacey, Ray. (Rickwood, Colin, Geoff Coates and Ray Stacey. "Managed Costs And The Capture Of Information," ABR, 1986-87, Vol. 17, No. 68, pp. 319-326.)

Stafford, Victor J. "Asset Base For Performance Evaluation," MA, 1968, Vol. 49, No. 6, pp. 21-25.

Stagliano, A. J. and Frederic M. Stiner, Jr. "Enrollments In Accounting Programs: Trends And Forecasts," JAED, 1985, Vol. 3, No. 1, pp. 145-163.

Stagliano, A. J. (Bedingfield, James P., Philip M. J. Reckers and A. J. Stagliano. "Assessing The Impact Of Mergers On Bank Performance," AIA, 1986, Vol. 3, pp. 149-170.)

Stagliano, A. J. (Freedman, Martin and A. J. Stagliano. "A

Variables With Common Stock Values," **AR**, 1965. Vol. 40, No. 1, pp. 119-134.

Staubus, George J. "The Dark Ages Of Cost Accounting: The Role Of Miscues In The Literature," **AHJ**, 1987, Vol. 14, No. 2, pp. 1-18.

Staubus, George J. "The Effects Of Price-Level Restatements On Earnings," **AR**, 1976, Vol. 51, No. 3, pp. 574-589.

Staubus, George J. "The Market Simulation Theory Of Accounting Measurement," **ABR**, 1985-86, Vol. 16, No. 62, pp. 117-132.

Staubus, George J. "The Measurement Of Assets And Liabilities," **ABR**, 1972-73, Vol. 3, No. 12, pp. 243-262.

Staubus, George J. "The Multiple-Criteria Approach To Making Accounting Decisions," **ABR**, 1975-76, Vol. 6, No. 24, pp. 276-288.

Staubus, George J. "The Residual Equity Point Of View In Accounting," **AR**, 1959, Vol. 34, No. 1, pp. 3-13.

Staubus, George J. "The Responsibility Of Accounting Teachers," **AR**, 1975, Vol. 50, No. 1, pp. 160-170.

Staub, Walter A. "Mode Of Conducting An Audit," **AR**, 1943, Vol. 18, No. 2, pp. 91-98.

Staub, Walter A. "The Cost Principle," **AR**, 1942, Vol. 17, No. 1, pp. 3-9.

Staub, Walter. "Contrasting Theories Of Profit: Comments," **AR**, 1936, Vol. 11, No. 1, pp. 15-17.

Stauffer, Ralph L. "What Bankers Like To Find In Audit Reports," **JOA**, 1951, Vol. 91, No. 3, pp. 416-421.

Staunton, J. J. "Realization: A Misapplied Concept In Accounting," **ABACUS**, 1973, Vol. 9, No. 2, pp. 193-200.

Staunton, J. J. (Brooker, R. P. and J. J. Staunton. "On The Independence Of Auditors," **ABACUS**, 1966, Vol. 2, No. 2, pp. 172-179.)

Steadman, G. T. (Moores, K. and G. T. Steadman. "The Comparative Viewpoints Of Groups Of Accountants: More On The Entity-Proprietary Debate," **AOS**, 1986, Vol. 11, No. 1, pp. 19-34.)

Stead, Gordon W. "Toward A Synthesis Of Accounting Doctrine," **AR**, 1948, Vol. 23, No. 4, pp. 355-359.

Stead, W. Edward. (McKee, Thomas E. and W. Edward Stead. "Managing The Professional Accountant," **JOA**, 1988, Vol. 166, No. 1, pp. 76-86.)

Steakley, Mark E. "Inflation Accounting Techniques: How They Compare," **MA**, 1979, Vol. 61, No. 3, pp. 16-18.

Stec, Stan. "Manufacturing Control Through Bar Coding At Target Products," **MA**, 1988, Vol. 69, No. 10, p. 47.

Steece, Bert M. (Moore, Michael L., Bert M. Steece and Charles W. Swenson. "An Analysis Of The Impact Of State Income Tax Rates And Bases On Foreign Investment," **AR**, 1987, Vol. 62, No. 4, pp. 671-685.)

Steece, Bert M. (Moore, Michael L., Bert M. Steece and Charles W. Swenson. "Some Empirical Evidence On Taxpayer Rationality," **AR**, 1985, Vol. 60, No. 1, pp. 18-32.)

Steedle, Lamont F. "Disclosure Of Segment Information - SFAS #14," **CPAJ**, 1983, Vol. 53, No. 10, pp. 34-47.

Steedle, Lamont F. "Has Productivity Measurement Outgrown Infancy?," **MA**, 1988, Vol. 70, No. 2, pp. 15-20.

Steele, Anthony and Jean Haworth. "Auditors' Views On The Truth And Fairness Of CCA," **ABR**, 1985-86, Vol. 16, No. 62, pp. 133-142.

Steele, Anthony. "Another Look At The Levels Of Assurance Issue In Auditing," **ABR**, 1983-84, Vol. 14, No. 54, pp. 147-156.

Steele, Anthony. "The Accuracy Of Chairmen's Non-Quantified Forecasts: An Exploratory Study," **ABR**, 1981-82, Vol. 12, No. 47, pp. 215-230.

Steele, A. "A Corrected Strategy For More Efficient Audit Sample Determination," **ABR**, 1985-86, Vol. 16, No. 61, pp. 53-58.

Steele, Charles G. and James J. Costello. "Summary Annual Reports: An Idea Whose Time Has Come," **CA**, 1984, Vol. 2, No. 4, pp. 4-11.

Steele, Charles G. "An Auditor Samples Statistics," **JOA**, 1962, Vol. 114, No. 3, pp. 50-56.

Steele, Henry M. "Managerial Uses And Limitations Of Uniform Dollar Accounting Data," **AR**, 1959, Vol. 34, No. 2, pp. 242-249.

Steffens, Larry. (Sprigg, William T., Alan Hanson and Larry Steffens. "Controlling And Tracking Unit Costs," **MA**, 1976, Vol. 58, No. 5, pp. 47-54.)

Steffler, Scott D. (Harwell, Jeff L. William S. Nichols, III and Scott D. Steffler. "Recent Developments In The Presentation Of Earnings Per Share," **AR**, 1974, Vol. 49, No. 4, pp. 852-853.)

Stehens, William L. (Harris, Le Brone C. and William L. Stephens. "The Learning Curve: A Case Study," **MA**, 1978, Vol. 59, No. 8, pp. 47-54.)

Stein, Lawrence J. (Coyner, Randolph S. and Lawrence J. Stein. "A Classification Scheme For Financial Footnotes," **MA**, 1981, Vol. 62, No. 11, pp. 43-47.)

Steinbart, Paul J. "Materiality: A Case Study Using Expert Systems," **AR**, 1987, Vol. 62, No. 1, pp. 97-116.

Steinbart, Paul J. (Loebbecke, James K. and Paul J. Steinbart. "An Investigation Of The Use Of Preliminary Analytical Review To Provide Substantive Audit Evidence," **AJPT**, 1986-87, Vol. 6, No. 2, pp. 74-89.)

Steinbart, Paul. (Dilley, Steven C., Randall B. Hayes and Paul Steinbart. "Development Of A Paradigm For Applied Accounting Research: A Way Of Coping With Subject-Matter Complexity," **AR**, 1983, Vol. 58, No. 2, pp. 405-416.)

Steinbart, Paul. (Gal, Graham and Paul Steinbart. "Artificial Intelligence And Research In Accounting Information Systems: Opportunities And Issues," **JIS**, 1987, Vol. 2, No. 1, pp. 54-62.)

Steinberg, Harold I. "A New Look At Governmental Accounting," **JOA**, 1979, Vol. 147, No. 3, pp. 46-55.

Steinberg, Harold I. (Meinhardt, Joan, Joseph F. Moraglio and Harold I. Steinberg. "Governmental Audits: An Action Plan For Excellence," **JOA**, 1987, Vol. 164, No. 1, pp. 86-91.)

Steinberg, Harold I., John R. Miller and Terrill E. Menzel. "The Single Audit In Government," **JOA**, 1981, Vol. 151, No. 6, pp. 56-67.

Steinberg, Richard M. (Livingstone, John Leslie and Richard M. Steinberg. "SEC's Proposed Internal Control Reporting Rules," **CPAJ**, 1979, Vol. 49, No. 12, pp. 39-43.)

Steinberg, Richard. (Biddle, Gary C. and Richard Steinberg. "Allocations Of Joint And Common Costs," **JAL**, 1984, Vol. 3, pp. 1-46.)

Steiner, Robert A. "An Analysis Of Income Tax Allocation," **JOA**, 1961, Vol. 111, No. 6, pp. 64-67.

Steinmetz, Lawrence L. (Bebee, Richard F., Lawrence L. Steinmetz and William D. Wilsted. "Managing The Income Number," **MA**, 1975, Vol. 56, No. 8, pp. 40-42.)

Steinmetz, Lawrence L. (Patten, Ronald J. and Lawrence L. Steinmetz. "What Do Students Think Of Your Elementary Course?," **AR**, 1966, Vol. 41, No. 4, pp. 767-772.)

Steinwurtzel, Samuel L. "A Uniform Report For State Regulatory Agencies," **CPAJ**, 1979, Vol. 49, No. 12, pp. 25-32.

Steinwurtzel, Samuel L. "The New 990," **CPAJ**, 1980, Vol. 50, No. 5, pp. 20-26.

Steinwurtzel, Samuel L. "The New 990 Of 1981 - Part II," **CPAJ**, 1982, Vol. 52, No. 4, pp. 37-41.

Steinwurtzel, Samuel L. "The New 990 Of 1981 - Part I," **CPAJ**, 1982, Vol. 52, No. 2, pp. 9-16.

Steinwurtzel, Samuel L. "The New 990 Of 1981 - Part III," **CPAJ**, 1982, Vol. 52, No. 5, pp. 36-44.

Stelson, Hugh E. and Ralph W. Snyder. "Note On Installment Loan Rebates," **AR**, 1954, Vol. 29, No. 1, pp. 72-73.

Stelson, Hugh E. and Ralph W. Snyder. "Finding The Rate Of Interest," **AR**, 1953, Vol. 28, No. 4, pp. 554-561.

Stelson, Hugh E. "Finding The Yield On A Bond," **AR**, 1951, Vol. 26, No. 4, pp. 538-539.

Stelson, Hugh E. "The Rate Of Interest In Instalment Payment Plans," **AR**, 1952, Vol. 27, No. 3, pp. 366-369.

Stelzer, Herbert J. "Evaluation Of Internal Control In Small Audits," **JOA**, 1964, Vol. 118, No. 5, pp. 55-61.

Stempf, Victor H. "A Critique Of The Tentative Statement Of Accounting Principles," **AR**, 1938, Vol. 13, No. 1, pp. 55-62.

Stempf, Victor H. "Termination And Renegotiation," **AR**, 1944, Vol. 19, No. 2, pp. 117-130.

Stening, Bruce W. (Davison, A. G., Bruce W. Stening and Wan Tai Wai. "Auditor Concentration And The Impact Of Interlocking Directorates," **JAR**, 1984, Vol. 22, No. 1, pp. 313-317.)

Stephan, Frederick F. "Faculty Advice About Statistical Sampling," **AR**, 1960, Vol. 35, No. 1, pp. 29-32.

Stephan, Jens. (Dyckman, Thomas, Donna Philbrick and Jens Stephan. "A Comparison Of Event Study Methodologies Using Daily Stock Returns: A Simulation Approach," **JAR**, 1984, Vol. 22, Supp., pp. 1-30.)

Stephenson, E. (Dangerfield, B. C. and E. Stephenson. "Stock Valuation Practices In Consumer Durables Manufacturing Industry," **ABR**, 1973-74, Vol. 4, No. 13, pp. 2-12.)

Stephenson, James C. and Harvey Smith. "A New Marketing Information System," **MA**, 1974, Vol. 56, No. 2, pp. 11-14.

Stephens, Alvis P. "Merger/Acquisition Valuation Approaches," **MA**, 1968, Vol. 49, No. 8, pp. 14-20.

Stephens, H. Virgil. "A Profit-Oriented Marketing Information System," **MA**, 1972, Vol. 54, No. 3, pp. 37-42.

Stephens, H. Virgil. "Efficiency And Effectiveness," **MA**, 1976, Vol. 57, No. 7, pp. 41-42.

Stephens, Matthew J. "Inseparability And The Valuation Of Convertible Bonds," **JOA**, 1971, Vol. 132, No. 2, pp. 54-62.

Stephens, Ray G. "An Investigation Of The Descriptiveness Of The General Theory Of Evidence And Auditing," **AJPT**, 1983-84, Vol. 3, No. 1, pp. 55-74.

Stephens, Ray G., Jesse F. Dillard and David K. Dennis. "Implications Of Formal Grammars For Accounting Policy Development," **JAPP**, 1985, Vol. 4, No. 2, pp. 123-148.

Stephens, R. J. "A Note On An Early Reference To Cost-Volume-Profit Relationships," **ABACUS**, 1966, Vol. 2, No. 1, pp. 78-83.

Stephens, William L. "Earnings Per Share: A Flow Approach To Teaching Concepts And Procedures: A Comment," **AR**, 1978, Vol. 53, No. 1, pp. 260-262.

Stephens, William L. (Dennis, David M. and William L. Stephens. "Recruitment And Utilization Of Minority Group Members," **JOA**, 1976, Vol. 141, No. 5, pp. 64-73.)

Stepp, James O. "Deferred Taxes: The Discounting Controversy," **JOA**, 1985, Vol. 160, No. 5, pp. 98-109.

Sterling, Robert R. and Raymond Radosevich. "A Valuation Experiment," **JAR**, 1969, Vol. 7, No. 1, pp. 90-95.

Sterling, Robert R. and Richard E. Flaherty. "The Role Of Liquidity In Exchange Valuation," **AR**, 1971, Vol. 46, No. 3, pp. 441-456.

Sterling, Robert R. "A Case Of Valuation And Learned Cognitive Dissonance," **AR**, 1967, Vol. 42, No. 2, pp. 376-378.

Sterling, Robert R. "A Test Of The Uniformity Hypothesis," **ABACUS**, 1969, Vol. 5, No. 1, pp. 37-47.

Sterling, Robert R. "Accounting Research, Education And Practice," **JOA**, 1973, Vol. 136, No. 3, pp. 44-52.

Sterling, Robert R. "An Explication And Analysis Of The Structure Of Accounting," **ABACUS**, 1971, Vol. 7, No. 2, pp. 137-152.

Sterling, Robert R. "An Explication And Analysis Of The Structure Of Accounting - Part Two," **ABACUS**, 1972, Vol.

8, No. 2, pp. 145-162.

Sterling, Robert R. "An Operational Analysis Of Traditional Accounting," **ABACUS**, 1966. Vol. 2, No. 2, pp. 119-136.

Sterling, Robert R. "Confessions Of A Failed Empiricist," **AIA**, 1988, Vol. 6, pp. 3-36.

Sterling, Robert R. "Conservatism: The Fundamental Principle Of Valuation In Traditional Accounting," **ABACUS**, 1967, Vol. 3, No. 2, pp. 109-132.

Sterling, Robert R. "Costs (Historical Versus Current) Versus Exit Values," **ABACUS**, 1981. Vol. 17, No. 2, pp. 93-129.

Sterling, Robert R. "Decision Oriented Financial Accounting," **ABR**, 1971-72, Vol. 2. No. 7, pp. 198-208.

Sterling, Robert R. "Determination Of Goodwill And Bonus On The Admission Of A Partner," **AR**, 1962. Vol. 37, No. 4, pp. 766-767.

Sterling, Robert R. "Elements Of Pure Accounting Theory," **AR**, 1967, Vol. 42. No. 1, pp. 62-73.

Sterling, Robert R. "On Identification Of Users And Firms." **ABR**, 1984-85, Vol. 15, No. 59, pp. 241-245.

Sterling, Robert R. "On Theory Construction And Verification," **AR**, 1970, Vol. 45, No. 3. pp. 444-457.

Sterling, Robert R. "Relevant Financial Reporting In An Age Of Price Changes," **JOA**, 1975, Vol. 139, No. 2, pp. 42-51.

Sterling, Robert R. "The Going Concern: An Examination," **AR**, 1968, Vol. 43, No. 3. pp. 481-502.

Sterling, Robert R., John O. Tollefson and Richard E. Flaherty. "Exchange Valuation: An Empirical Test," **AR**, 1972, Vol. 47, No. 4, pp. 709-721.

Sterling, R. R. "In Defence Of Accounting In The United States," **ABACUS**, 1966, Vol. 2, No. 2, pp. 180-183.

Stern, Harry L. "Planning For The Corporate Alternative Minimum Tax," **MA**, 1988, Vol. 69, No. 9, pp. 44-47.

Stern, Harry L. "The New Passive Activity Regulations," **MA**, 1988, Vol. 69, No. 12, pp. 37-40.

Stern, Harry L. "The New Statement On Accounting For Income Taxes," **MA**, 1988, No. 10, pp. 56-59.

Stern, Jerrold J. (Bathke, Allen W., Jr., Richard L. Rogers and Jerrold J. Stern. "The Security Market Reaction To Tax Legislation As Reflected In Bond Price Adjustments," **JATA**, 1985, Vol. 6, No. 2, pp. 37-49.)

Stern, Jerrold J. (Rogers, Richard L. and Jerrold J. Stern. "When Should LIFO Liquidated Inventories Be Replaced?," **MA**, 1986. Vol. 68, No. 5, pp. 53-57.)

Stern, Myles, Meryle Hirschland and Serge Matulich. "Comment And Reply - 'A Theoretical Deficiency In Accounting For Bonds'," **JAED**, 1986, Vol. 4, No. 2. pp. 147-151.

Stern, Myles. "Computer Conferencing For Accounting Instruction," **JAED**, 1985, Vol. 3. No. 1, pp. 69-79.

Stern, Roy D. "Accounting For Intracompany Inventory Transfers," **MA**, 1980, Vol. 62, No. 3, pp. 41-44.

Sternberg, Harry. "New Developments In Renegotiation Of Federal Government Contracts," **CPAJ**, 1973. Vol. 43, No. 6, pp. 481-486.

Sterner, Julie A. and Penelope J. Yunker. "Human Resource Accounting By Professional Sports Teams," **AIA**, 1986, Vol. 3, pp. 127-148.

Sterner, Julie A. "An Empirical Evaluation Of SFAS No. 55," **JAR**, 1983, Vol. 21, No. 2, pp. 623-628.

Sterner, Julie A. (Yunker, Penelope J., Julie A. Sterner and Michael Costigan. "Employment In Accounting: A Comparison Of Recruiter Perceptions With Student Expectations," **JAED**, 1986. Vol. 4, No. 1, pp. 95-112.)

Stettler, Howard F. and Chester B. Vanatta. "Our Changing Profession," **JOA**, 1963. Vol. 116, No. 4, pp. 53-56.

Stettler, Howard F. "Accreditation Of Collegiate Accounting Programs," **AR**, 1965, Vol. 40, No. 4. pp. 723-730.

Stettler, Howard F. "An Experiment In Education For The Profession," **AR**, 1972, Vol. 47, No. 3, pp. 614-617.

Stettler, Howard F. "Audit Objectives," **JOA**, 1956, Vol. 102, No. 4, pp. 56-59.

Stettler, Howard F. "Auditing And Accounting Systems: A Marriage Proposal," **AR**, 1964, Vol. 39, No. 1. pp. 173-175.

Stettler, Howard F. "Auditing Standards And Competence Of Evidential Matter," **AR**, 1954, Vol. 29, No. 1. pp. 121-126.

Stettler, Howard F. "Break-Even Analysis: Its Uses And Misuses," **AR**, 1962, Vol. 37. No. 3, pp. 460-463.

Stettler, Howard F. "Certificate Programs: Certified Internal Auditor," **AR**, 1975, Vol. 50, No. 4, pp. 904-907.

Stettler, Howard F. "Classification Of Auditing Questions," **AR**, 1943, Vol. 18, No. 4, pp. 293-306.

Stettler, Howard F. "CPAs/Auditing/2000," **JOA**, 1968. Vol. 125, No. 5, pp. 55-60.

Stettler, Howard F. "On Giving Guidance To The CPA Candidate," **AR**, 1978. Vol. 53. No. 2. pp. 510-516.

Stettler, Howard F. "Some Observations On Statistical Sampling In Auditing," **JOA**, 1966. Vol. 121, No. 4. pp. 55-60.

Stettler, Howard F. "Statistical Interpretation Of Test Checks," **JOA**, 1954, Vol. 97, No. 1, pp. 49-57.

Stettler, Howard F. (Reilly. Frank K. and Howard F. Stettler. "Factors Influencing Success On The CPA Exam," **JAR**, 1972, Vol. 10, No. 2, pp. 308-321.)

Stettler, Howard. (Smith, David B., Howard Stettler and William Beedles. "An Investigation Of The Information Content Of Foreign Sensitive Payment Disclosures," **JAEC**, 1984, Vol. 6, No. 2, pp. 153-162.)

Stettler, H. F. "Case Studies For Professional Accounting Training," **JOA**, 1959. Vol. 108, No. 5, pp. 60-64.

Steuer, Ralph E. (Balachandran, K. R. and Ralph E. Steuer.

"An Interactive Model For The CPA Firm Audit Staff Planning Problem With Multiple Objectives," **AR**, 1982, Vol. 57, No. 1, pp. 125-140.)

Stevelinck, Ernest. "Accounting In Ancient Times," **AHJ**, 1985. Vol. 12, No. 1, pp. 1-16.

Stevelinck, Ernest. "The Many Faces Of Luca Pacioli: Iconographic Research Over Thirty Years," **AHJ**, 1986, Vol. 13, No. 2. pp. 1-18.

Stevelinck, E. (Haulotte, R. and E. Stevelinck. "A Bit Of Accounting History: Adding The Pages In The Journal," **AHJ**, 1977, Vol. 4, No. 2, pp. 113-116.)

Stevens, Gerald N. "Accounting For Local Community Theater Groups," **MA**, 1975, Vol. 56, No. 7, pp. 16-19.

Stevens, Kathleen C. (Raabe, William A., Kathleen C. Stevens and William P. Stevens. "Tax Textbook Readability: An Application Of The Cloze Method," **JATA**, 1984, Vol. 6, No. 1, pp. 66-73.)

Stevens, Kathleen C. (Stevens, William P., Kathleen C. Stevens and William A. Raabe. "FASB Statements In The Classroom: A Study Of Readability," **AIA**, 1985, Vol. 2, pp. 89-100.)

Stevens, Kevin T. "Multi-State Apportionment Of Income: An Empirical Analysis," **AIT**, 1988, Vol. 2, pp. xx-xx.

Stevens, Robert G. "A Motivation Program To Increase The Effectiveness Of Accounting Courses," **AR**, 1956, Vol. 31, No. 4. pp. 666-671.

Stevens, Ross. "Product Line Cash Income: A Reliable Yardstick," **MA**, 1974, Vol. 56, No. 5, pp. 46-48.

Stevens, William P. "Market Reaction To Corporate Environmental Performance," **AIA**, 1984, Vol. 1, pp. 41-62.

Stevens, William P. (Raabe, William A. and William P. Stevens. "Who Is Educating Today's Accountants? Some Observations," **JAED**, 1985, Vol. 3, No. 2, pp. 147-154.)

Stevens, William P. (Raabe, William A., Kathleen C. Stevens and William P. Stevens. "Tax Textbook Readability: An Application Of The Cloze Method," **JATA**, 1984, Vol. 6. No. 1. pp. 66-73.)

Stevens, William P., Kathleen C. Stevens and William A. Raabe. "FASB Statements In The Classroom: A Study Of Readability," **AIA**, 1985, Vol. 2, pp. 89-100.

Stevens, William T. (Shannon, Donald S. and William T. Stevens. "How Debt Refunding Can Cause Decision Conflicts," **MA**, 1983, Vol. 65, No. 6, pp. 40-44.)

Stevenson, Francis L. "New Evidence On LIFO Adoptions: The Effects Of More Precise Event Dates," **JAR**, 1987, Vol. 25, No. 2. pp. 306-316.

Stevenson, Richard A. "Corporate Stock Reacquisitons," **AR**, 1966, Vol. 41, No. 2, pp. 312-317.

Stevenson, R. A. "Accounting In The Engineering Curriculum," **AR**, 1930, Vol. 5, No. 3, pp. 205-207.

Stevenson, R. A. "Avenues Of Entry To The Accounting Profession," **AR**, 1931, Vol. 6, No. 2, pp. 140-141.

Stevenson, R. A. "Short Tests In Accounting Theory And Practice," **AR**, 1930. Vol. 5, No. 2, pp. 182-187.

Stevenson, R. A. (Webb, J. T., R. A. Stevenson and W. R. Gray. "The Place Of Accounting In The Commerce Curriculum," **AR**, 1928, Vol. 3, No. 2, pp. 189-207.)

Stevenson, R. E. "Survey Of Petroleum-Accounting Course Offerings," **AR**, 1956, Vol. 31, No. 2, pp. 316-317.

Stevenson, Willis C. "An Information Model For Scrap Control," **MA**, 1970, Vol. 52, No. 3, pp. 38-40.

Stevenson, W. C. (Biel, Dennis H. and W. C. Stevenson. "Tax Shelters: A Primer For CPAs," **JOA**, 1982, Vol. 153, No. 6, pp. 54-71.)

Stevenson, W. C. (Weber, Richard P. and W. C. Stevenson. "Evaluations Of Accounting Journals And Department Quality," **AR**, 1981, Vol. 56, No. 3, pp. 596-612.)

Stewart, A. Frank. "Accounting Education - From The Viewpoint Of A Member Of A State Board Of Accountancy," **AR**, 1953, Vol. 28, No. 3, pp. 350-355.

Stewart, A. Frank. "Individual CPA Should Agree To Statement 23," **JOA**, 1951, Vol. 92, No. 5, pp. 588-590.

Stewart, A. Frank. "Liberal Disclosure Can Make Balance-Sheet More Useful: An Auditor's Recommendations," **JOA**, 1950, Vol. 89, No. 4, pp. 298-302.

Stewart, Barbara R. (Korb, Phillip J., Charles L. Martin, Jr., and Barbara R. Stewart. "Income And Expense Rules After Tax Reform: Helping Clients Cope," **JOA**, 1987. Vol. 164. No. 3, pp. 126-137.)

Stewart, Charles A. "The Nature And Prevention Of Fraud," **JOA**, 1959. Vol. 107, No. 2, pp. 41-46.

Stewart, Dave N. "Use Of LOGIT Analysis To Determine Employment Status For Tax Purposes," **JATA**, 1982, Vol. 4, No. 1. pp. 5-12.

Stewart, Dudley. "The Search For A Business Survival Coefficient: The Role Of ROI," **JOA**, 1967, Vol. 123. No. 4. pp. 59-63.

Stewart, I. C. "Mergers And The Institutional Environment In The UK 1960-1970," **ABR**, 1976-77, Vol. 7, No. 25, pp. 57-63.

Stewart, John E. and Benjamin S. Neuhausen. "Financial Instruments And Transactions: The CPA's Newest Challenge," **JOA**, 1986, Vol. 162, No. 2, pp. 102-113.

Stewart, John E. and Benjamin S. Neuhausen. "Understanding And Implementing The New Pension Rules," **CA**, 1987, Vol. 5. No. 1, pp. 41-50.

Stewart, John E. (Wyatt, Arthur R., Richard Dieter and John E. Stewart. "Tax Allocation Revisited," **CPAJ**, 1984. Vol. 54. No. 3. pp. 10-19.)

Stewart, Reuben F. (Bush, James L., Jr. and Reuben F. Stewart. "Vulcan Materials Automates Delivery Ticket Writing," **MA**, 1985, Vol. 67, No. 2, pp. 52-55.)

Stewart, R. D. "Canadian Taxation," **JOA**, 1957, Vol. 104, No. 5. pp. 37-41.

Stickel, Scott E. "The Effect Of Preferred Stock Rating

Changes On Preferred And Common Stock Prices," **JAEC**, 1986, Vol. 8, No. 3, pp. 197-215.

Stickney, Clyde P. and Victor E. McGee. "Effective Corporate Tax Rates: The Effect Of Size, Capital Intensity, Leverage, And Other Factors," **JAPP**, 1982, Vol. 1, No. 2, pp. 125-152.

Stickney, Clyde P. "A Note On Optimal Tax Depreciation Research," **AR**, 1981, Vol. 56, No. 3, pp. 622-625.

Stickney, Clyde P. "Current Issues In The Measurement And Disclosure Of Corporate Income Taxes," **AR**, 1979, Vol. 54, No. 2, pp. 421-433.

Stickney, Clyde P. (Aliber, Robert Z. and Clyde P. Stickney. "Accounting Measures Of Foreign Exchange Exposure: The Long And Short Of It," **AR**, 1975, Vol. 50, No. 1, pp. 44-57.)

Stickney, Clyde P. (Casey, Cornelius, Victor E. McGee and Clyde P. Stickney. "Discriminating Between Reorganized And Liquidated Firms In Bankruptcy," **AR**, 1986, Vol. 61, No. 2, pp. 249-262.)

Stickney, Clyde P. (Green, David O. and Clyde P. Stickney. "No Price Level Adjusted Statements, Please (Pleas)." **CPAJ**, 1974, Vol. 44, No. 1, pp. 25-33.)

Stickney, Clyde P. (Nurnberg, Hugo, Clyde P. Stickney and Roman L. Weil. "Combining Stockholders' Equity Accounts Under Pooling Of Interests Method," **AR**, 1975, Vol. 50, No. 1, pp. 179-183.)

Stickney, Clyde P. (Petri, Enrico and Clyde P. Stickney. "Business Combinations: Some Unresolved Issues," **JOA**, 1982, Vol. 153, No. 4, pp. 64-79.)

Stickney, Clyde P. (Selling, Thomas I. and Clyde P. Stickney. "Accounting Measures Of Unfunded Pension Liabilities And Expected Present Value Of Future Pension Cash Flows," **JAPP**, 1986, Vol. 5, No. 4, pp. 267-285.)

Stickney, Clyde P., Roman L. Weil and Mark A. Wolfson. "Income Taxes And Tax-Transfer Leases: General Electric's Accounting For A Molotov Cocktail," **AR**, 1983, Vol. 58, No. 2, pp. 439-459.

Stickney, Clyde. (Blocher, Edward and Clyde Stickney. "Duration And Risk Assessments In Capital Budgeting," **AR**, 1979, Vol. 54, No. 1, pp. 180-188.)

Stiglitz, Joseph E. and Mark A. Wolfson. "Taxation, Information, And Economic Organization," **JATA**, 1988, Vol. 9, No. 2, pp. 7-18.

Stiles, Kenneth. "Capital Expenditures," **JOA**, 1956, Vol. 102, No. 3, pp. 37-39.

Still, M. D. "The Readability Of Chairmen's Statements," **ABR**, 1972-73, Vol. 3, No. 9, pp. 36-39.

Stillabower, Linda. (Cowen, Scott S., Lawrence C. Phillips and Linda Stillabower. "Multinational Transfer Pricing," **MA**, 1979, Vol. 60, No. 7, pp. 17-22.)

Stillman, A. B. (Burrell, O. K. and A. B. Stillman. "An Aptitude Test For Accounting," **AR**, 1930, Vol. 5, No. 3, pp. 257-262.)

Stilwell, Martin C. and Robert K. Elliott. "A Model For Expanding The Attest Function," **JOA**, 1985, Vol. 159, No. 5, pp. 66-81.

Stilwell, Martin C. "Prospective Reporting And Small Business Clients," **JOA**, 1986, Vol. 161, No. 5, pp. 68-87.

Stiner, Frederic M., Jr. (Stagliano, A. J. and Frederic M. Stiner, Jr. "Enrollments In Accounting Programs: Trends And Forecasts," **JAED**, 1985, Vol. 3, No. 1, pp. 145-163.)

Stiner, Frederic M., Jr., John C. Williams and Adrian Sclawy. "Vanishing Accounting Journals Due To Paper Deterioration," **AHJ**, 1981, Vol. 8, No. 2, pp. 97-100.

Stobel, Caroline D. (Taylor, Martin E. and Caroline D. Stobel. "CPA's Responsibility To Notify Clients Of Tax Law Revisions," **JATA**, 1986, Vol. 8, No. 1, pp. 73-79.)

Stober, Thomas L. "The Incremental Information Content Of Financial Statement Disclosures: The Case Of LIFO Inventory Liquidations," **JAR**, 1986, Vol. 24, Supp., pp. 138-160.

Stockdale, Joanne L. "Do Accountants Make Good Small Business Owners?," **MA**, 1984, Vol. 66, No. 5, pp. 55-58.

Stocker, Frederick B., Jr. "Bankers Ask Help Of Accountants In Getting Wider Use Of Standard-Size Bank Checks," **JOA**, 1951, Vol. 91, No. 1, pp. 104-105.

Stocks, Kevin D. and Lynn J. McKell. "Accounting Education And Management Advisory Services," **JIS**, 1987, Vol. 2, No. 1, pp. 65-76.

Stocks, Kevin D. and Marshall B. Romney. "The Supply And Demand For IS/MAS Graduates," **JIS**, 1987, Vol. 1, No. 2, pp. 83-100.

Stocks, Kevin D. (Cherrington, J. Owen and Kevin D. Stocks. "Educating A Management Consultant," **JIS**, 1986, Vol. 1, No. 1, pp. 145-153.)

Stocks, Kevin D. (Hubbard, E. Dee, Kevin D. Stocks and John W. Hardy. "A Comprehensive Project For Managerial Accounting," **JAED**, 1984, Vol. 2, No. 1, pp. 111-125.)

Stocks, Kevin D. (McKell, Lynn J. and Kevin D. Stocks. "An Evaluation Of Computerized Accounting Practice Sets," **JAED**, 1986, Vol. 4, No. 1, pp. 177-190.)

Stocks, Kevin D. (Romney, Marshall B. and Kevin D. Stocks. "How To Buy A Small Computer System," **JOA**, 1985, Vol. 160, No. 1, pp. 46-63.)

Stock, Duane and Collin J. Watson. "Human Judgment Accuracy, Multidimensional Graphics, And Humans Versus Models," **JAR**, 1984, Vol. 22, No. 1, pp. 192-206.

Stock, William. "Using Time-Sharing Models In The Controller's Function," **MA**, 1982, Vol. 63, No. 8, pp. 50-53.

Stoddard, F. Don. "The Accountant's Role In Management," **MA**, 1978, Vol. 60, No. 1, pp. 42-45.

Stoeckel, Herbert J. "Loose-Leaf And Accounting," **AR**, 1946, Vol. 21, No. 4, pp. 380-385.

Stoeckenius, Jan. (Ng, David S. and Jan Stoeckenius. "Auditing: Incentives And Truthful Reporting," **JAR**, 1979, Vol. 17, Supp., pp. 1-24.)

Stokes, Charles J. (Gulden, Douglas J. and Charles J. Stokes. "Simultaneous Calculation Of Federal And State Income Taxes, A Suggested Method," **AR**, 1954, Vol. 29, No. 3, pp. 501-502.)

Stokes, Donald J. and Graham G. Sullivan. "Auditors' Responsibilities For Events Arising After Balance Date," **ABACUS**, 1988, Vol. 24, No. 2, pp. 132-144.

Stokes, Donald J. "The Nature And Extent Of Contemporary 'Audits' Of Directors' Reports," **ABACUS**, 1982, Vol. 18, No. 1, pp. 70-82.

Stokes, Donald J. (Francis, Jere R. and Donald J. Stokes. "Audit Prices, Product Differentiation, And Scale Economies: Further Evidence From The Australian Market," **JAR**, 1986, Vol. 24, No. 2, pp. 383-393.)

Stolen, Justin D. (Watanabe, Judith E., Virginia L. Bean and Justin D. Stolen. "An Empirical Study Of Complexity Experience By Taxpayers," **AIT**, 1987, Vol. 1, pp. 153-168.)

Stoler, Eugene Lyle. "Recent Cases And Rulings In Gift And Estate Taxation," **CPAJ**, 1973, Vol. 43, No. 12, pp. 1055-1062.

Stolle, Carlton D. and Philip W. Ljungdahl. "Lower Of Cost Or Market Decision Matrix," **AR**, 1974, Vol. 49, No. 4, pp. 841-843.

Stolle, Carlton D. "Perceived Differences Among Public Accounting Firms Which Affect Job Choices," **AR**, 1977, Vol. 52, No. 2, pp. 474-478.

Stolle, Carlton D. "Timing Of The Office Visit: A Factor In Public Accounting Job Selection," **AR**, 1976, Vol. 51, No. 1, pp. 139-141.

Stolle, Carlton D. (Bassichis, William H., D. Larry Crumbley and Carlton D. Stolle. "Caution: Teaching And Research Awards Ahead," **AIT**, 1987, Vol. 1, pp. 199-210.)

Stone, David R. (Wilson, Thomas M. and David R. Stone. "Project Management For An Architectural Firm," **MA**, 1980, Vol. 62, No. 4, pp. 25-28, 45-46.)

Stone, Donald E. "Computer Simulation In Financial Accounting," **AR**, 1973, Vol. 48, No. 2, pp. 398-409.

Stone, Donald E. "The Objective Of Financial Reporting In The Annual Report," **AR**, 1967, Vol. 42, No. 2, pp. 331-337.

Stone, Donald E. (Bower, Richard S., Christopher E. Nugent and Donald E. Stone. "Time-Shared Computers In Business Education At Dartmouth," **AR**, 1968, Vol. 43, No. 3, pp. 565-582.)

Stone, L. D. (Shonting, D. M. and L. D. Stone. "Auditing Electronic Systems," **JOA**, 1958, Vol. 106, No. 4, pp. 54-61.)

Stone, Marvin L. and Arthur E. Witte. "CPA Services For The CPA," **JOA**, 1962, Vol. 114, No. 1, pp. 31-39.

Stone, Marvin L. "Incorporated CPA Firms - A Modern Vehicle For A Dynamic Profession," **JOA**, 1967, Vol. 123, No. 3, pp. 53-57.

Stone, Marvin L. "Problems In Search Of Solutions Through Research," **JAR**, 1968, Vol. 6, Supp., pp. 59-66.

Stone, Marvin L. "Specialization In The Accounting Profession," **JOA**, 1968, Vol. 125, No. 2, pp. 25-29.

Stone, Mary and Bruce Bublitz. "An Analysis Of The Reliability Of The FASB Data Bank Of Changing Price And Pension Information," **AR**, 1984, Vol. 59, No. 3, pp. 469-473.

Stone, Mary and Robert W. Ingram. "The Effect Of Statement No. 87 On The Financial Reports Of Early Adopters," **AH**, 1988, Vol. 2, No. 3, pp. 48-61.

Stone, Mary S. "A Survey Of Research On The Effects Of Corporate Pension Plan Sponsorship: Implications For Accounting," **JAL**, 1982, Vol. 1, pp. 1-32.

Stone, Mary S. "Can Multiemployer Plans Fit Into FASB Pension Proposals?," **MA**, 1983, Vol. 65, No. 5, pp. 71-74.

Stone, Mary S. "The Changing Picture Of Pension Accounting," **CPAJ**, 1983, Vol. 53, No. 4, pp. 32-43.

Stone, Mary S. "The Pension Accounting Myth," **AHJ**, 1984, Vol. 11, No. 2, pp. 19-38.

Stone, Mary S., Thomas J. Frecka and Robert W. Jamison. "Multiemployer Pension Plan Amendments Act," **CPAJ**, 1981, Vol. 51, No. 12, pp. 34-40.

Stone, Mary S., Walter A. Robbins and David W. Phipps. "Disclosure Practices Of Public Employee Retirement Systems: An Analysis Of Incentives To Adopt Alternative Standards," **RIGNA**, 1987, Vol. 3, Part A, pp. 149-180.

Stone, Mary. "A Financing Explanation For Overfunded Pension Plan Terminations," **JAR**, 1987, Vol. 25, No. 2, pp. 317-326.

Stone, Peter F. and Mark L. Frigo. "The Neglected Management Letter," **CPAJ**, 1988, Vol. 58, No. 9, pp. 38-43.

Stone, Richard. "The International Harmonisation Of National Income Accounts," **ABR**, 1981-82, Vol. 12, No. 45, pp. 67-79.

Stone, Vernon W. "A Test For Reversing Entries," **AR**, 1960, Vol. 35, No. 2, pp. 318-320.

Stone, Williard E. "1794 - Middletown, Delaware - From Accounting Records," **AHJ**, 1979, Vol. 6, No. 1, pp. 39-52.

Stone, Williard E. "A 1794 Ledger Demonstrates An Economic Transition," **ABR**, 1980-81, Vol. 11, No. 43, pp. 243-248.

Stone, Williard E. "Abacists Versus Algorists," **JAR**, 1972, Vol. 10, No. 2, pp. 345-350.

Stone, Williard E. "Accounting Doctoral Programs In AACSB Colleges Of Business Administration," **AR**, 1965, Vol. 40, No. 1, pp. 190-195.

Stone, Williard E. "Accounting Records Reveal History: The Virginia Cobbler," JOA, 1976, Vol. 142, No. 1, pp. 60-66.

Stone, Williard E. "An Early English Cotton Mill Cost Accounting System: Charlton Mills, 1810-1889," ABR, 1973-74, Vol. 4, No. 13, pp. 71-78.

Stone, Williard E. "Antecedents Of The Accounting Profession," AR, 1969, Vol. 44, No. 2, pp. 284-291.

Stone, Williard E. "Barter: Development Of Accounting Practice And Theory," AHJ, 1985, Vol. 12, No. 2, pp. 95-108.

Stone, Williard E. "Can Accounting Meet The Challenge Of Liberalized Business Education?," AR, 1960, Vol. 35, No. 3, pp. 515-520.

Stone, Williard E. "Developments In Accounting Instruction," AR, 1961, Vol. 36, No. 3, pp. 474-477.

Stone, Williard E. "Grammateus Reappears In 1911," AHJ, 1978, Vol. 5, No. 1, pp. 67-68.

Stone, Williard E. "Intracompany Pricing." AR, 1956, Vol. 31, No. 4, pp. 625-627.

Stone, Williard E. "Legal Implications Of Intracompany Pricing," AR, 1964, Vol. 39, No. 1, pp. 38-42.

Stone, Williard E. "Managerial Accounting On The U.S. 1758 Frontier," AHJ, 1977, Vol. 4, No. 1, pp. 107-111.

Stone, Williard E. "Tax Considerations In Intra-Company Pricing," AR, 1960, Vol. 35, No. 1, pp. 45-50.

Stone, Williard E. "The Comphrehension Gap For Beginning Accounting Students," AR, 1954, Vol. 29, No. 1, pp. 138-140.

Stone, Williard E. "The Funds Statement As An Analysis Tool," AR, 1959, Vol. 34, No. 1, pp. 127-130.

Stone, Williard E. "The Tally: An Ancient Accounting Instrument," ABACUS, 1975, Vol. 11, No. 1, pp. 49-57.

Stone, Williard E. "Who Was Who In Accounting In 1909?," AHJ, 1975, Vol. 2, No. 1-4, pp. 6-10.

Stone, Williard E. (Coleman, Almand R., William G. Shenkir and Williard E. Stone. "Accounting In Colonial Virginia: A Case Study," JOA, 1974, Vol. 138, No. 1, pp. 32-43.)

Stone, Williard E. (Goldberg, Louis and Williard E. Stone. "John Caldwell Colt: A Notorious Accountant," AHJ, 1985, Vol. 12, No. 1, pp. 121-130.)

Stone, W. E. (Mepham, M. J. and W. E. Stone. "John Mair. M. A. : Author Of The First Classic Book-Keeping Series," ABR, 1976-77, Vol. 7, No. 26, pp. 128-134.)

Stoops, Barbara. (Hutton, Clifford E., Barbara Stoops and Michael J. Tucker. "Losses Caused By Drought," CPAJ, 1984, Vol. 54, No. 3, pp. 40-49.)

Storcy, J. (Hopper, T., J. Storey and H. Willmott. "Accounting For Accounting: Towards The Development Of A Dialectical View," AOS, 1987, Vol. 12, No. 5, pp. 437-456.)

Storey, Reed K. "Accounting Principles: AAA And AICPA," JOA, 1964, Vol. 117, No. 6, pp. 47-55.

Storey, Reed K. "Cash Movements And Periodic Income Determination," AR, 1960, Vol. 35, No. 3, pp. 449-454.

Storey, Reed K. "Revenue Realization, Going Concern And Measurement Of Income," AR, 1959, Vol. 34, No. 2, pp. 232-238.

Storey, Reed K. (Rosenfield, Paul H. and Reed K. Storey. "The Accounting Principles Board - A Correction," AR, 1966, Vol. 41, No. 2, pp. 327-330.)

Stoughton, Warner V. "Bringing Up Management Accountants," MA, 1978, Vol. 59, No. 12, pp. 55-59.

Stout, David E. and Donald E. Wygal. "Making By-Products A Main Product Of Discussion: A Challenge To Accounting Educators," JAED, 1988, Vol. 6, No. 2, pp. 219-233.

Stout, David E. and E. H. Bonfield. "Experimental Evidence On The Relationship Between Class Meeting Time Compression And Accounting Student Performance, Evaluations And Drop-Out Experience," JAED, 1986, Vol. 4, No. 2, pp. 51-62.

Stout, David E. (Schwartz, Bill N. and David E. Stout. "A Comparison Of Practitioner And Educator Opinions On Tax Education Requirements For Undergraduate Accounting Majors," IAE, 1987, Vol. 2, No. 2, pp. 112-126.)

Stout, David E. (Wygal, Donald E., David E. Stout and James Volpi. "Reporting Practices In Four Countries," MA, 1987, Vol. 69, No. 6, pp. 37-42.)

Stout, David E. (Wygal, Donald E. and David E. Stout. "Investment Income Reporting In The Property And Casualty Insurance Industry: A Critical Assessment," ACCHOR, 1987, Vol. 1, No. 4, pp. 51-62.)

Stout, David E., Donald E. Wygal and John J. Gorman. "Accounting Student Perceptions Of The Nature And Significance Of Extraordinary Items Data," JAED, 1987, Vol. 5, No. 1, pp. 13-25.

Stout, David E., Donald E. Wygal and James Volpi. "A Comparative Income Statement Approach To Integrating International Topics In The Financial Accounting Curriculum," AIIA, 1988, Vol. 2, pp. 147-166.

Stout, David E., Samuel Laibstain and Larry P. Bailey. "Managing Off-Balance-Sheet Financing," MA, 1988, Vol. 70, No. 1, pp. 32-39.

Stout, David F., E. H. Bonfield and Marianne S. Battista. "Additional Experimental Evidence On The Relationship Between Class Meeting Time Compression And Accounting Student Performance And Evaluations," JAED, 1987, Vol. 5, No. 2, pp. 339-348.

Stowe, Clifford W. "Audit, Conference, Appellate Procedures In Reorganized Bureau," JOA, 1952, Vol. 94, No. 3, pp. 298-301.

Stowe, Clifford W. "Moral Responsibility In Tax Practice: A Former IRS Official's View," JOA, 1959, Vol. 107, No. 4, pp. 36-39.

Stoy, John M. "Accountants And The Small Business Investment Act," JOA, 1959, Vol. 108, No. 1, pp. 28-30.

Stoy, John M. "Time-Record System For Smaller Accounting Firms," JOA, 1951, Vol. 91, No. 4, pp. 610-612.

Strahlem, Richard E. "Teaching Accounting With Microfilm," AR, 1941, Vol. 16, No. 1, pp. 107-108.

Strait, A. Marvin. "Expanding Your MAS Horizons," JOA, 1976, Vol. 141, No. 3, pp. 52-54.

Strand, Kenneth H. (Kross, William, Gordon Chapman and Kenneth H. Strand. "Fully Diluted Earnings Per Share And Security Returns: Some Additional Evidence," JAAF, 1980, Vol. 4, No. 1, pp. 36-46.)

Stratis, Gregory J. (Lammert, Thomas B. and Gregory J. Stratis. "Uniform Capitalization Rules Are Here To Stay," MA, 1987, Vol. 69, No. 6, pp. 31-33.)

Stratton, Richard A. (Barry, Hugh J. and Richard A. Stratton. "Maximizing The Tax And Financial Benefits Of Leveraged Buyouts," CA, 1984, Vol. 2, No. 1, pp. 16-22.)

Strauss, Norman N. and Alex T. Arcady. "A New Focus On The 'Bottom Line' And Its Components," JOA, 1981, Vol. 151, No. 5, pp. 66-77.

Strauss, Norman N. (Miller, Richard P. and Norman N. Strauss. "SFAS No. 52: The FASB Tackles Foreign Currency Translation...Again," CA, 1983, Vol. 1, No. 1, pp. 3-17.)

Strauss, Robert. (Simich, Stevan and Robert Strauss. "The Energy Audit." JOA, 1978, Vol. 146, No. 5, pp. 52-59.)

Strauss, Simon S. (Key, Stephen L. and Simon S. Strauss. "Allocating Purchase Price In An Acquisition: A Practical Guide," JOA, 1987, Vol. 164, No. 5, pp. 32-37.)

Strawser, Jerry R. (Harper, Robert M., Jr., William G. Mister and Jerry R. Strawser. "The Impact Of New Pension Disclosure Rules On Perception Of Debt," JAR, 1987, Vol. 25, No. 2, pp. 327-330.)

Strawser, Jerry R. (Okopny, D. Robert and Jerry R. Strawser. "A Management Guide To Prospective Financial Statements," CA, 1988, Vol. 6, No. 2, pp. 52-57.)

Strawser, Jerry R. (Pasewark, W. R., Jerry R. Strawser and Jack E. Wilkerson, Jr. "Empirical Evidence On The Association Between Characteristics Of Graduating Accounting Students And Recruiting Decisions," IAE, 1988, Vol. 3, No. 2, pp. 388-401.)

Strawser, Jerry R. (Vicknair, David P. and Jerry R. Strawser. "Reporting Discontinued Segments In A Cash Basis Statement Of Changes In Financial Position," ACCHOR, 1987, Vol. 1, No. 3, pp. 79-84.)

Strawser, Joyce A. (Scott, Diana J., Jane B. Adams and Joyce A. Strawser. "Retiree Welfare Benefits Come Out Of Hiding." CPAJ, 1988, Vol. 58, No. 11, pp. 26-34.)

Strawser, Robert H. (Alford, R. Mark, Mattie C. Porter and Robert H. Strawser. "Annual Reports Of Departments Of Accounting," IAE, 1985, No. 1, pp. 15-19.)

Strawser, Robert H. (Alford, R. Mark, Mattie C. Porter and Robert H. Strawser. "Forward Accounting - Past, Present And Future," CPAJ, 1981, Vol. 51, No. 2, pp. 40-47.)

Strawser, Robert H. (Benjamin, James J. and Robert H. Strawser. "The Publication Of Forecasts: An Experiment," ABACUS, 1974, Vol. 10 No. 2, pp. 138-146.)

Strawser, Robert H. (Benjamin, James A. and Robert H. Strawser. "Developments In Lease Accounting," CPAJ, 1976, Vol. 46, No. 11, pp. 33-36.)

Strawser, Robert H. (Brenner, Vincent C., Ronald M. Copeland, Paul E. Dascher, Arthur J. Francia. Ronald J. Patten and Robert H. Strawser. "Trials And Tribulations Of The Researcher: A Case Study," JAR, 1972, Vol. 10, No. 1, pp. 195-199.)

Strawser, Robert H. (Brenner, Vincent C. and Robert H. Strawser. "Some Observations On Required Continuing Education," CPAJ, 1972, Vol. 42, No. 6, pp. 469-474.)

Strawser, Robert H. (Carpenter, Charles G. and Robert H. Strawser. "Displacement Of Auditors When Clients Go Public," JOA, 1971, Vol. 131, No. 6, pp. 55-58.)

Strawser, Robert H. (Carpenter, Charles G. and Robert H. Strawser. "Disclosure Of Changes In Accounting Methods," JAR, 1972, Vol. 10, No. 1, pp. 209-216.)

Strawser, Robert H. (Carpenter, Charles G. and Robert H. Strawser. "Initial Experience With Satisfactory-Unsatisfactory Grading In Accounting Courses," AR, 1971, Vol. 46, No. 1, pp. 160-162.)

Strawser, Robert H. (Carpenter, Charles G. and Robert H. Strawser. "A Study Of The Job Satisfaction Of Academic Accountants," AR, 1971, Vol. 46, No. 3, pp. 509-518.)

Strawser, Robert H. (Copeland, Ronald M., Arthur J. Francia and Robert H. Strawser. "Students As Subjects In Behavioral Business Research," AR, 1973, Vol. 48, No. 2, pp. 365-372.)

Strawser, Robert H. (Copeland, Ronald M., Arthur J. Francia and Robert H. Strawser. "Further Comments On Students As Subjects In Behavioral Business Research," AR, 1974, Vol. 49, No. 3, pp. 534-537.)

Strawser, Robert H. (Cramer, Joe J., Jr. and Robert H. Strawser. "Perception Of Selected Job Related Factors By Black CPAs," CPAJ, 1972, Vol. 42, No. 2, pp. 127-130.)

Strawser, Robert H. (Crumbley, D. Larry and Robert H. Strawser. "Allocation Of Income Taxes In Segmented Financial Statements," CPAJ, 1974, Vol. 44, No. 7, pp. 35-38.)

Strawser, Robert H. (Crumbley, D. Larry, Robert H. Strawser and Herbert J. Jensen. "Accumulated Earnings: A New Court Calculation," JOA, 1977, Vol. 143, No. 3, pp. 75-78.)

Strawser, Robert H. (Daily, R. Austin and Robert H. Strawser. "Independent Audits And The Reporting Practices Of Banks," JOA, 1974, Vol. 138, No. 1, pp. 44-49.)

Strawser, Robert H. (Dascher, Paul E., Charles H. Smith and Robert H. Strawser. "Accounting Curriculum Implications Of The Multinational Corporation," IJAER, 1973, Vol. 9, No. 1, pp. 81-97.)

Strawser, Robert H. (Francia, Arthur J. and Robert H. Strawser. "Attitudes Of Management Accountants On The State Of The Art," MA, 1972, Vol. 53, No. 11, pp. 21-24.)

Strawser, Robert H. (Francia, Arthur J. and Robert H. Strawser. "Perceptions Of Financial Reporting Practices By Accounting Educators: An Empirical Study," AR, 1971, Vol. 46, No. 2, pp. 380-384.)

Strawser, Robert H. (Francia, Arthur J., Steven D. Grossman and Robert H. Strawser. "The Attitudes Of Management Accountants," MA, 1978, Vol. 60, No. 5, pp. 35-40.)

Strawser, Robert H. (Grossman, Steven D. and Robert H. Strawser. "Accounting And Behavioral Concepts: A Classroom Approach," AR, 1978, Vol. 53, No. 2, pp. 495-500.)

Strawser, Robert H. (Hubbard, Thomas D. and Robert H. Strawser. "A Test Of 'A Model For Integrating Sampling Objectives In Auditing'," JAR, 1972, Vol. 10, No. 2, pp. 404-406.)

Strawser, Robert H. (Hubbard, Thomas D. and Robert H. Strawser. "The Auditor And Statistical Sampling," CPAJ, 1973, Vol. 43, No. 8, pp. 670-673.)

Strawser, Robert H. (Licata, Michael P., Robert H. Strawser and Robert B. Welker. "A Note On Participation In Budgeting And Locus Of Control," AR, 1986, Vol. 61, No. 1, pp. 112-117.)

Strawser, Robert H. (Nelson, G. Kenneth and Robert H. Strawser. "A Note On APB Opinion No. 16," JAR, 1970, Vol. 8, No. 2, pp. 284-289.)

Strawser, Robert H. (Nickerson, Charles A., Larry Gene Pointer and Robert H. Strawser. "Attitudes Of Financial Executives Toward Interim Financial Statements," CPAJ, 1975, Vol. 45, No. 3, pp. 21-24.)

Strawser, Robert H. (Nickerson, Charles A. and Robert H. Strawser. "Photography As An Audit Tool," JOA, 1976, Vol. 142, No. 5, pp. 82-86.)

Strawser, Robert H. (Orbach, Kenneth N. and Robert H. Strawser. "Public Disclosure Requirements For CPA Firms?," CPAJ, 1979, Vol. 49, No. 2, pp. 15-22.)

Strawser, Robert H. (Robbins, Walter A., Nicholas G. Apostolou and Robert H. Strawser. "Municipal Annual Reports And The Information Needs Of Investors," JAAF, 1985, Vol. 8, No. 4, pp. 279-292.)

Strawser, Robert H. (Ryan, Frank, Arthur J. Francia and Robert H. Strawser. "Professional Football And Information Systems," MA, 1973, Vol. 54, No. 9, pp. 43-47.)

Strawser, Robert H. (Shenker, William G., Thomas L. Wheelen and Robert H. Strawser. "The Making Of An Accountant," CPAJ, 1973, Vol. 43, No. 3, pp. 218-221.)

Strawser, Robert H. (Shenkir, William G. and Robert H. Strawser. "Auditing And Management Advisory Services: A Conflict Of Roles," ABACUS, 1972, Vol. 8, No. 1, pp. 13-20.)

Strawser, Robert H. (Tummins, Marvin and Robert H. Strawser. "A Confidence Limits Table For Attribute Analysis," AR, 1976, Vol. 51, No. 4, pp. 907-912.)

Strawser, Robert H., John M. Ivancevich and Herbert L. Lyon. "A Note On The Job Satisfaction Of Accountants In Large And Small CPA Firms," JAR, 1969, Vol. 7, No. 2, pp. 339-345.

Strawser, Robert H., J. Patrick Kelly and Richard T. Hise. "What Causes Stress For Management Accountants?," MA, 1982, Vol. 63, No. 9, pp. 32-37.

Strawser, Robert. (Austin, Kenneth R., Robert Strawser and Henry Mixon. "Contingencies And Unasserted Claims: Adequate Answers?," CPAJ, 1985, Vol. 55, No. 9, pp. 48-58.)

Stray, S. J. (Newbould, G. D., S. J. Stray and K. W. Wilson. "Shareholders' Interests And Acquisition Activity," ABR, 1975-76, Vol. 6, No. 23, pp. 201-215.)

Strecker, Sister Mary F. "Accounting For The Not-For-Profit Organizations," MA, 1971, Vol. 53, No. 2, pp. 33-36.

Streer, Paul J. "Conforming Financial And Tax Accounting: Will The Conceptual Framework Help?," JAAF, 1979, Vol. 2, No. 4, pp. 329-338.

Streer, Paul J. "Obtaining And Preserving Tax-Exempt Status Under Section 501(c)(3): Judicially Developed Factors For Detecting The Presence Of Substantial Nonexempt Activities," JATA, 1985, Vol. 6, No. 2, pp. 63-75.

Strefeler, John M. and Jack P. Suyderhoud. "Piggybacking - A Free Ride With No Takers," JATA, 1980, Vol. 1, No. 2, pp. 42-48.

Strefeler, John M. (Jagolinzer, Philip and John M. Strefeler. "Marital Status And The Taxes We Pay," JOA, 1986, Vol. 161, No. 3, pp. 68-77.)

Streuling, G. Fred and Gary L. Holstrum. "Teaching Machines Versus Lectures In Accounting Education: An Experiment," AR, 1972, Vol. 47, No. 4, pp. 806-810.

Streuling, G. Fred and Thomas R. Harper. "Income Tax Questions On The CPA Exam: Recent Changes And Future Outlook," AR, 1973, Vol. 48, No. 2, pp. 429-432.

Streuling, G. Fred, James H. Boyd and Kenneth H. Heller. "Interrelationships Of Sections 731, 736, And 751: A Worksheet Approach," JATA, 1987, Vol. 8, No. 2. pp. 37-49.

Strickland, D. Gordon. "How An Investment Banker Prepares A Company For A Tender Offer," MA, 1980, Vol. 61, No. 8, pp. 26-28.

Stricklin, Wilma D. (Hoverland, H. Arthur and Wilma D. Stricklin. "Management And Accounting Concepts Of Control," MA, 1967, Vol. 48, No. 10, pp. 33-37.)

Stringer, Kenneth W. "A Statistical Technique For Analytical Review," JAR, 1975, Vol. 13, Supp., pp. 1-9.

Stringer, Kenneth W. "Some Basic Concepts Of Statistical Sampling In Auditing," JOA, 1961, Vol. 112, No. 5, pp. 63-69.

Strischek, Dev. "How To Determine The Value Of A Firm," MA, 1983, Vol. 64, No. 7, pp. 42-49.

Strobel, Caroline and Charles Caldwell. "Rehabilitation Credit Investment Incentives - ERTA 1981," CPAJ, 1982, Vol. 52, No. 9, pp. 40-44.

Strobel, Caroline D. and Ollie S. Powers. "Accounting For Inventories: Where We Stand," CPAJ, 1981, Vol. 51, No. 5, pp. 41-46.

Strock, Elizabeth. (Elgers, Pieter, Carolyn Callahan and Elizabeth Strock. "The Effect Of Earnings Yields Upon The Association Between Unexpected Earnings And Security Returns: A Re-Examination," AR, 1987, Vol. 62, No. 4, pp. 763-773.)

Stromsem, William R. (Bleyer, Stephen A. and William R. Stromsem. "Divorce - TRA Style," JOA, 1985, Vol. 159, No. 4, pp. 72-85.)

Stromsem, William R. (Johnson, Janice M. and William R. Stromsem. "The TRA And Individuals: A Year-End RX," JOA, 1986, Vol. 162, No. 6, pp. 172-177.)

Strowger, Richard J. "State-Financed Hospital Construction Programs," CPAJ, 1976, Vol. 46, No. 7, pp. 27-32.

Strum, Jay E. "Note On 'Two-Sided Shadow Prices'," JAR, 1969, Vol. 7, No. 1, pp. 160-162.

Strunck, Theodore P. "A County Controller Reviews His First Two Years In Office," JOA, 1954, Vol. 98, No. 1, pp. 54-57.

Strupeck, C. David. (Figlewicz, Raymond E., Donald T. Anderson and C. David Strupeck. "The Evolution And Current State Of Financial Accounting Concepts And Standards In The Nonbusiness Sector," AHJ, 1985, Vol. 12, No. 1, pp. 73-98.)

Struzziero, Ralph E. "Computer Application By A Concrete Block Manufacturer," MA, 1971, Vol. 52, No. 11, pp. 34-38.

Stuart, William T. (Enis, Charles R., William T. Stuart and John J. Hourihan. "Local Revenue Policy In Less Developed Countries: The Case For Energy Consumption Taxation," AIT, 1987, Vol. 1, pp. 85-108.)

Studdard, Kenneth. "Planning Effective Gifts - What-When-How-And To Whom?," JOA, 1967, Vol. 123, No. 6, pp. 45-53.

Stump, Evin J. "Composite Learning Curves For Fast Estimating," JCA, 1987, Vol. 4, No. 1, pp. 59-69.

Sturcke, H. Carl. "How To Prepare For Peer Review - Part I," CPAJ, 1979, Vol. 49, No. 6, pp. 19-22.

Sturcke, H. Carl. "How To Prepare For Peer Review - Part II," CPAJ, 1979, Vol. 49, No. 7, pp. 27-31.

Sturrock, Thomas. (Thies, Clifford F. and Thomas Sturrock. "What Did Inflation Accounting Tell Us?," JAAF, 1987, Vol. 2 (New Issues), No. 4, pp. 375-395.)

Stutler, Don C. "Cost Accounting For Sand Castings," MA, 1972, Vol. 53, No. 10, pp. 27-30.

Subotnik, Dan. "What Accounting Can Learn From Legal Education," IAE, 1987, Vol. 2, No. 2, pp. 313-324.

Subotnik, Dan. "Wisdom Or Widgets: Whither The School Of 'Business'?," ABACUS, 1988, Vol. 24, No. 2, pp. 95-106.

Sudreau, P. "The Reform Of The Enterprise," AOS, 1976, Vol. 1, No. 1, pp. 97-104.

Sugden, Keith F. "A History Of The Abacus," AHJ, 1981, Vol. 8, No. 2, pp. 1-21.

Sughrue, Robert N. "Issues Of Taxation In A Nonprofit Environment," MA, 1988, Vol. 70, No. 2, pp. 57-60.

Suh, Yoon S. "Collusion And Noncontrollable Cost Allocation," JAR, 1987, Vol. 25, Supp., pp. 22-46.

Suh, Yoon. "Noncontrollable Costs And Optimal Performance Measurement," JAR, 1988, Vol. 26, No. 1, pp. 154-168.

Sullivan, Brian. "An Introduction To 'Going Public'," JOA, 1965, Vol. 120, No. 5, pp. 48-60.

Sullivan, Frank E. "Professional Co-Operation In Estate Planning," JOA, 1964, Vol. 117, No. 3, pp. 48-50.

Sullivan, George E. "Modeling The University Budget," MA, 1971, Vol. 53, No. 5, pp. 47-50.

Sullivan, Graham. "Accounting And Legal Implications Of The Interposed Unit Trust Instrument," ABACUS, 1985, Vol. 21, No. 2, pp. 174-196.

Sullivan, Graham G. (Stokes, Donald J. and Graham G. Sullivan. "Auditors' Responsibilities For Events Arising After Balance Date," ABACUS, 1988, Vol. 24, No. 2, pp. 132-144.)

Sullivan, James A. (Leathers, Park E., James A. Sullivan and Jerome Bernstein. "The CPA Examination - Profile Of The Successful Candidate," AIA, 1984, Vol. 1, pp. 105-126.)

Sullivan, William G. and James M. Reeve. "Xventure: Expert Systems To The Rescue," MA, 1988, Vol. 70, No. 4, pp. 51-58.

Sullivan, William J. "Budget Reports At YSU," MA, 1972, Vol. 54, No. 2, pp. 43-46.

Sullivan, Jerry D. (Guy, Dan M. and Jerry D. Sullivan. "The Expectation Gap Auditing Standards," JOA, 1988, Vol. 165, No. 4, pp. 36-46.)

Summa, Don J. (Solari, Jerome P. and Don J. Summa. "Profile Of The CPA In Tax Practice," JOA, 1972, Vol. 133, No. 6, pp. 45-50.)

Summa, Jeffrey D. (Lubin, Millicent E. and Jeffrey D. Summa. "New Section 338 - History And Purpose," CPAJ, 1984, Vol. 54, No. 8, pp. 18-23.)

Summerhill, G. Winston. "Administrative Accounting In The Accounting Curriculum," AR, 1953, Vol. 28, No. 1, pp. 64-78.

Summers, Edward L. and James Wesley Deskins. "A Classification Schema Of Methods For Reporting Effects Of Resource

Price Changes (With Technical Appendix)," **IJAER**, 1970, Vol. 6, No. 1, pp. 101-120.

Summers, Edward L. and James Wesley Deskins. "A Classification Schema Of Methods For Reporting Effects Of Resource Price Changes," **JAR**, 1970, Vol. 8, No. 1, pp. 113-117.

Summers, Edward L. and Kenneth E. Knight. "The AICPA Studies MAS In CPA Firms," **JOA**, 1975, Vol. 139, No. 3, pp. 56-64.

Summers, Edward L. "Accountant's Productivity Increases In A Computer-Dependent Organization," **MA**, 1969, Vol. 50, No. 8, pp. 28-30.

Summers, Edward L. "Accounting Education's New Horizons," **JOA**, 1974, Vol. 138, No. 3, pp. 56-63.

Summers, Edward L. "Observation Of Effects Of Using Alternative Reporting Practices," **AR**, 1968, Vol. 43, No. 2, pp. 257-265.

Summers, Edward L. "The Audit Staff Assignment Problem: A Linear Programming Analysis," **AR**, 1972, Vol. 47, No. 3, pp. 443-453.

Summers, Edward L. (Chen, Kung H. and Edward L. Summers. "Should Accounting Data Be Single-Valued Measurements?," **IJAER**, 1977, Vol. 12, No. 2, pp. 109-125.)

Summers, Edward L. (Cruse, Rex B.. Jr. and Edward L. Summers. "Economics, Accounting Practice And Accounting Research Study No. 3," **AR**, 1965, Vol. 40.No.1,pp.82-88.)

Summers, Edward L. (Deakin, Edward B., III and Edward L. Summers. "A Survey Of Curriculum Topics Relevant To The Practice Of Management Accounting," **AR**, 1975, Vol. 50, No. 2, pp. 380-383.)

Summers, E. L. "The Audit Staff Assignment Problem: A Reply," **AR**, 1974, Vol. 49, No. 3, p. 575.

Summers, E. L. (Chen, K. H. and E. L. Summers. "A Study Of Reporting Probabilistic Accounting Figures," **AOS**, 1981, Vol. 6, No. 1, pp. 1-16.)

Summers, Warren D. (Fess, Philip E. and Warren D. Summers. "Comment On The Beamer Report's Recommendation On CPA Examination Qualifying Experience," **CPAJ**, 1972, Vol. 42, No. 9, pp. 745-748.)

Sumners, Glenn E. "Cost Benefit Evaluation Criteria For Public Projects," **JCA**, 1986, Vol. 3, No. 2, pp. 13-25.

Sumners, Glenn E. (Alderman, C. Wayne, Glenn E. Sumners and Mary Jeanne Welsh. "The Trend Toward Soft Data In Accounting," **MA**, 1983, Vol. 65, No. 6, pp. 34-39.)

Sumners, Glenn E. (Fields, Kent T., Heibatollah Sami and Glenn E. Sumners. "Quantification Of The Auditor's Evaluation Of Internal Control In Data Base Systems," **JIS**, 1986, Vol. 1, No. 1, pp. 24-47.)

Sumners, Glenn E., Richard A. White and Raymond J. Clay, Jr. "The Use Of Engagement Letters In Audit, Review, And Compilation Engagements: An Empirical Study," **AJPT**, 1986-87, Vol. 6, No. 2, pp. 116-122.

Sumutka, Alan R. and Maury R. Randall. "Some Tax Advantaged Investments - Part II," **CPAJ**, 1984, Vol. 54, No. 3, pp. 27-33.

Sumutka, Alan R. and Maury R. Randall. "Some Tax Advantaged Investments - Part I," **CPAJ**, 1984, Vol. 54, No. 2, pp. 10-15.

Sumutka, Alan R. "1980: Year Of Increased Audit Risk," **CPAJ**, 1980, Vol. 50, No. 12, pp. 21-28.

Sumutka, Alan R. "Questionable Payments And Practices: Why? How? Detection? Prevention?," **JOA**, 1980, Vol. 149, No. 3, pp. 50-63.

Sumutka, Alan R. "RA 87 And Personal Service Corporations," **CPAJ**, 1988, Vol. 58, No. 9, pp. 52-61.

Sundblad, Harry A. "Automobile Leasing," **MA**, 1975, Vol. 56, No. 9, pp. 53-55.

Sundem, Gary L. and W. L. Felix, Jr. "Tax Allocation And Security Prices: A Comment," **AR**, 1976, Vol. 51, No. 2, pp. 391-394.

Sundem, Gary L. "A Game Theory Model Of The Information Evaluator and The Decision Maker," **JAR**, 1979, Vol. 17, No. 1, pp. 243-261.

Sundem, Gary L. "Evaluating Simplified Capital Budgeting Models Using A Time-State Preference Metric," **AR**, 1974, Vol. 49, No. 2, pp. 306-320.

Sundem, Gary L. (Bowen, Robert M. and Gary L. Sundem. "Editorial And Publication Lags In The Accounting And Finance Literature," **AR**, 1982.Vol. 57,No. 4.pp.778-784.)

Sundem, Gary L. (May, Robert G. and Gary L. Sundem. "Research For Accounting Policy: An Overview," **AR**, 1976, Vol. 51, No. 4, pp. 747-763.)

Sundem, Gary L. (May, Robert G. and Gary L. Sundem. "Cost Of Information And Security Prices: A Reply," **AR**, 1974, Vol. 49, No. 4, pp. 791-793.)

Sundem, Gary L. (May, Robert G., and Gary L. Sundem. "Cost Of Information And Security Prices: Market Association Tests For Accounting Policy Decisions," **AR**, 1973, Vol. 48, No. 1, pp. 80-94.)

Sundem, Gary L. (Schall, Lawrence D. and Gary L. Sundem. "The Investment Tax Credit And The Leasing Industry," **JAPP**, 1982, Vol. 1, No. 2, pp. 83-94.)

Sunder, Shyam and Gregory Waymire. "Marginal Gains In Accuracy Of Valuation From Increasingly Specific Price Indexes: Empirical Evidence For The U.S. Economy," **JAR**, 1983, Vol. 21, No. 2, pp. 565-580.

Sunder, Shyam and Gregory Waymire. "Accuracy Of Exchange Valuation Rules: Additivity And Unbiased Estimation," **JAR**, 1984, Vol. 22, No. 1, pp. 396-405.

Sunder, Shyam. "A Note On Estimating The Economic Impact Of The LIFO Method Of Inventory Valuation," **AR**, 1976, Vol. 51, No. 2, pp. 287-291.

Sunder, Shyam. "Accuracy Of Exchange Valuation Rules," **JAR**, 1978, Vol. 16, No. 2, pp. 341-367.

Sunder, Shyam. "Optimal Choice Between FIFO And LIFO," **JAR**, 1976, Vol. 14, No. 2, pp. 277-300.

Sunder, Shyam. "Political Economy Of Accounting Standards," **JAL**, 1988, Vol. 7, pp. 31-41.

Sunder, Shyam. "Properties Of Accounting Numbers Under Full Costing And Successful-Efforts Costing In The Petroleum Industry," **AR**, 1976, Vol. 51, No. 1, pp. 1-18.

Sunder, Shyam. "Relationship Between Accounting Changes And Stock Prices: Problems Of Measurement And Some Empirical Evidence," **JAR**, 1973, Vol. 11, Supp., pp. 1-45.

Sunder, Shyam. "Simpson's Reversal Paradox And Cost Allocation," **JAR**, 1983, Vol. 21, No. 1, pp. 222-233.

Sunder, Shyam. "Stock Price And Risk Related To Accounting Changes In Inventory Valuation," **AR**, 1975, Vol. 50, No. 2, pp. 305-315.

Sunder, Shyam. (Amershi, Amin H. and Shyam Sunder. "Failure Of Stock Prices To Discipline Managers In A Rational Expectations Economy," **JAR**, 1987, Vol. 25, No. 2, pp. 177-195.)

Sunder, Shyam. (Dopuch, Nicholas and Shyam Sunder. "FASB's Statements On Objectives And Elements Of Financial Accounting: A Review," **AR**, 1980, Vol. 55, No. 1, pp. 1-21.)

Sunder, Shyam. (Joyce, Edward J., Robert Libby and Shyam Sunder. "Using The FASB's Qualitative Characterisitics In Accounting Policy Choices," **JAR**, 1982, Vol. 20, No. 2. Part II. pp. 654-675.)

Sunder, Shyam. (Lev, Baruch and Shyam Sunder. "Methodological Issues In The Use Of Financial Ratios," **JAEC**, 1979, Vol. 1, No. 3, pp. 187-210.)

Sunder, Shyam. (Prakash, Prem and Shyam Sunder. "The Case Against Separation Of Current Operating Profit And Holding Gain," **AR**, 1979, Vol. 54, No. 1, pp. 1-22.)

Sunder, Shyam. (Shih, Michael S. H. and Shyam Sunder. "Design And Tests Of An Efficient Search Algorithm For Accurate Linear Valuation Systems," **CAR**, 1987-88, Vol. 4, No. 1, pp. 16-31.)

Sunderland, Shirley A. (Treadway, James C.. Jr.. Jack L. Krogstad and Shirley A. Sunderland. "Financial Reporting And Public Confidence," **CA**, 1986, Vol. 4, No. 4.pp.4-8.)

Sunley, Emil M., Jr. "An Optimum Switch From Double-Declining Balance To Sum-Of-The-Years Digits Depreciation," **AR**, 1971, Vol. 46, No. 3, pp. 574-582.

Suojanen, Waino W. "Accounting Theory And The Large Corporation," **AR**, 1954, Vol. 29, No. 3, pp. 391-398.

Suojanen, Waino W. "Enterprise Theory And Corporate Balance Sheets," **AR**, 1958, Vol. 33, No. 1, pp. 56-65.

Suojanen, Waino W. "LIFO As A Spur To Inflation - The Recent Experience Of Copper," **AR**, 1957, Vol. 32, No. 1, pp. 42-50.

Surdick, John J. (Gaumnitz, Bruce R., Thomas R. Nunamaker, John J. Surdick and Michael F. Thomas. "Auditor Consensus In Internal Control Evaluation And Audit Program Planning," **JAR**, 1982, Vol. 20, No. 2, Part II, pp. 745-755.)

Surdick, John J. (Walker, John P. and John J. Surdick. "Controllers Vs. MIS Managers: Who Should Control Corporate Information Systems?," **MA**, 1988, Vol. 69, No. 11, pp. 22-26.)

Sussman, M. Richard. "Present-Value Short Cuts," **AR**, 1965, Vol. 40, No. 2, pp. 407-413.

Sussman, Paul E. and Samuel M. Watson. "Documentation For Wage/Price Compliance: Implications For The CPA," **CPAJ**, 1972, Vol. 42, No. 3, pp. 225-228.

Sutcliffe, Paul. "The Role Of Labour Variances In Harrington Emerson's 'New Gospel Of Efficiency' (1908)," **ABR**, 1981-82, Vol. 12, No. 46, pp. 115-123.

Sutcliffe, P. (Lewis, N. R.. L. D. Parker and P. Sutcliffe. "Financial Reporting To Employees: The Pattern Of Development 1919 To 1979," **AOS**, 1984, Vol. 9, No. 3/4, pp. 275-290.)

Sutcliffe, P. (Lewis, N. R., L. D. Parker, G. D. Pound and P. Sutcliffe. "Annual Report Readability: The Use Of Readability Techniques," **ABR**, 1985-86, Vol. 16, No. 63, pp. 199-214.)

Sutcliffe, P. (Lewis, N.. L. D. Parker and P. Sutcliffe. "Financial Reporting To Employees: Towards A Research Framework," **ABR**, 1983-84, Vol. 14, No. 55, pp. 229-240.)

Sutton, Michael H. (Beresford, Dennis R. and Michael H. Sutton. "Short-Term Debt Agreements - Classification Issues," **CPAJ**, 1983, Vol. 53, No. 8, pp. 32-37.)

Sutton, Michael H. (McDonald, Charles L. and Michael H. Sutton. "In-Substance Defeasance: Implementation Issues," **CA**, 1984, Vol. 2, No. 4, pp. 22-27.)

Sutton, Timothy G. "Management Accounting Needs A Data Base," **MA**, 1982, Vol. 63, No. 9, pp. 38-40.

Sutton, Timothy G. "The Proposed Introduction Of Current Cost Accounting In The U.K.: Determinants Of Corporate Preference," **JAEC**, 1988, Vol. 10, No. 2, pp. 127-149.

Sutton, T. G. "Lobbying Of Accounting Standard-Setting Bodies In The U.K. And The U.S.A.: A Downsian Analysis," **AOS**, 1984, Vol. 9, No. 1, pp. 81-98.

Sutton, T. G. "Physical Capital Maintenance In A Credit Economy," **ABR**, 1983-84, Vol. 14, No. 56, pp. 349-358.

Suver, James D. and Bruce R. Neumann. "Patient Mix And Breakeven Analysis," **MA**, 1977, Vol. 58, No. 7, pp.38-40.

Suver, James D. and Bruce R. Neumann. "Capital Budgeting For Hospitals," **MA**, 1978, Vol. 60, No. 6, pp. 48-50.

Suver, James D. and F. Theodore Helmer. "Developing Budgetary Models For Greater Hospital Efficiency," **MA**, 1979, Vol. 61, No. 1, pp. 34-36.

Suver, James D. (Neumann, Bruce R., James D. Suver and Ray L. Brown. "Accountants' Role In Zero-Base Budgeting," **CPAJ**, 1978, Vol. 48, No. 1, pp. 23-28.)

Suyderhoud, Jack P. (Strefeler, John M. and Jack P. Suyderhoud. "Piggybacking - A Free Ride With No Takers," **JATA**, 1980, Vol. 1, No. 2, pp. 42-48.)

Svensson, G. (Jonson, L. C., B. Jonsson and G. Svensson. "The Application Of Social Accounting To Absenteeism And Personnel Turnover," **AOS**, 1978, Vol. 3, No. 3/4, pp. 261-268.)

Swad, Randy G. and Bart P. Hartman. "Financial Accounting And Reporting Of ESOPs," **CPAJ**, 1980, Vol. 50, No. 1, pp. 37-42.

Swain, Frank S. "Reducing Domestic Barriers To A Strong Economy; A Small Business Agenda," **JOA**, 1987, Vol. 163, No. 6, pp. 110-119.

Swalley, Richard W. "Managing Your Inventory: New Use For An Old Tool," **MA**, 1984, Vol. 65, No. 11, pp. 52-56.

Swalley, Richard W. "The Benefits Of Direct Costing," **MA**, 1974, Vol. 56, No. 3, pp. 13-16.

Swan, Hugo. "Cash Conservation," **MA**, 1975, Vol. 57, No. 2, pp. 14-16.

Swann, Don M. "Where Did The Inventory Go?," **MA**, 1986, Vol. 67, No. 11, pp. 27-29.

Swanson, Edward P. and Keith A. Shriver. "The Accounting-For-Changing-Prices Experiment: A Valid Test Of Usefulness?," **ACCHOR**, 1987, Vol. 1, No. 3, pp. 69-78.

Swanson, Edward P. and Richard Vangermeersch. "Statement Of Financing And Investing Activities," **CPAJ**, 1981, Vol. 51, No. 11, pp. 32-43.

Swanson, Edward P. "Accounting For Changing Prices: Some Midcourse Corrections," **JOA**, 1984, Vol. 157, No. 4, pp. 78-93.

Swanson, Edward P. "Designing A Cash Flow Statement," **CPAJ**, 1986, Vol. 56, No. 1, pp. 38-45.

Swanson, Edward P. (Thomas, Lynn R. and Edward P. Swanson. "Additional Considerations When Using The FASB Data Bank Of Changing Price Information," **AR**, 1986, Vol. 61, No. 2, pp. 330-336.)

Swanson, Edward P., Winston T. Shearon and Lynn R. Thomas. "Predicting Current Cost Operating Profit Using Component Models Incorporating Analysts' Forecasts," **AR**, 1985, Vol. 60, No. 4, pp. 681-691.

Swanson, E. B. "The Two Faces Of Organizational Information," **AOS**, 1978, Vol. 3, No. 3/4, pp. 237-248.

Swanson, G. A. and John C. Gardner. "Not-For-Profit Accounting And Auditing In The Early Eighteenth Century: Some Archival Evidence," **AR**, 1988, Vol. 63, No. 3, pp. 436-447.

Swanson, G. A. and John C. Gardner. "The Inception And Evolution Of Financial Reporting In The Protestant Episcopal Church In The United States," **AHJ**, 1986, Vol. 13, No. 2, pp. 55-63.

Swanson, G. A. "An Inquiry Into The Utility Of A Parallel System For Providing Insights Into The Development Of An Accounting Conceptual System," **AIA**, 1987.Vol. 4.pp.3-12.

Swanson, G. A. "The 'Roots' Of Accounting," **AHJ**, 1984, Vol. 11, No. 2, pp. 111-116.

Swanson, G. A. (Gardner, John C. and G. A. Swanson. "From Bercu To Sperry - Significant Legal Landmarks In The Development Of Tax Practice," **JOA**, 1987, Vol. 163, No. 5, pp. 189-191.)

Swayze, W. S. "Internal Control In Industrial Organizations," **AR**, 1946, Vol. 21, No. 3, pp. 272-277.

Sweeney, Charles T. "Accounting Postulates: An Analysis Of The Tentative Statement Of Accounting Principles: Comments," **AR**, 1937, Vol. 12, No. 4, pp. 404-406.

Sweeney, C. T. "Accounting For Price Relief Under Capehart Amendment," **JOA**, 1952, Vol. 93, No. 5, pp. 550-556.

Sweeney, Henry W. "Capital," **AR**, 1933, Vol. 8, No. 3, pp. 185-199.

Sweeney, Henry W. "How Inflation Affects Balance Sheets," **AR**, 1934, Vol. 9, No. 4, pp. 275-299.

Sweeney, Henry W. "Income," **AR**, 1933, Vol. 8, No. 4 pp. 323-335.

Sweeney, Henry W. "Stabilized Appreciation," **AR**, 1932, Vol. 7, No. 2, pp. 115-121.

Sweeney, Henry W. "Stabilized Depreciation," **AR**, 1931, Vol. 6, No. 3, pp. 165-178.

Sweeney, Henry W. "The Technique Of Stabilized Accounting," **AR**, 1935, Vol. 10, No. 2, pp. 185-205.

Sweeney, H. W. "Maintenance Of Capital," **AR**, 1930, Vol. 5, No. 4, pp. 277-287.

Sweeney, Janet Lawson. (Swieringa, Robert J., Michael Gibbins, Lars Larsson and Janet Lawson Sweeney. "Experiments In The Heuristics Of Human Information Processing," **JAR**, 1976, Vol. 14, Supp., pp. 159-187.)

Sweeney, Robert B. "Business Use Of Linear Programming," **MA**, 1965, Vol. 47, No. 1, pp. 39-47.

Sweeney, Robert B. (Clark, Ronald L. and Robert B. Sweeney. "Admission To Accounting Programs: Using A Discriminant Model As A Classification Procedure," **AR**, 1985, Vol. 60, No. 3, pp. 508-518.)

Sweet, Franklyn H. "The Professional Accounting School And Natural School Year," **AR**, 1953, Vol. 28, No. 1, pp. 98-101.

Swenson, Charles W. and Michael L. Moore. "Use Of Input-Output Analysis In Tax Research," **AIT**, 1987, Vol. 1, pp. 49-84.

Swenson, Charles W. "An Analysis Of ACRS During Inflation Periods," **AR**, 1987, Vol. 62, No. 1, pp. 117-136.

Swenson, Charles W. "Taxpayer Behavior In Response To Taxation: An Experimental Analysis," **JAPP**, 1988, Vol. 7, No. 1, pp. 1-28.

Swenson, Charles W. (Davis, Jon S. and Charles W. Swenson. "The Role Of Experimental Economics In Tax Policy Research," **JATA**, 1988, Vol. 10, No. 1, pp. 40-59.)

Swenson, Charles W. (Moore, Michael L., Bert M. Steece and Charles W. Swenson. "An Analysis Of The Impact Of State Income Tax Rates And Bases On Foreign Investment," **AR**, 1987, Vol. 62, No. 4, pp. 671-685.)

Swenson, Charles W. (Moore, Michael L., Bert M. Steece and Charles W. Swenson. "Some Empirical Evidence On Taxpayer Rationality," **AR**, 1985, Vol. 60, No. 1, pp. 18-32.)

Swepston, Mary Anne. (Gentzel, Royce L. and Mary Anne Swepston. "The Cardinal Difference In Cash Management," **MA**, 1988, Vol. 69, No. 8, pp. 42-47.)

Swick, Ralph D. "Objectives Of Accounting Education," **AR**, 1961, Vol. 36, No. 4, pp. 626-630.

Swieringa, Robert J. and Dale Morse. "Accounting For Hybrid Convertible Debentures," **AR**, 1985, Vol. 60, No. 1, pp. 127-133.

Swieringa, Robert J. and D. R. Carmichael. "A Positional Analysis Of Internal Control," **JOA**, 1971, Vol. 131, No. 2, pp. 34-43.

Swieringa, Robert J. and Karl E. Weick. "An Assessment Of Laboratory Experiments In Accounting," **JAR**, 1982, Vol. 20, Supp., pp. 56-101.

Swieringa, Robert J. and Robert H. Moncur. "The Relationship Between Managers' Budget-Oriented Behavior And Selected Attitude, Position, Size, And Performance Measures," **JAR**, 1972, Vol. 10, Supp., pp. 194-209.

Swieringa, Robert J. "A Behavioral Approach To Participative Budgeting," **MA**, 1975, Vol. 56, No. 8, pp. 35-39.

Swieringa, Robert J. "The First 100 Days In The Life Of A New Board Member," **ACCHOR**, 1987, Vol. 1, No. 2, pp. 1-8.

Swieringa, Robert J. "The Silver-Lined Bonds Of Sunshine Mining," **AR**, 1981, Vol. 56, No. 1, pp. 166-176.

Swieringa, Robert J. "When Current Is Noncurrent And Vice Versa!," **AR**, 1984, Vol. 59, No. 1, pp. 123-130.

Swieringa, Robert J. (Demski, Joel S. and Robert J. Swieringa. "A Cooperative Formulation Of The Audit Choice Problem," **AR**, 1974, Vol. 49, No. 3, pp. 506-513.)

Swieringa, Robert J. (Elliott, John A. and Robert J. Swieringa. "Aetna, The SEC And Tax Benefits Of Loss Carryforwards," **AR**, 1985, Vol. 60, No. 3, pp. 531-546.)

Swieringa, Robert J. (Hilton, Ronald W. and Robert J. Swieringa. "Perception Of Initial Uncertainty As A Determinant Of Information Value," **JAR**, 1981, Vol. 19, No. 1, pp. 109-119.)

Swieringa, Robert J. (Hilton, Ronald W., Robert J. Swieringa and Martha J. Turner. "Product Pricing, Accounting Costs And Use Of Product-Costing Systems," **AR**, 1988, Vol. 63, No. 2, pp. 195-218.)

Swieringa, Robert J. (Hilton, Ronald W., Robert J. Swieringa and Robert E. Hoskin. "Perception Of Accuracy As A Determinant Of Information Value," **JAR**, 1981, Vol. 19, No. 1, pp. 86-108.)

Swieringa, Robert J., Michael Gibbins, Lars Larsson and Janet Lawson Sweeney. "Experiments In The Heuristics Of Human Information Processing," **JAR**, 1976, Vol. 14, Supp., pp. 159-187.

Swieringa, R. J. and J. H. Waterhouse. "Organizational Views Of Transfer Pricing," **AOS**, 1982, Vol. 7, No. 2, pp. 149-166.

Swieringa, R. J. and K. E. Weick. "Management Accounting And Action," **AOS**, 1987, Vol. 12, No. 3, pp. 293-308.

Swieringa, R. J. (Carmichael, D. R. and R. J. Swieringa. "The Compatibility Of Auditing Independence And Management Services - An Identification Of Issues," **AR**, 1968, Vol. 43, No. 4, pp. 697-705.)

Swieringa, R. J. (Dyckman, T. R., R. E. Hoskin and R. J. Swieringa. "An Accounting Change And Information Processing Changes," **AOS**, 1982, Vol. 7, No. 1, pp.1-2.)

Swigart, James A. "Corporate Acquisitions: Taxable Or Tax-Free?," **MA**, 1975, Vol. 57, No. 5, pp. 40-42.

Swindle, C. Bruce and Eldon R. Bailey. "Determining The Feasibility Of An Internship Program In Public Accounting," **JAED**, 1984, Vol. 2, No. 1, pp. 155-160.

Swingen, Judyth A. (Long, Susan B. and Judyth A. Swingen. "An Approach To The Measurement Of Tax Law Complexity," **JATA**, 1987, Vol. 8, No. 2, pp. 22-36.)

Swoboda, Peter. "Comparison Of Consolidated Financial Statements In The United States And West Germany," **IJAER**, 1966, Vol. 1, No. 2, pp. 9-24.

Swyers, Steven O. (Robbins, Barry P. and Steven O. Swyers. "Accounting For Income Taxes: Predicting Timing Difference Reversals," **JOA**, 1984, Vol. 158, No. 3, pp. 108-118.)

Swyers, William E. "A Computerized Approach To Timekeeping," **MA**, 1965, Vol. 47, No. 2, pp. 25-31.

Swyers, William E. "Employee Compensation Accounting In A Total Information System," **MA**, 1966, Vol. 47, No. 11, pp. 11-19.

Swyers, William E. "Integrated Information Systems And The Corporate Controllership Function," **MA**, 1968, Vol. 50, No. 2, pp. 18-21.

SyCip, Washington Sy. "Professional Practice In Developing Economies," **JOA**, 1967, Vol. 123, No. 1, pp. 41-45.

SyCip, Washington. "Auditors In A Developing Economy," **JOA**, 1963, Vol. 116, No. 1, pp. 46-48.

Sylvestre, Anne J. (Wood, Thomas D. and Anne J. Sylvestre. "The History Of Advertising By Accountants," **AHJ**, 1985, Vol. 12, No. 2, pp. 59-72.)

Symon, Iain W. (Grinyer, John R. and Iain W. Symon. "Maintenance Of Capital Intact: An Unnecessary Abstraction?," **ABR**, 1979-80, Vol. 10, No. 40, pp. 403-414.)

TTT

Tabb, J. B. and C. B. Frankham. "The Northern Steamship Company: The Depreciation Problem In Nineteenth Century," **AHJ**, 1986, Vol. 13, No. 2, pp. 37-53.

Tabb, J. B. "Reasons For The Emergence Of Contested Company Take-Overs In The 1950s," **ABR**, 1980-81, Vol. 11, No. 44,

Of Academic Accountants In Southern Business Administration Association Schools," **AIA**. 1988. Vol. 6. pp. 175-190.)

Taylor, Howard D. "Automatic Data Processing In The Internal Revenue Service." **JOA**, 1965. Vol. 119, No. 3, pp. 53-56.

Taylor, Jacob B. "A Program For Graduate Study Of Accounting," **AR**, 1932. Vol. 7, No. 1, pp. 42-47.

Taylor, Jacob B. "The Course In C.P.A. Problems." **AR**. 1935, Vol. 10, No. 1, pp. 21-23.

Taylor, James M. "Pitfalls And Your First Computer." **MA**. 1968, Vol. 49, No. 7, pp. 15-20.

Taylor, John L. "Lifo: A Different Approach." **JOA**. 1981. Vol. 151, No. 4, pp. 50-62.

Taylor, J. B. "Some Phases Of North Dakota's Experiment In Flour Mill Operation," **AR**, 1927, Vol. 2, No. 2, pp. 129-139.

Taylor, J. B. "The Field Work Plan," **AR**. 1933. Vol. 8, No. 4 pp. 348-350.

Taylor, J. Rowan. "A Plea For A Balanced Training Program For Accounting Students," **AR**, 1952. Vol. 27, No. 4, pp. 514-516.

Taylor, J. Roy. "Liquidation Of LIFO Inventories." **MA**, 1978, Vol. 59, No. 10, pp. 13-16.

Taylor, J. R. "Some Antecedents Of The Securities And Exchange Commission," **AR**, 1941, Vol. 16, No. 2, pp. 188-195.

Taylor, J. "The Use Of Accounting Concepts And Techniques In The Elementary Economics Course." **AR**. 1953, Vol. 28. No. 3, pp. 438-443.

Taylor, Kenneth W. (Lev. Baruch and Kenneth W. Taylor. "Accounting Recognition Of Imputed Interest On Equity: An Empirical Investigation," **JAAF**. 1979. Vol. 2, No. 3, pp. 232-243.)

Taylor, Martin E. and Caroline D. Stobel. "CPA's Responsibility To Notify Clients Of Tax Law Revisions," **JATA**. 1986, Vol. 8, No. 1, pp. 73-79.

Taylor, Martin E. and Robert L. Baker. "An Analysis Of The External Audit Fee," **ABR**, 1981-82. Vol. 12, No. 45. pp. 55-60.

Taylor, Martin E. (Bait-El-Mal. Mohamed M.. Charles H. Smith and Martin E. Taylor. "The Development Of Accounting In Libya." **IJAER**, 1973. Vol. 8. No. 2, pp. 83-101.)

Taylor, Martin E. (Evans, Thomas G. and Martin E. Taylor. "Bottom Line Compliance" With The IASC: A Comparative Analysis," **IJAER**. 1982. Vol. 18, No. 1, pp. 115-128.)

Taylor, Martin E. (Reckers, Philip M. J. and Martin E. Taylor. "Peer Review - At The State Level." **CPAJ**. 1979, Vol. 49, No. 1, pp. 35-41.)

Taylor, Martin E. (Reckers, Philip M. J. and Martin E. Taylor. "FAS No. 8 - Does It Distort Financial Statements?," **CPAJ**. 1978, Vol. 48. No. 8. pp. 31-34.)

Taylor, Martin E. (Reckers, Philip M. J. and Martin E. Taylor. "Consistency In Auditors' Evaluations Of Internal Accounting Controls." **JAAF**, 1979, Vol. 3. No. 1, pp. 42-55.)

Taylor, Martin E. (Schnee, Edward J. and Martin E. Taylor. "IRS Access To Accountants' Work Papers - The Rules May Be Changing," **JAAF**, 1981. Vol. 5, No. 1, pp. 18-29.)

Taylor, Martin E. (Schnee, Edward J. and Martin E. Taylor. "Accountants' Workpapers - Recent IRS Developments," **CPAJ**, 1980, Vol. 50, No. 2, pp 13-18.)

Taylor, Martin E. (Smith, Charles H.. Roy A. Lanier and Martin E. Taylor. "Comments On Survey Of Attitudes On Management Auditing: A Reply." **AR**, 1973. Vol. 48, No. 1, pp. 123-125.)

Taylor, Martin E. (Smith, Charles H.. Roy A. Lanier and Martin E. Taylor. "The Need For And Scope Of The Audit Of Management: A Survey Of Attitudes." **AR**, 1972. Vol. 47, No. 2, pp. 270-283.)

Taylor, Martin E., Thomas G. Evans and Arthur C. Joy. "The Impact Of IASC Accounting Standards On Comparability And Consistency Of International Accounting Reporting Practices," **IJAER**, 1986, Vol. 22. No. 1, pp. 1-9.

Taylor, Martin. (Harrell. Adrian. Eugene Chewning. and Martin Taylor. "Organizational-Professional Conflict And The Job Satisfaction And Turnover Intentions Of Internal Auditors," **AJPT**, 1985-86, Vol. 5, No. 2, pp. 111-121.)

Taylor, Paul C. "Value Of Establishing A System Of Standard Costs," **JOA**. 1951. Vol. 92. No. 6, pp. 688-693.

Taylor, Peter and Stuart Turley. "The Views Of Management On Accounting For Leases." **ABR**, 1985-86, Vol. 16. No. 61, pp. 59-68.

Taylor, P. C. "Aspects Of Public Utility Income And Expense." **AR**, 1927. Vol. 2. No. 1. pp. 28-36.

Taylor, Robert D. (Wright. Gail B. and Robert D. Taylor. "Reporting Materiality For Investors." **JAAF**. 1982. Vol. 5, No. 4, pp. 301-309.)

Taylor, Robert E. (Baker, Kenneth R. and Robert E. Taylor. "A Linear Programming Framework For Cost Allocation And External Acquisition When Reciprocal Services Exist," **AR**, 1979. Vol. 54. No. 4, pp. 784-790.)

Taylor, Robert G. "The Published Interim Report And The CPA." **JOA**, 1965, Vol. 120. No. 3, pp. 55-58.

Taylor, Ronald L. and Robert W. Ingram. "WORDS: A New Approach To Determining The Factors Affecting Tax Court Decisions Involving Real Estate Transactions," **JATA**. 1984, Vol. 5, No. 2. pp. 7-16.

Taylor, Ronald L. (Copeland. Ronald M.. Ronald L. Taylor and Shari H. Brown. "Observation Error And Bias In Accounting Research," **JAR**. 1981. Vol. 19. No. 1. pp. 197-207.)

Taylor, Russell H. (Crumbley. D. Larry and Russell H. Taylor. "Partial Liquidations And Subchapter S," **CPAJ**. 1973, Vol. 43, No. 12, pp. 1067-1072.)

Taylor, R. Emmett. "A Work-And-Study Program," **AR**, 1933. Vol. 8, No. 1, pp. 38-39.

Taylor, R. Emmett. "Pacioli," **AR**, 1935, Vol. 10, No. 2, pp. 168-173.

Taylor, R. Emmett. "The Name Of Pacioli," **AR**. 1944. Vol. 19. No. 1, pp. 69-75.

Taylor, R. G. "A Look At Published Interim Reports." **AR**. 1965, Vol. 40, No. 1, pp. 89-96.

Taylor, Stephen L. "International Accounting Standards: An Alternative Rationale," **ABACUS**, 1987, Vol. 23, No. 2. pp. 157-171.

Taylor, Thomas C. "A Comment On Smith's 'One Type Of Security'." **ABACUS**, 1976, Vol. 12, No. 2, pp. 166-167.

Taylor, Thomas C. "The Illusions Of Social Accounting." **CPAJ**, 1976, Vol. 46, No. 1, pp. 24-28.

Taylor, William M. and Jerry J. Weygandt. "Accounting For Stock-Based Awards Using The Minimum Value Method," **JAR**. 1982. Vol. 20, No. 2, Part I, pp. 497-502.

Taylor, W. Howard. (Maxwell, Arthur D. and W. Howard Taylor. "A Study Of Accounting Curricula," **AR**, 1942. Vol. 17, No. 2, pp. 141-149.)

Tearney, Michael G. "Accounting For Goodwill: A Realistic Approach." **JOA**. 1973. Vol. 136, No. 1. pp. 41-45.

Tearney, Michael G. "Compliance With AICPA Pronouncements On Accounting For Goodwill," **CPAJ**, 1973, Vol. 43, No. 2. pp. 121-125.

Tearney, Michael G. (Wolk. Harry I. and Michael G. Tearney. "Income Tax Allocation And Loss Carryforwards: Exploring Uncharted Ground," **AR**, 1973, Vol. 48, No. 2, pp. 292-299.)

Techavichit, Joseph V. (Buehlmann, David M. and Joseph V. Techavichit. "Factors Influencing Final Examination Performance In Large Versus Small Sections Of Accounting Principles." **JAED**, 1984. Vol. 2, No. 1, pp. 127-136.)

Teck, Alan. "Beyond FAS No. 8: Defining Other Exposures." **MA**. 1978, Vol. 60. No. 6, pp. 54-57.

Teck, Alan. "Financial Planning In Nations With Fluctuating Currencies." **MA**, 1970, Vol. 51, No. 7, pp. 25-28.

Teevan, John C. "C.P.A. Commercial Law Examinations," **AR**. 1936. Vol. 11. No. 3. pp. 229-233.

Tehranian, Hassan and James F. Waegelein. "Market Reaction To Short-Term Executive Compensation Plan Adoption," **JAEC**. 1985. Vol. 7, No. 1/3, pp. 131-144.

Tehranian, Hassan, Nickolaos G. Travlos and James F. Waegelein. "Management Compensation Contracts And Merger-Induced Abnormal Returns," **JAR**, 1987. Vol. 25. Supp.. pp. 51-76.

Teichman, Ronald J. (Dirsmith. Mark W. J., Edward Ketz and Ronald J. Teichman. "Vertical And Lateral Considerations Of Undergraduate Accounting Honors Programs," **AIA**. 1986. Vol. 3. pp. 301-322.)

Teitelbaum, Louis N. "Internal Auditing Developments In The Air Force." **AR**. 1954. Vol. 29. No. 3. pp. 399-408.

Teitelbaum, A. D. and C. F. Robinson. "The Real Risks In Audit Sampling." **JAR**. 1975. Vol. 13. Supp., pp. 70-91.

TeKolste, Elton. "Section 102," **AR**, 1954. Vol. 29. No. 1. pp. 100-105.

Telling, Raymond. (Derscheid, Vincent K., Raymond Telling and G. W. Tonkin. "Nontax Benefits Of The Incorporation Of A Practice," **JOA**. 1977. Vol. 143, No. 1, pp. 70-76.)

Temkin, Robert H. and Alan J. Winters. "SAS No. 55: The Auditor's New Responsibility For Internal Control," **JOA**. 1988, Vol. 165. No. 5, pp. 86-98.

Temkin, Robert H. "Automating Auditing: Auditing Will Never Be The Same." **CA**, 1986, Vol. 4. No. 4, pp. 56-59.

Ten Eyck, Ernest L. (Roussey. Robert S., Ernest L. Ten Eyck and Mimi Blanco-Best. "Three New SASs: Closing The Communications Gap," **JOA**, 1988, Vol. 166, No. 6. pp. 44-52.)

Tennant, Kirk and Charles Lawrence. "Teaching Strategies: Effects On Student Evaluations Of Teachers." **AR**. 1975. Vol. 50, No. 4, pp. 899-904.

Tennant, Kirk L. (Ferris, Kenneth R. and Kirk L. Tennant. "An Investigation Of The Impact Of The Qualitative Nature Of Compliance Errors On Internal Control Assessments," **AJPT**. 1983-84, Vol. 3, No. 2, pp. 31-43.)

Tenner, Irving. "Balance Sheets For The Federal Government." **AR**. 1950. Vol. 25. No. 4. pp. 420-424.

Tenner, Irving. "Difficulties Of A Terminologist," **AR**. 1941. Vol. 16. No. 4, pp. 349-357.

Tenner, Irving. "Municipal Budgeting In Wartime," **AR**. 1943. Vol. 18. No. 2. pp. 123-126.

Tenner, Irving. "The Manual Of Water Works Accounting." **AR**. 1939. Vol. 14. No. 2. pp. 184-186.

Tennyson B. Mack. (Frazier, Katherine Beal. Robert W. Ingram and B. Mack Tennyson. "A Methodology For The Analysis Of Narrative Accounting Disclosures," **JAR**. 1984. Vol. 22. No. 1. pp. 318-331.)

Teoh, H. Y. and G. Thong. "Another Look At Corporate Social Responsibility And Reporting: An Empirical Study In A Developing Country," **AOS**, 1984. Vol. 9, No. 2, pp. 189-206.

Tepperman, Fred L. "The Attest Function - Challenge Of The Eighties." **CPAJ**, 1981, Vol. 51, No. 12, pp. 17-21.

Terborgh, Eliot. "Evaluation Of Investment Center Performance." **MA**. 1969, Vol. 50, No. 7, pp. 42-46.

Terbrueggen, Jan E. "Can A Central Cash Pool Work For Transfer Pricing?." **MA**, 1986, Vol. 68. No. 1, pp. 31-33.

Terre, Norbert C., Dale W. Warnke and Albert P. Ameiss. "Cost/Benefit Analysis Of Public Projects," **MA**. 1973. Vol. 54. No. 7. pp. 34-37.

Terrell, Junius H. "A Conceptual Auditing Methodology - Interrelationships Between The Financial Statements. Internal Controls. And The Audit Program," **AR**, 1974. Vol. 49. No. 1, pp. 176-180.

Terrell, Junius H. "Areas For Error In Financial Accounting And Reporting," **CPAJ**, 1973, Vol. 43, No. 5, pp. 396-398.

Terrell, Junius H. "Minimum Standards For Unaudited Financial Statements," **JOA**, 1973, Vol. 135, No. 5, pp. 54-60.

Tersine, Richard J. and John S. Morris. "Materials Management: Futuristic Orientations," **JCA**, 1984, Vol. 1, No. 1, pp. 115-130.

Test, Darrell L., John D. Hawley and Michael F. Cortright. "Determining Strategic Value," **MA**, 1987, Vol. 68, No. 12, pp. 39-42.

Tewes, James A. "Valuing Bank Funds For Allocation And Pricing Decisions," **MA**, 1976, Vol. 58, No. 5, pp. 27-33.

Thacker, Ronald J. "Income Statement Form And Classification," **AR**, 1962, Vol. 37, No. 1, pp. 51-55.

Thakkar, Rashmi B. "The Association Between Market-Determined And Accounting-Determined Risk Measures: A Note," **JAR**, 1978, Vol. 16, No. 1, pp. 215-223.

Thakkar, Rashmi B., David R. Finley and Woody M. Liao. "A Stochastic Demand CVP Model With Return On Investment Criterion," **CAR**, 1984-85, Vol. 1, No. 1, pp. 77-86.

Theil, Henri. "How To Worry About Increased Expenditures," **AR**, 1969, Vol. 44, No. 1, pp. 27-37.

Theil, Henri. (Lev, Baruch and Henri Theil. "A Maximum Entropy Approach To The Choice Of Asset Depreciation," **JAR**, 1978, Vol. 16, No. 2, pp. 286-293.)

Theis, John A. (Mahoney, John J., Mark V. Sever and John A. Theis. "Cash Flow: FASB Opens The Floodgates," **JOA**, 1988, Vol. 165, No. 5, pp. 26-38.)

Theiss, Edwin L. "Accounting And Budgeting," **AR**, 1935, Vol. 10, No. 2, pp. 156-161.

Theiss, Edwin L. "The Beginnings Of Business Budgeting," **AR**, 1937, Vol. 12, No. 1, pp. 43-54.

Theiss, E. L. "Budgetary Procedure As A Means Of Administrative Control," **AR**, 1932, Vol. 7, No. 1, pp. 11-21.

Theiss, E. L. "Teaching Budgeting And Controllership," **AR**, 1952, Vol. 27, No. 4, pp. 554-555.

Theobald, Michael and John Whitman. "The Variabilities And Correlations Of Stock Market Indices," **ABR**, 1978-79, Vol. 9, No. 33, pp. 82-86.

Theobald, Michael. "Exclusion Period And Market Model Parameter Nonstationarities In Price Reaction Studies," **CAR**, 1985-86, Vol. 2, No. 1, pp. 1-45.

Theunisse, Hilda. "Accounting And Reporting In Belgium," **AIIA**, 1987, Vol. 1, pp. 191-248.

Thibadoux, Greg M., Nicholas Apostolou and Ira S. Greenberg. "The Development Of Not-For-Profit Hospital Cost Models," **JCA**, 1988, Vol. 5, No. 1, pp. 35-48.

Thibadoux, Greg. (Golen, Steven, James Worthington, Greg Thibadoux, William D. Cooper and Ira S. Greenberg. "Flowcharts & Graphics," **CPAJ**, 1986, Vol. 56, No. 3, pp. 12-23.)

Thierbach, Frederic D. "Making Dollars And Sense From Your Health Claims Management System," **CA**, 1986, Vol. 4, No. 2, pp. 17-21.

Thies, Clifford F. and Thomas Sturrock. "What Did Inflation Accounting Tell Us?," **JAAF**, 1987, Vol. 2 (New Issues), No. 4, pp. 375-395.

Thies, James B. and Lawrence Revsine. "Capital Expenditures Data For Inflation Accounting Studies," **AR**, 1977, Vol. 52, No. 1, pp. 216-221.

Thies, James B. (Ferrara, William L., James B. Thies and Mark W. Dirsmith. "The Lease-Purchase Decision," **MA**, 1980, Vol. 61, No. 11, pp. 57-58.)

Thies, James B. (Revsine, Lawrence and James B. Thies. "Price Level Adjusted Replacement Cost Data," **JOA**, 1977, Vol. 143, No. 5, pp. 71-75.)

Thies, James B. (Revsine, Lawrence and James B. Thies. "Productivity Changes And Alternative Income Series: A Simulation," **AR**, 1976, Vol. 51, No. 2, pp. 255-268.)

Thilman, E. Thomas. (Filippini, Thomas W. and E. Thomas Thilman. "The Insurance Crisis - An Opportunity," **CA**, 1987, Vol. 5, No. 2, pp. 10-12.)

Thirkell, J. E. M. (Jackson-Cox, J., J. E. M. Thirkell and J. McQueeney. "The Disclosure Of Company Information To Trade Unions: The Relevance Of The ACAS Code Of Practice On Disclosure," **AOS**, 1984, Vol. 9, No. 3/4, pp. 253-274.)

Thode, Stephen F., Ralph E. Drtina and James A. Largay, III. "Operating Cash Flows: A Growing Need For Separate Reporting," **JAAF**, 1986, Vol. 1 (New Series), No. 1, pp. 46-61.

Thokey, James W. "Practical Aspects Of Inventory Verification," **JOA**, 1954, Vol. 97, No. 2, pp. 195-200.

Thom, Harry. "Expressing Preferred Stock On The Balance Sheet," **AR**, 1927, Vol. 2, No. 1, pp. 1-9.

Thomas, Arthur L. "A Common Dollar Funds Statement," **AR**, 1965, Vol. 40, No. 1, pp. 223-230.

Thomas, Arthur L. "Arbitrary And Incorrigible Allocations: A Comment," **AR**, 1978, Vol. 53, No. 1, pp. 263-269.

Thomas, Arthur L. "Discounted Services Again: The Homogeneity Problem," **AR**, 1964, Vol. 39, No. 1, pp. 1-11.

Thomas, Arthur L. "Estimating The Effective Interest Rate," **AR**, 1968, Vol. 43, No. 3, pp. 589-591.

Thomas, Arthur L. "Evaluating The Effectiveness Of Social Programs," **JOA**, 1976, Vol. 141, No. 6, pp. 65-71.

Thomas, Arthur L. "Goals For Joint-Cost Allocation: An Incompatibility In The Literature," **ABACUS**, 1982, Vol. 18, No. 2, pp. 166-174.

Thomas, Arthur L. "North American College And University Uses Of Micro Computers In Teaching Accounting - 1983 Survey," **JAED**, 1984, Vol. 2, No. 2, pp. 31-41.

Thomas, Arthur L. "Precision And Discounted Services," **AR**, 1962, Vol. 37, No. 1, pp. 67-72.

Thomas, Arthur L. "The Amortization Problem: A Simplified Model And Some Unanswered Questions," **JAR**, 1965, Vol. 3,

No. 1, pp. 103-113.

Thomas, Arthur L. "The Chambers-Kennelly-McRae-Reilly-Weltmer Thesis: An Addendum," **ABACUS**, 1972, Vol. 8, No. 1, p. 75.

Thomas, Arthur L. "The FASB And The Allocation Fallacy," **JOA**, 1975, Vol. 140, No. 5, pp. 65-68.

Thomas, Arthur L. "Transfer Prices Of The Multinational Firm: When Will They Be Arbitrary?," **ABACUS**, 1971, Vol. 7, No. 1, pp. 40-53.

Thomas, Arthur L. "Use Of Microcomputer Spreadsheet Software In Preparing And Grading Complex Accounting Problems," **AR**, 1983, Vol. 58, No. 4, pp. 777-786.

Thomas, Arthur L. "Useful Arbitrary Allocations (With A Comment On the Neutrality Of Financial Accounting Reports)," **AR**, 1971, Vol. 46, No. 3, pp. 472-479.

Thomas, Arthur L. "Value-Itis' - An Impractical Theorist's Reply," **AR**, 1964, Vol. 39, No. 3, pp. 574-581.

Thomas, A. P. "The Contingency Theory Of Corporate Reporting: Some Empirical Evidence," **AOS**, 1986, Vol. 11, No. 3, pp. 253-270.

Thomas, Barbara S. "SEC Oversight Role In Self-Regulation," **CPAJ**, 1983, Vol. 53, No. 5, pp. 10-15.

Thomas, Donald R. "Data Processing Service Bureaus," **MA**, 1970, Vol. 51, No. 9, pp. 25-27.

Thomas, Donald R. "On Reliability Strategy In Electronic Data Processing," **MA**, 1969, Vol. 50, No. 5, pp. 39-42.

Thomas, D. A. (Brummet, R. L. and D. A. Thomas. "Accounting System For Home Builders Aids Control," **JOA**, 1952, Vol. 94, No. 5, pp. 570-575.)

Thomas, Jacob K. "Corporate Taxes And Defined Benefit Pension Plans," **JAEC**, 1988, Vol. 10, No. 3, pp. 199-237.

Thomas, Jacob K. (Imhoff, Eugene A. and Jacob K. Thomas. "Economic Consequences Of Accounting Standards: The Lease Disclosure Rule Change," **JAEC**, 1988, Vol. 10, No. 4, pp. 277-310.)

Thomas, Lynn R. and Edward P. Swanson. "Additional Considerations When Using The FASB Data Bank Of Changing Price Information," **AR**, 1986, Vol. 61, No. 2, pp. 330-336.

Thomas, Lynn R. (Swanson, Edward P., Winston T. Shearon and Lynn R. Thomas. "Predicting Current Cost Operating Profit Using Component Models Incorporating Analysts' Forecasts," **AR**, 1985, Vol. 60, No. 4, pp. 681-691.)

Thomas, Lynn. (Putnam, Karl and Lynn Thomas. "Does Predictability Change When GAAP Change?," **JAAF**, 1984, Vol. 8, No. 1, pp. 15-23.)

Thomas, L. L. "Methods Of Supervising Local Finances," **AR**, 1944, Vol. 19, No. 4, pp. 439-450.

Thomas, Michael F. (Gaumnitz, Bruce R., Thomas R. Nunamaker, John J. Surdick and Michael F. Thomas. "Auditor Consensus In Internal Control Evaluation And Audit Program Planning," **JAR**, 1982, Vol. 20, No. 2, Part II, pp. 745-755.)

Thomas, Mitchell T. "Another Look At Zero-Base Budgeting," **CPAJ**, 1979, Vol. 49, No. 8, pp. 37-43.

Thomas, Mitchell T. "Opportunities For The CPA In Cooperative Housing," **CPAJ**, 1981, Vol. 51, No. 5, pp. 34-40.

Thomas, Paula Bevels and Larry E. Farmer. "Accounting For Stock Options And SARs: The Equality Question," **JOA**, 1984, Vol. 157, No. 6, pp. 92-98.

Thomas, Paula B. and J. Larry Hagler. "Push Down Accounting: A Descriptive Assessment," **AH**, 1988, Vol. 2, No. 3, pp. 26-31.

Thomas, Paula B. and J. Larry Hagler. "Induced Conversions Of Convertible Debt: Beware Of The Pitfalls," **MA**, 1987, Vol. 68, No. 12, pp. 52-55.

Thomas, Robert E. "Government Fantasy Or Economic Reality?," **MA**, 1978, Vol. 60, No. 3, pp. 21-27.

Thomas, R. Douglas. "The Accountants International Study Group - The First Three Years," **IJAER**, 1970, Vol. 6, No. 1, pp. 59-65.

Thomas, William E. "One Approach To The Problem Of Communicating Accounting Information," **AR**, 1951, Vol. 26, No. 3, pp. 395-399.

Thomas, William E. "The Use Of Projected Visual Aids In The Teaching Of Cost Accounting," **AR**, 1952, Vol. 27, No. 1, pp. 94-99.

Thompson, David W. "How To Make Accounting Internship Program Work," **JOA**, 1951, Vol. 92, No. 6, pp. 694-696.

Thompson, David W. "Partnership Training Programs," **AR**, 1950, Vol. 25, No. 4, pp. 395-401.

Thompson, David W. "The Use Of Visual Aids In The Teaching Of Accounting," **AR**, 1948, Vol. 23, No. 3, pp. 276-281.

Thompson, Gerald L. (Ijiri, Yuji and Gerald L. Thompson. "Applications Of Mathematical Control Theory To Accounting And Budgeting (The Continuous Wheat Trading Model)," **AR**, 1970, Vol. 45, No. 2, pp. 246-258.)

Thompson, Gerald L. (Kaplan, Robert S. and Gerald L. Thompson. "Overhead Allocation Via Mathematical Programming Models," **AR**, 1971, Vol. 46, No. 2, pp. 352-364.)

Thompson, G. "Inflation Accounting In A Theory Of Calculation," **AOS**, 1987, Vol. 12, No. 5, pp. 523-544.

Thompson, Howard E. (Blakely, Edward J. and Howard E. Thompson. "Technological Change And Its Effects On Dollar-Value Lifo," **MA**, 1969, Vol. 51, No. 2, pp. 33-38.)

Thompson, James H. and Thomas E. Buttross. "Return To Cash Flow," **CPAJ**, 1988, Vol. 58, No. 3, pp. 30-41.

Thompson, James H. (Fields, Kent T., Gary L. Waters and James H. Thompson. "Accounting For The Costs Of Certain Computer Software," **CPAJ**, 1986, Vol. 56, No. 1, pp. 32-37.)

Thompson, James H., James S. Worthington and L. Murphy Smith. "An Inconsistency In The Method Of Accounting For Changes In Estimate: Variable Stock Plans," **ACCHOR**, 1987, Vol. 1, No. 4, pp. 29-34.

Thompson, Joel E. "Introducing The Capital Budgeting Problem," *JAED*, 1986, Vol. 4, No. 1, pp. 221-226.

Thompson, Joel E. (Gaumnitz, Bruce R. and Joel E. Thompson. "Establishing The Common Stock Equivalence Of Convertible Bonds," *AR*, 1987, Vol. 62. No. 3, pp. 601-622.)

Thompson, Joel E. (Gaumnitz, Bruce R. and Joel E. Thompson. "In-Substance Defeasance: Costs, Yes; Benefits, No," *JOA*, 1987, Vol. 163, No. 3, pp. 102-105.)

Thompson, Joel E. (Tanoury, Mark P. and Joel E. Thompson. "Accounting For Junior Stock: Another Look." *JOA*, 1985, Vol. 159, No. 4, pp. 86-93.)

Thompson, Kenneth L. "Long-Range Planning For A Growing Firm," *JOA*, 1960, Vol. 109, No. 3, pp. 39-43.

Thompson, Paul H. (Todd, John T., Paul H. Thompson and Gene Dalton. "Management Control Of Personnel," *JOA*, 1974, Vol. 137, No. 2, pp. 34-40.)

Thompson, Rex. "Comment On 'Standard Setting And Security Returns: A Time Series Analysis Of FAS No. 8 Events," *CAR*, 1986-87, Vol. 3, No. 1, pp. 242-250.

Thompson, Rex. (Lanen, William N. and Rex Thompson. "Stock Price Reactions As Surrogates For Net Cash Flow Effects Of Corporate Policy Decisions," *JAEC*, 1988, Vol. 10, No. 4, pp. 311-334.)

Thompson, Rex. (Richardson, Gordon, Stephan E. Sefcik and Rex Thompson. "Trading Volume Reactions To A Change In Dividend Policy: The Canadian Evidence," *CAR*, 1988, Vol. 5, No. 1, pp. 299-317.)

Thompson, Rex. (Schipper, Katherine and Rex Thompson. "The Impact Of Merger-Related Regulations On The Shareholders Of Acquiring Firms," *JAR*, 1983, Vol. 21, No. 1, pp. 184-221.)

Thompson, Rex. (Schipper, Katherine and Rex Thompson. "The Impact Of Merger-Related Regulations Using Exact Distributions Of Test Statistics," *JAR*, 1985, Vol. 23, No. 1, pp. 408-415.)

Thompson, Rex. (Sefcik, Stephan E. and Rex Thompson. "An Approach To Statistical Inference In Cross-Sectional Models With Security Abnormal Returns As Dependent Variable," *JAR*, 1986, Vol. 24, No. 2, pp. 316-334.)

Thompson, Richard E. (Boros, John L. and Richard E. Thompson. "Distribution Cost Accounting At PPG Industries," *MA*, 1983, Vol. 64, No. 7, pp. 54-59.)

Thompson, Robert B., II, Chris Olsen and J. Richard Dietrich. "Attributes Of News About Firms: An Analysis Of Firm-Specific News Reported In The Wall Street Journal Index," *JAR*, 1987, Vol. 25, No. 2, pp. 245-274.

Thompson, Robert B., II, Chris Olsen and J. Richard Dietrich. "The Influence Of Estimation Period News Events On Standardized Market Model Prediction Errors," *AR*, 1988, Vol. 63, No. 3, pp. 448-471.

Thompson, R. R. "Capital And Revenue Profits And Losses," *AR*, 1932, Vol. 7, No. 3, pp. 153-168.

Thompson, Steve. (Wright, Mike and Steve Thompson. "Divestment And The Control Of Divisionalised Firms," *ABR*, 1986-87, Vol. 17, No. 67, pp. 259-268.)

Thompson, William W., Jr. and Earl L. Kemper. "Probability Measures For Estimated Data," *AR*, 1965, Vol. 40, No. 3, pp. 574-578.

Thomsen, Carl J. "Management Systems In A Growth Company." *MA*, 1969, Vol. 50, No. 5, pp. 12-13.

Thomsen, C. Torben. "Continuous And Consistent Depreciation Formulas," *AR*, 1970, Vol. 45, No. 1, pp. 151-158.

Thomsen, C. Torben. "Dangers In Discounting," *MA*, 1984, Vol. 65, No. 7, pp. 37-40.

Thomsen, C. Torben. (Jensen, Robert E. and C. Torben Thomsen. "Statistical Analysis In Cost Measurement And Control," *AR*, 1968, Vol. 43, No. 1, pp. 83-93.)

Thong, G. (Teoh, H. Y. and G. Thong. "Another Look At Corporate Social Responsibility And Reporting: An Empirical Study In A Developing Country," *AOS*, 1984, Vol. 9, No. 2, pp. 189-206.)

Thor, Carl G. "Planning Your Productivity Efforts," *MA*, 1983, Vol. 64, No. 12, pp. 28-33.

Thorne, Jack F. "Tough Regulations For Tax Return Preparers," *CPAJ*, 1978, Vol. 48. No. 5, pp. 21-26.

Thornton, Daniel B. "Capital Values In Use Vs. Replacement Costs: Theory And Canadian Evidence," *CAR*, 1988, Vol. 5, No. 1, pp. 343-370.

Thornton, Daniel B. "Current Cost Disclosers And Nondisclosers: Canadian Evidence," *CAR*, 1986-87, Vol. 3, No. 1, pp. 1-34.

Thornton, Daniel B. "Theory And Metaphor In Accounting." *AH*, 1988, Vol. 2, No. 4, pp. 1-9.

Thornton, D. B. "Information And Institutions In The Capital Market," *AOS*, 1979, Vol. 4, No. 3, pp. 211-234.

Thornton, D. B. (Krinsky, I., W. D. Rotenberg and D. B. Thornton. "Takeovers: A Synthesis," *JAL*, 1988, Vol. 7, pp. 243-279.)

Thornton, John M., Jr. (Dixon, Lynwood J. and John M. Thornton, Jr. "The Costs Of Cleaning Up Pollution," *MA*, 1972, Vol. 54, No. 5, pp. 13-17.)

Thornton, John R. (DeNardo, Stephen and John R. Thornton. "Recruiting: The New Horizon," *JOA*, 1982, Vol. 154, No. 4, pp. 40-49.)

Thorson, John R. (Felix, W. L., Jr., Robert G. May, Marcia S. Niles and John R. Thorson. "SCAD: Something New In Auditing Education," *JAED*, 1985, Vol. 3, No. 2, pp. 5-14.)

Thralls, William H. (DuPree, Jean M., Al H. Hartgraves and William H. Thralls. "How Management Accountants Can Communicate Better," *MA*, 1987, Vol. 68, No. 8, pp. 40-43.)

Throckmorton, Jerry J. and John Talbott. "Computer-Supported Instruction In Financial Statement Analysis," *AR*, 1978, Vol. 53, No. 1, pp. 186-191.

Throckmorton, Jerry J. "Theoretical Concepts For Interpreting The Investment Credit," *JOA*, 1970, Vol. 129, No. 4, pp. 45-52.

Thrun, Walter J. Sr. "A Systems Approach To Cash Flow Determination," *MA*, 1973, Vol. 54, No. 8, pp. 29-31.

Thurman, Sam D., Jr. "Accountant-Attorney Cooperation," *AR*, 1944, Vol. 19. No. 3, pp. 283-289.

Tidwell, Victor H. and Robert W. Wyndelts. "Graduate Tax Education In AACSB Schools: Where We Stand Today," *AR*, 1977, Vol. 52. No. 4, pp. 963-970.

Tidwell, Victor H. "Collecting Investment Credit Data," *MA*, 1968, Vol. 50, No. 1, pp. 55-58.

Tidwell, V. H. (Lembke, V. C., J. H. Smith and V. H. Tidwell. "Compulsory Continuing Education For CPAs," *JOA*, 1970, Vol. 129, No. 4, pp. 61-65.)

Tidwell, V. H. (Smith, J. H., V. H. Tidwell and V. C. Lembke. "An Analysis Of Participation In Continuing Education," *JOA*, 1972, Vol. 133, No. 1, pp. 40-45.)

Tiedemann, Frank H. "Accounting And Auditing For Regulated Investment Companies," *JOA*, 1970, Vol. 129, No. 1, pp. 31-39.

Tierney, Cecilia V. "General Purchasing Power Myths," *JOA*, 1977, Vol. 144, No. 3, pp. 90-95.

Tierney, Cecilia. "Price-Level Adjustments - Problem In Perspective," *JOA*, 1963, Vol. 116, No. 5, pp. 56-60.

Tierney, Cornelius E. "No Quick Fix For Federal Finances," *JOA*, 1988, Vol. 165, No. 6, pp. 88-94.

Tiessen, Peter and Dennis M. Baker. "Human Information Processing, Decision Style Theory And Accounting Information Systems: A Comment," *AR*, 1977, Vol. 52, No. 4, pp. 984-987.

Tiessen, Peter and J. H. Waterhouse. "The Contingency Theory Of Managerial Accounting: A Comment," *AR*, 1978, Vol. 53, No. 2, pp. 523-529.

Tiessen, Pieter. (Colson, Robert H., Michael W. Maher. Amy J. Broman and Pieter Tiessen. "Auditing Pricing Models For Regulation Research: Reliability And Stability," *RIAR*, 1988, Vol. 2, pp. 61-79.)

Tiessen, P. and J. H. Waterhouse. "Towards A Descriptive Theory Of Management Accounting," *AOS*, 1983, Vol. 8, No. 2/3, pp. 251-268.

Tiessen, P. (Waterhouse, J. H. and P. Tiessen. "A Contingency Framework For Management Accounting Systems Research," *AOS*, 1978, Vol. 3, No. 1, pp. 65-76.)

Tietjen, A. Carl. "A Basis For Financial Reporting," *CPAJ*, 1973, Vol. 43, No. 1, pp. 37-44.

Tietjen, A. Carl. "Accounting Principles, Practices And Methods," *JOA*, 1963, Vol. 115, No. 4, pp. 65-68.

Tietjen, A. Carl. "Audit Examination Approach," *JOA*, 1956, Vol. 101, No. 4, pp. 65-72.

Tietjen, A. Carl. "Changes In Public Accounting," *JOA*, 1958, Vol. 105, No. 5, pp. 34-39.

Tietze, Armin R. and Delphine R. Shaw. "OPUS: A New Concept For Mastering Cost," *MA*, 1986, Vol. 68, No. 2, pp. 27-31.

Tiffany, Kenneth C. "The Future Of Accounting," *AR*, 1961, Vol. 36. No. 2, pp. 204-208.

Tiffany, K. C. "Reports For Management," *AR*, 1950, Vol. 25, No. 2, pp. 142-148.

Tiller, Mikel G. and Clinton White. "Are Accounting Majors Really Better? Evaluating Admission And Retention Standards For Undergraduate Accounting Programs," *JAED*, 1983, Vol. 1, No. 1, pp. 19-33.

Tiller, Mikel G. and Jan R. Williams. "Revenue Recognition Under New FASB Statements," *CPAJ*, 1982, Vol. 52, No. 1, pp. 43-47.

Tiller, Mikel G. and R. David Mautz. "The Impact Of State-Mandated Accounting And Auditing Requirements On Municipal Bond Ratings," *JAAF*, 1985, Vol. 8, No. 4, pp. 293-304.

Tiller, Mikel G. "The Dissonance Model Of Participative Budgeting: An Empirical Exploration," *JAR*, 1983, Vol. 21, No. 2, pp. 581-595.

Tiller, Mikel G. (Stanga, Keith G. and Mikel G. Tiller. "Needs Of Loan Officers For Accounting Information From Large Versus Small Companies," *ABR*, 1983-84, Vol. 14, No. 53. pp. 63-70.)

Tillett, J. William. (Dillon, Ray D. and J. William Tillett. "Containing The Costs Of Health Care," *JOA*, 1985. Vol. 159, No. 3, pp. 86-95.)

Tilley, Ian. "A Critique Of Historical Record Accounting," *ABR*, 1974-75, Vol. 5, No. 19, pp. 185-197.

Tilley, Ian. "Accounting As A Scientific Endeavour," *ABR*, 1971-72, Vol. 2, No. 8, pp. 287-297.

Tilly, Virgil S. "Depreciation - Does It Relate To Original Cost Or To Cost Of Replacement?," *AR*, 1958, Vol. 33, No. 4, pp. 622-624.

Tilly, Virgil S. "The Income Statement And Its Significance In Financial Reporting," *AR*, 1948, Vol. 23, No. 3, pp. 296-304.

Tilly, Virgil. "Professional Obligations Of The CPA," *JOA*, 1953, Vol. 95, No. 6, pp. 714-715.

Tilt, James T. and Martin M. Spencer. "Marriage Penalties Persist In Tax Laws," *CPAJ*, 1983, Vol. 53, No. 1, pp. 38-44.

Timmerman, John E. (Robinson, Michael A. and John E. Timmerman. "Vendor Analysis Supports JIT Manufacturing," *MA*, 1987, Vol. 69, No. 6, pp. 20-24.)

Tinius, David E. (Weis, William L. and David E. Tinius. "Does Anyone Understand Nonprofit Reports?," *MA*, 1980, Vol. 62, No. 5, pp. 25-29.)

Tinker, Anthony. "Theories Of The State And The State Accounting: Economic Reductionism And Political Voluntarism In Accounting Regulation Theory," *JAPP*, 1984, Vol. 3, No. 1, pp. 55-74.

Tinker, A. M. "Towards A Political Economy Of Accounting: An Empirical Illustration Of The Cambridge Controversies," **AOS**, 1980, Vol. 5, No. 1. pp. 147-160.

Tinker, A. M., B. D. Merino and M. D. Neimark. "The Normative Origins Of Positive Theories: Ideology And Accounting Thought," **AOS**, 1982, Vol. 7, No. 2. pp. 167-200.

Tinker, Tony. "Waiving Goodbye To The TWA Bus: 'Paper Prophets' And The Sraffian Critique Of Marginalism," **AIPIA**, 1988, Vol. 2. pp. 121-141.

Tinker, T. and M. Neimark. "The Role Of Annual Reports In Gender And Class Contradictions At General Motors: 1917-1976," **AOS**, 1987, Vol. 12. No. 1. pp. 71-88.

Tinker, T. "Panglossian Accounting Theories: The Science Of Apologising In Style," **AOS**, 1988, Vol. 13. No. 2. pp. 165-190.

Tinker, T. (Lehman, C. and T. Tinker. "The 'Real' Cultural Significance Of Accounts," **AOS**, 1987, Vol. 12, No. 5, pp. 503-522.)

Tinker, T. (Neimark, M. and T. Tinker. "The Social Construction Of Management Systems." **AOS**, 1986, Vol. 11, No. 4/5, pp. 369-396.)

Tipgos, Manuel A. and Robert P. Crum. "Applying Management Accounting Concepts To The Health Care Industry," **MA**, 1982, Vol. 64, No. 1, pp. 37-43.

Tipgos, Manuel A. "A Case Against The Social Audit," **MA**, 1976, Vol. 58, No. 9. pp. 23-26.

Tipgos, Manuel A. "A Comprehensive Model For Improving Accounting Education," **AIIA**, 1987, Vol. 1. pp. 383-404.

Tipgos, Manuel A. "Do We Need New Auditing Standards?," **CPAJ**, 1977. Vol. 47, No. 6. pp. 25-30.

Tipgos, Manuel A. "Offensive Auditing." **CPAJ**, 1976, Vol. 46, No. 9. pp. 19-24.

Tipgos, Manuel A. "Prior Year's Working Papers: Uses And Dangers," **CPAJ**, 1978. Vol. 48. No. 9. pp. 19-25.

Tipgos, Manuel A. "Reporting Corporate Performance In The Social Sphere," **MA**, 1976, Vol. 58. No. 2. pp. 15-18.

Tipgos, Manuel A. "Toward A Theory Of Corporate Social Accounting: A Comment," **AR**, 1977. Vol. 52, No. 4, pp. 977-983.

Tipgos, Manuel A. (Fern, Richard H. and Manuel A. Tipgos. "Controllers As Business Strategists: A Progress Report," **MA**, 1988, Vol. 69, No. 9, pp. 25-29.)

Tipgos, Manuel A., James R. Holmes and Gerald H. Lander. "The Management Accountant Today: A Status Report," **MA**, 1983, Vol. 65, No. 5, pp. 53-57.

Tippett, Mark. "Exchange Valuation Rules: Optimal Use Of Specific Price Indices," **ABR**, 1986-87, Vol. 17. No. 66. pp. 141-154.

Tippett, Mark. "On The Numerical Estimation Of The Loss From Holding Monetary Items," **ABR**, 1982-83, Vol. 13, No. 49, pp. 56-62.

Tippett, Mark. "The Axioms Of Accounting Measurement," **ABR**, 1977-78. Vol. 8, No. 32, pp. 266-278.

Tippett, Mark. "The 'Agio' Concept Of Interest And The A Priori Foundations Of Current Operating Profit." **ABACUS**, 1980. Vol. 16, No. 1, pp. 17-37.

Tippett, Mark. (Craig, Russell and Mark Tippett. "Estimating Current Cost Depreciation Expense Using Numerical Analysis And The STAPOL Technique: A Pedagogic Exposition." **ABACUS**, 1987, Vol. 23, No. 2. pp. 141-156.)

Tische, F. F. "The Development Of Accounting In The Tent And Awning Industry," **AR**, 1926. Vol. 1, No. 1. pp. 85-89.

Tishlias, Dennis P. and Peter Chalos. "Product Pricing Behaviour Under Different Costing Systems," **ABR**, 1988, Vol. 18, No. 71, pp. 257-265.

Titard, Pierre L. "Independence And MAS - Opinions Of Financial Statement Users," **JOA**, 1971. Vol. 132, No. 1, pp. 47-52.

Titman, Sheridan and Brett Trueman. "Information Quality And The Valuation Of New Issues," **JAEC**, 1986. Vol. 8. No. 2. pp. 159-172.

Titman, Sheridan. (Trueman, Brett and Sheridan Titman. "An Explanation For Accounting Income Smoothing," **JAR**, 1988, Vol. 26, Supp., pp. 127-139.)

Toal, Desmond J. (Silvern, David H. and Desmond J. Toal. "EDP - Choosing A Partner," **MA**, 1967, Vol. 48, No. 8, pp. 57-60.)

Toan, Arthur B., Jr. "Data Processing, Accounting And Business Administration," **JOA**, 1962. Vol. 114, No. 5, pp. 43-49.

Toan, Arthur B., Jr. "The Auditor And EDP," **JOA**, 1960. Vol. 109, No. 6, pp. 42-46.

Toan, A. B., Jr. "Auditing, Control, And Electronics," **JOA**, 1955. Vol. 99, No. 5, pp. 40-45.

Toba, Yoshihide. "A General Theory Of Evidence As The Conceptual Foundation In Auditing Theory: A Reply." **AR**, 1977. Vol. 52, No. 3. pp. 756-758.

Toba, Yoshihide. "A General Theory Of Evidence As The Conceptual Foundation In Auditing Theory." **AR**, 1975, Vol. 50, No. 1, pp. 7-24.

Toba, Yoshihide. "A Semantic Meaning Analysis Of The Ultimate Proposition To Be Verified By Independent Auditors," **AR**, 1980, Vol. 55, No. 4. pp. 604-619.

Todd, John O. "Employee Stock Ownership Trusts," **CPAJ**, 1976. Vol. 46. No. 2. pp. 22-24.

Todd, John T., Paul H. Thompson and Gene Dalton. "Management Control Of Personnel," **JOA**, 1974, Vol. 137, No. 2, pp. 34-40.

Todd, Kenneth R. "Reporting Equities In Estate Accounting," **JAR**, 1966, Vol. 4, No. 2. pp. 253-259.

Todd, Kenneth R., Jr. (Allardyce, Fred A. and Kenneth R. Todd, Jr. "Budgeting And Planning Implications Of Tax Credit Carryforwards," **MA**. 1969. Vol. 50.No.7,pp.51-56.)

Todd, Rebecca. (Chow, Chee W. and Rebecca Todd. "Consulting And Internship Opportunities For Accounting Faculty Members: Their Nature And Variables Associated With Their Attainment," **AIA**, 1987, Vol. 4, pp. 111-130.)

Todderud, James C. (Coonrod, Curtis L. and James C. Todderud. "Serving The Federal Election Campaign," **JOA**, 1982, Vol. 154, No. 3, pp. 80-90.)

Todres, Harry. "Bankruptcy And Insolvency: A Look At The Provisions And Procedures Of Chapter 11," **CA**, 1983, Vol. 1, No. 4, pp. 26-31.

Toepfer, Frederick. (Cismoski, David R. and Frederick Toepfer. "How To Allocate The College Budget Objectively." **MA**, 1979. Vol. 61, No. 6, pp. 45-50.)

Togo, Dennis F. "Risk Analysis For Accounting Models Utilizing An Advanced Electronic Spreadsheet Software," **JIS**. 1988, Vol. 2, No. 2, pp. 61-72.

Tokutani, Masao. (Arrington, C. Edward, Robert E. Jensen and Masao Tokutani. "Scaling Of Corporate Multivariate Performance Criteria: Subjective Composition Versus The Analytic Hierarchy Process," **JAPP**, 1982, Vol. 1, No. 2, pp. 95-123.)

Tokutani, M. and M. Kawano. "A Note On The Japanese Social Accounting Literature," **AOS**, 1978, Vol. 3, No. 2, pp. 183-188.

Tolan, Elizabeth M. (Schiff, Jonathan B. and Elizabeth M. Tolan. "Technical Inquiry Systems For The Accounting Profession." **CA**, 1987, Vol. 5, No. 2, pp. 51-53.)

Tollefson, John O. (Sterling, Robert R., John O. Tollefson and Richard E. Flaherty. "Exchange Valuation: An Empirical Test," **AR**, 1972, Vol. 47, No. 4, pp. 709-721.)

Tolman, Russell K. (Skousen, K. Fred, Robert A. Sharp and Russell K. Tolman. "Corporate Disclosure Of Budgetary Data," **JOA**, 1972, Vol. 133, No. 5, pp. 50-57.)

Tolstyka, William. "Fee Disputes: How Can We Solve Them?," **JOA**, 1980, Vol. 150, No. 6, pp. 47-50.

Tomassini, Lawrence A. "Assessing The Impact Of Human Resource Accounting: An Experimental Study Of Managerial Decision Preferences," **AR**, 1977, Vol. 52, No. 4, pp. 904-914.

Tomassini, Lawrence A. (Beck, Paul J., Ira Solomon and Lawrence A. Tomassini. "Subjective Prior Probability Distributions And Audit Risk," **JAR**, 1985, Vol. 23, No. 1, pp. 37-56.)

Tomassini, Lawrence A. (Harrison, Walter T., Jr., Lawrence A. Tomassini and J. Richard Dietrich. "The Use Of Control Groups In Capital Market Research." **JAR**, 1983. Vol. 21, No. 1, pp. 65-77.)

Tomassini, Lawrence A. (Solomon, Ira, Lawrence A. Tomassini, Marshall B. Romney and Jack L. Krogstad. "Probability Elicitation In Auditing: Additional Evidence On The Equivalent Prior Sample Method." **AIA**, 1984. Vol. 1, pp. 267-290.)

Tomassini, L. A. "Behavioral Research On Human Resource Accounting: A Contingency Framework," **AOS**, 1976, Vol. 1, No. 2/3, pp. 239-252.

Tomassini, L. A. (Solomon, I., J. L. Krogstad, M. B. Romney, and L. A. Tomassini. "Auditors' Prior Probability Distributions For Account Balances," **AOS**, 1982, Vol. 7, No. 1, pp. 27-42.)

Tomczyk, Stephen and Sangit Chatterjee. "The Impact Of Outliers And Influential Points On The Cost Variance-Investigation Decision," **IAE**, 1986, Vol. 1, No. 2, pp. 293-301.

Tomczyk, Stephen. (Read, William J. and Stephen Tomczyk. "An Argument For Complete Financial Disclosure By Public Accounting Firms," **ACCHOR**, 1988, Vol. 2, No. 2, pp. 39-46.)

Tomkins, C. and R. Groves. "The Everyday Accountant And Researching His Reality," **AOS**, 1983, Vol. 8, No. 4, pp. 361-374.

Tomkins, C. and R. Groves. "The Everyday Accountant and Researching His Reality: Further Thoughts'," **AOS**, 1983, Vol. 8, No. 4, pp. 407-418.

Tomkins, C. R. (Briston, R. J., C. R. Tomkins and D. King. "Shareholder Behaviour In The New Issue Market; A Preliminary Report," **ABR**, 1970-71, Vol. 1, No. 3, pp. 233-241.)

Tomkins, C. (Rosenberg, D., C. Tomkins and P. Day. "A Work Role Perspective Of Accountants In Local Government Service Departments," **AOS**, 1982, Vol. 7, No. 2, pp. 123-138.)

Tomkins, C., D. Rosenberg and I. Colville. "The Social Process Of Research: Some Reflections On Developing A Multi-Disciplinary Accounting Project," **AOS**, 1980, Vol. 5, No. 2, pp. 247-262.

Tomlinson, Allen, III. "Estate Planning And Administrative Expenses," **JOA**, 1964, Vol. 118, No. 4, pp. 47-52.

Tomlinson, Allen, III. "Gift Taxes And Tenancies By The Entirety," **JOA**, 1959, Vol. 108, No. 3, pp. 44-50.

Tomlinson, Allen. "Estate Tax Credit For Prior Transfers," **JOA**, 1957, Vol. 104, No. 4, pp. 31-37.

Tomlinson, Allen. "Tears Shed Over The Tier System," **JOA**, 1958, Vol. 106, No. 1, pp. 32-40.

Tomlinson, Allen. "The Gift Tax Credit Against The Estate Tax," **JOA**, 1960, Vol. 109, No. 5, pp. 52-57.

Tomlinson, Don. (Carter, Jack and Don Tomlinson. "Extending PERT/CPM Into Computerized LOB," **MA**, 1970, Vol. 51, No. 11. pp. 41-44.)

Tomlinson, Gregory B. (Knight, Roger N. and Gregory B. Tomlinson. "The Internal Auditor And The Annual Audit," **MA**, 1976, Vol. 58, No. 6. pp. 27-28.)

Tompkins, Daniel L. "Foreign Exchange Risk," **CA**, 1986, Vol. 4, No. 3. pp. 39-42.

Tondkar, Rasoul H. and Edward N. Coffman. "Teaching Foreign Currency Translation: A Flowchart Approach," **JAED**, 1984,

Vol. 2, No. 2, pp. 145-151.

Tondkar, Rasoul H. (Bishop, Ashton C. and Rasoul H. Tondkar. "Development Of A Professional Code Of Ethics," **JOA**, 1987, Vol. 163. No. 5, pp. 97-101.)

Tondkar, Rasoul H. (Lebow, Marc I. and Rasoul H. Tondkar. "Accounting In The Soviet Union," **IJAER**, 1986, Vol. 22, No. 1, pp. 61-79.)

Tonkin, G. W. (Derscheid, Vincent K., Raymond Telling and G. W. Tonkin. "Nontax Benefits Of The Incorporation Of A Practice," **JOA**, 1977, Vol. 143. No. 1. pp. 70-76.)

Toole, Howard R. (Chow, Chee W., Howard R. Toole and Adrian Wong-Boren. "Make Better Decisions: Divide And Conquer," **MA**. 1986, Vol. 68, No. 2, pp. 41-45.)

Toole, Howard R. (Lembke, Valdean C. and Howard R. Toole. "Differences In Depreciation Methods And The Analysis Of Supplemental Current-Cost And Replacement Cost Data," **JAAF**, 1981, Vol. 4, No. 2. pp. 128-135.)

Toole, Howard R. (Loy, L. David and Howard R. Toole. "Accounting For Discounted Convertible Bond Exchanges: A Survey Of Results," **JAAF**, 1980, Vol. 3, No. 3, pp. 227-243.)

Toolson, Richard B. "The Charitable Contribution Deduction: New Evidence Of A Strong Incentive Effect," **AIT**, 1988, Vol. 2, pp. xx-xx.

Topiol, Jack. "Accounting For Public Health Nursing Associations," **AR**, 1966, Vol. 41. No. 1. pp. 83-91.

Toppel, Heidi J. "Changes TRA '86 Makes In Executive Compensation," **CA**, 1987, Vol. 5. No. 3, pp. 20-25.

Tosh, David E. and Joseph C. Rue. "The Effects Of Unconsolidated Finance Subsidiary Debt On Market Estimates Of Systematic Risk," **JAL**, 1988, Vol. 7. pp. 157-173.

Tosh, David E. (Rue. Joseph C. and David E. Tosh. "Should We Consolidate Finance Subsidiaries?," **MA**, 1987. Vol. 68, No. 10, pp. 45-50.)

Tosh, David E. (Rue. Joseph C. and David E. Tosh. "Continuing Unresolved Issues Of Pension Accounting," **ACCHOR**, 1987, Vol. 1, No. 4, pp. 21-28.)

Tosh, David E. (Rue. Joseph C.. David E. Tosh and William B. Francis. "Accounting For Interest Rate Swaps," **MA**. 1988, Vol. 70, No. 1. pp. 43-49.)

Toussaint, Jack R. "The Problem With Hospital Accounting," **MA**, 1970. Vol. 52, No. 5. pp. 37-40.

Towles, Martin F. and Karl H. Silex. "Dollar-Value LIFO And Its Effect On Profits," **MA**. 1975. Vol. 57, No. 1, pp. 27-29.

Towles, Martin F. "Leases And The Relevant APB Opinions," **MA**, 1974, Vol. 55, No. 11. pp. 37-41.

Townsend, Lynn A. "A Career In Business Accounting." **AR**. 1967, Vol. 42. No. 1. pp. 1-6.

Townsend, Pamela G. "Tax Accounting In An Era Of Tax Reform," **MA**. 1987. Vol. 68. No. 9. pp. 26-31.

Townsend, Richard L. (Krueger. Charles A. and Richard L. Townsend. "The Controller's Role In Controlling Construction Costs," **MA**, 1988. Vol. 70. No. 6. pp. 38-42.)

Toy, Daniel R. (Milliron. Valerie C. and Daniel R. Toy. "Tax Compliance: An Investigation Of Key Features," **JATA**. 1988. Vol. 9, No. 2, pp. 84-104.)

Toy, James H. "Banking Relations And Short-Term Cash Management," **MA**. 1976. Vol. 58. No. 2. pp. 24-28.

Toy, James H. "Controlling Sales Goods Inventory," **MA**, 1972, Vol. 54, No. 3, pp. 48-51.

Toy, James H. "Responsibility Accounting: A Practical Application," **MA**, 1978. Vol. 59. No. 7. pp. 23-26.

Tracy, John A. "A Dissent To The General Price-Level Adjustment Proposal," **AR**. 1965. Vol. 40. No. 1. pp. 163-175.

Tracy, John A. "Accounting For Mutual Funds," **JOA**. 1963, Vol. 116, No. 3. pp. 50-57.

Tracy, John A. "Bayesian Statistical Confidence Intervals For Auditors," **JOA**. 1969, Vol. 128. No. 1. pp. 41-47.

Tracy, John A. "Bayesian Statistical Methods In Auditing." **AR**. 1969, Vol. 44. No. 1. pp. 90-98.

Tracy, John A. (Buchman. Thomas A. and John A. Tracy. "Obtaining Responses To Sensitive Questions: Conventional Questionnaire Versus Randomized Response Technique," **JAR**. 1982. Vol. 20. No. 1. pp. 263-271.)

Tracy, John A. (Monson. Norman P. and John A. Tracy. "Stock Rights And Accounting Wrongs." **AR**. 1964. Vol. 39. No. 4. pp. 890-893.)

Trader, Ramona L. and H. Fenwick Huss. "An Investigation Of The Possible Effects Of Nonsampling Error On Inference In Auditing: A Bayesian Analysis." **CAR**. 1987-88. Vol. 4, No. 1. pp. 227-239.

Trader, Ramona L. (Huss. H. Fenwick and Ramona L. Trader. "A Note On Optimal Sample Sizes In Compliance Tests Using A Formal Bayesian Decision Theoretic Approach For Finite And Infinite Populations," **JAR**. 1986. Vol. 24. No. 2. pp. 394-399.)

Traeger, Frank H. "Plant Accounting In The Apparel Industry," **MA**. 1966. Vol. 47. No. 8. pp. 43-50.

Trantanella, Charles J., Jr. "Group Dynamics," **MA**. 1972. Vol. 54, No. 5. pp. 25-28.

Trapani, Cosmo S. "Six Critical Areas In The Budgeting Process," **MA**. 1982. Vol. 64. No. 5. pp. 52-56.

Trapnell, Jerry E. (Glahn. Gerald L.. Kent T. Fields and Jerry E. Trapnell. "How To Evaluate Mixed Risk Capital Projects," **MA**. 1980. Vol. 62. No. 6. pp. 34-38.)

Trapnell, Jerry E. (Sami. Heibatollah and Jerry E. Trapnell. "Inflation-Adjusted Data And Security Prices: Some Empirical Evidence," **AIA**. 1987. Vol. 5. pp. 39-58.)

Trapnell, Jerry E. (Welsh. Mary Jeanne and Jerry E. Trapnell. "Labor Market Models And Employer Accounting For Pensions," **JAAF**. 1985. Vol. 8. No. 2. pp. 100-111.)

Traub, Jack. "Income Taxation Of Trusts," **CPAJ**. 1982. Vol.

Traub, Jack. "Regular Corporation Or Subchapter S Status," **CPAJ**. 1984. Vol. 54. No. 2. pp. 23-29.

Traub, Jack. "Subchapter S Corporations - The 1982 Law," **CPAJ**. 1983. Vol. 53. No. 7. pp. 24-29.

Travis, Arden L. (Burnet. Mary E. and Arden L. Travis. "A Cooperative Education Program In Public Accounting," **AR**. 1964. Vol. 39. No. 2. pp. 460-463.)

Travlos, Nickolaos G. (Tehranian, Hassan, Nickolaos G. Travlos and James F. Waegelein. "Management Compensation Contracts And Merger-Induced Abnormal Returns," **JAR**. 1987. Vol. 25. Supp.. pp. 51-76.)

Traxler, Arthur E. (Jacobs, Robert and Arthur E. Traxler. "What Manner Of Man Is The Average Accountant?," **JOA**. 1954. Vol. 97, No. 4. pp. 465-469.)

Traxler, Arthur E. (Kane. Robert L., Jr. and Arthur E. Traxler. "Predicting CPA Examination Results," **AR**. 1954. Vol. 29. No. 4. pp. 564-570.)

Traxler, Arthur E. (Wood. Ben D.. Arthur E. Traxler and Warren W. Nissley. "College Accounting Testing Program," **AR**. 1948. Vol. 23, No. 1. pp. 63-83.)

Treacy, John E. "For Direct Costing In The Steel Industry," **MA**. 1977. Vol. 58. No. 12. pp. 44-46.

Treadway. James C. "The National Commission On Fraudulent Financial Reporting: An Update," **MA**. 1986. Vol. 68. No. 3. pp. 24-27.

Treadway, James C., Jr., Jack L. Krogstad and Shirley A. Sunderland. "Financial Reporting And Public Confidence," **CA**. 1986. Vol. 4. No. 4. pp. 4-8.

Treffers, Henk C. "The Changing Nature Of The European Accounting Profession," **IJAER**. 1967, Vol. 3, No. 1. pp. 43-54.

Treiger, David L. (Newman, Barry and David L. Treiger. "Michelin And State Taxation Of Imports," **CPAJ**, 1976. Vol. 46. No. 7. pp. 33-36.)

Treloar, D. W. G. (Mauldon. R. G., Henry P. Schapper and D. W. G. Treloar. "A Managerial Accounting System For Australian Agriculture," **ABACUS**, 1968. Vol. 4, No. 1. pp. 39-50.)

Tremblay, Doria. (Holzer. H. Peter and Doria Tremblay. "Accounting And Economic Development: The Cases Of Thailand And Tunisia," **IJAER**. 1973, Vol. 9, No. 1. pp. 67-80.)

Trenholm, B. A. (Ritchie. P. C.. J. E. Rowcroft and B. A. Trenholm. "An Analytical Basis For The Treatment Of Corporate Income Tax," **AH**. 1988, Vol. 2, No. 4. pp. 29-40.)

Trentin. H. George and Monroe S. Kuttner. "The MAS Body Of Knowledge Study," **CPAJ**. 1976, Vol. 46. No. 8. pp. 15-22.

Trentin. H. G. "Sampling In Auditing - A Case Study," **JOA**. 1968. Vol. 125. No. 3. pp. 39-43.

Tress, R. B. (Coombes. R. J. and R. B. Tress. "The Financial Implications Of Corporate Share Reacquisitions," **ABACUS**, 1977. Vol. 13. No. 1. pp. 40-51.)

Trewin, Janet. "The Need And Opportunity For Field-Based Research In Accounting Information Systems," **JIS**, 1988. Vol. 3. No. 1. pp. 104-118.

Tricker, R. I. "Research In Accounting - Purpose, Process And Potential," **ABR** 1979-80. Vol. 10, No. 37, pp. 3-16.

Trienens, Howard J. "Legal Aspects Of Fair Value Accounting," **CPAJ**. 1973. Vol. 43, No. 5. pp. 369-374.

Trieschmann, James S. and E. J. Leverett. Jr. "What A CPA Needs To Know About General Liability Insurance," **CPAJ**. 1975. Vol. 45, No. 8. pp. 34-37.

Tripp, Thomas W. and Leonard A. Robinson. "The How And Why Of The Acquisition Decision," **MA**. 1983. Vol. 65. No. 1. pp. 48-53.

Tritschler, Charles A. "A Sociological Perspective On Accounting Innovation," **IJAER**. 1970, Vol. 5, No. 2, pp. 39-67.

Tritschler, Charles A. "Dilution And Counter-Dilution In Reporting For Deferred Equity," **ABR**. 1970-71. Vol. 1, No. 4. pp. 274-283.

Tritschler, Charles A. "Statistical Criteria For Asset Valuation By Specific Price Index," **AR**. 1969, Vol. 44, No. 1. pp. 99-123.

Troberg, Pontus. "Foreign Currency Translation: A Comparative Analysis Of Approaches," **AIIA**. 1987, Vol. 1, pp. 317-356.

Troester, J. Richard. "A Hobby - Or A Tax Shelter?," **MA**. 1974. Vol. 56, No. 5. pp. 31-32.

Troll, Stephan V. "Small Business Needs More Cost Accounting Information If It Is To Be Intelligently Run," **JOA**. 1950. Vol. 89, No. 1. pp. 39-41.

Trompeter, Gregory M. (Farmer, Timothy A., Larry E. Rittenberg and Gregory M. Trompeter. "An Investigation Of The Impact Of Economic And Organizational Factors On Auditor Independence," **AJPT**. 1987-88, Vol. 7, No. 1, pp. 1-14.)

Trone, Thomas N. (Chandler, John S. and Thomas N. Trone. "Bottom-Up' Budgeting And Control," **MA**. 1982. Vol. 63. No. 8. pp. 37-40.)

Trone, Thomas. (Chandler. John S.. Thomas Trone and Michael Weiland. "Decision Support Systems Are For Small Businesses," **MA**, 1983, Vol. 64, No. 10, pp. 34-39.)

Trotman, Ken T. and Ian R. Zimmer. "Revenue Recognition In The Construction Industry: An Experimental Study," **ABACUS**. 1986, Vol. 22, No. 2, pp. 136-147.

Trotman, Ken T. and Philip W. Yetton. "The Effect Of The Review Process On Auditor Judgments," **JAR**. 1985, Vol. 23. No. 1. pp. 256-267.

Trotman, Ken T. "The Review Process And The Accuracy Of Auditor Judgments," **JAR**. 1985, Vol. 23, No. 2, pp. 740-752.

Trotman, Ken T. (Campisi, Sam and Ken T. Trotman. "Auditor Consensus In Going Concern Judgments," **ABR**, 1984-85,

Vol. 15, No. 60, pp. 303-310.)

Trotman, Ken T., Philip W. Yetton and Ian R. Zimmer. "Individual And Group Judgments Of Internal Control Systems," **JAR**, 1983, Vol. 21, No. 1, pp. 286-292.

Trotman, K. T. and G. W. Bradley. "Associations Between Social Responsibility Disclosure And Characteristics Of Companies," **AOS**, 1981, Vol. 6, No. 4, pp. 355-362.

Trotman, K. T. "An Evaluation Of Accounting For Construction Contracts: An International Comparison," **IJAER**, 1982, Vol. 17. No. 2, pp. 151-166.

Trotta, Linda. (Katz, Adam M., Kevin O'Toole and Linda Trotta. "TRA-1986 And The Hotel/Restaurant Industry," **CPAJ**, 1987, Vol. 57, No. 7, pp. 46-51.)

Trowell, J. R. "Fixed Asset Prices And Economic Production Theory: Comment," **ABACUS**, 1981. Vol. 17, No. 1, pp. 8-12.

Troxel, Richard B. "Profit Analysis In The Grain Merchandising Industry," **MA**, 1968. Vol. 50, No. 4, pp. 30-32.

Troy, M. Frank. "Value Added By Manufacture." **MA**, 1970, Vol. 52, No. 4, pp. 51-54.

Trueblood, Robert M. and Robert J. Monteverde. "A Bibliography On The Application Of Statistical Methods To Accounting And Auditing," **AR**, 1954, Vol. 29, No. 2, pp. 251-254.

Trueblood, Robert M. and R. M. Cyert. "Statistical Sampling Applied To Aging Of Accounts Receivable," **JOA**, 1954, Vol. 97, No. 3, pp. 293-298.

Trueblood, Robert M. and W. W. Cooper. "Research And Practice In Statistical Applications To Accounting, Auditing, And Management Control," **AR**, 1955, Vol. 30, No. 2, pp. 221-229.

Trueblood, Robert M. "Accounting And New Management Attitudes," **JOA**, 1958, Vol. 106, No. 4, pp. 37-42.

Trueblood, Robert M. "Education For A Changing Profession." **JAR**, 1963, Vol. 1, No. 1, pp. 86-95.

Trueblood, Robert M. "Operations Research - A Challenge To Accounting," **JOA**, 1960, Vol. 109, No. 5, pp. 47-51.

Trueblood, Robert M. "Professional And Technical Practitioners In Accounting," **JOA**, 1960. Vol. 110, No. 3. pp. 57-62.

Trueblood, Robert M. "Rising Expectations." **JOA**, 1970, Vol. 130, No. 6, pp. 35-38.

Trueblood, Robert M. "Statistical Sampling," **JOA**, 1957, Vol. 103, No. 4, pp. 48-52.

Trueblood, Robert M. "The Management Service Function In Public Accounting," **JOA**, 1961, Vol. 112, No. 1, pp. 37-44.

Trueblood, Robert M. (Davidson, H. Justin and Robert M. Trueblood. "Accounting For Decision-Making." **AR**, 1961, Vol. 36, No. 4, pp. 577-582.)

Trueblood, Robert M. (David. Irwin T. and Robert M. Trueblood. "The Report Of The President's Commission On Budget Concepts," **JOA**, 1968, Vol. 125, No. 1, pp. 25-36.)

Trueblood, Robert. "Accounting Principles: The Board And Its Problems," **JAR**, 1966, Vol. 4. Supp., pp. 183-191.

Trueger, Paul M. "Contract Termination And Unabsorbed Overhead," **MA**, 1973, Vol. 54, No. 8, pp. 38-40.

Trueger, Paul M. "Contractor's Weighted Average Share In Cost Risk (CWAS)," **JOA**, 1967, Vol. 123, No. 5, pp. 47-55.

Trueger, Paul M. "Cost Or Pricing Data Under PL 87-653," **JOA**, 1968, Vol. 125, No. 5, pp. 47-54.

Trueger, Paul M. "Defense Contract Profits - Weighted Guidelines Method," **JOA**, 1965, Vol. 119, No. 2, pp. 45-50.

Trueger, Paul M. "Profit Guidelines On Defense Contracts." **JOA**, 1964, Vol. 117, No. 1, pp. 44-48.

Trueger, Paul M. "Renegotiation Is Not Negotiation." **JOA**, 1971, Vol. 131, No. 4, pp. 47-52.

Trueger, Paul M. "Renegotiation Is Here To Stay." **JOA**, 1955, Vol. 100, No. 1, pp. 30-35.

Trueger, Paul M. "Terminations - Cost Principles And Costing Procedures," **JOA**, 1970, Vol. 129, No. 6, pp. 59-64.

Trueger, Paul M. "Truth In Defense Contract Pricing (PL 87-653)," **MA**, 1969, Vol. 50, No. 8, pp. 52-54.

Trueger, P. M. "How To Get Price Redetermination On Government Contracts," **JOA**, 1952, Vol. 94, No. 4, pp. 442-447.

Trueman, Brett and Sheridan Titman. "An Explanation For Accounting Income Smoothing," **JAR**, 1988, Vol. 26. Supp., pp. 127-139.

Trueman, Brett. "Why Do Managers Voluntarily Release Earnings Forecasts?," **JAEC**, 1986. Vol. 8, No. 1, pp. 53-71.

Trueman, Brett. (Titman, Sheridan and Brett Trueman. "Information Quality And The Valuation Of New Issues," **JAEC**, 1986, Vol. 8. No. 2, pp. 159-172.)

Trueman, J. W. H. "Oil Company Accounts: Not So Comparable," **ABR**, 1974-75, Vol. 5. No. 18, pp. 127-132.

Truitt, Jack F. and Thomas R. Nunamaker. "Self-Insurance Should Be Accrued," **MA**, 1987, Vol. 68. No. 9, pp. 62-65.

Truitt, Jack F. "Capital Rationing: An Annualized Approach," **JCA**, 1988, Vol. 5. No. 1, pp. 63-75.

Truitt, Jack, Albert Frakes and John Fertakis. "A Survey Of The Cost/Managerial Sequence In AACSB Schools," **JAED**, 1983, Vol. 1, No. 1, pp. 131-135.

Truitt, Jack. "The Financial Theory Of The Firm: Capital Budgeting And Divisional Evaluation," **JCA**, 1986, Vol. 3, No. 1, pp. 25-31.

Trumbull, Wendell P. "Case Study In Writing Off Intangibles," **AR**, 1956, Vol. 31, No. 4, pp. 599-607.

Trumbull, Wendell P. "Differences Between Financial And Tax Depreciation," **AR**, 1968, Vol. 43, No. 3, pp. 459-468.

Trumbull, Wendell P. "Disclosure As A Standard Of Income Reporting," **AR**, 1953, Vol. 28, No. 4, pp. 471-481.

Trumbull, Wendell P. "Price-Level Depreciation And Replacement Cost," **AR**, 1958, Vol. 33, No. 1, pp. 26-34.

Trumbull, Wendell P. "Tax Allocation In Managerial Analysis." **JOA**, 1960, Vol. 110, No. 5, pp. 53-57.

Trumbull, Wendell P. "The All-Inclusive Standard," **AR**, 1952, Vol. 27, No. 1, pp. 3-14.

Trumbull, Wendell P. "When Is A Liability?," **AR**, 1963, Vol. 38. No. 1, pp. 46-51.

Tryfos, Peter. (Chan, K. Hung and Peter Tryfos. "Audit Sampling From Skewed Populations And Small Samples," **ABR**, 1983-84, Vol. 14. No. 56, pp. 311-318.)

Tsaklanganos, Angelos A. "Peers, Persuasion, And Horizontal Management," **MA**, 1978. Vol. 60, No. 2, pp. 33-37.

Tsay, Jeffrey J. "Human Resource Accounting: A Need For Relevance," **MA**, 1977, Vol. 58, No. 9, pp. 33-37.

Tsay, Jeffrey J. (Nichols, Donald R. and Jeffrey J. Tsay. "Security Price Reactions To Long-Range Executive Earnings Forecasts," **JAR**, 1979, Vol. 17, No. 1, pp. 140-155.)

Tsay, Jeffrey J. (Nichols, Donald R., Jeffrey J. Tsay and Paula D. Larkin. "Investor Trading Responses To Differing Characteristics Of Voluntarily Disclosed Earnings Forecasts," **AR**, 1979, Vol. 54, No. 2, pp. 376-382.)

Tschirhart, John T. (Hamlen, Susan S., William A. Hamlen, Jr. and John T. Tschirhart. "The Use Of Core Theory In Evaluating Joint Cost Allocation Schemes," **AR**, 1977, Vol. 52, No. 3, pp. 616-627.)

Tschirhart, John. (Hamlen, Susan S., William A. Hamlen, Jr. and John Tschirhart. "The Use Of The Generalized Shapley Allocation In Joint Cost Allocation," **AR**, 1980, Vol. 55. No. 2, pp. 269-287.)

Tse, Paul S. "Evaluating Performance In Multinationals," **MA**, 1979, Vol. 60, No. 12, pp. 21-25.

Tse, Senyo. "Intra-Year Trends In The Degree Of Association Between Accounting Numbers And Security Prices," **AR**, 1986, Vol. 61, No. 3, pp. 475-497.

Tse, Senyo. (Atiase, Rowland K. and Senyo Tse. "Stock Valuation Models And Accounting Information: A Review And Synthesis," **JAL**, 1986, Vol. 5, pp. 1-34.)

Tseng, M. S. (Smith, G. Stevenson and M. S. Tseng. "Benefit-Cost Analysis As A Performance Indicator," **MA**, 1986, Vol. 67, No. 12, pp. 44-49.)

Tsui, A. S. (Flamholtz, E. G., T. K. Das and A. S. Tsui. "Toward An Integrative Framework Of Organizational Control," **AOS**, 1985, Vol. 10, No. 1, pp. 35-50.)

Tsui, Kam-Wah, Ella Mae Matsumura and Kwok-Leung Tsui. "Multinomial-Dirichlet Bounds For Dollar-Unit Sampling In Auditing," **AR**, 1985, Vol. 60, No. 1, pp. 76-96.

Tsui, Kam-Wah. (Matsumura, Ella Mae and Kam-Wah Tsui. "Stein-Type Poisson Estimators In Audit Sampling," **JAR**, 1982, Vol. 20, No. 1, pp. 162-170.)

Tsui, Kwok-Leung. (Tsui, Kam-Wah, Ella Mae Matsumura and Kwok-Leung Tsui. "Multinomial-Dirichlet Bounds For Dollar-Unit Sampling In Auditing," **AR**, 1985, Vol. 60, No. 1, pp. 76-96.)

Tsui, Winston W. "Inflation Accounting And Foreign Currency Translation," **MA**, 1979, Vol. 61, No. 3, pp. 23-31.

Tuckerman, Bert. "Objective Consolidation Standards For Foreign Subsidiaries," **AR**, 1964, Vol. 39, No. 1, pp. 32-37.

Tuckerman, Bert. "Reporting Foreign Dividends," **MA**, 1965, Vol. 47. No. 3, pp. 51-55.

Tuckerman, Bert. "Reporting The Results Of Foreign Currency Fluctuation," **MA**, 1968, Vol. 49, No. 8, pp. 21-27.

Tucker, James J., III. "Government Oversight In 1917: The Shape Of Things To Come," **JOA**, 1987, Vol. 163, No. 5, pp. 73-77.

Tucker, James J., III. "The Economic Activity Of A Grain Mill Located In Bald Eagle Valley, Pennsylvania 1868 To 1872," **AHJ**, 1983, Vol. 10, No. 1, pp. 117-117.

Tucker, James J., III. "The Role Of Stock Dividends In Defining Income, Developing Capital Market Research And Exploring The Economic Consequences Of Accounting Policy Decisions," **AHJ**, 1985, Vol. 12, No. 2, pp. 73-94.

Tucker, John M. (Rose, Edward M. and John M. Tucker. "The CPA And The Media," **CPAJ**, 1985, Vol. 55, No. 3, pp. 11-17.)

Tucker, Joseph J. "Bookkeeping System Built Around Typewriter," **JOA**, 1954, Vol. 97, No. 2, pp. 188-194.

Tucker, Marvin W. "A Model For Accounting Flexibility," **AR**, 1971, Vol. 46, No. 4, pp. 801-802.

Tucker, Michael J. and Herbert F. Floyd. "Recent Cases Of Reallocation Of Income By IRS," **CPAJ**, 1987, Vol. 57, No. 12, pp. 62-67.

Tucker, Michael J. and Larry M. Parker. "Losses On Nonrecourse Loans - Tax Shelters," **CPAJ**, 1984, Vol. 54, No. 1, pp. 32-38.

Tucker, Michael J. (Horvitz, Jerome S. and Michael J. Tucker. "Clinical Practice Problems In Tax Education," **AR**, 1980, Vol. 55, No. 4, pp. 672-679.)

Tucker, Michael J. (Hutton, Clifford E., Barbara Stoops and Michael J. Tucker. "Losses Caused By Drought," **CPAJ**, 1984, Vol. 54, No. 3, pp. 40-49.)

Tucker, Michael J. (Parker, Larry M., John C. Corless and Michael J. Tucker. "Audit Firm Size And Internal Control Assessment: An Experiment," **RIAR**, 1988, Vol. 2, pp. 155-166.)

Tuggle, F. D. (Gordon, L. A., D. F. Larcker and F. D. Tuggle. "Strategic Decision Processes And The Design Of Accounting Information Systems: Conceptual Linkages," **AOS**, 1978, Vol. 3, No. 3/4, pp. 203-214.)

Tummins, Marvin and Hugh J. Watson. "Advantages Of Regression Analysis Over Ratio Analysis," **CPAJ**, 1975, Vol. 45, No. 5, pp. 35-38.

Tummins, Marvin and Percy Yeargan. "A Useful Worksheet For

Preparing Audit Applications Of Regression Analysis," **AR**, 1974, Vol. 49, No. 2, pp. 391-394.

Tummins, Marvin and Robert H. Strawser. "A Confidence Limits Table For Attribute Analysis," **AR**, 1976, Vol. 51, No. 4, pp. 907-912.

Tummins, Marvin. "Test-Checking And The Poisson Distribution," **AR**, 1954, Vol. 29, No. 4, pp. 605-613.

Tupy, L. T. "Purposes And Methods Of Accounting Instruction," **AR**, 1927, Vol. 2, No. 1, pp. 43-54.

Turk, Ivan. "Analysis Of Efficiency By Means Of Interrelated Indicators: A Yugoslav Approach," **IJAER**, 1982, Vol. 17, No. 2, pp. 89-102.

Turk, Ivan. "Recent Professional Statements Of Accounting Principles And Ethics In Yugoslavia," **IJAER**, 1976, Vol. 12, No. 1, pp. 111-120.

Turley, Stuart. (Moizer, Peter and Stuart Turley. "Surrogates For Audit Fees In Concentration Studies," **AJPT**, 1987-88, Vol. 7, No. 1, pp. 118-123.)

Turley, Stuart. (Moizer, Peter, Stuart Turley and David Walker. "Reliance On Other Auditors: A UK Study," **ABR**, 1985-86, Vol. 16, No. 64, pp. 343-352.)

Turley, Stuart. (Taylor, Peter and Stuart Turley. "The Views Of Management On Accounting For Leases," **ABR**, 1985-86, Vol. 16, No. 61, pp. 59-68.)

Turley, W. S. "International Harmonization Of Accounting: The Contribution Of The EEC Fourth Directive On Company Law," **IJAER**, 1983, Vol. 18, No. 2, pp. 13-27.

Turnbull, Shann. "Time-Limited Corporations," **ABACUS**, 1973, Vol. 9, No. 1, pp. 28-43.

Turnburke, H. M. "Accountancy - A Profession," **AR**, 1946, Vol. 21, No. 1, pp. 47-50.

Turnburke, H. M. "Accountancy: A Profession For Educated Men," **AR**, 1939, Vol. 14, No. 3, pp. 250-257.

Turner, Clifford L. "Significant Differences Between U.S. and Canadian Requirements For The C.P.A. And C.A. Certificates," **AR**, 1960, Vol. 35, No. 2, pp. 282-287.

Turner, Deborah H. (Hermanson, Roger H., Linda M. Dykes and Deborah H. Turner. "Enforced Competition In The Accounting Profession - Does It Make Sense?," **ACCHOR**, 1987, Vol. 1, No. 4, pp. 13-20.)

Turner, Jerry L. and Theodore J. Mock. "Economic Considerations In Designing Audit Programs," **JOA**, 1980, Vol. 149, No. 3, pp. 65-74.

Turner, Joanne H. and Daniel L. Jensen. "Recent Episodes In The 'Oversight Cycle' Of Accountancy Self-Regulation," **RIAR**, 1987, Vol. 1, pp. 35-50.

Turner, Joanne H. (Mutchler, Jane F., Joanne H. Turner and David D. Williams. "The Performance Of Female Versus Male Accounting Students," **IAE**, 1987, Vol. 2, No. 1, pp. 103-111.)

Turner, John N. "International Harmonization: A Professional Goal," **JOA**, 183, Vol. 155, No. 1, pp. 58-67.

Turner, Mark A. and Kenneth R. Lambert. "Why The Furor Over UBIT," **JOA**, 1988, Vol. 165, No. 5, pp. 78-84.

Turner, Martha J. (Hilton, Ronald W., Robert J. Swieringa and Martha J. Turner. "Product Pricing, Accounting Costs And Use Of Product-Costing Systems," **AR**, 1988, Vol. 63, No. 2, pp. 195-218.)

Turopolec, L. (Birnberg, J. G., L. Turopolec and S. M. Young. "The Organizational Context Of Accounting," **AOS**, 1983, Vol. 8, No. 2/3, pp. 111-130.)

Tussing, Robert T. and Glenn L. Helms. "Training Computer Audit Specialists," **JOA**, 1980, Vol. 150, No. 1, pp. 71-74.

Tuthill, William C. (Hartgraves, Al L. and William C. Tuthill. "How Cash Flow Reporting Should Be Changed," **MA**, 1986, Vol. 67, No. 10, pp. 41-45.)

Twark, Richard D. (Basi, Bart A., Kenneth J. Carey and Richard D. Twark. "A Comparison Of The Accuracy Of Corporate And Security Analysts' Forecasts Of Earnings: A Reply," **AR**, 1977, Vol. 52, No. 3, pp. 741-745.)

Twark, Richard D. (Basi, Bart A., Kenneth J. Carey and Richard D. Twark. "A Comparison Of The Accuracy Of Corporate And Security Analysts' Forecasts Of Earnings," **AR**, 1976, Vol. 51, No. 2, pp. 244-254.)

Twark, Richard D. (Kratchman, Stanley H., Robert E. Malcom and Richard D. Twark. "An Intra-Industry Comparison Of Alternative Income Concepts And Relative Performance Evaluations," **AR**, 1974, Vol. 49, No. 4, pp. 682-689.)

Twark, Richard D. (Kratchman, Stanley H., Robert E. Malcom and Richard D. Twark. "The Comparison Of Alternative Income Concepts: A Reply," **AR**, 1975, Vol. 50, No. 4, pp. 865-868.)

Twark, Richard D. (Kratchman, Stanley H., Robert E. Malcom and Richard D. Twark. "Alternative Income Concepts And Relative Performance Evaluations: A Reply," **AR**, 1976, Vol. 51, No. 2, pp. 421-426.)

Tweedie, D. P. "Cash Flows And Realisable Values: The Intuitive Accounting Concepts? An Empirical Test," **ABR**, 1977-78, Vol. 8, No. 29, pp. 2-13.

Tweedie, D. P. (Lee, T. A. and D. P. Tweedie. "Accounting Information: An Investigation Of Private Shareholders Understanding," **ABR**, 1975-76, Vol. 6, No. 21, pp. 3-17.)

Tweedie, D. P. (Lee, T. A. and D. P. Tweedie. "Accounting Information: An Investigation Of Private Shareholder Usage," **ABR**, 1974-75, Vol. 5, No. 20, pp. 280-291.)

Tweedie, D. (Lee, T. A. and D. Tweedie. "The Private Shareholder: His Sources Of Financial Information And His Understanding Of Reporting Practices," **ABR**, 1975-76, Vol. 6, No. 24, pp. 304-314.)

Twombly, John R. (Eggleton, Ian R. C., Stephen H. Penman and John R. Twombly. "Accounting Changes And Stock Prices: An Examination Of Selected Uncontrolled Variables," **JAR**, 1976, Vol. 14, No. 1, pp. 66-88.)

Twombly, John R. (Schipper, Katherine, John R. Twombly and

Roman L. Weil. "Financial Lease Evaluation Under Conditions Of Uncertainty: A Comment," **AR**, 1974, Vol. 49, No. 4, pp. 796-801.)

Tyndall, Gene R. (Busher, John R. and Gene R. Tyndall. "Logistics Excellence," **MA**, 1987, Vol. 69, No. 2, pp. 32-39.)

Tyra, Anita I. "Financial Disclosure Patterns In Four European Countries," **IJAER**, 1970, Vol. 5, No. 2, pp. 89-101.

Tyran, Michael R. "A Computerized Decision-Simulator Model," **MA**, 1971, Vol. 52, No. 9, pp. 19-26.

Tyran, Michael R. "A Financial Projection Plan," **MA**, 1973, Vol. 55, No. 1, pp. 19-24.

Tyran, Michael R. "Computerized Financial Data Banks: Transition From Conceptual Design To Reality," **MA**, 1968, Vol. 50, No. 1, pp. 36-43.

Tyran, Michael R. "Computerized Communication And Control Of Backlog Commitments: The 'Lifeblood' Of An Organization's Survival," **MA**, 1969, Vol. 51, No. 5, pp. 23-30.

Tyran, Michael R. "Computerized Cost Accumulation - A Must For Management's Effectiveness," **MA**, 1970, Vol. 51, No. 12, pp. 27-33.

Tyran, Michael R. "Management Information Technology In The Space Age," **MA**, 1967, Vol. 48, No. 8, pp. 3-13.

Tyran, Michael R. "Mechanical Verification Of Accounting Data Input," **MA**, 1966, Vol. 47, No. 6, pp. 36-48.

Tyran, Michael R. "Simulator Model Applications," **MA**, 1972, Vol. 54, No. 4, pp. 13-18.

Tyran, Michael R. "STARFIRE - An Advanced Financial Information System," **MA**, 1966, Vol. 47, No. 9, pp. 3-16.

Tyson, Thomas and Arjan T. Sadhwani. "Bar Codes Speed Factory Floor Reporting," **MA**, 1988, Vol. 69, No. 10, pp. 41-46.

Tyson, Thomas N. and Fred A. Jacobs. "Segment Reporting In The Banking Industry: Does It Meet The Criteria Of The Conceptual Framework?," **ACCHOR**, 1987, Vol. 1, No. 4, pp. 35-42.

Tyson, Thomas N. "A Government Cost Control Program For Private Industry," **MA**, 1988, Vol. 70, No. 1, pp. 55-58.

Tyson, Thomas N. "Energize Your Accounting Class With A Simulation That's Fun For Students," **JAED**, 1986, Vol. 4, No. 2, pp. 117-122.

Tyson, Thomas N. "Quality & Profitability: Have Controllers Made The Connection?," **MA**, 1987, Vol. 69, No.5,pp.38-41.

Tyson, Thomas. "The Nature And Function Of Cost Keeping In A Late Nineteenth Century Small Business," **AHJ**, 1988, Vol. 15, No. 1, pp. 29-44.

Tyson, William C. "Real Estate Tax Shelters - TRA 1986," **CPAJ**, 1987, Vol. 57, No. 1, pp. 56-63.

Tzur, Joseph. (Halperin, Robert and Joseph Tzur. "Monetary Compensation And Nontaxable Employee Benefits: An Analytical Perspective," **AR**, 1985, Vol. 60, No. 4, pp. 670-680.)

UUU

Uecker, Wilfred C. "A Behavioral Study Of Information System Choice," **JAR**, 1978, Vol. 16, No. 1, pp. 169-189.

Uecker, Wilfred C. "Behavioral Accounting Research As A Source For Experiential Teaching Aids: An Example," **AR**, 1981, Vol. 56, No. 2, pp. 366-382.

Uecker, Wilfred C. "The Effects Of Knowledge Of The User's Decision Model In Simplified Information Evaluation," **JAR**, 1980, Vol. 18, No. 1, pp. 191-213.

Uecker, Wilfred C. "The Quality Of Group Performance In Simplified Information Evaluation," **JAR**, 1982, Vol. 20, No. 2, Part I, pp. 388-402.

Uecker, Wilfred C. (DeJong, Douglas V., Robert Forsythe, Russell J. Lundholm and Wilfred C. Uecker. "A Laboratory Investigation Of The Moral Hazard Problem In An Agency Relationship," **JAR**, 1985, Vol. 23, Supp., pp. 81-120.)

Uecker, Wilfred C. (DeJong, Douglas V., Robert Forsythe and Wilfred C. Uecker. "The Methodology Of Laboratory Markets And Its Implications For Agency Research In Accounting And Auditing," **JAR**, 1985, Vol. 23, No. 2, pp. 753-793.)

Uecker, Wilfred C. (Kinney, William R., Jr. and Wilfred C. Uecker. "Mitigating The Consequences Of Anchoring In Auditor Judgments," **AR**, 1982, Vol. 57, No. 1, pp.55-69.)

Uecker, Wilfred C. (Madeo, Silvia A., Albert S. Schepanski and Wilfred C. Uecker. "Modeling Judgments Of Taxpayer Compliance," **AR**, 1987, Vol. 62, No. 2, pp. 323-342.)

Uecker, Wilfred C. (Salamon, Gerald L., Wilfred C. Uecker and Richard Simmons. "Prediction Achievement And Simulated Decision Makers As An Extension Of The Predictive Ability Criterion: Some Comments," **AR**, 1976, Vol. 51, No. 3, pp. 664-665.)

Uecker, Wilfred C., Arthur P. Brief and William R. Kinney, Jr. "Perception Of The Internal And External Auditor As A Deterrrent To Corporate Irregularities," **AR**, 1981, Vol. 56, No. 3, pp. 465-478.

Uecker, Wilfred, Albert Schepanski and Joon Shin. "Toward A Positive Theory Of Information Evaluation: Relevant Tests Of Competing Models In a Principal-Agency Setting," **AR**, 1985, Vol. 60, No. 3, pp. 430-457.

Uecker, Wilfred. (Schepanski, Albert and Wilfred Uecker. "Toward A Positive Theory Of Information Evaluation," **AR**, 1983, Vol. 58, No. 2, pp. 259-283.)

Uecker, W. C. and W. R. Kinney, Jr. "Judgmental Evaluation Of Sample Results: A Study Of The Type And Severity Of Errors Made By Practising CPAs," **AOS**, 1977, Vol. 2, No. 3, pp. 269-275.

Uecker, W. C. "An Inquiry Into The Need For Currently Feasible Extensions Of The Attest Function In Corporate

Annual Reports," **AOS**, 1977, Vol. 2, No. 1, pp. 47-58.

Uhl, Franklyn S. "Automated Capital Investment Decisions," **MA**, 1980, Vol. 61, No. 10, pp. 41-46.

Ullmann, A. A. "Corporate Social Reporting: Political Interests And Conflicts In Germany," **AOS**, 1979, Vol. 4, No. 1/2, pp. 123-134.

Ullmann, A. A. "The Corporate Environmental Accounting System: A Management Tool For Fighting Environmental Degradation," **AOS**, 1976, Vol. 1, No. 1, pp. 71-80.

Ullmann, John E. "The Reagan Administration: A New Issue, With Warmed-Over Ingredients." **AIPIA**, 1988, Vol. 2, pp. 167-178.

Ulrich, Thomas A. "The Financial Planning Implications Of Bank Loan Pricing," **JOA**, 1980, Vol. 150, No. 3.pp.64-72.

Ulrich, Thomas A. (Hanshaw, Nancy F., Thomas A. Ulrich and Charles J. Hollon. "Save Time, Money, And Taxes - Lease Your Employees," **MA**, 1986, Vol. 67, No. 10, pp. 30-36.)

Ulrich, Thomas A. (Kratchman, Stanley H., Richard T. Hise and Thomas A. Ulrich. "Management's Decision To Discontinue A Product," **JOA**, 1975, Vol. 139, No. 6, pp.50-54.)

Umapathy, Srinivasan. "Algorthm-Based Accounting Education: Opportunities And Risks," **IAE**, 1984, No. 1, pp. 136-143.

Umapathy, Srinivasan. "How Successful Firms Budget," **MA**, 1987, Vol. 68, No. 8, pp. 25-27.

Umapathy, Srinivasan. "Teaching Behavioral Aspects Of Performance Evaluation: An Experiential Approach," **AR**, 1985, Vol. 60, No. 1, pp. 97-108.

Umapathy, Srinivasan. (Abdolmohammadi. Mohammad J., Krishnagopal Menon, Thomas W. Oliver and Srinivasan Umapathy. "The Role Of The Doctoral Dissertation In Accounting Research Centers," **IAE**, 1985, No. 1, pp. 59-76.)

Umapathy, S. (Abdolmohammadi, M., K. Menon. T. Oliver and S. Umapathy. "Factors Motivating Academic Research In Accounting," **AIA**, 1988, Vol. 6, pp. 159-174.)

Underwood, William. "Is The Economist Trained To Use Accounting Data?," **AR**, 1941, Vol. 16, No. 3, pp. 262-268.

Ung, Swee-Im. (Standish, Peter E. M. and Swee-Im Ung. "Corporate Signaling, Asset Revaluations, And The Stock Prices Of British Companies," **AR**, 1982, Vol. 57, No. 4, pp. 701-715.)

Ungar, Meyer. (Flink, Solomon J., Assa Birati and Meyer Ungar. "The Impact Of Inflation On The Profits Of Listed Firms In Israel," **ABR**, 1977-78, Vol. 8, No. 32, pp. 253-257.)

Unger, David L. "The Activity Approach To Personal Financial Planning," **JOA**, 1985, Vol. 159, No. 4, pp. 94-103.

Unger, Frank J. "Indexing The Progressive Tax System," **MA**, 1978, Vol. 60, No. 4, pp. 55-57.

Uphoff, H. L. (Elliott, J. W. and H. L. Uphoff. "Predicting The Near Term Profit And Loss Statement With An Econometric Model: A Feasibility Study," **JAR**, 1972. Vol. 10, No. 2, pp. 259-274.)

Upson, Roger B. and James Fisher. "Sterling-Dollar Forward Exchange Rates," **ABACUS**, 1971. Vol. 7, No.2,pp.153-160.

Upton, Wayne S., Jr. and Carol Lynn Ostergaard. "The FASB Response To Small Business," **JOA**, 1986, Vol. 161, No. 5, pp. 94-101.

Upton, Wayne S., Jr. and Deborah K. Scott. "What You Should Know About The EITF," **JOA**, 1988, Vol. 165, No. 6, pp. 56-63.

Upton, Wayne S., Jr. "The FASB And Small Business: An Update," **JOA**, 1987, Vol. 163, No. 6, pp. 136-140.

Urbancic, Frank R. "University Library Collections Of Accounting Periodicals," **AR**, 1983, Vol. 58, No. 2, pp. 417-427.

Ureel, William L. "Nuclear Fuel Accounting," **MA**, 1973, Vol. 55, No. 1, pp. 14-16.

Uretsky, Myron. (Churchill. Neil C. and Myron Uretsky. "Management Accounting Tomorrow," **MA**, 1969, Vol. 50, No. 10, pp. 46-53.)

Ushman, Neal. (Morse, Dale and Neal Ushman. "The Effect Of Information Announcements On The Market Microstructure," **AR**, 1983, Vol. 58, No. 2, pp. 247-258.)

Usry, Milton F. and John L. Hess. "Planning And Control Of Research And Development Activities," **JOA**, 1967, Vol. 124, No. 5, pp. 43-48.

Usry, Milton F. "Cost Accounting In The CPA Examination - Updated," **AR**, 1971, Vol. 46, No. 4, pp. 791-796.

Usry, Milton F. "Cost Accounting On The CPA Examination," **AR**, 1966, Vol. 41, No. 4, pp. 754-762.

Usry, Milton F. "Cost Accounting In The CPA Examination - Updated," **AR**, 1976, Vol. 51, No. 3, pp. 633-636.

Usry, Milton F. "Developing The Relationship Between Process Cost Accounting Allocations And The Accounting Records," **AR**, 1963, Vol. 38, No. 3, pp. 614-619.

Usry, Milton F. "Recommended Design For Cost Courses," **AR**, 1965, Vol. 40, No. 3, pp. 656-659.

Usry, Milton F. "Standard Factory Overhead Variance Analysis," **AR**, 1974, Vol. 49, No. 1, pp. 180-181.

Usry, Milton F. (Anderson, Wilton T. and Milton F. Usry. "Use Of Theses And Reports In Master's Degree Programs," **AR**, 1970, Vol. 45, No. 3, pp. 579-584.)

Usry, Milton F. (Gossett, Thomas E. and Milton F. Usry. "Process Cost Accounting And Diagrammatical Outlines," **AR**, 1968, Vol. 43, No. 1, pp. 133-136.)

vvv

Vagge, Richard. "Toward Understanding Statistical Sampling," **CPAJ**, 1980, Vol. 50, No. 5, pp. 13-19.

Valine, Michael. (Weber, Joseph V., Alex T. Arcady and Michael Valine. "Junior Stock For Executive Compensation," **CPAJ**, 1984, Vol. 54, No. 6, pp. 22-29.)

Van Alstine, Robert W. and Alfred J. Maroli. "Proposed Accounting Model For State And Local Governments," **CPAJ**, 1983. Vol. 53, No. 2, pp. 42-51.

Van Alstine, Robert W. and Charles J. Schoff. "Auditing State And Local Governments," **CPAJ**, 1984, Vol. 54, No. 1, pp. 44-49.

Van Arsdell, Paul M. "Corporate Surplus Policy As A Function Of Monopoly," **AR**, 1940, Vol. 15, No. 3, pp.321-327.

Van Arsdell, Paul M. "Problems Of Corporate-Surplus Administration," **AR**, 1938, Vol. 13, No. 3, pp. 275-285.

Van Arsdell, Stephen C. "Criteria For Determining Materiality," **JOA**, 1975, Vol. 140, No. 4, pp. 72-78.

Van Breda, Michael F. "Capital Budgeting Using Terminal Values," **MA**, 1981, Vol. 63, No. 1, pp. 42-48.

Van Breda, Michael F. (Livingstone, J. Leslie and Michael F. Van Breda. "Relationship Between Accounting And The Internal Rate Of Return Measures: A Reply," **JAR**, 1976, Vol. 14, No. 1, pp. 187-188.)

Van Brunt, Roy T. and Robert C. Folbigg. "EDGAR - Informing The Public," **CA**, 1986, Vol. 4, No. 3, pp. 19-24.

Van Camp, John. (Perry, Raymond E. and John Van Camp. "The FASB Takes A Long-Awaited Look At Accounting For Corporate Income Taxes," **CA**, 1983, Vol. 1,No.4,pp.3-12.)

Van Daniker, Relmond P. "Measurement Of Certainty For 'Capitalize or Expense' Decisions," **CPAJ**, 1973, Vol. 43, No. 1, pp. 45-48.

Van Daniker, Relmond P. (Madden, Donald L., Levis D. McCullers and Relmond P. Van Daniker. "Classification Of Research And Development Expenditures: A Guide To Better Accounting." **CPAJ**, 1972, Vol. 42, No. 2, pp. 139-142.)

Van Daniker, Relmond P. (McCullers, Levis D. and Relmond P. Van Daniker. "Professionalism In Accounting," **CPAJ**, 1974, Vol. 44, No. 8, pp. 39-42.)

Van Den Bergh, R. J. A. and J. Fischer. "Human Resource Accounting - Some Problems In Implementation," **AOS**, 1976, Vol. 1, No. 2/3, pp. 265-270.

Van Der Tas, L. G. "Measuring Harmonisation Of Financial Reporting Practice," **ABR**, 1988, Vol. 18, No. 70, pp. 157-169.

Van Etten, A. T. II. "A CPA Puts On The Controller's Hat," **MA**, 1983, Vol. 64, No. 10, pp. 40-42.

Van Fleet, David D. and Daniel A. Wren. "History In Today's Business School," **AHJ**, 1982, Vol. 9, No. 1, pp. 111-118.

Van Horne, James C. "A Look At The Loss Carry-Forward," **AR**, 1963. Vol. 38, No. 1, pp. 56-60.

Van Horn, Lawrence. "An Experiment With The Case Method In Teaching Federal Income Taxes," **AR**, 1965, Vol. 40, No. 1. pp. 230-233.

Van Loon, Robert F. "Dialogue Makes The Difference Between Accountant And Management," **MA**, 1969, Vol. 51, No. 4, pp. 16-18.

Van Ness, Paul H. "To Reverse Or Not To Reverse?," **AR**, 1966. Vol. 41, No. 1, pp. 138-141.

Van Offeren, Dick H. "Replacement Value Accounting: Theory And Practice," **AIIA**, 1988, Vol. 2, pp. 23-50.

Van Pelt, John V. "Interim Reporting On Financial Statements," **MA**, 1970, Vol. 51, No. 8, pp. 9-13.

Van Pelt, John V., III. "Accounting For Acquisitions: What Should Be Done," **MA**, 1969, Vol. 50, No. 6. pp. 16-18.

Van Pelt, John V., III. "Accounting For Future Losses," **MA**, 1974. Vol. 55, No. 11, pp. 25-29.

Van Pelt, John V., III. "Developing Financial Executives," **MA**, 1969, Vol. 50, No. 8, pp. 18-19.

Van Pelt, John V., III. "Materiality," **MA**, 1975, Vol. 56, No. 12, pp. 13-15.

Van Pelt, John V., III. "Post Audit Of Capital Expenditures," **MA**, 1967, Vol. 49, No. 3, pp. 33-40.

Van Pelt, John V., III. "Reasons For Encouraging Broader Utilization Of Lifo," **JOA**, 1953, Vol. 96, No. 4, pp. 452-459.

Van Pelt, John V., III. "Some Basic Rules For Property Accounting In Manufacturing Companies," **MA**, 1968, Vol. 49. No. 9, pp 47-54.

Van Pelt, John V., III. "The Future Of Accepted Accounting Principles," **MA**, 1972, Vol. 53, No. 9, pp. 15-20.

Van Pelt, John V. III. "The Social Costs Of Social Benefits," **MA**, 1974, Vol. 56, No. 4, pp. 11-14.

Van Rensselaer, William H. (Ellyson, Robert C. and William H. Van Rensselaer. "Sunset - Is The Profession Ready For It?," **JOA**, 1980, Vol. 149, No. 6, pp. 52-61.)

Van Seventer, A. "An Unsettled Problem In The Theory Of Replacing Durable Assets: The Wemelsfelder-Traas Controversy," **IJAER**, 1974, Vol. 9, No. 2, pp. 45-81.

Van Seventer, A. "O. Ten Have (1899-1974)," **AHJ**, 1977, Vol. 4. No. 2, pp. 101-106.

Van Seventer, A. "Replacement Value Theory In Modern Dutch Accounting," **IJAER**, 1975, Vol. 11. No. 1, pp. 67-94.

Van Seventer, A. "The Continuity Postulate In The Dutch Theory Of Business Income," **IJAER**, 1969, Vol. 4, No. 2, pp. 1-19.

Van Sickle, C. L. "Discussion Of The Teaching Of Accounting In An Engineering School," **AR**, 1933, Vol. 8, No. 1, pp. 28-29.

Van Sickle, C. L. "Teaching Methods In Accounting Systems," **AR**, 1949, Vol. 24, No. 3, pp. 311-314.

Van Sickle, C. L. (Heckert, J. B., H. F. Taggart, C. L. Van Sickle, R. M. Mikesell, F. W. Woodbridge, Louis O. Foster and T. W. Leland. "Instruction In Methods Of Accounting Control: A Symposium," **AR**, 1937, Vol. 12, No. 2, pp. 114-122.)

Van Sickle, Robert W. and Sharon L. Mendus. "Producing Financial Statements Faster," **MA**, 1984, Vol. 66, No. 2, pp. 58-61.

Van Son, W. Peter and Alan J. Winters. "The Preaudit Conference: A Communication Tool," **JOA**, 1982, Vol. 154, No.

5. pp. 86-93.

Van Son, W. Peter, Dan M. Guy and J. Frank Betts. "Engagement Letters: What Practice Shows." **JOA,** 1982. Vol. 153, No. 6. pp. 72-81.

Van Tatenhove, James M. "Managing Indirect Costs In The Aerospace Industry." **MA,** 1969. Vol. 51, No. 3. pp.36-42.

Van Valkenburg, Marilyn. "Foreign Income And The Internal Revenue Code." **MA,** 1974. Vol. 55, No. 12. pp. 18-22.

Van Voorhis, Robert H. "A Practical Accounting Course For Non-Commerce Students." **AR,** 1954. Vol. 29, No. 1, pp. 132-138.

Van Voorhis, Robert H. "Changed Names Of Professional Organizations And Reference Thereto In Theses And Dissertations," **AR,** 1958. Vol. 33, No. 4. p. 675.

Van Voorhis, Robert H. "Coordinating Sections Of Courses In Elementary Accounting," **AR,** 1955. Vol. 30, No. 3. pp. 535-538.

Van Voorhis, Robert H. "Internal Auditing Courses In American Colleges," **AR,** 1952. Vol. 27, No. 4. pp. 484-489.

Van Voorhis, Robert H. "N.A.C.A. Forums Provide Practical Assistance In Teaching Cost Accounting At The University Of Alabama." **AR,** 1954. Vol. 29, No. 2. pp. 311-313.

Van Voorhis, Robert H. "Preparation For The CPA Examination - The University Of Alabama CPA Review Course." **AR,** 1956. Vol. 31, No. 1. pp. 99-103.

Van Voorhis, Robert H. "Should The Accounting Teacher Practice Accounting?." **AR,** 1956. Vol. 31, No. 4. pp. 608-616.

Van Voorhis, Robert H. "The Use Of 'Props' In Teaching Accounting." **AR,** 1953. Vol. 28, No. 2. pp. 285-286.

Van Vorhis, Robert H. "The Internal Auditing Course In The Accounting Curriculum," **AR,** 1958. Vol. 33, No. 1, pp. 111-117.

Van Zante, Neal R. "Educating Management Accountants: What Do CMAs Think?," **MA,** 1980. Vol. 62. No. 2. pp. 18-21.

Vanasse, Robert W. "Consolidated Position Statements: A Tabular Approach," **AR,** 1968. Vol. 43. No. 1. pp. 147-150.

Vanatta, Chester B. (Stettler, Howard F. and Chester B. Vanatta. "Our Changing Profession." **JOA,** 1963. Vol. 116. No. 4. pp. 53-56.)

Vance, G. Reese. "Inventory Simulation: Concepts, Implementation And Benefits." **MA,** 1968. Vol. 49. No. 11. pp. 43-49.

Vance, Lawrence L. "A Review Of Developments In Statistical Sampling For Accountants." **AR,** 1960. Vol. 35. No. 1. pp. 19-28.

Vance, Lawrence L. "An Experience With Small Random Samples In Auditing." **AR,** 1952. Vol. 27. No. 4. pp. 472-474.

Vance, Lawrence L. "Current Problems And Accounting Theory." **AR,** 1944. Vol. 19. No. 3. pp. 231-237.

Vance, Lawrence L. "Earning-Power Valuation Of Inventory." **AR,** 1942. Vol. 17. No. 4. pp. 376-383.

Vance, Lawrence L. "Education For Public Accounting." **AR,** 1956. Vol. 31. No. 4. pp. 573-580.

Vance, Lawrence L. "How Much Test Checking Is Enough?." **AR,** 1951. Vol. 26. No. 1, pp. 22-30.

Vance, Lawrence L. "The Authority Of History In Inventory Valuation." **AR,** 1943. Vol. 18. No. 3. pp. 219-227.

Vance, Lawrence L. "The Road To Reform Of Accounting Principles." **AR,** 1969. Vol. 44. No. 4. pp. 692-703.

Vance, L. L. "What The Editor Of An Academic Journal Expects From Authors." **AR,** 1966. Vol. 41. No. 1, pp. 48-51.

Vancil, Richard R. (McCosh, Andrew M. and Richard R. Vancil. "Reconciling Sandilands With Current Purchasing Power Adjustments." **ABR,** 1975-76, Vol. 6, No. 23. pp. 162-170.)

VanDaniker, Relmond P. (Madden, Donald L., Levis D. McCullers and Relmond P. VanDaniker. "The Materiality Of Research And Development Expenditures." **JAR,** 1972. Vol. 10. No. 2. pp. 417-420.)

VanDaniker, Relmond P. (McCullers, Levis D. and Relmond P. VanDaniker. "Socio-Economics And Accounting Education." **AR,** 1972. Vol. 47. No. 3. pp. 604-606.)

Vandendries, Rene. "Social Accounting And Its Applications In Peru." **IJAER,** 1970. Vol. 6. No. 1. pp. 91-99.

Vander Weele, Ray. "An MBO Perspective On Controllership." **MA,** 1976. Vol. 58. No. 2. pp. 13-14.

Vander Weele, Ray. "Catching China Fever: A Management Accountant's Perspective." **MA,** 1985. Vol. 67. No. 4. pp. 19-25.

Vander Weele, Ray. "Is This Merger Right For You?." **MA,** 1981. Vol. 62. No. 9. pp. 35-39.

VanderWeide, James H. (Brown, Lawrence D., John S. Hughes, Michael S. Rozeff and James H. VanderWeide. "Expectations Data And The Predictive Value Of Interim Reporting: A Comment," **JAR,** 1980. Vol. 18. No. 1. pp. 278-288.)

Vanecek, Michael T. and George Scott. "Data Bases - The Auditor's Dilemma," **CPAJ,** 1980. Vol. 50. No. 1. pp. 26-36.

Vanecek, Michael T. "An Overview Of Decision Theory For Management Accountants." **MA,** 1978. Vol. 59. No. 7. pp. 41-48.

Vanecek, Michael T. (Guynes, Carl Stephen, Michael T. Vanecek and Robert F. Zant. "Security Of Telecommunication Systems," **CPAJ,** 1979. Vol. 49. No. 10. pp. 31-34.)

Vanecek, Michael T., Robert F. Zant and Carl Stephen Guynes. "Distributed Data Processing: A New Tool For Accountants." **JOA,** 1980. Vol. 150. No. 4. pp. 75-83.

Vanecek, Mike. (White, Debra and Mike Vanecek. "Intended Use: A Uniform Tax Definition Of Software." **JAAF,** 1982. Vol. 5, No. 4, pp. 338-354.)

VanGundy, Sharon E. "Cost Accounting Standards And The Management Accountant," **MA,** 1973, Vol. 55, No. 3, pp. 51-54.

Vangermeersch, Richard and William T. Brosnan. "Enhancing Revenues Via Distribution Cost Control," **MA,** 1985, Vol. 67, No. 2, pp. 56-60.

Vangermeersch, Richard G. (Schwarzbach, Henry R. and Richard G. Vangermeersch. "Why We Should Account For The 4th Cost Of Manufacturing," **MA,** 1983, Vol. 65, No. 1, pp. 24-29.)

Vangermeersch, Richard. "A Comment On Some Remarks By Historians Of Cost Accounting On Engineering Contributions To The Subject," **AHJ,** 1984. Vol. 11, No. 1, pp. 135-140.

Vangermeersch, Richard. "An Improved Income Statement," **MA,** 1977. Vol. 58, No. 7, pp. 29-33.

Vangermeersch, Richard. "Let's Recognize Dissent In Standard-Making," **MA,** 1981, Vol. 63, No. 3, pp. 53-62.

Vangermeersch, Richard. "Renewing Our Heritage," **MA,** 1987, Vol. 69, No. 1, pp. 47-49.

Vangermeersch, Richard. "The Diagram Of The Cost System Of Hans Renold Ltd: A Blueprint For Accounting For Robots," **AHJ,** 1987. Vol. 14. No. 1, pp. 27-31.

Vangermeersch, Richard. "The Route Of The Seventh Directive Of The EEC On Consolidated Accounts - Slow, Steady, Studied, And Successful," **IJAER,** 1985, Vol. 20, No. 2, pp. 103-118.

Vangermeersch, Richard. (Swanson, Edward P. and Richard Vangermeersch. "Statement Of Financing And Investing Activities." **CPAJ,** 1981, Vol. 51, No. 11. pp. 32-43.)

Vannais, Leon E. "Service Centers And The CPA," **JOA,** 1959, Vol. 107. No. 2. pp. 47-59.

VanPelt, John V. "A Management Reaction To The Wheat Report On Accounting Principles," **CPAJ,** 1972, Vol. 42. No. 10, pp. 819-822.

Var, Turgut. "Bonsignori Family Estate Accounting 1461 - 1632." **AHJ,** 1981, Vol. 8, No. 2, pp. 23-35.

Var, Turgut. "Internal Control For Ottoman Foundations," **AHJ,** 1981. Vol. 8, No. 1, pp. 1-13.

Vargo, Richard J. "Municipal Service Charges - An Opportunity For CPAs," **CPAJ,** 1978, Vol. 48, No. 2, pp. 39-43.

Varner, Iris I. (Sanderson, Glen R. and Iris I. Varner. "What's Wrong With Corporate Codes Of Conduct?," **MA,** 1984. Vol. 66. No. 1, pp. 28-31.)

Varrone, James E. and Vincent E. Palmeri, Jr. "EDP Finds A Home At North Haven," **MA,** 1979, Vol. 60. No. 10, pp. 49-50.

Vasarhelyi, Miklos Antal. "Man-Machine Planning Systems: A Cognitive Style Examination Of Interactive Decision Making." **JAR,** 1977. Vol. 15, No. 1, pp. 138-153.

Vasarhelyi, Miklos Antal. "A Synthesis Of The Information Economics And Lens Models," **JAR,** 1978. Vol. 16, No. 2, pp. 414-423.)

Vasarhelyi, Miklos A. and W. Thomas Lin. "EDP Auditing Instruction Using An Interactive Generalized Audit Software." **JAED,** 1985, Vol. 3, No. 2, pp. 79-89.

Vasarhelyi, Miklos A. "Audit Automation: Online Technology And Auditing," **CPAJ,** 1985, Vol. 55, No. 4, pp. 10-17.

Vasarhelyi, Miklos A. "Automation And Changes In The Audit Process," **AJPT,** 1984-85, Vol. 4, No. 1, pp. 100-106.

Vasarhelyi, Miklos A. (Knauf, Janine B. and Miklos A. Vasarhelyi. "Empirical Characteristics Of Debenture Conversions The Issue Of Equivalency," **JAAF,** 1987, Vol. 2 (New Issues), No. 1, pp. 43-64.)

Vasarhelyi, Miklos A. (Mock, Theodore J., Teviah L. Estrin and Miklos A. Vasarhelyi. "Learning Patterns, Decision Approach, And Value Of Information," **JAR,** 1972, Vol. 10, No. 1. pp. 129-153.)

Vasarhelyi, Miklos, Da Hsein Bao and Joel Berk. "Trends In The Evolution Of Scholarly Accounting Thought: A Quantitative Examination," **AHJ,** 1988, Vol. 15, No. 1, pp. 45-64.

Vasarhelyi, M. A. (Bao, Ben-Hsien, Da-Hsien Bao and M. A. Vasarhelyi. "A Stochastic Model Of Professional Accountant Turnover," **AOS,** 1986, Vol. 11, No. 3, pp. 289-296.)

Vasarhelyi, M. A. (Brown, L. D., J. C. Gardner and M. A. Vasarhelyi. "An Analysis Of The Research Contributions Of 'Accounting, Organizations And Society': 1976-1984," **AOS,** 1987. Vol. 12, No. 2, pp. 193-204.)

Vasarhelyi, M. A. (Srinidhi, B. N. and M. A. Vasarhelyi. "Auditor Judgment Concerning Establishment Of Substantive Tests Based On Internal Control Reliability," **AJPT,** 1985-86, Vol. 5, No. 2, pp. 64-76.)

Vatter, William J. "Accounting And Statistics," **AR,** 1961, Vol. 36, No. 4, pp. 589-597.

Vatter, William J. "Another Look At The 1957 Statement," **AR,** 1962. Vol. 37, No. 4, pp. 660-669.

Vatter, William J. "Fund-Theory View Of Price-Level Adjustments." **AR,** 1962. Vol. 37, No. 2, pp. 189-207.

Vatter, William J. "Income Models, Book Yield, And Rate Of Return." **AR,** 1966. Vol. 41, No. 4, pp. 681-698.

Vatter, William J. "Limitations Of Overhead Allocation," **AR,** 1945. Vol. 20, No. 2, pp. 163-176.

Vatter, William J. "More About Leases: A Rejoinder To Professor Wolk," **JAR,** 1969, Vol. 7, No. 2. pp. 346-349.

Vatter, William J. "Postulates And Principles," **JAR,** 1963, Vol. 1, No. 2, pp. 179-197.

Vatter, William J. "Progress In The Pursuit Of Principles." **IJAER,** 1969. Vol. 5, No. 1, pp. 1-15.

Vatter, William J. "State Of The Art - Non-Business Accounting," **AR,** 1979, Vol. 54, No. 3, pp. 574-584.

Vatter, William J. "The Use Of Operations Research In American Companies," **AR,** 1967, Vol. 42, No. 4, pp. 721-730.

Vatter, William J. "'Time-Adjusted' Depreciation," **JAR,**

1969, Vol. 7, No. 1, pp. 163-164.

Vatter, Wm. J. "Sum Of (M3)i," **AR**, 1963, Vol. 38. No. 3, pp. 470-477.

Vatter, W. J. "Accounting Education For Controllership," **AR**, 1950, Vol. 25, No. 3, pp. 236-250.

Vatter, W. J. "Accounting For Leases," **JAR**, 1966, Vol. 4, No. 2, pp. 133-148.

Vatter, W. J. "The Accountant's Control Function Is A Part Of Management," **JOA**, 1952. Vol. 93. No. 6. pp. 705-710.

Vaughan, R. Allen. "This Hospital Service Forecasts Inflation For Its Fiscal Health," **MA**, 1978. Vol. 60. No. 6, pp. 44-47.

Vaughn, Donald E. and Ronald W. Melicher. "Capitalizing Net Lease Rentals," **MA**, 1974. Vol. 55. No. 7, pp. 27-33.

Vaughn, Donald E. "Sales Forecasting," **MA**, 1972. Vol. 53, No. 9, pp. 39-41.

Vaughn, Donald E. (Hoffman, William H., Jr. and Donald E. Vaughn. "Departmental And Item Profitability For Retailers," **JOA**, 1963, Vol. 116, No. 2, pp. 50-58.)

Vause, R. (Rands, C. A., R. Vause and K. G. Pemberton. "Using Computers In Small Company Cash Management," **ABR**, 1973-74, Vol. 4, No. 16, pp. 251-262.)

Vause, R. (Simmonds, K. and R. Vause. "Cost Estimating Under Uncertainty," **ABR**, 1970-71. Vol. 1, No. 1, pp. 3-10.)

Vavasour, John E. "The Third Generation Of Computers - New Tools For Management," **MA**, 1965. Vol. 47, No. 2. pp. 3-6.

Vecchio, Robert P. (Campbell, David K., James Gaertner and Robert P. Vecchio. "Perceptions Of Promotion And Tenure Criteria: A Survey Of Accounting Educators," **JAED**, 1983, Vol. 1, No. 1, pp. 83-92.)

Vejlupek, Judith R. and Betsy Hollowell Cropsey. "The Hidden Costs Of Postemployment Benefits." **JOA**, 1984. Vol. 158. No. 4. pp. 84-92.

Vendig, Richard E. "A Three-Part Transfer Price." **MA**, 1973. Vol. 55, No. 3, pp. 33-36.

Vent, Glenn A. (Milne, Ronald A. and Glenn A. Vent. "Publication Productivity: A Comparison Of Accounting Faculty Members Promoted In 1981 and 1984." **IAE**, 1987, Vol. 2. No. 1, pp. 94-102.)

Vent, Glenn A. (Milne, Ronald A., Glenn A. Vent and Reuben Neumann. "Accounting For Variable Stock Options," **JAED**, 1987, Vol. 5. No. 2. pp. 333-338.)

Vent, Glenn. "Accounting For Gold And Silver Mines: The Development Of Cost Accounting." **AHJ**. 1986. Vol. 13. No. 2. pp. 77-88.

Verbaere, Eric. (Ooghe, Hubert and Eric Verbaere. "Predicting Business Failure On The Basis Of Accounting Data: The Belgian Experience." **IJAER**, 1985, Vol. 20, No. 2, pp. 19-44.)

Vercio, Alan P. "Who Is The Customer?." **MA**, 1988. Vol. 70, No. 5, pp. 50-52.

Vermont, Paul A. "Is Your Production Plan Realistic?," **MA**, 1968, Vol. 50. No. 3. pp. 27-28.

Vernon, Thomas H. "Capital Budgeting And The Evaluation Process," **MA**, 1972. Vol. 54. No. 4. pp. 19-24.

Verreault, Kathryn. (Schroeder, Richard G. and Kathryn Verreault. "An Empirical Analysis Of Audit Withdrawal Decisions." **AIA**, 1987, Vol. 5. pp. 205-220.)

Verrecchia, Robert E. "An Analysis Of Two Cost Allocation Cases," **AR**, 1982. Vol. 57, No. 3. pp. 579-593.

Verrecchia, Robert E. "Discretionary Disclosure." **JAEC**, 1983, Vol. 5. No. 3. pp. 179-194.

Verrecchia, Robert E. "Managerial Discretion In The Choice Among Financial Reporting Alternatives." **JAEC**, 1986. Vol. 8. No. 3, pp. 175-195.

Verrecchia, Robert E. "On The Choice Of Accounting Method For Partnerships." **JAR**, 1978. Vol. 16. No. 1. pp. 150-168.

Verrecchia, Robert E. "On The Relationship Between Volume Reaction And Consensus Of Investors: Implications For Interpreting Tests Of Information Content." **JAR**, 1981. Vol. 19, No. 1. pp. 271-283.

Verrecchia, Robert E. "On The Theory Of Market Information Efficiency." **JAEC**, 1979. Vol. 1. No. 1, pp. 77-90.

Verrecchia, Robert E. "The Rapidity Of Price Adjustments To Information." **JAEC**, 1980, Vol. 2. No. 1, pp. 63-92.

Verrecchia, Robert E. "The Use Of Mathematical Models In Financial Accounting." **JAR**. 1982. Vol. 20.Supp.,pp.1-42.

Verrecchia, Robert E. (Billera. Louis J., David C. Heath and Robert E. Verrecchia. "A Unique Procedure For Allocating Common Costs From A Production Process." **JAR**, 1981, Vol. 19, No. 1, pp. 185-196.)

Verrecchia, Robert E. (Holthausen. Robert W. and Robert E. Verrecchia. "The Effect Of Sequential Information Releases On The Variance Of Price Changes In An Intertemporal Multi-Asset Market," **JAR**, 1988, Vol. 26. No. 1. pp. 82-106.)

Verrecchia, Robert E. (Lanen, William N. and Robert E. Verrecchia. "Operating Decisions And The Disclosure Of Management Accounting Information," **JAR**, 1987. Vol. 25. Supp., pp. 165-189.)

Verrecchia, Robert E. (Roth. Alvin E. and Robert E. Verrecchia. "The Shapley Value As Applied To Cost Allocations: A Reinterpretation," **JAR**. 1979. Vol. 17. No. 1, pp. 295-303.)

Verrecchia, R. (Manes. R. and R. Verrecchia. "A New Proposal For Setting Intra-Company Transfer Prices." **ABR**, 1981-82, Vol. 12. No. 46, pp. 97-104.)

Verschoor, Curtis C. "Personal Financial Planning And The CPA," **JOA**. 1985. Vol. 159. No. 1. pp. 52-59.

Vessey, Sean O. (Detweiler, John H., Sean O. Vessey and Arthur J. King. "A Model For Computing Shipyard Overhead," **JCA**, 1987. Vol. 4. No. 1. pp. 71-93.)

Vickers, Douglas. "On The Economics Of Break-Even," **AR**, 1960. Vol. 35, No. 3, pp. 405-412.

Vicknair, David B. (Curatola, A. P., D. B. Vicknair and Suzanne R. Pinac Ward. "Earnings Per Share: Alternative Interpretations Of The Three Percent Provision Of APB 15 In Intermediate Accounting Textbooks," **IAE**, 1988, Vol. 3, No. 1, pp. 17-26.)

Vicknair, David P. and Jerry R. Strawser. "Reporting Discontinued Segments In A Cash Basis Statement Of Changes In Financial Position," **ACCHOR**, 1987, Vol. 1, No. 3. pp. 79-84.

Vickrey, Don W. "General-Price-Level-Adjusted Historical-Cost Statements And The Ratio-Scale View," **AR**, 1976, Vol. 51, No. 1, pp. 31-40.

Vickrey, Don W. "Is Accounting A Measurement Discipline?," **AR**. 1970. Vol. 45, No. 4, pp. 731-742.

Vickrey, Don W. "Normative Information Qualities: A Contrast Between Information-Economics And FASB Perspectives." **ABACUS**, 1985, Vol. 21, No. 2, pp. 115-129.

Vickrey, Don W. "Two Views Of Current-Exit Values: Addition And Additivity," **IJAER**, 1976, Vol. 11, No. 2, pp. 51-57.

Vickrey, Don W. (Foster, Taylor W., III, D. Randall Jenkins and Don W. Vickrey. "The Incremental Information Content Of The Annual Report," **ABR**, 1985-86, Vol. 16, No. 62, pp. 91-98.)

Vickrey, Don. "A Comment On The Larson-Schattke And Chambers Debate Over The Additivity Of CCE," **AR**, 1975, Vol. 50. No. 1, pp. 140-146.

Vickrey, Don. (Barefield, Russell M., Taylor W. Foster, III and Don Vickrey. "Interpreting The API: A Comment And Extension." **AR**, 1976, Vol. 51, No. 1, pp. 172-175.)

Vickrey, Don. (Foster, Taylor W., III and Don Vickrey. "The Incremental Information Content Of The 10-K," **AR**, 1978, Vol. 53. No. 4, pp. 921-934.)

Vickrey, Don. (Foster, Taylor W., III and Don Vickrey. "The Information Content Of Stock Dividend Announcements," **AR**, 1978, Vol. 53, No. 2, pp. 360-370.)

Vickrey, Don. (Schroeder, Mary S., Ira Solomon, and Don Vickrey. "Audit Quality: The Perceptions Of Audit-Committee Chairpersons And Audit Partners," **AJPT**, 1985-86. Vol. 5. No. 2, pp. 86-94.)

Vickrey, D. W. "In Defense Of GPLAHCSATRSV," **AR**, 1979. Vol. 54. No. 4. pp. 830-839.

Vigeland, Robert L. "Dilution Of Earnings Per Share In An Option Pricing Framework," **AR**, 1982, Vol. 57, No. 2, pp. 348-357.

Vigeland, Robert L. "Instructional Usage Of The Compustat Data Files," **JAED**, 1983, Vol. 1, No. 2, pp. 123-133.

Vigeland, Robert L. "The Market Reaction To Statement Of Financial Accounting Standards No. 2," **AR**, 1981, Vol. 56. No. 2, pp. 309-325.

Vigeland, Robert L. (Daley, Lane A. and Robert L. Vigeland. "The Effects Of Debt Covenants And Political Costs On The Choice Of Accounting Methods: The Case Of Accounting For R&D Costs," **JAEC**, 1983, Vol. 5, No. 3, pp. 195-211.)

Vigeland, Robert L. (Daley, Lane A., David W. Senkow and Robert L. Vigeland. "Analysts' Forecasts, Earnings Variability, And Option Pricing: Empirical Evidence," **AR**, 1988. Vol. 63. No. 4, pp. 563-585.)

Vincent, Gay L. (Bamber, E. Michael, Linda S. Bamber and Gay L. Vincent. "Communication Can Improve Your Audit," **CPAJ**, 1985, Vol. 55, No. 3, pp. 34-38.)

Vincent, Janice I. (Armstrong, Mary Beth and Janice I. Vincent. "Public Accounting: A Profession At A Crossroads." **ACCHOR**, 1988, Vol. 2, No. 1, pp. 94-98.)

Vincent, Vern H. "The Graduate Curriculum In Accounting," **AR**. 1954. Vol. 29, No. 1, pp. 84-88.

Vincenzo, James J. "Replacement Cost Data: What Do You Do With It?." **MA**. 1978. Vol. 59. No. 12, pp. 22-26.

Violet, William J. "A Philosophical Perspective On The Development Of International Accounting Standards," **IJAER**, 1983, Vol. 19, No. 1, pp. 1-13.

Violet, William J. "The Development Of International Accounting Standards: An Anthropological Perspective," **IJAER**, 1983. Vol. 18. No. 2, pp. 1-12.

Virgil, Robert L. (Pankoff, Lyn D. and Robert L. Virgil. "Some Preliminary Findings From A Laboratory Experiment On The Usefulness Of Financial Accounting Information To Security Analysts," **JAR**, 1970, Vol. 8, Supp., pp. 1-48.)

Virgil, Robert L. (Pankoff. Lyn D. and Robert L. Virgil. "On The Usefulness Of Financial Statement Information: A Suggested Research Approach," **AR**, 1970, Vol. 45, No. 2, pp. 269-279.)

Virgil, Robert L. (Spiller, Earl A. and Robert L. Virgil. "Effectiveness Of APB Opinion No. 19 In Improving Funds Reporting." **JAR**, 1974, Vol. 12, No. 1, pp. 112-142.)

Virgil, Robert L., Walter R. Nord and Sterling H. Schoen. "A Classroom Experience In The Behavioral Implications Of Accounting Performance Evaluation Measurements," **AR**, 1973. Vol. 48. No. 2, pp. 410-418.

Vitalone, James W. "Replacement Cost Accounting: A Study Of Its Effect On Growth And Cyclical Stock Characteristics." **MA**, 1978. Vol. 59. No. 9, pp. 27-29.

Vogt, R. A. "A Corporate Strategy For Realizing Equal Employment Opportunity," **AOS**, 1977, Vol. 2, No. 1, pp. 59-80.

Volkan, Ara and Joseph Rue. "The Case Against Deferred Taxes," **MA**, 1985, Vol. 66, No. 9, pp. 30-35.

Volkan, Ara G. "Accounting For Unfunded Pension Costs," **MA**. 1982. Vol. 63. No. 11, pp. 30-38.

Volkan, Ara G. "National Economic Planning: Challenge Of The 1980s." **MA**, 1980. Vol. 62. No. 3, pp. 36-40.

Volkan, Ara G. (Bracken, Robert M. and Ara G. Volkan. "Cash Flows: A New Reporting Format For Turbulent Times," **MA**, 1988. Vol. 69, No. 7, pp. 38-41.)

170-182.

Walker, Michael A. "A Progress Report On The AICPA's New Quality Review Program," **CPAJ**, 1988, Vol. 58. No. 9, pp. 22-28.

Walker, Michael C. "Determining The Appropriate Discount Rate For Private, Not-For-Profit Organizations," **MA**, 1979, Vol. 60, No. 9, pp. 54-56.

Walker, M. (Board, J. L. G. and M. Walker. "Information Content Of SSAP 16 Earnings Changes," **ABR**, 1985-86. Vol. 16, No. 61, pp. 69-72.)

Walker, Norman R. and L. Tim Pierce. "The Price Waterhouse Audit: A State Of The Art Approach," **AJPT**, 1988, Vol. 8, No. 1, pp. 1-22.

Walker, Robert B. (Mayper, Alan G., Robert B. Walker and Casper E. Wiggins. "Accounting And Review Services: Perceptions Of The Message Within The CPA's Report," **AIA**, 1988, Vol. 6, pp. 219-232.)

Walker, R. G. and G. P. Whittred. "Bank Disclosures Of Secret Reserves. The Impact On The Australian Stock Market," **ABR**, 1982-83, Vol. 13, No. 50, pp. 131-142.

Walker, R. G. "An Evaluation Of The Information Conveyed By Consolidated Statements," **ABACUS**, 1976. Vol. 12, No. 2, pp. 77-115.

Walker, R. G. "Asset Classification And Asset Valuation," **ABR**, 1973-74, Vol. 4, No. 16, pp. 286-296.

Walker, R. G. "Australia's ASRB: A Case Study Of Political Activity And Regulatory 'Capture'." **ABR**, 1986-87, Vol. 17, No. 67, pp. 269-286.

Walker, R. G. "Disclosure By Diversified Companies," **ABACUS**, 1968, Vol. 4, No. 1, pp. 27-38.

Walker, R. G. "International Accounting Compromises: The Case Of Consolidation Accounting," **ABACUS**. 1978, Vol. 14, No. 2, pp. 97-111.

Walker, R. G. "The Governmental Budget As An Instrument Of Control," **AR**, 1926, Vol. 1, No. 2, pp. 33-47.

Walker, R. G. "The Hatry Affair." **ABACUS**. 1977, Vol. 13, No. 1, pp. 78-81.

Walker, R. G. (Ball, Ray, R. G. Walker and G. P. Whittred. "Audit Qualifications And Share Prices," **ABACUS**, 1979, Vol. 15, No. 1, pp. 23-34.)

Walker, R. G. (Birkett, W. P. and R. G. Walker. "Professional Ideas On Research In Accounting: Australia, 1930-49," **ABACUS**, 1972, Vol. 8, No. 1. pp. 35-60.)

Walker, R.G. (Birkett, W. P. and R. G. Walker. "Response Of The Australian Accounting Profession To Company Failures In The 1960s," **ABACUS**, 1971, Vol. 7, No. 2. pp. 97-136.)

Walker, R. G. (Sharpe, I. G. and R. G. Walker. "Asset Revaluations And Stock Market Prices," **JAR**. 1975, Vol. 13, No. 2, pp. 293-310.)

Walker, Scott T. "Visibility And Materiality In Interim Reporting," **MA**, 1973, Vol. 55. No. 6, pp. 23-27.

Walker, Warren E. "Costs Made To Order - A Company's Experience," **MA**, 1968, Vol. 50, No. 3, pp. 51-53.

Walker, W. A. "Internal Audit Procedures For Controlling Costs," **JOA**, 1950, Vol. 89, No. 5, pp. 382-386.

Wallace, Albert. "Budgetary Control In The Canvas Footwear Industry," **MA**, 1973, Vol. 55, No. 4, pp. 17-20.

Wallace, Albert. "Inventory Ownership Costs," **MA**, 1974, Vol. 56, No. 6, pp. 26-28.

Wallace, Edward L. "Some Comments On The Statement Of Planning Costs," **AR**, 1957, Vol. 32, No. 3, pp. 448-466.

Wallace, Edward L. (Gregory, Robert H. and Edward L. Wallace. "Work Sheet For Funds Statement Problems," **AR**, 1953, Vol. 28, No. 1, pp. 88-97.)

Wallace, George R. and Edward C. Christ. "Modern Accounting Can Help Save The Railroads," **MA**, 1970. Vol. 52, No. 6, pp. 15-18.

Wallace, Gerald O. "Controlling Expansion Costs: A Practical Guide," **MA**, 1975, Vol. 56, No. 10, pp. 43-46.

Wallace, John B., Jr. (Gleim, Irvin N. and John B. Wallace, Jr. "Probabilistically Answered Examinations: A Field Test," **AR**, 1974, Vol. 49, No. 2, pp. 363-366.)

Wallace, Michael E. "Behavioral Considerations In Budgeting," **MA**, 1966, Vol. 47, No. 12, pp. 3-8.

Wallace, R. S. O. "Corporate Financial Reporting In Nigeria," **ABR**, 1988, Vol. 18, No. 72, pp. 352-362.

Wallace, Wanda A. and Ronald L. Campbell. "State Boards Of Accountancy: Quality Review And Positive Enforcement Program," **RIAR**, 1988, Vol. 2, pp. 123-154.

Wallace, Wanda A. "Accounting Policies And The Measurement Of Urban Fiscal Strain," **RIGNA**, 1985, Vol. 1, pp. 181-212.

Wallace, Wanda A. "Agency Theory And Governmental And Nonprofit Sector Research," **RIGNA**, 1987, Vol. 3, Part B, pp. 51-70.

Wallace, Wanda A. "Analytical Review: Misconceptions, Applications And Experience - Part II," **CPAJ**, 1983, Vol. 53, No. 2, pp. 18-27.

Wallace, Wanda A. "Analytical Review: Misconceptions, Applications And Experience - Part I," **CPAJ**, 1983, Vol. 53, No. 1, pp. 24-37.

Wallace, Wanda A. "Enhancing Your Relationship With Internal Auditors," **CPAJ**, 1984, Vol. 54, No. 12, pp. 46-53.

Wallace, Wanda A. "Integrating Recent Developments In Attestation, Risk Evaluation, Technology, And Regulation Into The Ph.D. Auditing Seminar," **IAE**, 1987, Vol. 2, No. 2, pp. 325-348.

Wallace, Wanda A. "Internal Control Reporting Practices In The Municipal Sector," **AR**, 1981, Vol. 56, No. 3, pp. 666-689.

Wallace, Wanda A. "Internal Control Reporting - 950 Negative Responses," **CPAJ**, 1981, Vol. 51, No. 1, pp. 33-38.

Wallace, Wanda A. "More Effective Management Letters,"

CPAJ. 1983, Vol. 53, No. 12, pp. 18-29.

Wallace, Wanda A. "Objectives For The Governmental Accounting Standards Board," **RIGNA**, 1985, Vol. 1, pp. 33-76.

Wallace, Wanda A. "The Acceptability Of Regression Analysis As Evidence In A Courtroom - Implications For The Auditor." **AJPT**, 1982-83, Vol. 2, No. 2, pp. 66-90.

Wallace, Wanda A. "The Association Between Municipal Market Measures And Selected Financial Reporting Practices," **JAR**, 1981, Vol. 19, No. 2, pp. 502-520.

Wallace, Wanda A. "The Economic Role Of The Audit In Free And Regulated Markets: A Review," **RIAR**, 1987, Vol. 1, pp. 7-34.

Wallace, Wanda A. "The Effects Of Delays By Accounting Policy-Setters In Reconciling The Accounting Treatment Of Stock Options And Stock Appreciation Rights," **AR**, 1984, Vol. 59, No. 2, pp. 325-341.

Wallace, Wanda A. "The Irony Of Responding To Regulators' Pressures: The Case Of Management Letter Precautionary Representations," **ACCHOR**, 1988, Vol. 2, No. 1, pp. 88-93.

Wallace, Wanda A. "The Timing Of Initial Independent Audits Of Municipalities: An Empirical Analysis," **RIGNA**, 1986, Vol. 2, pp. 3-51.

Wallace, Wanda A. "Why Have Firms Withdrawn From An AICPA Section?," **CPAJ**, 1988, Vol. 58, No. 1, pp. 26-37.

Wallace, Wanda A. (Berry, Leonard Eugene and Wanda A. Wallace. "Governmental Auditing Research: An Analytic Framework. Assessment Of Past Work, And Future Directions." **RIGNA**, 1986, Vol. 2, pp. 89-115.)

Wallace, Wanda A. (Kreutzfeldt, Richard W. and Wanda A. Wallace. "Error Characteristics In Audit Populations: Their Profile And Relationship To Environmental Factors," **AJPT**, 1986-87, Vol. 6, No. 1, pp. 20-43.)

Waller, Thomas C. and Rebecca A. Gallun. "Microcomputer Competency Requirements In The Accounting Industry: A Pilot Study," **JAED**, 1985, Vol. 3, No. 2, pp. 31-40.

Waller, Thomas C. "Accounting For Stock Options," **MA**, 1976, Vol. 58. No. 6, pp. 29-31.

Waller, William and James Jiambalvo. "The Use Of Normative Models In Human Information Processing Research In Accounting," **JAL**, 1984. Vol. 3, pp. 201-226.

Waller, William S. and Chee W. Chow. "The Self-Selection And Effort Effects Of Standard-Based Employee Contracts: A Framework And Some Empirical Evidence," **AR**, 1985, Vol. 60, No. 3, pp. 458-476.

Waller, William S. and William L. Felix, Jr. "Auditors' Covariation Judgments," **AR**, 1987, Vol. 62, No. 2, pp. 275-292.

Waller, William S. and William L. Felix, Jr. "The Effects Of Incomplete Outcome Feedback On Auditors' Self-Perceptions Of Judgment Ability," **AR**, 1984, Vol. 59, No. 4, pp. 637-646.

Waller, William S. "Self-Selection And The Probability Of Quitting: A Contracting Approach To Employee Turnover In Public Accounting," **JAR**, 1985, Vol. 23, No. 2, pp. 817-828.

Waller, William S. (Chow, Chee W. and William S. Waller. "Management Accounting And Organizational Control," **MA**, 1982, Vol. 63, No. 10, pp. 36-41.)

Waller, William S. (Chow, Chee W., Jean C. Cooper and William S. Waller. "Participative Budgeting: Effects Of A Truth-Inducing Pay Scheme And Information Asymmetry On Slack And Performance," **AR**, 1988, Vol. 63, No. 1, pp. 111-122.)

Waller, William S. (Shields, Michael D., Ira Solomon and William S. Waller. "Auditors' Usage Of Unaudited Book Values When Making Presampling Audit Value Estimates," **CAR**, 1988, Vol. 5, No. 1, pp. 1-18.)

Waller, William S. (Smith, Vernon L., Jeffrey Schatzberg and William S. Waller. "Experimental Economics And Auditing." **AJPT**, 1987-88, Vol. 7, No. 1, pp. 71-93.)

Waller, William. (Jiambalvo, James and William Waller. "Decomposition And Assessments Of Audit Risk," **AJPT**, 1983-84, Vol. 3, No. 2, pp. 80-88.)

Waller, W. S. and W. L. Felix, Jr. "The Auditor And Learning From Experience: Some Conjectures," **AOS**, 1984, Vol. 9. No. 3/4, pp. 383-408.

Waller, W. S. "Slack In Participative Budgeting: The Joint Effect Of A Truth-Inducing Pay Scheme And Risk Preferences." **AOS**, 1988, Vol. 13, No. 1, pp. 87-100.

Waller, W. S. (Shields. M. D. and W. S. Waller. "A Behavioral Study Of Accounting Variables In Performance-Incentive Contracts," **AOS**, 1988, Vol. 13, No. 6, pp. 581-594.)

Waller, W. S. (Shields, M. D., I. Solomon and W. S. Waller. "Effects Of Alternative Sample Space Representations On The Accuracy Of Auditors' Uncertainty Judgments," **AOS**, 1987. Vol. 12, No. 3, pp. 375-388.)

Wallis, Charles T. "FASB Statement No. 87 And The Bottom Line." **CA**, 1987, Vol. 5, No. 4, pp. 38-41.

Wallis, Percy. "Wage Fund And Full Employment," **AR**, 1946, Vol. 21, No. 3, pp. 313-336.

Walsh, J. Anthony. "Empirical Evidence On Internal Control In Minicomputer-Based Accounting Information Systems," **ABR**, 1985-86, Vol. 16, No. 63, pp. 227-234.

Walsh, Lawrence M. "Accounting Education In Review," **AR**, 1960, Vol. 35, No. 2, pp. 183-189.

Walsh, Paul R. "Typesetting With A Time-Sharing Terminal," **MA**, 1973, Vol. 54, No. 12, pp. 42-44.

Waltemyer, Edward L. "The Professional Corporation," **MA**, 1973, Vol. 55, No. 6, pp. 31-32.

Walters, Michael J. (Barnickol, Karl R., Allan John Ross, Ronald O. Schowalter and Michael J. Walters. "Accounting For Litigation And Claims," **JOA**, 1985, Vol. 159, No. 6, pp. 56-69.)

Walters, R. M. "An Inheritance Tax In The United Kingdom,"
ABR, 1971-72, Vol. 2, No. 8, pp. 253-263.

Walters, William H. "Factoring," CPAJ, 1986, Vol. 56, No.
6, pp. 66-72.

Walter, Herbert E., II and J. Timothy Sale. "Financial
Reporting: A Two-Perspective Issue," MA, 1981, Vol. 62,
No. 12, pp. 32-37.

Walter, James E. "Last-In, First-Out," AR, 1950, Vol. 25,
No. 1, pp. 63-75.

Walter, James E. "Tax Notes As Liability Offsets," AR,
1953, Vol. 28, No. 4, pp. 545-549.

Walter, James E. "The Treatment Of 'Footnote' Liabilities,"
AR, 1955, Vol. 30, No. 1, pp. 95-102.

Walther, Larry M. "A Comparison Of Estimated And Reported
Historical Cost/Constant Dollar Data," AR, 1982, Vol.
57, No. 2, pp. 376-383.

Walther, Larry M. "Commodity Futures: What The Accountant
Should Know," JOA, 1982, Vol. 153, No. 3, pp. 68-81.

Walther, Larry M. (Snavely, H. Jim and Larry M. Walther.
"Earnings And The FASB - For Better Or Worse?," MA,
1983, Vol. 64, No. 8, pp. 28-33.)

Walton, Kenneth W. (Blagg, R. Raymond and Kenneth W.
Walton. "Functional Time Reporting: Shortcut To
Integrating Labor Data," MA, 1984, Vol. 65, No. 12, pp.
34-38.)

Walton, Peter. "The Export Of British Accounting Legislation To Commonwealth Countries," ABR, 1985-86, Vol. 16,
No. 64, pp. 353-358.

Walvoord, William. (Hartman, Bart P., David Laxton and
William Walvoord. "A Look At Employee Stock Ownership
Plans As Financing Tools," MA, 1977, Vol. 58, No. 9, pp.
23-28.)

Wankess, P. T. "Current Purchasing-Power Accounting: A
Study Of A Cooperative Venture," ABACUS, 1976, Vol. 12,
No. 1, pp. 61-72.

Wankess, P. T. "Reflections On Asset Valuation And Value To
The Firm," ABACUS, 1974, Vol. 10 No. 2, pp. 160-164.

Wansley, R. M. "How To Protect War-Inflated Cash Balance
Against Sec. 102," JOA, 1952, Vol. 93, No. 4, pp. 446-
450.

Ward, Bart H. "An Investigation Of The Materiality
Construct In Auditing," JAR, 1976, Vol. 14, No. 1, pp.
138-152.

Ward, Bart H. "Assessing Prior Distributions For Applying
Bayesian Statistics In Auditing: A Comment," AR, 1975,
Vol. 50, No. 1, pp. 155-157.

Ward, Bart H. (Knapp, Michael C. and Bart H. Ward. "An
Integrative Analysis Of Audit Conflict: Sources, Consequences And Resolution," AIA, 1987, Vol. 4, pp. 267-
286.)

Ward, Catherine R. (Jones, Wm. Jarell and Catherine R.
Ward. "Forecasts And Projections For Third-Party Use,"
JOA, 1986, Vol. 161, No. 4, pp. 100-102.)

Ward, C. W. R. "Property Lease-Or-Buy Decisions," ABR,
1982-83, Vol. 13, No. 50, pp. 143-150.

Ward, C. W. R. (Lee, S. L. and C. W. R. Ward. "The Investment Performance Of Property Unit Trusts Evaluated By
Stochastic Dominance," ABR, 1980-81, Vol. 11, No. 44,
pp. 303-308.)

Ward, C. W. R. (Peasnell, K. V., L. C. L. Skerratt and C.
W. R. Ward. "The Share Price Impact Of UK CCA Disclosures," ABR, 1987-88, Vol. 18. No. 69. pp. 3-16.)

Ward, C. W. R. (Skomp, Stephen E. and C. W. R. Ward. "The
Capital Structure Policies Of U.K. Companies: A Comparative Study," IJAER, 1983, Vol. 19, No. 1, pp. 55-64.)

Ward, D. Dewey and Jack C. Robertson. "Reliance On Internal
Auditors," JOA, 1980, Vol. 150, No. 4, pp. 62-74.

Ward, D. Dewey. (Arens, Alvin A. and D. Dewey Ward. "The
Use Of A Systems Understanding Aid In The Accounting
Curriculum," AR, 1984, Vol. 59, No. 1, pp. 98-108.)

Ward, D. Dewey. (Winckler, Susan W. and D. Dewey Ward. "Can
City Hall Go Broke? The Going Concern Issue?," JOA,
1984, Vol. 157, No. 5, pp. 90-100.)

Ward, Elizabeth G. (Scott, Richard A. and Elizabeth G.
Ward. "Carman G. Blough: His Personality And Formative
Years," AHJ, 1982, Vol. 9, No. 2, pp. 53-60.)

Ward, Gerald M. (Lutchen, Mark D. and Gerald M. Ward.
"Microcomputer Implementation: A Practical, Realistic,
And Surefire Strategy," CA, 1983, Vol. 1, No. 3, pp. 21-
25.)

Ward, James Gordon. "The Use And Usefulness Of Governmental
Financial Reports: The Perspective Of Public Sector
Labor Unions," RIGNA, 1987, Vol. 3, Part B, pp. 215-226.

Ward, James J., Jr. (Newton, Grant W. and James J. Ward,
Jr. "Valuation Of A Business In Bankruptcy," CPAJ, 1976,
Vol. 46, No. 8, pp. 26-32.)

Ward, Lewis B. and Russell H. Hassler. "A Critical Evaluation Of The Institute Personnel Selection & Testing
Program," JOA, 1950, Vol. 90, No. 2, pp. 113-121.

Ward, Suzanne R. Pinac. (Curatola, A. P., D. B. Vicknair
and S. R. Pinac Ward. "Earnings Per Share: Alternative
Interpretations Of The Three Percent Provision Of APB 15
In Intermediate Accounting Textbooks," IAE, 1988, Vol.
3, No. 1, pp.17-26.)

Warman, Alison. (Edwards, J. R. and Alison Warman.
"Discounted Cash Flow And Business Valuation In A Nineteenth Century Merger: A Note," AHJ, 1981, Vol. 8, No.
2, pp. 37-50.)

Warner, George H. "Depreciation On A Current Basis," AR,
1954, Vol. 29. No. 4, pp. 628-633.

Warner, Henry C. (Perry, William E. and Henry C. Warner.
"Systems Auditability: Friend Or Foe?," JOA, 1978, Vol.
145, No. 2, pp. 52-60.)

Warner, Jerold B. "Stock Market Reaction To Management
Incentive Plan Adoption: An Overview," JAEC, 1985, Vol.

7, No. 1/3, pp. 145-149.

Warner, Paul D. "EDP And Internal Control," CPAJ, 1976,
Vol. 46, No. 2, pp. 19-21.

Warner, Paul D. (Shuster, Harvey L. and Paul D. Warner.
"Micros For Small Business: The Time Is Now," MA, 1984,
Vol. 65, No. 9, pp. 45-48.)

Warner, Paul. "Audits Of Service-Center-Produced Records,"
CPAJ, 1975, Vol. 45, No. 1, pp. 25-28.

Warner, Robert S. "The Selection Of Accountants For Municipal Audit Work," JOA, 1954, Vol. 98, No. 4, pp. 483-490.

Warner, Ross T. "Problems In Taxing Partnerships," JOA,
1953, Vol. 96, No. 6, pp. 703-710.

Warner, Stanley E., Jr. and Frederick D. Whitehurst. "A
Graphical Approach To Lower Of Cost Or Market," AR,
1982, Vol. 57, No. 3, pp. 631-637.

Warner, Stanley E., Jr. and Frederick D. Whitehurst.
"Inconsistency In Inventory Loss Measurements Under The
LCM Rule," JAED, 1987, Vol. 5, No. 2, pp. 277-285.

Warner, Stanley E., Jr. and Frederick D. Whitehurst. "The
Educational Impact Of Unresolved Conceptual Issues In
Interest Capitalization," JAED, 1988, Vol. 6, No. 2, pp.
209-217.

Warne, Richard A. "A Controller Looks At Regulation," MA,
1982, Vol. 63, No. 12, pp. 14-20.

Warnke, Dale W. (Terre, Norbert C., Dale W. Warnke and
Albert P. Ameiss. "Cost/Benefit Analysis Of Public
Projects." MA, 1973, Vol. 54, No. 7, pp. 34-37.)

Warrell, C. J. "The Enterprise Value Concept Of Asset
Valuation," ABR, 1973-74, Vol. 4, No. 15, pp. 220-226.

Warren, Carl S. and Jack E. Wilkerson, Jr. "The Role Of
Observation, Inquiry And Reperformance," CPAJ, 1985,
Vol. 55, No. 8, pp. 46-49.

Warren, Carl S. "Audit Risk," JOA, 1979, Vol. 148, No. 2,
pp. 66-74.

Warren, Carl S. "Characteristics Of Firms Reporting Consistency Exceptions - A Cross-Sectional Analysis," AR,
1977, Vol. 52, No. 1, pp. 150-161.

Warren, Carl S. "Confirmation Informativeness," JAR, 1974,
Vol. 12. No. 1, pp. 158-177.

Warren, Carl S. "Uniformity Of Auditing Standards," JAR,
1975, Vol. 13, No. 1, pp. 162-176.

Warren, Carl S. "Uniformity Of Auditing Standards: A Replication." JAR, 1980, Vol. 18, No. 1, pp. 312-324.

Warren, Carl S. (Kiger, Jack E. and Carl S. Warren. "Visiting Professorships," AR, 1975, Vol. 50, No. 2, pp. 387-
391.)

Warren, Carl S. (Kinney, William R., Jr. and Carl S.
Warren. "The Decision-Theory Approach To Audit Sampling:
An Extension And Application To Receivables
Confirmation," JAR, 1979, Vol. 17, No. 1, pp. 275-285.)

Warren, Carl S., Stephen V. N. Yates and George R. Zuber.
"Audit Sampling: A Practical Approach," JOA, 1982, Vol.
153. No. 1, pp. 62-72.

Warren, Linda K. "Charting Staff Functions For Better
Management," MA, 1986, Vol. 68, No. 6, pp. 49-50.

Warriner, Philip. "How Statistical Analysis Can Serve
Accountants," AR, 1951, Vol. 26, No. 3, pp. 362-370.

Warthen, William H. F., Jr. "Mix Variances In Profit Rate
Analysis." MA, 1972, Vol. 53, No. 12, pp. 43-45.

Wasley, Robert S. "A Cash Budget For The Small Manufacturer," AR, 1954, Vol. 29, No. 3, pp. 409-412.

Wasley, Robert S. "A Revitalized Accounting Curriculum,"
AR, 1963, Vol. 38, No. 1, pp. 151-153.

Wasley, Robert S. "Sales Planning For The Small Manufacturer," AR, 1953, Vol. 28, No. 2, pp. 244-248.

Wasley, Robert S. "The Role Of Management Accounting In New
Zealand Business," IJAER, 1975, Vol. 10, No. 2, pp. 57-
74.

Wasley, R. S. "The Status Of Accountancy And Of Accounting
Practices In New Zealand," IJAER, 1968, Vol. 3, No. 2,
pp. 67-89.

Wasserman, Max J. "Accounting Instruction In France," AR,
1932, Vol. 7, No. 4, pp. 268-272.

Wasserman, Max J. "Accounting Practice In France During The
Period Of Monetary Inflation (1919-1927)," AR, 1931.
Vol. 6, No. 1, pp. 1-32.

Wasserman, Max J. "Costs And Volume In The Milk Pasteuriz-
ing Industry," AR, 1946, Vol. 21, No. 4, pp. 425-429.

Wasserman, Max J. "French Enterprise Under Inflation: A
Balance Sheet Analysis," AR, 1934, Vol. 9, No. 2, pp.
130-139.

Wasserman, Max J. "The Regulation Of Public Accounting In
France." AR, 1931, Vol. 6, No. 4, pp. 249-260.

Wasserman, William. (Hannum, William H. and William Wasserman. "General Adjustments And Price Level Measurement."
AR, 1968, Vol. 43, No. 2, pp. 295-302.)

Wasyluka, Ray. "Staff Motivation In The CPA Firm," JOA,
1966, Vol. 122, No. 2, pp. 37-40.

Wat, Leslie. (Barden, Ronald S., James E. Copeland, Jr.,
Roger H. Hermanson and Leslie Wat. "Going Public - What
It Involves," JOA, 1984, Vol. 157, No. 3, pp. 63-76.)

Watanabe, Judith E., Virginia L. Bean and Justin D. Stolen.
"An Empirical Study Of Complexity Experience By Taxpayers," AIT, 1987, Vol. 1, pp. 153-168.

Watanabe, Yoshiwo. "Accountancy Profession In Japan," AR,
1939, Vol. 14, No. 4, pp. 430-432.

Waterhouse, John H. (Bruns, William J., Jr. and John H.
Waterhouse. "Budgetary Control And Organization Structure." JAR, 1975, Vol. 13, No. 2, pp. 177-203.)

Waterhouse, J. H. and P. Tiessen. "A Contingency Framework
For Management Accounting Systems Research," AOS, 1978,
Vol. 3. No. 1. pp. 65-76.

Waterhouse, J. H. (Swieringa, R. J. and J. H. Waterhouse.
"Organizational Views Of Transfer Pricing," AOS, 1982,
Vol. 7, No. 2, pp. 149-166.)

Waterhouse, J. H. (Tiessen, Peter and J. H. Waterhouse. "The Contingency Theory Of Managerial Accounting: A Comment," **AR**, 1978, Vol. 53. No. 2, pp. 523-529.)

Waterhouse, J. H. (Tiessen, P. and J. H. Waterhouse. "Towards A Descriptive Theory Of Management Accounting." **AOS**, 1983, Vol. 8. No. 2/3, pp. 251-268.)

Waters, Gary L. (Fields, Kent T., Gary L. Waters and James H. Thompson. "Accounting For The Costs Of Certain Computer Software," **CPAJ**, 1986, Vol. 56, No. 1. pp. 32-37.)

Watkins, Paul R. "Multidimensional Scaling Measurement And Accounting Research," **JAR**, 1984, Vol. 22. No. 1, pp. 406-411.

Watkins, Paul R. (Biggs. Stanley F., Theodore J. Mock and Paul R. Watkins. "Auditor's Use Of Analytical Review In Audit Program Design," **AR**, 1988. Vol. 63. No. 1, pp. 148-161.)

Watkins, Paul R. (Driscoll, Donna A.. W. Thomas Lin and Paul R. Watkins. "Cost-Volume-Profit Analysis Under Uncertainty: A Synthesis And Framework For Evaluation." **JAL**, 1984. Vol. 3, pp. 85-116.)

Watkins, Paul R. (Milliron. Valerie C.. Paul R. Watkins and Stewart S. Karlinsky. "Policy Judgments Of Taxpayers: An Analysis Of Criteria Employed." **AIT**. 1988. Vol. 2, pp. xx-xx.)

Watne, Donald A. and Bruce A. Baldwin. "University-Level Education Of Accountants In The People's Republic Of China," **IAE**, 1988. Vol. 3. No. 1, pp. 139-155.)

Watson, Collin J. (Stock. Duane and Collin J. Watson. "Human Judgment Accuracy. Multidimensional Graphics, And Humans Versus Models," **JAR**, 1984, Vol. 22. No. 1, pp. 192-206.)

Watson, David J. H. and John V. Baumler. "Transfer Pricing: A Behavioral Context," **AR**, 1975, Vol. 50. No. 3, pp. 466-474.

Watson, David J. H. "Students As Surrogates In Behavioral Business Research: Some Comments." **AR**. 1974, Vol. 49. No. 3, pp. 530-533.

Watson, David J. H. "The Structure Of Project Teams Facing Differentiated Environments: An Exploratory Study In Public Accounting Firms," **AR**. 1975. Vol. 50. No. 2. pp. 259-273.

Watson, David J. H. (Albrecht, William Steve. Orace Johnson, Larry L. Lookabill and David J. H. Watson. "A Comparison Of The Accuracy Of Corporate And Security Analysts' Forecasts Of Earnings: A Comment." **AR**, 1977, Vol. 52. No. 3. pp. 736-740.)

Watson, Dorothy M. (Hoecker, Olivia J. and Dorothy M. Watson. "Risk Management: More Than Insurance." **MA**. 1984, Vol. 66, No. 2. pp. 22-29.)

Watson, D. J. H. (Jiambalvo. J.. D. J. H. Watson and J. V. Baumler. "An Examination Of Performance Evaluation Decisions In CPA Firm Subunits." **AOS**. 1983. Vol. 8, No. 1. pp. 13-30.)

Watson, Hugh J. (Tummins. Marvin and Hugh J. Watson. "Advantages Of Regression Analysis Over Ratio Analysis." **CPAJ**, 1975. Vol. 45. No. 5. pp. 35-38.)

Watson, J. Donald. "Annuities Illustrated By Diagrams." **AR**. 1936, Vol. 11, No. 2. pp. 192-194.

Watson, J. Donald. "Explaining Annuity Formulas." **AR**. 1936, Vol. 11, No. 4. pp. 388-389.

Watson, Peter L. "Accounting For Deferred Tax On Depreciable Assets," **ABR**, 1978-79. Vol. 9. No. 36. pp. 338-347.

Watson, Robert H. "A Course In Contemporary Literature For Accountants," **AR**, 1960, Vol. 35. No. 4. p. 732.

Watson, Robert H. "Investment Questions Which Involve The Method Of Distributing Partnership Profits." **AR**. 1952. Vol. 27, No. 1. pp. 136-137.

Watson, Robert H. "Two-Variate Analysis," **AR**, 1960, Vol. 35. No. 1. pp. 96-99.

Watson, Robert. (Keasey. Kevin and Robert Watson. "The Prediction Of Small Company Failure: Some Behavioural Evidence For The UK," **ABR**, 1986-87. Vol. 17. No. 65. pp. 49-58.)

Watson, R. (Keasey, K.. R. Watson and P. Wynarczyk. "The Small Company Audit Qualification: A Preliminary Investigation." **ABR**. 1988. Vol. 18. No. 72. pp. 323-333.)

Watson, Sameul M. (Sussman. Paul E. and Samuel M. Watson. "Documentation For Wage/Price Compliance: Implications For The CPA." **CPAJ**. 1972. Vol. 42. No. 3. pp. 225-228.)

Watson, Spencer C. "A Vote For R&D Profit Centers." **MA**. 1975. Vol. 56, No. 10. pp. 50-52.

Watts, Ross L. and Jerold L. Zimmerman. "Towards A Positive Theory Of The Determination Of Accounting Standards." **AR**, 1978. Vol. 53. No. 1, pp. 112-134.

Watts, Ross L. and Jerold L. Zimmerman. "On The Irrelevance Of Replacement Cost Disclosures For Security Prices." **JABC**, 1980, Vol. 2. No. 2. pp. 95-106.

Watts, Ross L. and Jerold L. Zimmerman. "The Demand For And Supply Of Accounting Theories: The Market For Excuses." **AR**, 1979. Vol. 54. No. 2. pp. 273-305.

Watts, Ross L. and Richard W. Leftwich. "The Time Series Of Annual Accounting Earnings," **JAR**, 1977, Vol. 15. No. 2, pp. 253-271.

Watts, Ross L. (Kothari, S. P.. Thomas Lys. Clifford W. Smith and Ross L. Watts. "Auditor Liability And Information Disclosure," **JAAF**, 1988. Vol. 3 (New Series). No. 4. pp. 307-339.)

Watts, Ross L. (Leftwich, Richard. Ross L. Watts and Jerold L. Zimmerman. "Voluntary Corporate Disclosure: The Case Of Interim Reporting." **JAR**. 1981. Vol. 19. Supp., pp. 50-84.)

Watts, Ross. (Ball, Ray, Baruch Lev and Ross Watts. "Income Variation And Balance Sheet Compositions." **JAR**. 1976. Vol. 14, No. 1, pp. 1-9.)

Watts, Ross. (Dopuch, Nicholas and Ross Watts. "Using Time-Series Models To Assess The Significance Of Accounting Changes," **JAR**, 1972, Vol. 10, No. 1, pp. 180-194.)

Watt, George C. "Toward Worldwide Accounting Principles," **CPAJ**. 1972. Vol. 42, No. 8, pp. 651-653.

Watt, George C. "Unrealized Foreign Exchange Gains And Losses," **MA**, 1968. Vol. 49. No. 8, pp. 31-38.

Watzlaff, R. H. "The Bubble Act Of 1720," **ABACUS**, 1971, Vol. 7. No. 1, pp. 8-28.

Waugh, James B. "The Interperiod Allocation Of Corporate Income Taxes: A Proposal," **AR**, 1968, Vol. 43. No. 3, pp. 535-539.

Wawro, James. "An Accountant's Guide To Leaky Shelters," **JOA**, 1978, Vol. 146. No. 5, pp. 60-64.

Waxman, Robert N. "Review Of APB Opinion No. 21 - Interest On Receivables And Payables," **CPAJ**, 1972, Vol. 42, No. 8, pp. 627-634.

Waymire, Gregory and Grace Pownall. "Some Evidence On Potential Effects Of Contemporaneous Earnings Disclosures In Tests Of Capital Market Effects Associated With FASB Exposure Draft No. 19," **JAR**, 1983. Vol. 21, No. 2, pp. 629-643.

Waymire, Gregory. "Additional Evidence On The Accuracy Of Analyst Forecasts Before And After Voluntary Management Earnings Forecasts," **AR**, 1986, Vol. 61. No. 1. pp. 129-142.

Waymire, Gregory. "Additional Evidence On The Information Content Of Management Earnings Forecasts," **JAR**, 1984, Vol. 22. No. 2, pp. 703-718.

Waymire, Gregory. "Earnings Volatility And Voluntary Management Forecast Disclosure," **JAR**, 1985, Vol. 23, No. 1. pp. 268-295.

Waymire, Gregory. (Sunder, Shyam and Gregory Waymire. "Marginal Gains In Accuracy Of Valuation From Increasingly Specific Price Indexes: Empirical Evidence For The U.S. Economy," **JAR**, 1983, Vol. 21, No. 2, pp. 565-580.)

Waymire, Gregory. (Sunder, Shyam and Gregory Waymire. "Accuracy Of Exchange Valuation Rules: Additivity And Unbiased Estimation," **JAR**, 1984, Vol. 22, No. 1, pp. 396-405.)

Weathers, Henry T. and Carole A. Cheatham. "Earnings Statement For Prediction, Comparison, And Evaluation," **MA**, 1976. Vol. 57. No. 9, pp. 17-18.

Weathers, Henry T. "An Eclectic Accounting Approach," **MA**, 1972. Vol. 54. No. 6, pp. 35-38.

Weathers, Henry T. "Managerial Profitability," **MA**, 1974, Vol. 56. No. 1. pp. 25-27.

Webber, David E. "Metrication And The Accountant," **MA**. 1976. Vol. 57. No. 12. pp. 49-50.

Webb, J. (Barnes. P. and J. Webb. "Management Information Changes And Functional Fixation: Some Experimental Evidence From The Public Sector," **AOS**, 1986, Vol. 11, No. 1. pp. 1-18.)

Webb, K. M. (Edwards J. R. and K. M. Webb. "The Development Of Group Accounting In The United Kingdom To 1933," **AHJ**, 1984. Vol. 11, No. 1, pp. 31-61.)

Webb, K. M. (Edwards. J. R. and K. M. Webb. "Use Of Table A By Companies Registering Under The Companies Act 1862," **ABR**. 1984-85. Vol. 15. No. 59, pp. 177-196.)

Webb, Richard D. "Audit Planning - EDP Considerations," **JOA**, 1979. Vol. 147. No. 5. pp. 65-75.

Webb, Richard. "AUDASSIST," **JOA**, 1970, Vol. 130. No. 5, pp. 53-58.

Weber, Charles. "Income Determination Theory: Some Mathematical And Graphical Approaches," **IJAER**, 1966, Vol. 2. No. 1. pp. 35-47.

Weber, Charles. "The Mathematics Of Variance Analysis." **AR**, 1963. Vol. 38. No. 3, pp. 534-539.

Weber, Fred. "Restrictions On Assets," **AR**, 1951, Vol. 26, No. 1. pp. 43-44.

Weber, G. Fred. "Price Level Accounting," **AR**, 1960. Vol. 35. No. 4, pp. 641-649.

Weber, John A. "Keeping Current On New Developments In Accounting," **IJAER**, 1971, Vol. 7, No. 1. pp. 115-123.

Weber, Joseph V. (Beresford, Dennis R., Lawrence C. Best and Joseph V. Weber. "Accounting For Income Taxes: Change Is Coming," **JOA**, 1984, Vol. 157. No. 1, pp. 72-79.)

Weber, Joseph V., Alex T. Arcady and Michael Valine. "Junior Stock For Executive Compensation," **CPAJ**, 1984, Vol. 54. No. 6, pp. 22-29.

Weber, Joseph V., John J. Mahoney, Jr. and Steven W. Hackett. "Inventory Costing Under TRA 86 - Part I," **CPAJ**, 1988. Vol. 58. No. 5. pp. 66-71.

Weber, Joseph V., John J. Mahoney, Jr. and Steven W. Hackett. "Inventory Costing Under TRA 86 - Part III," **CPAJ**. 1988. Vol. 58. No. 8. pp. 64-69.

Weber, Joseph V., John J. Mahoney, Jr. and Steven W. Hackett. "Inventory Costing Under TRA 86 - Part II," **CPAJ**. 1988. Vol. 58. No. 6. pp. 26-33.

Weber, Richard P. and W. C. Stevenson. "Evaluations Of Accounting Journals And Department Quality," **AR**, 1981, Vol. 56. No. 3. pp. 596-612.

Weber, Richard P. "Allocations Of Consolidated Taxes - Fiction In Financial Statements," **JATA**, 1985. Vol. 7, No. 1. pp. 44-51.

Weber, Richard P. "Misleading Tax Figures - A Problem For Accountants," **AR**, 1977. Vol. 52, No. 1, pp. 172-185.

Weber, Richard P. "Misleading Tax Figures - A Problem For Accountants: A Reply," **AR**, 1978, Vol. 53, No. 2, pp. 520-522.

Weber, Richard P. (Outslay, Edmund and Richard P. Weber. "Minimizing The Tax Cost Of Faculty Research Grants," **JATA**. 1986. Vol. 7, No. 2, pp. 48-59.)

Weber, Ron. "Audit Trail System Support In Advanced

Computer-Based Accounting Systems," **AR**, 1982, Vol. 57, No. 2, pp. 311-325.

Weber, **Ron**. "Auditor Decision Making On Overall System Reliability: Accuracy, Consensus, And The Usefulness Of A Simulation Decision Aid," **JAR**, 1978, Vol. 16, No. 2, pp. 368-388.

Weber, **Ron**. "Data Models Research In Accounting: An Evaluation Of Wholesale Distribution Software," **AR**, 1986, Vol. 61, No. 3, pp. 498-518.

Weber, **Ron**. "Some Characteristics Of The Free Recall Of Computer Controls By EDP Auditors," **JAR**, 1980, Vol. 18, No. 1, pp. 214-241.

Weber, **Ron**. "Toward A Theory Of Artifacts: A Paradigmatic Base For Information Systems Research," **JIS**, 1987, Vol. 1, No. 2, pp. 3-19.

Weber, **Ron**. (Davis, Gordon B. and Ron Weber. "The Impact Of Advanced Computer Systems On Controls And Audit Procedures: A Theory And An Empirical Test," **AJPT**, 1985-86, Vol. 5, No. 2, pp. 35-49.)

Weber, **Ron**. (Everest, Gordon C. and Ron Weber. "A Relational Approach To Accounting Models," **AR**, 1977, Vol. 52, No. 2, pp. 340-359.)

Weber, **Ron**. (Milne, Frank and Ron Weber. "Regulation And The Auditing Profession In The USA: The Metcalf Subcommittee's Recommendations Re-Examined," **ABR**, 1980-81, Vol. 11, No. 43, pp. 197-206.)

Webster, **Marshall W**. "Installing A New Direct Cost System," **MA**, 1971, Vol. 52, No. 9, pp. 31-34.

Webster, **Norman E**. "College Education As A Requirement For Certified Public Accountants - The New York Experience," **AR**, 1946, Vol. 21, No. 4, pp. 445-450.

Webster, **Norman E**. "Higher Education For Public Accountants," **AR**, 1938, Vol. 13, No. 2, pp. 117-123.

Webster, **Norman E**. "Shall I Become A Public Accountant?," **AR**, 1939, Vol. 14, No. 4, pp. 409-414.

Webster, **Norman E**. "Some Early Accountancy Examiners," **AR**, 1944, Vol. 19, No. 2, pp. 142-149.

Webster, **Norman E**. "The Examiner's Point Of View," **AR**, 1937, Vol. 12, No. 2, pp. 111-113.

Webster, **Norman E**. "The Meaning Of 'Public Accountant'," **AR**, 1944, Vol. 19, No. 4, pp. 366-376.

Webster, **Paul K**. "A Look At The New Look In Federal Taxation," **JOA**, 1955, Vol. 100, No. 4, pp. 43-49.

Webster, **Paul**. "Income Determination & Accounting For Emergency Facilities," **JOA**, 1953, Vol. 95, No. 5, pp. 580-587.

Webster, **Stuart K**. (Burger, Albert D. and Stuart K. Webster. "The Management Accountant Looks At EPS Vs. ROI: Conflict In Measuring Performance," **MA**, 1978, Vol. 60, No. 2, pp. 19-24.)

Wedemeyer, **Phil D**. (Roberts, Donald M. and Phil D. Wedemeyer. "Assessing The Likelihood Of Financial Statement Errors Using A Discriminant Model," **JAL**, 1988, Vol. 7, pp. 133-146.)

Wedick, **John L.**, **Jr**. "Electronic Filing At The IRS: The Goal Is Global," **JOA**, 1986, Vol. 162, No. 4, pp. 110-119.

Weed, **Ralph J**. "Financial Sources In The Public Sector," **MA**, 1978, Vol. 60, No. 4, pp. 23-28.

Weetman, **Pauline**. "Accounting Standards: A Pause For Reflection," **ABR**, 1976-77, Vol. 7, No. 27, pp. 168-176.

Wegener, **Steve M**. (Zikmund, William G., Ralph F. Catalanello and Steve M. Wegener. "The Accounting Student's Job-Rating Criteria: An Experiment," **AR**, 1977, Vol. 52, No. 3, pp. 729-735.)

Wehr, **P. N**. "How To Control, Establish, Eliminate Office Paperwork," **JOA**, 1952, Vol. 94, No. 1, pp. 74-77.

Wehr, **P. N.**, **Jr**. "Disclosing Fixed-Asset Commitments In Statements," **JOA**, 1951, Vol. 92, No. 3, pp. 322-325.

Wehr, **P. N.**, **Jr**. "Picking The Best Time To Audit An Account," **JOA**, 1954, Vol. 97, No. 1, pp. 58-61.

Wehr, **P. N.**, **Jr**. "What Are Alternative Procedures, And How Should The Auditor Use Them?," **JOA**, 1950, Vol. 89, No. 6, pp. 500-505.

Weicker, **Lowell P.**, **Jr**. "The Liability Insurance Crisis: Its Impact On Small Business," **JOA**, 1986, Vol. 161, No. 5, pp. 66-67.

Weick, **Karl E**. "Stress In Accounting Systems," **AR**, 1983, Vol. 58, No. 2, pp. 350-369.

Weick, **Karl E**. (Swieringa, Robert J. and Karl E. Weick. "An Assessment Of Laboratory Experiments In Accounting," **JAR**, 1982, Vol. 20, Supp., pp. 56-101.)

Weick, **K. E**. (Swieringa, R. J. and K. E. Weick. "Management Accounting And Action," **AOS**, 1987, Vol. 12, No. 3, pp. 293-308.)

Weidenbaum, **M. L**. "Measures Of The Government Spending Process," **AR**, 1960, Vol. 35, No. 2, pp. 238-245.

Weidenhammer, **Robert**. "The Accountant And The Securities Act," **AR**, 1933, Vol. 8, No. 4 pp. 272-278.

Weigand, **Robert E**. "The Accountant And Marketing Channels." **AR**, 1963. Vol. 38, No. 3, pp. 584-590.

Weigmann, **W**. "Legal And Economic Concepts Of The Balance Sheet In Germany," **AR**, 1932. Vol. 7, No. 2, pp. 103-106.

Weil, **Roman L**. "Managing Earnings Using An Insurance Subsidiary: A Case Of Restraint By Sears/Allstate," **AR**, 1980, Vol. 55, No. 4, pp. 680-684.

Weil, **Roman L**. "Reciprocal Or Mutual Holdings: Allocating Earnings And Selecting The Accounting Method," **AR**, 1973, Vol. 48, No. 4, pp. 749-758.

Weil, **Roman L**. "The Algorithm For Lower-Of-Cost-Or-Market Inventory Valuation: Mathematical Notation Makes It Easy," **AR**, 1973, Vol. 48, No. 3, p. 598.

Weil, **Roman L**. (Davidson, Sidney and Roman L. Weil. "On Holding Gains And Losses And The Evaluation Of Management: A Comment," **AR**, 1974, Vol. 49, No. 3, pp.524-527.)

Weil, **Roman L**. (Davidson, Sidney and Roman L. Weil. "Income Tax Implications Of Various Methods Of Accounting For Changing Prices," **JAR**, 1978, Vol. 16, Supp., pp. 154-233.)

Weil, **Roman L**. (Nurnberg, Hugo, Clyde P. Stickney and Roman L. Weil. "Combining Stockholders' Equity Accounts Under Pooling Of Interests Method," **AR**, 1975, Vol. 50, No. 1, pp. 179-183.)

Weil, **Roman L**. (Schipper, Katherine, John R. Twombly and Roman L. Weil. "Financial Lease Evaluation Under Conditions Of Uncertainty: A Comment," **AR**, 1974, Vol. 49, No. 4, pp. 796-801.)

Weil, **Roman L**. (Schipper, Katherine and Roman L. Weil. "Alternative Accounting Treatments For Pensions," **AR**, 1982, Vol. 57, No. 4, pp. 806-824.)

Weil, **Roman L**. (Shanno, David F. and Roman L. Weil. "The Separate Phases Method Of Accounting For Leveraged Leases: Properties Of The Allocating Rate And An Algorithm For Finding It," **JAR**, 1976, Vol. 14, No. 2, pp. 348-356.)

Weil, **Roman L**. (Stickney, Clyde P., Roman L. Weil and Mark A. Wolfson. "Income Taxes And Tax-Transfer Leases: General Electric's Accounting For A Molotov Cocktail," **AR**, 1983, Vol. 58, No. 2. pp. 439-459.)

Weil, **Roman**. (Dietrich, Richard and Roman Weil. "Partial Rank, Linear Management Information Systems," **AR**, 1974, Vol. 49, No. 4, pp. 846-851.)

Weiland, **Michael**. (Chandler, John S., Thomas Trone and Michael Weiland. "Decision Support Systems Are For Small Businesses," **MA**, 1983, Vol. 64, No. 10, pp. 34-39.)

Weimer, **Arthur M**. and Herman C. Miller. "The Attraction And Selection Of Accounting Teachers," **AR**, 1956, Vol. 31, No. 3, pp. 407-410.

Weinberg, **Seymour**. "Order Handling - A Computer Application For Small Companies," **MA**, 1966, Vol. 47, No. 12, pp. 44-48.

Weinberg, **Steven J**. "Why Choose An Accounting Software Package?," **MA**, 1980, Vol. 61, No. 8, pp. 44-47.

Weiner, **David P**. and Marc Lumer. "Accountants For The Public Interest: A Brief History," **CPAJ**, 1975, Vol. 45, No. 3, pp. 18-20.

Weiner, **David P**. "Do Private Universities Need Audit Committees?," **MA**, 1981, Vol. 62, No. 7, pp. 51-53.

Weiner, **Julian**. "Can Completed Contract Basis Be Used For Tax Purposes?," **JOA**, 1952, Vol. 94, No. 6, pp. 708-712.

Weiner, **Julian**. "Per Diem Costing In Hospitals," **JOA**, 1951, Vol. 91, No. 3, pp. 439-443.

Weingard, **Marvin**. "The Rockford Files: A Case For The Computer," **MA**, 1979, Vol. 60, No. 10, pp. 36-38.

Weingartner, **H. M**. "The Excess Present Value Index - A Theoretical Basis And Critque," **JAR**, 1963, Vol. 1, No. 2, pp. 213-224.

Weinstein, **Arnold K.**, Louis Corsini and Ronald Pawliczek. "The Big Eight In Europe," **IJAER**, 1978, Vol. 13, No. 2, pp. 57-71.

Weinstein, **Edward A**. and Bradford E. Smith. "Public Service And The Profession," **JOA**, 1985, Vol. 159, No. 5, pp. 114-120.

Weinstein, **Edward A**. "A Time Of Travail And Challenge," **CPAJ**, 1974, Vol. 44, No. 12, pp. 29-35.

Weinstein, **Edward A**. "Disclosure: Too Much Or Too Little?," **CPAJ**, 1977, Vol. 47, No. 4, pp. 27-32.

Weinstein, **Edward A**. "Forging Nonprofit Accounting Principles," **AR**, 1978, Vol. 53, No. 4, pp. 1005-1016.

Weinstein, **Edward A**. "Forging Nonprofit Accounting Principles - An Update," **AR**, 1980, Vol. 55, No. 4, pp. 685-691.

Weinstein, **Edward A**. "Government As A Client," **CPAJ**, 1977, Vol. 47, No. 11, pp. 19-24.

Weinstein, **Edward A**. "Let The Buyer Beware!," **JOA**, 1965, Vol. 119, No. 6, pp. 53-60.

Weinstein, **Edward A**. "Vacation Pay: Theory Vs. Practice," **CPAJ**, 1979, Vol. 49, No. 5, pp. 35-39.

Weinstein, **E. A**. "The Achilles Heel Of Retailing: Accounts Payable," **JOA**, 1969, Vol. 128, No. 1, pp. 48-52.

Weinstein, **George**. "Tax Aspects Of Professional Corporations." **MA**, 1972, Vol. 53, No. 7, pp. 19-24.

Weinstein, **Mark G**. (Brenner, Vincent C., Claude W. Carmack and Mark G. Weinstein. "An Empirical Test Of The Motivation-Hygiene Theory," **JAR**, 1971, Vol. 9, No. 2, pp. 359-366.)

Weinstock, **Irwin**. (Coe, Robert K. and Irwin Weinstock. "Evaluating The Accounting Professor's Journal Publications," **JAED**, 1983, Vol. 1, No. 1, pp. 127-129.)

Weintrop, **Joseph**. (Brown, Lawrence D., Ronald J. Huefner and Joseph Weintrop. "Financial Data Bases In Accounting Doctoral Programs," **IAE**, 1988, Vol. 3, No. 2, pp. 228-240.)

Weinwurm, **Ernest H**. "Modernizing The Goodwill Concept," **MA**, 1971, Vol. 53, No. 6, pp. 31-34.

Weinwurm, **Ernest H**. "Professional Accounting Examinations In Great Britain," **AR**, 1957, Vol. 32, No. 1, pp. 60-67.

Weinwurm, **Ernest H**. "The Importance Of Idle Capacity Costs," **AR**, 1961, Vol. 36, No. 3, pp. 418-421.

Weinwurm, **Ernest H**. (Langenderfer, Harold Q. and Ernest H. Weinwurm. "Bringing Accounting Curricula Up-To-Date," **AR**, 1956, Vol. 31, No. 3, pp. 423-430.)

Weirich, **Thomas R**. and Elizabeth J. Ringelberg. "Omitted Audit Procedures," **CPAJ**, 1984, Vol. 54, No. 3, pp. 34-39.

Weirich, **Thomas R**. and George M. Pintar. "Interpretation And Flowchart Of SSARS No. 1," **JOA**, 1979, Vol. 148, No. 5, pp. 60-66.

Weirich, **Thomas R**. "Auditing Standards Update," **CPAJ**, 1977, Vol. 47, No. 8, pp. 41-45.

Weirich, Thomas R., Clarence G. Avery and Henry R. Anderson. "International Accounting: Varying Definitions," IJAER, 1971, Vol. 7, No. 1, pp. 79-87.
Weisenburger, Sylvia. (Douglas, Patricia, Teresa Beed, Karen Clark and Sylvia Weisenburger. "Surviving Your First Job," MA, 1986, Vol. 67, No. 12, pp. 32-35.)
Weiser, Herbert J. "A Movement Toward Fair And Meaningful Reporting," MA, 1977, Vol. 58, No. 8, pp. 13-16.
Weiser, Herbert J. "Accounting Education - Present And Future," AR, 1966, Vol. 41, No. 3, pp. 518-524.
Weiser, Herbert J. "Break-Even Analysis: A Re-Evaluation," MA, 1969, Vol. 50, No. 6, pp. 36-41.
Weisman, Adam R. "The Prevention Of Fraud, Waste And Mismanagement In Defense Contracting," CPAJ, 1987, Vol. 57, No. 6, pp. 26-33.
Weiss, Allen. "Forecasting Collections Of Receivables," JOA, 1964, Vol. 118, No. 3, pp. 63-66.
Weiss, Arthur. "New Inventory Control System Speeds Orders," JOA, 1951, Vol. 91, No. 4, pp. 570-574.
Weiss, Charles J. "An Adjunct To The Accounting Curriculum: The Business Radio Series," AR, 1962, Vol. 37, No. 2, pp. 344-345.
Weiss, Debra. "Valuation Of Closely Held Stocks - A Recent Decision," CPAJ, 1987, Vol. 57, No. 6, pp. 40-47.
Weiss, Ira R. (Lientz, Bennet P. and Ira R. Weiss. "The Vulnerability Of Computer Auditing," CPAJ, 1977, Vol. 47, No. 3, pp. 17-22.)
Weiss, Ira R. (Pearson, Della A., Robert E. Seiler and Ira R. Weiss. "Why Do Management Accountants Feel Disliked?," MA, 1982, Vol. 63, No. 9, pp. 14-19.)
Weiss, Ira. (Brief, Richard P., Barbara Merino and Ira Weiss. "Cumulative Financial Statements," AR, 1980, Vol. 55, No. 3, pp. 480-490.)
Weiss, Jerold M. and Israel Blumenfrucht. "CPA Examination Tax Problems: An In-Depth Analysis," JATA, 1981, Vol. 3, No. 1, pp. 19-25.
Weiss, Madeline. "Taking Charge Of Stress," CA, 1987, Vol. 5, No. 4, pp. 49-58.
Weiss, Marvin. "Human Resource Accounting - A Neglected Area," CPAJ, 1972, Vol. 42, No. 9, pp. 735-744.
Weiss, Marvin. "Human Resource Accounting," MA, 1976, Vol. 57, No. 9, pp. 45-46.
Weiss, Stanley H. "An Introduction To Concepts Of Accountant's Liability," CPAJ, 1987, Vol. 57, No. 7, pp. 24-31.
Weiss, Stanley H. "Disclosures Surrounding A Change In Auditors: ASR 165," CPAJ, 1975, Vol. 45, No. 3, pp. 11-17.
Weiss, Steven P. and Ronald E. Grohe. "Complying With The Inventory Capitalization Rules," MA, 1988, Vol. 70, No. 2, pp. 44-49.
Weiss, Timothy J. (Fasci, Martha A., Timothy J. Weiss and Robert L. Worrall. "Everyone Can Use This Cost/Benefit Analysis System," MA, 1987, Vol. 68, No. 7, pp. 44-47.)
Weis, William L. and David E. Tinius. "Does Anyone Understand Nonprofit Reports?," MA, 1980, Vol. 62, No. 5, pp. 25-29.
Weis, William L. (Ramanathan, Kavasseri V. and William L. Weis. "How To Succeed In Nonbusiness (Without Really Trying): A University Case Study," JOA, 1980, Vol. 150, No. 4, pp. 46-53.)
Weis, W. L. (Ramanathan, K. V. and W. L. Weis. "Supplementing Collegiate Financial Statements With Across-Fund Aggregations: An Experimental Inquiry," AOS, 1981, Vol. 6, No. 2, pp. 143-152.)
Weitzel, John P. "Practice Before The Treasury," JOA, 1960, Vol. 109, No. 2, pp. 42-46.
Welam, Ulf Peter. (Kaplan, Robert S. and Ulf Peter Welam. "Overhead Allocation With Imperfect Markets And Nonlinear Technology," AR, 1974, Vol. 49, No. 3, pp. 477-484.)
Welch, G. D. (Metcalf, R. W. and G. D. Welch. "Basic Accounting Theory: A Set Of Three Postulates," MA, 1968, Vol. 49, No. 10, pp. 3-10.)
Welch, Paul R. "A Generalized Distributed Lag Model For Predicting Quarterly Earnings," JAR, 1984, Vol. 22, No. 2, pp. 744-757.
Welcker, William H. "The Public Accountant And Local Government Accounting," AR, 1934, Vol. 9, No. 1, pp. 53-57.
Welke, William R. and Karl G. King. "Using The Computer As An Audit Tool," CPAJ, 1972, Vol. 42, No. 11, pp. 930-935.
Welke, William R. "Accounting For 'Negative Salvage'," JAED, 1988, Vol. 6, No. 2, pp. 325-329.
Welke, William R. "Accounting Systems In The Curriculum," AR, 1966, Vol. 41, No. 2, pp. 253-256.
Welke, William R. "The Accounting Systems Course," AR, 1967, Vol. 42, No. 1, pp. 127-132.
Welker, Robert B. "Discriminant Analysis As An Aid To Employee Selection," AR, 1974, Vol. 49, No. 3, pp. 514-523.
Welker, Robert B. "Discriminant Analysis As An Aid To Employee Selection: A Reply," AR, 1975, Vol. 50, No. 3, pp. 593-594.
Welker, Robert B. (Anderson, Donald T., Harold I. Dycus and Robert B. Welker. "GAAS And The Small Business Audit," CPAJ, 1982, Vol. 52, No. 4, pp. 10-23.)
Welker, Robert B. (Apostolou, Nicholas G., Gary A. Giroux and Robert B. Welker. "The Information Content Of Municipal Spending Rate Data," JAR, 1985, Vol. 23, No. 2, pp. 853-858.)
Welker, Robert B. (Grossman, Steven D., Stanley H. Kratchman and Robert B. Welker. "Comment: The Effect Of Replacement Cost Disclosures On Security Prices," JAAF, 1981, Vol. 4, No. 2, pp. 136-143.)

Welker, Robert B. (Grossman, Steven D., Alan G. Mayper and Robert B. Welker. "Oil And Gas Disclosures - The FASB Reacts," CPAJ, 1983, Vol. 53, No. 5, pp. 24-29.)
Welker, Robert B. (Licata, Michael P., Robert H. Strawser and Robert B. Welker. "A Note On Participation In Budgeting And Locus Of Control," AR, 1986, Vol. 61, No. 1, pp. 112-117.)
Welker, Robert B. (Meixner, Wilda F. and Robert B. Welker. "Judgment Consensus And Auditor Experience: An Examination Of Organizational Relations," AR, 1988, Vol. 63, No. 3. pp. 505-513.)
Welker, R. (Crumbley, D. L., P. M. Davis and R. Welker. "A Subchapter S Corporation Is Taxable: Sometimes," CPAJ, 1977, Vol. 47, No. 12, pp. 23-28.)
Weller, Oren H. "Touch-Tone Attendance And Labor Reporting," MA, 1969, Vol. 51, No. 2, pp. 27-28.
Wellington, Roger. "Capital Budgeting," JOA, 1963, Vol. 115, No. 5, pp. 46-53.
Wellington, Roger. "Challenge Of Management Services," JOA, 1957, Vol. 104, No. 4, pp. 54-58.
Wellington, Roger. "Management Services," JOA, 1956, Vol. 101, No. 6, pp. 57-59.
Welling, P. "A Goal Programming Model For Human Resource Accounting In A CPA Firm," AOS, 1977, Vol. 2, No. 4, pp. 307-316.
Welling, P. "Introducing The MISA," MA, 1977, Vol. 58, No. 8. pp. 31-33.
Wells, Joseph T. "Red Flags: The Key To Reducing White-Collar Theft," CA, 1987, Vol. 5, No. 2, pp. 51-53.
Wells, Joseph T. "The Accountant's Role In The FBI," MA, 1975. Vol. 56, No. 10, pp. 24-26.
Wells, Murray C. "Costing For Activities," MA, 1976, Vol. 57, No. 11, pp. 31-37.
Wells, M. C. and W. D. J. Cotton. "Holding Gains On Fixed Assets," AR, 1965, Vol. 40, No. 4, pp. 829-833.
Wells, M. C. "A Note On The Amortization Of Fixed Assets," AR, 1968, Vol. 43, No. 2, pp. 373-376.
Wells, M. C. "A Pulseless, Inanimate And Boneless Thing," ABACUS, 1970, Vol. 6, No. 1, pp. 88-90.
Wells, M. C. "A Revolution In Accounting Thought?," AR, 1976, Vol. 51, No. 3, pp. 471-482.
Wells, M. C. "A Revolution In Accounting Thought?: A Reply," AR, 1977, Vol. 52, No. 3, pp. 748-750.
Wells, M. C. "Axioms For Historical Cost Valuation," JAR, 1971. Vol. 9, No. 1, pp. 171-180.
Wells, M. C. "Essays In British Accounting Research: A Review," ABR, 1982-83, Vol. 13, No. 50, pp. 151-158.
Wells, M. C. "Four Cost Accounting Classics: A Review," ABR, 1976-77, Vol. 7, No. 28, pp. 300-302.
Wells, M. C. "Management Attitudes," ABACUS, 1966, Vol. 2, No. 2, pp. 184-194.
Wells, M. C. "Profit Centres, Transfer Prices And Mysticism," ABACUS, 1968, Vol. 4, No. 2, pp. 174-181.
Wells, M. C. "Some Influences On The Development Of Cost," AHJ, 1977, Vol. 4, No. 2, pp. 47-61.
Wells, M. C. "Taylor's Contribution To Cost Accounting: A Comment," AHJ, 1982, Vol. 9, No. 2, pp. 69-77.
Wells, M. C. "Transfer Prices And Profit Centres? No," ABACUS, 1971, Vol. 7, No. 1, pp. 54-57.
Wells, M. C. (Bromwich, M. and M. C. Wells. "The Usefulness Of A Measure Of Wealth," ABACUS, 1983, Vol. 19, No. 2, pp. 119-129.)
Wells, M. C. (Gray, S. J. and M. C. Wells. "A Further Comment On Asset Values And Income Measurement," ABR, 1974-75, Vol. 5, No. 18, pp. 91-95.)
Wells, M. C. (Gray, S. J. and M. C. Wells. "Asset Values And Ex Post Income," ABR, 1972-73, Vol. 3, No. 11, pp. 163-167.)
Wells, Wayne R. (Schwieger, Bradley J., Wayne R. Wells and Ronald E. Carlson. "Solicitation - Where Do We Stand Today?," CPAJ, 1988, Vol. 58, No. 11, pp. 66-70.)
Wells, W. Howard, Jr. "Replacement Cost Accounting: How We Did It," MA, 1977, Vol. 59, No. 4, pp. 26-28.
Welsch, Glenn A. "A Fundamental Appraisal Of Profit Planning And Control," MA, 1969, Vol. 50, No. 7, pp. 22-27.
Welsch, Glenn A. "Budgeting For Management Planning And Control," JOA, 1961, Vol. 112, No. 4, pp. 37-41.
Welsch, Glenn A. "Serial Bond Redemption - Bonds Outstanding And Dollar-Period Methods," AR, 1954, Vol. 29, No. 4, pp. 689-691.
Welsch, Glenn A. "Some Challenges For Accounting Education," AR, 1964, Vol. 39, No. 4, pp. 1008-1013.
Welsch, Glenn A. "The Controller's Function In Top-Level Management," JOA, 1954, Vol. 98, No. 1, pp. 66-71.
Welsch, Glenn A. (Shenkir, William G., Glenn A. Welsch and James A. Bear, Jr. "Thomas Jefferson: Management Accountant," JOA, 1972, Vol. 133, No. 4, pp. 33-47.)
Welsh, John J. "Pre-Acquisition Audit: Verifying The Bottom Line," MA, 1983, Vol. 64, No. 7, pp. 32-41.
Welsh, Mary Jeanne and Jerry E. Trapnell. "Labor Market Models And Employer Accounting For Pensions," JAAF, 1985, Vol. 8, No. 2, pp. 100-111.
Welsh, Mary Jeanne. (Alderman, C. Wayne, Glenn E. Sumners and Mary Jeanne Welsh. "The Trend Toward Soft Data In Accounting," MA, 1983, Vol. 65, No. 6, pp. 34-39.)
Welsh, Wayne L. "PPBS And Proposal Formulation," MA, 1972, Vol. 53, No. 11, pp. 31-33.
Weltmer, W. Keith. (Chambers, R. J., John W. Kennelly, Thomas W. McRae, Frank K. Reilly and W. Keith Weltmer. "Historical Cost Accounting," ABACUS, 1971, Vol. 7, No. 1, p. 39.)
Welton, Ralph E. (Friedlob, G. Thomas, F. Ray Gray, Ralph E. Welton and James D. Sloan. "Combining LIFO And FIFO Inventory Disclosure," CPAJ, 1987, Vol. 57, No. 6, pp. 48-53.)

Welton, Ralph E., G. Thomas Friedlob, F. Ray Gray and James Sloan. "LIFO/FIFO: A Simple Solution To Inventory Disclosure Problems," **MA**, 1987, Vol. 69, No. 4, pp. 52-56.

Weltzin, James O. "Why Leave EDP In The Hands Of Specialists?," **MA**, 1970, Vol. 52, No. 4, pp. 9-10.

Wendell, Paul J. "Associations Of CPA Firms," **CPAJ**, 1976, Vol. 46, No. 9, pp. 25-28.

Wendell, Steve. (Bailes, Jack C., James F. Nielsen and Steve Wendell. "Capital Budgeting In The Forest Products Industry," **MA**, 1979, Vol. 61, No. 1, pp. 46-51.)

Wendt, A. P. "Wanted: Unambiguous Replacement For Term 'Earned Surplus'," **JOA**, 1953, Vol. 95, No. 2, pp. 206-209.

Wentz, Daniel J. "How We Match Costs And Revenues In A Service Business," **MA**, 1985, Vol. 67, No. 4, pp. 36-42.

Werbaneth, Louis A., Jr. (Kokkila, Leonard M. and Louis A. Werbaneth, Jr. "The Public Practice Of Accounting: An Experimental Program," **AR**, 1974, Vol. 49, No. 1, pp. 157-159.)

Werner, Charles A. and John W. Kostolansky. "Accounting Liabilities Under ERISA," **JAAF**, 1983, Vol. 7, No. 1, pp. 54-64.

Werner, Charles A. and John W. Kostolansky. "Accounting Liabilities Under The Multiemployer Pension Plan Amendments Act," **JAAF**, 1984, Vol. 7, No. 3, pp. 212-224.

Werner, Charles and John Kostolansky. "Legal Aspects Of Accounting For Post-Employment Health Care And Life Insurance Benefits," **JAAF**, 1988, Vol. 3 (New Series), No. 1, pp. 62-72.

Werner, Robert H. and Lennard J. Greenberg. "Audits Of CETA Programs," **CPAJ**, 1978, Vol. 48, No. 4, pp. 13-20.

Werner, Robert H. and Lennard J. Greenberg. "Auditing And Reporting For CETA Programs," **CPAJ**, 1978, Vol. 48, No. 6, pp. 27-28.

Werner, Robert H. "CPA Opportunities In Federally Assisted Programs," **CPAJ**, 1976, Vol. 46, No. 7, pp. 9-14.

Werne, Benjamin. "A Basic Statement Of WSB Regulations Governing Wage Rises," **JOA**, 1952, Vol. 93, No. 4, pp. 434-437.

Werntz, William W. "Accounting Education And The Ford And Carnegie Reports," **AR**, 1961, Vol. 36, No. 2, pp. 186-190.

Werntz, William W. "Accounting In Transition," **JOA**, 1958, Vol. 105, No. 2, pp. 33-36.

Werntz, William W. "Auditor's Responsibility In Corporate Reports," **JOA**, 1959, Vol. 107, No. 3, pp. 42-49.

Werntz, William W. "Comments On The Capital Principle," **AR**, 1942, Vol. 17, No. 1, pp. 35-59.

Werntz, William W. "Current Deficiencies In Financial Statements," **AR**, 1941, Vol. 16, No. 4, pp. 321-329.

Werntz, William W. "Dilemmas In Today's Reporting," **JOA**, 1955, Vol. 100, No. 5, pp. 44-50.

Werntz, William W. "Intangibles In Combinations," **JOA**, 1957, Vol. 103, No. 5, pp. 46-50.

Werntz, William W. "Recent Developments In Accounting," **AR**, 1947, Vol. 22, No. 2, pp. 131-140.

Werntz, William W. "Resurgence Of The Balance-Sheet," **JOA**, 1953, Vol. 96, No. 5, pp. 555-569.

Werntz, William W. "Some Current Problems In Accounting," **AR**, 1939, Vol. 14, No. 2, pp. 117-125.

Werntz, William W. "The Impact Of Federal Legislation Upon Accounting," **AR**, 1953, Vol. 28, No. 2, pp. 159-169.

Wertz, William F. and Anthony Donadio. "Collateralized Mortgage Obligations," **CPAJ**, 1987, Vol. 57, No. 11, pp. 68-71.

Wescott, Shari H. "Accounting Numbers And Socioeconomic Variables As Predictors Of Municipal General Obligation Bond Ratings," **JAR**, 1984, Vol. 22, No. 1, pp. 412-423.

Wescott, Shari H. "An Assessment Of The Ability Of Accounting Numbers To Predict Municipal General Obligation Bond Ratings," **RIGNA**, 1988, Vol. 4, pp. 79-102.

West, Marilyn. (Reilly, Frank K., David L. Morgenson and Marilyn West. "The Predictive Ability Of Alternative Parts Of Interim Financial Statements," **JAR**, 1972, Vol. 10, Supp., pp. 105-124.)

West, Owen D. (Borthick, A. Faye and Owen D. West. "Expert Systems - A New Tool For The Professional," **ACCHOR**, 1987, Vol. 1, No. 1, pp. 9-16.)

West, Phillip L. "The Reporting Of Earnings To Stockholders," **JOA**, 1959, Vol. 107, No. 2, pp. 27-32.

West, Richard R. "An Alternative Approach To Predicting Corporate Bond Ratings," **JAR**, 1970, Vol. 8, No. 1, pp. 118-125.

West, Richard R. (Hofstedt, Thomas R. and Richard R. West. "The APB, Yield Indices, And Predictive Ability," **AR**, 1971, Vol. 46, No. 2, pp. 329-337.)

West, Stephen G. (Harrison, Paul D., Stephen G. West and J. Hal Reneau. "Initial Attributions And Information-Seeking By Superiors And Subordinates In Production Variance Investigations," **AR**, 1988, Vol. 63, No. 2, pp. 307-320.)

West, W. H. "Message From The American Institute," **AR**, 1926, Vol. 1, No. 1, pp. 61-62.

Westbrook, L. Curtis, Jr. "Financing Real Estate Investment Trusts," **MA**, 1975, Vol. 56, No. 11, pp. 56-58.

Westerfield, Ray Bert. "Building Reserves By Overvaluation Of Assets," **AR**, 1954, Vol. 29, No. 1, pp. 45-51.

Western, Harold. (Smith, Jay M., Dale Taylor and Harold Western. "Experiment In Modularized Learning For Intermediate Accounting," **AR**, 1974, Vol. 49, No. 2, pp. 385-390.)

Weston, Frank T. "Accounting For Inflation," **CPAJ**, 1975, Vol. 45, No. 9, pp. 21-26.

Weston, J. Fred. "Consistency And Changing Price Levels,"

AR, 1949. Vol. 24, No. 4, pp. 379-386.

Weston, J. Fred. "Forecasting Financial Requirements," **AR**, 1958, Vol. 33, No. 3, pp. 427-440.

Weston, J. Fred. "Revaluations Of Fixed Assets," **AR**, 1953, Vol. 28. No. 4, pp. 482-490.

Westphal, William H. "The Future Of The CPA In Tax Practice," **JOA**, 1969, Vol. 127, No. 6, pp. 40-44.

Westphal, William H. "What Is Tax Reform?," **JOA**, 1970, Vol. 129, No. 2, pp. 55-59.

Westwick, C. A. "A Graphical Treatment Of Gearing," **JAR**, 1966, Vol. 4, No. 2, pp. 239-244.

Westwick, C. A. "The Lessons To Be Learned From The Development Of Inflation Accounting In The UK," **ABR**, 1979-80, Vol. 10, No. 40, pp. 353-374.

Westwick, C. A. "Towards A New Measure And Use Of Gearing," **ABR**, 1970-71, Vol. 1, No. 1, pp. 18-29.

Wetjen, John F. "A Not-For-Profit Nightmare," **MA**, 1982, Vol. 64, No. 2, pp. 21-23.

Wetterhall, R. C. "Pitfalls In Estimating Taxes," **JOA**, 1956, Vol. 101, No. 4, pp. 34-40.

Wetzel, Thomas S. (Norton, Curtis L. and Thomas S. Wetzel. "The Recognition And Measurement Guidelines Of FASB Concepts No. 5," **JAED**, 1986, Vol. 4, No. 2, pp. 75-84.)

Weygandt, Jerry J. "The CPA And His Duty To Silence," **AR**, 1970, Vol. 45, No. 1, pp. 69-75.

Weygandt, Jerry J. "Valuation Of Stock Option Contracts," **AR**, 1977, Vol. 52, No. 1, pp. 40-51.

Weygandt, Jerry J. (Bollom, William J. and Jerry J. Weygandt. "An Examination Of Some Interim Reporting Theories For A Seasonal Business," **AR**, 1972, Vol. 47, No. 1, pp. 75-84.)

Weygandt, Jerry J. (Deaton, William C. and Jerry J. Weygandt. "Disclosures Related To Pension Plans," **JOA**, 1975, Vol. 139, No. 1, pp. 44-51.)

Weygandt, Jerry J. (Dilley, Steven C. and Jerry J. Weygandt. "Measuring Social Responsibility: An Empirical Test," **JOA**, 1973, Vol. 136, No. 3, pp. 62-70.)

Weygandt, Jerry J. (Fess, Philip E. and Jerry J. Weygandt. "Cash-Flow Presentations - Trends, Recommendations," **JOA**, 1969, Vol. 128, No. 2, pp. 52-59.)

Weygandt, Jerry J. (Frank, Werner G. and Jerry J. Weygandt. "The APB, Yield Indices, And Predictive Ability: A Reply," **AR**, 1971, Vol. 46, No. 2, pp. 338-341.)

Weygandt, Jerry J. (Frank, Werner G. and Jerry J. Weygandt. "Convertible Debt And Earnings Per Share: Pragmatism Vs. Good Theory," **AR**, 1970, Vol. 45, No. 2, pp. 280-289.)

Weygandt, Jerry J. (Frank, Werner G. and Jerry J. Weygandt. "A Prediction Model For Convertible Debentures," **JAR**, 1971, Vol. 9, No. 1, pp. 116-126.)

Weygandt, Jerry J. (Hirschey, Mark and Jerry J. Weygandt. "Amortization Policy For Advertising And Research And Development Expenditures," **JAR**, 1985, Vol. 23, No. 1, pp. 326-335.)

Weygandt, Jerry J. (Imdieke, Leroy F. and Jerry J. Weygandt. "Accounting For That Imputed Discount Factor," **JOA**, 1970, Vol. 129, No. 6, pp. 54-58.)

Weygandt, Jerry J. (Imdieke, Leroy F. and Jerry J. Weygandt. "Classification Of Convertible Debt," **AR**, 1969, Vol. 44, No. 4, pp. 798-805.)

Weygandt, Jerry J. (Lloyd, B. Michl and Jerry J. Weygandt. "Market Value Information For Nonsubsidiary Investments," **AR**, 1971, Vol. 46, No. 4, pp. 756-764.)

Weygandt, Jerry J. (Nair, R. D. and Jerry J. Weygandt. "Let's Fix Deferred Taxes," **JOA**, 1981, Vol. 152, No. 5. pp. 87-94.)

Weygandt, Jerry J. (Olson, Steven K. and Jerry J. Weygandt. "Evolution Of Accounting Changes: Opinion No. 20," **AR**, 1973, Vol. 48, No. 2, pp. 428-429.)

Weygandt, Jerry J. (Revsine, Lawrence and Jerry J. Weygandt. "Accounting For Inflation: The Controversy," **JOA**, 1974, Vol. 138, No. 4, pp. 72-78.)

Weygandt, Jerry J. (Simons, Donald R. and Jerry J. Weygandt. "Stock Options Revised: Accounting For Option Buy-Outs," **CPAJ**, 1973, Vol. 43, No. 9, pp. 779-783.)

Weygandt, Jerry J. (Taylor, William M. and Jerry J. Weygandt. "Accounting For Stock-Based Awards Using The Minimum Value Method," **JAR**, 1982, Vol. 20, No. 2, Part I, pp. 497-502.)

Whalen, Hugh. (Abraham, Elizabeth, Carol Loughrey and Hugh Whalen. "Computerized Practice Set In Introductory Financial Accounting," **IAE**, 1987, Vol. 2, No. 1, pp. 1-12.)

Whaley, Robert E. and Joseph K. Cheung. "Anticipation Of Quarterly Earnings Announcements: A Test Of Option Market Efficiency," **JAEC**, 1982, Vol. 4, No. 2, pp. 57-83.

Wharton, Don. "Accounting And Reporting For Companies In The Development Stage," **JOA**, 1970, Vol. 130, No. 4, pp. 39-52.

Wharton, Don. (Hanson, Robert E. and Don Wharton. "A Local CPA Firm Plans For The Future," **JOA**, 1965, Vol. 120, No. 3, pp. 43-49.)

Wheatcroft, G. S. A. "Ethical Restraints On Tax Practice In Great Britain," **JOA**, 1961, Vol. 111, No. 2, pp. 59-66.

Wheatley, Edward W. "Auditing Your Marketing Performance," **JOA**, 1983, Vol. 156, No. 3, pp. 68-78.

Wheatley, John J. (Dilley, Steven and John J. Wheatley. "Tax Considerations In Research Grants To Faculty," **AR**, 1977, Vol. 52, No. 4, pp. 915-9201.)

Wheat, George C. and W. Paul Woodson. "A Case For Electronic Business Machines," **MA**, 1972, Vol. 54, No. 6, pp. 20-22.

Wheelen, Thomas L. (Shenker, William G., Thomas L. Wheelen and Robert H. Strawser. "The Making Of An Accountant," **CPAJ**, 1973, Vol. 43, No. 3, pp. 218-221.)

Wheeler, Dennie L. and Robert E. Shirley. "Minimizing The LIFO Pool Sample," **MA**, 1976, Vol. 58, No. 6, pp. 47-53.

Wheeler, James E. and Edmund Outslay. "The Phantom Federal Income Taxes Of General Dynamics Corporation," **AR**, 1986, Vol. 61, No. 4, pp. 760-774.

Wheeler, James E. (Outslay, Edmund and James E. Wheeler. "Separating The Annuity And Income Transfer Elements Of Social Security," **AR**, 1982, Vol. 57, No. 4, pp. 716-733.)

Wheeler, John T. "Accounting Theory And Research In Perspective," **AR**, 1970, Vol. 45, No. 1, pp. 1-10.

Wheeler, John T. (Aranya, Nissim and John T. Wheeler. "Accountants' Personality Types And Their Commitment To Organization And Profession," **CAR**, 1986-87, Vol. 3, No. 1, pp. 184-199.)

Wheeler, John T. (Cyert, Richard M. and John T. Wheeler. "A Proposal For An Integrated Course In Statistics And Accounting," **AR**, 1960, Vol. 35, No. 1, pp. 51-59.)

Wheeler, Robert C., Marlyn D. Felsing and Thomas F. Reilly. "Large Or Small CPA Firms: A Practitioners' Perspective," **CPAJ**, 1987, Vol. 57, No. 4, pp. 29-33.

Wheeler, Thomas R. "Flexible Benefits Work At Smaller Companies, Too," **MA**, 1987, Vol. 69, No. 4, pp. 37-41.

Wheelock, Alton R. (Benke, Ralph L., Jr., James Don Edwards and Alton R. Wheelock. "Applying An Opportunity Cost General Rule For Transfer Pricing," **MA**, 1982, Vol. 63, No. 12, pp. 43-51.)

Wheiler, Kent W. (George, William R. and Kent W. Wheiler. "Practice Development - A Services Marketing Perspective," **CPAJ**, 1986, Vol. 56, No. 10, pp. 30-43.)

Whinston, Andrew B. (Bailey, Andrew D., Jr., Gordon Leon Duke, James Gerlach, Chen-En Ko, Rayman D. Meservy and Andrew B. Whinston. "TICOM And The Analysis Of Internal Controls," **AR**, 1985, Vol. 60, No. 2, pp. 186-201.)

Whinston, Andrew B. (Bailey, Andrew D., R. Preston McAfee and Andrew B. Whinston. "An Application Of Complexity Theory To The Analysis Of Internal Control Systems," **AJPT**, 1981-82, Vol. 1, No. 1, pp. 38-52.)

Whinston, Andrew B. (Cash, James I. Jr., Andrew D. Bailey, Jr. and Andrew B. Whinston. "A Survey Of Techniques For Auditing EDP-Based Accounting Information Systems," **AR**, 1977, Vol. 52, No. 4, pp. 813-832.)

Whinston, Andrew B. (Haseman, William D. and Andrew B. Whinston. "Design Of A Multidimensional Accounting System," **AR**, 1976, Vol. 51, No. 1, pp. 65-79.)

Whinston, Andrew B. (Lieberman, Arthur Z. and Andrew B. Whinston. "A Structuring Of An Events-Accounting Information System," **AR**, 1975, Vol. 50, No. 2, pp. 246-258.)

Whinston, Andrew B. (Nusbaum, Edward E., Andrew D. Bailey, Jr. and Andrew B. Whinston. "Data-Base Management, Accounting, And Accountants," **MA**, 1978, Vol. 59, No. 11, pp. 35-38.)

Whinston, Andrew. (Colantoni, Claude S., Rene P. Manes and Andrew Whinston. "A Unified Approach To The Theory Of Accounting And Information Systems," **AR**, 1971, Vol. 46, No. 1, pp. 90-102.)

Whinston, Andrew. (Colantoni, Claude S., Rene P. Manes and Andrew Whinston. "Programming, Profit Rates And Pricing Decisions," **AR**, 1969, Vol. 44, No. 3, pp. 467-481.)

Whipp, Richard. (Smith, Chris, Richard Whipp and Hugh Willmott. "Case-Study Research In Accounting: Methodological Breakthrough Or Ideological Weapon?," **AIPIA**, 1988, Vol. 2, pp. 95-120.)

Whisler, Thomas L. "The Manager And The Computer," **JOA**, 1965, Vol. 119, No. 1, pp. 27-32.

Whisnant, Susan R. and J. W. Martin. "What Is Cycle Auditing?," **MA**, 1982, Vol. 64, No. 4, pp. 52-55.

Whisnant, Susan R. (Martin, J. W. and Susan R. Whisnant. "Why Johnny Can't Audit," **CPAJ**, 1982, Vol. 52, No. 11, pp. 10-17.)

White, B. Frank. "An Appeal To Accountants For Aid In Tax Administration," **JOA**, 1954, Vol. 98, No. 2, pp. 197-200.

White, Clinton E. (Covaleski, Mark A., Mark W. Dirsmith and Clinton E. White. "Economic Consequences: The Relationship Between Financial Reporting And Strategic Planning, Mgmt. And Oper. Control Decisions," **CAR**, 1986-87, Vol. 3, No. 2, pp. 408-429.)

White, Clinton E., Jr. (Kunitake, Walter K. and Clinton E. White, Jr. "Ethics For Independent Auditors," **JAAF**, 1986, Vol. 1 (New Series), No. 3, pp. 222-231.)

White, Clinton. (Tiller, Mikel G. and Clinton White. "Are Accounting Majors Really Better? Evaluating Admission And Retention Standards For Undergraduate Accounting Programs," **JAED**, 1983, Vol. 1, No. 1, pp. 19-33.)

White, Debra and Mike Vanecek. "Intended Use: A Uniform Tax Definition Of Software," **JAAF**, 1982, Vol. 5, No. 4, pp. 338-354.

White, Debra M. and James W. Giese. "Federal Tax Clinic Practice For Accounting Students," **JATA**, 1982, Vol. 4, No. 1, pp. 33-35.

White, Denis W. "How A Safety Program Affects The Bottom Line," **MA**, 1979, Vol. 60, No. 8, pp. 42-46.

White, Edward. "The Income Tax - Statistical Aspects," **AR**, 1928, Vol. 3, No. 1, pp. 14-17.

White, Gary E. and Phillip F. Ostwald. "Life Cycle Costing," **MA**, 1976, Vol. 57, No. 7, pp. 39-40.

White, Gary E. and Thomas Buchman. "The Continuing Education Requirement: How Effective?," **CPAJ**, 1977, Vol. 47, No. 12, pp. 11-16.

White, Gary E. "Discretionary Accounting Decisions And Income Normalization," **JAR**, 1970, Vol. 8, No. 2, pp. 260-273.

White, Gary E. "Effects Of Discretionary Accounting Policy On Variable And Declining Performance Trends," **JAR**, 1972, Vol. 10, No. 2, pp. 351-358.

White, Gary E. (Moores, Tommy and Gary E. White. "Perceptions Of The Control And Effectiveness Of Schools Of Accountancy," **IAE**, 1985, No. 1, pp. 20-27.)

White, Gerald I. "Pension Accounting: A Challenge For The FASB," **CA**, 1984, Vol. 2, No. 2, pp. 4-12.

White, Godwin T. (Wyer, Jean C., Godwin T. White and Ernest C. Janson. "Audits Of Public Companies By Smaller CPA Firms: Clients, Reports, And Quality," **AJPT**, 1988, Vol. 7, No. 2, pp. 164-173.)

White, Godwin T., Jean C. Wyer and Ernest C. Janson. "Uncertainty Reporting - Impact Of Proposed Changes," **CPAJ**, 1987, Vol. 57, No. 9, pp. 46-53.

White, Godwin T., Jean C. Wyer and Ernest C. Janson. "Peer Review: Proposed Regulations And Current Compliance," **ACCHOR**, 1988, Vol. 2, No. 2, pp. 27-30.

White, Harold C. "A Leadership Audit," **MA**, 1973, Vol. 55, No. 2, pp. 39-41.

White, H. Warren. "Management-Technician Dichotomy," **MA**, 1971, Vol. 53, No. 3, pp. 19-21.

White, H. Warren. "The Man-Machine Relationship In Business Systems," **MA**, 1966, Vol. 47, No. 9, pp. 19-26.

White, James C. "Teaching Of Accounting In Schools Of Engineering," **AR**, 1930, Vol. 5, No. 3, pp. 208-212.

White, James K. (DeMaagd, Gerald R. and James K. White. "Financing Private Capital With IDBs," **MA**, 1985, Vol. 66, No. 7, pp. 49-52.)

White, John Arch. "Accounting Research," **AR**, 1955, Vol. 30, No. 3, pp. 522-532.

White, John A. "Accounting Research," **AR**, 1954, Vol. 29, No. 4, pp. 661-670.

White, Lawrence. (Nelson, Julianne, Joshua Ronen and Lawrence White. "Legal Liabilities And The Market For Auditing Services," **JAAF**, 1988, Vol. 3 (New Series), No. 3, pp. 255-295.)

White, Mick. (Juchau, Roger, Mick White and Roger Hopkins. "Tertiary Education Strategies For Accounting In Developing Societies - The Southwest Pacific As A Case Study," **IJAER**, 1986, Vol. 21, No. 2, pp. 145-160.)

White, Richard A. "Employee Preferences For Nontaxable Compensation Offered In A Cafeteria Compensation Plan: An Empirical Study," **AR**, 1983, Vol. 58, No. 3, pp. 539-561.

White, Richard A. (Golen, Stephen P. and Richard A. White. "Communicating Effectively With Clients," **CPAJ**, 1983, Vol. 53, No. 12, pp. 12-17.)

White, Richard A. (Golen, Steven P., Stephen W. Looney and Richard A. White. "An Empirical Examination Of CPA Perceptions Of Communication Barriers Between Auditor And Client," **AIA**, 1988, Vol. 6, pp. 233-250.)

White, Richard A. (Hartman, Bart P. and Richard A. White. "Why Not Try A Cafeteria Compensation Plan?," **MA**, 1984, Vol. 66, No. 4, pp. 44-47.)

White, Richard A. (Hoffman, Michael J. R. and Richard A. White. "Tax Planning For Employee Home Offices - Part II," **CPAJ**, 1985, Vol. 55, No. 12, pp. 50-55.)

White, Richard A. (Hoffman, Michael J. R. and Richard A. White. "Tax Planning For Employee Home Offices - Part I," **CPAJ**, 1985, Vol. 55, No. 11, pp. 48-56.)

White, Richard A. (Sumners, Glenn E., Richard A. White and Raymond J. Clay, Jr. "The Use Of Engagement Letters In Audit, Review, And Compilation Engagements: An Empirical Study," **AJPT**, 1986-87, Vol. 6, No. 2, pp. 116-122.)

White, Richard. (Johnson, Douglas A., Kurt Pany and Richard White. "Audit Reports And The Loan Decision: Actions And Perceptions," **AJPT**, 1982-83, Vol. 2, No. 2, pp. 38-51.)

White, Robert A. "The Admission Of A Partner By Investment," **AR**, 1937, Vol. 12, No. 4, pp. 427-430.

White, Robert H. "Municipal Budgets," **JOA**, 1960, Vol. 109, No. 4, pp. 55-61.

White, Wayne. "Depreciation Under The Tax Reform Act Of 1969," **MA**, 1972, Vol. 54, No. 4, pp. 29-33.

White, Wilford L. "Problems In Determining Total Costs Of Distribution," **AR**, 1934, Vol. 9, No. 1, pp. 15-21.

White, William C. (Knowles, Asa S. and William C. White. "Teaching Load Of Accounting Instructors," **AR**, 1940, Vol. 15, No. 2, pp. 166-169.)

Whitehead, Charles N. "Business Expenses And Deductions For Corporations And Individuals," **JOA**, 1954, Vol. 98, No. 3, pp. 303-308.

Whitehead, Harold B. (Carruth, J. H., H. B. Whitehead and K. E. Anderson. "Maximizing Contributions To Retirement And Deferred Compensation Plans Under Sections 403(b), 401(k), And 457: A Linear Programming Approach," **JATA**, 1986, Vol. 8, No. 1, pp. 49-72.)

Whitehead, J. Paul, III. "Changes To Installment Sales Provisions Under TRA 86 And The Revenue Act Of 1987," **CPAJ**, 1988, Vol. 58, No. 4, pp. 44-53.

Whitehurst, Frederick D. "The Predictability Of Investor Cash Return From Historical Income Trends Of Common Stocks," **AR**, 1970, Vol. 45, No. 3, pp. 553-564.

Whitehurst, Frederick D. (Warner, Stanley E., Jr. and Frederick D. Whitehurst. "A Graphical Approach To Lower Of Cost Or Market," **AR**, 1982, Vol. 57, No. 3, pp. 631-637.)

Whitehurst, Frederick D. (Warner, Stanley E., Jr. and Frederick D. Whitehurst. "Inconsistency In Inventory Loss Measurements Under The LCM Rule," **JAED**, 1987, Vol. 5, No. 2, pp. 277-285.)

Whitehurst, Frederick D. (Warner, Stanley E., Jr. and Frederick D. Whitehurst. "The Educational Impact Of Unresolved Conceptual Issues In Interest Capitalization," **JAED**, 1988, Vol. 6, No. 2, pp. 209-217.)

Whiteman, Michael J. and Anthony T. Krzystofik. "401(k) Plans: A Time To Act," **MA**, 1986, Vol. 68, No. 3, pp. 33-35.

Whiteman, Michael J., Anthony T. Krzystofik and Joseph E. Finnerty. "Interest Ruling - Questions For Lenders And Borrowers." **CPAJ,** 1984. Vol. 54. No. 1. pp. 39-43.

Whitford, David T. (Gentry, James A., Paul Newbold and David T. Whitford. "Classifying Bankrupt Firms With Funds Flow Components," **JAR,** 1985. Vol. 23. No. 1, pp. 146-160.)

Whiting, Grafton. "Uniform Accounting In A Trade Association," **AR,** 1926. Vol. 1. No. 1. pp. 74-82.

Whitley, R. "The Transformation Of Business Finance Into Financial Economics: The Roles Of Academic Expansion And Changes In U.S. Capital Markets," **AOS,** 1986. Vol. 11. No. 2, pp. 171-192.

Whitman, John. (Theobald, Michael and John Whitman. "The Variabilities And Correlations Of Stock Market Indices." **ABR,** 1978-79, Vol. 9, No. 33. pp. 82-86.)

Whitman, W. Tate. "Liquidation Of Partnerships In Installments," **AR,** 1953. Vol. 28, No. 4, pp. 576-577.

Whitmire, Kathryn J. and Philip B. Scheps. "Municipal Pension Plans: The Long Road Back To Financial Soundness." **MA,** 1979, Vol. 61. No. 4, pp. 30-33.

Whitney, William H. "Deferred Income Tax Liability." **AR,** 1958. Vol. 33, No. 2, pp. 305-309.

Whitney, William H. "Insurance Reserves In The Accounts Of Non-Insurance Companies," **AR,** 1959. Vol. 34. No. 1, pp. 37-45.

Whitney, William H. "Introducing Accounting Majors To Auditing." **AR,** 1949, Vol. 24. No. 1. pp. 89-94.

Whitney, William H. "The Human Side Of The Deflated Dollar Bias," **AR,** 1957. Vol. 32, No. 3, pp. 419-427.

Whitney, W. H. "Accounting For Investments In Life Insurance," **AR,** 1939, Vol. 14, No. 4, pp. 381-390.

Whitsell, Gary M. (Rhode, John Grant, Gary M. Whitsell and Richard L. Kelsey. "An Analysis Of Client-Industry Concentrations For Large Public Accounting Firms." **AR,** 1974, Vol. 49, No. 4, pp. 772-788.)

Whitt, Jerry D. (Whitt, Sue Y. and Jerry D. Whitt. "What Professional Services Firms Can Learn From Manufacturing." **MA,** 1988, Vol. 70. No. 5. pp. 39-42.)

Whitt, John D. "Making An Investment In Mexico." **MA,** 1974, Vol. 56, No. 5, pp. 43-45.

Whitt, John D. "Motivating Lower-Level Management Of Mexican Affiliates." **MA,** 1979. Vol. 60. No. 12. pp. 46-49.

Whitt, John D. "Multinationals In Latin America: An Accent On Control," **MA,** 1977. Vol. 58. No. 8, pp. 49-50.

Whitt, Sue Y. and Jerry D. Whitt. "What Professional Services Firms Can Learn From Manufacturing." **MA,** 1988. Vol. 70, No. 5. pp. 39-42.

Whittaker, Edmund. "Economic Considerations Of Obsolescence," **AR,** 1937, Vol. 12, No. 4. pp. 337-344.

Whittaker, Edmund. "Realism And Cost Accounting." **AR,** 1946, Vol. 21, No. 1, pp. 13-18.

Whittenburg, Gerald E. (Adams. Steven J. and Gerald E. Whittenburg. "How The Energy Tax Act Affects Capital Budgeting," **MA,** 1981, Vol. 63, No. 5. pp. 34-39.)

Whittenburg, Gerald E. (Chow, C. W., M. D. Shields and G. E. Whittenburg. "The Quality Of Tax Practitioners' Judgments Regarding Substantial Authority: Potential Research Directions And An Exploratory Empirical Investigation," **AIT,** 1988, Vol. 2. pp.)

Whittenburg, Gerald. (Whittington, Ray and Gerald Whittenburg. "Judicial Classification Of Debt Versus Equity - An Empirical Study." **AR,** 1980. Vol. 55. No. 3. pp. 409-418.)

Whittenburg, G. E. (Wright, Penny, Ray Whittington and G. E. Whittenburg. "Student Ratings Of Teaching Effectiveness: What The Research Reveals." **JAED,** 1984, Vol. 2. No. 2. pp. 5-30.)

Whittington, Geoffrey. "A Tower Of Babel?." **ABR,** 1980-81. Vol. 11, No. 43, pp. 249-252.

Whittington, Geoffrey. "Accounting For State Regulated Enterprises." **ABR,** 1984-85, Vol. 15. No. 60. pp.311-326.

Whittington, Geoffrey. "On The Use Of The Accounting Rate Of Return In Empirical Research." **ABR,** 1978-79. Vol. 9. No. 35. pp. 201-208.

Whittington, Geoffrey. "Pioneers Of Income Measurement And Price-Level Accounting: A Review Article." **ABR,** 1979-80, Vol. 10, No. 38, pp. 232-240.

Whittington, Geoffrey. "The Usefulness Of Accounting Data In Measuring The Economic Performance Of Firms." **JAPP,** 1988, Vol. 7, No. 4, pp. 261-266.

Whittington, G. "Asset Valuation. Income Measurement And Accounting Income," **ABR,** 1973-74. Vol. 4. No. 14, pp. 96-101.

Whittington, G. "Indexation: A Review Article." **ABR,** 1975-76, Vol. 6, No. 23, pp. 171-176.

Whittington, G. "Positive Accounting Theory: A Review Article." **ABR,** 1986-87, Vol. 17. No. 68. pp. 327-336.

Whittington, Oliver Ray, III. (Horvitz, Jerome S. and Oliver Ray Whittington. III. "Responsibilities In Tax Practice." **CPAJ,** 1978. Vol. 48. No. 10. pp. 26-31.)

Whittington, O. Ray and Steven J. Adams. "Temporary Breakdowns Of Internal Control: Implications For External And Internal Auditors." **JAAF,** 1982. Vol. 5. No. 4, pp. 310-319.

Whittington, O. Ray. (Ballew, Van Bennett and O. Ray Whittington. "Litigation Support Engagements - A Growing Practice." **CPAJ,** 1988. Vol. 58. No. 2, pp. 42-47.)

Whittington, O. Ray. (Skekel, Ted D. and O. Ray Whittington. "Management Reports' On Financial Statements." **CPAJ,** 1979, Vol. 49, No. 7, pp. 32-37.)

Whittington, Ray and Gerald Whittenburg. "Judicial Classification Of Debt Versus Equity - An Empirical Study." **AR,** 1980, Vol. 55. No. 3. pp. 409-418.

Whittington, Ray, Marilyn Zulinski and James W. Ledwith. "Completeness - The Elusive Assertion," **JOA,** 1983, Vol. 156, No. 2. pp. 82-92.

Whittington, Ray, Van Bennett Ballew and Doyle Z. Williams. "Selecting An Auditor: Times Have Changed," **MA,** 1984, Vol. 65, No. 8, pp. 62-67.

Whittington, Ray. "Social Accounting And The Tragedy Of The Commons." **MA,** 1977, Vol. 58, No. 10, pp. 32-34.

Whittington, Ray. (Ballew, Van Bennett, Ray Whittington and Marilyn Zulinski. "Shared Audit Engagements," **CPAJ,** 1983, Vol. 53, No. 2, pp. 28-35.)

Whittington, Ray. (Carmichael, D. R. and Ray Whittington. "The Auditor's Changing Role In Financial Reporting," **JAAF,** 1984, Vol. 7, No. 4, pp. 347-361.)

Whittington, Ray. (Wright, Penny, Ray Whittington and G. E. Whittenburg. "Student Ratings Of Teaching Effectiveness: What The Research Reveals," **JAED,** 1984, Vol. 2, No. 2, pp. 5-30.)

Whittred, Greg and Ian Zimmer. "Timeliness Of Financial Reporting And Financial Distress," **AR,** 1984, Vol. 59, No. 2. pp. 287-295.

Whittred, Greg. "The Derived Demand For Consolidated Financial Reporting," **JAEC,** 1987, Vol. 9, No. 3, pp. 259-285.

Whittred, Greg. "The Evolution Of Consolidated Financial Reporting In Australia," **ABACUS,** 1986, Vol. 22, No. 2, pp. 103-120.

Whittred, G. P. "Accounting For The Extractive Industries: Use Or Abuse Of The Matching Principle?," **ABACUS,** 1978. Vol. 14. No. 2, pp. 154-159.

Whittred, G. P. "Audit Qualification And The Timeliness Of Corporate Annual Reports," **AR,** 1980, Vol. 55, No. 4, pp. 563-577.

Whittred, G. P. "The Timeliness Of The Australian Annual Report: 1972-1977," **JAR,** 1980, Vol. 18, No. 2, pp. 623-628.

Whittred, G. P. (Ball, Ray, R. G. Walker and G. P. Whittred. "Audit Qualifications And Share Prices," **ABACUS,** 1979. Vol. 15. No. 1, pp. 23-34.)

Whittred, G. P. (Davies, B. and G. P. Whittred. "The Association Between Selected Corporate Attributes And Timeliness In Corporate Reporting: Further Analysis," **ABACUS,** 1980, Vol. 16, No. 1, pp. 48-60.)

Whittred, G. P. (Walker, R. G. and G. P. Whittred. "Bank Disclosures Of Secret Reserves: The Impact On The Australian Stock Market," **ABR,** 1982-83, Vol. 13, No. 50, pp. 131-142.)

Wichmann, Henry, Jr. "SBA Update," **CPAJ,** 1979, Vol. 49, No. 7. pp. 23-26.

Wichmann, Henry, Jr. (Nix, Harold M. and Henry Wichmann, Jr. "The Governmental Audit Report," **JAAF,** 1983, Vol. 6. No. 4, pp. 341-352.)

Wiebe, Frank A. (Briner, Russell F., Frank A. Wiebe and Shaker A. Zahra. "Management Accountants: Don't Overlook Quality Circles," **MA,** 1984, Vol. 66, No. 6, pp. 45-49.)

Wiemans, Corstiaan. "George's Business Problems - Continued." **MA,** 1976, Vol. 57, No. 11, pp. 22-24.

Wiener, Julius. "Separation Of Fixed And Variable Costs," **AR,** 1960. Vol. 35, No. 4, pp. 686-690.

Wiener, Julius. "The Cost Structure Of The Industrial Enterprise: Pattern Of Analysis," **AR,** 1962, Vol. 37, No. 3. pp. 438-451.

Wiese, Donald C. and Kelly Polich. "The Revenue Act Of 1987: Revenue-Raising Snippets," **JOA,** 1988, Vol. 165, No. 3. pp. 30-37.

Wiese, Donald C. "The Fiscal Year: An Endangered Species Under Tax Reform," **JOA,** 1987, Vol. 163, No. 1, pp. 78-86.

Wiesen, Jeremy and D. R. Carmichael. "High Tech: A Challenge For CPAs," **JOA,** 1983, Vol. 156, No. 2, pp. 67-73.

Wiesen, Jeremy and Richard Eng. "Corporate Perks: Disclosure And Tax Considerations," **JAAF,** 1979, Vol. 2, No. 2. pp. 101-121.

Wiesen, Jeremy L. (Schiff, Michael, George H. Sorter and Jeremy L. Wiesen. "The Evolving Role Of Corporate Audit Committees." **JAAF,** 1977, Vol. 1, No. 1. pp. 19-44.)

Wiesen, Jeremy. "Reporting Concepts For The 1980s," **JAAF,** 1981. Vol. 4. No. 4, pp. 309-324.

Wiesner, Philip J. and Sherri P. Nadeau. "Alternative Minimum Tax (Part 2): More Headaches Than Aspirin," **JOA,** 1988. Vol. 165, No. 2, pp. 54-63.

Wiesner, Philip J. "Real Estate Syndications: Is There Life After Tax Reform?," **JOA,** 1986, Vol. 162, No. 5, pp. 116-127.

Wiesner, Philip J. "The TRA's Alternative Minimum Tax (Part 1): How Book Income Can Increase Tax Liability," **JOA,** 1988. Vol. 165, No. 1, pp. 28-37.

Wiggins, James E. (Benjamin, James J., Steven D. Grossman and Casper E. Wiggins. "The Impact Of Foreign Currency Translation On Reporting During The Phase-In Of SFAS No. 52." **JAAF,** 1986, Vol. 1 (New Series), No. 3, pp. 177-184.)

Wiggins, Casper E. (Crumbley, D. Larry, Nicholas G. Apostolou and Casper E. Wiggins. "Tax-Sheltered Plans In Educational And Other Organizations," **CPAJ,** 1984, Vol. 54, No. 4, pp. 22-31.)

Wiggins, Casper E. (Mayper, Alan G., Robert B. Walker and Casper E. Wiggins. "Accounting And Review Services: Perceptions Of The Message Within The CPA's Report," **AIA,** 1988, Vol. 6, pp. 219-232.)

Wiggins, Casper E., D. Larry Crumbley and Nicholas G. Apostolou. "A Critical Analysis Of The Marriage Tax Penalty," **JATA,** 1986, Vol. 7, No. 2, pp. 60-75.

Wiggins, Casper E., Jr. and L. Murphy Smith. "A Generalized Audit Simulation Tool For Evaluating The Reliability Of

Internal Controls," **CAR**, 1986-87. Vol. 3, No. 2, pp. 316-337.

Wiggins, Casper. (Giroux, Gary and Casper Wiggins. "Intergovernmental Grants And Local Needs," **JAPP**, 1987. Vol. 6, No. 3, pp. 169-183.)

Wiggins, C. Don. (Kare, Dilip D. and C. Don Wiggins. "How To Estimate The Effect Of A Stock Repurchase." **MA**, 1987, Vol. 68, No. 11, pp. 55-57.)

Wilcox, Earl A. (Green, Gary I. and Earl A. Wilcox. "Find The Right Software Through Specifications." **MA**, 1982, Vol. 63, No. 7, pp. 43-50.)

Wilcox, Edward B. "Business Combinations: An Analysis Of Mergers, Purchases, And Related Accounting Procedure," **JOA**, 1950, Vol. 89, No. 2, pp. 102-107.

Wilcox, Edward B. "Ethics: The Profession On Trial," **JOA**, 1955, Vol. 100, No. 5, pp. 72-79.

Wilcox, Edward B. "Qualifications For A Professional Career," **AR**, 1944. Vol. 19, No. 1. pp. 1-6.

Wilcox, Ed. B. and Howard C. Greer. "The Case Against Price-Level Adjustments In Income Determination." **JOA**, 1950, Vol. 90, No. 6, pp. 492-503.

Wilcox, E. B. "Accountant's Responsibility For Disclosure Of Events After Balance-Sheet Date." **JOA**, 1950, Vol. 89, No. 4, pp. 286-297.

Wilcox, E. B. "Comments On 'An Introduction To Corporate Accounting Standards'," **AR**, 1941. Vol. 16. No. 1. pp. 75-81.

Wilcox, E. B. "Dissent From Current Practice In Accounting For Stock Dividends," **JOA**, 1953. Vol. 96. No. 2. pp. 176-181.

Wilcox, E. B. "Restoration Of Fixed Asset Values To The Balance Sheet," **AR**, 1947. Vol. 22. No. 2. pp. 206-208.

Wilcox, James B. (Kiger, Jack E., James B. Wilcox and Jan R. Williams. "Intraperiod Income Tax Allocation With Differential Rates," **AR**, 1977. Vol. 52. No. 3, pp. 716-720.)

Wilcox, Jarrod W. "A Prediction Of Business Failure Using Accounting Data," **JAR**, 1973. Vol. 11, Supp.. pp. 163-179.

Wilcox, Jarrod W. "A Simple Theory Of Financial Ratios As Predictors Of Failure," **JAR**. 1971. Vol. 9, No. 2. pp. 389-395.

Wilcox, K. A. and C. H. Smith. "Role Discrepancies And The Auditor - Client Relationship." **AOS**, 1977, Vol. 2, No. 1, pp. 81-97.

Wild, John J. "The Prediction Performance Of A Structural Model Of Accounting Numbers." **JAR**, 1987. Vol. 25, No. 1, pp. 139-160.

Wild, John J. (Biggs, Stanley F. and John J. Wild. "A Note On The Practice Of Analytical Review." **AJPT**, 1983-84, Vol. 3, No. 2. pp. 68-79.)

Wild, John J. (Biggs, Stanley F. and John J. Wild. "An Investigation Of Auditor Judgment In Analytical Review." **AR**, 1985, Vol. 60, No. 4, pp. 607-633.)

Wildavsky, A. "Policy Analysis Is What Information Systems Are Not," **AOS**, 1978, Vol. 3. No. 1. pp. 77-88.

Wilder, Harrison W. (Edwards, H. R., Myron S. Kem and Harrison W. Wilder. "The Use Of Accounting In Business Policy Determination," **AR**, 1947. Vol. 22. No. 4, pp. 394-404.)

Wildman, John R. "Appreciation From The Point Of View Of The Certified Public Accountant," **AR**, 1928. Vol. 3. No. 4, pp. 397-406.

Wildman, John R. "Classification Of Accountancy Services." **AR**, 1928, Vol. 3. No. 2. pp. 124-130.

Wildman, J. R. "A Research Program." **AR**. 1926. Vol. 1. No. 1, pp. 43-54.

Wildman, J. R. "Comments On Is Appreciation A Depreciating Element?," **AR**, 1930, Vol. 5. No. 1. pp. 54-55.

Wildman, J. R. "Comments On Is Appreciation Available For Dividends." **AR**, 1930, Vol. 5. No. 1. pp. 27-28.

Wildman, J. R. "Comments On Should Appreciation Be Brought Into The Accounts?," **AR**, 1930. Vol. 5. No. 1. p. 34.

Wildman, J. R. "Comments On What Is Appreciation." **AR**. 1930. Vol. 5. No. 1. pp. 14-15.

Wilgus, Ralph E. "Improving Auditor-Client Co-Operation." **JOA**, 1960. Vol. 109, No. 1. pp. 46-50.

Wilhelm, Maurice F., Jr. "Purchase Or Lease: That Is The Question," **MA**, 1969, Vol. 51. No. 1. pp. 43-46.

Wilkerson, Jack E., Jr. "Selecting Experimental And Comparison Samples For Use In Studies Of Auditor Reporting Decisions." **JAR**, 1987. Vol. 25. No. 1. pp. 161-167.

Wilkerson, Jack E., Jr. (Pasewark. W. R., J. R. Strawser and J. E. Wilkerson. Jr. "Empirical Evidence On The Association Between Characteristics Of Graduating Accounting Students And Recruiting Decisions." **IAE**. 1988, Vol. 3, No. 2. pp. 388-401.)

Wilkerson, Jack E., Jr. (Warren, Carl S. and Jack E. Wilkerson, Jr. "The Role Of Observation. Inquiry And Reperformance," **CPAJ**. 1985. Vol. 55. No. 8. pp. 46-49.)

Wilkie, Patrick J. "Corporate Average Effective Tax Rates And Inferences About Relative Tax Preferences," **JATA**, 1988, Vol. 10, No. 1, pp. 75-88.

Wilkie, Patrick J. (Boley, Richard and Patrick J. Wilkie. "Practitioners' Views Of The Common Body Of Tax Knowledge For Persons Entering Public Accounting," **JATA**. 1986, Vol. 8, No. 1, pp. 80-97.)

Wilkie, Patrick J. (Fellingham, John C., Stephen T. Limberg and Patrick J. Wilkie. "Tax Rates, Tax Shelters And Optimal Portfolios," **AIT**. 1987. Vol. 1. pp. 23-48.)

Wilking, S. Vincent, Melvin L. Braun and William M. Gips. "Pay And Price Control - Phase II," **CPAJ**, 1972, Vol. 42, No. 2. pp. 115-122.

Wilkins, Edwin N. "Forecasting Cash Flow: Some Problems And Some Applications," **MA**, 1967, Vol. 49, No. 2. pp. 26-30.

Wilkins, Trevor and Ian Zimmer. "The Effect Of Leasing And Different Methods Of Accounting For Leases On Credit Evaluations," **AR**, 1983, Vol. 58, No. 4, pp. 749-764.

Wilkins, Trevor and Ian Zimmer. "The Effects Of Alternative Methods Of Accounting For Leases - An Experimental Study," **ABACUS**, 1983, Vol. 19, No. 1, pp. 64-75.

Wilkins, T. A. "A Behavioural Investigation Of Alternative Methods Of Financing Capital Acquisitions And Lease Capitalisation," **ABR**, 1983-84, Vol. 14, No. 56, pp. 359-366.

Wilkinson, James R. and Lloyd D. Doney. "Extending Audit And Reporting Boundaries," **AR**, 1965, Vol. 40, No. 4, pp. 753-756.

Wilkinson, Jeffrey M. (Hartman, Bart P., Vincent C. Brenner, Richard A. Lydecker and Jeffrey M. Wilkinson. "Mission Control Starts In The Controller's Department," **MA**, 1981, Vol. 63, No. 3. pp. 27-32.)

Wilkinson, Joseph W. "Designing A Computer-Based Information System: An 'Intermediate' Systems Course," **AR**, 1971. Vol. 46. No. 4, pp. 797-799.

Wilkinson, Joseph W. "The Meanings Of Measurements," **MA**. 1975, Vol. 57. No. 1, pp. 49-52.

Wilkinson, Joseph W. (Davall, Bernard M. and Joseph W. Wilkinson. "Simulating An Accounting Information System Model." **MA**, 1971, Vol. 52. No. 7, pp. 26-30.)

Wilkinson, Joseph W. (Kneer, Dan C. and Joseph W. Wilkinson. "Data-Base Management Systems: Do You Know Enough To Choose?," **MA**, 1984, Vol. 66, No. 3, pp. 30-38.)

Wilkinson, Theodore L. "Can Accounting Be An International Language?," **AR**, 1964, Vol. 39, No. 1, pp. 133-139.

Wilkinson, Theodore L. "United States Accounting As Viewed By Accountants Of Other Countries," **IJAER**, 1965, Vol. 1, No. 1. pp. 3-14.

Will, Hartmut J. "Computerized Accounting: International Issues." **IJAER**, 1980, Vol. 16, No. 1, pp. 169-207.

Will, Hart. (Ahituv, Niv, Jonathan Halpern and Hart Will. "Audit Planning: An Algorithmic Approach," **CAR**, 1985-86. Vol. 2. No. 1, pp. 95-110.)

Will, H. J. "Auditing In Systems Perspective," **AR**, 1974. Vol. 49, No. 4, pp. 690-706.

Willard, Bruce K. "Cost Distribution Using Infinitely Variable Averages," **MA**, 1969, Vol. 51, No. 4, pp. 12-15.

Willard, Bruce K. "Integrating Project Planning With Periodic Planning And Reporting," **MA**, 1968, Vol. 50, No. 3. pp. 34-35.

Willard, Dorothy G. "Accountant's Responsibilities In Income-Tax Work," **JOA**, 1951, Vol. 91, No. 4, pp. 549-553.

Willard, William C. "Instant Banking - A Tiger By The Tail." **MA**, 1968, Vol. 49, No. 7, pp. 3-8.

Willens, Robert and Thomas G. Butler. "Tax Ramifications Of Selling A Business - Part I," **CPAJ**, 1986, Vol. 56, No. 3. pp. 30-35.

Willens, Robert and Thomas G. Butler. "Tax Ramifications Of Selling A Business - Part II," **CPAJ**, 1986, Vol. 56, No. 4. pp. 24-29.

Willens, Robert. "Consolidated Returns And Affiliated Groups (With A Nod To Wall Street)," **JOA**, 1986, Vol. 161. No. 2, pp. 60-69.

Willens, Robert. "Corporate Provisions Of The TRA Of 1984," **JOA**. 1985, Vol. 159, No. 2, pp. 54-63.

Willens, Robert. "General Utilities Is Dead: The TRA Of '86 Ends An Era," **JOA**, 1986, Vol. 162, No. 5, pp. 102-115.

Willens, Robert. "Mutual Funds After Tax Reform: Hedging Your Bets," **JOA**, 1987, Vol. 164, No. 4, pp. 110-115.

Willens, Robert. "M&As: The CPA As Tax Adviser," **JOA**, 1988. Vol. 166, No. 2, pp. 44-52.

Willens, Robert. "Section 355: The Minefield Of Subchapter C." **CPAJ**. 1980. Vol. 50, No. 3, pp. 23-28.

Willens, Robert. "Taxes And Takeovers," **JOA**, 1986, Vol. 162. No. 1, pp. 86-96.

Willens, Robert. "The Revenue Act Of 1987: Why Companies Can Breathe Easier," **JOA**, 1988, Vol. 165, No. 3. pp. 22-29.

Willens, Robert. "The Technical Corrections Act: What Corporations Should Know Now," **JOA**, 1988, Vol. 166, No. 1. pp. 46-49.

Willens, Robert. (Ivy, Madie and Robert Willens. "Final Sec. 385 Regs.: Debt V. Equity." **CPAJ**, 1981, Vol. 51, No. 7. pp. 16-22.)

Willens, Robert. (Ivy, Madie and Robert Willens. "Proposed Section 385 Regs. Bring Order From Chaos," **CPAJ**, 1980. Vol. 50, No. 10, pp. 13-20.)

Willett, R. J. "An Axiomatic Theory Of Accounting Measurement." **ABR**. 1986-87, Vol. 17, No. 66, pp. 155-172.

Willey, Russell W. "In Defense Of FAS No. 8," **MA**, 1979, Vol. 61. No. 6. pp. 36-40.

Williams, Albert S. "Starting A CPA Firm," **JOA**, 183, Vol. 155. No. 6. pp. 80-89.

Williams, Allan. (Silverstone, Rosalie and Allan Williams. "Recruitment, Training, Employment And Careers Of Women Chartered Accountants In England And Wales," **ABR**, 1978-79. Vol. 9, No. 34, pp. 105-122.)

Williams, Bernard C. (Bhaskar, Krish N. and Bernard C. Williams. "Audit And Control Issues For The Small Computerised Business," **ABR**, 1986-87, Vol. 17, No. 65. pp. 13-20.)

Williams, Bruce R. "Measuring Costs: Full Absorption Cost Or Direct Cost?," **MA**, 1976, Vol. 57, No. 7, pp. 23-24.

Williams, Charles M. "Small Business And EDP," **MA**, 1971. Vol. 52. No. 8. pp. 44-47.

Williams, David D. (Haskins, Mark E. and David D. Williams. "The Association Between Client Factors And Audit Fees: A Comparison By Country And By Firm," **ABR**, 1988, Vol. 18. No. 70, pp. 183-192.)

Williams, David D. (Haskins, Mark E. and David D. Williams. "Corporate Mergers And Auditors' Client Portfolios," **ACCHOR**, 1988, Vol. 2, No. 1, pp. 77-87.)

Williams, David D. (Haskins, Mark E. and David D. Williams. "A Genealogy Of Today's Contributors To Accounting Research," **AHJ**, 1986, Vol. 13, No. 1, pp. 93-101.)

Williams, David D. (Mutchler, Jane F., Joanne H. Turner and David D. Williams. "The Performance Of Female Versus Male Accounting Students," **IAE**. 1987, Vol. 2. No. 1, pp. 103-111.)

Williams, David J. and Anne Lillis. "EDP Audits Of Operating Systems - An Exploratory Study Of The Determinants Of The Prior Probability Of Risk," **AJPT**, 1984-85. Vol. 4, No. 2, pp. 110-117.

Williams, David J. and John O. S. Kennedy. "A Unique Procedure For Allocating Joint Costs From A Production Process?," **JAR**, 1983, Vol. 21, No. 2, pp. 644-645.

Williams, David J. "Operating System Audits: Their Importance And Use," **ABR**, 1983-84, Vol. 14, No. 56, pp. 367-372.

Williams, Doyle Z. and Sexton Adams. "Computer Technology And Organizational Change," **MA**, 1968, Vol. 50, No. 1, pp. 44-48.

Williams, Doyle Z. "A Profile Of CPA Candidates." **AR**. 1969, Vol. 44, No. 1, pp. 153-164.

Williams, Doyle Z. "A Seminar On The Teaching Of Accounting," **AR**, 1966, Vol. 41, No. 3, pp. 541-549.

Williams, Doyle Z. "Reporting Loss Carryovers In Financial Statements," **AR**, 1966, Vol. 41, No. 2, pp. 226-234.

Williams, Doyle Z. "Schools Of Accounting: Anatomy Of A Movement," **IAE**, 1984, No. 1, pp. 13-32.

Williams, Doyle Z. (Dock, V. Thomas. Dan M. Guy and Doyle Z. Williams. "Integrating The Computer In The Classroom: An Approach In Auditing," **AR**, 1974. Vol. 49. No. 1, pp. 149-153.)

Williams, Doyle Z. (Guy, Dan M.. Patricia E. Harris and Doyle Z. Williams. "Client Perceptions Of A Local CPA Firm." **CPAJ**, 1979, Vol. 49. No. 3. pp. 17-22.)

Williams, Doyle Z. (Holder, William W., E. John Larsen and Doyle Z. Williams. "Educational Requirements For Public Accounting," **CPAJ**, 1985, Vol. 55. No. 12. pp. 36-49.)

Williams, Doyle Z. (Krzystofik. Anthony T.. Stephen E. Loeb and Doyle Z. Williams. "How To Review Audit Training." **CPAJ**, 1978, Vol. 48, No. 7. pp. 11-16.)

Williams, Doyle Z. (Lewis, Merrill T., W. Thomas Lin and Doyle Z. Williams. "The Economic Status Of Accounting Educators: An Empirical Study." **AIA**. 1984. Vol. 1. pp. 127-144.)

Williams, Doyle Z. (Whittington. Ray. Van Bennett Ballew and Doyle Z. Williams. "Selecting An Auditor: Times Have Changed," **MA**, 1984, Vol. 65. No. 8. pp. 62-67.)

Williams, D. D. and M. W. Dirsmith. "The Effects Of Audit Technology On Auditor Efficiency: Auditing And The Timeliness Of Client Earnings Announcements." **AOS**. 1988. Vol. 13. No. 5, pp. 487-507.

Williams, D. J. "Shareholder Bonding In Financial Mutuals: An Exploratory Study Of The Relative Effects Of Altruism And Agency," **AOS**. 1986. Vol. 11. No. 3. pp. 271-288.

Williams, D. J. (Peasnell, K. V. and D. J. Williams. "Ersatz Academics And Scholar-Saints: The Supply Of Financial Accounting Research," **ABACUS**. 1986. Vol. 22. No. 2. pp. 121-135.)

Williams, Edward E. and M. Chapman Findlay, III. "Is Common Stock Obsolete?," **ABACUS**. 1983. Vol. 19, No. 1, pp. 39-55.

Williams, Edward E. and M. Chapman Findlay, III. "Beyond Neoclassical Economic Theory As A Foundation For Financial Accounting," **ABACUS**. 1980. Vol. 16. No. 2, pp. 133-141.

Williams, E. E. (Findlay, M. C. and E. E. Williams. "Toward A Positive Theory Of Corporate Financial Policy." **ABACUS**, 1987, Vol. 23. No. 2. pp. 107-121.)

Williams, Harold M. "Audit Committees - The Public Sector's View," **JOA**, 1977, Vol. 144, No. 3. pp. 71-75.

Williams, Harold M. "Financial Reporting In A Changing Economic Environment," **MA**, 1979. Vol. 61, No. 3, pp. 11-15.

Williams, H. James. "Practitioners' Perspectives On Going-Concern Issues," **CPAJ**, 1984. Vol. 54, No. 12. pp. 12-19.

Williams, H. James. (Ricchiute, David N. and H. James Williams. "Heuristics, Biases. And Decision Making In Accounting," **IAE**, 1985. No. 1, pp. 51-58.)

Williams, James M. (Klasny. Edward M. and James M. Williams. "Tracking Current Governmental Standards." **JOA**. 1982. Vol. 154. No. 1. pp. 60-73.)

Williams, Jan Robert. "Differing Opinions On Accounting Objectives," **CPAJ**. 1973. Vol. 43. No. 8. pp. 651-656.

Williams, Jan R. "The Accounting Lyceum Of The Federation Of Schools Of Accountancy." **JAED**, 1983, Vol. 1, No. 1, pp. 141-144.

Williams, Jan R. "Time And Use Depreciation." **MA**. 1972. Vol. 53, No. 7. pp. 28-30.

Williams, Jan R. (Arnold, Jerry L.. William W. Holder and Jan R. Williams. "FASB Should Establish An Accounting Laboratory," **MA**, 1983, Vol. 64. No. 9. pp. 52-55.)

Williams, Jan R. (Clay, Raymond J.. Jr. and Jan R. Williams. "Preparation Guide For Price-Level-Adjusted Financial Statements," **CPAJ**, 1975, Vol. 45. No. 10. pp. 37-44.)

Williams, Jan R. (Kiger, Jack E., James B. Wilcox and Jan R. Williams. "Intraperiod Income Tax Allocation With Differential Rates," **AR**, 1977. Vol. 52. No. 3. pp. 716-720.)

Williams, Jan R. (Kiger. Jack E. and Jan R. Williams. "An Emerging Concept Of Income Presentation," **AHJ**. 1977.

Vol. 4, No. 2, pp. 63-77.)

Williams, Jan R. (Stanga, Keith G. and Jan R. Williams. "The FASB's Objectives Of Financial Reporting," **CPAJ**, 1979, Vol. 49, No. 5, pp. 30-34.)

Williams, Jan R. (Tiller, Mikel G. and Jan R. Williams. "Revenue Recognition Under New FASB Statements," **CPAJ**. 1982. Vol. 52, No. 1, pp. 43-47.)

Williams, John C. (Stiner, Frederic M., Jr., John C. Williams and Adrian Sclawy. "Vanishing Accounting Journals Due To Paper Deterioration," **AHJ**, 1981, Vol. 8, No. 2, pp. 97-100.)

Williams, John Daniel. (Gibson, Charles H. and John Daniel Williams. "Should Common Stock Equivalents Be Considered In Earnings Per Share?," **CPAJ**, 1973, Vol. 43, No. 3, pp. 209-213.)

Williams, John J. "A New Perspective On The Evolution Of Double-Entry Bookkeeping," **AHJ**, 1978, Vol. 5, No. 1, pp. 29-39.

Williams, J. J. and C. R. Hinings. "A Note On Matching Control System Implications With Organizational Characteristics: ZBB And MBO Revisited," **AOS**, 1988, Vol. 13, No. 2, pp. 191-200.

Williams, J. J. "Zero-Base Budgeting: Prospects For Developing A Semi-Confusing Budgeting Information System." **AOS**, 1981, Vol. 6, No. 2, pp. 153-166.

Williams, J. J., J. D. Newton and E. A. Morgan. "The Integration Of Zero-Based Budgeting With Management-By-Objectives: An Empirical Inquiry," **AOS**, 1985, Vol. 10, No. 4. pp. 457-478.

Williams, Kathy. "A Novel Approach To Accounting: The Case Of The Purloined Pagoda," **MA**, 1988, Vol. 70, No. 6, pp. 19-23.

Williams, Louise R. "Internal Auditing: Hamilton County," **MA**. 1972, Vol. 53, No. 7, pp. 49-51.

Williams, Paul F. "A Descriptive Analysis Of Authorship In The Accounting Review," **AR**, 1985, Vol. 60, No. 2, pp. 300-313.

Williams, Paul F. "The Evaluative Relevance Of Social Data." **AR**. 1980, Vol. 55, No. 1, pp. 62-77.

Williams, Paul F. (Arrington, C. Edward, William A. Hillison and Paul F. Williams. "The Psychology Of Expectations Gaps: Why Is There So Much Dispute About Auditor Responsibility?," **ABR**, 1982-83, Vol. 13, No. 52, pp. 243-250.)

Williams, Paul F. (Hillison, William A. and Paul F. Williams. "Confidentiality Of Student Records: The Professor's Obligation," **JAED**, 1983, Vol. 1, No. 1, pp. 55-62.)

Williams, P. F. "The Legitimate Concern With Fairness," **AOS**, 1987, Vol. 12, No. 2, pp. 169-192.

Williams, P. F. "The Predictive Ability Paradox In Behavioral Accounting Research," **AOS**, 1982, Vol. 7, No. 4. pp. 405-410.

Williams, P. F. (Rockness, J. and P. F. Williams. "A Descriptive Study Of Social Responsibility Mutual Funds." **AOS**, 1988, Vol. 13, No. 4, pp. 397-414.)

Williams, Richard E. "Converting To A Direct Costing System." **MA**, 1968. Vol. 49, No. 5, pp. 23-34.

Williams, Robert L. "Poor Internal Control Leads To Fraud. Unreliable Data," **JOA**, 1952, Vol. 94, No. 5, pp. 580-585.

Williams, Robert W. and Robert I. Leonard. "Financial Reporting By Nonprofit Organizations," **JOA**, 1962, Vol. 113. No. 4, pp. 46-50.

Williams, Robert W. (Campbell, David R. and Robert W. Williams. "Accreditation Of Accounting Programs: Administrators' Perceptions Of Proposed AACSB Standards," **IAE**, 1983, No. 1, pp. 60-70.)

Williams, Thomas H. and Charles H. Griffin. "Matrix Theory And Cost Allocation," **AR**, 1964, Vol. 39, No. 3, pp. 671-678.

Williams, Thomas H. and Charles H. Griffin. "On The Nature Of Empirical Verification In Accounting," **ABACUS**, 1969. Vol. 5. No. 2, pp. 143-180.

Williams, Thomas H. and Charles H. Griffin. "Accountancy And Professional Development," **AR**, 1961. Vol. 36, No. 4. pp. 637-641.

Williams, Thomas H. and Charles H. Griffin. "MAS And The Expanded Meaning Of Accounting Education," **IJAER**. 1973. Vol. 8. No. 2. pp. 33-43.

Williams, Thomas H. and Charles H. Griffin. "Income Definition And Measurement: A Structural Approach," **AR**, 1967. Vol. 42. No. 4, pp. 642-649.

Williams, Thomas H. (Griffin, Charles H. and Thomas H. Williams. "Measuring Adequate Disclosure," **JOA**, 1960, Vol. 109. No. 4. pp. 43-48.)

Williams, Thomas H. (Griffin, Charles H. and Thomas H. Williams. "Simulation In Business Education," **AR**, 1964. Vol. 39. No. 1, pp. 160-163.)

Williams, Thomas H. (Griffin, Charles H. and Thomas H. Williams. "A Comparative Analysis Of Accounting And Mathematics," **AR**, 1962. Vol. 37, No. 3. pp. 410-414.)

Williams, Thomas H. (Roller, Julius and Thomas H. Williams. "Professional Schools Of Accounting," **AR**, 1967, Vol. 42. No. 2, pp. 349-355.)

Williams, Wade S. "Illegal Payments: The Legislative Outlook," **JOA**, 1977. Vol. 143. No. 1, pp. 58-62.

Williams, William J., Gerald Fuller and Roger W. Payne. "Improving Cost Management By Forming An Alliance," **CA**. 1986. Vol. 4. No. 1. pp. 54-61.

Williamson, James E. "The Effects Of Measurement Concepts On The Investment Decisions Of Trustees," **AR**, 1971, Vol. 46. No. 1, pp. 139-148.

Williamson, J. Peter. (Bower, Richard S., Frank C. Herringer and J. Peter Williamson. "Lease Evaluation,"

AR, 1966, Vol. 41, No. 2, pp. 257-265.)

Williamson, Robert W. "Evidence On Selective Reporting Of Financial Ratios," **AR**, 1984, Vol. 59, No. 2, pp. 296-299.

Williamson, Robert W. "Measuring Divisional Profitability," **MA**, 1975, Vol. 56, No. 7, pp. 29-30.

Williamson, Robert W. "Presenting Information Economics To Students," **AR**, 1982, Vol. 57, No. 2, pp. 414-419.

Williford, Edith S. (Wilson, M. Allen and Edith S. Williford. "S Corporation: The New Corporate Tax Planning Weapon," **MA**, 1987, Vol. 69, No. 3, pp. 46-50.)

Willinger, G. Lee. "A Contingent Claims Model For Pension Costs," **JAR**, 1985, Vol. 23, No. 1, pp. 351-359.

Willingham, John and James Parks. "Internal Control Analysis - A Solution," **CPAJ**, 1982, Vol. 52, No. 5, pp. 24-35.

Willingham, John J. and D. R. Carmichael. "The Professional Auditing Subculture," **ABACUS**, 1968, Vol. 4, No. 2, pp. 153-163.

Willingham, John J. and James E. Sorensen. "The Behavioral Science Milieu Of Accounting," **IJAER**, 1971, Vol. 7, No. 1, pp. 49-63.

Willingham, John J. and William F. Wright. "Financial Statement Errors And Internal Control Judgments," **AJPT**, 1985-86, Vol. 5, No. 1, pp. 57-70.

Willingham, John J. "The Accounting Entity: A Conceptual Model," **AR**, 1964, Vol. 39, No. 3, pp. 543-552.

Willingham, John J. (Ashton, Robert H., John J. Willingham and Robert K. Elliott. "An Empirical Analysis Of Audit Delay," **JAR**, 1987, Vol. 25, No. 2, pp. 275-292.)

Willingham, John J. (Blocher, Edward, Robert S. Esposito and John J. Willingham. "Auditors' Analytical Review Judgments For Payroll Expense," **AJPT**, 1983-84, Vol. 3, No. 1, pp. 75-91.)

Willingham, John J. (Carmichael, D. R. and John J. Willingham. "New Directions In Auditing Education: A Proposal For The Undergraduate Course," **AR**, 1969, Vol. 44, No. 3, pp. 611-615.)

Willingham, John J. (Collins, Frank and John J. Willingham. "Contingency Management Approach To Budgeting," **MA**, 1977, Vol. 59, No. 3, pp. 45-48.)

Willingham, John J. (Libby, Robert, James T. Artman and John J. Willingham. "Process Susceptibility, Control Risk, And Audit Planning," **AR**, 1985, Vol. 60, No. 2, pp. 212-230.)

Willingham, John J. (Mock, Theodore J. and John J. Willingham. "An Improved Method Of Documenting And Evaluating A System Of Internal Accounting Controls," **AJPT**, 1982-83, Vol. 2, No. 2, pp. 91-99.)

Willingham, John J. (Schrader, William J., Robert E. Malcom and John J. Willingham. "A Partitioned Events View Of Financial Reporting," **AH**, 1988, Vol. 2, No. 4, pp. 10-20.)

Willingham, John. (Gray, Jack, John Willingham and Kenneth Johnston. "A Business Game For The Introductory Course In Accounting," **AR**, 1963, Vol. 38, No. 2, pp. 336-346.)

Willis, Carl G. (Dockweiler, Raymond C. and Carl G. Willis. "On The Use Of Entry Requirements For Undergraduate Accounting Programs," **AR**, 1984, Vol. 59, No. 3, pp. 496-504.)

Willis, Eugene. "Computation Of Gain On Disposition Of Section 1250 Property," **AR**, 1977, Vol. 52, No. 3, pp. 727-728.

Willis, Eugene. "The Amount Of A Charitable Contribution Of Property," **AR**, 1977, Vol. 52, No. 2, pp. 498-502.

Willis, Eugene. (Hreha, Karen S., Robert F. Sharp and Eugene Willis. "An Analysis Of Two Proposed Cost Recovery Systems," **JATA**, 1986, Vol. 7, No. 2, pp. 76-84.)

Willis, Eugene. (Raabe, William, Jr. and Eugene Willis. "The Conformity Requirement," **CPAJ**, 1977, Vol. 47, No. 7, pp. 33-36.)

Willis, G. W. K. (Egenolf, Robert and G. W. K. Willis. "Status Of Public Sector Accounting Education," **JAED**, 1983, Vol. 1, No. 1, pp. 63-69.)

Willis, James T. (Tabor, Richard H. and James T. Willis. "Empirical Evidence On The Changing Role Of Analytical Review Procedures," **AJPT**, 1984-85, Vol. 4, No. 2, pp. 93-109.)

Willis, J. R. M. (Sandford, C. T., J. R. M. Willis and D. J. Ironside. "An Accessions Tax The Problem Of Trusts," **ABR**, 1972-73, Vol. 3, No. 12, pp. 263-281.)

Willits, Stephen D. (Munter, Paul and Stephen D. Willits. "Understanding The New Pension Math," **MA**, 1986, Vol. 68, No. 6, pp. 34-39.)

Willits, Stephen D., Donald K. Clancy and Robert J. Freeman. "Public Employee Retirement System Reports: A Study Of Knowledgable User Information Processing Ability," **RIGNA**, 1988, Vol. 4, pp. 3-48.

Willmer, M. A. P. "A Mathematical Approach To Complex Fraud Problems," **ABR**, 1976-77, Vol. 7, No. 26, pp. 120-123.

Willmott, Hugh. (Smith, Chris, Richard Whipp and Hugh Willmott. "Case-Study Research In Accounting: Methodological Breakthrough Or Ideological Weapon?," **AIPIA**, 1988, Vol. 2, pp. 95-120.)

Willmott, H. C. "Paradigms For Accounting Research: Critical Reflections On Tomkins And Groves' 'Everyday Accountant And Researching His Reality'," **AOS**, 1983, Vol. 8, No. 4, pp. 389-406.

Willmott, H. C. (Puxty, A. G., H. C. Willmott, D. J. Cooper and T. Lowe. "Modes Of Regulation In Advanced Capitalism: Locating Accountancy In Four Countries," **AOS**, 1987, Vol. 12, No. 3, pp. 273-292.)

Willmott, H. "Organising The Profession: A Theoretical And Historical Examination Of The Development Of The Major Accountancy Bodies In The U.K.," **AOS**, 1986, Vol. 11, No. 6, pp. 555-582.

Willmott, H. (Hopper, T., J. Storey and H. Willmott. "Accounting For Accounting: Towards The Development Of A Dialectical View," **AOS**, 1987, Vol. 12, No. 5, pp. 437-456.)

Willson, James D. and Steven J. Root. "A Practical Guide To Operational Auditing," **CA**, 1983, Vol. 1, No. 2, pp. 13-19.

Wilner, Neil A. "A Simple Teaching Approach For Process Costing Using Logic And Pictures," **IAE**, 1987, Vol. 2, No. 2, pp. 388-396.

Wilner, Neil. (Jiambalvo, James and Neil Wilner. "Auditor Evaluation Of Contingent Claims," **AJPT**, 1985-86, Vol. 5, No. 1, pp. 1-11.)

Wilner, N. A. "SFAS 8 And Information Inductance: An Experiment," **AOS**, 1982, Vol. 7, No. 1, pp. 43-52.

Wilner, N. and J. Birnberg. "Methodological Problems In Functional Fixation Research: Criticism And Suggestions," **AOS**, 1986, Vol. 11, No. 1, pp. 71-82.

Wilson, Arlette C., G. William Glezen and Timothy P. Cronan. "Forecasting Accounting Information For Auditors' Use In Analytical Reviews," **AIA**, 1988, Vol. 6, pp. 267-276.

Wilson, Charles J. "The Operating Lease And The Risk Of Obsolescence," **MA**, 1973, Vol. 55, No. 6, pp. 41-44.

Wilson, David A. "A Note On Environmental Complexity And Financial Reports," **AR**, 1973, Vol. 48, No. 3, pp. 586-588.

Wilson, David A. "On The Pedagogy Of Financial Accounting," **AR**, 1979, Vol. 54, No. 2, pp. 396-401.

Wilson, Earl R. and R. Penny Marquette. "Evaluating The Effects Of Multicollinearity: A Note On The Use Of Ridge Regression," **AIA**, 1988, Vol. 6, pp. 143-158.

Wilson, Earl R. and Thomas P. Howard. "Information For Municipal Bond Investment Decisions: Synthesis Of Prior Research, An Extension And Policy Implications," **RIGNA**, 1985, Vol. 1, pp. 213-263.

Wilson, Earl R. and Thomas P. Howard. "The Association Between Municipal Market Measures And Selected Financial Reporting Practices: Additional Evidence," **JAR**, 1984, Vol. 22, No. 1, pp. 207-224.

Wilson, Earl R. (Francis, Jere R. and Earl R. Wilson. "Auditor Changes: A Joint Test Of Theories Relating To Agency Costs And Auditor Differentiation," **AR**, 1988, Vol. 63, No. 4, pp. 663-682.)

Wilson, Earl R. (Ingram, Robert W. and Earl R. Wilson. "Governmental Capital Markets Research In Accounting: A Review," **RIGNA**, 1987, Vol. 3, Part B, pp. 111-126.)

Wilson, Earl R. (Lomax, Victor W., Jr. and Earl R. Wilson. "Predicting Failure Of Private Colleges: Financial And Nonfinancial Determinants," **RIGNA**, 1986, Vol. 2, pp. 213-232.)

Wilson, Earl R. (Marks, Barry R., K. K. Raman and Earl R. Wilson. "Toward Understanding The Determinants Of Pension Underfunding In The Public Sector," **JAPP**, 1988, Vol. 7, No. 3, pp. 157-183.)

Wilson, E. Lee. "Data Processing Output Devices," **MA**, 1975, Vol. 57, No. 5, p. 45.

Wilson, Gerald E. "Theory Z: Implications For Management Accountants," **MA**, 1983, Vol. 65, No. 5, pp. 58-62.

Wilson, G. Peter. "The Incremental Information Content Of The Accrual And Funds Components Of Earnings After Controlling For Earnings," **AR**, 1987, Vol. 62, No. 2, pp. 293-322.

Wilson, G. Peter. "The Relative Information Content Of Accruals And Cash Flows: Combined Evidence At The Earnings Announcement And Annual Report Release Date," **JAR**, 1986, Vol. 24, Supp., pp. 165-200.

Wilson, G. Peter. (McNichols, Maureen and G. Peter Wilson. "Evidence Of Earnings Management From The Provision For Bad Debts," **JAR**, 1988, Vol. 26, Supp., pp. 1-31.)

Wilson, Jack O. "How To Cure Small Business Automation Headaches," **MA**, 1983, Vol. 64, No. 11, pp. 46-49.

Wilson, John M. "Integer Programming Approaches To Resource Allocation And Profit Budgeting," **ABR**, 1984-85, Vol. 15, No. 57, pp. 33-36.

Wilson, K. W. (Newbould, G. D., S. J. Stray and K. W. Wilson. "Shareholders' Interests And Acquisition Activity," **ABR**, 1975-76, Vol. 6, No. 23, pp. 201-215.)

Wilson, M. Allen and Edith S. Williford. "S Corporation: The New Corporate Tax Planning Weapon," **MA**, 1987, Vol. 69, No. 3, pp. 46-50.

Wilson, Robert. "Auditing: Perspectives From Multiperson Decision Theory," **AR**, 1983, Vol. 58, No. 2, pp. 305-318.

Wilson, Susan B. (Cornick, Michael, William D. Cooper and Susan B. Wilson. "How Do Companies Analyze Overhead?," **MA**, 1988, Vol. 69, No. 12, pp. 41-43.)

Wilson, Thomas M. and David R. Stone. "Project Management For An Architectural Firm," **MA**, 1980, Vol. 62, No. 4, pp. 25-28, 45-46.

Wilsted, William D. (Bebee, Richard F., Lawrence L. Steinmetz and William D. Wilsted. "Managing The Income Number," **MA**, 1975, Vol. 56, No. 8, pp. 40-42.)

Winakor, Arthur H. and Daniel Borth. "Documentation In Accounting Literature," **AR**, 1934, Vol. 9, No. 1, pp. 61-68.

Winakor, Arthur H. "Creditors' Protection And Stockholders' Responsibility," **AR**, 1934, Vol. 9, No. 3, pp. 247-253.

Winakor, Arthur H. "Incidence Of Expenses In Accounting," **AR**, 1934, Vol. 9, No. 4, pp. 312-318.

Winakor, Arthur H. "Limitations On Assets," **AR**, 1936, Vol. 11, No. 1, pp. 40-48.

Winakor, Arthur H. (Borth, Daniel and Arthur H. Winakor. "Some Reflections Of The Scope Of Auditing," **AR**, 1935,

Vol. 10, No. 2, pp. 174-184.)

Winarchick, James S. and Robert E. Malcom. "General Purchasing Power Accounting," **MA**, 1976, Vol. 58, No. 1, pp. 38-40.

Winborne, Marilyn G. "The Operating Cycle Concept - Accepted?," **AR**, 1964, Vol. 39, No. 3, pp. 622-626.

Winborne, Marilynn G. and Dee L. Kleespie. "Tax Allocation In Perspective," **AR**, 1966, Vol. 41, No. 4, pp. 737-744.

Winborne, M. G. "A Wrinkle On An Intellectual Groove," **JAR**, 1966, Vol. 4, No. 2, pp. 245-252.

Winckler, Susan W. and D. Dewey Ward. "Can City Hall Go Broke? The Going Concern Issue?," **JOA**, 1984, Vol. 157, No. 5, pp. 90-100.

Windal, Floyd W. "Analysis Of Changes In Gross Profit," **AR**, 1963, Vol. 38, No. 3, pp. 619-622.

Windal, Floyd W. "Dynamic Programming: An Introduction," **MA**, 1969, Vol. 51, No. 1, pp. 47-49.

Windal, Floyd W. "Legal Background For The Accounting Concept Of Realization," **AR**, 1963, Vol. 38, No. 1, pp. 29-36.

Windal, Floyd W. "Publishing For A Varied Public: An Empirical Study," **AR**, 1981, Vol. 56, No. 3, pp. 653-658.

Windal, Floyd W. "Slaying The Quantitative Goliath," **AR**, 1968, Vol. 43, No. 4, pp. 779-781.

Windal, Floyd W. "The Accounting Concept Of Realization," **AR**, 1961, Vol. 36, No. 2, pp. 249-258.

Windal, Floyd W. (Engstrom, John H. and Floyd W. Windal. "Accounting Education For MBA Students: A Survey," **JAED**, 1985, Vol. 3, No. 1, pp. 107-121.)

Winetroub, David. (Capelli, Andrew J. and David Winetroub. "Multiemployer Pension Plans: Uncertain Impact On Financial Reporting," **CA**, 1983, Vol. 1, No. 1, pp. 18-23.)

Winjum, James O. "Accounting And The Rise Of Capitalism: An Accountant's View," **JAR**, 1971, Vol. 9, No. 2, pp. 333-350.

Winjum, James O. "Income Tax Administration In Great Britain," **IJAER**, 1972, Vol. 8, No. 1, pp. 109-116.

Winjum, James O. "The Journal Of Thomas Gresham," **AR**, 1971, Vol. 46, No. 1, pp. 149-155.

Winjum, James. "Accounting In Its Age Of Stagnation," **AR**, 1970, Vol. 45, No. 4, pp. 743-761.

Winkler, Othmar W. "Secret Allies?," **MA**, 1985, Vol. 66, No. 12, pp. 48-53.

Winkworth, John W. "Profit Analysis In The Ready-Mixed Concrete Industry," **MA**, 1976, Vol. 57, No. 9, pp. 34-36.

Winsen, Joseph K. "Capital Market Behaviour And Accounting Policy Decisions," **ABR**, 1976-77, Vol. 7, No. 26, pp. 100-110.

Winslow, Charles D. "Clerical Work Measurement Techniques In A Control System," **MA**, 1969, Vol. 50, No. 5, pp. 43-47.

Winslow, Rex S. "Relationships And Responsibilities Of Teaching Staffs To Executive Development Programs," **AR**, 1958, Vol. 33, No. 4, pp. 568-572.

Winston, Ralph J. "The U.S. Accountant Goes To The Orient," **MA**, 1969, Vol. 50, No. 4, pp. 39-44.

Winter, Elmer L. "What The Corporate President Wants From His Accounting Firm," **JOA**, 1972, Vol. 134, No. 1, pp. 56-60.

Winter, Sidney G. "Accountancy For The General Business Student," **AR**, 1933, Vol. 8, No. 2, pp. 105-109.

Winter, Sidney G. "Comments On 'Attracting And Maintaining A Supply Of Effective Accounting Teachers'," **AR**, 1956, Vol. 31, No. 2, pp. 223-226.

Winter, Sidney G. "What Is Proper Training For Accountants?," **AR**, 1941, Vol. 16, No. 2, pp. 183-187.

Winter, S. G. "Accounting Instruction At Iowa," **AR**, 1927, Vol. 2, No. 2, pp. 178-181.

Winter, S. G. "The C.P.A. Review Course," **AR**, 1935, Vol. 10, No. 1, pp. 23-26.

Winter, S. G. "The Next Decade In Accounting," **AR**, 1928, Vol. 3, No. 3, pp. 311-322.

Winters, Alan J. "Avoiding Malpractice Liability Suits," **JOA**, 1981, Vol. 152, No. 2, pp. 69-74.

Winters, Alan J. "Banker Perceptions Of Unaudited Financial Statements," **CPAJ**, 1975, Vol. 45, No. 8, pp. 29-33.

Winters, Alan J. "Looking At The Auditor Rotation Issue," **MA**, 1976, Vol. 57, No. 9, pp. 29-30.

Winters, Alan J. "Unaudited Statements: Review Procedures And Disclosures," **JOA**, 1976, Vol. 142, No. 1, pp. 52-59.

Winters, Alan J. (Guy, Dan M. and Alan J. Winters. "Unaudited Financial Statements: A Survey," **JOA**, 1972, Vol. 134, No. 6, pp. 46-53.)

Winters, Alan J. (Lightner, Sharon M., James J. Leisenring and Alan J. Winters. "Underreporting Chargeable Time," **JOA**, 183, Vol. 155, No. 1, pp. 52-57.)

Winters, Alan J. (Spiceland, J. David and Alan J. Winters. "Market Response Of Stock Distributions: The Effects Of Magnitude, Anticipation, And Cash Returns," **ABR**, 1985-86, Vol. 16, No. 63, pp. 221-226.)

Winters, Alan J. (Temkin, Robert H. and Alan J. Winters. "SAS No. 55: The Auditor's New Responsibility For Internal Control," **JOA**, 1988, Vol. 165, No. 5, pp. 86-98.)

Winters, Alan J. (Van Son, W. Peter and Alan J. Winters. "The Preaudit Conference: A Communication Tool," **JOA**, 1982, Vol. 154, No. 5, pp. 86-93.)

Winters, Arthur Lee. (Most, Kenneth S. and Arthur Lee Winters. "Focus On Standard Setting - From Trueblood To The FASB," **JOA**, 1977, Vol. 143, No. 2, pp. 67-75.)

Wise, John A. and Dennis C. Johnson. "Carryover Basis: To Be Given A 'Fresh Start'?," **JOA**, 1979, Vol. 148, No. 2, pp. 59-64.

Wise, Ronald L. "Cost Reporting For The Small And Medium Size Job-Shop Operation," **MA**, 1970, Vol. 51, No. 8, pp. 20-22.

Wise, Trevor D. (Aitken, Michael J. and Trevor D. Wise. "The Real Objective Of The International Accounting Standards Committee," **IJAER**, 1984, Vol. 20, No. 1, pp. 171-177.)

Wiseman, Dorsey E. "A Review Of Improvements In Federal Government Accounting," **AR**, 1953, Vol. 28, No. 4, pp. 570-575.

Wiseman, J. "An Evaluation Of Environmental Disclosures Made In Corporate Annual Reports," **AOS**, 1982, Vol. 7, No. 1, pp. 53-64.

Wishon, Keith and Lorin S. Chevalier. "Interest Rate Swaps - Your Rate Or Mine?," **JOA**, 1985, Vol. 160, No. 3, pp. 63-84.

Wishon, Keith and Robert P. Roche. "Making The Switch: Corporation To Partnership," **JOA**, 1987, Vol. 163, No. 3, pp. 90-95.

Wishon, Keith. "Plugging The Gaps In GAAP: The FASB's Emerging Issues Task Force," **JOA**, 1986, Vol. 161, No. 6, pp. 96-107.

Witham, Robert B. "Controlling Computer Results," **MA**, 1973, Vol. 55, No. 4, pp. 48-51.

Withey, Howard A. and Guy Holman. "Standards Of Accounting For Voluntary Health-Welfare Agencies," **JOA**, 1965, Vol. 120, No. 2, pp. 47-56.

Withey, Howard A. "Financial Reporting For Nonprofit Organizations," **JOA**, 1967, Vol. 124, No. 6, pp. 40-53.

Withey, Howard A. (Johns, Ralph S. and Howard A. Withey. "Authoritative Accounting Guide For Colleges And Universities," **JOA**, 1969, Vol. 127, No. 3, pp. 55-59.)

Witschey, Robert E. "CPAs And Noncertified Practitioners," **JOA**, 1960, Vol. 110, No. 6, pp. 63-71.

Witschey, Robert E. "The Accounting Function For Small Business," **JOA**, 1958, Vol. 106, No. 6, pp. 30-39.

Witschey, Robert E. "The Business Need For Better Accounting Principles," **JOA**, 1964, Vol. 117, No. 1, pp. 27-31.

Witschey, Robert E. "The Future Of The Local Practitioner," **JOA**, 1962, Vol. 113, No. 6, pp. 31-36.

Witschey, Robert E. "Three Challenges To CPA Serving Small Local Client," **JOA**, 1953, Vol. 95, No. 3, pp. 320-324.

Witschey, Robert E. "What Does It Take To Be A Successful CPA," **JOA**, 1954, Vol. 97, No. 1, pp. 64-70.

Witt, Raymond C. (Grant, Edward B. and Raymond C. Witt. "A Look At Leveraged Leases Under FAS No. 13," **MA**, 1979, Vol. 60, No. 8, pp. 49-52.)

Witt, Wallace E. "Work Measurement Of Indirect Labor," **MA**, 1971, Vol. 53, No. 5, pp. 31-34.

Witte, Arthur E. "Management Auditing: The Present State Of The Art," **JOA**, 1967, Vol. 124, No. 2, pp. 54-58.

Witte, Arthur E. "The Income Statement As A Management Tool," **JOA**, 1959, Vol. 108, No. 4, pp. 44-48.

Witte, Arthur E. (Stone, Marvin L. and Arthur E. Witte. "CPA Services For The CPA," **JOA**, 1962, Vol. 114, No. 1, pp. 31-39.)

Wittenbach, James L. and Ken Milani. "A Profile Of The CPA In Tax Practice: An Update," **JOA**, 1982, Vol. 154, No. 4, pp. 65-76.

Wittenbach, James L. and Stephen J. Mayer. "A Flowchart Of The Charitable Contribution Rules," **JOA**, 1974, Vol. 138, No. 5, pp. 63-67.

Wittenbach, James L. "Vacation Home Deductibility - Part II," **CPAJ**, 1983, Vol. 53, No. 1, pp. 45-51.

Wittenbach, James L. "Vacation Home Deductibility - Part I," **CPAJ**, 1982, Vol. 52, No. 12, pp. 18-23.

Wittenbach, James L. (Morris, Michael H. and James L. Wittenbach. "The First Year Of Safe Harbor Leasing Activity: A Look At Objectives And Results," **AIT**, 1987, Vol. 1, pp. 131-152.)

Wittus, Erwin Bud. "A CPA Firm's Experience With Punched Tape," **JOA**, 1961, Vol. 112, No. 3, pp. 65-70.

Wittus, Erwin Bud. "Business Combinations In The Health Care Industry," **CPAJ**, 1988, Vol. 58, No. 3, pp. 42-45.

Witwer, John L. (Currie, Edward M. and John L. Witwer. "Gaining A Foothold In Systems Education," **AR**, 1969, Vol. 44, No. 3, pp. 618-623.)

Wixon, Rufus. "Legal Requirements And Accounting Standards," **AR**, 1945, Vol. 20, No. 2, pp. 139-147.

Wixon, Rufus. "The Measurement And Administration Of Income," **AR**, 1949, Vol. 24, No. 2, pp. 184-190.

Woelfel, Charles J. and William R. Woelfel. "Fraud: The Inside Criminal," **CPAJ**, 1987, Vol. 57, No. 3, pp. 41-45.

Woelfel, Charles J. "Understanding The Multinationals," **IJAER**, 1976, Vol. 11, No. 2, pp. 133-142.

Woelfel, Charles J. (Morgan, Robert G., Jalaleddin Soroosh and Charles J. Woelfel. "Are Ethics Dangerous To Your Job?," **MA**, 1985, Vol. 66, No. 8, pp. 24-32.)

Woelfel, Robert C. "How Brunswick Accomplished Constant Dollar Accounting," **MA**, 1980, Vol. 62, No. 6, pp. 44-48.

Woelfel, William R. (Woelfel, Charles J. and William R. Woelfel. "Fraud: The Inside Criminal," **CPAJ**, 1987, Vol. 57, No. 3, pp. 41-45.)

Wojciechowski, Stanley R. "Du Pont Evaluates FAS 52," **MA**, 1982, Vol. 64, No. 1, pp. 31-36.

Wojdak, Joseph F. and D. Larry Crumbley. "Introducing Important Tax Provisions Into Advanced Accounting," **AR**, 1969, Vol. 44, No. 1, pp. 173-175.

Wojdak, Joseph F. "A Theoretical Foundation For Leases And Other Executory Contracts," **AR**, 1969, Vol. 44, No. 3, pp. 562-570.

Wojdak, Joseph F. "Holding Gains And Losses On Executory Contracts," **MA**, 1969, Vol. 50, No. 5, pp. 55-58.

Wojdak, Joseph F. "Levels Of Objectivity In The Accounting Process," **AR**, 1970, Vol. 45, No. 1, pp. 88-97.

Wojdak, Joseph F. (Copeland, Ronald M. and Joseph F. Wojdak. "Income Manipulation And The Purchase-Pooling Choice," **JAR**, 1969, Vol. 7, No. 2, pp. 188-195.)

Wokutch, Richard E. and Liam Fahey. "A Value Explicit Approach For Evaluating Corporate Social Performance." **JAPP**, 1986, Vol. 5, No. 3. pp. 191-214.

Wolf, Arthur E. "Education Revisited," **MA**, 1971, Vol. 52, No. 7, pp. 14-15.

Wolf, Frank M. "The Nature Of Managerial Work: An Investigation Of The Work Of The Audit Manager," **AR**, 1981, Vol. 56, No. 4. pp. 861-881.

Wolf, Frank M. "The Nature Of Managerial Work - The Case For Unobtrusive Measures Revisited' - A Reply." **AR**, 1981, Vol. 56, No. 4, pp. 971-974.

Wolf, Frank M. (Gibbins, Michael and Frank M. Wolf. "Auditors' Subjective Decision Environment - The Case Of A Normal External Audit," **AR**, 1982. Vol. 57, No. 1. pp. 105-124.)

Wolf, Frederick D. (Miller, John R. and Frederick D. Wolf. "A Look At The New Yellow Book: Tomorrow's Government Audits," **JOA**, 1988. Vol. 166. No. 5, pp. 64-80.)

Wolf, F. (Cooper, D. J., D. Hayes and F. Wolf. "Accounting In Organized Anarchies: Understanding And Designing Accounting Systems In Ambiguous Situations." **AOS**, 1981, Vol. 6, No. 3, pp. 175-192.)

Wolf, G. (Young, S. M., M. D. Shields and G. Wolf. "Manufacturing Controls And Performance: An Experiment." **AOS**, 1988, Vol. 13, No. 6, pp. 607-618.)

Wolf, Henry C. "Funding Postretirement Welfare Benefit Plans," **CA**, 1988, Vol. 6. No. 2, pp. 3-10.

Wolf, Richard G. "Being Audited? Making It Easier Is Up To You." **MA**, 1976, Vol. 57, No. 9, pp. 27-28.

Wolf, Warren G. "Developing A Cost System For Today's Decision Making," **MA**, 1982. Vol. 64, No. 6, pp. 19-23.

Wolfangel, Claire P. (Bruegelmann, Thomas M., Gaile A. Haessly, Claire P. Wolfangel and Michael Schiff. "How Variable Costing Is Used In Pricing Decisions." **MA**, 1985, Vol. 66, No. 10. pp. 58-61.)

Wolfe, Donald N. and Gerald Smith. "Planning The Audit In A Distressed Industry," **CPAJ**, 1988, Vol. 58. No. 10. pp. 46-50.

Wolff, Joel C. "Business Logistics And The Bottom Line," **CA**, 1987, Vol. 5, No. 2, pp. 58-64.

Wolfram, Harold W. "Taxpayer Can Lose Benefit Of Statute Of Limitations," **JOA**, 1951, Vol. 91. No. 4, pp. 580-585.

Wolfson, Mark A. (Amershi, Amin H., Joel S. Demski and Mark A. Wolfson. "Strategic Behavior And Regulation Research In Accounting," **JAPP**, 1982. Vol. 1, No. 1. pp. 19-32.)

Wolfson, Mark A. (Beaver, William H. and Mark A. Wolfson. "Foreign Currency Translation And Changing Prices In Perfect And Complete Markets," **JAR**, 1982. Vol. 20, No. 2, Part II. pp. 528-550.)

Wolfson, Mark A. (Demski. Joel S., James M. Patell and Mark A. Wolfson. "Decentralized Choice Of Monitoring Systems," **AR**, 1984. Vol. 59, No. 1. pp. 16-34.)

Wolfson, Mark A. (Fellingham. John C. and Mark A. Wolfson. "Taxes And Risk Sharing," **AR**, 1985, Vol. 60, No. 1. pp. 10-17.)

Wolfson, Mark A. (M.M. Laurentius.J.M. Patell and M.A. Wolfson. "The Experimental Design Of Classification Models: An Application Of Recursive Partitioning And Bootstrapping To Commercial Bank Loan Classifications," **JAR**,1984,Vol.22,Supp.,pp. 87-114.)

Wolfson, Mark A. (Patell, James M. and Mark A. Wolfson. "The Ex Ante And Ex Post Price Effects Of Quarterly Earnings Announcements Reflected In Option And Stock Prices," **JAR**, 1981, Vol. 19, No. 2, pp. 434-458.)

Wolfson, Mark A. (Patell, James M. and Mark A. Wolfson. "Anticipated Information Releases Reflected In Call Option Prices," **JAEC**, 1979, Vol. 1, No. 2. pp. 117-140.)

Wolfson, Mark A. (Patell, James M. and Mark A. Wolfson. "Good News, Bad News, And The Intraday Timing Of Corporate Disclosures," **AR**, 1982. Vol. 57, No. 3, pp. 509-527.)

Wolfson, Mark A. (Stickney. Clyde P., Roman L. Weil and Mark A. Wolfson. "Income Taxes And Tax-Transfer Leases: General Electric's Accounting For A Molotov Cocktail." **AR**, 1983, Vol. 58, No. 2, pp. 439-459.)

Wolfson, Mark A. (Stiglitz, Joseph E. and Mark A. Wolfson. "Taxation, Information, And Economic Organization." **JATA**, 1988, Vol. 9, No. 2, pp. 7-18.)

Wolfson, Mark. (Noreen, Eric and Mark Wolfson. "Equilibrium Warrant Pricing Models And Accounting For Executive Stock Options," **JAR**, 1981, Vol. 19, No. 2. pp. 384-398.)

Wolinsky, Daniel and Arthur L. Breakstone. "Reporting For The Rehabilitation And Sheltered Workshop." **JOA**, 1975, Vol. 140, No. 1, pp. 56-62.

Wolitzer, Philip and Stewart Sandman. "Bridges Between Accounting Educators And Practitioners," **CPAJ**, 1976, Vol. 46, No. 8, pp. 23-25.

Wolk, Harry I. and A. Douglas Hillman. "Materials Mix And Yield Variances: A Suggested Improvement." **AR**, 1972, Vol. 47, No. 3, pp. 549-555.

Wolk, Harry I. and Michael G. Tearney. "Income Tax Allocation And Loss Carryforwards: Exploring Uncharted Ground," **AR**, 1973, Vol. 48. No. 2, pp. 292-299.

Wolk, Harry I. and Roger W. Briggs. "Accounting Research, Professors, And Practitioners: A Perspective," **IJAER**, 1975, Vol. 10, No. 2, pp. 47-56.

Wolk, Harry I. "Accounting For Leases: A Further Examination Of The Issues," **JAR**, 1968. Vol. 6. No. 1, pp. 153-157.

Wolk, Harry I. "Current Value Depreciation: A Conceptual Clarification," **AR**, 1970, Vol. 45, No. 3, pp. 544-552.

Wolk, Harry I. (Metcalf. Richard W. and Harry I. Wolk. "Applied Fixed Overhead Accounting: A Proposal," **MA**, 1971, Vol. 52, No. 8, pp. 25-27.)

Wolkstein, Harry W. "Criteria For Tax Exemption As A Religious. Educational, Or Philanthropic Organization," **JOA**, 1950, Vol. 89, No. 5, pp. 404-412.

Wollman, Jack B. (Istvan, Donald F. and Jack B. Wollman. "Turnover In CPA Firms," **CPAJ**, 1976, Vol. 46, No. 7, pp. 21-26.)

Wollstadt, Roger D. "The Challenge Of The Sandilands Report," **MA**, 1976, Vol. 58, No. 1, pp. 15-22.

Wolnizer, P. W. "Independence In Auditing: An Imcomplete Notion," **ABACUS**, 1978, Vol. 14, No. 1, pp. 31-52.

Wolnizer, P. W. "Market Prices V. Cost Indexation In Accounting For Steel Inventories," **ABACUS**, 1983, Vol. 19, No. 2, pp. 171-188.

Wolnizer, P. W. "Primary Production Inventories Under Current Value Accounting," **ABR**, 1976-77, Vol. 7, No. 28, pp. 303-310.

Womer, Norman Keith and Ronald C. J. Marcotte. "Airframe Cost Estimation Using An Error Components Model," **JCA**, 1986, Vol. 3, No. 1, pp. 41-62.

Womer, Norman Keith. (Camm, Jeffrey D., Thomas R. Gulledge, Jr. and Norman Keith Womer. "Production Rate And Contractor Behavior," **JCA**, 1987, Vol. 4, No. 1, pp. 27-37.)

Wong, Jilnaught. "Economic Incentives For The Voluntary Disclosure Of Current Cost Financial Statements," **JAEC**, 1988, Vol. 10, No. 2, pp. 151-167.

Wong, Jilnaught. "Political Costs And An Intraperiod Accounting Choice For Export Tax Credits," **JAEC**, 1988, Vol. 10, No. 1, pp. 37-51.

Wong-Boren, Adrian and Andrew H. Barnett. "Mexican Market Efficiency: A Study Of The Information Content Of Accounting Numbers," **IJAER**, 1984, Vol. 20, No. 1, pp. 45-70.

Wong-Boren, Adrian. (Chow, Chee W., Howard R. Toole and Adrian Wong-Boren. "Make Better Decisions: Divide And Conquer," **MA**, 1986, Vol. 68, No. 2, pp. 41-45.)

Wong-Boren, Adrian. (Chow, Chee W. and Adrian Wong-Boren. "Voluntary Financial Disclosure By Mexican Corporations." **AR**, 1987, Vol. 62, No. 3, pp. 533-541.)

Wong-Boren, Adrian. (Chow, Chee W. and Adrian Wong-Boren. "Audit Firm Size And Audit Quality: Some Evidence From Mexico," **IJAER**, 1986, Vol. 21, No. 2, pp. 1-25.)

Wong-Boren, Adrian. (Chow, Chee W., Michael D. Shields and Adrian Wong-Boren. "A Compilation Of Recent Surveys And Company-Specific Descriptions Of Management Accounting Practices," **JAED**, 1988, Vol. 6, No. 2, pp. 183-207.)

Wong-On-Wing, Bernard. "User Involvement In Systems Development: An Attributional Approach," **JIS**, 1988, Vol. 2, No. 2, pp. 3-14.

Wonnacott, Ronald. "U.S. Investment And The Recipient Country," **IJAER**, 1972, Vol. 7, No. 2, pp. 45-54.

Woo, John C. H. "Accounting For Inflation: Some International Models," **MA**, 1978, Vol. 59, No. 8, pp. 37-43.

Wood, Ben D., Arthur E. Traxler and Warren W. Nissley. "College Accounting Testing Program," **AR**, 1948, Vol. 23, No. 1. pp. 63-83.

Wood, D. R. (Precious, J. R. and D. R. Wood. "Corporate Modelling: When Success Can Be A Long-Term Forecast," **ABR**, 1974-75, Vol. 5, No. 20, pp. 254-272.)

Wood, Edwin A. and Robert G. Murdick. "A Practical Solution To Forecasting Problems," **MA**, 1980, Vol. 61, No. 11, pp. 45-48.

Wood, James H. "How RJR Put Its New MIS On-Line," **MA**, 1979, Vol. 60, No. 10, pp. 17-23.

Wood, John P. and Elson P. Dolliver. "Silver Spoons," **MA**, 1975, Vol. 57, No. 1, pp. 18-19.

Wood, Thomas D. and Anne J. Sylvestre. "The History Of Advertising By Accountants," **AHJ**, 1985, Vol. 12, No. 2, pp. 59-72.

Wood, Thomas D. and Donald A. Ball. "New Rule 502 And Effective Advertising By CPAs," **JOA**, 1978, Vol. 145, No. 6, pp. 65-71.

Wood, Thomas D. "An Audit Program For Compliance With Pollution Control Laws," **CPAJ**, 1974, Vol. 44, No. 4, pp. 63-66.

Wood, Thomas D. "Auditors' Concern For Compliance With Laws," **CPAJ**, 1978, Vol. 48, No. 1, pp. 17-22.

Wood, Venita M. and Daniel L. Kovlak. "What Is The GASB?," **CPAJ**, 1987, Vol. 57, No. 3, pp. 18-23.

Wood, William B. "Tax Problems Of Partnerships," **JOA**, 1959, Vol. 107, No. 2, pp. 33-40.

Woodall, Robert L. (Clements, Joel and Robert L. Woodall. "Controlled Disbursements: A Cash Management Tool For Growing Concerns," **MA**, 1983, Vol. 64, No. 11, pp. 53-55.)

Woodard, Gerald D. "Controlling Office Payroll," **MA**, 1966, Vol. 47, No. 5, pp. 19-26.

Woodbridge, F. W. "Time As A Factor In Determining Debt-Paying Ability," **AR**, 1939, Vol. 14, No. 3, pp. 236-249.

Woodbridge, F. W. (Heckert, J. B., H. F. Taggart, C. L. Van Sickle. R. M. Mikesell, F. W. Woodbridge, Louis O. Foster and T. W. Leland. "Instruction In Methods Of Accounting Control: A Symposium," **AR**, 1937, Vol. 12, No. 2, pp. 114-122.)

Woodburne, Lloyd S. "The Evaluation Of Faculty Services," **AR**, 1957, Vol. 32, No. 2, pp. 235-238.

Woodbury, W. F. "A Treatment Of Distribution Costs," **AR**, 1927, Vol. 2, No. 2, pp. 124-128.

Woodham, Jack. "CCA - A Proposal For Reform," **ABR**, 1983-84, Vol. 14, No. 55, pp. 257-266.

Woods, J. H. "Recording Obsolescence: A Note," **JAR**, 1965, Vol. 3. No. 2, pp. 261-263.

Woods, L. Milton. "The Oil Venture - An Exercise In Accounting," **AR**, 1958, Vol. 33, No. 4, pp. 632-636.

Woods, Milton. "Law And/Or Accounting - A Footnote," **AR**, 1962, Vol. 37, No. 3, p. 556.

Woods, Richard S. "Content Of The Accounting Systems Course," **AR**, 1960, Vol. 35, No. 4, pp. 720-726.

Woods, Richard S. "Some Dimensions Of Integrated Systems," **AR**, 1964, Vol. 39, No. 3, pp. 598-614.

Woods, Richard S. "Theory And Practice In The Capitalization Of Selling Costs," **AR**, 1959, Vol. 34, No. 4, pp. 564-569.

Woodside, Perry. (Henry, James B., Perry Woodside and James B. Edwards. "Public Sector Leasing In South Carolina," **MA**, 1979, Vol. 61, No. 4, pp. 43-49.)

Woodson, W. Paul. (Wheat, George C. and W. Paul Woodson. "A Case For Electronic Business Machines," **MA**, 1972, Vol. 54, No. 6, pp. 20-22.)

Woodward, P. D. "Depreciation - The Development Of An Accounting Concept," **AR**, 1956, Vol. 31, No. 1, pp. 71-76.

Woolf, Jack J. "A Management Action Reporting System (MARS)," **MA**, 1967, Vol. 48, No. 9, pp. 35-40.

Wooller, Jeff. (Grinyer, Peter H. and Jeff Wooller. "An Overview Of A Decade Of Corporate Modelling In The UK," **ABR**, 1980-81, Vol. 11, No. 41, pp. 41-50.)

Woolsey, Sam M. "Approach To Solving The Materiality Problem," **JOA**, 1973, Vol. 135, No. 3, pp. 47-50.

Woolsey, Sam M. "Criteria For Judging Materiality," **JOA**, 1954, Vol. 97, No. 2, pp. 167-173.

Woolsey, Sam M. "Improving The Quality Of Advanced Accounting Instruction," **AR**, 1959, Vol. 34, No. 2, pp. 303-305.

Woolsey, Sam M. "Materiality In Determining Requirements For Full Disclosure," **JOA**, 1954, Vol. 98, No. 6, pp. 745-750.

Woolsey, Sam M. "Materiality In Financial Reports," **MA**, 1975, Vol. 56, No. 8, pp. 23-26.

Woolsey, Sam M. "Teaching Accounting By Television," **AR**, 1957, Vol. 32, No. 1, pp. 119-123.

Woolsey, S. M. "Accounting For Investment Credit," **AR**, 1963, Vol. 38, No. 4, pp. 709-713.

Woomer, Donald B. "LIFO As A Method Of Determining Depreciation," **AR**, 1949, Vol. 24, No. 3, pp. 290-295.

Wormley, James T. "Ensuring The Profit Contribution Of A Corporate Data Processing Department," **MA**, 1967, Vol. 48, No. 5, pp. 3-12.

Worrall, Robert L. (Fasci, Martha A., Timothy J. Weiss and Robert L. Worrall. "Everyone Can Use This Cost/Benefit Analysis System," **MA**, 1987, Vol. 68, No. 7, pp. 44-47.)

Worrell, Dwight. "Cost Of Sales: A Budgeting Priority," **MA**, 1983, Vol. 65, No. 2, pp. 67-70.

Worthington, James S. "And Now We Have....," **MA**, 1977, Vol. 59, No. 2, pp. 30-32.

Worthington, James S. "Footnotes: Readability Or Liability," **CPAJ**, 1978, Vol. 48, No. 5, pp. 27-32.

Worthington, James S. (Thompson, James H., James S. Worthington and L. Murphy Smith. "An Inconsistency In The Method Of Accounting For Changes In Estimate: Variable Stock Plans," **ACCHOR**, 1987, Vol. 1, No. 4, pp. 29-34.)

Worthington, James. (Golen, Steven, James Worthington, Greg Thibadoux, William D. Cooper and Ira S. Greenberg. "Flowcharts & Graphics," **CPAJ**, 1986, Vol. 56, No. 3, pp. 12-23.)

Worthington, Judi L. (Reardon, Thomas E. and Judi L. Worthington. "Magnetic Media Reporting: A Solution To Small Business Paperwork?," **JOA**, 1987, Vol. 163, No. 6, pp. 130-135.)

Worthley, Stephen G. and Christopher Skaar, Jr. "Managing Information Through Banks," **MA**, 1982, Vol. 64, No. 2, pp. 52-58.

Wragge, John H. (Abdel-Khalik, A. Rashad, Doug A. Snowball and John H. Wragge. "The Effects Of Certain Internal Audit Variables On The Planning Of External Audit Programs," **AR**, 1983, Vol. 58, No. 2, pp. 215-227.)

Wragge, John H. (Gillespie, Jackson F., Janis R. Reeder and John H. Wragge. "Safeguarding Your Spreadsheet," **MA**, 1985, Vol. 66, No. 11, pp. 38-42.)

Wrege, William T. and R. Penny Marquette. "Measurement Focus And Basis Of Accounting (GASB)," **CPAJ**, 1988, Vol. 58, No. 12, pp. 64-70.

Wren, Daniel A. (Van Fleet, David D. and Daniel A. Wren. "History In Today's Business School," **AHJ**, 1982, Vol. 9, No. 1, pp. 111-118.)

Wren, Melvin C. "The Chamber Of The City Of London, 1633-1642," **AR**, 1949, Vol. 24, No. 2, pp. 191-198.

Wright, Albert W. "Earnings Per Share: Sensitizing The Numerator," **MA**, 1971, Vol. 52, No. 11, pp. 19-21.

Wright, Albert W. "Maintaining Balance In Financial Position," **MA**, 1969, Vol. 51, No. 3, pp. 14-16.

Wright, Albert W. "Periodic Net Income And Extraordinary Items," **MA**, 1967, Vol. 47, No. 9, pp. 35-42.

Wright, Arnold and Mohammad Abdolmohammadi. "Modeling Auditor Weights Of Key Critria In Evaluating Alternative Sampling Aproaches: A Guide For Researchers," **AIA**, 1987, Vol. 4, pp. 287-302.

Wright, Arnold and Theodore J. Mock. "Towards A Contingency View Of Audit Evidence," **AJPT**, 1985-86, Vol. 5, No. 1, pp. 91-100.

Wright, Arnold M. "On The Use Of An Available Prior Examination Policy," **IAE**, 1986, Vol. 1, No. 1, pp. 24-36.

Wright, Arnold. "An Investigation Of The Engagement Evaluation Process For Staff Auditors," **JAR**, 1982, Vol. 20, No. 1, pp. 227-239.

Wright, Arnold. "Performance Appraisal Of Staff Auditors," **CPAJ**, 1980, Vol. 50, No. 11, pp. 37-44.

Wright, Arnold. "Performance Evaluation Of Staff Auditors: A Behaviorally Anchored Rating Scale," **AJPT**, 1985-86, Vol. 5, No. 2, pp. 95-110.

Wright, Arnold. "Rating The Raters: Indications Of Seniors'

Performance In Evaluating Staff Auditors," **AIA**, 1985, Vol. 2, pp. 185-198.

Wright, Arnold. "The Comparative Performance Of MBAs Vs. Undergraduate Accounting Majors In Public Accounting," **AR**, 1988, Vol. 63, No. 1, pp. 123-136.

Wright, Arnold. "The Impact Of CPA Firm Size On Auditor Disclosure Preferences," **AR**, 1983, Vol. 58, No. 3, pp. 621-632.

Wright, Arnold. (Abdolmohammadi, Mohammad and Arnold Wright. "An Examination Of The Effects Of Experience And Task Complexity On Audit Judgments," **AR**, 1987, Vol. 62, No. 1, pp. 1-13.)

Wright, Arnold. (Lin, W. Thomas, Theodore J. Mock and Arnold Wright. "The Use Of The Analytic Hierarchy Process As An Aid In Planning The Nature And Extent Of Audit Procedures," **AJPT**, 1984-85, Vol. 4, No. 1, pp. 89-99.)

Wright, Arnold. (Mock, Theodore J. and Arnold Wright. "Evaluating The Effectiveness Of Audit Procedures," **AJPT**, 1982-83, Vol. 2, No. 1, pp. 33-44.)

Wright, A. "The Impact Of Prior Working Papers On Auditor Evidential Planning Judgments," **AOS**, 1988, Vol. 13, No. 6, pp. 595-605.

Wright, Charlotte J. and James E. Groff. "Uses Of Indexes And Data Bases For Information Release Analysis," **AR**, 1986, Vol. 61, No. 1, pp. 91-100.

Wright, C. T. (Richardson, Frederick M. and C. T. Wright. "Standards Overload: A Case For Accountant Judgment," **CPAJ**, 1986, Vol. 56, No. 10, pp. 44-53.)

Wright, D. L. (Chambers, D. J., H. S. Singhal, B. D. Taylor and D. L. Wright. "Developing Dividend And Financing Policies With A Computer Terminal," **ABR**, 1970-71, Vol. 1, No. 4, pp. 267-273.)

Wright, D. M. "Inflation Accounting In The Nationalised Industries: A Survey And Appraisal," **ABR**, 1979-80, Vol. 10, No. 37, pp. 65-73.

Wright, F. Kenneth. "Depreciation Theory And The Cost Of Funds," **AR**, 1963, Vol. 38, No. 1, pp. 87-90.

Wright, F. Kenneth. "Measuring Project Profitability: Rate Of Return Or Present Value?," **AR**, 1962, Vol. 37, No. 3, pp. 433-437.

Wright, F. K. "A Theory Of Inventory Measurement," **ABACUS**, 1965, Vol. 1, No. 2, pp. 150-155.

Wright, F. K. "An Evaluation Of Ladelle's Theory Of Depreciation," **JAR**, 1967, Vol. 5, No. 2, pp. 173-179.

Wright, F. K. "Capacity For Adaptation And The Asset Measurement Problem," **ABACUS**, 1967, Vol. 3, No. 1, pp. 74-79.

Wright, F. K. "Depreciation And Obsolescence In Current Value Accounting," **JAR**, 1965, Vol. 3, No. 2, pp. 167-181.

Wright, F. K. "Dual Variables In Inventory Measurement," **AR**, 1970, Vol. 45, No. 1, pp. 129-133.

Wright, F. K. "Managerial Controls Of Accounts Receivable: A Comment," **JAR**, 1966, Vol. 4, No. 1, pp. 127-130.

Wright, F. K. "Measuring Asset Services: A Linear Programming Approach," **JAR**, 1968, Vol. 6, No. 2, pp. 222-236.

Wright, F. K. "On The Linear Programming Approach To Asset Valuation," **JAR**, 1969, Vol. 7, No. 2, pp. 183-187.

Wright, F. K. "The Valuation Of Tax-Depreciable Assets," **IJAER**, 1973, Vol. 8, No. 2, pp. 45-57.

Wright, F. K. "Towards A General Theory Of Depreciation," **JAR**, 1964, Vol. 2, No. 1, pp. 80-90.

Wright, F. K. "Value To The Owner: A Clarification," **ABACUS**, 1971, Vol. 7, No. 1, pp. 58-61.

Wright, Gail B. and Robert D. Taylor. "Reporting Materiality For Investors," **JAAF**, 1982, Vol. 5, No. 4, pp. 301-309.

Wright, Gail B. (Oglesbee, Tom W., Larry N. Bitner and Gail B. Wright. "Measurement Of Incremental Benefits In Computer Enhanced Instruction," **IAE**, 1988, Vol. 3, No. 2, pp. 365-377.)

Wright, Howard W. "A Case Of Valuation," **AR**, 1966, Vol. 41, No. 3, pp. 559-560.

Wright, Howard W. "Allocation Of General And Administrative Expenses," **AR**, 1966, Vol. 41, No. 4, pp. 626-633.

Wright, Howard W. "Federal Accountants Offer Cooperation," **AR**, 1951, Vol. 26, No. 4, pp. 579-581.

Wright, Howard W. "Generally Accepted Accounting Principles And Practices In Relation To Defense Contracts," **AR**, 1953, Vol. 28, No. 3, pp. 385-391.

Wright, Howard W. "New Records Clause In Cost-Type Defense Contracts," **JOA**, 1953, Vol. 96, No. 1, pp. 56-61.

Wright, Howard W. "Tentative Statement On Government Accounting," **AR**, 1958, Vol. 33, No. 2, pp. 210-213.

Wright, H. W. "An Informal Accounting System For Administrative Costs," **JOA**, 1952, Vol. 93, No. 6, pp. 694-697.

Wright, H. W. "When To Use Standard Cost In Price Procurement Contracts," **JOA**, 1952, Vol. 94, No. 2, pp. 178-183.

Wright, Ivor B. "Guidelines For First-Time Audits," **CPAJ**, 1972, Vol. 42, No. 3, pp. 197-204.

Wright, Ivor B. "Review Of APB Opinion No. 27 - 'Accounting For Lease Transactions By Manufacturer Or Dealer Lessors'," **CPAJ**, 1973, Vol. 43, No. 7, pp. 563-566.

Wright, James M. and Gerard T. Mazurkiewicz. "Accounting For Contract Revenue: Builders' Burden?," **MA**, 1988, Vol. 69, No. 7, pp. 49-54.

Wright, Michael A. and John W. Jonez. "Material Burdening: Management Accounting CAN Support Competitive Strategy," **MA**, 1987, Vol. 69, No. 2, pp. 27-31.

Wright, Mike and Steve Thompson. "Divestment And The Control Of Divisionalised Firms," **ABR**, 1986-87, Vol. 17, No. 67, pp. 259-268.

Wright, Mike. "Audit Qualifications On The Accounts Of Nationalised Industries," **ABR**, 1984-85, Vol. 15, No. 58,

pp. 134-143.

Wright, Penny, Ray Whittington and G. E. Whittenburg. "Student Ratings Of Teaching Effectiveness: What The Research Reveals," **JAED**, 1984, Vol. 2, No. 2, pp. 5-30.

Wright, Raymond E. "Preparing Proposals For Expansion In Foreign Markets," **MA**, 1970, Vol. 52, No. 4, pp. 46-50.

Wright, Robert F. and Stephen R. Helpern. "Corporate Business Combinations - A New Look At The Basic Tax And Accounting Considerations," **CPAJ**, 1973, Vol. 43, No. 5, pp. 361-368.

Wright, Robert F. (Gaffney, Francis M. and Robert F. Wright. "Compensating The Executive In Today's Economic Climate," **CPAJ**, 1975, Vol. 45, No. 9, pp. 27-30.)

Wright, Robert G. "Changing Concepts In EDP Feasibility Studies," **JOA**, 1962, Vol. 113, No. 6, pp. 47-51.

Wright, Roger L. (Roshwalb, Alan, Roger L. Wright, and James Godfrey. "A New Approach For Stratified Sampling In Inventory Cost Estimation," **AJPT**, 1987-88, Vol. 7, No. 1, pp. 54-70.)

Wright, William F. "Empirical Comparison Of Subjective Probability Elicitation Methods," **CAR**, 1988, Vol. 5, No. 1, pp. 47-57.

Wright, William F. "Financial Information Processing Models: An Empirical Study," **AR**, 1977, Vol. 52, No. 3, pp. 676-689.

Wright, William F. (Beaver, William H., Roger Clarke and William F. Wright. "The Association Between Unsystematic Security Returns And The Magnitude Of Earnings Forecast Errors," **JAR**, 1979, Vol. 17, No. 2, pp. 316-340.)

Wright, William F. (Hamilton, Robert E. and William F. Wright. "Internal Control Judgments And Effects Of Experience Replications And Extensions," **JAR**, 1982, Vol. 20, No. 2, Part II, pp. 756-765.)

Wright, William F. (Willingham, John J. and William F. Wright. "Financial Statement Errors And Internal Control Judgments," **AJPT**, 1985-86, Vol. 5, No. 1, pp. 57-70.)

Wright, William. "An Empirical Study Of The Professional Socialization Of Accounting Students," **IJAER**, 1977, Vol. 13, No. 1, pp. 53-76.

Wright, Wilmer. "Use Of Standard Direct Costing," **MA**, 1967, Vol. 48, No. 5, pp. 39-46.

Wright, Wilmer. "Why Direct Costing Is Rapidly Gaining Acceptance," **JOA**, 1962, Vol. 114, No. 1, pp. 40-46.

Wright, W. F. "Comparison Of The Lens And Subjective Probability Paradigms For Financial Research Purposes," **AOS**, 1982, Vol. 7, No. 1, pp. 65-78.

Wright, W. F. "Self-Insight Into The Cognitive Processing Of Financial Information," **AOS**, 1977, Vol. 2, No. 4, pp. 323-332.

Wright, W. H. "Observations Of An American Cost Accountant Abroad," **AR**, 1957, Vol. 32, No. 1, pp. 107-111.

Wu, Chunchi. (Lee, Cheng F. and Chunchi Wu. "Expectation Formation And Financial Ratio Adjustment Processes," **AR**, 1988, Vol. 63, No. 2, pp. 292-306.)

Wu, Frederick H. and Donald W. Hackett. "The Internationalization Of U.S. Public Accounting Firms: An Empirical Study," **IJAER**, 1977, Vol. 12, No. 2, pp. 81-91.

Wu, Frederick H. and Douglas Sharp. "An Empirical Study Of Transfer Pricing Practice," **IJAER**, 1979, Vol. 14, No. 2, pp. 71-99.

Wu, Frederick H. and Ronald A. Safran. "A Practical Approach For Evaluating EDP Controls," **CPAJ**, 1987, Vol. 57, No. 10, pp. 58-69.

Wu, Frederick H. "Expanding The Profit Contribution Approach," **MA**, 1975, Vol. 56, No. 12, pp. 39-42.

Wu, Frederick H. "Incremental Budgeting: A Decision Model," **MA**, 1976, Vol. 57, No. 11, pp. 46-48.

Wu, Frederick H. "Small Business Computers For CPA Firms," **CPAJ**, 1983, Vol. 53, No. 11, pp. 46-56.

Wu, Frederick H. "Spreadsheet Software: A Tool For Teaching Managerial (Cost) And Financial Accounting," **JIS**, 1986, Vol. 1, No. 1, pp. 121-136.

Wu, Frederick H. "Teaching Accounting Information Systems: A Synthesis," **IAE**, 1983, No. 1, pp. 132-145.

Wu, Frederick H. "Teaching Managerial (Cost) Accounting With Electronic Spreadsheet Software," **IAE**, 1984, No. 1, pp. 81-97.

Wuchina, Stephen W. "Program Control Network: A Tool For Month End Closing," **MA**, 1969, Vol. 51, No. 1, pp. 38-42.

Wucinich, William J. "Financial Management For Small Contractors," **MA**, 1975, Vol. 57, No. 1, pp. 23-26.

Wucinich, William. "How To Finance A Small Business," **MA**, 1979, Vol. 61, No. 5, pp. 16-18.

Wunder, Haroldene F. (Carper. Wm. Brent, M. Frank Barton, Jr. and Haroldene F. Wunder. "The Future Of Forecasting," **MA**, 1979, Vol. 61, No. 2, pp. 27-31.)

Wyatt, Arthur R. and Elmer B. Staats. "Who Should Set Governmental Accounting Standards?," **JOA**, 1979, Vol. 147, No. 3, pp. 65-70.

Wyatt, Arthur R. "Accounting For Business Combinations: What Next?," **AR**, 1965, Vol. 40, No. 3, pp. 527-535.

Wyatt, Arthur R. "Comparability In Accounting," **MA**, 1969, Vol. 51, No. 1, pp. 10-14.

Wyatt, Arthur R. "Efficient Market Theory: Its Impact On Accounting," **JOA**, 183, Vol. 155, No. 2, pp. 56-65.

Wyatt, Arthur R. "Leases Should Be Capitalized," **CPAJ**, 1974, Vol. 44, No. 9, pp. 35-38.

Wyatt, Arthur R. "Professional Education In Accounting," **AR**, 1959, Vol. 34, No. 2, pp. 200-206.

Wyatt, Arthur R. "Professionalism In Standard-Setting," **CPAJ**, 1988, Vol. 57, No. 7, pp. 20-33.

Wyatt, Arthur R. "Tradition And Accounting," **AR**, 1956, Vol. 31, No. 3, pp. 395-400.

Wyatt, Arthur R. (Bows, Albert J. and Arthur R. Wyatt. "Improving Interim Financial Reporting," **JOA**, 1973, Vol.

136, No. 4, pp. 54-59.)

Wyatt, Arthur R. (Ketz, J. Edward and Arthur R. Wyatt. "The FASB In A World With Partially Efficient Markets," **JAAF**, 1983, Vol. 7, No. 1, pp. 29-43.)

Wyatt, Arthur R., Richard Dieter and John E. Stewart. "Tax Allocation Revisited," **CPAJ**, 1984, Vol. 54, No. 3, pp. 10-19.

Wycoff, David W. "Direct And Idle-Time Cost Accounting," **MA**, 1974, Vol. 56, No. 6, pp. 36-38.

Wycoff, David W. "Profit Determinants," **MA**, 1977, Vol. 58, No. 8, pp. 47-48.

Wycoff, David W. "Profitability Measurement In Margin Dollars Per Hour," **MA**, 1975, Vol. 56, No. 12, pp. 37-38.

Wyer, Jean C. "Conceptual V. Procedural: A Developmental Approach," **JAED**, 1984, Vol. 2, No. 1, pp. 5-18.

Wyer, Jean C. (White, Godwin T., Jean C. Wyer and Ernest C. Janson. "Peer Review: Proposed Regulations And Current Compliance," **ACCHOR**, 1988, Vol. 2, No. 2, pp. 27-30.)

Wyer, Jean C. (White, Godwin T., Jean C. Wyer and Ernest C. Janson. "Uncertainty Reporting - Impact Of Proposed Changes," **CPAJ**, 1987, Vol. 57, No. 9, pp. 46-53.)

Wyer, Jean C., Godwin T. White and Ernest C. Janson. "Audits Of Public Companies By Smaller CPA Firms: Clients, Reports, And Quality," **AJPT**, 1988, Vol. 7, No. 2, pp. 164-173.

Wygal, Donald E. and David E. Stout. "Investment Income Reporting In The Property And Casualty Insurance Industry: A Critical Assessment," **ACCHOR**, 1987, Vol. 1, No. 4, pp. 51-62.

Wygal, Donald E. (Stout, David E. and Donald E. Wygal. "Making By-Products A Main Product Of Discussion: A Challenge To Accounting Educators," **JAED**, 1988, Vol. 6, No. 2, pp. 219-233.)

Wygal, Donald E. (Stout, David E., Donald E. Wygal and John J. Gorman. "Accounting Student Perceptions Of The Nature And Significance Of Extraordinary Items Data," **JAED**, 1987, Vol. 5, No. 1, pp. 13-25.)

Wygal, Donald E. (Stout, David E., Donald E. Wygal and James Volpi. "A Comparative Income Statement Approach To Integrating International Topics In The Financial Accounting Curriculum," **AIIA**, 1988, Vol. 2, pp. 147-166.)

Wygal, Donald E., David E. Stout and James Volpi. "Reporting Practices In Four Countries," **MA**, 1987, Vol. 69, No. 6, pp. 37-42.

Wyler, Richard S. "Tax Court Says Goodwill Attaches To Accounting Practice, And May Be Sold," **JOA**, 1950, Vol. 90, No. 3, pp. 242-248.

Wyman, Harold E. and J. Edgar McFarland. "Financial Investments And The True Rate Of Return," **MA**, 1977, Vol. 59, No. 2, pp. 41-45.

Wyman, Harold E. and Wesley T. Andrews, Jr. "Classifying The Receivable In A Lease Transaction: A Dilemma," **AR**, 1975, Vol. 50, No. 4, pp. 908-909.

Wyman, Harold E. "Analysis Of Gains And Losses From Foreign Monetary Items: An Application Of Purchasing Power Parity Concepts," **AR**, 1976, Vol. 51, No. 3, pp. 545-558.

Wyman, Harold E. "Financial Lease Evaluation Under Conditions Of Uncertainty: A Reply," **AR**, 1974, Vol. 49, No. 4, pp. 802-806.

Wyman, Harold E. "Financial Lease Evaluation Under Conditions Of Uncertainty," **AR**, 1973, Vol. 48, No. 3, pp. 489-493.

Wyman, Harold E. "Formulas For Depreciation," **MA**, 1972, Vol. 54, No. 6, pp. 45-47.

Wyman, Harold E. "Pascal's Triangle," **MA**, 1974, Vol. 56, No. 4, pp. 27-28.

Wyman, Harold E. "Standardized Debt Coverage Ratios," **AR**, 1977, Vol. 52, No. 2, pp. 503-507.

Wyman, Harold E. (Bavishi, Vinod B. and Harold E. Wyman. "Foreign Operations Disclosures By U.S.-Based Multinational Corporations: Are They Adequate?," **IJAER**, 1980, Vol. 16, No. 1, pp. 153-168.)

Wyman, Harold. (Kochanek, Richard, Bimal Prodhan and Harold Wyman. "CMAs Can Learn From The U.K. Experience," **MA**, 1985, Vol. 67, No. 5, pp. 38-42.)

Wynant, Larry. "Project Financing For Extractive Ventures," **MA**, 1978, Vol. 60, No. 4, pp. 29-35.

Wynarczyk, P. (Keasey, K., R. Watson and P. Wynarczyk. "The Small Company Audit Qualification: A Preliminary Investigation," **ABR**, 1988, Vol. 18, No. 72, pp. 323-333.)

Wyndelts, Robert W. and Anna C. Fowler. "Installment Sales: Temporary Regulations Inconsistent With Judicial Definition Of Payment," **JATA**, 1981, Vol. 3, No. 1, pp. 26-31.

Wyndelts, Robert W. (Jensen, Herbert L. and Robert W. Wyndelts. "Through The Looking Glass: An Empirical Look At Discrimination In The Federal Income Tax Rate Structure," **AR**, 1976, Vol. 51, No. 4, pp. 846-853.)

Wyndelts, Robert W. (Sanders, Debra L. and Robert W. Wyndelts. "An Examination Of Tax Practitioners' Decisions Under Uncertainty," **AIT**, 1988, Vol. 2, pp. xx-xx.)

Wyndelts, Robert W. (Tidwell, Victor H. and Robert W. Wyndelts. "Graduate Tax Education In AACSB Schools: Where We Stand Today," **AR**, 1977, Vol. 52, No. 4, pp. 963-970.)

Wynne, Robert C. and Alan Frotman. "Microcomputers: Helping Make Practice Perfect," **JOA**, 1981, Vol. 152, No. 6, pp. 34-39.

YYY

Yager, E. Ben. "An Aid In Explaining 'Funds Provided By Operations'," **AR**, 1963, Vol. 38, No. 1, pp. 154-156.

Crossroads," **ACCHOR**, 1987. Vol. 1. No. 3. pp. 17-24.)

Young, S. Mark. "Participative Budgeting: The Effects Of Risk Aversion And Asymmetric Information On Budgetary Slack," **JAR**, 1985, Vol. 23, No. 2, pp. 829-842.

Young, S. Mark. (Lewis, Barry, Michael D. Shields and S. Mark Young. "Evaluating Human Judgments And Decision Aids," **JAR**, 1983, Vol. 21, No. 1, pp. 271-285.)

Young, S. M. (Birnberg, J. G., L. Turopolec and S. M. Young. "The Organizational Context Of Accounting," **AOS**, 1983, Vol. 8, No. 2/3, pp. 111-130.)

Young, S. M., M. D. Shields and G. Wolf. "Manufacturing Controls And Performance: An Experiment," **AOS**, 1988, Vol. 13, No. 6, pp. 607-618.

Young, T. N. and C. G. Pierson. "Depreciation - Future Service Basis," **AR**, 1967, Vol. 42, No. 2, pp. 338-341.

Young, Walter. "A Method Of Securing A Statement Of Application Of Funds," **AR**, 1935, Vol. 10, No. 3, pp. 287-293.

Yu, Seongjae and John Neter. "A Stochastic Model Of The Internal Control System," **JAR**, 1973, Vol. 11, No. 2, pp. 273-295.

Yu, S. C. "A Flow-Of-Resources Statement For Business Enterprises," **AR**, 1969, Vol. 44, No. 3, pp. 571-582.

Yu, S. C. "A Reexamination Of The Going Concern Postulate," **IJAER**, 1971, Vol. 6, No. 2, pp. 37-58.

Yu, S. C. "Is The New U.S. Budget A More Understandable Document?," **IJAER**, 1968, Vol. 3, No. 2, pp. 45-66.

Yu, S. C. "Macroaccounting And Some Of Its Basic Problems," **AR**, 1957, Vol. 32, No. 2, pp. 264-272.

Yu, S. C. "Microaccounting And Macroaccounting," **AR**, 1966, Vol. 41, No. 1, pp. 8-20.

Yu, S. C. "National Position Statement: A Proposal On Operational Principles And Process," **AR**, 1959, Vol. 34, No. 1, pp. 74-83.

Yu, S. C. "The Several Modes Of Normative Accounting Thought: A Critical Examination," **IJAER**, 1974, Vol. 9, No. 2, pp. 83-104.

Yunker, Penelope J. (Sterner, Julie A. and Penelope J. Yunker. "Human Resource Accounting By Professional Sports Teams," **AIA**, 1986, Vol. 3, pp. 127-148.)

Yunker, Penelope J., Julie A. Sterner and Michael Costigan. "Employment In Accounting: A Comparison Of Recruiter Perceptions With Student Expectations," **JAED**, 1986, Vol. 4, No. 1, pp. 95-112.

Yurko, Allen M. "Managing Change Through Human Resource Development," **MA**, 1982, Vol. 63, No. 12. pp. 36-42.

ZZZ

Zachry, Benny R. "An Investigation Into The Status Of Public Community College Tax Curricula," **JAED**, 1987, Vol. 5, No. 2, pp. 323-332.

Zack, David. "How The New Code Will Affect The Individual Taxpayer," **JOA**, 1954, Vol. 98, No. 3, pp. 294-302.

Zahorsky, Alyce. (Peterson, Raymond H. and Alyce Zahorsky. "Telephone Company Develops New Cost Standards," **MA**, 1988, Vol. 70, No. 6, pp. 47-49.)

Zahra Shaker A. (Briner, Russell F., Frank A. Wiebe and Shaker A. Zahra. "Management Accountants: Don't Overlook Quality Circles," **MA**, 1984, Vol. 66, No. 6, pp. 45-49.)

Zaiden, Dennis J. "Some Legal Aspects Of EDP," **MA**, 1972, Vol. 54, No. 1, pp. 51-52.

Zald, M. N. "The Sociology Of Enterprise, Accounting And Budget Rules: Implications For Organizational Theory," **AOS**, 1986, Vol. 11, No. 4/5, pp. 327-340.

Zannetos, Zenon S. "Depreciation And Funds Statements," **AR**, 1962, Vol. 37, No. 2, pp. 300-307.

Zannetos, Zenon S. "Mathematics As A Tool Of Accounting Instruction And Research," **AR**, 1963, Vol. 38, No. 2, pp. 326-335.

Zannetos, Zenon S. "On The Mathematics Of Variance Analysis," **AR**, 1963, Vol. 38, No. 3, pp. 528-533.

Zannetos, Zenon S. "Programmed Instruction And Computer Technology," **AR**, 1967, Vol. 42, No. 3, pp. 566-571.

Zannetos, Zenon S. "Some Thoughts On Internal Control Systems Of The Firm," **AR**, 1964, Vol. 39, No. 4, pp. 860-868.

Zannetos, Zenon S. "Standard Costs As A First Step To Probabilistic Control: A Theoretical Justification. An Extension And Implications," **AR**, 1964, Vol. 39, No. 2, pp. 296-304.

Zannetos, Zenon S. "Statistical Attributes Of Group Depreciation," **AR**, 1962, Vol. 37, No. 4, pp. 713-720.

Zant, Robert F. (Guynes, Carl Stephen, Michael T. Vanecek and Robert F. Zant. "Security Of Telecommunication Systems," **CPAJ**, 1979, Vol. 49, No. 10, pp. 31-34.)

Zant, Robert F. (Vanecek, Michael T., Robert F. Zant and Carl Stephen Guynes. "Distributed Data Processing: A New Tool For Accountants," **JOA**, 1980, Vol. 150, No. 4, pp. 75-83.)

Zappala, Frederick J. "The Current State Of The Accounting Profession In Italy," **IJAER**, 1973, Vol. 8, No. 2, pp. 111-121.

Zarowin, Paul. "Non-Linearities And Nominal Contracting Effects: The Case Of The Depreciation Tax Shield," **JAEC**, 1988, Vol. 10, No. 2, pp. 89-110.

Zaunbrecher, Hilary C. (Spiceland, J. David and Hilary C. Zaunbrecher. "Human Resource Accounting: An Historical Perspective," **AHJ**, 1976, Vol. 3, No. 1-4, pp. 43-49.)

Zaunbrecher, H. C. (Hartman, Bart P. and H. C. Zaunbrecher. "Comparability And Objectivity Of Exit Value Accounting: A Comment," **AR**, 1976, Vol. 51, No. 4, pp. 927-929.)

Zaunbrecher, H. C. (Spiceland, J. D. and H. C. Zaunbrecher. "The Usefulness Of Human Resource Accounting In Personnel Selection," **MA**, 1977, Vol. 58, No. 8, pp. 29-30.)

Zavgren, Christine V. "The Prediction Of Corporate Failure: The State Of The Art," **JAL**, 1983, Vol. 2, pp. 1-38.

Zavgren, Christine V. (Dugan, Michael T. and Christine V. Zavgren. "Bankruptcy Prediction Research: A Valuable Instructional Tool," **IAE**, 1988, Vol. 3, No. 1, pp. 48-64.)

Zazoff, Alan. (Ferguson, Florence J. and Alan Zazoff. "How You Can Control Unemployment Insurance Costs," **MA**, 1985, Vol. 66, No. 9, pp. 48-53.)

Zebda, Awni. "Stochastic Audit Planning And Control Using GERT Simulation," **ABR**, 1985-86, Vol. 16, No. 63, pp. 235-244.

Zebda, Awni. "The Choice Of Management Accounting Normative Models: A Synthesis," **AIA**, 1987, Vol. 5, pp. 73-98.

Zebley, John H., Jr. "Challenges To The Accounting Profession." **AR**, 1956, Vol. 31, No. 2, pp. 173-181.

Zebley, John H., Jr. "The Standard C.P.A. Examination," **AR**, 1941, Vol. 16, No. 1, pp. 82-86.

Zebley, John H., Jr. "The Standard C.P.A. Examination," **AR**, 1942, Vol. 17, No. 2, pp. 119-124.

Zeff, Stephen A. and Robert L. Fossum. "An Analysis Of Large Audit Clients," **AR**, 1967, Vol. 42, No. 2, pp. 298-320.

Zeff, Stephen A. and Sven-Erik Johansson. "The Curious Accounting Treatment Of The Swedish Government Loan To Uddeholm," **AR**, 1984, Vol. 59, No. 2, pp. 342-350.

Zeff, Stephen A. and W. David Maxwell. "Holding Gains On Fixed Assets - A Demurrer," **AR**, 1965, Vol. 40, No. 1, pp. 65-75.

Zeff, Stephen A. "Accounting Journals In Business School Libraries: A Survey," **AR**, 1968, Vol. 43, No. 1, pp. 150-153.

Zeff, Stephen A. "Big Eight Firms And The Accounting Literature: The Falloff In Advocacy Writing," **JAAF**, 1986. Vol. 1 (New Series), No. 2, pp. 131-154.

Zeff, Stephen A. "Chronology Of Significant Developments In The Establishment Of Accounting Principles In The United States, 1926-1972," **JAR**, 1972, Vol. 10, No. 1, pp. 217-227.

Zeff, Stephen A. "Comments On The NIDA Program," **IJAER**, 1968, Vol. 4, No. 1, pp. 141-143.

Zeff, Stephen A. "Debating Accounting Theory," **AR**, 1963, Vol. 38, No. 3, pp. 622-626.

Zeff, Stephen A. "Does The CPA Belong To A Profession?," **ACCHOR**, 1987, Vol. 1, No. 2, pp. 65-68.

Zeff, Stephen A. "Economic Consequences In Intermediate Textbooks: A Review After Eight Years," **IAE**, 1988, Vol. 3, No. 2, pp. 433-444.

Zeff, Stephen A. "F. R. M. de Paula," **AHJ**, 1974, Vol. 1, No. 1-4, pp. 31-34.

Zeff, Stephen A. "In Appreciation Of Ray Chambers, An Australian Original," **ABACUS**, 1982, Vol. 18, No. 2, pp. 179-181.

Zeff, Stephen A. "Leaders Of The Accounting Profession: 14 Who Made A Difference," **JOA**, 1987, Vol. 163, No. 5, pp. 46-71.

Zeff, Stephen A. "Replacement Cost: Member Of The Family, Welcome Guest, Or Intruder?," **AR**, 1962, Vol. 37, No. 4, pp. 611-625.

Zeff, Stephen A. "Right Of Offset Vs. Partnership Act In Winding-Up Process," **AR**, 1957, Vol. 32, No. 1, pp. 68-70.

Zeff, Stephen A. "Some Junctures In The Evolution Of The Process Of Establishing Accountng Principles In The U.S.A.: 1917-1972," **AR**, 1984, Vol. 59, No. 3, pp. 447-468.

Zeff, Stephen A. "The Rise Of 'Economic Consequences'," **JOA**, 1978, Vol. 146, No. 6, pp. 56-63.

Zeff, Stephen A. "Truth In Accounting: The Ordeal Of Kenneth MacNeal," **AR**, 1982, Vol. 57, No. 3, pp. 528-553.

Zeff, Stephen A. "'Price-Level' Should Be Taught...In The Introductory Course," **AR**, 1961, Vol. 36, No. 4, pp. 642-645.

Zeff, Stephen A. (Boudreaux, Kenneth J. and Stephen A. Zeff. "A Note On The Measure Of Compensation Implicit In Employee Stock Options," **JAR**, 1976, Vol. 14, No. 1, pp. 158-162.)

Zeff, Stephen A. (Dyckman, Thomas R. and Stephen A. Zeff. "Two Decades Of The Journal Of Accounting Research," **JAR**, 1984, Vol. 22, No. 1, pp. 225-297.)

Zega, Cheryl Ann. "The New Statement Of Cash Flows," **MA**, 1988, Vol. 70, No. 3, pp. 54-59.

Zeghal, Daniel. "Industry, Market Structure, And The Informational Content Of Financial Statements," **JAPP**, 1983, Vol. 2, No. 2, pp. 115-131.

Zeghal, Daniel. (Ahmed, Sadrudin A. and Daniel Zeghal. "Industry Segment Identification And Social Responsibility Information Disclosure In Selected Canadian Companies," **IJAER**, 1987, Vol. 22, No. 2, pp. 153-167.)

Zeisel, Gerald and Ralph W. Estes. "Accounting And Public Service," **AR**, 1979, Vol. 54, No. 2, pp. 402-408.

Zell, Gary A. "Streamlined SEC Registration System," **CPAJ**, 1982, Vol. 52, No. 11, pp. 18-23.

Zellner, Joseph E. "Nomographs - Aids For Decision Makers," **MA**, 1966, Vol. 47, No. 9, pp. 56-60.

Zenker, David M. "The PC As Prototype Problem-Solver," **MA**, 1987, Vol. 68, No. 11, pp. 30-33.

Zenker, Richard J. "Effect Of TRA '86 On Business Combinations," **CA**, 1987, Vol. 5, No. 3, pp. 3-9.

Zhijun, Lin. "A Survey Of Current Developments In Chinese Accounting," **AIIA**, 1988, Vol. 2, pp. 99-110.

Zhou, Zhong Hui. "Chinese Accounting Systems And Practices." **AOS**, 1988, Vol. 13, No. 2, pp. 207-224.

Zick, Harold F. "The Investment Of Idle Cash Funds," **MA**, 1974, Vol. 55, No. 8, pp. 27-28.

Ziebart, **David A.** and David H. Kim. "An Examination Of The Market Reactions Associated With SFAS No. 8 And SFAS No. 52," **AR**, 1987, Vol. 62, No. 2, pp. 343-357.

Ziebart, **David A.** "Control Of Beta Reliability In Studies Of Abnormal Return Magnitudes: A Methodological Note," **JAR**, 1985, Vol. 23, No. 2, pp. 920-926.

Ziebart, **David A.** "Exchange Rates And Purchasing Power Parity: Evidence Regarding The Failure Of SFAS No. 52 To Consider Exchange Risk In Hyper-Inflationary Countries," **IJAER**, 1985, Vol. 21, No. 1, pp. 39-51.

Ziegler, **Francis, S. J.** and John M. Ivanoff. "A Study Of A Maturity Factor Between Freshman And Sophomore Accounting Students," **AR**, 1964, Vol. 39, No. 1, pp. 155-160.

Ziegler, **John H.** "Current Trends In The Teaching Of Auditing," **AR**, 1972, Vol. 47, No. 1, pp. 167-170.

Ziegler, **Richard E.** (Bedford, Norton M. and Richard E. Ziegler. "The Contributions Of A. C. Littleton To Accounting Thought And Practice," **AR**, 1975, Vol. 50, No. 3, pp. 435-443.)

Ziegler, **R. E.** "Willard J. Graham," **AHJ**, 1976, Vol. 3, No. 1-4, pp. 76-81.

Zieha, **Eugene L.** and Thomas T. Cheng. "Proposing A More Appropriate Dividend Policy," **MA**, 1979, Vol. 61, No. 3, pp. 32-36.

Zieha, **Eugene L.** "Accounting Under Conditions Of Changing Prices From The Debtor And Creditor Viewpoint," **AR**, 1953, Vol. 28, No. 4, pp. 528-533.

Zieha, **Eugene L.** "Computer-Generated Accounting Assignments," **AR**, 1974, Vol. 49, No. 3, pp. 600-602.

Zieha, **Eugene L.** (Duangploy, Orapin, Eugene L. Zieha and Dahli Gray. "SFAS No. 52 And The Statement Of Changes In Financial Position: A Survey And Proposal For Change," **IJAER**, 1987, Vol. 22, No. 2, pp. 25-40.)

Zikmund, **William G.,** Ralph F. Catalanello and Steve M. Wegener. "The Accounting Student's Job-Rating Criteria: An Experiment," **AR**, 1977, Vol. 52, No. 3, pp. 729-735.

Zimering, **Max.** "Teaching And Solving Installment Sales Problems," **AR**, 1952, Vol. 27, No. 3, pp. 376-382.

Zimmer, **Ian R.** (Trotman, Ken T. and Ian R. Zimmer. "Revenue Recognition In The Construction Industry: An Experimental Study," **ABACUS**, 1986, Vol. 22, No. 2, pp. 136-147.)

Zimmer, **Ian R.** (Trotman, Ken T., Philip W. Yetton and Ian R. Zimmer. "Individual And Group Judgments Of Internal Control Systems," **JAR**, 1983, Vol. 21, No. 1, pp. 286-292.)

Zimmer, **Ian.** "A Lens Study Of The Prediction Of Corporate Failure By Bank Loan Officers," **JAR**, 1980, Vol. 18, No. 2, pp. 629-636.

Zimmer, **Ian.** "Accounting For Interest By Real Estate Developers," **JAEC**, 1986, Vol. 8, No. 1, pp. 37-51.

Zimmer, **Ian.** "Modelling Lenders' Assessments Of The Ability Of Corporate Borrowers To Repay," **ABACUS**, 1981, Vol. 17, No. 2, pp. 145-160.

Zimmer, **Ian.** (Whittred, Greg and Ian Zimmer. "Timeliness Of Financial Reporting And Financial Distress," **AR**, 1984, Vol. 59, No. 2, pp. 287-295.)

Zimmer, **Ian.** (Wilkins, Trevor and Ian Zimmer. "The Effect Of Leasing And Different Methods Of Accounting For Leases On Credit Evaluations," **AR**, 1983, Vol. 58, No. 4, pp. 749-764.)

Zimmer, **Ian.** (Wilkins, Trevor and Ian Zimmer. "The Effects Of Alternative Methods Of Accounting For Leases - An Experimental Study," **ABACUS**, 1983, Vol. 19, No. 1, pp. 64-75.)

Zimmer, **Robert K.** (Skousen, K. Fred and Robert K. Zimmer. "Controllership Obsolescence: Fact Or Fiction," **MA**, 1970, Vol. 51, No. 12, pp. 20-23.)

Zimmerman, **Guenter.** "Short-Term Forecasts In Industry," **JOA**, 1958, Vol. 105, No. 5, pp. 48-54.

Zimmerman, **Jerold J.** (Liberty, Susan E. and Jerold J. Zimmerman. "Labor Union Contract Negotiations And Accounting Choices," **AR**, 1986, Vol. 61, No. 4, pp. 692-712.)

Zimmerman, **Jerold L.** "Budget Uncertainty And The Allocation Decision In A Nonprofit Organization," **JAR**, 1976, Vol. 14, No. 2, pp. 301-319.

Zimmerman, **Jerold L.** "Taxes And Firm Size," **JAEC**, 1983, Vol. 5, No. 2, pp. 119-149.

Zimmerman, **Jerold L.** "The Costs And Benefits Of Cost Allocations," **AR**, 1979, Vol. 54, No. 3, pp. 504-521.

Zimmerman, **Jerold L.** "The Municipal Accounting Maze: An Analysis Of Political Incentives," **JAR**, 1977, Vol. 15, Supp., pp. 107-144.

Zimmerman, **Jerold L.** (Jensen, Michael C. and Jerold L. Zimmerman. "Management Compensation And The Managerial Labor Market," **JAEC**, 1985, Vol. 7, No. 1/3, pp. 3-9.)

Zimmerman, **Jerold L.** (Leftwich, Richard, Ross L. Watts and Jerold L. Zimmerman. "Voluntary Corporate Disclosure: The Case Of Interim Reporting," **JAR**, 1981, Vol. 19, Supp., pp. 50-84.)

Zimmerman, **Jerold L.** (Meckling, William H. and Jerold L. Zimmerman. "Schools Of Accountancy - Accomplish Little," **CPAJ**, 1976, Vol. 46, No. 10, pp. 25-30.)

Zimmerman, **Jerold L.** (Smith, Clifford W., Jr. and Jerold L. Zimmerman. "Valuing Employee Stock Option Plans Using Option Pricing Models," **JAR**, 1976, Vol. 14, No. 2, pp. 357-364.)

Zimmerman, **Jerold L.** (Watts, Ross L. and Jerold L. Zimmerman. "On The Irrelevance Of Replacement Cost Disclosures For Security Prices," **JAEC**, 1980, Vol. 2, No. 2, pp. 95-106.)

Zimmerman, **Jerold L.** (Watts, Ross L. and Jerold L. Zimmerman. "Towards A Positive Theory Of The Determination Of Accounting Standards," **AR**, 1978, Vol. 53, No. 1, pp. 112-134.)

Zimmerman, **Jerold L.** (Watts, Ross L. and Jerold L. Zimmerman. "The Demand For And Supply Of Accounting Theories: The Market For Excuses," **AR**, 1979, Vol. 54, No. 2, pp. 273-305.)

Zimmerman, **Jerold.** "Price-Level Restatements: A Technical Note," **JAR**, 1974, Vol. 12, No. 2, pp. 372-382.

Zimmerman, **John.** "Accountant's Guide To Tax Resources," **CPAJ**, 1986, Vol. 56, No. 6, pp. 56-65.

Zimmerman, **John.** "The Flat Tax: A Closer Look," **CPAJ**, 1984, Vol. 54, No. 2, pp. 30-35.

Zimmerman, **Philip.** (Fusaro, Frank G., Robert A. Gaida and Philip Zimmerman. "Senior Turnover - Seniors Speak Out," **CPAJ**, 1984, Vol. 54, No. 7, pp. 26-35.)

Zimmerman, **Stephen B.** (Goldstein, Robert H. and Stephen B. Zimmerman. "Help For Small-To-Medium-Size Distributors," **CPAJ**, 1978, Vol. 48, No. 10, pp. 21-25.)

Zimmerman, **Vernon K.** "Adding Flexibility To The Accounting Curriculum: An Accelerated Program," **AR**, 1959, Vol. 34, No. 4, pp. 658-660.

Zimmerman, **V. K.** "The Long Shadow Of A Scholar," **IJAER**, 1967, Vol. 2, No. 2, pp. 1-20.

Zimmerman, **V. K.** (Kafer, Karl and V. K. Zimmerman. "Notes On The Evolution Of The Statement Of Sources And Applications Of Funds," **IJAER**, 1967, Vol. 2, No. 2, pp. 89-121.)

Zircher, **James R.** "The EDP Technician, The Accountant, And Internal Control," **MA**, 1975, Vol. 57, No. 3, pp. 38-40.

Zises, **Alvin.** "Disclosure Of Long-Term Leases," **JOA**, 1961, Vol. 111, No. 2, pp. 37-47.

Zitmore, **Irving.** "How To Decide Whether To Microfilm Business Records, And How To Go About It," **JOA**, 1951, Vol. 91, No. 2, pp. 276-281.

Zlaktovich, **Charles.** "How Research Projects Can Help Guide The Profession," **JOA**, 1952, Vol. 94, No. 2, pp. 208-214.

Zlatkovich, **Charles T.** "A New Accounting Theory Statement," **JOA**, 1966, Vol. 122, No. 2, pp. 31-36.

Zlatkovich, **Charles T.** "Some Principles Of Accounting Systems Design," **AR**, 1958, Vol. 33, No. 3, pp. 419-422.

Zlatkovich, **Charles T.** "Teaching The Application Of Funds Statement," **AR**, 1949, Vol. 24, No. 2, pp. 206-208.

Zlatkovich, **Charles T.** "Training For An Accounting Career: An Educator's View," **AR**, 1958, Vol. 33, No. 2, pp. 193-197.

Zmijewski, **Mark E.** and Robert L. Hagerman. "An Income Strategy Approach To The Positive Theory Of Accounting Standard Setting/Choice," **JAEC**, 1981, Vol. 3, No. 2, pp. 129-149.

Zmijewski, **Mark E.** "Methodological Issues Related To The Estimation Of Financial Distress Prediction Models," **JAR**, 1984, Vol. 22, Supp., pp. 59-82.

Zmijewski, **Mark E.** (Brown, Lawrence D., Paul A. Griffin, Robert L. Hagerman and Mark E. Zmijewski. "An Evaluation Of Alternative Proxies For The Market's Assessment Of Unexpected Earnings," **JAEC**, 1987, Vol. 9, No. 2, pp. 159-193.)

Zmijewski, **Mark E.** (Brown, Lawrence D., Robert L. Hagerman, Paul A. Griffin and Mark E. Zmijewski. "Security Analyst Superiority Relative To Univariate Time-Series Models In Forecasting Quarterly Earnings," **JAEC**, 1987, Vol. 9, No. 1, pp. 61-87.)

Zmijewski, **Mark E.** (Brown, Lawrence D. and Mark E. Zmijewski. "The Effect Of Labor Strikes On Security Analysts' Forecast Superiority And On The Assoc. Between Risk-Adjusted Stock Returns And Unexpected," **CAR**, 1987-88, Vol. 4, No. 1, pp. 61-75.)

Zmijewski, **Mark E.** (Hagerman, Robert L. and Mark E. Zmijewski. "Some Economic Determinants Of Accounting Policy Choice," **JAEC**, 1979, Vol. 1, No. 2, pp. 141-161.)

Zmijewski, **Mark E.** (Hagerman, Robert L., Mark E. Zmijewski and Pravin Shah. "The Association Between The Magnitude Of Quarterly Earnings Forecast Errors And Risk-Adjusted Stock Returns," **JAR**, 1984, Vol. 22, No. 2, pp. 526-540.)

Zmud, **R. W.** (Blocher, E., R. P. Moffie and R. W. Zmud. "Report Format And Task Complexity: Interaction In Risk Judgments," **AOS**, 1986, Vol. 11, No. 6, pp. 457-470.)

Zoffer, **H. J.** "Accounting Education And Educated Accountants," **MA**, 1978, Vol. 59, No. 9, pp. 19-23.

Zolfo, **Frank J.** and Barry N. Cooper. "Considering The LIFO Election," **MA**, 1977, Vol. 58, No. 12, pp. 41-43.

Zoltners, **Andris A.** (Balachandran, Bala V. and Andris A. Zoltners. "An Interactive Audit-Staff Scheduling Decision Support System," **AR**, 1981, Vol. 56, No. 4, pp. 801-812.)

Zook, **Donald R.** (Knight, Royal E. and Donald R. Zook. "Controllers And CPAs Evaluate Relevance Of Education Topics," **MA**, 1982, Vol. 64, No. 5, pp. 30-35.)

Zraick, **Louis E.** "Air Transport Accounting," **AR**, 1946, Vol. 21, No. 2, pp. 166-171.

Zraick, **Louis E.** "Packing Housing Accounting," **AR**, 1947, Vol. 22, No. 3, pp. 299-303.

Zraick, **Louis E.** "The Audit Of Overhead In Companies Handling Both Commercial And Government Contracts," **AR**, 1950, Vol. 25, No. 2, pp. 180-183.

Zuber, **George Russell.** (Akresh, Abraham D. and George Russell Zuber. "Exploring Statistical Sampling," **JOA**, 1981, Vol. 151, No. 2, pp. 50-56.)

Zuber, **George R.** "What Auditors Should Know About FASB Statement No. 87," **JOA**, 1988, Vol. 165, No. 3, pp.38-48.

Zuber, **George R.** (Loebbecke, James K. and George R. Zuber. "Evaluating Internal Control," **JOA**, 1980, Vol. 149, No. 2, pp. 49-57.)

Zuber, **George R.** (Loebbecke, James K., John F. Mullarkey and George R. Zuber. "Auditing In A Computer Environment," **JOA**, 183, Vol. 155, No. 1, pp. 68-78.)

Zuber, George R. (Warren, Carl S., Stephen V. N. Yates and George R. Zuber. "Audit Sampling: A Practical Approach," **JOA**, 1982, Vol. 153, No. 1, pp. 62-72.)

Zuber, George R., Robert K. Elliott, William R. Kinney, Jr., and James J. Leisenring. "Using Materiality In Audit Planning," **JOA**, 183, Vol. 155, No. 3, pp. 42-55.

Zuckerman, Gilroy J. (Bublitz, Bruce O. and Gilroy J. Zuckerman. "Discounting Deferred Taxes: A New Approach," **AIA**, 1988, Vol. 6, pp. 55-70.)

Zuckerman, Gilroy J. (Messere, Carl J. and Gilroy J. Zuckerman. "An Alternative Approach To Depreciation Switches," **AR**, 1981, Vol. 56, No. 3, pp. 642-652.)

Zuckert, Donald M. "Think About Your Advertising Program," **CPAJ**, 1977, Vol. 47, No. 10, pp. 11-14.

Zug, Harry C. "Rigid Courses Of Study For CPA Certificates Are Opposed," **JOA**, 1951, Vol. 92, No. 2, pp. 175-179.

Zukowska, Wilhelmina H. "Essential Subject Matter For A One-Year Basic Accounting Course Offered To Non-Accounting Majors," **AR**, 1961, Vol.36, No.3, pp. 481-487.

Zukowska, Wilhelmina H. "Determination Of Goodwill Or Bonus On The Admission Of A Partner - An Alternative Approach," **AR**, 1964, Vol. 39, No. 2, pp. 457-460.

Zulinski, Marilyn. (Ballew, Van Bennett, Ray Whittington and Marilyn Zulinski. "Shared Audit Engagements," **CPAJ**, 1983, Vol. 53, No. 2, pp. 28-35.)

Zulinski, Marilyn. (Raiborn, D. D., Dan M. Guy and Marilyn Zulinski. "Solving Audit Problems In Small Business Engagements," **JOA**, No. 183, Vol. 155, No. 4, pp. 50-59.)

Zulinski, Marilyn. (Whittington, Ray, Marilyn Zulinski and James W. Ledwith "Completeness - The Elusive Assertion," **JOA**, 1983, Vol. 156, No. 2, pp. 82-92.)

Zulli, Ronald. (Kissin, Warren and Ronald Zulli. "Valuation Of A Closely Held Business," **JOA**, 1988, Vol. 165, No. 6, pp. 38-48.)

Zweig, Jeanne. "Administrative Skills - A Prerequisite For The Smallest Of CPA Firms," **JOA**, 1966, Vol. 122, No. 6, pp. 53-55.

MONTHLY AND SEASONAL DESIGNATIONS
USED FOR EACH JOURNAL ISSUE

Abacus

1965-66 (2) Sep, Dec
1967-68 (2) Aug, Dec
1969-70 (2) Sep, Dec
1971-84 (2) Jun, Dec
1985-88 (2) Mar, Sep

Accounting and Business Research

1970/71-1988/89 (4) Winter/Spring, Summer, Fall

The Accounting Historians Journal

1974-76 (1) No Designation
1977-88 (2) Spring, Fall

Accounting Horizons

1987-88 (4) Mar, Jun, Sep, Dec

Accounting, Organizations and Society

1976-88 (4) No Designation

The Accounting Review

1926-41 (4) Mar, Jun, Sep, Dec
1942-88 (4) Jan, Apr, Jul, Oct

Advances in Accounting

1984-88 (1) No Designation

Advances in International Accounting

1987-88 (1) No Designation

Advances in Public Interest Accounting

1986 (1) No Designation
1987 No Issue
1988 (1) No Designation

Advances in Taxation

1987-88 (1) No Designation

Auditing: A Journal of Practice and Theory

1981/82 (2) Summer/Winter
1982/83 (2) Fall/Winter
1983/84-1988/89 (2) Fall/Spring

Contemporary Accounting Research

1984/85-1988/89 (2) Fall, Spring

Corporate Accounting

1983-88 (4) Winter, Spring, Summer, Fall

The CPA Journal

1972-88 (12) Jan, Feb, ... , Nov, Dec

International Journal of Accounting

1965/66-1988/89 (2) Fall, Spring

Issues in Accounting Education

1983-85 (1) No Designation & No Volume #
1986-88 (2) Spring, Fall

Journal of Accountancy

1950-88 (12) Odd Vol. #'s Jan, Feb, Mar, Apr, May, Jun
Even Vol. #'s Jul, Aug, Sep, Oct, Nov, Dec

Journal of Accounting and Economics

1979-81 (3) Mar, Aug, Dec
1982 (3) Jul, Oct, Dec
1983-85 (3) Apr, Aug, Dec
1986 (3) Mar, Jun, Oct
1987 (3) Apr, Jul, Dec
1988 (4) Jan, Apr, Jul, Dec

Journal of Accounting and Public Policy

1982 (2) No Designation, Winter
1983-88 (4) Spring, Summer, Fall, Winter

Journal of Accounting, Auditing and Finance

1977/78-1983/84 (4) Fall/Winter, Spring, Summer
1984/85 (5) Fall/Spring, Summer, Fall, Winter(Vol.9)
1986-88 (4) Spring, Summer, Fall, Winter

Journal of Accounting Education

1983-88 (2) Spring, Fall

Journal of Accounting Literature

1982-85 (1) Spring
1986-88 (1) No Designation

Journal of Accounting Research

1963-88 (3) Spring, Autumn, Supplement

Journal of Cost Analysis

1984-85 (1) Spring
1986 (2) Spring, Fall
1987-88 (1) Summer

Journal of Information Systems

1986/87-1988/89 (2) Fall/Spring

Journal of the American Taxation Association

1979/80-1981/82 (2) Spring/Winter
1982/83 (2) Summer/Spring
1983/84-1988/89 (2) Fall/Spring

Management Accounting

1965/66-1967/68 (12) Sep, Oct, ... , Jul, Aug
1968/69 (10) Sep, Oct, ... , May, Jun
1969/70-1988/89 (12) Jul, Aug, ... , May, Jun

Research in Accounting Regulation

1987-88 (1) No Designation

Research in Governmental and Nonprofit Accounting

1985-88 (1) No Designation

The number in parentheses indicates the number of issues in that journal year. Years separated by a dash, 1984-85 for example, designates the years 1984 through 1985. Those years separated by a slash, 1984/85 for example, designates that the volume spans from one calendar year into another. Thus, 1984-87 includes 1984, 1985, 1986, and 1987. And 1981/82-1983/84 includes the three journal years of 1981/82, 1982/83 and 1983/84.